The Oxford Dictionary of

Architecture

THIRD EDITION

JAMES STEVENS CURL

with line-drawings by the author

and contributions on landscape architecture by
SUSAN WILSON

OXFORD
UNIVERSITY PRESS

OXFORD
UNIVERSITY PRESS

Great Clarendon Street, Oxford, OX2 6DP,
United Kingdom

Oxford University Press is a department of the University of Oxford.
It furthers the University's objective of excellence in research, scholarship,
and education by publishing worldwide. Oxford is a registered trade mark of
Oxford University Press in the UK and in certain other countries

First published as *The Dictionary of Architecture* 1999
First issued as an Oxford University Press paperback 2000
Second edition published 2006
Third edition published as a hardback 2015
Third edition published as an Oxford University Press paperback 2016

Impression: 6

Published in the United States of America by Oxford University Press
198 Madison Avenue, New York, NY 10016, United States of America

British Library Cataloguing in Publication Data
Data available

Library of Congress Control Number: 2015952461

ISBN 978-0-19-967499-2

Printed and bound by
Clays Ltd, St Ives plc

In Memoriam

Stephen Ernest Dykes Bower
18 April 1903–11 November 1994

and

James Edmund Kennedy Esdaile
21 September 1910–18 January 1994

It is the fate of those who toil at the lower employments of life ...
to be exposed to censure, without hope of praise; to be disgraced by
miscarriage, or punished by neglect ...
Among these unhappy mortals is the writer of dictionaries ...
Every other author may aspire to praise; the lexicographer can only hope to
escape reproach.

Samuel Johnson (1709–84): *A Dictionary of the English Language* (1755),
Preface.

Preface to the Second Edition

To make dictionaries is dull work.

Samuel Johnson (1709–84): *A Dictionary of the English Language* (1755), definition no. 8 of 'dull'.

Dictionaries, unlike Athene, do not spring, fully accoutred, from the heads of their begetters. They draw on numerous sources. Although one would not go so far as Dr Johnson in identifying the labour involved as 'dull', his definition of a lexicographer in his own *Dictionary* as a 'writer of dictionaries, a harmless drudge' has struck the occasional chord.

Entries in a dictionary must be succinct, attempt to avoid distortion, and require discipline of a very different kind to the techniques involved in writing more extended narratives. Edmund Burke (1729–97), in his influential *On the Sublime and Beautiful* (1757), observed that he had no 'great opinion of a definition, the celebrated remedy for the cure of... uncertainty and confusion', and Desiderius Erasmus (*c.*1469–1536), in his *Adagia* (1500), went further, declaring that 'every definition is dangerous'. Thomas Hobbes (1588–1679), in *Leviathan* (1651), however, noted that in Geometry (a science closely connected to Architecture, after all) 'men begin at setting the significations of their words, ... which they call Definitions'[1]. Samuel Butler (1835–1902), in *Notebooks* (1912), created more worries when he described a definition as 'the enclosing' of a 'wilderness of idea within a wall of words'[2]. Some quotes concerning dictionaries and definitions, therefore, could easily frighten off the faint-hearted. However, in spite of the caveats, admonitions, and reservations, the present work attempts to define architectural terms and much else, bearing in mind the view of Dr Johnson that 'dictionaries are like watches; the worst is better than none, and the best cannot be expected to run quite true'. Ben Jonson (*c.*1573–1637), in *Volpone* (1606), raised another problem when he described a definition as 'a mere term... invented to awe fools'[3]. One-upmanship, let it be said with firmness, has no place here.

The primary sources for the contents of this *Dictionary* have been personal experience and study of architecture for a working life over more than half a century. As a student, faced with a bewildering and daunting array of unfamiliar words necessary to describe buildings and architectural detail, the author haunted dusty second-hand and antiquarian bookshops (almost all of which have closed), and was fortunate to acquire certain volumes, including the very useful *Glossary of Terms used in Grecian, Roman, Italian, and Gothic Architecture* by John Henry Parker (1806–84) in the 1850 edition, *An Attempt to Discriminate the Styles of Architecture in England* by Thomas Rickman (1776–1841) in Parker's 1848 edition, and *The Principles of Gothic Ecclesiastical Architecture* by Matthew Holbeche Bloxam (1805–88) in the 1882 edition, which helped to establish a familiarity with terms, but, more especially, encouraged an understanding of and an admiration for English medieval ecclesiastical architecture that have never faded or palled. Later acquisitions added to an already vast cornucopia of architectural terminology. Among them may be mentioned *A Dictionary of Architecture* by 'Robert Stuart' (actually Robert Stuart Meikleham [1786–1871]), published in three volumes in London (1832); *Rudimentary Dictionary of Terms used in Architecture*, etc., published in 1849–50 by John Weale (1791–1862), which went into further editions (that of 1860 was a great improvement on the first); *The Carpenter and Joiner's Assistant*, etc. (1880) by James Newlands (1813–71); *A Synopsis of Architecture*, etc. (1826) by Charles Edward Papendiek (1801–35); *An Encylopædia of Architecture, Historical, Theoretical, and Practical*, by Joseph Gwilt (1784–1863), originally published in 1842, in the edition revised by the indefatigable Wyatt Angelicus van Sandau Papworth (1822–94); *An Architectural and Engineering Dictionary*, etc. by Peter Nicholson (1765–1844), in the 1835 edition; *A Treatise on the Decorative Part of Civil Architecture* by Sir William Chambers (1723–96) in the Gwilt Edition of 1825; *A Dictionary of Architecture*, edited by Wyatt Papworth and issued by The Architectural Publication Society between 1852 and 1892; and that extraordinary mine of information, *An Encyclopædia of Cottage, Farm, and Villa Architecture and Furniture* by John Claudius Loudon (1783–1843) in the

[1] Pt. 1, Ch. 4.
[2] Ch. 14.
[3] Act 3, Sc. 7.

1834 edition. These formed the beginnings of the sources on which this dictionary has drawn, but a lifetime spent working with historic buildings and architectural conservation has meant that, of necessity, a comprehensive specialist terminology has been acquired, for ancient fabric, as in churches, cannot be described without access to an appropriate vocabulary and language.

Terms are one thing, biographies another. Judgements have to be made concerning who is to be included on grounds of importance, contributions, quality, and so on. Many personalities (however unattractive) have entries because, by common consent, they are reckoned to be or to have been of significance for good or ill. Others are included because of publications, perhaps a very small but important output in terms of buildings (or unrealized designs), and others for reasons of quality, influence, or other matters. A biography's presence does not mean approval or disapproval by the compiler: it is there because in the author's judgement it has to be. Some may find fault with inclusions or omissions, length or brevity of entries, and, in some instances, failure to join in fashionable choruses of uncritical admiration. No compiler can please everyone, but this dictionary is an attempt to provide as informative a resource as is possible within the parameters set by the publishers. It is hoped that this second and expanded volume, which includes more material on landscape architecture, will prove to be useful. However, anybody familiar with historical research will know that such a work is only a staging-post on an endless journey: errors are inevitable, and the indulgence of those who find any is humbly asked, although it is hoped that intelligence of them will be passed on to the author.

Certain volumes have provided the foundations for the biographical entries. *The Dictionary of National Biography*, the various comparable dictionaries of other countries (e.g. the German *Allgemeines Künstler-Lexikon*, the Danish *Weilbachs Dansk Kunstnerleksikon*, and *Dictionary of American Architects*) have been used. For architects in the British Isles Sir Howard Colvin's definitive *A Biographical Dictionary of British Architects 1600–1840* (1995), John Harvey's *English Mediæval Architects: A Biographical Dictionary down to 1550* (1987), Sarah Bendall's *Dictionary of Land Surveyors and Local Map-Makers of Great Britain and Ireland, 1530–1850* (1997), Rolf Loeber's *A Biographical Dictionary of Architects in Ireland 1600–1720* (1981), A.Stuart Gray's *Edwardian Architecture: A Biographical Dictionary* (1985), Brodie, Felstead, Franklin, Pinfield, and Oldfield's *Dictionary of British Architects 1834–1914* (2001), A.W.Skempton's *A Biographical Dictionary of Civil Engineers in Great Britain and Ireland 1500–1830* (2002), and the many monographs are essential, and these publications have been drawn upon (with acknowledgement) where appropriate. Among other useful volumes are Stanisław Łoza's *Architekci i Budowniczowie w Polsce* (1954), Ray Desmond's *Dictionary of British and Irish Botanists and Horticulturalists including Plant Collectors, Flower Painters, and Garden Designers* (1994), Hadfield, Harling, and Highton's *British Gardeners: A Biographical Dictionary* (1980), Chilvers, Osborne, and Farr's *The Oxford Dictionary of Art* (1988), and Maud Rosinski's *Architects of Nova Scotia: A Biographical Dictionary 1605–1950* (1994). Essential for the overlap between architecture and monuments is Rupert Gunnis's *Dictionary of British Sculptors 1660–1851* (1968). Many articles in the *Macmillan Encylopedia of Architects*, edited by Adolf K.Placzek (1982), are almost short monographs with substantial bibliographies far more comprehensive than can be hoped for in a Concise Dictionary, so readers are referred to this work as Placzek (1982), where the article in question provides information (especially references) impossible to include at any length in the present edition. Other publications, including *Contemporary Architects*, edited by Muriel Emanuel (1980, 1994) and Ann Lee Morgan and Colin Naylor (1987), and *International Dictionary of Architects and Architecture*, edited by Randall J.van Vynckt (1993) contain lists of buildings, bibliographies, and other published matter (including some illustrations) that are more expansive than is possible in the present work. A major source of information on architecture, styles, architects, artists, and so on, came out in 1996 in the form of *The Dictionary of Art*, edited by Jane Shoaf Turner, reprinted with minor corrections in 1998.

Apart from the scholarly books devoted to single individual architects (and they increase in number each year, although it has to be said that some veer perilously close to what might be called 'vanity publishing'), more information has been extracted from many general books. For example, French architects of the eighteenth and nineteenth centuries are discussed in useful works such as Allan Braham's *The Architecture of the French Enlightenment* (1980) and Robin Middleton and David Watkin's *Neoclassical and 19th-Century Architecture* (1987); Italian architecture is well-served by Carroll L.V.Meeks's excellent volume (1996); and an enormous amount of information on German architecture is enshrined in David Watkin and Tilman Mellinghoff's *German Architecture and the Classical Ideal 1740–1840* (1987). However, in many instances entries are based on personal knowledge, or on information kindly provided by individuals. In all cases, sources for biographies are given at the end of each entry, although citations also contain recommendations for further reading intended to guide, rather than indicate the origins of the material.

There are many fine books which are important to any student of the subject. For example, William Bell Dinsmoor's *The Architecture of Greece* (1950) and D.S.Robertson's *Handbook of Greek and Roman*

Architecture (1945) remain useful sources for information on architectural matters from Classical Antiquity. R.W.Brunskill's work on *Vernacular Architecture* (1978) and *Brick Buildings in Britain* (1990) are extremely helpful, crammed with all sorts of fascinating information, although Nathaniel Lloyd's *A History of English Brickwork* (1925) is still a standard (and desirable) volume for any student to have on his or her shelves. Alcock, Barley, Dixon, and Meeson's *Practical Handbook in Archæology No. 5, Recording Timber-Framed Buildings: An Illustrated Glossary*, published by the Council for British Archeology (1996), is invaluable when trying to understand the arcane mysteries of timber-framed structures, and should be read with Brunskill's work to provide a suitable grounding in the topic.

For ornament, many admirable sources exist, but among the best are F.S.Meyer's *A Handbook of Ornament* (1896), A.Speltz's *The Styles of Ornament* (1910), R.Glazier's *A Manual of Historic Ornament* (1926), O.Jones's *The Grammar of Ornament* (1868), and an especially helpful volume, Lewis and Darley's *Dictionary of Ornament* (1986), which contains highly informative and scholarly entries graced with over 1,300 illustrations, and also includes useful biographies of those who influenced the development, use, or invention of ornament.

The Penguin Dictionary of Design and Designers by Simon Jervis (1984) contains biographical notes and essential information about designers. Twentieth century art-historical terms and movements have mushroomed, and it is difficult to determine what permanence, if any, can be assured. Those movements and terms that appear to have had some significance, however short, are included in this *Dictionary*, but entries dealing with them are necessarily brief: fuller accounts of the second half of the twentieth century may be consulted in John A.Walker's *Glossary of Art, Architecture, and Design since 1945* (1992), a thorough and scholarly tome with comprehensive bibliographies for all those who wish to further pursue things. The considerable oeuvre of Charles Jencks also attempts to classify various stylistic and other movements in twentieth-century architecture.

No lexicographer, 'harmless drudge' or otherwise, can afford not to consult the *Oxford English Dictionary*: here the 1933 edition has been used. Other standard foreign-language dictionaries have been involved, including P.G.W.Glare's *Oxford Latin Dictionary* (1985) and Cassell's various dictionaries of European languages. The *Oxford Companion* volumes dealing with *Art*, the *Decorative Arts*, *Christian Art and Architecture*, and *Classical Literature* have proved helpful. Several exhaustive American publications dealing with architectural terms deserve citations for thoroughness of scholarship and fullness of coverage: *Dictionary of Architecture and Construction* (1975), *Illustrated Dictionary of Historic Architecture* (1987), and *American Architecture: An Illustrated Encyclopedia* (1998), all by or edited by Cyril M.Harris, are essential reference books. Ernest Burden's *Illustrated Dictionary of Architecture* (2002) is very useful for its illustrations, although the definitions are perhaps rather excessively condensed. A.L.Osborne's *Dictionary of English Domestic Architecture* (1954) is worth consulting, not least for its handsome illustrations. Glen L.Pride's *Glossary of Scottish Building* (1975), revised and expanded as *Dictionary of Scottish Building* (1996), is essential for terms used in the North.

This *Dictionary* is intended to help the subject of architecture to become more accessible to the general public, but it is also hoped that students and even professionals will turn to it for helpful information. It does not have pretensions to completeness, for that is not possible in a Concise Dictionary, but it does provide a wide range of entries, including biographies of architects and others who have made contributions to architecture, architectural terms, architectural styles, building types, and certain regional and national movements. There are no essays on the architecture of individual countries, for such entries are more suited to an encyclopedia than to a dictionary, and to include such material would have been impossible within the requirements of the publishers. Whilst the scope of the *Dictionary* has been restricted to Europe, the British Isles, the United States of America, Canada, Australia, and Latin America, aspects of the subject associated with the Indian subcontinent, the Near and Far East, and former Colonial architecture are included when deemed necessary. In particular, those influences on exoticism (Buddhism, China, India, Islam, and Japan) in Western architecture are mentioned, although no attempt has been made to include the vast terminology of Chinese and Japanese architecture that would itself fill volumes. The inclusion of some architects from Japan and elsewhere needs explanation: those who are listed have made an acknowledged contribution to the increasingly international nature of architecture, and their work has been perceived as influential. Essential information on Islamic architecture is included, for obvious reasons. Illustrations are provided where appropriate, for pictures can do so much more than words to clarify meaning.

During the preparation of the first edition, patient and good humoured guidance was provided by Mr Angus Phillips, Senior Commissioning Editor, Trade Books, of Oxford University Press. Similar help was forthcoming from Miss Ruth Langley, Commissioning Editor, when the second edition was on the stocks, and thanks are also due to Miss Carol Alexander, Mr Ben Denne, Mr Richard Lawrence, and Mr John Mackrell for all their sterling work, much of which must have been exceedingly tedious.

When the project was first mooted in 1992, it was intended that the author's former colleague, collaborator, and friend, Mr John Sambrook (1933–2001), should prepare the line-drawings, but, in the event, he was only able to produce a portion of what was required. So, in order to give greater homogeneity to the appearance of the edition, all Mr Sambrook's drawings have been superseded by new ones by the author, several of whose original drawings have also been replaced, and many additional images have also been prepared. Where drawings are based on the work of others, this is acknowledged in the captions: *after Parker*, for example, means that drawings are by the author, based on J.H.Parker's *Glossary* in the 1850 edition, *after JJS* acknowledges that the illustration is based on a drawing by the late Mr Sambrook, and *after Normand* indicates that the author's drawing is based on Charles Normand's *Parallèle* of 1852. In a few instances, Mr Sambrook's drawings in the first edition have been used as the basis for new illustrations (and the fact acknowledged), but in very many cases the illustrations are based on the author's own observations and sketches. Mr Sambrook also made several useful suggestions relating to items included in the *Dictionary*, and that help is gratefully remembered: his early death is deeply regretted.

For the first edition, Mr Ashley Barker, Professor Charles MacCallum, the late Professor Newton Watson, and Professor Michael Welbank gave welcome support. Financial assistance towards the costs of research and preparation was given by a Royal Institute of British Architects Research Award made in 1993 which continued until the end of 1996: the author expresses his gratitude to the RIBA Historical Research Trust for helping to fund the project. Further financial assistance came in the form of a Small Personal Research Grant from The British Academy, and grants from The Worshipful Company of Tylers and Bricklayers and The Worshipful Company of Chartered Architects: to The British Academy and to those two Livery Companies of the City of London warmest thanks is extended. Mr Mark Le Fanu and Mr Gareth Shannon of The Society of Authors courteously assisted in many ways, as did Miss Ingrid Curl, District Judge Ronald Dudley, Fru Lisbeth Ehlers, Lady Freeman, Dr Timothy Mowl, Mr John Simpson, Mrs Jane Thorniley-Walker of The Council for British Archaeology, and Professor David Watkin. For the second edition, The Authors' Foundation, Society of Authors, provided a welcome and timely grant, which is gratefully acknowledged. More financial help was given by The Worshipful Company of Chartered Architects.

The compiler of a dictionary such as this incurs many other obligations, not least to his sources. However, he is also indebted to fellow-scholars (who helped with suggestions, information, and in other ways), archivists, librarians, and many other people. Use has been made of various libraries, including The Bodleian Library of the University of Oxford, The British Library, The RIBA Library, and The Perne Library of Peterhouse, University of Cambridge. A considerable debt is owed to the staffs of all those great collections, and especial thanks are due to Mrs Karen Latimer and Mr Dan Holden, of the Library of The Queen's University of Belfast, who were immensely helpful in tracking down elusive bibliographical information. Mrs Ann Perry and Mrs Mary Weston, formerly of the Kimberlin Library, De Montfort University, Leicester, also rendered valuable assistance, and Mr Lucas Elkin of Cambridge University Library patiently put up with, and answered, many queries, as did Miss Rose Marney and Mrs Carol Morgan of the Institution of Civil Engineers Library, London. Mr Simon Edwards, Mrs Anna Gagliano, Mr Malcolm Green, Miss Dawn Humm, Miss Claudia Mernick, Mr Paul Nash, Miss Jane Oldfield, Mr Richard Reed, Mr Trevor Todd, Miss Helen Wade, and Miss Karen Wilman, all of whom work or worked at the RIBA, obtained much valuable material. Professor Gavin Stamp most generously lent his notes on various architects, and granted permission to use them, an act of a true friend and colleague. Professors Peter Swallow, David Walker, and Richard Weston made many thoughtful and immensely helpful suggestions, as did Dr R.W.Brunskill, Lady Freeman, and Mevr Petra Maclot (who very kindly and generously provided comprehensive notes which were of great assistance), so have the author's gratitude: Lady Freeman, Mevr Maclot, Professor Stamp, and Professor Weston even generously drafted some outlines for entries. Among many others who assisted in various ways, Dr N.W. Alcock, Mr Victor Belcher, Mr Peter Bezodis, Mr Eric Cartwright, Sir Howard Colvin, the Reverend James Douglas, Frau Eva Eissmann, Mr John Fisher, Mr John Greenacombe, Mr Paul Grinke, Mr Ralph Hyde, Mr Ian Johnson, Herr Dr Georg Friedrich Kempter, Mr Joseph Kilner, Dr Karin Kryger, Professor Stanisław Mossakowski, Mr Stephen Oliver, Mr Warwick Pethers, Mr Richard Sidwell, Professor Georg Graf zu Solms, the late Sir John Summerson, and Mr Henry Vivian-Neal, deserve mention and are thanked for individual acts of kindness. Mrs Margaret Reed, of Starword, heroically prepared the typescripts and disks, and her sterling work is hereby acknowledged.

In the *Dictionary* there are references by author and date at the end of most entries: some of these references are given to guide those wishing to delve further, while others refer to sources, or to material connected with the entry in some other way. All items are listed alphabetically by journal name or surname. As far as names are concerned, surnames including 'de', 'du', 'Le', 'van', 'von', etc., are given under the main name: de Soissons is placed under S, Le Corbusier under C, and von Klenze under K, for the same reason that no reasonable person would ever expect to see the Duke of Buckingham under O. Further information on using these references is provided in the following notes on abbreviations.

Work on the second edition began during residence at Peterhouse, University of Cambridge, where the author was Visiting Fellow from January to June 2002. Thanks are due to the Master, Fellows, and Governing Body of that College, and an appreciation of the many kindnesses of the Fellows who became friends and of the College staff who made the period of residence so agreeable is here recorded.

Finally, the *Dictionary* is dedicated to the memory of Stephen Dykes Bower and Edmund Esdaile, who corresponded with the author for more than a quarter of a century, and who loved architecture, words, and the English language. The many happy hours spent in their company are remembered with a mixture of pleasure in their recollection and sadness that they cannot be repeated.

J. S. C.

Burley-on-the-Hill, Rutland; Peterhouse, Cambridge; and Holywood, Co. Down
1993–2005

Preface to the Third Edition

And let a scholar all Earth's volumes carry,
He will be but a walking Dictionary.

George Chapman (1559/60–1634): *The Tears of Peace* (1609), l. 530.

New editions (and this *Dictionary* is far more than that) require new Prefaces, although the Preface to the previous edition still stands and is also presented here. Six decades studying real architecture (rather than what is too often miscalled by that term) and working with old buildings have driven home the fact that modern architectural education does not equip students for any interventions concerning existing fabric, be it of individual historic structures or established urban patterns: the *tabula rasa* is assumed or made, and designs pay no heed whatsoever to context. Architecture is probably one of the most politicized of professions, and, regrettably, one not strong in terms of intellectual content. Too often bullying and shouting have replaced rational argument (though the bullies and shouters ludicrously claim affinities with 'objectivity' and 'rationalism'): the rot seems to have set in during the C19 when 'moral' arguments were used to enforce the adoption of architectural styles, and similar techniques were employed by devotees of International Modernism to insist that a limited set of *clichés* was universally embraced, but those *clichés* never added up to a *vocabulary*, let alone a coherent *language* of architecture.

The first edition of this *Dictionary* (1999) was centred on architecture, and the second (2006) included material on landscape architecture, although the emphasis on architecture remained. This third edition differs from the previous two. First of all, a decision was taken not to include individual biographies of living persons (though some are mentioned in relation to movements/style/building-types where appropriate) because many modern practices are huge, and any attempted entry is obsolete as soon as it is written (let alone published), and, furthermore, it is impossible to form rounded judgements about somebody's life's work before it is complete. Second, it was recognized that the imbalance between architecture and landscape architecture (highlighted when a thematic key was constructed) had to be addressed; there are now many more entries on landscape than in earlier editions.

Oxford University Press's requirements to electronically track revisions and account for words (added, deleted, or revised) exposed the need for a collaborator. Following a constructive meeting in convivial surroundings with Ms Judith Wilson, Commissioning Editor at OUP, in January 2012, when the author was attending a conference at St Hugh's College, Oxford, it was agreed to omit specific entries on living persons and strengthen the historical content (not just with terms, but biographies of architects and landscape architects). Later, over dinner at St Hugh's, the author was fortunate to meet Dr Susan Wilson, landscape-historian, and possibilities of some sort of collaboration were discussed, followed up by several months of correspondence, then a meeting in the summer, and a fortnight of preliminary work together to test the waters, as it were. Collaboration began in earnest in October 2012, with many months of intensive work lasting as much as twelve hours a day, six days a week (and sometimes seven): the bulk of the task was completed by the end of March 2014. The complicated business of the Excel sheets (including categories, word-counts, etc.), was handled by Dr Wilson, but Mr Richard Golding also rendered generous help, sorting out problems with his accountant's skills: he is gratefully thanked for all his efforts.

The new edition, therefore, has been greatly expanded to include almost 1,000 new entries, 50% of which are related to landscape, and for this transformation a mighty debt is owed to Dr Wilson, who not only researched and prepared many articles on landscape architects, architecture, and gardens, but organized a vast amount of material relating to the Excel sheets, thematic keys (applied to the primary activity or discipline of the topic/subject), and word-counts: the author could not have had a more dedicated collaborator and friend, whose devotion to what has proved to be a daunting task has been exemplary. She has the compiler's gratitude for her many contributions, reliability, many suggestions, and support, unstintingly given. Her name, deservedly, now graces the title-page. Thus this volume contains much more information on landscape (ideas, people, styles, and terms), and many more entries on historical architecture are included, replacing biographies of living practitioners. This should prove useful for those involved in assessment, study, practice, conservation, and preservation in both disciplines, and for others interested in architecture and landscape in general. Illustrations are provided when appropriate, for pictures can do so much more than words to clarify matters. All drawings are by the author, and some new drawings, also by him, have been added.

A word of warning is necessary about sections on 'architects': in the Middle Ages many master-masons were actually architects, and until the C19 architects were skilled in surveying, and several were structurally inventive, so were also engineers. Compartmentalization of expertise is therefore comparatively recent, for many 'engineers' and 'surveyors' also had architectural knowledge and ability: even the official positions of 'Surveyor' to London Livery Companies or the City of London were filled by persons skilled in architecture. Similarly, the term 'landscape architect' includes garden-designers, gardeners, horticulturalists, etc., given that it is of relatively recent general acceptance.

In addition to the sources mentioned in the earlier Preface, Colvin's *Biographical Dictionary* in its 2008 manifestation has been invaluable, and other works consulted include *A Dictionary of Architecture and Building: Biographical Historical, and Descriptive* by Russell Sturgis (1836-1909) published by Macmillan (1901-2); Brendan O Donoghue's *The Irish County Surveyors 1834-1944* (2007); the companion-volume to Skempton's *Biographical Dictionary of Civil Engineers* for the period 1830-90, edited by P.S.M.Cross-Rudkin *et al.* (2008); the excellent online *Dictionaries* of *Scottish Architects* and *Irish Architects 1720-1840*; *A Biographical Dictionary of Sculptors in Britain 1660-1851* edited by Ingrid Roscoe *et al.* (2009), based on Rupert Gunnis's *Dictionary of British Sculptors 1660-1851* (1968); *The Oxford Companion to the Garden*, edited by Patrick Taylor (2006); *Pioneers of American Landscape Design*, edited by Charles A.Birnbaum and Robin Karson (2000); *Shaping the American Landscape*, edited by Charles A.Birnbaum and Stephanie S.Foell (2009); *Chicago Botanic Garden Encyclopedia of Gardens: History and Design*, edited by Candice A.Shoemaker (2001); *Encyclopedia of 20th-Century Architecture*, edited by R.Stephen Sennott (2004); *Bouwkundige Termen: Verklarend woordenboek van de westerse architectuur—en bouwhistorie*, edited by E.J.Haslinghuis and H.Janse (2005—which gives Dutch, English, and German equivalents); Edward Cresy's enormous and staggeringly full *An Encyclopaedia of Civil Engineering, Historical, Theoretical, and Practical* (1861); the *Oxford Dictionary of National Biography* (2004—with later online updates); *Dictionary of Irish Biography* (2009); Jane Loudon's updated versions of J.C.Loudon's *Encyclopaedia of Cottage, Farm, and Villa Architecture* (from 1846); and last, but not least, Loudon's massive *Encyclopaedia of Gardening* (1835). Other sources consulted are listed in the Bibliography. However, the compiler and his collaborator are aware that the amount of material available on architecture and architects is enormous compared with that for landscape architecture and landscape architects (a trawl through the bibliography of the present work shows this very clearly), and suggest that a comprehensive dictionary of landscape architects/architecture is something that is sorely needed.

From April 2013 the author was appointed Professor at the Department of Architecture and Design, University of Ulster. Thanks are due to Professor Peter Walker, Head of the Department, for his understanding of the time needed to carry out the work on the new edition: the appointment enabled Dr Wilson to be retained as research assistant, without whose input the Dictionary could not have taken its present form, so the author records here his gratitude to Professor Walker for helping to ease the creative processes.

For the third edition Ms Judith Wilson, Mr Jamie Crowther (Assistant Commissioning Editor), and Ms Abigail Humphries Robertson of Oxford University Press have provided speedy, courteous help and encouragement, and are warmly thanked for their patience, help, and understanding. The Worshipful Company of Chartered Architects made a small personal grant available, and this is acknowledged with thanks. In addition to individuals mentioned in this and the previous Preface, the following have given generously of their time, advice, and general support, all much appreciated: Dr Tatiana Abramzon helped with matters Russian; Dr Timothy Brittain-Catlin was of assistance over several points; Mr Lucas Elkin of Cambridge University Library helped to find elusive bibliographical information; the author's wife, Professor Dorota Iwaniec, tolerated late meals (which she kindly provided), and, realizing that time was limited and long periods of concentrated work were necessary, created conditions that hugely eased pressures; Professor Gavin Stamp suggested additions and generously provided notes; the Reverend Anthony Symondson SJ kindly made suggestions concerning Dykes Bower; Mr Trevor Todd took the trouble to supply lists of omissions which he felt should be made good, and these were all taken on board and implemented; and Professor David Walker once again came up with very helpful comments in writing.

Some words are necessary concerning the arrangement of the *Dictionary*. When an entry incorporates a term defined in its own right, this is indicated by an asterisk before the term at its first mention (e.g. *spandrel in the entry for **apron**). However, a rigorous adherence to this system would involve too many asterisks in an entry and thus make it difficult (and irritating) to read. The commonest terms (e.g. **arch, architect, architecture, brick, cathedral, chapel, church, column, door, garden, hall, house,**

landscape, monument, park, roof, theatre, tomb, tower, walk, wall, and **window**) are only cross-referenced where it is considered helpful for the reader to turn to those specific entries. *Italics* are used to draw attention to alternative names or otherwise employed for clarity. In instances where a term has more than one meaning each has been prefixed by a number in **bold** type (**1.**, **2.**, **3.**, etc.), with the most usual meaning given first, and the least usual given last: in some cases, however, the numbering has no particular significance, as where two or more meanings carry equal weight.

The compiler and his collaborator embrace the idea that the intellectual content of the *Dictionary* might be made available through other contemporary means, in addition to the online version currently offered in parallel to the printed book itself.

Finally, the *Dictionary*'s Dedication to two remarkable men remains unchanged: memories of them both are undimmed.

J. S. C.

Holywood, Co. Down
2012–14

Contents

Notes on Abbreviations

States in the USA

For States in the United States of America, the abbreviations follow the standard American usage rather than the old-fashioned forms (e.g. MA instead of the archaic Mass., CT instead of Conn.):

AL	Alabama	MT	Montana
AK	Alaska	NE	Nebraska
AZ	Arizona	NV	Nevada
AR	Arkansas	NH	New Hampshire
CA	California	NJ	New Jersey
CO	Colorado	NM	New Mexico
CT	Connecticut	NY	New York
DE	Delaware	NC	North Carolina
DC	District of Columbia	ND	North Dakota
FL	Florida	OH	Ohio
GA	Georgia	OK	Oklahoma
HI	Hawaii	OR	Oregon
ID	Idaho	PA	Pennsylvania
IL	Illinois	RI	Rhode Island
IN	Indiana	SC	South Carolina
IA	Iowa	SD	South Dakota
KS	Kansas	TN	Tennessee
KY	Kentucky	TX	Texas
LA	Louisiana	UT	Utah
ME	Maine	VT	Vermont
MD	Maryland	VA	Virginia
MA	Massachusetts	WA	Washington
MI	Michigan	WV	West Virginia
MN	Minnesota	WI	Wisconsin
MS	Mississippi	WY	Wyoming
MO	Missouri		

English Counties

Abbreviations of English counties are given thus:

Beds.	Bedfordshire	Essex	Unabbreviated
Berks.	Royal County of Berkshire	Glos.	Gloucestershire
Bucks.	Buckinghamshire	Hants.	Hampshire (includes Isle of Wight, but the Isle (IoW) is given separately for clarity)
Cambs.	Cambridgeshire		
Ches.	Cheshire		
Cornwall	Unabbreviated	Herefs.	Herefordshire
Cumb.	Cumberland	Herts.	Hertfordshire
Derbys.	Derbyshire	Hunts.	Huntingdonshire (now absorbed by Cambridgeshire)
Devon	Unabbreviated, but formerly was called Devonshire		
		Kent	Unabbreviated
Dorset	Unabbreviated	Lancs.	Lancashire
Durham	Co. Durham	Leics.	Leicestershire

Lincs.	Lincolnshire	Staffs.	Staffordshire
Mddx.	Middlesex	Suffolk	Unabbreviated
Norfolk	Unabbreviated	Surrey	Unabbreviated
Northants.	Northamptonshire	Sussex	Unabbreviated
Northum.	Northumberland	Warwicks.	Warwickshire
Notts.	Nottinghamshire	Westmd.	Westmorland
Oxon.	Oxfordshire	Wilts.	Wiltshire
Rut.	Rutland, formerly Rutlandshire	Worcs.	Worcestershire
Salop.	Shropshire	Yorks.	Yorkshire
Som.	Somerset		

Other abbreviations

Please note that the bibliographies at the end of entries suggest further reading by giving author names and the publication date of the relevant work. Some author's surnames have been shortened to abbreviations, which are listed here (for an expanded list of these authors and works, please see the select bibliography online: http://www.oxfordreference.com/page/architect). Where two authors in this bibliography share the same surname, then an initial is included in the reference at the end of the entry. If there is more than one author with the same initial and same surname, then more than one initial, part of the first name, or a full first name have been given to aid identification. A reference (for example 'J.T') may sometimes therefore refer to an abbreviated surname ('T' for Turner) and then give an extra initial 'J.' to indicate that this is Jane Shoaf Turner rather than Paul Venable Turner.

Other abbreviations used in texts and references are:

A	Amsoneit	AHe	*Architectural Heritage*
A	*L'Architecture*	AHR	*American Historical Review*
AA	Architectural Association	AIA	American Institute of Architects
A & A	*Art and Architecture* or *Arts and Architecture*	AJ	*Architects' Journal*
		aka	also known as
AAAB	*American Association of Architectural Bibliographers*	ALA	American Landscape Architect
		AM	*Arquitectura México*
AAF	*Archives de l'Art Français*	AmA	American Architect
AAJ	*Architectural Association Journal*	An	Ackerman
AAM	*Archives d'Architecture Moderne*	A & O	Auty & Oblensky (eds)
AAQ	*Architectural Association Quarterly*	AQC	*Ars Quatuor Coronatorum*
Ab	Abercrombie	*A.QJBS*	*Albion: A Quarterly Journal Concerned with British Studies*
AB	*Art Bulletin*		
A & B	Andersson & Bedoire	AR	*Architectural Review*
ABDM	Alcock, Barley, Dixon, & Meeson	Ar & Bi	Arnell & Bickford (eds)
ABN	*The Architect & Building News*	Arch.	Architect or Architectural
ABSA	*Annual of the British School at Athens*	ARe	*Architectural Record*
		ArtH	*Art History*
ACGB	Arts Council of Great Britain	ASLA	American Society of Landscape Architects
AD	Anno Domini (In the Year of (Our) Lord), i.e. any year since the reputed birth of Christ (actually c.4BC) from AD 1 onwards		
		Assn.	Association
		ATSN	*Alexander Thomson Society Newsletter*
AD	*Architectural Design*	AulV	Architekten und Ingenieur-Verein
Ad'A	*L'architecture d'aujourd'hui*	A & U	*Architecture and Urbanism*
ADB	*Australian Dictionary of Biography* <http://adb.anu.edu.au/>	A & W	Atterbury & Wainwright
		AYB	*Architects' Year Book*
AdK	Akademie der Künste	B	*Builder*
Ae	Allibone	B	Braham
AF	*Architectural Forum*	B et al.	Brodie, Felstead, Franklin, Pinfield, & Oldfield
AH	*Architectural History* (Journal of the Society of Architectural Historians of Great Britain)	BA	*British Architect*
		Ba	Banham

Bad	Badovici
Bae	Baedeker
BaLa	Badisches Landesmuseum
B-B	Bush-Brown
B & B	Blair & Bloom
B.C.	British Columbia
BC	Before Christ, i.e. the years before AD 1
B-C	Brittain-Catlin or information kindly provided by Timothy B-C
B & C	Bond & Camm
BD	*Building Design*
Be	Berckenhagen
Ben	Benevolo
B & F	Birnbaum & Foell (eds)
B & G	Borsi & Godoli
B-H	Bohle-Heintzenberg
BJ	Blundell Jones
B-J	Bence-Jones
B & K	Birnbaum & Karson (eds)
BL	The British Library
Bl & Ro	Bletter & Robinson
BM	British Museum
B-M	Brown-Manrique
B & M	Baldon & Melchior
BN	Bassegoda Nonell
BN	*Building News*
Bo	Bognar
BoE	*Buildings of England Series*
Boh	Bohigas
BoI	*Buildings of Ireland Series*
BoS	*Buildings of Scotland Series*
Bou	Bourke
BoW	*Buildings of Wales Series*
Br	Blaser
B & R	Bindmann & Riemann
Bru	Brunskill
B-S	Börsch-Supan
BSP	Borisova, Sternin, & Palmin
BSHAF	*Bulletin de la Société de l'histoire de l'art français*
Bt	Blunt
Bu	Buchanan
BuMa	*Burlington Magazine*
B & V	Bentivoglio & Valtieri
BW	*Building World*
B + W	*Bauen + Wohnen*
B & W-P	Boëthius & Ward-Perkins
By	*Byggmästeren*
C	Century, so C20 = twentieth century
c.	*circa*
Ca	Caldenby *et al.*
CBA	By permission of the Council for British Archaeology
C & C	Collins & Collins
CCS	Cambridge Camden Society
Cd'ÉSdlR	Centre d'Études Supérieures de la Renaissance
CdSAÉ	Commisson des Sciences et Arts d'Égypte

C-E	Coudenhove-Erthal
CFRS	Information kindly provided by Herr Christoph Fischer and Frau Renate Schein
CG	Chueca Goitia
C & G	Chastel & Guillaume
Ck	Cruickshank *or* Cruickshank (ed.)
CL	*Country Life*
CLA	*Country Life Annual*
Cm	Cunningham
CM	Information kindly provided by Miss Claudia Mernick of the RIBA
C & M	Conrads & Marschall
Co	Colvin
CoE	Council of Europe
COF	Chilvers, Osborne, & Farr (eds)
C & P	Crook & Port
C-R	Cross-Rudkin *et al.* (eds)
C & R	Casey & Rowan
C & S	Conrads & Sperlich
Ct	Condit
C-T	Clifton-Taylor
Cu	Curtis
D	Dinsmoor
DAB	*Dictionary of American Biography*
DB	*Deutsche Bauzeitung*
DBI	*Dizionario biografico degli italiani*
DdA	Dézallier d'Argenville
D & E	Desmond & Ellwood
De	Debenedetti
Di	Diamonstein (ed.)
DIA	*Dictionary of Irish Architects 1720–1840* <http://www.dia.ie/>
DIB	*Dictionary of Irish Biography*
DK	*Dekorative Kunst*
DKuD	*Deutsche Kunst und Dekoration*
DKuDe	*Deutsche Kunst und Denkmalpflege*
D & M	Dixon & Muthesius
Do	Doumato
D & P	Danesi & Patetta (eds)
DQ	*Design Quarterly*
Dr	Drexler
D & S	Downing & Scully
DSA	*Dictionary of Scottish Architects* <http://www.scottisharchitects.org.uk/>
DW	*Das Werk*
DW	Information kindly provided by Professor David Walker
E	Emanuel (ed.)
Ea	Eastlake
EB	*Encyclopaedia Britannica*
ed., eds	editor, editors
edn	edition
EH	English Heritage
EHThe	English Heritage Thesauri <http://thesaurus.english-heritage.org.uk/>
É & J	Éri & Jobbágyi
EM	*Engineering Magazine*
E & P	Elliott & Pritchard (eds)

esp.	especially
F	Frampton
FA	Information kindly provided by Dr Frank Albo
FdA	Fagiolo dell'Arco
FdA & C	Fagiolo dell'Arco & Carandini
Fe	Feuchtmüller
F & C	Fransen & Cook
F & H	Fischer & Höpfner
FHL	Fraser, Hibbard, & Lewine (eds)
fl.	*floruit* = flourished
FL	Flores Lopez
Fr	Frommel
FR	Fraser Reekie
F & S	Fröhlich & Sperlich
F & T	Fiore & Tafuri (eds)
Fu	Futagawa (ed.)
G	Germann
Ga	Gallet
G & B	Gloag & Bridgwater
Gd	Girouard
GdBA	*Gazette des Beaux-Arts*
G & D	Gelder & Duverger (eds)
G & G	Gayle & Gillon
GGJ	*The Georgian Group Journal*
Gh	Greenhalgh (ed.)
GH	*Garden History* (Journal of the Garden History Society, not to be confused with the *Journal of Garden History* (*JGH*))
Gi	Grodecki
G & I	Gubotosi & Izzo (eds)
GJ & L	Gomme, Jenner, & Little
GLC	Greater London Council
GM	Geffrye Museum
GMcW & W	Gifford, McWilliam, & Walker
Gn	Giedion
G-R	Goodhart-Rendel
GS	Information kindly provided by Professor Gavin Stamp
G & TK	Gerson & Ter Kuile
gv	Gardenvisit.com, The Garden and Landscape Guide <http://www.gardenvisit.com/>
Gw	Gwilt
G & W	Gomme & Walker
H	Hamilton
Ha	Hautecœur
Hd	Hibbard
He	Heydenreich
HHH	Hadfield, Harling, & Highton
H & H	Hennebo & Hoffmann
H & H	*House & Home*
HHS	Hart, Henn, & Sontag
Hi	Hitchcock
H & J	Haslinghuis & Janse (eds)
H & K	Haiko & Krimmel
Hl & Su	Howell & Sutton (eds)
H & M	Headley & Meulenkamp
Hn	Herrmann
Ho	Hoffmann
H-O	Horn-Oncken
H & P	Hegemann & Peets
HPZ	Humbert, Pantazzi, & Ziegler
Hr	Hilbersheimer
Hs	Harris
H & S	Hornblower & Spawforth
Hs & T	Harris & Tait
Ht	Hazlehurst
Hu & Sch	Hubala & Schweikhart (eds)
H & W	Hunt & Willis (eds)
IA	*Irish Architect*
IAR(Y)	*Irish Arts Review (Yearbook)*
ID	*Industrial Design*
IGSB	*Irish Georgian Society Bulletin*
Inst.	Institute or Institution
Inst. CA	Institute of Classical Architecture
intr.	introduction
IoM	Isle of Man
IoW	Isle of Wight
ISR	*Interdisciplinary Science Reviews*
IV	*L'illustrazione vaticana*
J	Jodidio
J.	*Journal*
JAIA	*Journal of the American Institute of Architects*
JAIP	*Journal of the American Institute of Planners*
JAPA	*Journal of the American Planning Association*
JARCE	*Journal of the American Research Center in Egypt*
J & C	Jensen & Conway
JD	Information kindly provided by The Reverend James Douglas
Je	Joedicke
JF	Information kindly provided by Lady Freeman
J-G	Jeanneret-Gris
JGH	*Journal of Garden History* (not to be confused with *Garden History* (*GH*))
JIGS	*Journal of the Irish Georgian Society*
JJS	After a drawing by the late John Sambrook
JK	Information kindly provided by the late Mr Joseph Kilner
JRAIC	*Journal of the Royal Architectural Institute of Canada*
JRSA	*Journal of the Royal Society of Arts*
JRSUA	*Journal of the Royal Society of Ulster Architects*
JRWAHS	*Journal of the Royal Western Australian Historical Society*
Js	Jencks
JSAH	*Journal of the Society of Architectural Historians* (American, not to be confused with *Architectural History* (British (*AH*))

J.T	Jane Turner (ed.) (1996). If given as J.T (2013) it signifies the online version (post-1996) <http://www.oxfordartonline.com/>
JUH	*Journal of Urban History*
Jun.	junior
J & W	Johnson & Wigley
JWCI	*Journal of the Warburg and Courtauld Institutes*
K	Kalman
Ka	Kaufmann
K & B	Kurtz & Boardman
K-C	Kentgens-Craig
KiDR	*Kunst im Deutschen Reich*
KK	Information kindly provided by Dr Karin Kryger
K & K	Kunst & Künstler
K-K	Kamm-Kyburz
K & L	Kalnein & Levey
K-M	Khan-Magomedov
Ko	Kobayashi *et al.*
K-PO-B	Königlich-Preussischen Ober-Baudeputation (ed.)
Kr	Kreytenberg
K-R & F	Kahn-Rossi & Franciolli
Kra	Krautheimer
Ks	Koulermos
K-S	Kidder-Smith
K & S	Kubler & Soria
Ku	Kurokawa
Kz	Karpowicz
L	Lampugnani (ed.)
LA	*Landscape Architecture*
La	Lawrence
L & C	Lindsay & Cosh
LCC	London County Council
Lb & D	Lieb & Dieth
LD	*Landscape Design*
L-D	Landale-Drummond
L & D	Lewis & Darley
Le	Leatherbarrow
LeG & S	LeGates & Stout (eds)
L & G	Leuthäuser & Gössel (eds)
L & H	Lever & Harris
LH & A	*Lincolnshire History and Archaeology*
Li	Leśnikowski (ed.)
L & M	Lloyd & Müller
Ln	Lieberman
L & R	Lorentz & Rottermund
L-S	Lévi-Strauss
Ly	Lissitzky
M	Muthesius
Ma	Malave
MacD	MacDonald
MacG & R	MacGibbon & Ross
McP	McParland
MacR & A	MacRea & Adamson
MfBuS	*Monatshefte für Baukunst und Städtebau*
mag.	magazine
MC	Information kindly provided by the late Mr Martin Charles
M & C	Morselli & Corti
McK	Information kindly provided by the late Mr Robert McKinstry
Me	Mezzanotte
M & E	Mowl & Earnshaw
MFOKGC	*Magazine of the Friends of Kensal Green Cemetery*
M & G	Miller & Gray
MGA	Mitchell Giurgola Architects
Mi	Millech
M & M	Maguire & Murray
MM & T	Moore, Mitchell, & Turnbull
MM & Wa	Montgomery-Massingberd & Watkin
M & N	Morgan & Naylor (eds)
Mr	Meyhöfer
M & P	Michel & Pasricha
M & R	Mosser & Rabreau
Ms	Meeks
M & T	Mosser & Teyssot (eds)
Mu	Murray
M.W	Information kindly provided by Mr Min (W. G. M.) Wood
M & Wa	Middleton & Watkin
Mx	Maxwell
My	Macartney
N	Nicholson
Nat.	National
NDB	*Neue Deutsche Biographie*
Ne	Nerdinger (ed.)
Nn	Neumann
N & R	Nicolin & Repishti
NRO	Northumberland County Record Office
n.s.	new series
N-S	Norberg-Schulz
NSW	New South Wales (AU)
NUHG	*Newsletter of the Urban History Group*
NY	New York State
NYC	New York City
NYRB	*The New York Review of Books*
O	Osborne (ed.)
OAO	*Oxford Art Online* <http://www.oxfordartonline.com/>
ODNB	*Oxford Dictionary of National Biography* (2004). If given as *ODNB* (2013) it signifies the online version <http://www.oxforddnb.com/>
OED	*Oxford English Dictionary*
On	Oechslin
ÖZK & D	*Österreichische Zeitschrift für Kunst und Denkmalpflege*
P	Placzek (ed.)
PA	*Progressive Architecture*
Pa	Papworth

PAIA	*Proceedings of the American Institute of Architects*
Pa & Pl	Parreaux & Plaisant (eds)
P & D	Physick & Darby
PdM	Pérouse de Montclos
Pe	Pevsner *or* Pevsner (ed.)
Perp.	Perpendicular
p & g	Parks and Gardens UK <http://www.parksandgardens.org/>
P-H	Pope-Hennessy
Pi	Portoghesi
P & J	Pierson & Jordy
P:JRSUA	*Perspective: Journal of the Royal Society of Ulster Architects*
Pk *or* pk	personal knowledge
PM	Information kindly provided by Mevr Petra Maclot
P & M	Pearson & Meeson (eds)
Pn	Paavilainen (ed.)
PN	Information kindly provided by Mr Paul Nash of the RIBA
Po	Powers
PoA	*Perspectives on Architecture*
Poly	Polytechnic
P & P	Paatz & Paatz
PPR	Information kindly provided by Dr Pamela Pomerance Steiner
Pe & R	Pevsner & Richards (eds)
Proc.	Proceedings
Prof	Professor
PS	Information kindly provided by Professor Peter Swallow
PSR	*Prairie School Review*
P & V	Parent & Verroust
P & W	Papadakis & Watson (eds)
Q	Quantrill
QBIGS	*Quarterly Bulletin of The Irish Georgian Society*
QdQ	Quatremère de Quincy
QUB	The Queen's University of Belfast
R	Robertson
r.	reigned
RA	Royal Academy
RAM	*after* R.A.Meeson
RC	Roman Catholic
r.c.	reinforced concrete
RdP	Ruffinière du Prey
REB	Rogers, Eustis, & Bidwell
RfK	*Repertorium für Kunstwissenschaft*
Ri	Richards
RIASQ	*Royal Incorporation of Architects in Scotland Quarterly*
RIBA	Royal Institute of British Architects
RIBAJ	*RIBA Journal* (Journal of the Royal Institute of British Architects)
RJfK	*Römisches Jahrbüch für Kunstgeschichte*
R & K	Rowe & Koetter
R & L	Romero & Larkin
Rn	Richardson
Ro	Rossi
R & R	Robertson & Robertson
RSTK	Rosenberg, Slive, & Ter Kuile
RUA	*Revue Universelle des Arts*
RW	Information kindly provided by Professor Richard Weston
Ry	Rykwert
Ry & Ry	Rykwert & Rykwert
S	Sturgis *et al. or* Sturgis
SAAR	*South African Architectural Review*
SAR	*Scottish Art Review*
S & B	Steinmann & Boga (eds)
SBL	*Svenska Biografiskt Leksikon*
Se	Service
Sen.	senior
Sg	Singelenberg
Sh	Sheppard (ed.)
Shoe	Shoemaker (ed.)
Shv	Shvidkovsky
Sk	Skempton *et al.* (eds)
S & M	Shinohara & Matsunaga
Sn	Smithson
Soc.	Society
SoD	Society of Dilettanti
Sp	Spence
Sr	Schumacher
SS	Saumarez Smith
S & R	Stuart & Revett
S & S	Sky & Stone
St	Stanton
Su	Summerson *or* Summerson (ed.)
Sw	Swenarton
Sy	Scully
T	Turner (J.T= Jane Shoaf Turner (ed.))
Ta	Tavernor
T & B	Thieme & Becker
T & DC	Tafuri & Dal Co
Tay	P.Taylor (ed.)
Tg	Trachtenberg
THB	Information kindly provided by Mr Thomas Hall Beeby
THI	Tinley, Humphreys, & Irving
T-M	Tschudi-Madsen
TPR	*Town Planning Review*
tr.	translator *or* translated by
Trans.	*Transactions*
UA	*Ulster Architect*
UK	United Kingdom
US	United States
USA	United States of America
US NPS	United States National Park Service
V	Vidler
Va	Varriano
V & A	Victoria & Albert Museum
V & AMB	*Victoria & Albert Museum Bulletin*
Ve	Veronesi
Vi	Venturi

V-l-D	Viollet-le-Duc	W-P	Ward-Perkins
VP	Vitruvius Pollio	W-R	Wagner-Rieger
VSBI	Venturi, Scott Brown, & Izenour	WRH	Williamson, Riches, & Higgs
VTB	Vlaamse Toeristen-bond	*W-R-J*	*Wallraf-Richartz-Jahrbuch*
vV	van Vynckt (ed.)	W & S	Walker & Simo
V & V	Vale & Vale	Wy	Wycherley
W	Wasmuth (ed.)	Wz	Warsaw
Wa	Watkin	Y	Yorke
Wa & M	Watkin & Mellinghoff	YGS	York Georgian Society
We	Weilbach	YRM	Yorke, Rosenberg, & Mardall
W-E	Wilton-Ely *or* Wilton-Ely (ed.)	Z	van Zanten
W-H	Windisch-Hojnacki	Za	Zabalbeasoa *et al.* (eds)
Wi	Wittkower	*ZdB*	*Zentralblatt der Bauverwaltung*
WJ	Wilson Jones	*ZdÖIuAV*	*Zeitschrift des Österreichischen*
W-J	Ward-Jackson		*Ingenieur-und-Architekten-*
WJfK	*Wiener Jahrbuch für*		*Vereines*
	Kunstgeschichte	*ZfB*	*Zeitschrift für Bauwesen*
W & K	Whiffen & Koeper	*ZfGdB*	*Zeitschrift für Geschichte der*
Wl	Wackernagel		*Baukunst*
Wi.Cu	William Curtis	*ZfK*	*Zeitschrift für Kunstgeschichte*
W-L	Windsor-Liscombe	Z-J	Personal information from
WMfB	*Wasmuths Monatshefte für*		Pani Katarzyna Zachwatowicz-
	Baukunst		Jasiénka
Wn	Wiebenson	Zu	Zukowsky
Wo	Wodehouse	Z & Z	Zapatka & Zardini

A

Aalto, Hugo Alvar Henrik (1898–1976) Finnish architect, he started as a *Neo-Classicist in Jyväskylä (1923–7), but, influenced by *CIAM and by **Aino Marsio** (1894–1949—his wife and partner from 1925), became involved in *International *Modernism after he resettled in Turku. The Standard Apartment Block, Turku (1927–9), incorporated prefabricated *concrete units, while the *Turun Sanomat* Building (1928–30) was the first of his designs to embrace Le *Corbusier's *Five Points for a New Architecture*. Among his early buildings were the Viipuri Library (1927, 1930–5) and the Paimio Tuberculosis Sanatorium (1928–33), which established his credentials as an architect with distinctive idiosyncrasies. Aalto's reputation grew, not least because of his designs for bent-plywood furniture: his three-legged stacking-stool (1938) is ubiquitous. Timber also enjoyed a growing role in his architecture, as in his country's Pavilion at the Paris *Exposition Universelle* (1937) and the *Villa Mairea* at Noormarkku (1937–9). His more personal style, in which curved walls, monopitched roofs, and brick-and-timber construction were prominent, evolved after the 1939–45 war: examples include the Baker House Halls of Residence at Massachusetts Institute of Technology, Cambridge, MA, with its curved walls and projecting staircases (1946–9); the Town Hall at Säynätsalo (1949–52); and the Finlandia Conference Centre and Concert Hall, Helsinki (1962–75). Aalto married (1952) **Elissa Mäkiniemi** (1922–94), who took over the practice after his death. For a brief period **Kristian Valter Gullichsen** (1932–) worked in his office before establishing (1961) his own practice.

Cuito (ed.) (2002a); Fleig (ed.) (1963–78); W.Miller (1984); Ne (1999); P (1982); Pn (1982); Pallasmaa (ed.) (from 2003); Porphyrios (1982); Q (1983, 1995); Ray (2005); P.Reed (ed.) (1998); RW; Schildt (1994, 1998); J.T (1996); Trencher (1996); Tuukanen (ed.) (2002); Weston (1995)

Aaron's rod 1. Ornament in the form of a staff with budding leaves. 2. Rod with a serpent twined around it, not to be confused with *caduceus.

abaciscus 1. Small *abacus* or *abaculus*. 2. Border enclosing part or the entire pattern of a *mosaic. 3. *Tessera or *abaculus*. 4. Small *tile.

abaculus *Abaciscus (**1**) or (**3**).

abacus (*pl.* abaci) 1. Flat-topped plate or *tailloir*, the upper member of a column *capital supporting the *architrave. The *Greek–*Doric abacus is the simplest, consisting of a square unmoulded block, called *plinthus*, but abaci vary with each *Order. 2. Flat slab supported on a *podium or legs, used as a sideboard or for the display of plate, etc., in Antiquity. 3. *Panel on an *Antique wall.

Abadie, Paul (1783–1868) French architect, he joined (1805) *Percier's office in Paris, and became (1818) Architect to the City of Angoulême and the *Département de Charente*. He designed the *Palais de Justice* (1825), *Hôtel* of the Prefecture (1828), the School, and the Grain Market, all in Angoulême. His son, also **Paul Abadie** (1812–84), became (1848) Diocesan Architect to Angoulême, Périgueux, and La Rochelle, and Inspector-General of Diocesan buildings (1861). He designed the *Hôtel de Ville* at Angoulême, but is best known for his over-restorations of the Cathedral Church of *St-Pierre* (1854–82), Angoulême, and the Byzantino-*Romanesque *St-Front*, Périgueux (1852–1901), both of which owe more to conjecture than archaeology. He used the same style for *Sacré-Cœur*, Montmartre, Paris (1874–1919). He succeeded (1874) *Viollet-le-Duc as Architect of *Notre Dame*, Paris.

Ha (1943–57); Laroche (ed.) (1988)

abamurus *Buttress or reinforcing wall.

abated Stone surface cut away, leaving a design in low *relief (e.g. a *Greek-*Doric *metope).

abat-jour 1. Anything that serves to throw daylight in a given direction, such as a sloped or bevelled *cill, or splayed *jambs. 2. Skylight set in a sloping aperture. *Related terms include*:
abat-son: 1. anything to reflect sound downwards or outwards, such as a *louvre; 2. series of sloping louvres in a *belfry;
abat-vent: louvre in an external wall, such as is found in the belfry-*stage of a *steeple, acting as a baffle to the elements, permitting the admission of light and air and the emission of sound;

abat-voix: *tester or *canopy over a *pulpit to reflect sound, common in late-C17 churches, e.g. those of *Wren in the City of London.

abaton 1. Inaccessible place. **2.** Building containing *trophies erected by **Artemisia** (*fl*.C4 BC) in Rhodes, closed to all but a select few.

abbey *See* MONASTERY.

Abbott, Stanley William (1908–75) Influential American designer of the Blue Ridge Parkway (1935–87) linking the Shenandoah National Park to the Great Smoky Mountains National Park in the Appalachians.

US Dept. Commerce (1966); US NPS (1964); Zapatka (1995)

ABC Architectural journal published in Switzerland as part of the *Neues Bauen* movement, edited by **Hans Schmidt** (1893–1972) in association with *Stam and Emil *Roth, with contributions from El *Lissitzky, so associated with *Constructivism.

Ingberman (1994)

Abel, John (*c*.1578–1675) English architect/master-carpenter, he designed and built several elaborate *timber-framed structures in the English and Welsh Border Counties, e.g. the Market Halls at Brecon, Wales (1624—demolished), Kington, Herefs. (1654—demolished 1820), and Leominster, Herefs. (1633—dismantled 1861 and reconstructed as a house named Grange Court). He also built the stone Grammar School at Kington (1625), and (probably) the *Caroline timber *screen at Abbey Dore Church, Herefs. (1633).

Co (2008)

Abele, Julian Francis (1881–1950) Afro-American graduate (1902) of the University of Pennsylvania, he joined (1906) the firm of Horace *Trumbauer, becoming (1909) chief designer (and from 1938) partner, in which capacity he was responsible for numerous buildings, including the French-*château*-inspired residence (1912) on 5th Avenue and East 78th Street, NYC (later the Institute of Fine Arts of NYU); the Widener Memorial Library, Harvard University (1912–15); and the Free Library of Philadelphia (1911–27). Abele's masterpiece, the campus of Duke University, NC, was designed (1924–54) in an English-*Gothic style, and his greatest work there is recognized as the Chapel, the tower of which is based on *Wastell's 'Bell Harry' at Canterbury, Kent (1494–1505).

North Carolina Architects & Builders: A Biographical Dictionary (2009)

<http://ncarchitects.lib.ncsu.edu/people/P000277> accessed 1 Dec. 2012; Penn University Archives & Records Center

<http://www.archives.upenn.edu/people/1800s/abele_julian_fra_wm.html> accessed 1 Dec. 2012

Abelin, Carl Rudolf Zacharias (1864–1961) Swedish-born innovative landscape-designer/writer/pioneer of Swedish garden-culture at a time when Swedish professionals in the field were few. Informing his work was his belief that Nature was the 'Mother of Art', a concept he held had to be integral to any garden-plan for its success: some 35 of his garden-projects in Sweden were founded on this premise. He acquired several prestigious awards for reform in horticulture, arguing the economic importance of the *kitchen-garden, and the renaissance of the country estate. His own lands at Norrviken (from 1906) provided an eclectic ensemble of gardening styles, open to all as an educative tool in the understanding of perspective, colour, and the importance of line following the contour of the ground. The inclusion of a *cemetery (the 'Valley of Death') in his garden aimed to evoke peace and confidence through murmuring waters and birdsong.

Shoe (2001)

Abercrombie, Sir (Leslie) Patrick (1879–1957) British architect/town-planner. He worked at the University of Liverpool (1907–9) under *Reilly and *Adshead, edited the *Town Planning Review*, and produced a series of studies on the growth and condition of several European cities. After Adshead was appointed to the Chair of Town Planning at University College London, Abercrombie became (1915) Professor of Civic Design at Liverpool, a post he held until 1935, when he succeeded Adshead in London. During those years Abercrombie produced a multitude of reports on many areas in England and Wales, and published (1926) a study which led to the formation of the Council for the Preservation of Rural England (CPRE). He championed the idea of a Green Belt around London, and contributed to the Royal Commission on the Distribution of the Industrial Population, resulting in the *Barlow Report* (1940). In association with **John Henry Forshaw** (1895–1973), he was appointed to prepare plans for post-war rebuilding in and around London. The progeny were the *County of London Plan* (1943) and the *Greater London Plan* (1944) which provided the basic skeleton of development policies from 1946, including the *New Towns programme.

Ab (1926, 1933, 1959); G.Cherry (ed.) (1981); *ODNB* (2004); Stephenson & Pool (1944)

Aberdeen bond *See* MASONRY.

ablaq *See* MASONRY.

aboon, abowne, abune 1. Above. **2.** In an upper *storey.

Abraham, Pol Hippolyte (1891–1966) French architect whose early works were influenced by *Art Deco. At Sables-d'Or-les-Pins and Val-André (Côtes-du-Nord), he designed, with others, many buildings from 1923, including the *Villa Miramar* (1928) and the *Villa Ramona* (1929). In partnership with **Henry-Jacques Le Même** (1897–1997), he designed (1931–4) several hospitals, including three at Plateau d'Assy (Haute-Savoie). He attacked (1934) *Viollet-le-Duc's insistence on the 'rational' nature of *Gothic construction, especially the absurd notion that *vault *ribs were structural, when it was obvious from ruins that often *webs stayed up after the ribs had fallen away. Abraham was to undertake experiments in constructional *masonry, notably in Brittany, where he drew on local *vernacular motifs, and at Orléans he tested heavy-wall construction and partial *prefabrication. He believed, erroneously, that a rational approach to construction would transcend style.

Annals of Science lvii/4 (1 Oct. 2000), 447–53; *GdBA* vi/ v/pt.11 (May 1934), 257–71; Heyman (1995), 66, 88

Abraham, Raimund Johann (1933–2010) Austrian-born American architect. Prompted by the idea of 'collision' in architecture, much of his work was theoretical and utopian, although he built several houses (e.g. Pless, Vienna (1960–4); Dellacher, Oberwarth (1963–7); and Prefabricated Houses, RI, USA (1968–70)). He designed a residential and office building, *Friedrichstrasse*, Berlin (1986–7), apartments, *Traviatagasse*, Vienna (1987–92), and a residential and commercial complex, Graz, Austria (1992). His Austrian Cultural Forum, 11 East 52nd Street, New York City (1992–2002—which he himself likened to 'a curtain-wall that falls down like a guillotine'), has been admired. His circular House for Music, *Museum-Insel*, Hombroich, Rhine County, Neuss, Germany, was unfinished when he died.

P.Cook (1970); *New York Times* (6 March 2010); Noever & Prix (eds) (2011)

Abraham, Robert (1775–1850) English architect/surveyor. Competent in various styles, he seems to have had a professional relationship with *Nash, contributing to the development of Regent Street, London, designing the County Fire Office (1819—demolished 1924) and nos. 176–86 (1820—demolished). Employed by **Bernard Edward Howard** (1765–1842—**12th Duke of Norfolk** from 1815) to design alterations to Norfolk House, St James's Square (1819–20—demolished 1938), and new stables in Charles Street, he was commissioned by other members of the RC aristocracy for various works (e.g. Worksop Manor, Notts., and Glossop Hall, Derbys.), and for the Norfolks he designed the Town Hall (1836) and repaired the Fitzalan Chapel (1836) and the Castle (1842–5), all at Arundel, Sussex. For J.C.*Loudon's father, **William** (d.1809), he designed Kenton Lane Farm, Wealdstone, and Woodhall Farm, Pinner (both c.1808–9, both Mddx., and both demolished). He designed (1820s) various garden-buildings at Alton Towers, Staffs. His son, **Henry Robert Abraham** (1800/4–77) also worked for the Howards, but was dismissed (1858) for dishonesty.

Co (2008); *ODNB* (2004)

Abramovitz, Max (1908–2004) Chicago-born architect, educated in the USA and at the *École des *Beaux-Arts*, Paris, he worked with W.K. *Harrison and J.-A.*Fouilhoux, and was Harrison's partner 1945–76. He was responsible for the Philharmonic (now Avery Fisher) Hall, Lincoln Center, NYC (1962), and for the Assembly Hall (1963) and Krannert Center, University of Illinois, Urbana-Champaign (1969), among many other projects.

Abramovitz (1963)

abrevoir 1. Joint between stones in *masonry. **2.** Elaborate water-tank.

Absolute architecture The antithesis of *Functionalism, it was proposed (1960s) as a purposeless architecture by **Walter Pichler** (1936–2012) and Hans *Hollein, the opposite of objectivity (*Sachlichkeit*). Its forms were to be created by imagination without consideration of need. It was also used to describe *Goff's investigations of structure and space.

A (1994); *AR*, clxxii/1030 (Dec. 1982), 53–71; Conrads (ed.) (1970); Klotz (1988); Long (1977, 1988); Pettena (ed.) (1988); J.T (1996); J.Walker (1992)

absorption Transition between a wall-surface or a *pier and the springing of a *vault or vault-ribs in *Gothic architecture, where the vault seems to flow into (or be absorbed by) the wall or pier.

abstraction Omission or severe simplification of details in drawings of a building or landscape, leaving essentials of massing, form, and solids, so that the basis of a design can be explained.

Abstract Representation Synthesis of *Late-*Modernism and *Post-Modernism in which analogies, associations, ornament, and symbolism were suggested rather than clearly quoted.

Js (ed.) (1983)

abuse Violation of established uses or corruption of form in Classical architecture. *Palladio included among abuses *brackets, *consoles, or *modillions supporting (or seeming to support) a structural load, e.g. a column; broken or open-topped *pediments; exaggerated overhangs of *cornices; and *rusticated or banded columns (*see* BAND). *Perrault and others identified others: *pilasters and columns physically joined, especially at the corner of a building; *coupled columns (which Perrault himself employed at the east front of the Louvre, Paris); distortion of *metopes in abnormally wide *intercolumniations; omission of the bottom part of the *Ionic *abacus; *Giant instead of an *assemblage of *Orders; an inverted *cavetto between a column-base *plinth and a *pedestal-cornice; architrave-cornices (as in *Hellenistic *Ionic); and *entablatures broken or interrupted above a column. Many abuses featured in Mannerist and *Baroque architecture.

Gw (1903); W.Pa (1852)

abutment 1. Any solid structure, e.g. *pier, which receives the thrust of an arch or *vault. **2.** Point at which a roof-structure rests on a wall.

abutment-piece *Cill or *sole-plate (*see* SOLE-PIECE).

academy 1. Garden of Akademos near Athens where **Plato** (*c*.429–347 BC) taught. **2.** Institution of higher learning for the arts and sciences. **3.** Place of training in skill, e.g. riding. **4.** Society/institution for the promotion of art, science, etc.

acanthus Conventionalized representation of the leaf of the *Acanthus spinosus* plant, found on the lower parts of *Corinthian and *Composite *capitals, also used as enrichment in Classical architecture. *Vitruvius records how a basket with a *tile on top, placed over a grave in Corinth, became festooned in acanthus stalks and leaves: *Callimachus created the Corinthian capital in stylized form using this as his model.

Stylized form of acanthus leaf. Acanthus-leaves over an astragal moulding.

accessory Aesthetically enhancing element in a composition, inessential (unlike an *accompaniment (2)) to a building's use or character.

accolade Two *ogee curves meeting above or within an arch, and rising to a *finial, usually associated with late-*Gothic work, e.g. over a *doorway or in a *screen.

accompaniment 1. Ornament further enriching another ornament. **2.** Building or ornament closely connected with, or essential to, the completeness of the design, such as the *wings of a *Palladian *villa. *See* ACCESSORY.

accouplement Pair of *coupled columns or *pilasters.

accumulation Collection of features derived from different periods used to suggest a chronological sequence of building even though construction may have taken place at the one time. *See* ADDITIVE.

Achaemenian, Achaemenid Period in Persian architecture from the time of **Cyrus the Great** (d.529 BC) until the death of **Darius III** (330 BC). Its most elaborate buildings include the vast *palace complex at Persepolis (518–*c*.460 BC) which included large relief decorations, while the *apadana (or Hall of the Hundred Columns) had elaborate *capitals with vertical *volutes and animal-heads. *Reliefs of green, yellow, and blue glazed bricks were employed at the palaces of Susa, and the rock-cut tombs at Naksh-i-Rustam have similar capitals to those at Persepolis, with door-surrounds derived from Egyptian precedents.

Ck (1996); L & M (1986)

Achievement of Arms Collected armorial ensigns consisting of *shield of arms, crest, helm, mantling,* and *motto,* with *supporters* and *heraldic badge* as appropriate. It is corrupted as *hatchment,* and this term denotes an *Achievement of Arms* painted on a diamond-shaped frame hung on a house following a death (and thereafter displayed in a church).

Norroy and Ulster King of Arms

achromatic Architecture without colour, or only with white and black, or white and gold, commonly found in early examples of the *Greek Revival.

Ackermann, Rudolph (1764–1834) German-born British (from 1809) publisher/patron, he opened (1795) a drawing school in London which ran for a decade. His importance lies in his patronage of artists such as **William Henry Pyne** (1770–1843) and A.C.*Pugin. His illustrated *Microcosm of London* (1808–10); *The History of the Abbey Church of St Peter's, Westminster* (1812); and *The Repository of the Arts* (1809–28) are superb examples of his work with magnificent illustrations, many hand-coloured. Embracing innovations and paying great attention to detail and quality, his lavish publication on *Nash's Royal Pavilion, Brighton (1826), is very fine by any standards. His topographical productions remain major sourcebooks on the *Regency period, and he was a significant publisher of architectural designs (e.g. J.B.*Papworth's *Hints . . .* (1823)).

ODNB (2004); J.B.Pa (1823); J.T (1996)

acorn *Finial or other *termination representing the fruit or seed of the oak-tree, often used instead of an *urn or *pine-cone.

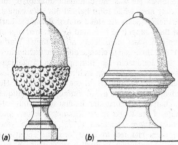

(a) _____   (b) _____

acorn (a) Acorn-shaped cast-iron finial (c.1820), Mecklenburgh Square, London. (after JJS); (b) conventional stone or stucco acorn ornament of stone or stucco.

acoustic vases Earthenware pots or vases were embedded in structures to improve the acoustics. Examples include the dome of *San Vitale* (c.540–48), and the Orthodox Baptistery (c.400–50), both in Ravenna, but in both cases the base of each vase fits into the mouth of the vase below, forming structural ribs or tubes, the spaces between filled with *concrete. Earthenware pots are found embedded in the walls of many medieval churches, e.g. in the South of France, in Normandy, in Cologne, and in The Netherlands. *Also called* DOME-POT

acrolithus, acrolith *Antique or Neo-Classical statue of wood (concealed by drapery), with *marble hands, feet, and face.

acropodium 1. *Pedestal, usually elaborate and high, supporting a statue. **2.** Terminal pedestal resting on representations of feet.

acropolis Elevated part of the city, or the citadel, in Ancient Greece, especially the Athenian acropolis (from *acro-* (highest), and *polis* (city)).

D (1950)

acrostolium Part of the prow of an *Antique warship, often circular, spiral, or shaped to resemble an animal: representations occur on e.g. the *columna rostrata.

acroter, acroterion, acroterium (*pl.* acroteria) **1.** *Plinth or *fastigium,* one placed over the *apex and those (*acroteria angularia*) over each end of a *Classical *pediment, left unadorned but often carrying a statue or ornament. **2.** Ornament or statue with no *plinth (or forming one object with its plinth) in those positions. **3.** *Ridge of a

Classical *temple. **4.** *Horn or *ear of an *altar, *stele, or *sarcophagus.

D (1950)

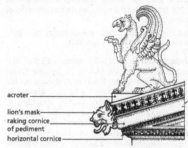

acroter _____

lion's mask _____
raking cornice _____
of pediment
horizontal cornice _____

acroter One of two *acroteria angularia*, Temple of Aphaia, Aegina (early C5 BC).

Action architecture 1. Architecture evolved from sketches without precise working-drawings and using materials ready to hand. **2.** Creation of form through constant repetition and evolution of one concept. An example of Action architecture is Boston City Hall, MA (1964–9), by **Kallmann, McKinnell, & Knowles**.

P.Collins (1965); Js (1973a); Kallmann (1959)

Adair, Arthur Charles (c.1824–1903) Irish architect/engineer, trained by *Lanyon, who worked on railway construction in Canada before returning to Ireland to become (1855) Clare County Surveyor. His major building was the *Italianate Lunatic Asylum at Ennis (1866–70), designed with the architect **William Fogerty** (c.1833–78). He moved to Co. Tyrone (1867) then to Co. Londonderry (1874), where he made additions to the *Greek-Revival court-house in Londonderry (1896–8), originally designed by *Bowden.

O Donoghue (2007)

Adam, James (1732–94) Scots architect and third son of William *Adam, he toured Italy (1760–3) with George *Richardson, before joining the family firm in London. While in Italy he met *Clérisseau, and travelled with him to Rome. Adam visited Naples and *Paestum, but plans to see Sicily and Greece did not materialize. His studies of *Pompeian decorations and *grotesques influenced his interior designs, as *The Works in Architecture of Robert and James Adam* (1773–1822) proves. Although, by the time he returned to England, his brother **Robert** had established the vocabulary of the 'Adam style', James must share credit for many buildings under their joint authorship. In his own right he was responsible for the *Ionic gateway at Cullen House, Banff (1767), Hertford Shire and Town

Hall (1767-9), the unified *façades of Portland Place, London (1776) incorporating *stucco details for the central elements of each block on either side, and several buildings in Glasgow. In 1769 James succeeded his brother as Architect of the King's Works.

R.Adam & J.Adam (1975); Bolton (1922); Co (2008); D.King (1991, 2001); Ry & Ry (1985)

Adam, John (1721-92) Scots architect, and eldest son of William *Adam, he became (1748) Master-Mason to the Board of Ordnance on the death of his father. With his brother, **Robert**, he completed the impressive military structures at Fort George and elsewhere in the Highlands begun by William in the aftermath of the Jacobite Rising (1745-6). A competent designer who drew on the vocabulary of *Palladianism, John was nevertheless business-manager of the partnership, which survived until 1758 when Robert set up his own London practice. Works identifiable as by John and Robert were illustrated in *Vitruvius Scoticus*, published (1811) by John's son **William** (1751-1839): John's buildings include the completion of Hopetoun House, West Lothian (1750-6), the Adam family *mausoleum in Greyfriars Churchyard, Edinburgh (1753), the Court House and other structures at Inveraray, Argyll (1755-61), and Moffat House, Moffat, Dumfries (1761). By the 1770s John had retired from practice, but was closely involved in the business affairs of his brothers **James** and Robert. When the Adelphi speculation, Strand, London, got into difficulties (1772), John mortgaged the family seat (Blair Adam) to avoid bankruptcy.

W.Adam (2011); Co (2008); J.Fleming (1962); D.King (1991, 2001)

Adam, Robert (1728-92) One of the most celebrated of British architects/decorators/interior designers in the later C18 and second surviving son of William *Adam, he matriculated at Edinburgh University, and knew leading Scottish Enlightenment figures such as David Hume (1711-76) and Adam Smith (1723-90). On William's death, he entered into partnership with his brother **John**, and by 1754 had enough capital to set out on the *Grand Tour. In Italy Adam studied Antiquities and met *Piranesi (who incorporated a monument to him in his *Antichità Romane* (1756) and dedicated his *Campo Marzio* (1762) to 'Roberto Adam'). *Clérisseau joined the young Scot in his travels, instructed him in draughtsmanship, and encouraged an appreciation of *Neo-Classicism. Adam and Clérisseau visited (1755) Naples and *Herculaneum to see the excavations, and proceeded (1757) to Spalato (Split *or* Spljet), where they surveyed the Roman Palace: their *Ruins of the Palace of Emperor Diocletian at Spalatro in Dalmatia* appeared (1764), with fine engravings.

Adam settled in London (1758), was joined by his brothers **James** and **William** (1738-1822), and set out to establish himself as the leading British architect. He was the dominant director of the family firm, while **John** helped out with capital. His fellow-Scots the **Duke of Argyll** and the **Earl of Bute** supported him, and he obtained one of the two posts of Architect of the King's Works (1761). He began to change domestic architecture (then dominated by *Burlingtonian *Palladianism) by providing fresh architectural vocabularies drawn from Antiquity to the *Cinquecento*. He advertised himself as an authority on *Antique Roman architecture, and the first sumptuous volume of the *Works in Architecture of Robert and James Adam* appeared (1773), in which the brothers claimed to have 'brought about...a kind of revolution' in English architecture. At Kedleston Hall, Derbys., for example, the Adam Brothers took over and completed the house after Matthew *Brettingham and James *Paine had started the central *block and the *quadrants: the Adams were responsible for the domed *Pantheon-like *saloon and the *triumphal arch applied to the south front, while the Palladian marble-hall was a reworking of Paine's version of *Palladio's reconstruction of *Vitruvius's *Egyptian hall. Indeed, it was in interior design that the Adam Brothers had their greatest influence: essentially, they eschewed a violent change of established canons, but they succeeded in evolving an elegant Neo-Classical style that avoided Greek severity or old-fashioned Palladianism and drew upon a vast eclectic range of decorative elements. Ceilings were often enriched with painted panels by Italian artists, while **Joseph Rose Sen.** (*c.*1723-80) and **Jun.** (1745-99) created their designs for plasterwork. The firm employed several draughtsmen: among them were George *Richardson, Joseph *Bonomi, and **Antonio Zucchi** (1726-96). The Adams juxtaposed room-plans of various shapes and forms that had their origins in Antique interiors from Spalato and from Roman *thermae*: such variations of form and the judicious use of *apses, *niches, and *colonnaded *screens created spatial complexities.

At Syon House, Isleworth, Mddx., the remodelled interiors (1762-9) demonstrate the exploitation of varied geometrical forms, and the ante-room displays an eclectic *Antique Roman Neo-Classical *polychrome treatment incorporating detached Greek-*Ionic columns (with blue-grey *marble *shafts rescued from the bed of the River Tiber and *capitals based on those of the Athenian *Erechtheion*) supporting an elegant *entablature, over which are gilded statues. Other fine Adam interiors include Osterley Park, Mddx. (1763-80), Newby Hall, Yorks. (*c.*1770-*c.*1780), and the beautiful Library at Kenwood House, Hampstead (1767-9). As far as ingenious planning is concerned, the most intricate examples are at two London houses: 20 St James's Square and 20 Portman Square, although the decorative details are shallow compared with earlier works.

Perhaps because of a frustrated desire to 'raise a great public building...in the monumental manner', the brothers began (1768) their scheme to erect 24 first-rate houses between the north bank of the Thames and The Strand, the whole set on a mighty *podium of vaulted areas intended as warehouses. Called The Adelphi, the speculation was ruined by a national credit crisis, and the Adams were forced to stave off bankruptcy by disposing of the property in a lottery. Other unified *terrace-house designs include Charlotte Square, Edinburgh (1791-1807), and the south and east sides of Fitzroy Square, London (1790-4)—the latter with attenuated Grecian detail.

In the last years of his life Robert Adam obtained a number of commissions for large buildings, including the Register House, Edinburgh (1774-92), Edinburgh University (1789-93), and *Picturesque houses in the *Castle style (that is, with elements derived from medieval castle architecture, but with Classical interiors), including Culzean Castle, Ayrshire (1777-92), and Seton Castle, East Lothian (1790-1). Adam also designed distinguished *mausolea, among which may be cited the rectangular Templetown mausoleum, capped with an *urn and two ash-chests, at Castle Upton, Co. Antrim (1789), and the *Doric drum of the Hume monument at Calton Old Burying Ground, Edinburgh (1778).

The Adam firm was wound up (1794), although William (bankrupted 1801) produced (1815) designs for the completion of Edinburgh University, then sold (1818-21) all his brothers' possessions. While the *Works...* provided a definitive account of the 'Adam style', details designed by Robert and his brothers were pirated even during their lifetimes, and there was an Adam Revival dating from 1862 which still goes on, though often as a travesty.

R.Adam & J.Adam (1975); Bolton (1922); Co (2008); J.Fleming (1962); E.Hs (2001); King (1991, 2001); Parissien (1992); P (1982); Rowan (1985); Ry & Ry (1985); Stillman (1966, 1988); Su (1993); Tait (1992); J.T (1996)

Adam, Robert (1948-) *See* NEW CLASSICISM.

Adam, William (1689-1748) As a Presbyterian Whig, Adam was acceptable both to the aristocracy and to the protagonists of the Enlightenment in post-1715 Scotland, and quickly established himself as the leading architect in Scotland. A successful entrepreneur, he invested in Edinburgh property, purchased a country-estate at Blair Crambeth, Kinross (renamed Blair Adam), became Clerk and Storekeeper of the Works in Scotland (1728), and (from 1730) was appointed Mason to

the Board of Ordnance in North Britain (which brought him many lucrative building-contracts for *forts and other structures after 1745). As an architect he drew on numerous precedents, creating an eclectic mix that was lively and often startlingly original. While he imbibed much from *Gibbs and *Vanbrugh, he knew something of Continental *Baroque architecture from a visit to The Netherlands. Adam endeavoured to publicize his own designs and those of other Scots architects in a book, but *Vitruvius Scoticus* was only published as plates without an explanatory text (1811).

Adam was the founder of the famous Adam dynasty, including **Robert** and **James**. His most important buildings include Hopetoun House, West Lothian (1723-48), Haddo House, Aberdeenshire (1732-5), the erection of Inveraray Castle, Argyll, to designs by Roger *Morris (1745-8), Mavisbank House, Loanhead, Midlothian (1723-7), and Floors Castle, Roxburghshire (1721-6).

W.Adam (2011); Co (2008); J.Fleming (1962); Gifford (1989); D.Howard (ed.) (1990)

Adams, Charles Gibbs (1884-1953) American landscape architect, he advocated using local, desert, and succulent plants in his designs. He was among the first to promote the *patio as outdoor living-space, believing it to be of Spanish/Mexican origin. Among his works was *The Succulent Garden*, Arabian Horse Ranch, Pomona, CA.

B & F (2009)

Adams, Henry Percy (1865-1930) English architect, who took over **Stephen Salter's** (1825-96) practice, which in 1913 became **Adams, Holden, & Pearson** (*see* HOLDEN, CHARLES HENRY).

A.S.Gray (1985)

Adams, Maurice Bingham (1849-1933) English architect, best-remembered for his part in the making of Bedford Park, Chiswick, the artists' colony founded 1875, where he designed several of the houses (illustrated in *Artists' Homes* (1883)), supervised the erection of Norman *Shaw's St Michael and All Angels, and designed the north aisle and parish-hall (1887). He was also responsible for the exquisite Chapel of All Souls, added to St Michael's (1909). He designed several public libraries for **John Passmore Edwards** (1823-1911), the philanthropist. His work is generally in a free *Arts-and-Crafts style. He wrote *Modern Cottage Architecture* (1904).

M.Adams (1883, 1904); A.S.Gray (1985); Greeves (1975)

Adaro Magro, Eduardo (1848-1906) Spanish architect, influenced by the French *Beaux-Arts style, he could be described as an eclectic Classicist. Among his works may be cited the *Banco de España, Paseo del Prado*, Madrid

(1882–91), designed with **Severiano Sáinz de la Lastra** (d.1884), **Lorenzo Álvarez Capra** (1848–1901), **José María Aguilar** (*fl.*1880s), et al. He also designed numerous monuments.

Navascués Palacio (1973)

Addison, Joseph (1672–1719) English writer, who influenced the design of the landscape-garden by praising 'informality' in showing a 'Genius in Works of... Nature', and can be regarded as one of the begetters of the so-called *jardin *anglo-chinois*, of the *Picturesque, and of the *Elysium found in C18 gardens, complete with *fabriques.

M & T (1991), 231–41; Wa (1982a)

additive A method of *agglutinative* or *serial* design involving asymmetrical plans and elevations, where the interior spaces and volumes are suggested by, and even dictate, the exterior treatment of projections, roofs, and other features. Derived from the theories of A.W.N.*Pugin, *additive design* can also include *accumulation (suggesting a sequence of building additions of different styles and periods). *See* ARTICULATION; CONCATENATION.

addorsed Opposite of *affronted. Set back-to-back, such as two identical figures facing in opposite directions.

addorsed (*after Normand*).

Adelcrantz, Carl Fredrik (1716–96) Swedish architect, son of the architect **Göran Josuae Adelcrantz** (1668–1739), he was a pupil of **Carl Gustav Tessin** (*see* TESSIN, NICODEMUS THE YOUNGER). Appointed Supervisor of Court Buildings in Stockholm (1741), he remodelled the riding-master's quarters at Ulriksdal as a theatre in the *Rococo style (1753). Drawing on *Chambers's *Designs for Chinese Buildings* (1757), he created the charming *Chinoiserie *pavilion at Drottningholm (1763–9), and designed two more theatres (Drottningholm (1764–6) and the Royal Opera in Stockholm (1777–82)). In Stockholm (1768–74) he built the Adolf-Fredrik Church, much influenced by French *Classicism, and remodelled other buildings in a Neo-Classical style.

A & B (1986); Fogelmarck (1957)

Adhocism Architectural design resembling a *collage, where many components made of different materials and methods of construction

are employed in deliberately untidy ways, and every part of a building or each element of a building complex, is designed with scant regard for the whole, often involving disparate artefacts taken from catalogues. The Belgian architect, **Lucien Kroll** (1927–), who believed *Functionalism no longer functions and that *Modernism is essentially totalitarian barbarism, developed an architecture of 'controlled anarchy', as in the Medical Faculty Housing, *Université Catholique*, Woluvé-St-Lambert, Brussels (1970–82).

E (1994); Js (1968, 1972, 1977); L.Kroll (1983, 1987, 1996, 1996a, (2001); Loo (ed.) (2003); Mikellides (ed.) (1980)

adit Entrance of a building or the approach to it.

Adler, Dankmar (1844–1900) German-born American architect/engineer, he gained experience under **Augustus Bauer** (1827–94), in Chicago, IL, and after the disastrous fire there (1871) collaborated with **Edward Burling** (1818–92) on numerous Chicago buildings including the First National Bank (1871) and the Methodist Church block (1872). After he and Burling parted company (1879), Adler designed the Central Music Hall (1879—destroyed 1900), which combined an office-block, multi-purpose auditorium, and shops. Many private houses and commercial buildings followed, and by 1881 Adler's staff included Louis *Sullivan, who designed the ornament on the Borden Block (1881—destroyed 1916). Sullivan became Adler's partner (1883), and the firm designed the Auditorium Building (1886–9), although the overall conception was Adler's. After the partnership (which had briefly employed the young F.L.L.*Wright) dissolved (1895), Adler made his son, **Abraham** (1876–1914), a partner, designing Morgan Park Academy Dormitories (1896, destroyed *c.*1970) and the Isaiah Temple (1898). He devoted many of his later years to promoting architecture as a learned profession. Pragmatic and creative, he encouraged a multi-disciplinary approach to design.

Adler (1983); Do (1985); J.T (1996); Twombly (1986); *Wisconsin Architect* (1967), xxxviii (July), 15–19; (September), 10–14; (November), 16–19

Adler, David (1882–1949) Versatile American architect, competent in various styles, he studied at the Munich *Polytechnikum* (1904–6) and the *École des *Beaux-Arts* (1908–11). He worked in the Chicago office of the *Arts-and-Crafts architect, **Howard Van Doren Shore** (1869–1926), before setting up in practice with **Henry Corwith Dangler** (1881–1917). One of the first of their great country-houses was at Lake Bluff, IL (1912), with which the *Loire-*château* style came to the Prairie. After Dangler's untimely death Adler went on to create some superb houses, including Castle Hill, Ipswich, MA (mid-1920s—drawing on late-C17 English sources); House-on-

Hill, Hillsborough, CA (1930—Elizabethan, featuring finely-crafted timber-framing filled with brick *nogging); and the Reed House, Lake Forrest, IL (1931—Pennsylvanian-Dutch, designed with **Frances Elkins** (1888-1953)). His attention to detail was exemplary.

Pratt (1970); Salny (2001); Sennott (ed.) (2004)

Adler, Johann Heinrich Friedrich (1827-1908) German architect/archaeologist/writer, he oversaw the construction of several buildings by *Strack, including *Schloss Babelsberg*, Potsdam. From 1877 he became responsible for the building of churches in Prussia: his *Thomaskirche*, Berlin (1865-9), merged medieval and *Renaissance detail, and proved to be influential. Inspired by the works of *Bötticher, his syntheses of *Romanesque, *Gothic, and *Classical elements in church-design were paradigms followed by many architects in Germany, especially where there was a tradition of building in brick, and his restorations included works at Schleswig Cathedral (1888-94) and the *Schlosskirche* at Wittenberg (1890s). In 1874-81 he took part in excavations at Olympia under **Ernst Curtius** (1814-96), and designed the original archaeological museum there (1883). He published works on the Roman Pantheon (1871) and the Mausoleum at Halicarnassus (1900), and was one of the first to appreciate the importance of **Johann Ludwig Heinrich Julius Schliemann's** (1822-90) excavations at Troy.

Hammerschmidt (1985)

adobe Sun-dried unburned clay or earth building-brick or -block (*clay-bat*) made with straw, found in England, Spain, Latin America, The Netherlands, the southern USA, the Middle East (e.g. high-rise buildings in Yemen), bronze-age Mesopotamia, Africa, etc. *Compare* COB; PISÉ de terre; TABIA.

Bourgeois (1989); Davey (1961); Dethier (1983); R & L (1994)

Adshead, Stanley Davenport (1868-1946) English architect, he moved to London (1890) and worked with *Flockhart for whom he superintended the building of Rosehaugh, Avoch, Ross and Cromarty, a vast mansion of great magnificence. He set up his own practice (1898): his most successful work (in partnership with **Stanley Churchill Ramsay** (1882-1968)) is undoubtedly the delightful Neo-*Regency Duchy of Cornwall Estate, Kennington, South London (1913), modelled on modest early-C19 stock-brick London housing. He was appointed to the Leverhulme Chair of Civic Design at the University of Liverpool (1912), and to the Chair of Town Planning at the University of London (1914).

A.S.Gray (1985); *ODNB* (2004); Po (ed.) (1981)

advanced work Fortifications in front of the main defensive building.

advice-stane Stone *lintel over a *doorway with an inscription cut into it.

Advocacy planning Coined (1965) by the American planner **Paul Davidoff** (1930-84), meaning architectural design and planning for powerless, inarticulate inner-city groups, notably when resisting destructive schemes by planning authorities, government agencies, etc. Among its early practitioners were ARCH (Architects' Renewal Committee in Harlem), founded (1964) by **C.Richard Hatch**.

Davidoff (1965); Lopen (1965)

adyton, adytum Innermost unlit chamber of a Greek *temple whence oracles were delivered. *See* SECOS.

aedes, aedis Small *Antique dedicated (not consecrated) *shrine or building, often circular on plan, either *monopteral or a *rotunda with *peristyle.

aedicule, aedicula (*pl.* aedicules, aediculae) **1.** *Shrine or *sacellum within a *temple *cella, either a large *niche or a *pedestal supporting two or more columns carrying an *entablature and *pediment thus forming a frame or *canopied housing for a cult-statue. **2.** Architectural frame around a *doorway, niche, or window-aperture consisting of two columns or *pilasters over which is an entablature with pediment, like a miniature *distyle* building: such an opening is said to be *aediculated*.

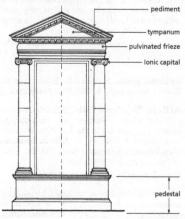

— pediment

— tympanum

— pulvinated frieze

— Ionic capital

pedestal

aedicule Example with Roman Ionic Order, pulvinated frieze, and triangular pediment.

aegicrane, aegicranium (*pl.* **aegicranes, aegicrania**) Classical ornament of sculpted ram's or goat's head or skull. Not *aegricane. See* BUCRANIUM.

Aelric (*fl.c.*1124–53) Northumbrian master-mason, probably of Saxon origin, he was perhaps the designer of the Abbey Church at Dunfermline, Scotland (*c.*1125–50).

J.Harvey (1987)

Aeolic *Primitive type of *Ionic *capital with *volutes seeming to grow from the *shaft, and a *palmette between the volutes.

Two proto-Ionic capitals:
(*left*) from Larissa;
(*right*) from Neandria.

Aesthetic Movement British and American artistic reaction against overblown Victorian design which enjoyed a vogue from *c.*1870, associated with the cult of the Beautiful and 'Art for Art's Sake'. Plain materials and surfaces were preferred to profuse ornament. Influenced by the arts of Japan and China, it was closely connected with the *Arts-and-Crafts movement, *Art Nouveau, *Japonaiserie, and the *Queen-Anne Revival. The architect most connected with the Movement was E.W.*Godwin, but its main manifestations were in late-Victorian decorative arts and painting, often influenced by exotic orientalism, giving it a somewhat perfumed, decadent flavour.

Aslin (1969); D.Burke *et al.* (1986); Kornwolf (1986); Lambourne (1996); L & D (1986); Soros (2000); J.T (1996)

aetoma, aetos 1. *Ridge of a Classical *temple. 2. Apex *acroterium. 3. *Pediment *tympanum.

Affleck, Raymond Tait (1922–89) Canadian architect, whose interests in multi-purpose spaces are expressed in the vast *Place Bonaventure*, Montréal (1964–8), by **Affleck Desbarats Dimakopoulos Lebensold Sise** (1955–69): a forbidding example of *Brutalism.

K (1994); PA lxx/7 (July 1989), 20; J.T (1996)

affronted Opposite of *addorsed. Identical figures or animals facing each other on each side of an opening, as in the tower of Alexander 'Greek' *Thomson's St Vincent Street Church, Glasgow (1857–9).

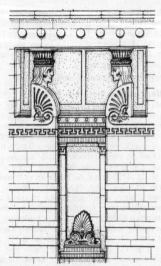

affronted Detail from St Vincent Street Church, Glasgow.

Agache, Donat-Alfred (1875–1934) French architect/planner, and pupil of *Laloux, he is said to have invented the term *urbanisme*, and prepared master-plans for several towns, including Poitiers (1928) and Rio de Janeiro (1930). At the Paris *Exposition Internationale des Arts-Décoratifs et Industriels Modernes* (1924–5), his model dwelling, the *Maison de Tous*, demonstrated the influence of Tony *Garnier.

Les Cahiers de la recherche architecturale viii (April 1981), 31–49

Agg, James (*c.*1758–1828) Lieutenant of the Bengal Engineers, he designed St John's Church, Calcutta (1787), loosely based on *Gibbs's St Martin-in-the-Fields, London (1722–6), but without the western *temple-front, the main entrance and *portico being at the *east* end. This arrangement was due to the presence of several tombs and *mausolea to the west, later (1802) demolished. Subsequently (1811), Roman-*Doric porticoes were added on the north and south sides, and the main entrance moved to the west end. It was this building, rather than Gibbs's original, which influenced the design of many Anglican churches in India.

Historic Churches, xix (2012), 2–3

agger 1. Mound or *rampart formed by earth and stones excavated from a ditch. 2. *Piers carrying the domed structures of a *Byzantine church. 3. Roman road-foundation.

agglutinative See ADDITIVE.

aggregate Material (e.g. crushed bricks, *tiles, stones, and sand) added to *lime to make *concrete.

agora Public open space in a Greek city, surrounded by fine architecture. See FORUM.

Wy (1962)

Agostino di Duccio (1418–81) Florentine sculptor/architect, he worked (c.1450–7) on *Alberti's *Tempio Malatestiano* at Rimini, where he created refined *personifications of the Liberal Arts. He designed the early-*Renaissance *façade of the *Oratorio di San Bernardino*, Perugia (1457–61), on which both coloured *marble and *terracotta are effectively used. He was also responsible for decorations on the monumental *Porta San Pietro* in the same city (1473–81).

S.Hesse (1992); He (1996); P-H (1958)

agrafe, agraffe *Keystone decorated with relief sculpture.

Agrest & Gandelsonas See ANALYTICAL DECOMPOSITION.

Agricultural Order Type of *Corinthian *capital with *volutes replaced by representations of animal-heads, *acanthus-leaves replaced by those of mangel-wurzel and turnip, and other allusions to agriculture (see DONTHORN).

aguilla *Obelisk, *spire, or similar.

Aguilonius, Franciscus (1567–1617) Flemish architect of Spanish descent, he designed the Jesuit Church, Antwerp (St Carolus Borromeus), begun 1615, which owed something to Il Gesù, Rome: it was completed under the direction of Peter *Huyssens and decorated by Sir Peter Paul *Rubens.

J.T (1996)

Ahmad, Ustad (Ustad Ahmad Lahori) (c.1580–1649) **Master Ahmad** of Lahore, also known as **Ahmad Mi'mar** (**Ahmad the Architect**), served **Shah Jahan** (r.1628–58). Credited with the design of the huge Red Fort at Delhi (1639–48), he may have designed the *Tāj Mahal* (*mausoleum of **Arjumand Banu Begum**, *known as* **Mumtaz Mahal** (d.1631)) at Agra (1631–48 and later). If these attributions are correct, he was one of the greatest C17 architects.

M & P (2011); P (1982)

Aichel, Jan Blažej Santini- (1667–1723) See SANTINI-AICHEL, JAN BLAŽEJ.

Aida, Takefumi (1937–) See ARCHITEXT.

Aigner, Chrystian Piotr (1756–1841) Leading architect/theorist of Polish *Neo-Classicism, he designed the *façade of St Anna's Church,

Warsaw (1786), the Marynka Palace, Puławy (1790), and the *Garden of Allusions at Puławy (1798 onwards, with various *fabriques including circular *temple of the Sybil, *Gothic house, Chinese *pavilion, and *rotunda-church (1800–3) with *portico based on the *Pantheon, Rome). He was responsible for the *orangery and *Neo-Gothic elevation of the castle at Łańcut, and at Wilanów, Warsaw, he landscaped the grounds and erected the Gothic gallery and Morysinek Rotunda (1802–12). He reworked (1806–8) the house at Natolin originally designed by *Zug, making it more severe. Later, he rebuilt the Namiestnikowski Palace (1818–19), and designed the Pantheon-like St Aleksander's Church (1818–25), both in Warsaw.

Łoza (1954); L & R (1984); J.T (1996)

aileron Half-*gable or half-*pediment concealing a *lean-to roof, *aisle-roof, or similar.

Aillaud, Émile (1902–88) French architect. He attempted to counter the rigid effects of using prefabricated *concrete panel-construction by arranging masses of building on curving snake-like plans, as at Les Courtillières, Pantin (1955–60). His La Grande Borne, Grigny, near Evry (1964–71), included contrasting densities, visual surprises, and enclosed, secluded spaces. He attempted to give interest to low-cost mass housing, as at La Noë, Chanteloup-les-Vignes (1971–5), and the Quartier Picasso, Nanterre (1974–8).

Dhuys (1983); J.T (1996)

aip-house 1. *Beehive. 2. *Louvre or *lantern in the shape of a beehive.

air-brick Perforated brick, *terracotta, or metal brick-sized element, with its outer face formed like a grating, to allow the passage of air to ventilate an interior, space under a timber floor, etc.

air-conditioning Mechanical treatment of air to a desired state of purity, temperature, and humidity. Systems pioneered in the USA included the use of ice (Carnegie Hall, NYC, in the 1890s) and ammonia (New York Stock Exchange, 1904). In 1902–6 **Willis Haviland Carrier** (1876–1950) of Buffalo, NY, devised the 'dew-point control', by which air was washed and saturated, the temperature being controlled automatically, thus determining the air's moisture content. The first building to be fully air-conditioned was the Milam office-block, San Antonio, TX (1928), closely followed by the Philadelphia Saving Fund Society offices (1929–32), by *Howe & *Lescaze.

C.Elliott (1992); Ingels (1952)

airgh, argh, ergh Hollow: concave surface requiring filling to make it level.

air-grating Grille or grating to admit air.

air-hole Void to ventilate, e.g. a cellar.

airie Building in which farm-labourers lodge.

Aislabie, William (1699/1700–81) English landscape-designer/landowner, his gardening career began (from 1724) at Kirkby Fleetham, Yorks., where he embellished his estate with *pavilions and extensive planting—an approach he later brought (from 1741) to Studley Royal, Yorks., where the gardens (a World Heritage site from 1987) were established by his father, **John** (1670–1742). Aislabie's approach was perfected from *c*.1750 at Hackfall, Yorks., where rugged topography was exploited to enhance *Sublime aspects. Acquisition (1760s) of the ruined Cistercian *abbey on the neighbouring estate of Fountains provided him with a romantic canvas—one he improved whilst always aware of the need to preserve historic fabric.

GH, vii/4 (1987), 307–411; *ODNB* (2013)

aislar, astlayr, astler, estlar, ezlar, islare As *ashlar, especially polished and cut to form very tight joints.

aisle 1. Part of a church on either side of the *nave or *choir, divided from them by *arcades, *colonnades, or *piers supporting the *clerestorey. Aisles are commonly of less height than the nave, and the normal *basilican form consists of a clerestoreyed nave with *lean-to aisles on each side, sometimes doubled so that there are two aisles on each side, but in England there are countless medieval churches with single aisles. *Transepts (called *cross-aisles*) may also have aisles to the liturgical east or west, those on the east accommodating chapels. In German *hall-churches (*Hallenkirchen*) nave and aisles are the same height, so there are no clerestoreys, but aisle-windows are tall. Some churches are *aisleless*: those with aisles are *aisled*. Aisle-galleries are over the aisles, as in C18 London churches, usually necessitating windows in the side-walls under and over the galleries. 2. Compartment of a *timber-framed barn, hall, or house, defined by a row of *posts separating it from the main body of the building. 3. Walk or passage in a theatre, church, or hall giving access to rows of seats. 4. Covered and enclosed burial-place (*see* MORTUARY-CHAPEL (**1**)) attached to a church. 5. Flanking *wing of a building.

Aitchison, George, Sen. (1792–1861) British architect, pupil from 1813 of H.H.*Seward, he became (1823) principal clerk to Thomas *Hardwick, and was appointed (1827) Clerk of Works to the St Katharine's Dock Company, to which the architect was Philip *Hardwick. He designed and built *warehouses and dockyard structures under Hardwick's direction, and succeeded him (1830). Competent as an architect/engineer/surveyor, Aitchison often exhibited at the RA, and designed

several stations for the London & Birmingham Railway Company. His son, George *Aitchison, Jun., became his professional partner (1859).

Co (2008); Sk (2002)

Aitchison, George, Jun. (1825–1910) British architect, son of George *Aitchison. His finest work is the house he designed for **Frederic, Baron Leighton of Stretton** (1830–96), at Holland Park Road, Kensington, which includes the Arab Hall (added 1877–9, built to display Leighton's collection of glazed *tiles acquired during his visits to the East) and the artist's studio. Aitchison enjoyed a considerable reputation, being Professor of Architecture at the Royal Academy (1887–1905) and President of the RIBA (1896–9). He opposed too slavish a following of historical styles: many of his furniture designs were published, and he brought out (1892) a new edition of **James Ward's** (1851–1927) *Principles of Ornament*.

Jervis (1984); M.Rn (1980); *ODNB* (2004)

ajaraca Spanish ornament on brick walls formed of patterns a half-brick in depth.

ajimez, aximez Window-aperture in *Moorish architecture with *colonnettes or *mullions dividing it into arch-headed *lights.

ajour, à jour, ajouré Pierced *panel of some material, e.g. *marble, to allow the admission of air and light.

ala (*pl.* alae) 1. Rectangular room on each side of the *cella of an *Etruscan *temple, each with its own door, approached from a deep *portico. 2. Small room or *alcove on each side of a *vestibule or *atrium in a Roman house. 3. Space between the *naos and flanking *colonnade of a Greek temple.

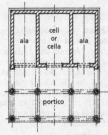

ala Plan of Etruscan temple (*after Vitruvius*).

alabaster Massive, fine-grained partly translucent type of *gypsum* (calcium sulphate), coloured white, yellow, red, and brown, called *bastard alabaster*, often employed for church fittings and monuments. *Oriental* or *calcareous alabaster* is a translucent calcium carbonate, yellowish-white in colour, broken with milky veins: thin slabs were often used in window-*lights (especially in Italy), and the *sarcophagus of **Pharaoh Seti I** (r.1290–c.1279 BC), now in Sir John *Soane's Museum, London, is made of this material.

Alan of Walsingham (fl.1314–64) See WALSINGHAM, ALAN OF.

Álava, Juan de (c.1480–1537) Spanish master-mason involved in the building of the Cathedrals at Salamanca (1512) and Seville (1513). Later, he worked with members of the *Colonia family at Plasencia Cathedral (notably around the *crossing), and from 1521 he built the *cloisters of San-tiago de Compostela, in the *Plateresque style, which are among the largest and most beautiful in Spain. From 1524 he was engaged in building San Esteban, Salamanca (completed 1610), and was in charge of the works at Salamanca Cathedral from 1526. His work spans a late flowering of *Gothic to early *Renaissance styles.

K & S (1959)

Alavoine, Jean-Antoine (1778–1834) French architect, he rebuilt the central *spire of Rouen Cathedral after it burned down (1822), and designed the Colonne de Juillet, Place de la Bastille, Paris, modified and completed by L.-J.*Duc. He pioneered the use of cast iron as a building material, as in his restorations of the Cathedrals of Sées (1817–23) and Rouen (from 1823).

Chirol (1920)

albanega *Spandrel between a *Moorish horse-shoe arch and a rectangular *frame (alfiz) around it.

Alberic (fl.1249–53). English master-mason, he oversaw the building of the east *cloister at Westminster Abbey (1249–53), and was engaged in the construction of the *chapter-house there. He probably worked under Henry de *Reyns.

J.Harvey (1987)

Albert, Prince Francis (Albert) Charles Augustus Emmanuel, Duke of Saxony and Prince of Saxe-Coburg and Gotha (1819–61) Born at Schloss Rosenau, near Coburg, Prince Albert married (1840) **Queen Victoria** (r.1837–1901), and was created Prince Consort (1857). He chaired (1841) the Royal Commission to oversee the decorations of the new Palace of Westminster that were to act as a catalyst to improve the quality of British art, design, and manufactures. The Prince joined the Society of Arts and became its President (1843); in this capacity he encouraged the application of science and art to industrial purposes. Around this time two important figures, (Sir) Henry *Cole and **Professor Ludwig Grüner** (1801–82), became closely involved with the Prince: the latter acted as art-adviser, encouraging a taste for *Renaissance *polychromy, *grotesques, and the *Rundbogenstil that were to

be influential in the buildings at South Kensington, and the former became Chairman of the Society of Arts, promoting model designs commissioned from artists, hence the term 'art manufactures'. Cole was an energetic organizer, becoming Prince Albert's chief lieutenant for the Great Exhibition (1851) in *Paxton's Crystal Palace.

Albert was also President of the **Society for Improving the Condition of the Labouring Classes**, and encouraged the building of exemplary dwellings: the Society erected four 'Model Houses for Families' as part of the 1851 Exhibition, designed by Henry *Roberts and paid for by the Prince. Later, Albert proposed using the profits of the Great Exhibition to found an establishment where science and art could be applied to industry of all nations. This was the beginning of 'South Kensington', a complex of museums, scientific institutions, and places of learning, known as Albertopolis, which had at its nucleus the Schools of Design. The Victoria & Albert Museum is probably the Prince's greatest memorial.

As an influence on architecture the Prince was significant. Not only was polychromy favoured from the late 1840s, but many of Grüner's other Italianizing enthusiasms took root. Albert himself was involved in a number of design-projects, including the *Italianate Osborne House, IoW (with the London builder Thomas *Cubitt from 1845), the Royal Dairy at the Model Farms at Windsor (1858–61 with **John Thomas** (1813–62)), and Balmoral Castle (in the *Scottish Baronial style executed by **William Smith** (1817–91) of Aberdeen). However, Prince Albert's importance in the history of design lies in the immense improvements that became apparent from the time of the 1862 London Exhibition, which he encouraged, but did not live to see realized.

Ames (1967); J.Curl (1983, 2007); Hobhouse (1983); ODNB (2004); Rhodes James (1983); Scheele (1977)

Alberti, Leon Battista (1404–72) Uomo uni-versale of the Italian early *Renaissance, and architect of genius (though never involved in the actual building of his designs), he was the first architectural theorist of the Renaissance, and established the intellectual essence of architecture.

Born in Genoa, educated at Padua and Bologna, he visited Florence (1428) where he became acquainted with leading practitioners: in his De Pictura (the Italian version (1436) is dedicated to *Brunelleschi) he provided the first written description of the principles of *perspective. His admiration of the achievements of Brunelleschi and his appreciation of architecture in the revitalization of the spirit of Antiquity led him to a study of theoretical and archaeological bases, and therefore to Rome, where he became closely involved in the Papal Court from 1431. In Descriptio urbis Romanae (1443), a key work of Roman topography, his understanding of Antiquity and of

Renaissance principles of *proportion is displayed. He became an intimate of **Tommaso Parentucelli** (b.1397, **Pope Nicholas V** (r.1447–55)), and Alberti became architectural consultant to the Papacy. He presented (1452) his *De re aedificatoria* to the Pope: the book (published complete 1486), intended to be a modern equivalent of *Vitruvius's treatise, encapsulated concerns with the *Orders and proportion, extolled *Antique architecture, gave practical advice, and explained the principles of Roman civic-design and how they had contemporary significance. It was translated into English by *Leoni and published (1726–9) as *The Architecture of L.B.Alberti*, with subsequent editions (1739; 1753–5).

Alberti prepared plans (from 1450) for the transformation of the medieval *San Francesco*, Rimini, into a *mortuary-chapel-cum-*mausoleum for **Sigismondo Malatesta** (1417–68), **Lord of Rimini**. He encased the *Gothic structure in Classical *ashlar, with an unfinished front (the first Renaissance example of a Classical west front on a *basilican church), the lower part of which is based on a Roman *triumphal arch (symbolizing Christian triumph over death). This *Tempio Malatestiano* was a deeply serious building, evoking the severity of Ancient Roman architecture.

C15 perception of the *Romanesque *San Miniato al Monte*, Florence, as Antique probably inspired Alberti in his designs for the west front of the Gothic *Santa Maria Novella* in that city (1456–70), executed in a skin of coloured *marble applied to the brick structure behind. This was an attempted solution to the problem of providing a Classical *façade for the traditional basilican shape of a *clerestoreyed *nave with *lean-to *aisles. The Orders framing the central doorway (itself based on that of the Roman *Pantheon) and the *blind *arcading merge the triumphal-arch theme with echoes of *San Miniato*'s façade: above, the crowning *pediment is carried on an *entablature and four *pilasters, suggesting a *temple-front, and large *scrolls hide the roofs of the aisles. There are clear geometrical relationships between the various parts of the façade and the whole, and these complex interconnections are early manifestations of *harmonic proportions; this scheme was prepared for **Giovanni Rucellai** (1403–81), for whom Alberti also designed the façade of the *palazzo* (c.1460) erected under the direction of **Bernardo di Matteo Gambarelli**, *called* **Rossellino**. The latter was the first domestic Renaissance building in which each *storey was defined by an *Order (but influenced by Brunelleschi's *Palazzo di Parte Guelfa*).

Alberti again served the Papacy under **Pope Pius II** (r.1458–64), for whom he may have played a part in the rebuilding of Pienza, and was probably involved in the design of the Benediction Loggia at the Vatican. He was very likely responsible for the barrel-vaulted mortuary-chapel

(*Cappella Rucellai*) at *San Pancrazio*, Florence (1460–7), and certainly designed the exquisite marble shrine (c.1467) of the Holy Sepulchre for that chapel. Also of the 1460s is Alberti's *San Sebastiano*, Mantua, built on a Greek-cross plan not unlike that of the Greek Library of Hadrian's Villa at Tivoli, and with an entrance temple-front originally intended to have six pilasters carrying a broken entablature and pediment: the arch linking the two parts of the pediment and the elimination of two of the pilasters suggest the triumphal arch of **Tiberius** (r. AD 14–37) at Orange (late C1 BC), but the real model is probably **Diocletian's** (r.284–305) Palace at Spalato (c.300) and the Antique façades of the tombs of **Annia Regilla** (near the *Via Appia*) and of the **Cercenii** (south of Rome—the plan of which is similar to that of *San Sebastiano*). Alberti was involved (1470) in the construction of the *rotunda of *Santissima Annunziata*, which is derived from *Santa Maria degli Angeli*, also in Florence (1434), in turn influenced by the so-called temple of 'Minerva Medica' in Rome (c.250), although *Michelozzo di Bartolommeo was involved earlier. On the death of Pius II, however, he devoted himself to serving the **Gonzaga** family of Mantua for whom he designed *Sant'Andrea* (commenced 1470), where the influence of Roman exemplars is clear. The nave is roofed with a gigantic barrel-*vault (the largest and heaviest to be erected since Antiquity): to carry this, Alberti drew on the structural principles of Roman *thermae, and formed massive *abutments at right angles to the axis of the nave, between which he created large barrel-vaulted and smaller domed chapels in what would have been the 'aisles' of a normal basilican arrangement. Furthermore, the elevation of the nave arcades consists of three interlocked triumphal arches, and the west front combines an Antique temple-front with a triumphal arch that echoes the arches of the interior as well as the massive barrel-vault within. The grand interior with chapels instead of aisles was the precedent for many Counter-Reformation churches.

Alberti (1988); F.Borsi (1989); Boschetto (2000); Gadol (1969); Grafton (2000); He (1996); Ry (ed.) (1966); Ry & Engel (1994); Ta (1998); J.T (1996); Wi (1998)

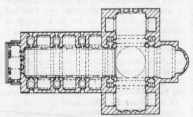

Plan of *Sant'Andrea*, Mantua: massive internal buttresses (wall-piers) subdivide aisles into chapels.

Albini, Franco (1905–77) Influential Italian architect, born near Como, Albini rose to eminence in the 1930s. His first important building was the Pavilion for the *Istituto Nazionale della Assicurazione* at the Milan Congress (1935). He had considerable success as a designer of exhibitions, and won the silver medal at the Paris International Exhibition (1937) with the **Fabio Filzi** housing project, Milan (1936—designed with **Renato Càmus** (1891–1971) and **Giancarlo Palanti** (1906–77)). After the 1939–45 war his renovation of the *Palazzo Bianco* Museum (1950–61) and the *Tesoro di San Lorenzo* (1952), both in Genoa, brought him new fame. His remarkably sophisticated Department Store, *La Rinascente*, *Piazza Fiume*, Rome (1957–62—with **Franca Helg** (1920–89)), suggested elements (e.g. the crowning *cornice) of a *Renaissance *palazzo, although the construction was a matt-black steel frame with reddish infill panels. From 1945–6, with Palanti, he was editor of *Casabella*, and was a member of *CIAM for many years. His work was eclectic, and reflected the independence of Italian design from the tyrannies of *Modernist orthodoxy.

Albini (1981); L (1988); Leet (ed.) (1990); Ma (1984b); Moschini (1979a); Piva (1998); Ro Prodi (1996)

alcázar Spanish fortress or *palace (from the Arabic).

Alchimia Italian 'New Wave' co-operative design group (1976–91), founded in Milan by **Alessandro Guerriero** (1943–), **Alessandro Mendini** (1931–), *Sottsass, et al., also called *Studio Alchymia*. One of its aims was to make and market designs, many of which employed historical styles, ironically used. It rejected the *Modern Movement, made clear by the whimsical *Bau Haus* collection (exhibited 1975).

Branzi (1984); Casciani & Bontempi (1985); J (1995a); Poletti (1994); Radice (1980)

alcove 1. Large *niche. **2.** Recess or part of a chamber defined by an *estrade, partition, or *balustrade, for a bed. **3.** Arched recess or niche in the wall of any building or room. **4.** Covered retreat, bower, summer-house, or recess in a wall or hedge in a garden or pleasure-ground provided with seats. From the Arabic for 'vaulted chamber'.

Aldrich, Henry (1648–1710) Canon and Dean of Christ Church, Oxford, polymath/virtuoso/ forerunner of *Palladianism/architect of several Oxford buildings/author of a *Vitruvian-Palladian book on architecture, *Elementa Architecturae Civilis* (not published until 1789). He designed Peckwater *Quadrangle at Christ Church (1707–14), built by William *Townesend (which anticipates *Wood's Queen Square, Bath, by two decades, and is the first Palladian *palace-fronted composition in England); (probably) the Fellows'

Building (1706–12), Corpus Christi College (which shows certain affinities with Peckwater Quad); and possibly All Saints' Church (1701–10), although the *steeple was a compromise between an original design and an alternative by *Hawksmoor.

H.Aldrich (1789); Co (2008); Hiscock (1960); *ODNB* (2004)

Aleijadinho, Antônio Francisco Lisboa, *known as* **O** (1738–1814) Leading practitioner of *Baroque and *Rococo in Brazil, born the illegitimate son of the Portuguese architect **Manoel Francisco Lisboa** (*fl.c.*1720–*before* 1767) near Ouro Prêto, Brazil. The 'little cripple' (as *O Aleijadinho* means) suffered from a disease that gradually cost him his toes, fingers, sight, and skin. In spite of these disadvantages he transformed traditional types of Lusitanian church-architecture by means of richly imaginative applied decoration, much of it carved by himself in the soft soapstone found in the interior captaincy of Minas Gerais, where gold and diamonds were mined. Ouro Prêto acquired numerous chapels, *altars, *doorways, and *façades by Aleijadinho, and his masterpieces in and near the town are *São Francisco de Assis* (1766–94—with twin cylindrical towers set on either side of a curved front in which is a sumptuous carved *door-case, while the interior is remarkably unified, undulating, and elegant); and *Bom Jesus de Matozinhos* in Congonhas do Campo (1777–1805—with 12 carved figures guarding the entrance, while the rest of the ensemble is a synthesis of dramatic, powerful, and richly plastic elements).

Bazin (1963); Brétas (1951); K & S (1959); N-S (1986a) J.T (1996)

Alen, William van (1883–1954) Born in Brooklyn, he studied at the *École des *Beaux-Arts*, Paris, before establishing his architectural practice in NYC. The firm became known for its tall commercial buildings in which Classical allusions to *base, *shaft, and *capital were abandoned. Van Alen's most celebrated work is the Chrysler Building, NYC (1928–30), a monument not only to **Walter P. Chrysler** (1875–1940), but also to corporate advertising. The *Art Deco upper part of this *skyscraper incorporates eagle-head and radiator-cap *gargoyles as well as a series of semicircular forms recalling hub-caps.

Bl & Ro (1975); Nat. Inst. for Arch. Education (1964); P (1982)

Aleotti, Giovanni Battista (1546–1636) Italian architect, he designed several churches in Ferrara (including *Santa Barbara* (1586–8)), and *Santa Maria del Quartiere* (1604–19), Parma, a curious composition with an exterior built up in layers like a *pagoda. He restored numerous buildings in Ferrara damaged in earthquakes (1570), including the castle, the *Palazzo del*

Regione, and the *Palazzo del Paradiso* (which housed (1586-1962) the University). His most imposing work of military architecture was the fortress in Ferrara. His masterpiece was the *Teatro Farnese*, Parma (1617-19—damaged 1944, and restored 1960-2), in which he combined a U-shaped *auditorium with architectural elements derived from the works of *Palladio and *Scamozzi: it was the most sumptuous theatre erected up to that time.

Il Carrobbio, ix (1983), 197-208, and xi (1985), 114-21; *JSAH*, xxi/3 (Oct. 1962), 116-28; Magagnato (1954)

Alessi, Galeazzo (1512-72) Perugia-born, trained in Rome (where he was influenced by *Michelangelo), he became the leading mid-C16 architect in Genoa and Milan. His first important building was *Santa Maria Assunta in Carignano*, Genoa (1549-1603): a Greek-*cross on plan within a square, with a projecting *apse and a *dome surrounded by four smaller domes, it was clearly based on *Bramante's scheme for *San Pietro*, Rome. His domestic architecture, especially the *Villa Cambiaso* (1548), has elements derived from the *Palazzo Farnese*, Rome, but some of the exterior elevational treatment is very rich, with open-topped *pediments and *Michelangeloesque window-surrounds. The Doge of Genoa ordered (1550) the construction of the *Strada Nuova* (1558-70), which was laid out by Alessi, and lined with *palaces: it was the first planned street of independent *blocks of the period, each designed by a different architect, but with an overall control of certain architectural features, heights, and scale to ensure a degree of harmony. It became internationally known after the publication of *Rubens's *Palazzi di Genova* (1622-52). Alessi's enormous *Palazzo Marino* (1557), Milan, had sumptuous elevations, and its *cortile displayed fine examples of *Mannerist decoration. His *Santi Barnaba e Paolo* (1561) and *Santa Maria presso San Celso* (1568) in Milan deserve note, the former for the distinct divisions between *nave, *presbytery, and *choir, and the latter for its size and decorations, completed by Martino *Bassi after Alessi's death.

Alessi (1974); N.Brown (1982); Rott (2003); J.T (1996)

alette 1. *Ala or *wing of a building. 2. *Jamb or *piedroit. 3. In Classical architecture the visible parts of a *pier flanking *engaged columns or *pilasters, usually forming *abutment of arches. 4. Semi-visible rear pilaster among several columnar elements.

Alexander, Christopher Wolfgang (1936-) *See* CHERMAYEFF; COMMUNITY ARCHITECTURE; DECONSTRUCTIVISM.

Alexander, Daniel Asher (1768-1846) English architect/engineer/surveyor, known for his work for the London Docks Company from 1794. By the time *Rennie was appointed Engineer to the Company (1801), Alexander had already prepared plans for the docks and warehouses, and realized works appear to have been by Alexander, including the Tobacco Warehouse with its unusual branched cast-iron columnar supports. He also designed Dartmoor (1806-9—much altered) and Maidstone (1811-19—mostly demolished) Gaols; additions and flanking colonnades at the Queen's House, Greenwich (1807-10); and various lighthouses for Trinity House, including examples at the South Stack, Anglesey (1809), Heligoland (1811), and Harwich (1820).

Co (2008); Sk (2002)

Alexander the Mason III (*fl.c.*1235-57) English? master-mason. An important and innovative designer, his works at Lincoln Cathedral (1237-c.1258) had a profound influence on English *Gothic, and included (probably) the *nave (with lierne *vaults which led to the evolution of patterned vaulting in Europe), polygonal vaulted *chapter-house, and the *Galilee, together with the *screen-front at the west and the rebuilding of the lower stage of the *crossing-tower. Among other innovations were the trellis-patterns on the west front and central tower. He may also have designed the lower *stages of the towers of the Churches of St Wulfram, Grantham, Lincs., and St Mary Magdalene, Newark, Notts. He was probably the same Alexander (*fl.c.*1224-40), master-mason at Worcester Cathedral (which also had a polygonal chapter-house), who was involved in works at Le Mans Cathedral, France.

J.Harvey (1987)

alexandrian work *See* OPUS ALEXANDRINUM.

Alfieri, Benedetto Innocente (1699-1767) Piedmontese Roman-born lawyer-turned-architect, he succeeded (1739) *Juvarra as architect in Turin, completing the latter's *Palazzo Reale*. His main secular works were the *Palazzo Ghilini*, Alessandria (1732), the *Teatro Regio* (1736-40—celebrated for its acoustics and sight-lines), the *Segretario di Stato* (1739-67), the *Piazza d'Erbe*, and the *Carceri Senatoriali*, all in Turin. His *Santi Remigio e Giovanni*, Carignano (1757-64), has an odd plan, a spectacularly enriched interior, and a contrasting plain *façade. His design for the west front of the Cathedral of *St-Pierre*, Geneva (1752-6), is in an advanced *Neo-Classical style. He published (1740) *Il nuovo teatro regia di Torino*.

A.Bellini (1978); Cancro (1992); Macera (ed.) (1992); Pommer (1967)

alfiz *See* ALBANEGA.

Algardi, Alessandro (1598-1654) Bologna-born architect/sculptor, he settled in Rome, designing the *Villa Doria-Pamphilj* (1640s), situated in beautiful gardens outside the *Porta San Pancrazio*.

Montagu (1985)

Algarotti, Francesco (1712–64) Influential Venetian figure of the Enlightenment, he became artistic adviser to **King Friedrich II ('the Great') of Prussia** (*r*.1740–86), and was largely responsible for introducing *Palladianism to Potsdam and Berlin. His writings on architecture (influenced by *Lodoli) were of considerable importance in the development of architectural theory, and include *Il Newtonianismo per le Dame ovvero Dialoghi sopra la Luce e i Colori* (actually a treatise on optics—1737) and *Opere del Conte Algarotti* (1791–4).

JSAH, iv/2 (Apr. 1944), 23–9; Kaufman (1998); E.Ka (1955); Ry (1980)

algorithmic design Method of designing in a prescribed set of computational procedures for solving problems. Known as a/d, it can be a set of equations or a series of mechanical processes (e.g. analogue or digital). The algorithms are in essence instructions or patterns for the efficient completion of a task, so a/d involves steps taken in code to reach a result.

Goodrich & Tamassia (2002); Kleinberg & Tardos (2006); Skiena (2010)

Alhambra 1. One of the most exquisite and richly ornamented of all *Moorish buildings in Spain (mostly 1338–90—probably a *madrasa rather than a *palace), it consists of a series of joined *pavilions, with two great *courts set at right angles to each other. Channels of water, linking pools with fountains, add to the overall effect of an earthly Paradise. 2. Garden-building in a Moresque style, such as *Chambers's 'Alhambra' at Kew Gardens (1758), named after the complex in Granada.

B & B (1994); Irwin (2004)

alicatado Wall-finish of uniformly shaped coloured glazed *tiles (*azulejos*) commonly found framing tilework in Spain and Latin America. *See* LACERÍA.

aliform 1. Wing-shaped. 2. Building with additions resembling wings.

alignment, alinement 1. Line laid down to enable a road, street, or building to be constructed. 2. Lines establishing positions of any construction. 3. Any arrangement of trees, columns, standing-stones, etc., set up in a straight line.

Alison, Archibald (1757–1839) Scots clergyman/botanist/ornithologist/zoologist/writer on aesthetics, his *Essays on the Nature and Principles of Taste* (1790) argued that Taste is a

consequence of the imagination's responses to objects seen (a notion earlier floated by *Chambers), not instinctive (as *Burke had suggested), but through an **association** of ideas in the mind prompted by observation. As J.-J.*Rousseau had experienced, a response in its most intense form induced a dreamlike 'state of reverie' facilitating romantic euphoria. Alison argued that perceptions concerned with the *Beautiful (prompted by pleasure) and the *Sublime (prompted by apprehension) determined the 'emotion of Taste'. He held that Beauty in architecture was dependent upon mental associations of fitness for function of form, size, and scale, so proportion was variable, not a constant. Certain proportions look agreeable because we **associate** them with stability (which is one reason why *Deconstructivism is so unnerving). *See* ASSOCIATIONISM.

Alison (1790); *ODNB* (2004); Rousseau (1782)

allars 1. Garden-walk. 2. *See* ALLEY; ALURA.

Allason, Thomas (1790–1852) English architect. After visiting Greece (from 1814), he published *Picturesque Views of the Antiquities of Pola in Istria* (1817), and claimed he was the first to spot *entasis on the *shafts of Greek columns, although C.R.*Cockerell and *Haller von Hallerstein, whom Allason had met while in Athens, had also observed this. His main work was the Alliance Fire Office, Bartholomew Lane, London (1841—demolished), and he planned and carried out designs for houses on the Ladbroke Estate, Kensington, in a severe, *stripped Classical style from 1823: his own house in Linden Gardens (demolished) was illustrated in *Loudon's *Encyclopaedia of Cottage, Farm, and Villa Architecture* (1846), and he designed a studio for the artist **William Mulready** (1786–1863) at Linden Grove, Bayswater (1827). He oversaw the development of the Pitt Estate, Kensington (from 1844), and was involved in the d'Este Estate, Ramsgate, Kent.

Co (2008); W.Pa (1852); Sh (1973)

allée *See* ALLEY.

allège 1. Thinner part of a wall, e.g. between a window-cill and the floor. 2. *Cill. *See* APPUI.

allering, *also* **alaryne, alerin, alleringe, allure, aloring, alrine, alring, alryne** 1. *Battlement or *parapet-wall: *aluryt* means 'with a parapet' or 'battlemented'. 2. Gutter, *galery, or passage behind a parapet at the top of a building. 3. *Alura, or *clerestorey gallery (e.g. at Ely Cathedral). 4. Uppermost part of a wall on which the roof-structure rests. 5. *Cloister walkway. 6. Highest part of a building.

alley 1. Allée, allars, or long straight gravel or grass garden-walk, usually defined by trees, shrubs, or hedges on each side, sometimes terminated by an *eye-catcher. An *allée couverte* has planting trained to have branches meeting overhead. **2.** Any garden-walk bordered with bushes, etc., e.g. in a *maze. **3.** Long, narrow area for open-air games. **4.** *Aisle. **5.** Pedestrian passage between houses or walls. **6.** Passage between rows of seats, as in a church. *See* ALURA.

Allinger, Gustav (1891–1974) German land-scape-designer of numerous gardens, parks, cemeteries, sports-grounds, and garden exhibitions. Apprenticed under *Encke in Cologne, after the 1914–18 war he joined the Parks and Cemeteries Department, Dortmund, before heading the gar-den-design office of the Ludwig Späth Nursery, Berlin (1921–25). He won (1926) the *Jubiläums-Gartenbau-Ausstellung* competition, Dresden, which established him as a landscape-designer who integrated con-temporary and traditional trends. He was later (1928–31) Garden Director for the new town of Hindenburg prior to founding (1932) his own design firm. He closely associated himself with Nazi ideals, and undertook many projects for organizations associated with the *Reich*, working with Alwin *Seifert on the landscaping of the new *Autobahnen*, and designing camouflage. After the 1939–45 war, Allinger held an academic post at the Institute for Garden Art and Landscape Design, Berlin (1952–9), and published on land-scape architecture.

Allinger (1926); *Die Gartenkunst*, **xxxvii** (1924), **xli/9** (1928), **xlvi/9** (1933); Shoe (2001)

Allio, Domenico dell' (1505–63) Italian architect/engineer, he fortified several towns in Styria, Carinthia, Slovenia, and Croatia against the Turks. His most important architectural work is the *Landhaus*, Graz (1556–63), two sides of the court-yard of which are embellished with three super-imposed ranges of *arcades, one of the earliest assured Italian *Renaissance designs in Austria.

Sitwell & Schneiders (1959); J.T (1996)

Allio, Donato Felice d' (1677–1761) Des-cended from a family of Italians settled in Austria, he was the architect of the Salesian *convent and church (1717–28), Vienna, an assured *Baroque ensemble with a two-storey church-façade of the *scroll type and a plan consisting of an ellipse on the long axis. His greatest, but unfinished, work is *Klosterneuburg* (begun 1730), modified by **Joseph Emanuel Fischer von Erlach** (1695–1742).

Bou (1962); J.T (1996)

Alliprandi, Giovanni Battista (1665–1720) Architect of the Garden Palace of Liblice (1699–1706) and the *Palais Lobkowicz*, Prague (1702–5), he explored curved bow-centrepieces, and con-tributed to the richness of Bohemian *Baroque.

J.Nn (1970); N-S (1986a); J.T (1996)

Allom, Thomas (1804–72) London-born architect, articled to Francis *Goodwin, Allom's skills gained him employment as a topographical artist: he was a frequent exhibitor at the RA, and often produced exquisite drawings for his fellow architects. His designs include St Peter's Church, Kensington Park Road, London (1855–7), and some spectacular ranges of *stucco-faced houses in Kensington Park Gardens (1850s).

B *et al.* (2001); Brooks (ed.) (1998); *ODNB* (2004); Sh (1973)

allotment Found throughout Europe and referred to in North America as a 'community-garden', it is a designated area of land, not attached to a house, providing facilities for people to grow produce, or to develop small pleasure-gardens. Allotments were recognized (1887 with subsequent legislation) in English law, which required local authorities to provide them where need demanded.

Crouch & Ward (1997); EHThe accessed 8 June 2013; Tay (2006)

allure Misspelling of *alura. See* ALLERING.

almena Upright solid part of a *battlement shaped like a trapezium with serrated sides, char-acteristic of *Moorish architecture.

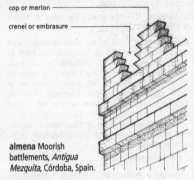

cop or merlon

crenel or embrasure

almena Moorish battlements, *Antigua Mezquita*, Córdoba, Spain.

almery *Aumbry.

almond The 'egg' in *egg-and-dart mouldings, defined by a *fillet around it.

almonry *See* ALMSHOUSE.

Almqvist, Osvald (1884–1950) Swedish archi-tect. With *Lewerentz et al., he founded an inde-pendent architectural school, studying traditions of *vernacular architecture as part of the search for a national style, but became a pioneering non-*Historicist with such designs as the industrial village, Berglagsby, Domnarvet, Dalecarlia (1916–20), and the hydro-electric power-stations of Forshuvudfors (1917–21), Hammarfors (1925–8), and Krångfors (1925–8).

A & B (1986); Ca (1998); Linn (1967)

almshouse 1. Establishment founded and endowed by private charity for the reception, housing, and support of aged poor. Almshouses often consisted of groups of dwellings, sometimes with a chapel and dining-hall. Many English almshouses were erected following the dissolution of the monasteries (1535–41): some are very simple *terraces of houses, but others, e.g. the Beauchamp Almshouses at Newland, Worcs. (1862–4—complete with church), have architectural pretensions. 2. *Almonry* where alms of a *monastery were dispensed: the term is also given to the residence of an *almoner* or to the building in, e.g., a *monastery, where food and gifts for the poor were received, usually associated with the almoner's rooms.

Bailey (1988); Godfrey (1955)

aloring, alorying See ALLERING; ALURA.

Alphand, Jean-Charles-Adolphe (1817–91) French landscape architect/civil-engineer. Under *Haussmann, Alphand, with **Jean-Pierre Barillet-Deschamps** (1824–75), designed many public gardens and parks, including those of the *Bois de Boulogne* (1854), *Bois de Vincennes* (1860), *Buttes-Chaumont* (1864–9), and *Montsouris* (1869). Of these, *Buttes-Chaumont* was the most elaborate, with a lake, streams, a waterfall, and artificial *grottoes. With Barillet-Deschamps and É.-F.*André, he created the botanic gardens at *La Muette* (1860—moved to Boulogne in 1895), and became (1867) supervisor of the public ways of Paris. After 1871 he was in charge of all public works, including cemeteries (e.g. Bagneux of 1886), and oversaw layouts and landscaping of the International Exhibitions in Paris (1867, 1878, 1889).

W.Robinson (1869); J.T (1996)

Alpine garden See ROCK-GARDEN. An *Alpine house* is a garden-building with ventilation but no heating, suitable for the cultivation of Alpine species: it may also refer to a *Swiss cottage or *châlet.

altana *Loggia*, covered roof-terrace, or *belvedere*, common in medieval Venice and *Renaissance Rome.

altar Block, *pedestal, stand, or table on which to place or sacrifice offerings to a deity. Jewish altars had *horn-like ornaments at each corner, and this type of decoration also occurred in Classical Antiquity, with simplified horns or *ears, also known as *acroteria. Classical altar-tops have similarities to *cinerarium- and *sarcophagus-lids, and influenced the design of Neo-Classical gate-piers, tops of *door-cases, and the like. Christian altars, consecrated for celebration of the Eucharist, are elevated tables with a plane (usually stone) top (*mensa*) incised with crosses representing the Five Wounds of Christ, and (in pre-Reformation and RC altars) with a Relic embedded in the stone (after the Reformation, altars were replaced with wooden *Communion- or Holy-tables). In a church the *high-altar is the chief altar sited at the east end of the *chancel. *Sides (*horns*) of altars are termed *Epistle (south) and *Gospel (north). *Compounds include*:

altar-facing: detachable finish or cover for the front part of an altar, facing the *nave, often of fabric woven into intricate designs, also called *altar-frontal* or *antependium*. If continued around the sides of the altar it is a *paliotto*;

altar-niche: recess for an altar, often given an architectural frame, e.g. an *aedicule*;

altar of credence: *credence-table, or table of *prothesis*;

altar of repose: *niche or side-altar where the Host rests from Maundy Thursday until Good Friday. See EASTER SEPULCHRE;

altar-piece: painting or sculpture set above and behind an altar;

altar-rail: *rail, dividing the rest of the chancel from the *sacrarium, at which Communicants kneel during the Eucharist;

altar-screen: *altar-wall* separating the *presbytery or *sacrarium* from the *ambulatory to the east;

altar-slab, altar-stone: slab of stone (*mensa*) forming the top of an altar;

altar-stair, altar-steps: steps up to the elevated area where an altar stands;

altar-table: timber 'Holy Table', used instead of stone altars in post-Reformation churches;

altar-tomb: monumental tomb-chest, or *high tomb*, resembling an altar, but never used as such, sometimes supporting recumbent *effigies or with memorial brasses on top, and occasionally embellished with *weepers in niches around its sides. Altar-tombs are often protected by ornate canopies.

alternating system Where circular alternate with compound *Romanesque *piers, as in Durham Cathedral, this is termed an *alternating system*.

alternative architecture Dwellings constructed with parts of motor-vehicles or other recycled material, sometimes based on *geodesic principles, in the 1960s, esp. in the USA. Some doubt if it is architecture.

alto-rilievo Carved work projecting by at least half its true proportions from the background on which it is sculpted.

aluminium, aluminum Light, silvery metal first named (though not then isolated) by **Sir Humphry Davy** (1778–1829). **Hans Christian Oersted** (1777–1851) was the first to produce the metal (1825), but a practical electrolytic method

of isolating aluminium was not employed until
1886. The alloy *duralumin* was discovered
(1909) by **Alfred Wilm** (1869-1937): consisting
of 94% aluminium, 4% copper, 1% magnesium,
and 1% manganese, *duralumin* can be greatly
strengthened by heat treatment (just as steel is
hardened by tempering and quenching), and
owes its special qualities to the association of
magnesium with the silicon present as an impu-
rity in aluminium. Other strong aluminium alloys
include the addition of iron, nickel, chromium,
and other metals. Duralumin may be spun,
pressed, riveted, machined, etc., but, like aluminium and its other alloys, duralumin cannot be
effectively soldered or welded. Heat-treated
duralumin is resistant to corrosion, is ductile,
and will carry heavy loads, and strength per unit
of weight is high compared with nickel steel or
nickel chrome steel: the alloy is especially suited
to the construction of aircraft (airships such as the
German craft designed by **Ferdinand, Graf von
Zeppelin** (1838-1917), would not have been possible without duralumin) and internal-combus-
tion engines. *Fuller used duralumin for the
Dymaxion House (designed 1927, realized 1945-
6); **Alfred Lawrence Kocher** (1885-1969) and
*Frey employed it in their Aluminaire House
(1931), built for an exhibition in NYC, subsequently used by W.K.*Harrison as a summer-
house at Syosset, Long Island, NY, later
reconstructed at the New York Institute of Technology; and it was an essential part of the project
to provide prefabricated dwellings after the
1939-45 war in both the UK and USA. *Prouvé
used it in his Aluminium House (1953), and it is
often found in recent work.

R.Anderson (1925); Pawley (1990); Peter (1956);
Schäpke *et al.* (1991)

alura, alure, ailure Gangway, *gallery, garden-walk, passage, walkway, or *allering behind
*battlements. A *clerestorey gallery, as at Ely
Cathedral, the passages in a *cloister, or other
covered passage or *ambulatory.

Álvares, Baltazar (*fl.*1570-1624) Portuguese
architect, partly responsible for the fine *St Vicente de Fora* (begun 1582), Lisbon, the west front of
which (designed 1615) is entirely his work,
although **Filippo Terzi** (*c.*1520-97) planned the
building, mindful of *Il Gèsu*, Rome, as a precedent. He designed several churches for the
Jesuits, including the splendid *Mannerist *façade
of *St Lourenço*, Oporto (begun 1614). His uncle,
Afonso (*fl.*1550-75), designed the *hall-church
Cathedrals of Leiria (1559-74) and Portalegre
(begun 1556), and contributed to the designs of
the Jesuit churches of *Espírito Santo* (1567-74),
Évora, and *St Rocque* (1567), Lisbon.

Kubler (1972); K & S (1959); J.T (1996)

Álvarez, Augusto Harold (1914-95) Mexican architect, his early works were influenced by
designs of Le *Corbusier and *Mies van der Rohe,
and by theories of *Gropius. His devotion to the
*International-Modern Movement is exemplified
by the Jaysour Building (1961), IBM Building
(1971-2), and *La Mitra* offices (1972-3), México
City.

Creixell (1996); A.Leon *et al.* (1998)

Álvarez, Mario Roberto (1913-2011) Argen-
tinian architect, he promoted the *Modern
Movement, developing prefabrication techniques, engineering, and town-planning. His
buildings include the San Martín Sanatorium
(1936-7), Buenos Aires, the San Martín Cultural
Centre (1953-60), Corrientes, and the IBM Argentina Headquarters (1979-84), Catalinas Norte. His
SOMISA building (1966-77), Buenos Aires, was
the first in Argentina constructed entirely of steel
and glass, and one of the first to be wholly welded.

E (1994); Trabucco (1965); J.T (1996)

Amadeo, Homodeo, Homodeus, *or* **Omo-
deo, Giovanni Antonio** (*c.*1447-1522) Italian
architect/engineer/sculptor. Pavia-born, he assisted in the decoration of the *chiostro* of the
Certosa there from 1466, and designed the portal
of the small *cloister (*c.*1470) as well as the *terracotta *lavabo. His first significant architectural
work was the Colleoni *mortuary-chapel at *Santa
Maria Maggiore*, Bergamo (1470-3), for which he
also designed the tomb of **Bartolomeo Colleoni**
(*c.*1470-5): the chapel is derived from *Michelozzi's
Portinari Chapel, *Sant' Eustorgio*, Milan, and
Bergamo Cathedral (possibly by *Filarete).
The elaborate, even fantastic, encrustation of the
Cappella Colleone *façade is also a theme found in
Amadeo's work on the front of the *Certosa*, Pavia, a
project with which he was first associated (1474),
and given responsibility for the whole (1491).
These designs fuse Classical principles favoured
by Tuscan architects with a love of decoration
found in Northern Italy. The *polychrome *Renaissance *screen-façade of the *Certosa* (carried out
with **Antonio** (d.1495) and **Cristofero** (d.*c.*1481)
Mantegazza) conceals the *basilican form behind.
As chief architect to Milan Cathedral he, with
Giovanni Giacomo Dolcebuono (1440-1506),
was involved in the construction of the Gothic
domical vault and lantern (*tiburio*), but the
design reflected the views of *Giorgio Martini
and *Bramante, who considered that the architecture must conform to the *Duomo*'s Gothic style.
Amadeo also worked on the *cupola of *Santa
Maria presso San Celso* (from 1494), the *Ospedale
Maggiore* (1493-4), and Bramante's *choir at
Santa Maria delle Grazie (from 1498), all in Milan.

He (1996); Schofield *et al.* (1989); Shell & Castelfranchi
(eds) (1993); J.T (1996)

ambitus 1. Consecrated area surrounding a grave, tomb, or burial-ground attached to a church. **2.** Space in a *catacomb* or *hypogeum* *loculus* surrounding the body or coffin, or around a funerary *urn* or *cinerarium* in a *columbarium* or tomb.

ambo, ambon (*pl.* ambones) *Gradus, lectorium, lectricium,* or *lectern* or *pulpit,* properly a singing-desk, approached by steps, particularly associated with *Early-Christian churches, where there were often two *ambones,* one on the north (for reading or chanting the *Gospel) and one on the south (for the *Epistle) side of the *choir or *presbytery: in *San Clemente,* Rome, the *ambones* balance each other on either side, attached to the *cancelli* or low *screen-walls defining the choir.

ambry *See* AUMBRY.

ambulacrum 1. *Atrium,* *court, or *parvis, sometimes with a *fountain in the centre, surrounded by *arcades or *colonnades, and often planted with trees, in front of a *basilica. **2.** Any walk or avenue with formally arranged tree-planting.

ambulatio (*pl.* ambulationes) **1.** Promenade, or *xystum open to the sky. **2.** Covered promenade, or *xystus,* defined by fragrant formal planting, by a *colonnade, or both. **3.** *Ambulatory, volume, or walkway bounded by a temple-*peristyle and the *cella-wall.

ambulatory 1. Any place in which to process or promenade, whether partially or totally covered or uncovered, e.g. *ambulatio or *cloister. **2.** *Aisle linking the *chancel-aisles behind the *high-altar in a large church: it can be canted, semicircular, or straight on plan, with chapels to the east and the *sanctuary to the west.

ambulatory church 1. Church with an *ambulatory between the *sanctuary and chapels to the east. **2.** *Early-Christian or *Byzantine church with a domed area bounded on at least three sides by *aisles and *galleries, so forming a cross on plan, also known as a *cross-domed church.

American bond *See* BRICK.

American Directory *See* DIRECTOIRE.

American garden Garden planted with species from North America. In the C18 seeds were collected and sent to subscribers in England: these included magnolias, kalmias, and rhododendrons, which flourished in shady dells and peaty soils. *Beckford introduced extensive American planting at Fonthill, Wilts. (1780s), whilst H. *Repton reinvented the *wilderness at Bulstrode, Bucks., as an American garden in the woodland style: he later took a more artificial approach at Ashridge, Herts. (1813)—thus two schools of

planting developed. By the mid-C18 the style became loosely associated with the term *gardenesque as seen in *Loudon's American garden at Coleshill, Warwicks. (1843).

Shoe (2001); Symes (2006)

American Order *Capital resembling that of the *Corinthian *Order with *acanthus leaves replaced by *corn-cobs, corn-ears, and tobacco-leaves, invented by *Latrobe for the US Capitol in Washington, DC.

Ammanati *or* **Ammannati, Bartolomeo** (1511–92) Born near Florence, Ammanati was a gifted *Mannerist sculptor, but he also designed buildings, including the *Ponte Santa Trinità* in Florence (1567–70—rebuilt after destruction (1944)). He was involved in the making of the sunken *cortile and fountain *grottoes at the *Villa Giulia,* Rome (1551–5), with *Vignola and *Vasari, and later extended the *Palazzo Pitti,* Florence (1558–70), for which he designed the heavily *rusticated garden-front and *cortile,* where the influence of the Venetian Mint by *Sansovino (with whom Ammanati had worked earlier) is overt. He supervised the construction of (and may have partly designed) *Michelangelo's entrance *vestibule and staircase to the Library of *San Lorenzo,* Florence (1524–50s). Among his designs for churches were *San Giovannino,* Florence (1579–85), and *Santa Maria in Gradi,* Arezzo (1592), both of which were influenced by *Il Gesù,* Rome. His connection with the *Collegio Romano* is tentative, for it was designed by **Giuseppe Valeriano** (1542–96). He probably built most of the *Palazzo Provinciale,* Lucca (1577–81), in which the centrepiece is a *Serlian *loggia derived from that employed by Vasari at the Uffizi, Florence.

Fossi (1967); He (1996); Kiene (1995); Lotz (1977); J.T (1996)

Ammann, Gustav (1885–1955) Influential Swiss landscape architect, he was taught by, among others, Leberecht *Migge. He became (1911) executive garden-designer for *Froebels Erben, and worked for the firm until 1933, during which time he taught many, including Ernst *Cramer, and his designs influenced *Neutra (who began his career with Froebel in 1918). Ammann established (1934) his own firm in Zürich, working with numerous architects, and was responsible for the landscapes for the Swiss *Werkbund* project at Niebühl (1929–32) and the Swiss National Exhibition (1939). He designed Hoenggerherg Cemetery, Zürich (1948), and wrote on his profession for numerous journals.

Bucher (1996); Shoe (2001)

Ammann, Othmar Hermann (1879–1965) Swiss-born engineer, he settled (1904) in the USA, and over 35 years designed bridges in the

NY area. He joined (1925) the Port of New York Authority and made his name with the Bayonne Bridge, a graceful *parabolic two-hinged steel-arch structure (opened 1931). In the same year his George Washington Bridge was opened, with twice the span of any then existing suspension-bridge, and steel-framed towers suggesting vestigial *Classicism. His elegant Bronx–Whitestone suspension-bridge was the first to use shallow plate-*girders as stiffeners instead of the more usual deep *trusses. He formed (1946) a partnership with **Charles S. Whitney** (1892–1959), establishing one of the leading engineering firms in the world. The majestic Verrazano-Narrows Bridge, NYC (completed 1964), was even longer than his earlier structures.

Billington (1983); Rastorfer (2000); Stüssi (1974)

ammer-tree, emmertree Timber beam or iron bar (from which chains are suspended for cooking-pots) set in a *chimney over a fire.

Ammonite Order Type of *capital similar to the *Ionic Order, first used 1788-9, according to some authorities, by George *Dance, Jun., on **Alderman John Boydell**'s (1719-1804) Shakespeare Gallery, 52 Pall Mall, London (demolished 1868-9), but possibly derived from designs by *Piranesi. It was employed by the architect-developers Amon and Amon Henry *Wilds (probably as a kind of 'signature') to embellish early C19 domestic architecture in Kent and Sussex, with *volutes resembling the whorled chambered fossilized shells, called *snake-stones*, of a genus of cephalopods, once supposed to be coiled petrified snakes, and were so called from their resemblance to the *Cornu Ammonis*, or involuted horn of **Jupiter Ammon**.

Co (2008); Dale (1947)

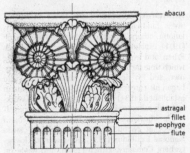

Ammonite capital As used by the Wilds at Brighton (1820s), and in groups of houses in London, e.g. New Cross Road, Southwark (c.1829).

Amoretto (*pl.* **Amoretti, Amorettoes**) *See* AMORINO.

Amorino (*pl.* **Amorini**) Winged male baby (unlike a wingless *putto), or young child, often chubby and knowing, *also called* **Amoretto, Little Love, *Cherub, or *Cupid**.

amphi- Prefix, meaning on both sides, or the same at front and rear. *For example*:
amphi-antis: Classical *temple with an *in-antis* (*see* ANTA) *portico at each end;
amphi-prostyle: *apteral temple without flanking *colonnades, but with a *prostyle portico at each end of the *cella;
amphitheatre: **1.** Roman building-type resembling two theatres joined together to form an *arena, elliptical on plan (viz. the Colosseum, Rome); **2.** Bowl-like garden feature with tiers, planted or not, sometimes used for open-air performances;
amphithura: veil or curtain, opening at the sides, in the *iconostasis of a Greek church.

ampullae niche **1.** Niche associated with the *credence-table and often with the *piscina in a church containing consecrated oil, holy water, etc. **2.** Recess or space in which the *font stands, so a *baptistery.

Amsterdam School Group of Netherlands architects influenced by E.G.H.H.*Cuijpers, *Berlage, and F.L.L.*Wright, including van der *Mey, *Kramer, and de *Klerk, who designed brick structures much influenced by *Expressionism and by Dutch *vernacular traditions (c.1912-36). The antithesis of work by the *De-*Stijl* group, it was publicized in *Wendingen* ('Turnings'—1918-31), edited by *Wijdeveld.

Amsterdam School (1975); Casciato (1996); Derwig *et al.* (1991); Hewitt *et al.* (1980); Sennott (ed.) (2004)

amusement-park C20 development that emerged from medieval European *pleasure-gardens featuring live entertainment, fireworks, dancing, games, and amusement-rides. The 1893 Columbian Exposition, Chicago, IL, was a US commercial development of this historic tradition where popularized leisure activities (usually strolling or walking manifest in rural cemeteries, city-parks, and rooftop gardens) embraced new technological devices such as the carousel, roller-coaster, and Ferris-wheel. The Exposition's temporary White City, with grounds designed by *Olmsted and buildings by *Sullivan and F.L.L.*Wright, was an important precedent for developments, providing a unified landscape that functioned as an escapist oasis. Later exemplars veered more towards amusement than aesthetic beauty: the idea was taken further (1956) by **Walt Disney** (1901-66) in CA—a permanent theme-park named Disneyland (then Disney World (1965)), with other progeny elsewhere. From this emerged Experimental Prototype Community of Tomorrow in 1982. *See* EPCOT.

Shoe (2001)

Analogical architecture Aldo *Rossi's term for his 1970s work in which he saw analogies with historic buildings, *vernacular architecture, etc.

Ferlenga (1987)

Analytical Decomposition Term used by Argentine-born American architects, **Diana Agrest** (1944–) and **Mario Gandelsonas** (1938–), possibly suggested by the work of the Russian film-maker, **Sergei Eisenstein** (1898–1948), in which the spectator moves through a series of carefully disposed scenes. It suggests something between memory and amnesia, where the architecture 'resists stylistic, typological, or linguistic classification', drifting between abstractions and real forms, and 'between convention and idiosyncrasy'. With their house at Sag Pond, Sagaponack, Long Island, NY (1990–4), they demonstrated the architectural possibilities of this with disparate elements, using timber cladding, and suggesting a tradition that was only half-remembered. It owes something to the compositional techniques of **Piet(er) Cornelis Mondrian** (1872–1944) and *Rietveld, but with injections of traditional construction and vernacular techniques.

J (1996); V (1995a)

anastylosis Term for rebuilding a structure with its original materials and structural system, employing new materials only when absolutely necessary, and ensuring they cannot be confused with original fabric.

anathyrosis Smooth *dressing of the margin of *ashlar *masonry or of the *drums comprising the *shaft of a Classical column to ensure accurate joints.

anchor 1. Misnomer for the arrow-head, dart, or tongue-like ornament alternating with the *egg-like form enriching e.g. *ovolo *mouldings or the *echinus of *Ionic *capitals. **2.** Exposed head of a metal tie or *anchor-beam* preventing the bulging of walls, often with a circular plate, or **S, X,** or **Y** shapes on the external face of a wall. **3.** *Attribute of Faith, later of Hope.

anchorage *Cell or retreat of an *anchorite*, or person who has withdrawn from this world. They are often found over *vestries on the north side of *chancels in the North of England, but could be sited elsewhere, usually in churchyards.

ancon, anconis (*pl.* **ancones**) **1.** *Console, *crossette, shouldering-piece, or *truss resembling a scrolled bracket, supporting each end of a *cornice over the *antepagmenta* of apertures in Classical architecture, narrower at the bottom than at the top (so wedge-shaped), although the term is loosely given to parallel-sided *consoles, parotides*, or *prothyrides*. **2.** Keystone, often ornamented. **3.** *Quoin or two adjacent sides of a

rectangle. **4.** Cramp employed in *masonry to join two stones. **5.** Projection left on a column-shaft *drum to enable it to be lifted by ropes.

ander, andor 1. *Porch, *vestibule, or lobby. **2.** Space between the top of a wall and the sloping roof.

Anderson, John MacVicar (1835–1915) Scots architect, articled to his uncle, William *Burn, whose partner he became: he continued to practise after Burn's death. As well as carrying out additions to various London clubs, he was responsible for the handsome Classical *façade of Coutts's Bank in the centre of the *Nash terrace at The Strand, London (demolished 1973), and the British Linen Bank (now Bank of Scotland), Threadneedle Street (both 1902–4).

DSA (2013); A.S.Gray (1985)

Anderson, Sir Robert Rowand (1834–1921) One of the most gifted architects Scotland has produced, trained in the office of **John Lessels** (1808–83). Among his buildings are All Saints' Church, Edinburgh (1864–78), the Catholic Apostolic Church, Edinburgh (1871–94), the Medical School (1874–86) and McEwan Hall (1884–90), Edinburgh University, the Central Station Hotel, Glasgow (1878–84—influenced by Scandinavian C17 precedents), and Govan Parish Church (1884–8): the last is one of the finest works of the *Gothic Revival in Scotland. He designed the *wings and *terrace at Pollok House, Glasgow (1890s), and the Pearce Institute, Govan (1903–5). A meticulous conservationist, his sensitive work at e.g. Iona (1874–6), Paisley (1898–1907), and Sweetheart (near Dumfries—1911–14) Abbeys, may be cited. Among his many designs, Mount Stuart, Rothesay, Bute (from 1878), and the National Portrait Gallery and Museum of Antiquities, Edinburgh (1884–9), are of considerable interest. His Revivalism was scrupulous and scholarly, he published works on French and Italian medieval architecture (1870–5), and, with others, edited a volume dealing with Scottish architecture (C12–C17).

McKinstry (1991); *ODNB* (2004); Paterson (1921); Savage (1980)

Andersson, Sven-Ingar (1927–2007) Swedish horticulturalist/art-historian, he succeeded *Sørensen as Professor of landscape architecture, Royal Academy of Fine Arts, Copenhagen (1963–94). His publications discussed principles of restoration in garden-art, identifying the *locus amoenus* (the garden as a place for sensual pleasure), the *genius loci* (the garden as the realization of the potential of the place), and *teatrum orbi* (the garden as a stage for life) as essentials for success. His approach was evident in projects at Sophienholm, Denmark (from 1967), Ronneby, Sweden

(1980s), and Damsgaards Have, Norway (c.1983). His concept of 'free-renewal', founded on archaeological evidence and his own creative skills, was evident in his reconstruction (1990s) of **Tycho Brahe**'s (1546-1601) observatory at Uraniborg, Hven. Prizewinning designs include the *Karlsplatz-Resselpark*, Vienna (1991-8).

Shoe (2001)

André, Édouard-François (1840-1911) French landscape architect, he assisted *Alphand in laying out the parks of Paris, and worked with **J.-P. Barillet-Deschamps** (1824-75) on the horticultural gardens at *La Muette*, Paris. On his own account he worked in England (e.g. Sefton Park, Liverpool (1867-72)), The Netherlands (he revived the C17 style of Dutch gardens), Italy, and Lithuania (where he promoted English landscape-design). He published *L'Art des Jardins* (1879), in which many themes found in the English landscape-garden were advocated for use in *public parks.

Imbert (1993)

André, Émile (1871-1933) French architect, pupil of *Laloux. With **Henri Gutton** (1873-1963) he designed the *Parc de Saurupt* housing development outside Nancy, in which *Art Nouveau features were mingled in a *Picturesque composition. He designed the double villa (1903) between the arch *abutments of the Strasbourg-Paris railway-line, and the **Vaxelaire** and **Pignot** department-stores (1901—to which his father, **Charles André** (1841-1928), and **Eugène Vallin** (1856-1922) contributed).

J.T (1996)

André, Louis-Jules (1819-90) French architect, pupil of *Lebas, he is best known for the reptile gallery (1870-4), zoology galleries (1877-89), and central hall (a master-work of cast-iron and glass architecture) in the *Musée d'Histoire Naturelle*, Paris. He took over *Labrouste's atelier (1855) and was an influential teacher.

J.T (1996)

Andrea di Cione (*fl.*1343-68) *See* ORCAGNA, ANDREA.

Andronikos of Kyrrhos, or Andronicus Cyrrhestes (*fl.*late-C2 BC–mid-C1 BC) Greek astronomer/architect, named by *Vitruvius, and known for one building, the Tower of the Winds or *Horologium*, Athens—a small octagonal structure intended as a sundial and weather-vane, and containing a water-clock. The *Order of the columns at the entrance was influential, especially in England during the late C18 and early C19 (*see* CAPITAL).

Crook (1972*a*); D (1950); D.S.R (1945)

Androuet *See* CERCEAU.

angel light Small, roughly triangular *light between subordinate arched window-*tracery, especially in *Perp. work.

Angell, Samuel (1800-66) English architect, pupil of Thomas *Hardwick, he later (1821-3) travelled in Sicily and Italy with William *Harris, and, with **Thomas Evans** (c.1784-1874), published (1826) *Sculptured Metopes discovered amongst the Ruins of the Temples of the Ancient City of Selinus in Sicily*. Appointed (1824) Surveyor to The Clothworkers' Company, he laid out (from 1846) that Company's estate in Islington. He designed Clothworkers' Hall, Mincing Lane (1856-60), in an *Italianate style (destroyed 1940), and various other buildings including several on the Clothworkers' estates in Co. Londonderry, notably The Clothworkers' Arms Hotel, Waterside, Coleraine, Formoyle Parish Church, and the layout and several pretty Classical houses at Castlerock in the 1840s. Angell was from 1831 one of the London District Surveyors, and was also Surveyor to The Saddlers' Company. He advised on the architectural competition for the Foreign Office in the 1850s. **Frederick William Porter** (1820-1901) succeeded to Angell's practice and designed the Parish Church at Castlerock.

Co (2008); J.Curl (1986)

angle Degree of inclination of two lines meeting at a point. *Compounds include*:

angle-bead: **1.** beaded *angle-staff*, consisting of a single *bead at the corner of joiner's work; **2.** upright *staff-bead* at the external angle of, and flush with, plasterer's work;

angle-buttress: *see* BUTTRESS;

angle-capital: *capital at the corner of a *colonnade or *portico. In the *Ionic *Order the front and side of a normal capital differ, so to obtain *volutes on *both* sides of the corner those at the external angle are splayed outwards at 45° (or 135° to the planes of the front and side elevations). Not to be confused with *angular capital*;

angle-fillet: *fillet to define an external angle and make it read clearly: it is more vulnerable to damage than a *bead;

angle-leaf: one of four carved claws, griffes, leaves, or *spurs projecting from the lower *torus of a *pier-base in medieval architecture covering one of the corners of the *plinth below. *See* SPUR;

angle-modillion: *modillion set diagonally at the external corner of a Classical *cornice, properly regarded as an *abuse, although known in Roman Antiquity;

angle-post: vertical *post at the corner of a *timber-framed structure: if one storey high, as in jettied construction, it is a *storey-post*;

angle-roll: *bowtell (plain rounded *moulding);

angle-round: *battlemented *parapet on continuous *corbelling set over a curved corner of a tower or wall, esp. in C17 Scottish architecture;

angle-shaft: **1.** decorative *colonnette at a building's external corner; **2.** colonnette in the *jamb of a *Romanesque aperture;

angle-stone: *quoin;

angle-tie: **1.** *angle-brace, dragon-tie*, or *horizontal brace* linking wall-plates at the corner of a hipped roof or supporting one end of a *dragon-beam (the other set on the mitring of the wall-plates); **2.** any timber *tie between two other timbers to stop them spreading;

angle-volute: spiral form at the corners of *Composite, *Corinthian, and Ionic capitals, also found in their medieval, especially *Romanesque, derivations.

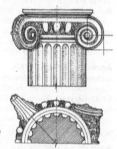

angle- *or* **corner-capital** Temple of *Fortuna Virilis*, Rome (*after Langley*).

anglo-chinois French term for a type of irregular informal landscape-garden supposedly evolved from Chinese prototypes and embellished with buildings in the Chinese Taste popularized by *Chambers. *See* CHINESE GARDEN; CHINOISERIE; SHARAWADGI.

Anglo-Saxon architecture English architecture from the end of C6 to the Norman Conquest (1066), *also called* **Saxon**. Much Anglo-Saxon building was of timber, but from *c.*672 significant structures were of *masonry, usually *rag or *rubble. Later, freestone *dressings, including *quoins set alternately horizontally and on end (*long-and-short work), raised *lesenes (as at Earl's Barton Church, Northants.), horizontal *string-courses, *blind arcades with lesenes, paired semicircular-headed openings separated by *baluster-like *colonnettes in towers, triangular-topped openings, and roughly carved outsized elements framing doorways, were common. Raised lesenes, strings, and long-and-short work suggest that rubble panels set back were originally intended to be *rendered. Occasionally, rubble was laid in *herring-bone patterns. Window-openings were usually small. Churches

consisted of a *nave (sometimes with a storey over) and a *chancel divided from the nave by an arch (e.g. Wittering, Soke of Peterborough) or by three arches (e.g. Bradwell-juxta-Mare, Essex). Northern chancels were usually square-ended, but in the South were often *apsidal. All Saints Church, Brixworth, Northants., has nave-arcades partly made of recycled Roman bricks and *tiles: this suggests a *basilica, but it appears the 'aisles' were subdivided by walls to form chambers, called *porticūs, although there seems to have been an *apse at one end and a two-storeyed porch at the other, with chambers on each side. Thus Brixworth is one of the grandest surviving examples of Anglo-Saxon architecture, although certain structures, such as the New *Minster at Winchester, Hants. (begun 903—destroyed), seem to have been more ambitious, owing much to *Carolingian precedent.

Ck (1996); Stoll (1967)

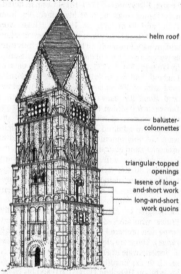

- helm roof
- baluster-colonnettes
- triangular-topped openings
- lesene of long-and-short work
- long-and-short work quoins

Composite church-tower incorporating typical Anglo-Saxon motifs from All Saints, Earls Barton, Northants., St Mary, Sompting, W.Sussex, and St Mary, Deerhurst, Glos.

angular Noun describing the vertical timber fixed at its base to a ceiling-*joist and at its top to a *rafter.

angular capital Type of *Ionic 'diagonal' *capital, with four identical faces and therefore eight *volutes, supposedly an *abuse invented by *Scamozzi, and known as the *Modern* or *Scamozzian* Ionic *Order. Thus, if it is used, no special *angle-capital is needed at the return angle of a *portico.

However, it had *Antique origins, for it occurs at the top part of *Composite capitals, and indeed existed independently as the 'diagonal' Ionic capital, fashionable in *Pompeii, and conspicuous on the Temple of Saturn, Rome (c.AD 320).

angular *or* **Scamozzi capital** (*after Langley*).

Anhalt-Dessau, Leopold III Friedrich Franz, Fürst von (1740-1817) German hereditary Prince (reigning over his Principality from 1758, and from 1807 as **Herzog** (Duke) **von Anhalt-Dessau**), he was a patron of architecture and, more importantly, of landscape architecture, as well as a protector of the Craft of *Freemasonry. In 1763-4, 1768-9, 1775, and 1785, he travelled in England, and began (1764) work to transform a total area of 300 square kilometres of meadowland along the banks of the River Elbe into a *Gartenreich* (Garden Realm) to evoke, by means of landscapes, gardens, and *fabriques*, the England he admired. Essentially, these gardens were not only mnemonic, but were intended as exemplary and educational: different styles in the buildings were to improve taste, and over thirty solutions to the technical problems of bridge-building were demonstrated in the structures over the waters. As a centrepiece to the gardens at Wörlitz, an Anglo-Palladian house was erected to designs by *Erdmannsdorff (friend of the Prince, who advised on the design of the landscape and prepared drawings of the various *fabriques*). There are allusions to the *Ile des Peupliers* at Ermenonville in France (the tomb of J.-J.*Rousseau); to the English diplomat and archaeologist **Sir William Hamilton** (1730-1803) and his collection of Greek vases in Naples in the 'Villa Hamilton' and rockwork 'Vesuvius'; to modernity in the form of the Iron Bridge (a quarter-scale version of *Pritchard's original at Coalbrookdale, Salop. (1775-9)); to *Walpole's Strawberry Hill at Twickenham, Mddx., (1750-76) in the Gothic House; to *Chambers's Casino at Wilton, Wilts. (c.1759) in the Temple of Flora; and much else influenced by *Clérisseau, *Winckelmann, and others. The various allusions in the *Gartenreich* (or 'England-by-the-Elbe') suggested an approach to life that was open-minded and free from all bigotry: the presence of the *Synagogue said as much. Apart from Erdmannsdorff, the gardeners involved were J.L.L.*Schoch, J.G.G.*Schoch, and J.F.*Eyserbeck: they created an enchanting place.

R.Alex (ed.) (1986, 1988); *AQC*, cxvi (2004) 83–126; Buttlar (1989); Günther (ed.) (1993); D.Hempel (ed.) (1987); Kleinschmidt & Bufe (1997); Quilitzsch *et al.* (1997); Ringkamp & Janssen (eds) (2000); Trauzettel (2000); Trauzettel & Winkler (1992)

annex(e) 1. *Wing of a building. **2.** Supplementary building or outbuildings providing additional accommodation. **3.** Addition to a building: if in front, it is an *avant-corps*, and if behind, an *arrière-corps*.

annular Ring-shaped. Annular *vaults spring from two concentric walls circular on plan, as in *Santa Costanza*, Rome (c.AD 325).

annulet 1. Horizontal *shaft-ring, *band, or *fillet encircling a *colonnette or column, especially that repeated three to five times under the *echinus of a Greek-*Doric *capital: thus *annulated* means with a ring or rings, e.g. a *Gothic *band securing a *shaft to a *pier. **2.** *List, *listella*, or vertical fillet between column-*flutes.

Anreith, Anton (1754-1822) German-born architect/sculptor/woodcarver, he settled in Cape Colony, South Africa (1776), bringing South-German *Rococo to the region. He built the less successful *Neo-Classical *façade of the Lutheran Church, Cape Town.

Bosdari (1954); Meintjes (1951)

anse de panier *See* ARCH.

anta (*pl.* **antae**) **1.** Square or rectangular *pier formed by the thickening of the end of a wall, e.g. in Greek *temples, where the projecting lateral walls of the *naos terminate. When *porticoes were formed by extending side-walls beyond the front wall of the naos and placing columns in a line between the antae, the columns, portico, and temple are described as *in antis*. Greek antae can have *capitals and *bases differing from those of the *Order proper, unlike Roman *pilasters, which are usually identical to the columns save for having rectangular plans. Antae have either very slight or no *entasis. **2.** Another term for an *antepagmentum.

ante- Prefix, meaning before or in front of. *Compounds include:*

ante-chamber: room leading to an apartment beyond, often used as a waiting-room;

ante-chapel: part of a chapel situated at its west end, like *transepts, serving as a volume before the chapel proper, e.g. Magdalen College Chapel, Oxford;

ante-choir: fore-choir, or area corresponding to the thickness of the *pulpitum*, e.g. Southwell *Minster, Notts. (c.1320-40);

ante-church: ante-nave, fore-church, or *narthex at the west end of a church, with *aisles and *nave, sometimes a few *bays long, e.g. the five-aisled *Galilee, Durham Cathedral (*c.*1170–80);

ante-court: first *court of a great house, preceding the *cour d'honneur, giving access to service-wings;

antefix, antefixum (*pl.* antefixes, antefixa): **1.** Decorative termination (often featuring *anthemion) of the covering-tiles over the joints of roof-tiles placed on the *eaves-tiles or on top of the *cyma of the *cornice, and sometimes on the *ridge-crest of a Greek temple; **2.** Ornament on the *frieze of early Classical temples, or over *pediment *acroteria, often of *terracotta. *Antefixum* (not *antefixa*) seems to have been an erroneous term for lions'-heads on the *cymatium of temples;

ante-mural(e): defensive breastworks, outworks, or walls before a city-wall, castle, or fortress, such as *barbican;

ante-nave: see ANTE-CHURCH;

antepagment, antepagmentum (*pl.* antepagments, antepagmenta): **1.** face of a *jamb of an aperture, or a moulded *architrave. Its top horizontal part, *supercilium* or *antepagmentum superius* is really a *moulding over the *lintel, and has a *section identical to that of the vertical parts of the architrave: it is often expressed as a lintel by means of a *crossette (**1**) projecting slightly beyond the tops of the *antepagmenta*: mouldings return at the ends, forming *ears, elbows, lugs, or shoulders*; **2.** *anta or *pilaster.

antependium: see ALTAR-FACING.

antefix from the *Parthenon*, Athens.

Antelami, *or* Antelmi, Benedetto degli

(*fl.*1178–1233) Italian sculptor/architect, responsible for the towering octagonal *Romanesque *Baptistry at Parma (1196–1216, completed 1270): the exterior features four tiers of open *colonnaded *galleries. Also attributed to him are the *pilgrimage-church of *Borgo San Donnino*, Fidenza (late-C12/early-C13), and the Church of *Sant'Andrea*, Vercelli (1219–26), in which the transition from *Romanesque to *Gothic is expressed.

K.Forster (1961); Quintavalle (1990)

anteris, anteridos (*pl.* anterides) **1.** *Buttress, *counter-fort, *erisma, sperone*, or *spur supporting or strengthening a wall. **2.** Type of *anta or *pilaster, called *sperone*, resembling a *lesene.

anthemion (*pl.* anthemia) **1.** Decorative group of leafy forms resembling a radiating cluster of flowers on the same plant, and called by some a honeysuckle: it occurs in Classical architecture above *acroteria, on *antefixa, on *cornices, on the *hypotrachelium of some varieties of the Greek-*Ionic *Order, and elsewhere, often used alternately with the *palmette or lotus in horizontal embellishments such as *friezes, and sometimes instead of the *fleuron on the *Corinthian *capital. **2.** William *Wilkins, in *Prolusiones Architectonicae* (1837), erroneously suggested it referred to the *Ionic *volute.

anthemion and **palmette** from the *Erechtheion*, Athens.

Anthemios of Tralles (*fl.* first half of C6) Greek mathematician/theorist, celebrated for the *Byzantine Church of *Hagia Sophia*, Constantinople (532–7). Commissioned by **Emperor Justinian I** (*r.*527–65) to design this huge structure (largely because of his reputation as an engineer), his building employed four massive *buttresses and two hemi-domes to contain the outward thrust of the low saucer-dome on *pendentives. He was assisted at *Hagia Sophia* by *Isidorus of Miletus.

Huxley (1959); Kra (1986); Mainstone (1988); Mango (1972, 1986); R.Mark & Çakmak (1992)

Anthon, George David (1714–81) Danish architect. Appointed Professor of Architecture at the Old Academy, Copenhagen (1748), and Royal Building Inspector (1751), he became (1760) Master-Builder to the Royal Court. He supervised construction at *Eigtved's Frederik's Hospital, and directed building works at Christian's Church after Eigtved's death, although he himself was responsible for the design of the *spire (1769). He prepared (1756) designs (unrealized) for Frederik's Church which were developments of proposals by Eigtved and *Jardin. Other works included the Castle of Bregentved, essentially after Eigtved's designs (1754), restoration at Kronborg Castle (1761), and building at Fredensborg (1762). He published (1759) *Anvisning til Civil-*

Bygningskunsten (Directions for Civic Architecture), which went into further editions (1772, 1818).

S (1901–2); We (1947–)

antic 1. *Grotesque ornamental representation of human, animal, and floral forms bizarrely mingled. **2.** Deliberately monstrous, fantastic, and caricatured representations of fauna and flora used in decorations. **3.** *Caryatid(e) or other humanoid representation, incongruously formed and inappropriately positioned. **4.** Distorted, leering mask, suggesting irrational, wild nature, and the realm of unreason.

anticlastic Of a double-curved surface, of which the two curvatures (transverse to each other) lie in opposite directions, convex in length and concave in breadth, or vice versa. This condition can be seen in e.g. a *hyperbolic *paraboloid roof. *See* SYNCLASTIC.

anticum 1. Latin equivalent of *pronaos, the space between the front of the *cella and the *colonnade of a *portico. **2.** Gate or a front door, or a variety of porch in front of a main door. **3.** *Temple-front. **4.** *Anta, but its use for this is erroneous.

Antique Pertaining to the Classical civilizations of Graeco-Roman Antiquity.

antis, in *See* ANTA.

Antistates (*fl.*C6 BC) One of the architects (the others were **Antimachides, Kallaeschros,** and **Porinos**) engaged by **Peisistratos** (560–527 BC) to build the Temple of Jupiter Olympius, Athens, mentioned by *Vitruvius.

D (1950); La (1983)

Antoine, Jacques-Denis (1733–1801) French architect, active in the *Louis-Seize period, appointed (1766) to build the *Neo-Classical *Hôtel des Monnaies, Quai de Conti,* Paris (1768–75), reckoned by *Quatremère de Quincy to be one of the finest French public buildings. He completed the *Barrières des Fermiers Généraux,* Paris, after *Ledoux was dismissed (1787). His town-houses for the aristocracy (including the rigorously plain *Hôtel Brochet de Saint-Prest* later *École des Ponts-et-Chaussées* (c.1768–74), and the *Hôtel de Jaucourt, Rue de Varennes* (1770)), and his country residences (e.g. *Château de Herces,* Berchères-sur-Vesgres, near Houdan (1770–2)), are in a severe Neo-Classical style. As architect to the *Révérends Pères de la Charité,* he built hospitals, including the *Hôpital de la Charité,* Paris (c.1760s), probably the first building with a baseless Greek-*Doric *portico in the French capital.

B (1980); Ha (1952); M & Wa (1987); P (1982); J.T (1996)

Antolini, Giovanni Antonio (1756–1841) Italian architect, much influenced by French *Neo-Classicism, as his monumental scheme for the *Foro Buonaparte,* Milan (1801), shows, but his realized projects are few.

Antolini (1806); Me (1966); Ms (1966); M & Wa (1987)

Antonelli, Alessandro (1798–1888) Professor of Architecture at Turin (1836–57). Addicted to the *temple-front, he employed it in several buildings, including the Sanctuary at Boca (from 1830), and the Parish Church, Oleggio (1853–8). He is regarded as one of the last great masters of *Neo-Classicism in Italy, and is famed for the *Mole Antonelliana* (a former *synagogue), Turin (1863–84), one of the tallest *masonry structures ever erected: rising in a series of stages defined by *Orders, it was crowned by a *pagoda-like *spire. It was completed by his son, **Costanzo** (1844–1923). He also added the very tall *cupola and *lantern over the *crossing of *San Gaudenzio* (from 1841) and remodelled the *Duomo* (1854–69—essentially a *basilica, but using columns extensively, inside and out), both in Novara.

Brino (1972); Gabetti (1989); Ms (1966); Rosso (1989)

Antonine column Monumental *Tuscan-*Doric column (similar to the earlier *Trajanic column) in Rome, supposedly commemorating **Emperor Antoninus Pius** (*r.*AD 138–61). Set on a large *pedestal, its *shaft is embellished with a spiral band of sculptured reliefs, and contains a circular staircase. It actually celebrates **Emperor Marcus Aurelius Antoninus** (*r.*AD 161–80), hence the confusion.

Antonio di Vicenzo (c.1350–1401/2) *See* VICENZO.

Antunes, João (1643–1712) Portuguese architect. His *Sta Engrácia,* Lisbon (begun 1682), has a centralized Greek-cross plan, four apsidal ends to the arms of the cross, and towers between each of the apsidal arms: it is therefore a variation on *Bramante's and *Peruzzi's designs for *San Pietro,* Rome. Antunes's other works in and around Lisbon (he was appointed (1699) Royal Architect) are of superlative quality, and include the enormous tomb of the **Infanta Joana** and the interior of the ante-choir of the convent-church of *Jesus in Aveiro* (1699–1711) in which the tomb stands.

Carvalho (1960–2); Kubler (1972)

apadana, apadhana Square porticoed, free-standing *hypostyle hall such as that in Persepolis built by **Darius I** (*r.*522–486 BC). *See* ACHAEMENIAN, ACHAEMENID.

apartment Self-contained set of rooms for domestic use (aka *flat*), on one floor, usually one of several in a large building (if extending over more than one floor it is called a *duplex).

Apartments were known in Ancient Rome, and were common in C17 Paris. Glasgow and Edinburgh have many outstandingly fine C18 and C19 apartments within handsome stone-built edifices. Numerous tall blocks containing apartments were built in NYC from the 1890s, and the type evolved when *elevators/lifts were developed. C20 apartment-blocks of note include the Lake Shore Drive Apartments, Chicago, IL (1950–1— with steel frames), by *Mies van der Rohe and Florin Court, Charterhouse Square, London (1935–7), by **Guy Morgan & Partners**.

Geist & Kurvers (1989); Loyer (1987)

aperture Opening in a wall for access, the admission of light or air (or both), or for defence or aesthetic reasons. Its sides are *jambs, its top a *head, *lintel, or arch; and its bottom the *cill.

apex Top of a cone, *gable, *obelisk, *pediment, or *pyramid. The *saddle- or apex-stone is the topmost stone at the apex of a gable or pediment.

apiary Place where *beehives are housed. At the beginning of the C19 the *apiary* entered the architectural pattern-book as a garden **fabrique*: J.B.*Papworth included it in *Hints on Ornamental Gardening* first published by *Ackermann in *The Repository* (1818–20). An example of Chinese-style beehives can be seen at Biddick Hall, Co. Durham. *See* AIP-HOUSE, BEE-BOLE, BEEHIVE.

J.B.Pa (1832); W.Pa (1852); Symes (2006)

Apolline Type of decoration drawing on the *attributes of the Greek sun-god **Apollo**, found in Classical Antiquity and revived during the *Renaissance and *Baroque periods, especially during the reign of *Louis Quatorze (1643–1715). Common motifs were the head of Apollo surrounded by sun-rays (the *sunburst), the chariot, the lyre, and the sun.

Apollodorus of Damascus (*fl.*AD 98–*c.*125) Architect to **Emperor Trajan** (*r.*98–117), credited with most of the Imperial buildings of the latter's reign, including the *thermae* and forum of Trajan, the enormous Ulpian *basilica, Trajan's column, and the nearby market complex. He seems to have given the Roman *thermae* their definitive form, was an important influence on the Roman Imperial style, and brought knowledge of advanced constructional techniques to bear on his various projects (not least of which was the huge bridge over the fast-flowing Danube, near Turnu Severin, Romania, constructed in *c.*104). It would be tempting to connect Apollodorus with the building of the *Pantheon and the *Villa Adriana*, Tivoli, in the time of **Hadrian** (*r.*117–38), but the evidence is lacking. He wrote several technical treatises, now lost, and enjoyed a considerable reputation in his lifetime, although disagreements

with Hadrian concerning the Temple of Venus and Rome may have cost him his life.

W.MacD (1965–86); W-P (1981, 1986)

apophyge, apophysis, apothesis 1. Outward curve, called *congé or scape, connecting the *shaft of a Classical column to the *fillets over the *base and under the *astragal beneath the *capital. **2.** *Hypotrachelium of the *Tuscan capital or the slightly concave *trachelium beneath the *echinus of certain archaic Greek-*Doric capitals.

applied 1. *Moulding, etc., planted on to a surface (*appliqué*). **2.** *Engaged, as a column.

approach Road leading from an estate entrance to the house, either a winding *drive* offering views within the landscape approaching the house from an angle, or a straight *avenue* (long, broad, tree-lined, and offering a sight of a point of view from a distance). A typical sweeping H.*Repton *approach* is at Port Eliot, Cornwall (1792–3).

W.Pa (1852); Symes (2006)

appui, appuy 1. *Base, support, *buttress, or *cill. It commonly refers to the narrower (because of the level to throw off water) top part of the *allège* forming the cill. **2.** Hand-*rail.

apron 1. Panel below a window-*cill, often enriched. **2.** In an apron- or *curtain-wall, a *spandrel or infill-panel between a window-cill above and a window-head below. **3.** Ornamental work below the *cornice or *eaves of a *verandah, i.e. *valance.

apse, apsis (*pl.* apses, apsides) Recess, generally semicircular on plan, and *vaulted, projecting from an external wall. It often terminates the *nave of a *basilica, and contains the *high-altar. Apses forming chapels were built on the eastern sides of *transepts of larger churches (e.g. Lincoln Cathedral), and some, termed *apse-chapels*, were arranged round a semicircular *apse-aisle* or *ambulatory* as in the complex *chevet* form of larger French churches. Some apses are canted.

apsidiole *Apse-chapel, or small apsidal chapel projecting from a larger apse.

apteral 1. Adjective describing a Classical *temple with a *portico at one or both ends, with no flanking *colonnades. **2.** Said of a church without *aisles, and especially of a liturgical west front with gabled top and no lean-to aisle-walls sloping to meet the *nave.

aqueduct Structure for artificially conveying a constant supply of water, consisting of a channel (usually covered to prevent evaporation and/or pollution) supported on *piers over valleys, roads, etc., and cut through hills. Numerous *Antique remains of aqueducts survive, the most impressive being the huge arcaded structures over the Roman *Campagna*, and that over the River Gard in France. Some C19 canal aqueducts, e.g. *Telford's Pont-y-Cysyllte (1795–1805) over the River Dee, Vale of Llangollen, Denbighshire, Clwyd, Wales, consist of cast-iron structures carried on massive piers.

Sk (2002); W-P (1981)

ara (*pl.* **arae**) Roman *altar. It could be a large, public, commemorative structure, like the sumptuous *Ara Pacis* (erected by **Emperor Augustus** (*r.* 27 BC–AD 14) to mark the establishment of Imperial power and the coming of peace in 13 BC), or a small altar in a private house by which protection of deities was invoked.

arabesque Decorative *scroll-ornament derived from branches, leaves, tendrils, and vegetation, inaccurately called *Moresque*, arranged in intertwined symmetrical geometrical patterns. Usually defined as free from human or animal figures, it is distinct from *grotesque ornament.

W-J (1967a)

(a)   (b)

arabesque (*a*) from C17 Flemish pattern-book; (*b*) C16 example from The Louvre, Paris.

Arabian Vague term suggesting *Moorish or other architecture of Islamic origin.

araeostyle *See* INTERCOLUMNIATION.

ARAU (*Atelier de Recherche et d'Action Urbaine*) Belgian architectural pressure-group formed in 1968 by **Maurice Culot** (1939–) to study problems posed by drastic urban redevelopment (especially arguing for *conservation and *restoration). It was publicized in *Archives d'Architecture Moderne* from 1975.

AD, **xlvii/3** (1977), 187–99; Culot & Meade (eds) (1996); Loo (ed.) (2003); J.T (1996); J.Walker (1992)

arbalestina, arbalesteria *See* BALISTRARIA.

Arbeitsrat für Kunst (Work-Council for Art) Group of German architects founded (1918) by Bruno *Taut, including Otto *Bartning, Walter *Gropius, Erich *Mendelsohn, and Max *Taut. Gropius took over leadership in 1919 and when he moved to the Weimar *Bauhaus, the programme there reflected the group's (disbanded 1921) ideals; a fusion of the arts under the wing of architecture (the *Bauprojekt*).

Boyd Whyte (1982)

arboretum 1. Garden containing a collection of trees. **2.** Tree nursery. *See* PINETUM.

arbor vitae *Thuja articulata*, or *white cedar*, with figured parts called *Tigerwood* and *Pantherwood*, used for *inlay and other fine work (e.g. the *retablo* in Seville Cathedral (1482–1550)).

arbour Garden-building of timber, lattice-work, and wicker-work, intended to be covered with climbing plants.

arca, archa 1. Space in a vaulted chamber for sepulchral purposes, e.g. *arcosolium* or *loculus*. **2.** Excavation before the basement-walls of a building. **3.** Mortuary-chest, shrine, pyx, or receptacle for Relics. **4.** *Prison or secure chamber. **5.** *Caisson for building bridges. **6.** Roof-beam with a groove running its length.

arcade 1. Series of arches on the same plane, supported by *colonnettes, columns, *piers, or *pilasters. *Varieties of arcade include*:
alternating: with arches springing from the ends of two-column *colonnades, resembling a series of overlapping *serlianas;
blind: arcade *engaged with (attached to) a wall, also called *surface-* or *wall-arcade*;
coupled: carried on *coupled columns;
interlacing or intersecting: overlapping arcades, e.g. *Romanesque overlapping arcades, producing a series of pointed arches, as in Southwell *Minster, Notts. (C12);
nave: series of arches on *piers separating *nave from *aisle and supporting the *clerestorey in a church;
regular: any series of repetitive arches, also called a *simple* arcade;
screen: arcade standing on its own as a feature, or used as a *screen;
simple: *see* REGULAR;
surface: *see* BLIND;
syncopated: two rows of arcade, one in front of the other, with the colonnette shafts of one set in front of the centres of the arches behind, as in Lincoln Cathedral;

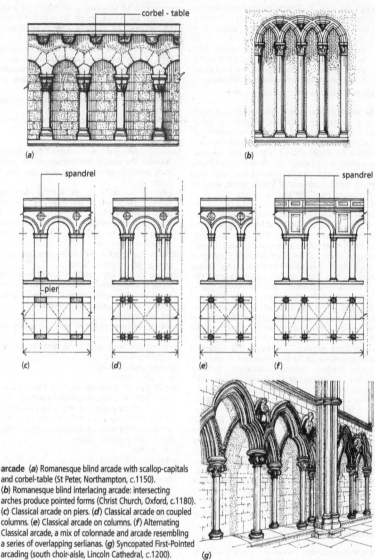

arcade (*a*) Romanesque blind arcade with scallop-capitals and corbel-table (St Peter, Northampton, c.1150). (*b*) Romanesque blind interlacing arcade: intersecting arches produce pointed forms (Christ Church, Oxford, c.1180). (*c*) Classical arcade on piers. (*d*) Classical arcade on coupled columns. (*e*) Classical arcade on columns. (*f*) Alternating Classical arcade, a mix of colonnade and arcade resembling a series of overlapping serlianas. (*g*) Syncopated First-Pointed arcading (south choir-aisle, Lincoln Cathedral, c.1200).

wall: see BLIND. **2.** Row of vertical *arcade-posts* carrying the *arcade-plate*, set between the nave or central area and aisles of a *timber-framed aisled building. **3.** Top-lit roofed passage with shops on either side, known as a *shopping-arcade*, equivalent to the *galerie, galleria*, or *passage* on the Continent. **4.** Avenue arched over with trees and shrubs.

ABDM (1996); Geist (1983); MacKeith (1986)

Arcadia Central area of Peloponnesus, shut off from the coast by mountains, inhabited in Antiquity by shepherds and hunters worshipping the nature-deities Pan, Hermes, and Artemis. Immortalized by **Virgil** (70–19 BC), Arcadia became perceived as a peaceful, beautiful, secluded landscape in which simple, pastoral lives were enjoyed. Printed editions of Virgil's works were in circulation from the middle of the C15, with themes re-emerging in literary works such as **Jacopo Sannazaro**'s (1458–1530) popular verse-eclogues, *Arcadia* (1504), and **Sir Philip Sidney**'s (1554–86) prose-romance (1590). Sannazaro suggested far more than a sweetened pastoral landscape: scenery was revealed with darker emotions emphasized in waterfalls and precipices, caves, and the like. The Arcadian ideal prompted the evolution of rural retreats in Roman times, epitomized in the *villa urbana* described by *Pliny the Younger: uncultivated ground evoked surprise, and his seaside Laurentine retreat offered views of woods and meadows with mountain backdrops. This prompted concepts of viewing landscape from windows, *porticos, and sheltered seating-areas, popular in numerous C17 and C18 garden-designs, although Arcadian lyricism became the subject of C17 Dutch, French, and Italian landscape-painters and poets *before* it penetrated other genres such as theatre, architecture, and garden-art. These characteristics underpinned the experimental process of the C18 English landscape-garden, transforming Arcadian concepts producing garden-paradigms studded with Classical, Gothic, and *rustic *fabriques* set against backgrounds of 'wild nature': Studley Royal, Yorks., Stourhead, Wilts., and Stowe, Bucks., were the three great English gardens that impacted most on European garden-design.

Morley (1993); Mowl (2000); Pliny the Younger (1751); RdR (1994); Sannazaro (1504); Schama (1995); VP (1567)

arc-boutant See ARCH-BUTTRESS.

arch Construction, known as an *arch-ring*, made of truncated wedge-shaped *blocks (*arch-stones* or *voussoirs*) that by mutual pressure stay in place, set out in a curved form to span an opening and carry a superimposed load, as an alternative to a *lintel: it is termed *arcuated*, as opposed to *trabeated*. *Terms associated with an arch include:*

abutment: solid structure from which an arch springs, and which resists the outward *thrust* (all arches will collapse unless adequately supported);

archivolt: concentric ring of *mouldings round an arch, like an *architrave bent around the top;

chord: horizontal distance between *abutments* taken from the *springing-line* on one side to that of the other, also called the *span*;

crown: highest point of the *intrados*, also called *vertex*;

extrados: upper curve of each *voussoir* or outer extremity of the *archivolt*;

flank: see HAUNCH;

haunch: curved part on the top of the section between the *crown*, the portion of the arch itself, and the extremity of the *span*, also called *flank*;

height: *rise* of an arch, or vertical distance between the *chord* to the *crown* or highest point of the *intrados*;

impost: projecting member, often moulded, from which an arch *springs*, e.g. a *block, *bracket, *corbel, or *dosseret*;

intrados: lower curve of each *voussoir*, i.e. coinciding with the arch's *soffit*;

keystone: central large wedge-shaped *voussoir* in an arch, often elaborately carved as an *ancon*;

section of the cavity: vertical plane figure bounded by the *span* and the *intrados*;

span: see CHORD;

springing: point at which an arch unites with its support;

springing-line: horizontal plane from which an arch begins to rise.

Types of arch include:

acute: see LANCET-;

anse de panier: *three-centred*, resembling a basket-handle, also known as *basket-handled*, usually formed by a segment of a circle connected to two other segments with smaller radii, but sometimes constructed using five or seven centres to give a similar shape;

back: see REAR;

basket: see ANSE DE PANIER;

bell: arch supported on two *corbels with curved faces above the reveals, so that the resulting compound curve of the opening resembles a bell;

Caernarfon: see WELSH;

camber: *flat* with a slight upward curve to the intrados, or a very low *segmental*;

canted: similar to a *corbel*, but with straight haunches set at an angle of 45°;

catenary: formed like an inverted *catenary, similar to *parabolic*, but less sharp and more elegant;

compound: *Order* or *recessed* consisting of several concentric arches with vertical supports, successively placed within and behind each other, each smaller than that in front, as in a *Romanesque doorway;

contrasted: as *ogee*;

corbel: *false* or *pseudo-* formed by means of horizontal blocks corbelled out from each side of the opening to be bridged until the last is closed;

cusped: *see FOIL*;

depressed: *see ANSE-DE-PANIER, FOUR-CENTRED*, and *THREE-CENTRED*;

diaphragm: *transverse* across a nave supporting a gable between sections of a timber roof to prevent the spread of fire;

diminished: *segmental*, lower than a *semicircular*;

discharging: *see RELIEVING*;

drop: *pointed* with its centres on the springing-line and with the *span* longer than the radius;

Dutch: triangular *false* constructed of bricks laid on a slope of 45° starting from a *skew-back at each *jamb and meeting at an *apex;

elliptical: formed as half an ellipse with its axis coinciding with the springing-line;

equilateral: *pointed two-centred* of two arcs, the radii of which are equal to the span;

false: *see CORBEL* and *DUTCH*;

flat: *straight* with a level or slightly *cambered* soffit, the *voussoirs* seeming to form a lintel;

Florentine: *semicircular* with extrados and intrados struck from different centres, so that the *voussoirs* increase in length towards the top;

foil: *cusped* or *foliated* associated with *Gothic, *Moorish, and *Islamic styles. Foil-arches can have *trefoils, *cinquefoils*, or *multifoils* within a *pointed* arch, can have a series of small arcs cut in the intrados, as in the *Moorish multifoil* or *scalloped* arch, or can themselves be in the form of *foils, such as the *pointed trefoil* or *round trefoil* arch;

foliated: *see FOIL*;

four-centred: *depressed*, the characteristic form of late-*Perp. openings, with upper central arcs with centres below the springing-line, flanked by two arcs with centres on the springing-line;

French: *Dutch*;

gauged: *flat*, with a slightly *cambered *soffit, formed of voussoirs made of precisely cut stones, or, more usually, finely rubbed bricks (known as *rubbers*), with very fine lime-putty joints;

horseshoe: usually associated with Islamic styles, such arches are *horseshoe* (semicircular, narrowing towards the base below the springing-line, on straight piers), *pointed horseshoe* (pointed with arcs continuing to narrow the opening below the springing-line), and *round horseshoe* (semicircular with arcs continuing to narrow the opening below the springing-line);

interlacing: *intersecting* semicircular *Romanesque arches in a *blind *arcade, overlapping and forming pointed arches;

inverted: built upside-down, used in foundations;

Italian pointed: with intrados and extrados struck from different centres, and *voussoirs* increasing in size towards the apex. Similar to *Florentine*, but *pointed*;

jack: *segmental* brick arch spanning between iron beams, thus forming a vault;

keel: *see OGEE*;

lancet: sharply pointed *two-centred* or *acute* type with the radii greater than the span;

mitre: triangular *pseudo*-arch of two flat stone slabs leaning together at a mitred apex, common in *Anglo-Saxon architecture; also called *pediment* arch;

Moorish: *horseshoe*-shaped, sometimes with a pointed top;

Moorish multifoil: *see FOIL*;

nodding-ogee: *see OGEE*;

obtuse-angled: pointed type formed of arcs with centres on either side of the centre-line;

ogee: pointed *keel*-arch of four arcs with two centres outside it and two inside, thus producing two **S**-shaped curves, first occurring *c.*1300. A *nodding ogee* has its apex projecting beyond the *naked of the wall, so it is a double *ogee in elevation and a single in section;

Order: *see COMPOUND*;

parabolic: shaped like the intersection of a cone with a plane parallel to its vertical axis, sometimes confused with a *catenary*, but sharper and less elegant;

pediment: *see MITRE*;

pointed: any pointed arch, but especially *equilateral*. Proportions of pointed arches are governed by the positions of the centre-points from which the arcs are struck. *See ACUTE, DROP, EQUILATERAL, FOIL, FOUR-CENTRED, HORSESHOE, ITALIAN POINTED, LANCET, OBTUSE-ANGLED, OGEE, SARACENIC, SEGMENTAL POINTED*, and *TUDOR*;

pseudo-four-centred: *see TUDOR*;

pseudo-three-centred: *depressed* type consisting of two arcs struck from the springing-line supporting a central *flat* or *straight pseudo*-arch of *voussoirs* with joints struck from a point well below the springing-line;

raking: *rampant* with one impost higher than the other;

rampant: *see RAKING*;

rear: *arrière voussure, back*, or *secondary* spanning an opening on the inside of a thick wall, as when there is a lintel on the outside, but a splayed arched reveal inside;

recessed: *see COMPOUND*;

relieving: *discharging* or *safety*, it is usually *segmental*, built flush with the wall-surface over a lintel to relieve the latter from the weight of *masonry above, and to discharge the forces away from the lintel;

round horseshoe: *see HORSESHOE*;

round trefoil: *see FOIL*;

rowlock: has small *voussoirs* laid in a series of concentric rings;

safety: *see RELIEVING*;

Saracenic: pointed *stilted, striped* with alternate *voussoirs* of contrasting colours;

scalloped: see FOIL;

scheme: *segmental* or *skene*;

secondary: see REAR;

segmental: with its centre below the springing-line. A *segmental pointed* arch has two centres below the springing-line;

semicircular: with its centre on the springing-line;

shouldered: flat arch or lintel carried on *quadrant-ended corbels over jambs;

skene: see SCHEME;

skew: has jambs at an angle other than 90° to its face, or one spanning something obliquely. The beds of the courses of a *skew* arch consist of spiral lines wound, as it were, around a cylinder, every part of which cuts the axis at a different angle, the angle being greatest at the keystone and least at the springing: when viewed from beneath the courses appear as straight lines. *Skew* is a slope, as in the abutment of a gauged-brick *flat* or *straight* arch. *Skewback* is the part of the abutment giving support to the arch;

soldier: *flat pseudo*-arch of uncut ungauged bricks laid on end and supported by some means such as on an L-shaped metal angle;

squinch: diagonal arch or arches (see TRUMPET-arch) in the internal angle of a tower supporting an octagonal *spire, or used instead of pendentives to carry a dome over a square compartment;

stilted: with its springing-line raised on piers above the level of the impost;

straight: see FLAT;

strainer: one constructed between piers or walls to prevent them moving inwards towards each other, as at the *crossing of Wells Cathedral, Som.;

sub-: subsidiary minor arch enclosed and framed within a larger structural arch. In *Gothic work it consisted of two inferior arches, under the main arch, rising naturally from the middle *mullion and forming two independent arches filled with *tracery;

surbased: rises less than half its span;

surmounted: rises higher than half its span;

Syrian: series of small arches above a series of wider arches, centred on the arches and piers below;

three-centred: *depressed* with two arcs struck from the springing-line with a central arc struck from below it. A *depressed three-centred* arch has the central arc struck from a point very much lower than the springing-line;

transverse: divides a compartment of a vault from another, spanning from wall to wall or from wall to pier, forming a *bay;

trefoil: see FOIL;

triangular: see MITRE;

triumphal: monumental arched free-standing structure, invented by the Romans, and a significant precedent for later *façade treatments in which *columnar-and-*trabeated elements were mixed with *arcuated forms. Many Roman examples survive, including that of **Septimius Severus** (*r.*AD 193–211), with two smaller arches flanking a wider central arch with a richly coffered vault. The form was revived during the *Renaissance period, and there are many fine Neo-Classical examples, including the Carrousel arch, Paris, by *Percier and *Fontaine (1806–7);

trumpet-: *squinch*-like part of a cone, i.e. with the arches getting wider and higher towards the extremities;

Tudor: *pseudo-four-centred* late-*Perp. arch, similar to the *four-centred* type, but with shanks starting as quarter-circles (with centres on the springing-line) continuing as straight lines to the apex. It is very *depressed*, and often expressed as a single lintel;

two-centred: *acute* or *lancet*;

Venetian: *semicircular* framing two semicircular-headed *lights separated by a colonnette above which is a *roundel in the space between the tops of the smaller arches and the main intrados;

Welsh: *Caernarfon*, comprising a wide keystone resting on two corbels shaped to fit the keystone.

Compounds include:

arch-band: raised *band or strip (*arc-doubleau*) below the soffit of an arch or vault;

arch-bar: metal rectangular bar under a *flat*- or *soldier*-arch supporting the voussoirs;

arch-beam: curved beam or *collar-brace*;

arch-brace: curved brace in timber-framed work found in pairs forming an arched shape;

arch-brick: wedge-shaped brick (called *compass-brick, feather-edged brick*, or *voussoir*) for constructing an arch or a wall curved on plan;

arch-buttant: as *arch-buttress*;

arch-buttress: flying *buttress, *arch-buttant*, *arched butment*, or *arc-boutant*;

arch-façade: screen-wall into which are set deep, plain arches, as at the west front of Lincoln Cathedral;

arch Order: **1.** engaged columns, bases, *pedestals, and *entablature attached to an arcuated structure as in a triumphal arch, or a series of superimposed Orders and arches as in the Roman Colosseum; **2.** successive planes of diminishing concentric arches with colonnettes, as in a compound arch or a Romanesque doorway;

arch-rib: vault-rib across a *nave or *aisle at right angles to the main axis;

arch-ring: load-bearing curved part of an arched structure made of *voussoirs;

arch-stone: voussoir or keystone;

arch-truss: *truss with an arched upper chord (the lower side of which is concave) and a lower horizontal member, with vertical hangers between the chords.

Bland (1839); Gw (1903); W.Pa (1852); J.Parker (1850); S (1901–2)

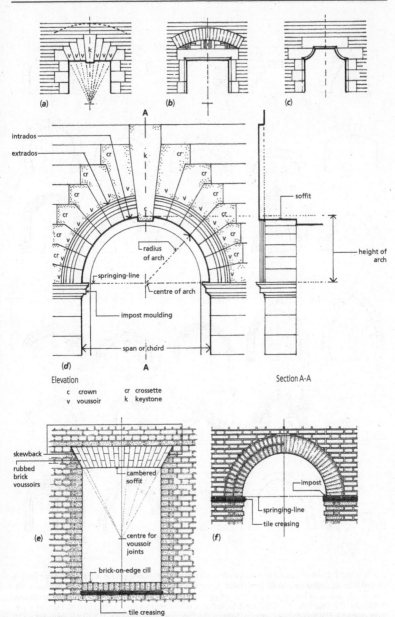

intrados
extrados
soffit
radius
of arch
height of
arch
springing-line
centre of arch
impost moulding
span or chord
(d)
A
Elevation   Section A-A

  c crown   cr crossette
  v voussoir k keystone

skewback
rubbed
brick
voussoirs
cambered
soffit
impost
springing-line
tile creasing
centre for
voussoir
joints
(e)
brick-on-edge cill
tile creasing
(f)

arch (**a**) Flat arch with keystone and voussoirs. (**b**) Segmental relieving arch over lintel. (**c**) Shouldered false 'arch' (lintel carried on shaped corbels). (**d**) Classical arch. (**e**) 'Flat' or 'straight' arch of gauged brick rubbers. (**f**) Semicircular brick arch springing from imposts of tile creasing: (*left*) rowlock arch of special bricks; (*right*) arch of brick rubbers.

arch (a = arch.) (1) Anglo-Saxon triangular pseudo-a. (2) Corbelled *or* stepped pseudo-a. (3) Bell-shaped pseudo-a. (shaped lintel on shaped corbels). (4) Semicircular a. (5) Semicircular stilted a. (6) Segmental a. (7) Elliptical a. (8) Florentine a. (9) Circular horseshoe a. (10) True horseshoe a. (11) Italian pointed a. (12) Lancet a. (13) Equilateral a. (14) Drop a. (15) Four-centred a. (16) Pointed horseshoe a. (17) Pointed Saracenic a. (18) Moorish multifoil a. (19) Three-centred a. (20) Pseudo-four-centred *or* Tudor a. (21) Depressed three-centred a. (22) Gothic cinquefoil a. (23) Gothic ogee a. (24) Pointed trefoil a. (25) Pointed segmental a. (26) False three-centred a. (27) Parabolic a. (28) 'Flat' or straight a. (29) Rampant a. (30) Venetian a.

archaeology Scientific study of remains and monuments of earlier periods. Revivals of architectural styles usually have an archaeological phase in which accurate recording of extant buildings informs architectural design, e.g. *Greek Revival.

archaic 1. Primitive. 2. Marked by the characteristics of an earlier period, e.g. *Aeolic *capital compared with the *Ionic Order.

Archer, John Lee (1791–1852) English architect, John *Rennie's draughtsman (from 1812) until he established (1818) his own architectural/engineering practice. Appointed (1826) Civil Engineer to the Government of Van Diemen's Land, he designed several distinguished Classical buildings in Hobart, including the Custom (later Parliament) House and the Churches of St George (1837–8) and St John (1834–5).

Co (2008); Ko (1996); E.G.R (1970); R.S.Smith (1962)

Archer, Thomas (*c.*1668–1743) English architect, who made the *Grand Tour and absorbed lessons from works of *Bernini and *Borromini. His reputation rests upon a handful of accomplished *Baroque buildings, including the north front of, and *cascade-house at, Chatsworth, Derbys. (1704–5), the garden-pavilion at Wrest Park, Beds. (1709–11), and three churches (St Philip, Birmingham (now the Cathedral of 1710–15), St Paul, Deptford (1713–30), and St John, Smith Square, Westminster (1713–28)). The last-named building (damaged in the 1939–45 war), has four Baroque towers worthy of Borromini, and open-topped *pediments framing *aedicules. St Paul's, Deptford, is his finest surviving church, with a centralized space, powerfully modelled wall-surfaces and *entablatures, and an elegant tower.

Co (2008); Downes (1966); Friedman (2011); Su (1993); Whiffen (1950a)

archery-house *Archeria,* or long, narrow *aperture, with much-splayed sides, for the discharge of a long-bow. If fitted with a horizontal slit (*see* BALISTRARIA), it was probably intended for use with a cross-bow, requiring an even wider splay of the *embrasures.

Archigram Group of English designers formed by (**Sir**) **Peter Frederic Chester Cook** (1936–), *Herron, **Warren Chalk** (1927–88), et al. (1960–75), influenced by Cedric *Price (especially his Fun Palace (1961)). Archigram provided precedents for the so-called *High-Tech style, and promoted architectural ideas through futuristic graphics, exhibitions, and the magazine *Archigram*: buildings designed resembled machines or machine-parts, and structures exhibited their services and structural elements picked out in strong colours. The group's vision of disposable, flexible, easily extended constructions was influential,

although very few of its projects were realized. Some of R.G.Rogers's (1933–) architecture derived from Archigram ideas, while Price's notions of expendability influenced Japanese *Metabolism.

Archigram (1961–70, 1994); *AD*, **xxxv**/11 (Nov. 1965), 534–5; R.Ba (1994); P.Cook (1970); P.Cook *et al.* (eds) (1999); Crompton & Johnston (1994); Crompton (ed.) (1998); Klotz (ed.) (1986); J.T (1996)

architect *See* ARCHITECTURE.

architectonic 1. Pertaining to architecture or to the arrangement of knowledge. 2. Suggesting in e.g. music or sculpture the qualities of architecture. 3. In the plural, the science of architecture or the systematic ordering of knowledge.

Architect's Collaborative (**TAC**) *See* GROPIUS, WALTER.

Architects' Co-Partnership Firm of English architects, founded 1939 and restructured 1945, it fostered team-work and often used industrialized components. Its most celebrated building was the Rubber Factory at Bryn Mawr (1946–9), with which *Arup was associated. It also designed several schools, study-bedrooms on hexagonal plans at St John's College, Oxford (1960), and St Paul's Cathedral Choir School, London (1967).

E (1994); Melvin (1999)

architecture *Ruskin, in his *Seven Lamps* (1849), stated that architecture was the 'art which so disposes and adorns the edifices raised by man ... that the sight of them' contributes 'to his mental health, power, and pleasure', which proposes aesthetic, beneficial, and spiritual aspects rather than a utilitarian or *Functionalist agenda. He also opined that 'architecture' should be confined to 'that art which, ... admitting ... the necessities and common uses' of a building 'impresses on its form certain characters venerable or beautiful, but otherwise unnecessary'. He stated that it would be 'unreasonable to call battlements or machicolations architectural features, so long as they consist only of an advanced gallery supported on projecting masses, with open intervals beneath for offence. But if these projecting masses be carved beneath into rounded courses, which are useless, and if the headings of the intervals be arched and trefoiled, which is useless, that is Architecture.' Such a simplistic, prolix, and arguably wrong-headed definition is revealing of Ruskin's attitudes, which, to a large extent, became the general view of the subject for the next eighty years or so.

Architecture is (or historically was) concerned with the creation of *order* out of *chaos*, a respect for organization, the manipulation of geometry, and the creation of a work in which aesthetics plays a far greater role than anything likely to be found in a humdrum building. *Wotton's statement that 'well building hath three conditions:

Commodity, Firmness, and Delight' seems to have originated from *Vitruvius, who insisted that architecture derives from *order, arrangement, eurythmy* (or *harmony* of *proportion*), *symmetry, propriety*, and *economy*, and *Wren spoke of 'Beauty, Firmness, and Convenience': these definitions suggest that many C21 buildings cannot be architecture at all. Architecture might be described as the art and science of designing a building having qualities of beauty, geometry, emotional and spiritual power, intellectual content and complexity, soundness of construction, convenient planning, many virtues of different kinds, durable and pleasing materials, agreeable colouring and decorations, serenity and dynamism, good proportions and acceptable scale, and many mnemonic associations drawing on a great range of precedents. An essential element must be *stability* (*see* PATMORE), expressed in the architecture: visual lack of it (as in *Deconstructivism) creates a sense of unease. Doubtless there are many more aspects that some would consider essential other than those suggested previously: Philip *Johnson, in the *New York Times* (1964), went so far as to claim that 'architecture is the art of how to waste space'. In C21 many buildings have been increasingly concerned with *advertising* or *image*, and the devaluing of symbols has led some to question their status as architecture.

An *architect* or *master-builder* has been defined as a skilled professor of the art of building, one who designs and frames any complex structure, capable of preparing *plans, *elevations, and *sections of a sophisticated building with an aesthetic content and to supervise its construction in accordance with drawings and specifications. *Soane described an architect's business as that of making 'designs and estimates', directing 'the works', and valuing 'the different parts': he declared the architect as the 'intermediate agent between the employer, whose honour and interest he is to study, and the mechanic, whose rights he is to defend'. Soane emphasized the architect's position as implying great trust, being 'responsible for the mistakes, negligences, and ignorance of those he employs'. With the development of computers and changes in patronage, however, the role of the architect is changing, and indeed many architects are now concerned *only* with image, and have even distanced themselves from the design of structure and detail (having in the past discarded surveying and engineering), to the detriment of the profession.

B-C (2014); Co (2008); Gw (1903); N (1835); W.Pa (1852); Ruskin: *Seven Lamps*, ch.1 (1849); S (1901–2); J.T (1996)

Architecture Machine Title of book by the Greek-American **Nicholas Negroponte** (1943–) in which artificial intelligence in architectural design was proposed, involving computers that would eventually function like colleagues.

Negroponte (1970)

architecture parlante Architecture expressive of its purpose by means of its form, a term first used in print by L. *Vaudoyer in respect of the French C18 Neo-Classicists, notably *Ledoux.

Bergdoll (1994a)

ArchiteXt Anti-*Metabolism informal grouping of Japanese architects (**Takefumi Aida** (1937–), **Takamitsu Azuma** (1933–), **Mayumi Miyawaki** (1936–), **Makoto Suzuki** (1935–), and **Minoru Takeyama** (1934–86)). They published the magazine *ArchiteXt*, the name of which was a comment on Modernist dogmas and theories. Especially concerned with the links of individuals to tradition and to the environment, they argued for *Pluralism, as opposed to the incipient totalitarianism of *Modernism.

Aida exploited unusual relationships of elements in a building to each other (as in his Artist's House, Kunitachi, Tokyo (1967)), and the 'encounters' of disparate parts of a structure (e.g. the Nirvana House, Fujisawa (1972) and the PL Institute Kindergarten, Osaka (1974)), phenomena he called 'oppositional harmonies'. Inspired by children's building-blocks, he designed a series of 'toy-block' dwellings near Tokyo (1978–84), intended to bring delight back to housing. His Kazama House, Kawaguchi (1987) consisted of a series of parallel walls between which rooms were defined by screens. Other works by him included the Memorial Park for Tokyo War Dead (1988). He exploited ideas of 'defensive living' in urban settings, as in his own Tower House, Tokyo (1967), and the Seijin Nursery School, Kyoto (1974). Among other works by him were the K Flat Housing (1991–2) Mejiro, Tokyo (with **Rie Azuma**, his daughter). Miyawaki also drew on the notion of creating defended volumes against hostile external environments, notably with the use of *concrete 'boxes' and manipulation of cubic forms (e.g. Blue Box, Tokyo (1971), and Yoshimi Box, Yokohama (1979)). Suzuki combined simple geometries, finely crafted concrete finishes, and traditional architectural elements: his work included the Yamano House, Himeji (1970). Takeyama saw in architecture the possibilities of using signs and language: among his buildings may be cited Ichiban-kan and Niban-kan, Tokyo (1969–70), the 'Renaissance' complex, Kyoto (1983–6), and Tokyo International Port Terminal (1989–91).

Aida (1990); ArchiteXt (1976); Bo (1985, 1990, 1990–2); E (1994); *Japan Architect*, li/232 (1976), 19, 80; Ross (1978); J.T (1996)

architrave 1. Essentially a formalized beam or *lintel, it is the lowest of the three main parts of an *entablature, itself often divided into *fasciae*. An *architrave-cornice* is an entablature (usually of the *Ionic *Order) with no *frieze. 2. *Antepagmentum* consisting of plain or elaborate *mouldings framing a doorway, *niche, panel, window-aperture, or other opening, properly with the same *section and number of *fasciae as on an entablature architrave. If the vertical mouldings of the architrave turn outwards horizontally as though at the ends of a lintel, then turn vertically, then run horizontally again across the top of the opening, they comprise an *eared*, or *lugged*, architrave; and if the vertical mouldings turn outwards horizontally, again as though at the ends of a lintel, then turn vertically, then run horizontally for a distance equal to the short vertical run, then drop vertically, then run horizontally along the top, they comprise a *shouldered* architrave, and the projecting shoulders are called *crossettes. Architraves often stop against an *architrave-*, *plinth-*, or *skirting*-block against which a *plinth or *skirting also stops. An architrave narrower at the top than at the bottom, i.e. with *battered sides, is called a *Vitruvian opening*.

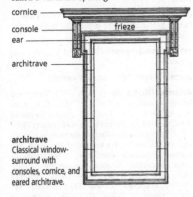

cornice

console

ear

architrave

frieze

architrave
Classical window-surround with consoles, cornice, and eared architrave.

archivolt 1. Collection of *fasciae* and other *mouldings in a concentric ring forming a curved *band around a Classical arch terminating on a *platband at the springing: it is really an *architrave bent around the head of an arch. 2. Erroneous term for the intrados or *soffit of an arch or *vault.

Archizoom (*Studio Archizoom Associati*) Group of Florentine architects, founded 1966, devoted to anti-*Functionalism, employing elements from popular 'culture' and even from *Kitsch. Associated with *Supersensualism, anti-design, and so-called 'banal' design, it was promoted in *Casabella, Domus*, and *Architectural Design. See* ALCHIMIA.

Branzi (1984); Hays (ed.) (1998); Pettena (1996); J.Walker (1992)

Arciniega, Claudio de (*c.*1520–93) Spanish architect/sculptor. He worked with Gil de *Hontañon before settling in México, where he designed the Cathedral in México City (1563–1667) and, probably, the Cathedral of Puebla (1557–1649), for which *Becerra was for a time the Clerk of Works.

Marco Dorta (1951); K & S (1959)

Arcology Combination of architecture and ecology supported by *Soleri as a solution to urban living involving the building of *megastructures able to contain up to three million people. Arcosanti, a future self-sufficient community powered by solar energy in the desert of Arizona, was commenced (1970s) and has been under construction ever since.

LeG & S (1996); Soleri (1969); Wall (1971)

arcosolium (*pl.* arcosolia) *Loculus* with an arched or vaulted top in a Roman *catacomb, *hypogeum, or other type of tomb, usually big enough to contain a *sarcophagus.

arcuated Structure with arches, as opposed to a *columnar-and-*trabeated system.

arcus 1. Roman arch. 2. Entrance to a *basilica, or a *porch or gateway to a church. 3. Area in front of a basilica. 4. *Apse. *Other combinations include*:
arcus choralis: 1. *screen between the *choir and *nave in a basilica, often of *lattice-work; 2. arch between choir and nave, called *arcus ecclesiae* or *arcus presbyterii*;
arcus toralis: as *arcus choralis* (1);
arcus triumphalis: 1. *triumphal arch; 2. arch between the *nave and *sanctuary in a *basilica.

arena 1. Central area of an *amphitheatre surrounded by seats for spectators where public competitions, displays, or games take place. 2. Building for public performances, contests, or displays, usually in the open. 3. Theatre without a *proscenium, loosely called 'theatre-in-the-round'. 4. Part of a theatre used by the performers. 5. The main body of a church.

Arens, Johann August (1757–1806) Hamburg-born architect, he studied with *Harsdorff and de *Wailly. Through *Goethe he was called to Weimar to rebuild the *Schloss* (1789–92), but his most remarkable building there is the so-called Roman House in the Park, with its primitivist *Doric columns at the lower level supporting a temple-like structure (1790–2). Much of his output is in Hamburg, where, with C.F.*Hansen, he practised a refined and mature *Neo-Classicism.

Grundmann (1957); Wa & M (1987); Wietek (1972)

Arets, Wiel (1955–) *See* CALVINIST AUSTERITY.

Ariss, John (*c.*1725–99) English-born, he settled in Maryland *c.*1751, and seems to have been among the first professional architects to work in the American Colonies. Steeped in English *Palladianism and in the architectural language of *Gibbs, he was probably responsible for some of the more imposing Virginian houses, such as Mount Airey, Richmond County.

P & J (1970–86); Waterman (1945); W & K (1983)

ark 1. Receptacle for storing the scrolls in a *synagogue. See ECHAL. **2.** Cupboard in a church for hanging vestments.

armarium 1. Cupboard or closet. **2.** Library. **3.** *Aumbry. **4.** Place where weapons were kept.

armature Iron bars used in *tracery, to support *canopies, *bosses, etc., or to otherwise strengthen parts of a building. Iron was not infrequently used in medieval buildings.

Arnold von Westfalen (c.1425–80) German architect. As *Oberlandbaumeister* he directed building-works in numerous Electoral properties in Saxony. His major works were the *Albrechtsburg* (1471–1525—one of the most important German late-Gothic buildings, with its celebrated and fanciful *vaults in the Great Hall), and the west end and towers of the Cathedral (begun 1479), both in Meissen. He was also involved in works at the Church of *Unsere Liebe Frau auf dem Berge*, Penig (c.1472), Leipzig Castle (1478–80), and Zwickau Cathedral.

Mrusek (1972); Nussbaum (1994); J.T (1996)

Arnolfo di Cambio (c.1245–c.1302) Master-mason/sculptor, perhaps born in Tuscany, but also referred to (early C16) as German, he assisted Nicola *Pisano of Siena (1260s), before going to Rome (1277), where he designed several sepulchral monuments. His most important surviving tomb is that of **Cardinal de Braye** (d.1282) in *San Domenico*, Orvieto. He evolved a type of tomb designed to be set against a wall, with a *gabled *canopy carried on *colonnettes protecting an *effigy on a *sarcophagus, which established the precedent for a century or so. He designed several handsome *ciboria*, including those over the *high-altars at *San Paolo fuori le mura* (1285) and *Santa Cecilia in Trastévere* (1293), both in Rome. He was probably familiar with French *Gothic, was master-mason for the new Cathedral in Florence (begun 1294–6), responsible for the *nave and *aisles, and for an earlier version of the present east end, possibly influenced by Rhineland precedents (especially Cologne Cathedral). His other Florentine designs (according to *Vasari) include *Santa Croce* (begun 1294–5), the *choir of the *Badia* (begun 1284), and perhaps the tower of the *Palazzo Vecchio* (c.1310).

Romanini (1980); J.T (1996); Vasari (1568); J.White (1987)

aronade *Battlement with, on the centres of straight-topped merlons, round-topped narrower uprights.

Aronco, Raimondo d' (1857–1932) Italian architect responsible for buildings at the Turin International Exposition of Decorative Arts (1902), where *Art Nouveau (called in Italy *Stile Liberty*), was vigorously in evidence. The central rotunda at Turin was an ebullient design, much ornamented, with low symmetrical wings. D'Aronco's buildings marked a stylistic climax, even though his particular architectural language was greatly influenced by the *Sezession in its Austrian manifestation. The d'Aronco mausoleum at Udine (1898), with *battered walls, Egyptianizing heads, and influences from *Wagner and *Viollet-le-Duc, demonstrated other facets of his eclecticism.

Barillari (1995); Freni & Varnier (1983); Ms (1966); T-M (1967)

Arras, Mathias of (fl.1342–52) French architect of the *Gothic Cathedral of St Vitus in Prague, Bohemia, commenced 1342, influenced by the Cathedrals of Narbonne, Rodez, and Toulouse.

S (1901–2); J.T (1996)

arris Sharp crease-like edge where two surfaces join, e.g. the corner of a brick or between the *flutes of a Greek-*Doric column.

arrow-head Pointed element in *egg-and-dart ornament.

arrow-loop *Balistraria or *loophole.

Arruda, Diogo de (c.1470–1531) Portuguese architect working within the *Manueline style, responsible for the *nave and *chapter-house of the Church of the Order of Christ at Tomar (1510–14): it has a mass of exuberant decoration, including net-like *vaults over the two-storey space, and external ornament combining Royal coats-of-arms, emblems, musical instruments, ropes, sails, and marine flora and fauna. Arruda's brother, **Francisco** (c.1480–1547), designed the exotic tower at Belém (1515–20), erected to defend the approaches to Lisbon.

K & S (1959); J.T (1996)

arsenal 1. Building for the manufacture and storage (or storage alone) of weapons and ammunition of all kinds, e.g. the vast building in Venice. **2.** Dockyard with buildings for the reception, construction, and repair of ships.

Art Deco Style of European and American design and interior decoration (also known as the *Style Moderne*) fashionable in the period immediately before and after the 1914–18 war. In the 1920s and 1930s it evolved further, and took its name from the Paris *Exposition Internationale des Arts-Décoratifs et Industriels Modernes* (1924–5): the official 12-volume publication of the Exposition (*Encyclopédie des arts décoratifs et industriels modernes au XXième siècle*) disseminated the elements of a style derived from severe geometrical patterns evolved as a reaction to *Art Nouveau. Archaeological aspects also influenced the style: the discovery (1922) of Pharaoh Tutankhamun's (r. c.1332–c.1323 BC) tomb led to a new enthusiasm for Ancient-Egyptian motifs and themes such as strong colouring, pyramidal compositions, and stepped forms. However, the canted arch, *chevron, stepped corbelled arch, and stepped *gable (themselves pyramidal compositions) owed more to what C18 designers imagined was Egyptian, derived from publications such as *Piranesi's *Diverse maniere d'adornare i cammini* (Different Ways of Decorating Fireplaces—1769) and from exotic *Egyptian-Revival stage-sets. Investigations of *Aztec and other *Meso-American architecture with its stepped forms were also influential. Late Art Deco designs were often concerned with aerodynamics, speed, and *streamlining to emphasize the style's Modern pretensions. *Mallet-Stevens was the most important of the French architects working with Art Deco elements, but the style also flourished in the USA, where van *Alen's Chrysler Building, NYC (1928-30), is its most celebrated architectural example. Vulgarized elements of Art Deco entered *Post-Modern designs from the 1960s.

Bayer (1992); C.Benton *et al.* (eds) (2003); Bl & Ro (1975); Brunhammer (1984); J.Curl (2005); Hillier (1985); Hillier & Escritt (1997)

Hoover Factory entrance, Western Avenue, London (1931–3), by Wallis, Gilbert, & Partners, with chevron and other motifs of the Art Deco style.

articulation Architectural composition in which elements and parts of the building are expressed logically, distinctly, and consistently, with clear joints.

Artinatural Style lying between the formal and informal, defined by Batty *Langley in his *Practical Geometry* (1726) and *New Principles of Gardening* (1728) as 'regular irregularity': in landscape-gardens this signified a symmetrical geometry overlaid by asymmetrical elements such as *serpentine paths.

Symes (2006)

Artisan Mannerism English architecture created by masons (rather than architects) in the period *c.*1615–75, based on *Mannerist *pattern-books. Such craftsmen were not trained in the theory and vocabulary of the Classical language of architecture, so their creations often have a curious scale, are strangely proportioned, and frequently display an ignorance of how elements are put together (which some commentators have found refreshing and others distressing).

M & E (1995); Su (1993); Wüsten (1951)

Art Nouveau Style of architecture/decorative arts that flourished (*c.*1888–1914) in Europe and the USA, featuring asymmetrical compositions; attenuated blooms, foliage, roots, and stems with sinuous flowing lines, as though floating in water; the dream-maiden (female figure with long wavy tendril-like hair known as *femme-fleur*); stylized *rose-bowls; intertwining plant-forms; and indeterminate *whiplash curved tendrils. It evolved from some late-*Gothic-Revival patterns, and owed something, perhaps, to *Auricular and *Rococo ornament. Prototypical Art-Nouveau *capitals at Blackfriars Railway Bridge (1862-4) and Holborn Viaduct (1863-9), both in London, demonstrate that the essence of the style was in place in the early 1860s, while the illustrations in *Viollet-le-Duc's influential *Entretiens sur l'Architecture* (1872) spread images of free-flowing curved forms throughout Europe and America. Certain artists associated with the *Arts-and-Crafts movement, notably *Mackmurdo, William *Morris, and C.F.A.*Voysey, produced celebrated designs that fall firmly within the style. Named after the Paris shop (*Maison de l'Art Nouveau*) of the art-dealer **Siegfried Bing** (1838-1905—which stocked artefacts that were not reproductions of styles of earlier periods, but were modern and often oriental, and had interiors designed by Henry van de *Velde (1896)), the style was associated first with the *Aesthetic Movement, and then with modernity (in France it was also known as the *Style Moderne*, in Spain as *Modernismo*, *Estilo Modernista*, or *Modernisme* (Catalan), in The Netherlands as *Nieuwe Kunst*, in Germany, Austria-Hungary, and Scandinavia as

Jugendstil (Youth style), and in Italy as *Stile* *Floreale* or *Stile Liberty* (from Liberty's shop in London which stocked Art Nouveau objects), so its new, youthful, and modern associations were emphasized by its various names). In architecture the style reached its heights of virtuosity with the buildings of d'*Aronco in Milan, *Eisenstein in Riga, *Gaudí in Barcelona, *Guimard in Paris, *Horta in Brussels, and *Shekhtel' in Moscow. Drawings by **Aubrey Beardsley** (1872–98), furniture by **Louis Majorelle** (1859–1926), designs by **Margaret Macdonald** (1865–1933) and her husband C.R.*Mackintosh, graphic work by **Alphonse Mucha** (1860–1939), glassware by **Louis Comfort Tiffany** (1848–1913), and architectural designs by Émile *André, *Basile, *Hankar, *Hoffmann, *Jourdain, **Jules Lavirotte** (1864–1924), *Olbrich, and Louis *Sullivan, all display characteristic Art Nouveau elements. Journals such as *L'Art Décoratif, Die Jugend, Kunst und Kunsthandwerk, Pan,* and *The Studio* disseminated the style, which was also promoted in German-speaking countries by various *Sezession* groups (in Austria-Hungary the preferred term was *Sezessionstil* rather than *Jugendstil*). In the Ottoman Empire traditional Muslim and Turkish motifs and ways of handling space blended with new ideas from Western Europe, so that some extraordinary Art Nouveau works were erected in Istanbul *c.*1900: they are not well-known in Europe or America.

Arwas (2000); Barillari & Godoli (2002); Borisova & Kazhdan (1971); BSP (1988); Dierkens-Aubry & van den Breelen (1991); Escritt (2000); Gh (2000); J.Howard (1996); Latham (ed.) (1980); Loyer (1986, 1986a, 1991, 1997); Nicoletti (1978); Ogata (2002); P & R (1973); F.Russell (ed.) (1979); Shinomura (1992); Tahara *et al.* (2000); T-M (1967); J.T (1996)

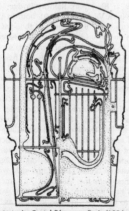

Metal gate to *Le Castel Béranger*, Paris (1894–8), by Hector Guimard, typical of the Art Nouveau style.

Arts-and-Crafts Influential late-C19 English movement that attempted to re-establish craftsmanship threatened by mass-production. Whilst the medieval craft-guilds were revered as ideals, the movement had its origins in the ideas of J.-J. *Rousseau, who proposed that manual skills should be acquired by everybody, no matter from what social class, but owed its immediate impetus to the polemical publications and widespread influence of *Pugin and *Ruskin. The last founded the Guild of St George in 1871 to promote the transition from theory to practice, but the most important personality associated with the Arts-and-Crafts movement was William *Morris, who sought to revive medieval standards and methods of making artefacts while holding truth to materials, constructional methods, and function to be the essence of design. Learning the problems and solutions of providing designs for objects in his own living-accommodation, Morris set up a company (1861) capable of undertaking any species of decoration, from pictures to a consideration of the smallest work in which artistic beauty could be incorporated. **Morris, Marshall, Faulkner, & Co,** with which **Ford Madox Brown** (1821–93), **Dante Gabriel Rossetti** (1828–82), **Edward Burne-Jones** (1833–98), and Philip *Webb were closely associated, embraced medieval craftsmanship as the ideal, opposed mass-production, and encouraged design and decoration intricately allied to the properties of materials and logical methods of construction, drawing on traditional and *vernacular precedents. The movement gave rise to the Century Guild (founded by *Mackmurdo in 1882), the *Art-Workers' Guild (1884), the Guild of Handicraft (founded by *Ashbee (1888)), and the Arts-and-Crafts Exhibition Society (1888). Soon the movement was taken up on the Continent, notably in Austria-Hungary (where the *Sezession* and *Wiener Werkstätte* were two of its most obvious offspring), Belgium, Germany, The Netherlands, and Scandinavia (where it is still influential at the beginning of C21). Other key figures were **Walter Crane** (1845–1915), W.R. *Lethaby (who had an enormous influence on education, was appointed Principal of the Central School of Arts and Crafts in London in 1896, and was the mentor of the *Barnsley brothers and Ernest *Gimson), and E.S.*Prior.

The chief legacy of the movement to architecture was the appreciation of *vernacular buildings leading to elements derived from them being widely used in the *Domestic Revival (which grew out of the *Gothic Revival and aspects of the *Picturesque). Important developments in housing such as at Bedford Park, Chiswick (from the 1870s), Bournville, near Birmingham, Warwicks. (from the 1890s), Letchworth, Herts. (from 1903), and Port Sunlight, Ches. (from the 1880s), all employed themes drawn from vernacular architecture and set the agenda for domestic architecture in Britain until 1939. So admired was English domestic architecture that a major study of it by Hermann *Muthesius was published as *Das Englische Haus* (1904/5), and regular articles also appeared in architectural journals as well as in the art journal *The Studio* (which strongly supported the Arts-and-Crafts movement as a whole). Two American disciples of Morris, **Elbert Hubbard** (1856–1915) and **Gustav Stickley** (1857–1942), helped to promote the movement in the USA. Finally, the movement was in the vanguard of recording, studying, and preserving old buildings, and argued for the careful *conservation of ancient fabric rather than wholesale or drastic 'restorations'. Morris himself founded the Society for the Protection of Ancient Buildings (SPAB) which has been an influential agent ever since.

Anscombe (1996); Carruthers (1992); Cumming & Kaplan (1991); P.Davey (1980, 1995); Haigh (1995); Hawkes (1986); Kaplan (1987); C.Kelley (2001); Kornwolf (1972); L & D (1986); Latham (ed.) (1980); M (2007); M.Rn (1983); Stansky (1996); R.Winter (ed.) (1997)

Arts-and-Crafts gardening There was no fixed approach to style in *Arts-and-Crafts garden-design, although ordered geometry (e.g. in the work of *Lutyens) might co-exist with themes drawn from informal *cottage-gardens. Many architects, however, considered *contexts* of their buildings, inside and out, ironically often *precluding* creative contributions from craftspeople. R.*Blomfield and *Sedding advocated, like William *Morris, that house and garden should be viewed as one architectural entity—a creed opposed by horticulturalists such as *Jekyll and W.*Robinson, who promoted a wild, informal style of garden planting (in harmony with, but not necessarily closely related to the architecture of the house), resonating with exponents who identified the cottage-garden as an embodiment of the *vernacular style. These opposing views and practices were upheld in parallel until Jekyll struck up a partnership with Lutyens, collaborating in commissions that drew together the ideologies of both, wedding geometry to informality. A master of the style was Thomas *Mawson. Among important Arts-and-Crafts gardens are Rodmarton Manor, Glos. (1912–26); Hidcote, Glos. (1920s and later); and Sissinghurst, Kent (from 1930—influenced by Hidcote).

Blomfield (1892); Mawson (1900); Shoe (2001); Symes (2006); Tay (2006)

Art-Workers' Guild Founded 1884 as a forum for discussion for architects, craftsmen, and designers, it promoted *Arts-and-Crafts ideals, and still continues at the beginning of C21. Its Masters have included *Lutyens, *Morris, *Sedding, and *Gradidge.

Platman (2009); Stansky (1996)

Arup, Sir Ove Nyquist (1895–1988) Anglo-Danish engineer, he became (1934) chief designer/director with **J.L.Kier & Co.**, and worked with *Tecton in London on such projects as Highpoint (1936–8), the Penguin Pool at the Zoo (1939), and Finsbury Health Centre (1938–9). In 1938 he left Kier to found, with his cousin, **Arne Arup**, the engineering and consultancy firm of **Arup & Arup**, and during the 1939–45 war designed air-raid shelters and parts of the Mulberry Harbour, which, in 1944, made the Normandy Landing possible. He was one of the first in England to design load-bearing *concrete walls using slip-form *shuttering (moulds that can be moved and reused as work progresses). He established (1946) a practice which became **Ove Arup & Partners**, expanding as **Arup Associates** (1963) to become a multi-professional team famed for its elegant approach to design problems: key figures were South-African-born (Sir) **Philip Manning Dowson** (1924–2014), **Ronald William Hobbs** (1923–2006), et al. Works included the Maltings Concert Hall, Snape, Suffolk (1965–7—with acoustics consultant **Derek Sugden** (1924–2015)), the IBM Process Assembly Plant, Havant, Hants. (1966–72), and the Sir Thomas White Building, St John's College, Oxford (1970–6—with *precast-concrete frame). From the beginning Arup was a *Modernist, a founding member of *MARS: he worked with the *Smithsons on the School at Hunstanton, Norfolk (1949, 1952–4 (*see* BRUTALISM), with *Utzon on Sydney Opera House (1956–74), with Renzo Piano (1937–) and Richard George Rogers (1933–) on the *Centre Pompidou*, Paris (1971–7—called *Beaubourg*), and with Norman Robert Foster (1935–) on the Hong Kong & Shanghai Bank, Hong Kong (1979–86). His own command of elegance in structure can best be seen in his Kingsgate footbridge over the River Wear at Durham (1963). The firm was also involved in the Broadgate scheme, Liverpool Street (1984–8 and 1988–91); Rogers's Lloyd's Headquarters, City of London (1978–86); Munich Airport (1993–6—with *Murphy/Jahn); and many other projects.

Brawne (1983); Dobney (ed.) (1994); Dunster (ed.) (1997); E (1994); Hawkes & W.Forster (2002); Morreau (ed.) (1995); *ODNB* (2004); P.Rice (1994); D.Sommer *et al.* (1994); *see also* Arup Journal (various years)

Asam Brothers (Cosmas Damian (1686–1739) *and* Egid Quirin (1692–1750)) Although C.D. Asam was primarily a painter of *frescoes, and his brother a sculptor, together they created some of the foremost examples of Bavarian *Baroque architecture. Supported by the Abbot of Tegernsee who sent them on a study-visit to

Rome after the death of their father **Georg Asam** (1649-1711), on their return they were employed as decorators of several churches, especially after C.D.Asam demonstrated his mastery of theatrical effects and dramatic perspectives in the ceiling-frescoes of the *Dreifaltigkeitskirche*, Munich (1715). In 1714 he started work on the *Benedictine Abbey of Weltenburg, where Roman influences are plainly demonstrated, for the *nave of the church is an ellipse on plan, light-sources are difficult to discern, and the rich colouring and gilding are reminiscent of *Bernini's *Sant'Andrea al Quirinale*. However, Bernini placed the *high-altar on the shorter axis of the ellipse, whereas at Weltenburg Asam set it on the longer. E.Q.Asam also contributed to the works at Weltenburg from 1721, and the collaboration created a stunning work, the climax of which is the stage-like *aedicule of *Solomonic columns within which an equestrian St George, bathed in yellow light that pours from above and behind, slays a fearsome dragon. A smiling sculptured figure of C.D.Asam leans elegantly over the gallery high above the elliptical nave.

The brothers decorated many churches, including the *Pfarrkirche* (now *Dom* of *St Jakobi*, Innsbruck (1722-3)), but it was in the few they designed and built that they demonstrated their mastery of spatial illusion, lighting effects, and other melodramatic aspects of design they had learned in Rome. Weltenburg is sensational, but so is the Augustinian Priory Church at Rohr (1717-25), where the Virgin rises from her coffin, carried up to Heaven by angels within an *aedicule, the broken *pediment of which features in its centre clouds, *putti, and a *sunburst of glory. At the tiny *St Johann Nepomuk* (aka *Asamkirche*), Munich (1733-40), lighting, drama, theatrical effects, and intensity of expression reached new heights, while the delicate and fanciful *Ursulinenkirche*, Straubing (1736-41), built on a quatrefoil plan, also employs dramatic lighting sources from on high, and makes more overt the visual expression of earthly and heavenly realms. Masters of drama and illusion, the Asams rarely failed to delight the eye and move the emotions.

Bou (1962); Bushart & Rupprecht (eds) (1996); K.Harries (1983); Hi (1968a); C.Powell (1959); Rupprecht & Mülbe (1987); Sauermost (1986)

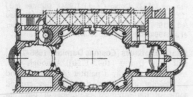

Plan of the Benedictine Abbey Church, Weltenburg, showing elliptical nave and, behind the high-altar, the apse from which light floods.

asbestos Mineral (actually impure hydrous magnesium silicate) of fibrous texture, capable of being woven or compressed into an incombustible fabric or sheet. By the second half of C19 fire-resistant fabrics made of asbestos were being made, and later, by the first decade of C20, the material, combined with cement, was used to make *asbestos cement* moulded into pipes, sheets, and insulating material. Corrugated asbestos cement sheets were in widespread use from the 1914-18 war, and asbestos-cement pipes were being manufactured in large quantities from the 1920s. Unfortunately, asbestos causes lung-disease and malignant tumours, so has been superseded by other materials, notably GRC (glass-reinforced concrete).

W.McKay (1957); Mitchell (1953)

ascent, ascendant In *masonry and *joinery the upright part of the border, frame, or dressings of an *aperture. The part across the top is the *traverse. See CHAMBRANLE.

Ash, Maurice Anthony (1917-2003) Indian -born English planner, impassioned critic of post-1939-45 bleak, high-rise housing-estates, he declared that the mess made of British cities in the 1940s, '50s, '60s, and '70s was a mirror of the values held by those in power. A supporter of the British *New-Towns programme of 1946-67, Ash was drawn to the Town & Country Planning Association, but was dismayed when he saw that the Government was using the New Towns as vehicles for public-housing policies while at the same time conniving at massive erosion of the Green Belt. He was also concerned by the change of direction of the Association, which became increasingly embroiled in public inquiries concerning airports and nuclear energy. He greatly feared (with sound reason) the collapse of civilization, perceiving the architectural, environmental, and social problems of post-war Britain as symptoms of a greater malady.

Pk; *The Times* (6 Feb. 2003), 33

Ashbee, Charles Robert (1863-1942) English *Arts-and-Crafts architect with some sixty buildings, most of them houses, to his credit. Influenced by *Morris, *Ruskin, and idealistic Socialism, he worked for a time with *Bodley, and founded (1888) the School and Guild of Handicraft (which exhibited at the 1889 and later Arts-and-Crafts exhibitions), and worked for a time in the East End of London. Ashbee designed (1893-4) a house (destroyed 1968) for his mother at 37 Cheyne Walk, London, the interiors of which were decorated by the Guild, and this was followed by other houses (notably 72-3 (destroyed) and 38-9 Cheyne Walk) in the *Queen-Anne Revival style (1897-1903). The Guild designed furniture (1898) for Baillie *Scott's house for **Ernst Ludwig** (*r.*1892–1918) **Grand Duke of Hesse** at Darmstadt, exhibited at the Vienna **Sezession* (1900), moved to Chipping Campden, Glos. (1901), but failed (1905). Ashbee was in the forefront of *conservation, and carried out many sensitive restorations, new buildings, and extensions, notably his adaptation of a ruined chapel of *c.*1100 as a dwelling-house at Broad Campden (*c.*1906–7). He was in the vanguard of endeavour to bring order and care to the planning of towns and cities: mindful of the huge losses of historic buildings through redevelopment, he began a process of surveying London buildings that led to the important *Survey of London* volumes. He published *A Book of Cottages and Little Houses* (1906).

A.Crawford (1985); *ODNB* (2004); Se (ed.) (1975); Se (1977)

ash-chest *See* CINERARIUM.

ash-hole, ash-pit 1. An *ash-hole* is a cavity beneath a fireplace or furnace into which ashes fall. **2.** An *ash-pit* is a hole into which ashes and household refuse are thrown; medieval and other examples can reveal much when excavated.

ashlar 1. *Masonry consisting of blocks of accurately cut, dressed, squared, and finished stone (Roman **opus quadratum*), with clean, sharp *arrises, forming perfect courses, laid in lime-mortar. *Compare* RUBBLE. Thin slabs of similar masonry, used as a facing to a brick wall or as paving slabs, were also termed *ashlar*, although *bastard ashlar* is preferred. Finished work featuring the *faces of each stone projecting beyond the line of the joints is *rusticated ashlar*. *See* RUSTICATION. **2.** Large clay-based block larger than a brick, such as **faïence* or **ter-racotta* (US).

ashlar-piece *See* ASHLERING.

ashlering Series of short, upright timber *ash-lar-pieces* or *ashlar-posts*, fixed in *garrets between floor-joists and *rafters in order to cut off the useless acute angle and receive the wall-finish.

Ashlin, George Coppinger (1837–1921) Pupil, then partner (1860–9) of E.W.*Pugin, whose sister he married. He later formed a partnership with **Peter Paul Pugin** (1851–1904) and **Cuthbert Welby Pugin** (1840–1928), and later still (1902–21) with **Thomas Aloysius Coleman** (1865–1950). He designed numerous buildings for the RC Church, but his masterpiece is the RC Cathedral, Cobh, Co. Cork (1867–1902), designed with E.W.Pugin, beautifully sited above the harbour. Ashlin's rich screens and other fittings within the RC Cathedral at Armagh were partially destroyed (1977–82) during the insensitive re-ordering following Vatican 2. His Lombardic *choir with *apse and side-chapels at the RC

Cathedral, Skibbereen, Co. Cork, and handsome *steeple at St Eugene's RC Cathedral, Londonderry (1900), deserve note. He completed A.W.N.*Pugin's RC Cathedral at Killarney, including the spire, and embellished J.J.*McCarthy's Lombardic *Roman-esque RC Cathedral in Thurles, Co Tipperary. His output was prodigious.

Mulligan (2013); Williams (1994).

Ashurst, John (1937–2008) English architect, he promoted proper training in the repair and *conservation of historic buildings and ancient monuments, especially the care of *masonry. He published *Mortars, Plasters, and Renders in Con-servation* (1983), and his technical notes for the staff of English Heritage were published in five volumes as *Practical Building Conservation* (1988–9). His *The Conservation of Ruins* (2007) remains a seminal work.

RIBAJ (December 2008), 64

Asiatic base *Base of the *Ionic *Order, con-sisting of a lower *fluted and *reeded cylinder with reeded *torus above. *Compare* ATTIC BASE.

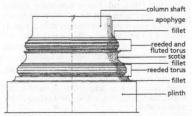

column shaft
apophyge
fillet
reeded and fluted torus
scotia
fillet
reeded torus
fillet
plinth

Asiatic base Ionic *or* Asiatic base, *Erechtheion*, Athens.

Aslin, Charles Herbert (1893–1959) Pioneer of C20 *prefabrication: as Herts. County Architect (1945–58) he used standardized components for the County school-building programme.

E (1980)

aspersorium *See* STOUP.

asphalt(e) 1. Black or chocolate-brown lime-stone impregnated with *bitumen* or natural pitch. Fine grit is added at high temperatures, and the result cast into blocks. When reheated, the melted asphalt can form an impervious barrier to water, so is used for damp-proof courses and as a cov-ering for 'flat' roofs. **2.** Inferior *artificial asphalt* is a mixture of tar with *aggregates (such as sand and gravel) and pitch, unsuitable for waterproof-ing, but employed to finish road surfaces and walkways.

W.McKay (1957)

Asplund, Erik Gunnar (1885–1940) Swedish architect. His early works show the influence of *National Romanticism (the villas Selander (1913) and Ruth (1914)), but his mastery of the *Neo-Classicism he absorbed during his time in Germany was demonstrated in Stockholm at the Skandia Cinema (1922–3—with *Pompeian interior colouring), in the Public Library (1920–8—with its *drum rising up from the simple, blocky mass of the rest of the building expressing the shape of the reading-room), and in the Swedish Pavilion (for the 1924–5 *Exposition* in Paris). For the Woodland Cemetery, part of Stockholm South Cemetery, he and *Lewerentz subtly mingled Neo-Classicism and *Romanticism: the austere funerary Chapel, for example, set in a movingly serene wooded landscape, combined *vernacular themes with *Classicism. For the Stockholm Exhibition (1930), Asplund demonstrated that he had become a Modernist, and his handling of steel and glass was greatly admired for its elegance and lightness. Other Modernist buildings include the Bredenberg Department Store, Stockholm (1933–7), but his extension to Nicodemus *Tessin's 1672 Göteborg Town Hall (1934–7, designed in 1925) mixed *stripped Neo-Classicism and a modern structural grid. His over-rated Crematorium, Stockholm South Cemetery (1935–40), has a beautifully crafted *portico contrasting with the solemn main chapel behind, demonstrating his incorporation of aspects of historical architecture with contemporary design, and his ability to anchor his buildings within a partly natural and partly contrived landscape.

Ahlberg (1943); A & B (1986); Asplund (1985, 1988); Asplund *et al.* (1931); Ca (1986); Constant (1994); Ck (1988); Holmdahl *et al.* (eds) (1981); Johansson & Galli (1996); Maré (1955); Nagy (1974); C.Wilson (ed.) (1988); Wrede (1980)

Asprucci, Antonio (1723–1808) *Neo-Classical architect, the first Italian to revive the Greek-*Doric style. His best-known works are the sumptuous interiors of the *Villa Borghese*, Rome (from the 1780s), including the Egyptian Room. With his son, **Mario Asprucci** (1764–1804), he designed various Neo-Classical *fabriques* for the *Villa Borghese* Gardens (the first 'English' landscape-garden in Rome) in the 1780s and 1790s (the plan of which was by the Scots landscape-painter, **Jacob More** (*c.*1740–93)). Mario Asprucci was responsible for the original designs for Ickworth House, Suffolk (*c.*1795), executed, from 1796, with some modifications, by Francis *Sandys.

J.Curl (2011a); *Lavagnino* (1961); Ms (1966); Rankin (1972)

Assche, Simon van (*fl.*C15) Flemish architect of the *Gothic Cloth Hall at Gent, Belgium (1426–41).

Bae: *Belgium* (1931)

assemblage of Orders Arrangement of superimposed *Orders on a Classical *façade, set one above the other with the vertical axes of the columns lining up, defining the *storeys, also called *supercolumniation*. The hierarchy places *Tuscan at the lowest storey, then *Doric, *Ionic, *Corinthian, and finally *Composite. The *Antique precedent was the Colosseum in Rome, its external *arcuated wall having Doric, Ionic, and Corinthian *engaged Orders with columns, but the topmost storey (over the Corinthian columnar Order) had Corinthian *pilasters. *Serlio codified the five Orders in his *L'Architettura*, which had appeared in six parts (1537–51), with illustrations augmenting the information (1575), and so the five Orders set above each other (in the hierarchy described previously) was essentially a *Renaissance invention, and was widely disseminated.

J.Curl (2001)

assembly-room Large room or suite of rooms for the reception of large parties, for concerts, dinners, balls, etc. A good example is the assembly-room at York by *Burlington (1731–2). Assembly-rooms were an important part of C18 and early C19 social life in England and were often associated with *spas.

J.Curl (2010)

asses' ears Type of *ear or *horn.

Associationism Theory that *associations* of ideas are the bases of all mental activity. *Alison argued that Taste is a consequence of associations prompted by observation (e.g. a building is *perceived* as pleasant because it *looks* stable and fit for its purpose). *See* BEAUTIFUL; DECONSTRUCTIVISM; PATMORE; PICTURESQUE.

Alison (1790)

Assyrian architecture When the Assyrians of Northern Mesopotamia became dominant in the region towards the end of the second millennium BC they adopted design principles established by their *Sumerian predecessors: they used brilliant colouring (usually by means of coloured glazed bricks), and sculptured decorations in relief. The great Palace of Sargon at Khorsabad (C8 BC) incorporated many repeated motifs such as arches, winged lions and bulls with humanoid heads, gigantic *reedings, and two-stepped crenellations, although columns were little used: it stood on a vast brick *plinth, and was approached by *ramps and *stairs. Assyrian temple-platforms resembled flat-topped stepped *pyramids, with the 'steps' formed of a continuous ramp that led around the square plan to reach the summit. Vaulting and even domed construction were apparently known to the Assyrians.

Ck (1996); L & M (1986)

astragal, astragulus 1. *Baguette, *bead, chaplet, small convex moulding, or *roundel, especially the ring of semicircular section at the top of the *shaft of most Classical columns (except Greek *Doric), defining the bottom of the *capital, or a similar moulding, often ornamented, usually with *bead-and-reel (called *astragulum Lesbium*), further defining *architrave *fasciae. **2.** In Scotland, glazing-bars in a window-frame, dividing the *lights into *panes.

astreated Decorated with stars.

astylar With no columns or *pilasters.

Atelier 5 Group of Swiss architects established at Berne in 1955 by **Erwin Fritz** (1927–92), **Samuel Gerber** (1932–98), **Rolf Hesterberg** (1927–2013), **Hans Hostettler** (1925–, retired 1990), and **Alfredo Pini** (1932–), best-known for housing developments in Switzerland, the most celebrated of which is the unified Halen complex at Herrenschwanden, near Bern (1955–61), influenced by Le *Corbusier's unrealized project for *La Sainte-Baume* (1948), but also incorporating a grid-plan similar to that of the old town of Bern. Atelier 5's later work includes extensions to the Court House, Bern (1976–81), students' accommodation, University of Stuttgart, Vaihingen, Germany (1966–72), and housing developments including Flamatt 3 (1988), and Ried, Niederwangen (1990).

Achleitner (ed.) (2000); Atelier 5 (1986, 1994, 2000); Br (1982); E (1994)

Atget, Jean-Eugène-Auguste (1857–1927) French photographer, he made a unique and comprehensive record of historic fabric and royal parks in and around Paris as they were before they were radically altered or destroyed (late-C19–early-C20). His shots, carefully timed and composed, were tinged with melancholy, yet are evocative records of the old, untidy city.

Shoe (2001); Szarkowski & Hambourg (1981–5)

Athens Charter In 1933, the fourth *CIAM congress 'investigated' 33 major cities, and evolved principles based on Le *Corbusier's notions of the distribution and ordering of functions, including rigid *zoning, housing in high-rise blocks, and wholesale destruction of existing urban fabric. Le Corbusier published (1943) the dogma of Modernist urban planning in his *La Charte d'Athènes*, in which such functions were treated simplistically and crudely. Great damage was inflicted on countless towns and cities through the widespread acceptance of the pernicious dogmas enshrined in the Charter, prompting the reactions of *New Urbanism and a dawning realization among a few that the supposed panaceas applied after the 1939–45 war were leading to the destruction of civilized urban living.

J.Jacobs (1961); J-G (1973)

Atkinson, Peter (1735–1805) As *Carr's assistant, he worked at Buxton, Derbys., and Harewood, Yorks., and succeeded to Carr's practice. Among his works are 51, Bootham, York (1803–4), the gateway and farm-buildings at Harewood House (c.1803), and Brockfield Hall, Warthill, Yorks. (1804–7). His son (also **Peter** (1780–1843)), succeeded (1805) to the practice, and designed several competent buildings in the *Greek-Revival style and several less successful *Gothic churches. His works include the Female Prison, now the Castle Museum (1802), the Subscription Library, St Helen's Square (1811–12), and South Parade (1824–8), all in York.

Co (2008)

Atkinson, Robert Frank (1871–1923) Articled to John Francis *Doyle (1840–1913), Atkinson later opened an office in London, and designed the Midland Adelphi Hotel, Liverpool (built 1911–14 in modified form under **Stanley Hinge Hamp** (1877–1968)). He collaborated with the Chicago-based *Burnham on the design of the steel-framed *Beaux-Arts* Classical Selfridges Store in Oxford Street, London (1907–9), although the architect of the *façade was *Swales, who placed a *Giant *Order of *Ionic columns (based on de l'*Orme's Tuileries Palace, Paris), with panels of metal and glass between them, on the ground-floor base. This building set the style for British stores and offices until 1939.

A.S.Gray (1985)

Atkinson, Thomas (c.1729–98) Capable of competent work in *Gothic (e.g. Bishopthorpe Palace (1763–9), and the *chancel of Coxwold church (1774–77)) and *Classical (e.g. Constable *mausoleum at Halsham (1792–1802) and the symmetrical Houghton Hall, Sancton (c.1765–8)) styles, this architect was also an able monumental sculptor (e.g., the Prickett monument, All Saints church, Kilham (c.1780s)), all Yorks.

Co (2008); Roscoe et al. (2009)

Atkinson, William (c.1774–1839) Pupil of James *Wyatt, he published (1805) *Views of Picturesque Cottages*. He invented 'Atkinson's Cement', used for external *rendering and to form *mouldings, and succeeded Wyatt as Architect to the Board of Ordnance (1813). He seems to have specialized in the design of asymmetrical *Gothick country-houses: these include Scone Palace, Perthshire (1803–12), Mulgrave Castle, Yorks. (c.1804–16), Abbotsford, Roxburghshire (1814–24), and extensive Gothic additions at Taymouth Castle, Perthshire (1818–21, 1826–8). He carried out important alterations at The Deepdene, nr. Dorking, Surrey, for Thomas *Hope (1818–19, 1823—all demolished).

Co (2008); Wa (1968); Wa & Hewat-Jaboor (eds) (2008)

atlantes *See* ATLAS.

atlas, atlantis (*pl.* **atlantes, atlantides**) Well-developed, sculptured, male figure, often occurring in *Baroque architecture, especially in Central Europe, supporting an *entablature or other architectural element (e.g. *balcony). Atlantes are carved to suggest they strain to sustain great burdens, and the arms and shoulders are used to hold up the superstructure, unlike *canephorae*, *caryatides*, or *telamones*, which support loads on their heads. Some sources state that *atlantes* (or *gigantes*) were Greek equivalents of Roman *telamones*, and that they were also called *Persians*, but male standing figures dressed in oriental fashion, *telamones* (often with Egyptianizing attributes), *canephorae*, and *caryatides* are always straight and unbowed, and are wholly unlike *atlantes*. The Greek temple of *Zeus Olympius*, Agraces (*or* Agrigentum), had *atlantes* standing on screen-walls between *engaged *Doric columns to give additional support with heads *and arms* to the entablature (*c.*480 BC).

J.Curl (2001); D (1950)

atrium (*pl.* **atria**) **1.** Small *court or principal room in a Roman house, called *cavaedium* or *cavum aedium*, with the *compluvium* or roofless opening in the centre, usually surrounded by a colonnaded roofed area. Rainwater was channelled into an *impluvium*, *cistern, pool, or tank set under the opening in the floor. *Types of domestic atrium include*:

atrium Corinthium: with more than four columns (i.e. a *peristyle*) supporting the edge of the roof surrounding the *compluvium*;

atrium displuvatium: with the roof sloping away from the *compluvium*, rainwater being removed in gutters and pipes;

atrium testudinatum: with no *compluvium*, but covered with an arched *vault (*testudo*);

atrium tetrastylum: with four columns, one at each corner supporting the roof around the *compluvium*;

atrium Tuscanicum: insignificant and *astylar with the roof carried on two beams with two short *trimmers.

2. Open court surrounded by a roofed *arcaded or *colonnaded walk, laid out before the west end of an *Early-Christian, *Byzantine, or medieval church, sometimes planted with trees, and often with a fountain in the centre. An interesting survival is at *Sant'Ambrogio*, Milan (*c.*1140). In this sense, the atrium was the forerunner of the *cloister. **3.** Top-lit internal space surrounded by several storeys, e.g. Portman's Hyatt Regency Hotel, Atlanta, GA (1967–71).

Br (1985); D.S.R (1945); Saxon (1994)

attached *See* ENGAGED.

Attic 1. Of or pertaining to Attica, or to its capital, Athens. **2.** Marked by Classical elegance, peculiarly Athenian. *Compounds include*:

Attic base: commonest *base of a Classical column (used with all *Orders except Greek *Doric and (properly) *Tuscan) consisting of (usually) a *plinth over which is a large convex *torus ring, a *fillet, then a concave *scotia, then another fillet above which is a torus smaller than the lower ring, then a fillet, then the *apophyge and the *shaft. *Compare* ASIATIC BASE;

Attic door-case: *battered or *Vitruvian opening, its dimension at the threshold wider than at the top, the whole framed by an *architrave, often with *fasciae (VP **iv. vi.** 1, 2, 6);

Attic Order: subordinate *Order, perhaps of *pilasters, adorning the front of an Attic storey over the main *entablature, lining up with the Orders below;

Attic storey: in Classical architecture, a *storey over the main *entablature, often with an Attic *Order relating to the Orders below, but sometimes treated very plainly, as in a *triumphal arch, or the *Choragic Monument of Thrasyllus, Athens (added 279 BC). It should not be confused with a *garret. A room within an Attic storey proper is an *Attic-chamber*.

Atticurges, Atticurgic: seems to refer to anything 'in the Athenian style', and might allude to an Attic base or door-case.

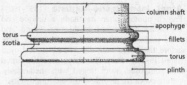

torus
scotia

column shaft
apophyge
fillets
torus
plinth

Attic base Theatre of Marcellus, Rome.

Attiret, Jean-Denis (1702–68) French Jesuit artist, he went to China (1737), where he prepared descriptions and illustrations of the Imperial Gardens, published (1752) in English. These were close to C18 ideas concerning so-called *Picturesque and *rustic landscape-design in England, and may explain the French label, '*jardin *anglo-chinois*'. His work informed *Chambers's descriptions, and promoted the introduction of orientalizing garden-*fabriques*.

Attiret (1982); Gothein (1966); Wiebenson (1978)

attribute Object expressing the authority or character of a personage (mythical or otherwise) or a deity, used associated with a building's use (e.g. lyre for **Apollo**, a dove **Venus**, a grid-iron **St Lawrence**, a flaying-knife **St Bartholomew**, and a trident **Neptune**). Thus lyres occur on concert-halls and tridents on buildings associated with marine affairs.

Atwood, Charles Bowler (1849-95) MA-born and -educated architect, he worked for *Ware and **van Brunt** from 1866 before opening (1872) his own office, later (1891) joining *Burnham in Chicago, IL. His 1880s work showed an ever-developing fluency in *Classicism, and this got him appointed chief designer for the World's Columbian Exposition, Chicago, 1893. The power of his Classical architecture was apparent at the Exposition's Terminal Railroad Station, based on Roman *thermae, which influenced subsequent designs of many railway stations in the United States. His Fine Arts Building (1893—later Museum of Science and Industry) was a noble essay in the Graeco-Roman *Neo-Classical style. Atwood applied a logical and scholarly architectural language to tall structures, including the Reliance (1894-5) and the Fisher (1895-6) Buildings, two of the most important works of the *Chicago School: towers clad in glass and *terracotta, they represent a significant step in the evolution of the metal-framed *skyscraper, the outside skin of which was visibly non-structural.

C.Jenkins (1895); Woltersdorf (1924)

Atwood, Thomas Warr (*c*.1733-75) Architect/builder who played a significant part in directing the building policies of Bath. He erected The Paragon (1768) and Oxford Row (1773), and designed the new prison in Grove Street (1772-3). He was also responsible for the Guildhall completed by Thomas *Baldwin. He produced several examples of street-elevations informed by *Palladianism.

Co (2008); Ison (1969)

Atwood, William (*fl.*1490-1557). English *freemason, master-mason at Wells Cathedral, Som., from 1490, who rebuilt the south *cloister there (completed 1508).

J.Harvey (1987)

Aubert, Jean (*fl.*1702-41) French architect, he worked for *Hardouin-Mansart before being taken up by the **Bourbon-Condé** family for whom he remodelled the *château* of *Saint-Maur-des-Fosses*, near Paris (1709-10). At Chantilly (Oise) he designed the stables for the *château* (1719-35), and in Paris he was responsible for the *Palais Bourbon* (1724—destroyed). Two of his finest Parisian works were the *Hôtel de Lassay* (1724-8) and the *Hôtel Peyrenc de Moras* (1728-32). His interiors of the *Petit Château*, Chantilly (1718-22), are exquisite. He used powerful horizontal channelling on his rusticated wall-surfaces, and his interiors typified the elegant *Régence style.

Kalnein (1995); K & L (1972)

auditorium (*pl.* **auditoria**) **1.** *Nave of a church (*see* AUDITORY). **2.** Part of a concert-hall, theatre, etc., occupied by the audience. **3.** Reception-room in a *monastery. **4.** Building for concerts, theatrical performances, etc.

auditory 1. Ancient name for a church *nave, where the Gospel could be heard. **2.** From C17, churches of the Reformed religion adopted a wide, almost square, plan so that the *lectern and *pulpit were more clearly visible and the Word could be heard: they were called *auditory churches.*

L-D (1934)

aula (*pl. aulae*) **1.** Inner *court, *atrium, or entrance-hall in a Greek or Roman house. **2.** Hall in a house, *palace, or *temple. **3.** Main hall or assembly-room in an educational building.

Aulenti, Gae(tana) (1927-2012) Italian architect. From 1956, when she commenced practice, her work developed within the richly diverse atmosphere in Milan. Her best-known building is the conversion of the redundant *Gare d'Orsay* railway-terminus in Paris (1896-1900—by *Laloux) to the *Musée d'Orsay* (1980-6). She was also responsible for the restoration and conversion of the *Palazzo Grassi*, Venice, for use as a musical *auditorium and exhibition-centre (1985-6). She restored the *Palazzo Muti-Bussi*, Rome (1991), planned the Feshane Museum of Modern and Contemporary Art, Istanbul, Turkey (1992), and converted San Francisco's Neo-Classical Main Library into the Museum of Asian Art (2003). She was closely associated with the *Neo-Liberty Movement, and was critical of expensively outlandish structures (notably those influenced by *Deconstructivism) for museums and art galleries.

E (1994); *The Times* (19 Nov. 2012), 44

aumbry, *also called* **almerie, almery, almory, ambry, amry, aumerie, aumery, aumrie 1.** Recess in a church wall in which sacred vessels are kept, usually near an *altar. **2.** Store for food, cooking-utensils, etc.: food-cupboard or larder. **3.** Recessed cupboard in a wall. **4.** As *almonry.

aureole Halo or Glory surrounding the figure of Christ, the Virgin, or a Saint. If almond-shaped, it is formed of two interlocking segmental arcs, called a *mandorla or *vesica piscis. A circular *halo surrounding a head only is termed *nimbus.*

Auricular Style of C16 and C17 ornament featuring curved, smooth, undulating forms with flowing lines and ripple-like elements suggesting the human ear. Called *Cartilaginous, Dutch Grotesque, Lobate,* or *Oleaginous* style, it occurred in *antic, *grotesque, and *Mannerist ornament, and probably influenced *Rococo and *Art Nouveau detail.

Aust, Franz (1885-1963) American landscape architect, he prepared numerous schemes in WI. Concerned with the *conservation of the

American landscape, he was active as a lobbyist/educator, and promoted studies in rural planning, soil conservation, outdoor advertising, and roadside developments.

B & F (2009)

Austin, Geoffrey Langshaw (1884-1971) *See* SHARPE, EDMUND.

Austin, Henry (1804-91) CT-born architect, he trained with *Town & *Davis, mastering several historical styles. His works at New Haven, CT, include the Yale Library (now Dwight Chapel, of 1842-5), based on King's College Chapel, Cambridge; the *Egyptian-Revival gateway at Grove Street Cemetery (1848-9); the Railway Station (1848-9—featuring *Italianate, *Chinoiserie, and *Indian styles); and City Hall (1861-2—*High-*Victorian *Gothic Revival). He exploited exotic styles in a number of *villas, one of the best of which was the Moses Yale Beach House, Wallingford, CT (1850), in which Indian and Italian motifs mingled. In his last years in practice he designed several timber houses using the *Stick style (e.g. the W.J. Clark House, Stony Creek, Branford, CT (1879-80)).

Austin (1985); E.Brown (1976); Carrott (1978); P (1982)

Austin, Hubert James (1841-1915) *See* SHARPE, EDMUND.

automata Water-, wind-, or clockwork-propelled mechanical devices rooted in ancient traditions—again in vogue during the Italian *Renaissance—facilitating movement such as transporting large amounts of water to power garden-features (*fountains/*cascades), or driving outdoor curiosities incorporating motion, sound, music, and/or light. Interest in *hydraulics and pneumatics inspired literature, including Salomon de *Caus's *Les raisons...* (1615), which demonstrated schemes for *pleasure-gardens with *grottoes and fountains. A good example is the *Villa d'Este*, Tivoli, Italy (1550-72).

Caus (1615); Dernie & Carew-Cox (1996); Shoe (2001); Symes (2006)

avant-corps *Porch, *pavilion, etc., projecting from the *corps de logis*.

avenue 1. Parallel lines of trees, with or without a path or road between them. 2. Main approach to a country-house with regularly-planted trees on either side, a term imported from France by John *Evelyn. 3. Wide, handsome street, with or without trees.

O'Malley et al. (eds) (1998)

Averlino, Antonio (c.1400-69) *See* FILARETE.

aviary House, enclosure, or large cage for keeping, breeding, and displaying birds. Known in Antiquity, aviaries enjoyed a revival during the *Renaissance, for beautiful birds and their songs could enhance enjoyment of the landscape. Aviaries became essential elements of gardens, impacting French taste, while the occasional aviary appeared in C18 English *landscape-gardens ('Capability' *Brown designed one at Melton Constable, Norfolk). With the introduction of many more exotic birds in England during C19, aviaries became regular features of *public parks and private gardens: **Gabriel Thouin** (1747-1829) published one in his *Plans raisonnés de toutes les espèces de jardins* (1820), and J.B.*Papworth illustrated an example in his *Hints...* (1818-20). Outstanding exotic aviaries were built at Waddesdon (1888-90—of cast iron and glass), and Dropmore (mid-C19), both Bucks.

J.B.Pa (1823), 101, pl. xxi; W.Pa (1852); Symes (2006); Tay (2006); Thouin (1820)

awning 1. Tent-like projection from the face of a building, roofed with copper, zinc, etc. imitative of the curved form of a canvas covering, common in *Regency dwellings. 2. Temporary tent-like structure. 3. Retractable canvas shelter above a shop-window.

axial Layout disposed symmetrically about an *axis, e.g. a *basilican church.

axis 1. Straight guide-line on either side of which elements of a plan are symmetrically disposed: in a sphere it runs through the centre *see* AXIAL. 2. Thickness of the thinnest portion of the *Ionic *volute cushion, i.e. the *fillet. 3. Hanging-*stile of a *door.

axonometric projection Geometrical architectural drawing, useful to give an idea of three-dimensional form, more or less to scale, which can be exploded to show the interior, etc. Its plan is produced to *scale, but moved round at an angle of 60° and 30° to the normal *axis (or set at 45°, whichever is convenient or creates the best impression). Vertical lines to scale are then also projected from the plan, thus the only parts distorted and not to scale are curves and diagonals.

FR (1946); Seidenberg (1956)

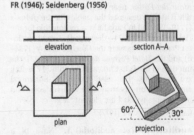

axonometric projection

Aylmer, John (c.1471–1548) English master-mason, partner of John *Vertue, he contracted (1506) to build the *vault of St George's Chapel, Windsor, Berks., including flying *buttresses, cresting, etc. He also built the Savoy Hospital, London (1512–19), and carried out works at the Tower of London.

J.Harvey (1987)

Aymonino, Carlo (1926–2010) Rome-born architect, he edited *Casabella-Continuità* (1959–64), but is perhaps best known for his writings on *typology, cities, and *urbanism. He designed the *Monte Amiata* housing development, Gallaratese, Milan (built 1967–73), in collaboration with other architects (including Aldo *Rossi): blocks of apart-ments (mostly seven *storeys high) were arranged geometrically around a vast space. Aymonino was involved in several city-centre planning schemes, including those at Bologna and Turin (both 1962), Reggio Emilia (1971—with **Constantino Dardi** (1936–91)), and Florence (1978—with Rossi).

Aymonino (1971, 1975, & (ed.) 1975a); Conforti (1980); Eisenman (ed.) (1996); Ma (1984); Pitzalis (ed.) (2000)

Azéma, Léon (1888–1978) French architect. With **Louis-Hippolyte Boileau** (1878–1948) and **Jacques Carlu** (1890–1976) he designed the *Palais de Chaillot*, Paris (completed 1937), in a mon-umental stripped Classical style. Among other works the forbidding Ossuary at Douaumont (1923–7—containing bones of unidentifiable dead at Verdun in the 1914–18 war), by Azéma et al., and his solo design for *St-Antoine de Padoue*, Paris (1933–6), may be cited.

J.Curl (2002a); P (1982)

Aztec architecture A people who settled on the island of Texcoco c.1325, the Aztecs soon came to dominate Meso-America in what is now México. The previously dominant people, the Tol-tecs, built storeyed *pyramids adorned with fear-some sculpture, and the Aztecs seem to have adopted their architecture, adding the double pyramid to the repertoire of building types. Their capital, Tenochtitlán (now México City), and the city of Cholula were adorned with pyra-mids and temples. The surviving pyramid at Te-nayuca (c.1450–1500) has a steep stair on one side, and rows of sculptured serpent-heads on the base on the three other sides. An early C16 pyramid at El Tepozteco and the rock-cut struc-tures at Malinalco of the same period represent the chief architectural remains. Aztec architecture inspired the *Art-Deco style.

Ck (1996); Gendrop & Heyden (1986); Kubler (1984)

azulejo 1. Glazed earthenware lustrous *tile, brightly coloured and ornamented with geomet-rical and floral patterns, found in *alicatado* work in the Iberian Peninsula and Latin America. **2.** Dutch or Delft glazed tiles in which the pre-dominant colour is blue.

Azuma, Takamitsu (1933–) *See* ARCHITEXT.

Babb, George Fletcher (1836–1915) American architect, responsible for several buildings in NJ before forming (1877) a partnership with **Walter Cook** (1846–1916) in NYC: **Babb & Cook** designed the cast-iron office-building, 55 Broadway, NYC (1881—demolished). They were joined (1884) by **Daniel Wheelock Willard** (1849–after 1902): as **Babb, Cook, & Willard**, the firm's most celebrated design was the De Vinne Press Building, Lafayette Street, NYC (1885-6), one of many works, mostly in NYC.

Schull (1980); V.J.Sy (1971)

Babcock, Charles (1829-1913) American architect, he worked with *Upjohn (1853–8), was one of the founding-members of the American Institute of Architects, and later designed a number of buildings for Cornell University, Ithaca, NY, including the *Gothic house for the University's President (1871) and Franklin Hall (1881).

Wo (1976)

Bābur (Ẓahīr al-Dīn Muhammad Bābur) (*r.* 1526-30) Founder of the Mughal Dynasty of India (1526-1857—originally from Uzbekistan), and wrote the important *Bābur-nama*, which includes details of contemporary gardens and plants. After the loss (1494) of his patrimony in Ferghana, by the late 1520s he had established his rule over much of northern India. He laid out several gardens in Afghanistan and India, including the *Bāgh-i-Nilufar*, Jhor, near Dholpur (begun 1527 to designs perhaps by **Ustad Shah Muhammad** (*fl.*1520s)), and other gardens in the vicinity of Agra with *pavilions and stretches of water intended to provide settings for pleasure and reflection (*see* BĀGH) which appear to have been influenced by memories of earlier gardens of Bābur's ancestors, the Timurids. Many such formal gardens were subsequently associated with grand *mausolea (*see* MUGHAL GARDEN, PARADISE GARDEN).

A.S.Beveridge (1922); M & P (2011); Shoe (2001); Thakston; J.T (1996)

Babylonian architecture Mesopotamian architecture *c.*4000-1250 BC. Early inhabitants of the region were the Sumerians, who, by the fourth millennium, had evolved a sophisticated architecture using brick, and who set the architectural agenda, virtually until *Hellenistic times. They built arches with *voussoirs and *vaults, and used cedar-wood in great quantities. In important buildings, walls were decorated with coloured *terracotta cones placed in geometrical patterns, while other characteristic elements were walls with slightly projecting decorative *buttresses, vertical channelling, and stepped or triangular *battlements. Towers, known as *ziggurats, consisting of a series of superimposed *stages, each smaller than that below, were associated with *temples: an impressive example was the enormous ziggurat at Ur (C22 BC), with huge staircases giving access to the sanctuary on top. Aspects of Babylonian architecture were absorbed by the *Assyrians near the end of the second millennium BC.

Ck (1996); L & M (1986)

Bacchic ornament Associated with Bacchus, Roman deity of wine and fertility, among whose *attributes are asses, grapevines, laurels, panthers, rams, serpents, and tigers, it was found in Antiquity, and from *Renaissance times was used when associations with sensual pleasure were desired. Regarded as the opposite of *Apolline decoration, it appeared in *Neo-Classical designs.

L & D (1986)

Bachelier, Nicolas (1500-57) French *Renaissance architect, he designed the *Hôtel de Bagis*, Toulouse (1538-46), and the *châteaux* at Pibrac (1540-5), Castelnau d'Estrétefonds (1539-44), and Lasserre-les-Montastruc (1555-6).

Bt (1982); Graillot (1914); Ha (1943–57)

bacino (*pl.* bacini) Coloured glazed earthenware plates and roundels set into the exterior walls of Italian *Romanesque buildings.

back 1. *Principal *rafter in a roof. **2.** Top or visible part of, e.g. a *slate. **3.** Rear or hidden side of something.

back-aisle Portion of a church forming an appendage to the main building, e.g. a *chantry-chapel projecting from a *chancel-aisle.

back-house 1. Part of a house or building lying behind, usually subsidiary to the front or main part, or forming an appendage. **2.** Brew- or bake-house (also *baikhouse*). **3.** Privy, separated from the main building.

Backsteingotik Simplified medieval *Gothic architecture constructed of brick, e.g. the town-halls of Lübeck or Toruń, or the vast churches of Northern Germany and Poland.

Backström, Sven Mauritz (1903–92) Swedish architect, partner of **Leif Axel Reinius** (1907–95): they designed some of the most influential buildings of the 1940s, when Sweden's relative isolation encouraged the evolution of an indigenous style using natural materials (e.g. timber) and traditional roof-forms. The firm invented the **Y**-shaped housing-block with three arms joined to a central circulation-core, as at Gröndal, Stockholm (1943–5), and planned the suburb of Vällingby (1956–7), among other projects.

A & B (1986); E (1980)

back-to-back housing Houses built in *blocks (**3**), with the backs of one block forming the backs of the others. Common in British C19 industrial towns, they must not be confused with *terrace-housing (**5**) with walled rear *yards and a *path between those yards. Most true back-to-back housing has long been demolished.

J.Curl (1983); Tarn (1971)

Bacon, Edmund Norwood (1910–2005) American architect/planner, born in Philadelphia, PA, where much of his work was done, who authored numerous works on planning. A supporter of *urban renewal, much of his work was adversely criticized.

E.Bacon (1974)

Bacon, Francis (1561–1626—**1st Viscount St Alban** from 1621) English essayist/gardener/statesman: *Mason thought him a prophet and *Hirschfeld noted how his views on gardens anticipated those in *Milton's *Paradise Lost* (1667). In his rejection of *knot-gardens, *topiary (both common in the early C17), and his insistence on *mounts (though then rather old-fashioned) from which to view 'abroad into the fields', he was in many respects a century ahead of *Kent and *Pope, but, like *Temple and *Wotton, Bacon was familiar with the Dutch School of land-scape-painting, and all wrote about gardens, advocating the importance of using the country-side as backdrops. His essay (**xlvi**), *Of Gardens* (to him 'the Purest of Humane pleasures'), recommended diversity, variety, and horticultural profusion (with flowers, herbs, and trees, including evergreens, to bring beauty and colour throughout the year), mindful of a metaphysical longing to realize a mythical *Ver Perpetuum*, for, after all, 'God *Almightie* first Planted a *Garden*': his

'natural *wilderness' would be treeless, but have thickets of sweet-briar, honeysuckle, and wild vine. His ideal garden should not be of less than 30 acres (12 hectares) and of three parts: a lawn of four acres in front of the house; a main garden (12 acres, with *alleys on both sides); then a '*Heath* or *Desart*' of six acres beyond the main garden. On either side of the lawn should be covered walks, with 'Carpenters Worke' some twelve feet high, with plants trained to climb on it and provide shade. The main garden should be square, surrounded on all sides with a '*Stately Arched Hedge*', the arches set on timber columns or *piers, ten feet high and six feet wide, with *hedges over the arches some four feet high: over every arch he suggested a little *turret 'with a *Belly*' (concavity) large enough to receive a bird-cage, and over every space, between the arches, some 'little *Figure*', with 'Broad Plates of *Round Coloured Glasse*, gilt', to catch and reflect the sun's rays. This hedge would be set on a bank planted with flowers, and, beyond the square enclosed thus, there should be a 'diversity of *Side Alleys*' approached from the two covered walks flanking the lawn. However, no obstructions at the ends of the alleys should block views over the '*Desart*'. His garden had fruit trees, sunny areas, and agreeable *arbours, but he disapproved of 'unwholesome' ponds, despite the fact that his own garden, Gorhambury, Herts. (*c.*1608—destroyed), included *water-gardens and statuary, and a square pond with a central island adorned with a *banqueting-house 'of Roman architecture' set on a mount. There were also a *terrace, a *grotto, and an arbour covered with roses. At Twickenham House, Mddx., he created (1590s) elaborate geometrical gardens with mounts at each corner (drawn *c.*1609 by R.*Smythson), and he improved (from 1597) the gardens at Gray's Inn, London, again with a ban-queting-house on a mount. He seems to have taken a utilitarian attitude to the design of houses 'built to live in, and not to look on; therefore let use be preferred before uniformity' in his 1625 essay (**xlv**), *Of Building*. He was also critical of excessively large windows.

Bacon (1858–74); *GH*, **xvii**/1 (Spring 1989), 41-67; *GH*, **xx**/2 (Autumn 1992), 116–31; Gothein, I (1966), 446-8; H & W (1988); Shoe (2001); Strong (1979); Tay (2006)

Bacon, Henry (1866-1924) IL-born American architect, much influenced by his elder brother, **Francis Henry Bacon** (1856-1940), architect, who had been involved (1880s) in archaeological expeditions in Asia Minor. Henry Bacon himself travelled (1889) in Greece and Asia Minor, before returning to the prestigious firm of *McKim, Mead, & White, where he contributed to several current projects, including the J.P.Morgan Library (1902-6). He set up his own practice (1897), producing scholarly and exquisitely detailed buildings, including a large number of monuments and *mausolea. His expertise in this field led to the commission to design the Lincoln Memorial in Washington, DC (1911–22), which terminates the axis of the Mall at the Potomac River: it is one of the finest examples of *Greek-Revival designs anywhere.

Hi (1977); Kidney (1974); V.J.Sy (1988)

Badger, Daniel D. (1806–84) American designer, he established in NYC one of the USA's largest iron foundries, where he manufactured cast-iron kits of parts for entire buildings, including the Haughwout Store, Broadway, NYC (1856).

G & G (1974); Handlin (1985)

Badovici, Jean (1893–1956) Romanian architect, he edited *L'Architecture Vivante* (1923–5), the Paris journal that promoted *Modernism. He built two houses for himself, at Vézelay (1924) and near the *Pont de Sèvres*, Paris (1934), and collaborated with Eileen *Gray on 'E-1027', the *Maison en Bord de Mer* at Roquebrune-Cap-Martin in the South of France (1926–9—a whole issue of *L'Architecture Vivante* was devoted to it). Badovici was a friend of Le *Corbusier (who painted murals in the Roquebrune-Cap-Martin house in 1929).

Bad (1923, 1925, 1926–30, 1931, 1937); Bad (ed.) (1975); Bad & Gray (1929)

Baerwald, Alexander (1877–1930) German architect, he assisted *Ihne during the building of the *Neo-Baroque *Königliche Bibliothek* (1908–13—now the *Staatsbibliothek zu Berlin*), and designed several other works in the German capital, as well as the Technion University buildings (1912–24) and the Arthur Biram Reali School (1910–14), both in Haifa (now Israel), essays in *Historicism with a strong infusion of Islamic motifs and Jewish symbolism. He settled (1925) in Palestine, and was responsible for numerous buildings there, including the Anglo-Palestine Bank (1924), a dwelling for **Hermann Struck** (1876–1944), and several other buildings in Haifa (including the Phillips House (1929–30)). As Professor of Architecture at the Technion, he brought Prussian academic discipline, rigour, and academically based architecture to his adopted country.

J.T (1996)

baffle-entry See ENTRY.

bāgh Enclosed garden of Persian origin. A *chahar bāgh* or *chār-bāgh* is a garden subdivided into four parts by canals and paths, e.g. the *Paradise-garden of the *Tāj Mahal* at Agra.

bagnet, bagnette See BAGUET.

bague See BAGUET.

baguet, baguette, *also* **bagnet, bagnette 1.** Small convex *moulding with a semicircular *section, similar to a *bead or an *astragal (called *chaplet* when ornamented). **2.** Frame ornamented with a bead-moulding.

Bähr, Georg (1666–1738) Trained as a carpenter, he became (1705) *Ratszimmermeister* (Master Carpenter) to the City of Dresden, and then developed skills as a gifted architect of German *Baroque. Responsible for Loschwitz *Pfarrkirche*, near Dresden (1705–8—the plan of which was a distorted octagon), *Dreifaltigkeitskirche*, Schmiedeberg, south of Dresden (1713–16), and the *Dorfkirche*, Forchheim, near Chemnitz (1719–26), the last two with plans based on the Greek *cross, his reputation rests on the *Frauenkirche*, Dresden (1722–43), the finest Protestant *auditory church ever conceived on a *centralized plan. On the strength of that one building (one of the most grievous losses of the 1944–5 bombing, but happily rebuilt 1996–2005), Bähr must be considered a master of the Baroque style, fully in control of complex geometries and structure, who gave Dresden a great domed church, rising majestically by the banks of the Elbe. The plan was, in essence, circular, but set inside a square, the *chancel inside part of an *ellipse, and *staircases, capped with elegant *turrets, placed diagonally in relation to the square four corners. Eight massive *piers supported the very high stone-vaulted *dome with its huge *lantern, and, between those piers, three tiers of *galleries were fitted, the fronts of the lowest tier being glazed, and known as *Bettstübchen* (Little Bedrooms), *Hoflogen* (Court Boxes), or *Ranglogen* (Gallery Boxes). The *altar was given prominence by being raised on a platform, while the organ-pipes rose up behind it, increasing the theatrical effects of a stunning interior.

Birne (2001); E.Hempel (1965); L-D (1934); H.Popp (1924); Sponsel (1893)

bailey 1. External wall or defences surrounding a *keep or *motte of a medieval *castle. **2.** Area between the circuits of walls or defences of a castle, also called a *ward, or any *court within the walls, hence *outer bailey* or *inner bailey*.

Baillargé (*or* **Baillairgé**) **Family** Dynasty of French-Canadian architects active in Québec for two centuries. **Jean** (1726–1805) and **François** (1759–1830) were responsible for the first phases of the reconstruction of Notre-Dame Cathedral, Québec (1768–1818), while **Thomas** (1791–1859) designed the severe front (1843). The last, as Diocesan Architect of Québec, conceived the elegant interior of *St-François-de-Sales*, Île d'Orléans (1835–44), and made alterations to the *façade of the *Ste-Famille*, Île d'Orléans, including the central *clocher (1843). Among his other churches are *Sainte-Croix de Lotbinière* (1835) and *Saint-François-Xavier* at Saint-François-du-Lac (1835–49), *Sainte-Geneviève* at Pierrefonds (1837–44), and *Saint-Joseph* at Lauzon (1830–2).

Charles-Philippe-Ferdinand (1826–1906), architect/civil-engineer/surveyor, was influenced by the publications of *Lafever, as demonstrated in his designs for the *Greek-Revival Music Hall, Québec (1851–3). He designed many buildings, including *Saint-Romuald*, Québec (1854–6), and the New Québec Prison (1860–3). He had a fine architectural library and published much.

Baillairgé (1899, 1900, 1979); C.Cameron (1989); K (1994); Noppen *et al.* (1979)

Baillie Scott, Mackay Hugh (1865–1945) *See* SCOTT.

Bailly, Antoine-Nicolas-Louis (1810–92) Pupil of *Debret and *Duban, he specialized in the French-*Renaissance Revival. He was appointed by *Haussmann to design the *Tribunal de Commerce*, Paris (1858–64), based on Brescia Town Hall, which contained a sumptuous vaulted *staircase. His *Mairie* of the fourth *arrondissement* (1862–7) is probably his best work, owing much to C17 precedent.

Ha (1957); M & Wa (1987)

Baird, John (1798–1859) Scots architect, his Glasgow practice was second only in importance to that of David *Hamilton. He rarely strayed from a sedate *Classicism, although there were forays into *Jacobethan (Cairnhill House, Airdrie, 1841) and *Tudor Revival (Urie House, Fetteresso, Kincardineshire, 1855). He is remembered today primarily for his experiments with metal, including the *cast-iron *hammer-beam roof of the Argyll (formerly Argyle) Arcade (1827–8), and the cast-iron fronted Gardner's Warehouse, 36 Jamaica Street (1855–6), both in Glasgow. Baird was assisted by **James Thomson** (1835–1905), who became his partner, and Alexander 'Greek' *Thomson worked in the office (1836–48).

Co (2008); G & W (1987)

Baird, John (1816–93) *See* THOMSON.

Bakema, Jakob Berend (1914–81) Dutch architect, he worked under van *Eesteren and for the municipality of Rotterdam before setting up (1948) in partnership with **Johannes Hendrik van den Broek** (1898–1978). Bakema joined (1947) *CIAM, and (1963) *Team X, and was joint editor (1959–64) of *Forum* (which promoted the cause of *Structuralism). Both partners favoured *Modernism, attacking conservative craft-orientated beliefs of the *Delft School. Their *Lijnbaan* Centre, Rotterdam (1949–54—which has not worn gracefully), was a precedent

for many *shopping-malls, while their Civic Centre, Marl, Germany (1958–62—four tower-blocks linked by lower slab-blocks) was representative of a type that became common over the following decades. The partnership's Town Hall, Terneuzen (1968), and Psychiatric Hospital, Middelharnis (1973–4), both have nods to *Constructivism. The firm influenced developments in Britain and Germany, but Bakema's assertion that architecture is the three-dimensional expression of human behaviour savours of the *cliché*, while his campaigns to jettison craft traditions and historical references have done much damage.

M.Gray (ed.) (1981); G & I (eds) (1976); Ibelings (ed.) (2000); J.Je (1976); J.Je (ed.) (1963a)

Baker, Charles (1791–1861) Architect/engineer/surveyor, based in Glos., he was in partnership (1834–43) with **Edwin Hugh Shellard** (1815–85), with whom he designed the layout of the Bayshill Estate, Cheltenham (*c.*1835), and perhaps some of the street-elevations (e.g. The Royal Well and Bayshills Terraces, St George's Road (1837–40)).

Co (2008)

Baker, Sir Herbert (1862–1946) Kent-born architect, he worked (1882–7) for *George and *Peto before opening his own office and then emigrating to Cape Colony, South Africa. He quickly became a protégé of **Cecil John Rhodes** (1853–1902) and **Lord Milner** (1854–1925), under whose aegis he began to create a distinctive architecture for British South Africa, drawing together English *vernacular elements, aspects of the *Arts-and-Crafts movement, Dutch-*Colonial architecture, *Wrenaissance, and much else. He adapted his eclectic style for later buildings in Rhodesia, Kenya, India, and England. For Rhodes he built the house known as *Groote Schuur*, Rondebosch (1893–8), in which Dutch-Colonial elements were well to the fore, followed by Government Buildings, Bloemfontein, and the masterly Union Buildings, Pretoria (1909–13—with twin *cupolas derived from Wren's work at Greenwich). Baker was then appointed joint architect (with *Lutyens) for the design of the Imperial Capital, New Delhi, India, and designed (from 1913) the north and south Secretariat Blocks as well as the circular Legislative Building. He introduced Indian architectural features such as *chattris*, and successfully combined Western and Eastern elements. Baker established (1912) an office in London, and was appointed (1917) Principal Architect to the Imperial War Graves Commission, in which capacity he encouraged design of the highest calibre. However, he was responsible for some grandiose London developments, including the enormous Bank of England works (1921–39—which destroyed *Soane's building (apart from the *screen-wall)), India House, Aldwych (1928–30), and South Africa House, Trafalgar Square (1930–5). These buildings cannot really be described as wholly successful, for Baker seems to have been happier using *Classicism with a strong dose of *Arts-and-Crafts influence: in this respect his beautifully articulated war-memorial cloister at Winchester College, Hants. (1922–5), demonstrates a sensitivity absent in his grander buildings.

H.Baker (1934, 1944); A.S.Gray (1985); Greig (1970); Irving (1981); Keath (1992); Stamp (1977)

Baker, Ian Crampton (1923–2010) English architect, associated with *New Humanism. Partner of **Leonard Manasseh** (1916–2017) for half a century, he designed (with **Elizabeth Chesterton** (1915–2002)) the National Motor Museum, Beaulieu, Hants. (completed 1972), as well as the surrounding landscaped grounds. He was also involved in the Rutherford School, Marylebone (completed 1960) and the Teachers' Training College, Tooting (1960–5), both in London; King's Lynn Law Courts, Norfolk (completed 1981); and works at the *New Towns of Harlow and Basildon, Essex.

The Guardian (20 May 2010), Obits; *C20 Newsletter* (Autumn 2010), 37

Baker, Laurence ('Laurie') **Wilfred** (1917–2007) British-born architect, he settled (1945) in India, specializing in cost-effective energy-efficient architecture to promote 'sustainable' buildings. Believing that homes should be made with local materials found within five miles of any site, he encouraged improvisation, recycling, and resistance to expensive fads such as *High Tech, Corbusian *Modernism, and *Deconstructivism. Among his works may be cited the Narayan House, Trivandrum (1973), the hexagonal house in Manvila (1982), and St John's Cathedral, Tiruvella (1974).

Bhatia (1991)

Baker, William (1705–71) English architect/surveyor active in Salop., Staffs., and adjoining counties. His works include the Butter Cross, Ludlow, Salop. (1743–4—influenced by *Gibbs), the Market-Hall, Montgomery (1748—partially rebuilt 1828), and the stable-block at Aldenham House, Morville, Salop. (1750–1). He designed several funerary monuments, including the Acton Memorial in Acton Scott Church, Salop. (1750–1). Survival of his account book and diary for 1748–59 has shed light on English provincial Georgian architectural practice.

Bold & Chaney (eds) (1993): Co (2008)

balanced sash Window-frame with two vertically sliding *sashes hung on chains/cords draped over pulleys in the boxed frame and fixed at the other end to weights balancing the sashes and facilitating easy movement.

balanced winder *Dancer (**2**) or winder of a curving section or *turn* of a *stair, with the narrowest parts of the wedge-shaped treads the same size as those of a straight flight in the same stair.

Balat, Alphonse-Hubert-François (1818–95) Appointed (1852) architect to the **Duke of Brabant** (the future **King Leopold II of the Belgians** (*r.*1865–1909)), and influenced by *Viollet-le-Duc in his search for a rational approach to design, he drew on the immense vocabulary of *Classicism whilst also experimenting with advances in engineering, which influenced his pupil *Horta and other exponents of *Art Nouveau. His Classicism struck the right note with the Belgian nobility, who commissioned him to carry out numerous works (e.g. the van Assche Palace, *Wetenschapsstraat*, Brussels (1856–8—with its *Italianate *astylar *façade)). His best buildings were Royal commissions, including the Riding-School and Winter-Garden (1873–4) and the celebrated *glass-houses (1883–7) at Laeken, and the grand *stair and several State Rooms (e.g. Throne-Room, Marble Hall, Grand Gallery) as well as the garden-elevation of the Royal Palace, Brussels. His masterpiece is reckoned to be the *Neo-Classical *Palais des Beaux-Arts* (now the *Musée d'Art Ancien*), Brussels (1875–88).

Loo (ed.) (2003); P (1982); PM; J.T (1996)

balcon 1. Curved row of theatre-seats projecting beyond a stack of *boxes above the pit. **2.** Boxes situated on the *proscenium of a theatre.

balcone Large group of windows forming an architectural feature.

balconet, balconette 1. Railing at the outer plane of a window-opening reaching to the floor, and having, when the window is open, the *appearance* of a *balcony. Common in France, Spain, and Italy. **2.** Ornamental *vignette on a window-*cill to prevent flower-pots from falling.

balcony 1. Platform or open *gallery built out from the *naked of a wall, supported on *brackets, *consoles, *corbels, or columns, or *cantilevered. Normally constructed in front of windows or other apertures, it is unroofed, with a *balustrade, *parapet, or *rail around the platform, is capable of bearing the weight of one or more persons, and is usually slightly below the floor-level within. **2.** Projecting gallery with seats in an *auditorium at a higher level than the *stalls.

baldachin, baldachino, baldacchino, baldaquin Permanent *canopy, especially over an *altar, throne, or tomb, usually supported on columns. *Compare* CIBORIUM.

Baldessari, Luciano (1896–1982) Italian architect, who, with *Figini and **Gino Pollini** (1903–82), designed the Rationalist De Angeli Building (1929–32), and, with *Ponti, the Cima Chocolate Factory, (1932–3), both in Milan. He worked on many exhibition-buildings, notably the Breda Pavilions for the Milan Trade Fair (1933, 1951, 1952, 1953, and 1954). An exponent of *Rationalism, he retreated from *Functionalism early in his career. He built an *apartment-block in the Hansa Quarter, Berlin (1957–8), and the Fratelli Fontana Technical Institute, Rovereto (1961–73).

L (1988); J.T (1996); Ve (1957)

Baldwin, Thomas (c.1750–1820) Clerk to Thomas Warr *Atwood, he supervised the building of the Markets and Guildhall, Bath, Som., completing the latter and designing two *elevations (1775–9). Appointed (1776) City Surveyor, he became one of the principal architects of the Georgian city, designing in a *Palladian style with *Neo-Classical touches influenced by work of the *Adam Brothers. He was responsible for the Cross Bath and Pump Room (1783–4), the Pump-Room Colonnade (1786), Great Pulteney Street (c.1789), 1–14 Sydney Place, and houses in Southwick Street (1788–92), Union Street (c.1790), and several buildings in Wilts., including the Town Hall, Devizes (1806–8).

Co (2008); Ison (1969)

bale Type of tomb found in the Cotswolds, England, essentially an *altar-tomb supporting a stone half-cylinder resembling a woollen bale.

balection *See* BOLECTION.

balistraria *or* **ballistraria** (*pl.* **balistrariae**) **1.** Arbalestina, arbalisteria, arrow-loop, *loop-hole, or similar aperture, frequently cruciform, in a medieval wall through which bowmen (*arbalesters*) fired arrows or bolts. **2.** Store-room for *arbalests* (crossbows) or similar.

balistraria

balk, baulk 1. Any large piece of squared timber. **2.** *Lintel or *summer-beam. **3.** Upper roof-*tie, or balk-tie, between *rafters. **4.** Earthen ridge dividing areas of land.

ball-flower Characteristic *Second-Pointed C14 *Gothic ornament resembling a small ball, just visible, enclosed within a broken ball with a trefoil or quatrefoil opening, normally placed at regular intervals in a continuous hollow *moulding.

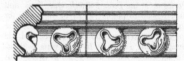

ball-flower String-course, St Nicholas's, Kiddington, Oxon. (*after Parker*).

balloon 1. Large ball, *ballon*, globe, or sphere placed above a column or *pier as a termination. **2.** Globe under a cross on a church *spire or *dome. **3.** System of *timber-framed construction common in Scandinavia and the USA in which the corner *posts and *studs are continuous in one piece from *cill or *sole-plate to roof-plate, the intermediate floor-joists being secured to them without mortises and tenons.

Ct (1968); Giordano (1964); F.Peterson (1992)

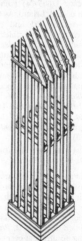

balloon-framing Typical American type.

Ballu, Théodore (1817–85) French architect, renowned for the early *Renaissance-style *La Trinité* (1861–7), near *Gare St-Lazare*, Paris. He completed *Gau's *Ste-Clotilde* (1846–57), the first *Gothic-Revival church in the capital; restored the *Tour St-Jacques de la Boucherie* (1854–8);

and designed the *Flamboyant-Revival free-standing tower, and restored the rest of the fabric of *St-Germain l'Auxerrois*, beside *Hittorff's *Mairie du Ier* (1858–63). He also built the *Hôtel de Ville*, Paris (1874–82).

Ballu (1868); Ben (1971); Deconchy (1875); Delaborde (1887); Ha (1957); Sédille (1886)

Baltard, Louis-Pierre (1764–1846) French architect/academic/theorist. He became (1796) Professor at the *École Polytechnique*, Paris, and later helped to prepare many of the plates for the Napoléonic *Description de l'Égypte*, the major sourcebook of the *Egyptian Revival. He designed the *Palais de Justice*, Lyons, with its *façade composed of a long line of twenty-four huge *Corinthian columns (1835–41), and the *Salle des Pas Perdus* consisting of a series of low-domed spaces: the design is typical of the type of official architecture, promoted by *Quatremère de Quincy, based on Roman Antiquity. He was also responsible for the *prison of the *Quartier Perrache* (1830), the artillery arsenal (1840–6), and other buildings in Lyons. His publications include *Recueil des Monuments Antiques* (1801).

L-P.Baltard (1818, 1875); J.Curl (2005); Egbert (1980); Ha (1952–5); E.Ka (1955); M & Wa (1987); S (1901–2)

Baltard, Victor (1805–74) French architect/academic, son of L.-P.*Baltard. As City Architect of Paris, he redecorated and rebuilt many Parisian churches, but his chief works were the iron-and-glass *Halles Centrales*, Paris (1852–9—demolished)—with **Félix-Emmanuel Callet** (1792–1854)—and the remarkable *St-Augustin* (1860–71)—with *cast-iron columns inside and a French-*Renaissance-Revival exterior. He also added the *Chapelle des Catéchismes* (1853) to *Chalgrin's *St-Philippe-du-Roule* (1768–84). He published *Villa Médicis à Rome* (1847) and, with Callet, *Monographie des halles centrales de Paris* (1863 and 1873).

V.Baltard & Callet (1863); Ben (1971); Deconchy (1875); C.Garteus (1874); M & Wa (1987)

balteus 1. Strap-like element around the *baluster-side, *cushion, coussinet, or *volute of the *Ionic *capital: it refers both to the central strap visible at the side of the capital and to those seeming to join the volutes at the ends of the cushion visible on the fronts. **2.** *Praecentio*, wide step, or landing occurring at every eighth seat in an *Antique theatre or *amphitheatre, affording a passage for spectators so that those seated would not be disturbed.

baluster Upright support in a balustrade: it may be a square, circular, turned, or ornamented bar or rod, very small in thickness (as in a *stair balustrade), a miniature column, or the bellied,

bulbed type of *colonnette (*columella*) with *base, *shaft, and *capital, circular, polygonal, or square on plan, with elaborate profiles, in some cases given distinctive features depending on which *Order is used elsewhere. The thickest part of a baluster is the *belly*, and the thin part the *sleeve*. *Banister* is sometimes used instead of *baluster*, while *banisters* signifies a balustrade. *See* STAIR. *Associated terms include*:

baluster-shaft: **1.** short, thick *colonnette with pronounced *entasis between openings (usually in towers) in *Anglo-Saxon architecture; **2.** *baluster-column* in Italian *campanili*;

baluster-side: form like a rolled-up mattress, like a baluster laid on its side, also known as a *bolster, *cushion, *pulvin, or pulvinus, joining the *volutes of an *Ionic *capital;

balustrade: **1.** row of balusters supporting a hand-rail of a stair; **2.** series of balusters between *pedestals, *plinths, and *copings or *cornices, forming a type of *parapet;

balustrade-Order: Order of balustrade columns, actually miniature versions of Classical *Orders;

balustrata: *chancel-*screen;

balustrum: *altar-rail, *cancelli, or chancel-screen. The last is more usually termed *balustrata*, while *balustrum* usually refers to the low *balustrade* or wall defining a *choir, as in *San Clemente*, Rome.

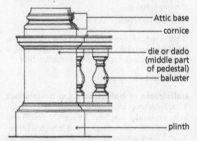

Labels: Attic base; cornice; die or dado (middle part of pedestal); baluster; plinth

baluster Balustrade terminating in a pedestal supporting a column with an Attic base.

banal-mill Also *bannal-mill*, a corn-mill where feudal tenants were obliged to have their corn ground: they also had to have their bread baked in a *banal-oven* for the benefit of the landlord.

Bancroft, John (1928–2011) English architect, he joined (1957) the LCC Schools Division: his best-known work was the *Brutalist Pimlico School, London (built 1964–5), set deep into the site, but large areas of glazing caused the usual problems of overheating, and it was demolished (2008).

C20 Newsletter (Autumn 2011), 50

band 1. Flat raised horizontal strip on a *façade, occasionally ornamented, sometimes coinciding with *cills or floor-levels, also called a *band-course, band-moulding, belt-course,* or *string-course.* The term can therefore be applied to the *fasciae on an *architrave, and sometimes (though rarely) to a *fillet, *list, or *taenia. In Classical *Orders *dentils and *modillions project from such bands called *dentil-* or *modillion-bands.* 2. Plain *block interrupting an architectural element, such as a column: in this sense, *banded* is used to describe the condition. *Examples are*:

banded architrave: one with projecting blocks placed at regular intervals between which the architrave is visible, as in a *Gibbs surround;

banded, blocked, ringed, or *rusticated column*: with shaft interrupted by plain or *rusticated square or cylindrical blocks, although some authorities prefer to use *banded* to mean a column-shaft made up of alternating larger and smaller drums, and *blocked* to indicate square blocks alternating with circular shaft-drums;

banded impost: formed by horizontal *mouldings, etc., at the springing of the arch when the *section of a medieval *pier is identical to that of the arch above;

banded pilaster: pilaster-shaft interrupted by rectangular blocks at intervals, corresponding to *banded columns*;

banded rustication: smooth *ashlar alternating with rusticated bands or blocks projecting beyond the *naked of the wall.

Other associated terms include:
banderole, bannerol (sculptured band, often inscribed, especially resembling a *ribbon or continuous spiral *scroll, or an enriched *string-course); and *band-work* (type of *arabesque, also occurring in *Rococo C-scroll frames and in *parterres). 3. *Bond,* in Scots, hence *inband* (header) and *outband* (*stretcher or *quoin with long side on face and short on reveals).

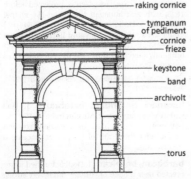

raking cornice
tympanum of pediment
cornice
frieze
keystone
band
archivolt
torus

band Gateway with banded Tuscan columns.

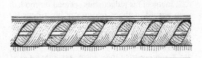

banderol *or* ribbon-moulding.

bandelet, bandlet 1. Small flat plain *moulding, greater than a *fillet and smaller than a *band or *fascia, e.g. the *taenia of the *Doric *Order. 2. *Annulet.

band of a shaft *Annulet, *bandelet, bandlet, or *shaft-ring around *colonnettes and slender *shafts in *Gothic architecture, at the junctions of *monolithic lengths, often tying the shafts to the *pier behind, as in a *cluster arrangement.

band of a shaft

band-stand Platform or open-sided *pavilion, often polygonal, where a band of musicians can play in a *public park.

Banfi, Gianluigi (1910–45) *See* BBPR.

Banham, Peter Reyner (1922–88) British architectural critic/historian/polemicist, promoter/chronicler of New *Brutalism and the *Machine Aesthetic in *AR* and elsewhere. His *Theory and Design in the First Machine Age* (1960) was a reassessment of the history of the *Modern Movement: it was followed by *The New Brutalism* (1966); *The Architecture of the Well-Tempered Environment* (1969—in which he described architecture determined by its mechanical services); *Los Angeles: The Architecture of Four Ecologies* (1971); *Age of the Masters* (1975); and *Megastructure* (1976). He moved (1976) to the USA, after which he published *Scenes in America Deserta* (1982) and enthusiastic interpretations of American life and urban developments. He was vitriolic about the retreat from the Modern Movement known as *Neo-Liberty in Italy, which he described as 'infantile regression'. Believing that the design of a machine could be subjected to the same processes of research and analysis as any building or painting, he combined attention to source-material (learned from

*Pevsner) with his ability to look at problems from new positions. However, by the beginning of the C21, many of his judgements seemed outmoded, even absurd, perhaps because of his ardour for what was new, trendy, and supposedly futuristic in the 1960s and 1970s.

AD, xxx/9 (1960), 375–6; *AR* cxxv/747 (April 1959), 231–5 and cxxvi/754 (Dec. 1959), 341–4; M.Ba *et al.* (eds) (1997); R.Ba (1959, 1960, 1966, 1971, 1975, 1976, 1994); *ODNB* (2004); S.Rn (1987a); Whiteley (2002)

banister *See* BALUSTER.

banner Ornament in the form of a pole with flag, found on metal railings, and, with a counter-balance, used as a *weather-vane or *banneret*.

banquet, banquette 1. Narrow footpath beside an *aqueduct or road. **2.** Raised standing-place or platform behind a *rampart. **3.** Window-seat or long seat against a wall or recessed into it. **4.** Ceremonial or State feast. *Associated terms include*:

banquet-hall, banqueting-hall: large room designed for festive or State occasions, especially formal feasts (*banquets* (**4**)), equivalent to the French *Salle des Fêtes*;

banquet- or banqueting-house: **1.** large room or building for audiences of State or the reception of ambassadors, usually a *wing of a *palace (e.g. Inigo *Jones's building in Whitehall, London); **2.** garden-room or -building, sited away from the main house and commanding a view, for entertainment and light refreshment (e.g. the *Gothic structure, Gibside, Co. Durham (1741–3)). Francis *Bacon caused two such buildings to be erected: one at Gorhambury, Herts., and one at Gray's Inn, London. As a building-type it is often difficult to distinguish it from other garden-buildings (e.g. *gazebos). Small banqueting-houses were sometimes erected on rooftops (e.g. Longleat, Wilts.).

banqueting-room: **1.** apartment in which fruits, wines, etc. (called *refection*) were displayed and served, occasionally used for performances of plays or masques; **2.** as *banquet-hall*.

W.Pa (1852); S (1901–2); Shoe (2001); Symes (2006); J.T (1996)

baptistery, baptistry, baptisterium Building or part of a church containing the *font used for the Sacrament of Baptism, modelled on the *cold-bath, or *baptisterium*, of a Roman *frigidarium* in a *therma*, often consisting of a sunken pool in a circular building. Baptisteries such as those in Parma and Pisa were detached, one polygonal and the other circular, and the form was recalled in some apsidal baptisteries physically joined to churches. Fonts in churches are often found (usually at the west end), not screened off in any way, but if the area used for

Baptism is demarcated by, e.g., a *baptistery screen*, or placed within an architectural element distinct from the *nave or *aisles, it is referred to as a *baptismal enclosure*.

bar 1. Single piece of wood or metal, of any shape in *section, placed horizontally, like the rail of a *gate, to form an obstruction, or latch-bar dropped into a mortise behind a *door or *shutter to fasten it. **2.** Horizontal timber ledge fixed to the back of a *barred or ledged door to which the door-finish and the hinges are fixed. **3.** *Gateway or *gate-house (e.g. Micklegate, York), barrier, or toll-gate (*toll-bar*) on a highway. **4.** Enclosure or barrier in a *court of justice marking off the precinct of a judge's seat, at which prisoners are stationed for arraignment, trial, and sentence, or a particular court of law; or a barrier separating the seats of the benchers or readers from the rest of a hall, to which students were 'called' (hence barristers 'called to the bar'). **5.** Barrier or counter over which drink (or food) is served in an *inn, *hotel, etc., or the room in which it is installed. **6.** Pieces of timber forming the horizontal and vertical glazed divisions of a *sash in a window, called *bar of a sash, glazing-, sash-*, or *window-bar*. At the junction of two planes of a canted *bay-window the upright is the *angle-bar*. **7.** Flowing patterns in *Gothic *tracery, all the stonework having moulded *sections the same as the *mullions from which they rise, create *bar-tracery*, because the patterns are similar to those capable of being formed using wrought-iron bars.

Barabino, Carlo Francesco (1768–1835) Italian *Neo-Classical architect, he became (1818) City Architect of Genoa. His *Teatro Carlo Felice*, Genoa (1825–32), is an important early Italian example of the Greek-*Doric Revival. He designed several *temple-fronts for Genoese churches (Rosary (1824), *San Siro* (1820–1), and *Santissima Annunziata* (1830–43)), and was responsible for the *Cimitero di Staglieno*, Genoa, projected before 1825, with its competent *Pantheon-like chapel (with Greek-Doric *portico), erected (1844–61) under the direction of **Giovanni Battista Resasco** (1799–1872). This *cemetery is one of the most brilliantly sited in Europe, and its conception was entirely Barabino's.

J.Curl (2002a); Me (1966); Ms (1966); Negri (1977); Resasco (1892)

baradari, barahdari, barahdurri 1. Hall with twelve entrances in Muslim India. **2.** *Palace, but more often applied to a garden-*pavilion which, after the death of its builder, became a *mausoleum.

barbacan, barbican 1. Double fortified tower erected over a *gate or *bridge, often very strong and high, serving as a *watch-tower. **2.** Advanced outwork or structure flanking the approach to a fortified *gateway. **3.** *Balistraria, in the sense of a *loop-hole.

Barbaro, Daniele (1514–70) Italian patron/architect/theorist, he translated *Vitruvius into Italian (1556), and provided a learned commentary, which, with *Palladio's illustrations, made *I dieci libri* one of the most useful editions ever published, as well as containing a treatise by Barbaro on *Harmonic Proportions. He published (1568) a book on *perspective (*La pratica della perspettiva*), and probably was responsible for some aspects of Palladio's *villa at Maser (1550s) and the *Palazzo Trevisan*, Murano (completed 1557).

J.T (1996)

Barbet, Jean (1591–c.1650) French architect, he worked for **Cardinal Richelieu** (1585–1642). His *Livre d'Architecture d'Autels et de Cheminées* (1632) illustrated *altar- and *chimney-pieces, many in an elaborate *Mannerist style. Inigo *Jones was influenced by Barbet's designs, some of which reappeared in **Robert Pricke's** (c.1642–1708) *The Architects Store-House* (1674).

Jervis (1984); L & D (1986)

Barbier, Jules (c.1865–1910) Belgian architect, his works include the *Galerie Leroy*, *Groote Hertstraat*, Brussels (1900), and a house in the *Ijzerlaan*, Etterbeek, Brussels (1905–6), both freely composed, finely crafted, and including an eclectic selection of motifs.

Loo (ed.) (2003)

Barbon, Nicholas (c.1638–98) London-born, he not only became one of the most important developers there after the Great Fire (1666), but instituted fire insurance. He built houses at Red Lion Fields, near Gray's Inn, and (1690s) carried out improvements at Chancery Lane and Lincoln's Inn. It is unclear whether or not he was his own architect, but his housing developments set the pattern for London *terrace-housing for years to come. After the Temple was destroyed by fire (1678/9) he was involved in its rebuilding (Roger *North was concerned in an architectural capacity). Barbon's designs for the *cloisters in Pump Court, Middle Temple (1679), however, were rejected in favour of a 'model' prepared by *Wren.

Barbon (1976); Co (2008); ODNB (2004); Su (2003)

Bardi, (Achil) Lina Bo (1914–92) Italian-born Brazilian architect, she founded/edited *Habitat* (1949–53), and designed the *Museu de Arte da São Paulo* (1958–68). She was also responsible for the *Museu de Arte Popular do Unhão*, Salvador, Bahia (1960s), for the Vera Cruz Centre, *São*

Bernardo do Campo, São Paulo (1977–91), and for plans to restore the historic centre of Salvador, Bahia (1986–8).

AR, cxii/669 (Sept. 1952), 160–3; E (1994); J.T (1996)

Bardwell, William (1795–1890) Suffolk-born, he worked under *Debret on the *Chapelle Expiatoire* in the *crypt of Saint-Denis, but was back in England (1830s) when he submitted unsuccessful entries for the competitions to design the new Palace of Westminster, London, the Fitzwilliam Museum, Cambridge, and buildings at Kensal Green Cemetery, London. He drew up plans (1832) to improve Westminster, which also proved abortive, although they anticipated the layout of Victoria Street (opened 1851). Among his works may be cited Glenstal Castle, Co. Limerick (1838–9–*Neo-Norman), and Model Dwellings at Shooter's Hill, Kent (1840s). He published *Temples, Ancient and Modern, or, Notes, on Church Architecture* (1837); *Westminster Improvements* (1839); *Healthy Homes* (1858); and *What A House Should Be* (1875). His family's monument in the churchyard of St Edmund, King and Martyr, Southwold, Suffolk, is an eclectic concoction.

Co (2008); J.Curl (ed.) (2001); J.Loudon (ed.) (1846), 237–8, 853, 877

Barelli, Agostino (1627–79) Bologna-born architect, he designed the Theatine Church of *San Bartolomeo* there (1653). He introduced the Italian *Baroque style to Bavaria, notably with his designs for the *Theatinerkirche*, Munich (1663–90—completed by *Zuccalli), modelled on *Sant'Andrea della Valle*, Rome, the Order's mother-church. Barelli was also responsible for the central block with the high roof at *Schloss Nymphenburg*, Munich (from 1663), altered by *Effner and Cuvilliés.

Bou (1962); Lieb (1988); C.Powell (1959)

barge 1. Coping on a *gable, so a *barge-stone* is one forming a gable's raked top. **2.** Projecting ledge or drip at the base of a chimney following the line of the pitched roof, also called a *watertable. *Associated terms include*:

barge-board: inclined board (often decorated), also called *berge-*, *gable-*, *parge-*, *verge-*, or *wind-board*, above a gable under the *barge-course* and covering the *barge-couples* or used instead of the last;

barge-couple: *rafters under the *barge-course* serving as grounds for *barge-boards* and to which the *soffits are fixed, or supporting the roof over the *gable if there are no barge-boards;

barge-course: **1.** part of a tiled roof projecting beyond the *barge-boards*, or, if the latter are omitted, projecting over the gable and sealed with *mortar or *parging, called *parged *verge; **2.** brick *tumbling-course *coping on a gable roof.

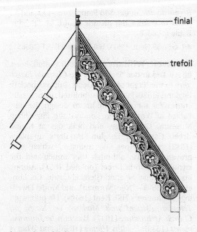
finial

trefoil

barge-board (*after A.W.N.Pugin*).

bark 1. Outer sheath of tree trunks and branches, used in C18/19 for cladding/roofing garden-buildings to create a *rustic effect. **2.** Structural timber with bark attached, used to construct a *bark-house* or -*hut*.

Barker, John (1668–1727) Architect/builder active in the northern Midlands in the early C18. He probably designed the stable-block at Belvoir Castle, Leics. (1704–5), as well as St Ann's Church, Manchester (1709–12), and the similar St Alkmund's, Whitchurch, Salop. (1712–13), possibly influenced by *Aldrich's All Saints, Oxford (1701–10).

Co (2008)

barley-sugar Twisted column or *colonnette like a corkscrew, or a *spiral column.

Barlow, William Henry (1812–1902) Woolwich-born and, as consulting engineer to the Midland Railway, responsible (with *Ordish) for the design of the iron-and-glass terminus-shed at St Pancras, London (1864–8), an immense pointed structure that was widely copied. An advocate of the use of steel, he published papers on a wide variety of engineering and scientific subjects, and advised on the reconstruction of the Tay Bridge (1882–7) after the 1879 disaster.

ODNB (2004)

barn Building to store and protect agricultural produce, especially grain. Medieval barns often had architectural pretensions: examples include the C12 barley-barn at Cressing Temple, Essex, which has a timber *nave-and-*aisle interior.

Endersby *et al.* (1992); Kirk (1994)

Barnes, Edward Larrabee (1915–2004) Chicago-born architect, he studied under *Gropius and *Breuer at Harvard, later opening an office in NYC. He employed bold geometries, evoking forms used by Le *Corbusier, but, influenced by *vernacular architecture, his designs began to respond to their surroundings (e.g. Haystack Mountain School of Crafts, Deer Island, ME (1958–62)). Indeed, Barnes was one of the first *Modernist architects to become a proponent of *contextual design. His Walker Art Center in Minneapolis, MN (1971–4), employed the simplest of forms, and he designed (1988) an urban *sculpture-garden to enhance it. His *museum interiors are treated as simply as possible, but the exteriors are given a civic presence, as at the Dallas Museum of Art, TX (1983–4). Later work of his office became more *Historicist, as with the Allen Library at the University of Washington in Seattle (1991), with *Neo-Gothic *gables and *finials, and the Judicial Office Building, Washington, DC, which had Neo-Classical and *Beaux-Arts influences. His planning expertise was demonstrated at the State University of New York *campus at Purchase, NY (1966–77), derived from *Jefferson's work at Charlottesville, VA. With the Equitable Tower West, NYC (1987), came a venture into *Post-Modernism.

Blake (1994); Di (1980, 1985); E (1994); Morton *et al.* (eds) (1994); J.T (1996); vV (1993)

Barnet, James J. (1827–1904) Scots-born, he was Colonial Architect for New South Wales (1862–90), and produced numerous competent buildings, including the Venice-inspired General Post Office, Sydney (1865–74); the *palazzo*-like *Renaissance-Revival Lands Department, Sydney (1876–90); the Court House and Government Buildings, Bathurst (1878–80); and the arcaded Court House, Goulburn (1887). He also designed the *Gothic railway stations associated with Rookwood Cemetery, Sydney (1868).

Bridges & D.McDonald (1988); Ck (1996); J.Curl (2002a, 2004)

Barnsley, Edward (1900–87) English architect: the son of Sidney *Barnsley, he continued his father's work at Bedales after the latter's death, and settled in Froxfield, near Petersfield, Hants., where he made furniture.

Carruthers (1992)

Barnsley, Ernest Arthur (1863–1926) English architect articled to *Sedding, later entering into partnership with *Gimson. He designed a number of buildings in the *Arts-and-Crafts *vernacular manner (some with his brother, S.H.*Barnsley), including the Village Hall, Sapperton, Glos. (1910–14—with **Norman Jewson** (1884–1974)— an essay in the C17 gabled style). His largest building was Rodmarton Manor, near Cirencester (1912–26), completed by Jewson and held by some to be the last great country-house built in England.

A.S.Gray (1985)

Barnsley, Sidney Howard (1865–1926) English architect, he was articled to Norman *Shaw, and travelled in Greece with Robert Schultz *Weir, with whom he collaborated on *Byzantine Architecture in Greece* (1901). His finest work is the Church of St Sophia, Lower Kingswood, Surrey (1891), in a free *Byzantine style, which includes several *Antique fragments. Barnsley joined his brother (E.A.*Barnsley) and *Gimson, settling at Sapperton, Glos., where Sidney designed his own cottage (Beechanger) and several buildings in an *Arts-and-Crafts *vernacular style. He superintended the completion of works at Bedales School, near Petersfield, Hants., after Gimson's death, and when his brother died he worked on Rodmarton Manor, near Cirencester, Glos. He carried out tactful work at Gyde Almshouses, Painswick, Glos. (1912–13).

Carruthers (1992); A.S.Gray (1985)

Baronial *See* SCOTTISH BARONIAL.

Baroque Style of C17 and C18 European architecture derived from late-*Renaissance *Mannerism and evolving into *Rococo before *Neo-Classicism eclipsed it. Theatrical and exuberant, it employed convex-concave flowing curves in *plan, *elevation, and *section, optical illusions, interpenetrating ellipses in plans that were often extensions of the centralized type, complicated geometries and relationships between volumes of different shapes and sizes, emphatic overstatement, daring colour, exaggerated modelling, and much architectural and symbolic rhetoric. Associated with the Counter-Reformation, the style reached maturity with the C17 works of *Bernini and *Borromini: it achieved heights of inventiveness and beauty in Central Europe, especially Austria, Bavaria, and Bohemia (e.g. the churches of the *Asams and the *Dientzenhofers); the epitome of exotic over-ornamentation in the Iberian peninsula and Latin America; and a chasteness where a strong *Classicism was never far away in France. In England, however, where the Counter-Reformation had little direct architectural impact, the curved, swaying, swelling forms were generally eschewed in favour of emphasized modelling of wall-surfaces, as in the work of *Hawksmoor. There was a European Baroque Revival that was evident in the years immediately before and after 1900 (*see* WRENAISSANCE). In landscape-design, the Baroque style was associated especially with the huge formal gardens of France, notably at Versailles.

Bl (1973); N-S (1986, 1986a); Pe (1960)

Baroque garden Style of garden based on geometrical and symmetrical layouts, often incorporating broad, straight axes leading into the distance (usually crossed by subsidiary axes); several levels; *parterres; long, broad *canals or pools; and elaborate *fountains. Statues and other elements played important roles, and splendour, pomp, drama, movement, and monumental scale were all evident. The grandest gardens were those associated with **King Louis XIV** (*r.*1643–1715), designed by Le *Nôtre (e.g. Vaux-le-Vicomte (1656–61) and Versailles (1661–87)). English exemplars were illustrated by *Kip and *Knijff, and included work by *London and *Wise. An important sourcebook on the subject was *Dézallier d'Argenville's *Théorie* (1709).

DdA (1709); Hazelhurst (1966, 1974, 1980); Laird (1992); Shoe (2001); Tay (2006); T.T (1986)

barrack Originally a soldier's *tent or *cabin, it came to mean a building for the lodgement of troops. It is usually given in the plural (*barracks*), indicating substantial establishments.

Barragán, Luis (1902–88) Mexican architect, he trained as an engineer and settled (1936) in México City. His early work drew on the precedents of Mexican *vernacular domestic architecture, and also on *Islamic themes. However, he embraced (1936) the *International style and dogmas of Le *Corbusier, and by 1940 evolved a personal architectural language in which simple geometrical forms were associated with water, planting, and the use of colour (his own house in Tacubaya, México City (1947), shows his mixing of Corbusian motifs with vernacular elements). The house and stud-farm at *San Cristóbal*, Los Clubes, México City (1967–8), is a good example of his late work, almost dream-like in its imagery: their simplicity and bareness implied connections with *Minimalism. The *Parque Residencial Jardines del Pedregal de San Angel* (1945–50) was a transformation of an unpromising area into tropical gardens with *courts, water, *fountains, and buildings. Among his other works the Houses Gilardi, Tacubaya (1976), and Valder, Monterrey (1982), are cited.

Ambasz (1976); Arets & van der Bergh (1990); Buendia *et al.* (1997); Burri (2000); E (1994); Ma (1983); Noelle (ed.) (1995); Pauly *et al.* (2002); Riggen Martinez *et al.* (1996); Rispa (ed.) (1996); Saito (2001); J.T (1996); W & S (1994); Zanco (ed.) (2001)

Barre, Eloy de la (1764–1833) French architect, pupil of J.-D. *Antoine and *Chalgrin, he succeeded *Brongniart as architect of the Paris *Bourse*, completing it. He played a significant part in architectural developments in Paris from c.1810.

S (1901–2)

Barré, Jean-Benoît-Vincent (c.1732–1824) French architect. The best of his town-houses (e.g. *Hôtel Grimod de la Reynière, Champs-Élysées,* Paris (1769)), are known only through drawings, but his ingeniously planned *Château Montgeoffroy* (1771–6), Anjou, survives. He designed some of the **fabriques* in the celebrated *Parc de Méréville,* and built the *Château du Marais,* Remarde, south of Paris. He designed the *Place Royale,* Brussels, Belgium, realized (1770s) by **Gilles-Barnabé Guimard** (c.1734–92).

Saur (1993)

Barre, William Joseph (1830–67) Irish architect, he assisted *Duff until the latter's death, and established (1850) his own practice, later (1860) moving to Belfast, where he designed the *Italianate Ulster Hall (1859–62—one of the largest music-halls in the British Isles when built), the *Second-Pointed Duncairn Presbyterian Church (1860–2), the *polychrome round-arched Moat, Old Holywood Road (1863–4), Clanwilliam (later Danesfort) House (1864), the polychrome Lombardic-Romanesque Methodist Church, University Road (1864–5), the Venetian **palazzo* of Bryson House, Bedford Street (1865–7), the *Gothic-Revival Albert Memorial clock-tower (1865–9—beautifully restored 2000–2), and the emphatic round-arched former Bank at Castle Junction (1864–9), encrusted with lavishly carved detail.

Brett (1967); D.Dunlop (ed.) (1868); Larmour (1987)

barrel Describes a form (*barrel-vault*) like a half-cylinder or extruded semicircular arch with a smooth underside. A *barrel-ceiling* is like the underside of a true barrel-vault.

Barrett, Nathan F. (1845–1919) American landscape architect. With *Beman he designed the garden-suburb near Chicago, IL (1880–84), for the factory-workers of the railway industrialist *Pullman. Like Lever's Port Sunlight, near Birkenhead, Ches., Pullman was a model settlement run by a company (*see* COMPANY TOWN), but discontent led to its annexation by Chicago (1889), although the Pullman Corporation continued to hold most of the property until 1910.

M.Crawford (1995)

barrier 1. Fence or material obstruction to bar the advance of persons or objects, or to prevent access. 2. *Passage de queue,* to break the rush of persons entering, e.g. a theatre. 3. External defence, *palisade, or stockade. 4. *Gate at which tolls or custom-duties were collected. 5. Boundary.

barrier-free Design for those with physical or other disabilities, involving the provision of alternative means of access to steps (e.g. *ramps and *elevators). It is also called *universal* or *barrier-free* design.

Goldsmith (1976); Holmes-Siedle (1996); Peloquin (1994)

barrow *Tumulus, or large mound of stones and earth over a burial. A *long barrow* or *long cairn* may be a long, rectangular mound covering wooden or stone burial chambers for communal entombment. A good example is the long barrow at Belas Knap, near Cheltenham, Glos.

Grinsell (1975, 1982)

Barry, Sir Charles (1795–1860) English architect. In Italy he studied *Renaissance architecture, and this was to be of great importance in his development. He established his London practice, and designed several competent *Gothic-Revival churches including St Peter's, Brighton (1824–8), and Holy Trinity, Cloudesley Square, Islington (1826–8), before turning his attention to public buildings, where he would demonstrate his mastery of *Classicism. The Royal Institution of Fine Arts (now the City Art Gallery), Manchester (1824–35), in a Grecian style, was followed by the Travellers' Club, Pall Mall, London (1829–32—in a refined **Quattrocentro* style pioneered by von *Klenze in Munich a decade earlier), which was to mark the beginning of the **Italianate-*Renaissance* Revival. The Reform Club, next door to the Travellers', followed (1838–41), a vast **Cinquecento *palazzo,* which has a fine glass-roofed *cortile of the greatest sumptuousness, and signals Barry's transition from the use of low to robust high relief, culminating in his Bridgewater House, Green Park, London (1846–51). He experimented with Northern-Renaissance architecture, the most outstanding examples being the *Jacobethan Highclere Castle, Hants. (1842–c.1850), and Free-*Cinquecento* Halifax Town Hall (1859–62), the latter completed by his son, E.M.*Barry.

Barry's most celebrated building is the Palace of Westminster and Houses of Parliament (1835–60), the ingenious and complex plan of which is essentially Classical. Barry would have preferred an Italianate design, but was obliged to use Gothic or *Elizabethan styles by the rules of the competition. Indeed, the *façade to the river is symmetrical, in a late-*Georgian manner (it could easily have been clothed in Classical garb), but the overall composition is *Picturesque, with exquisite *Perp. detail inside and out (mostly designed by A.W.N.*Pugin). The choice of style for such a prestigious building gave considerable impetus to the Gothic Revival, while the work earned Barry his Knighthood (1852).

Barry's rich clients enabled him to produce grand and opulently detailed architecture after 1840: some of his later buildings, however, tended to be over-lavish. His was a significant figure in garden-history: he placed sumptuous flower-gardens around the mansions he designed, thus replacing the subtle Georgian concept of the house set within a *Picturesque landscape.

Barry (1867); Co (2008); Co (ed.) (1973); Hi (1954, 1977); *ODNB* (2004); Port (ed.) (1976); Whiffen (1950)

Barry, Edward Middleton (1830–80) Son of Sir Charles *Barry, he worked in the office of T.H.*Wyatt before joining his father's office where he helped prepare drawings for the Palace of Westminster. He was a competent architect, responsible for some opulent Victorian buildings, including the Royal Opera House (1857–8) and Floral Hall (1858–60), Covent Garden, and Charing Cross Station Hotel (1864), all in London. He completed the Palace of Westminster, the eclectic Halifax Town Hall (1859–62), and *Basevi's Fitzwilliam Museum, Cambridge (1870–5).

D & M (1985); *ODNB* (2004); Port (ed.) (1976); Su (1970)

Barth, Erwin (1880–1933) German landscape architect. Graduating in horticulture (1902, 1906), he worked briefly in the Hanover parks department under **Julius Trip** (1857–1907—who had been active in organizing the first professional body of German landscape architects from 1887), before designing open spaces in Lübeck (1908–11—highlighting architectural aspects of the city). As head of the Charlottenburg parks department (1912–25) Barth designed several public spaces of outstanding quality, as well as Wilmersdorf Cemetery, Berlin (1921). Appointed (1926) head of Greater Berlin parks department, he reviewed all open spaces, and from 1929 served as first professor of garden-art at the Agricultural University, Berlin. He planned schemes to manage traffic, improve public amenities, and served on the German body in charge of war cemeteries. When National Socialism gained power (1933) he killed himself.

Shoe (2001); Tay (2006)

Barthélemy, Jacques-Eugène (1799–1882) French architect, his *Notre-Dame de Bon-Sé-cours*, near Rouen (1840–7), is one of the most important early examples of the Revival of C13 *Gothic in France. As Rouen Diocesan Architect, he carried out numerous restorations, including work at *St-Maclou*.

Saur (1993)

Bartholomew, Alfred (1801–45) Architect of the *Italianate Finsbury Savings Bank, Sekforde Street, Clerkenwell, London (1840), he is mostly remembered for his perceptive *Essay on the*

Decline of Excellence in the Structure of Modern English Buildings, an appendix to his *Specifications for Practical Architecture* (1840, 1846), and *Hints Relative to the Construction of Fire-Proof Buildings* (1839). He was for a time Editor of *The Builder*, and became (1844) District Surveyor of Hornsey.

Co (2008); Ea (1970)

bartisan, bartizan *Battlemented unroofed *turret or *parapet, circular or square, projecting on *corbels or *machicolations from an angle at the top of a tower or wall. *See* TOURELLE.

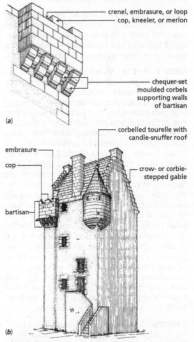

(a)

(b)

bartisan (*a*) Bartisan with plain crenellation. (*b*) Coxton Tower, Lhanbryde, near Elgin, Morayshire, Scotland (C16), with bartisan and tourelle (*after MacG & R, 1887*).

Bartning, Otto (1883–1959) German architect/Lutheran theologian, he began his career as an *Expressionist, and later directed (1926–30) the *Hochschule für Handwerk und Baukunst*, Weimar, which took over the functions of the *Bauhaus after it moved. In his role as Director, Bartning attempted to revive *Arts-and-Crafts traditions that had been destroyed by the *Gropius régime there. A Christian traditionalist, he is best known as a designer of Protestant churches, nearly all centrally planned. His *Pressa* Church, or *Stahlkirche*, Cologne (1928), was designed with a steel frame and glazed walls using a *hyperbola on plan set on a low square base, whereas the Church of the Resurrection, or *Rundkirche*, Essen (1930), was circular. Both owe much to C18 prototypes, at least in their overall arrangement, although the architecture was stark. After the 1939–45 war Bartning was involved in programmes to provide prefabricated timber churches for the German Evangelical Relief Organization.

Bartning (1959); Bredow & Lerch (1983); H.Mayer (1958); Pollak (1926); Siemon (ed.) (1958)

bascule Apparatus acting on the principle of the lever or pulley, whereby one end is raised when the other is depressed, especially a *drawbridge balanced by a counterpoise rising or falling when the element is lowered or raised. *See* BRIDGE.

base 1. Anything on which an object rests, the term is given primarily to the foot or lowest member of a *colonnette, column, or *pier on which the *shaft or mass of construction sits. The *base of a column* is therefore that part between the bottom of the shaft and the pavement, *pedestal, or *plinth. Bases differ according to the *Order used, although the *Attic base is commonly used on all Orders except the Greek *Doric (which has no base) and the *Tuscan (except in impure Tuscan Orders). *See* ASIATIC BASE. Typical bases of the *Ionic, *Corinthian, and *Composite Orders are also called *spira. Bases of *pilasters are usually identical to those of the columns used in the same *portico or building, and may continue with the same profile when used as a continuous skirting or wall-base, but the bases of *antae may differ. Medieval bases have far greater variety: pierbases, for example, are invariably set on a circular, polygonal, or square plinth, and have many *mouldings. **2.** Lowest, thickest part of a wall, such as a *plinth or a *skirting, or the lowest visible element of a building, like a platform, plinth, or *podium called the *basement.

basement 1. Lower part of the walls of a building, especially if distinguished by *rustication or *battering, as in Palladian compositions. **2.** *Storey behind such walls, above the ground or wholly or partly underneath it.

basement-table *See* STEREOBATA.

Basevi, Elias George (1794–1845) Londonborn architect related to the Jewish families of **Disraeli** and *Ricardo, and a pupil of *Soane. After a tour of Greece and Italy (1816), he returned to London well-equipped to provide an eclectic architecture then in growing demand. From 1820, when he established his practice, he designed several London *squares and *terraces,

including Belgrave (1825–40), Alexander (1827–30), and Thurloe (c.1839–45) Squares, and (from 1833) Pelham Crescent, Pelham Place, Egerton Crescent, and Walton Place for the trustees of the Smith's Charity Estate. In these developments he reinterpreted the late-C18 domestic architecture of London, giving it a new freshness without slavish archaeological or antiquarian bias. Like many of his contemporaries, Basevi was capable of designing in many styles, including *Gothic (e.g. the *Tudor-Revival Dr Fryer's *Almshouses and Truesdale's Hospital, Stamford, Lincs. (1832), both agreeable essays in that style). His best-known work is the Fitzwilliam Museum, Cambridge (1836–45), completed by C.R.*Cockerell and E.M.*Barry, which eloquently demonstrates the shift from *Regency to *Victorian taste: an opulence, far removed from the chilly *Greek Revival that had been *de rigueur* for public buildings since 1815, was evident in a noble synthesis of Graeco-Roman and *Renaissance themes. The monumental *portico with its flanking *colonnades terminating in end-*pavilions was derived from *Antique precedent at Brescia, and further *gravitas* was given by the *Attic storey over the *pediment. In collaboration with Sydney *Smirke he designed the Conservative Club in St James's Street (1843–4). Had he not fallen to his premature death while inspecting the west tower of Ely Cathedral, Cambs., he could well have been the greatest Classical architect of his generation.

Bolton (1925); Co (2008); Sh (1983); J.T (1996)

Basile, Ernesto (1857–1932) Palermo-born architect, he designed many buildings in Rome and Sicily, including those for the Palermo Exhibition (1891–2). One of the chief protagonists of the *Stile Liberty*, his work was shown at the Turin Exhibition (1902), the Venice Biennale (1903), and in *The Studio* (1904). His elegantly linear *Art Nouveau architecture is perhaps best represented by the *Villino Florio* (1899–1902), the *Hotel Villa Igiea* (1899–1901), and the Utveggio House (1901) in Palermo. One of his most impressive buildings was his extension to *Bernini's Montecitorio Palace, Rome (1902–27), in a sumptuous *Renaissance style. After the 1914–18 war his architecture became more Classical, as at the *Istituto Provinciale Antitubercolare* (1920–5) and the *Albergo Diorno* (1925), both in Palermo, with which he demonstrated his opposition to the baleful influence of *Functionalism.

F.Borsi (1966); Caronia Roberti (1935); Ms (1966); Nicoletti (1978); Pirrone (1971); J.T (1996); Zevi (1973)

Basile, Giovanni Battista Filippo (1825–91) Palermo-born architect. Primarily a *Neo-Classicist, perhaps his greatest work was the *Teatro Massimo*, Palermo (1875–97), completed by his son, Ernesto *Basile. Among his many distinguished works the *Giardino Inglesi* (1851–3), *Piazza Marina* (1861–4), and *Palazzino Favaloro* (1889–91), all in Palermo, may be cited. In the last building, with its allusions to the exotic, Sicilian *Art Nouveau first appeared. He also designed the *cemetery at Monreale (1865) and the Italian Pavilion, *Exposition Universelle*, Paris (1878).

Lo Nardo (1995); Samona (1988); J.T (1996)

basilica (*pl.* **basilicas** *or* **basilicae**) Roman building-type with *clerestoreyed *nave, two or more lower lean-to *aisles on each side of the nave, and an *apse at the end of the nave, originally for public functions, but later adapted for Christian worship, and the precedent for medieval church-design. Early basilicas include that of Trajan in Rome (*c.* AD 113), and the very important Constantinian basilica of *San Pietro*, Rome (begun *c.*333—the model for Christian churches for nearly two millennia): the latter had two aisles on each side of the nave and a lateral *transept between the apse and the nave to accommodate the large numbers of pilgrims wishing to venerate the shrine over the *martyrium containing the remains of the Apostle; a *narthex in front of the nave and aisles; and a very large colonnaded *atrium with a central *fountain for ritual washing. Attached to the south transept were two *mausolea, both *rotundas. Thus *San Pietro* (destroyed to make way for the present church) had all the prototypes of a medieval cathedral, including the *chapter-house attached to the transept, and the *cloisters. *Basilican* therefore means having the characteristics of a basilica.

Kra (1986); W-P (1981)

Hypothetical section through clerestoreyed *nave* and lean-to double *aisles* looking towards the *high-altar* and *Solomonic* columns seen through the great arch.
Constantinian basilica of *San Pietro*, Rome (begun *c.*333).

basin 1. Bowl for water in a *fountain, or an artificial pool fed by *cascades or *fountains. **2.** Large ornamental pond.

basket 1. *Bell of a *Corinthian *capital. **2.** *Byzantine/*Romanesque capital carved with interwoven strips resembling *basket-weave. **3.** *Corbeil, or ornament resembling a basket filled with fruit and flowers, often with *festoons. **4.** Type of arch, as in *basket-handled* arch.

basket-weave Pattern resembling interweaving rushes, etc. *See* BRICK.

bas-relief *See* RELIEF.

Bassae Order Greek-*Ionic Order with *capital similar to an *angular capital, that is with *volutes on all sides, but with a high curved join set under the *abacus between volutes. Developed by C.R. *Cockerell from his studies of the *temple of *Apollo Epicurius*, Bassae.

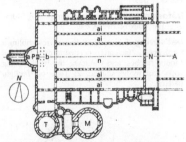

Basilican plan, the model for later medieval churches (although orientation differs from the usual one of *altar* at the east end). It consists of a *nave* (n) flanked by two *aisles* (ai) on each side, a *transeptal* arrangement in which stood the *high-altar* on a *bema* (b) over the Shrine of St Peter (P), an *apse* (a), a *narthex* (N) or entrance-porch, and an *atrium* (A). Attached to the church were circular mausolea of Honorius (later the tomb of St Petronilla (T)) and another (later *Santa Maria della Febbre* (M)).

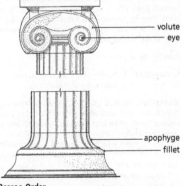

volute
eye

apophyge
fillet

Bassae Order

Bassi, Martino (1542–91) Milanese architect, he succeeded *Alessi at *Santa Maria presso San Celso*, and from 1573 was engaged in the rebuilding of the *Early Christian *rotunda of *San Lorenzo*, Milan. He also worked on Milan Cathedral from 1587, and at the *Sacro Monte*, Varallo, from 1578.

M.Bassi (1572); Lotz (1977); Wi (1974)

Bastard Brothers (**John** (1688–1770) *and* **William** (*c.*1689–1766)) English architects/builders, they rebuilt Blandford Forum, Dorset, in a *vernacular *Baroque style from 1731 after that town had been destroyed by fire. They employed the *capital with *volutes turned inwards (*see* BORROMINI CAPITAL) favoured by *Archer, derived from *Borromini, as well as exploiting *Rococo motifs. Among their more important buildings are the Town Hall (1734), the Church (1735–9), and two *inns (1734–5).

Co (2008); P (1982); Su (1993)

bastel, bastle Mid-C16 to mid-C17 fortified farmhouse, with accommodation for livestock on the *vaulted ground-floor, usually found in the Border counties of Scotland and England.

bastide 1. As *bastel. 2. Country-house in southern France. 3. Medieval fortified new town in South-West France, usually with a regular grid-like plan with a market-place in the centre. Examples include Monpazier (founded 1284 by **King Edward I** of England (*r.*1272–1307)).

Lauret *et al.* (1988)

bastille 1. *As* BASTION (1). 2. Fortified tower. 3. Small *fortress. 4. Name of the C14 Parisian prison-fortress destroyed 1789, so synonymous with *prison.

bastion 1. Defensive projection, usually canted on plan and with *battered sides, at an angle of a fortress from which the ground in front of *ramparts may be viewed and raked with fire. 2. In gardens, a vantage-point in a corner, or a raised projection, like an arrow-head bastion.

bastle *See* BASTEL.

batardeau 1. *Coffer-dam. 2. Wall across the ditch or moat around a fortification.

Bateman, James (1811–97) English botanist/landowner, and authority on orchids. He purchased (early 1840s) an estate at Biddulph Moor, near Knypersley, Staffs., and there built Biddulph Grange, around which he created a remarkable garden containing allusions to China, among other places: the *Egyptian garden is a place of extraordinary atmosphere.

J.Curl (2005); HHH (1980)

Bateman, Hon. Richard (1705–73) English connoisseur/collector/architectural patron, he appreciated Chinese aesthetics and promoted *Sharawadgi. Introduced to things *Gothic by *Walpole, he caused the Church of St John the Evangelist, Shobdon, Herefs., to be rebuilt (1749–56) in Strawberry-Hill *Gothick, incorporating elements derived from *Kent, *Langley, and others (possibly including Richard *Bentley, *Flitcroft, *Garrett, William *Robinson, and *Vardy).

Brooks & Pe (2012); Co (2008); J.Curl (2011a); McCarthy (1987)

Batey, Mavis, *née* **Lever** (1921–2013) English garden-historian, a prolific writer for, e.g. *CL* and *GH*, she was passionately interested in the *conservation of designed landscapes. Steeped in German *Romanticism, she worked as a codebreaker at Bletchley Park during the 1939–45 war.

Pk; *The Times* (15 Nov. 2013), 69

bath-house 1. C18 garden-feature, often erected over a spring, and containing changing-rooms and *fireplaces as well as a bath. 2. Building containing bath- and dressing-rooms: public bathing establishments were known throughout Europe, also called *bagnios*. 3. Because of the association with dissipation, the term *bagnio* became synonymous with *brothel*. See also THERMAE.

Bath Stone Oölitic *limestone easily worked when first quarried, but hard after exposure to air, ranging from white to light cream or yellow-ochre, found in the area around Bath, Som., and elsewhere in England.

W.McKay (1957)

bâtons rompus *Mouldings comprising *Romanesque *chevron or *zig-zag.

bat's-wing 1. Fluted half-*patera, resembling a semicircular *fan, often occurring over late-C18 *doors, *niches, and windows, the *flutes being wide and wedge-shaped. 2. Type of *fanlight pattern.

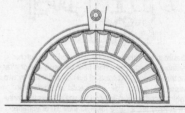

bat's-wing Suffolk Place, London (1820s), by Nash.

batten 1. Vertical board in a door secured to horizontal boards called *ledges* (*see* DOOR). 2. Piece of squared timber used for flooring. **3.** Small squared timbers used to provide fixings for *tiles or *slates on roofs, or to support *laths for plastering. **4.** Any thin, narrow strip of wood, e.g. used to cover joints between boards cladding a framed building.

batter Slope, or inclination from the perpendicular, as in a *Vitruvian opening or on a retaining-wall or battered Egyptian *pylon-tower.

battery Raised strip in a garden overlooking a view, resembling a *bastion or gun-batteries. Garden-batteries were sometimes embellished with real cannon.

Batteux, Abbé Charles (1713–80) French writer, his *Les beaux arts réduits à un même principe* (1746) was an influential text on aesthetics, countering the opinion that art could be judged in non-artistic terms (e.g. morality), and holding that imitation of the beauties of Nature distinguished the Fine Arts (his response to claims that they were subject to too many rules). His *Cours de belles-lettres* (1747–8—which included his previously published theory) became a standard text on the Humanities, particularly in German-speaking countries.

Batteux (1746); Dankelmann (1903); Lühe (1979); J.T (1996)

battle-garden Of all garden-types, battle-gardens must be the most unfamiliar: they represented battle-formations, battlefield topography, or military architecture and engineering. Conceived in the C16, when Hermetic and other ideas were stimuli to intellectual movements, most seem to have had connections with specific military engagements. *Wise laid out a garden to commemorate the victory at Blenheim (1704) at Windsor Castle, Berks., already furnished with a precedent marking the Siege of Maastricht (1673) constructed below the long terrace with *bastions, *horn-works, *palisades, *ramparts, etc., shown in a view by *Kip. Wise was also involved at Blenheim Palace, Oxon., where a *mur de retranchement* was constructed, and avenues of trees were planted perhaps representing opposing armies. One of the oddest battle-gardens was formed at Kilwarlin, Co. Down (early 1840s), a re-creation of the Battles of Thermopylae (480 and 279 BC), as a talisman to keep the Turks at bay: it succeeded. See MILITARY GARDEN.

GH, xi/1 (Spring 1983), 65–9; D.Green (1956); Hooghe (1685); ISR, xiii/3 (1988), 265–81

battlement *Parapet with higher and lower alternate parts. Indentations between the higher parts are the *carnels, crenels, embrasures, loops*, or *wheelers*, and the uprights between the indentations are the *cops, kneelers*, or *merlons*: a *crenellated* or *embattled* wall is therefore one with

battlements, on *Perp. churches often ornamented with quatrefoils (*see* FOIL). Miniature decorative battlements occur in a number of places in architecture including the *transoms of *tracery and the *capitals of *piers in *Perp.: even *Tudor *chimney-pots have them. An *almena is a merlon with sloping, notched sides. A *Guelphic* or *swallowtail* battlement, common in medieval Italian architecture, has merlons with V-shaped notches, giving a horn-like effect.

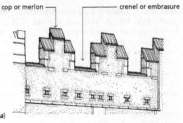

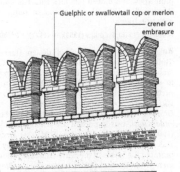

battlement (*a*) Irish crenellation (with extra step on cop), Coolhull Castle, Co. Wexford (late C16). (*b*) Guelphic crenellation, Verona: also known as *Scaliger, La Scala*, or *swallowtail*.

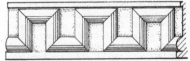

battlement Romanesque embattled moulding, Lincoln Cathedral (mid–C12) (*after Parker*).

Baud, Benjamin (*c.*1807–75) English architect, *Wyatville's assistant during the remodelling (1824–30) of Windsor Castle, Berks. He won (1838) the competition to design the West London and Westminster Cemetery, Brompton, London, which contained so many buildings for *catacomb 'burial' that the founding Company never had any possibility of recouping capital expended. After disastrous litigation with the Company, Baud carried on a minor architectural practice: he designed the eccentric *mausoleum in Lowther churchyard, Westmd. (1857), for **William Lowther** (1787–1872—**2nd Earl of Lonsdale** from 1844). With Michael *Gandy he published *Architectural Illustrations of Windsor Castle* (1842—text by John *Britton).

Co (2008); J.Curl (2004, 2007); Sh (1983)

Baudot, Joseph-Eugène-Anatole de

(1834–1915) French architect, pioneer of `*reinforced-concrete construction, and pupil of *Labrouste and *Viollet-le-Duc. He is remembered primarily for *St-Jean de Montmartre*, Paris (1894–1902), in which *concrete and brick reinforced with steel rods were used: influenced by Viollet-le-Duc's *Entretiens* (1863–72), it demonstrated Baudot's search for a rational architecture in which structure would be expressed. Even then, *St-Jean* owes much to medieval *Gothic prototypes, and indeed Baudot's earlier *St-Lubin*, Rambouillet (1865–9), was Gothic in spirit, but with iron *piers.

A.Baudot (1916); P.Collins (1959); Hi (1977); J.T (1996)

Bauhaus

German school of design (literally 'Building House'), its influence dominated C20 architecture after the 1914–18 war, yet contrary to widespread belief it had no Department of Architecture until 1927. In 1919 the *Grossherzogliche Sächsische Kunstgewerbeschule* and the *Grossherzogliche Sächsische Hochschule für Bildende Kunst*, two important art schools founded (1906) by **Wilhelm Ernst** (1873–1923) **Grand Duke of Saxe-Weimar** (r.1901–18), expressly to promote the ideals of the *Arts-and-Crafts movement, were merged (1919) to become the *Staatliches Bauhaus Weimar*. Walter *Gropius had been proposed (1915) by Henry van de *Velde (*see* KESSLER) to succeed him as Director, but Gropius was serving in the army, and was unable to take up the post until 1919. Under his leadership the School rapidly moved away from its Arts-and-Crafts ideals (although Gropius claimed his policies were derived from notions promoted by the *Deutscher Werkbund), and the Bauhaus became a centre for *Modernist theorizing, especially from 1922, when van *Doesburg was there, propagating *Constructivist and De-*Stijl themes. Thereafter, self-dramatization was the *forte* of the institution, for although the Bauhaus claimed to be inspired by notions of unifying art and technology, it did nothing of the sort: its protagonists accelerated the sundering of 'design' from craftsmanship, and, with an emphasis on 'industrial design', abandoned any pretence that hand-crafts had a part to play in the Bauhaus-envisaged future. As a state-subsidized but overtly left-wing institution, it began (unsurprisingly) to be perceived as a threat to local private craft workshops, and opposition grew so intense it was disbanded (1925), and its functions taken over by the *Hochschule für Handwerk und Baukunst* (High-School for Handicrafts and Architecture), directed by Otto *Bartning, who was more sympathetic to Arts-and-Crafts ideals. It should be emphasized that it was not Nazis (who were relatively unimportant then) who objected to the scandalously mismanaged and pretentious Bauhaus, but traditional craftsmen and designers.

After Weimar had proved hostile, the industrial town of Dessau became host to the Bauhaus, and a new building, designed by Gropius, was erected there (1925–6), which became a paradigm of the *International-Modern style: the complex included three wings, a large glass-fronted workshop *block, and residences for the 'Masters', or professors, at the institution. The Bauhaus became the Anhalt State School of Art, and a department of architecture was established (1927) under the direction of Hannes *Meyer, who promoted a Collectivist and Socialist agenda, especially after he succeeded (1928) Gropius as Director. Meyer's insistence (backed by Ludwig *Hilberseimer) that building was not an aesthetic process, and that everything depended on the marriage between function and economy, led to dissent. Eventually the *Bürgermeister* of Dessau was obliged (1930) to remove Meyer from his post. Meyer's successor, *Mies van der Rohe, demanded rigorous standards of quality as well as a ferocious work ethic concentrated on building and development: this regime alienated leftists, and the ensuing uproar led to the Bauhaus being shut down, partly because of the (by then) increasing influence of the National Socialist German Workers' Party. Under Mies (who attempted a rapprochement with the Nazis) it moved (1932) to Berlin-Steglitz, but finally closed (1933). One of Meyer's and Mies's students designed parts of the 'camp' at Auschwitz–Birkenau.

Emigration of Bauhaus members led to the spread of its anti-crafts and anti-*Historicist programmes throughout the world: in the USA its message was promoted at Harvard by Gropius and *Breuer, at Chicago by *Moholy-Nagy, and at the Armour Institute, Chicago (now Institute of Technology), by Mies and others. Bauhaus mythology was promoted by *Giedion and by *Pevsner (who saw it as the Modernist educational ideal *par excellence*). At the Ulm *Hochschule für Gestaltung*, founded 1950, *Bill revived the Bauhaus programme.

Argan (1975); H.Bayer (1938, 1968); Wi.Cu (1996); Droste (1998); Engelmann & Schädlich (1991); Fiedler *et al.* (eds) (2000); Forgács (1995); Friedewald (2009); Gropius (1965); Herdeg (1985); Jervis (1984); K-C (1998, 1999); Lupton & J.Miller (eds) (1993); A.Meyer (1925);

U.Meyer *et al.* (2001); G.Naylor (1985); E.Nn (ed.) (1993); Strasser (2009); Wingler (1969); Wolfe (1993)

baulk-tie *See* ROOF.

Baumeister, Reinhard (1833–1917) German architect/engineer/town-planning theorist. His *Stadt-Erweiterungen in technischer, baupolizeilicher, und wirtschaftlicher Beziehung*, published 1876, attempted to establish a rational scientific basis for urban design. He designed (1860s, 1870s) several railways in south-west Germany, the *Ringstrasse*, Wiesbaden (1871), and the hospital, Karlsruhe (1888–90). His main concerns were to find a balance between freedom to build and official interference with individuals' rights, and to promote 'artistic' town-planning, anticipating ideas of *Sitte.

Baumeister (1876, 1902); C & C (1986); J.T (1996)

Baurscheit, Jan Pieter van (1699–1768) Son of German-born sculptor **Jan Pieter van Baurscheit** (1669–1728), he was his father's pupil, assisting him on works for the Jesuit Church of *St Carolus Borromeus*, Antwerp (1718–28), and other projects. Influenced by *Marot, he evolved an architectural language in which Flemish and German decorative devices were mingled. His works include the *Beeldenhuis*, Vlissingen (1730), the Fraula house, Antwerp (1737—largely destroyed, apart from its reconstructed *façade), and the castle of 'Gravenwezel (*c.*1730–37—near Antwerp), all in the *Régence* style, the *Rococo Town Hall, Lier (1740–4), and several Antwerp town-houses, including *van Susteren-Roose* (1745–8) and *Grooten Robijn* (1745–50), with magnificent interiors. His *Van de Perre* house, Vlissingen (1763–5—now the Court of Justice), is an essay in early *Neo-Classicism.

Baudouin (1995); Breedveldt (2003)

Bautista, Francisco (1594–1679) Spanish Jesuit priest/architect, responsible for *San Salvador del Mundo* and *San Isidro el Real*, Madrid (1626–51), based on *Il Gesù*, Rome, and precedents for many churches in Spain and Latin America of the *Gesù* type.

K & S (1959)

Bawa, Geoffrey (1919–2003) English-educated Sri Lankan architect/lawyer, his architecture mixed modern techniques with Sri Lankan *vernacular themes. The da Silva house, Colombo (1962) was the first of his designs to fuse traditional Sinhalese domestic architecture with open planning, and showed how outdoor spaces could be enjoyed within confined urban plots. His own house in Colombo, an inward-looking oasis within a noisy urban environment, was created around a series of *courts, *verandahs, and *loggie*, developed by linking four existing

*bungalows, and its tower afforded views over the rooftops of the city. Among other projects were Parliament Building at Kotte (1979–82), Ruhuna University, Matara (1980–6), and the minimalist Jayawardene House (1999–2002) set on a cliff overlooking the ocean. Over half a century he created a series of episodes in a garden within a wilderness at Lunganga, Bentota.

E (1994); Khan (1995); D.Robson (2002); B.Taylor (1986).

bawn Walled enclosure protected by circular, polygonal, or square *flankers (low towers) at the corners, and associated with fortified houses, especially in C17 Ulster.

J.Curl (1986)

Baxter, John (*fl.*1767–98) Scots architect, son of **John Baxter** (*fl.*1722–69), he studied in Rome and became (1766) an honorary member of St Luke's Academy. His Town-House, Peterhead, Aberdeenshire (1788), and Bellie Church, Fochabers, Moray (1795–7—the centre-piece of a new town he designed for **Alexander Gordon** (1743–1827—**4th Duke of Gordon** from 1752)), owed something to *Gibbs, while his Merchants' Hall, 3–4 Hunter Square, Edinburgh (1788), was in the *Adam style. He carried out various works on Scottish country houses, including the remodelling of Gordon Castle, Moray (1769–82—*castellated), and designed numerous *bridges, including that at Kenmore, Loch Tay (1774).

Co (2008); Sk (2002)

bay 1. Regular *structural* subdivision of a building, such as a church: in the latter case the building is divided along its long axis by *bays* defined by the *buttresses, *piers, and *vaults, with windows inserted into the *curtain-wall of each bay. In Classical buildings bays may be marked by *Orders, vaults, roof-*trusses, or beams, but it is erroneous to describe, say, an C18 Georgian domestic *façade in terms of 'bays', as the *number of windows* may not relate to *structure*: *five windows wide* would be more correct. **2.** Part of a framed building between the main supporting timbers. The term describes units, such as a *two-bay hall*, or a *half-bay* used as a *cross-entry. **3.** Free or *light-space* in a *sash-window. *Compounds include*:
bay-window: projection from a house-front, circular, rectangular, segmental, or canted on plan, largely filled with windows. A segmental bay is defined as a *bow, common in the *Regency period. A bay-window on an upper floor only is an *oriel.

Bayer, Herbert (1900–85) Austrian designer, he studied architecture before joining (1921) the Weimar *Bauhaus. In 1925, as head of the typographical workshops at Dessau, he designed the journal *Bauhaus*, promoted a single-alphabet sans-serif typography, and invented the typeface *Universal*. He established (1928) his own firm in Berlin, working with *Gropius, *Breuer, and others on the Paris *Deutscher Werkbund* Exhibition (1930). He emigrated to the USA (1938), helped with the Museum of Modern Art's Bauhaus exhibition of that year, and became (1946) a design consultant in Aspen, CO.

Bayer (1938); Jervis (1984); E.Nn (ed.) (1993); Widder (2001)

bay-leaf Classical decoration based on the bay-leaf, often in *garlands, and usually applied to a *torus moulding or a *pulvinated *frieze.

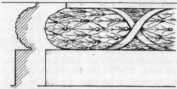

bay-leaf garland

Baylis, Douglas (1915-71) American landscape architect of the so-called *California School, he began his career with *Church. From 1946 he established his own practice with his wife, and designed the Civic Center Plaza and Washington Square, San Francisco, the Monterey Freeway, and the gardens of IBM Headquarters, San José, all in CA. He was a regular contributor to *Landscape Architecture*.

B & F (2009); W & S (1994)

bazaar, bazar 1. Oriental market-place or permanent market, usually consisting of ranges of shops or stalls in *alleys, roofed over, and capable of being locked after hours. *Mosques and/or *madrasas, financed by the rent paid by stall-holders or shopkeepers, were often associated with bazaars (e.g. mosque and madrasa of Sultan Hassan, Cairo, Egypt (c.1356-63)). The huge bazaar at Isfahan, Iran (early C17—with a commercial area over a mile long (approx. 2 km.)), was embellished with arched galleries, examples of the *charsu over various crossings, and a *caravanserai. 2. C19 fair for the sale of articles on behalf of charities, etc. 3. Any large shop or collection of shops selling mainly fancy goods.

Ck (1996); K.Morrison (2003); *OED* (1933); *OED Supplement*, I (1987), 222

Bazhenov, Vasily Ivanovich (1737-99) Russian architect and pupil of de *Wailly, his contribution to *Neo-Classicism is of considerable importance. He was put in charge (1767) of the reconstruction of the Kremlin in Moscow, his team including *Kazakov (whose Senate Building (1776) is an outstanding memorial to the whole

aborted scheme). Bazhenov produced a design (1775-6) for a *Gothic *palace (with much *polychrome lace-like detail) at Tsaritsyno, and appears to have been responsible for a series of eclectic garden-*fabriques, including the Figurny Bridge (1776). A convinced *Freemason, his severe *Neo-Classicism has parallels with the work of other known Freemason-architects throughout Europe. The best surviving buildings attributed to him are the Dolgov and Yushkov Houses, the belltower of the Skorbyashchenskaya Church, and Pashkov Palace (1784-6), all in Moscow. His last great building was the moated St Michael or Engineer's *fortress at St Petersburg, with its golden *flèche and detached *pavilions, though it seems *Brenna was largely responsible for the finished work.

G.H (1983); M & Wa (1987); Shv (2007); J.T (1996)

Bazzani, Cesare (1873-1939) Italian architect, he worked in Rome and created the *Museo d'Arte Moderne* there for the 1911 Exhibition. His style was eclectic *Historicist, and his buildings include the *Biblioteca Nazionale*, Florence (1907-35), and the *Ministero dell' Educazione Nazionale*, Rome (1913-28).

F.Borsi (1966); Giorgini & Tocchi (1988); Ms (1966)

BBPR Architectural Partnership founded (1932) in Milan by **Gianluigi Banfi** (1910-45), **Lodovico Barbiano di Belgiojoso** (1909-2004), **Enrico Peressutti** (1908-76), and Ernesto Nathan *Rogers. Like many Italian Modernists, BBPR backed Fascism, hoping it would continue to favour 'progressive' architecture, and many early works are associated with that *régime*. The firm's restoration of the *cloisters of *San Simpliciano* *monastery, Milan (1940—which included offices for the firm), was indicative of sympathy for historic buildings that ran counter to orthodox *Modernism. As Fascist Italy became tightly bound to the Nazi Axis, any 'progressive' tendencies vanished in Italy, although BBPR managed to erect the Central Post Office Complex in the EUR Quarter of Rome (1940), the only building there not to succumb to the *stripped *Classicism of *Piacentini: such bravado led to BBPR's falling from favour. After the 1939-45 war BBPR's search for severe geometry that could yet express emotion led to the memorial erected in the *Cimitero Monumentale*, Milan (1946), to concentration-camp victims (Banfi perished at Mauthausen). Conversion of the Sforza Castle into a museum (1954-6) again demonstrated sensitivity to older fabric, but the *Torre Velasca*, Milan (1954-8—with its projecting upper storeys reminiscent of a medieval tower) signalled rejection of rigid dogmas, arousing consternation among adherents of *International Modernism over the building's allusive qualities.

Belgiojoso (1979); M & N (1987); P (1982); J.T (1996)

bead 1. Convex *moulding, often of semicircular *section, also called *astragal, *baguet(te), half-round, or *roundel. If ornamented, it is a *chaplet*. A *bead-moulding* is one that does not project, also called a *reed if several occur together in parallel lines. *Beading* is enrichment consisting of a row of small balls resembling a string of beads, called *beadwork,* or *pearling*, common in *Romanesque work, and revived in C18. **2.** Prayer (referring to beads on a string as mnemonics for prayers), so a *bead-* or *bede-house* was a type of *almshouse, the inmates of which were required to pray in an adjacent chapel or church for the founder's soul.

bead-and-reel *Astragal carved to resemble a continuous row of bead-like and spool- or reel-like elements, arranged (usually) with one bead then two reels, then a bead, in series.

bead-and-reel

beak-head *Romanesque carving of a series of animal, bird (*birds'-heads*), or humanoid heads with long pointed beaks (or tongues) curving around a lower *roll-moulding, as in a church doorway. Heads with stumpier cone-like beaks are *cats'-heads*.

Romanesque *beak-head* ornament, St Ebbe's, Oxford.

Romanesque *cat's-head* ornament, Sts Peter and Paul, Tickencote, Rut. (*after Parker*).

beak-moulding Pendent *fillet on the edge of a *larmier, with a channel or curved groove behind, as on a *Doric *anta *capital.

beam Horizontal structural element supported at each end by some means, such as walls, columns, *piers, etc. A beam employed as a *lintel supports a weight. Beams are further defined by adjectives, as in *tie-beam. *See* TRUSS.

bearing 1. Part of a *truss or *beam resting on a support. **2.** The distance between two such supports (i.e. the *span* of the void). **3.** Figure copied from the *Antique. **4.** In heraldry an *Achievement of Arms, or supporters of a coat of arms.

Beaudouin, Eugène-Elie (1898–1983) French architect, he specialized in low-cost housing, notably at *Cité de la Muette,* Drancy (from 1934), employing industrialized components. Among his other works the *Maison du Peuple,* Clichy (1937–9—with *Prouvé), and extensions to the *Palais des Nations,* Geneva, Switzerland (1967–73—with *Nervi and others), should be cited. His work produced hard, uncompromising environments.

J.T (1996)

Beaugrant, Guyot de (c.1500–49) Sculptor of French origins, he worked in Brugge and Mechelen, Flanders, before moving to Spain (1530s), where he created several elaborate *retables (e.g. Santiago, Bilbao). He seems to have carved the early *Renaissance *façade of the *Hôtel de Savoie* (later Law Courts), Mechelen (1517–26). *See* KELDERMAN.

J.T (1996)

Beautiful One of three C18 aesthetic categories, with the *Picturesque and the *Sublime. *Burke, in his *Philosophical Enquiry...*(1756), perhaps the most influential C18 English work on aesthetics (esp. the 1757 expanded edn), did not accept that architectural Beauty was connected with proportions of an idealized human body, denied that there was any 'inner sense' of Beauty, and argued against the 'notion of mathematical means of measuring it. Beauty gave pleasure (*Alison defined it as the 'emotion of Taste', and held that architectural Beauty of proportion was dependent upon *association*), its essence lying in relative smallness, smoothness, delicacy, absence of angularity, harmoniousness, and brightness and clarity of colour. Uvedale *Price and Payne *Knight claimed the Beautiful suggested a smooth, undulating appearance, with no harshness, surprises, or broken lines; a concept they applied to landscapes. *See* ASSOCIATIONISM; KANT.

E.Burke (1757); H.O (1970); Symes (1993, 2012); Watkins & Cowell (2012)

Beaux-Arts Florid Classical style evolved in the *École Nationale Supérieure des Beaux-Arts,* the main official art-school in France (founded 1795), when it became a separate institution from the old *Académie Royale.* The School was influential, and often gave young architects starts in their careers with the award of the *Prix de Rome* (from 1723), intended to perpetuate academic traditions of training. The *Beaux-Arts style* evolved in the second half of the C19, especially in Paris, where most important architects trained, including several (e.g. *Hunt, *McKim, and *Richardson) from the USA. Examples of that style include *Garnier's *Opéra,* Paris (1861–75), *Poelaert's *Palais de Justice,* Brussels (1866–83), and

*Girault's *Petit Palais*, Paris (1897–1900): scholarly, self-confident, grand, and lush, it was perfectly attuned to the mood of Europe and America in the two decades before 1914.

COF (1988); Dr (ed.) (1977); Egbert (1980); Middleton (ed.) (1982)

beaver-tail *Tile, the exposed part of which is shaped like a beaver's tail.

Beazley, Samuel (1786–1851) English architect/playwright/novelist/wit and leading designer of theatres of his time: among his works were the Royal Lyceum, London (1816, rebuilt 1831–4, reconstructed 1902, leaving the *portico), the Theatre Royal, Birmingham (1820—demolished 1956), the County Library and Reading Rooms, Leamington Spa, Warwicks. (1820–1), Drury Lane Theatre, London (1822, with *Ionic *colonnade added in 1831), and many other theatres in Belgium, Latin America, and India. He designed the new town at Ashford, Kent, for employees of the North Kent Railway (1851), the Lord Warden Hotel, Dover (1848–53), several country-houses, commercial buildings, etc., and published on many subjects.

Co (2008); Harbron (1936)

Becerra, Francisco (c.1545–1605) Spanish-born architect, he settled (1573) in México, where he worked on the Cathedral of Puebla, probably to designs by *Arciniega. He was mostly responsible for the design of the Cathedrals of Cuzco (1582–1654) and Lima (1582–1662), both in Peru. Becerra adopted the somewhat severe style of mid-C16 Spain, although the *façade of Cuzco Cathedral was an ornate, somewhat clumsy *Baroque.

K & S (1959); Marco Dorta (1951)

Beckford, William Thomas (1760–1844) English connoisseur/writer, he inherited (1770) Fonthill Splendens, Wilts., a Palladian house and large estate. Coached by *Chambers and *Cozens in architecture and drawing, he acquired a taste for the exotic and landscape-painting, and (in Switzerland from 1777) for *Sublime scenery (as well as for writings of, e.g., *Gessner, *Goethe, *Rousseau, and the stupendous visions of *Piranesi (which may have stimulated Beckford when writing his 'Gothic' romance, *Vathek* (1786)). He visited *Grande Chartreuse* (where, as the custodian of the site of the earliest (1182) English Carthusian House, Witham Friary, Som., he was welcomed), and this, together with other medieval buildings he saw on the Continent (e.g. Batalha *monastery, Portugal), appears to have prompted the building of a vast 'Abbey' in the grounds of his Wilts. house. This was accomplished (1796–1812) to designs by James *Wyatt, and is perhaps the best example of ecclesiastical

*Gothic used in a secular building: it included an astonishing *steeple (276.5 feet (84 metres) high), which collapsed (1825). Beckford sold Fonthill Abbey and moved to Bath, Som., where he created (1826–8) another eclectic building, Lansdown Tower, using a local architect, **Henry Edmund Goodridge** (1797–1864): it was a mix of *Greek Revival, *Italianate, *Neo-Classicism, and *Romanesque in one *Picturesque composition, intended as a retreat and also as a terminating feature of an idyllic *landscape-garden that linked the Tower with Beckford's house in Lansdown Crescent and included a 'Moorish' *kiosk. At Sintra, Portugal, Beckford also formed (1794–1809) a garden containing a *cascade, *rill, and Gothic garden buildings.

B.Alexander (1954); G.Chapman (1928); Chapman & Hodgkin (1930); Co (2008); Fothergill (1979); Lees-Milne (1976); Mowl (1998); *ODNB* (2004); Ostergard (2001); Tay (2006); J.T (1996)

Beckhard, Herbert (1926–2003) American architect, he was in partnership with *Breuer for a time after the 1939–45 war, and remodelled (1981) the latter's own house at New Canaan, CT.

C.Jones (ed.) (1962)

bed 1. Prepared horizontal surface with a layer of *mortar on which bricks, stones, *tiles, etc., lie; also the under-surface in contact with the mortar-layer. The *bed-joint* is therefore where those surfaces meet, and the term is also applied to the joints between the *voussoirs of an arch. In Classical architecture the *bed-moulding* is part of the *entablature, lying between the *corona and the *frieze, or any moulding over which any horizontal moulding projects. **2.** Plot of land for growing flowers, shrubs, vegetables, etc.

bedding-out 1. Art, dating from the 1830s, of planting flowers (especially annuals) in garden-beds, having raised them from seeds or cuttings. It facilitates the changing of floral displays two or three times each year in the same *beds. **2.** Bedding schemes, often featuring colourful symmetrical patterns, can be seen in public parks, on road roundabouts, etc.

Symes (2006); Tay (2006)

bede *See* BEAD.

Bedford, Eric (1909–2001) English *Modernist architect, he designed the British Telecom Tower, London (1961–4), at the top of which were a revolving restaurant, bars, a kitchen, and two observation platforms. He supervised the design of various elements for the 1953 Coronation, the residence of the British Ambassador in Warsaw (1964), and the Marsham Street development, Westminster (1965–70), a building which pleased few and performed badly: a spectacular failure, it was deservedly demolished (2002-3).

Bradley & Pe (2003); *The Daily Telegraph* (8 Aug. 2001), Obits

Bedford, Francis Octavius (1784-1858) English architect. With J.P.*Gandy and William *Wilkins he was engaged by the Society of *Dilettanti to accompany *Gell on a tour of Greece and Asia Minor to collect material leading to the publication (1817) of The *Unedited Antiquities of Attica* and (1840) the third volume of *The Antiquities of Ionia.* Much later (1912) the fifth part of *The Antiquities of Ionia,* containing work by Bedford, Gandy, and Gell, was published, edited by *Lethaby. As an architect he produced some fine churches in the *Greek-Revival style, including St John, Waterloo Road, Lambeth (1823-4), St George, Camberwell (1822-4—gutted), Holy Trinity, Southwark (1823-4—converted by *Arup Associates as the Henry Wood Hall), and St Luke, West Norwood (1823-5—altered by *Street (1870-9)), all in London. His pre-ecclesiological *Gothic-Revival churches are thin and spindly.

B.Cherry & Pe (1983); Co (2008); Crook (1972a)

bee-bole Recess or *niche in a garden-wall to house a straw or wooden *beehive.

Beeby, Thomas Hall (1941-) See NEW CLASSICISM.

beehive 1. Case or box of straw-work, timber, etc., in which bees are kept, also called *bee-skep.* **2.** *Dome-shaped, like an old-fashioned beehive, e.g., structure of coursed *rubble on a circular plan, each successive course smaller in diameter and slightly *corbelled over the course below, so that, as each course is completed, a roughly conical or beehive-shaped *thole* or *tholos* is formed. The finest *Antique example is the C13 BC *Mycenaean 'Treasury of Atreus'. Inhabited beehive-houses in Southern Italy are called *trulli:* prehistoric Sardinian versions are *nuraghi.*

ABSA, lxxvii (1982), 65-77; Antiquity, xxxiv (1960), 166-76; La (1996)

Beer Family Family of architects active mostly in South Germany and Switzerland, which created some of the finest *Baroque churches in the area. Although a **Georg Beer** (1527-1600) was working in Stuttgart in C16, the Beers came from the Bregenzerwald, and, with the *Moosbruggers and *Thumbs, were important protagonists of the *Vorarlberg School. **Michael Beer** (c.1605-66) was the first member to come to eminence in the C17 with his work at the Abbey Church of *St Lorenz,* Kempten (1652-66), which on plan is a mixture of the longitudinal and centralized type, with a domed octagon set between *chancel and *nave. His son, **Franz** (1660-1726), earned his apprenticeship at the prototypical Vorarlberg

Abbey Church at Obermarchtal (1686-92), a *Wandpfeiler* building with slightly projecting transeptal bay, three-bay nave, and three-bay *choir, designed by Michael *Thumb. Franz Beer's next building (much under the Thumb influence) was the former *Benedictine Abbey Church, Irsee (1699-1704), another *Wandpfeiler* building with transeptal chapels, apsidal *choir, and twin-towered *façade: inside is the charming *pulpit in the form of a ship, complete with sail and *putti* climbing rope-ladders. Also *Wandpfeiler* was his *Heiligenkreuzkirche,* Donauwörth (1717-22), completed by Josef *Schmutzer. Beer's most brilliant work can be found in Switzerland, starting with the former Benedictine Rheinau Abbey Church, near Schaffhausen (1704-11), again of the *Wandpfeiler* type with twin-towered *façade. Inside, *galleries are set back from the *piers, so that *bays and verticality are emphasized. Beer's masterpiece is the former Cistercian Abbey Church of St Urban, near Langenthal (1711-36), with double *pilasters on the wall-piers, and, like Rheinau, set-back galleries. Beer was involved in the designs of the Benedictine Abbey Church of Weingarten, north of Lake Constance (1714-24), not far from which, near Ravensburg, he designed Weissenau Premonstratensian Church (1717-24). **Johann Michael Beer** (1700-67) was responsible (with his nephew, **Johann Ferdinand Beer** (1731-89)) for the handsome twin-towered façade (and probably the *choir) of the former Benedictine Abbey Church (now Cathedral), St Gallen, Switzerland (1760s).

Bou (1962); Lb & D (1976); On (1973); J.T (1996)

Begg, John (1866-1937) Scots architect and pupil of *Blanc before working with *Waterhouse and *Edis. He settled (1901) in India and succeeded (1908) **James Ransome** (1865-1944) as consulting architect to the government there. His best works are the General Post Office, Bombay (1903-9—an eclectic essay incorporating Indian motifs); the Council-House Secretariat (1909), and Stationery Office (1912), Calcutta; and the Lady Hardinge Medical College and Hospital, New Delhi (1915-16—with elements reminiscent of *Lutyens's work). He returned to Edinburgh (1921) to practise, designing several houses in the suburbs of that city in partnership with **Alexander Lorne Campbell** (1871-1944): their Edinburgh Dental Hospital, Chambers Street (1925-7), was in a 'tired Renaissance' style.

Davies (1985); GMcW & W (1984); JRSA cxxix (1981), 358-79; RIBAJ xliv (1937), 466, 519

beguinage Establishment of, or house for, *Beguines,* members of a lay sisterhood formed (C12) in The Netherlands.

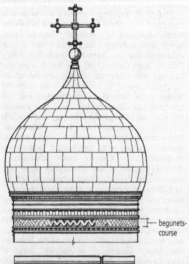

Elevation of begunets-course with brick cogging.

Construction of brick/tile begunets-course with brick cogging.

begunets Typical upper part of Russian church-tower with begunets.

begunets In Russian medieval churches, *string-course or *frieze of bricks laid on ends at angles, stretcher-sides flush with the wall behind, and touching at the tops to form a series of indented triangular recesses. Often associated with brick *cogging (called *porebrik*), it was sometimes made of *masonry, forming repeated carved depressions.

Behne, Adolf (1885–1948) German architect/theorist/critic, he was involved in the *Deutscher

*Werkbund, *Arbeitsrat für Kunst*, and *Gläserne Kette*, all of which he promoted in *Die Wiederkehr der Kunst* (1919). He used the telling term *Reklamerarchitektur* (Advertising Architecture) to describe works of *Mendelsohn et al. He published (1920) *Ruf zum Bauen*, and his best-known book (1923–5), *Der moderne Zweckbau*, which promoted *Functionalism and the *Modern Movement. In his *Entartete Kunst* he described art and architecture banned by the Nazis, and continued to publish polemics until his death.

Behne (1919, 1920, 1926, 1988, 1994, 1998); Saur (1994)

Behnisch, Günter (1922–2010) German architect, his Stuttgart firm was responsible for the *Olympiapark*, Munich (1967–72): **Frei Otto** (1925–2015) collaborated in the design of the tent-roof covering the stadium, sports-hall, and swimming pool. Other works included the *Hohenstaufen-Gymnasium*, Göppingen (1956–9), the Secondary School, Lorch (1973), Lutheran Study Centre, Stuttgart-Birkach (1977–80), the Technical School, Bruchsal (1983), Catholic University Library, Eichstätt (1987), German Postal Museum, Frankfurt-am-Main (1990), Central Bank of Bavaria, Schwabing, Munich (1992), and the former Federal Parliament Building in Bonn (1992).

Behnisch & Partner (1996); BJ (2000); E (1994); Gauzin-Müller (1997); L (1988); Mr (1995); J-K.Schmidt & Zeller (1992)

Behrendt, Walter Curt (1884–1945) German-born American architect/writer. He worked with the Ministry for Housing and Town Planning (1919–26) and in the Ministry of Finance (1927–33), in which positions he promoted the *Modern Movement in public-building projects in Prussia and throughout the Weimar Republic. He was involved in the *Deutscher Werkbund, and later joined Der *Ring. He left Germany (1934) and settled in the USA, where he taught at Buffalo, NY (1937–41), Dartmouth College, Hanover (1941–5), and elsewhere. His writings include *Der Sieg des neuen Baustils* (1927), *Modern Building: Its Nature, Problems, and Forms* (1937), and *Roots of Contemporary American Architecture* (1972).

Behrendt (1920, 1937); Saur (1994)

Behrens, Peter (1868–1940) German artist, he became an architect prompted by William *Morris's teachings. A founder-member (1893) of the Munich *Sezession, his graphic work was influenced by *Art Nouveau. From 1898 he became interested in the problems of designing mass-produced artefacts. Invited (1899) to Darmstadt by **Ernst Ludwig** (1868–1937—**Grand Duke of Hesse**, *r.*1892–1918), he designed his own house at the artists' colony of *Mathildenhöhe*:

incorporating severe geometry with *Gothic *ogee *gable and dormer-windows, it was designed inside and out, drawing on ideas of van de *Velde and *Mackintosh. From 1907 his work became more *Neo-Classical: the crematorium at Delstern, Hagen, Westphalia (1906–7), is a good example. A founder of the *Deutscher Werkbund, he was appointed architect to the first electrical company in Berlin, the AEG, for which he designed the turbine-hall (1908–10), factories, offices, shops, workers' housing, and all manner of artefacts until 1914.

His Berlin office gained an international reputation, and in c.1910 Le *Corbusier, W.*Gropius, and *Mies all worked there. There was much that was Neo-Classical in his AEG work, and the influence of *Schinkel was strong in his *Haus Schröder*, Hagen-Eppenhausen, Westphalia (1908), and *Haus Wiegand*, Berlin (1911–13). The Imperial German Embassy in St Petersburg (1911–12), a powerful essay in *stripped Classicism, influenced many architects, including the Scandinavian Neo-Classicists of the 1920s and 1930s. In 1920–4 he built offices for the I.G. Farben (now Höchst) Dyeworks in Frankfurt-am-Main, an *Expressionist essay with touches of proto-*Art Deco.

Behrens was Director of the School of Architecture, Vienna Academy of Arts (1922–36), and then headed the Department of Architecture, Prussian Academy of Arts, Berlin. He designed one house in England: 'New Ways', 508 Wellingborough Road, Northampton (1923–5), for **Wenman Joseph Bassett-Lowke** (1877–1953), which incorporated an earlier (1907) room from 78 Derngate by *Mackintosh. He designed the *Werkbund*'s exhibition-house at the *Weissenhofsiedlung, Stuttgart (1927), the *Villa Lewin*, Schlachtsee, Berlin (1929–30), an *apartment-house at Westend, Berlin (1930), and the *Villa Ganz*, Kronberg-in-Taunus (1931–4), all with influences from the *International-Modern style, which he also employed in the Austrian State Tobacco Administration block, Linz (1936—with **Alexander Popp** (1891–1945)). In 1937–9 he prepared a design for *Speer's north–south axis in Berlin: it was to be for a new AEG administration-building in a *stripped-Classical style.

S.Anderson (2000); Behrens (1901); Buddensieg & Rogge (1984); Darmstadt (ed.) (2000–4); Weber (1966); Windsor (1981)

Bélanger, François-Joseph (1744–1818) French architect, the most important landscape architect and the most refined of the *Louis-Seize *Neo-Classicists. Appointed (1767) *Dessinateur des Menus-Plaisirs du Roi*, he met (1769) Charles-Joseph, Prince de *Ligne, for whom he designed *fabriques for the celebrated gardens at Belœil (now Belgium). He created (1770–1)

the lovely *pavillon à l'antique* at the **Comte de Lauragais**'s *Hôtel de Brancas*, Paris. For **Charles-Philippe, Comte d'Artois** (1757–1836—later King **Charles X** (r.1824–30)—to whom he had become *premier architecte*), his design for the exquisite *Parva sed Apta* Neo-Classical *Pavillon de Bagatelle* in the *Bois de Boulogne*, Paris, was erected (1777) in 64 days to win a bet with **Marie-Antoinette** (1755–93—Queen of France from 1774). The main bedroom was designed as a *tent, and the whole building set in the most celebrated 'English' garden of the period (1778–80), with many *Gothick, *Chinoiserie, and other *fabriques, designed by Bélanger and created by the Scots landscape-gardener *Blaikie. At Neuilly, the *Folie Saint-James* (c.1780) was placed in a large *jardin *anglo-chinois in which were many famous *fabriques, including *kiosks, *grottoes, Chinese *pavilions, and a massive artificial rock (the *Grand Rocher*, known as the Eighth Wonder of the World) containing a bathroom, reservoir, grotto, and art-gallery. He designed (from 1784) the extraordinary gardens and *fabriques at Méréville, near Étampes, for the Court Banker, **Jean-Joseph, Marquis de Laborde** (1724–94), held to be superior to anything by *Kent, and was succeeded there by Hubert *Robert, who claimed the designs were his alone. Bélanger's *dome of the *Halle au Blé*, Paris (1808–13), probably the first such iron-and-glass structure in the world, replaced the timber-and-glass dome by *Legrand and *Molinos (1782).

B (1980); Deming (1984); M & Wa (1987); Racine (ed.) (2001); M & T (1991)

Belcher, John (1841–1913) Distinguished late-Victorian/Edwardian British architect, he joined (1865) his father, **John** (c.1816–90), in practice in London, remaining until 1875. He made his name with the Genoese-inspired *Mannerist *Baroque Hall of the Incorporated Chartered Accountants, Great Swan Alley, London (1888–93), designed with *Pite. The building was adorned with a lively *frieze carved by (Sir) **William Hamo Thorneycroft** (1850–1925), while **Harry Bates** (1850–99) designed the *terms and *corbels. The ideals of revived *Classicism and the *Arts-and-Crafts movement were fused in the building, as they were in Belcher's own career, for he was responsive to the spirit of the Italian *Renaissance (and especially Genoese *palazzi*), and was also a founder-member of the *Art-Workers' Guild. His office produced Colchester Town Hall (1898–1902) with a fine *campanile and vigorous main *façade, enlivened by a *Giant *Order carrying broken *pediments. *Joass joined Belcher (1897), becoming his partner (1905), and the firm evolved an assured and robust Baroque, culminating in the massive *Wrenaissance Ashton Memorial, Lancaster (1904–9). He published *Essentials in*

Architecture (1893), and with *Macartney, a collection of photographs and drawings in *Later Renaissance Architecture in England* (1901), which influenced contemporary architecture. Belcher and Joass designed the Franco-British White City Exhibition in 1908, displaying their mastery of opulent late-Baroque.

A.S.Gray (1985); *ODNB* (2004); Se (ed.) (1975); Se (1977)

belection *See* BOLECTION.

Belfast *See* TRUSS.

belfry 1. Bell-tower, usually attached to a church or other building, and sometimes freestanding. 2. *Stage of a tower in which bells are hung and from which the sound is emitted, called the *belfry-stage*, identified by its (usually) *louvred openings. 3. Framing on which bells are supported.

Belgiojoso, Lodovico Barbiano di (1909–2004) *See* BBPR.

bell 1. Ancient Egyptian bell-like *capital. 2. *Basket, *corbeille, or vase-like solid part of a *Corinthian and *Composite capital from which leaves, scrolls, etc., spring. 3. Bell-shaped *First-Pointed *Gothic capital 4. One of many small bell-shaped forms (*campanulae*) suspended from the *eaves of *pagodas, etc., in *Chinoiserie buildings. 5. *Gutta of the *Doric *Order. *Compounds include:*
bell-arch: arch springing from curved-ended *corbels, creating a bell-shaped aperture;
bell-cage: structure supporting bells in a *belfry;
bell-canopy: roof to protect a bell or bells, often with a *gable;
bell-capital: see BELL (1, 2, 3);
bell-cast: 1. sprocketed *eaves with *sprockets or *cocking-pieces* fixed to the top of the common *rafters immediately above the eaves so that the part of the roof over has a flatter pitch; 2. projecting finish, or *bell-cast piece*, at the bottom of *harling, *render, or *roughcast finish on a wall, resembling the base of a bell, forming a *drip;
bell-chamber: room containing one or more bells hung from their *cage or frame. Some bell-chambers are in buildings detached from churches, and near the ground (e.g. *bell-house*, East Bergholt, Suffolk);
bell-cote or *bell-gable*: small gable, usually set over the west wall of a church or over the east wall of the *nave immediately above the *chancel-arch, containing a bell or bells suspended within arched openings. Over the chancel-arch a bell-cote is called a *Sanctecote*, as it carries the *Sanctus* bell;
bell-roof: roof with exterior profile resembling a bell;
bell-tower: tower, attached to or detached from a building such as a church, called *campanile in Italian, with a *belfry-stage containing bells.

bell-cote Typical C13 Rut. type, All Saints' Church, Little Casterton, Rut.

Bell, Edward Ingress (1837–1914) *See* WEBB, SIR ASTON.

Bell, Henry (1647–1711) English gentleman-architect, he appears to have been partly responsible for the replanning and rebuilding of Northampton after the fire (1675), and to have designed All Saints' Church there (1677–80) as well as some of the *façades of houses in the Market Place. Bell's other works are all in King's Lynn, Norfolk: they include the charming Customs House (1683), built as an Exchange; the Market Cross (1707–10)—demolished; two altarpieces; probably the Duke's Head Inn (c.1684); and various houses. He was also responsible for North Runcton Church, Norfolk (1703–13), and may have designed other buildings in Hunts., Norfolk, and Suffolk.

Co (2008)

Bell, John (*fl.*1478–88) English master-mason, he worked on the upper *stages of the *crossing-tower at Durham Cathedral (1483–90). He may be the same Bell employed (1472) at York *Minster, at King's College Chapel, Cambridge (1480s), and at Great St Mary's Church, Cambridge (until 1503).

J.Harvey (1987)

bell-flower *See* HUSK.

Bellot, Dom Paul (1876–1944) French *Benedictine monk/architect, a disciple of *Choisy and *Viollet-le-Duc, and trained (1894–1901) at the *École des *Beaux-Arts*, Paris. He designed many buildings in Belgium, England, France, The Netherlands, and Portugal. His Benedictine Monastery of *St-Paul-de-Wisques*, Oosterhout, Brabant, The Netherlands (1906–20) greatly impressed *Berlage. Quarr Abbey, IoW (1907–14), his outstanding architectural achievement, is a master-work of *Expressionism in brick, with a church of 1911–12 that is wholly original, having a short, low *nave, a long *choir, and a stunning eastern tower with brick arches inspired, perhaps, by *Moorish architecture of Spain: it astonished *Pevsner. Bellot explored architectural possibilities of load-bearing brick parabolic arches and corbelling, arguing that such investigations were more in the spirit of medieval architecture than in archaeologically based *Gothic Revival. Among his finest buildings are the *polychrome *Notre-Dame-des-Trévois*, Troyes (1931–4), *Ste-Bathilde*, Vanves (1933–6), both in France, and the lovely Church at Bloemendaal (1923–4), in The Netherlands.

He visited (1934) Montréal, Canada, to give a series of lectures (published 1939) in which he stressed that the modern architect should emulate, not imitate, the lessons of the Middle Ages, and also in which he roundly denounced Le *Corbusier as an *'architecte bolchéviste militant'*: these lectures promoted the building of several churches in what became known as the 'Dom-Bellot style', featuring parabolic arches, polychrome brickwork, and powerful geometries. Bellot's disciple **Adrian Dufresne** (1904–82) designed *Ste-Thérèse-de-Lisieux*, Beauport, near Québec City (1936), partly influenced by Bellot's own Church at Noordhoek, The Netherlands (1921–2). Bellot himself, with **Félix Racicot** (1903–73) and another architect-monk, **Dom Claude-Marie Côté**, designed (1935) additions to the *Abbaye de St-Benoît-du-Lac*, begun 1939, dramatically composed works, with brick *cloisters again featuring parabolic arches. At the *Oratoire St-Joseph*, Montréal, he worked with **Lucien Parent** (1893–1956) on the completion of the building, his principal contribution being the polygonal *concrete *dome and the canted arches of the interior.

Bellot (1948); Culot & Meade (1996); K (1994); *PoA*, **xxvii** (Feb.-Mar. 1997), 54–7; P.Willis (1997)

Belluš, Emil (1899–1979). Slovak *International-Modernist architect. Among his works National House, Banská Bystrica (1925), covered *bridge, Piešťany (1932), the flour mill, Trnava (1936), and the National Bank, Bratislava (1938), are cited. He carried out restoration-work at the Slovak National Council Building and the *Baroque Grassalkovich Palace (both 1940, both in Bratislava). He designed the Trnava Water-Works (1946), and various buildings for the Slovak Technical University, Bratislava (1948, etc.).

Kusý (1984); J.T (1996)

Belluschi, Pietro (1899–1994) Italian-born architect/engineer, he settled (1920s) in the USA, and joined (1925) the Portland, OR, office of the architect **Albert Ernest Doyle** (1877–1928),

which he reorganized (1943) under his own name (it was later absorbed by *SOM). Belluschi established his reputation with several buildings, among which the Art Museum (1931–8), Sutor House (1937–8), and St Thomas More's Church (1939–41), all in Portland, should be mentioned. With his US National Bank of Oregon, Salem (1940–1), he showed an inclination to *International Modernism, a tendency reinforced with his Equitable Life Assurance Building, Portland (1944–8), one of the first examples of an aluminium-and-glass *curtain-wall enclosing a *concrete-framed tower, a building-type that became common thereafter. Fond of the phrase 'eliminate, refine, and integrate', he built up a huge commercial practice, and collaborated with others (while also involved in teaching at MIT), notably with Walter *Gropius and Emery *Roth for the PanAm building (1962—which has dated), and with **Eduardo Catalano** (1917–2010) and **Helge Westermann** (*c.*1916–2010) for the Juilliard School of Music and Alice Tully Hall at the Lincoln Center (1955–70), both NYC. On relinquishing (1965) his MIT position, he re-established himself in Portland, again working with other architects. Among later works are numerous churches, the San Francisco Symphony Hall, CA (with SOM—1980), and the Baltimore Symphony Hall, MD (with **Jung, Brannen, Associates**—1982).

Clausen (1992, 1994); G & I (1974); Heyer (1978); Stubblebine (1953)

belt 1. Series of trees planted around estate perimeters, sometimes associated with a *drive. *Switzer published designs for belts, and 'Capability' *Brown often employed them, as at Petworth, Sussex (late 1750s). Belts defining boundaries were the antitheses of designs by *Kent, who created views outwards into the countryside. **2.** Perimeter drive affording changing views over an estate.

Symes (2006)

belt-course *See* BAND.

Beltrami, Luca (1854–1933) Italian architect/writer. He published many studies of C15 buildings in Lombardy, and restored several, including the *Certosa di Pavia* (1891). His rigorous researches informed the *eclecticism of his architecture: among his best-known works were the new *façade of *Alessi's *Palazzo Marino, Piazza Scala* (1890), restoration of *Santa Maria delle Grazie* (1892–5), the transformation of the *Castello Sforzesco* (1893–1911), the *Palazzo per l'Esposizione Permanente di Belle Arti* (1896—in a *Renaissance-Revival style (which he also employed in the *Palazzo Venezia delle Assicurazioni Generali di Milano* (1897–99), *Casa Dario-*

Biandrà (1902), offices for the *Corriere della Sera* (1904), and *Banca Commerciale Italiana* (1907)), all in Milan. From 1920 he lived in Rome and carried out important works at the Vatican after his friend **Ambrogio Damiano Achille Ratti** (b.1857) was elected as **Pope Pius XI** (*r.*1922–39): among them were the restoration of *Michelangelo and della *Porta's *dome and of *Bramante's *Cortile del Belvedere* (both 1928–9), and the building of the huge new library (1929–33). The last, with its beautiful proportions, is an elegant testimony to his abilities. He founded the review *Edilizia Moderna* (1891–1914).

Baldrighi (ed.) (1997); Ms (1966); J.T (1996)

belvedere Any raised structure or tower erected over the roof of a dwelling-house or on a vantage-point in a landscape from which pleasant scenery may be viewed. Such a building in a garden might be in the form of a Classical *temple, and is also termed a *gazebo, *mirador*, or *summer-house.

bema 1. Platform, *rostrum, or raised floor in the *apse of a *basilica. **2.** *Chancel, *sanctuary, or elevated part of a church containing the *altar. **3.** Raised part of the *nave, enclosed by a balustrade, *cancelli*, or *screen, allotted to the clergy. **4.** Elevated *pulpit in *synagogues for readings.

Beman, Solon Spencer (1853–1914) American architect, trained in *Upjohn's office, he designed the model industrial towns of Pullman, IL (1880–95—with *Barrett) and Ivorydale, OH (1883–9), and was a contributor to the achievements of the *Chicago School. Uninhibited by squeamishness, he employed a wide stylistic range, as in the houses in Florence Square, South Forestville, Chicago, IL. He designed the Grand Central Station, Chicago (1890), a large iron-and-glass train-shed with a *Neo-Romanesque clock-tower, which was a successful integration of architecture and engineering. His Mines and Mining and Merchant Tailors *pavilions at the World's Columbian Exposition, Chicago (1893), were suitably grand, after which his work became more soberly Classical (e.g. the First Church of Christ Scientist, Chicago (1897), in which the *Greek Revival was dominant). His Studebaker (now Brunswick Fine Arts) Building, Chicago (1895), employed finely articulated glazing and *terracotta Gothicizing detail.

Chicago Architectural Journal, **v** (1986), 9–31; J.T (1996)

bench *Pew. A *bench-end* is therefore the terminal timber facing of a church-pew, frequently decorated with *poppy-heads, *blind tracery, and the like. A *bench-table* or *bench-table stone* is a low projecting course of *masonry, its lowest part chamfered, forming a seat against medieval walls in e.g. *cloisters.

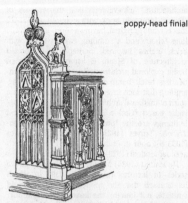

poppy-head finial

bench-end Medieval example with blind tracery panels, poppy-head finial, and figures in ogee-headed niches, Holy Trinity, Blythburgh, Suffolk.

Benedetto da Maiano (1442–97) *See* MAIANO.

Benedictine Monastic Order based on the rules of **St Benedict** (480–543), who established the Abbey at *Monte Cassino* from which the arts of agriculture, architecture, and writing were disseminated. In C9 the Rule was regularized, and the Order confined its activities to Western Europe. An exemplary plan for the Benedictine Monastery of St Gall in Switzerland survives, and demonstrates the sophistication of the architecture as early as *c.*820: the plan of the church itself is similar to that used for several later churches.

Eschapasse (1963); J.Evans (1972)

Bengal cottage Mid-C19 European garden-building with *cob (or similar) walls, bamboo doors and window-frames, and a reed-covered roof.

bénitier *See* STOUP.

Benjamin, Asher (1771–1845) American architect, he published *The Country Builder's Assistant* (1797) and *The American Builder's Companion* (1806), among other works, the sources of the design of countless buildings in New England. Five other titles followed, and Benjamin's books went into many edns: they were clear, practical, and well-illustrated volumes containing examples of various architectural styles from late-*Georgian to *Greek Revival. Benjamin thought highly of the *Federal-style architecture of Charles *Bulfinch. He practised as an architect in Boston, MA, from 1803, and several of his buildings may still be seen there, including the African Meeting House

(1805), West Church (1806), and Charles Street Meeting House (1807). He was responsible for the reticent and handsome 54-5 and 70-5 Beacon Street. Benjamin was the architect for many buildings in MA, VT, CT, RI, and NH, while his *Practical House Carpenter* (1830) was the most popular architectural book in C19 USA, and the source for an enormous range of buildings and street-furniture. He also published *Elements of Architecture* (1843), which includes technological information, including notes on the uses of cast iron. Most of his writings have been reprinted.

Benjamin (1838, 1854, 1972, 1972a 1976, 1976a–c); Embury (1917)

Benoît-Lévy, Georges (1880–1971) French theorist, founder of the *Association Française des Cités-Jardins* (1903), based on Ebenezer *Howard's ideas in England for *Garden Cities. It achieved a few pleasant garden-suburbs, but little more. Benoit-Lévy was a prolific writer, however, and his thought was widely disseminated.

Benoît-Lévy (1911, 1932)

Benš, Adolf (1894–1982) Czech architect. He designed numerous buildings in the crisp *International-Modern style, e.g. Electric Administration Building, Holešovice District, Prague (1926–35—with **Josef Kříž** (1895-1935)), a villa at Troja, Prague (1928), and his own house in the Baba District, Prague (1937). His best-known work was Prague Airport (1931-5). He was Professor of Architecture at the School of Industrial Arts in Prague (1945–70).

Li (1996); Šlapeta (1978); Vondrová *et al.* (1978)

Benson, William (1682–1754) English architect, he designed Wilbury House, Wilts. (1710), the first example of the Revival of the 'stile' of Inigo *Jones's domestic architecture in C18 England, derived in this case from John *Webb's Amesbury House, Wilts. (1661). Wilbury was illustrated in *Vitruvius Britannicus* (1715—i, plates 51–2—where it was spelled 'Wilberry'). Benson provided a system of piped water-supply for Shaftesbury, Dorset (1715), and designed waterworks for the gardens of Herrenhausen, near Hanover, for **King George I** (*r*.1714-27). He curried such favour that he was appointed (1718) to the Surveyorship of the Works, having had the octogenarian *Wren dismissed. In the fifteen months he held the post he managed to remove any subordinate with talent, although he appointed Colen *Campbell as his Deputy. Benson and Campbell seem to have planned to have the Houses of Parliament demolished (by claiming the House of Lords was structurally unsound) in order to further their plans to design a huge new Palladian building, but were dismissed (1719), though not before new State Rooms at

Kensington Palace (1718-20) were commenced, probably to Campbell's designs. *Hawksmoor claimed that Benson got more in one year for 'confusing the King's Works' than Wren obtained in forty years of 'honest endeavours'. Benson seems to have been involved in the building of Campbell's Stourhead, Wilts., and a new *chancel of the Parish Church at Quarley, Hants. (1723).

Co (2008); *ODNB* (2004)

Bentley, John Francis (1839–1902) English architect. He joined *Clutton's London office, working on the Jesuit Church in Farm Street and on the delightful little St Francis of Assisi, Notting Dale, London, where he designed the *high-altar, *baptistery, and much else. He converted (1862) to Roman Catholicism and set up his own practice, obtaining much work from his Church, including the Holy Rood, Watford, Herts. (1883-90), a firmly English mix of *Second and Third *Pointed, with an exquisite high-altar, *reredos, *Rood-loft, and Rood. His eclectic *tour-de-force* is Westminster Cathedral (1894–1903), a fusion of *Byzantine and *Romanesque elements, with a red-and-white striped exterior influenced partly by Norman *Shaw's New Scotland Yard: other precedents were *San Marco*, Venice, *San Vitale*, Ravenna, the Romanesque *Duomo*, Pisa, the *Domkirche*, Speier, *Sant'Ambrogio*, Milan, the *Certosa*, Pavia, and *Hagia Sophia*, Constantinople (Istanbul). The plan is not unlike *Vignola's *Il Gesù*, Rome, and the series of saucer-domes (constructed of *concrete) recall those of *St-Front*, Périgueux.

Browne & Dean (1995); Hôpital (1919); *ODNB* (2004); Scott-Moncrieff (1924)

Bentley, Richard (1708–82) Member of *Walpole's 'Committee of Taste' advising on the building of Strawberry Hill, Twickenham, Mddx.: he was responsible for the hall, *staircase, *screen in the 'Holbein Chamber', several *chimney-pieces, and other details (1751-61). He also designed the 'Gothic Cloister' at Richard *Bateman's *villa at Old Windsor, Berks. (dismantled after 1774), and (1758) the *Gothick monument to **Galfridus Mann** (d.1756) in St Nicholas's, Linton, Kent. His illustrations for the first anthology of poems (1753) by **Thomas Gray** (1716-71) were much admired. Apart from essays in *Gothick, he also did the occasional *Chinoiserie confection.

Co (2008); Newman (2012); *ODNB* (2004)

berceau 1. *Arbour of *trellises covered with plants. **2.** Trees trained in *espalier fashion, with branches arched to form an arbour.

Berg, Max (1870-1947) German architect, he became City Architect of Breslau (now Wrocław), where he designed the gigantic *Jahrhunderthalle* (1910-13), one of the first buildings in which the

*arcuated possibilities of *reinforced *concrete were exploited on a large scale in the huge ribbed *dome with rings of *clerestorey-lights rising up above. It was intended as the centrepiece of a park laid out to commemorate the centenary of the defeat of **Napoléon** at the Battle of Leipzig, hence its name He also designed many buildings in and around Breslau to cope with the increase in population when the creation of the Polish Corridor drove many Germans into Silesia after 1918.

Biegański (1972); Konwiarz (1926); Pehnt (1973); J.T (1996)

Berg, Wilfred Clement von (1894–1978) British architect, he joined (1919) the Imperial War Graves Commission, working under *Blomfield, *Lutyens, and *Holden, and designing nearly 40 *cemeteries. He practised for a time at St Raphael, France, collaborating with *Goodhart-Rendel, before moving to South Africa (1931).

Stamp (1977)

Berlage, Hendrik Petrus (1856–1934) Distinguished Dutch architect, influenced by the work of *Sullivan and *Wright. He went into partnership (1884) with **Theodorus Sanders** (1847–1927), and opened his own office (1889). Early works were in the *Renaissance-Revival style, but he produced (1890s) several *Art-Nouveau designs, culminating in the *Villa Henny*, The Hague (1898), with furnishings informed by design philosophies of *Morris and *Pugin. Berlage's most celebrated building is the Amsterdam Merchants' Exchange (*Koopmansbeurs*—1897–1903), which revealed his respect for the expressive power of constructional arched brickwork: robust detailing and clear expressive functions (such as the *kneelers from which the segmental arches in the hall spring, and the junctions between load-bearing structure and metal *trusses) made him a precursor of the *Amsterdam School, while his writings earned him the respect of the young, aspiring members of the *avant-garde*. Berlage, like *Behrens, designed furniture, graphics, and all manner of artefacts: he was also an important town-planner. Although he was a delegate to *CIAM (1928), he never actually joined, and claims for him as a proto-Modernist are nonsensical: in fact, when *Rietveld asked him to join a group (that included Le *Corbusier, *Lurçat, Hannes *Meyer, et al.) to have a photograph taken at the 1929 CIAM conference, Berlage refused, stating unequivocally that everything he had created was being destroyed by the same people.

Berlage (1996); Derwig & Wert (1994); Polano (ed.) (1988); Reinink (1975); Sg (1972); Sg & Bock (1975)

berm 1. Horizontal surface lying between a *moat and the slope of a *rampart in military architecture. **2.** Area between a ditch and a

bank. **3.** Continuously sloping bank of earth against a wall, as in a fortified city-wall.

Bernard, Oliver Percy (1881–1939) Architect and designer of Scots descent. He did sets for **Wilhelm Richard Wagner's** (1813–83) *Ring* cycle at Covent Garden (1921), and carried out works for the British Empire Exhibition at Wembley (1924–5). His interiors for J. Lyons & Co., the London hotel and catering firm, included the stunning *Art-Deco entrance to the Strand Palace Hotel (1930–1—later dismantled and now in the Victoria & Albert Museum) and the Regent Palace Hotel, near Piccadilly Circus (1934–5).

J.Curl (2005); *J.* of the Thirties Soc., v (1985), 2–7; *ODNB* (2004); J.T (1996)

Bernard de Soissons (*fl.*C13) *See* soissons.

Bernini, Giovanni Lorenzo (1598–1680). Neapolitan sculptor/architect/painter/poet, he made an outstanding contribution to the evolution of *Baroque in Rome, where his family settled (*c.*1605), and where he spent the rest of his life. By the age of 20 he was famous, and from the election of **Maffeo Barberini** (b.1568) as **Pope Urban VIII** (*r.*1623–44) his rise was meteoric: he began work (1624) on his gigantic *baldacchino in *San Pietro*, Rome, a *tour-de-force* with four *barley-sugar columns that alluded to the columns supposedly taken from the Herodian Temple in Jerusalem (but actually presented (*c.*324–30) by **Emperor Constantine 'the Great'** (*r.*324–37) and set up over the tomb of the Apostle in the *basilica that preceded the later church). Those columns, and the extravagant grandeur of the object, made clear the continuity of the Church from the Old Testament, and celebrated the Counter-Reformation Church Triumphant.

Bernini was a master of the theatrical, as his sensational Cornaro Chapel in *Santa Maria della Vittoria*, Rome (1645–52), demonstrates: in the *Ecstasy of St Teresa*, a smiling angel thrusts its spear into the bosom of the swooning Saint, carried aloft in clouds, illuminated by gilded-rod *sunbursts and concealed lighting, and placed within an *aedicule above the *altar. The whole vision is viewed by members of the Cornaro family, as though in theatre-boxes: it is an unforgettable creation (though deeply disturbing to puritanical dispositions). He also used theatrical techniques of false *perspective, concealed lighting, and optical devices at the *Scala Regia*, Vatican Palace (1663–6), to emphasize the illusion of great length and size.

He designed the Four Rivers Fountain (1648–51) in the *Piazza Navona*, Rome (a powerful *base for the Roman Egyptianizing *obelisk (*c.*81–96) recovered from excavations), and the (1667) elephant carrying another *Antique obelisk from Saïs (*c.*685–525 BC) on its back outside *Santa Maria sopra Minerva*. His designs for Papal tombs in *San Pietro* (**Urban VIII**, 1627–47, and **Alexander VII**,

1671-8) employed essentially pyramidal compositions where the figures were set against fat obelisk-forms: these were the precedents for countless such pyramidal funerary monuments throughout Europe thereafter (there are many examples in England).

As an architect, Bernini was also outstanding. His finest church is *Sant'Andrea al Quirinale* (1658-70), an *ellipse with the *high-altar set on the short axis, and a series of chapels off the centralized volume. A triumphant, vigorous, richly coloured space, it was influential in RC countries during the Baroque period, notably in Central Europe. Also elliptical was his *Piazza di San Pietro* (1656-67), with the Ancient-Egyptian obelisk (*c.*1290-1279 BC—re-erected 1586 by Domenico *Fontana) at its centre, on the main axis of the *basilica: the *colonnades of the severe *Tuscan *Order around the wider parts of the ellipse become straight as they approach *Maderno's façade, but they are not parallel, being closer together as they branch off from the ellipse. These points, and the fact that the ground rises up to the steps before the façade, employ theatrical techniques to make the approach to the church seem longer and more impressive, while creating the illusion that Maderno's somewhat weak front is taller. There is a symbolic aspect too, for the great curved arms of the colonnade reach out to embrace the faithful to the bosom of Mother Church.

In secular architecture he was equally influential. His *Palazzo Chigi* (1664-6—later *Odescalchi*), which has a centrepiece of eight *Giant *pilasters with rusticated *wings on either side, provided a model for many European princely *palaces. At the same time he produced proposals for the east side of the Louvre in Paris: although never realized, it was an important precedent.

Avery (1997); F.Borsi (1984); Brauer & Wi (1970); FdA & C (1977–8); Lavin (1980); Lavin *et al.* (1981); Marder (1998); Va (1986); Waddy (1990); Wi (1981, 1982)

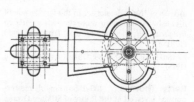

Diagrammatic plan of the Basilica and *Piazza* of *San Pietro*, Rome, showing Bernini's ellipse and converging colonnades.

Berthault, Louis-Martin (1770–1823) French architect/landscape architect, pupil of *Percier, he decorated a house on the *Rue du Mont-Blanc*, Paris, and designed a celebrated garden at Raincy which included a Russian House, a *grotto, and an iron *bridge (all 1790s and early 1800s). His garden at *Les Fontaines*, near Chantilly (1792–1822), had *Picturesque and *Neo-Classical features (e.g. Fisherman's House, Boat-House, Sepulchre, and Obelisk on an island), and is known from images by **Constant Bourgeois** (1767–1841) and Berthault's uncle, **Pierre-Gabriel Berthault** (1737–1831), published in *Suite de Vingt-Quatre Vues de Jardins Anglais* (1812). Berthault transformed several French gardens into less formal arrangements, notably at Courson (from 1820). He became (1805) Chief Architect to the **Empress Joséphine** (1763-1814), for whom he carried out works at the *Malmaison* gardens. Other parks on which he worked were those at *St-Leu-Taverny*, Beauregard (near Villeneuve-St-George), and Compiègne. His eclectic use of a wide variety of exotic shrubs and trees created a rich, sometimes overwhelming effect.

Arneville (1981); M & T (1991); Racine (ed.) (2001)

Bertotti-Scamozzi, Ottavio (1719-90) Doyen of the *Palladian Revival in Italy, he edited Palladio's work, producing the important *Le fabbriche e i disegni di Andrea Palladio raccolti e illustrati* (1776-83) and *Le terme dei Romani, disegnate da A.Palladio* (1785), publications which have tended to obscure his own architectural significance. He was well-connected, and knew such figures as *Algarotti and *Quarenghi, while he seems to have been sought-after as *cicerone* by *cognoscenti* on the *Grand Tour, producing (1761) a guide-book to the architectural sights of Vicenza. His own buildings in and around Vicenza, unsurprisingly, are strongly influenced by Palladianism: his *Casa Muzzi*, Riello (1770), is based on the *Villino Cerato di Montecchio Precalcino* (1540s), while the *Palazzo Franceschini a San Marco*, Vicenza (1770), though essentially Palladian in composition, betrays certain tentative

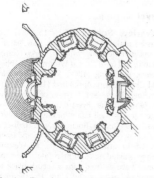

Plan showing elliptical *nave* surrounded by chapels with *high-altar* on the short axis opposite the entrance, *Sant'Andrea al Quirinale*, Rome.

aspects of *Neo-Classicism. In the last decade of his life his work became more severe (e.g. *Palazzo Braghetta sul Corso* (1780) and *Teatro Eretenio* (1781–4)).

Bertotti-Scamozzi (1776–83, 1797); K-K (1983); Olivato (1975)

Berty, Thomas (*c*.1485–1555) English master-mason, engaged at the Priory of St Mary Overie, Southwark, including the top *stage of what is now the tower of Southwark Cathedral. He worked (1530s) on the *vaults of the *presbytery *aisles of Winchester Cathedral, Hants., was in charge of Royal building-works at Calshot Castle and Cowes Castle, IoW, and built Hurst Castle (1540s). He seems to have been a key figure in the transformation of *Perp. into *Tudor-*Renaissance, as can be seen in the *chantry-chapels of **Bishops Fox** and **Gardiner**, Winchester Cathedral.

J.Harvey (1987)

Bestelmeyer, German (1874–1942) German traditionalist architect, best known as one of the founders of *Der *Block*, and as a critic of *Modernism. A pupil of *Thiersch, he designed several buildings, remodelled existing ones at the University of Munich (1906–22), was responsible for the German Pavilion at the International Art Exhibition, Rome (1911), and extended the *Germanisches Nationalmuseum*, Nuremberg (1914–19). He won the competition to design a House of Friendship, Istanbul, Turkey (1916—unrealized), and during the inter-war period designed several large projects, including the *Luftwaffe* District Headquarters Building, Munich (1933–9), all simplified Neo-Classical in style.

Hegemann (1929); Lane (1985); Rittich (1938); Heinz Thiersch (1961)

Béthune, Jean-Baptiste-Charles-François, Baron (1821–94) Belgian architect, known as the '*Pugin of Belgium', because of his *Gothic-Revival expertise and his associations with the Pugin clan. He established a team of craftsmen which executed his designs, and gave the Revival in Belgium its own Flemish character, while maintaining contacts with other Goths in England, France, Germany, Austria, and Italy. Two of his best creations are the *Vivenkapelle* complex, near Brugge (1860–9), and the Castle of *Caloen-de-Gourcy*, Loppem (1857–63), but his chief importance lies in the training and encouragement he gave to others in promoting the Revival in his country.

BN, xxxvi (1879), 350; *Handelingen van de Koninklijke Geschieden Oudheidkundige Kring van Kortrijk*, xxxiv (1965), 3–101, and lxvii (1979), 267–355; Helbig (1906); Loo (ed.) (2003); J.Maeyer (ed.) (1998); PM

Betjeman, Sir John (1906–84) English poet/writer, his *Ghastly Good Taste* (1933) reflected concerns about the destruction of fine buildings, Victorian churches, railway stations, and leafy suburbs. He was among those who founded (1958) The Victorian Society, which sought to preserve buildings such as Philip *Hardwick's *Doric *propylaeum*, Euston Station (1836–40—philistinely demolished 1962), and 'Great' *Scott's Midland Grand Hotel, St Pancras (1868–74—saved). His celebration of incense-scented polychrome Anglican churches, Victorian architecture generally, and the hitherto unsung charms of 'Metroland' (the suburbs served by London's railways) touched chords, and his poetry enjoyed phenomenal success.

Hillier (2002); *ODNB* (2004); J.T (1996)

béton *Concrete. *Béton brut* is raw concrete, exposed after the *formwork is struck, sometimes showing impressions of the timber boards of which formwork is constructed.

Bettino, Antonio (*fl*.1650–80) Italian architect who designed *San Filippo Neri*, Chieri (1664–73), and *Santi Maurizio e Lazzaro*, Turin (1679–1704—generally agreed to be his greatest work). He was also responsible for *San Filippo Neri*, Turin (begun 1675), but *Guarini took this over.

Pommer (1967); Tamburini (1968)

Betto, Giovanni (*known as* **Jean**) (1647–1722) The Betto family provided architects who practised in and around Nancy, Lorraine, in C17 and C18. Jean is the most celebrated, remembered as architect to the *Benedictine Order in Lorraine, and for the interior design of the Cathedral (1699–1736), but his son and grandson also practised in the Nancy area.

Bauchal (1887); Ha (1950)

bevel *See* CHAMFER.

Beverley, Robert of (*fl*.1253–85) English master-mason, he worked on the *choir and *transept of Beverley *Minster, Yorks. (completed *c*.1260), and from 1253 at Westminster Abbey and Palace, becoming (1260) King's Master-Mason and Chief Mason. Appointed (1271) Surveyor of the Royal Works at the Tower of London (where he designed the Byward and Middle towers, together with their beautiful internal *vaults), the *castles of Windsor, Rochester, and Hadleigh, and the manors of Guildford, Kempton, and Havering, his works and contributions at Westminster Abbey (including the first four *bays of the *nave) have assured him a secure place in the history of English architecture. He was no mean sculptor, either, and was responsible for the image (1276) of **King Henry III** (*r*.1216–72) from which the famous *effigy was copied.

J.Harvey (1987)

Beyaert, Henri (1823–94) Belgian architect, who, like his contemporary *Balat, made an eclectic contribution to *fin-de-siècle* architecture in Brussels: he often employed a harmonious blending of white-and-blue *masonry and brick, and was particularly interested in the use of iron in architecture. He was fluent in the *Renaissance-Revival style, drawing on French and Flemish precedents. Among his works may be mentioned the *'Hier is't in der Kater en de Kat'*, *Adolphe Max-laan*, Brussels (1874), Tournai (Doornik) Railway Station (1874–9), and his masterpiece, the *Banque Nationale*, Brussels (1875–9—with *turrets, *lucarnes, and steeply-pitched roofs). His assistants included *Hankar and *Horta.

Beyaert (1880–92); Kennes *et al.* (1978); Loo (ed.) (2003); Martiny (1980); PM; Puttemans *et al.* (1976); Vanderperren & Victoir (1992)

Bianchi, Pietro (1787–1849) Italian Neo-Classical architect. A pupil of *Cagnola, he was responsible for *San Francesco di Paola*, Naples (1817–31), with its high windowless *drum, *Pantheon-like *dome, and serenely beautiful interior. Much influenced by French precedent, the curved *colonnades on either side of the *portico, based on *Bernini's *Piazza di San Pietro* in Rome, were designed by **Leopoldo Laperuta** (1771–1858) and **Antonio de Simone** (1759–1822) from 1808 for an earlier scheme proposed under the French occupation.

Ms (1966); M & Wa (1987); Ossana Cavadini (1995)

Bianco *or* **Bianchi, Bartolommeo** (*c*.1590–1657) Como-born architect who worked in the *Baroque style in Genoa. His Jesuit College, now the University (1630–6), built on a dramatically sloping site, has a staircase rising from the vaulted entrance-vestibule to the *arcaded *cortile* at the far end of which is a splendid symmetrical double *stair rising the full height of the building. The chief influence on Bianco was *Alessi, who also constructed *palazzi* on sloping sites.

D.Wa (1986); Wi (1982)

Bibiena *See* GALLI DA BIBIENA.

Bicknell, Julian (1945–) *See* NEW CLASSICISM.

bicocca Small *castle or tower on a hill.

Bidlake, William Henry (1861–1938) Son of Wolverhampton church-architect **George Bidlake** (1829–92), he established a Birmingham practice (1887) with **John Cotton** (1844–after

1914). He designed several fine late *Arts-and-Crafts houses, one of which (his own), 'Woodgate', 37 Hartopp Road, Sutton Coldfield, was published in *Muthesius's *Das Englische Haus*.

A.S.Gray (1985); H.M (1979, 2007)

Bidonville Shanty town built of oil-drums, petrol-tins, etc. (from *bidon*, meaning an oil-drum or petrol-tin): by association, any collection of houses or shelters constructed of scrap-metal.

OED Supplement, I (1987), 254

Biedermeier Central European style of architecture, decorative arts, painting, and interior design (*c*.1815–*c*.1860), especially in Berlin, Vienna, and Munich. The name derives from the fictional (1854) character, **Wieland Gottlieb Biedermaier**, a comfortable, middle-class figure of fun, *Bieder* meaning virtuous, and *Maier* being a common German surname. The style was robustly comfortable, decently proportioned, essentially *Neo-Classical, with *Empire and *Regency touches.

COF (1988); Gentil (ed.) (1990)

Biegański, Piotr (1905–86) Polish architect, he contributed to the restoration of Warsaw's Old Town (1947–54), and helped, with *Zachwatowicz, to evolve Polish theories of *conservation. He prepared (1952) prizewinning designs for the new opera house in Leipzig, Germany, but the building erected (1956–60) under the direction of the German architects **Kunz Nierade** (1901–76) and **Kurt Hemmerling** (1898–1977) owed little to his work. He wrote on many aspects of historic buildings.

Biegański (1972); Puget (ed.) (1994); Wz Poly (1967)

biforate window Type of medieval window, common in Italy, with a *colonnette subdividing it into two arched *lights, also called a *Venetian arch or *bifore*.

biforis, biforus (*pl.* **bifora**) **1.** *Antique two-leaved *door or window according to *Vitruvius. **2.** Building or room with two doors or other openings.

Bigelow, Jacob (1786–1879) Rumford Professor of Medicine at Harvard University, responsible for the design of Mount Auburn Cemetery, Cambridge, MA, with its *Egyptian-Revival gateway and lodges (1831–42). It was the first *garden-cemetery in the USA.

Carrott (1978); J.Curl (2005); Linden (2007)

Bigio, Nanni di Baccio (1512/13–68) Florentine architect, he settled (1540s) in Rome, and designed the *Porta del Pòpolo* (1561–5), unquestionably his best work. Appointed (1567) Architect to the Papal Palace for life, he supervised construction of the *Castel Sant'Angelo*, various fortifications, and *San Martino degli Svizzeri* (1568).

An (1986); Wi & Jaffé (eds) (1972)

Bijhouwer, Jan Thijs Pieter (1898–1974) *Modernist landscape architect, among the first in The Netherlands (aware of uneasy ambiguities between Modernism and landscape), who studied under **H.F.Hartogh Heys van Zouteveen** (1870–1943—pioneer of scientific approaches to the subject), giving him a greater understanding of the reactions of plants to soil conditions. He joined the Rotterdam planning department and the local branch of *CIAM (a curious move which seemed to run counter to his belief in 'back to nature and native art'). Sympathetic to the *Delft School (notably the work of *Granpré Molière at the *Garden Suburb of Vreewijk (1913–21)), Bijhouwer contributed (from 1932) a course on Dutch landscapes at the *Technische Hogeschool*, Delft, as well as collaborating with Granpré Molière on the *Wieringermeer*, the first of the new *Ijsselmeer* *polders. He published (1938) theories about the relationships between buildings and landscapes in *De 8 en Opbouw*, and had special interests in planting design based on phytogeographic principles (the geography of plant distribution), becoming (1946) the first professor of garden and landscape architecture in The Netherlands. Works included the *Hoge Veluwe* National Park and Kröller-Müller *sculpture-garden; Resistance Cemetery, Overveen; Memorial Garden, Putten; and *Het Nederlandse Landschap* (1972).

Bijhouwer (1972); Shoe (2001); Tay (2006); Wolschke-Bulmahn (1997)

bilection *See* BOLECTION.

Bill, Max (1908–94) Swiss architect, he trained at the Dessau *Bauhaus (1927–9) and designed (1940s) many timber houses, but also revived (from 1950) the Bauhaus programme at the *Hochschule für Gestaltung*, Ulm, Germany, for which he designed a new building (1950–5). Other work included the Swiss Pavilions at the World's Fair, New York (1938), the Milan *Triennale* (1951), and the Venice *Biennale* (1952); the Ulm City Pavilion, Baden-Württemberg Exhibition, Stuttgart (1955); and the *Bilden und Gestalten* section, Swiss National Exhibition, Lausanne (1964). He published prolix material on aspects of *Modernism.

Bill (1945, 1949, 1952, 1955, 1969); Frei (1991); Hüttinger (1977); Maldonado (1955); Staber (1964)

billet One of a series of short chamfered, cylindrical (resembling short lengths of dowel), prismatic, rectangular, segmental, or square projecting members in, or forming, a decorative continuous *moulding, its axis parallel to the direction of the series, with

sometimes two or more rows of this ornament placed one above the other, with the billets of one row alternating with those of the other, characteristic of *Romanesque architecture.

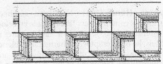

alternating cubical billets, St Augustine, Canterbury, Kent.

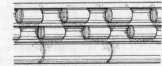

cylindrical billets, Binham Priory, Norfolk.

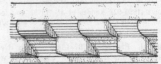

half-cylindrical and prismatic billets, St Mary de Castro, Leicester.

billet (*after Parker*).

Billing, Hermann (1867–1946) German architect of houses and fine interiors in the early C20, often in a zestful *Jugendstil* manner. He evolved a massive simplified *Rundbogenstil* shortly afterwards. His buildings include the *Rathaus*, Kiel (1907–11), the powerful *Kunsthalle*, Mannheim (1905–7), and University buildings, Freiburgim-Breisgau (1907–11). In the 1920s he turned to a simplified *Neo-Classicism.

Billing (1904); K.Martin (1930)

Billings, Robert William (1813–74) English architect, known for his fine draughtsmanship, e.g. *History and Description of St Paul's Cathedral* (1837), *Churches of London* (1839), and *Durham Cathedral* (1843). His most celebrated work was *Baronial and Ecclesiastical Antiquities of Scotland* (1845–52), a major sourcebook of the *Scottish-Baronial style. He also published on *Gothic architecture, and had an extensive practice, specializing in restoration. He designed Castle Wemyss, Renfrewshire, various works at Dalzell Castle, Motherwell, Lanarkshire (1859), the inventive Church of St John, Crosby-on-Eden, Cumb. (1854), and a fine monument to Peter *Nicholson (1856) in Carlisle Cemetery.

Billings (1845–52); Hyde & Pe (2010); *ODNB* (2004)

binder Main *binding-beam* or *-joist* supported on walls, *piers, *girders, or *breastsummers, carrying the bridging-joists above and ceiling-joists below.

Bindesbøll, Michael Gottlieb Birkner (1800–56) Danish Neo-Classical architect. In Paris (1820s) he was influenced by the new theories of Classical *polychromy, and after a period working as an architectural assistant and studying in Copenhagen (1824–33), he spent several years travelling before returning to the Danish capital to work on his masterpiece, the museum in Copenhagen (1839–47) to house **Bertel Thorvaldsen's** (1770–1844) sculptures. Bindesbøll's designs were selected and finalized (1839–40): the completed building has five Graeco-Egyptian *battered or *Vitruvian openings on the entrance-front, set *in antis*, as it were, between *antae and under an *Ionic *entablature from which the *frieze has been elided. This *portico seems to have been derived from a synthesis of *Schinkel's first project for the *Neue Wache, Unter den Linden* (1816), mixed with his *Lustgarten* Museum-front, both in Berlin. Similar battered motifs are repeated (to a smaller scale) on two storeys around the windows of the side-walls. The *stucco exterior is painted ochre, with architectural elements picked out in blue, green, and white, and the vaulted interiors painted red, green, and ochre are admirable settings for the white *marble sculptures. The airy central courtyard (in which Thorvaldsen's body was buried) has its surrounding walls painted with images of trees: these murals create a memorable backdrop to the sculptor's grave. On three sides of the building is a painted frieze, set just above the *plinth, that depicts the transportation of the exhibits from Rome to Copenhagen. The Museum made an important contribution to the C19 debate about polychromy in Classical architecture. Bindesbøll also designed a lunatic-asylum near Aarhus, a complex of simple brick buildings set in a specially created landscape intended to benefit patients by its serenity (1850–1); another mental hospital at Oringa, Zeeland (1854–7); the Town Halls of Thisted (1851–3), Flensburg (1852), Stege (1853–4), and Naestved (1855–6); and the Medical Association housing-block, Copenhagen (1853–5), all of which were accomplished works. His son, **Thorvald** (1846–1908), was also an architect, and became the most prolific of designers in the *Art-Nouveau style: he also designed the Carlsberg Lager-Beer label.

Bramsen (1959); Bruun & Fenger (1892); Mi (1960); Wanscher (1903)

biomorph Form based on a living object. *Animal, Biomorphic*, or *Zoömorphic architecture* draws on non-geometrical naturally occurring forms, as in certain aspects of *Organic architecture. An example is **Santiago Calatrava Valls's**

(1951–) Milwaukee Art Museum, WI (2000–3), based on the wings of a bird in flight. In such architecture grids were replaced by blobs (*see* BLOBISMUS), and the rigid lines of *International Modernism gave way to curving forms and undulating roofs. In some cases critics detected allusions to specific creatures, e.g. the reptilian exterior of **Future Systems's** Selfridge's Store, Birmingham (2003) *see* KAPLICKY.

Aldersley-Williams (2003); Field (1999); Future Systems (1996); Pawley (1994)

Biotecture Architecture influenced by biology, e.g. the work of *Soleri. *See* ARCOLOGY.

bipeda *Tile two Roman feet long.

bird-cage *or* **-house** *See* AVIARY.

bird's-beak *Moulding, the *section of which consists of an *ovolo at the top under which is an *ogee or hollow, forming a sharp point at the junction of the two: the section resembles a *bird's beak*. Common in *Renaissance work. *Related terms include*:

bird's-head: *see* BEAK-HEAD;

bird's-mouth: triangular right-angled notch formed in the end of a timber (e.g. *rafter) to enable it to be securely fixed to a rectangular timber (e.g. a wall-plate).

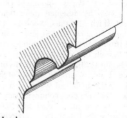

bird's-beak

bitumen 1. Type of mineral pitch used for *mortar and waterproofing, similar to *asphalt(e), called *bitumen judaicum*. **2.** Natural pitchy substance similar to tar consisting mostly of hydrocarbons varying in colour and hardness, which melts when heated and sets hard. When it is mixed (either naturally occurring or artificially) with *limestone, shale, etc., it is called *rock asphalt* and has been used for road-surfacing from the late C18.

W.McKay (1957)

Blackburn, James (1803–54) English-born Australian architect. Transported (1835) to Van Diemen's Land for forging a cheque, he was employed by the Department of Roads and Bridges, and directed much road-building and engineering work. From 1839 he designed numerous buildings in which an *Italianate style influenced by *Loudon's publications was much in evidence, notably in the Rosedale extension of Campbell Town (1848–50). His Lady Franklin Museum, Hobart (1842–3), was a distinguished essay in Greek *Doric, but he could turn his hand to *Gothic (influenced by the works of J.L.*Archer), and *Norman Revival (influenced by *Ferrey and others). He moved to Melbourne (1849), where he became City Surveyor, in which capacity he designed the Town Hall. His large and eclectic library was one of the first major architectural collections to be formed in Australia.

Kobayashi *et al.* (1996); Tanner (ed.) (1981); J.T (1996).

Blackburn, William (1750–90) English architect, he made his name as a designer of prisons following the Penitentiary Act (1779—19 Geo.III, c.74): They include the County Gaols at Oxford (c.1785–1805), Ipswich, Suffolk (1786–90), Monmouth (1788–90), and Dorchester, Dorset (1789–95). He was also responsible for the Houses of Correction at Northleach (1787–91), and Horsley (1787–91), both Glos., among others.

Co (2008); *ODNB* (2004)

Blacket, Edmund Thomas (1817–83) English-born architect who settled (1842) in Sydney, and became a leading member of the profession in New South Wales. Appointed Diocesan Architect (1847), he designed more than fifty churches, of which All Saints, Woollahra (1874), St Mark, Darling Point (1847–75), and St Andrew's Cathedral (from c.1847, all in Sydney, and the Cathedral Church of St George, Perth, Western Australia (begun 1879), may be cited. His masterpiece is the *Tudor-*Gothic University of Sydney (1854–60), the great hall of which is based on Westminster Hall, London, complete with *hammer-beam roof structure. He also designed St Paul's College at the University, also Gothic, but he could turn his hand to *Classicism as well, as at his extensions to Sydney Grammar School (1856). From the 1850s his office became an important factor in the training of young Australian architects. In later years he was assisted by his son, **Cyril** (1857–1937), and the practice continued until the 1930s.

Ck (1996); Herman (1954, 1963); *Jnl. Proc. Royal Australian Hist. Soc.*, xxxii (1946), 145–72; Kerr (1983); J.T (1996); Vine Hall (1983)

black house House of turf, without windows or chimney, usually thatched, found in the Western Isles of Scotland.

blade 1. *Back or principal *rafter. **2.** Main element of a *cruck *truss.

Blaikie, Thomas (1750–1838) Scots botanist/ landscape-gardener, mentioned in *Loudon's *Encyclopaedia* as an important gardener in France, having established himself in Paris (1776). Associated with the creation of several celebrated French gardens, notably those at *Bagatelle* (with *Bélanger), *Monceau*, and *Le Petit Trianon*, he was also significant as a collector of Alpine plants for **Dr John Fothergill** (1712–80) and **Dr William Pitcairn** (1711–91), and contributed many pieces to Loudon's *Gardener's Magazine.*

HHH (1980); Racine (ed.) (2001); Patricia Taylor (2001)

Blair, John (1820–1906) Scots-born landscape-gardener, he emigrated (1851) to North America, where (1854) he was commissioned to design gardens for a new house at Rockford, IL (which later passed to the ownership of **Robert Tinker** (1836–1924—landscape-designer), and is known for its large (27-room) *Swiss cottage (1856—now a museum). Blair's horticultural exhibit in Chicago, IL (1865), brought him to the notice of *Olmsted et al., and he was appointed superintendent of Chicago parks, creating the West Side system. He also designed gardens in the Chicago suburb of Oak Park, including his own home and that of **Henry Warren Austin** (1828–89) with whom he travelled (1871) to Colorado Springs. There he was introduced to **General William Jackson Palmer** (1836–1909), railway magnate and founder of that city, who commissioned him to design the layout, including parks, *cemeteries, roads, and Palmer's own estate, Glen Eyrie, using rocks, trees, water, and *rustic features to create a 'natural' landscape. A trained mason, he built a *bridge and designed a road through the Garden of the Gods between Manitou Springs and Glen Eyrie. Blair finally settled (1881) in Victoria, B.C., where he designed Beacon Hill Park and other works.

B & K (2000); pk

Blanc, Hippolyte-Jean (1844–1917) Scots architect, son of French parents. Articled to David *Rhind, he subsequently joined (1864) the Office of Works, and won (1875) the competition to design Christ Church, Morningside, Edinburgh, followed by Mayfield Free Church (built 1876–9), both in a French-*Gothic style. His masterpiece is Coats Memorial Baptist Church, Paisley (1885), with *crossing-tower topped by a *crown *spire. His Parish Church of St Cuthbert, Edinburgh (1892–5—in a mixed *Renaissance style, retaining the C18 *steeple of its predecessor), contains sumptuous furnishings. Other buildings include Mayville Gardens, Trinity, Edinburgh (1881); works at Edinburgh Castle; panels for John Knox House in the Royal Mile (1880s); and from the same period St Cuthbert's Wholesale Association Offices, Fountainbridge (*Baronial: turreted and dormered). He was one of the most interesting architects working in late-C19 Scotland.

GMcW & W (1984)

Bland, William (c.1796–1869) Kentish land-owner, author of a book dealing with principles of building arches, *buttresses, *piers, etc., based on a series of articles published in *Loudon's *Architectural Magazine*. It also discusses several works in Rochester, Kent, including *bridges, the Cathedral, and various churches (e.g. Sittingbourne).

Bland (1839)

blank *Blind, meaning with no openings. *Blank door* or *window* is a sealed recess with the appearance of a door or window placed to create symmetry in a *façade. A *blank, blind,* or *dead wall* has no apertures.

blazon Written description of armorial bear-ings. *See* ACHIEVEMENT OF ARMS.

blind 1. As *blank. Anything *engaged or attached to a wall, with no openings or glazing, used decoratively, such as an *arcade or *tracery, is described as *blind*, as in a *blind arcade* or *blind tracery*. A *blind storey* is a wall *façade at the top of a building, essentially a raised *parapet, with-out rooms behind it, and unroofed, employed for architectural effect to conceal, e.g., a roof. It also can refer to a *tribune in a church. **2.** Device for partially or wholly preventing light from passing through an opening, such as a piece of flexible material attached at the top to a roller on which it is unwound or wound, or a *screen with fixed or moveable slats (*Venetian blind*).

Blobismus, Blobism Late-C20–early-C21 fash-ion for anti-urban, anti-contextual buildings resem-bling large blobs with reptile-like carapaces: they may have scales, but lack scale. *See* BIOMORPH.

J.Waters (2003)

blocage Mass of *rubble-stones of various sizes mixed with *mortar, often used inside the *dressed faces of *Romanesque walls and *piers. It was not always stable.

block 1. Piece of *masonry, *terracotta, etc., prepared for building and bigger than a brick. **2.** In Classical detailing, rectangular plain element at the bottom of a door-architrave, also stopping the *skirt or *plinth. **3.** Row or mass of buildings connected together, as in a *terrace, set against a street on the front and bounded by other streets, often of mixed use. **4.** Most significant building in an architectural composition, e.g. a *corps-de-logis with *wings. **5.** One of a series of projecting blocks on *architraves, columns, or *pilasters as in a *Gibbs surround: in such cases the architrave, column, or pilaster is said to be *banded* or *blocked. See* BAND. **6.** Small triangular piece of

timber in the angle between two other timbers, e.g. at the top of two *cruck *blades. *Related terms include*:

block-capital: *cushion *capital;

block-cornice: Italian *Renaissance *entablature with a series of plain undecorated *modillions treated as *corbels supporting a normal *cor-nice, often with the *bed-mouldings suppressed, or converted into a simplified architrave;

blocked: column, pilaster, Gibbs surround, etc., in which projecting blocks interrupt and pro-ject from the column, pilaster, or architrave. *See* BAND, GIBBS SURROUND;

blocking-course: **1.** *masonry or brickwork laid on a cornice to hold the latter down, as large pro-jecting cornices are effectively *cantilevers, and need weights to anchor them; **2.** course of stone or brick forming a projecting band with-out *mouldings at the base of a building, i.e. an unmoulded *plinth; **3.** plain band or *string-course;

blocking-out: **1.** *boasting in masonry; **2.** prepara-tion for a finish on a wall by means of timber grounds or *battens;

block-plan: drawing of buildings and layouts in simplified, undetailed form.

Block, Der Group of German traditionalist architects formed (1928) to resist the *Modernist *Ring group. Its origins lay in acrimony that arose when *Bonatz prepared a plan at the behest of the *Deutscher Werkbund* for its housing exhibition in Stuttgart, in which buildings with pitched roofs were proposed, but, following ferocious disputes, *Mies van der Rohe's *Weissenhofsiedlung* flat-roofed solution was accepted. Bonatz and his colleague, **Paul Schmitthenner** (1884–1972), withdrew in protest, and, with other architects, including *Bestelmeyer and Paul *Schultze-Naumburg, formed *Der Block*, proposing an architecture *responsive to regional and national conditions*, and suited to the tastes and needs of ordinary people rather than ideologically imposed upon an unwilling populace by a Leftist coterie.

T & DC (1986); Teut (ed.) (1967)

block-house Structure, frequently of timber, often for defensive purposes, constructed of logs.

Blom, Holger (1906–96) Swedish landscape architect. As Director of Parks in Stockholm, he instituted a comprehensive plan for landscaping the city (1937–72). His ideas have been widely adopted since the 1939–45 war.

E (1994)

Blom, Piet (1934–99) Amsterdam-born archi-tect who became one of the most important protagonists of Dutch *Structuralism. He is best known for the '*Kasbah*' housing at Hengelo

(1965–73) and *'t Speelhuis* centre and housing at Helmond (1975–8).

E (1994)

Blomfield, Sir Arthur William (1829–99) English architect. After the obligatory Continental tour, he established a successful London practice. His best-known works are the skilful rebuilding of the *nave and south *transept of St Mary Overie (now Southwark Cathedral), in the *Gothic style (1890–7—after its execrable treatment (1839–40) at the clumsy hands of **Henry Rose** (d.1853), caricatured by *Pugin in *Contrasts* (1836)); the *Italianate *basilica of St Barnabas, Jericho, Oxford, with a fine *Gothic *campanile* (1869–87); and the Chapel at Tyntesfield, Som. (1873–5—inspired by *Sainte-Chapelle*, Paris, and 'Great' *Scott's Exeter College Chapel, Oxford).

ODNB (2004)

Blomfield, Charles James (1862–1932) Eldest son/pupil of Sir Arthur *Blomfield, he carried out sensitive works at St Cross, Winchester 1899–1904), and his new buildings include the dining hall, etc., at Wellington College, Crowthorne, Berks. (1906–7—in a Free-*Renaissance style).

A.S.Gray (1985)

Blomfield, Sir Reginald Theodore (1856–1942) Cousin of C.J.*Blomfield, he entered (1881) the office of his uncle, Sir Arthur *Blomfield, before setting up (1884) his own London practice. He began writing and drawing for publication, and was involved in the founding of the *Art-Workers' Guild. He designed the warehouse at Greycoat Place, Westminster, for the Army and Navy Stores (1895), various buildings at Lady Margaret Hall, Oxford (1896–1915), the former United Universities Club, Suffolk Street, London (1906–7—in his *Champs-Élysées* style), and the Regent Street Quadrant and part of Piccadilly Circus, London (1917–28). Other works were the 'Cross of Sacrifice' erected in numerous war cemeteries (with the design of which he was also involved) and the Menin Gate, Ieper, Belgium (1922–6). His writings include *The Formal Garden in England* (1892); *A History of Renaissance Architecture in England, 1500–1800* (1897—a sourcebook for the *Wrenaissance and *Georgian Revival); *A History of French Architecture, 1494–1774* (1911–21); *Memoirs of an Architect* (1932); and elegant studies of *Vauban (1938) and Norman *Shaw (1940). He published a scathingly witty attack on fashionable *International *Modernism then being promoted by the *AR*: it was called, appropriately, *Modernismus* (1934). His garden-designs were the antitheses of styles promoted by *Jekyll and William *Robinson.

Blomfield (1892, 1897, 1932, 1934, 1938, 1940, 1974); Fellows (1985); A.S.Gray (1985); *ODNB* (2004)

Blomstedt, Aulis (1906–79) Finnish architect/theoretician, whose architecture has been influential. His apartment-blocks and *terrace-houses at Tapiola, Espoo (1962–5), are boldly conceived, with strong, rhythmic patterns.

Pallasmaa (ed.) (1980); Salokorpi (1970); Tempel (1968)

Blond, Jean-Baptiste-Alexandre Le (1679–1719) French architect, trained in Paris, where he built the *Hôtel de Clermont, Rue de Varennes* (1708–14). His architecture is perhaps best appreciated in the Reynault House, Châtillon-sur-Bagneux (c.1709–14). He was engaged (1716–17) by **Tsar Peter I** ('the Great'—r.1682–1725) to superintend works at St Petersburg, Russia, where he introduced the *Rococo style at the palace of *Peterhof (later extended by *Rastrelli). A fine draughtsman, he prepared illustrations for **Michel Félibien**'s (1666–1719) history of *Saint-Denis* (1706), *Dézallier d'Argenville's *La Théorie et le Pratique du Jardinage* (1709), and **Augustin-Charles d'Aviler's** (1653–1701) *Cours complet d'architecture…* in the 1710 edn, which he edited.

Ga (1972, 1972a); Ha (1950); Kimball (1980); Mariette (1927–9); J.T (1996)

Blondel, Jacques-François (1705–74) French architect/teacher/theorist/writer, he revered French architecture, especially works of *Gabriel, *Mansart, and *Perrault. His School of Architecture, opened in Paris (1743), included among its students *Boullée, *Chambers, *Ledoux, and de *Wailly. Appointed (1762) Professor at the *Académie Royale d'Architecture*, his lectures and theories were set out in his *Cours d'architecture* (1771–7), completed by *Patte. His many books included the encyclopedia of French buildings, *L'Architecture Françoise…* (1752–6), and *Discours sur la Manière d'étudier l'Architecture* (1747, 1754). Among his surviving works are part of the *Place des Armes*, Metz (1760s), and a *screen in Strasbourg Cathedral (c.1767). His son, **Georges-François Blondel** (c.1730–92), was an engraver whose work helped to popularize views of Romantic ruins, and even of unfashionable *Baroque architecture; and another architect-son, **Jean-Baptiste Blondel** (1764–1825), worked for the City of Paris.

Blondel & Patte (1771–7); B (1980); Eriksen (1974); Ga (1972a); Ha (1950); Hn (1962); E.Ka (1955); Picon (1992); Prost (1860); Ry (1980)

Blondel, Jean-François (1683–1756) French architect/engineer, he designed (early 1720s) the *Hôtel Mallet, Place St-Pierre*, and the Lullin House, both in Geneva, Switzerland: these and other designs by him were published in *L'Architecture Française* (1727–38), by **Jean Mariette**

(*c.*1654–1742). His work is regarded as exemplary *Régence*.

Mariette (1927–9)

Blondel, Nicolas-François (1617–86) French military-engineer/mathematician, he became the first Director of the Royal Academy of Architecture and *Ingénieur du Roi*. His *Cours d'Architecture* (1675, 1683, and 1698) was an important architectural textbook in which the *Orders were given prominence, and the principles of *Classicism and rational approaches to architecture were promoted and explained. He did not design many buildings but was responsible for the huge monumental Parisian *Portes*, those of *St-Antoine*, *St-Bernard*, and *St-Denis* (all 1671).

Blondel (1698); Bt (1982); Ha (1948); Hn (1973); Mauclair *et al.* (1983); Teyssèdre (1967)

Blore, Edward (1787–1879) English architect, he contributed to the designs of **Sir Walter Scott's** (1771–1832) Abbotsford, Roxburghshire (although the lion's share was by William *Atkinson), provided the architectural drawings for *The Provincial Antiquities and Picturesque Scenery of Scotland*, and published *The Monumental Remains of Noble and Eminent Persons* (1824). He established himself as a reliable architect, designing the Mall front (destroyed) and other works at Buckingham Palace (1832–7), becoming Surveyor to Westminster Abbey (1827–49), and carrying out alterations at Hampton Court and Windsor Castle. He built up an enormous practice, designing country-houses in *Tudor and *Elizabethan styles (Crom Castle, Co. Fermanagh, Ireland (1838–41), is a good example), and building and restoring churches. Among his most important designs were the completion of the north wing of Daniel *Robertson's University Press, Walton Street, Oxford (1829–30), Trinity Hospital, Retford, Lincs. (1832–3), the Watt Institution and Library, Union Street, Greenock (1846), the Preacher's and Pensioner's Courts, Charterhouse, London (1839–42), Freeland House, Perthshire (1825–6—later Strathallan School), and sundry others listed by *Colvin.

Blore (1826); Co (2008); *ODNB* (2004); Temple (2010)

Blouet, Guillaume-Abel (1795–1853) French architect/theorist. He travelled to Greece (1828) and prepared studies of the *Doric temple at Aegina (published 1838), showing the building brilliantly coloured (with *Gilbert and *Hittorff, Blouet was an important protagonist in arguments concerning colour in Greek architecture). His reputation as a scholar was further enhanced by his *Restauration des thermes d'Antonin Caracalla à Rome* (1828). He worked with Gilbert in Rome and later in Paris, where he was appointed (1831) architect to *Chalgrin's *Arc de Triomphe*

de l'Étoile (with Gilbert as his deputy): he added the *Attic storey, supervised the sculpture, and altered the *Empire* character to a more energetic *Classicism.

Blouet determined to use architecture to further social and moral aims, and his ideas were developed from those of **François-Marie-Charles Fourier** (1772–1837) and **Claude-Henri de Rouvroy, Comte de Saint-Simon** (1760–1825). He toured (1836) America to look at *prisons, and on his return (1839) designed several corrective institutions, including the penal farm colony at Mettray, near Tours, and he became recognized as an authority on prison design. His utilitarian aims were promoted through his teaching, and he succeeded (1846) L.-P.*Baltard as Professor of the Theory of Architecture at the *École des *Beaux-Arts*, a post he held until his death. He commenced work (1847) on the *Supplément à la traité théorique et pratique de l'art de bâtir de Jean Rondelet*, essentially a catalogue of early C19 achievements in engineering.

Ha (1943–57); M & Wa (1987); J.T (1996)

Blow, Detmar Jellings (1867–1939) London-born *Arts-and-Crafts architect, he travelled to Italy with *Ruskin (1888), and then worked (1892) for Philip *Webb on St Mary's Church, East Knoyle, Wilts. A member of the *Art-Workers' Guild from 1892, he was Clerk of Works (1897–8) for three cottages by *Gimson in Leics., and then acted in the same capacity for *Lethaby at All Saints Church, Brockhampton, Herefs. (1901–2). He designed a building for the Cheap Cottages Exhibition, Letchworth, Herts. (1905), and from 1906 (when he was in partnership with the *Beaux-Arts* architect **Fernand Billerey** (1878–1951)) worked on numerous town- and country-houses, notably on the **Duke of Westminster's** estates. He designed Wilsford Manor, near Salisbury, Wilts. (1904–6—his best house in the Arts-and-Crafts style), and Happisburgh Manor, Cromer, Norfolk (1900—a flint-and-brick house on a *butterfly plan with thatched roof), as well as carrying out repairs and alterations to numerous churches.

A.S.Gray (1985); Me.Miller (2002); *ODNB* (2004); J.T (1996)

Bloxam, Matthew Holbeche (1805–88) English antiquary, and a major authority on ecclesiological/liturgiological matters. Influenced by *Rickman, he published (1829) the first edition of *The Principles of Gothic Ecclesiastical Architecture*, a remarkable achievement for one in his twenties: several years earlier than *Pugin's publications, and twenty years ahead of those of J.H. *Parker, it went into many edns and assured Bloxam's place in the *Gothic Revival. Prompted by 'Great' *Scott, Bloxam revised and expanded the work, and the eleventh edition was published in London (1882): illustrated with numerous admirable woodcuts by **Thomas Orlando Sheldon Jewitt** (1799–1869), it stands as one of the most scholarly texts of *Ecclesiology and the Revival.

Bloxam (1882); J.Curl (2002, 2007); *ODNB* (2004)

Blum, Hans (*fl.*1550) German compiler of an influential, much-published work on the *Orders based on *Serlio, *Quinque Columnarum exacta descriptio atque deliniatio cum symmetrica earum distributione* (1550), later published in London as *The Book of Five Collumnes of Architecture... Gathered... by H. Bloome out of Antiquities*, of which the 1608 edn was probably the finest. Some German edns also contained *designs* by Blum.

H.Blum (1550); E.Hs (1990)

Bo & Wohlert Danish architectural firm established by **Jørgen Bo** (1919–99) and **Vilhelm Wohlert** (1920–2007). Among their works were the Louisiana Museum, Humlebæk, near Elsinore (1958—with subsequent enlargements (1960s, 1980s)); terrace housing at Piniehøj (1962), Rungsted (1964), and Kirstineparken, Hørsholm (1964); the Danish Embassy, Brasília (1973); and the Bochum Museum, Germany (1977–83). Bo designed the IBM Training Centre, Brussels (1969–75—with **Anders Hegelund** (1938–)), and Wohlert carried out several major restoration projects, including *Hansen's Cathedral of Our Lady, Copenhagen (1979).

J.T (1996)

board Thin, long plank of timber no more than 5 cm thick.

board-marked concrete *See* BÉTON.

boast 1. To cut material, especially stone, to the general form, leaving it for later carving into, say, a *capital: such a form, awaiting fine *dressing, is called *boasted* or *bossage*. **2.** To dress stone with a *boaster* or *drove* (a broad chisel): *boasted* or *droved* dressings have regular marks like ribands or small chequers; irregular rough dressings are *random-tooled* or *random-droved*.

boat-house Building near water in which boats are kept. Prominent locations (e.g. beside a lake or river) provided opportunities to make such buildings waterside *eye-catchers (e.g. the *crenellated *Gothic *barge-boarded exemplar at Crom, Co. Fermanagh (*c.*1850), by **George Sudden** (*fl.*1830–50), and the exquisite *Gothick building (1769–70—demolished), Enville, Staffs., with a *banqueting-house* (*see* BANQUET).

Mowl & Barre (2009); Sherriff (2008); Symes (2006)

Boberg, Ferdinand (1860–1946) Swedish architect. His early designs were influenced by

*Viollet-le-Duc's theories as well as by works of H.H.*Richardson and *Sullivan, but his most important achievements were several large civic buildings, including the Central Post Office, Stockholm (1898–1904). He designed the Baltic Exposition Building, Malmö (1914), and numerous private houses, notably the *Villa Bergsgarden* (1905–6). His mature designs were rich in decoration and materials, with simple, bold massing in the Swedish *Neo-Classical tradition, but with exotic allusions in his interpretation of *Art Nouveau. His reputation has been largely eclipsed by the works of *Asplund, *Lewerentz, *Östberg, and *Tengbom, but he was one of the major architectural figures of *National Romanticism in Scandinavia (1884–1915). From the time he closed his office (1915) he recorded much of Sweden's historical architecture in portfolios supported by subscription.

A & B (1986); Ca (1998); Eaton (1972); J.T (1996); Walton (1994)

Böblinger Family South-German mastermasons among whom **Hans** (1412–82) and his son **Matthäus** (d.1505) were the most important. Hans worked under *Ensinger on the *Frauenkirche*, Esslingen on the Neckar. Matthäus, who seems to have been apprenticed at Cologne, joined his father at Esslingen, later becoming master-mason at Ulm *Minster (*c.*1480), where he succeeded Ensinger and designed the upper stages of the spectacular western tower. However, the beautiful octagon and perforated *masonry *spire (the tallest such ensemble in Europe) were only completed (1890s—according to Böblinger's drawings) under **August von Beyer** (1834–99).

Baum (1956); Bucher (1979)

Bodley, George Frederick (1827–1907) English architect, one of the most successful and sensitive of the *Gothic Revival. A student (1840s) of 'Great' *Scott, his first churches include St Michael and All Angels, Brighton (1859–61), an essay in C13 *polychromy of the *'muscular' kind; All Saints', Jesus Lane, Cambridge (1862–9), which marks Bodley's rejection of Continental influences in favour of English *Second Pointed; and St John the Baptist, Tue Brook, Liverpool (1868–71), representing a glowingly refined English C14 Second-Pointed revival of the utmost delicacy, with glorious colour all over the walls, roof, and furnishings (beautifully restored by *Dykes Bower). Bodley was in partnership (1869–97) with Thomas *Garner, designing several churches, including the exquisite and scholarly Holy Angels, Hoar Cross, Staffs. (1872–1900); St Augustine's, Pendlebury, Manchester (1870–4—with the internal *buttress arrangement of Albi Cathedral translated into English Second

Pointed (the *buttresses pierced to form *aisle-passages)); and St Mary the Virgin, Clumber Park, Notts. (1886–9), a cruciform church with a central tower and spire, the ensemble being in Bodley's most elegant flowing Second-Pointed style. Bodley designed most of Clumber on his own, as he did with St Mary's, Eccleston, Ches. (1894–9), again nominally C14 in style, with stone rib-vaulting throughout. His Holy Trinity, Prince Consort Road, Kensington, London (1902), is light and airy, quite unlike his earlier work. His last great church was the Cathedral of Sts Peter and Paul, Washington, DC (1906–76, completed 1990).

B.Clarke (1969); J.Curl (2002, 2007); D & M (1985); Ea (1970); *ODNB* (2004)

Bodley, Sir Josias (c.1550–1617) Exeter-born military engineer, brother of the founder of the Bodleian Library, Oxford. He saw service in Ireland from 1598 in the war (ended 1603) against **Hugh, The O'Neill, 'Great' Earl of Tyrone** (c.1540–1616). Appointed by the Privy Council as Superintendent of Castles in Ireland, he was entrusted (1609) with the survey for the Plantation of Ulster, and became Director-General of the Fortifications and Buildings in Ireland (1612). His largest works were the *ramparts and fortifications of the City of London's new town of Coleraine in the specially created County of Londonderry (colonized by the City and its Livery Companies).

J.Curl (1986, 2000); Loeber (1981)

Bodt, Jean de (1670–1745) Huguenot military engineer/architect who left France after 1685, trained in The Netherlands, arrived in England (1688), served in **King William III**'s (r.1689–1702) army in Ireland (1690–1) and in Flanders (1692–5), and worked for a while in England, producing grand *Baroque designs for Whitehall and Greenwich Palaces (1698), neither of which was realized. He eventually moved (1699) to Berlin (where he was known as **Johann von Bodt** or **von Bott**). He completed (c.1706) the *Baroque *Zeughaus* on *Unter den Linden* (begun by *Nering, with sculptures by *Schlüter), built the great Fortuna Gate of the *Stadtschloss*, Potsdam (1701), and added the *steeple (resembling *Wren's work at St Vedast, Foster Lane, London) to Nering's *Pfarrkirche*, Potsdam (1695–1703). **Thomas Wentworth, Lord Raby** (1672–1739), British envoy to Prussia (1703–11), who had also been involved in King William's many military campaigns, obtained designs from Bodt from which the east wing of Stainborough Hall (Wentworth Castle), Yorks., was built (c.1710–20): the elevation is almost pure Franco-Prussian in style, a considerable rarity in England. Although much of his work in Prussia was concerned with fortifications, he also designed several fine houses,

including the *Schwerin* (1700–2) and *Rademacher* (1701–4) Palaces, Berlin, and *Friedrichstein* (1709–14) and *Dönhoffstadt* (1710–16) *Schlösser*, East Prussia. Bodt moved (1728) to Dresden as Superintendent of the Royal Works, and oversaw construction of Pöppelmann's extensions and restorations of the Dutch (later Japanese) Palace (c.1730). He also designed parts of the castle of *Königstein*, near Dresden (1734–6).

AR, cxxx (July 1961), 34–5; Co (2008); Colombier (1956); E.Hempel (1965); Lorck (1972); J.T (1996)

Boehmer (**Bomer** *after* 1915), **Edward** (1861–1940) PA-born architect, educated in Stuttgart, Hamburg, and Berlin. He set up a practice in London (1889) with **Percy Christian Gibbs** (1864–1904), designing Harley House, Marylebone Road (1904), and Portland Court, 160–200 Great Portland Street (1904–12), both impressive blocks of mansion-flats. 80 Portland Place (1909) has a distinguished Classical *façade with strong French and American influences.

A.S.Gray (1985)

Boer, Willem (**Wim**) **Christiaan Johannes** (1922–2000) Dutch landscape architect, pupil of, among others, *Bijhouwer, and influenced by *Modernists, *CIAM dogma in general, and *Giedion in particular. He worked for the Rotterdam planning department after the 1939–45 war, proposing green open spaces as social areas within settlements and distinct routes for pedestrians and cyclists. His plans for the Pendrecht and Alexanderpolder districts were informed by *De-*Stijl* patterns, and he was an early advocate of 'ecological planting', nurturing a more 'natural' aesthetic. He carried out some 400 projects in town (e.g. The Green Heart, Kampen (1958–79)) and country; private, public, and institutional gardens; *cemeteries (including Doorn (1952) and Epe (1964)); and multi-functional urban spaces in town centres.

Shoe (2001); Tay (2006); Vroom (1995); Vroom & Meeius (eds) (1990)

Boffrand, Gabriel-Germain (1667–1754) French sculptor/architect, he made a fortune designing/building Parisian *hôtels* on ingenious plans with complicated geometries, among them the *Hôtels d'Amelot* (1712–14) and *de Torcy* (1713–15). His *Rococo style was of the utmost refinement, and can best be seen in the charming elliptical rooms he created at the *Hôtel de Soubise*, Paris (1732–9—later the *Archives Nationales*): these were decorated by **François Boucher** (1703–70), **Charles-Joseph Natoire** (1700–77), and **Charles Andrew van Loo** (1705–65). Boffrand's exteriors are deceptively simple and reticent, influenced by *Bernini's *Palazzo Chigi-Odescalchi*, Rome, and his frequent use of the *ellipse in planning also recalls the great Italian master's work. He was consulted by *Neumann about the plans of the *Residenz*, Würzburg, and made designs for **Elector Maximilian II Emmanuel of Bavaria** (*r.*1679–1704 & 1715–26). For the Ducal Court of Lorraine he designed the *Palais Ducal*, Nancy (1715–22), and the *château* (1708–22) and chapel at Lunéville (1720–3): the last was influenced by *Hardouin-Mansart's chapel at Versailles, and also by *Cordemoy's suggestions for an ideal church with free-standing columns and straight *entablature—its quality of gracious lightness looks forward to *Soufflot's *Ste-Geneviève* in Paris. Both *château* and chapel were badly damaged by fire (2003). The enchanting house at St-Ouen, near Paris, with *pavilion in a *court surrounded by guest-wings and offices, was one of his most felicitous creations (1717), but, like much of his work, no longer survives. *His Livre d'architecture contenant les principes généraux de cet art* (1745) is an important collection of theoretical essays.

Ga & Garms (1986); Ha (1950); K & L (1972); Morey (1866); J.T (1996)

Bogardus, James (1800–74) American inventor/engineer/industrialist. He exhibited (1847) a model of a prefabricated iron factory, and was commissioned (1848) to make an ornamental five-storey iron *façade for **Dr John Milhau**'s (1785–1874) drug-store on Broadway, NYC (the first of several other fronts), which had a profound influence on the development of *cast-iron construction, prefabricated structural frames, and kits of parts that could be quickly assembled on site. He proposed an exhibition-house for the 1853 New York Exposition which was to have had a roof suspended from a central tower. He published *Cast Iron Buildings: Their Construction and Advantages* (1856, revised 1858). Most of his works have been destroyed, but a few survive: two in Manhattan and one in Cooperstown, NY.

Ben (1971); Bogardus (1856); Ct (1968); G & G (1974)

bog-garden Bog (from the Irish *bogach*) is a *morass*, *moss*, or wet, spongy ground, consisting of decaying vegetable matter, so a *bog-garden* (described by William *Robinson in his magazine, *The Garden* (1871), and then in his *English Flower Garden* (1883)) is one created where the soil is permanently saturated, but where the water does not rise above the surface to form pools. Soil in such conditions is peaty and acidic, and plants are permitted to grow and naturally reproduce. Bog-gardens were featured (late-C19) in the Botanic Gardens, Glasnevin, Dublin: interest in them and in *wild gardens was renewed in the late-C20.

W.Robinson (1883); Shoe (2000); Symes (2006)

Böhm, Dominikus (1880–1955) German ecclesiastical architect, his early works had references to historical styles, but from the 1920s, although his plans remained conventional, his work contained first *Expressionist elements and then abstract *Gothic (as in the Freilingsdorf *Pfarrkirche*, near Cologne (1926–7)). Perhaps one of his best churches is *St Johann*, Neu-Ulm (1921–7), with its banded *façade of brick and *masonry, and squat centrepiece pierced by three pointed arches. He experimented with centralized planning in order to bring the congregation nearer the *altar, using elliptical or circular plans, anticipating liturgical changes made in RC worship by the Second Vatican Council (1962–5). Among other buildings, *St Engelbert*, Köln-Riehl (1930–3), and *St Maria-Königin*, Köln-Marienburg (1951–4), may be cited. From 1928 his architecture became more Modernist in character, but he fell into disfavour under the Nazis. After 1945 he and his son **Gottfried** (1920–) restored damaged churches and built many new ones: Gottfried's Church of Mary, Queen of Peace, Neviges, near Velbert (1963–8), resembled a craggy rock formation, and his *Rathaus*, Bensberg (1963–9), connected to the ruins of a medieval *Schloss*, was another example of his dramatic use of irregular pointed forms. The restoration of the Saarbrücken *Schloss* (1979–89) demonstrated his sureness of touch in mixing old and new fabric.

Böhm (ed.) (2001); E (1994); Habbel (ed.) (1943); Höff *et al.* (1962); M & M (1965); Pehnt (1999); Raev (1982, 1987); S.Rn (1987); Stalling (1974)

Böhm, Gottfried (1920–) *See* BÖHM, DOMINIKUS.

Boileau, Louis-Auguste (1812–96) French architect, an early user of iron for church construction, as at Mattaincourt (Vosges), where even the *pews were of cast iron. His *St-Eugène*, Paris (1854–5), with thin cast-iron columns, *vault-ribs, and even *tracery, was a paraphrase of *Gothic, but aroused the wrath of critics such as *Daly. This was followed (1864–9) by *St-Paul*, Montluçon (Allier), which was *First-Pointed in style, but nevertheless very spidery. He published *La nouvelle forme architecturale* (1854), which illustrated an extraordinary iron church with a weird system of segmental ribs and arches piled up in a nightmarish debauch that mercifully was not realized. However, he warmed further to the theme in *Les principes et exemples d'architecture ferronière* (1881), and indulged in further literary propaganda. With his son, **Louis-Charles** (1837–1910), he built the *Magasins de Bon Marché*, Paris (1867–1876), designed by **Jean-Alexandre Laplanche** (1839–1910). Louis-Charles's *Ste-Marguerite*, Le Vésinet (Seine-et-Oise—1862–5), also had an iron frame and was in a spiky Gothic style, but the 'masonry' was of *Coignet's patented *clinker concrete, and an early type of *reinforced *concrete (also a Coignet patent) in the vaults. However, water-penetration and poor adhesion caused innumerable problems, probably due to the use of clinker.

Behnisch & G. Hartung (1982); Hi (1977); Marrey (1989); Marrey (ed.) (2002); M & Wa (1987); J.T (1996)

boiserie 1. *Wainscoting. 2. Wooden panelling, usually from floor to ceiling, on interior walls, embellished with carvings in low relief, gilding, inlay, etc., common in C17 and C18. Excellent *Rococo *boiseries* include work by **François-Antoine Vassé** (1681–1736), **Jacques Verberckt** (1704–71), and **Jules Degoullons** (*c.*1671–1737), which clearly influenced *Cuvilliés and *Knobelsdorff at Munich and Berlin. Some of the finest *boiseries* were those for the *Amalienburg*, *Nymphenburg*, Munich, designed by Cuvilliés and made (1734–9) by **Wenzeslaus Miroffsky** (*fl.*1726–59) and **Johann Joachim Dietrich** (1690–1753), with *stucco-work by J.B.*Zimmermann. Such French-inspired work reached heights of exquisite delicacy in Germany.

Bt (1978); Pons (1986, 1997); J.T (1996)

Boisserée, Sulpiz Melchior Dominicus (1783–1854) German scholar, important in the history of *Romanesque and *Gothic Revivals. He began (1818) to measure Cologne Cathedral, and submitted (1813) the results of his survey to **Crown Prince Friedrich Wilhelm of Prussia** (1795–1861—whose influence prompted the start (1823) of restoration of the medieval fabric following a detailed report from *Schinkel), although Boisserée's *Domwerk*, showing seductive views of the interior and exterior of Cologne's *Dom* as it would look when finished, had appeared from 1821, and undoubtedly was a catalyst for the whole affair. Sulpiz, his brother **Melchior Hermann Josef Georg** (1786–1851), and Georg *Moller discovered medieval drawings of the building on which he based his proposals. He also published *Geschichte und Beschreibung des Doms von Köln* (1823–32) with text in German and French, as well as sundry works on aspects of medieval architecture: *Geschichte* was an important volume, and its influence spread far beyond the boundaries of Germany. His efforts led to the appointment (1833) of *Zwirner as *Dombaumeister*, and when the Prince became **King Friedrich Wilhelm IV** (1840) he gave orders that the building should be completed (accomplished later in C19).

Berliner Museen, liii (1931), 39–45; Boisserée (1833); Borger (ed.) (1980); G (1972); W-R-J, ix (1936), 181–204

Boito, Camillo (1836–1914) Italian architect/nationalist/theorist, influenced by *Viollet-le-Duc. Among his early works are the buildings of the *cemetery (1865—of brick with stone *dressings, in a round-arched style), and the somewhat harsh and acidic *Ospedale Civico* (1869–74), both at Gallarate, north of Milan. More ebullient is his *Palazzo delle Debite*, Padua (1872–4), in a Venetian round-arched style that, with its richness and modelling, heralded the *Stile Boito*, the Italian equivalent of *High-Victorian architecture. Also round-arched is the Municipal Museum, Padua (1879), but in Milan he built the *Gothic *Casa Riposo per i Musicisti*, or *Casa Verdi* (1899–1913), which included the colourful tomb-chamber of the composer **Giuseppe Verdi** (1813–1901), whose librettist **Arrigo** (1862–1918), was Boito's brother. The mixing of elements from several periods and the use of constructional colour point to influences in the *Floreale* style. Boito restored *Sant'Antonio*, Padua (1892–6): in his many writings he urged that historical truth should underpin all interventions in historic buildings, and that restoration projects should be fully documented to aid future generations. Among his publications were *Questioni practiche di belle arti* (1893), *I principii del disegno e gli stili dell'ornamento* (1882), and *Architettura del Medio Evo in Italia* (1880).

Boito (1880, 1882); F.Borsi (1966); DBI, xi (1969), 237–41; Ms (1966); M & Wa (1987); Restauro, xv (1975), 5–88, and xliii (1980), 5–76; Zucconi (1997)

bole 1. Recess in a wall (*see* BEE-BOLE). 2. Unglazed opening in a wall to admit light and air, called *window-bole*, usually closed with *shutters.

bolection, bolexion *Moulding covering a joint between elements where one is recessed, as in a panel set in a door-frame, where the bolection projects beyond the surface of the *stile. *See* PANEL.

bollard 1. Low robust post, fixed to quays of harbours, in order to secure the moorings of ships. 2. Street-furniture, often of cast iron, usually in the form of a small column conforming to the *Doric *Order, or resembling a cannon, fixed in a road, footpath, or boundary to prevent vehicles from passing.

Bolotov, Andrey Timofeyevich (1738–1833) Russian horticulturalist/surveyor/writer, his work affected garden aesthetics, agriculture, forestry, and the development of botanical studies in his native land. A creature of the *Enlightenment, his reputation remained secure, even during the Soviet era, although physical manifestations of his career suffered badly, save for his garden at *Bogoroditske*, Tula (1784–6—the *palace there was by *Starov), influenced by *Hirschfeld and supplied with numerous *fabriques*, yet planted with birch and other locally available trees to create a specifically Russian 'national' landscape. He disseminated foreign ideas too, publishing translations by non-Russian authors (some 4,000 articles with references) in *Ekonomichesky Magazin* (1780–89).

Floryan (1996); Liubchenko (1988); Shoe (2001); Shv (2007)

bolster 1. *Baluster-side. **2.** Bellied profile of a *pulvinated *frieze. **3.** *Bolster-, cushion-,* or *pillow-work* refers to *rusticated *masonry, each course of which is bowed out, as in Roman *aqueduct-*piers. **4.** Timber *corbel or *plate supporting a *truss, etc.

Bon *or* **Bono, Bartolomeo** (*c.*1463–1529) Lombard architect (also called **Bergamasco**) who worked in Venice, where he designed the ground-floor of the early *Renaissance *Scuola di San Rocco* (1516–24), completed by others. He designed the upper *stages of the *campanile in the *Piazza di San Marco* (1510–14), rebuilt 1905–11.

Arslan (1971); D.Howard (1980); Ln (1982); McAndrew (1980)

Bon, Bono, *or* **Buon, Bartolomeo** (*c.*1405–67) Venetian architect/sculptor who worked with his father, **Giovanni** (*c.*1362–1443), on the celebrated *Gothic *palazzo known as the *Ca'd'Oro* (1421–40), and subsequently on the west wing (facing the *Piazzetta*) of the Doge's Palace (1424–43) in which their Gothic style reached perfection. The *Porta della Carta* (1438–43), which lies between the palace and the *basilica, makes a transition between Gothic and early *Renaissance. Bartolomeo was responsible for the west *portals of *Santi Giovanni e Páolo* (1458–63) and *San Cristofero Martire* (also known as *Madonna dell'Orto*), both essentially Classical, as is his east end of the *Porta della Carta*, known as the *Arco Foscari* (*c.*1440–64/67). To judge from the lowest *storey of the *Ca' del Duca Sforza* (now *Palazzo Corner*), the building, (1456–7), had it been finished, would have been a very advanced and early Renaissance *palazzo*. Also attributed to him is the gateway of the Arsenal (1460), one of the earliest Renaissance structures in Venice.

Arslan (1971); D.Howard (1980); Ln (1982); McAndrew (1980)

Bon, Christoph Rudolf (1921–99) *See* CHAMBERLIN, POWELL, & BON.

Bonanus *or* **Bonanno of Pisa** (*fl.*1179–86) Italian architect/sculptor. He made three pairs of bronze doors: for the *Porta Regia* of the west front (1180—destroyed), the *Porta di San Ranieri* (*c.*1180) of the south *transept at Pisa Cathedral, and for the west portal of Monreale Cathedral, Sicily (the last signed and dated 1186). He may have designed the *campanile (or 'leaning tower') of Pisa (1174–1271). His part in the creation of the Pisan *Duomo* and Baptistery is the subject of much debate.

DBI (1969)

Bonatz, Paul Michael Nikolaus (1877–1956) Lothringen(Lorraine)-born architect, he studied in Munich, and assisted Theodor *Fischer (1902–6) at the *Technische Hochschule*, Stuttgart, before himself becoming a professor (1908). In partnership (1913–27) with **Friedrich Eugen Scholer** (1874–1949) he designed the City Hall, Hanover (1911–14), and the *Hauptbahnhof*, Stuttgart (1911–28), which may owe something to *Saarinen's Helsinki terminus as well as to *Behrens's AEG buildings, Berlin. The partnership also designed locks, *bridges, weirs, and other structures on the Neckar Canal (1926–36), the *Graf Zeppelin Hotel*, Stuttgart (1929–31), the Henkel warehouses, Biebrich (1908–9), and the University Library, Tübingen (1910–12). Later, Bonatz was consultant to *Todt for the design of the *Autobahnen* and their handsome bridges (1935–41). He was a signatory of the *Block manifesto, and most of his domestic work was rooted in traditional forms. With **Paul Schmitthenner** (1884–1972) and **Heinz Wetzel** (1882–1945), Bonatz built up the Stuttgart School of Architecture as a bastion of traditionalism against the ferocious onslaught of *International Modernism, and so it was no accident that the *Weissenhofsiedlung was established at Stuttgart as a challenge and almost a declaration of war. The response of Bonatz and his colleagues, in collaboration with the local timber industry, was to build the *Kochenhofsiedlung* (1933—the name suggested basic realities (*Kochen* = 'cooking') as opposed to the white impracticalities of the rival *Siedlung* (settlement, colony, or housing-estate)), drawing on regional vernacular architecture, traditional timber construction, and craftsmanship, as a *riposte* to the alien imagery favoured by *Mies van der Rohe et al.

Under National Socialism Bonatz prepared schemes for the Naval High Command (1939–43) as part of *Speer's reordering of Berlin, and for the *Hauptbahnhof*, Munich (1939–42)—both unrealized. He also designed the War Memorial Chapel, Heilbronn (1930–6), the Stumm Company Building, Düsseldorf (1935—with Scholer), and the *Kunstmuseum*, Basel, Switzerland (1936). Disheartened by lack of recognition and by the dearth of building commissions during the 1939–45 war, he emigrated (1943) to Turkey, where he was appointed City Architect of Ankara, and became (1946) Professor at the Technical University, Istanbul (the State Opera House, Ankara (1948), was erected to his designs). On his return to Stuttgart (1953) he concentrated on repairing war-damage suffered by his earlier projects, published (1950) *Leben und Bauen* (Life and Buildings), and worked on the reconstruction of the opera house at Düsseldorf (1950s).

Bonatz (1950); Bongartz *et al*. (1977); Graupner (1931); Lane (1985); *Lotus International*, **xlvii** (1985), 70–91; Rittich (1938); Roser (1991); J.T (1996)

bond Placing of bricks, *masonry, etc., in a construction, breaking joints in every direction, so that each separate brick, stone, *tile, etc., holds in and retains its neighbour in its place, and in return is also held. This ensures strength and stability, while the pattern of the bond on the face of the wall makes a major contribution to the aesthetic quality of the building. In masonry a *bond-header, bonder, bond-stone*, or *through-stone* (*inband* in Scots) extends the width of a stone wall, tying it together. *See* BRICK.

Bru (1990); N.Lloyd (1925)

bone-house *See* CHARNEL-HOUSE, OSSUARY.

bonnet 1. *Cone-* or *curved hip-tile* used to cover the junctions of plain *tiles on the *hip of a roof. **2.** Chimney-cap.

bonnet-top Broken, scrolled *pediment.

Bonneuil, Étienne de (*fl*.1287-8) French architect of the *ambulatory and radiating chapels at the Cathedral of the Holy Trinity, Uppsala, Sweden (from 1287), the largest church in Scandinavia.

Boëthius & Romdahl (1935)

Bono *See* BON.

Bonomi, Joseph (1739-1808) Italian-born architect, educated in Rome. He studied for a period with *Asprucci and *Clérisseau before settling (1767) in England to work for the *Adam Brothers, afterwards apparently assisting *Leverton in the building of Bedford Square, London. For **Heneage Finch** (1751-1812—**4th Earl of Aylesford** from 1777) he designed the Neo-Classical interiors at Packington Hall (1785-8), and St James's Church, Great Packington (1789-90), both Warwicks. A severe brick building with *lunette windows, the church is a rare English example of the advanced *stripped *Neo-Classicism favoured on the Continent. He also designed the pyramidal *mausoleum at Blickling, Norfolk (1794-6). A regular exhibitor at the RA, he was also a fashionable architect for country-houses (e.g. Lambton Hall, Co. Durham (1796-7)), and is mentioned in chapter 36 of **Jane Austen's** (1775-1817) *Sense and Sensibility* (1811).

His second surviving son, **Ignatius** (1787-1870), built up an extensive practice around Newcastle upon Tyne: he built one of the first railway-bridges in England, at Skerne, near Darlington (1824), and was a competent and prolific designer in many styles. His Burn Hall, Co.

Durham (1821-34), was in an advanced French Classical style, while his *Romanesque-Revival Oxenhope Church, Yorks. (1849), had reasonably authentic detail. His pupil and assistant (1831-41) was J.L. *Pearson. Joseph's youngest son, also **Joseph** (1796-1878), was a distinguished Egyptologist who became curator of Sir John *Soane's Museum: his works included Temple Mills, Marshall Street, Leeds (1842—in a scholarly *Egyptian-Revival style); the Egyptianizing *gate-houses and *gates at Abney Park Cemetery, Stoke Newington, London (1840); and the Egyptian Court, Crystal Palace, Sydenham (with Owen *Jones), completed 1854 (destroyed).

Co (2008); J.Gosby (1987); J.Curl (2004, 2005, 2011a); Meadows (1988); Stillman (1988)

bonsai Japanese term meaning the art/practice of growing plants in *containers to suggest natural scenery in miniature. It originated in China as *shanshui penjing*. *See* MINIATURE GARDEN.

Bester (tr.) (2003); Koreshoff (1984); Tay (2006)

Booth, John (1759-1843) English architect/surveyor, closely associated with The Drapers' Company. For the Lloyd-Baker Estate in Clerkenwell, London, he designed the layout and remarkably inventive pairs and terrace houses of Lloyd Square, Lloyd-Baker Street, and Wharton Street (*c*.1819-40). He remodelled the Church of St George, Queen Square, London (1817-18).

Co (2008)

Booth, William Joseph (*c*.1796-1871) English architect, son of John *Booth. He became Surveyor to The Drapers' Company (1822), and carried out numerous works on the Company's estates in Co. Londonderry, including the very severe Presbyterian Meeting-House (1843—a remarkable essay in stripped *Neo-Classicism) and Market-House (1839) at Draperstown, and at Moneymore the monumental Corn-Store, Market-House, and outbuildings (1839), numerous houses (some in a C17 *Gothic style), the Common Barn (1843), Second Presbyterian Church (1829-32), and the large Parish Church of St John (1830-32—in a massive *Romanesque style). He produced several accomplished watercolours of aspects of the estate, lithographs of which were published.

J.Curl (1986)

Bor, Walter George (1916-99) *See* DAVIES, RICHARD LLEWELYN.

border 1. Long strip of ground forming a fringe to the general area of a garden, often reserved for flowers. **2.** *Plate-bande* of French C17 *Baroque gardens, although such strips were not flat, but mounded lengthways, rising either to a crest (*dos de carpe* ('carp's back')) or rounded (*dos d'âne* ('donkey's back')). Designs for *parterres* often included borders edged with trimmed box, and examples were given in **André Mollet**'s (*fl.*1620–64) *Jardin de Plaisir* (1651). The restored *Privy Garden, Hampton Court Palace (in which *Marot, who also worked at *Het Loo*, The Netherlands, probably had a hand), contained elaborately ornamented strips featuring clipped yew, hollies, and flowers. **3.** Late-C19 and early-C20 herbaceous borders planted with perennials were influenced by work of William *Robinson and *Jekyll.

Laird (1999); Mollet (1651); Symes (2006); Tay (2006)

Borra, Giovanni Battista (1713–70) Piedmontese architect/draughtsman (a pupil of *Vittone), aka *Il Torquelino*, he accompanied **Robert Wood** (1716–71) and **James Dawkins** (1722–57) to Asia Minor (1750–1): he was in England from 1751 preparing drawings for *The Ruins of Palmyra* (1753) and *The Ruins of Balbec* (1757). He probably designed (1755) the main rooms in the **Duke of Norfolk**'s house in St James's Square (by *Brettingham) which had motifs derived from *Antique remains at Palmyra mixed with Italian-*Rococo themes. Similar devices occur in the Racconigi Palace, Turin (1756–7), in Stratfield Saye, Hants., and Stowe, Bucks. Borra redecorated the State Bedroom and Dressing Room at Stowe (1760) and *Neo-Classicized several *fabriques* there (he made designs for the Temple of Concord and Victory, and altered the *Rotunda (1752), the Boycott Pavilions (1758), the Oxford Gate (1760–1), and the Lake Pavilions (*c.*1761)). **Richard Chandler**'s (1737–1810) expedition (1764–6) to collect material for *Ionian Antiquities* (1769) included *Revett and **William Edmund Pars** (1742–82—who was influenced by Borra's work).

Co (2008); E.Hs (1990); Zoller (1996)

Borromini capital Type of *Composite *capital with incurving *volutes used by the *Bastards at Blandford Forum, Dorset, (1730s), and by Thomas *Archer (1720s). It was derived from capitals favoured by *Borromini.

Borromini capital Variant as used by the Bastards at Blandford Forum, Dorset.

Borromini, Francesco (1599–1667) One of the greatest *Baroque architects in C17 Rome, he was born **Francesco Castello** near Como, studied sculpture in Milan (where he probably met masons working on late-*Gothic forms at the *Duomo*), and was apprenticed to his relative, *Maderno, from *c.*1620, before assisting (1629–33) *Bernini (of whom he was critical and jealous) at *San Pietro*, Rome. Fascinated by the teachings of **Galileo Galilei** (1564–1642—who held that mathematics was the key to Nature, and that geometrical figures were Nature's pictographs), Borromini developed his architecture through highly complex interlinked geometries, creating powerful, restless, dynamic forms totally different from the *concatenated method of *Renaissance design. Other sources included *Antique buildings such as Hadrian's *villa at Tivoli.

Borromini set up (1633) on his own, and was involved in a number of designs for *palazzi* and *villas, although he is best known for his churches. He was commissioned (1634) to design the *monastery of *San Carlo alle Quattro Fontane* (1634–43) for the Order of Spanish Discalced Trinitarians: in spite of its smallness, the complex of *cloister and church is ingenious in the extreme, illustrating Borromini's concerns with geometrical intricacies. The church has an elliptical, central space that merges with other *ellipses, the *Orders being placed on contraflexed curves on plan, so that wall-surfaces bow inwards and outwards. The whole front (from 1665) of the building seems to be in motion, with its concave-convex-concave plan for the lower *Ionic storey and a concave-concave-concave plan for the upper *Composite *façade. The miniature *Orders for the *aedicules recall *Michelangelo's (Borromini's hero) work on the Capitol. Shortly after beginning work on *San Carlo*, Borromini was appointed to design the *Casa e Oratorio dei Filippini* (1637–50), the façade of which curves slightly, as though it had been bent, but the plan is ingenious and has a wonderful logic. The monastery of the *Oblate Agostiniane*, including *Santa Maria dei Sette Dolori* (1642–9), remained unfinished, but has several interesting features: *vestibule, church, and the space before the concave façade determine each other's shape, for a concave in one creates a convex in the other, giving an impression of elasticity.

The plan of *Sant'Ivo alla Sapienza* (1642–62) is based on six circles drawn on a six-pointed star evolved from two superimposed equilateral triangles. The resultant space is extraordinary and dynamic, carried up within the *dome which is capped by a *lantern (the shape of which resembles the late-Roman temple of Venus at Baalbek), topped by a spiral tower (which may refer to the Tower of Babel) above which is the flame of Truth. The plan resembles the shape of a bee, the heraldic device of **Matteo Barberini** (b.1568—**Pope Urban VIII** (*r.*1623-44)), who appointed Borromini architect to the ancient University (the *Sapienza*). There are references to the Wisdom of Solomon (and therefore to the Temple) in the Cherubims, palms, pomegranates, and stars within the dome, eclectic symbolism having few architectural precedents. The *Biblioteca Alessandrina alla Sapienza* (1660-6) was the model for many later monastic and university libraries.

These Baroque masterpieces led to other ecclesiastical commissions (largely through **Giambattista Pamfili** (b.1574—**Pope Innocent X** (*r.*1644-55)), including the renovation and modernization of the ancient *basilica of San Giovanni in Laterano* where he clothed the *nave and *aisles in Baroque garb, using overlapping *triumphal-arch themes that *Alberti had earlier employed in *Sant'Andrea* in Mantua. The work involved rearranging and adapting the many funerary monuments within the new setting, and this Borromini did with skill, adding *putti and Baroque decorations to give coherence. However, his intended *vaulting over the nave was never realized. He was commissioned to complete *Rainaldi's unfinished *Sant'Agnese in Agone* in the *Piazza Navona* (1653-7). The building was a Greek *cross on plan, which Borromini kept in essence, but raised the *drum of the *dome and vigorously articulated the concave front between two inventive towers: this design seems to draw the onlooker within the generous space, the High-Baroque version of the centralized plan of *San Pietro*. *Sant'Agnese* was influential, especially in Austria (*see* FISCHER VON ERLACH). From 1647 Borromini worked on the *Collegio di Propaganda Fide*, the main façade of which has a *Giant *Order of *pilasters (with *capitals reduced to five *flutes) between which strange *Doric *aedicules burst from the plane of the wall. The *cornice, part straight and part swaying, is carried on larger *mutules, and the whole effect is surreal and oppressive. Inside the complex is the *Cappella dei Re Magi* (1660-4), roofed with rib-vaults connected to the Giant Order of pilasters, giving a *Gothic flavour to what is essentially a Baroque ensemble.

Borromini's commissions dried up on the death (1655) of his Papal patron, and, in spite of a moderately successful decade, he committed suicide. His style, which fused Gothic and late-Renaissance elements, successfully mixing flowing forms with vigorous sculpture, was unconventional, but his experiments with swaying walls and interpenetrating ellipses were influential in C18 Central Europe.

Bosel & C.Fr (2000); Bt (1979); Connors (1980); C.Fr (ed.) (2000); E.Hempel (1924); N-S (1986, 1986a); Pi (1982, 1990); Raspe (1994); Sinisgalli *et al.* (2000); Va (1986); Wi (1982)

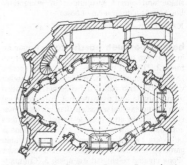

Plan of *San Carlo alle Quattro Fontane*, Rome, showing the centres from which arcs describing the circles and ellipse are struck, and the geometrical relationships of those centres to elements within the plan. Note the concave–convex–concave arrangement of the entrance-front.

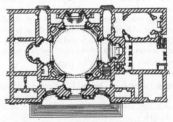

Plan of *Sant'Agnese in Agone*, Piazza Navona, Rome, showing the concave front and centralized space.

borrowed landscape Garden-composition drawing countryside into the prospect, or incorporating a distant feature (e.g. a hill or *steeple): C17 examples included work by *Bruce (e.g. inclusion of the *ruin of Lochleven Castle into views at Kinross House, Perth and Kinross (1686-93)), and in C18 *Addison, *Kent, and *Switzer advocated such an approach, facilitated, of course, by the *ha-ha. *See* JAPANESE GARDEN; JIE JING; SHARAWADGI.

Bond (ed.) (1987); Kraushaar (ed.) (2010); Switzer (1980); Tay (2006)

bosco (*pl.* **boschi**) **1.** Dense wood with walks and clearings within it, close to the spirit of the formal *wilderness. The *sacro bosco* (sacred wood) contained groves suggesting those inhabited by deities in Antiquity, and was associated with a perilous journey, so carved figures and various structures were set among the trees, as at Bomarzo, near Viterbo (begun 1552). *See* BOSKET; ORSINI. **2.** Wood or *grove, often a place of shade and retreat surrounded by evergreens. *Boschetto* is a diminutive of *bosco*.

JGH, **iv**/1 (Jan.–Mar. 1984), whole issue.

bosket, bosquet, boschetto 1. Plantation in a garden, park, etc., of underwood and small trees. **2.** *Thicket or *grove of the same species (e.g. hornbeam, privet, phillyrea) cut through with walks, also called a *wilderness, intended to give shade and pleasure, not to be confused with an uncultivated wasteland. It might be a looser element within an otherwise formal layout, thus anticipating a more 'natural' style of gardening. Le *Nôtre formed many organized spaces within gardens, and both *Bridgeman and Alexander *Pope created celebrated examples. **3.** Compartment in a garden enclosed by a formal *palisade **(4)**, thus becoming an interior grassed space, or *cabinet de verdure*, sometimes containing buildings (e.g. *summer-houses) or monuments as mnemonics of ideas, feelings, or people, not uncommon in C18 Continental landscape-design. Some *bosquets* were complex, with subsidiary *cabinets* off them, decorated with statues, urns, or single trees in the centres, lined with flower-beds and with trees planted behind the palisades. *Dézallier d'Argenville devoted a whole chapter of his *Théorie . . .* (1709) to *bosquets*. *See also* BOSCO.

DdA (1709); Symes (2006); Tay (2006)

boss *formerly* **boce 1.** Carved convex block, often richly decorated, at the junction of *vault-ribs, etc., in medieval architecture. **2.** *See* BOAST **(1)**.

boss Medieval Gothic vault-boss, Oxford Cathedral, C13 (*after Parker*).

bossage *See* BOAST.

Bossan, Pierre-Marie (1814–88) French architect, pupil of *Labrouste. Appointed (1844) Diocesan Architect of Lyons, he designed several revivalist churches including *St-Georges* (1844).

From 1852 he produced designs in a *Byzantinesque *Néo-Grec* style, including *Ste-Philomène*, Ars (1862–5), *St-Jean-François Régis*, Lalouvesc (1865), and the massive *Notre-Dame-de-Fourvière*, Lyons (1871–96), completed by **Saint-Marie Perrin** (1835–1917).

Perrin (1889, 1912); Thollier (1891)

bossing Space under a window where the wall is thinner than on either side (*see* ALLÈGE).

botanic garden Collection of plants having several purposes: botanic/horticultural education; scientific study and experiment; public recreation; *conservation; and nurture of indigenous and foreign specimens. A specialist type is the *arboretum*. Botanical gardens are of considerable antiquity: they existed in C11 Islamic Spain (Toledo and Seville), and probably a lot earlier in Hellenistic and Roman civilizations. Exemplars were known during the *Renaissance, notably in Pisa (*c.*1543), Padua (1545), Leipzig (1580), Leiden (1592), Montpellier (1593), and Paris (1635). The 'Physick Garden', Oxford, was established (1620s), and the Chelsea Physick Garden, London, and Royal Botanic Garden, Edinburgh, were founded (1670s). **Carl von Linné (Linnaeus)** (1707–78), the Swedish botanist, developed a system of classification of plants, with principles for defining genera and species, and so established a logical use of specific names. With the enormous upsurge of interest in botany during the C18, many new varieties were introduced into northern climes: this necessitated special buildings (*conservatories) in which they could be cultivated. Important C18 botanic gardens included those at Kew. Inventions involving the structural possibilities of *iron and *glass enabled many new building types to emerge, not least through the writings of *Loudon, who also promoted the botanic garden as a resource for public education. Numerous botanic gardens were established during the C19 in many cities, often with splendidly inventive conservatories (e.g. Belfast's Palm House (1839–40 and 1852— by *Lanyon and Richard *Turner). In the 1980s numerous botanic gardens worldwide were recorded, the best of which not only inform, but delight.

Henderson (1983); J.C.Loudon (1834); Shoe (2001); Symes (2006); Tay (2006)

bothan 1. *Shebeen* or unlicensed drinking-house. **2.** Circular building with *corbel-vaulted roof.

bothy, bothe, bothie, buith 1. Rough *hut used as a shelter or for temporary accommodation for shepherds, mountaineers, etc. **2.** Living-quarters, temporary or permanent, for unmarried male farm-workers, servants, etc. Usually of one *storey, built of *rubble or turf (often finished with *render), it occasionally acquired an upper storey as sleeping-quarters. This type of *vernacular architecture gradually attracted the attention of late-C18 designers, becoming the inspiration for agricultural housing and *rustic buildings in landscape-gardens illustrated in numerous contemporary *pattern-books.

OED (2013); W.Pa (1852); Pride (1996)

Botta, Mario (1943–) *See* NEO-RATIONALISM, RATIONAL ARCHITECTURE, TENDENZA, TICINESE SCHOOL.

Bötticher, Karl Gottlieb Wilhelm (1806–89) German architect/scholar, his *Holzarchitektur des Mittelalters* (1835–40) was an important early study of *timber-framed medieval buildings, while his *Der Tektonik der Hellenen* (1844–52, 1869) was of significance in the understanding of *Greek architecture, though he attempted to explain it *entirely* in structural terms.

Arenhövel *et al.* (1979); B-S (1977); S (1901–2); J.T (1996)

bottle-dungeon Repulsive *cell, narrow at the top through which a prisoner would be dropped, the *section of which was similar to that of a bottle. Form of *oubliette.

bouleuterion Meeting-place/debating-chamber for a senate in a Greek city.

boulevard 1. Broad street, *promenade, or walk, planted with rows of trees, e.g. those laid out by *Haussmann in C19 Paris. **2.** Horizontal portion of a *rampart, hence the promenade laid out on demolished fortifications, e.g. the *Ring* streets around many German cities. One of the first boulevards (1670) was created on the line of walls flattened by *Vauban in Paris, running from the *Porte St-Denis* to the *Bastille*, intended as a promenade for pedestrians only. **3.** Any wide main street, especially in the USA.

Goulty (1991); Symes (2006)

Boullée, Étienne-Louis (1728–99) Parisian architect, whose importance lies in his theoretical writings and visionary drawings, for he taught generations of pupils, including *Brongniart, *Chalgrin, and *Durand. He imbibed the great French Classical traditions of C17 and C18 from *Blondel and Le *Geay, and designed (1762–78) several private houses, most of which no longer exist, although the *Hôtel Alexandre*, Paris (1763–6), survives. With *Ledoux, *Peyre, and de *Wailly, Boullée pioneered severity in domestic architecture: he monumentalized main *blocks with *Giant *Orders and concealed the *wings behind *trellises or walls to give emphasis to the composition's centrepiece. In the vanguard of the anti-*Rococo decorators, he gained a reputation as an interior designer, exploiting lighting effects with considerable success. He produced (1778–88) a great range of visionary drawings based on those he used for teaching purposes and others made to enter architectural competitions. He responded to *Laugier's reductionist themes by stripping all unnecessary ornament from stereometrically pure forms inflated to a megalomaniac scale (influenced by *Piranesi), repeating elements such as columns in huge ranges, and making his architecture expressive of its purpose (*architecture parlante*). His most successful (though unrealized) schemes of visionary architecture are those for tombs, *mausolea, *cenotaphs, and *cemeteries, including the huge 'Cenotaph of Newton' (a vast sphere set in a circular base topped with cypresses). His treatise (1790s), *Architecture. Essai sur l'art*, was not published until the C20.

B (1980); Jacques & Mouilleseaux (1988); Kalnein (1995); E.Ka (1952); Lankeit (1973); Madec (1986); PdM (1974); Rosenau (1953, 1976); A.Ro (ed.) (1967); Vogt (1969)

Boumann, Johann (**Jan**) (1706–76) Amsterdam-born architect, called (1732) to Prussia by **King Friedrich Wilhelm I** (*r.*1713–40), he laid out the Dutch Quarter (1734–42) and designed (1753) the *Rathaus*, based on *Palladio's unrealized *Palazzo Angarano*, all in Potsdam. His Lutheran Cathedral (1747–50) was remodelled (1816) by *Schinkel, but destroyed (1890s), and he worked with *Büring on St Hedwig's RC Cathedral (1770–3), both in Berlin. His son, **Georg Friedrich Boumann** (1737–*c.*1812), executed *Unger's design for the Royal Library, *Forum Fridericianum*, Berlin (1774–80), and another son, **Michael Philipp Daniel** (1747–1803), designed the Neo-Classical *Schloss Bellevue*.

Wa & M (1987)

boundary-stone Tablet, post, etc., erected to mark the extent of an estate, parish, or other boundary.

Bourdon, Eugène (1870–1916) French-born architect, trained under *Daumet and *Girault at the *École des *Beaux-Arts. He became an inspector (1896–1900) for the *Exposition Universelle*, and then went to New York before returning to Europe to work with Girault on the *Parc du Cinquantenaire*, Brussels. As first (from 1904) Professor of Architectural Design at the new, joint, Glasgow School of Architecture, he directed a generation of students towards *Beaux-Arts* *Classicism (perceived as progressive because *Art Nouveau was by then passé). His appointment was probably prompted by J.J.*Burnet et al. to counter the influence of so-called 'New Art', and undoubtedly helped to eclipse the careers of *Mackintosh and *Salmon. His pupils included **Andrew Graham Henderson** (1882–1963), **Edward Grigg Wylie** (1885–1954), and **Richard M.M.Gunn** (1889–1933—architect of the present Bank of Scotland,

110-20 St Vincent Street, Glasgow (1924-7—a splendid example of American-influenced Classicism, featuring an *Ionic Order)). Bourdon was killed on the first day of the Battle of the Somme.

Stamp (2004)

Bourgeau, Victor (1809-88) French-Canadian Diocesan Architect of Montréal, he carried out major renovations to *Notre Dame* (1872-80) to create a more convincing *Gothic-Revival interior (only one of his 23 remodellings of existing churches). In addition, he designed over 20 new churches: the grandest in the Gothic-Revival style is *St-Pierre-Apôtre*, Montréal (1851-3). Subsequently, his designs became less Gothic, possibly because of the enthusiastic reception of that style by English Protestant Canadians. His *St-Barthélémy*, Berthier, Québec (1866-7), for example, was Classical, with a twin-towered western *façade recalling the work of *Baillargé. When Montréal Cathedral was destroyed by fire (1854), the Bishop determined to replace it with a version of the *basilica of San Pietro, Rome. Accordingly, Bourgeau was sent to Europe to study various churches, but returned after only a week in Rome, convinced that a reproduction of the basilica would be a mistake. The Bishop then appointed **Father Joseph Michaud** (1823-1902) to design the replica and construction began (1870), but Michaud's lack of expertise led to Bourgeau being reappointed, and the Cathedral-Basilica of *Saint-Jacques-le-Majeur* (now *Marie-Reine-de-la-Monde*) was completed (1894), partly under the direction of **Étienne-Alcibiade Leprohon** (c.1842-1902).

K (1994)

Bourgeois, Victor (1897-1962) Belgian architect/planner, he practised in Brussels from 1920, and, as Vice-President of *CIAM became the leading Belgian disciple of Le *Corbusier, advocating the adoption of *International *Modernism. His most celebrated work was the municipal housing scheme or *Cité Moderne*, Sint-Agatha Berchem, near Brussels (1922-5), influenced by Tony *Garnier's *Cité Industrielle* and by F.L.L.*Wright. Other works include a house at the *Weissenhofsiedlung*, Stuttgart (1927).

V.Bourgeois (1946, 1955, 1971); Flouquet (1952); Linze (1959); Loo (ed.) (2003)

Bourla, Pierre Bruno (1783-1866) Paris-born architect, he brought a distinguished *Neo-Classical style to Belgium. His finest achievement was the *Théâtre Royal Français*, Antwerp (1829-34), with a stunning foyer on its first floor, and a chaste, even noble, exterior.

Loo (ed.) (2003)

bow 1. Part of a wall projecting from its face, a partial *ellipse, semicircle, or segment on *plan, usually with a window set in it or extending the full width, known as a *bow-* or *compass-window*. If the plan is canted (or part of a polygon), or rectangular, it is not called a *bow*, but rather a *bay*, so a projecting window would be a *canted bay-window* or *a rectangular* or *square bay-window*. See BAY-WINDOW. **2.** Arched form, therefore part of a flying *buttress. **3.** *Attribute of the goddess Diana, so associated with hunting.

Bowden, John (*fl.*1798-1821) Architect to the Board of *First Fruits in Ireland (therefore designer of numerous Anglican churches), he also had a large secular practice. Among works based on his standard *Gothic designs were the Parish Churches of Aghanloo (1823), Bovevagh (1823), Faughanvale (Eglinton) (1821), Fahan (1820), and Maghera (1819), all in Co. Londonderry. He also designed the handsome *Greek-Revival Court-House, Londonderry (1813, completed 1817), and Foyle College, Londonderry (1808-14). He was responsible for the design of St George's Parish Church, Belfast (1811), with its handsome *Corinthian *portico recycled from the great house at Ballyscullion, Co. Londonderry (built (from 1787) for **Frederick Augustus Hervey** (1730-1803—**4th Earl of Bristol** from 1779 and **Bishop of Derry** from 1768), probably designed by *Sandys, *Shanahan, and Sandys's brother **Joseph**). With **Edward** *or* **Robert Parke** (*fl.*1787-1818—who designed the west façade and *Ionic *colonnade of the House of Commons (now Bank of Ireland), Dublin (1787-94)) he was responsible for the severe Greek-*Doric Court-House, Dundalk, Co. Louth (1813-18), and, with *Welland, for St Stephen's, Dublin, a fine Greek-Revival Anglican church, with distyle *in antis* portico (consecrated 1824, but subsequently altered inside).

Brett (1967, 1973); M.Craig (1982); J.Curl (1986, 2000); DIB (2009)

bower 1. Room in medieval houses for the exclusive use of women, therefore the precursor of the *boudoir*. **2.** Small dwelling in the country, or a cottage, therefore a *cottage orné* or deliberately *rustic building in a Romantic, *Picturesque landscape. **3.** *Gazebo or other similar garden-building. **4.** Shady recess, leafy covert, or place closed in or overarched with branches, deliberately created to look 'natural' in a garden or landscape.

bowl 1. Surface of a sloping *auditorium floor, sometimes, for acoustic reasons, in the form of part of an inverted cone. **2.** *Basin, as of a *fountain. **3.** Plain *capital like a bowl or basin.

bowling-alley 1. *Alley or long, narrow track along which bowls are rolled or skittles played.

Some C18 examples survive as decorative level lawns with *borders. **2.** Building for the same purpose.

bowstring *See* TRUSS.

bowtell, bowtelle 1. Plain *moulding, larger than an *astragal or *bead, with a convex *section, such as a *roll-moulding, *ovolo, or *torus, also called *boltel, bottle, boultel, boultin.* **2.** *Colonnette or *shaft of a medieval *clustered *pier.

box 1. Small unpretentious rural house, usually for temporary use, such as a *shooting-box* for sportsmen. **2.** Compartment, enclosed at the sides and back, with seats for a small number of people in a theatre. **3.** *Box-pew. **4.** Small dwarf evergreen shrub with dark green leaves used for the edgings of flower-beds: larger varieties of box are used to form dense *hedges.

Box, John (*fl.*1333-75) English mason, he worked on Westminster Palace and Christ Church Priory, Canterbury, Kent. He probably designed the fine early *Perp. funerary monument (*c.*1350) in Canterbury Cathedral to **John Stratford** (*c.*1275-1348—**Archbishop of Canterbury** from 1333), and also worked with *Yeveley on the *chantry-chapel of **Edward, Prince of Wales and Aquitaine** (1330-76—known as the **Black Prince**) in the Cathedral *crypt (*after* 1363).

J.Harvey (1987)

box-beam Rectangular beam constructed of four sheets of wrought iron or steel to form a long box, also called *box-girder.*

box-frame 1. Type of construction resembling a series of boxes, involving structural walls at right angles to the *façade (called *cross-walls*): its repetitive nature limits its use to hotel-bedrooms, small *flats, hostels, etc. **2.** Type of *timber-framed structure where roof-*trusses are supported on a frame of *posts, tie-beams, and wall-plates.

ABDM (1996)

box-frame Typical C20 box-frame, on pilotis.

box-pew Common English (and American) C18 *pew type (some big enough for entire families) surrounded by tall timber-panelled partitions with a hinged door.

Boyceau, Jacques de la Barauderie (*c.*1562-*c.*1634) French garden-designer/theorist. As Superintendent of the King's Gardens under **Louis XIII** (*r.*1610-43) he exerted considerable influence on French taste. His *Traité du jardinage* (1638) not only summarized the history of French gardening, but established garden-design as something to be taken very seriously, complete with its own theory: in particular, it suggested a mode of training to include architecture, art, draughtsmanship, geometry, horticulture, and hydraulics. It did not avoid a discussion of the siting of statues, *eye-catchers, *fountains, and so on. He was probably responsible for the design of the gardens of the Luxembourg Gardens, Paris (*c.*1611-29—with *Mollet), which seems to have contained the first *parterre de broderie.* In collaboration with his nephew, **Jacques de Menours** (1591-1637), he laid out the gardens of the first Versailles (*c.*1631-6), and probably contributed to the creation of the *parterre* designs at Fontainebleau, Saint-Germain-en-Laye, the Louvre, and the Tuileries (the last two in Paris).

Ht (1966); Racine (ed.) (2001)

Boyle *See* BURLINGTON.

Boyne, Donald Arthur Colin Aydon (1921-2006) British architectural journalist, whose dogmatic adherence to *Modernism was promoted through the *AJ* and *AR* for some forty years. His rule at the Architectural Press helped to form received opinion: indeed, like the *Ecclesiologist* in C19, the Press could make or break architectural reputations. Boyne never practised architecture, but he is included here because his belief in Modernism was a faith; a social determinant akin to religious fundamentalism.

The Times (18 Oct. 2006), 72; pk

Boytac, Diogo (*fl.*1490-1525) French master-mason who worked on *Santa Maria,* Belém, Lisbon (begun 1502), one of the first examples of the *Manueline style of Portugal, and also Christ Church at Setúbal (1494-8), which commemorates Portuguese voyages of discovery in its form and detail.

Ck (1996)

brace 1. Subsidiary structural timber, curved or straight, placed at an angle between vertical and horizontal members to complete a triangle and thus stiffen a *timber frame. If supporting a *rafter, it is called a *strut. *See* TRUSS. **2.** *See* BRACKET-MOULDING.

bracket 1. Member (essentially a type of *brace) projecting from the *naked of a wall to support by means of *leverage* an element that overhangs. **2.** *Ancon, *console, *corbel, *modillion, *mutule, or other element expressing a support, or even a *cantilever principle.

bracket-moulding 1. *Brace in the form of a double *ogee. **2.** *Moulding of two ogee-forms joining at a point and supporting, e.g., a *finial.

Bradford, William (1845–1919) English architect, he specialized in breweries, designing or altering over seventy of them, including Hole's Castle Brewery, Newark-on-Trent, Notts. (1882—a rich French-Renaissance composition of stone, enlivened by *vermiculation, and with a large clock tower), and the Hook Norton Brewery, Oxon. (c.1870—an extraordinary pile of brick, *ironstone, *cast iron, timber, and *weatherboarding). The firm continued under his sons, **W. Stovin** (author of a paper on 'The Architecture of Breweries') and **J.W.Bradford**, designing several lavishly ornamented *public houses.

J. Inst. Brewing, **xxxviii/2** (1932), 190–4; L.Pearson (1999); PS

Braem, Renaat (1910–2001) Belgian architect, influenced by Russian *Constructivism and Le *Corbusier (with whom he worked 1936–7), and member of *CIAM from 1939. He designed the Kiel district (1949–58—which has not improved with age), and the huge tower of the Administrative Centre, *Schoenmarkt* (1951), both in Antwerp; the *Sint Martensdal* district of Leuven; low-cost housing at Boom (1965–70); the *Gemeentebibliotheek van Schoten* (1968–74); and the administrative building for the Free University of Brussels (1971–8). His career was marked by the extreme Utopian stances he adopted.

Loo (ed.) (2003); PM; Strauven (1983); J.T (1996)

Bragard, René (1892–1971) English-born Belgian architect. Influenced by *Hankar, he designed several fine houses (e.g. that in the *Molièrelaan*, Uccle, Brussels (1923)).

Loo (ed.) (2003)

Bramante, Donato *or* **Donato di Angelo di Pascuccio d'Antonio** (1444–1514) The only architect of the High *Renaissance (with the exception of *Raphael) respected by his peers and successors as the equal of the Ancients, it was he, above all, who revealed the power, emotional possibilities, and gravity of *Antique Roman architecture. Born near Urbino, he trained as a painter, and perhaps knew **Piero della Francesca** (c.1410/20–92) and Francesco di *Giorgio at the Court of **Federigo da Montefeltro** (r.1444–82) in that city, but his first documented appearance was as a painter of *frescoes at the *Palazzo del Podestà*, Bergamo (1477). Around 1479 he

entered the service of **Ludovico Sforza** (1452–1508) in Milan, where he turned his attention to architecture, and met *Leonardo da Vinci, who alerted him to the problems of designing centralized churches. Bramante's first significant church was *Santa Maria presso San Satiro*, Milan (begun c.1481), where he erected the first *coffered dome since Antiquity, made the shallow east end appear as a deep *chancel by means of theatrical *perspective techniques, placed a barrel-*vault over the *nave (influenced by *Alberti) and reworked the C9 chapel of *San Satiro* as a *drum (embellished with *pilasters and *niches). He also planned, with Leonardo, a centralized arrangement at *Santa Maria delle Grazie*, Milan (1490s), which has a *drum with *dome on *pendentives rising over it.

The fall of the Sforzas forced Bramante to abandon Milan for Rome, where he designed the elegant *cloister of *Santa Maria della Pace* (1500–4—more refined than his earlier effort at *Sant'Ambrogio*, Milan (1492)). The *Pace* cloister has arches springing from *piers (embellished with *Ionic *pilasters (a motif based on the Colosseum)) carrying a continuous *entablature with an inscription on the *frieze, while above is an open *colonnaded gallery with slim columns set between pilastered piers (the gallery *Order is vaguely *Corinthian, another nod to the Colosseum). Then (1502–10) came the astonishing *Tempietto* in the *chiostro* (*cloister) of *San Pietro in Montorio*, a drum surmounted by a dome and surrounded by a *peristyle of *Tuscan columns carrying a Roman-*Doric entablature: the effect is graceful, serene, and *Antique. Tuscan Doric was used because of its association with the strong masculine character of St Peter, on the supposed site of whose Martyrdom the *Tempietto* was erected. Indeed *Serlio credited Bramante with adapting the Doric *temple for Christian purposes, for *Vitruvius, no less, had recommended Doric as appropriate for heroic, masculine deities. Circular plans were based upon Antique temples, but they also have important precedents in the *martyria* of Early-Christian churches: thus Bramante, in this tiny building, linked Christian *martyria*, Roman circular temples, and Classical architecture in the first great building of the High *Renaissance.

With the election of **Giuliano della Rovere** (b.1453, **Pope Julius II** (r.1503–13)), Bramante acquired a patron with ambitions to build, and he drew up plans for the Vatican and the Basilica of *San Pietro*. One range of buildings with three superimposed arcades was subsequently incorporated within the *Cortile di San Damaso*, and then came the vast *Cortile del Belvedere* of which only the spiral ramp (c.1505) remains relatively intact. However, the greatest work was the rebuilding of *San Pietro*. The huge *Hagia Sophia*, Constantinople, had fallen to Islam in the mid-C15, and it became politically and symbolically important to replace the Constantinian *basilica (which was really a *martyrium* over the tomb of the Apostle) with a great centrally-planned church. Bramante proposed a mighty Greek *cross (with each arm terminating in an *apse) in the corners of which would be four smaller Greek crosses (each covered by a minor dome), the centre covered by a dome to rival that of the Roman *Pantheon, but carried on a huge colonnaded drum. Bramante's design was derived from the *Tempietto*, and he was designing a *martyrium*, with reference to Constantine's other foundations (the Holy Sepulchre and the Church of the Nativity), and to the mathematical perfection of a centralized plan that symbolized the Perfection of God. The building was only partially begun when he and the Pope died, but the massive piers of the *crossing and the arches carry the dome of the present building. His other works include the choir of *Santa Maria del Pòpolo* (1505–9), with a huge coffered vault and *apse, and the *Palazzo Caprini* (House of Raphael (1508–9)) which had (it has been virtually obliterated) an arcaded and heavily rusticated base, with coupled Tuscan-Doric columns above, an arrangement that was greatly admired by *Palladio (who drew the building), and was influential among later generations of architects, notably *Burlington.

An (1954); Bruschi (1977); He (1996); P (1982); Patetta (1987); Serlio (1964); J.T (1996); Vasari (1912–15)

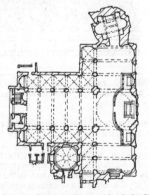

Plan of church of *Santa Maria presso San Satiro*, Milan. Note the chapel of *San Satiro* at the top, and the very shallow chancel in the church itself.

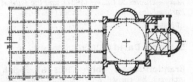

Centralized east end of *Santa Maria delle Grazie*, Milan.

Bramantino (*fl.*1503–36) *See* SUARDI.

Branca, Alexander, Freiherr von (1919–2011) Munich-born architect, he established (1950) his own practice in the Bavarian capital, and produced many distinguished buildings in which his beliefs in the necessity of continuity through tradition and in the symbolic value of 'supertemporal' architecture were expressed. His religious buildings, including the Monastery and Church (1965–8), Chapel and School (1973–77), Guest-House and *Mortuary Chapel (1980–2), and Father Joseph Kentneich Reception-Hall (1982–3), all at Schönstatt, are powerful compositions (the Mortuary Chapel is particularly moving), while his *conservation work at Regensburg *Altstadt* (from 1981) demonstrated his sensitive approach. His *Neue Pinakothek*, Munich (1973–81), is boldly modelled with excellent lighting. Other works include the Church and Parish-Centre of St Thomas More, Neusäss, Augsburg (1970–4), the Library, University of Regensburg (1970–4), the RC Academy of St Ulrich, Augsburg (1971–5), the Woodland Cemetery, Leutkirch (1977–82), the German Embassy to the Holy See, Vatican City (1979–84), and the Municipal Hall, Frankenthal (1989). To von Branca, architecture involved a high seriousness of purpose, for architecture lives and can reveal much about life, as well as enhancing it (conversely, of course, bad architecture depresses life and destroys pleasure). His many prizes and honours testified to his distinguished contribution to German C20 architecture, yet his work is not well known in the UK or USA.

E (1994); *Pantheon*, ii (1981), 104–9; Stark (1998); Walz (ed.) (1996); pk

branch 1. *Gothic *vault-*rib that continues from the top of a *pier without interruption, there being no pier-*capital. **2.** Any Gothic vault-rib. *See* TRACERY.

Branco, Cassiano (1897–1970) Portuguese Modernistic architect. He designed the Eden Cinema, Lisbon (1930–1—an impressive essay in *Art Deco), and the *Hotel Vitória, Avenida da Liberdade* (1934—a powerful example of *Rationalism). Other works include 179A *Rua do Salitre* (1934), 44–8 *Avenida Alvares Cabral* (1936), 27

Rua Defensores de Chaves (1937), and the *Parque Portugal dos Pequenitos*, Coimbra (1937–44).

J.T (1996)

Brandon, David (1813–97) *See* WYATT, T. H.

Brandon-Jones, John (1908–99) English architect, he carried on *Arts-and-Crafts traditions through a long, bleak period, ensuring his pupils were informed about late-C19 and early-C20 architects who had been so important in giving that movement life, yet whose existence was ignored by *Modernists. Opposed to what he called 'style-mongering', he stressed the importance of 'doing it well and getting it right'. From 1933, when he joined **Charles Cowles Voysey** (1889–1981—son of C.F.A.*Voysey) as an assistant (later partner), he devoted his life to architecture. He designed town halls for Bromley (Kent—1937–9), Watford (Herts.—1939–40), and Worthing (Sussex—*c*.1935), the Guildhall in Cambridge (1936–7), and the Festival House in Hull (1949–53). After war-service, he returned to practice with Voysey, and was joined by **Robert Ashton** (1906–1995) and **John Desmond Broadbent** (1920–94), rebuilding Morley College (1958—which had been bombed), and designing several municipal offices (including the superb County Offices at Winchester, Hants. (1959–60—later disfigured by hideously insensitive Modernist extensions)). He was a regular attender at the *Art-Workers' Guild, which he served as Master.

Pk; *The Times* (11 June 1999), 27.

Brandt, Gudmund Nyeland (1878–1945) Danish landscape architect, influenced by Italian-*Renaissance gardens, the gentle Danish countryside, and works by *Jekyll, *Lutyens, and William *Robinson. Much of his *oeuvre* was structured as a series of 'garden-rooms' connected by *bowling-alley-like areas: his Hellerup Coastal Path, Copenhagen (1912–18) has spaces for differing uses defined by *hedges and rows of trees. At Marienlyst Castle, Helsingør, he retained (1919–21) the outer *enclosures of linden trees (created under the direction of N.-H.*Jardin), but within them designed two *lawns (bounded by hedges flanking a middle section) enriched with *Greek-key *parterres. His *cemetery-designs (e.g. Ordrup (1919–30) and Mariebjerg (1926–36)) combined Classical enclosures of hedges and trees with informal planting. At the *Villa Svastika*, Rungsted (1925), formal spacing, divisions, and flowering plants were placed within a forested landscape, reminiscent of Robinson's *wild and H.*Repton's later gardens. Brandt's Classical vocabulary of regular walks and enclosures heralded his successors' later experiments in *abstraction derived from the work of **Piet Mondrian** (1872–1944).

JGH, **ix**/2 (April–June 1989), 53–70; A.Lund (2003); Shoe (2001); Stephensen (2007); Tay (2006)

brass 1. Mixed metal, an alloy of copper and zinc, capable of taking a high polish. **2.** In the sense of an engraved plate let into a slab of stone or set on top of an *altar-tomb, it is not true brass, but an alloy of copper and tin, creating *bronze or *latten, and examples abound with incised figures, *town-canopies, and inscriptions, often with infill of black resin, enamels, and mastic. The monumental or memorial 'brass' once again became popular in the C19 *Gothic Revival, using true brass.

brattice 1. *Bartizan. **2.** Timber construction overhanging a wall on a fortification.

brattishing 1. Ornamental *parapet, especially a *battlement. **2.** Decorative *Gothic *cress on top of a *cornice, parapet, *screen, etc., generally of *openwork consisting of stylized foliate and floral enrichment, often the *Tudor flower.

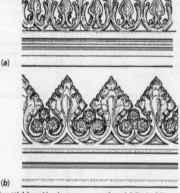

(a)

(b)

brattishing *Also known as* **cresting.** (*a*) Typical Perp. type. (*b*) Tudor-flower type, early C16, Henry VII's Chapel, Westminster.

breastsummer, bressummer, brest summer Horizontal *beam, *cill, *lintel, or *plate over an opening in an external wall or a fireplace-opening, or set forward from the lower part of a building to support an entire *jettied wall in *timber-framed construction. In the latter case (*jetty-bressummer*) it sometimes rests on the *cantilevered floor-*joists, sometimes secured to the joists tenoned into it, and is also carried on jetty-brackets: in turn, the bressummer supports the *posts of the jettied upper front wall. On occasion cantilevered *jetty construction is disguised

behind an ornamental *fascia-board often mis-
taken for a true bressummer.

ABDM (1996)

breeze-block *Breeze* was small cinders and
cinder-dust, essentially extinguished partially
burned coal, used in burning bricks, and obtained
from gasworks and coke-ovens. The material (6–8
parts, in crushed form) was mixed with *cement
(1 part), cast in wooden moulds, and made into
blocks for building walls or partitions not destined
to carry heavy loads. A variant was the *clinker-
block*, made from cement and *clinker* (mineral
matter or ash from furnaces formed by the fusion
of earthy impurities of coal, limestone, iron-ore,
etc., aka *slag*). Breeze and clinker, because of their
high sulphur content, proved to be unsuitable as
*aggregates for *concrete as they caused rapid,
extensive corrosion of steel-work and spalling of
the concrete's surface.

W.McKay (1957)

Brenna, Vincenzo (1745–1820) Florence-born
architect, he settled in Rome by 1767, and, with
Franciszek Smuglewicz (1745–1807), produced
drawings of Roman wall-paintings and other
remains, published as *Vestigia delle Terme di
Tito* (1776–8). Employed by **Count Stanisław
Kostka Potocki** (1755–1821), he moved to Poland
(1777), painting *Neo-Classical *grotesques for
Princess Lubomirska, the **Potockis**, and **King
Stanisław II Augustus Poniatowski** (*r.*1764–95):
some of his best Polish interiors are at Lańcut for
*Aigner. He then went on to St Petersburg, where
he worked as a decorative painter on schemes by
*Cameron, from whom he learned architectural
skills, and whom he succeeded (1796) as Court
Architect. His main works are at Gatčina, where
he designed many Neo-Classical interiors, developing a showy Imperial style from his earlier
archaeological studies.

Łoza (1954); L & R (1984); Polanowska (2009); J.T (1996)

bressummer *See* BREASTSUMMER.

**bretess, bretesse, bretex, bretise, bret-
tisse, brettys 1.** Battlement, so *bretexed*
means *crenellated* or *embattled*. **2.** *Brattice.

Breton, Gilles Le (*c.*1500–52) French master-
mason in charge (from 1527) of * **François Ier**'s
(*r.*1515–47) works at *Fontainebleau, surviving
designs at which include the *Porte Dorée*, with
superimposed *loggie* (1528–40), the entrance to
the *Cour Ovale* (from *c.*1531—with *portico and
staircase also by Le Breton), and the north side of
the *Cour du Cheval-Blanc*. His relatively straightforward *Renaissance *Classicism was influenced
by *Serlio, and in turn was a precedent for the
work of *Lescot.

Bt (1982); D.Wa (1986)

Brett, Sir Charles Edward Bainbridge
(1928–2005) Belfast solicitor/architectural historian, he founded with others (1967) the Ulster
Architectural Heritage Society at a time when
that city was losing one fine historic building
after another, and, with his *Buildings of Belfast*
(1967), drew attention to a remarkable legacy of
*Victorian architecture. His excellent series of
books on the buildings of Counties Antrim,
Armagh, and North Down, and his pioneering
works on *Mulholland and Ulster court- and market-houses remain exemplary. He set up the
HEARTH Revolving Fund and Housing Association (early 1970s), bodies which restored many
buildings for social housing or resale, and under
his energetic chairmanship the Housing Executive of Northern Ireland built over 50,000 properties, often admirably suited to their contexts.

Brett (1967, 1973, 1976, 1996, 1999, 2002); *ODNB*
(2013); pk

Brettingham Family. Matthew (1699–
1769) developed a large East Anglian practice as
an architect/builder/surveyor, and from 1734
supervised the building of *Kent's *Palladian
mansion of Holkham Hall, published as *The
Plans, Elevations, and Sections of Holkham in
Norfolk, the Seat of the late Earl of Leicester*
(1761), the plates of which attribute the designs
to him as 'Architect', Kent's name being omitted.
Holkham led to other commissions, including
Norfolk House, St James's Square (1748–52),
York House, Pall Mall (1761–3), neither of which
survives, and 5 St James's Square (1748–9), which
does. One of his most important works was
Kedleston Hall, Derbys. (*c.*1758), another great
essay in Palladianism. Only the *wings were built
as part of *Paine's revised design, but Paine was in
turn replaced by Robert *Adam, who completed
the house.

His son, **Matthew** (1725–1803), was responsible
for the *Neo-Classical work at Charlton House,
Wilts. (1772–6). **Robert William Furze Brettingham** (*c.*1750–1820), grandson of the older Matthew Brettingham, designed several *prisons,
including (probably) the noble front to Downpatrick Gaol, Co. Down (1789–96), and was perhaps
responsible (with **S. Woolley**) for the charming
*Gothick *choir refurbishment in the Cathedral of
the Holy and Undivided Trinity, Downpatrick
(1795), although **Charles Lilly** (*fl.*1781–1809)
may also have been involved. For **Arthur Hill**
(1753–1801—**2nd Marquess of Downshire** from
1793), he carried out enlargements of Hillsborough House, Co. Down (*c.*1795–97), drawings for
which were exhibited (1797) at the Royal Academy. His pupils included George *Smith.

Brett (2002); Co (2008); W.Pa (1852); J.F.Rankin (1997);
Su (1993); J.T (1996)

Breuer, Marcel Lajos (1902–81) American (from 1944) *Modernist architect/designer, born in Pécs, Hungary. He became (1924) Director of the furniture department at the Weimar *Bauhaus, designing furniture using structural frames of bent-steel chrome-finished tubes realized in the Dessau Bauhaus. He established (1928) an architectural practice in Berlin, producing the Harnischmacher House, Wiesbaden, and (with the *Roth brothers) the Doldertal Apartments, Zürich (1935–6), for *Giedion. He moved to London and a partnership with F.R.S.*Yorke (1935), but crossed the Atlantic (1937) to Harvard, where he became *Gropius's partner (1937–40), and also worked with him as associate professor, numbering among his students Philip *Johnson and Paul *Rudolph. After setting up an office in Cambridge, MA (1941), he moved (1946) to NYC. His career as an independent architect only really began after 1945, when he designed several private houses in New England (including his own at New Canaan, CT (1947)), in which *rubble and timber played no small part. With *Nervi and *Zehrfuss he worked on designs of the UNESCO Headquarters in Paris (1952–8) and, with **Abraham Elzas** (1907–95), on the *De Bijenkorf* Store, Rotterdam (1953–7). Stylistically his work became less *International-Modernist from this time, e.g. St John's Abbey and University, Collegeville, MN (1953–70, with **Hamilton P.Smith** (1925–)). Later works included the IBM Research Centre, La Gaude, Var, France (1961 with **Robert F.Gatje** (1927–)), and the Whitney Museum of American Art, New York (with Smith, 1963–6). He published a prolix and self-regarding book (1955).

Argan (1957); Blake (1949); Breuer (1955); C.Y.Jones (ed.) (1962); Masello (1993); P (1982); Papachristou (1970); J.T (1996)

Brewer, Cecil Claude (1871–1918) *See* SMITH, ARNOLD DUNBAR.

bric-à-brac Pejorative term for *Renaissance-Revival buildings based on French precedents and overloaded with busy ornament.

brick Solid, hollow, or indented building element, usually rectangular, but also other shapes for special purposes, manufactured from clay, *concrete, sand, *lime, or other materials, formed in a mould, then burnt, set, or cured. Its advantage over *masonry lies in the ease of mass-producing bricks to standard sizes, and in the fact that a brick can be lifted and laid using one hand, leaving the other free for holding a trowel for manipulation of *mortar. *Terms to describe bricks include:*
Accrington: see ENGINEERING BRICK;
air-: with regular perforations to allow air to pass through a wall;

angle-: see DOGLEG;
arch-, also called *tapered headers* or *tapered stretchers*: special brick tapered along its length to serve as a *voussoir* in an arch;
bat: half (*c*), *three-quarter* (*d*), *large-bevelled* (*e*), or *small-bevelled* (*f*) part of a brick greater than a quarter-brick, with the cut made across its *width*. It is used as an alternative to a *closer* in bonding to make up the dimensions in the courses of a wall;
bird's mouth: with a wide angular notch in one of the header faces;
brick tile: see MATHEMATICAL TILE;
brindle: attractive brown-purple brick, or bricks discoloured with stripes;
bullnose: with a rounded edge instead of an *arris (*single bullnose*, used where arrises are vulnerable) or with two rounded edges (*double bullnose* (*n*), for *copings*);
calcium silicate: brick, also called *flint-lime* or *sand-lime* brick made from sand or crushed *flint mixed with hydrated lime, then pressed into a mould and permitted to harden, usually in an autoclave;
cant: moulded brick with one corner (*single-cant*) or two corners (*double-cant*) cut off with a diagonal;
capping: shaped brick laid on edge on the top of a wall but not projecting beyond its faces. It can be a *half-round, bull-nosed, saddleback* (triangular), or *segmental* type;
clinker: **1.** brick the surface of which is *vitrified* by exposure to intense heat in the kiln or clamp; **2.** hard pale brick made in The Netherlands, used for paving;
circular: curved on plan, for curved walls;
closer: brick cut or moulded lengthways, exposing an uncut stretcher-face and a half-header, used to close the course at the return of the wall or at an opening in it, and to keep the *bond. *Closers are of various types*: bevelled closer (*j*)—with splayed stretcher-face, a half-header at one end, and a whole header at the other; *king-closer* (*i*)—three-quarter *bat* with concealed splayed corner, and exposed half-header; *mitred closer* (*k*)—with one end sharply splayed and the header-face removed, leaving a half or three-quarter stretcher, used where adjacent bricks join at an angle; and *queen-closer* (usually next to the first brick in a header-course, consisting of half a brick *half queen-closer* (*g*)—or a quarter brick *quarter queen-closer* (*h*));
closure: brick *slip*, smaller than a *bat*, used with a header to make up the full width of an early eleven-inch cavity-wall, where the two leaves were to be bonded, as in *Loudon's hollow wall*;
common: cheap bricks used where appearance or strength are not critical;

compass: also *radial* or *radiating brick*, it is tapered for use in arches, circular windows, or patterns;

concrete: moulded brick made from cement, sand, and crushed stone, etc., used instead of common bricks;

coping: like a *capping-brick*, used for copings, with bullnose, canted, saddle-back, segmental, or semicircular tops, laid on-edge, and made so that the ends project beyond the face of the wall to throw water clear of it;

Cossey white: very pale *gault* brick from Costessey, Norfolk, common in Norwich and environs, *c*.1830;

course: horizontal layer or row of bricks;

cownose: semicircular at one end only;

cut and rubbed: brick cut to shape with a bolster then rubbed to a fine finish with a *rubber* brick;

cutter: brick made from natural or mixed sandy loams (of uniform texture). When burnt they can be cut and rubbed to precise shapes;

dogleg: *angle-brick* (**o**) used to ensure a good bond at *quoins which are not right angles. A better job than *mitred closers*;

dry-dipped enamelled: moulded, dried, burnt, cooled, coloured, glazed, and reburnt *biscuitware*;

Dutch clinker: small yellowish brick often found in East-Anglian walls and pavements, called *klinkart*;

engineering: very dense, durable, strong, and water-resistant, used for *bridges, *piers, sewers, and other engineering construction. Commonest types are *Accringtons* (bright orange-red, pressed, and smooth), *Hunzikers* (crushed flint and lime), *Southwaters* (pressed and wire-cut), and *Staffordshire Blues* (blue, wire-cut, and handmade, often used for *plinths, as dampproof courses, and for copings);

facing: superior brick selected to be seen on the exposed face of a wall;

flare: *see* VITRIFIED BRICK;

Flemish: thin brick imported from Flanders or The Netherlands or made to imitate this type;

Fletton: made from Knotts clay found near Peterborough, Cambs., containing a large proportion of finely distributed combustible matter, with a resulting economy of fuel when being fired. A mass-produced *common* brick;

gault: dense brick made from limy or calcareous clay-beds found between the upper and lower greensands and containing sufficient chalk to render the brick pale yellow or white when burnt, often with bluish tinges;

glass: square glass *block, unlike the shape of normal bricks, hollow or solid;

glazed: usually of fireclay or shale, and accurate in size and shape, with exceptionally straight arrises, it is waterproof, *enamelled*, or *salt*-glazed. Useful for *dados, *plinths, and other surfaces requiring to be kept clean, or for lightwells where good qualities of clean, reflective surfaces are needed;

header (**a**): laid with its short face exposed;

Hitch: *see* RAT-TRAP BOND;

hollow: clay walling-block, larger than a true brick, useful for quickness of construction and properties of insulation;

Hunziker: *see* ENGINEERING BRICK;

klinkart: *see* DUTCH CLINKER;

London stock: yellowish-brown *stock-brick* made from London clay, often with the admixture of clinker from the coal used in previous firings, giving the finished brick dark spots with attractive patches of blue and red;

malm: almost white brick made from marly (limy or calcareous) clay to which chalk is added, common in Cambs., Lincs., and Suffolk;

mathematical tile: aka *brick tile* or *wall tile*, a tile with one face moulded to resemble the appearance and dimensions of a brick, laid in mortar and nailed to battens on a rough wall or timber-frame, then *pointed* so that the finished work resembles brickwork (*see* MATHEMATICAL TILE);

multi-coloured: known as a *multi*, used for facing work, it has faces attractively coloured with bright red, dark red, blue, yellow, etc., and is most satisfactory with *white pointing*;

perforated: has several small vertical cylinders of clay taken out from its core, leaving the faces indistinguishable from solid bricks;

Pether's patent moulded: pale buff moulded brick with very sharp detail much used in C19, notably by *Butterfield (e.g. at St Augustine's, Queen's Gate, London), and in countless Victorian terraces as *lintels and *string-courses;

pistol-: used to form a smooth curve between wall and floor, especially where good hygiene is necessary and there is regular washing out;

plinth: usually moulded or splayed at the top;

purpose-made: *special* brick for unusual or nonstandard work;

rubber: also known as a *cutter*, coloured soft red, white, or buff, it is formed from clean clay containing a lot of sand, moulded, then baked (not burnt). It is carved, cut, or rubbed with ease, and used for *gauged* arches, etc., with fine joints of *lime-putty*;

sand-faced: with sand sprinkled on the clay before firing. Used to enhance the appearance of inferior clays (e.g. *Flettons*) and usually applied to one stretcher- and one header-face only;

sand-lime: *see* CALCIUM SILICATE. It is usually employed in internal or below-ground work;

shaped: any type of brick other than a normal rectangular unit, e.g. *pistol*-brick;

slip: small *closure* (*p*), or piece of brick smaller than a *bat*;

snapped header: broken in half and laid so that its short face only appears in the wall-surface, suggesting a wall thicker than half a brick wide, so deceptive in terms of structural stability;

soldier: with its stretcher-face set vertically;

Southwater: *see* ENGINEERING BRICK;

special: made specially for a job (*purpose-made*), or a standard *shaped* brick;

splay (*l, m*): with a bevelled top, used for *plinths or *cills;

Staffordshire: *see* ENGINEERING BRICK;

stock: originally hand-made on a *stock-board*, but now machine-moulded. The term is also applied to any characteristic local facing-brick;

stretcher (**a**): laid so that its longest face is exposed;

vitrified: also a *flare*, it is often a very dark-blue or blue-black colour, usually with a shiny, glazed surface brought about by extremely high temperatures during firing, and is frequently found, often *snapped*, in walls forming *chequer-board, diaper, lettered,* or *numerical* designs;

wire-cut: formed by extruding clay through a rectangular die from the end of which individual bricks are cut off mechanically by serrated wires.

Terms associated with bricks or brickwork include:

arris: sharp edge between two adjacent brick faces;

bed: lower surface. A *bed-joint* is the horizontal mortar-joint;

cogging: as *dog-tooth*;

course: complete horizontal layer of bricks—a *brick-on-edge* course has bricks laid on their stretcher-faces; a *brick-on-end* or *soldier* course is one of bricks laid on their header-faces, the stretcher-faces being then vertical; a *heading* or *header course* consists of headers, and a *stretching* or *stretcher*-course of stretchers;

dentilation: alternate projecting headers, also called *toothing*, to carry a projecting course or *cornice. See* DOG-TOOTH;

dog-tooth: also *hound's tooth* or *mouse-tooth*, it is a course of projecting bricks laid diagonally to carry a projecting *course* or *cornice*, giving a jagged saw-tooth effect, called *cogging*, achieved by the exposure of one corner. It is an alternative to *dentilation*;

face: exposed surface;

fair-faced: unplastered brickwork, usually with flat or flush joints, as used for internal walls, whether painted or not;

frog: indentation or *kick* on the bed or the uppermost surface (**b**) or both—one-frog bricks laid with frog down save weight, work, and mortar, but they are usually laid frog up so that mortar fills the frog to ensure that the wall is strong;

gauged: fine, precise brickwork, as in an arch of soft *rubbers*, often a bright red or creamy colour contrasting with the rest of the wall, used around window- and door-openings and for arches;

indentation: *see* TOOTHING;

lap: horizontal distance between a vertical joint in one course and the joint in the course above or below it;

leaf: thin brick wall forming part of a cavity-wall. There is an inner and outer leaf on either side of the cavity;

nogging: brick infill panel in *timber-framed construction;

perpend: vertical line through superimposed vertical joints;

quoin: external angle of a wall;

sinking: *see* TOOTHING;

stopped end: also *closed end*, a square end of a wall the same thickness as that wall, finished with the aid of *closers*;

toothing: *dentilation*, or projections of alternate courses at the end of a wall to provide a *bond* for a later addition, leaving *indentation* or *sinking* in each alternate course. Dentilation is also used in a different sense, as part of a *cornice* support.

Brick bonds (patterns formed by arranging the courses with bricks overlapping the joints to provide a sound structure) are many and varied, and are often confused. *Listed here are attempts to describe the commonest types of bond*:

American: US term for a type of *English garden-wall bond*, but with a course of headers to every five or six courses of stretchers;

American with Flemish: *see* FLEMISH STRETCHER BOND;

basket-weave: three soldiers alternating with three stretchers in squares with no bond, forming a *chequerboard* pattern;

bastard: *see* HEADER BOND;

block: US term for *Flemish bond* or *common bond*;

block bonding (**a**): several courses of brick used to join one wall or part of a wall to another, e.g. where facing-bricks are bonded to common bricks of different sizes. The several courses may give the effect of *quoins where they interlock with the different brickwork;

chequered: bond formed by e.g. *Flemish bond* in which the headers are vitrified (a darker colour than the rest, and glazed), giving a regular chequered pattern. Flint or other materials may be used instead of vitrified headers to give the same effect;

Chinese: *see* RAT-TRAP BOND;

common: see ENGLISH GARDEN-WALL BOND;

Dearn's (**b**): variation on *English bond* where stretcher courses are bedded on edge (i.e. on their face) with a cavity between, the header courses laid normally on their beds, bonding the leaves together, and saving bricks by a slight gain in height for every course of stretchers. *Dearn's bond is often confused with *rat-trap* or *Silverlock's bond*. Dearn (incorrectly Dearne) also designed a bond with a course of headers, then a course of stretchers cut along their lengths giving a final appearance of ordinary English bond, but leaving unseen continuous cavities between the stretchers that could be heated (e.g. by connecting them from a stove to a flue) for use in conservatories;

diaper: bonding involving the creation of patterns using bricks of a different colour set in the wall, such as *vitrified* headers, forming diamond, square, lozenge, and other designs;

Dutch (**c**): also *staggered Flemish bond*, it is a variation on *Flemish bond*, with alternate headers and stretchers in each course, the courses being moved half a header on each course to left or right, giving a zig-zag effect called *staggered Flemish* in the USA. Another type of Dutch bond is actually a modification of *English bond*, and consists of alternate rows of headers and stretchers, but each stretcher-course begins at the quoin with a three-quarter bat and every alternate stretcher-course has a header placed next to the quoin three-quarter bat, causing the stretchers to break joint in alternate courses, the quoin three-quarter bats rendering the queen-closers of normal English bond redundant;

English (**d**): strong bond of alternate courses of headers and stretchers;

English cross- (**e**): also *St Andrew's bond*, it is similar to English bond, with alternate rows of stretchers and headers, and *queen-closers* next to the quoin-headers. Each alternate stretcher-course is moved half a stretcher to right or left to give a stepped effect to the joints. Aka *Dutch bond*;

English garden-wall (**f**): also *American bond*, *common bond*, or *Liverpool bond*, it has one course of headers to every three to (usually) five stretcher-courses, with a *queen-closer* introduced next to the quoin-header in the header course. Other variations occur;

facing: thin fine bricks employed to face a thicker wall of *common bricks*. In many C18 and C19 brick walls, outer skins of normal-sized *facing bricks* often did not bond with the *common-brick* backing except when an occasional tie was included: the *headers* of such walls in *Flemish bond* would then be *snapped* or *snap-headers*;

Flemish (**g**): alternate headers and stretchers in *each* course with closers next to the header quoins—variants may have three or five stretchers to each header. *Double Flemish bond* shows the bond on both faces of the wall;

Flemish cross-: as *Flemish bond*, but with additional headers at intervals instead of stretchers;

Flemish garden-wall (**h**): also *Scotch* or *Sussex bond*, it has courses of three or five stretchers between each pair of headers, continued along each course and contrived so that the header lies over the central one of the group of stretchers in the course above and below;

Flemish stretcher- (**i**): also called *American with Flemish bond*, it has courses of alternate headers and stretchers, sandwiching several courses of stretchers. Sometimes there can be anything from one to six courses of stretchers instead of the commoner three courses;

flying: see MONK BOND;

header (**j**): also *bastard* or *heading bond*, it has only headers on the wall-surfaces, is very strong, and is useful for engineering work or for curved walls. However, where the *header bond* is the outer leaf of a *cavity-wall*, the bricks might be *snapped* or *snap-headers*;

heading: see HEADER BOND;

herringbone: bricks laid in diagonal zig-zag fashion, with each course laid at right angles to the one below;

honeycomb (**k**): brickwork with the omission (usually) of headers in a pattern to permit ventilation, or for decoration;

hoop-iron: reinforced brickwork in which flat iron bars dipped in tar and sanded are laid in every sixth course;

irregular (**l**): bond using headers, but with no particular or consistent pattern, with broken vertical joints;

lacing (**m**): one or more courses of bricks or tiles establishing a regular reinforcement and bond in a wall of flint, cobbles, etc.;

Liverpool: see ENGLISH GARDEN-WALL BOND;

Loudon's hollow wall (**n**): brick wall of two *leaves each of *Flemish bond*, the stretchers of which have a gap between them two inches (5.08 cm) apart, so the *headers* require a two-inch *closer* brick to make up the full width of the wall. A variant was to lay the headers without the closers, or to lay them so that they were only one inch back from each face, thus providing excellent *keys for plaster or *stucco rendering. Invented by J.C.*Loudon, it was both strong and aesthetically acceptable, and allowed heat to pass through the cavity, so was ideal where certain plants were to be trained against it, as in a garden-wall, *kitchen-garden, *greenhouse, or *conservatory. Loudon also invented variations on other types of hollow

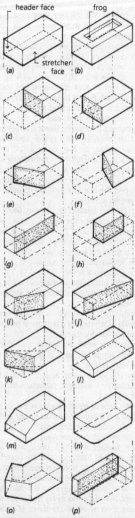

Pether's patent moulded brick, St Augustine's, Queen's Gate, London.

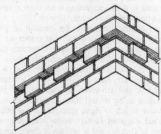

Dentilated brickwork.

brick Some types of brick: (*a*) standard full-size; (*b*) pressed with frog; (*c*) half bat; (*d*) three-quarter bat; (*e*) large bevelled bat; (*f*) small bevelled bat; (*g*) queen closer (half); (*h*) queen closer (quarter); (*i*) king closer: may also be a three-quarter bat with diagonal cut-back; (*j*) bevelled closer; (*k*) mitred closer; (*l*) splayed *or* splay-stretcher, *also known as* plinth-brick; (*m*) splayed *or* splay-header, *also known as* plinth-brick; (*n*) double bullnose; (*o*) dogleg; (*p*) slip.

wall, including improvements to *Dearn's* and *Silverlock's* bonds;

mixed garden (**o**): also called *mixed garden-wall bond*, it is essentially a variant on *Flemish bond*, but with two to five courses of stretchers, then a course of stretcher-header-stretcher, then three to five more of stretchers. Headers are not placed directly above each other in any regular pattern;

Monk (**p**): also called *flying bond* or *Yorkshire bond*, it is a variant on *Flemish bond*, with each course consisting of two stretchers rather than one between each pair of headers, each header placed over the joint between pairs of stretchers. Closers are required;

quarter: *see* RAKING STRETCHER BOND;

quetta: variant on Flemish bond with continuous vertical gaps left inside the wall thickness filled with reinforcement and mortar;

raking: courses laid alternately in different directions, such as *herringbone*;

raking stretcher (**q**): also *quarter bonding* or *quarter bond*, a variant on *stretcher bond* with each brick overlapping the brick below by a quarter brick;

rat-trap (**r**): also *Chinese*, *rowlock*, or *Silverlock's* bond, a variant on Flemish or Sussex bond with courses of alternate headers and stretchers in each course laid on edge rather than on bed, the stretchers forming outer and inner leaves of bricks laid on edge with a cavity between them,

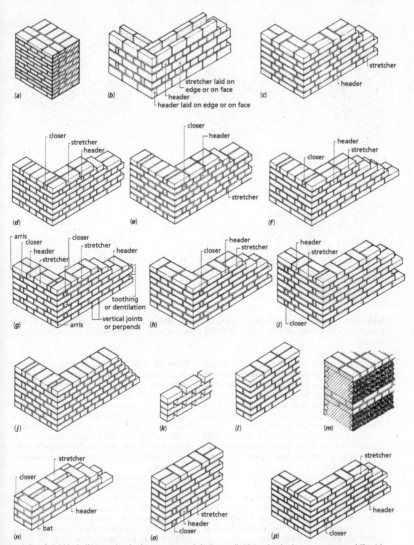

brick bonds (*a*) block; (*b*) Dearn's, *also known as* Dearn's hollow wall; (*c*) Dutch, *also known as* staggered Flemish (USA); (*d*) English; (*e*) English cross-bond, *also known as* St Andrew's; (*f*) English garden-wall, American, common, *or* Liverpool; (*g*) Flemish; (*h*) Flemish garden-wall, Scotch, *or* Sussex; (*i*) Flemish stretcher, *or* American with Flemish; (*j*) header, heading, *or* bastard; (*k*) honeycomb; (*l*) irregular; (*m*) lacing, *or* courses in flint-faced wall; (*n*) Loudon's hollow wall; (*o*) mixed garden, *or* mixed garden-wall; (*p*) Monk, flying, *or* Yorkshire;

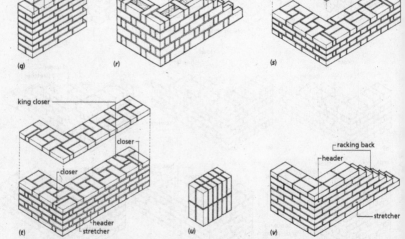

brick bonds (*q*) quarter, quarter-bonding, *or* raking stretcher; (*r*) rat-trap, Chinese, rowlock, *or* Silverlock's; (*s*) single Flemish exploded to show alternate courses; (*t*) double Flemish exploded to show alternate courses; (*u*) stack; (*v*) stretcher.

and the headers (laid on the centre of each stretcher-on-edge) acting as bonders. Although economical, it is not watertight, so if used for dwellings has to be rendered on the outside. The main virtue was that its hollow centre could be heated and used for walls against which plants could be grown. In the vicinity of Ware, Herts., what appears to be rat-trap bond may be a wall of *Hitch* hollow bricks of complex interlocking forms invented (1828) by **Caleb Hitch** (*fl.*1810–51);

Scotch: *see* FLEMISH GARDEN-WALL BOND;

Silverlock's: *see* RAT-TRAP BOND;

single Flemish (*s*): with the appearance of Flemish bond on the outside face of a wall more than one brick-length thick. *Double Flemish bond* (*t*) is contrived to look like Flemish bond on both the inner and outer faces;

stack (*u*): bricks laid on end with continuous vertical joints and no bond, so unsuitable for structural load-bearing walls;

staggered Flemish: *see* DUTCH BOND;

stretcher- (*v*): stretchers only, each lap being half a stretcher, commonly found in cavity walls;

Sussex: also called *Sussex garden-wall bond*, the same as *Flemish garden-wall bond*;

Yorkshire: as *Monk bond.*

Types and colours of pointing (application of a superior mortar-finish to the raked-out joints (mortar between adjacent bricks, horizontally and vertically)) of ordinary mortar in brickwork are very important for appearance, stability, and weathering. ***Some common examples of pointing include:***

bag-rubbed: flush pointing slightly recessed in the middle, so a type of *rubbed* joint;

bastard tuck-: imitation *tuck-pointing* of mortar only, with a profile similar to that of real tuck-pointing;

ribbon-: mortar standing proud of the stones. It is both unsightly and traps water, which damages the wall when it freezes, and became a common problem in the second half of the C20 when untrained 'masons' were allowed to get away with it (or encouraged by the ignorant);

tuck-: mortar the same colour as the brickwork set flush in the joints, with a groove formed along the centre of each joint into which is *tucked* a precise band of lime-putty to which a small amount of silver sand is added: this putty projects a few millimetres, and the top and bottom edges are trimmed in straight lines. In first-class work the vertical *tucks* are slightly narrower than the horizontal;

vee-: **V**-shaped channel formed in a *flush* joint.

Some common joints include:

bucket-handled: *see* KEYED JOINT;

flush: mortar flush with the brick faces;

hungry: deeply recessed pointing to enable the outline of every brick or stone to be emphasized;

keyed: called a *bucket-handled joint*, the mortar is indented with a segmental profile. Also a joint raked out to give a key to plaster or *stucco;

overhand struck: straight joint struck diagonally downwards, starting flush with the upper course;

raked-out: joint cleared of mortar to a depth of 10–15 mm from the face of the brickwork for decorative purposes, to provide a key for plaster, or to permit a different type of pointing;

recessed: set back from the face;

rubbed: flush joint made by rubbing excess mortar off the surface with a rag, rubber, etc.;

ruled: also *scored joint*, in which grooves are ruled by running the point of a trowel against a straight-edge to give the appearance of very precise work;

struck: straight joint struck diagonally, the bottom set back, and the top flush with the course below;

weathered: straight joint struck diagonally, the top set back, and the bottom *flush* with the course below.

Bru (1990); J.Campbell & Pryce (2004); N.Lloyd (1925); Lynch (1990, 1994–6); W.McKay (1957); JK

bridal door Portal at the side of a church where weddings took place (e.g. *Brautportal*, St Sebald, Nuremberg).

bridge Structure by means of which a *path, road, etc., is carried over a ravine, valley, river, etc., affording passage between two points at a height above the ground level, and allowing free passage through its one or more open intervals beneath. Bridges vary in complexity of structure from a simple plank, log, or slab of stone supported at each end (or a single arch spanning from bank to bank, say), to a far more elaborate structure with architectural pretensions, featuring *piers, arches, *girders, chains, tubes, and many other elements. Early bridges were made of ropes, while timber bridges of various types have a long ancestry. Arched bridges of brick or stone go back to *Antiquity, and some spectacular Roman bridges survive, such as the *Pons Fabricius* (62 BC), *Pons Milvius* (109 BC), and the *Pons Aelius* (now *Ponte Sant'Angelo*, completed AD 134), in Rome, but the *Puente del Diablo* near Martorell in Spain is even earlier (*c.*219 BC), although much restored, and seems to be one of the oldest still in existence. Also in Spain is the celebrated bridge over the Tagus at Alcántara (AD 105), with its six impressive arches. Many fine bridges were erected in medieval times (e.g. the fortified *Pont Valentré* over the Lot at Cahors, France

(1308–80); and London Bridge over the Thames (demolished), on which habitable buildings stood, erected 1176–1209 to designs by **Peter**, chaplain of Cole Church. Elegant C17 and C18 Classical structures (essentially based on Roman precedents) were built (e.g. *Telford's Tay Bridge, Dunkeld, Perthshire (1806–9)). *Cast iron was first used for bridge-construction in C18 at Ironbridge, Salop. (1777–9). The development of *canals and railways led to considerable advances in bridge-design, notably the suspension-bridge over the Menai Straits in Wales (1819–26) by Telford, the tubular-girder-bridge also over the Menai Straits (1844–50) by *Stephenson, and the Clifton suspension-bridge, Bristol (1831–64), by the younger *Brunel. Other important designers of C19 bridges included *Eiffel and *Roebling. In C20 *reinforced *concrete was used to great effect by many designers, including *Freyssinet, *Hennebique, *Maillart, and other elegant structures were erected by *Ammann, *Arup, and *Bonatz, among others.

The main types of bridge are:

aqueduct: for conveying water (such as a canal). Good examples are the Roman *Pont du Gard*, near Nîmes, France (C1 BC) and Telford's *Pont-y-Cysyllte* aqueduct (1795–1805);

arch-: carried on arches or *vaults;

bascule: type of *cantilever that can be raised to allow ships to pass under, e.g. London's Tower Bridge;

cantilever: arm projecting from a pier, or with two arms projecting from piers and connected in the centre;

clapper: stone bridge of piers with slabs of stone spanning between them;

draw: one that can be drawn up or let down, hinged like a flap;

girder: consisting of straight beam-like elements carried on piers, columns, or other supports;

Palladian: bridge with colonnaded superstructure (e.g. at Wilton, Wilts. (1735–7));

suspension: hung from chains or cables suspended from elevated piers;

swing: swivelling bridge which revolves horizontally on a pivot;

tubular: very large hollow girder, carried on piers, through which traffic passes (e.g. *Stephenson's Menai Straits railway bridge (1844–50));

viaduct: long structure carrying a road or a railway over a valley.

Bennett (1997); Billington (1979, 1983, 1990, 1997); Jurecka (1986); Leonhardt (1984); Mainstone (1975); Pearce & Jobson (2002)

Bridgeman, Charles (1690–1738) English landscape architect, he influenced the design of the informal English garden, introducing features that preceded the looser plans of *Brown and *Kent. He is credited with an early use (1719) of the French *ha-ha at Stowe, Bucks., and later used it in the simple form commonly found during C18. He also used the French *pattes d'oie* (literally 'goose-foot', but meaning avenues crossing each other) that drew attention towards various *eye-catchers. Bridgeman first came to notice before 1709 when he appears to have worked under *Vanbrugh and Henry *Wise at Blenheim, Oxon. He began to work (1714) for **Lord Cobham** (c.1669–1749) at Stowe, the most celebrated land-scaped garden of the time, with its 'informal' walks, carefully contrived planting, use of water, and numerous *fabriques*, most with literary, mythological, political, or historical allusions. He collaborated with many architects, including *Gibbs and Kent, and worked on several gardens, including those at Claremont (Surrey), Eastbury (Dorset), Rousham (Oxon.), and Wimpole Hall (Cambs.) (all 1720s). He may have advised Alexander *Pope on his garden at Twickenham, and was possibly involved in the creation of *Burlington's garden at Chiswick. In 1727, with Wise, he began a report on the management of the Royal gardens, and succeeded (1728) Wise as Royal Gardener to **King George II** (r.1727–60), working on numerous gardens, including Hampton Court, Kensington Palace, St James's Park, Richmond Park, and Hyde Park (all c.1727–38).

HHH (1980); J.T (1996); vV (1993); P.Willis (2002)

Brierley, Walter Henry (1862–1926) English architect, leading protagonist of the *Wrenaissance style in the North-East, his fine *Arts-and-Crafts house, The Close, Northallerton, Yorks. (1895–1904), was mentioned by *Muthesius.

A.S.Gray (1985); Nuttgens (1984)

Brinkman, Johannes Andreas (1902–49) Rotterdam-born architect, he was in partnership (1925–36) with **Leendert Cornelius van der Vlugt** (1894–1936) and (1937–48), with van den *Broek. The firm produced the van Nelle tobacco factory, Rotterdam (1926–30), on which *Stam also worked: regarded as one of the purest *Constructivist buildings of the period, as well as a pioneering example of Modern architecture, it was a mushroom-columned *reinforced-*concrete structure with large areas of *curtain-walling, and ramped connections between the factory-block and the warehouse in glazed elevated *bridges. Brinkman and van der Vlugt collaborated with **Willem van Tijen** (1894–1974) on the design of the slab-shaped *Bergpolder* high-rise residential block in Rotterdam (1933–4), with an early *piloti*-base (to be made obligatory by Le *Corbusier and his disciples).

Wi.Cu (1996); Geurst & Molenaar (1993); J.Je (1963a, 1976); M & N (1987)

brise-soleil Baffle or check of vertical or horizontal *louvres, fixed or swivelling, or other elements attached to or part of a building to protect windows from excessive solar light and heat.

Britannic Order *See* GERMAN ORDER.

Britton, John (1771–1857) English architectural/topographical writer. In partnership with **Edward Wedlake Brayley** (1773–1854), he produced *The Beauties of England and Wales* (starting with *Wiltshire* (1801)), a compilation which took 20 years to complete and ran to 27 volumes. His *Architectural Antiquities of Great Britain* (1807–26), *Specimens of Gothic Architecture* (1820–25), and *Cathedral Antiquities of England* (1814–35) were major sourcebooks for the *Gothic Revival: E.J.*Willson was among several contributors. He taught R.W.*Billings. *See* PUGIN, A. C.

Britton (1807–26); ODNB (2004)

broach 1. To remove the marks of rough scraping from a stone face, thus finishing it as broached work. **2.** To drill holes in stone in a quarry and then cut between them to free the *blocks. **3.** *Spire, more particularly one on a tower without *parapets, requiring extra *masonry to effect the transition between the square tower and the octagonal spire-base: the partial pyramidal forms are *broaches.* Broach-spires were usually *First Pointed, and occasionally *Second Pointed. **4.** A pointed ornamental structure, e.g. an *obelisk. **5.** Junction (*broach-stop* or *chamfer*) between a chamfered and squared edge by which the bevel merges into a right angle.

broch Prehistoric dry-stone circular structure with cells (presumably for habitation) in the wall, surrounding an open space (presumably for livestock), as found in Scotland.

Brodie, John Alexander (1858–1934) British civil-engineer/town-planner, pioneer of *prefabrication for cheap housing (e.g. the block of flats at the corner of Eldon Street and Vauxhall Road, Liverpool (1904–5—demolished)), he planned New Delhi from 1912, work for which *Lutyens held him in high regard. As City Engineer of Liverpool he was responsible for numerous improvements and innovations, including the Mersey Tunnel (1925–34), one of the great engineering feats of the time.

Sharples (2004)

Brodrick, Cuthbert (1821–1905) English architect, he won (1852) the competition to design Leeds Town Hall (the assessor was Charles *Barry): this fine civic building shows a pronounced French influence (*Brongniart's Paris *Bourse*) in the ranges of columns, as well as an acknowledgement of *Elmes's St Georges Hall, Liverpool. His Corn Exchange, Leeds (1860–3), is Italian-*Renaissance in style, with an elliptical plan and an ingeniously arranged roof-structure of iron (perhaps influenced by the *Halle au Blé*, Paris). Brodrick's Cliffs (now Grand) Hotel, Scarborough, Yorks. (1863-7), is much more overtly French Renaissance, with a massive *Second-Empire style roof.

Hi (1977); Linstrum (1978, 1999); J.T (1996); T.B.Wilson (1937)

Broek, Johannes Hendrik van den (1898-1978) *See* BAKEMA.

broken Signifies interruption of an element, e.g. *broken arch* (usually segmental with its centre filled by a carved motif), *broken ashlar* (random *masonry laid in irregular courses), *broken column* (with the shaft broken off, symbolizing death, a recurring theme in commemorative art), *broken pediment* (*see* PEDIMENT), and *broken rangework* (*masonry laid in courses but with *blocks of different heights, thus breaking the horizontal joints).

Brongniart, Alexandre-Théodore (1739-1813) One of the most distinguished French exponents of *Neo-Classicism, pupil of *Blondel and *Boullée, his Parisian town-houses, e.g. *Hôtel de Monaco, Rue St-Dominique* (1774-7), *Hôtel de Bourbon-Condé, Rue Monsieur* (1780-3), and *Hôtel de Montesquiou, Rue Monsieur* (1782), were in a simple, elegant, Neo-Classical style, influenced by de *Wailly, but he also evolved a severe *primitive type of architecture. He used an unfluted baseless *Doric *colonnade at the *cloister of the Monastery of *St-Louis d'Antin, Paris (1779-83), now the *Lycée Condorcet*, and at *St-Germain l'Auxerrois*, Romainville, Paris (1785-7), he was influenced by *Chalgrin's *St-Philippe-du-Roule* (1768-84), although he used sturdy Doric columns in the *nave. Primitivist, too, was his 'ruined' stepped *pyramid into which was set a tough Doric tetrastyle *portico carrying a segmental *pediment: he also designed the park, or *Élysée*, at Maupertuis, in which the 'ruined' pyramid stood. From 1804 Brongniart worked on designs for *Père-Lachaise* Cemetery, Paris, in which the *jardin *anglo-chinois* became a burial-ground, a conception that had a profound effect on the design of *cemeteries thereafter. His influential Paris *Bourse* (1807-13), with ranges of *Corinthian columns, satisfied Napoléonic tastes for Roman Imperial grandeur and embodied many theories of *Cordemoy and *Perrault.

B (1980); Brongniart (1986); J.Curl (2004, 2005, 2011); Eriksen (1974); Etlin (1984); Ha (1952-3); K & L (1972); E.Ka (1955); M & Wa (1987); Rosenblum (1967)

bronze Alloy of copper and tin used for architectural ornament, doors and door-furniture, funerary monuments, grilles and railings, wall-plaques (commemorative or not), window-frames, etc. It is also used in *masonry for cramps, dowels, etc. *See* BRASS.

Brookes, William McIntosh (1800-49) Architect educated at Peterhouse, Cambridge, he designed Gisborne Court at that college (1825-6—*Tudor *Gothic), the County Gaol, Ipswich, Suffolk (1836-7—also Tudor Gothic), Albury Church, Surrey (1840-1—*Romanesque Revival), and the Catholic Apostolic (Irvingite) Church, also in Albury (*c.*1837—*Perp., with William *Wilkins).

Co (2008)

Brooks, James (1825-1901) One of England's most distinguished *Gothic-Revival church-architects, he established his own practice (1851). He favoured Burgundian C13 *First-Pointed, and worked mostly in London, often using brick. Some of his churches follow the ideal of urban *Minsters established by *Butterfield at All Saints', Margaret Street, and include the powerful St Chad (begun 1867) and St Columba, Kingsland Road (1865-74), both in Haggerston: the latter is on a large scale, light admitted to the impressive interior through a *clerestorey of plate-traceried windows and *lancets at the east and west. Later churches include The Ascension, Lavender Hill (1874), and The Transfiguration, Lewisham (1880s). All Hallows', Gospel Oak (begun 1891), was intended to have stone *vaulting, but the 1914-18 war prevented this; at St John the Baptist, Holland Road, Kensington (1872-1911), however, stone vaulting was erected throughout the church. He was in partnership with his son, **James Martin Brooks** (1852-1903).

B.Clarke (1966, 1969); J.Curl (2002, 2007); D & M (1985); Ea (1970)

Brosse, Salomon de (*c.*1571-1626) French architect, important figure in the transition from *Mannerism to *Classicism. The son and grandson of architects (his grandfather was J.A.du *Cerceau), he settled (1590s) in Paris. His work tended to eschew Mannerist decorative effects, and was more architectonic, sober, and monumental than that of his immediate predecessors. Of his three *châteaux at Blérancourt, Aisne (1611-19), Coulommiers-en-Brie, Seine-et-Marne (1613), and Luxembourg, Paris (from 1614), only the last and a *pavilion at Blérancourt survive. The Luxembourg was *rustication over the whole of the *façades, presumably to emulate the *Palazzo Pitti* in Florence, the childhood home of de Brosse's client, **Maria de' Medici** (1573-1642), widow of **King Henri IV** of France (*r.*1589-1610). De Brosse's other surviving works include the *Palais de Justice de Bretagne*, Rennes (designed 1618), perhaps the very first manifestation of true French Classicism, influenced by architecture at *Fontainebleau and by *Vignola, built under the direction of **Germain Gaultier** (1571–1624). The handsome west front of *St-Gervais*, Paris (1616–23), with its *superimposed unengaged *Orders, is reminiscent of Vignola's *Il Gesù* façade, Rome, and also of de l'*Orme's *frontispiece at Anet: designed by de Brosse, it probably found its final form at the hands of J.-C.*Métezeau, who was the contractor, yet no mean architect himself. De Brosse's Protestant *Temple at Charenton (1623—destroyed) seems to have impinged on the design of Northern-European Protestant churches.

Blomfield (1974); Bt (1982); Coope (1972); J.T (1996)

Brown (*née* **Giles**), **Doris Jocelyn** (1898–1971) Australian landscape-gardener, she married (1920—in England) NZ architect, **Alfred John Brown** (1893–1976), then working with L.-E.-J.-G. de *Soissons at Welwyn *Garden City, Herts. They settled in Sydney, Australia, where A.J.Brown moved towards town planning, and, drawing on his English experience, published on the subject (1951) promoting the Garden-City ideal. D.J.Brown, also influenced by experiences in Herts., began to design gardens in Sydney, including Comely, Woollahra (1930–5), Fountains, Killara (1937–41—with the house designed by her husband), and Greenwood, St Ives (1941–5), and published (1939–42) numerous articles in *The Home* magazine, complete with plans, diagrams, and her own drawings of flowers. The *Arts-and-Crafts Movement and *Jekyll influenced her work.

ADB, xiii (1993); Brown & Sherrard (1951); Shoe (2001)

Brown, Joseph (1733–85) American amateur architect, he designed several important buildings at Providence, RI, including the First Baptist Meeting House (1774–5), the *spire of which is based on the illustrations in *Gibbs's *Book of Architecture* (1728). Among other works are University Hall (1770–1), the Market House (1773–7), and the Brown House (1786–8).

Cady (1957); Downing (1937); Hi (1939)

Brown, Lancelot *called* **Capability** (1716–83) One of the most influential English landscape architects who has ever lived, he was also an architect. He became (1741) head-gardener at Stowe, Bucks., where, with *Bridgeman and *Kent, he realized the 'naturalization' of the park. This much-admired work enabled Brown to set up on his own from 1749, and, for the next thirty years, he created many landscapes with artificial lakes, apparently randomly disposed *clumps of trees, and expanses of grass providing settings for the *Palladian mansions that were such a feature of the period. Country-houses,

which had once dominated the park, now tended to nestle in composed landscapes, and Brown's famed 'natural' parks (where untidy Nature was tamed and carefully composed) became enormously popular throughout England as well as influential on the Continent. His nickname is said to have originated in his reputed habit of telling clients that their estates were 'capable' of or had 'capabilities' for improvement. His finest existing landscape-gardens, perhaps, are at Berrington Hall, Herefs. (1780s), Croome Court, Worcs. (1751–2), Bowood, Wilts. (1760s), and Nuneham Park, Oxon. (1778–82). Landscapes influenced by his work and ideas are referred to as *Brownian*. He also designed buildings, and much of his work was executed by **Henry Holland** of Fulham (1712–85). He took the latter's son Henry *Holland (who became (1773) his son-in-law) into partnership (1771) and gradually handed over the architectural side of his practice. Brown's architectural works include Croome Court, Worcs. (1751–2), the *bridge, ice-house, and chapel, Compton Verney, Warwicks. (1770–8), and Claremont House, Esher, Surrey (1771–4, with Holland).

Co (1995); J.Curl (2011a); HHH (1980); Hinde (1986); Mowl (2000); Stroud (1966, 1975); R.T (1999); D.Wa (1982a); P.Willis (2002)

Brown, Richard (*fl.*1804–45) Probably from Devon, Brown established an architectural practice, but his main claim to fame was as a teacher of drawing and a writer. His pupils included M.A. *Nicholson, and he wrote *The Principles of Practical Perspective . . .* (1815), the indiscriminately eclectic *Domestic Architecture* (1842), *Sacred Architecture* (1845), and *The Rudiments of Drawing Cabinet and Upholstery Furniture* (1822 and 1835), one of the most handsome of early C19 English furniture *pattern-books, in which *Neo-Classical taste is well to the fore.

Co (2008); J.Curl (2005)

Browne, George (1811–85) Belfast-born architect, he practised in Canada from 1830. His best-known works were St George's Church, Kingston, Ontario (1859), a variant on *Gibbs's St Martin-in-the-Fields, and the City Hall and Market Building, also in Kingston (1842–4), in a robust mixture of *Neo-Classicism and late-*Georgian styles that looks back, perhaps, to the *Baroque of *Hawksmoor and *Vanbrugh, although *Gandon's work in Dublin is called to mind.

K (1994); J.T (1996)

Browne, Sir George Washington (1853–1939) Scots architect, he was Rowand *Anderson's junior partner (1881–95), having worked in London with *Nesfield who greatly influenced his later development. He won (1887) the competition to design Edinburgh's Central Library (completed 1890) with an essay in the *François Ier* style at George IV Bridge, and used the same style for the British Linen Bank (1902–5—now Bank of Scotland), at the corner of George and Frederick Streets, Edinburgh. Among his other works the Braid (former United Presbyterian) Church, Morningside (1886), the cheerful Hospital for Sick Children (1892), the National Memorial to Edward VII at Holyrood (1912–22), and the fine YMCA Building, St Andrew Street (1914–15), all in Edinburgh, should be cited. He was in partnership (*c.*1895–1907) with J.M.D.*Peddie.

AHe, iii (1992), 52–63; DW; *RIBAJ*, ser. 3 **xlvi**/376 (1939), 141–3

Browne, Kenneth George (1917–2009) English architect/artist/caricaturist. From 1958 he was for many years Townscape editor of *AR*, the proprietor-editor of which, H. de Cronin *Hastings, believed (correctly) that the consequences of a lack of visual education in Britain would create a hideous world termed *Subtopia (unfortunately, the magazine (despite its concerns for *townscape), simultaneously promoted a *Modernism that did enormous damage). Browne (et al.) produced *Civilia: the End of sub-Urban Man* (1971), a passionate attempt, using photomontage and drawings, to propose an ideal city, but the realization of such ambitions in Britain has proved chimærical. Perhaps Browne's wisest remark was that 'planning' on paper, based solely on finance, could not create a humane environment.

The Guardian (9 April 2009), 37

Browne, Sir Thomas (1605–82) English physician/writer, his *Garden of Cyrus* (1658) outlined the history of ancient gardens (starting with that of Eden), and went into considerable detail concerning the *quincunx in garden-design (described by **Xenophon** (*c.*430–*after* 355BC) in his plantation in Sardis, Lydia), architecture, numerology, and much else.

Browne (1658); *ODNB* (2004)

Brownian See BROWN, LANCELOT.

Browning, Bryan (1773–1856) Born in Lincs., he was active as an architect by 1817, and worked in London (*c.*1820–30) with builder/surveyor **George Woolcot** (*c.*1785–1853), with whom he built Strensham Court, Worcs. (1824) to designs by **George Maddox** (1760–1843). By 1834, however, Browning was back in Lincs., where (1821) he had designed the fine Sessions House at Bourne in which an external staircase and columnar screen recall the entrance to the Rasumovsky Palace, Moscow (1801–3). Established (1838) in

Stamford, he designed the powerful Graeco-Egyptian Stamford Institute, St Peter's Hill (1842), and Grant's Foundry, Wharf Road (1845—only the portal survives). One of his best works was the House of Correction, Folkingham, Lincs. (1824–5—demolished except for the entrance-gatehouse). He was responsible for several *workhouses in the 1830s and for Stoke Dry Rectory, Rutland (1840—*Tudor *Gothic). Towards the end of his life he was in partnership with his son, **Edward Browning** (1816–82): they rebuilt Stamford Bridge and adjoining Toll-House (1847–9).

Apollo (April 1998), 55; Co (2008)

brownstone Dark red-brown sandstone much used in the eastern USA in the mid- and late C19, hence the typical brownstone-faced *terrace-houses of NYC.

Bruant *or* **Bruand, Libéral** (*c.*1635–97) Architect of the *Hôtel des Invalides* (1670–7—with its severely *Antique arcaded *cour d'honneur* and *St-Louis des Invalides* (the *Dôme* was added later by *Mansart)), and Chapel of *St-Louis* in the *Salpêtrière* Hospital (*c.*1670—with a *rotunda surrounded by four compartments forming a Greek-*cross on plan, and four chapels at the angles of the central space, allowing different categories of inmate to follow services conducted at the central *altar), all in Paris.

Bt (1982); Ha (1948); Reutersvärd (1965); J.T (1996)

Bruce, Sir William (*c.*1630–1710) Founder of Classical architecture in Scotland. A Perthshire laird, he became Surveyor-General and Overseer of the King's Buildings (1671–8), advising **Robert Mylne** (1633–1710) on the rebuilding (1671–9) of Holyroodhouse, Edinburgh, with its symmetrical Frenchified *façade. He was consulted by members of the Scottish aristocracy wishing to improve their residences. At Kinross House (1686–93) he adopted the highly accomplished manner of *Pratt and *Webb, and the architecture is enhanced by its formal setting. The main vista is terminated by the ruins of Lochleven Castle, so Bruce, like *Vanbrugh, has a position in the history of the *Picturesque. He designed Lauder Church, Berwickshire (1673), Hopetoun House, West Lothian (1699–1710), the Town House, Stirling (1703–5), and (probably) the Hope Aisle, Abercorn Church, West Lothian (1707–8).

Co (2008); Dunbar (1970, 1978); Fenwick (1970); J.T (1996)

Brückwald, Otto (1841–1904) Saxon Court Architect, and designer of the innovatory *Festspielhaus*, Bayreuth, Bavaria, for **Richard Wagner** (1813–83), much influenced by the work of *Semper and Wagner himself. There is a huge stage, and the *auditorium seating is arranged like a segment of a circle, with the orchestra placed out of sight partially under the stage.

Mallgrave (1996); pk

Brukalski, Stanisław (1894–1967) He and his wife, **Barbara** (1899–1980), were pioneers of *International *Modernism in Poland, specializing in public-housing developments, and were members of *CIAM. They also designed the interiors of passenger-liners, including the *Batory, Piłsudski, Sobieski,* and *Chrobry* (1927–38). Among their works the Warsaw Housing Co-operative Housing Colony VII, Warsaw-Żoliborz (1930–4), deserves mention.

Li (1996); Wisłocka (1968)

Brun, Charles Le (1619–90) French artist/designer, responsible for much of the interior decoration of the *Château* at Versailles (including the sumptuous allegorical paintings in the *Galerie des Glaces* (1678–84)), as well as the programme of sculpture in the gardens. His work encapsulates the essence of the *Louis-Quatorze* style.

Montagu & Thuillier (1963); J.T (1996)

Brunel, Isambard Kingdom (1806–59) One of the most distinguished and imaginative C19 engineers, Brunel was the son of French-born engineer **Sir Marc Isambard Brunel** (1769–1849). Educated privately and at the *Lycée Henri Quatre,* Paris, he entered (1823) his father's office where he was involved in the construction of the Thames Tunnel from Wapping to Rotherhithe. He designed (1829) the suspension-*bridge over the Avon at Clifton (built in modified form 1836–64). Appointed (1833) engineer for the Great Western Railway, he not only surveyed the route, but designed the Box Tunnel between Chippenham and Bath, the bridge over the Thames at Maidenhead, and introduced a limited standardization for the design of station-buildings on the line between London and Bristol. He was responsible for Temple Meads Station, Bristol (1839–40); Paddington Terminus, London (1850–5—to which M.D.*Wyatt and Owen *Jones contributed); the Royal Albert Bridge over the Tamar at Saltash (1857–9—his most celebrated iron structure); the Railway's *Company town, Swindon, Wilts. (again with Wyatt); a prefabricated hospital (complete with tarred wooden sewers and mechanical ventilation, for Renkioi in the Crimea (1855—possibly suggested by the success of the Crystal Palace, for he was a zealous promoter of the Great Exhibition (1851)); and ocean-going steamships (e.g. the *Great Eastern* (1858)) that were larger and more technically advanced than any previously known.

Binding (1997); R.A.Buchanan (2002); Falconer (1995); Kentley *et al.* (eds) (2000); Noble (1938); *ODNB* (2004); Pugsley (ed.) (1980); Rolt (1957); Sk (2002)

Brunelleschi, Filippo (1377–1446) Florentine architect, the first of the *Renaissance, who trained as a sculptor and goldsmith, learned geometry, and developed laws and principles of *perspective. Gradually he became more interested in architecture, and from 1417 advised on the proposed *cupola for the Cathedral of *Santa Maria del Fiore,* Florence. His inspiration for his architecture was certainly from earlier buildings, but it came from Tuscan *Romanesque and *proto-Renaissance buildings rather than from the remains of Imperial Roman architecture, for structures such as *San Miniato al Monte* and the *baptistery, Florence (both C11 and C12), were thought at the time to be much older than they were. Indeed, he was less of an antiquarian than those who followed him (notably *Alberti and *Michelozzo), and seems to have been more interested in problems of construction, definition of architectural elements by linear means, and control and management of volume. He began to build (1420) the Cathedral cupola (in collaboration with *Ghiberti), a vast octagonal structure crowned by an enormous *lantern designed by Brunelleschi alone (1436–67). The octagon, double shell, and pointed profile were settled before Brunelleschi's involvement, but the use of spiralling courses of herringbone brickwork, iron chains and sloping masonry-rings to bind the dome together, and ribs joining the shells are his inventions, although owe much to his studies of Roman structures. Brunelleschi's genius lay in his abilities to combine ancient and modern aesthetic, architectural, and engineering principles.

His *Ospedale degli Innocenti,* Florence (1419–44), with its elegant *arcades on *Corinthian columns, glazed *terracotta *medallions in the *spandrels, *architrave dividing first and second floors, and small rectangular windows over which are *pediments, is reckoned to be the very first truly Renaissance building, but its sources are local. Brunelleschi designed two *basilican churches (*San Lorenzo* (from 1418) and *Santo Spirito* (from 1436)): both have *nave-arcades with Classical columns carrying fragmentary *entablatures from which the arches spring, and both have domed crossings with *transepts, although at *Santo Spirito* the *aisles and semicircular side-chapels carried all round the church give a rhythmic unity not present at *San Lorenzo.* At the latter Brunelleschi designed the Old Sacristy, also the *mortuary-chapel of the **Medicis,** as a cube roofed by a *dome with ribs radiating from the central lantern giving an impression of sail-like forms over ribs. The entire interior was painted white with bands of grey on the dominant architectural motifs, the first time such a decorative scheme was employed. Brunelleschi may have designed the Pazzi Chapel in the *cloister of *Santa Croce*, Florence (1429–61), where Old-Sacristy themes are developed with a central domed space flanked on two sides by barrel-vaulted side bays and on the third by a small domed recess set behind an arch. The chapel is approached through an entrance-*loggia* consisting of two groups of three Corinthian columns carrying an entablature between which is an arch: behind is a saucer-dome. The fine interior is articulated by means of *pilasters, entablatures, *archivolts, and other architectural elements, all in local grey stone (*pietra serena*), set against the white walls, while glazed *terracotta *roundels complete the scheme.

The uncompleted *oratory of the Camaldulensian convent of *Santa Maria degli Angeli* (1434–7) is the first truly centrally-planned Renaissance building, with a domed octagon set on eight *piers which also provide the divisions between the radiating chapels: it is quite clearly based on *Antique precedent, notably the so-called Temple of *Minerva Medica*, Rome. The *astylar rusticated *Palazzo Pitti*, Florence, may have been partially designed by Brunelleschi, for its severe *Antique quality and carefully ordered proportions suggest at the very least his influence. Brunelleschi used simple proportional relationships throughout his buildings, giving his architecture its pleasing harmonious quality.

Argan (1978); Battisti (1981); Braunfels (1981); Cable (1981); Do (1980); R.King (1999); Klotz (1970); Luporini (1964); P (1982); Prager & Scaglia (1970); Ragghianti (1977); Saalman (1980, 1993)

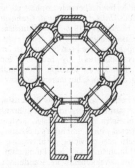

Plan of *Santa Maria degli Angeli*, Florence.

Brunfaut, Fernand (1886–1972) Belgian architect, he designed public and private housing in Brussels, the *Maison du Peuple*, Dinant (1922), and, in his capacity as a member of Parliament, was responsible for a law (1949) controlling the development of working-class housing in Belgium. From 1930 his buildings were designed in collaboration with his son, **Maxime** (1909–2003— pupil of *Horta), and include the offices of the newspapers *Vooruit* in Gent (1930) and *Le Peuple*, Brussels (1931). Maxime completed Horta's Central Station, Brussels (1946–53). Fernand's brother, **Gaston** (1894–1974), was an *International Modernist: his Children's Home, Oostduinkerke (1933–9), and the *Instituts Jules Bordet et Paul Héger*, Brussels (1937–9—with **Stanislas Jasinski** (1901–78)) are examples of his work. Through his editorship of *Le Document* he influenced Belgian architecture.

Loo (ed.) (2003); Puttemans *et al.* (1976); J.T (1996)

Brunfaut, Jules (1852–1942) Belgian architect, he worked for a time with *Beyaert, and then concentrated on designing houses for middle-class clients, larger houses for the rich, industrial buildings, and exhibitions. His finest work is the *Hôtel Hannon, Rue de la Jonction*, Brussels (1902), in the *Art-Nouveau style. He ran the influential architectural journal *L'Emulation* (1885–90).

Annuaire de l'Académie royale de Belgique, **cxvi** (1950), 137–65

Brunt, van *See* WARE & VAN BRUNT.

Brutalism Term so loosely used it could mean anything intended by those employing it. It seems mainly to have signified a C20 architectural style where exposed rough concrete finishes and chunky, blocky forms coexisted, especially in works influenced by Le *Corbusier from 1945 (where *béton brut* was treated particularly uncompromisingly, with *formwork patterns not

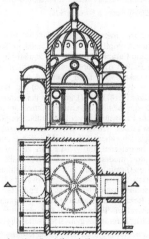

Plan and section, *Pazzi Chapel, Florence.*

only visible, but deliberately emphasized, as in Le Corbusier's *Unité d'Habitation de Grandeur Conforme*, Marseilles (1948–54)). Brutalism was widely fashionable from the 1950s, when the term appears to have been first used in England. Architects influenced by Brutalism included *Kahn, *Mayekawa, *Rudolph, the *Smithsons, *Stirling, and *Tange, but there were many others as well.

What became known as **New Brutalism**, however, was particularly associated with British supposed disciples of Le Corbusier, perhaps not unconnected with P. Smithson's nickname, 'Brutus', whilst also providing an alternative to the *New Humanism and *New Empiricism influenced by developments in Scandinavia. The Smithson's Smithdon High (formerly Secondary Modern) School, Hunstanton, Norfolk (1949–53), was described (somewhat curiously) as 'Brutalist', even though it clearly owed more to *Mies van der Rohe than to Le Corbusier, and its construction was exposed steelwork with panels of glass and yellow brick: *Pevsner described the building as 'ruthlessly perfect and ruthlessly symmetrical', so the use of that term for a building not made of *concrete would appear in this case to refer to supposed rigour, the exposure of structure and services, and work by or influenced by the Smithsons (who portentously described New Brutalism as an 'ethic, not an aesthetic', conjuring associations with absurd Puginian–Ruskinian 'moral' stances). Critics pointed out that this 'ethical' approach overlooked major problems (the exposed steel frame was subject to warping, and classrooms suffered from severe solar-heat gain, so claims to be 'Functionalist' had no credibility). *New Brutalism* probably came into use as obeisance to the Smithsons: Peter Smithson claimed of one of his unexecuted designs (a house featuring brick, wood, and exposed concrete) that it would have been the first example of New Brutalism in England (as it was the intention to have the structure entirely exposed, without internal finishes): by what appears to have been a process of association, or even of osmosis, therefore, the school became associated with New Brutalism because of what its creators *might have done*, had their work been realized. Thus, if *New Brutalism* seems vague and a curiously catch-all term, loosely applied, it could nevertheless be a label attached to buildings in which raw, exposed concrete was used (e.g. the Yale University Art Gallery (1951–3), by Kahn, and the Ham Common *flats (1955–8), by Stirling & Gowan—who loathed the term as it (unsurprisingly) put clients off), especially those where over-sized rough concrete elements, crudely colliding with each other, were visible, while aspects of mechanical engineering (e.g. service-ducts, ventilation-towers, etc.) were visible and even emphasized. Examples would include the Hayward Gallery, Queen Elizabeth Hall, and surrounding walkways, *parapets, and *stairs at London's South Bank (1968–9). *Banham held that 'the ultimate disgrace of Brutalism . . . [was] . . . to be seen in the innumerable blocks of flats built throughout the world that use the prestige of Le Corbusier's *béton brut* as an excuse for low-cost surface treatments'. The intellectual confusion surrounding New Brutalism was symptomatic of a serious malaise: rigour and 'ethics' played no part in suspect claims and shaky pedigrees.

AD, xxiii (Dec. 1953) 342; *AJ*, cxliv/26 (28 Dec. 1966) 1590–1; *AR*, cxviii/708 (Dec. 1955), 355–61; R.Ba (1966); *OED Supplement*, i (1987), 371; Sn (ed.) (1968); J.T (1996); M.Webb (1969)

Bryce, David (1803–76) Scots architect, pupil and assistant of *Burn. He designed several distinguished buildings, including the *Scottish-Baronial Royal Infirmary (1870–9); Fettes College (1863–70); the Head Office of the Bank of Scotland (1864–71); St George's West Church (1867–9); and the British Linen Bank, St Andrew Square (a fine *palazzo*, 1846–51), all in Edinburgh. He is best-known for his country-houses, most of which are in the Scottish-Baronial style, influenced by *Billings's *Baronial Antiquities* (1845–52): one of his best houses in that style is Kinnaird Castle, Brechin, Angus (1853–7). He designed the enormous Classical Hamilton Palace *Mausoleum, Lanarkshire (1848–51). His brother, **John** (1805–51), practised in Glasgow, where he designed monuments in the Necropolis including the McGavin memorial (1830s), and several ranges of Classical houses, including Queen's Crescent (1840).

Co (2008); Fiddes & Rowan (1976)

Brydon, John McKean (1840–1901) Scots architect, pupil of *Bryce, he joined J.J.*Stevenson and **Campbell Douglas** (1828–1910) in Glasgow (c.1863–6) before settling in London where he worked with Eden *Nesfield and Norman *Shaw. He set up in practice (1880) with **William Wallace** (*fl.*1871–1907), and won the competition to design the new Government Offices at the corner of Parliament Street and Parliament Square, Westminster (1898–1912), a fine ensemble in which *Chambers, *Wren, and *Webb influences can be detected, and Wren's work also informed his more modest Chelsea Town Hall (1885–7—in a 'Free-Classic' style). In a series of lectures and articles, Brydon called for the revival of Classical discipline in architecture as an antidote to the free-for-all of late-Victorian times, and promoted a revival of *Palladianism and elements from English *Baroque, as in his Bath Guildhall (1890s).

A.S.Gray (1985); P & D (1973); Stamp & Amery (1980); J.T (1996)

Bryggman, Erik William (1891-1955) Finnish architect, he practised in Turku (1923): Aino and Alvar *Aalto worked with him for a brief period, their collaboration producing designs for the 1929 Exhibition to celebrate seven centuries of the city's existence. Bryggman won (1930) the Grand Prix at the Antwerp World Fair for his Finnish *pavilion, an essay in birch plywood, and in 1938 his well-known *cemetery-chapel at Turku was commenced (completed 1941). Other works include Vierumäki sports-club (1931-6) and the library of Åbo Academy, Turku (1933-6).

Nikula *et al.* (1991); J.M.Ri (1978); J.T (1996); Wickberg (1962)

Buchanan, Sir Colin (1907-2001) Scots architect/planner. He published (1958) *Mixed Blessing: The Motor in Britain*, resulting in his appointment (by the then Conservative government) as planning advisor to the Ministry of Transport to study long-term problems of urban traffic. The resulting 'Buchanan Report' (entitled *Traffic in Towns*) had the rare accolade of being published (1963) as a book by Penguin, and marked the beginning of an era when urban 'planning' was not to be completely dominated by traffic-engineers (as had been the case). Appointed (1963) Professor of Transport at Imperial College, University of London, Buchanan set up his own planning consultancy (**Colin Buchanan & Partners**), producing development-plans for cities in the UK and abroad. Many lessons learned from his work in the 1950s and 1960s seem to be disregarded in C21.

The Times (10 December 2001), 15

Buchsbaum, Hans von (*c.*1390-*c.*1456) German architect, he worked in the Danube area, first at Ulm (1418), then at Steyr (1440s), where he built the *Pfarrkirche*. He probably worked (1430s) at the *Stephansdom*, Vienna, before being appointed (1446) Master of the Works there, supervising construction of the *nave *vaults.

Grimschitz (1947); Koepf (1969)

buckler 1. *Acrostolium*. 2. *Pelta* ornament common on Classical *friezes (especially in the Roman-*Doric *Order according to *Vignola), consisting of a wide shield-like form with its extremities on either side returning as heads or scrolls. 3. Circular shield of small size.

Buckler, John (1770-1851) English draughtsman/architect, he left records of much that was subsequently altered or destroyed, notably in Bucks., Herts., Oxon., Som., Staffs., Wilts., and Yorks. He designed some funerary tablets, but his most substantial architectural works were Halkin Castle, Flintshire (1824-7—*Tudor *Gothic), and (probably) the charming Gothic remodelling of Blithfield Hall, Staffs. (1822-3). His architect-son, **John Chessell Buckler** (1793-

1894), published (1822) *Views of the Cathedral Churches of England and Wales*, and (1827) *Sixty Views of Endowed Grammar Schools*. J.C.Buckler designed Costessey Hall, Norfolk (1826-—*Tudor *Gothic, demolished 1920), carried out restorations at Adderbury Church, Oxon. (1831-4), and won (1836) second prize in the competition for rebuilding the Palace of Westminster. Other works included Butleigh Court, Som. (1845), Dunston Hall, Norfolk (1859), and the Turl frontage of Jesus College (1854-6) and Choristers' Hall, Magdalen College (1849-51—now the Library), both in Oxford. His restorations included several Oxford colleges, Lincoln Cathedral, and Hengrave Hall, Suffolk. *His* son, **Charles Alban Buckler** (1824-1905), became an RC, and worked mostly for clients of that religious persuasion. His major work was the remodelling of Arundel Castle, Sussex (1890-1903), for **Henry Fitzalan-Howard** (1847-1917—**15th Duke of Norfolk** from 1860), and his best-known church is Our Lady and St Dominic, Haverstock Hill, London (1874-83).

Co (2008); *ODNB* (2004)

Bucklin, James Champlin (1801-90) Born in RI, USA, he is remembered as an architect of monumental buildings in the *Greek-Revival style including the Westminster Street front to Providence Arcade (1828) and Manning Hall, Brown University (1833), both in Providence, RI.

Hi (1939); P & J (1970-86); J.T (1996)

bucrane, bucranium (*pl.* **bucranes, bucrania**) Ornament in the form of an ox-skull or -head frequently associated with *festoons and *garlands, found especially on the *metopes of the Roman-*Doric *Order. *See also* AEGICRANE.

bucranium (*left*) Hung with bellflower or husk-garlands; (*right*) hung with inverted flambeaux.

bud In the *Corinthian *capital the bud-like form at the top of the stalks out of which the *volutes grow.

Buddhist railing Stone barrier resembling a timber *fence, with the horizontals running through the vertical *posts, usually surrounding a *stupa.

buffet d'eau *Fountain shaped like a stepped cake-stand, with a *basin underneath.

Buffington, LeRoy Sunderland (1847–1931) American architect, he established (1873) himself in Minneapolis, MN, where he designed numerous buildings in several styles, notably *Queen Anne and the round-arched style for which *Richardson became famous. His mansion for **Charles Pettit** (1874) was much influenced by *Visconti's and *Lefuel's additions to the Louvre in Paris (1852–7), and by *Hunt's house for the Wetmore family, Newport, RI (1872–3). His West Hotel (1881–4—destroyed), the Pillsbury 'A' Mill (1880–3), and the Pillsbury (1887) and Gale (1888) residences, all in Minneapolis, received much critical attention. Buffington invented (1880–1, 1883–4) a system of metal *skeleton construction to make the building of *skyscrapers (he called them 'cloudscrapers') possible: in 1888 he patented it, but attempts to claim royalties through litigation were unsuccessful.

AB, xx (1935), 48–70, and xxvi (1944), 3–12, 267–76; J.T (1996); E.Upjohn (1935)

building line Line beyond which a building may not encroach: it might, for instance, define the frontage of *façades in a street.

buitenplaats (*pl.* **buitenplaatsen**) Literally 'outside place', Dutch for a small country house or retreat. Common in the C17, *buitenplaatsen* or *buitenhuizen* were summer homes for merchants/burghers, easily accessible from towns, and often sited along the banks of rivers such as the Amstel, Vecht, etc. By the end of the C18 many *buitenplaatsen* had been built, set in gardens (often with 'stiff *parterres', as *Beckford described them).

Haslinghuis & Janse (eds) (2005)

Bulfinch, Charles (1763–1844) One of the USA's first native-born professional architects. His work combined *Colonial-*Georgian and *Adam styles in a frugal *Neo-Classicism, prompted by his tour of Europe (1785–7). He designed the old State House, Hartford, CT (1793–6), followed by the Massachusetts State House, Boston, MA (1795–7), influenced by *Chambers's Somerset House, London (1776–86). He also designed several groups of *terrace-houses and some churches (including the Church of Christ, Lancaster, MA (1816)), but much has been demolished. He was architect to the Federal Capitol in Washington, DC (1818–30).

Bulfinch (1973); *JSAH*, xxix/2 (May 1970), 124–31; Kirker (1969); P & J (1970–86); Place (1968); J.T (1996); W & K (1983)

Bulgarian architecture See BYZANTINE ARCHITECTURE.

Bullant, Jean (*c.*1515–78) French *Renaissance architect, much influenced by de l'*Orme, who introduced the *Giant *Order to France at the entrance-*portico on the south side of the *château* at Ecouen, Seine-et-Oise (*c.*1560). He designed the monumental gallery at Fère-en-Tardenois (1552–62) to connect the fortified *château* to its dependent buildings, placing it on a tall series of arches (giving the impression of a Roman *aqueduct), and the small *château* at Chantilly (*c.*1560—with a *frontispiece featuring a monumental arch carried on the Mannerist device of *coupled columns to enliven the *façade). He also completed the *gallery over de l'Orme's bridge at Chenonceaux (1576–8) for **Catherine de' Medici** (1519–89), the Queen Mother: again Mannerist devices and rhythms recur. His *Mannerism came close to that of du *Cerceau the Elder. Bullant's publications include *Reigle Générale d'Architecture* (1563) and *Petit Traicté de Géometrie* (1564).

Blomfield (1974); Bt (1982); J.T (1996); D.Wa (1986)

Bullard, Helen Elise (1896–1987) American landscape architect, she insisted that modern architecture needed associated landscapes designed with 'directional lines' to evoke a sense of movement: it is unclear what this actually meant, but she rejected 'classic forms'. Her works included *public parks, Calumet, MI (1921–3); State parks and *parkways, Long Island, NY (1931–5); and landscape designs for the World's Fair, NYC (1939).

Shoe (2001)

Bullet, Pierre (1639–1716) French architect (pupil of N.-F.*Blondel), author of *Livre Nouveau de Cheminées and L'Architecture Pratique* (1691), he practised in Paris from 1672. His *Hôtels Crozat* (now the Ritz) and *d'Evreux* in the *Place Vendôme*, Paris (1702–7), were precedents in their interior arrangement for later Parisian houses. His son, **Jean-Baptiste Bullet de Chamblain** (1665–1726), assisted him in the construction of the *Place Vendôme* houses, but on his own he designed the *Hôtel Poisson de Bourvalais* (1703–7). His *Château de Champs* (1703–7) had an elliptical salon exposed in a protruding *bow on the garden-front, while his *Hôtel Dodun*, Paris (after 1715), had *Rococo interiors.

Bt (1982); Ha (1948, 1950); K & L (1972); Langenskiöld (1959); Strandberg (1971); J.T (1996)

bull's-eye See ŒIL-DE-BŒUF.

Buls, Charles (Karel) François Gommaire (1837–1914) Belgian town-planner/educationalist. Influenced by the German art-historians **Karl Schnaase** (1798–1875) and **Wilhelm Lübke** (1826–93) and by the theories of *Semper, he promoted rationalist and nationalist-traditionalist views concerning the decorative arts. Prompted by *Sitte's writings, he opposed some grandiose schemes favoured by **King Leopold II** (r.1865–1909), arguing for development respecting scale and existing fabric that had been features of historic cities, and helped to reverse tendencies to clear huge areas of Brussels (his *conservation of the *Grand Place* won him international renown). He advised on conservation projects for the *Piazza Navona*, Rome.

Loo (ed.) (2003); J.T (1996)

bundle *Gothic *pier resembling a tight bundle of *colonnettes in which the latter are not actually detached, but grow from the undulating plan-form. *Compare* clustered or compound pier at CLUSTER.

bungaloid growth Pejorative term for developments of speculative *bungalows without aesthetic or architectural qualities: although mostly associated with suburbs (e.g. the fringes of Golders Green, London), a famous example is Peacehaven, East Sussex, built immediately after the 1914–18 war, and sometimes known as 'New-Anzac-on-Sea', because of its resemblance to Antipodean suburbs.

A.King (1982); Lancaster (1985)

bungalow Corruption of the Hindustani *bangla*, meaning 'belonging to Bengal', applied to one-storey, lightly built, detached dwellings, often with thatched roofs and surrounded by a *verandah. The word appears (1676) as *Bungales* in relation to housing for servants of the East India Company, but as *bungalow* by 1711: it later described single-storey houses throughout the British Empire and in the USA, and became usual to indicate any single-storey detached house (often a second home by the seaside or a first house in a suburb, especially immediately after the 1914–18 war). Nevertheless, some large isolated bungalows were erected on land owned by J.P.*Seddon at Birchington, North-East Kent, from the late 1860s, to designs by **John Taylor** and Seddon himself: the Indian idiom was preserved, with broad overhanging roofs and side verandahs, in Tower Bungalows (1880s—which also had *sgraffito* decoration between the *applied* timber decorations).

A.King (1982); Lancaster (1985)

Bunney, Michael Frank Wharlton (1875–1926) English architect, he became assistant to Horace *Field before setting up (1902) his own practice, and from 1905 was in partnership with **Clifford Copeman Makins** (1876–1963). Bunney is remembered for his modest houses, especially those he designed for Hampstead *Garden Suburb (1907–14), all modelled on C17 *vernacular Herts. buildings. Bunney and Field collaborated on *English Domestic Architecture of the XVIIth and XVIIIth Centuries* (1905, 1928), an invaluable compendium of undervalued buildings.

A.S.Gray (1985)

Bunning, James Bunstone (1802–63) London architect/surveyor to several organizations, including the London Cemetery Company and The Haberdashers' Company. He designed the *Egyptian-Revival *avenue* (not *circle*) and other structures at Highgate Cemetery, and the Classical Grecian *lodges and *gates at Nunhead Cemetery (1839–43). He was appointed (1843) 'Clerk to the City's Works' (the title was changed (1847) to 'City Architect'), and was responsible for several street improvements, including the first plans for Holborn Viaduct (1848). His masterpiece (demolished 1962) was the London Coal Exchange (1846–9), an internal top-lit *cast-iron galleried *rotunda within an *Italianate exterior. He also designed the handsome Italianate Metropolitan Cattle Market, Caledonian Road (1855—only the clock-tower and corner-pubs survive), and the *castellated Holloway Prison (1849–52—largely demolished). He published *Designs for Tombs and Monuments* (1839).

J.Curl (2004, 2007); D & M (1985); *ODNB* (2004)

Bunshaft, Gordon (1909–90) American architect. He joined (1937) *SOM, and, influenced by European *International *Modernism (esp. *Gropius's work), introduced that style to the firm. As an SOM partner from 1949 he made his name with Lever House, NYC (1950–2), which, with its prefabricated aluminium/plate-glass *curtain-walls, was the precedent for a huge number of high-rise buildings in America and throughout the world. Among other SOM buildings credited to Bunshaft the *Banque Lambert*, Brussels (1961–6), extension to the Albright-Knox Art Gallery, Buffalo, NY (1960–2), and the L.B.Johnson Library and S.W.Richardson Hall, University of Texas, Austin, TX (1969–71), may be cited.

AR, cxxxix/829 (Mar. 1966), 193–200; E (1994); Krinsky (1988); J.T (1996)

Buon, Bartolomeo (c.1405–67) *See* BON, BARTOLOMEO.

Buonarotti *See* MICHELANGELO.

Buontalenti delle Girandole, Bernardo (1531–1608) Florentine architect/painter/sculptor, he also designed masques, pyrotechnics (*Girandole* means Catherine-wheel), and other amusements for his patrons, the **Medici Grand Dukes**. His *Mannerist detailing is best seen at the *Porta delle Suppliche*, Uffizi, Florence (1580—where a broken segmental *pediment has its *scrolls reversed to form a wing-like element supporting the bust of **Cosimo de'Medici** (r.as **Duke**

of Florence 1537-69 and as **Grand Duke of Tuscany** 1569-74)), and at the new *altar-steps for *Santa Trinità* (1574-6—now in *Santo Stefano*— where the **trompe l'oeil* carved steps are unusable, and the real stairs were placed, invisible, on each side). He designed a fantastic *grotto for the Bóboli Gardens (1583-8—where pumicestone encrustations submerge the entrance, and the interior, with its hidden sources of light and eerie figures, is a *tour-de-force* of theatricality). He created the Uffizi *Tribuna* (1574-89), the decorations and lavish gardens at the Medici *villa at Pratolino (destroyed), and the *Casino Mediceo* (*Casino di San Marco*), Florence (1574). Much more restrained is the *façade of *Santa Trinità* (1593-4), with four *Giant *pilasters carrying an *entablature, over which is a pedimented *Attic-storey flanked by scrolls. Elegant and simple too is the *Fortezza di Belvedere* (1590s) set high on a hill to protect the Pitti Palace. Buontalenti designed and built fortifications, engineering works, and a *canal, and his Mannerist, distorted, melting-mask decorations anticipated *Auricular ornament.

Berti (1967); Botto (1968); *DBI* (1972); Fara (1979, 1988, 1990)

Burgee, John (1933-) *See* JOHNSON, PHILIP CORTELYOU.

Burges, William (1827-81) London-born architect, one of the least restrained of *Gothic Revivalists, he was articled to *Blore (1844) before moving (1849) to the office of M.D.*Wyatt. He joined (1851) Henry *Clutton, later becoming his partner, and assisted in the preparation of *Domestic Architecture of France* (1853). They won (1854) the competition to design the new Cathedral at Lille with an essay in robust C13 *Gothic (not realized). After a quarrel, Burges established his own practice, and won the competition (1857) for the Crimea Memorial Church in Constantinople, a *polychrome essay in the C13 style, again not executed. He designed furniture based on C13 French prototypes (illustrated in *Viollet-le-Duc's publications), and his work was shown in London at the Architectural Exhibition (1859), the year in which his *muscular east end of Waltham Abbey, Essex, was begun. His great Anglican Cathedral of St Fin Barre was erected in Cork, Ireland (1863-1904), with its three *spires, the whole in a convincing French C13 style, with a noble, powerful interior, and many allusions to *Freemasonry (he was an active member of the Craft).

From 1866 his alterations, extensions, and additions were designed and built at Cardiff Castle, and the reconstruction and decoration of *Castell Coch*, Glamorganshire, Wales, were carried out (1872-91) for **John Patrick Crichton-Stuart**

(1847-1900—**3rd Marquess of Bute** from 1848). These works are extraordinary for the richness of their polychromy and French-Gothic style, although the so-called Arab Hall at Cardiff Castle (1881) betrays *Islamic influences. For **John McConnochie** (1823-89—Chief Engineer of the Bute Docks, Cardiff, from 1862) he designed and built a Gothic house, Park Place, Cardiff (1871-80), and at Melbury Road, Kensington, Burges built his own Tower House (1875-81), a Gothic building of red brick with a circular tower: decorated and furnished to designs by its architect-owner, it was an instant success, admired for its medievalism and massive construction. Each room had its own iconography, and symbols and allegories were present throughout. Perhaps partly because of these designs, Burges has a claim to be regarded as a herald of the *Arts-and-Crafts movement.

Massive, tough detail is evident in the two churches he built in Yorks.: Christ the Consoler, Skelton-on-Ure (1870-6), and St Mary, Aldford-cum-Studley (1870-8). Skelton marked a move from French to English Gothic Revival of *c.*1270, but the French elements are still present, notably in the details of the *spire and in the *balcony of the organ-loft: the richly beautiful *chancel is one of the most remarkable of C19. At Studley, French and English sources again mix, and *piers are derived from English medieval precedents, but the whole is marvellously rich and integrated, with a complicated iconography concerning Paradise Lost and Regained. Burges's ecclesiastical master-work, it is probably the most perfect of his *muscular-Gothic buildings, freely and imaginatively treated, yet backed by genuine scholarship. His designs for Trinity College, Hartford, CT (1873-82), were only partly realized in watered-down form. However, his work influenced the executant architect for Trinity College, his American pupil **Francis Hatch Kimball** (1845-1919), and may also have impressed itself upon H.H.*Richardson.

FA; Crook (1981); J.Curl (2007); Lawrence & Wilson (2006); J.T (1996)

Burgess, Edward (*c.*1850-1929) English architect, he worked mostly in Leics.: many of his buildings were of considerable distinction. Some were in the *Domestic-Revival style (the former Wyggeston Girls' School (1877-8) and the coffeehouses (1880s) he designed for the Leicester Cocoa and Coffee Company), but others were in *Neo-Renaissance (e.g. the *terracotta-faced Alexandra House, Rutland Street (1895-8), one of the handsomest *warehouses in England). Other works of quality included the Reference Library, Bishop Street (1904), the former High Cross Coffee House, High Street (1880s), the *Gothic former Savings Bank, Greyfriars (later Bank of Ireland)

(1873), Nos. 8-10 Millstone Lane (1864), the former Liberal Club, Bishop Street (1885-8), some schools (e.g. the Hazel Primary, Hazel Street (1880)), and houses (e.g. No. 6 Ratcliffe Road (1880)), all in Leicester.

Pe,Williamson, & Brandwood (1984)

Burgh, Thomas (1670-1730) Irish military-engineer, he worked under Surveyor-General William *Robinson, succeeding him in 1700. His Dublin buildings include the Library at Trinity College (1709-33), the Royal Barracks (1701-7), various other buildings at Trinity, and Dr Steevens's Hospital (from 1718). His only essay in tentative *Palladianism seems to have been at his own house at Oldtown, Co. Kildare (c.1715).

M.Craig (1969, 1982); Loeber (1981); McP (2001)

Burghausen, Hans von (d.1432) *See* STETHAIMER.

Büring, Johann Gottfried (1723-*after* 1788) German architect, responsible for the *Neues Palais* (1763-8), with a main *elevation based on *Vanbrugh's Castle Howard, Yorks.; the Chinese Tea House (1754-7); and No. 5, *Am Neuen Markt* (1753-5), based on *Palladio's *Palazzo Thiene*, Vicenza, all in Potsdam. He also worked with *Boumann on the building of St Hedwig's RC Cathedral, Berlin (1772-3), and designed the exquisite picture-gallery at *Sans Souci*, Potsdam (1755-63).

Wa & M (1987)

Burke, Edmund (1729-97) Irish-born statesman/writer. His *A Philosophical Enquiry into the Origin of our Ideas of the Sublime and Beautiful* (1757) was of enormous importance in creating a move from *Classicism to *Romanticism, and in the history of aesthetics greatly influenced German philosophers of the Enlightenment, notably Immanuel *Kant. His discussion of the aesthetic categories of the *Beautiful and the *Sublime were especially significant.

E.Burke (1757); *ODNB* (2004)

Bürklein, Georg Christian Friedrich (1813-72) German architect, he assisted *Gärtner with the formation of the *Ludwigstrasse*, Munich. He designed the *Rathaus*, Fürth (1840-3), based on the *Palazzo Vecchio*, Florence, and the *Rundbogenstil *polychromatic Hauptbahnhof*, Munich (1847-9—destroyed). His new architectural style for the *Maximilianstrasse* was a brick-and-*terracotta version of English, German, and Italian *Gothic (1852-75).

Hederer (1976, 1976a); Ne (1987)

Burle Marx, Roberto (1909-94) Brazilian landscape architect, he studied botany at Dahlem, Berlin (1928), and became Director of Parks at Recife, Brazil, from 1934, setting up (1937) his own practice. As a champion of Brazilian flora, he used native species in his designs, composing his palettes of colour with scientific care. He collaborated with *Niemeyer and others in the designs of the gardens of the Ministry of Education and Health, Rio de Janeiro (1938), and with Niemeyer and *Costa at Brasília. His bay-front at Glória-Flamengo Park (1961) and the designs for the pavements along Copacabana Beach (1970), both in Rio de Janeiro, demonstrate his use of Brazilian stone and rocks with native plants, but his most celebrated creation is the *Odette Monteiro* garden, Correas, Rio de Janeiro (1947-8).

Adams (1991); Bardi (1964); Eliovson (1991); Montero (2001); J.T (1996); W & S (1994)

Burlington, Richard Boyle (1694-1753), **3rd Earl of,** *and* 4th Earl of Cork from 1704). Immensely rich, from c.1716 he took up the cudgels on behalf of *Palladianism, a movement of which he was to become undisputed leader and arbiter of taste. He studied *Palladio's work in and around Vicenza (1719), returning later that year with *Kent, whom he retained as a painter of historical scenes. Burlington had employed (1716) *Gibbs to transform his town-house in Piccadilly, but replaced him with Colen *Campbell, while Kent was to be responsible for the interiors. From the early 1720s Burlington made his own architectural designs, assisted by *Flitcroft, and (1722) commenced his first public building, the dormitory of Westminster School, intended as an exemplar in his campaign to restore to England *Vitruvian principles of architecture, as embodied in the works of Palladio, *Scamozzi, and Inigo *Jones. His sources were Palladio's drawings and published works, and drawings by Jones and *Webb. Now Jones's *first Palladian Revival* was associated with the reigns of the Stuart **James I & VI** (r.1603-25) and **Charles I** (r.1625-49), so the *second Palladian Revival* provided an element of continuity after an interruption (perhaps associated with the need to give legitimacy to the Hanoverian succession (from 1714) that was not universally popular, and had received a jolt as a result of the Jacobite Rebellion (1715)), but it could have signified a hedging of bets in case the Stuarts returned. To further his campaign, Burlington arranged for publication by Kent of drawings by Jones and Webb as *Designs of Inigo Jones* (1727) with some 'few Designs' by Burlington himself. He also published drawings by Palladio in *Fabbriche Antiche disegnate da Andrea Palladio* (1730). Virtually all the motifs of English Palladianism recurred (1720s, 1730s) in Burlington's designs: at Tottenham Park, Wilts. (from 1721), the *pavilion-towers based on Wilton were pierced by *serlianas; the *villa (influenced by Palladio's *Villa Capra* near

Vicenza) at Chiswick, Mddx. (c.1723-9), had serlianas set in semicircular-headed recesses; and at York, the Vitruvian Palladian *Egyptian Hall was recreated at the Assembly Rooms (1731-2). The *rusticated lower storey, the taller and more important *piano nobile* (complete with *portico and windows with *dressings set in large expanses of wall) became common, and not only for country-houses, but in public buildings as well: by the 1730s, in fact, Anglo-Palladian conventions had become *de rigueur* for English country-houses.

Burlington was one of the most potent influences on the development of English architecture in its entire history, and was the key figure in the rejection of *Baroque in favour of a more austere *Classicism: as high-priest of absolute standards and architectural rules, he was consulted to ensure that Good Taste was not contravened. His protégés were given influential posts in the Office of Works (Kent, for example, became an architect in his own right); and as a catalyst for the evolution of English *Neo-Classicism he should not be underestimated.

Dana Arnold (ed.) (1994); T.Barnard & J.Clark (1995); Burlington (1730); C.Campbell (1728-9, 1967-72); Carré (1994); Co (2008); Corp (ed.) (1998); J.Curl (2001, 2011a); J.Hs (1981, 1994); Kingsbury (1995); Su (1993); D.Wa (1979, 1986); S.Weber (ed.) (2013); M.Wilson (1984); Wi (1974a)

Burn, William (1789-1870) Scots architect, he worked in Robert *Smirke's London office (1808-11), before returning to Edinburgh to join his father, **Robert Burn** (1752-1815), designer of the Nelson Monument on Calton Hill (1807-16). Young Burn's earliest commissions included the Custom House, Greenock (1817-18), the *Ledoux-like Gasworks, Tanfield, Canonmills (1824, drawn by *Schinkel (1826)), and County Hall, Inverness (1834-5), but his large and successful practice consisted mainly of commissions for country-houses (Blairquhan, Ayrshire (c.1820-4), is an example of his *Tudor-*Gothic style, but by c.1825 Burn was designing in a *Jacobethan manner that became his speciality. Scottish *vernacular architecture and *tower-houses were added to his sources from 1829 (Faskally, Perthshire, and Tyninghame House, East Lothian), but, from his completion of *Salvin's great Harlaxton Manor, Lincs. (from 1838), his work became more ebullient, leading to his best houses, including Falkland House, Fife (1839-44), Whitehill Hall, Midlothian (1839-44), Stoke Rochford House (1841—badly damaged by fire 2005) and Revesby Abbey (1844), both in Lincs., Dartrey, Co. Monaghan (1844-6—demolished), and Bangor Castle, Co. Down (1847—perhaps with interventions by *Salvin), all Jacobethan, but including other styles

(e.g. the castellated Castlewellan, Co. Down (1854)). He also designed in the *Scottish-Baronial manner in which his pupil (and later partner), *Bryce, became adept: e.g. Helen's Tower, Clandeboye, Co. Down (1848-62). Although prolific, Burn perhaps never quite rose to great architecture: his work was competent, often agreeable, but sometimes dull. He took his nephew, J. MacVicar *Anderson, into partnership, who continued the practice after Burn's death. Pupils included Eden *Nesfield and Norman *Shaw.

N.Allen (ed.) (1984), 3-35; Co (2008); DW; J.Fawcett (ed.) (1976), 8-31; Fiddes & Rowan (eds) (1976); Gd (1979); Macaulay (1975, 1987); ODNB (2004); Youngson (1966)

Burnacini, Lodovico Ottavio (1636-1707) Designer (assisted by *Fischer von Erlach) of the *Dreifaltigkeitssäule, Graben*, Vienna (erected 1687-93), a *Baroque monument showing the vanquishing of Plague. He was Architect to the Imperial Court, but most of his work was as an engineer or for the theatre.

H.Aurenhammer (1973); J.T (1996)

Burnet, John (1814-1901) Scots architect, he practised in Glasgow from 1844. His early work was modestly Classical, including Elgin Place Congregational Church (1856) and the *Italianate 61-3 Miller Street (1854) but later designs include the exuberant Italian-*Renaissance Clydesdale Bank, St Vincent Place (1870), and the restrained Cleveden Crescent (1876). Burnet designed the Italian-*Gothic Glasgow Stock Exchange (1874), Woodlands Parish Church (also 1874), and Lanarkshire House, Ingram Street (1876), an *Italianate-*Mannerist design of great verve, with an unevenly spaced *pilastrade and a *colonnade on the two upper floors.

G & W (1987); WRH (1990)

Burnet, Sir John James (1857-1938) Glasgow-born son of John *Burnet, educated at the *École des *Beaux-Arts*, Paris, he joined his father's office (1878). His Fine Arts Institute, Sauchiehall Street, Glasgow (1879-80—demolished 1967), was an essay in restrained *Greek Revival, and anticipated the Classical Revival in England by many years. Another French-trained Scot, J.A.*Campbell, became (1886) Burnet's partner, and they won the competition to design the Barony Church, Glasgow (1886-9, 1898-1900—now the ceremonial hall of Strathclyde University), influenced by Dunblane and Gerona Cathedrals, and by the work of *Pearson (who was adjudicator during the competition). A series of low, broad-eavesed churches followed, including Shiskine, Arran (1887), the Gardner Memorial Church, Brechin (1896-1900), and the McLaren Memorial Church and Manse, Stenhousemuir (1897-1907). The firm also produced the fantastically eclectic

Charing Cross Mansions, Glasgow (1891), in which C16 French themes predominate. During a visit to the USA (1895), Burnet met Charles *McKim and Louis *Sullivan, and almost immediately his work became influenced by American precedents (e.g. Atlantic Chambers, Hope Street, and Waterloo Chambers, Waterloo Street (both in Glasgow and both 1899, by which time the partnership had been dissolved (1897)).

Burnet was commissioned (1903) to design the extension to the British Museum, the King Edward VII Galleries, which had a *Giant *Order of three-quarters *engaged *Ionic columns that Burnet tilted slightly inwards so that the *flutes ran parallel to the *naked of the wall, avoiding awkward junctions. This *Beaux-Arts* building, one of the first of the Edwardian *Neo-Classical reactions to the *Baroque Revival and *Wrenaissance, made his reputation, and he was knighted (1914). By that time a London office had been opened, and the Glasgow practice became a separate partnership (1909) under Paris-trained **Norman Aitken Dick** (1883–1948). Burnet appointed (1903) Thomas S. *Tait as his personal assistant, and by 1910 the latter was a significant figure in the London office, becoming (1918) a partner. A fine essay in *Beaux-Arts* elevational treatment at General Buildings, 99 Aldwych (1909), demonstrates Tait's influence, while Kodak House, 65 Kingsway (1910–12—designed by Tait), admitted its steel frame and eschewed all overt references to the *Orders. Adelaide House, London Bridge (1920–5), was one of the first large buildings of the 1920s to be consciously modelled on a monumental Egyptianizing style, and yet owed something to Sullivan: again, Tait was mostly responsible. By far the most impressive work of the firm (it had become (1930) **Burnet, Tait, & Lorne** when **Francis Lorne** (1889–1963) became a partner) between the wars was St Andrew's House, Edinburgh (1934–9), to accommodate the Scottish Office: a symmetrical composition in the *Beaux-Arts* tradition, it was mainly the work of Tait.

AJ, lvii/1486 (27 June 1923), 1066–1110; *AR*, liv (Aug. 1923), 66–9; Crook (1972); J.Curl (2001, 2005); DW; Eaton (1972); G & W (1987); A.S.Gray (1985); *ODNB* (2004); *RIBAJ*, xlv/17 (18 Jul. 1938), 893–6, xlv/18 (15 Aug. 1938), 941–3; Se (ed.) (1975); J.T (1996)

Burnham, Daniel Hudson (1846–1912) American architect/first-class administrator/entrepreneur, he could also bring out the best in those with whom he collaborated. He entered the office of Loring & *Jenney (1867–8) where he acquired some architectural experience, and formed a partnership (1873) with **John Wellborn Root** (1850–91). As **Burnham & Root**, the firm was significant in the creation of the *Chicago School: their first *skyscraper was the (demolished) Montauk Building, Chicago, IL (1881–2), and other tall buildings followed in which load-bearing walls were mixed with framed structures. Then came the sixteen-storey Monadnock Building, Chicago (1889–91), with load-bearing walls, tiers of canted *bay-windows, and huge crowning coved *cornice, and the (demolished) Masonic Temple, Chicago (1890–2), with twenty-two storeys and a steel *skeleton. After Root's early death Burnham set up (1891) with *Atwood, and built up one of the largest practices in the USA. The firm produced the Reliance Building, Chicago (1891–4), which further developed architecture using a metal skeleton: a fourteen-storey tower with glass and *terracotta cladding, it looked forward to C20 developments in which structural *frames would be clearly expressed. Burnham was appointed the co-ordinator of the World's Columbian Exposition in Chicago (1890–3), and began to promote a *Beaux-Arts* *Classicism for the buildings, which had a profound effect on American architecture/planning for many years to come. In Burnham's firm's own work (e.g. the Fuller ('Flat-Iron') Building, NYC (1902–3), and Wanamaker's Store, Philadelphia, PA (1909)), elements of *Renaissance architecture were grafted on. Burnham's fame, connected with his impressive *Beaux-Arts* Classicism, caused him to be employed as consultant to Selfridges Store for the new building (1907) in Oxford Street, London (by *Atkinson and *Swales): it was as innovative and as grand as *Burnet's contemporary extension to the British Museum. *Beaux-Arts* principles of powerful axes, symmetry, and confident use of Classical motifs were adopted for proposals for the *City Beautiful in which Burnham attempted to bring uniformity and an academic approach to urban America: his plan for Washington, DC, attempted to restore the eroded parts of L'*Enfant's design. The firm's Union Station, Washington, DC (1903–7), was its first fully developed *Beaux-Arts* design, with a *façade of five huge *bays and a triple-arched entrance leading to a *barrel-*vaulted space worthy of Roman *thermae. Burnham's plan for Chicago (1906–9), informed by his success with the Exposition, was influential at the time. His publications include *The World's Columbian Exposition: The Final Report of the Director of Works* (1898), and (with English-born **Edward Herbert Bennett** (1874–1954)) *Plan of Chicago* (1909). When he died Burnham's name was widely respected, and his plans for Chicago and Washington, DC, determined the development of both until the 1950s. However, as *International *Modernism gained the upper hand after the 1939–45 war, his reputation fell, but in C21 his work seems infinitely preferable to the urban devastation created by those who decried his work.

Ct (1952, 1961, 1964, 1968, 1973); Hines (1974); D.Ho (ed.) (1967); D.Ho (1973); Monroe (1966); C.Moore (1968); P (1982); Roessel (1996); J.T (1996); Zu (ed.) (1987, 1993)

Bürolandschaft Type of office-planning (literally 'office-landscape') evolved (1950s and 1960s) in Germany by **Eberhard** (1921–97) and **Wolfgang** (1930–2005) **Schnelle**, based on open-plan offices developed in the USA in the 1940s. Freed from partitions, large spaces could be designed that were decently lit and serviced: informal layouts suggested a landscape, enhanced by fashionable placing of plants in pots.

Boje (1972); F.Duffy (1969)

Burton, Decimus (1800–81) British architect, tenth son of **James Burton** (or **Haliburton**) (1761–1837), Scots builder/surveyor who settled in London. James developed the Foundling Hospital's, Skinners', and Bedford (including Russell Square (1800–14)) Estates in Bloomsbury, and laid out the new town of St Leonard's-on-Sea, Sussex (1828–32—a development in which advanced *Neo-Classical buildings can be found as well as an eclectic stylistic mixture). Decimus trained with his father, worked with **George Maddox** (1760–1843), entered (1817) the Royal Academy Schools, and went on to design several distinguished *Greek-Revival buildings. Under *Nash's supervision he designed Cornwall and Clarence Terraces, Regent's Park, then the Colosseum, Regent's Park (1823–7), a vast *Pantheon-like structure with *dome bigger than that of St Paul's Cathedral and a Greek-*Doric *portico. Important commissions followed: the *Ionic *screen at Hyde Park Corner, *lodges at Cumberland, Grosvenor, and Stanhope Gates (1824–5), and then the prestigious Athenaeum Club, Waterloo Place (1827–30), with its fine *frieze and handsome interiors. His dignified arch on Constitution Hill (1827–8—intended as a Royal entrance to Buckingham Palace from the north), was moved to its present position (1883).

Decimus enjoyed success as a designer of *villas and small country-houses: he laid out the enchanting Calverley Estate, Tunbridge Wells, Kent (from 1828), in which the Classical and the *Picturesque, derived from works of Nash, are judiciously mingled. He designed the new town, including St Peter's Church, the North-East Hotel, Queen's Terrace, Custom House, and two lighthouses, at Fleetwood, Lancs. (1836–43), which fell on hard times when the railway was extended to Carlisle and Scotland, passing it by. He was also involved at Beulah Spa, Upper Norwood, Surrey (1828–31). Burton was interested in the problems of design using iron and glass: his finest essays were the (demolished) Great Stove or *conservatory, Chatsworth (1836–40, with *Paxton); the conservatory (1845–6, with Richard *Turner

(demolished)), Regent's Park; and the palm-house (1845–8—again with Turner); Royal Botanic Gardens, Kew.

Britton (1829); Co (2008); J.Curl (2010); Funnell (1982); Hyde (1982); Miller (1981); *ODNB* (2004); Su (1993); Whitbourn (2003)

Busby, Charles Augustin (1786–1834) English architect, he published (1808 (later edn 1835)) a volume of designs for *villas and country houses followed (1810) by another on fittings for such buildings. He designed several villas before building the Commercial Rooms, Bristol (1810), with a Classical *temple-front and an interior lit by means of a lantern supported by *caryatides. In the USA (1817), he designed a theatre in Virginia, but returned to England, where he worked with *Goodwin, later settling in Brighton, where he formed a partnership with Amon Henry *Wilds. The firm laid out the Kemp Town and Brunswick Estates there, Busby providing the designs and Wilds acting as contractor. His best work is Sussex Square, Lewes Crescent, Arundel Terrace, and Chichester Terrace (1823–c.1850), Kemp Town, and Brunswick Square, Brunswick Terrace, Brunswick Street East and West, Lower Brunswick Place, Lansdowne Place, and Lansdowne Square, Hove (1823–c.1834).

N.Bingham (1991); Busby (1810, 1835); Co (2008); Dale (1947)

Busch, Johann (John) (c.1725–95) German nurseryman-gardener, he settled (1740s) in England, gaining fame by translating Philip *Miller's *Dictionary* (Nuremberg, 1750–8) into German. He opened (1753) a nursery in Hackney, and by the 1760s had become the most important provider of seeds and plants (notably trees) for German aristocratic patrons (**Freiherr von Münchausen** (1716–74) promoted forestry in landscape-design in his *Der Hausvater* (1764–8)). Busch's influence as a teacher of botany ensured that by 1770 his reputation was established, leading to his appointment (1771) as Court Gardener in Russia (he sold his Hackney concern to *Loddiges). Sent to *Tsarskoye Selo* (1772), he worked with *Cameron (who married Busch's daughter) and *Quarenghi to create gardens in the *anglo-chinois style (influenced by ideas of *Chambers) for **Catherine II** ('the Great', *r.*1762–96). He also collaborated with the English gardener, **James Meader** (*fl.*1779–90), and the German botanist/zoologist, **Peter Simon Pallas** (1741–1811). Busch's expertise ensured a proliferation of *glass-houses and *landscape-gardens in Russia. After he returned to England, his Russian post passed to his son, **Joseph Busch** (1760–1838), who worked on several Russian Court projects, including the park-village at *Tsarskoye Selo* and the gardens of Alexander Palace (1792–6—by Quarenghi). Joseph left Russia *c.*1811–12, but after the

Napoléonic wars designed the gardens at Jelagin Island (1817-30s—influenced by the work of H.*Repton), the Theatre Garden, Stone Island (1828-30), and the Forest Academy and *arboretum (1830), all St Petersburg.

JGH, **xliii/3** (July-Sept. 1993), 172-81; Miller (1731-9); München hausen (1764-8); Shoe (2001); D.Shv (1996, 2007); Solman (1995)

Buscheto *or* **Busketus** (*fl*.1063-1110) Architect of the *Romanesque Cathedral at Pisa (1063-1116), whose name is recorded in an inscription there.

Sanpaolesi (1975)

bush-hammered 1. Finish on *concrete (usually *in situ*) made with a mechanical *bush-hammer* fitted with a strong grooved head: the flat plane left after the concrete has set is hammered away to partially reveal the coarser aggregate, leaving a rough-textured surface. **2.** Stone *dressing obtained using a hammer with square ends divided into a number of pyramidal points.

business park Landscaped area in which are built offices, buildings for light industry, and the like, served by roads, and where development is controlled by a master-plan. A good example is Stockley Park, Heathrow, Hillingdon, London, by *Arup Associates, and containing buildings by Arup, *SOM, et al. Other business parks include the Cambridge Science Park (1970s), and Aztec West, near Bristol (1980s).

A.Phillips (1993)

Butler, Lady Charlotte Eleanor (*c*.1739-1829) Reclusive Irish diarist, descended from the **Dukes of Ormond**, she met (1768) **Sarah** ('Sally') **Ponsonby** (1755-1831) with whom she formed an immediate bond, having mutual interests in art and in J.-J.*Rousseau's pastoral ideals. The pair settled (1778) in the Vale of Llangollen, Wales, where they transformed a cottage into an exotic *Gothick retreat, called *Plas Newydd*, furnished with a large library and having a garden with wild planting, *rustic timber structures, *dell with stream, pools, and a *cascade. Their home became a popular attraction, not least because of the eccentricities of the two women: visitors included **William Wordsworth** (1770-1850), **Sir Walter Scott** (1771-1832), and J.C.*Loudon.

DIB (2009); Hubbard (1986)

Butler, John Dixon (1861-1920) London architect, appointed (1895) Architect and Surveyor to the Metropolitan Police. He collaborated with Norman *Shaw on the extensions to New Scotland Yard (1904-6), and himself designed the Police Court and Station, Old Street, Shoreditch (1906), a *Mannerist building with a *Baroque centrepiece.

A.S.Gray (1985)

Butler, Ronald Morley (1929-2012) Investigator for the Royal Commission on Historical Monuments, one of several scholars who made an inventory of ancient fabric of York, setting standards for future urban surveys. He also contributed to the Dorset and Cambs. studies, and was the prime author of *A Matter of Time* (1960).

The Times (17 Feb. 2012), 63

butler's pantry Room in which the plate, linens, etc., for the table are kept. Also called *housemaid's pantry*.

Butterfield, William (1814-1900) Prolific and original English *Gothic Revivalist, he worked with the *Inwoods before opening (1840) his own practice. From 1842 he was closely involved with the *Cambridge Camden Society, contributing designs to *The Ecclesiologist* (1842-68) and *Instrumenta Ecclesiastica* (1850-2). His first church and parsonage were at Coalpit Heath, Glos. (St Saviour's, 1844-5), an essay in *Second Pointed much influenced by *Pugin, and decidedly plain. The parsonage was an important precedent for the free domestic compositions of W.E.*Nesfield, Norman *Shaw, and Philip *Webb, because *fenestration was planned where needed, and all traces of the tyranny of symmetry vanished. Butterfield's mastery of grouping disparate elements together is best seen at the College of the Holy Spirit and Cathedral of the Isles at Millport, Greater Cumbrae, Scotland (1849-51), demonstrating Pugin's ideal of a 'True Picturesque' composition.

The *Ecclesiologists determined to build a model church that would fulfil the requirements of ritual, and would set standards for urban Anglican churches in the future. Butterfield was appointed architect, and designed the church, clergy-house, and school of All Saints, Margaret Street, London (1849-59). The buildings were of *polychrome brickwork, considerably influenced by Continental-*Gothic precedents. Here was a modern church designed to stand up to the rigorous climate of a Victorian city, a citadel of faith, an urban *minster. The hard, sharp architecture of the interior was coloured with glazed bricks and tiles, and it marked the beginning of the so-called *High-Victorian Gothic Revival. Many other churches with polychromatic interiors followed: among them should be mentioned All Saints, Babbacombe, Devon (1865-74), St Augustine, Penarth, Glamorganshire (1864-6), and St Mark's, Dundela, Belfast (1876-91). Keble College, Oxford (1867-83), and Rugby School chapel (completed 1872—the climax of which is the massive tower) are excellent examples of his work. He was *the* High-Victorian Goth, using materials with honesty of expression, glorying in structural polychromy, expressing his plans in three-dimensional forms, and obeying Pugin's call to build with clarity and truth. His grander houses include Milton Ernest Hall, Beds. (1853–6), a large Gothic pile of startling boldness, anticipating Shaw's Cragside and other examples later in the century: the whole ensemble has a pronounced Continental and un-English air. Butterfield also designed the County Hospital, Winchester, Hants. (1863–4—mutilated in C20), and carried out many works of restoration, notably at St Cross Hospital, Winchester (1864–5), and the Church of St Mary, Ottery St Mary, Devon (1947–50—where he designed a beautiful *font).

AH, **viii** (1965), 73–9; *AJ*, **cxci**/25 (20 June 1990), 36–55; J.Curl (2007); Hersey (1972); Hi (1977); P.Thompson (1971)

butterfly plan Popular during the *Arts-and-Crafts period, it had *wings projecting symmetrically at angles from a central core, resembling a butterfly, as in the work of *Prior.

buttery 1. Store-room for beer and other liquor. **2.** Later, a store-room for provisions, especially bread, butter, cheese, etc., directly behind the *screen of a great hall in a medieval dwelling or college, etc.

Button, Stephen Decatur (1813–97) CT-born American architect known for his work in Philadelphia, PA, and Camden, NJ. His State Capitol, Montgomery, AL (1847), and Pennsylvania Railroad Building (1856–8) no longer exist. He designed many houses in and around Hoboken, NJ, the Spring Garden Lutheran Church, Philadelphia (*c.*1859), and the City Hall, Camden (1874–5).

Teitelman & Longstreth (1974); J.Webster (ed.) (1976)

buttress *Pier-like projection of brick, *masonry, etc., built either in close connection with a wall needing extra stability, or standing isolated, to counter the outward thrust of an arch, *vault, or other elements. *Types of buttress are*:

angle- (*c*): one of a pair of buttresses at the corner of a building set at an angle of 90° to each other and to the walls to which they are attached;

Anglo-Saxon: not really a buttress at all, but more a thin freestone *lesene or *pilaster- strip dividing a wall-surface into *rubble panels originally *rendered. See* ANGLO-SAXON ARCHITECTURE;

arch-: known as an *arc-boutant*;

buttress-tower: tower seeming to function as a buttress, as on either side of a gateway, but mostly for defence;

clasping (*b*): massive buttress, square on plan, at the corner of a building, usually of the *Romanesque or *First-Pointed period;

Decorated: see SECOND-POINTED BUTTRESS;

diagonal (*e*): set at the corner of a building, forming an angle of 135° with the walls, and usually of the *Second-Pointed period;

Early English: see FIRST-POINTED BUTTRESS;

First-Pointed or *Early-English*: C13 type, often of formidable depth, frequently chamfered, and staged, each *stage defined by *off-sets, and the whole structure surmounted with steep triangular *gables;

flying, also called *arc-boutant* or *arch-buttress* (*f*): consists of an arched structure extending from the upper part of a wall to a massive *pier in order to convey the outward thrust of (usually) the stone vault safely to the ground;

hanging: type of slender support, carried on a *corbel;

lateral: attached to a corner of a structure, seeming to be a continuation of one of the walls;

Perp. or *Third-Pointed*: late-*Gothic type with elaborately panelled faces, and, often, crocketed *finials of great elegance;

pier- (*f*): detached external pier by which an arch or vault is prevented from spreading, as in the *chapter-house of Lincoln Cathedral, where *flying buttresses* are used. Pier-buttresses are often constructed with a heavy superstructure rising higher than the springing of the flying-buttress arch;

Romanesque (*a*): C11 and C12 wide *lesene* of little projection, it defines *bays;

Second-Pointed or *Decorated*: C14 type constructed in stages, frequently elaborately enriched, and surmounted by crocketed gables, *pinnacles, finials, and even crocketed *spirelets. Many were further embellished with canopied *niches for statuary;

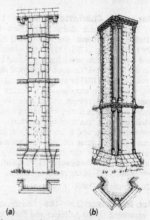

(*a*)   (*b*)

(*a*) Plan/perspective, *Romanesque* buttress (or *lesene*), Fountains Abbey, Yorks. (second half of C12).
(*b*) Plan/perspective, Romanesque *clasping buttress* with angle-shafts and chevron ornament, St Mary de Castro, Leicester (*c.*1150).

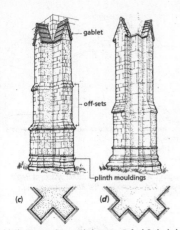

(c) Plan/perspective, *angle buttress*, Oxford Cathedral.
(d) Plan/perspective, early-C13 *set-back buttress*, St Mary's, Higham Ferrers, Northants.

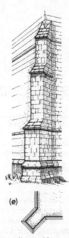

(e) Plan/perspective, *diagonal buttress* with off-sets, St Botolph's, Church Brampton, Northants.

set-back: (*d*) resembling an *angle-buttress*, but not built immediately at the corner, so does not touch the set-back buttress on the return-wall, thus the quoin of the building remains visible. *See also* SPIRE.

Bland (1839)

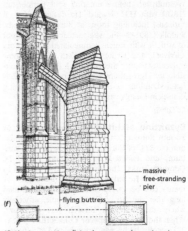

(f) Plan/perspective, *flying buttress* and massive pier, C13 chapter-house, Lincoln Cathedral.

Buzás, Stefan (1915–2008) Hungarian-born Vienna-educated architect, he settled (1938) in Britain and was associated with *New Humanism. Australian-born **James William Archibald Cubitt** (1914–83) established (1947) his architectural practice in London with **Fello Atkinson** (1919–82), **Dick Maitland** (1918–69), and Buzás, designing several educational buildings, including works in Yorks. and Nigeria, as well as in Herts. under *Aslin. Buzás's 1950s projects included the South African Tourist Office and Qantas Airways Office, Piccadilly, London; a pair of small houses, Ham Common, Surrey (1951); and a section on Earth Sciences in the Dome of Discovery, *Festival of Britain.

The Guardian (23 Oct. 2008), Obits

Bye, Arthur Edwin (1919–2001) Dutch-born American landscape architect. Influenced by F.L.L.*Wright's work at Falling Water, Connelsville, PA (1935–48), he thereafter limited his palette to plants indigenous to the site, enhancing natural features through subtle changes: coherence and unified composition are terms best describing his work. His *Art into Landscape, Landscape into Art* (1983) records his output, which might be compared with that of Jens *Jensen, influencing *New Perennials or Dutch Wave planting and the evolution of *New American landscape.

B & F (2009); Bye (1983); A.Wilson (2005)

Byfield, George (c.1756–1813) Apprenticed (1771) to *Plaw, he became (1803) Surveyor to the estates of the Dean and Chapter of

Westminster, before entering into partnership (1810) with H.H.*Seward. He designed several *prisons, including those at Bury St Edmunds, Suffolk (1801–3—the spectacular entrance-front of which, with much vermiculated *rustication, survives), and Canterbury, Kent (1806–8—now university lecture theatres, etc.). He was responsible for Hurlingham House (now a Club), Fulham, London (1797–8), and for completing houses in Dean's Yard, Westminster (1809).

Co (2008)

Byzantine architecture The Byzantine, or Eastern Roman, Empire, began with the foundation (AD 324) of Constantinople (formerly Byzantium) and ended with its capture (1453) by Ottoman Turks. The *Byzantine style* evolved in the age of *Justinian* (r.527–65), although elements can be found from C4, and continued long after the fall of Constantinople, especially where the Orthodox Church was dominant. When the Roman **Emperor Constantine** (r.324–37) established his new Imperial and administrative capital on the Bosphorus, the seeds were sown for a division of the Empire into Eastern and Western parts, with Greek becoming dominant in the former and Latin in the latter. The division was exacerbated in C11 with the *Great Schism*, dividing Christendom into Orthodox and RC Churches (the latter centred on Rome). When Constantinople was founded, every effort was made to create a new Rome in the East. Many Roman buildings were plundered to enrich the city, and the Classical *Orders were familiar there, as well as the style of architecture which we call *Early Christian. However, two building-types played an important part in the evolution of a specifically Byzantine church architecture: the *basilica and the circular *temple. The latter was known in pagan times, but acquired greater complexity in C4 when circular *clerestoreyed domed structures (e.g. *Santa Costanza*, Rome) were developed first as tombs, then centrally planned *martyria*. It is clear the *martyrium was planned in a different way from an ordinary church, and from C4 *martyria* were known to have been constructed as octagons with radiating arms to produce cruciform plans.

The basilican type of church can be seen at *Sant'Apollinare in Classe*, Ravenna (534–49), where the *clerestorey is carried on *arcades set on rows of columns on rectangular *pedestals and with curiously un-Classical *capitals based on the *Composite type. Above the *abaci are *blocks or *dosserets from which the arches spring. Yet this building is essentially Italian, whereas *San Vitale*, also in Ravenna (c.532–48), is very different: centrally planned, it has a clerestoreyed vaulted octagon carried on *piers, a lower galleried *aisle, and an apsidal *chancel. Columns have block-like

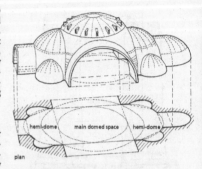

Diagram of geometry and structural system of *Hagia Sophia*, Constantinople (*after Rosengarten* et al.).

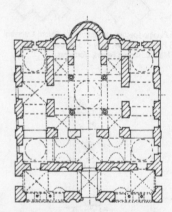

Plan of the Holy Apostles, Thessalonika (1310–14), a variation on the *quincunx* and *cross-in-square* plan.

Byzantine architecture

*capitals, making the transition from circular *shafts to square dosseret, and have virtually no connection with Classicism, while the bases are stepped and octagonal. *San Vitale* appears to have been a *martyrium*, and, architecturally, derives from the Church of *Sts Sergios and Bacchos*, Constantinople (c.525–c.536), which has a clerestoreyed octagon and beautiful lace-like capitals with only a suggestion of the Classical about them.

Hagia Sophia, Constantinople (c.532–7), designed by the scientists/mathematicians *Anthemios of Tralles and *Isidorus of Miletus, was the greatest achievement of Byzantine architecture. Various themes familiar at the time were synthesized and combined in one design, as though the basic form of *Sts Sergios and Bacchos* had been cut in two, greatly inflated, and built on either side of a gigantic square space covered with a low saucer-dome carried on **pendentives*. Such a huge *dome on a square space and constructed thus was unprecedented, and the complete synthesis of the basilican and centralized plan can be found in that great building. The church's interior was enriched with a skin of coloured *marbles, porphyry, and other stones, while the *vaults and domes were covered with the *mosaics that were such a glorious feature of Byzantine churches.

After *Hagia Sophia* the next-largest church in Constantinople was *Hagia Irene*, begun 532, rebuilt 564 and 740 (the C8 rebuilding included an additional dome over the nave, creating a more longitudinal plan). By C11, the typical Byzantine church-plan was a *Greek *cross within a square, roofed with a central dome flanked by four barrel-vaults and with domed squares in the corners. The plan is also known as the **quincunx*, and there were further variations on it (often consisting of three *apses to the east and one or more *narthexes to the west—a good example is the *Holy Apostles*, Thessalonika (early C14), where **cloisonné*, *herring-bone, and other patterns occur). Exteriors of earlier Byzantine churches often give the impression of having been left to their own devices, as though they were merely the result of the need to encase the rich interiors. Later churches, however, had greater care lavished on their outsides: clerestoreyed drums of domes are taller, walls are often given **cloisonné* treatment, while motifs based on the *Kufic alphabet are introduced in bands on the wall-surface. A typical example is the *Theotokos* Church of the *monastery of *Hosios Loukas*, Phocis (C10 or C11), probably the earliest representative of architectural themes that were to dominate in Byzantine architecture in Greece.

With the spread of Christianity northwards, tall drums with domes recurred in the Ukraine and *Russia: *Hagia Sophia*, Kiev (C11), had the rectangular cross-in-square plan, but there were five naves each with its own apse, and thirteen domes arranged in a pyramidal formation crowned the composition. Byzantine churches in Russia generally consisted of the cross-in-square, with many variants, as at *Hagia Sophia*, Novgorod (1045–50), and the Cathedral of the Transfiguration, Černigov (c.1036). However, after C11 Byzantine themes were elaborated upon, and architecture became more identified as having national or regional styles. Among characteristic Russian themes are walls subdivided into *bays by means of large blind arcades, and the 'onion' cappings that evolved from helmet-like forms in C13. A variation on the *quincunx* plan occurred in the C11 Church of *San Marco*, Venice, with a dome over the centre of the nave and over each of the four arms:

modelled on Justinian's Church of the Holy Apostles in Constantinople, it was deliberately antiquarian, as it was intended to enshrine the Relics of St Mark in a church that was as important as the *Apostoleion* in Constantinople (which contained the Relics of Sts Andrew and Luke).

From C7 the Eastern Empire was threatened from within and without, and fatally weakened by the Crusaders' sack of Constantinople (1204), an event which deepened rifts between RC and Orthodox Christendom. Paradoxically, as the Empire contracted, missionary activity seems to have increased, and the Byzantine style proliferated over a wide area. In both Armenia and Georgia (Christian from C4), basilican and centralized churches were erected in numbers, although from the end of C6 the domed centralized plan, much influenced by architecture in Syria, began to reach heights of elaboration. In both Armenia and Georgia, a domed interior surrounded by four apses roofed with hemi-domes (the '*tetraconch*' arrangement), the whole enclosed in a rectangle, was common. It is best represented by St Ripsime, Echmiadzin, Armenia (618–30), and Holy Cross, Džvari, Georgia (before 605). It is unclear how certain Western-European buildings were influenced by (or influenced) some Armenian architecture, but certainly by the early C11 domed basilicas (such as at Ani (988–1000)) began to acquire *bundle-like *piers, vaulting systems, and architectural features reminiscent of Western *Romanesque forms. However, Transcaucasia (Armenia and Georgia) developed a characteristic type of church architecture that had a surprisingly long life, usually based on the *tetraconch* plan with a high polygonal central drum pierced with windows. An example is Holy Cross, Aght'amar, Armenia (915–21), which also has the exterior enriched with figures and stylized ornament carved in low relief. In Bulgaria impressive Byzantine architecture evolved, including the extraordinary circular church at Preslav (a twelve-sided rotunda of c.900 with radiating *niches, a projecting apse, a ring of internal columns on which the dome was supported, a western narthex flanked by circular towers, and an *atrium surrounded by columns and with its deep walls enriched with niches). At the Black Sea town of Mesembria (Nesebŭr), known as the 'Bulgarian Ravenna', there are several Byzantine churches, including St John the Baptist (probably C10, a cross-in-square plan with barrel-vaulted aisles).

Serbian churches can be classified in three Schools: Raška (1170–1282); Byzantine Serbia (1282–1355); and the Morava (1355 until Turkish domination beginning 1459). The first School combined Romanesque elements (notably in the treatment of *gable-tops and *eaves, *fenestration, and *arcading) with Byzantine domes and decorations. Good examples are the Church of the Virgin, Studenica, the Monastery at Sopočani (both C13), and the backward-looking Monastery Church of Dečani (1327–35). Later, the cross-in-square type of church acquired a pyramidal pile-up of domes: for example, the Monastery Church of Gračanica (c.1318–21), where the upper array of barrel-vaults has pointed arches. The Morava School may be represented by the Church of the Ascension, Ravanica (c.1375)—another five-domed structure, the elongated drums of which have deeply recessed arches—and by the church (1406–18) within the fortress of Resava (Mana-sija). In Moldavia and Wallachia (Romania), Byzantine influences acquired a rich exoticism. The Church of the Episcopal Monastery at Curtea de Arges (C16) is an offspring of the Morava School, where the main body of the church is a trefoil, with a huge narthex given an *ambulatory plan. The Monastic Church of Dealu (1502) is also a descendant of the Morava School, derived from the plan of the Church at Cozia (1386). Moldavian C16 and C17 churches are less overtly

Byzantine in inspiration, but are uniquely deco-rated: among the best was the Monastery Church of Voronet (c.1488). It had a large rectangular narthex covered by a domical vault, and a trefoil nave with a tall drum in the centre. The three apses of the trefoil plan were treated with tall *blind arcades, and the exterior was deco-rated with elaborate frescoes protected by wide overhanging eaves. A similar arrangement was given to the Monastery Church at Sucevita (c.1602–4).

A *Byzantine Revival* was spurred by scholarly publications in C19 following the independence of Greece and the Balkan States. Works include the Greek-Orthodox Cathedral of *Hagia Sophia*, Moscow Road, Bayswater, London (1877–82), by John Oldrid *Scott (1841–1913), and Westmin-ster Cathedral (1895–1903), by John Francis *Bentley.

Buchwald (1999); Ck (1996); G.H (1983); Kra (1986); Mango (1972, 1986); Ousterhout (1999); Peña (1996); Runciman (1975); J.T (1996); D.Wa (1986)

Cabanel, Rudolph(e) (*c.*1763–1839) A native of Aachen or Liège, he lived for most of his life in England, specializing in theatre-architecture. Among his works were the Royal Cobourg Theatre (later the 'Old Vic'), Waterloo Road, Lambeth (1816–18—reconstructed 1924), and the upgrading of Sadler's Wells Theatre in the early 1800s (with circle and *galleries supported by slender *cast-iron columns). He invented a roof structure named after him, as well as theatre-machinery.

Co (2008); J.Curl (2010); *ODNB* (2004)

cabin **1.** Small, single-roomed primitive dwelling. **2.** Contrived *rustic retreat in a *Picturesque landscape, often ornamental, but much simpler than a *cottage orné.*

cabinet **1.** *Cabin. **2.** Relatively small room used for interviews or private conferences by e.g. a sovereign. **3.** Small room, often richly ornamented, designed for the display of valuable objects. The 'porcelain cabinets' of *Rococo palaces in Germany (e.g. in the *Residenz,* Ansbach (1739–40)) are examples. **4.** Garden-compartment or *arbour.

cabinet *or* **salle de verdure** Small area enclosed by clipped hedges within a *bosquet (e.g. the C18 example in the garden of the *Musée Jean-Jacques Rousseau,* Montmorency, France), sometimes containing a statue, *parterre, or pool; or a space within a *berceau sited within or at the end of a tunnel.

Symes (2006); Tay (2006)

cabinet-window Projecting shop-window common in early C19, usually with curved sides.

cable **1.** *Rope-moulding* carved to look like a rope, with twisted strands, found in Roman Antiquity (e.g. *Corinthian *Order of the *thermae, Nîmes), but mostly associated with *Romanesque architecture, especially around arches. **2.** *Cabled fluting, cabling, ribbed fluting, rudenture,* or *stopped flute,* consisting of convex *mouldings set in the *flutes of Classical column- or *pilaster-*shafts, between the *fillets but not projecting beyond their faces, and seldom carried up higher than a third of the height of the shaft. Cabling occurs occasionally on unfluted shafts, so the cables are in relief, as in *Borromini's *Sant'Ivo della Sapienza,* Rome (1643–60). For *cable structures see* TENSILE ARCHITECTURE.

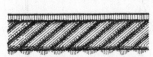

cable Romsey Abbey, Hants. (*after Parker*).

cabochon **1.** Protruding circular element, notably in *guilloche or *strapwork ornament. **2.** Small *cartouche and frame.

Cabot, Edward Clarke (1818–1901) American architect, a leading figure in the Boston architectural world after his *Athenaeum* (1846–9—influenced by Charles *Barry's *Italianate clubhouses in London) was built. *Gilman was his associate (1850s), and he produced (1870s) several distinguished *Queen-Anne houses. Some of his later designs shared affinities with those of H.H.*Richardson.

P (1982)

Cachemaille-Day, Nugent Francis *See* DAY.

CAD *See* COMPUTER-AIDED DESIGN.

Cadbury-Brown, Henry Thomas (aka 'Jim') (1913–2009) *See* CASSON; LYONS.

caduceus (*pl.* caducei) **1.** Winged rod with two *serpents and leaves wound around it, called the *Wand of Hermes* (of which deity it is an *attribute). *Compare* AARON'S ROD. **2.** Herald's rod, or wreathed olive-branch, originally wingless.

Caen Soft, fine-grained, easily-worked *limestone from near Caen, Normandy, used in several English medieval buildings (e.g. Canterbury and Norwich Cathedrals).

Caernarfon Welsh arch.

cage **1.** Enclosure formed mostly of *tracery, e.g. *screens surrounding *chantry-chapels, as in

Winchester Cathedral. **2.** Framework of a building in *timber- or steel-framed construction.

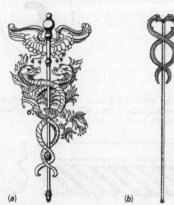

(a)   (b)

caduceus (*a*) As 1; (*b*) Leafless Aaron's rod 2.

Cagnola, Marchese Luigi (1762–1833) Italian Neo-Classical architect, in Milan he built the *Ionic *Porta Ticinese* (1801–14) and *Arco del Sempione or della Pace* (1806–38), the latter a beautifully proportioned and detailed *triumphal arch based on Roman precedents. His own house, the *Villa Cagnola*, Inverigo (c.1813–33), is a severe Neo-Classical work with a low domed circular entrance-hall and ranges of Ionic columns outside. His *Pantheon-like *San Lorenzo* (known as *La Rotonda*), Ghisalba (1822–33), is a pure example of the *Antique form. Although he did not design the Ghisalba *campanile, he was responsible for the free-standing five-stage tower, Urgnano (1824–9), with *caryatides supporting the domed top. *See* MOOSBRUGGER.

DBI (1973); Me (1966); Ms (1966); M & Wa (1987)

caher *See* CASHEL.

Cain, Michael (1930–2008) English architect, partner of *Casson for many years, he was closely involved in the Sidgwick Avenue buildings from the 1950s, and was largely responsible for the Lady Mitchell Hall, Oriental Studies building, Museum of Classical Archaeology, and McDonald Institute, all in Cambridge. He also worked on plans for the University of Warwick and the Ismaili Centre, South Kensington, London (1978–83).

RIBAJ (Oct. 2009), 14

cairn *Tumulus of undressed stones, chamfered or solid, and usually of a sepulchral or commemorative character.

caisson 1. Watertight chamber in which underwater construction work takes place. **2.** Device for sinking foundations under water or in waterlogged conditions, in the form of an airtight box the size of the *pier to be built, which is sunk to bedrock, or other surface on which it is to remain, then filled with *concrete. **3.** *Coffer in ceilings, *cupolas, *soffits, and *vaults.

Caius, John (1510–73) Refounder of Gonville and Caius College, Cambridge (1557), where he built (1560s and 1570s) the three Gates of Honour, Humility, and Virtue, remarkable for the refinement and correctness of their early *Classical detail, derived from *Serlio, and designed with the assistance of the architect and sculptor **Theodore de Have**, or **Haveus** (*fl.*1562–76), of Cleve (Clèves), Germany.

ODNB (2004); E.Roberts (ed.) (1912); D.Wa (1986)

calathus *See* CAMPANA.

caldarium (*pl.* **caldaria**) Hot- and vapourbaths in Roman *thermae, or the building in which they were situated.

Calderini, Guglielmo (1837–1916) Influential architect of the huge, eclectic, and majestic *Palazzo di Giustizia*, Rome (1888–1910), and other *Renaissance-Revival buildings in the decades before the 1914–18 war. As Director of Monuments for Rome, Aquila, and Chieti, his restorations, including the *chiostro* of *San Giovanni in Laterano*, were exemplary. He designed the grandiose *façade of the *Duomo*, Savona (1880–6), influenced by *Alessi's works; the *quadriportico* at *San Paolo fuori le Mura*, Rome (1893–1910); and two *palazzi* in Perugia (*Bianchi* and *Cesaroni*).

Ms (1966)

Caldwell, Alfred (1903–98) American landscape architect, he worked with *Mies van der Rohe on the Illinois Institute of Technology (from 1938), and with *Hilbersheimer at Lafayette Park, Detroit, MI (1955–9). From Jens *Jensen he adopted the latter's so-called *Prairie style, which he used at Lincoln Park, Chicago, IL (c.1936–7), and from Hilbersheimer he acquired theories of regionalism, decentralization, and low-rise high-density developments. He wrote *Architecture and Nature* (1984).

Caldwell (1984)

calefactory Artificially heated chamber in a *monastery, usually the common-room.

calf's tongue Medieval decorative *moulding featuring a long continuous series of tongue-like forms with parallel axes, or coinciding with the radii if embellishing an arch.

calidarium *See* CALDARIUM.

caliduct Means by which hot air is distributed.

California School Term used to group some American landscape architects, all working independently, but responding to Californian demands for gardens with amenities such as swimming-pools and terraces allowing the living-rooms to extend outwards. *Baylis, *Church, *Eckbo, and *Halprin were associated with it, and their work proved influential outside CA.

Church (1955, 1969); W & S (1994)

calion, calyon 1. *Flint nodule, boulder, or pebble. **2.** Flint panel in *flush-work.

Callicrates C5 BC Athenian architect, responsible with *Ictinus for the Greek-*Doric *temple known as the *Parthenon* (447–436 BC), and on his own (probably) for the small *Ionic temple of *Nike Apteros* (c.426–4 BC) on the Bastion outside the *Propylaea*. He supervised part of the construction of the walls between Athens and Piraeus, and may have restored the Athenian city-walls.

Carpenter (1970); D (1950)

Callimachus (c.430–400 BC) Athenian credited by *Vitruvius with the invention of the *Corinthian *capital. *See* ACANTHUS.

VP (1955–6)

calotte Low segmental *dome, circular on plan, without a *drum, so called from its resemblance to a clerical skull-cap e.g. *Pantheon-dome.

Calvary 1. *Rock-work on which three *crosses are erected, or a sculptured representation of the Crucifixion. **2.** *Rood.

Calvinist austerity Sharp, hard-edged late-C20 and early-C21 architecture, esp. associated with The Netherlands, notably **Wiel Arets**'s (1955–), *apartment-blocks in Tilburg (1992–4) and KNSM Island, Amsterdam (1990–6).

S.Allen & Zwarts (1999); Boc (1999); X.Costa *et al.* (eds) (2002); RW

calyon *See* CALION.

calyx (*pl.* calyces) Ornament resembling a cup-like (properly *calix*) flower, as in the *Corinthian *capital, or on the neck of the Roman *Doric capital.

camarín Chapel or *shrine set above and behind the *high-altar in Spanish churches, but visible from the body of the church.

camber Very shallow, scarcely perceptible upward curve, often apparent on the underside of *collar-and-*tie beams in a *truss. A *camber-arch* is therefore the *soffit of a 'flat' arch of brick *rubbers* achieved by using a camber-strip as a support for the *intrados* during construction.

Cambio, Arnolfo di (c.1245–c.1310) *See* ARNOLFO DI CAMBIO.

cambogé Type of *brise-soleil* with transverse openings permitting ventilation but providing shade from direct sunlight.

Cambridge Camden Society Founded (1839) as the Cambridge Society for the Study of Church Architecture, and named after the antiquary, **William Camden** (1551–1623), it was more than an antiquarian body. A pressure-group which set out to encourage scholarly restoration of decayed churches and the building of new ones that would provide suitable settings for a revived liturgy, it was a major factor in promoting the *Gothic Revival, and became (1845) the Ecclesiological Society. Its ideals were set out in numerous publications, of which the *Ecclesiologist* (from 1841), was the most important: it remained influential long after publication ceased (1868), and as an organ for architectural criticism, it could make or break reputations. *See* ECCLESIOLOGY.

J.Curl (2007); Webster & Elliott (eds) (2000)

came Cast, extruded, or milled lead rods with a section like an **H**, also called *lattice, used in *leaded *lights (e.g. stained-glass windows) to frame and secure the *panes or regular lozenge-shaped glass *quarrels.

Camelot, Robert (1903–92) *See* ZEHRFUSS.

camera, *also* **camara** Curved or *vaulted ceiling: *camerated* is applied to a ceiling with the *appearance* of a *vault, the term implying a false ceiling. *Compounds include*:

camera lucida: instrument by which rays of light from an object are refracted by a prism producing an image on paper, thus facilitating an accurate drawing of the object;

camera obscura: darkened box or chamber into which light is admitted through a double convex lens, thus forming an image of external objects, a view, etc., on a surface placed at the focus of the lens.

Cameron, Charles (1745–1812) London-born architect of Scots descent whose significance lies in his accomplished and refined *Neo-Classicism and in his introduction to Russia of the *Greek-Revival style and the naturalistic English *landscape-garden. Apprenticed (1760) to his father, **Walter Cameron** (*fl.*1740–80), he became a pupil of Isaac *Ware, on the death (1766) of whom Cameron determined to realize Ware's project for a new edition of *Burlington's *Fabbriche Antiche* (1730), and went to Rome to correct and finish the unsatisfactory drawings of Roman *thermae* by *Palladio used by Burlington. His *Baths of the Romans Explained and Illustrated, with the Restorations of Palladio Corrected* *and Improved* (French and English texts (1772)) was an important source for Neo-Classical ornament, and went into further editions (1774, 1775).

At some time (1770s) he may have been in Ireland, but by 1779 he was Architect to **Empress Catherine II ('the Great') of Russia** (*r.*1762–96), for whom he made many additions to the Palace of *Tsarskoye Selo* (now *Pushkin*), near St Petersburg (1779–85), including the colonnaded Cameron Gallery, the Cold Baths, the Agate *Pavilion, the private apartments, and the Church of *St Sophia*, where he demonstrated his skill as a designer of refined Neo-Classical interiors, among the most beautiful of their kind and date in Europe. His use of colour is especially felicitous: in the Agate Pavilion, for example, the red-agate columns with gilt-bronze *capitals set against a background of green-jasper walls create a stunningly opulent effect. He designed and built (1782–5) the Palace at Pavlovsk for **Grand Duke Paul** (1754–1801—**Tsar Paul I** from 1796) as well as many other buildings there, including the theatre, town-hall, and the *temples in the English Park. The circular *Doric Temple of Friendship (*c.*1780) is an important pioneering exemplar of the *Greek Revival. Also in the 1780s he produced various designs for the Imperial Palace at Bakhtchi-Serai in the Crimea, including a *triumphal arch, a drawing of which, by **John Linnell Bond** (1764–1837), was exhibited at the Royal Academy in London (1793). Cameron fell from favour after Catherine's death, and was superseded as Chief Architect to the Imperial Court by *Brenna. However, he remained in Russia, and worked for several patrons, including the Razumovskys at Baturin, Ukraine (1799–1802). At Pavlovsk (1800) he designed the *Ionic Pavilion of the Three Graces. Appointed (1803) Architect to the Admiralty, he designed various buildings at the Imperial naval base of Kronstadt, including the barracks and hospital.

In many ways his compositions are essentially Palladian, but his precise knowledge of the *Antique sources of Neo-Classicism led him (like *Adam) to design details and furnishings for his buildings. He was responsible for importing Scots craftsmen to Russia, including *Menelaws, and collaborated with *Busch in the design of gardens.

C.Cameron (1772); Co (2008); CoE (1972); Kuchumov (1976); Loukomski (1943); T.Rice & Tait (1967–8); D.Shv (1996); J.T (1996); Tait (ed.) (1967)

camp 1. Ceiling resembling the interior of a truncated *pyramidal form. 2. Ceiling within a roofspace or *garret with sloping sides formed by the positions of the *rafters. 3. *Comb* ceiling with sides, like those of a *tent, also called a *tent ceiling*.

Camp Standing out from the background, or theatrical posturing. Camp taste is concerned with affectation, artificiality, and playfulness, and historically is therefore associated with vogues for *Chinoiserie*, *Gothick, and the *exotic: in C20 it included *Art Nouveau, *Art Deco, *Baroque, *Kitsch, and *Rococo, as well as the outrageously amusing. Some critics have even detected *High, Middle,* or *Low Camp* in architecture: e.g. Baroque = High Camp, while aspects of *Post-Modernist *Kitsch* = Low Camp.

M.Booth (1983); Js (1973a)

campagna Open countryside (*Walpole's 'champaign'), as depicted, e.g., in the paintings of **Claude Lorraine** (1600–82), **Nicolas Poussin** (1594–1665), and **Gaspard Dughet** (*called* **Poussin**—1615–75). Such images profoundly affected C18 landscape-design in Britain.

Symes (2006)

campana *Bell-shaped (*campaniform* or *campanular*) core of a *Corinthian *capital.

campanile (*pl.* **campanili**) Italian bell-tower, usually free-standing.

campanula (*pl.* **campanulae**) Miniature bell-shaped form, such as conic *guttae in the *Doric *Order, or the elements beneath the *eaves of a *pagoda or *Chinoiserie buildings.

Campbell, Colen (1676–1729) Scots lawyer/landowner who became a leader of *Palladianism and one of the most distinguished figures in early-C18 English architecture. His metamorphosis into architect is shrouded in obscurity, but he does seem to have had some association with the Scots architect James *Smith, and may have been taught by him. Campbell's first (and most important) house in England was Wanstead, Essex (*c.*1714–20, demolished 1820), the precedent for large Classical country-houses of virtually the whole *Georgian period. Campbell published (1715) the first volume of *Vitruvius Britannicus*, which promoted the virtues of 'Antique Simplicity' (as opposed to 'affected and licentious' *Baroque architecture), lauded the 'renowned Palladio' and the 'famous Inigo Jones', and advertised his own expertise as an architect, in much the same way as *Palladio had done in *Quattro Libri* (1570).

Campbell was appointed (1718) Chief Clerk and Deputy Surveyor-General under *Benson, but in the following year both he and Benson were removed from office, which precluded the possibility of the Palladian Revival being led from within the Office of Works. However, Campbell became (1719) architect to **George Augustus, Prince of Wales** (1683–1760—*r.* as **King George II** from 1727), and was also appointed by *Burlington to re-fashion his town-house in Piccadilly in the Palladian style. Subsequently, Burlington transferred his favours to *Flitcroft and *Kent, dropping Campbell, but the last had no shortage of rich and influential patrons, attracted, no doubt, by his sumptuous *Vitruvius Britannicus*, the second and third volumes of which appeared in 1717 and 1725. They contained illustrations of all his designs, and he addressed many projects to eminent Whigs: he dedicated volume i to **King George I** (*r.*1714–27).

Campbell's patrons included **Sir Robert Walpole** (1676–1745), for whom he designed Houghton Hall, Norfolk (begun 1722); **Henry Hoare** (1677–1725), for whom he built Stourhead, Wilts. (*c.*1718–24); and many others. Newby (now Baldersby) Park, Yorks. (1720–8), was an important precedent for the neo-Palladian villa, while Mereworth Castle, Kent (*c.*1722–5), was a distinguished version of Palladio's *Villa Capra*, Vicenza. Campbell was the designer of many of the most important buildings of the whole Palladian movement, and in the decade after the publication of volume i of *Vitruvius Britannicus* he created many models from which the English *second Palladian Revival* evolved. Campbell was appointed (1726) Surveyor of Greenwich Hospital in succession to *Vanbrugh. He brought out (1728) a version of the first book of Palladio's *Quattro Libri*, which was revised and published (1729) as *The Five Orders of Architecture* with extra plates featuring some of his own designs.

C.Campbell (1728–9, 1967–72); Co (22008); Co & J.Hs (1970); E.Hs (1990); Stutchbury (1967); Su (1993); J.T (1996)

Campbell, John Archibald (1859–1909) Scots architect, he commenced practice in Glasgow (1886) with J.J.*Burnet, and practised alone (1897–1909) until he entered into partnership with **Alexander David Hislop** (1876–1966). Shawlands Old Parish Church, Pollokshaws Road (1885–9), is an essay in *First Pointed, with a defensive street-elevation and a dramatic north *elevation facing Shawlands Cross in which parts of Dunblane Cathedral were quoted, but the Barony Church (1886–9—now the ceremonial hall of Strathclyde University) is a masterpiece of First Pointed, much influenced by the work of *Pearson (who was adjudicator during the architectural competition) and again with quotations from Dunblane: in both of these Glaswegian works Burnet was deeply involved. On his own account Campbell designed the mighty office-building at 157–67 Hope Street, on the corner with West George Street (1902–3), the great height of which relies on load-bearing *masonry with *cast-iron columns supporting steel beams spanning between internal brick *piers. His last independent work was the office-building at 84–94 St Vincent Street, Glasgow, the city's first steel-framed building, with a *Portland-Stone front.

DW; WRH (1990)

Campbell, Kenneth John (1909–2002) English architect, from 1949 Deputy Architect in the LCC (later GLC) Schools Division, and (1958) Deputy Housing Architect in charge of the largest office of its kind in the UK. Forced to implement Government guidelines, he opposed the official view that prefabricated systems were more economical than traditional methods, but nevertheless his department was responsible for the erection of many residential tower-blocks. He was responsible for saving and converting into *apartments some derelict warehouses by the Thames at Deptford, the best part of the Pepys Estate there.

The Times (30 July 2002), 30

Campbell, Oran (1941–2004) Scots architect/conservationist, he worked from 1969 with *Jebb before establishing (1971) his own London practice. From 1976 he was Regional Architect for East Anglia and then for South-East England and South London at the Department of the Environment's Directorate of Ancient Monuments and Historic Buildings (absorbed 1984 into **English Heritage**). He became (1989–97) head of the conservation department of **Broadway Malyan**, where he undertook work for, among others, The National Trust, English Heritage, and the Almshouse Association, and from 1999 he was director and partner at **Lincoln & Campbell**, Edinburgh. He restored the Shell *Grotto at Painshill, Surrey.

The Scotsman (5 Nov. 2004), Obits; pk

Campen, Jacob van (1595–1657) Chief exponent of *Classicism in The Netherlands, he was influenced by the work of *Scamozzi and *Palladio, and with his Coymans House on the *Keizersgracht*, Amsterdam (1624), he introduced the *Palladian style to The Netherlands. His most refined work is the *Mauritshuis* in The Hague (1633–5), which has a Palladian plan, elevations featuring a *Giant *Order of *Ionic *pilasters set on a plain base, a *pedimented central section given little emphasis, and a hipped roof. Much grander is the Town Hall (now Royal Palace), Amsterdam (1648–55): it has two internal courtyards separated by a huge central hall, *façades with two superimposed Giant Orders of pilasters, and a large projecting pedimented central section over which is a domed *lantern. His *Nieuwe Kerk*, Haarlem (1645–9), is based on the *quincunx plan (essentially a Greek *cross within a square), with square Ionic crossing-piers and a *groin-vault over the *crossing. He was responsible for the *Accijnshuis*, Amsterdam (1638), the *Noordeinde Palace*, The Hague (1640), and, with others, the decorations of *Post's *Huis-den-Bosch*, Maarssen, near Utrecht (*c.*1628). His secular architecture influenced van 's *Gravesande and *Vingboons, and was introduced to England by Hugh *May and his contemporaries.

Fremantle (1959); Kuyper (1980); RSTK (1977); Swillens (1961)

Campionesi C19 term for a group of sculptors/architects active in Lombardy (mid-C12–late-C14): the name derives from Campione da Lugano, their place of origin. The *Rood-screen (late-C12) in Modena Cathedral is attributed to **Anselmo da Campione**; the *altar, *crypt *capitals, main *façade (including the circular window), and the *Porta Regia* on the south flank of the *nave (1209–31—which has a porch incorporating one hexagonal and one twisted column) to his followers, including his son, **Ottavio**; and the completion of the Ghirlandina *campanile* (1319) and nave-*pulpit to **Enrico**. **Giovanni da Campione** designed the *Baptistery at *Santa Maria Maggiore*, Bergamo (1340), and the south porch of the church (1351). **Bonino da Campione** (*fl.*1357–97) signed the extraordinary tomb of **Cansignorio della Scala** (d.1375) at *Santa Maria Antica*, Verona, and **Matteo da Campione** (d.1396) carried out major works at Monza and Milan Cathedrals.

Romanini (1964); J.T (1996)

Camporese Family Pietro **Camporese** (1726–81) and his sons **Giulio** (1754–1840) and **Giuseppe** (1763–1822) were the architects for the remodelling of *Santa Scolastica*, Subiaco, of the *Galleria dei Candelabri* (1786–88), and for the completion of the Neo-Classical *atrium* of the *Quattro Cancelli*, *Museo Pio-Clementino*, in Rome (1793). **Pietro the Younger** (1792–1873) was an important scholar of antiquities, and became a member of the Commission formed to study the problems of planning the enlargement of Rome. He was responsible for *Renaissance-Revival work in the *Piazza Nicosia palazzetto*, for the colonnaded *Portico di Veio*, *Palazzo Wedekind*, facing the *Piazza Colonna* (1838), and for the *façade of the Hospital of *San Giacomo degli Incurabili* (1843), in Rome, among other works.

Ms (1966); M & Wa (1987)

campo santo Italian *cemetery surrounded by *arcaded *cloisters or roofed *galleries containing funerary monuments (e.g. Pisa (1278–83), designed by **Giovanni da Pisa** (*c.*1240–1320)).

camp-shedding Facing of piles and boards along a river bank to protect it from collapsing due to action of the current. Also *camp-shot*, *camp-sheeting, camp-sheathing*.

campus 1. Grounds of a college or university, or a separate, discrete part of such an institution. **2.** Large expanse of parkland containing a series of buildings used for academic purposes.

3. Arrangement of such buildings around a large open grassed area, as at Downing College, Cambridge (from 1806), by *Wilkins, which replaced the plan featuring the smaller medieval *court or *quad for collegiate buildings. One of the most celebrated campuses is *Jefferson's University of Virginia at Charlottesville (1817–26), the precedent for many others in the USA. *See* COLLEGE GARDEN.

Dober (1992); Shoe (2001); P.T (1987)

Camus de Mézières, Nicolas Le (1721–93) French architect of the huge circular *Halle au Blé*, Paris (1763–7), and author of *Le Génie de l'architecture; ou, l'analogie de cet art avec nos sensations* (1780) in which the new idea that architecture should be pleasing to the senses and induce elevating impressions on the heart and mind was floated. This led to the notion of *architecture parlante* adopted by *Boullée and others, and to the belief that architectural character can be created by the mysterious effects of light, a notion taken up by many important architects, not least *Soane. He also published *Le Guide de ceux qui veulent bâtir* (1781) and *Traité de la force des bois* (1782). His namesake, **Louis-Denis Le Camus** (*fl.*1742–75), designed the *Chinoiserie tower or *pagoda in the gardens of the *chateau at Chanteloup (1775–8), and also the *Colisée, Champs-Elysées*, Paris (1769–71), a vast and complex building, with a huge *dome in which spectacular lighting effects were achieved.

Camus de Mézières (1780); M & Wa (1987); M & T (1991)

canal 1. *Channel, gutter, or pipe to convey liquid, usually water. **2.** Long, narrow, artificially created water-course for the ornamentation of a park, or for inland navigation. **3.** *Flute in the *shaft of a column or *pilaster. **4.** Spiral channel (*canalis*) flanked by small convex *mouldings from the eye following the revolutions of the *volute, and carrying over to the other volute between the *abacus and *echinus of the *Ionic *capital.

canaliculus (*pl.* **canaliculi**) *Channel or groove on a *triglyph in the *Doric *Order.

cancellus (*pl.* **cancelli**) **1.** *Latticed *screen, especially one (*cancello*) that divides the *sacrarium* or *presbyterium* from the rest of the church, hence *chancel. **2.** In the plural, *balustrades or *rails defining the *choir, usually attached to *ambones, as at *San Clemente*, Rome (C6).

candelabrum (*pl.* **candelabra**) **1.** Stand on which lamps are supported. **2.** *Chandelier. **3.** Branched candlestick.

Candela Outeriño, Félix (1910–97) Madrid-born and -educated naturalized American

architect. Influenced by the structures of *Torroja, he developed a lifelong interest in *shell-
vaulting. He emigrated to México (1939), where
he formed the firm of **Cubiertas Ala** with his
brother **Antonio.** His advocacy of shell-vaults
brought him commissions, including the Cos-
mic-Ray Pavilion, University City, México City
(1951–2), with its *hyperbolic *paraboloid *concrete roof, much of which is only 15 mm thick, set
on legs. His Church of the Miraculous Virgin,
México City (1953–5), with **Enrique de la Mora
y Palomar** (1907–78), is *Expressionist in style,
influenced by *Gothic and by the work of
*Gaudí. He again worked with Mora on the chapel
of *San Vicente de Paul,* Coyoacán, México City
(1960), which has an inverted **U**-shaped canopy
set on *rubble walls. He used mushroom-shaped
umbrella-like forms at the John Lewis warehouse,
Stevenage, Herts. (1963), designed with *Yorke,
Rosenberg, & Mardall. He was also involved in
the design of the Olympic Stadium, México City
(1968).

E (1994); C.Faber (1963); Henn (ed.) (1992); Segui Bon-
aventura (1994); C.B.Smith (1967); Starczewski (1992);
Tonda (2000)

Candid, Peter, *also known as* **Peter de Wit** *or*
Witte (1548–1628) Netherlandish architect/
painter, he worked under *Vasari at the Vatican
before settling in Munich (1586), where he laboured on the frescoes in the *Grottenhalle* in the
Residenz designed by *Sustris: indeed, he also
appears to have acted as architect. From 1611 he
was recognized as the leading painter at the
Court, designed many tapestries and *grotesques,
and was responsible for painted decorative
schemes at the *Altes Schloss,* Schleissheim (1617),
and *Goldener Saal, Rathaus,* Augsburg (1619).

Hi (1981); Jervis (1984)

Candilis, Georges (1913–95) Azerbaijan-born,
naturalized French architect, disciple of Le *Corbusier, for whom he worked (1945–50), supervising construction of the first *Unité d'Habitation.*
He collaborated with **Shadrach Woods** (1923–73)
and **Vladimir Bodiansky** (1894–1966), before
they set up with **Alexis Josic** (1921–2011) as **Can-
dilis-Josic-Woods** in Paris (1955–63). With Bodiansky and Woods he produced the master-plan
for Casablanca (1952–4), and with Woods and
Josic he worked on the new towns of Bagnols-sur-
Cèze (1956–61) and Toulouse-le-Mirail (1960–77).
Responsible for many master-plans (e.g. Free
University of Berlin-Dahlem (1963–79)), the firm
adhered to dogmas of the *Athens Charter and
*CIAM, and it shows in the results.

Candilis (1973, 1977); S.Woods (ed.) (1968)

Cane, Stephen Percival (Percy) (1881–1976)
English landscape architect/writer. Inspired by

*Peto's garden (1902) at Easton Lodge, Essex, he
established (by 1919) in London what was to
become an international practice. He drew on
elements of later *Arts-and-Crafts gardens (merging stonework (e.g. steps) with formal woodland
*glades), the *Italianate gardens of Peto, and the
aesthetics of Japanese exemplars. Among his gardens may be cited Dartington Hall, Devon (from
1945), Falkland Palace, Fife (from 1947), and
Westfields, Oakley, Beds. (1953–64). Mindful of
the need to create harmonious relationships
between buildings, gardens, and the surrounding
scenery, his designs were influential, as were
his copious writings. He taught **Frank Clark**
(1902–71) and *Tunnard.

Cane (1926–7, 1934, 1967); *ODNB* (2004); Shoe (2001);
Snell (1989); Tay (2006); Webber (1975)

Canella, Guido (1931–2009) Italian architect
responsible for stark and controversial buildings,
including the Pieve Emanuele Civic Centre,
Lombardy (1971–81), a complex that expresses
his ideas about defence, historical allusions, and
composition in a design of towers, massive walls,
and powerful modelling.

E (1994)

canephora (*pl.* **canephorae**) *See* CARYATID.

Canevale, Isidore Marcel Armand (1730–
86) French architect. Trained under *Servandoni,
he settled in Austria (1760), where he designed
the *triumphal arch in Innsbruck (1765). As Court
Architect in Vienna he was responsible for, *inter
alia,* the *Allgemeines Krankenhaus* (1783) and
the Military College of Surgery and Medicine
(the *Josephinum,* 1783–5). His masterpiece is the
Cathedral, Vác, Hungary (1763–77), the central
*dome, coffered ceiling, and vast *Corinthian
*portico of which are as advanced works of
*Neo-Classicism as anywhere else in Europe at
that time. He designed gardens at Bernolákovo,
Slovakia (1763), and Laxenburg, Austria (from
1782—in which the English style of landscape
was employed).

W.Pa (1852); J.T (1996)

Canina, Luigi (1795–1856) Italian *Neo-Classical architect. With *Valadier, he was important as
a protagonist of archaeologically correct *Neo-
Classicism in early-C19 Rome. He succeeded *Asprucci at the *Villa Borghese* Gardens, where his
scholarly Egyptian Gate (completed 1828, with
*pylon-towers (the first in Italy, it seems), and
*obelisks) is a good example of the *Egyptian
Revival, and he also designed the archaeologi-
cally-correct *Ionic *in antis* *lodges at the *Piazza
Flaminia* entrance, influenced, no doubt, by
*Cagnola's *Porta Ticinese* in Milan (1801–14).
His works at the Borghese Gardens included
the Fountain of Esculapius and the *astylar

*triumphal arch (both 1818–28), the latter recalling *Chalgrin's work in Paris. As an architectural historian he produced *Gli edifizi di Roma antica* ...(1848–56) and *Le nuove fabbriche della Villa Borghese*...(1828), and was responsible for major archaeological excavations in the Forum, Appian Way, and Campagna (1823–46).

Canina (1828, 1846, 1852); J.Curl (2005); Ms (1966); Raggi (1857)

canister 1. Basket for flowers or fruit, so found represented on the heads of *canephorae*. **2.** Metal vessel to hold the wafers before consecration for Communion.

cannon 1. Component of the *Empire* and *Federal styles, *military decoration, *trophies, etc. **2.** Element of architecture, often found with cannon-balls, powder-kegs, etc. **3.** Cannon-shaped *bollard. **4.** Projecting water-spout shaped like a cannon-barrel.

Cano, Alonso (1601–67) Spanish painter/architect. During the 1620s he assisted his father with the design of *altar-pieces, but his west front of Granada Cathedral (from 1667) is stupendous, recalling arched *Romanesque fronts (e.g. Lincoln Cathedral). Consisting of three huge arches, it does not employ the *Orders, but rather species of *pilasters, panels, and layers of planes.

K & S (1959); Rosenthal (1961)

Canonica, Cristoforo Maria Luigi (1762–1844) Born in the Ticino, he was trained by *Piermarini. Before settling in Milan, where he made his mark by creating spacious layouts, modernizing the street system, and erecting many public buildings in a refined *Neo-Classical style, including the *Palazzo Brentani-Greppi* (1829–31) and the *Palazzo Anguissola-Traversi* (1829–30), both on the *Via Manzoni*. His largest work was the Civic Arena near the Castello (1806–13), with a Neo-Classical Roman-*Doric entrance (1813), and a battered perimeter-wall pierced at intervals with semicircular arches, the whole effect being powerful, worthy of *Piranesi, but probably influenced by *Fischer von Erlach's *Entwurff* (1721) and by the projects for public spaces by **Giovanni Antonio Antolini** (1753–1841) and **Giuseppe Pistocchi** (1744–1841). With **Innocenzo Giusti** he enlarged (1814) *La Scala* Opera House.

Ms (1966); M & Wa (1987)

Canopus 1. Alexandrian town in Ancient Egypt, celebrated for its *canals and beauty. **2.** *Canopic* bulbous ovoid Ancient Egyptian jar, usually of stone, to contain the internal organs of the dead after disembowelling during the mummification process, with the lid shaped like a head. The jar containing the liver had a humanoid head

Canopus (*a*) Canopic jars, properly called *visceral jars*, they have the heads of the Sons of Horus as stoppers. They are (*left to right*) *Imsety* (humanoid, for the liver); *Qebehsenuef* (hawk, for intestines); *Hapy* (baboon, for lungs); and *Duamutef* (jackal, for the stomach). (*b*) Decorative *canopic* ornament: the head, with lotus-bud, is Antique and the rest is heavily restored strigillated work. Probably from the *Canopus* of the *Villa Adriana*, Tivoli, so largely Roman work in the Egyptian Taste.

of **Imsety**, son of **Horus**, and it was this type that was widely copied for ornaments of the *Neo-Classical period and *Egyptian-Revival style, though the 'lids' were usually fixed. **3.** Part of the gardens of **Hadrian**'s *villa at Tivoli (*Tibur*), near Rome, laid out AD 134–8 around a *Euripus (canal) lined with Egyptianizing statues and complete with sculptured crocodiles and an elephant, intended as a mnemonic of the Nilotic landscape and of Canopus itself.

J.Curl (2005); Roullet (1972)

canopy 1. Roof-like ornamented *hood surmounting an *altar, *doorway, *font, *niche, *pulpit (where it is called a *tester), *stall, statue, *tabernacle, throne, tomb, window-aperture, etc., supported on *brackets, *colonnettes, etc., or suspended. **2.** *Canopy of honour, ceele, ceilure, celure, cellure,* or *seele,* is a richly coloured, often gilded, and panelled ceiling above an altar, *chancel, *chantry-chapel, *mortuary-chapel, etc. **3.** *Town canopy* is a structure resembling an arcaded *gabled opening, often with elaborate *pinnacles, *finials, etc., like a model building, set on top of a niche or protecting a statue: the motif was adapted in funerary architecture, often shown in three dimensions, but horizontal (90° from the usual vertical position as a protection from the weather) on tomb-chests over the heads of *effigies, and was later depicted on *incised slabs and funerary *brasses. A canopy over an altar is usually called *baldachin* or *ciborium*.

cant 1. Angle or inclination of a piece, member, or plane to another, especially to the horizontal. **2.** Oblique surface cutting off the corner of a square, or an oblique face of a polygon, hence a polygonal plan is *canted* (e.g. canted *bay-window).

Canterbury, Michael of (*fl.*1275-1321) Medieval master-mason, he worked at Canterbury Cathedral, Kent, and at St Stephen's Chapel, Palace of Westminster (from 1292). He was of great importance in the evolution of the *Second-Pointed style, esp. through his use of the *ogee. He designed the Eleanor Cross at Cheapside, London (1291-4—destroyed); the *canopied tombs of **Prince Edmund Crouchback** (1245-96—**1st Earl of Leicester** and **1st Earl of Lancaster** from 1276) and his wife, **Aveline de Forz** (d.1274), in Westminster Abbey (*c.*1296); probably the Chapel of St Etheldreda, Ely Place, London (1290-8); the *Lady Chapel in St Paul's Cathedral, London (*c.*1307-12—destroyed); and the tomb (1292-1300) of **Archbishop John Pecham** (Peckham) (*fl.c.*1230-92), Canterbury Cathedral.

J.Harvey (1987); *ODNB* (2004)

Canterbury, Thomas of (*fl.*1323-35) Master-mason who worked (1323) under Walter of *Canterbury at the Palace of Westmínster and the Tower of London. Around 1326 he was building the new chapel at Guildhall, London, and was master-mason (1331) in charge of the upper chapel at St Stephen's Chapel, Westminster, the epitome of English *Second Pointed. He may have been partly responsible for the tomb of **Prince John of Eltham** (1316-36—**Earl of Cornwall** from 1328), Westminster Abbey, and for several works at Canterbury, including the gate-house of St Augustine's Abbey (*c.*1308), *parclose-*screens around the *choir in the Cathedral (1304-*c.*1320), the tomb of **Archbishop Simon Mepham** (*c.*1275-1333), and the great window in St Anselm's Chapel (1336).

J.Harvey (1987); *ODNB* (2004)

Canterbury, Walter of (*fl.*1319-27) Master-mason. He rebuilt the outer *curtain-wall at the Tower of London beside the Traitors' Gate (1324-5), and about the same time was engaged on work at the lower part of St Stephen's Chapel, Palace of Westminster, where he probably designed the *vaults and window-*tracery (completed 1327).

His masterpiece is the tomb (*c.*1325-30) of **Aymer de Valence** (*fl.*1275-1324) in Westminster Abbey.

J.Harvey (1987)

canterius, cantherius *Principal *rafter in Antiquity.

cantharus Basin or *fountain for ablutions in the *atrium of an *Early-Christian or medieval *basilica.

cantilever Horizontal member projecting from a wall, etc., without supports at any point in its entire projection, capable of sustaining loads, and prevented from falling by means of a heavy dead-weight on the opposite side of its *fulcrum. Any *bracket, *corbel, *modillion, or *mutule carrying a *canopy, *cornice, or *eaves (for example) is essentially a cantilever.

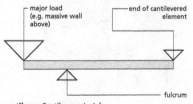

cantilever Cantilever principle

canton *Pier or other projection at an angle of a building, such as *antae, columns, *pilasters, or *rusticated *quoins. Any work of architecture with this condition is said to be *cantoned*, from the French *cantonné*. A *cantoned pier* (*pilier cantonné*) is found in *Gothic architecture, otherwise a *compound pier* with a massive core and four projecting piers or *shafts connecting to the transverse *vaults over *nave and *aisle and the nave-*arcade.

cantoria Italian term for a *gallery or *tribune used by singers, often on the north (*cantoris*) side of the *choir.

Cantwell, Robert (*c.*1792-1858) London architect/surveyor, whose works included the layout of the southern part of the Norland Estate, Northern Kensington, and the design of Royal Crescent there (1839-43). He also designed 2-6 and 24-28 Holland Park Avenue (1826-8), and 1-4 Ladbroke Terrace (1826), on the Ladbroke Estate.

Co (2008); Sh (1973)

cap 1. Abbreviation of *capital*. **2.** *Capital, *cope, *cornice, or crowning or *terminal feature, fitting closely on any member, or extending beyond it in horizontal dimensions. **3.** Domical roof on a windmill. *Related terms include*:

cap-house: upper enclosed part of a *stair giving access to a walk behind a *parapet or an upper *gallery: in Scotland (*capehouse*) it is sometimes in the form of a square top to a circular stair-tower, hence its name;

cap-moulding: cornice-like finish of a *dado, *pedestal, door-*lintel, handrail, or other architectural feature;

capping: *see* COPE; COPING;

cap-stone: **1.** *lintel-stone or large flat stone laid horizontally on two or more upright stones in a *dolmen; **2.** cap of a *staddle-stone; **3.** *cope.

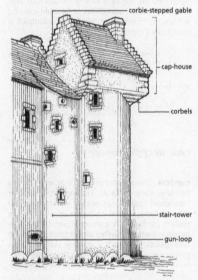

— corbie-stepped gable

— cap-house

— corbels

— stair-tower

— gun-loop

cap-house Rectangular cap-house on a circular tower, Claypotts, Broughty Ferry, Angus (1519–88) (*after MacG & R*).

capital *Chapiter*, *cap, head, or topmost member of an *anta, *colonnette, column, *pilaster, *pier, etc., defined by distinct architectural treatment, often ornamented. *Types include*:

Aeolic: primitive type of *Ionic (*see* AEOLIC);

basket: *Byzantine *bell-type (*a*), ornamented with carving resembling wicker-work or basket-weave;

bell: inverted bell-like form, found in Ancient-*Egyptian architecture (*e*) and *First Pointed (*b*). It forms the essential shape of the *basket-capital* and *core* of the *Corinthian capital;

block: *see* CUSHION;

bud: Ancient-Egyptian type (*f*) based on a *lotus-bud;

Composite: *see* COMPOSITE ORDER;

Corinthian: *see* CORINTHIAN ORDER;

crocket: *Gothic capital (*c*) with stylized rolled leaves resembling small *volutes;

cube: *see* CUSHION;

cushion, also *block* or *cube* capital: *Byzantine and *Romanesque (*d*) form, essentially a cube with its lower corners shaved off and rounded in order to accommodate the transition from square *abacus to circular *shaft, its four faces reduced to semicircular *lunettes*;

Doric: *see* DORIC ORDER;

Hathor-headed: Ancient-Egyptian type (*e*) carved on each face with an image of the goddess **Hathor** and having a large block-like abacus, also carved with a variety of images;

Ionic: *see* IONIC ORDER;

lotus: Ancient-Egyptian type in the form of a lotus-bud (*f*) or decorated with lotus-flowers;

moulded: any capital shaped with horizontal *mouldings, e.g. in the *Perp. style (*i*);

palm: Ancient-Egyptian type (*g*) like the top of a *palm-tree (*palmiform), surrounded by closely arranged vertical palm-fronds and leaves, the column-shaft frequently having vertical bands or large convex reed-like forms. A variant is the Greek-*Corinthian capital from the Tower of the Winds, Athens (*c*.50 BC), with one row of *acanthus-leaves and an upper row of palm-leaves under a square abacus (*h*);

protome, protoma: with upper part of figures, mostly animals, projecting from the angles, usually in Romanesque work;

scallop: Romanesque type (*j*), like the *cushion*, with the curved lower part further shaped with conical forms resembling trumpets (*k*);

stiff-leaf: late-C12 and early C13 Gothic or *Transitional type with stylized leaves, usually with large projections (*l*);

Tuscan: *see* TUSCAN ORDER;

volute: usually associated with the Ionic Order, variants can also be found in Egyptian (*m*) and medieval work;

water-leaf: late-C12 Transitional or early Gothic type with big, wide, unribbed leaves growing outwards above the convex moulding on top of the shaft, turning upwards and inwards at the corners to the abacus (*n*).

caracol, caracole See STAIR.

Caramuel de Lobkowitz, Juan (1606–82) Spanish-born architectural theorist, he saw architecture as part of a vast system embracing all branches of knowledge, and his major work of theory was *Architectura civil, recta y obliqua, considerada y dibuxada en el Templo de Ierusalem* (1678–81), also published in Latin as *Templum*

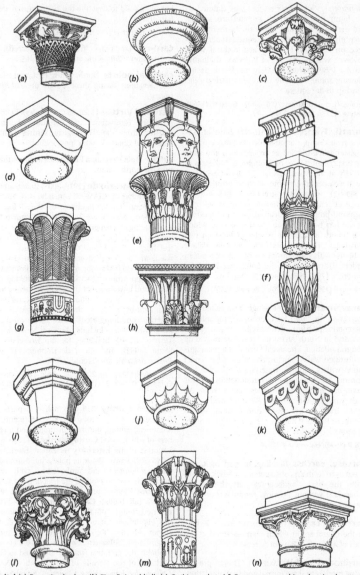

capital (*a*) Byzantine basket; (*b*) First-Pointed bell; (*c*) Gothic crocket; (*d*) Romanesque cushion showing lunettes; (*e*) Ancient-Egyptian Hathor-headed on bell-capital, Philae; (*f*) Ancient-Egyptian lotus-bud, with column and gorge-cornice; (*g*) Ancient Egyptian palm; (*h*) Ancient Greek Corinthian palm, Tower of the Winds, Athens; (*i*) Moulded Perp.; (*j*) Romanesque scallop; (*k*) Romanesque trumpet (scallop variant); (*l*) First-Pointed stiff-leaf, Galilee porch, Ely Cathedral; (*m*) Ancient-Egyptian volute, Philae; (*n*) Transitional water-leaf, Galilee, Durham Cathedral.

Salomonis . . . Solomon's temple was claimed as the fount from which all architecture sprang, and the book included much on mathematical-scientific problems: it was a considerable influence on *Guarini. His only architectural work, however, was the *façade of Vigevano Cathedral (1673–*c*.1680) in Northern Italy, an eclectic design showing some virtuosity in its geometrical relationship to the square.

Caramuel de Lobkowitz (1678–81); Guarini (1968); Pastine (1975); Tadisi (1760)

Caratti, Francesco (*c*.1615–77) Born at Bissone near Como, Caratti settled in Prague where he established himself as an architect, and used the first *Giant *Order of *Composite *pilasters in the city at the Nostitz (Nostic) Palace (1658–60). He developed the theme at the Černin Palace (1669–92), where the street-front has a huge range of *engaged Composite columns set over diamond-pointed *rustication, and the garden-façade has two enormous *serlianas over which is a *blind *arcade, the whole set between two *pavilions. He designed the Michna Palace (*c*.1640), with its centrepiece of *superimposed Orders. He worked on the Lobkowitz Palace at Roudnice (1652–6) and several churches.

E.Hempel (1965); J.Nn (1970); C.Powell (1959)

caravanserai Place of refuge (also called *funduq, khan*, or *ribat*) for caravans (companies of merchants, pilgrims, etc., travelling in groups for security) in North Africa or West Asia providing accommodation. The usual form was a rectangular fortified walled enclosure with a large *court (often with a garden), water-supply, kitchens, a *mosque, and sleeping-accommodation, so was larger and had more functions than a *serai. An early *caravanserai* was the *Ribat-i-Sharaf* (1114, 1155), Iran, on the route from Central Asia to Northern Persia: it had four *iwans and was richly decorated.

B & B (1994); Hillenbrand (1994)

carcase, carcass Building, or part of it, finished as to its main construction, or *shell, essentially the basic loadbearing part (framed or otherwise) without flooring, roofing-cover, window-frames, or finishes.

carcer (*pl.* **carceres**) **1.** Roman *prison. **2.** One of the chambers in which chariots stood at the start of a race in a Roman *circus.

cardboard architecture 1. Design-process using models to show formal and spatial relationships without taking into account the materials or functions of the final buildings. **2.** Models with flat surfaces pierced by plain black holes resembling a series of cardboard boxes. The term in this sense has been used to describe the 1960s work of certain architects.

Frampton *et al.* (1975); Sharp (1978)

card-cut Low-relief *fret (but unpierced) in (especially) *Chinoiserie and *Gothick *friezes.

cardinal points North, south, east, and west, so *elevations facing these points are *cardinal fronts*.

Cardinal Virtues (*Virtutes Cardinales*) Justice, Prudence, Temperance, and Fortitude, as distinguished from the Theological Virtues (Faith, Hope, and Charity), often *personified.

cardo Main street in a Roman *castrum or town running north–south.

Carlo, Giancarlo de (1919–2005) Italian architect, member of *CIAM (of which he was critical, denouncing crude rigidities of the *Modern Movement) and *Team X. He is best known for his buildings on superb sites (which may be seen as sensitive to the *genius loci*, exemplars of *Critical Regionalism before the term became overused) at the Free University of Urbino (1973–9 and later). He had strong affinities with Francesco di *Giorgio, whose great spiral ramp linking the upper and lower parts of Urbino he reopened and restored. His career embraced academic appointments on both sides of the Atlantic, as well as a practice combining architecture and town-planning. Other works include Matteotti New Village, Terni (1972–6), buildings for the University of Siena (1982), and the redevelopment of the *Piazza della Mostra*, Trento (1990).

AR, ccxviii/1301 (July 2005), 30; Carlo (1965, 1970); Colombo (1964); E (1994); McKean (2004); Zucchi (1993)

Carlone Family C16–C18 Italian dynasty of Central-European masons/stuccoers/painters/architects, among the most distinguished members of which were: **Carl(o) Martin(o)** (1616–67), architect of the **Esterházy** residence, Eisenstadt (1663–72), a vast *Baroque palace built around a *cour d'honneur* and embellished with twin towers. He also worked on the *Hofburg* and *Servitenkirche*, Vienna, and *Schloss Petronell*, Lower Austria (all 1660s). **Carlo Antonio** (1635–1708) planned (1686–1708) the Abbey of St Florian and the Pilgrimage Chapel at Christkindl (1702–9), Upper Austria, both completed by his pupil *Prandtauer. **Silvestro Carlone** (1610–71) was probably the architect (usually attributed to C.A. Carlone) of the *façade of the Church of *Neun Chören der Engel* (Nine Choirs of Angels), *Am Hof*, Vienna (1662), with projecting *wings and central balcony behind which the *Baroque front of the church rises. This arrangement is partially derived from *Mansart's Baroque

Minimes Church, Paris, and integrates the front of the church with the flanking palatial façades. He also contributed to the design of the *Schotten-kirche*, Vienna (1638–48).

Bou (1962); Brucker (1983); C.Powell (1959); J.T (1996)

Carmontelle, Louis Carrogis, aka (1717–1806) French dilettante/designer of several gardens, including the *jardin *anglo-chinois Parc Monceau*, Paris (1773–8), with its many diversions in the form of **fabriques*, including 'ruins', a 'Dutch windmill', a 'Tartar tent', and similar *conceits. One of its most unusual features was the *Bois des Tombeaux* containing fabriques in the form of tombs (*pyramids, etc.). Thomas *Blaikie, the Scots landscape-gardener, was brought in (*c.*1781) to simplify Carmontelle's somewhat overladen scheme, but the work was an important catalyst in the transformation of the garden, embellished with monuments, to the *cemetery.

W.Adams (1979); Carrogis (1779); J.Curl (2011); Etlin (1984)

carnel *See* BATTLEMENT.

Caröe, Martin Bragg (1933–99) Third-generation (grandson of W.D.*Caröe) British architect to the Deans and Chapters of Brecon and St David's Cathedrals, Wales, and Rochester, Kent. He carried out (1982–4) meticulous *conservation work at Kingston Lacy, Dorset, for the National Trust, and at the Tower of London (1991–8) he made careful surveys of the fabric, restoring the White Tower and a pair of pre-Fire houses at 4 and 5 Tower Green. One of his most controversial projects was the conservation of the west front of Wells Cathedral, Som. (1974–86), involving poultices to extract dirt and consolidation with lime-water.

COPAC Newsletter, xvi (May 2000), 11–12; *Independent* (9 Dec. 1999), Obits

Caröe, William Douglas (1857–1938) Son of the Danish Consul in Liverpool, he was a versatile church architect and pioneer of building *conservation, who also designed country-houses, educational buildings, offices, remarkably inventive furniture, embroideries, memorials, monuments, and metalwork (e.g. the *high-altar *cross for the Cathedral at Bury St Edmunds, Suffolk). He was architect to five cathedrals (notably St David's and Brecon in Wales) and to the Ecclesiastical Commissioners in England (1895–1938). Among his best works are St David, Exeter, Devon (1897–1900—with passage-aisles derived from *Bodley's work at Pendlebury); St Barnabas, Walthamstow (1902–23—which forms a felicitous composition with its charming *Queen-Anne tile-hung vicarage and adjoining hall); St Ninian, Douglas, IoM (1913); the beautifully composed St Helen, St Helen's, Lancs. (1920–6); St George, Troodos,

Cyprus (1928–30); St Bartholomew, Beltinge, Herne Bay, Kent (1908–31—described by *Pevsner as 'Caröe at his larkiest'); and the exquisite chapels in St Mary's Church, Gillingham, Dorset (1921), and Holy Trinity, Eccleshall, Staffs. (1929–31). His repairs to St Thomas à Becket Church, Fairfield, Romney Marsh, Kent (1912–13), and St Ishow (or Issui), Partrishow, Breconshire (now Powys), Wales (1908–9), are outstanding. Secular works include the robust 75–83 Duke Street, London (1890–4), the elegant offices of the Ecclesiastical Commissioners at 1 Millbank, London (1903–6), the considerable extensions to his own house, Vann, near Hambledon, Surrey (1907–30), and his winter home, Latomia, Kyrenia, Cyprus (1933).

Freeman (1990); A.S.Gray (1985); JF; Se (ed.) (1975); Se (1977).

carol *See* CARREL.

Carolean Period of King **Charles II** (*r.*1660–85). *Caroline* refers to the reign of **King Charles I** (*r.*1625–49).

Carolingian Term describing the style of architecture associated with the reign of **Emperor Charlemagne** (800–14). Carolingian architecture is generally accepted as dating from late C8 to early C10, and examples were erected in The Netherlands, France, and Germany, especially in the areas bounding the Rhine. Stylistically, Carolingian architecture looked back to *Early-Christian *basilicas of the time of the Roman **Emperor Constantine** (*r.*324–37), and included the first building of the Abbey Churches of St-Denis (*c.*754–75) and Fulda (790/2–819), the latter based on the Constantinian basilica of *San Pietro* in Rome (begun *c.*333). At Aachen, the Palatine Chapel (792–805) is based on *San Vitale,* Ravenna, and was probably designed by Odo of *Metz. At Lorsch in the Rhineland (late C8) is a *gate-house and guest-hall with *engaged *Composite columns and arches (a motif derived from Roman Antiquity) above which is a range of fluted *pilasters supporting a series of triangles instead of arches (a theme taken from Roman *sarcophagi). In 790–9 was built the Abbey Church of St-Riquier (Centula), with a *nave, *lean-to *aisles, two sets of *transepts (the west of which had a low entrance-*narthex with a chapel above called a *west-work), four round towers, an apsidal east end, and towers over each of the *crossings. Similar plans were developed in the *Romanesque period in the Rhineland (Worms, for example), while an impressive west-work can be found at Corvey-on-the-Weser (873–85).

Conant (1979); D.Wa (1986)

carolitic, carolytic Properly *corollitic,* column with foliated *shaft embellished with branches and leaves winding spirally around it.

Carpenter, Richard Cromwell (1812-55) English architect, friend and admirer of A.W.N. *Pugin, he was one of the first architects of the *Gothic Revival to meet with the approval of *Ecclesiologists, notably with his Churches of St Paul, Brighton (1846-8), and St Mary Magdalene, Munster Square, London (1849-52), both in a sober and scholarly *Middle-Pointed style. He designed (1848) the Anglican College of St Nicholas at Lancing in Sussex, begun (1854) in a variety of Gothic that owed much to Continental precedent of C13, completed by his son, **Richard Herbert Carpenter** (1841-93), with other work by his pupil and partner **William Slater** (1818/19-72—who seems to have contributed more to the design than was thought), and, later, S.E.*Dykes Bower.

AH, xxxix (1996), 114–23; B.Clarke (1969); J.Curl (2007); D & M (1985)

Carpenter's Gothic(k) 1. Whimsical, unscholarly *Gothick derived from *pattern-books of e.g. Batty *Langley. 2. C19 timber buildings in the USA with Gothicizing tendencies, e.g. in *barge-boards.

McArdle & Bartlett (1978)

carpentry 1. Trade of selecting, cutting, and joining timber for structural purposes. 2. Timber-work constructed by a carpenter: an assemblage of pieces of wood connected by means of joints, etc., distinct from *joinery.

carpet-bedding C19 version of a *parterre de broderie* in which the areas for planting were filled with low-growing colourful plants: the effect was often somewhat garish.

Carr, John (1723-1807) English architect, a competent and prolific practitioner, in Yorks. (where he was Surveyor of Bridges, first for the West Riding (1760-73), and then for the North Riding (from 1772)) and the North of England, of the *Palladianism he had learned while building Kirby Hall, Ouseburn, Yorks., by *Burlington and *Morris (1747-c.1755). His reliability gained him favour among the gentry, and many of his works were featured in *Vitruvius Britannicus* (vols. **iv, v**) and in *New Vitruvius Britannicus*. He was also influenced by Robert *Adam's *Neo-Classicism, and could turn his hand to *Gothic when required. Among his works may be mentioned his many *bridges, his domestic architecture (e.g. Constable Burton, North Riding (c.1762-8), illustrated in *Vitruvius Britannicus*, **v**), his public buildings, and his churches (e.g. Kirkleatham, North Riding (c.1760-3)). The Assize Courts (1773-7) and Prison for Females (1780-3) at York Castle are accomplished *palace-fronted compositions, while the Assembly Rooms and Crescent, Buxton, Derbys. (1780-90), have an

elevational treatment derived from Inigo *Jones's arcaded Covent Garden *piazza* and a variation of the younger *Wood's Royal *Crescent at Bath. His public buildings include the Palladian Town Hall and Assembly Rooms at Newark, Notts. (1773-6).

Bradshaw & I.Hall (1973); Co (2008); J.Curl (2011a); Su (1993); Wragg (2000); YGS (1973)

Carrara Quarried in Northern Italy, a type of close-textured *marble, suited for funerary monuments and other sculpture.

carrel, carol, carrol 1. *Aisle divided into chapels, or the *screens dividing it, or the divisions themselves. 2. Small enclosure, room, *niche, or compartment in a *cloister or any other small space used for study, as in a library, etc. 3. *Light in a *Gothic window defined by *tracery *bars. 4. *Bay-window. 5. Any precinct, or space defined by *rails, etc. 6. Pane of glass secured by *cames in a leaded *light.

Carrère, John Merven (1858-1911) Brazilian-born American architect. He studied at the *École des *Beaux-Arts*, Paris, before joining (1883) *McKim, Mead, & White in NYC. He opened (1886) an office with **Thomas Hastings** (1860-1929): the firm, **Carrère & Hastings**, was responsible for many buildings, including the New York Public Library (1902-11), but started with the *Ponce de Léon* Hotel, St Augustine, FL (1886-8), an eclectic mix of *Moorish, Spanish, and *Renaissance elements, constructed of *concrete using shell and coral *aggregate. Nearly all the work (and it was extremely varied) of the 1890s was elaborately ornamented, but gradually turned to more restrained French *Classicism and American *Colonial *Georgian for inspiration. Later tall buildings, influenced by Chicago architecture, included the Blair Building, NYC (1902), and the Traders' Block, Toronto, Canada (1905). The Royal Bank of Canada retained Carrère & Hastings for their architecture (e.g. Bank, Main Street, Montréal (1909-12), a restrained *Italianate job).

K (1994); H.Reed (1986); J.T (1996); vV (1993)

carriage Timber framework on which the steps of a *stair are supported. One such *rough-string* is called a *carriage-piece*.

Carrier, Willis Haviland (1876-1950) *See* AIR-CONDITIONING.

Carstensen, Georg Johan Bernhard (1812-57) Danish publisher/entrepreneur/founder of the Tivoli Gardens (1842-3) and the Casino (1845-7—the first commercial theatre in the Danish capital), both in Copenhagen. On both these projects he worked with the architect *Stilling, although the unique *Chinoiserie* fantasy, the Tivoli Pantomime Theatre, was designed by *Dahlerup and Ove *Petersen. Carstensen resided

(1852–5) in NYC, USA, where he designed the *polychrome Crystal Palace (1853–4—burnt 1858) with the German architect **Karl** (or Charles) **Gildemeister** (1820–69).

Arkitekten, **vii** (1992), 188–90; Carstensen & Gildemeister (1854); Mi (1951)

Carter, John (1748–1817) English pioneer of scholarly studies of *Gothic. A fine draughtsman, he contributed an imaginative range of designs for *The Builder's Magazine* (1774–86) and drawings of medieval antiquities for several publications, including Gough's *Sepulchral Monuments* (1786). His major work was *The Ancient Architecture of England* (1795–1814), which attempted to set out the 'Orders of Architecture during the British, Roman, Saxon, and Norman Æras'. He had a reputation in his lifetime as an antiquarian: his Argyll-Campbell-Conway monument in St Mary's Church, Sundridge, Kent (*c*.1810), is an early example of *Gothic Revival based on archaeologically correct precedents.

Co (2008); Crook (1995); Ea (1970); Jervis (1984); *ODNB* (2004)

Carthusian Of or belonging to a religious Order of monks founded (1084 *or* 1086) by **St Bruno** (*c*.1030–1101) at Chartreuse, Dauphiné, as a more severe interpretation of *Benedictine rule. Each monk, devoted to the spirit of contemplation, had individual living-accommodation, generally grouped around *courts or *cloisters, communal activities being confined to the religious Offices and Holy Days. Architecture was unadorned, and the Order flourished, especially in Germany, France, Italy, and Spain. Good examples of Carthusian monastery-buildings are the *Certosa*, Pavia (1396–1497), the *Certosa di Val d'Ema*, near Florence (founded 1341), and the *Cartuja de Miraflores*, Burgos (C15—built to designs by members of the *Colonia family). In England, a Carthusian establishment was called *Charter House*, hence the name of the school founded in London on the site of the *Carthusian* monastery.

W.Pa (1852)

Cartilaginous *See* OLEAGINOUS STYLE.

carton-pierre Paper-pulp mixed with resin and glue, pressed into moulds and backed with sheets of glued paper. It was used for roofing, and is not the same as *papier-mâché*.

cartoon Full-size scale drawing on stout paper, for a work in, e.g., stained-glass, mosaic, etc.

cartouche 1. Carved element resembling a sheet of parchment, with its ends or corners rolled, usually carrying an inscription. 2. Ornamental or inscribed *tablet, as in a mural funerary memorial, with an elaborate *scroll-like frame resembling curling pieces of parchment, common

cartouche (2) C17 funerary cartouche of Sir Walter Curl (d. 1678), St Peter's, Soberton, Hants.

in *Baroque work. 3. Any ornament in the form of a scroll, e.g. *console or *Ionic *volute. 4. *Ancon, *console, *modillion, *mutule, or *truss supporting an *entablature instead of a column, especially an ornamented keystone of an arch touching the entablature above. 5. Ring-like frame around figures or characters expressing Royal or Divine titles in Egyptian hieroglyphs.

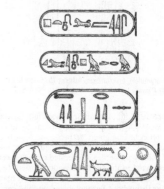

cartouche (5) Egyptian cartouches, reading (*top to bottom*) PTOLMYS, KLEOPATRA, TIBERIUS, TRAJAN.

Carvalho, Eugenio dos Santos de (1711–60) Portuguese architect responsible for the handsome rebuilding, on a regular street plan, of the area between *Terreiro do Paço* (*Praça do Commercio*) and *O Rocío*, Lisbon, after the earthquake (1755), carried out under the aegis of **Sebastião José de Carvalho e Mello**, later **Marquess of Pombal** (1699–1782), all in a sober, restrained French *Neo-Classical style, among the most impressive of all late-C18 town-planning schemes.

Franca (1965); K & S (1959); R.C.Smith (1968)

caryatid(e) (*pl.* **caryatid(e)s**) Carved, draped, straight, standing female figure (*cora*), on its head an *astragal (enriched with *bead-and-reel), *ovolo (enriched with *egg-and-dart), and square *abacus, used as a column substitute, supporting an *entablature. Examples from Greek Antiquity include those of the south porch of the *Erechtheion*, Athens (*c.*421–407 BC), where six figures supported the roof. A similar draped female figure with a basket-like form over the head instead of the astragal-ovolo-abacus *capital arrangement is a *canephora* (*pl.* *canephorae*). See ATLAS, HERM, PERSIAN, TELAMON, TERM.

D (1950)

(*a*)   (*b*)

(*a*) Caryatid(e), *Erechtheion*, Athens; (*b*) Canephora (*after Piranesi*).

cascade Natural or artificial waterfall. Cascading water, a feature of *Mughal gardens, for example, often linking green *terraces, has long been appreciated for its appearance, soothing sounds, and cooling properties. Celebrated cascades were constructed in Italian *Renaissance gardens (e.g. *Villa d'Este*, Tivoli (from 1559)), followed by many others throughout Europe, including the *Grande Cascade*, Saint-Cloud (*c.*1662–5), by Le *Pautre; the double-cascade and pool, Sceaux, (1673–7) by Le *Nôtre; and the 24-step example at Chatsworth, Derbys. (completed 1696 to designs by **Grillet** (pupil of Le Nôtre)), where each step was of a different height and width to vary the sounds emitted. Other exemplars include those at *Peterhof*, St Petersburg, Russia (1704–15—by Le *Blond), and the *Palazzo Reale*, Caserta, near Naples (1752–70—by *Vanvitelli). Many C18 cascades were inspired by *La Rivière de Marly*, Yvelines (1697–9—by *Hardouin-Mansart and **Sébastien Truchet** (1657–1729)). Formal (1724–7) and informal (1740s) cascades were constructed at Gnoll, Neath, Glamorgan: in many British C18 landscape-gardens informal falls, often linking lakes, were made, sometimes associated with *bridges. 'Capability' *Brown created some 'naturalistic' ones, e.g. at Blenheim, Oxon. At Shute House, near Shaftesbury, Dorset, *Jellicoe designed a cascade of four falls over V-shaped pieces of metal, thereby attempting (unsuccessfully) to produce harmonic chords, and (also in the 1960s) *Halprin formed several cascades in the USA. A *cascade-house* is a building from which flows a cascade, e.g. Thomas *Archer's *Baroque exemplar surmounted by a stepped *dome topped by a circular *temple-like *lantern at Chatsworth, Derbys. (1702): it has a front with banded *pilasters (the larger rusticated *blocks with *congelation) and a couple of dolphins.

EHThe accessed 9 July 2013; Symes (2006); Tay (2006)

case 1. Solid frame of a *door or window. **2.** Wooden covering of anything, e.g. a *girder.

casemate 1. In fortifications, a vaulted and blast-resistant chamber with an *embrasure in the outer wall, used as a gun-emplacement, usually within the general constructions comprising the defences. A *casemate* or *casemated wall* is a fortification with a series of casemates between strong outside and inside walls, with massive cross-walls acting as stiffeners between them. **2.** *Cavetto* *moulding not exceeding a quarter-round.

casement 1. Window-frame with hinged or pivoted opening-*lights or *sashes hung from a vertical member of the fixed frame. **2.** *Casemate, or wide hollow *moulding, such as in late-*Gothic *jambs or *bundle-piers, not exceeding a quarter-round.

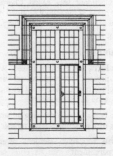

casement C17 oak cross-casement (with leaded lights and one wrought-iron opening-sash) set in an aperture in a brick wall with stone dressings, protected by a *hood-moulding* terminating in *label-stops*.

Case Study houses Campaign by the American journal *Arts and Architecture* started after the 1939-45 war in order to promote architecturally superior yet inexpensive dwellings, employing up-to-date building methods and modern materials. The leading light was **John Dymock Entenza** (1903-84), editor/publisher, and the most widely publicized houses were by *Eames, *Ellwood, and *Koenig (whose Case Study houses 21 and 22 (1958-60), Hollywood, CA, made his name, partly through *Shulman's photography).

Gössel (ed.) (2002); McCoy (1962, 1968, 1977); McCoy & E.Smith (1988); E.Smith (2002)

cashel Irish ring-fort or enclosure of dry-stone masonry, also called a *caher*.

casing, casting 1. *Plaster thrown against the *laths of *timber-framed buildings, either *roughcast or brought to a fair face with a trowel, then, while still wet, patterned. **2.** External plastering lined to imitate the joints of *ashlar.

casino (*pl.* **casinos**) **1.** Small country-house, lightly fortified. **2.** Pleasure-*pavilion, *summerhouse, *villa, etc., in the grounds of a large country-house. **3.** Place of recreation, public or semi-private, with facilities for various activities (e.g. concerts). **4.** Building or part of a building where gambling takes place. **5.** Dwelling appearing to be one storey high, but not necessarily so.

Gw (1903); W.Pa (1852); S (1901-2); Symes (2006)

casita Small *pavilion resembling a *loggia*.

Cassels, *also* **Cassel** *or* **Castle, Richard** (*c.*1690-1751) German-born architect, possibly of Huguenot descent, whose original surname seems to have been **de Ricardi**. He settled in Ireland (1720s) under the aegis of **Sir Gustavus Hume** (1689-1731—**3rd Baronet** from 1695), and from 1728 worked for *Pearce (from whom he inherited a considerable practice, also succeeding him as Surveyor-General of the Newry Canal, for which he designed the first summit-level system in the British Isles). Reared in the European *Baroque tradition, he nevertheless became an exponent of *Palladianism. Cassels's first independent Dublin work was the Printing House, Trinity College (1734), with a *Doric *temple-front, but his most important buildings in the Irish capital were Tyrone House, Marlborough Street (1740-5—which incorporates his favourite Palladian motif of a *serliana surmounted by a *blind arch), and Leinster House (1745-51), probably inspired by Burlington House, London. Ballyhaise, Co. Cavan (1733), is one of Cassels's earliest country-houses, and has two important features: a stone *frontispiece with superimposed Doric and *Ionic *pilasters; and a semi-elliptical projection or *bow on the rear elevation,

suggesting Continental Baroque exemplars, and indicating the elliptical *saloon behind (an. innovation anticipating English elliptical saloons by some four decades). Russborough, Blessington, Co. Wicklow (*c.*1741-55), is one of his most mature Palladian buildings, with exquisite Baroque and *Rococo plaster-work inside.

B-J (1988); M.Craig (1969, 1982); *DIB* (2009); Glin (1964); McP (2001); *ODNB* (2004); Su (1993)

Casson, Sir Hugh Maxwell (1910-99) English architect. Appointed Director of Architecture at the *Festival of Britain (1948-51), he was joined by **Hugh Neville Conder** (1922-2003), who headed the section concerned with education. The Casson **Conder Partnership** was formally established (1956): works included the Royal College of Art, Kensington Gore (1962—with **Henry Thomas Cadbury-Brown** (1913-2009) as principal architect (whose wife, **Elizabeth** (1922-2002), also contributed)), buildings at Worcester College, Oxford (1963), the Elephant and Rhinoceros House, London Zoo (1964), the Ismaili Centre, South Kensington, London (1984), and the Sidgwick Avenue buildings for the Faculty of Arts, University of Cambridge (1952-70). The Lady Mitchell Hall, the Museum of Classical Archaeology, and Oriental Studies building, all on the Sidgwick site, were largely the work of *Cain, who worked with the partnership for over forty years. Casson was President of the Royal Academy of Arts (1875-84), and was a fine watercolourist.

E (1994); Manser (2000); *ODNB* (2004); *The Times* (17 Aug. 1999, 27; 24 June 2003, 24)

cast Reproduction of the form of any object, usually in a material that hardens after a time. It is essentially an object made by running liquid (such as molten metal) or forcing a plastic substance (such as plaster) into a mould or shape which then sets.

Castellamonte, Carlo Conte di (1550/60-1639/40) Trained in Rome, he settled in Turin, working first with *Vitozzi, becoming architect/engineer to **Carlo Emanuele I** (*r.*1580-1630 as **Duke of Savoy**) on *Vitozzi's death (1615), and taking over responsibilities (1627) for fortifications. Castellamonte made an immense contribution to Turin's development, where his Churches of *San Carlo* (1619) and *Santa Cristina* (1635-8) form a festive entrance to his handsome *Piazza San Carlo*, a grand square enlivened by elegant *palazzi*. He also designed the *Piazza San Giovanni* (1630s) and a number of fortresses influenced by French precedents. His son, **Amedeo** (1610-80), succeeded him in his Court appointments, and designed (1656) the Chapel of the Holy Shroud (*SS Sindone*), completed later by *Guarini. Amedeo was also responsible for the

castellated

154

*façade of the *Palazzo Reale,* Turin (1658), and designed the late-*Mannerist *Palazzo Beggiono di Sant'Albano* (1665), as well as numerous fine church-altars.

Brayda et al. (1966); Brino et al. (1966); Wi (1982)

castellated With *battlements (*crenels, crenelles*). A *castellated* building is one with battlements, *turrets, *balistraria, etc., to give it the appearance of a castle, common in the late C18 and early C19, often a *folly.

Castell, Robert (*fl.*1727-28) His accounts of *Pliny's *villas were published posthumously (1729) as *The Villas of the Ancients Illustrated,* serious attempts to reconstruct them from literary evidence. The superb plates showed the villas in their settings, demonstrating strong affinities with English landscape-design of the period.

Co (2008); Hs (1990); RdP (1994)

casting *See* CASING.

cast iron Also known as *grey iron,* it is *cast in moulds (usually fine compacted sand), and has enjoyed much use in architecture since C17 for *street-furniture, railings, *screens, *gates, and decoration, all of which are reproduced from moulds taken from an original model (often of wood). Strong in compression (but weak in tension) it could be used for columns, but for beams it was problematic. In the second half of C18 it began to be used to support *galleries in churches, and was employed to great effect by *Nash at Carlton House Terrace, London (1827-33), for the row of Greek-*Doric columns on The Mall front (which would have been far more expensive to make individually of stone). It began to be used structurally from the time of the building of the Iron Bridge in Salop. (1777-9) (*see* IRON). Whole *façades were made of cast iron (and kits of parts) to designs by *Badger, *Baird, and *Bogardus in C19. Vast quantities of cast-iron lamps, street-furniture, railings, urinals, architectural decorations, *grilles, gates, etc., were produced by firms such as the Scottish Carron and Saracen foundries and the Coalbrookdale Ironworks, Salop., exported all over the British Empire. Cast-iron components contributed an enormous amount to the interest of *townscape, which has been impoverished by the loss of so much (especially in the UK during the 1939-45 war, which was more to do with social-engineering/propaganda than with the war effort).

Aitchison (1960); Fairbairn (1869, 1870); G & G (1974); Loudon (1834); W.Pa (ed.) (1852); E.G.R & J.R (1994); S (1901-2)

castle 1. Large, strong, fortified structure or complex of buildings used for defence against an attacker. In the Middle Ages the most important part of a castle was the *donjon or *keep (*Bergfried* in German), essentially a strong tower with living quarters. The keep, in France and England, might also include the hall for gatherings, in which case it was called a *hall-keep.* The Tower of London has a hall-keep of great magnificence (1077-97) and includes an apsidal-ended *Romanesque chapel. The most usual Continental arrangement was for the hall-range to be separate and not within the keep: perhaps the most impressive C14 hall-ranges are those at *Malbork* (*Marienburg*) in Poland, built by the Teutonic Order. The keep was set within the *inner *bailey* or *ward,* itself protected by walls, either in a corner or the centre of the space. Outside the inner bailey was the *outer bailey,* often containing stables and other offices, so it was a distinct space surrounded by walls. The outer ring of walls had *battlemented tops and walks, with towers at intervals—with *curtain-walls between towers. Gates leading from the outside to the baileys or from bailey to bailey were protected by towers and *portcullises. An entrance to a castle could also have the extra defence of a *barbican. Around the walls, themselves often raised on sloping *embankments or *ramparts (*valla*) were usually *fossae* or *ditches, sometimes filled with water (*moat), and over the moat was a drawbridge that could be raised. Smaller, less important castles might have the central keep (of modest proportions) set on a *motte* surrounded by a bailey contained within palisaded *earthworks and surrounded by a ditch. **2.** Country-house, named after a feudal castle, or a large country mansion looking vaguely like a castle. *See* CASTLE STYLE.

Boase (1967)

Castle *See* CASSELS.

Castle style Type of C18 architecture employing *battlements, *loop-holes (used decoratively), and *turrets to create the *impression* of a fortified dwelling, even though the plan might be regular and Classical as in some buildings by Robert *Adam (e.g. Culzean Castle, Ayrshire (1777-92)). Elements derived from medieval military or fortified architecture were also employed for C18 *follies, gateways, *Picturesque cottages, and fake 'ruins', loosely described as *crenellated.

Macaulay (1975); Rowan (1985)

castrum (*pl.* **castra**) Roman fortified *camp, rectangular in plan, and standardized throughout the Empire. It had two main thoroughfares at right angles, the *cardo maximus* and *via decumana,* which each joined two *gates set in towers with walls and towers around the whole.

cast stone Fine stone dust or *aggregate mixed with *mortar and set in a mould, not unknown in the medieval period and earlier.

cat 1. Strong movable *penthouse to protect besiegers. 2. Lofty work used in fortifications and sieges. 3. Double tripod with six legs. *Associated terms include*:

cat-slide: *see* ROOF;

cat-stones: *crow-steps;

cat-walk: narrow footway, as on a *bridge, or to give access to high-level parts of a building, e.g. sky-lights or *gutters.

catacomb 1. Single subterranean *crypt, *gallery, or passage cut into and hollowed out of rock and lined with rectangular recesses (*loculi*) or arched *niches (*arcosolia*) for the entombment of corpses. *Catacomb* is properly the name given to the public underground *cemetery beneath the *basilica of *San Sebastiano*, on the *Via Appia*, outside Rome, but may also relate to the *atrium* in front of an early church *portico in which the dead were permitted to be buried. It is also used to describe any built basement used for the entombment of coffined bodies, usually associated with C19 cemeteries or cemetery-chapels: there is a good brick-vaulted example under the Anglican chapel at the General Cemetery of All Souls, Kensal Green, London (1837). A small underground burial-place with rock-cut *loculi*, etc., intended for one group or family, was called *hypogeum* in Antiquity, while a large *chamber (often elaborately decorated) in a public catacomb was called *cubiculum*. 2. The plural, *catacombs*, is the term for a large subterranean public cemetery of great size, labyrinthine, and on many levels, such as those in the vicinity of Rome.

Co (1991); J.Curl (ed.) (2001); Kra (1986); Toynbee (1971)

catafalque, catafalco Stage or platform on which a coffin or effigy of a deceased person is placed. It may take the form of a temporary structure, decorated or hung with draperies, used in funeral ceremonies, or as a permanent one, with rollers on top to facilitate the sliding of coffins, and capable of being lowered, as in the fine example (1838) in the Anglican Chapel, General Cemetery of All Souls, Kensal Green, London, where it could carry the coffin down to the *catacomb below. The Kensal Green catafalque also has a swivelling top to aid the handling of the coffin. Permanent catafalques are features found in crematoria, while impermanent examples have been features of elaborate funeral ceremonies.

J.Curl (ed.) (2001); Popelka (1994)

Cataneo, Pietro (*c*.1510–*c*.1574) Sienese architect/military-engineer, possibly a pupil of *Peruzzi. He was the author of *I Quattro Primi Libri di Architettura* (1554), later expanded with four more books, and brought out (1573) as *L'Architettura*, in which civil and military architecture were considered together, and the city plan was revealed as part of a defence-system associated with fortifications. Cataneo saw the design of towns as the task of the architect, emphasizing the importance of geometry in layouts.

AB, xlii (1960), 263–90; Cataneo (1964); *DBI* (1979); Kruft (1994)

catena d'acqua Artificial *cascade with a series of steps.

catenary Curve described by e.g. a rope hung from two points on the same horizontal plane. *See* ARCH. *Catenate* is therefore: 1. to connect like the links of a chain, forming a series, as of linked buildings; 2. to ornament with suspended chain-like forms.

cathedra 1. Chair or seat of a Bishop in his church. In Early Christian times it was placed in the *apse of a *basilica behind the *altar, but later, in the medieval period, it was situated in the *choir, associated with *stalls. 2. *Episcopal See* or dignity.

cathedral Principal church of the *See* or *Diocese* containing the *cathedra.

Cathedral style Early-C19 *Gothic Revival (*c*.1810–*c*.1840), in which motifs were used in an unarchaeological, unscholarly way before the advent of *Ecclesiology.

Catherine-wheel Circular *Gothic *marigold- or *wheel-window, the radiating *colonnettes suggesting spokes. *See* ROSE.

cathetus 1. Axis of an *Ionic *volute-eye. 2. Axis of any cylinder or *drum, such as a column-*shaft or *colonnette.

cat-house 1. As cat (1). 2. Brothel.

caul, caulcole, caulicole, cauliculus (*pl.* cauliculae*), **caulis** (*pl.* caules*) *Caules* are principal stalks rising behind the upper row of *acanthus-leaves in a *Corinthian *capital. From these *caules* spring lesser branches (*caulicoles* or *cauliculae*) supporting the *volutes or helices.

caulking, calking Means by which joints in, e.g., log-built houses, boats, etc., are made watertight with oakum, resin, and pitch.

Caus, *or* **Caux, Isaac de** (*fl*.1612–55) Born in Dieppe, a relative of Salomon de *Caux, he settled in England, working mainly as a garden-architect/hydraulics engineer, but was also described as an architect. Associated with Inigo *Jones, he designed a *grotto in the basement of the Whitehall Banqueting House (1623–4), and supervised the erection of Jones's houses around the 'Piazza' at Covent Garden (1631–7). He also designed grottoes at Somerset House (1630–3) and Woburn

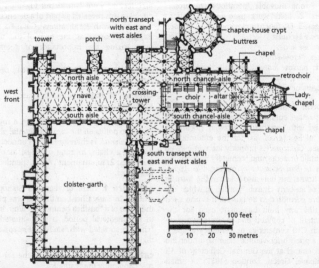

north transept
with east and
west aisles

chapter-house crypt

buttress

chapel

tower

porch

north aisle

north chancel-aisle

retrochoir

west
front

crossing-
tower

choir · altar

Lady-
chapel

south aisle

south chancel-aisle

chapel

south transept with
east and west aisles

N

cloister-garth

0   50   100 feet

0   10   20   30 metres

cathedral Wells, Som.

Abbey, Beds. (1630). De Caux then moved to the service of **Philip Herbert** (1584–1650—**4th Earl of Pembroke** from 1630), for whom he rebuilt the south front of Wilton House, Wilts., and laid out gardens (1635–7): a *Palladianesque composition with *pavilion-towers, probably derived from *Scamozzi's *Idea della Architettura Universale* (1615), Jones was likely involved as consultant. De Caux prepared designs for Stalbridge Park, Dorset (1638), and published (1644) a book on *hydraulics.

Co (2008); J.Hs & T (1979); M & E (1995); Strong (1979)

Caus, *or* **Caux, Salomon de** (c.1577–1626) French hydraulics engineer and garden-designer, he laid out the formal grounds at Heidelberg (described in his *Hortus Palatinus* . . . , published (1620) in Frankfurt by De Bry) for **Frederick V** (1596–1632—**Elector Palatine of the Rhine** (r.1610–20) and his consort, **Princess Elizabeth of Great Britain** (1596–1662). These extraordinary gardens (only known from the *Hortus Palatinus*, as they were systematically destroyed during the Thirty Years War) contained ingenious waterworks and fantastic *grottoes similar to those illustrated in his *Les raisons des forces mouvantes,* published (1615) in Frankfurt by Norton and in Paris (1624) by Sevestre and Droüart.

Co (2008); *JGH,* I/1 (January–March 1981), 67–104, and I/2 (April–June 1981), 179–202; Maks (1935)

causeway 1. Pathway or road formed on a *causey* or mound, so a raised road across a low or wet place. **2.** Mole or landing-pier extending into water. **3.** Paved highway, or ancient way, e.g. Roman or military road.

Cautley, Marjorie Sewell (1892–1954) American landscape architect, she established her NJ practice when women were less than welcome in the profession, unusually combining design *and* site supervision. Influenced by Ebenezer *Howard's ideas, she was concerned with planning for the community and with the need to provide low-cost schemes for open spaces (e.g. her work at Sunnyside Gardens, Queens, NY (1924–8), and Radburn, Fairlawn, NJ (1928–30)). Cautley articulated (1943) her thinking (using site-specific arguments) on the huge problems of city planning, urban blight, and the necessity to transform city neighbourhoods, emphasizing the need to create opportunities and communal social activities, although her ideas were not really accepted until half a century later, long after *'urban renewal' had devastated many US towns and cities, ruining lives and creating dystopias. Embracing the ideals of the *Garden City and *Garden Suburb, she applied them to the needs of neglected urban neighbourhoods. She published (1935) a book on garden-design.

B & K (2000); Cautley (1935); Shoe (2001)

cavaedium *Cavum aedium,* partially roofed main room or **atrium* of a Roman house, with a rectangular opening to the sky (*compluvium*) in the centre, and a pool or cistern (*impluvium*) set in the floor.

cavalier Elevated platform used as a look-out or a gun-emplacement in a fortress.

cavation, cavazion 1. Excavation of earth to form a *cellar or *basement. 2. Trench or excavation to accommodate the foundation of a building.

Cave, Adrian (1935–2012) English architect, he specialized in the design of disabled access, notably in historic buildings (e.g. Westminster Abbey, Strawberry Hill, and the Royal Hospital, Chelsea).

The Times (1 Feb. 2012), 49

Cave-Brown-Cave, Anthony (1925–2011) English architect of numerous restoration schemes, notably Ragley Hall, Warwicks., and other commissions in Glos., Oxon., and Warwicks. (e.g. conversion of Alveston Manor, Stratford-upon-Avon, into a hotel).

The Times (18 Nov. 2011), 76

cavetto (*pl.* **cavetti**) Concave *chamfer, gorge, hollow, throat,* or *trochilus* *moulding the *section of which is a quarter-round, often used on *cornices, distinguished from the **scotia,* the section of which is a half-circle, half-ellipse, or more. It normally has a **torus* beneath, and, in Ancient-*Egyptian architecture, was the main element of a *cornice, plain or decorated with upright stylized leaf forms.

Cave, Walter Frederick (1863–1939) English architect, articled to A.W.*Blomfield, he established a London practice (1889). As Surveyor to the Gunter Estate, Brompton, he laid out the model estate at Tamworth Street, Fulham. He designed several cottage-houses at Walton-on-Thames, Surrey, and built some fine *Arts-and-Crafts houses, two of which were mentioned by *Muthesius in *Das Englische Haus* (1904–5). Cave's most celebrated building is Burberry's in the Haymarket, London (1912), with a handsome **Beaux-Arts* front and superimposed *Orders applied to a framed structure.

A.S.Gray (1985); Patrick (2012)

cavity-wall Wall constructed of two leaves or *skins* (two walls), with a cavity between them, invented to improve insulation and damp-proofing: the leaves are given strength by being joined together with metal ties. Certain types of cavity-wall are used for *conservatories etc., where it is possible to introduce hot air into the gap. *See* BRICK.

ceil 1. To furnish with a *canopy or *screen. A *ceiling* is therefore the visible covering of the underside of a floor which provides the roofing of a room or other space below, and can take many forms. 2. To cover with a lining of woodwork, e.g. a *wainscot.

ceiling-cornice *Cavetto *cornice at the junction of the vertical and overhead surfaces of a room.

ceilure *See* CELURE.

Celer (*fl.*AD 64) *See* SEVERUS.

cell 1. Small *apartment of any sort, such as a room in a *dormitory or *inn, but especially a confined study-bedroom allotted to a monk or nun in a *monastery. 2. Medieval cell in which penitents were immured. 3. Secure room with bed or beds in a prison. 4. Any small cavity or room. 5. *Cella or *naos. 6. *Web* of a *vault framed by the *ribs, or one surface of a *groin* vault. 7. In *timber-framed structures, one room or unit. A *single-cell* plan is one volume, while a *two-cell* plan may have a *cross-entry or *cross-passage, and a *three-cell* plan will have a cross-passage, cross-entry, or *lobby-entry.

cella (*pl.* **cellae**) 1. *Cell, in the sense of a monastic study-bedroom. 2. Enclosed part of a Greek or Roman *temple including the sacred chamber and *vestibule, in fact everything within the walls. In Greek, **naos.*

cellar Subterranean or partly underground room or rooms within a building, normally without windows, for the storage of fuel, provisions, wines, etc., rather than as living-space. *Compare* BASEMENT.

Celtic Epithet of the peoples now identified as Bretons, Cornish, Irish, Manx, and Scots Gaels, originally Aryans. Early Celtic art seems to have become widespread, or widely influential, from *c.* C5 BC throughout the Rhineland, Central Europe, the Balkans, and Northern Italy, then in France, Ireland, and Britain *c.*C3 BC. Later, during the first millennium AD, its art-forms embraced influences from *Byzantium, *Early-Christian, *Etruscan, *Greek, Oriental, and Syrian precedents. Characteristic elements are abstract patterns such as the *triquetrac* (triangular three-lobed form of interlaced crescents), *triskele* (Y-shaped forms), and *trumpet-pattern* (trumpet shapes with sinuous forms between), complex interlaced stalks and ribbons, knots, spirals, and highly stylized *flora* and *fauna*. Celtic art influenced other styles, especially *Anglo-Saxon, *Hiberno-Romanesque, and *Romanesque architectural enrichment, and reached its highest architectural development (*c.*650–*c.*1150) with masterpieces such as the Bewcastle Cross, Cumb. (C7).

L & D (1986); J.T (1996)

Celtic cross Monumental carved stone *cross consisting of a vertical shaft and horizontal arms with a circlet, its centre at the intersection, linking the blocky forms at the extremities of the arms with the shaft and the base of the shrine-like superstructure with pitched roof that crowns the composition. Also called *wheel-head cross*.

Vallance (1920)

Celtic Revival was a C19 revival of *Celtic art, mostly in Britain and Ireland, which sparked the *Hiberno-Romanesque Revival in architecture, and influenced the *Arts-and-Crafts movement as well as the development of *Art Nouveau. An example of Celtic-Revival ornament can be seen at the Watts Chapel, Compton, Surrey (from 1896).

Larmour (1992)

celura, celure, ceilure, cellure Part of the roof (especially a wagon-roof) of a church, panelled, decorated, and coloured, immediately above an *altar or *Rood. *See also* ABAT-VOIX; CANOPY; TESTER.

cement 1. Substance to bind together the materials in *concrete, *mortar, etc., hardening it to a solid. **2.** *Render used to provide a finish to external walls, also called *stucco. C18 types of cement-render included *Liardet's Cement* (which included oil), extensively used by the *Adam Brothers, but it did not last, and fell off. More satisfactory was *Parker's* (also called *Roman or *Sheppey) Cement, discovered 1796, which was widely used by *Nash and his contemporaries, but it was a dark brown colour, so was sometimes called *black cement*: it did have one great advantage, however, in that it was waterproof. *Atkinson's Cement*, also called *Yorkshire* or *Mulgrave Cement*, was a better, lighter colour than Roman Cement, but was inclined to shrink and crack unless plenty of sand was used in the mix. *Portland Cement*, discovered (1794) by **Joseph Aspdin** (1779–1855) and patented by him (1824), was also widely used as a render, but again it had to be very weak and mixed with plenty of sand otherwise it cracked.

N.Davey (1961); Gw (1903); W.Pa (1853–92)

cemetery 1. Burial-ground, especially a large landscaped park or ground laid out expressly for the deposition/interment of the dead, not being a churchyard attached to a place of worship. The first Christian examples of cemeteries physically detached from churches were established by Protestants for two reasons: decency (because of the disgusting state of overcrowded churchyards in towns); and doctrine (the desire to weaken RC belief in Purgatory by sundering the living from the dead). Examples are those at Geneva (1536), Kassel (1526), and Marburg (1530, 1568). During C18 several suburban walled cemeteries of limited extent were formed, in RC as well as

Protestant countries, from sheer necessity (e.g. Paris, Vienna, Berlin, Dessau, Belfast, all 1780s and 1790s). However, Europeans had been burying in cemeteries in India in C17, and erecting monuments over their graves (e.g. Surat), and in Calcutta the South Park Street Cemetery was established (1767), a true *necropolis, with streets of fine Classical *mausolea and monuments far more magnificent than anything in Europe at that time. Attempts to bring major reforms to European cities were sporadic, generally unsatisfactory, and aesthetically dreadful until, by a complex process prompted by a new sensibility forged through poetry and literature, the English landscape-garden fused with the necessity of burying the dead in decent and hygienic ways, and, as a result of the Decree of *23 Prairial*, Year XII (12 June 1804), cemeteries were to be established in France outside urban limits. *Brongniart was entrusted with the design of a great cemetery at *Mont-Louis*, east of the city of Paris, which became *Père-Lachaise*; this was to become world-famous and enormously influential, for nothing short of a revolution had occurred. Liverpool's St James's Cemetery was created in a disused quarry (1825–9—by *Foster); Glasgow's Necropolis (1831–2) followed, and, after Asiatic Cholera arrived (1831), London's first great *garden-cemeteries were established at Kensal Green (1833), Norwood (1837), Highgate (1839), Nunhead (1840), Brompton (1840), Abney Park (1840), and City of London and Tower Hamlets (1841), all of which were landscaped and embellished with architecture. No major town or city in Europe or the USA could function properly without a cemetery or cemeteries, and many of great quality were designed. Fine examples in the USA include Mount Auburn, Boston, MA (1831—a superbly landscaped cemetery by *Bigelow et al.), Laurel Hill, Philadelphia, PA (1839—by *Notman, again a stunning layout with an *arboretum), Hollywood, Richmond, VA (1848—also by Notman, who must be regarded as one of the founding-fathers of American landscape-architecture), Green-Wood, Brooklyn, NYC (from 1838—a marvellously landscaped cemetery laid out by *Douglass), and Albany Rural Cemetery, Menands, NY (from 1844—the apotheosis of the large garden-cemetery, also by Douglass). However, the proliferation of monuments inhibited the maintenance of the grounds, and *Downing suggested that memorials should be designed in a way that would not hinder upkeep. One of the first of the so-called 'Lawn Cemeteries' was created (1855) at Cincinatti, OH, by Adolphus *Strauch.

In Italy cemeteries tended to be more of the *campo-santo* type, but very much larger than the medieval Pisan prototype. Examples were the *Certosa*, Bologna (1801–15), Brescia (1814–49), Verona (1828) and the superlative *Staglieno*,

Genoa (1844–51—with its *Neo-Classical galleries and Rotunda by *Barabino and *Resasco). C20 cemeteries include the war cemeteries established after the 1914–18 war, with contributions from *Lutyens, *Baker, and others; the fine Woodlands Cemetery near Stockholm by *Asplund and *Lewerentz (1917–41); the Slovene National Cemetery, Žale (1937–40—by *Plečnik, who created a masterpiece); the San Cataldo Cemetery, Modena (1971–6 and 1980–90— by *Rossi); the Brion Cemetery, San Vito d'Altivole, near Treviso, Italy (1970–2—by *Scarpa); the Woodland Cemetery, Leutkirch (1977–82—by von *Branca); and the Cemetery for the Unknown, Mirasaka Sousa, Hiroshima, Japan (1998–2002—by **Hideki Yoshimatsu** (1958–) + **Archipro** (founded 1987)—a moving meditation on nature, loss, and death). **2.** *Catacombs. **3.** Consecrated enclosure for burial of the dead.

AR, ccxii/1270 (Dec. 2002), 42–5; Ariès (1981); Berresford *et al.* (2004); Co (1991); J.Curl (2002a, 2004); J.Curl (ed.) (2001); Etlin (1984); Linden (2007); Loudon (1981); Ms (1966); Stannard (ed.) (1975); Vernon (2011)

cenotaph Empty sepulchre, or funerary monument to the dead whose bodies lie elsewhere. *Lutyens's Cenotaph, Whitehall, London (1919–20), is an example of such a symbolic tomb.

Centerbrook Architects *See* MOORE, CHARLES WILLARD.

centering Timber framework or mould to support arches or *vaults during construction, removed (struck) after the setting of the *mortar and completion of the arched form.

centralized plan One arranged around a *centre, rather than an *axial plan (as in a *basilican church), e.g. a *tholos, the Roman *Pantheon, or *Palladio's *Villa Capra*, Vicenza.

centre Point around which a circle is described, or the middle point of a sphere. A *centrally-planned* building is one arranged around a central point, as opposed to an *axial plan:* a *drum or octagonal structure is centrally planned, while a *basilica is axially planned. A *centrepiece* is a central ornamental element, e.g. an elaborate doorway and its superstructure in the middle of a *façade, or a ceiling *rose.

Cerceau, Du, Family Group of French architects/decorators founded by **Jacques Androuet Du Cerceau the Elder** (1510/12–85), whose *Les Trois Livres d'Architecture* (1559–72) was influential. The first volume (1559) was essentially a *pattern-book of domestic architecture, some of which was influenced by *Serlio; the second (1561) contained highly decorated features; and the third (1572) followed the treatises of Philibert de L'*Orme and *Palladio. These volumes became

important sources of *grotesque ornament and *Mannerist designs in France and Northern Europe. His *Les plus excellents bastiments de France* (1576–9) remains a fine record of French-*Renaissance *châteaux. He has been credited with the design of the *château* of Verneuil (1568), clearly influenced by Italian Mannerists working at *Fontainebleau.

Du Cerceau's son **Baptiste** (1544/7–90) became a major architect working in Paris at the end of C16, and entered royal service (1575). He succeeded (1578) *Lescot as architect at the Louvre, completing the west part of the south wing of the Square Court (1582). He made designs for the *Pont Neuf* (1578), but later fled Paris as a Protestant refugee (1585). Baptiste's brother **Jacques** (*c.*1550–1614) became architect to **King Henri IV** (*r.*1589–1610) and was very likely responsible for the *pavilions in the *Place des Vosges*. Baptiste's son, **Jean** (*c.*1585–*c.*1649), was appointed (1617) architect to **King Louis XIII** (*r.*1610–43), having trained with his cousin, de *Brosse, with whom he worked on the *Palais du Luxembourg*, Paris. He was involved in the development of the *Marais* and *Île St-Louis* areas (1620s–1640s), and was responsible for the *Hôtel Sully* (now *Béthune-Sully*—1625–9) and the *Hôtel de Bretonvilliers* (1637–43), in Paris, both extraordinary for their cunningly contrived axes and richly carved decorations. Jean also rebuilt de L'Orme's *staircase in the *Cour du Cheval Blanc* at Fontainebleau with a complicated horseshoe-shaped arrangement.

Androuet du Cerceau (1611, 1972); Bt (1982); Chevalley (1973); Coope (1972); Geymüller (1887); Har (1943–57); W.Ward (1976)

Cerdá, Ildefonso (1815–76) Catalan architect, he studied civil-engineering in Madrid (1835–41), and worked as an engineer for the State (1841–9). From 1849 he devoted himself to the theory of urbanization, and planned the expansion of Barcelona on a grid-iron plan (1859) intersected by two diagonal avenues, each block of the grid-iron having *chamfered sides. Originally each block (*c.*100 metres square) was to be built up on two sides only, leaving a central green space, but as a result of increased land-values the remaining areas have been developed. Cerdá influenced Arturo *Soria y Mata in his philosophy of ruralizing the city and urbanizing the countryside (the Linear City). He was the first to attempt to apply scientific principles to urban and rural planning, and was the author of the important *Teoría general de la urbanización* (1867). His work at Barcelona was the model for other Spanish city enlargements, including Madrid and Bilbao.

Cerdá (1968); Estape (1971); Soria y Puig (1979)

Certosa Italian *Carthusian monastery.

chahar bāgh *or* **charbāgh** From the Persian, meaning 'four gardens', it is a garden-type divided into four parts by means of walks and water-courses intersecting in the centre, so is a formal geometrical design symbolizing both the organization of territory and the idea of the Celestial Gardens of *Paradise. Such gardens were associated with *Mughal *palaces and *mausolea. *See* BAGH; COMPARTIMENT; MUGHAL GARDEN; PARADISE GARDEN.

J.Brookes (1987); Lehrman (1980); M & P (2011); MM & T (1998); Moynihan (1980); Petruccioli (ed.) (1997); Ruggles (2008)

chain 1. *Romanesque *moulding carved to resemble a chain. **2.** Piece of timber or metal built into a brick wall to increase its stability and cohesion, called *chain-bond*. **3.** Bond course of stone with one or more cramps connecting each pair of stones. **4.** Complete circlet formed of a chain, used to prevent a circular work of *masonry from spreading, e.g. in the *dome of St Paul's Cathedral, London (begun 1675). **5.** Chain-tie used to connect the heads of *piers, etc., while *vaults and arches are constructed. **6.** If used to tie in bulging brickwork, an *anchor is fixed to the end of the chain or rod, visible on the outside of the wall.

chaînes *Masonry *pier-like elements on a *façade (sometimes with parallel sides, and sometimes with alternating wide and narrow blocks (like the normal arrangement of *quoins)), subdividing it into panels of brick. Common in C17 French architecture, good examples exist in the *Place des Vosges*, Paris (early C17). In England they were alluded to in the vertical strips of brick-work differing from the colours of the panels between that became fashionable from the time of *Wren, common in architecture of the *Queen-Anne period and its C19 revival.

chair-rail *Cornice of a continuous *pedestal-like arrangement around the walls of a room, called *dado-rail.

châlet Wooden dwelling-house of a type common in Switzerland, with a broad, low-pitched roof with wide overhanging *eaves, and often timber balconies and external stairs.

Chalgrin, Jean-François-Thérèse (1739–1811) Paris-born architect who studied with *Servandoni and *Boullée, and worked for a while as *Inspecteur des Travaux de la Ville de Paris* (from 1763) under *Moreau-Desproux: he erected the *Hôtel St-Florentin*, Paris (1767–70), to plans by *Gabriel, but he was responsible for the Neo-Classical courtyard-screen, portal, and interior décor. An important *Neo-Classicist, he designed the *basilican *St-Philippe-du-Roule*, Paris (1768–74), in a severe *Antique style, much influenced

by *Cordemoy, *Laugier, and *Contant d'Ivry, with interior free-standing *Ionic columns (defining the barrel-*vaulted *nave and continuing in a curve around the *apse), while the entrance-*portico featured the *Tuscan *Order. *St-Philippe* was contemporary with similar buildings by *Potain and *Trouard: *Quatremère de Quincy praised it (1816) as a model for French architects to follow because it adopted the *Early-Christian basilica and avoided *Baroque excess. While working on *St-Philippe*, Chalgrin completed Servandoni's *St-Sulpice*, building the north tower (1776–8), changing Servandoni's unfluted proposals for the west front to a fluted arrangement, and carrying out other works, including the *baptistry and organ-case. He also designed several gardens, as well as the exquisite *Pavillon de Musique*, Versailles (1784), with its *rotunda containing a *trompe-l'œil* painting that suggests the room is set in a garden. He remodelled the *Palais du Luxembourg*, Paris (1787–1807), creating the impressive Neo-Classical *Salle du Sénat* and grand *staircase (1803–7), and designed the enormous *astylar *Arc de Triomphe de l'Étoile*, Paris (1806), completed by *Blouet (1836), which has two main axes instead of just one.

B (1980); Gaehtgens (1974); Ga (1972); M & Wa (1987)

Chalk, Warren (1927–88) *See* ARCHIGRAM.

chalk-line Cord impregnated with chalk used for laying down straight lines on material prior to cutting.

Chamberlin, Powell, & Bon London-based partnership established by **Peter Hugh Girard Chamberlin** (known as 'Joe'—1919–78), **Geoffry Charles Hamilton Powell** (1920–99), and Swiss-born **Christoph Rudolf Bon** (1921–99). When Powell won the competition for the Golden Lane housing scheme in the City of London (1951–63), the firm was established, and shortly afterwards the Corporation of London invited the firm to submit ideas for some 35 acres of land which led to the commission to design the Barbican development (1955–83), arguably the best example in the British Isles of a high-density urban scheme, incorporating cultural, residential, and educational uses, influenced by Le *Corbusier's theories. Other works included the *Mies-van-der-Rohe-inspired Bousfield Jun. and Infant School, The Boltons, South Kensington, London (1953–6—where co-loured panels in the *cladding were supposed to have a didactic purpose, but the excessive amounts of glass caused problems with solar heat-gain and glare (a common problem with *Modernist buildings at that time)); buildings at New Hall, Cambridge (1962–6—where the hall *dome and circular stair-towers were criticized for having historical allusions); the University of

Leeds, Yorks. (1959-74); and the Vanbrugh Park Housing at Greenwich (1960s).

E (1994); Harwood (2011); information from Philippa Cooper

Chambers, Sir William (1723-96) Important British Classical architect. Son of a Scottish merchant, he was born at Göteborg, Sweden, educated in Yorks., and went to India and China with the Swedish East India Company (1740-9). He enrolled (1749) in J.-F.*Blondel's *École des Arts*, Paris, and travelled to Italy (1750), where he spent five years, was taught drawing skills by *Clérisseau et al., and studied *Antique and contemporary buildings. During his European sojourns he absorbed ideas that were to lead to *Neo-Classicism in the second half of C18.

He established a practice in London (1755), and became (1756) architectural tutor to the **Prince of Wales** (later **King George III** (*r.*1760-1820)). Commissioned (1757) to lay out the grounds of the **Dowager Princess of Wales**'s (**Augusta of Saxe-Gotha** (1719-72)) house at Kew, he ornamented the gardens with an exotic array of garden-buildings. There, he had no stylistic inhibitions, building an Alhambra, *Moorish 'mosque', and buildings in the Chinese style (including the celebrated Pagoda (1761-2)), as well as more conventional Classical structures: he seems to have intended to provide the Gardens with a sort of encyclopedia of architectural styles. It should be remembered that he was the only architect in England at the time who had seen the real architecture of Cathay. He had published *Designs of Chinese Buildings* . . . (1757—which was regarded as a source for pictures of Chinese architecture even though by then the fashion for *Chinoiserie* had almost ended). Later, his *Dissertation on Oriental Gardening* (1772—which was in reality an attack on the manner of landscape-design promoted by 'Capability' *Brown), was misinterpreted as an apology for the Chinese garden as an exemplar, and earned him opprobrium (1773 *see* MASON, WILLIAM). In the Old Deer Park he also designed the King's Observatory (1767-9), set in landscape designed by Brown, and surrounded by a mound, probably as protection against flooding.

Chambers's *Treatise on Civil Architecture* (1759) became a standard work dealing with the *Orders and their uses, going into further editions (1768, 1791 (when it became (much expanded and amended) *A Treatise on the Decorative Part of Civil Architecture*). One of the two architects (the other was Robert *Adam) appointed by the Crown in the Office of Works (1761), his career thereafter was assured : his *Plans, Elevations, Sections, and Perspective Views of the Garden Buildings at Kew in Surrey* came out (1763—tactfully dedicated to his Royal patroness); he succeeded *Flitcroft as Comptroller of the Works (1769); and

was appointed Surveyor-General and Comptroller (1782), in which position he rapidly showed himself to be a first-rate administrator as well as a great official architect. His architecture combined English *Palladianism and French Neo-Classicism, as can be seen at the Casino, Marino, near Dublin (1758-76), built on a Greek-cross plan, and at his masterpiece, Somerset House, London (1776-96), arguably the grandest official building ever erected in the capital: John *Webb's Queen's Gallery, Somerset House (1662), which had an arched *rusticated ground-floor and a *Giant *Order rising through the first and second floors, was quoted in the new building. Duddingston House, Midlothian, a country house by Chambers near Edinburgh (1763-8), is not unlike *Campbell's Stourhead, Wilts., but has no rusticated *basement and the *Corinthian *portico sits on a platform only four steps high. Chambers also designed (1775) the Theatre (built 1777-86) and Chapel (built 1787-*c.*1800) at Trinity College, Dublin, two of the most distinguished buildings of the College. However, Chambers, it seems, had a blind spot concerning Greek architecture, referring to 'Attic Deformity', but he designed Milton Abbey House, Dorset (1771-6), in the *Gothic style, and indeed seems to have planned a treatise on Gothic for publication. He may have been responsible for the layout of the model village at Milton Abbas (*c.*1774-80). His pupils included *Gandon.

W.Chambers (1759, 1968, 1969, 1972); Co (2008); J.Hs (1970); J.Hs & Snodin (eds) (1996); M.McCarthy (1987); P (1982); D.Wa (2004)

Chambiges, Martin (*c.*1465-1532) French *Gothic architect, he designed the *transept *façades at Sens (*c.*1489-95) and Beauvais (*c.*1499-1532) Cathedrals, and the exquisite west front of Troyes Cathedral (from *c.*1502). His work had canopied *niches, intricate *tracery, and subtle treatments of *piers and *buttresses. His son, **Pierre** (*fl.*1509-44), was associated with his father at Troyes and Beauvais, worked on the old *Hôtel de Ville*, Paris (1533-4), and built the *Château* at St-Germain-en-Laye from 1539.

Berty (1860); Guiffrey (1915); P (1982); Sanfaçon (1971); J.T (1996); Vachon (1907)

chambranle Frame-like embellishments around apertures such as doors, fireplaces, *niches, and windows, the equivalent of an *architrave, and having the same profile as the *entablature architrave. Its vertical sides are *ascendants* and the *lintel-top is the *traverse*.

chamfer *Bevel, cant,* or oblique surface produced by cutting away an *arris or corner at an angle (usually 45°), not as big as a *splay. Thus a piece of stone or wood (e.g. beam) so treated is *chamfered*. Chamfers can be hollowed out, or concave, called *chamferet, chamfret,* or *hollow* *chamfer*, as in a *flute, and can be *beaded* (with a convex bead-like moulding projecting from the chamfer). When the chamfer does not extend the whole length of the object (e.g. *beam or splayed *jamb), it is a *stopped chamfer*, sometimes simply treated, but often ornamented (*chamfer-stop—see* STOP). *Rustication includes *chamfered rustication*. *Swelled chamfer* is a *Vitruvian scroll.

Chamoust, Ribart de (*fl.*1776–83) *See* RIBART DE CHAMOUST.

champ, champe *Field* or *ground* on which carving is raised.

Champneys, Basil (1842–1935) English architect, he began practice (1867), designing many important buildings, including the Selwyn Divinity School, Cambridge (1878–9), in an early-*Tudor style, and Mansfield College, Oxford (1887–9), in *Gothic Revival. At the Indian Institute, Oxford (1883–96), he mixed early English-*Renaissance and Flemish detail. His finest buildings are the John Rylands Library, Manchester (1890–1905), a good example of *Arts-and-Crafts *Second Pointed, with tierceron *vaulting, and Newnham College, Cambridge (1874–1910), in red brick, with *Queen-Anne and Dutch *Domestic-Revival elements.

B.Champneys (1875, 1901); A.S.Gray (1985); *ODNB* (2004); Se (ed.) (1975); Se (1977)

chancel Liturgical eastern part of a church, used by those officiating in the services, and often defined by a *cancellus* (from which the term is derived) or *screen. It contains the *sanctuary and *altar, and often embraces the *choir, especially in larger churches where the chancel is part of the main body of the building east of the *crossing. *Compounds include*:

chancel-aisle: *aisle parallel to a chancel, often continuing behind the *high-altar as an *ambulatory, connecting with the chancel-aisle on the other side;

chancel-arch: *arch at the liturgical east of the *nave, separating nave from chancel, carrying a *gabled wall above, often an object of some magnificence, in the Middle Ages sometimes adorned with a *Doom on the surface above the arch facing the nave. Above the roof (usually higher or lower than that of the nave), the gable was often crowned with a *bell- or *Sancte-cote;

chancel-rail: *balustrade, barrier, *cancelli*, or low wall defining or separating the chancel from the nave, sometimes doubling as an *altar-rail;

chancel-screen: *screen separating chancel from nave. A large stone chancel-screen is a *pulpitum*. Many English wooden examples exist with *brattishing on top of elaborately carved, traceried, and vaulted screens: they have *galleries,

are approached by narrow *stairs (many of which have survived the screens themselves), and originally supported a *Rood, so are often referred to as *Rood-screens;

F.Bond (1916); B & C (1909); Vallance (1947)

chandelier Ornamental branched support or frame to hold several lights (originally candles), and suspended from a ceiling.

chandelle Type of *cable in *flutes of columns, etc., often ornamented with foliage.

channel 1. *Canal, as in the *shaft of a column. 2. *Canaliculus* of a *Doric *triglyph. 3. *Bevelled channelling* or grooves in *rustication. 4. Furrow, groove, or gutter sunk for carrying off water from a surface.

Chantrell, Robert Dennis (1793–1872) English architect, pupil of *Soane, he settled (1819) in Leeds, Yorks., where he commenced his successful practice with a series of *Greek-Revival public buildings, most of which have been demolished. He is of considerable significance as the designer of churches (1823–50): St Peter's, Leeds (1837–41), his masterpiece, is an essay in *Gothic that for its date was unusual in its size and quality, and was recognized as such in *The Ecclesiologist* (1847).

Co (2008); Linstrum (1978); Webster (2010)

chantry Establishment, endowment, or foundation for the daily or frequent saying of Masses on behalf of the souls of the founder, founders, or other persons: a *chantry-chapel* was therefore a chapel or separate part of a church established for this purpose, often enclosed by a *screen (with or without a *canopy), and frequently erected over the burial-place of the founder. It might incorporate an *altar, tomb-chest, and *effigy (e.g. the medieval examples in Winchester Cathedral).

chapel 1. Building for Christian worship, not a parish-church or cathedral, often without certain privileges normally those of a parish-church. 2. Room or building for worship in or attached to a *castle, college, great house, *monastery, *palace, school, or other institution. 3. *Oratory in a burial-aisle, *mausoleum, *mortuary-chapel, or elsewhere, with an *altar where Masses might be chanted (i.e. *chantry-chapel), often with funerary monuments. 4. Screened compartment in a large church, usually in *aisles, to the east of *transepts, or to the east of the *high-altar, with its own altar, separately dedicated, and often of great magnificence (e.g. *Lady-chapels for veneration of the Blessed Virgin Mary, as at Westminster Abbey). A chapel with its main axis on that of the *nave of the church is called an *axial chapel;* those grouped around a semicircular end of a *choir on radii of the apsidal east end are *radiating chapels,* as in a *chevet arrangement; and those disposed parallel to each other at the east end of a church, but not on the same alignment (as in Wells Cathedral (see CATHEDRAL)), are echelon chapels. **5.** Place of worship subordinate to the parish-church, created for the convenience of parishioners, such as a chapel-of-ease, when the parish was very large and distances great, or where populations increased. **6.** Place of Christian worship other than buildings of the Established Church in England, so usually applied to a Nonconformist establishment. In Ireland and Scotland it may refer to an RC church, even in the early C21.

chapiter *Capital.

chaplet *Moulding resembling a string of beads, as on an *astragal, also called pearling.

chaplet

chapter-house Building for assemblies, business, meeting, maintenance of discipline, etc., associated with cathedral, *collegiate, and conventual churches, often situated on the east side of the *cloisters, but sometimes on the north side of the church with access through a *vestibule or *trisantia. In English cathedrals or large churches, chapter-houses were often polygonal on plan (e.g. Wells—see CATHEDRAL), with or without central *piers supporting the *vaults, with *stalls around the perimeter. Polygonal examples sited on the north side perhaps were suggested by the plan of the Constantinian *basilica of San Pietro, Rome (begun c.333).

chaptrel 1. *Capital of a *pier supporting the springing or an arch or *vault, or any capital *engaged to a wall, such as those of an *anta or *pilaster. **2.** *Impost.

charbāgh See CHAHAR BĀGH.

Charbonnier, Martin (c.1655–1720) French-born *Baroque landscape-gardener, pupil of Le *Nôtre, employed by the Electoral House of Hanover, his works include the Residenzgarten, Schloss Osnabrück (1674), the garden of Lustschloss Salzdahlum, near Wolfenbüttel (1689), the Grosser Garten, Herrenhausen, Hanover (from 1682—incorporating French, Dutch, and Italian influences, and containing a hedged theatre and a *maze), and the garden of the Ducal Hunting-Lodge, Linsburg, Nienburg/Weser (1696), all in Lower Saxony.

Gothein (1979); Tay (2006); J.T (1996)

Chareau, Pierre (1883–1950) French architect/furniture-designer, he came to public notice with his remodelling of an apartment in the Rue St-Germain, Paris (1918–19), which included furniture (some of which featured plywood, metal tubing, and ebony), exhibited (1919) at the Salon d'Automne. He showed furniture at the 1924–5 Exposition International des Arts-Décoratifs, and designed (1928) a house in the Rue St-Guillaume, Paris, in which glass blocks were widely employed (pre-dating Le *Corbusier's use of them), giving the work its name, Maison de Verre (completed 1932 in collaboration with **Bernard Bijvoet** (1889–1979), his associate (1925–35)): it also had an exposed steel structure. In 1940 Chareau emigrated to the USA where he built a studio at East Hampton, NY (1948—destroyed).

Chareau (1929); B.Taylor (1992); Vellay (1985)

charge 1. Any device or bearing, charged, or carried on an *escutcheon. **2.** Ornament projecting from the face or soffit of, e.g., a piece of *masonry.

Charles, Frederick William Bolton (1912–2002) English expert on *timber-framed (especially *cruck) construction. Considering the 'patina of time' and 'layering of history' were unimportant, his approach to restoring old buildings often raised hackles. When he proposed shifting condemned timber-framed buildings in Coventry to one site (Spon Street), he ran foul of the Society for the Protection of Ancient Buildings (SPAB): the final result was perhaps unconvincing, but had they not been moved, the buildings would have been destroyed. More successful among his interventions, perhaps, were Bear Steps, Shrewsbury, Salop., Boring Mill Cottage, Ironbridge, Salop., and the Ancient High House, Stafford. He was also a key figure in the formation of the Avoncroft Museum of Historic Buildings, Worcs., and his reconstruction of the C14 Bredon Tithe Barn, Worcs. (for the National Trust after a disastrous fire (1980)), changed the Trust's attitude to making good damaged buildings. His Medieval Cruck Building and its Derivatives (1967) was influential, but his main published legacy is Conservation of Timber Buildings (1984), written with his second wife, **Mary.**

F.Charles (1967, 1984, 1997); MC; The Times (12 Sept. 2002), 37

Charles, Martin Bolton (1940–2012) English architectural photographer (son of F.W.B.*Charles), among Europe's best. His work graced the Masters of Building series published in AJ as well as numerous books and papers. An ideal collaborator with authors, his sensitivity and discriminating eye were greatly valued.

C20 Magazine (Spring 2012), 62–3; pk.

charmille *Arbour, bower, or tall clipped hornbeam hedge.

charnel-house 1. Building, *crypt, *ossuary, or *vault where the bones of disinterred dead are stored as new graves are required in a churchyard. Once very common in medieval England, charnel-houses became unusual from C16 as religious practices concerned with the dead changed with the Reformation, although a three-bay charnel-house of brick with stone dressings was built at the end of C17 in St Nicholas's churchyard, Deptford Green, London. Charnel-houses may be found on the Continent today, especially where burial-space is limited, as in Alpine churchyards, and several decorative charnel-houses exist, where walls and ceilings are covered with bones arranged in patterns (e.g. Capuchin Church, Rome). **2.** Place of deposit for dead bodies which dry out in certain conditions, as in Palermo, Sicily.

Ariès (1981); Litten (1991)

charsu In *Islamic architecture, a structure in a *bazaar centred around a domed space, e.g. where two *alleys cross in a market (e.g. the C16 *Taqi-Zargaran,* Bukhara, Uzbekistan).

B & B (1994)

Charterhouse *Carthusian monastery, *Certosa,* or *Chartreuse* (French).

chasing Technique of engraving raised metalwork. *See* REPOUSSÉ.

château 1. French *castle. **2.** Large French country-house, in C16 often retaining allusions to fortifications, as in the deep *ditch and corner towers of e.g. Chambord, and various *châteaux* in the Loire Valley. **3.** Any large French country-house, with allusions to castles or not.

Châteauneuf, Alexis de (1799–1853) Hamburg-born architect of noble French parentage, he trained under *Weinbrenner, *Wimmel, and others. Settling in his native city, he designed buildings in which North-German brick-built traditions were combined with *Rundbogenstil* and *Renaissance elements. His work owed much to *Percier & *Fontaine and *Schinkel, and was itself influential; buildings included the City Post Office (1830s—destroyed), a fine house on the *Neu-Jungfernstieg* (c.1835—destroyed), and an asylum consisting of detached *pavilions in a park near Kiel (1842). He remodelled part of Hamburg around the Alster Lake after the 1842 conflagration, and designed numerous structures, including buildings for the Guild of Cabinetmakers, the Hall for the Guild of Tailors, and the *Peterskirche.* With his assistant, **Andreas Friedrich Wilhelm von Hanno** (1826–82), he built Trinity Church, Oslo, Norway (1850–8), a *Gothic centralized building on an octagonal plan with projecting *porch, *transepts, and *chancel. His publications included *Architectura Domestica* and *The Country House* (both 1843).

Châteauneuf (1839, 1860); Lange (1965); T-M (1965)

château style C19 revival of the style of architecture of the reign of *François Ier of France (1515–47), epitomized by Fontainebleau *château,* or a revival incorporating *Gothic and *Renaissance elements *derived* from Fontainebleau.

chatri Indian *pavilion consisting of a horizontal slab carried on four *colonnettes, recurring in *Hindoo orientalizing architecture in the West, also called *chavada,* often with an *ogee-shaped roof.

chatta, chattra *Masonry parasol-like form. *See* CHAT(T)RA.

chat(t)ra Umbrella-like (from Hindu for umbrella, *chatta*) form on a horizontal slab carried by a post (*chattrayashti*), which, if supporting three umbrellas set each above the other, is termed *chattraval(l)i.* Indian-Revival or *Hindoo architecture may have *pavilion-like forms (*chavada*) on which *chatris are set.

chatri *or* chavada   chattravalli Set on a *stupa.*

checker *See* CHEQUER.

Chedanne, Georges (1861–1940) French architect. At the *École des *Beaux-Arts,* Paris, he came to notice with drawings for the restoration of the *Pantheon, Rome (1887). As an architect, some designs had debts to *Art Nouveau, while others exploited the possibilities of exposed iron structures and glass infill (e.g. the elegant *Parisien Libéré* Office Building, 124 *Rue de Réaumur,* Paris (1903–4)). His *Galeries Lafayettes* in Paris was one of the most impressive of the great department-stores, with a framed structure using iron.

Emery (1971); *Byggekunst,* liv/6 (1972), 190–1

chedi A *stupa in Thailand, rarely occurring in orientalizing architecture in the West.

cheek Narrow vertical face, usually one of two corresponding opposite faces, as in the sides of an opening or of a projection (e.g. a *buttress, *dormer-window, or *chimney-breast).

Chelles, Jean *and* **Pierre de** (*fl.*C13 and C14) **Jean de Chelles** was the master-mason who built part of the *transepts of *Notre Dame*, Paris: work on the north transept was carried out (1240s) and on the south transept (1258). Pierre de *Montreuil worked with de Chelles and succeeded him as master-mason or architect (1265). A relative, **Pierre de Chelles**, was master-mason at *Notre Dame* in the early part of C14, and worked on the Cathedral at Chartres.

Branner (1965); Frankl (2000); S (1901–2)

Chen, Congzhou (1918–2000) Distinguished Chinese architectural/garden historian, active in the *conservation of the natural environment and in the restoration of much historic fabric. Some of his many publications on traditional Chinese buildings and gardens were translated into English. *See* CHINESE GARDEN.

Chen (1984, 2003, 2008)

cheneau 1. *Eaves-gutter with the profile of an elaborate *cornice. 2. Ornamented *crest, as on the *ridge of a roof, or associated with a gutter at the eaves.

chequer, checker 1. Pattern involving the division of a surface into equal squares (*chequers*) treated alternately in different ways, such as in colour or texture: it is commonly found in tile or stone pavements resembling a chessboard and called *chequer-work*. 2. Type of *diaper-work in which the compartments are all square, as in late-*Romanesque and *Gothic surface-carving.

chequer-set *or* **staggered corbelling** Row of *corbels or *machicolations placed so that each alternate projection is higher or lower than its neighbour, i.e. set *chequerwise*.

Chermayeff, Serge Ivan (1900–96) Russian-born as **Sergius Ivanovich Issakovich**, he emigrated (1910) to England, and set up his architectural practice (1930): among his works at that time were interiors of the Cambridge Theatre (1930), and of the BBC (1932), both in London. He formed a partnership with Erich *Mendelsohn (1933–6) which produced several classic *Modern-Movement buildings, including the De La Warr Pavilion, Bexhill-on-Sea, Sussex (1934–5), Shrub's Wood, Chalfont St Giles, Bucks. (1934–5), and another house at 64 Old Church Street, Chelsea, London (1935–6). His elegant house at Bentley Wood, Halland, Sussex (1938–9), looked forward to his period in America (from 1940), and his use of *timber-framed structures: his house at New Haven, CT (1962–3), is probably his most successful work in the USA. With **Christopher Wolfgang Alexander** (1936–) he published *Community and Privacy* (1963), and with **Alexander Tzonis** (1937–), *Shape of Community* (1971).

Chermayeff & C.Alexander (1963); Chermayeff & Tzonis (1971); E (1994); *ODNB* (2004); Plunz (ed.) (1982); Po (2001)

Chersiphron (*fl.c.*560 BC) Crete-born architect (with *Theodoros of Samos) of the foundations and *colonnades of the archaic *Ionic *temple of Artemis at Ephesus (*c.*565–550 BC). His son, *Metagenes, continued the work and erected the *entablature. These architects wrote a treatise (now lost) on the building.

Ashmole (1972); Coulton (1977); D (1950); La (1983)

chert Stone resembling *flint.

cherub Chubby winged male infant, or a winged infant's head, also called *Cupid*, similar to the *Antique and *Renaissance *Amorino* or *Love*, found in profusion in *Baroque architecture and decoration. *Compare* PUTTO.

Cherubim Figures with wings over the mercy-seat in the Jewish temple, later members of the second of the *Nine Orders of Angels with attributes of the knowledge and contemplation of Divine things. Thus representations of an adult figure with wings.

Chevakinsky, Savva Ivanovich (1713–c.1774–8) Russian architect, he designed the Maritime Cathedral of St Nicholas, St Petersburg (1753–62), arguably the best late-*Baroque church in Russia. He was also involved from 1745 in the early designs of the development of *Tsarskoye Selo* before *Rastrelli took over. His later work was influenced by *Neo-Classicism.

H (1983); D.Shv (2007); J.T (1996)

chevaux de frise Defensive arrangement of sharp obstacles set in the ground before a fortification to deter or slow a frontal assault.

chevet Apsidal liturgical east end of a large church, with the *ambulatory around the semicircular end of the *choir off which the chapels radiate.

chevron 1. V-shaped *Romanesque ornament used in series to form a *dancette* or *zig-zag*, usually on *archivolts and *string-courses. It is mostly

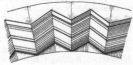

chevron Romanesque type, as around a doorway. Church of St Lawrence, North Hinksey, Oxon. (formerly Berks.) (*after Parker*).

of part-circular *section, so-called 'broken sticks' (*bâtons rompus*), but may also be composed of convex and concave elements. **2.** The **V**-form commonly occurring in *Art-Deco design, either alone or in series. It is also found in series in Roman decorative work, notably in *mosaic.

Chiattone, Mario (1891–1957) Italian architect. With *Sant'Elia he exhibited drawings for a 'modern metropolis' that were among the seminal images of Italian *Futurism. His 1930s work, associated with the *Novocento Italiano* group, turned increasingly to stripped *Neo-Classicism.

Ve (1965)

Chiaveri, Gaetano (1689–1770) Rome-born architect who worked mostly in St Petersburg (1717–27—where he assisted *Trezzini), Warsaw (where he designed the Salesian Church (1728–33)), and Dresden (1737–48), where his *Katholische Hofkirche* (1737–53) was built as a foil to *Bähr's Lutheran *Frauenkirche*, and is one of the most elegant and accomplished late-*Baroque masterpieces in all Europe (restored 1971–84 after severe war-damage), with a beautiful tower (reminiscent of *Borromini's work at *Santa Agnese in Agone*, Rome), and elevations influenced by the Royal Chapel at Versailles. Chiaveri also prepared plans for the Vistula frontage of the Royal Palace in Warsaw (1740), and for another Royal Palace (late 1740s) in Dresden: both unrealized schemes had a rare refinement of Baroque detail. He published *Ornamenti Diversi di Porte e Finestre* (1743–4), influenced by works of Roman Baroque masters.

Chiaveri (1743–4); E.Hempel (1955, 1965); J.T (1996)

Chicago School 1. Group of architects working mostly in Chicago, IL, in the last quarter of C19. **2.** Group of high-rise commercial and office-buildings erected in Chicago (*c*.1875–*c*.1910).

It is claimed the *skyscraper was born in Chicago, exploiting the invention of the *elevator (*lift*) and *metal-framed structures. *Jenney's pioneering use of steel *skeletons led to other developments, notably those of *Burnham & Root. One of the most important early buildings of the Chicago School was the Marshall Field Wholesale Store (1885–7—demolished) by H.H.*Richardson, a massive round-arched building clad in rock-faced *rustication, the precedent for a new type of monumental architecture, freed from Classical or *Renaissance *Historicism. *Adler and *Sullivan's Auditorium Building (1887–9) clearly owed much stylistically to Richardson's model, but the structure was much more innovative. **Burnham & Root**'s Monadnock Building (1889–91) was the last of the tall buildings with *load-bearing outer walls almost devoid of ornament. The metal frame for skyscrapers was first expressed on the elegant exterior in **Burnham & Co.**'s Reliance

Building (1894–5), the designer of which was *Atwood. Sullivan's Schlesinger & Mayer Department Store of 1899 and 1903–4 (later Carson, Pirie, & Scott) was probably one of the most important buildings of the Chicago School expressing the underlying skeleton and exploiting the *Chicago window to the full.

Charernbhak (1984); Ct (1952, 1960, 1961, 1964, 1968); Peisch (1964); Randall (1949); Tallmadge (1941); J.T (1996)

Chicago window Horizontal window consisting of a large square fixed central pane with narrow vertical sliding-sashes on either side, as in the Carson, Pirie, & Scott Store, Chicago, by *Sullivan (1899–1904). It is usually the full width of a structural *bay.

chien-assis Medieval miniature pitched-roof *dormer, with unglazed foiled opening, resembling a miniature dog-kennel on a slope of a roof. It permits air and light to enter a roof-space.

chigi Terminations of *gables on a Japanese roof, like scissors, or projecting *barge-couples, called *forked finials*, sometimes found in orientalizing garden-buildings in the West.

chimney 1. Fireplace or hearth. **2.** Fireplace with flue and vent over it, so including the structure rising above a roof or outside the building. A *chimney-stack* could be a large structure surrounded by a *timber-framed building (where it helped to stabilize the structure as well as providing heat), could be erected over the *gable-end, or placed in series along a *façade, as in a medieval hospital or *almshouse (e.g. St John's Hospital, Lichfield, Staffs. (late C15), with its array of stacks). In *Elizabethan and *Jacobethan *prodigy-houses chimney-stacks contributed to the complex *skylines.

The following terms are associated with chimneys: *fireplace* (opening of a chimney into a room, whether decorated or not); *gathering* (part of the flue that contracts with the ascent); *hearth* (floor of the fireplace); and *inglenook* (small space beside the chimney, often containing seats, sometimes illuminated by means of a small window, and occasionally having a lower ceiling than in the rest of the room, hence its other name, *roofed ingle*). *Compounds include*:

chimney-arch: arch over the fireplace-opening, supporting the *chimney-breast*;

chimney-back: **1.** *fireback*, or rear wall of the *fireplace*, often protected by a decorative cast-iron plate; **2.** rear of *chimney-stack* projecting outwards from the exterior wall of a building;

chimney-bar: support or *lintel for the *chimney-breast*, often a metal flat, **H**-, or **T**-section, or a massive timber beam (*mantel-tree*), carried on the *chimney-cheeks*;

chimney-breast: **1.** front wall, from base to top, necessary to house a *chimney*, containing the *fireplace*; **2.** wall over the fireplace, whether or not projecting from the wall, carried on the *arch, bar, mantle,* or *tree*: it is essentially that part of the wall facing the room and forming one side of the chimney;

chimney-can: **1.** metal pipe set on the top of the flue to increase the up-draught; **2.** *chimney-pot*;

chimney-cap: *abacus or *cornice crowning a *chimney-stack*;

chimney-cheek: side of a *fireplace-opening*, really the *face* of a *pier providing the support for the *arch, bar, mantle,* or *tree*, and the *chimney-breast*;

chimney-corner: corner or side of a large open projecting or retreating *fireplace* or *hearth*, or the seat on each end of the *fire-grate*. Variations include the *inglenook* or *roofed ingle*;

chimney-crane: swivelling metal bar, hooked at one end, from which cooking-pots may be suspended and swung over the fire, also called *chimney-crook* or *chimney-hook*;

chimney-cricket: protective structure erected over a roof where a chimney-stack penetrates it, to improve water-proofing;

chimney-crook or -hook: *chimney-crane*;

chimney-flue: hollow part of the chimney through which smoke passes. It starts with the *funnel*, tube, or cavity leading upwards from the *fireplace*;

chimney-head: top of a *chimney-stack*;

chimney-hood: metal or *masonry hood-like structure projecting from a *chimney-breast* over a *fireplace* to collect the smoke, common in the Middle Ages;

chimney-jamb: wall projecting from the back to form one side of the enclosure of a *fireplace*, carrying the *arch, bar, mantle,* or *tree*;

chimney-mantle: **1.** horizontal part of the *chimney-piece*; **2.** beam or any horizontal support carrying the *breast*;

chimney-piece: dressing or surround of a *fireplace*. The horizontal part is the *mantle-* or *mantel-piece*, and the ensemble can have considerable architectural magnificence;

chimney-pot: cylindrical, polygonal, or square element of brick, metal, or *terracotta fixed on top of a *chimney-stack* to extend the flue and improve the extraction (*draught*) of smoke;

chimney-shaft: as *stalk*, but more often a *chimney-stack* containing only one flue;

chimney-stack: mass of brickwork or masonry containing one or more flues separated by *withs* or *withes*, projecting above the roof;

chimney-stalk or -tun: any very lofty *chimney*, or that part of a chimney which rises from a roof;

chimney-throat: part of the *chimney-flue* which contracts as it ascends is the *gathering* or *gathering of the wings*, and that part where the gathering and the flue meet each other is the *throat* or *waist* because it is the narrowest part;

chimney-top: crowning parts of a *chimney-stack* or *-stalk*;

chimney-waist: as *chimney-throat*;

chimney-wing: one of the sides or lateral cheeks of the *gathering*, by which the narrowing towards the *chimney-throat* is achieved.

Chinese fret *Lattice ornament on *balustrades, *gates, *friezes, and *rails, made of square-sectioned timber, and forming square and rectangular patterns, with diagonals adding triangular and other shapes. It was common in C18 *Chinoiserie-inspired design.

Chinese fret

Chinese garden-design This entry attempts to provide a synoptic overview of the subject, the rationale being that, from the time it first impinged on European sensibilities in C17, it profoundly influenced developments in the West to an extent underestimated in the past. The eminent C20 scholar, Professor *Chen, revealed much concerning the history and development of Chinese gardens.

By the beginning of the **Ming** period (1368–1644), Confucian philosophical systems were widely accepted, and principles of garden-design were firmly established, with especial reference to theories of *feng shui. Key elements were the symbolic attachment to mountains (*shan*) and water (*shui*) which had to be balanced, so *shan-shui* means 'landscape': equilibrium between the male *yang* (found in rocks and wood) and female *yin* (found in water) principles was regarded as all-important, and old, gnarled trees were prized, notably gingko and pine. By the late **Ming** and **Qing** (1644–1911) periods, itinerant professional garden-designers, trained as painters, conceived their works in pictorial terms, and codified the subject. Nearly all surviving Chinese gardens date from this last period. Principles of Chinese garden-design were set out in *Ji's *Craft of Gardens* (1631–4): in this, he concerned himself with composition, overall impressions, the expression of emotion, the selection of rock types, respect for the *genius loci, and, especially, architecture. Such gardens were enclosed, private, and even secret, evidenced only by trees and tops of pavilions visible from the outside. Ji likened walls to art paper against which plants and rocks were sketched. He also included detailed information on planning; walls punctured with shaped openings (see DI XUE); building construction; *balustrades; *screens; *lattice-work designs; *shutters; paving patterns and materials; *rock-work; water; and inclusion of natural scenery, though with little information on planting.

Chinese garden-design evolved over at least three millennia, and by Ji's time was steeped in tradition, imbued with a deep reverence for Nature and for the antiquity of Chinese culture. Early designs derived from hunting-parks, emerging in the **Shang** period (c.1600–c.1046 BC), called *you: they contained built mounds (features of Chinese gardens ever since) on which the Emperor would perform rituals. In the **Zhou** period (1046–221 BC), certain plants were accorded meanings: peach, for example, was associated with Heaven, mulberry with the Sun, and yarrow with Divination. During a period of instability (475–221 BC) the contrast between Confucian ideals of participation in society and the Taoist notion of retreat into solitariness began to shape subsequent gardens: therein, philosophers, poets, and scholars could read and meditate in garden-pavilions on themes that included connecting to ancestors, intellectual work, and self-cultivation.

From the start of the **Qin** Dynasty (221 BC) China became more centralized and settled, and the *you* was gradually transformed into the **yuan*, which included forests, pastures, lakes, and pavilions placed throughout the whole landscape. From the **Han** Dynasty (206 BC–AD 220) the three-mountains-one-lake model of the garden developed, later found throughout the Empire, and pictograms indicated enclosed gardens with water, plants, and large stones (suggesting distant mountains): indeed, as advances in construction and transport techniques evolved, rocks were transported great distances alluding to far-off lands. Following the C3 fall of the **Han** Dynasty, the garden became a place of refuge, retreat, and contemplation, enclosed and safe. With decentralization, the northern **Wei Kingdom** (220–65) acquired 'mountains' of rocks in elaborately constructed configurations, but in the south, a taste for 'natural' gardens to be lived in as extensions to dwellings encouraged an appreciation of pastoral ideals and celebrations of the gentler beauties of landscape. Under the **Shui** (581–618), two traditions merged, combining winding paths, secluded spots, beautiful scenery, and the three-mountains-one-lake, integrating the private scholar's garden-ideal with the grander showpiece: this Imperial style was termed Xi Yuan.

During the **Tang** (618–907) and **Song** (960–1279) periods, the scholar's garden provided peaceful settings for the solitary thinker. One such was that of the poet **Wang Wei** (699–759)

at Chang'an: conceived as sequences of garden-scenes (*jing*) viewed on walks and composed like landscape-paintings, dominants were water and rocks, with sparing notes of strong colour in each scene. Plants were chosen for their symbolism and relevance to scholarly virtues: bamboo for straightness; pine for resilience; plum-blossom leading the way as an early bloom; and the lotus, growing pure and white from muddy ground.

Invaders of China absorbed much of its culture, and that included garden-design. The Mongol **Yuan** Dynasty (1270–1368), for example, combined *you* themes with the nomadic tent (an ornate pavilion described by **Marco Polo** (c.1254–1324)) at Shang-tu (Xanadu). Absorption was not confined to invaders: thanks to trade, aspects of Chinese garden-design made their way across the oceans, and had a huge impact on Japan and then the West. *See* CHINOISERIE; JARDIN ANGLO-CHINOIS; SHARAWADGI.

Addison (1712); Chen (1984, 2003, 2008); Conner (1979); Cooper (1709, 1714); Goodrich & Chaoying Fang (eds) (1976); Gothein (1979); Ji (2012); Keswick (1986); Krafft (1809–10); E.Morris (1983); Laar (1802); Mason (1768); Osbeck (1771); Pope (1713, 1732); Rouge (1776–88); Sellers (n.d.); Sennott (ed.) (2004); Shoe (2001); Sirén (1949, 1990); Temple (1690); Wang (1998); Wiebenson (1978)

chink Gap between the timbers of a log-house: to *chink* is to fill those gaps up (see CAULKING).

Chinoiserie Style of European architecture and artefacts in the Chinese Taste, intended to evoke Cathay, first appearing in C17, and reaching heights of delicacy and inventiveness in C18 and early C19. *Chinese garden-design and its informal traditions seem to have influenced Japan a millennium before they made an impact on C17 Western Europe: partly through trading connections of the Dutch East India Company (which included the establishment of a factory at Deshima, Nagasaki), together with Western writings (e.g. those of Sir William *Temple), they began to impinge on European sensibilities, and their influence became widespread (almost a mania), in C18. Other contemporary Western authors who helped to cultivate an attitude towards a more irregular, less formal, style of garden-design included *Addison (1712), A.A. *Cooper (1709), Alexander *Pope (1713, 1732), and *Switzer (1718). The C18 *jardin *anglo-chinois*, therefore, was informal and irregularly planned, in which *Chinoiserie* touches could be found. Moreover, the impact of Chinese garden-buildings was manifest in English architectural publications at a time when buildings in the Chinese taste and *Gothick style were regarded as relaxations from *Classicism, and were treated as a branch of exotic *Rococo (e.g. *Halfpenny's *New Designs for Chinese Temples ...* (1750), *Chinese* *and Gothic Architecture*...(1752), and *Rural Architecture in the Chinese Taste* (1752, 1755); *Chambers's publications (1757, 1772) detailed numerous *Chinoiserie* buildings influencing contemporary trends in English landscape aesthetics; and *Over's *Ornamental Gardening* (1758)). Realized examples of *Chinoiserie* in garden-architecture include *bridges (often with *Chinese-fret *balustrades), *summer-houses and tea-houses (e.g. the exemplar at Shugborough, Staffs. (1747)), and the celebrated *pagoda by Chambers at Kew Gardens (1761–2). Some interiors at Brighton Pavilion have *Chinoiserie* elements, including gaudy decorations by **Frederick Crace** (1779–1859).

Other early European manifestations of buildings in the Chinese taste include the Tea House in the grounds of the palaces at Potsdam (1754–7) designed by **King Friedrich II ('the Great') of Prussia** (*r.*1740–86) and *Büring, and the Chinese House, Drottningholm, Sweden (1763–9), by *Adelcrantz. Chinese-inspired elements also appeared in French *fabriques (e.g. the pagoda, Chanteloup, Amboise (1775–8), and the *Maison Chinoise*, Retz (1774–5)), and many designs were published (1776–88) by Le *Rouge and (1809–10) **Johann Carl Krafft** (1764–1833). Other important influences on the evolution of the **jardin anglo-chinois* were *Watelet (1774) and *Hirschfeld (1779–85—which may have partly prompted the building of the Chinese Village, Wilhelmshöhe, Kassel (1780s–'90s)). Chinese-inspired *fabriques* were also erected at Steinfort, near Münster, Westphalia (1780–7). Other European countries adopted the Chinese taste for *fabriques*, including Hungary, The Netherlands (where **Gijsbert van Laar** (1767–1820) published a volume well illustrated with inventive buildings, many in the Chinese style), Poland, Russia, and Sicily. In the USA 'Chinese Manner' described both architecture and gardens: *Loudon wrote about Chinese themes, and almost simultaneously *Downing did the same in the USA, although by then Chinese architecture and gardens were understood from a more archaeological rather than fanciful perspective. *Strickland designed the Pagoda and Labyrinth Garden, Philadelphia, PA (1823–8), and there were many instances where English pattern-books informed forays into American *Chinoiserie. See* CHINESE GARDEN-DESIGN; JARDIN ANGLO-CHINOIS; SHARAWADGI.

Addison (1712); Chen (1984, 2003, 2008); Conner (1979); Cooper (1709, 1714); Goodrich & Chaoying Fang (eds) (1976); Gothein (1979); Halfpenny (1968a & c); Honour (1961); Impey (1977); Jacobson (1993); Ji (2012); Krafft (1809–10); E.Morris (1983); Laar (1802); Mason (1768); Osbeck (1771); Over (1758); A.Pope (1713, 1732); Rouge (1776–88); Sellers (n.d.); Shoe (2001); Sirén (1949, 1990); Temple (1690); Vance (1985); Wiebenson (1978)

Chochol, Josef (1880–1956) Influenced by the work of Otto *Wagner through the latter's pupil *Kotěra, Chochol became an important figure in Bohemia and Moravia. Before 1914 he dabbled with *Expressionism, notably in the apartment-block in Neklan Street, Prague (1913), where prismatic shapes and inclined planes predominate. He was a leading practitioner of *Cubism in architecture, as his *villa below Vyšehrad Hill, Prague (1912–14), demonstrates. The applied decoration has no right angles, and virtually no surface is parallel to the outlines of the plan. His elimination of *Historicism and reduction of *façades to elementary shapes led him to experiment with *Constructivism in the 1920s.

Li (1996); P (1982); J.T (1996); Vegesack (ed.) (1992)

chock Wedge-shaped timber or metal used to fill frames, shores, and other rough constructions.

choir *or* **quire** 1. Part of a large church appropriated for the singers, with *stalls, situated to the liturgical east of the *nave, often partially screened. 2. In a cruciform church that part east of the *crossing, including choir, *presbytery, and *sanctuary around the *high-altar, wholly or partially screened. *Compounds include*:

choir-aisle: *aisle parallel to the nave of the choir, sometimes joined at right angles or in a semicircle behind the high-altar, thus becoming an *ambulatory or *deambulatory, often with chapels to the east;

choir-loft: *balcony in the choir, or the upper part of a *choir-screen* or *pulpitum;

choir-rail: *rail, low *balustrade, or *cancelli separating choir from nave;

choir-screen or *-enclosure*: partition, rail, *screen, or wall separating a choir from *choir-aisles*, *ambulatory*, *retrochoir, and, sometimes, the nave, although chancel-screen, *jubé, *Rood-screen, or *pulpitum* were formerly preferred to describe the last case;

choir-stall: raised seat, one of a series of fixed *stalls in a choir, backing on to a *choir-screen* (where there are *choir-aisles*) and on to a *pulpitum* where that exists. In cathedrals choir-stalls have rich canopies of *open-work, enhanced with *pinnacles and ornament. Seats were usually hinged, with brackets (*misericords) underneath;

choir-wall: as *choir-screen*, but a *masonry wall between *choir* and *choir-aisles*.

Choisy, Auguste (1841–1904) French archaeologist/architectural historian, Chief Engineer of the *Département des Ponts et Chaussées* for several years, his reputation rests on his considerable published output. Influenced by the work of *Viollet-le-Duc, his analyses of form and structure—not the results of chance or taste but representative of the essence of society—were attractive to later architects such as Le *Corbusier and *Perret. His beautifully illustrated *Histoire de l'Architecture* (1899) described the evolution of construction, and it was that which appealed to the following generation: the book contained a précis of Viollet-le-Duc's and other architectural theories by boiling them down to neat phrases and diagrams. His arguments supported utilitarian views of architecture as developing from practicalities best seen in the work of engineers: reducing architecture to structure, he claimed that this was more realistic than any style or art.

Choisy (1873, 1883, 1883a, 1899, 1904, 1910); Pouillon (1994)

choragic Pertaining to the leader (*choragus*) of a Greek chorus, so a *choragic monument* (such as that of **Lysicrates** (334 BC) or **Thrasyllus** (319–279 BC) in Athens) was one created in honour of a *choragus*, and supported a bronze tripod given as a prize.

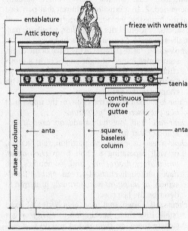

entablature —
— Attic storey
frieze with wreaths —
— taenia
continuous row of guttae
anta — — square, baseless column — anta
antae and column

choragic monument of Thrasyllus, Athens. Version at the Bazouin mausoleum, *Père-Lachaise* Cemetery, Paris. This design provided Neo-Classical architects with a useful precedent for door-cases, window-surrounds, etc.

chord 1. Straight line joining two points on an arc. **2.** Span of an arch. **3.** Diameter of an *apse or a semicircular arch. **4.** Principal member of a *truss, usually one of a pair extending along the top and bottom. **5.** Lower straight part of a *Belfast* or *bowstring* truss.

Chrismon The sacred monogram ✸, an arrangement of the first three Greek letters (*Chi, Rho,* and *Iota*) of ΧΡΙΣΤΟΣ, Christ's name, also called *Christogram,* which suggests the *Cross as well as *pax*

(peace). Another version is ✳, the initial letters of Ἰησούς Χριστός (Jesus Christ) and the first two letters of ἰχθύς, the Greek for 'fish', a symbol of the Faith and of Baptism. Other sacred symbols associated with Christ are **A** (*Alpha*) and **Ω** (*Omega*)—the Beginning and the End; **INRI** (*Iesus Nazarenus Rex Iudaeorum* (Jesus of Nazareth King of the Jews), or *In Nobis Regnat Iesus* (Jesus Reigns In Us), or *Igne Natura Renovatur Integra* (Nature is Regenerated by Fire—referring to the Spirit and to Redemption)); **IHS** (variously explained as the first two and last Greek capital letters of ΙΗΣΟΥΣ, Christ's first name (**IHC,** the *Iota, Eta,* and *Sigma,* given as Σ, **C,** or the Latin **S**), *Iesus Hominum Salvator* (Jesus the Saviour of Man), *In Hoc Signo* (In This Sign [Thou Shalt Conquer]), and *In Hac Salus* (In This [Cross] is Salvation).

Dirsztay (1978); G.Ferguson (1961); Whone (1990)

Christian, Ewan (1814–95) British architect, he established his own practice (1842), and was architect and consultant to the Ecclesiastical Commissioners from 1850. His churches tend to be robust and powerful works of the *Gothic Revival, and include St Mark's, Leicester (1869–72). His best-known building is the National Portrait Gallery, London (1890–5), in an Italian-*Renaissance style. He carried out various restorations of medieval buildings, some more drastic than others. His major works at Southwell Minster, Notts. (1848–88), included the two pyramidal roofs that cap the western towers.

Brooke (1997); B.Bu & Hulme (1996); J.Curl (2007); D & M (1985)

Christo & Jeanne-Claude Bulgarian and French Americans, **Christo Vladimirov Javacheff** (1935–2020) and **Jeanne-Claude,** *née* **Denat de Guil-lebon** (1935–2009), formed (1960s) a partnership to create large ephemeral outdoor installations. Preferring to conceal and separate elements rather than alter or destroy them, they argued their work was a method of seeing objects in new ways. Associated with *Land Art, their outputs included *Surrounded Miami Islands* (1983), *Wrapped Reichstag* (1995), *Verhüllte Bäume* (1998), and *The Gates* (2005). Their work has been described as 'revelation through concealment', though some take different views.

N & R (2003); Tay (2006)

chromium Metallic element discovered independently (1798) by **Louis-Nicolas Vauquelin** (1763–1829) and **Martin Heinrich Klaproth** (1743–1817), but not isolated until 1859 by **Friedrich Wöhler** (1800–82). Despite its attractive, bright, shiny, silvery appearance, and its reluctance to corrode, it was not much used until it was employed in the armaments industry during the 1914–18 war. From the 1920s it was produced commercially, and was used for plating on steel or copper (notably for the automobile industry), and was favoured by several *Modernist architects for both buildings (e.g. *Mies van der Rohe for the casings of columns in both the Barcelona Pavilion and the Tugendhat House) and furniture (e.g. the tubular steel frames of chairs of the period). It was widely used for *Art-Deco work.

C.Benton et al. (eds) (2003)

chryselephantine 1. Literally, made of gold and ivory, it also described *Antique wooden sculptures overlaid with those materials, the draperies being covered with gold and the nude parts of the figure covered with ivory (e.g. the *Athena Parthenos* of **Phidias** (c.490–430 BC). *Quatremère de Quincy studied chryselephantine sculpture (1814) which was the starting-point for *Hittorff's work on Classical *polychromy. **2.** The term was sparingly applied to the chaste white-and-gilt colour-schemes of early *Greek-Revival interiors before polychromy was introduced.

D (1950); Metcalf (1977)

chujjah, chiyjah In Indian architecture, or the *Hindoo style, a *cornice with a considerable projection.

church Edifice for public Christian worship, distinguished from a *chapel or *oratory, which in some respects are not public in the wider sense. Church-plans are of two basic types: the *basilican form with *clerestoreyed *nave, lean-to *aisles, apsidal east end, and some kind of *porch or *narthex; and the *centralized plan derived from *Byzantine domed spaces and from circular or polygonal *mausolea associated with important tombs and *martyria. The simplest type of church-plan (e.g. in *Anglo-Saxon times)

consisted of a nave (for the worshippers) and the smaller *chancel (for the clergy) containing the *altar and approached through an arch. Larger, more important churches had several chapels, two or four *transepts, towers, and other structures such as *cloisters, porches, a *baptistery, and a *chapter-house.

Church, Thomas Dolliver (1902–78) American landscape architect, influenced by the *Modern Movement, and especially by *Aalto. His use of curved forms, as at the Donnell garden, Sonoma, CA (1947–9), with its kidney-shaped swimming pool, proved to be a model for the Californian upper middle classes. His major projects in CA were the Park Merced, San Francisco (1941–50); *campus plans for the University of CA, Berkeley (1961), and Santa Cruz (1963); Harvey Mudd (1963) and Scripps (1969) Colleges, Claremont (1963); and Stanford University, Palo Alto (1965). Among other works the landscape-designs for General Motors Research Center, Detroit, MI (1949–59), and *Wurster's Valencia Public Housing, San Francisco (1939–43), may be cited. Acknowledged as the leader of the *Californian School of landscape design, his ideas were disseminated through his writings and assistants (including *Baylis, *Eckbo, and *Halprin).

Church (1955, 1983, 1969); LA, lxvii/2 (1977), 128–139, 170–1; LD, ci (1973), 8–12; Tischler (ed.) (1989); W & S (1994)

Churriguera Family Three Catalan architect-brothers, **José Benito de Churriguera** (1665–1725), **Joaquín de Churriguera** (1674–1724), and **Alberto de Churriguera** (1676–1750), they made substantial contributions to *Baroque C17 and C18 art and architecture in Spain and Latin America. They started professionally by creating elaborate carved *retables for churches, including

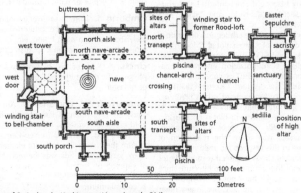

church Plan of St Andrew's, Heckington, Lincs. (mostly C14).

those in the Ayala chapel, Segovia Cathedral (1686-7), *San Esteban*, Salamanca (1692-4), and *San Salvador*, Leganñes (1701-4). José Benito turned his attention to architectural matters when he designed the town of Nuevo Baztán (1709-13) with a main axis broken by three impressive *plazas*. Joaquín designed part of the *Colegio de Anaya* (1715) and the *Colegio de Cala-trava* (1717)—both in Salamanca—in a more restrained manner, and Alberto was responsible for the *Plaza Mayor*, Salamanca, with its contin-uous *arcade (1728 onwards), and the *Rococo church at Orgaz (1738). He designed the main *façade of the Church of the Assumption at Rueda (1738-47) with its portal flanked by two massive towers. The family gave its name (*Chur-rigueresque*) to richly elaborate Baroque architec-ture prevalent (late-C17–early-C18) in Spain and its colonies (especially México).

CG (1951); Gutiérrez de Ceballos (1971); K & S (1959); Pla Dalmáu (1951)

Chute, John (1701-76) English amateur archi-tect, he played important parts in the genesis of Strawberry Hill, Twickenham (*Walpole referred to him as 'the genius that presided over poor Strawberry!'). His best work in the *Gothick style was Donnington Grove, near Newbury, Berks. (1763). The staircase he designed for his own seat, The Vyne, Hants., was a theatrical master-piece (1770).

Co (2008)

chymol Hinge, *gemel, or *gimmer*.

CIAM (*Congrès Internationaux d'Architecture Moderne*) At the request (1928) of a rich patron of architects, **Madame Hélène de Mandrot** (1867-1948), *Giedion organized a meeting of leading Modern architects including *Berlage (who quickly became disenchanted), Le *Corbu-sier, El *Lissitzky, *Rietveld, and *Stam. Karl *Moser was elected as the first president of CIAM, which became the arbiter and dissemina-tor of the dogma of *International *Modernism until its dissolution (1959). It promoted (1930s) *Functionalism, standardization, and rationaliza-tion, dominated first by the Germans, and then by Le Corbusier. The *Athens Charter (1933) set down the primary functions of urban planning, including rigid functional zones with green belts between, high-rise apartment-blocks for housing, provision for traffic, and space for recreation. *Costa's Brasília was to be the realization of CIAM's aims in this respect, but rigid adherence to the dogmas of CIAM has been responsible for huge problems in planning and architecture since 1945, and the results have not been happy aes-thetically, socially, functionally, nor in any other ways. Furthermore, the insistence on rectangular

structures has resulted in plenty of wasteful *SLOAP. After 1959 some, e.g. *Bakema (*see* DELFT SCHOOL) and the *Smithsons attempted to take *Modernism further with *Team X.

J-G (1973); L (1988); Mumford (2000); Sn (1968); Sn & Sn (1991); Steinmann (1979)

ciborium (*pl.* **ciboria**) Fixed *canopy over a Christian *altar, usually supported on four col-umns. It resembles an inverted cup, or the vessel in which the Eucharist is Reserved, with its domed cover, so the canopy itself has a similar domed top. *Compare* BALDACCHINO.

Cibot, Pierre-Martial (1727-80) French Jesuit, he arrived (1760) in Beijing, where he was retained, with others, at the Imperial Court. He wrote on Chinese *flora*, and contributed *Essai sur l'antiquité des Chinois* to the huge *Mémoires ...* edited by **Charles Batteux** (1713-80) et al. (1776-1814), an important source of information concerning China at the time.

Batteux *et al.* (eds) (1776–1814); Herbermann *et al.* (eds) (1907–22)

cill, *or* **sill, sole, sule 1.** Horizontal timber (usually called a *cill-beam, ground-cill, or sole-piece or -plate) at the bottom of a *timber-framed wall into which *posts and *studs are tenoned. A *cill-wall is a low wall of brick or stone supporting the cill-beam. In *timber-framed construction, an *interrupted cill* runs between main posts and is tenoned into them. **2.** Lower horizontal projecting element below an aperture (e.g. doorway or win-dow), to throw water off the *naked of the wall below. **3.** Lower horizontal member of a door- or window-frame.

cima *See* CYMA.

cimbia 1. *Band or *fillet around a column-shaft. **2.** *Cornice or band formed of fillets.

cimborio 1. *Lantern set over a roof permitting light to enter. **2.** *Cupola or other device immedi-ately above a *high-altar, *choir, etc., or any struc-ture over the *crossing in a Spanish church.

cincture *Fillet or *list that receives the *apo-phyge at the extremities of the *shaft of a column or *pilaster.

cinerarium (*pl.* **cineraria**) **1.** *Antique ash-chest or *urn, often of considerable beauty, to hold cremated remains. Lids of the square box-like types had *horns, so in Neo-Classical archi-tecture the *cinerarium lid*, with elements drawn from *sarcophagus-lids, was the model for a type of capping on funerary monuments, gate-piers, and *pedestals. **2.** Building to contain ash-chests: a *columbarium.

Toynbee (1971)

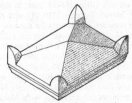

cinerarium lid capping with *cat's-ear horns*.

Cinquecento Italian term, literally 'five hundred', applied to C16 *High-Renaissance art and architecture, or C19 revivals.

cinquefoil *See* FOIL.

Ciołek, Gerard (1909–69) Polish architect/landscape architect/historian/town-planner, he pioneered the *conservation of historic gardens, including several projects at Arkadia, Nieborów, Puławy, and Wilanów. His *Ogrody polskie* (Polish gardens—1954) remains a fine introduction to the subject, and, with **W.Plapis** (1905–68), he published (1968) a book of material for a dictionary of Polish garden-creators.

Ciołek (1978); Ciołek & Plapis (1968); Tay (2006)

cippus (*pl.* **cippi**) **1.** Short stone column or *pillar, usually rectangular on plan, used in Antiquity as a milliary-marker, direction-post, or boundary-stone. Sometimes used to mark the extent of a burial-ground, it was also employed as a grave-marker, e.g. *stele, or as the *pedestal for *herms. **2.** *Keep or *prison of a *castle.

circus (*pl.* **circuses**) **1.** Oblong roofless enclosure, or *hippodrome, semicircular at one end, having tiered seats for spectators on both sides and round the curved end, and a central barrier (*spina*) on which stood *obelisks, monuments, etc. It was used for Roman chariot-races and other spectacles, so had *carceres* or starting-gates arranged in a curve with its centre a point on the axis of the track the horses would take at the start of the race, thus ensuring each competitor had an equal distance to travel to the centre of the broad route. **2.** Unified group of buildings, with concave *façades, fronting a circular open space, as in C18 town-planning schemes by *Wood in Bath and *Nash in London. **3.** Circular road or junction from which streets radiate.

cist Box-like prehistoric grave made of rectangular slabs of stone set on edge, often concealed under a *cairn.

Cistercian Monastic Order founded at Cîteaux, Burgundy (1098), as an offshoot of the *Benedictine rule. Cistercian architecture was international, and *plans and *elevations were severely simple. *Chancels had straight, rather than apsidal, ends, and *transept-chapels were also squared off. The earliest surviving complete Cistercian church is Fontenay (1139–47), while one of the finest is Pontigny (*c*.1160–1200), both in Burgundy. Impressive ruins of large establishments can be found at Byland, Fountains, Kirkstall, and Rievaulx (all Yorks.), Furness (North Lancs.), and Greyabbey (Co. Down). Other Cistercian houses include Fossanova (Italy), Heiligenkreuz, and Zwettl (both Austria).

Braunfels (1972); P.Fergusson (1984); C.Norton & Park (1986); Stalley (1987); Tobin (1996)

cistern 1. Reservoir for storage of water, especially a tank in a high part of a building feeding taps. **2.** Vessel in which to bathe. **3.** Pond in a garden. **4.** Water-tank where grain is soaked in malting.

citadel Fortress with *bastions (usually four or six) sited within a fortified town, usually on an eminence.

City Beautiful American movement led by architects, landscape architects, and others to make cities in the USA as attractive as those in Europe. Stimulated by the World's Columbian Exposition in Chicago, IL (1893), the development of metropolitan park systems (e.g. those of *Olmsted and *Vaux), and the founding of art societies in many cities, it gathered momentum, and, with the unveiling of the plan by *Burnham, *McKim, and the younger Olmsted for Washington, DC (1901–2), became of national importance. **Charles Mulford Robinson** (1869–1917) published (1903) his *Modern Civic Art or the City Made Beautiful*, and he became spokesman for the movement, advising municipalities and tirelessly promoting the cause, which had nothing to do with social reform, but only with beautification in order to enhance prestige and attract wealth. Cass *Gilbert designed a new setting for the State Capitol in St Paul, MN (1903–6), and there were many other schemes to improve city-centres with *Beaux-Arts-inspired *boulevards, squares, and buildings (mostly paid for by public subscription). The culmination of the movement was the Plan for Chicago (1906–9) by Burnham and **Edward H. Bennett** (1874–1954), which proposed radial avenues, ring-roads, a complete reorganization of the rail-network, an ambitious system of parks and *parkways, and a vast and handsome civic-centre. By the end of the 1914–18 war most of the protagonists were coming to the ends of their careers, but the movement exercised a powerful effect on American town-planning for many years until *International *Modernism killed it stone dead.

Hines (1974); Reps (1967); C.Robinson (1903); J.T (1996); W.Wilson (1989)

clachan Small Gaelic settlement of dwellings informally arranged.

cladding Visible non-structural external finish of a building, such as a thin face of *ashlar, *clap-boarding on a frame, or a *curtain-wall. *Cleading* is rough boarding on a roof.

Brookes (1998); Rostron (1964)

claire-voie, clairevoyée (*pl.* **claires-voies**) Open-work fence, gate, or grille at the end of a vista permitting a view of the landscape beyond. It can occur as a panel in a solid wall.

clamp 1. Large mass of dried bricks or *limestone arranged for burning. **2.** Metal bar for binding together stones in a building. **3.** Timber receiving in a groove on one side the rebated ends of other timbers, as in shutters. **4.** As clasping *buttress.

clap-board Riven (rather than sawn) horizontal *feather-edged timber boards used for external *cladding, also called *bevel-siding, lap-siding,* or *weather-boarding, although the latter is properly sawn parallel-sided boards.

clapper-bridge *See* BRIDGE.

Clark, H.Fuller (1869–*after* 1905) *See* FULLER-CLARK, HERBERT.

Clark, Kenneth Mackenzie (1903–83) British art historian, he directed (1934–45) the National Gallery in London, after which he concentrated on writing, enjoying phenomenal success with his television programmes and book entitled *Civilisation* (the broadcasts began in 1969). Although he claimed *Ruskin was a major influence on his thought, he delivered his own messages with lucidity, elegance, and aplomb, never wallowing in purple prose or exaggeration (faults painfully evident in Ruskin's work): however, his major achievement was to make art accessible to the public through the medium of television. Apart from books on art, his early volume (1928) on the *Gothic Revival (a work which greatly helped the appreciation of *Georgian *Gothick, A.W.N. *Pugin, and *Victorian architecture (all greatly underrated at the time by others)), may prove to have been his most influential creation, changing perceptions and taste. He was created a Baron (1969).

K.Clark (1974); *ODNB* (2004)

Clarke, George (1661–1736) Oxford-educated, he is mostly remembered as a virtuoso, consulted by those involved in design and building after the death of *Aldrich. He was involved in the genesis (1710) of the Clarendon Building, Oxford, and was responsible for revisions to Aldrich's proposals for the south side of Peckwater Quadrangle at Christ Church from 1716: indeed, Christ Church Library, based on Michelangelo's Capitoline Palace, was largely Clarke's design (1717–38). He had a significant role (with *Hawksmoor) in the planning of Queen's College (1710–21), and appears to have provided the designs for the new buildings at Magdalen College, begun (1733) by *Townesend. He probably designed and built the Warden's House at All Souls, and proposed a *quadrangle that was eventually realized to Hawksmoor's plans (1715–40). Clarke was the patron and collaborator of Hawksmoor, and collected architectural drawings: with Aldrich, he can be regarded as an early protagonist of the second English *Palladian Revival.

Co (2008)

Clarke, George Somers Leigh (1825–82) British architect, pupil of Charles *Barry, he was an ingenious designer of office buildings on restricted sites. His General Credit and Discount Company Building, Lothbury, London (1866), is an attractive composition in a *Venetian-*Gothic style, but he was equally fluent in *Cinquecento, *Elizabethan, *François Ier, and Oriental styles. One of his best houses was Wyfold Court, Oxon. (1873–4). His nephew, **George Somers Clarke** (1841–1926), was also an architect, among whose works are extensions to Holy Trinity Church, Ardington, Berks. (1887): he was in partnership (1876–92) with *Micklethwaite.

D & M (1985)

Clarke, Gilmore David (1892–1982) American landscape architect, he designed the first *parkway from Bronx Park to Kensico Dam, NY (1913–25), and was responsible for the Merritt Parkway, CT (1934–40), the Palisades Inter-State Highway, NJ (1945–50), and the Westchester Park north of NYC (1923–33). He laid out the World's Fairs, NYC (1939 and 1964), and the gardens of the UN HQ, NYC (1948–52).

Radde (1993); Zapatka (1995)

Clason, Isak Gustaf (1856–1930) Swedish architect, whose works drew on the *Arts-and-Crafts movement and on *Historicism. His Nordisk Museum, Stockholm (1890–1907), is an essay in the free Northern *Renaissance-Revival style. Other works include Östermalms Market Hall (1885–9), Carpenters' Hall, Stockholm (1915–27), and Mårbacka House, Värmland (1920–2). He influenced *National Romanticism.

Edestrand & Lundberg (1968)

CLASP (Consortium of Local Authorities Special Programme) Several English local education authorities combined resources (1957) to develop a system of prefabricated school-building devised in Notts. and evolved under *Aslin in Herts.

L (1988)

clasping *See* BUTTRESS.

Classicism The principles of Greek and Roman art and architecture, so Classical architecture is derived from *Antique precedents that were respected as having some kind of authoritative excellence. Later revivals of Classicism were associated not only with a desire to emulate the magnificence of *Antique architecture, but to establish laws, order, and rules in artistic matters. The first Classical revival is associated with the *Carolingian period (not unconnected with ambitions to re-establish Imperial power), and the next with the C11 Tuscan *proto-*Renaissance, which influenced early Renaissance architects, e.g. *Brunelleschi. From C16 Renaissance architecture and publications had even more of an impact on design than Antique models, for new theoretical writings appeared prompted by the work of *Vitruvius, and there was much written about the canonical nature of the Roman *Orders of architecture. In the late C17 a tendency towards a more severe Classicism was apparent in the works of *Mansart and *Perrault, and in the early C18 a revival of Vitruvian, Antique, and Italian-*Renaissance architecture took place, under the aegis of *Burlington, prompted by the works of *Campbell, although the chief models were the oeuvres of *Palladio and Inigo *Jones. Burlington and his circle (including *Flitcroft and *Kent) established a veritable tyranny of Taste, with very precise rules about proportions, details, and precedents, called *Palladianism*, which was the predominant movement in British architecture for most of C18 from 1714, a reaction to the *Baroque of *Wren, *Vanbrugh, and *Hawksmoor. It was no accident that Palladianism (or, more accurately, the *second Palladian Revival*) coincided with the arrival of the Hanoverian dynasty and the ascendancy of the Whig Oligarchy from 1714, and indeed Burlington's championship of Palladianism may have been a form of architectural continuity from the *first Palladian Revival* in the reign of **King James I & VI** (1603-25) after the Baroque interlude of c.1660-1714. Some writers have viewed Palladianism as a stylistic cleansing after 'excessive' Baroque exuberance, a notion that was particularly held some 60 years ago, but it should not be forgotten that Baroque architecture was based on Classical precedents, and there were also examples of Antique Roman architecture that displayed similar tendencies to Baroque, especially in C2.

Palladianism has been seen as an early type of *Neo-Classicism, but the latter properly started in the mid-C18 when architects and artists began to study *original* Antique buildings anew rather than derive their Classicism from Renaissance exemplars (as Burlington and Campbell had done). *Piranesi's engravings revealed and exaggerated the grandeur of Roman architecture, while the excavations at *Herculaneum, *Pompeii, and Stabia revealed many aspects of Roman architecture and design that quickly entered into the architectural repertoire. Scholarly archaeology became a primary source for design. Inspired by *Winckelmann, Greek architecture began to be appreciated, and the tough, rugged, masculine qualities of the powerful *Doric of the temples at *Paestum touched chords in those who thought that architecture, like Mankind, was superior when it was at a stage of primitive simplicity. The search for archaeologically correct motifs from Roman architecture was extended to include Greek exemplars, and so surveys were made of Greek buildings, notably by *Stuart and *Revett, whose *Antiquities of Athens*, one of the prime sourcebooks for the *Greek Revival, began to come out from 1762. Influenced by the writings of *Cordemoy, *Laugier, and *Lodoli, architects sought a cleansed and purified architecture that looked to Antiquity and even to *primitive forms for appropriate precedents, and this led not just to Greece, but to stereometrically pure forms such as the cone, cube, pyramid, and sphere, exploited initially by architects such as *Boullée, *Gilly, and *Ledoux. Simple geometries, clearly expressed, encouraged some extraordinary syntheses of Antique themes, drawing Ancient-Egyptian elements into architecture, while decoration became sparse and was sometimes completely avoided. The Orders, if used, were structural, supporting *entablatures or primitive *lintels, and not *engaged. Neo-Classicism was severe, even chilly, the antithesis of the Baroque.

By the early C19 Neo-Classicism mellowed in favour of a greater opulence, while compositions became more free, drew on the *Picturesque, and had powerful archaeological, emotional, and allusory aspects. Imperial Rome, Greece, and Egypt provided a rich vocabulary for the inventive *Empire* style of Napoléonic France and *Regency England. The reaction from 1815 led to a widespread *Greek Revival in Europe and America, while in Prussia *Schinkel created an architecture that combined refinement, scholarship, inventiveness, and richness of effect using the simplest of means, though strongly based on Neo-Classical principles, including clarity of expression, logic in structural development, truthfulness in the use of materials, and expression of volumes both outside and inside. In the middle of the century taste again moved towards Renaissance show, expressed in the Paris of the Second Empire (1852-70) and in the Vienna of **Kaiser Franz Joseph** (r.1848-1916), followed by a Baroque Revival. In England this was associated with the *Wrenaissance, but in France and the USA with the *Beaux-Arts* style, which once more led to a reaction in a C20 Neo-Classical Revival in which an architectural language, stripped down to its elements, and free of excess, evolved. This stark

Neo-Classicism was widespread in the 1920s and 1930s, notably in Scandinavia, France, and the USA, but it was also found in Fascist Italy, Nazi Germany, and the Soviet Union, which gained it opprobrium in spite of the fact that it had many distinguished practitioners in the democracies. In recent times elements of Classicism have reappeared in the disparate architecture that has been categorized as anything from *New Classicism to *Post-Modernism.

J.Curl (2001); P & W (1990); Pn (1982); Wn (1969)

Claude-glass Miniature dark or coloured convex hand-mirror, named after **Claude Gellée** (the landscape painter *called* **Lorraine** (1600–82)), used to reflect landscapes in mellow tones, without detail or colour. Popular in C17 and 18, it was used by, e.g., **Thomas Gray** (1716–71) when studying the *Picturesque, and in C19 was employed by **Jean-Baptiste-Camille Corot** (1796–1875) who sought tonal unity in painting.

COF (1988); Symes (2006); pk

claustrum (*pl.* **claustra**) Panel pierced with geometrical designs, e.g. as employed by *Perret in several of his *reinforced-concrete buildings.

clausura, clausure *Convent or *monastery, especially the parts occupied by the monks or nuns to which the laity was not admitted.

clavis *Keystone.

cleat Small timber block fixed to principals to help to secure them to purlins, or fixed to posts to form a bearing when timbers are not housed into them.

clerestor(e)y, clearstor(e)y, overstorey Upper parts of walls carried on *arcades or *colonnades in the *nave, *choir, or *transepts of a church, rising higher than the *lean-to roofs of the *aisles and pierced with windows to allow light to penetrate.

Clérisseau, Charles-Louis (1721–1820) Paris-born draughtsman/scholar/architect, pupil of *Boffrand: his importance was as a teacher/artist/archaeologist who had a profound effect on the evolution of *Neo-Classicism. He instructed James and Robert *Adam in draughtsmanship, and assisted in the survey of **Diocletian**'s (*r.*284–305) Palace at Spalato (Split, Croatia), later supervising the engraving of the plates for Adam's *Ruins of the Palace of the Emperor Diocletian at Spalatro in Dalmatia* (1764). He also gave lessons in drawing to *Chambers (with whom he quarrelled), and knew or met many architectural personalities of the time, including *Piranesi and *Erdmannsdorff. More than his relatively few realized works (e.g. the *Palais du Gouverneur*, Metz, France (1776–89)), his many drawings of *Antique

decorative schemes and details, real and imaginary ruins, and designs for buildings in the Ancient style helped to form the language of *Neo-Classicism. Later, he produced design-drawings for a 'Roman villa' (unrealized) for the Russian **Empress Catherine II** ('the Great'—*r.*1762–96), and advised *Jefferson on the design of the Virginia State Capitol. He published *Monumens des Nismes* in Part I of *Antiquités de la France* (1778).

B (1980); Chevtchenko *et al.* (eds) (1995); Clérisseau (1778); CoE (1972); Kalnein (1995); K & L (1972); T.McCormick (1990)

Clerk, Sir John (1676–1755) Clerk of Penicuik was a leading figure in learned Edinburgh circles. With William *Adam he designed (1722) a new house for his estate at Mavisbank, an important precedent for the *Palladian-style *villa in Scotland. Clerk visited *Burlington at Chiswick (1727) and saw several Palladian houses, after which he published *The Country Seat*, a long poem in which Burlingtonian principles were expounded. Indeed, he seems to have become Burlington's Caledonian equivalent, influencing the design of Arniston, Midlothian (1726–38), and Haddo House, Aberdeenshire (1732–5), both of which were built by William *Adam, and promoting Palladian restraint throughout the land. His son, **Sir James Clerk** (1709–82), was also a cultivated amateur architect, and designed Penicuik House in a Palladian style (1761–9).

Co (2008); *ODNB* (2004)

Clerk, Simon (*fl.*1434–89) English master-mason, he worked on Bury St Edmunds Abbey, Suffolk, from 1445, and later at Eton College (*c.*1453–61). He is known to have been employed (1477–85) at King's College Chapel, Cambridge, where he worked with John *Wastell, and helped to create the celebrated fan-*vault. He may have designed the tower of Lavenham Church, Suffolk (*c.*1486–1525), and was probably responsible, with Wastell, for the *naves at Lavenham and at Great St Mary's, Cambridge. He also worked on St Mary's Church, Saffron Walden, Essex.

J.Harvey (1987)

Cleveland, Horace William Shaler (1814–1900) American landscape architect, in partnership from 1854 with *Copeland, with whom he designed several *cemeteries, including Oak Grove, Gloucester, MA (1854), and Sleepy Hollow, Concord, MA (1855). He worked with *Olmsted on Prospect Park, Brooklyn, NYC, from 1865 before moving (1869) to Chicago, IL, where he set up a new firm with **William Merchant French** (1843–1914), working on Drexel Boulevard, South Parks, and Graceland Cemetery. The 1870s saw his most creative period: he published *Landscape*

Architecture as applied to the Wants of the West (1873) in which he argued for the need to lay out broad tree-lined *boulevards in order to beautify the towns of the Mid-West, and defined landscape architecture as the art of ordering land conveniently, economically, and beautifully to best adapt it to the needs of society. He moved (1886) to Minneapolis, MN, where he designed the St Paul Minneapolis Park System (1877–95), argued for the preservation of the Minnehaha Falls, and made an enormous contribution to civic design. He also presented a paper on *The Influence of Parks on the Character of Children* (1898), believing in the beneficial effects of landscape-design.

LA, xx (1929), 99–110; Shoe (2001); J.T (1996)

Cleverly, Charles Peter (1923–2002) English architect. Disgusted by the damage being inflicted (1960s) by *Corbusian- and *CIAM-inspired developments, he left London to practise in Suffolk. He created the North Quad of Pembroke College, Oxford (1956–64), from a disparate series of houses backing on to Beef Lane. Specializing in conserving churches and ancient houses, he collaborated with the National Trust, carrying out restoration work at Felbrigg Hall, Norfolk, the Rotunda at Ickworth, Suffolk, Thorington Hall, Stoke by Nayland, Suffolk, Flatford Mill, Essex, Bourne Mill, Essex, and Paycocke's, Coggeshall, Essex, among other places. Some 85 medieval churches were in his care, and he campaigned for sensitive conversion of East-Anglian barns as dwellings. His great-grandfather, **Charles St George Cleverly** (1819–97) was responsible for the original layout of Hong Kong, and his grandfather **Professor Frederick Moore Simpson** (1855–1928) wrote *A History of Architectural Development* (1905–11).

The Times (8 July 2002), 34

clicket Key, possibly resembling a latch-key, for opening a *wicket.

clinker block See BREEZE-BLOCK.

clipeus, clypeus Disc-like ornament resembling a *buckler shield fixed to an *architrave or *frieze in Roman architecture.

clochan Irish circular structure with rings of corbelled stones constructed to form a beehive-shaped building, like a primitive *tholos.

clocher French bell-tower.

cloisonné 1. Type of coloured wall-construction consisting of stones of one colour individually framed all round with bricks of another, laid in courses, especially in *Byzantine architecture, such as the *Katholikon, Hosios Lukas*, Styris

(*c.*1020). **2.** Surface formed of coloured enamel panels defined by *fillets.

cloister Enclosed *court, attached to a monastic or *collegiate church, consisting of a roofed *ambulatory, often (but not always) south of the *nave and west of the *transept, around an open area (*garth*), the walls (*panes*) facing the *garth constructed with plain or traceried openings (sometimes glazed or shuttered). It served as a way of communication between different buildings (e.g. *chapter-house, *refectory), and was often equipped with *carrels, seats, and a *lavatorium* in which to perform ablutions before entering the refectory. In *basilican and *Early-Christian churches the cloister was at the west end, often with a fountain for washing in the garth, and was called an *atrium*, with one side either doubling as or leading to the *narthex. This type of cloister, not intended as a means of communication between conventual buildings, was sometimes used for burial, and in due course became a detached building-type, used as a walled cemetery, such as the *Campo Santo*, Pisa, with memorials set around the walls.

Braunfels (1972); Rey (1955)

cloister-garden *Garth, sometimes an ornamental garden surrounded by an arcaded or colonnaded *ambulatory. *Antique exemplars include the House of the Vettii, Pompeii (early AD C1), and *Early-Christian churches (e.g. the *atrium* (with *fountain for ritual washing) of the Constantinian *basilica of *San Pietro*, Rome (begun *c.*333)). Medieval gardens are poorly documented, although the famous plan of the monastery of St Gall, Switzerland (*c.*820) shows a square cloister-garden subdivided into four parts by two intersecting paths, and some sort of central feature (perhaps a well or fountain). Other images exist for a few cloister-gardens (e.g. Canterbury, *c.*1165, which shows part of the garth used as a *herbary*).

Crisp (1924); Harvey (1981); Hennebo (1987); Symes (2006)

cloister-vault See VAULT; COVED VAULT.

close 1. *Court, *quad, or yard. **2.** Precinct of a cathedral.

Close, Samuel Patrick (1842–1925) Irish architect, articled (1862) to *Lanyon, Lynn, & Lanyon, he supervised the building of their *Gothic Sheils Almshouses, Carrickfergus, Co. Antrim (1868), and under his mentor, W.H. *Lynn, he was involved in realizing Chester Town Hall (designed 1864). He joined **Alexander Tate** (1823–1904—County Surveyor of Antrim from 1861), before establishing his own Belfast practice. Among his surviving works are Runkerry

House, Bushmills (1883–5—with subdued Scottish motifs); the round tower (1887–8), Larne, commemorating **James Chaine** (1841–85—leading light in the development of the port and harbour), all Co. Antrim; and Trinity Presbyterian Church, Bangor, Co. Down (1887–9). During the 1890s Close designed eight new *Gothic-Revival Belfast churches, including St Patrick's, Ballymacarrett (1891–3—with tower based on that of Magdalen College, Oxford), St Peter's, Antrim Road (1898–1900—with several Irish details); and Fisherwick Presbyterian (1898–1901). His son, **Richard Mills Close** (1880–1949), joined him (1910) in practice.

Brett (1996); *DIA; P:JRSUA*, **vi**/5 (May–June 1998), 72–5; O Donoghue (2007)

closet 1. Private audience-chamber. **2.** *Oratory. **3.** Dressing-room adjacent to a larger room. **4.** Cupboard. **5.** Secluded study. **6.** Private *pew in a church. **7.** Store. **8.** Water-closet.

close walk Shady walk, usually between tall hedges.

cloth-hall Exchange, often of some magnificence, where buyers and sellers of woollen cloth met to transact business, e.g. the Cloth Hall, Brugge, Belgium.

clump Cluster (*massif* in French) of trees, often features of C18 English and American *landscape-gardens, as used by *Kent at Holkham, Norfolk. 'Capability' *Brown employed clumps on hills or slopes, e.g. at Petworth, Sussex. Sometimes formed of single species (*Whately advised trees should be planted irregularly to suggest 'naturalness', a notion *Hirschfeld adopted), clumps could also be mixtures of trees, shrubs, etc. (as advised in America by **Bernard MacMahon** (*c.*1775–1806)).

MacMahon (1806); O'Malley *et al.* (2010); Symes (2006); Whately (1770)

Cluny By the early part of C12 the *Benedictine *abbey of Cluny in Burgundy (destroyed) had the largest *Romanesque church in Europe, with double *aisles, double *transepts with apsidal chapels, an *ambulatory with radiating chapels, and a huge barrel-vaulted *nave. This type of plan, devised to permit more *altars to be placed in chapels, proved influential. The double transept is known as the *Cluniac transept.*

Conant (1979); Eschapasse (1963); J.Evans (1972)

cluster 1. Vertical support, or *cantoned *pier (*pilier cantonné*), consisting of a cluster of columns or *shafts joined together, *inosculated, or *engaged with a central pier. **2.** *Annulated, clustered, or compound pier with *colonnettes or shafts attached to it and each other by means of *bands of a shaft, as distinct (according to some sources) from a *bundle pier. Other sources claim the shafts can be attached or detached, or appear as demi- or engaged shafts against a pier or core: however, the problem arises from the fact that on the Continent the minor shafts were almost always engaged with the central mass, but in English *First-Pointed examples they were detached, and often of dark *Purbeck marble, tied together at intervals by bands of a shaft.

cluster-block Several storeys of apartments grouped around a central service-tower containing *stairs, *elevators, etc.

Clutton, Henry (1819–93) British architect, pupil of *Blore (1835–40), he commenced independent practice (1844) and won first place in the Lille Cathedral competition with William *Burges (his partner 1851–56). His pupil/assistant was John Francis *Bentley, with whom he built the delightful little RC Church of St Francis of Assisi, Notting Hill, London (1859–60). Clutton designed the *Romanesque *cloister at the Birmingham Oratory (1860).

D & M (1985); Sh (1973)

Cluysenaar, Jean-Pierre (1811–80) Accomplished Belgian eclectic architect, his *Galerie Saint-Hubert*, Brussels (1837–47), with its glazed barrel-vaulted roof, was an elegant *Renaissance-Revival *shopping-arcade. He designed the Royal Music Conservatory, Brussels (1872–7), the Theatre and Casino, Homburg, Germany (1851–66), and the *Parkmarkt, Congresplein*, Brussels (1847).

Geist (1983); Loo (ed.) (2003)

Clyve, John (*fl.*1362–92) English mason, he worked at Windsor Castle, Berks. (1362–3), and was master-mason of Worcester Cathedral Priory (1366–7). He was probably responsible for the *chapter-house, east *cloister (1386–96), and south *arcade and *vault of the *nave at Worcester, all in high-quality early Perp.

J.Harvey (1987)

coach-house Building, subservient to the main house, for carriages.

Coade stone Fine, hard, water-resistant, artificial stone, made in Lambeth from 1769 by a firm run by **Mrs Eleanor Coade** (1733–1821). Consisting of China clay, sand, and crushed material that had already been fired, it was used for architectural ornaments and components (e.g. *capitals, keystones, funerary monuments, etc.). Also called *Lithodipyra,* meaning twice-fired stone, its stability during firing enabled the finished size of an artefact to be accurately estimated during modelling.

A.Kelly (1990); *ODNB* (2004)

coastal garden Garden by the sea requiring protection (provided by belts of shrubs) for plants to take hold and thrive. **Derek Jarman** (1942–94) created such a garden (1986–94) on a desolate expanse of shingle at Dungeness, Kent, enlivened with flints, shells, driftwood, flotsam, etc., interspersed among salt-loving indigenous plants and other shrubs introduced by Jarman himself.

Jarman (1995)

Coates, Wells Wintemute (1895–1958) Tokyo-born son of a Canadian missionary, he studied arts, science, and engineering in Canada, and moved to London (1920). From 1927 he worked on many aspects of design, influenced by Le *Corbusier and others. With **Jack Pritchard** (1899–1992) of the **Venesta Plywood Company**, he formed (1931) the **Isokon Company** to design houses, apartments, furniture, and fittings. The Lawn Road flats, Belsize Park, Hampstead (1932–4—rehabilitated (2003–5) by **John Allan** of **Avanti Architects**), was a pioneering development of 'minimum dwellings' for tenants with few possessions: among early inhabitants were *Breuer and *Gropius. Coates also designed flats at 10 Palace Gate, Kensington, London (completed 1939, refurbished (2003–5) by **Alan Brown** of **John McAslan & Partners**), a variation on a theme by *Scharoun of a decade earlier. His Embassy Court, Brighton, Sussex (1936), underwent refurbishment by **Paul Zara** of **Conran & Partners** from 2004. Coates was one of the founders of the *MARS Group, and (1930s) was in the vanguard of *International *Modernism in England.

Cantacuzino (1978); Cohn (ed.) (1979); Darling (2012); E (1980); Jervis (1984)

cob Composition containing clay, gravel, sand, straw, and water, thoroughly mixed until consistent and plastic, and applied in layers (without *formwork) to make walls, then finished with a roof and several coats of lime-wash. Commonly found in south-west England, it offered a cheap way of building, and, provided it was protected from the rain, was stable. *Compare* ADOBE; PISÉ; TABIA; WICHERT.

Cobbett, William (1763–1835) English political journalist/farmer, admirer of J.-J.*Rousseau. The distressed state of English agriculture after the Napoléonic Wars led him to publish *Cottage Economy* (1821), giving practical advice on brewing, bee-keeping, and fattening of pigs: it also prompted travels throughout the land (1821–6) and the publication of his *Rural Rides* (1830) containing vivid accounts of the dire condition of a rural England exacerbated by the Industrial Revolution. He saw London as the 'Great Wen', consuming the country's produce and creating national economic and social imbalance. His writings on gardening include *The American Gardener* (1821) and *The English Gardener* (1829): then his devastating critique, *History of the Protestant Reformation* (1824–7), argued that the State had dispossessed the English poor, beginning with the Crown's appropriation of Church lands, something which struck chords with many, including A.W.N.*Pugin. His publications were appreciated by *Loudon. He established a tree nursery in Kensington, where he championed sweetcorn among other imported varieties.

ODNB (2004); Shoe (2001)

Coberger (*or* **Coeberger, Coebergher**), **Wenceslas** (*or* **Wensel, Wenzel**) (c.1560–1634) Flemish architect/painter/antiquarian/engineer. After a successful career as a painter in Italy, he became (1605) '*architecte et ingeniaire*' to **Archduke Albert** (1559–1621) in Brussels, for whom he carried out numerous commissions. His masterpiece, the Church of *Onze Lieve Vrouwe*, Scherpenheuvel, Brabant (1606–24), introduced the Italian-*Baroque *façade, derived from *Il Gesù*, Rome, to the southern Netherlands, as well as the centrally planned domed arrangement. Appointed (1618) General Superintendent of public pawn shops, a concept (based on the *Monti di Pietà* of Italy) he championed, he designed several of the *Bergen van Barmhartigheid* himself (e.g. Gent (1622), Arras (1624), and Lille (1628)—in which Baroque features may be found).

PM; Soetart (1986); J.T (1996); W.Thomas & Duerloo (eds) (1998)

cochlea 1. Newel *stair. **2.** Tower containing such a stair.

Cockerell, Charles Robert (1788–1863) One of the most gifted, scholarly, C19 architects working in England within the Classical tradition, his work was bold yet fastidious, thoroughly based on archaeologically proven precedents yet unpedantic, and full of refinements while achieving noble monumentality. London-born, son of S.P.*Cockerell (with whom he trained before moving (1809) to Robert *Smirke's office), he travelled with John *Foster to Athens, where they met the German archaeologists *Haller and **Jakob Linckh** (1786–1841), and together they discovered (1811) the Aegina marbles (now in Munich), studied the temple of *Apollo Epicurius* at Bassae, Arcadia (in particular the *Bassae *Order of *Ionic), and found the Phigaleian marbles. With Haller, Cockerell observed *entasis on Greek column-*shafts (*see* ALLASON; PENNETHORNE; PENROSE). He visited (1811–16) Asia Minor, the Peloponnesos and the Archipelago, Rome, and Florence before returning to London where he set up his own practice (1817) and succeeded (1819) his father to the Surveyorship of St Paul's Cathedral. Receptive to

*Wren's work, he also admired the compositions of *Hawksmoor and *Vanbrugh. His designs were a judicious mix of *Greek Revival, *Renaissance, and *Baroque, with a refinement of detail acquired from his archaeological research. A splendid example of his work is the Ashmolean Museum and Taylorian Institution, Oxford (1841-5), where the Bassae Order is much in evidence but the columns stand forward of the *façade in the manner of a Roman *triumphal arch, while Italian Renaissance influences are strong, notably in the robust *cornice.

Cockerell succeeded (1833) *Soane as Architect to the Bank of England for which he designed distinguished work, including Bank branches in Bristol (1844-6) and Liverpool (1844-7), where Greek, Roman, and Renaissance features were confidently and intelligently used. He also designed the University Library, Cambridge (1837-40—where the Bassae Order was again incorporated, in conjunction with a *coffered barrel-*vault), and completed the interiors of both the Fitzwilliam Museum, Cambridge (1845-7), after *Basevi's death, and St George's Hall, Liverpool (1851-64), after *Elmes died.

Elected (1829) to the Royal Academy, Cockerell became Professor of Architecture there (1840). Awarded the Gold Medal of the RIBA (1840), he was the Institute's first professional President (1860), and was honoured by many European academies. His works included *Antiquities of Athens and other Places of Greece, Sicily, etc.* (1830—a supplementary volume to *Stuart and *Revett's *The Antiquities of Athens*); *The Temple of Jupiter Olympius at Agrigentum* (1830); works on William of *Wykeham's contributions to Winchester Cathedral (1845), on the sculptures at Lincoln Cathedral (1848), on the west front of Wells Cathedral (1851, 1862), and on colour in *Antique architecture (1859); *The Temples of Jupiter Panhellenius at Aegina and of Apollo Epicurius at Bassae* (1860); and *Travels in Southern Europe and the Levant 1810-1817* (1903).

Cockerell (1830, 1860); Co (2008); *ODNB* (2004); P (1982); J.T (1996); Wa (1974)

Cockerell, Samuel Pepys (1753-1827) English architect, pupil of Sir Robert *Taylor, he held several important official posts from 1774. On Taylor's death, he became Surveyor to the Foundling and Pulteney Estates in London: he was also Surveyor to the Victualling Office (from 1791), to the East India Company (from 1806), to the See of Canterbury, and to St Paul's Cathedral (1811-19). He was responsible for laying out the Bloomsbury Estate for the Governors of the Foundling Hospital, London (from 1790), and developed a large and prosperous practice. His pupils included his son, C.R.*Cockerell, *Latrobe, *Porden, and *Tatham. His architecture was eclectic and varied from work of an advanced French Neo-Classical type to the exotic. Tickencote Church, Rut. (1792), incorporating a C12 *chancel, is in a harsh *Romanesque style, while his Sezincote House, Glos. (c.1805), is a country-house with exotic *Hindoo details, the first example of that style in England.

Co (2008); J.Curl (2011a); *ODNB* (2004); Su (1993); J.T (1996)

cocking-piece *See* SPROCKET.

Cockrill, John William (1849-1924) English architect, known for works in Great Yarmouth, Norfolk, where he was appointed (1882) Borough Surveyor. Some of his buildings incorporated tiles manufactured by **Doulton** and patented by him (1893): the tiles (giving an impervious finish to walls) were laid in courses and spaces between them filled with *concrete, the same operation repeated as the structure rose. He also experimented with *terracotta, and designed layouts for suburbs and landscaped areas (e.g. Wellington Gardens).

Ferry (ed.) (2009)

Coderch y de Sentmenat, José Antonio (1913-84) Catalan *Modernist architect, member of *Team X, he rejected traditionalism. His work included the *Casa Garriga-Nogués*, Sitges (1947), the *Casa Ugalde*, Caldetes (1951), the Trade Office Building (1968—with influences from *Mies van der Rohe), and the School of Architecture (1978-84), all in Barcelona.

E (1994); J.T (1996)

Coducci *or* **Codussi, Mauro** (c.1440-1504) The greatest *Quattrocento architect working in Venice from c.1469. An inventive technician, he knew the works of *Alberti, clearly revered Venetian *Byzantine architecture, and was largely responsible for introducing a style that was a synthesis of *Renaissance and earlier forms. His *San Michele in Isola* (1469-78), was the first Renaissance church in Venice, with a *façade influenced by Alberti's *San Francesco*, Rimini, but with a crowning semicircular *pediment with *volutes and flanking segmental *gables concealing the *aisle roofs. He completed (1480-1500) *San Zaccaria*, a church built from 1458 to designs by Antonio *Gambello, with a façade topped by paired columns and a huge ornate semicircular *pediment again flanked by volutes. Coducci seems to have been fascinated by the Byzantine *quincunx plan (found at *San Marco*), and employed it with variations at *Santa Maria Formosa* (1492-1504), and *San Giovanni Crisostomo* (1497-1504).

Coducci was probably responsible for the *Palazzo Corner-Spinelli* (c.1493) and *Palazzo Véndramin-Calergi* (c.1500-9), although the latter (prototypical of the grander secular architecture of Venice, with a façade of three superimposed *Orders and an array of *Venetian arches) is said to have been begun by Pietro *Lombardo. Coducci was the architect of the spectacular double staircase with smooth barrel-*vaults, flights, and domed landings in the *Scuola di San Giovanni Evangelista* (1498–1504), the *campanile of *San Pietro di Castello* (1482–8), the great staircase (destroyed) and completion of the façade of the *Scuola Grande di San Marco* (the crowning storey of semicircular gables), and (probably) of the *Torre dell'Orolozio* (1496–9), which closes the vista in the *Piazzetta San Marco*.

D.Howard (1980); Lieberman (1982); McAndrew (1980); Polli (1993); Puppi & Puppi (1977); J.T (1996)

Coecke (*or* **Coucke**) **van Aelst, Pieter** (*or* **Peter**) (1502–50) South Netherlandish painter/architect/linguist. After extensive travels he settled in Antwerp, where he published (1539) a Flemish translation of *Vitruvius's *De Architectura* and (1539–53) *Serlio's multi-volume treatise into Flemish, French, and High German. He can be credited with introducing a Classicizing architecture to Antwerp and Brussels.

Guillaume (ed.) (1988); PM; *Quaerendo*, **vi**/2 (1976), 167–94

coenobite Member of a religious community as opposed to an *anchorite* living in solitude.

coffer 1. *Caisson* or *lacuna*, i.e. deep panel sunk in a ceiling, *dome, *soffit, or *vault, often decorated in the centre with a stylized flower or similar embellishment, as on the undersides of *Composite and *Corinthian *cornices. A ceiling, etc., with coffers is said to be *coffered*, and *coffering* is an arrangement of coffers. **2.** Cavity in a thick wall, *pier, etc., filled with *rubble and other material, often box-like compartments formed by the facing-stones and cross- or bonding-stones.

coffer-dam Watertight enclosure constructed of two rows of *piles with clay packed between them used when constructing a bridge-pier, etc., in water.

Coffin, David Robbins (1918–2003) American art-historian, he made an invaluable contribution to the history of landscape architecture, especially that of the *Renaissance. Insisting on a rigorous approach to documentary sources, he did much to enhance literature dealing with Italian *villas, making an early mark with his book, *The Villa d'Este at Tivoli* (1961—the subject of his Doctoral Dissertation at Princeton (1954), in which he wrote perceptively about Pirro *Ligorio, sympathetically investigated in a subsequent biography (2004)), followed by *The Villa in the Life of Renaissance Rome* (1979—in which he discussed *villeggiatura* at length). Other volumes on the gardens of Papal Rome (1991) and on the

English Garden (1994—with an emphasis on the significance of transience) further enhanced his reputation.

D.Coffin (1960, 1979, 1991, 1994, 2004); *JSAH*, **lxiii**/2 (June 2004), 248–54

Coffin, Marian Cruger (1876–1957) American landscape architect, the first woman to establish a practice in the field. Her major works were the *campuses for Delaware College and the Women's College of the University of Delaware (1918–52), and the Botanical Garden, Winterthur, DE. She also designed numerous gardens for wealthy clients in the eastern USA.

M.Coffin (1940); N.Fleming (1995)

cog 1. Projection or *tenon* at the end of a beam received into a corresponding notch or *mortice* in another beam. A *cog-hold* is therefore a connection using a cog. **2.** Brick projecting and laid diagonally. *See* COGGING.

cogging Course of projecting bricks laid diagonally to give a saw-like effect in a *cornice or *string-course: a variant on *toothing* (*see* BRICK; TOOTH).

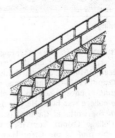

cogging

Coia, Jack (**Giacomo**) **Antonio** (1898–1981) *See* GILLESPIE, KIDD, & COIA.

coign *See* QUOIN.

Coignet, François (1814–88) French pioneer of experimental *concrete construction, who, with his brothers, **Louis** (*fl.*1819–46) and **Stéphane** (1820–66), took over the family's chemical works in Lyon (1846). He patented (1854) a concrete with a *clinker *aggregate, and opened a new factory at St-Denis, itself built of pre-cast clinker-blocks, to manufacture it. To advertise his products he built (1853) a house (designed by **Théodore Lachèz** (*fl.*1820–60)) at St-Denis which was entirely of artificial stone. From that time he concentrated his energies to the study of concrete and similar materials. One of his largest projects

coin 182

was the construction of the *aqueduct of the Vanne (1867–74), nearly 140 km (87 miles) long, and with some arches as high as 40 metres, and he built the sea-wall at *Saint-Jean-de-Luz* (1857–93). He provided concrete elements for L.-C. *Boileau's Church of *Ste-Marguerite*, Le Vésinet (Seine-et-Oise—1862–5), but Boileau complained of poor adhesion and water-penetration. His son, **Edmond Coignet** (1856–1915), was also an inventor, and with the architect *Hermant, erected two of the first Parisian *reinforced-concrete buildings: *Le Magasin des Classes Laborieuses* department-store, *Rue St-Martin*, and the *Salle Gaveau* concert-hall, *Rue St-Honoré* (1906–7). Edmond Coignet patented (1892) his system.

Ck (1996); Marrey (1989); Marrey (ed.) (2002); J.T (1996)

coin 1. Disc used in a series of overlapping coin-like forms, resembling *guilloche, set in horizontal or vertical strips called *coin-mouldings* or *money-patterns*. **2.** *Quoin.

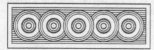

coin-moulding

Coke, Humphrey (*fl*.1496–1531) English master-carpenter. He worked on the *cloisters at Eton College (1510–11), and on Corpus Christi College, Oxford (1514–18): he seems, with William *Vertue, to have drawn up the plans from which the college was built. He was one of the masters of the works at Cardinal (later Christ Church) College, Oxford, from 1525, where he designed the roof of the Great Hall, the last and finest work of medieval carpentry. There is no doubt that his skills included architectural expertise.

J.Harvey (1987)

Cola (di Matteuccio) da Caprarola (*fl*.1494–1518) Italian architect. He worked with *Sangallo the Elder on the Papal palace and fortifications of *La Rocca*, Città Castellana (1494–1500), and carried out other works on the fortifications of Nepi. He was involved in the building of *Santa Maria della Consolazione*, Todi (1508–12—a *centrally planned church probably derived from sketches by *Leonardo da Vinci and from *Bramante's designs for *San Pietro*, Rome). He restored Foligno *Duomo* (1512–15), and built the fortress at *Porto Ercole* (*c*.1518–21).

He (1996); Pedretti (1985); J.T (1996)

colarin, colarino *See* HYPOTRACHELION.

Colchester, William (*fl*.1385–1420) English mason. He worked at Southampton Castle (1385–8) before becoming (1400) chief mason for the *nave at Westminster Abbey. Appointed (1407) to rebuild the fallen *belfry at York *Minster, he remained in charge of the works there until 1418 when he was appointed King's master-mason at Westminster Palace and the Tower of London. His most notable works are the stone *screens at the entrance to the *choir-*aisles, the *buttresses at the eastern *piers of the tower, and the stone altar-screen, all in York Minster.

J.Harvey (1987)

cold-bath C18 fashions for coastal and *spa bathing (followed by those in search of health, pleasure, and longevity) led to the construction of cold-baths and plunge-pools (containers fed with water from natural sources) located within the main house or inside structures in landscape-gardens (often doubling as aesthetically agreeable *fabriques). Early advocates of the cold-bath were **John Locke** (1632–1704) in his *Some Thoughts Concerning Education* (1693, with later, esp. 1703, edns) and **Sir John Floyer** (1649–1734) in *An Enquiry into the Right Uses and Abuses of the Hot, Cold, and Temperate Baths in England* (1697). Good examples of cold-baths as *fabriques* in landscapes include the plunge-pool and grotto, Stourhead, Wilts. (with statue of Neptune), and the *Gothick exemplar (1761–3) by 'Capability' *Brown, remodelled by *Nash (1790s), Corsham Court, Wilts.

J.Curl (2010); Hickman (2010)

Cole, Sir Henry (1808–82) English industrial-designer/museum-director/art-administrator, he reformed the Public Record Office (1823–38), helped to introduce the Penny Post (1838–42), and commissioned (1843) **John Calcott 'Clothes' Horsley** (1817–1903) to design the first commercial Christmas card. Under the pseudonym 'Felix Summerly' he wrote children's books, tourist guides, and papers on many subjects, and designed (1846) the Felix Summerly Tea Service, made by **Herbert Minton** (1793–1858), which was such a success that Cole established (1847) Felix Summerly's Art-Manufactures with the object of improving industrial design (and the execrable taste of the general public) by commissioning work from artists. Soon Cole was to realize that teaching in Government Schools of Design was not up to much, and prompted a Select Committee of the House of Commons to look into the matter (1848) whilst airing the problem in the *Journal of Design and Manufactures* (1849–52). Through the Royal Society of Arts he met Prince *Albert, and was entrusted (1850) with the organization of the 1851 Great Exhibition: the result was a triumph; the first of a series of major C19 exhibitions. Cole was made head of the newly-created Department of Practical Art, and also established a *museum containing various exhibits shown in 1851 to provide suitable models for students as well as raising the level of public taste. Almost immediately his department was called upon to design the funeral-car and bier for the exequies (1852) of **Arthur Wellesley** (1769-1852—**1st Duke of Wellington** from 1814): with men of the calibre of *Semper at his side, the result was another triumph. When Cole began his stint as General Superintendent of what became (1853) the Department of Art and Science, there were only 36 provincial art schools, but by 1861 there were 91, and there is no question he had a huge impact on design throughout the Kingdom (and therefore throughout the Empire). So successful had the Great Exhibition been, even in terms of profit, that Cole's department was able to move to new premises in South Kensington, and in due course became (1899) the Victoria and Albert Museum. He was adviser to the London exhibition at South Kensington (1862), and was the proposer of a huge hall to be erected as part of the National Memorial to Prince Albert (d.1861). Cole threw himself with his customary energy into realizing the scheme, and (1867) the foundation-stone of what was to become the Royal Albert Hall was laid (the building, designed by *Fowke and H.Y.D.*Scott, opened 1871). He was active in starting the National Training School for Music (1876—from 1883 the Royal College of Music). The fine building was designed by his son, **Henry Hardy Cole** (1843-1916), and later became the Royal College of Organists: its extraordinary *sgraffito decorations were by **Francis Wollaston Moody** (1824-86).

Bonython & Burton (2003); *ODNB* (2004); P & D (1973); Sh (1975); J.T (1996)

Cole, John (*fl.*1501-4) English master-mason, he built the elegant *spire at the church in Louth, Lincs. (1501-4), and, with *Scune, carried out works there and at Ripon *Minster, Yorks.

J.Harvey (1987)

Coles, George (1884-1963) Versatile English architect, he became (1912) a partner of **Percy Henry Adams** (1870-1934), and the firm gained a reputation for cinema-design (e.g. the Carlton, Upton Park, and Carlton, Islington (1928-30), with their Egyptianizing frontages). For **Oscar Deutsch** (1893-1941) Coles designed several *Odeon* cinemas, starting with that at Welling, Kent. Among his best *Odeon* designs were Isleworth, Southall (Mddx.), Muswell Hill (London—a particularly fine essay), the superb Woolwich (London—with its *streamlined features and Egyptianizing *torchère*), and Acton (London), all 1935-6.

Atwell (1981); Eyles (2002)

collage Work constructed of assemblages of disparate fragments, e.g. a picture made from scraps of paper, newspaper cuttings, and oddments pasted onto a backing. In architecture it is associated with *Adhocism.

collar Transverse horizontal straight, cambered, or cranked timber connecting pairs of *cruck-blades or *rafters in a position above their feet and below the apex of the roof, also called a *collar-beam, span-beam, spar-piece, top-beam,* or *wind-beam,* thus a *collar-beam roof* or *collar-roof* has collars used in its construction. A *collar-* or *arch-brace* is a structural timber to stiffen a roof-*truss. An *extended collar* extends beyond its principal to a gable-wall in roofs with large *gables, often with the lower part of the principal omitted. A *collar-plate, collar-purlin,* or *crown-plate* is a horizontal timber *plate resting on collars to tie trusses together, set above a *crown-*post.

collarino See HYPOTRACHELION.

Collcutt, Thomas Edward (1840-1924) English architect who worked in *Street's office before establishing (1869) his own London practice. Collcutt's work was in a Free-*Renaissance style, of which the *façades of the Royal English Opera House (later Palace Theatre), Cambridge Circus, London (1889), and the very fine Imperial Institute, London (1887-93—lamentably demolished (1950s) except for the handsome tower), were the best examples. He also worked in a relaxed *Arts-and-Crafts style, designing houses at Totteridge, Herts. (1904), and various buildings at Mill Hill School, London (of the same period). From 1906 he was in partnership with **Stanley Hinge Hamp** (1877-1968), with whom he designed parts of the Savoy Hotel, London, in a simplified *Renaissance manner much influenced by American precedents.

D & M (1985); Gd (1977); A.S.Gray (1985); Se (ed.) (1975); Se (1977)

college garden Unlike many European universities (Paris, Prague, etc.), English college foundations at Oxford and Cambridge were established in what were small hamlets distant from the capital, and so had gardens, and even extensive meadows (Christ Church, Oxford) attached to them. College buildings were grouped around spaces (*quads in Oxford and *courts in Cambridge), some huge (Trinity, Cambridge), some small (Merton, Oxford; Peterhouse, Cambridge). A few colleges possess gardens with ancient features (e.g. the *mount, New College, Oxford), and Worcester College, Oxford, had a C19 *Picturesque garden with lake. At Cambridge, several colleges have gardens behind them (The Backs) with the River Cam flowing through them. In North America the universities of Harvard and

Yale were also founded in rural surroundings (Cambridge, MA, and New Haven, CT), but with C19 developments, the creation of naturalistic gardens often accompanied the construction of new university buildings (e.g. Stanford and Berkeley) where the hand of *Olmsted is evident. *See* CAMPUS.

Shoe (2001); Symes (2006)

Collegiate church Church endowed for a body corporate, or chapter, of dean and canons, attached to it.

Collegiate Gothic Secular *Gothic, e.g. that of Oxford and Cambridge colleges, as revived in C19 educational and other institutional foundations, especially *Tudor Gothic.

colombier *Dovecote or *columbarium.

colonia Roman farm or farmhouse, also called *colonica.*

Colonia Family Juan de Colonia (*c.*1410–81), as his name suggests, came from Cologne (aka **Hans of Cologne**): he settled in Burgos, Spain, where his family was associated with the building of the Cathedral (*c.*1440–*c.*1540). He built the *spires of the western towers (1442–58), which are of the German *tracery type, and *La Cartuja de Miraflores,* near Burgos (from 1441). Juan's sculptor-architect son, **Simón** (*fl.*1481–1511), succeeded (1481) his father at Burgos Cathedral, and designed the spectacular *Plateresque or *Isabellino late-*Gothic *Capilla del Condestable* (1482–94), with its huge *escutcheons and eight-pointed star-*vault with tracery infill similar to the western spires of the Cathedral. Simón was also responsible for the elaborate *façade of *San Pablo,* Valladolid (1486–1504), an example of a church-front designed to look like a *reredos (common in Spain and in Latin America), and was appointed (1497) master-mason of Seville Cathedral. His son, **Francisco** (*fl.*1511–42) worked with Simón on the decorations of the *San Pablo* façade, and designed and made the Gothic *retable of *San Nicolás,* Burgos (*c.*1503–5), where there are early *Renaissance motifs. Francisco (who succeeded (1511) his father as master-mason) worked with **Juan de Vallejo** (*c.*1500–69) on the *crossing-tower (Gothic) from 1540 and himself made the *Puerta de la Pellejería* (early Renaissance, 1516), both at Burgos Cathedral. He also worked with Juan de *Álava at the Cathedrals of Plasencia and Salamanca.

CG (1953, 1965); Dezzi Bardeschi (1965); K & S (1959); Lamperez-y-Romea (1904)

Colonial Applied to styles of architecture derived from those of the motherland in a colony. *American Colonial* is a modification of the English-*Georgian or *Queen-Anne styles, of

particular interest because frequently *pattern-book designs were reinterpreted for *timber-framed structures, or otherwise altered, often by very subtle means. Although originally associated with the thirteen British colonies in North America, the essentials of American Colonial architecture were often revived well into C20 all over the USA. *Colonial Revival* is a term given to architecture of the late C19 and early C20, especially in the USA, South Africa, and Australia. Attention had been drawn to the qualities of colonial architecture in various publications from the 1840s, and several writers advocated its revival, the catalyst for which was the Centennial International Exhibition, Philadelphia, PA (1876), at which the New England Log House and the Connecticut House attracted particular attention, as did two *half-timbered buildings (the British Executive Commissioner and Delegate Residence) by the British *Rogue, **Thomas Harris** (1830–1900), which encouraged an interest in *vernacular architecture. The Colonial Revival was taken up by *Peabody & Stearns (e.g. Denny House, Brush Hill, Milton, MA (1878), and the influential Massachusetts Building for the World's Columbian Exposition, Chicago, IL (1893—the model for a nationwide revival)). Firms such as *McKim, Mead, & White designed in both Colonial-Revival and *Shingle styles. A fine example of the Colonial Revival in the USA is the *clap-boarded Mary Perkins Quincy House, Litchfield, CT (1904), by John Mead *Howells and **Isaac Newton Phelps Stokes** (1867–1944). American Colonial Revival influenced some developments elsewhere, e.g. *Lutyens's work at Hampstead *Garden-Suburb, London (designed 1908–10), and de *Soissons's designs (from the 1920s) at Welwyn *Garden City, Herts. Two further variations of Colonial Revival evolved on the West Coast of the USA: *Mission Revival (from the 1890s) and Spanish Colonial Revival (from just after the 1914–18 war). A good example of the latter style is Sherwood House, La Jolla, CA (1925–8), by **George Washington Smith** (1876–1930—who could turn his hand to villas in medieval, Islamic, and Mediterranean modes as well).

In Australia, following the creation of a unified country at the beginning of C20, a need for a national style was urged, and the late-*Georgian domestic architecture of Australia was selected as offering suitable models. The main practitioners of the Australian Colonial Revival (featuring colonnaded *verandahs, sash-windows with shutters, and *fanlights over doors) were W.H.*Wilson (e.g. Eryldene, Gordon, Sydney (1913–14)), **Robin Dods** (1868–1920—e.g. several fine houses in Brisbane), and **Leslie Wilkinson** (1882–1973—who mixed Mediterranean features in with Australian Colonial elements, e.g. 'Greenway', Vaucluse, Sydney (1923)). In South Africa, the so-called *Dutch Colonial* or *Cape Dutch* style, which had developed from C17, was revived by *Baker at *Groote Schuur*, Rondebosch (1893-8—built for **Cecil John Rhodes** (1853-1902), and was quickly adopted by other South African architects. *Spanish Colonial* was also revived in Latin America as well as in the USA, and both it and *Dutch Colonial* evolved as separate styles from those found in Spain and The Netherlands. The Colonial Revival has enjoyed further revivals and interpretations at the end of C20 and the beginning of C21.

Axelrod (ed.) (1985); J.T (1996)

colonial siding Wide *weather-boarding of pieces of timber the same thickness (unlike *clap-boarding), square-edged, and fixed with each board overlapping that below, often with a roll-moulding along the bottom edge of each board.

Colonna, Fra Francesco (1433-1527) Venetian author/cleric, his *Hypnerotomachia Polifili*, written (1467) and published (1499) by **Aldus Manutius** (1450-1515) in Venice, was a work of imagination, but it contains descriptions of hieroglyphs and many buildings of Classical Antiquity, clearly drawing on *Antique literature (including *Vitruvius) and on contemporary *Renaissance architectural concerns. Manutius's celebrated edition contained fanciful woodcut illustrations that were very influential for long afterwards, not least in connection with garden-design. *Bernini's elephant carrying an *obelisk and the common theme of an obelisk on top of a *pyramid are but two of the images that recur after 1499.

Colonna (1999); J.Curl (2005); Jervis (1984); Pe (1968)

colonnade Series of columns in a straight line supporting an *entablature: when standing before a building, carrying a roof, and serving as a porch, it is a *portico, and if it is carried around three or four sides of a building exterior or round a *court or garden it is a *peristyle. A colonnade is defined in terms of its number of columns (*see* PORTICO) and in terms of spaces between columns (*see* INTERCOLUMNIATION). *See* TEMPLE.

colonnette Small column, *baluster, or slender circular *shaft, as in an *annulated *pier.

Colossal Order *See* GIANT ORDER.

colour 1. The subject of colour in architecture is huge, and can only be briefly mentioned here. Colour was used in many ancient cultures, not least by the Egyptians, many of whose decorative schemes in tomb-chambers survive in remarkable states of preservation. The Greeks, too, coloured their buildings with stylized decorations, the subject of much C19 controversy until the notion (promoted by *Winckelmann that Greek architecture was pristine and white) was firmly rejected when *Hittorff, *Penrose, *Zanth, et al. proved *polychromy was usual. The Romans used colour: wall paintings, *mosaics, etc., have partially survived from C18 *Pompeian excavations, and *Antique decorations in *grotte* (*see* GROTESQUE) were rediscovered (1488). *Byzantine interiors were enriched with mosaics, and during the *Romanesque and *Gothic periods colour was liberally applied to church-interiors, not only in stylized repetitive painted ornament, but in pictorial representations of Biblical scenes, on *canopies and tomb-effigies, and, of course, in stained-glass windows, while colour seems also to have enlivened some exteriors, perhaps startlingly (e.g. the west front of Wells Cathedral, Som.). The *Renaissance saw revivals of Roman decorations, such as *grotesques, as well as inventive interpretations of Classical ornament and detail. *Baroque and *Rococo decorations, notably in the churches of southern Germany, achieved an exquisite, joyful, subtle, porcelain-like delicacy, with much gilding, pinks, and blues, and *fresco ceilings of astonishing liveliness and virtuosity. Secular colour schemes, e.g. those of the *Amalienburg*, near Munich, by *Cuvilliés and *Zimmermann, featured silver and yellow, among other colours, and the *Adam Brothers provided elegant and harmonious colour schemes to embellish their attenuated, refined interior designs. Later C18 and C19 *Neo-Classical interiors, especially those of the *Empire and *Regency periods, were enriched with much strong colour and gilding, providing a robust, sometimes exotic, eclectic opulence, with occasional touches of *Chinoiserie* (as at the Royal Pavilion, Brighton) and Egyptianizing motifs (e.g. the work of *Percier and *Fontaine). C19 architecture was often brightly coloured, especially at the height of the *Gothic Revival, when *structural* *polychromy appeared, inside and out, as in the work of *Butterfield. In that century, too, the manufacture of *terracotta, *faïence, and glazed, patterned *tiles made permanent colour in architecture cheaply available, and was widely advocated, especially by architects such as *Ricardo, who used strongly coloured designs by **William Frend de Morgan** (1839-1917). Late-Victorian/Edwardian schemes of decoration were often highly coloured, and Arts-and-Crafts work, prompted by, e.g., William *Morris, was anything but subdued. *Japonaiserie* also informed design, and *Art Nouveau, in its various manifestations, employed colour and decorative motifs culled from a *mélange* of sources, freely treated. *Art Deco embraced strong hues again, such as vermilions, yellows, greens, and blacks, set off with chrome and gold, with more than a small injection of Egyptian and

*Aztec allusions. Later uses of colour have included banishing it altogether; strident primary colours used by, e.g. the De-*Stijl movement; and bright, harsh colours prompted by *Cubism, Le *Corbusier, et al. **2.** Colour is introduced to gardens by plant selection and/or painted structures (e.g. the Chinese Bridge at Biddulph Grange, Staffs., or the 'Turkish Tent', *Désert de Retz*, France), and plays an essential rôle in garden-design. Before C18 colour ranges were limited, but by the time *Loudon was writing about the subject, notably concerning *Loddiges, the choice was immense, thanks to the C18 importations of huge numbers of new varieties, and the effects could be somewhat garish. A more harmonious approach was adopted in the second half of C19, when the 'natural' aspects of the *cottage-garden began to be explored as part of *Arts-and-Crafts gardening, achieving great subtlety and pleasing blends of less strident colouring, as in the work of, e.g. William *Robinson and *Jekyll. The theorist **Michel-Eugène Chevreul** (1786–1889), in his *Principles of Harmony* ... (1839) had a profound influence on garden-design, and in recent times **Penelope Hobhouse** (1929–) explored all aspects of colour in gardens, challenging beliefs held by many that it is only provided by flowers. Other significant designers have incorporated exotic plants in the hotter climes in which they worked, e.g. Burle *Marx and *Barragán, while artists such as **Johannes Itten** (1888–1967) contributed to theory. The softer, harmonious legacies of Arts-and-Crafts approaches to colour in gardens were described in works such as Tinley, Humphreys, & Irving's *Colour Planning* ... (1924), and displayed in, e.g., Sissinghurst, near Cranbrook, Kent, where 'Vita' *Sackville-West created a 'garden of *rooms', with beautifully judged colour, from 1930.

Bristow (1996); J.Brown (1994); Chevreul (1967); Cornforth (1978, 2000, 2004); Hittorff (1851); Hittorff & Zanth (1835); P.Hobhouse (2003); Itten (1973); O.Jones (1868); Loudon (1834a, 1981); Mason (1768); Penrose (1851); Shoe (2001); Thornton (1984); THI (1924); J.T (1996)

Columbani, Placido (fl.1744–1800) Italian architect who spent most of his working life in England. He published *The Chimney-piece Maker's Daily Assistant* (1766), *Vases and Tripods* (n.d.), *A New Book of Ornaments* (1775), and *Variety of Capitals, Friezes, and Corniches* (1776). He added a *Doric *portico (c.1780–2) to Mount Clare, near Roehampton, Surrey; laid out a garden at Audley End, Essex (from 1781); supervised works at Downhill, Co. Londonderry (1783–5); prepared layouts for the garden and made working drawings for a lodge at Antony House, Torpoint, Cornwall (1793–4), by Humphry *Repton; and designed a *villa at Lower Park, Putney Lane, Surrey (1793). His furniture designs were

influential in the later C18, and popularized the Neo-Classical style of the *Adam brothers.

AH, **xxvii** (1984), 259–60; Co (2008); Rankin (1972)

columbarium (*pl.* **columbaria**) **1.** *Colombier or *dovecote, a substantial building commonly on a circular plan, with *niches (*columbaria*) in tiers around the walls of the structure for nesting doves or pigeons, and an aperture or apertures to allow the birds to fly in and out. **2.** Building or subterranean excavated tomb lined with niches to receive *cineraria* or *urns holding Roman cremated remains, so-called from its resemblance to a dovecote, or any C19 or C20 building designed to contain such remains. **3.** *Putlog-hole, from its resemblance to a niche in a dovecote.

J.Curl (2002a); Toynbee (1971)

columella (*pl.* **columellae**) **1.** *Baluster. **2.** *Colonnette.

column 1. Detached rather slender vertical structural element, sometimes *monolithic, usually circular (but sometimes square or polygonal) on plan, normally carrying an *entablature or *lintel, but sometimes standing on its own with a statue on top as a monument. In the Classical *Orders, a column consists of a *base, *shaft, and *capital (except for the Greek *Doric *Order, which has no base), and the shaft tapers towards the top in a gentle curve called *entasis. Columns are distinct from *piers and *pillars. **2.** Any relatively slender vertical structural member in compression, supporting a load acting near the direction of its main axis. *See* ANGULAR; ANTONINE; BAND; BARLEY-SUGAR; BLOCK; CAROLITIC; CLUSTER; COLONNADE; COLUMNIATION; COMPOSITE; CORINTHIAN; DETACHED; DORIC; ENGAGED; GROUPED; INTERCOLUMNIATION; IONIC; ORDER; PORTICO; SOLOMONIC; SPIRAL; TORSO; TRAJANIC; TRIUMPHAL; TUSCAN; TWISTED. **Other terms include**:

column figure: carved figure attached to a column or shaft, normally on each side of a *doorway or other opening;

columna caelata: column with shaft adorned with carving, as in a *carolitic column;

columna cochlis: monumental *triumphal column* such as the *Antonine or *Trajanic column with an internal spiral staircase and an external *spiral band of continuous sculpture;

columnar and trabeated: type of construction consisting of vertical columns or *posts supporting horizontal *beams or lintels, as opposed to *arcuated construction;

columna rostrata (*pl.* *columnae rostratae* or *rostral columns*): *Tuscan column on a *pedestal, its shaft embellished with sculpted prows (*rostra*) of *Antique Roman warships, originally to honour naval victories. The type was revived in C17 and C18;

columna triumphalis: *triumphal column (as *columna cochlis*);
columniation: arrangement of columns. *See* INTERCOLUMNIATION; PORTICO; TEMPLE.

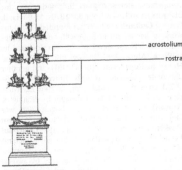

columna rostrata

Colvin, Brenda (1897–1981) English landscape architect. She specialized in private gardens (1922–39), but after the 1939–45 war made her reputation with landscape designs for power stations, reservoirs, universities, hospitals, factories, and mineral-workings. From 1962 she worked at Gale Common, Eggborough, Yorks., using waste from coal-fired power stations to form a hilly area. She designed a series of 'ecological environments', including Rugeley Power Station, Staffs. (1962). Her book, *Land and Landscape* (1948) emphasized that ecological and conservation factors were essential to design.

S.Harvey (ed.) (1987); J.T (1996)

Colvin, Sir Howard Montagu (1919–2007) English architectural historian. His meticulous attention to documentary research, rather than a reliance on stylistic attributions, transformed British architectural history. His *Biographical Dictionary of English Architects 1660–1840* (1954), much enlarged as *Biographical Dictionary of British Architects 1600–1840* (1978, 1995, and 2008), is the standard work on British architects of the period. He was general editor and part-author of the *History of the King's Works* (1963–82).

Co (1991, 1995, 2008); pk; *The Times* (1 Jan.2008), 47

comb *See* CAMP.

commandery 1. Ecclesiastical or other benefice held *in commendam* (i.e. given to the charge of a qualified clerk or layman pending the appointment of an incumbent, or a benefice held by a bishop or other dignitary). 2. Landed estate or manor belonging to an Order of Knights (e.g. of St John of Jerusalem) under the charge of a

Commander. 3. Conventual priory or non-military religious order. 4. The buildings of certain abbeys, priories, etc.

Commissioners' churches Following the Napoléonic Wars, it was feared that England might suffer upheavals similar to those of France, and, faced with irreligion, Nonconformity, and an increasing population (much of it restive and uncivilized), the authorities determined to build Anglican churches, numbers of which (also known as *Waterloo churches*) were erected under the aegis of the Commissioners for Building New Churches appointed under *An Act for Promoting the Building of Additional Churches in Populous Parishes* (58 Geo. III, c.45), 1818. Most were cheap, utilitarian preaching-boxes, with any architectural pretensions reserved for the west end. Designs were Classical or in a thin, lean, unscholarly *Gothic, with low-pitched roofs, *galleried interiors, and *Pointed windows set in *bays marked by *buttresses: the last type was known as *Commissioners' Gothic*.

B.Clarke (1969); J.Curl (2007); Ea (1970)

common *Compounds and derivatives include*:
common ashlar: Hammer- or pick-dressed stone;
common bond: also *American, English garden-wall*, or *Liverpool bond*, it has four or five courses of *stretchers* to every one of *headers* (*see* BRICK);
common joist: structural floor-joist spanning from wall to wall;
common rafter: one of a series of *rafters of uniform size regularly spaced along the length of a pitched roof, or placed as intermediates between *principals, with one end attached to the wall-plate and the other to the opposite common rafter at the *ridge. A *pair* of common rafters is a *couple;
common roof: one consisting of *common rafters* only, with or without *purlins, also called *coupled-rafter roof*;
common round: *roll-*moulding.

common-house *Calefactory, or heated room in a *monastery, also called the *common-room*. Precedent for university common-rooms.

Communion-rail *Altar-rail.

Communion-table Wooden table in Protestant churches, replacing the stone *altar, introduced as a deliberate denial of the doctrine of Transubstantiation.

community architecture English housing-movement involving participation in design of users of buildings. The term was probably coined by **Charles Knevitt** (1952–2016) in an article in *Building Design* (1975). Walter *Segal pioneered (1970s) the movement with his system of *timber-framed housing, followed by several instances of rehabilitation of older dwellings as well as new buildings (1980s). **Christopher Wolfgang Alexander**'s (1936–) arguments for relatively simple labour-intensive housing have been associated with community architecture, as have concepts of public participation in the design-process.

BD (11 July 1975), 8; Hackney (1990); Lozand (1991); J.McKean (1989); Towers (1995); Wates & Knevitt (1987)

Company-town Planned development to house factory workers. Early examples include the *Saline de Chaux* (or *du Roi*), Arc-et-Senans (1773–8), by *Ledoux, and New Lanark, on the Clyde, in Scotland, commenced (1785) by **David Dale** (1739–1806), who made provision for the education of the children of those he employed in his cotton mills and also housed. Dale sold (1799) New Lanark to a Manchester concern which appointed **Robert Owen** (1771–1856) its manager. Owen (who married Dale's daughter) developed this Company-town, adding a nursery, communal buildings, an Institution for the Formation of Character (1812), and the New Institution (1816), which were intended to educate and raise the tone of working classes employed and living there.

Nonconformists were in the vanguard of experiments to create Company-towns: a good example was **John Grubb Richardson** (1813/14–90), a Quaker who established (1846) Bessbrook, Co. Armagh, Ireland, as an alcohol-free village with amenities (e.g. schools, dispensary, community centre, etc.) for those who worked in his linen mill. Bessbrook was to prove an inspiration to other Quakers, including the **Cadburys** and the **Rowntrees**. Paternalistic and philanthropically-minded industrialists, such as **Colonel Edward Akroyd** (1810–87—who laid out estates for his mill-workers at Copley Hill (1847–65—complete with school, church, and library) and Akroydon (from *c.*1859—with one of 'Great' *Scott's finest churches (All Souls, Haley Hill)), both near Halifax, Yorks.), and **Sir Titus Salt** (1803–76—who believed that 'drink and lust' were at the root of all problems among the lower orders—whose noble Saltaire, at Shipley, on the River Aire, Yorks., was built 1851–76, and contained schools, bath-houses, almshouses, a hospital, and a club), demonstrated what could be done to improve the lot of the workers. Akroyd's architect for his two developments were *Crossland and 'Great' Scott, and Salt's architects were *Lockwood & Mawson of Bradford. In France, **J.-B.-A.Godin-Lemaire** (1817–89), influenced by **François-Marie-Charles Fourier** (1772–1837) and, indirectly, by Owen, built his *Familistère* (1859–77), or workmen's home, attached to his iron-foundry at Guise, not far from St-Quentin. Influenced by the writings of Henry *Roberts, the *Cité Ouvrière*, Mulhouse, Haut-Rhin, France (1852–97), was built under the

aegis of the *Société Industrielle de Mulhouse* (of which the leading light was **Jean Dollfus** (1800–87)) to designs by Émile *Muller. In Germany, the industrialist **Alfried Felix Alwyn Krupp** (1812–87—known as the 'Cannon King') built housing, co-operative stores, schools, infirmaries, etc., for his workers in Essen from the 1870s. In England, **George Cadbury** (1839–1922) founded (1879) his workers' settlement at Bournville, near Birmingham (much of the development was designed by **William Alexander Harvey** (1874–1951) and **Henry Bedford Tylor** (1871–1915)), and another chocolate magnate, **Joseph Rowntree** (1836–1925), created the model village of New Earswick, near York (from 1901, to designs by *Parker & *Unwin). Port Sunlight, Ches., begun 1888, was laid out for the soap-manufacturer **William Hesketh Lever** (1851–1925—later (1922) **Viscount Leverhulme**), who planned the general layout himself, later amended by Segar *Owen and *Lomax-Simpson; the very fine housing was by several architects, including William and Segar Owen, *Douglas & **J.P.Fordham** (1843–99), *Grayson & Ould, and others, including Lomax-Simpson and C.H.*Reilly. S.S.*Beman designed Pullman, the Company-town outside Chicago, IL (1880–95), for the railway-magnate: N.F.*Barrett designed the layout. Near Brno (Brünn), in what was then Austria-Hungary, *Kotěra designed the industrial town of Zlín (later in Czechoslovakia) for the Baťa concern: it was influenced by the ideas of Ebenezer *Howard. Later, Zlín's architecture was informed by the skeletal frames evolved in Chicago, IL: the main architectural protagonists were **František Lydie Gahura** (1891–1958—from 1927) and *Karfík (from 1930), who employed the *International-Modern style. In Finland *Aalto designed (1937) residential areas and an industrial complex for the cellulose industry, Sunila, near Kotka.

M.Crawford (1995); J.Curl (1983, 2007); Darley (1975); Garner (1984)

compartiment *Bed, patterned with designs formed with, e.g., box. The word tended to replace the English *plat*, *plot*, *quarter*, or *square*, yet was not really equivalent to any of these. To *compartition* a garden was to lay it out with *compartiments*. A *parterre de compartiment* is an embroidered *parterre symmetrical about two axes. The *compartiment* system dominated European garden-design from the late-C15 through C16: *compartiments* or *compartimenti* were ornamental subdivisions of a larger design, usually involving clipped box, knots, beds, borders, and walks. They functioned as independent designs, yet were arranged in groups of four or eight to comprise larger pictures. Aspects of medieval gardens were carried through for compartiment systems, involving lattice-fences, raised beds, arbours, and mazes. *See also* BAGH; CHAHAR BAGH; HEDGE; MUGHAL GARDEN; PARADISE GARDEN.

Crisp (1924); *GH*, **xxvii**/1 (Summer 1999), 32–53

compartment 1. Clearly defined area within a garden, often hedged or walled in. 2. Room in a building, or an area partitioned off. 3. Subdivision of a larger division in a building. 4. *Coffer in a ceiling.

compass-roof *See* ROOF.

compass-window *Bay-window.

Comper, Sir John Ninian (1864–1960) Aberdeen-born British architect. Whilst in the office of *Bodley and *Garner (1882–7), he learnt the intricacies and subtleties of late English *Gothic. In partnership (1888–1905) with **William Bucknall** (1851–1944), he designed the exquisite St Cyprian's, Clarence Gate, London (1902–3), in which the *altar is visible from all parts of the church and the sanctuary is defined using gilded *screens influenced by C14 English prototypes favoured by Bodley. A scholar of *Ecclesiology, Comper revived the *English altar with its *riddel-posts at St Wilfrid's, Cantley, Yorks. (1892–4—where he also designed the north *arcade and *aisle, *Rood-screen and loft, *parclose-screens, *reredos, and altar-canopy, all in an archaeologically correct late-Gothic style), and became a prolific designer of and authority on church fittings, furnishings, and, especially, stained glass. His richest creation is St Mary's, Wellingborough, Northants. (1904–31), in which Classical elements made their appearance, notably in the *ciborium, and the plaster-vaulting in the *nave has *pendants. He moved towards giving the altar a new dominance in Anglican church-architecture, and was a major influence on the liturgical revival: with St Philip, Cosham, Portsmouth, Hants. (1936–7), his ideal of 'unity by inclusion', drawing on various styles, combined with a free-standing sanctuary to realize a solution to church planning which accomplished the supremacy of the altar. One of his last works was the altar and reredos in *Craze's Shrine of Our Lady of Walsingham, Norfolk (1959).

Anson (1965); C.Brooks & Saint (eds) (1995); Buckley (1993); Comper (1893, 1897, 1933, 1940, 1950); J.Curl (2007); *ODNB* (2004); Symondson (1988)

compluvium *See* CAVAEDIUM.

Composite Order Grandest of the Roman *Orders, essentially an ornate version of the eight-voluted *Ionic capital known as the *angular capital or *Scamozzi Order under which are added two tiers of *acanthus-leaves. Its *entablature is also very ornate. It bears a resemblance to the *Corinthian Order and is also called the *Compound Order*.

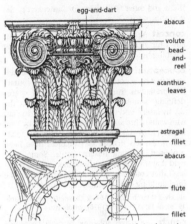

Composite Order Plan and elevation of circular and square capital (*after Langley*).

composition *or* **compo** 1. Type of *putty* made of whiting, glue, linseed-oil, and resin, subjected for two hours to the action of steam, and forced under pressure into moulds for ceiling ornaments, *mouldings on *boiserie, etc. 2. C18 *plaster mixes (normally consisting of *gypsum* and *size*) used instead of *stucco.

compound arch *See* ARCH.

compound pier *See* CLUSTER.

computer-aided design Also CAD or CAM (computer-aided manufacture). From the 1970s computers have been used in design as representations of complicated three-dimensional forms can be easily stored and manipulated. Images can be printed, architectural projections produced, and interiors explored in virtual reality. Details can be stored for reuse, avoiding the drudgery of repetitive hand-made drawings. To a certain extent the design-process has changed, but CAD may not be appropriate for all eventualities, especially when highly specialized knowledge of historic buildings is required.

Burger & Gillies (1989); Franke (1985); Jankel & Morton (1984); N.Johnson (1991); Lewell (1985); May (1985); Penman (1989); Penz (1992); Perkins (1989); Raker & H.Rice (1992); R.Reynolds (1987)

concatenation Union by *chaining* parts together, as with separate architectural elements in a long *façade (each with its own roof and separate composition), the fronts being brought forward or recessed, also called *staccato* composition. Concatenated façades were favoured by

*Kent and other *Palladians for *articulation. *See also* ADDITIVE.

conceit Agreeable *fabrique in a garden, usually whimsical, such as a *bridge not spanning anything but there purely for ornament.

conceptual architecture Architectural designs that have not been realized are 'conceptual'. Interpretations from the 1960s involved space-defining, simulated images projected into the sky by lasers, and volumes roofed by moving air, with walls of fire and water (e.g. proposals by **Yves Klein** (1928–62) and **Werner Ruhnau** (1922–2015)). Air-jets instead of structures have been proposed, creating instant forms. Some have held that it is the *process* (limitless and directionless) that counts in architecture, rather than the final building, which some might question.

AD, xlv/3 (March 1975), 187–8; *Casabella*, ccccxl (March 1976), 8–13; *DQ*, 78/79 (1970), whole issue

conch 1. Quarter-spherical *cupola or *dome over an *apse or *niche. **2.** *Pendentive. **3.** Shell motif over a *niche, etc.

concourse 1. Large space in e.g. a railway terminus or airport to accommodate many people. **2.** Place where several paths or roads meet in a park, e.g. *rond-point.

concrete Building material made by mixing fragments of hard material (*aggregate—usually broken stone) with *mortar (fine aggregate—usually sand, water, and a binding-agent—now usually *Portland *cement). Historically, concrete was made with lime, sand, and water, with brick-dust, crushed volcanic rock, and other materials. A type of concrete was used in Roman construction called **opus caementicium*, consisting of undressed stones bedded in a mix of lime and *pozzolan, which dried out quickly, so had to be laid in courses. By C1 AD the drying-out process could be retarded, thanks to the evolution of slow-drying mixes, and this facilitated the evolution of huge vaulted structures covering vast spaces. The Romans used types of concrete made of lime, with *tufa* (porous, light, volcanic rock found around Rome) and other aggregates for these *vaults, often in association with brick or stone reinforcement, and this created architecture where inner volumes were more important, perhaps, than the exteriors. Early examples of Roman architecture covered by concrete vaults are the *Domus Aurea* by *Severus, and the enormous *Pantheon in Rome, with its *coffered *dome.

Types of concrete were in use for *Byzantine structures but fell from favour until revived in C18, notably in France and England. Concrete was used by *Smirke in the structure of the British Museum, and concrete laid over hollow-brick

vaulting was used by Henry *Roberts for fire-proof construction in working-class housing (1850s). The discovery by **Joseph Aspdin** (1779–1855) of Portland cement made from lime and clay facilitated the development of immensely strong concrete structures as well as the evolution of a scientifically based theory. Strong in compression, concrete is weak in tension, so the weakness has to be eliminated if concrete is to be used in members subjected to tension, such as *beams. Reinforcement with metal was experimented with in the early C19, and *Loudon (1832) recorded concrete floors reinforced with interlacing iron bars. Other pioneers include *Coignet, *Monier, and **Louis-Joseph Vicat** (1786–1861—who produced cements that set under water, and classified them as 'hydraulic'), **William E.Ward** (1821–1906—who built a concrete house at Chester, NY, in 1873), and **Thaddeus Hyatt** (1816–1901). The last two published (1870s) theoretical works in the USA, but the theoretical basis for reinforced concrete evolved from the early work of **William Boutland Wilkinson** (1819–1902—who patented (1854) a reinforced-concrete floor system), and **Joseph-Louis Lambot** (1814–87—who exhibited his system of wire-mesh reinforced concrete at the 1855 *Exposition Universelle*, Paris). Monier licensed his patents in Germany (1885) through **Gustav Adolf Wayss** (1850–1917), who in turn commissioned **Matthias Koenen** (1849–1924) to research the theory of reinforced concrete, but a major advance came when *Hennebique developed concrete reinforced with steel (1892). In the USA advances were made by **Ernest L.Ransome** (1884–1911) and Albert *Kahn, leading to standardization and the mass-production of building components.

*Baudot's *St-Jean de Montmartre*, Paris (1894–1902), employed steel reinforcement in its brick-and-concrete construction, and *Maillart evolved designs for reinforced-concrete buildings from 1905, developing the theme of unified *pier and *vault known as 'mushroom slabs'. Max *Berg constructed (1910–13) the huge *Jahrhunderthalle*, Breslau (now Wrocław), of reinforced concrete, and *Perret began using reinforced concrete almost from the beginning of his career with the *Rue Franklin* flats, Paris (1903–4). The Royal Liver Building, Liverpool (1908–10), by **W.Aubrey Thomas** (1859–1934), is an early British example of reinforced-concrete construction on the Hennebique principle, while the same architect's Tower Buildings, near by (1908), expresses the frame more clearly, and is clad in *faïence. Reinforced concrete enabled very large *cantilevers to be constructed, but its major advantages were that it was capable of withstanding great compressive *and* tensile loads (as steel can), but with the important advantage of a high degree of fire-resistance. The evolution of complex reinforced-concrete structures was pioneered by *Freyssinet with his *bridges and *parabolic vaults. In later times, *Candela and *Nervi further developed reinforced-concrete structures (see BÉTON).

A.Allen (1988, 1992); Bennett (2001, 2002); P.Collins (1959); N.Davey (1961); J.Faber & Alsop (1976); B.Fröhlich (2002); Kind-Barkáuskas et al. (2002); S.Macdonald (ed.) (2003); W.McKay (1957); Mainstone (1975); Mallinson (1986); Newby (ed.) (2001); Stanley (1979); J.T (1996)

Concrete Regionalism Concrete used in ways supposedly responding to local conditions yet aspiring to meaning, monumentality, and symbolic architectural language.

Slessor (2000).

Conder, Hugh Neville (1922–2003) See CASSON.

Conder, Josiah (1852–1920) English architect, he worked with **Thomas Roger Smith** (1830–1903), and later with *Burges. He settled (1876) in Tokyo where he was appointed Professor of Architecture, and instructed the first generation of Japanese architects in the Western traditions, although he also inculcated a respect for ancient Japanese buildings, publishing several works on them and on indigenous landscape architecture.

ODNB (2004)

conditivum, conditorium Roman sepulchre containing *sarcophagi.

condominium Large development in which individual *apartments are privately owned, but all owners are bound by restrictive covenants. It is usual in major housing schemes, where for aesthetic and social reasons the fabric cannot be altered and communal spaces are shared.

conduit 1. Artificial *channel or pipe to convey water or other liquids; *aqueduct; *canal. 2. Structure, often elaborate, from which water issues from a pipe, e.g. Hobson's Conduit, Cambridge (1614). 3. Large *basin or laver.

cone 1. Cone-shaped building enclosing a tile-kiln, glass-furnace, etc. 2. Conical structure (e.g. the brick cone supporting the *lantern in St Paul's Cathedral, London).

Conefroy, Abbé Pierre (1752–1816) French-Canadian RC Vicar-General for the Montréal region of the Diocese of Québec. He devised a standardized plan for churches, based on mid-C17 prototypes, in which the apsidal *chancel was narrower than the *nave, and transeptal chapels were provided. The gabled west front was pierced by a central door, with a smaller door on each side, and single or twin *clochers were provided. Examples of his work are Ste-Marguerite,

L'Acadie, Québec (1800–1), and Ste-Famille, Boucherville (1801). Such conservative (even backward-looking) architecture emphasized cultural and religious identity.

K (1994)

cone mosaic Repetitive zigzag or lozenge patterns formed by embedding many clay cones around 10 cm (nearly 4 inches) long, with black, red, or buff heads, in mud walls, as at the Sumerian temples of Uruk (now Warka, Iraq), dating from c.3500–3000 BC, so a very early type of architectural enrichment.

J.T (1996)

confessio Place where the body of a Martyr or Confessor is kept, or the *crypt or *shrine under an *altar, in which such Relics are placed. By extension, the whole chapel or church, called *confession, confessional,* or *confessionary.*

confessional Booth, box, or cubicle in a church where confessions of penitents are heard.

conge *Echinus or similar *moulding (*swelling conge*), or a *cavetto (*hollow conge*).

congé, congee 1. *Apophyge, scape, or outward concave curves at the top and bottom of a Classical column-*shaft terminating in *fillets. 2. *Sanitary shoe,* or concave junction between a floor and a wall, used where a right-angled junction would be difficult to clean.

congelation *Rustication resembling icicles, as on *cascade-houses,*fountains, and *grottoes, also called *frosted.*

Connell, Amyas Douglas (1901–80) New Zealand-born architect, he practised in London from 1929 and entered into partnership (1932) with **Basil Robert Ward** (1902–78), joined (1933–39) by **Colin Anderson Lucas** (1906–84). As **Connell, Ward, & Lucas,** they designed (1930s) a whole series of advanced *International-Modern houses in England, much influenced by Le *Corbusier. Connell's most celebrated house was 'High and Over', Amersham, Bucks. (1928), built with a *reinforced-concrete frame on a three-pointed star-shaped plan. 'New Farm', Grayswood, Surrey (1932–3), displayed a series of cubic forms attached to a central circulation area. The firm's later work included the Tarburn House, Temple Gardens, Moor Park, Herts. (1937–8), the Walford House, Frognal, Hampstead (1937), 'Potcraft', Sutton, Surrey (1938), and the Proudman House, Roehampton, London (1938–9).

E (1994); Sharp (1967a, 2003)

conoid Form resembling a cone, as in the springing of a *Gothic *vault where the *ribs branch out.

consecration cross *See* CROSS.

conservation Retention of existing buildings or groups of buildings, landscapes, etc., taking care not to alter or destroy character or detail, even though repairs or changes may be necessary. Sensitive conservation (pioneered by *Morris and others connected with the *Arts-and-Crafts movement) is concerned to preserve as much original fabric as possible, making overt what is new. Conservation does not necessarily mean preservation: it can involve considerable intervention, even much new building, but the key to success is in respecting existing character, and even *enhancing* it. A *conservation area* is one designated as of special architectural or historic interest, where all changes should *enhance*, rather than *detract from*, its character. *Compounds include*:

conservation-based: project in which precedence is given to the retention of historic fabric and features held to be of interest or value: when there is a requirement to give priority to such retention, the project is said to be *conservation-driven*;

conservation-minded: philosophically inclined towards the retention of historic fabric held to be of interest or value.

JF; Huxtable (1970, 1986, 1986a); Weston (2003)

conservative wall Garden-wall against which glass structures are built to enable plants to be grown.

conservatory 1. Grander and more ornamental version of a *glass-house, *greenhouse, or *hot-house used for conserving plants, detached or joined to a dwelling, heated and kept humid. Early conservatories were of conventional construction, with large windows, but the finest examples date from C19 when iron-and-glass structures evolved in terms of invention and elegance. While there were early iron-and-glass conservatories in C18, including that at Hohenheim, near Stuttgart, J.C.*Loudon invented a curved bendable sash-bar of iron that made further developments possible, including the Great Stove at Chatsworth, Derbys. (1836–40) by *Burton and *Paxton. 2. Public building devoted to the cultivation of, and instruction in, any branch of art or science, especially music.

Hix (1996); Kohlmaier & von Sartory (1986); Koppelkamm (1981); Loudon (1834); Marston (1992); M.Woods & Warren (1988)

console Type of Classical bracket or *corbel with parallel sides, usually an *ogee curve terminating in a *volute at the top and bottom surmounted by a horizontal slab, often moulded, fixed upright to a wall with the greater projection at the top. Called *ancon, *crossette, *parotis, *shoulder, or *truss, it is commonly found e.g.

on each side of the top of a door- or window-*architrave, supporting the *cornice. In a horizontal position, the curved part downwards and the bigger scroll at the end fixed to a wall, it appears to carry an element, e.g. a *balcony, and thus suggests a *cantilevered form. Horizontal consoles fixed to the *soffits of a building's crowning cornice and appearing to support it are *modillions. Wedge-shaped (sides not parallel) consoles or *key-stones are *ancones.

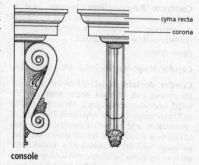

cyma recta
corona

console

Constructivism Anti-aesthetic, anti-art, supposedly pro-technology (in that it favoured the use of man-made industrial materials and processes e.g. welding), Left-wing movement originating in the USSR from *c.*1920, later promoted in the West, notably at the *Bauhaus. Although its scope varied, and was never very clearly defined, many Constructivists insisted that architecture was simply the means of expressing a structure made using industrial processes and machine-made parts, with no hint of craftsmanship, and tended to stress utilitarian aspects, especially the function of elements of the building. The best-known Russian Constructivist projects were *Tatlin's huge monument to the Third International (1920), a distorted *frustum in the form of a diminishing spiral; *Mel'nikov's Rusakov Club, Moscow (1927–8), with *cantilevered *concrete lecture-halls expressed on the main *elevation (and yet some commentators would deny that Mel'nikov was a Constructivist at all, seeing him more as a 'Productivist' (anti-aesthetic technician) concerned with timber structures, as in his pavilions for the Moscow Exhibition (1923) and the Paris *Exposition* (1924–5)); and *Vesnin's project for the *Leningradskaya Pravda* building in Moscow (1923), with advertising signs, clocks, loudspeakers, lifts, and a searchlight all incorporated and expressed as integral elements of the design. One of the key figures was El *Lissitzky, who was the link between Russian Constructivism and Western Europeans such as *Duiker, *Gropius, *Meyer, and *Stam. The last worked on *Brinkman and van der Vlugt's *Van Nelle* factory, Rotterdam, held by some to be the best example of Constructivism in the West. The movement gave rise to many sub-theories and factions, some more extreme than others, and Constructivist themes have re-emerged in recent years in the work of **Richard George Rogers** (1933-), notably the *Centre Pompidou*, Paris (1972–7), and Lloyd's Building, London (1978–86). Russian Constructivism's anti-environmentalist aspects, jagged overlapping diagonal forms, expression of mechanical elements (such as services, lifts, etc.), have proved to be potent precedents for *High-Tech architecture, and, more recently, for the followers of *Deconstructivism.

Ingberman (1994); Js (2002); J & W (1988); K-M (1975, 1986, 1991); Kopp (1970); L (1988); Ly (1970, 1981); Ly-Küppers (1980); Lodder (1983); Margolin (1997); Richter (1958); Salingaros et al. (2004); O.Shv (1970)

container From at least Ancient Egyptian times, plants were transported in *containers*, and the practice continued into the times of the Greeks and Romans: evidence from *Pompeii and *Herculaneum suggests that *atria* had plant containers arranged around central pools. Containers for plants therefore have impressive histories: as ornaments and as means of moving plants over long or short distances, they have been features of gardens for millennia. During the *Renaissance period containers themselves became more elaborate, and were used to embellish gardens: various publications demonstrated how containers could be arranged, and by the *Baroque period they were ubiquitous in Europe. In C17 gardens, container-pots were often disposed in symmetrical patterns in *parterres*, placed on walls set along *terraces, etc.: plants could be moved into *conservatories during winter. The arrival of exotic plants from the Americas and elsewhere from C17 (and especially C18) stimulated the use of containers and the building of conservatories. Manufacturing processes in C19 produced vast numbers of containers made of many different materials, often brightly coloured. The widespread use of containers is termed *container gardening*.

Crisp (1924); Shoe (2001); Tay (2006)

Contamin, Victor (1840–93) French architect/engineer. He assisted *Dutert in the design of the *Galerie des Machines, Exposition Universelle*, Paris (1889).

J.T (1996)

Contant d'Ivry, Pierre (1698–1777) Parisian architect, who was the first to develop *Cordemoy's theories. His Churches of *St-Vasnon*, Condé-sur-L'Escaut (1751), and *St-Vaast*, Arras (1775–7—completed 1833), had continuous rows of columns carrying *entablatures from which sprang *vaults, while his *Abbaye Royale de Penthémont* (104–6 *Rue de Grenelle*, Paris (1747–56)) also demonstrated his interest in refined constructional techniques. His grand staircase at the *Palais Royal*, Paris (1756–70), was one of the most elegant of its period, and his only partially executed design for the *Madeleine*, Paris (1761), exploited columns and entablatures carrying vaults in a manner similar to that adopted by *Soufflot at *Ste-Geneviève*.

Contant d'Ivry (1769); F.Kretzschmar (1981); M & Wa (1987)

Contemporary style Style of design prevalent in Britain (*c*.1945–56). In architecture it included the type of light structures of the 1951 *Festival of Britain, and many of that Exhibition's design-motifs were adopted as *clichés* of the period. It evolved from late-1930s styling and the post-war technologies of laminates and alloys.

M.Ba & Hillier (eds) (1976); Sissons & French (eds) (1964)

contextual architecture Also called *Contextualism*, the term suggests an architecture that responds to its surroundings by respecting what is already there, unlike *Constructivism or *Deconstructivism which deliberately work against established geometries and fabric.

K.Ray (ed.) (1980); Tugnutt & M.R (1987)

contractura Tapered *diminution of a column-shaft from top to bottom, without *entasis, and wider at the top, as in Ancient Crete.

conurbation Term coined by *Geddes *c*.1915 for an aggregate of towns linked up to form one built-up area, e.g. the Potteries district of Staffs., or Greater London.

convent Building housing a company of men or women living in the discipline of a religious Order and under one Superior, more usually referring to a *nunnery*, i.e. for women only.

Cook, Sir Peter Frederic Chester (1936-)
See ARCHIGRAM; ZOÖMORPHIC.

Cooley, Thomas (*c*.1740–84) English architect, he gained early experience in Robert *Mylne's office, and won the competition to design the Royal Exchange (now City Hall), Dublin (1769–79), which encouraged him to move to the Irish capital. Appointed (1775) Clerk and Inspector of Civil Buildings in Dublin, he was the most important figure in the profession for a few years, and was significant in the creation of Irish *Neo-Classicism. He designed Caledon House, Co. Tyrone (1779), later (1812) extended by *Nash, and, with

Francis *Johnston, designed several buildings in the Archdiocese of Armagh for **Richard Robinson** (1709–94—**Archbishop of Armagh** from 1765), including the Primate's Chapel (1781–5), and Public Library (1770–1—later extended by others), both in Armagh. He was involved in the design of several country-houses, and was responsible for the Public Offices (1776–84), the *Sublime (now demolished) Newgate Gaol (1775–81), and early plans for the Four Courts (all in Dublin). By 1781 Cooley was overshadowed by *Gandon, who was to complete the Four Courts (1786–1802) and many other important Dublin public buildings.

M.Craig (1969, 1982); McP (2001); Mulligan (2013)

Cooper, Anthony Ashley (1671–1713—**3rd Earl of Shaftesbury** from 1699) English writer/philosopher/politician, influenced by **John Locke** (1632–1704). Following an extended Continental tour (which, with his friendship with **Robert Molesworth** (1656–1725), confirmed his Whig sympathies), he wrote *A Letter Concerning the Art, or Science of Design* (c.1712), in which he argued for a 'National Taste' avoiding corrupting influences, notably Absolutism and Roman Catholicism: it was published in the 1714 illustrated edition of his *Characteristicks*... His writings had a profound impact on taste in architecture, painting, and gardens well into C18, and also impacted on several important writers in the British Isles (e.g. *Pope and **Francis Hutcheson** (1694–1746)) and on the Continent (e.g. **Denis Diderot** (1713–84) and **Gotthold Ephraim Lessing** (1729–81)).

Cooper (1714); Mowl (2000); *ODNB* (2004)

Cooper, Sir Thomas Edwin (1874–1942) English architect, partner (1903–10) of **Samuel Bridgman Russell** (1864–1955), with whom he designed the Guildhall and Law Courts, Hull (1905–14); the *Neo-Georgian Royal Grammar School, Newcastle upon Tyne (1904–7), and other fine *Edwardian buildings. When the partnership ended, Cooper went on to design St Marylebone Town Hall and Library, London (1911–39); the imposing headquarters of the Port of London Authority, Trinity Square, London (1912–22); and the offices of Lloyd's, Leadenhall Street (1925–8—destroyed), among other buildings. His work was essentially Classical, and sometimes powerfully *Baroque.

A.S.Gray (1985); *ODNB* (2004)

cop Merlon. *See* BATTLEMENT.

cope, coping Top course (*capping*) of *masonry, brick, etc., usually sloping, of a *chimney, *gable, parapet, or wall, formed of *cap-stones, *copstones, copestones,* or *coping-stones* to throw off water. *Feather-edged* coping is thinner on one

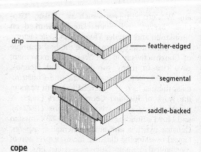

cope

side than on the other, and *saddle-back* coping has a triangular section with a *ridge.

Copeland, Robert Morris (1830–74) American landscape architect, he was first a scientific farmer (like *Olmsted) before setting up (1854) a practice in landscape and ornamental gardening with *Cleveland, with whom he designed Oak Grove Cemetery, Gloucester (1855), and Sleepy Hollow Cemetery, Concord (1855–6), both MA. His *Country Life: A Book of Agriculture, Horticulture, and Landscape Gardening* (1859) emphasized technical sides of farming and artistic aspects of landscape-design, what he called the 'Useful and the Beautiful'. Advanced for the time, he advocated the connection of parks, weaving them through urban fabric: in his *The Most Beautiful City in America: Essay and Plan for the Improvement of the City of Boston* (1872) he developed these ideas regionally, and although Olmsted is usually given credit for the Boston park system, Copeland was among its creators.

Copeland (2009); Shoe (2001)

Coppedè, Florentine Gino (1866–1927) Italian master of *Stile Liberty. He designed the *Neo-Gothic *Castello Mackenzie* (1896–1906), the *Mannerist *Palazzo Zuccarino* (1907), and several family tombs in as well as the entrance (1904) to the English *cemetery at the *Staglieno*, all in Genoa. Responsible for the brilliant *Quartiere Coppedè*, around the *Piazza Mincio*, Rome (1921–7), he demonstrated how new urban fabric can have a richness of decorative treatment as interesting as anything in the older parts of the city: this he achieved by a *collage of features drawn from various periods and in different styles to give his buildings a kind of fictional history, as well as a humane scale, which prompted sour *Modernist labelling of his work as 'irrelevant' and 'not of today', despite its obvious success. His brother, **Adolfo** (1871–1951), with **Dario Carbone** (1857–1934), designed the *Neo-Baroque *Palazzo Borsa*, Genoa (1907–12), and was also responsible for the *Casa del Fascio*, Signa, Florence (1928).

Architecture (Nov. 1984), 76–8; Capellini & Poleggi (1998); Etlin (1991); GS

coppice Small wood or thicket of deciduous trees (e.g. oak, hazel, sweet chestnut, and willow) grown for the purpose of periodical rotational cutting (*coppicing*) down to a low stump (*coppice-stool*) to encourage the growth of long, thin uprights used for basket-making, fences, hurdles, thatching, etc. In recent years willow has emerged as a desirable organic material in the fine and applied arts, not least for its flexibility.

Darvill (2003); Goulty (1991); Symes (2006)

Coptic architecture Christian Egyptian architecture consisting of *coenobitic cells, funerary monuments, and monastic and urban churches. The Coptic Church developed separately from 451. Among the most impressive works of Coptic architecture was the Cathedral at Hermopolis Magna (*c.*430–40), with an *apse, apsidal *transepts, a gallery, and an *atrium: three apses recur at the White and Red Monasteries, near Sohag (C5 and C6 respectively). The *basilican plan with variations was used, and *capitals based on *Corinthian and *Byzantine basket types recurred. *Domes and *vaults were commonly employed (e.g. the Holy Martyrs, Esna (C11), and the monastery of Deïr-el-Baramus, Wadi Natrun (C12)). *See also* ETHIOPIAN ARCHITECTURE.

A.Butler (1970); Kra (1986); J.T (1996)

coquillage Carved representations of shell-forms, e.g. at *niche-heads or in *rocaille decorations.

cora (*pl.* **corae**) Any column in the form of a young woman (as in the *prostasis* of the *Erechtheion*, Athens), also called *caryatid.

Corazzi, Antonio (1792–1877) Italian-born leading C19 architect in Warsaw responsible for many distinguished *Neo-Classical buildings, including the Grand Theatre (1826–33), the Stock Exchange, now Polish Bank (1828–30), the Staszic Palace (1820–3), and the County Headquarters at Radom (1822–7).

L & R (1984)

corbeil, corbeille 1. Architectural element resembling a basket containing flowers and fruit, often in relief or placed on *pedestals as terminal ornaments. 2. *Capital in the form of a basket over heads of *canephorae or *corae, varying in size and type. 3. *Campana or *calathus*.

corbel Projection from a wall-face consisting of a *block built into it, supporting any superincumbent load such as an arch, *beam, *parapet, *truss, etc., so essentially a *cantilever. *Corbelling*

consists of successive courses of corbels forming a pseudo-*vault or supporting an element projecting over the wall below, such as a *tourelle. *See also* BARTISAN; CHEQUER-SET; MACHICOLATION.

Compounds include:

corbel-arch: pseudo-arch formed of successive corbels, really cantilevers, anchored back, each projecting over the corbel below;

corbel-course: continuous uninterrupted *course of corbels forming a projection or projecting *moulding;

corbel-gable: incorrect term for a *crow-stepped *gable;

corbel-piece: *bolster-work, suggesting a stone projecting face, as in *rustication;

corbel-ring: old term for *band of a shaft or a *shaft-ring;

corbel-table: row of corbels, often with carved heads on them, set at intervals, sometimes carrying connecting arches (*Lombardy frieze), but more often simply supporting a projecting wall, especially a *battlement or *parapet. *See also* ARCADE;

corbel-vault: vault built using the same technique as in a corbel-arch.

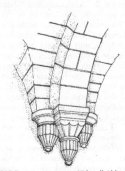

corbel C12 Romanesque type, Kirkstall Abbey, Yorks. (*after Parker*).

Corbie, Pierre de (*fl.*1215–50) French master-mason, called **Petrus de Corbeis** by *Villard de Honnecourt, and mentioned by *Viollet-le-Duc in his *Dictionnaire* as having designed several churches in Picardy. He may have made designs for parts of Rheims (1215) and Cambrai (1230–43) Cathedrals.

W.Pa (1852); S (1901–2); Viollet-le-Duc (1875)

corbie-step *See* CROW-STEPS.

Corbusier, Le Pseudonym (from 1920— meaning 'the crow-like one') of Swiss-born architect **Charles-Édouard Jeanneret-Gris** (1887–1965), who was probably the most influential (and not

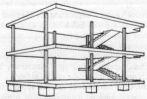

Dom-Ino skeleton showing floor-slabs supported on columns (*after Le Corbusier*).

entirely beneficial) figure in C20 architecture. He built (with **René Chapallaz** (1881–1976)) his first house, the *Villa Fallet*, La Chaux-de-Fonds, Switzerland (1906–7), partly influenced by *vernacular architecture, before setting off on one of a series of educational journeys. His visits (1907–8) took him to the medieval *Carthusian monastery (*Certosa di Val d'Ema*—which impressed as an example of how repetitive living-quarters could be organized within one monumental composition), and he appears to have met leading Viennese architects, including *Hoffmann. He also designed the *Jacquemet* and *Stotzer* villas, La Chaux-de-Fonds, then worked briefly (1908–9) with *Perret in Paris before making a study-visit to Germany, working in *Behrens's Berlin office (1910–11), and meeting leading German figures in the *Arts-and-Crafts movement and *Deutscher Werkbund*, including *Muthesius and *Tessenow. At that time he absorbed the works of *Viollet-le-Duc, *Sitte, and *Choisy, and wrote a report on the decorative-art movement in Germany (published 1912), in which his admiration for German organization was expressed. He travelled (1911) down the Danube to Istanbul, returning through Greece and Italy, which profoundly affected his perceptions, and made him more aware of the power of the primitive, the rugged, and the ruined, while awakening his appreciation of the qualities of southern light. At the end of 1911 he returned to Switzerland, was involved in teaching and in the Swiss equivalent of the *Werkbund*, but, more especially, designed several buildings, including the *Villas Jeanneret* (1911–12), *Favre-Jacot* (1912–13), and *Schwob* (1916–17). This last was one of his first *reinforced-concrete houses, clearly influenced by Perret and Behrens in its *stripped Neo-Classical form: it gained him recognition, and was published. During this period at La Chaux-de-Fonds he evolved (1914–15) the low-cost *Maison Dom-Ino*, the name of which evolved from the Latin *domus* (house) and the *innovative* reinforced-concrete column-grid that suggested the patterns of a *domino*-piece. Essentially, columns supported floor-slabs, and the design offered a prototype for industrialized living-units, giving

freedom in matters of room-arrangement and elevational treatment: non-structural partitions could be placed where desired, and the elevations filled with any design of glazing and solid uninhibited by structural requirements because the columns were not placed around the edges of the slabs, but back from the perimeters.

Jeanneret-Gris settled in Paris (1916), where he developed skills as a self-publicist. Through Perret he met the painter *Ozenfant, and, having absorbed *Cubism and *Futurism, together they invented *Purism, where the primacy of the objects was insisted upon, disposed on canvas using a proportioning device based on the *Golden Section, and depicted by means of a limited range of pure colours. Purism was promulgated in the manifesto *Après le Cubisme* (1918) and *L'Esprit Nouveau* (1920–5), a journal edited by Jeanneret-Gris and Ozenfant which also contained ideas on architecture, published under the pseudonym 'Le Corbusier': those contributions were collected in *Vers une architecture* (1923), translated as *Towards a New Architecture* (1927), and became influential texts. Their heady brew of the latest technology, messianic slogans proclaiming the supposed moral and hygienic virtues of the architectural language, and dodgy claims that ideas therein derived from Antiquity, attracted uncritical devotees. In his writings Le Corbusier defined architecture as a play of masses brought together in light, and advocated that buildings should be as practically constructed as a modern machine, with 'rational' planning, and capable of being erected using mass-produced components.

Another study-visit to Italy (1922) was followed by the exhibition of his *Maison Citrohan*: it started (1919) as a box-like form with the structural walls along the long sides, but evolved with the introduction of *pilotis* to raise the building from the ground. The name suggests the **Citroën** motor-car, with its connotations of mass-production and industrialization, logical evolution, economy, and efficiency. From 1921 Le Corbusier collaborated with his cousin, A.-A.-P.*Jeanneret-Gris, and their Paris office attracted many architects, for from it flowed *Modernist polemics and designs for experimental housing in which simple forms and smooth surfaces were expressed. The *Citrohan* houses were published in *L'Esprit Nouveau* and *Vers une architecture*, and were the precedents for the realized designs at the *Villa Besnus*, Vaucresson (1922–3), followed by many more, including the influential *Villa Stein* at Garches (1927), two houses at the *Weissenhofsiedlung*, Stuttgart (1927), and the *Villa Savoie*, Poissy (1928–31). The last was the definitive exemplar of the famous *Five Points for a New Architecture*, and, with its formal architectural language, *pilotis*, linkage of external and internal spaces, long strip-windows, and crisp, uncompromising lines, became a powerful paradigm for C20 supposed *Rationalism. The *cinq points*, with other ideas, were expounded in Alfred *Roth's *Zwei Wohnhäuser von Le Corbusier und Pierre Jeanneret* (1927): they were, in essence, the use of *pilotis* as structural elements, lifting the building and leaving a space under it; columnar-and-slab construction enabling floor-plans to be left as free and adaptable as possible, partitions (if required) not being structural; the creation of a roof-garden at the top, affording better light and air than on the ground; the mode of construction facilitating long continuous strips of windows; and complete freedom of façade-design.

At the *Exposition International des Arts-Décoratifs et Industriels Modernes*, Paris (1924–5), Le Corbusier and Jeanneret-Gris presented their *Pavillon de l'Esprit Nouveau*. A white box derived from an L-shaped variant of the *Citrohan* type, it contained a model of the so-called *Plan Voisin* for Paris, an architectural and town-planning time-bomb, proposing the complete destruction of part of Paris east of the Louvre, between Montmartre and the Seine, and its replacement with eighteen gigantic *skyscrapers. Earlier (1910), Le Corbusier had prepared *La Construction des Villes*, much influenced by *Sitte, in which he analysed town-planning taking into account the existing historic cores, but this approach was to be wholly jettisoned by 1925 when *Urbanisme* came out (translated as *The City of Tomorrow and Its Planning*, 1929). The *Ville Contemporaine*, a design for a city of 3 million inhabitants (1922), and the *Plan Voisin* provided the imagery for redevelopment and new towns that was to be almost universally adopted (largely through the influence of *CIAM, with which Le Corbusier and Jeanneret-Gris were to be intimately connected from its beginnings (1928)) after the 1939–45 war with such disastrous results for countless towns and cities.

His pernicious mis-titled book, *La Ville Radieuse* (1935), contains demands for a Utopian city in which buildings conforming to his aesthetic would be erected. In the 1930s, indeed, he was able to build paradigmatic structures in Paris, including the *Pavillon Suisse, Cité Universitaire* (1930–3), and the *Cité de Refuge* (1929–33). These slab-blocks of framed construction were designed with large areas of glass (the *curtain-wall) that caused difficulties with solar-heat gain and glare as well as heat-loss, yet were to be progenitors of countless problematic slab-blocks thereafter solely because of *image* and pseudo-religious belief. Such facts can only be explained by obsessions about glass (perhaps derived from the slogans of *Taut) as an indicator of 'modernity', 'progressiveness', and 'cleanliness'. Large-scale projects also occupied Le Corbusier from the late 1920s, including the competition designs

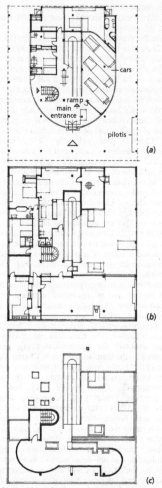

Corbusier Plans of *Villa Savoie* (*Savoye*), Poissy, near Paris (*after Le Corbusier*). (*a*) Ground-floor showing pilotis, car-parking arrangements, entrance, central ramp, and stair. (*b*) First floor. (*c*) Second floor.

for the League of Nations Palace, Geneva (1927), and the Palace of the Soviets, Moscow (1931). With Soviet disciples, he built (1928–36) the *Tsentrosoyuz* Building, Moscow, and prepared other designs, including the Ministry of Education and Health, Rio de Janeiro, Brazil (executed by *Costa, *Niemeyer, and *Reidy, 1936–43), and a preliminary project for the United Nations Building, NYC (final design and execution by *Harrison and *Abramovitz, 1947–50).

For the *Exposition Internationale*, Paris (1937), Le Corbusier built the *Pavillon des Temps Nouveaux* of steel, with a *tent-like canvas roof, the whole derived from an image of the Jewish Tabernacle in the Wilderness mixed with elements of aeroplane structures. The slogan over the rostrum evoked the Popular Front (a union of Communist, Socialist, and Radical parties), and inside, like the Ten Commandments, were CIAM principles, some of which would be incorporated in the *Athens Charter. Thus, politically, Le Corbusier's brand of *Modernism appeared to be allied with the Left, but his position throughout the 1930s was ambivalent, for he was also involved with the Syndicalists (who had affiliations with Fascism), and sympathized with the Vichy régime, which affected his relationships with both Jeanneret-Gris and *Perriand, but had no effect whatsoever on his hero-worshipping disciples.

After 1945 Le Corbusier abandoned the smooth images with which he had been associated, and produced a series of aggressive, massively constructed buildings, beginning with the huge *Unité d'Habitation*, Marseilles (1946–52). Originally a steel frame had been proposed, but shortages led to the use of reinforced concrete, with board-marked *béton-brut, much use of the *brise-soleil, and a system of proportions based on Le Corbusier's *Modulor, derived from the *Golden Section. The *Unité* was conceived as a huge structure for autonomous living, partly inspired by the Utopian theories of **Charles Fourier** (1772–1837), with a shopping-street, hotel, gymnasium, crèche, community services, and running-track. Other *Unités* were built at Nantes-Rezé (1952–7), Charlottenburg, Berlin (1956–8), Meaux (1957–9), Briey-en-Fôret (1957–60), and Firminy-Vert (1962–8): apartments within them were two-storey living units with double-height living space, linked by internal 'streets'. The *images* of the *Unités* were copied in a ludicrously scaled-down form at Roehampton Park by the LCC's Department of Architecture (1952–5), but the immediate international influence was in the use of raw, unfaced concrete in countless buildings, giving rise to the style known as New *Brutalism. Powerful, chunky forms of *béton-brut* recurred at the Dominican Monastery of *Ste-Marie-de-la-Tourette* at Eveux-sur-Arbresle, near Lyons (1953–9).

Le Corbusier's Pilgrimage Church of *Notre-Dame-du-Haut* at Ronchamp (1950–4), with its *battered walls filled with rubble and sprayed with *Gunnite* (a patent rough-cast finish), silo-like tower, windows of many shapes and sizes piercing the walls at random, and distorted boat-like roof apparently floating over the walls,

seemed to suggest a complete shift towards anti-*Rationalism (causing infantile consternation in CIAM). At the *Maisons Jaoul*, Neuilly-sur-Seine (1952–6), coarsely laid brickwork, oversized concrete beams, and segmental *vaults influenced architects such as *Spence and *Stirling.

With *Drew, *Fry, and others, Le Corbusier laid out (1950s) Chandigarh as the administrative capital of the Punjab, India, and built several gigantic public buildings (using excessively heavy, oversized, chunky, raw concrete) that were influential, notably in Japan, and were (like the *Unités*) attempts to create a spurious 'monumentality' (a tendency denounced as early as 1929 by *Teige). One of his last significant buildings was the Carpenter Center for the Visual Arts, Harvard University, Cambridge, MA (1960–3). Some commentators have defended Corbusier from charges of totalitarianism: however, his adoption of a pseudonym is uncomfortably reminiscent of other, hardly liberal-minded dictators (*see* BELLOT).

AA (2003); P.Baker (1996, 1996a); Besset (1976); Birksted (2009); Boesiger (ed.) (1966–70, 1972); H.Brooks (ed.) (1982, 1987, 1987a); Choay (1960); Wi.Cu (1995a); E.Darling (2000); Etlin (1994); F (2001; 2002a); Franclieu (ed.) (1981–2); D.Gans (2000); J-G (1964, 1968, 1973, 1973–7); J-G & J-G (1999); Js (1973, 2000); Jenger (1996); Lucan (ed.) (1987); Moos (2009); Murray & Osley (eds) (2009); Ozenfant & J-G (1975); P (1982); Raeburn & W.Wilson (eds) (1987); T & DC (1986); Tzonis (2001); Walden (ed.) (1977)

Cordemoy, Abbé Jean-Louis de (*c.*1660–1713) French priest/architectural theorist (not to be confused with **L.-G.de Cordemoy** (1651–1722)). His *Nouveau Traité de Toute l'Architecture* (1706) was an important influence on the search for truth, simplicity, and honest expression of form, drawing on the works of *Perrault, and demonstrating an early understanding of the sophistication of *Gothic structures. His argument was essentially in favour of Classical clarity with the *Orders *used structurally*, all unnecessary ornament eschewed, design that drew upon Nature and Antiquity, and buildings that *expressed their purpose*. An influence on *Laugier, he was a precursor of *Neo-Classicism.

Cordemoy (1714); Hn (1962); *JWCI*, xxv (1962), 278–320, and xxvi (1963), 90–123; Ry (1980)

cordon 1. *String- or belt-course, usually a *band, projecting slightly from a wall, normally used in connection with fortifications. **2.** Slightly projecting step or riser at the lower edge of each part of a stepped ramp so that each section between steps has less of an inclination than the ramp as a whole (called *scala cordonata* or *scala a cordoni*), for surer footing, essentially a step-division in an inclined plane.

coretti *Galleries resembling theatre-boxes in the *choirs of *Baroque churches.

Corinthian Order Classical *Order of architecture, *third* of the Greek Orders and *fourth* of the Roman. Slender and elegant, it consists of a *base (usually of the *Attic type, often with further enrichment, or a more elaborately moulded variety, called *spira*) on a *plinth; a tall *shaft (fluted or plain); a *capital (the distinguishing feature, consisting of two rows of *acanthus-leaves over the *astragal, with *caules rising from the acanthus-leaves and sprouting *helices or *volutes from each *calyx with *bud) with concave-sided *abacus (with chamfered or pointed corners) in the centre of each face of which is a *fleuron in the Roman version and sometimes an *anthemion or *palmette in the Greek; and an *entablature, often of great magnificence, with *bead-and-reel between *fasciae of the *architrave, *frieze

ornamented with continuous sculpture, and *cornice with ornate *coffers and richly carved *modillions.

Supposedly invented by *Callimachus, the capital is essentially a bell-like core (*campana) from which the acanthus-leaves, caules, helices, etc., sprout, reflecting its origin as vegetation growing from a basket capped with a slab. Among the earliest examples of the *Greek Corinthian Order* were the three (or possibly only one) at the end of the *naos of the temple of *Apollo Epicurius*, *Bassae (*c.*429–*c.*400 BC), but the beautiful capitals of the *Choragic Monument of Lysicrates, Athens (334 BC), were among the most elegant ever designed (and probably the first to be used externally): they were much admired and copied after being recorded by *Stuart and *Revett in *The Antiquities of Athens* (1762). The Lysicrates capital is taller than most other examples of the Order, with the shaft *fillets terminating in leaf- or

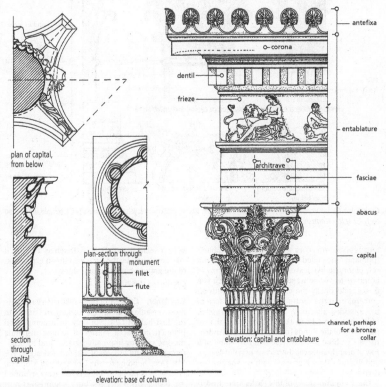

plan of capital, from below

plan-section through monument
— fillet
— flute

section through capital

elevation: base of column

elevation: capital and entablature

— antefixa

O—corona

dentil—
frieze—

— entablature

architrave
— fasciae

— abacus

— capital

— channel, perhaps for a bronze collar

Corinthian Order Greek-Corinthian Order, Choragic Monument of Lysicrates (334 BC) (*after Normand*).

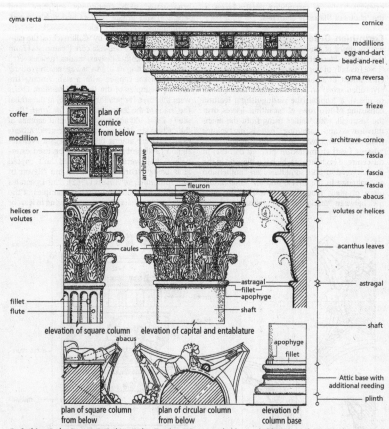

cyma recta — ⎯ cornice
— modillions
— egg-and-dart
— bead-and-reel
— cyma reversa

coffer —
plan of cornice from below
— frieze

modillion —
— architrave-cornice
— fascia
— fascia
— fascia
fleuron
— abacus

helices or volutes
— volutes or helices

caules
— acanthus leaves

astragal
fillet
apophyge
— astragal

fillet
flute
shaft
— shaft

elevation of square column from below   elevation of capital and entablature

abacus
apophyge
fillet

— Attic base with additional reeding
— plinth

plan of square column from below   plan of circular column from below   elevation of column base

Corinthian Order Roman-Corinthian Order, *Pantheon*, Rome, probably recycled from an early C1 temple, re-erected early C2 (*after Normand*).

tongue-like forms over which is a recessed band (probably once filled with a metal collar), then a row of tongue-like leaves above which is a row of acanthus-leaves between each pair of which is a flower, and finally the exquisite volutes with an anthemion in the centre of each concave face of the moulded abacus. A simpler type of capital, often found in C18 work in Britain, was that of the Tower of the Winds (or *Horologium* of **Andronicus Cyrrhus**), Athens (*c*.50 BC), consisting of a row of acanthus-leaves then a row of palm-leaves, and finally a square abacus, with no volutes (*see* CAPITAL).

Greek column-shafts of this Order were invariably fluted. Not surprisingly, the Order has always

been associated with Beauty. Taken as a whole, it was developed by the Romans into an expression of the grandest architectural show.

C.Normand (1852)

Cormier, Ernest (1885–1980) Perhaps the most versatile of architects working in Canada in the first half of C20. Not only an accomplished planner, he was a master of joining disparate masses, creating impressive spaces, and incorporating beautiful ornament within his designs. His *Art-Deco building for the University of Montréal (1928–35) is probably his greatest work, planned on *Beaux-Arts principles, but his Supreme Court Building, Ottawa (1938–50), draws on stripped

*Classicism and French C17 precedents, notably in its steeply pitched roofs. Cormier's own house in Montréal (1930–1) was influenced by contemporary European *Modernism, with Art-Deco-inspired interiors, while his National Printing Bureau, Hull, Québec (1950–8), incorporated technical innovations such as the *curtain-wall.

K (1994)

Cormont, Thomas de (*fl.*1235–50) French master-mason, he assisted *Luzarches at Amiens Cathedral, succeeding him as architect (*c.*1235), and supervising the construction of the *nave up to the springing of the *vaults. His son, **Regnault** *or* **Reynaud**, succeeded him at Amiens (*c.*1250), completing the vaults, and probably building the *choir, *Lady Chapel, and northern *transept with *rose-window. He began the south transept, completed 1296.

W.Pa (1852); J.T (1996)

corn-cob Carving of the woody receptacle to which the grains are attached in an ear of maize, used in a variation of the *Corinthian *Order invented by *Latrobe for the US Capitol Building, Washington, DC, after 1814, and called the *American Order. Corn-cobs recur as C19 *finials, popularized by Latrobe's design.

corner Angle, so meeting of two converging walls forming an angular extremity: therefore *quoin. *Compounds include*:

corner-bead: angle-bead forming the corner of plastered walls to avoid a vulnerable *arris;

corner-brace: short *brace set horizontally between a *tie-beam and a wall-plate, stiffening the structure;

corner-capital: angle-capital;

corner-post: structural upright at the corner of a *timber-framed building;

corner-stone: **a.** *quoin; **b.** foundation-stone.

Cornforth, John Lewley (1937–2004) English writer, he worked for *Country Life* for over 40 years, establishing interior decoration as a worthy subject for art historians. With Oliver *Hill, he published *Caroline: 1625–1685* (1966), a success which encouraged him in his researches concerning C17 and C18 country-houses. John *Fowler collaborated with him for *English Decoration in the 18th Century* (1974), one of the first books on the subject based on documentary research as well as on study of surviving exemplars. Cornforth followed with his own *English Interiors, 1790–1848* (1978), and what was perhaps his most original work, *The Inspiration of the Past* (1985). His polemic, *The Country Houses of England: Can they Survive?* (1974), was a catalyst for the influential exhibition at the Victoria & Albert Museum, *Destruction of the Country House* (1975–6). He

wrote many guides to country-houses (e.g. Berrington Hall, Herefs.), and his *London Interiors* (2000) was a memorial to his abiding affection for the capital. His posthumously published (2004) *Early Georgian Interiors* was one of his finest achievements.

Cornforth (1974, 1978, 1985, 2000, 2004); Fowler & Cornforth (1974); *The Guardian* (8 May 2004), Obits.; Hill & Cornforth (1966); *Independent* (8 May 2004), Obits.; pk

cornice 1. Uppermost division of a Classical *entablature. **2.** Crowning projecting moulded horizontal top of a building (if very large and crowning the main *façade of e.g. a *palazzo, it is termed *cornicione) or part of a building (e.g. a *pedestal (where it is the *cap), or a wall, termed *wall-cornice). It is an *eaves-cornice* if it occurs where a roof overhangs a wall and forms *eaves with a Classical *moulding, or a *crown-moulding* if at the junction of an internal wall and ceiling. A cornice continuing around a corner or in a different direction is a *cornice-return*, and one faced with e.g. *terracotta or some other material is an *encased* cornice. On sloping sides of a *pediment the cornices are *raking*. A *block-cornice* has simple blocks (instead of *modillions) projecting from rudimentary *bed-mouldings.

cornicione Italian *Renaissance *wall-cornice* proportioned to be a suitable crowning feature of the entire *façade and mass of a large building, usually *astylar, such as a *palazzo, e.g. Palazzo Strozzi, Florence.

cornucopia Large goat's 'Horn of Plenty' represented in Classical architecture as overflowing with flowers, fruit, and corn, and a symbol of concord, fruitfulness, and happiness: it is also found as an object in a garden, filled with real plants.

corona (*pl.* **coronae**) **1.** Part of a Classical *cornice, called *larmier*, above the *bed-moulding and below the *cymatium, with a broad vertical face, usually of considerable projection, with its underside recessed and forming a drip protecting the *frieze under it. **2.** Circlet or hoop hanging from above, as over an *altar: usually carrying candles, it is called a *corona lucis* (e.g. as in Aachen Cathedral).

coronet Suggestion of a *pediment or some other crowning element (e.g. *scroll-patterns over an aperture), usually in relief and not projecting like a true *cornice or pediment. Von *Klenze employed it.

Corporate Modernism *International-Modern architecture adopted by large corporations, e.g. Lever House by *Bunshaft of *SOM (1950–2), NYC. Many glass-and-metal-faced office-blocks were built in mid-C20 by corporations hopeful of demonstrating 'progressiveness' and 'modernity', usually resulting in tedious conformity.

Dr (1959); Ruttenbaum (1986)

corps-de-logis Main dominant *block of a major building, e.g. a country-house, distinct from subsidiary blocks, *pavilions, or *wings.

Correalism Term invented (1939) by *Kiesler. He dismissed *Functionalism as the 'mysticism of hygiene', and argued for an alternative visionary architecture related to spirals, infinity, and eternity. Forms he perceived as points where apparent known forces met invisible, secret, spiritual ones, and that reality was really the interaction of these forces. The nature of their relationships and of the connections between humans, forms, space, time, and the world he called *Correalism*.

Conrads (ed.) (1970); Kiesler (1964, 1966); L.Phillips et al. (1989)

corsa 1. *Fascia of a Classical *architrave. **2.** *String-course higher than its projection.

cortile (*pl.* **cortili**) Internal area (*cortis*) or *courtyard of a *palazzo, often with *arcades or *colonnades rising several storeys, and open to the sky (as in various Florentine *palazzi*) or roofed (e.g. *Barry's Reform Club, London (1837–41)).

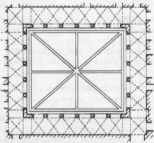

cortile *Palazzo Ducale*, Urbino (C15), showing Renaissance attention to geometry in providing an arcaded walk around the open space.

Cortona, Pietro Berrettini da (1596–1669) With *Bernini and *Borromini, one of the masters of Roman *Baroque. Trained as a painter, Cortona settled in Rome (c.1611), where he was patronized by the **Sacchettis**, for whom he designed the *Palazzetto del Pigneto* (1626–36). Although the building no longer exists, it made his reputation, for it was approached through a

series of *ramps and *terraces leading up to the entrance *exedra*, a design influenced, no doubt, by the Roman temple of Fortuna at Palestrina (Praeneste), and containing other *Antique allusions, including semicircular *apses screened by columns and derived from Roman *thermae*. The *façade was one of the first curved fronts in Rome. He came to the notice of **Cardinal Francesco Barberini** (1597–1679), for whom he created the sensational Baroque ceiling-*fresco (completed 1639) in the *saloon of the *Palazzo Barberini*. His first church was *Sts Luca e Martina* (1634–69) in the Forum: the central part of the front has a convex plan, and columns are sunk into the wall in the manner of *Michelangelo's Laurentian library-vestibule in Florence. Inside the church (a Greek *cross on plan) the walls are articulated by means of *Ionic columns and *pilasters (the capitals are of the *angular type), giving a unity to the entire composition enhanced by the lack of colour (the interior is painted white).

Under **Pope Alexander VII** (*r.*1655–67) da Cortona built two of the finest Baroque church façades in Rome. The front of *Santa Maria della Pace* (1656–9) has a half-elliptical porch of paired *Tuscan columns and an upper storey with a recessed convex central section: the plastic qualities recall Michelangelo at his *Mannerist best. Da Cortona carried the main elements of the façade over the adjacent buildings, creating a unified *piazza* resembling a theatre with boxes, with the church-front appearing as the backdrop. With the façade of *Santa Maria in Via Lata* (1658–62) in the *Corso*, da Cortona achieved a deceptive simplicity and grandeur with an *in antis* (*see* ANTA) *porch and upper storey featuring an arch continuing the profile of the *entablature. The design was reminiscent of elements from **Diocletian**'s Palace at Spalato and the temples at Baalbek.

Briganti (1962); N-S (1986); P (1982); J.T (1996); Va (1986); Wi (1982)

Cosmati Family of C12 and C13 Roman *marmorarii* (workers in *marble), taking their name from the leading member, **Cosma**, or **Cosmatus**. *Cosmati-work*, known as *Cosmatesca* or *Cosmatesque*, consists of inlaid geometrical *polychrome patterns of stone, glass, mosaic, and gilding set in marble. Good examples survive in Westminster Abbey: the pavements of the *presbytery (1268) and *feretory (1267–8), the base of the *shrine of the Confessor (1270), and the tomb-chest (c.1280) of **King Henry III** (*r.*1216–72). *Cosmatesque* is also a style of architectural decoration deriving from southern Italian, Sicilian, and *Byzantine work.

Hutton (1950)

Costa, Lúcio (1902-98) Brazilian architect/ planner influenced by *Warchavchik. He headed a team (all disciples of Le *Corbusier) designing the building for the Ministry of Education and Health in Rio de Janeiro (1936–43), for which Le Corbusier was consultant architect and *Burle Marx was landscape architect. Costa and *Niemeyer designed the Brazilian Pavilion at the World's Fair, NYC (1939), and he himself was responsible for the *Eduardo Guinle* apartmentblock, Rio (1948–54), and the Brazilian Pavilion at the *Cité Universitaire*, Paris (1955). The attention of the world was captured (1956–7) by his plan for the new capital, Brasília, and construction moved rapidly ahead. The plan is formal, in the shape of a bow and arrow, and it encapsulates many principles laid down by *CIAM in the *Athens Charter: it has not lived up to absurdly over-optimistic expectations.

Bullrich (1969); L.Costa (1962); Gazeneo & Scarone (1959); Guimaraens (1996)

cot 1. Humble small rural cottage, especially with wattled sides and a thatched roof, or a structure in a garden or park in imitation of it, but used as a retreat, *summer-house, or similar. **2.** *Dovecote. *Related terms include*:

cottage: **1.** dwelling-house of small size and humble character (*cot*), such as that occupied by *cottars* (farm- or other labourers), built of cheap materials such as *adobe, *cob, *pisé, *rubble, etc., and roofed with *thatch, turf, etc., although it could also be constructed of brick, or even *timber-framed with appropriate *nogging. It might also be a small, single-storey dwelling, sometimes with sleeping-quarters in the roof-space, inhabited by agricultural workers, or even a temporary shelter, hut, or shed. During C17 many cottages were built for weavers, and some survive, with provision for looms and storage, e.g. at Sapperton, Stroud, Glos. The cottage was the subject of C18 reform and attracted architects' attention leading to aestheticizing of the type as the *cottage orné*: simultaneously, Romantic notions of simplicity/idealized rural life led to the conscious design of *rustic cottages and their gardens in country parks (e.g.*Repton's work at Blaise Castle, Bristol (1795–7)). C19 oriental and cottage-style buildings constructed with a variety of materials were often associated with quasi-national styles: they included the *Bengal and *Swiss cottage, and the *Danish and *Polish hut; **2.** USA summer residence by the sea, in the country, etc., often quite substantial and well equipped; **3.** small country-house or detached suburban house, adapted to a modest scale of living, thus divested of any associations with poverty, yet free from pretensions or show; **4.** public convenience;

cottage orné: small late-C18 or early-C19 dwelling in the country or in a park, often asymmetrical and irregular, with small *leaded lights, *hips, *gables, and *dormers, fretted *barge-boards, large ornamental *chimneys, and rough timber *verandahs supported by tree-trunks, part of the cult of the *Picturesque. Construction was of brick, timber (or half-timbering), rubble (sometimes rendered and painted), etc., and roofs were often thatched. So the genuine *vernacular architecture of the cottage was taken up and transformed by architects, who created deliberately rustic buildings for aesthetic reasons: the results were superior in finish to their models, but less ostentatious than the more formal *villa. The fashion for the *cottage orné* was promoted in many *pattern-books (including those by *Plaw), largely in *Regency Britain, but it also influenced *Carpenter's Gothic in the USA. However, an early pioneer of the *cottage orné* was Thomas *Wright, whose work at Badminton, Glos. (1740s), is still extant. *Soane fused cottage elements with primitive *Doric, notably in the *dairy he designed (1781–3) at Hamels, Herts., for **The Hon. Philip Yorke** (1757–1834—later **3rd Earl of Hardwicke** from 1790). The once-unregarded *vernacular architecture of the cottage was celebrated by **James Malton** (1765–1803) in his *An Essay on British Cottage Architecture . . .* (1798, 1804), and *Collection of Designs for Rural Retreats . . .* (1802), which established him as a pioneer of the type. Other sources for such designs included J.B.*Papworth's *Rural Residences . . .* (1818, 1832), and there were others. Taking a cue from Plaw's pattern-books, *Nash and G.S. *Repton created examples of the *cottage orné* at Blaise Hamlet, Henbury, near Bristol (1810–11—emphasizing outhouses, *pentices, and chimneys, and adding thatch to *porches and *bay-windows), arranging buildings around a green with a *sundial in the centre: this was a philanthropic venture, treated in the Picturesque manner. Nash may also have been responsible for the 'Swiss Cottage' at Cahir, Co. Tipperary (*c.*1810), a very early example in which traces of the exotic were added to the mix. The *cottage orné* should not be confused with the *ferme ornée*. During the latter part of C19, elements of cottage architecture were used in the design of dwellings by architects of the *Arts-and-Crafts and *Domestic-Revival movements, but the results were far removed from the playful, witty character of the *cottage orné*, and were often associated with housing for the labouring classes.

J.Archer (1985); Barley (1961); C-T (1987); J.Curl (1983); Darley (1975); Hussey (1967, 1967a); Lyall (1988); Malton (1798, 1802); J.B.Pa (1832); Plaw (1785, 1795, 1800); Shoe (2001); Su (1980a, 1993); Tay (2006); D.Wa (1982a)

cottage-garden Garden cultivated to blend mixtures of plants, growing together, as if naturally. This requires an understanding of how individual plants propagate so as to sustain a controlled yet natural-looking aesthetic. Various C18 and early-C19 British writers advocated the cultivation of cottage-gardens to grow food (especially during the French Wars), and made suggestions (e.g. encouraging climbers, especially roses, to grow freely over walls, thus helping to blend humble buildings with their surroundings) to generally improve the appearance of cottages, as, e.g., *Loudon advocated. The aesthetic of the useful garden with a great variety of plants therein, appealed to sensibilities attuned to the idea of a rural idyll, and was adopted as a suitable setting for the vernacular-inspired *cottage orné*. Seemingly 'natural' cottage-gardens actually designed to *look* thus were created, therefore, and developed as a late-C19 style, for aesthetic rather than utilitarian reasons, influencing *Arts-and-Crafts gardening, and especially designers such as William *Robinson, *Jekyll, and Thomas *Mawson.

J.Archer (1985); G.W.Johnson (1846, 1857); Loudon (1834, 1834a); Shoe (2001); Tay (2006); pk

Cotte, Robert de (1657-1735) French architect/town planner, probably the most influential of *Rococo designers during the *Régence. Brother-in-law and pupil-assistant of *Hardouin-Mansart, he promoted French architecture throughout Europe, notably in the German-speaking lands. He succeeded (1709) Hardouin-Mansart as *Premier Architecte*, and carried out his first independent work, the *Hôtel du Lude*, Paris, in the following year (destroyed 1861). He designed the *Hôtel d'Éstrées, Rue de Grenelle*, Paris (1711-13—a *Palladian composition), and the episcopal palaces at Châlons-sur-Marne (1719-20—not completed), Verdun (1724-35—altered in execution), and Strasbourg (*Palais Rohan* (1727-42—a fine example of the *noble simplicité* of C18 French Rococo). His *façade of St-Roche*, Paris (1728-38), completed one of the city's great *basilicas. His designs for the *Thurn-und-Taxis* palace, Frankfurt-am-Main (1727-36—partly destroyed), *Schloss Clemensruhe*, Poppelsdorf, Bonn (1715-18), and the Electoral Palace, Bonn (1713-23), deserve mention. He was also consulted about the designs of *Schloss Brühl, Schloss Schleissheim*, and the *Residenz*, Würzburg, but his influence there was of little account.

J-F.Blondel (1752-6); K & L (1972); Neuman (1994)

Cottinelli Telmo, José Ângelo (1897-1948) Portuguese architect who carried out most of his best work during the *Estado Novo* (New State)—the corporatist authoritarian Second Republic (1933-74)—including numerous buildings for

the railway system (e.g. the station at *Vila Real de Santo António*). His most celebrated work is the dramatic *Monumento aos Descobrimentos*, with sculpture by **Leopoldo de Almeida** (1898-1975), created (1940) for the *Exposição do Mundo Português*, re-erected in Lisbon (1960).

Fernandes (1993)

Cottingham, Lewis Nockalls (1787-1847) English architect/antiquary, pioneer of the *Gothic Revival, he carried out numerous works of restoration to medieval churches, notably at Theberton, Suffolk (1836—where his sensitive colouring and detailing of the south *aisle deserve respect), Ashbourne, Derbys. (1839-40), and St Mary's, Bury St Edmunds, Suffolk (1840-3). He refitted Magdalen College Chapel, Oxford (1830-2), virtually rebuilt St Patrick's Cathedral, Armagh (1834-7), and carried out careful restorations at Hereford Cathedral (from 1841). Among his buildings were Snelston Hall, Derbys., a Gothic house (1828—demolished), the former Savings Bank in Crown Street, Bury St Edmunds (1846—*Tudor Gothic), and an extensive estate at Waterloo Bridge Road, London (from 1825). He established a fine collection of medieval architectural details (a descriptive memoir of which was published (1850), later incorporated into the collections of the South Kensington Museum. He published several books, including *Plans, etc. of Westminster Hall* (1822), *Plans, etc. of King Henry VII's Chapel* (1822-9), *The Ornamental Metal Worker's Director* (1823—with later editions), *Working Drawings of Gothic Ornaments* (1824), and *Grecian and Roman Architecture* (1820).

Co (2008); J.Curl (2013); Mulligan (2013); Myles (1996); ODNB (2004)

Couchman, Henry (1738-1803) Kent-born, he was employed by Matthew *Brettingham, who sent him (1766) to Great Packington, Warwicks., to supervise the reconstruction (completed 1772) of the Hall for **Heneage Finch** (1715-77—**3rd Earl of Aylesford** from 1757), whose patronage ensured Couchman's future career as architect/surveyor in Warwicks. Employed by *Newdigate to complete the comprehensive Gothicization of Arbury Hall, Warwicks., he also worked on Harefield Lodge, Mddx., for the same client (completed 1786). Other works include the octagonal crossing-tower of St Mary's Church, Atherstone, Warwicks. (1792), and the rebuilding of St Peter's Church, Higham-on-the-Hill, Leics. (1791). The *elevation of the former gaol to Barrack Street, Warwick (1784-93), by him, was retained when the complex became the offices of the County Council (1929-32).

Co (2008)

counter Opposite, or against, hence used as a noun for a long narrow flat-topped construction to separate staff from customers in a bank, inn, or shop. *Compounds include*:

counter-apse: *apse opposite another, as in the east and west ends of German churches (e.g. Worms Cathedral);

counter-arch: *arch opposing another's outward force, the principle of a flying *buttress;

counter-brace: *brace counteracting the strain of another, as in a *timber-framed structure;

counter-change: pattern formed by repetitive figures but alternating in colour or texture, the basic type of which is the *chequer;

counter-fort: **1.** *buttress or other projection (e.g. *spur-wall or *pier), built against a wall in order to prevent it from moving or bulging; **2.** *sconce;

counter-lath: **1.** *batten or *lath laid by eye between every two battens or laths laid at measured (*gauged*) distances apart; **2.** where one side of a partition was plastered, or the outside of a roof was finished, the other side was said to be *counter-lathed* when prepared for plastering; **3.** one of a number of laths laid at right angles over another set of laths or battens to provide a better backing for plaster, and render it less likely to crack;

counter-mure: **1.** in fortifications, a wall (*contra-mure*) behind another as a reserve defence, in case of the first wall being breached, or an outer wall to prevent an attacker from getting at the first wall; **2.** breakwater;

counter-poise: weight balancing another weight or force, as in a *counter-poise* or *counter-weight* *bridge, e.g. a *bascule* bridge;

counter-scarp: **1.** outer wall or slope of the ditch in a fortification; **2.** area between the *parapet and *glacis, also in a fortification; **3.** the term sometimes includes the *glacis*;

counter-vault: inverted arch or *vault, used e.g. in *foundations.

couple Pair of common *rafters. A *couple-roof* therefore consists of couples resting on wall-plates and pitched together at the *ridge, with or without *purlins. A *close-couple* roof has couples with *ties above their feet, thus forming triangles, preventing the feet from spreading.

coupled columns *Accouplement, or columns placed in a *colonnade (or *arcade) in line in very closely spaced pairs, as in the east front of the Louvre, Paris, or in pairs at 90° to the line of the *entablature.

cour d'honneur Principal *court, often the *fore-court*, of a grand house or palace, often enclosed between the principal front of the *corps-de-logis*, the projecting *wings and *colonnades, and the fourth side composed of very low buildings, lodges, etc., or a wall or railing: e.g. Burley-on-the-Hill, Rut. (1696–1704).

course Any horizontal level range of bricks, *masonry, etc., placed according to some rule or order in the construction of a wall, laid evenly. *Coursed* *rubble, for example, is roughly dressed stones of the same height laid in courses, unlike *random* rubble, which is uncoursed and requires ingenuity in getting the stones to bond. Thus *coursed* masonry has courses of dressed stones (*ashlar) of the same height, yet each course may vary in height. Courses may be described by position or function: *base* or *plinth*, *blocking* (plain course above a *cornice weighing down the ends of the cantilevered sections of stone), *bond* (with every stone, or stones at regular intervals, bonding a wall), *lacing* (as *bond*, but with continuous ranges of brick or *tile, and with *piers every two metres or so, used in a *flint wall for bonding, levelling, and strengthening), and *string-courses are some examples.

court **1.** Clear area enclosed by walls or surrounded by buildings, such as a space left for the admission of light and air, an area around a *castle *keep, a fore-court or *cour d'honneur* in front of a grand house, a *cortile*, a Cambridge college *quadrangle, or a *cloister. **2.** Princely or Royal residence (as at Hampton Court Palace). **3.** Building where legal tribunals sit.

Court style Earliest phase of the *Rayonnant* style of French *Gothic, closely associated with the reign of **King Louis IX** (1226–70). It was characterized by the dissolution of walls in favour of huge areas of windows subdivided by thin, wire-like *tracery, the piercing of the wall of the *triforium-gallery with windows, and the introduction of masses of *colonnettes corresponding to the ribs in the *vault. The most glorious examples of the Court style are *Ste-Chapelle, Paris (1243–8), the *Collegiate Church of *St-Urbain, Troyes (begun 1262), and the east end of Sées Cathedral, Normandy (*c.*1270).

Branner (1965); Gi (1986); D.Wa (1986)

Courtonne, Jean (1671–1739) French architect. His *Hôtel de Noirmoutier* and *Hôtel de Matignon*, Paris (both 1720–4), are models of elegance and restraint. They have continuous *astylar wall-surfaces punctuated by tall windows (some with semicircular and others with segmental heads). His chief importance lies in his treatise on architectural perspective (1725), which also contained numerous remarks on architecture, including his insistence that the exterior of a building should be derived from the forms of the interior.

Courtonne (1725); Ha (1950); K & L (1972)

courtyard Open area surrounded by walls or buildings within the precincts of a farm, castle, large house, prison, etc. It applies to something less grand than *court (**1**).

coussinet 1. Cushion of the *Ionic *capital, including the two *volutes and their connecting bands, like a rolled mattress. **2.** Lowest *voussoir of an arch resting on the *impost.

Covarrubias, Alonso de (1488–1570) Spanish mason/sculptor, he worked at Salamanca Cathedral (1512) before carrying out decorations at Sigüenza. His most important work was *El Alcázar*, Toledo (1537–53—badly damaged during the Civil War, 1936–9), where the top storey is rusticated and the two lower storeys plain (an inversion of the normal Classical arrangement), and Italian forms were applied to a large plain *ashlar *façade for decorative purposes. As master-mason to Toledo Cathedral, he was responsible for the chapel of the New Kings (1531–4).

CG (1953); K & S (1959); J.T (1996)

cove, coving 1. Surface of concave, more or less quarter-cylindrical form, usually applied to the *cavetto *moulding between a wall and *coved ceiling*, called *coving*. In many cases the coving is heavily ornamented. **2.** Large concave part of a *chancel-*screen under the *gallery, often with the appearance of *vaulting. **3.** Curved transition between an exterior wall and the *eaves, called *coved eaves*.

coved vault *Cloistered* arch or *vault, composed of four triangular *coves rising from a square plan in *corbelled *courses to an apex and meeting in vertical diagonal planes, the axial *sections being arcs, but actually *pseudo-vaults*.

cover Anything finishing a join, e.g. a *cover-fillet*, *cover-moulding*, or *cover-strip* moulding concealing a joint in panelling, or the part of a tile or slate covered by the overlap of the course above.

covie, covey *Pantry or *closet.

coving *See* COVE.

cowan 1. Person uninitiated in *Freemasonry. **2.** *Rough-setter *or* -mason.

cowl *Cap, hood, etc. for covering the open top of a chimney-flue and improving the draught, often with a wind-vane allowing it to rotate. A *cowl-dormer* is a *dormer, the roof of which is shaped like a cowl projecting in front of the window.

Cowlishaw, William Harrison (1869–1957) English *Arts-and-Crafts architect and disciple of William *Morris. He is remembered for two charming buildings: The Cearne, Kent Hatch, Crockham Hill, Kent (1896), and the summer-school known as The Cloisters, Barrington Road,

Letchworth *Garden City, Herts. (1908), an eclectic and romantic building. He worked for the Imperial War Graves Commission, and later for *Holden.

A.S.Gray (1985); Miller (2002)

Cowper, John (*fl*.1453–84) English mason, he worked at Eton College (1450s), Tattershall Church, Lincs. (1478), and around the same time built Kirby Muxloe Castle, Leics., where the resident clerk of the works was **Robert Steynforth** (*fl*.1480s). Cowper may also have been responsible for the gatehouse-tower at Esher, Surrey (*c*.1475–80), the school at Wainfleet, Lincs. (1484), and the great tower at the Bishop's Palace, Buckden, Hunts. (also 1480s). Cowper is important in the development of *Tudor brick-built architecture which was to become fashionable. He appears to have finished his career in the service of **King James IV** of Scotland (*r*.1488–1513), for a John Cowper was in charge of the works at Rothesay Castle, Bute (1512), where he was paid handsomely, so must have enjoyed considerable status.

J.Harvey (1987)

Cox, Oliver Jasper (1920–2010) Like many of his generation, this English architect became (1930s) a convinced *Modernist and Leftist, and joined Herts. County Council before moving (1950) to LCC. He was involved in the housing development at Alton East, Roehampton, and led the LCC team planning a *New Town at Hook, Hants. (1956–7), a typical product of its time (not implemented). Cox set up (1966) **Shankland Cox** with **Colin Graeme Lindsay-Shankland** (1918–94—*known as* **Graeme Shankland**, a convinced Communist, who had worked in the planning department of LCC, notably on the South Bank and Elephant & Castle schemes). Shankland had already secured the contract to re-plan the centre of Liverpool, and was a protagonist of *urban renewal, a paradoxical position given his trumpeted devotion to the legacy of William *Morris. Numerous lucrative planning commissions followed, many involving loss of urban fabric (much of which could have been conserved). Cox rejected the *Systems architecture fashionable in the 1960s.

AH, lvii (2014), 393–422; *The Guardian* (2 June 2010), obits.

coyn *See* QUOIN.

Cozens, Alexander (1717–86) Major English artist, he devoted himself almost entirely to imaginary landscape painting, usually in monochrome, with intense lights and darks suggesting the *Sublime power of Nature, which did much to popularize C18 notions of aesthetics. He gained a reputation as an artist/teacher, and published

Essay to Facilitate the Inventing of Landskips, Intended for Students in the Art (1759): in it he explained how compositions might be aided by observing accidents of nature. He developed these ideas in *The Various Species of Landscape, &c. in Nature* (mid-1770s) and in *A New Method of Assisting the Invention in Drawing Original Compositions of Landscape* (1785-6). Among his pupils was *Beckford, with whom he travelled to Italy (1762), and on whom his insights impinged: both *Gilpin and *Mason experimented with his techniques.

His son, **John Robert Cozens** (1752-97), made numerous topographical drawings in which rough, craggy landscapes predominated. He accompanied Payne *Knight on a Continental tour (1776-9) during which he made many watercolours of mountainous Swiss scenery, and (1782-3) travelled with Beckford to Italy, producing a series of accomplished pictures. Both father and son were aware of the effects on viewers' sensibilities that could be stimulated by scenery, and imparted this to men like Beckford and Knight (clearly influencing their ideas about landscape composition on their respective estates at Fonthill and Downton Castle), so are significant figures in the histories of the *Picturesque and the Sublime.

ODNB (2004); Oppé (1952); Sloan *et al.* (1986); J.T (1996)

Crabtree, William (1905-91) English architect. His reputation rests mainly on his Peter Jones Department Store, Sloane Square, London (1932-7—designed for **Spedan Lewis** (1885-1963—founder of the John Lewis Partnership)) in collaboration with **Slater & Moberly**, with C.H.*Reilly (Crabtree's former mentor at Liverpool University) as consultant. It was one of the first C20 uses of the glass *curtain-wall in England, was influenced by the work of *Mendelsohn (Schocken department-stores in Chemnitz and Stuttgart), and is one of the most distinguished *Modern-Movement buildings in Britain. He subsequently worked with *Abercrombie on the reconstruction of Plymouth and Southampton after the 1939-45 war, and designed several buildings in Basildon and Harlow New Towns, Essex, and elsewhere, but never again was he to build anything to match in quality the Peter Jones store.

AR, lxxxv (June 1939), 291-8; and clxxxvii/1115 (Jan. 1990), 75-9; pk

cradle 1. Light structure or framework (cradling) to support a *plaster *cornice or *vault. **2.** *Corbeil. **3.** *Caisson.

cradle-roof Form of timber roof more or less arched on the underside, as when *braces were used.

cradle-vault Improper term for a *barrel-*vault.

Craig, James (1744-95) Edinburgh-born architect, he achieved fame with his design for Edinburgh New Town (1766), and published *Plan for improving the City of Edinburgh* (1786). He was the architect of St James Square (1773—demolished), the *Palladian Physicians' Hall, George Street (1775—demolished), and the Old Observatory, Calton Hill (1776-92).

Co (2008); J.Craig (1786); Youngson (1966)

Craig, Maurice (1919-2011) Irish architectural historian, whose books on Dublin (1952), Irish houses, and the architecture of Ireland established him as one of the finest writers on the built fabric of his country. He was especially interested in *mausolea, and photographically recorded a vast range of buildings, leaving a unique archive on Irish architecture.

M.Craig (1969, 1982, 2009); *Irish Times* (13 May 2011), Obits

Craig, Vincent (1869-1925) Irish architect, brother of **James Craig** (1871-1940—1st Prime Minister of Northern Ireland, **1st Viscount Craigavon** from 1927), who trained (1885-9) with W.H. *Lynn before establishing (1891) his own Belfast practice. His works include the former Belmont School (1890-2); St John's Presbyterian Church, Ormeau Road (1890-2—*Gothic); the former Trustee Savings Bank, Arthur Street (1894—an Italian *Renaissance *palazzo, originally offices of Dunville's Whiskey Distillers), all in Belfast; and a charming *Arts-and-Crafts house (Rathmoyle (formerly Eldon Green), Helen's Bay, Co. Down (1901)), which he built for himself. He also designed the Arts-and-Crafts–Gothic Presbyterian Churches at Hillhall, Co. Down (1902), and Portstewart, Co. Londonderry (1905—with more elaborate *tracery).

Brett (2002), 126; *DIA*; Larmour (1987)

Cram, Ralph Adams (1863-1942) Leading American *Gothic Revivalist, influenced by the works of *Bodley, *Morris, and *Ruskin. He went into partnership (1889) with **Charles Francis Wentworth** (1861-97), and together they built the Episcopalian Church of All Saints, Ashmont, Dorchester, Boston, MA (1891-1913). This brought them fame and attracted the gifted **Bertram Grosvenor Goodhue** (1869-1924) to join the firm, renamed **Cram, Wentworth, & Goodhue** (1892-1914). After Wentworth's early death, **Frank Ferguson** (1861-1926) became a partner, and **Cram, Goodhue, & Ferguson** rose to national pre-eminence with two important commissions: the master-plan and chapel for the US Military Academy, West Point, NY (1903-14), and the Church of St Thomas, Fifth Avenue, NYC (1906-

14). The latter is one of the finest works of *Arts-and-Crafts *Gothic Revival in America. The Graduate School Complex and Chapel at Princeton University (1911–29) were sophisticated designs, but Cram's greatest achievement (1915–41) is undoubtedly the project for the completion and Gothicizing of the Cathedral of St John the Divine, Morningside Heights, NYC, begun (1892) in a *Byzantine-*Romanesque style to designs by *Heins and Lafarge. Cram published *Church Building* (1901) and *The Substance of Gothic* (1917) among other works.

Cram (1924, 1925, 1930, 1966, 1967, 1969); A.Daniel (1980); Muccigrosso (1980); North (1931); Shand-Tucci (1975, 1990); D.Wa (1986)

Cramer, Ernst Friedrich (1898–1980) Swiss landscape architect, pupil of Gustav *Ammann at **Froebels Erben**, Zürich (1914–17), he founded (1929) his own practice, designing numerous informal *Wohngärten*, sometimes leavened with influences from the Ticino region of southern Switzerland (e.g. the *Vogel-Sulzer* garden, Itschnach, Zürich (1933), and the *Forrer-Sulzer* garden, Moscia, Ticino (1942–8), both of which are in the 'rustic' style). As a member of the *Werkbund (headed by Max *Bill and **Johannes Itten** (1888–1967)), he dramatically changed tack in the 1950s, embracing *Modernism and including geometrical *concrete shapes: his *Garten des Poeten* for the first national garden show, Zürich (1959), contrasted with his earlier designs, and was described as a 'sculpture to walk through… abstract shapes… with sharp arrises foreign to the nature of their material', and indeed subsequent designs were more sculpture than garden, setting the agenda for modern Swiss landscape architecture. He influenced *Minimalism and *Land Art. Some works were aesthetically unsuccessful (e.g. the *concrete structures resembling abstractions of ski-slopes, with coloured concrete paving in undulating patterns at the Central Post and Administration Building, Vaduz, Liechtenstein (1972–8), demolished).

Kassler (1984); Shoe (2001)

cramp Piece of metal used to hold stones together in the same *course.

Cranbrook The Cranbrook Academy of Art, Bloomfield Hills, MI, was founded (1920s) under the influence of the *Arts-and-Crafts movement. Buildings for its *campus were designed by the *Saarinens. Its importance lies in its promotion of modern design, many practitioners having been associated with it over the years.

Gaidos (ed.) (1972)

Craze, Romilly Bernard (1892–1974) English ecclesiastical architect, much of whose output consists of replacements of, or draconian repairs to, churches destroyed or damaged during the 1939–45 war. Among his works St Luke, Farnborough Way, Camberwell (1953–4), St Cuthbert, Watford Road, Wembley (1958–9), and All Saints, Waltham Avenue, Kingsbury (1954), may be cited. He carried out many re-orderings of churches in the Diocese of London, rebuilt (1953–63) *Pugin's RC Cathedral of St George, Southwark (erected 1841–8), on the original plan, with details in a desiccated *Arts-and-Crafts Free *Gothic, and carried out repairs (not often elegantly) to numerous churches, including *Keeling's St George, Aubrey Walk, Kensington (1947–9). His Shrine of Our Lady of Walsingham, Norfolk (1931–7), however, is vaguely *Italianate, but the interior is spatially complex for such a small building, and contains a fine *reredos by *Comper. The land on which the Shrine was built was donated by **Sir William Frederick Victor Mordaunt Milner** (1896–1960—**8th Baronet** from 1931), Craze's professional partner in the architectural firm of **Milner & Craze**.

Pk; Sh (1973)

credence Table or shelf (called *prothesis*) on the south side of the *sanctuary of a church, near the *altar (where the Sacred Elements were placed before the Oblation), often given architectural treatment, and sometimes associated with the *piscina.

cremone, cremorne *Casement bolts with a rack-and-pinion mechanism controlled by a rotary handle: two sliding rods, fixed to one leaf of e.g. a *French window, are moved up and down in opposite directions into sockets in a frame in order to lock it. A variant is called the *espagnolette*, where the bolt-rods have hooks on the ends that engage in slots at the top and bottom of the main frame, locking and tightening the opening-light.

crenel, crenelle *See* BATTLEMENT.

crepido 1. Greek foundation of a building. 2. Elevated base, *crepis*, or platform on which e.g. an *obelisk, *altar, or esp. *temple stands: if the base of a temple, it was called *crepidoma*, normally of three steps, the topmost platform surface of which was termed *stylobate. 3. Raised footpath parallel to a Roman street. 4. Projecting ornamental parts of a Classical building, e.g. a *cornice.

crescent 1. Building or series of buildings of which the frontage stands in plan on the concave arc of a circle or of an ellipse, generally facing a garden or *promenade. The earliest examples are the Royal Crescent, Bath (1767–75), by *Wood the Younger, and the semicircular Crescent at Buxton, Derbys. (1780–90), by *Carr of York. Camden Crescent (*c.*1788) by **John Eveleigh** (*fl.*1756–1800) and Lansdown Crescent (1789–93) by **John**

Palmer (*c.*1738–1817), both in Bath, are two further examples of a type of development that became common in C19. A range of buildings with the front on a plan part of a circle is called a *quadrant*. **2.** Type of arch.

cress, crest, cresting 1. A *crest* is a figure placed on a wreath, coronet, or chapeau, borne above the shield and helmet in a coat of arms. **2.** *Finial. **3.** Any plain or ornamental work, often perforated, running continuously in a horizontal direction, as on a *canopy, *ridge, *screen, or wall, although *brattishing is preferred for screens. **4.** Bed of *mortar in which ridge-tiles were set (probably the origin of the word *creasing). **5.** *Cope, called a *crest-table* in the Middle Ages. **6.** *Battlement.

cresset Iron frame holding pitched rope, etc., to be burned for light, usually set on a pole or building or suspended from a roof.

Creswell, Harry Bulkeley (1869–1960) British architect, articled to Aston *Webb before setting up his own practice (1899). In addition to his work as Inspecting Engineer for the Crown Agents for the Colonies, he designed the turbine-factory at Queensferry, Flint (1901–6), with its huge *pylon-like tower and *battered Egyptianizing *piers articulating each *bay. Creswell was a contributor to *AR*, and the author of *The Honeywood File* (1929) and *The Honeywood Settlement* (1930), both witty and humorous 'fictional' correspondence between architect, client, quantity-surveyor, and builder.

Creswell (1929, 1930, 1931, 1935, 1942, 1943); A.S.Gray (1985)

Cresy, Edward (1792–1858) Kent-born architect/engineer (he deplored the sundering of the professions), apprenticed to James Thompson Parkinson (*fl.*1795–1840s), he later (1814) joined George *Smith, Surveyor to The Mercers' Company. With G.L.*Taylor, Cresy undertook a walking tour of England (1816) to study medieval buildings, and they travelled on the Continent with John *Sanders (1817). The results were the publication of *The Architectural Antiquities of Rome* (1821–2) and *The Architecture of the Middle Ages in Italy* (1829). His architectural works include 6 Suffolk Street, London (1824), the Square d'Orléans, IXième Arondissement, Paris (1829–33), the layout of Serpentine Terrace (later Rutland Gate), Knightsbridge (and probably the detailed design of No. 10—1836–42), and the black marble *Gothic tomb-chest (1842) of **Lord Henry Thomas Howard Molyneux Howard** (1766–1824) in St Nicholas's Church, Arundel, Sussex. Other publications included *An Analytical Index to an Historical Essay on Architecture by the late Thomas Hope* (1836), *A Practical Treatise on*

Bridge-Building (1839), and *Encyclopaedia of Civil Engineering, Historical, Theoretical, and Practical* (1847—illustrated with over 3000 engravings by **Robert Edward Branston** (1803–77) from original drawings mostly by Cresy's son, also **Edward** (1824–70)). Interested in urban hygiene, he gave evidence to the Commission of Enquiry into the State of Large Towns (1844). With **Cuthbert William Johnson** (1799–1878) he published *On the Cottages of Agricultural Labourers . . .* (1847).

Burfield (2003); Co (2008); C-R (2008); *ODNB* (2004)

Cret, Paul Philippe (1876–1945) French-born American architect. He trained at the *Écoles des *Beaux-Arts* in Lyons and Paris, before emigrating (1903) to the United States where he taught at the University of Pennsylvania and set up (1907) his own practice. Under his aegis Penn's School of Architecture achieved an outstanding reputation, and produced many graduates of distinction, including L.I.*Kahn. Cret's monumental Pan-American Union Building, Washington, DC (1907–10), reveals his *Beaux-Arts* training. The Public Library, Indianapolis, IN (1914–17), has massive blocky *pavilions on either side of a severe *Doric *colonnade, but with the Folger Shakespeare Library, Washington, DC (1928–32), Cret's style became more stripped and powerful. His most moving works in a simplified Classical idiom are his memorials to the dead of the 1914–18 war, e.g. the Aisne-Marne Memorial, near Château-Thierry, France (1926–33).

Grossman (1996); Hoak & Church (1930); T.White (1973)

Cretan architecture Large palace complexes, designed in the second millennium BC and later replaced with even grander structures planned on asymmetrical lines, with vast corridors, many chambers, *courts, and columned halls, are known to have been built at Knossos and Phaestos, Crete. At the 'Palace of King Minos' at Knossos there was a formal axially planned arrangement with a great stair leading to the state rooms (so-called 'Minoan' architecture). Painted decorations were plentiful, vigorous, and strongly coloured, while *contractura* columns (often of cypress-wood) were set with the smaller diameter at the base, so the taper was downwards, without *entasis, a curious reversal of natural form. The *primitive character of Cretan architectural detail attracted some C20 architects, notably *Plečnik.

Ck (1996); D (1950); T (1996)

Crewe, Bertie (*c.*1860–1937) English architect, he became an important and prolific designer, responsible for over 100 theatres and music-halls as well as several early cinemas. His buildings include the New Prince's (later Shaftesbury)

Theatre, London (1911), the Hippodrome, Golders Green (1910), and the first 'super-cinema' in England, the New Tivoli, Strand (1923—demolished 1957).

A.S.Gray (1985)

Crickmer, Courtenay Melville (1879–1971) London-born architect, he began work (1907) at Letchworth *Garden City, Herts., then being developed by *Parker & *Unwin, where he designed single and groups of houses, schools, and other buildings, all in a restrained *vernacular style. He was responsible for several houses at Hampstead *Garden Suburb, and was appointed resident architect at the new munitions town of Gretna, Scotland during the 1914–18 war.

A.S.Gray (1985); M & G (1992)

crinkle-crankle, crinkum-crankum Garden-wall, usually aligned east-west so that one side faces south, on a plan of elongated S-shaped curves joined in a continuous *ribbon* or *serpentine* form that stiffens the wall, enabling it to be less thick than a straight wall would have to be for stability, and removing the need for *buttresses.

criosphinx Ancient Egyptian *sphinx-like form, but with a ram's head on a lion's body.

Critical Regionalism Supposedly a strategy for achieving a more humane architecture as an antidote to widespread employment of international *clichés* and universally held abstractions by drawing on elements not necessarily from context, but used in unfamiliar ways, the term was coined (1981) by **Alexander Tzonis** (1937–) and **Liane Lefaivre**. It was later employed by **Kenneth Brian Frampton** (1930–), who argued that instead of designing buildings that conformed to a global uniformity, employing 'consumerist iconography masquerading as culture', architects should 'mediate the impact' with themes drawn indirectly from the individual 'peculiarities of a particular place', taking into account local topography and climate. He saw Critical Regionalism as adopting *Modernism for its 'progressive' qualities while placing a value on the geographical context. He opposed drawing on *vernacular architecture or *Historicism, and proposed 'autochthonous elements with paradigms drawn from alien sources', which, when one thinks about it, is what *Modernists had been doing for nearly a century, giving the *genius loci* not much chance of survival. Frampton's writings often seem to hold that the totalitarian Le *Corbusier's architecture was somehow 'humanist' (as he described the competition project for the League of Nations, Geneva (1937)), yet they also point out that *Kahn's work at Dacca and Le Corbusier's at Chandigarh ignored the technological facts for their locations, both designed for 'automobiles . . .

where many, as yet, still lack a bicycle'. He also cited works by *Aalto (the inevitable Säynätsalo) and *Utzon (Bagsvaerd Church) as examples in which the local and the general were synthesized. Therein might appear to lie massive contradictions.

AD, xxxviii (1968), 134–6; Amourgis (ed.) (1991); W.Cu (1996); H.Foster (ed.) (1983); F (1980, 1982, 1995, 2002)

Crittall windows Metal *casement-windows developed in the period immediately after the 1914–18 war by a British company of that name. They were features of many *Art-Deco and *Modernistic (*see* MODERNIST) buildings, as well as of countless dwellings.

PS

crocket 1. *Gothic ornament, generally a bud, flower, leaf, or bunch of foliage, placed at regular intervals on the external edges of *canopies, *gables, gablets, *hood-moulds, *pinnacles, *spires, etc. The largest bunches at the top, standing on an upright stem (*finial), are properly called *crops. **2.** Crockets also occur on the corners of foliated *Gothic *capitals, based, no doubt, on the *Corinthian *Order. **3.** *Foil, as in a *crocket-arch* with foils on the intrados.

croft *See* CRYPT.

croisée *See* FRENCH WINDOW.

croisette *See* CROSSETTE.

cromlech *See* DOLMEN.

Cronaca, Simone del Pollaiuolo *called* **Il** (1457–1508) Florentine architect. He worked with Giuliano da *Sangallo on the octagonal *sacristy of *Santo Spirito*, and with Benedetto da *Maiano on the *Palazzo Strozzi*, where he was responsible for the grand *cornicione* (c.1489–1504). He completed (1504) the monastery-church of *San Salvatore* (or *San Francesco*) *al Monte*, admired by *Michelangelo. Cronaca has been credited with the design of the *Palazzo Guadagni* (1504–6).

Goldthwaite (1980); He (1996)

crop, crope *Gothic *knop* of sculptured unfolding leaf-like forms surmounting a *finial, *gable, *spire, etc. A more rounded, less leafy, ball-like finial is a *pommel.

cross Very ancient ornamental form consisting primarily of two straight or nearly straight members, set at 90° to each other, one vertical and the other horizontal, but also with many variations. *Varieties of cross include:*

alisée patée: like a circle with four curved, spear-headed slices taken out of it;

Ankh: Ancient Egyptian T-form topped by a halo-like loop, signifying Life and Resurrection, and

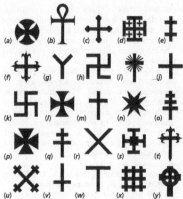

cross (*a*) *Alisée patée* or *pattée*; (*b*) Ancient Egyptian *Ankh*; (*c*) *bottonée* or *clover-leaf*; (*d*) *Crusader's* or *Jerusalem*. Without the four small crosses it is *potent*; (*e*) *double*; (*f*) *fleurée* or *fleury*. with the centre-leaf of each arm omitted, it is *Moline*; (*g*) *forked*; (*h*) *fylfot* or *swastika*; (*i*) *glory*; (*j*) *Greek*; (*k*) *Hakenkreuz* or *potent rotated*; (*l*) *iron* or *Eiserneskreuz* of Prussia; (*m*) *Latin*; (*n*) *Maltese*; (*o*) *papal*; (*p*) *patée formée*; (*q*) *patriarchal*; (*r*) *St Andrew's* or *saltire*; (*s*) *St Chad's*; (*t*) *St James's*; (*u*) *St Julian's*; (*v*) *St Peter's*; (*w*) *Tau* or *St Anthony's*; (*x*) *triparted*; (*y*) *wheel-head* or *Celtic*.

therefore a prototype of a Crucifixion symbol. With *serif*-like (splayed) ends to the three arms (instead of being *sans-serif*), the *Ankh*-form becomes a *crux ansata*;

bottonée: *Greek* cross with each arm terminating in a trefoil-like form resembling a clover-leaf;

Calvary: large stone cross erected on three steps representing Faith, Hope, and Charity;

cantonée: *Greek* cross with a small *Greek* cross in each of the areas bounded by the arms;

churchyard: large stone cross standing on a stepped base in a churchyard to indicate the ground was consecrated, and from the base of which itinerant friars would preach;

city: see MARKET;

clover-leaf: as *bottonée*;

consecration: cross painted or carved on a church wall indicating where chrism was to be applied during the consecration of the building. There were 12 in all, and many have survived as permanent interior decoration;

Crusader's: *potent* cross with four *Greek* crosses added to the areas bounded by the arms;

crux ansata: see *Ankh*;

double: two *Greek* crosses, one set above the other, with the two verticals joined;

Eiserneskreuz: Prussian *iron* cross, designed by *Schinkel as a form of *patée* cross, but with

the ends of the arms straight, so like a square from which four wide curved-sided sections like spear-heads have been taken out of the diagonals;

Eleanor: one of the 12 tall *Gothic memorial structures resembling a variety of ornate *spire set over a stepped base, erected to commemorate the funeral route of **Queen Eleanor** (d.1290), consort of **King Edward I** of England (*r.*1272–1307). Three survive (Geddington, Northants.; Northampton; and Waltham Cross, Herts.). The monument at Charing Cross, London, is a C19 revival of the type;

fleury or *fleurée*: *Greek* cross with each arm terminating in three leaves resembling the *fleur-de-lys*. If the centre-leaf of each termination is missing, it is a *moline* cross;

forked: **Y**-shaped;

fylfot: *Greek* cross, with the arms cranked at 90°, the ends pointing anti-clockwise, an ancient symbol associated with good fortune and the sun, called *swastika*, related to the *Greek-key, *fret, or *labyrinth, and to the *potent* cross;

glory: *Latin* cross with radiating lines like a *sunburst projecting from the centre of the cross where the two arms intersect, symbolizing glory;

Greek: with arms of equal length, representing the miraculous powers of Christ, and used as the basic form of *Byzantine and some *Renaissance church-plans;

Hakenkreuz: *potent rotated* cross, like the *fylfot* or *swastika*, but with the cranked arms pointing clockwise, used by the National Socialist German Workers' Party (*Nazis*). Its association with misfortune is C20 propaganda;

iron: see *Eiserneskreuz*;

Jerusalem: as *Crusader's* cross;

Latin: with three equally long topmost arms, though sometimes the vertical arm may be shorter than the two horizontals, and a much longer bottom arm. Used as the basic form for many Western *cruciform* church-plans from the *Romanesque period;

Latin cross fleurée: as *Latin* cross, but with a three-leafed termination to each arm resembling the *fleur-de-lys*;

Lorraine: resembles the *patriarchal* cross, but the lower, longer arm is set further down the vertical element;

Maltese: like four identical acute-angled triangles or arrow-heads meeting at their most acute points, with **V**-shaped notches taken out of the ends of each equal arm;

market: large structure in the principal marketplace of a town, consisting of a raised platform with a high and elaborate superstructure, sometimes acting as a *canopy over the platform. A good example is the *Gothic *city*- or *market*-cross, Chichester, Sussex (1501);

moline: *see fleury*;

papal: like a *Latin* cross, but with three horizontals set across the vertical, the lowest longer than the one above, which is in turn longer than the topmost member. If the lowest arm is set diagonally, it is a *Russian Orthodox* cross;

patée or pattée: *see alisée patée*;

patée formée: like a square from which four sharp straight-sided triangular notches have been removed from the diagonals, so like the *Eiserneskreuz* but with straight-sided arms;

patriarchal: like a *Latin* cross but with two horizontals set across the vertical, the lower longer than the top and set roughly half-way up the vertical;

pommée: *Greek* cross with each arm terminating in a circular blob;

potent: *Greek* cross with each arm a T;

potent rotated: *see Hakenkreuz*;

Rood: cross set above the western entrance to a *chancel, on a *screen, on a *Roodbeam, or suspended. Roods often have a representation of the Crucifixion with Sts Mary and John on either side;

St Andrew: X or *saltire* cross;

St Anthony: T or *Tau* cross;

St James: *Latin* cross *fleurée*, with each arm terminating in three leaves, like the *fleur-de-lys*, although the base is usually pointed;

St Julian: X or *saltire* cross with each arm terminating in a *Latin* cross;

St Peter: Latin cross set upside-down;

saltire: X-shaped cross, also known as *St Andrew's* cross. If each arm terminates in a *Latin* cross, it is a *St Julian's* cross;

Tau: T-shaped cross, also known as *St Anthony's* cross.

The Cross is the emblem of the Christian religion, and is employed architecturally, not merely in the plan of *cruciform* churches with *transepts, but on grave-slabs and tombs and on crowning features on *cupolas, *gables, *spires, etc. It was also placed surmounting a monument, such as a *churchyard-, Eleanor-*, or *market*-cross. *The word also recurs with others. Examples include*:

cross-aisle: **1.** *transept; **2.** passage between rows of *pews; **3.** clearway to exits set parallel to rows of seats in a theatre;

cross-banded: veneered, with the grain at right angles to the length of an object, especially the handrail of a *stair-*balustrade;

cross-bar: *transom;

cross-beam: transverse *beam spanning from wall to wall;

cross-bond: Flemish bond (*see* BRICK);

cross-brace: crossing or intersecting *braces in a timber roof;

cross-church: cruciform church with *transepts;

cross-domed: type of *Early-Christian or *Byzantine church on a cruciform plan with a *dome over the crossing and four barrel-*vaults over the arms, also known as an *ambulatory* church. The centre had galleried *aisles on three sides;

cross-entry: *see* ENTRY;

cross-gable: one parallel to the roof-ridge of the main part of a building, as on a *cross-wing*;

cross-in-square: common *Byzantine church-plan consisting of a large central domed square (with the dome supported on four *piers or columns), four corner (domed or barrel-vaulted) squares, and four rectangular barrel-vaulted *bays, the whole called *cross- inscribed, croix inscrite*, or *quincunx*;

cross-passage: *see* ENTRY;

cross-quarter: quatrefoil (*see* FOIL), its lobes set diagonally, usually in series as a *band;

cross-rail: in *timber-framed construction, the main horizontal mid-rail parallel to the *cill and wall-plate;

cross-rib: transverse *rib in a *vault, i.e. at right angles to the main axis of a *nave or *aisle;

cross-springer: diagonal rib in a vault. Some authorities use the term for *transverse* rib;

cross-tree: *cross-* or *tie-beam*;

cross-vault: intersecting *barrel-vaults* forming a *groin-vault*;

cross-window: window with *lights defined by a *mullion and *transom forming a cross;

cross-wing: *wing attached to the hall-range of a medieval house, its axis at right angles to the hall-range, often gabled.

Dirsztay (1978); G.Ferguson (1961); Seymour (1898)

crossette. Also *croisette* or *crosette*. **1.** Projection on each side of the top of a Classical *architrave around an aperture at the junction of the *lintel and *jamb, where the *supercilium projects beyond the *antepagments, and the *mouldings return, forming *ears, elbows, *knees, *lugs, or *shoulders. **2.** *Console set on each flank at the top of an architrave around an aperture, supporting a *cornice: consoles are also called *ancones, ears, elbows, hawksbills (or beaks), knees, lugs,

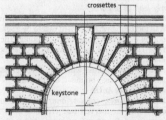

crossette Crossettes in V-jointed masonry

prothyrides, or *trusses. **3.** *Shoulder, ledged* projection, ear, *joggle, or lug in a *voussoir of a flat arch, segmental arch, or architrave constructed of voussoirs, fitting into a recess in the adjacent voussoir for stability. **4.** Ledged or joggled voussoir resting on a neighbouring voussoir, as in *rusticated *ashlar over an aperture or in an *arcade on *piers.

crossing Volume formed on a square plan by the intersection of *chancel, *nave, and *transepts of a *cruciform church, often with a tower, *flèche, or other architectural feature, such as a *cupola, over it.

Crossland, William Henry (1835-1908) English architect, pupil of 'Great' Scott, with whom he worked on the *Company-town of Akroydon (now Boothtown), Halifax, Yorks. (from c.1859). Establishing himself in Yorks., he designed numerous churches (e.g. St Chad, Far Headingley, Leeds (1866-8), with **Edmund Beckett Denison** (1816-1905—**1st Baron Grimthorpe** from 1886)), and restored others, as well as producing secular buildings, including the magnificent Town Hall, Rochdale, Lancs. (1864-71—the tower (1885-7) is a replacement by *Waterhouse). Echoes of this building reappeared in the former Franco-Flemish Holloway Sanatorium, Virginia Water, Surrey (1872-85—now Virginia Park housing development), designed with **John Philpot Jones** (fl.1857-75). His masterpiece is the ebullient Royal Holloway College, Egham, Surrey (1879-87), in a *Loire-château style. He died penniless.

Elliott (1996); *ODNB* (2004)

croud, croude, crowd, crowde *See* CRYPT.

Crowe, Dame Sylvia (1901-97) Influential English landscape architect, she trained under **Edward White** (1872-1952) of **Milner White & Son** before joining the **William Cutbush** nurseries, Barnet, Herts. After service in the 1939-45 war she commenced practice, sharing an office (but not as a partner) with Brenda *Colvin, many of whose ideas she adopted. One of her first jobs was the reclamation of sand dunes in Lincs. damaged during the war. She was also influenced by *Jellicoe, esp. in her work for the post-war *New Towns (e.g. Basildon, Harlow) and power stations. As consultant (1964-76) to the Forestry Commission, she attempted to balance needs for timber production with aesthetic, recreational, and *conservation considerations, and from 1969 she was involved in landscaping around reservoirs (e.g. Empingham, Rut.). She designed the master-plan for the Commonwealth Gardens, Canberra, Australia.

Collens & Powell (eds) (1999); Crowe (1956, 1958, 1966); Crowe (ed.) (1961); Crowe & Miller (eds) (1964); Crowe & Mitchell (1988); S.Harvey (ed.) (1987); *ODNB* (2004); J.T (1996)

crown 1. Head of any part of a building, especially of an arch or *vault (including the *keystone and about the middle third of the arc), called *crown of an arch,* and embracing both *intrados* and *extrados.* **2.** *Apse at the east end of a church. **3.** *See* SPIRE. *Compounds include*:

crown cornice: **1.** main *cornice and *frieze defining the top of a *façade, i.e. a *cornicione*; **2.** upper part of a cornice, including the *corona and anything over it;

crown-moulding: any *moulding that crowns anything, e.g. the *corona of a cornice;

crown-plate: longitudinal timber in a *crown-post roof,* supported on *crown-posts* and bearing the *collars, also called a *collar-purlin* or *collar-plate*;

crown-post: upright timber set on a *tie-beam, or occasionally on a collar, supporting the *crown-plate* and not rising above a collar;

crown-steeple: decorative termination in which a *spire is replaced by four flying *buttresses rising from *pinnacles at the corners of a tower, meeting in the middle and supporting a slender *spirelet that rests entirely upon the buttresses: a good example is at St Giles Cathedral, Edinburgh (c.1486);

crown-strut: upright timber resembling a *crown-post,* but not supporting a *plate;

crown-tile: *ridge-tile or -cresting.

crown glass Fine English window-glass with a brilliant, fine-finish lustre, in general use until the mid-C19. *See* GLASS.

crow-steps *Corbel-, *cat-, *craw-, or *corbie-steps forming the stepped tops of a *gable, the *crow-stone being the topmost stone at the apex. *Crow-stepped* (or *cat-stepped*) gables were common in Flemish, Netherlandish, North-German, and Scandinavian architecture, and influenced the design of buildings in East Anglia and Eastern Scotland.

Croxton, John (fl.1411-47) English mason, he worked at Guildhall, London (1411), when that structure was begun, and was associated with it for most of his career. He was undoubtedly the architect, and the *crypt and porch were fine examples of the *Perp. style.

J.Harvey (1987)

Croyland, William (fl.1392-1427) English master-mason responsible for most of the *Perp. work at Croyland Abbey, Lincs., including the north *aisle, tower, and *nave-*screen. His other very considerable buildings there have all been destroyed.

J.Harvey (1987)

cruciform *Cross-shaped: e.g. a church with *transepts.

cruck *Blade or inclined curved timber, meeting a similar timber to form an approximately triangular frame on which the subsidiary structure rests. A *full* or *true cruck* (**c**) has two blades serving as the *principals of a roof, rising from near ground level to the *ridge, and supporting both walls and roof. A *cruck-truss* has two blades with a transverse timber that could be a *tie-beam (at or below the top level of the walls), a *collar (at high level), a *saddle (just under the apex), or a *yoke (just below the apex). A *cruck-framed* structure is therefore one constructed of crucks instead of boxframes. ***Types of cruck include***:

base- (**e**): rises from just above ground level to just under the first transverse member, and provides the main upright for the wall;

end-: cruck-blade in the centre of a *gable-wall of a cruck-framed building supporting the ridge-timber;

jointed (**d**): cruck-truss made of two or more pieces of timber, the lowest of which rises from just above ground level and doubles as a wall-post at the top of which the cruck is jointed and changes direction to follow the slope of the roof;

middle-: the same as a *raised cruck* (**b**);

raised (**b**): cruck with its feet set in solid walls, with the blades reaching down the walls (if the blades reach half-way down the walls, they are *middle-crucks*);

two-tier: supporting a small pair of cruck-shaped blades over the collar;

upper (**a**): cruck with its feet resting on a first-floor *ceiling-beam* that is not a *tie-beam*.

Alcock (1981); ABDM (1996); Charles (1967)

Crucy, Mathurin (1749–1826) Architect/surveyor of Nantes, he created many fine buildings and public spaces, including the *Grand Théâtre* and *Place Graslin* (1784–7), *Place d'Armes* (1786–90), *Place Royale* (1787), *Bourse* (1790–1814), and Textile Exchange (1821). His civic designs were conceived on a grand scale, and are good examples of Greek-inspired French *Neo-Classicism.

Lelievre (1942)

Crundale, Richard (*fl.*1281–93) English master-mason he worked under Robert of *Beverley at the Tower of London (1281–3), and was at Westminster Abbey 1284–5, where he succeeded Beverley as King's Chief Mason for London Works. He designed the Eleanor Cross at Charing Cross (1290—replaced by the later work by E.M. *Barry), and the beautiful tomb of **Queen Eleanor** (d.1290) in Westminster Abbey. His brother, **Roger** (*fl.*1290–8), completed Charing Cross, and worked with **Nicholas Dyminge de Reyns**

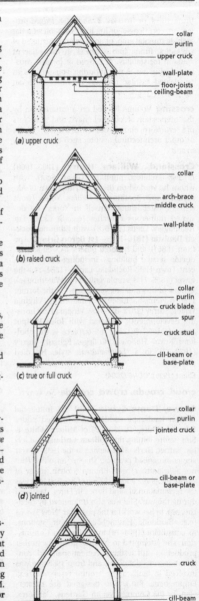

(*a*) upper cruck

(*b*) raised cruck

(*c*) true or full cruck

(*d*) jointed

(*e*) base cruck

(*fl*.1290s) on the designs and making of the tomb of Queen Eleanor's viscera in Lincoln Cathedral (1291-4—destroyed) and the Eleanor Cross at Waltham, Herts. (which survives).

J.Harvey (1987)

Crunden, John (*c*.1741-1835) English architect, known for his *pattern-books (influential, notably in America), one of which, *Convenient and Ornamental Architecture, consisting of Original Designs (from) the Farm House ... to the Most Grand and Magnificent Villa* (1767), went into seven later editions, and was the most successful of its type, containing designs for a range of Palladianesque buildings. He collaborated with **J.H.Morris** to produce *The Carpenter's Companion ... for ... Chinese Railing and Gates* (1765), and also designed in the *Gothick style, including a garden-pavilion illustrated in Krafft's *Plans des plus beaux jardins pittoresques* (1809). His architectural works are not numerous, but include Boodle's Club, St James's Street, London (1775-6), which is influenced by the work of Robert *Adam.

Co (2008); Crunden (1767); E.Hs (1990)

Crusader castles C12 military architecture in the Middle East, consisting of pilgrims' forts, coastal fortifications, and large castles (e.g. *Krak des Chevaliers* (1150-1200)).

Folda (1995); H.Kennedy (1994); Kühnel (1994)

crypt 1. Large vaulted chamber (*croft, croud, croude, crowd, crowde, shroud*, or *undercroft*) beneath a church, wholly or partly underground, usually under the *chancel, often divided into *nave, *aisles, and chapels, equipped with *altars, and used for religious services and burials beneath the floor. They often had some degree of natural light, and were generally bigger than a *confessio, though very small crypts, such as the *Anglo-Saxon example at Hexham (C7) were little more than *Relic-chambers*. *Ring-crypts* were semi-circular crypts inside and below an *apse, originating with the *basilica of *San Pietro*, Rome: outer ring-crypts (called *ambulatories) were characteristic of the *Carolingian and *Ottonian periods, but a very early example, pre-dating those on the Continent, existed at All Saints Church, Brixworth, Northants. (*c*.C8 or later). **2.** Burial-chamber.

crypta 1. Long narrow *vault, wholly or partly underground, associated with a Roman farm, used for storage. **2.** Long narrow *gallery with windows on each side, the larger openings being on the side next to the sea or an especially fine view, used for walking and conversation, attached to a Roman *villa, called *cryptoporticus*.

C-scroll C- and S-scrolls were elements of *Rococo ornament, especially in frames around *cartouches*, mirrors, etc.

cubicle Small compartment, e.g. changing-room, shower-compartment, or w.c. cubicle.

cubiculum (*pl*. **cubicula**) *See* CATACOMB.

Cubism Movement in art originating with the work of **Pablo Picasso** (1881-1973) and **Georges Braque** (1882-1963), mainly *c*.1905-14. Cubism departed from the notion of art as an imitation of Nature that had been paramount in Europe from *Renaissance times, and also abandoned traditional *perspective. Instead it attempted to achieve the illusion of three-dimensionsal forms in a different way by showing solids and volumes in two-dimensional flat planes to suggest space. To do this, many aspects of familiar objects were represented all at once, their forms shown on various geometrical planes redrawn from many vantage-points to create new combinations. Thus it claimed to be a new way of seeing, and tried to indicate that which was visible as well as everything known about the item depicted.

The relationship of Cubism and architecture was at best tentative, often involving the application of Cubist decorations to *stripped Neo-Classical buildings. Hints of Cubist themes are found in *Art-Deco and *Modernist work: however, even in Prague, the Czech Cubist group (including *Chochol and *Gočár) did little more than treat *façades with *Expressionistic *prismatic ornament. The fundamentals of Cubism, including asymmetrical composition, interpenetration of volumes, transparency, and perception simultaneously from various points of view, became enshrined in the *Modern Movement.

Barr (1936); Blau & Troy (eds) (1997); Burkhardt & Lamarová (1982); COF (1988); Golding (1988); Svácha (1995); Vegesack (ed.) (1992)

Cubitt, Lewis (1799-1883) English architect. Apprenticed (1815) to his eldest brother, Thomas *Cubitt, he worked in *Kendall's office before entering into partnership with his brothers (1824) and setting up on his own (1830s). He designed many houses in Belgravia and Bloomsbury built by the Cubitts, and designed and built the *Italianate houses on the south side of Lowndes Square, London (1837-9). In the 1840s he became a successful railway architect, and was responsible for the terminus of the Great Northern Railway, King's Cross (1851-2).

Co (2008); Hobhouse (1995)

Cubitt, Thomas (1788-1855) English master-carpenter. He entered into partnership (*c*.1814) with his brother, **William** (1791-1863), and set up (1815) a building establishment to encompass all the trades, engaging in speculative developments on a huge scale in London. From 1824, he built large parts of the Bedford Estate, Bloomsbury, all to an excellent standard of workmanship, and all designed 'in-house', largely by his brother, Lewis *Cubitt. He developed substantial areas of Belgravia and Pimlico, and much of Kemp Town, Brighton. He also erected several large, substantial, and well-built houses to his own designs: these were sub-*Palladian or *Italianate, and the most celebrated is Osborne House, IoW (1845–8), to which Prince *Albert also contributed. Cubitt was active in promoting public hygiene, *public parks, better building regulations, and smoke abatement.

Co (2008); Hobhouse (1995); *ODNB* (2004); Su (1993)

Cuijpers *or* **Cuypers, Eduard Gerard Hendrik Hubert** (1859–1927) Dutch architect, nephew of P.J.H.*Cuijpers, under whom he trained before establishing (1878) his Amsterdam practice, specializing in housing. He founded (1903) the periodical *Het Huis* (re-named *Het Huis oud en nieuw* (1905–27)) which included articles on historic buildings and reflected Cuijpers's eclectic tastes. His office was a training-ground for members of the *Amsterdam School.

Sennott (ed.) (2004); J.T (1996)

Cuijpers *or* **Cuypers, Petrus Josephus Hubertus** (1827–1921) Dutch architect, he designed many *Neo-Gothic churches in The Netherlands, and in *St Willibrordus-buiten-de-Veste*, Amsterdam (1864), demonstrated his interest in honesty of materials and construction derived from study of *Viollet-le-Duc. As an RC from the province of Limburg he was ideally placed when the RC episcopal hierarchy was restored (1853), and an ambitious programme of church-building began. His best-known works are the *Rijksmuseum* (State Museum—1877–85) and the Central Station (1881–9), in Amsterdam, both powerfully symmetrical, in a free style, and with lively skylines. The *Rijksmuseum* was influenced by the University Museum, Oxford, even in respect of its iron roofs and interior galleries. His *Picturesque compositions and principles of truth to materials and expression caused him to be labelled the 'Dutch *Viollet-le-Duc'. Among his finest *polychrome works were the *Heilige Hart*, *Vondelstraat* (1870–3), and the *Maria Magdalenekerk*, Amsterdam (1889–91—destroyed). The sophistication of his brick polychromy demonstrates that his work was at least as original as anything by *Butterfield or *Street.

Cuypers (1917); Hoogewoud *et al.* (1985); H.Rosenberg (1972); J.T (1996)

cul-de-four 1. Half-dome, as used over an *apse or a *niche. **2.** Incorrectly held to mean a hemispherical vault on a circular or elliptical plan.

cul-de-lampe 1. Pendent ornament shaped like a *pyramid or a cone. **2.** *Corbel formed like a half-cone.

cul-de-sac Alley, lane, passage, street, etc., closed at one end.

Cullen, Thomas Gordon (1914–94) English architect/town-planner. He started his career (1933) assisting *McGrath before joining *Tecton (1936–8) to work on the Finsbury Health Centre and Highpoint, Highgate. He became (1946) assistant art-editor of the *AR*, gaining *Hastings's confidence, for whom he produced many seductive drawings intended as compositional rules for new urban centres, even though the sort of architecture increasingly promoted by the *AR* ensured they would be ignored. His *Townscape* (1961) attempted to promote visual pleasure in urban developments, but the poverty of language in the architecture of the time ensured that such well-meaning campaigns would never succeed in creating anything like an aesthetically agreeable environment.

ODNB (2004); J.T (1996)

Culot, Maurice (1939–) *See* ARAU.

cultural tourism Term reflecting specific interest in visiting sites of architectural and historic interest: it may cause damage to those sites if excessive, so any gain in income should be offset by the costs of making good wear, deliberate damage, or theft.

JF

culver-hole Aperture in a wall to receive the end of a timber-member. *Putlog-hole.

culver-house *Columbarium in the sense of a *dovecote.

culvert Tunnel or passage through which water passes under a road, building, etc.

Cumberland, Frederic William (1820–81) One of the most accomplished *Gothic Revivalists working in Canada, he designed St James's Cathedral, Toronto (1852–3), in the *Gothic style, working in partnership with **William G. Storm** (1826–92) during the construction of the church. With Storm he also designed University College, University of Toronto (1856), a demonstration of *Ruskinian principles of design that is arguably a superior composition to *Deane & Woodward's University Museum, Oxford. The Toronto building has central and corner towers, and is a fine example of *High-Victorian *Picturesque.

K (1994); J.T (1996)

Cundy, Thomas (1765–1825) Cornwall-born architect, he became (1821) Surveyor to Lord Grosvenor's Estates in Belgravia and Pimlico,

London. He designed numerous country-houses in a *Picturesque *Gothic style, e.g. Wytham Abbey (1809–10) and All Saints Church (1811–12), Wytham, Berks., and Middleton Stoney Rectory, Oxon. (1816–17).

Co (2008); *ODNB* (2004)

Cundy, Thomas, Jun. II (1790–1867) London-born architect, he worked in his father's office and succeeded him to the practice and the Surveyorship of the Grosvenor Estate. He oversaw the development of Belgravia and Pimlico, largely by Thomas *Cubitt. His Normanton Church, Rut. (1826), has a tower derived from *Archer's *Baroque towers at St John's, Smith Square, Westminster. From the late 1840s Cundy was joined by *his* son, **Thomas III** (1820–95), who also succeeded to the practice and Surveyorship. Thomas II and III seem to have been jointly responsible for a number of *Gothic-Revival churches, including St Barnabas, Pimlico (1847–50—said by the St Paul's Ecclesiological Society to be the 'most sumptuous and correctly fitted church erected in England since the Reformation'). Thomas III designed some of the tall *stucco-fronted terraces in Kensington, in a free *Italianate manner that was widely imitated. His best houses are arguably 22–4 Queen's Gate (1858–60), and Cornwall Gardens (1866–79).

Co (2008); Hobhouse (ed.) (1986); *ODNB* (2004); J.T (1996)

cuneus 1. Wedge or *voussoir. 2. Part of a Classical theatre *auditorium, shaped like a wedge, containing seating and defined by the gangways, passages, etc. 3. Species of *zig-zag or *fret painted on flat *bands, a variation on *Greek key.

Cunningham, Ivor Richard (1928–2007) English architect/landscape architect, he worked with B.*Colvin, S.*Crowe, and **Erik Anjou** in Sweden, before joining (1955) Eric *Lyons in practice, becoming a partner in SPAN (1962). The first fruits of their collaboration were at Blackheath: Cunningham's approach to landscape there, involving respect for existing features such as mature trees, integrating spaces between the buildings with the more open public areas, and designing the architecture and the landscape as one entity, set the agenda for subsequent developments by the firm. After Lyons's death, Cunningham completed the SPAN project, Mallard Place, Twickenham (1984).

RIBAJ (5 May 2007), 94; *The Times* (29 March 2007), 79

cupboard 1. Properly, a board or table on which to place cups and other vessels. 2. Piece of furniture for the display of plate, etc. 3. A sideboard. 4. Closet or cabinet with shelves for the storage of dishes, cups, etc. In some cases (**1**) was combined with (**4**), the board forming the door of the cupboard, which, when lowered on its hinges,

stood on a folding leg and provided a table. A *cupboard-bed* was one either fitted within a recess, or capable of being folded away.

Cupid God of Love, usually depicted as a winged male child with bow and arrow, as distinct from an unarmed *cherub or wingless *putto. See AMORINO.

cupola 1. Bowl-shaped *vault on a circular, elliptical, or polygonal plan. 2. Underside or *soffit of a *dome. 3. Bowl-shaped element carried on columns set as a *canopy over a tomb, etc., or a *ciborium. 4. Small dome on the *lantern over the eye of a large dome, or the dome plus lantern, or any diminutive domed form, visible above a roof. 5. Revolving dome of an *observatory, or an armoured revolving dome over the guns of a fortress.

curb-roof See ROOF.

curstable Course of stones forming a *string, with *mouldings.

curtail 1. In a *stair, the outward curving or *scroll-shaped part of the handrail, and the outer end of the lowest step. In grander stairs the first flight, detached from a wall, may have a *curtail-* or *scroll*-step with curved parts at each end of the *balustrades and lowest step, often curving around the centre-line of the *newels. See STAIR. 2. The scrolled shape gives the term *curlicue* or *curleycue* to a façade with scrolled *gable, otherwise known as a *curtail* *façade, common in Belgium and The Netherlands.

curtain-wall 1. Part of a straight wall constructed between two advancing structures, such as *bastions, *buttresses, or *piers. In a fortification it is the weakest element, and in a church it is pierced with large windows, as in a *Perp. *aisle. 2. Any plain enclosing screen-wall not supporting a roof. 3. Partition between two rooms, or subdividing a space. 4. In modern construction, a thin subordinate wall between piers or other structural members, the curtain being a filling, having no share in the support of other parts of the building. This principle was extended to the provision of entire external non-loadbearing skins, supported

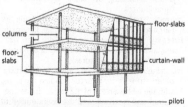

curtain-wall on column-and-slab construction.

by the structure, and usually made of metal, glass, or some other type of *cladding.
HHS (1985)

curved brace In many medieval *timber-framed structures and *trusses the *braces were curved, as in *knee-braces or arch-braces. Sometimes the *principals themselves were curved.

Curvilinear *See* TRACERY.

cushion 1. Convex projection (*pulvinus*) of part of a building, e.g. a *frieze apparently bulging outwards as if under pressure, called *cushion-course*, *cushioned*, or *pulvinated* frieze, or even a *bolster or *pulvin. **2.** Stone block on an *impost, being the *springer of an arch. **3.** *Corbel or *pad-stone. *Other compounds include*:
cushion-capital: *see* CAPITAL;
cushion-course: *pulvinated *frieze.

cusp Point made by the intersection of two curved lines or members, e.g. the projecting point between the small arcs or *foils in *Gothic *tracery, or the enrichment on the intrados of a Gothic arch provided by foliation, the curves of which touch the inner edge of the main arch (*cusped* arch). *Cuspidation* is a series of cusps, as on the *intrados of a Gothic arch.

cussom(e) Large heavy *slate, or stone slab, bedded in *mortar and laid as part of a *course, slightly inclined, immediately above the *eaves of a pitched roof above the gutter, thus providing an overhanging *soffit and avoiding the necessity of *sprockets, timber *fasciae, or soffit-linings.

cutaway Drawing (usually an *axonometric or *isometric projection) showing a building or part of a building with a part cut away to reveal the interior, a *section through the structure, and the exterior. *As a derivative of* cut *compounds include*:
cut brackets: **1.** piece of board cut with a profile resembling a *corbel or *console, used to support a shelf, or a larger timber, cut similarly, supporting overhanging *eaves; **2.** board, further enriched, under the returned nosing of each step on the outer string of a *stair, sometimes resembling the sides of *consoles or *modillions;
cut-roof: *roof with the appearance of having the part above the *collars removed, i.e. flattened;
cut splay: obliquely cut corners of bricks in walling, as in *gables before the placing of *copes, or the *reveals of apertures;
cut-string stairs: open-string *stairs in which the outer *string is cut to accommodate the steps, with the treads on top of the string, the nosings mitred and returned, and the risers mitred to the string.

cut-water: *starling, or sharply pointed bridge-*pier to reduce the pressure on it when a river is in flood.

cut-work Flower-beds cut into elaborate patterns outlined in turf, separated by narrow sanded *paths in a *parterre, fashionable in C17, and sometimes edged with box.

cut-work parterre Elaborate example (*after Crisp*).

Cuvilliés, Jean-François-Vincent-Joseph (1695–1768) *Rococo architect of the utmost refinement. Born near Brussels, as Court Dwarf he entered (1708) the service of **Max II Emanuel, Elector of Bavaria** (*r.*1679–1704 & 1715–26), who was then in exile. As a member of the Electoral household, Cuvilliés was exposed to the latest French tastes in architecture. When the Court returned to Munich (1715), Cuvilliés worked under *Effner, a pupil of *Boffrand, and, in due course, the budding architect Cuvilliés was also sent to Paris, where he studied briefly under **Jean-François Blondel** (1683–1756). Back in the Bavarian capital, he worked with Effner, and, when **Karl Albrecht** succeeded as Elector (*r.*1726–45), seems to have been treated as the older architect's equal, although the prize of *Oberhofbaumeister* eluded him until 1763. For the new Elector's brother, **Clemens August** (1700–61—**Elector/Prince-Archbishop of Cologne** from 1723), Cuvilliés designed Rococo interiors (1728–30) at *Schloss Brühl* near Cologne (newly-built to designs by *Schlaun), as well as the charming hunting-lodge of Falkenlust (1729–37), with interiors gaily decorated with *Chinoiserie and other orientalizing motifs judiciously mingled with Rococo ornament. Cuvilliés also may have been responsible for the *chinesisches Haus* for the

219   **cyma, cima**

Pheasantry in the Park (c.1730). He was called in as
a consultant by the Archbishop to advise on the
building of the *Collegiate Church of St Michael,
at Berg-am-Laim, Munich (1738–51), J.M.*Fischer
being the architect, and, c.1737, designed the lovely
*high-altar for the former Augustinian (now Parish)
Church at Diessen, also by Fischer.

Dissemination of the Rococo style throughout
Bavaria was largely the result of Cuvilliés's creations. His *Reiche Zimmer* in the Munich *Residenz*
(1730–7) was acclaimed as among the finest of
European Rococo achievements before being
badly damaged during the 1939–45 war. From
1733 he was involved in the building of the Archiepiscopal *Palais Königsfeld* (or *Holnstein*), Munich (completed 1737), and, at the same time, in
preparing the plans of the Premonstratensian
Abbey of Schäftlarn, south of Munich. However,
his finest creation is unquestionably the *Amalienburg* in the grounds of *Schloss Nymphenburg*
(1734–9): this is an exquisite single-storey hunt-
ing-*pavilion with a balcony (a *tir aux faisans*
from which pheasants could be shot) over the
central circular *saloon, part of which extends
outwards in a *bow in the centre of the
entrance-façade. The enchanting Rococo interior
decorations, with blue, yellow, and straw-co-
loured walls enriched with refined silvered
embellishments, and enlivened with mirrors and
Chinoiserie motifs, are outstanding, although J.B.
*Zimmermann was responsible for the *stucco-
work.

The *Livre de Cartouches* marked the start of a
series of publications by Cuvilliés from 1738 featuring illustrations of ornamental designs for *cartouches, ceilings, frames, and entire rooms, with
furnishings and panels. Other publications, featuring designs for mirrors, chandeliers, and a
great deal more, followed from 1745, and from
1756 yet another series, this time featuring architectural designs, came out. These works were
hugely influential in Central Europe. By the mid-
1740s his advice was being sought by many
patrons, and he was involved in the designs for
Schlösser at Haimhausen, near Munich (from
1747), and Wilhelmsthal, near Kassel (from
1750—a restrained Classical design), but his finest
works were in and around Munich. His *Residenz-
Theater*, Munich (1750–3), is one of the most
beautiful small theatres in the world, bursting
with the type of ornament he had published in
various *Livres*: it was badly damaged (1944), but
was reconstructed (1958), albeit on a different site
within the *Residenz* complex. His appointment as
Oberhofbaumeister by the **Elector Maximilian III
Joseph** (r.1745–77) came late in his career, after
he had rebuilt the central room at *Schloss Nymphenburg* (1756–7), and he did not live long after.
His last work was the completion of the *façade of
the *Theatinerkirche St Kajetan*, Munich (1767).

His son, **François-Joseph-Ludwig** (1731–77), produced many of the illustrations for his father's
publications, and seems to have been largely
responsible for the third series of the 1750s in
which Rococo and *Neo-Classicism merged. He
reissued many of his father's designs in his *École
de l'Architecture Bavaroise* (from 1770).

Bou (1962); Braunfels (1938, 1986); Hi (1968a); Jervis
(1984); Lieb (1992); F. Wolf (1967)

Cuypers *See* CUIJPERS.

cyclopean 1. *Masonry composed of irregularly shaped very large blocks, sometimes approximating to polygons, dressed sufficiently for them
to fit tightly together, without *mortar, called
Megalithic or *Pelasgic*. Found in Antiquity, it was
also occasionally used by later architects to suggest very early origins, or rock-like foundations, as
in the *plinth of 'Greek' *Thomson's Caledonia
Road Church, Glasgow (1856). **2.** *Rock-faced*
masonry, intended to appear like roughly quarried stones, but in fact dressed with rough surfaces for effect.

cyclostyle Circular *peristyle of columns surrounding a wall-less volume, i.e. a *monopteral
*temple, often found in C18 parks.

cyma, cima (*pl.* **cymae**) Projecting *moulding,
common in Classical architecture, with an *ogee
*section, usually of equal convex and concave arcs,
with a plain *fillet above and below it. There are
two main types: the *cyma recta*, or *Doric cyma*,
usually found at the top of a *cornice, with the
concave part uppermost (called cymatium), and
the *cyma reversa, Lesbian cymatium*, or *reverse
ogee*, with the convex part uppermost, usually
part of the bed-mouldings of a cornice or the
exterior moulding of *architraves. *Cymatium* refers
to a *crown-moulding of a Classical cornice, commonly of the cyma type, but sometimes an *ovolo
(in some *Tuscan *Orders) and sometimes a
*cavetto (in the *Doric Order).

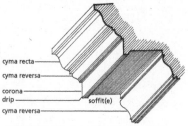

cyma Cornice with *cyma recta* and *cyma reversa*
profiles.

cynocephalus Beast with the body of an ape, and a dog-like head, probably derived from baboons, found in Ancient Egyptian and Roman work.

cynocephalus Roman Egyptianizing statuette.

cypher Capital letters of the alphabet interwoven in one symmetrical design, or two capitals together, one reversed (e.g. JL) and surrounded by wreaths, etc., commonly found in schemes of architectural decoration, especially from the time of *Louis Quatorze*.

cyrtostyle 1. *Portico on a semicircular plan projecting from a *façade. **2.** Curved *colonnade.

cyzicene hall *Oecus Cyzicenus*, or large hall overlooking a garden in an Ancient-Greek house.

Czech Renaissance style Late-C19 style of architecture associated with Czech nationalism, the hallmarks of which were the use of *sgraffito* and *fresco*, notably in works by *Wiehl and his contemporaries, influenced by C16 work in Prague, etc.

dado 1. *Die or flat-faced plain block of a Classical *pedestal between the *base and *cap. **2.** Surface of an internal wall like an extended pedestal all the way round a room between a *skirting (base or *plinth) and *chair-rail (*cornice), called a *chair- or dado-rail. A *wainscot is a panelled timber dado. *Dado* is not used to describe an external pedestal-course. **3.** To cut or form with a groove of rectangular section, so the groove itself is also called a *dado*.

Daedalus 'Cunning artificer' of Greek mythology, inventor/artist/architect, he was responsible for the *labyrinth at Knossos, Crete. Medieval architects identified with Daedalus as his heirs, and his legends are associated with those of *Freemasonry.

J.Curl (2011); H & S (1996)

dagger *Light with both ends pointed, the larger of which is an *ogee: it resembles a dagger in *Second-Pointed *tracery (*see* TRACERY). Symmetrical about the long axis, and straight, it is distinct from the curved *mouchette*, rounded at one end, resembling a *tadpole*.

dagoba *Stupa, consisting of a low *drum surmounted by a bell-shaped or *dome-like form above which is a square platform or *tee*, or several umbrella-forms. Associated with Buddhist architecture, its name may have been the origin of the curious word *pagoda*.

Dahlerup, Jens Vilhelm (1836–1907) Danish architect, pupil of *Hetsch and *Nebelong, also influenced by T. von *Hansen's and *Schinkel's architecture, he turned more to a rich Italian-*Renaissance style, persuaded in that direction by the works of *Semper. He designed numerous important buildings: among them the Agriculture School at Lyngby, the Royal Theatre, Copenhagen (1872–4—with Ove *Petersen), the Pantomime Theatre, Tivoli Gardens, Copenhagen (1870s), the New Carlsberg Brewery Building (1880–3), the *Jesuskirken* at Valby, the Royal Museum of Art (1888–96—with **Georg Møller**), the *Glyptotek* (1891–5), and many private houses in and around Copenhagen. The Vejlefjord Sanatorium (1899) was also built to his designs. He was one of the last of the academic architects of *Historicism in

Denmark, and something of a *virtuoso* in his use of architectural language.

Saur (1991–); We (1947)

dairy Building where milk and cream are kept, sold, or made into cheese, often divided into rooms for each process, and separated from cow-houses and milking-places. Necessity dictated it should be well insulated, so *thatch was often used for the roof, and interiors were of stone and/or tiled. Functioning dairies were transmogrified into *fabriques* in landscaped parks, and, like the cottage, treated decoratively, appearing in numerous books of designs, including those by *Plaw of 1785 and **Johann Karl Krafft** (1764–1833) of 1809-10. An early example was the *Laiterie* at Chantilly, by *Hardouin-Mansart (1689–94): C18 ornamental dairies include those at Hohenheim, near Stuttgart, Württemberg, Germany (*c*.1782); the *Laiterie de la Reine* at the *Hameau*, Versailles, by *Mique (1783–5—which mingled the rustic with Classical statuary); the magnificent *Neo-Classical *Laiterie*, Rambouillet (1785—by **Jacques-Jean Thévenin** (1732-1813 and Hubert *Robert)); and the *Ermitage*, Arlesheim, Basel, Switzerland (*c*.1787). Other examples include *Soane's building at Hamels, Herts. (1781–3—with primitive *Doric columns); the Chinese Dairy, Woburn, Beds. (1787–1802—by Henry *Holland); James *Wyatt's chapel-like *Gothic Dairy (1795) at Cobham, Kent; the thatched dairy at Blaise Castle, Bristol (*c*.1804), by G.S.*Repton, with probable input from *Nash; the octagonal building with *loggia at Endsleigh, Milton Abbot, Devon (*c*.1814—by *Wyatville); the C19 octagonal structure at Kilruddery, Bray, Co. Wicklow, Ireland, by **Sir George Frederick John Hodson** (1806–88—**3rd Baronet** from 1831); and the Gothic confection featuring *marbles and *alabaster, Buxley Farm, Manderston House, near Duns, Berwickshire (1897–1900—by **John Kinross** (1855–1931)).

CL, clxxxiv/4 (25 Jan. 1990), 88-91; Krafft (1809–10); W.Pa (1852); Pückler-Muskau (1832); J.M.Robinson (1983); Symes (2006)

daïs 1. *Estrade, footpace, halpace*, or platform in a *banqueting-hall on which a high-table is situated. **2.** Any similar platform, as in a lecture-theatre. **3.** The high-table itself. **4.** *Canopy over such a table or platform. **5.** *Tester or protective top over a throne, etc.

Dakin, James Harrison (1806–52) Born in NYC, he became one of the most distinguished American architects of his time, equally fluent in *Egyptian, *Greek, or *Gothic styles. He joined *Town & *Davis (1829), becoming a partner (1832), and, with Ithiel *Town, he designed New York University (1833–7), one of the first examples of *Collegiate Gothic in America. He set up (1833) in independent practice, and designed several distinguished *Greek-Revival buildings, including the First Presbyterian Church, Troy, NY (1834), Bank of Louisville, KY (1834–6), and University of Louisiana (1847–55), later Tulane University. His Louisiana State Capitol, Baton Rouge (1847–52), is a daring *Gothic-Revival essay. He influenced *Lafever and produced drawings for several plates in two of the latter's books.

Lafever (1968, 1969); Patrick (1980); P (1982); A.Sy (1973)

dalle 1. Flat slab of stone, *marble, *terracotta, etc., used in floors. **2.** Ornamental or coloured slab for pavements in churches, etc., so *dallage* is flooring with *dalles*. **3.** Narrow box-gutter.

Dalton, John (1927–2007). Yorks.-born Australian architect. He contributed to the creation of an architecture drawing on simple forms responsive to the climatic conditions of Queensland by controlling solar-heat gain and providing cross-ventilation to counteract the problems of humidity. His University House, Griffith University (1975), and Halls of Residence, Kelvin Grove College of Technology and Further Education (1977), both in Brisbane, are among his larger works, but many of his houses, with their *louvres, *verandahs, and other features that reflect the climate, deserve notice. Among his houses the Mount Manning Homestead, Darling Downs (1982), and the Beach House, Point Lookout (1988), both in Queensland, reflect his architectural philosophy.

E (1994); Freeland (1968); I.McKay & R.Boyd (1971); Tanner (1976)

Daly, César-Denis (1811–93) The most important French architectural editor and journalist of the second half of C19. He was brought up in England, studied architecture under *Duban, and later directed the *Revue Générale de L'Architecture et des Traveaux Publics* (1839–90), France's first illustrated architectural journal, and *La Semaine des Constructeurs* (1876–97). His most influential work was *L'Architecture privée au XIXme siècle* (1864–77), a many-volumed *pattern-book of domestic architecture in the era of **Napoléon III** (r.1852–70) and after. *L'Architecture Funéraire Contemporaine* (1871) is a richly illustrated record of French *cemetery art of the period. He was responsible for the restoration of Albi Cathedral (1844–77). During his career, he gave critical support to *Barry, *Duc, *Garnier, *Labrouste, and *Vaudoyer, among others, and he was an admirer of **François-Marie-Charles Fourier** (1772–1885), the social theorist: indeed, Daly had been involved with the Fourierists since the 1830s, and had contributed articles and money to *La Phalange, La Démocratie Pacifique*, and other journals. As early as 1833 he proposed a scheme for *phalanstères* (buildings housing *phalanxes* or socialistic communities) for 400 children: during 1849 plans were made to found a Fourierist colony in TX, and *La Réunion*, near Dallas, was founded in 1855. Daly travelled to TX, and was a member of the Board of Directors, but did not remain long, probably because of internal dissent. He visited Central America (1856) where he discovered important pre-Columbian ruins, and returned to Paris (1857) a changed man, his pro-Fourierist notions dissipated. Thereafter he promoted the single-family suburban villa as the ideal home rather than the *phalanstère*. He and *Viollet-le-Duc were founding members of the *Société d'Ethnographie Americaine et Orientale* (1858), charged with encouraging pre-Columbian archaeology in México.

Becherer (1984); Daly (1840–90, 1848, 1864, 1869, 1871, 1871a, 1877, 1880, n.d.); Daly & Davioud (1874); Lipstadt & Mendelsohn (1980)

dam 1. Bank or barrier of earth, *masonry, etc., built across a stream to obstruct its flow and raise its level, to form a reservoir, or to make water available to turn a mill-wheel, etc. **2.** *Causeway over swampy ground.

Damascene-work Designs incised into metal and filled with gold, silver, or copper, often of the *arabesque type.

Damesme *or* **Damême, Louis-Emmanuel-Aimé** (1757–1822) French architect, he supervised the erection of *Ledoux's *barrières* (toll-collecting offices) in Paris (1780s), and followed the master's severe Neo-Classical style. He designed several mansions and apartment-blocks in Paris and the theatre of the *Société Olympique* which so impressed **Tsar Alexander I of Russia** (r.1801–25) that he requested a set of the drawings for it. He also designed the *Théâtre Royale de la Monnaie*, Brussels (1813–18), with its octastyle *Ionic *portico.

Ga (1972); Krafft (1801–3)

Dammartin Family French architects. **Guy, Gui,** or **Guiot de Dammartin** (d.1398) worked with Raymond du *Temple on the Louvre, Paris (1362–72), and (1367–72) was employed by **Jean de France, Duc de Berry** (1340–1416), to oversee his ambitious building plans. He designed the Palace of Bourges (1375–85) with an *enfilade* system of planning, an innovative arrangement for the time in an *hôtel*. He designed two *Saintes-Chapelles*, at Riom (1382–8) and Bourges (1392–8), and remodelled the *châteaux* of Mehun-sur-Yèvre, Riom, and Poitiers as grand mansions, excising *battlements and constructing *dormers, windows, and architectural embellishments (all 1380s). His brother, **Drouet de Dammartin** (d.1413), also contributed to building operations at the Louvre and the *Hôtel de Nesle* (the latter for the **Duc de Berry**), Paris. Later (1380s), he became Master of the Works for the **Duc de Bourgogne**, and built the *Sainte-Chapelle*, Dijon (1387), as well as a *Carthusian monastery. Drouet's son, **Jean de Dammartin** (d.1454), was supervising architect at the Cathedral of St-Julien, Le Mans, from 1421, where he built the north *transept and *rose-window. Appointed (1432) Master of the Works at Tours Cathedral, he completed the *nave and the west portal.

Champeaux & Gauchery (1894); Lehoux (1966–8)

Damon, Isaac (1781–1862) American architect/ builder, he came to Northampton, MA (1811), to work on the Fourth Meeting-House (aka First Church of Christ—destroyed) designed by *Benjamin, and built Benjamin's Center Church, New Haven, CT (1813–14), a variant on *Gibbs's St Martin-in-the-Fields, London. Associated with *Town (with whom he became involved in *bridge construction, a speciality which he practised until the end of his career), he became the leading architect in Western MA for over three decades, designing at least thirteen churches as well as nearly all the town halls and court-houses in the region. Among his works may be cited the church at Springfield (1818–19), and his own house at Bridge Street, Northampton (1813).

Historic Northampton Museum & Education Center, MA

<http://www.historic-northampton.org/highlights/damon.html> accessed 5 Nov. 2012

Dance, George, Sen. (1695–1768) London mason/monumental-sculptor/builder/architect, he collaborated with his father-in-law, **James Gould** (*fl*.1720–34), in erecting St Botolph's Church, Bishopsgate (1725–8). Appointed Clerk of the Works to the City of London (1735), he designed the Mansion House (1739–42) with its grand *Egyptian Hall, probably his best work. His other buildings have influences from *Gibbs, *Palladianism, and *Wren, of which St Leonard's Church, Shoreditch (1736–40), with a *steeple design clearly based on the precedent of Wren's St Mary-le-Bow (completed 1680), is an example. He also rebuilt the *nave of St Mary's

Church, Faversham, Kent (1754–5), and designed the Market House, Coleraine, Co. Londonderry, for The Honourable The Irish Society (*c*.1740–3—demolished).

Co (2008); J.Curl (1986, 2000); GM (1972); Perks (1922); Stroud (1971)

Dance, George, Jun. (1741–1825) Youngest son of George *Dance, Sen. He set off for Italy (1758), met up with his brother **Nathaniel** (1735–1811) in Florence, and arrived in Rome (1759), where he acquired his skills as a draughtsman and absorbed the essentials of *Neo-Classicism, returning to England (1764). His first commission was All Hallows Church, London Wall (1765–7), an advanced Neo-Classical building with a barrel-vaulted interior and a bare exterior that perhaps shows influences of *Laugier and other French writers. He succeeded (1768) his father as Clerk of the Works, and designed the outstanding Newgate Gaol (1768–85—demolished 1902), a powerful and *Sublime composition with massive windowless *rusticated walls based on precedents by *Palladio and Giulio *Romano, and certain elements reminiscent of *Piranesi's imaginary prisons. It was one of the few works of architecture by an Englishman to be illustrated in *Durand's *Recueil . . .* (1799), and was architecture expressive of retribution (*architecture parlante*). Dance effected various town-planning improvements that altered many of the medieval street-plans of London, and, with Sir Robert *Taylor, drafted the *Building Act* (1774), which had a profound effect on the character of the London street-façade for the subsequent seven decades by setting down the thickness of front walls and ensuring no timbers such as *sash-frames were exposed but set back behind the brickwork. He remodelled part of the Mansion House, roofing over the *cortile, removing the grand staircase, lowering the roof of the *Egyptian Hall and erecting a coffered ceiling (1795–6). He rebuilt (1788–9) the south *façade of Guildhall in a *Hindoo-*Gothic style with Greek detailing, later to be lampooned by A.W.N. *Pugin. His most distinguished pupil was *Soane, who was influenced by Dance's designs (e.g. the low dome of the Council Chamber at Guildhall (1737–8—demolished 1908)). Some of Dance's work anticipated the *Greek Revival, e.g. the severe *portico at Stratton Park, Hants. (1803–6), and the Royal College of Surgeons, Lincoln's Inn Fields, London (1806–13), where the portico is all that survives the rebuilding by *Barry, who fluted the columns (1835–7).

Co (2008); GM (1972); Jeffery (1993); Pugin (1973); Stroud (1971); Su (1963)

dancer 1. Curved or spiral *stair. **2.** Wedge-shaped step in a curved stair with the narrow end widened, also known as *danced* or *dancing step*, or *balanced winder*.

dancette *Romanesque *chevron.

dancing step *See* DANCER.

Daneri, Luigi Carlo (1900–72) Italian architect of the circular *San Marcellino* (1932–5—with *concrete *dome by *Nervi). He designed some of the best 1930s *Rationalist buildings, including the *'Nicola Bonservi' Casa del Fascio*, Sturlo (1937–8). Other works include the *Villa Venturini* (1934–40), the *Villa Vitale*, Genoa (1934–40), the *Piazza R. Rossetti* (1936–55); Condominium Apartments, Quinto (1951–2), the *INA Casa* Residential Unit, *Villa Bernabo Brea*, Genoa (1952–3), and the huge *Quartiere Forte Quezzi* (or *'Biscione'*) (1956–7), high above Genoa.

Cevini (1989); D & P (eds) (1976); Gregotti (1968)

Daniell, Thomas (1749–1840) English artist: his views of topographical subjects in India, produced in collaboration with his nephew, **William Daniell** (1769–1837), were published in *Oriental Scenery* (1808) and *Picturesque Voyage to India* (1810) which greatly influenced the *Hindoo and *Indian styles during C19.

ODNB (2004)

Danish hut *See* BENGAL COTTAGE.

Danish knot Complicated intertwining tendrils of foliate *Anglo-Saxon and *Celtic ornament. Also called *Runic knot.*

Dantesque C19 revival of the austere *Gothic styles prevalent in Italy during the lifetime of **Dante Alighieri** (1265–1321).

Danyell, Thomas (*fl.*1461–87) English mason, appointed (1482) King's Master-Mason: he carried out works at London Bridge, Deptford, Greenwich, and The Mote, Maidstone, Kent, where he seems to have been involved in major construction.

J.Harvey (1987)

Daphnis of Miletus (d.*c.*300 BC) Architect (with *Paeonius of Ephesus) of the *Ionic temple of Apollo at Didyma (begun *c.*313 BC), one of the largest temples in Asia Minor.

D (1950); VP (1955–6)

Darbishire, Henry Astley (1825–99) English architect mostly associated with philanthropic schemes, including the *Gothic Columbia Market (1866) and the Gothic working-class housing-scheme at Columbia Square (1857–60), both in Bethnal Green, London, financed by **Miss Angela Georgina** (later Baroness) **Burdett-Coutts** (1814–1906), but both demolished. For the same client he designed the *Picturesque-Gothic Holly Village,

Highgate, London (1865), a group of modest houses round a green, influenced no doubt by *Nash's Blaise Hamlet, Som. Darbishire produced a standard design for five-storey apartment-blocks (the planning of which was derived from Henry *Roberts's pioneering schemes of the 1850s) for the Peabody Trust (set up in 1862 to ameliorate the condition of the London poor). Many of these *Italianate blocks survive in London.

J.Curl (1983); D & M (1985); Tarn (1971)

Darbourne & Darke English architectural firm founded by **John William Charles Darbourne** (1935–91) and **Geoffrey James Darke** (1929–2011), who met when working in *Lyons's office where they absorbed concerns for better integration of architecture and landscape and for more humane public housing. Indeed, it was with housing that the practice made its mark when it won (1960) the competition to design Lillington Gardens, Pimlico, London (built 1964–72): this showed that *low-rise* dwellings could provide the same *high densities* as tower-blocks and uniform slabs favoured by *Modernists. Employing complex and ingenious *sections, traditional materials, and clever landscaping, the scheme was a triumph, but later housing at Marquess Road, Islington (1966–77), quickly developed major problems with drug-users and gangs, and was largely demolished (2001). Other designs included the public library (1974–5) and housing off Head Street, Pershore, Worcs. (1975–7). The firm also carried out works in Germany and Italy.

J.T (1996); *The Times* (10 Dec. 2011), 105

Darke, Geoffrey James (1929–2011) *See* DARBOURNE & DARKE.

Darling, Frank (1850–1923) Canadian architect, he trained with *Street and Arthur *Blomfield in London before setting up in practice in Toronto. His early works, including his Anglican churches, were influenced by *Pearson and Street, but he is best remembered for his fine *Beaux-Arts* Classical Banks (designed with his partner (from 1895) **John A. Pearson** (1867–1940)), notably the Canadian Bank of Commerce, Winnipeg, Manitoba (1910–11), and a series of prefabricated timber banks that could be erected on site in a day. The firm also designed the Sun Life Assurance Company Building, Montréal (1914–31), one of the tallest buildings in the British Empire at the time.

K (1994)

Darly, Matthias *or* **Matthew** (*fl.*1741–78) English engraver/caricaturist/designer, his publications include *A New Book of Chinese Designs* (1754), *A New Book of Ceilings* (1760), *The Ornamental Architect ... consisting of the Five Orders*

drawn with their Embellishments (1770—reissued as *A Compleat Body of Architecture* (1773)).

Co (2008); E.Hs (1990)

D'Aronco, Raimondo (1857–1932) *See* ARONCO.

dart Part of the *egg-and-dart or egg-and-anchor ornament.

date-stone Stone built into a wall on which the date of a building is cut. A date-anchor also has a date, and is the exposed head of a metal tie (usually of cast iron). *See* ANCHOR (**2**).

daub Mud, clay, etc., placed on a backing. *See also* WATTLE-AND-DAUB.

Daukes, Samuel Whitfield (1811–80) *See* HAMILTON & MEDLAND.

Daumet, Pierre-Gérôme-Honoré (1826–1911) French architect, he worked with and succeeded L.-J.*Duc on the *Palais de Justice*, Paris, and rebuilt the *Grand Château*, Chantilly (1875–82), in which eclectic virtuosity was displayed. He taught *Girault (who realized many of his projects) and C.F.*McKim, among others.

J.T (1996)

David, Charles (1552–1650) French architect, son-in-law of **Nicholas Lemercier** (*see* LEMERCIER, PIERRE), he succeeded (1585) his father-in-law as architect of *St-Eustache*, Paris, and was involved in the construction of the *choir and *nave (completed 1637).

S (1901–2)

Davies, Richard Llewelyn (1912–81) Leftist British architect, he worked for the London, Midland, & Scottish Railway from 1942, where he met **John Weeks** (1921–2005), and together they designed prefabricated steel stations, becoming collaborators thereafter. Involved (from 1948) in hospital research, they advocated industrialized systems of construction. Convinced that architecture was intellectually undeveloped compared with other professions, Davies held this could only be remedied by interdisciplinary systematic research and a supposedly rationalist 'scientific' *Modernism: his stance soon gained him credence within government circles, and his was a leading voice in the transformation of architectural education from a *Beaux-Arts approach to one derived from *Gropius-*Bauhäusler* tendencies established in American universities, the results of which are depressingly obvious. Appointed to the Chair of Architecture at University College London (1960), he destroyed the ethos established by Sir Albert *Richardson, and, with Weeks, developed a large practice, especially in hospital design. One of their earliest works was the estate-village at Rushbrooke, Suffolk

(1955–63), followed by Northwick Park Hospital, Harrow, Mddx. (1961–5), the flexibly planned prototype of several more, including Westmead, Sydney, Australia (1975–7). The practice was joined (1966) by former Austrian **Walter George Bor** (1916–99—born **Bukbinder**), and, as **Llewelyn Davies, Weeks, Forestier-Walker, & Bor**, planned Washington *New Town, Co. Durham (designated 1964—which has not proved to be a great success, least of all in architectural terms), and Milton Keynes, Bucks. (1969–71—which represented the importation of the American car-based, dispersed settlement, marked by flexibility, repetitions, and absence of any coherent aesthetic). He was created **Baron Llewelyn-Davies** (1963).

Crinson & Lubbock (1994); Esher (1981); *The Independent* (30 June 2005), Obits; Llewelyn-Davies (1961); *ODNB* (2004); Saint (1987)

Davioud, Gabriel-Jean-Antoine (1823–81) French architect, he studied with *Viollet-le-Duc and *Vaudoyer, then worked on the *Halles Centrales*, Paris, with *Baltard, who recommended him for the post of *Inspecteur des Promenades*. He built *pavilions and *lodges in the *Picturesque style for the *Bois de Boulogne* (1855–9), and designed structures for other Parisian parks, including the *Parc Monceau*, where the railings and gates, suggested by *Héré de Corny's work at Nancy, show him at his best. He designed the circus and *panorama for the *Champs Élysées*, and four large fountains for Paris (*Saint-Michel*, *Boulevard Saint-Michel* (1858—much praised by *Daly); *Château d'Eau* (1867–74); *l'Observatoire* (1870–5); and *Place du Théâtre-Français* (1872–4)). He was also responsible for the *Théâtre du Châtelet* (1860–2) and *Théâtre Lyrique* (1860–2, later *Théâtre de la Ville*). He was the architect of the *Magasins Réunis* Department Store, *Place de la République* (1865–7); the *Mairie du XIXe* (1876–8), and the *Trocadéro* for the Paris Exhibition (1876–8). His eclecticism (especially in theatre design) is identified with the *Rageur style.

Daly (1840–90); Daly & Davioud (1874); M & Wa (1987)

Davis, Alexander Jackson (1803–92) American architect, one of the most imaginative of his generation. His Highwood, a house at New Haven, CT (1829–31), brought him recognition, and, as a result, Ithiel *Town invited him to become a partner in his office. **Town & Davis** evolved a bold *Greek-Revival style, and designed a series of public buildings that are among the most distinguished Greek-inspired works of architecture in the USA: a good example is the Indiana State Capitol, Indianapolis (1831–5), with its *octastyle Greek-*Doric *porticoes, long side elevations of *antae-*piers, and domed *drum set over the centre of the roof. The firm also designed the NC State Capitol, Raleigh (1833–40), and several Greek-Revival churches with *distyle in-antis* fronts. The powerful range of *antae*-piers was used again at the New York Custom House (1833–42—now the Federal Hall Memorial Museum). Davis invented a variety of multi-storey *fenestration in which the windows were set in recesses with panels between them at floor-levels, anticipating later developments. This *Davisean window* (as he called it) appears to have been used first between the *antae*-piers at the Lyceum of Natural History, NYC (1835–6).

The partnership was dissolved (1835), after which Davis mostly practised on his own, designing several *Picturesque houses, such as the influential *cottage orné* at Blithewood, Barrytown, NY (1836). He commenced (1836) *Rural Residences,* the first American book on the subject that really marks the birth of the Picturesque movement in the USA: it was illustrated with ingeniously planned eclectic designs, although only two parts were published (1838). He also provided (1838–50) illustrations for A.J.*Downing's works. Thereafter, for some twenty years, Davis ran a successful practice, generally favouring *Gothic and *Italianate styles. His first large villa was Lyndhurst, Tarrytown, NY (1838–42—later expanded (1865–7)), which, with its asymmetry and Gothic style, was widely admired. In his many commissions Davis also re-interpreted the English *cottage style, although he returned to *Neo-Classicism for Montgomery Place, Barrytown, NY (1843–67), and the refined and beautiful Greek-Revival John Cox Stevens House, NYC (1845–8). Davis saw possibilities in cast-iron construction and kits of parts (he designed (1835) a cast-iron shop-front). Among his other works the *Tuscan Town Hall and Court House, Bridgeport, CT (1853–4), and the estate of villas and cottages at Llewellyn Park, West Orange, NJ (1857–66), deserve mention.

W.Andrews (1955); A.Davis (1980); A.J.Downing (1967, 1967a, 1968); Newton (1942); Peck (ed.) (1992); P & J (1970–86)

Davis, Arthur Joseph (1878–1951) English architect, trained at the *École des *Beaux-Arts,* he joined (1900) the practice of the Parisian C.F. *Mewès. **Mewès & Davis** brought Parisian *Beaux-Arts* *Classicism to London with their Ritz Hotel, Piccadilly (1903–9), an early steel-framed building. Their next work was Inveresk House, Aldwych, Strand (1906–8), followed by the Royal Automobile Club, Pall Mall (1908–11). After Mewès's death, Davis and others designed the *palazzo* of the Cunard Building, Pier Head, Liverpool (1914–16), which was a foretaste of his Italian-*Renaissance buildings in London, including the London County and Westminster Bank, Threadneedle Street (1922).

A.S.Gray (1985); MM & Wa (1980); Se (ed.) (1975); Se (1977)

Dawber, Sir Edward Guy (1861–1938) English architect, he worked with *George & *Peto from 1882 before establishing his own practice (1890). He earned his reputation as a designer of small well-mannered country-houses, some of which were published in *Muthesius's *Das Englische Haus* (1904–5). Among his designs Conkwell Grange, Bradford-on-Avon, Wilts. (1907), deserves note. He wrote *Old Cottages and Farmhouses in Kent and Sussex* (1900) and *Old Cottages, Farmhouses, and Other Stone Buildings in the Cotswolds* (1905).

A.S.Gray (1985)

Dawson, Matthew James (1875–1943) British architect, he designed several houses at Hampstead *Garden Suburb, London (1909–14), all variations on *vernacular themes, including 87–9 Hampstead Way.

A.S.Gray (1985); M & G (1992)

day *See* LIGHT.

Day, Nugent Francis Cachemaille- (1896–1976) English architect, he worked (1920s) with L.-E.-J.-G. de *Soissons at Welwyn Garden City, Herts., then with *Goodhart-Rendel, before establishing a practice with **Felix J. Lander** (1898–1960), joined (1930) by **Herbert Archibald Welch** (1889–1953). On his own from 1935, as consultant to the LCC after the 1939–45 war he designed numerous schools and apartment blocks. He is best known as a church architect (e.g. St Nicholas, Burnage, Manchester (1931–2); St Saviour's, Eltham, Kent (1932–3); St Michael and All Angels, Wythenshaw, Manchester (1937); and All Saints, Hanworth, Mddx. (1952–8)), all of which were influenced by Continental (especially German) trends).

ODNB (2004); pk; *Thirties Society J.* **vii** (1991), 2–7

dead 1. Without variety or features, e.g. a *blank unrelieved wall. 2. *Dead-light* (window or part of a window that does not open), or *blank or *blind window (sealed up or designed to look like a window but actually blocked up). 3. Flat or dull, without brilliance, as in finishes. 4. Useless, or not used for its original purpose, e.g. a *chimney-flue.

dead-house 1. *Mortuary, in the sense of a building for the temporary accommodation of corpses before disposal; 2. *Ossuary.

deal 1. Softwood (e.g. pine). 2. Fir or pine board of a standard size.

deambulatory 1. Covered walk, esp. continuous around something, such as a *cloister around a *garth. 2. *Aisle or *ambulatory joining the liturgical east ends of *chancel-aisles behind the *high-altar, especially in an apsidal arrangement with radiating chapels on one side.

Deane, Sir Thomas Newenham (1828-99) Irish architect, son of **Sir Thomas Deane** (1792-1871), who founded one of the most successful Irish architectural practices, designing the Commercial Buildings, Cork (1811-13), and the castellated *Tudor-style Dromore Castle, Kenmare (1831-6). Sir Thomas Deane was joined (1841) by **Benjamin Woodward** (1815-61), and the latter, a disciple of *Pugin, seems to have been the moving force behind the *Ruskin-inspired buildings for which the firm (**Deane & Woodward**) is mainly known: they designed The Queen's College (now University College), Cork (1845-9). T.N. Deane became active in the partnership from 1850: soon afterwards, Deane & Woodward designed the beautiful Trinity College Museum, Dublin (1852-7), which established their reputation and, moreover, gained the approval of Ruskin, who admired the vigorous carvings of the **O'Shea** brothers that enriched the detail. The Oxford University Museum (1855-61) followed, a monumental secular *Gothic edifice with pronounced Continental features: it has a *cortile, roofed with a structure of iron, timber, and glass, surrounded by *Venetian-Gothic *cloisters. The firm also designed the Debating Room of the Oxford Union Society (1857), the former Kildare Street Club, Dublin (1858-61), and, after Woodward's death, T.N.Deane built the Meadow Buildings, Christ Church, Oxford (1862-6). Deane & Woodward were important in the history of the *Gothic Revival in England, and were the first significant followers of Ruskin's ideas. From 1871, T.N.Deane continued in practice, and was joined (1876) by his son, **Thomas Manby Deane** (1851-1933). They designed the National Library and Museum, Dublin (1885-90), which earned T.N.Deane his knighthood, and forms part of the handsome group of buildings (also designed by the firm) around Leinster House. T.N.Deane was active in preserving Ireland's ancient buildings. T.M.Deane, a pupil of *Burges, was in partnership (1884-99) with his father, and then with Aston *Webb. He, too, was knighted (1911).

Acland & Ruskin (1859); Blau (1982); *DIB* (2009); D & M (1985); Ea (1970); Hersey (1972); Hi (1954); S.M (1972); *ODNB* (2004); O'Dwyer (1997)

Dearborn, Henry Alexander Scammell (1783-1851) American landscape-designer/polymath. He supervised fortifications of Portland, ME (then MA), during the 1812 war, founded the MA Horticultural Society, researched/illustrated a treatise on Greek architecture (1829), and was involved in the *conservation of the site of the battle of Bunker's Hill. His chief claim to fame was his promotion of the USA's first 'rural' *garden-cemetery, prompted by the writings of *Evelyn and the considerable literature on the *cemetery of *Père-Lachaise, Paris. This was Mount Auburn,

near Boston, MA (opened 1831), with which *Wadsworth was also concerned, but the final designs were by *Bigelow. Dearborn supplied 1,300 trees for the cemetery from his own nurseries, and, like *Loudon, saw the cemetery as providing the means to educate gardeners in the science and practicalities of horticulture. Dearborn was also the promoter of Forest Hills Cemetery, Roxbury, MA, when he was Mayor of that town (1847-51): it was spaciously laid out, with ingenious well-wooded landscaping (it had over 30,000 native and European trees planted under Dearborn's aegis). He was buried there, appropriately on Mount Dearborn.

B & K (2000); J.Curl (2004); N.P.Willis (1839)

dearn, dern 1. *See* DURN. 2. *Threshold.

Dearn, Thomas Downes Wilmot (1777-1853) Son of **Prince Henry Frederick** (1745-90), **Duke of Cumberland and Strathearn**, and **Anne Horton** (*née* Luttrell—1743-1808), whom the Prince married (1771—though his brother, **King George III** (*r.*1760-1820), refused to recognize the union). Apprenticed (1793) to William *Thomas, he succeeded (1800) his master as Architect to **Prince William Henry** (1765-1837— **Duke of Clarence** from 1788, **King William IV** (*r.*1830-7). His importance lies in his handsome publications, including *Sketches in Architecture* (1806), *Designs for Cottages and Rural Dwellings* (1807), and *Designs for Lodges and Entrances to Parks*, etc. (1811, 1823). He settled (*c.*1800) in Cranbrook, Kent, where he designed houses and the spectacular front of Providence Chapel (1828). He also published *An Historical, Topographical, and Descriptive Account of the Weald of Kent* (1814), and invented a *brick bond named after him. *See* BRICK.

Co (2008); Dearn (1806, 1811); Donovan (2005); Stell (2002)

death-lantern In a churchyard or *cemetery, a column surmounted by a lantern (usually behind an *ajouré panel) and a cross. Intended to deflect evil spirits, it sometimes had a staircase within the structure, and a *lectern or *pulpit at the base. In certain situations they also served as beacons (e.g. Visby, Gotland). Some were incorporated within chapels (e.g. Cemetery of the Innocents, Paris).

PM

de Bodt, Jean (1670-1745) *See* BODT.

Debret, François (1777-1850) French architect, pupil of *Percier, he became an important teacher of many architects destined to transform Paris under *Haussmann. A controversial and over-zealous restorer of historic buildings, he had worked on the *basilica of *St-Denis for many years when he started (1839) his dramatic transformation of the west front, adding details to the north tower unsupported by *archaeology. When the tower began to collapse (1846), Debret was dismissed, to the delight of those protagonists of the *Gothic Revival who saw him as a reactionary in favour of academic *Classicism: the disputes that raged at the time greatly promoted the cause of the Revival in France, notably with the building of *Ste-Clotilde*, Paris (1846–57) by *Gau and *Ballu.

M & Wa (1987)

de Brosse, Salomon (*c.*1571–1626) *See* BROSSE.

Decalogue Parts of a *reredos in a church on which the Ten Commandments are set out, commonly found in England from C17. It may also be in the form of separate framed panels on a church-wall.

de Carlo, Giancarlo (1919–2005) *See* CARLO.

decastyle *See* PORTICO.

de Caus *See* CAUS.

Decker, Paul (*fl.*1750s) Perhaps a pseudonym, he was credited as author of *Chinese Architecture, Civil and Ornamental . . .* , and *Gothic Architecture Decorated*, both 1759 and both indebted to earlier publications.

Co (2008)

Decker, Paulus (1677–1713) Nuremberg-born, he worked under *Schlüter during the building of the *Schloss*, Berlin, then became (1707) Court Architect at Bayreuth. He is remembered as an architectural theorist and for his imaginative *Baroque designs, published in his *Fürstlicher Baumeister* (1711–16), which influenced the design of C18 German aristocratic residences. A second edition was published (1885), and his book of ornament, *Architectura Theoretica-Practica*, came out (1720–22).

Decker (1711–16); E.Schneider (1937).

declination Angle formed between the *naked of a wall and the inclined *mutules of the *Doric *Order.

Deconstructivism *or* **Deconstructionism** Late-C20 tendencies in architecture having certain formal similarities to aspects of Russian *Constructivism, such as diagonal overlappings of rectangular or trapezoidal elements, and the use of warped planes, as in the works of *Lissitzky, *Malevich, and *Tatlin, although many critics and protagonists have denied those similarities. Deconstructivist 'architecture' has been held to embrace works of **Peter D.Eisenman** (1932–), **Frank Owen Gehry** (1929–), **Zaha Hadid** (1950–2016), **Daniel Libeskind** (1946–), and **Bernard Tschumi** (1944–), among others

(though not all might wish to be associated with the label). Deconstructivism induces a sense of dislocation both within buildings and between buildings and their contexts (which Deconstructivists ignore). By breaking continuity, disturbing relationships between interior and exterior, fracturing connections between exterior and context, Deconstructivism undermines harmony, unity, and perceived stability (which *Patmore identified as crucial to successful architecture). An example was the noisy City Edge project, Berlin (1987), by Libeskind, which ripped through established geometries of urban fabric, responding to the Berlin Wall by slicing up territory. However, Deconstructivism is hardly a new movement, nor is it a coherent style: rather it perhaps exposes the unfamiliar and the disturbing by means of deformity, distortion, fragmentation, and the awkward superimposition of jarring, disparate grids. If *Deconstructivism* took *Russian Constructivism* as its starting-point, *Deconstructionism* was linked to the theories of **Jacques Derrida** (1930–2004), and presupposed that, if architecture were a language, it was therefore capable of communicating meaning, and of receiving treatment by methods of linguistic philosophy: that raises certain difficulties, as it is arguable if late-C20 and early-C21 architecture possesses claims to any *vocabulary*, let alone a *language*. Nevertheless, some (e.g. **Charles Alexander Jencks** (1939–2019)) have claimed Deconstructivism as a 'new paradigm', but others have questioned this (**Christopher Wolfgang Alexander** (1936–) called it 'nonsensical'), mindful of the impact it has on the built environment: those who are concerned about Deconstructivism's legacy have perceived it as fundamentally destructive, because of its rejection of all that went before and its failure to provide clear values as replacements. Indeed, Deconstructivism has been seen as intentional aggression on human senses, abusing perceptive mechanisms in order to generate anxiety and discomfort. If this is a new paradigm, it could be cause for deep concern.

Abram *et al.* (1999); AD, **xlvii**/5 (1977), *Profile* 5, 315–27; AD, **lx**/9–10 (1990), 32–49; A (1994); Broadbent (1991); Brunette & Wills (eds) (1994); Cuito (ed.) (2002*b*); Wi.Cu (1996); J (1995*a*); Js (2002); J & W (1988); L (1988); Norris (1987); Norris & Benjamin (1988); S.Rn (1989); Salingaros *et al.* (2004)

Decorated style *See* SECOND POINTED.

de Cotte, Robert (1656–1735) *See* COTTE.

découpage Decoration of a surface with applied paper cut-outs resembling lace.

dedication cross Consecration *cross.

deercote, deerpen, deershed, deershelter Building for sheltering/protecting deer, often given architectural treatment, esp. in C18 and C19 landscaped parks, e.g. the fine *Gothic arcaded exemplar (like a *cloister facing outwards) at Auckland Castle Park, Bishop Auckland, Co. Durham (1767, attributed to Thomas *Wright): it also contains a room for watching the deer inside a pinnacled tower. Other examples exist at Sudbury, Derbys. (before 1751), Dunham Massey, Ches. (1740), and a Palladian effort at Heath Hall, near Wakefield, Yorks. (mid-C18, possibly by *Carr of York).

Symes (2006); Wragg (2000)

deer-house 1. As *deercote. **2.** Accommodation for a gamekeeper (e.g. the *Gothick *eyecatcher (*c.*1768) at Scampston Park, Ryedale, Yorks., possibly by *Carr of York).

deer-park 1. Enclosed park for keeping deer, examples of which were known in Anglo-Saxon times, and were used for hunting. Medieval examples were concerned with food production and sport, and were sometimes surrounded with ditches, having entrances called 'deer-leaps' by which the animals could enter but not leave. **2.** Seen as a precursor to the *landscape-park, and as a place of beauty in its own right, it was often transformed in C18, many examples being by 'Capability' *Brown. American authors have treated it as a sub-category of the term *park, as only a few American deer-parks existed, usually to suggest wealth and status, but sometimes to contain the deer to prevent them damaging crops (e.g. Mount Vernon, VA (late C18)).

O'Malley (2010); Symes (2006); Tay (2006)

defensive architecture 1. Military architecture, e.g. castles, city walls, and fortifications. **2.** Architecture that looks inwards, giving protection from hostile urban environments (e.g. Greek or Roman houses in Antiquity, or some of the works of modern Japanese architects).

Defoe, Daniel (*c.*1660–1731) English writer, important in this context for his descriptions of country estates, many of them in the course of improvement when he recorded them in his *A Tour thro' the Whole Island of Great Britain* (from 1724 (when the French Taste was still dominant)) with many later edns (when newer 'natural' landscapes (e.g. Painshill, Surrey) were coming into vogue).

Defoe (1724–7); H & W (1988); ODNB (2004)

dégagement 1. Restricted space forming a connection between two rooms, or between a room and a passage, for privacy, the equivalent of a lobby or *vestibule. **2.** The opposite of *engaged, so applied to free-standing columns.

degree *Step of a *stair.

Deilmann, Harald (1920–2008) German architect. He did much to re-establish *Modernism in Germany after the 1939–45 war, and strove for informality (e.g. the *Stadttheater*, Münster (1952–6), designed with **Max Clemens von Hausen** (1919–95), **Ortwin Rave** (1921–92), and **Werner Ruhnau** (1922–2015)). Other works include the *Volkswohlbund* Building, Münster (1967), the *Clemens-Sel-Museum*, Neuss (1972), and the *Neues Rathaus*, Minden (1974–9).

E (1994); Ma (1985c); J.T (1996)

Deinocrates (*fl.*mid-C4 BC) *Hellenistic architect, supposedly the designer of the city of Alexandria, laid out on lavish lines. *Vitruvius reported he proposed reconstructing Mount Athos into a gigantic carved image of **Alexander the Great**. He may have been (with *Paeonius) the architect of the last great *Ionic temple of Artemis at Ephesus (from 356 BC).

R.Martin (1956); VP (1955–6)

de Key, Lieven (*c.* 1560–1627) *See* KEY.

de Keyser, Hendrick (1565–1621) *See* KEYSER.

de Klerk, Michel (1884–1923) *See* KLERK.

Delafosse, Jean-Charles (1734–91) French architect, one of the creators of the *Louis-Seize* style, as the ornament in his *Iconologie*, featuring *Greek keys, *garlands, and much other Classical ornament, demonstrates. He also published a treatise on the five *Orders, and designed two *hôtels at 58–60 *Rue du Faubourg Poissonnière*, Paris (1776–83).

B (1980); GdBA, vi/61 (1963–4), 157; Ka (1955)

Delany, Mary (*née* **Granville**) (1700–88) English gardener/writer, she married (1743) **Patrick Delany** (1685/6–1768) and settled with him in Ireland. P.D.Delany knew *Addison, *Pope, and other writers, and made a *Rococo garden at his estate, Delville, Glasnevin, near Dublin, which his wife improved. Her importance lies in the descriptions she left of C18 Irish and English gardens in her letters, published 1861, in which eminent figures, e.g. J.-J.*Rousseau, also appear. After her husband's death, she moved back to England, and spent most of her Summers at Bulstrode, Bucks., the country home of **Margaret Cavendish Bentinck** (1715–85—**Duchess of Portland** from 1734), where the two women enhanced the gardens and collected botanical specimens. From 1774 Delany began making 'paper mosaics' (exquisite cut-paper *collages of flowers and plants), and by 1784 had completed 1,000 pages of her *Hortus Siccus*. She also made *shell-work interiors (e.g. at Killala, Co. Mayo), but little of her work survives.

Delany (1861); Laird & Weisberg-Roberts (eds) (2009); ODNB (2004); Tay (2006)

del Duca, Giacomo (*c.*1520–1604) *See* DUCA.

Delft School Group of Dutch architects associated (1920s–50s) with the *Technische Hogeschool*, Delft, and especially with *Granpré Molière, who objected, like *Berlage, to the dogma and pretensions of 'unprincipled' *Nieuwe Zakelijkheid* (*see* NEUE SACHLICHKEIT) and the *International style with its obsessions about industrial processes (usually only images *suggesting* those). Valuing sensitivity to context (especially landscape), natural materials, and traditional techniques, the protagonists of the Delft School were attacked by Modernists, and after Granpré Molière retired (1953) the *Technische Hogeschool* changed direction, influenced by *Bakema, *Eesteren, and other *CIAM enthusiasts.

Kuiper (1991); *Plan*, vi (1972), whole issue; J.T (1996)

Delille, Abbé Jacques (**Jacques Montanier,** *called*) (1738–1813) French poet, his reputation was made through his translation of **Virgil**'s *Georgics* (1769), but his importance in the context of late-C18 garden-design, esp. the C19 genesis of the *garden-cemetery, lies in his publications, e.g. *Les Jardins* (1782), *L'homme des champs* (1800), and *Les trois règnes de la nature* (1808).

J.Curl (2011); Delille (1782); Etlin (1984); Wiebenson (1978)

dell Small, deep, well-planted natural hollow or vale, adopted as an aesthetic feature of C18 English garden-design, as in, e.g. *Shenstone's The Leasowes, now Worcs. Hence *dell-garden.*

della Porta, Giacomo (1533–1602) *See* PORTA.

Delorme *See* ORME.

de L'Orme, Philibert (*c.*1510–70) *See* ORME.

demesne 1. Possession of real estate by free tenure. 2. An estate, including house and land: the term is common in Ireland (pronounced *dimayne*).

demi-column *Engaged half-column, not to be confused with a *pilaster.

demilune *Ravelin, or projecting outwork of a fortification beyond the *bastions and *curtain-wall, semicircular or segmental on *plan rather than the more usual triangular arrangement, facilitating the turning of guns.

demi-metope Fragmentary or half *metope* at an external angle or a *re-entrant internal angle of a Roman *Doric *frieze, found in *Renaissance and C18 work, sometimes regarded as an *abuse.

Demmler, Georg Adolph (1804–86) German architect, pupil of *Schinkel, he was Court Architect to the **Grand Dukes of Mecklenburg-Schwerin,** for whom he transformed the *Schloss*, Schwerin, into a *Picturesque pile of the Northern-*Renaissance Revival (1844–57), although

*Stüler and *Strack were responsible for its completion, and the overall scheme owed something to an earlier project (1842) by *Semper. Like Schinkel, Demmler cunningly mixed medieval and Classical elements, notably in the Schwerin *Rathaus* (1835) and *Zeughaus* (1840–4).

Ende (1971); Ohle (1960); Stüler et al. (1869)

Denby, Elizabeth (1893–1965) *See* FRY, EDWIN MAXWELL.

Denham, Sir John (1615–69) English poet/courtier/administrator, Surveyor-General of the King's Works (1660–9), with John *Webb as his deputy at Greenwich Palace: *Wren was appointed Denham's sole deputy (1669), and succeeded him on the latter's death two weeks later. Although he does not appear to have designed anything, Denham was probably a competent administrator, and, as the holder of the same position as Inigo *Jones and Wren, deserves mention.

Co (2008); *ODNB* (2004)

Denon, Baron Dominique Vivant (1747–1825) French *savant*, he accompanied the Napoléonic expedition to Egypt (1798) as leader of the Commission on the Sciences and Arts to study Ancient-Egyptian buildings and architecture, heralding the birth of modern Egyptology. He published his *Voyage dans la Basse et la Haute Égypte pendant les campagnes du général Bonaparte* (1802): an accurate sourcebook of Ancient-Egyptian architecture, it had an extraordinary impact, triggering the C19 *Egyptian Revival that at first was correctly described as 'Egyptomania'. Denon was Director-General of Museums, and was in charge of the *Musée Napoléon* (now the Louvre). He supervised the design and production of the *Sèvres Service Égyptien* (a dinner-service sumptuously decorated with Ancient-Egyptian themes and motifs), one of the high points of the Egyptian Revival, and was a major influence on the *Empire* style, *Neo-Classicism, and the work of *Percier and *Fontaine.

J.Curl (2005); Denon (1802); Humbert (1989); Humbert (ed.) (1996); HPZ (1994)

dentil Small block forming one of a long close-set horizontal series under *cornices, associated with the *bed-mouldings of the *Composite, *Corinthian, *Ionic, and (sometimes) Roman-*Doric *Orders. An *entablature with dentils is said to be *dentilated* or *denticulated.* Early-Greek dentils include those of the *caryatid porch of the *Erechtheion* (C5 BC) and the *Choragic Monument of Lysicrates (C4 BC), both in Athens. In better work dentils should stop at the angle of a building, forming a *re-entrant, and there should not be a dentil at the angle itself: they should also be arranged so that the dentil above a column should be on its centre-line. *Associated terms include*:

231   Destailleur, Hippolyte-Alexandre-Gabriel-Walter

dentilation: **1.** with, or an arrangement of, dentils; **2.** *toothing;

dentil-band: plain *moulding of square or rectangular section forming part of the bed-mouldings of an entablature, that could be cut to form dentils, but is left as a *band, as on *Scamozzi's version of the *Ionic *Order.

dependency C18 American term for an outbuilding or group of outbuildings on an estate, including quarters for slaves, schools, etc.

depressed *See* ARCH.

Dereham *or* **Durham, Elias of** (*fl.*1188–1245) Canon of Salisbury and Wells, he may have designed the *shrine of **St Thomas à Becket** (*c.*1118–70) in Canterbury Cathedral, Kent (completed 1220), which, by all accounts, was of great magnificence. He seems to have been involved in the building of Salisbury Cathedral, Wilts., from *c.*1220, where he was described as being the director of the new fabric, and supervised at least the erection of the *Lady Chapel (1225) and the eastern arm of the Cathedral (1237). He was in charge of the King's Works at Winchester Castle, Hants. (1233). Reading between the lines he was probably an informed amateur, a forerunner of the C18 dilettante architect, perhaps a kind of C13 *Burlington.

J.Harvey (1987)

Derneford, Nicholas de (*fl.*1309–31) English mason. He seems to have been a specialist in military architecture and fortification, was master-mason at Beaumaris Castle (from 1316), and Master of the Works at Caernarfon, Conway, Criccieth, and Harlech Castles in Wales from 1323. He was also put in charge (1327) of the castles at Aberystwyth, Cardigan, and Carmarthen. In addition, he may have designed the exquisite *choir (1298–1340) at Bristol Cathedral, Som., in which case he was an architect of great originality.

J.Harvey (1987)

de Rossi, Giovanni Antonio (1616–95) *See* ROSSI.

Derrida, Jacques (1930–2004) *See* DECONSTRUCTIVISM.

de Sanctis, Francesco (1693–1740) *See* SANCTIS.

desert C18 landscape *designed* to look wild, forsaken, and uncultivated, with 'ruined' buildings, giving the impression of having been abandoned, and conducive to melancholy, e.g. the *Désert de Retz,* Chambourcy, Yvelines, France (1774–85), with *folly in the form of a huge overscaled ruined column (*colonne brisée*) containing several floors of apartments arranged around a central top-lit spiral stair, the rooms illuminated through glazed 'cracks' and windows set in the 'flutes'. It was the creation of **François-Nicolas-Henri Racine de Monville** (1734–97). A *desert garden,* however, is a cultivated landscape with desert *flora* (arid-land plants, e.g. agaves, cacti, yuccas, etc., native to Central and America and to the south-west USA). Examples include The Huntingdon Desert Garden, San Marino, CA (from 1907–9) and the Desert Botanical Garden, Phoenix, AZ (established 1930s).

W.Adams (1979); M & T (1991); Racine (ed.) (2001); Tay (2006)

Desgodets *or* **Desgodetz, Antoine Babuty** (1653–1728) Paris-born architect, he recorded many ancient structures in Rome, which he published in *Les Édifices Antiques de Rome* (1682), later brought out in English (1771–95): it made his reputation, for it was the most accurate printed source for *Antique Roman architecture to date, a source for details of many significant C18 buildings (e.g. *Kent's entrance-hall at Holkham Hall, Norfolk), and was an important influence on C18 styles, especially *Neo-Classicism.

Desgodetz (1771–95); Ha (1948–50); K & L (1972); Wn (1969)

Desornamentado Austere style of Spanish-*Renaissance architecture in the reign of **King Philip II** (1556–98), of which *Herrera's *Escorial,* near Madrid (1559–84), is a good example.

Kubler (1982); K & S (1959)

Desprez, Jean-Louis (1743–1804) French architect/illustrator/stage-designer, he settled (1784) in Sweden and produced severe Neo-Classical and Egyptianizing designs for tombs. His buildings include the Uppsala *Botanicum* (1788), with its low octastyle Greek-*Doric *portico, and Egyptianesque *capitals.

A & B (1986); J.Curl (2005); HPZ (1994); Rosenblum (1967)

Destailleur, Hippolyte-Alexandre-Gabriel-Walter (1822–93) French architect of several town and country-houses in a *Renaissance-Revival style, including the *Château du Duc de Massa,* Franconville, Oise (1880–5), Waddesdon Manor, near Aylesbury, Bucks. (1888–90), and the *Palais d'Albert de Rothschild, Prinz Eugen Strasse,* Vienna (1876–82). He designed the priory and *mausoleum for **Emperor Napoléon III** (*r.*1852–70) and his family, Farnborough, Hants. (1887–9—in a *Flamboyant*-Gothic style), and various mausolea and memorials, including the Hersent tomb, *Père-Lachaise* Cemetery (1861), and the Collard tomb, Montparnasse Cemetery (1864), both in Paris. His published works include *Recueil d'estampes relatives à l'ornamentation des appartements aux XVIe, XVIIe, et XVIIIe siècles* (1858–71), and he designed furniture and interiors.

Be (1976); D & M (1985); *Hampshire: The County Magazine,* **xxix/9** (1983), 36–9

De Stijl *See* STIJL.

detached *Insulated or free-standing, the opposite of *engaged, as with a column.

Deutscher Werkbund Organization founded (1907) in Munich to improve design of products through the joint efforts of artists, craftsmen, and manufacturers: its leading lights were *Behrens, Theodor *Fischer, Hermann *Muthesius, and Fritz *Schumacher. It organized (1914) a major exhibition in Cologne, with buildings by *Gropius, *Taut, and van de *Velde, but a debate was sparked in which Muthesius argued for industrialized design while van de Velde spoke up for the creative artist/craftsman. After the 1914–18 war the *Werkbund* moved away from anything redolent of an *Arts-and-Crafts position towards the *Modern Movement, as is clear from the journal *Die Form* (Design) published 1925–34. It held a housing exhibition in Stuttgart, the *Weissenhof-siedlung* (1927), under the directorship of *Mies van der Rohe, which included work by Le *Corbusier, *Oud, and *Stam: further exhibitions were held in Paris (1930) and Berlin (1931), but it disbanded (1934). Revived after the 1939–45 war, largely to promote *Modernist ideology, it published *Werk und Zeit* from 1952. The *Werkbund* inspired further organizations in Austria (1912), Switzerland (1913), Sweden (1913), and England (Design and Industries Association of 1915).

Burckhardt (1980); L (1988); Pommer & Otto (1991); Schwartz (1997)

Devětsil Group Founded 1920, it was the focus for the *avant-garde* of the new Czechoslovak Republic after 1918, and embraced *International *Modernism. It promoted work by *Chochol, *Krejcar, and *Teige, evolved close relations with German and Austrian Modernists, and promoted ideas from the Soviet Union.

Li (1996)

Devey, George (1820–86) London-born architect, he promoted the *Domestic Revival using *vernacular elements in his buildings. His first commission was at Penshurst, Kent, where he designed cottages and various estate buildings from 1850 in a C15 style. His larger buildings, which often look as though they were developed and added to over a long period, include Bette-shanger House (1856–82), St Alban's Court, Non-ington (1874–8), and Denne Hill (1871–5), all in Kent. A good example of his *additive style is Smithills Hall, Bolton, South Lancs. (1874–86), a medieval house which he extended. He influenced his pupil, *Voysey, and was an important precursor of the *Arts-and-Crafts movement.

Ae (1991); Gd (1979)

de Wailly, Charles (1730–98) *See* WAILLY.

dextral stair Circular *stair ascending from left to right.

Dézallier d'Argenville, Antoine-Joseph (1680–1765) French writer/engraver, his important *La Théorie et la pratique du jardinage* (1709) codified the formal French garden, and in subsequent edns (including French and German translations) disseminated principles and evolution of French garden-design of the first half of C18. It contained illustrations of *parterres* by Le *Blond. His son, **Antoine-Nicolas Dézallier d'Argenville** (1723–96), wrote books on gardening, including *Manuel de jardinier* (1772) and *Dictionnaire du jardinage* (1777). He also published two books (1749, 1755) describing places of architectural and historic interest in and around Paris, and completed his father's work on the lives of celebrated architects and sculptors (1787).

DdA (1709); Ketcham (1994); Racine (ed.) (2001); Rouge (1776–88); J.T (1996)

diaconicon *Sacristy in or near an *Early-Christian or *Byzantine church used as a treasury and library.

diagonal *See* BUTTRESS; VAULT.

diameter *See* MODULE.

diamond-faced *See* RUSTICATION.

diamond-fret *Lozenge-*fret of intersecting *fillets or thin beads forming diamond-shaped patterns repeated in series. It occurs in *Romanesque work as a variation on *chevron or *zig-zag *mouldings (using round rod-like elements) and in C18 *Chinoiserie and *Gothick (using flat strips, fillets, or square sections).

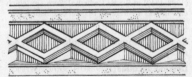

diamond-fret Sts Peter and Paul, Tickencote, Rut. (*after Parker*).

diaper Decorative pattern on a plain, flat, unbroken surface consisting of the constant repetition of simple figures (such as squares, lozenges, or polygons) closely connected with each other, sometimes with embellishments in the form of stylized flowers. It may be lightly carved, as on the *Gothic *pulpitum* (*c.*1320–40) in Southwell *Minster, Notts.; painted on a wall; or formed of dark bricks laid in diagonal patterns on a lighter brick wall, commonly found in *Tudor brickwork and in *Butterfield's architecture.

Tudor brick diaper-work with darker vitrified bricks.

diaphragm *See* ARCH.

diastyle *See* INTERCOLUMNIATION.

diazoma, diazomata Passage or *aisle in a Greek theatre concentric with the outer wall and with the *orchaestra, communicating with the radial aisles.

Dickenson, Christopher (*fl.*1528–40) English *Freemason. Appointed (1528) master-mason at Windsor Castle, Berks., on the death of Henry *Redman, he became (1531) master-bricklayer at Westminster (Whitehall) Palace, and supervised works at Hampton Court Palace (1536). He was put in charge (1539) of the castles at Deal, Sandown, and Walmer, Kent, all remarkable examples of *Tudor military architecture.

J.Harvey (1987)

die 1. *Dado. 2. *Abacus.

Dientzenhofer Family Master-masons/architects originally from Bad Aibling, near Rosenheim, Bavaria, they made an enormous contribution to the complexities of *Baroque architecture in Germany and Bohemia. **Georg** (1643–89) built the Cistercian Abbey-Church at Waldsassen (1682–1704) to designs by *Leuthner (who seems to have given the Dientzenhofer clan their chance to rise above artisan status, possibly for family reasons, as he married (1678) **Anna Dientzenhofer**). Georg also designed the *Wallfahrtskirche, Kappel, near Waldsassen (1684–9), with a triapsidal plan and three slender cylindrical towers, an unusual arrangement clearly intended to symbolize the Trinity. It was completed by his brother **Christoph** (1655–1722), who was strongly influenced by the geometries of *Guarini (published in 1686), and who designed several churches of great splendour in Bohemia, including *St Joseph*, Oboříště (1699–1712), the Chapel in the Castle, Smiřice (1700–11), *Sv Mikuláš, Malá Strana*, Prague (1703–11), and *Sv Markéta*, Břevnov, near Prague (1708–15). Christoph's uses of ellipses mixed with the *Wandpfeiler arrangement made

his interiors particularly complex, and demonstrate how he synthesized motifs drawn from *Borromini and Guarini. His beautiful *façade of the monastery of Our Lady of Loreto, Hradčany, Prague (1717–23), has a central belfry, one of the most elegant in Central Europe.

Wolfgang (1648–1706) is remembered for several buildings, notably the Abbey Church of Speinshart (1691–1706) and the *pilgrimage church, Straubing (1705–7), while **Leonhard** (1660–1707) was responsible for the abbeys at Ebrach (1686–1704) and Banz (1695–1705). However, **Johann** (1663–1726) completed Banz, designing the Abbey Church there (1710–19) in which complex interlocking ellipses (not unlike Christoph's scheme at Oboříště) again feature, contributing to an interior of great beauty, arguably the finest design by any Dientzenhofer. Johann's first great church was the *Stiftskirche* (now *Dom*), Fulda (1704–12), with echoes of St Peter's, *Il Gesù, Sant'Ignazio*, and (especially) Borromini's remodelling of *San Giovanni in Laterano*, all in Rome. Johann Dientzenhofer worked at Pommersfelden, near Bamberg (1711), and there, for **Lothar Franz, Graf von Schönborn** (1655–1729), **Prince-Bishop of Bamberg** from 1693, **Elector-Archbishop of Mainz**, and **Chancellor of the Empire** from 1695, built *Schloss Weissenstein*, one of the noblest Baroque palaces in Franconia (1711–18), with a stupendous symmetrical *Treppenhaus* (partly designed by *Hildebrandt and von Schönborn himself) rising in a vast galleried hall the full height of the building.

Christoph's son, **Kilian Ignaz** (1689–1751), trained with his father and with Hildebrandt. He may have been partly responsible for completing the latter's stunning *Maria Treu*, Vienna, but the first building for which he was solely responsible was the *Villa Amerika*, Prague (1715–20), which has obvious Hildebrandtian echoes. He collaborated with his father in the building of the Prague *Loreto*, Hradčany (1721–4). His Ursuline *St Johann Nepomuk*, Hradčany (1720) and the pilgrimage church, Nitzau (Nicov—1720–6), represent his earliest independently designed churches, but in both buildings Hildebrandt's Guarini-influenced plan for St Lawrence, Gabel, is synthesized with the Dientzenhofer family's much-used *Wandpfeiler* theme. At the noble *St Johann Nepomuk am Felsen* (*Sv Jan na Scalce*), Prague (1729–39), Kilian Ignaz's mastery of Baroque rhetoric, drama, and plastic modelling is admirably expressed. His *Sv Mikuláš, Staré Město*, Prague (1732–7), has astonishing originality and fluency, with a complex central space surrounded by ellipses: the twin-towered façade is parallel to the long axis. Elliptical elements again form the basis of the plan of *Sv Majdaléna*, Karlovy Vary (1732–6). He added the beautiful *cupola (1750–2) and tower (1755) to his father's

Sv Mikuláš, Malá Strana, Prague. Among his last churches, *St Florian*, Kladno (1746–8), and St John the Baptist, Paštiky (1748–51), show a tendency towards restraint and simplification.

Bou (1962); Büchner (1964); Dientzenhofer (1991); H.Franz (1942, 1943, 1943a, 1962); H.Hegemann (1943); E.Hempel (1965); Kreisel (1953); N-S (1968, 1986, 1986a); Swoboda (ed.) (1964); J.T (1996); Vilímková & Brucker (1989)

Dietterlin, Wendel (1551–99) German *Renaissance architect, his fame rests on his *Architectura und Ausztheilung/Symmetria und Proportion der Fünff Seulen* (1593–4), an exotic collection of plates showing architectural features derived from Flemish *Mannerist details with the *Orders, *strapwork, and fantastic ornament, called *Ditterling.

Dietterlin (1598); Jervis (1984); L & D (1986); Ohnesorge (1893); Pirr (1940); P (1968)

digital architecture Derives from computer modelling, simulation, and imaging to arrive at virtual forms. It may not involve the use of real materials, but relies upon numbers stored electronically to create simulations corresponding to material performance. It can be used to develop 'skins' that can alter the appearance of such 'architecture', and to suggest spaces that do not have many affinities with real architectural volumes. The complexities it makes possible have resulted in the evolution of forms that owe nothing to context, creating alien notes within the established grain of towns and cities, facilitating *Blobismus, *Deconstructivism, and *Zoömorphic architecture.

International Journal of Architectural Computing, ix/4 (2011), 437–61; *Journal of Architectural Education*, lvi/2 (2002), 7-13; Lynn (1999); Oxman & Oxman (2010)

diglyph *Doric *triglyph with only two vertical channels, omitting the two half-grooves at its sides, regarded by some as an *abuse.

dike 1. Ditch, trench, or *fosse. 2. Embankment, wall, or *causeway. 3. Defensive wall. 4. Low wall or fence of turf or stone marking a division or acting as an enclosure, e.g. of a field. 5. Ridge or *dam to resist encroachment by the sea. 6. *Jetty or *pier. 7. Raised causeway over marshy ground. 8. Barrier. *See also* DYKE.

dike-house 1. Shelter for a *diker* (one who tends sea-walls or dikes). 2. Store for materials needed to repair dikes.

Dilettanti, Society of Originally a convivial gathering of rich young men who had been on the *Grand Tour, it met in London from 1732, and developed as a serious supporter of architectural and archaeological explorations of Greece, the Middle East, and Italy, thereby laying the foundation for a systematic scholarly study of Classical

antiquities, financing expeditions and publishing the results. Notable successes were *The Antiquities of Athens* (1762–1814) and *Antiquities of Ionia* (1769–1814). It was a powerful stimulus for late C18 *Neo-Classicism, especially the *Greek Revival.

COF (1988); Crook (1972a); SoD (1814)

diminished 1. For *diminished* arch, *see* ARCH. 2. In a sash-window, a *diminished bar* is a *glazing-bar* moulded or shaped to present a finer, thinner appearance inside a room than it would appear if unshaped. 3. *Diminishing* or *graduated courses* are layers or rows of *slates that are of the same length in each course, but diminishing in height with each course from *eaves to *ridge.

diminution *Contractura* or reduction of the diameter of a column-shaft with height: in Antiquity it began from the lowest part of the *shaft, but C18 practice began it from about a third of the height. Associated with *entasis.

Dinkeloo, John Gerard (1918–81) American architect. With Irish-born **Eamonn Kevin Roche** (1922–2019) he worked with Eero *Saarinen (1950s) before establishing (1961) **Roche & Dinkeloo**. Their first work was the Oakland Museum, CA (1961–8), a huge building covering four city blocks and constructed of sandblasted *concrete both inside and out, with a series of gardens (1965–9) by *Kiley contained within the complex. The Cummins Engine Plant, Darlington, Co. Durham, England (1963–5), constructed of steel with the H-sections exposed externally, was a paradigm for its day, and exposed steelwork was again used at the Ford Foundation Headquarters, 42nd Street, NYC (1963–8), with a 12-storey indoor garden or office *atrium that became influential. In 1967–85 came the extensions to the Metropolitan Museum of Art, NYC, including the Pavilion for the Ancient-Egyptian temple of Dendur. After Dinkeloo's death Roche followed the reaction against the *Modern Movement, designing the E.F. Hutton Building, NYC (1980—with a stone *colonnade and *mansard roofs), and other works with Classical references. More recently the firm has built the enormous World Headquarters of Merck & Company, Whitehouse Station, NJ (1993).

Dal Co (ed.) (1985); E (1994); Fu (1975a); Stern (1977)

Dinocrates *See* DEINOCRATES.

Diocletian window Semicircular opening (usually a window) subdivided by two plain *mullions into three compartments. Named after its use in the *thermae of **Diocletian** (*r*.284–305), Rome, its alternative name is *thermal window*, commonly found in *Palladian and *Neo-Classical architecture.

Diocletian *or* **thermal window**

diorama 1. Large picture given additional reality by optical illusions and illumination, viewed through an aperture in a dark room. It underwent repeated changes by the operation of modified light on its transparent and semi-transparent surface. 2. Building specially constructed for 1., sometimes with a revolving circular room for spectators.

Diotisalvi (*fl.*C12) Probable architect of the circular *Romanesque*baptistery at Pisa (1152–1265). He may also have designed the octagonal *San Sepolcro*, Pisa (from 1153), and worked at *Santa Maria Maggiore*, Florence. His likely name was **Diotisalvi de Petroni.**

W.Pa (1852); S (1901–2)

dipteral Classical *temple with two rows of columns forming the *peristyle around the *cella, so with a minimum of eight columns (*octastyle*) beneath the *pedimented ends.

diptych *Altar-piece of two leaves that close like a book.

Directoire Austere, simplified *Neo-Classicism favoured during the *Directoire* (1795–9) in France sparingly ornamented with motifs associated with the Revolution (e.g. *Phrygian cap*), and after 1798 including Egyptian elements (e.g. *lotus and *sphinx). Taste demanded more opulent decoration by 1800, and the following *Empire* style embraced more Egyptianizing detail, especially after the publication of *Denon's account of Egypt and Nubia (1802). *Directoire* provided the inspiration for *American Directory* (*c.*1805–30—a variant on the USA *Federal style (1776–*c.*1830)) in general terms, except that the favoured motifs in the USA were those of *Freemasonry.

COF (1988); J.Curl (2005); L & D (1986)

Directory *See* DIRECTOIRE.

disc 1. Flat, circular, raised ornament, like a thin slice of a pole, carved as a series of discs adjacent to each other, found in *Romanesque work (e.g. Canterbury Cathedral, *c.*1100). 2. Any disc-like ornament. *See also* COIN.

discharging *See* ARCH.

distemper Cheap type of paint for walls and ceilings, consisting of whiting (e.g. ground chalk) mixed with size (i.e. weak glue), and water,

sometimes tinted. It was also used on *façades, but needed frequent renewal.

distyle *See* PORTICO.

ditch *See* DIKE.

ditriglyph *See* INTERCOLUMNIATION.

Ditterling Northern-European Mannerist fantastic ornament based on *grotesques and *strapwork in *Dietterlin's publications, occurring (late-C16 and early-C17) in England and the Low Countries.

Dietterlin (1598); L & D (1986); Ohnesorge (1893)

diwan *or* **divan** Islamic hall, court, council-chamber, court of justice, or audience-chamber.

di xue Chinese term for *moon-door (circular doorway in a garden-wall framing a view), also adopted in the West. *See* CHINESE GARDEN-DESIGN.

Dobson, John (1787–1865) Gifted and prolific architect / engineer / surveyor working in north-east England in the first half of C19, his best architecture was in a restrained *Neo-Classical style. With the builder Richard *Grainger he was responsible for the area bounded by Grey, Market, and Grainger Streets (*c.*1835–7), Newcastle upon Tyne, one of the most distinguished urban developments in the England of **King William IV** (*r.*1830–7), although Eldon Square was wantonly destroyed (late 1960s). His Central Railway Station, Newcastle (1847–50), built on a gently curving plan, combined *Greek-Revival architecture with an iron-and-glass station roof, while his entrances to Jesmond Old Cemetery (1836) are as severe and stark as any Continental architecture of the period. His best country-houses are Nunnykirk (1825) and Meldon Park (1832) in Northumberland. He advised *Monck at Belsay Castle (1807–17).

Co (2008); Dobson (1885); Faulkner & Greg (1987); Loudon (1981); Wilkes (1980); Wilkes & Dodds (1964)

dodecastyle *See* PORTICO.

Dodington, John (*fl.*1412–27) English mason, he was in charge of the works during the construction of many new buildings at King's Hall (now Trinity College), Cambridge, including the range of buildings projecting north behind the Great Court (1417–22), aka King's Hostel. In 1427 work began on the new Gate Tower (completed 1432) forming the south entrance to the College, but later (1599–1600) taken down and re-created on the north side of the Great Court west of the Chapel. Known as King Edward's Gate, it is the prototype of the Cambridge college gate-tower with corner *turrets.

J.Harvey (1987)

Doesburg, Theo van (1883–1931) Born **Christian Emil Maries Küpper** in Utrecht, Netherlands: though not an architect, he had considerable influence on modern architecture. With *Oud and others he established the periodical *De *Stijl*, taught at the *Bauhaus, Weimar (1921–4), and, with van *Eesteren, designed houses for a *De-Stijl* exhibition in Paris (1923). With the painter **Hans Peter Wilhelm Arp** (1886–1966) and Arp's wife, **Sophie Taeuber-Arp** (1889–1943), he decorated the interior of the *Café de l'Aubette*, Strasbourg (1926–8—destroyed). He also designed a studio and house at Meudon-Val-Fleury, France (1929–31 —incomplete), based on Le *Corbusier's *Citrohan* houses of the early 1920s. He influenced *Rietveld's *Elementarist Schroeder House, Utrecht.

COF (1988); Danzker *et al.* (eds) (2000); Doig (1986); Hedrik (1980); Straaten *et al.* (1993); Straaten (1994)

dog-ear *Acroterion.

dog-kennel Buildings for packs of hounds associated with hunting were often large and complex, with yards for exercise, cooking facilities, storage of straw, etc.: they often doubled as features in the landscape (e.g. the kennels at Milton Park, Cambs. (1767), looking like a ruined medieval *gate-house). *See also* CHIEN-ASSIS.

dog-leg *See* STAIR.

dog-tooth 1. Ornament resembling a *pyramid with **V**-shaped notches on each face pointing towards the apex, forming one of a closely spaced series within a *cavetto* moulding. It is characteristic of *First *Pointed, and is also found enriched with stylized foliage. **2.** Brick laid diagonally with a corner corbelled out and projecting from the *naked of a wall below, one of a series of adjacent similar bricks forming a continuous saw-toothed *band on a *string-course or part of a *cornice (*see* COGGING).

dog-tooth C13 First-Pointed example, Lincoln Cathedral.

dog-wheel Cylinder, *spit*, or *treadwheel*, turned by a dog treading inside it, commonly used to turn a spit in a kitchen.

Doll, Charles Fitzroy (1850–1929) English architect, educated in Germany and in Sir Matthew Digby *Wyatt's office, where he worked on the India Office, Whitehall, London (1866–8). Appointed Surveyor to the Bedford Estates in Bloomsbury and Covent Garden, London (1885), he designed the Hotel Russell (1898), a luxuriant

essay in the *François-Ier* style, based on the *Château de Madrid*, Paris (1528–1785), clad in *thé-au-lait *terracotta; and the Imperial Hotel, of a few years later, which *Pevsner described as a 'vicious mixture of Art Nouveau Gothic and Art Nouveau Tudor', to which he might have added 'Bavarian spires' (replaced with tawdry *Modernist banalities, late-1960s), both in Russell Square. Doll was also responsible for the exquisitely detailed Flemish Franco-*Gothic terrace of shops with apartments over them in Torrington Place (1907). His practice continued under his son, **Christian Charles Tyler Doll** (1880–1955), who was partly responsible for reconstructing the grand staircase of the Palace of King Minos, Knossos, Crete.

A.S.Gray (1985); Cherry & Pe(1998)

dolly 1. Short length of timber or metal on top of a *pile acting as a buffer between it and the *ram* or *monkey* (striking-head of a *pile-driver*). **2.** The same, used to make the pile longer if driven beyond the reach of the ram.

dolmen Prehistoric enclosure (usually a *tomb-chamber*) formed by three or more upright *megaliths supporting a large flat horizontal stone usually covered with earth to form a *tumulus. Also known as a *cromlech*.

dome *Cupola, essentially a species of *vault, constructed on a circular, elliptical, or polygonal *plan, bulbous, segmental, semicircular, or pointed in vertical *section. It can be built on top of a structure the plan of which is identical to that of the dome: if that structure's wall is circular or elliptical it is a *drum* (often pierced with windows) as in a *rotunda. However, domes usually provide a covering for a square- or rectangular-planned building or compartment, so adjustments are made to facilitate the transition from the square to the circular, elliptical, or polygonal base of the cupola or dome. This is achieved by means of *pendentives* (fragments (*b*) of a *sail-vault* (*a*,*c*) resembling a species of concave, distorted, almost triangular *spandrels, rising up from the corner at the top of the right-angled compartment to the circular or elliptical base of the drum or cupola) or (*d*) *squinches* (small arch or series of parallel arches of increasing radius spanning the angle of the square compartment). Both the drum and cupola will have a diameter the same dimension as the side of the square on which the whole structure stands. *Types of dome include*:

calotte: low cupola or saucer-dome of segmental vertical section, like a skull-cap;

cloister-vault: as *domical vault*;

domical vault: *cloister-vault*, not a true dome, but formed of four or more (depending on the shape of the base) *cells* or *webs* forming *groins* where they touch vertically and rising to a point;

melon: as *parachute*;

Pantheon: low dome on the exterior, often stepped, resembling that of the *Pantheon in Rome, and coffered on the interior, widely copied by Neo-Classical architects;

parachute: *melon*, *pumpkin*, or *umbrella* dome standing on a scalloped circular base and formed of individual *webs*, segmental on plan, joining in *groins* or *ribs*. Each web has a concave interior and convex exterior so it resembles a parachute, rather than an umbrella;

pumpkin: as *parachute*;

sail-dome (*a*): dome resembling a billowing sail over a square compartment with its diameter the same dimension as the *diagonal* instead of the side of the square below, enabling the structure to rise as though on *pendentives* but continuing without interruption. Pendentives are really parts of a sail-dome and themselves are a species of *sail-vault*;

umbrella: as *parachute*.

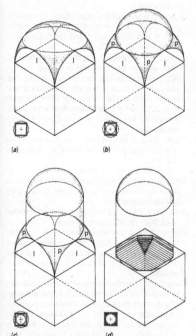

(a)   (b)

(c)   (d)

dome (*a*) Sail. (*b*) On pendentives, on square base. (*c*) On drum on pendentives, on square base. (*d*) On squinches on square base. l = lunette, p = pendentive.

Domènech i Montaner, Lluís (1850–1923) Like *Gaudí, inventive practitioner of *Modernisme*, the Catalan variant of *Art Nouveau at the turn of C19. He drew on *Romanesque and *Gothic themes as well as the ideas of *Viollet-le-Duc, and as early as 1878 published an article in which he argued for a specifically national Catalan architecture that would be a transformation of *eclecticism into something new, yet distinctive, clearly an early manifestation of *Critical Regionalism. His café-restaurant for the Barcelona Universal Exposition (1887–8) drew on medieval models, but in the *Palau de la Música Catalana* (1905–8), Barcelona, he drew on modern technology with a structure of interlaced iron to produce his master-work.

Boh (1968, 1991); Borràs (1970); Pe & R (1973); Sack (1995); T-M (1967)

Domenig, Günther (1934–2012). Austrian architect, leader of the **Graz School**, countering *Historicist traditions and promoting individualistic buildings no matter what the context. His *Zentralsparkasse, Favoritenstrasse*, Vienna (1974–9), was designed with a front that seemed to be folding and crumpling. Among other works were the Documentation Centre, Nazi-Party-Rally area, Nuremberg (1996–8), and the *Steinhaus*, Steindorf, near Klagenfurt (1980–2002). His buildings influenced younger Austrian architects.

Domenig (2002); E (1994)

dome-pot Earthenware vase, pipe, or pot, the base of one fitted into the top of another, so forming a curved series of ribs acting as the frame for the construction of a *concrete *vault (e.g. *San Vitale*, Ravenna). See ACOUSTIC VASES.

Domestic Revival Offshoot of the cult of the *Picturesque and the *Gothic Revival, it was essentially a style of domestic architecture that incorporated forms, details, and materials found in English *vernacular buildings, including steeply-pitched tiled roofs, *dormers, *timber-framing and jettied construction, small-paned *mullioned and *transomed windows (often with leaded *lights), tile-hung walls, tall chimneys (often of the *Tudor type in carved and moulded brick), and carefully contrived asymmetrical compositions. Aka *Old English style. See also COT.

J.Curl (1990); D & M (1985); Gd (1977)

domical vault See VAULT.

domus Roman house for a single wealthy family. See ATRIUM; ROMAN ARCHITECTURE.

Donaldson, Thomas Leverton (1795–1885) London-born architect, first Professor of Architecture at University College London (1842–65), his work includes the noble Classical Library of UCL (1848–9), and the uninspired *Gothic Holy

Trinity Church, Brompton, London (1826–9). Author of *Architectural Maxims and Theorems* (1847) and *Architectura Numismatica* (1859), he contributed to the supplementary volume (1830) of *Antiquities of Athens*, and to the *Dictionary of the Architectural Publication Society* (1852–92). He was one of the founders of the Institute of British Architects.

Co (2008); Hi (1954); *ODNB* (2004); W.Pa (1852)

donjon 1. Strongest part of a medieval *castle, usually a tower or *keep* containing the best rooms and living-quarters, capable of being defended even if the outer walls were breached. 2. Lowest storey in a keep, usually a basement. 3. Prison of several compartments, or one cell, wholly or partly below ground level.

Donthorn, William John (1799–1859) English architect, pupil of *Wyatville, whose manner of *Picturesque composition he adopted. He established an extensive practice, designing country-houses and *parsonages, but most of his Neo-Classical works recalling the designs of *Dance the Younger and *Soane have been demolished. His severe *Neo-Classicism can best be appreciated from his drawings in the RIBA British Architectural Library Drawings Collection, and from a handful of buildings (e.g. the stable-block, High House, West Acre, Norfolk (*c.*1823–9), and Upton Hall, near Southwell, Notts. (*c.*1830)). He designed the Leicester Testimonial at Holkham, Norfolk, a column of the *Agricultural Order (with mangel-wurzel and turnip-leaves instead of *acanthus), and the romantic *Gothic Highcliffe Castle, Hants. (1830–4), which incorporated medieval fragments from the *Grande Manoir des Andelys* (C15) and the *Romanesque Abbey of Jumièges, both in Normandy, while the interiors contained *Louis-Quinze* panelling and *Empire décor*. His output of *Tudor Gothic was prolific, and he made forays into Norman Revival (e.g. Gaol and Session House, Peterborough (1841–2)). He was a founder-member of the Institute of British Architects.

AH, xxi (1978), 83–92; Co (2008)

doocot, ducat Scots term for *dovecote: it can be of the attached (i.e. incorporated with other outbuildings), *beehive, *drum, *lectern (square on plan with monopitched roof), polygonal, or square (with pitched or pyramidal roof) type.

Doom Medieval pictorial representation of the Last Judgement: it often took the form of a mural over a church *chancel-arch, with Christ in the middle, Hell and the damned on His left (the south or right when seen from the *nave), and the Blessed on His right (north). It was also a subject for stained-glass windows: a spectacular glass Doom survives in St Mary's Church, Fairford, Glos. (late C15 and early C16).

E.Duffy (1992)

door Moveable lockable barrier of wood or other material consisting of one piece, or of several pieces framed together, usually turning on hinges or sliding in a groove, serving to permit or bar access through a doorway. Commonly supported on hinges secured to the *door-post* or *door-frame*, a door may also turn on pivots at the top and bottom (an arrangement usual in Antiquity), slide, or roll up horizontally or vertically, and itself can be divided into more folds, or *valves*, hinged to the frame or each other. In traditional *timber-framed* doors the horizontal timbers are called *rails*, the verticals at the sides *stiles*, and the vertical in the centre *muntin*. **Types of traditional door include**:

batten: see LEDGED;

bivalve: with two leaves meeting in the middle;

blind: with fixed or moveable slats having the character of, and serving as, a *blind. Also a *sham* door;

casement: with a glazed part above the middle rail, usually with *diminishing stiles* on either side of the glazed part (itself subdivided with *glazing-bars*);

crapaudine: turning on a pivot at top and bottom;

double: divided into two folds or valves;

double margin: looking as though it has two leaves with a *muntin* looking like a *stile* in the centre, twice as wide as the side stiles, but with its centre beaded or otherwise finished to make it resemble two stiles, therefore showing a double margin;

Dutch: divided horizontally into two pieces so that the lower part can be kept shut, also called *half-door*;

false: immoveable; imitation;

flap: small vertical door hinged at the bottom to open downwards, or one placed horizontally and opening up;

flush: with its construction concealed behind plain flush faces, usually plywood;

folding: divided into two or more valves hinged to the frame or to each other, properly called *bivalve*, *quadrivalve*, etc. In larger, heavier doors, the valves should be supported on wheels;

framed: with a timber frame all round, consisting of vertical *stiles* (one of which is the *hanging-stile* to which the hinges are fixed) and horizontal rails top and bottom. An additional *middle-* or *lock-*rail (in which the locks are fixed) is usual, while in panelled doors a central vertical element, the *muntin*, is found;

framed, ledged, braced, and battened: with top, middle, and bottom *rail* mortised and tenoned

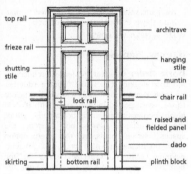

top rail

architrave

frieze rail

hanging
stile

shutting
stile

muntin

lock rail

chair rail

raised and
fielded panel

dado

skirting

bottom rail

plinth block

Framed door.

into two *stiles*, and two braces housed into the
rails rising diagonally from the hinged side,
clad on the outside with vertical boards or
battens;

half: one half of a *Dutch* door, or the entire Dutch
door, or a door less high than the doorway, with
an opening top and bottom;

Holy: to the *iconostasis* in a church;

jib: hinged, *flush*, set in a wall or panelling without a visible frame, designed to be almost invisible to preserve the appearance of a wall, etc.,
where a visible door would be unacceptable;

ledged and battened: with horizontal rails or
ledges (to which hinges and other ironmongery
can be fixed), clad with vertical boards or battens outside;

ledged, braced, and battened: as *ledged and battened*, but stiffened by means of braces or struts
set diagonally (in better work mortised and
tenoned into the ledges) and rising from the
hanging side;

overhung: hinged at the top and swinging outwards;

panelled: *framed*, with one or more *panels.
As with a *framed* door the frame consists of
horizontal *top* and *bottom* rails (for one panel),
a *middle* or *lock* rail (for four or more panels)
to which the handles, locks, etc. are fixed,
and a *frieze* rail (where there are six panels)
near the top, with vertical *stiles* (one *hanging*
(to which the hinges are fixed) and the
other *shutting*). Where there are four or more
panels a central vertical *muntin* is placed
between the rails. In panelled doors the
frame is exposed and expressed, surrounding
the panels, which can be *plain*, *decorated*,
raised, or *fielded*;

revolving: four flaps or valves fixed at right angles
to each other and hung from a central pivot at
the axis of a cylinder within which the doors
revolve. The outer edges of the valves are

finished with rubber or other materials so that
close contact is maintained with the cylindrical
shell. Access is like a turnstile. It helps to conserve energy and prevent draughts;

rolling: type of *shutter consisting of slats joined
together and rolling on a suspended axle;

sash: see CASEMENT;

sham: finished on one side and set into a wall or
partition to look like a door for reasons of
appearance or symmetry, really a kind of *blind*
door;

sliding: one sliding horizontally on tracks, often
suspended from wheeled brackets, and sometimes designed to be housed within a wall;

storm: extra outer doors to give added protection
in cold weather;

swing: with no striking-piece, commonly with
double-action spring hinges, used e.g. for
doors between kitchen and dining-room in a
restaurant;

trap: fitted to a horizontal surface to give access
to a cellar or roof;

wicket: small door forming part of a very large
one, as in a big church-door.

Compounds include:

door-case: case or frame lining a door-opening,
from which a door is hung, consisting of *architraves, panels,etc., and sometimes with a *cill;

door-frame: *frame to which a door is hung set in
a *reveal in a *doorway*. The verticals of the
frame are the *door-checks, -jambs*, or *-posts*,
and the top part is the *door-head*. Frames can
sometimes include cills. Door-frames are often
associated with a *door-case*;

door-furniture: hinges, locks, handles, etc., fitted
to doors;

door-handle: lever by which a door is opened;

door-jamb: vertical side of a door-aperture, usually with a *door-post*;

door-knob: circular or elliptical knob, which,
when turned, allows a door to open;

door-knocker: heavy metal hinged lever (often
elaborately decorated) which, if banged on the
plate to which it is attached (and which is fixed
to the door), alerts those inside the house;

door-post: upright on either side of doorway, to
one of which the door is hung;

doorway: opening for an entrance to a building,
part of a building, or an enclosure, together with
its immediate structure and surroundings, often
of considerable architectural magnificence.
Classical *Antique doorways were mostly rectangular (occasionally *battered), surrounded by
*mouldings, normally the architrave, conform-
ing with the architrave of the *entablature in
*section, and often with *ears, *lugs, or *tabs.
Above the architrave there was sometimes a
*cornice supported on *ancones or *consoles.
A Classical doorway could also be framed by
an arrangement of columns, *pilasters, and

entablature (often with a *pediment), in which case the opening would be said to be *aediculated. *Renaissance doorways were sometimes arched. A doorway can often be treated architecturally to enhance its importance in a *façade, as in a church, where symbolic aspects play a great part in the design. *Romanesque doorways, for example, usually have semicircular heads, and may consist of several parallel arched layers, each with its own *Order of *colonnettes, *chevron, *beak-head, *billet, or other mouldings. *Gothic doorways have pointed heads, and grander types have several Orders, lush ornament (e.g. *dog-tooth), *Purbeck-marble colonnettes, and, in the centre of the opening, a vertical post (*trumeau) dividing it into two parts, with an elaborate sculptured *tympanum above, framed by the pointed arch.

W.McKay (1957); W.Pa (1852)

d'Orbay, François See ORBAY.

Doric Order Classical *Order of architecture found in distinct *Greek and *Roman varieties, probably evolved from timber prototypes before C6 BC, as suggested by the *frieze with its *triglyphs perhaps representing beam-ends, *guttae the constructional dowels, and *metopes the spaces between beams, but this interpretation is by no means accepted as gospel. Ancient-Egyptian columns, especially those at the Beni-Hasan rock-cut tombs (c.1900 BC) and the

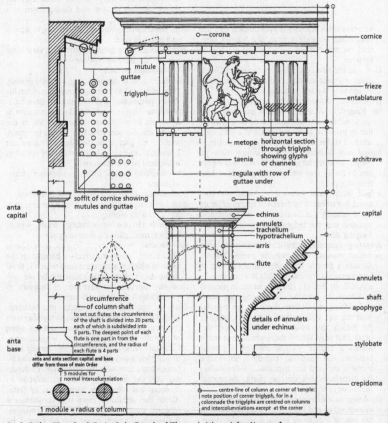

Doric Order C5 BC Greek-Doric, Order Temple of 'Theseus', Athens (*after Normand*).

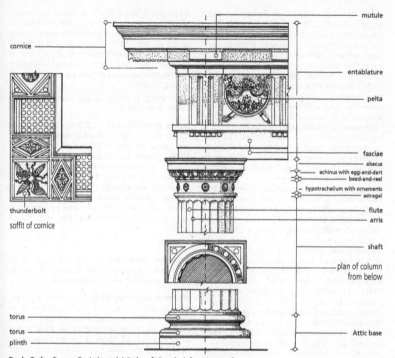

cornice

mutule

entablature

pelta

fasciae
abacus
echinus with egg-and-dart
bead-and-reel
hypotrachelium with ornaments
astragal
flute
arris

thunderbolt

soffit of cornice

shaft

plan of column
from below

torus

torus
plinth

Attic base

Doric Order Roman-Doric 'mutule' Order of Vignola (*after Normand*).

sixteen-sided columns at the *temple of **Queen Hatshepsut**, Deïr-el-Bahari (*c*.1479–*c*.1458 BC), also have been seen as prototypes of the Doric column. The Greek-Doric Order comprises a baseless shaft (normally cut with *flutes separated by *arrises, but occasionally unfluted (probably because unfinished), as in the temple of Apollo, Delos (*c*.325–300 BC)), rising directly from the *stylobate, diminishing in diameter from bottom to top (*diminution) in a delicate outward curve called *entasis (very pronounced in the Orders used at *Paestum (*c*.565–*c*.450 BC)), terminating in the *trachelion (part of the shaft between the horizontal grooves circumscribing the shaft (*hypotrachelion) and the *annulets); a *capital consisting of 3–5 annulets (rings) that stop the shaft and its flutes and form the base of the cushion-like *echinus (again pronounced in the Paestum temples) supporting the unornamented square *abacus; and an *entablature, approximately a quarter the height of the entire Order, consisting of a flat *architrave (*lintel) carrying the frieze and crowning *cornice. Immediately over the

architrave is a plain *band or *taenia* under which, lining up with the triglyphs above, is a series of narrow bands (*regulae*) with 6 *guttae* or cone-like drops hanging beneath them. Over the *taenia* is the frieze, consisting of a series of alternating triglyphs (flat upright slabs, incised with two vertical **V**-shaped *glyphs (channels) and a half-glyph on each side, at the top of which is a plain projecting band) and approximately square metopes set back from the face of the triglyphs and often embellished with sculpture in *relief (earlier with painted *terracotta panels). Triglyphs are normally set over the centre-line of each column and over the centre-line of each *intercolumniation in *Hellenic buildings (where one triglyph only is set between each column centre-line), but in *Hellenistic buildings the intercolumniation is usually wider, so two or more triglyphs occurred. However, the Athenian *propylaea (C5 BC) had two triglyphs over the centre intercolumniation. In Greek Doric the triglyphs invariably terminate a frieze, so touch at the angle of a building: as a column set on the centre-line of the triglyph would have an unacceptably clumsy projection at a corner it is therefore set back, and the centre-line rule is broken at the angle, resulting in narrower intercolumniations between the corner-columns and their immediate neighbours. Set over the frieze is the cornice with inclined projecting *mutules on the *soffit placed over the triglyphs and centre-lines of the metopes, so there is insufficient space for ornamentation of the soffit except for the guttae on the undersides of the mutules and (sometimes) an *anthemion or other enrichment at the corner of the soffit, where there are no mutules. The paradigm of Greek Doric is held by some to be the Athenian *Parthenon (447–438 BC), although the type was established by the temple of Aphaia at Aegina (c.495 BC).

In the Roman version of Doric, there may be a rudimentary *base, but the shaft is generally more slenderly proportioned, and the entablature is only an eighth the height of the Order (as at the *prostyle tetrastyle temple at Cori in Latium (C1 BC)), giving a somewhat feeble effect. Under the Roman Empire Doric really ceased to be used, and what we call *Roman Doric* is really a variety of *Tuscan Order to which triglyphs and other embellishments were added. This so-called Doric was codified and developed during the *Renaissance, and consists of a base, a shaft (fluted or unfluted) more slenderly proportioned than in Greek Doric, and a capital consisting of an *astragal (sometimes ornamented with *bead-and-reel) joined to the shaft by an *apophyge, a frieze-like *hypotrachelium* (often ornamented), an *echinus (sometimes enriched with *egg-and-dart), and a square *abacus* with a crowning *moulding. Architraves are sometimes plain, but usually have two *fasciae* separated by mouldings, and the frieze has triglyphs that do not occur off-centre in relation to columns because they do not touch at the angles. There is instead a demi-metope at the corner, a solution proposed by *Vitruvius, who probably got it from a Hellenistic theorist: Roman-Doric columns are therefore always equidistant, with identical intercolumniations, even at the corners, though the spacing is invariably wide, with two or more triglyphs over each intercolumniation although there are some exceptions, such as *Hawksmoor's Mausoleum at Castle Howard, Yorks. (1729–36), where the intercolumniation is deliberately narrow, to add to the *gravitas* of the architecture. Metopes are often ornamented with *bucrania* and other devices derived from Hellenistic models, especially from Asia Minor. Mutules are usually set over the triglyphs only, giving scope for additional inventive ornamentation on the soffit, and have a slight slope and very modest projection (usually only the guttae) below the cornice. The powerful *Mutule Order* of *Vignola has horizontal mutules that

do project, giving a highly modelled soffit additionally ornamented with lozenges and thunderbolts. *Scamozzi and Vignola both used *dentils associated with the *bed-mouldings of their versions, clearly derived from the *Antique Order of the *thermae* of Diocletian, Rome (AD 306), which has a continuous band of *fret-like ornament suggesting *dentils.

J.Curl (2001); D (1950); Hersey (1988); C.Normand (1852); Onians (1988)

Doric Revival Until c.1570 the Greek *Doric *Order was virtually unknown, and, even when the Greek temples at *Paestum began to be taken seriously by *Winckelmann et al. in C18, aroused controversy, as they were perceived to be deformed and ugly by eyes accustomed to *Palladian refinements. Only when primitive, *Antique themes began to be explored was Greek Doric appreciated, and became a powerful element in *Neo-Classicism and the *Greek Revival.

Pe (1968)

dorman, dormant 1. Large horizontal structural timber or *summer-tree*. 2. Main beam supporting smaller ones. 3. *Dormer-window.

dormer Projecting framed structure set vertically on the *rafters of a pitched roof, with its own roof (pitched or flat), sides (*dormer cheeks*), and a window set vertically in the front. It will often have a small *gable or *pediment (*dormer-head*) over the window if its roof is pitched at right angles to the main roof, but if the roof is a *cat-slide it will have a flat top. Not to be confused with a *lucarne rising directly over the *eaves from the *naked of the main wall below.

Dormer, Henry (fl.1680–1727) Architect / surveyor active in Leics. and Northants. He carried out works (1686) at Lamport Hall, Northants., and made designs to rebuild the Chapel of St Mary in Arden, Market Harborough, Leics. (1693–4). From 1694 he was employed by **Daniel Finch** (1647–1730—**2nd Earl of Nottingham** from 1682 and **7th Earl of Winchilsea** from 1729) to supervise the building of the new house at Burley-on-the-Hill, Rut., but his duties were taken over by *Lumley from 1697.

Co (2008); *Studies in Local History* (1955), 148ff.

dormitory 1. Large sleeping-room (or *dorter) with many beds (sometimes placed in separate cubicles). 2. College hostel.

dormitory-suburb Suburban development where most residents work somewhere else. So a *dormitory-town* is the same, only bigger.

dorse *Canopy or *dorsel.

dorsel, dossal, dossel 1. *Reredos. 2. Embroidered cloth suspended over the rear of an *altar. 3. Ornamental hanging suspended at the backs of *sedilia or elsewhere at the sides of a *chancel. 4. *Stall with a back to it, as in a *Collegiate church or cathedral. 5. High *wainscoting or panelling.

dorter, dortour Sleeping-room, bed-chamber, or *dormitory, esp. in a *monastery.

Dortsman, Adriaan *or* **Adriaen** (1625–82) Dutch architect/military-engineer, practising in Amsterdam from 1665. He designed the *Nieuwe Lutherse Kerk* (1668–71—a domed church with an *ambulatory around half its circumference), supervised the construction of defences at Amsterdam and Naarden, and built several groups of houses on, the *Heerengracht* and *Keizersgracht*, Amsterdam (1665–72), in a refined, plain, stripped style, the only architectural emphases being on door-cases, balconies, and crowning elements.

Kuyper (1980); L-D (1934); RSTK (1977)

Doshi, Balkrishna Vithaldas (1927–2010). Indian architect/planner. Influenced by Le *Corbusier (with whom he worked in France, Chandigarh, and Ahmadabad) and *Kahn (e.g. Centre for Environmental Planning and Technology, Ahmadabad (1967–81)), he later evolved a more personal style, as at his own studio, Sangath, near Ahmadabad (1981), a series of barrel-vaulted structures, partially submerged in the ground, set amongst landscaped terraces and water-cascades. Similar themes were explored in his Gandhi Labour Institute, Ahmadabad (1980–4). Among his other works may be cited the Indian Institute of Management, Bangalore (1977–85), the National Institute of Fashion Technology, New Delhi (1991–5), the Maharashtra Institute of Development Administration, Pune (1991), a town-plan for Vidhyadhar Nagar, near Jaipur (1984–6), and low-cost housing at Indore (1983–6).

Ashraf & Belluardo (eds) (1998); W.J.R.Cu (1988); E (1994); Steele (ed.) (1998)

dossal, dossel *See* DORSEL.

dosseret 1. Supplementary cubical block or *super-abacus*, often taller than the *capital itself, placed over an *abacus of *Early-Christian, *Byzantine, and *Romanesque capitals, really an *impost-block* from which arches spring. 2. Block formed like a section of *entablature over a column or *pier. 3. Small projection on a *jamb, forming a *pilaster-like member supporting e.g. a *lintel.

Dotti, Carlo Francesco (1670–1759) Como-born, he settled in Bologna, where he became the leading *Baroque architect. His most

celebrated designs are the dramatically sited *pilgrimage church of the *Madonna di San Luca*, near Bologna (1723–57—a vast domed church on an elliptical plan), and the Meloncello arch (1722).

Matteucci (1969); ZfK, **xxxiv**/3 (1971), 208–39

dou In Chinese and Japanese architecture, notched wooden block supporting a bracket in a timber system in which many brackets are employed.

double Any repeated two-fold building, architectural feature, or motif, forming a pair.
Compounds of double *include*:
double arch: *arch erected from two centres, with radii shorter than half the span, sometimes occurring in *Romanesque work;
double bead: two *beads parallel to each other, one of which is generally smaller, with *quirks;
double-bellied: *baluster shaped like two long-bows (weapons, as in archery), one mirroring the other, identical above and below its middle and on either side of its centre-line;
double cloister: *ambulatory divided in two by a range of columns or *piers;
double cone: *Romanesque *moulding consisting of a series of truncated cones laid on their sides, set with bases joined and truncated tops together, forming a continuous horizontal ornament in a *cavetto;

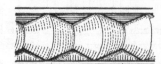

double cone St Mary's, Stoneleigh, Warwicks. (C12).

double floor: one consisting of three horizontal ranges of timbers (boards laid on flooring- or bridging-joists which are carried on binding-joists, to the underside of which the ceiling-joists are fixed);
double-framed roof: *see* TRUSS;
double-fronted: house with a centre door, its front symmetrical about an axis through the door (e.g. Pembridge Square, Northern Kensington, London (1857–79));
double hammer-beam: *see* TRUSS;
double-hung sashes: window with two *sashes hung with pulleys, lines, and weights, each moveable up and down in the same frame;
double lancet: 1. *Gothic window consisting of two *lancet-lights separated by a *mullion, often with a small circular or lozenge-shaped light above; 2. two lancets placed close together;

double-margin door: *door looking like a pair of doors with its central *muntin divided vertically by a *bead;

double ressaunt: *moulding consisting of two *ogees meeting in a *fillet;

double-return stair: *see* STAIR;

double vault: two *vaults carried up with a space between them, as in the dome at *San Pietro*, Rome (1546–90).

double window: window with two *lights within one architectural entity, as in *Gothic work, the lights separated by a *mullion.

double church 1. Two-storeyed church, i.e. with a church on each storey, as in the *Romanesque example, Schwarz-Rheindorf, Rhineland, Germany (C12). **2.** Church with two distinct *naves joined together at a centre point, as at the L-shaped Lutheran Church, Freudenstadt, Germany (1601–8).

double-pile house *Pile is a row of rooms: *single-pile* house therefore has a single row of rooms; *double-pile* house is two rooms deep, sometimes, but not always, with a corridor between the two rows. One of the earliest double-pile houses to survive is Whitehall, Shrewsbury, Salop. (1578–82), and *Pratt's Coleshill, Berks. (*c*.1650–62—demolished 1952) was an excellent example of an English C17 double-pile plan.

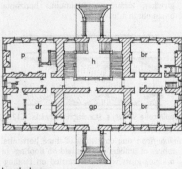

br	bedroom
dr	drawing-room
gp	great parlour
h	hall
p	parlour

double-pile house Coleshill, Berks.

doucine *Cyma recta*.

Douglas, Campbell (1828–1910) *See* SELLARS, JAMES.

Douglas, John (1829–1911) English architect. He set up in Chester and influenced a regional style of *vernacular architecture, featuring timber-framing. His best works (as **Douglas & Fordham**

(with **J.P.Fordham** (1843–99)) are the cottages, houses, and model farms on the Westminster Estates at Eaton Hall, Ches., and several fine buildings at Port Sunlight, including the Lyceum (1894–6). He designed St Chad's Church, Hopwas, Staffs. (1881), in which he introduced *timber-framed construction, giving the building a domestic air.

Hartwell *et al.* (2011); Darley (1975); Davison (1916); A.S.Gray (1985); Hubbard (1991)

Douglass, David Bates (1790–1849) American military-engineer who designed the layouts of Green-Wood Cemetery, Brooklyn, NYC (1838–48—four times the size of *Père-Lachaise*, Paris), and Albany Rural Cemetery, Menands, NY (1841–5). He deserves to be considered as one of America's foremost pioneers of landscape-architecture in the first half of C19.

J.Curl (2004)

Doultonware High-fired vitrified non-porous salt-glazed ceramic made of a hard grey-brown material (stoneware) on which designs were drawn, a part or the whole then being richly coloured. Produced in the **Doulton Works**, Lambeth, London, founded by **John Doulton** (1793–1873), it was invented and patented by **Sir Henry Doulton** (1820–97), and exhibited (1871) as *sgraffito*-ware. He then developed *Lambeth faïence* (brightly coloured glazed blocks) and *Doulton impasto* (glazed earthenware, the colour applied thickly). Both products were used for festive *façades, such as the fronts of *public-houses, bar-fronts, and the like. Hard-wearing and easily washed, Doultonware's heyday was the late C19 to *c*.1914.

ODNB (2004)

dovecot(e), dovehouse Circular, polygonal, rectangular, or square building, like a short tower, called *colombier* or *columbarium*, the interior of which is fitted with small niches (*columbaria*) all round the walls for nesting pigeons or doves. If it is a tall building it is called a *dove-tower*. *See* DOOCOT.

dovetail 1. *See* SWALLOWTAIL. **2.** Wedge-shaped projection at one end of a timber designed to fit into a similarly-shaped recess in another piece to join them together.

Dow, Alden Ball (1904–83) American architect. He worked (1933) with F.L.L.*Wright before establishing his own practice. Most of his works are in or near Midland, MI, and have been noted for their influences from or rejection of Wright's designs. Midland Country Club (1930), built before he moved to work with Wright; his own studio, Midland (1935), much influenced by Wright; and the Midland Center for the Arts (1970), which represents rejection of Wright, may be cited.

Dow (1965, 1970, c.1970); E (1994); S.Robinson (1983)

dowel(l) Headless peg, pin, or bolt of wood, metal or other material, used to fasten two members together by being set into each part. *See* CRAMP.

Dowland, Thomas (*fl.*1490s) English mason. He built the west tower of the Holy Cross Guild Chapel at Stratford-on-Avon, Warwicks. (begun 1496), and may have been responsible for the *chancel and *clerestorey of the Parish Church in the same town (*c.*1465–*c.*1495). To judge from the stylistic similarities he seems to have worked on several churches in Warwicks. and Worcs., especially towers.

J.Harvey (1987)

Downing, Andrew Jackson (1815–52) Leading American writer/landscape-designer of the first half of C19. His *A Treatise on the Theory and Practice of Landscape Gardening Adapted to North America* (1841) drew on *Loudon and *Repton, while his *Cottage Residences* (1842) and *The Architecture of Country Houses* (1850) helped to disseminate his ideas and designs, which owed much to the skills of A.J.*Davis (who made professional drawings for Downing's publications (1839–50)), but, when his proposals to form a partnership with Davis failed, he took on the Englishman *Vaux (1850). Through his editorials in *The Horticulturist* (the 'Journal of Rural Art and Rural Taste') he had a profound effect on architecture and landscape-design, and can be compared with Loudon in importance. He was the father of the American *public park, and his visions were given substance by Vaux and *Olmsted in Central Park, NYC (1857–60). Among his designs for gardens, those at Springside, Poughkeepsie, NY (1850–2), and The White House, Washington, DC (1851–2), should be mentioned. He also promoted an American type of timber-framed house, with large *verandahs and bracketed *eaves, a precursor of the *Stick style, and later adapted by architects such as Davis and *Notman.

A.Downing (1841, 1866, 1868); Haley (ed.) (1988); Hi (1977); Major (1997); P (1982); D.Schuyler (1996); Sweeting (1996); Tatum & MacDougall (1989)

downpipe Drainpipe conveying water from a roof-gutter, or from a water-tank.

Dowson, Sir Philip Henry Manning (1924–2014) *See* ARUP.

Doxiadis, Constantinos Apostolos (1913–75) Greek architect/engineer/town-planner, he became influential, and formed (1939) the Office for National, Regional, and Town Planning Studies and Research. Intimately involved with the reconstruction of Greece after the 1939–45 war, he founded (1951) his own architectural/consulting/engineering firm, which quickly won an international reputation. He is remembered primarily for the theory of *Ekistics, and for his books, *Ekistics: Introduction to the Science of Human Settlements* (1968) and *Ecumenopolis* (1979).

Deane (1965); Doxiadis (1963, 1966, 1966a, 1968, 1972); Doxiadis & Papaioannou (1974); E (1994)

Doyle, Albert Ernest (1877–1928) California-born, he founded (1907) his architectural firm in Oregon with **William B. Patterson** (*fl.*1900–30) as his partner, and designed a ten-storey extension to the Meier and Frank Department Store in Portland. The firm's commercial designs were eclectic, largely in Revival styles, but its simpler seaside houses (e.g. Wantz Studio House, Neahkahnie, OR (1916)), were inspirations for *Belluschi and others who worked with Doyle.

Architect and Engineer, viii/1 (1919), 38–96

Doyle, James Francis (1840–1913) Influential Liverpool architect, his churches were in a scholarly *Gothic Revival, but his commercial buildings, notably the Royal Insurance Offices, Dale Street, Liverpool (1896–1903), were assured *Baroque compositions. He supervised construction of Norman *Shaw's White Star Building, Pier Head (1894–6), which resembles New Scotland Yard, London. He also designed a number of houses for the prosperous classes of the area, but most have been demolished or unsympathetically altered.

A.S.Gray (1985); Sharples (2004)

draft, draught Regular *dressed *drafted margin* the width of the chisel, also called a *border*, along the edges of the face of a squared stone.

dragon *or* **dragging** Timber set at an angle in *timber-framed and roof- construction. ***Compounds include*:**
dragon-beam: in timber-framed buildings, a *beam set diagonally to support jetties on two adjacent *façades at an angle of an upper storey, or to carry the foot of a hip-*rafter;
dragon-bracket: *bracket, often shaped or curved, supporting the corner of a *jetty and set at an angle of 135° from a *corner-post;
dragon-piece, dragging-piece: short length of horizontal timber (really a small *dragon-beam*) set diagonally at an angle, one end on the junction of two adjacent wall-plates and the other on a *dragon-tie*, to support the foot of a hip-rafter;
dragon-tie: **1.** horizontal timber *angle-brace* between a *tie-beam and a *wall-plate; **2.** the same, but between adjacent wall-plates at the angle of a hipped roof, especially when it supports one end of a *dragon-piece*, the other supported on the angle of the wall-plates.

Dragon style Style of decoration influenced by Scandinavian Viking art, a Norwegian revival of which took place in the second half of C19. Certain motifs were incorporated within the *Celtic Revival and *Art Nouveau.

T-M (1967)

Drake, Gordon (1917–52) American architect, he designed several exemplary houses in CA, understood the complex relationships between design and structure, and was intensely aware of the impact buildings can have on the environment. Sensitive to Nature, he often used timber. His last buildings (1951), the Unit House, East Bay, Oakland, CA (with *Baylis as landscape architect), and the Berns House, Malibu, were paradigms, demonstrating his responses to environmental problems. Much of his *oeuvre* was exquisitely photographed by *Shulman.

Baylis & Parry (1956)

drapery *Swag of drapery instead of a *festoon, suspended from an object, e.g. *bucranium*, in Classical ornament.

drapery panel As *linenfold.

Dravidian architecture Architecture in the southern part of the Indian Subcontinent.

drawbridge 1. Bridge over a moat, ditch, river, etc., hinged at one end, like a flap, fixed to chains at the other end, capable of being raised and lowered to prevent or permit passage over it, especially in fortifications. 2. The same, but over a waterway, raised to permit the passage of ships beneath it. In such cases the flap is often matched with an identical flap on the other side, and each rotates about an axis, counterweighted at the other side of the axis. See BASCULE.

Dreghorn, Allan (1706–65) Scots architect, involved in the building of the Town Hall, Trongate, Glasgow (1736–8—demolished), but his most important architectural work was St Andrew's Church, Glasgow (1740–56), a variant on *Gibbs's St Martin-in-the-Fields, with *steeple based on another Gibbsian design.

Co (2008)

dressed Describes the operation a stone has undergone before it is built into a wall. A *dressed stone* is therefore one finished. See DRESSINGS.

Dresser, Christopher (1834–1904) Glasgow-born, one of the most distinguished inventive C19 industrial designers, his publications include *Botany as Adapted to the Arts and Art Manufactures* (1857–8), *The Art of Decorative Design* (1862), *The Principles of Decorative Design* (1873), *Japan, its Architecture, Art, and Art Manufactures* (1882), and *Modern Ornamentation* (1886). Many of his designs for incised ornament and cast-iron artefacts were widely copied. He was profoundly influenced by the natural world, by A.W.N.*Pugin, by Owen *Jones, and by Japanese artefacts.

Dennis & Jesse (1972); Dresser (1862, 1873, 1882); Durant (1993); Halen (1993); *ODNB* (2004)

dressings Term for all finishes, *mouldings, ornaments, *dressed stones, and the like (often projecting) around an aperture (e.g. *door or window), distinguished from the rest of the *naked of a wall. A *façade of brick or *rubble with *stone dressings*, therefore, has most of the wall-surface of those materials, but *quoins, *architraves, and the like are of dressed stone so that door- and window-frames can be accurately fixed.

Drew, (Dame) Jane (Joyce) Beverley (1911–96) British *Modernist architect, she was a founder-partner (1945) with *Fry (her husband from 1942) of **Fry, Drew, & Partners,** London, of which *Lasdun became a partner (1951). The firm worked extensively in West Africa, and was the force behind the establishment of the first School of Tropical Architecture by the Architectural Association of London. From the 1950s Drew and her colleagues worked on the designs for the new capital of the Punjab, India, at Chandigarh, in association with Le *Corbusier (with whom she became emotionally connected) and Pierre *Jeanneret. Drew was involved in the genesis of colleges, health-centres, housing, shopping areas, and schools. She also designed (1960s) buildings in Iran, Ceylon (now Sri Lanka), and Ghana, as well as housing for Harlow (Essex), Welwyn, and Hatfield (both Herts.), and was responsible for the Open University buildings at Milton Keynes, Bucks. (1969–77). A member of the *MARS group, she also published various works including *Architecture for Children* (1944) and *Kitchen Planning* (1945), as well as works on tropical architecture with Fry.

Bristol Centre for the Advancement of Architecture (1986); Brockman (1978); Fry & Drew (1947, 1956, 1964, 1976); K.Parker (1993); *The Times* (1 Aug. 1996) Obits

Drew, Sir Thomas (1838–1910) Irish architect, he trained under *Lanyon from 1854, and established his practice in Dublin (1875). He gained a reputation as a writer and antiquarian (he was President of the Royal Society of the Antiquaries of Ireland), and was noted for his virile *Gothic. His best work is the nave of St Anne's Anglican Cathedral, Belfast (1898–1904), in a tough *Romanesque Revival. As Diocesan Architect for Down, Connor, and Dromore, he designed many churches, including the fine Kilmore Church, Crossgar, Co. Down (1866–8); St Jude's Church, Ormeau Road, Belfast (1869–75); and St Donard's Church, Dundrum, Co. Down (1886). He carried out major works at St Patrick's, Dublin (1899–1904), and Armagh (1893–7) Cathedrals.

Brett (1996, 2002); J.Curl (2013); Larmour (1987); Mulligan (2013); *ODNB* (2004); *P:JRSUA*, iv/5 (May/June 1996), 61–3

drift Thrust or outward pressure of an arch or *vault requiring the counter-thrust of a *buttress.

drip 1. Any projection shaped to throw rainwater off and stop it running back to the wall, usually with a channel or *throating underneath. **2.** *Head- or hood-mould, *label, or weathermoulding over the head of an aperture.
Compounds include:
drip-cap: horizontal head-moulding or label over an opening to divert rainwater, causing it to drip on either side;
drip-channel: throating under the drip;
drip-course, dripstone-course: continuous horizontal *drip-mould on a wall;
drip-joint: joint between two metal sheets on, e.g., a roof, which carries the water away and is watertight;
drip-mould, drip-moulding: *moulding or *hood performing as a drip;
dripping eaves: *eaves without *gutters, overhanging a wall, throwing rainwater to the ground;
dripstone: hood-moulding or *label, especially in *Gothic work on an exterior, convex on top and returning to the wall underneath by deep hollows or throatings. If used inside a building, *label* or *hood-mould* would be preferred terms.

drive Route originally laid out for horse-drawn carriages within a park, an important component of English C18 landscape-design, intended to provide changing views of the scenery, especially in work by *Repton: it entered American usage in the second quarter of C19, although *Downing distinguished it from an *approach which led from a public road to the house, and a drive was a way along which visitors could be conveyed around an estate. *See* APPROACH; WALK.

O'Malley (2010); Symes (2006)

dromos 1. Long, narrow passage, partly open and partly within a mound, giving access to Aegean chamber- or *tholos-tombs. **2.** Straight, formal entrance-avenue of great magnificence, lined on each side by columns, *sphinxes, statues, *obelisks, etc., as existed in the *Serapeion* at Delos (C1 BC), and especially at the huge *Isaeum Campense*, Rome (AD C1–C4). This long axial formal plan leading to a Holy of Holies and associated with courts, *porticoes, and *colonnades got its name from a Greek race-course. A *dromic* or *dromical* church was a term for an Eastern *basilican church, the plan of which resembled the Greek *dromos* arrangement of *Isaea*. **3.** Open space with room to move freely, such as a forecourt.

J.Curl (2005); D (1950); Roullet (1972)

drop 1. Type of arch. **2.** *Gutta, *campanula, droplet, or lachryma (tear-drop) in the *Doric *Order, or any small pendant. **3.** Pendent ornament hanging from the base of a *newel-post or beneath a *jetty in *timber-framed construction. **4.** Outlet from an *eaves-gutter to a *downpipe.
Compounds include:
drop-ornament: pendent ornamental form like a tear-drop on the intrados of *Gothic arches, really an enriched *cusp;
drop-point slating: diagonal slating, i.e. roof laid with slates turned so that their diagonals are horizontal, and one sharp corner faces downwards;
drop-tracery: fragmental Gothic *tracery suspended from the *soffit of an arch.

druid's cell *or* **cave** C18 *rustic structure in a *landscape-garden, e.g. at Stourhead, Wilts., reflecting a contemporary interest in British Antiquity, archaeological theories, *ruins, and *Romanticism. Published designs included those of Thomas *Wright (influenced by his studies of Irish historic remains). *See* HERMITAGE.

Roden (2005); Symes (2006); Wright (1748)

druid's temple C18 garden structure imitating prehistoric circles of upright stones (*megaliths*), prompted by the writings of, e.g. **William Stukeley** (1687–1765), who incorrectly believed that monuments e.g. Stonehenge were 'Druidic': examples occurred at Hagley, Worcs. (*c.*1740s); Piercefield Park, near Chepstow, Monmouthshire (*after* 1750); Temple Combe, Henley-on-Thames, Berks. (1785—a relocation of a real Neolithic chambered tomb); and Ilton, Yorks. (1820s). Associated with mystery, melancholy, solemnity, and darkness, they resonated with *Romanticism and *Gothic fantasies.

Darvill (2003); *GH*, xxxv/supp.1 (2007), 108; Hirschfeld (2001); Symes (2006)

drum 1. One of the nearly cylindrical pieces of which a column-shaft is constructed. **2.** Vertical wall on a circular or polygonal plan, usually carrying a *cupola or *dome, and often pierced with windows. **3.** *Bell or core of a *Composite or *Corinthian *capital.

dry area 1. Gap excavated between a basement-wall of a building (lower than the floor-level) and the adjacent soil to prevent water-penetration and allow light and air to enter. **2.** Space between a *retaining-wall and the wall of a *basement commencing at least as low as the foundations, drained and ventilated to prevent moisture seeping through into the building.

dry masonry Stones (usually *rubble) laid without *mortar in a wall (*dry-stone walling*).

Dryopic Pertaining to the Dryopians, held to be one of the earliest settlers in Ancient Greece, hence prehistoric columnar structures pre-dating Classical Antiquity, such as those of Euboea.

Duany & Plater-Zyberk, Inc. *See* NEW UR-BANISM.

Duban, Félix-Louis-Jacques (1797–1870) Parisian architect, he was in the vanguard (with *Duc, *Labrouste, and *Vaudoyer) of the younger generation that came to eminence in the 1830s, and he won a reputation as a restorer of lavish interiors. Appointed (1832) architect to the *École des *Beaux-Arts, he incorporated *Picturesque techniques in his composition, and his details were refined. With *Lassus and *Viollet-le-Duc he restored the C13 *Sainte-Chapelle*, with its powerful colouring attracting the favour of *Pugin, although he seems to have been more at ease with Italian *Classicism. His best work is probably the *Salle de Melpomène* (1860–3) at the *École des Beaux-Arts*, and the richly opulent resuscitation of the salons in the Louvre. From 1845 he worked on the restorations of the *Châteaux at Blois, Chantilly, Dampierre, and Fontainebleau.

Bellenger & Hamon (eds) (1996); Middleton (ed.) (1982); M & Wa (1987); P (1982); Questel (1872)

Dubois, Nicolas (*c*.1665–1735) Huguenot architect/military-engineer, he translated *Leoni's *The Architecture of A. Palladio* (1715–18), a key book of English *Palladianism. He established an architectural practice (1718) with *Galilei, but the latter returned to Italy (1719), and Dubois was appointed Master Mason in the Office of Works. He was also involved in speculative building in London, developing part of Hanover Square and St George Street (1717–20), as well as certain elements on Lord *Burlington's estate. He carried out works at various country-houses: he designed Stanmer Park, Sussex (1722–7), and built Eastwick Park, Great Bookham, Surrey (1720s—demolished), and the bridge at Lewes, Sussex (1727—widened 1932).

Co (2008)

Duc, Gabriel Le (1623/5–96) French architect of several houses in Paris, mostly destroyed: he is best known for his work at the *Val-de-Grâce*, Paris (1649–67), where, with Le *Muet, he constructed the *vaults, *dome, and other upper parts of the church, refining and improving the designs of *Mansart and *Lemercier. His *baldacchino there is sumptuously *Baroque.

W.Pa (1852); S (1901–2)

Duc, Louis-Joseph (1802–79) French architect, he restored and extended the *Palais de Justice*, Paris (1840–79): the *Cour des Assises*, *Salles des Pas Perdus*, and the *façade on the *Rue de Harlay* (1857–68) are particularly robust, anticipating *Beaux-Arts *Classicism of forty years later. With *Duban, *Labrouste, and *Vaudoyer he was one of the more radical architects of the 1830s. He was responsible for completing the *Colonne de Juillet, Place de la Bastille*, Paris (1835–40—originally designed by J.-A.*Alavoine), an eclectic mix of *Egyptian, *Greek, *Roman, and *Renaissance motifs, and designed the *Lycée Michelet*, Vanves (1862), in a *Lombardic *Gothic style.

Daly (1840–90); Delaborde (1879); M & Wa (1987)

Duca, Giacomo del (*c*.1520–1604) Known also as **Jacopo Siciliano** *or* **Ciciliano**, he was born in Cefalù, Sicily, and eventually became a pupil of *Michelangelo in Rome. He completed the Master's *Porta Pia* (1562–5), and designed the *Porta San Giovanni* (1573–4). He also completed the *drum, *dome, and *lantern of *Santa Maria di Loreto* (1573–7), near Trajan's column, and designed parts of the *piazza* before the *Palazzo Farnese*, Caprarola (1584–6), including the curved ramps and upper garden with elaborate waterchain of contorted dolphins.

S.Benedetti (1973); W.Pa (1852)

Du Cerceau Family *See* CERCEAU.

Duchêne, Henri (1841–1902) French engineer/horticulturalist/garden-designer, initially he followed *Alphand's lead, but turned to restoring French-*Baroque gardens from *c*.1882, even where very little remained of the original layouts. With his son, **Achille** (1866–1947), he restored the gardens at *Champs-sur-Marne* (1895–99) and *Vaux-le-Vicomte* (1875–1939), both Seine-et-Marne. Achille extended the scope to creating new formal gardens, e.g. Voisins, Île-de-France (1903–25), and elsewhere in many places outside France. Achille contributed to the literature of gardens (e.g. *Les jardins de l'avenir: Hier, aujourd'hui, demain* (1935)).

M & T (1991); Shoe (2001); Tay (2006)

Dudok, Willem Marinus (1884–1974) Amsterdam-born Dutch military-engineer, he became one of the most influential architects working in The Netherlands between the two World Wars. In 1915 he was appointed Director of Public Works at Hilversum, near Amsterdam, where he designed around 250 buildings, most of some distinction, and drew up the expansion-plan inspired by the English *Garden-City movement. Initially, he was influenced by *Berlage, then by the *Amsterdam School, and, from *c*.1920, by De *Stijl. His masterpiece is Hilversum Town Hall (1924–30), which has certain similarities with the work of F.L.L.*Wright, and was particularly admired in Britain in the 1930s.

Bergeijk (1995); *CLA* (1972), 104–7; Cramer *et al.* (1981); Hi (1977); Jappelli & Menna (1997); Langmead (1996); Magnée (1954); Mattie (1994); Michon *et al.* (1993); Oosterman (ed.) (1995); pk

Duff, Thomas (*c.*1792–1848) Irish architect, he designed and built the first scholarly *Gothic-Revival buildings in that country. He practised from Newry, Co. Down, and formed a partnership with Thomas *Jackson of Belfast. His masterpiece is the RC Pro-Cathedral of St Patrick, Dundalk, Co. Louth (1835–47), in the English *Perp. style. In 1838 he prepared designs for St Patrick's RC Cathedral, Armagh (also Perp.), but *McCarthy completed the building in the *Second-Pointed style, leaving Duff's incongruous Perp. *nave-*piers supporting *stylistically earlier* elements. With *Jackson, he designed the *Greek-Revival Old Museum, College Square North, Belfast (1830–1). He was also responsible for a number of Classical (e.g. extensions to Hillsborough Castle, Co. Down (*c.*1830–40)) and *Tudorbethan (e.g. Parkanaur, Castlecaulfeild, Co. Tyrone (1839–48), and Narrow Water Castle, Warrenpoint, Co. Down (*c.*1831–7)) country-houses, as well as court- and market-houses, the latter usually in a sober Classical style (e.g. Hilltown (1828) and Newry (1841), Co. Down). His assistant was W.J.*Barre.

B-J (1988); Brett (1967, 1973, 1999); C & R (1993); Larmour (1987); Sheehy (1977)

dug work Patterns of late-C17 and early-C18 flower-beds. *See* PARTERRE.

Duiker, Johannes (1890–1935) Dutch architect, influenced first by F.L.L.*Wright and then by *De *Stijl*. He was editor of, and a regular contributor to, the architectural journal *De 8 en Opbouw* (1932–5), and was one of the leading Modernists of the inter-war period. *Zonnestraal Sanatorium*, Hilversum (1926–8), was a good example of *International *Modernism, and his *Handelsblad-Cineac* Cinema, Amsterdam (1934–6), with its huge *sky-sign, owed much to *Constructivism and to Le *Corbusier. His last work, completed by his partner, **Bernard Bijvoet** (1889–1979), was the *Grand Hotel Gooiland*, Hilversum (1934–6).

AR, cii/610 (Oct. 1947), 128–30; Duiker (1930); Molema (1989); vV (1993)

Dülfer, Martin (1859–1942) German architect, he taught in Dresden and acquired a formidable reputation as a theatre-designer. His works include the Dortmund Municipal Theatre (1903), the Dresdner Bank, Leipzig (1910–12), and the *Technische Hochschule*, Dresden (1912–14). He used massive *rock-faced *masonry, certain motifs derived from *Jugendstil, and powerful,

blocky forms in his compositions that stand comparison with those of *Bonatz and *Kreis.

Dülfer (1914); Licht (ed.) (1910)

dungeon *See* DONJON.

Dunn, William Newton (1859–1934) British architect, an early advocate of *reinforced *concrete. With **Robert Watson** (1865–1916), he continued *MacLaren's practice after the latter's death. The firm designed competent *Arts-and-Crafts *vernacular-revival buildings, but could also produce excellent essays in *Classicism. A good example of the latter is the Scottish Provident Institution's Building, 16–17 Pall Mall, London (partly designed by Curtis *Green, who became a partner in 1900), which incorporated Michelangeloesque Mannerist devices derived from the New Sacristy at *San Lorenzo*, Florence.

A.S.Gray (1985)

Dupérac, Étienne (1520–1607) Paris-born architect/painter/engraver/landscape architect credited with introducing *parterres* to French gardens. He is mostly remembered for his drawings of *Antique Roman ruins made during his stay there (1550–70): he published (1570) views of the *Villa d'Este* gardens, Tivoli, and designed gardens at Anet, St-Germain-en-Laye, and Fontainebleau (all 1580s and 90s).

Dupérac (1973); Ehrle (1908); MacDougall & Hazlehurst (eds) (1974)

duplex *Apartment in a block of flats on two floors, with its own internal stair.

Durand, Jean-Nicolas-Louis (1760–1834) Paris-born architect, one of the most important early-C19 theorists and teachers. He worked for *Boullée, and for the civil-engineer **Jean-Rodolphe Perronet** (1708–94—who designed the *Pont de la Concorde*, Paris), and became (1795) Professor of Architecture at the *École Polytechnique*. His lectures were published as *Précis des leçons d'architecture données à l'école polytechnique* (1802–5), and were widely influential, notably in Prussia, and his *Recueil et parallèle des édifices de tout genre* (1800) was the first book organized by building type to deal with historical architecture, and with illustrations reproduced to the same scale. He was a significant figure in *Neo-Classicism, and his system of design using simplified, repetitive, modular elements anticipated *industrialized building components.

B (1980); Durand (1802–9, 1809); Ha (1953); Hi (1977); M & Wa (1987); Rondelet (1835); Szambien (1984); Villari (1990); D.Wa (1986)

Durbar Hall or space used for private audiences with rulers in India.

Durham *See* DEREHAM.

durn 1. Timber cut from a piece with a grown angle from which e.g. a door-frame with a shaped arched head can be formed: a symmetrical arched frame was usually made from paired durns sawn from a single baulk. **2.** Door-post made of solid timber.

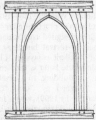

durn Doorway of opposed durns.

Du Ry, Paul (1640–1714) *See* RY.

Dutch arch *See* ARCH.

Dutch barn Type of C17 and C18 front-gabled almost square barn erected by Dutch settlers in the Hudson Valley and NJ. It had a steeply-pitched roof supported on wall-plates and *purlins, and was sheathed with bevelled overlapping planks.

Dutch gable Tall *gable with sweeping *ogee sides ending in *volute *scrolls, called *klauwstuk*, crowned by a triangular *pediment. Not to be confused with a *shaped gable.

Dutch garden *or* **style** Adapted from and influenced by French formal gardens, Dutch manifestations were flat, compact, enclosed, with emphases on *canals, raised *beds, *hedges, *topiary, lead statuary, flowering bulbs, and shrubs. An example in The Netherlands is the garden of the palace of *Het Loo*, Apeldoorn (1680s). The style was imported to England when **William of Orange** became **King William III** (*r.*1689–1702). An English example of a water-garden in the Dutch style is Westbury Court, Glos. (1696–1705): in America the Dutch style emerged during the early Colonial period. *Loudon published designs (1826) for Dutch-style *parterres,, emphasizing their compartmental character, describing the strongly geometrical arrangements of Dutch gardens, and the importance of water in layouts.

Loudon (1834); O'Malley (2010); Symes (2006)

Dutch Wave *See* NEW PERENNIALS.

Dutert, Charles-Louis-Ferdinand (1845–1906) French architect of the *Galerie des Machines* at the International Exposition in Paris (1889—demolished 1905), a huge development of the metal-and-glass structures that proliferated in C19, designed in collaboration with *Contamin.

It had an unprecedented span of 114 metres, with the principal *trusses in the form of four-centred arches (*see* ARCH) hinged at the apices and bases. He designed the new galleries for the Museum of Natural History, Paris (1896), which had its metal structure expressed.

Durant (1994); M & Wa (1987)

Duthoit, Edmond-Armand-Marie (1837–89) French architect, pupil of *Viollet-le-Duc, he acquired a formidable architectural eclectic vocabulary from his studies of historic buildings. His most celebrated design is the colourful *basilica of *Notre-Dame-de-Brebières*, at Albert, Somme (1884–96). His *Château du Roquetaillade*, near Langon, in the Gironde (1864–70), continued work begun by Viollet-le-Duc, but it is mostly Duthoit's: it is an exotic confection of *Gothic, but leavened with Arabic and *Byzantine themes, continuing a trend he had evolved at the reconstruction of the C15 *Château d'Arragori*, near Hendaye, Basses-Pyrénées (*c.*1864–79). It is almost as luxuriant as contemporary work by *Burges.

Middleton (ed.) (1982); M & Wa (1987)

Düttmann, Werner (1921–83) German architect. As City Architect of Berlin (1960s) he was a leading light in the *conservation movement to save Berlin's heritage of stucco-fronted C19 apartments, but he was also a prime mover in the campaign to persuade *Mies van der Rohe to return to Berlin and build the *Nationalgalerie*, which, predictably, with the *Philharmonie* by *Scharoun, ignored the historic plan of the city in that area. He was responsible for some major developments, including low-density housing at *Heiligensee* (1975) and apartment-blocks at *Märkisches Viertel*, Wittenau, both in Berlin (1970).

E (1994)

dwarf gallery External covered passage or *ambulatory with an *arcade on one side, as at the *Romanesque church at Schwarz-Rheindorf, Germany (C12), where it ran virtually all round the upper church. *Compounds include*:

dwarf wainscoting: *dado;

dwarf wall: low perforated wall giving intermediate support to floor-joists that would otherwise be liable to deflect.

Dyer, Charles (1794–1848) Bristol-born architect, his grandest building was the Victoria Rooms, Bristol, (1838–42—now part of the University of Bristol), with octastyle *Corinthian *portico. Other Bristolian works include Oakfield House, Oakfield Road (1831—a substantial *villa); Christ Church, Clifton Down Road (begun 1841—*First Pointed, with additions by Ewan *Christian and **John Norton** (1823–1904)); Litfield House (1829–

30); Engineers' (formally Camp) House (1830–1); and a villa (1842), the last four at Clifton.

Co (2008)

dyke *Dry-stone *rubble wall.

Dykes Bower, Stephen Ernest (1903–94) English scholar-architect, he believed passionately in continuity of historical memory, in using natural materials, and encouraging fine craftsmanship. He continued the best traditions of the *Gothic Revival, and was in the front rank of ecclesiastical architects/decorators. His churches include All Saints, Hockerill, near Bishops Stortford, Herts. (1935–7—incorporating remains of earlier fire-damaged fabric), St John's, Newbury, Berks. (1950–7—a robust *Rundbogenstil* essay), and numerous alterations, additions, and restorations, including *Bodley's *polychrome scheme (1867–70) in St John's, Tue Brook, Liverpool (1966–71—a particularly felicitous achievement). With **Walter Godfrey Allen** (1891–1986—Cathedral Surveyor (1931–56)), he designed the vigorous *Baroque *high-altar and *ciborium in St Paul's Cathedral, London (1948–55). He restored St Vedast's, Foster Lane, London (1948–62—incorporating *Wren furnishings from redundant City churches) and, as Surveyor to Westminster Abbey (1951–72), he carried out a massive programme of stone cleaning/restoration, with reinstatement of colour. From 1943 he worked on St Edmundsbury Cathedral, Bury St Edmunds, Suffolk, designing the new *quire from 1953, and left funds to complete the north *transept. Work on the building continued into C21 under the **Gothic Design Practice**, headed by his former assistant, **Warwick Pethers** (1959–), who designed the upper stages of the *crossing-tower (based on precedents from Long Melford, Suffolk (1903), Cattistock, Dorset (1876), and *Wastell's 'Bell Harry' tower at Canterbury (1494–1501). Pethers's work there was regarded as a triumph of scholarly architecture, but hostile elements succeeded in severing (2006) Pethers's involvement, a sorry tale recorded by Symondson (2011), and one reminiscent of earlier treatment suffered by Dykes Bower himself, notably at the hands of offensively doctrinaire Modernists in Cambridge. In 1979 R.C.*Carpenter's Lancing College Chapel, Sussex, was completed to Dykes Bower's designs: it has the largest *rose-window to be built in England since those medieval examples in the *transepts of Westminster Abbey.

Dykes Bower *et al.* (1985); *Independent* (14 Nov. 1994), 14; pk; Symondson (2011)

Dymaxion *See* FULLER, RICHARD BUCKMINSTER.

dyostyle **1.** As distyle. *See* PORTICO. **2.** Having coupled columns.

Eads, James Buchanan (1820–87) American engineer, he pioneered the use of structural steel with the Eads Bridge, St Louis, MO (1867–74). He also invented tests for compression and tension in steel, and devised ironclad ships for the Union side in the Civil War.

Scott & Miller (1979); Vollmar (1974)

eagle 1. From the Latin *aquila* (meaning the bird, it also refers to a *gable, *pediment, or, esp., the *tympanum*), ultimately deriving from the Greek Ἀετός, Ἀέτωμα. **2.** Reading-desk or *lectern in a church, often in the form of an eagle (believed to be the only bird that could fly directly into the sun without closing its eyes, thus a *symbol of the Word (leading man with open eyes to God) and of St John the Evangelist).

JD

Eames, Charles Ormond (1907–78) American designer, one of the most versatile of his time. His reputation as an architect rests on his own dwelling at Pacific Palisades, Santa Monica, CA (1945–9—one of *Entenza's *Case Study houses), a steel-framed structure owing something to the work of *Mies van der Rohe: it was an example of *industrialized building. He was even better-known as a designer of moulded plywood chairs and other furniture, especially the Eames Chair (1940–1), produced with Eero *Saarinen (whom he met while at *Cranbook Academy). With his second wife, **Bernice Alexandra 'Ray' Kaiser** (1912–88), he shared credit for all his design projects from 1941.

Albrecht *et al.* (1997); Wi.Cu (1996); Demetrios (2001); *DQ*, **xcviii–xcix** (1975), 20–29; Dr (1973); E (1994); Kirkham (1995); Neuhart (1989); Sennott (ed.) (2004); Steele (ed.) (1994b); Stungo (2000)

Eames, John Heagan (1900–2002) Stylistically eclectic American architect, he had early success with a design which won the Gold Medal in a competition organized by 'Better Homes in America' after he joined the office of **Dwight James Baum** (1886–1939), a congenial firm which carried out scholarly work in *Colonial, *Georgian, *Italianate, and other styles for numerous private houses.

Independent (31 May 2002), Obits

ear 1. *Acroter or *horn of an *altar, *sarcophagus, or *stele. **2.** *Crossette. **3.** *Lug or *tab.

Early-Christian architecture An integral part of the architecture of the Roman Empire, the most important buildings are of three types: churches, commemorative structures, and covered cemeteries. The exemplar of churches after the recognition of Christianity in C4 was the Roman *basilica, of which *San Pietro*, Rome (*c.*320–30—demolished early C16), was an influential example because seen by countless pilgrims. The form reached its standard in *Santa Maria Maggiore*, Rome (423–40), with the *clerestoreyed *nave, lean-to *aisles, and apsidal end. Old St Peter's was built over a *cemetery, and its funereal character was emphasized by the large mausolea attached to the tall *transeptal structure on one side. Another circular *mausoleum, that of *Santa Costanza*, Rome (*c.*350), is a clerestoreyed domed structure surrounded by an *annular *barrel-vault. Originally it was attached to the covered cemetery of *Santa Agnese* (*c.*340). Early-Christian basilicas had nave-*arcades incorporating columns taken from early buildings, or nave-*colonnades where even the *entablatures were recycled. Openings were almost invariably semicircular-headed.

Aspects of Early-Christian architecture were revived in C19, especially as part of the *Rundbogenstil* pioneered by von *Klenze, *Gärtner, and others. Good examples can be found in England too (e.g. *Wild's Christ Church, Streatham Hill, London (1840–2), and *Losh's St Mary, Wreay, Cumb. (begun 1842)).

Co (1991); Kra (1986); Mango (1986); J.T (1996)

Early English *See* FIRST POINTED.

earth *and* **earth-work architecture** There are long traditions of buildings made of earth or mud (*see* ADOBE, COB, PISÉ DE TERRE). In the 1960s proposals were mooted to create buildings by pouring *concrete on to mounds of earth which would be excavated once the concrete had set, thus creating cave-like forms called *earth-work architecture*.

Dethier (1983)

earth-table *Grass-* or *ground-table*, or *foot-stall*, meaning the base-course or **plinth* of a building in **Gothic* work, or the lowest visible course of stone above the ground projecting in front of the **naked* of a wall.

earthwork 1. Mound, **rampart*, etc., of earth, as in fortifications. **2.** Work done in removing earth, etc.

Easter Sepulchre The ritual 'burial' of Christ was a solemn observance in medieval times, and required a 'tomb'. At the end of the liturgies of Good Friday (including the Creeping to and Adoration of the Cross), the Priest, in bare feet and clad in his surplice, carried a **Pyx* containing the third Host (consecrated on Maundy Thursday) and the Cross, both wrapped in linen, to the north side of the **chancel*, where a temporary 'sepulchre' (usually of timber, draped with a pall) was made ready, and laid them within. The 'sepulchre' was censed, and numerous candles glowed before it, a continuous watch being kept to protect both the Host and the Pyx (which was usually of high quality). Early on Easter Morning, the church was illuminated with candles; clergy processed to the 'sepulchre', which was censed; the Host was removed to the Pyx above the **high-altar*; and the Cross was raised from the 'sepulchre' and carried in procession round the church while bells chimed and the Resurrection was celebrated. The Cross was then set on an **altar* on the north side of the church, where it was again venerated. The now empty 'sepulchre' remained an object of devotion (being censed, having illuminated candles in front of it, etc.) for the days after Holy Week. The Easter Sepulchre often found more permanent architectural expression as a **masonry* recess, usually canopied, over a tomb-chest. Wealthy patrons, desiring association with the annual Easter mysteries, often built tombs for themselves that doubled as Easter Sepulchres (e.g. Clopton tomb, Long Melford, Suffolk (*c.*1497), and Sackville tomb, Westhampnett, West Sussex (*c.*1535)). Other Easter Sepulchres were just that, not associated with human tombs: a richly decorated example survives at Heckington, Lincs. (*c.*1330), complete with somnolent soldiers, the three Marys and the Angel, and, above, the Risen Christ, the whole exquisitely carved (but mutilated in C16).

N.Brooks (1921); E.Duffy (1992); Nairn & Pe (1965); Pe, Hs, & Antram (1989); Pe & Radcliffe (1974)

Eastlake, Charles Locke (1836–1906) English architect, better known for his work as a journalist and writer. His *Hints on Household Taste in Furniture, Upholstery, and Other Details* (1868) popularized design derived from the work of **Seddon*, **Shaw*, and **Street*, especially in the USA where a style of **Gothic* domestic architecture with

oversized elements, rich ornament, and a general toughness is called the Eastlake or **Stick* style. His *A History of the Gothic Revival* (1872) is an important and perceptive study.

Ea (1970); *ODNB* (2004)

Eastwick-Field, John & Elizabeth (*both* 1919–2003) British architects, they established a London practice (1949) with **John Stillman** (1920–), at first designing schools and housing, and then hospitals and university buildings. Among their completed works were the West of England School for the Partially Sighted, Exeter (1966), Trevelyan College, Durham (1968), Princess Marina Psychiatric Hospital, Northants. (1972), and primary schools at Market Harborough, Leics. (1966), and Allington Park, Kent (1970).

RIBAJ (6 June 2003), xv

eave (*pl.* **eaves**) Sheltered area under **eaves*.

eaves edge or lowest part of a pitched roof projecting beyond the **naked* of the wall below.
Related terms include:
eaves-board: **fascia-board*, or board fixed under the overhanging **tiles* or **slates* of the eaves to which a **gutter* can be fixed;
eaves-bracket: **bracket* supporting the eaves, or appearing to do so, often paired, and sometimes treated like simplified **modillions*;
eaves-cornice: Classical **cornice* forming the transition between the **naked* of a wall and the edge of the roof above;
eaves-drip: end of a pitched roof where the water drips off, usually into a **gutter*, but sometimes dripping to the ground;
eaves-gutter: one fixed at the edge of a pitched roof to convey water away from the *eaves-drip*, usually fixed to a fascia-board or supported on metal brackets;
eaves overhang: amount by which eaves project beyond the naked of a wall.

Ecclesiology Study of churches, church-history, traditions, decorations, and furnishings. The Ecclesiological Society was a powerful force in the English **Gothic* Revival, and its journal, *The Ecclesiologist* (1841–68), was influential, especially in the making (or breaking) of architectural reputations. *See* CAMBRIDGE CAMDEN SOCIETY.

CCS (1842–68, 1847); J.Curl (2007); Ea (1970); Webster & Elliott (eds) (2000)

echal Enclosure for the Ark containing the scrolls in a **synagogue*.

échauguette **Turret*, **watch-tower*, etc., corbelled out from a **curtain-wall* or **salient angle*, open or roofed. **Bartisan* or angle-turret.

echinus Plain circular cushion-like convex *moulding between the *abacus and *annulets of the Greek-*Doric *capital, between the abacus and *hypotrachelium of the *Tuscan and Roman Doric Orders, and beneath the *pulvinus joining the *volutes of the *Ionic capital where it is enriched with *egg-and-dart (so occurs in the upper part of a *Composite capital, always enriched).

Eckbo, Garrett (1910–2000) American landscape-architect. Influenced by *Gropius, he predictably rejected historical styles of garden-design, and attempted to create a 'modern' style on a *tabula rasa*. From 1945, with **Robert Royston** (1918–2008—until 1958) and **Edward A. Williams** (1914–84—until 1973), he designed many gardens in CA, using exotic plants, so his work was associated with the *California School. Most of his later designs were for housing developments, settings for factories, *campuses, *parkways, and urban spaces, mostly in CA: they include the Downtown Mall, Fresno (1963), Union Bank Square, Los Angeles (1964–8), and landscape-designs for the University of NM at Albuquerque (1962–78). He wrote *Landscape for Living* (1950) and much else.

B & F (2009); Treib & Imbert (1997); W & S (1994)

eclecticism 1. Design drawing freely on forms, motifs, and details selected from historical styles and different periods. 2. The practice of selecting from a wide range of sources what elements, styles, motifs, details, etc., that may appear to be sound, acceptable, functional, and beautiful, in order to create an architectural effect.

Porphyrios (1982)

École des Beaux-Arts *See* BEAUX-ARTS.

ecological architecture Aims to respond to declining energy resources, e.g. using energy conservation, efficient insulation, rainwater, solar radiation, wind power, and recycling as much as possible. The term was coined in the 1970s.

AD, xliv/11 (1974), 681–9; Cuito (ed.) (2000); K.Daniels (1997); Goldstein (ed.) (1977); Ryn & Cowan (1996); Stitt (ed.) (1999); Yeang (1995)

ecphora Projection of one part over another, e.g. a Classical column-*base projecting beyond the *shaft; or a *plinth before the *naked of a wall.

EDAW Acronym for a firm of landscape-architects that evolved from a partnership formed by *Eckbo, **Francis Dean**, **Donald B. Austin** (1933–2004), and **Edward A. Williams** (1914–84): it established offices throughout the world, carrying out work from small gardens to proposals for *conserving huge areas of natural landscape. Among schemes may be cited the redesign of the centre of Washington, DC (from 1976),

EuroDisney, Marne-la-Vallée, France (early 1990s), and Eco City, Tokyo, Japan (1992–4).

B & F (2009); W & S (1994)

edge *Eave or eaves, or the line in which two surfaces join, or a border or *verge. Compounds include:

edge-moulding: medieval *moulding often used on *string-courses, with a convex top and a *cavetto underneath, often with a sharp edge at the junction;

edge-roll: convex moulding, such as a *bowtell, *ovolo, or *torus;

edge-shaft: common *Romanesque arrangement of an *engaged half-shaft attached to a *pier, usually the element from which an *arch springs.

Edge, Charles (c.1801–67) Birmingham architect (c.1827–60s): when *Hansom and *Welch were bankrupted (1834), Edge completed (1849) the Town Hall. He designed several Banks (e.g. Bank of Birmingham, Bennett's Hill (c.1832), Birmingham and Midland, Union Street (1836), and National Provincial, Bennett's Hill (c.1840)). His grandest work was The Crescent, Filey, Yorks. (1835–8), though the detailed design of the buildings appears to have been by **John Barry** (1803–66), with some of the blocks of the 1850s perhaps by **John Petch** (fl.1840–74). Edge designed the General or Key Hill Cemetery, Hockley, Birmingham (1835–6), with its impressive range of *catacombs and a *Greek-Revival chapel (demolished 1966).

Co (2008)

edicula *See* AEDICULE.

Edis, Sir Robert William (1839–1927) English architect, best known as a protagonist of the *Queen-Anne style. His works included houses at 31–3 Tite Street, Chelsea (1879–81), additions to Sandringham House, Norfolk (1891–2), the Constitutional Club, Northumberland Avenue, London (1884–6), and the Great Central Railway Hotel, Marylebone Station, London (1897–9).

Edis (1973); Gd (1977)

Edmeston, James, Sen. (1791–1867) Hymn-writer/architect, his works included Hackney Grammar School (c.1830—*Gothic); St Barnabas's School, Homerton (1855–6), and St Paul's Church, Onslow Square, London (1859–60). Among his pupils were **James Edmeston, Jun.** (c.1823–98), 'Great' *Scott, and *Moffatt (Scott's partner (1835–44)). The younger Edmeston designed St Michael's Church, Ladbroke Grove (1870–1—gritty Rhineland *Romanesque), with *his* son, **James Stanning Edmeston** (1844–87).

Co (2008); Scott (1995)

Edward, Alexander (1651–1708) Scots architect/landscape-gardener, he prepared drawings for Sir William *Bruce's seat at Kinross, was also involved at Melville House (1697), both in Fife, and at Kinnaird (1698), Kellie (1699–1705), and Brechin (1696–1708) Castles, all in Angus. He helped Bruce to design the gardens at Hopetoun House, West Lothian, and planned gardens at Hamilton Palace, Lanarkshire (1708). Other works include alterations at Ashton Hall, Lancs. (1708), and the impressive monument to **John Murray** (1631–1703—**1st Marquess of Atholl** from 1676) in Dunkeld Cathedral, Perthshire (1704–5). On behalf of several Scots noblemen, Edward studied architecture and land improvements in London, France, and The Netherlands (1701–2).

Co (2008); Lowrey (1987)

Edwardian architecture Architecture of the British Empire in the reign of **King Edward VII** (1901–10), often characterized by an opulent *Baroque revival or *Wrenaissance (e.g. *Belcher's Ashton Memorial, Lancaster (1906)). However, another aspect was the enormous amount of fine domestic design, including much influenced by the *Arts-and-Crafts movement, that was greatly admired on the Continent, notably as a result of the work of *Muthesius.

Airs (ed.) (2000); A.S.Gray (1985); Fellows (1995, 1999); H.M (1979); Se (ed.) (1975); Se (1977)

Edwardine Of the time of **King Edward VI** (r.1547–53).

Eesteren, Cor(nelis) van (1897–1988) Dutch architect, much influenced by *Bauhaus ideas and by van *Doesburg (with whom he drew up the architectural principles of *Neo-Plasticism and the manifesto *Vers une construction collective* (1924—also signed by *Rietveld)): he was involved in the De-*Stijl movement, and by 1929 was firmly within the Modernist camp that envisaged high-rise blocks and huge traffic arteries to replace traditional cities. As Chief Architect of the Town Planning Department for nearly half a century, he was responsible for the General Extension plan for Amsterdam (1936). He was president of *CIAM (1930–47). *See* DELFT SCHOOL.

Blijstra (1962, 1971); Bock (2001); M.Friedman (ed.) (1982); L (1988)

effigy Sculptured representation of a figure, normally shown clothed or in armour, lying on its back on a *tomb-chest.

Crossley (1921); Esdaile (1946); W.Pa (1852)

Effner, Joseph (1687–1745) Court Architect of Bavaria, he introduced fashionable French styles of architecture/decoration to that country, having studied in Paris, probably under *Boffrand, during the **Elector Max II Emanuel's** (r.1679–1704 & 1715–26) exile there. He worked on the Electoral palaces of *Nymphenburg* (1715–23—adding the *wing-pavilions to *Barelli's existing building), and *Schleissheim* (1719–25—begun by *Zuccalli). He designed the *Chinoiserie Pagodenburg* (1716–19), Roman *Badenburg* (1718–21), and *Picturesque *Magdalenklause* (1725–8), all *pavilions in *Nymphenburg* park. He worked with J.B.*Zimmermann and *Cuvilliés on several of his projects, making a major contribution to the evolution of Bavarian *Rococo, but was gradually eclipsed by the latter.

D.Frank (1985); L.Hager (1955); Hager & Hojer (1976); M.Hauttmann (1913); E.Hempel (1965); Hi (1968a); Schmid (1987); Thon (1977); Vits (1973)

Egas, Enrique de (fl.1480–1534) Castilian architect, his style was a synthesis of late *Gothic and *Plateresque. As Master of the Works at Toledo Cathedral, he redesigned the sanctuary *(Capilla Major—1500–4)* and built the *Capilla Mozárabe* (1519). His most celebrated achievements are the cruciform hospitals of *Santiago de Compostela* (1501–11) and Holy Cross, Toledo (1504–15), where Italian-*Renaissance influences are evident. He worked at Plasencia (1490s), Seville (1512–15), Malaga (1528), Salamanca (1523–34), and Segovia (1529) Cathedrals, and contributed to the design of the Royal Chapel, Granada, from 1506, as well as the Cathedral there from 1523.

Azcárate (1958); CG (1951, 1953); Gallego y Burin (1952); K & S (1959); Rosenthal (1961); J.T (1996)

egg-and-dart Classical ornament on convex rounded *mouldings (e.g. *echinus or other *ovolos) consisting of a series of vertical oviform elements (with their tops cut off) surrounded by a groove and raised rim, between which rims are inserted, one between each pair of 'eggs', a sharply pointed dart-like or anchor form, sometimes resembling a tongue. Thus the egg and dart alternate in series. Also called, depending on the shape of the 'dart', *egg-and-anchor*, *egg-and-tongue*, or *nut-and-husk*.

egg-and-dart

Eginhard (fl.c.800–20) German abbot/architect, credited with the famous plan of the *monastery of St Gall in Switzerland, with its double-apsed *basilican church and well-organized disposition of parts.

W.Pa (1852); S (1901–2)

Egyptian architecture Ancient-Egyptian architecture was mostly that of the monumental *temple and tomb, and featured *obelisks, *battered walls, *pylon-towers, *pyramids, *cavetto (or *gorge*) *cornices, large columns with *lotus, *papyrus, *palm, and other *capitals, *hypostyle halls, *courts, vast processional axes (called *dromos, flanked by *sphinxes), stylized sculpture, and hieroglyphs. It was an architecture of the *columnar-and-*trabeated type. The early stone-built funerary complex at Saqqara (c.2630–c.2611 BC—designed by *Imhotep) had many buildings including a stepped pyramid, processional hall with reeded and fluted *engaged columns, courts, and a vast wall containing the whole. Stepped pyramids were superseded by the smooth-sided type e.g. the Gizeh exemplars (mid-third millennium BC). The big temple complex at Deïr-el-Bahari (mid-second millennium BC) was designed with three main levels approached by *ramps and having long *façades of plain square columns that were greatly influential in C20 *Neo-Classicism and *Rational architecture. The temple-groups of Karnak and Luxor were also started around the same time, and their remaining ruins are still impressive. There are many surviving buildings of the Graeco-Roman period (332 BC–AD 395), including the Philae and Edfu temples. Egyptian architecture influenced other styles: the rock-cut tombs at Beni-Hasan, for example, have *proto-*Doric columns; very many Egyptian motifs were absorbed by the *Hellenistic Greek cultures and by the Roman Empire; and Neo-Classicism, *Art Deco, Rational architecture, and *Post-Modernism drew on Ancient-Egyptian motifs.

D.Arnold (2003); Ck (1996); J.Curl (2005); L & M (1986); W.S.Smith (1998); Stafford-Deitsch (2001); J.T (1996)

Egyptian garden 1. Ancient Egypt was the source of some of the oldest illustrations of gardens, going back to the third millennium BC. The Nile provided essential water, which the Egyptians were adept at using functionally and decoratively, and trees were planted to provide essential shade. Layouts were geometrical, and gardens were set among walls and buildings, therefore enclosed. The visitor to Egypt today sees *temples and tombs out of context, for they once had shady gardens near them, formally related to the architecture, with pools, walks, *pavilions, etc. It should also be remembered that much of Egyptian *architectural* detail (e.g. *bud-, *lotus-, *palm-, and *papyrus capitals) was derived from plants. The Temple at Karnak (c.1440 BC) seems to have had some sort of botanical garden, well stocked with specimens. We also know that during the Graeco-Roman period (C4 BC–AD C7) gardens were part of the great public and royal building complexes, and were also associated with tombs. **2.** Egyptianizing features

(e.g. sphinxes in various guises) are often found in Western gardens (e.g. *Burlington's *villa, Chiswick, London, by *Kent); pyramids were employed as garden buildings (e.g. Castle Howard, Yorks. (1729, by *Hawksmoor), Stowe, Bucks. (c.1719–25, by *Vanbrugh), and doubling as *mausolea (e.g. at Blickling, Norfolk (1794–6, by Joseph *Bonomi)); and obelisks recur in many landscapes. However, an Egyptian garden at Biddulph Grange, Staffs. (1840s–56) went further: with sphinxes flanking a tomb-like entrance set in clipped yew cut to suggest gloomy architecture, and statue of the god **Bes** at the end of a dark tunnel, it is an extraordinarily evocative place, laid out by **James Bateman** (1811–97) with the assistance of **Edward William Cooke** (1811–80).

J.Curl (2005); Symes (2006); Tay (2006)

Egyptian gorge *Cavetto *cornice between a flat horizontal slab-like element at the top and a *torus, often enriched, below.

Egyptian hall Type of grand rectangular public room, neither its style nor form having any connection with Egypt. It was evolved by *Palladio based on descriptions in *Vitruvius, its essential elements being an internal *peristyle carrying a smaller upper *Order or *pilastered *clerestorey above the *entablature. The Order used was *Corinthian, and the form was referred to as an *oecus*. A good Palladian example is the Assembly Rooms, York (1731–2), designed by *Burlington.

J.Curl (2001, 2011a)

Egyptian Revival Elements of Ancient-Egyptian architecture occurred in *Hellenistic and *Roman architecture. After Egypt became part of the Roman Empire and Egyptian deities (especially the goddess **Isis** and her consort **Osiris** (Greek and Roman **Serapis**)) were venerated by the Romans the process accelerated: not only were many Egyptian artefacts, including *obelisks, brought to Rome and re-erected to embellish Roman buildings, but countless objects in the *Egyptian style* were made in Europe. Ancient obelisks were again set up in *Renaissance Rome, where they can be seen in several locations today, and huge numbers of Egyptian and Egyptianizing artefacts re-emerged to grace the collections in the Vatican and elsewhere. During the latter half of C18, Egyptian motifs began to intrigue designers in the West. *Piranesi designed an 'Egyptian' interior for the *Caffè degl'Inglesi, Piazza di Spagna,* Rome (c.1768), which he published together with a number of fireplaces in an 'Egyptian' style, in *Diverse Maniere d'adornare i Cammini* (Different Ways of Decorating Chimneypieces, 1769). This work included illustrations of the Roman *telamones* and figure of **Antinoüs**

(c.AD 110-130) from the *Villa Adriana*, Tivoli (all C2), bogus hieroglyphs, Apis-bulls, various Nilotic motifs, and also corbelled pseudo-arches of stepped form which passed into Western consciousness as 'Egyptian'. At the time, many architects, influenced by French theorists such as *Laugier, began to discard architectural ornament deemed to be inessential, and, prompted by a growing admiration for the *primitive, explored the possibilities of basic geometries that would bring clarity, severity, and integrity to their compositions. Ancient-Egyptian forms such as *battered rectilinear buildings, obelisks, and *pyramids were combined with cubes, spheres, etc., in the developing language of *Neo-Classicism. C18 archaeological activity that encouraged a scholarly and accurate approach to Antiquity, especially the study of buildings in Rome, *Pompeii, *Herculaneum, Greece, Sicily, and *Paestum, encouraged by *Winckelmann among others, also turned to Egypt. The Napoléonic investigations of Egyptian architecture, published by *Denon (1802) and the *Commission des Sciences et Arts d'Égypte* (1809-29), did for Egyptian architecture what *Stuart and *Revett had done for Greek. *Empire and *Regency designs were permeated with Egyptianizing influences after the Franco-British campaigns in Egypt (1798-1801) and the subsequent division of information and objects: so great was the enthusiasm for Egypt that *l'Égyptomanie* played an enormous role in early C19 taste in both France and Britain. The Egyptian style was used for several buildings in France, notably a series of fountains (e.g. *Place du Châtelet*, Paris (1807)), while elsewhere the Egyptian Revival spawned progeny (P.F.*Robinson's *Egyptian Hall*, Piccadilly, London (1811-12); *Canina's *Egyptian Gate*, Borghese Gardens, Rome (c.1825-8); J.*Haviland's 'Tombs' Gaol, NYC (1835-8), and the same architect's New Jersey State Penitentiary, Trenton (1843-6); the entrance-gates and lodges of Abney Park Cemetery, London (1840), by *Hosking and *Bonomi, and the last's Temple Mills, Marshall Street, Leeds, Yorks. (1842) are examples). Egyptianizing motifs are common in European and American design: they include battered square chimney-pots with Egyptian cornices, lotus-buds and leaves, obelisks, pyramids, and sphinxes. Battered towers resembling Egyptian temple pylons were ideally suited for suspension bridges, while battered retaining walls and dams frequently had *sections derived from Ancient-Egyptian precedents. Funerary architecture was often in the Egyptian style, especially 1820-50. C20 Egyptology, including the discovery of **Tutankhamun's** (*r. c.1332-c.1323 BC) tomb (1922), influenced a further revival of the Egyptian style spurred by the 1925 Paris exhibition in which Egyptian and *Aztec archaeology influenced the burgeoning *Art-Deco style, though many elements were derived from *Piranesi.

More recently both *Post-Modernism and *Rational architecture have incorporated aspects of Egyptian architecture.

Carrott (1978); Clayton (1982); CdSAÉ (1820–30); Ck (1996); J.Curl (2001, 2005, 2007, 2011, 2011a); Denon (1802); Humbert (1989); Humbert (ed.) (1996); HPZ (1994); Piranesi (1769); Roullet (1972); J.T (1996)

Egyptian triangle The 3-4-5 triangle, fundamental to architecture and surveying because it enables a right angle to be constructed.

Ehn, Karl (1884-1957) Austrian architect, he studied under *Wagner, became City Architect of Vienna, and was responsible for many public housing-schemes in the 1920s and 1930s. Initially he was attracted by the English *Garden-City movement, as his development at *Hermeswiese* shows (1923), but at the *Lindenhof* project (1924) he was influenced by housing in Amsterdam. His most celebrated works are the *Bebelhof* (1925), the huge *Expressionist *Karl-Marx-Hof*, Heiligenstadt (1927), and the more *Modernist *Adelheid-Popp-Hof* (1932). The housing-block at Heiligenstadt is nearly half a mile long, designed with 1,382 apartments, offices, laundries, a library, and a clinic, so is a *Unité d'Habitation*, a forerunner of works by Le *Corbusier, and a descendant of C19 ideas, such as those of **Charles Fourier** (1772-1837). It has simplified *façades, powerful cubic, blocky masses, and highly organized geometries.

H.Hautmann & R.Hautmann (1980); Mang (1977)

Ehrenkrantz, Ezra David (1932-2001) American architect, inventor of standardized prefabricated components for low-cost school-buildings with adaptable plans (e.g. School Construction System Development, Pilot Unit, Stanford, CA (1964)). He restored the *Art-Deco Woolworth Tower, NYC (1980), and designed many educational buildings (e.g. Canaday Hall, Harvard University, Cambridge, MA (1974), and Henle Student Village, Georgetown University, Washington, DC (1980)).

E (1994)

Ehrensvärd, Carl August (1745-1800) Swedish Neo-Classical architect. His storehouse at the dockyard at Karlskrona (1784) is one of the most severe late-C18 buildings. After a visit to *Paestum in the 1780s (recorded in his *Journey to Italy 1780, 1781, 1782* (1786)) he designed a primitivist *Doric project for an entrance-gate to the dockyard that influenced *Stirling in his *Staatsgalerie*, Stuttgart (1977-84). His architectural designs, including a *pyramid and an extremely squat Doric Order, were as advanced as any at the time, and his polemical works heralded C20 *Functionalism.

CoE (1972); J.Curl (2005); Ehrensvärd (1786, 1922–5, 1948); Frykenstedt (1965); Josephson (1963); *Konsthistorisk Tidskrift*, **xxxii** (1964), 1–20; Rosenblum (1967); J.T (1996); Warburg (1893)

Eichler, Joseph L. (1900–74) American property developer, he elevated the architectural quality of mass-produced low-cost houses, using talented architects to achieve his aims, and, by the time he died his firm, **Eichler Homes, Inc.**, had built some 11,000 single-family, affordable homes in the San Francisco Bay area, CA. Among his works were houses designed by Archibald Quincy *Jones, including the US Gypsum Research House, Barrington Woods, Barrington, IL (1995), which employed steel in the construction, and expressed it. Other designs by Jones for Eichler were the X-100 house at San Mateo, CA (1956), and the Steelaire Fifth-Avenue house, Pittsburgh, PA (1957). Eichler also employed Raphael Simon *Soriano, who had worked with *Neutra, to design a steel-framed house at Palo Alto, CA (1955), which received much publicity.

Adamson & Arbunich (2002); N.Jackson (1996); *J. of Architecture*, **vi**/1 (Spring 2001), 1–25

Eidlitz, Cyrus Lazelle Warner (1853–1921) American architect, son of Leopold *Eidlitz. He made his reputation with the *Rundbogenstil* Dearborn Station, Chicago, IL (1883–5—altered), and Buffalo Public Library, NY (1884–7—destroyed). His *New York Times* Building (1903–5) had *Renaissance and *Gothic *terracotta *cladding.

J.T (1996); Wo (1976)

Eidlitz, Leopold (1823–1908) Prague-born American *Romanesque and *Gothic Revivalist, influenced by works of von *Gärtner in Munich, Richard *Upjohn (with whom he briefly collaborated) in NYC, and by the writings of *Pugin and *Ruskin. St George's Church, NYC (1846–8), was his first major commission, for which he designed a large *Rundbogenstil* galleried hall, clearly influenced by Munich architecture. His later Gothic work is of the *muscular type, best seen in the Albany State Capitol Assembly Chamber, Albany, NY (1875–85), designed with *Richardson and *Olmsted. His *The Nature and Function of Art* (1881) was influential, notably on *Furness and Richardson, and he published many papers in sundry journals, but few of his fine buildings have survived.

Eidlitz (1977); Jordy & Coe (eds) (1961); P (1982); J.T (1996)

Eiermann, Egon Fritz Wilhelm (1904–70) German architect, a pupil of *Poelzig and *Tessenow, his architecture was always firmly within *Rationalism. Before the 1939–45 war he worked on the exhibition and propaganda film *Gebt mir vier Jahre Zeit* (Give me Four Years—1936–7), and

designed many administrative and industrial buildings, notably for *Dega AG*, Berlin (1937–9). After the war he designed several major buildings, including the handkerchief-factory at Blumberg (1949–51), the *Burda-Moden* Buildings, Offenburg (1953–5), and the *Neckermann KG* Mail Order Building, Frankfurt (1958–61), all in collaboration with **Robert Hilgers** (1912–77). His best-known buildings were the German Pavilion at the Brussels World's Fair (1958, with **Sep Ruf** (1908–82)), the German Embassy in Washington, DC (1958–64), and the *Kaiser Wilhelm Gedächtniskirche*, Berlin (1957–63—named the 'egg-crate' ('*Eiermann*' means 'Eggsman') by Berliners), beside the ruins of the *Neo-Romanesque church by *Schwechten. His administrative-building for Olivetti in Frankfurt (1968–72) was more elegantly modelled.

Feireiss (ed.) (1994); Hildebrand (1999); L (1988); Ma (1985b); P (1982); Schirmer (ed.) (1984); J.T (1996); vV (1993)

Eiffel, Gustave (1832–1923) French engineer, best known for the iron tower bearing his name erected for the 1889 Paris Exhibition. Whilst the Eiffel Tower was an important step in the use of exposed metal for architectural purposes, Eiffel made other significant contributions, notably in bridge-building throughout Europe, South America, and Indo-China (his railway-bridge over the Truyère at Garabit, France (1880–4), was an example of his technical mastery). He was consultant for the Paris Exhibitions (1867 and 1878), and devised a theory of how wrought-iron construction performed that enabled precision of design to be achieved. He worked with *Boileau on the *Bon Marché* Department Store, Paris (1876), and designed the internal structural framework for the Statue of Liberty, NYC (1885).

Barthes (1964); Besset (1957); Bonet (ed.) (2003); Harriss (1989); Lemoine (1984, 1986); Poncetton (1939); Prévost (1929); J.T (1996)

Eigtved, Nils, Niels, *or* **Nicolai** (1701–54) Danish architect, he trained (1725–33) under **Carl Friedrich Pöppelmann** (*c.*1697–1750) in Dresden and Warsaw before returning to Copenhagen, where he became Court Architect and was largely responsible for laying out the *Frederiksstaden* Quarter, with its octagonal Amalienborg Square (1750–5), the finest and most noble composition of its time in Denmark, influenced by the work of *Juvarra and by Parisian *hôtels. He also designed the Royal Theatre (1750), Frederik Hospital (1752), and several *Rococo interiors and other works at Christiansborg Palace (1755–6—destroyed by fire in 1794, apart from the charming entrance-pavilions and bridge). His work is exquisitely refined and delicate.

N-S (1986a); J.T (1996); Voss (1971)

Einhart (*c.*770–837). German patron/writer. He appears to have worked in some kind of overseeing capacity on the *Carolingian palace and chapel at Aachen, in which case he was of considerable importance. He built Steinbach monastery (consecrated 827) and Seligenstadt Abbey (831–40).

S (1901–2); J.T (1996)

Eisenmann, John (1851–1924) American architect, best-known for the Cleveland Arcade, Ohio (1882–90), with its two nine-storey round-arched blocks flanking a galleried iron-and-glass arcade.

JSAH, xxv/4 (Dec. 1966), 281–91

Eisenman, Peter D. (1932–) *See* NEO-RATIONALISM; NEW YORK FIVE.

Eisenstein *or* **Eizenštein, Mikhail Osipovich** (1867–1921) Russian architect/engineer of German-Jewish descent, celebrated for remarkable *Jugendstil *apartment-blocks in Riga, Latvia (from 1903), notably 2a, 4, and 8 Alberta iela, and 10/10b Elizabetes iela. However, he also designed lavishly eclectic buildings in which *Baroque and *Classical elements recur in profusion, such as the apartment-block at 33 Elizabetes iela (1901) and the former private school at 4a Strelnieku iela (1905). His son was the film director, **Sergei Eisenstein** (1898–1948).

Sīlis (2012)

Ekistics The science and study of human settlements, invented by *Doxiadis.

Doxiadis (1963, 1966, 1968)

elbow *See* CROSSETTE.

Eldem, Sedad Hakki (1908–88) Turkish architect, pupil (1929–30) of *Poelzig, he attempted to make *Modernism relevant to his native land. Early works include the State Monopolies General Directorate, Ankara (1934–7), the Faculty of Arts and Sciences, Istanbul (1942–3), and the Faculty of Sciences, Ankara (1943–5). The last two were influenced by *Bonatz, with whom Eldem worked. His *Taşlık* Coffee-House (1947–8—destroyed) attempted to interpret C17 timber-framed Ottoman domestic architecture in C20 *reinforced-concrete form. He won international recognition for his Zeyrek Social Security Agency, Istanbul (1962–4), and designed numerous buildings along the banks of the Bosphorus in which the influence of traditional Ottoman architecture, as illustrated in his magisterial *Türk Evi* (Turkish House) of 1984–7, is clear. A good example is the *Rahmi Koç* villa, Tarabya (1975–80). He also designed several embassy buildings in Ankara (1964–77).

J.T (1996)

Eldon-Jones, Peter (1927–2013) English architect, he joined (1954) the then LCC, becoming deputy schools architect (1960) and town-development architect/planner (1965) responsible for Thamesmead, Andover, and Thetford. He was among those responsible for saving/restoring *Fowler's Covent Garden Market (opened 1980s), and was involved in the design and construction of the Thames Barrier (opened 1984).

RIBAJ (Dec. 2013), 52; *The Times* (4 Dec. 2013), 59

electrographic architecture Term coined by the American writer **Tom Wolfe** (1930–) in *c.*1969 to describe structures supporting electric advertising signs or *sky-signs.

AD, xxxix/7 (1969), 379–82; Proulx (1977)

Elementarism Term used by van *Doesberg to describe the use of planes and colours in architecture, notably by *Mies van der Rohe, van *Eesteren, and *Rietveld. Examples are the Schröder House, Utrecht (1921–4), and Mies van der Rohe's brick villa (1923) and Barcelona Pavilion (1928–9).

Doig (1986)

elevation 1. Accurate geometrical projection, drawn to scale, of a building's *façade or any other visible external or internal part on a plane vertical (at a right angle) to the horizon. **2.** Any external façade.

FR (1946)

elevator Means by which loads or people can be moved vertically in a chamber within a shaft from one floor of a building to another, called *lift* in the UK. Although primitive lifts were known in the early C19 (e.g. in the Bunker Hill Monument, Charlestown, MA (1824–42, by *Willard)), more sophisticated USA elevators were in use by the 1850s, and *Post's Equitable Life Assurance Building, NYC (1868–70—demolished) was one of the first office buildings to be so equipped. Hydraulic power was used for a time, but by the 1880s electrically powered lifts were evolving, so that by the end of C19 their use was widespread, facilitating the development of tall buildings. *See also* GRAIN ELEVATOR.

C.Elliott (1992)

Elias of Dereham *or* **Durham** (*fl.*1188–1245) *See* DEREHAM.

Eliot, Charles William (1859–97) *See* PARKWAY.

elision Omission of part of an architectural element. If a *frieze is *elided from an *entablature, an *architrave-cornice* is created.

Elizabethan architecture Architecture of the reign of **Queen Elizabeth I of England** (1558–1603), regarded as within the last phase of the *Tudor period, but showing the influence of

European-*Renaissance styles, though often somewhat provincial in treatment. Elizabethan England was relatively isolated from mainstream developments on the Continent, partly because of religious schism, but essentially because the Queen's legitimacy and rights to the Throne were not accepted by major European RC powers. Architectural trends were therefore slow in arriving, and were mostly disseminated through publications. Initially, Renaissance motifs were largely treated as surface decoration. The first major building to incorporate reasonably accurate French-Renaissance elements, old Somerset House, London, was not built until 1547-52, and was derived from work by Philibert de l'*Orme and Jean *Bullant. In 1550 John *Shute was sent to Italy to study *Antique and modern architecture, after which he published *The First and Chief Groundes of Architecture* (1563), derived from *Serlio and *Vignola, and the first book on the Classical *Orders in English. Thereafter, several great *prodigy-houses were built, including Burghley House, near Stamford, Lincs. (1550s-80s), Longleat, Wilts. (1572-80), and Hardwick Hall, Derbys. (1590-6). Late-*Gothic features, such as large *mullioned and *transomed windows, the *E-shaped late-Tudor plan, elaborate upper-works such as arrays of tall chimneys, *turrets, etc., and even the occasional *spire, were mixed promiscuously with the *Orders (often used as an *assemblage or even as chimneys), much *strapwork, *grotesque ornament, and *obelisks (upright and inverted, often with *herms). Sources were often French, especially the school of *Fontainebleau's *Mannerism which had such a profound influence on North-European Renaissance and Mannerist designs, notably those of *Dietterlin and de *Vries: indeed, the so-called *Ditterling ornament was often strongly represented. The Gate of Honour, Gonville and *Caius College, Cambridge (1572-3), has an *arch derived in form from late-Tudor examples, but set within a Classical ensemble of Roman-*Doric over which is an *engaged *temple-front flanked by obelisks, the whole crowned by a hexagonal superstructure with a domical vaulted top. It is clearly derived from Serlio, and from Flemish Renaissance designs: indeed its architect was **Theodore de Have**, or **Haveus** (*fl.*1562-76), a Fleming or German from Cleve (Cleves), who settled (1562) in England. However, van *Paesschen, who was involved in the design of Burghley House, Theobald's Palace (Herts.), Bach-y-Graig (Flintshire), and the Royal Exchange (London) in the 1560s, has a claim to be regarded as the first architect to design buildings in England that were Italian rather than French in style.

Elizabethan architecture was often ebullient, notably in *chimney-pieces, *frontispieces, and funerary monuments (the last often with spectacular structural *polychromy, i.e. the colour provided by the materials used in the construction e.g. Kelway monument (1580s), Church of Sts Peter and Paul, Exton, Rut., and the Cecil tomb (late C16), perhaps by **Cornelius Cure** (*fl.c.*1574-c.1609), in the Church of St Martin, Stamford, Lincs.). The essence of the Elizabethan style continued into *Jacobean architecture, and there was a C19 revival.

Airs (1975, 1995); Ck (1996); Gd (1966, 1983); Pe: *BoE* series (1951-); Su (1993); D.Wa (1986)

Elizabethan Revival During the 1830s *Elizabethan architecture provided precedents for those in search of an English *national* style: associated with a period of great creativity, wealth, and naval/military power, unlike *Gothic it had no connections with pre-Reformation religion. In 1835 the recommendations for the rebuilding of the Palace of Westminster stipulated that the designs should be either Elizabethan or Gothic, and the accession of **Queen Victoria** (*r.*1837-1901) prompted hopes of a new 'Elizabethan' age. The revival of the style therefore dates from these times: Harlaxton Manor, Lincs. (1831-7), Highclere Castle, Hants. (1842-9), and Mentmore Towers, Bucks. (1851-4), are good examples of the Revival, which also had occasional manifestations in the USA. A second revival occurred in the 1920s and 1930s, although it drew more on *timber-framed and *vernacular exemplars for domestic architecture and *public-houses.

J.Curl (2007); D & M (1985); Gd (1979); Hi (1954)

ell 1. Measure of length, in England once 45 inches. **2.** Extension or *wing added at right angles to the principal mass of the original building (USA).

Ellerton, Henry de (*fl.*1304-22) English mason, he became (1309) Master of the Works at Caernarfon Castle, Wales, and (1318) Master and Surveyor of the King's Works in the castles of North Wales. He designed the King's Gate at Caernarfon as well as the northern walls.

J.Harvey (1987)

Elliot, Archibald (1760-1823) Scots architect. With his brother, **James** (1770-1810), he formed one of the leading early-C19 Edinburgh practices. He designed Regent Bridge (1815-19) in the *Greek-Revival style, but his country-houses were usually *castellated with *Gothic detail (e.g. Taymouth Castle, Perthshire (1806-10)). His Grecian Forbes *mausoleum, Callendar House, Stirlingshire (1816), is a distinguished variation on the circular-*temple theme, while Waterloo Place, Edinburgh (1815-19), demonstrates his expertise in civic design. The practice continued under his son, **Archibald Jun.** (*fl.*1817-43), architect of the handsome Greek-Revival Royal Bank of Scotland, Glasgow (1827).

Co (2008); GMcW & W (1984); G & W (1987); WRH (1990)

Elliot, James (1770–1810) *See* ELLIOT, ARCHIBALD.

ellipse Figure formed by *section made by a plane passing obliquely through the axis of a regular cone. Unlike an *oval, it is identical at each end, i.e. on both sides of its dividing axes. *See* ARCH.

Ellis, Harvey (1852–1904) American architect. His *eclecticism was typical of the period, but his chief claim to importance lies in his drawings, especially *perspectives published in *American Architect and Building News* etc.: he produced illustrations for *Buffington that helped the latter's claims as a pioneer of the steel-framed *skyscraper. From 1902 until his death he was editor of *The Craftsman.*

P (1982); Rochester (1972)

Ellis, Peter (1804–84) English architect, known for two office-buildings in Liverpool: Oriel Chambers, Water Street (1864), has a cast-iron frame supporting shallow brick-vaulted floors and stone-faced elevations with canted *oriel-windows of metal and glass; 16 Cook Street (1866) has a rear elevation of iron and glass with a spiral staircase set within an iron-and-glass *curtain-wall remarkable for its time.

Ainsworth & Jones (2013); Hi (1977); Hughes (1964); Sharples (2004)

Ellwood, Craig (1922–92) American architect, he made his name with the *Case Study house, 1811 Bel Air Road (1951–2), followed by two more Case Study houses at 9554 Hidden Valley Road (1954) and 1129 Mirdero Road (1955), all in Los Angeles, CA. An exponent of the rectangular grid based on a steel-framed structure, he developed the *parti of *Mies van der Rohe with his Smith House, Crestwood Hills (1957–8), and his Rosen House, 910 Oakmount Drive, Brentwood (1961–3), both in Los Angeles. In his later buildings he exploited exposed steel trusses, notably with the Art Center School, Pasadena, CA (1970–5), which is essentially a bridge spanning between two hills.

E (1994); N.Jackson (2002); McCoy (1962, 1968); Perez-Mendez (2002); S.Rn (1987b)

Elmes, Harvey Lonsdale (1814–47) English architect, son of James *Elmes. He won the competition to design St George's Hall, Liverpool (1839), extended the following year to include the Assize Courts. Arguably the finest Neo-Classical building in England, it was completed (1847–54) by *Rawlinson and C.R.*Cockerell. The design may have been influenced in part by published works of von *Klenze and *Schinkel, some of whose

monumental buildings Elmes saw during a study-visit (1842). Other works by him include the *façades of houses in Ennismore Gardens and Prince's Gate, Kensington, London (*c.*1843–6), some houses in Wallasey, Ches. (*c.*1845), and the Lancashire County Lunatic Asylum, Rainhill, Lancs. (1847–51).

Co (2008); Sh (1975); J.T (1996); D.Wa (1974)

Elmes, James (1782–1862) Father of H.L. *Elmes, known for his writings, especially as editor of **Thomas Hosmer Shepherd**'s (1793–1864) *Metropolitan Improvements* (1827–9) and for *Memoirs of the Life and Works of Sir Chr. Wren* (1823). Other works included *Hints for the Improvement of Prisons* (1817) and *A Topographical Dictionary of London and its Environs* (1831). He also practised as an architect/surveyor: a list of his works is given by *Colvin.

Co (2008)

Elmslie, George Grant (1871–1952) *See* PURCELL & ELMSLIE.

Elsaesser, Martin (1884–1957) German architect, he studied under *Bonatz and Theodor *Fischer, from whom he gained his interest in historical styles. He was an important educator, and published *Einführung in das Entwerfen* (1950) and *Wohnung und Lebensgefühl* (1955). Many of his designs were published (1933): most have simple forms, pitched roofs, and agreeable proportions.

P (1982)

Elsam, Richard (*c.*1772–*c.*1838) English architect, author of several architectural books. A pupil of **Robert Browne** (1756–1827), Clerk of the Works at Kew Palace, his career was marked by disagreements with clients and others. Elsam settled in Ireland (1804), and when working in Londonderry published *The Gentleman and Builder's Assistant* (1808). After a time in Dublin he was bankrupted (1815), and returned to England where he was recorded (1818) Surveyor to the Corporation of Dover, and was still there some twenty years later. He exhibited designs at the Society of Artists, Dublin, and published *Hints for Improving the Condition of the Peasantry, with . . . Designs for Cottages* (1816). This was followed by *A Brief Treatise on Prisons, Illustrated with . . . the New Gaol about to be Erected at Dover* (1818) and *The Practical Builder's Perpetual Price-Book* (1825). He designed gaols for Cavan (1810—demolished 1930s) and Monaghan (1814): the last was unrealized, but the building went up (1814–21) to plans by **John Behan** (*fl.* early C19). Elsam seems to have been involved in the design of Urney Parish Church, Cavan (1815).

Co (2008); *DIA* (website) accessed 2 Dec. 2012; Mulligan (2013)

Ely, Reginald *or* **Reynold of** (*fl.*1438–71) As one of the English master-masons working at King's College Chapel, Cambridge, from its commencement, he is a likely candidate as its architect, and must be regarded as one of the greatest C15 English architects. His name is first associated (1438) with Peterhouse, Cambridge, where he built the stair to the library at the west side of the medieval *court and may have worked on the kitchen-wing at the west end of the Hall. Commissioned (1444) to find craftsmen for building works at King's College, work began (1446) on the Chapel, **King Henry VI** (*r.*1422–71) laying the foundation-stone. Reginald Ely seems to have been the man on the spot, and was involved at the Chapel until work stopped (1461). He was probably the designer of the *elevations, but it is doubtful if he was responsible for the *tracery patterns except for the east window of the easternmost chapel on the north side, unusual for its *Curvilinear design differing from the tracery of the rest of the chapels which is all firmly *Perp. King's Chapel was designed to have a *lierne* rather than a *fan-vaulted* ceiling, as is clear from the design of the *piers in the *choir. He may have designed Burwell Church, Cambs. (1454–64), and Queen's College, Cambridge (from 1446).

J.Harvey (1987)

Elysium, Elyzium 1. Land of the dead in Classical Antiquity. 2. Place where a state of ideal or perfect happiness may be achieved, so, by extension, a charming, exquisitely beautiful, tenderly elegiac landscaped garden, often embellished with monuments and even real tombs, as at C18 *Elysées* of Maupertuis and Ermenonville, France. 3. Landscaped *Picturesque *cemetery, such as *Père-Lachaise*, Paris (from 1804), and Mount Auburn, Cambridge, MA (1831).

Bazin (1990); Etlin (1984); Racine (ed.) (2001); Symes (2006)

embankment 1. Artificial long ridge sometimes made from the material excavated when forming artificial lakes, etc., on which a *terrace or walk is made from which views may be enjoyed. 2. The same, but used to carry an elevated road or railway. 3. Barrier to confine a river, etc., within fixed limits (e.g. the Albert (1868), Victoria (1870), and Chelsea (1874) Embankments, London). *See* MOTTE; MOUNT.

embattled *See* BATTLEMENT.

Emberton, Joseph (1889–1956) English architect, he worked (1918–22) with *Burnet and *Tait before establishing a practice with **Percy James Westwood** (1878–1958). The firm introduced a vaguely *Islamic style to the various *kiosks for the British Empire Exhibition, Wembley, Mddx. (1924–5—demolished). They also designed

Summit House, Holborn (1925), for Austin Reed, which showed Burnet & Tait's influence. He refaced/extended (1929–30) the Olympia exhibition-halls, Hammersmith Road, London, in a 'grim and sensational' *Modernistic style, as *Pevsner put it, which looks like *concrete, but is, in fact, of steel and rendered brick, the details 'borrowed from progressive Continental buildings such as the Einstein Tower', Potsdam, by *Mendelsohn. To the rear, the new entrance-hall towards Sinclair Road (1936) is 'quieter' and 'well-proportioned'. This tendency towards conventional *International *Modernism continued with the Royal Corinthian Yacht Club, Burnham-on-Crouch, Essex (1930–1), followed by Simpson's Department Store, Piccadilly, London (1935–6), which Pevsner pronounced 'progressive', with the 'new idiom' handled 'with conviction': the building has a pioneering welded-steel frame. Clearly Mendelsohn was the main influence on Emberton, as can be seen from 363–7 Oxford Street, London (1938–9), and the Casino, South Shore, Blackpool, North Lancs. (1937–8).

AAQ, viii/3 (1976), 51–9; Ind (1983); *ODNB* (2004); Cherry & Pe (1991); Bradley & Pe (2003)

emblem 1. Picture, sign, or device expressing a moral allegory. 2. Picture of an object serving as a symbolic representation of an abstraction. 3. Device used as a badge of a person, family, Saint, etc. C16 and C17 emblems were often connected with hidden meanings: books of emblematic designs were important sources of architectural decoration.

embrasure 1. Space between *cops in a *battlement. 2. Splayed enlargement of an aperture creating a larger opening on the inside of a wall than outside, thus affording an extended range of vision from within while keeping the aperture small. This allowed more light in as well as improving defence.

Emerson, Sir William (1843–1924) English architect, he worked (1860s) with *Burges, then moved to Bombay, where he designed the Crawford Market (1865–71), clearly influenced by Burges's work, and with decorations by **John Lockwood Kipling** (1837–1911), father of **Rudyard**. He returned (1869) to London and practised, but his best work remained on paper: among his few English buildings was the sturdy *Gothic-Revival Sts Mary & James Church, Brighton, Sussex (1877–9). His Indian practice flourished, however, and his work there includes the Cathedral (1869–93) and the eclectic Muir College (1872–8), both in Allahabad; the vast Maharajah's Palace, Bhaunagar (1894–5); and that epitome of *Edwardian *Baroque, the Queen Victoria Memorial, Calcutta (1903–21).

A.S.Gray (1985); *ODNB* (2004)

Emerson, William Ralph (1833–1917) American architect, his late-C19 domestic architecture, especially in the *Shingle and *Stick styles, was significant, although he also produced elegant *Queen-Anne and *Colonial-Revival designs. The Forbes House, Milton, MA (1876), is reckoned to be his finest building in the Stick style, while his Shingle-style houses include the C.J. Morrill House, Bar Harbor, ME (1879), and Loring House, Pride's Crossing, MA (1881).

V.J.Sy (1971, 1974, 1989); J.T (1996); Zaitzevsky (1969)

Emler, Lawrence (*fl.*1492–1506) German carver/designer. He made the exquisite head of the funerary *effigy of **Queen Elizabeth of York** (*r.*1485–1503) in Westminster Abbey (1503), and may have designed the fine bronze *screen around the tomb of **King Henry VII** (*r.*1485–1509) and his Queen in the *Lady Chapel.

J.Harvey (1987)

Empire Neo-Classical style of decoration and interior design evolved in the Napoléonic period in France in the first fifteen years of C19, corresponding to British *Regency and American *Directory styles. It was largely the creation of *Percier and *Fontaine, and it drew on *Egyptian, *Etruscan, *Greek, *Pompeian, and *Roman motifs, treated with extraordinary verve, synthesized in a satisfactory whole. Motifs such as eagles, the letter N, wreaths, lotuses, winged discs, and other ornaments, gilded, were set against fine, rich woods. The style had a profound effect on taste in Britain, Prussia, Russia, and the USA, although in the last-named country Greek forms and Freemasonic symbols played more of a role.

CoE (1972); L & D (1986)

encarpus Sculptured *festoons of fruit, flowers, leaves, and drapery in Classical architecture.

encaustic 1. Fixed by heat, with reference to e.g. painting with wax colours and fixing them during firing so that the colours are burnt in. 2. Type of *tile of one colour decorated with inlaid patterns formed with different coloured clay, then fired, and usually glazed. Encaustic tiles with yellowish patterns on a dark red ground were commonly used in medieval and *Gothic-Revival churches.

enceinte 1. Wall or *rampart surrounding a fortified enclosure. 2. Area bounded or defined by such a wall or rampart. 3. Central, best-defended part of a fortification in the middle.

Encke, Friedrich August Ernst (*known as* **Fritz**) (1861–1931) German landscape architect, responsible for many parks and gardens, he was a passionate advocate of social benefits to be gained from properly designed green spaces in towns. He taught (1890–1903) at Potsdam,

published (1898) an important book on the laying out of gardens, and gained several Royal appointments before moving to Cologne where he was in charge of all gardens (1903–26), designing the Beethoven, Blücher, Humboldt, Klettenberg, and Rhein Parks, as well as numerous other schemes. After the 1914–18 war, with the support of **Konrad Adenauer** (1876–1967—Mayor of Cologne from 1917) and Fritz *Schumacher (who had designed the Hamburg *Stadtpark*), he created a series of *green belts around the city. He worked on parks in Berlin, and taught several landscape architects, including *Allinger. His son, **Fritz Joseph Encke** (1904–2002) followed the same profession, and was also an author: much of his work was in Frankfurt-am-Main.

Encke (1898); Encke & Schiller (1975)

enclosure, inclosure 1. Marking off or surrounding land with *fences, walls, or other barriers to prevent ingress/egress, or to delineate ownership. Walls, hedges, etc., can conceal views, but they also define space, creating *'rooms' with their own identity, so are essential elements in landscape-design, and are extensions of architecture, as in *Chinese gardens. Two types of enclosure are used in landscape-design: plants (hedges, belts of trees, etc.) and man-made structures (walls, fences, *embankments, etc.). Hedges, of course, require regular attention, but can provide dark colouring as well as possibilities for shaping, e.g. yew, against which other colours stand out. Walls are important parts of urban or village design, and buildings themselves can enclose space. An invisible barrier, the *ha-ha, was employed in C18 parks as a means of obtaining uninterrupted views over countryside yet preventing cattle, etc., from getting close to the house. 2. State of being enclosed, as in a *monastery. 3. Buildings around a *court, *quad, etc. 4. Space within boundaries. 5. Conversion of common land into private property achieved under many Acts of Parliament which removed existing rights (e.g. to graze animals or cultivate land) and even caused whole villages to be destroyed. Most of these Acts were passed in C18, consolidated under 41 Geo.III, c.109 (1801). The process of 'inclosure' began in C16 and accelerated in C18, leading to the Agricultural Revolution and the creation of large private holdings. The effects marked the beginning of the end for subsistence farming (because of the amalgamation of scattered holdings of strips of land into individual farms that could be managed independently), the rise of the bourgeoisie, and the creation of much of the landscape seen in England today. In a century and a half about one acre in every seven in England was enclosed. The movement stopped with a growing realization of the importance of protecting public health, and the value of commons as open spaces in populous areas: attempts to enclose the commons of Epsom and Wimbledon led to the *Inclosures Act* (1866—29 & 30 Vict.c.29) and the *Metropolitan Commons Act* of the same year (29 & 30 Vict., c.122) which prevented further enclosures within the Metropolitan area, and led to the protection of such amenities as Hampstead Heath (1871—under 34 & 35 Vict., c.77 (local)) and Epping Forest (1878—under 41 & 42 Vict., c.71). *See* HORTUS CONCLUSUS.

DdA (1709); Fairbrother (1974); Switzer (1980); Thacker (1979); Shoe (2001); Whitehead (1966)

end Term used to denote the distinctions between private and service rooms in a medieval *timber-framed house, with the *upper* or *high end* the private part of a hall and the *lower end* containing the *entry and near the services.

en délit *Gothic detached stone *shaft or *colonnette with vertical grain.

Endell, Ernst Moritz August (1871-1925) German *Arts-and-Crafts architect, connected with the Munich *Sezession*. His first significant architectural work was the Elvira Photographic Studio, Munich (1896-7), the *façade of which was decorated with swirling masses of marine-like forms of *stucco set beneath an *Egyptian *gorge-cornice: it was one of the most celebrated of *Jugendstil* designs. He developed a successful Berlin practice from 1901, and argued for sensitivity to spiritual values in *Die Schönheit der grossen Stadt* (1908). He was a supporter of van de *Velde's stance in favour of individualism in design against *Muthesius's arguments for standardization in the 1914 debate within the *Deutscher Werkbund*. He moved (1918) to Breslau (now Wrocław) to head the Academy of Art.

Benton *et al.* (eds) (1975); Bröcker *et al.* (2012); Endell (1896); Gh (2000); Killy *et al.* (1965)

end lobby-entry See ENTRY.

Enfant, Pierre-Charles L' (1754-1825) A Frenchman, he served as a volunteer with the American forces during the War of Independence from 1777, and designed a large Neo-Classical *pavilion in Philadelphia to commemorate the birth of the Dauphin (1782). He remodelled the City Hall, NYC, as the Congress or Federal Hall of the USA (1788-9—demolished 1812). From 1789 he was involved in the design of the new Federal Capital of Washington, DC, where the plan was on the grandest lines, owing something to *Baroque precedents, especially Versailles.

Caemmerer (1970); Kite (ed.) (1929); Reiff (1977); Reps (1967); W & K (1983)

enfilade *Baroque alignment of all the doorways (usually sited near the window-walls) in a series or suite of rooms so as to create a vista when the doors were open, as in a palace. It avoided corridors, privacy provided by e.g. the hangings around a bed.

engaged Applied, attached, semi-engaged, *inserted, or seemingly partly buried in a wall or *pier, such as a column with half or more of its *shaft visible, quite distinct from a *pilaster. A fluted engaged column with more or less than half its shaft exposed creates difficulties at the junction with the wall because of the *entasis unless the whole shaft is tilted back towards the wall, as *Burnet did with the *Ionic columns at the *Edwardian extension to the British Museum, London (1904-14).

Engel, Carl Ludvig (1778-1840) German architect, he trained under F.*Gilly and further developed his *Neo-Classicism in St Petersburg, Russia. He settled (1816) in Helsinki, Finland, having been appointed architect for the new capital of the then Grand Duchy, and designed many important buildings there, including the Senate House (1818-22), Lutheran Cathedral (1830-40), University Library (1836-45), and City Hall (1827-33). In 1824 he was appointed Controller of Public Works, leading to the dissemination of his Neo-Classical language throughout Finland. His architectural output was prolific and usually distinguished.

Engel (1990); Lilius *et al.* (1990); M & Wa (1987); Suo-lahti (1973); J.T (1996); Wickberg (1962, 1970)

Engelberger, Burkhard (*c.*1450-1512) One of the most important architects working (late C15-early C16) in southern Germany and Switzerland. As consultant architect (1493-1508) at Ulm *Minster, he strengthened the tower and transformed the side-aisles with intricate net-vaults. He also designed the *vaults at St Georg, Nördlingen (1490s). For many years (1477-1512) he worked on the Church of *Sts Ulrich and Afra*, Augsburg, where his masterly *Bogenstückwerk* (net-vaults with intersecting fragments of arched *ribs (often pierced and truncated)) may best be seen in the Simpertus *arch in the south aisle (1493-6).

W.Pa (1852); S (1901-2); J.T (1996)

English altar Type of late-medieval *altar arrangement with *riddells, riddell-posts, and, sometimes, a *tester. *See* COMPER.

English bond See BRICK.

English cottage *Picturesque rural cottage, also called *cottage orné*.

English garden Informal, asymmetrical, 'natural' type of landscape evolved in C18, associated with L.*Brown, H.*Repton, and others, and widely copied in Europe, where it was called *jardin *anglo-chinois* because of its apparent haphazard design. It was associated with the *Picturesque and *Sharawadgi.

D.Coffin (1994); D.Wa (1982a)

Englishman, William the   (*fl.*1174–1214) English master-mason, he worked under William of *Sens on the rebuilding of Canterbury Cathedral, Kent, from 1174, and continued the works (1177–84) after Sens was injured, including the Trinity Chapel and the Corona (circular chapel at the east). He may also have been involved at Chichester Cathedral (1187–99), and the Abbey of St Radigund, Dover, Kent.

J.Harvey (1987)

English style   Term coined (1984) to describe a type of English and North-American late-C20 interior design in which antique and modern, the odd and the familiar, the permanent and the ephemeral, and above all, fine quality, were synthesized.

E.Dickson (1989); Slesin & Cliff (1984)

Enlightenment   C18 European and North American intellectual climate in which belief in reason as a means to ensure human progress was combined with a questioning of tradition and authority, the systematic collection and categorizing of facts, and the study of nature on a scientific basis. In German-speaking countries it was called the *Aufklärung*. Its architectural manifestations were a reaction to *Baroque and *Rococo, the adoption of *Rationalism and therefore a return to the principles of *Classicism. International *Neo-Classicism began to be established in the French Academy in Rome, and led to an increasing severity, prompted by writers such as *Laugier: it was also sustained by developments in *archaeology, which gave a solid basis upon which it could develop. *Winckelmann and others drew attention to the art of Ancient Greece, while French scholars argued for even greater severity which led to the beginnings of Egyptology after 1798. In addition, C18 investigations and explorations encouraged sympathetic appropriations of other than European cultures, made manifest in burgeoning *eclecticism, often expressed in the design of *fabriques* in landscaped gardens, one of the finest being Wörlitz in Sachsen-Anhalt (late C18), by *Erdmannsdorff, *Eyserbeck, and others. So the Enlightenment also influenced the design of *Picturesque gardens, and the *jardin *anglo-chinois* was more than fashion, for it suggested an admiration for English resistance to Absolutism, and the cultivation of a civilized, ironic detachment, leading to an attempt to give visual expression to a wide range of ideas and themes.

Etlin (1994a); Picon (1992); J.T (1996); V (1987); D.Wa (2004)

enneastyle   *Portico with nine columns in a line.

enrichment   Any ornamentation on *mouldings, such as the *egg-and-dart on *ovolos.

Ensingen, Ulrich von   (*c.*1350–1419) One of the greatest German medieval master-masons, he worked for many years (from 1392) at the *Minster, Ulm, where he designed the beautiful *Sondergotik tower and west porch, though the upper stages were built by *Böblinger. He was also the architect of the elegant octagonal stage of the tower at Strasbourg Cathedral, France, with its cage of intricate *tracery (from 1399). He worked at the *Frauenkirche*, Esslingen (from 1398), and the convent at Pforzheim (from 1409). He also appears to have acted as a consultant at Milan Cathedral in the early 1390s.

Frankl (1960, 2000); Mojon (1967); Recht (ed.) (1989); J.T (1996); Wortmann (1977)

Ensinger, Matthäus   (*c.*1390–1463) Son of Ulrich von *Ensingen, he worked under his father at Strasbourg and Ulm before moving to Bern, Switzerland, where he designed the Cathedral (begun 1421). He also became master-mason for the *Frauenkirche*, Esslingen (1429) and the *Minster, Ulm (from 1446). Like his father, he ranks high among German medieval master-masons.

Frankl (1960, 2000); Mojon (1967); Recht (ed.) (1989); J.T (1996); Wortmann (1977)

entablature   In Classical *Orders the entire horizontal mass of material carried on columns and *pilasters above the *abaci*. Normally it consists of three main horizontal divisions, the *architrave (essentially the *lintel spanning between the columns), the *frieze (occasionally elided (omitted), as in certain examples of the *Ionic Order, especially *Hellenistic versions), and *cornice. An entablature on the top of an *astylar *façade, as in a Florentine-*Renaissance *palazzo*, is called *cornicione*. Entablatures are also found at the tops of Classical rooms, between ceiling and wall.

entasis   In Classical architecture *shafts of columns have a greater diameter at the bottom than at the top: the *diminution does not result in slightly *battered straight inclining slides, but a subtly convex curved swelling called *entasis*. In the Greek-*Doric Order from *Paestum shafts are much smaller at the tops than the bases, so entasis is obvious, at first offending Palladian sensibilities. Entasis can also be found on walls, *spires, and towers. Entasis in Greek shafts may have been noticed first by *Allason in *c.*1814, but it was subsequently confirmed by C.R.*Cockerell and *Haller von Hallerstein. Allason published a paper in the *Quarterly Journal of Science and Arts* (1821) on the subject (but was indebted to

Cockerell for material), and F.C.*Penrose followed with detailed discussions in the 1850s.

Entenza, John Dymock (1903–84) *See* CASE STUDY HOUSES.

enterclose, interclose 1. *Partition. **2.** Passage between two rooms in a house.

entrelac (*pl.* **entrelacs**) In landscape-design, an interlacing band found in *knot- and ornamental-gardens.

entresol *See* MEZZANINE.

entry. Term used to describe the position of the main entrance to a medieval *timber-framed house. *Types include*:

baffle-entry: entry to a lobby in front of an axial chimney-stack, without doors;

cross-entry: entry to a hall through opposite doors, without any partition;

cross-passage: similar to a *cross-entry*, but with a partition forming a passage screening the hall;

end lobby-entry: like a *lobby-entry* but at the end of a side-wall, with access to one room only;

gable-entry: situated in a gable-wall;

lobby-entry: with door leading to a lobby at the rear of which is the axial chimney-stack, with doors on either side.

ABDM (1996)

envelope 1. Roof, outer walls, etc., of a building enclosing/protecting interior volumes. **2.** Light, waterproof protective *cladding, e.g. glazed metal frames, as in *curtain-walling. **3.** In geometry, the covering of a solid with a thin pliable substance. **4.** In fortifications, earthworks enclosing an area.

environmental art Art form that emerged in the 1960s, conceived as a complete space, an invasion of the architecture around it, rather than as an object on display in a room or on a wall. Supposedly new, it might be challenged by suggesting, e.g., that *Baroque church interiors, which surround the visitor with a plethora of images (sculptures, frescoes, architectural decorations, etc.), might also be considered as environmental art.

Lippard (ed.) (1997)

environmental design Aspects of building design connected with environmental control within them (e.g. heat, quality of air, humidity, etc.). *Passive* control might involve thick, well-insulated walls, but *active* control suggests *air-conditioning by mechanical means, regulation of temperature, humidity, lighting, and so on (termed *environmental control*). *Integrated Environmental Design* (*IED*) involves control of solar heat-gain, artificial lighting-systems with supplementary back-ups capable of functioning by day and by night, and means of reducing energy-consumption by means of computers (giving rise to the term *intelligent buildings*).

Baggs & Baggs (1996); Day (1990); Hawkes & W.Forster (2002); Hawkes,McDonald, & Steemers (2002); Knowles (1974)

Environmentally Responsible Architecture Also *Green* or *Sustainable Architecture*, it developed from the 1960s in response to mounting ecological and environmental worries: it involved experiments with energy-efficient natural materials (e.g. timber or earth), providing well-insulated buildings, and drawing on solar and wind power, and other sources of energy (e.g. decomposition of wastes). It also included care of and respect for sites. It should be emphasized that *International-Modernist architecture was anything but environmentally responsible, devoured energy, leaked it, and was subject to extremes of temperature because of solar-heat gain. Houses built partly underground (in order to reduce the impact on the landscape and improve insulation) have pointed the way forward, but have not been much loved by the public. *Soleri's projects at Arcosanti, AZ, employing his idea of an architecture compatible with ecology (*Arcology), have been created from the 1970s, and the Center for Maximum Potential Building Systems, Austin, TX, has pioneered developments. Unlike the Modern Movement, Environmentally Responsible Architecture attempts to involve itself in the *retention* of old buildings (recognizing they are resources, and to destroy them is wasteful) to make them 'sustainable' (e.g. the Audubon Building, NYC, of 1891, by *Post, restored and adapted by the National Audubon Society, a group concerned to protect and manage habitats, ecosystems, and worthy buildings).

Baggs & Baggs (1996); B.Edwards (1996); Egan (2004); St John (ed.) (1993); V & V (1991); Yeang (1995, 1997)

Eosander, Johann Friedrich, Freiherr von Göthe (1670–1729) Scandinavian-born Court Architect in Berlin, succeeding *Schlüter as architect of the Berlin *Schloss*: he worked there (1707–13), adding the west side with the *triumphal-arch portal and part of the frontage facing the *Lustgarten* (all destroyed). He designed part of the main block, the *cupola with *drum, and the chapel at Charlottenburg Palace, Berlin, from 1702. Other works included the *Schloss* (from 1704), Schönhausen and the *Schloss* (1706–9), Oranienburg (both near Berlin), and the central block of the Garden-Palace *Monbijou*, Berlin (from 1708). He built a mansion at Altlandsberg, near Frankfurt-on-the-Oder (1709—destroyed), and the *Schloss* at Übigau, near Dresden (1724–6).

Biederstedt (1961); E.Hempel (1965); Peschken (1993); Peschken & Klünner (1982)

EPCOT (Experimental Prototype Community of Tomorrow) A development in the USA of the *amusement- or theme-park, including housing developments, water parks, a monorail system, a conservation area, artificial lakes, canals, streams, hotels, resorts, parking spaces, a *wilderness area, 'ancient cities', modern shopping areas, and topiary whimsically clipped into Disney characters.

Shoe (2001)

épi *Spire-shaped termination, as on a hipped roof.

epinaos In a Greek *temple, the rear open *vestibule to the *naos.

Epistle side South side of a church or *altar.

epitaph Inscription on a funerary monument, tombstone, etc.

epithedes Upper member of an *entablature, or *cyma.

E-plan English country-house plan shaped like an **E**, formed of a principal range attached to two parallel *wings extending at right angles to it, and with a central projecting porch. Barrington Court, Som. (from 1514), is a good example.

equilateral 1. *See* ARCH. **2.** An *equilateral roof* has 60° pitches, and thus in *section the timbers form an equilateral triangle.

Erdmannsdorff, Friedrich Wilhelm, Freiherr von (1736–1800) German Neo-Classical architect and *Freemason. He travelled with his friend/patron, the Prince of *Anhalt-Dessau, in the British Isles (1763–4—where he imbibed *Palladianism and aspects of the *Picturesque (especially from English landscaped gardens)), and Italy (1761–3, 1765–6, and 1770–1—where he absorbed *Neo-Classicism (notably from *Winckelmann and *Clérisseau)). His English experiences stood him in good stead when designing the Neo-Palladian *Schloss* at Wörlitz, near Dessau (1769–73—which resembles Claremont in Surrey (1771–4) by Capability *Brown and *Holland), and some of the *fabriques* in the park there. Interiors of the *Schloss* include *Pompeian elements, while the park (laid out by *Eyserbeck and the *Schochs) has many allusions to England (e.g. the Iron Bridge (a quarter-scale version of *Pritchard's original (1775–9) at Coalbrookdale, Salop.); Gothic House (with *Hesekiel, an allusion to *Walpole's Strawberry Hill, Twickenham, Mddx., of 1750–76); Temple of Flora (derived from *Chambers's Casino at Wilton, Wilts. (*c.*1759), and much else). In fact, the park incorporates many influences from Kew, near Richmond, Rousham (Oxon.), Stourhead (Wilts.), and Stowe (Bucks.), and was an attempt to create England-

by-the-Elbe, not just out of caprice, but as an exemplary and educational programme to raise the tone of the Principality to one of *Enlightenment and Progress. Erdmannsdorff also designed *Schloss Luisium*, near Dessau (1775–80), the Court Theatre, Dessau (1777), and many other buildings in the Prince's *Gartenreich* (Garden Realm). In 1786 he was called to Berlin to contribute to the new Royal Academy there, and designed Neo-Classical interiors at *Sanssouci*, Potsdam, and the *Schloss*, Berlin. He designed (1787) the new *cemetery and *portal, Dessau, and from 1791 contributed further to the fabric of Dessau, Magdeburg, and Wörlitz. On his memorial-altar in the Wörlitz park is the inscription (in German), which might be translated as 'Wanderer, heed Nature and Art, and protect their works'.

R.Alex (ed.) (1986, 1988); J.Curl (2011); Harksen (1973); D.Hempel (ed.) (1987); Kadatz (1986); Quilitzsch et al. (1997); Trauzettel (2000); Trauzettel & Winkler (1992)

ergonomics Study of relationships between working humans and e.g. tools, machinery, and instrument panels to ensure efficiency and usability of designs.

Murrell (1965); Sanders & E.McCormick (1993)

Erickson, Arthur Charles (1924–2009) Canadian architect, he gained international recognition with the Simon Fraser University, Burnaby, Vancouver (1963–5), designed with London-born **Geoffrey Massey** (1924–), and influenced by work of Le *Corbusier, *Kahn, and *Rudolph. Erickson's expression of *columnar and trabeated architecture is best seen at the Smith House, West Vancouver (1965), and the Museum of Anthropology, University of B.C. (1973–6). His Provincial Government Offices and Court House complex, Robson Square, Vancouver (1973–9), is a formal essay in *urban design, landscaped with trees and water. The Canadian Chancery, Washington, DC (1983–9), demonstrates a response to Washington's *Classicism, with its huge courtyard and *rotunda. In 2002–3 his Museum of Glass, Tacoma, WA, was built (with **Thomas Cook Reed Reinvald Architects**).

Erickson (1988); Iglauer (1981); K (1994)

Erith, Raymond Charles (1904–73) English traditionalist Classical architect. In partnership (1929–39) with **Bertram Stewart Hume** (1901–77), he designed a house at Dedham, Essex, followed by lodges at the approach to Royal Lodge, Windsor, Berks. (1939), both in the idiom of *c.*1800. He started (1946) his own practice, designing the Classical Provost's Lodging, Queen's College (1955), followed by the new library and residential block at Lady Margaret Hall (1960–6), both in Oxford. He reconstructed 10, 11, and 12

Downing Street, London (1958–63). His *Gothick Jack Straw's Castle, Hampstead (a large *public-house (1963–4)), the common-room building at Gray's Inn (1971–2), and various residential buildings (e.g. the Palladian *villa at Wivenhoe New Park, Essex, of 1962–4) demonstrate his mastery of English historical styles. He took Quinlan *Terry into partnership (1962).

Archer (1985); *ODNB* (2004)

Erlach, Johann Bernhard Fischer von (1656–1723) *See* FISCHER.

ermitage *See* HERMITAGE.

Ersatz architecture Indiscriminately eclectic architecture with diverse motifs not copied with exactitude, understanding, or scholarship, verging on *Kitsch*, e.g. many examples of *Post-Modernism. The term seems to be one of many inventions (*c.*1973) of **Charles Alexander Jencks** (1939–2019).

AD, xliii/9 (1973), 596–601

Erskine, John (1675–1732), **22nd** *or* **6th Earl of Mar** from 1689, Jacobite **Duke of Mar** from 1722, architect, and landscape-gardener: as *Gibbs's patron he was of immense importance in the history of British architecture. He proposed, as early as 1726, bridges on the northern and southern sides of the Old Town of Edinburgh, as well as the siting of George Street, the spine of *Craig's New Town (1766). Active with architectural/planning proposals while in exile in Europe, it is clear he was familiar with the works of numerous architects e.g. *Bramante, *Guarini, and *Palladio. An admirer of Classical Antiquity, some of his views heralded *Neo-Classicism.

Co (2008); *ODNB* (2004)

Erskine, Ralph (1914–2005) London-born architect, he emigrated (1939) to Sweden, where he began to specialize in the design of low-cost housing, notably at Gyttorp (1945–55), Fors in Dalecarlia (1950–3—with cardboard-factory of modelled brickwork), and Tibro (1959–64). His housing-scheme at Byker, Newcastle upon Tyne (1969–82), arranged behind a huge eight-storey wall a kilometre long, was designed with the participation of residents. He also designed the Postgraduate College, Clare Hall, Cambridge (1967–9), housing at Killingworth, Northum. (1969–72), and the Eaglestone Estate, Milton Keynes, Bucks. (1973–7). The Larson Office Building (called 'The Ark'), Hammersmith, London (1988–91—with **Vernon Gracie**) is a major development near the Hammersmith flyover. Other projects included the Students' Centre, Auditorium, and Library, Stockholm University (1979–82), and the Skanska office building, Göteborg (1989). He was a member of *Team X from 1959.

Ca (1998); Collymore (1994); Egelius (1988); E (1994); Lasdun (ed.) (1984); Pearman *et al.* (1993); S.Ray (1978)

Ervi, Aarne Adrian (1910–77) Finnish architect, he worked for *Aalto before setting up his own practice (1938), designing power-stations, industrial, and university buildings. Ervi won the competition to lay out Tapiola *Garden City, Espoo, and realized (1954–64) his projects for the town centre, houses, and apartments there, making use of the natural features of the site.

J.M.Ri (1978); Salokorpi (1970); J.T (1996); Tempel (1968); vV(1993); Wickberg (1962)

Erwin von Steinbach (*fl.*1275–1318) *See* STEINBACH.

escalator Type of stepped conveyor belt or moving stairway to convey passengers from one floor to another. Patented (1892), the American Otis Elevator Company exhibited its version in Paris (1900).

C.Elliott (1992)

escape *Apophyge.

escarp, escarpment 1. Steep bank or wall immediately in front of and below the *rampart in fortification. **2.** Ground formed like an escarp as a garden-feature.

Eschwege, Wilhelm Ludwig, Baron von (1777–1855) German military-engineer, he settled in Portugal, and designed the *Palácio da Pena* (1839–49), near Sintra, which involved rebuilding and enlarging the ruined monastery of *Nossa Senhora da Pena*: influenced by contemporary English and German *Gothic Revival, it also embraced *Manueline themes from Sintra and Tomar, so is an early C19 example of Portuguese *eclecticism.

GS; Pereira & Carneiro (1999); J.T (1996)

escoinson 1. Corner of a *jamb, essentially to accommodate something, especially in medieval work, sometimes enriched with a *shaft or *colonnette. **2.** *Squinch. **3.** *Arch over a window-opening with splayed *reveals. **4.** Part of the reveal of an aperture where a window is set.

escutcheon, scutcheon 1. Shield or shield-shaped surface on which a coat of arms is depicted. **2.** *Hatchment, also known as *funeral escutcheon*. **3.** Shield-shaped ornament, usually on *Gothic buildings, on *bosses, etc. **4.** Plate over a keyhole. **5.** *Escutcheon of pretence* is a small escutcheon (**1**) bearing the arms of an heiress in the centre of her husband's shield, also called *inescutcheon*. In the arms of a Baronet, the inescutcheon is borne in *chief* and *charged* with the Red Hand of Ulster (because the Dignity of Baronets was instituted (1610) to raise capital for the settlement and securing of Ulster by means of fines paid for the Dignity by armigerous families with lands to their name).

Eseler, *or* **Essler, Nikolaus** (c.1400–92) German architect, involved in the building of the fine *Gothic *hall-churches at Nördlingen (from 1442) and Dinkelsbühl (from 1448). He also worked at Rothenburg-ob-der-Tauber (1453–67), and was from 1463 Master of the Works at Mainz Cathedral. His son, also **Nikolaus**, worked at Dinkelsbühl (1492–9).

Pa (1852); J.T (1996)

esonarthex *Narthex within a church, separated from *nave and *aisles by columns or some other means.

espagnolette *See* CREMONE.

espalier 1. *Lattice-work *trellis upon which tree-branches are trained in horizontal directions. **2.** Row of trees so trained, without the trellis.

esplanade 1. Level walk or *promenade laid out with planting by a river, lake, or seashore. **2.** *Glacis or open ground between a fortress and a town, or the glacis of the *counter-scarp.

esquillage *See* SHELL.

Essenwein, August Ottmar von (1831–92) German architect/historian. He enlarged the *Germanisches Nationalmuseum*, Nuremberg (1860s), and restored churches in Nuremberg, Cologne, Bonn, and elsewhere. He acquired a reputation as an expert on *Romanesque architecture, and published extensively. Among his works were *Die mittelalterlichen Kunstdenkmäler der Stadt Krakau* (1869) and *Nord-Deutschlands Backsteinbau im Mittelalter* (1877).

S (1901–2); J.T (1996)

Essex, James (1722–84) English architect, one of the best of the early *Gothic Revivalists. He designed many works in a Classical style in Cambridge, but is important as among the very first to understand the structural properties of *Gothic, publishing several pioneering papers on medieval buildings in the *Journal* of the Society of Antiquaries of London, and writing an (unpublished) history of Gothic architecture in England. He designed the Beauclerk Tower and Gothic Gate at Strawberry Hill, Twickenham, Mddx. (1776), for *Walpole, and carried out restorations at Lincoln (1762–5) and Ely (1757–62) Cathedrals that were far more scholarly than anything attempted by his contemporaries (or some of his successors).

Co (2008); Mowl (1996); *ODNB* (2004)

Estilo Modernista Spanish *Art Nouveau.

estípite *Pilaster or square column, often tapered so that it is smaller at the bottom than

the top, lavishly enriched with geometrical patterns, low reliefs, intermediate *capital-like mouldings, and *cartouches derived from *pattern-books e.g. those of *Dietterlin and North-European Mannerists. It occurs in Spanish *Baroque and *Churrigueresque architecture.

Pla Dalmáu (1951)

estrade Low raised platform or *daïs, usually with a *balustrade.

étang Small lake.

Etchells, Frederick (1886–1973) English architect/painter/pioneer of *International *Modernism, evident in his Crawford's Advertising Building, 223 High Holborn, London (1929–30): with chamfered corners, long uninterrupted bands of windows subdivided by steel *mullions, and white cement-rendered walls, it was one of the earliest paradigms of the style to be built in England. Etchells also designed 38 Chapel Street, Westminster (1934), and several buildings on the Grosvenor Estate, Westminster. He is best remembered for translating Le *Corbusier's *Vers une architecture* as *Towards a New Architecture* (1927) and *Urbanisme* as *The City of Tomorrow and Its Planning* (1929): the changes of titles enhanced the messianic/polemical texts. With the Dean of Chester, **George William Outram Addleshaw** (1906–82), he wrote *The Architectural Setting of Anglican Worship* (1948), a thoughtful book that became a classic.

Etchells (1947, 1989); Etchells & Addleshaw (1948)

Ethiopian architecture C5 and C4 BC stone-built *temples in the Melazo region and in Yeha, and the large *Ta'aka Maryam* palace, Aksum (c.C1 BC–AD C5—with a central *pavilion on a high *podium approached by monumental stairs surrounded by ranges of subsidiary buildings on all four sides), have been excavated. The city of Aksum also possessed large *necropoleis, with many granite *stelai*. From c.C10 to C15 or later, *rock-cut churches were created, and hundreds survive, the most sophisticated of which are free-standing *monoliths (e.g. the church of *Beta Giyorgis*, with a Greek-cross plan, crosses in relief on its flat roof, and some *ogee-headed windows, the whole set in a deep pit). Such buildings are sometimes called *Coptic.

J.T (1996)

étoile French for *star*, so a *circus where several straight paths converge, esp. in a wood. *See* ROND-POINT.

Etruscan architecture Surviving buildings of ancient Etruria (now approximating to Tuscany and part of central Italy) are not numerous, but Etruscan design is important for the part it played in the evolution of *Roman architecture.

Structures were mostly of wood, clay, *rubble, and *terracotta, stone being reserved for *temple-bases, fortifications, and tombs. The finest surviving Etruscan architecture consists of city-walls and *rock-cut tombs (of which the best examples (C6 to C4 BC) are at Cervéteri, Chiusi, Corneto Tarquinia, and Perugia): a few arched town-gateways still stand, e.g. *Falerium Novum* (Fáleri—c.250 BC) and Perugia (c.300 BC). From C6 BC a temple type evolved consisting of a central *cella flanked by two *alae and a very deep *portico, often *tetrastyle, and with widely spaced timber columns (normally short and without *flutes) carrying a low-pitched wooden roof structure. These columns were the prototypes of the Roman-*Tuscan *Order, and the very wide *intercolumniation made possible by timber construction clearly influenced Roman column spacing. Superstructures were often enriched with terracotta *claddings (e.g. Portonaccio Temple, Veii (late C6 BC)). Tombs were richly decorated and coloured, and constitute the most substantial Etruscan architectural legacy. The '*Etruscan style*' was prompted by widespread C18 archaeological activity associated with *Neo-Classicism (e.g. at *Herculaneum and *Pompeii). Many collections were made of black-and-red vases (then thought to be Etruscan, but many were actually Greek), greatly admired for their elegance, shape, decorations, and, not least, for the ithyphallic aspects of many of the figures: images of them, notably by **Francesco Bartoli** (*fl.*1706-30), the **Comte de Caylus** (1692-1765), and **Bernard de Montfaucon** (1655-1741), were published, making them familiar throught Europe. In particular de Caylus's *Recueil d'antiquités égyptiennes, étrusques, grecques, romaines et gauloises* (1752-67) had an enormous influence on the development of Neo-Classicism and on the evolution of the *Egyptian and *Greek Revivals as well as the creation of the 'Etruscan' style of interior decoration, involving the use of much red, black, and white, with griffins, harpies, lions, *sphinxes, *medallions, *festoons, *bell-flowers, tripods, *urns, chimeras, and light, delicate details derived from *Antique sources and *Renaissance *grotesque ornament. The C18 *Etruscan style* first emerged in France in the reign of *Louis Seize*, and was used by Robert *Adam for the Etruscan Room, Osterley House, Middlesex (1775). By then, what was known as the *style étrusque* owed much to Pompeii and Herculaneum, with some Greek influences: the actual Etruscan influence was tenuous.

B & W-P (1970); COF (1988); G.Dennis (1883); H.Gray (1840); D.S.R (1945); L & D (1986); Toynbee (1971); J.T (1996)

Etty, John (c.1634-1708) York architect/builder involved at Londesborough House (1672-3), Temple Newsam, Leeds (1674), Newby Hall

(1693), Acomb Grange (1694-6), and Sprotborough Hall (c.1696-1700), all Yorks. His third son, **William Etty** (c.1675-1734), acted as Clerk of Works for Colen *Campbell at Newby (now Baldersby) Park (1720-1), and for *Vanbrugh at Castle Howard, Yorks. (from 1701) and Seaton Delaval, Northum. (from 1719). He laid out the park at Temple Newsam (1712), and designed the front of Barrowby Hall, Yorks. (1718-20). On his death, *Hawksmoor arranged for **John Etty** (1705-38) to be employed at Castle Howard.

Co (2008)

eucharistic window *Hagioscope or *lychnoscope.

Eulalius (*fl.*C6) Possible inventor of the *Byzantine cross-plan or *quincunx with five domes, at the Church of the Holy Apostles, Constantinople (536-45—destroyed), the prototype of *San Marco*, Venice (begun c.1063).

Drachmann (1963); Mango (1986)

Eupolemos of Argos (*fl.*430-410 BC) Architect of the *Doric *Heraion*, Argos, Greece (c.416 BC), of which only the foundations survive.

D (1950)

Euripus 1. Formal stretch of water in a Roman garden, often flanked by architectural constructions, statuary, etc., as at the *Canopus* of the *Villa Adriana*, Tivoli (134-8). 2. Ditch or *canal around an arena in a Roman *amphitheatre to deter the escape of wild animals and to separate spectacle from spectators.

J.Curl (2005); Roullet (1972)

eustyle *See* INTERCOLUMNIATION.

Eveleigh, John (*fl.*1756-after 1825) Possibly the 'Eveley' apprenticed to *Paine (1756), he established himself as an architect/builder in Bath, where he worked independently and sometimes with *Baldwin. Uninhibited stylistically, he often designed for speculative builders: works included Camden Crescent (c.1787-8); Somerset Place (begun 1790); and parts of Upper Camden Place (early C19). He was also responsible for Bailbrook House, Batheaston, Som. (1789-93); a house in Englishcombe, Som. (1789); and a row of houses at Trowbridge, Wilts. (c.1788). Bankrupted (1793), he moved to Plymouth, Devon, where he designed the *Gothic Guildhall (1800—demolished 1941).

Co (2008); Ison (1969)

Evelyn, John (1620-1706) English scholar/diarist/gardener/founder-member of The Royal Society. Having judiciously removed himself from England during the Civil War, he travelled on the Continent (1643-7, 1649-52), where he absorbed much information. He settled in Sayes Court, Deptford (then Kent), where he landscaped the grounds: he also designed gardens for his brother's property at Wotton House, Surrey, and laid out (from 1677) gardens at Albury Park, Surrey. He was involved at Cornbury House, Oxon. (1664, 1680s), and Euston Hall, Suffolk (1671), where he employed straight *avenues (a term he promoted). Very little of these works survives. In his *Fumifugium; or the inconveniencies of the aer and smoak of London dissipated, together with some remedies...* (1661) he proposed expelling noxious trades from the City of London, forming extra-mural *cemeteries, and designing urban squares planted with trees and sweet-smelling flowers. His *Sylva* (1664), a treatise on arboriculture, was probably intended as part of an ambitious encyclopaedia of gardening, and in the same year he published *A Parallel of Ancient Architecture with the Modern* (a translation of *Fréart de Chambray's Parallèle...*) in which he argued for the formal teaching of architecture: it also included a glossary of terms. He advised (1666) *Wren on the rebuilding of St Paul's Cathedral, and prepared a plan for a new City of London after the Fire which included using the rubble to extend the City into the Thames, straighten the shoreline, and create grand buildings along the river-front: his proposals fell on deaf ears. He published translations of various French works on the subject of gardens and gardening, and prepared a vast work, 'Elysium Britannicum', published posthumously. His son, **John Evelyn** (1655–99) published (1672) *Of Gardens*, a translation of **René Rapin**'s (1621–87) volume.

H & W (1988); *ODNB* (2004); O'Malley *et al.* (eds) (1998); Shoe (2001); Tay (2006)

Everard, Robert (*fl.*1440–85) English master-mason, he seems to have succeeded *Woderofe at Norwich Cathedral (*c.*1453), where he designed the stone *spire and the *nave *vault (*c.*1463–72). His *Perp. *lierne* vaults are widely regarded as among the finest of their type.

J.Harvey (1987)

excubitorium 1. Roman *dormitory for *vigiles* (night-watchmen). **2.** As *watching-loft.

exedra, exhedra 1. Passage, *colonnade, *portico, or other outdoor element, often fitted with seats, where debate/conversation could occur. **2.** Large semicircular *niche-like building with stone seats ranged around the walls, sometimes with a hemi-dome over, resembling a large *apse, often with its axis related to a larger space. **3.** Semicircular low wall with seats on the concave side so that the wall acts as the seat-backs.

4. Place in a garden partially enclosed by a semi-circular hedge, walls, etc.

exonarthex *Narthex outside the main *façade of a church, usually part of a colonnaded or arcaded *atrium or *quadriporticus.

exotic Belonging to, or suggesting, another, distant, unfamiliar country, so introduced from abroad; not indigenous, e.g. *Chinoiserie, *Hindoo, *Japonaiserie, etc.

Experimental architecture Architecture that questions concepts/limitations, committed to experimentation with form, materials, technology, constructional methodology, and even social structure. The title of a book (1970) by **Peter Frederic Chester Cook** (1936–), it identified certain architects, including *Goff, *Price, the *Smithsons, *Soleri, and groups (e.g. *Archigram), as involved in Experimental architecture.

J.Burns (1976z); P.Cook (1970); *DQ*, lxxviii/lxxix (1970), 29–30; Feuerstein (1988); Haus-Rucker-Co (1984)

Expressionism Artistic movement (*c.*1905–*c.*1930) in Northern Europe, especially in Germany and The Netherlands, it was concerned in architecture not to emphasize *function*, but to create free and powerful sculptural forms, often crystalline, sometimes sharply angular, and occasionally stalactitic. In The Netherlands it was associated with the *Amsterdam School, and characteristic works were housing by de *Klerk and the *Scheepvaarthuis* (1913–17) in Amsterdam. In Denmark an Expressionist manifestation (with a pronounced *Gothic flavour) was the Grundtvig Church, Copenhagen (1913–26), by *Jensen-Klint. In Germany, however, there were several outstanding examples: the water-tower and exhibition-hall (1911) at Posen (now Poznań), with a polygonal steel structure resembling crystalline hexagonal forms, by *Poelzig; the glass pavilion, *Werkbund Exhibition, Cologne (1914), by Bruno *Taut; the *Grosses Schauspielhaus*, Berlin (1918–19—destroyed), with its interior resembling a cave of stalactites, by Poelzig; the Einstein Tower, Potsdam (1919–21), by *Mendelsohn; the *Chile-Haus*, Hamburg (1922–3), by *Höger; the administrative building of the Hoechst Dyeworks (1920–5), by *Behrens; the churches of *Bartning; some churches by Dominikus *Böhm; certain works by *Bellot; and the farm buildings, Gut Garkau, by *Häring. The *Goetheanum*, Dornach, Switzerland (1924–8), by Rudolf *Steiner, was one of the greatest works of the movement. Some of Gottfried *Böhm's architectural language derived from Expressionism.

COF (1988); L (1988); Pehnt (1973); U.Schneider (1999); Sharp (1967); Wit & Casciato (1986)

external angle When two lines meet at an angle an *internal (*re-entrant) angle and an *external* angle (*salient) are formed.

extrados *See* ARCH.

extruded corner Projection from the inner corner of a *court or at the junction of a main block and a projecting *wing, often containing a *stair, carried above the roof-line. Also called *angle-tower*, common in C16 and C17 architecture.

Eyck, Aldo van (1918–99) Dutch architect, he set up his own practice (1952), and entered into partnership (1971–82) with **Theo Bosch** (1940–94). A committed *Modernist (a member of *Team X), he insisted on structural and practical adaptability, as in his Municipal Orphanage, Amsterdam (1957–60), which embraced forms of various sizes flowing into each other within a quadrangular frame, creating a complex mnemonic of various urban spaces. Other works include the Arnhem Sculpture Pavilion, in which the circular plan was subdivided by straight and semicircular partitions (1966), the *Pastoor van Arskerk*, The Hague (1968–70), and a Conference Centre and Restaurant, Noordwijk (1984–9). His work has been classified within *Structuralism, and he published many polemical articles.

Blijstra (1962); P.Bu (1989); Wi.Cu (1996); Js (1973a); Lefaivre & Tzonis (1999); Ligtelijn (1999); Strauven (1998)

eye 1. *Oculus, or any circular element placed in the centre of something, e.g. a bull's-eye circular window in the middle of the *tympanum of a *pediment. **2.** Circular or nearly circular central part of a *volute, as in an *Ionic *capital. **3.** Very small, more or less triangular, light in *Gothic *tracery. **4.** Circular base or rim of a *cupola, i.e. the circle from which the domed part springs. *Compounds include*:

eyebrow: **1.** *fillet; **2.** *hood-moulding or *label; **3.** low *dormer with no cheeks or sides on a pitched roof, the roof-covering rising in a concave curve, then convex over its top, then falling away in a concave curve on the other side, like an eyebrow;

eyebrow window: **1.** window in an *eyebrow dormer; **2.** window-light hinged at the bottom in a semicircular-topped opening;

eye-form: *vesica piscis or *fish-bladder form serving as small *lights in *Gothic *tracery of the *Second-Pointed *Curvilinear and *Flamboyant styles;

eyelet: small aperture in a wall, such as a miniature *loop-hole.

eye-catcher *folly, *ruin, *temple, or other structure in a landscape, such as a *gloriette*, drawing the eye to a desired point.

Eynsham, Henry de (*fl.*1290s–1345) English mason, he worked at Caernarfon Castle, Wales, in the first years of C14, and was in charge of important repairs at Clarendon Palace (1316–17) before building a great tower at Pontefract Castle, Yorks. (1323–6). Engaged (from *c.*1328) in building at Spalding Priory, Lincs., he seems to have remained there for the rest of his life. He was versatile, being engaged in architectural work for military/civil/ecclesiastical buildings. He probably began his career at the *Benedictine Abbey, Eynsham, Oxon., in the early 1290s, hence his surname.

J.Harvey (1987)

Eyre, Wilson (1858–1944) American architect, he worked with **James Peacock Sims** (1849–82) in Philadelphia, PA, when he was influenced by Norman *Shaw and the *Queen-Anne movement in England, as can be seen in the design of The Anglecot, 401 East Evergreen Avenue, Philadelphia (1883—much altered). By the late 1880s his work was becoming more free, influenced by the *Shingle style (e.g. the C.B.Moore house, 1321 Locust Street, Philadelphia (1891)). He also employed an agreeably eclectic *Arts-and-Crafts manner, as in the Mask and Wig Club, 311 South Camac Street, Philadelphia, and turned to *Colonial Revival (e.g. Neill and Mauran houses, 315–17 South 22nd Street, Philadelphia (1891)). More grand yet *Picturesque was his Jeffords house, Glen Riddle, PA (1917). His work exercised a powerful influence on subsequent generations of architects in Pennsylvania.

V.J.Sy (1971); J.T (1996); Tatman & Moss (1985)

Eyserbeck, Johann Friedrich (1734–1818) German landscape-gardener, known primarily for his work at the *park of *Schloss Wörlitz*, near Dessau. This was one of the most important and beautiful of the C18 *Enlightenment, designed for the Prince of *Anhalt-Dessau in collaboration with *Erdmannsdorff and the gardeners *Schoch: the intention was exemplary and mnemonic with its series of allusions in its *fabriques*, including an iron bridge based on the original by T.F.*Pritchard in Salop. (1775–9), a *Rousseauinsel* based on the *Île des Peupliers* at Ermenonville, France, and a *Synagogue (to demonstrate freedom from bigotry).

R.Alex (ed.) (1986, 1988); J.Curl (2011); *GH*, xxiv/2 (1996), 221–36; Kleinschmidt & Bufe (1997)

Eyton, William de (*fl.c.*1310–36) English master-mason, he worked at Lichfield Cathedral, Staffs., at least from *c.*1310 when the *Lady Chapel was designed, with its *vault and the eastern *bays of the *chancel-*aisles.

J.Harvey (1987)

Fabiani, Max (1865-1962) Slovenian architect, pupil of Otto *Wagner: from 1899 he was a senior member of Wagner's office, mostly responsible for the *Portois & Fix* Department Store (1899) and the *Artaria* Apartment Block (1900), both in Vienna. As personal architectural adviser to the heir to the Throne, **Archduke Franz Ferdinand** (1863-1914), he had considerable influence. Most of his important buildings, however, were designed after the 1914-18 war in Ljubljana and Trieste, and he prepared master-plans for Ljubljana, Gorizia (near Trieste), and elsewhere.

Pozzetto (1966, 1979)

fabric 1. Structural parts of a building, as opposed to furniture or movable fittings. **2.** Building, including windows, doors, and finishes. *Urban fabric* means the streets, buildings, open spaces, etc., making up a town or part of a town. **3.** Factory.

fabrique Building in a landscaped garden, such as an *eye-catcher, *folly, *temple, etc. A French term (*c.*1770), it suggests a small *Picturesque building intended as an ornament in a park in the English style, and stems from images of buildings in landscape-paintings: importantly, it had emotional and mnemonic aspects, intended to trigger associations and allusions, and although some English examples (e.g. at Stowe, Bucks.) were also intended to do the same, the emphasis was greater on the Continent.

façade External *face or *elevation of a building, especially the principal front.

Façadism Retention of the front or exterior of a building even though the interior is completely gutted: this may be because of the contribution the exterior or the *façade makes to street or *townscape. Purists might question the wisdom of Façadism, but there is no doubt that places such as the terraces around Regent's Park, London, would be the poorer had the works by *Nash and others been completely demolished.

J.Ri (1994)

face Dressed or finished external plane of a wall, piece of *masonry, brick, etc., intended to be seen.

face-work *or* **facing** Better type of material and finish masking an inferior one, generally applied in a thin layer, such as *ashlar (known as *bastard ashlar*) to brickwork, etc.

factable Erroneous term for *fractable.

Fahrenkamp, Emil (1885-1966) German architect, assistant to and then successor of *Kreis at the School of Applied Arts and the Academy of Arts, Düsseldorf. He designed factories and administration buildings for the Rhine Steel Corporation in several cities (1920s), the *I.G.Farben* power-station, Frankfurt-am-Main (1945-56), and several churches, including those for the Lutherans at Düsseldorf (1926) and Essen (1927).

Heuter (2002); Hoff (1928); Rittich (1938)

Faid'herbe, Lucas (1617-97) Architect, trained in Rubens's studio in Antwerp. He designed the Church of *Onze-Lieve-Vrouw van Hanswijk* (1663-87) and other *Baroque churches in Mechelen, Belgium.

PM; Nein *et al.* (eds) (1997)

faïence Earthenware, essentially a type of *terracotta, covered with an opaque coating called *enamel*, usually coloured, glazed, and twice fired, used for *face-work.

Fairbairn, Sir William, Bt. (1789-1874) Scots engineer, he assisted Robert *Stephenson in the design of the bridges over the Menai Straits and at Conway, describing his contributions in *An Account of the Construction of the Britannia and Conway Tubular Bridges . . .* (1849). His numerous publications on various practical matters concerned with iron construction contributed to advances in engineering.

Fairbairn (1849, 1869, 1870); Fairbairn & Pole (1970); *ODNB* (2004)

falchion As *mouchette*.

Falconetto, Giovanni Maria (1468-1535) Verona-born architect/painter. His work suggests the Roman *Classicism of *Bramante and *Raphael, and he was an important practitioner of the style in Northern Italy. His garden-houses, the *Loggia Cornaro* and *Odeon* (1524), now part of the *Palazzo Giustiniani*, Padua, pre-date designs by *Palladio and *Sansovino, yet have architectural characteristics of the later masters' works. He was involved in the design of the *Villa dei Vescovi*, Luvigliano, near Padua (*c.*1529–35), which has a sophisticated arched loggia of remarkable architectural quality. He designed the handsome town-gates (*Porta di San Giovanni* (1528) and *Porta di Savonarola* (1530)) and worked on the *Cappella del Santo* (from 1533) in *Sant'Antonio*, all in Padua.

Boucher (1998); He (1996); Lotz (1977); P.Mu (1986); Puppi *et al.* (eds) (1994)

Falkner, Harold (1875–1963) English architect, most of whose work was realized in the Farnham-Godalming area of Surrey. An *Arts-and-Crafts designer, his work evolved into a *Colonial-Revival *Neo-Georgian style of fine quality, and then veered towards a *Free-*Tudor *vernacular (e.g. nine houses (1921–63) at Dippenhall, Farnham, some incorporating genuine *timber-framed buildings brought from elsewhere, including two Glos. barns placed end to end, called Burles (completed 1937)). Among Falkner's works may be cited the Town Hall (1930–4), the Lutyensque Swimming Pool (1897), the *Surrey & Hants News* office (1930s), all in Farnham; North Munstead farm, Munstead (*c.*1920); and Tancredsford, Tilford (*c.*1920). All his work was of the highest quality. He was a voluble critic of the *Modern Movement, and frequently attacked the architectural Establishment.

Osmond (2003)

false Anything that seems to be what it is not, such as a false or *pseudo-arch, false *Attic (wall concealing a roof, but not containing rooms), false door, or false front (*façade extending beyond the side walls and/or roof of the building to make a building seem grander than it is).

fan Shaped like the sector of a circle. *Compounds include*:

fan-light: **1.** glazed *light over a door, often with a semicircular or other type of curved top, with radiating glazing-bars suggesting the shape of an open fan, also called *sunburst-light*, common in British C18 houses. From *c.*1800 *batswing and teardrop designs were introduced; **2.** any glazed light over a door, fan-shaped or not, or any upper part of a window hinged to open;

fan-palm: palm with *palmate* leaves (*palmetto*);

fan-tracery: see TRACERY;

fan-vaulting: see VAULT.

Sambrook (1989)

fane 1. Pagan *temple, therefore a C18 garden *fabrique. **2.** *Weather-cock or -vane.

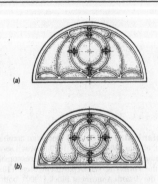

(a)

(b)

(c)

fanlight (*a*) Bat's-wing pattern, *c.*1820 (*after IJS*). (*b*) Teardrop, *c.*1820 (*after IJS*). (*c*) Grander C18 type over door set between margent-ornamented pilasters with margin-lights.

Fantastic architecture Eccentric, imaginative architecture, such as the later work of *Gaudí, Bruno *Taut, or Hans *Poelzig; futuristic high-technology megastructures (*see* HIGH TECH); *follies of an outlandish sort; or irrational structures, defying logic or considerations of use.

C & S (1960, 1962); Schuyt & Elffers (1980); Vostell & Higgins (1969)

Fanzago, Cosimo (1591–1678) Born in Clusone, near Bergamo, he became the most important exponent of *Baroque architecture in Naples from 1612, especially in his designs for *altars. He created a series of exuberant *façades for existing churches, notably the *Certosa di San Martino* (1623–56), with its *triumphal arch, *Santa Maria della Sapienza* (1638–53), with its triple-arched

275

Fathy, Hassan

loggia, and *San Giuseppe degli Scalzi*, Pontecorvo (1643-60). His huge unfinished but very original *Palazzo Donn'Anna*, Posilipo, near Naples (1642-4), is a gigantic *belvedere* of three stories of *loggie*, and has bevelled corners. His elaborate *Guglia di San Gennaro* monument (1637-60) is typical of his confidently triumphalist style.

Bt (1975); Fogaccia (1945); Winther (1973); Wi (1982)

Farleigh, Richard of (*fl.*1332-65) English mason, in charge of work at the Abbeys of Reading, Berks., and Bath, Som., before 1334, when he was appointed Master-Mason of Salisbury Cathedral. He probably built the great *tower and *spire at Salisbury, and may also have been responsible for the tower of Pershore Abbey, Worcs., as well as St Anne's Gate and Chapel at the Close, Salisbury (1350-4). He was Master of the Works at Exeter Cathedral, Devon (1352-3).

J.Harvey (1987)

Farnham, Richard de (*fl.*1242-7) Probably master-mason of the Chapel of the Nine Altars, Durham Cathedral (begun 1242), the design of which is attributed to Elias de *Dereham. He is described as *architector nove fabrice Dunelm* in a contemporary document, which points to considerable importance.

J.Harvey (1987)

Farrand, Beatrix Jones (1872-1959) American landscape-architect, niece of the writer **Edith Wharton** (1862-1937), who taught her about European gardens, she established (1896) her practice in NYC. She merged *Italianate and *English garden-design, as at Princeton University, NJ (1913-41), and Dumbarton Oaks, Washington, DC (1922-33). She designed The Eyrie, Seal Harbour, ME (1926-*c.*1939—which includes a moon-gate (**di xue*) and other allusions to *Chinese gardens), the grounds of Dartington Hall, Devon (1933-8), and the *campus of Yale University, New Haven, CT (1924-47).

B & K (2000); Brown (1995); McGuire & Fern (eds) (1982)

Farrer, Reginald John (1880-1920) English traveller/plant-collector, when very young he redesigned the Alpine-garden at the family home, Ingleborough, Clapham, Yorks. At Oxford (1898-1902) he assisted in the formation of the *rock-garden, St John's College, before setting off on the first of his journeys which led to the publication of *The Garden of Asia* (1904). This was followed by *My Rock Garden* (1907) and other books, culminating in the enormous *English Rock Garden* (1919), both of which helped to popularize such gardens and Alpines.

Farrer (1904, 1907, 1919); *ODNB* (2004); Tay (2006)

fasces Bundle of straight rods bound together, often around an axe. Roman emblem of legal power: it was frequently used in *Empire and Neo-Classical design, and was revived as an emblem of *Fascism* (which gets its name from *fasces*) in Italy.

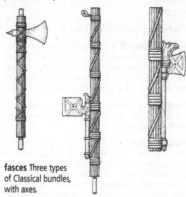

fasces Three types of Classical bundles, with axes.

fascia (*pl.* fasciae) 1. One of two or three *bands on a Classical *architrave, each projecting slightly beyond the one below, often separated by enriched *mouldings. 2. Any *band or belt with a plain vertical *face, such as a fascia-board at *eaves-level. 3. Deep board over a shop-front on which lettering is placed.

fastigium 1. Slope or fall of any surface or plane. 2. *Gable or *pediment. 3. Raking *mouldings, especially the *cyma, of a pediment. 4. *Canopy carried on four columns, esp. with a pedimented top. 5. *Ridge on a pitched roof. 6. *Acroterion block.

Fathy, Hassan (1900-89) Egyptian architect, he used traditional materials, means of construction, and *vernacular styles in his search for an inexpensive architecture for the poor. At New Gourna, Luxor (from 1945), he created a model village made of sun-dried bricks, and exploited traditional methods to encourage natural convection of cool air. He founded the International Institute for Appropriate Technology, Cairo (1977), intended to develop his ideas. His writings include *Architecture for the Poor* (1973) and *Natural Energy and Vernacular Architecture* (1986), and his individual dwellings include several houses (1945-79) outside Cairo. He also designed the Presidential Rest-House, Gharf Hussain (1981), and the Greiss house, Abu Sier (1984).

Hezel (1993); J.M.Ri *et al.* (1985); Sennott (ed.) (2004); Steele (ed.) (1994a, 1997)

Fatimid Islamic dynasty which ruled Egypt (969–1171). It founded the city of Cairo, and built the monumental *al-Azhar* (960–73) and *al-Hakim* (990–1013) *mosques, among many other works of architecture, including palaces (destroyed).

J.T (1996)

faubourg Medieval extra-mural suburb.

feather-edged 1. Horizontal timber board thicker at the bottom than at the top, i.e. tapered in *section, normally used for *clap-boarding. **2.** Type of *coping with one edge thicker than the other, draining in one direction.

feathering Arrangement of small *foils separated by *cusps, usually on the inner *mouldings of *Gothic arches.

Federal style Style of architecture/decoration prevalent in the USA from the Declaration of Independence (1776) to *c.*1830. It drew on aspects of *Palladianism, *Georgian architecture, the work of Robert *Adam, Freemasonic symbolism, and French styles, and, promoted by *Jefferson, *Neo-Classicism. *American Directoire* or *Directory* describes styles from *c.*1805–30 influenced by French *Directoire* and *Empire* taste.

L.Craig (1978); Franco (ed.) (1976); Garrett (1992); L & D (1986)

Fehling, Hermann (1909–96) German architect, he established (1953) a practice with **Daniel Gogel** (1927–97) in Berlin. Their Max Planck Institute for Educational Research, Berlin-Dahlem (1965–74), and European Southern Observatory, Garching, near Munich (1976–80), suggest aspects of *Expressionism and certain influences from *Scharoun, but the firm's work was stylistically varied.

E (1994); Pehnt (1970)

Fehn, Sverre (1924–2009) Norwegian architect. With *Korsmo and others he was a founder-member of the Norwegian division of *CIAM, the main aim of which was to oppose *New Empiricism and further the *Modern Movement. With **Geir Grung** (1926–89), he designed the House of Crafts, Maihaugen, Lillehammer (1949–56), and the Økern Home for the Elderly, Oslo (1955): the latter was conceived as a large, low-set concrete-and-glass block set in a mature park. In contrast, the Skådalen Residential School, Oslo (1976–7), was designed as a series of small blocks, constructed of red brick, timber, and *concrete. His *Hadmarksmuseet*, Hamar (1973), consisted of an addition to fragments of a medieval building, perhaps not as successful as some have claimed. He was responsible for the Norwegian Pavilion at the *Exposition Universelle*, Brussels (1958), and for the Scandinavian Pavilions at the Venice Biennales of 1959 and 1964.

N-S (1986b, 1997); N-S & Postiglione (1997); Sennott (ed.) (2004); Stiller (ed.) (2001); J.T (1996)

Feilden, Sir Bernard Melchior (1919–2008) English *conservation architect. He established (1952), with **David Mawson** (1924–2013), the Norwich practice of **Feilden & Mawson**. An early project (1962), was the saving of the *spire of Norwich Cathedral using stainless-steel wires, and this was followed by conservation-works at York Minister and St Paul's Cathedral, London (where he created a memorial chamber in the *crypt for the Empire's field-marshals). At Chesterfield, Derbys., he rescued the historic core of the town from destruction, and for this was awarded the Europa Nostra Silver Medal (1982). Involved throughout the 1960s and '70s at the Institute of Advanced Architectural Studies in the King's Manor, University of York (which his firm converted for this purpose from 1963), he was also connected with the Intergovernmental International Centre for the Study of the Preservation and Restoration of Cultural Property in Rome (ICCROM), and was a leading light in establishing (1972) the Conference on Training in Architectural Conservation (COTAC). Concerned with conservation projects throughout the world, he wrote several books, including *The Conservation of Historic Buildings* (1982), *An Introduction to Conservation* (1980), and *A Manual for the Management of World Cultural Heritage Sites* (1993). He was knighted (1985).

The Times (2 Dec. 2008), 66; pk

Feilden, Richard John Robert (1950–2005) English architect specializing in schools and promotion of *Environmentally Responsible Design. He established (1978) **Feilden Clegg** with **Peter Alexander Clegg** (1950–), later enlarged as **Feilden Clegg Bradley** when **Keith Bradley** became a partner. Among their works were the National Trust building at Swindon, Wilts., the Yorkshire Sculpture Park Centre, and the Arrivals Building, Earth Centre, Doncaster, Yorks. Feilden was also interested in Urban Regeneration.

The Guardian (12 Jan. 2005), Obits

Feldman, Anthony (1953–2005) Multi-talented South-Africa-born architect/interior designer/composer. Eclectic in tastes, and temperamentally unsympathetic to *Minimalism, an example of his work was for the Royal Asiatic Society's premises in Pentonville. London, in which the diluted spirit of *Soane could be detected by some, but he also designed a Cube House, Hampstead, London, and a dwelling in *Art-Nouveau style in Budapest.

The Times (18 Jan. 2006), 65

Félibien des Avaux, André (1619-95) French architect/writer, his *Des Principes de l'architecture...avec un dictionnaire des termes propres...*(1676) was one of the most important reference works of its time. His son, **Jean-François Félibien des Avaux** (*c.*1656-1733), published (1699) a somewhat unreliable work on the lives and works of celebrated architects, which, nevertheless, contained a synoptic discussion of *Gothic and *Islamic architecture, one of the first printed attempts to do so.

Félibien (1687, 1699); Ha (1948)

Fellner, Ferdinand (1847-1916) Viennese architect/critic. He specialized in theatre design, and, influenced by *Semper, used *Renaissance and *Baroque languages, and, later, *Jugendstil. He designed and built some fifty theatres and concert-halls, including the *Deutsches Volkstheater*, Vienna (1887-9), the *Stadttheater*, Graz (1898-9), the *Jubiläums-Stadttheater*, Baden-bei-Wien (1908-9), and the *Stadttheater*, Klagenfurt (1909-10), all in Austria, and all with **Hermann Gottlieb Helmer** (1849-1919).

Dienes (ed.) (1999); H-C.Ho (1966); Wurm-Arnkreuz (1919)

femerall, femerell, fomerell, fumerell *Louvred *lantern or other device placed on a roof over a hall for ventilation or to permit the escape of smoke (a common medieval arrangement before *chimneys became usual).

femme-fleur *Dream-maiden* with long strands of hair resembling vegetation tendrils, often intertwined with marine-like plant-forms, found in *Art-Nouveau designs.

T-M (1967)

femur Flat vertical *face of a *Doric *triglyph between pairs of channels (*glyphs*).

fence 1. Defence, bulwark, or means of providing security. **2.** *Enclosure or barrier (e.g. *rail, *palisade, etc.) along the boundary of a park, field, etc., or any place to protect it from intruders or to define limits. It can take various forms and be made of many materials, and may display stylistic motifs, e.g. *Chinese fret.

fenestella 1. Small opening (*cataracta* or *foramen*) in an *altar or *shrine affording a view of the Relics within. **2.** *Niche in the south wall of a *chancel containing the *piscina and (sometimes) *credence-table. **3.** Opening for a bell in a *bellcote over a *gable.

fenestral 1. Window-blind of paper or oiled cloth in place of *glass. **2.** *Shutter.

fenestration Pattern formed by or arrangement of windows in a building *façade.

feng shui Literally 'wind-water', it refers to ancient Chinese beliefs (called *geomancy*) that vital currents present within the earth can influence the quality of human life, and so should be taken into account when designing, siting, and orientating buildings, especially houses or tombs. Dwellings, for example, should be protected from the west and should have their main *façades to the south; there must be heavy barriers to prevent the entry of evil spirits (which are held to proceed in straight lines); and buildings should respond to the surrounding topography as well as to winds and waters. Interestingly, many aspects of C21 *environmental design in the West would appear to support certain principles of *feng shui*.

Keswick (1986); Lip (1995); Sennott (ed.) (2004); J.T (1996); Wang (1998); Waring (1993)

Fenoglio, Pietro (1865-1927) Italian architect, he designed the *Casa Besozzi, Corso Siccardi*, Turin (1904—a *Renaissance-style *palazzo* flanked by *castellated *pavilions with *Neo-Romanesque openings), and numerous essays in the *Stile Liberty*, of which the *Palazzina Scott, Corso Lanza*, and *Casa Fenoglio, Corso Francia/Via Principi d'Acaja* (both Turin, and both 1902-3), are examples.

Bolletino della Società Piemontese di Archeologia e Belle Arti, n.s., **xiv/xv** (1960-1), 125-34; Nelva & Signorelli (1979)

fereter 1. Permanent or portable *shrine containing Relics. **2.** Construction of a funerary type or association, such as a *catafalque or tomb-chest. A *feretory*, therefore, is a place in a church or chapel, usually defined, e.g. with a *screen, containing a fereter.

Fergusson, James (1808-86) Scots architectural writer, his first books were *Illustrations of the Rock-Cut Temples of India* (1845), and *Picturesque Illustrations of Ancient Architecture in Hindostan* (1847): he prepared his own illustrations (including measured drawings), establishing a name for himself as an authority on Indian architecture. He published (1849) *Historical Inquiry into the True Principles of Beauty in Art, more especially with reference to architecture*: it included some of the earliest expositions of themes he was later to develop, e.g. the means by which Greek temples were illuminated. He brought out (1840s and 50s) papers on fortifications as well as on the topography of Jerusalem which prompted surveys of the city: later (1878), he published a book on Jewish *temples and other buildings. His major work was *A History of Architecture in All Countries*. This began as *Illustrated Handbook of Architecture* (1855) and *History of the Modern Styles* (1862), which were revised and brought out as the 2-volume *History* (1865-7), later augmented by a volume on Indian and

Eastern architecture (1876), and a re-working of *Modern Styles*. The first comprehensive study of the subject, it was appreciated for its accuracy, and especially for the quality of its many excellent illustrations, even though Fergusson was given to speculation and dogmatic opinions: he held, e.g., that structure was the prose and ornament the poetry of architecture. He denounced 'servile copying', thought the *Gothic Revival a 'standing insult' to the age, felt industrial architecture and engineering (notably lighthouses) encapsulated architectural achievements of the time, and believed architects had 'ceased to think' (what he would have made of C21 architects can only be guessed). He designed the North Gallery in the Royal Botanic Gardens, Kew, Richmond upon Thames (1879-82), paid for by **Marianne North** (1830-90) to house her own rather wonderful 848 botanical paintings (1872-85), and demonstrating his theory of lighting temples through *clerestoreys. The building also has a *verandah around three sides of the exterior, suggested to both Fergusson and North by their experiences in India. Awarded (1871) the Gold Medal of the RIBA, by the end of his life Fergusson was being compared with *Vitruvius: **Heinrich Schliemann** (1822-90), archaeologist and discoverer of Troy, dedicated his book on Tiryns to Fergusson.

J.Fergusson (1845, 1847, 1847a, 1849, 1851, 1855, 1862, 1865-7, 1874, 1876, 1878, 1883); *JSAH*, **xvii**/4 (Winter 1958), 25-30; MacLeod (1971); *ODNB* (2004)

ferme ornée Farm designed for both utility and beauty, the buildings treated decoratively and contributing to the aesthetic effect within a *Picturesque landscape. *See* COT.

fernery, fern-house, *or* **filicetum** 1. *Collection* of ferns, or the *place* where ferns are grown, especially *rock- and *woodland-gardens, popular in the *Victorian period. 2. *Glass-house or *conservatory to house ferns brought from warm climes: exemplars include structures at Tatton Park, Ches. (*c.*1859—by *Paxton); Ashridge Park, Herts. (1864—by M.Digby *Wyatt); Ascog Hall, Bute (*c.*1879—a glass-roofed *grotto, probably by **Edward La Trobe Bateman** (1816-97), restored 1995-6); and the building at Rippon Lea, Melbourne, Australia (*from* 1874—created on his estate by **Sir Frederick Thomas Sargood** (1834-1903)).

Shoe (2001); Symes (2006); Tay (2006)

Ferrey, Benjamin (1810-80) English architect, he became a zealous pioneer of the *Gothic Revival, much influenced by A.W.N.*Pugin, having been articled (1825) to A.C.*Pugin. His Church of St Stephen, Westminster (1847-50), was one of the most significant ecclesiastical buildings of the early Revival, its hard interior a model for later work, and was justly appreciated by *The*

Ecclesiologist, which recognized him as one of the ablest contemporary Goths. St Michael's, Chetwynd, Salop. (1865-7), demonstrated his *archaeological approach, drawing on elements derived from several historic buildings. He wrote *Recollections of A.W.N.Pugin* (1861). His son, **Edmund Benjamin Ferrey** (*c.*1845-1900), worked with him (1862-9) before joining 'Great' *Scott and then establishing his own practice.

B *et al.* (2001); B.Clarke (1969); J.Curl (2007); D & M (1985); Ea (1970)

Ferriss, Hugh (1889-1962) Distinguished American architectural visionary draughtsman, his images of *skyscrapers in which ornament was suppressed were influential, and best seen in *The Metropolis of Tomorrow* (1929). His *Power in Buildings: An Artist's View of Contemporary Architecture* (1953) was an important record of some of his later work.

Ferriss (1929, 1953); Leich (1980); Sennott (ed.) (2004)

ferro-concrete *See* REINFORCED CONCRETE.

Ferstel, Heinrich, Freiherr von (1828-83) Austrian architect, he designed the twin-towered *Gothic Revival *Votivkirche* (1856-82) and various other *Historicist buildings, including the vast Italian *Renaissance-Revival University (1873-84), Vienna. Much of his important work (where the influence of *Semper is often clear) was done for the area adjoining the *Ringstrasse*, but he also designed many buildings throughout the Austro-Hungarian Empire. An advocate of housing reform, he admired English low-density developments, which influenced the *Cottageverein* (Cottage Association), Vienna (1872-4), responsible for building small single-family houses. Ferstel also promoted the laying out of the *Türkenschanzpark*, a *public park on English lines (from 1883). Among his publications, *Über Styl und Mode* (1883) is revealing of his attitudes.

Eitelberger & Ferstel (1860); W-R (1970); Wibiral & Mikula (1974)

Festival of Britain National celebratory event throughout the United Kingdom (1951) which brought *Modernism to the attention of the public, popularizing certain aspects and motifs that recurred in design over the following decade. Plans were laid by the then Labour Government, and (Sir) **Gerald Reid Barry** (1898-1968) was appointed Director-General. Partly inspired by the success of the 1851 Great Exhibition, the Festival was later said to be a 'manifestation of gaiety and ordered imagination in a world ... short of both'. Its centrepiece was a major exhibition on the South Bank of the Thames in London housed in various purpose-built structures, the whole architectural development under the direction of *Casson. While the exhibition was intended to encourage national achievements, inventions, and so on, attracting custom from abroad, thereby improving morale and the economy after the economic doldrums following the 1939–45 war, it also offered an opportunity to show off modern architecture, design, and planning principles. Of all the structures on the site, only the Royal Festival Hall (by Leslie *Martin, Robert *Matthew, and a large team) remains, although the riverfront was later extended and altered. The main buildings were the Dome of Discovery (**Ralph Tubbs** (1912–96)), the administrative block (*Fry, *Drew, and **Edward David Mills** (1915–98)), the Skylon (*Powell & Moya with *Samuely), the Minerals and Land Pavilion (*Architects' Co-Partnership), the Natural Scene and the Country (*O'Rorke and **Frederick Henri Kay Henrion** (1914–90)), the Power and Production Pavilion (*Grenfell Baines and **Heinz J. Reifenberg** (1894–1968)), the Sea and Ships Pavilion (*Spence), the Transport exhibit (**Arcon**), the Lion and Unicorn Pavilion (**Robert Yorke Goodden** (1909–2002) and **Richard Drew Russell** (1903–81)), and the Land of Britain (**Henry Thomas Cadbury-Brown** (1913–2009)).

Ba & Hillier (eds) (1976)

festoon Classical ornament representing drapes, flowers, foliage, and fruit, depicted as a *swag hanging in a natural *catenary curve from two points on the same horizontal plane, and tied at each end with ribbons. It is light and narrow at the points of suspension and thick and heavy in the middle.

festoon (*after Normand*).

Feszl, Frigyes (1821–84) Hungarian architect, pupil of von *Klenze and *Gärtner (1839–41), he returned to Hungary where he built several houses in Budapest (e.g. Balassovits House, 57 Váci Street, Pest (1848–9)). He favoured an exotic version of the *Rundbogenstil he had absorbed when in Munich, mingling it with *Moorish and other elements, as in the Municipal Concert Hall, Budapest (1859–64). He was in partnership (1845–54) with **Lipót Kauser** (1818–77) and **Károly Gerster** (1819–67).

Merényi (1970); Rados (1975)

Feuerstein, Bedřich (1892–1936) Czech architect, associated with *Behne, *Chochol, and other members of the Prague avant-garde, he designed several important buildings after the formation of Czechoslovakia, including the Military Geographic Institute, Prague-Bubenec (1921–2), a somewhat heavy version of vaguely *stripped Classicism. His Nymburk Crematorium (1921–3—with **Bohumil Sláma** (1887–1961)) is regarded as one of his best buildings, reminiscent of the severe, stripped stereometrically pure forms advocated in the late C18, and influenced by *Purism. He later worked with *Perret in Paris and *Raymond in Tokyo (where he designed the Soviet Embassy (1928) and St Lucas Hospital (1928–30)).

Li (1996); Masaryková (1967)

Field, Horace (1861–1948) English architect, his work was often in a refined *Wrenaissance manner, e.g. Lloyd's Bank, Rosslyn Hill, London (1891), and the offices for the North Eastern Railway Company, York (1898–1906). With *Bunney, he compiled *English Domestic Architecture of the XVIIth and XVIIIth Centuries* (1905, 1928). He designed houses at Letchworth *Garden City, Herts., and Hampstead *Garden Suburb (with **Charles Evelyn Simmons** (1879–1952)), as well as churches at Eastriggs and Gretna in Scotland.

B-C (2014); A.S.Gray (1985); Me.Miller (2002); M & G (1992)

fielded Flat central raised part of a *panel thicker than the bevelled edges or margin.

fieldstone US term for *rubble.

Figini, Luigi (1903–84) Italian architect, a leading figure in *Rationalisim, he formed (1929) a partnership with **Gino Pollini** (1903–91), and, with *Terragni and others, founded (1926) *Gruppo 7*. He and Pollini were involved (1934–57) in the design and extension of the Olivetti Factory, Ivrea, where *Modern-Movement principles were applied. Their *Madonna dei Poveri* (1952–4), Milan, had themes drawn from industrial and administrative architecture adapted to a basilican arrangement.

Blasi (1963); E (1994); Savi (1980); Seta (1978)

Figueroa, Leonardo de (1650–1730) *Baroque architect, all his known buildings are in Seville, Spain, and feature yellow or white cut brickwork framed with red, glazed tiles. He favoured *Solomonic columns, *estípites, elaborately contorted *cornices, and much statuary and carved decoration, all mingled in unbridled freedom, with occasional touches of *mudéjar ornament. Examples of his designs include the *Hospital de los Venerables Sacerdotes* (1687–97) and the Churches of *La Magdalena* (1691–1709) and *San Salvador* (1696–1711). He was responsible for the west door of *San Telmo* (1724–34), and may have designed the outstandingly ornate and centralized *San Luis* (1699–1731—in which influences from *Borromini and *Rainaldi may be detected). His son, **Ambrosio** (1700–75), also worked in an ornate Baroque style in Seville (he designed *Santa Catalina* (1732)), and his grandson, **Antonio Matías** (c.1734–96), was responsible for the *campanile of *La Palma del Condado* (c.1780).

Bazin (1964); K & S (1959)

Figurative architecture Term apparently coined by Portoghesi to describe architectural design from the 1970s, influenced by *Graves, *Rossi, and others, in which attempts were made to restore the obscured meaning of *types found in traditional architecture, as in walls, columns, door-cases, *pediments, etc., after the jettisoning of so much by the *Modern Movement.

C.MacD et al. (1986); Pi (1983)

Filarete, Il (Antonio di Pietro Averlino (c.1400–69)) Florentine sculptor/architect, his pseudonym means 'Lover of Virtue' (or *Virtù*). His importance lies in his promotion of the early *Renaissance style, and in his *Trattato d'architettura* or *Libro architettonico* (1461–4), which was widely circulated, though not published until C19: *Vasari had no high opinion of it. It includes plans for ideal cities (*Sforzinda* and *Plousiapolis*) as well as an ingenious ten-storey House of Vice and Virtue complete with whore-house and *observatory. It also proposed (perhaps taking the basic idea from *Vitruvius) using the Greek *Orders to suggest social classes, a form of *Associationism. He seems to have designed Bergamo Cathedral (from 1455—extensively rebuilt in C17), but his major architectural work was the *Ospedale Maggiore (Cà Granda)*, Milan, designed on a complex symmetrical plan, only part of which was built, including *arcades (1456) rather coarser than *Brunelleschi's work in Florence. However, the idea of designing for the isolation of patients into wards probably makes the Milan building the first scientific modern hospital of our era, and was influential in the following centuries. He may have been involved in the design of the *Cà del Duca*, Venice (1445–61).

Filarete (1965); He (1996); *JWCI*, xxxiv (1971), 96–114, xxxv (1972), 391–7; P.Mu (1986); Onians (1988); Patetta (1987); Tigler (1963); E.Welch (1995)

fillet Small, narrow, flat *moulding, usually a plain *band in a group of mouldings, either of projecting rectangular *section or simply a flat surface between other mouldings, such as *flutes of a column-*shaft, or one of the elements of an *Attic base between the *torus* and *scotia*. It often defines, emphasizes, and clarifies mouldings, as at the top of a *cornice, above the *cyma recta*, where it is termed *list* or *listel*. An *annulet* is a

very small fillet, e.g. between the channels under the *echinus* of a *Doric *capital.

finger-plate Plate (of metal, porcelain, etc.) to protect the shutting-stile of a door from fingermarks. It may be associated with the door-knob or handle, or be separate.

finial *Boss, *crop, crope, *knob, or *pommel at the top of e.g. a *bench-end, canopy, *gable, *pinnacle, or *spire, usually decorated.

Gothic C14 finial, Wimborne, Dorset.

finial (*left*) Pine-cone. (*right*) Acorn.

Finlay, Ian Hamilton (1925–2006). Scots poet/garden-designer. From 1966 at Stonypath, near Dunsyre, Lanarkshire, in the Pentland Hills south-west of Edinburgh, this 'avant-gardener' (as he called himself) and his wife made a landscape-garden in which water, trees, and plants set off *fabriques, inscriptions cut in stone, architectural fragments, sundials, etc., creating an evocative place with many mnemonic triggers linking his work to C18 *Gardens of Allusion. Finlay called (1983) it 'Little Sparta', a sly reference to rivalry between Athens and Sparta, as Edinburgh was known as the 'Athens of the North'. Carving and fine lettering on the monuments were carried out by various artists, including **Michael Harvey** (1931–2013) and **Alexander Stoddart** (1959–). Extensions included a small English park (1990s) and a *hortus conclusus* (from 2006).

Finlay also created a 'Sacred Grove' in the grounds of the Kröller-Müller Museum, Otterloo, The Netherlands (1982), and *Fleur de l'Air*, a garden in Provence which, like Little Sparta, is haunted by the icy idealism of the French Revolution, so Beauty and Violence are juxtaposed.

Abrioux (1992); Finlay (2004); *The Guardian* (17 Nov. 2012), Obits; *JGH*, I/2 (April–June 1981), 113–144; Hunt (2008); Simig *et al.* (1995); Tay (2006); *The Times* (28 March 2006), 64

Finsterlin, Hermann (1887-1973) German designer of visionary buildings, many of which were published by Bruno *Taut and promoted by *Arbeitsrat für Kunst. Interest in his work was revived in the 1960s.

Frühlicht, iii (1922), 73ff.; P (1982); Ul.Schneider (1999)

Fioravanti, Aristotele (*c*.1415–86) Bolognese architect/engineer, he worked on many engineering problems in Bologna, Mantua, Venice, Rome, and Naples, and was in the service of the Sforzas in Milan (1458–64). In 1467 he was in Hungary, and spent the last decade of his life in Russia, working on various projects, including the Cathedral of the Dormition (or Assumption), Kremlin, Moscow (1475-9), in the *Byzantine style.

Arte Lombarda, xliv–xlv (1976), 35–70, 79–82; Beltrami (1912); J.T (1996)

fireplace Place created for the making of fires, especially open fires of coal, peat, timber, etc. Unlike the furnaces, stoves, or *hypocausts of the Romans, it was the hearth in the middle of an area. In an enclosed space of earlier times, the smoke escaped through openings of its covering (*see* FEMERALL; LOUVRE), and later through a smoke-shaft, or *chimney. The term implies a recess in a wall connecting with a flue above, although sometimes no recess was constructed: instead, a large *hood with a flue above projected from the *naked of the wall behind. Decoration of the fireplace was important from late-medieval and early-*Renaissance times.

Pa (from 1852); S (1901)

fire-temple There are about 50 fire-temples in Iran, associated with fire-worshipping Zoroastrianism. Generally square on plan, they consist of four massive *piers carrying an arch on each side (so called *chahār tāq*, meaning 'four-arched'), the whole composition roofed over with a *dome supported on *squinches. They are likely to be of the *Sassanian period. After the C7 Moslem invasion, many fire-temples were destroyed, but a few were converted into *mosques, and indeed some may have been the prototypes of prayer-halls.

J.T (1996)

firring, furring 1. Strips, usually of wood, applied to uneven walls, sagging *beams, etc., to support a finish, e.g. *plaster, to create a more even and uniform level surface. **2.** Short pieces of timber fixed to the feet of *rafters to project the *eaves beyond the *naked of the wall.

First Fruits Papal dues, subsequently paid to the Crown, essentially the first year's income of a *cure* (parish or other sphere of spiritual ministration), plus annual payment of a twentieth part of that income. Abolished in England (1704), in Ireland a **Board of First Fruits** was established (largely through the influence of **Jonathan Swift** (1667-1745)) to fund building and repair of churches and glebe-houses (parsonages) of the Church of Ireland (the Established (until 1871 by 32 & 33 Vict.,*c*.42) Anglican Church). The Board received substantial grants from the Irish Parliament during the late C18 and early C19, enabling an impressive building-programme to be undertaken. The functions and income of the Board passed (1833) to the Ecclesiastical Commissioners with the Whig Government's momentous *Church Temporalities (Ireland) Act* (3 & 4 Will. IV, *c*.37).

First Pointed Earliest (late-C12–late-C13) of the *Gothic styles, known in England as *Early English*. Good examples include much of Wells (from 1180), Lincoln (from 1192), and Salisbury (from 1220) Cathedrals. Gothic is characterized by the pointed arch and *vault. Windows started as apertures in a wall of the *lancet type, often very sharply pointed, or with blunter heads formed of equilateral arches. *Foil-arches occurred in some locations, and grander doorways (with numerous *Orders) were often divided in two with a central *pier or *shaft (*trumeau*) supporting a *tympanum ornamented with sculpture and associated with an almond-shaped (*mandala*) or *quatrefoil panel. *Mouldings of arches were often composed of contrasting concave and convex forms in *section, sometimes with *fillets, giving emphasis to light and shade, while detached *colonnettes or shafts of black or grey *marble, secured to piers at vertical intervals by *bands of a shaft*, enriched the architectural effect and accentuated verticality. Common ornament of horizontal mouldings (often on *capitals) was *nail-head, while the larger, sharper *dogtooth ornament usually occurred in *cavetto mouldings around doorways, windows, *niches, etc. Capitals, in their simplest form, were shaped like an inverted *bell, but more frequently were ornamented with vigorous stylized foliage of the *stiff-leaf, trefoil-leaf, or *volute type, deeply under-cut. *Bases of colonnettes or piers consisted of cylindrical forms with *torus mouldings and the occasional cavetto, displaying a debt to Classical architecture, just as the bell- and volute-capitals clearly were derived from *Antique Roman precedents. Vaulting was often employed

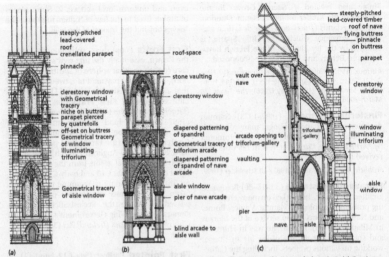

First Pointed Typical bay, Westminster Abbey, London. (*a*) External elevation. (*b*) Internal elevation. (*c*) Section.

for ceilings, ribbed vaults first occurring probably at Durham or in Lombardy: the pointed vault overcame the problems of covering rectangular areas using semicircular arches because the curved forms meeting at an apex were far more flexible and adaptable, the pointed apex being effectively the 'hinge', enabling arches to span from apex to springing without the awkward geometry and junctions inevitable when the *Romanesque semicircular arch was used. *Bosses were the usual ornament at the intersection of ribs. The outward-thrusting forces of heavy vaults had to be counteracted by means of deep *buttresses, which divided *façades into *bays, and were themselves capped by *gablets or *pinnacles designed as *clustered piers. Roofs, like Romanesque roofs, were steeply pitched, and in some cases (e.g. Lincoln Cathedral) increased in pitch to 70° or thereabouts. Circular windows of the *wheel* type were used, especially in *gables (e.g. north and south *transept walls), while other windows started out as the lancet, then evolved as two lancet-lights with a *roundel over, as in early plate-*tracery. Starting with Rheims Cathedral (1211), the moulded *bar *mullion was used to separate *lights, with the bars forming decorative patterns above, beginning with the simple *Geometrical type featuring circles, foils, and approximately triangular elements. By the time Geometrical bar-tracery was fully developed, the style merged with *Middle Pointed.

Gi (1986); J.Parker (1850); Rickman (1848)

Fischer, Heinrich Karl von (1782–1820) German architect, he settled in Munich (1796), where he designed the *Prinz-Karl-Palais* (1803–6), the first great Neo-Classical building in the Bavarian capital, with a fine *portico. He contributed to the considerable improvements in the planning of the city under **King Maximilian I Joseph** (*r*.1806–25), including the *Karolinenplatz* (1808–12), and the *Hoftheater* (1810–18—destroyed 1823 and rebuilt by von *Klenze, who retained parts of the exterior, then destroyed again in the 1939–45 war, and rebuilt as the *Nationaltheater*).

Hederer (1960); Ne (1982*a*)

Fischer, Johann Michael (1692–1766) German architect responsible for 32 churches, 23 monasteries, and many secular buildings in Bavaria in the *Rococo style. His *Benedictine Abbey-Churches of Zwiefalten (1741–64) and Ottobeuren (1748–68) are his masterworks, with two of the most frothy and exquisite Rococo interiors in all Germany (*stucco-work by **J.M.Feichtmayr** (1696–1772)), but each shows a powerful command of architectural form that is not lost in a welter of ornament. He fused longitudinal axes with central spaces at Rott-am-Inn (1759–63) and Berg-am-Laim (1738–51), and created a series of interpenetrating volumes each formed on elliptical or circular plans at Ottobeuren. At Zwiefalten, wall-piers define the chapels, *transepts flank the crossing-dome, and *choir and *sanctuary are set in an elongated space beyond the *crossing: galleries sway out into the *nave between the pairs of *engaged *scagliola columns. Other works include the churches at Altomünster (1763-6); Diessen (1732-9—with *high-altar by *Cuvilliés); Fürstenzell (1739-48); and Osterhofen (1726-40—with decorations by the *Asam brothers). Without exception, his churches are worthy of the closest study.

Bou (1962); Dischinger & Peter (eds) (1995, 1997); Hi (1968a); Lieb (1982)

Fischer, Theodor (1862-1938) German architect/teacher, a founding member of the *Werkbund (1907). His architecture often drew on *vernacular forms, as in the housing at Gmindersdorf, near Reutlingen (1903-8), and he insisted that the local landscapes and indigenous architectural character should be respected and enhanced. In this his ideas were related to those of *Sitte, but wholly repudiated by the *Modern Movement. He carried out expansion plans for several German cities, including Mannheim (1916) and Augsburg (1926), and designed workers' housing for various sites, including *Weberstrasse*, Stuttgart (1904-6), Langensalza (1907-8), and *Neu-Westend*, Munich (1909-10). He influenced *Bonatz, Bruno *Taut, *Mendelsohn, and *Oud. In his *Für die deutsche Baukunst* (1917) he advocated the study of construction and crafts, and denounced the excessive emphasis on mathematics, natural sciences, draughtsmanship, and 'design' in architectural education as it failed to inculcate any understanding of the handling of volumes. He was closely associated with *Heimatstil*, a South-German and Swiss *Arts-and-Crafts movement which reacted against the bullying dictatorship of *International Modernism.

T.Fischer (1903, 1917); Karlinger (1932); Ne (1988); Pfister (1968)

Fischer von Erlach, Johann Bernhard (1656-1723) Distinguished Austrian *Baroque architect, he studied in Rome from 1671, where he became acquainted with the work of *Bernini and Carlo *Fontana, and developed an interest in *Antique objects and architecture. After the defeat of the Turks (1683) and the rise of Austria as a European power, Fischer settled in Vienna. He designed *Schloss Frain*, Moravia (1688-95), with its elliptical hall clearly influenced by his Roman stay, and shortly afterwards he developed the theme in three Salzburg churches. At the elliptical *Dreifaltigkeitskirche* (1694-1702) the long axis is that of the entrance-*high-altar, while (owing a debt to *Guarini) twin towers flank a concave front (a theme derived from *Borromini and

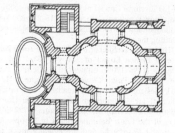

Plan of *Dreifaltigkeitskirche*, Salzburg, showing the concave front and elliptical space within.

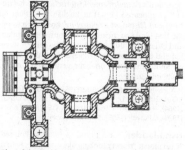

Plan of the *Karlskirche*, Vienna, showing the wide front with towers and *Solomonic/Trajanic* columns, *prostyle hexastyle portico* on a *podium*, and central ellipse.

*Rainaldi's *Santa Agnese*, Rome, although the middle of the *façade was influenced by the work of *Hardouin-Mansart, and the basic plan by *Vignola's *Santa Anna dei Palafrenieri*, Rome). His mastery of synthesis was demonstrated, and he may also have been influenced by *Zuccalli's Salzburg churches. Then came the *Kollegienkirche* (1694-1707—a mixture of the longitudinal and central church-plan, with a soaring *cupola over the central space) and the *Johannesspitalkirche* (1699-1704—where influences from Borromini are again apparent). While in Salzburg he designed the exquisite *high-altar (1709) for the *Franziskanerkirche*. The *Ursulinenkirche* (1699-1705) is also attributed to him. These Salzburg buildings, in a sense, were trial runs for the *Karlskirche*, Vienna (from 1715), with its *Antique Roman *portico, biblical allusions to the Temple of Solomon (enhanced by the twin *Trajanic columns doubling as the Pillars of Hercules and Jachin and Boaz), elliptical central space crowned by a cupola, and wide front, one of the most original and powerful designs of the entire Baroque period. Mention should also be made of his Electoral Chapel next to the *choir of Bre-slau (now Wrocław) Cathedral (1715–24): it mixes Palladian and Borrominiesque themes, again exploiting the ellipse.

His secular architecture includes the Town Palace of **Prince Eugen of Savoy** (1663–1736) in Vienna (1696–1700), influenced by Bernini and Le *Vau, the *Palais Clam-Gallas*, Prague (1713–25), designs (only partly realized, and much altered) for Schönbrunn Palace, Vienna (from 1696), and the *Hofbibliothek*, Vienna (1722–30), one of the finest Baroque rooms in Europe. At both the *Karlskirche* and the *Hofburg* much of the work was carried out by his son, **Joseph Emanuel Fischer von Erlach** (1695–1742). Johann Bernhard's *Entwurff einer historischen Architektur* (1721) appeared (1730) in English as *A Plan of Civil and Historical Architecture*, and was among the first books to include illustrations of Egyptian and Oriental buildings, although the images were fanciful in the extreme. Nevertheless, they had a profound influence on later generations, especially on *Boullée.

H.Aurenhammer (1973); Bou (1962); Brucker (1983); J.Curl (2005, 2011); Dotson (2012); Fischer von Erlach (1964); Fuhrmann (1950); Lorenz (1992); Polleross (1995); C.Powell (1959); Sedlmayr (1996)

fish-bladder Form found in *Second-Pointed *Curvilinear *tracery looking like a tadpole, with a round or pointed head and a curving pointed tail, also called *mouchette*: apparently from the German *Fischblase*, referring to comma shapes in *Sondergotik* tracery.

fishing-house Waterside *pavilion, often with architectural pretensions, from which persons could fish. Examples include the Palladian 'tabernacles' at Studley Royal, Yorks. (1727). R.*Adam's combined fishing- and boat-house at Kedleston, Derbys. (1771), also contains a cold bath.

fishpond, fishpool Artificial reservoir or controlled pool, fed from a stream, in which fish were kept for food. Sometimes formed in series, they were features (*called* **stewponds**) of religious foundations (e.g. *abbeys) or grand country-houses. Later they transmogrified into purely ornamental ponds stocked with, e.g., goldfish, often incorporating small *fountains.

Fisker, Kay Otto (1893–1965) Danish architect, his inspiration came from *vernacular buildings and from German *Modernism. He was best known for Aarhus University (1932–45—with *Stegmann and C.F.*Møller), in which traditional materials (e.g. bricks) and simple forms were used. He had a considerable reputation as a designer of public and private housing, notably the Co-operative Building Society Housing, *Borups Allé* and *Stefansgade*, Copenhagen (1918–21); the *Voldparken* Housing and School, Husum (1945); and many other schemes, including *Interbau* Housing, Berlin (1956–7). His *Modern Danish Architecture* (1927—with **Francis Rowland Yerbury** (1885–1970)) disseminated Danish achievements in Britain and America.

T.Faber (1966); T.Faber et al. (1995); Fisker & Yerbury (1927); Lankilde (1960); Sennott (ed.) (2004)

Five Points *See* CORBUSIER, LE.

flag *or* **flagstone** Large stone slab for paving, etc.

Flagg, Ernest (1857–1947) American architect, he promoted French *Beaux-Arts ideals in the USA, and is best-known for the Singer Loft Building (1902–4), and the Singer Tower (1906–8—demolished), NYC. In those works he promoted the idea of structural rationality he had absorbed from his studies of *Viollet-le-Duc. Among his other works may be cited the Corcoran Gallery of Art, Washington, DC (1892–7), the US Naval Academy, Annapolis, MD (1896–8) (in both of which his mastery of academic *Classicism was displayed), and Bowcot (1916–18) and Wallcot (1918–22)—two fine houses on Staten Island.

Bacon (1986); *DAB* (1974); P (1982)

Flamboyant Late style of Continental *Gothic (c.1375–mid-C16) that evolved from *Second-Pointed *Curvilinear work, especially the flowing forms of the *tracery: it gets its name from the flame-like shapes bounded by the curved *bars. In France its most outstanding manifestations were at the west porch of *St-Maclou, Rouen (c.1500–14), and the west front of Troyes Cathedral (early C16) by *Chambiges. Flamboyant tracery occurs elsewhere, including the British Isles (e.g. west window of York *Minster).

flank 1. Lateral *face of a structure: an end or side as distinguished from the front or back (e.g. side of a *bastion). 2. *Party-wall between *terrace-houses. 3. *Haunch of an arch. 4. *Valley of a roof. *Related terms include*:

flanker: one of several (3 or 4) circular, polygonal, or square projections at the corner of a *bawn to defend the straight *curtain-wall linking them;

flanking window: framed *margin-, *side-, or *wing-*light on either side of a *door or window.

flashing Metal (usually lead) set into brickwork joints, or *raglets in *masonry, where e.g. a pitched roof is pierced by a *chimney-stack. It provides a watertight joint.

285 fleuron

flat *See* APARTMENT.

flat arch *See* ARCH.

flèche 1. *Spire. **2.** *Spirelet surmounting a roof, especially over the *crossing of a French *Gothic cathedral.

Flemish bond *See* BRICK.

Flemish Mannerism North-European mutation and *mélange* of *Flamboyant *Gothic, *High-*Renaissance Italian-*Mannerist, and French-Renaissance *Fontainebleau styles. It exploited *cartouches, *caryatides, *grotesque ornament, *herms, *banded *pilasters, *obelisks, and *strap-work, composed with a freedom bordering on licentiousness. The style was disseminated in *pattern-books by *Dietterlin, de *Vries, and others, notably in England and C18 Spain, where it had a profound effect on *Baroque details such as the *estípite. Examples of the style include some of the guild-houses in the *Grand' Place*, Brussels (from the 1690s), and the Town Hall, Leiden (1597).

Flemish Revival *See* PONT-STREET DUTCH.

Fletcher, Banister (1833–99) English architect/surveyor. He designed several industrial buildings in Newcastle upon Tyne before settling (1870) in London, where he published *Model Houses for the Industrial Classes* (1871) in which the influence of Henry *Roberts can be detected. He built up an extensive architectural/surveying practice in which he was assisted by his sons, **Banister Flight** and **Herbert Phillips Fletcher** (1872–1916). Appointed (1890) to a Chair at King's College, London, he did much to further architectural education. Indefatigably industrious, he published many works, including *Dilapidations* (1872), *Compensations* (1874), *Arbitrations* (1875), *Quantities* (1877), *Light and Air* (1879), *The Metropolitan Building Acts* (1882), and, with his son, **Banister**, his celebrated *A History of Architecture* (1896), which rapidly went into further editions, and became the standard work for generations of students.

Ck (1996); *ODNB* (2004)

Fletcher, Sir Banister Flight (1866–1953) British architect/barrister-at-law/architectural historian, son of Banister *Fletcher, he joined his father's office (1884). His early work was noted for its quality: it included 111–25 Oxford Street, London (1887); part of King's College School, Wimbledon (1899); 20 and 46 Harley Street and 30 Wimpole Street, London (1890); Goslett's, 127–31 Charing Cross Road, London (1897); the charming monument to his father in Hampstead Cemetery (*c*.1900); St Ann's Vestry Hall, Carter Lane, City of London (1905); 'Seldown', 23 The Avenue, and 'Tiverton', pleasant houses in Potters

Bar, Herts. (1909); and the handsome former Westminster Bank, Hythe, Kent (1912). After the 1914–18 war the works at Roan School, Greenwich (1926–8); the extensions to Morden College, Blackheath (1933); and the monumental Gillette Factory, Osterley (1936–7—which *Pevsner described as having an 'incongruous, timidly modernistic grandeur') deserve note (on the whole, Pevsner adopted a respectful tone when commenting on Banister Fletcher's work). Accomplished though his architecture was, Fletcher is better-known as an author (jointly, with his father), of *A History of Architecture on the Comparative Method* (1896). The 1921 edn was rewritten by him and his first wife, **Alice Maud Mary** (d.1932), and illustrated with the famous line-drawings by **George Gilbert Woodward** (1861–*c*.1936) and others: it remained the basis for the 1924 and 1928 edns, and underwent textual revisions for the 1931 edn. The tenth edn (1938), with its successors (only slightly revised), was definitive until **Reginald Annandale Cordingley**'s (1896–1962) edn (1961), followed by others (1975, 1987, 1996). This informative book, of vast scope (described by Pevsner as the 'indispensable historical compilation of architectural history'), was used by countless students of architecture, and translated into various languages. Other works by Fletcher include a much-criticized study of *Palladio (1902), and books written with his brother, **Herbert Phillips Fletcher** (1872–1916)—*Architectural Hygiene* (1899), and *Carpentry and Joinery* (1898). The last volume and his *Architectural Work* (1934) were illustrated with his accomplished sketches. He did much to further the profession and education, and gave generously to the RIBA and the University of London. He was knighted (1919).

A.S.Gray (1985); Hanneford Smith (1934); *ODNB* (2004)

Flettner *or* **Flötner, Peter** (*c*.1485–1546) German *Renaissance architect/sculptor. He designed the *fountain, *Marktplatz*, Mainz (1526), and the *Hirschvogelsaal*, Nuremberg (1534—destroyed). His *Kunstbuch* (1549) contained elaborate and masterly designs for *arabesques and one design for *grotesque ornament that remained influential long after his death.

Angerer (1984); Hi (1981); Jervis (1984)

fleur-de-lis *or* **-lys** Ornament consisting of three leaf-like pointed members above and three or one below a horizontal cross-bar: essentially a stylized lily, it is often found in late-*Gothic *tracery and as poppy-head *finials on medieval *bench-ends. It is especially associated with the Virgin Mary and France.

fleuron 1. Ornamental termination of the apex of a roof, such as a *crop, *finial, or *épi. **2.** Stylized four-leafed square floral ornament, used in late-*Gothic *cresting, *tiles, *crockets, and *cavetto *mouldings. **3.** Ornament in the middle of each concave *face of the *Corinthian *abacus. **4.** *Anthemion.

fleuron Called *tablet-flower*, C14 Lady Chapel, Wells Cathedral, Som. (*after Parker*).

flight Continuous straight series of steps, uninterrupted by landings, in a *stair, e.g. from landing to landing.

flint Hard steely-grey stone occurring in nodules of a varying size, usually covered with a white encrustation. It is used for building in combination with brick or stone *dressings. It is easily split, or *knapped, and is used in *flush-work with *freestone dressings.

S.Hart (2000)

Flitcroft, Henry (1697–1769) English architect, he became draughtsman to *Burlington, and produced drawings for *Kent's *The Designs of Inigo Jones* (1727). Burlington had him installed in the Office of Works, and for the rest of his life 'Burlington Harry' was made, becoming Master-Mason and Deputy Surveyor in succession to Kent, then Comptroller of the Works in succession to *Ripley. He was a competent practitioner of *Palladianism, and his designs for decorative features showed he had made a careful study of Inigo *Jones. His St Giles-in-the-Fields, London (1731–4), follows the *type established by *Gibbs at St Martin-in-the-Fields. He designed the east front and wings of Wentworth Woodhouse, Yorks. (c.1735–c.1770), the longest Palladian composition in England, and Woburn Abbey, Beds. (1747–61).

Co (2008); *ODNB* (2004)

Flockhart, William (1854–1913) Scots architect, he set up a practice (1881) in London, and produced several competently designed buildings. His Lansdowne House, Flats, and Studios, at 11 and 13 Lansdowne Road, London, were in a free *Renaissance style. His best work was probably Rosehaugh, Avoch, Ross and Cromarty (1890s), a vast house, the site-architect for which was the young *Adshead. His 108 and 110

Old Brompton Road (1885–6) are finely-crafted buildings.

A.S.Gray (1985)

floor 1. Division between one storey and another. In the UK ground-, first-, second-, etc., described the storeys, but in many countries 'first-floor' means the 'ground-floor', etc. **2.** Set of rooms and landings, on the same level, i.e. in one storey. **3.** Layer of boards, etc., on which people tread, and i.e. the surface of the floor in the room.

floor-slab Stone funerary monument in a church in the form of a coffin-lid or a flat slab, inscribed and sometimes incised, set in the floor.

floral- *or* flower-clock C20 feature of *public parks and seaside resorts, with the face planted with low-growing flowers, etc., and the moving hands (controlled by an underground motor) also decorated with foliage. An early example was designed by **John Wilson McHattie** (*fl.*1900–23) for Princes Street Gardens, Edinburgh (1903).

Floreale Style of exuberant decorative architecture used particularly for the dwellings of the prosperous Italian *bourgeoisie*, and essentially a branch of *Art Nouveau, derived from America, Belgium, Britain, France (notably *Viollet-le-Duc), and (especially) Austria. It featured distorted *mouldings, ribbons like tape-worms, and luxuriant plant-forms. It reached its apogee in the 1902 Turin Exposition of Decorative Arts, in the works of d'*Aronco, and its legacy was ubiquitous, Italian architecture (c.1898–1914) being often ornamented with lushly decorated *bands, garlands, and growths of flowers and fruit. *Sommaruga's *Palazzo Castiglioni*, Milan (1901–3), is generally regarded as the apotheosis of the *Stile Floreale*. *Basile's dining-room in the *Villa Igiea*, Palermo (1901), was also a fine example, with ornament in such abundance it seemed almost capable of consuming room and diners.

Ms (1966); Pica (1903)

Florentine arch *See* ARCH.

floriate Type of ornament resembling flowers or leaves and foliage.

Florid style Highly ornamented work of the late-C14 and early-C15, notably in France, England, Germany, and Spain.

Floris, Cornelis (1514–75) Antwerp-born Cornelis Floris II *or* Floris de Vriendt made his name as a designer/sculptor of funerary monuments, notably that of **King Christian III of Denmark** (*r.*1535–59), Roskilde Cathedral (c.1568–75); the work commissioned (c.1549) by **Duke Albrecht I of Prussia** (*r.*1525–68) for his wife, **Dorothea**, with additions for his second wife, **Anna Maria**

(*c.*1570); and that for the Duke himself (1569–73—destroyed) (the last in the *Domkirche*, Königsberg (*now* Kaliningrad). After a visit to Rome he became the most influential designer of *Renaissance and Mannerist ornament in Flanders. The Town Hall in Antwerp (1561–6) was an important step in the assimilation of Italian sources into Northern Europe, and incorporated features derived from *Bramante and *Serlio such as coupled columns and *triumphal arches in its six-storey frontispiece. However, there is some doubt as to whether Floris himself was the architect of the building, as he was primarily a sculptor: the designer appears to have been van *Paesschen, who also may have designed the *Hanzehuis* (Hanseatic House), Antwerp (1564–8), attributed to Floris de Vriendt. The latter designed and made the *Rood-screen in Tournai Cathedral (1573–4), and the stone tabernacle in the *St Leonarduskerk*, Zoutleeuw (1550–2), both in Belgium. His decorative style was much disseminated by de *Vries, influenced designers in the northern Netherlands, and his monuments were made familiar by the engravings published (1557) by **Hieronymus Cock** (*c.*1510–70). His work was typical of Antwerp *Mannerism.

G & D (1954); G & TK (1960); Hedicke (1913); Huysmans *et al.* (1996); Millar (1987)

Flötner *See* FLETTNER.

flowing *See* TRACERY.

flue-wall Garden or *conservatory-wall containing flues for hot air from a boiler-house, e.g. *Dearn's* or *rat-trap bond*. *See* BRICK.

Flügelaltar *See* TRIPTYCH.

flush 1. Even with or in the same plane as something else, e.g. a *panel with its surface on the same plane with its surrounding frame, or flush-*pointing. **2.** Stones or bricks bedded closely in *mortar with very small joints. *Compounds include*:

flush-bead moulding: double-*quirked *bead, its face level with the plane of the surfaces on either side. *See* MOULDING;

flush-pointing: mortar on the same plane as (flush with) the *face of brickwork;

flushwork: knapped *flint, with the split (*spaultered*) dark sides of the flint facing outwards, built into finely-jointed panels framed by *freestone *dressings resembling *tracery, all finished faces of flint and stone in the same plane.

S.Hart (2000)

flute Channel (*stria*) of semicircular, segmental, or partially elliptical *section, one of many set parallel (or nearly so) to each other (collectively known as *fluting*) as in Classical column-*shafts, where they occur in all save the *Tuscan *Order.

flushwork East-Anglian knapped flint with limestone dressings.

In the Greek-*Doric Order segmental flutes are separated by *arrises and stopped by *annulets, while those in other Orders are deeper, separated by *fillets, and terminate in quarter-spherical forms. In some instances flutes may have convex *mouldings or *beads (*cables) set within them to one-third the height of the shaft (called *cabled fluting* or *cabling*). Small horizontal flutes, as on the *Asiatic *base of the *Ionic Order, are *reeds. If ornamenting a flat *band, set vertically, flutes are *strigils, while flutes cut in elongated **S**-shapes (as on the sides of Roman *sarcophagi) are collectively referred to as *strigillation.

flying buttress *See* BUTTRESS.

flying façade As *false *façade.

foil In *Gothic *tracery any circular *lobe tangent to the inner side of a larger arc or arch, meeting other lobes in points called *cusps projecting inwards from the arch: prefixes are used to describe how many foils occur—*tre*foil (3), *qua*trefoil (4), *cinque*foil (5), *sex*foil (6), *multi*foil, etc. A *quatrefoil*, therefore, has four lobes, separated by cusps, in the shape of a flower with four leaves the axes of which are vertical and horizontal. Bands of quatrefoils were much used for *enrichment during the *Perp. period. Quatrefoils placed with the axes set diagonally are cross-*quarters. *Related terms include*:

foliate: **1.** adorned with foils; **2.** ornament resembling leaves, as on a *capital;

foliated: **1.** decorated with leaf-ornament; **2.** with foils separated by cusps in apertures or tracery;

foliate mask: sculpted human face or *mask (called *Green Man*, *masque feuillu*, or *tête de* *feuilles*), amid foliage, some of which sprouts from the mouth and nose.

folly *Eye-catcher, usually a building in a contrived landscape, often otherwise useless. It might be in the form of a sham *ruin, Classical *temple, oriental tent, *Chinoiserie *pagoda, or other charming *fabrique set in a *Picturesque garden. It might provide seats and shelter from which an agreeable view can be enjoyed, but more often simply demands attention/gives pleasure by its eccentricity. One of the oddest follies in Britain is the giant pineapple at Dunmore Park, Stirlingshire, Scotland (1761). More recently the term has been given to buildings that are out of the ordinary, do not conform to any of the recognized styles, and are not necessarily placed in a landscape. The delightful King's Coffee House, King Street, Knutsford, Ches. (1907–8), built by R.H. *Watt to designs by **William Longworth**, could be regarded as a folly, as could the complex of open-work turrets of steel covered with broken pottery and glass, seashells, and other detritus by **Simon** (Sam) **Rodia** (1879–1965), known as Watts Towers, Los Angeles, CA. Other C20 follies include the Bottle Village, Simo, Santa Susana, CA (c.1950–1970s), built by *Prisbrey of bottles set in concrete to house her curious collection scavenged from rubbish-dumps: Esther *McCoy wrote lovingly (1974) about 'Grandma's Bottle Village'. Mention should also be made of the *Palais Ideal*, Hauterives, Drôme, France (1879–1905), a fantastic dreamlike castle of concrete and stone embellished with much decoration, built to a plan of great complexity by **Facteur Ferdinand Cheval** (1836–1924), who also designed and built his own *mausoleum in Hauterives Cemetery (1913–15). Other inventions demonstrate the folly is more than whimsical: it encapsulates creative longing, often in the realms of fantasy, with many allusions, far removed from the prim, joyless *Modern Movement.

A & A, lxviii (July 1951), 23–5; H & M (1986); Howley (1993); Ba.Jones (1974); M & T (1991); Mott *et al.* (1989); Prisbrey (1967); Schuyt & Elffers (1980); Walker Art Center (1974)

Fomin, Ivan Aleksandrovich (1872–1936) Russian architect, he worked for a time with *Shekhtel', but by 1910 was a convinced Classicist, and his work evolved into *stripped Classicism (called *Proletarian Classicism* after the creation of the Soviet Union). Among his buildings may be cited the House of the Soviets, Bryansk (1924), the Industrial Bank, Yekaterinburg (1925), the Polytechnic, Ivanovo-Voznesensk (1927–32), the HQ of the Moscow Soviet (1928), and the Dynamo Sports Club, Moscow (also 1928). He designed the *Lermontovskaya* (1935)

and *Teatral'naya* (1938) metro-stations, Moscow, in a sombre, palatial, Classical style.

K-M (1987); J.T (1996)

Fonoyll, Raynard (*fl.*1331–62) English mastermason, he built the south *cloister of the *Monastery of *Santes Creus*, Catalonia, Spain (1331–41), and *Santa Maria*, Montblanch, Spain (from 1352). He also seems to have worked at Tarragona and Lérida Cathedrals, the Royal Monasteries of Pedralbes at Barcelona and Poblet, and the Town Church of Morella. He is of importance in the history of Spanish architecture because his work is the earliest-known *Curvilinear-*Gothic in the Iberian peninsula.

J.Harvey (1987)

font Basin for consecrated water used during the Sacrament of Baptism. Commonly formed from a large block of stone, hollowed out and elaborately carved with Christian symbols, it is supported on a short *pier or cluster of *colonnettes set on a stepped *plinth or platform. *Font-covers* adorned with *pinnacles and *finials, raised on ropes and pulleys, and sometimes coloured, were not unusual in the medieval period.

Bond (1908); Paley (1844)

Fontaine, Pierre-François-Léonard (1762–1853) French architect/interior-designer, he studied under *Peyre, in whose *atélier* he met *Percier, with whose name his was to be so intimately linked. He went to Rome (1786), where he was joined by Percier, and there absorbed principles of *Neo-Classicism. Together, they worked on decorations for the *Opéra* (1792), and designed furniture for the *Convention* (1793). Drawing on their Roman experiences, they produced their first book, *Recueil des palais, maisons, et autres édifices modernes dessinés à Rome* (1798). By that time Fontaine had established a reputation as a furniture-designer, and his contacts led to an introduction to **Napoléon Bonaparte** (1769–1821): Percier and Fontaine were appointed to design the interiors of *Malmaison* (1800–2), in which exquisite work they effectively created the *Empire* style. From that time, they were virtually Napoléon's official architects, and their influence was widespread, especially after their *Recueil de décorations intérieures* was published (1801—reissued 1812, 1827, and in an enlarged Italian edn (1843)), in which their developed eclectic Neo-Classical style, embracing Egyptian, Greek, Roman, and Renaissance ornament, was enticingly displayed. They restored many palaces (e.g. *Saint-Cloud* and the *Tuileries*) that had been vandalized at the time of the Revolution, and designed settings for two great Napoléonic events: the Coronation (1804) and the Emperor's second marriage (1810, to **Marie**

Louise of Habsburg-Lorraine (1791-1847)). However, the partners did not confine their activities to providing *Empire* interiors, for their buildings (though few) were also beautifully proportioned and elegant: they include the *Arc du Carrousel*, Paris (1806-8—modelled on the Arch of **Septimius Severus** (*r.*193-211), Rome, but treated polychromatically); a whole series of transformations of Paris, of which the *Rue de Rivoli* and *Place des Pyramides* (1802-3) are the best-known, although they prepared a huge scheme including a *Palais de Chaillot*, larger than Versailles, linked on a vast *axis to a huge complex of buildings, including a University, *École des Beaux-Arts*, and Archives, not executed.

After Napoléon's fall, Fontaine became architect to **King Louis XVIII** (*r.*1814-24), for whom he built the *Chapelle Expiatoire*, Paris (1815-26), on the site of the burial of **King Louis XVI** and **Queen Marie Antoinette** (both *r.*1774-92, d.1793). He also restored the *Palais Royal* (1814-31) and the *Hôtel-Dieu*, Pontoise (1823-7). He published *Le Palais-Royal* (1829) and *Résidences de Souverains* (1833). In the words of obituarists, Percier and Fontaine 'never married', and are buried in the same grave in *Père-Lachaise* Cemetery, Paris.

Biver (1964); B (1980); M & Wa (1987); D.Wa (1986)

Fontainebleau Style of architectural decoration at the French Royal *Château* created 1528-58 by Italian (notably **Rosso Fiorentino** (1495-1540), **Francesco Primaticcio** (1504/5-70), *Serlio, and *Vignola), French, and Flemish artists for *François Ier. It was an eclectic mutation of *High *Renaissance design into a distinct form of *Mannerism featuring lavish *cartouches, *caryatides, *grotesques, *scrolls, *strapwork, and etiolated *stucco figures. Fontainebleau influenced French design until the end of C16, but the style was widely disseminated through printed sources emanating from Antwerp, and influenced *Flemish Mannerism and architecture in England, Germany, and the Netherlands.

Bt (1982); COF (1988); Shearman (1967)

Fontana, Carlo (1638-1714) Italian *Baroque architect. Born near Como, he lived in Rome from the early 1650s, and assisted *Cortona, *Rainaldi, and *Bernini. For the last he worked on the design of the *Piazza di San Pietro*, the *Scala Regia*, and other projects, and was to succeed (1697) the master as architect of St Peter's. Fontana was prolific, and his fame was based on the series of works starting 1671: the *Cappella Ginetti, Sant'Andrea della Valle*, has a rich interior of coloured *marble, and there were other chapels, but the *Cappella Cibo, Santa Maria del Pòpolo* (1682-4), is perhaps the finest of them. At the same time he built the concave *façade of *San Marcello al Corso*. His remodelling of the

Baptismal Chapel in St Peter's (1692-8) involved ingenious high-level lighting. He transformed and enlarged the *Palazzo di Montecitorio* (1694-6), left unfinished by Bernini, made additions to the *Ospizio di San Michele* (1700-11), and remodelled the façade and *porch of *Santa Maria in Trastévere* (1702). Fontana also published books on St Peter's (1694), the Baptismal Chapel (1697), and other subjects. As the leading architect in Rome towards the end of his long life, he was highly influential, not least because he taught men of genius who carried his ideas far and wide: those pupils numbered among them *Fischer von Erlach, *Hildebrandt, and *Gibbs.

B & H.Hager (1977); N-S (1986, 1986a); Wi (1982)

Fontana, Domenico (1543-1607) Architect/ engineer, born in the Ticino, Switzerland, he settled in Rome, where he worked for **Cardinal Montalto** (1520-90—later **Pope Sixtus V** (*r.* from 1585)), for whom he designed the *villa on the Quirinal (1576-88). He made his name (1585-6) by re-erecting the Egyptian red-granite *obelisk from the *Circus Gai et Neronis* (but originally in Alexandria), in the centre of the *piazza* in front of St Peter's *basilica, and also re-erected the ancient obelisks at *Santa Maria Maggiore* (1587), *San Giovanni in Laterano* (1587-8), and *Piazza del Pòpolo* (1589). Thereafter he built the Lateran Palace (1585-9), the Vatican Library (1587-90), and supervised the erection of the dome of St Peter's under della *Porta (1588-90). His other major contributions in Rome were the laying out of new streets, including the *Via Felice* (1585-9), and other town-planning improvements ordered by Sixtus V. In 1593 he moved to Naples, where he built the *Palazzo Reale* (1600-2).

AR, cxi/644 (April 1952), 217-26; J.Curl (2005); D.Fontana (1604); Muñoz (1944); Roullet (1972); Wi (1982)

Fontana, Giacomo (1710-73) Italian architect, he made a major contribution in Poland during the reign (1764-95) of **King Stanisław Augustus Poniatowski**, working in a refined early Neo-Classical style. He designed the *façade of the Church of the Holy Cross (1756), and the interiors of the Krasiński Palace, both in Warsaw (1766-73).

L & R (1984)

footings Projecting courses at the bottom of a wall or *pier: those below walls are *continuous footings*, and *single-column footings* are those under point-loads such as columns or piers. Footings, being wider than the walls or piers, distribute the loads.

W.McKay (1957)

foot-pace 1. *Daïs or raised floor at the upper end of a hall. 2. Raised floor in a church-

*sanctuary where the *altar is sited. **3.** Landing in a *stair (*see* PACE).

foot-stall 1. *Pedestal. **2.** *Base of a column or *pier.

Forbes, William Nairn (1796–1855) Military-engineer with the rank of Major-General, he designed the *Gothic St Paul's Church, Calcutta (1839–47), which became the Cathedral. Originally, the *tower and *spire were modelled on those of Norwich Cathedral, but after two earthquakes (1897, 1934) they were re-cast to resemble *Wastell's Bell Harry Tower at Canterbury. Forbes designed the *Greek-Revival Silver Mint (1831) with *portico based on that of the Athenian *Parthenon.

Historic Churches, **xix** (2012), 3–4

Förderer, Walter-Maria (1928–2003) Swiss architect, his works include the Commercial High School, St Gallen (1957–63—with **Rolf Georg Otto** (1924–2003) and **Hans Zwimpfer** (1930–2017), in which *concrete forms are boldly expressed. His Church Centre, Hérémence (1963–71), has been admired for its late-flowering *Expressionism, and was perhaps his most adventurous essay.

Burckhardt & Förderer (1968); Förderer (1964, 1975)

fore Situated in front of something else, and usually used as a prefix. *Examples include*:
fore-choir: *ante-choir;
fore-church: *ante-church, like a *narthex, but with *nave and *aisles;
fore-court: outer court of a large building or assemblage of buildings, in grander ensembles a *cour d'honneur;
fore-front: principal *façade or entrance-front of a building.

Forestier, Jean-Claude-Nicolas (1861–1930) French landscape-architect, he began his career assisting *Alphand on works in Paris, e.g. *Bois de Vincennes* (from 1887), and subsequently designed part of the *Champ de Mars* (1908–28) and other open spaces. For the *Exposition des Arts Décoratifs*, Paris (1925), he was director of the exhibition of gardens designed by others, e.g. *Mallet-Stevens. He also laid out the park in Barcelona where the International Exhibition was held (1929–30). He designed part of Buenos Aires, Argentina, the spacious *Avenue Costanera* by the banks of the *Rio de la Plata*. His influential book on large cities and park-systems was published (1908).

Imbert (1993); Leclerc (ed.) (1990)

foreyn 1. Drain or cess-pool. **2.** Reservoir.

forma 1. *Stall. **2.** Mould, pattern, or *template. **3.** *Gothic, *tracery, hence *form-piece.

formal Geometrical, regular, symmetrical, usually with long axes, as in *Renaissance and *Baroque designs, usually associated with *Dutch, *French, and *Italian gardens.

Forman, John (*fl.*1515–58) English mason, he worked under *Lebons at Hampton Court Palace, and (*c.*1523) was appointed master-mason at York *Minster. From 1525 he built St Michael-le-Belfry, York (completed 1536). He was involved in the redecoration of York Minster when Roman Catholicism was briefly restored (1557) under **Queen Mary I** (*r.*1553–8).

J.Harvey (1987)

formeret *Gothic arch-rib in a *vault *engaged with the wall, called *wall-rib,* smaller than the rest of the ribs of the vault-compartment.

form-piece Piece of stone from which *Gothic *tracery is constructed.

formwork Temporary metal or timber *shuttering* constructed as the mould for *concrete. When removed (*struck*) after the concrete has set, the imprint of the formwork is left on the face of the concrete: timber boarding can be made to leave a rugged *board-marked* finish, much sought after (1950s, 1960s) as part of *Brutalism.

Förster, Christian Friedrich Ludwig, Ritter von (1799–1863) Bavarian-born architect, he designed the *Ringstrasse* (begun 1858) and the *Romanesque-*Byzantine-Revival Arsenal (1850–6—with Theophil von *Hansen), Vienna. As Professor at the Vienna Academy (1843–6), he influenced the following generation of Viennese architects through the *Allgemeine Bauzeitung* (founded 1836) and his own studio. His son, **Emil von Förster** (1838–1909), worked with him for a time, and then for the State, remodelling the *Hofburg* and the *Burgtheater* (1895–7), and designing the *Allgemeine Österreichische Baugesellschaft* (1872–4) and the *Dorotheum* (1898–1901), all in Vienna. *See* HASENAUER; SEMPER.

Eggert (1976); Niemann & Feldegg (1893); W-R (1970, 1980)

fort 1. Fortified camp or base for an army. **2.** *Folly or *fabrique* like a sham *castle in a garden. *Associated terms include*:
fortalice: small fort or minor outwork to a fort;
fortified church churches designed like *donjons (square, circular, or polygonal), e.g. in Southern France or Denmark, or with fortified elements, e.g. in the Dordogne or Languedoc. In Alsace-Lorraine several *Romanesque and *Gothic *Kirchenburgen* were attached to city-walls, with the space above the vaulted ceilings serving as *redoubts;
fortress: **1.** castle, or strong defensive military structure of *bastions, earthworks, *ramparts,

walls, etc., far grander than a fort; **2.** town or city with a *citadel, surrounded by fortifications.

forum (*pl.* **fora**) Public market-place, open square, or place of assembly for judicial and other public business in a Roman town or city, surrounded by important buildings, *colonnades, and *porticoes, and ornamented with monuments. Imperial *fora* were symmetrical, formal, and axially planned, owing much to *Hellenistic precedent.

foss, fosse Defensive wet or dry ditch. A *fosse commune* is a common grave in a *cemetery, cleared every seven years or so and re-used.

Foster, James (*c.*1748–1823) Bristolian pupil of *Paty, he mixed architectural activities with those of a *statuary. From early C19, he was joined by his son, **James Jun.** (d.1836), who later practised with his brother, **Thomas** (1792/3–1849), and (until 1840) with **William Ignatius Okely.** After Thomas's death the firm continued under his son, **John** (d.1880), and **Joseph Wood** (*fl.*1848–1905). They designed the *Greek-Revival Upper and Lower Arcades (1824–5), and *terrace-houses at Clifton Vale, Caledonia Place, and New Mall, as well as the Royal Promenade, Victoria Square (*c.*1845–7), all in Clifton (*c.*1840); and the Byzantinesque Colston Hall (1864–73) and Burgundian-*Gothic Foster's Almshouses (1861–83—converted to flats in 2006) in Bristol. They also designed numerous churches and church-alterations, mostly Gothic (e.g. the *Perp. *nave and *aisles of Holy Trinity, Minchinhampton, Glos. (1841–3)), but some *Neo-Romanesque (e.g. St Mary's, Bute Street, Cardiff (1841–3)).

Co (2008); GJ & L (1979); Ison (1978)

Foster, John (*c.*1759–1827) English architect. As Surveyor to the Corporation of Liverpool from 1790, he became a powerful figure in that city's architectural concerns, especially after he added the Surveyorship of the Docks to his portfolio. He built many well-mannered houses in Liverpool as well as most of the late-Georgian public buildings, including the Exchange (1789–1811—now Town Hall, designed with James *Wyatt), his most impressive work. Foster's achievements have been eclipsed by those of his second son, **John Foster** (*c.*1787–1846), a pupil of Jeffry and (probably) James *Wyatt. Foster Jun. travelled abroad (1809), and worked with *Haller, **Jakob Linckh** (1786–1841), and C.R.*Cockerell on excavations in Greece before returning to Liverpool (1816). He succeeded (1824) his father as Architect and Surveyor to Liverpool Corporation, designing many of the most significant buildings in that city, mostly in a competent *Greek-Revival style, many of which have been destroyed. St James's Cemetery, Liverpool (1823–4—partly

cleared and comprehensively vandalized), laid out in a disused quarry, was one of his most distinguished designs, and included the surviving *Doric *mortuary-chapel, entrance arch, superintendent's house, and *mausoleum (1834) of **William Huskisson**, MP (1770–1830—killed at the opening of the Liverpool and Manchester Railway (15 September 1830)). His greatest work was Liverpool Custom House (1828–35—destroyed in the 1939–45 war).

Co (2008); W.Pa (1852); Picton (1875)

Foster of Thames Bank, Norman Robert, Lord (1935–) *See* ARUP; HIGH TECH.

Foster, Peter (1919–2010) English architect, Surveyor (1973–88) of Westminster Abbey, whose works included many church-restorations, garden-*fabriques*, and numerous watercolours and pencil drawings. On qualifying, he joined **Marshall Sisson** (1897–1978) in practice, later becoming a partner, and then (1971) sole principal. Among Foster's works were the restoration of *Archer's great Church of St Paul, Deptford, *Hawksmoor's St Alphege, Greenwich, and the removal of *Wren's Church of St Mary Aldermanbury to Westminster College, Fulton, MO (1965–9). He also converted Archer's St John's, Smith Square, Westminster, into a concert-hall (1965–9). His most charming *fabriques* were at Abbots Ripton Hall, Hunts., and Staunton Hall, Notts. His exquisitely lettered memorials include several in Westminster Abbey.

The Times (30 Mar. 2010), 65; pk

Fouilhoux, Jacques-André (1879–1945) French architect, he became (1924) a partner of Raymond *Hood, with whom he designed the St Vincent de Paul Asylum, Tarrytown, NY (1924), the Masonic Temple, Scranton, PA (1929), the McGraw-Hill *skyscraper, NYC (1930–2), and other buildings. He was also partly responsible for the Rockefeller Center, NYC (1931–4). When Hood died (1934), Fouilhoux joined Wallace K. *Harrison, and continued working on the Rockefeller Center. He also contributed to the New York World's Fair (1938–9) and worked (1940s) on the Fort Greene and Clinton Hill housing-schemes, NYC.

AF, lxxxiii/2 (1945), 86; Krinsky (1978)

Foulston, John (1772–1842) English architect, he established himself in Plymouth, Devon, where he became the leading practitioner. His Royal Hotel, Assembly Rooms, and Theatre (1811–22—demolished) employed much cast and wrought iron in its construction, and was made all the more interesting for the grouping of three buildings into one coherent composition. Most of his work was in the Classical manner of the *Regency period, with Greek *Orders and detail applied to *stucco terraces, but at Ker Street, Devonport, Plymouth, he created an eclectic *Picturesque group of buildings, including an *Egyptian-Revival Library (1823), a Baptist Chapel in the *Hindoo style (1824), a Greek-*Doric Town Hall (1821-3), and a Doric Column (1824). He published *The Public Buildings erected in the West of England, as designed by J.Foulston* (1838), and was in partnership with *Wightwick from c.1830.

Co (2008); Crook (1987); J.Curl (2005); Nettleton (1836)

foundation 1. That upon which a structure is erected, e.g. the solid ground beneath a building. **2.** Lowest part of a building, below the ground level, providing a firm base for what is above, by which the load is transferred to the ground underneath. Very heavy buildings, such as *high-rise, normally require deep foundations on *piles, but for lighter structures, such as one- or two-storey houses, trenches into which *concrete is poured to provide a base for the *footings of the walls will usually suffice. Certain ground conditions might require a reinforced-concrete 'raft', which covers the site and evenly distributes the load.

fountain 1. Source of water issuing from the earth and collecting in a natural or artificial basin. **2.** Jet or stream of water made to rise or spout up artificially, sourced from a reservoir at a higher level before the advent of mechanical pumps (which permitted recycling of water as well as spectacular effects, e.g. height of jet or complexity of sprays). See HYDRAULICS. **3.** Structure from which water flows or spouts, often treated with architectural verve, e.g. the Trevi Fountain, Rome (1732-7), by *Salvi. See CONDUIT. **4.** Fountains are often found in town-squares and parks, doubling as commemorations of individuals or events (e.g. the Shaftesbury Memorial (1886-93), Piccadilly Circus, London, by **Alfred Gilbert** (1854-1934)).

Downing (1849); W.Pa (1852); pk; Switzer (1729); J.T (1996)

four-centred See ARCH.

Fourier, François-Marie-Charles (1772-1837) See COMPANY TOWN.

four-leafed flower See FLEURON.

Fowke, Captain Francis (1823-65) Ulsterborn military-engineer, he designed Raglan Barracks, Devonport, Plymouth (1853-5—demolished), to an advanced hygienic specification. Ingenious and inventive, his ideas were usually blocked by conservative military and naval establishments, but his opportunity arrived when, under the aegis of Henry *Cole, he was appointed (1856) Superintendent of Buildings for 'Albertopolis', the cultural complex in South Kensington, London. His buildings, of brick and *terracotta,

were in the *Rundbogenstil, influenced by German precedents (notably by von *Gärtner and *Semper), and include the galleries, courts, and lecture-theatre of the South Kensington (now Victoria & Albert) Museum (1856-65—with **Godfrey Sykes** (1824-66)), the buildings for the International Exhibition, South Kensington, London (1862—demolished 1863-4), and the Royal Albert Hall (1867-71—with Lt.-Col. Henry *Scott). He also designed (1858) the handsome Royal Scottish Museum, Edinburgh (begun 1861), a grand Lombardic-*Renaissance essay, with an elegant galleried iron-and-glass Great Hall, and improved and enlarged the National Gallery, Dublin (also 1860s). His designs have been underrated, but there can be little argument about his finesse in building large, impressive public buildings. Fowke patented (1856) a folding camera, and following further research, developed the large 'bellows' camera, which came into general use, widely employed for architectural photography. See also ALBERT, PRINCE.

GMcW & W (1984); ODNB (2004); Physick (1982); P & D (1973); Sh (1975).

Fowler, Charles (1792-1867) English architect, he established (1818) his practice in London, where his Covent Garden Market Buildings (1828-30) and masterly iron-and-glass conservatory at Syon House, Isleworth, Mddx. (1827-30) established his reputation. Hungerford Market, London (1831-3), and Lower Market, Exeter, Devon (1835-7)—both demolished—demonstrated his understanding of elegant iron structures as well as his grasp of a simplified straightforward *Neo-Classicism derived from *Durand. He also designed Totnes Bridge, Devon (1826-8). *Loudon praised his work for its rational qualities and freedom from slavish adherence to antiquated rules and precedents. His pupils included Henry *Roberts.

Co (2008); ODNB (2004)

Fowler, John Beresford (1906-77) English interior-decorator, he learned his trade with **Thornton Smith** in London, then joined the decorative-painting studio of **Margaret Kunzer**, after which he set up his own practice (1934). His work caught the eye of **Sibyl Sophie Julie, Lady Colefax** (1874-1950), who recruited him (1938) for her firm, which became **Colefax & Fowler**, with a growing number of fashionable patrons. After the 1939-45 war, American-born **Nancy Keene Tree** (*née* **Perkins**—1897-1994), acquired the business as a gift from her then husband, **Arthur Ronald Lambert Field Tree** (1897-1976): from 1948 she was known as **Nancy Lancaster**, and she was closely associated with the firm until 1977, although she and Fowler were described by one wit as 'the most unhappy unmarried couple in England'. Together, they adorned many English country-houses and gardens, and acquired an enviable reputation for stylish elegance, comfort, and taste. With *Cornforth Fowler wrote *English Decoration in the 18th Century* (1974).

Becker (1996); Fowler & Cornforth (1974); Hughes (ed.) (2005); C.Jones (2000); *ODNB* (2004); M.A.Wood (2005, 2007)

foyer 1. Lobby or entrance-hall of a theatre or other public building. **2.** Area outside the *auditorium for the audience to meet, promenade, mingle, talk, etc. It acts as a sound-barrier between exterior and interior. **3.** Any public area in a large public or civic building between the exterior and the main parts of the building, i.e. an extended entrance-hall. **4.** Room for gatherings or meetings. **5.** Room for meetings, especially of actors and performers, in a theatre.

fractable *Cope on a *gable-wall carried up as a *parapet. The term is especially appropriate for scrolled, shaped, or stepped gables: the horizontal part at the base of the gable is the *foot*-table; the curved parts are *boltels* or *bottles*; and a step is a *square*.

frame 1. Skeletal structure of *concrete, metal, or timber on which floors, roof, and external *cladding are placed to form the building, as opposed to a structure of heavy *load-bearing walls. **2.** Frame of a *door. **3.** Surround of an opening, usually an *architrave, trim, or border. A **frame-house** is a dwelling constructed of a *timber frame, clad with *clap- or *weatherboarding, or with *shingles, found on the east coast of the USA.

Frampton, Kenneth Brian (1930–) *See* CRIT-ICAL REGIONALISM.

Francesco Maurizio di Giorgio Martini (1439–1501/2) *See* GIORGIO.

Francini family Florentine dynasty of hydraulic-engineers, involved in creating aspects of some of the greatest C17 French gardens. **Tommaso Francini** (1571–1651—who appears to have worked on water-powered *automata* at the Medici Villa, Pratolino) and his brother, **Alessandro** (*fl.*1599–1649), settled in France at the end of C16, and designed water-features at Saint-Germain-en-Laye (from 1598). Tommaso also worked on water-supplies at the Luxembourg Palace, Paris (though Alessandro was responsible for the *Fontaine de Médicis* in the gardens), designing (with J.-C.*Métezeau) the *aqueduct (1613–23) and reservoir (this still exists under the *Maison des Fontaniers, Rue de l'Observatoire*): Tommaso created the lovely *nymphaeum, Château de Wideville*, Yvelines (1635). Alessandro also worked for many years at Fontainebleau from 1602. Names of Tomasso's sons were gallicized as **François** (1617–88) and **Pierre** (1621–86) **de Francine**, and both worked at Versailles, bringing water from high ground at Clagny to serve the fountains and gadgets there (including a twittering-machine and an organ). François's son, **Pierre-François de Francine** (1654–1720), succeeded his father as *Intendant des Eaux et Fontaines* at Versailles.

Tay (2006); K.Woodbridge (1986)

Francke, Paul (1538–1615) Important German architect of the late-*Renaissance period. He designed the University Buildings, Helmstedt (1592–7), and the *Marienkirche*, Wolfenbüttel (1604–26).

Fink & Appuhn (1965); E.Hempel (1965)

François Ier, *or* **François Premier** King of France (*r.*1515–47), he gave his name to the style of *High-*Renaissance and *Mannerist architecture and decoration that emerged at *Fontainebleau. It enjoyed a C19 revival sometimes called the *Château* style.

Frank, Josef (1885–1967) Austrian architect. Before the 1914–18 war he designed several Viennese *villas, e.g. *Hoch* (1912), *Scholl* (1913–14), and *Wassermann* (1914). He was involved in the *Garden-City movement and in the formation of cooperatively run *Garden Suburbs: after the war he designed a series of housing-projects for the City of Vienna, including the *Wiedenhofer-Hof* (1924–5) and the *Winarsky-Hof* (1924–6). Other works included the *Villa Beer* (1930) and the *Leopoldine-Glöckel-Hof* (1932), both in Vienna. He designed a house for the *Weissenhofsiedlung*, Stuttgart (1927), with colourful interiors that attracted opprobrium as 'bourgeois' and worse. A member of the *Werkbund, he warned against the bullying, dogmatic attitudes emanating from the German *Bauhaus, from Le *Corbusier, and from *CIAM. In 1933 he prudently settled in Sweden.

Sennott (ed.) (2004); J.T (1996)

Fraser, James (1793–1863) Scots landscape-gardener/writer, he worked at Trinity College Botanic Garden, Dublin, and became *Loudon's Irish Correspondent for the *Gardener's Magazine*. He established (1829) himself in Dublin, laying out numerous estates, including Curraghmore, Co. Waterford (1843), and Saunderscourt, Co. Wexford (*c.*1840). He published (1838–53) travel-guides for Ireland.

D & E (1994); *DIA*; Malins & Bowe (1980); Reeves-Smith (2001)

frater, fratery, fraterhouse Monastic *refectory.

Fréart de Chambray, Roland (1606–76) French exponent of *Classicism, his *Parallèle de l'Architecture Antique et de la Moderne* (1650) was an important source for students of the works of *Palladio, *Scamozzi, *Serlio, *Vignola, and others. It appeared in English in a translation by John *Evelyn as *A Parallel of the Ancient Architecture with the Modern* (1664).

Fréart de Chambray (1650)

Free Classicism Late-C19 English style, not adhering strictly to historical precedents or rules, essentially a mixture of *Classical, *Mannerist, *Renaissance, and *Baroque motifs, e.g. John McKean *Brydon's Chelsea Town Hall, London (1885–7), and Government Offices, Whitehall, London (1898–1912), the latter perhaps more *Baroque. The term *Free Classical style* was given to the *Queen-Anne style or Revival. *Other compounds include*:

Free Gothic: **1.** revival of *Gothic forms and motifs, freely used in an eclectic mix, as in the Midland Grand Hotel, St Pancras Station, London (1868–74), by 'Great' *Scott; **2.** late-C19 style, in which *Arts-and-Crafts and other influences were mingled, creating a non-archaeological, scholarly, yet highly individual style. Examples include work by *Caröe, Temple *Moore, Charles *Nicholson, *Sedding, *Shaw, and others;

Free style: late-C19 style in which *Classical, *Domestic-Revival, *Gothic, *Queen-Anne, and *vernacular themes, motifs, and elements were mingled promiscuously in eclectic compositions, sometimes with additional *Elizabethan or *Renaissance allusions added, as in the works of Philip *Webb (especially 'Clouds', East Knoyle, Wilts. (1879–91));

Free Tudor: late-C19 and early-C20 style in which late-*Perp., *Tudor, or Elizabethan forms are freely mixed, e.g. the work of Leonard *Stokes.

Crook (1987); Gd (1977); Latham (ed.) (1980)

Freed, James Ingo (1930–2005) German-born American architect, a pupil of *Mies van der Rohe, who joined (1956) **Ieoh Ming Pei** (1917–2019) as a partner. Among the projects with which he was associated may be cited the Jacob Javits Convention Center, NYC (1985–6), the Holocaust Memorial Museum, Washington, DC (1986–93), and the San Francisco Public Library, CA (1992–6). The firm became **Pei Cobb Freed**, the other member of the triumvirate being **Henry N. Cobb** (1926–).

Di (ed.) (1980, 1985); J (1997)

Freemason 1. Craftsman capable of hewing, dressing, and setting *freestones. **2.** Person 'Free' of the Masons' Guilds, i.e. a Freeman. **3.** Itinerant mason, emancipated, so able to travel widely to carry out work, enjoying an élite status among craftsmen. **4.** Member of a fraternity called, more fully, Free and Accepted Masons. *See* FREEMASONRY.

Freemasonry System of morality, veiled in allegory, and illustrated by symbols (many of them associated with architecture and working with stone): it is an organization based on a Lodge, with unique and elaborate rituals and secrets. In its 'speculative' form (i.e. indirectly connected with actual building-works) it seems to have originated in Scotland, and came south with the Stuart Court (1603).

J.Curl (2011); Knoop & G.Jones (1949); D.Stevenson (1988)

freestone Stone that can be easily cut and worked in any direction, such as fine *limestone or *sandstone.

Frémin, Michel de (*fl.* early C18) French critic, author of *Mémoires critiques d'architecture* (1702), which argued for a rational approach to design, drawing attention to restrictions suggested by the site, materials, costs, and needs of the users. He stated that the *Orders and rules of *Classicism were of no great significance, and viewed medieval Parisian *Gothic buildings such as *Sainte-Chapelle* and *Notre Dame* as more logical works of architecture than Classical buildings such as *St-Sulpice*. He was an influence on *Neo-Classicism. *See also* PRIMITIVE HUT.

M & Wa (1987); D.Wa (1986)

French garden Reaching its apogee (C17 and early-C18), it was characterized by symmetry and regular geometry; *parterres adjacent to the house planted with flowers, etc., in carefully contrived *beds; *fountains, waterworks, *cascades, and *canals; *terraces with decorative statuary; high clipped *hedges, *topiary, and *espalier arrangements, with or without *trellises; *grottoes; *boskets with walks; and long, broad avenues laid out in grids, with sometimes diagonal walks cutting across them. The design was all about controlling Nature, and it was primarily associated with the reign of **Louis XIV** (1643–1715), with Versailles, and with the designer of the gardens there, Le *Nôtre. It was widely emulated throughout Europe.

J.-F.Blondel (1737–8); DdA (1709); Hirschfeld (1779–85, 2001); Symes (2006); Tay (2006)

French Order 1. *Corinthian *capital featuring the cock and *fleur-de-lys. **2.** Type of *Order invented by de l'*Orme with *bands of sculptured leaves concealing the *shaft-*drums; **3.** Classical Order consisting of three columns set at the points of an equilateral triangular plan (∴), with creepers trailing in spiral forms around the shafts (reminiscent of *Solomonic or spiral columns), invented by *Ribart de Chamoust (1783).

J.Curl (2011); L & D (1986)

French Renaissance Revival C19 revival of C16 styles, exemplars of which are the enlargements to the Louvre, Paris (from 1853).

French roof *See* ROOF.

French Second Empire style Eclectic mixture of *Baroque, *Empire, *François Ier, *Louis Quatorze, *Louis Seize, *Neo-Classical, and *Renaissance styles prevalent in the France of **Emperor Napoléon III** (*r*.1852–70).

French window *Casement-window, also called *croisée*, carried down to floor-level, and opening like two-leafed glazed doors to a garden, *verandah, or *terrace.

fresco Mural painting on *plaster while still wet and fresh (*buon fresco*). A wall-painting on dry plaster (*secco*) is a poor substitute, as the paint peels and pigments fade.

fret, frette, fretwork 1. *Meander, or *band-like ornament of shallow short *fillets touching each other at right angles, called variously angular *guilloche, *Greek key, or *lattice, depending on the type. If some fillets are set diagonally it is called *Chinese fret*, found in *Chinoiserie and *Regency work. 2. *Trellis-work. 3. Any interlacing raised work. 4. Complex patterns of ribs on a *Gothic *vault. 5. Net-like forms, as in *tracery.

Frey, Albert (1903–98) Swiss-born American architect, uncritical disciple of Le *Corbusier, he worked on the *Villa Savoie*, Passy (1928–31), and the *Tsentrosoyuz* Building, Moscow (1919–34). Back in the USA he designed the 'Aluminaire House' for the 1931 Allied Arts and Building Products Exhibition, NYC, reminiscent of Corbusier's *Maison Citrohan* (1915–21): it is now reassembled at the NY Institute of Technology, Islip, Long Island. In partnership (1934–57) with **John Porter Clark** (1905–91—whose own house at Palm Springs, CA (1939) was a paradigm of *International Modernism), work included the Frey 1 (1940) and Loewy (1947) Houses, City Hall (1957), and Frey 2 (1965) House, all in Palm Springs.

N.Jackson (1996); Rosa (1999); Sennott (ed.) (2004);

Freyssinet, Eugène (1879–1962) French engineer, pioneer of *reinforced-concrete construction. He designed several *bridges, including Plougastel (1924–30), five bridges over the Marne (1947–51), and the Saint-Michel Bridge, Toulouse (1959–62). During the 1914–18 war he designed industrial buildings with reinforced-concrete roofs, followed by two huge parabolic-arched airship-hangars at Orly (1916–24). He developed *prestressed concrete (patented 1928), and published (1921–54) much on his ideas and methods, including *Une Révolution dans les techniques du béton* (1936).

Fernández Ordóñez (1978); Günschel (1966); *J. of the Prestressed Concrete Institution*, xxi/5 (1976), 48–71

Frézier,   Amédée-François   (1682–1773) French military-engineer, known primarily for his championship of *arcuated rather than *columnar-and-trabeated structures, and for his perceptive writings on *Gothic architecture, especially his *La Théorie et la pratique de la coupe des pierres et des bois pour la construction des voûtes... ou, traité de stéréotomie, à l'usage de l'architecture*, first published 1737–9. He noted that Gothic structures were accurately conceived, depending upon carefully balanced systems of thrust and counter-thrust, and in his formal analysis he revealed the principles of order and construction in Gothic architecture, although he did not favour reintroducing its forms into contemporary work. He opposed *Cordemoy's views, and can be said to have been a prophet of *Romantic Classicism. He published (1738) a book on the *Orders of Architecture.

Frézier (1716, 1737–9, 1738, 1747); Hoefer (ed.) (1857); *JWCI*, xxv (1962), 278–320, xxvi (1963), 90–123

frieze 1. Horizontal central *band of a Classical *entablature below the *cornice and over the *architrave, occasionally omitted in the Greek-*Ionic *Order. It is a flat unornamented band in the *Tuscan Order; it is broken up into *metopes and *triglyphs in the *Doric Order; and is plain or enriched with sculptured reliefs in the Ionic, *Corinthian, and *Composite Orders. It can have a convex profile (i.e. be *pulvinated*), usually in variations of the Ionic and Composite Orders. 2. *Hypotrachelion of some Ionic Orders resembling a frieze under the *capital. 3. Strip or *band under the cornice of an internal wall over the picture-rail. A *frieze-rail* is the intermediate rail below the top-rail of a six-panelled framed door.

frigidarium Large, handsomely decorated cold room in Roman *thermae*, containing a large pool.

Frisoni, Donato Giuseppe (1683–1735) North-Italian architect, he worked in Germany, where he laid out Ludwigsburg, Württemberg (1715–35), with its regular streets and gardens. He remodelled the Ducal Palace (*Schloss Ludwigsburg—*1714–35) carefully integrating it with the planned town, having taken over from the previous architect, **Johann Friedrich Nette** (1672–1714). He also designed the *Favorite* Banqueting Hall at Ludwigsburg (from 1718), and was responsible for the *façade, *gable, *dome, upper storeys of the towers, and some *altars of the great

*Benedictine Abbey of Weingarten (1715–24), shaping it to its present form.

Bou (1962); E.Hempel (1965); Lieb (1992)

Fritsch, Theodor (1853–1933) German theorist, he published (1896) *Die Stadt der Zukunft* which anticipated by two years Ebenezer *Howard's *Tomorrow: a Peaceful Path to Real Reform*. However, half of the circular plan of Fritsch's design was given over to parkland, and he proposed large living-quarters with communal gardens, underground services, and industrial estates.

J.T (1996)

Froebel family Three generations of successful Swiss landscape-architects/plantsmen. German-born **Theodor Froebel** (1810–93) became (1835) Head Gardener at the University of Zürich where he established the *botanic- and *rock-gardens, as well as an office for designing landscape-gardens which he headed until 1890, publishing many papers on hybridization. He designed several *public parks for Zürich, including a children's playground inspired by the theories of his uncle, **Friedrich Wilhelm August Froebel** (1782–1852), educationalist and inventor of the *Kindergarten*. **Theodor**'s son, **Otto** (1844–1906), continued his father's work, designing private and public parks, and excelling in hybridization, winning many prizes. *His* son, **Robert** (1878–1966), specialized in laying out institutional gardens for schools, hospitals, etc.: one of his last works was the ZUGA garden-exhibition, Zürich (1933), before the firm closed (1934).

Schweizer Garten, v (1943); Shoe (2001)

front 1. *Façade of a building, as in *garden-front*, but especially the most important façade, e.g. street-front. **2.** East end of a church.

frontal 1. *Antependium*, movable or fixed, in front of a church-altar from the table downwards. It is often an embroidered cloth, but can be carved or painted. **2.** Small *pediment or other decorative top to a door-case, *niche, etc., but this usage may be a corruption of *fronton*.

Frontinus, Sextus Julius (*c*.35–105) Roman author of a major, clearly written, uncluttered treatise (*De Aquaeductibus Urbis Romae*) on the water-supply of the city as well as another on surveying (which survives in fragments). He provided descriptions of *aqueducts, as well as of methods used to provide linings for the *conduits.

H & S (1996)

frontispiece 1. Principal *front or *façade of a building. **2.** Elaborate entrance, centrepiece, or gateway embellishing the centre of a main façade.

fronton *Frontal (**2**).

frosted, frostwork *See* RUSTICATION.

fruit-wall As *crinkle-crankle or *serpentine wall.

frustum 1. Slice of a solid body, especially a form produced by cutting through a *cone or *pyramid between the base and a parallel plane, or between any two planes. **2.** Drum of a column-*shaft.

Fry, Edwin Maxwell (1899–1987) English *Modernist architect. Encouraged by Wells *Coates he abandoned the *Classicism absorbed at the Liverpool School under *Reilly, and became a disciple of Le *Corbusier, becoming involved in *MARS, the English branch of *CIAM. He established (1934) his own practice in London, demonstrating his final acceptance of *International *Modernism with Sassoon House, Peckham (a block of working-class flats—1934), and two private dwellings that made his name—the Sun House, Frognal Lane, Hampstead (1936), and Miramonte, Kingston upon Thames (1937), where the influence of *Mies's Tugendhat House, Brno, was evident. With **Elizabeth Denby** (1893–1965) and others, he designed Kensal House, Ladbroke Grove, London (1936–7), a *Modern-Movement block of workers' flats, much publicized for its 'progressiveness' by Fry's clients, The Gas Light and Coke Company. Fry helped *Gropius when he arrived in England (1934), and revised the German's designs for Impington Village College, Cambs. (1936–7), overseeing its construction. Fry was responsible for the MARS Group Exhibition (1937) which promoted the CIAM line and publicized International Modernism. He married (1942) 'Jane' *Drew with whom he wrote several books, including *Tropical Architecture in the Dry and Humid Zones* (1966). A Fry-Drew partnership was established (1945), later joined by *Lasdun: among its works were the Passfield Flats, Lewisham (1949), the Riverside Restaurant for the *Festival of Britain South Bank Exhibition site (1951), and numerous projects in Africa, including University College, Ibadan, Nigeria (1953–9). Fry and Drew were appointed (1951) to the design team for Chandigarh, the new capital of the Punjab, and were largely responsible for bringing in Le Corbusier and *Jeanneret-Gris as architects for some of the major buildings. Fry designed the Pilkington Brothers headquarters, St Helen's, Lancs. (1959–65), and a derivative crematorium, Coychurch, Mid-Glamorgan, Wales (1966–70). He wrote *Autobiographical Sketches* (1975).

Brockman (1978); Fry (1944, 1969, 1975); Fry & Drew (1947, 1956, 1964, 1976); Hitchins (ed.) (1978); *ODNB* (2004)

Fuchs, Bohuslav (1895-1972) Pupil of *Kotěra, he became a leading *avant-garde* architect in Brno, Moravia, Czechoslovakia, where he settled (1923), designing the influential *Modernist Avion Hotel (1927-8). At the Czechoslovak *Werkbund* Exhibition, Brno (1928), he and **Josef Štěpánek** (1889-1964) built an acclaimed 'triple house'. He designed a house for himself in Brno (1928-9); the Special School for Girls, Brno-Pisárky (1929-30—with **Josef Poláŝek** (1899-1946)), held to be a paradigm of the *International-Modern style; the Moravská Bank, Brno (1929-31—with *Wiesner); and the Green Frog Thermal Bath Building, Trenčianske Teplice (1936-7).

Kubinszky (1977); Kuděkka (1966); Li (1996); T (1996)

Fuga, Ferdinando (1699-1781) Florence-born architect, his early works were in Rome, where he designed the ingeniously planned *Palazzo della Consulta* (1732-7) at the *Quirinal*, the *Palazzo Corsini* (1736-54), the handsome, even ebullient, *façade of *Santa Maria Maggiore* (1741-3), and the Church of *Sant'Apollinare* (1742-8). In 1750 he left Rome for Naples, where his huge *Albergo de'Poveri* (1751-81), a gigantic poor-house for 8,000 inhabitants, was one of the grandest architectural projects of C18, and one that anticipated the boldest *Neo-Classicism of *Boullée. In Naples he also designed the façade of the *Chiesa dei Gerolomini*, and the *Palazzo Giordano* (both *c*.1780).

Bianchi (1955); Bt (1975); F.Borsi (1975); Kieven (ed.) (1988); Matthiae (1952); Pane (1956)

fulcrum Prop, support, or fixed point about which a lever rotates. It is the point beyond which a *cantilever extends in one direction into space, its other end anchored on the opposite side of the fulcrum.

Fuller, Richard Buckminster (1895-1983) American inventor of the *Dymaxion* House (1927), evolved from aircraft and motor-car construction techniques, intended for mass-production, and of the prefabricated modular bathroom (1929—patented 1936). While he was much concerned with the design of cheap living-units, he also developed means of covering large areas by means of *geodesic 'domes' constructed on the *space-frame principle, using timber, plywood, metal, *concrete, and other materials: these did not require elaborate foundations as their structural integrity was such that they only needed to be anchored to the ground. This system could enable huge clear-span structures to be made, and therefore whole cities could be roofed over, with considerable possibilities for environmental control and saving of energy. A collection of his breathless writings was published (1970).

Baldwin (1996); Fuller (1971, 1975, 1979, 1981); A.Hatch (1974); Krausse & Lichtenstein (eds) (1999); R.Marks (1973); McHale (1962); Pawley (1990a); D.W.R (1974); Sennott (ed.) (2004); Sieden (1989); Vance (1987); J.Ward & Tomkins (1984)

Fuller, Thomas (1823-98) English architect, he settled in Canada (1857), where he formed a partnership with Canadian-born **Chilion Jones** (1835-1912). They designed St Stephen's-in-the-Fields, Toronto (1858), in the *Gothic style, before building their grandest work, the Parliament Building, Ottawa (1859-67), the *Gothic-Revival style of which emphasized the connection between the traditions of Great Britain and British Canada. Only the library-block (reminiscent of a medieval *chapter-house) survives, as the building was destroyed (1916) by fire and reconstructed on simpler lines by **J.Omar Marchand** (1873-1936) and **John A. Pearson** (1867-1940). Fuller won (1863) the competition to design the New York State Capitol, Albany, later altered by *Eidlitz and *Richardson after Fuller and his then partner **Augustus Laver** (1834-98) were dismissed after a newly formed Advisory Board recommended major changes to plans and style. Fuller & Laver won the competition to design the San Francisco City House and Law Courts (1871—destroyed 1906), but its construction was fraught with difficulties, and Fuller returned to Canada (1881) as Chief Architect of the Department of Public Works, and under his aegis some 140 buildings were erected.

K (1994); Roseberry (1964); J.T (1996)

Fuller-Clark, Herbert (1869-*after* 1912) English *Arts-and-Crafts architect responsible for the rich interior of the ground-floor of the *Black Friar* *public-house, Blackfriars, London (1905), with **Henry Poole** (1878-1928). He also designed Boulting's Offices at Riding House Street, a free composition, and 40 and 41a Foley Street, both in London (*c*.1908). He appears to have been in Jamaica, West Indies, in 1912.

A.S.Gray (1985)

Functionalism Theory that good design results from or is identical with functional efficiency, i.e. architecture should be determined by function alone. It is of considerable antiquity, and was promoted by *Viollet-le-Duc and other C19 architects before Louis *Sullivan coined his 'form follows function' slogan (1896). It was used by e.g. *Giedion and *Pevsner to justify *International Modernism, a style believed to *suggest* it, even though that style was no more 'functional' than any other, and in many ways less so.

R.Ba (1960); L (1988); J.M.Ri (1958); Sartoris (1936); J.T (1996); Zurko (1957)

funeral board *See* ACHIEVEMENT OF ARMS.

Furness, Frank (1839-1912) American architect, dominant figure in Philadelphia's architectural world from 1866, when he settled there, having worked in *Hunt's office. He designed almost 400 buildings, mostly in and around Philadelphia, many of which are rather fierce and full of character. *Sullivan worked briefly in his office, and some of Furness's inventiveness rubbed off on him. Furness's first success was the Philadelphia Academy of Fine Arts (1871-6), in which Continental *polychrome *Gothic is treated with rumbustious zest, demonstrating his penchant for elephantine eclectic motifs that almost puts him in the category of a *Rogue Goth. Influenced by *Ruskin and *Viollet-le-Duc, Furness absorbed their lessons, and transformed them in works of bold and aggressive creativity. Apart from the synthesis of architectural influences, he adapted detail and geometrical ornament from many published sources, notably the works of *Dresser, who reached Philadelphia (1876) en route for Japan, and returned there the following year with a collection of artefacts for **Tiffany & Co.** of NYC and **Londros & Co.** of London. A series of banks (designed from *c.*1870 to early C20) brought in new clients, and when **Allen Evans** (1849-1925) became his partner (1881), the firm (**Furness & Evans**) enjoyed considerable success, thanks partly to Evans's sociability. The Furness Library for the University of Pennsylvania (1888-91), intelligently planned and boldly detailed, is perhaps the crowning achievement of his career.

Handlin (1985); Hi (1977); M.Lewis (2001); O'Gorman (1987); G.Thomas *et al.* (1996); J.T (1996); vV (1993)

furring See FIRRING.

Furttenbach, Josef (1591-1667) German architect, he prepared a guide-book for Italy (1626) and made his base in Ulm, where he wrote several books on architecture, including *Architectura Civilis* (1628), *Architectura Navalis* (1629), *Architectura Martialis* (1630), *Architectura Universalis* (1635), and *Architectura Recreationis* (1640). He became director of the *Stadtbauamt*, Ulm, and designed the *Brechhaus* (1634), a hospital designed on the latest Italian lines, and a theatre with seats for 1,000 people (1641). He introduced *High-Renaissance architecture to Germany.

E.Hempel (1965); Hewitt (ed.) (1958); Hi (1981); W.Pa (1852)

fusarole Ring of semicircular *section under the *echinus of the Roman-*Doric, *Ionic, and *Composite *Orders, often ornamented.

fust 1. Column-*shaft or *pilaster-trunk. **2.** *Ridge of a roof.

fusuma Sliding *screen in a Japanese house.

Future Systems See KAPLICKY, JAN.

Futurism Italian architectural movement founded (1909) by **Filippo Tommaso Marinetti** (1876-1944). It exploited images derived from industrial buildings (dams, hydro-electric schemes, silos, etc), *skyscrapers, multi-level highways, and factories with curved ends, and it glorified machines, speed, violence, and war. The chief architectural exponents were **Antonio Sant'Elia** (1888-1916) and **Mario Chiattone** (1891-1957), who produced visions of the metropolis of the future, with forms that anticipated work by certain architects, e.g. *Mendelsohn. The movement became closely associated with Fascism, and many of its ideas were absorbed by the *avant-garde*, notably Russian *Constructivists, Le *Corbusier, and *Archigram.

R.Ba (1960); Caramel & Longatti (1988); Hulten (1987); Martin (1977); E.D.C.Meyer (1995); J.T (1996); Tisdall & Bozzolla (1977)

fylfot See CROSS.

Gabetti, Roberto (1925-2000) Italian architect. In partnership with **Aimaro Oreglia d'Isola** (1928-), he designed the influential *Borsa Valori* (1953) and *Bottega d'Erasmo* (1953-6), both in Turin. The latter was seen as an example of *Neo-Liberty (it owes more to *Art Deco), and indeed **Gabetti & d'Isola** declared their rejection of the ideals and doctrines of the *Modern Movement, preferring to explore developments of local building-traditions, thereby incurring the wrath of fundamentalist believers, e.g. *Banham, but nevertheless continued to produce architecture that distanced itself from a tired and discredited style. Among other works may be mentioned the *Società Ippica Torinese*, Turin (1959-60), the *Conca Bianca* *condominium, Sestrière (1976-9), the Orbessano flats, Turin (1982-5), the *monastery at Quart, Val d'Aosta (1984-9), and offices and gardens for SNAM, *San Donato*, Milan (1985-91).

Cellini & D'Amato (eds) (1985); Dal Co *et al.* (1996a); Guerra *et al.* (1996); Olmo *et al.* (1993); Zermani (1989)

Gabio, Jean-Michel del *also* **Dalgabio** (1788-*after* 1828) French architect, pupil of *Vaudoyer, he subscribed to his master's rational views. As Town Architect of St-Étienne, Loire, he taught at the School of Architecture there and designed the Cemetery Chapel, Abattoirs, Exchange (1820), Town Hall, Prison, Corn-Market, Barracks, and other municipal buildings (1821-8). He also restored the Churches of *Ste-Marie* and *St-Thomas*.

W.Pa (1852)

gable, gavel Wall (*gable-end*), of a building, closing the end of a pitched roof: its top may be bounded by the two slopes of the roof forming *parged *verges or *overhangs with *bargeboards, or it may be a *parapet following (more or less) the slopes of the roof behind. Thus *Romanesque gables were steep, and often ornamented (as at Southwell *Minster, Notts.), while *First-Pointed gables (e.g. Lincoln Cathedral) were extremely steep and pierced with windows to illuminate the space behind. Later English medieval gables were usually very steep on domestic architecture, but in churches were almost invariably very slightly sloped, and had *battlemented parapets, often richly decorated.

Brick gables are sometimes finished with *tumbling-courses, and the *cope or tumbling-course is usually prevented from sliding or moving by means of a *gable-springer*, also called *gable-shoulder*, *kneeler, *skew-block, or *skew-butt, at the foot of the gable. Not all gables are triangular. *Other types of gable include*:

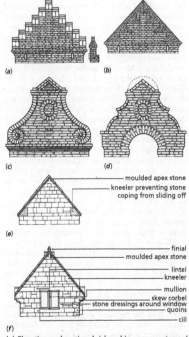

(*a*) Elevation and section, brick corbie- or crow-stepped gable, Kent (*c.*1540). (*b*) Brick gable with tumbled brickwork. (*c*) Shaped brick gable, Kent, *c.*1691 (*after* Lloyd). (*d*) Brick Dutch gable based on Kent and Sussex details. (*e*) Basic stone gable. (*f*) More elaborate stone gable.

crow-stepped: with a stepped top, also called *corbie-stepped*;

Dutch: with curved (often scrolled) sides (*klauwstukken*) and a *pediment on top;

hipped: with the top crowned by a small hipped roof;

shaped: with the sides composed of convex and concave curves, usually with steps between them, and a semicircular or segmental top.

Elaborate gables with windows were features of North-European (especially Flemish and German) C16 and C17 domestic architecture, revived in C19.

gable-entry *See* ENTRY.

gable-shoulder *See* GABLE.

gablet 1. Small *gable-shaped top to e.g. a *buttress, common in early *Gothic architecture. **2.** Type of roof (*gambrel-* or *gablet-*roof) with a small gable rising up from a hipped roof.

Gabriel, Ange-Jacques (1698–1782) One of the greatest French C18 architects, he trained under his father, whom he succeeded as *Contrôleur* of Versailles (1735) and as *Premier Architecte* and Director of the Academy (1742). He was responsible for some of the most distinguished Classical buildings of the *Louis-Quinze* period, continuing and refining the architectural language established by François *Mansart as in the *Grand Pavillon*, Fontainebleau (1749). As Architect to the King, Gabriel carried out extensive alterations and extensions to the Royal Palaces, notably the Opera House at Versailles (1761–8). His largest schemes were for the *École Militaire*, Paris (1750–68), and the *Place Louis XV* (now *Place de la Concorde*), Paris (1755–74): in the latter he created two elegant Classical monumental *façades (the *Hôtel de Coislin* (now Crillon) and the *Gardemeuble* (later *Ministère de la Marine*)) with screens set between end-pavilions owing much to *Perrault's east front of the Louvre of a century earlier. His smaller buildings, including the *Pavillon Français*, Versailles (1749–50), *Le Butard*, Vaucresson, near Versailles (1749–50), *Pavillon de la Muette*, near St-Germain (1753–4) and the *Petit Château*, Choisy (1754–6), all attest to his ability in finding an expression of *noble simplicité*. His masterpiece is the *Petit Trianon*, Versailles (1761–8), which may partly derive from *Palladianism, but its continuous horizontals, absence of curved elements, and ultra-refinement give the building a gracious nobility and serene authority far removed from the *Rococo, a harbinger, perhaps, of *Neo-Classicism.

J-F.Blondel (1752–6); Blondel & Patte (1771–7); Bottineau (1962); B (1980); Ga & Bottineau (1982); Ha (1943–57); Tadgell (1978)

Gabriel, Jacques-Jules (1667–1742) French architect, father of Ange-Jacques *Gabriel, he assisted *Hardouin-Mansart and succeeded de

*Cotte as *Premier Architecte* (1734) and Director of the Academy (1735). He designed several *hôtels in Paris (including the *Hôtel Peyrenne de Moras—later *Musée Rodin*), the *Place d'Armes*, Rennes, and the *Place Royale*, Bordeaux (from 1728), which is probably one of his finest achievements.

Ha (1943–57); Tadgell (1978)

Gabrieli, Gabriel de' (1671–1747) Italian architect, he completed *Palais Liechtenstein*, Vienna (1691–1705), where the stunning *Treppenhaus* is his design. Called to Ansbach (1694), he designed various buildings, most importantly the *Residenz*, completed by the von *Zochas and *Retti. Gabrieli settled (1714) in Eichstätt, where he remodelled part of the Cathedral (1716–18), designed the *Residenz* of the Prince-Bishop (1735–7), and contributed to the planning of the town. He was also responsible for the *Schönbornhof*, the *Weldenpalast*, and the Bishop's Palace, Hirschberg. His work was influenced by that of *Fischer von Erlach and, to a lesser extent, of von *Hildebrandt.

Collectaneen, iv (2001), 110–29; *Heimgarten*, xxiii/2 (1952); *Sammelblatt des Historischen Vereins Eichstätt*, ix (1962–4), 113–6, lxii (1967–8), 33f, lxxi-ii (1978–9), 54–60, lxxxi-ii (1988–9), 83–132, xc (1997), 57–83; *Der Zwiebelturm*, vii (1952), 162–7

Gaddi, Taddeo (*c*.1297–*after* 1366) Consultant architect to the Cathedral in Florence (where he probably completed *Giotto's *campanile from 1337), he also appears to have been responsible for the rebuilding of the *Ponte Vecchio* (1333–45). He may also have worked at the *Palazzo Vecchio* (*c*.1333). **Agnolo Gaddi** (*fl*. second half of C14), presumably Taddeo's son, may have designed several Florentine buildings, but the evidence is confused.

W.Pa (1852); S (1901–2); Vasari (1568)

gadroon, godroon One of a series of *thumbmouldings* like fat fingers joined side by side on the upper surface of a convex moulding. *Gadrooning* (also *knulled* or *lobed decoration*) means ornamented with convex rods or *lobes*.

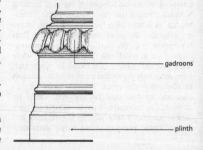

gadroons

plinth

Gahura, František Lydie (1891-1958) *See* COMPANY TOWN.

gaine *Pedestal or *herm (usually the lower part).

Galilee *Narthex or large room between the exterior and the west end of the *nave where penitents and women were admitted, corpses laid out before burial, and monks collected before or after processions. At Durham Cathedral the Galilee is divided into *aisles. Also called *Paradise.

Galilei, Alessandro Maria Gaetano (1691-1737) One of a number of gifted Italian architects active in the first half of C18 whose work moved away from *Baroque towards *Neo-Classicism. He arrived in the British Isles as the chosen architect of the 'New Junta for Architecture', a group of connoisseurs who wished to encourage a Classical style. He designed (1718-19) the *palazzo*-like country-house of Castletown, Celbridge, Co. Kildare, for **Speaker William Conolly** (1662-1729)—begun 1722 under the direction of *Pearce—and the *Doric *portico (1718-19) on the east front of Kimbolton Castle, Hunts., for **Charles Montagu** (*c.*1660-1722—**1st Duke of Manchester** from 1719). He returned to Italy (1719), and was responsible for the splendid *façade (1732-6) of and the lavish Corsini Chapel (1731-3) in *San Giovanni in Laterano*, as well as the front of *San Giovanni dei Fiorentini* (1733-5), Rome.

Co (2008); *CL*, cxlv/3760-2 (1969), 722-6, 798-802, 882-5; Wi (1982)

gallery 1. Large internal passage, often a grand room on the upper floor of an *Elizabethan or *Jacobean house, called *long gallery, extending the full length of a *façade, and used to display pictures and tapestries, for recreation, and as a connecting corridor. Good examples exist at Hardwick and Haddon Halls, both in Derbys. **2.** Large room in which pictures, etc., are hung so that they can be viewed to advantage, often with plain walls and illumination from above, hence a building containing such rooms. **3.** *Arcade, *passage* or *galerie*, in the French sense, top-lit, with shops on either side, also serving as a pedestrian way from street to street. **4.** Passage leading to a burial-chamber (*gallery-grave*) within a *tumulus, the equivalent of the *dromos*. **5.** *Triforium over the *aisles in a large church above the *nave *arcade. **6.** *Scaffold or extra floor for seating in a church placed at the west end and over the aisles. **7.** *Mezzanine at the end of a large hall or room for access between rooms or to accommodate musicians, etc. **8.** Upper level of seating in a theatre. **9.** Passage on top of a *Rood-screen, *choir-screen, or *pulpitum. **10.** Any narrow passage intimately connected with the *fabric of a large building, especially a church. *See* DWARF GALLERY. **11.** Any *arcaded or *colonnaded long passage, not wide or deep, such as an *ambulatory in a *cloister or a passage leading from one building to another.

gallet One of several slivers of stone, splinters of *flint, spalls, or small pebbles inserted in the mortar-joints of a *rubble wall to fill the gaps between stones and leave less *mortar exposed. Hence *galleting* or *garreting*.

Galleting with roughly squared rubble and dressed quoins with chamfered joints, Holy Trinity, Waringstown, Co. Down.

Galli da Bibiena Family Italian *quadratura* painters/theatrical designers/architects. **Ferdinando** (1657-1743) was architect of *Sant'Antonio Abbate*, Parma (1712-60), and author of *L'Architettura civile...* (1711), a text that describes various means of creating spatial illusion. **Francesco** (1659-1739), Ferdinando's brother, designed several theatres (none survives intact), but **Giuseppe** (1695-1747), Ferdinando's son, designed the enchanting *Rococo interior of the *Markgräfliches Opernhaus*, Bayreuth, Bavaria (1745-8), one of the loveliest *auditoria in Europe, completed under the direction of Giuseppe's son, **Carlo Ignazio** (1728-87). Another son of Ferdinando, **Antonio** (1697-*c.*1774), designed the *Nuovo Teatro Pubblico* (now *Teatro Communale*), Bologna (1755-63), the *Teatro Scientifico*, Mantua (1767-9—inspired by *Palladio's *Teatro Olimpico*, Vicenza, but destroyed), and the Church, *Villa Pasquali*, near Sabbioneta (1765-84), with its delicate *trellis-like *stucco-work under the *dome. He also completed the *presbytery, designed the *high-altar, and frescoed the *vault of the *choir of the *Peterskirche*, Vienna (1730-2). A third son, **Alessandro** (1686-1748), became Court Architect to the Electors Palatinate at Mannheim, in which capacity he designed the *Jesuitenkirche* (1738-48), one of the most important *Baroque churches in South-West Germany before it was badly damaged in the 1939-45 war.

Galli da Bibiena (1703-8, 1711); Hadamowsky (1962); Mayor (1945); Muraro & Povoledo (eds) (1970); Wi (1982)

Gallier, James, sen. (1798-1868) Irish-born architect, he designed the 'Chinese Bridge' at Godmanchester, near Huntingdon, England (1827—replaced with a replica, 1960), and several houses in South Street, Mayfair, London, before emigrating (1832) to the USA where he worked for a while in NYC, formed a short-lived partnership with *Lafever, and published *The American Builder's General Price Book and Estimator* (1833). He settled (1834) in New Orleans, in partnership with **Charles Bingley Dakin** (1811–39—joined the following year by J.H.*Dakin), and established a successful practice, designing many important buildings, all in a *Greek-Revival style. The partnership broke up (1836), and Gallier continued on his own, designing the City Hall, New Orleans, LA (1845–50), a handsome building with a Greek *Ionic *portico. He published his autobiography (1864).

Christovich *et al.* (1972–7); Co (2008); Gallier (1973)

Gallo, Francesco (1672–1750) Italian architect, he designed over 100 known works in his native Piedmont, including the *Assunta Carrù* (1702–25), *Sant'Ambrogio*, Cuneo (1710–43), *Santa Chiara*, Mondovi (1712), *Santa Croce*, Cavallermaggiore (1737–43), *San Giovanni Battista*, Racconigi (1719–30), and the elliptical *drum and *dome on *Vitozzi's *Santuario di Vico*, Mondovi (1728–33). The last is probably his greatest achievement.

P (1982); Pommer (1967)

Gambello, Antonio di Marco (*fl.*1458–81) Italian architect/sculptor. Appointed chief architect to *San Zaccaria*, Venice (1458), he worked there all his life (it was completed by *Coducci).

L.O.Puppi & L.Puppi (1977)

gambrel *See* ROOF.

Gameren, Tilman *or* **Tylman van** (*c.*1630–1706) Dutch architect/painter, he became the foremost C17 *Baroque architect in Poland, having been invited (*c.*1660) to settle there, and took the surname **Gamerski**. He designed the villa at Puławy (1671–2), the first with a *pediment on an *Order in Poland. Three rooms designed by him for the *pavilion within the Ujazdów area survive in the Łazienki Palace, and he was also responsible for the Church of the Nuns of the Holy Sacrament in Warsaw's New Town (1688–92—one of the most perfect centralized churches in Europe), and for the Bernardine Church at Czerniaków, Warsaw (1687–92—on a Greek-cross plan with octagonal sanctuary). His Krasiński Palace, Warsaw (1688–95), was an outstanding achievement, and incorporated a *Giant Order for the first time in Poland. He designed some 75 buildings in all, and remodelled the Palace at Nieborów (1695–7).

Kz (1991); Mossakowski (1973); *Zfk*, lvii/2 (1994), 201–18

Ganay, Ernest, Comte de (1880–1963) French garden-historian, his publications include a bibliography of garden-art (1989) and a work on Le *Nôtre.

Ganay (1962, 1989)

Gandelsonas, Mario (1938–) *See* ANALYTICAL DECOMPOSITION.

Gandon, James (1742–1823) English architect, apprenticed to *Chambers, he established his own practice *c.*1765. With the Irishman **John Woolfe** (*fl.*1750–93) he produced the fourth and fifth volumes of *Vitruvius Britannicus* (1767, 1771), published *Six Designs of Frizes* (1767), and two volumes on ornament (1778). He designed Nottingham County Hall (1770), and went to Dublin (1781) to oversee the erection of his Custom House, the design of which owes much to Chambers's Somerset House in London. His excellent contacts ensured he had plenty of work, including the Four Courts (1786–1802) and the new *portico and screen-wall for the Parliament House (1785–9), Dublin. His architecture was influenced by French *Neo-Classicism (through Chambers), but he also admired *Wren. He created some of Ireland's most outstanding buildings.

Co (2008); M.Craig (1969, 1982); H.Duffy (1999); Gandon (1969); McP (1985); Mulvany (1969); Su (1993)

Gandy Brothers English architects/draughtsmen. **Joseph Michael** (1771–1843) travelled to Italy (1794–7) with *Tatham, and became a draughtsman in *Soane's office. Thereafter, even though he established (1801) his own practice, he undertook work for Soane (making fine renderings of Soane's designs), and produced accomplished and eclectic architectural fantasies (1789–1838). He published *The Rural Architect* and *Designs for Cottages, Cottage Farms and other Rural Buildings* (1805). As an architect, Gandy perhaps lacked the discipline to make a success of practice, but he produced some competent work, including the completion of *Harrison's Courts and Gaol, Lancaster (1802–21), the 'Doric House', Sion Hill, Bath (*c.*1810–12—a remarkable severe Grecian building), and Storrs Hall and Boat House, Windermere, Westmd. (1804–11).

Michael (1778–1862) studied under his brother and became James *Wyatt's assistant before travelling in India and China. He was later employed as a draughtsman by *Wyatville, and, with *Baud and *Britton, published *Architectural Illustrations of Windsor Castle* (1842). **John Peter** (1787–1850)—who changed his name (1828) to **Deering**—was a pupil of James Wyatt, and travelled (1811–13) to Greece and Asia Minor with *Gell and *Bedford for the Society of *Dilettanti: the results of the journey were published as *Unedited Antiquities of Attica* (1817) and Volume iii of *Antiquities of Ionia* (1840). He co-authored (with Gell) *Pompeiana* (1817–19), an important work on the excavations. He was regarded as an authority on Greek architecture, and designed the handsome St Mark's Church, North Audley Street, London (1825–8), which was typical of his scholarly approach. Other works by him include the *Tudor-Gothic Infirmary, Stamford, Lincs. (1826–8), the County Gaol, Cardiff, Glamorgan (1827–32), and houses in South Street, Mayfair, London (*c.*1828–30).

Co (2008); Lukacher (2002); Su (1963); W-L (1980)

Ganghofer, Jörg (*fl.*1441–88). German architect, also known as **Jörg von Halsbach** or as **Maurer von Polling**. He became City Architect of Munich (1468), where he designed the *Gothic Frauenkirche. He also contributed to the works at the *Rathaus* in the same city.

Frankl (2000); J.T (1996)

gantry 1. Stand for barrels, shelves, racks, etc., often treated with elaborate architectural enrichment and mirrors, behind a *bar in a public-house. **2.** Frame/platform for a travelling crane, etc.

Garbett, Edward Lacy (*fl.*1840–1900). English architectural theorist, author of *Rudimentary Architecture for the Use of Beginners and Students, the Principles of Design in Architecture as Deducible from Nature and Exemplified in the Works of the Greek and Gothic Architects* (1850), he argued that style was linked to construction, and that modern methods of building would lead to non-*Historicist styles.

AR, clii/908 (Oct. 1972), 239–41; JSAH, xvii/4 (Winter 1958), 25–30

Gardella, Ignazio (1909–99) Italian architect, his work was steeped in *Rationalism, and he made his name with the Anti-Tuberculosis Dispensary, Alessandria (1936–8). His *Regina Isabella* Thermal Baths, Lacco Ameno, Ischia (1950–3), and Gallery of Contemporary Art, *Villa Reale*, Milan (1951–4), were admired for their rigour and clarity. The School of Architecture, University of Genoa (1975–90), drew on traditional forms.

Argan (1959); E (1994); Ry (1994); J.T (1996); Zermani (1991)

garden 1. Enclosed piece of ground devoted to the cultivation of flowers, fruit, vegetables, etc., often preceded by a defining word, e.g. flower-, fruit-, kitchen-, market-, etc. **2.** Ornamental grounds, again with a defining word, e.g. *botanical, *pleasure-, zoological-, etc. **3.** Bordered or enclosed area with lawns, *terraces, *parterres, etc., contiguous to a dwelling, used for enjoyment.

Gardens for perambulation, spiritual succour, pleasure, and recreation have been known since ancient times: some had religious significance, and water (in channels, rivulets, or fountains) helped to enhance them. Certain gardens where the architectural content was huge, e.g. those of the *Villa d'Este* at Tivoli (1565–72—by *Ligorio), were designed to link the present to the past, and contained complex programmes to trigger historical, philosophical, and religious musings. Rigid geometrical planning of gardens was known in *Islamic architecture, but in France, the formal *Baroque garden, with features such as *parterres, was created on a grand scale by designers such as Le *Nôtre. There was a reaction against such formality, notably in England, where the *landscape-garden, laid out in a more 'natural' manner to form compositions in the *Picturesque fashion, often with *fabriques, became influential.

Tay (2006)

garden-cemetery Known in the USA as *rural cemetery*, it combined the landscaped park with the *cemetery, enhancing Nature with Art (an idea promoted by *Loudon), and was the precursor in America of the *public park.

Garden City *and* **Garden Suburb** The 'Garden City', devised in England by Ebenezer *Howard (theoretically to combine the benefits of town and country), involved the creation of a town built in the countryside with all facilities, places of work, etc. Influenced by the Garden Suburbs (low-density developments that were essentially derived from the *Picturesque tradition of houses in gardens evolved by *Nash and others at, e.g., Blaise Hamlet near Bristol), the first Garden City was at Letchworth, Herts. (begun 1903), designed by *Parker and *Unwin. The *vernacular-revival style of houses at Letchworth was influenced by the earlier Garden Suburb, Bedford Park, Chiswick, London (from 1877), and by housing-developments and settlements such as Port Sunlight (from 1888) and Bournville, Birmingham (from 1879). Hampstead Garden Suburb (from 1906) was an excellent example of low-density development in which the *Domestic Revival featured prominently, but it was essentially a *dormitory-suburb as opposed to a Garden City, which was, in theory, largely self-contained. Germany acquired an important development at Hellerau, near Dresden, designed by *Riemerschmid and *Tessenow (begun 1907), and in Belgium, influenced by *Geddes, **Louis van der Swaelmen** (1883–1929—author of *Préliminaires d'art civique* (1916)) played a major part in planning the first Garden Cities at Selzaete, near Gent (1921–3), Kapelleveld (1923–6), and three more near Brussels, including the *Cité*

Floreal and Boitefort. *Stein promoted Howard's ideas in the USA.

K-P.Arnold (1991); Beevers (1988); Benoît-Levy (1911, 1932); Creese (ed.) (1967, 1992); Darley (1975); Fishman (1977); E.Howard (1898, 1902, 1946, 1965); Loo (ed.) (2003); Meacham (1999); Me.Miller (1992, 2002); M & G (1992); Parsons & D.Schuyler (eds) (2002); S.Ward (ed.) (1992)

gardeners' tunnel *See* SERVANTS' TUNNEL.

Gardenesque 1. Design-style identified by *Loudon (1832) as going further than *Repton in *improving* on Nature and displaying the art of a garden: it is a style of laying out a garden, contrasted with the *Picturesque (where trees, shrubs, and flowers were indiscriminately mixed, and crowded together, though forming groups or masses pleasing to admirers of landscape) or with the rigid geometries of the *Baroque. In Gardenesque schemes the uniqueness and beauty of individual plants could be appreciated, and they also had an educational purpose. The style was introduced to the USA by *Downing. William *Robinson reassessed Gardenesque principles, and the *Arts-and-Crafts movement also encouraged their development. *See* NATURESQUE; PICTURESQUE. **2.** Ornament or architecture suited to, or which enhances, a garden.

JGH, ii/2 (April–June 1982), 175–88; MacDougall (1980); J.K.Major (1997); O'Malley *et al.* (2010); Tay (2006); M.W

Garden of Allusions Garden consciously designed and embellished with many and varied *fabriques* intended to imply covert references, perhaps to trigger thoughts in visitors walking through it about architecture, civilizations, culture, history, ideas, personalities, or even a journey through Life itself. The type was a complex mnemonic device, prompting emotional, historical, and literary associations (*see* ASSOCIATIONISM), all imbued with feeling.

J.Curl (2011)

garderobe 1. Place where garments were stored. **2.** Medieval latrine.

Gardiner, Stephen (1924–2007) English architect, he worked first with Wells *Coates, then with other *Modernists, including Jane *Drew, *Fry (on the *Festival of Britain), and *Sheppard. He taught for many years at the Oxford School of Architecture. In private practice with **Christopher Shirley Knight** (1925–2013), he designed a new house (1963–5) at Stratton Park, East Stratton, Hants., to replace another by *Dance the Younger (demolished 1960), retaining the *tetrastyle unfluted Greek-*Doric *portico. Gardiner wrote a monograph on Le *Corbusier (1974), and was Architectural Correspondent of *The Observer* (1970–93).

The Times (16 Feb. 2007), 76; pk

gargoyle Spout to take water from a *gutter behind a *parapet away from a wall to spew it on the ground. Medieval gargoyles (sometimes mere ornaments) are frequently of stone, imaginatively sculpted in the form of devils, composite animals, etc.

garland 1. Wreath-like ornament of flowers, leaves, etc. **2.** *Festoon. **3.** Ornamental *band around a *Gothic *spire etc.

Garner, Thomas (1839–1906) English *Gothic Revival architect, pupil of 'Great' *Scott. In partnership (1869–97) with G.F.*Bodley, he made a major contribution to the work of the firm, notably at St Augustine, Pendlebury, Manchester (1870–4), and the exquisite Holy Angels, Hoar Cross, Staffs. (1872–6). After the partnership was dissolved, Garner carried out works at Yarnton Manor, Oxon., and Moreton House, Hampstead (1896–7), among other commissions. *Bentley considered him a designer of genius, and there is certainly a warmth in the buildings he erected in collaboration with Bodley that is lacking when the latter worked on his own. He wrote *The Domestic Architecture of England during the Tudor Period* (1908–11), with **Arthur James Stratton** (1872–1955). Garner (who became an RC) designed the *chancel at Downside Abbey, Som. (1901–5), as fine a work of liturgiological and ecclesiological scholarship as may be found in England.

J.Curl (2007); D & M (1985); J.Fawcett (ed.) (1976); *RIBAJ*, 3 ser. xvii (10 Feb. 1910), 305–40

Garnier, Jean-Louis-Charles (1825–98) French architect, a student of *Lebas. During his time as a *pensionnaire* in Rome (1848–54) he visited Greece and Turkey, and seems to have been more enchanted with *Byzantine and other styles than he was with Ancient-Greek architecture, although he investigated the Temple of Aphaia, Aegina, largely from the point of view of its colouring in Antiquity. When he returned to Paris he worked for a period under *Ballu, but took on what private commissions he could obtain. He made his name with his designs (won in competition) for the *Opéra* in Paris (1861–75), the most luxuriant building of the *Second-Empire *Beaux-Arts* style, yet one in which the disposition of the main elements is immediately clear from the exterior. Garnier drew his inspiration from the Italian *Renaissance, notably the architectural visions of **Paolo Veronese** (1528–88), the Venetian painter, while echoes of *Sansovino are detectable (the lavish staircase mingled *Baroque and Venetian Renaissance themes). The *Opéra* was immensely successful and influential, its confident brashness finally laying the drier aspects of French *Rationalism to rest, and setting the agenda for public architectural style in France until 1914, but it has tended to overshadow Garnier's many other architectural achievements. His ebullient interpretation of Italian- and French-Renaissance styles can be seen in a number of his works, including the *Cercle de la Librairie* (1878–9), 117 *Boulevard St-Germain*, the *Maison Hachette* apartment-block at 195 on the same *Boulevard* (1878–80), and, especially, the *Casino*, Monte Carlo (1876/8–9). The last, a lushly festive concoction, influenced the style of buildings along the Riviera and in other seaside resorts. In the 1890s, however, the *Casino* theatre was altered to enable large-scale operatic performances to take place, and Garnier protested (1897), in vain, to the architect **Henri Schmit** (1851–1904) about the changes to his work.

He published his theory of theatre-design in *Le Théâtre* (1871) and *Nouvel Opéra de Paris* (1878–81). His reconstruction of the Aegina *temple (complete with *polychrome decorations) was published in *Le Temple de Jupiter Panhellénien à Égine* (1884), and he also published works on domestic architecture in *Constructions élevées aux Champs de Mars* (1890) and *L'Habitation humaine* (1892).

Dr (ed.) (1977); C.Garnier (1871, 1878–81); Kliczkowski (ed.) (2003); Mead (ed.) (1991); Patureau (1992); Steinhauser (1970)

Garnier, Tony (1869–1948) Born in Lyons, he was City Architect there (1905–19) before setting up his own practice. He designed the huge *Abattoirs de la Mouche*, Lyons (1909–13), with a gigantic top-lit open hall constructed of large steel trusses recalling *Dutert's *Galerie des Machines* in Paris (1889). He was also responsible for the *Stadium (1913–16), the *Hôpital Édouard Herriot* (1915–20), and the low-cost housing district, *États-Unis* (1928–35), all in Lyons. He is remembered primarily for his unrealized *Cité Industrielle*, a design for a model town of 35,000 people, which he mostly conceived while a student in Rome: it was exhibited (1904), and published (1918). While the idea for the *Cité* owed something to English ideas (low density, zoning of function, etc.) and the Utopian notions of *Fourier et al., the architecture was to be uncompromisingly non-derivative, most of the structure was to be of *reinforced concrete, and the town-planning principles as taught by the *École des *Beaux-Arts were jettisoned. The *Cité Industrielle* influenced Le *Corbusier and other Modernists. Garnier continued to build monuments, schools, and other buildings until the 1939–45 war, but his chief legacy was in forming C20 ideas about architecture and planning.

T.Garnier (1920, 1932, 1938, 1951); Guiheux *et al.* (eds) (1989); Hi (1977); Jullian (1989); Pawlowski (1967); Ve (1947); Wn (1970)

garret Space in a building beneath the roof-covering and above the uppermost storey of flat-ceilinged rooms, therefore with sloping sides. It may be unlit, or illuminated with roof-lights, *dormers, etc. Not to be confused with an *Attic.

garreting *See* GALLET.

Garrett, Daniel (*fl.*1727–53). English builder/architect, *protégé* of *Burlington, he acted as clerk of works for many projects before establishing (*c.*1735) his own practice, designing numerous schemes in the North of England, e.g. the steps, balustrades, and outer court for *Hawksmoor's *mausoleum at Castle Howard, Yorks. (1737–42). Not averse to using *Rococo plasterwork or to designing in the *Gothick taste (e.g. Banqueting House, Gibside, Co. Durham (1751)), he brought out the pioneering *Designs and Estimates of Farm-Houses, etc*...(1747). He may have been related to, or had business connections with, *Paine, who succeeded him as architect in many locations (e.g. Gibside).

Co (2008)

garth 1. Planted *enclosure. **2.** Open area surrounded by the *ambulatory of a *cloister.

Gärtner, Friedrich von (1792–1847) German Romantic Neo-Classical architect: he and von *Klenze were the most distinguished practitioners working in Munich in the first half of C19, and influenced later generations. Gärtner trained (1808–12) under K. von *Fischer in Munich, *Weinbrenner in Karlsruhe (1812–13), and *Percier and *Fontaine in Paris (1814), before making the obligatory tour of Italy (1814–17) followed by a visit to The Netherlands and England, where he was fascinated by industrial architecture and problems of industrialization. He then settled in the Bavarian capital and taught at the Academy. He published (1819) his *Ansichten der am meisten erhaltnen griechischen Monumente Siciliens*. Not until after he had met (1827) the future **King Ludwig I** (*r.*1825–48) was he commissioned to design buildings, starting with the Court and State Library (1827–43) and *Ludwigskirche* (1829–44) in the *Ludwigstrasse*, both in the *Rundbogenstil* derived from Florentine *palazzi* and Italian *Early-Christian and *Romanesque architecture. Semicircular-arched Florentine *Renaissance was used for the Institute for the Blind (1835), the Women's Charitable Foundation (1835–9), and the Offices of the Salt Works (1838–43), all in the *Ludwigstrasse*. At the Salt Works Gärtner employed exposed brickwork, suggested by buildings in Bologna he had seen on his Italian tour. He also designed the *Universitätsplatz*, including the University (1835–40), *Georgianum* (1835–40), and Girls' School (1837). This rich urban scheme was further embellished by the

Siegestor (1843-54), a *triumphal arch derived from the Arch of **Constantine** (*r*.324-37), Rome. For the other end of the *Ludwigstrasse* Gärtner designed the *Feldherrnhalle* (1841-3), a copy of the *Loggia dei Lanzi*, Florence. This mix of Florentine medieval and Romanesque architecture with Classical elements was not accidental, but was a component of the King of Bavaria's policy to make Munich a cultural and national capital of European significance. Perhaps Gärtner's finest composition was the 'Pompeian House', Aschaffenburg (1842-6), based on the house of Castor and Pollux, Pompeii, which inventively alludes to Antiquity. He also designed the *Villa Ludwigshöhe*, near Edenkoben, Palatinate—an *Italianate *villa that has reminiscences of *Palladio's *Palazzo Chiericati*, Vicenza—and the *Kursaal*, Bad Kissingen (1834).

When **Prince Otto of Bavaria** (1815-67), Ludwig's second son, became **King Othon of Greece** (*r*.1833-62), Gärtner travelled to that country in order to design the new Royal Palace in Athens (1836-41), a Neo-Classical building with fine interiors, many in the *Pompeian style. Gärtner also planned part of the new Athens that was to acquire so many distinguished Neo-Classical buildings by the *Hansens and others.

Eggert (1963); Hederer (1976); Hi (1977); Ne (1987, 1992); Wa & M (1987)

gate 1. Opening in a wall, *fence, etc., allowing admission and exit, capable of being closed by a moveable barrier, to afford defence/containment of what is within. **2.** The barrier itself, turning on pivots or hinges, or sliding in a groove, usually constructed of wood or of metal, or a combination of these. **3.** Monumental entrance to a large building, city, etc., e.g. Brandenburg Gate, Berlin (1789-94), by *Langhans. **4.** Name of a way, road, path, or street (as in *Gallowgate*, *Micklegate*, etc.).

gate-house 1. Dwelling or office at or over the entrance to a park, *cemetery, country-estate, etc., e.g. a *lodge. **2.** Apartment over the *gate of a city, palace, etc.

gate-post Upright upon which a *gate hangs or against which it shuts.

gateway 1. Passage capable of being closed by a *gate, i.e. an opening in a *fence or wall. **2.** *Frame or arched opening in which a gate is hung. **3.** Structure built over a gate, for defence or for architectural reasons, e.g. gateway to an Oxbridge college. Medieval gateways were often large and architecturally ambitious structures erected over the principal entrances to the precincts of religious establishments (e.g. those of the *abbey at Bury St Edmunds, Suffolk (*c*.1120-48, *c*.1327-53), colleges, *courts of houses, *castles, etc.). They frequently had a large archway for

horse-drawn vehicles and smaller entrances for pedestrians, and strong gates were fitted to inner and outer arches. Ceilings of entrance-ways were commonly vaulted.

Gau, Franz Christian (1790-1853) German-born architect, he settled (1810) in Paris, travelled in Italy and Egypt, and published his *Antiquités de la Nubie* (1822-7) as well as important work on *Pompeii (1829, 1838). He was appointed (1839) architect for the distinguished and scholarly *Gothic-Revival *Ste-Clotilde*, Paris (begun 1846), completed by *Ballu.

Gau (1822-7, 1829-38); M & Wa (1987)

Gaudí y Cornet, Antonio (1852-1926) Catalan architect, he worked all his life in and around Barcelona, where he was part of the *Renaixensa* or renascence of Catalan patriotism, expressed in a strange and wilful architecture drawing on Islamic and *Gothic monuments of Spain. His first important work was the *Casa Vicens* (1878-85), Barcelona, a riotously *polychrome *villa in which Gothic and *Moorish themes were overtly expressed. This was followed by *El Capricho* (1883-5), a summer villa at Comillas, near Santander, again uninhibited in its exploitation of geometry and colour. His patron from the early 1880s was the industrialist, **Baron Eusebi Güell i Bacigalupi** (1847-1918), for whom Gaudí designed the *Palacio Güell*, Barcelona (1885-9), a complex building, its street *façade reminiscent of a vaguely Venetian-Gothic prototype, with parabolic arches and a roof embellished with tile-encrusted chimneys and ventilators. Tile-encrusted too were the serpentine seats of the *Parque Güell* (from 1900).

From 1883 Gaudí worked on the design of the Expiatory Church of the *Sagrada Familia*, which started as a Gothic structure, but was gradually transformed into a very free composition owing something to Gothic, but more to an imagination fired by *Art-Nouveau tendencies and the structural possibilities of parabolic forms and inclined *piers. In order to evolve a structure in equilibrium, Gaudí designed *catenary cord models with weights that transformed the hanging curves into funicular polygons from which masons could take measurements. Even more startling was the *Modernismo* apartment-block, the *Casa Batlló* (1904-6), a remodelling of an earlier structure, with a façade of bony stone uprights carrying free arched openings over which is a ceramic-faced front from which project mask-like balconies resembling human pelvic-bones. More extreme is the *Casa Milá* (1906-10), a layered pile-up of inwardly inclining stone *piers carrying I-beams between which spring tile *vaults, the whole capped by a surreal collection of tiled chimneys, etc. Internal planning avoids right-angled rooms, and the block is one of the most extraordinary creations of its time. He collaborated with *Jujol on these and other projects. It was proposed (1998) that Gaudí should be beatified, an unusual fate for an architect.

BN (1979, 2000); BN *et al.* (2002); Bergos Masso *et al.* (1999); Boh (1968); Boh *et al.* (1991); Carmel-Arthur (1999); Casanelles (1968); G.Collins (1960, 1973); G.Collins & BN (1983); Descharnes (1982); Hensbergen (2001); Kent & Prindle (1993); Martinell (1975); Pane (1964); P (1982); J.Sweeney & Sert (1970); Thiébaut (2002); T-M (1967)

gavel *See* GABLE.

Gay, William (1814–93) ?English landscape-gardener/surveyor, he designed several *public parks, but is best known for *cemetery layouts. Appointed Superintendent of Welford Road Cemetery, Leicester (1842–9), he was profoundly influenced by *Hamilton & Medland's landscape-design (which was in turn informed by the theories of *Loudon), and helped to realize this. He designed cemeteries at Undercliffe, Bradford, Yorks. (1852–5—with **John Dale** (1821–70)); Lancaster (1855—with E.G.*Paley); Toxteth Park, Liverpool (1856); Belfast City (1866–9); Philips Park, East Manchester (1864–7—with **Oliver Ayliffe** (*fl.*1860–70) and **Henry John Paull** (*fl.*1860–88)); Pudsey, Yorks. (1875); and Lawnswood, Leeds, Yorks. (opened 1875—a project in which he assisted **George Corson** (1829–1910)). He was also involved in design for several public parks, including Saltaire, Shipley, near Bradford, Yorks. (1870–1).

Bentley (1926); Chapple (ed.) (1982); Clark & Davison (2004); Conway (1985, 1991); *GH*, xxxiii/1(Summer 2005), 61–86; Hartley (2010)

gazebo 1. Garden-house built at the corner of a garden-wall with windows on all sides commanding views. 2. *Turret, *lantern, or look-out on the roof of a house or a *belvedere or *summer-house in a garden commanding an extensive prospect. 3. Projecting *balcony or window with a view.

Geary, Stephen (1797–1854) ?English architect/civil engineer/inventor, he designed King's Cross, Battle Bridge, London (1830–6, lampooned (1836) by A.W.N.*Pugin, demolished 1845), but is best known as the original architect for Highgate Cemetery, London (from 1837), where he designed the *Egyptian and *Gothic-Revival *catacombs, among other works. He published *Designs for Tombs and Cenotaphs* (1840) in which he was credited with the founding of other cemeteries in the London area. He is supposed to have designed the first *gin-palace in London (*c.*1829).

Co (2008); J.Curl (2004, 2005); Pugin (1973)

Geay, Jean-Laurent Le (*c.*1710–*c.*1786) French architect, he won (1732) the *Grand Prix d'Architecture*, and worked at the French Academy in Rome (1738–42), returning to Paris, where he gained a reputation as a Neo-Classicist. With *Knobelsdorff he prepared plans (1747–8) for St Hedwig's RC Cathedral, Berlin (executed (1772–3) with modifications by *Boumann and Bühring). After a spell (from1748) as Architect to **Christian Ludwig II** (1683–1756—**Duke of Mecklenburg-Schwerin** from 1747), during which he designed a water-garden at Schwerin and a larger (unexecuted) project for *Ludwigslust*, he was appointed (1756) *Premier Architecte* to **King Friedrich II** (**'the Great'**) **of Prussia** (*r.*1740–86), for whom he designed the elegant *Communs* (or service-wing), in the form of semicircular *colonnades flanked by domed and porticoed *pavilions, standing before the *Neues Palais*, Potsdam, realized later to slightly altered designs by *Gontard. After quarrelling with the King (1763), he seems to have built little, but published etchings of fountains, ruins, tombs, and vases collected as *Collection de Divers Sujets de Vases, Tombeaux, Ruines, et Fontaines Utiles aux Artistes Inventée et Gravée par J.-L. Le Geay, Architecte* (1770), providing a large array of Neo-Classical motifs, many of which were based on the work of *Piranesi. Le Geay taught *Boullée, *Moreaux-Desproux, *Peyre, and de *Wailly, and through them spread the Neo-Classical gospel.

Jervis (1984); Wa & M (1987)

Geddes, Norman Bel (1893–1958) American designer, he became identified with the style known as 'streamlining', based on aerodynamics. He designed the Toledo Scale Company Building, Ohio (1929), General Motors Pavilion at the New York World's Fair (1939), and produced a scheme of prefabricated housing systems for the Housing Corporation of America (1940). He published *Magic Motorways* (1940), and was responsible for many interiors.

N.Geddes (1932, 1940, 1940a); W.Kelley (ed.) (1960); Welter (2002)

Geddes, Sir Patrick (1854–1932) Scots town-planning theorist, he gave emphasis to preliminary surveys and analyses (including sociological research) before any action should be taken. His study of Dunfermline, described by *Abercrombie as the first town-planning report ever undertaken, was published as *City Development* (1904). He organized the influential 'Cities and Town-Planning Exhibition' in London (1910), and later prepared numerous reports on cities in India. His designs included the first hall of residence for students at Edinburgh University (1892) and the Outlook Tower (1895) in the same city. He was one of the first in Britain to call himself (1907) a landscape architect.

Boardman (1978); P.Geddes (1918, 1973); LeG & S (1996); Meller (1990); *ODNB* (2004); Tyrwhitt (ed.) (1947)

Gehry (*originally* **Goldberg**), **Frank Owen** (1929–) *See* DECONSTRUCTIVISM.

geison 1. Stone block forming part of a Classical *cornice and its subordinate *mouldings. 2. *Cope projecting from a wall. 3. Horizontal cornice of a *pediment, often with a very deep shelf-like top to permit statuary to be placed in the *tympanum.

Gell, Sir William (1777–1836) English archaeologist/antiquarian. His publications include *Topography of Troy* (1804), *Geography and Antiquities of Ithaca* (1807), *Itinerary of Greece* (1810), and *Itinerary of the Morea* (1817). With J.P.*Gandy (later **Deering**) he published *Pompeiana* (1817), and later (1832) *Pompeiana: the Topography, Ornaments, etc.*, showing the results of excavations at *Pompeii since 1819. His work is of particular interest because he drew the excavations and artefacts with the aid of a *camera lucida*, so the images are remarkably accurate. His work influenced late *Neo-Classicism, the *Néo-Grec* style, and many designers, e.g. Owen *Jones.

Gell & Gandy (1852); *ODNB* (2004)

gemel, gemmel(e), gimmer Anything paired, e.g. a *hinge, or a pair of window-openings. *See* CHYMOL.

Genelli, Hans Christian (1763–1823) German architect/archaeologist, pioneer of the *Greek Revival, he proposed (1786) a severe Greek-*Doric *temple as a monument to **King Friedrich II** ('**the Great**') **of Prussia** (*r*.1740–86), a revolutionary idea that influenced F.*Gilly when designing his later (1797) proposals for Berlin. He published a reconstruction of the *Mausoleum at Halicarnassus in an edition of *Vitruvius (1801), a commentary on Vitruvius (1801–4), and a study of the theatre in Athens (1818). He designed *Haus Ziebingen* near Frankfurt-on-the-Oder (*c*.1800), one of the most severe Neo-Classical *villas of the period.

Wa & M (1987)

Genga, Girolamo (*c*.1476–1551) Born in Urbino, where he spent most of his life, his architecture was influenced by *Bramante and *Raphael, notably at the *Monte dei Imperiale* villa, Pesaro (begun 1530), which in turn influenced the design of the *Villa Giulia*, Rome. He carried out alterations and additions to the Ducal Palace, Urbino, from 1523, and designed *Santa Maria delle Grazie*, Sinigaglia (from 1535), and *San Giovanni Battista*, Pesaro (from 1543).

Groblewski (1976); Pinelli (1971); Tafuri (1966); J.T (1996)

genius loci Latin term meaning 'the genius of the place', referring to the presiding deity or spirit. Every place has its own unique qualities, not only in terms of its physical makeup, but of how it is perceived, so it ought to be (but far too often is not) the responsibilities of the architect or landscape-designer to be sensitive to those unique qualities, to enhance them rather than to destroy them. Alexander *Pope, in *Epistle IV* (1731) of his *Moral Essays*, addressed to *Burlington, states in his *Argument* that, 'instanced in architecture and gardening, . . . all must be adapted to the genius of the place, and . . . beauties not forced into it, but resulting from it'.

Batey (1999); Goulty (1991); N-S (1980a)

genlese, gentese Apparently same as FEATHERING.

gentrification Migration of middle classes into former working-class areas, with a resulting change of character, e.g. modernization/repair of old property.

Gentz, Heinrich (1766–1811) German architect, he studied under *Gontard, and was a leading light of spartan Franco-Prussian *Neo-Classicism. He became *Hofbaumeister* in Berlin (1795), and won praise for his entry to the 1797 competition for a monument to **King Friedrich II** ('**the Great**') **of Prussia** (*r*.1740–86). His severe, uncompromising style was demonstrated in the New Mint, Berlin (1798–1800), which also contained (1799–1806) the *Bauakademie*, where he and Friedrich *Gilly, his brother-in-law, taught. At the *Schloss*, Weimar, Gentz designed some fine Neo-Classical interiors, including the staircase of the East Wing (an early example of the *Greek Revival), the *Festsaal*, Cedar Room, and Falcon Gallery (1800–3). He also designed an extension to the *Prinzessinpalais*, Berlin (1810), and (with *Schinkel) the Greek-*Doric *mausoleum for the beloved **Queen Luise of Prussia** (*r*.1797–1810), Charlottenburg (also 1810).

Doebber (1911); Doebber (ed.) (1916); Jericke & Dolgner (1975); Wa & M (1987)

geode Piece of rock having a *druse*, or cavity lined with crystals, or a rounded hollow ironstone nodule used e.g. in *rock-rash facings.

geodesic dome Half-spherical *space-frame made of linked lightweight elements arranged in hexagonal figures. *See* BUCKMINSTER FULLER.

Geoffrey de Noiers (*fl.c*.1200) *See* NOIERS.

geometric *See* STAIR.

Geometrical *See* STAIR; TRACERY.

George, Sir Ernest (1839–1922) English architect, he set up a practice first (1861–71) with

Thomas Vaughan (1836–74), then (1876–92) with H.A.*Peto, and last (1892–1919) with **Alfred Bowman Yeates** (1867–1944). The firm specialized in expensive domestic architecture, often of brick with *terracotta dressings, in a *Free style derived from North-European late-*Gothic and *Renaissance architecture. Good examples include Harrington Gardens and Collingham Gardens, South Kensington (1880–90), and houses on the Cadogan Estate, London, notably in Pont Street, which gave the style the name *Pont-Street Dutch. Herbert *Baker, *Lutyens, and Weir *Schultz all worked in his prestigious office. Other buildings include Golders Green Crematorium (1901–5—in a Lombardic style), and the Ossington Coffee Palace, Newark, Notts. (1882— a charming building with gables and a variety of *Ipswich window).

A.S.Gray (1985); Grainger (2011); Hobhouse (ed.) (1986); *ODNB* (2004)

Georgian architecture English architecture during the reigns of the first four **Georges** (1714–1830), which saw the rise of *Palladianism, the varied and elegant work of Robert *Adam, and fashions for *Rococo, *Chinoiserie, *Gothick, and *Hindoo styles. It also embraced early *Gothic and *Greek Revivals, the *Picturesque, *eclecticism, *Neo-Classicism, and the taste for *Etruscan and *Pompeian design, as well as the new, elemental, powerful architecture of the canals, railways, and industry, so it included much that was *Sublime. 'Georgian' often describes a type of C18 and early C19 domestic architecture with unadorned window-apertures, double-hung *sashes, and *door-cases (often with *fan-lights), sometimes embellished with columns, *pilasters, *entablatures, *pediments, and *consoles, but there was far more to it than that.

B.Clarke (1963); Ck (1985); J.Curl (2011a); Su (1980a, 1986, 1988, 1993, 2003); Su *et al.* (1983)

Gerbier, Sir Balthazar (1592–1663) Born in Middelburg, Netherlands, descended from French Huguenots, he settled (1616) in England, becoming naturalized 1629. As adviser to **George Villiers** (1592–1628—**1st Duke of Buckingham** from 1623), he carried out extensive alterations at York House, Strand, London, and New Hall, Essex, in 1624–5 (both destroyed). The Water Gate on Embankment Gardens, London (1626–7—formerly at York House, and derived from the *Fontaine des Médicis*, Luxembourg Palace, Paris), has been attributed to him, but Inigo *Jones and Nicholas *Stone also have claims to authorship. Gerbier may have introduced Netherlandish *Baroque and *Mannerist themes to England, but these were overshadowed by Jones's *Palladianism. He published *A Brief Discourse concerning the Three Chief Principles of Magnificent Building*

(1662) and *Counsel and Advise to All Builders* (1663). The large *Jacobean house at Hampstead Marshall, Berks. (started 1662, completed (1688) by William *Winde), was remodelled by him (destroyed).

Co (2008); Croft-Murray & Hulton (1960); Su (1993); H.Williamson (1949)

Gerlach, Philipp (1679–1748) Born in Spandau, Brandenburg, he became head of the State Building Administration (1720), and laid out the Berlin district of Friedrichstadt (1732–6), complete with square, octagonal, and circular urban spaces. He designed a number of the most important buildings for this quarter, including the *Palais von Marschall* (1735–6—destroyed), and the *Kammergericht* (1733–5), where the dominant influence was French. His Garrison Church, Potsdam (1731–5), had the finest *Baroque tower in Northern Germany before its destruction in the 1939–45 war.

E.Hempel (1965); Reuther (1969); Zucker (1959)

German Order Type of C18 *Corinthian *Order, also called the *Britannic Order*, the *volutes replaced by winged lions and unicorns and the *fleuron superseded by the Crown. Its incorporation of Royal emblems led to its association with the House of Hanover, hence its name.

German tile *Tile with concave upper edge fitting into a corresponding groove in the lower edge of the tile above. *German siding* is timber boarding with similar upper and lower edges to those described previously.

Gesellius, Herman (1874–1916) Finnish architect, he designed (with Eliel *Saarinen) the Helsinki and Viipuri Railway Stations (from 1904). His work was in the *National-Romantic style, of which the Villa at Hvitträsk (1901–3) and National Museum, Helsinki (1902–5), both designed with *Lindgren and Saarinen, are good examples, drawing on stylistic aspects from Britain, the USA, and Vienna. His work was also influenced by *Jugendstil* tendencies, but his Wuorio Office Building, Helsinki (1908–10), designed independently, was free from both *Jugendstil* and National Romanticism.

Wi.Cu (1996); J.M.Ri (1978); Salokorpi (1970); J.B.Smith (1975)

Gesner, Conrad *or* **Konrad von** (1516–65) Swiss naturalist, his *Historia Animalium* (1551–8) is considered to herald modern Zoology. In *Libellus de Lacte et operibus lactariis* (On Milk and Substances produced from Milk—1541) he published appreciation of mountains for botanical studies and exercise of body and mind, themes to which he returned in *Descriptio Montis Fracti sive Mantis Pilati* (1555). He claimed the senses were heightened in contemplation of mountainous scenery, and so was one of the very first to write positively about it: he also appears to have been the first to record the term *châlet*, locating it in its Swiss context.

J.Curl (2011); Gesner (1541–1555)

Gessner, Salomon (1730–88) Swiss etcher/ painter/poet, he extolled the benefits of 'natural' landscapes compared with *Baroque regimenta- tion. His importance here lies in his *Idyllen* (1756), which enjoyed sensational success: his 'weeping pastorals' suggested tombs in gardens where the dead would be kept 'alive' in thought and spirit. His was therefore an influence on the transformation of the *landscape-garden to the *garden-cemetery.

J.Curl (2011); Gessner (1756, 1776, 1802)

gesso *Plaster of Paris*, or *gypsum*, mixed with *glue* and *whiting* (ground chalk) used to prepare a flat surface for painting, or to raise parts of the surface to enhance enrichment of a painting, as in the exquisite late-medieval panels of the *chan- cel-screen in St Edmund's Church, Southwold, Suffolk. *Gesso duro* is of superior quality, used for making bas-reliefs which are then painted to resemble *terracotta* or *faïence*.

N (1835)

Gherardi, Antonio (1644–1702) Italian paint- er/architect, he remodelled the Avila Chapel, *Santa Maria in Trastévere*, Rome (*c.*1686), in which space is magically extended in all direc- tions, notably upwards, where angels carry a ring under the *cupola. Even richer is his Chapel of *Santa Cecilia*, *San Carlo ai Catinari* (1691– 1702). Works of *Bernini, *Borromini, and *Guar- ini influenced his architecture.

Pi (1970); Wi (1982)

Ghiberti, Lorenzo (*c.*1378–1455) Florentine goldsmith, he designed bronze doors for the Bap- tistery, Florence (1403–24, 1424–32), and from 1420 was appointed supervisor (with *Brunelleschi and **Battista d'Antonio**) for the building of the great *dome at Florence Cathedral, a position he held until 1436. He claimed in his autobiographi- cal *Commentaries* to have executed the dome with Brunelleschi and at the same salary.

Ghiberti (1947); He (1996); Kra *et al.* (1956)

Gianotti, Bernardino (*fl.*1520–41) (*see* ZANOBI DE GIANOTIS).

Giant Order Classical *Order of architecture, the *pilasters or columns of which rise from the ground or *plinth through more than one *storey. Also called *Colossal Order*. *See* GIGANTIC ORDER.

giardino segreto *See* HORTUS CONCLUSUS.

gib *or* **jib** Door with the same continuity of surface as that of the *partition or wall in which it is set, i.e. in panelling, to preserve uniformity or symmetry that would be destroyed if the door were overtly displayed.

Gibberd, Sir Frederick Ernest (1908–84) English architect/town-planner/landscape archi- tect, one of the first in England to adhere to *International Modernism after he met F.R.S. *Yorke. He set up in practice (1930), designing Pulman Court, Streatham, London (1934–6), low-cost housing which established his reputa- tion. After the 1939–45 war, he designed (1949– 51) the Lansbury Shopping Centre and Market, Poplar, London (perversely called 'dainty' by *Pevsner), in the style promoted at the *Festival of Britain South-Bank Exhibition (1951). He was also appointed (1946–72) Architect/Planner of Harlow New Town, Essex. Other buildings by him include Heathrow Airport, London (1950– 69), Didcot Power Station, Berks. (1964–8), Ulster Hospital, Belfast (1953–61), Liverpool RC Cathe- dral (1960–7), Coutts's Bank, The Strand, London (1966–75), and the Central Mosque, Regent's Park (1969–70), none of which could be regarded as great architecture. His eclectic garden created from 1956 at his own house in Harlow was aes- thetically more successful.

E (1994); Gibberd (1952, 1968, 1970, 1980); Gibberd & Yorke (1978); *ODNB* (2004)

Gibbs, James (1682–1754) Scots RC, he turned to architecture (1704) while training for the priest- hood in Rome, became a pupil of Carlo *Fontana, and returned (1709) to Britain, having acquired a thorough knowledge of Roman *Baroque. Partly through *Wren's good offices, he became (1713) one of the two Surveyors to the Commissioners for Building Fifty New Churches in London, and designed the masterly St Mary-le-Strand (1714– 24), with its powerfully Roman side elevations and modelling recalling works by *Cortona and *Borromini, which made his reputation. With **Queen Anne**'s death (1714) and the new régime of **King George I** (*r.*1714–27) and Whiggery, Gibbs, who, as a Tory, Scot, and Papist, was sus- pect, was dismissed. He was then patronized by *Burlington, but shortly afterwards superseded by *Campbell as architect of Burlington House. Campbell's machinations also led to the omission of any mention of Gibbs from *Vitruvius Britanni- cus*. Through **John Campbell** (1680–1743—**2nd Duke of Argyll** from 1719), he was employed to design Sudbrooke House, Petersham, Surrey (*c.*1717–20), and in 1720 designed St Martin-in- the-Fields, London (1722–6), with its Roman *temple-front, *steeple derived from the works of Wren, and galleried rectangular body with two rows of windows, which became the prototype for urban Anglican churches for the next century, being widely copied even across the Atlantic. He also designed Derby Cathedral (1723–5), the *mausoleum at Kirkleatham Church, Yorks. (1739–40), and St Nicholas Church West, Aberdeen (1741–55).

His secular buildings were many, and his training in Italy gave him advantages over his rivals, compensating for difficulties of birth and religion. He designed the Senate House, Cambridge (1722–30), Fellows' Building, King's College, Cambridge (1724–49), and the Radcliffe Library, Oxford (1737–8—the last owes much to earlier designs by *Hawksmoor, but as completed shows Italian influences unthinkable in the Englishman's designs). Among other works are the *cupolas at Houghton Hall, Norfolk (1725–8), and various *fabriques at Stowe, Bucks., including the *Gothic Temple of Liberty (1741–4), Temple of Friendship (1739), and Belvedere (1726–8—demolished). He also designed funerary monuments, including several in Westminster Abbey (e.g. **John Dryden** (1631–1700), 1720). Gibbs advertised his work in *A Book of Architecture* (1728, 1739), which spread his influence far and wide, and was probably the most used architectural book of C18. He also published *Rules for Drawing the Several Parts of Architecture* (1732—with further edns (1736, 1738, and 1753)).

Co (2008); T.Friedman (1984, 2011); Gibbs (1728, 1732, 1747); E.Hs (1990); Little (1955); Su (1993)

Gibbs surround *Banded *architrave around a *door-case, *niche, or window, usually with a massive *keystone and *voussoirs breaking into the top of the architrave. Named after *Gibbs (who illustrated and often employed it) it was widely used by other C18 and later architects.

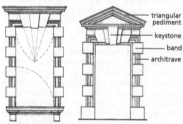

Gibbs surround (*left*) Window, (*right*) Door-case.

Gibson, Jesse (*c.*1748–1828) English architect, he was District Surveyor, Eastern Division, City of London (1774–1828), and Surveyor to The Saddlers' (from 1774) and Drapers' (from 1797) Companies. For The Vintners' Company he designed *almshouses, Mile End Road, London (1802—demolished), and for The Drapers' Company he

was responsible for many buildings in Moneymore, Co. Londonderry (1818–23), including the Lancastrian Schools, Inn, Court House, and other structures.

Co (2008); J.Curl (1986)

Gibson, John (1817–92) English architect, he trained with *Hansom and Charles *Barry: most of his work was for banks, using the *Italianate *palazzo treatment learnt from Barry. Typical of his work was the National Provincial Bank, Bishopsgate, London (1864–5). He designed the impressive Todmorden Town Hall, Yorks. (1860–75—essentially a Roman *temple with an *engaged *Composite *Order set on a *podium) and the *Rundbogenstil Central Baptist Chapel, Bloomsbury, London (1845–8).

J.Curl (1990); D & M (1985)

Giedion, Sigfried (1888–1968) Swiss art-historian, advocate of the *Modern Movement, his influence was widespread, largely through his power-base as an *apparatchik* of *CIAM (for which he served as Secretary-General until 1956) and his perniciously selective *Space, Time, and Architecture* (1941—*de rigueur* in Schools of Architecture from the 1940s). Other works included *Mechanization Takes Command* (1948), *The Eternal Present* (1964), and *Architecture and the Phenomena of Transition* (1970).

Giedion (1922, 1928, 1954, 1954a, 1958, 1962–4, 1967, 1969, 1971)

Gigantic Order *Tuscan *Order, according to *Scamozzi. Not to be confused with the Colossal or *Giant Order.

Gigliardi, Gilardi, Gilliardi, *or* **Zhilyardi, Domenico** (1788–1845) Italian-born architect, he settled in Moscow with his father, **Giovanni Battista** (1755–1819). They built the Widows' House (1818–23—with its impressive octastyle *portico of unfluted Greek-*Doric columns) and the Guardianship Council Building (1821–6—with its portico of *Ionic columns and vaulted staircase-hall with two tiers of unfluted columns). Probably his finest work is the Lunin House (1818–23), but his largest commission was the reconstruction (1817–19) of *Kazakov's Moscow University, where he replaced the Ionic Order on the entrance-portico with a tougher Greek-Doric Order, and remodelled the side-*pavilions to render them more severe. He designed the Khrushchev (1814) and Lopukhin (1817–22) Houses, both essentially *Palladian, but with *Empire enrichments. His main importance lies in the bold *Neo-Classicism he promoted, and in his influence on Russian architecture that, to some extent, paralleled that of *Gilly in Prussia. He altered Kazakov's Music Pavilion of the Equerry on the Kuzminki Estate (1819), and completed

Kazakov's and *Quarenghi's Suburban Palace (begun 1788), in the 1820s.

G.H (1983); M & Wa (1987); D.Shv (2007); J.T (1996)

Gil de Hontañon Family See HONTAÑON.

Gilbert, Cass (1859–1934) American architect, he designed the Minnesota State Capitol, St Paul, MN (1895–1903), a vast *Beaux-Arts pile with a *dome based on *Michelàngelo's at *San Pietro*, Rome, which made his reputation, gaining him commissions to design the US Custom House (1901–7) and the Florentine *palazzo* of the Union Club (1902), both in NYC. He later built a *Gothic *skyscraper on West Street, NYC (1905–7), the trial run for the huge Woolworth Building, NYC (1911–13—clad in lightweight fire-resistant *faïence*). The pyramidal composition of the New York Life Insurance Building (1925–8) was crowned with a vaguely Gothic *spire. His later buildings were nearly all Classical.

Christen & Flanders (eds) (2001); Heilbrun (ed.) (2000); Ed.Ka (ed.) (1970); P & J (1970–86)

Gilbert, Émile-Narcisse-Jacques (1793–1874) French architect, pupil of *Durand, he became an expert on the design of hospitals, asylums, and prisons. He was influenced by *Hittorff (e.g. his severe Greek-*Doric chapel with *polychrome interior at the enormous lunatic asylum (*Asile d'Aliénés*), Charenton (1838–45—consisting of a series of elongated blocks linked by colonnaded walkways)). His buildings were expressions of humanitarian reform and its administration: they include the *Préfecture de la Police, Île de la Cité*, Paris (1862–76), and the impressive *Hôtel-Dieu* nearby, designed with his son-in-law, **Arthur-Stanislas Diet** (1827–90), built 1864–76.

M & Wa (1987); J.T (1996)

Gill, Irving John (1870–1936) American architect, he trained under *Sullivan and worked with *Wright before setting up on his own (1893). His early buildings owed much to the *Arts-and-Crafts, *Shingle, and *vernacular styles, but he began (1907) to experiment with *concrete construction, perfecting a system by 1912, and by 1915 inventing an insulation-core to concrete panels to eliminate condensation and heat-loss. His Laughlin House, Los Angeles (1907), employed concrete, while his Dodge House, Los Angeles (1914–16—demolished), and Horatio West Court, Santa Monica (1919), were in a crisp, cubic style owing nothing to period precedent, remarkably advanced for their time, showing that *Modernism was manifest in the USA at least as early as in Europe, and in Gill's case his buildings look as though they ought to date from the 1920s, so he was unquestionably a pioneer of Modern Architecture and of building using concrete.

Gebhard (1965); Hines (2000); Kamerling (1979); Kaplan (1987); McCoy (1975); P & J (1970–86); Starr (1973)

Gilles le Breton (*c*.1500–52) See BRETON.

Gillespie, Kidd, & Coia Glasgow-based firm of architects evolved from *Salmon's office under **Jack (Giacomo) Antonio Coia** (1898–1981—of Italian parentage), who was apprenticed (1915–19) to **John Gaff Gillespie** (1870–1926). Following Gillespie's death, the latter's partner, **William Alexander Kidd** (1879–1928), invited Coia to join him, so by the end of 1928, the young man was sole partner in the firm of what was now **Gillespie, Kidd, & Coia**. Several commissions for RC churches made Coia's reputation: all were faced with brick (a foreign building-material in a Glasgow largely built of brown and red *sandstone), and drew on round-arched styles, yet influenced by modern Continental design. Among them were St Anne, Dennistoun (1931–3), St Columbkille, Rutherglen (1934–40), St Patrick, Greenock (1935), and St Columba, Maryhill (1937): the last two were not untouched by *Expressionism. In 1937 Coia was joined as partner by **Warnett Kennedy** (1911–99), who was later to claim that he had been mostly responsible for the Church of St Peter in Chains, Ardrossan (1938—with echoes of works by *Behrens, *Östberg, and *Dudok), and for the RC Pavilion at the Empire Exhibition in Glasgow (also 1938): the last and the Palace of Industries North at the same exhibition marked stylistic changes in the firm's work.

During the 1939–45 war, Coia, as the son of an 'enemy alien', had to close his office: when it reopened (1945), Berlin-born **Isi Metzstein** (1928–2012) joined him as an apprentice, and he designed several more churches, but perhaps only St Laurence, Greenock (1951–4—with its pointed internal arches), is in any way comparable with the pre-war buildings (St Michael's, Dumbarton (1952), is unquestionably a child of the *Festival of Britain). During the 1950s the firm became exponents of the *Modern Movement, especially after **Andrew MacMillan** (1928–2014) joined it (1954). A series of churches, necessary because of the expansion of Glasgow and the building of *New Towns, followed, all reflecting modern liturgical ideas: St Paul, Glenrothes, Fife (1956–7), St Charles, Kelvinside (1959–60—influenced by the work of *Perret), and Our Lady of Good Counsel, Dennistoun (1964–6) may be cited. The firm also designed St Peter's College, Cardross (1958–66—abandoned), as well as numerous schools, public housing in Cumbernauld and East Kilbride (which has not aged gracefully), etc. It designed extensions to Wadham College, Oxford (1969–70—including the former Blackwell's Music Shop in Holywell Street), and Robinson College, Cambridge (1978–81). Virtually every building from the Glenrothes church onwards was essentially the work of Metzstein and MacMillan.

GS; *ODNB* (2004); Rogerson (1986)

Gilly, David (1748–1808) German architect, his Huguenot forebears settled (1689) in Pomerania. Successful in the State Examination in architecture (1770), he became Director of Building in Pomerania, founding (1783) an architectural academy in Stettin (*now* Szczecin). With *Erdmannsdorff and *Langhans, he was called (1788) to Berlin by **King Friedrich Wilhelm II of Prussia** (*r*.1786–97) to help establish a new style of architecture removed from the Francophilia of **Friedrich II** ('the Great' (*r*.1740–86)). Gilly founded (1793) the Building School in Berlin, re-established (1799) as the *Bauakademie*, which became one of the most important architectural schools in Europe, numbering *Schinkel, von *Klenze, *Weinbrenner, *Engel, and *Haller von Hallerstein among its illustrious students. Gilly founded *Sammlung nützlicher Aufsätze und Nachrichten, die Baukunst betreffend*, one of the first German architectural journals, published (1797–1806) in Berlin. He designed *Schloss Paretz*, near Potsdam (1796–1800), *Schloss Freienwalde*, north of Berlin (1798–9), and Vieweg House, Brunswick (1800–7), all in a severe Neo-Classical style.

D.Gilly (1797, 1797–8); D.Gilly (ed.) (1797–1806); Hn (1977); Lammert (1964); Wa & M (1987)

Gilly, Friedrich (1772–1800) Son of David *Gilly, he learned practice and theory with his father in Stettin (*now* Szczecin), before settling in Berlin (1788). Aged only 16, he developed his skills while also acting as Inspector in the Royal Buildings Department, working under *Erdmannsdorff and *Langhans. His own designs began to experiment with stereometrically pure forms and primitivist, elemental architecture, while his studies (1794) of the medieval *Marienburg* (now *Malbork*, Poland) fortress in Prussia led to the beginnings of a *conservation programme for that *Sublime building as well as to a growing appreciation of North-German *Backsteingotik*.

The Academy of Fine Arts, Berlin, announced (1796) a competition for a monument to **King Friedrich II** ('the Great') of Prussia (*r*.1740–86), and Gilly's design (1797), set in a re-ordered *Leipzigerplatz*, and incorporating a powerful monumental gate, *sarcophagi*-lids, *obelisks, and a *Doric *temple (suggested in a project (1786) by *Genelli) on a massive *podium, was exhibited. With this seductive image, Gilly won the admiration of younger architects, including von *Klenze, *Schinkel, *Strack, and *Stüler. Gilly was profoundly influenced by French theories and buildings (notably those of *Bélanger, *Legrand, and *Molinos), and was closely associated with his

brother-in-law, *Gentz, whose Mint (1798–1800) had a *frieze designed by Gilly. His later unrealized designs, e.g. those for a National Theatre, Berlin, with its primitive Doric *portico, *Diocletian windows, and clearly defined bare masses, were among the most advanced of the period, later impressing *Semper. His stark (also unrealized) designs for a Stonehenge-like *mausoleum are unprecedented in their stripped severity. He was Professor of Optics and Perspective at the new *Bauakademie* until his untimely death.

Bothe & Reelfs (eds) (1984); F.Gilly (1994); F.Gilly & Frick (1965); Hederer (1976a); Hn (1977); H-O (1981); E.Ka (1952); M & Wa (1987); Oncken (1935); Simson (1976); Wa & M (1987)

Gilman, Arthur Delavan (1821–82) American architect, influenced by contemporary trends in England and France, he first rose to prominence (1840s) with a series of articles in the *North American Review*. His friendship with Charles *Barry may explain aspects of E.C.*Cabot's designs for Boston's *Athenaeum* (1846–9), and indeed Gilman was (1857) an Associate in Cabot's firm. His best-known work is Arlington Street Church, Boston, MA (1859–61—derived from *Gibbs's Church of St Martin-in-the-Fields, London), a late example of Gibbs's long-lived influence in the USA. His Equitable Life Assurance Company Building, NYC (1867–70—destroyed), was an early office-building served by *elevators. He collaborated with **Gridley James Fox Bryant** (1816–99) on the design of Boston City Hall (1861–5), where the *Second Empire style was employed with *élan*. He was prominent in early moves to conserve Boston's architectural heritage.

DAB (1943); Hi & Seale (1976); *JSAH*, **xx**/4 (1961), 191–7; Landau & Ct (1996); Whitehill (1968)

Gilpin, Revd William (1724–1804) English garden-theorist, he published (1748) a 'dialogue' on the gardens at Stowe, Bucks., in which he drew distinctions between 'moral' and 'picturesque' beauty in natural scenery and *ruins, and contrasted formality with informality. He made numerous tours of Britain, recording landscapes using a *Claude-glass. He defined (1768) the *Picturesque as a 'term expressive of that peculiar kind of beauty, which is agreeable in a picture', a theme on which he expounded further in works published 1782–1809, illustrated with aquatint reproductions of his own pen-and-wash drawings. He explained that *roughness* was the essential difference between the *Beautiful and the Picturesque. His nephew, the English landscape-painter and -gardener, **William Sawrey Gilpin** (1761/2–1843), provided some illustrations for him (e.g. *Observations on the River Wye* … (1782)). W.S.Gilpin met (1799) Uvedale *Price, which proved crucial to his future career as a landscape-gardener, advising on hundreds of properties, and publishing (1832) *Practical Hints upon Landscape Gardening* in which he advocated 'picturesque improvement' (a term coined by *Loudon (1806)) based on principles of landscape-painting. In particular, Gilpin called for the reinstatement of 'architectural foregrounds' of *terrace-walks, *parterres*, and *balustrades, elements which had tended to be discarded in the late C18. Works include the grounds of Scotney Castle, Kent (with *Salvin); Bowhill, Selkirk; Sudbury Hall, Derbys.; Crom Castle, Co. Fermanagh; and Gorhambury, Herts. (all 1820s-30s).

GH, xxii/2 (Winter 1994), 175–96; W.Gilpin (1768, 1782, 1792, 1808, 1973, 1976); W.S.Gilpin (1832); Hussey (1967a); Malins & Bowe (1980); *ODNB* (2004); Shoe (2001); Tait (1980); Tay (2006)

Gilpin, William Sawrey (1761/2–1843) *See* GILPIN, REVD. WILLIAM.

Gimson, Ernest William (1864–1919) English architect, admirer of William *Morris, he worked (1885–8) with *Sedding before forming an association with the *Barnsley brothers (1893), and moving to Sapperton, Glos., where he designed The Leasowes Cottage (*c.*1901—much altered) and various artefacts. He was a convinced follower of the *Arts-and-Crafts movement: his houses include Inglewood, Ratcliffe Road (1892), and The White House, North Avenue (1897), both in Leicester, and Stoneywell and Lea Cottages, Charnwood Forest, Leics., two remarkable essays in the *vernacular-cottage style. He designed the Hall and War-Memorial Library, Bedales School, Steep, Hants., after 1919.

Carruthers (1978); Comino (1980); D & M (1985); Gimson (1924); A.S.Gray (1985); Jervis (1984); G.Naylor (1971); *ODNB* (2004)

gingang, gin-case, gin-house, gin-rink Farm-building, circular or polygonal on plan, containing a horse-engine to operate the threshing-mill. Also called *mill-course, mill-gang,* or *mill-rink.*

ginnell Narrow passage between two buildings or walls, probably related to *vennel*: an *alley, or *wynd*. Also *jitty, gitty,* meaning a passage between two rows of *terrace-houses or a fenced or hedged pathway linking two areas of, e.g., a village.

gin-palace Ornate *public-house evolved in Britain in the 1830s, featuring plate- and mirror-glass, a *bar, *gantry, showy elaborate fittings, and illuminated by gas-flares and lights. **Thompson & Fearon's** gin-palace, Holborn, London (1829-31), seems to have been among the earliest, and Stephen *Geary had a reputation as a designer of the type.

Gd (1979a); Loudon (1834)

Ginzburg, Moisei Yakovlevich (1892–1946) Pioneer Russian *Constructivist/engineer. The author of *Ritm v Arkhitektura* (Rhythm in Architecture—1923) and *Stil' i Epokha* (Style and Epoch—1924), among other works, he founded (1926) with *Vesnin the influential Soviet architectural journal *Sovremennaye Arkhitektura* (Contemporary Architecture). From 1927 he specialized in mass-housing, building experimental blocks in Moscow (1928–9) and Sverdlovsk (1928–9). He was involved in avant-garde planning, notably the proposal for a linear Green City, Moscow (1930), and remained active in architecture and planning until his death.

Ginzburg (1982); K-M (1975, 1986, 1987); Kopp (1970); Ly (1970); O.A.Shv (1970); J.T (1996)

giochi d'acqua Italian for 'water-games' or '-jokes' (*jeux d'eau* in French), they were features of Italian-*Renaissance gardens, triggered by unsuspecting visitors or set in motion by concealed servants, often spraying perambulators. Some (e.g. at Pratolino) involved water-powered *automata which emitted noises or music as well as water-jets. Good examples may be found in the gardens of *Schloss Hellbrunn*, near Salzburg, Austria, the summer-residence (designed by *Solari) of **Prince-Archbishop Marcus Sitticus von Hohenems** (*r.*1612–19), further embellished in C18. *See* HYDRAULICS.

Symes (2006); Tay (2006); J.T (1996)

Giocondo, Fra Giovanni (1433–1515) Verona-born architect/engineer, he made his name with an early woodcut-illustrated edition of *Vitruvius' *Ten Books of Architecture* (1511). He succeeded *Maiano as architect at Poggioreale, Naples, completing it in 1485, and worked (1495-1505) for the Kings of France, designing the *Pont Notre Dame* over the Seine (*c.*1499-1512—destroyed). On his return to Italy he designed the fortifications at Treviso (1509-11) with rounded (rather than canted) gun-platform bastions. He worked with da *Sangallo and *Raphael on St Peter's, Rome, from 1514.

Croix (1972); V.Fontana (1988); He (1996); Vagnetti (ed.) (1978)

Giorgio Martini (Pollaiolo), Francesco Maurizio di (1439–1501/2) Sienese architect/theorist/engineer. His architectural tracts (1475-92) and version of *Vitruvius were influential in C16. He proposed a complete theory for *Renaissance architecture based on that of Antiquity, argued for the placing of *altars in centralized church-plans, gave a rational explanation of ecclesiastical symbolism, and invented fortifications that were a defence against gunfire. On moving to Urbino (1476) he contributed (possibly the refined *loggia) to the design of the *Palazzo*

Ducale (1476-82) and other works. He designed *Santa Maria della Grazie al Calcinaio*, near Cortona (1484-1516), an accomplished Renaissance building; (probably) the *Palazzo degli Anziani*, Ancona (completed 1493—destroyed), and the severe *Palazzo del Comune*, Iesi (completed 1503). Many other buildings have been attributed to him, including *Santo Spirito*, Siena (1498-1509). *Vasari held him in high regard.

Croix (1972); F & T (1993); Giorgio di Martini (1967); He (1996); Papini (1946); Rotondi (1950-1, 1970); vV (1993); Weller (1943)

Giotto di Bondone (1267-1337) Florentine painter/architect. He probably designed the *Gothic *campanile* beside the Cathedral (from 1334), completed by *Gaddi, *Pisano, and *Talenti. Only the first stage of the *base or *socle appears to have been completed by the time of his death.

Gioseffi (1963); M.Tg (1971); J.White (1987)

Girard, Dominique (*c.*1680-1738) French landscape-designer/engineer trained under Le *Nôtre at Versailles before entering the service (1714) of **Elector Maximilian II Emanuel of Bavaria** (*r.*1779-1704, 1715-26) as *Brunnmeister* (Fountain Engineer). With **Charles Carbonet** (*fl.*1700-15) he created formal gardens, *canals, and *fountains on the central axis of the park at *Nymphenburg*. He also worked at Schleissheim and (1717-22) at *Schloss Belvedere*, Vienna, where he and *Hildebrandt laid out the gardens and water-works. Girard also designed the park at *Schloss Brühl* (with *Cuvilliés) for **Clemens August, Elector-Archbishop of Cologne** from 1723. His works were influenced by *Dézallier d'Argenville and his master, Le Nôtre.

Shoe (2001); Tay (2006); J.T (1996)

Girardin, René-Louis, Marquis de (1735-1808) French writer/designer of landscapes. He saw several English landscape-gardens during his travels in the early 1760s, and in 1766 settled at Ermenonville, Oise, where he laid out the influential landscape-garden. He published his *De la composition des paysages* (1777) in which he described the garden and set out his own theories. He was strongly aware of the importance of *associations* in gardens, used to trigger memories, stimulate ideas, and create a narrative. His friend, J.-J.*Rousseau, died on his estate, and was buried on the *Île des Peupliers* in the *Élysée* which Girardin had created. Views of this funerary island were published, and the image was an important stimulus to the *cemetery movement of C19, as well as to other estate owners, notably the Prince of *Anhalt-Dessau.

J.Curl (2011); Ermenonville (1788); Girardin (1777); JGH, xiv/2 (Summer 1994), 92–118; Wn (1978)

Girault, Charles-Louis (1851-1932) French *Beaux-Arts* architect, his work is among the most splendid, festive, and rich late-C19 and early-C20 Neo-*Baroque architecture. He designed the *Petit Palais*, Paris (1897-1900), for the 1900 International Exhibition, the triumphal *Arc du Cinquantenaire, Palais du Cinquantenaire*, Brussels (1905), and the *Musée du Congo Belge*, Tervueren, Belgium (1904-11). One of his richest and most colourful designs is the tomb of **Louis Pasteur** (1822-95) in the Pasteur Institute, Paris (1896), embellished with *mosaics in the *Early-Christian style.

L'Architecture, xlvi (1933), 253–62; Loo (ed.) (2003)

girder 1. Main timber beam of great size supporting subsidiary beams at right angles to it. **2.** Beam built up for additional strength to support a floor, road, etc. A *plate-girder* is constructed of plates of rolled iron or steel, consisting of vertical webs with flat plates fixed to the upper and lower parts.

girt 1. *Fillet, *list, or small *scantling. **2.** Small timber *girder, e.g. a horizontal member half-way between a wall-plate and the *cill in a *timber frame. **3.** Measure of timber.

girt-light *Casement frame with *mullions and *transoms.

gitty *See* GINNELL.

Giuliano da Maiano (1432-90) *See* MAIANO.

Giulio Romano (*c.*1499-1546) Italian architect, one of the major figures of the late *Renaissance. Called **Giulio Pippi** *or* **Giuliano Giannuzzi**, he became a pupil of *Raphael and trained amidst the *High-Renaissance reverence for Classical antiquities. He completed Raphael's *Villa Lante al Gianicolo*, Rome (1523), and designed the *Palazzo Maccarani, Piazza Sant'Eustachio*, Rome (*c.*1520-4), where his originality was demonstrated in the ambiguous capital-less *pilasters and the windows that rest uneasily on a *stringcourse. His bending of the rules of Classical propriety led him to extremes, and he became one of the most interesting Mannerist architects, especially after he settled in Mantua (1524), where he worked for **Duke Federigo II Gonzaga** (*r.*1519-40). His extraordinary *Palazzo del Tè* (1525-32), Mantua, one of the first Mannerist buildings, is a single-storey building around a courtyard. The vestibule of the main entrance mixes elements from the Basilica of **Maxentius** (*r.*306-12), Rome, and a plan taken from *Giocondo's edition of *Vitruvius (1511). In the courtyard finely finished *ashlar is contrasted with deliberately 'unfinished' work, and on two *elevations some of the *triglyphs are designed to appear to 'drop' from the *entablature, giving a feeling of instability, probably suggested to the architect by Roman ruins in which the *frieze had broken up: such a ruin (the *Basilica Aemilia* in the *Forum Romanum*) had been drawn by *Sangallo. The gardenfront is composed of overlaid *serlianas and the garden itself is enclosed, terminating in a semicircular pilastered *colonnade. The plan is a clever mixture of an *Antique *villa and Raphael's *Villa Madama* (itself influenced by Roman *thermae*). As a result of his success with the *Palazzo del Tè*, Giulio was ennobled and presented with a house in Mantua, on the *façade of which (1538-44) he reworked the themes of the House of Raphael (*Palazzo Caprini*) by *Bramante. His *Cortile della Mostra* (or *Cavallerizza*) in the *Palazzo Ducale*, Mantua (1538-9), employs tortured, engaged, irregular spiral columns on *pedestals carried on chunky rusticated *consoles, while the rusticated façades have arches that are not quite semicircles, nor are they segments of circles. It is a distortion of themes from Bramante's House of Raphael and the Colosseum, with allusions to the *Solomonic columns in *San Pietro*, Rome. Such preoccupations with Antiquity and with the gravitas of the great Bramante suggest that, far from acting with a disregard for *Classicism, as some have suggested, Giulio was scholarly and witty, drawing on many sources to give his buildings authority. He prepared designs for the marketsquare in Vicenza from 1542: the *Palazzo Thiene*, Vicenza, with its overt quotations from Ancient Rome, may owe more to him than to *Palladio, who completed it. He restored the Abbey of *San Benedetto al Polirone*, near Mantua (1540-6), and remodelled the Cathedral, Mantua (1544-6) with double aisles incorporating massive *Corinthian columns. The *Residenz*, Landshut, Bavaria (begun 1536), was influenced by his architecture, but was not by him. He was also a famous painter: his *frescoes in the Vatican (*Stanza dell'Incendio di Borgo* (1514-17)) and at Mantua helped to make him celebrated in his lifetime.

Ferrari & Belluzzi (1992); C.Fr (1973); C.Fr *et al*. (1989); Giulio Romano (1991); Hartt (1958); He (1996); *JSAH*, xxx/4 (Dec. 1971), 267-93; T.Ka (1995); Lotz (1977); Pettena (ed.) (1981); Verheyen (1977)

Giurgola, Romaldo (1920-2016) *See* MITCH-ELL, EHRMAN BURKMAN.

glacis 1. Steep slope of ground falling from one level to another in a landscaped garden. **2.** The same, sloping from the bottom of a fortress wall or from the top of a trench, so that it presents a clear view for defenders and gunners. **3.** Sloping upper surface of a *battlement, *cope, *cornice, or *parapet to promote the descent of rainwater.

glade Clearing (open space or passage) in a wood or forest, natural or created by cutting down trees, either sunny or providing shade.

Gläserne Kette German group (*The Glass Chain*) founded (1919) by Bruno *Taut, including *Gropius and *Scharoun, favouring forms derived from crystals, shells, and plants, using glass, steel, and concrete. Several members later joined the *Ring.

Boyd Whyte (1982, 1985)

Glasgow School Name given to late-C19-early-C20 Glasgow architects/designers, especially C.R.*Mackintosh, **Margaret** (1865-1933) and **Frances** (1874-1921) **Macdonald**, and **Herbert McNair** (1868-1953). They employed calligraphic elements of *Art Nouveau, including the *femme-fleur*, *rose-ball, and long, flowing tendrils, earning them the collective title of 'Glasgow Spook School'. They exhibited on the Continent, and had a considerable impact on the *Sezession, especially in Vienna, where *Hoffmann particularly admired their work. In architecture Art Nouveau was synthesized with aspects of *vernacular buildings and the English *Arts-and-Crafts movement, perhaps best seen at Mackintosh's Hill House (1902), Helensburgh, and the Willow Tea Rooms (1903), Sauchiehall Street, Glasgow.

Howarth (1977); L & D (1986); R.MacLeod (1983); Steele (1994)

glass Semi- or fully transparent hard, brittle, lustrous material made by igneous fusion of silica (usually sand) with an alkaline sodium or potassium salt and added ingredients, such as lime, alumina, lead oxide, etc. Colour may be added by the addition of metallic oxides. It appears to have come into use for glazing the windows of grander buildings during the Roman Empire. In the Middle Ages coloured and painted glass, used in small pieces because of the difficulties of manufacturing larger expanses, was set in lead *cames, commonly in churches: surviving examples (e.g. Chartres Cathedral, King's College Chapel, Cambridge, and Fairford, Glos.) are among the glories of medieval art. Glass used for domestic architecture also had to be set in lead cames or in *sashes subdivided by glazing-bars. *Types of glass include*:

acid-etched: treated with wax or a similar substance into which a design is cut, then subjected to action by hydrofluoric acid which etches into the unprotected surface to create a design. Much used from Victorian times for decorative windows for public-houses, etc.;

armourplate: thick toughened polished *plate glass* used for large windows, doors, etc.;

broad: blown in cylinders which are then cut open and flattened, called *muff* or *window-glass*;

Crown: blown from a glass tube into a bulb then opened and spun rapidly, the outer part thin, clear, and lustrous, but the centre or hub of thick glass (*bottle, bullion, or bull's eye*) largely opaque and never used for good work. It was the commonest type of glass found in British domestic architecture until the mid-1830s;

flint: made from white sand, potash, nitre, red lead, and ground window-glass, used where refraction is desired, as on decorative *altar-pieces, etc.;

ground: with a rough surface, usually ground, to make it lose transparency;

iridescent: with a coating to give it the appearance of the surface of a soap-bubble with rainbow colours;

jealous: roughened to allow the light to pass through, but with a loss of transparency;

laminated: toughened, made by a laminated process;

plate: poured on to a cast-iron table, rolled with a heavy roller, and polished on both sides;

sheet: made by blowing into a cylinder of glass which increases in diameter before being cut lengthways, flattened, and polished. It was a refinement of *broad* or *muff* glass, invented by **Messrs. Chance**, near Birmingham (1832-8), and had a finish comparable to that of *Crown* glass, but cheaper and capable of being made in larger sheets, thus making glazing-bars in *sashes obsolete;

stained: coloured throughout its mass or with the colour applied or *flashed*. Crimson is produced with oxides of copper or tin, blue with cobalt, purple with manganese, and other colours using various combinations of chemicals;

toughened: thick, made in a variety of ways;

wire: with a network of wire enclosed within it to improve security.

Used as a major component of external walls first in *conservatories and *green houses, and then as a roofing material with glazing-bars of wood and, later, of iron, the evolution of railway termini and major exhibition-buildings (e.g. *Paxton's Crystal Palace, London (1851)) revealed glass's architectural possibilities, leading to *Dutert's *Galerie des Machines*, Paris (1889). Glazed *curtain-walls were suggested by conservatories and used by architects such as *Ellis, later exploited by *Behrens, *Gropius, et al. Later developments have included solar-reflective and tinted glass for large expanses, while blocks of glass, glass tubes, and glass slabs were used widely in C20.

H.Berger (1996); Br (1980); Button & Pye (1993); Hix (1996); Kohlmaier & vonSartory (1986); Koppelkamm (1981); Korn (1967); McGrath & Frost (1937); W.Pa (1852); Parissien (1997); Schild (1983); S (1901–2); Wigginton (1996)

glass-house 1. Building in which *glass is manufactured. **2.** Building with walls and roof mainly of glass: a *conservatory, *greenhouse, *hot-house, or *orangery.

glazed brick Brick with a ceramic coating or finish applied then fixed in a second firing. Earthenware so treated can be brightly coloured and useful in decorative *façades. *Polychrome glazed bricks were used in *Assyrian and *Babylonian architecture, notably at Khorsabad (C8 BC), Babylon itself (C6 BC), and Susa (C5 BC).

Andrae (1925); Bru (1990); L & M (1986); W.McKay (1957)

glazing-bars Lengths of wood or metal (*sash-bars* or *astragals, usually chamfered or moulded (e.g. with *lambs'-tongue to make them elegant and as unobtrusive as possible)), dividing the void within the frame of a window-*sash into rectangles to receive panes of *glass. *See* BAR; GLASS; SASH; WINDOW.

Glemme, Erik (1905–59) Swedish landscape architect responsible (under Holger *Blom) for the Norr Malstrand *promenade (1941–3) along the lakeshore (which included various buildings), the Tegner Grove garden (early 1940s), and the Vasa Park (late 1940s), all in Stockholm.

Tay (2006); pk

gloriette *Eye-catcher, or *pavilion in a garden from which views may be enjoyed, e.g. *Hohenburg's *Gloriette* at Schönbrunn, Vienna (1775).

Gloucester, John of (*fl.c.*1245–60) English mason. From 1255 he carried out works at the Tower of London and Windsor Castle, Berks., and at the same time appears to have been in charge of works at Westminster Abbey. He was a man of some substance, and his activities and responsibilities ranged far and wide, especially in regard to the Royal Castles, for he was involved at Oxford, Winchester, Gloucester, Porchester, and Salisbury Castles.

J.Harvey (1987)

glyph Channel, *flute, or groove, normally vertical, as in a *Doric *frieze, where the blocks framing *metopes are the *triglyphs so called because they each have two *glyphs* and two *half-glyphs*.

glyptotheca Sculpture-gallery.

Go Pejorative term used by some Victorian commentators (e.g. *Street) to describe work of *Rogue Goths that was restless, animated, 'acrobatic', and embarrassing. It implied empty fashion, hamfistedness, clumsiness, discord, clashing colours, excessive liveliness, coarseness, loudness, decadence, furious vigour, recklessness, exaggeration, vulgarity, and generally something overdone for purposes of self-advertisement (so could easily be applied to some fashionable architects of the early C21).

J.Curl (2007)

Gočár, Josef (1880-1945) Czech architect. He experimented with *Cubism and with attempts to introduce a National style into his work, as at the Czechoslovak Legion Bank, Prague (1921-3), heavily decorated with cubes, cylinders, and squares, giving the building a backward-looking appearance for its date. His High School, Hradec Králové (1924), owed much to *stripped Classicism and to Dutch brick architecture, but his Czechoslovak Pavilion at the *Exposition Internationale des Arts-Décoratifs*, Paris (1924-5), attempted to use the architectural language of *Modernism, somewhat uneasily mixed with decorative elements. With the Baba Hill housing development exhibition of the Czechoslovak *Werkbund*, Prague (1932-3), however, Gočár's work became more *International-*Modern in style (*Mauk* and *Glücklich* Houses, 1932), and he went further with the *Sochor* House, Dvůr Králové (c.1934).

Benešová (1971); Gočár (1930); Li (1996); Wirth (1930)

Goddard, Henry Langton (1866-1944) English architect, son of Joseph *Goddard. His most distinguished work was the basilican Church of St James the Greater, London Road, Leicester (1899-1914), a noble essay in the Italian-*Renaissance style. He designed many of the charming *Arts-and-Crafts *vernacular-revival houses at Horninghold, Leics. (1903-14), and was responsible for Gilroes Cemetery and Crematorium, Leicester (1901-2). He also designed the Carnegie Library, Kettering, Northants. (1903), and many commercial buildings in the English Midlands.

Brandwood & M.Cherry (1990); A.S.Gray (1985)

Goddard, Joseph (1839/40-1900) English architect, the most distinguished of the *Gothic Revival working in Leicester in the second half of C19. He designed the *polychrome brick church of St Andrew, Tur Langton, Leics. (1865-6), the Leicestershire (later Midland) Bank, Granby Street, Leicester—in a Continental-Gothic polychrome manner—(1872-4), the ornate Gothic clock-tower, Leicester (1868), and numerous houses and other buildings in and around Leicester.

Brandwood & M.Cherry (1990); Pe, Williamson, & Brandwood (1984)

Godde, Étienne-Hippolyte (1781-1869) French architect. As Chief Architect of the City of Paris (1813-48) he carried out many restorations and alterations, notably (1840-5) at the *Hôtel de Ville* (with **Jean-Baptiste-Ciceron Lesueur** (1794-1883)). He improved the layouts of the Cemeteries of *Père-Lachaise* (where he designed the *mortuary-chapel) and Montparnasse (1840-5). Other works by him include the Chapel

and Seminary, *St-Sulpice* (1820-8), and the Churches of *St-Pierre-du-Gros-Caillou* (1822), *Notre-Dame-de-Bonne-Nouvelle* (1823-30), *St-Denis-du-Saint-Sacrement* (1823-35), and *St-Pierre-de Chaillot* (1823-35), all in Paris.

Bae: *Paris* (1904); M & Wa (1987)

Godefroy, Jean Maur Maximilien (c.1765-1840) French architect, influenced by *Blondel and *Durand, he, with *Latrobe, introduced the latest *Neo-Classicism to the USA, where he settled (1805-19). Most of his work was in Baltimore, and included the *Gothic St Mary's Chapel (1806-8), the Commercial and Farmers' Bank (1812-13—destroyed), the Unitarian Church (1817-18), and the Egyptianizing Battle Monument (1810-27), the first civic monument to be erected in the USA. He returned to France by 1827 after a few years (from 1819) in London (where he designed the RC Charities School, Clarendon Square (1825-6—demolished)). His later works included the Hospice des Aliénés, Nayenne (1829-36), and a new wing to the *Palais de Justice* (1829-33) and the *Préfecture* (1831-40), both at Laval.

R.Alexander (1974); Carrott (1978); Co (2008); vV (1993)

Godwin, Edward William (1833-86) English architect/designer/writer, from Bristol, who received his early training under **William Armstrong** (c.1781-1858). He joined (1856) his brother **Joseph Lucas Godwin** (1823-82), civil engineer, in the North of Ireland, and designed three *Gothic RC churches whilst there, all in Co. Donegal: St Johnstown (1857-60—unsympathetically modernized (1970s)); Newtowncunningham (1857-61); and Tory Island (1857-61). By 1858, on the death of Armstrong, he was back in Bristol, where he designed a huge round-arched warehouse at Merchant Street (1856-8), another warehouse at 104 Stokes Croft (1860), and the Jacob Street Brewery (1863-5). He made his name with Northampton Town Hall (1861-4—won in competition), an accomplished Anglo-Franco-Italian *Gothic-Revival *polychrome essay (influenced by *Ruskin) for which he designed all the decorations and fittings (sensitively restored (1992-3) by *Gradidge). He took **Henry Crisp** (1825-96) into partnership to enable him to concentrate on competitions, but although the new firm was awarded the first premium in several, in only one case, Congleton, Ches. (1864-6—again Ruskinian, but more French in character), did the win lead to a realized building. His career seemed set fair when he received two important commissions for country-houses in Ireland: Dromore Castle, Pallaskenry, Co. Limerick (1866-73—ruined), and Glenbeigh Towers, Glenbeigh, Co. Kerry (1867-71—burnt 1922). The latter was a fortress-house in the form of a massive *keep, and the former was a composition of exceptional quality, not only archaeologically correct, but beautifully composed and partly designed for defence (the period of building was the time of the Fenian disturbances). Godwin also introduced a Japanese flavour into the décor of Dromore, which established him as one of the earliest designers of the *Aesthetic Movement. Regrettably, both buildings leaked, and at Dromore the water-penetration was so bad that the wall-paintings by **Henry Stacy Marks** (1829-98) on the subject of **Spenser's** *Faerie Queen* were destroyed. These disasters damaged Godwin's reputation. Nevertheless, he designed Beauvale House, Newthorpe, Northants. (1872-3), Nos. 1, 2, 3, 5, 7, 9, 12, 14, 16, 18, 37, and 39 The Avenue, and other houses at Bedford Park, Chiswick (1875-7), and several *avant-garde* dwellings in Chelsea. The last include the White House, Tite Street (1877-9—demolished), for **James Abbott McNeill Whistler** (1834-1903); the studio-house at 44 Tite Street (1878-9), for the artist **George Francis** ('Frank') **Miles** (1852-91); the Tower House, 46 Tite Street (1881-5); and interiors of 16 Tite Street (1884-5), for **Oscar Wilde** (1854-1900), exemplifying the ideal of the 'House Beautiful'.

Godwin was one of the most original designers of his time; a pioneer in the evolution of Anglo-Japanese styles of decoration and furnishing. His furniture designs were widely copied, notably in the USA, and his was a considerable influence on German and Austrian taste. Despite this, his considerable output as an architectural journalist, and his work for the theatre designing costumes and sets (he lived with (1868-75) the actress **Ellen Terry** (1847-1928), with whom he had two children, one of whom was the theatrical designer **Edward Gordon Craig** (1872-1966)), his income was inadequate and he died in debt.

Aslin (1969, 1986); B-J (1988); Harbron (1949); Soros (2000); J.T (1996); N.Williamson (1992)

Godwin, George (1813-88) English architect, son of the architect **George Godwin** (1789-1863), he is remembered as the editor (1844-83) of *The Builder*, the most important British C19 architectural journal. He also practised with his brothers **Sidney** (1828-1916) and **Henry** ((1831-1917), designing the Churches of St Mary Boltons (1849-50), St Luke's, Redcliffe Square (1872-4), and St Jude's, Courtfield Gardens (1870-9), as well as Redcliffe Mansions (1871), all in Kensington, London). He published papers on *concrete (1835), *The Churches of London* (1838-9), and *History in Ruins* (1853). He was also active in attempts to ameliorate housing-conditions of the working classes.

D & M (1985); Hobhouse (ed.) (1986); *ODNB* (2004)

Goethe, Johann Wolfgang von (1749-1832) German polymath, towering figure of the *Aufklärung* (*see* ENLIGHTENMENT), celebrated particularly for his poetry. His visit (1770) to Strasbourg sparked the idea that *Gothic (epitomized in the Cathedral there) was a symbol of the German national ideal, prompting his *Von deutscher Baukunst* (1770-3), in which he wrote glowingly of the achievements of von *Steinbach. Profoundly influenced by Edward *Young's *Night Thoughts*, he became interested in Youngian themes. He often visited the *Gartenreich* (Garden-Realm) of the Prince of *Anhalt-Dessau, which he found 'infinitely beautiful': it informed many of the scenes concerning the laying out of a garden around a lake in his tenderly wistful novella, *Die Wahlverwandtschaften* (1809), which includes a description of the building of a *fabrique* that is unquestionably an allusion to *Freemasonry (Goethe himself was a *Freemason, as was *Erdmannsdorff, architect of many buildings in the *Gartenreich*). He was also significant as a forerunner of **Charles Robert Darwin** (1809-82) in his works on botany and biology which might be described as 'organic evolution'. His visit to Italy (1786-8) made profound impressions on him, and he was appreciative of Ancient Greek architecture, especially when he saw *Paestum (1787): indeed, Goethe's *Italian Journey* is one of the most perceptive accounts of any C18 travels in that country.

Prince Karl August (1757-1828—**Duke** (from 1775) and **Grand Duke** (from 1815) **of Saxe-Weimar-Eisenach**) met Goethe (1774), and called him (with other intellectuals) to Weimar where he was to remain for the rest of his life. Goethe's interest in landscape, prompted partly by the writings of *Hirschfeld and his appreciation of Anhalt-Dessau's creations, especially at Wörlitz, influenced the design of the splendid gardens at Weimar (which included an 'English' landscape; a *Schneckenberg* (spiral or *snail's *mount); a *hermitage; *ruins; winding paths set among trees, bushes, and brooks with *bridges; a *temple; and the so-called 'Roman House' with primitivist *Doric columns (1790-2—by *Arens)). Goethe should be seen as a pivotal figure of *Romantic Classicism.*

J.Curl (2011, 2011a); Goethe (1809); Gothein (1966); J.T (1996)

Goff, Bruce Alonzo (1904-82) Idiosyncratic American, originally influenced by F.L.L.*Wright, identified as an exponent of *Experimental architecture, he evolved a free style of his own, employing unconventional materials (e.g. coal, ropes, objects retrieved from rubbish-dumps, and bits of aircraft) in his buildings. At the Bavinger House, Norman, OK (1950-5), he created a spiral *rubble wall enclosing a volume illuminated from above, while subsidiary volumes were hung from a central mast. Other works included the Price House, Bartlesville, OK (1956–8), the Glen Harder House, near Mountain Lake, MN (1970–2), and the Barby House, Tucson, AZ (1974–6).

J.Cook (1978); P.Cook (1970); Fu (ed.) (1975); Long (1977, 1988); Mead (ed.) (1989a, 1991a); Mohri (1970); Murphy & Muller (1970); Saliga & Woolever (1995)

goffer To create a wavy pattern or rippling effect by means of indentations, incisions, or impressions, so the object thus treated is referred to as *goffered*.

Gogel, Daniel (1927–97) *See* FEHLING.

Goldberg, Bertrand (1913–97) German-born American architect, he attended (1930s) the *Bauhaus, and emigrated (1934) to Chicago, IL. He designed *prefabricated housing and industrial buildings for the Government, and was responsible for the Marina City Towers, Chicago (1959–64), with *concrete *shell construction, earning them the nickname of the 'Corn-Cobs'. He used similar forms in the Raymond Hilliard Housing (1964–6) and the Prentice Women's Hospital (1970–5).

Goldberg (1992); L.Legner (1974); Zu (ed.) (1993)

Golden House *Domus Aurea* built by **Emperor Nero** (*r.*54–68) to designs by *Severus and **Celer** (mid-C1) on the Esquiline Hill, Rome. A large *palace with landscaped gardens, it was remarkable for its complex plan with rooms of different geometrical shapes, many *vaulted and sumptuously decorated.

S (1901–2); Segala & Sciortino (1999)

golden rectangle The basis of standardized sizes of components, in which the ratio of width to length is the same as that of length to the sum of the width and length.

golden section Also called the *golden cut* or *mean,* or *harmonic proportional ratio,* it may have originated in the circle of **Pythagoras** (*fl.* mid-C6 BC), was certainly known during the time of **Euclid** (*c.*325–*c.*250 BC), and was held to be divine by several *Renaissance theorists, especially **Luca Pacioli** (*c.*1445–*c.*1514) in his *De Divina Proportione,* written 1497 and published in Venice (1509). It can be expressed as a straight line (or as a rectangle) divided into two parts so that the ratio of the shorter part (**a**) to the longer (**b**) is the same as the ratio of the longer (**b**) to the sum of the shorter and longer parts, or **a: b = b: a + b,** or that the ratio of the smaller part is to the longer as the latter is to the whole. The ratio is expressed in algebra as Φ (*Phi,* the first letter of the name of the Greek sculptor **Phidias,** or **Pheidias** (*c.*490–430

BC)) = $(1 + \sqrt{5})/2$, which comes to 1.61803. Thus the ratio is approximately 8: 13.

Borrisavlievitch (1970); Ghyka (1976); Hagenmaier (1977); Huntley (1970)

Goldfinger, Ernö (1902–87) Hungarian-born British architect. He worked in Paris before settling (1934) in England. His best-known building is 1–3 Willow Road, Hampstead, London (1937), a *terrace of three houses, one of which was his own dwelling, the first *Modern-Movement house to be taken over by the National Trust. With *Perriand he designed the French Government Tourist Offices in London at 66 Haymarket (1958) and 177 Piccadilly (1963). Other works include the office-building at 45–6 Albemarle Street (1956), Alexander Fleming House, Elephant and Castle (1962–6), Rowlett Street Housing, St Leonard's Road (1966–78), and Edenham Street Housing, Cheltenham Estate, Golborne Road (1968–9), all in London.

AD, xxxiii/1 (Jan. 1963), whole issue; Elwall (1996); E (1994); Warburton (2003)

Goldie, Edward (1856–1921) English RC architect, he was articled to his father, and designed several important buildings for the Church, including (with **Charles Edwin Child** (1843–1911)) St James's, Spanish Place, London (1885–90), a learned work of the *Gothic Revival, much influenced by Continental precedents, and especially by *Pearson. Other buildings include Ashorne Hill House, Newbold Pacey, Warwicks. (1895–7), St Alban's, Larkhill, Blackburn, Lancs. (1900–1), and St Mary's Priory, Storrington, Sussex (1904). He was in partnership with his son, **Joseph** (1882–1953), until his death.

D & M (1985); A.S.Gray (1985)

Goldie, George (1828–87) English architect, grandson of Joseph *Bonomi, he was articled to, and later a partner of, the RC architects *Hadfield & *Weightman of Sheffield before setting up (1861) his own practice, later joined by his son, **Edward,** and **Charles Edwin Child** (1843–1911). His churches include the heavy *Gothic-Revival St Wilfred's, York (1862–4), the Abbey of St Scholastica, Teignmouth, Devon (1863), St Augustine's, Stamford, Lincs. (1864), the Assumption, Kensington Square, London (1875), and St Joseph's, Durban, South Africa (1878), in all of which Continental, rather than English, Gothic was dominant.

D & M (1985); Ea (1970)

Golding, Francis (1944–2013) English *townscape consultant, his book, *Building in Context: New Development in Historic Areas* (2001), was influential, and he steered controversial schemes through planning processes. One New Change and the so-called 'Walkie-Talkie', Fenchurch Street, both in the City of London, were among the buildings he supported, but approval of them has not been universal.

F.Golding (2001); *The Times* (25 Nov. 2013), 49

Goldsmith, Selwyn (1932–2011) English architect/writer, he pioneered design for the physically disabled. Partially paralysed, he published *Designing for the Disabled* (1963—expanded 1967, 1976).

Goldsmith (1976); *RIBAJ* (June 2011), 16

Golgotha 1. Burial-ground or *charnel-house. 2. Carved timber base of a *Rood from which the figures of the Crucified Christ, St Mary, and St John rise, as at St Andrew's Church, Cullompton, Devon.

Gollins, Melvin, Ward Partnership established in London (1947) by **Frank Gollins** (1910–2008), **James Melvin** (1912–79), and **Edmund Ward** (1912–98), it built (1957) offices at New Cavendish Street, London, incorporating an early use of *curtain-walling in England: Castrol House, Marylebone Road, London (1960), was an even more confident example. The firm designed additions to the Royal Opera House, Covent Garden, London (1975), and was responsible for many office-buildings throughout its history. GMW Partnership (as it became) designed the St Enoch Centre, Glasgow (1988), and the headquarters of Barclays Bank, Lombard Street, London (1993).

E (1994); Gollins, Melvin, & Ward (1974)

Golosov, Ilya Aleksandrovich (1883–1945) Moscow architect, he worked with his brother, **Pantelemon** (1882–1945), who was first a Neo-Classicist and then a Constructivist: Ilya's Zuyev Workers' Club, Moscow (1926–8), was one of the bolder essays in *Constructivism. When the Stalinist era insisted on 'Socialist Realism' and a return to *Neo-Classicism, Ilya designed in that mode. He was in charge of the redevelopment of Moscow from 1933, responsible for numerous housing-schemes and public buildings. His work includes the Theatre, Minsk (1934), the Hydro-Electric Station, Gorky (1936–40), and collective housing on the Yausky Boulevard, Moscow (1934). His monumental designs for battle memorials of the 1940s were firmly traditionalist, drawing on historical allusions.

CoE (1995); Kopp (1970, 1978); O.Shv (1970)

Gómez de Mora, Juan (*c*.1580–1648) Spanish architect, he designed the Church of the Royal Convent of the *Encarnación*, Madrid (1611–16), a model for monastic churches in Spain and Latin America, and planned the *Clerecía*, or Jesuit College and Church (*Seminario Conciliar*),

Salamanca (1616–1750), based on *Il Gesù*, Rome. Much influenced by the work of de *Herrera, he succeeded his uncle, **Francisco de Mora** (*c*.1553–1610) as architect to the *Escorial* and as Court Architect. He worked on the development of the *Plaza Mayor*, Madrid (1617–19), designing the ground-level *arcades and *façades.

N-S (1986); W.Pa (1852); vV (1993)

Gondoin *or* **Gondouin, Jacques** (1737–1818) French architect. Trained under J.-F.*Blondel, he designed the *École de Chirurgie* (later *École de Médecine*), Paris (1769–75), one of the most influential buildings of French *Neo-Classicism, with an *Ionic *colonnade on the street elevation and *triumphal arch in the centre leading to a *court off which was a semicircular top-lit anatomy-theatre roofed with a coffered hemi-dome resembling that of the *Pantheon*, Rome. The severe *Antique character of the theatre was the precedent for the Chamber of Deputies, Paris (1795–7), and for aspects of *Latrobe's interiors in the Capitol, Washington, DC. With *Lepère he designed the *Colonne Vendôme*, Paris (1806–10), based on *Antonine and *Trajanic exemplars.

B (1980); M & Wa (1987)

Gontard, Karl Philipp Christian von (1731–91) German architect. He studied under J.-F.*Blondel in Paris, and travelled in Italy (1754–5) with the **Margrave** and **Margravine of Bayreuth**. Called (1763) to Potsdam by the **Margravine's** brother, **King Friedrich II** ('the Great') **of Prussia** (*r*.1740–86), he became responsible for all Royal buildings. He built the *Communs* in front of the *Neues Palais* to designs by Le *Geay, as well as the Temples of Friendship and Antiquity (1768–70) in *Sanssouci* park. With G.C.*Unger he designed the handsome Brandenburg Gate, Potsdam (1770), a Frenchified version of the *triumphal arch reminiscent of the works of *Perrault. His most important contributions to the urban fabric of Berlin were the tall *cupolas he added to the French Protestant Church (by **Jean-Louis Cayart** (1645–1702) of 1701–5) and the New Church (by **Giovanni Simonetti** (1652–1716) to designs by **Martin Grünberg** (1665–1707) of 1701–8) in the *Gendarmenmarkt*, while his works at the *Marmorpalais*, Potsdam, and Berlin *Schloss* (both 1786–9) were influenced by English *Neo-Classicism.

Borrmann (1893); Gersberg (1986); E.Hempel (1965); Wa & M (1987); Zieler (1913)

González de León, Teodoro (1926–2016) *See* ZABLUDOVSKY KRAVESKI, ABRAHAM.

Goodhart-Rendel, Harry Stuart (1887–1959) English architect of great originality, whose best building is arguably the *Art-Deco Hay's Wharf Building, Tooley Street, London

(1929–31). Other works include Broad Oak End, Bramfield, Herts. (1921–3), and the churches of St Wilfrid, Brighton, Sussex (1932–4), St John the Evangelist, St Leonards, Sussex (1946–58), Holy Trinity, Dockhead, Bermondsey, London (1957–9), and Our Lady of the Rosary, Marylebone Road, London (1958). He published *Nicholas Hawksmoor* (1924), *Vitruvian Nights* (1932), and *English Architecture since the Regency* (1953). He coined the term *'Rogue Goths'.

AD, **xlix**/10–11 (1979), 44–51; *AR*, cxxxviii/824 (Oct. 1965), 259–64; G-R (1924, 1949, 1989); *ODNB* (2004); *RIBAJ*, ser. 3, lvi/6 (Apr. 1949), 251–9

Goodhue, Bertram Grosvenor (1869–1924) American architect. In partnership (1892–1913) with *Cram, they designed All Saints' Church, Ashmont, MA (1892–1941), a robustly scholarly work that established their reputation, consolidated with the US Military Academy, West Point, NY (1903–10), and St Thomas's Church, NYC (1906–13—a distinguished work of the *Gothic Revival). After the partnership was dissolved, Goodhue designed the Cathedral of the Incarnation, Baltimore, MO (1911–24—partly influenced by Giles Gilbert *Scott's Anglican Cathedral, Liverpool, which Goodhue saw (1913) being built), St Vincent Ferrer Church, NYC (1914–19), St Bartholomew's Church, NYC (1914–18—in a *Byzantine-*Romanesque style influenced by *Bentley's Westminster Cathedral, London), and the Rockefeller Chapel, University of Chicago, IL (1918–28—a very handsome achievement). Probably his greatest work is the Nebraska State Capitol, Lincoln (1920–32), in a free style, vigorously composed, and with a central tower reminiscent of *skyscraper designs. He designed the National Academy of Sciences, Washington, DC (1919–24), in a simplified Classical style.

J.Baker (1915); R.Oliver (1983); Whitaker (ed.) (1925)

Goodwin, Francis (1784–1835) English architect, he established a practice (1819) and designed a number of churches in a late-*Gothic style as well as several Classical buildings of which the *Greek-Revival Town Hall at Manchester (1822–5—demolished) was the most accomplished. He published *Domestic Architecture* (1833–4), reissued (1835) as *Rural Architecture*. His unrealized designs for a 'Grand National Cemetery' for London (1830) were in a spectacular monumental Greek-Revival style. His masterpiece was Lissadell, Co. Sligo (1831–2—the finest Neo-Classical house in Ireland).

AH, **I** (1958), 60–72; Co (2008); J.Curl (2011a); Goodwin (1850)

goose-foot *See* PATTE D'OIE.

gopura Tall, ornate *gateway to a Hindu temple-enclosure.

gorge 1. Shallow part-elliptical *cavetto. **2.** *Neck (*gorgerin*) of a column-*shaft at the top, as in the *Tuscan and *Roman-*Doric *Orders. **3.** *Cyma. **4.** *Apophyge. *Associated terms include*:

gorge-cornice: large cavetto in *cornices of Ancient-Egyptian *pylon-towers;

gorgerin: collarino, gorge, *hypotrachelium, or neck separating a *capital from a shaft, such as the *frieze-like collar above the *astragal and below the *annulets and *echinus of the Roman-Doric Order.

gorge-cornice Ancient-Egyptian type, with *winged globe* and rearing *uraei*, with *torus* below.

Gospel side North side of an *altar or church.

Gotch, John Alfred (1852–1942) English architect/architectural historian, he studied in London and Zürich before commencing (1878) independent practice in Northants. and London, then with **Charles Saunders** (*fl.*1868–1928), and later with **Henry Ralph Surridge** (1885/6–1954). Among his works were major alterations to Quenby Hall, Leics. (*c.*1908–13—he was an expert on the *Jacobean style), the impressive Irthlingborough Viaduct over the Nene Valley, Northants. (1930s), and numerous buildings for the Midland Bank. Gotch's books include works on *Thomas Tresham* (1883), *Kirby Hall*, and *Haddon Hall* (both 1889), the two-volume *Architecture of the Renaissance in England* (1891), and several studies concerning old houses in Northants.

ODNB (2004)

Göthe *See* EOSANDER VON GÖTHE.

Gothein, Marie Luise (*née* **Schroeter**) (1863–1931) German scholar/gardener, author of works on **John Keats** (1795–1821), **William Wordsworth** (1770–1850), Indian gardens, and the life/work of her husband, **Eberhard Gothein** (1853–1923), her *Geschichte der Gartenkunst* (1914), sumptuously produced in an updated 1926 edn by **Eugen Diederichs** (1867–1930) of Jena, translated as *History of Garden Art* by **Laura Archer-Hind** for the English edn (1928), edited by **Walter Page Wright** (1864–1940), is a great achievement.

Gothein (1926, 1966)

Gothic Architectural style, properly called *Pointed, evolved in Europe (starting with France) from the late C12 until C16, even lingering until C17 and C18 in some places (e.g. Oxford and certain provincial areas). As its correct name suggests, it is the architecture of the *pointed* arch, *pointed* rib-*vaults, *piers with *clusters of *shafts, deep *buttresses (some of the *flying* type), window-*tracery, *pinnacles, *spires, *battlements, and a soaring verticality. While Ancient-*Egyptian and *Greek architecture is *columnar and* *trabeated, Gothic is *arcuated, giving an impression of dynamic thrust and counter-thrust. Certain elements of Gothic church-architecture, such as the *triforium, *clerestorey, and *Orders found in doorways, had developed in *Romanesque architecture. Pointed rib-vaults had been used in Burgundy and Durham, while half-arches or half-barrel-vaults used as buttresses were exploited by English and French Romanesque builders. Fully developed Gothic, however, was not a matter of eclectic motifs being gathered together: it was a remarkably coherent style of logical arcuated forms in which forces were expressed and resisted, and non-structural walls were dissolved into huge areas of glazed window.

*First Pointed (*Early English*) was used from the end of C12 to the end of C13, though most of its characteristics were present in the lower part of the *chevet of the Abbey Church of St-Denis, near Paris (*c*.1135–44). Windows were first of all *lancets, but later contained elementary tracery of the *plate* type (*see* TRACERY), then got larger, divided into *lights by means of *Geometrical* *bar-tracery. Once First Pointed evolved with *Geometrical* tracery it became known as *Middle Pointed. *Second-Pointed work of C14 saw an ever-increasing invention in bar-tracery of the *Curvilinear, Flowing,* and *Reticulated* types, where the possibilities of the *ogee form were fully exploited in canopies, tracery, and *niches, culminating in the *Flamboyant style (from *c*.1375) of the Continent. Second Pointed was relatively short-lived in England, and was superseded by *Perp. (or *Third Pointed*) from *c*.1332, although the two styles overlapped for some time. On the Continent, however (where Perp. was unknown), lace-like patterns of tracery evolved, and churches of great height were erected with highly complex vaulting, as at the Church of St Barbara, Kutná Hora, Bohemia (1512). The Gothic style embraced a complete system of dynamic structure with developed geometries and daring experiments with stone, especially in the final flowering of *Flamboyant* in Central Europe. Although Gothic was superseded by a revival of interest in the language of *Classicism from the *Renaissance period, it enjoyed a widespread and scholarly revival in C19. *See* GOTHIC REVIVAL.

Branner (1965); Co (1999); Frankl (1960, 2000); Gi (1986); H.O (1970); J.Parker (1850); Rickman (1848); Toman (ed.) (1998); V-I-D (1875)

Gothic bond Term for **Flemish bond** (*see* BRICK).

Gothic cornice C18 *Gothick *cornice or *frieze consisting of a series of interlacing pointed arches not carried on anything, but with *pendants hanging from where the arches would normally spring. A curious C20 use of the motif was under the cornice of Ideal (Palladium) House, Great Marlborough Street, London (1928), by Raymond *Hood.

Gothick C18 style only vaguely based on archaeologically correct *Gothic, and more connected with a taste for the exotic, so really a branch of *Rococo frivolity. It was largely associated with Sanderson *Miller's work, with *Walpole's Strawberry Hill (1750–70), and especially with Batty *Langley's *pattern-books, *Ancient Architecture Restored...* (1741–2) and *Gothic Architecture...* (1747). Gothick, sometimes curiously intermingled with *Chinoiserie* motifs, was an aspect of *Georgian *eclecticism, and was often treated with great delicacy, so it was pretty, ideal for interiors, garden-*fabriques, and built *'ruins'. It was a significant part of the *Picturesque. Although originating in England, Gothick influenced architecture in Germany (the Gothic House, Wörlitz (*c*.1773)), Poland (the *fabrique* at Arkadia (1797)), and other European countries.

J.Curl (2011a); K.Clark (1974); Ck (1985); T.Davis (1974); Ea (1970); *GH*, xxiii/1 (Summer 1995), 91–112; G (1972); B.Langley (1747); Macaulay (1975); M.McCarthy (1987)

Gothic Revival Conscious movement that began in England to revive *Gothic forms, mostly in the second half of C18 and throughout C19. It was one of the most influential artistic movements ever to spring from England, and from it grew the *Domestic Revival, the *Arts-and-Crafts and *Aesthetic movements, and many other developments in art and architecture. *Hawksmoor's All Souls' College, Oxford (1716–35), and western towers at Westminster Abbey (1734), were among the earliest *Georgian examples, followed by *Gibbs's *Gothick Temple, Stowe, Bucks. (1741–4), Sanderson *Miller's work (1740s), and *Keene's designs (1760s). Miller and Keene both advised *Newdigate about the Gothic work at Arbury Hall, Warwicks. (*c*.1750–2), which, with *Walpole's Strawberry Hill, Twickenham (*c*.1760–76), made the style fashionable, and it was adopted in Germany, France, Italy, Russia, America, and elsewhere. While many 'Gothic' churches were built in the early C19, they were often unconvincing in archaeological terms, and do not resemble medieval buildings: the *Friedrich Werderschekirche,* Berlin (1821–31), by *Schinkel, is one example, and in England there were many simple Georgian *Commissioners' churches with rudimentary *Perp. or *First-Pointed windows that only purported to be Gothic. What might be called the archaeological phase of the Gothic

Revival in which *real* medieval buildings provided the precedents for design began in England with *Bloxam, *Carter, *Rickman, and *Pugin, and was triggered partly by *Ecclesiology and partly by the popular success of the Palace of Westminster by *Barry and Pugin (from 1836). From that time a growing body of scholarship informed the Gothic Revival, and an ambitious programme of Victorian church-building was served by architects thoroughly immersed in the style. The building-industry, manufacturers, and craftsmen had to be trained too, for all manner of artefacts, carvings, stained-glass, and the like had to be provided. In France the main protagonist of the Revival was *Viollet-le-Duc, whose restoration of *Sainte Chapelle*, Paris (1840-9—with *Duban and *Lassus), had such an influence on Pugin. Indeed, the very considerable C19 programme of restoration of medieval buildings throughout Europe (especially in the UK, France, and Germany), prompted partly by national pride and partly by the religious revival after the *Enlightenment experiment, had a powerful impact, encouraging scholarship, archaeological investigations, accurate surveys of extant buildings, and the production of illustrated books. Experience gained in restoration increased confidence in the use of the style for modern buildings. Very soon the Revival was embraced throughout Europe and America. The C19 main Gothic Revival in Britain began with a resurrection of Perp.; turned to *Second Pointed (English first, then Continental) in the 1840s, largely due to the arguments of Pugin and the Ecclesiologists who perceived C14 Gothic as fully developed with advantages over both the 'undeveloped' *lancet style and 'decadent' Perp.; then embraced Continental Gothic, especially that of Italy, where the possibility of structural *polychromy had attracted many commentators, the most effective of whom were *Ruskin and *Street. The 'High Victorian' Gothic Revival of the 1850s and early 1860s was thus often coloured, incorporating polished granites, marbles, many-coloured brick- and tile-work, becoming more free in expression and less archaeologically derivative in the process. As with *Neo-Classicism's search for the *primitive early forms, Gothic-Revivalists also sought a more robust and 'primitive' Gothic, and so turned to the powerful First-Pointed Burgundian precedents of C13, giving birth to the *muscular Gothic of *Brooks, Street, and *Pearson. 'Great' *Scott drew on eclectic elements of Continental Gothic for his Midland Grand Hotel, St Pancras, London (1868-74), *Waterhouse also paraphrased European precedents for Manchester Town Hall (1868-76), and there were many other examples. Towards the end of the British and American Revivals *Bodley and other architects once more used Second-Pointed sources, and Perp. was also restored to favour, as in *Sedding's Holy Trinity,

Sloane Street, London (1888-90). Other major buildings of the Revival include *Gau's and *Ballu's *Ste-Clotilde*, Paris (1846-57), von *Schmidt's *Rathaus*, Vienna (1872-83), *Steindl's Hungarian Parliament Building, Budapest (1883-1902), Giles Gilbert *Scott's Anglican Cathedral, Liverpool (from 1902), and *Cram's Cathedral of St John the Divine, NYC (begun 1911).

M.Aldrich (1994); W.Andrews (1975); Baur (1981); Blau (1982); Bloxam (1882); Bremner (2013); C.Brooks (1999); K.Clark (1974); B.Clarke (1958, 1969); J.Curl (2007, 2011a); D & M (1985); Ea (1970); Frankl (1960, 2000); G (1972); Hersey (1972); M.Lewis (1993, 2002); Macaulay (1975); M.McCarthy (1987)

Gothic Survival Continuation of *Gothic elements in architecture in C16 and C17, of which *St-Eustache*, Paris (1532-1640), the Chapel at Lincoln's Inn, London (1619-23), the Cathedral of St Columb, Londonderry (1628-33), and the Hall staircase, Christ Church, Oxford (*c*.1640), are important examples. In England, the tradition of Gothic, designed and built by masons, continued, having survived both the Reformation and the upheavals of the Civil War and the Commonwealth. One of those places was Oxford, but there were plenty of churches or parts of churches that were erected in Gothic elsewhere: examples include Low Ham Church, Som. (consecrated 1669), the tower of Condover Church, Salop. (1662-79), and the central tower of Sherston Church, Wilts. (1730-3—by **Thomas Sumsion** (*c*.1672-1744)). In London, however, after the fire of 1666, the monopoly of the Company of Masons was undermined because many artisans (not associated with that Company) had to be employed in the works, and they laboured under *Wren's direction using the architectural language of *Classicism from Europe, not the ancient language of Gothic. Gothic survived in areas where there was good building stone (the West, the North, and parts of the Midlands), and was kept alive by masons working on repairs to churches or building new ecclesiastical work. Gothic certainly survived as a living tradition well into C18: it was the fact that masons lost ground to architects, that architects pushed the new-fangled Classicism from the Continent, and that when architects turned their hands to Gothic the results bore little resemblance to that real Gothic tradition which had been kept going by masons, which spelled the end of Gothic Survival. Acceptance of *International Modernism by C20 architects had an even more devastating effect on traditional craftsmanship and skills. When the *Gothic Revival proper got under way, Gothic had to be relearned, and only gradually was lost ground recovered, largely through painstaking scholarship, such as that of *Bloxam and *Rickman.

Co (1999); J.Curl (1986, 2007, 2011a); Ea (1970)

Gough, Alexander Dick (1804-71) English architect. Partner of R.L.Roumieu, he designed the curiously sinister Milner Square, Islington (*c.*1840), in a stripped, vaguely Classical style. His son, **Hugh Roumieu Gough** (1843-1904), designed St Paul's, Hammersmith, London (1882-7—with J.P.*Seddon), and, his masterpiece, the *Gothic-Revival St Cuthbert's, Philbeach Gardens, Kensington, London (1884-8).

J.Curl (2007); D & M (1985)

Gowan, James (1923-2015) *See* STIRLING, JAMES.

Gradidge, John Roderick Warlow (1929-2000) English architect. At the Architectural Association, London (1949-53), he refused to conform to **Robert Furneaux Jordan's** (1905-78) dogmatic insistence on *International Modernism: thereafter he was hostile to the *Modern Movement. He carried out numerous sympathetic restorations/alterations of *public-house interiors, holding that 'Modernism never sold a pint of bitter'. His interventions in Victorian churches were intelligent: among them were the reordering of A.W.N.*Pugin's St Augustine, Ramsgate (1970), and the re-erecting in the Anglican Church of the Most Holy Trinity, Reading, Berks., of Pugin's fine screen which had been crassly removed from St Chad's RC Cathedral, Birmingham. He restored (1992-3) the colourful interior of E.W.*Godwin's Guildhall, Northampton, and designed (1986) the witty decorations for the National Portrait Gallery at Bodelwyddan Castle, Flintshire (Clwyd), Wales. Perhaps one of his most successful new interiors was the library at Easton Neston, Northants., realized (1964) with **David Nightingale Hicks** (1929-98). His *Dream Houses* (1980) extolled the virtues of the late-Victorian and Edwardian *Arts-and-Crafts houses of England; *Edwin Lutyens: Architect Laureate* (1981) assisted in reviving the reputation of a great architect; and *The Surrey Style* (1991) celebrated the *Domestic Revival in his favourite county. Gradidge (who was Master of the *Art-Workers' Guild, 1987-8) firmly believed in 'keeping in keeping' (contrasted with the *Modernist approach), as his extension (1974-6) to *Lutyens's Fulbrook, Surrey, and his superb virtual rebuilding of the Old Rectory, Wiggonholt, Pulborough, West Sussex, demonstrate. Some of his best work can be found in St Mary's Church, Bourne Street, Westminster, including the *columbarium (1999), where his own calcined remains rest.

GS; Gradidge (1980, 1981, 1991); pk

gradino, gradine *See* PREDELLA.

Graham, Bruce (1925-2010) American architect of Scots-Canadian-Peruvian descent. He joined (1951) *SOM, and added several high-rise buildings to Chicago's skyline, including the Sears (1974—now Willis), Hancock (1970), and Quaker (1987) Towers. He headed (1980s) two significant projects as part of London's urban renaissance: the Canary Wharf (Isle of Dogs) and Broadgate developments (the latter included Exchange House which spanned the railway terminating in Liverpool Street). His innovations included structural 'tubes' in which the loads were carried by the *façades (leaving the interiors of *skyscrapers free of columns).

The Times (6 April 2010), 57

Graham, James Gillespie (1776-1855) Scots architect, he specialized in *castellated country-houses and *Gothic churches. The former were essentially symmetrical, with a nod to the *Picturesque by means of round towers to one side, but had plainish exteriors, although interiors frequently had impressive Gothic treatments. Among his houses Achnacarry, Inverness-shire (1802-5), Armadale Castle, Skye (1814-22), Duns Castle, Berwickshire (1818-22), and Dunninald, Craig, Angus (1823-4), may be mentioned. His best Gothic works are probably the RC Cathedral, Glasgow (1814-22), and the *steeple at Montrose, Angus (1832-4—based on a precedent at Louth, Lincs.). His most distinguished Classical essays are Gray's Hospital, Elgin, Morayshire (1812-5), the layout and design of the Moray Estate, Edinburgh New Town (1821-8—with the polygonal Moray Place), and a street-plan for Birkenhead, Ches. (1825-8), of which only Hamilton Square appears to have been developed according to his designs (1825-44). He was probably the first to use the term *Baronial (1813, 1846). He appears to have had some sort of business arrangement with David *Rhind.

Co (2008); Macaulay (1975); *ODNB* (2004); Youngson (1966)

grain elevator Silo (tall, cylindrical tower) with mechanical lifting-machinery for the storage of grain. Large r.c. elevators were erected in the USA, and these unlikely structures were regarded as exemplary by certain architects such as *Mendelsohn (who made many sketches of them) and *Gropius (who claimed to find them as impressive as Ancient-Egyptian architecture).

R.Ba (1976); Gropius (1913); Mahar-Keplinger (1993); Müller-Wülckow (1929); Torbert (1958)

Grainger, Richard (1797-1861) English speculative builder who carried out distinguished developments in Newcastle upon Tyne, starting with Eldon Square (1825—destroyed), continuing with Leazes Crescent and Terrace (1829-34), then culminating in the sequence of streets (Grey, Grainger, Market, Clayton, Nun, Nelson, and others (1834-42)). He was also responsible for the Markets, Theatre Royal, Exchange, Royal

Arcade, the Branch Bank of England, Lambton's Bank, and Salem Methodist Chapel. Clearly an enlightened developer/town-planner of considerable skill, he collaborated with several architects, including John *Dobson, **Thomas Oliver** (1791-1857—the designer of Leazes Crescent and Terrace), **John** (1787-1852) and **Benjamin** (1813-58) **Green** (who designed the Theatre Royal), **John Wardle** (c.1795-1860—responsible for parts of Grey, Market, and Grainger Streets), and **George Walker** (fl.1835-68). Grainger himself must be regarded as an architect.

Co (2008); *ODNB* (2004); Wilkes & Dodds (1964)

Grandjean de Montigny, Auguste-Henri-Victor (1776-1850) French Neo-Classicist, he studied with *Percier and *Fontaine, and was architect to **Napoléon**'s brother, **Jérôme (King of Westphalia**, r.1807-13). He settled in Brazil as part of the artistic mission introduced by **King John VI** (r.1816-26) to elevate public taste, and designed the Roman Arch (1816), Customs House (1819-26), and many eclectically *Classical buildings in Rio de Janeiro. The first Professor of Architecture at the Imperial Academy of Fine Arts in Rio, he introduced a *Beaux-Arts* curriculum. He wrote *Recueil des plus beaux Tombeaux exécutés en Italie pendant les XVe et XVIe siècles* (1813), and *Architecture de la Toscane* (1815).

Castedo (1969); Morales de Los Rios Filho (1942)

Grand Manner Style of C17 academic history-painting, so applied to large-scale *Baroque Continental gardens (e.g. those of Le *Nôtre). In Britain formal gardens also tended to incorporate views of surrounding countryside.

A.A.Cooper (1714); Symes (2006); J.T (1996)

Grand Tour Obligatory Continental journey, especially taking in Italy and France, regarded as an essential part of the education of a young gentleman from the British Isles in the C18. It encouraged a sophisticated taste among the aristocracy and landed gentry, led to the formation of many great collections, gave much work to the compilers and publishers of guide-books, and promoted the cause of *Palladianism and *Neo-Classicism. It frequently lasted a year or more. Certain persons who had been on the Grand Tour founded the Society of *Dilettanti in London (1732).

H.O (1970)

granite Coarse-grained hard igneous crystalline rock composed of feldspar, mica, and quartz, usually grey or dark red, and capable of taking a high polish. Used by the Ancient Egyptians (e.g. for *obelisks), it was also employed by the Romans for, e.g. the shafts of columns. As industrialized methods of cutting stone developed in C19, the material was frequently used for *ashlar

work, and especially for funerary monuments in the new *cemeteries.

N.Davey (1961); W.McKay (1957); W.Pa (1852)

Granpré Molière, Marinus Jan (1883-1972) Dutch architect/planner, best known for the creation of Vreewijk (1913-21), the urban extension of Rotterdam, laid out on *Garden-City principles, with *Berlage et al. Believing in the cultural and artistic significance of architecture and planning, he was appointed (1924) professor at the *Technische Hogeschool*, Delft, where he rejected much of the theorizing associated with contemporary architecture, and opposed the dogmatic assumptions of *CIAM and the *Modern Movement, favouring a more subtle and complex approach involving the typologies of Dutch architecture and drawing on traditional forms as catalysts for modern design. He was a leading light of the *Delft School.

Kuiper (1991); *Plan*, **vi** (1972), whole issue; J.T (1996)

Granville, Walter Long Bozzi (1819-74) Englishman who went to India (1858) as architect to the Eastern Bengal Railway, and was consulting architect to the Government of Bengal (1864-9). He designed several distinguished *Classical buildings, including the General Post Office (1868), Indian Museum (1875), and the University buildings (1861-72—destroyed 1961), all in Calcutta. His High Court (1872), Calcutta, mixed Flemish and Venetian *Gothic, modelled on 'Great' *Scott's designs for the Hamburg *Rathaus* (1854-5), which themselves owed debts to the medieval Cloth Hall in Ieper.

Stamp (1981a)

grapevine See TRAIL.

Grassi, Giorgio (1935-) See NEO-RATIONALISM; RATIONAL ARCHITECTURE; TENDENZA.

Graves, Michael (1934-2015) See NEW YORK FIVE; POST-MODERNISM.

Gravesande, Arent van 's (c.1600-62) Municipal architect to several Netherlandish towns, including The Hague, Leiden, and Middelburg, he was a leading Classicist and disciple of van *Campen. His best work is in Leiden, including the *Bibliotheca Thysiana* (1655), *Laeckenhalle* (1639-40), and octagonal *Marekerk* (1639-49—with *Ionic columns carrying the *dome). He completed the *Oostkerk*, Middelburg (1646—a variation on the *Marekerk*), and designed the *Sebastiansdoelen*, The Hague (1636).

Kuyper (1980)

Gray, Eileen (1879-1976) Irish-born designer, her *International-Modernist architectural work included the 'E-1027' House, Roquebrune, France (1926-9), the *Badovici Apartment, Paris (1930-1), the *Tempe à Pailla* House, Castellar,

France (1932–4), and a cultural centre exhibited at the 1937 Paris Exhibition by Le *Corbusier in his *Pavillon des Temps Nouveaux*. She was also a gifted furniture-designer, starting with her lacquer-work, influenced by Japanese precedent. After the 1914–18 war she became an interior designer, anticipating aspects of *De-*Stijl* themes, and designing furniture using chromed steel, aluminium, and mirror-glass.

P.Adam (2000); F.Baudot (1998); Constant (2000); Garner (2006); Hecker & C.Müller (1993); Jervis (1984); J.S. Johnson (1980); Loye (1984)

Grayson, George Enoch (*c.*1833–1912) Liverpool architect, in partnership with **Edward Augustus Lyle Ould** (1852–1909) he built up a successful practice, later joined (1897) by **George Hastwell Grayson** (1871–1951). The firm designed several distinguished groups of houses at Port Sunlight, Ches., including those with stepped gables in Wood Street (1895) and the *Gothic houses of hard *terracotta and brick (1896). At Cambridge, Grayson & Ould designed the Hall at Selwyn College (1907) and buildings at Trinity Hall (1910).

Davison (1916); A.S.Gray (1985)

Gréber, Jacques (1882–1962) French urban designer. He prepared the plan for the national capital of Canada at Ottawa, including parks and gardens.

JRAIC, **xxvi**/12 (December 1949), 395–445

Greek architecture Cradle of *Classicism, Greece perfected and refined *columnar-and-*trabeated architecture, each part of which was expressive of a long tradition of such construction, and related to the whole by subtle systems of proportion. Greek architecture was related to human scale, expressive of its structural elements, yet was perfected in the *temples, the greatest achievements of Greek architects, as habitations for the deities. The three Greek *Orders (*Doric, *Ionic, and *Corinthian) were evolved, each with its own characteristics and rules, refinements of detail and appropriate ornament, and these Orders were adapted by the Romans, providing the essentials of everything known as Classical architecture thereafter. The Corinthian Order is often thought to be no more than a variant of Ionic with a different capital, but there are, in fact, subtle differences.

Greek architecture was a petrified and ultra-refined development of timber-construction from the period after C6 BC, so much of the ornament (e.g. the Doric Order) that appears merely decorative had its origins in carpentry, *triglyphs suggesting the ends of beams, *guttae the dowels, and *metopes the planes (or even voids) between the beams. It appears to have derived much from

Ancient-Egyptian architecture, notably the *columnar-and-trabeated elements, but also the basic forms of the Doric Order have precedents of sorts in the Egyptian rock-cut tombs at Beni-Hasan (early second millennium BC) and in the Mortuary Temple of Queen Hatshepsut (*r. c.*1479–*c.*1458 BC) at Deïr-el-Bahari. However, the Greek-Doric temple, which may have been derived partly from the Mycenaean *megaron and partly from Egyptian columnar-and-trabeated models, was a unified, original, and entirely Greek invention, and was established in C7 BC. Among early Doric temples may be mentioned that of Apollo, Thermum (*c.*640 BC); the *Heraeum*, Olympia (before 600 BC—and originally with timber columns later replaced with stone); the fragmentary Temple of Artemis at Corcyra (Corfu) of *c.*580–570 BC (which was lavishly embellished with sculpture); the first Temple of Hera at *Paestum (*c.*550 BC); the Temple of Aphaia at Aegina (*c.*500–495 BC); and the huge Temple of *Zeus Olympios* at Acragas (Agrigentum), Sicily (*c.*510–409 BC). These buildings had sturdy, even stocky, columns, and, at Paestum especially, the columns had an exaggerated *entasis and wide overhanging capitals admired for their powerful, even *primitive, evocations by C18 Neo-Classicists. Indeed, the severity, toughness, roughness (emphasized by the loss of the smooth *stucco rendering that covered the heavily textured stone), and sturdiness of Paestum-Doric suggested masculine strength, and was used for expressive purposes by C18 and C19 Neo-Classical architects. Much more refined were the *Hephaesteion* ('*Theseion*'), Athens (449–444 BC), and the *Parthenon, Athens (447–438 BC), regarded by many commentators as one of the finest works of architecture ever created because of its elegant proportions, equilibrium between sculpture and structure, and subtle optical corrections to ensure serenity and repose (although there are many details such as the relationships of columns to *soffits that are less than satisfactory). Mention should also be made of the *Propylaea, the plural name given to the whole structure of formal gateway to the Acropolis with its wings, designed by *Mnesicles, constructed 437–432 BC: the central *intercolumniation of the Doric Order was wider than the others to facilitate the passage of processions and sacrificial beasts, and the Ionic Order was used to flank the central roadway inside the structure.

The Ionic Temples of *Athene Nike* (*Nike Apteros*—*c.*448–421 BC) and the *Erechtheion* (421–405 BC), both on the Athenian Acropolis, were among the most refined inventions, and are therefore important exemplars. The latter, with its *caryatid porch and exquisite Order incorporating a *frieze around the neck of the columns, was widely admired during the *Greek Revival: its asymmetrical composition was of particular interest. Among other important Ionic buildings were the Temples of Artemis at Ephesus in Asia Minor (c.560–450 BC and c.356–236 BC) and the Mausoleum at Halicarnassus (355–330 BC).

All three Orders were used in the Temple of *Apollo Epicurius* at *Bassae (c.450–425 BC): the external Order was Doric; the internal Ionic Order was unusual in that it had a unique *capital with adjoining *volutes, columns were attached to or *engaged with *piers or spur-walls along the inner walls of the naos; and at the southern end one isolated Corinthian column stood between two spur-walls that had an engaged Ionic, or, some authorities say, an engaged Corinthian, Order attached to each of them. The use of a Corinthian Order for interiors only as at Bassae was normal until the *Hellenistic period: examples include the *Tholos at Epidaurus (c.350 BC) and the Temple of *Athena Alea* at Tegea (c.350 BC). However, a refined Corinthian was used on the exterior of the exquisite little *Choragic Monument of Lysicrates, Athens (334 BC), and was much admired in C18, as the many quotations from it demonstrate.

Apart from temples, monuments, and tombs, the Greeks perfected the design of theatres, of which those of Dionysus, Athens (C5 BC), and Epidaurus (C4 BC) were the most impressive, and were influential, notably in Asia Minor. The Greeks also evolved designs for the *stadium, the *stoa, and other building-types. Elaborate public monuments were also vehicles for Greek architecture: a distinguished example was the Great Altar of Zeus, Pergamon (early C2 BC), with its vigorous sculpted *podium and Ionic superstructure, now in Berlin.

Camp (2001); J.Curl (2001); D (1950); Fyfe (1936); La (1996); R.Martin (1956, 1986); C.Normand (1852); D.S.R. (1945)

Greek cross See CROSS.

Greek key Geometrical ornament consisting of horizontal and vertical *fillets joining at angles, a variety of *fret called *grecque* or *labyrinthine*, like a series of key-like shapes on *bands (usually *friezes and *string-courses).

Greek key Two types of *Greek key* or *labyrinthine fret*.

Greek Revival Style of architecture in which accurate copies of Ancient-*Greek motifs were incorporated in the design of buildings from the 1750s. It was essentially part of *Neo-Classicism in that it drew upon scholarly studies of *Antique buildings, especially the work of *Stuart (who designed the early *Doric garden-temple at Hagley, Worcs. (1758), the first example of the *Doric Revival) and *Revett in the *Antiquities of Athens* (from 1762). In the mid-C18 Greece and most of what had been Greek territories were part of the Ottoman Empire, and therefore relatively unknown in the West. Curiously, the accessible Greek *temples at *Paestum in Italy and in Sicily had never really been studied, and were not taken seriously until relatively late, because baseless Greek Doric was seen as uncouthly *primitive. Early admirers of Greek architecture included *Winckelmann, *Ledoux, and *Soane, but the Revival was not universally adopted until after the Napoléonic wars, when it was associated with national aspirations: unlike other styles, it was not tainted with discredited ideas or regimes, and was widely used in the USA, the British Isles, Prussia, and Bavaria. Among its most accomplished practitioners were *Hamilton, *Hansen, von *Klenze, *Playfair, *Schinkel, *Smirke, *Strickland, *Thomson, and *Wilkins.

Crook (1972a); J.Curl (2001, 2011a); Honour (1977, 1979); Kennedy (1989); M & Wa (1987); W-L (1980)

green 1. Grass-covered land, especially that common to a village or small town, sometimes used for recreation, e.g. bowling or cricket. **2.** The same, but once used for bleaching in areas where linen was manufactured, e.g. Ulster, where many survive, called *bleach-greens*.

Green, David John (1912–98) See TAYLER, HERBERT.

Green, John (1787–1852) English architect/civil-engineer. His two sons, **John** (c.1807–68) and **Benjamin** (1813–58) were also architects, and Benjamin, a pupil of A.C.*Pugin, worked (c.1831–52) with his father. They designed numerous undistinguished churches and altered medieval fabric in an unscholarly way. Their best work was for the railways, and includes the wrought-iron suspension-bridge, Whorlton, near Barnard Castle, Co. Durham (1829–31), and Tynemouth Railway Station, Northum. (1847). In Newcastle upon Tyne they designed the Literary and Philosophical Society's Library (1822–5), the Theatre (1836–7), the Grey Column (1837–8), the Corn Exchange and Cloth Market (1838–9—demolished 1854 and 1972), the Corn Warehouse (1848), and the United Secession Meeting-House (1821–2). One of their best works was the Greek- *Doric temple, Penshaw Hill (1840).

Co (2008); *ODNB* (2004)

Green, Leslie William (1875–1908) English architect, he made his name as Architect to the Underground Electric Railways Company of London Ltd., working with **Harry Wharton Ford** (1875–1947), Staff Architect to the Company (1899–1911). He designed stations for the Baker Street and Waterloo Railway, the Great Northern, Piccadilly, and Brompton Railway, and the Charing Cross, Euston, and Hampstead Railway, all in a clean, clear, practical manner, using *glazed bricks and tiles in a simple, uncomplicated way.

A.S.Gray (1985); Leboff (2002)

Green, William Curtis (1875–1960) English architect, pupil of *Belcher, he set up a practice (1898) and designed a number of electricity-generating stations, houses, and cottages (notably at Letchworth *Garden City and Hampstead *Garden Suburb). He became a partner (1912) in the London firm of *Dunn and Watson, responsible for several accomplished Classical buildings, including Wolseley House (1921—later Barclays Bank) and the National Westminster Bank (with details derived from *Peruzzi), both in Piccadilly, and the Scottish Provident Institution, Pall Mall (with elements derived from *Michelangelo's New Sacristy, *San Lorenzo*, Florence). In the 1930s he designed the exterior and interiors of the Dorchester Hotel, London, the structure of which was by Owen *Williams. He also designed churches (e.g. St Christopher, Cove, Hants. (1934)).

A.S.Gray (1985); J.Lloyd (ed.) (1978); Me.Miller (1992, 2002); M & G (1992); *ODNB* (2004); Reilly (1931)

Green architecture 1. Formal, *Picturesque gardens that are closely related to buildings, or where landscape and architecture coalesce. **2.** Buildings designed according to energy-saving criteria and the reduction of pollution. *See also* ENVIRONMENTALLY RESPONSIBLE ARCHITECTURE.

AR, clxxxvii/1123 (Sept. 1990), whole issue; J (ed.) (2000); Solomon (1988); V & V (1991)

green belt Undeveloped agricultural land, forest, heath-land, wild country, etc., around a town or city, protected to prevent it being developed. *Loudon proposed such a benefit for London, partly to contain its sprawl, as early as the 1820s, and the idea was subsequently adopted by the promoters of *Garden Cities and *New Towns. The green belt around London preserved areas of countryside in several counties where otherwise development would have been difficult to resist: in C21, however, it is under threat for short-term political ends. *See* STEIN, CLARENCE.

Me.Miller (1992, 2002)

Greenberg, Allan (1938–) *See* NEW CLASSICISM.

Greene, Charles Sumner (1868–1957) and **Greene, Henry Matthew** (1870–1954) **Greene & Greene** were important American *Arts-and-Crafts architects who established their practice in Pasadena, CA, exciting attention with their Kinney-Kendall Building (1896): it had simplified *façades of *mullions, wide *friezes, and a crowning *entablature. Thereafter, however, their work was almost entirely in domestic architecture, with low-pitched roofs reminiscent of Swiss *châlets, the *Italianate style of *Schinkel and *Thomson, and the *Prairie houses of F.L.L. *Wright. Examples of their work were the Robert C.Blacker House (1907), the David B.Gamble House (1908), and the S.S.Crow House (1909), all in Pasadena. In all three, massive over-sized timbers, overhanging roofs, and a careful relationship with the landscape were hallmarks of their style.

Bosley (2000); Current (1974); Greene & Greene (1977); Jordy (1976); McCoy (1975); Makinson (1974, 1977–9, 1998); B.Smith (1998); R.Winter (ed.) (1997)

Greene, Colonel Godfrey T. (1807–86) Director of Engineering and Architectural Works for the British Admiralty (1850–64), he was responsible for the factory, smithy, foundry, ship-fitting shop, and boat-store at Sheerness, Kent (1856–7), all remarkably straightforward well-crafted buildings with no stylistic pretensions. The boat-store appears to be the very first four-storeyed lightly clad iron-framed structure.

Ck (1996); J.Newman (2012)

greenhouse *Glass-house in which plants are reared, affording protection from cold yet permitting maximum sun-penetration. As a building-type it was perfected in C19 with improvements in the manufacture of iron-and-glass structures prompted by early inventions by J.C.*Loudon. *See* CONSERVATORY; HOT-HOUSE; ORANGERY; PINERY; WINTER GARDEN.

Greenough, Horatio (1805–52) American sculptor/aesthetic-theorist, he demanded American art/architecture be 'cleansed' of 'archaic' and 'corrupt' European influences to make it appropriate for a new nation. He shared views with **Ralph Waldo Emerson** (1803–82), including the importance of 'truth' in design, the discarding of meaningless ornament, and fitness of creations to subject and place, sometimes called the 'organic principle'. In turn, his ideas inspired works by landscape architects *Cleveland and *Copeland (e.g. Sleepy Hollow Cemetery, Concord, MA).

Shoe (2001); J.T (1996); N.Wright (ed.) (1975)

green roof Roof of a building with plants growing on it, designed to be environmentally and aesthetically pleasing. The Anglo-Hispanic roof-garden (1937-8) of the former **Derry & Toms** store, Kensington High Street, London (1929-31), by **Bernard George** (1894-1964), is one of the earliest of its kind in England.

PS

Greenway, Francis Howard (1777-1837) English architect. A pupil of *Nash, he set up in business in Bristol (*c.*1805) with his builder and stonemason brothers, himself providing the architectural expertise. The firm built the Hotel and Assembly Rooms, The Mall, Clifton, and erected many housing developments. He was found guilty of forgery in connection with a contract, and was transported (1812) to Australia. He became (1816) Civil Architect to the Government of New South Wales, designing many public buildings in Sydney, including St James's Church (1819-24), the Barracks (1817-19), the Macquarie Tower, and the stables of Government House. The last were in the *castellated style, but most of his other buildings were competent essays in *Classicism. He also designed St Matthew's Church, Windsor (1817-20), and St Luke's Church, Liverpool (1818), both in New South Wales.

Co (2008); Ellis (1966); Herman (1954); Kobayashi *et al.* (1996)

grees, grese, gryce 1. *Steps. **2.** *Staircase.

Greeves, Thomas Affleck (1917-97) British architectural conservationist/draughtsman. A founder-member of the Victorian Society (1957), he was active in resisting wholesale demolition of quality buildings, and was particularly involved in *conservation at Bedford Park, Chiswick, West London, the C19 *Arts-and-Crafts development by Norman *Shaw and others. He appreciated Victorian urban fabric before it became fashionable, and when those who look with their ears were involved in plans for its destruction. Influenced by visions of *Piranesi and by his own experiences viewing the decaying buildings of the British Raj in India, he began to produce beautifully drawn architectural fantasies of great imaginative power, often showing Victorian buildings in a state of decay, composed in the form of the C18 *capriccio.* His publications include *Bedford Park* (1975) and *Ruined Cities of the Imagination* (1994).

Daily Telegraph (29 Sept. 1997), 23; Greeves (1975); pk; *The Times* (27 Sept. 1997), 25

Gregotti, Vittorio (1927-) *See* NEO-LIBERTY; NEO-RATIONALISM.

Greisch, René (1929-2000) Belgian architect/ engineer, celebrated for his many *bridges in Belgium and Luxembourg, and for his search for harmony between aesthetics and technical innovation. Among his suspension-bridges may be cited that over the Maas and the Albert Canal, Wandre (1989), and another over the Albert Canal at Hermalle-sous-Argenteau (1983)

Loo (ed.) (2003)

Grenfell-Baines, Sir George (1908-2003) English architect. He founded (1961) **Building Design Partnership (BDP)**, an early British multi-disciplinary design-team, and anticipated the globalization of architecture earlier than most. He designed the Power and Production Pavilion for the *Festival of Britain (1951), and offices for the Shell Company at Stanlow, Ches. (1956—a sub-Corbusian essay). He claimed to be influenced primarily by the *Bauhaus and by his own Leftist beliefs, specializing in large-scale public and industrial works, e.g. buildings for British Nuclear Fuels at Sellafield, Cumb. (1970s).

The Times (14 May 2003), 38

Greppi, Giovanni (1884-1960) Italian architect. With sculptor **Giannino Castiglioni** (1884-1971) he created two of the most successful memorials to the dead of the 1914-18 war: the *Sacrario Militare del Monte Grappa* (1932-5), a vast circular tiered *podium (with *loculi containing the remains of the dead) crowned by a circular chapel; and the *Sacrario di Redipuglia* (inaugurated 1938) at Monte Sei Busi, near Udine-Monfalcone, a series of massive steps (the Stairs of the Hundred-Thousand Dead) with the word PRESENTE repeated in relief many times and the huge *sarcophagus of the army-commander, **Emanuele Filiberto, Duke of Aosta** (1869-1931). Greppi also worked at the *Companytown of Dalmine (1934-40), and designed the Giuseppe Sinigaglia Stadium, Como (1925-7). His architecture suggests that universal condemnation of buildings erected under Fascism is not based on evaluation of the architecture at all, but is merely posturing.

J.Curl (2002*a*); pk; Stamp (1977)

grese *See* GREES.

grid, gridiron 1. Network of one lot of equidistant parallel lines laid at right angles over a similar set forming squares, establishing the pattern for a plan, e.g. of a building using, say, a *columnar-and-*trabeated framework, the columns placed at the intersections, or of a city with streets regularly spaced and crossing each other at right angles. **2.** *Mullioned and *transomed window (grid- *tracery), or a *grille of metal or wood in a *screen.

griffe *See* SPUR.

Griffin, Walter Burley (1876–1937) IL-born American architect, he worked in *Chicago (1899–1901) and for F.L.L.*Wright (1901–5) before being appointed (1913) Director for the design and construction of the Federal Capital at Canberra, Australia. The formal geometry of his plan was successfully imposed upon a natural landscape of great beauty, perhaps reflecting Griffin's interest in the *Steiner movement of **Anthroposophy**. Among his best designs are Newman College, University of Melbourne (1917), the Capitol Theatre, Melbourne (1924), and several houses in Australia. He designed and patented a system of construction involving interlocking components he called **Knitlock**. He produced an enormous number of designs for his adopted country, many of which were realized. Griffin's wife, **Marion Lucy Mahony** (1871–1961), worked in Wright's Oak Park Studio, Chicago (1898–1909), and was responsible for many drawings in the influential *Ausgeführte Bauten und Entwürfe von Frank Lloyd Wright*, published by **Wasmuth** (1910).

Birrell (1964); H.Brooks (1972); E (1980); D.L.Johnson (1977); Ko (1996); Maldre (1996); Peisch (1964); Z (ed.) (1970)

Griffith, John (1796–1888). English architect, he designed the *Greek-Revival buildings at the General Cemetery of All Souls, Kensal Green, London (consecrated 1833), including the *Ionic Dissenters' Chapel (1833–4), the *Doric Anglican Chapel, *catacomb, and *colonnades (1836–8), the Terrace catacomb and colonnade (1832–3), the wall and railings surrounding the ground (with gates), the arched entrance-gate and lodges (1833–4), and the overall layout and planting of the grounds.

J.Curl (ed.) (2001)

Griffith, John William (c.1790–1855) Surveyor to the Parish of St Botolph, Aldersgate, London (the church of which he may have enlarged and enhanced (c.1830)), and to the London estates of St John's College Cambridge. He designed the Islington Parochial Schools (1815), and many houses in Highgate, Hornsey, Islington, and Kentish Town (1816–55). His architect-son, **William Pettit Griffith** (1815–84), was an antiquary, publishing books on *Gothic architecture, geometrical proportions, etc.

Co (2008); Pinks (1880); *ODNB* (2004)

Griggs, Frederick Landseer Maur (1876–1938) English architect/illustrator, he was in great demand as a perspectivist for many of the leading architects and landscape architects of the *Arts-and-Crafts fraternity. He settled in Chipping Campden, Glos., spent much of his time restoring traditional Cotswold buildings on principles established by *Morris, and built himself New Dover's House in the town. His etchings were much admired, and many of them decorated numerous books. He was Master of the *Art-Workers' Guild (1934).

J.Moore (2000)

grille *Lattice or *screen of *openwork, usually metal. *See also* CLAIR-VOIE

Grimaldi, Giovanni Francesco (1606–80) Italian painter/architect. He was site-architect (1645–7) for *Algardi's *Villa Doria-Pamphili*; Rome, and he may have contributed to the garden-layout. He probably designed the Chapel of the Immaculate Conception in Tivoli Cathedral (1656–9), and painted numerous decorative *frescoes, e.g. at the *Villa Falconieri*, Frascati (1672).

J.T (1996)

Grimshaw, Sir Nicholas (1939–) *See* HIGH TECH.

grisaille 1. Style of painting in grey monochrome to represent solid objects in *relief, the objects being supposedly white and the shadows they project properly depicted by various grey tints. It was used on the external leaves of medieval *triptych *altar-pieces. In Neo-Classical schemes of decoration it represents e.g. figures in *Etruscan or *Pompeian interiors. **2.** Grey-tinted stained glass.

gritstone Strong, hard, sandstones, e.g. Berristall (Derbys.), Bramley Fall (Leeds, Yorks.), Dunn House, (Darlington, Co. Durham).

groin *Arris formed by the *salient between two intersecting *vaults, as in two barrel-vaults joined at right angles.

Gropius, Georg Walter Adolf (1883–1969) German-born naturalized American architect, best known for promoting *International Modernism both as practitioner and educator. He worked with *Behrens in Berlin (1907–10) before setting up his own practice. His earliest significant work (with A.*Meyer) was the Fagus Factory, Alfeld-an-der-Leine (1911), a three-storeyed steel-framed structure with glass *curtain-walls, one of the first buildings in which the beginnings of the International-Modern style were displayed. For the *Deutscher Werkbund* Exhibition, Cologne (1914—again with Meyer), he designed the administrative building with curved glazed towers enclosing the staircases (an influential motif throughout the 1920s and 1930s), but otherwise the building had a stripped Neo-Classical simplicity, certain aspects of it were reminiscent of F.L.L. *Wright's work, and its plan resembled the Ptolemaïc temple of Horus, Edfu, Egypt. Through van de *Velde, Gropius was given the opportunity (1915) to direct the *Grossherzoglich-Sächsische Kunstgewerbeschule* at Weimar, but was prevented by the war from taking this up. Gropius joined in the euphoria following the collapse of the monarchial system (1918), and, with *Taut, was active in promoting Modernist ideas: he was involved in the *Novembergruppe* and *Arbeitsrat für Kunst* which combined efforts, out of which grew *Die *Gläserne Kette*. Seeing the Weimar possibilities as a means by which he could promote Leftist ideology, he sought those who might be able to confirm the 1915 offer, and in 1919 became Director not only of the former Grand-Ducal *Kunstgewerbeschule*, but of the *Hochschule für Bildende Kunst*, which he amalgamated under the new title of *Das Staatliche Bauhaus Weimar*. Influenced by the *De-*Stijl* movement and by his own belief in industrialization and mass-production, the Bauhaus moved inexorably away from a craft-oriented ethos.

When the *Bauhaus moved to Dessau, Gropius designed the buildings (completed 1926), paradigms for the International-Modernist style. Even while at the Bauhaus, Gropius continued in practice with Meyer, designing the Sommerfeld House, Berlin-Dahlem (1921-2—made of teak from a scrapped warship); an *Expressionist memorial at Weimar (1922); and the Jena State Theatre (1923). He designed buildings for the *Weissenhofsiedlung*, Stuttgart (1927), resigned as Bauhaus Director (1928), and laid out the Siemensstadt Housing Estate, Berlin (1929-30), designing two of the apartment-blocks himself: with long strip-windows set in smooth rendered walls, they were widely imitated. As an active member of *CIAM his proposals for high-rise housing in green areas were disseminated, and became part of Modernist orthodoxy. His own moderate left-wing views and the more overtly Communist political stance adopted by Hannes *Meyer at the Bauhaus had repercussions, and even though he registered with the Nazi-created *Reichskulturkammer* and designed a recreational and cultural centre (unrealized) for the *Kraft durch Freude* Nazi movement (a project that invoked images of gigantic Party junketings worthy of a Nuremberg Rally), he failed to obtain major commissions.

He settled (1934) in England where he lived in Lawn Road Flats, Hampstead, designed by Wells *Coates, was involved in the *MARS group, and worked with *Fry, designing the film laboratories at Denham, Bucks. (1936), Wood House, Shipbourne, Kent (1937), 66 Old Church Street, Chelsea (1935-6), and Impington Village College, Cambs. (1936), the last his main contribution to architecture in England. He was also consultant (1934-5) to the Isokon Company, headed by Jack

Pritchard (1899-1992), which had built the Hampstead flats to Coates's designs. Gropius accepted (1937) the offer of a post in the Graduate School of Design, Harvard University, USA, and became (1938) Chairman of the Department of Architecture there, at once expunging all *Beaux-Arts traditions, an event followed at architectural schools throughout the USA. With *Breuer he designed the Gropius House, Lincoln, MA (1938), the first monument of International Modernism in New England, which was followed by several more private houses, culminating in the Frank House, near Pittsburgh, PA (1939). With *Wachsmann, Gropius evolved systems for constructing prefabricated houses (1943-5).

After the 1939-45 war Gropius went into partnership with several younger architects, forming **The Architects' Collaborative (TAC)**, which produced the Harvard Graduate Center, Cambridge, MA (1949-50). For the *Hansaviertel*, Berlin, Gropius designed an apartment-block (1957), and in the 1960s the new town of Britz-Buckow-Rudow, Berlin, was laid out to plans by him. He was probably the most influential architectural pedagogue of all time, but many aspects of his pronouncements and teachings were being questioned in the late C20 and early C21, as the environments created as a result of his influence have not proved to be either agreeable or functional.

Argan (1975); Berdini (1994); Fitch (1960); Franciscono (1971); Gropius (1913, 1945, 1952, 1962, 1965, 1968); Gropius & Harkness (eds) (1966); Herdeg (1985); F.Hesse (1964); Hüter (1976); Isaacs (1983-4); K-C (1999); K-C (ed.) (1998); Lane (1985); O'Neal (ed.) (1966); Probst & Schädlich (1986-8); Sharp (1993); H.Weber (1961); Wingler (1969)

Gropius, Martin Philipp (1824-80) Influential German architect/teacher, he studied at the Berlin *Bauakademie*, where he became familiar with the Grecianized *Classicism evolved by *Schinkel. He later became Professor there, Director of the Berlin Art School, and supervisor of all Prussian Art Schools. He designed the Lunatic Asylum at Neustadt-Eberswalde (1862-3), the hospitals at Friedrichshain (1867-71) and Tempelhof (1875-8), and the Art-Industrial Museum, one of his best buildings, now the *Martin-Gropius-Bau* (1881), Berlin. The clarity of his planning and structural systems owes much to Schinkel, while the *terracotta and red-and-yellow brick he favoured created an opulent *polychrome architecture. From 1866 he was in partnership with **Heino Schmieden** (1835-1913).

Körte (2013); Schliepmann (1892); J.T (1996)

Grosch, Christian Henrik (1801-65) Danish architect of German descent, he made a significant contribution to North-European

*Neo-Classicism. He worked under C.F.*Hansen, from whom he acquired his severe Neo-Classical style. He settled (c.1825) in Christiana (Oslo), Norway, where he assisted *Linstow in connection with the building of the Royal Palace (1824–7), taught for a while at the Royal Drawing School, and became City Architect (1828) then Inspector for Buildings (1833). He produced a huge amount of architecture, including the Greek *Doric *Børs* (1826–52), the Norwegian Bank (1826–30), Immanuel Church, Halden in Østfold (1827–33—influenced by Hansen's *Vor Frue Kirke* in Copenhagen), and the monumental Oslo University (1838), plans of which were shown to *Schinkel for comment, with the result that the finished buildings incorporate several Schinkelesque themes, including wall-articulation derived from the Berlin *Schauspielhaus*. Grosch also designed the Market Halls (1840–59) and Fire Station (1854–6), Oslo, in a red-brick *Rundbogenstil*. Fifty-nine churches were built after his designs, together with many houses and other buildings. He also designed numerous timber buildings based on Norwegian *vernacular architecture.

M & Wa (1987); J.T (1996); We (1947)

grotesque 1. Capricious Classical ornament (properly *grottesque*) consisting of animals, figures, flowers, foliage, fruits, and *sphinxes, all connected together, and distinct from *arabesques which do not have animal or humanoid representations. It is so called after the *Antique decorations rediscovered (1488) during the *Renaissance period in buried ruins of Roman buildings called *grotte*. Grotesques as a type of decoration were revived by *Raphael (so sometimes called *Raphaelesques*), and were used at the Vatican *Loggie* (from c.1515) and the *Villa Madama*, Rome (1520–1). Designs for grotesques were made available in publications, and, with *strapwork, were common in *Renaissance and *Mannerist schemes of decoration, especially in Northern Europe. **2.** *Picturesque irregular landscape, often with *grottoes.

Chastel (1988); Dacos (1969); L & D (1986); W-J (1967, 1967a)

grotto 1. Artificial cave/cavern in a *Picturesque landscape. **2.** Built structure of *rockwork, or an excavation imitating a rocky cavern, often adorned with broken pottery and shells arrayed in patterns (sometimes with fountains and water-cascades), serving as a cool retreat. Grottoes were not unknown in *Antique Roman gardens, and were often revived during the *Renaissance, *Mannerist, and *Baroque periods (in the last they were sometimes features of the lowest or entrance-floor of palaces, such as *Schloss Weissenstein*, Pommersfelden, Germany

(1711–20)). Some grottoes were further embellished with *congelated *rustication. Many were features of *landscape-gardens: architects (such as Thomas *Wright) and influential writers on gardens (such as *Hirschfeld) published designs for 'grottos'.

Batey (1999); Bazin (1990); D.Coffin (1994); He (1996); B.Jones (1974); M & T (1991); N.Miller (1982)

ground-plan *See* PLAN.

Grounds, Sir Roy Burman (1905–81) Australian architect, he made *Modernism acceptable in that country with his early houses (1950s) and the Academy of Science Building, Canberra (1957–9). Among his later works, the Arts Centre, Melbourne (1959–84), may be mentioned.

Tanner (ed.) (1981)

grouped 1. Two columns or *pilasters used in pairs are *coupled (as on the east front of the Louvre, Paris). More than two closely placed on one *base, *pedestal, or *plinth are grouped. **2.** *Clustered *pier.

grout Fluid *mortar, with added water, employed to fill holes or joints.

grove Group of trees (naturally occurring or planted), providing shade or wind-breaks, or forming avenues or walks. Valued in Ancient Greece, they were planted near *temples, and were places where discourses took place. Also associated with deities, images might be set up within them: they were also placed around graves to protect them from desecration. C17 groves were often symmetrically planted and could be designed as 'close' or 'open', as defined by Philip *Miller in his *Gardener's Dictionary* (1731–9): open groves had large trees, the branches of which formed canopies, and close groves were under-planted with shrubs. Groves became important ingredients of formal C17 and C18 gardens, and known as *boscages*, *boskets*, *bosquets*, *coppices*, *thickets*, *wildernesses*, etc., becoming *woodlands* in the time of C18 'improvers' such as 'Capability *Brown.

P.Miller (1731–9); O'Malley *et al.* (2010); Shoe (2001); Symes (2006); Tay (2006)

Gruen, Victor David (1903–80) Viennese architect, born **Grünbaum**, he settled (1938) in the USA. He established (1951) himself in Los Angeles, specializing in out-of-town *shopping-centres including the Northland Center, Detroit, MI (1954), the Southdale Center, Minneapolis, MN (1956), and the first inner-city enclosed *shopping-mall at Midtown Plaza, Rochester, NY (1962). His ideas (e.g. the mid-C20 shopping-mall) are encapsulated in his *The Heart of Our*

Cities (1964), but have been questioned by several commentators.

Fitch (1961); Gruen (1964, 1973); Gruen & L.Smith (1960); Hardwick (2004); J.Jacobs (1961); Tunnard & Pushkarev (1981)

Grumbold Family C16-18 masons active in Cambs./Northants., associated with quarries at Raunds and Weldon. **William Grumbold** (*fl.* 1570-95) worked for **Sir Thomas Tresham** (1543-1605) of Rushton, building the Market-House, Rothwell (1578), and in the 1590s 'Grumbolds' were constructing the New Building, Lyveden, all Northants. William Grumbold was involved in the erection of Fotheringhay Bridge (1573-4) and, with **Robert** and **John Grumbold**, worked at Great St Mary's Church, Cambridge (1593-4). **Arthur Grumbold** (1603-70) leased the Weldon quarries, and left his name on a house in Weldon's main street (1654). A **Thomas Grumbold** (d.1657) worked at St John's College Library (1625), Clare Hall (1639-40), and King's College (1651), all in Cambridge. **Robert Grumbold** (1639-1720) surveyed Worcester Cathedral (1677-8), and in 1669 he and another mason, one **Bradwell**, executed stonework for the west range of Clare College, Cambridge: from 1674 he was building St Catherine's College which he probably designed. He was master-mason from 1676 at *Wren's Library, extended (1680-2) Nevile's Court, and built the 'Tribunal' (a Classical feature on the eastern side of the Court, almost certainly designed by Wren), all at Trinity College. The north range of Clare Hall was designed/built by him (1682-6), and he was responsible for the bridge and gate-piers at St John's College (completed 1712). Other works include the west front of Clare Hall (1705-6); the north and south *cloisters on either side of the chapel at Peterhouse (1709); rebuilding of the *fountain at Trinity College (1716); and the beginnings of the Westmorland Building, Emmanuel College, under John *Lumley. Outside Cambridge, Grumbold worked at Audley End, Essex (1681); Great Park House, Ampthill, Beds. (1687-9); Wrest Park, Beds. (1693-5); and Ely Cathedral (1699—the new doorway to the north *transept resembling that of St Mary-le-Bow, City of London, may have been approved by Wren). As *Colvin observed, Robert Grumbold was 'the principal figure in Cambridge architecture' at the end of C17, and 'although he never learned the full discipline of classical architecture he achieved an attractive vernacular style' in which *Artisan Mannerism and *Baroque elements 'picked up from Wren and others' were evident.

BuMa (Dec.1925–Jan.1926); Co (2008); *RIBAJ* (17 Oct. 1936), 1069–70; Willis & Clark (1988)

Gruppo 7 Association (formed 1926) of Italian architects (**Ubaldo Castagnoli** (1882–*after* 1926— soon replaced by *Libera), *Figini, **Guido Frette** (1901–84), **Sebastiano Larco** (1901-   ), *Pollini, **Carlo Enrico Rava** (1903–85), and *Terragni), which, in their exhibition at Monza (1927) and manifesto (1926–7) in *La Rassegna Italiana*, promoted a supposed *Rationalism in which attempts were made to balance the Classical heritage of Italy and a *machine aesthetic derived from Le *Corbusier. The *Movimento Italiano per L'Architettura Razionale* (*MIAR) developed from Gruppo 7 (1930). Works associated with the group include Terragni's *Novocomum* Apartment Block, Como (1927–9), Libera's *façade for the Exhibition of the Fascist Revolution, Rome (1932), and the *Città Universitaria*, Rome (1930s). Most Gruppo 7 members were closely associated with Fascism.

AD, IV/1–2 (1981), 5–8; Etlin (1991); *Oppositions*, vi (1976), 86–102; Savi (1980)

gryce See GREES.

Guadet, Julien Azais (1834–1908) French architect/writer. A pupil of *Labrouste, he was associated with the *École des *Beaux-Arts for virtually all his life. Among his few buildings the *Hôtel des Postes, Rue du Louvre*, Paris (1878–84), a stone-faced work with a partly metallic structure behind, may be mentioned. As a theorist he is regarded as of some importance because of his promotion of rationalist approaches to architecture, as set out in his *Éléments et théories de l'Architecture* (1901–4, with later edns): this work covered an enormous range of problems and solutions, and included a comprehensive study of building-types from many periods in history. He argued that the architect should always establish the *content* from which he would arrive at the design of the *container* of that content. Taken out of context this remark gave his writings a spurious position in the canon of *Functionalism, but he also advocated providing buildings with any historical garb demanded by the client (a fact that tends to be overlooked). His pupils included Tony *Garnier and *Perret. The latter collaborated with Guadet's son, **Paul** (1873–1931), in the building of a pioneering *concrete house in Paris (1912). Paul Guadet also worked with his father on the reconstruction of L.-N.-V.*Louis's *Comédie Française* theatre, which had burned down in 1900.

P.Collins (1965); Dr (ed.) (1977); Egbert (1980)

Guarini, Guarino (1624–83) Born in Modena, baptized **Camillo**, he became a mathematician, Theatine priest, and one of the most original architects of the late C17. A sophisticated geometrician, as is clear from his *Placita Philosophica*

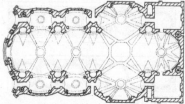

Plan of *Santa Maria della Divina Providenza* (*after Guarini*).

(1665), *Euclides Adauctus* (1671), and *Architettura Civile* (1686—not published until 1737), his work anticipated that of **Gaspard Monge** (1746–1818—who is usually credited with the invention of descriptive geometry). His understanding of *stereotomy helps to explain the great complexity of his buildings. His main architectural influences derived from *Bernini, *Borromini, and *Cortona: the deeply modelled *façades of the *Collegio di Nobili*, Turin (1679–83), clearly owe a debt to Borromini; while the *Palazzo Carignano* (also 1679–83) was influenced by Bernini's proposals for the Louvre, Paris (1665), with elements drawn from Borromini's *San Carlo alle Quattro Fontane*, Rome. All his most interesting surviving work is in Turin, where he developed openwork systems of intersecting ribs instead of solid domes, derived, perhaps, from Borromini's Oratory and *Propaganda Fide* chapels in Rome. At Turin Cathedral Guarini built the *Cappella della SS Sindone* to house the Holy Shroud, with a cone-shaped *dome (1667–90) composed of diminishing tiers of segmental rib-arches piled up upon one another and framing windows (severely damaged 1997). His *San Lorenzo*, Turin (1668–80), has an approximately octagonal central space each side of which curves inwards and is composed of a *serliana motif, while the dome above is formed of interlocking semicircular ribs disposed to form an eight-pointed star with an open octagon in the centre. The parallel to these arrangements can be found in the *Moorish architecture of Spain, such as the Mosque at Córdoba (c.965), and in French *Gothic cathedrals. Indeed, his *Architettura Civile* (1737) contains an intelligent appraisal of Gothic architecture, and his work seems to have exercised a considerable influence in Central Europe, notably on von *Hildebrandt, the *Dientzenhofers, *Fischer von Erlach, *Neumann, J.M.*Fischer, and, above all, *Santini-Aichel, for he made designs for St Maria, Altötting, Prague (1679), while his project for *Santa Maria della Divina Providenza*, Lisbon (1679 or 1681), has a plan remarkably similar to that of Neumann's *pilgrimage-church of *Vierzehnheiligen*, Franconia, Germany (1740s).

Brinckmann (1931, 1932); Guarini (1660, 1665, 1671, 1674, 1675, 1676, 1678, 1683, 1966, 1968); Meek (1988); N-S (1986, 1986a); On (1970); Pommer (1967); Pi (1956); Wi (1982)

Guas, Juan (*c*.1433–96) One of the greatest architects working in late-*Gothic Spain, he drew on Flemish medieval elements imaginatively mixed with *Moorish themes from Toledo. His was a major influence on the *Isabelline style. He designed the Franciscan Monastery of *San Juan de los Reyes*, Toledo (from 1476), which incorporates *muqarnas* under the springing of the *vaults. His style can best be seen at the castle of *El Real de Manzanares*, near Madrid (1475–9), with vigorously modelled *muqarnas* *cornice, and at the Palace of *El Infantado*, Guadalajara (1480–3), where the *façade is enriched with projecting diamond-shaped stones arranged in a rhomboid grid all over the wall: above is an arcaded *gallery with corbelled *balconies. He worked at the Cathedrals of Segovia and Toledo, and designed the Chapel of the Dominican College of *San Gregorio*, Valladolid (1487–9).

CG (1965); Herrera Casado (1975); K & S (1959); Layna Serrano (1941)

Gucewicz, Wawrzyniec (1753–98) Polish Neo-Classicist, he prepared designs for the monumental Wilno (now Vilnius) Cathedral (1777–1801), with a huge Roman-*Doric *portico and long side *colonnades: it was as impressive an exercise in Neo-Classical taste as anywhere else in Europe. For the same city he designed a Town Hall with a vast *Tuscan column as its tower (1785–6), and the Bishop's Palace (also 1780s). His was a strong influence on the architecture of Vilnius and its region until well into C19.

L & R (1984); Łoza (1954); D.Wa (1986)

Guedes, Joaquim Manuel Sobrinho (1932–2008). Brazilian architect. Critical of the stranglehold of Le *Corbusier and *Niemeyer's dogmas in Brazil since the late 1930s, he advocated architecture more attuned to climatic and economic realities in his plan for the new town of Caraíba (from 1976) which drew on traditional urban models and a study of vehicle and pedestrian circulation-patterns. His own house at São Paulo (1974) has a series of crisp planes and an elegantly minimal structure. Later work included the State Primary and High School, Jandira, São Paulo (1991), the Botanical Gardens Pavilions, Rio de Janeiro (1993), and the Mesquita House, São Paulo (1994).

Bullrich (1969); E (1994); J.T (1996)

Guelphic crenellation *See* BATTLEMENT.

Guêpière, Pierre-Louis-Philippe de la (*c*.1715–73) French architect: with *Pigage he introduced the *Louis-Seize* style to Germany. He worked on the *Neues Schloss*, Stuttgart, with Leopoldo *Retti, built 1746-68 (destroyed), and designed *Schloss Solitude* (with **Johann Friedrich Weyhing** (1716-81)), above Stuttgart (1763-7), a charming single-storey building with two wings extending from a central elliptical domed element. He was also responsible for *Monrepos* (1760-7), an enchanting Classical lakeside building near Ludwigsburg. All three buildings were for **Duke Karl Eugen of Württemberg** (*r.*1744-93). Following his retirement (1768), he designed the *Hôtel de Ville*, Montbéliard, erected in modified form after his death in the late 1770s. He published *Recueil de projets d'architecture* (1750) and *Recueil d'esquisses d'architecture* (1759).

Colombier (1955); Guêpière (1759); Ha (1950); Klaiber (1959); Wa & M (1987); Wörner (1979)

Guévrékian, Gabriel (1900-70) American architect of Armenian birth, he studied in Vienna and settled (1920) in Paris. He gained recognition with designs for a *Boutique Simultanée* and for the *Art-Deco *Jardin d'Eau et de Lumière* at the *Exposition Internationale des Arts-Décoratifs* (1924-5), as a result of which he was commissioned to lay out the garden for the *Villa Noailles* (designed by *Mallet-Stevens), Hyères, Var (reconstructed 1991, 1997), in which, like the *Exposition* exhibit, the influence of *Cubism was apparent. He designed the *Villa Heim*, Neuilly, outside Paris (1927-8), where the garden was broken up into small areas, including part on the roof. He became (1928) Secretary-General of *CIAM, but resigned (1933) when he was appointed by the **Shah** City Architect and Planner of Teheran, beginning that city's transformation into a modern capital. He worked with *Connell, Ward, & Lucas in England for a brief period from 1937, and after the 1939-45 war collaborated with *Pingusson on the reconstruction of Saarbrücken. He emigrated to the USA (1948). *See* MODERNIST GARDEN.

Imbert (1993); M & T (1991); J.T (1996); Vitou *et al.* (1987); A.Wilson (2005)

guglia, guglio 1. *Obelisk, needle, or *spire, sometimes confused with a thin *pyramid or *pinnacle. 2. *Meta sudans* ('sweating spire'): an obelisk, thin pyramid, or conical upright with water flowing down its sides.

guildhall 1. Hall in which a guild or livery-company met. 2. Meeting place for a corporation (in the case of the City of London, drawn from Livery Companies, so known as *Guildhall*). Many guildhalls survive, e.g. in Belgium.

guilloche 1. Classical ornament, or *plait-band*, usually composed of a series of equidistant circular elements all of the same diameter surrounded by curved bands, enriched with single or double

Two types of guilloche.

*fillets that overlap each other in a continuous strip. Each circle can also be enriched with a flower or can be plain. It is related to a *fret, but with curves instead of right angles. 2. Inaccurate term for a *fret.

Guimard, Héctor (1867-1942) French *Art-Nouveau architect, he was influenced by *Viollet-le-Duc and *Horta. He designed *Castel Béranger*, 16 *Rue de la Fontaine*, Paris (1894-9), an apartment-block of *rubble, coloured brick, stone, and *faïence, with an entrance in a fully developed Art-Nouveau style, causing the building to be christened *Castel Dérangé* (Mad Castle). His Paris *Métro*-Station entrances (1899-1913), featuring metal that seemed to grow from the stone, modular prefabricated construction, and bizarre, almost surreal lamps, made his works familiar, although many have been destroyed. The decorations of his own house, the *Hôtel Guimard, Avenue Mozart*, Paris (1912), perhaps were his most exquisite creations.

Brunhammer *et al.* (1975); Brunhammer & Naylor (1978); Graham (1970); Guimard (1907, 1992); Rheims & Vigne (1988); T-M (1967); Thiébaut (1992)

Gumpp, Johann Martin (1643-1729) Son of **Christoph Gumpp the Younger** (1600-72), Court Architect to the Tyrolean Habsburgs and designer of the *façade (1635) of the *Jesuitenkirche* and the centrally planned *Mariahilfkirche* (1647-9), both in Innsbruck. J.M. Gumpp designed the Fugger-Taxis Palace (1679-80), reworked Government House (1690-2), and designed the *Spitalkirche* (1700-5), all in Innsbruck. He, his father, and his son (**Georg Anton** (1682-1754)) all contributed to the transformation of the Abbey of Stams with *Baroque overlays (1719-25 and 1729-32), while Georg Anton alone designed the adjoining *Heiligenblutkapelle* (1715-17), the distinguished *St Johann am Innrain* (1729-35), and the *Landhaus* of the Tyrolean Estates (1724-8). The Gumpps were pioneers of the Baroque style in the Tyrol, working on a number of projects in the area, including the *Stiftskirche*, Wilten (from 1649). **Johann Martin Gumpp** the Younger (1686-1765) designed the south wing of the *Hofburg*, Innsbruck (1754-6).

J.Bou (1962); Frodl-Kraft (1955); E.Hempel (1965); Krapf (1979); J.T (1996)

gun-loop Aperture, often of horizontal elliptical form, in a wall to enable fire to be directed over a wide angle, found in Scots architecture, even in C19 revivals.

Gunnis, Rupert Forbes (1899–1965) English historian of British sculpture, from 1942 he began to build up an index of information about monumental sculptors and statuaries, and his *Dictionary of British Sculptors, 1660–1851* appeared in 1953 (revised edn 1968, hugely expanded in 2009).

ODNB (2004); Roscoe *et al.* (2009)

Gurlitt, Cornelius (1850–1938) German architect/architectural historian. He wrote nearly 100 books and many more articles, but he is remembered as the first effective champion of *Baroque art and architecture which, in C19, had been out of favour. Rejecting the language of *Schinkel and his followers, he favoured *Semper, *Wallot, and others who turned to a richer, less restrained architecture. His *magnum opus* was the influential *Geschichte des Barockstiles, des Rococo und des Klassizismus* (1887–9).

Mallgrave (1996); P (1982)

gutta (*pl.* **guttae**) Pendent ornament resembling a truncated cone under the *soffits of the *mutules and *regulae of the Greek-*Doric *Order. In *Renaissance and later versions of Doric, guttae are often cylindrical, or like truncated pyramids. There are usually 18 under each *mutule, set in three rows, and 6 under the *regula, but the number may vary. A *guttae band*, therefore, is the *regula or *listel from which guttae are suspended, directly under the *taenia and lining up with the *triglyph above. In the Athenian *Choragic Monument of Thrasyllus (319 BC) a continuous series of guttae was set above the *architrave under the taenia, with no regulae at all: this was often revived in C19 during the *Greek Revival, notably by *Schinkel at *Charlottenhof, and the *Neue Wache, Unter den Linden, Berlin (1816–18). Guttae are also called *campanulae, drops, lachrymae, nails,* or *trunnels.*

gutter Channel for taking water away, e.g. at the *eaves of a roof. It may take several forms, e.g. be shaped like a *cyma-recta *moulding, and is usually of metal.

Gwathmey, Charles (1938–2009). American architect, one of the *New York Five. He established (1966) a practice in NYC, later (1971) forming a partnership with **Robert Siegel** (1939–). Most of his works are private houses (e.g. Gwathmey House, Amagansett (1965–7), Steel House, Bridgehampton (1968–9), Cogan House, East Hampton (1971–2), and De Menil House, East Hampton (1979–84), all NY). Larger projects

include Fogg Art Museum, Harvard University, Cambridge, MA (1989–90), Disney World Convention Center, Orlando, FL (1990–1), and the Guggenheim Museum Extension and Refurbishment, NYC (1991–2). The **Gwathmey/Siegel** design for the Chen Residence, Taipei, Taiwan (1992–4), is a distillation of a limited Modernist architectural vocabulary.

Ar & Bi (eds) (1984a); Cheviakoff (ed.) (2003); B.Collins (ed.) (2000); B.Collins & Kasprowicz (eds) (1993); Dobney (ed.) (1998); E (1994); F *et al.* (1975); J (1993)

Gwilt, Joseph (1784–1863) English architect, younger son of **George Gwilt** (1746–1807): he designed in various eclectic styles, but is better-known as a writer. His works include *A Treatise on the Equilibrium of Arches* (1811); an edition of *Chambers's *Treatise on the Decorative Part of Civil Architecture* (1825—which included a new section on Ancient Greece); a translation of *Vitruvius (1826); and *Rudiments of Architecture* (also 1826). His most important book was *An Encyclopaedia of Architecture, Historical, Theoretical, and Practical* (1842—partly by his son, **John Sebastian Gwilt** (1811–90)), with many subsequent editions, the last three of which were enlarged by Wyatt *Papworth. His brother, **George Gwilt** (1775–1856), rebuilt the *steeple of *Wren's Church of St Mary-le-Bow, London (1818–20), and carried out works at Southwark Cathedral (then the Church of St Mary Overie) in 1818–33.

Co (2008); Gw (1811, 1818, 1822, 1825, 1826, 1826a, 1837, 1848, 1903); *ODNB* (2004); Pe (1972)

Gwynne, Alban Patrick (1913–2003) English Modernist architect, who worked with *Lasdun in the office of Wells *Coates. With Coates he designed The Homewood, Esher, Surrey (completed 1938), for his parents, a house on *Corbusian *pilotis which was comprehensively published (1939) in *AR.* After the 1939–45 war he designed several private houses for wealthy clients (e.g. the Jack Hawkins House, Bournemouth). Other works included the remodelling of and extensions to the Theatre Royal, York (1967).

E (1994); *The Times* (8 May 2003), 39

Gwynn, John (1713–86) Salop.-born architect, he designed Atcham Bridge, Salop. (1769–71), Worcester Bridge (1771–80), Magdalen Bridge, Oxford (1772–90), and the English Bridge, Shrewsbury, Salop. (1769–74—rebuilt 1925–7). He was a leading light in attempts (1755) to found a Royal Academy 'for the improvement of Painting, Sculpture, and Architecture', and published an *Essay on Design* (1749) and *London and Westminster Improved* (1766—a remarkably forward-looking and enlightened book, proposing, among other things, the Thames Embankment, the formation of urban open space where Trafalgar Square is now, and a new bridge (where Waterloo Bridge was subsequently erected)).

Co (2008); E.Harris (1990), 214–7; *ODNB* (2004); Skempton *et al.* (2002)

gymnasium (*pl.* **gymnasia**) **1.** Place for physical exercise and teaching in Ancient Greece, also known as *palaestra. **2.** School of the highest

grade designed to prepare students for University, esp. in Germany.

Delorme (1960); D (1950)

gynaeceum, gynaecium, gynaeconitis
1. Part of a house in Ancient Greece or Rome reserved for women. **2.** Any building set apart for women. **3.** Roman textile manufactory. **4.** Women's *gallery in a *Byzantine church.

Habershon, Matthew (1789–1852) English architect, he published *The Ancient Half-Timbered Houses of England* (1836), and gave A.W.N.*Pugin's *Contrasts* a hostile reception. In Jerusalem (1842–3), he superintended the erection of the Anglican Cathedral, designed by **James Wood Johns** (c.1810–63), and himself designed St Peter's Church, Belper, Derbys. (1824), the Town Hall and Market, Derby (1828–30—partially destroyed), model cottages at Brampton, Hunts. (c.1837), and Burbage Church, Leics. (1842). Among his pupils were Ewan *Christian and his son, **William Gilbee Habershon** (1818/19–91), who was in partnership (1863–78) with **Alfred Robert Pite** (1832–1911).

Co (2008)

habitacle 1. Dwelling. 2. *Niche for a statue.

Hablik, Wenzel August (1881–1934) Bohemian *Arts-and-Crafts designer. His influential drawings of crystalline structures were exhibited (1912), and he produced several powerful architectural fantasies after the 1914–18 war, some in association with *Arbeitsrat für Kunst and *Die Gläserne Kette*. He envisaged airborne settlements in the future, as in *Cyklus Architektur* (1925). His work had some influence on German *Expressionism.

AAQ, xii/3 (1980), 18–24; G.Collins (ed.) (1979); Rossow et al. (1980); Ungers (ed.) (1963); M.Urban (1960)

Hadfield, George (1763–1826) English architect, pupil of James *Wyatt, he settled (1795) in the USA to superintend the building of the Capitol in Washington, DC, in succession to *Hallet, but was dismissed (1798), having fought a losing battle with ignorant, incompetent officials and workmen. He designed several Neo-Classical buildings in Washington, including City Hall (1820–6—later the District of Columbia Court House), the unfluted *Paestum-*Doric *portico of the Custis-Lee Mansion, Arlington (1818), the Assembly Rooms (1822), and the J.P.van Ness *mausoleum, Oak Hill Cemetery, Georgetown (1826). With *Godefroy and *Latrobe, he can be credited with introducing the *Greek Revival to the USA.

Co (2008); Goode (1979); Maddex (1973); Reiff (1977); W & K (1983)

Hadfield, Matthew Ellison (1812–85) *See* WEIGHTMAN.

Hadid, Zaha (1950–2016) *See* DECONSTRUCTIVISM.

Haesler, Otto (1880–1962) German pioneer of industrialized housing construction and member of *Der* *Ring from 1926. He designed buildings on the Dammerstock Estate, Karlsruhe (1927–8), collaborating with *Gropius, and numerous *Modern-Movement developments at Celle (1920–31), Kassel (1929–31), Misburg (1931) and Rathenow (1946–51).

Haesler (1930, 1957); Lane (1985); Oelker (2002)

hagioscope Squint, *loricula*, or aperture cut obliquely in a wall (usually of a *chancel), affording a visual connection between the *high-altar and the *aisles or side-chapels. One of its functions was to enable the celebrant at a side-altar (e.g. in a *chantry-chapel) to see if the Priest at the high-altar had reached the sacring, to ensure sacrings would not occur simultaneously, but the main purpose was probably for security.

Bloxam (1882); E.Duffy (1992); J.Parker (1850)

ha-ha In landscape-gardening, garden-boundary designed not to interrupt a view from e.g. a country-house. Consisting of a ditch with side or *revetment nearest the viewpoint perpendicular (or slightly *battered), faced with brick or stone, and the other side sloped and turfed, it kept animals away from the area contiguous to the house, yet was concealed. It was probably a French invention called *ah, ah* (an exclamation of surprise, but more likely to be derived from a corruption of 'hedge' in Old English), described as having *un fosse sec au pied* in *Dézallier d'Argenville's *Théorie…du Jardinage* (1709), and may have been first used (c.1698) in England by **Guillaume Beaumont** (*fl.* late C17 and early C18) at Levens Hall, Westmd. It was used in many English landscape gardens, notably by *Bridgeman and *Kent.

DdA (1709); Goulty (1991); HHH (1980); Symes (2006)

Hakewill, Henry (1771–1830) English architect, he designed two distinguished *Greek-Revival buildings: *Coed Coch*, Denbighshire, Wales (1804), a country-house with a diagonally placed *portico (demolished) and *stair; and St Peter's Church, Eaton Square, London (1824–7—rebuilt after a fire in 1987). He had a large practice, mostly concerned with country-houses, and published an account of the Roman *villa at Northleigh, Oxon. (1823). His brother, **James** (1778–1843), also a competent architect, is known primarily for his many architectural/topographical publications, including a work on the abattoirs of Paris (1828) and *Views ... in the Regent's Park, laid out from the Designs of Decimus Burton* (1831).

Co (2008); *ODNB* (2004)

half If applied to a *baluster or a column, it means *engaged, so *half-column* is an engaged column. *Other compounds include*:

half-figure: *term;

half-moon: *see* DEMILUNE;

half-pace: **1.** landing where two flights of a *stair meet at 180°; **2.** *daïs or step forming the floor in a *bay-window.

half-bat Snapped header (*see* BRICK).

Halfpenny, William (*fl.*1720–55) English architect/carpenter (*alias* **Michael Hoare**), author of several *pattern-books for domestic buildings, among the first of which was *Practical Architecture* (*c.*1724), a cheap, clear guide to the *Orders and various architectural elements drawing on *Campbell's *Vitruvius Britannicus* (1715). He disseminated *Gothick and *Chinoiserie designs in *Rural Architecture in the Gothic Taste, Chinese and Gothic Architecture properly ornamented* (both 1752 and both with his son, **John Halfpenny** (*fl.* mid-C18) and *Rural Architecture in the Chinese Taste* (1752–5—parts of which were by John). With these, *Improvements in Architecture and Carpentry* (1754), *The Art of Sound Building* (1725), and other publications, he and *Langley dominated the pattern-book market of the time. In *A New and Compleat System of Architecture* (1749–59) there are indications he may have known the Irish *Palladian architect *Pearce, and indeed he seems to have been involved in designing in Ireland, notably a horse-barracks at Hillsborough, Co. Down (1732), and Waterford (1739—where he surveyed the cathedral and made drawings for a new Classical building (not realized)). In spite of his debt to Campbell, Halfpenny was never a polished Palladian, and his work drew on *Baroque elements. His publications clearly had a profound effect on the appearance of many cathedral- and market-towns throughout England, while his *Twelve Beautiful Designs for Farm Houses* (1750) and other publications showed he was capable of designing for the countryside as well (e.g. Chinese bridge at Croome Court, Worcs. (*c.*1752)). From *c.*1730 he settled in Bristol (whence he probably travelled to

Ireland), and designed several buildings there (including the Redland Chapel (*c.*1740–3)), although none is particularly distinguished. He or his son may have been responsible for the charming Gothick *orangery at Frampton-on-Severn, Glos. (*c.*1750). At least twelve of his publications were known in the American colonies before 1776, so his work was influential in the USA.

Co (2008); Ck (1985); J.Curl (2011a); Halfpenny (1731, 1747, 1748, 1749, 1752, 1752a, 1752b, 1757, 1774, 1965, 1968, 1968a, 1968b, 1968c), E.Hs (ed.) (1990)

half-timbering 1. Obsolete term for a *timber-framed building, the gaps between the members of the frame filled with some other material, e.g. brick *nogging or plaster on *wattles or laths. **2.** Building with stone or brick lower storey and upper storeys (or parts of them, e.g. *gables), timber-framed, and visible as such. **3.** Building constructed of brick, block, etc., with timber *applied* to it in parts suggesting timber-framing, but in fact false.

hall 1. Main room of a medieval house or the large, communal room of a college, etc., often an *open hall, sometimes with an *open hearth. **2.** Large room or building for the transaction of public business, the holding of courts of justice, or any public assembly, meeting, or entertainment (e.g. *music-hall). **3.** Building for a guild or fraternity, such as a London Livery Company Hall (e.g. Hall of The Fishmongers' Company), or for a municipal body (e.g. city- or town-hall). **4.** Principal messuage of a manor, i.e. the residence of a territorial proprietor. **5.** University building set aside for the residence or instruction of students. **6.** Common-room in a mansion in which servants dined. **7.** Any large roofed volume. **8.** Entrance-room (or -hall).

ABDM (1996); Gw (1903); W.Pa (1852); M.Thompson (1995)

Hall, William Hammond (1846–1934) American landscape architect. He designed the Golden Gate Park, San Francisco, CA (1865–76), laid out on sand dunes, the first *public park in the USA after Central Park, NYC.

B & K (2000); Clary (1979)

hall-church Church with *aisles but without a *clerestorey, the *nave and *aisles being of the same or about the same height. It is a characteristic German *Gothic type, called *Hallenkirche*, with very tall windows illuminating the aisles, no *transepts, and, sometimes, with the *chancel defined only by the furnishings rather than by a separate architectural compartment. Examples include the churches at Nördlingen (1427–1505), Dinkelsbühl (1444–92), and Pirna (consecrated 1546).

S (1901–2); J.T (1996)

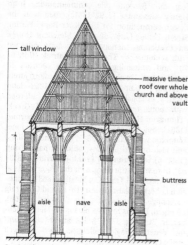

tall window

massive timber roof over whole church and above vault

buttress

aisle nave aisle

Section through nave and aisles of typical German hall-church.

Hallenkirche See HALL-CHURCH.

Haller, Fritz (1924–2012) Swiss architect, he designed building-systems using steel (*Maxi* for large spans and *Midi* for medium-span, e.g. Swiss Railways Training-Centre, Löwenberg, Murten (1978–82)). Other buildings include the Wagsenring School, Basel (1951, 1962), and the Higher Technical Training Centre, Brugg-Windisch (1961–6).

B & W, **xxxvi**/7/8 (1981); Br (1982)

Haller, Karl Christoph Joachim, Freiherr von Hallerstein (1774–1817) German architect, pupil of David *Gilly, he was one of the first (with T.*Allason and C.R.*Cockerell) to note *entasis on Greek columns. With *Foster, **Jakob Linckh** (1786–1841), and Cockerell he discovered the Aegina marbles (1811), and helped to survey the *temple of *Apollo Epicurius* at Bassae. He submitted a design for the *Walhalla*, near Regensburg (1814–15), consisting of a massive series of battered platforms, a *propylaeum* with three *pylon-towers, and a *Greek-Revival temple on top, obviously inspired by F.*Gilly's monument (1797) to **Friedrich II ('the Great') of Prussia** (*r*.1740–86). His unrealized proposals for the Munich *Glyptothek* (1814) combined Greek and Egyptian elements. Von *Klenze built both projects to his own designs, retaining Haller's platform at *Walhalla*.

Co (2008); Wa & M (1987)

Hallerstein See HALLER.

Hallet, Étienne-Sulpice, *called* **Stephen** (*c*.1760–1825) French architect, he settled (1786) in the USA, and from 1793 supervised the building of the Capitol, Washington, DC, to *Thornton's designs, which he modified slightly in building, but was dismissed (1794) and succeeded by *Hadfield.

Art Studies, **i** (1923), 76–92; G.Brown (1970); *DAB* (1932); Padover (ed.) (1946)

hall-house Obsolete term for an *open hall.

Halprin, Lawrence (1916–2009). American architect/landscape architect/planner, pupil of *Breuer, T.D.*Church, *Gropius, and *Tunnard. His wife, dancer **Anna Schuman** (1920–), helped to shape his ideas about landscape and the development of graphic techniques in design, as evidenced in his many publications (e.g. *Cities* (1963), *RSVP Cycles* (1970), and *Notebooks 1959–1971* (1972)) in which process, space-time, and motion in relation to landscape were discussed. He collaborated with **George Rockrise** (1917–2000) on the Dewey Donnell garden, Sonoma, CA (1948), before establishing his own office (1949). Aiming to create landscapes which responded to human needs, environmental concerns, and problems of accessibility and quality of life in urban contexts, he insisted on public participation in the design process. His plans for the 5,000-acre Sea Ranch *condominium (1962–7) on the Pacific coast north of San Francisco responded to the problems of soil-erosion, and were perceived as a critique of (and alternative to) typical suburban planning (the development included buildings by *Moore et al.). Other works included Ghirardelli Square (1962–8), Embarcadero Plaza (1962–72), and Levi Strauss Plaza (1982), all in San Francisco, CA; Nicolett Mall, Minneapolis, MN (1962–7); Lovejoy Plaza. Pettigrove Park, Auditorium Forecourt, and Transit Mall, all in Portland, OR (1965–78); the Freeway Park, Seattle, WA (1970–6); and Roosevelt Memorial Garden, Washington, DC (1974–8). His gardens for private houses are examples of the *California School.

B & F (2009); Halprin (1970, 1972); Lyall (1991); N & R (2003); Tay (2006); Tunnard (1938); W & S (1994)

hameau (*pl.* **hameaux**) Hamlet, but applied to a cluster of purpose-made intentionally 'rural' buildings (e.g. *dairy, etc.) erected in a French *landscape-garden (*c*.1770–93) to enable the upper echelons of society to engage in 'pastoral' play-acting, influenced by the writings of J.-J. *Rousseau: a celebrated example was *Mique's *Hameau du Trianon*, Versailles (1772–82), a kind of 'toy-village' linked to a 'Norman Farm' (begun 1783), designed for **Marie Antoinette**

(1755–93—**Queen of France** from 1774), but there were others at Chantilly (from 1775—which included a billiard-room, dairy, dining-hall, grange, kitchen, mill, and stable, all centred on a green); Franconville-la-Garenne (*c.*1780–7—strongly Swiss in flavour); and Ermenonville (from *c.*1762). English 'hamlets' intended to house estate-workers were located outside park-boundaries to provide *Picturesque scenes as appetizers for full enjoyment of the landscape-gardens: examples include Blaise Hamlet, Som. (1810–11), and Old Warden, Beds. (1830s).

Wa (1982*a*); Wn (1978)

Hamilton, Hon. Charles (1704–86) Anglo-Irish landscape-gardener, inspired by paintings of **Claude Gellée** (1600–82), **Nicolas Poussin** (1594–1665), and **Salvator Rosa** (1615–73). He gained a position (1738–47) in the household of **Frederick Lewis** (1707–51—**Prince of Wales** from 1729), enabling him to acquire some 200 acres of desolate heathland sloping down to the River Mole near Cobham, Surrey, which he transformed into Painshill Park, including a circuit through wooded grounds around a *serpentine lake with island-*grotto, a *hermitage, and various ornamental garden-buildings (including a *Gothick *rotunda, a Roman arch, a Turkish tent, a *temple of Bacchus, and a *bath-house). Recognized in his lifetime as a major contributor to the essentials of the new 'naturalistic' style of English landscape-design, his advice was sought for the gardens at Stourhead, Bowood, and (probably) Fonthill (all Wilts.), and Hagley (Worcs.).

ODNB (2004); Tay (2006)

Hamilton, Craig (1961–) *See* NEW CLASSICISM.

Hamilton, David (1768–1843) Glasgow architect, he designed the Neo-Classical Hutcheson's Hospital, Ingram Street (1802–5), and became a fluent *Greek Revivalist. His former Royal Exchange (1829–30) is in sumptuous Graeco-Roman *Corinthian, while his Western Club, Buchanan Street (1840), is *Italianate. He designed the 'Bridge of Sighs' at the Glasgow Necropolis (1833–9). His country-houses were eclectic, and he designed with facility in *Jacobean (e.g. Dunlop House, Ayrshire, 1832–4), *Gothic (e.g. Castle House, Dunoon, Argyll, 1823–4), and even *Romanesque (e.g. Lennox Castle, Lennoxtown, Stirlingshire, 1838–41). His son, **James Hamilton** (1818–61), who became his partner, contributed to many of his schemes. After his death, James continued working with his brother-in-law, **James Smith** (1808–63).

Co (2008); G & W (1987); *ODNB* (2004); WRH (1990)

Hamilton, James (*c.*1826–94) Scots architect, articled to **Alexander Kirkland** (1824–92). He designed funerary monuments in Glasgow Necropolis

(e.g. the *Baroque pile commemorating **John Henry Alexander** (1792–1851)), then won the design-competition for the Ulster Bank, Waring Street, Belfast (1857–60—now Merchant Hotel), an exuberant *Renaissance *palazzo adorned with sculpture by **Thomas Fitzpatrick** (*fl.*1856–70) and containing a sumptuous centrally lit banking-hall. He also designed the Bedford Street Weaving Company warehouse (1869—later Ewart's establishment, now derelict), adorned with motifs reminiscent of the work of 'Greek' *Thomson. Hamilton became Kirkland's partner (1861), but the arrangement did not last long: Hamilton was assisted (1864–7) by James *Sellars, and also opened a Belfast office in partnership (1863–6) with **Francis** ('**Frank**') **Stirrat** (*c.*1833–95), from which the designs for the Ulster Banks at Sligo (1862) and Trim (Co. Meath—1863), a mansion at Fort William, Belfast (1871), and Glencraig Parsonage, Craigavad, Co. Down (1866), emerged. He was responsible for the Tillie & Henderson Building, 37–51 Miller Street (1854), and the Venetian Eagle Buildings, 205–9 Bothwell Street (1854), both in Glasgow.

G & W (1987); Larmour (1987); pk

Hamilton, John R. (*fl.*1840–66) *See* HAMILTON & MEDLAND.

Hamilton & Medland English architectural practice developed from that established (*c.*1837) by **Samuel Whitfield Daukes** (1811–80), a pupil of *Pritchett. He entered into partnership (1841) with **John R. Hamilton** (*fl.*1840–66) and later with **James Medland** (1808–94—another Pritchett *protégé*). Daukes moved (1848) to London (he designed Middlesex County Asylum (later Colney Hatch Lunatic Asylum), Friern Barnet (built 1849–51)), and the practice (which produced competent buildings in a variety of styles) became **Hamilton & Medland**: as such it designed several *cemeteries, including the chapels, lodges, and landscapes (e.g. Welford Road Leicester (1842–9), Warstone Lane, Birmingham (1847–8), and Ford Park, Plymouth, Devon (also 1847–8), all with *Gothic buildings). The catalyst for their cemetery-landscapes was *Loudon, and *Gay in turn was influenced by their work at Leicester. Hamilton emigrated to America (1850), settling in Cincinnati, OH.

B *et al*. (2001); pk

Hamilton, Thomas (1784–1858) Distinguished Scots Neo-Classical architect, he worked mostly in Edinburgh, and success began when he won (1818) the competition to design the Burns Monument, Alloway, Ayrshire (1820–3), an open circular temple freely adapted from the *Choragic Monument of Lysicrates (334 BC), illustrated in *Stuart and *Revett's *Antiquities of*

Athens (1762). He was commissioned to design a second Burns monument for Regent Road, Edinburgh, on the edge of Calton Hill (built 1830–2), an enlarged version of the Lysicrates monument with a ring of columns set round a cylindrical *cella which once contained a statue (1822) of the poet by **John Flaxman** (1755–1826) now in the National Portrait Gallery. Hamilton's Royal High School (1825–9), on the southern slope of Calton Hill opposite the Burns Monument, one of the most brilliant essays of the *Greek Revival, is of international importance, with its *Theseion*-like temple, flanking *colonnades, *pylon-like pavilions, and stepped platforms recalling *Haller's designs for *Walhalla*. Hamilton placed windows high in the walls of the main 'temple' (one of the main difficulties with the Greek Revival was how to adapt the windowless *type of the Greek temple for modern use) and treated the composition in a *Picturesque manner. His Edinburgh buildings include the Orphan Hospital at the Dean Bridge (1831–3—now the Dean Gallery of the National Galleries of Scotland (1996–9—designed by **Sir Terry Farrell** (1938–)), in which the high chimneys suggest the *Baroque of *Vanbrugh, and the elegant Neo-Classical Royal College of Physicians, Queen Street (1844–6). He also designed the George IV Bridge, providing the southern approach to the Old Town (1827–34). Outside Edinburgh he designed the Greek-*Doric John Knox Memorial, Glasgow Necropolis (1825), the new assembly-rooms in Ayr (1828–31—with an elegant *steeple suggesting an elongated version of a design by *Gibbs), and various schools, villas, and churches. Although a distinguished Greek Revivalist, Hamilton's essays in the Gothic, *Romanesque, and *Jacobethan styles are less impressive.

Co (2008); Crook (1972*a*); GMcW & W (1984); GS; Rock (1984); Youngson (1966)

hammam Islamic bath-complex, usually containing changing-rooms, latrines, and a steam-room heated by the *hypocaust method. A good example was the *Khirbat al-Mafjar*, Jordan (late C8). One of the finest public baths in Istanbul is the *Hasseki Hurrem* (1556), attributed to *Sinan, with its four domes aligned on one single axis. So-called 'Turkish Baths', complete with lavish decorations in the Islamic style, tiled, marbled, and mosaiced, became popular throughout Europe and America in the second half of C19.

B & B (1994); Hillenbrand (1994)

Hammerbacher, Herta (1900–85) German landscape architect/influential teacher, she made some 3,000 designs for gardens, parks, cemeteries, etc., as well as numerous settings for private houses. Trained at Potsdam and Berlin, from 1928 she collaborated with **Hermann Mattern** (1902–

71—her husband until 1935) and **Karl Foerster** (1874–1970—who was influenced by the works of William *Robinson and *Jekyll) before establishing her own practice (1934/5), working with several architects associated with *Neue Sachlichkeit* (e.g. *Eiermann, *Neutra, and *Scharoun). Strongly influenced by the views of *Lange (who favoured indigenous plants, informal layouts, and 'natural' garden-design, all acceptable to the 'Blood-and-Soil' ideology of National Socialism) and by those of the anti-semitic Alwin *Seifert, she designed exhibits for the Reich Garden Expositions in Dresden (1936) and Stuttgart (1939). After the 1939–45 war she resumed practice, laying out the *Waldfriedhof*, Berlin-Zehlendorf (1946–7), and taught in Berlin.

JGH, **xii/3** (July–Sept. 1992), whole issue; Shoe (2001); *Stadt und Grün* I/1 (2001); Tay (2006)

hammer-beam Transverse timber in the position of a tie-beam, but short, not spanning the space, essentially a bracket supported on a wall and brace and carrying the hammer-post (upright timber *post set on the end of a hammer-beam and forming one side of a triangle with the principal and hammer-beam). A *false hammer-beam* is like a true hammer-beam, but does not have the hammer-post above: rather it is braced below and supports the base of the *principal* or *collar*. See TRUSS.

Hammond Beeby & Babka Inc. See NEW CLASSICISM.

Hammond, James Wright (1918–86) See NEW CLASSICISM.

hanging Tapestry, paper, or other material for covering and decorating walls of a room.

hanging-buttress Not a true *buttress, but put there to maintain a sequence or series, and carried on a *corbel. It might also help in the construction of a *vault, and in such a case will have elements responding to the *ribs.

hanging gardens Gardens planted in a series of stepped hillside *terraces. The paradigm (one of the *Seven Wonders of the Ancient World), was the 'Hanging Gardens of Babylon', although it appears there were exemplars at Nineveh laid out under the Assyrian **Sennacherib** (*r*.705–681 BC): constructed on an artificial hill and featuring running water (supplied by an *aqueduct and raised by bronze screws to higher levels), trees, and colonnaded walkways providing views. **Nebuchadnezzar** (*r*.604–562 BC) *may* have drawn on the Nineveh precedent to create another exemplar at Babylon, but archaeological evidence is sparse. Recent (2003–4) investigations at Lisburn Castle Gardens, Co. Antrim, have revealed a C17 four-terrace (three of brick) garden, with double-flight *perron, bowling-green, and *banquet-house, on a slope running down to the River Lagan: the terraces have been partially restored.

Clayton & Price (eds) (1988); Dalley (2013); Finkel & Seymour (eds) (2008); *Lisburn Historical Society Journal* x (2005–6); Tay (2006)

hanging-post Post from which a *door or gate is hung.

hanging step Step with one end built into a wall and *cantilevered, or perhaps resting on the step underneath.

Hankar, Paul (1859–1901) Belgian architect. Influenced by *Beyaert and *Viollet-le-Duc, he later became a protagonist of *Art Nouveau. His buildings were exquisitely detailed, and include the *Hôtel Zegers-Regnard* (1888), *Hôtel Hankar* (1893), and the superbly crafted *Hôtel Ciamberlani* (1897), all in Brussels. Informed by Japanese art, his work in turn influenced Otto *Wagner, who saw some of Hankar's lushly inventive interiors in 1897.

F.Borsi & Wieser (1971); Loo (ed.) (2003); Loyer (1991); C.Maeyer (1963); T-M (1967)

Hansen, Christian Frederik (1756–1845) Leading architect of the Danish *Greek Revival. Trained under *Harsdorff, he assisted the latter at **Frederik V**'s (*r.*1746–66) Chapel (completed 1825), Roskilde Cathedral, before visiting Italy (1782–4). His finest work is *Vor Frue Kirke*, Copenhagen (1808–29), with a *portico in which the primitive *Paestum *Doric *Order was adapted. He also designed the Copenhagen Law Courts, Prison, and Town Hall, with archways (1803–16), in the severe Neo-Classical style also developed by *Gilly and others in Germany. In his capacity as Surveyor for Holstein, he designed the Schleswig Mental Hospital (1818–20), a serene, symmetrical complex of buildings in a rural setting that aroused much interest. His works include various delightful Classical buildings in Altona, Hamburg (e.g. his own house (1803–4) at 116 Palmaille), and along the banks of the Elbe (e.g. *Hirschparkhaus*, *c.*1798), as well as the churches at Husum (1828–33) and Neumünster, Germany (1828–34). He was the chief arbiter of architectural taste in Denmark 1784–1844.

Hedinger (ed.) (2000); Langberg (1950); Lund & Küster (1968); Lund & Thygesen (1995); Wa & M (1987)

Hansen, Hans Christian (1803–83) Danish Neo-Classicist, brother of T.E.*Hansen, he was influenced early in his career by C.F.*Hansen (to whom he was not related), and by *Hetsch, who introduced *Schinkel's work to the Danish architectural world. Hansen completed his studies by travelling in Italy and Greece, and became (1834) Architect to the Greek Court in Athens, where he remained for eighteen years, making archaeological investigations (he reconstructed the Temple of *Nike Apteros* and, with **Eduard Schaubert** (1804–60) and **Joseph Hoffer** (*c.*1810–*before* 1851), compiled the material for Hoffer's account of horizontal curvature and optical corrections in Greek temples (1838)), and designing many important buildings, including the Mint (1834–6), and University (1839–50), in a refined Schinkelian *Greek Revival. With C.R.*Cockerell et al. he designed the Anglican Church of St Paul, Athens (1841). Other works include the *Byzantine-*Rundbogenstil* City Hospital (1856–63), the Observatory (1859–61), and the Zoological Museum, (1863–70), all in Copenhagen. He was a pioneer in the study and application of *polychromy in architecture.

M & Wa (1987); P (1982); vV (1993); We (1947)

Hansen, Theophilus Edvard von (1813–91) Brother of H.C.*Hansen (who taught him), he trained in Copenhagen, where the dominant figures were C.F.*Hansen (no relation) and *Hetsch, who imparted a robust *Neo-Classicism to the aspiring architect. Hansen travelled in Germany and then Greece, where he joined his brother in Athens, designing the Demetrios House (1842–3—later a hotel, demolished 1958), Academy of Sciences (1859–87), and National Library (1859–91). He settled in Vienna (1846) at the invitation of *Förster, whose daughter he married (1851). Influenced by French *Neo-Classicism, by *Schinkel's architecture, and by his studies of Greek *Antique and *Byzantine architecture, he created many of the most distinguished buildings of his time in the Austrian capital. He collaborated with Förster on *Byzantine-*Rundbogenstil* designs for the Army Museum in the Arsenal (1850–6), and contributed to the developments on the *Ringstrasse*, including his masterpiece, the *Parliamentsgebäude* (1874–83), a handsome composition in the spirit of Greek Antiquity with some of the finest *Greek-Revival interiors ever conceived. After a visit to Italy (1856) his style turned to a luxuriant Italian *Renaissance (e.g. Protestant School, *Karlsplatz* (1859), and the *Heinrichshof* on the *Ringstrasse* (1861), which set the *Cinquecento* flavour of many apartment-blocks on the *Ringstrasse* over the following years). However, Hansen also became a leader in the use of *polychromy, influenced no doubt by *Semper, and synthesized Greek and *Renaissance themes in his beautiful *Musikvereinsgebäude* (1869–70) and Academy of Fine Arts (1872–7), Vienna.

Anzeiger der österreichischen Akademie der Wissenschaften, cxiv (1977), 260–76; Lhotsky (1941); M & Wa (1987); Niemann & Feldegg (1893); Russack (1942); Strobl (1961); Traulos (1967); W-R (1970, 1980)

Hansom, Joseph Aloysius (1803–82) English architect, he entered into partnership with **Edward Welch** (1806–68), and designed Birmingham Town Hall (1830–4), a large *peripteral *Corinthian Roman *temple on a high rusticated *podium, completed (1849) by Charles *Edge (c.1801–67). Bankrupted by the Birmingham venture (1834), the partnership was dissolved and Hansom turned to invention (he designed the *Hansom Cab*) and business (he founded (1842) *The Builder*). Welch practised in Liverpool (1837–49), and patented various heating-systems for houses (1850 and 1865). Hansom resumed architectural practice, designing the robustly Classical Particular Baptist Chapel, Belvoir Street, Leicester (1845), now in secular use and known as the 'Pork-Pie', but is better known for his *Gothic RC churches, including St Walburga, Preston, Lancs. (1850), the Holy Name of Jesus, Manchester (1869–71), and St Philip Neri, now the Cathedral of Our Lady and St Philip Howard, Arundel, Sussex (1870–3).

J.Curl (2007); J.Curl (ed.) (2001); D & M (1985); P.Harris (2010); Peers (2012)

Hara, Hiroshi (1936–2007) Japanese architect, his work includes the Yamato International Building, Tokyo (1985–7), the Umeda Sky Building, Osaka (1988–93), and the Kyoto JR Station, Shimogyo, Kyoto (1991–7), demonstrating his skills in handling sophisticated technologies and complex structures.

Bo (2001); Fu (1993); J (1997a); J.T (1996)

Hard architecture Tough, impersonal, windowless buildings with *graffiti*-resistant walls, usually associated with *prisons, mental-hospitals, and other secure structures.

R.Sommer (1974, 1983)

Hardenbergh, Henry Janeway (1847–1918) American architect. After he built an apartment-block on West 55th Street, NYC, called *The Vancorlear* (1879), he was commissioned by the Singer Sewing Machine Co. to design a housing-development to include luxury and lower-middle-class apartments, with some *terrace-houses (1880–6): part of this scheme (in an eclectic style) became the Dakota Apartments, Eighth Avenue. Thereafter he specialized in large and luxurious *hotels.

ARe, **vi** (1897), 335–75 and **xliv** (1918), 91–3; *JSAH*, **xxxiv/1** (Mar. 1975), 19–36

Hardouin-Mansart, Jules (1646–1708) French architect, trained by his great-uncle, F.*Mansart. Master of the *Louis-Quatorze style, imbibing architectural ideas from Le *Vau and *Bruant, he was eventually appointed to important State offices associated with building, becoming *Premier Architecte* (1681) and *Surintendant des Bâtiments du Roi* (1699). He worked (1670s) with Bruant on *St-Louis des Invalides, Paris, but himself designed and built the noble *Dôme des Invalides* (c.1677–91), where *Baroque and Classical tendencies are serenely balanced, the whole constructed on a Greek-cross plan influenced by F.Mansart's unexecuted designs for the Bourbon *mortuary-chapel at *St-Denis. From 1673 he worked at Versailles, taking charge (1678), and filling in Le Vau's Garden-Court to form the *Galerie des Glaces* (1678–89), the epitome of the *Louis-Quatorze* style. He also designed the *Grand Trianon* (again 1678–89), several *fountains in the grounds, and the Chapel (1688–after 1708). The last, with its steeply pitched roof, looks like a Classicized medieval building, but the beautiful interior, with its *arcade carrying an elegant *screen of *Corinthian columns, is almost a harbinger of *Neo-Classicism, and was completed by de *Cotte. In much of his work he was also assisted by *Lassurance and **Pierre Le *Pautre** (1648–1716)—who was the leading interior decorator at Versailles, responsible for the *Salon de l'Œil de Bœuf* (1701), and the finishings of the Chapel. Hardouin-Mansart's *Place Vendôme* (from 1698) has handsome, unified façades on an arcaded *rez-de-chaussée*, and is one of the French capital's most distinguished urban spaces. His circular *Place des Victoires* only partially survives. His grandson, **Jean Hardouin-Mansart de Jouy** (1700–84), rebuilt the west *façade of *St-Eustache, Paris (1733–88).

B (1982); Bourget & Cattaui (1960); B & Smith (1973); Do (1981); Ha (1948); Marie & Marie (1972)

Hardouin-Mansart de Levi, Jacques, Comte de Sagonne (1703–58) French architect, grandson of Jules *Hardouin-Mansart, he became (1742) *Architecte du Roi*. His Parisian domestic designs include the *Maison des Dames de Saint-Chaumont* (1754—destroyed) and the *Hôtel Mansart de Sagonne* (1743), both of which were essentially *Rococo in style. His masterpiece is the elegant *St-Louis*, Versailles (1743–54), with its noble *cupola and assured architectural enrichment. He also designed a hospital at Marseilles (1753).

Ga (1972); K & L (1972); J.T (1996)

Hardwick, Philip (1792–1870) English architect, he commenced practice with his father, Thomas *Hardwick. From 1816 he held several official posts, and was a competent and eclectic designer. He is best known for the monumental *Doric *propylaeum at Euston Station, London (1836–40—needlessly demolished 1962), and mastered a plain, robust *Neo-Classicism, as in his utilitarian brick St Katharine's Docks and Warehouses, London (1827–9). His *Tuscan Dock

Traffic Office, Albert Dock, Liverpool (1846-7), is a powerful design, and he also collaborated with *Hartley on the designs of the warehouses there. His Goldsmiths' Hall, Foster Lane (1829-35), and City Club, Old Broad Street (1833-4), both in London, are typical of his robust *Baroque and Classical styles. With his son, P.C.*Hardwick, he was responsible for the *Tudor-*Gothic Hall and Library, Lincoln's Inn, London (1843-5), an accomplished design for its date, on which the young *Pearson also worked.

Co (2008); D & M (1985); *ODNB* (2004); Sn & Sn (1968)

Hardwick, Philip Charles (1822-92) Son of Philip *Hardwick, pupil of *Blore, he joined his father in practice (1843). He designed the majestic Great Hall at Euston Station, London (1846-9—demolished), the huge Great Western Hotel, Paddington Station (1851-3), and the exquisite *Gothic-Revival Beauchamp Almshouses and Chapel, Newland, Worcs. (1862-4).

J.Curl (2007); D & M (1985)

Hardwick, Thomas (1752-1829) Son of master-mason **Thomas Hardwick** (1725-98—who had worked for the *Adam brothers), he became (1767) a pupil of *Chambers. In the 1770s he visited Italy where he made measured drawings of many *Antique remains before returning (1779) to London, where he made his living as an estate-surveyor, designing churches and minor public buildings. He restored (1796-8) Inigo *Jones's St Paul's Church, Covent Garden, after a fire; saved the surviving part of St Bartholomew-the-Great, Smithfield, from demolition by carrying out careful repairs (1790-1, 1808); and designed St Marylebone Church (1813-17—his best-known work). He was also responsible for Wanstead Church, Essex (1787-90), and St John's Church, Workington, Cumb. (1822-3). His pupils included *Angell, *Foulston, his son, Philip *Hardwick, and (briefly) J.M.W.*Turner.

Co (2008)

Hardy, Thomas (1840-1928) Although known as a novelist, Hardy trained as an architect from 1856 with **John Hicks** (1815-69) of Dorchester, working on numerous church-'restorations', often involving destruction of ancient fabric (which led to his interest in *conservation). Hardy settled (1862) in London, where he worked under A.W.*Blomfield, and won (1863) the RIBA Silver Medal with a paper on the 'application of coloured bricks and terra cotta to modern architecture'. During his time with Blomfield he oversaw (1866-7) the exhumation of vast amounts of human remains from the burial-grounds adjacent to Old St Pancras Church occasioned by the construction of the railway: this led him to write *The Levelled Churchyard*. He resumed working with

Hicks in Dorset, after whose death he joined the Weymouth architect, **George Rackstrow Crickmay** (1830-1907), until 1872. Hardy's architectural works included Max Gate, his own house in Dorchester (1885); the *capitals in St Mary's Church, Turnworth (1869-70); Talbothays Lodge and Cottage, West Stafford (1890s); and interventions at St Peter's Church, West Knighton (1894), all in Dorset.

Beatty (2004); Emery & Wooldridge (2011); *ODNB* (2004)

Hare, Henry Thomas (1861-1921) English architect, he designed the *Renaissance-Revival Town Hall, Oxford (1893-7), with *Elizabethan *gables derived from Kirby Hall, Northants. At University College, Bangor, Wales (1907-10), and Westminster College, Cambridge (1897-9), he used a late *Tudor-*Gothic style, but he was also capable of powerful *Mannerist and *Baroque essays, e.g. the Central Library, Islington (1905-8).

D & M (1985); A.S.Gray (1985)

Häring, Hugo (1882-1958) German architect, pupil of Theodor *Fischer. He became Secretary of *Der *Ring, an early participant in *CIAM, and designer of Modernist buildings for Berlin-Zehlendorf (1926-7) and Berlin-Siemensstadt (1929-31). Later, he gradually evolved theories concerning *Organic architecture, which in his terms seems to have meant fitness for purpose and an abandonment of preconceived aesthetic ideas or forms, although some of his buildings had flavours of *Expressionism. Among his works were farm-buildings, Gut Garkau, near Lübeck (1923-5); the Tobacco Goods Factory, Neustadt, Holstein (1925); Behrendt House, Berlin (1930); the von Prittwitz Building, Tutzing (1937-41); *Kunst und Werk* School, Berlin (1942); and Schmitz House, Biberach (1949-50).

BJ (1999, 2001, 2002); J.Je & Lauterbach (eds) (1964); Kremer (1995); M & N (1987); Schirren *et al.* (2001); vV (1993)

Hårleman, Carl (1700-53) Swedish architect, son of Johan *Hårleman, educated in Paris (partly by **Claude Desgots** (*or* **Desgotz**)—*fl.*1670-1732, a relative of Le *Nôtre), before travelling to Italy (1726-7). Called back to Stockholm, he worked on the Royal Palace, originally designed by *Tessin the Younger (whom he succeeded as Superintendent of Royal Buildings). He visited France (1731-2, 1744-5) to recruit craftsmen to work on the interiors there and at Drottningholm (in both of which palaces he introduced *Rococo decorations). He designed various country-houses based on *Blondel's ideas (which influenced *Adelcrantz et al.). He carried out (1740s) sensitive interventions at the Carolinian *mortuary-chapel (*Karolinska Grafkoret*), Riddarholms Church,

Stockholm (originally designed by *Tessin the Elder). Among other works were the exquisite *maison de plaisance*, Svartsjö (1735–9), Övedskloster Manor, Scania (1750s—with *cour d'honneur*), and the East India Company warehouse, Göteborg (c.1740—an industrial building with *Sublime qualities). He fused French *formal gardens with a proto-landscape-garden style, e.g. at the transformation of the *parterre into a lawn at Svartsjö (c.1730s) and the *boskets at Ulriksdal (c.1740s).

A & B (1986); Shoe (2001); Stavenow (1927); Tay (2006); J.T (1996)

Hårleman, Johan (1662–1707) Swedish garden-designer, active for 25 years with Royal gardens and most private estates in the country, he often worked with *Tessin the Younger, who appears to have prompted his first tour (1680–5) of Europe after which he was appointed (1688) Inspector of all Royal gardens. Among his works were the gardens at Drottningholm (notably the embroidered *parterres (1695–6)), Ulriksdal, Strömsholm, Kungsträdgården, Läckö, Höjentorp, and Ekolsund. His second European tour (1699–1700) led to a meeting with Le *Nôtre, whose style he embraced in designs, e.g. at Noor, south of Uppsala (from c.1690). He designed *orangeries at Drottningholm, Karlberg, Ulriksdal, Kungsträdgården, Östanå, and Noor (all early 1700s).

A & B (1986); Shoe (2001); Stavenow (1927); Tay (2006)

harling Rough-cast *render on a wall, made with sand, *lime, water, and fine gravel.

harmonic division *or* **proportion** Relation of successive numbers in a series, the reciprocals of which are in arithmetical progression, the numbers being proportional to the lengths of twanged cords that sound harmonious. Rooms with measurements 1: 2, 2: 3, and 3: 4 were held by *Renaissance theorists to be harmonious: some, including *Alberti, argued that this was the basis for satisfactory relationships of dimension and form in Classical architecture, and indeed the key to understanding Nature and the Universe. *Palladio and others evolved further complex proportions including ratios of 5: 6 and others.

OED (1933); Wi (1988)

Harris, Emanuel Vincent (1876–1971) English architect. For the LCC (1901–7) he designed a series of austere transformer-stations for the tramway system, of which one of the best was that at Upper Street, Islington (1905–6), probably influenced by *Dance's Newgate Gaol (demolished 1902). He won the competition for Glamorgan County Hall, Cardiff (1908), a confident essay in *Beaux-Arts *Classicism, completed 1912, which launched him as a successful architect

of public buildings in the Grand Manner. At first he was in partnership with **John Stanley Towse** (1875–1951), and then (1909–11) with **Thomas Anderson Moodie** (1874–1948). He won (1914) the competition for the Board of Trade building in Whitehall, London, which, as a much larger structure, became known as the 'Whitehall Monster', completed (1959) for the Ministry of Defence (*Pevsner thought it a 'monument of tiredness'). After the 1914–18 war, Harris demonstrated his undoubted skills with a series of public buildings, including Sheffield City Hall (1920–34), Braintree Town Hall, Essex (1926–8), Leeds Civic Hall (1930–3), Som. County Hall, Taunton (1932–6), and Nottingham County Hall, Trent Bridge (1935–50). His best works were unquestionably the extension to the Town Hall (1925–38—in a hybrid style that nevertheless responds admirably to *Waterhouse's great *Gothic building) and circular Classical Central Library (1925–38), Manchester: the extension is linked to the *Victorian building by elegant bridges, and the walk between the extension and the library is one of the most thrilling urban spaces in Britain. He also designed the long, curved Bristol Council House (1935–9), and the Central Library, Kensington, London (1955–60), both of which are faced largely in brick. He created the fine master-plan (1931—wrecked by *Holford from 1953) for University College of the South West (now Exeter University), and (with **Sidney Kyffin Greenslade** (1866–1955)) designed some of the simplified *Tudor-Gothic and *Neo-Georgian buildings there. He himself considered 2 Duke Street, St James's, London (1910–12), his best building.

A.S.Gray (1985); GS; *RIBAJ*, 3 ser., lviii (Feb. 1951), 149–152; Stamp & Harte (1979)

Harris, John (1919–2008) English architect, who, following his success in the competition to design the new State Hospital, Doha, Qatar (1952—an early example where climatic and environmental concerns played no small part in the finished proposals), developed one of the first truly global architectural practices, drawing up a master-plan for Dubai (1960) laying its foundation as a modern city. Other works include the Dubai World Trade Centre (1970—the tallest building in the Arab world for some twenty years) and Tuen Mun Hospital, Hong Kong (1980s).

The Times (22 March 2008), 75

Harris, William (*fl.*1835–50) One of Bristol's District Surveyors from 1840, he designed the *Greek-Revival Market-Houses in Penzance (1836), Helston (1837–8), and Bodmin (1839), all Cornwall. Clearly a competent and scholarly architect when designing in the Grecian style, he was shakier with *Neo-Romanesque (e.g. work at

St Mary's Church, Chepstow, Monmouthshire) and *Tudor *Gothic (*workhouse, St Clement's, Truro, Cornwall (1849–50)).

Co (2008); Crook (1972a); Morrison (1999)

Harrison, Peter (1716–75) English architect, he settled (1740) in America, and designed various distinguished buildings of the *Colonial period. His *Palladianism was gleaned from various standard works: he drew on *Gibbs for his King's Chapel, Boston, MA (1749–58), and Christ Church, Cambridge, MA (1760–1), and on Gibbs and *Kent for the Touro Synagogue, Newport, RI (1759–63). For his Brick Market, Newport, RI (1761–73), he was influenced by Old Somerset House, illustrated in *Campbell's *Vitruvius Britannicus*. The clarity of his remarkably advanced Redwood Library, Newport, RI (1748–50), points to *Neo-Classicism, and appears to have inspired *Jefferson. He was the most talented architect working in America at the time, and possessed a fine architectural library, destroyed (1775) by an anti-Loyalist mob.

Bridenbaugh (1949); *DAB* (1943); D & S (1967); P (1982)

Harrison, Thomas (1744–1829) English architect, he designed the Lyceum, Bold Street, Liverpool (1800–3), the Portico Library, Mosley Street, Manchester (1802–6), and his masterpiece, the Castle, County Courts, Prison, Armoury, Barracks, Exchequer, and *Propylaeum*, Chester (1788–1822), in all of which he demonstrated his talents as a creator of monumental Neo-Classical buildings. The Chester Castle group is arguably the finest *Greek-Revival ensemble in the British Isles. He also designed two huge *Doric columns commemorating distinguished soldiers of the Napoleonic Wars: one to **Rowland Hill** (1772–1842—**1st Viscount** from 1842) in Shrewsbury, Salop. (1814–16), and the other celebrating **Henry William Paget** (1768–1854—**1st Marquess of Anglesey** from 1815) at Llanfairpwll, Anglesey (1816). With *Gothic, however, Harrison was less impressive, although at Lancaster Castle (1788–99) he composed some fine buildings, notably the polygonal Shire Hall, but his engineering abilities were also formidable: his Skerton Bridge, Lancaster (1783–8), was the first large *masonry *bridge in Britain carrying a flat road from bank to bank, while his Grosvenor Bridge, Chester (1827–9), his largest such structure, was the biggest stone arch in the world when it was built. He also designed some visionary national monuments as severe as any, and he was highly regarded in his lifetime, notably by C.R.*Cockerell. Among his many works of domestic architecture may be mentioned Broomhall, Fife (1796–9), and The Citadel, Hawkstone, Salop. (1824–5). Had he not lived in relative isolation in Chester he would conceivably have outshone *Soane and *Smirke.

Co (2008); *CL*, cxlix/3853 (15 Apr. 1971), 876–9, 3854 (22 Apr.), 944–7, 3856 (6 May), 1088–91, 3862 (1 Jun.), 1539; Crook (1972a); *ODNB* (2004); P (1982)

Harrison, Wallace Kirkman (1895–1981) American architect, he formed one of the largest practices in the USA. With Raymond *Hood et al. he worked on the Rockefeller Center, NYC (1929–33), and was joined by *Abramovitz (1941). As Harrison, *Foulhoux, and Abramovitz, the firm expanded the Rockefeller Center, work continuing until 1974. After Fouilhoux's death (1945), the firm became **Harrison & Abramovitz** and, with Le *Corbusier, *Niemeyer, and *Markelius, designed the United Nations Headquarters, NYC (1947–53), with the Secretariat, one of the city's first *curtain-walled *skyscrapers. Then came the Glass Center and Administrative Building, Corning, NY (1955–6), followed by the Phoenix Mutual Life Insurance Building, Hartford, CT (1960–4). A much more formal style was adopted for the *Travertine-clad Lincoln Center, NYC (1959–66), with its Metropolitan Opera House and Philharmonic (now Avery Fisher) Hall: the style is an extremely stripped minimalist type that cannot really be called 'Neo-Classical'. The gigantic South Mall, Albany, NY (1963–78), was supposedly influenced by the Dalai Lama's Palace at Lhasa, Tibet.

Krinsky (1978); Newhouse (1989); Stern *et al.* (1995); E.Young (1980)

Harsdorff, Caspar Frederik (1735–99) Danish architect, pupil of N.-H.*Jardin and J.-F. *Blondel, he was an accomplished Neo-Classicist, responsible for the *Mortuary Chapel of **King Frederik V** (*r.*1746–66), Roskilde Cathedral (1768–78), one of the purest works of *Neo-Classicism in Europe for its date, with octagonal coffering derived from the *basilica of **Maxentius** (*r.*306–12), Rome. For this project he was assisted by C.F.*Hansen, his pupil for several years, who completed the work (1821–5). He also designed the *propylaea* between the Royal Palaces, the *Doric Hercules *pavilion, and a house in *Kongens Nytorv* (1770s), all in Copenhagen. The house, intended as an exemplar of Neo-Classicism, is extraordinary for its *engaged *Ionic *capitals that show not the usual fronts of the *volutes on the *façade, but the *pulvins or *baluster-sides.

M & Wa (1987); J.T (1996)

Hartley, Jesse (1780–1860) English Surveyor to the Liverpool Dock Trustees (1824–60), in which capacity he designed (with contributions from P.C.*Hardwick) the Albert Dock (1843–5), a *Sublime exercise in utilitarian brick carried on massive unfluted cast-iron *Doric columns. He also designed the Brunswick (1832), Waterloo (1834), Stanley (1850–7), Wapping (1855), and West Canada (1858) Docks, all in Liverpool.

Co (2008); C-R (2008); J.Curl (2007); D & M (1985)

Hartung, Hugo (1855–1932) German architect, primarily a designer of domestic architecture, much of it with medieval *vernacular motifs, steep roofs, and *turrets. His *Motive der mittelalterlichen Baukunst in Deutschland* (1896–1902) and *Ziele und Ergebnisse der italienischen Gotik* (1912) prompted some early-C20 architects to explore medieval architecture as a catalyst for contemporary design. His drawings of Egyptian buildings (published 1907) influenced *Behrens and others who sought to simplify design into blocky cubic forms. His own house and others at the *Villencolonie*, Grünewald, Berlin, of the early 1900s, deserve mention.

H.Hartung (1896–1902, 1902, 1912); *ZdB*, **xx** (1900), 4–6, 16–17, **xxvii** (1907), 566–9, 578–80

Harvard architecture Work of architects (e.g. E.L.*Barnes, Philip *Johnson, and Paul *Rudolph) trained in *Bauhaus principles by *Gropius and *Breuer at Harvard University's Graduate School of Design (1940s and 1950s).

Herdeg (1985)

Harvey, John Hooper (1911–97) English writer, he made a major contribution over many years to several aspects of garden and medieval architectural history, but his greatest achievement was his magisterial *English Mediaeval Architects: A Biographical Dictionary down to 1550* (1954, with subsequent revisions). Based on documentary sources, it illumines the English medieval architectural world with gracefully presented facts.

GH, **xxvi/1** (Summer 1998), 102–5; J.Harvey (1987); pk

Haschenperg, Stephan von (*fl.*1539–43) German military engineer, he was employed by **King Henry VIII of England** (*r.*1509–47) to design part of the new coastal defences, including Sandgate, Deal, and Walmer Castles, Kent, all remarkably coherent geometrical examples of C16 military architecture. He carried out surveys at Calais (completed 1540), and was in charge of the works at St Mawes Castle, Cornwall. He also fortified Carlisle against the Scots before returning to Central Europe, where he worked for the Bishop of Olmütz (now Olomouc).

J.Harvey (1987)

Hasenauer, Karl, Freiherr von (1833–94) Austrian architect, he was involved with the building of *Semper's Museums of Art and Natural History in Vienna (1872–9), and realized the gigantic proposals of van der *Nüll and *Siccard von Siccardsburg for the Great Exhibition in Vienna (1873), a huge rectangle with central *rotunda and, on both sides, 32 *pavilions. He built the *Burgtheater*, Vienna (1874–8), to Semper's designs, and supervised the Imperial Forum

complex after Semper's death, including the grandiose *Neue Burg* (completed 1913). He also designed the *Villa Zang*, Neidling (1864), the Lützow Palace (1870), and the *Hermesvilla*, Lainz (1882–6), all in or near Vienna, and all on cunningly contrived plans, with *Renaissance-inspired interior decorations. The interiors of the *Kunsthistorisches Museum* and of the *Burgtheater* are by him, and are among the finest in Vienna of the time.

Beetz (1929); Bernhard (1992); Eggert (1976); Lhotsky (1941); Mallgrave (1996)

Hastings, Hubert de Cronin (1902–86) English editor, he joined (1918) the Architectural Press (of which he later became the proprietor), and edited (1927–32, 1935–7) *AR*, introducing innovations in content, graphic design, and page layouts. He also edited (1932–7) *AJ* and was a founder-member of the *MARS Group. Despite professed sympathies for the *genius loci* and the *Picturesque, the Press promoted a rigid *Modernist party-line that ignored both, and sat uncomfortably with Hastings's campaigns to promote an appreciation of *townscape (aided by the draughtsmanship of *Browne, *Cullen, et al.). Hastings adopted the pseudonym **Ivor de Wolfe**, and published two books on town-design: *The Italian Townscape* (1962) and *Civilia: the End of sub-Urban Man* (1971), which advocated ideas and images the antitheses of the sort of architecture/planning seen in much of the Press's output.

ODNB (2004); J.T (1996)

hatchment *See* ACHIEVEMENT OF ARMS.

haunch 1. Indefinite roughly triangular portion or *flank* between the *crown* and *abutments of an arch, i.e. between the crown and the *springing* on the *piers. 2. Timber slightly arched or concave on its underside under a *lintel. 3. Part of a beam projecting below a floor, usually slightly cambered.

Haussmann, Baron Georges-Eugène (1809–91) French *Préfet* of the *Département* of the Seine (from 1853), he directed the improvements of the City of Paris during the *Second Empire of **Napoléon III** (*r.*1852–70). His models were those established by **Henri IV** (*r.*1589–1610), **Louis XIV** (*r.*1643–1715), **Napoléon I** (*r.*1804–14, 1815), and late-C18 types of Classical layout involving straight avenues meeting at circular spaces (*rond-points*), while his brief was to make Paris a capital suitable for an Imperial power; to modernize it for an expanding population and the needs of industrialization; to solve the problems of traffic (especially by connecting the railway-termini by means of wide streets and boulevards); and to create vistas of Roman grandeur terminating in monumental buildings. In a mere 17 years of wholesale clearance and rebuilding Paris got nearly 100 miles of brand-new streets, thousands of buildings, over 4,000 acres of parks (see ALP-HAND), nearly 400 miles of sewers, and means by which millions of gallons of clean water flowed daily to the city. He encouraged modern methods of construction, such as the use of iron and glass by *Baltard and others, and he managed to ensure the erection of a homogeneous *Renaissance-Revival urban fabric. His *Mémoires* (1890-3) are a valuable record of his career and ideas, while under his patronage several monumental works on the history and architecture of Paris were published (1867-73). Some critics have been harsh about his destruction of old buildings and whole quarters, while others have seen his work as inimical to the urban proletariat: nevertheless, he created an elegant and beautiful city, laid out on principles established at the *École des *Beaux-Arts*, and his systems of streets worked well until excessive numbers of motor-vehicles created such immense problems of traffic-jams and pollution from the 1960s. His work was influential, especially in France and the USA, and had a profound effect on the planning of Vienna.

Chapman & Chapman (1957); Gaillard (1977); Haussmann (1890-3); Lavedan (1975); Loyer (1987); Malet (1973); M & Wa (1987); Pinkney (1958); Reau *et al.* (1954); Saalman (1971); vV (1993)

Haviland, John (1792-1852) English architect, pupil of James *Elmes, he settled (1816) in the USA, where he designed several buildings, including the Franklin Institute, Philadelphia, PA (1825-6), with a severe *Greek-Revival front based on the *Choragic Monument of Thrasyllus, Athens. He published *The Builder's Assistant* (1818-21), intended, like his other publishing and teaching activities, to augment his meagre earnings as an architect: it was the first American publication in which the Greek *Orders were depicted, and was re-issued (1830) in four volumes. He designed the first prison in the USA built in accordance with the ideas of English reformers (Eastern State Penitentiary, Philadelphia, PA (1821-37)), using a *Gothic *castellated style. He published a new edition (1830) of **Owen Biddle**'s (1737-99) *Young Carpenter's Assistant* (1805), embellished with new plates, including an illustration of his Miner's Bank, Pottsville, PA (1830-1—demolished), with its *façade covered with iron plates made to resemble *ashlar. His many churches and private houses were mostly in the Greek-Revival style, but his building housing the New York City Halls of Justice and House of Detention, known as the 'Tombs' (1835-8), was in the *Egyptian-Revival style, calculated to instil awe and terror in all who saw it. He first used Egyptianizing details at the New Jersey State Penitentiary, near Trenton (1832-6), partly for reasons of economy, but partly to suggest, with its large areas of blank

walls and sinister *portico set between two *pylons, the 'misery which awaits the unhappy being' unfortunate enough to be incarcerated. Egyptianesque, too, was his Essex County Court House and Gaol, Newark, NJ (1836-8). Haviland has been called the greatest American Egyptian-Revival architect.

Carrott (1978); Hamlin (1964); Haviland (1830, 1830a); Hi (1976); *JSAH*, xxiii/2 (May 1964), 101-5, xxv/3 (Sept. 1966), 197-208, xxvi/4 (Dec. 1967), 307-9; Kennedy (1989); Tatman & Moss (1985); Teeters & Shearer (1957); W & K (1983)

Havlíček, Josef (1899-1961). Czechoslovak promoter of *CIAM and Le *Corbusier's dogmas, with **Karel Honzík** (1900-66) he designed the *International-*Modernist Ministry of Pensions, Prague (1926-35). Mercifully, his proposal (1950s), in line with CIAM orthodoxy, to demolish Prague's New Town, replacing it with pyramidal *skyscrapers, was not realized. Other works include an apartment-block, Prague-Letná (1937-8), a sanatorium at Poděbrady (1936-40), and two *apartment blocks in Prague (1937-8).

Havlíček (1964); Li (1996); J.T (1996)

hawksbeak, hawksbill 1. *Romanesque *ovolo *moulding enriched with *beak-heads. **2.** Any moulding with a convex top and a concave underside meeting at a point, in *section resembling the beak of a bird of prey, as on a *stringcourse. **3.** *Doric moulding related to the *cyma recta. **4.** *Crossette in the sense of a *volute at the upper corner of a door- or window-*architrave.

hawksbell *Ballflower ornament.

Hawksmoor, Nicholas (1661-1736) One of the two most imaginative English *Baroque architects (the other was *Vanbrugh), he worked with *Wren from c.1684, notably on the Chelsea Hospital, St Paul's Cathedral, and the City Churches, all in London. He was Clerk of Works (1689-1715) at Kensington Palace (where he supervised the building of the *Orangery (1704-5—probably designed by Wren, with revisions by Vanbrugh and Hawksmoor)), and was Clerk of Works (1698-1735) at Greenwich Hospital, where he played a major role in the design of the east range of Queen Anne's Court and the dormitories in King William's Court. He also became (1715) Clerk of the Works at Whitehall, Westminster, and St James's, as well as Secretary to the Board of Works. Vanbrugh engaged his services at Castle Howard, Yorks., and Blenheim Palace, Oxon., and it is now clear that the skills Hawksmoor had acquired under Wren enabled the architecturally untrained Vanbrugh's schemes to come to fruition. By 1700 Hawksmoor had evolved his original style, as is evident from Easton Neston, Northants. (c.1695-1702), a large country-house (in the design of which, however, *Talman may have played a greater role than recognized hitherto), and over the next decades demonstrated his assured knowledge of the Classical vocabulary as well as its imaginative application. He understood the tensions and possibilities of the juxtaposition of masses of *masonry, and exploited the drama and power of modelling, light, and dark in his vigorous designs.

Hawksmoor was appointed one of the two Surveyors (the other was *Gibbs) to the Commissioners for Building Fifty New Churches in London under the 1711 Act, and in that capacity he designed six of the most original churches in and near the capital: the body of St Alphege, Greenwich (1712–14), St Anne, Limehouse (1714–30), St George-in-the East, Wapping (1714–29), Christ Church, Spitalfields (1714–29), St Mary Woolnoth, City of London (1716–24), and St George, Bloomsbury (1716–31). St Alphege's is in the form of a *temple, with a huge *serliana at the east end; St Anne's has a powerful tower with a crowning *lantern like a medieval element in Classical clothes; St George-in-the-East has four pepper-pot staircase-towers and a curious top to the western tower formed of *altar-like drums; Christ Church, Spitalfields, has a *broach spire set above a gigantic serliana porch; St Mary Woolnoth has powerful Baroque modelling; while St George Bloomsbury has an immense Roman temple *portico and a tower crowned with a stepped *pyramid derived from descriptions of the *Mausoleum at Halicarnassus. From these buildings the interests of Hawksmoor may be deduced. He was bookish (he had a considerable library), steeped in a love of Antiquity, fascinated by English medieval architecture, and intrigued by the possibilities of freely interpreting the great buildings of the past from descriptions. Some of his work is derived from earlier French publications showing images of supposedly *Antique buildings, which partially explains the element of fantasy in his designs. He often introduced powerful emotional contents: at the Mausoleum, Castle Howard (1729–42), for example, the *peristyle of his circular temple-form is a Roman-*Doric Order, but the unfluted columns have only one *triglyph over each *intercolumniation, giving a brooding solemnity to the architecture, influenced perhaps by *Bramante's *tempietto* at *San Pietro in Montorio*, Rome. The Clarendon Building, Oxford (1712–65), also employs closely packed unfluted Roman-Doric columns as well as inventively oversized keystones and oddly-placed *guttae. He also designed in the *Gothic style, as at All Souls College, Oxford (1716–35), and the western towers at Westminster Abbey, London (designed 1734 and completed by J.*James (c.1745)). Some of his inventions, such as the Carrmire Gate, Castle Howard (c.1730), with its

steep pyramids, powerful modelling derived from *Serlio, and emphatic qualities, combine the *primitive, allusions to Antiquity, and a fascination with geometry, anticipating the most robust and stripped language of late-C18 *Neo-Classicism. He also designed the Pyramid *eye-catcher at Castle Howard (1728), the *obelisk in the Market Place, Ripon, Yorks. (1702), and (with James) the Church of St Luke, Old Street, London (1727–33), with its obelisk-spire. In its essentials, Hawksmoor's architecture is primarily a demonstration that in geometry lies the key to all order, all creation. One of his last designs to be realized (with modifications by its builder, *Townesend) was the screen-wall and entrance at Queen's College, Oxford (1733–6).

CL, **cxcix**/34 (25 Aug. 2005), 52–5; Co (2008); Co (ed.) 1976); Downes (1966, 1980); Friedman (2011); G-R (1924); V.Hart (2002); P (1982); RdP (2000); Su (1993); J.T (1996)

Hayberger, Johann Gotthard (1695–1764) With *Hüber, Hayberger is credited with the design of the *Baroque library of Admont *Benedictine Abbey (c.1745–66—completed (1776) by Hüber). He was also responsible for the library of St Florian Abbey (1744–50—based on *Prandtauer's plans), and designed the *Rathaus* (1765–78—a *Rococo palace with a handsome tower), and several town houses in Steyr.

Brucker (1983); C.Powell (1959); J.T (1996)

head 1. Top or upper part of anything, e.g. a *doorway or window-aperture. 2. Roofing-tile forming part of the first course of a roof at the *eaves. 3. Any stone so finished as to have one end exposed on the face of a wall as a *header in brickwork. 4. Upper part of a chimney-stack. 5. Small cistern at the top of a rainwater-pipe receiving water from the gutter called a *rainwater- or hopper-head. *Compounds include*:
head-mould: *hood-mould, *drip-stone, *label, or *weather-moulding set above the head of any aperture;
head-stone: 1. upright inscribed memorial stone at the head of a grave in a burial-ground; 2. corner- or foundation-stone; 3. *keystone in an arch.

header Brick or stone with its longer dimension buried within the wall and the smaller *face exposed. *See* BRICK.

hearse, herce, herse 1. Falling door of grated construction, i.e. *portcullis. 2. Horizontal grating, flat or curved, fixed with *prickets for candles to commemorate the dead. 3. Open metal framework over a sepulchral memorial, usually to support the pall, as in the Beauchamp chapel, St Mary's Church, Warwick. An iron hearse, with prickets, survives over the Marmion tomb, St Nicholas's Church, West Tanfield, Yorks. (c.1387).

The Beauchamp hearse (3), St Mary's, Warwick.

heath-hut *See* MOSS-HUT.

hecatomped Measuring 100 Attic feet in length, e.g. the width of the octastyle front and the length of the *naos* of the *Parthenon*, Athens. *Hecatompedon* is a *temple in which 100 feet is an essential element of proportion (100 Attic feet = 101.241 English feet, according to *Penrose).

hedge Row of trees/shrubs planted closely to form a thick *screen between parts of, or at the boundary of, a garden, in order to block views, afford protection, or form 'walls' for walks or *compartments. It may be composed of evergreen (e.g. box, holly, privet, yew, etc.) or deciduous (e.g. beech, hornbeam, lime, etc.) species, depending on purpose, colour requirements, and climate. Some evergreens (e.g. yew) can be clipped to form *topiary. Hedges also occur at the sides of roads, commonly used instead of *fences, to contain animals, deter intruders, etc.: some English hedges are of considerable antiquity.

Darvill (2003); *GH,* xxvii/1 (Summer 1999), 32–53; O'Malley (2010); Tay (2006)

Hegemann, Werner Manfred Maria Ellis (1881–1936) German architect/planner, he designed (in association with Elbert *Peets) several *Garden Suburbs in the USA, and (again with Peets), published The *American Vitruvius: An Architects' Handbook of Civic Art* (1922), an important work in city-planning literature in which *Beaux-Arts* ideas and the influence of *Sitte are clear. In Berlin from 1922 he edited and wrote prolifically for *Wasmuths Monatshefte für Baukunst und Städtebau,* but returned to the USA having fallen foul of Nazism, which he denounced in 1933.

W.Hegemann (1911, 1911–13, 1923, 1929, 1929a, 1936–8, 1976); H & P (1972)

Heideloff, Karl Alexander von (1789–1865) German architect, Professor at the *Polytechnische Schule,* Nuremberg, from 1823. He wrote several important studies, including *Bauhütte des Mittelalters in Deutschland* (1844) and *Kunst des Mittelalters in Schwaben* (1855), and carried out numerous restorations of medieval buildings, including Bamberg Cathedral (1831–4),

and *Jakobskirche,* Rothenburg-ob-der-Tauber (1854–7). Among his designs for new churches, based on late-*Gothic and geometrical principles owing much to *Neo-Classicism, the *Peterskirche, Sonneberg, in the former Dukedom of Saxe-Meiningen (1843–4), is probably the best surviving example.

Heideloff (1838–55, 1844, 1855, 1855a); Hensoldt (1845); *Mailande,* xvi (1965), 65–88; Mittig & Plagemann (eds) (1972)

Heidenreich family German architects. **Erhard Heidenreich** (*fl.*1509–24) worked at Regensburg Cathedral under *Roriczer, whom he succeeded (1514) as architect after the latter's execution. He probably designed the six windows in the *cloister which have early-*Renaissance details. He worked on the tower of the *Martinskirche,* Amberg, and on *Unsere Liebe Frau,* Ingolstadt (1509–24—where he and his son **Ulrich** (*fl.*1520s) were responsible for the net-*vaults, one of the glories of late German *Gothic).

Nussbaum (1994); J.T (1996)

Heins & La Farge American architects. **George Lewis Heins** (1860–1907) and **Christopher Grant La Farge** (1862–1938) formed a partnership (1886), and won the competition (1891) to design the Cathedral of St John the Divine in NYC with an entry mixing a round-arched style influenced by the work of H.H.*Richardson and *Byzantine architecture. From 1911, *Cram, Goodhue, & Ferguson took over and transformed the building into a masterpiece of *Gothic Revival, the original style having fallen from favour. Heins & La Farge also designed St Matthew's RC Cathedral, Washington, DC (from 1893), the subway stations for the New York Rapid Transit Commission (from 1904), and buildings in the New York Zoological Park (from 1899). La Farge continued to practise after Heins's death, and, with **Benjamin Wistar Morris** (1870–1944), designed St James's RC Cathedral, Seattle, WA (from 1905), and St Patrick's Church, Philadelphia, PA (completed 1915).

Muccigrosso (1980); P (1982); J.T (1996); Wickersham (1977); Wo (1976)

Heinzelmann, Konrad (c.1390–1454) German late-*Gothic architect, he worked (1420s) at Ulm *Minster and on the great *hall-church of St Georg, Nördlingen, Bavaria (1427–38). In Rothenburg-ob-der-Tauber (1438), he oversaw works at the *Jakobskirche,* and from 1439 until his death was building the *choir of the *Lorenzkirche,* Nuremberg (completed by *Roriczer).

RfK, xxxii (1909), 1–30, xxxiv (1911), 232–54

Hejduk, John Quentin (1929–2000) American architect, with **Michael Graves** (1934–2015), **Peter D. Eisenman** (1932-), **Richard Alan Meier** (1934-), and *Gwathmey one of the *New York Five. Works include the Demlin House, Locust Valley, Long Island, NY (1960), the Hommel Apartment, NYC (1969), and the Cooper Union Foundation Building restoration, NYC (1974-5). Later, he designed the Tegel Development and Kreuzberg Tower and Wings, *IBA Social Housing, Berlin (1987-8), and the Tower of Cards project, Groningen, The Netherlands (1990). Hejduk was best known through his theoretical writings/projects, including the *Lancaster/Hanover Masque* (1982-3), an experiment in town-planning containing 'dwellings' for a variety of inhabitants: these include the *House of the Suicide* and the *House of the Mother of the Suicide*, in which were exhibited his didactic strivings to push space to the limits.

A & U, liii (1975), 73–154; Di (1985); E (1994); F et al. (1975); Hejduk (1985); JSAH, xxxviii/2 (May 1979), 205–7; Moneo (ed.) (1987); vV (1993)

helioscene Type of external blind with *louvres, ensuring adequate ventilation, yet keeping out excessive light.

helix (*pl.* **helices**) **1.** Small *volute or *urilla under the *abacus of the *Corinthian *capital, of which there are 16 (2 at each angle, and 2 on each face) connected to the stalks. According to some authorities the 8 inner spiral forms are the *helices*, while those at the angles are *volutes*. **2.** Any volute, as on an *Ionic or *Composite capital, a *console, or a *modillion. **3.** Handrail of a stair balustrade forming a helix over the *newel.

Hellenic *Greek architecture and culture from C10 BC to *c.*323 BC.

Wy (1962)

Hellenistic *Greek architecture and culture from the consolidation of Macedonian supremacy under **Alexander the Great** (*r.*336-323 BC) to the foundation of the Roman Empire under **Augustus** in 27 BC and after in the Eastern Mediterranean. The Hellenistic period therefore coincided with the relative decline of Greece and the evolution of centres of art and patronage in the Greek Kingdoms of Asia Minor and Egypt. Hellenistic architecture is characterized by a greater variation of influence than was apparent in *Hellenic buildings, and was often more opulent, elegant, and graceful. Furthermore, Hellenistic structures gained in lightness of effect through a wider *intercolumniation than in Hellenic work. The *Doric *Order, for example, became more attenuated and less severe (often with two or more *triglyphs over each intercolumniation), becoming less 'pure' in the process and acquiring certain features from the *Ionic Order: an example was the Temple of *Hera Basileia*, Pergamon (mid-C2 BC), with very slender columns (7½ diameters high) and a relatively low *entablature. Among

the finest Hellenistic buildings incorporating the Ionic Order, much embellished with vigorous sculpture, were the Mausoleum at Halicarnassus and the Temple of Artemis at Ephesus (both mid-C4 BC, and both 'Wonders' of the Ancient World). Features of the Hellenistic Ionic Order included the *Asiatic base and the omission of the *frieze, as in the Temple of *Athena Polias*, Priene (from *c.*335 BC). The *Corinthian Order was represented by the *Choragic Monument of Lysicrates, Athens (a very beautiful and delicate version of this Order—334 BC), and by the Temple of *Zeus Olympios* (later the *Olympeion*), Athens (started 174 BC), the latter the first external use of that Order for a major building.

Whilst cities like Ephesus, Priene, and Pergamon were graced by spectacular and elegant Hellenistic religious buildings (including the huge and opulent public *altar of Zeus, Pergamon (*c.*180 BC—now in Berlin), many structures were of a civic nature, and regular gridiron town-planning became usual, as at Miletus and Priene, while the huge city of Alexandria in Egypt not only had a grid plan but vast processional avenues and monumental buildings of which virtually nothing survives. Pergamon had a library, theatre, palace, the altar, and other buildings composed as a sequence (C2 BC), and the effects of vistas of *scenography anticipated Imperial Roman planning. Among the most elaborate civic buildings was the *Bouleuterion*, Miletus (175-164 BC), with its seating arranged like that of a theatre.

Hellenistic fortifications, gates, public buildings, and monuments drew on eclectic motifs and themes, and often displayed dazzling technique and bravura. Dwelling-houses were often of considerable magnificence, anticipating the luxurious Roman *villa. Arches and *vaults were also employed, notably for tombs and subterranean structures, again pointing the way for Roman architecture, which absorbed many aspects of Hellenistic design, as is demonstrated by the temple-complex of Baalbek, Lebanon (AD C1 and 2).

D (1950); Fyfe (1936); Onians (1979); D.S.R (1945); Wy (1962)

helm 1. *Spire on a square tower each side of which is crowned with a *gable (*see* ROOF). **2.** Bulbous termination of a tower or turret, commonly occurring in Central and Eastern Europe.

Helmer, Hermann Gottlieb (1849–1919) *See* FELLNER, FERDINAND.

Helpeston, William de (*fl.*1319–75) English mason, he worked at Caernarfon Castle, Wales (1319-20), and built 12 chapels at the east end of Vale Royal Abbey, Delamere, Ches., from 1359, the plans of which were similar to aspects of

Toledo Cathedral, Spain. Helpeston was also in charge of the walls at Chester.

J.Harvey (1987)

hemi- Greek word meaning 'half'. It prefixes other words in architectural terminology. *Examples include*:

hemi-cycle: semicircular room, part of a room, or area off a *court, *forum, garden, large *exedra, semicircular *vault, arch, etc.;

hemi-dome: half-dome, e.g. over an *apse or *niche;

hemi-glyph: half-glyph or chamfer on each side of a *triglyph in the *Doric *Order;

hemi-sphaerium: *dome;

hemi-triglyph: half-triglyph-block as in an internal corner of a *frieze, touching another.

Hénard, Eugène-Alfred (1849–1923) French architect, regarded as one of the founding fathers of *urbanism, he made important contributions to the City of Paris. He was involved in planning the 1889 and 1900 *Expositions*, and throughout his career worked to conserve the best of the historic fabric, helping to formulate legislation to facilitate the preservation of whole areas, such as the banks of the Seine and various squares. He also headed the Commission for extending and improving the city (1908–12).

Bardet (1978); Hénard (1903–9); P.Wolf (1969)

henge, hengle 1. *Hinge. **2.** Class of ancient monument consisting of a bank and internal ditch enclosing a circular area, e.g. 'Giant's Ring', near Belfast. **3.** Prehistoric stone circle with 'hanging' elements, e.g. the *lintels at Stonehenge, Wilts.

Hennebique, François (1842–1921) French engineer, he developed (1892–4) a system of *concrete reinforced with steel bars and hooked connections, evolving earlier patents by *Monier (he called it *ferro-concrete). His first experiments seem to have been for a house at Lombartzyde, Belgium (1879), but progress was rapid, and he designed the first *reinforced-concrete *bridge at Viggen, Switzerland (1894), followed by *grain-elevators and factories built of the same material (including the spinning-mill, Tourcoing, France (1895), incorporating an early use of a framed structure in ferro-concrete), and he gained further publicity with his *cantilevered concrete structure for an exhibition in Geneva (1896), followed by staircases at the *Petit Palais*, Paris (1897–1900). He revolutionized theatre-design with the use of cantilevered galleries at Morges (1899): his *Schauspielhaus*, Munich (1901–3), was one of the first buildings to have an exposed concrete *frame, while his own house at Bourg-la-Reine (1904) was a remarkable example of the sculptural possibilities of the material. His in-

house journal, *Le Béton Armé* (1898–1921) contains records of his designs.

Christophe (1902); P.Collins (1959); Delhumeau (1999); Hennebique (1908); Pe (1976); vV (1993)

henostyle With one column: *henostyle in antis* = with one column between *antae. See CHORAGIC.

Henri II (Deux) Architecture in France (1547–59) following the reign of *François Ier. Italian *Renaissance influences became stronger, and *arabesques were favoured, although *Gothic traces were never entirely eliminated. Philibert de L'*Orme was an active protagonist of the period, notably at Anet, while *Bullant also contributed. The *style Henri-Deux* was revived in C19.

L & D (1986); D.Wa (1986)

Henri IV (Quatre) Architectural style in France (c.1589–1610) of which the *Place des Vosges*, Paris (1605–12), is a good example, with its private houses set over uniform vaulted *arcades (a theme derived from Italian precedents), brick *façades with *limestone *dressings and *chaînes, and tall hipped roofs like *pavilions with *lucarnes. Another fine example of the style is the *Château de Grosbois*, Seine-et-Marne (c.1600). The *style Henri-Quatre* was revived in C19.

Ck (1996); Ha (1943–57); S (1901–2)

Henry of Reyns (*fl.* mid-C13) *See* REYNS.

Henselmann, Hermann (1905–95) German architect/theorist, perhaps the most influential in the former German Democratic Republic (GDR). He directed the *Hochschule für Baukunst und Bildende Künste*, Weimar (1945–50), and was later in charge (1951–72) of planning East Berlin, in which capacity he was one of the main architects (1949–61) of the *Stalinallee* (later *Karl-Marx-Allee*). He was responsible for *Punkthaus an der Weberwiese*, Berlin (1951—the first example of the so-called 'National Tradition' style (a coarse, stripped-down architecture loosely based on *Classicism) required by the Communist authorities); for the main buildings in Berlin's *Strausberger Platz* (1952–3) and *Frankfurter Tor* (1955–6); and, as Chief Architect (1966–72) of the *Institut für Städtebau und Architektur*, for attempts to create structures with 'personalities' as urban centre-pieces, though these had little relevance to history in devastated cities. Among his works were the first glass and steel-framed high-rise building in the former GDR (the *Haus des Lehrers* (1962–4)), the Congress Centre (1964), and the *Fernsehturm* (1969—known as the 'Pope's Revenge' because when the sun shone on the ball at the top, it beamed a cross into the West), all near *Alexanderplatz*, Berlin. Henselmann was also responsible for the University Complex at Leipzig (1969–74), and for the cylindrical multi-storey Research Building at the University of Jena (1969–75). He was not unaware of the importance of historical references: his design for the elliptical *Strausberger Platz* owed much to *Möhring's plans (1920), and the twin *cupolas at the *Frankfurter Tor* were clearly derived from *Gontard's handsome additions to the *Gendarmenmarkt* (1780–5). Most of Henselmann's works from 1949 depended on *industrialized *prefabrication.

Schache (1995); Siepelt & Eckhardt (eds) (1982); J.T (1996).

Hentrich, Helmut (1905–2001) German architect, principal of **Hentrich-Petschnigg & Partners** (HPP), Düsseldorf, responsible for many gigantic buildings for large corporations, all in the style of *International Modernism. The bestknown works of the firm are the *Thyssenhaus*, Düsseldorf (1957–60); the *Europa-Centre*, Berlin (1964); the Dietrich-Bonhoeffer Church, Düsseldorf-Garath (1964–5); the *Finnlandhaus*, Hamburg (the first high block in Europe constructed on the suspension system (1966)); the Standard Bank Centre, Johannesburg, South Africa (with *Arup (1967–70)); and the *Konzerthalle*, Düsseldorf (1978).

H-B.Adams (ed.) (1989); E (1994); Hentrich (1995); Hentrich-Petschnigg (1969, 1975); Tunkers (2000)

heptastyle *See* PORTICO.

herald's rod *See* CADUCEUS.

herbarium 1. Systematic collection of preserved dried plants (e.g. that of Philip *Miller). **2.** Building, room, or case containing it. **3.** *Herbgarden, *arbour, or *herber.

herber 1. Medieval pleasure-ground. **2.** *arbour.

Herbert, Henry (*c.*1693–1751—**9th Earl of Pembroke** from 1733). Owner of Wilton House, Wilts., he studied at Christ Church College, Oxford, in the time of *Aldrich, and was active in promoting the *Palladianism Inigo *Jones had introduced, revived in Herbert's lifetime under *Burlington's aegis. He became an important amateur, probably more faithful to Palladian principles than either Burlington or *Kent. He and Roger *Morris appear to have designed the elegant bridge at Wilton (1736–7), Marble Hill, Twickenham (1724–9), White Lodge, Richmond New Park (1727–8), and other works. *Campbell also worked for or with Herbert, notably in connection with the latter's house in Whitehall, London (1724), and, it seems, Marble Hill. It is probable that Herbert, lacking practical architectural skills, called in Morris as his amanuensis.

Co (2008); *ODNB* (2004)

herb-garden 1. Garden for growing herbs for culinary, medicinal (*see* PHYSIC-GARDEN), or other purposes (e.g. dyeing cloth or making perfume), usual in *monasteries (e.g. C9 plan of St Gall, Switzerland). **2.** C20 ornamental garden-feature, e.g. at Long Barn (from 1915) and Sissinghurst (from 1930), both in Kent, created by the Hon. Victoria Mary ('Vita') *Sackville-West. Historically based herb-gardens have been re-created (e.g. Hall Place, Bexley, London).

Rohde (1926); Sanecki (1992); Symes (2006); Tay (2006)

Herculaneum Roman city, buried after the eruption (AD 79) of Vesuvius. Its rediscovery and excavation (from 1738) proved to be a potent catalyst in *Neo-Classicism, especially as the finds were documented in *Le Antichità di Ercolano* (1757–92), sumptuously illustrated. The artefacts were particularly influential because they revealed much about domestic furnishings and the lives of ordinary Romans. As with *Pompeii (found later than Herculaneum), excavations provided countless motifs for designers as ingredients of Neo-Classicism, notably the *Etruscan, *Pompeian, *Adam, *Empire, and *Regency styles. *Die schönsten Ornamente und merkwürdigsten Gemälde aus Pompeji, Herkulanum und Stabiae* (1828–59—with many chromolithographed plates) by **Wilhelm Zahn** (1800–71) provided a rich and accurate source for C19 designers.

H & S (1996); L & D (1986)

Héré de Corny, Emmanuel (1705–63) French architect (from 1738) to **Stanisław Leszczyński** (1677–1766), **King of Poland** (1704–9, 1733–4), and **Duke of Lorraine and Bar** (1736–66), for whom he produced many elegant designs for *châteaux* and garden-buildings in Lorraine, but his masterpiece is the sequence of urban spaces in Nancy—the *Place Royale* (now *Place Stanislaus*), the promenade or *Place de la Carrière*, and the *Hemicycle* (1752–6), that together form exquisite and impressive works of *Rococo urban planning. Héré published his designs in *Recueil* (1753–6) and *Plans et élévations de la place royale de Nancy & des autres edifices à l'environment bâtis par les ordres du Roy de Pologne duc de Lorraine* (1753). Earlier, he designed *Notre Dame de Bon-Secours*, Nancy (1738–41), as a mortuary-church for the Duke and his family. He also designed a series of gardens and *fabriques* at the Duke's estates of Chantehéux, Commercy, Einville, Lunéville, and Malgrange: Héré was among the first to build exotic *fabriques*, including the influential Turkish and Chinese Kiosks at Lunéville (1737 and 1740). At Lunéville he also built a *rocher* or *rock-work structure (1742–52—early for its type), and completed the Church of St-Jacques (1743–7).

Boyé (1910); Conner (1979); France-Lanord (1984); Héré de Corny (1753, 1753–6); P.Marot (1954, 1966); Rau (1973); J.T (1996); Wn (1978)

Hereford, Walter of (*fl.*1277–1309) English mason, Master of the Works at Vale Royal Abbey, Delamere, Ches. (1278–90), he later ran building-operations at Caernarfon Castle, Wales, from 1304, and was the principal master-architect employed by the Crown (1285–1309). He designed Grey Friars' Church, Newgate, London (from 1306), and probably influenced the design of St Thomas's, Winchelsea, Sussex, and Holy Trinity, Hull (1295–1300). He may have planned Denbigh Castle, including the gate-house, begun *c.*1300.

J.Harvey (1987)

Herholdt, Johan Daniel (1818–1902) Danish architect, pupil of *Bindesbøll and *Hetsch, he studied old brick buildings in Denmark and *Renaissance architecture in Northern Italy, amalgamating aspects of both in his designs. It was partly through his influence that brickwork became fashionable for grander C19 Danish buildings, and he was a pioneer in the use of exposed structural cast-iron members. His most celebrated work is the University Library, Copenhagen (1857–61), in a robust brick *Rundbogenstil with elegant exposed ironwork inside. The Main Railway Station, Copenhagen (1863–4—demolished 1917), was also fine. Perhaps his most significant building is the National Bank (1865–70) in which the influence of C15 Florentine-Renaissance architecture was strong. In Odense he designed the Town Hall (1881–3—with **Carl William Frederik Lendorf** (1839–1918)). In his many *villas and other private houses he was influenced by developments in England, especially the *Domestic Revival, and he in turn influenced the following generation, notably Martin *Nyrop.

T.Faber (1963); Mi (1951); Rasmussen (1940); We (1947)

Herigoyen, Emanuel Joseph von (1746–1817) Portuguese architect, he designed the gardens at Schönbusch, near Aschaffenburg, in the 'English' style, and built there a Neo-Classical *pavilion (1778–9). He was responsible for the staircase at Aschaffenburg *Schloss*, and designed the churches at Esselbach (1779) and Sulzbach-am-Main (1786). Later, at Regensburg, he built the Theatre (1804—destroyed 1849), the circular Kepler Memorial (1808), and other works. In Munich he designed the *Volkstheater* (destroyed), the *Greek-Revival entrance to the Botanical Gardens (1812), and the *Palais Montgelas* (1810–11).

J.T (1996)

heritage asset Denotes structures, features, and objects of historic interest and value that are potentially viable as attractions.

Herland, Hugh (*c.*1330–*c.*1411) English carpenter, possibly the son of William *Herland. He worked on the Chapel *stalls at Windsor Castle,

Berks. (1350), and was employed (1360s) at Westminster Palace and the Tower of London. He designed and made the *tester over the tomb of **Queen Philippa** (*r.*1328–69—consort of **King Edward III** (*r.*1327–77)) in Westminster Abbey. He was put in charge (1375) of the King's Works 'touching the art or mastery of carpentry', and was in command of building operations at Rochester Castle, Kent (1378). Around this time he designed the tester over the tomb of **King Edward III**, foreshadowing his design for the ceiling of Winchester College Chapel, Hants., ten years later. He worked at Rochester, Leeds, and Portchester Castles (1380s), and for William of *Wykeham at New College, Oxford (*c.*1384). Engaged (1390s) at Westminster Hall, he designed and built the outstanding *hammer-beam roof, one of the greatest achievements of medieval carpentry. Herland may also have done the ceiling of the Fitzalan Chapel, Arundel, Sussex (*c.*1380–1400).

J.Harvey (1987)

Herland, William (*fl.*1332–75) English carpenter, he was making moulds for St Stephen's Chapel, Westminster (1332), worked (1350) at Eltham and Windsor Castles, and seems to have been appointed (1354) King's Chief Carpenter. He supervised carpentry works at the Tower of London and Westminster Palace, and designed the Great Hall roof and other works at Windsor Castle, Berks. (1355–7). He was also involved at Hadleigh Castle, Essex, Rotherhithe Manor, near London, Rochester Castle, Kent, and the Tower of London.

J.Harvey (1987)

herm, hermes Statue found in *Antiquity, comprising head and neck or head and shoulders (often representing **Hermes** *or* **Mercury**) joined to a quadrangular shaft proportioned to be the same height as a human body and slightly tapered

(a)   (b)

herm (*a*) Ancient-Greek ithyphallic type. (*b*) Front and side elevations, C16 term-pilaster, *Villa Cambiaso*, Genoa.

downwards, frequently with the male reproductive organs protruding from its front. The form was revived from *Renaissance times, often used for garden-ornaments (e.g. at the *Palazzo Farnese*, Caprarola (1547-9)), and from C18 became a common motif, often with female head and frequently with the feet showing at the base (since Antiquity the phallic imagery has normally been avoided). Herms are distinct from *terms in that they do not have torsos or waists, have no arms, and may have volute-like forms instead of shoulders.

J.Curl (2005); L & D (1986)

Hermant, Jacques (1855-1930) French architect, son of **Pierre-Antoine-Achille Hermant** (1823-1903—who designed the Reformatory in Nanterre (1874-81), a model for late-C19 French penal establishments). Jacques was an uninhibited eclecticist, and won fame with his French *pavilions at the World's Columbian Exposition, Chicago, IL (1893), and the *Exposition Internationale*, Brussels (1897). Although he used the *Louis-Seize* style for his *Salle Gaveau* concert-hall, the building was remarkable for its *reinforced-concrete construction (the first in Paris), designed with *Coignet, with whom he also designed *Le Magasin des Classes Laborieuses, Rue St-Martin*, Paris (1898). He was responsible for the *Société Générale* office, *Boulevard Haussmann*, Paris, tucked in behind three existing *façades: with its central banking-hall (under a glazed roof) surrounded by offices and its sumptuous *Art-Nouveau decorations, it was a remarkable ensemble. It is curious his name is not better known.

Delaire (1907); Emery (1971); J.T (1996)

Hermelin, Sven (1900-84) Swedish landscape architect, he designed the park at Sundbyberg, Stockholm (1935-7), for the Marabou Chocolate Factory, and several churchyards and *cemeteries.

Pk; Tay (2006)

hermitage, ermitage 1. Dwelling of a hermit or religious recluse, in the medieval period often associated with religious foundations, endowed for an *anchorite* in a churchyard or some other place, often attached to a monastery, and frequently associated with an *oratory. **2.** C18 habitation in a lonely situation, often in a landscaped park, occupied by a paid 'hermit'. **3.** *Cottage orné*, *primitive hut, or rustic residence in a landscape intended as a mnemonic of a hermit's house. **4.** *Bower, *gazebo, or secluded place, often associated with a *grotto or cave, artificial *rock-work, or some such construction in a C18 elegiac landscape.

G.Campbell (2013); Gw (1903); W.Pa (1852); Symes (2008); D.Wa (1982a)

Hermogenes (*fl.c.*220-190 BC) *Hellenistic architect/theorist, mentioned by *Vitruvius, he designed the *temples of Dionysus, Teos (*c.*220-205 BC), and Artemis, Magnesia on the Meander (*c.*205-190 BC). He favoured *Ionic, objecting to *Doric because of the problem of combining equal *intercolumniation with the *triglyph *frieze at the corners. He seems to have promoted the *pseudodipteral plan (large temples in Ionia had been built with two rows of columns surrounding the cell, but Hermogenes omitted the inner *colonnade, providing a very wide, open, airy space, surrounded by the *peristyle). He also promoted *eustyle* intercolumniation, giving a stable yet elegant appearance to the colonnade.

D (1950); Gerkan (1929); Humann (1904); La (1983); Onians (1979); P (1982)

Herrera, Juan de (1530-97) Celebrated Spanish architect, he introduced an austere *Classicism (known as *estilo desornamentado*) to that country. He became assistant (1563) to de *Toledo, and when the latter died Herrera rose to a position of eminence, confirmed (1579) in his appointment as Architect to **King Philip II** (*r.*1556-98). Herrera's career was closely bound up with the building of the Royal Monastery, Palace, and *Mausoleum of *El Escorial*, near Madrid, the plan of which is not unlike various reconstructions of the Temple of Solomon, especially that of the Jesuits **Hieronymo Prado** (1547-95) and *Villalpando, and has various astrological, magical, religious, geometrical, and symbolic allusions discussed elsewhere. The form of the complex, with its gridiron plan and four angle-towers, may be an allusion to the martyrdom of **St Laurence** (d.258): **Pope Gregory XIII** (*r.*1572-85) presented some of that Saint's supposed melted fat to the King, thus St Laurence is Patron of the church there. Herrera's other Royal buildings include the completion of the *Alcázar*, Toledo (1585), work on the Palace at Aranjuez (1571-86—which has many of the *Escorial* motifs), the elegant *Lonja* (Exchange), Seville (1582-98), and part of the Cathedral of Valladolid (1585-97). The last, though incomplete when Herrera died, was widely copied, notably at Salamanca, Mexico City, Puebla, and Lima Cathedrals.

CG (1953); J.Curl (2011); FHL (1967); Kubler (1982); K & S (1959); P (1982); Ruiz de Arcaute (1936); J.T (1996); Wilkinson-Zerner (1994)

herring-bone Bricks, stones, tiles, or wood-blocks laid aslant in alternate rows or courses at 45° to the general direction of the course or row, and at 90° to the adjoining courses or rows, thus each course or row slopes in a different direction to those on either side or above and below, forming a *zig-zag pattern.

Herron, Ronald (Ron) James (1930–94) English architect, associated (1960s) with *Archigram, partly responsible, when working for the GLC, for the conception of the South Bank Arts Complex, London (early 1960s). His best-known work was probably the refurbishment of an existing office-building in Store Street, Bloomsbury, London (1989), for Imagination Ltd., involving covering a courtyard with a stretched-fabric roof.

Cook et al. (1999); E (1994)

Hertfordshire spike *Flèche or short *spire rising from a church-tower, its base concealed by a *parapet, common in Herts., England.

Hesekiel, Georg Christoph (1732–1818) German architect, he designed the *Gothic-Revival *Peterskirche* (1804–10), Wörlitz, Anhalt, the *steeple of which alludes to English types such as that of St James's Church, Louth, Lincs. (c.1440–5, 1501–5). With *Erdmannsdorff, he designed the Gothic House in the *Gartenreich* (Garden-Realm) at Wörlitz (1773–1813). Both were key buildings in German *Gothic Revival, underlining the Anglophilia of the reigning Prince of *Anhalt-Dessau.

J.Curl (2011); *AQC,* cxvi (2004), 83–126; Ringkamp & Janssen (eds) (2000); Trauzettel (2000); Trauzettel & Winkler (1992)

Hesse, Ludwig Ferdinand (1795–1876) German architect, he worked under *Schinkel in Berlin, where he detailed/supervised the building of the *Gothic *Friedrich Werderschekirche* (1825–31). He became *Hofbaumeister* in Potsdam (1831), and worked with *Persius, whose *villas were models for his own buildings. He designed the extension to the *mausoleum of **Queen Luise of Prussia** (*r.*1797–1810), Charlottenburg, Berlin (1841), the *Teehaus* (1847), the *Belvedere, Pfingstenberg* (1847–52), and the *Orangery and Terraces (1851–60), all at *Sanssouci*. The last two projects (designed with *Stüler) were derived from C16 *Renaissance precedents (e.g. *Villa Madama* and *Villa Pamphili*, Rome).

B-S (1977); Dehio (1961); L.Hesse (1854–5, 1854–6); P (1982)

Hetsch, Gustav Friedrich (1788–1864) German architect, he trained in Germany and in Paris (with *Percier and *Fontaine) before settling (1815) in Copenhagen, Denmark, where he worked with C.F.*Hansen, whose daughter he married. He designed the RC Church of St Ansgar (1840–1) and the Synagogue (1829–33), both in Copenhagen. He is better known for his furniture designs, metalwork, ceramics, and publications (many of which proved influential). As a representative of late *Classicism, his work was severe, rational, and finely detailed. Among his many pupils was *Herholdt.

We (1947)

Hewett, Cecil Alec (1926–98) English craftsman/carpentry-historian. Realizing (early 1960s) that 'conventional wisdom' was reluctant to attribute *timber-framed buildings to any period before C15, and that nobody seemed to accept that techniques of jointing timbers might actually have *evolved* over centuries, he revolutionized dating of English timber-framed architecture. His examinations of the Knights Templars' Barley and Wheat Barns, Cressing Temple, Essex (which the Royal Commission on Historical Monuments (1922) dated to C16, despite the Templars having been suppressed at the beginning of C14), included examinations of carpentry joints, and he proved an *evolution* of such joints, identifying features of archaic carpentry (some of which had been noted by the French scholar, **Henri-Louis Deneux** (1874–1969), as dating from C11 to C13). Hewett's theories were confirmed by carbon-14 dating, which estimated timber-felling for the Barley Barn as c.1205–30, and that for the Wheat Barn as c.1257–80. Despite reasoned analyses, his ideas were treated with contempt in 'academic' circles, but, aided by his own clear drawings, his theories were accepted in Germany, Scandinavia, and the USA, then, reluctantly and tardily, in his own country; but recognition came very late, long after he was severely incapacitated by a massive stroke.

Hewett (1969, 1980, 1982); *Independent* (30 Sept. 1998), Obits.; pk

hewn Cut, prepared, dressed stone, or *ashlar.

hexastyle See PORTICO.

Hiberno-Romanesque Style of Irish ecclesiastical buildings (C10–C12) characterized by simple rectangular structures, detached circular towers with conical roofs, semicircular-headed openings, and the usual array of *Romanesque ornament, with such structures as *Celtic crosses sumptuously carved (e.g. Monasterboice, Co. Louth (C9 or C10)). Some of the most outstanding buildings are those at Devenish, Co. Fermanagh (C10–C12), and Cormac's Chapel, Cashel, Co. Tipperary (1127–34). The style was resurrected (C19) as part of the *Celtic Revival (*see* LYNN), its most common manifestations being carved *high memorial-crosses in *cemeteries and numerous churches, including some C20 exemplars (e.g. those designed by **Pádraig Bernard Gregory** (1886–1967)). Aspects of Hiberno-Romanesque/Celtic design informed *Art Nouveau and the *Arts-and-Crafts movement. Also called *Hiberno-Saxon* as there were similarities between Irish and *Anglo-Saxon decoration.

A.Champneys (1910); M.Craig (1982); L & D (1986); Petrie (1845); Stokes (1878)

Higgins, Harold Cassius (1926–2011) English architect, he believed architecture was a determinant of society and a branch of the social sciences, so early work (as **Higgins, Ney, & Partners**) was mostly for low-cost housing, e.g. the 'High-Deck' development at Reporton Road, Fulham, London (1964–8). The firm also designed expensive private houses (e.g. Heathbrow, Spaniards End, Hampstead (1959–61), and 8a Fitzroy Park, Highgate (1964)); the interior of The Museum of London (1980s); and The Bank of England Museum which involved the reconstruction of *Soane's Bank Stock Office (1986–8).

RIBAJ (Feb. 2012), 16

high-altar Main *altar of a church sited on the main axis at the east of the *choir or *chancel.

high cross Free-standing detached sculpted stone *cross, usually *Celtic or *Anglo-Saxon (e.g. Monasterboice, Co. Louth (C9 or C10), Ruthwell, near Dumfries (C7), and the magnificent Bewcastle Cross, Cumb. (C7)).

C & R (1993); Gifford (1996); Hyde & Pe (2010)

High Gothic 1. *Gothic architecture (*c.*1195–*c.*1350), known in German as *Hochgotik*. 2. Supposedly 'classic' period of Gothic architecture, embracing Northern French Cathedrals erected *c.*1195–*c.*1230 (e.g. Chartres, Rheims, Amiens, and Soissons). The term is problematic: it raises the question of what is 'Low Gothic', and tends to devalue the extraordinary achievements of later Gothic, especially English *Perp.

Bony (1982); Frankl (1960, 2000); Gi (1986); Kimpel & Suckale (1985)

high relief *Alto-rilievo*, i.e. sculpture in relief projecting more than half its form from its background.

High Renaissance Early C16 Italian-*Renaissance style at the height of its development, called *Cinquecento*.

high-rise Tall structure of several floors, or a *skyscraper.

High Tech Style (some would deny it is anything of the sort) expressive of structures, technologies, and services by exposing and emphasizing them, or *appearing* to do so (the so-called *Machine Aesthetic). Some erroneously hold that High Tech originated in C19 iron-and-glass structures such as *Paxton's Crystal Palace (1851), but its aggressive imagery owes more to Buckminster *Fuller, *Archigram, and even *Futurism and New *Brutalism. The *Centre Pompidou*, Paris (1977), by **Renzo Piano** (1937–) and **Richard Rogers** (1933–); the Lloyd's Building, London (1986), again by **Rogers**; the Hong Kong and Shanghai Bank, Hong Kong (1986), by **Norman Foster** (1935–); Schlumberger Research Laboratories, Cambridge (1985), by **Michael Hopkins** (1935–); and the *Financial Times* Printing Works, Docklands, London (1988), by **Nicholas Grimshaw** (1939–) are among paradigmatic High-Tech structures. Also known as the *Industrial Aesthetic, it is really about *image* (called, appropriately, *Slick Style* by **Charles Jencks** (1939–2019)), and is expensive to construct/maintain.

Amery (1995); *AR*, clxl/693 (May 1977), 270–94, clxxix/1037 (Jul. 1983), 14–59; *AR Supp.* (Sept. 2000); *CL*, cxcvii/33 (14 Aug. 2003), 38–43; K.Daniels (1998); C.Davies (1988, 1993); C.Davies *et al.* (2001); Forester (1987); Js (1988); Kron & Slesin (1979); Mr (1995); R.Moore (ed.) (1995); NGP; Pearman (2000); J.T (1996)

High Victorian Style of somewhat harsh *polychrome structures of the *Gothic Revival (1850s–1860s) when *Ruskin held sway as arbiter of Taste. Like *High Gothic it is an unsatisfactory term, as it poses the question as to what is 'Low Victorian'. 'Mid-Victorian' would, perhaps, be better, but precise dates and description of styles would be more so.

Blau (1982); J.Curl (2007); Hersey (1972); Jervis (1983)

Hilbersheimer, Ludwig Karl (1885–1967) German-born American architect, he taught at the *Bauhaus, and was involved with *Arbeitsrat für Kunst*, the *Expressionist *Der* *Sturm, and *Der* *Ring. He joined *CIAM and was Director (1931) of the *Deutscher Werkbund, so his *International-Modernist credentials were impeccable, and indeed he was one of the founders of that style. His project for a 'skyscraper city' (1924) evolved from Le *Corbusier's ideas, and he built a house for the *Weissenhofsiedlung*, Stuttgart (1927), where he was closely associated with *Mies van der Rohe, a connection that led to his joining (1938) the Illinois Institute of Technology (then the Armour Institute). He published *Grossstadtbauten* (1925), *Grossstadt Architektur* (1927), *Contemporary Architecture: Its Roots and Trends* (1964), and many other polemical works intended to further International Modernism.

E (1994); Hays (1992); Hilbersheimer (1925, 1927, 1927a, 1929, 1944, 1949, 1955, 1956, 1963, 1963a); P (1982); Pommer (1988); Spaeth (1981); J.T (1996)

Hild, József (1789–1867) Hungarian architect, one of the most successful during the first half of C19. He commenced practice (1820s) in Pest, designing numerous *Neo-Classical residential blocks there, but became (1830s) an important church-architect, designing Eger Cathedral (1831–7), with a *Corinthian *portico, a *dome, and towers on either side of the *chancel. After *Packh's death (1839) he took over responsibility for the building of the Archiepiscopal Cathedral of St Adalbert,

Esztergom (1822–69—originally planned by *Kühnel), designing the dome on its colonnaded drum.

J.T (1996); Zádor (1985)

Hildebrandt, Johann Lukas von (1668–1745) Genoa-born military-engineer, he became one of Austria's most distinguished and inventive early-C18 *Baroque architects (with *Fischer von Erlach). Studying in Rome with Carlo *Fontana, he absorbed much from the works of *Borromini and *Guarini, notably the possibilities of interpenetrating elliptical plans and undulating *façades. During military campaigns (1690s) he met his future patron, the great commander **Prince Eugen of Savoy** (1663–1736), and settled (1696) in Vienna, becoming (1700) Court Engineer. He was concerned with the design of the *Mansfeld-Fondi* (later *Schwarzenberg*) Palace, Vienna (1697–1715), where influences from Borromini and Guarini are overt, notably in the two-storey elliptical salon that bows outwards on the garden-front. The axial garden-layout, with *ramps, changes of level, and *terraces, derives from Italian prototypes, especially the *Villa Giulia*, Rome, and, with the Palace, demonstrates syntheses of Italian, French, and German sources that suggest such features of Hildebrandt's style, for there are traces of Le *Vau's *Vaux-le-Vicomte*, Guarini's *Palazzo Carignano*, and *Bernini's project for the east wing of the Louvre, Paris. Hildebrandt's admiration for Guarini was even clearer at the Dominican Chapel of St Laurenz, Gabel, North Bohemia (1699–1711), with its concave corners, convex balconies, and plan of a circle flanked by two ellipses with chapels placed on the diagonals. This church-plan was to be influential, especially on the work of the *Dientzenhofers.

Hildebrandt took over responsibility (1703) for the design of the *Peterskirche*, Vienna (begun 1702 by **Gabriele Montani** (*fl.* early C18)), planned as a longitudinal ellipse crowned by a *cupola, flanked by two rectangular compartments and an apsidal *choir: the tall entrance-front is flanked by twin towers set at angles, giving great drama to the composition (**Franz Jänggl** (1650–1734) was involved in the building's construction). A variant of the *Peterskirche* plan was used for the *Seminarkirche*, Linz (1717–25). From 1698 Hildebrandt worked (possibly with a contribution from K.I. *Dientzenhofer) on the beautiful *Piaristenkirche Maria Treu*, Vienna (built by Jänggl, 1716–31), which has a similar plan to that of the Gabel church. Completed (1751–3) by the Piarist **Matthias Gerl** (1712–65), the church is by far the lightest and most joyous in a city where Baroque tends to the sombre. Hildebrandt's greatest work is arguably the *Belvedere*, Vienna (1714–24), the dream-palace of **Prince Eugen**, with almost oriental roofs and frothy façades with shaped pediments and corner-towers. There are, in fact, two

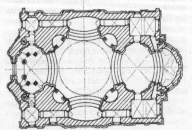

Laurenzkirche, Gabel.

buildings—the Upper and Lower (1714–16) Belvedere—linked by a series of terraced gardens, with statuary and planting. The Upper Palace contains the most celebrated of Hildebrandt's staircases where massive, struggling *atlantes carry heavy vaulting: he also designed the *Treppenhaus* (with *urns and *putti) at *Schloss Mirabell*, Salzburg (1721–7). Other fine staircases can be found at the *Palais Daun-Kinsky*, Vienna (1713–16), and *Schloss Weissenstein*, Pommersfelden (1711–15—where he also designed the central *pavilion). He collaborated (1720–23, 1729–44) with *Neumann on the *Residenz* of the Prince-Bishop at Würzburg: his hand is evident in the shaped *pediments of the central pavilion as well as in the *Kaisersaal* and Chapel. He was involved in the rebuilding of *Stift* Göttweig (from 1719): his plans were ambitious but never fully realized, although the building containing the *Kaiserstiege* (1738) is as splendid as anything he conceived.

G.Aurenhammer (ed.) (1969); Brucker (1983); H.Franz (1942, 1943, 1943a, 1962); Freeden (1952); Grimschitz (1947a, 1959); E.Hempel (1965); W.Ho (1968); O.Kerber (1947); Kreisel (1953); P (1982); Sedlmayr (1930); J.T (1996); *WJfK*, xvi (1954), 205–11, xvii (1955), 49–62, xxix (1976), 121–56

Hill, Oliver Falvey (1887–1968) English architect, pupil of *Flockhart. He reconstructed the house and *Italianate garden at Moor Close, Binfield, Berks. (1911–14, 1922—later (from 1945) Newbold College), and designed a series of houses, including Cour House, Argyll (1921–3—influenced by late-C19 *Lutyens); Cockrock Croyde, Devon (1925—informed by *vernacular architecture and *Voysey's work); and Joldwynds, Holmbury St Mary, Surrey (1930–4—in the *International-Modern style, replacing a house by Philip *Webb). One of his most remarkable buildings was the Midland Hotel, Morecambe, Lancs. (1932–3), the first Modernist hotel to be built in England, the client for which was the **London Midland and Scottish Railway**: the structure is not merely interesting in itself, but was significant for the art-works by **Arthur Eric Rowton Gill**

(1882–1940), **Marion V. Dorn** (1896–1964), **Eric William Ravilious** (1903–44), and **Denis Tegetmeier** (1909–87). The building was renovated (2005–8) by **Urban Splash**. Hill drew up plans for the development of the Park at Frinton-on-Sea, Essex, from 1934, and designed several buildings there, including the Round House, Cliff Way (1934–5), 55 & 57 Quendon Way, 16 Warley Way, and 1 & 2 Easton Way. After the 1939–45 war Hill was neglected, although his 1937 design for the bus station, Newbury Park, London Borough of Redbridge, was built (1947–8), and he was responsible for the Library and War Memorial, Uppingham School, Rutland (1948–9). With John *Cornforth he wrote *Caroline: 1625–1685* (1966).

Bettley & Pe (2007); *ODNB* (2004); *C20 Newsletter* (Spring 2003), 2–3

Hill *or* **Hyll, Thomas** (1529–76) English writer on gardens, his *A Most Briefe and Pleasaunte Treatyse, Teachyng how to Dresse, Sowe, and Set a Garden* (1558) was published in several edns, with changed (1568) title, *The Proffitable Arte of Gardening*. His *Gardeners Labyrinth* (1577) appeared under the pseudonym **Didymus Mountaine**, completed by **Henry Dethick** (*fl.*1577–1613) with woodcuts of garden-designs and much else. He drew on the works of others, not least the late-C4–early-C5 Roman author, **Rutilius Taurus Aemilius Palladius**.

Dethick (ed.) (1577); Hoyles (1994); Shoe (2001); Tay (2006); Thacker (1994)

Hill, William (1827–89) English architect of several chapels for the Methodist New Connexion, including those at Woodhouse Lane, Leeds (1853–8—with later (1887) school-buildings); Salem, Halifax (1871–4); Mount Tabor, Stockport (1865–8—with *prostyle tetrastyle *portico); and Mannville, Bradford (1875). For the Connexion he also designed Ranmore College, Sheffield (1862–4). Success in competitions led to commissions for the Classical Corn-Exchanges at Devizes, Wilts. (1856–7), Banbury, Oxon. (1857), and Hertford, Herts. (1858–9). He designed two lavish Classical Town-Halls: those at Bolton (1863–73—influenced by *Brodrick's work at Leeds) and the even grander one at Portsmouth, Hants. (1886–90). He was also interested in cemetery-design.

Webster (ed.) (2012)

Hindoo Exotic orientalizing architectural style, part of the *eclecticism associated with the C18 *Picturesque. One of its earliest manifestations was the Hindoo *Gothick *façade, Guildhall, London (1788–9), by *Dance. The Hindoo or *Indian style gained momentum with the publication of the various views of India by *Hodges and the *Daniells. Sezincote, Glos. (c.1805), a country-

house by S.P.*Cockerell, is perhaps the finest example of the style.

Conner (1979); L & D (1986)

hinge Movable joint by which a *door, *gate, opening-*light, or *sash is hung to a fixed post or frame so as to be opened or shut by being turned upon it. Medieval hinges were especially decorative and conspicuous, with graceful *scroll-work. *See also* GEMEL, HENGE.

Hiorne Family Based in Warwick, architect/builder **Francis Hiorne** (1744–89) created several buildings in the *Gothick taste including St Mary's Church, Tetbury, Glos. (1771–81), with its elegant *piers of timber containing iron cores. He designed the Classical St Anne's Church, Belfast (1772–6—demolished 1900). His father, **William** (c.1712–76), and his uncle, **David** (1715–58), worked for William *Smith whom they succeeded in business, carrying out numerous works in the English Midlands. **William Hiorne** was the executant architect (from c.1748) for *Newdigate's Gothick Arbury Hall, Warwicks., and the brothers designed and built Holy Cross Church, Daventry, Northants. (1752–8), in a Classical style. They also erected several buildings to Sanderson *Miller's designs, including Shire Hall, Warwick (1754–8), and the stable-block, Packington Hall, Warwicks. (1756–8).

Brown (ed.) (1985); Co (2008)

hip 1. Sloping *salient angle of a roof where two sides (*skirts*) join. **2.** *Rafter at this angle. *Associated terms include*:

hip-bevel: **1.** angle between two slopes of a roof separated by a hip; **2.** bevel on the end of a *hip-rafter*;

hip-knob: *finial where the *ridge and hips of a roof meet;

hip-rafter: rafter at the angle of a hipped roof to which the upper ends of other rafters are fixed;

hip-roll: long rounded piece of timber fixed above the *hip-rafter* over which lead or other metal is dressed to render the hip watertight;

hip-roof: roof with all sides sloping and meeting at hips;

hip-tile: curved or angled tile laid in series over hips.

hippocamp *Sea-horse*, with the upper body of a horse and lower of a fish-like creature, often used in Classical decorations.

Hippodamus of Miletus (*fl.c.*500–440 BC) Greek architect/town-planner, he proposed that rational, geometrically clear, grid-patterned town layouts could express social order. He may have designed Miletus, Asia Minor (from c.475 BC), Piraeus, near Athens (c.470 BC), and Thurii (Thourioi), Italy (c.443 BC), but he is remembered as one of the earliest theorists of the *Ideal City, and through **Aristotle's** (384–322 BC) writings influenced later thinkers, notably during the *Renaissance.

Castagnoli (1956, 1971); Greco et al. (1983); R.Martin (1956); P (1982); W-P (1974); Wy (1962)

hippodrome Place used by the Greeks for horse- and chariot-races, or for equestrian exercises.

Hirsau style Type of German *Romanesque architecture derived from the great Abbey of Cluny, France, and developed at Hirsau (from 1082). Hirsau-type churches had *ante-churches, two west towers, *nave-arcades with columnar *piers rather than massive square structures, plain block-*capitals, and slender towers over the eastern *bays of the *aisles.

Conant (1979); J.T (1996)

Hirschfeld, Christian Cay (Caius) Lorenz (1742–92) German intellectual. His publications promoted the design of landscape-gardens, starting with *Anmerkungen über die Landhäuser und die Gartenkunst* (1773) and *Theorie der Gartenkunst* (1775). These were followed by the huge five-volume *Theorie der Gartenkunst* (1779–85— which also came out in French as *Théorie de l'Art des Jardins*). Drawing heavily on English writers, he described exemplary gardens, contrasting them with *Baroque French types (which he firmly associated with Absolutism), and he emphasized the value of gardens with their *fabriques* in the triggering of memory, associations, moods, and feelings. He was particularly interested in gardens as places of education, to raise the tone of society, and generally improve minds. In particular, he advocated *public parks as places where the moral improvement of the populace would be achieved. His works were a major source by which English concepts of landscape-gardens were disseminated in the German-speaking lands. Indirectly, too, his publications helped to promote ideas that led to the formation of the first *garden-*cemeteries.

Breckwoldt (1995); Hirschfeld (1779–85); JGH, **xiv**/2 (Summer 1994), 92–118; Kehn (1992); Schepers (1980)

Hispano-Moresque Architectural style based upon that of C8–C15 *Moorish buildings in the Iberian peninsula. Earlier work was contemporary with *Romanesque and was called *Mozarabic. Later architecture infused with *Gothic is known as *Mudéjar. The *Alhambra*, Granada (mostly 1338–90), is a fine example of the style, which was revived elsewhere in Europe in C19 and C20, often for *synagogues. It was also an ingredient of Catalan *Modernisme.

L & D (1986)

historic character Used in planning parlance to describe structures and features of architectural and historic interest. The term might be extended to a whole street, block, or area.

Historicism 1. Architecture strongly influenced by the past, especially Revivalist architecture (*Greek, *Gothic, *Early Christian, *Romanesque, *Italianate, *Renaissance, the various *Henri and *Louis styles, *Rundbogenstil, *Elizabethan, *Jacobethan, *Tudor, and other Revivals). **2.** Term used to describe a tendency among some architects to insist their work was part of a *continuous* process of cultural evolution that was capable of historical analysis. Revivals were facilitated by the many lavish and scholarly publications, notably those based on archaeology and meticulous measured drawings that were such a feature of the late C18 and C19, collections of architectural casts and details, and the desire to enter into the essence of a style or styles. Virtually all the way through C19, concerns to find a style appropriate to the time (and for the many new and unprecedented building-types) were voiced (notably by *Hübsch), and by the time *Shaw, *Webb, and others were working in the 1870s a theory evolved that, by mixing styles in a free, eclectic way, some kind of new style would emerge from the *mélange*. Although conventional wisdom holds that the so-called *Queen-Anne and *Free styles were relatively free from Historicism, such a view is demonstrably false, while *Art Nouveau, supposedly a reaction against historical revivals, was too firmly embedded in late Gothic and *Celtic Revivals, and even (obviously) in *Rococo, to be regarded as such, in spite of the claims of its protagonists and its later apologists. The *International Modernists' rejection of history (and, supposedly, of all styles (save their own)) in turn created in C20 reactions, where certain architects, perceiving that a serious disruption had taken place, attempted to consider the nature of their own relationship with history, and to rebuild bridges to a great cultural past that had been arrogantly dismissed as 'irrelevant'.

AHR, lix (1954), 568–77; (1987); Crook (1987); Döhmer (1976); Hn (1992); Pe (1960, 1968); Streich (1984); J.T (1996); D.Wa (1977)

Hitchcock, Henry-Russell (1903–87) American architectural critic/historian. He published (1929) *Modern Architecture*, the first English-language book on the subject, and he and Philip *Johnson organized (1932) the celebrated exhibition at MoMA, NYC, which brought European architects such as Le *Corbusier, *Gropius, *Oud, and *Mies to the notice of the American public. In the same year Hitchcock and Johnson published *The International Style: Architecture since 1922*: the term *International Style was coined by **Alfred**

H. Barr (1902–81—Director of MoMA, who had invited Hitchcock and Johnson to organize the exhibition) and Hitchcock. Having written about F.L.L.*Wright (1928, 1942), Oud (1931), and H.H. *Richardson (1936), Hitchcock turned his attention to C19 architecture with *Early Victorian Architecture* (1954) and *Architecture: Nineteenth and Twentieth Centuries* (1958). Later still he wrote perceptively about South-German *Rococo (1968), and near the end of his life his first book on German-*Renaissance architecture was published (1981). The scope of his scholarship and interests was vast, and his output enormous.

Hi (1931, 1938, 1939, 1954, 1966, 1966a, 1966b, 1968, 1968a, 1973, 1976, 1977, 1981, 1993); Hi & Johnson (1966); Hi & Seale (1976); Searing (ed.) (1983)

Hittorff, Jakob Ignaz, *known as* **Jacques-Ignace** (1792–1867) German-born architect/ scholar, he settled in Paris (1811), and studied under *Percier from whom he acquired his 'liberal' *Classicism and eclectic philosophy. He worked with *Bélanger on the creation of the iron-and-glass *dome of the *Halle au Blé*, Paris (1808–13), during which he met **Joseph Lecointe** (1783–1858), which led to the two men being appointed Architects for all ceremonial occasions after Bélanger's death (1818): they quickly became fashionable, designing interiors for wealthy patrons. Hittorff travelled in England, Germany, and Italy (1820–4) during which he became interested in the problem of *polychromy in Ancient-Greek architecture and, with *Zanth, published *Architecture antique de la Sicile* (1827): this had accounts of traces of painted decorations on Greek temples, yet the book was publicly attacked. However, he became one of the leaders of the *Société Libre des Beaux-Arts*, publicized his ideas, and obtained various important commissions, including alterations to the *Place de la Concorde* (1832–40) and the *Champs-Élysées* (1834–40). His first great Parisian building was *St-Vincent-de-Paul*, sketched out first by **Jean-Baptiste Lepère** (1761–1844) in 1824 (the year in which Lepère became Hittorff's father-in-law), but completely redesigned and built by Hittorff (1830–48). It is a particularly beautiful *basilica in the *Early-Christian style, with two rows of superimposed *colonnades carrying the timber *trusses of the roof, an apsidal *chancel, and the whole interior strongly coloured in a manner Hittorff insisted was a *modern expression* of Greek Antiquity: its exterior has an *Ionic *portico set against a plain *façade flanked by two square towers, and the church is not only important for its use of colour, but because it anticipates late-C19 *Beaux-Arts *Classicism. Hittorff wished to extend polychromy to the exterior, proposing *Lave emaillée* (enamelled fired metal panels, invented 1827, and manufactured by **Hachette & Cie**

from 1833 for fire-surrounds, table-tops, and even *altar-facings) for the wall of the portico as well as lavish colour elsewhere, but the plans were blocked by *Haussmann after he inspected a trial section. Nevertheless, *St-Vincent-de-Paul* was an important landmark in the development of a free *eclecticism that was to be of such significance in C19 French architecture. His most innovative structures, however, were *Rotonde des Panoramas* (1838–9—destroyed 1857), with its suspended roof, the *Cirque National* (1839–41), with elegant lattice-trusses, and the *Cirque Napoléon* (1851–2—later *Cirque d'Hiver*) also with lattice-trusses, which established his reputation as an innovative architect.

A renewal of interest in polychromy (1850s) encouraged Hittorff to bring out his *Architecture polychrome chez les Grecs* (1851) which silenced his enemies. He enjoyed favour under the new regime of **Napoléon III** (*r*.1852–70), designing a series of handsome houses in Paris in the vicinity of the *Place de l'Étoile* (1852–5), the *Mairie* of the First *Arrondissement* (1855–61), the *Grand Hôtel du Louvre*, *Place du Théâtre Français* (1856–9—with **Alfred Armand** (1805–88), J.-A.-F.-A.Pellechet (1829–1903), and C.*Rohault de Fleury), and, finally, his best-known building, the *Gare du Nord* (1859–66), where his main contribution appears to have been a 'tidying-up' of what was essentially a design by the Railway Company's engineers. Nevertheless, it is an excellent example of how the new *Beaux-Arts* Classicism could be used in conjunction with iron-and-glass structures: some trusses were based on designs by **Antoine-Rémi Polonceau** (1778–1847), and all the castings done in Glasgow.

Hammer (1968); Hi (1977); Hittorff (1851, 1987); Hittorff & Lecointe (1827); Hittorff & Zanth (1827, 1835); P (1982); D.Schneider (1977)

Hitzig, Georg Heinrich Friedrich (1811–81) German architect, pupil of *Schinkel, he spent time in Paris where he absorbed influences from *Percier and *Fontaine. With *Knoblauch et al. he helped to consolidate the style of Berlin's domestic architecture in a series of exquisite *villas (1840s–50s). He also used brick to considerable effect, taking his cue from Schinkel's *Bauakademie* (1831). Most of his buildings have been destroyed, including the Kronenberg Palace, Warsaw (1866–70), and the *Börse*, Berlin (1859–64), on both of which he published monographs (1875 and 1867 respectively).

B-S (1977); Hitzig (1850–9, 1867, 1875)

Hoare, Henry (1705–85) English banker/patron, he inherited Stourhead, Wilts., from his father, **Henry Hoare** (1677–1725), and from 1743 transformed the gardens into a Claudian landscape (historically important as an early exemplar of the **jardin anglais*), creating a lake by damming the River Stour, and employing *Flitcroft to design the *temples of Flora (1745), Apollo (1765), and the Pantheon (1753–4—**John Michael Rysbrack** (1694–1770) contributed statues of Hercules (1747–52) and Flora (1759–60) for the Pantheon). Hoare's grandson, **Richard Colt Hoare** (1758–1838—2nd Baronet from 1787), added some buildings, removed others, and planted many exotic trees and shrubs, thereby radically altering the aesthetic of the garden.

Mowl (2000); *ODNB* (2004); Tay (2006)

Hoban, James (1758–1831) Irish-born, he emigrated (1785) to America. He won the competition to design the President's House, Washington, DC, with a proposal (1792) originally based on Leinster House, Dublin, but altered at the request of Washington and *Jefferson. As built, the White House, (1793–1801, rebuilt 1814–29) was derived from plate 41 of *Gibbs's *A Book of Architecture* (1728). His other Washington buildings (hotels, houses, and Government buildings) no longer exist.

Architecture, **xi** (1981), 66–82; *ARe*, **xi** (1901), 581–9; *DAB* (1932); Goode (1979); *JSAH*, **xxviii**/2 (May 1969), 135–6; Maddex (1973); Reiff (1977); Ryan & Guinness (1980)

Hodges, Desmond (1928–2012) Irish architect, appointed (1972) Director of the Edinburgh New Town Conservation Committee, in which capacity he used his diplomatic skills to ensure no further damage was done to that masterpiece of *Georgian town-planning. The first project, 23 Fettes Row, was completed (1975), and by 1994 (when Hodges retired) he had overseen over 1,000 refurbishments and preserved the integrity of a part of the city that, prior to 1972, had started to be badly damaged by crass new developments and insensitive alterations. He co-authored a book on care and *conservation of Georgian houses.

Davey *et al.* (1978); *The Herald* (13 Feb. 2013), Obits; Hodges (1982); *The Scotsman* (8 Dec. 2012), Obits

Hodges, William (1744–97) English painter, specializing in topographical views, he accompanied **Captain James Cook** (1728–79) on his expedition to the South Seas (1772–5) as the official artist. Under the aegis of **Warren Hastings** (1732–1818) he went to India (1779) and published *Select Views in India* (1785–8) followed by *Travels in India* (1793) which had a considerable impact, popularizing *Hindoo and *Indian architecture.

ODNB (2004); J.T (1996)

Hoff, Robert van't (1887–1979) Dutch architect, he studied in England, where he was first influenced by the *Arts-and-Crafts Movement, by the *Glasgow School, *Lethaby, and then by more radical ideas. His first realized designs were a house/studio for **Augustus John** (1878–1961) at 28 Mallord Street, Chelsea, London (1913–14), and *Løvdalla*, Huis ter Heide, near Utrecht (1911). He visited the USA (1914), where he saw buildings by F.L.L.*Wright, notably the Unity Temple and various houses at Oak Park, Chicago, IL. On his return to Europe the influence of Wright is clear in van't Hoff's summer-house for **J.N.Verloop** (1914) and the *villa for **A.B.Henny** (1915–19), both at Huis ter Heide: the latter established his reputation. From 1917 he was closely associated with *De* *Stijl, giving the movement monetary help and contributing articles to the journal. He became (1918) a Communist, and believed that the architectural/artistic 'avant-garde' would unite with the 'proletariat' to create an improbable artistic paradise, but when the great 'revolution' failed to occur, he abandoned *De Stijl*, and settled in England (1933) with a commune of anarchists. He died in Hants.

Bouw, **xii** (1979), 6–8, **xiii** (1979), 17–23; *De Stijl*, **i**/5 (1918), 57–9, **i**/6 (1918), 71–2, **ii**/3 (1919), 31–2, **ii**/4 (1919), 40–2, **ii**/5 (1919), 54–5, **ii**/10 (1919), 114–6; Fanelli (1968); Jaffé (1956); Rijksmuseum (1975); Zevi (1974)

Hoffmann, Josef Franz Maria (1870–1956) Austro-Hungarian architect, he studied with *Hasenauer and *Wagner in Vienna. He became involved in the Vienna *Sezession (he greatly admired, and was friendly with, C.R.*Mackintosh) and, with **Koloman Moser** (1868–1918) and **Fritz Wärndorfer** (1868–1923), founded (1903) the **Wiener Werkstätte*. He absorbed *Beaux-Arts methods of composition, the Classically inspired style of Wagner, the freer style of the British *Arts-and-Crafts movement, and early in the C20 began to simplify and purify his architecture, moving away from the *Art Nouveau of the early *Sezession*. His white cubic building at the Purkersdorf Sanatorium (1903–5) led to a blocky style, the most developed example of which was the *Adolphe Stoclet* house, Brussels (1904–11): for this Hoffmann and other artists of the *Werkstätte* designed virtually everything (the building was sumptuously finished in panels of *marble framed with bronze, while some of the interiors (notably the dining-room) were also finished in marble, with glittering mosaics designed by **Gustav Klimt** (1862–1918)). His *Ast* (1909–11) and *Skywa-Primavesi* (1913–15) houses, both in Vienna, showed a profound shift towards *Neo-Classicism that was a general tendency of the time. Later works were never again of such distinction: they included the Austrian Pavilion, *Exposition Internationale des Arts-Décoratifs*, Paris (1924–5), an asymmetrical composition with strong horizontal bandings on the walls; the *Ast* House, near Velden, Austria (1923–4), and the

Austrian Pavilion, Venice Biennale (1934–5). In 1953–4 he designed housing on the *Heiligenstädterstrasse*, Vienna.

Kleiner (1927); Noever & Oberhuber (1987); P (1982); Rochowanski (1950); Sekler (1985); J.T (1996); Ve (1956); Weiser (1930)

Höger, Johann Friedrich, *called* **Fritz** (1877–1949) German Expressionist architect, he was a student of the *Backstein* (brick) architecture of North Germany, particularly interested in the decorative traditions of brickwork and the effects of light and shade on brick buildings. He helped to evolve the Hamburg *Kontorhaus* style, notably with his *Klostertorhof Kontorhaus* (1910–11), and (especially) the *Chilehaus* (1923–4), a vast 12-storey block with curved *façades and a ship-like form. He also designed the *Sprinkenhof Kontorhaus*, Hamburg (1927–43), the *Rathaus*, Wilhelmshaven-Rüstringen (1928–9), the *Evangelischekirche*, *Hohenzollernplatz*, Wilmersdorf, Berlin (1929–30), the City Hospital, Delmenhorst (1930), and the Siebetsburg Housing, Wilhelmshaven (1935–8).

Be (ed.) (1977); Pehnt (1973); J.T (1996); Westphal (ed.) (1938)

hoggin *or* **hogging 1.** Siftings or screenings separated by a sieve from the stones of rough pit-gravel, used for *paths, while the larger stones are employed in carriage-ways. **2.** *Camber of a road.

Hohenberg, Johann Ferdinand Hetzendorf von (1732–1816) Architect of the arcaded *Gloriette*, the celebrated *eye-catcher in the park at *Schönbrunn*, Vienna (1773–5), an early revival of the *Cinquecento* style, as well as the 'Roman Ruin' (1778), inspired by *Piranesi. He redesigned (1772) the *landscape-garden at *Schönbrunn*, and is credited with the interior of the theatre at *Schloss Schönbrunn*. He designed gardens at Vöslau (from 1774) and Schönau (from 1796), where *grottoes are among the various *fabriques. His *Maison de Caprice*, Laxenburg (1799), is an outstanding *fabrique* in a variety of styles (including *Gothic and *Egyptian Revival): indeed, Hohenberg was a master of many styles, anticipating C19 *eclecticism. His *Neo-Classical church, Austerlitz, Moravia (1786) is remarkably pure, but his *Palais Fries-Pallavicini*, *Josefsplatz*, Vienna (1783–4), attracted criticism because of its austere *façade.

J.T (1996); W-R (1970)

Holabird & Roche American architects. **William Holabird** (1854–1923) settled in Chicago, IL, where he worked (1875) in *Jenney's office before establishing (1880) a practice with O.C. *Simonds, joined the following year by **Martin Roche** (1853–1927). The firm was commissioned (1886) to design the 12-storey Tacoma Building (completed 1889—demolished 1929), with a structure of cast-iron columns, wrought-iron beams, brickwork, concrete, and steel, the whole clad in *terracotta and glass: it established a skeletal structure for *skyscrapers and the *Chicago School style. The firm's office-buildings had external walls employing the *Chicago window, continuous *piers, recessed panels, and terracotta ornament. Good examples are the Marquette (1894–5) Brooks (1909–10), and McClurg (1899–1900) Buildings.

Br (1992); Bruegmann (1991, 1997); Ct (1964, 1973); *JSAH*, xviii/4 (Dec. 1959), 126–39; Mujica (1929); J.T (1996); Zu (ed.) (1987, 1993).

Holabird & Root Successor-firm to *Holabird & Roche, founded (1927) by **John Augur Holabird** (1886–1945) and **John Wellborn Root, Jr.** (1887–1963). They designed several *Art-Deco *skyscrapers including the Palmolive (1928–9), Board of Trade (1929–30), *Daily News* (1928–9), and Travel and Transport (1930–3) Buildings, all Chicago, IL. Later, they were responsible for the Illinois Bell Telephone Company Building, Northbrook (1970–3), the Hollister Incorporated Building, Libertyville (1979–81), and the Motorola Center, Schaumberg (1990–4), all in IL.

Br (1992)

Holden, Charles Henry (1875–1960) English architect, he worked for a while with *Ashbee before joining (1899) H.P.*Adams as an assistant, becoming a partner (1907). Among their earliest buildings was the Belgrave Hospital for Children, Clapham Road, Lambeth, London (1900–3), a complex composition on a tight site, with elevations in an *Arts-and-Crafts style influenced by Philip *Webb and Henry *Wilson. His Central Reference Library, Deanery Street, Bristol (1906), avoided fashionable *Neo-Baroque for stripped *Neo-Tudor, and at the new Library (1902–4) for the Incorporated Law Society, Chancery Lane, London, an assured understanding of *Mannerism was displayed. The King Edward VII Sanatorium, Midhurst, Sussex (1903–6), followed, by which time **Lionel Godfrey Pearson** (1879–1953) had joined the firm. Adams & Holden's Headquarters for the British Medical Association (later Zimbabwe House) in The Strand (1906–8) developed Mannerist themes, with nude sculptured figures (mutilated) by (Sir) **Jacob Epstein** (1880–1959—with whom Holden also collaborated in the design of **Oscar Wilde's** (1854–1900) tomb (1911–12), *Père-Lachaise* Cemetery, Paris). The firm became **Adams, Holden, & Pearson** (1913), and Holden was appointed one of the four principal architects of the Imperial War Graves Commission for which he designed 67 cemeteries. From 1924 Holden worked with **Frank Pick** (1878–1941) to design more than 50 London Underground Railway Stations that represent a peak of rational English design: much influenced by Scandinavian and Netherlandish architecture, they have a clear, uncluttered geometry, and include Arnos Grove (1932), Boston Manor (1934), Southgate (1935), and Sudbury Town (1930-1). Holden also designed shelters, signs, lamp-standards, platforms, and much else for the London Passenger Transport Board.

The firm could be relied upon to create monumental effects by piling up blocky, cubic masses, as in Pearson's designs for the Royal Artillery Memorial, Hyde Park Corner (1921-5), with sculptures by **Charles Sergeant Jagger** (1885-1934), but Holden's Headquarters Building for London Transport at 55 Broadway, Westminster (1927-9), is an even more sophisticated essay in massing: Epstein, **Eric Gill** (1882-1940), and **Henry Moore** (1898-1986) were responsible for the external sculpture. From 1931 he designed new buildings for the University of London, including the Senate House (which lacks the sculpture intended for it), and from the 1939-45 war was involved in redevelopment plans for London, working with *Holford and Myles *Wright.

AR, clviii/946 (Dec. 1975), 349-56; Artifex, iii (1969), 35-53; B, cxli (1931), 396-401; A.S.Gray (1985); Karol & Ae (1988); ODNB (2004); Pe (1968); P (1982); Se (ed.) (1975), 386-92; Stamp (1977); J.T (1996); vV (1993)

Holford, William Graham, Lord (1907-75) South-African born, he trained under *Reilly at Liverpool. During the 1939-45 war he helped to form the framework of British town-planning legislation, and was involved with *Abercrombie in creating the County and Greater London Plans. He proposed development plans for the Universities of Liverpool (1949-54), Exeter (1955-75—which destroyed *Harris's far more sensitive scheme), and Kent (1958), and, with *Holden, the Plan for the City of London (1946-7). His less than satisfactory designs for the precinct of St Paul's Cathedral, London (1956), did not stand the test of time, and the area was redeveloped from the end of C20. Nevertheless, his influence as an architect/planner was widespread in the UK during the first three decades after 1945, but his reputation, while dazzling his contemporaries, failed to outlive him for long.

G.Cherry (1986); E (1994); ODNB (2004); J.T (1996)

Holl, Elias (1573-1646) Leading German *Renaissance architect: after a visit to Italy (1600-1), he was responsible for the city of Augsburg's official buildings from 1602, designing the Giesshaus (1601), Zeughaus (1602-7), Siegelhaus (1604-6—destroyed 1809), Metzge (1609), and many other structures. His most important building was the Rathaus (1614-20), the central section of which has all the verticality of a gabled German house, but on either side the elevations are more Classical and serene. His Heilige Geist Spital (1626-30) is marked by clear cubic forms, a separation of individual elements, the subordination of decoration, and a two-storey *arcade around a *court. Among his works outside Augsburg, his designs for the Willibaldsburg, Eichstätt (1609-10), are the most significant.

Architectura, xv (1985), 1-12; E.Hempel (1965); Hieber (1923); Hi (1981); Roeck (1985, 1985a); Schürer (1938); J.T (1996); R.Walter (1972)

Hollamby, Edward (1921-99) English architect. A lifelong devotee of William *Morris, he purchased (1952) Philip *Webb's Red House, Bexley Heath (1859-60), which he meticulously restored. He worked in local-authority offices, first with the LCC (1949-62), and then with the London Borough of Lambeth, for which he was director of architecture, planning, and development (1969-81). During his time with the LCC he worked on numerous housing-schemes, including Thamesmead, and at Lambeth he began to promote low-rise estates. Appointed chief architect/planner to the London Docklands Development Commission (1981), he drew up a design-guide for the Isle of Dogs, promoting Docklands Light Railway, and preparing strategies for the Royal Docks.

The Guardian (24 Jan. 2000), Obits

Holland, Henry (1745-1806) Leading English *Georgian architect, he became (1771) the partner of Lancelot 'Capability' *Brown, whose daughter he married, and with whom he built Claremont House, Esher, Surrey (1771-4). He evolved an elegant Neo-Classical style to rival that of the *Adams, as can be seen at Brooks's Club, 60 St James's Street, London (1776-8). The success of this building made his name known in aristocratic circles, and he designed a number of pleasing country-houses, including Berrington Hall, near Leominster, Herefs. (1778-81); the remodelling of Woburn Abbey, Beds. (1787-1802), including the entrance *portico (demolished), conservatory (later sculpture-gallery), and Chinese *dairy; the remodelling of Althorp, Northants. (1787-9—including *cladding the building with *mathematical tiles); and alterations at Broadlands, Hants. (1788-92), and Southill, Beds. (1796-1800). His greatest work was probably the remodelling of Carlton House, Pall Mall, London (1783-96), including the *Corinthian portico and *Ionic screen (all demolished, 1827-8). He also designed The Albany, Piccadilly, London (1803-4), and developed Hans Town, Chelsea, from 1771, including Sloane Street, Cadogan Place, and the polygonal Hans Place, but the fabric has mostly been redeveloped. As an architect he was influenced by French sources, notably *Gondouin,

*Patte, and *Peyre, but, unlike *Chambers, he used *Greek elements in his designs.

Co (2008); Stroud (1950, 1966); J.T (1996)

Hollein, Hans (1934–2014). Austrian architect. He established his reputation with small, well-crafted shops, including the Retti Candle Shop (1964–5), Schullin Jewellery Shop with its 'cracked' front (1972–4), and the Austrian State Travel Agency with its palm-tree supports (1976–8), all in Vienna, which employ materials such as marble, brass, stainless steel, and chrome, detailed with meticulous care. Less happy, however, is the relationship of the new fronts with the existing façades into which they are set, while the use of themes such as the apparently haphazard crack suggests tension and disruption of perfection. Much admired have been the Städtisches Museum, Abteiberg, Mönchengladbach (1972–82), with a grid structure that breaks down in the corner, and the Museum of Modern Art, Frankfurt (1987–91). The Haas House, near the Cathedral in Vienna (1987–90), might suggest that ideas that work on the scale of a shop-front are less successful on a large, prominent building on a key site within a historic urban centre. His last European project was the cone-shaped Vulcania (Museum of Volcanology), Auvergne, France (2002).

A (1994); AR, clxxii/1030 (Dec. 1982), 53–71; E (1994); Klotz (1988); Pettena (ed.) (1988); The Times (6 May 2014), 50; J.T (1996)

hollow gorge *Cavetto or *Egyptian *gorge. *Other compounds include*:

hollow moulding: *trochilus, *cavetto, or *scotia;
hollow square: *Romanesque *moulding consisting of a series of indented *pyramids, the base coinciding with the *face.

hollow walls See BRICK.

Holy Loft *Rood-loft, -beam, or -screen.

Holy Sepulchre The Church of the Holy Sepulchre, or *Anastasis* (Resurrection), Jerusalem, was one of **Emperor Constantine**'s (*r.*324–37) most important church foundations. Essentially a *rotunda (an inner ring of columns and *piers carrying the *dome) with an *annular *ambulatory contained by a wall from which three *apses projected, it was not unlike Imperial *mausolea such as *Santa Costanza*, Rome. It contained a tiny temple-like structure encasing the tomb itself. Both church and shrine were destroyed (1009), but rebuilt (C11) in a *Byzantine-*Romanesque style, the plan remaining similar. The basic form was the precedent for many cemetery-chapels, *martyria*, and churches (notably the round churches at Cambridge, the Temple (London), and Northampton), while the shrine inspired progeny, including *Alberti's *Rucellai Chapel, San Pancrazio*, Florence (1460–7).

N.Brooks (1921)

Holy-water stone *or* **stock** See STOUP.

Holzmeister, Clemens (1886–1983) Austrian architect, much of his work drew on historical precedent, even when he was attracted to *Expressionism, as in the City Crematorium, Vienna (1921–3). His Eichmann Country House, Litzlberg, Seewalchen (1926–8), was almost Arcadian in its relation to nature, but his more monumental buildings, such as those for the Government in Ankara, Turkey (1931–4), show his grasp of a tradition based on *Classicism. He was responsible for developing the *Festspielhaus*, *Hofstallgasse*, Salzburg (1926–60), tucked in between a rocky eminence and *Fischer von Erlach's *Kollegienkirche*, and built many churches, among which *Maria Hilf*, Bregenz-Vorkloster (1924–31), *Judas Thaddeus in der Krim*, Vienna (1924–32), *St Adalbert*, Berlin (1933), *Seipel-Dollfuss* Memorial, Vienna (1933–4), and the Evangelical Church, Kitzbühel (1960–2), may be mentioned.

P.Becker (1966); E (1994); Gregor (1953); Holzmeister (1937, 1976); Rigele & Loewit (eds) (2000); Weiser (1927)

Honeyman, John (1831–1914) Scots architect, he practised in Glasgow from 1854, later joined (1885) by **John Keppie** (1862–1945) and C.R. *Mackintosh (1904). The firm became **Keppie & Henderson** (1945). Honeyman's works include the *First-Pointed Lansdowne United Presbyterian Church, Great Western Road, Glasgow (1862–3), with an extremely tall, thin spire; Smith's Warehouse, later the *Ca d'Oro*, Gordon and Union Streets (with its upper *façade of iron and glass—1872); Westbourne Church (1881); the refronting of the Mitchell Street *façade of the *Glasgow Herald* Building (with Keppie and Mackintosh—1893–5); and many other fine buildings, including the Martyr's Public School (1896–8—with Keppie and Mackintosh). He published *Open Spaces in Towns* (1883) and works on municipal improvements and working-class housing.

DW; G & W (1987); WRH (1990)

honeysuckle Greek enrichment resembling a honeysuckle flower, and called *anthemion* or *palmette*.

Hontañon Family Father and son, they worked on some of the last *Gothic buildings in Spain. **Juan Gil de Hontañon** (*c.*1480–1526) worked on Sigüenza Cathedral, and designed and built *mortuary-chapels in the *hall-church of *San Antolin, Medina del Campo*, Valladolid, and the Church of *Santa Clara*, Briviesca, Burgos (both *c.*1503–*c.*1523). He worked (1505–16) on the *cloister and *chapter-house of Palencia Cathedral, and was appointed (1512) Master-Mason at Salamanca Cathedral: by 1520 the building had risen to the *vaults of the side-chapels.

He designed the new *crossing-lantern at Seville Cathedral with its complicated rib-vaults (1513-19) to replace *Colonia's structure that had collapsed. From 1524 he was engaged at Segovia Cathedral, the building of which was carried out by his son, **Rodrigo Gil de Hontañon** (1500-77), who seems to have worked at Santiago, probably with *Álava (1521), and was consulted at Valladolid before becoming Master-Mason (1530) at Astorga Cathedral, where he probably built the *nave. He then worked on the *transepts at Salamanca from 1537, and then, or simultaneously, at the cloisters of Santiago. He also contributed at Plasencia and designed the *chevet of Segovia Cathedral (from c.1560). At Salamanca he introduced *Renaissance ideas, and at the *façade of the College of *San Ildefonso*, Alcalá de Henares, near Madrid (1537-53), the style is entirely Renaissance, of the *Plateresque* type. He designed Monterey Palace (1539-41), the *Monasterio de Bernardas de Jesús* (from 1542), both in Salamanca, and the Church of *La Magdalena*, Valladolid (1566-72). He wrote *Compendio de Arquitectura y Simetria* (c.1560s), which exists in a distorted copy made (1681) by one **Simon Garcia**.

Aznar (ed.) (1941); CG (1951, 1953); *JSAH*, **xli/4** (Dec. 1982), 281-93; K & S (1959); Pereda de la Reguera (ed.) (1951); J.T (1996)

hood 1. Projecting cover to a fireplace to increase the draught and remove smoke, attached to the wall behind. **2.** Canopy or cover above an aperture, such as a *doorway, to protect it from the weather. **3.** *Drip-stone or *label over the *heads of apertures, arched or rectangular, usually with label-stops at each end.

Hood, Raymond Mathewson (1881-1934) American architect. With John Mead *Howells he won the competition (1922) to design the *Chicago Tribune* Tower, Chicago, IL. (built 1923-5), a high point of *Beaux-Arts* *eclecticism with a *Gothic superstructure (Hood had studied (1905-6, 1908-10) in Paris). From 1924 he was in partnership with **Frederick A. Godley** (1886-1961) and *Fouilhoux, and from 1931 with Fouilhoux only. The *Tribune* Building was followed by the American Radiator Company Building, NYC (1923-5—now the Bryant Park hotel, converted by **David Chipperfield Architects** (1998-2001)) with a black exterior and gilded *pinnacles and trims, and the Masonic Temple, Scranton, PA (1929), again Gothic. With **Stanley Gordon Jeeves** (c.1888-1964) he designed Ideal (later Palladium) House, at the corner of Argyll and Great Marlborough Streets, London (1929), a building completely clad in black Swedish granite with cast-bronze gilded and enamelled *Art-Deco detailing. The *Daily News* Building, NYC (1929-30—with

Howells), was devoid of any historical references, and was a *skyscraper with vertical window-strips set between continuous vertical solid strips, a design that was to be influential for the next three decades, notably at the Rockefeller Center, NYC (1931-4), for which he and Fouilhoux acted as consultants. The McGraw-Hill Building, NYC (1930-2) (with Fouilhoux and others), combined bold horizontal bands with central vertical strips, paving the way for lighter cladding and the *International style in skyscraper design.

AA Files, **vii** (1984), 30-43; *AF*, **lxii** (1935), 127-33; J.Curl (2005); Hood (1931); Kilham (1974); P (1982); Schwartzmann (1962); Stern (1982); J.T (1996)

Hooke, Robert (1635-1703) English scientist and colleague of *Wren, he became one of the three Surveyors (the others were *Jerman and Peter *Mills) for the reconstruction of the City of London after the Great Fire (1666), and was the author of a plan (now lost) for a new layout (not implemented). He seems, with Wren, to have designed the Monument (1671-6), and collaborated on some of the City churches (he was probably responsible for St Benet, Paul's Wharf (1678-84)). He designed Bethlehem Hospital, Moorfields, London (1675-6—demolished), Escot House, Devon (1677-88 demolished, illustrated in vol. **i** of *Vitruvius Britannicus*); the Royal College of Physicians, Warwick Lane, London (1672-8—demolished); Ragley Hall, Warwicks. (1679-83), subsequently altered by *Gibbs (1750-5) and James *Wyatt (c.1780); and many other buildings, most of which have been demolished or altered beyond recognition. His planning was strongly influenced by French precedents. He was one of the first to assert the true principles of *arcuated construction, notably in relation to *catenary curves and ellipses.

Bradley & Pe (1997); Co (2008); Downes (1966); *Early Science in Oxford*, **x** (1935), 69-265; 'Espinasse (1962); Jardine (2003); Keynes (1960); *ODNB* (2004)

hoop-tie Metal chain or loop tying the lower part of a *dome or *cupola to prevent it spreading, thus avoiding *buttresses.

Hope, Alexander James Beresford (1820-87) English writer/collector/patron, son of Thomas *Hope. At Cambridge he befriended **Benjamin Webb** (1819-85), co-founder (with **John Mason Neale** (1818-66)) of the *Cambridge Camden Society (*see* ECCLESIOLOGY). On inheriting the English estate of his stepfather, **General William Carr Beresford** (1768-1854—**1st Viscount Beresford** from 1823), he changed his name to **Beresford Hope**. He became the most energetic and influential lay-member of the Society, helped to edit *The Ecclesiologist*, and promoted 'urban minsters' using tough materials and structural *polychromy: his was the guiding force that helped to create the Society's exemplary All Saints, Margaret Street, London (1849–59), by *Butterfield. His *The English Cathedral of the Nineteenth Century* (1861) and other writings were important influences on the development of the *Gothic Revival, on the planning of Anglican churches, and on the growing High-Church party with its emphasis on symbolism and ritual within an appropriate architectural setting. He was President of the RIBA (1865–7).

AH, viii (1965), 73–9; C.Brooks (1999); J.Curl (2007); *ODNB* (2004); J.T (1996); J.White (1962)

Hope, Thomas (1769–1831) British connoisseur/virtuoso, avid collector of antiques as well as modern Neo-Classical sculpture, he became an arbiter of Taste by exhibiting his collections and publishing books including *Household Furniture and Interior Decoration* (1807), *Costumes of the Ancients* (1809), *An Historical Essay on Architecture* (1835), and *Anastasius, or Memoirs of a Modern Greek, written at the Close of the Eighteenth Century* (1819). A member of the Society of *Dilettanti, he was asked to comment on James *Wyatt's designs for Downing College, Cambridge, and published his opinions in *Observations on the Plans and Elevations . . . for Downing College . . .* (1804) which favoured the *Greek Revival: the result was the building of *Wilkins's College in chaste Greek garb, and the establishment of Hope as a champion of modernity.

Influenced by the example of his second cousin, **Henry Hope** (1735–1811), Hope designed two remarkable houses for his collections. At Duchess Street, Portland Place, London, he altered and enlarged (1799–1804, 1819) a house designed by Robert *Adam (demolished 1851), adding picture- and sculpture-galleries, with other rooms (decorated in *Hindoo, *Egyptian-Revival, Greek, and Neo-Classical styles) to display Greek vases, Graeco-Egyptian furniture designed by Hope, and other objects. These interiors were published in *Household Furniture* (1807). Like *Soane's house, the building was open to the public, and played no small part in popularizing *Neo-Classicism (the picture-gallery was one of the earliest English interiors to be articulated with the Greek-*Doric Order). The other house was The Deepdene, near Dorking, Surrey, enlarged (1818–19, 1823—with the assistance of William *Atkinson) in an asymmetrical *Picturesque yet Classical manner, and containing much Egyptian ornament, including a bed derived from published French sources. Many of Hope's designs were related to the *Empire style of *Percier and *Fontaine.

Apollo (Sept. 1987), 162–77; Co (2008); J.Curl (2005); Hope (1804, 1835, 1962, 1971); *ODNB* (2004); J.T (1996); D.Wa (1968); D.Wa & Hewat-Jaboor (eds) (2008)

Hopkins, Sir Michael (1935–) *See* HIGH TECH.

Hopper, Thomas (1776–1856) English eclectic *Regency architect, his extensive works at Craven Cottage, Fulham, London (1806—demolished), included an exotic *Egyptian-Revival room and a *Gothic dining-room. He designed the Gothic *conservatory at Carlton House, Pall Mall (1807—demolished 1827-8), in the manner of **Henry VII**'s (*r.*1485–1509) chapel at Westminster Abbey, but with cast-iron *tracery-panels of the bogus fan-vaulting filled with coloured glass: it should be recognized as a pioneering work of metal-and-glass construction. Thereafter he had a successful practice as a country-house architect, designing in a number of styles (he insisted it was the architect's business to 'understand all styles, and to be prejudiced in favour of none'): the buildings include Leigh Court, near Bristol, Som. (1814—Greek *Ionic), Gosford Castle, Co. Armagh (1819–21—*Romanesque Revival), Penrhyn Castle, Caernarfonshire (*c.*1819–*c.*1844—again Romanesque Revival), Margam Abbey, Glamorgan (1830–5—*Tudor Gothic), Wivenhoe Park, Essex (1846–9—*Jacobethan), and Amesbury House, Wilts. (1834–40—*Palladian). Other works included The County Gaol, Springfield, Chelmsford, Essex (1819–26 and 1845–8—with a sombre *Tuscan Order); the Carlton Club, 69–70 St James's Street, London (1826–7—in a *Palladian manner); the Church of St John the Baptist, Southend, Essex (1841–2—*Gothic Revival); and the Church of St Thomas, Butterton, Staffs. (1844–5—substantial *Neo-Norman).

R.Brown (ed.) (1985); Co (2008); Crook & Port (1973); J.Curl (2005, 2011a); Hussey (1958, 1965); J.T (1996)

hopper-head *See* RAINWATER-HEAD.

Horder, Percy Richard Morley (1870–1944) English architect, trained by *Devey. From *c.*1902 his domestic designs were published, and he worked (1919–25) in partnership with **Bryant Alfred Poulter** (1881–1972). Horder's houses were cleverly and practically planned; he took enormous care to relate his houses to their gardens; and his handling of building-materials was extremely sensitive (e.g. *Ard na Sidhe*, near Killorglin, Co. Kerry (1915)). His own dwelling was the medieval (*c.*1400) Court House, East Meon, Hants., which he meticulously restored. He also designed Cheshunt College (1913), the National Institute of Agricultural Botany (1919), both in Cambridge; new works for Somerville College (1934) in Oxford; and a group of buildings in Italian-*Renaissance style (1925–8) at Nottingham University. His pupils called him 'Holy Murder', but he was a good, if underestimated, architect.

A.S.Gray (1985); *ODNB* (2004); pk

Horeau, Héctor (1801–72) French architect, he built little, but published designs for urban improvements, including iron-and-glass structures, early proposals for the markets in Paris (1844), a *jardin d'hiver* at Lyons (1846–7), and a (1849) design for a vast iron glazed building for London's 1851 exhibition, thus pre-dating *Paxton's realized scheme. He designed Pippingford Park, Nutley, Sussex (1857–8—in a *Second-Empire style—destroyed), and published the spectacular coloured *Panorama d'Égypte et de Nubie* (1841–6).

Boudon *et al.* (1979); Dufournet (1981); Hix (1996); Horeau (1841–6); Koppelkamm (1981); M & Wa (1987); Pe (1976); J.T (1996)

horizontal cornice Lower, *unraked* *cornice of a *pediment.

horn 1. *Composite, *Corinthian, or (especially) *Ionic *volute. **2.** Strong-stemmed projections ending in stiff leaves commonly found on C13 *Gothic *capitals or *crockets. **3.** Projection at each corner of an *altar, ash-chest, *sarcophagus, or *stele, also called *acroterium or *ear. **4.** Each of four projecting portions of any *abacus curved on plan. **5.** *Cornucopia* or Horn of Plenty. **6.** Projection of one member in framed work, as in the head of a door-frame, or the horn of a C19 *sash-window.

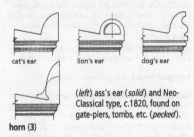

cat's ear   lion's ear   dog's ear

(*left*) ass's ear (*solid*) and Neo-Classical type, *c.*1820, found on gate-piers, tombs, etc. (*pecked*).

horn (3)

horn-work In fortifications, an outer defence of two half-*bastions linked to the main fortress.

horseshoe *See* ARCH.

Horta, Baron Victor (1861–1947) Belgian architect, one of the most brilliant protagonists of *Art Nouveau in Brussels. He absorbed *Viollet-le-Duc's theories, admired the works of *Eiffel and *Boileau, and learned about iron-and-glass from his mentor *Balat. He made his name with the exquisite *Hôtel Tassel*, 6 *Rue Paul-Émile Janson* (1892–3), in which the exposed ironwork and curvaceous decorations showed Art Nouveau at its most inventive and refined. The success of the *Hôtel Tassel* brought other commissions for

buildings, including the *Huis van Eetvelde, Palmerstonlaan* (1895–7), the ingenious and beautiful *Hôtel Solvay*, 224 *Avenue Louise* (1894–1900), and the brilliant *Maison du Peuple, Place Émile van de Velde* (1895–9—shamefully demolished 1964), with its curved iron, glass and *masonry *façade, and a light-filled interior with exposed ironwork and much fine detailing. His own house at 22–23 *Rue Américaine* (1898–1901—now the *Musée Horta*) and the *Hôtel Aubecq*, 520 *Avenue Louise* (1899–1900), were ingeniously planned and marvellously detailed, with metal and masonry meticulously joined. Thereafter, Horta's work became more pedestrian: his Central Railway Station (1911–37), and his *Palais des Beaux-Arts* (1919–28), have reinforced-concrete structures, and lack all the grace and charm of the Art-Nouveau work. He designed numerous funerary and other monuments.

Aubry *et al.* (1996); F.Borsi (1969); Delevoy (1958); Dernie *et al.* (1995); Hoppenbrouwers *et al.* (1975); Hustache (1994); Loo (ed.) (2003); Loyer (1986); P (1982); T-M (1967); J.T (1996)

hortus conclusus Enclosed (referring to Virginity), inviolate, or *secret garden* (*giardino segreto*—a reference to the *Song of Solomon*), often within a bigger garden, associated with the *Garden of Eden*, but also an attribute of the **Virgin Mary** (so planted with roses and lilies, and provided with *fountains (all Marian attributes)), and furnished with walks, *arbours, and turfed seats. Medieval 'Mary Gardens' were surrounded by *hedges, wattle-*fences, or walls, and had raised beds planted with scented flowers and herbs (each with its own meaning): the term *herber was often used synonymously. Some such gardens were ecclesiastical, others were secular, and were used for contemplation and enjoyment.

ISR, xlii/3 (Sept.1988), 264–81; Tay (2006)

Hosking, William (1800–61). English architect. With **John Jenkins** (*c.*1798–1844) he published *A Selection of Architectural and Other Ornaments, Greek, Roman, and Italian* (1827). He became Engineer to the **Birmingham, Bristol, and Thames Junction Railway Company** (1834), and was appointed Professor at King's College, London (1840). His publications include *The Principles and Practice of Architecture* (1842); *The Theory, Practice, and Architecture of Bridges* (1843—with **James Hann** (1799–1856)—which became the standard work); and documents connected with building regulations in towns. However, he is best remembered as the architect of Abney Park Cemetery, Stoke Newington, London (1839–43), for which Joseph *Bonomi was consultant for the *Egyptian-Revival entrance-gates and lodges: conceived as an *arboretum as well as a *cemetery, Abney Park had an educational agenda, and its scheme of planting was influenced by *Loudon (*see* LODDIGES). Later (1849), he proposed a circular *Pantheon-like building (published 1850) filling in the quadrangle of the British Museum, which may have prompted the realized circular reading-room (1854–7) by S.*Smirke.

Co (2008); J.Curl (2004, 2005); *ODNB* (2004)

Hôste, Huib (1881–1957) Pioneer of *International Modernism in Belgium, as demonstrated in his house in Zele (1931) and the *Villa Fouarge*, *Sint-Janslaan*, Sint-Pieters-Woluwe, Brussels (1935).

Loo (ed.) (2003); Smets (1972)

hôtel 1. Large private residence, or town-house, in France. **2.** Official residence of a public figure or official. **3.** University hostel. **4.** Building for accommodation of strangers, really a superior *inn, since the C19 a very large and luxurious establishment with bedrooms, dining-rooms, and other facilities, usually spelled without the circumflex accent. *Other compounds include*:
hôtel de ville: town-hall in Francophone countries;
hôtel-Dieu: French hospital;
hôtel particulier: French town-house of considerable grandeur, the basic form of which was invented by *Serlio and consisted of a *corps de logis* flanked by lower projecting *wings on either side forming a *court enclosed on the street side by a wall in which was the entrance-gate, often with an enclosed garden on the other side of the main block. The plans of the *Hôtel Carnavalet* (*c.*1545 and later additions) by *Lescot, remodelled by *Mansart (1660–1), and Mansart's *Hôtel de la Vrillière* (1635–45—destroyed), both in Paris, are examples.

Contet (1914–34); Ga (1964, 1972, 1972a); Loyer (1987); S (1901–2)

hot-house Heated *greenhouse for plants needing plenty of warmth. *See* CONSERVATORY; GLASS-HOUSE; GREENHOUSE; ORANGERY; TEMPERATE HOUSE.

Houghton, Thomas de (*fl.*1288–1318) English carpenter/engineer, involved (1288) in building-works at Westminster Palace: he made (1292) a carved timber *screen and canopy for the tomb of **Queen Eleanor** (*r.*1272–90) in Westminster Abbey. For the rest of his career he was in the King's service, working at Beaumaris, Edinburgh, Linlithgow, Dover, and Carlisle Castles, as well as the Tower of London. He was with the English army (1298–1318), involved not only with building-work, but with supply, transportation, and building of military equipment for the wars against the Scots.

J.Harvey (1987)

Howard, Sir Ebenezer (1850–1928) English begetter of the *Garden-City movement. Inspired by **Edward Bellamy**'s (1850–98) Utopian book *Looking Backward 2000–1887* (1888) which prophesied a transformation of society in an industrial age made possible by co-operative ventures, he wrote *To-morrow: A Peaceful Path to Real Reform* (1898), later republished as *Garden Cities of Tomorrow* (1902). Howard envisaged curing the ills of densely packed urban living and rural decline by merging the best of town and country into Garden Cities of limited size. His ideas were taken up, and the Garden City Association was formed (1899) which led to the creation of Letchworth Garden City, Herts. (from 1903), and the second experiment, Welwyn Garden City, also Herts. (from 1919). Low densities, separation of housing and industries, and the provision of all amenities were essential ingredients. Howard's ideas led to the *New Towns policy adopted in Britain after the 1939–45 war, and had influence earlier elsewhere, notably in France, Germany, and the USA.

Beevers (1988); Bellamy (1967); Fishman (1977); P.Hall & C.Ward (1998); E.Howard (1898, 1902, 1946, 1965); LeG & S (eds) (1996); MacFadyen (1970); Me.Miller (1992, 2002); M & G (1992); *ODNB* (2004); Parsons & D.Schuyler (eds) (2002)

Howard, John Galen (1864–1931) American architect, educated at the *École des *Beaux-Arts*, Paris (1891–3), he worked with H.H.*Richardson and *McKim, Mead, & White. He moved (1901) to CA, where he designed the Hearst Mining Building (1901–7), Greek Theater (1920–3), California Hall (1903–5), Architecture Building (1906–12), Doe Library (1907–17), Sather Gate (1908–10), Boalt Hall (1908–11), Sather Tower (1911–14), Hilgard Hall (1916–17), Stephens Hall (1921–3), and the Women's Faculty Club (1923), all for the University of CA. He also designed several houses in the Bay Area of San Francisco. His commercial and public buildings exhibited an assured approach to *Classicism, informed by his studies in France.

ARe, xxiii (1908), 269–93; Partridge (1978)

Howard, John George (1803–90) Born **John Corby** in England, he emigrated (1832) to Canada, settling in Toronto, where he had a successful practice. He established *Neo-Classicism as the style for commercial and public buildings (e.g. the Bank of British North America (1845), the Lunatic Asylum (1846–9), and the Third Gaol (1838)—all destroyed). His finest surviving building is the Leeds and Greenville County Court House, Brockville, Ontario (1841–5—with a handsome *Ionic *portico). He also designed several *Gothic-Revival churches, e.g. Christ Church, Holland Landing (1843).

K (1994); J.T (1996)

Howe, George (1886-1955) American architect, he designed High Hollow, Chestnut Hill, Philadelphia, PA (1914-17), which evidenced influences from his *Beaux-Arts* training in Paris (1908-13), his European travels (notably Italy), and *vernacular architecture of PA. A partner (1916-28) in the firm of **Mellor, Meigs, & Howe**, he specialized in houses influenced by the work of *Lutyens, by American-*Colonial buildings, and by the English *Arts-and-Crafts movement. A monograph (1923) contains illustrations of houses designed at that time (also illustrated in **Arthur Ingersoll Meigs**'s (1882-1956) *An American Country-House* (1925)). Following a visit to the *Exposition Internationale des Arts-Décoratifs* in Paris (1924-5), Howe began to abandon his architectural stance, adopting *International Modernism, and, with *Lescaze, designed the Philadelphia Saving Fund Society Office (1929-32), the paradigm of an International-Modernist *skyscraper. Howe promoted Modernism in the USA throughout the 1930s, but broke with Lescaze (1935) and returned to designing private houses, merging traditional plans with Modernist forms and local materials (e.g. Square Shadows, Whitemarsh, PA (1932-4), and Fortune Rock, Mount Desert Island, ME (1937-9). He entered into brief associations with L.I.*Kahn and others (1940), and became (1950) Chairman of the Department of Architecture, Yale University.

JSAH, **xxi**/2 (May 1962), 47–102; P (1982); Stern (1975)

Howell, Killick, Partridge, & Amis British architectural firm established (1959) by **William Gough Howell** (1922-74), **John Alexander Wentzel Killick** (1924-71), **John Albert Partridge** (1924-2016), and **Stanley Frederick Amis** (1924-). With the LCC Architects' Department they designed the Roehampton Lane Housing, London (1951-60), with blocks based on greatly scaled-down *images* of Le *Corbusier's *Unités*. Work included buildings at St Anne's College, Oxford, using precast concrete elements (1960-9), the new Hall and Common Rooms, St Antony's College, Oxford (1966-71), and various buildings in Cambridge, including the combination-room, hall, and kitchens at Downing College (1965-70). Later works include the Warrington Crown and County Court House, Ches. (1992).

Arena, **lxxxii** (1966), 95–119; E (1994); Js (1980)

Howells, John Mead (1868-1959) American architect, he worked with *McKim, Mead, & White before establishing (1897) an office with **Isaac Newton Phelps Stokes** (1867-1944) in NYC. The firm designed the Madison Square Church Mission House, NYC (1898), and Woodbridge Hall, Yale University, New Haven, CT (1901), the latter resembling an C18 Parisian *hôtel*. Generally, their work was restrained,

eclectic, and sensitive to context. The First Congregationalist Church, Danbury, CT (1909), reflected Howells's affection for American-*Colonial C18 architecture. Stokes developed interests in philanthropic work, notably the housing of the working classes, and published *The Iconography of Manhattan Island, 1498-1909* (1915-28). The partnership was dissolved (1917), but Howells designed (with Raymond *Hood and J.A.*Fouilhoux) the *Chicago Tribune* Tower, Chicago, IL (1922-5), drawing on French *Flamboyant* precedents. Howells and Hood collaborated on the *Daily News* Building, NYC (1929-30), and Howells himself was responsible for the Panhellenic (later Beekman) Tower, NYC (1928), with *Art Deco modelling. He was a sensitive restorer of early American architecture, and wrote much, including *Lost Examples of Colonial Architecture* (1931) and *The Architectural Heritage of the Merrimack* (1941).

Bunting & Nylander (1973); Goldstone & Dalrymple (1974); E.Ka (ed.) (1970)

H-plan *Plan shaped like an **H**, as in *Elizabethan houses such as Montacute House, Som. (finished 1599). It was a variation on the *E-plan in that it was like two **E**s placed back to back, with the wings extending symmetrically in both directions.

Hüber, Joseph (1716-87) Austrian architect, he completed (1776) *Hayberger's library at *Stift* Admont (*c.*1745-66), and was probably responsible for the the interior. Hüber designed and built the elegant twin-towered façade of the *Mariahilfkirche*, Graz (1742-4), and worked on other buildings in Styria, including the churches of *St Veit-am-Vorgau* (1748-51) and the *Weizbergkirche* (1756-8).

J.T (1996)

Hübsch, Gottlieb Heinrich Christian (1795-1863) Accomplished German practitioner of the *Rundbogenstil*, and author (1828) of *In welchem Stil sollen wir bauen?* (In What Style Shall We Build?), which created a climate of opinion antagonistic to the *Neo-Classicism dominant in Baden and Prussia. Prompted by rational French arguments, notably those of *Durand, Hübsch argued that style should be derived from carefully considered structural methods and realistic approaches to cost. His plumping for *Byzantine-*Romanesque round-arched forms was based less on style than on the qualities of brick. His best building is arguably the elegant *Trinkhalle*, Baden-Baden (1837-40), with segmental *arcades. He succeeded (1827) *Weinbrenner (under whom he had studied) as *Baurat* at Karlsruhe, Baden.

Döhmer (1976); Valdenaire (1926); Wa & M (1987)

Hughes, James Quentin (1920–2004) English architect, founding-editor of the journal *Fort*, and leading preservationist of fortresses. He also worked on numerous *conservation projects, including Bridge Street, Chester (1962–4), Neston, Wirral (1967), and Greenbank House, Sefton Park, Liverpool (1969). He published *The Buildings of Malta 1530–1795* (1956); *Seaport: Architecture and Town Planning in Liverpool* (1964—later published as *Liverpool: City of Architecture*); *Fortress: Architecture and Military History in Malta* (1969); and *Military Architecture* (1974). He did much for the historic architecture of Liverpool.

Hughes (1964); *The Times* (8 June 2004), 57

Hulle, Robert (*fl.*1400–42) English mason, he was engaged (1400) on works at Winchester College and St Cross Hospital, Winchester, Hants., and was Master-Mason of Winchester Cathedral (1411–12). He worked on the *Rood-loft at St John's, Glastonbury, Som., and supervised construction at St John's Hospital, Sherborne, Dorset (1439–40).

J.Harvey (1987)

Hültz, Johann (*c.*1390–1449) Architect of the north tower of Strasbourg Cathedral after the death of von *Ensingen (1419). Hültz designed the *tracery *spire and spiral staircase rising from the octagonal *stage (completed 1439).

Białostocki (1972); *Œil*, clxxiv–clxxv (1969), 26–33

Humane Modernism *See* NEW HUMANISM.

Humanism Devotion to those studies promoting human culture, esp. developments relating to the revival of Classical literature/learning (including architecture) in Europe (*c.*1300–*c.*1600) known as the *Renaissance.

Burckhardt (1990); Chastel (1959); J.T (1996); Weiss (1969)

Humboldt, Karl Wilhelm, Freiherr von (1767–1835) Prussian philologist/writer/authority on aesthetics. In letters (1799) to *Goethe he described *Lenoir's Museum, observing that a perception of history can best be understood through a study of *monuments* from the past rather than relying solely on *historical texts*. During his time as a diplomat in Rome (1802–9), he mixed with the artistic community (including *Schinkel), and collected sculptures and other artefacts. In London (1817–18) he saw the Elgin Marbles, which greatly impressed him, and in Berlin he commissioned Schinkel to design *Schloss Tegel* (1820–4), his home there. His brother, **Friedrich Heinrich Alexander, Freiherr von Humboldt** (1769–1859), was a distinguished scientist and traveller (notably in Latin America (his work there influenced Schinkel's stage-sets) and the Russian Empire).

Flitner & Giel (eds) (1960–81); P.R.Sweet (1978–80)

Hundertwasser, Friedensreich (1928–2000) Austrian artist/architect, born **Friedrich Stowasser**, he abhorred the rigid crudities of *Modernism, ensuring he became a target of abuse hurled by its devotees: his *Hundertwasserhaus*, at the junction of *Kegelgasse* and *Löwengasse*, Vienna (1977–86), with irregular *fenestration, bands of colour, onion-domes, and plantation of trees on the roof, demonstrated his skills as an extraordinarily inventive designer, which did not go down well in certain quarters. He brought the same verve to a motorway service-station, Bad Fischau (1989–90), and a new district-heating plant in Vienna (1988–92). Other projects include the Rueff factory, Muntlix, Vorarlberg (1982–8), the renovation of St Barbara's Church, Bärnbach, Styria (1984–8), the *Kunst-Haus*, Vienna (1989–91), the Village near the *Hundertwasserhaus*, Vienna (1990–1), and housing-developments at Bad Soden-am-Taunus (1990–3) and Plockingen-am-Neckar (1990–4). He believed that architecture should be humane and in harmony with nature, but architects were no longer capable of creating beautiful buildings, having uncritically swallowed shallow Modernist slogans to the exclusion of all else.

Hundertwasser (1997); Taschen (ed.) (1997); pk

Hungarian Activism Movement associated with *Constructivism, *Cubism, *Expressionism, and *Bauhaus ideas, influenced also by *Futurism and Leftist ideologies. It published *MA* (Today) in Budapest (1916–19) and in Vienna (1920–5), which influenced architects such as *Breuer. Among those loosely associated with the movement were El *Lissitzky, *Oud, *Molnár, *Tatlin, and the *Tauts.

Benson & Forgács (eds) (2002); L (1988)

hungry Deeply recessed raked-out *mortar-joints in brickwork leaving the outline of each brick clearly defined: they weather badly, so are not recommended.

hunting-lodge Building providing a viewing-point for the chase, or to accommodate and refresh guests during the hunting-season (also known as a **hunting-box**). Grand hunting-lodges or -seats also had kitchens, stable, kennels, and rooms for servants: one of the grandest was *Juvarra's *Stupinigi*, near Turin (1729–33). *See* LODGE.

hunting-park Enclosed area of parkland used almost exclusively for the hunting of deer. *See* PARK.

Hunt, Richard Morris (1827–95) American architect, the first to be trained at the *École des *Beaux-Arts*, Paris (from 1846). He worked in the office of *Lefuel, and assisted during construction at the Louvre from 1854, designing the *Pavillon de* *la Bibliothèque.* He returned (1855) to the USA where he used his knowledge of French *Renaissance-Revival architecture to great effect. His works included the Tribune Building (1873–6—one of the first tall buildings equipped with 'elevators'—demolished), NYC, and a series of grand private houses, including the French *Gothic Vanderbilt Mansion (Biltmore House), Asheville, NC (1888–95), and several at Newport, RI, including the *Stick-style Griswold House (1861–3), and the Neo-Classical Vanderbilt Mansion (Marble House, 1888–92). Even though he was the most nationally and internationally honoured American architect of the time, a great many of his buildings have been demolished. His grand *Beaux-Arts Classical entrance-wing of the Metropolitan Museum of Art, NYC (1894–1902), was completed by his son, **Richard Howland Hunt** (1862–1931).

ARe, v/2 (1895), 97–180; P.Baker (1980); P (1982); Stein (ed.) (1986)

Hunt, Thomas Frederick (*c.*1791–1831) He published on the *Picturesque *Tudor style, including *Half-a-Dozen Hints on Picturesque Domestic Architecture* ... (1825, with subsequent editions), *Designs for Parsonage-Houses,* etc. (1827), and *Exemplars of Tudor Architecture* ... (1830, 1841). He designed (1815) the *Neo-Classical *mausoleum of **Robert Burns** (1759–96), St Michael's churchyard, Dumfries, and (1815–17) the Old Episcopal (later Wesleyan) Church in Buccleuch Street, also in Dumfries, with an *Ionic *portico.

Co (2008)

Hurley, William (*fl.*1319–54) English carpenter, he worked (1323–4) at Ely Cathedral, Cambs., where he designed the octagon over the *crossing, making him one of the most outstanding medieval structural inventors. He also designed *stalls: his works at Windsor and St Stephen's Chapel, Westminster, have not survived, but those at Ely do. He was active at the Tower of London (1324), Caerphilly Castle, Wales, and Guildhall, London (where he was in charge until its completion (1337)). The roof of the Great Hall, Penshurst Place, Kent (1341–9), may be by him.

J.Harvey (1987)

Hurtado Izquierdo, Francisco de (1669–1725) Spanish *Baroque architect responsible for some of the most ornate interiors of the period: many are in Granada, including the *Sagrario* Chapel of the *Cartuja* (1702–20), with a *polychrome central tabernacle on *Solomonic columns, and the Sacristy of the *Cartuja* (1724–64), the masterwork of Spanish Baroque with *piers encrusted with 45 different motifs, giving

a rich, jewel-like effect: the building was completed under the direction of **Luís de Arévalo** (*fl.* mid-C18), and contains exquisite inlaid *cómodas* (cabinets) by **José** or **F.Manuel Vázquez** (1730–64). Also remarkable is the *Sagrario* of the *Cartuja* of *Nuestra Señora del Paular,* near Segovia (from 1718), with a capricious *marble and *lapis-lazuli *camarín.*

Archivo Español de Arte, xxxv (1962), 135–73; *AB,* xxxii (1950), 25–61; Gallego y Burín (1956); K & S (1959); vV (1993)

husk Classical ornament in the form of a stylized bell-flower, *nut-shell,* or *wheat-ear,* usually in series, linked together in *drops, *festoons, *garlands, or *strings. When composed to form a *husk-garland,* the vertical parts 'hanging' on each side often have nut-shells diminishing in size towards the bottom, although, like festoons, they increase in size towards the centre of the *catenary curve.

Bell-flower, husk, nut-shell, or *wheat-ear garland* with *margents* around an elliptical Neo-Classical *medallion* (*after Robert Adam*).

Husly, Jacob Otten (1738–96) Dutch architect, his work was influenced by *Palladianism, and then by *Neo-Classicism, of which he appears to have been among the earliest practitioners in The Netherlands. He designed the Town Halls at Weesp (1771–6) and Groningen (1793–1810), van Teyler's Museum interiors, Haarlem (1780), and the Felix Meritis Society Building, Amsterdam (1781–8), all in The Netherlands.

RSTK (1977); Vriend (1949)

Hussey, Christopher Edward Clive (1899–1970) English architectural historian. From 1917 he established a relationship with *Country Life,* contributing numerous articles on country-houses and other matters (including *conservation and landscape) for the rest of his life (a list of his publications is given in *Architectural History*): he edited the magazine 1933–40. His concerns regarding the future of the country-house led to the National Trust's country-houses scheme, and among his most important books were a trilogy on Georgian country-houses, biographies of *Lorimer and *Lutyens, and an excellent volume on the *Picturesque which laid solid foundations for later explorations of the subject, especially in garden-history. He was active in the National Trust, the Historic Buildings Council for England, and the Society of Architectural Historians of Great Britain, among other organizations.

AH, xiii (1970), 5–29; Hussey (1931, 1967, 1983, 1988, 1989); *ODNB* (2004)

hut *See* HERMITAGE *and* PRIMITIVE HUT.

Hutchinson, Henry (1800–31) English architect, pupil and later (1821) partner of *Rickman, he made a major contribution to the firm's success. His works include the *Gothic bridge at St John's College, Cambridge (1827), and he was active as a designer (1819–30), until he fell ill, probably with tuberculosis.

Co (2008)

Huvé, Jean-Jacques-Marie (1783–1852) French architect, pupil of his father, **Jean-Jacques Huvé** (1742–1808), and *Percier, he later worked with *Vignon at the *Temple de la Gloire*, Paris, and later became sole architect, completing it (1817–42) as the *Madeleine*, a sumptuous Roman *temple. He was Architect to the Paris *hospices* and to the postal service.

M & Wa (1987); D.Wa (1986)

Huxtable (*née* **Landman**), **Ada Louise** (1921–2013). American architectural critic, she established her reputation with a series of trenchant articles in the *New York Times* from 1963, but before then published her monograph on *Nervi (1960) and many articles in various journals. Her love of her native city was expressed in *Classic New York: Georgian Gentility to Greek Elegance* (1964), and her forthright writings assailed the insupportable hideousness of many aspects of American cities: indeed, her *Will They Ever Finish Bruckner Boulevard?* (1970) has been described as a 'Primer on Urbicide'. A passionate conservationist, she was a major figure in the creation (1965) of a Landmarks Preservation Commission for NYC to resist the 'blind mutilation', as she called it, 'in the name of *urban renewal'. She also championed excellence in contemporary architecture, denouncing the 'big, the expedient, and the deathlessly ordinary', and making plain her exasperation with the General Services Administration (the body in charge of all Federal construction in the USA) for proliferating banality. She called the *skyscraper one of the 'great technological and architectural achievements of our civilization': *The Tall Building Artistically Considered: The Search for a Skyscraper Style* (1982, 1984) is a major study of the subject. *Pevsner

described her as 'the best architectural critic' of his time.

Huxtable (1960, 1960a, 1961, 1964, 1970, 1976, 1984, 1986, 1986a, 1997)

Huyssens, Peter (1577–1637) Flemish Jesuit architect. He designed (1606–13) the Church and other buildings for the Jesuit College at Maastricht, and completed (1617–22) *St Carolus Borromeus*, Antwerp, after *Aguilonius's death. He prepared designs for two more churches: *St Walburga*, Brugge, 1619, and *St-Loup*, Namur, 1621, both unfinished when Huyssens died. Following a study-visit to Italy (1626–7), he designed the building that is now *St-Pieterskerk*, Gent, begun 1629, the *choir of which was influenced by Roman exemplars. The building, completed in C18, was not fully realized in accordance with his plans.

PM; J.T (1996)

hydraulics 1. Science concerned with conveying water through pipes or other artificial channels, and with the various mechanical means by which water is forced upwards or activates machinery. Water was brought great distances in Roman *aqueducts, but hydraulics reached heights of invention during the Italian *Renaissance and in French *Baroque gardens of the time of **Louis XIV** (*r.*1643–1715). **2.** *Hydraulic* is applied to various mechanical contrivances operated by water power, e.g. *hydraulic elevator, engine, organ, ram*, etc. **3.** Also applied to substances which harden under water and become impervious to it, e.g. *hydraulic cement, lime, mortar*, etc. *See* AUTOMATA; FOUNTAIN; GIOCHI D'ACQUA; WATER-WORKS.

Hyndeley, Thomas (*fl.*1401–33) English mason, he worked at Durham Cathedral Priory from 1401, including the *cloisters, and became chief mason (1416). He designed an octagonal *lavatory in the centre of the *cloister (1433), and was in charge of works at Scarborough Castle, Yorks. (1420s).

J.Harvey (1987)

Hyndeley, William (*fl.*1466–1505) English mason, he became (1473) Master-Mason at York *Minster, where he constructed the *battlements on the south side. He seems to have been greatly esteemed, in spite of having spent some time in gaol on suspicion of murdering a tiler, one **John Partrik**, and was buried in the Minster under one of the towers.

J.Harvey (1987)

hypaethral Structure without a roof, or partly open to the sky. *Related terms include*:
hypaethron: **1.** open *court or enclosure; **2.** part of a building open to the sky;
hypaethros, hypaethrus: **1.** building open to the sky, but especially a promenade between

*porticoes or *colonnades in a garden; **2.** *Antique *temple with its middle part un-roofed; **3.** Antique temple with a two-storey *peristyle in the middle, often of superimposed *Orders;

hypaethrum: Roman *fanlight of *lattice-work over a door and within a *doorway *architrave: more properly *hyperthri lumen*.

hyperbola Conic *section formed by the inter-section of a plane with both branches of a double cone (two identical cones on either side of the same vertex or pointed top). *Hyperboloid* is there-fore a solid figure, some of the plane *sections of which are hyperbolas.

hyperbolic parabola Continuous flowing double-curved form, used for *concrete shell-roofs, wing-like in *elevation, starting from a par-abolic arch and progressing to an upside-down *parabola of similar size, often doubled, as a mir-ror-image. Its geometry, although seemingly complex, is actually very simple, and its construc-tion is largely dependent on straight lines. It was pioneered by *Nowicki.

Mainstone (1975); *OED* (1933)

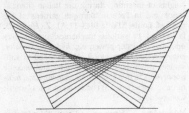

hyperbolic parabola

hyperthyris *Lintel or *supercilium* of an *architrave over a Classical *doorway or other aperture. *Hyperthyrum* is the *frieze between architrave and *cornice in a similar position.

hypocaust Hollow space under the floor of a Roman building through which hot air passes by convection to heat the rooms.

hypogaeum, hypogeum **1.** Antique *build-ing or part of a building below ground, i.e. a cellar, basement, etc. **2.** Underground rock-cut or built tomb with *niches for cremated remains or *loculi for bodies. Smaller than *catacombs, it was usu-ally intended for one family or group.

Toynbee (1971)

hypophyge *Apophyge.

hypopodium Second or lower *podium, defined horizontally by *strings, *bands, etc.

hypostyle Any roofed *colonnade, or series of colonnades, as in an Ancient-Egyptian *temple. A *hypostyle hall* is therefore a large room with a flat roof carried on many columns in rows, the middle rows often having taller columns to accommodate a *clerestorey. Examples are those of the cult-temples of Ancient-*Egypt, including the temple of Amun at Karnak (*c.*1570–*c.*1200 BC, with additions to *c.*323 BC).

Ck (1996); Phillips (2002); J.T (1996)

hypostyle hall Great Temple, Karnak, showing bell-capitals supporting taller element with clerestorey, and bud-capitals carrying the rest of the roof (*after various sources*).

hypotrachelion(um) In Classical architec-ture, a member or part between the *capital proper and the *shaft of an *Order, meaning lit-erally 'below the neck' or the 'lower part of the neck'. Its exact meaning seems to have varied slightly according to the source consulted or the Order used. *Vitruvius appears to suggest it refers to the *apophyge, but *Renaissance commenta-tors on Vitruvius, while accepting the apophyge/ apophysis connection, also applied it to the lower part of the capital between the *astragal and the *echinus, so it meant the *frieze-like *collarino*, *gorgerin, or *neck of the Tuscan, Roman-*Doric, and Greek-*Ionic (*Erechtheion*) Orders. In the Greek-Doric Order it meant the horizontal grooves, *reeds, or *fillets encircling the column, the part of the column above, with *flutes, termi-nating in the *annulets under the echinus being the *trachelion(um). However, in certain archaic Greek-Doric Orders (e.g. the C6 BC 'Basilica' at *Paestum) the hollow 'necklace' of vertical styl-ized leaf-like forms is defined as the *hypotrache-lion(um)*.

J.Curl (2001); D (1950)

I'Anson, Edward (1775–1853) London architect/surveyor, partner of D.A.*Alexander, on whose retirement he continued the practice, acting as surveyor to estates in the City of London and Southwark, designing several handsome *warehouses. His son, **Edward I'Anson** (1812–88), joined him in practice, and built Royal Exchange Buildings for Magdalen College, Oxford, at Cornhill, City of London (1842–6—largely demolished except for No. 22 Finch Lane), one of the first office-blocks in the City.

Co (2008); *ODNB* (2004)

IBA (Internationale Bau-Ausstellung (International Building Exhibition)) To mark the 750th anniversary (1987) of the founding of the city, the West Berlin authorities decided (1978) to hold an international exhibition to promote a series of exemplary permanent housing initiatives. *Kleihues was appointed (1979) Director of Planning, and several architects contributed, including *Rossi and *Stirling. Examples of exhibits may be seen, e.g., in *Schlossstrasse* and *Rönnestrasse*, Charlottenburg.

CFRS; pk

ice-house 1. Building for the storage of ice collected during the winter for use in summer, usually wholly or partly underground, often of two walls insulated with sawdust or other material, fitted with a drain at the base, and frequently of circular *vaulted form. They were not uncommon on larger estates in C18 and C19, often with *fabriques on top. An advanced design by J.B.*Papworth was published in his *Rural Residences* (1818). They were sometimes found in the basements of town-houses (e.g. C16 Antwerp). **2.** Eskimo igloo (*iglugeak*), a circular domed or pseudo-domed structure built of ice, often of complex plan, usually with a barrel-vaulted entrance-tunnel.

N (1835); W.Pa (1852); PM

icicle 1. Representation of icicles or falling water occurs in *rustication and is known as *congelation: it is often a feature of *fountains, *grottoes, *hermitages, *nymphaea, etc. **2.** Motif in *Rococo ornament, often associated with *Chinoiserie, resembling icicles.

icon 1. Image, figure, or representation. **2.** Monumental figure, or statue. **3.** Stylized representation of a sacred personage, itself also regarded as sacred, especially in the Orthodox Churches. *Related terms include*:

iconic: **1.** of or pertaining to an icon; **2.** work of architecture uncritically admired: the term is so over-used (and *misused*) as to be almost meaningless;

iconostasis (*pl. iconostases*): in Greek and Russian Orthodox churches, *screen (often hung with icons and other images) between the *sanctuary and the body of the church, with three *doorways.

iconography Branch of knowledge dealing with representations of people/objects, hence symbolism in a design.

Ictinus, *or* **Iktinos** (*fl.*C5 BC) Active in Periclean Athens, he (with *Callicrates) designed the *Parthenon (447–432 BC), and wrote a description of the building (with **Carpion**) that has not survived. He prepared a scheme for the *Telesterion*, Eleusis (*c.*440 BC), and may have designed the *temple of *Apollo Epicurius*, Bassae (*c.*429–*c.*400 BC), which was remarkable in that it had a *Doric *Order outside, an Ionic *engaged Order (*see* BASSAE ORDER) inside, and a *Corinthian Order at the end of the *naos.

Berve & Gruben (1963); Carpenter (1970); D (1950); P (1982); D.S.R (1945); J.T (1996)

ideal Concept of something perfect, sometimes equated with works that attempt to reproduce the best of natural forms but improve upon them, ironing out imperfections. In Europe it was the art of Classical Antiquity from the *Renaissance until *Modernism rejected it.

Ideal City City existing as an idea or an archetype, conceived as perfect, or as an object to be aimed at as a standard of excellence. The term suggests something whole and complete, as in many of the geometrical symmetrical plans for such cities in the *Renaissance period, all of which are variants on patterns established by *Vitruvius, who in turn may have derived his typology from earlier sources, now lost. Renaissance designers of the *città ideale* froze elements into formal patterns as an expression of Order in which Man imposed ideals and heroic dimensions, often with a central structure as an expression of the social order. Such perfect geometrical plans also symbolized the yearning for *Utopia*, the perfect state, and even the *City of God*, the *New Jerusalem*.

Rosenau (1975)

igloo *See* ICE-HOUSE.

Ihne, Ernst Eberhard (1848–1917) German architect, he popularized English domestic architecture (later comprehensively published by *Muthesius), and was one of the protagonists of the *Neo-Baroque style. At *Schloss Friedrichshof* (1889–94), Kronberg-im-Taunus (now a hotel), he introduced English influences, a tactful gesture as the building was to be the residence of the **Empress Frederick** (*r.*1888—formerly **Victoria, Princess Royal of England** (1840–1901)). Ihne very soon became the most important official architect in Germany, and was ennobled (1906) by **Kaiser Wilhelm II** (*r.*1888–1918). Among his works, the *Kaiser-Friedrich Museum* (1898–1903—now the *Bodemuseum*), the *Königliche Bibliothek* (1908–13—with *Baerwald), and the *Kaiser-Wilhelm Institut* (1914–15), all in Berlin, were examples of *Beaux-Arts*-inspired Neo-Baroque style.

J.T (1996)

IHS *See* CHRISMON.

imbrex (*pl.* **imbrices**) Bent or curved *tile like a half-cylinder used for *gutters or for covering the junction of adjacent concave or flat tiles with upstands.

imbrication Scale-pattern, or petal-diaper ornament resembling a surface covered with scale-like curved roofing-tiles, found on *Antique *sarcophagus*-lids and on the roof of the *Choragic Monument of Lysicrates, Athens (334 BC). It is also used on *terracotta panels, *screens, *tracery, etc., and resembles a construction of *imbrices* (*see* IMBREX) piled on top of each other.

Imhotep (*fl.c.*2620–*c.*2590 BC) Ancient-Egyptian courtier/priest/architect to **King Zoser** (**Djoser**—*r. c.*2630–*c.*2611 BC). He was deified later as **Architect of the Universe**, and one of the Trinity, with **Horus** and **Isis**. He was 'son of Ptah', and identified with **Asclepius**. As designer of the huge and sophisticated step-pyramid and complex at Saqqara, he must be regarded as an important innovator of *masonry.

J.Curl (2005, 2011); Hurry (1928); Sethe (1902); W.S. Smith (1998); Wildung (1977)

Imperial stair *See* STAIR.

impluvium *See* ATRIUM.

imposition Something laid or superimposed on, e.g., an existing building.

impost *See* ARCH.

improvement C18 term for land rendered more productive by *enclosure, cultivation, etc., later applied to landscaping, carefully considered planting, erection of buildings, etc.

improver 1. C18 term for a landscaper, e.g. 'Capability' *Brown or H.*Repton, not always used as a compliment. **2.** C19 architectural assistant, working wholly or partly *gratis*, in order to enhance knowledge and skills.

in antis *See* ANTA.

in cavetto Impressed ornament, like *relief in reverse.

incertum opus *See* OPUS ANTIQUUM.

incident Garden-feature (e.g. *fabrique*) adding interest on a garden-circuit.

incised slab Stone slab with a design cut into its surface, commonly a funerary monument featuring human figures representing *effigies, inscriptions, emblems, etc., the incised work often enhanced with black or coloured filling. A variation is a more comprehensive series of *indents filled with *brass or *latten sheets cut to fit and themselves incised and inlaid.

Greenhill (1976)

incrustation Finish consisting of one material fixed to another, e.g. *marble applied to a wall.

indent Shape cut out in a stone slab to receive *brass or *latten *inlaid work, e.g. an *effigy or inscription.

Indian style Cultural/commercial links with India from C16 led to manifestations of *Hindoo and *Mughal architecture in the British Isles from C18: by the end of C16 and during C17 Hindu architecture began to be known and appreciated by Englishmen, and by the second half of C17 the great buildings of Mughal India started to be admired, notably *mausolea* such as the *Tāj Mahal*, Agra, set in its geometrical gardens. Yet an *Indian Revival* as such was a short episode in the history of Taste. Unlike *Chinoiserie (which permeated European sensibilities only gradually), aspects of 'Hindoo' and 'Mughal' art and architecture arrived in the last quarter of C18, and were phenomena at first largely confined to Britain: it was most evident during the *Regency and *Victorian periods as a variation on themes of *Picturesque eclectic *Orientalism. Under the aegis of **Warren Hastings** (1732–1818) William *Hodges began to record (1779–83) the architecture and landscapes of the Subcontinent, publishing *Select Views in India* (1785–8), *Dissertation on* *the Prototypes of Architecture: Hindoo, Moorish, Gothic* (1787), and *Travels in India during the Years 1780, 1781, 1782, 1783* (1793—which also came out in a French edn). Indian topography was also made familiar in the publications of Thomas *Daniell and his nephew **William** (1769–1837): Hodges and the Daniells revealed the 'Barbaric Splendour' of Indian buildings to the West. However, Indian referencing in architecture, like 'Chinee', Egyptianiesque, 'Gothick', 'Moorish', 'Turkish', and other styles, was often in the form of loose interpretations, part of that late-Georgian phenomenon of a counter-culture to the Classical tradition. One of the first fruits of the linking of Indian and Gothic forms was *Dance the Younger's south *façade of the Guildhall, City of London (1788–9), and nods to Indian architecture were also made by Dance at Stratton Park, Hants. (1803–6), and Coleorton Hall, Leics. (1804–8). For Hastings, S.P.*Cockerell carried out works at Daylesford House, Glos. (1788–93), which had oblique references to India (including chimney-pieces by **Thomas Banks** (1735–1805)); Stanmore Hall, Mddx., had an octagonal *temple (1793) with Hindoo sculptures within its grounds; at Melchet Park, on the Hants/Wilts. border, a 'Hindoo temple' (based on images by Daniell of the temple at Bihar) was built of artificial stone by **John Charles Felix Rossi** (1762–1839); and there was an Indian Room at Thomas *Hope's house in Duchess Street, London (1800–4), with pictures by Thomas Daniell showing both *Islamic and Hindu architecture. Then, at Sezincote, Glos., manifestations of Indian architecture were spectacularly realized: **Charles Cockerell** (1755–1837—**1st Baronet** from 1809, who had served with the East India Company) acquired the estate after his brother **John**'s death (1798), and called in another brother, S.P.Cockerell, with H.*Repton and the Daniells, to create a house and grounds with allusions to the Subcontinent. Work began in 1805, the predominant influence being Mughal, with well-observed details, including onion-domes, *chattra-topped *pinnacles, and multifoil *arches, but the grounds, too, have Indianesque *fabriques, including a Hindoo *temple, a bridge with *shafts copied from the Elephanta caves and *Brahminee* bulls, a three-headed serpent (originally a *fountain) coiled around a tree in the middle of a pool, and farm-buildings (stables, *dairy, gardener's house, and surrounding wall). In the mid-1960s a formal *Paradise-garden was added south of the house.

Contemporary with Sezincote were the Hindoo-style stables, riding-school, and coach house, the Pavilion, Brighton, Sussex (1804–8), by *Porden. *Nash's Royal Pavilion, Brighton (1815–21), promiscuously mixed *Chinoiserie and Hindoo styles in a lush display of wildly extravagant *Regency Taste. Indian-style designs

for *villas appeared in *pattern-books by several architects, including **Robert Lugar** (*c*.1773–1855) and **Edmund Aikin** (1780–1820), and H.Repton published Indianesque details in connection with his proposals for Brighton Pavilion. *Foulston, too, used Indian references at Mount Zion Chapel, Devonport (1823–4), and *Loudon recorded (1834) Indian *fabriques* at Alton Towers, Staffs., by *Robert Abraham. Other instances of an Indian Revival occurred at Clifton Baths, Gravesend, Kent (1835—probably by **Amon Henry Wilds** (1784–1857)), and there is a very pretty Indo-Gothick gateway at Dromana, Co. Waterford (*c*.1830). After the Great Exhibition (1851) the Indian style became influential, given the importance of the Subcontinent in the British Empire, and Owen *Jones in his *Grammar of Ornament* (1856) praised India's contributions. The style appeared in numerous interiors, including smoking-rooms and Turkish baths, especially after **Queen Victoria** (*r*.1837–1901) was proclaimed **Empress of India** (1877). A good example is the Indian Hall, Elveden Hall, Suffolk (1890s), by William *Young and his son **Clyde Francis Young** (1871–1948), added to the house designed by **John Norton** (1823–1904), who had also incorporated certain Indian features in the work of 1863–70. Earlier, the Indian style had appeared in the USA, notably at **Phineas Taylor Barnum**'s (1810–91) house at Bridgeport, CT (1846–8), designed by Leopold *Eidlitz and based on Nash's work at Brighton. This influenced Henry *Austin when designing the New Haven Railroad Station (1851). Samuel *Sloan's *The Model Architect* (1852–3) included designs with Indian flavours (e.g. the 'Oriental Villa'), clearly the model for his Longwood Villa (Nutt's Folly), Natchez, MS (1854–61), a polygonal house crowned with an onion-dome. This may have influenced the New York Crystal Palace (1853–4) by *Carstensen and Gildemeister, a *polychrome structure of iron and glass. In the C20 *Lutyens's Viceroy's House, New Delhi (1912–31), combined *Classicism with themes derived from Indian architecture.

Antram & Pe (2012); Conner (1979); J.Curl (2011a); Handlin (1985); Hunt (2012); L & D (1986); Stamp (1976); Verey & Brooks (1999); Wa & Hewat-Jaboor (eds) (2008)

Industrial Aesthetic Buildings in which the structure (or what *appears* to be that) is given dominance, emphasizing engineering (e.g. suspended structures, bridge-like buildings, etc.), or when not only the structure but the services are exposed. *See also* BRUTALISM; HIGH TECH.

industrial architecture Architecture to house manufactures, e.g. mills, engineering works, potteries, etc.

industrialized building Architecture and constructional techniques dependent on *prefabrication. Mass-produced building components were available from C18, while the iron-foundries made many and varied artefacts (e.g. balcony-fronts, *balusters, *crests, railings, etc.). Cast-iron *Greek-*Doric columns (far cheaper than stone and easy to make because repetitive) were used by *Nash at Carlton House Terrace, London (1827–33), *Barry employed mass-produced metal window-frames and cast-iron roof-panels at the Palace of Westminster (1839–60), and *Paxton's Crystal Palace, London (1851), was almost entirely built of prefabricated parts assembled within a *modular system. *Curtain-walling designs, panel systems, *precast concrete, and many other aspects of industrialized building speeded C20 building processes. Charles *Eames, Buckminster *Fuller, *Gropius, *Nervi, *Perret, *Prouvé, and *Wachsmann were in the forefront of developments in C20 industrialized building. In England, *Aslin and *CLASP evolved systems for building, while *Arup and others raised industrialized building techniques to some degree of refinement.

G.Herbert (1978, 1984); Hix (1996); Klotz (ed.) (1986); Pawley (1990); Pe (1976); Russell (1981)

industrial park Area planned as an estate for industrial use, e.g. Trafford Park, Manchester (late C19). In the mid-C20, industrial estates were established on the outskirts of many towns, especially for light industry and advanced technology uses, allowing for 'landscaping' between buildings. The amount of space so used has been phenomenal.

inflatable architecture See PNEUMATIC ARCHITECTURE.

informal Irregular, asymmetrical, ungeometrical design or planting.

ingle-nook 1. Corner of a large fireplace where the opening of the *chimney was far larger than needed, and there was space where persons could sit. **2.** Area off a room, containing the fireplace, often with a small window, fitted with seats between *chimney-breast and wall.

ingo, ingoing *Reveal or return face of a wall in a recess, such as a *niche, *doorway, or window.

inlaid work Decoration made by inserting one material within an incision, *indent, or depression cut into another material to the same depth and finished *flush. This may be accomplished using hard materials, such as black *marble set in white, wood of one colour laid in wood of another colour (*marquetry*), one metal set in another, e.g. gold in steel (*damascening*), or *brass set in polished tortoiseshell (*boule* or *buhl* work). Surfaces made up of very small pieces fitted together are properly *mosaics because they are laid *on* and not *in* the background, although wood of various colours laid within a surface in Italian-*Renaissance designs does qualify as inlaid work and is called *intarsia, intarstatura,* or *tarsia.* Soft materials, such as paint, mastic, or coloured pastes, which harden after a while, really fall into the category of *incised rather than inlaid work.

inn 1. *Public-house kept for the lodging and entertainment of travellers, so a *hostelry* or *hotel* (**4**). The word is erroneously used to describe a *tavern* which does not provide accommodation. **2.** Houses or sets of London buildings, originally places of residence for law students. **3.** Groups of buildings in London belonging to the four legal societies (Inner Temple, Middle Temple, Lincoln's Inn, Gray's Inn) having the right to admit lawyers to practise at the *bar.

inosculating column *Cluster column.

INRI See CHRISMON.

inserted *Engaged.

in situ In position or location. It refers to work done on site, e.g. *concrete poured on site rather than pre-cast in a factory.

insula 1. Group of buildings in a Roman town bounded by four streets, so an isolated *block containing one large structure or several smaller ones joined together. **2.** Detached house in Antiquity.

insulated 1. Building, column, or other work standing *detached so that all sides are visible, as in the *peristyles* of *Greek *temples, but unlike a *pseudo-*peripteral Roman temple where the columns around the *cella* are *engaged. **2.** Kept apart and separate, to assist sound-proofing, retention of heat, prevent contamination, etc.

intelligent building Building in which the services (e.g. heating), environmental design, security, performance, maintenance, outbreaks of fire, leaks, etc., are controlled by computers.

Hakser et al. (1992)

interclose See ENTERCLOSE.

intercolumniation Space between the lower parts of the *shafts of adjacent columns in a Classical *colonnade or *portico defined by *modules the same size as the shaft-diameters (*d*). *Vitruvius described its commonest varieties*:

1½*d*: pycnostyle (used only with the *Ionic and *Corinthian *Orders);

2*d*: systyle;

2¼*d*: eustyle (usual Roman and *Renaissance spacing, with 3*d* used for wider central portico intercolumniations);

3d: *diastyle*;
more than 3d: *araeostyle*.

*Perrault is supposed to have invented *araeosystyle*, an arrangement with two columns ½d apart followed by a space of 3½d used at the east front of the Louvre, Paris, and also by *Wren at St Paul's Cathedral, London. *Doric intercolumniation is not controlled by diameters, but by the relationships of *triglyphs* and *metopes*. *Greek-*Doric *Hellenic intercolumniation normally had one triglyph over the space *between* columns (therefore of the *monotriglyph* type), and, of course, one on the centre-line of each column, although the Athenian *Propylaea had two over the central entrance. *Hellenistic intercolumniation (even Doric) was generally wider, often with two (*ditriglyph*) or more triglyphs above, giving a lighter, more elegant appearance. At the angles of Greek-Doric porticoes, however, because the end triglyphs must terminate each *frieze and therefore touch at the corner, the corner-columns cannot be placed on the centre-line of the triglyphs, and have to be moved inwards, so that the adjoining intercolumniations are smaller. This problem does not exist in Roman- or Renaissance-Doric, as triglyphs do not touch at the corners, so the corner-columns can be on the centre-lines of both corner-triglyphs, and a half-metope is set on each face of the angle.

J.Curl (2001); D (1950); Gw (1903); D.S.R (1945); VP (1567)

interlace Carved ornament of crossed and re-crossed cords or bands arranged like a single piece of flexible material returning upon itself, resembling unravelled knots. Called *entrelacs*, it is common in *Anglo-Saxon, *Celtic, and some *Romanesque art. *Interlacement* or *interlacing band* is *guilloche*.

Glazier (1926); O.Jones (1868); L & D (1986)

interlacing arch See ARCH.

internal angle Figure formed when two walls meet each other at an angle, as in the corner of a room, called a *re-entrant.

International Modern *or* **International style** C20 architectural style which emerged just before the 1914–18 war: the term appears to have been coined by **Alfred Hamilton Barr** (1902–81—Director of MoMA), later publicized by H.-R.*Hitchcock and Philip *Johnson *c.*1932. It is generally accepted as having originated in Germany with work by W.*Gropius et al., and, because its image discarded allusions to the past, it was embraced by those with pretensions to appear *avant-garde* after 1918, first in Central Europe, then elsewhere. Its main characteristics were asymmetry; severe, blocky, cubic shapes; smooth, flat, plain, undecorated surfaces (often

painted white); elimination of *mouldings and ornament; 'flat' roofs; large expanses of glass held in steel frames (often in the form of long horizontal bands or *curtain-walling); and free planning made possible by the adoption of steel-framed or *reinforced-concrete post-and-slab construction (with a series of slab-floors and a roof-slab carried on concrete posts) enabling partitions to be erected where desired as they played no part in the structure.

Paradigms of International Modernism include Gropius's *Bauhaus building, Dessau (1925–6), Le *Corbusier's *Pavillon Suisse* (1930–2), Paris, and *Mies van der Rohe's housing-blocks at the *Weissenhofsiedlung*, Stuttgart, Germany (1926–7). Regarded as indicative of 'progressive' Leftist ideologies, its so-called *Machine Aesthetic was used in both the Fascist headquarters, Como, Italy, by *Terragni, and the Soviet Union in the 1920s. It was adopted universally after 1945, especially in Western Europe, Britain, and the USA. *See* NEW HUMANISM; MODERN MOVEMENT.

Hi (1993); Hi & Johnson (1995); Khan (ed.) (1998); Korn (1967); L & G (1990)

interrupted 1. Architectural element from which part has been omitted (*see* ELISION). **2.** *Broken or *open *pediment.

intersecting *See* ARCH; TRACERY.

intersectio Space between *dentils *or *triglyphs (i.e. *metope*) in a *Doric *entablature.

interstitium Volume or space on a square plan at the *crossing of a *cruciform church.

intertriglyph *Metope.

intrados *See* ARCH.

Inwood, William (*c.*1771–1843) English surveyor/architect, author of *Tables for the Purchasing of Estates* (1811 and several edns thereafter). He designed many houses, barracks, and warehouses in collaboration with his son, **Henry William** (1794–1843), who brought his scholarly understanding of the *Greek Revival to their buildings. There were two other sons, both architects: **Charles Frederick** (1799–1840—designer of All Saints' Church, Marlow, Bucks. (1832–5)), and **Edward** (1802–40). Henry William travelled in Italy and Greece (1818–19), and published *The Erechtheion at Athens: Fragments of Athenian Architecture and a few remains in Attica, Megara, and Epirus* (1827), the standard work on the great Greek *temple. His undoubted scholarship was displayed in St Pancras New Church, London (1819), one of the finest monuments of the Greek Revival, which adapted *Gibbs's *type of Anglican church using Greek motifs (*portico, *caryatides, and windows from the *Erechtheion*, and a *steeple derived from the Tower of the Winds). It was designed in collaboration with his father, with whom he also built All Saints, Camden Town (1822–4), and St Peter's, Regent Square (1822–5—demolished). They designed St Mary's Chapel, Somers Town (1824–7), a thin, unscholarly *Gothic effort lampooned by A.W.N.*Pugin in *Contrasts* (1836). W.H.Inwood also published *The Resources of Design in the Architecture of Greece, Egypt, and other Countries* (1834). He died when the ship on which he was travelling to Spain foundered.

Crook (1972a); Co (2008); J.Curl (2001, 2011a); Inwood (1827, 1834); *ODNB* (2004); Su (1993, 2003)

Ionic Order Classical *Order of architecture, the second *Greek and the third *Roman, primarily identified by its *capital, with its rolled-up cushion-like form on either side creating distinctive *volutes. It has a base of the *Asiatic or *Attic type (the latter favoured by the Romans), and the *shaft is more slender in proportion than in the *Doric Order: Greek-Ionic shafts are almost invariably fluted with *fillets separating the flutes (although *Hellenistic columns often have the lower part of the shaft faceted or plain, as in the **stoa*, Priene (*c*.158–156 BC)), but Roman shafts are often wholly unfluted. *Astragal (sometimes embellished with *bead-and-reel), **echinus* (enriched with *egg-and-dart), and fillet occur in both Greek and Roman capitals: the particularly elegant capitals of the Athenian *Erechtheion* (*c*.421–407 BC) also have a **hypotrachelion* with a continuous *frieze of **anthemion* motifs, while

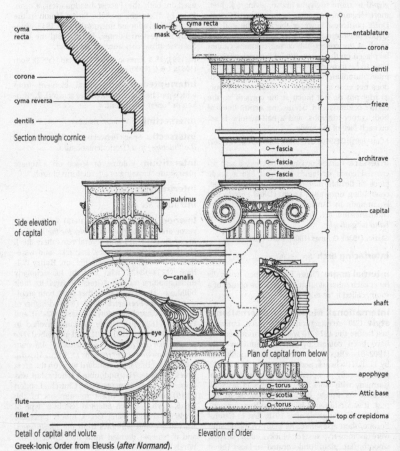

Detail of capital and volute   Elevation of Order

Greek-Ionic Order from Eleusis (*after Normand*).

Labels (clockwise): cyma recta, corona, cyma reversa, dentils — Section through cornice; lion-mask, cyma recta; entablature, corona, dentil, frieze, architrave, capital, shaft; fascia, fascia, fascia; pulvinus — Side elevation of capital; canalis, eye, flute, fillet; Plan of capital from below; apophyge, torus, scotia, torus — Attic base; top of crepidoma

the astragal below has bead-and-reel and the moulded *abacus* is ornamented with egg-and-dart. Indeed, *abaci* (much smaller than Doric) are always moulded, usually plain, but sometimes enriched. *Entablatures* consist of *architrave* (usually divided into *fasciae*), *frieze* (sometimes omitted, particularly in *Hellenistic buildings), and *cornice*. The frieze has no *metopes* or *triglyphs*, so the *intercolumniation discipline inherent in Doric does not exist, and spacing can be wider. Furthermore, the Ionic frieze may be a plain *band, can be richly ornamented with continuous sculpture either in relief (as with Roman work), or as applied in different coloured stone (e.g. *Erechtheion), and may also be *pulvinated (as in the *thermae* of **Diocletian** (*r*.284–305), Rome). Cornice-mouldings can be rich, with bed-mouldings including *dentil-courses, egg-and-dart, or other ornament, as in the temple of *Fortuna Virilis*, Rome (*c*.40 BC). Additional *mouldings of bead-and-reel occur between the architrave *fasciae* in richer versions of the Order. One of the main problems when using Ionic is the capital, with its two distinct *elevations—one with the two volutes (desirable on a front), and the other with the *baluster-side or *pulvinus (not desirable on a *façade): in Greek temples, therefore, a 'special' had to be designed so that two adjacent volutes would appear on two faces at the external angle of a *portico by pulling the corner volutes out with concave curved faces at 45° (135° to each façade). This *angle-capital also had two adjacent partial volutes at the inner angle within the portico. This somewhat clumsy arrangement was superseded by the Romans, who invented a capital with four identical faces, the eight volutes projecting under the four corners of the abacus thus doing away with the need for a 'special' as all the capitals were the same on all four sides. This *angular capital* (also known as the *Scamozzi Order*) was used at the temple of Saturn, Rome (*c*.42 BC, rebuilt *c*.AD 320), and was the basis for the upper part of the *Composite capital. *See* AMMONITE.

J.Curl (2001); D (1950); C.Normand (1852)

Ipswich window C17 *oriel window, with convex sides between the wall and *mullions; *transoms two-thirds of the height of the convex side-*lights; and an arched centre-light with small lights on either side of an elaborate *ancon, the lights leaded, and the mullions and panels beneath the cills heavily encrusted with ornament. Good examples survive at Sparrowe's House, Buttermarket, Ipswich, Suffolk (*c*.1670). R.N.*Shaw used it at New Zealand Chambers, London (1871-3—demolished), and elsewhere.

Saint (1976)

iron Widely used in architecture. There are two basic types: *cast iron*—strong in compression, but weak in tension, used for columns, *bollards, railings, and decorative features; and *wrought iron*—employed for *gates, ornamental *scrolls, filigree-work, and the like. Some fine medieval ironwork survives, notably associated with tombs and *chantry-chapels in English cathedrals. Later, iron was widely used for balcony-fronts, railings, etc., in C18. Exposed cast iron was used for components in whole *façades in C19, notably by John *Baird in Glasgow, and wrought iron was employed to construct large *trusses spanning wide spaces. Many C19 catalogues of cast-iron components, notably by *Badger in the USA and the Saracen Factory, Glasgow, survive. *Fairbairn's *On the Application of Cast and Wrought Iron to Building Purposes* (1854) was an important publication. Iron-and-glass structures were developed for *conservatories, railway-stations, exhibition-buildings, etc., notably by *Loudon, *Paxton, et al. Iron was used structurally, starting with late-C18 bridges such as at Coalbrookdale, Salop. (1777-9), Sunderland (1793-6), and Buildwas, Salop. (1795-6), and then for factories and warehouses, notably at **William Strutt**'s (1756–1830) Mill, Derby (1792), and the Marshall, Benyon, & Bage Mill, Shrewsbury, Salop. (1796), both of which had cast-iron columns carrying beams from which sprang brick vaults. Developments in iron structures occurred when composite girders and columns were made, using rivets, and gradually framed buildings were evolved, permitting speed of erection, great heights, and light claddings. Ultimately, the steel frame permitted the building of *skyscrapers. *See also* METAL STRUCTURES.

J.Curl (2007, 2011a); Fairbairn (1849, 1869, 1870); Fairbairn & Pole (1970); G & B (1948); G & G (1974); G.Hartung (1983); Lemoine (1986); Loudon (1834); Mainstone (1975); R & R (1994); S (1901–2)

ironstone Stone containing iron-ore, which influences colour (e.g. brown, brownish-red, etc.).

Isabelline *or* **Isabellino style 1.** Style of late-*Gothic architecture in the Spain of **Ferdinand and Isabella** (1474–1516), contemporary with the *Manueline style of Portugal, and characterized by a love of ornament. A good example is *San Juan de los Reyes*, Toledo (from 1477) by Juan *Guas. Essentially a fusion of Netherlandish forms with the *Mudéjar style of Castile, it was particularly associated with Toledo, Burgos, Palencia, and Valladolid (where Italian-*Renaissance elements first began to penetrate). The term **Hispano-Flemish** style is preferred to avoid confusion with (**2**). **2.** Style prevalent in Spain and Latin America during the reign of **Isabella II** (1830–68).

J.T (1996)

Isidorus of Miletus (*fl.*C6) Greek architect/
engineer/geometer/universal man, he worked
with *Anthemios of Tralles on the design and
construction of the great *Byzantine Church of
Hagia Sophia, Constantinople (532–7). They may
also have worked on the Church of the Holy
Apostles, Constantinople (*c.*536–550—destroyed—
the model for *San Marco*, Venice (begun 1063)).
When the *dome of *Hagia Sophia* collapsed (558),
it was rebuilt to a modified design by **Isidorus the
Younger**, also from Miletus, probably the elder
man's nephew.

Krautheimer (1986); Mango (1972, 1986); D.Wa (1986)

Islamic architecture Term associated with
buildings connected with the followers (Muslims)
of **Mohammed** (*c.*570–632). Islamic architecture
has several characteristic features, including the
pointed, multifoil, low, wide, four-centred, and
horseshoe *arch, the *muqarna* or stalactite *corbel, cladding of coloured glazed earthenware and
patterned tilework, fretted *gables of stone, *marble, or *stucco, and, above all, coherent and
serene geometry. *Domes, *minarets, *cloisters,
and elaborate *battlements, often of the *almena*
type, are commonly associated with Islamic
buildings. Islamic architecture probably influenced design in the West, notably the pointed
arch and *cusping in the medieval period (though
some deny this), and the stylistic aspects of so-
called *Moresque* architecture in which elements of
Islamic, especially *Moorish (e.g. the Alhambra,
Granada, Spain), architecture were used as part of
the European enchantment with exotic oriental
styles in the C18 (e.g. the work of *Chambers at
Kew) and C19 (e.g. *Persius's steam-engine house
at Potsdam (1841–2), and *Aitchison's Arab Hall in
Kensington (1877–9)). *See* MOORISH ARCHITECTURE.

Ashraf & Belluardo (eds) (1998); B & B (1994); Conner
(1979); Ck (1996); Ettinghausen & Grabar (1988); Hillenbrand (1994); Hoag (1986); L & D (1986); M & P
(2011); Petersen (1996); J.T (1996)

Islamic garden Found in Asia, the Middle
East, North Africa, Spain, and Turkey, albeit with
regional variations, the constants were geometrical layouts, the presence of water, shade, quiet,
enclosure, and a basis in religion, the model originating in Persia (modern Iran). Many gardens
were associated with funerary structures (e.g. the
grand *mausolea of Mughal India), but they were
also connected with *madrasas, *mosques, *palaces, and even quite modest houses. Essentially
introverted, they displayed ordered unity and
equilibrium: nearly always rectangular, with
paths and water-channels (sophisticated systems
of *hydraulics fed the central pools and *channels
(e.g. Alhambra, Granada, Spain)) laid out in geometrically ordered patterns, they were cool,
shady, delightful oases; protected microclimates

in the hostile, dry lands usual in many areas
where Islam held sway. *See* BĀGH; CHAHAR-BĀGH;
MUGHAL GARDEN; PARADISE GARDEN.

Gharipour (2013); Hunt (2012); MacDougall & Ettinghausen (eds) (1976); Pothorn (1971); Shoe (2001)

isodomon, isodomum 1. *Masonry consisting of blocks of stone of equal length laid in
courses of equal height, each vertical joint
centred on the block in the course below.
2. Masonry in which all the courses are of equal
height, but the alignment of vertical joints is irregular. *See* PSEUDISODOMON.

OED (1933); W.Pa (1852)

isometric projection Method of showing a
building with an illusion of three-dimensional
form by drawing a *plan to scale but not with
right angles (being set at 30° to the horizontal),
and projecting the vertical axes to scale. Thus the
plan is slightly distorted, but the effect is more
realistic than in an *axonometric projection,
although diagonals and curved lines are not accurately depicted.

FR (1946)

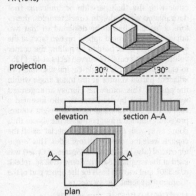

isometric projection

Italianate Style of C19 architecture modelled
on the *astylar Italian *palazzo*, represented by
the *Palazzo Farnese*, Rome (1517–89), by da *Sangallo the Younger and *Michelangelo. The plain
*façade had window-apertures framed by *aedi-
cules, *quoins were emphasized and the whole
front was topped by a large *cornicione*. Typical
are Charles *Barry's Travellers' (1829–32) and
Reform (1837–41) Clubs, Pall Mall, London, the
Northern (formerly Belfast) Bank Head Office,
Belfast (1845), by *Lanyon, and Osborne House,
IoW (1845–51), by Thomas *Cubitt and Prince
*Albert. Following such a Royal *imprimatur* Italianate *stucco ornament was widely used to

enrich the façades of *terrace-houses in areas such as Kensington, London, from the mid-C19. The style was widely used in Germany (especially Berlin, Dresden, and Munich) and in the USA. The term **Italianate garden** refers to gardens outside Italy influenced by Italian exemplars, e.g. the spectacular Shrubland Park, Suffolk (1848–52), also by Barry, the western garden of which has *terraces reminiscent of the *Villa d'Este*, Tivoli, and included a *gloriette* in *Cinquecento* style.

Bazin (1990); J.Curl (2007); D & M (1985); Hunt (ed.) 1996); L & H (1993); M & Wa (1987); Sh (1973)

Italian garden Garden-design in Italy was influenced by literary sources (e.g. *Pliny the Younger and *Vitruvius) giving information on *Roman gardens, reinterpreted during the *Renaissance, *Mannerist, and *Baroque periods. Spectacular C16 gardens (such as major exemplars in and around Rome, the *Villa d'Este*, Tivoli, and the *Villa Lante*, Bagnaia) depended on formal, geometrical layouts, with much architectural intervention (steps, *terraces, *balustrades, statuary, etc.), and, of course, elaborate *cascades, *fountains, and waterworks made possible by sophisticated developments in *hydraulics: they influenced garden-design elsewhere in Europe. Some gardens, e.g. the *Sacro Bosco*, *Villa Orsini*, Bomarzo, near Viterbo (from *c*.1552), have extraordinary, sometimes distorted, *fabriques as part of a complex iconographic programme of multifarious allusions. *See* PHILOSOPHER'S GARDEN.

Bazin (1990); Coffin (1960, 1979, 1991, 2004); Conan (ed.) (1999); Hunt (ed.) 1996); Hunt (2012); *JGH*, **iv**/1 (Jan. –March 1984), whole issue; Masson (1987); M & T (1991); Platt (1993); Tay (2006); J.T (1996); M.Woods (1996)

Italian roof Low-pitched *hip-roof covered with *pan-and-roll tiles.

Italian Villa style Eclectic style used for C19 domestic buildings originating with *Nash and other architects. Its main characteristics were very low-pitched roofs (sometimes hipped) with wide overhanging *eaves (often supported on ornamented *brackets or *mutules), asymmetrical compositions, windows that were sometimes treated as *aedicules but just as often had semicircular heads influenced by the fashionable *Rundbogenstil, square towers, often with a *loggia, and an *arcaded or *colonnaded element connecting it with the garden. Nash's Cronkhill, Salop. (*c*.1802), *Schinkel's and *Persius's Court Gardener's House, Potsdam (1829–33), and 'Greek' *Thomson's villas in and around Glasgow are good examples.

G & W (1987); Wa & M (1987)

Ittar, Henryk (1773–1850) Polish Neo-Classical architect of Italian extraction, he designed several of the *fabriques in the *Garden of Allusions at Arkadia, near Nieborów, Poland, including the Circus (1801) and Amphitheatre (*c*.1805) influenced by *Piranesi's visionary engravings. The Circus perhaps alluded to the Imperial Palace on the Palatine Hill, Rome (AD C1), but was otherwise unprecedented in European gardens. He was also responsible for the Isle of Poplars (complete with Rousseauesque 'tomb'). Some of his designs for buildings at Arkadia are among the most severe conceptions of their time.

AQC, **cxvi** (2004) 83–126; Ciołek (1978); J.Curl (2011); *GH*, **xxiii**/1 (1995), 91–112; L & R (1984); Piwkowski (1998)

Ivanov-Shits, Illarion Aleksandrovich (1865–1937) Russian architect, by the 1890s one of the most fashionable working in Moscow, where his Belkin and Martyanov houses made his name. From *c*.1898 his work was strongly influenced by that of Otto *Wagner, notably at the Hirsh Theatre and Restaurant (1898–1902—destroyed), the superb Merchants' Club (1905–9), and the State Savings Bank (1913–14—with a huge glass-roofed banking-hall). From 1900 he was a member of Moscow City's Construction Council, which was primarily concerned to meet the needs of the poor: among his works for those purposes may be cited the House of the People (1901–3), the Tea-Room Theatre, Lefortovo District, and other buildings with auditoria (all of similar dates). His other Classicizing-*Jugendstil* essays include the Shanyavsky People's University (1910–13), and the *Soldatenkovskaya* (later *Botkinskaya*) City Hospital (1908–12). From *c*.1911 his architecture became more severe and Neo-Classical (e.g. Cas'yanov and Orlov houses), Moscow City Bank (1922–5), and the Weisbrot Hospital (1923–6). He flirted with *Constructivism with the Sanatorium, Barvikh, near Moscow (1920s), but reverted to *Neo-Classicism from *c*.1930 (e.g. his work on *Ton's (1838–49) Andreyevsky and Aleksandrovsky Halls in the Kremlin Palace (1932–4), which became the Assembly Hall of the Supreme Soviet). He was clearly able to accommodate himself successfully to working from the 1890s to the 1930s, under very different régimes. He is one of the most seriously underrated Russian architects, whose work is virtually unknown in the West.

Raeburn (ed.) (1991); *Stroitel'stvo: arkhitektura Moskvy*, **iv** (1986), 24–6; J.T (1996)

iwan In *Islamic architecture, a vaulted space used as an entrance, or, if closed at one end, a hall facing a *court in a *madrasa or *mosque. From C11 four iwans disposed on axes on each side of a *court became usual in mosques, madrasas, and *caravanserais. *Vaults could be plain, half-elliptical barrels, or more elaborately decorated with *muqarnas. An impressive pre-Islamic precedent was that at the *Sassanian Palace, Ctesiphon, Iraq (C4 or C6).

B & B (1994); Ck (1996); Hillenbrand (1994)

Ixnard, Pierre-Michel d' (1723–95) French architect (originally **Pierre Michel**). An early protagonist of *Neo-Classicism in Germany, he made a career by passing himself off as an academically trained architect with an aristocratically resonant name (he was actually a joiner who had worked on e.g. stage-scenery) and by employing competent draughtsmen to work up designs into presentation drawings. Employed (1764) by **Prince Joseph Wilhelm von Hohenzollern-Hechingen** (1717–98) to remodel various interiors (destroyed), he designed sundry works for the Swabian aristocracy. His big chance came when he was commissioned to rebuild the *Benedictine *monastery and church of St Blasius, Waldshut, Black Forest (begun 1772). With its domed space surrounded by free-standing *Corinthian columns and *choir also featuring columns, the inspiration was clearly the Chapel at Versailles and the *Pantheon: St Blasius was the first significant Neo-Classical building in Southern Germany, and was completed under the direction of *Pigage when d'Ixnard's contract was cancelled

(1774). D'Ixnard designed the Church of Sts Cornelius and Cyprian, Bad Buchau (1773–6), and was commissioned (1777) by **Prince Clemens Wenzeslaus of Saxony** (1739–1812), **Archbishop-Elector of Trier** (1768–1803), to prepare designs for a vast *Residenz* at Koblenz, with a *Giant Order of columns and pilasters to unify the scheme, and a dome over the *corps-de-logis*. Although work started (1778), the architecture was adversely criticized, and a reduced version of the palace was erected from 1779 to designs by A.-F.*Peyre. D'Ixnard also prepared drawings for a series of *crescents and *circuses within a *grid-plan for Clemensstadt, later Neustadt, Koblenz (1777), a spacious new town, also for the Archbishop-Elector, only partly realized. His proposals for the *Residenz* were published in his *Recueil d'Architecture* (1791). Other works by D'Ixnard include the Merchants' Guildhall, *Zum Spiegel*, Strasbourg (1782–5), the church at Hechingen, near Stuttgart (1780–3), the library of the *Collège Royal*, Colmar (1785–7), and the Church at Epfig (1790–1).

E.Franz (1985); Ixnard (1791); *Jahrbuch der staatlichen Kunstsammlungen in Baden-Württemberg*, vi (1969), 161–8; J.T (1996); Wa & M (1987); *W-R-J*, liii (1992), 155–75

jack 1. *Rafter set obliquely where two roofs meet (e.g. in *dormers or *valleys). **2.** Short *common rafter* (e.g. between *eaves and a *hip).

jack arch *See* ARCH.

Jackson, John (*c*.1602–63) English master-mason active in Oxford, he oversaw the building of Canterbury Quadrangle, St John's College (from 1634). The unusual south porch at the Church of St Mary the Virgin (1637), with *Solomonic columns and other *Baroque effects curiously co-existing with the *Perp. fan-vaulting of the ceiling, is a *tour-de-force*, and is known to have been *built* by him, although Nicholas *Stone's name has been associated with the *design*. He was consulted about the tower and gateway of University College (1635–6), and superintended the building of the new Chapel and Library of Brasenose College (1656–66), where late-*Gothic and *Renaissance elements are again mixed with great *élan*. He may have designed Welford Park, Berks. (*c*.1660—later remodelled).

Co (2008)

Jackson, Thomas (1807–90) Accomplished Irish architect, he was in partnership with *Duff of Newry, Co. Down, with whom he designed the *Greek-Revival Old Museum, College Square North, Belfast (1830–1). He settled in Belfast where he laid out an estate of Grecian *villas on the Cliftonville Road, Belfast (1831–2), and designed several fine Neo-Classical houses, including Graymount (1835), a pair of villas at Mount Charles (1842), and Clonard House (1843). He was probably responsible for 4–30 University Square, but his masterpiece is the charming *Tudor-Gothic RC Church of St Malachy (1840–4), with its beautiful *plaster fan-*vault. He designed a series of ambitious *Italianate villas, including Glenmachan Tower (1860s), Altona (1864), and Craigavon (1870), all in Belfast. He took his son, **Anthony Thomas Jackson** (1838–1917) into practice as **Thomas Jackson & Son**, and together they designed the first purpose-made insurance-offices in Belfast in the form of a Venetian *palazzo* at 10 Victoria Street (1863) as well as the round-arched former Town Hall, Victoria Street (1869–71).

Brett (1967, 1996); *DIA;* Dixon (1978); Larmour (1987); McClenaghan (1983); *P: JRSUA,* iii/2 (Nov/Dec 1994), 57–9; J.Williams (1994)

Jackson, Sir Thomas Graham (1835–1924) English architect, pupil of 'Great' *Scott, he commenced practice in 1862. Works include the *Jacobethan Examination Schools (1876–82); the vaguely *Gothic New Buildings, Brasenose College (1909–11); Girls' High School, Banbury Road (1879); Boys' High School, George Street (1880–1); and new buildings for Hertford College (1887–1914—including the chapel and the 'bridge of sighs', in a style Jackson himself called 'refined English Renaissance'), all in Oxford. Other works include the Science Block, Uppingham School, Rut. (1894–7), extensions (including the Chapel) to Radley College, Berks. (1891–1910), and the Chapel at Giggleswick, Yorks. (1897). He published much, including *Reason in Architecture* (1906), *Byzantine and Romanesque Architecture* (1913), and *Gothic Architecture in France, England, and Italy* (1915).

D & M (1985); A.S.Gray (1985); T.Jackson (2003)

Jacobean architecture Style of English architecture of the reign of **King James I & VI** (1603–25), not greatly differing from *Elizabethan architecture, and largely continuing into the reign of **Charles I** (1625–49). It was essentially a *mélange* of Flemish, French, and Italian-*Renaissance influences, with pronounced emphases on themes drawn from Flemish *Mannerism, including *jewelled *strapwork and *grotesque ornament. *Assemblages of Orders, emblems, heraldic devices, *herms, *obelisks, and curved and Dutch *gables were also favoured. Traces of *Gothic, especially *Perp., architecture remained, notably the continuing use of mullioned and transomed windows, and the late-medieval **E-** and **H-**plans were also used. Examples of Jacobean architecture are Hatfield House, Herts. (1607–12), Bramshill, Surrey (1605–12), and Audley End, Essex (1603–16). However, Inigo *Jones's contributions also took place in the reigns of James I & VI and Charles I, but his sophisticated Palladian style is not described as 'Jacobean'.

There was a *Jacobean Revival* in C19, notably in country-houses, and it was also mixed with the *Queen-Anne style to produce hybrids (e.g. R.N.*Shaw's New Zealand Chambers, London (1872–3—demolished)).

Airs (1995); Ck (1996); L & D (1986); Mowl (1993); Pe: *BoE* (1951–); S (1901–2); Su (1993)

Jacobean Mannerist garden Until 1603, when **James VI of Scotland** ascended the Throne as King of England, Scotland, and Ireland (*r.* until 1625), England had been to some extent isolated from artistic developments on the Continent during the reign of **Elizabeth I** (1558–1603). With the accession of the Stuarts, however, contacts were renewed with Italian art as the Court (in which the Queen, **Anne of Denmark** (1574–1619) played no small part) set the fashion after years of frugality. The inspiration for the Mannerist *fountain-and-*grotto mania which gripped *Jacobean England was the celebrated garden of Pratolino, outside Florence, filtered through French gardens such as those at *Fontainebleau and St Germain-en-Laye, and the key figure was the Huguenot Salomon de *Caus, who knew the gardens of the *Villa d'Este*, Tivoli, and Frascati, and was an expert on *hydraulics and *automata. The Queen appointed de Caus to design the gardens of her London home, Somerset House, which contained a huge grotto-fountain alluding to Mount Parnassus. Jacobean gardens retained certain earlier aspects (e.g. the *hortus conclusus*, *knots, *topiary, and so on), but new elaborate features introduced by de Caus set the scene for a new generation of English gardens in which esoteric symbols, elaborate water-features, and 'grots' were all the rage (e.g. Richmond Palace, Surrey (1610–12), Hatfield House, Herts. (1607–12), and other exemplars). Isaac de *Caus, sometimes collaborating with Inigo *Jones, also developed Mannerist gardens at, e.g. Moor Park, Herts. (*c.*1617–27), and Wilton, Wilts. (*c.*1633). From *c.*1615 such gardens also acquired sculpture in the form of statues, but the Mannerist garden in England was essentially a place of 'conceits', with geometrical layouts based on circles, squares, and triangles, intended to be read symbolically or as puzzles: it was a garden of *incident, not yet embracing a distant *point de vue*, and largely inward-looking. *See* MANNERISM.

Bazin (1990); Strong (1979); Symes (2006)

Jacobethan Revivalist architecture of C19 and early C20, in which *Elizabethan and *Jacobean elements were freely mixed. William *Burn specialized in the style for his country-houses.

Co (2008); L & D (1986); L & H (1993)

Jacob, Sir Samuel Swinton (1841–1917) English architect/engineer/writer, Chief Engineer to Jaipur State, India, where he spent most of his working life. He published *Jeypore Portfolio of Architectural Details* (1890)—an enormous collection which became an important reference-work. Among his best buildings were the Anglican Church (1870–5), Albert Hall and Museum, Jaipur (1876–87), and many civic and educational buildings in Lucknow. When he returned to England (1911) he advised on Indian materials and details during the planning stage of the Indian capital at New Delhi.

Builder, **cxiii** (14 Dec. 1917), 345; Davies (1985); *RIBAJ*, n.s.3, **xxv** (1918), 72; J.T (1996)

Jacobsen, Arne Emil (1902–71) Danish architect, he was influenced by *International Modernism, as is demonstrated in his own house (1928) and in the Bellavista Estate, Klampenborg (1934), both in Copenhagen, where he embraced the style of the Stuttgart *Weissenhofsiedlung*. *Asplund's architecture informed his designs for Aarhus (1937–42—with **Svend Erik Møller** (1909–2002)) and Søllerød (1940–2—with **Flemming Lassen** (1902–84)) Town Halls. He used refined *curtain-walls from the 1950s, examples of which were the Jespersen Building (1955), and Rødovre Town Hall (1955), both in Copenhagen. Attention to detail (including furnishings and fittings) was clear in St Catherine's College, Oxford (1960–4—with **Knud Helmuth Holscher** (1930–)), where the brickwork and *precast concrete were meticulously detailed in every respect. He was responsible for the Danish Embassy, Sloane Street, London (1969–77), which, like his *Rathaus*, Mainz, Germany (1970–3), was completed by his colleagues **Hans Oluf Dissing** (1926–98) and **Otto Weitling** (1930–).

Dyssegaard (1972); E (1994); Faber (1964); Kastholm (1968); pk; Sheridan (2003); Skriver et al. (1971); Thau & Vindum (1998, 2001); Tøjner & Vindum (1996); J.T (1996)

Jacobsen, Holger Alfred (1876–1960) Danish architect, he designed Bispebjerg Crematorium, Copenhagen (1905–7), drawing on eclectic motifs, which made his name. Later he worked on the Police Headquarters, Copenhagen (1918–24—with **Anton Frederiksen** (1884–1967), *Kampmann, and *Rafn), an important C20 Neo-Classical building. His most significant work was the *Nye Scene*, a major extension to the Royal Theatre, Copenhagen (designed 1919, completed 1931), in which *Mannerism and stripped *Neo-Classicism are evident, although the interior has touches of colourful *Art Deco, without parallel in Denmark. His Neo-Classical *villas of the 1920s (including his own house, Copenhagen (1926)) combined a rational approach to planning with a scholarly refinement of detail.

Pn (1982); J.T (1996); We (1949)

Jacobsen, Theodore (*fl.*1730–72) English architect of German descent, he worked in London, where his best-known building was the Foundling Hospital (1742–52—demolished 1928). He is remembered today for the main quadrangle, Trinity College, Dublin (1752–9).

Co (2008); *ODNB* (2004)

Jacobs, Jane Butzner (1916–2006) American critic, she began her career (1952) as a writer with *Architectural Forum*. Believing cities provide the foundation for civilization, she made her name with *The Death and Life of Great American Cities* (1961), a sustained attack on so-called *'*urban renewal' being promoted by architects and centralized agencies, arguing that such policies were killing the living organism that was the city, and demanding a new respect for self-generating urban forces to create social and economic diversity and well-being. Her realization that the orthodoxies of *CIAM and the *Athens Charter (e.g. zoning and a free-for-all for motor-cars), which had permeated Government and professional circles, were strangling and ruining cities led to an important chapter in *The Exploding Metropolis* (1958) in which she argued that 'Downtown is for People' at a time when traditional urban centres were dying. Her studies convinced her that when the principles advocated by Le *Corbusier (on one hand) and Ebenezer *Howard (on the other) were applied (as they almost invariably were), they not only failed to stop decay, but actually made matters worse, causing immense social and economic problems: drabness and uniformity were imposed where once there was charm and variety. She rightly saw that cities were far more complex, like living organisms, than insensitive simplistic notions of Modernists would allow, and advocated that forces advancing social and economic *diversity* should be *encouraged* rather than *obstructed*. She illustrated her points with real case-histories, pointing out that *high density* was not the same as *overcrowding*, and drawing attention to why certain areas were pleasant in which to live and work, while others were not. In her *The Economy of Cities* (1969) she showed how manufacturing and trade helped the economies of rural areas, and why some cities flourished and others stagnated. Again she emphasized the importance of *diversity*, stressing that economic well-being rests with many small, innovative, different businesses rather than with grand conglomerations and monopolies. While her work became accepted and widely read, she herself complained that very little had changed and that the same mistakes were being 'compulsively repeated', not least because of unintelligent 'urban studies' and the use of myriad statistics to justify the same old panaceas, which were nothing of the sort. Her

work encouraged the *conservation movement, and many of her heretical ideas were adopted, despite vicious attacks on her by *Banham et al.

J.Jacobs (1961, 1969, 1984, 1992, 1996)

Jadot de Ville Issey, Jean-Nicolas (1710–61) French architect, trained by *Boffrand, he settled in Vienna under the aegis of **Francis Stephen, Duke of Lorraine** (1708–65—consort of **Maria Theresia** (*r.*1740–80)). He designed the *Arco San Gallo*, Florence (1738–9), to commemorate Francis Stephen's accession to the Grand Duchy of Tuscany (1739), and, after he arrived in Vienna, was the architect of the *Alte Aula*, or Old University (later *Akademie der Wissenschaften*—1753–5), and the *Schönbrunn Menagerie*, both in the *Louis-Quinze* style. He may have been responsible for the plan for the Royal Palace in Budapest (1749).

Kalnein (1995); *Römische historische Mitteilungen*, xxxi (1989), 319–38

Jäger, Hermann (1815–90) German horticulturalist, trained in Weimar and Paris, he studied gardens throughout Europe and England (1830s and '40s) before becoming (1845) Court Gardener to the **Grand Duchy of Saxe-Weimar-Eisenach**. He is remembered for books and articles (published from the 1850s until his death) in which influences from *Downing, *Hirschfeld, *Loudon, *Pückler-Muskau, *Repton, *Sckell, and *Whately, among others, may be detected: they include *Lehrbuch der Gartenkunst* (1877—in which he gave equal value to 'natural' and 'artificial' styles), and *Gartenkunst und Gärten Sonnst und Jetzt* (1888—a history of landscape architecture from Classical Antiquity to the 1880s). From 1857 he co-edited *Gartenflora*.

Shoe (2001)

Jahn, Helmut (1940–) *See* MURPHY/JAHN.

jalousie 1. External slatted or *louvred shutter. **2.** Grille protecting a *gallery in a church.

jamb Vertical side of an aperture, such as a window or doorway, essentially that part on which a superincumbent load is sustained. That part of the jamb between the *outer* wall and the door- or window-frame is the *reveal*. A *jamb-shaft* is a *colonnette or *shaft, often *detached, set against or part of the junction of a jamb and an internal or external wall in medieval architecture.

James, John (*c.*1672–1746) English architect, he was joint Clerk of the Works at Greenwich with *Hawksmoor, and became (1715) Assistant Surveyor to *Wren at St Paul's Cathedral, London, succeeding to the Surveyorship on Wren's death (1723). When *Gibbs was dismissed, James became (1716) Hawksmoor's colleague as Surveyor to the Commissioners for Building Fifty

New Churches, and designed St George's, Hanover Square, London (1720–5), with its handsome *Corinthian *portico (the precedent for Gibbs's St Martin-in-the-Fields). With Hawksmoor he designed St Luke's, Old Street, London, with its original *obelisk-spire (1727–33—converted into a Music Centre for the London Symphony Orchestra to designs by **Levitt, Bernstein, & Associates** 1999–2003), and St John's, Horselydown, Southwark (1727–33—demolished). On Hawksmoor's death (1736) James became Surveyor to the Dean and Chapter of Westminster, and completed the western towers of Westminster Abbey to Hawksmoor's designs. He also added the not entirely satisfactory *steeple to Hawksmoor's otherwise robust St Alphege's, Greenwich (1730). He published several works, including *Rules and Examples of Perspective* (1707, 1725) translated from *Pozzo's original (1693) and *A Treatise on the Five Orders of Columns* (1708) from *Perrault's original (1683).

Co (2008); J.Curl (2011a); Downes (1966, 1980); Friedman (2011); *GGJ* (1994), 4–10; E.Hs (ed.) (1990); Lees-Milne (1970); *ODNB* (2004); Su (1993)

jami *Mosque serving the population of an area, also called *masjid al-jami*.

Janyns, Henry (*fl.*1453–83) English mason, son of Robert *Janyns, appointed (*c.*1475) Chief Mason of the Works at the Chapel of St George, Windsor Castle, Berks., and responsible for the foundations and early stages of the building. He may have designed the tomb of **Cardinal-Archbishop Thomas Bourchier** (*c.*1411–86) in Canterbury Cathedral and the monument of **King Edward IV** (*r.*1461–83) in Windsor.

J.Harvey (1987)

Janyns, Robert (*fl.*1438–64) English mason, Warden of the Masons at All Souls College, Oxford (1438–43), master-mason during the building of the bell-tower at Merton College, Oxford (1448–51), and Warden of the Masons, Eton College. He was also involved in the building of the Divinity Schools, Oxford (1452–3). He made and fixed the carving above the *gateway of Merton College (1463–4).

J.Harvey (1987)

Janyns, Robert, jun. (*fl.*1499–1506) English mason, son of Robert *Janyns, Chief Mason during the building of **King Henry VII's** (*r.*1485–1509) polygonal tower at Windsor Castle, Berks. (1499), where he remained until 1505. He may have designed the *Lady Chapel, Burford Church, Oxon. (1490s), the four-centred windows of which resemble those at St George's Chapel, Windsor, and was probably in charge of building at the Royal Palace, Richmond, Surrey, after 1497 (destroyed).

J.Harvey (1987)

Japanese garden-design Of volcanic origins, the Japanese archipelago (more than a thousand islands rising from the sea and possessing a great many steeply sided valleys) was blessed with a wide range of *flora*. The inhabitants early acquired acute sensitivities to natural sites, creating gardens in which rigid geometries were avoided and stylization of features was evident. Long before ideas about garden-design were imported from China and Korea, Japanese gardens featured boulders, ponds, large trees, and waterfalls, perceived as 'points of connection' through which contacts with *kami* (deities) were possible, so areas around such features were regarded as sacred. Animistic perceptions of the natural world by which living souls and vital principles were associated with inanimate objects and natural phenomena were essential ingredients of design.

Detailed expositions of the complexities of the subject cannot be attempted here, given the impact of Buddhism and Shintoism, so only an outline of basic principles will be set out. The first of these is the *miniaturization* of idealized views of Nature (rocks = mountains or islands; ponds = seas; sand = water); the second is the art of *concealment* behind trees, hills, groves, walls, or buildings, so that scenes are only *revealed* during a walk through a garden; the third is *asymmetry*, eschewing straight axes and any single feature dominating the landscape; the fourth consists of *borrowed landscapes* beyond the confines of the immediate enclosed garden; and the fifth is the careful *placing of buildings*, often beautifully constructed of timber, with possibilities of opening whole sides for the enjoyment of the garden without (they were unlike often heavily ornamented Chinese garden-buildings sited next to or over water). Japanese gardens featuring sea-worn pebbles or rocks, set in white sand to suggest the sea, were contrasted with Chinese gardens alluding to mountains and inland scenery.

So, rooted in a tradition of stylized idealized landscapes designed for pleasure, recreation, or contemplation, types included the meditative *rock-, dry-, or *zen-garden (*karesansui*), where empty spaces were as important as the objects (e.g. boulders), and raked sand representing the sea often featured; the *roji* *rustic garden with buildings for the formalized tea-ceremony; the garden for promenading (*kaiyu-shiki-teien*) in which composed landscapes were revealed during the walk; and the small, enclosed, exquisite, courtyard-garden. Japan has long been able to absorb influences from outside, historically from China, and the single view, the lake, the island, the *bridge, falling water, trees, and elaborate stonework were imports, but given a distinctive Nipponese flavour. Religious meanings of hills, stones, trees, boulders, and so on triggered associations with real landscapes, suggesting profound symbolism for contemplation and the exercise of the imagination. Traditions of Japanese gardens were passed down through apprentices, but fortunately there were garden-treatises, e.g. the C11 *Sakuteiki* (Records of Garden-Making), supposedly by *Tachibana-no-Tohshitsuna (in which both Chinese and Korean influences are detectable); **Kokan Shiren**'s (1278-1347) work on a Miniature Landscape-Garden (*c.*1300); the C15 *Senzui Narabi ni Yagko no Zu* (Illustrations for designing Mountain, Water, and Hillside-Filled Landscapes); and the C18 *Tsukiyama Teizoden* (Building Mountains and Making Gardens) which tell us a great deal about the subject.

It appears to have been through trade involving 'factories' of Western organizations such as the Dutch East India Company (which had premises at Deshima, Nagasaki, in C17) that ideas about irregular, asymmetrical design (*see* SHARAWADGI) began to filter Westwards. Towards the end of the **Edo** dynasty (1600-1868) and the commencement of the **Meiji** period (1868-1912), Japanese culture became accessible to the West, prompting an enthusiasm for things Japanese (*see* JAPONAISERIE). Apart from earlier notions of irregularity in design sparked by the writings of, e.g., Sir William *Temple, Japanese gardens were lauded by authors such as JOSIAH *CONDER. Japanese-inspired gardens included those of Heale House, Woodford, Wilts. (early C20); the Huntingdon Library Japanese Garden, San Marino, CA, USA (1912); Park Japoński, Szczytnicki, Wrocław (1912-13); the Japanese Garden, Tully, Co. Kildare (1906-10—with bridge, stone lanterns, and a teak 'geisha-house', all designed by **Tassa Eida**); and an exemplar at *Greene & Greene's Blacker House, Pasadena, CA (1907), carefully related to the building. **Samuel Newsom** (1899-1996) brought his interpretations of Japanese gardening into North America in the 1930s with a series of books, and later Western interest in Zen Buddhism encouraged further Japanese themes in gardens. The Japanese-American, ISAMU *NOGUCHI, produced numerous designs, including the *courtyards and *roof-garden of the Beinicke Rare Book and Manuscript Library, Yale University, New Haven, CT (1960-4), mingling Japanese principles of garden-design with Westernized symbolism, used perhaps with a touch of irony. His work demonstrates a response to his roots in the context of a different culture, although deeper philosophical and symbolic meanings, very much part of Japanese approaches to landscape-design (in, say, the significant placing of a boulder, or the way in which a tree might be trained), challenge Western eyes and understanding.

Post-1945 Japan tended to move away from traditional approaches to garden-design, but trends have subsequently emerged that seem to suggest attempts to re-incorporate them within contemporary environments.

Conder (1964); Gothein (1966); Hunt (2012); Keane (1996); Kuck (1996); Kuitert (2002); Newson (1939, 1955, 1965); Nitschke (2007); Reeves-Smyth (2001); Shoe (2001); Slawson & Myer (1987); Symes (2006); Tachibana-no-Toshitsuna (1985); Takei & Keane (2001); Tay (2006); Wichman (1999); Young & Young (2005)

Japelli, *or* **Jappelli, Giuseppe** (1783-1852) Unusually eclectic Italian architect, he trained under *Selva before designing his most celebrated work, the *Caffè Pedrocchi*, Padua (1816-31), reckoned by H.-R.*Hitchcock to be the 'handsomest C19 café in the world' and the 'finest Romantic Classical edifice in Italy'. It is an essay in *Neo-Classicism with Greek-*Doric, *Corinthian, *Empire, *Palladian, *Gothic, *Moorish, and *Egyptian-esque themes: *Il Pedrocchino*, an 1837 extension, is Venetian-*Gothic in style. From 1816 he worked on the *Villa dei Conti Cittadella Vigodarsere*, Saonara, near Padua, with a *Pantheon-like dome over the chapel, and a strong whiff of *Palladianism throughout. The gardens of the *villa were in the English style, complete with *Picturesque compositions and *fabriques in several styles. He also designed the garden for the *Villa dei Baroni Treves de' Bonfili*, Padua (late 1810s and 1820s). Other works include the severe *Greek-Revival Meat Market, Padua (1819-24), *Moorish conservatory, *Villa Torlonia*, Rome (1830s—where the park was also in the *giardino inglesi* style), and the Neo-*Empire *Rococo *Teatro Nuovo*, Padua (1846-7). Among his other garden-designs were those at Castelguelfo, near Parma (early 1830s), at Tradate, near Varese, at Vaccarino, near Padua, and at Precenicco, Friuli (all 1830s).

Bussadori *et al.* (1983); Fiocco (1931); Hi (1977); Lavagnino (1961); Mazza (1978); Mazzi (ed.) (1982); Ms (1966); M & Wa (1987); Li.Puppi (1980a); J.T (1996)

Japonaiserie Late-C19 term (interchangeable with **Japonisme**), counterpart of *Chinoiserie, meaning design influenced by the arts of Japan. Until the mid-C19 Japan was largely closed to the West. After the USA (followed by European nations) signed a trade agreement (1858) with that country, Japanese artefacts became more familiar, and greatly influenced Western *Aesthetic, *Art Nouveau, *Arts-and-Crafts, and even *International-Modernist designers of furniture and buildings (among those to draw inspiration from Japan were E.W.*Godwin and *Mies van der Rohe (e.g. Farnsworth House, Plano, IL (1946-50)). Fashionable taste appreciated the simplicity of Japanese objects after various exhibitions (e.g. London (1862) and Paris (1867)), and by the 1870s *Japonaiserie* permeated art and architecture, especially in Britain, France, and the USA. Various publications helped to make it familiar, including **Sir Rutherford Alcock**'s (1809-97) *Art and Art Industries of Japan* (1878), **T.W.Cutler**'s (1841/2-1909) *Grammar of Japanese Ornament and Design* (1880), **Louis Gonse**'s (1846-1921) *L'Art Japonais* (1883), and **Siegfried** (*not* Samuel) **Bing**'s (1838-1905) *Artistic Japan* (1888-91—with French and German editions). Bing's shops in Paris popularized *Japonaiserie*, while his connections with the firm of **Tiffany** in NYC contributed to the spread of the style to the USA. A further catalyst was provided by *Dresser, who not only knew Japan and supplied Tiffany & Co. with Japanese *objets d'art*, but married a Japanese woman, and published *Japan, its Architecture, Art, and Manufactures* (1882).

Gh (2000); Jervis (1984); L & D (1986); Soros (2000); Wichmann (1999)

Jardin, Nicolas-Henri (1720-99) French Neo-Classical architect, he moved to Denmark (1754), where, as Professor at the Royal Academy, he was influential. He continued the *Frederikskirke*, Copenhagen (1749-1894), a fine, domed Neo-Classical essay, begun by *Eigtved, completing the lower part and the eastern portal: the church was finished by *Harsdorff, *Meldahl, et al. Jardin's dining-room (1755-7) in the Amalienborg Palace, Copenhagen, was described by Eriksen as probably designed the 'earliest surviving room decorated entirely in the Neo-Classical style by a French architect'.

Eriksen (1974); Ha (1946); Høller (1973); M & Wa (1987); J.T (1996)

jardin anglais Term used on the Continent to describe the 'natural' type of C18 garden with winding *paths, *clumps of trees, etc., pioneered in England.

Pa & Pl (eds) (1977); Racine (ed.) (2001); Symes (2006)

jardin anglo-chinois French term for the informal type of 'natural' garden. *See also* SHARAWADGI.

M & T (1991); Pa & Pl (eds) (1977)

jardinet Large ornamental circular basin for growing plants, e.g. on a *terrace. *See* CONTAINER.

jardinière Ornamental receptacle for growing flowers indoors or on *balconies, window-cills, etc. *See* CONTAINER.

Jarman, Derek (1942-94) *See* COASTAL GARDEN.

Jarvis, Geoffrey (1928-2009) Scots architect who conserved many historic buildings in his native land, including Robert *Adam's Culzean Castle, Ayrshire, converting (1972) the Home Farm into a Visitors' Centre. Other works included the Clan Donald Centre, Armadale, Skye (early 1980s), and a restoration of William *Adam's heavily rusticated hunting-lodge known as the 'Dogg-Kennels' (1731-43), Chatelherault,

Lanarkshire. He promoted *conservation and *regeneration in Glasgow, often in the teeth of philistine political opposition.

Guardian (15 June 2009), Obits

jaspé, jaspered Marbled, mottled, veined, and coloured paint finish to represent *marble, as on a *dado or column-*shaft.

Jay, William (c.1793-1837) English architect, his Albion Chapel, Moorfields, London (1815-16—demolished) was admired by James *Elmes. Jay, however, emigrated (1817) to Savannah, GA, USA, where he designed some of the earliest *Greek-Revival houses (e.g. Owen Thomas House Museum, Telfair House, and Scarborough House (1818, 1820)). He returned to England (1822), and probably designed houses in Columbia Place, Winchcombe Street, Cheltenham, Glos. He was responsible for Watermoor House, Cirencester, Glos. (1825-7), and for two houses in Pittville Parade (now Evesham Road), Cheltenham.

Co (2008); *JSAH*, xxii/4, (Dec. 1963), 225-7

Jean de Chelles (*fl*.C13) *See* CHELLES.

Jean d'Orbais (*fl*.C13) *See* ORBAIS.

Jeanneret-Gris, Arnold-André-Pierre (1896-1967) Swiss architect, he joined the office of *Perret in Paris, before establishing an office (1921-40) with his cousin, Le *Corbusier, which became a magnet for the aspiring young, not only because of the well-publicized *Modern-Movement designs produced there, but because of published Modernist polemics (a few of which were signed jointly by both men, including the *Five Points of Architecture*, the basis for their theory of design). Their combined efforts produced paradigms of the Modern Movement, including the *Villa Besnus*, Vaucresson (1922), the *Pavillon de L'Esprit Nouveau* for the *Exposition Internationale des Arts-Décoratifs et Industriels Modernes*, Paris (1924-5), houses for the *Weissenhofsiedlung, Stuttgart (1927), the *Maison Stein*, Garches (1927-9), the *Villa Savoie*, Poissy (1928-31), the *Tsentrosoyuz* Building, Moscow (1928-36), the *Cité de Refuge*, Paris (1929-33), the *Maison Suisse, Cité Universitaire*, Paris (1930-3), and the Apartment House *Clarté*, Geneva (1930-2). Although they jointly produced designs, Jeanneret-Gris seems to have been more closely involved in resolving details and supervising construction. Both men participated in debate, meetings, and events that helped to form the ideology of Modernism, such as *CIAM (from 1928).

After the Fall of France (1940) the two went their separate ways, not least because the authoritarian Le Corbusier had strong affinities with, and leanings towards, the Nazi-collaborationist Vichy *régime*. Jeanneret-Gris established an office in Grenoble where (with *Prouvé and others) he designed prefabricated systems for housing. He returned to Paris (1944), and designed (1946-7—unrealized) a large apartment-building which anticipated Le Corbusier's *Unités d'Habitation*, although the apartments were planned to permit more daylight to enter the interior than Le Corbusier was able to achieve. However, his collaboration with Le Corbusier was re-established when he began to work with him, *Fry, and *Drew (1951) on plans for a new capital of the Punjab at Chandigarh, India, and supervised the construction of designs by Le Corbusier, including the Supreme Court. He himself designed numerous buildings there, including hospitals, housing, offices, schools, and shops, as well as the grander State Library, City Hall, Governor's Palace, and much else, often working with Indian colleagues. From 1961 he worked on the new University of the Punjab. In particular, he experimented with non-mechanical methods of environmental control.

Jeanneret-Gris's name has been overshadowed by Corbusier's, who was the more charismatic publicist, but it is clear he was of enormous importance in the genesis of paradigms with which the pseudonym of his cousin is solely associated in the popular mind.

Bulletin d'information architecturales, cxiv (1987); *Design*, viii/9 (1964), 17–24; E (1994); J-G & Jeanneret (1999); P (1982); *PA*, xlv/2 (1964), 148–53; A.Roth (1977); *Werk*, lv/6 (1968), 377–96; *see also* references after the Corbusier entry.

Jebb, Philip Vincent Belloc (1927-95) English architect, brother-in-law of Francis *Pollen, with whom he established a practice (1956). At 44 Berkeley Square, London, by *Kent, he designed the Clermont Club and Annabel's in conjunction with *Fowler of *Colefax & Fowler, an association which created fine work at Daylesford House, Glos. (1960-3) and Cornbury Park, Oxon. (from 1967), and continued until Fowler's death in 1977. For **John Victor Aspinall** (1926-2000), founder of the Clermont Club, he designed the *Gorillarium* at 'Howlett's' (Aspinall's Zoo), and the Curzon House Club, Mayfair, London (with **David Mlinaric** (1939-) with whom he collaborated on work at Woolbeding House, Sussex, and Ashdown House, Berks.). Jebb also worked on various National Trust properties, including Chartwell, Kent; Claremont, Surrey; and Nymans, Sussex; and on the restoration of small buildings acquired by the Landmark Trust to be let to holidaymakers: projects included the Pavilion, Ingestre, Staffs. Among other works were North Port House, Lennoxlove, Lothian (1978), and restoration of large houses (e.g. Badminton, Glos. (from 1984)). Clients included the Devonshires at Chatsworth, Derbys.

Independent (13 April 1995), Obits; pk

Jeckyll *or* **Jeckell, Thomas** (1827-81) English architect, pioneer of *Japonaiserie*, he designed (1876) the 'Peacock Room', 49 Princes Gate, London, decorated by **James Abbott McNeill Whistler** (1834-1903), now in the Freer Gallery, Washington DC, so was significant in the *Aesthetic Movement. His ecclesiastical work included St Mary's, Stapleford Abbots, Essex (1862—*Pevsner thought it 'hideous'); the *polychrome *First-Pointed Methodist Church, Holt (1862-3); and Holy Trinity, Hautbois (1864), the last two in Norfolk. He also designed 118-120 Queenstown Road, Battersea, London (1875). By 1876 he was insane, dying in the madhouse.

Soros & Arbuthnott (2004)

Jeeves, Stanley Gordon (c.1888-1964) *See* HOOD, RAYMOND MATHEWSON.

Jefferson, Thomas (1743-1826) American self-taught architect, he excelled in many things, and was one of the founding fathers and third President of the USA (1801-9). He had a fine library of architectural books, and it was largely from these (e.g. *Gibbs and *Leoni) that he acquired his skills. One of his first buildings was *Monticello*, his own house near Charlottesville, VA (1768-82—remodelled 1796-1809), the plans of which were a variation on a design in Robert *Morris's *Select Architecture* (1755), with additional elements derived from Gibbs, and a dash of *Palladio taken from Leoni's edition of the *Quattro Libri*. Indeed, Monticello was Palladian in layout, intelligently altered to accommodate the most convenient internal arrangements, but in its final version it suggested the *Antique *villa transformed by French *Neo-Classicism (e.g. *Hôtel de Salm*, Paris (1783)). Jefferson was appointed (1784) Second American Minister to Paris, a stroke of good luck enabling him to absorb up-to-date architectural ideas at first hand. He was also conveniently placed to visit England (1786), expressly to study *Picturesque gardens that attracted the admiration of Europe at that time. In France he admired the top-lighting at the *Château de Chaville* (1764-6—destroyed) by *Boullée, as well as *Legrand and *Molinos's *dome of the *Halle au Blé*, Paris (1782-3). When it was decided to build a State Capitol in Richmond, VA, Jefferson chaired the Committee charged with arranging for this, and he himself proposed a building based on the *Corinthian Roman *temple, the *Maison Carrée*, Nîmes (16 BC—to which building he had been introduced by *Clérisseau's *Antiquités de France* (1778), and which he greatly admired): thus he was the first to reintroduce the rectangular temple-form into public architecture (as opposed to small garden *fabriques*, e.g. at Stowe, Bucks.) in the West since Classical Antiquity. In the event, the State Capitol (1785-99), which was designed by Jefferson with Clérisseau as adviser, employed the *Ionic *Order with *angular capitals of the *Scamozzi type, and had *pilasters rather than *engaged columns as on the *cella of the Maison Carrée.

When he returned to the USA (1789), he became Secretary of State in Washington's Government, and involved himself in the planning and architecture of the new Federal capital, promoting French ideas when he could. Jefferson's greatest architectural achievement, however, was the University of Virginia, Charlottesville (1817-26), a series of porticoed *pavilions (each with an *Order from a different Roman building) linked by *colonnades, on either side of a long rectangular lawn (the *campus plan) with a scaled-down version of the Roman *Pantheon on the long axis at one end. While *Latrobe helped Jefferson with this design, the main scheme was Jefferson's own, though possibly based on Marly-le-Roi, the *château of Louis XIV (r.1643-1715). The *Rotunda at the University contained the most remarkable elliptical rooms in America, an arrangement possibly derived from the *Doric column-base in the Désert de Retz near Paris, which Jefferson had seen. The University is arguably the most beautiful architectural ensemble in the American Continent. Like Monticello and the Virginia Capitol, it was more than a fine work of Classical architecture: all three were intended as exemplars from which Americans would learn the rules of architecture and civic design.

W.Adams (1976, 1983); J.Boyd (ed.) (from 1950); Brawne (1994); Kimball (1966, 1968); Lehman (1980); Malone (1948-74); Mayo (ed.) (1970); Nichols (ed.) (1978); Nichols & Bear (1967); Nichols & Griswold (1978); O'Neal (1960); P (1982); J.T (1996)

Jekyll, Gertrude (1843-1932) English gardendesigner/writer, particularly remembered for her books on horticulture (profoundly influenced by William *Robinson) and for the various gardens she planned with *Lutyens (whom she first met in 1889, and was instrumental in introducing the budding architect to his first clients). Lutyens designed Munstead Wood, Surrey (1896-9), for her, where, prompted by her *Arts-and-Crafts background (she knew *Ruskin), she laid out a cottage-style garden of old-fashioned flowers, doing away with carpet-bedding, topiary-work, box-edging, and so on, in favour of a completely informal approach. She made the herbaceous border famous, and she herself became a household name, not least through her influential Wood and Garden (1899—illustrated with her own photographs). She designed some 300 gardens, about 100 of them with Lutyens (good examples of which were Deanery Garden, Sonning, Berks. (1899-1901), Orchards, Munstead, near Godalming, Surrey (1897-9), and Hestercombe, Taunton,

Som. (1903-6)). One of her best gardens, designed independently of Lutyens, was Barrington Court, Som. (1916-17).

Bisgrove (1992); J.Brown (1982, 1986, 1996); JGH, ii/3 (July–Sept. 1982), 285–92; Tooley (ed.) (1994)

Jellicoe, Sir Geoffrey Alan (1900-96) English architect/landscape architect/writer, he published (1925) his first book, Italian Gardens of the Renaissance (with **John Chiene Shepherd** (1896-1978)). During the 1930s his was a powerful influence in the establishment of the Institute of Landscape Architects. He prepared a village plan for Broadway, Worcs. (1933), and (1934) with Russell *Page, the restaurant and visitors' centre at Cheddar Gorge, Som., one of the first examples of *International Modernism in England. Among his pre-war gardens may be mentioned Ditchley Park, Oxon. (1935-9), Royal Lodge, Windsor Park, Berks. (1936-9), and Mottisfont, Hants. (1936-9). He also worked on housing-estates (e.g. in Acton (1934-5) and Bestwood, Notts. (1938-40)) and industrial installations (e.g. Calverton Colliery, Notts. (1937-40), where he demonstrated that the effects of industry on the landscape need not be catastrophic). He was responsible for conversions of sites where clay and gravel had been extracted, turning them into recreational amenities, notably the Hope Valley, Derbys. After the 1939-45 war he received many commissions for landscape/planning schemes, including Hemel Hempstead, Herts. (1947-50), and the John F. Kennedy Memorial, Runnymede, Berks. (1963-5). His interventions in the centre of Gloucester have not worn well, and indeed several of his public planning works (e.g. for English *motorways (1964-72)) quickly dated. He published Motopia (1961), a proposal for a town where cars would travel on raised roads and helicopters would be the main means of travel, delivering people directly to their front doors, which is equally dated. In 1980-4 he landscaped the garden at Sutton Place, Guildford, Surrey (an allegory of creation and aspiration in life), and carried out two large garden-designs for Modena and Brescia in Italy. He also prepared designs for the Moody Historical Gardens, Galveston, TX (1984-92—in which the history of landscape-architecture was alluded to by association). His garden at Shute House, Donhead St Mary, Wilts. (1968-75), has been admired. Among his other publications, Baroque Gardens of Austria (1932), Studies in Landscape Design (1960-70), The Guelph Lectures on Landscape Design (1983), and The Studies of a Landscape Designer over 80 Years (1993-6) should be mentioned. Late in life he claimed not to know about plants, and that he 'loathed' gardens.

AR, clxxxvi/1111 (Mar.1989), 85–92; E (1994); House & Garden, xlvi/11 (1991), 130–3; Jellicoe (1932, 1960-70,

1983, 1988, 1993–6); Jellicoe & Jellicoe (1995); *JSAH*, lvii/3e (Sept. 1998), 345–7; Shepherd & Jellicoe (1925); Spens (1994); *Daily Telegraph* (9 July 1996), Obits; A.Wilson (2002)

Jencks, Charles Alexander (1939–2019) *See*

ABSTRACT REPRESENTATION; ACTION ARCHITECTURE; ADHOCISM; CAMP; CARDBOARD ARCHITECTURE; ERSATZ ARCHITECTURE; HIGH TECH; LATE-MODERN ARCHITECTURE; MODERN MOVEMENT; NEO-CLASSICISM; NEO-VERNACULAR; POP ARCHITECTURE; POST-MODERNISM; RATIONAL ARCHITECTURE; SEMIOLOGICAL SCHOOL; SNAIL-MOUNT; SUPERSENSUALISM; SYMBOLIC ARCHITECTURE; and entries in the BIBLIOGRAPHY.

Jenney, William Le Baron (1832–1907)

American architect. Unusually, he studied (1853–6) at the *École Centrale des Arts et Manufactures*, Paris, where empirical and pragmatic approaches to design problems were stressed rather than the 'art' of 'design' (emphasized at the *École des *Beaux-Arts*). After the American Civil War he established (1868) his practice in Chicago, IL, and began to consider the design of office-buildings, making structures more economical/efficient, and enlarging fenestration. The success of his Portland Block (1872—destroyed) drew young architects to his office (including *Burnham, *Holabird, **Martin Roche** (1853–1927), and *Sullivan). His innovative first Leiter Building (1879—destroyed) had an internal skeleton of *iron, with slender iron columns embedded in the exterior wall (which exposed something of the frame behind), and in the Home Insurance Building (1883–5—destroyed 1931) columns were of cast and wrought iron, girders and floor-beams were of wrought iron up to the sixth floor, and girders were of steel above that, apparently the first major use of structural steel in a building (as opposed to a bridge or other work of pure engineering). With the engineer **Louis E. Ritter** (1864–1934) he took matters further in the Manhattan Building, 431 S. Dearborn Street (1889-90), using an iron-and-steel frame for the whole building, with diagonal wind-bracing. Then, with the Sears, Roebuck, & Company Store, State and Van Buren Streets (1889–81), he expressed the iron and steel frame behind the granite-clad exterior. Jenney went into partnership (1891) with **William B. Mundie** (1863–1939), and the firm designed the Ludington Building (1891—probably its most elegant work), the Montgomery Ward Store (1891-2—destroyed), the Morton Building (1896), and the Chicago Garment Center (1904–5). Jenney's firm created proto-*skyscrapers, and its work was an important step in the evolution of constructional principles leading to the achievements of the *Chicago School. Jenney published papers on problems of designing tall buildings.

Ct (1952, 1964, 1968); *DAB* (1943); *JSAH*, xxlx/1 (Mar. 1970), 40–7; Mujica (1929); P (1982); Randall (1949); Turak (1968); J.T (1996); Zu (ed.) (1987)

Jensen, Albert Christian (1847–1913) Dan-

ish architect responsible, usually in collaboration with *Meldahl, for several important Copenhagen buildings. They completed (1874–94) the *Frederikskirke* (*or* Marble Church) begun by *Eigtved and *Jardin, and Jensen designed Charlottenborg Art Gallery (1880–3), *Hagemanns Kollegium* (1908), and *Magasin du Nord* Department Store on the *Kongens Nytorv* which emulated Parisian prototypes even to the extent of having pavilion-roofs. Active in the Society of Architects, he was instrumental in starting the journal *Architekten*.

We (1995)

Jensen, Jens (1860–1951) Danish-born Ameri-

can landscape architect: employed (1886) by the City Parks Department, Chicago, IL, he designed the American Garden in Union Park (1888). Subsequently, he reshaped Union, Humboldt, Garfield, and Douglas Parks, and his design of Columbus Park (1916) has been regarded as the finest in the Chicago West Parks system: his work led to the making of the Forest Preserve around Chicago and the IL State Park system. Through his friendship with architects of the *Prairie School, he designed gardens for private clients (e.g. Coonley House, Riverside, IL (1908–12), by F.L. L.*Wright) in which he used indigenous Mid-West flora. Jensen's large public works include the Lincoln Memorial Garden, Springfield, IL (begun 1933). An early advocate of natural gardens, he influenced designers e.g. *Bye, **Wolfgang Oehme** (1930–2011), **James van Sweden** (1935–2013), and other protagonists of the *New American landscape.

ALA, ii/1 (1930), 34–8; Eaton (1964); Grese (1992); Wilhelm Miller (2002); J.T (1996); A.Wilson (2005)

Jensen-Klint, Peder Vilhelm (1853–1930)

Danish architect, pupil of *Herholdt, his most celebrated building is Grundtvig's Church, Bispebjerg, Copenhagen (designed 1913, built 1919–26, and soundly based on configurations found in the brick *Gothic churches of Northern Europe). It has a steep, stepped, gabled brick front, resembling organ-pipes, and its style is balanced between C19 *Historicism and C20 *Expressionism. The surrounding buildings form one composition with the church, and were completed (1940) by Jensen-Klint's son, **Kaare** (1888–1954).

Jørgensen (1979); Mi (1951); We (from 1947)

jerkinhead Hipped roof above a part-gable. The *gable-wall is *clipped* about half-way up its raked part, the pitched roof terminating in *barge-boards and then becoming a hipped roof, the *verges merging with *eaves. Also called *shread-head*.

Jerman *or* **Jarman, Edward** (*c*.1605–68) London surveyor/carpenter, he was one of three Surveyors appointed to control rebuilding in the City of London after the Fire (1666), the other two being *Hooke and *Mills. He worked on several Livery Company Halls and the Royal Exchange (1667–71—demolished), a handsome building with tower rising from a *triumphal arch (*see* PAESSCHEN).

Co (2008); Collins (2004)

Jerusalem 1. *See* CROSS. **2.** The Ideal or Holy City, a symbol of *Paradise as the goal of a pilgrim (or indeed of any Christian), and therefore represented by the centre of a medieval *labyrinth or *maze cut in turf or inlaid in a church floor (as in the *nave of Chartres Cathedral, France) used for ritual pilgrimages/penances.

Jesse Genealogical tree depicting the genealogy of Christ, a common medieval motif. It is usually in the form of a winding trunk of a tree or vine springing out of the recumbent body of the patriarch **Jesse**, with figures denoting his descendants (as given in the Bible) standing on the ends of its branches, the Virgin and Child forming the fruit at the top. A good example survives in the *tracery of the Abbey Church of Sts Peter and Paul, Dorchester, Oxon. (*c*.1340).

Jesuit architecture A distinct architectural style may be detected in Jesuit churches from the end of C16. The **Society of Jesus** played an important role in the evolution of *Baroque architecture, starting with *Vignola and della *Porta's *Il Gesù*, Rome, which served as a precedent for countless buildings (e.g. *St-Roch*, Paris, *St Carolus Borromeus*, Antwerp (1615–24)). Theatrical interiors and two-storey *façades were essential elements.

Delen (1946); Moisy (1958); PM; Wi & Jaffé (eds) (1972)

jetty, jettie, jutty 1. Projection of a *timber-framed upper storey overhanging a wall beneath, usually formed by *cantilevered floor-joists and beams supporting the *bressummer above which the projecting wall rises. *Associated with the jetty are*:

hewn jetty: wall-post thickened above the lower storey.

jetty-bracket: curved bracket under a jetty, usually associated with a support for the bressummer or *dragon-beam;

jetty-bressummer: *cill-beam on the ends of jettied beams or joists, often given additional support by jetty-brackets;

jetty-plate: wall-plate of the storey on which the jetty rests;

2. Construction carried out from land into deep water to protect a harbour and act as a landing-stage.

ABDM (1996)

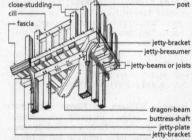

Typical corner of East-Anglian jettied construction (*RAM, ABDM, CBA*).

Jewell, Richard Roach (1810–96) English-born architect, he settled in Western Australia (1852), where he became Foreman then Supervisor of Public Works. He designed many public buildings in Perth, including the Court House and Gaol (1854), Pensioner's Barracks (1863), Trinity Church (1864), Town Hall (1867), the Old Treasury (1874), and the Girls' School (1877).

Morison & J.White (eds) (1979); Oldham & Oldham (1978)

jewelled Late-C16–early-C17 complex *strapwork enriched with half-spheres or *lozenges (*prismatic ornament) suggesting jewels.

jib *See* GIB.

Ji Cheng (1582–*after* 1634) Chinese landscape-painter/garden-designer/writer, influenced by **Jing Hao**, *also called* **Hongguzi** (*c*.855–915), and the latter's pupil, **Guan Tong** (*c*.906–60), painter of monochrome landscapes in Northern China. Ji Cheng designed numerous private gardens in southern China, and wrote one of the earliest surviving books (1631–4) on garden-design (*Yuan Ye* (The Craft of Gardens)), which gives detailed practical advice on many aspects of the subject.

Goodrich & Chaoying Fang (eds) (1976); Ji Cheng (2012); Mi Fu (1964); pk

jie jing Chinese term (properly *jièjǐng*) meaning 'borrowed views', it refers to the inclusion of background natural landscape outside a garden or *courtyard into the composition. Called *shakkei* in Japanese, it is used to enhance small urban gardens. *See* BORROWED LANDSCAPE.

Kraushaar (ed.) (2010); Tay (2006)

jitty *See* GINNELL.

Joass, John James (1868–1952) Scots architect, he worked with *Burnet, Son, & Campbell in Glasgow, and then (1889) in Rowand *Anderson's Edinburgh office. He joined (1893) the progressive office of Sir Ernest *George, then left to work with *Belcher, becoming the latter's partner (1905–13). One of the most distinguished buildings of the partnership was the Royal Insurance Office at the corner of Piccadilly and St James's Street, London (1907–9), a robust essay in C20 *Mannerism. Other Joass/Belcher buildings included the former Mappin & Webb Building, Oxford Street, London (1906–8), and the opulent *Wrenaissance Ashton Memorial, Williamson Park, Lancaster (1907–9).

A.S.Gray (1985); Se (1977); J.T (1996)

joggle, joggling 1. Joint at the meeting of two adjacent pieces of stone to prevent them from sliding: it consists of a projection in one piece fitting into a notch in another, and is especially used in flat arches or built-up *lintels made of several pieces, sometimes called *crossette. 2. Rebated joints in timber construction, especially braces joining an upright *post.

Johann, Meister (*fl*.C14) Designer of the hall-choir of the *Cistercian Abbey of Zwettl, Lower Austria (1343–83), which has the *chevet arrangement of *ambulatory and radiating chapels, probably influenced by the work of the *Parler family.

Bae: *Austria* (1929); Gi (1986)

Johansen, John Maclane (1916–2012) American architect, he worked with *Breuer and *SOM before establishing an office (1948). At the circular Chancellery for the US Embassy, Dublin (1958–64), he employed precast-concrete frames. Around the same time he experimented with the fragmentation of form, the climax of which was the Mummers' Theater, Oklahoma City (1970–1), actually three theatres loosely linked together by tubes containing passages and services, perhaps influenced by images of *Archigram, *Constructivism, and *Brutalism. Other works include the Johansen House, Stamfordville, NY (1974), the Ellsworth House, Salisbury, CT (1976), and the Barna House, Bedford, NY (1979).

AF, cxxxiv/2 (1971), 30–7; E (1994); Heyer (1978)

John of Ramsey (*fl*. early C14). See RAMSEY.

Johnson, Francis (1911–95) English architect, he established (1934) his practice in Bridlington, Yorks., specializing in scholarly restorations of C18 buildings (he had an unrivalled knowledge of C18 *pattern-books). Notable successes included *Carr's Fairfax House, Castlegate, York (1975–80), and the Long Gallery, Burton Agnes, Yorks. (1975). He carried out important works at York and Howden *Minsters, Belton House,

Lincs., and Heath Hall, Wakefield, during his long career, and built new houses, including several in Yorks., and Strathconan, Muir of Ord, Ross and Cromarty, Scotland (1980s). He designed St Margaret's Church, Hilston, Yorks. (1956–7), in a style reminiscent of the Free *Romanesque of Scandinavia. He refused to be cowed by aggressive *Modernists or critical neglect.

Po (1987); Robinson & Neave (2001); *The Times* (13 Oct. 1995), Obits

Johnson, George William (1802–86) English writer on gardening, he contributed (from 1826) to *Loudon's *Gardener's Magazine.* His first book (1829) was *A History of English Gardening*, and, after a period in India (1839–42), he returned to England, edited the *Gardeners' Almanack* (1844–66), and wrote *The Principles of Practical Gardening* (1845—later (1862) revised as *The Science and Practice of Gardening*) and *A Dictionary of Modern Gardening* (1846—with several subsequent edns (until 1917) entitled *Johnson's Gardening Dictionary*). From 1847 he brought out 12 issues of *The Gardener's Monthly Volume*, and from 1848 the weekly *Cottage Gardener*, later (from 1861) *Journal of Horticulture and Cottage Gardener*, which ran until 1915.

ODNB (2004)

Johnson, James (*fl*.1790–1807) Architect to the War Office Barrack Department (1794–1805), he designed Cavalry Barracks, including those at Fulford Road, York (1795—with *Sanders—unnecessarily demolished 1970s). Appointed (1794) Surveyor to the Royal Mint, he designed the handsome building at Tower Hill, London (erected 1807–12 under the direction of Robert *Smirke).

Co (2008); J.Curl (2011a); Douet (1998)

Johnson, John (1732–1814) English architect, he built up a considerable practice. He became (1782) Essex County Surveyor, and in that capacity designed Shire Hall, Chelmsford (1789–91). He was responsible for the handsome County Rooms (formerly a hotel), Hotel Street, Leicester (1792–1800).

Briggs (1991); Co (2008)

Johnson, Philip Cortelyou (1906–2005) American architect with an aloof disdain for the opinions of the masses, his independence of mind, flair for publicity, and political skills established a powerful position in the architectural world, both as designer and critic. While a student of philosophy at Harvard he met **Alfred Hamilton Barr** (1902–81), who pointed him towards an architectural career. Barr created (from 1928) the Museum of Modern Art (MoMA), NYC (of which he was Director 1929–67), and called in several young men to assist: Johnson was one of them, but Barr asked him first to travel in Europe to learn about trends in modern architecture. Joining forces with H.-R.*Hitchcock, Johnson met leading members of the European *avant-garde*, including *Mies van der Rohe (who was invited to design Johnson's Manhattan *apartment). When Johnson returned to NYC, he worked at MoMA while also completing his degree at Harvard, before officially taking up his post as head of the Department of Architecture at MoMA (1932). There, Johnson, Hitchcock, and Barr organized the exhibition which publicized work by Le *Corbusier, *Gropius, Mies, *Oud, and others. The term *International style was accepted into the general vocabulary of architecture from the publication (1932) of Johnson and Hitchcock's *The International Style: Architecture since 1922*.

Johnson gave up (1934) his MoMA post to begin a short-lived career in right-wing politics, assisting those opposed to **Franklin Delano Roosevelt** (1882–1945—32nd President of the USA, 1933–45). Johnson had heard (1933) **Adolf Hitler** (1889–1945) speak, and thereafter increasingly joined in the widespread adulation accorded to Nazi Germany (1933–45). He supported Mies in attempts to get the Nazis to embrace the International style: after all, both Gropius and Mies entered the competition to design the *Reichsbank*, one of many suppressed aspects of their careers (recognizing the close connection between Power and Modernism, Johnson himself said that *Speer would have made a great architect of *skyscrapers). He returned to Harvard (late 1940) to study architecture under *Breuer and Gropius, and resumed (1945) his position at MoMA, organizing (1947) an influential exhibition and publishing a monograph on Mies's work (which he admired for its purity and tenuous connections with *Classicism), although he avoided discussion of Mies's attempted *rapprochement* with the Hitler *régime*.

In partnership (1946–51) with **Landis Gores** (1919–91), Johnson soon made his name with the Mies-inspired Glass House, New Canaan, CT (1949): with Mies's Farnsworth House, Plano, IL (1946–51), the Glass House was seen as a paradigm of Modernism at the time, although Johnson perversely claimed he had been influenced by Le Corbusier, *Ledoux, *Malevich, *Schinkel, and De *Stijl when designing it. Associated with Mies and others during the design of the Seagram Building, NYC (1954–8), once the International style became universally accepted in America, he turned away from it: about this time, his position became complex, for he seemed to be interpreting Modernism while at the same time stripping it of its supposed *Functionalism, its claims to 'social responsibility', and its fraudulent morality

(Johnson had no fears about exposing the shallow hypocrisy of the architectural profession). Rejecting all the claims that Modernism was a social, cultural, and economic movement, he firmly labelled it for what it was: *a style*. For a time, however, he became the impresario of the International style before he began to twist its tail, sending up the puritanical European Modernists and (especially) their servile British followers (his views on some of them were particularly scathing). He loathed his former teacher, Gropius, who, in turn, detested him.

In the guest-house at New Canaan (1952) he introduced *vaults with a hint of *Soane above them, and thereafter (in partnership in the 1960s with **Richard Foster** (1919–2002)) he turned to a feeble monumentality (e.g. New York State Theater, Lincoln Center, NYC (1962–4), and the extension to the Boston Public Library (1964–73)). In partnership (1967–91) with **John Henry Burgee** (1933–) they sent shock-waves through the cosy world of orthodox *Modernism with their American Telephone and Telegraph *skyscraper, NYC (1978–83—now the Sony Building—a *masonry-clad structure with powerful mullions set on a stripped variation of a *serliana-cum-*triumphal arch, and capped by a paraphrase of an open-topped *pediment), described variously as the first Post-Modern building, as 'flippant', as an 'inflated and simplistic reference to history' (*Huxtable), or (ignorantly) as 'pseudo-classical'. Later works (sometimes in collaboration with other architects) included the Investors Diversified Services Building, Minneapolis, MN (1970–3), and Pennzoil Place, Houston, TX (1970–6). Then followed the Crystal Cathedral, Garden Grove, CA (1976–80), the Republic Bank Center, Houston, TX (1980–4—with reminiscences of *crow-stepped *Gothic *gables from Northern Europe), the Transco Tower, also in Houston (1981–5—with a hint of the *Classicism of *Goodhue), the Pittsburgh Plate Glass HQ, Pittsburgh, PA (1983–4—also with quirky 'historical' allusions), and the School of Architecture, Houston, TX (1983–6).

In 1988 Johnson again confounded critics by returning to MoMA as guest-curator of the exhibition *Deconstructivist Architecture*, billed as 'development post-dating post-modernism': it brought architects such as **Zaha Hadid** (1950–2016) and **Daniel Libeskind** (1946–) to media attention, and demonstrated again his capabilities in knowing (and even *creating*) 'celebrity culture'. In fact, his career demonstrates he was a taste-former, insisting that architecture is not about social engineering or 'making life better', but should be viewed as an *aesthetic experience*. He himself designed the Gate House, New Canaan (1994–5—a *pavilion without any right angles, his own homage to *Deconstructivism), and experimented with developing ideas from German *Expressionism. It seems as though, having shocked, Johnson then went on to do something else, almost gleefully, leaving critics floundering in his wake: he promoted, then subverted the International style, did the same to *Post-Modernism, and repeated the feat with Deconstructivism, all of which adds up to quite a comment on his times. He often described himself as a 'whore', as he exposed pretence and exercised his influence with cynicism and puckish disregard for what might be thought of his stance (which changed so much nobody could actually pin him down (to the intense annoyance of (especially) fatuous British critics)). Amazingly, he admitted he was 'not a good architect', and indeed some of his work might bear out his admission: it is often superficial, lacks depth, and could be considered unusually brittle, suggesting he could not think architecturally (he could not draw either). However, he was as successful in creating new trends and forming opinions as he was in deflating the pretensions of adherents to once-fashionable (and frequently untenable) orthodoxies: his greatest achievement was to expose the fake morality of Modernism, and indeed the bogusness of major trends in C20 and C21 architecture.

Blake (1996); Fox *et al.* (2002); Goldberger (ed.) (2002); Hi (1996a); Hi & Johnson (1995); Jacobus (1962); Jenkins & Mohney (2001); J (1997); J & W (1988); Kipnis (1996); Lewis & O'Connor (1994); Nory Miller (1979); Nakamura (ed.) (2000); Petit (ed.) (2009); Salingaros *et al.* (2004); Schulze (1994); Stern (ed.) (1979); *The Times* (28 Jan. 2005), 70; Welch (2000); Whitney & Kipnis (1994)

Johnson, Thomas (*c.*1740s–1800) English architect, he designed the County Gaol, Warwick (1779–82—now the County Council offices), one of the earliest uses of Greek *Doric in an English public building. He also built St Nicholas's Church, Warwick (1778–9), and rebuilt St Mary's, Hanbury, Worcs. (1792–5), both *Gothic. The Warwick church was reputedly designed by his son, **John Lees Johnson** (1762–*after* 1781), who was then not 16 years old: he seems to have predeceased his father, but designed (1781) *fabriques* for Bowood House, Wilts.

Co (2008)

Johnston, Francis (1760–1829) Irish architect, trained under *Cooley, he worked for **Richard Robinson** (1709–94), **Archbishop of Armagh** (from 1765), for whom he completed (*c.*1785) the exquisite Primate's Chapel, Armagh. Influenced by James *Wyatt and *Gandon, his work was eclectic, and includes St George's Church, Dublin (1802–17—which had echoes of work by *Gibbs), the austere but beautifully proportioned Neo-Classical Townley Hall, Drogheda, Co. Louth (1790s—probably his best work), the grim

Richmond Penitentiary (now part of St Brendan's Hospital), Grangegorman, Dublin (1812–16), and the very pretty Strawberry-Hill *Gothick house, Charleville Forest, Tullamore, Co. Offaly (1800–12—the finest early-C19 *Picturesque house in Ireland). He was largely responsible for converting *Pearce's Parliament House, Dublin, to the Bank of Ireland (1804–8), for the Chapel Royal, Dublin Castle (1807–14), and for the Court House, Armagh (from 1809). He designed the handsome *Greek-Revival General Post Office, Dublin (1814–18), completed (1817) Gandon's King's Inns, Dublin, and built the Royal Hibernian Academy (1824–6).

B-J (1988); Casey (2005); Casey & Rowan (1993); *DIA*; *DIB* (2009); M.Craig (1982); McP (1969, 1971–2); Mulligan (2013)

joinery The framing or joining of wood for internal and external finishes: thus the covering and lining of rough walls, the covering of rough timbers, the manufacture of doors, shutters, windows, stairs, cupboards, panelling, etc., i.e. betterclass work than *carpentry.

N (1835)

jointing Completion of joints in brickwork or *masonry while the *mortar is still soft, in contrast to *pointing. *See* BRICK.

Bru (1990)

joist One of a series of horizontal timbers, spanning the space between walls, *beams, etc., supporting a floor-finish and a ceiling. *Types of joist include*:

cogged: joist supported and held in a notch in a transverse beam;

cross: one of a series of joists in a section of floor running at right angles to the direction of joists in other sections of the same floor;

lodged: joist resting on a beam;

trimmer: also *trimmed joist*, spanning between two joists and supporting the ends of short joists, e.g. to permit an opening to be formed in a floor.

ABDM (1996); W.McKay (1957)

Joly, Jules-Jean-Baptiste de (1788–1865) French architect, pupil of *Percier and *Fontaine, he designed the *Chambre des Députés*, vestibule, *Salon du Roi*, and sumptuous Library (1821–33) in the *Palais Bourbon*, Paris, published (1840) as *Plans, coupes, élévations et détails de la restauration de la Chambre des Députés*.

M & Wa (1987)

Jones, Archibald Quincy (1913–79) American architect, he assisted (1936–7) **Douglas Honnold** (1901–74) and **George Vernon Russell** (1905–89), and then (1937–9) **Burton A. Schutt** (1906–54), before collaborating (1939–40) with Paul R.*Williams on projects in the Palm Springs area. He opened (1945) his own office in Los Angeles, CA, and soon began working with *Eichler, an arrangement that continued until the latter's death. In partnership (1950–69) with **Frederick Earl Emmons** (1907–99), he designed low-cost dwellings for Eichler, often incorporating park-like common areas in layouts, and carefully integrating buildings with landscape, mostly in the San Francisco Bay area, CA. Jones participated in the *Case Study programme of **John Dymock Entenza** (1903–84).

Adamson & Arbunich (2002); Buckner (2002)

Jones, Euine Fay (1921–2004) American architect, well-known in AR (both **William Jefferson** ('**Bill**') **Clinton** (1946–) and his future wife, **Hillary Diane Rodham** (1947–), lived in houses designed by him), he was a disciple of F.L.L. *Wright and of *Goff (with whom he had collaborated). Perhaps his best works were his own house at Fayetteville, AR (1956), the Orval Faubus house, AR (1964), and the Thorncrown Chapel near Eureka Springs, AR (1978–80—acclaimed as one of the five best buildings designed by any C20 US architect).

Ivy (1992); *The Times* (28 Sept. 2004), 63

Jones, Sir Horace (1819–97) English architect, he commenced practice in London (1843), and designed numerous commercial buildings, before being elected (1864) Architect and Surveyor to the City of London in succession to *Bunning. Responsible for the Central Meat Market (1866–7) and the General Market, Smithfield (1879–83— with the American 'Phoenix' system of rolled channelled iron columns (patented 1862) in its construction); Billingsgate Fish Market (1874–8— converted (1985–9) into offices by the **Richard Rogers Partnership**); and the charming Leadenhall Market (1880–2—brilliantly integrating shops and arcades into an ancient system of alleyways); he also designed the former Guildhall Library and Museum, Basinghall Street (1870–2), and (to mark the site of Temple Bar, Fleet Street) the memorial (1880) surmounted by a rampant bronze dragon by **Charles Bell Birch** (1832–93— the statues are by **Sir Joseph Edgar Boehm, Bt.** (1834–90)). His twelve-sided iron-framed Council Chamber at Guildhall (1883–4) was destroyed (1940). When proposals were made (1877) for a *bridge over the Thames at the Tower of London, Jones collaborated with the engineer **(Sir) John Wolfe Wolfe-Barry** (1836–1918), but concepts of how it (completed 1894) would operate and of its architectural treatment were Jones's alone. Part suspension- and part bascule-bridge, the towers, containing *elevators and supporting high-level footbridges (for use when the bascules were open), are of steel clad with stone, so look like

*Gothic city-gates with towers over. Jones and Wolfe-Barry came in for predictable denunciation for the 'untruthfulness' of the architecture, but the Gothic garb was insisted upon by Parliament, in deference to the neighbouring Tower of London: however, what *Modernist critics failed to note was that the towers were among the first steel-framed structures in London. Jones's last important work was the former Guildhall School of Music (1885–7) on the Thames Embankment, three façades of which survive, one with pretty *terracotta panels facing south to Tallis Street.

Bradley & Pe (1997); Freeman (1981, 2003); JF; *ODNB* (2004); J.Smith & J.Clarke (2003)

Jones, Inigo (1573–1652) London-born architect of Welsh origin, he was largely responsible for introducing the *Palladian style to *Jacobean England, and indeed for begetting the *first Palladian Revival.* He staged (1605–40) over 50 masques, plays, etc. (often in collaboration with **Ben Jonson** (1572–1637)) for the Courts of **Kings James I & VI** (*r.*1603–25) and **Charles I** (*r.*1625–49). From *c.*1606 he produced designs for structures in which his partially digested understanding of *Classicism taken from sources such as *Palladio, *Sangallo, and *Serlio was apparent, yet surviving drawings by him show he had acquired an acquaintance with up-to-date Italian architecture by 1609. Appointed (1610) Surveyor to **Henry, Prince of Wales** (1593/4–1612), he was granted (1613) the reversion of the place of Surveyor of the King's Works after the Prince's death. He had visited Italy before 1603, but his second trip to that country (1613–14) was important in forming his architectural tastes, for he met *Scamozzi and saw buildings illustrated in Palladio's *Quattro Libri.* Armed at last with the necessary architectural expertise, he became (1615) Surveyor of the King's Works, and built the Queen's House, Greenwich (1616–35), the Banqueting House, Whitehall (1619–22), and the Queen's Chapel, St James's (1623–5), all of which survive as a testimony to careful study of buildings by Italian masters and his understanding of Classical design principles. Nothing resembling them had been built in England before, and indeed in a Europe dominated at the time by *Baroque they had no contemporary equivalents across the Channel. Although not immediately influential, and perhaps oddities when Jacobean *Mannerism was *de rigueur,* they became exemplars for a type of *astylar house that came into favour after 1660, and indeed led to the C18 *second Palladian Revival* of *Campbell, *Burlington, et al. He also designed the Prince's Lodgings, Newmarket, Cambs. (1619–22—destroyed), which influenced the appearance of many red-brick houses with stone *dressings and hipped roofs throughout the second half of C17.

Jones worked (1625–40) on the Classicization of old St Paul's Cathedral, London, clothing the medieval fabric in new garb, and adding a huge prostyle *Corinthian *portico, the grandest north of the Alps at that time, which demonstrated the power, scale, and possibilities inherent in Roman architecture, providing a potent precedent for *Wren when rebuilding the Cathedral after 1666. For **Francis Russell** (1539–1641—**4th Earl of Bedford** from 1627), he designed the *Piazza*, Covent Garden (1631–7), the first London Square, with unified *façades consisting of arcaded ground floors over which was a *Giant Order of *pilasters, perhaps suggested partly by the *piazza and church in Livorno (Leghorn) and partly by the *Henri-Quatre Place des Vosges, Paris (1605–12). It was an enormously influential development, anticipating much C18 British urban planning and domestic architecture. He designed St Paul's Church, Covent Garden (1631–3), the first complete Classical church in England, with a *Tuscan portico taken from **Daniele Barbaro**'s (1514–70) version of *Vitruvius. His design for a huge new palace at Whitehall (c.1638) reveals that he was unimpressive as an architect of large complexes, although his work influenced developments at Whitehall until the end of C17.

Jones seems to have acted as a consultant for the south front of Wilton House, Wilts. (c.1636), designed by Isaac de *Caus, but his supposedly prolific activities as a country-house architect (a hare apparently started by Colen *Campbell) are now, through modern research, largely exploded as myths: among works attributed to him were Byfleet House, Surrey (c.1617), Coleshill House, Berks. (from 1647), Houghton House, Houghton Conquest, Beds. (*after* 1615), and Stoke Park, Stoke Bruern, Northants. (c.1630), but documentation is inadequate. He did, however, design a very handsome Classical *choir-screen for Winchester Cathedral, Hants. (1637–8), during the episcopacy (1632–45) of **Walter Curll** (1575–1647), who made it his business to decorate and improve the interior: the *screen was dismantled (1820), but the central part is now in the Museum of Archaeology, University of Cambridge. He was an important influence on his pupil and nephew, John *Webb, through whom Jones's collection of drawings were passed down to subsequent generations. Many of the drawings in Burlington's collection were published in *Kent's *The Designs of Inigo Jones* (1727), *Ware's *Designs of Inigo Jones and Others* (1731), and *Vardy's *Designs of Mr. Inigo Jones and Mr. William Kent* (1744). All Jones's known drawings were listed in Harris and Higgott's *Inigo Jones: Complete Architectural Drawings* (1989). *See also* PAESSCHEN.

Co (2008); J.Curl (2001, 2011a); Hart (2011); E.Hs (ed.) (1990); J.Hs & Higgott (1989); J.Hs,Orgel, & Strong (1973); J.Hs & Tait (1979); Leapman (2003); Lees-Milne (1953); Millar (1987); M & E (1995); P (1982); Su (1966, 1993)

Jones, Owen (1809–74) London-born architect of Welsh descent, he travelled extensively, afterwards producing *Views on the Nile* (1843) and (with **Jules Goury** (1803–34)) *Plans, Elevations, Sections, and Details of the Alhambra* (1836–45), which established him as an authority on *Moorish architecture, ornament, and colour. He was in demand as a designer of *tiles, publishing *Designs for Mosaics and Tessellated Pavements* (1842) and *Encaustic Tiles* (1843). As well as designing two Moresque houses at 8 and 24 Kensington Palace Gardens, London (1845–7), he was appointed (1850) joint architect of the Great Exhibition in Hyde Park, and was responsible for the colour-scheme of red, blue, and yellow in *Paxton's Crystal Palace (1851). The success of this led to his employment as director of decorations for the new Crystal Palace at Sydenham (opened 1854). With *Semper, Digby *Wyatt, and Joseph *Bonomi jun., Jones was involved in the creation of 'Courts' illustrating various historical architectural styles as part of a permanent exhibition there. The Egyptian Court (1854), designed with Bonomi, was spectacular, polychrome, and scholarly. Jones was very influential in his own lifetime, especially in the evolution of *polychromatic ornament: he decorated the interior of *Wild's Christ Church, Streatham (1841), and the apse of All Saints' Ennismore Gardens (1850). He taught at the Department of Science and Art in the South Kensington Museum, London, from 1852. His *Grammar of Ornament* (1856), based on his theories and lectures, illustrated all the known historical styles of ornament in colour, became a sourcebook of international importance, and showed the potential of non-European, particularly *Islamic, schemes of decoration.

Architectura, **iv** (1974), 53–75; J.Curl (2005. 2007); Jervis (1984); O.Jones (1843, 1854, 1863, 1868); O.Jones & Bonomi (1854); O.Jones & Goury (1836–54); P & D (1973); P (1982); Sh (1973); J.T (1996); Z (1977)

Jones, William (*fl.*1730–57) British architect remembered for one outstanding building, the Rotunda in Ranelagh Gardens, Chelsea, London (1740–2—demolished 1805), a large circular structure with a very pretty, light, galleried interior, really a glorified concert-hall and place for drinking tea: it showed rare originality for the period. Much of his realized work has also been demolished, although Alresford House, Hants. (1749–51), survives. He published (1739) designs for doors, gateways, and other architectural elements.

Co (2008); J.Curl (2010)

Jourdain, Frantz Calixte Raphaël (1847–1935) Antwerp-born architect, influential as the designer of the *Art-Nouveau *La Samaritaine* department store, Paris (1905-10), extended by him (1914, 1926-8). He saw Art Nouveau as the C19 equivalent of C18 French *Rococo, and argued for gracious ornament to bring elegance to buildings. His fulminations against a slavish adherence to *Beaux-Arts *Classicism before 1914 were influential at the time, and were associated with the search for a renewal of French culture. His son, **Francis** (1876-1958), was a *Modern-Movement interior-designer, exhibiting at the Paris exhibitions (1925, 1937).

Barre-Despond & Tisé (1991); B & G (1978); Clausen (1987); Jervis (1984); Jourdain (1893, 1895, 1902, 1914); Rey (1923)

jowl Part of a *post in *timber-framed construction at the top or bottom, wider than the rest of the post on one face, to house *tie-beams, wall-plates, etc. Tops of *crown-posts are often jowled.

Joy, William (*fl*.1329-47) English mason, appointed (1329) Master-Mason at Wells Cathedral, Som., where he appears to have been responsible for substantial building-works at the eastern arm of the church, including the refashioning of the *First-Pointed *choir, the erection of the *presbytery and new *vaults, the *retrochoir, *pulpitum, and the celebrated strainer-arches of the *crossing-tower. He also carried out (1340s) works at the gate-houses and wards of the Close at Wells, and may have made designs for the *Collegiate Church, Ottery St Mary, Devon (1337-45). Joy's designs have affinities with aspects of St Augustine's Abbey, Bristol (now the Cathedral), and he probably came from that area.

J.Harvey (1987)

Juan de Álava (*c*.1480-1537) *See* ÁLAVA, JUAN DE.

Juan de Colonia (*c*.1410-81) *See* COLONIA FAMILY.

jube, jubé 1. *Pulpitum, or *screen at the west end of the *choir in a French church. **2.** *Rood-loft or *gallery in the same position, often forming part of the screen. One of the finest surviving *jubés* is in the church of *St-Étienne-du-Mont*, Paris (*c*.1545), with its twin spiral stairs winding round *piers.

judas Small aperture, peep-hole, or lattice in a door or shutter through which a person may look without being observed from the other side.

Jugendstil Literally 'youth-style', German version of *Art Nouveau, it was named after the journal *Die Jugend* (1896-1914) which publicized it. More angular and less curvaceous than its French or Belgian counterparts, it had a Classicalizing element, and was associated with the various *Sezession movements, notably in Vienna (where it was called *Sezessionstil*), Munich, and Dresden. It had considerable influence on

Scandinavia and Russia. Its chief architectural protagonists were *Eisenstein, *Endell, *Hoffmann, *Kotěra, *Olbrich, and O.*Wagner.

BSP (1988); Wiener Sezession (1972)

Jujol (i Gibert), Josep Maria (1879-1949) Catalan architect, who, in his early years, was *Gaudí's collaborator (1906-10), and with whom he formed the studio of the **Sagrada Família**. Among Gaudí's works (in the creation of which he had a significant part) the *Casa Batlló* (1904-6), the *Casa Milá* (1901-10), and the *Parque Güell* (1900-14), all in Barcelona, and the choir of Palma Cathedral, Mallorca (1904-14), may be cited. His own architecture employed unusual and eclectic motifs from diverse sources, and so resembled a type of *collage as a means of transforming and combining elements in his compositions: a good example of this is his *Torre Bofarull*, Els Palleresos, Tarragona (1914-30). He also designed several churches and shrines, including those at Vistabella, Tarragona (1918-23—arguably one of his best buildings), and Montserrat in Montferri (1926-9). In his later years, as with many of his contemporaries, he turned to *Classicism. He was a gifted draughtsman and painter.

BN *et al.* (2002); Christ (1996); Flores (1982); Fontanals Rafols *et al.* (1974); Ligtelijn *et al.* (1996); Llinas Carmona (1992); M & N (1987)

Jurković, Dušan (1868-1947) Slovak architect. Inspired by *vernacular timber architecture, he first absorbed *Jugendstil elements, but his finest work is the Classical Štefánik monument, near Bradlo, Slovakia (1926-8).

J.T (1996)

Jury, Percy Morgan (1875-1945) Belfast architect, he formed (*c*.1901) a partnership with **William Blackwood Blackwood** (1876-1951), later (1934) joined by **Arthur Edward Jury** (*fl*.1924-76). P.M.Jury was architect to the united dioceses of Down, Connor, and Dromore (*c*.1926-after 1939). Among his works may be cited Castle Buildings, 10-16 Castle Place (1904-7—with an *Art Nouveau *façade clad in cream and pale-green 'Carraware' *faïence by **Doulton** of Lambeth); the extension to Ulster Buildings in Skipper Street (1929); Mayfair Building, Arthur Square (1906); Ulster Bank, Albertbridge Road (1908-10); 276 Malone Road (1916-17—*Old English *Domestic Revival); and St Clement's Church, Templemore Avenue (1928-30), all in Belfast.

Irish Builder & Engineer (19 Nov. 1904), 772, (20 May 1905), 341, (3 Nov. 1906) 890; Larmour (1987)

Jussow, Heinrich Christoph (1754-1825) German Neo-Classical architect, pupil of S.-L. du *Ry from whom he acquired a *Palladianism derived from England, but he evolved a simpler, more severe style discovered during his time with

C.de*Wailly in Paris (1784). He completed du Ry's work at *Schloss Wilhelmshöhe*, Kassel (1791-8), including the massive central block and the creation of the *Picturesque garden complete with water-works and exotic *fabriques*. Also at Kassel he designed *Schloss Löwenburg* (1793-8—an early example of the *Gothic Revival in Germany, much influenced by English precedents, Picturesquely composed) and many other buildings, including the charming *Doric *mausoleum of **Wilhelmine Karoline of Denmark** (1747-1820—from 1803 *Kurfürstin* of Hesse-Kassel), *Altstädter Friedhof*, Kassel (1820).

Biehn (1965); Dittscheid (1987); Honour (1979); M & T (1991); Paetow (1929); Schweikhart & Adler (eds) (1983); J.T (1996); H.Vogel (ed.) (1958-9); Wa & M (1987)

Juvarra, Filippo (1678-1736) Pupil of Carlo *Fontana, he was arguably the most gifted Italian architect of his time, and continued a late-*Baroque tradition evolved by *Bernini. His architecture is characterized by its pellucid forms, sustained invention, and perfectly balanced massing, while his command of decorative devices was extensive and inventive. Appointed (1714) Architect to **Vittorio Amedeo II** (1666-1732— **Duke of Savoy** from 1675, **King of Sicily and Piedmont** from 1713), he realized that monarch's ambition to elevate Turin into a Royal capital by designing and building a vast range of churches, lodges, palaces, and villas, as well as planning extensions to the city. His masterpiece is the Church and Monastery of *Superga*, Turin (1716-31), with its temple-portico, tall, elegant *cupola, and delightful twin *campanili*, but *San Filippo Neri* (1717, 1730-6—a variation on *Alberti's *Sant'Andrea*, Mantua) and the emphatic *façade added to *Castellamonte's *Santa Cristina* (1715) demonstrated his mastery of the Baroque style. Other works included the *Castello*, Venaria Reale (1714-26—with its spectacular chapel (1716-21)), the *Palazzo Birago di Borgaro* (1716), the *Palazzo Madama* (1718-21), and the *Castello Reale*, Rivoli (1718-21). His greatest palace for the King was the *Palazzina di Caccia*, Stupinigi, near Turin (1729-35), with an elliptical nucleus and four radiating wings: it is the grandest *hunting-lodge in Europe, with its remarkable *salone* decorated in the richest possible fashion. Juvarra also designed the garden-front of the *La Granja* Palace, San Ildefonso, near Segovia, Spain, and was working on the Royal Palace, Madrid, when he died. This last owed much to Bernini's third design for the Louvre in Paris, and was completed by *Sacchetti.

Boscarino (1973); Carboneri (ed.) (1979); Cormoli & Griseri (eds) (1995); A.Correa *et al.* (1998); Gritella (1992); H.Hager (1970); Millon (1984); P (1982); Pommer (1967); Rovere *et al.* (1973); Severo (ed.) (1996); J.T (1996); Viale (ed.) (1966); Wittkower (1982)

Kaftantzoglou, Lysandros (1811–86) Greek architect, educated in Rome and France, he settled (1838) in Athens where he made a major contribution to the promotion/acceptance of *Neo-Classicism. He executed a number of buildings by other architects, including T.*Hansen's Eye Clinic, which, on the instructions of the Bavarian-born **King Otto** (*or* **Othon**) (*r.*1832–62), he altered to *Rundbogenstil* during its construction (1844–54). Among his best buildings were the *Arsakeion* School (1845–52), the *Tositseion* School (1865—destroyed), the National Technical University of Athens (1861–76), and the Churches of St Irene (1846–92), and St Constantine (1869–93).

J.T (1996)

Kahn, Albert (1869–1942) German-born American architect, he founded (1902) the most prolific architectural practice of its time in the USA with his brothers **Julius** (1874–1942) and **Moritz** (1881–*c.*1939). Their Packard Motor Car Company Plant, Detroit, MI (1903–10), was an early example of an overt *reinforced-concrete structure. From 1905 the firm pioneered standardization/modularization for factory-design, and for the George N.Pierce Company, Buffalo, NY, makers of the Pierce-Arrow motor-car, designed (1906) a top-lit factory, thus avoiding wall-windows, and allowing the plan to expand to suit the manufacturing sequence. In 1909 Moritz Kahn established a British division of the Trussed Concrete Steel Company in order to market the Kahns' 'Truscon' system of reinforced concrete: *Wallis, Gilbert, & Partners, established 1914, worked with the Americans, specializing in industrial architecture. In 1908 Kahn was employed by **Henry Ford** (1863–1947) to design a factory at Highland Park, Detroit (demolished), to manufacture the famous **Model T**, and evolved (1913) systems of assembly-line methods there which were developed for the vast single-storey Ford Rouge Plant, Dearborn, MI (1917–39). Erected with great speed, it was planned to accommodate huge assembly lines, had a steel frame, top-lighting, and *curtain-walling, and was made of standardized prefabricated components. The Kahns continued to develop designs for factories to make mass-produced goods efficiently: the

Dodge Half-Ton Truck Plant, Warren, MI (1937–8), was the logical conclusion of their methods, with its wide column-spacings, use of steel *cantilevers, and sloping glazed roofs. Kahn also worked for General Motors, the Chrysler Corporation, Glenn Martin Aircraft, and other concerns, and during his long and remarkable career he designed over 2,000 factories. He also set up (1932) an office run by Moritz Kahn in the Soviet Union, training many Soviet architects and designing over 500 factories.

Not all the Kahns' buildings were industrial, however. Their Clements Library, University of Michigan, Ann Arbor (1922), was in the *Neo-Classical style, and other non-industrial works included the Engineering Building (1903), the Hill Auditorium (1913), and Angell Hall (1922), all at Ann Arbor. As an adaptable pragmatist with a mind uncluttered by cant, Albert Khan had no time for *International *Modernism, which he found unintelligent, doubting if it qualified as architecture at all.

Bucci (1993); Ferry (ed.) (1987); G.Hildebrand (1974); A.Kahn (1948); L.Roth (1980)

Kahn, Ely Jacques (1884–1972) American architect. Educated in NYC and the *École des *Beaux-Arts, Paris, he later (1919) became a partner in the firm of **Buchman & Fox**, NYC (subsequently **Buchman & Kahn**, and later still (1942) **Kahn & Jacobs**). He designed (1920s–30s) several NYC *Art-Deco *skyscrapers. Among his best-known works are 2 Park Avenue (1924–7—with external treatment designed with **L.V.Solon** (1872–1953)), Insurance Center Building (1926–7), Bergdorf Goodman Store Building (1926–7), Squibb Building (1928–9), and 1400 and 1410 Broadway (1930–1), all well-organized and technically advanced. The entrance-lobbies in the office buildings at the corner of 29th street and Fifth Avenue (*c.*1929) and 2 Park Avenue were particularly fine examples of his Art-Deco style. From the 1950s the office turned from the inventive verve of exuberant Art Deco to conformity with *International Modernism. The firm executed (and partially planned) the Seagram Building, NYC, designed by *Mies van der Rohe (1954–8—with Philip *Johnson). Cultivated and with wide interests, Kahn published several works, including *Design in Art and Industry* (1935) and *A Building Goes Up* (1969).

Architecture, lxiv (1931), 65–70; C.Benton *et al.* (eds) (2003); Bl & Ro (1975); Bollack & Killian (eds) (1995); Duncan (1988); E (1994); E.Kahn (1935, 1969); P (1982); J.T (1996)

Kahn, Louis Isadore (1901–74) Estonia-born architect, he settled (1905) in the USA, only becoming (1950s) internationally renowned with Yale University Art Gallery, New Haven, CT (1951–3). Then came (1957–64) the influential Alfred Newton Richards Medical Research Building, University of Pennsylvania, Philadelphia, where the laboratories were clearly separated from the services stacked in slim towers. Kahn's insistence that there should be a distinction between *served* and *serving* volumes was taken a stage further with the Salk Institute for Biological Studies, La Jolla, CA (1959–65), where ducts were placed horizontally in the structure spanning the laboratory, while towers housed study-areas. For the Performing Arts Theater, Fort Wayne, IN (1965–74), Kahn used segmental brick arches springing from *concrete blocks, an image that signified his return to a more humane and expressive architecture. Highly controlled geometries and meticulous detailing gave the Phillips Exeter Academy Library, NH (1967–72), a sense of order and dignity that marked Kahn's later work. His brick detailing in his Indian Institute of Management Studies, Ahmadabad (1962–74), drew on Roman and other precedents to produce a work of rare quality. Other buildings by Kahn include the Erdman Dormitory Block, Bryn Mawr College, PA (1960–5), the Kimbell Art Museum, Fort Worth, TX (1967–72), and the Mellon Center for British Art and Studies, Yale University (1969–77). At the end of his life he designed the National Assembly of Bangladesh, Dacca (1962–83), which drew on many historical/traditional allusions, but he had problems in getting paid, with the result that his office ran into severe financial difficulties. His work marked a significant move away from *International *Modernism.

Ashraf (1994); D.B.Brownlee & Long (1992); Büttiker (1993); Gast (1998, 1999); Giurgola & Mehta (1975); L.Kahn (1969, 1973, 1975, 1977); Klotz (1988); K.Larson *et al.* (2000); P (1982); D.Robinson (1997); Ronner *et al.* (1987); V.J.Sy (1962); Tafuri (1980); Tyng (1984); Wurman (ed.) (1986)

Kallikrates *See* CALLICRATES.

Kampen *See* CAMPEN.

Kampmann, Hack (1856–1920) Danish architect, protagonist of the *National-Romantic movement that drew on traditional and *vernacular forms as well as on themes from the *Rundbogenstil. He designed the Regional Archives, Viborg

(1889–91), and the Custom House (1895–7), Theatre (1897–1901—with touches of *Jugendstil), and State Library (1898–1902), all in Aarhus. Influenced by the strong Danish tradition of *Neo-Classicism, he was responsible for the New Carlsberg *Glyptotek*, Copenhagen (1901–6—with a stepped pyramidal roof over the centrepiece), and, with **Anton Frederiksen** (1884–1967), Holger *Jacobsen, and *Rafn, designed the Copenhagen Police Headquarters (1919–24), one of the finest C20 Neo-Classical essays in Scandinavia. His son, **Christian Peter Georg Kampmann** (1890–1955), designed the distinguished State School, Viborg (1918–26), combining Neo-Classicism with aspects of *Modernism. He was also responsible for the Railway Station, Teheran, Iran (*c.*1935).

Pn (1982); J.T (1996); We (1995)

Kamsetzer, Jan Chrystian (1753–95) Important Neo-Classical architect, he worked in the Poland of **King Stanisław Poniatowski** (*r.*1764–95), designing a number of stylish interiors at the Royal Palace, Warsaw (1777–82), and Mielżyńskich Palace, Pawłowice (1789–92), and collaborated with *Merlini on the exquisite Łazienki Palace, Warsaw (1784–93). Kamsetzer designed the austere Roman *Doric Guard-House, Poznań (1787), the Tyszkiewicz Palace, Warsaw (1785–92), and the robustly severe Church of St Dorothy, Petrykozy (1791–5).

L & R (1984)

Kant, Immanuel (1724–1804) German philosopher. His *Observations on the Feeling of the Beautiful and Sublime* (1764) and *Critique of Judgement* (1790) laid the foundations of much aesthetic theory, especially in relation to the *Beautiful and the *Sublime discussed earlier by Edmund *Burke.

COF (1988); H.O (1970); J.T (1996)

Kanvinde, Achyut (1916–2002) Indian architect, pupil of *Gropius, his works include the Institute of Technology, Kanpur (1959–65), Nehru Science Centre, Bombay (1971–82), and the National Science Centre, New Delhi (1975–84), all in strict conformity with *International Modernism.

J.T (1996)

Kaplicky, Jan (1937–2009) Prague-born, he worked with *Lasdun, *Soissons, **Richard Rogers** (1933–), **Renzo Piano** (1937–), and **Norman Foster** (1935–), on various projects before founding (1979) **Future Systems** in London with **David Nixon**: later, he married **Amanda Levete** (1955–), who joined him in partnership (1989). Work included the Media Centre, Lord's Cricket Ground, London (1999), and Selfridge's Store,

Bull Ring, Birmingham (2003—having a reptilian exterior covered with anodized aluminium discs, rejecting the scale, materials, and geometry of surrounding buildings). *See* BIOMORPH; BLOBISMUS; ZOÖMORPHIC *or* NEW ANIMAL ARCHITECTURE. The firm designed (2005) the Maserati Museum in the grounds of Enzo Ferrari House, Modena, Italy (completed 2010), with a dominant curved roof and *façade paying tribute to the bonnet and radiator of a motorcar, a connection that is, perhaps, visually tenuous.

Field (1999); Future Systems (1996); Pawley (1994); *RIBAJ* (March 2009), 16; *The Times* (19 Jan. 2009), 52

Karfík, Vladimír (1901–85) Czechoslovak Modernist architect, he worked for *Holabird & Root and F.L.L.*Wright in the USA (1926–9), became influenced by Le *Corbusier, and joined *CIAM. Head of the Architecture Department of the Baťa Company from 1930, he designed new settlements on the *Garden-City principle at Zlín, Partizánske, and Otrokovice, with Modernist aesthetics well to the fore. Other designs for Baťa included a hotel (1932) and 17-storey office-building in Zlín (1937–8—with a *reinforced-concrete frame influenced by his work in Chicago), department-stores in Brno (1930) and elsewhere, and housing at Belcamp, MD, and East Tilbury, Thurrock, Essex (1932–8). He designed the first prefabricated residential buildings in post-war Bratislava.

Bauforum, xvii/103 (1984), 21–31; Li (1996); vV (1993)

Karmi Family Israeli architects. **Dov Karmi** (1905–62) established (1936) his Tel Aviv practice, designing residential buildings influenced by Le *Corbusier (with *brises-soleils, *pilotis, etc.), and promoting *Modernism, designing the Histadrut HQ, Tel Aviv (1950–6), and Knesset (Parliament) Building, Jerusalem (1955–66—with **Joseph Klarwein** (1893–1970)). His son, **Ram** (1931–2013), with **Zvi Melzer**, joined the firm (1956), and several buildings followed, featuring exposed *reinforced concrete and natural timber (an example is the *El Al* office, Tel Aviv (1962–3)); his daughter, **Ada Karmi-Melamede** (1936–) also joined **Karmi Associates** (1964). The Hadar Dafna offices (1964–8) and the Lady Davies Amal Technical School (1970–4), both in Tel Aviv, display the influence of the *Brutalism with which Ram Karmi had been influenced during his studies in London, but the Israel Supreme Court Building, Jerusalem (1986–93), with walls pierced by rectangular and arched openings, and water-features recalling those of the Alhambra, Granada, marked an attempt to return to architecture based on Classical geometries.

E (1994); J.T (1996)

Katayama, Tokuma (1854–1917) Japanese architect, he designed the National Museums in Nara (1894), Kyoto (1908), and Tokyo (1909), all in a Neo-Classical style with a pronounced *Beaux-Arts* flavour. His Akasaka Palace, Tokyo (1903–9—now the State Guest House), was influenced by the work of *Hasenauer and *Semper in Vienna (which city Katayama had visited earlier), and by the Louvre in Paris.

P (1982); J.T (1996)

Kauffmann, Richard (**Yitzchak**) (1887–1958) German-born Israeli architect, he worked on houses for Krupp at *Margaretenhöhe*, Essen, before the 1914–18 war, after which (1920) he emigrated to Palestine, where he was involved in planning agricultural settlements for immigrant Jews, combining Zionist ideals with elements of the *Garden-City movement. Indeed, he designed some 80 developments for the Palestine Land Development Company, including Ramat-Gan, Herzliya, and Bat-Yam, and about 160 *kibbutzim* for the Zionist organization. His design for Nahalal agricultural settlement (early 1920s) was conceived using strict geometries.

P (1982); J.T (1996)

Kay, Joseph (1775–1847) English architect, pupil of S.P.*Cockerell, he later travelled on the Continent (for part of the time with Robert *Smirke), and married (1807) the eldest daughter of *Porden, for whom he acted as assistant during the building of the *Gothic-Revival Eaton Hall, Ches. (1804–12—demolished). He designed the handsome range of houses on the east side of Mecklenburgh Square, London (1810–21), the Post Office, Waterloo Place, Edinburgh (1818–19), and Nelson Street and the Market, Greenwich, London (1829). His masterpiece is the elegant Pelham Crescent (with the Church of St Mary-in-the-Castle in the centre), Hastings, Sussex (1824–8): the church is top-lit and has an *Ionic *prostyle *portico, while beneath the terrace in front of the whole composition is an ingenious structure intended for shops and services. His eldest son, **William Porden Kay** (1809–97) emigrated to Australia (1842) where he was Director of Public Works.

Co (2008)

Kazakov, Matvey Feodorovich (1738–1812) Russian Neo-Classical architect, influential in giving a Classical character to late-C18 and early-C19 Moscow. He studied with **Dmitri Vasil'yevich Ukhtomski** (1719–74), later assisting **Pyotr Romanovich Nikitin** (1735–c.1790) in the rebuilding (1763–7) of Tver' after the fire (1762): Kazakov was responsible for the design of the Town Hall, Gentry Club, School, and Salt Store, which were formed on more severely Classical lines than the *Baroque which previously had been *de rigueur*. He worked (1768–74) with *Bazhenov et al. on the enormous Kremlin Palace project and (probably) the Pashkov Palace, Moscow (1784–6—a boldly articulated Classical design) before setting up on his own in Moscow, creating palaces, hospitals, official buildings, and churches in a pure Classical style. His Senate Building, Kremlin, Moscow (1776–87), was designed with a *Doric *rotunda containing an internal *Corinthian Order, and is a distinguished work of Russian *Neo-Classicism. Kazakov travelled in France and Italy, and developed a taste for the works of *Palladio, as is evident in his Golitsyn Hospital (1794–1801), Demidov House (1789–91), and Batashev House (1798–1802). Other works include the Churches of St Philip the Metropolitan (1777–88—a rotunda), Sts Cosmas and Damian (1780s), and the Ascension (1780s), the 'Old' University (1786—later remodelled), and the impressive Hall of the Noblemen's Assembly (Hall of Columns—1784–6). Kazakov collaborated with *Quarenghi and others on the Sheremetev Palace, Ostankino (1791–8), one of the grandest houses of the time, with an opulent theatre and various pavilions in the grounds, including 'Italian' and even 'Egyptian' *fabriques*. As a Goth he produced curious effects, as in the Petrovsky Palace, near Moscow (1775–82).

G.H (1983); M & Wa (1987); D.Shv (2007); J.T (1996)

Keay, Sir Lancelot Herman (1883–1974) English architect, he worked (1906–15) in Norwich where he restored several historic buildings and designed small housing-schemes. From 1921 he developed more than 16,000 houses for Birmingham Corporation, and in 1925 moved to Liverpool Corporation, where, from 1926 he was involved in the Housing Department, of which he was Director from 1929 until appointed City Architect (1938–48). He oversaw more than 35,000 new flats and houses in the city and suburbs, including developments at Speke, although his vision of creating a self-contained community was never realized, so Speke remained an isolated, deprived, working-class suburb. Many of his larger blocks have been demolished, though St Andrew's Gardens and Myrtle Gardens remain, influenced by the work of Bruno *Taut. He was Chairman of both Basildon and Bracknell New Town Development Corporations from 1948.

Harwood & Powers (eds) (2008), 37–50; *ODNB* (2004); Pollard & Pe (2006)

keel Common *First- and *Second-Pointed *moulding on *vault-ribs and elsewhere, resembling a ship's keel, in section consisting of two *ogees or convex curves meeting at an arris (a definition preferred by some), and sometimes at a *fillet (which is more keel-like).

keel-arch *Ogee arch.

Keeling, Enoch Bassett (1837–86) English *Rogue *Gothic-Revival architect. He built several churches in London with violent *polychrome brick interiors, but none survives intact. His most extraordinary creation was the eclectic, debauched, eccentric, and outrageous Strand Music-Hall, London (1864—demolished).

AH, xvi (1973), 60–9; xlii (1999), 307–15; J.Curl (2012)

Keene, Henry (1726–76) English architect, Surveyor to the Dean and Chapter of Westminster from 1746 and Surveyor to the Fabric of Westminster Abbey from 1752. He may have refined *Jacobsen's designs for the west front of Trinity College, Dublin. One of the first exponents of C18 *Gothic Revival, as early as 1749 Keene assisted Sanderson *Miller to prepare drawings for Hagley, Worcs., and in *c*.1750 he fitted out the chapel at Hartlebury Castle, Worcs., in the *Gothick style. He designed the octagonal Hartwell Church, Bucks. (1753–5), and *Newdigate employed him on the remodelling of Arbury Hall, Warwicks., from 1761, where some details were copied from Westminster Abbey. He was also responsible for the handsome Classical Guildhall, High Wycombe, Bucks. (1757), and the Provost's Lodgings, Worcester College, Oxford (1773–6).

Co (2008); J. Curl (2011a); M.McCarthy (1987); *ODNB* (2004)

Keene's cement Gypsum (sulphate of lime or *plaster of Paris) steeped in a solution of alum (double sulphate of aluminium and potassium) then subjected to intense heat, ground to a powder, and sifted. Invented *c*.1840, and also called **Martin's** or **Parian cement**, it was exceptionally hard when dry, took a high polish, and could also be coloured. Easily cleaned, it was often used for skirtings, *dados, mouldings, and even floor-surfaces. It was combined with *marble for parts of the interior of *Butterfield's Church of All Saints, Margaret Street, London (1848–59).

AJ, cxci/25 (20 June 1990), 36–55; W.Pa (1852)

keep Inner and strongest portion (*donjon) of a medieval *castle or citadel, also the residence of the lord.

Kelderman van Mansdale *or* **Keldermans** Family of C15 and C16 architects from Mechelen, Belgium. The most distinguished members were **Anthonis I 'the Elder'** (1450–1512) and **Rombout II** (*c*.1460–1531). Anthonis designed the tower of the *Stadhuis*, Middelburg, The Netherlands (1507–12), and worked on the *choir of *Sint-Laurenskerk*, Alkmaar (1497–1512), among other projects, while Rombout worked with *Waghemakere on the *Stadhuis*, Gent, Belgium (1517–33). Rombout designed the *Flamboyant

*Gothic *Hôtel de Savoie*, Mechelen (1515–17), to which *Beaugrant applied the first *Renaissance *façade in Belgium (1517–26). Rombout also completed the great tower of *St-Rombout, Mechelen.

Janse *et al.* (1987); P (1982); J.T (1996)

Kellum, John (1809–71) American architect best known for his iron buildings in NYC. These included the cast-iron ferry-houses for Fulton Ferry and South Ferry (1864—demolished), the Cary Building, 105 Chambers Street (1856–7), and the boldly modelled A.T.Stewart (later Wanamaker's) Department Store, Broadway (1859–62—demolished). He designed Stewart's Model Town, or *Garden City, Long Island, NY (from 1870).

ARe , cxx/3 (1956), 273–9; Francis (1980); G & G (1974); P (1982)

Kemp, Edward (1817–91) English garden-designer, pupil of *Paxton (1830s) at Chatsworth, Derbys., and supervisor of his master's designs at Birkenhead People's Park, Ches. (1843–7), where he remained for 40 years as Superintendent, also running a private practice. Birkenhead, with its *serpentine paths, concealed views, artificial mounds, lakes, and *fabriques, had a didactic purpose, a response to ideas floated earlier by *Loudon, and influenced *Olmsted, who used it as the model for Central Park, NYC. Other commissions included the landscaping of Anfield Cemetery, Liverpool (1856), Hesketh Park, Southport, Lancs. (1864–8—complete with *cascade and *fountains), Stanley Park, Liverpool (1868), and the *terrace-garden, Knightshayes, Devon (1874). In much of his work he continued using Paxtonesque *formal styling and viewing-terraces. One of the gardens influenced by his own publications (in which debts to Uvedale *Price and Loudon are clear) was that at Biddulph Grange, Staffs., laid out from 1856 by James *Bateman and **Edward William Cooke** (1822–80). Much of his work could be described as *gardenesque.

B.Elliott (1986); *GH*, xxiii/2 (Winter 1995), 201–11; E.Kemp (1851, 1862, 1864); Shoe (2001); Tay (2006); Thacker (1994)

Kemp, George Meikle (1795–1844) Scots self-taught *Gothic-Revival architect, he worked (1831–2) as a draughtsman for William *Burn, and prepared drawings (1834) for the restoration of St Mungo's Cathedral, Glasgow, that formed the basis for Gillespie *Graham's scheme published in *Plans and Elevations of the Proposed Restorations and Additions to the Cathedral of Glasgow* (1836), though Graham caddishly failed to acknowledge Kemp at all. In the event, *Blore got the job. Kemp won (1838) the second competition to design the monument to **Sir Walter Scott** (1771–1832), Princes Street, Edinburgh, with proposals derived from meticulous study (built

1840–6): it is one of the finest and earliest Gothic-Revival canopied monuments, although the seated figure of Scott it protects (by **John Steell** (1804–91)) is far too small. The success of the Scott monument augured well for an architectural career, but Kemp fell into a canal and drowned (1844) while the building was under construction.

Bonnar (1892); Colston (1881); Co (2008); GMcW & W (1984)

Kempthorne, Sampson (1809–73) English architect, trained by A.*Voysey. Appointed Architect to the Poor Law Commissioners (whose *First Report* (1835) contains his designs for *workhouses, exemplars for many built in the 1830s and 1840s), he was responsible for several such buildings in the south of England, assisted by the young George Gilbert *Scott. Kempthorne also produced several designs, some of which appear in *Rules to be Observed in Planning and Fitting Up Schools* (1839–40), published by the Committee of the Council of Education; and for the Church Missionary Society he designed (1836) a church for North Waimate, New Zealand, to which country he emigrated (1841–2).

Bremner (2013); Co (2008); Morrison (1999), 60; G.G. Scott (1995)

Kendall, Henry Edward (1776–1875) English architect, pupil of *Leverton and (probably) *Nash, he had a successful and varied practice. His Sessions-House and House of Correction, Spilsby, Lincs. (1824–6), is a handsome essay in *Greek Revival, but he was equally at home with *Gothic, as at the Carr's Hospital, Sleaford, Lincs. (1830–46), and his winning (but unrealized) designs for Kensal Green Cemetery, London (1832). With his son, **Henry Edward Kendall** (1805–85—also a successful architect), he laid out the Esplanade and Tunnel, Kemp Town, Brighton, Sussex (1828–30). Among Kendall Jun.'s works were Shuckburgh Hall, Warwicks. (1844), the *Tudor-Gothic 'Pope's Villa', Crossdeep, Twickenham, Mddx. (*c.*1845), the gritty round-arched St John's Church, Kensal Green (1844—*Pevsner thought it 'atrocious'), and the splendid *Egyptian-Revival wandering *mausoleum of **Francis Jack Needham** (1787–1880—**2nd Earl of Kilmorey** from 1832) and his mistress, **Priscilla Hoste** (d.1854) at Gordon House, Isleworth, Mddx., originally built (1854) in Brompton Cemetery, London, then moved (1862) to Woburn Park, Chertsey, and finally brought (1870) to rest in Isleworth.

Cherry & Pe (1991); Co (2008); J.Curl (2005); J.Curl (ed.) (2001); Pe,Hs, & Antram (1989)

Kennedy, T. Warnett (1911–2000) *See* GILLESPIE, KIDD, & COIA.

Kent, William (c.1685-1748) English painter/landscape architect/architect. Taken up by the nobility early in his career, he travelled to Rome (1709), where he met many English grandees, including *Burlington, whose *protégé* he became. Kent edited the *Designs of Inigo Jones with some Additional Designs* (1727), the 'additions' being by Burlington and himself, drawn by *Flitcroft. Kent did not practise as an architect until the 1730s, at a time when the second *Palladian Revival* was in full swing, but he was not stylistically restricted, for some of his schemes of interior decorations (and his furniture-designs) are sumptuous, looking back towards the *Baroque he had admired in Italy: 22 Arlington Street (1741) and 44 Berkeley Square (1742-4—with a noble staircase), both in London, contained some of his most successful interiors. Burlington got his man into the Office of Works (1726), and Kent became (1735) Master-Mason and Deputy Surveyor. His best-known buildings are the Treasury (1733-7) and the Horse Guards (1748-59—completed by *Vardy), both in Whitehall, London, but he also designed several *fabriques* at Stowe, Bucks. (including the Temple of Venus (before 1732), the Temple of Ancient Virtue (c.1734), the celebrated Temple of British Worthies (c.1735) in the 'Elysian Fields' (also his creation), Congreve's Monument (1736), and other buildings). Of considerable significance in the history of *Palladianism was Holkham Hall, Norfolk (1734-65—for which M.*Brettingham was the executive architect), the most splendid Palladian house in England (Burlington had a hand in its design): its lavish marble apsidal entrance-hall (an amalgam of a Roman *basilica and a Vitruvian *Egyptian Hall), with coffered ceiling and magnificent stair leading to the *piano-nobile* level, is one of the grandest rooms of the period. Holkham is an excellent example of *concatenation, of which Kent was a master (e.g. Horse Guards, London).

An important figure in garden-history, Kent was in the vanguard of the revolution against formal C17 gardens, and combined Palladian architecture with the contrived 'naturalness' of the park. He created landscapes comparable to pictures of **Claude Gellée** (1600-82—*called Lorraine**) (as at Rousham, Oxon. (1738-41)), and so must be regarded as a pioneer of the *Picturesque in English landscape-design (famously, he 'leapt the fence and saw that all Nature was a garden'). He also designed in the *Gothick style, notably the choir-screen, Gloucester Cathedral (1741—destroyed), and the pulpit at York *Minster (1741—burned, 1829), published by John *Vardy (1744), which may have been the source of some Gothick elements in St John's Church, Shobdon, Herefs. (1746-56).

Kent's mastery of Baroque is best seen in funerary monuments, e.g. the huge memorial (1730-3)

to **John Churchill** (1650-1722—**1st Duke of Marlborough** from 1702), Blenheim Palace Chapel, Oxon., carved by **John Michael Rysbrack.** (1694-1770).

Co (2008); J.Curl (2011a); Hunt (1987); Hunt & Willis (eds) (1989); M.McCarthy (1987); *ODNB* (2004); Roscoe *et al.* (2009); J.T (1996); S.Weber (ed.) (2013); M.Wilson (1984)

Kentish rag Hard compact grey-white *limestone used in polygonal *rubble rough- or close-pitched walling, often on *Gothic-Revival London churches, where it was usually a facing to common brick walls. Its irregular forms create a network of mortar-joints.

Kentish tracery *See* TRACERY.

Keppie, John (1863-1945) Glasgow architect, he joined John *Honeyman (1889), and, with C.R.*Mackintosh, became a partner when Honeyman retired (1900). Keppie worked on the remodelling of the *Glasgow Herald* Building, Mitchell Street (1893-5), and remained with **Keppie, Henderson, & Partners** until 1937.

G & W (1987); A.S.Gray (1985); WRH (1990)

Kerr, Robert (1823-1904) Combative Scots architect, major figure in C19 debates about style: he perceptively observed of the *Queen-Anne 'School' that it would 'pass into a phase of the French Renaissance', and the 'ultimate result' would be a 'more refined species of Classicism'. His *Newleafe Discourses* (1846) was a critique of pretentiously nonsensical architectural writings, and *The Gentleman's House* (1864) was an analysis of country-house design. He opposed *Ruskin and all that he stood for, exposing in no uncertain terms absurdities and inconsistencies in his works. His architecture was an eclectic mix of *Renaissance, *Jacobethan, and *Second-Empire styles (e.g. Bearwood, Berks. (1865-74) and the formidable Greathed (formerly Ford) Manor, Surrey (1868)).

AH, **xxiv** (1981), 83-91; *BN*, **xxvi** (26 June 1874), 691; Crook (1987); Kerr (1846, 1864); J.T (1996)

Kessler, George Edward (1862-1923) German-born and educated American landscape architect, he was recommended by F.L.*Olmsted, Jun., to take charge of the Kansas City, Fort Scott, & Gulf Railroad Company's park, Merriam, Kansas, and his work there led to commissions for Kansas City, MO (1887), Roland Park, Baltimore (1891), Fairlawn Cemetery, Oklahoma City (1892), parks in Memphis, TN (1900), and the landscape-design of the Louisiana Purchase Exposition (1904). He opened an office in St Louis, where he was joined by **Eda Sutermeister** (1878-1929) and Henry *Wright: the firm carried out numerous projects in the American

Mid-West, including a complex park-system for Cincinnati, OH (from 1906), which introduced the idea of the city as a park in itself, surpassing in scale and complexity anything of its kind previously proposed for any American city. His name is associated with the *City Beautiful movement.

B & K (2000); W.H.Wilson (1989, 1990)

Kessler, Harry Clément Ulrich, Graf von (1868-1937) German-Anglo-Irish diplomat/patron/writer, appointed (1903) Director of the *Grossherzogliche Museum für Kunst und Kunstgewerbe*, Weimar, where, prompted by *Nietzsche's sister, **Therese Elisabeth Alexandra Förster-Nietzsche** (1846-1935), curator of her brother's archive, he called to Weimar Henry van de *Velde, who designed a stadium and monument to the philosopher (unrealized), and built and directed the two important Schools founded by **Wilhelm Ernst** (1873-1923—**Grand Duke of Saxe-Weimar-Eisenach** (*r.*1901-18)). Kessler's influence at the time is still being assessed, but as a catalyst his was a major force in the transformation of art and architecture in Germany in the two decades before the catastrophe of 1914-18.

Easton (2002)

key 1. Rough surface of brick, stone, etc., the interstices of which, being entered by *plaster or *stucco, ensure sound adherence of one material to the other. **2.** 'Key' relates to the central stone at the top of an arch, an essential element in stabilizing the structure. *Compounds include*:
key-block: *keystone* or *sagitta* (*see* ARCH);
key-brick: tapered brick or *voussoir (*see* ARCH), not to be confused with a *keyed brick*, i.e. one with a *stretcher-surface* indented to act as a key for plaster or stucco;
key-console: *console-shaped *keystone* (properly *ancon) sometimes functioning as a base for a statue, etc.;
key-course: more than one *keystone* in an arch of great depth, or stones in the *crown of a barrel-*vault;
keystone: wedge-shaped *key-block* at the crown of an arch to consolidate it.

Key, Lieven de (*c.*1560-1627) Born in Gent, he settled (1590) in Haarlem, where he became Town Mason and Carpenter: he and de *Keyser were the most prominent architects working in The Netherlands in the *Renaissance style at that time. He designed the *façade of the *Stadhuis*, Leiden (1594-7), the scrolled *strapwork gables, downward tapering *pilasters, and *obelisks of which show a pronounced influence from the *pattern-books of de *Vries. He also designed the spectacular stepped-gabled *Vleeshal*, Haarlem (1601-5), with an exterior of brick with stone *dressings, the whole much decorated with

*scrolls, *festoons, and *cartouches derived from de Vries. He built the exotic tower for the *Nieuwe Kerk* of St Anna (1613—destroyed), the front of the side-wing of the *Stadhuis* (1620), and the *Waaghuis* (1598), all in Haarlem.

RSTK (1977); Vermeulen (1941); vV (1993)

key pattern *Greek key, *labyrinthine *fret, or *meander.

Keyser, Hendrick Cornelis de (1565-1621) One of two important early-C17 architects working in The Netherlands, the other being de *Key. De Keyser was appointed (1594) Municipal Mason and Sculptor (effectively City Architect) to Amsterdam, where he built the *Zuiderkerk* (1606-14) and the *Westerkerk* (1620-31), both models for Protestant churches in The Netherlands and Northern Germany, partly through their publication in *Architectura Moderna* (1631) by **Salomon de Bray** (1597-1664). Both have handsome *steeples that may have had some influence, disseminated through the publication, on *Wren's designs for the London City churches. At the *Westerkerk*, built on a Greek-cross plan, his style reached maturity, moving away from Dutch *Mannerism towards the *Classicism of van *Campen. His most important secular work was the handsome *Stadhuis*, Delft (1618-20), and he invented a type of gable for Amsterdam houses (e.g. on the *Herengracht*) that was less busy and more Classical than earlier examples. His son-in-law and pupil was Nicholas *Stone, with whom de Keyser's son, **Willem** (1603-78), worked when living in London.

L & D (1934); RSTK (1977); vV (1993)

khan Unfurnished building for the accommodation of travellers in the Middle East, etc. A *caravanserai.

khanaqah Hostel for Muslim mystics (*Sufis*), usually in the form of a *court with individual cells around three sides of the perimeter, with an assembly-hall on the fourth (*qibla) side. An example is in the complex of *Baybars al-Jashankir*, Cairo (early C14). At the shrine of *Char Bakr*, near Bukhara (1559-69), the *khanaqah* is placed between the *mosque and the *madrasa, linking them in one grand architectural ensemble.

B & B (1994); J.T (1996)

kheker, khekher 1. Ancient-Egyptian decorative *frieze consisting of repetitive upright motifs resembling *papyrus-stalks bundled together with the floral parts at the top, or the fringes of a carpet. **2.** Cavetto *gorge-cornice carved or painted with vertical leaf-shapes over a *torus moulding.

khekher (1) Ancient-Egyptian frieze.

kibbutz (*pl.* **kibbutzim**) Communally-owned collective rural settlement in Palestine (later Israel) established by Jewish immigrants from early C20. Some were designed by European-born architects (e.g. *Kauffmann).

Kienast, Dieter (1945-98) Swiss landscape architect, he researched spontaneous urban vegetation, underpinning later work in Switzerland. Advocating variety, diversity, and heterogeneity over uniformity, he held the unoriginal view that design is an expression of the culture of the times, but that the site should always be respected, even though he avoided naturalistic references, applying rigorous geometrical compositions so that there was always a clear distinction between what was 'nature' and 'garden'. Realized works included *Et in Arcadia Ego*, Uetliberg (1989-94); the grounds of the Psychiatric Clinic, Chur (1990-6); and *Mimesis*, Greifensee (1995), all in Switzerland; and *Nature n'existe pas*, Chaumont-sur-Loire, France (1996), typical of his *Minimalism.

Bauwelt, xc/4 (1999), 150; Kienast (1997, 2000, 2002); N & P (2003); Weilacher (1996)

Kiesler, Frederick John (1890-1965) Vienna-born American visionary architect. In the 1920s he worked for a while with *Loos and joined *De *Stijl, later producing designs in which endless curves and continuous wall- and ceiling-planes contrasted with the grid, rectangle, and flat wall then generally favoured. His *Endless House* (from 1923, with revisions as late as the 1960s) encapsulated his ideas of improving the human condition by means of an architecture derived from organic forms he perceived as 'visible trading-posts' of seen and unseen forces. He claimed that reality consists of those forms interacting in a way he dubbed *Correalism, arguing that humans react continuously with their environment, and that space and time are continuous, endless, and capable of expanding architectural possibilities. He published *Inside the Endless House: Art, People, and Architecture* (1966). Described (1960) by *Huxtable as the 'greatest non-building architect' of his time, his *Shrine of the Book*, Hebrew

University, Jerusalem (1959-65), is perhaps his most impressive realized work, although his theatre stage-sets (1920s-1940s) were innovative.

ARe, lxxxvi (Sept. 1939), 60-75; C & S (1962); E (1994); Gohr & Luyken (eds) (1996); Huxtable (1960); Kiesler (1964, 1966)

Kikutake, Kiyonori (1928-2011) Japanese architect, leading light in *Metabolism, committed to adaptability, as expressed in his visionary designs for cities. His *Sky-House*, Tokyo (1958-9—a single volume elevated on *piers with scope for hanging future rooms when needed below it), made his reputation, while his *Tower Shaped Community* (1958), with a spine-like element for services to which cylinders containing the living-apartments could be fixed, was publicized in *Metabolism: Proposals for a New Urbanism* (1960), a document which also displayed *Marine City*, an extension of Tokyo into the sea. Arguing that elements most likely to change should be designed for ease of replacement, he disposed services around the open living-space of the *Sky-House*, and attached the bathroom-units to the external walls of the Pacific Hotel, Chigasaki (1966). At *Aquapolis*, Okinawa (1975), the concept of extending cities into the sea was partially realized. Other works include Miyakonoyo Civic Hall (1966—with a light, collapsible roof-structure), the Administration Building, Shrine of Izumo (1963), and Tokoen Hotel, Yonago (1964). Like their *Archigram colleagues in Britain, the Metabolists proposed prefabricated pods and cells which could be fixed to frames or some kind of central structure, the pods (as variables) being given insubstantial architectural treatment. Other works include the Pasadena Heights terrace-housing, Mishima (1972-4), and the huge Edo-Tokyo Museum, Tokyo (1980-92). In 1978 he published *Kiyonori Kikutake: Concepts and Planning*.

Bo (1985, 1990, 1995); R.Boyd (1968); Wi.Cu (1996); E (1994); Kikutake (1973, 1997); Ku (1972, 1977); P (1982); Ross (1978); J.T (1996)

Kiley, Daniel Urban (1912-2004) American landscape architect, disciple of *Olmsted. He collaborated (1947) with Eero *Saarinen on the competition to design the Jefferson Memorial Park, St Louis, MO, but the realized scheme (including the Gateway Arch) was Saarinen's. He designed landscaping at Saarinen's Irwin Miller House, Columbus, IN (1955-7); approaches to the same architect's Dulles Airport, Washington, DC (1955-8); the terrace and roof-gardens of Roche & *Dinkeloo's Oakland Museum, CA (1961-9); and the water-garden for **Ieoh Ming Pei**'s (1917-2019) Fountain Place, Dallas, TX (mid-1980s). Other works include the Henry Moore Sculpture Garden, Nelson Atkins Museum of Art, Kansas City, MO

(1987-9); the Scholar Garden, Rockefeller University, Manhattan, NYC (early 1990s); the interior *atria* of the National Gallery of Art, Washington, DC (1970-7); the European Court of Human Rights, Strasbourg, France (1991-2—with **Richard George Rogers** (1933-)); and the National Sculpture Garden, Washington, DC (1982-3—with *SOM). One of his earlier works as an architect was the Court for the Nuremberg Trials (1945). He pioneered a break with American tendencies to draw on European precedents (although he claimed an interest in Le *Nôtre's work), and urged a greater sensitivity to local and regional American topography in modern landscape-design.

Cerver (1995); E (1994); Hilderbrand *et al.* (1999); Kiley & Amidon (1999); N & R (2003); Rainey & Treib (eds) (2009); W.Saunders (ed.) (1999); Shoe (2001); *The Times* (9 Mar. 2004) 33; W & S (1994): A.Wilson (2005)

Kinetic architecture Architecture evolved in the belief that static, permanent forms of architecture were no longer suitable for use in times of change. It was supposed to be dynamic, adaptable, capable of being added to or reduced, and even disposable. *Archigram, *Futurism, *Metabolism, and works by **Yona Friedman** (1923-) and *Fuller have been associated with it.

Mutnjakovic (1995); Zuk & R.Clark (1971)

king-pendant Vertical timber in a *truss between the *ridge and projecting below the lowest transverse member.

king-post *See* TRUSS.

King, William (*fl.*1770s-1800) Landscape-designer active in the North of Ireland during the latter part of the C18. He laid out the parks of Castle Coole and Florencecourt, Co. Fermanagh; Downhill, Co. Londonderry; and Mount Stewart, Co. Down, among others.

Reeves-Smyth (2001)

kiosk 1. Oriental summer-palace or *pavilion for temporary resort. **2.** Small open or partly open free-standing structure, the roof (often tent-like) carried on posts or a light *colonnade, used as a garden-*pavilion, *band-stand, or *summer-house, often with an orientalizing character, in the *Moorish, *Hindoo, or other exotic style. **3.** Public telephone-box or a small stall for the sale of newspapers, etc.

Kip, Johannes (1653-1722) Dutch artist/engraver, settled in England after 1688, he is best known for his topographical engravings of country-mansions published (1708) as *Britannia Illustrata: Or Views of Several of the Queen's Palaces, as Also of the Principal Seats of the Nobility and Gentry of Great Britain*, etc., which is among the most important English topographical publications of C18, with engravings executed after drawings by **Leonard** *or* **Leendert Knyff** *or* **Knijff** (1650-1722). Kip's plates for *The Ancient and Present State of Gloucestershire* (1712) by **Sir Robert Atkyns** (1647-1711) are outstanding.

Atkyns (1712); Hs & Jackson-Stops (eds) (1984); *ODNB* (2004); J.T (1996)

kitchen-garden Garden (also known as *potager*) in which fruit and vegetables are grown. Of great antiquity, kitchen-gardens have existed as long as civilization: ideally, they should be in warm, sheltered enclosures, laid out in grid-like patterns, and capable of being easily irrigated, so often incorporated central pools of wells, water-channels, etc. Skills associated with kitchen-gardening were passed down through the monastic Orders, and in France and esp. The Netherlands C17 advances in fruit-growing were introduced to kitchen-gardens, including dwarf varieties, with trees grown in *espalier* formations trained against south-facing walls, while at the same time the kitchen-garden became detached from flower-gardens and pleasure-grounds. Advanced C17 exemplars acquired heated *glass-houses, often built as lean-to structures, and later further *green- and *hot-houses were constructed for a wide variety of plants, many imported from the Americas and elsewhere. Walled kitchen-gardens within a large estate could serve both practical and aesthetic purposes, as at Ickworth, Suffolk, where **Sir John Hervey** (1665-1751—**Baron Hervey** from 1703 and **1st Earl of Bristol** from 1714) caused a charming *Queen-Anne (1) *summer-house to be built against the kitchen-garden wall, commanding views over the lake. Such gardens, once visited and walked in, went out of vogue and were neglected in the mid-C20, but in more recent times a growing interest in fresh organic produce has seen a renaissance of the type (e.g. the examples at Audley End, Essex (1750s, restored 1998-2000, with long wall heated by smoke-flues, built (1822) by **Richard Ward**; and Heligan, St Ewe, Cornwall (C18, restored from 1991)).

Campbell (2006); *GH*, x/1 (Spring 1982), 1-16; G.W. Johnson (1846, 1857); O'Malley (2010); Parkinson (1629); Shoe (2001); Symes (2006); Tay (2006); C.A.Wilson (ed.) (2003)

Kitsch German term meaning rubbishy pretentious trash; anything that is shoddy, tawdry, mawkishly sentimental, and in bad taste. When applied to any of the arts it suggests false, superficial, spurious imitation of real artistic creations, so implies that *Kitsch* art apes something without any understanding or depth whilst at the same time endeavouring to please, soothe, and reassure. However, it has also been described as the cultural revenge of the proletariat, identified as an aspect of *Camp taste that values the outrageously hideous for its own sake. Much architectural *Post-Modernism possessed *Kitsch*-like aspects (notably the allusions to *Classicism made without any evidence of scholarship), but some designers have deliberately introduced reflections of *Kitsch* in their work for populist commercial reasons.

C.Brown (1976); Dorfles (ed.) (1969); Giesz (1971); Saisselin (1985); Steinberg (ed.) (1975); Sternberg (1971); P.Ward (1991)

Kleanthis, Stamatis (1802–62) Greek architect, pupil of *Schinkel. With **Eduard Schaubert** (1804–68) he produced (1832) a plan for the development of Athens which contained important suggestions for the preservation of ancient monuments, but private interests frustrated its implementation. He designed the Byzantine Museum, Athens (mid-C19).

J.T (1996)

Kleihues, Josef Paul (1933–2004) German architect. His early work was influenced by New *Brutalism and by *Structuralism, but in the 1960s *Neo-Rationalism began to change his architecture. His buildings include the Main Workshops of the Berlin Sanitation Service, Berlin-Tempelhof (1969–83), the Hospital in Berlin Neukölln (from 1973), and the Museum Complex at Solingen, near Düsseldorf (1981–5). A protagonist (with *Ungers) for an architecture of severe clarity, pure geometry, and reason in Germany, he was appointed (1979) Director of Planning for the *IBA, Berlin. He designed the *Museum für Vor- und Frühgeschichte*, Frankfurt-am-Main (1981–9), the *Stadtmuseum*, Kornwestheim (1990), the Museum of Contemporary Art, Chicago, IL (1991–5), and the galleries in the former *Hamburger Bahnhof*, Berlin (late 1980s). His beliefs in the old Prussian virtues of austerity, simplicity, and fine craftsmanship were clear from his work.

E (1994); Shkapich (ed.) (1989); J.T (1996)

Klengel, Wolf Caspar von (1630–91) German architect. As Inspector-General of Works in Saxony, he restored buildings that had been damaged during the Thirty Years War (1618–48), including the *Schloss* at Zwickau. He designed the chapel (1661–72) at *Moritzburg*, and the *Kommödienhaus* (1664–7—destroyed), the *Ballhaus* (from 1668), the *Reithaus* (1667–78), and alterations to the *Schloss* (1674–8), all in Dresden. He rebuilt (from 1685) that part of Dresden north of the Elbe (now *Neustadt*) and made major contributions to Saxon *Baroque architecture.

Dresdner Geschichtsblätter, **xxii** (1913), 35–56; J.T (1996)

Klenze, (Franz) Leo(pold Karl) von (1784–1864) German architect, he created some of the finest C19 buildings in Bavaria, notably in Munich, which he helped to transform into a beautiful Capital City. Trained in Berlin (1800–3—where he was influenced by architecture of the *Gillys), he worked with *Percier and *Fontaine in Paris (where he also absorbed much of *Durand's approach), and then became Court Architect to **Jérôme** (1784–1860), **Napoléon Bonaparte**'s (1769–1821) brother, **King of Westphalia** (*r.*1807–13): for Jérôme he designed the Court Theatre, Wilhelmshöhe, Kassel (1812). Called to Munich (1816) at the behest of **Crown Prince Ludwig** (1786–1868—later **King Ludwig I of Bavaria** (*r.*1825–48)), Klenze created many of the city's noblest buildings, starting with the *Glyptothek* (1816–31), built to house *Antique sculptures, including parts of the Greek *temple at Aegina, discovered (1811) by *Haller von Hallerstein et al. Although Haller had produced a ravishing Graeco-Egyptian design, and *Fischer a severe project with a *Pantheon-dome, Klenze's realized building is a synthesis of Greek, Roman, and Italian-*Renaissance styles. Originally the vaulted interiors (destroyed in the 1939–45 war and unhappily not reinstated) had mural and ceiling decorations in the manner of *Raphael's *grotesques, providing an explanatory *iconography for the collection.

Klenze designed (1816) the Leuchtenberg Palace (the first scholarly *Italianate building in C19 Germany) as well as several *façades (many of which had Florentine allusions) on the wide, straight, new *Ludwigstrasse* running north from the *Residenz*. Then came the Neo-Renaissance *Pinakothek* (1822–36), to display the Royal Collection: the architecture drew on the *Palazzo Cancellaria*, Rome, and on the Belvedere *cortile* in the Vatican, but the clear, logical plan and top-lit galleries were influential. When Ludwig ascended the Throne, Klenze was commissioned to add various buildings to the *Residenz*: these were the *Königsbau* (1826–35), in which elements of the *Palazzo Pitti* and *Palazzo Rucellai*, both in Florence, were mixed; the *Allerheiligenhofkirche* (1826–37), an important essay in the *Rundbogenstil*, with quotations from the Palatine Chapel, Palermo, *San Marco*, Venice, and Lombardic *Romanesque; and the remodelling of the north front, the *Festsaalbau* (1832–42).

Klenze's greatest buildings are his public monuments, which testify to his deep feeling for the architecture of Greek Antiquity. *Walhalla*, near Regensburg (1830–42), is a *Greek-Revival *temple, based on the *Parthenon* and set on a high stepped platform derived partly from the image of F.*Gilly's proposed monument (1797) to **Friedrich II of Prussia** ('the Great'—*r.*1740–86), and partly from an earlier scheme for the site by Haller (1814–15). The rich *polychrome interior, illuminated from above, is not unlike C.R.*Cockerell's sensitive and scholarly drawings of the Temple of *Apollo Epicurius* at Bassae, while the exposed decorated roof-trusses recall *Hittorff's contemporary work at *St-Vincent-de-Paul*, Paris. Then came the *Propyläen, Königsplatz*, Munich (1846-60), with Graeco-Egyptian *pylon-towers flanking the Greek-*Doric *porticoes; the *Ruhmeshalle*, Munich (1843-54), a Greek-Doric *stoa-like *colonnade terminating at each end in projecting pedimented wings, essentially a shelter for portrait-busts of eminent Bavarians (it is particularly interesting in that its composition is similar to that of the *Hellenistic Great Altar of Pergamon, which had not been discovered when Klenze designed the *Ruhmeshalle*, so he is revealed as an architect with a natural affinity for Ancient-Greek buildings); and the *Befreiungshalle* (originally designed by *Gärtner), near Kelheim (1842-63), a drum surrounded by buttresses, with a Roman-Doric *colonnade around the upper part. These four monuments are among the noblest works of C19 architecture in all Europe.

When **Prince Otto of Bavaria** (1815-67), second son of King Ludwig I, was chosen (1832) as King of Greece, Klenze prepared an ambitious plan for Athens, including a vast new museum and elaborate proposals for the protection of ancient monuments, but only the RC Cathedral of St Dionysus (1844-53), a *Neo-Renaissance *basilica, was built. Klenze was more fortunate in his dealings with the Russians, for whom he demonstrated his skills in the huge Neo-Classical addition he designed for the Hermitage Museum, St Petersburg (1839-51), one of the very finest buildings of the European Classical Revival. He was a master of synthesis of styles, and was equally at home with most of them. As a Neo-Classicist, however, he was in the first rank.

Hederer (1964); Honour (1979); Klenze (1830–50, 1833, 1843); Lieb & Hufnagel (eds) (1979); Ne (1980, 1987); Wa & M (1987)

Klerk, Michel de (1884–1923) Dutch architect, member of the *Amsterdam School, he is best known for his *Expressionist designs carried out in collaboration with *Kramer, notably the *Scheepvaarthuis*, Amsterdam (with van der *Mey, 1911-16), and the *De Dageraad* housing-estate, Amstellaan (1920-2). His *Eigen Haard* housing-estate, *Spaarndammerbuurt*, Amsterdam West (1913-20), in which towers, turrets, different types of windows, and finely crafted brickwork suggested the richness of a medieval town, reflects the architect's aim to avoid barrack-like tenements for working-class Socialist housing.

Bock *et al.* (1997); Fanelli (1968); S.Frank (1984); Millon & Nochlin (1978); Pehnt (1973); P (1982); Sharp (1967)

Klint *See* JENSEN-KLINT.

knap To *snap* or *break* stones, so split *flint is *knapped* and laid with the smooth dark surfaces exposed on the surface of the wall, set *flush with *freestone patterns of *tracery, initials, etc., as in medieval *flushwork.

S.Hart (2000)

knee 1. Short *brace or bracket between a *post and a *tie-beam, post and *rafter, or any stiffener in a similar position in a *timber frame. **2.** *Corbel or other projection supporting a *beam. **3.** Bend of 90° such as that at the top of a Classical *architrave round a *doorway suggesting the ends of a *lintel, *called *ear, elbow, *lug, etc. *See* CROSSETTE. **4.** *Label-stop, especially if the *label or *hood-mould is cranked at 90°. **5.** Kneeler. **6.** Length of *stair-*balustrade handrail bent in a convex curve where a flight arrives at a landing: opposite of the concave *ramp*. *Terms include*:

knee-brace: *as* knee (**1**);

kneeler, knee, knee-stone: **1.** large, approximately triangular stone at the foot of a *gable, cut to have a horizontal bed and a top conforming, wholly or in part, to the slope of the gable: it (called *foot-stone, gable-springer*, or *skewtable*) stops the *raked *cope from sliding off; **2.** stone securely bedded with one side cut at an angle or skew forming the *springing of an arch or *vault; **3.** *cop in a *battlement; **4.** square return of a *label over a late-*Gothic aperture.

Knight, Richard Payne (1751–1824) English landscape-theorist/member of the Society of *Dilettanti/connoisseur, he designed (with help from T.F.*Pritchard) Downton Castle, Herefs. (1772-8), a *Picturesque composition in the *Gothic style (though *Neo-Classicism dominated the interiors) in which symmetry was avoided in overall planning, but not in individual rooms. This asymmetry made Downton revolutionary, and influenced many English and Continental architects. Knight claimed the house was designed to resemble buildings in landscapes by **Claude Gellée** (1600–82): he questioned 'Capability' *Brown's style of landscape-design in *The Landscape—A Didactic Poem* (1794), helping to create a climate in which asymmetrical, serene, reposeful, and informal aspects of much architecture and landscape-design developed in C19, and his *Analytical Enquiry into the Principles of Taste* (1805) contained important discussions on contemporary architectural ideas, notably the Picturesque. When **Thomas Bruce** (1766–1841)—**7th Earl of Elgin** from 1771) had sculptures from the Athenian *Parthenon* exhibited in London Knight made a fool of himself by dogmatically declaring they were Roman of the time of **Hadrian** (*r.*AD 117-138), and led other members of the Dilettanti in the controversy about their artistic worth. He also courted controversy when the Dilettanti published (1786) his *Account of the Remains of the Worship of Priapus*, regarded by the prissy as obscene.

Ballantyne (1997); COF (1988); M.Clarke & Penny (eds) (1992); Co & J.Hs (eds) (1970); Knight (1794, 1972); Pe (1968); Wa (1982a)

Knijff, Leendert, *or* **Knyff, Leonard** (1650-1722) *See* KIP, JOHANNES.

knob, knop *Finial or *boss.

Knobelsdorff, Georg Wenzeslaus, Freiherr von (1699-1753) Prussian aristocrat/architect/soldier, friend of **Crown Prince Friedrich of Prussia** (1712-86—later **King Friedrich II** ('the Great', *r*.1740-86)), for whom he built the circular *Tuscan *temple of Apollo in the gardens of *Amalthée*, Neu-Ruppin, Brandenburg (1735). After a journey in Italy (1736-7), Knobelsdorff enlarged *Schloss Rheinsberg*, near Neu-Ruppin, introducing a pronounced French note with coupled columns derived from *Perrault's east front of the Louvre. When Friedrich became King, Knobelsdorff was appointed *Oberintendant* of Buildings and Gardens. He added a new wing to *Schloss Monbijou* (1740-2), and another at *Schloss Charlottenburg* (1740-3), with a sumptuous *Rococo interior, and designed the new Opera House, *Unter den Linden* (1740-3), all in Berlin. The last was the first example of *Palladian Revival in Prussia, with a design closely derived from Colen *Campbell's Wanstead House, Essex, illustrated in *Vitruvius Britannicus* (1715 and 1725).

When the King moved his Court to Potsdam, Knobelsdorff remodelled the *Stadtschloss* there (1744-51), with Rococo interiors (destroyed). The enchanting *Schloss Sanssouci*, Potsdam (1745-7—also known as the *Weinberg-Schloss* because it stands above a series of glazed *terraces forming *conservatories for growing vines), survives: an exquisite single-storey building with an elliptical Neo-Classical *Marmorsaal* in the centre, it has paired *terms instead of *pilasters on the exterior. He also designed St Hedwig's RC Cathedral, Berlin, built by *Boumann and *Büring (1742-73), renovated the *Schloss* at Dessau, Anhalt (1747-51), and designed other buildings in Potsdam.

E.Hempel (1965); Kadatz (1983); Streichhan (1932); J.T (1996); vV (1993); Wa & M (1987)

Knoblauch, Carl Heinrich Eduard (1801-65) German architect, pupil of *Schinkel, he designed several houses in Berlin, and indeed, with *Hitzig and *Stüler, evolved a refined *Italianate style for mid-C19 domestic architecture in the Prussian capital. He also designed country-houses, some in the *castellated style of Schinkel's

Babelsberg. The Synagogue, *Orianienburger-strasse*, Berlin (1859-66—in a *Moorish-medieval style) was by him, but completed by his son, **Gustav** (1833-1916), and Stüler (destroyed 1943-45, but partially reconstructed 1988-93). He edited *Zeitschrift für Bauwesen* for many years. Another son, **Edmund** (1841-83), also became a Berlin architect.

B-S (1977); Knoblauch & Hollen (1878); J.T (1996)

Knöffel, Johann Christoph (1686-1752) German architect, much influenced by French *Classicism, as at his *Wackerbarth Palais*, Dresden (1723-6—destroyed 1945, rebuilt 1962). A pupil of *Longuelune, he spent most of his professional life in Dresden, where he became *Ober-landbaumeister* (1734). Nearly all his fine and considerable work has been obliterated, but he completed *Chiaveri's exquisite *Hofkirche* (now the RC Cathedral), Dresden, after 1748 (restored 1980s) after severe damage (1945)), and finished Longuelune's *Blockhaus* (so called because a timber customs-house once stood on the site), or Guard House, Dresden (1749). He designed the *hunting-lodge of *Hubertusburg*, Wermsdorf (1743-51). His pupils included *Krubsacius.

E.Hempel (1965); Hentschel & May (1973); Wa & M (1987)

knoll Small rounded hill, eminence, or *mount, sometimes artificial.

knop *Finial or swelling termination to anything.

knot 1. *Boss or *finial. 2. Ornament resembling a bunch of leaves or flowers. 3. Architectural treatment resembling tied ropes, as in a *knotted shaft. 4. *Strapwork.

knot-garden Garden containing intricate knot-like patterns of low-growing *hedges of box, rosemary, thyme, etc., common in C16 and C17, with spaces between the hedges filled with flowers, coloured gravels, or herbs of different colours to the varieties used in the hedges. Early detailed descriptions occur in **Francesco Colonna**'s (*c*.1433-1527) *Hypnerotomachia Poliphili* (1499): knot-gardens became popular in C16 France (with varieties illustrated in Du *Cerceau's *Les Plus Excellents Bastiments de France* (1576-9)) and *Tudor England. Modern re-creations include those at Hatfield House, Herts., Hampton Court, Mddx., and the Museum of Garden History, Lambeth, London.

Crisp (1924); Shoe (2001); Symes (2006); Tay (2006)

Knott, Ralph (1879-1929) English architect, he assisted Aston *Webb and won (1908) the competition to design London's County Hall, a massive building in which *Baroque, *Neo-Classicism, and even *Mannerism play parts. Shortly afterwards Knott took **Ernest Stone Collins** (1874-1942) into partnership, and together they produced several well-mannered buildings, including 21 Upper Grosvenor Street, London (1913). Knott collaborated with *Thorneley on the designs for the *Greek-Revival Parliament Buildings, Stormont, Northern Ireland, and he and Collins designed the Speaker's House, Stormont (1926) in the years preceding his early death.

A.S.Gray (1985)

knotted shaft *Romanesque column-shaft carved to look as though tied in a knot. Good C12 or C13 examples survive in Würzburg Cathedral, Germany, and similar *shafts can be found at the *Broletto, Como, Italy (c.1215).

Ck (1996); J.Curl (2011)

knotwork *Interlacing carved cord or *ribbon-ornament, occurring at many times and in many styles. Obvious examples are the intricate patterns in *Anglo-Saxon and *Celtic design, but it also occurs in *arabesque, *Art Nouveau, *Moorish architecture, and *strapwork, to name but a few examples.

L & D (1986)

Knowles, James Thomas, Sen. (1806-84) English architect, he designed a great number of competently composed houses, including the handsome *Italianate *palazzo, 15 Kensington Palace Gardens, London (1854). Together with his son, (**Sir**) **James Thomas Knowles** (1831-1908), he was responsible for the Grosvenor Hotel, Victoria Station, London (1860-2). Knowles jun. laid out the Cedars Estate, Clapham, London (1860), the Park Town Estate, Battersea, London (1863-6), and other developments. He also edited *Contemporary Review* and founded *The Nineteenth Century*.

D & M (1985); Metcalf (1978, 1980); *ODNB* (2004); Sh (1973)

knull 1. Type of *gadroon. **2.** Variety of *bead-and-reel with the components apparently squashed, so that they are very thin and close together.

Kobori Enshū (1579-1647) Japanese architect of numerous houses and gardens. Using finely finished woods, richly carved *transoms, decorative *alcoves, sliding-doors and wall-panels, he created a style that was influential thereafter, even into C21. His gardens were intimately connected to his buildings, and he exploited distant vistas, so his work was very unusual for C17. A master of the tea ceremony, he created spacious settings for that ritual.

J.T (1996)

Koch, Alexander (1848-1911) Swiss-born architect, not to be confused with *Koch of

Darmstadt. Zürich-trained, he later worked under *Semper on projects for the *Ringstrasse, Vienna, and after further studies (1870-1) in Berlin, he established a Zürich practice (c.1871-85) as **Koch & Ernst** (with **Heinrich Ernst** (1846-1916)), designing a children's hospital, several mansions on the *Alpenquai*, and much else. He settled (1885) in London, and, as a Visitor, studied methods of training and design at South Kensington. From 1889 he edited/published *Academy Architecture and Architectural Review* (an invaluable record) and from 1905 *British Competitions in Architecture* (both in collaboration with Munich-trained architect/perspectivist **Charles William English** (1862-1932), with whom he also submitted designs for various European architectural competitions). His sons changed their names to **Martin-Kaye** during the 1914-18 war: **Hugh Martin-Kaye** (1878-1954) founded *Architecture Illustrated*, and continued publishing *Academy Architecture* until 1931; **Douglas Neil Martin-Kaye** (1891-1954) practised architecture in the Southend area of Essex.

B, **c** (12 May 1911), 598, and **clxxxvii** (3 Dec. 1954), 909; A.S.Gray (1985); A.Koch (ed.) (1907, 1908, 1931); Saur (from 1991)

Koch, Alexander (1860-1939) German publisher, influential in promoting new architecture and design from the 1880s, not to be confused with **Alexander *Koch** of Zürich and London. He established his firm (1880s), bringing out successful journals such as *Fachblatt für Innen-Dekoration* (from 1890), and *Deutsche Kunst und Dekoration* (from 1897), the first journal to report on the work of the *Wiener Werkstätte* (publishing (1904-11) 12 issues on its achievements). Friendly with **Ernst Ludwig, Grand Duke of Hesse** (*r*.1892-1918), Koch inspired him and the Hessian authorities to found (1899) the famous artists' colony at the *Mathildenhöhe* in Darmstadt to which *Behrens and *Olbrich (among others) contributed designs: the idea was to produce exemplary work to improve the quality of design in Hessian industries. Koch published a record of the important exhibition (which promoted *Jugendstil*, held (1901) under the aegis of the Grand Duke in Darmstadt, and also brought out *Meister der Innenkunst* (1902—edited by *Muthesius), which included the series of prizewinning designs for *Das Haus eines Kunstfreundes* competition which he had announced in and sponsored through *Innen-Dekoration*: the book contained the celebrated designs by Baillie *Scott and *Mackintosh. Following the success of the Darmstadt exhibition, Koch was appointed adviser to the *Esposizione Internazionale d'Arte Decorativa*, Turin (1902), which promoted the *Stile floreale* and *Stile Liberty* in Italy. Other important and influential publications of Koch include *Moderne*

Innen-Architektur und innerer Aufbau (1899), and *Handbuch neuzeitlicher Wohnungskultur* (1914), a survey of recently completed German domestic interiors, some of which were very up-to-date indeed, and at first glance could easily have been post-1918. Koch's son (also **Alexander**) continued the publishing interests after his father's death.

Darmstadt (ed.) (2000–4); A.Koch (1901, 1902); Thornton (1984); J.T (1996)

Koch, Gaetano (1849–1910) Italian architect, he designed mostly in a refined *Cinquecento* style in Rome. His works include the *Palazzo Voghera, Via Nazionale* (1870s), the splendid *Piazza dell'Esedra* (1880), with its quadrant *façades, the Palazzo Boncompagni, Largo Goldoni* (1886–90), the tiny *Museo Barracco* (from 1902), and his masterpiece, the *Palazzo Margherita, Via Veneto* (1886). He helped to complete *Sacconi's monument (1885–1911) to **Victor Emmanuel II** (*r.*1861–78 as **King of Italy**).

Hi (1977); Ms (1966); Pi (1968); J.T (1996)

Koenig, Pierre (1925–2004) American architect, known for his exploitation of the steel frame and industrialized building techniques, he made his name with two *Case-Study houses in Los Angeles, CA (No. 21 of 1958 at 9038 Wonderland Park Avenue, and No. 22 of 1959 at 1635 Woods Drive, the latter cantilevered from a clifftop overlooking the city). Later works include the Gantert House, Hollywood, CA (1981), the Koenig House, Los Angeles (1984–5), and the Schwartz House, Santa Monica, CA (1991).

E (1994); McCoy (1962); Steele & D.Jenkins (1998); *Zodiac,* v (1960), 156–63

Koninck, Louis Herman de (1896–1984) Belgian architect, an early devotee of *International Modernism, influenced by Le *Corbusier, *Gropius, etc. Among his works may be mentioned the house at *Vronerodelaan*, Uccele, Brussels (1924), the *Ley Villa, Prins van Oranjelaan*, Brussels (1934), and the standardized rationalized kitchen he exhibited at *CIAM (1930). He was influential as Belgian correspondent for *L'Architecture d'aujourd'hui* (from 1934).

Loo (ed.) (2003); Mierop *et al.* (eds) (1989)

Konstantinidis, Aris (1913–93) Greek architect, he sought to harness tradition, technology, and simplicity in his work, employing clear geometries. His buildings include the *Ciné-News* Cinema, Athens (1940), various housing developments in Greece, *Hotel Xenia*, Mykonos (1960), a holiday-house, Anavyssos, near Athens (1962), and the Museum, Komotini (1967).

E (1994); Leatherbarrow (2000); J.T (1996)

Korb, Hermann (1656–1735) German architect/carpenter to **Ferdinand Albrecht II** (1680–

1735—**Duke of Brunswick-Wolfenbüttel** from 1687), he supervised construction of the huge, largely timber *Schloss Salzdahlum*, designed by **Johann Balthasar Lauterbach** (1660–94—demolished), with architectural motifs anticipating work of *Hildebrandt at the *Belvedere*, Vienna. He probably designed the elliptical library at Wolfenbüttel (1706–13), but his only remaining work is the *Dreifaltigkeitskirche*, Wolfenbüttel (1716–22), with tiers of *galleries opening to an octagonal space.

Gerkens (1974); E.Hempel (1965)

Korn, Arthur (1891–1978) German-born architect, he worked with *Mendelsohn in Berlin (from 1919) before establishing a partnership (1922) with **Siegfried Weitzmann** (1886–1960), with whom he built *Villa Goldstein*, Grünewald (1922), *Kopp & Joseph* shops (1922–30), *Ullstein* Building (1930), *Fromm* Factory, Köpenick (1928), and *Intourist* shop, *Unter den Linden* (1929), among other works, all in Berlin. The *Fromm* Factory had a steel frame, painted red, exposed, and emphasized, and it was this building, more than any other, that was the spark for *Mies van der Rohe's development of the theme. He published (1929) *Glas im Bau und als Gebrauchsgegenstand*, which was influential, but his most important years were arguably spent in England. He chaired the *MARS Group, which produced a plan for London that encapsulated his Hegelian and Marxist ideas (he had been a member of *Der *Ring*), and worked with *Fry and *Yorke (1938–41). As a teacher, first at the Oxford School of Architecture (1941–5) and then at the Architectural Association (1945–65), he influenced the course of architecture and town-planning until well into the 1980s.

E (1994); Korn (1953, 1967); pk; J.T (1996)

Korsmo, Arne (1900–68) Norwegian architect, one of the first to build in the *International style in that country. In partnership with **Sverre Aasland** (1899–1992) from 1929, he designed the *Frøen* housing-development (1929–30), the apartment-block at *Pavels Gate* 6, Oslo (1930), the *Havna* development, Oslo (which included the *Villa Dammann* (1930–2)), and that building-type so beloved of *Modernists, the *grain-elevator, Kristiansand (1933–6). Both the *Dammann* and *Hansen* (1935) houses, Oslo, were influenced by the works of *Dudok and *Mendelsohn. From 1935 Korsmo worked independently, producing the *Benjamin* (1935) and *Heyerdahl* (1935–6) houses, both in Oslo, and designing the Norwegian Pavilion for the Paris *Exposition* (1937), by which time the influence of Le *Corbusier on his work was clear, notably in the *Villa Stenersen*, Oslo (1937–9), where inevitable *pilotis* appeared. At the invitation of *Giedion ·he formed (1950)

PAGON (Progressive Architects Group of Norway), the Norwegian branch of *CIAM, which he led until 1956: other members included *Norberg-Schulz, *Fehn, and **Geir Grung** (1926–89), while *Utzon was associated with them as a 'guest' member. With Norberg-Schulz he designed the *Alfredheim* Home for Young Girls, Tåsen (1951–2), and the Terrace Houses, Planetveien (1952–5), both in Oslo. In collaboration with **Terje Moe** (1933–2009) he designed the *Hotel Britannia*, Trondheim (1961–3). He influenced architectural education after 1945.

Boe (2001); E (1980); N–S (1986*b* & *c*)

Kotěra, Jan (1871–1923) Brno-born, he studied with Otto *Wagner in Vienna. Profoundly influenced (*c.*1898–1905) by the *Sezession, he designed with *Jugendstil* themes well to the fore, while also taking a lively interest in the folk-art of his native land and drawing upon ideas and themes connected with the English *Arts-and-Crafts movement. His early work was published in *Meine und meiner Schüler Arbeiten: 1898–1901* (1902), dominant flavours of which were Arts-and-Crafts and *Jugendstil*. Typical of his designs at that time were the *Peterka* House, Wenceslas Square, Prague (1899–1900), and the National House, Prostějov (1905–7). A journey to the USA (1903) brought him into contact with the work of F.L.L.*Wright, and visits to The Netherlands and England led him to introduce an architecture of brick to Bohemia, as well as Wrightian ideas of space as in the Hradec Králové Town Museum (1906–12). He was an influential teacher, numbering *Fuchs, *Gočár, and *Krejcar among his pupils (although they turned away from the elegance of his work in favour of Modernism). He made a design for the *Company Town for Bat'a at Zlín, which was influenced by the ideas of Ebenezer *Howard.

Kotěra (1902, 2001); Mádl (1922); F.Russell (ed.) (1979); J.T (1996)

Krakauer, Leopold (1890–1954) Austrian-born Israeli architect, he experimented with *Expressionism before emigrating to Palestine (1925) where he worked briefly for *Baerwald. His severe architecture, influenced by De *Stijl and *Purism, suited the *kibbutzim, for which he designed many buildings. He also designed private houses as well as the Megiddo Hotel, Haifa (1930s). His restaurant at the *Tel-Yosef kibbutz* (1933), with its two cubes colliding at an angle of 45° heralded aspects of *Deconstructivism.

J.T (1996)

Kramer, Piet(er) Lodewijk (1881–1961) Dutch architect of the *Amsterdam School. He worked with van der *Mey and de *Klerk on the *Scheepvaarthuis*, Amsterdam (1911–16), and

collaborated with de Klerk at the *De Dageraad* housing-complex, Amsterdam South (1925–6), in which the brick walls were modelled in flowing curved forms regarded as important examples of *Expressionism. He designed the *De Bijenkorf* store, The Hague (1924–6), again with a carefully modelled *façade. Most of his works were *bridges for the Amsterdam Department of Public Works (1917–28).

Casciato (1996); Kohlenbach (1994); Retera (1928); Vriend (1949–50)

Krebs, Konrad (1491–1540) German architect, he designed the *Johann-Friedrichs-Bau* (1533–6), *Schloss Hartenfels*, Torgau, one of the earliest and finest *Renaissance ensembles in Saxony, with a central open stair-tower.

Hi (1981); J.T (1996)

Kreis, Wilhelm (1873–1955) German architect, influenced by a growing taste in Wilhelmian Germany (1888–1918) for national monuments of elemental, aggressive character (e.g. work of *Schmitz), he rose to the occasion with many towers commemorating **Otto von Bismarck** (1815–98) erected to his designs. He was responsible for the Provincial Museum of Prehistory, Halle (1911–16), complete with massive *cyclopean *masonry and corner-towers slightly resembling the Roman *Porta Nigra*, Trier (probably early-C4). After the 1914–18 war some of his work leant towards *Expressionism, e.g. the exhibition-buildings and art-museum by the banks of the Rhine at Düsseldorf (1925–6), including the circular *Rheinhalle* with lozenge-patterned brickwork, *buttresses, openings topped by inverted Vs, and a *stalactite *vault inside recalling *Poelzig's work. In the 1930s Kreis turned to a monumental stripped Neo-Classical style for buildings proposed for *Speer's new plan for Berlin, and he looked to *Boullée and *Gilly for precedents for his gigantic smoking cones and other memorials (*Totenburgen*) designed (but never realized) to commemorate German 'sacrifice and victory' of the 1939–45 war.

Ellenius (1971); Kreis (1927, 1944); L.Krier (ed.) (1985); Lane (1985); Larsson (1983); Mayer & Rehder (1953); Meissner (1925); Ne & Mai (eds) (1994); Preiss (1993); Stephan (1939, 1944); Troost (ed.) (1942–3)

Krejcar, Jaromír (1895–1949) Czechoslovak Modernist architect. With *Teige, he was one of the protagonists of the *Devětsil group*, and edited *Život II* (1922), which promoted *Constructivism and *Purism. His works include the Olympic Department Store, Prague (1924–6—one of the first *reinforced-concrete framed structures in Czechoslovakia), the *Machnáč* Sanatorium, Trenčianské Teplice (1929–32—a paradigm of *International *Modernism), and the Czechoslovak

Pavilion, Paris International Exhibition (1937—destroyed).

AAJ, lxv (1949–50), 89–90; Krejcar (ed.) (1928); Li (1996); Teige (1933)

Kremlin Russian *fortress or *citadel within a town, especially that in Moscow, established 1156, more strongly fortified with stone walls from 1367 and brick walls and towers (1489–95), and beautified with many fine buildings from C15.

Kreschaty Type of *vault over a domed *cruci-form church without *piers, with *barrel-vaults over the arms of the cross and segments of dom-ical vaults over the corner-cells, e.g. Church of the Conception of St Anne in the Corner, Moscow (1478–83).

Krieger, Johann Cornelius (1683–1755) Danish architect/landscape architect, he de-signed (1719–22) the summer-residence of the Danish Court, Fredensborg, and laid out the park there (1720–35). His finest works were reck-oned to be the gardens of *Frederiksborg* Castle (1720–5), much influenced by designs of Le *Nôtre.

J.T (1996)

Krier, Léon (1946–) *See* NEO-RATIONALISM; NEW CLASSICISM; NEW URBANISM; RATIONAL ARCHITECTURE.

Krier, Rob(ert) (1938–) *See* NEO-RATIONALISM; NEW URBANISM; RATIONAL ARCHITECTURE.

Kroll, Lucien (1927–) *See* ADHOCISM.

Krubsacius, Friedrich August (1718–89) German architect/theorist, pupil of *Longuelune and *Bodt: appointed (1764) Professor at the Academy of Arts, he became (1776) *Oberhofbau-meister* in Dresden. In his *Betrachtungen über den wahren Geschmack der Alten in der Baukunst* (1747), he proposed (drawing on French sources) that the proportions of the human body should be the basis of architectural invention, and in another book (1759) that the *Baroque style should be replaced by something purer. In spite of this his own designs in and around Dresden were largely Baroque in flavour, but nearly all his work has been destroyed or damaged, although the *Landhaus*, Dresden (1770–6), has been partly restored and contains a fine *Rococo *staircase. He also carried out (1760s) works at the *Schlösser* of *Neschwitz* and *Otterwisch*, little of which has survived. He published the interesting studies of *Pliny the Younger's villas in *Warscheinlicher Entwurf von des jüngern Plinius Landhause und Gartens Laurens* (1760) and a further (1763) vol-ume on the Tuscan *villa. Krubsacius was also an important figure in landscape-design.

Gottsched (1760); Krubsacius (1760, 1768); Lüttichau (1983); RdP (1994); J.T (1996); Wa & M (1987)

Krumpper, Johann (Hans) (c.1570–1635) Architect of the somewhat ungainly *Renaissance *façade of *Sustris's *Hofkirche* of St Michael, Munich (1583–97). Other works include the tower of the *Stiftskirche*, Polling, the *high-altar of the Charterhouse at Prüll, near Regensburg (1607), the *Paulanerkirche*, Munich (1621–3—destroyed), the *Pfarrkirche*, Dachau (1624–5), and several funerary monuments, notably that of **Duke Ludwig IV** (d.1347) in the *Frauenkirche*, Munich (1621–2).

J.T (1996)

Kufic Characters employed in stonework and *tile inscriptions in *Islamic architecture. Kufic inscriptions were sometimes employed decora-tively (and meaninglessly) in *Hispano-Moresque architecture in much the same way as Egyptian hieroglyphs were used before they could be read and understood by C18 and C19 designers. They were widely employed in C19 revivalist architec-ture of the *Moorish or orientalizing type.

L & D (1986)

Kurokawa, Kisho Noriaki (1934–2007) Prominent in *Metabolism, he was among the first Japanese architects to question the basis of the *International-*Modern Movement, promoting the argument that life-sciences had more rele-vance to architecture than the so-called *Machine Aesthetic. The Nagakin Capsule-Tower, Tokyo (1972), demonstrated his concept of sophisticated buildings incorporating the latest technology yet capable of being changed. Active in fusing Eastern and Western cultural currents, his search for an inter-cultural architecture led him to an *eclecti-cism ranging from the Neo-Classical extension to the Japanese Embassy, Berlin (1988), to the gigan-tic Pacific Tower, *La Défense*, Paris (1991). Other works included the National Museum of Ethnol-ogy, Osaka (1978), Saitama Museum of Modern Art, Urawa (1982), Museum of Modern Art, Nagoya (1987), City Museum of Contemporary Art, Hiro-shima (1988), and City Museum of Photography, Nara (1992).

Bo (1985); Chaslin (1988); Drew (1972); E (1994); Gui-heux *et al.* (1997); Ku (1972, 1977, 1988, 1990, 1992, 1993, 1995, 1995a, 1995b, 1996, 2000); Sharp (ed.) (1998, 2001, 2002)

Kympton, Hugh (*fl.*1343–88) English master-mason involved in building castles at Windsor, Berks., Porchester, Hants. (where he took instruc-tions from *Yeveley), and Southampton, Hants.

J.Harvey (1987)

label 1. *Hood-moulding across the top of a late-*Perp. or *Tudor aperture, returning downwards vertically on each side and terminating in label-stops, often elaborately carved. While the term is mostly applied to rectangular *drip-mouldings (often forming *spandrels between a low four-centred or Tudor arch and the label), it can also be applied to certain curved hood-mouldings. 2. Rectangular tablet, framed or plain, with wedge-shaped tab-projections on each side, commonly found in Neo-Classical architecture, having its origins in Roman work, where it was often inscribed. *Related terms include*:

label-stop: 1. *knee, or termination of a drip-stone, hood-mould, or label by cranking the *moulding horizontally for a short length; 2. decorative feature as a termination of a label, hood-mould, or *string-course. If resembling a human head, it is a *head-stop*.

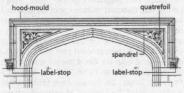

(1) Typical late-Gothic arch with spandrels, hood-mould, and label-stops.

(2) Classical label, often inscribed.

Laborde, Jean-Joseph, Marquis de (1724–94) French *fermier-général* (1759–67), he acquired the estate at Méréville, Essonne, where his interpretation of the fashionable *jardin anglais* was realized (1784–94) under *Bélanger and Hubert *Robert with numerous *fabriques,* including a *Chinoiserie *pavilion, *Gothick *ruins, a *rostral column, and much else. He was guillotined (1794), but his son, **Louis-Joseph-Alexandre, Comte de Laborde** (1773–1842), published a massive work, with outstanding illustrations by **Florent-Fidèle-Constant Bourgeois** (1767–1841), of numerous French gardens (including those at Méréville) created in the latter days of the *ancient régime*: it influenced Humphrey *Repton, among others.

J.Curl (2011); Laborde (1808–15); M & T (1991); Racine (ed.) (2001)

Labrouste, Pierre-François-Henri (1801–75) French architect, he studied under A.-L.-T. *Vaudoyer and L.-H.*Lebas, and then at the French Academy, Rome. His theoretical reconstruction (based on accurate site-surveys) of *Doric *temples at *Paestum (1829) was described by *Viollet-le-Duc as a 'revolution on several folio sheets of paper' because it proposed a re-ordering of the accepted historical sequence of the temples and suggested that the architectural *type was adapted to new environmental, social, and political conditions in a colonial setting, thereby upsetting Received Opinion. Indeed, this work (which included the application of colour) is considered to be a watershed in French architecture, heralding a challenge to the supremacy of *Classicism. When he returned to Paris he opened (1830) an *atelier* which promoted rationalist ideas. His reputation rests on his *Bibliothèque Ste-Geneviève*, Paris (1838–50), in which an elegant iron structure seems to have been slotted into the cage of *masonry: it was one of the first monumental (rather than utilitarian) public buildings to have an exposed iron frame. The masonry exterior is a powerful *Cinquecento* essay employing a range of semicircular-headed windows to illuminate the library space, but it has mnemonic aspects too, for there are allusions to *Alberti's *Tempio Malatestiano*, Rimini, *Sansovino's *Biblioteca Marciano*, Venice, and *Wren's Trinity College Library, Cambridge. The *Bibliothèque* placed him in the highest echelons of French Government architects, and he created (1854–75) the iron-and-glass interior of the Reading-Room at the *Bibliothèque Nationale, Rue Richelieu*, Paris, and built the stack-rooms, again employing iron. He published (1877) his work on Paestum, and designed other buildings, including tombs in Montmartre and Montparnasse Cemeteries, Paris. His brother, **François-Marie-Théodore** (1799–1885), also an architect, trained under Vaudoyer and Lebas, and was architect-in-chief to the hospitals of Paris in succession to *Gau from 1845.

Bergdoll *et al.* (2012); Dr (ed.) (1977); Hi (1977); H.Labrouste (1877); L.Labrouste (1885, 1902); M & Wa (1987); Millet (1882); Saddy (1977); J.T (1996); Z (1977, 1987)

labyrinth 1. *Key-pattern, *maze (some authorities make a distinction between mazes and labyrinths), or *meander. **2.** Planting in a garden arranged as *hedges between labyrinthine *paths leading to a centre, a feature of C17 garden-design, e.g. Hampton Court. **3.** Place laid out for ritual pilgrimage in a church (e.g. the *inlaid labyrinth of blue and white stones in the *nave-floor of Chartres Cathedral, France, the centre of which was the *Jerusalem or *Paradise, the Holy City of God to which the pilgrim aspired). **4.** Figure cut in turf, as at Wing, Rut., and Saffron Walden, Essex, England, similar in design to labyrinths in churches, which has led to a Christian interpretation being placed upon them, but they may have a non-Christian origin. **3** and **4** all lead to the centre, but the single winding path from entrance to centre is much longer than it would be in a direct line. See TROY-TOWN.

Bord (1976); Coate *et al.* (1986); A.Fisher & Gerster (1990); A.Fisher & Loxton (1997); Kern (2000); Ladendorff (1963); Matthews (1970); Pennick (1990)

labyrinth 13 metres in diameter, formed of inlays in the nave-floor of Chartres Cathedral, associated with ritual pilgrimages: the circuitous path is 230 metres long.

labyrinthine fret *Key-pattern, *Greek key, or *meander, resembling a *labyrinth.

laced valley *Valley formed of *tiles or *slates without a valley-gutter where two sloping roofs meet at an angle.

laced windows Vertical series of window-apertures with *dressings, e.g. bright-red brick rubbers contrasting with the rest of the wall, common in early C18 England.

lacería Geometrical *Islamic decoration in glazed tiles (called *alicatado geométrico*) consisting of intersecting polygons and star-shapes, much used by *Mudéjar craftsmen in the Iberian peninsula.

lacería *or* **alicatado geométrico** Based on an example from Granada, Spain.

lacertine *Celtic *interlacing scrolling ornament, with dragon-like head biting its tail.

lacing-course Course of brick or *tile, or several such courses collectively, built, often at regular intervals, in rough or *rubble walls as a *bond- or bonding-course, and to assist the creation of level horizontals. In walls of *knapped or unknapped *flint pebbles, lacing-courses are essential for stability, and are usually combined with *piers of brick, tile, or stone to secure panels of facings bound to the core of a wall.

Bru (1990); S.Hart (2000)

Lacoste, Henry (1885–1968) Belgian architect, his work defies description, as it did not conform to any recognized style, and remained untouched by *International Modernism. The Queen Elisabeth Medical Institute, *Jean-Jacques Crocqlaan*, Jette, Brussels (1927), possessed certain elements of *Art Deco, but the Pion House, a chunky structure of *rubble and brick in the *Rue de l'Enclos*

Saint-Martin, Tournai (Doornik) (1935), not only drew on traditional materials, but on over-emphasis of parts as well, perhaps influenced by aspects of building in the Belgian Congo. This influence was also present in the portal of the Church at Beringen (1938–48), where strong patterns and vivid modelling are reminiscent of *Bellot's idiosyncratic work.

Loo (ed.) (2003)

lacuna (*pl.* **lacunae**) Literally a gap, applied to a Classical *coffer in a ceiling, *cornice-*soffit, or any flat, level horizontal underside, a coffer under a *cupola being a *caisson. Lacunae are often elaborately ornamented with *egg-and-dart, *bead-and-reel, etc., and *laquear is used to express the effect of *mouldings separating the margins of *panels in coffering. *Related terms include*:
lacunar: **1.** coffer in a flat *soffit, ceiling, etc.; **2.** ceiling with coffers; **3.** soffit, as under a cornice, with coffers or lacunae; **4.** *beams enclosing a coffer;
lacunarium (*pl. lacunaria*): system of lacunae or coffers. The plural is given to the coffered ceiling of an *ambulatory or *peridrome between the *peristyle and the *cell-walls of an *Antique *temple, as well as to the soffit of the main cornice.

Lady-chapel Chapel in a larger church, expressly for venerating the Virgin Mary, often situated to the east of the *chancel or *choir, as in Westminster Abbey (1503–*c*.1512) and Hereford Cathedral (*c*.1220–40), but in Parish or other Churches often to the east of one or other chancel-*aisle. At Long Melford, Suffolk, the Lady Chapel (1496) is virtually a separate building to the east of the church proper. Even grander is the chapel at Ely Cathedral, Cambs. (*c*.1321–53), a huge rectangular *Second-Pointed building to the north of the choir, mostly free-standing, but entered via the north *transept.

Lafever, Minard (1798–1854) American architect. His NYC practice produced a wide range of buildings in a variety of styles, but his importance lies in his dissemination of *Greek and *Gothic Revivals through many publications, including *The Young Builder's General Instructor* (1829), *The Modern Builder's Guide* (1833), *The Beauties of Modern Architecture* (1835), *The Modern Practice of Staircase and Handrail Construction* (1838), and *The Architectural Instructor* (1856). Lafever himself drew heavily on *Stuart and *Revett's *Antiquities of Athens* and the various publications of Peter *Nicholson, but his own Grecian work was inventive, going far beyond archaeological exactness, and there are interesting parallels with some of 'Greek' *Thomson's details and those of Lafever (which came first). His major

NYC buildings were Gothic-Revival churches, including the handsome Holy Trinity (1844–7) and the Church of the Saviour (First Unitarian Church, 1842–4), both in Brooklyn Heights. He also designed in the *Egyptian-Revival (Shields *obelisk, Greenwood Cemetery, Brooklyn, 1845, and the Whalers' First Presbyterian Church, Sag Harbour, Long Island, 1843–4), *Italianate, and *Renaissance styles.

Carrott (1978); Hamlin (1964); Lafever (1829, 1838, 1856, 1968, 1969, 1969a); Landy (1970); Stamp & McKinstry (eds) (1994)

Laing, David (1774–1856) London-born architect, he was articled to *Soane before publishing *Hints for Dwellings* (1800) that contained original designs for various types of house, and became (1810) Surveyor to the Customs, designing the Custom House, Plymouth, Devon (1810), a refined Neo-Classical building clearly derived from a study of French architecture. His vast London Custom House (1813–17), on the bank of the Thames, was also Neo-Classical, but the collapse (1825) of the central portion ruined him, and R.*Smirke was called in to reconstruct the building.

AH, vi (1963), 91–101; Co (2008)

laiterie *See* DAIRY.

Lajta, Béla (1873–1920) Hungarian architect, otherwise **Leitersdorfer**, Pupil of *Steindl, *Lechner, et al., he worked briefly under Norman *Shaw (1898–9). Among his works the Institute for Blind Jews (1905–8), various sepulchral monuments and the mortuary in the *Salgótarján* Street Jewish Cemetery (1908), the Jewish Charity Home (1909–11), the School in *Vas* Street (1909–12), the severe *apartment-block, *Népszinház* Street (1911), and the *Rózsavölgyi* Building, *Szervita* Square (1911–12), all in Budapest, should be cited. With Lechner he designed the exotic *mausoleum* of **Sándor Schmidl** (d.1899) in the *Rákoskeresztúr* Cemetery, Budapest (1903).

É & J (1990); J.T (1996)

lake Large expanse of (usually fresh) water, entirely surrounded by land: it should be sufficiently extensive to form a geographical feature, as opposed to a small *pond* or *pool*. Artificial lakes, created by damming or diverting streams, were often features of C18 parks, e.g. 'Capability' *Brown's fine example at Blenheim Palace, Oxon.

Goulty (1991); *OED* (1933); Symes (2006)

Laloux, Victor-Alexandre-Frédéric (1850–1937) French architect. Early in his career he published a book on Greek architecture (1888), and with **Paul Monceaux** (1859–1941), another tome on Olympia (1889). Perhaps, as a result of these studies, his *Beaux-Arts *Classicism was dignified and serious, avoiding the *Baroque extravagances of C.*Garnier and his followers. He designed the *Gare du Quai d'Orsay*, Paris (1896-1900), and the Station at Tours (1895-8): both are scholarly, handsome, and competent works. Some of his most distinguished work was in Tours, his birthplace, including the Byzantino-*Romanesque *Basilique St-Martin* (1887-1924—his first major building, reminiscent of designs by *Abadie) and the *Hôtel de Ville* (1896-1904).

Laloux (1888); Lemaresquier (1938)

Lamb, Edward Buckton (1806-69) English *Rogue-*Gothic Revivalist, who trained under *Cottingham, his elephantine churches tend to have centralized plans and frenetically busy timber roofs: examples are St Margaret's, Leiston, Suffolk (1853), and St Mary Magdalene, Canning Road, Addiscombe, Croydon, Surrey (1868-70). His work attracted opprobrium, notably in *The Ecclesiologist*, and he seems to have been untouched by more conventional tastes of the time. He produced many drawings for *Loudon's *Encyclopaedia* (1833), and published books on *Gothic Ornament* (1830), *Ancient Domestic Architecture* (1846), and articles in *Architectural Magazine* (1834-8), as well as a memoir of Loudon. He refashioned Hughenden Manor, Bucks. (1863-6), for **Benjamin Disraeli** (1804-81), and designed the Town Halls in Eye, Suffolk (1857—*Pevsner thought it 'horrible'), and Berkhamsted, Herts. (1859).

J.Curl (2007); D & M (1985); Gd (1979); Loudon (1834, 1981); *RIBAJ*, ser.3, lvi/6 (Apr. 1949), 251-9

lambrequin Horizontal ornamental *band, fringed, lobed, and notched on the underside, like a series of aprons and tassels, often found under *cornices.

L & D (1986)

lamb's tongue 1. Regency *glazing-bar with a *section of two long *ogees separated by a *fillet (*see* KEEL), very fine and deep compared with its width. 2. Tapering tongue-like end to a *stair handrail rising in a concave curve and joining the handrail in a convex sweep.

lancet *First-Pointed tall, narrow window-aperture with a pointed arched *head, either a single insert in a wall or one of several *lights of similar shape in a window. The *Lancet style* is First-Pointed late-C12 work before the introduction of *tracery.

Lanchester, Henry Vaughan (1863-1953) English architect, he established his practice (1887), taking (1896) **James S. Stewart** (1865-1904) and E.A.*Rickards into partnership. They won the competition to design the City Hall and Law Courts, Cathays Park, Cardiff (1898-1906), with **Beaux-Arts* planning and exuberant *Baroque *façades, and followed this success with the even more splendid Wesleyan Central

Hall, Westminster (1905-11). **Thomas Geoffrey Lucas** (1872-1947), who had built several houses at Letchworth *Garden City and Hampstead *Garden Suburb, joined (1919) the partnership, followed (1923) by **Thomas A. Lodge** (1879-1967). As **Lanchester, Lucas, & Lodge**, the firm enjoyed great success, and when Lucas retired, it continued as **Lanchester & Lodge**, designing many university buildings, hospitals, and other major works.

A.S.Gray (1985)

Land art As part of the 1960s rejection of concepts of art-galleries and *museums, a movement evolved concerned with site-specific creations within the natural environment using organic materials: the landscape itself was the 'canvas' on which the artist imposed his or her explorations. Experiments were made with earth-moving equipment to form works, often ephemeral because of erosion and the elements: in part they were attempts to return to primitive art-forms, e.g. the cutting of figures, horses, etc., into the ground. **Robert Smithson** (1938-73) created his *Spiral Jetty*, a huge spiral of rocks, earth, and salt crystals at Rozel Point, in the Great Salt Lake, UT. *Christo and Jeanne-Claude experimented with their *Running Fence*, a meandering construct of white nylon, nearly 40 km (nearly 25 miles) long, running across part of CA and into the Pacific Ocean (1972-6), and other examples of Land art (they were also known for wrapping buildings, e.g. the *Pont Neuf*, Paris (1975-85), and the *Reichstag*, Berlin (1971-95)).

Beardsley (1978); Betsky (2002); Bye (1983); Lippard (ed.) (1997); Tay (2006); J.T (1996); Weilacher (1996)

landscape architecture Multidisciplinary, it is concerned with the design, planning, realization, and management of landscapes, often with architectural aspects, informed by aesthetic, associational, philosophical, and many other facets. Evolved from ancient agricultural practices, it embraces garden-design, rural improvements, and urban planning, often in association with buildings, water-features, roads, etc., to provide places that can be enjoyed within and without. A *landscape architect* is therefore a practitioner of *landscape architecture*. However, agreement about nomenclature is by no means universal: *Olmsted called it 'miserable', and **Charles Eliot** (1859-97) saw it as broader than *landscape-gardening* which he saw as *part of landscape architecture*. Many American practitioners had an affinity with English practices of landscape-gardening, a term seemingly coined mid-C18 by *Shenstone and adopted by Humphry *Repton. The French exponent of the English style of landscape-gardening, *Morel, is credited with the formulation of the term *architecte-paysagiste*.

Gilbert Laing Meason (1769–1832) first used (1828) the compound 'landscape architecture', and *Loudon incorporated it (1840) in the title of his book on Repton; Loudon followed Meason in using it to refer to architecture set within landscape, rather than Repton's practice, consistently called *landscape-gardening*. *Downing and other C19 American protagonists paved the way for development of landscape architecture as a profession—notably continuing Meason's foundation of referring to architecture in landscape or rural contexts, but he preferred 'landscape-gardening' to 'landscape architecture'. By the mid-C19, at least one English practitioner, W.A. *Nesfield, was referred to as a 'landscape architect', but the term was the exception until the early C20, when it was used by Patrick *Geddes and T.H.*Mawson. In 1852 **Louis-Sulpice Varé** (1802–83) was appointed *jardinier paysagiste* for improvements to the *Bois de Boulogne*, Paris, and given the title *architecte-paysagiste*: he was replaced by *Alphand and Jean-Pierre Barrilet-Deschamps (1824–75), but his identification as a landscape architect is important as the *Bois de Boulogne* was a significant precedent for later parks including Central Park, NYC. Olmsted, once appointed for the last, was called 'Architect-in-Chief and Superintendent' (1858), while *Vaux was called 'Consulting Architect'. Olmsted visited (1859) Paris and other European cities with parks, at a time when landscape-gardening was seen as an essential part of town-planning and infrastructure-improvements. In spite of the fact that he was not entirely happy with the terminology, he used the term 'landscape architect' in writing in 1860, and it was used in connection with the extension of NYC in northern Manhattan, so the 'landscape architect' was charged with the design of the shape of the city itself rather than with mere gardening. By 1865 'landscape architect' had become an accepted term in the USA, even though Olmsted felt the French terms were more satisfactory, but no helpful English equivalent could be suggested. **The American Society of Landscape Architects** (ASLA), was the first body (1899) of the profession advocating practices of urban order and infrastructural arrangement, though many were uncomfortable with the terminology: *Farrand, e.g., preferred the English compound 'landscape-gardener'. Professional identity in Britain was consolidated through the foundation of **The Institute of Landscape Architects** (ILA—1929—later Landscape Institute) and the **International Federation of Landscape Architects** (1948), though many, including *Jellicoe, continued to express anxieties. However, many C20 landscape architects became concerned with ecological and *conservation problems, notably in the design of industrial sites, *motorways, etc. (e.g. *Colvin and Jellicoe): professionals have expressed a

growing commitment to landscape *as architecture*, revitalizing landscape-design as a means by which the contemporary city can be improved in very many ways.

B & K (2000); Bull (2002); Cleveland (2002); G.Cooper & G.Taylor (2000); *Harvard Design Magazine* xxxvi (2013), 178–20; Holden (1996, 2003); Jellicoe (1988); Jellicoe & Jellicoe (1995); Jellicoe *et al.* (1996); Lazzaro (1990); Lyall (1991); Meason (1828); Pennypacker *et al.* (1990); Shoe (2001); Simonds (2000); Steenbergen *et al.* (1996); Tay (2006); Thacker (1979); W & S (1994); Weilacher (1996); Z & Z (1995)

landscape-garden *Landscape-gardening* is defined as the art of laying out grounds to create the effect of natural scenery, hence *landscape-gardener* (aka *landscapist*)/*landscape-garden*. A *landscape-garden* could take the form of a park, often inspired by paintings of Classical landscapes by **Claude Gellée** (1600–82—*called* **Lorraine**), etc., with land modelled with contours, *clumps or plantations of trees carefully conceived, water in the form of a *lake or a river, and sometimes strategically placed **fabriques*. Distant views might extend over farmland that was worked, so the farm-buildings could be designed as features (**ferme ornée*), but the overall composition was asymmetrical. Such gardens in England (e.g. Stourhead, Wilts., and Stowe, Bucks.), may have been prompted by Sir William *Temple, who, in *Upon the Garden of Epicurus* (1685), contrasted the 'symmetries, or uniformities' of formal European with irregular and asymmetrical so-called *Chinese gardens (which he described as 'without any order or disposition of parts', called **Sharawadgi*). Not long afterwards, A.A.*Cooper, in *The Moralists* (1709), scorned the 'formal mockery' of what he described as 'princely' gardens, contrasting them with the beauties of natural landscapes, the 'genuine order' of which was uncorrupted by artifice or 'caprice'. In *The Moralists* and *Characteristics of Men, Manners, Opinions, and Times* (1711) he associated aesthetics with a moral sense, praised 'wildernesses' as divine creations, and argued that in gardens true Order, the work of God, could be found outside the rigidities of formal layouts—philosophical bases for the design of naturalism in *Georgian gardens, anticipating later writers. For example, *Addison deplored excesses of *topiary, and condemned French formality; *Pope attacked (1713) fashionable formality and topiary, advocating a return to the 'amiable simplicity of unadorned nature', and a respect for the *genius loci*. Soon, landscape-gardens were perceived as superior to formal exemplars from aesthetic, moral, and political points of view: they represented Freedom and Liberty, contrasted with Absolutism. *Switzer pioneered the landscape-garden in England at Castle Howard, Yorks. and Grimsthorpe, Lincs. As the author of

Ichonographia Rustica (1715-18), he pointed out that entire estates, with gardens, woodlands, and farmland, should be designed with respect for natural features, and that the 'useful and profitable' parts of an estate could also contribute to the aesthetic pleasures of the garden as a whole (e.g. *ferme ornée*). Other C18 books gave practical advice on the design of gardens and *fabriques*, but further transformations were prompted by: *Shenstone at his *ferme ornée*, The Leasowes, Worcs., and through his *Unconnected Thoughts on Gardening* (1764); *Mason's *The English Garden* (1772-81); *Walpole's *On Modern Gardening* (1780), later (1785) published as *Essay on Modern Gardening*; and *Knight's and *Price's important observations on the *Picturesque. It became widely accepted that the *genius loci* should always be respected when 'improving' a landscape. *Bridgeman was another early practitioner (with Switzer), but *Kent took things further, using devices such as the *ha-ha to make his gardens flow seamlessly into the surrounding landscape, and the country-house did not dominate the landscape-garden. 'Capability' *Brown developed designs with woodland clusters in fields and by lakes: not everyone was convinced, e.g. *Chambers (who promoted what he said was a 'Chinese' style, complete with *Chinoiserie fabriques*) and enthusiasts for the Picturesque, who felt Brown's work was too bland and predictable, urging greater variety, even roughness, at times. *Repton reverted to formal *terraces, symmetrical flower-beds, and the like, with occasional *avenues of trees, and merged aspects of Brown's method with a more rigid geometry. The presence of allusions to commemoration (e.g. the urn in Shenstone's garden), and the various garden-buildings at Stowe, caused a gradual transformation. Buildings, memorials, and cenotaphs in landscape-gardens could enhance them and trigger memories. As the English landscape-garden impacted on the Continent (partly through translations of Addison, Pope, and Shaftesbury), it went through subtle metamorphoses. An important 'wild' or 'natural' garden (an *Élysée*) was described by J.-J.*Rousseau in La *Nouvelle Héloïse* (1761), which influenced the design of *Girardin's gardens at Ermenonville, Oise (1766-76), explained in the Marquis's own *De la composition des paysages* (1777). Rousseau, born a Protestant, was regarded as a 'heretic', and when he died at Ermenonville, the Marquis had him buried on the *Île des Peupliers* in the *Élysée* as an act of friendship and public statement of open-mindedness and lack of bigotry in response to *Young's description of 'Narcissa's Burial' in *Night Thoughts*, which had come out in French (1769), and which described the anguish of having to bury a loved one surreptitiously by night because of RC attitudes towards 'heretics'. Published

images of Rousseau's island-grave were influential, and encouraged the idea of not only commemorating ideas and the dead in gardens, but burying them under monuments in gardens to make a political and philosophical point (the cenotaph of **Admiral de Coligny** (1517-72—murdered during the St Bartholomew's Day excesses in France) at Maupertuis is one example, and the tomb of **Antoine Court de Gébelin** (1725-84) in the gardens of **Claude-Camille-François, Comte d'Albon** (1753-89) at Franconville-la-Garenne is another). Various theoretical writings followed, emphasizing the idea of gardens as agents of mnemonics and association: these included *Observations on Modern Gardening* (1770) by Thomas *Whately; *Essai sur les Jardins* (1774) by *Watelet; *Theorie der Gartenkunst* (1779-85) by *Hirschfeld; *Théories des jardins* (1776) by **Jean-Marie Morel** (1728-1810—particularly interesting on *fabriques*); and *Jardins anglo-chinois ou détails des nouveaux jardins à la mode* (1776-87) by Georges-Louis Le *Rouge. At Wörlitz at *Anhalt-Dessau's 'England-by-the-Elbe', ideas from England and France (e.g. the *Rousseau-Insel* or *Île des Peupliers* from Ermenonville) were merged with associationist themes to create a *Gartenreich* (Garden-Realm) of great beauty and evocative power. Landscape-gardens at, e.g. *Pavlovsk* and *Tsarskoye Selo* (1780s—by *Cameron and others); *Powązki*, near Warsaw (1770s—by *Zug and **J.P.Norblin de la Gourdaine** (1745-1830), now the cemetery); *Arkadia*, near Nieborów, Poland (1777-early C19—by Zug, *Ittar, Norblin, et al.—which also had an *Île des Peupliers*); the English Garden, Munich (from 1789—by *Rumford and *Sckell—it was probably the first example where the English landscape-garden style was adopted for a *public park); the *jardin anglais*, Bagatelle, Paris (1778-80—by *Bélanger, realized by *Blaikie); and others, influenced later developments, including *campus design, *cemeteries, *Garden Cities, and suburbs, public parks, etc. *Loudon was a towering figure in the understanding of the landscape-garden.

AQC, cxvi (2004) 83–126; Buttlar (1982, 1989); D.Chambers (1993); D & E (1994); Gothein (1966); Hunt (1992, 2002); Hunt & P.Willis (eds) (1989); *JGH*, xiv/2 (Summer 1994), 92–118; Loudon (1834, 1835, 1838, 1981); M & T (1991); Racine (ed.) (2001); Sieveking (ed.) (1908); O.Sirén (1990); Wn (1978)

Lane, Joseph (1717-84) English maker of landscape-features, esp. *grottoes, he worked at Stourhead, Wilts., and Painshill and Oatlands, Surrey, among other places. His son, **Josiah Lane** (1753-1833), assisted him, and then, on his own, he constructed grottoes at Bowood (*c*.1785), Wardour Castle (1792), and Fonthill (*c*.1794), all Wilts.

D & E (1994); Jacques (1983); p & g

Lange, Willy (1864–1941) German landscape architect, he frequently referred to *Goethe, F.H.A.von *Humboldt, J.-J.*Rousseau, and **Johann Christoph Friedrich von Schiller** (1759–1805) in his works promoting 'natural' garden-design as a 'biological aesthetic'; an expression of Nordic associations with race and culture. Opposed to modern international trends, his ideas gained acceptance among those for whom connections between Germans and their landscape were part of the *Blut und Boden* ideology. His theories were disseminated in *Deutsche Gartenkunst* (1939) and carried weight in the USA, notably with **Frank Albert Waugh** (1869–1943), who believed that styles of landscape-gardening could reflect nationhood/race. Some commentators have noted interesting parallels to interpretations of 'natural' gardens designed by Lange and William *Robinson. Lange designed numerous gardens for private houses designed by **Otto Stahn** (1859–1930) at Berlin-Wannsee.

Hasler (1939); *JGH*, xii/1 (Jan.–March 1992), 73–80, and xii/3 (July–Sept. 1992), 183–206; Lange (1910, 1913, 1919); Shoe (2001)

Langhans, Carl Gotthard (1732–1808) German architect from Silesia (now in Poland), he became *Oberbaurat* in Breslau (now Wrocław), designing a number of Palladianesque buildings influenced by *Erdmannsdorff's work at *Schloss Wörlitz*. These included a new wing for the *Palais Hatzfeld*, Breslau (1765–75—destroyed); the *Samotwór* Palace (1776–81), with a *serliana as the frontispiece-porch; the noble Mielżyński Palace, Pawłowice (1779–87), with its *corps-de-logis* linked to the handsome *service-wings by arcaded *quadrants; and several elliptical Protestant churches. In 1788 **King Friedrich Wilhelm II of Prussia** (*r.*1786–97) summoned Langhans to Berlin (with David *Gilly and Erdmannsdorff) in order to make the capital a major cultural centre. There, Langhans created one of the pioneering monuments of the *Greek Revival, the Brandenburg Gate (1789–94), inspired by Le *Roy's reconstruction of the Athenian *Propylaea* in *Ruines des plus beaux monuments de la Grèce* (1758), and the first building based on the *Antique prototype. The gate was greatly admired by all who saw it, influencing Thomas *Hope when he argued for a Greek-Revival design at Downing College, Cambridge. It was also a precedent for Thomas *Harrison's *propylaeum* at Chester Castle (1811–13), and von *Klenze's *Propyläen, Königsplatz*, Munich (1817, built 1846–60).

Langhans designed several theatres, including the State Theatre, Potsdam (1795), which had a severely Neo-Classical *façade, and the unadventurous Royal Theatre, *Gendarmenmarkt*, Berlin (1800–2—which burned down (1817) and was replaced by *Schinkel's *Schauspielhaus*). He designed the *Gothick top for the tower of the *Marienkirche*, Berlin (1789–90).

Arenhövel *et al.* (1979); Bauch (1966); Hinrichs (1909); Kalinowski (1977); L & R (1984); J.T (1996); Wa & M (1987)

Langhans, Karl Ferdinand (1781–1869) Son of C.G.*Langhans, he studied in Berlin under his father and David *Gilly, and settled (1815) in Breslau (now Wrocław), where his own dwelling and other buildings were clearly influenced by the austere *Neo-Classicism of *Gentz and F.*Gilly. He published several works on theatre-design, and was among the first to examine the science of acoustics as an influence on the planning of *auditoria, outlined in a book on the subject (1810). He designed several theatres, including Breslau (1838–41), Liegnitz (now Legnica, 1841–2), Stettin (now Szczecin, 1846–9), Dessau (1855–6), and Leipzig (1864–8). He was responsible for several buildings in Berlin, including the Palace of **Prince Wilhelm**, *Unter den Linden* (1834–6). Much of his work no longer exists.

B-S (1977); Kalinowski (1977); Langhans (1810); Rohe (1934); Schneider & Langhans (1845); J.T (1996)

Langley, Batty (1696–1751) English landscape-gardener/architect/prolific producer of architectural books (including *Practical Geometry* (1726), *The Builder's Chest Book* (1727 and 1739), *New Principles of Gardening* (1728), *The Landed Gentleman's Useful Companion* (1741), *A Sure Guide to Builders* (1729), *The Young Builder's Rudiments* (1730 and 1734), and *The City and Country Builder's and Workman's Treasury of Designs* (1740 and further editions)). His grandest book, with 500 or so plates (most looted from other sources), probably the largest English *pattern-book, was *Ancient Masonry* (1736). His publications are full of sensible advice on how to set about drawing and constructing various elements. He is remembered today primarily for *Ancient Architecture Restored and Improved by a Great Variety of Grand and Usefull Designs, Entirely New in the Gothick Mode* (1741–2), reissued as *Gothic Architecture, Improved by Rules and Proportions in Many Grand Designs* (1747), an attempt to systematize *Gothic on the lines of five Classical *Orders. There was virtually nothing of real Gothic in the books, for Langley's sources were more an early *Georgian *Gothick invented by people like *Kent, so his work was ridiculed. However, 'Langley', 'Carpenter's', or 'Sham Gothick' had considerable success, and his designs were widely copied. Sanderson *Miller and Horace *Walpole were indebted to Langley for some of their Gothick, though they were more than reluctant to say so. A pioneer of what he described as the *Artinatural, or 'regular irregularities', he must be counted as one of the earliest to espouse the 'natural' landscape that was to be such a feature of C18, and he was also an advocate of the *Rococo, presumably as an antidote to *Palladianism. His importance as an influence on *Georgian architecture cannot be overestimated.

Co (2008); Crook (ed.) (1983); J.Curl (2011a); E.Hs (1990); B.Langley (1724, 1726, 1728, 1729, 1729a, 1734, 1736, 1738, 1739, 1742, 1745, 1747, 1756, 1970, 1970a, 1971)

languet Tongue-shaped upright ornament like a **U** reproduced in series on Classical enrichment, e.g. *frieze.

Lankester, Jack (1921–2007) Isle-of-Man-born architect/surveyor, he became Surveyor to the University of Oxford (1955–84), a position enabling him to make many contributions to the city's fabric. He was instrumental in realizing Arne *Jacobsen's vision for the new St Catherine's College (1960–4), but the main function of his office was to repair, maintain, and adapt existing buildings and to design new ones for University use: to this end he built up a professional organization capable of carrying out exemplary work. One of his earliest jobs was the conversion of the Malthouse, Tidmarsh Lane, providing accommodation for his department (1956). Other works included the reading-room at the Radcliffe Science Library (1975), now named after him; the Mathematical Institute, St Giles (1964–6); and accommodation at Green College (1979–81).

The Times (10 Dec. 2007), 52; pk

lantern 1. Any structure rising above the roof of a building and having apertures in its sides by which the interior of the building is ventilated or illuminated, e.g. the octagonal lantern at Ely Cathedral (1322–c.1344). **2.** Any such structure whether lighting an interior or not, such as the upper part of cathedral- or church-towers, especially those treated in a light, almost transparent way, usually octagonal uppermost stages (e.g. St Mary and All Saints, Fotheringhay, Northants. (late C15), and the *crossing-tower of St-Ouen, Rouen, France (C15)). **3.** By extension, the upper structure on top of a *cupola (e.g. Florence Cathedral (C15), *San Pietro*, Rome (C16), and St Paul's Cathedral, London (C17)). *Compounds include*:

lantern-cross: medieval stone churchyard-cross with a top carved to resemble a lantern, in the sense of a structure surrounding and protecting an artificial light;

lantern-light: lantern (**1**);

lantern-tower: tall *crossing-tower with *lights or any tower with an elegant, usually octagonal, upper storey, as in St Botolph, Boston, Lincs. (c.1510–20).

Lanyon, Sir Charles (1813–89) English-born architect/engineer/surveyor, he settled in Ireland, where he became County Surveyor of Antrim (1836–60), building the breathtaking Antrim Coast Road (originally planned and begun by **William Bald** (1789–1857)) from Larne to Ballycastle, and designing the handsome Glendun Viaduct (1837). In his official capacity he also designed the powerful Crumlin Road Gaol, Belfast (1841–5—influenced by the planning of Pentonville Gaol, London) and the noble *Italianate Court House opposite the Gaol (1848–50—in 2014 derelict). Lanyon established a successful practice, carrying out a huge range of works in numerous styles, as well as acting as engineer for several railway companies, designing stations and routes. His Palm House, Botanic Gardens, Belfast (1839–40 and 1852), is an early and elegant example of curvilinear iron-and-glass construction, and was built with Richard *Turner of Dublin, predating Turner's collaboration with *Burton at Regent's Park and Kew Gardens, London. Lanyon also designed the *Tudorbethan Institute for the Deaf, Dumb, and Blind (1843–5—lamentably destroyed 1965); the *Tudor-Gothic Queen's College (1846–9—now the Lanyon Building of The Queen's University); the remodelling of Sir Robert *Taylor's Exchange and Assembly Rooms for the Belfast Banking Company (1844–6—in an *Italianate *palazzo* style derived from the work of *Barry); the Presbyterian (later Union Theological) College (1852–3—with a powerful Roman-*Doric *engaged *portico and a *Baroque *Attic storey); and the former Head Office of the Northern Bank (1851–2), all in Belfast. He employed the Italian *palazzo* style for several buildings, notably the very grand Custom House, Belfast (1854–7). He reworked Killyleagh Castle, Co. Down, in a robust Franco-Scottish style (1849–51), providing an amazing vision when first viewed across the drumlin landscape, and designed the powerful *campanile* at Trinity College, Dublin (1852–4).

In 1854 Lanyon took his pupil, W.H.*Lynn, into partnership, and the firm, as **Lanyon & Lynn**, designed many fine Victorian buildings, including the Lombardic-*Gothic Sinclair Seamen's Church, Corporation Square, Belfast (1856–7), and the charming Venetian Gothic Banks at Newtownards, Co. Down, and Dungannon, Co. Tyrone (both c.1855). In 1860 the firm became **Lanyon, Lynn, & Lanyon** when Charles's son, **John** (1839–1900) became a partner. Several distinguished buildings followed, including the *polychrome *Venetian-Gothic Clarence Place Hall (1865–6), the former warehouse of Richardson, Sons, & Owden, Donegall Square (1865–9—now Marks & Spencer), both in Belfast, and the exquisite *Hiberno-Romanesque St Patrick's Church, Jordanstown, Co. Antrim, complete with round tower (1865–8).

Brett (1967, 2000); *DIB* (2009); *IAR* (1989), 200–7; Larmour (1987); *ODNB* (2004); *P:JRSUA*, ii/5 (May–June 1994), 53–4; J.T (1996)

La Padula, Ernesto Bruno (1902-69) *See* PADULA.

Lapidus, Morris (1902-2001) Russian-born American architect, he specialized (1927-45) in the design of shop-fronts and -interiors, including the Parisian Bootery (1928), Herbert's Home of Blue White Diamonds (1930), and the offices of Swank Jewellers (1931), all *Art Deco, and all in NYC. He then experimented with theatrical lighting, e.g. at Doubleday Doran Book Shop, NYC (1934), and Schwobilt Clothing Store, Tampa, FL (1936). His flair was again apparent in the designs for the Fontainebleau Hotel, Miami Beach, FL (1952-4), so spectacular it was used in the Bond film *Goldfinger*. Other works included the Summit (1957-61), and Americana (1964-6) Hotels, both NYC. He published *An Architecture of Joy* (1979), *Architecture: A Profession and a Business* (1967), and other works.

Duttmann & M.Schneider (eds) (1992); P (1982); J.T (1996)

Iaquear *See* LACUNA. Also perhaps a net-like form of decoration used on ceilings, etc., in *Antique *grottoes. Passages in **Virgil** (70-19 BC) suggest chain-like forms, but other sources using the term are vague.

Iararium (*pl.* **Iararia**) **1.** Small room or *niche in a Roman house used as a type of private chapel/*shrine where images of the *lares* and *penates* were placed for devotional observances. **Emperor Alexander Severus** (*r.*222-35) furnished his *Iararia* with an eclectic collection of the principal Roman deities to which he added Abraham, Achilles, Alexander the Great, Christ, Cicero, Orpheus, and Virgil. **2.** Place for the display of *Antique statuettes, as in Thomas *Hope's celebrated house in Duchess Street, London (1799-1819).

Iarmier 1. Classical *corona or similar horizontal *moulding acting as a *drip, also called *lorimer*. **2.** Medieval moulding curved on top with a deep concave underside, called *ressaunt lorymer*, acting as a drip or based on a drip-stone.

Larsen, Henning Göbel (1925-2013) Danish architect, he established (1956) his practice in Copenhagen, developing an approach to architecture that allowed change and adaptation. Among his works were the Primary School, Søllerød (1958—each classroom a separate *pavilion with its own courtyard), Høje Tåstrup Grammar School, near Copenhagen (1978-82), Gentofte Library, Copenhagen (1979-84), the Danish Embassy, Riyadh, Saudi Arabia (1982-6), the Faculty Building, Free University, Berlin (1982-8), Congress Centre, Esbjerg (1982-8), and Conference Centre, Churchill College, Cambridge (1994). He won the competition to design the Opera House, Compton Verney, near Kineton, Warwicks. (1989—unrealized).

E (1994); N-O.Lund (1996); H.Moller (2000); J.T (1996)

Lasdun, Sir Denys Louis (1914-2001) British architect, he worked with Wells *Coates (1935-7), then joined *Tecton, remaining there until 1948, when he founded his own practice. Clearly influenced by *Lubetkin and other Modernists, he designed a house at 32 Newton Road, Paddington, London (1937-8), which was indebted to Le Corbusier's *Maison Cook* of over a decade earlier. He built *cluster-blocks of flats in Bethnal Green, the living-apartments joined to a central core for circulation and services (1952-5). Then came the apartment-block at 26 St James's Place (1958), one side of which overlooks Green Park: the Royal College of Physicians (1960) also has a sensitive position, overlooking Regent's Park, London. In the 1960s Lasdun's firm designed several major projects, including the University of East Anglia, Norwich (1962-8); Charles Wilson Building, University of Leicester (1963); School of Oriental and African Studies, the Institute of Education, Institute of Advanced Legal Studies, University of London, Bloomsbury (1965); the National Theatre, by Waterloo Bridge (1967-76); IBM Central London Marketing Centre, South Bank (1978-84); and the City of London Real Property Company Offices, Fenchurch Street (1980-5), all in London. Other works include the European Investment Bank, Luxembourg (1973), and an office-block, Milton Gate, Chiswell Street, London (1986-91).

Wi.Cu (1995, 1996); E (1994); Lasdun (ed.) (1984); Lasdun & Partners (1976)

Lassurance (*real name* **Pierre Cailleteau**) (1650-1724) Assistant to J.*Hardouin-Mansart, he worked at Versailles (1684-1700), where he seems to have been behind the effective disposition of mirrors as part of the interior decoration. In Paris he designed several *hôtels, illustrated by *Blondel, with many features that influenced *Boffrand and de *Cotte. Among his essays of the *hôtel particulier type were the *Hôtel des Marets, Rue de St-Marc* (1704), *Hôtel de Montbazon, Rue St-Honoré* (1719), and *Hôtel de Roquelaure, Rue St-Dominique* (1722).

J-F.Blondel (1752-6); Ha (1950); Kalnein (1995); K & L (1972); Kimball (1980)

Lassus, Jean-Baptiste-Antoine (1807-57) French architect, pupil of *Lebas and *Labrouste, he was an early student of *Gothic. He worked on the restoration of *Sainte-Chapelle*, Paris (from 1838), especially its influential *polychrome decorations (hailed in 1844 by A.W.N.*Pugin as 'glorious'), with *Duban and *Viollet-le-Duc: from 1849 he was in sole charge, and designed the elegant **flèche*. From 1844 he collaborated with Viollet on the huge programme of restoration at the Cathedral of *Notre-Dame*, Paris, where many significant French Gothic Revivalists acquired their skills. He was an active conservator, working in the Dioceses of Paris, Le Mans, and Chartres (where he restored the Cathedral *spires). A scholar, he contributed numerous learned papers to various publications, including *The Ecclesiologist* (1856). Although his designs for the Lille Cathedral competition (1855) were placed third, they were the ones partially realized. He designed several other Gothic-Revival churches, including *Sacré-Cœur*, Moulins (from 1849), *St-Jean-Baptiste-de-Belleville*, Paris (1854–9), *St-Nicolas*, Nantes (1844–69), and *St-Pierre*, Dijon (1853–8).

G (1972); Lassus (1842–67, 1858); Léon (1951); M & Wa (1987); Troche (1857)

Last Judgement *See* DOOM.

Late-Modern architecture Architecture in which images, ideas, and motifs of the *Modern Movement were taken to extremes, structure, technology, and services being grossly overstated at a time when Modernism was being questioned. The work of **Renzo Piano** (1937–) and **Richard Rogers** (1933–) at the *Centre Pompidou*, Paris (1971–7), has been cited as an example, although it has also been seen as *High Tech.

Js (1980, 1990)

later (*pl.* **lateris**) Roman brick or *tile.

laterite Red, porous, ferruginous (i.e. containing iron) rock, found in India and parts of South-East Asia. It is easy to cut when first excavated, but soon becomes extremely hard on exposure to air. It was used in blocks for walls, with no *mortar, but surfaces had to be clad with softer stone or plastered as it was too hard to carve.

Geographical Review, xxxi (1941), 177–202; W.Pa (1852)

lath 1. Narrow, thin strip of wood used as a base for a *plaster finish. 2. Slightly larger timber, more a *batten or *firring-strip* secured to *beams, *rafters, *studs, etc., as a fixing for *slates, *tiles, or other finish.

Latin cross *See* CROSS.

Latrobe, Benjamin Henry Boneval (1764–1820) English-born Moravian architect of French descent, educated in England and Saxony (where he absorbed many advanced ideas, partly through *Freemasonry), who introduced an advanced, austere *Neo-Classicism to the USA. A pupil of S.P.*Cockerell, he set up his own office (1790) from which he designed Hammerwood Lodge, East Grinstead, Sussex (1792), an essay in Neo-Classicism with an unfluted version of the 'primitive' *Paestum *Order of *Doric, much influenced by French architects such as *Ledoux. He also designed Ashdown House, Forest Row, Sussex (1793), a beautiful building having a projecting Greek *Ionic circular porch with *Coade-stone details. These are two of the most remarkable houses for their date in the British Isles, and show Latrobe to have been in the vanguard of English Neo-Classicism, far more adventurous than any of his better-known contemporaries.

He emigrated to America (1796), where, through his Freemasonic connections, he met **George Washington** (1732–99—1st President of the USA) and acquired a wide circle of influential friends. He made his mark with the very advanced Richmond Penitentiary (1797), which incorporated many of *Jefferson's ideas, and then with the Bank of Pennsylvania, Philadelphia (1798), the first great monument of the *Greek Revival in the USA. In the following year he designed Sedgeley, a house for **William Crammond** (1754–1843) on the banks of the River Schuylkill, the first *Gothic-Revival domestic building in the USA (destroyed). Appointed (1803) Surveyor of Public Buildings by Jefferson, he worked on the Capitol in Washington, DC, creating some of the finest Neo-Classical rooms in America (reconstructed with modifications after its destruction by the British in the War of 1812–15), and inventing *American Classical *Orders such as the *corn-cob and tobacco *capitals. He also advised Jefferson on the design of the University of Virginia (1817–26), and should be given credit for what is one of the most beautiful architectural ensembles in the USA. His best complete work is the RC Cathedral, Baltimore (1804–18), with segmental coffered *vaults, minimalist *Classicism, and shallow-domed ceilings as severe as any of their date. He contributed to the design of gardens, including that of the White House, Washington, DC. The Louisiana State Bank, New Orleans (1820), was his last building, but it was still faithful to the dignified polished Classicism he had introduced to his adopted country. His pupils included *Mills and *Strickland.

G.Brown (1970); E.Carter *et al.* (eds) (1977, 1980); J.Cohen & Brownell (1994); Co (2008); Hamlin (1955, 1964); Hi (1977); R.Kennedy (1989); Latrobe (1971); P.Norton (1977); Padover (ed.) (1946); W & K (1983)

latten Pale-yellow metal resembling *brass, an alloy of copper and tin, much used for medieval funerary monuments (the so-called 'brasses' in churches, *incised, coloured, and *inlaid in stone slabs).

lattice 1. *Came. 2. System of small, light *bars crossing each other at intervals, often made of *laths, or light slips of wood forming regular square- or *lozenge-shaped openings. Lattices formed of square-sectioned wood arranged in square, rectangular, and diagonal patterns were a common feature of C18 and C19 *Chinoiserie. **3.** Undivided part of a C18 theatre *auditorium between the *boxes and the pit. *Compounds include*:

lattice-girder: metal *girder with *webs uniting the flanges by means of a *trellis of diagonal *braces crossing each other, or with a web of a single series of braces arranged in a zig-zag pattern;

lattice-moulding: *reticulated or net-like arrangements of diagonal *fillets or other straight *mouldings crossing each other diagonally, resembling a lattice;

lattice-window: any window, fixed or with an opening *sash, the *lights filled with *lozenge-shaped glass *panes set in lead *cames.

Laudian rails *Altar- or *communion-rails, often with *balusters, usually of oak, dating from the time (1633–40) when **William Laud** (1573–1645) was Archbishop of Canterbury, and endeavoured to restore dignity to Anglican worship.

Laugier, Abbé Marc-Antoine (1713–69) French Jesuit, he became one of the earliest and most important theorists of *Neo-Classicism. His *Essai sur l'Architecture* (1753) was profoundly influential, setting out a rational interpretation of *Classicism as a logical expression of the need for shelter, derived from the *Primitive Hut of tree-trunks supporting a structure. He extolled the need for columns as opposed to those of the *engaged variety or *pilasters, and argued for a return to *Antique principles as an antidote to all the accretions from the *Renaissance period onwards that had hidden the essence of the origins of *columnar and *trabeated construction. The immediate influence of his views was on *Soufflot, but translations into English and German carried them throughout Europe. In his *Observations sur l'Architecture* (1765) he recognized the grace of *Gothic.

B (1980); Fichet (ed.) (1979); Hn (1962); Laugier (1753, 1753a, 1765); M & Wa (1987); P (1982); Ry (1980)

Laurana, Luciano (*c*.1420–79) Born in Dalmatia, a key figure in the transition from *Renaissance to the *High Renaissance of *Leonardo and *Bramante. He provided (1465) a design for the *Palazzo Ducale*, Urbino, and built the elegant arcaded *cortile* (1465–79). Many of the exquisite details (e.g. door-cases, chimney-pieces, etc.) in the palace were also by him.

He (1996); Lutz (1995); P (1982); Rotondi (1950–1)

Lautner, John (1911–94) American architect, pupil (1933–9) of F.L.L.*Wright. He established a practice in Los Angeles, designing some private

houses, including the Arango House, Acapulco, México, of 1973 (where *terraces exploit the views over the bay below), and the Sheats Goldstein House, Beverley Hills, CA, of 1960–3 (which seems to grow out of the rocks and is covered with a massive folded *concrete roof). Perhaps his best-known buildings are the Malin House, or 'Chemosphere', Torreyson Drive, Los Angeles (1960), with the entire structure carried on one *pier, and the Elrod House, Palm Springs (1968), with a *concrete wheel-like roof of massive 'spokes' framing wedge-shaped windows. Esther *McCoy called him a 'lyrical technologist'.

E (1994); Escher (1994); Gössel (ed.) (1999, 2002); Hess (2000)

Lauweriks, Johannes Ludovicus Mathieu (1864–1932) Dutch theorist, he evolved a proportional system that he connected with his occult beliefs, and produced intricate designs of cubes, squares, and rectangles that influenced *Behrens, notably in his design for the crematorium at Hagen (1906–7), and later Le *Corbusier in his *Modulor system. The journal *Der Ring* (1909) published his designs.

P (1982); Tummers (1968); J.T (1996)

lavabo 1. Basin used by a priest for ritual washing at the Offertory during Mass. **2.** Stone trough or *lavatory used for washing in medieval monasteries: some were free-standing (e.g. at Mellifont Abbey (*c*.1200), Co. Louth), and some were inside the *cloister-wall (e.g. Gloucester Cathedral C14). **3.** Washstand.

lavatory, lavatorium 1. Vessel for washing, or place in which to wash. **2.** *Piscina. **3.** As *lavabo (2). **4.** Room furnished with basins for washing the hands and face, in C19 and C20 usage also including water-closets. **5.** Laundry.

Laves, Georg Ludwig Friedrich (1788–1864) German architect, pupil of *Jussow, he became (1814) Court Architect in Hanover, where he remodelled the *Leineschloss* (1817–35—destroyed, but rebuilt 1959–62), and designed the *Bibliothek-Pavillon*, Herrenhausen (1818–19), *Wangenheim Palais* (1829–33—which had a semicircular glazed winter-garden on the first floor), the *Waterlooplatz* and column (1825–32—influenced by *Nash's London developments), Opera House (1845–52—his greatest work), and *Mausoleum at Herrenhausen (1842–6). He specialized in a Neo-Classical style derived from the work of *Schinkel and *Persius and in a half-century he transformed Hanover into a fine Neo-Classical capital-city to rival Berlin, but much of his work was destroyed in the 1939–45 war. He planned the *Oststadt* and *Nordstadt* suburbs of Hanover, and laid out the workers' estate at Linden (1853–4). His fine

Ernst-August quarter (planned from 1843) was very grand and spacious (it is now the city centre), but very little of the fabric there today is by him. He was also involved in iron-and-glass construction, and made several designs for 'crystal palaces', including a proposal (1850) for a prefabricated structure at the 1851 London Exhibition made out of old railway-lines. He invented (1839) a type of *trussed *beam that involved cutting a timber beam in two along its length, fixing each end together with straps, and placing blocks between the two parts so that the beam-truss ended up as convex on the top and bottom. Its advantage was that it was much stronger than it was before treatment, did not deflect much, and was extremely economical.

AR, **cxlviii**/1884 (Oct. 1970), 257; Dolgner (1971, 1993); Hoeltje (1964); Kokkelink (ed.) (1964); W.Pa (1852); Wa & M (1987)

lawn **1.** Open space or *glade (laund)* between woods. **2.** Stretch of untilled land, or an extent of grass-covered ground. **3.** C18 term for an area of a garden or *pleasure-ground turfed or sown with grass, camomile, etc., to give a sense of openness. **4.** Area covered with meadow-grass in a park grazed by cattle, deer, etc. The concept of an open lawn blending into the landscape beyond was fundamental to the aesthetic of the English landscaped park, made possible by the *ha-ha*. In American usage, 'lawn' occurs in descriptions of residential landscapes, but it also had social and symbolic significance as a sign of improved or cultivated space. Well-tended lawns also suggested connections between cultured landed gentry and real worth, both financial and moral. Later, it also suggested civic order and responsibility.

OED (1933); O'Malley (2010); Shoe (2001); Symes (2006); Tay (2006)

Lawson, William (1553/4–1635) English clergyman/writer, his only book, *A New Orchard and Garden* ... (1618), was published by **Roger Jackson** (*fl.*1600–25): its second section, *The Countrie Housewifes Garden* ..., was the first horticultural work written specifically for women. While its emphasis was on *kitchen-gardens, it included designs for *knot-gardens.

Lawson (1618); *ODNB* (2004); Shoe (2001)

Layens, Matthieu de (*fl.*C15) Master-Mason of the *Flamboyant *Gothic Town Hall at Leuven, Belgium (1448–63), one of the most perfect of late-Gothic secular buildings in Northern Europe. His work was particularly harmonious and controlled in its use of Gothic ornament and motifs, and resembles contemporary architecture at Brugge, Gent, Brussels, and Oudenaarde, but surpasses in its richness of detail. He also designed the *choir of *St-Waudru, Mons, Belgium (1450–1502), and other works.

W.Pa (1852)

Layer, William (*fl.*1419–44) English mason involved in repairs to the *Lady Chapel at Ely Cathedral (1439–40): he may have designed the fine *nave of St Mary's Church, Bury St Edmunds (1424–44), and the tower of Rougham Church, both in Suffolk.

J.Harvey (1987)

lazaretto Originally a *lazar-house* where lepers were confined, but later any hospital for contagious diseases.

lead Heavy, silvery-grey metal, easily beaten, bent, and joined by heat as its melting-point is low. Used as a roof-covering in the Middle Ages, it was also employed for joints between roofs and, e.g., chimneys, and for rainwater-pipes, water-cisterns, etc. In Antiquity it was used to convey water, but the fact that it could pollute drinking water was recognized by the Romans.

Leadbetter, Stiff (*c.*1705–66) English architect, he succeeded (1756) *Flitcroft as Surveyor of St Paul's Cathedral. He designed several country-houses based on Palladian principles, often using canted *bays similar to those employed by Sir Robert *Taylor. Works include Langley Park, Langley Marish, Bucks. (1756–8); Hatchlands, Surrey (1756–8); and the Radcliffe Infirmary, Oxford (1759–67). He had numerous aristocratic clients to whom he may have been introduced by his patron, **Francis Godolphin** (1678–1766—**2nd Earl of Godolphin** from 1712).

Co (2008); *ODNB* (2004)

leaded lights Any windows, fixed or opening, in which the *panes or *quarrels (quarries) of *glass are secured in lead *cames, often arranged in *lattice patterns, usually lozenges.

leaf **1.** Part of a *door, *panel, or *shutter that folds, i.e. is hung on hinges or pivoted. **2.** One of two skins of brick or *block forming a *cavity-wall. **3.** Ornament derived from the leaves of plants, such as the *acanthus, *bay, laurel, olive, *palm, or other plant; *see* WATER-LEAF. **4.** Very thin finish, such as a *veneer*, or *gilding*.

leaf-and-dart moulding

lean-to Structure with a monopitch roof sloping from a taller building or wall, e.g. an *aisle of a *basilica, leaving the *clerestorey rising above. *See also* PENT.

Lebas, Louis-Hippolyte (1782–1867) French architect trained by A.-L.-T.*Vaudoyer, *Percier, and *Fontaine. He designed *Notre-Dame-de-*

Lorette, Paris (1823-36), on a *basilican plan with a noble *portico of the *Corinthian Order and a multi-coloured interior entirely *Early-Christian in style. The *clerestorey is carried on an *Ionic *colonnade, the ceiling is *coffered, and the east end is *apsidal. He won (1825) the competition to design a model prison on the site of *La Roquette*, Paris, in the form of a huge hexagon with six *wings linked to the central chapel (destroyed 1973). Among his pupils were the *Labrouste brothers and Charles *Garnier.

M & Wa (1987); J.T (1996)

Le Blond, Jean-Baptiste-Alexandre (1679-1719) *See* BLOND.

Lebons, John (*fl*.1506-29) English master-mason. With *Janyns and *Vertue he was involved in preparing estimates for the new *Lady Chapel at Westminster Abbey for **King Henry VII** (*r*.1485-1509). He was employed by **Thomas Wolsey** (1470/1-1530—Cardinal from 1515) at Hampton Court, and by 1525 was resident master-mason at Cardinal (now Christ Church) College, Oxford. He also carried out works at Balliol College, Oxford, and Windsor Castle, Berks. There is evidence that he was a designer, as paper for 'platts' (i.e. plans) was accounted (1515) for his use.

J.Harvey (1987)

Le Breton, Gilles (*c*.1500-53) *See* BRETON.

Le Brun, Charles (1619-90) *See* BRUN, CHARLES LE.

Lechner, Ödön (1845-1914) Hungarian architect, a master of the exotic national version of *Jugendstil*, with strong injections of folk-art and certain *Gothic *Moorish *Rundbogenstil themes reminiscent of *Gaudí's work and Barcelona *Modernisme generally. His most celebrated buildings are the Museum of Applied Arts (1891-6), Institute of Geology (1898-9), Post Office Savings Bank (1899-1901), and *György Zala* studio (1905), all in Budapest. He taught *Lajta.

Bakonyi & Kubinszky (1981); É & J (1990); Kismarty-Lechner (1961)

Lecointe, Jean-François-Joseph (1783-1858) French architect, an early associate of *Hittorff, he worked with *Gilbert on the design of *La Nouvelle Force*, the prison at Mazas (commenced 1843), and designed several *villas and theatres, including the *Salle-Favart* (1825) and *Ambigù-Comique* (both destroyed).

Ha (1955); W.Pa (1852)

Le Corbusier (1887-1965) *See* CORBUSIER.

lectern 1. High sloping reading-desk, especially in a church, placed on the *Epistle side, often consisting of a columnar or *pedestal arrangement supporting a globe on which stands an *eagle with outstretched wings, a symbol of **St John the Evangelist. 2.** *Ambo. **3.** Small rectangular or square building with a monopitched roof (e.g. *dovecote).

ledge 1. *Course of stone, etc., especially one projecting, as a *plinth. **2.** Structural timber placed horizontally on the inner side of a wooden *door, as in *ledged, braced,* and *battened* door.
Related terms include:
ledger: **1.** large flat stone slab used as the top of a structure, e.g. an *altar-tomb, or covering a brick-lined grave, usually *incised or *inlaid with e.g. *brasses; **2.** any member intended to occupy a horizontal position, as in scaffolding or a *door;
ledgment, legement, ligament: *string-course, or horizontal suit of *mouldings, e.g. *basement (1).

Ledoux, Claude-Nicolas (1736-1806) Prolific French Neo-Classicist, he is regarded as one of the greatest architects of his time, although very few of his works survive. He studied under J.-F. *Blondel, and his earliest works were elegant paradigms of the *Louis-Seize style. These include the *Hôtel d'Hallwyl, Rue Michael-le-Comte*, Paris (1766), the *Château de Bénouville*, Normandy (*c*.1764-*c*.1770), the exquisite *Hôtel d'Uzès, Rue Montmartre*, Paris (1768), and the ingenious *Hôtel de Montmorency*, facing the *Boulevard Montmartre* and the *Chaussée d'Antin* (1769-71—with a diagonal axis and elliptical salon). From 1771, however, he worked for **Madame du Barry** (1746-93) for whom he built the charming *Pavillon de Louveciennes* (1771-3), one of his first essays in a pure Neo-Classical style, with interior decorations perfect examples of their time. At the *Hôtel Thélusson*, between the *Rue de Provence* and *Rue de Chantereine*, Paris (1778-83—demolished), he created an approach via a gigantic rusticated *astylar *Doric arch, and surrounded the house with an informal garden in the 'English' style, complete with *rock-work *fabriques. His command of stark geometry evolved further at the semicircular theatre at Besançon (1775-80—burnt 1957), with its Greek-Doric *colonnade inside, and at the extraordinarily tough *Salines* (Salt-Works) *d'Arc-et-Senans* (1773-8), built in his role as *Inspecteur des Salines de la Franche-Comté*. Banded columns, simplified rigid geometry, and *primitivist qualities emphasized by unfluted *Greek-*Doric columns were something new. The complex formed the centre-piece for his Utopian town of Chaux (published in *L'architecture considerée sous le rapport de l'art, des mœurs, et de la législation* (1804, 1847)), in which simplified, stripped *Neo-Classicism was

the language, with allusions to all sorts of stereo-metrically pure geometries, including Egyptian *pyramids, a phallus-shaped brothel, a hoop-shaped house for a cooper, and even spherical structures. Allied to this were routes passing through various mnemonic devices, clearly Free-masonic in origin and intent. Although Chaux (meaning 'lime', the binding agency of *masonry and therefore an allusion to a programme of Free-masonic connections) remained mostly a strange and wonderful dream, Ledoux was able to realize many of his most advanced ideas in the series of Barrières or toll-houses erected around Paris (1785-9), including the Rotonde de la Villette, with its mighty drum on unfluted Greek-Doric *serlianas, set over a square plan to each elevation of which are attached square Doric columns, and the grimly powerful Barrières of Passy, Long-champ, l'Observation, and Chopinette. Here was 'primitive' Neo-Classicism at its starkest and most sophisticated, among the greatest architectural creations of C18.

B (1980); J.Curl (2011); Ga (1980, 1992); E.Ka (1952); M & Wa (1987); P (1982); Rabreau (2000); J.T (1996); V (1987, 1990, 1995)

Lee or **Alee, John** (fl.1487-1522) English mas-ter-mason, with *Wastell he was involved in the final phase of building at King's College Chapel, Cambridge, from 1506. He probably designed the Ramryge *chantry-chapel in St Alban's Cathedral, Herts. (c.1521).

J.Harvey (1987)

Lee, Richard (fl.1525-35) English master-mason, probably the son of John *Lee. He made (1525-33) the tomb of **John Fisher** (c.1469-1535—**Bishop of Rochester** from 1504) intended for St John's College Chapel, Cambridge, but de-stroyed. It had early *Renaissance features, like those of **Nicholas West**'s (fl.1478-1533—**Bishop of Ely** from 1515) *chantry-chapel, Ely Cathedral. He was therefore among the first to use Renais-sance motifs in England.

J.Harvey (1987)

Lee, Sir Richard (c.1513-75) English architect/military engineer, probably grandson of John *Lee, he was the first English architect to be knighted. Surveyor of Fortifications at Calais (1536-42) he also worked (1558-65) on the impressive defences at Berwick-on-Tweed, Northum. He seems to have designed Sandown Castle, IoW (1540s) and Upnor Castle on the River Medway, Kent (1560s).

J.Harvey (1987)

Leeds, William Henry (1786-1866) English architectural critic, his essays on public improve-ments in the Companion to the Almanac (1838-50) were important. He published Moller's Memorials of German Gothic (1836), a Supple-ment in *Britton and A.C.*Pugin's Illustrations of the Public Buildings of London (1838), The Travellers' Club House...and the Revival of the Italian Style (1839), Railway Architecture (1848), and edited A Treatise on the Decorative Part of Civil Architecture by William Chambers (1862). His work on The Travellers' Club did much to publicize the *Italianate style of *Barry, and he introduced words such as *cornicione to architectural vocabulary.

Co (2008); Hi (1954); Leeds (ed.) (1836, 1839, 1862, 1904)

Lefuel, Hector-Martin (1810-80) French architect, he succeeded L.*Visconti as architect of the Louvre and Tuileries (1854-80), where he was assisted by R.M.*Hunt. His tall *mansard roofs and rich (even excessive) *Renaissance-Revival decorations were the epitome of the *Second-Empire style, and influential. He also designed the theatre at *Fontainebleau (1853) in an C18 style, and the buildings for the 1855 Paris International Exhibition.

Ha (1957); Hi (1977); M & Wa (1987)

Legeay, Jean-Laurent (c.1710-c.1786) See GEAY.

legement See LEDGMENT.

Legorreta Vilchis, Ricardo (1931-2011) Mexican architect, protégé of *Barragán, best known for adaptations of pre-Columbian and Spanish-Colonial references, often mixed with vivid colouring, and even including nods to *Moorish Spain with the use of *mashrabiya *lattice-work. Becoming aware of limitations, rigidities, and lack of warmth in so-called *Func-tionalism, his work gave expression to walls as major architectural elements (with emphasis on solids rather than voids), reflecting Mexican architecture before the invasion of *International *Modernism and its uninteresting clichés. He fused tradition and modernity in his Camino Real *hotels (e.g. at México City (1968), Cancún, Quintana Roo (1975-9), and Ixtapa, Guerrero (1981)). Other examples of his work are the Con-temporary Art Museum, Paloma, México (1991); the series of buildings for the Westlake/Southlake Development, Solana, near Dallas, TX (including the Village Center, the Real Estate Office Building, and the IBM Offices (all 1980s)); the Greenberg House, Los Angeles, CA (1991); Managua Cathe-dral, Nicaragua (1993); and the Fashion & Textile Museum, Bermondsey, London, for the fashion-designer **Zandra Lindsey Rhodes** (1940-). His son, **Victor** (1966-), continued running the firm.

Attoe (ed.) (1990); Cuito (2002c); E (1994); Mutlow (ed.) (1997); N & R (2003); Novodzelsky (ed.) (2000); Q et al. (eds.) (2000); Sennott (ed.) (2004); Slessor (2000)

Legrand, Jacques-Guillaume (1743–1808) French architect, student of J.-F.*Blondel, he became *Clérisseau's son-in-law. With *Molinos he built the *dome, using timber construction, over the central *court of the *Halle au Blé, Paris (1782–3), by Le *Camus de Mézières. This was likened to the Roman *Pantheon at the time, and was greatly admired for its bold geometry. He re-sited and remodelled Goujon and *Lescot's *Fontaine des Innocents* (1788) when the *cemetery closed, and published several books, including *Parallèle de l'architecture* (1789).

Etlin (1984); M & Wa (1987)

Leicester, John (*fl.*1349–51) English mason, he built a *postern at the Tower of London (1349–51), and was ordainer of all the King's Works there.

J.Harvey (1987)

Leith, George Esslemont Gordon (1885–1965) South-African architect working in the Classical language established in that country by Herbert *Baker. He was assistant-architect to the Imperial War Graves Commission (1918–20) in England before returning to South Africa where he set up his practice. His works include the Calais Southern War Cemetery, France (1918–20), the Central Railway Station, Johannesburg (1927–32), the Town Hall, Bloemfontein (1920–40), and the South-African Reserve Bank, Johannesburg (1938), all in a stripped Neo-Classical style reminiscent of *Holden's architecture.

P (1982); *South African ARe*, xxxi (1946), 279–86; Stamp (1977)

Leitner von Grund, Abraham (*c.*1639–1701) *See* LEUTHNER VON GRUND.

Lemercier, Jacques (*c.*1585–1654) Important mid-C17 French architect, he worked on the Square Court of the Louvre in Paris, begun by *Lescot, and was responsible for the *Pavillon de l'Horloge* (completed 1641) in which he introduced an *Order of *caryatids above the *Attic carrying a triangular *pediment, containing smaller triangular and segmental pediments, derived from della *Porta's *façade of *Il Gesù*, Rome. Lemercier was architect to **Cardinal Richelieu** (1585–1642) for whom he built the *Palais Cardinal* (later *Royal*), Paris (1624–36—destroyed, apart from a piece of external wall), and the domed Church of the *Sorbonne*, Paris (begun 1626—probably based on *San Carlo ai Catinari*, Rome), with a fine *Corinthian *portico on the courtyard side. He designed the handsome *dome at the *Val-de-Grâce* (from 1646), with its *drum surrounded by powerful *buttresses, treated as Classical *Orders, giving it lively modelling. From 1631 he designed and laid out the Town of Richelieu, near Chinon, the latter a strict essay in

formal rectilinear planning (which survives virtually intact). Also for Richelieu he enlarged the *Château* (mostly demolished), laid out the superb formal gardens, and built the Church at Rueil (from 1633). Lemercier is also remembered as the architect of some *hôtels particuliers* in Paris, including the *Hôtel de Liancourt* (1623–destroyed), which Marot published (1655).

Babelon (1991); Blomfield (1974); Bt (1982); Cramail (1888); Marot (1969, 1970)

Lemercier, Pierre (*fl.*1532–52) French architect, supposedly the designer of *St-Eustache*, Paris (begun 1532), an interesting building on a typical French *Gothic plan with apsidal east end, *ambulatory, *radiating chapels, and *transepts, but almost entirely *Renaissance in detail, including *tracery, which, though superficially Gothic, is transformed by the patterns and ornament. He was commissioned (1552) to complete the tower of *St-Maclou*, Pontoise. His works at *St-Eustache* and *St-Maclou* were continued by his son, **Nicolas Lemercier** (1541–1637), who worked mainly on the *nave of the Paris church (1578–80). Nicolas's son was the great Jacques *Lemercier.

S (1901–2)

Le Muet, Pierre (1591–1669) *See* MUET.

Lemyinge *or* **Liminge, Robert** (*fl.*1600–28) Carpenter employed to design and supervise the building of Hatfield House, Herts. (1607–12), for which Inigo *Jones was consulted about the south front. Lemyinge also designed Blickling Hall, Norfolk (1616–17).

Co (2008)

L'Enfant, Pierre-Charles (1754–1825) *See* ENFANT.

Lenginour, Richard (*fl.*1272–1315) English military-engineer involved in the building of Flint and Rhuddlan Castles (*c.*1277–82), but his greatest works were the Castle and fortifications at Conway, Wales. He carried out major building operations at Chester Castle (1290–1312), and probably designed the *choir of Chester Cathedral (*c.*1305–15). He was an important figure in the creation and upkeep of the military architecture of **Edward I** (*r.*1274–1307).

J.Harvey (1987)

Lengynour, Robert (*fl.*1308–27) English master-mason, he worked at Glastonbury Abbey, Som., for some 19 years, where he was in charge of (and probably designed) the major part of the great church (mostly destroyed).

J.Harvey (1987)

Lenné, Peter Joseph (1789–1866) German landscape architect/urban-designer, trained under his father, **Peter Joseph Lenné** (1756–1821), and

J.-N.-L.*Durand. He worked at Laxenburg, near Vienna (1814-15), before settling in Potsdam, where he became (1854) General Director of Gardens. He laid out the grounds of the *Pfaueninsel* (1818) and *Schloss Charlottenburg* (1819), and after a visit to England (1822) he introduced the English *landscape-garden to Prussia on a grand scale, influenced by the work of *Kent and *Sckell, notably at the *Volksgarten*, Magdeburg (1824). Lenné collaborated with *Schinkel and the latter's pupils, especially *Persius, on numerous schemes, notably the gardens contiguous to *Charlottenhof* (from 1825—where there were allusions to Antiquity and to the Alhambra, Granada), and the grounds of *Schloss Glienecke* and *Schloss Babelsberg* (although both parks were strongly influenced from 1843 by the views of *Pückler-Muskau, who had no high opinion of Lenné's work). He prepared (from 1833) an ambitious scheme for the landscaping and general improvement of the whole Potsdam-Sanssouci district adjoining the Havel Lake, transforming it into one of the most enchanting landscapes in all Europe, with reciprocal vistas, panoramic views, and intimate enclosures. He redesigned the *Tiergarten*, Berlin, into an informal landscape, enlarged (1840s) to encompass the zoo: the entire ensemble became a *public park. He also prepared plans for Berlin and its suburbs, including *Moabit* and *Tempelhof*, and (1850s) advised on the planning of several cities, including Dresden, Leipzig, and Munich. Lenné's designs should be seen as complementary to the architecture of Schinkel (especially in the area round *Charlottenhof*, the Court Gardener's House, and the 'Roman Baths', Potsdam), and as playing no small part in *Romantic Classicism. His work was very influential in C19 Germany, especially through his pupil's (Gustav *Meyer) *Lehrbuch der schönen Gartenkunst* (1860).

Bergdoll (1994); Giersberg & Schendel (1982); Günther (1985); G.Hinz (1989); Meyer (1860); Tay (2006); G-H. Vogel (1992)

Lennox, Edward James (1854-1933) Canadian architect. In 1911 he was still designing in a vaguely late-Victorian manner, as with his *Scottish-Baronial *Casa Loma*, Toronto, but drew on themes from the USA for his earlier Toronto City Hall and Court House (1887-99), much influenced by *Richardson's round-arched Allegheny County Court House and Gaol, Pittsburgh (1884-8). His work therefore mixed British and American influences, but he was also capable of impressive *Beaux-Arts *Classicism, as with the Toronto Power Generating Station, Niagara Falls, Ontario (1903-13).

K (1994)

Lenoir, Alexandre-Marie (1761-1839) French archaeologist/writer/museum official. Recognizing the historical/artistic importance of artefacts removed from the religious houses of France after they were closed and their contents confiscated (from 1789), he saved many from destruction. A prime mover in the reconstruction of dismembered monuments, notably the royal tombs from *Saint-Denis* Abbey, thanks to his efforts (often in the face of fanatical revolutionary vandalism) many wonderful objects were rescued and placed in the *Musée des Antiquités et Monuments Français* (opened 1796). Influenced by the ideas of *Winckelmann, Lenoir was a major influence on a C19 scholarly appreciation of French art and architecture.

Courajod (1878-87); P.Léon (1951)

Le Nôtre, André (1613-1700) *See* NÔTRE.

Leonardo da Vinci (1452-1519) *Uomo Universale* of the Italian *Renaissance, he made important contributions to architectural theory and town-planning. Involved in preliminary studies for the *crossing of Milan Cathedral (*c*.1487), he, with di *Giorgio, was consulted (*c*.1490) about the building of Pavia Cathedral. He provided plans for Milan's new buildings and expansion (1490s), and produced sketches in which his interest in relating buildings geometrically to streets, squares, and gardens using axes is demonstrated. Like others of his time, he was fascinated by the possibilities of centrally planned domed buildings, and in this respect his relationship with *Bramante in Milan is important, for the two men developed their ideas under the aegis of the **Sforza** family. Leonardo was involved with Bramante in the design of the domed *crossing and *chancel of *Santa Maria delle Grazie*, Milan (1490s), intended as a *mausoleum for the **Sforzas**, and painted his beautiful *Last Supper* (which contains an architectural setting of remarkable modernity for its date, almost anticipating *Palladio) in the *refectory (*c*.1495). It would seem that the maturing of Bramante's style to the *gravitas* of his *Tempietto* at *San Pietro in Montorio*, Rome, and his development of centralized geometries at the *basilica of *San Pietro*, Rome, may be due in no small part to Leonardo's influence.

Leonardo's notebooks give a fascinating glimpse of his architectural interests. Apart from his important scientific and mechanical drawings, his lively mind often experimented with the Classical vocabulary in a way that looked forward to much later developments. Fortifications, centralized plans, and technology were all his concerns, but there are also studies of designs for *villas (*c*.1506) that anticipate *Palladianism, and even *Mannerism, with columns *inserted* in recesses, something *Michelangelo was to do years later. With Bramante, he seems to have acted as some kind of adviser for the Church of *Santa Maria* *della Consolazione* at Todi (1508), begun by *Cola da Caprarola. In his last years Leonardo worked in France, planning a vast Royal residence and settlement at Romorantin (*c*.1517-19), complete with huge canals linking the English Channel to the Mediterranean.

Arata (1953); Firpo (ed.) (1963); He (1996); P.Mu (1969, 1986); Pedretti (1985); P (1982); J.T (1996)

Leoni, Giacomo (*c*.1686-1746) Supposedly Venetian, he spent most of his life in England from *c*.1713. Before that he was in Düsseldorf, where he assisted in the design of *Schloss Bensberg*, near Cologne (1705-16): while in Germany he worked on a treatise on the Five Roman *Orders of architecture which indicates that the idea of publishing a version of *Palladio's *Quattro Libri* was already in his mind before he settled in England and did just that. Texts were translated by Nicolas *Dubois, and Leoni prepared drawings on which the engravings were based: the results appeared as *The Architecture of A.Palladio, Revis'd, Design'd and Publish'd by Giacomo Leoni, a Venetian: Architect to his most Serene Highness, the Elector Palatine* with texts in English, French, and Italian (1715-18). It was the first English edition, illustrated with large engraved plates instead of the rather crude woodcuts used by Palladio himself, and was an outstanding and immediate success, helping to promote *Palladianism and probably sparking *Burlington's interest in the cause. He also published *The Architecture of Leon Battista Alberti* (1726-9). Leoni designed several houses (e.g. Queensberry House, Burlington Gardens, London (1721—an important prototypical Palladian town-house), Lyme Park, Ches. (*c*.1725-35), Argyll House, King's Road, Chelsea, London (1723), Clandon Park, Surrey (*c*.1730-3), and Alkrington Hall, Lancs. (1735-6)). All had borrowings from Inigo *Jones and Palladio, but Leoni was no purist, and there is more than an echo of the *Baroque in his work, suggesting a position closer to that of *Gibbs than of *Campbell. It is arguable that he was more influenced by than influencing British architecture.

J.Brown (ed.) (1985); Co (2008); E.Hs (1990); Leoni (1742, 1755); Su (1993); J.T (1996)

Leonidov, Ivan Ilich (1902-59) Russian architect, a figure in *Constructivism influenced by *Vesnin. His unrealized project for a Lenin Institute, with glass-clad suspended elements and an elevated monorail communications network, looked forward to the kind of adaptable open-ended structures envisaged by *Archigram et al. His only significant built work was the landscaped *amphitheatre and stairway for *Ordzhonikidze Sanatorium*, Kislovodsk (1937).

Wi.Cu (1996); Gozak & Leonidov (1988); K-M (1987); Kopp (1970); Quilici & Scolari (eds) (1975); O.Shv (1970)

Le Pautre, Antoine (1621-79) *See* PAUTRE.

leper window, *also called* **leper's squint** *See* LYCHNOSCOPE.

Lepère, Jean-Baptiste (1761-1844) *Savant* who accompanied **Napoléon Bonaparte** (1769-1821) to Egypt (1798), he was involved in the preparation of *Description de l'Égypte,* one of the most important sourcebooks of C19 Egyptology. He designed the exquisite *surtout* of the Sèvres *Service Égyptien* (1811-12) representing the *Kiosk* at Philae, obelisks from Luxor, and the *pylon-towers of the temple at Edfu. He also designed many of the medals struck to glorify episodes in the history of the *Empire* of **Napoléon I** (*r*.1804-14, 1815). With *Percier and *Fontaine, he was involved (1802) in the design of *Malmaison*, and, with *Gondouin, was responsible for the *Colonne Vendôme*, Paris (1806-10), based on the *Trajanic exemplar. He prepared the earliest designs for St-Vincent-de-Paul, Paris (1824), in the style of *Chalgrin's *St-Philippe-du-Roule* (1768-84). He was *Hittorff's father-in-law.

CdSAÉ (1820-30); J.Curl (2005); Ha (1952, 1957); Hi (1977); HPZ (1994); M & Wa (1987); D.Schneider (1977)

Lequeu, Jean-Jacques (1757-1826) French visionary Neo-Classicist, he is known for the extraordinary drawings that survive in the *Bibliothèque Nationale*, Paris. These include a weird 'Gothic House' that has nothing *Gothic about it, but is in fact a design for a route for supposedly 'Freemasonic' trials by Fire, Water, Earth, and Air, clearly derived from descriptions in the **Abbé Jean Terrasson**'s (1670-1750) prolix novel *Séthos* (1731) which were also sources for the libretto of **Wolfgang Amadeus Mozart**'s (1756-91) *Die Zauberflöte* (1791). Other designs include Egyptianizing *temples, *fabriques, spherical buildings, phallic erections, and even a *dairy in the shape of a gigantic cow. His grotesque obscene drawings (*figures lascives*) suggest that he was at least very odd. None of his buildings survives, but he built a country-house known as the *Temple of Silence* (1786), actually a Roman temple with *engaged columns along the side, embellished with dogs, turtles, owls and much else. Inside was what appears to have been a Freemasonic Lodge.

B (1980); J.Curl (2011); Duboy (1987); Jacques & Mouilleseaux (1998)

Leroy, Julien-David (1724-1803) *See* ROY.

Lesbian cymatium *See* CYMA.

Lescaze, William Edmond (1896-1969) Swiss-born architect, an important figure in bringing *International Modernism to the USA, where he established (1923) his NYC practice. His early work included essays in *Neo-Classicism and *Art Deco before he went into partnership

(1929) with George *Howe. The firm designed the Philadelphia Saving Fund Society Bank and Office (1929–33), regarded as the pioneering International-Modern *skyscraper of the time. The partnership was dissolved (1933), but Lescaze continued to work under the joint names until 1935 when he once again set up in independent practice. Among his works of that period were the Headmaster's House at Dartington Hall, Totnes, Devon, England (1930–2), the Churston Estate Housing Development, Devon (1932–6), and the Lescaze House, NYC (1933–4—which A.L.*Huxtable said was the first modern house built in the USA. Its success led to further commissions). His Longfellow Building, the first International-style work in Washington, DC, was commenced 1939 (completed 1941). During the 1939–45 war Lescaze designed prefabricated buildings using experimental materials, and later produced several large public, office-, and apartment-buildings, including the Swiss Embassy Chancellery, Washington, DC (1959), the Christian Peace Building, United Nations, NYC (1961), and the Chatham Center, Pittsburgh (1964).

E (1994); Hubert & Shapiro (1982); Lescaze (1942); P & J (1970–86); Stern (1975)

Lescot, Pierre (*c*.1500/10–78) French architect, possibly of Scots descent, credited with introducing *Renaissance *Classicism to France. He collaborated with the sculptor/architect **Jean Goujon** (*c*.1510–68) for nearly 20 years. One of their earliest works is the *Fontaine des Innocents*, Paris (1547–9), wholly rebuilt (1788) and re-worked by *Legrand and others. He also collaborated with Jean *Bullant at the *Hôtel de Ligneris* (later *Carnavalet*—*c*.1545–50). Appointed (1546) to design part of the Louvre, he was responsible for the south-western corner of the Square Court there (1546–51, with Goujon), with *façades of great refinement, lacking the monumental quality of Italian work, but introducing a delicate ornamental quality that was peculiarly French. However, Goujon may have been responsible for the entire architectural embellishments of the Louvre façades, with Lescot primarily in charge of the planning and disposition of the main elements.

Androuet du Cerceau (1972); Bt (1982); Colombier (1949); Ha (1943); J.T (1996); vV (1993)

lesene Vertical strip resembling a *pilaster, but without a *base or *capital. It is a feature of *Anglo-Saxon (e.g. Earls Barton church-tower, Northants. (early C10)) and *Romanesque architecture. Anglo-Saxon *lesenes* were composed of bonding-stones (often *long-and-short work) in *rubble walls, and subdivided wall-surfaces into framed plastered panels. Also called *stripwork*.

Lesser, Ludwig (1869–1957) German landscape architect, he designed (1908–14) open spaces (e.g. *Zeltingerplatz* and the *cemetery) at Frohnau *Villenkolonie* north of Berlin, where influences of *Olmsted's Riverside Suburb, Chicago, IL (1867–70), have been detected. Lesser founded the *Deutscher Volksparkbund*, intended to make landscaped open spaces available for ordinary people, and taught garden-art and horticulture at the *Humboldt-Hochschule* (a further-education establishment for adults, closed (1933) by the Nazis). He served on the Board of the *Deutsche-Gartenbau-Gesellschaft* from 1919, becoming its President (1923–33) and saving its great library from dispersal: today it is one of the finest resources for landscape architecture in Germany. His Berlin practice produced designs for some 700 open spaces, including private parks and gardens. He published an important treatise on *public parks (1927). Prudently, he settled in Sweden (1939), becoming a citizen (1948).

Lesser (1927); Shoe (2001)

Lesyngham, Robert (*fl*.1376–94) English master-mason, he designed the *cloisters (destroyed), the upper part of the screen on the west front, and the east window at Exeter Cathedral, Devon (1376–94). He may have designed the cloisters at Gloucester Cathedral.

J.Harvey (1987)

Lethaby, William Richard (1857–1931) English architect/educator/theorist, he trained with Norman *Shaw before establishing his own office (1889). Influenced by William *Morris, *Ruskin, and Philip *Webb, he was an important figure in the *Arts-and-Crafts movement, being a founder-member of the *Art-Workers' Guild (1884). He built in a *Free style, not without historical references, and among his houses are Avon Tyrrell, Christchurch, Hants. (1891–2), High Coxlease, Lyndhurst, Hants. (1898), and the fine Melsetter, Hoy, Orkney (1898–1900). His beautiful All Saints' Church, Brockhampton, Herefs. (1901–2), while having *Gothic allusions, is a free Arts-and-Crafts interpretation of church architecture, while the Eagle Insurance Building, Colmore Row, Birmingham (1899–1900), shows Webb's influence, although it is boldly personal. Lethaby helped to found the Central School of Arts and Crafts, London (1894—which had craft-teaching facilities and workshops), and was its first Principal. He was a leading member of the Society for the Protection of Ancient Buildings and wrote several books including *Architecture, Mysticism, and Myth* (1892), *Mediaeval Art* (1904), *Architecture* (1912), *Form in Civilization* (1922), and *Westminster Abbey* (1906, 1925).

Backemeyer & Gronberg (eds) (1984); Garnham (1994); A.S.Gray (1985); Hi (1977); Lethaby (1935); H.M (1979); *ODNB* (2004); Rubens (1986)

Leuthner *or* **Leitner von Grund, Abraham** (*c*.1639–1701) Austrian architect, he became active in Bohemia when Italian influence was in decline, and from the 1680s supervised the construction of fortifications there. He built the Černín Palace, Prague (1669–92), to plans by *Caratti, and designed the Cistercian Abbey Church, Waldsassen, Bavaria (1681–1704), although Georg and Christoph *Dientzenhofer (whose sister Anna was married to Leuthner) seem to have had more than a little influence in shaping the completed building. He published (1677) an architectural treatise containing many designs of *fountains, *portals, etc., that appears to have been used by the Dientzenhofers (whose careers he promoted) and *Fischer von Erlach.

Bou (1962); Knox (1962); Leutheusser (1993); Morper (1940); J.Nn (1970); P (1982); C.Powell (1959); WI (1915)

Levasseur Family Noël (1680–1740) and his cousin **Pierre-Noël Levasseur** (1690–1770) were French designers/craftsmen working in Québec, Canada. They carried out the *altars, *retables, and architectural sculptures for the Chapel of the Ursuline Convent in Québec (1726–36), for which the architect was the Parisian **François de Lajoüe** (*c*.1656–*c*.1719). The *high-altar of *St-François- de-Sales, Île d'Orléans, Québec (1734–6), was designed and made by **François-Noël Levasseur** (1703–94).

K (1994)

Le Vau, Louis (1612–70) *See* VAU.

levecel, levesel Small *lean-to roof or *pent over a *door, window, etc.

Leverton, Thomas (1743–1824) English architect/builder, he was a successful developer in late-C18 London. There is no evidence that he planned Bedford Square, Bloomsbury, London (1775–80), but he certainly decorated some of the houses there (1, 6, 10, and 13). Leverton's style was influenced by that of the fashionable *Adam brothers, as the Neo-Classical interiors of Watton Wood Hall (now Woodhall Park), Herts. (1777–81), and Plaistow Lodge, Bromley, Kent (1780), demonstrated. Leverton built 65 Lincoln's Inn Fields, London (1772), for the banker, **Henry Kendall**, who had originally 'enabled' Leverton to 'perfect' his knowledge of architecture. In turn, Leverton took on Kendall's son, Henry Edward *Kendall, as a pupil. He laid out Hamilton Place, Piccadilly, London (1806), for the Crown.

Co (2008); *ODNB* (2004); W.Pa (1852); Su (1988, 1993)

Levi, Rino (1901–65) Brazilian Modernist architect, he designed the first large *International-style apartment-building, the Columbus block, São Paulo (1928–32). Later works include the UFA Art Palacio Cinema (1936), and the Central

Cancer Hospital (1948), both in São Paulo. He adopted *Brutalism in the 1960s, as in the *Parahyba* Dairies, São João dos Campos (1963–7), and the *Santo André* Civic Centre, São Paulo (1965).

Levi (1974); M & N (1987); J.T (1996)

Levittown American suburban development at Hicksville, NY, built after the 1939–45 war for demobilized servicemen by **Levitt & Son**. Conceived with winding roads, accommodation for cars, and detached houses, it was followed by other developments in PA and NJ, and influenced countless *dormitory suburbs.

Dobriner (ed.) (1958); H.Gans (1969); Halberstam (1993)

Lewerentz, Sigurd (1885–1975) Swedish architect, he worked (1908–10) with *Fischer, *Möhring, and *Riemerschmid in Germany, and became a protagonist of *National Romanticism, as with his influential but unrealized project for the Hälsingborg Crematorium (1913–14), and indeed it was in cemetery and crematorium design that he made his name. In the Hälsingborg project the relationships of building, water, and landscape were carefully and sensitively considered, and this was to be true of other works designed around the time of the 1914–18 war when he worked with **Torsten Stubelius** (1883–1963). He began (1915) a long collaboration with *Asplund in the design of the Woodland Cemetery, Stockholm, which was to last until his death: there, he designed the landscapes and the exquisite Neo-Classical Resurrection Chapel (1922–8), one of Sweden's finest and most subtle essays in C20 *Neo-Classicism. Other commissions for cemeteries included that for Malmö's Eastern Cemetery, work on which likewise extended from the 1920s until the end of his life: the buildings, with their severe geometries, recall Roman *Antiquity and late-C18 Neo-Classicism. For the mortuary-chapel, Stora Tuna (1928), Lewerentz employed the simplest of means to give it dignity.

Lewerentz designed *sans-serif* lettering, posters, and many *pavilions for the 1930 Stockholm Exhibition, marking a change of direction in his style. For his two late churches, St Mark's at Skarpnäck, Stockholm (1956–60), and St Peter's, Klippan (1963–6), he used naked, unadorned brick to great effect, and virtually all historical references were absent.

Ahlin (1987); A & B (1986); Ca (1998); Constant (1994); E (1994); Flora *et al.* (eds) (2002); Johansson & Galli (1996); Pn (ed.) (1982); *SBL* (1979)

Lewis, Michael (1927–2011) South African-born engineer, he joined (1950) *Arup's firm, and was appointed (1962) to lead the engineering team for *Utzon's Sydney Opera House, seeing the project through the fraught period of its construction (1960s–70s). Later, he headed the design team proposing an alternative route for the then approved Channel Tunnel Rail Link: after much lobbying, Lewis's plan (the *Arup Alignment*) was accepted.

The Times (10 Dec. 2011), 104

LeWitt, Solomon ('Sol') (1928–2007) American artist of Russian-Jewish stock, he is included here because of his design for a **parterre*-garden (1981) realized posthumously at Fairmount Park, Philadelphia, PA (2011). Entitled *Lines in Four Directions in Flowers*, its geometry and colour-control reflected his affinity for creating variation within rigid structures, with species chosen to bloom sequentially.

The Guardian (10 April 2007), Obits

Lewyn, John (*fl.*1364–98) English master-mason, he was principal mason at Durham Cathedral in the latter part of C14, and carried out many works in the North, including the great kitchen at Durham (completed 1374), repairs to Bamburgh Castle (1368–72), the new **keep at Durham Castle, works at Carlisle and Roxburgh Castles (from 1378), various structures at Bolton Castle, Yorks., and major alterations to Dunstanburgh Castle (1380–7). He was unquestionably the most important provincial architect working in the North of England at the time.

J.Harvey (1987)

Liang Ssu-ch'eng (Sicheng) (1901–72) American-educated Chinese architect/historian, revered as a pioneer of research into and exploration of Chinese architecture/planning (notably **conservation/preservation of ancient monuments/historic buildings), and as the author of the first modern history of Chinese architecture. His wife was the English- and American-educated architect/poet, **Lin Huiyin** (1904–55—otherwise known as **Phyllis Lin**), aunt of the Chinese-American architect/artist, **Maya Ying Lin** (1959–), who designed the Vietnam Veterans Memorial, Washington DC (1980–2). With others, he discovered/analysed some of the oldest timber structures still extant in China, and attempted to record the grammar of traditional timber-framed architecture which survived largely in oral form. He designed several buildings in a National Style (e.g. Ganjin Memorial Hall, Yangzhou), and restored many more (e.g. Wenyuan Chamber, Forbidden City, Beijing), thus predictably fell foul of the Communist Party, and suffered under the 'Cultural Revolution', though was posthumously 'rehabilitated', for what that was worth.

Liang (2005); Sennott (ed.) (2004); J.T (1996)

Libera, Adalberto (1903–63) Italian architect, he joined (1927) **Gruppo 7*, and was involved with **Rationalism which he sought to promote

as the architectural language of Fascism. He exhibited at **Mies van der Rohe's **Weissenhofsiedlung*, Stuttgart (1927), and organized the first exposition of Rationalism in architecture in Rome (1928). The *Villa Malaparte*, Capri (1938), was an interesting attempt to marry architecture to its natural rocky site. While he designed the Olympic Village, Rome, with others (1959–60), and a few buildings (e.g. *Palazzo della Regione Trentina*, Trento (1954)), nothing of his later years compares with the designs for the monumental *Mostra della Rivoluzione Fascisto* (1932), intended by **Benito Mussolini** (1883–1945) to promote, predictably, a 'contemporary style, very modern and audacious, without melancholy references to the decorative styles of the past'. The exhibition was influenced by **Futurism and **Constructivism as well as by **Stripped Classicism, and had considerable influence thereafter, even into the post-war years. His masterpiece is the *Palazzo dei Congressi, Città Giardino EUR*, Rome (1937–40), and for *E'42* (the exhibition planned by Mussolini for 1942, but cancelled) he designed a huge arched gateway which influenced Eero **Saarinen for his Gateway to the West, St Louis, MO (1954).

Argan (1976); Etlin (1991); Garofalo & Veresani (eds) (1992); P (1982); Rivalta (2000); Seta (1978); Talamona (1992)

Libergié *or* **Libergier, Hue** *or* **Hugues** (*fl.*1231–63) French master-mason, he designed the **Benedictine Abbey Church of *St-Nicaise*, Rheims (1231–63—destroyed), with an exquisite west front incorporating a **tracery screen and a gigantic twin-**lancet with **oculus rather than the **rose-window usual at that time. He is commemorated by an **incised slab in Rheims Cathedral, on which he is shown holding a model and a staff of office, while a square and compasses are drawn on either side of his feet.

Branner (1965); Givelet (1897); Svanberg (1983)

Liberty 1. Allegorical female figure frequently depicted by French Revolutionary artists, complete with flaming torch and Phrygian cap. **2.** Italian **Art Nouveau, called **Stile Liberty*.

Libeskind, Daniel (1946–) *See* DECONSTRUCTIVISM.

lich-gate *See* LYCH-GATE.

Licht, Hugo (1841–1923) German architect, he trained in Berlin and under von **Ferstel in Vienna. As Director of Municipal Building, Leipzig (1879–1906), he built a series of monumental buildings including the Music Conservatory (1885–7), Police Headquarters (1889–90), Grassi Museum (1892–5), and the new *Rathaus* (1898–1912). The last is eclectic, drawing on aspects of medieval architecture, and with **masonry treated in a powerful, oversized way recalling the work of *Richardson in the USA. Licht was important for his many publications, notably those produced for Wasmuth Verlag, which included *Die Architektur des XX. Jahrhunderts: Zeitschrift für moderne Baukunst* (1901–14), a lavishly illustrated mine of information on the period, which promoted the careers of many architects.

Licht (1877, 1879–82, 1886–1900, 1900, 1901–6); Licht (ed.) (1901–14)

Liddell, The Hon. Thomas (1800–56) English architect, son of **Sir Thomas Henry Liddell** (1775–1855—**1st Baron Ravensworth** from 1821), he supervised the latter stages of the building of Ravensworth Castle, County Durham, erected from 1808 to designs by *Nash (demolished 1952–3). Liddell designed a *Gothic gate-lodge at Ravensworth (illustrated in *Loudon (1846)) and (probably) Beckett Park, Berks. (1831), though William *Atkinson's name has been suggested: he was also involved at The Deepdene, Surrey (1835–41), with *Roos. Liddell advised on landscape-design for Kensal Green Cemetery, London (1830–1).

Co (2008); J.Curl (ed.) (2001); *GGJ*, xv (2005/6), 11–68; Jane Loudon (ed.) (1846)

Lienau, Detlef (1818–87) Born in Schleswig-Holstein, trained in Germany and in Paris (under *Labrouste, from whom he derived his *Classicism), he settled (1848) in the USA where he developed a thriving practice in NYC. His work was eclectic, ranging through *Rundbogenstil*, *Gothic, French *Second Empire, *Italianate, *Picturesque asymmetrical, to a nondescript, even dour manner from which French influences, however, were not entirely obliterated. He designed several large blocks of town-houses in NYC, including the Rebecca Jones group, Fifth Avenue and 55th Street (1868–79—destroyed), which were influential. In the 1870s and 1880s his career was closely bound up with the rapid growth of Manhattan.

JSAH, xiv/1 (Mar. 1955), 18–25; P (1982); J.T (1996)

lierne See VAULT.

lift See ELEVATOR.

ligement See LEDGE.

light Aperture (called *day*) through which daylight passes, e.g. a *pane of *glass, an area around which are *mullions or *transoms, or an opening defined by *tracery-bars.

Light, Colonel William (1786–1839) Surveyor-General of South Australia, he founded and laid out Adelaide from 1837 on a generous plan with six large squares, the whole development surrounded by a *green belt of parkland, the first to be realized on any scale.

ODNB (2004)

Lightoler, Timothy (1727–69) Lancastrian architect, he settled in Warwick, where he worked as a carver/joiner (e.g. *Gothick *altarpiece in the Beauchamp Chapel, St Mary's Church (c.1760)), and introduced Neo-*Jacobean motifs at Burton Constable, Yorks. (c.1757–68). Other works include (probably) the *spire of Holy Trinity Church, Stratford-upon-Avon, Warwicks. (1763–4—sometimes attributed to William *Hiorn(e)), and the Octagon Chapel, Milsom Street, Bath, Som. (1766–7). Hired (1757) by **Robert Sayer** (1724/5–94) to complete *The Modern Builder's Assistant* after the deaths (1755 and 1754 respectively) of William *Halfpenny and Robert *Morris, he prepared (1762) *The Gentleman and Farmer's Assistant*, which included designs for *parsonages, farm-buildings (some in the Chinese Taste), *façades 'to place before disagreeable objects', and artificial *ruins in the manner of Sanderson *Miller. He also provided illustrations of country-houses for *A Complete History of the English Peerage* (1763) by **William Guthrie** (1708–70).

Co (2008); E.Hs (1990); Ison (1969)

light-well Unroofed space in a building, really a small *court with high buildings around it, providing light and air to the windows that open to it.

Ligne, Charles-Joseph, Prince de (1735–1814) French garden-theorist and landowner, he inherited the *Château de Beloeil*, Haincourt (now in Belgium), from his father, **Prince Claude-Lamoral II de Ligne** (1685–1766—who created the *Baroque gardens there), adding *Picturesque elements, including *fabriques* and *ruins. With his son, **Prince Charles-Joseph-Emmanuel de Ligne** (1759–92) he operated an important publishing-house at Beloeil, from which he issued his famous *Coup d'oeil* (1781), in which many other European gardens as well as his own were described, including the *Gartenreich* of the Prince of *Anhalt-Dessau.

Mansel (2003); Ligne (1781); Tay (2006; J.T (1996)

Ligorio, Pirro (c.1513–1583) Italian architect/archaeologist/librarian/painter, he settled in Rome (1534) after which he explored and recorded antiquities and remains, and began to collect material for his huge encylopedias of Classical artefacts. He brought out a volume on Roman antiquities (1553), the only publication in his lifetime disseminating his vast knowledge. In this respect, his work is an invaluable source of information on what *Antique remains were known at the time. Appointed (1549) archaeologist to **Cardinal Ippolito d'Este** (1509–72), he carried out major works at the old Franciscan monastery, Tivoli, creating the *Villa d'Este* and its gardens (1550–72), greatly influenced by the nearby *Villa*

Adriana which Ligorio had recorded. The *fountains, *cascades, and *waterworks at the *Villa d'Este* contributed to the making of one of the finest C16 European gardens. He began (1558) work on a summer-house for **Pope Paul IV** (*r.*1555-9) in the Vatican Gardens: work on this resumed (1560) after the election of **Pope Pius IV** (*r.*1559-65), and by 1562 the exquisite *Casino di Pio IV*, one of the most affecting creations of *Mannerism, was complete. **Jacob Burckhardt** (1818-97), the Swiss art-historian, called it the most beautiful 'afternoon retreat' ever created. It drew on the *type of the *Antique *diaeta*, or auxiliary building used for the *otium* (rest- or leisure-time). At the same time Ligorio began work on *Bramante's *Belvedere* Court at the Vatican, with the addition of curved seating at the lower terrace's south side, making changes to the *exedra* to the north so that it formed an enormous *niche. He also designed the *astylar rusticated Lancellotti Palace (*c.*1560), restored the *Pantheon (1561), and built the Cenci Palace (*c.*1564), all in Rome. He succeeded (1564) *Michelangelo as Architect of *San Pietro*, but in the following year was accused of fraud and theft, thus ending his Papal career. Once more he turned his attention to the gardens at Tivoli, supervising the works and designing several fountains. He moved to Ferrara (1569), where he was placed in charge of the Duke's collection of antiquities.

An (1954); D.Coffin (1960, 1979, 1991, 2004); Dernie & Carew-Cox (1996); Gaston (ed.) (1988); He (1996); Lamb (1966); Lazzaro (1990); Lotz (1977); Mandowsky & Mitchell (eds) (1963); P (1982); G.Smith (1977); J.T (1996)

Li Jie (1065-1110) Chinese architect/engineer, Superintendent for State Buildings, he was in charge of all State building construction from 1092, but he is remembered primarily as the author of *Yingzao Fashi* (State Building Standards—1100, published 1103), the oldest surviving Chinese technical manual on architecture. An edn of 1145 was re-issued (1919, with subsequent edns), sparking a worldwide interest in ancient Chinese buildings.

AH, xli (1998), 1-13

lime When *limestone is burned it produces *quicklime* (*calcium oxide*), which, when *slaked* with water, becomes *calcium hydroxide*. Lime is the chief ingredient of *mortar, *plaster, *stucco, etc.

W.Pa (1852)

limestone Sedimentary rock consisting mostly of *calcium carbonate*, which, when burned, produces *lime. Limestones were and are employed for building. Granular crystalline limestone is *marble.

W.McKay (1957)

Liminge See LEMYINGE.

Lindgren, Armas Eliel (1874-1929) Finnish architect, he formed (1896) a partnership with *Gesellius and Eliel *Saarinen. The firm's work was eclectic, drawing on *Arts-and-Crafts, medieval, *vernacular, and *Art-Nouveau styles, and was regarded as part of *National Romanticism: it includes the Pohjola Insurance Building, Helsinki (1900-1), the Studio and House, Kirkkonummi (1902-3), and the National Museum, Helsinki (1902-5). The partnership was dissolved (1905), and he established a new one with one of Finland's first female architects, **Wivi Lönn** (1872-1966), designing the Vanemuinen Theatre, Tartu (1906), and the Estonia Theatre, Tallinn (1912), both in Estonia, and both *Jugendstil*. Some of his other works merged *Renaissance elements with a subdued *Jugendstil*, as in the *Suomi* (1911) and *Kaleva* (1913) Insurance Companies' buildings, Helsinki. His later work drew on medieval precedents, notably in his restoration of Turku Cathedral (1923-8), and in the churches at Säynätsalo and Valkeala (both 1926 with **Bertel Liljeqvist** (1885-1954)). He also designed housing, mostly in Helsinki.

J.M.Ri (1978); Salokorpi (1970); J.B.Smith (1975)

Lindsay (*née* **Bourke**), **Norah Mary Madeleine** (1873-1948) Self-taught British gardener, she created two large garden-*rooms' (Long- and Persian- (or Jewel-) Garden, screened from each other by high walls covered in climbing plants) and a wild garden at her manor-house, Sutton Courtenay, Oxon. There, she permitted self-set seedlings to proliferate (creating jungles of mixed flowers contained within low box-*hedges and clipped yews) and experimented with one-colour gardens or planting with strident contrasting colours: she thus demonstrated her independence from prevalent ideas of *Jekyll et al. Admired by arbiters of taste such as *Hussey, she carried out planting-schemes at several English country-houses, collaborating with **Lawrence Johnston** (1871-1958) on the garden at Hidcote Manor, Glos., just before the 1939-45 war.

J.Brown (1990); *CL*, lxix (16 May 1931), 610-16; Hayward (2007); *ODNB* (2004)

linear planning Urban development laid out on either side of a central transport-spine consisting of roads, railways, and services (with variants consisting of additions of canals, etc.). Although formalized by *Soria y Mata as the **Ciudad Lineal** (1894), variants were in operation along main roads out of C19 cities where tramlines and railways facilitated development (now destroyed by the requirements of the motor-car).

linenfold *Parchemin plié* or *linen-pattern*, a late-*Gothic ornamental finish to a *panel, resembling linen with vertical loose folds. It evolved in Flanders from C15, and is very common in architecture of the *Tudor period. Linenfold was revived in C19.

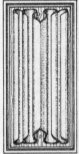

linenfold or napkin-pattern C16 example, Layer Marney Hall, Essex (after Parker).

Linstow, Hans Ditlev Frants (or **Franciscus**) (1787–1851) Danish-born architect of the Neo-Classical Royal Palace, Oslo, Norway (1824–48), one of the most distinguished of Greek-inspired buildings in that country, with an impressive *Ionic *portico: it was influenced by German exemplars, especially the works of *Schinkel, who advised on the design. Linstow's assistant (1824–7) for this work was the Danish architect *Grosch, who made Oslo his home from 1825. From the 1840s Linstow promoted an architecture of timber, based on *vernacular precedents, which he identified with nationalist aspirations.

We (1995)

Linstrum, Derek (1925–2009) Yorkshire-born architectural historian/conservationist, he published studies of *Brodrick, *Wyatville, the architecture of West Yorkshire, and the Victoria Memorial Hall, Calcutta. He founded the Leeds Civic Trust, taught at the Institute of Advanced Architectural Studies, University of York (from 1971), and was active in the International Centre for Conservation (ICOMOS), based in Rome.

The Times (14 July 2009), 52; pk

lintel *Beam over an aperture carrying the wall above and spanning between *jambs or columns (hence *post-and-lintel or *trabeated construction). *Compounds include*:
lintel-course: *string-course or *band continuing the lines of a lintel along a *façade.

lion 1. Carved representation of lions' masks in Classical architecture, especially on *cornices (e.g. *temple of Aphaia, Aegina (c.490 BC)). 2. Emblem of **St Mark**, so common in Christian *iconography.

Lisboa, António Francisco (1738–1814) See ALEIJADINHO.

Lissitzky, Eleazar (Lazar' called El) Markevich (1890–1941) Russian architect/graphic-designer/painter/polemicist, an early devotee of *Suprematism before embracing *Constructivism. He studied at Darmstadt from 1909, travelled, and graduated in architecture at Riga (1915), after which (1919) he worked with **Marc Chagall** (1887–1985) at the Vitebsk School of Art, where he evolved the idea of a work of art as an 'interchange station' between painting and architecture. This he termed *Proun* (an acronym for the Russian meaning 'Project for the Affirmation of the New'), and his paintings of the time have a resemblance to plans for three-dimensional structures. Influenced to some extent by the painter **Kasimir Malevich** (1878–1935) and *Tatlin, Lissitzky helped to organize Malevich's *New System of Art* (1919), the manifesto of Suprematism, and later designed the *Lenin Tribune* project (1920), a precedent for *Vesnin's *Pravda* (Truth) Building in Leningrad (1923). Through his Western contacts van *Doesburg, *Stam, and others, his ideas were disseminated within the *De-*Stijl* group and at the *Bauhaus. He designed several rooms for exhibitions, including the *Proun* Room for the Greater Berlin Art Exhibition (1923—reconstructed at the *Stedelijk Museum*, Eindhoven, Netherlands) and the Exhibition Cabinet (room) for the International Art Exhibition, Dresden (1926), and Hanover (1928—recreated at the *Landesmuseum*, Hanover). His images and, especially, his graphics, have been widely influential, especially in the late C20, and fragmentation apparent in his work has informed *Deconstructivism.

AYB, **xii** (1968), 253–68; Debbaut et al. (eds) (1990–1); Jervis (1984); Ly (1970, 1981); Ly-Küppers (1980); Margolin (1997); P (1982); Richter (1958)

list, listel, listella *Annulet or *fillet crowning or separating other *mouldings.

Littlewood, Maudie Joan (1914–2002) See PRICE, CEDRIC JOHN.

Liturgical Movement C20 Movement the object of which was an increasing involvement of the laity in worship. It brought the *altar nearer the congregation, physically and visually, and involved considerable 'reordering' of church interiors, often (but not always) to the detriment of the architecture.

J.Curl (2007); Dearmer (1911, 1931); Etchells & Addleshaw (1948)

liturgical orientation See ORIENTATION.

Liturgiology The study of liturgy or liturgies leading to a revival (or interpretation) of liturgical forms, especially in relation to the **Eucharist**.

It played an important part in late-C19 and C20 ecclesiastical architecture, notably in the work of *Comper, *Micklethwaite, and *Sedding.

J.Curl (2002, 2007); Dearmer (1911, 1931); Maskell (ed.) (1846–7, 1882)

liwan See IWAN.

Llewelyn Davies, Richard (1912–81) See DAVIES, RICHARD LLEWELYN.

Lloyd, Jeremy Sampson (*known as* **Sam**) (1930–2009) Grandson of Curtis *Green, steeped in the *Lutyens *Arts-and-Crafts traditions, he became chief designer in the London architectural firm of **Green Lloyd** (later **Green Lloyd Adams**). Later stylistic inclinations were evident when he drew on *Modernism in his work, e.g. the headquarters of Barclays Bank, Manchester (1965), the British Oxygen Building, Hammersmith, London (1975), and No. 1 Porchester Gate (1988—in which arched stone elevations hinted at a return to traditionalism)). Strong social convictions informed his designs for housing for the less well-off, e.g. Swan Bank Court, Willow Bank, Fulham (1981—sheltered housing); Cunningham House, Bessborough Road, Harrow (1975); and Evelyn Fox Court, Wallingford Avenue, Kensington (1984–5—for the Kensington Housing Trust). Other works include St Paul's Church, Robert Adam Street, St Marylebone (1970); the conversion of Ulster Terrace, Regent's Park (1975—with touches of Roguishness tinged with hints of Orientalism); and the gabled, tile-hung Chiswick Staithe, Chiswick (1964–5). His firm sensitively intervened at Somerset House, the Strand, London (1980s).

Bradley & Pe (2003); Cherry & Pe (1991); *The Guardian* (14 Oct. 2009), Obits; pk

load-bearing Type of construction in which walls, blank or punctuated with openings, support the floors, roofs, etc., as opposed to a structure based on the *frame principle, as in *timber-framed construction.

lobby-entry See ENTRY.

lobe 1. Small arch, arc, or *foil in medieval architecture, separated by a *cusp from another lobe or foil. Thus *lobed* describes anything such as an arch or *tracery with lobes and cusps. **2.** *Gadroon.

Lock, Adam (*fl.*1215–29) English master-mason, known for his work at Wells Cathedral, Som. He was in charge of the building of the second work of the *nave, west of the north porch, and he probably carved the detail of the first *Lady Chapel at St Augustine's Abbey (now Cathedral), Bristol (1218–20).

J.Harvey (1987)

Lockwood, Henry Francis (1811–78) English architect, articled to P.F.*Robinson before he established (1834) his own office in Hull, Yorks. He moved to Bradford, Yorks. (1849), then a rapidly expanding town, where he formed a partnership with **Richard** (1834–1904) and **William** (1828–89) **Mawson**. As **Lockwood & Mawson** they designed some of the most distinguished Bradford buildings, including St George's Hall (1851–2), the impressive *Venetian-*Gothic Wool Exchange (1864–7), and the very fine C13 Continental *Gothic-Revival Town Hall (1869–73). They also laid out and designed the Mill, Model Town, and Church at Saltaire, near Bradford (1851–76), one of the most important examples of a philanthropic industrial and housing development (*Company town) in the world for its date, all in an *Italianate Classical style. Lockwood trained *Brodrick. When the partnership was dissolved (1874) Lockwood moved to London, where he designed the Methodist City Temple, Holborn Viaduct (1873–4), and St Stephen's Church, Cowbridge Park, East Twickenham, Mddx. (1874).

J.Curl (2007); D & M (1985); Hi (1954); Linstrum (1978, 1999); P & D (1973)

loculus (*pl.* **loculi**) **1.** In a *catacomb, *hypogeum, *mausoleum, or other place of entombment, a recess large enough to receive a human corpse, with or without a coffin or *sarcophagus. An arched recess is termed *arcosolium. **2.** *Cinerarium or *ollarium of impressive dimensions. **3.** *Sarcophagus.

Loddiges, Joachim Conrad (1738–1826) Hackney(London)-based nurseryman from Hanover, who introduced many unfamiliar plants to England. His son, **George** (1786–1846) published *The Botanical Cabinet* (1817–34), with many fine plates of botanical specimens produced in conjunction with **George Cooke** (1781–1834). George Loddiges (possibly assisted by Cooke's son, **Edward William Cooke** (1811–80)), created the famous *arboretum at Abney Park *Cemetery (1840), Stoke Newington, and planted there some 2,500 varieties of trees and shrubs. *Loudon approved, and called it 'the most highly ornamental cemetery' near London, where trees and shrubs were labelled for the enlightenment of all who walked there. Thus Abney Park was the first Victorian *garden-cemetery* that can really be called by the name, designed to instruct the populace.

J.Curl (2004); Solman (1995)

lodge 1. Medieval masons' workshop, *refectory, *tracing-house, and living-quarters erected during the building of a great work. In very large projects, such as a cathedral, it was often a permanent structure, with a resident master-mason, associated with the building and maintenance of the *fabric. **2.** Place where *Freemasons assemble, representing the lost Temple of Solomon and an ideal. **3.** Small, usually decorative, building at the gateway to an estate or park, serving as the accommodation and office for a gatekeeper or porter. Such buildings were often in pairs, disposed symmetrically on either side of the *gates. **4.** Dwelling in the grounds of a large country-house, usually substantial, granted as a permanent residence for e.g. minor Royalty. **5.** Quarters for the porter, as in the entrance to a collegiate establishment or a club. **6.** Building in mountainous or wild country, used by e.g. hunting, shooting, or fishing parties.

Booz (1956); Bucher (1979); Colombier (1953); J.Curl (2011); J.Dean (1994); Gw (1903); M & E (1985); W.Pa (1852); S (1901–2); Svanberg (1983)

lodge-books 1. Book containing regulations or ordinances for masons, including rules for training and certification in the Craft. **2.** Books of designs and construction drawings.

Bucher (1979); J.T (1996)

Lodoli, Fra Carlo (Cristoforo Ignazio Antonio) (1690-1761) Venetian Franciscan/architectural theorist whose ideas may have influenced *Neo-Classicism from the time they were (rather inaccurately) propounded in *Algarotti's *Saggio sopra l'Architettura* (1753). Later, **Andrea Memmo** (1729–93) published *Elementi d'architettura Lodoliana* (1786), but it was incomplete until **Lucia Mocenigo** (1770–1854), Memmo's daughter, organized a fuller edition, including other hitherto unpublished texts (1833–4). Among other things, Lodoli insisted that 'proper function and form are the only final, scientific aims of civil architecture', merged in an 'indivisible entity', and that when a fully suitable material is *openly* used in accordance with its characteristics and the purpose of the building, a strong, well-proportioned, and convenient building will *always* result. He designed the Pilgrim's Quarters at the *Monastery of *San Francesco della Vigna*, Venice (*c.*1740), with curiously carved *cills and plain utilitarian raking *hoods, but its significance is perhaps overrated, for Lodoli's one known design was unpublished and unvisited until C20 when Italian *Rationalism rediscovered him and his works, although his *writings* may have struck chords with *Laugier and *Piranesi.

AB, xlvi/2 (1964), 159–75; CoE (1972); L.Grassi (1966); Hn (1962); E.Ka (1955); Memmo (1973); Ry (1980); Torcellan (1963); Wi (1982)

Lods, Marcel-Gabriel (1891-1978) French architect, in partnership (1925–40) with *Beaudouin, and on his own from 1945 in Paris. The Lods–Beaudouin partnership was responsible for early prefabricated housing-schemes at the *Cité de la Muette*, Drancy, Paris (1934—unfortunately remembered mostly as the transit-centre for French Jews on their way 'to the East'), and (with **Vladimir Bodiansky** (1894–1966) and *Prouvé) the *Maison du Peuple*, Clichy (1939). It also designed the layout of the World's Fair, Paris (1937). After the 1939–45 war Lods argued for the planning of *all* land and towns on *CIAM principles, but the fierce opposition of German authorities saved the ancient city of Mainz from the catastrophe Lods intended for it (1946–8).

E (1994); M & N (1987); J.T (1996)

Loewy, Raymond Fernand (1893-1986) French-born American industrial designer. After a chequered career he was retained (1929) by the Gestetner firm to restyle their products, and his success prompted other firms to employ him (e.g. BP, Co-op, Exxon, Lockheed, Shell, Studebaker). He designed automobile bodies, railway-engines and passenger-cars, refrigerators, the famous Greyhound buses, the **Coca-Cola** bottle, and various corporate identity packages. Among later works were the interiors of the *Skylab* for NASA (1967–73). He published *Never Leave Well Enough Alone* (1951), and was a considerable influence on the late-C20 Western environment.

L'Ad'A, ccxlvii (Oct. 1986), 96–8; Jodard (1994); Loewy (1937, 1951, 1975, 1988); Schönberger (ed.) (1990)

loft 1. Formerly, any upper floor, but now the volume contained by the pitched roof of a building and the supports for the ceiling of the topmost floor bounded by the walls. Essentially a *garret, but used for storage, without any finishes. **2.** Elevated platform, staging, or *gallery within a larger room or hall, such as an *excubitorium* or *watching-loft* (e.g. in St Alban's Abbey, Herts.), *Rood-loft, or *organ-loft in a church.

log Type of construction in which walls are formed of straight tree-trunks each placed horizontally on top of another, overlapping at the corners of the building. Joints were filled with mud, dung, moss, etc.

Hansen (1971); Jordan (1985); S (1901–2)

loggia (*pl.* **loggie**) **1.** Roofed structure, open on at least one side, essentially a *gallery, *arcade, or *colonnade, affording a protected seating-place with a view, common in Italy, often with architectural pretensions. It is usually part of a building, and subsidiary to the whole, although there are some *loggie* that have immense scale and overwhelming presence, such as the *Sala Terrena*, *Valdštejn* Gardens, Prague (C17). **2.** *Lodge, in the sense of a building in a park.

Loire-château *or* **Touraine style** Type of C19 architecture based on the French *Renaissance

C16 *châteaux* of the Loire valley in the time of *François Ier. Examples include *Destailleur's Waddesdon Manor, Bucks. (1874–90), and *Crossland's Royal Holloway College, Egham, Surrey (1879–87).

D & M (1985); Pe *et al.* (2003); Nairn *et al.* (1971)

Lomax-Simpson, James (1882–1977) British architect, his finest works are the late-*Arts-and-Crafts *Domestic-Revival houses he designed from 1910 at Port Sunlight, Ches., as Architect to Lever Brothers, including virtually all the buildings facing The Diamond (1–22 King George's Drive, 8–12 The Causeway, 25–50 Queen Mary's Drive, and 13–17 The Causeway) of 1913; those in The Ginnel, 60–2 Bolton Road, and 2–4 Water Street (*c.*1914); the Duke of York's Cottages (1933); Jubilee Crescent (*c.*1938); and many other houses and structures (e.g. the Social Centre, King George's Drive (1913), the Rose Garden and Arch (*c.*1937), and the axial vista at Windy Bank). Other works are St George's Church (1906–7), handsome additions to Thornton House (1906), the Smithy (1905), and houses, all at Thornton Hough, Ches. With Sir John *Burnet, *Tait, & Lorne, he designed the Unilever Building, New Bridge Street, London (1930–1).

Hartwell *et al.* (2011); pk

Lombardo, Pietro Solari, *called* (*c.*1435–1515) One of the most important architect/sculptors working in Venice from *c.*1467. He laboured from 1471 on embellishments for the *chancel of *San Giobbe*, which has stylistic affinities with the work of *Brunelleschi in Florence. Florentine-inspired too are the large funerary monuments he designed for *Santi Giovanni e Paolo*: conceived as compositions in the *Renaissance style, the tomb (1481) of **Doge Pietro Mocenigo** (1406–76) is his finest achievement in this genre. He designed and built *Santa Maria dei Miracoli* (1481–9), an aisleless *nave with a barrel-vaulted timber ceiling and a raised chancel set under a *cupola on *pendentives, the whole exterior treated with a two-storey arrangement of *engaged *Orders, the uppermost carrying a *blind *arcade. Inside is *marble panelling, and the combination of rich Byzantinesque wall-decorations and Renaissance detailing is impressive. The *chancel-arch is approached from a flight of steps, and this creates the appearance of greater size. *Trompe l'œil effects were also employed on the *façade of Lombardo's *Scuola di San Marco* (from 1489), built as a confraternity hall: on the ground floor are panels treated as perspective views of architectonic spaces (upper parts of the front were completed by *Coducci). Lombardo's name is associated with various Venetian *palazzi*, notably the beginnings of *Véndramin-Calergi* (*c.*1500), and the *Ca'Dario* (*c.*1488), the decorative work

of which is not unlike that of *Santa Maria dei Miracoli*. In much of his work Lombardo was assisted by his sons **Antonio** (*c.*1458–1516) and **Tullio** (*c.*1455–1532).

D.Howard (1980); Luciani (1987); McAndrew (1980); vV (1993)

Lombard style Essentially an amalgam of *Early Christian and *Romanesque, it flourished in Northern Italy (e.g. *Sant'Abbondio*, Como (C11)). It was revived in C19 as part of the *Rundbogenstil*, and enjoyed a further American Revival, especially for churches.

Lombardy frieze Arched *corbel-*table or series of small arches under *eaves and supported on corbels, as at *Sant'Abbondio*, Como (C11).

London, George (*c.*1640–1714) English garden-designer in partnership with Henry *Wise, with whom he edited *The Compleat Gard'ner* (1699) and *The Retir'd Gard'ner* (1706). As Master Gardener and Deputy Superintendent of the Royal Gardens, he carried out works at Kensington and Hampton Court Palaces, and also designed ostentatious gardens for aristocratic clients at Chatsworth, Derbys., Longleat, Wilts., Wimpole Hall, Cambs., and Staunton Harold, Leics. Although nearly all his work was subsequently obliterated, much of it was recorded in views (e.g. *Kip & Knyff's *Britannia illustrata* (1707)). His garden at Melbourne Hall, Derbys. (1704–6), partially survives, and the Privy Garden at Hampton Court has been recreated.

AH, **xxviii** (1985), 40–70; J.Hs (1982); J.T (1996)

Long, Robert Cary (1810–49) American architect, he set up in Baltimore, MD (1835–6), designing in the Classical, *Egyptian, and *Gothic styles: he was responsible for Greenmount Cemetery, where he built the Gothic entrance (1840) and an *Egyptian-Revival *mausoleum. Among other Baltimore works, the Perine House (1839), **Jérôme Napoléon Bonaparte** (1805–70) Town House (1844), and the distinguished *Greek-Revival Church of St Peter the Apostle (1843–4) deserve mention. He published many articles on architecture, as well as *The Ancient Architecture of America* (1849).

Carrott (1978); Howland *et al.* (1953); P (1982); St (1968)

long-and-short work *Anglo-Saxon *masonry consisting of tall thin verticals and short lengths of horizontal blocks, both of *freestone, used as *dressings in *rubble walls, set alternately one on the other as *quoins and *lesenes, the shorts set deep into the wall to help bind it together. Lesenes were formed by creating a raised vertical strip on the long-and-short work which, with the raised quoins, provided a frame for the *render concealing the rubble beneath.

long gallery Room or *gallery in an *Elizabethan/*Jacobean house of the *prodigy *type, sometimes the width of a *façade, as at Hatfield House, Herts. (1607–11), and Hardwick Hall, Derbys. (1590–7), well-lit by means of lavish windows and sumptuously appointed with chimney-surrounds, panelling, moulded ceilings, etc., used to hang tapestries and pictures, and for entertainment.

Longhena, Baldassare (1596–1682) The most distinguished Venetian architect of the *Baroque period, he is said to have trained under *Scamozzi. Early in his career he designed the *Palazzo Giustinian-Lolin* on the Grand Canal (1620–3), which was a taste of things to come in its lively invention. Longhena won (1630) the competition to design the splendid votive Church of *Santa Maria della Salute* on which he was to work for the remainder of his life. Its plan is an octagonal domed space surrounded by lower *aisles off which are six rectangular chapels illuminated by *Diocletian windows, with a domed *chancel on either side of which are *apses. The *clerestorey carrying the *dome is linked to the radiating chapels by means of vast *buttresses in the form of *scrolls, and a *triumphal-arch motif is used on the entrance-façade. The Church is sited at the entrance to the Grand Canal opposite the *Piazzetta* and Doge's Palace and on the axes of *Palladio's Churches of *San Giorgio Maggiore* and *Il Redentore*. The connection with *scenography is continued inside with telescoping views from the great central space, creating an architectural experience at once powerful and satisfying. Almost identical in plan is the Philippine Church, Gostyń, Poland (from 1679), for which Longhena provided drawings, realized by **Andrea** (c.1640–1701) and **Giorgio** (fl.1640–86) **Catenazzi** and completed (1728) by **Pompeo Ferrari** (c.1660–1736). Longhena's mastery of theatrical effects was also demonstrated in the influential double staircase he designed for the *Benedictine Monastery of *San Giorgio Maggiore* (1643–5).

His domestic designs were many, but his finest achievements in the field were the *Palazzo Pésaro* (1649/52–82—completed by his disciple, **Antonio Gaspari** (c.1658–1738)), with its diamond-rusticated *plinth, two superimposed *Orders, and an arrangement of arched windows carried on subsidiary Orders. It is arguably one of the most carefully composed of all Venetian *palazzi*, with a deeply layered *façade, the main *Orders standing in front of the 'real' structural wall. He also began (1666) the *Palazzo Bon* (later *Rezzonico*), with a façade (completed 1759 by *Massari) regularly arranged as wall and pier over a plinth

derived from *Sanmicheli's *Porta Palio*, Verona (1548–9), the upper part evolved from *Sansovino's *Biblioteca Marciana* (1536–60), and a total composition with a precedent in Sansovino's *Palazzo Corner della Ca'Grande* (begun 1537). His façade of the Chapel of the *Ospedaletto* (1670–4) was elaborately embellished, a precursor of late-Baroque tendencies. Apart from the scenographic triumph of *Santa Maria della Salute*, his greatest town-planning achievement was the completion of Scamozzi's *Procuratie Nuove, Piazza di San Marco* (1640–63).

Cristinelli (1978); Hopkins (2012); D.Howard (1980); Kz (1991); D.Lewis (1979); P (1982); Puppi *et al.* (eds) (1982); J.T (1996); vV (1993)

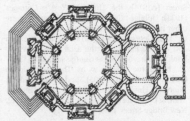

Plan of *Santa Maria della Salute*, Venice.

Longhi Family Group of C16 and C17 architects active mostly in Rome. **Martino Longhi the Elder** (c.1534–91) appears to have settled there c.1569, where he worked for the Papacy, notably at the Vatican and Quirinal Palaces, the rebuilding of the *portico of *Santa Maria Maggiore* (1575), and the new *campanile on the *Palazzo del Senatore* (1578). He designed the well-mannered but unadventurous *façade of *San Girolamo degli Schiavoni* (1588–9). His son, **Onorio** (1568–1619), who seems to have been an odd character, fled Rome (1606) for his part in a murder, but returned (1611) after a Papal Pardon. He designed the huge *Santi Ambrogio e Carlo al Corso* (1612–19), completed by his son, **Martino the Younger** (1602–60), the most gifted of the tribe, who designed *Sant'Antonio dei Portoghesi* (1630–8), with its lively façade. It was as a designer of church-fronts that the younger Martino excelled: his masterpiece is the façade of *Santi Vincenzo ed Anastasio* (1646–50). He introduced three new features to Roman *Mannerism: detached columns accentuating unhesitant verticality; the mixing of triangular, segmental, open-topped, and open-bedded pediments; and the layering of planes, with the *scrolls merging with other sculpture as part of *scenographic effects. The assured rhetoric of Roman *Baroque had arrived.

Arco (ed.) (1972); J.Curl (2001); J.Hess (ed.) (1934); Koksa (1971); Pascoli (1965); P (1982); J.T (1996); Va (1986); Wi (1982)

long-house 1. Domestic building including living-quarters, byres, etc., under one roof, with access by a single *entry-passage. 2. Very large prehistoric timber structure, apparently used for many purposes, the remains of which have been found in several sites in Western Europe. 3. Large timber structure raised above the ground on posts, and divided into *apartments, found in Malaysia and Indonesia. 4. Communal dwelling or meeting-house of Native Americans.

ABDM (1996); Dawson & Gallow (1994); P.Oliver (ed.) (1997)

Longuelune, Zacharias (1669-1748) French architect, he worked on the *Zeughaus*, Berlin (c.1698), under de *Bodt, travelled in Italy, and settled in Dresden (1715), rising to become *Oberlandbaumeister*. His best work was the formal park at Gross-Sedlitz (1723-6), and part of the Dutch Palace (later *Japanisches Palais*), Dresden (from 1729 with *Pöppelmann). The *Blockhaus* (so called because it stood above a timber customs-house once stood on the site), Dresden-Neustadt (1728-31), employed his favourite devices of shallow *ressaults, *lesenes, and horizontal *bands: it was completed by *Knöffel. His designs in a rather dry French Classical style had some influence in Saxony and Poland, and he proposed schemes for an enormous Saxon Palace in Warsaw (1717—with Pöppelmann) and for *Schloss Pillnitz*, near Dresden.

Colombier (1956); H.Franz (1953) J.T (1996)

look-out *See* PROSPECT TOWER.

loop 1. Long, narrow, vertical aperture with splayed *jambs set in a *parapet (sometimes in the *merlon of a *battlement) or wall for the discharge of arrows, etc., also called *arrow-loop*, *loop-window*, or *loop-hole*, occasionally with a shorter horizontal aperture across it forming a cruciform opening. The terminations of the apertures (little more than slits in the wall) were often widened into circular holes, and occasionally the point at which the slits crossed was enlarged to a circular opening as well. *See* GUN-LOOP.

Loop-hole also refers to a vertical series of doors each set above the other in a warehouse wall in tiers, usually with hinged drop-platforms and with a pulley above the series so that goods could be hoisted up and swung through the doors into storage. 2. Merlon.

Loos, Adolf (1870-1933) Austro-Hungarian architect, born in Brno, Moravia, he studied in Dresden, where *Semper's ideas made a great impression on him. He visited (1893) the USA, where he absorbed the lessons of the *Chicago School, and was impressed by an essay of *Sullivan (1892) in which the latter advocated refraining from all ornament for a period, so that

architects could concentrate on the design of buildings 'well-formed and comely in the nude'. He was also influenced by the work of F.L.L. *Wright (whom he also met), by the English *Arts-and-Crafts movement, and by the designs of Otto *Wagner. Loos settled in Vienna, and in a series of articles denounced the ornamenting tendencies of *Jugendstil*, notably in the works of *Hoffmann and *Olbrich, so he was opposed to aspects of the *Sezession. He likened extravagance and dishonesty in architecture to the fake fronts of streets in towns erected for show by **Grigory Aleksandrovich Potemkin** (1739-91) in Russia, publishing (1898) his views in the important journal *Ver Sacrum*.

Ornament und Verbrechen was published (1908), in which he claimed that lack of ornament was a sign of spiritual strength: this has led to his beatification as a 'pioneer' of the *Modern Movement, but he was nothing of the sort, for his designs of the period are almost entirely Neo-Classical in spirit, reflecting his admiration for Greek architecture and for *Schinkel. A prime example of this stripped Classicizing tendency is the *Goldman & Salatsch* block on the *Michaelerplatz*, Vienna (1909-11), with its simplified *Tuscan columns and unornamented *façades using the finest materials, but nearly two years before, (1907-8), his *Kärntner Bar*, Vienna, had demonstrated a type of *stripped *Classicism, using fine materials. The Steiner House, *St-Veit-Gasse*, Vienna (1910), is usually shown in a view from the garden, but the street-front, an almost single-storey symmetrical composition with a great curved roof, is hardly ever illustrated because it shows how Loos was deeply rooted in tradition, as it is an interpretation of a small *Baroque building stripped of ornament and with its curved roof simplified.

In both the Steiner and Scheu (*Larochegasse* 3, Hietzing—1912-13) Houses, Loos employed exposed timber beams (they were not always *structural* either), and drew heavily on the Arts-and-Crafts tradition of England (a country he greatly admired), with *ingle-nooks, brick fireplaces, and wooden panelling. His reverence for Greek architecture was expressed in his competition entry (1923) for the *Chicago Tribune* Building: his design was a *skyscraper shaped like a gigantic Greek-*Doric column. For a brief period (1920-2) he was the Chief Architect for the City of Vienna's Housing Department, and produced proposals for a model estate at Heuberg. He also designed a 'row-house with one wall' which he patented.

He spent the next five years in Paris, where he made contact with the leading figures of the avant-garde and built the celebrated house for **Tristan Tzara** (1896-1963) (*Avenue Junot* 15, Paris XVIII—1925-6), which, like the *Michaelerplatz* building, had an innovative plan with the volumes divided up to form rooms of differing heights, but the architectural language was more stark, and followed Modernist tendencies. After he returned to Vienna (1928) Loos designed a few dwellings, including the Moller, *Starkfriedgasse* 19, Pötzleinsdorf, Vienna (1927–8), and Müller, *Střešovická* 33, Prague (1929–30), Houses, both of which had complex interiors and smooth rendered walls that were very much *de rigueur* as *International *Modernism acquired its poverty-stricken language. He designed (1931) houses for the *Werkbund* at *Woinovichgasse* 13-15-17-19, Vienna, also with stark geometries and white rendered walls: these late works appear to have influenced the younger generation of architects. Both *Neutra and *Schindler were among those who were affected by Loos's ideas before the 1914–18 war. His early writings on architecture and design (1897–1900) were collected as *Ins Leere Gesprochen* (Spoken into the Void—1921) and his later works (1900–30) as *Trotzdem* (In Spite Of—1931).

ACGB (1985); R.Ba (1960); Duzer & Kleinman (1994); Gravagnuolo (1982); Hi (1977); Kristan (ed.) (2001, 2001a); Kulka (ed.) (1931); Li (ed.) (1986); Loos (1962); Lustenberger (1994); Münz & Künstler (1966); Opel (eds) (2003); Safran & Wang (eds) (1985); Schezen *et al.* (1996); Schweighofer (2000); J.Stewart (2000); Tournikiotis (1994); Trevisiol (1995); J.T (1996)

loricula *See* HAGIOSCOPE.

lorimer *See* LARMIER.

Lorimer, Sir Robert Stodart (1864–1929) Scots architect, articled to Rowand *Anderson, he later worked with *Bodley and *MacLaren. He commenced practice in Edinburgh (1893) and established his reputation with a series of cottages in the *vernacular style, so much so that he was recognized by Hermann *Muthesius as one of the most significant architects of his time, doing for Scotland what R.N.*Shaw and his contemporaries had done for England a generation before. His interest in the *Arts-and-Crafts movement led him to design several distinguished country-houses (e.g. Rowallan, Ayrshire (1903), and Ardkinglass, Argyll (1906)), and by 1905 he was unassailable as the top architect in Scotland for restorations, renovations, garden-design, and new houses. He designed (1906) his first important church, St Peter's, Morningside, Edinburgh (completed 1929), followed by the Chapel of the Knights of the Thistle, St Giles's Cathedral, Edinburgh (1909—an exquisite work, earning him his Knighthood (1911)). He designed several memorials and war-cemeteries, but his undisputed masterpiece is the Free-*Gothic Scottish National War Memorial Chapel, Castle Rock, Edinburgh (1922–7).

J.Curl (2002a); *GH*, v/2 (1977), 30–34; A.S.Gray (1985); GMcW & W (1984); Hussey (1931); Jervis (1984); P (1982); *ODNB* (2004); *RIBAJ*, ser. 3, **xxxviii/8** (21 Feb. 1931), 239–49; Savage (1980)

L'Orme, Philibert de (1514–70) *See* ORME.

Losh, Sara (1785–1853) English architect, she designed St Mary's Church, Wreay, Cumb. (consecrated 1842), an extraordinary mixture of French, Italian, and Rhineland-*Romanesque. She was also responsible for the *mausoleum of her sister, **Katherine** (1788–1835), a robustly primitive, severe structure of large blocks of stone, with deliberately rough surfaces, called 'Druidical' or even 'Attic-Cyclopean' by some observers. They are two of the most original buildings of their time in England.

ODNB (2004); Pe (1967); Uglow (2012)

Lote, Stephen (*fl.*1381–1417/18) English mason, warden under *Yeveley of the *lodge of St Paul's Cathedral, London (1381–2). He worked with Yeveley on the tombs of **King Richard II** (*r.*1377–99) and his first Queen (**Anne of Bohemia** (1366–94)) in Westminster Abbey (1394–5). In 1400 he became the King's Master-Mason at Westminster and the Tower of London, and completed the *nave, built the *cloisters, continued work on the *transepts, and probably designed the *pulpitum (*c.*1410) and tomb of **King Henry IV** (*r.*1399–1413) at Canterbury Cathedral, Kent. He carried out works at Maidstone Church, Kent, and Rochester Bridge in the same county. He may have designed the *choir (destroyed) of Fotheringhay Church, Northants. Lote made the tomb of **Edward, Duke of York** (killed at Agincourt, 1415), for Fotheringhay (destroyed) and, also, with Yeveley, the tomb of **Simon Langham** (*fl.*1339–76—**Archbishop of Canterbury** (1366–8)), in Westminster Abbey (1379). He is also referred to as a 'latoner', indicating he made monumental funerary *brasses as well as stone tombs.

J.Harvey (1987)

Lotti, Cosimo (1571–1643) Italian architect/landscape architect/engineer, he collaborated (1593) with *Buontalenti on the Bóboli Gardens, Florence, and designed hydraulic systems for the Pratolino and Castello Gardens. Sent (1626) to the Court of **King Philip IV of Spain** (*r.*1621–65), he renovated the Royal gardens (which had decayed following the expulsion of Moorish engineers) and designed theatres. His works at *Aranjuez* were based on those at Bóboli, and had *parterres, copses, and many water-features, much-praised by contemporaries. Other works were at *El Pardo* and *Zarzuela*. At *Buen Retiro*, Madrid, he created a lavish centre for Court entertainment, with dismountable stage-systems (*c.*1633) and optical tricks exploiting aspects of *scenography.

Barghahn (1986); Brown & Elliott (1986); Gothein (1966); J.T (1996)

lotus Ornament based on one of several water-plants, including the Egyptian water-lily, the source of much architectural enrichment of the stylized, bud, flower, and leaf type. Ancient-Egyptian *capitals decorated with both bud and flower motifs were common, and were revived in *Egyptian-Revival design. The lotus is related to a great number of common decorative devices, including the *fleur-de-lys, *palmette, and sundry Classical and medieval motifs.

J.Curl (2005); Glazier (1926); O.Jones (1868)

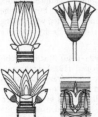

(*top left*) Ancient-Egyptian lotus-bud. (*top right*) Ancient-Egyptian stylized lotus-flower.
(   ) Ancient-Egyptian lotus-flower.
(   ) Ancient-Greek stylized lotus-flower and -buds.

Loudon, John Claudius (1782–1843) Scots agriculturist, encyclopedist, landscape-gardener, horticulturist, expert on *cemeteries, architect, influential critic, he settled (1803) in London and began a career of frenetic literary activity. His *Observations on the Formation and Management of Useful and Ornamental Plantations, on the Theory and Practice of Landscape Gardening . . . etc.* (1804) was followed by *A Short Treatise on Several Improvements Recently Made in Hothouses* (1805), and *A Treatise on Forming, Improving, and Managing Country Residences* (1806—in which he revealed a passionate interest in architecture). About that time he began to do architectural work: on the death of his father he designed a Neo-Classical monument in Pin-ner churchyard, Mddx. (1809), a vertical mass with two battered sides from which a *sarcophagus projects, as advanced as any architectural scheme could be for its date, *primitive, severe, and stripped.

He invented (1811) an iron *glazing-bar that made curved glazing possible and erected various prototype *hot-houses incorporating his structural and other practical ideas: *Remarks on the Construction of Hothouses* (1817), *Sketches of Curvilinear Hothouses*, and *A Comparative View of the Common and Curvilinear Modes of Roofing Hothouses* followed (1818). The principles that Loudon developed became the basis of famous works by *Paxton at Chatsworth (and ultimately at the 1851 Great Exhibition), of *Lanyon and Richard *Turner at Belfast, and of Turner

and *Burton at Kew (1845–8): they were applied to countless *conservatories and exhibition-buildings throughout C19 Europe and America.

Work then began on the enormous and immediately successful *Encylopaedia of Gardening* (1822), which enabled Loudon to design and build the 'double detached villa' for himself at 3 and 5 Porchester Terrace, London (1823–4), an advanced and convenient building of *Italianate Classical appearance: he also established (1826) *The Gardener's Magazine*, which had a profound effect on taste and expertise. He proposed (1829) a *green belt half-a-mile broad around London, urged the formation of national schools for compulsory education, and advocated the beneficial use of sewage for agricultural purposes: as if these activities were not enough, he published (1830) the first part of *Illustrations of Landscape-Gardening and Garden Architecture*, laid out the Botanic Gardens in Birmingham, and married the remarkable **Jane Webb** (1807–58), author of a futuristic novel (1827) about C21 England bedevilled by universal air-travel, world-wide instant communication systems, intolerable burdens of taxation, and endemic inflation. John and Jane Loudon worked together on the *Encylopaedia of Cottage, Farm, and Villa Architecture* (1833): with its numerous illustrations (many by E.B.*Lamb) it played an important part in the formation of *Victorian suburban architectural taste as well as recording much that has proved ephemeral. The Loudons also published (1834–8) *The Architectural Magazine*, the first British periodical solely devoted to architecture. As a landscape-architect Loudon was influenced by Payne *Knight, *Repton, and Uvedale *Price, and himself advocated the *Gardenesque style in which the *Picturesque was combined with the display of trees and plants chosen for their botanical, scientific, and horticultural qualities. More than anyone he established the character of the Victorian garden, *public park, and *arboretum, and his design for the Derby Arboretum (1839–41) was a good example of his style.

His *On the Laying Out, Planting, and Managing of Cemeteries; and on the Improvement of Churchyards* (1843) is the most exhaustive book ever written on the subject, and includes detailed ideas for landscaping cemeteries that were very widely followed. Loudon's idea of the cemetery as a *landscape-garden/*arboretum, with all plants labelled, was part of his concept of mass-education and improvement of society. He produced designs for three cemeteries: Histon Road, Cambridge, Bath Abbey, and Old Southampton (all 1842–3).

J.Curl (2002a, 2004,); J.Curl (ed.) (2001); Jervis (1984); Loudon (1834, 1835, 1838, 1981); Jane Loudon (ed.) (1846); MacDougall (1980); Simo (1988) J.T (1996)

Loudon's hollow wall See BRICK.

Louis, Louis-Nicolas-Victor (1731–1800) French Neo-Classical architect, he designed (1765) several interiors in the *Louis-Quinze* style for the Royal Palace, Warsaw, after which he returned to France and built the Governor's Residence, Besançon (1770–6), and several *hôtels*. His most influential building was the *Grand Théâtre*, Bordeaux (1773–80), with a huge *colonnade of the *Corinthian *Order running the width of the *façade and a high *foyer with symmetrical *staircase, the grandest in any theatre to that date. The *auditorium was a truncated circle on plan, surrounded by a *Giant *Composite Order, and there was an elliptical concert-room over the *vestibule. There was much in the design that influenced the planning of later theatres, notably *Garnier's *Opéra*, Paris. He built several town- and country-houses, and designed the elegant colonnades and enclosing buildings for the *Palais Royal* Gardens, Paris (1780–5). His *Théâtre du Palais Royal*, later the *Comédie-Française* (1786–90—rebuilt), had wrought-iron trusses and hollow-clay-pot floors set in *concrete, an early use of fire-resistant structure.

B (1980); Ha (1952); Kalnein (1995); L & R (1984); M & Wa (1987); Pariset (1980); Taillard (1993)

Louis Quatorze Style of French *Baroque and Classical architecture of the reign of **King Louis XIV** (1643–1715), beginning in the 1660s. Its great monuments are the Churches of the *Sorbonne* and the *Val-de-Grâce*, the *Institut de France*, and the east front of the Louvre, all in Paris, and, of course, the *Château of Versailles.

Louis Quinze Style of French Classical, *Rococo and early Neo-Classical architecture of the reign of **King Louis XV** (1715–74), characterized by its charm, lightness, and elegance. Apart from several exquisite schemes of Rococo interior-decoration the characteristic buildings are the interior of the Chapel at Versailles, the *Châteaux* at Nancy and Lunéville, the *Panthéon*, Paris, and the *palace-fronted buildings of the *Place de la Concorde*, Paris.

Louis Revivals C19 and C20 revivals of all four *Louis styles.

Louis Seize Style of Neo-Classical architecture that really began during the reign of **King Louis XV**, but evolved in that of **Louis XVI** (1774–92). It was marked by simplicity, even severity, manifest in its more extreme forms in the *barrières* of *Ledoux and in the same architect's *Salines* (Salt Works) *d'Arc-et-Senans* (1775–80). It also included refined detail in schemes of interior design, much less exuberant in its use of ornament than during the previous reign.

Louis Treize Style of French-*Renaissance architecture coinciding with the reign of **King Louis XIII** (1610–43), but continuing until the 1660s, as *Le style *Louis Quartorze* did not really evolve until then. The best-known buildings of the period are the *Luxembourg* Palace and the west front of *St-Gervais*, both in Paris.

louvre, louver, luffer 1. Outlet for smoke in a roof. 2. *Lantern or *femerell over such an outlet with openings at its sides. 3. Structure on a roof for ventilation fitted with horizontal fixed lever-, *louvre-*, or *luffer-boards* sloping downwards and outwards, each board lapping over the one below, with a space between to exclude rain but allow the passage of air. 4. Any opening fitted with sloping boards or *louvres*, especially the *belfry-stage of a church-tower.

Löwitsch, Franz (1894–1946) Austrian architect/engineer, he published (1928) a paper in which he explained contemporary tendencies in architecture to open interiors of dwellings to the outside, and to relate rooms to each other. He worked (1927–9) with *Mendelsohn on the *Schocken* store, Chemnitz (built 1927–30) and other projects, and developed theories concerning the 'sensations' of space, not unconnected with the work of **Sigmund Freud** (1856–1939).

The Journal of Architecture, xvii/2 (2012), 251–72

low-side window See LYCHNOSCOPE.

Low Tech Antithesis of *High Tech, it involves the recycling of materials and components and the use of traditional construction, insulation, and natural means of heating and ventilation. Low Tech recognizes the environmental damage done by High Tech through excessive use of resources, and has been applied to the circumstances of poverty-stricken areas, where it has been termed 'alternative', 'intermediate' and even 'utopian' technology. It might involve the harnessing of solar energy or the use of human wastes to generate energy and nutrient for soil.

Ball & Cox (1982); Daniels (1997, 1998); D.Dickson (1974); Papanek (1985)

lozenge *Diamond-* or *rhomboid*-shaped equilateral parallelogram with two opposite angles more acute than the other two. Lozenges occur in *mouldings, on *diaper-patterns, in *jewelled *strapwork, in window-*lights subdivided by lead *cames (*see* LATTICE), and as small lights over *Gothic *lancet-lights in *tracery, in net-*vaults, and in many other instances. *Lozenge-fret* is *diamond-fret*, or moulding of repeated lozenges, like a double *chevron occurring in *Romanesque or *Romanesque-Revival work.

Lubetkin, Berthold Romanovitch (1901–90) Russian-born, he was the most influential

Socialist architectural immigrant to Britain in the 1930s, bringing *International Modernism with him. He studied in Russia (1920s), then in Berlin and Warsaw, and finally with *Perret in Paris (1925-7). He worked (1927-30) with **Jean Ernest Ginsberg** (1905-83) in Paris, where the apartment-block at 25 *Avenue de Versailles*, with its aggressive horizontal bands of windows, attracted hostility. Nevertheless, it was the prototype of Lubetkin's 1930s style. He settled (1931) in London, and became (1932) senior partner of *Tecton, a firm composed of former Architectural Association students. A founder-member of the *MARS Group, he was also involved with *CIAM. Tecton built the Gorilla House, London Zoo (1932-3), followed by the elegant Penguin Pool with its spiral *concrete *ramps designed with Ove *Arup (1934): other Zoo buildings at Whipsnade, Beds. (1933-6), and Dudley, Staffs. (1936-7), followed. The influential apartment-block, *Highpoint I* (1933-5), Highgate, London, again designed with Arup, was a paradigm for similar developments, followed by *Highpoint II* (1936-8), which, with elevations of patterns of brick, *glass, and *tile, suggested Tecton realized the white-painted flat surfaces of the International Modernist style were unsuited to London. The entrance-canopy seemed to be supported by a cast of one of the *caryatids from the Athenian *Erechtheion*, which some saw as a witty reference to *Classicism, but to others was either a vulgar manifestation of *Kitsch* or a betrayal of Modernism. Tecton's most celebrated building of the period was the Finsbury Health Centre, London (1935-8), an axially planned building that was widely photographed in a way that disguised its very small size. Both the Priory Green (1937-51) and Spa Green (1938-46) Estates in London were early paradigmatic slab-blocks. Lubetkin was appointed (1948) Chief Architect to Peterlee New Town Development Corporation, Co. Durham, but his ideas for high-density development were not realized and he resigned (1950).

AAQ, viii/3 (1976), 40-50; Allan (1992); Allan *et al.* (2002); Coe & Reading (1981); E (1994); *ODNB* (2004); Reading & Coe (1992); J.T (1996); vV (1993)

lucarne, luthern 1. Elliptical, rectangular, segmental-headed, or semicircular-headed window, to illuminate a volume within a pitched roof. Its front is usually built of the same material as the wall of the building's main *façade, is constructed on that wall, lines up with the *naked of the wall, so often is a strong architectural feature (Flemish *gable*), and is positioned over the *entablature. It is distinct from a *dormer, which rises from the slope of a roof and is normally of light construction. **2.** Small gabled aperture on the sloping sides of a *Gothic *spire, constructed of the same material.

Lucas, Colin Anderson (1906-84) English architect, pioneer of *reinforced-concrete construction. He formed a company to build *concrete structures in the style of *International Modernism, including Noah's House at Spade Oak Reach, Bourne End, Bucks. (1930), and Hop Field House, St Mary's Platt, Wrotham, Kent (1933—with *Connell and **Basil Ward** (1902-76)). In 1933 he joined Connell and Ward to form **Connell, Ward, & Lucas,** and brought his expertise to the creation of a whole series of International-Modernist houses (e.g. four houses, High and Over Estate, Amersham, Bucks. (1934), the Gunn House, The Ridgeway, Westbury-on-Trym, Bristol (1936), the Tarburn House, Temple Gardens, Moor Park, Herts. (1937-8), Walford House, 66 Frognal, Hampstead, London (1937) and Potcraft, Thomas House, Sutton, Surrey (1938)) unparalleled elsewhere in the country. After the 1939-45 war he worked in the Architects' Department of the LCC, heading a team of young Modernists who designed, among much else, the Alton Estate West at Roehampton, London (1951-78), where the slab-blocks are on a very small scale *superficially* resembling Le *Corbusier's *Unités d'Habitation*.

E (1994); *The Times* (29 August 1984), Obits

Lucas, Thomas Geoffrey (1872-1947) *See* LANCHESTER; MOUNTFORD.

Luckhardt Brothers Hans (1890-1954) and **Wassili** (1889-1972) worked mostly in Berlin, and were associated (1920s, 1930s) with Bruno *Taut. After the 1914-18 war they shared their theoretical, *Expressionist ideas with others through the *Gläserne Kette* circle, and practised as architects (1921-54). They designed one of the first *Modern-Movement housing estates at Dahlem-Berlin (1924), rapidly evolving an architecture of rectangular blocks with bands of horizontal windows that were such a feature of the *International-Modern style. Their houses at *Schorlemerallee*, Berlin (1925-8), and three houses in *Am Rupenhorn* (1928) were constructed with steel frames and large areas of glazing. Their ideas were publicized in *Zur neuen Wohnform* (1930). Their Berlin Pavilion at the *Constructa* exhibition, Hanover (1951), was built of steel and glass in the manner of *Mies van der Rohe. After the death of Hans, his brother continued in practice, building the Bavarian Social Welfare Administration Centre, Munich (1957), the Plant Physiology and Veterinary Medicine Institute, Free University of Berlin (1962-70), and the Deputies' Assembly Hall, Bremen (1962-9).

B.Fischer (1995); Kliemann (1973); Kulturmann (1958); Nowitzki (1991); J.T (1996)

Ludovice, João Frederico German-born as **Johann Friedrich Ludwig** (1670–1752), he brought Italian *Baroque to Portugal, and became the leading C18 architect in that country. His greatest work was the Convent Palace at Mafra, near Lisbon (1717–30). The plan resembles that of the *Escorial*, Madrid, and, of course, reconstructions of Solomon's Temple in Jerusalem, but there are echoes of Central-European designs in the scheme, notably the *monasteries of Weingarten, Einsiedeln, and Göttweig. The Church at Mafra influenced other designs in Lisbon and Rio de Janeiro. He was also responsible for the sumptuous Library at the University of Coimbra (1716–23), and for the *apse at Évora Cathedral (1716–29), both in Portugal.

Carvalho (1960–2); K & S (1959); J.T (1996)

luffer See LOUVRE.

lug 1. Projecting plate, *ear, or *tab on either side of a pipe for fixing it to a wall. **2.** *Crossette.

lumber Timber sawn and split for use.

Lumley, John (1654–1721) Northants. master-mason/surveyor, he succeeded (1697) *Dormer during the building of the great house at Burley-on-the-Hill, Rutland, for **Daniel Finch** (1647–1730—**2nd Earl of Nottingham** from 1682 and **7th Earl of Winchilsea** from 1729), largely completed by 1705. Lumley was also involved (1704–7) in Great Park House, Ampthill, Beds., and at Apethorpe, Aynho Park, and Cottesbrooke Hall, all in Northants. He prepared (1719) designs for the south range of Front Court, Emmanuel College, Cambridge (known as the Westmorland Building, worked on by Robert *Grumbold).

Co (2008); *Studies in Local History* (1955), 148ff.

lunette 1. Portion of a vertical plane beneath a segmental or semicircular *vault running into it, bounded by the intrados and springing-line. **2.** Similar-shaped aperture bounded by an arch or vault, e.g. in a wall at the end of a barrel-vault or above a *door set in an arched opening, possibly a *fanlight. **3.** *Tympanum in a segmental or semicircular *pediment. **4.** In a fortification a detached *bastion, usually shaped like a half-moon. **5.** Semicircular face of a *Romanesque *cushion-*capital formed by the shaping of its lower part to fit the circular *shaft.

Lurago Family Italian architects, active in Bohemia. **Carlo** (*c.*1618–84) designed the *monastery at Kladno (1663–8) and the *Collegium Clementinum*, Prague (1654–8). The best-known member of the family was **Anselmo Martino** (1701–65), active in Prague. The Luragos were important for the evolution of Bohemian *Baroque and *Rococo architecture.

J.T (1996)

Lurago, Giovanni (*c.*1548–71) Genoese sculptor/stone-mason, who carried out works in *Alessi's *Strada Nuova*, notably the *façade (1564–6) of the *Palazzo Grimaldi* (later *Municipio*). His brother, **Rocco** (*fl.*1558–97), has been credited with the design of the *Palazzo del Municipio* (built 1564–75), cleverly planned as a series of *terraces built on the steep hillside joined by grand staircases, but documentary evidence proves that the architects were **Domenico** (*fl.*1548–71) and **Giovanni Ponzello** (*fl.*1549–96).

J.T (1996)

Lurçat, André Émile Lucien (1894–1970) French architect, he embraced doctrines of Le *Corbusier et al., designing several *villas and studios in the approved manner, including the Huggler House, *Cité Seurat*, Paris (1925–6), the *Villa Michel*, Versailles (1926), and the *Guggenbuhl* House, Paris (1927), and was a founding-member of *CIAM. A prolific polemicist, he zealously promoted both Communism and Modernism, and at the *École Karl-Marx*, Villejuif (1931–3), attempted to associate architectural forms with the revolutionary workers' movement. Invited to Moscow (1934), he carried *Bauhaus and *CIAM theories with him, only to find they did not fit into Stalinist Socialist Realism in which powerful, stripped *Neo-Classicism loomed large. He therefore seems to have accepted that Form Followed what was Demanded during the Stalin era (1925–53), as his many buildings at St-Denis and Maubeuge (1946–50), demonstrate.

J-L.Cohen (1995); Gn (1928); Hilaire (1994); Joly (1995); Lurçat (1929, 1953–7); Piccinato (1965); Sartoris (1936); T & DC (1986); J.T (1996); vV (1993)

luthern See LUCARNE.

Lutyens, Sir Edwin Landseer (1869–1944) English architect held by some as the greatest since *Wren. He began his career in the office of *George and *Peto, where he met Herbert *Baker. He set up his own practice (1889), and designed the house, gardens, and stables at Crooksbury, Surrey, influenced by works of George, Norman *Shaw, and Philip *Webb. Indeed, his early houses were pleasant *Arts-and-Crafts buildings incorporating Surrey *vernacular elements, e.g. steeply pitched tiled roofs, tall brick chimneys, and *casement-windows with *leaded *lights, but he began to achieve real distinction shortly after he met and began to collaborate with *Jekyll, the artist and gardener, who was to work with him on the design of many gardens over the next two decades. She commissioned Munstead Wood, Munstead, Surrey (1896–9), where Lutyens's use of finely crafted traditional building-materials and the subtle relationship between house and garden demonstrate a new sensitivity prompted by her *Ruskin-inspired beliefs. Among his best houses of the late-Victorian period are Fulbrook, near Elstead (1897-9), Orchards, Munstead, near Godalming (1897-9), both in Surrey, and Roseneath, Dumbartonshire, Scotland (1898). At *Les Bois des Moutiers*, Varengeville-sur-Mer, France (1897-8), certain elements, such as the tall windows, pre-empted some of *Mackintosh's work, notably the Library windows at the Glasgow School of Art (1907-9).

With Tigbourne Court, Witley, Surrey (1899-1901), a new theme of Classically composed formal symmetry began to emerge. He again used vernacular motifs at Deanery Garden, Sonning, Berks. (1899-1902), but the prominent axes connecting elements inside and outside the building had a similarity to ideas then being pursued by F.L.L.*Wright. For the same client, **Edward Burgess Hudson** (1854-1936), founder (1897) of *Country Life*, Lutyens reconstructed and re-worked Lindisfarne Castle, Holy Island, Northum. (1903-4). From around this time his work began to draw on a wider range of styles. At Little Thakeham, Sussex (1902), for example, the exterior continued the vernacular late-*Tudor manner, but the interior, with its double-height hall and stair, contains Classical Mannerist elements. Classical *pilasters graced Homewood, Knebworth, Herts. (1901), and aspects of *Mannerism were explored at Overstrand Hall, Cromer, Norfolk (1899-1901).

Then, with Heathcote, Ilkley, Yorks. (1906), came a change of direction. The house is a *palazzo*, with the *Doric *Order as used by *Sanmichele at the *Porta Palio*, Verona (c.1545), but Lutyens made the *antae* of the Order disappear into the walls, re-emerging only as *base and *capital (a device (which infuriated *Pevsner) also used with *pilasters on many of his buildings, including the Midland Bank, Poultry, London (1924-39)). Heathcote marked the period when Lutyens was fired with enthusiasm for what he called the 'big game, the high game', of Classical architecture. He employed a *William-and-Mary style at Folly Farm, Sulhampstead, Berks. (1906), while Nashdom, Taplow, Bucks. (1905-8), was a vast pile in the early *Neo-Georgian style, and William-and-Mary was used with great sensitivity at The Salutation, Sandwich, Kent (1911), one of his most serene creations. Castle Drogo, Drewsteignton, Devon (1910-32), however, is an allusion to medieval domestic architecture, built of granite, with mullioned and transomed windows and powerfully composed interiors and stairs. For Hudson's *Country Life* offices at Tavistock Street, Covent Garden, London (1904), Lutyens drew on Wren's work at Hampton Court Palace for the *façade, and at Hampstead *Garden Suburb, London (1908-10), he designed the formal centre with two Churches, the Institute, and surrounding houses.

In 1912 Lutyens was appointed architect for the planning of New Delhi, India, and was joined by Baker, who was to design several of the buildings there. Together they created a magnificent *Beaux-Arts*-inspired work of civic design centred on the huge Viceroy's House by Lutyens (1912-31): the latter, with its Private and State Rooms, planned with unerring skill, is an eloquent testament to Lutyens's greatness. Certain Indian architectural elements were incorporated, such as the *chatris and *chujjah; the *dome was derived from a *stupa; and Lutyens invented a 'Delhi Order', a version of Roman Doric of different heights, the capitals all at one level, but the bases not. The gardens, too, were an ingenious synthesis of Eastern and Western themes.

Lutyens became one of the chief architects (with Baker, Reginald *Blomfield, and *Holden) to the Imperial War Graves Commission (from 1917). He designed many of the Cemeteries, including that at Étaples, France (1923-4), with twin arched *pavilions carrying stone sculptured military standards and *cenotaphs on high *catafalques. He was also responsible for the Cenotaph, Whitehall, London (1919-20—a tall *podium with subtle *entasis carrying a tomb-chest); for the Stone of Remembrance to be erected in the War Cemeteries; and for Memorials to the Missing, including that to the Missing of the Somme, at Thiepval (1927-32), a metamorphosis of the *triumphal arch with its subordinate sides also triumphal arches.

During the 1920s Lutyens's practice changed direction towards commercial buildings. His works included the Midland Bank, Piccadilly, London (1921-5); Britannic House, Finsbury Circus, London (1920-4); the Midland Bank, Manchester (late 1920s); and Offices in Pall Mall, London (1929). For the British Embassy, Washington, DC (1927-8), he employed an American *Colonial-*Georgian style, and designed subtly detailed buildings at Magdalene College, Cambridge (1928-32), and Campion Hall, Oxford (1935-42). His later years were devoted to the design of the RC Cathedral, Liverpool (from 1929), to be a huge building based on similar ideas to those of the Thiepval Memorial, the whole composition crowned by an enormous dome larger than that of *San Pietro*, Rome. Only part of the *crypt was built (1933-41), but the *Sublime dark-brick vaults, inventive Orders, and Mannerist details (including a key-stone 'bending' a *transome) are impressive. Lutyens's greatest design was abandoned after the 1939-45 war, and *Gibberd's hesitantly-detailed circular structure was erected instead, uneasily perched on its *podium. Lutyens also designed the Beatty and Jellicoe Memorial Fountains, Trafalgar Square, London (1937-9), and the Irish National War Memorial, Phoenix Park, Dublin (1930).

After his death Lutyens's reputation declined with the rise of *International Modernism, but began to revive after major exhibitions in NYC (1978) and London (1981).

Amery *et al.* (1982); *AR,* clxx/1077 (Nov. 1981), 311–18; J.Brown (1982, 1996); A.S.J.Butler (1950); Gradidge (1980, 1981); Hussey (1989); Inskip (1979); Lutyens (1991); P (1982); Ridley (2002); Stamp (1976, 1977, 2001); Stamp & Hopkins (eds) (2002); J.T (1996); Weaver (1981); Wilhide (2000)

Luzarches, Robert de (*fl.c.*1220–40) Master-mason, presumably architect, of Amiens Cathedral from 1220. He started the *nave, and was succeeded (*c.*1235) by **Thomas de Cormont**, who designed the west front and upper parts of the nave. He, in turn, was succeeded by his son, **Regnault de Cormont** (master-mason *c.*1240–88), who was responsible for the *choir above the *tribune, crossing-vault, and *transept elevations, all in the *Rayonnant style of *Gothic.

Branner (1965); S (1901–2)

L'vov, Nikolay Aleksandrovich (1751–1804) Russian architect, he designed the Neva Gate, Peter and Paul Fortress, St Petersburg (1780–7); the Cathedral, Mogilyov (1780–98); and the church in the monastery of Sts Boris and Gleb, Torzhok (1785–96), all monumental and spare, heralding C19 *Neo-Classicism. Other works include the Post Office, St Petersburg (1782–9); the Church of the Blessed Mother of God's Entry into the Shrine, Vvedenskoye; the mansion and outbuildings of the Glebov Estate, Znamenskoye-Rayok; and numerous *fabriques in parks. He published a translation of the first book of *Palladio's treatises (1798), though he was selective about adopting *Palladianism to Russian conditions.

D.Shv (2007); J.T (1996)

lych-gate Gateway, usually protected by a wide spreading pitched roof, sited at the main entrance to a burial-ground. It was customary for bearers carrying the coffin to rest beneath the gate while awaiting the officiating clergy.

lychnoscope *Leper's squint, low-side window, or offertory-window*: aperture set low in the south side of a *chancel-wall of a church near its west end, or sometimes on both sides of the chancel, or even occasionally in an *aisle-wall. Lychnoscopes are found in a great variety of shape and form, but there is no evidence that any were ever glazed. Instead, they were *shuttered from within and often protected by an iron grille without. The *cill of the opening on the inside was sometimes adapted as a seat (e.g. at Elsfield, Oxon.). They very often commanded a view of a *chantry-altar. Various explanations have been given as to the use of a lychnoscope: hearing confessions and

giving Communion to lepers or other persons not permitted for whatever reason to enter the church; distributing alms; for sounding a bell during the Manifestation of the Host; and even for ventilation.

Lyming *See* LEMYINGE.

Lynch-Robinson, Henry (1920–84) Ulster architect, the most controversial of those who brought *Modernism to the Province after the 1939–45 war. Among his early houses, 110 Malone Road, Belfast (1949), and his own single-storey house by the shore of Lough Neagh (1952) may be cited. For a brief period he was in partnership with *McKinstry, with whom he designed Greenwood School, Upper Newtownards Road, Belfast (1954–7). He was appointed local adviser on Production and Design during *Festival of Britain Year (1951), and his office designed the Farmhouse of the Future (on stilts) at the Farm and Factory Exhibition. He designed several fire-stations, e.g. the headquarters of the Northern Ireland Fire Authority, Lisburn, Co. Antrim. Much of his *œuvre* proved ephemeral, especially lounge-bars and cafés (e.g. *Susan's,* a typically 1950s ensemble in Howard Street, Belfast). He was in charge of hospital design in Ghana (1966–early 1970s), but contracted polyneuritis and never walked again.

McK; pk

Lynn, Jack Basil (1926–2013) English Modernist architect, he worked under **John Lewis Womersley** (1910–89) in Sheffield Architects' Department, designing (with **Ivor Smith**) the *Corbusier-inspired Park Hill Estate, a huge development rapturously received by critics (notably *Banham) when completed (1961). With its 'streets-in-the-sky' and other features, it rapidly degenerated, exemplifying for many the failure of both an architectural and social experiment, but from 2008 it was completely re-vamped for more affluent inhabitants than those originally intended. Influenced by the *Smithsons, Lynn went on to produce the master-plan for the University of Newcastle upon Tyne (1966).

The Times (7 Nov. 2013), Obits.

Lynn, William Henry (1829–1915) Irish architect, apprenticed (1846) to *Lanyon in Belfast, he became (1854–72) the latter's partner. The charming Banks at Newtownards, Co. Down, and Dungannon, Co. Tyrone (both 1855), may be cited as two of the earliest examples of the *Venetian-*Gothic style in Ireland, and indeed many of the Italian-inspired buildings in Belfast that originated in the office of **Lanyon & Lynn** and **Lanyon, Lynn, & Lanyon** owed much to his skills (*see* LANYON). Among his works with Lanyon the Church of St Andrew, Dublin (1860), the delightful *Hiberno-Romanesque Church of St Patrick, Jordanstown, Co. Antrim (1865-8—complete with round tower), and Chester Town Hall, Ches. (1863-9), should be mentioned. Probably his finest design on his own account was the *First-Pointed Carlisle Memorial Methodist Church, Carlisle Circus, Belfast (1872-5—in 2014 derelict). He was also responsible for the Central Library (1883-8—Classical), the Bank Buildings (1895-1900—Classical), and Campbell College (1891-4—*Tudor Gothic), all in Belfast, and designed the Town Halls in Paisley, Scotland (1875-82), and Barrow-in-Furness, North Lancs. (1882-7—Gothic), as well as the tactful extension (1891-5) to the *Italianate Harbour Office, Belfast. He continued the work of construction at St Anne's Cathedral, Belfast, after *Drew's death, designing the beautiful apsidal *baptistery (1915-24).

Brett (1967); D.Evans & Larmour (1995); Larmour (1987); *P:JRSUA*, li/6 (July/Aug. 1994), 35–6; *QBIGS*, xvii/1–2 (Jan/June 1974), 25–30; J.T (1996)

Lyons, Eric Alfred (1912-80) English *Modern-Movement architect, he worked with other professionals (including *Fry and *Gropius) before establishing (1938) an office with **Geoffrey Paulson Townsend** (1911-2002). After the 1939-45 war, Lyons re-formed (1948) his practice with Townsend, and designed Oaklands, a block of flats in Twickenham, Middlesex, the first of around 60 speculative housing-developments set in fine landscaping. As the practice evolved, Townsend acted as developer, and the partnership became **SPAN Ltd.** Parkleys, Ham Common, London (completed 1956), consolidated Lyons's standing, and in the following year the first of nineteen SPAN schemes in the Blackheath area was completed. A local builder, **Lesley Bilsby,** joined SPAN at that time, and the firm was further strengthened when *Cunningham joined it (1955) as landscape architect, becoming a partner in 1962. Integrated approaches to architecture and landscape were apparent at Templemere, Weybridge, Surrey (1964-5), and the largest SPAN work was a whole village at New Ash Green, Kent (from 1966). Lyons collaborated with *Cadbury-Brown for the World's End Estate in Chelsea (completed 1977). After Lyons died, Cunningham oversaw the completion (1984) of the last SPAN project, Mallard Place, Twickenham.

E (1994); *ODNB* (2004); *The Times* (2 Oct. 2002, 31, and 29 March 2007,79)

M

Macartney, Sir Mervyn Edmund (1853–1932) London-born of a Co. Armagh, Ireland, family, pupil of Norman *Shaw, he was a founder of the *Art-Workers' Guild. He began practice (1882), his work showing Shaw's influence with a strong dash of late-C17 and early-C18 architectural elements. Among his buildings, 169 Queen's Gate (1899), 1–6 Egerton Place (1893), and the Public Library, Essex Road, Islington (1916), all in London, may be mentioned, but he was better known for his publications, including *The Practical Exemplar of Architecture* (1908–27) and (with *Belcher) *Later Renaissance Architecture in England* (1898–1901), which celebrated the riches of English architecture in the age of *Wren. He was Editor of *AR* (1905–20), and, as Surveyor to St Paul's Cathedral, London, carried out important works of *conservation on Wren's building (1906–31), including the strengthening of the *dome.

P.Davey (1980); A.S.Gray (1985); My (1907–27, 1908); My & Belcher (1901); Ward (1998)

McCarthy, James Joseph (1817–82) Called the 'Irish Pugin', he flourished during the impressive building-programme of the Irish RC Church after 'Catholic Emancipation' (1829), designing in a *First- and *Second-Pointed style, following the leads of Pugin and English Ecclesiologists. He may have been in England during the early 1840s, but work started (1846) on his Church of St Kevin, Glendalough, Co. Wicklow: in a severe First-Pointed style, it was an early attempt by a native-born Irish architect to build a church on *Ecclesiological principles. McCarthy was one of the three joint-secretaries of the Irish Ecclesiological Society (founded 1849), and published *Suggestions on the Arrangement and Characteristics of Parish Churches* (1851). Appointed (1853) Architect to Armagh RC Cathedral in succession to *Duff, he abandoned Duff's *Perp. for Second Pointed in accordance with Ecclesiological preferences (even though the building was well advanced), added the two western *steeples, omitted the *crossing-tower, and increased the pitch of the roof. In the process he changed the character from English to French Gothic, reflecting his growing Irish Nationalism by adopting non-English exemplars, even though the *stylistically* earlier* work on top of *stylistically later* architecture is visually absurd, and the realized building has a certain hardness that is unattractive. He designed many churches in Dublin (St Saviour's, Dominic Street, is the finest) and Co. Kerry, drawing on the great wealth of Irish ecclesiastical remains for certain elements. Occasionally he made forays into *Romanesque, as at the chapel, Glasnevin Cemetery, Dublin (finished 1878), and the Cathedral of the Assumption, Thurles, Co. Tipperary (1865–72), but most of his work is assured Continental Gothic, as at St Patrick's, Dungannon, Co. Tyrone (1870–6), the Chapel, Maynooth College, Co. Kildare (1875–1903), and St Macartan's Cathedral, Monaghan (1861–92).

DIB (2009); Sheehy (1977); J.T (1996)

McCormick, William (Liam) Henry Dunlevy (1916–96) Irish architect, he made his reputation with a series of *Modernist churches for the RC Church, including the circular St Aengus, Burt (1964–7), the fan-shaped St Michael, Creeslough (1970–1), both in Co. Donegal, the circular St Patrick, Clogher, Co. Tyrone (1979), and the rectangularly planned St Conal, Glenties, Co. Donegal (1974–5).

DIB (2009); *IA*, lxxxiii (Mar./Apr. 1991), 60–4; *P:JRSUA*, v/2 (Nov./Dec. 1996), 30–43

McCoy, Esther (1904–89) American self-taught architectural historian/critic, she worked in *Schindler's office, which gave her architectural insights, before publishing *Five California Architects* and *Richard Neutra* (1960), which established her name, encouraging her to produce further work on the California *avant-garde* from the early C20. She was also a novelist, and contributed hundreds of articles to various books, journals, and exhibition catalogues, all demonstrating her mastery of taut prose. She was successful in relating social history to architecture, and argued that the *Modern Movement developed in America at least as early as in Europe. In her work on Californian architecture she showed how important modest architecture can be.

McCoy (1960, 1962, 1968, 1974, 1975, 1977, 1979, 1983, 1990); McCoy & Goldstein (1982); McCoy & Smith (1988); *PA*, lxxi/2 (Feb. 1990), 118–19; E.Smith (2002)

MacDougall, Elisabeth (*née* **Blair**) (1925-2003) American architectural and landscape-historian. With *Coffin she helped to transform garden-history into an academic discipline, esp. with her work on C16 and 17 French and Italian gardens. Her mentors included **John P. Coolidge** (1913-93—whose influence was clear in her work on Roman *villa-gardens, esp. in relation to the role of the C16 Roman patriciate). As first director of studies in landscape architecture at Dumbarton Oaks (1972-88) she made an outstanding contribution. She wrote perceptively about *Loudon.

JSAH, lxiii/2 (June 2004), 248-54; MacDougall (1980, 1986); MacDougall & Hazlehurst (eds) (1974); MacDougall & Ettinghausen (eds) (1976)

McGrath, Raymond Herbert (1903-77) Australian architect, he designed the *Modernist interior of Fischer's Restaurant, New Bond Street, London (1932), and, with *Chermayeff and *Coates, the interiors of BBC Broadcasting House, London. He published *Twentieth Century Houses* (1934—which promoted *International Modernism for domestic architecture), and, with **Albert Childerstone Frost**, *Glass in Architecture and Decoration* (1937). His best houses are St Anne's Hill, Chertsey, Surrey, a *reinforced-concrete building (1937-8), and Carrygate, Galby, Leics. (1938-42). In 1940 he joined the Office of Public Works, Dublin, becoming Principal Architect (1948-68), after which he returned to private practice. He designed a house, St Anne's, Carrickmines, Co. Dublin (1974), and the new Headquarters of the Royal Hibernian Academy, Dublin (1979).

AR, clxii/695 (July 1977), 58-64; *Architecture Australia*, lxvii (May 1978) 72; *DIB* (2009); McGrath (1934); McGrath & Frost (1937); O'Donovan (1995)

McHarg, Ian Lennox (1920-2001) Scots-born American landscape architect, he founded (1963) **Wallace, McHarg, Roberts, & Todd** in Philadelphia, PA. Although involved mostly in urban design (e.g. Inner Harbor and Municipal Center, Baltimore, MD, and the *New Town, Woodlands, Houston, TX (1970-4)), McHarg was an important influence on the climate of awareness that recognized the damage being done to the environment by short-sighted economic and political considerations. Advocating active cooperation with Nature and a respect for ecology, his work influenced *Green or *Sustainable architecture.

Duhl (eds) (1963); *JRSA*, cxxviii (Feb. 1980), 132-143; McHarg (1969, 1971); W & S (1994)

machicolation 1. Opening between *corbels carrying a *parapet that is set in front of the *naked of a fortified wall or tower to enable missiles to be dropped on any attacker. **2.** Structure containing a range of such openings.

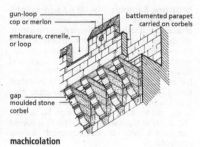

machicolation

Machin, Francis (1949-2007) English architect, son of the sculptor, **Arnold Machin** (1911-99), he worked first with R.*Seifert, but his interests led him to design *grottoes and gardens: with his father he created the gardens at Offley Rock and Garmelow Farm (both Staffs.). He is best known for the **Machin Conservatories** (built of aluminium, with an *ogee *section), and created a *gazebo with a tapering roof-structure. A keen conservationist, he preserved and adapted old buildings and derelict landscapes, demonstrating how they could be rescued and used. He designed the first of the Battersea Riverside conversions at Ransome's Dock, and one of the earliest warehouse transformations at Denmark House, Smithfield, London.

The Times (27 April 2007), 76

Machine Aesthetic Architecture *suggesting* something machine-made, acknowledging industrialization, mass-production, and engineering, or that copied elements of metal structures (ships, aeroplanes, motor-cars, etc.) in an eclectic fashion, more a matter of arriving at an *appearance* than of actually *being* what it seemed, a fact that contradicted demands for 'honesty' and 'truth' in architecture, and denied the logic of structural principles (e.g. *International Modernism favoured smooth wall-finishes and long strips of metal-framed windows suggested by ocean-going liners of the *Titanic* vintage, but the walls were often of *rendered brickwork).

AR, lxxviii (Dec. 1935), 211-18; R.Ba (1960); Gn (1969); P.Johnson (1969); Sparke (ed.) (1981); J.T (1996); R.Wilson *et al.* (1986)

Machuca, Pedro (*c*.1485-1550) Spanish architect, he designed the Palace of **Emperor Charles V** (*r*.1519-55, d.1558) in the Alhambra, Granada (1527-68), in an accomplished Italian-*Renaissance style (revised by *Herrera) worthy of *Raphael or *Bramante. The circular colonnaded *court (begun 1540) is especially fine.

CG (1953); Rosenthal (1985); J.T (1996)

McIntire, Samuel (1757–1811) American architect/builder, he worked in and near Salem, MA, producing a number of well-mannered houses in an elegant late-*Georgian style, mostly of three storeys. His sources appear to have been pattern-books, including those of *Langley and *Ware, and he was familiar with *Palladianism, for he used that style at the Peirce-Nichols House (1782). The influence of *Bulfinch, from whose work he seems to have been introduced to the *Adam style, was evident in his designs (e.g. the John Gardner House (1804–5), a refined composition with an entrance-porch bowing outwards).

Kimball (1966a); Labaree (ed.) (1957); J.T (1996); W & K (1983)

Mackenzie, Alexander Marshall (1848–1933) Scots architect, he practised with **James Matthews** (1820–98) in Aberdeen from 1877, designing Greyfriars Church (1906) and the Marischal College (1904–6) in that city, the latter an extraordinarily hard essay in *Perp., all in granite. Joined (1903) by his Paris-trained son, **Alexander George Robertson Mackenzie** (1879–1963), they designed the fine *Beaux-Arts Classical Waldorf Hotel (1906–7) and Australia House (1913–18), Aldwych, London. The latter was in the Imperial-Classical style that was widely used throughout the Empire, notably by *Palmer & Turner.

DSA (2013); A.Ś.Gray (1985); J.T (1996)

McKim, Mead, & White American architectural partnership, the most distinguished of its time, based in NYC. **Charles Follen McKim** (1847–1909), **William Rutherford Mead** (1846–1928), and **Stanford White** (1853–1906) were in the vanguard of a return to *Classicism in the USA. McKim and White had worked in *Richardson's office, and McKim had attended the *École des *Beaux-Arts, Paris. At first the firm's work drew on American-*Colonial architecture and then Italian High-*Renaissance was added to the palette of styles, as was evidenced by the six houses for **Henry Villard** (1835–1900), Madison Avenue, NYC (1882–5). However, White's taste for the *Picturesque and for variety in colour and texture led to the creation of many buildings in the *Shingle style, partly derived from American-Colonial prototypes, and influenced by the English *Domestic Revival of the *Arts-and-Crafts movement, with a dash of rural French medieval buildings. The study of Renaissance buildings led to geometries becoming more formal, as in the beautiful **William G.Low** House, Bristol, RI (1886–7—demolished 1962).

Then came the Boston Public Library (1887–8), with a *façade treatment derived from *Labrouste's *Bibliothèque Ste-Geneviève*, Paris, but given a more Italo-Roman flavour. This celebrated design made the firm's reputation. Madison Square Garden, NYC (1887–91—demolished), had pronounced Sevillian notes in its tall tower, but the Rhode Island State Capitol, Providence (1891–1903), was influenced by the Federal Capitol in Washington, DC, with a *Wrenaissance *dome. At Columbia University, NYC (1893–4), both the New Sorbonne in Paris and *Jefferson's University of Virginia, Charlottesville, were precedents for the plan, and the Library Building, with its *Pantheon-dome and long *portico of *Ionic columns, entered the language of *Neo-Classicism. This growing interest in Antiquity reached its apogee in the enormous and brilliant Pennsylvania Station, NYC (1902–11—destroyed), with gigantic hall based on the *thermae of **Caracalla** (r.212–217), Rome. It not only worked extremely well, but was the most *Sublime work of architecture in the USA—its destruction was a grievous loss, as was the demolition of the perfect Madison Square Presbyterian Church, NYC (1904–6), another variant on the Pantheon theme, but with *polychrome enrichment. The *Georgian-Revival Symphony Hall, Boston (1892–1901), was much more subdued, but the series of great works of the three decades 1880–1910 (including the very fine J.Pierpont Morgan Library, NYC (1902–7)) put McKim, Mead, & White in the forefront of world architects of their time.

Stanford White was shot dead (1906) in public in Madison Square Garden by a jealous rival in amorous matters: the ensuing publicity did enormous damage. However, the firm itself survived well into the second half of C20, and its achievements were celebrated in *A Monograph of the Works of McKim, Mead, & White, 1879–1915* (1915 and 1973).

ARe, xx (1906), 153–246; P.Baker (1989); C.Baldwin (1976); Broderick (2010); Hi (1977); Lessard (1997); P (1982); Reilly (1972); A.Roth (ed.) (1973, 1983); J.T (1996); S.White (1998); R.G.Wilson (1983); Wo (1988)

McKinstry, Robert James (1925–2012) Ulster architect, he worked (1950s) with *Lynch-Robinson before establishing (1956) his own Belfast practice. Among his works may be cited Ashfield Girls' (1973) and Boys' (1975) Secondary Schools, extensions to Portora Royal School, Enniskillen (1964–72), Regional Headquarters for the Open University, University Road, and Headquarters for the Royal Society of Ulster Architects at 2 Mount Charles, Belfast (1976 and 1982 respectively—replica replacements of Grecian buildings damaged by terrorist bombs), and the new Council Chamber, Canada Room, and Extra Mural Department in the centre section of the *Lanyon Building, The Queen's University of Belfast (1986). Best-known for his restoration-work (he was Consultant Architect to The National

Trust (1971–83)), his most important works in the field were the restoration and upgrading of *Matcham's Grand Opera House, Belfast (1980—with Tiepoloesque ceiling by his wife, **Cherith Rosalind,** née **Boyd** (1928–2004)), **E. & J.Byrne's** rumbustious Crown Liquor Saloon, Belfast (1983), his own house at Chrome Hill, Lambeg, Co. Down (from 1967), Ardress House, Co. Armagh (1962—for The National Trust), the Temple, Castleward, Co. Down (1971), and the total rebuilding of Malone House, Belfast (1983). He completed the north *transept of St Anne's Cathedral, Belfast (1981).

CL, cxcv/37 (13 September 2001), 168–173; McK; pk

Mackintosh, Charles Rennie (1868–1928) Scots architect/interior designer/watercolourist, he worked mostly in and around Glasgow. He joined (1889) *Honeyman & *Keppie and studied at the Glasgow School of Art before travelling in Italy (1891), and in the following year, with **Margaret** (1865–1933) and **Frances** (1874–1921) **Macdonald** and **Herbert J.McNair** (1868–1955), began to produce watercolours, posters, and artefacts. The friends became known as 'The Four', 'The Mac Group', the *Glasgow School, or the 'Spook School' (the last because of the attenuated *femme-fleur, long tendrils, *rose-balls, and other slightly sinister elements that were an integral part of their *Art-Nouveau-inspired style): they gained recognition (1897) in *The Studio,* which made their work widely known.

Mackintosh's first realized building for Honeyman & Keppie seems to have been the tower of the *Glasgow Herald* Building, Mitchell Street, Glasgow (1893). This was followed by Queen Margaret's Medical College (1894–6) and the Martyrs' Public School (1895), both traditionally constructed, but in a free style. Mackintosh began to draw on Scottish *vernacular buildings for his inspiration, often looking to medieval towerhouses and fortified dwellings (which he misnamed *Scottish Baronial) for his themes. His sources were not exclusively Scottish, however, and in later buildings his *eclecticism ranged widely: in essence, Mackintosh was an *Arts-and-Crafts designer who used Art-Nouveau decorative devices, but always employed *traditional* forms of Scottish construction.

Honeyman & Keppie won (1896) the competition for the new Glasgow School of Art, but the design was Mackintosh's. The plan worked well, and the studios were lit by large north-facing windows, while the centrepiece had vernacular canted bay-windows derived from Dorset (or perhaps from *Voysey's work), Art-Nouveau elements, and an arched feature paraphrasing certain English *Wrenaissance motifs. When the School was being erected (1897–9), Mackintosh was commissioned to design fittings and

decorations for Miss Cranston's Tea Rooms, and this was followed by Queen's Cross Church, Garscube Road (1897–1900), in a free Arts-and-Crafts *Gothic style with touches of Art Nouveau. His first important house was Windy Hill, Kilmacolm, Renfrewshire (1899–1902), and some of his furniture-designs were published in *Dekorative Kunst* (1898, 1899). Mackintosh married (1900) Margaret Macdonald, and the couple decorated their apartment at 120 Mains (now Blythswood) Street, Glasgow, with white, elegant furniture and all fittings designed by themselves (now in the Hunterian Art Gallery, University of Glasgow). Together, they participated in the *Sezession Exhibition, Vienna, where their work was well received, and they became friendly with *Hoffmann and others. The *Sezession* journal, *Ver Sacrum,* publicized (1901) Glasgow and Mackintosh, and the latter won a special prize for his *Haus eines Kunstfreundes* in a competition organized (1900) by *Koch, publisher of *Zeitschrift für Innen-Dekoration*: this project (to which Margaret Macdonald contributed) was published (1902), and built at Bellahouston Park, Glasgow, in the 1980s and 1990s.

Having worked on the Scottish section at the International Exhibition of Decorative Art, Turin (1902), Mackintosh was commissioned to design The Hill House, Helensburgh, probably his finest achievement in domestic architecture. The exterior is completely harled (finished with rough *render), and beautiful interiors have panelled or stencilled walls: the white bedroom is one of Mackintosh's most felicitous creations. Then came the Willow Tea Rooms of Miss Cranston, the first of which (1903–19) was in Sauchiehall Street, Glasgow. Mackintosh's domestic work was featured in *Muthesius's *Das Englische Haus* (1904–5, 1908–11), while Muthesius and other commentators wrote up Mackintosh's designs in *Deutsche Kunst und Dekoration* and *Dekorative Kunst,* all of which made his name and the Glasgow School widely known.

Perhaps influenced by the Germans and Austrians, Mackintosh began to adopt a more formal, angular geometry *c.*1904, gradually discarding the curving lines of Art Nouveau. For example, his Scotland Street School, Glasgow (1904), was influenced by castle architecture, and is a symmetrical building with two conical-roofed staircase-towers flanking the stone front: the traditional arrangement is reversed, however, for the *curtain-wall is solid, pierced by windows, and the towers are glazed. In 1906 it was decided to complete the Glasgow School of Art, and Mackintosh revised the original design for the west end, with tall vertical *oriel windows perhaps suggested by *Lutyens's *Les-Bois-des-Moutiers* (1898), while on the south side the windows were recessed, and a *cantilevered *conservatory was introduced, suggested, no doubt, by Scots *bartisans. This western extension contains Mackintosh's library, badly damaged by fire, where his angular style is eloquently exhibited in the galleried timber construction, suggesting an almost Japanese economy of means.

Mackintosh became a partner in the firm (probably 1902), although this was not made public until 1904 when **Honeyman, Keppie, & Mackintosh** was established, but by 1909 his career as an architect was foundering, not least because his criticism of the profession alienated his colleagues. He was also suspect among English Arts-and-Crafts architects because his work was tainted with 'decadent' Art Nouveau, and because he does not appear to have been overly concerned with 'honesty' or soundness in construction, and so offended purists who held to the views promoted by A.W.N.*Pugin, William *Morris, and others. He left the practice (1913), and after a period in Walberswick, Suffolk (1914–15), the Mackintoshes settled in Chelsea, London.

'CRM' was commissioned (1916) by **Wenman Joseph Bassett-Lowke** (1877–1953) to alter and furnish his house at 78 Derngate, Northampton: he introduced a repeated triangular motif suggested by trends in Viennese design. The guest-bedroom (c.1919—now in the Hunterian Art Gallery, Glasgow), with its startling linear, striped, and black-white-ultramarine colour-scheme, was illustrated in *The Ideal Home* (1920), and had affinities with designs by *Loos and *Behrens. Some of the triangular stencilled patterns for Derngate may have been suggested by F.L.L. *Wright's Dana House, Springfield, IL (1903), published in Berlin (1911). From 1914 Mackintosh had been producing exquisite drawings and watercolours, and from 1923 concentrated on painting.

He has been proclaimed since the 1930s as a kind of proto-Modernist, but this does not stand up to serious examination: he had far more in common with *fin-de-siècle *Jugendstil and the Sezessionists in Vienna, Berlin, and Munich, and it was there that his work was best appreciated.

Billcliffe (1977); J.Cooper (ed.) (1984); A.Crawford (1995); F.Davidson (1998); *DSA* (1913); H.Ferguson (1995); Fiell (1995); Howarth (1977); Kaplan (ed.) (1996); Macaulay (1993); J.McKean (1999, 2000, 2002); McLeod (1983); Nuttgens (ed.) (1988); P (1982); P.R (1995); Steele (ed.) (1994); J.T (1996); vV (1993); Wilhide (1995); A.Young (1968)

Mackmurdo, Arthur Heygate (1851–1942) London-born architect, his first work was influenced by Norman *Shaw, but he also drew on Italian-*Renaissance, *Queen-Anne, and *Wrenaissance styles. He founded (1882) the **Century Guild**, based on *Arts-and-Crafts principles, which made well-designed artefacts, including

furniture. These were featured in *The Hobby Horse* from 1884, which influenced *Voysey and *Mackintosh. In some of his designs, notably the title-page of Wren's *City Churches* (1883), early *Art-Nouveau forms were overt. His buildings included 6 (1874–6—demolished) and 8 (1883) Private Road, Enfield, 16 Redington Road, Hampstead (1889), 12 Hans Road, Chelsea (1894), 25 Cadogan Gardens, Chelsea (1893–4), and 109–13 Charterhouse Street (1900), all in London.

Lambourne (1980); Pe (1968); P & R (1973); Stansky (1996)

MacLaren, James Marjoribanks (1853–90) Scots *Arts-and-Crafts architect, he established (1886) a London practice with **Richard Coad** (1825–1900), following a short stay in E.W.*Godwin's office. After a new wing for Stirling High School, Scotland (1887–8), MacLaren designed several farm-buildings and cottages at Fortingall, Perthshire (1889–90—including the tenant-farmer's house), and Aberfeldy Town Hall, in all of which the Scottish-*vernacular roots of the designs were clear, providing precedents for *Mackintosh's domestic work. He designed some original houses, including 10–12 Palace Court, Bayswater, London (1889–90), and Heatherwood, Crawley Down, Sussex (1890–1). W.N.*Dunn and **Robert Watson** (1865–1916) continued the practice as **Dunn & Watson**, later taking W.Curtis *Green into partnership (1900).

Calder (2003); D & M (1985); *DSA* (1913); Se (1977); Se (ed.) (1975)

Maclure, Samuel (1860–1929) Canadian architect, he designed a large number of interesting houses in the *Shingle style in and around Victoria, British Columbia, from 1890 until his death. He later favoured Tudoresque *Arts-and-Crafts detailing, and the best examples that survive include the Biggerstaff-Wilson House (1905–6), with its natural materials, careful siting, and plan of two axes meeting in the stairway and hall. With **Cecil Croker Fox** (1879–1916), who had worked in *Voysey's office, he designed several successful houses, including the Huntting House, Vancouver, British Columbia (1911). After the 1914–18 war the office was run by his former pupil, **Ross Anthony Lort** (1889–1968), who was influenced by the Classical work of *Lutyens. Maclure was also important for his garden and landscape design.

J.Bingham (1985); Eaton (1971); K (1994); Segger (1986); J.T (1996)

McMorran & Whitby British firm of architects (**Donald Hanks McMorran** (1904–65) and **George Frederick Whitby** (1916–73)) which produced work of real architectural distinction after the 1939–45 war. Influenced partly by Vincent

*Harris (for whom McMorran worked (1927–35)) and mostly by *Lutyens, the firm's architecture could best be described as undoctrinaire *Classicism. Good examples include Devon County Hall, Exeter (1954–63), and Shire-Hall Police-Station and Library, Bury St Edmunds, Suffolk (1957–68). Their housing-estate at Lammas Green, Sydenham Hill (1955–7), London, used traditional materials and had a village-like character totally different from that of contemporary local-authority estates elsewhere in London, while their Holloway Estate, Islington (1959–75), London, was also far more successful (both socially and architecturally) than the much-publicized *Modern-Movement developments of the time. Among McMorran & Whitby's works of the 1950s were the designs for the University of Nottingham (Cripps and Lenton Halls and the Education Block for Social Sciences), which employed a *stripped Classical manner inspired by *Soane, with a baseless *Ionic Order at the entrance to the internal courtyard, and a fine bell-tower with Lutyensian echoes over the Refectory. Other buildings include those in the City of London: the Police Station, Wood Street (1959–66), and the extension to the Central Criminal Court in the Old Bailey (1968–72). Although their work was largely ignored by the architectural press, they were masters of a progressive Classicism that is beginning to be admired.

Denison (2009); GS; pk; Stamp (1991)

Maderno, Carlo (c.1556–1629) Leading architect working in Rome from the mid-1570s, before *Bernini, *Borromini, and *Cortona developed the *Baroque style to its greatest potential. He started under D.*Fontana, his uncle, and was involved in the re-erection of the Ancient-Egyptian *obelisks at *Piazza di San Pietro* (1586), *Piazza dell'Esquilino* (1587), *Piazza di San Giovanni in Laterano* (1588), and *Piazza del Pòpolo* (1589). He worked on a number of engineering projects before designing his masterpiece, the remodelling of *Santa Susanna* on the Quirinal Hill (1593–1603), with a dramatic *façade based on that of *Il Gesù*, but with an *engaged lower *Order and *scrolls linking the narrower upper *pilaster *façade to the wider front below. Emphasis was more decisive and vertical than at *Il Gesù*. After the election of **Pope Paul V** (r.1605–21) Maderno was appointed Architect to St Peter's, where he constructed the *nave (1609–16), began work on the decorations of the *crossing, built the curving stairs leading to the *confessio, designed the façade facing the *Piazza* (its great width was occasioned by the enforced requirement to add two *campanili of which only the first two stages were built), and created the *fountain (later moved to the cross-axis of the *obelisk and duplicated with a twin by Bernini).

At the Mother-Church of the Theatines, *Sant' Andrea della Valle*, Maderno completed the nave, added the *transepts and *chancel, and constructed the distinguished and beautiful *dome with *lantern (1608–c.1628). He also designed the façade, begun in the mid-1620s, and completed (1660s) with modifications by *Rainaldi. He was responsible for the *Palazzo Mattei di Giove*, Rome (1598–1617), and the *Villa Aldobrandini*, Frascati (1603–c.1620), including the superb semicircular water-theatre featuring arched *niches with *grottoes and fountains fed by a chain of stepped *cascades at the top of which is a pair of spiral columns. One of his last works was the *Palazzo Barberini*, Rome (1626–8), completed by Bernini.

Hd (1971); P.Mu (1969, 1986); P (1982); J.T (1996); vV (1993); Waddy (1990)

Madin, John Hardcastle Dalton (1924–2012) Birmingham-born, he reshaped his native city with the zeal of the true *Modernist, determined to obliterate the past. The results included the *Birmingham Post and Mail* Tower (1961–6—prompted by *SOM's Lever House, NYC), the BBC Pebble Mill Studios (1971), and the *Brutalist Birmingham Central Library (1974—bearing a passing resemblance to an inverted *ziggurat). He was responsible for some two-thousand high-density dwellings at the Calthorpe Estate, Edgbaston (from 1957), and planned Dawley New Town in the early 1960s (which became Telford, Salop.). Other works included a building for the Engineering Employers Federation (1954–7—supposedly influenced by Le *Corbusier's *Villa Savoie*); the Birmingham Chamber of Commerce (1958–60); and Warwickshire Masonic Temple (1970). By 2005 several of his best-known buildings were partly or wholly demolished.

Clawley (2011); A.Foster (2005); *RIBAJ* (May 2012), 16; *The Times* (24 Jan. 2012), 47

madrasa, madrassa, madraseh, medresseh Islamic theological/legal place of instruction, usually with a *court with *iwan, accommodation, and study-cells. The grandest madrasas resembled four-*iwan *mosque plans, with cells on two storeys ranged around the court (e.g. *Madrasa al-Nuriya al-Kubra*, Damascus, Syria (1171–2), and the Madrasas of Ulughbeg (1417–20), Samarkand, Uzbekistan). In some cases the open court was replaced by a smaller covered, domed space (e.g. the *Inje Minare Madrasa*, Konya, Turkey (c.1260–5)), and in others they were part of much larger complexes (e.g. the *Süleymaniye Mosque*, Istanbul, Turkey (1550–7), by *Sinan). The *Madrasa Madar-I-Shah*, Isfahan, Iran (1706–14), was a late and very beautiful example of the four-*iwan* madrasa, complete with high, pointed domes, and two-storey *arcades and a garden-court crossed by axial canals (the true *paradise garden).

B & B (1994); Hillenbrand (1994); M & P (2011)

Maekawa *or* **Mayekawa, Kunio** (1905–86) Japanese architect, he worked for Le *Corbusier and *Raymond before setting up on his own (1935). He brought *International Modernism to Japan, and was a pioneer there of *reinforced-concrete construction, prompted by the ideas of *Nervi. His work was strongly modelled, including Kyoto Cultural Hall (1958–60) and Tokyo Metropolitan Festival Hall (1958–61), and influenced later generations including *Tange. Other buildings include the City Museum, Fukuoka (1979), the Prefectural Museum, Miyagi (1980), and the Concert Hall, Kunitachi College (1983).

Altherr (1968); E (1994); L (1988); J.Reynolds (2001); vV (1993)

Magot Seated obese male figure, often with crossed legs, found in *Chinoiserie decorations, also known as a *Pagod* or *Poussah*, associated with Contentment and the Chinese deity **Pu-T'ai**.

Maher, George Washington (1864–1926) American architect of the *Prairie School, influenced by the English *Arts-and-Crafts movement and by developments in Austria (e.g. *Olbrich's architecture). His work, mostly domestic (e.g. The Farson House, Oak Park, IL (1897)), was refined, well-made, and decently composed, some reminiscent of *Greene & Greene's, and some of F.L.L. *Wright's work.

H.Brooks (1972, 1984); Kaplan (1987)

Maiano Brothers C15 Florentine architects. **Giuliano da Maiano** (1432–90) designed the Chapel of *Santa Fina* in the *Collegiata*, San Gimignano (1466–8), where he was influenced by *Brunelleschi and *Michelozzo, and the *Palazzo Spannocchi*, Siena (1473–5), where the watered-down themes derived from *Alberti's *Palazzo Rucellai*, Florence. In Florence itself he probably designed the *portico of Brunelleschi's *Pazzi* Chapel (1472), and was called to Faenza (1474) where he designed the Cathedral. From 1485 he worked in Naples and built the *Porta Capuana* and the *Villa di Poggio Reale* (c.1488—destroyed), one of the most important early *Renaissance villas derived from Classical sources which later influenced *Peruzzi at the *Villa Farnesina*, Rome (1509–11).

Giuliano had two brothers, **Giovanni** (1439–78) and **Benedetto** (1442–97). The latter collaborated with Giuliano at the Gimignano Chapel, may have designed the portico of *Santa Maria delle Grazie*, Arezzo (1490–1), and was involved in the construction of the *Palazzo Strozzi*, Florence, which was mostly *Cronaca's work.

He (1996); Lamberini *et al.* (1994); Pampaloni (1963); P (1982); Quinterio (1996); vV (1993)

maidan, maydan 1. Open space in or just outside an Indian or Central Asian town, used for ceremonial occasions, parades, etc. 2. *Esplanade. 3. Market-place.

Maillart, Robert (1872–1940) Swiss engineer who evolved designs for *bridges using curved *reinforced-concrete members. He also designed columns with mushroom-shaped tops to support floor-slabs which he used in the Giesshübel Warehouse, Zürich (1910). It is for his bridges that he will be remembered, notably the Rhine, Tavanasa (1905), Valtschielbach, Donath (1925), and Salginatobel, Schiers (1930), bridges, all in Switzerland.

Abel *et al.* (eds) (1973); Bill (1969); Billington (1979, 1990, 1997); G.Collins (1973a); M & N (1987)

Maillou, *called* **Desmoulins, Jean-Baptiste** (1668–1753) French-Canadian, he became the principal architect, with the title of King's Architect of New France, working in Québec in the first half of C18. His buildings included the *Hôpital-Général*, Québec (1710–12), the *façade of *St-Laurent, Île d'Orléans* (1708), the Church and Vestry of *St-Nicolas*, Québec (c.1720), and many fortifications and other buildings.

Gowans (1955); K (1994)

maisonnette 1. Small house. 2. Part of a residential building, let separately, distinguished from an *apartment or *flat by not being all on one floor, i.e. a *duplex* arrangement.

Maitani, Lorenzo (c.1270–1330) Sienese architect, he worked under *Pisano at the Cathedral there before being called to Orvieto Cathedral (1310), where he enlarged the *transepts and designed the west front, a fine example of Italian *Gothic. He carried out other commissions, and was to all intents and purposes City Architect of Orvieto.

J.White (1987)

Majewski, Hilary (1837–92) Polish architect of most of the vast and extraordinary Poznański cotton-factory and housing complex, Łódź, Poland (from 1872), in a mixture of *Rundbogenstil and *Gothic. The entrance-gates had stunted, massive, deformed, vaguely *Tuscan columns carrying the pointed arches over which were brick *battlements and other decorations.

Ck (1996); Łoza (1954)

majolica 1. Fine Italian pottery coated with opaque white enamel ornamented with metallic colours. 2. Any kind of glazed coloured earthenware or *faïence, also called *Raffaella* ware.

Quinterio (1990)

Major, Joshua (1786–1866) English landscape-gardener, born in Owston, Yorks., on the estate for which Humphry *Repton had prepared a 'Red Book' (and where his father, **Richard Major** (1736–1809), was a labourer). He founded a nursery-garden at Knowsthorpe, Leeds, Yorks. (c.1810), and won (1845) first premium for the design of the earliest *public parks in Manchester: results were manifest in Peel, Philips, and Queen's Parks. Other works included Hanover Square, Leeds (1824), Derwent Hall, Derbys. (1833), Oakes Park, Sheffield (1834) and the People's Pleasure-Ground, Meltham, Yorks. (c.1860). He wrote several books, including The Theory and Practice of Landscape Gardening (1852), and contributed regularly to *Loudon's Gardener's Magazine, especially on garden-layouts for Victorian *villas. Aware of the controversies concerning the *Picturesque (1790s), he disagreed with Payne *Knight and Uvedale *Price, leaning more to the principles of Repton as developed by Loudon.

D.Baldwin (1987); Conway (1985, 1991); D & E (1994); B.Elliott (1986, 1986a); Major (1852); ODNB (2004); Wyborn (1994)

Maki, Fumihiko (1928–) See METABOLISM.

Makovecz, Imre (1935–2011) Hungarian architect, influenced by the work of F.L.L. *Wright and by the ideas of *Steiner. The RC Church, Paks, Hungary (1987–90), seems to grow from the earth within a huge *ogee-shaped roof pierced by pointed windows: three spires, carrying a crescent, a symbol of the sun, and a Latin cross, rise up from the almost *biomorphic form. His work drew on primitive shapes and naturally occurring elements, and included the Naturata Shop Restaurant, Überlingen, Germany (1992).

J.Cook (1996); E (1994); Dvorszky (ed.) (1991); Gáborjani (ed.) (1991); Gerle (ed.) (1996); Mr (1995); Tischhauser (2001)

Malevich, Kazimir Severinovich (1878–1935) Russian artist, a pioneer of *Suprematism, he built many architectural models (arkhitektoniki) of projects that were difficult to show graphically. He influenced El *Lissitzky, activities in the *Bauhaus, and, indirectly, aspects of *Deconstructivism.

Malevich (1959); Zhadova (1982)

mall 1. *Alley in which pall-mall (involving hitting a boxwood ball with a mallet through an iron ring) was played from C16. 2. Fashionable C18 promenade, usually lined with trees: in the USA it was a feature of most towns along the East Coast.

O'Malley (2010); Symes (2006)

Mallet-Stevens, Rob(ert) (1886–1945) French architect, he collaborated with *Bourgeois, *Chareau, and *Jourdain on various projects

before setting up his own practice (1920). He was influenced by *Hoffmann and *Mackintosh before the 1914–18 war, but the Pavilion of Tourism at the Paris Exposition International des Arts-Décoratifs (1924–5) gained him a position as one of the leading exponents of *Art Deco. He is best known for his apartments and other buildings in the Rue Mallet-Stevens, Paris (1926–7), where certain *Cubist elements occurred, and later he was a pioneer of *International Modernism.

E (1994); Mallet-Stevens (1922, 1929, 1937); Pinchon (1990); J.T (1996)

Mallows, Charles Edward (1864–1915) English *Arts-and-Crafts architect practising from 1892 in Bedford. A gifted draughtsman, he produced many architectural perspectives, and in 1898 he took **George H.Grocock** (fl.1892–1904) into partnership. His finest work was domestic, including Three Gables, King's Corner, and White Cottage, all at Biddenham, Bedford (1899–1900), and Tirley Garth, Tarporley, Ches. (1907).

A.S.Gray (1985)

Maltese cross See CROSS.

Malton, Thomas, Sen. (1726–1801) London-born, he taught *perspective, publishing The Royal Road to Geometry (1776) and A Compleat Treatise on Perspective (1775). Following financial difficulties, he settled in Dublin. His elder son, **Thomas Malton, Jun.** (1752–1804) also taught perspective and became a skilled topographical artist, one of the first to make use of the newly invented process of Aquatinta. He published (1792–1801) A Picturesque Tour through the Cities of London and Westminster which remains a valuable and fascinating record of the *Georgian fabric. Just before he died he was working on a similar project for Oxford, and made aquatint views of various buildings by Sir Robert *Taylor. **James Malton** (1765–1803), Malton Sen.'s younger son, wrote on perspective, and practised as an architectural draughtsman, working for a time with *Gandon in Dublin. His 'irregularities' led to his dismissal and return to London, where, like his brother, he earned his living as a topographical artist. He published (1797) A Descriptive View of Dublin, and (1798 and 1802 respectively) An Essay on British Cottage Architecture and A Collection of Designs for Rural Retreats . . . principally in the Gothic and Castle Styles of Architecture, both works on *Picturesque cottages which demonstrated he was a competent designer of the cottage orné. His exhibits at the RA showed he was in the vanguard of designing in the *Neo-Romanesque style.

Co (2008); H.Duffy (1999); J.Malton (1798,1802); Mulvany (1969); ODNB (2004); Strickland (1969)

Malton, William de (*fl.*1335-8) English master-mason at Beverley *Minster, Yorks., from 1335, where he supervised the completion of the *nave. He appears to have designed the tomb of **Lady Eleanor Percy** there (1340), reckoned to be one of the finest creations of English C14 funerary architecture of its type before the Black Death. He built the north *aisle and wall-*arcade at Beverley, and may also have worked (1320s) at York Minster and Bainton Church, Yorks.

J.Harvey (1987)

mandala Geometrical figure with a centre, such as a circle, or polygon, or a square, often in the form of a *labyrinth or *maze with symbolic meanings.

mandapa Hall in a Hindu temple, sometimes with a pyramidal superstructure, and with columns supporting intricate ceilings (often consisting of concentric rings of corbelled *masonry). The temples at Dilwara, Mount Abu, Rajasthan (C12) have good examples.

Ck (1996)

mandorla Almond-shaped figure composed of two vertical arcs each passing through the other's centre, enclosing a panel, called *aureole, halo, or *vesica piscis, and often found in a *Gothic *tympanum of a *doorway.

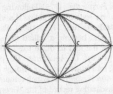

mandorla Diagram showing how almond-shaped form (related to equilateral triangles) is described. c: centres of two circles passing through each other.

Mangiarotti, Angelo (1921-2012). Italian architect, influenced by *Mies van der Rohe and *Nervi, he evolved refined systems for building using prefabricated concrete units. With **Bruno Morassutti** (1920-2008) he designed the starkly simple *Mater Misericordiae* Church, Baranzate (1957), and on his own the Marmi and Machine Offices and Exhibition Building, Carrara (1989-92).

E (1994); Nardi (1997)

Mannerism C16 style of architecture from the period of *Michelangelo identified by the employment of Classical elements in a strange or abnormal way (*see* ABUSE), or out of context, such as slipping *triglyphs or keystones, columns *inserted in deep apertures in walls and seemingly supported on *consoles, and distortion of *aedicules and other features, as in *Giulio Romano's

buildings in Mantua or *Michelangelo's work at *San Lorenzo*, Florence. In Northern Europe the works carried out by the School of *Fontainebleau contributed to a peculiarly inventive Mannerism evolved in the Low Countries (especially in Antwerp and Flanders generally), where *cartouches, *grotesque decoration, *herms, *swags, and *terms were used in abundance, and examples published in *pattern-books, influencing design in Germany, the British Isles, and elsewhere.

He (1996); Jervis (1984); L & D (1986); Lotz (1977); M & E (1995); Shearman (1967); Stenvert (1990); J.T (1996); Wüsten (1951)

Mannerist garden Style of garden evolved between the *Renaissance and *Baroque periods, created in Italy during a time of anxiety and change, characterized by a growing importance of architectural (e.g. *grottoes, etc.) and water features (e.g. *cascades and jokes), combined with allusion, novelty, and surprise. *Pratolino*, Florence (1568-81) was an example, but perhaps the most extraordinary were the unsettling *Parco dei Mostri*, Bomarzo, near Viterbo (begun 1552) (*see* ORSINI), and the beautiful *Villa Lante*, Bagnaia (begun 1560s), with its strangely crustacean *catena d'acqua* and much else.

Bazin (1990); *JGH*, **iv**/1 (Jan–Mar 1984), whole issue

Manning, Eleanor (1884-1973) American architect. With **Lois Howe** (1864-1964) she established a successful partnership, later joined by **Mary Almy** (1883-1967). The firm became known for its low-cost housing, e.g. at Mariemont, OH, the industrial suburb of Cincinnati, planned by **John Nolen** (1869-1937). Other housing-schemes included Old Harbour Village, Boston, MA (1934-7).

Susana Torre (ed.) (1977)

Manning, Warren Henry (1861-1935) American planner who published proposals for a system of interstate *motorways linking the east and west coasts of the USA. He designed the Milwaukee, Minneapolis, and Cincinnati *parkway system.

Z & Z (1995)

manor-house House in a district in medieval England over which the Court of the Lord of the Manor had authority, or on the land belonging to that nobleman: it was usually unfortified, of medium size, and architecturally unpretentious.

O.Cook & E.Smith (1983); Wood (1965)

mansard *See* ROOF.

Mansart, François (1598-1666) Leading French Classical architect. Establishing his own practice by 1624, he evolved a style influenced by de *Brosse and du *Cerceau. One of his most important works was the *Val-de-Grâce*, Paris (from 1645), completed by *Lemercier and others when building had reached the *nave *entablature: the original design was probably a derivation of *Palladio's *Il Redentore*, Venice. One of his earliest works was the *Château de Balleroy*, near Bayeux, Calvados (*c.*1626), with single-storey *pavilion-*wings set in front of a massive central block, the whole composed with assurance. With the *Orléans* wing, *Château de Blois* (1635–8), Mansart reached a mature architectural style derived from de Brosse but distinguished by purity of detail giving the building an unfussy Classical dignity. Later elevations were modelled more elaborately, as in his *Château de Maisons*, near Paris (1642–51), a serene, very French composition, with elliptical rooms set in the projecting wings. Elevations are treated as a regular grid with planes defined by *pilasters, unengaged columns, *entablatures, and *architraves. The centrepiece has three superimposed *Orders.

He also designed *Ste-Marie-de-la-Visitation*, Paris (1632–4), a circular domed church surrounded by small chapels, and prepared designs (unrealized) for a huge domed *mausoleum for the Bourbons at *St-Denis* (1665), complete with chapels set around the main circular space. However, the design demonstrates that Mansart was an architect of genius: it influenced J.*Hardouin-Mansart's dome of the *Invalides*. Ingenuity and assured geometries were also demonstrated in Mansart's Parisian *hôtels*, although most of his work has been destroyed. However, his remodelling of the *Hôtel Carnavalet* (1660–1) survives in part: there he placed rooms all round the *court, eliminating the usual wall with gate on the streetfrontage. His ambitious schemes for the Louvre (1660s) survive only on paper.

Babelon & Mignot (eds) (1988); Bt (1941, 1982); B & Smith (1973); Ha (1948); P (1982); J.T (1996)

Mansart, Jules Hardouin (1646–1708) *See* HARDOUIN-MANSART.

manse Ecclesiastical residence, especially a dwelling of a Presbyterian Minister.

Mansfeld, Alfred (1912–2004) Russian-born Israeli architect, one of the first to introduce European Modernism to Palestine, where he settled (1935). With **Munio Gitia Weinraub** (1909–70) he designed the Institute of Hebrew Studies, Hebrew University, Jerusalem (1956), his own house, Mount Carmel, Haifa (1957), and the Hydrotechnical Institute, Technion, Haifa (1957). With **Dora Gat** (1912–2003) he designed the Israel Museum, Jerusalem (1960–5).

Ma (1985*d*); J.T (1996)

mantel 1. Structure supporting *masonry above a fireplace-opening, either arched or a beam (*mantel-tree*). **2.** Projecting *hood above a fireplace to collect the smoke. **3.** Finish to the outer *face of a wall, covering the structure, and of a material differing from that of the wall itself.

mantelpiece 1. *Mantel with its supports, i.e. the fireplace *jambs. **2.** Shelf in front of the mantel. **3.** Ornamental structure and frame around a fireplace-opening, including the shelf, concealing the mantel and structure, and often surmounted by an *over-mantel*.

Manueline Portuguese late-*Gothic style of the reign of **King Manoel I** (1495–1521): highly decorative, it included *ropes, corals, twisted *piers, and the Cross of the Military Order of Christ, best seen at the Cristo Monastery at Tomar (from 1510). There was a C19 Revival.

Ck (1996); L & D (1986); D.Wa (1986)

Mapilton, Thomas (*fl.*1408–38). English master-mason, he built the *cloisters at Durham Cathedral (1408–16), and (1416–18) was employed at Westminster Abbey and the Tower of London. He may have been in Florence (1420), acting as a consultant for the design of the *dome of the Cathedral there, but was promoted (1421) to the office of King's Master-Mason in London. He designed the south-west tower of Canterbury Cathedral (1423–34), and may have been responsible for the Lollards' Tower at Lambeth Palace, London (begun 1434). He built St Stephen's Church, Walbrook, London (1429–39—replaced by *Wren's church after the Great Fire (1666)). He gave advice at the Abbey of Bury St Edmunds, Suffolk (1429–30—destroyed), and may have been involved in the planning of St Bernard's (now St John's) and All Souls Colleges, Oxford, just before his death.

J.Harvey (1987)

maqsura 1. Enclosure in a *mosque, situated near the *mihrab and *minbar, defined by a metal or timber *screen, for protection and status (e.g. the Great Mosque, Qairouan, Tunisia (C11)). **2.** Large domed room used for communal prayer (e.g. Mosque of Baybars, Cairo (C13)).

B & B (1994); Hillenbrand (1994); M & P (2011)

marble Crystalline or granular *limestone, capable of taking a polish: it varies greatly in colour, and may be veined, depending on its constituent elements. Widely employed in Antiquity, the white varieties (e.g. Carrara) were used for sculpture. It deteriorates rapidly in polluted acidic atmospheres, as may be seen in *cemeteries of the British Isles.

Borghini (ed.) (1989); Castelnuovo (1992); N.Davey (1961); Mannoni & Mannoni (1985); W.Pa (1852) marble-stucco   466

marble-stucco *Stucco with crushed *marble in the mix.

marbling Process, practice, craft, or finish (of considerable antiquity) by which, using paint, a *marble finish is suggested. Trained painters/decorators can produce some astonishingly convincing effects, e.g. on column-shafts, *dados, etc.

W.Pa (1852)

March, Otto (1845–1913) German architect, he became (1878) *Regierungsbaumeister* in Berlin, responsible for several Government buildings, theatres, and private houses (he also built up a prosperous practice). The Municipal Theatre, Worms (1889–90), had hefty structural forms, and the *Neue Friedrichstrasse* Store, Berlin (1895), with its three-storey bays of iron and glass, anticipated work by W.*Gropius. His private houses usually had steep roofs, projecting *bays, and a plan grouped around a double-height hall: the best examples were the *Landhaus Vörster*, Cologne (1891–4—where English influences were pronounced), *Landhaus Holtz*, Eisenach (1892–4), and Twin House, *Villenkolonie*, Grüne-wald, Berlin (1892–4). He also designed the *Schillertheater*, Charlottenburg (c.1895), and the Siemens Residence, Potsdam (c.1900).

S.M (1974); P (1982); *ZdB*, xxxiii (1913), 199–200

March, Werner (1894–1976) German architect, son of Otto *March. He designed in a powerful, stripped Neo-Classical style. He is remembered for his impressive *Olympiastadion* (1934–6), grounds, and various buildings of the *Reichssportfeld*, Berlin, created for the 1936 Olympic Games from the earlier *Deutsches Sportforum* (1925–8), which he and his brother **Walter** (1898–1969) had designed. Other works included *Karinhall*, Prussia (1935–6), for **Hermann Goering** (1893–1946), the *Landeszentralbank*, Münster, Westphalia (1949), and a plan for Wetzlar (1952).

P.Adam (1992); Lane (1985); March (1936); Petsch (1978); Rittich (1938); Rohrbach (1936); T.Schmidt (1992); J.T (1996); Troost (ed.) (1942–3); *WMfB*, **xii** (1928), 187–91, and **xlv** (1930), 13–21

Marchi, Virgilio (1895–1960) Italian *Futurist architect/polemicist, his *Architettura Futurista* (1924) and *Italia Nuova, Architettura Nuova* (1931) extolled speed, modern techniques, and the 'formal exaltation' of machinery. He conceived architecture as sculpture to be inhabited, in visions of gigantic spaces and megalomaniac perspectives. He designed the *Casa d'arte Bragaglia e Teatro degli Indipendenti*, Rome (1921), probably the first Futurist work of architecture, and *Il Teatro dei Piccoli di Vittoria Prodecca* at the *Teatro Odescalchi*, Rome (1924–5).

AD, II/1–2 (1981), whole issue; Amico & Damesi (eds) (1977); Clough (1961); Marchi (1924, 1931); Pehnt (1973)

Marchionni, Carlo (1702–86) Italian architect/decorator, he is best known for his work at the *Villa Albani* (later *Torlonia*), Rome (from 1746), including the *casino, coffee-house, temples, and fountains, which demonstrate his mastery of scenographic effects. While the casino's arcaded front owes much to *Michelangelo's *Palazzo dei Conservatori*, Rome, the temples show the influence of *Winckelmann's *Neo-Classicism, especially the *Tempietto Diruto* (1751–67), an artificial ruin composed of *Antique fragments. He designed the new Sacristy, St Peter's, Rome (1776–83).

De (1988); P (1982); J.T (1996)

Maré, Eric Samuel de (1910–2002) English architectural photographer of Swedish-Huguenot descent. He edited (1943–6) the *AJ*, later worked for the *AR*, and published (1948) *New Empiricism*. His images, notably of early industrial buildings, made a considerable impact.

ODNB (2009)

margent Vertical ornament of flowers and leaves (called *wheat-ear drops* or *husks*) suspended from a bow, *mask, *patera, ring, or *rosette, usually derived from the *festoon (with which it is often found), on either side of an aperture or in the centre of a *panel.

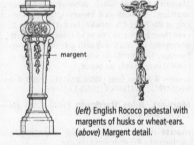

margent

(left) English Rococo pedestal with margents of husks or wheat-ears. *(above)* Margent detail.

margin-draft *Dressed band the width of a chisel all around the *face of an *ashlar-block, contrasting with the rest of the exposed stone.

margin-light 1. Tall, narrow flanking-window or wing-light on either side of a wider door or window, often found in late-C18 and early C19 British houses of the grander sort (*see* FANLIGHT). **2.** Narrow *lights defined by glazing-bars around the edges of a *sash-window, often with coloured glass, and common in C19 *Greek-Revival architecture or that influenced by a taste for a wider, squatter proportion of rectangular window fashionable c.1810.

Maria, Walter De (1935–2013) American pioneer of *Land art, esp. in NM, where he created *Lightning Field* (1971–7), using 400 six-metre-high stainless-steel rods, placed upright at regular intervals, aligned to reflect sunlight and attract lightning strikes. The observer/consumer was encouraged to consider mankind's relationship with the Earth and Universe.

N & R (2007); *OAO* (2013)

marigold Formalized circular floral decoration in *Greek architecture, resembling a *rosette, but more like a chrysanthemum or marigold, repeated in series, e.g. on the *architrave of the north *portico of the *Erechtheion*, Athens.

marigold window Medieval circular window, its area subdivided into segments by radiating *bars of *tracery, sometimes resembling a marigold, and sometimes more like a rose, if more complicated, so called *rose-window.

marine decoration Classical ornament suggesting the sea or navigation, including *anchors, the *columna rostrata*, dolphins, fish, *hippocamps, mermaids, Neptune with his *attribute (trident), nets, ropes, sea-shells, and tritons, often associated with *grottoes.

L & D (1986)

mark 1. Land held in common by, e.g., a village community. **2.** Proper name of certain principalities, e.g., Mark of Brandenburg. **3.** Indicator of a boundary, e.g. a post or stone *marker*. **4.** *Masonry monument. **5.** Sign or token. **6.** Device or incised character indicating ownership or origin, e.g. *mason's mark*, used to identify work done, as in medieval buildings. **7.** In *Freemasonry, a designation of a grade, degree, or rank of a *mark-mason*: a *mark-lodge* is therefore a *lodge of mark-masons. **8.** Denomination of weight (mostly for gold or silver), therefore a monetary value which, in the Middle Ages, was about two-thirds of a Pound Sterling.

Markelius, Sven Gottfrid (1889–1972) Swedish architect/town-planner, he worked for *Östberg before becoming influenced by Le *Corbusier and joining *CIAM (1928). He won the competition to design Hälsingborg Concert Hall (1925, built 1932–4), and made his reputation with the Swedish Pavilion, New York World's Fair (1939—with Ralph *Pomerance). As Director of Stockholm Planning Commission (1944–54) he implemented a policy of building 'town-sections' fully integrated with the city, including Vällingby (from 1953) with central pedestrian zone. He was consulting architect for the UN Building, NYC, and the UNESCO Building, Paris.

A & B (1986); Ca (1998); E (1994); S.Ray (1969, 1989); Rudberg (1989); PPS

market 1. Periodic gathering of people to buy and sell goods. **2.** Building, public place (e.g. market-square), etc., used for such gatherings, e.g. *fish-market*. **3.** Privilege granted to the lord of a *manor, municipality, etc., to establish a market (**1**).

market-cross Stone *cross on a tall upright, indicating 'market-peace', found in North-West Europe since C12, set up as a reminder of fair dealing and probity where *markets were held. A partly *Romanesque example survives in Trier, Germany. Some 'crosses' became buildings (e.g. the octagonal market-cross, Chichester, Sussex (1501), with a central *pier and external *arcade articulated with *buttresses, and hexagonal C15 'Poultry' Cross, Salisbury, Wilts.).

Marot, Daniel (1661–1752) Son of **Jean Marot** (1619–79—who produced *L'Architecture Française* (known as *Grand Marot—c.*1670) and *Recueils des plans* (known as *Petit Marot—c.*1654–60) both of which show plans, elevations, and sections of the most important buildings in Paris and its environs), he was born in Paris, but fled to The Netherlands after the Revocation (1685) of the **Edict of Nantes** (1598) that had guaranteed the rights and citizenship of French Protestants (Huguenots). His engravings, published as *Livre d'Ornemens, Nouveau Livre de Placfond*, and *Livre d'Appartement* over some 15 years from 1687, subsequently collected as *Oeuvres du Sieur D. Marot* (1703, 1713, and later), are a complete record of the *Louis-Quatorze* style. His work was influential in The Netherlands, Germany, Austria, Denmark, Sweden, and England.

Marot settled in The Hague and collaborated with the Leiden architect Jacob *Roman on the design of **William** and **Mary**'s palace and garden, *Het Loo*, near Apeldoorn (1690s), and remodelled the audience-chamber in the *Binnenhof*, The Hague (1695–8). He accompanied William and Mary to England (1688), where he appears to have designed part of the gardens (*Grand Parterre*) and perhaps some of the interiors at Hampton Court Palace, Mddx. (1689–98) but his precise role is unclear. His name has been associated with work at Boughton House, Northants, Montagu House, London, and Petworth House, Sussex (all *c.*1689–96), while Schomberg House, Pall Mall, London (*c.*1698), appears to owe much to his style, although documentary evidence is lacking. He enlarged *Huis ten Bosch*, near The Hague (1734–9), and built the *Huis Schuylenburch* (1715), *Huis Wassenaer-Obdam* (1716–17), a new wing of the *Stadhuis* (1734–5), and *Huis Huguetan* (1734–7), all in The Hague. He was assisted for many years by his son, **Daniel Marot the Younger** (1695–1769).

Jessen (1892); Kuyper (1980); Mauban (1944); Ozinga (1939); P (1982); RSTK (1977); Thornton (1984)

marouflage 1. Process of pasting/attaching a painted canvas to a wall with *maroufle* (adhesive made of white lead ground in oil, or a paste of rye-flour to which several heads of garlic were added). **2.** Mural or ceiling finish consisting of painted decorations on a strong impermeable canvas, giving the appearance of being the real surface. It has the advantage of permitting the preparation of the decorations off site, and enabling the canvas to be peeled off and removed for cleaning/repair.

JF; *OED Supplement* (1976), ii, 838; W.Pa (1852), v, 39–40

marquetry, marqueterie *Inlaid work consisting of thin veneers of hardwood, ivory, or other costly materials, usually fixed to a timber backing.

marquise 1. Tent-like *canopy. **2.** By association, a more permanent protective canopy, usually of metal or metal-and-glass.

MARS (Modern Architectural Research) Group Group of architects (including *Arup, *Coates, and *Lubetkin) founded (1933) to promote *International Modernism and *Rationalism in the United Kingdom (it was the UK branch of *CIAM). Taking its cue from Le *Corbusier's *Plan Voisin* and other theoretical ideas, it proposed (1942) widespread destruction and rebuilding of London. It was disbanded (1957).

Korn (1953); Reading (1986); T & DC (1986).

Martellange, Étienne (1568/9–1641) French architect who designed the Jesuit Novitiate, Paris (1630—destroyed), and followed (with *Lemercier) the refined *Classicism later illustrated in *Parallèle de l'Architecture* (1650) by Roland *Fréart de Chambray (1606–76). Martellange exerted much influence on French C17 and C18 ecclesiastical architecture.

Babelon (1991); Bt (1982); J.T (1996)

Martello tower *Battered two-storeyed circular/elliptical fortified tower named after *Cape Mortella*, Corsica, where a watchtower of similar form was occupied by a British garrison (1794); several were constructed on coasts of the British Isles from 1804 under the direction of **General William Twiss** (1745–1827) and **Captain William Henry Ford** (1773–1829) as precautions against invasion by the French. Good examples survive, e.g. on the Suffolk coast between Aldeburgh and Bawdsey.

Sutcliffe (1973)

Martienssen, Rex Distin (1905–42) South-African pioneer *International Modernist, who quoted liberally from the works of Le *Corbusier, *Gropius, and *Mies van der Rohe: his buildings include the Stern House, Houghton (1934–5), and the Martienssen House, Greenside (1939–40),

both Johannesburg. He published numerous articles in the *South African Architectural Record* (1931–3), and *The Idea of Space in Greek Architecture: with Special Reference to the Doric Temple and its Setting* (1956) seems to have influenced some American writers.

AAQ, ix/2–3 (1977); E (1994); *SAAR, ii* (1942), whole issue

Martin, Leonard (1869–1935) English architect, he practised (1890–1910) in London with H.J.*Treadwell, producing elaborately modelled buildings in the West End, notably in New Bond Street and Jermyn Street. *Tudor, *Baroque, and *Art-Nouveau styles were used very freely. After Treadwell's death Martin practised on his own, designing houses in Ilchester Place, Kensington, and many other places.

A.S.Gray (1985)

Martin, Sir (John) Leslie (1908–2000) English architect. As Deputy Architect of the LCC under Robert *Matthew, he designed his best-known work, the Royal Festival Hall (1948–51—with Peter *Moro, **Edwin Williams** (1896–1976), et al.), and succeeded Matthew as Architect to the LCC (1953). Appointed (1956) Professor of Architecture at Cambridge University, he established his own practice in the same year. He designed Harvey Court, Gonville and Caius College, Cambridge (1957–62), the Library at Manor Road, Oxford (1959–64—with Colin St John *Wilson and **Patrick Hodgkinson** (1930–2016)), the William Stone Building, Peterhouse, Cambridge (1960–4—also with Wilson), the Zoology/Psychology Building, Oxford (1964–70), and the Royal Concert Hall, Glasgow (1983–90—with **Ivor Richards** (1943–)). There is no doubt that, through the tenure of the Chair at Cambridge (until 1972 and afterwards as Emeritus Professor) he exercised enormous influence on architecture and planning, although his attempts to emphasize measurable and supposedly rational elements of architecture cannot be regarded as successful.

Carolin & Dannatt (eds) (1996); E (1994); J.McKean (2001); J.T (1996)

Martinelli, Anton Erhard (1684–1747) Austrian architect/master-builder, he was involved in the erection of many of the most important early-C18 Viennese buildings, notably *Fischer von Erlach's *Karlskirche* (1715–37) and Fischer and von *Hildenbrandt's *Schwarzenberg Palais* (begun 1697). He designed the *Invalidenhaus* (later Town Hall), Pest (1721–37), and carried out numerous works for the **Esterházy** family.

List (1726) of works in *Baumeistergenossenschaft*, Vienna

Martinelli, Domenico (1650–1718) Italian architect, he worked with Carlo *Fontana in

Rome from 1678. His importance lies in his influence on the *Baroque style in Central Europe, notably with the *Stadtpalais Liechtenstein*, Vienna (1692–1705), which includes an elaborate staircase, and was as a whole derived from *Bernini's *Chigi-Odescalchi* Palace, Rome. He probably designed the *Palais Harrach* (c.1690), the *Gartenpalais Liechtenstein*, Vienna (1694–1711), and the *Kaunitz* Palace, Slavkov (Austerlitz), where he introduced the *cour d'honneur* (from 1698— only partially completed).

Grimschitz (1947a); Lorenz (1991); J.Nn (1970)

Martorell y Montells, Joan (1833–1906) Catalan disciple of *Viollet-le-Duc, one of the most distinguished architects of the eclectic Barcelona school. His *Gothic work was influenced by English architects, especially *Butterfield. His most outstanding building is the Church of the Salesas (1882–5), where Gothic, *Romanesque, and *Mudéjar styles merge. His Mercantile Credit Society Building, Barcelona (1896–1900), was influenced by *Neo-Classicism and other trends of the time. He taught *Gaudí.

Boh (1968); Boh *et al.* (1991)

martyrium (*pl.* **martyria**) **1.** Structure, usually circular or polygonal, built over the tomb of a Christian martyr, so essentially a *mausoleum. Hundreds of Christian churches owe their existence to *martyria*, which took their form from well-established Roman funerary types (*exedrae*, octagons, *rotundas, etc.). The complex *martyrium* at Hierapolis in Phrygia, Turkey (early C5), had a plan derived from **Nero's** (r.54–68) Golden House, Rome (C1). **2.** Place in a church where Relics are deposited. **3.** Structure on a site where witness to Christian faith occurred.

Co (1991); Ck (1996); Grabar (1972)

Maruscelli *or* **Marucelli, Paolo** (1596–1649) Italian *Baroque architect, contemporary of *Bernini, *Borromini, and *Cortona. He designed the *Chiesa Nuova*, Perugia (1629–65), and the *Casa dei Filippini*, Rome (1622–36), which Borromini transformed after 1637. At the *Palazzo Medici-Madama*, Rome (1637–42), he enlarged the building and composed the impressive *façade (1638–9), loosely derived from the *Palazzo Farnese*. From 1633 until his death he was involved in the rebuilding of the *Palazzo Spada-Capodiferro*, and was architect for several buildings, notably the Theatine House, *Sant'Andrea della Valle* (from 1629), the Sacristy of *Santa Maria dell'Anima* (1636–44), and a *wing attached to the *cloister of *Santa Maria sopra Minerva* (1638–42), all in Rome.

Connors (1980); J.T (1996)

Marvell, Andrew (1621–78) English poet, his *Upon Appleton House* (written 1650s, published 1681), based on his observations of the gardens at Nun Appleton, Yorks. (seat of **Thomas Fairfax** (1612–71—**3rd Lord Fairfax of Cameron** from 1648)), when tutoring Fairfax's daughter, **Mary** (1638–1704), revealed aspects of English garden-design before it was transformed by influences from France and The Netherlands. These included the importance of a ruined nunnery (an early exemplar of *ruins in a landscape-garden), a flower-garden formed like a *fort (a type of *military garden, perhaps), appreciation of the *genius loci*, and delight in real 'landskips' beyond the garden itself, again an early example of 'leaping the fence' to embrace natural scenery.

H & W (1988); *ODNB* (2004)

Marville, Charles (1816–c.1879) French illustrator/photographer. His inclusion here is because he collaborated with several architects (e.g. *Abadie) to record the various stages during the erection of major Parisian buildings. His most important work was the book containing over 400 photographs of Paris streets destroyed by *Haussmann's replanning of the city.

Mellot (1995); de Thézy (1993, 1994)

Marvuglia, Giuseppe Venanzio (1729–1814) Sicilian architect. He designed the *tepidarium* and *caldarium* (1789) in a *stripped Neo-Classical style at the Botanic Gardens, Palermo, using the Greek-*Doric *Order. Other designs incorporated *Baroque and Classical elements, e.g. the Monastery of *San Martino delle Scale*, Palermo (1762–74), and the *Palladian *Villa Belmonte all'Acquasanta*, Palermo (from 1801). His most extraordinary building is *La Favorita (Palazzina Cinese*—1799–1802), a partly Classical and partly *Chinoiserie confection, which may have been partly designed by **Giuseppe Patricola** (*fl.*1846–84). Marvuglia also designed the *Doric Hercules Fountain at the *Villa della Favorita*, Palermo (c.1814).

Bt (1968); Ms (1966); M & Wa (1987)

mascaron Representation of a human or partly human face, more or less caricatured, used as an architectural ornament, e.g. on a *keystone over an arch.

Mascherino, Ottaviano (1536–1606) Bolognese by birth, he settled in Rome (1574), where he made additions to *Bramante's *Cortile di Belvedere* (1578–85), probably built *San Salvatore in Lauro* (1591–1600), and restructured the *Palazzo del Quirinale* (1583–5). He designed the *façades of *Santa Maria della Scala* (1592) and *Santo Spirito dei Napoletani* (1593), both in Rome.

AB, **xlv**/3 (1963), 205–44; An (1954); Wi (1982)

mashrabiya, meshrebeeyah, mushrabeyeh, *or* **shanasheel** Timber *lattice-work (often intricate, geometrical, and beautiful) in *Islamic architecture, once common in the Ottoman Empire: the term is usually applied to a projecting *balcony or *bay protected by such a *screen so that those inside can see without being seen.

Hillenbrand (1994); S (1901–2)

masjid Literally a place of prostration, a *mosque for daily prayers.

mask 1. Representation of a human, animal, or fantastic face used in architectural ornament, often part of *grotesque decoration. See MASCARON. **2.** *Label-stop (2) carved to resemble a head, called *head-* or *mask-*stop.

Mason, Hilda (1880–1955) English architect (with *Erith) of St Andrew's Church, Felixstowe, Suffolk (1929–31), an intermingling of late-*Gothic Suffolk wool-churches (e.g. Blythburgh and Lavenham) with the *reinforced-concrete-and-glass language of *Perret's *Notre-Dame*, Le Raincy (1922–4): nods to *Perp. were made overt by four-centred flattened arches. She also designed King's Knoll, Woodbridge, Suffolk (1933), a house in the *International-Modern style.

EH

<http://www.english-heritage.org.uk/content/imported-docs/f-j/women-architects-early-20th-century.pdf> accessed 8 Jan 2013

Mason, William (1725–97) English clergyman/poet/garden-designer, a pivotal figure between Augustan Classicism and Romanticism by way of the *Picturesque, whose *English Garden* (1772–81—modelled on **Virgil**'s *Georgics*), celebrated the English *landscape-garden. He synthesized influences from 'Capability' *Brown, *Gilpin, *Kent, J.-J.*Rousseau, et al., and was a progenitor of the *Gardenesque, and an influence on *Loudon. In *An Heroic Epistle to Sir William *Chambers* (1773) he ridiculed the fashion for *Chinoiserie. He designed (1772–3, 1784) the walled flower-garden at Nuneham Park, Oxon., for **George Simon Harcourt** (1736–1809—**2nd Earl Harcourt** from 1777), in which inscriptions, etc., helped to engender spiritual refreshment/aesthetic contemplation.

CL, cxliv/3732 (12 Sept 1968), 640–2; *GH, I/2 (Feb 1973), 11–25; GH, xviii/2 (Autumn 1990), 103–54; Laird (1999); Mowl (2000); ODNB (2004); Tay (2006)

masonry 1. Art, craft, and practice of building with natural or artificial stone, involving its quarrying, cutting, *dressing, jointing, and laying. **2.** Work produced by a mason, such as an *ashlar wall, stone dressings, and the like. *Types of masonry include*:

Aberdeen bond: type of masonry developed in Aberdeenshire, and exported to Canada, it

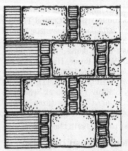

masonry Aberdeen bond.

consists of courses of large, roughly-dressed, rectangular blocks between which are two or three smaller stones, like large *gallets, often of a contrasting colour;

ablaq: alternating courses of masonry in contrasting colours;

ashlar: stone cut and dressed to accurate shapes with right-angled corners, laid in true courses with *mortar on flat beds, and with fine joints, carefully bonded;

cyclopean: **1.** any polygonal masonry, but especially masonry of large irregularly shaped stones; **2.** rusticated masonry dressed to appear as naturally rough *rock-faced work straight from the quarry;

rubble: stonework of undressed or roughly dressed stones including *coursed rubble* (stones laid in courses, so requiring some preparation to ensure that joints are horizontal and stones properly bedded), *dry-stone* (rough stones laid without mortar), *random rubble* (very rough stones, uncoursed), and *squared rubble* (stones cut roughly to have verticals at right angles to the horizontals);

rusticated: masonry laid with joints exaggerated by chamfering, etc., the surface projecting beyond the joints. See RUSTICATION.

3. Brickwork or any load-bearing structure such as blockwork, but the term is not recommended in this sense.

4. With a capital M (see FREEMASON (**4**)).

mason's lodge See LODGE.

mason's mark Device carved in stones by a mason to identify his work, often found in medieval buildings.

B.E.Jones (1956)

mason's mitre When stone *mouldings, *cills, *string-courses, etc., are continued around an angle, the point where they change direction must not coincide with the joint because an acutely angled piece of stone is subject to damage and easily snapped off. The joint, therefore, is formed at right angles to the *naked of the wall at a distance from the angle, the change of direction of the moulding effected by cutting it to shape. See REPRISE.

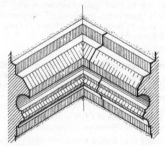

mason's mitre

mass Body of coherent matter of relatively large bulk, a solid physical object, so applied to built forms, as in the *mass of the building*.

Massari, Giorgio (1687-1766) Venetian architect, he designed the *Chiesa dei Gesuati* (*Santa Maria del Rosario*—1725-36), elements of which are derived from *Palladio's *Il Redentore*, but with *Rococo elements: it is positioned diagonally across the *Giudecca* from *Il Redentore*. He designed (1735) *Santa Maria della Pietà*, completed *Longhena's *Palazzo* (*Ca'*) *Rezzonico* (1748-66) and designed the *Palazzo Grassi* (1748-60) with its sober Neo-Classical *façade and plan containing a four-columned *atrium.

D.Howard (1980); Massari (1971); J.T (1996)

massif See CLUMP.

mastaba Ancient-Egyptian *mausoleum, the exterior of which has *battered sides, a flat roof, and is otherwise plain. The tomb-chamber was cut far underground. The step-*pyramid at Saqqara evolved from a mastaba-form.

mastin See MESTLING.

Matas, Niccolò (1799-1872) Italian architect of the *polychrome *Gothic *façade of *Santa Croce*, Florence (1857-63). He worked on several other buildings in Florence, and contributed to the design of the *cemetery at *San Miniato al Monte* (1848-59).

Bae: *Northern Italy* (1913); J.T (1996)

Matcham, Frank (1854-1920) Leading English theatre and music-hall architect, his designs were festive, opulent, often elephantine (even blowsy), with distorted *Orders. His best-known works are the Grand Opera House, Belfast (1894-5—with pronounced *Indian flavours), the London Coliseum (1902-5), Buxton Opera

House, Derbys. (1902-3), and the London Palladium (1909-10).

A.S.Gray (1985); B.Walker (1980)

matchboard Timber board cut with a *tongue on one edge and a groove on the other, often with bevels on either side of the face to be exposed, so that when the boards are fixed they have **V**-joints between them, forming decorative *dados, ceilings, *panels, walls, etc., called *matchboarding*.

mathematical tiles Small facing-tiles designed to look like *brick *headers with joints, used to clad *timber-framed fronts to give the appearance of top-quality brickwork. C18 examples abound in Lewes, Sussex. *Stretcher-like tiles are also found.

Bru (1990)

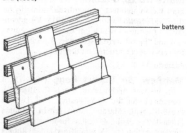

mathematical tiles (Lewes, Sussex).

Mather, Rick (1937-2013) American-born architect, he made his name with extensions to C.R.*Cockerell's Ashmolean Museum, Oxford; *Soane's Dulwich Picture Gallery (1995); **Thomas Benjamin Ambler's** (1819-75) Hertford House, Manchester Square, London (2000); D.A.*Alexander's National Maritime Museum, Greenwich (1999); and the Virginia Museum of Fine Arts, Richmond, VA (completed 2010). He carried out several prestigious commissions, including the Arco Building, Keble College, Oxford.

Maxwell *et al.* (2006); *The Times* (24 April 2013), 50

Mathey, Jean-Baptiste (*c.*1630-95) Born in Dijon, France, Mathey worked in Prague (1675-94), and designed the Troja Palace there (1679-96), with its central *block and *perron*, and two *wings linking the main building to symmetrically disposed *pavilions: it combines French ideas about the planning of *châteaux* with Italian detailing. He designed the *Kreuzherrenkirche* (1679-88) and the Toskana Palace (1689-90), both in Prague. His church-architecture influenced *Fischer von Erlach.

E.Hempel (1965); J.Nn (1970); J.T (1996)

Mattern, Hermann (1902–71) German land-scape architect, exposed to *Modernism through contacts with *Häring, *Korn, et al., he worked with *Migge at Worpswede (1926) before joining (1927) **Karl Foerster** (1874–1970) as Director of his design-studio, Bornim, near Potsdam. He developed a style of garden-design in which powerful geometries, architectonic treatments, and influences from *Jekyll and William *Robinson coalesced, and wild plants and grasses were introduced. Alwin *Seifert engaged him (1936) to work on the landscaping of the *Autobahn* system. After 1945 he designed numerous landscapes, including *cemeteries, worked to re-establish professional/academic organizations disbanded or corrupted under National Socialism, and published much.

Heinrich (ed.) (1982); Shoe (2001)

Matté-Trucco, Giacomo (1869–1934) French-born Italian architect, remembered primarily for the *Fiat Lingotto* Factory, Turin (1914–26), a *concrete structure in which influences from *Futurism and *Perret were discernible. A testing-track for cars was constructed on the roof.

Pozzetto (1975)

Matthew, Sir Robert Hogg (1906–75) A Scot, he was Architect to the LCC (1946–53), responsible for the Royal Festival Hall, London (1948–51, with *Martin, *Moro, **Edwin Williams** (1896–1976), et al.), as well as for housing-developments of that era. He established (1953) **Robert Matthew, Johnson-Marshall, & Partners**, designing the University of York (1963) and many other major projects throughout the United Kingdom, including the University buildings, Coleraine, Co. Londonderry (1970s). The *Neo-Vernacular Hillingdon Civic Centre, Uxbridge, near London (1973–8), was a significant change of direction for the firm.

ODNB (2004); vV (1993)

Matthias of Arras (*fl.* 1342–52) *See* ARRAS.

Maufe, Sir Edward Brantwood (1883–1974) English architect of simplified *Gothic churches influenced by developments in Scandinavia, he is best known for Guildford Cathedral, Surrey (1932–66). Other works include Kelling Hall, Norfolk (1912–14—an *Arts-and-Crafts house with *flint walls), St Bede's Church, Clapham, London (1922–3), St Saviour's Church, Acton, London (1924—which had reminiscences of *Tengbom's Högalid Church, Stockholm (1917–23), much admired by Maufe), Yaffle Hill, Broadstone, Dorset (a house of 1929), the Playhouse Theatre, Oxford (1937–8), and Chapel Court and North Court, St John's College, Cambridge (1937–9). He rebuilt Gray's Inn and the Middle Temple, London, in a *Neo-Georgian

style after the 1939–45 war. With **John McGeagh** (1901–85) he designed the Sir William Whitla Hall, The Queen's University of Belfast (designed 1937, built 1938–49). He was involved (1943–69) with the Imperial (later Commonwealth) War Graves Commission, and designed many memorials (e.g. the Royal Air Force Memorial, Coopers Hill, Runnymede, Surrey (1949–51)).

ODNB (2004)

mausoleum (*pl.* **mausolea**) Any roofed building used as a tomb, detached or joined to another building (e.g. a church), containing coffins, *sarcophagi, or *urns, often on shelves. The term originated with the C4 BC *Hellenistic *Ionic tomb of **King Mausolos of Caria** at Halicarnassus, one of the *Seven Wonders of the Ancient World.

Co (1991); J.Curl (2002a); Hillenbrand (1994); Toynbee (1971)

Mawson, William (1828–89) *See* LOCKWOOD.

Mawson, Thomas Hayton (1861–1933) English landscape architect (one of the first in England to use the term). He specialized in *public parks (e.g. at Blackpool, Bolton (Leverhulme Park), Burslem, Newport, Preston (Haslam Park), Southgate (Broomfield Park), Stoke-on-Trent (Hanley Park), Tipton, Walsall, Wednesbury, and Wolverhampton). His private gardens include Graythwaite Hall, Windermere (1889), Lindeth Fell, Bowness-on-Windermere (1907–8), Rivington Hall, Lancs. and Thornton Manor, Ches. (both 1905–10), and Bodelwyddan Castle (1910). He planned the gardens of the Royal Palace, Athens, and the area around the Acropolis (before 1914). He also designed town-planning schemes and gardens in Canada (e.g. at Banff, Calgary, Ottawa, Regina, and Vancouver), Denmark, Greece (e.g. Salonika), and The Netherlands (Palace of Peace, The Hague). He published *The Art and Craft of Garden Making* (1900), *Civic Art* (1911), and *The Life and Work of an English Landscape Architect* (1927). His son, **Edward Prentice Mawson** (1885–1954), took over the management of his father's firm.

Chadwick (1966); D & E (1994); B.Elliott (1986); HHH (1980); Kissack (2006); Mawson (1900, 1927); *ODNB* (2004)

Maxwell, Edward (1867–1923) Canadian architect, he was skilled at mixing the round-arched and *Italianate styles (e.g. Henry Birks Store, Montréal, 1893–4). He entered into partnership (1902) with his brother, **William Sutherland Maxwell** (1874–1952—who had trained at the *École des *Beaux-Arts, Paris), and together they produced many confident *Classical designs (e.g. the Saskatchewan Legislative Building, Regina (1907–10), the J.K.L.Ross House, Montréal (1908–9), and the Montréal Art Association

Gallery (1910-12)). Their additions to **Bruce Price**'s (1845-1903) *Château Frontenac* Hotel, Québec (1892-3), included the *St-Louis* Wing and Tower Block (1920-4), in which a mixture of the French *château style and elements derived from Scots fortified houses encapsulated the importance of Scots settlers and French colonization in the history of Canada. The firm had an enormous and successful practice, designing many commercial and other building-types.

K (1968, 1994); J.T (1996)

Maxwell, Francis (Frank) William (1863-1941) *See* MAXWELL & TUKE.

Maxwell, James (1838-93) *See* MAXWELL & TUKE.

Maxwell & Tuke English architectural firm founded (1865) by **James Maxwell** (1838-93) and **William Charles Tuke** (1843-93). Located first in Bury, Lancs., it rose to prominence with Cambridge Hall, Southport, Lancs. (1871-4), began to experiment with cast-iron construction, planned the resort of St Anne's-on-the-Sea, Lancs. (from 1874), relocated (1884) to Manchester to design buildings for the Royal Jubilee Exhibition (1887), and won (1883) the competition to design the Ulster Reform Club, Belfast (1883-5, in a *Free style). **Francis William (Frank) Maxwell** (1863-1941) joined (late-1880s) the practice, and was closely involved with its best-known work, Blackpool Tower (1891-4), inspired by *Eiffel's Tower, Paris. At the same time the firm carried out designs relating to Marine Drive, Isle of Man, a tramway with *viaducts. After 1893 the practice continued under Frank Maxwell, designing New Brighton Tower, Wallasey, Ches. (1895-8), even larger than the Blackpool version (demolished). Other works included buildings at Whitworth Cemetery, Lancs. (1877-9—layout by **Thomas Holt** (*fl.*1870s)), the dome of Rhyl Pavilion (1908), and Whitehead Clock-Tower, Bury (1914).

ODNB (website) accessed 25 April 2013

May, Edward John (1853-1941) Pupil of Decimus *Burton, he worked for Eden *Nesfield and Norman *Shaw, for whom he designed (1870s, 1880s) several buildings at the Bedford Park Estate, Chiswick, near London, including the Vicarage (*c.*1882), the Club House (1879), Hogg House, Priory Gardens (1883), and Queen Anne's Grove (1883).

A.S.Gray (1985); Hi (1977)

May, Ernst (1886-1970) German architect, disciple of the *Garden-City movement, he studied in London (1907-8) and Darmstadt (1908-10) before working with *Unwin (1910-12), completing his studies in Munich under *Fischer and *Thiersch (1912-13). Director (1919-25) of the Silesian Building Department, Breslau (now Wrocław), he produced the Development Plan for the City to cope with the huge influx of German refugees from the 'Polish Corridor'. He was *Stadtbaurat* at Frankfurt-am-Main (1925-30), where he designed the famous *Römerstadt* Housing Development (1926-30) and other schemes incorporating English low-density ideas with the architectural language of the *International Modernism, using prefabricated *industrialized systems. He edited (1926-30) *Das neue Frankfurt* and promoted his ideas about housing, transport, and pollution as well as publishing proposals for Berlin and planning generally. He moved to the Soviet Union (1930), where he planned a series of new towns (the 'May' towns), and then (1934-45) was in Africa, farming in Tanganyika and practising as an architect-planner in Kenya, but was interned as an enemy alien (1940-2). Returning to Europe (1953), he carried out many housing developments in Hamburg and elsewhere in West Germany. He edited *Das schlesische Heim* (1919-25) and *Die Neue Heimat* (1954-60).

AAQ, xi/1 (1979), 39-62; Buekschmitt (1963); E (1994); F & H (1986); Herrel (2001); Korn (1953); Me.Miller (1992); J.T (1996)

May, Hugh (1621-84) English architect of the period between the first Palladian Revival of Inigo *Jones and the *Baroque style of *Vanbrugh and *Hawksmoor. He became (1668) Comptroller of the Works, and was one of those appointed to supervise the rebuilding of the City after the 1666 Fire. He seems to have been responsible for introducing well-mannered Dutch *Palladianism into England and, with *Pratt, for establishing what became known (inaccurately) as the *Wren style. Apart from the *double-pile Eltham Lodge, Kent (1664—apparently influenced by the work of *Vingboons), however, his only major surviving works are the east front, stables, and chapel at Cornbury House, Oxon. (1663-8). He remodelled the Upper Ward, St George's Hall, and the King's Chapel at Windsor Castle, Berks. (1675-84), with paintings by **Antonio Verrio** (*c.*1639-1707) and carvings by **Grinling Gibbons** (1648-1721), creating what was once the most complete Baroque ensemble in England, now virtually obliterated.

Co (2008); Downes (1966); Hill & Cornforth (1966); J.T (1996); vV (1993)

Mayan architecture A *Meso-American people, the Maya built (*c.*C2 BC–C.AD 900) very steep *battered platforms on which monumental structures were created. The remains of many such temples have *corbelled *vaults inside (*c.*C4), but most openings have *lintels or triangular *heads. Mayan and *Aztec architecture influenced European *Art Deco in the 1920s and 1930s.

Ck (1996); J.T (1996)

Maybeck, Bernard Ralph (1862–1957) American eclectic architect, he made a distinctive contribution to domestic design. Educated in Paris, he was influenced by *Viollet-le-Duc's theories, and in 1886 returned to New York to work with *Carrère & Hastings before setting up on his own (1902) in CA, where he worked mostly in the *Stick style. In his First Church of Christ Scientist, Berkeley, CA (1910–12), he mixed *Gothic, *vernacular, the Stick style, and more than a hint of Japanese-inspired timber-work. His many houses had similar qualities, but at the A.C.Lawson House, Berkeley (1907), he also used *reinforced concrete, an early example of this material. He employed *Beaux-Arts *Classicism too, notably in the Palace of Fine Arts, San Francisco (1913–15), built for the International Exposition.

ARe, ciii (1948), 72–9; Bosley (1994); Cardwell (1977); Longstreth (1983); McCoy (1975); P (1982); J.T (1996); R.Winter (ed.) (1977); S.Woodbridge (1992)

Mayekawa, Kunio (1905–86) See MAEKAWA.

maze *Fret, *Greek key, *labyrinth, *meander, but esp. a complex system of winding interconnecting paths defined by trimmed hedges in a garden, with dead-ends at certain points which force the perambulator to retrace steps. Some authorities hold a maze is distinct from a labyrinth (which has circuitous winding paths, but no dead-ends).

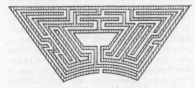

maze From a late-C17 example at Hampton Court Palace, probably originally formed of clipped hornbeam hedges.

Mazotti, Vincenzo de (1756–98) Rome-born architect of the gardens, palace (1783–9), *mortuary-chapel (a *rotunda, completed 1814), and church (a *basilican arrangement, built 1851–4) at Varakļāni, now Latvia (but then Polish Lavonia), for **Michał Jan Borch** (1753–1811). The garden was one of several in Poland influenced by the vogue for 'English' landscape-gardens, and was embellished with several *fabriques, including a circular granary with conical roof, a *pyramid (commemorating Mazotti), and a monument to Borch's dog. The inspiration was partly Stowe, Bucks.

Łoza (1954); Mākslas Vēsture & Teorija, xvi (2013), 18–26

Mead, William Rutherford (1846–1928) See MCKIM, MEAD, & WHITE.

meander *Band-like progressive ornament composed of straight lines joining at right angles or cut diagonally (as in the *fret and *key patterns), or curving (as in the *Vitruvian scroll, *running-dog, or *wave-scroll). It is used on *friezes, *string-courses, etc.

Mebes, Paul (1872–1938) C20 German housing architect/theorist, whose designs for apartments were influential. He published *Um 1800. Architektur und Kunsthandwerke im letzten Jahrhundert ihrer traditionellen Entwicklung* (1908) which dealt with German *Biedermeier architecture, and argued that simple, stripped *Neo-Classicism was more adaptable for modern needs than *Jugendstil or any of the other styles in vogue at the time. His views influenced *Behrens, *Bonatz, and *Troost, and others. Among his housing developments may be cited those at Pankow (1907–9), Zehlendorf (1912–33), Lichterfelde (1920–9), Reinickendorf (1920–9), Tempelhof (1920–9), and Weissensee (1930–2), all in Greater Berlin.

AR, clii, 907 (Sept. 1972), 176–80; Lane (1985); Mebes & Behrendt (1920); E.Meyer (1972); WMfB, xvi (1932), 49–56, 115–22, 429–35, 515–16, xxii (1938), 177–84, 233–40; Zeitler (ed.) (1966)

medallion 1. *Panel or *tablet, usually circular, elliptical, oval, or sometimes square, bearing a portrait or figures in *relief, really like a large medal, used for Classical architectural decoration. **2.** Repeated circular ornament, e.g. in a *frieze (especially in *Romanesque work).

Medd, David Leslie (1917–2009) English architect, claiming affinities with *Arts and Crafts *and* *Modernism (he worked with *Lubetkin on the Finsbury Health Centre, London), associated with the post-war school-building programme in Herts. (where the Education Officer was (Sir) **John Hubert Newsom** (1910–71), working with the architect **Mary Crowley** (1907–2005)). Newsom's ideas about education became realizable from 1945 when C.H.*Aslin was appointed County Architect, but it was the assembly of a team including Medd and Crowley (and Medd's wife from 1949) by Aslin's Deputy, (Sir) **Stirrat Andrew William Johnson-Marshall** (1912–81—who believed that *prefabrication would solve the need for speedy erection of cheap buildings), that enabled the programme to develop. The Medds became influential in school-design, and when Johnson-Marshall left Herts. (1949) to found the Ministry of Education research/development group (which included *Ventris), they joined him, and prototype schools (starting with the exemplar at Wokingham, Berks.) were erected using a version of system-building evolved in Herts.

However, the Medds realized that prefabricated, industrialized approaches had limitations, and turned to simple *brick structures. D.L.Medd wrote extensively on school-building and was critical of modern procurement procedures.

The Guardian (14 April 2009), Obits; *RIBAJ* (Jan 2010), 13; pk

Medd, Henry Alexander Nesbitt (1892–1977) English architect. From 1919 he was the man on the spot in India, interpreting and adapting Herbert *Baker's drawings, but in fact designing most of the details of the Secretariats and Legislative buildings, New Delhi. On his own account, as the result of wins in competitions, he designed the Anglican Church (now Cathedral) of the Redemption, New Delhi (1928–31—a masterly domed building clearly influenced partly by *Lutyens's work at Hampstead Garden Suburb, London, and partly by the work of *Wren), and the RC Church of the Sacred Heart, also in New Delhi (designed 1927, built 1930-4—with a twin-towered liturgical west *façade, a *dome over the *crossing, and long side-elevations with horizontals, the whole Sublimely Lutyensesque). Medd also designed the High Court building at Nagpur (1935–42—in a style very similar to that of Lutyens's Viceroy's House (he himself said it was 'all cribbed')), and the Mint in Calcutta (1940–49), a nobly Neo-Classical composition featuring the Roman *Doric Order. Like *Shoosmith, Medd was shamefully neglected when he returned to an England where his work and the Empire were out of favour, and so worked as a draughtsman. He was Master of the *Art-Workers' Guild (1959).

ODNB (2013); GS; Stamp (1976)

Medd, Mary (*née* **Crowley**) (1907–2005) *See* MEDD, DAVID LESLIE.

medieval architecture Architecture of Europe in the Middle Ages from the end of C8 to the first half of C16, thus including the *Romanesque and *Gothic (or *Pointed) styles.

medieval garden European *monasteries incorporated buildings with *cloisters, the roofed *ambulatory around the *garth derived from the Roman *atrium surrounded by a *peristyle: *Early-Christian religious foundations had such attributes, and herb- and vegetable-gardens were part of C6 *Benedictine monastic establishments. Under **Charlemagne** (Roman Emperor 800–14) the *Capitulare de Villis* (*c*.800) contained information on gardens: the famous idealized C9 plan in the Benedictine Abbey of St Gall, Switzerland doubtless owed something to the *Capitulare*, as well as to the Classical *philosopher's garden, the *academe*. Apart from evidence in woodcuts/illuminated miniatures (mostly C15 Flemish), however, information about medieval gardens is tantalizingly elusive: most images feature enclosed gardens, with *trellises, *topiary, herbs, *arbours, *paths, and occasionally pools and *fountains, many associated with the Virgin Mary (the *hortus conclusus*), but some writings provided a limited amount of information (e.g. *De proprietatibus rerum* (*c*.1240) part of which was devoted to plants, by **Bartholomew de Glanville** (*fl*.1220–50), which, in turn, informed *De Vegetabilibus et plantis* (*c*.1260) by **Albertus Magnus** (*c*.1193–1280); and the gardening manual, *Liber Ruralium Commodorum* (*c*.1304–9), by **Pietro de'Crescenzi** (*c*.1233–*c*.1320)). Some *Islamic gardens (C10–C14) in which elaborate hydraulic systems were employed (e.g. *Madinat al-Zahra*, near Córdoba, Spain (C10)), were among the finest of the time in Europe. There appears to have been an enclosed park at Woodstock, Oxon. (*c*.1100), which included a *menagerie, and a *water-garden was laid out there (later C12). A *herber and ornamental gardens existed at Windsor Castle, Berks., and **Guillaume de Machaut** (1310–77) described (1330s) a large park at Hesdin, near Arras, which had canals and *automata, presumably of Islamic origin, perhaps from Sicily.

Co (1999); Crisp (1924); Harvey (1981); Hennebo (1987); Hyams (1971); Landsberg (1998); MacDougall (ed.) (1986); Ruggles (2000, 2008); Shoe (2001); Stokstad & Stannard (1983); Tay (2006)

Medland, James (1808–94) *See* HAMILTON & MEDLAND.

medresseh *See* MADRASA.

meeting-house Building for Nonconformist (usually Presbyterian or Quaker) religious observances.

megalith Large block of undressed or partially dressed stone used singly or with other megaliths as prehistoric monuments (*c*.4000–*c*.1000 BC). A single standing-stone is a *menhir, sometimes arranged in regular rows (as at Carnac, Brittany). Megaliths are also found set in a circle, as at Stonehenge, Wilts. (*c*.1800 BC), with *lintels forming a continuous band around the tops. Structures formed of uprights supporting a large flat slab were usually chamber-tombs, known as *cromlechs* or *dolmens.

Burl (1976, 1995); G.Daniel (1972); Joussaume (1988); Mohen (1989); Reden (1982); Rudofsky (1977); Teichmann (1983)

megalopolis Very large urban region formed of a *metropolis that has far outgrown itself and swallowed many towns and villages, or a series of *metropoleis* that have joined up (e.g. the urban sprawl between Washington, DC and NYC).

Eldredge (ed.) (1967); L.Mumford (1938, 1946, 1961)

megaron 1. Principal men's room or hall in an Ancient-Greek house, or a room in a *temple where only the priest could enter. **2.** Square or rectangular room often with a raised central hearth, and four columns supporting the roof. The side-walls projected beyond the front wall and partly enclosed a columned *porch, probably the precedent for a *Doric temple.

D (1950); D.S.R (1945)

megastructure Gigantic, entirely enclosed, complex of buildings, usually with many functions under one or several roofs. Examples include work by the *Metabolists and *Soleri's *Arcology.

R.Ba (1976); Dahinden (1972)

Megaw, Arthur Hubert Stanley (*known as* **Peter**) (1910–2006) Dublin-born to a distinguished Belfast family, he became an archaeologist and scholar, as well as a highly competent administrator, appointed (1936) to the new Department of Antiquities of Cyprus from which he promoted the *conservation of numerous buildings and artefacts. His achievements in Crusader and *Byzantine Studies were immense.

The Times (4 Aug 2006), 62

Meier, Richard Alan (1934–) *See* NEW YORK FIVE; WHITES.

Meissonnier, Juste-Aurèle (1695–1750) Turin-born, of French descent, he established himself in Paris (*c.*1714) as an interior-designer/architect, eschewing straight lines, symmetry, and blandness in his polished *Rococo designs. The ingenious house for **Léon de Bréthous** (1693–1751), Bayonne, France (1733), demonstrated his mastery of irregular plans and fondness for sweeping curves. Most of his work has been destroyed, but can be studied in *Oeuvre de Juste-Aurèle Meissonnier*, published (*c.*1750) by **Gabriel Huquier** (1695–1772).

Fitzgerald *et al.* (1963); Ha (1950); Jervis (1984); K & L (1972); Kimball (1980); Nyberg (ed.) (1969)

Meldahl, Ferdinand (1827–1908) Danish architect, influenced especially by the work of *Persius, *Schinkel, and *Semper, he became the leading proponent of *Historicism in Denmark. At the Manor House, Pederstrup, Lolland (1859–62), he drew on French-*Renaissance prototypes, and at the School for Navigation (later Life Assurance Institution), Copenhagen (1864–5), he quoted the *façade of *Lombardo's *Palazzo Véndramin-Calergi*, Venice (*c.*1500–9). Other works include the Town Halls at Ålborg (1857–61) and Fredericia (1859–60), the Royal Mint (1872–3), and the triumphant completion (1878–94) of the *Baroque *Frederikskirke* or Marble Church (both in Copenhagen), originally designed by *Jardin and *Eigtved, with its noble *cupola.

Mi (1951); J.T (1996); We (1995)

Mellinghoff, Götz-Tilman *See* NEW CLASSICISM.

Mel'nikov, Konstantin Stepanovich (1890–1974) Russian architect who rose to eminence (1920s) in the Soviet Union. His early work was influenced by *Tatlin, and he evolved an architecture partly informed by traditional rural timber buildings using roughly sawn members (e.g. the USSR Pavilion at the Paris Exposition (1925), a split rectangle slashed by powerful diagonals (perhaps anticipating aspects of *Deconstructivism), which gained him international celebrity among the 'avant-garde'). Although his work has been associated by some with *Constructivism, he was more connected with the **Productivists**, who saw themselves as anti-artistic Constructivist technicians. He is best known for his Workers' Factory Clubs in Moscow, including the Frunze (1927), Rubber (1927), Rusakov (1927), Svoboda (1927–8), and Stormy Petrel (1929). The Rusakov Club has auditoria and circulation-spaces externally expressed in strong elemental forms. His own house in Moscow essentially consisted of two interlocking cylinders (1927–9), a theme he explored in other buildings.

K-M (1987); Pallasmaa Gozak (1996); S.F.Starr (1978)

melon-dome *See* DOME.

membrane structures *See* TENSILE STRUCTURES.

menagerie Place in a garden housing exotic and curious animals. Menageries were known in medieval and earlier times, but during the *Renaissance and *Baroque periods several spectacular examples were built, notably that at Saint-Germain-en-Laye by Philibert de l'*Orme (1548) and at Versailles by Louis Le *Vaux. A good C18 example was at Horton Hall, Northants. (*after* 1739), possibly by Thomas *Wright.

Mendelsohn, Eric(h) (1887–1953) German-born naturalized American architect, he started as an *Expressionist, producing many images of structures with streamlined curves while serving in the German Imperial Army (1914–18). His Einstein Tower, Potsdam (1919–24), resembles aspects of the early typological sketches: built of concrete-rendered *brick and *block, it had the *appearance* of being made of *reinforced concrete, and is popularly believed to be so constructed. The plan owed much to South-German *Baroque staircase designs of C18. Expressionist, too, was the *Steinberg-Hermann* Hat Factory, Luckenwalde (1921–3), with its jagged, angular forms, but curved walls were also used in some of his other buildings, notably the *WOGA* Complex with *Universum* Cinema, Berlin (1925–8), and the *Schocken* Department Stores at Stuttgart

(1926) and Chemnitz (1927-30). The cinema was the precedent for many such buildings in Europe and America in the 1930s, while the long strips of horizontal windows at the stores made a considerable impact.

*International Modernism impinged more and more on Mendelsohn's work. He settled in England (1933) where he joined *Chermayeff, designing the celebrated de la Warr Pavilion, Bexhill-on-Sea, Sussex (1933-5), which has bands of windows and a streamlined curved glass enclosure for the staircase derived from the *Schocken Store*, Stuttgart. With Chermayeff he also designed Shrub's Wood, Chalfont St Giles, Bucks. (1934-5), and 64 Old Church Street, Chelsea, London (1936—unfortunately altered in the 1990s), both important Modernist houses. In the late 1930s he moved to Palestine, where he designed buildings for the Hebrew University, Jerusalem (1937-9), and in 1941 emigrated to the USA, where his work lacked the power of his German designs. The Russell House, Pacific Heights, San Francisco (1950-1), was probably his best work in America.

Aschenbach (ed.) (1987); Eckardt (1960); Evenden (ed.) (1994); Hi (1977); K.James (1997); Pehnt (1973); Stephan (ed.) (1999); Whittick (1956); Zevi (1985, 1999)

Menelaws, Adam (*c.*1749-1831) Scots architect, one of several who settled in Russia at the invitation of *Cameron. By 1818 he had taken Cameron's place as the leading Court-architect. He designed a country-house with *Gothic interiors at Alexandria (Gulf of Finland) from 1825, and several ornamental buildings in the Alexander Park, *Tsarskoye Selo* (e.g. the Ruined Chapel (1827), Turkish Elephant-House (1828), and the wholly extraordinary Egyptian Gate (1827-30), with its *pylon-towers covered with cast-iron plates decorated with Egyptianizing hieroglyphs designed by **Vasily Ivanovich Demut-Malinovsky** (1779-1846)).

Co (2008); HPZ (1994)

Mengoni, Giuseppe (1829-77) Italian architect. His best work is the cruciform *Galleria Vittorio Emanuele*, Milan (1861-77), one of the largest and most impressive iron-and-glass covered *arcades of C19, in the Italian *Renaissance style, with an important elevation facing the *Piazza del Duomo*. He also designed the handsome *Palazzo della Cassa di Risparmio* (1868-76) and the impressive Classical arcades of the *Campo Santo* (1860s), both in Bologna.

Geist (1983); Ms (1966); J.T (1996)

menhir *See* MEGALITH.

mensa Upper slab of stone forming the top of an *altar in a church.

mensole *Keystone.

meridian Line running north-south, i.e. where the great circle passing through the poles reaches the earth's surface. Some meridians have been marked on church floors (e.g. *Santa Maria del Fiore*, Florence, and *Santa Maria degli Angeli*, Rome), complete with signs of the zodiac and graduations.

W.Pa (1852)

Merlini, Domenico (1730-97) Italian-born Court Architect to **King Stanisław August Poniatowski** (*r.*1764-95) of Poland from 1773. He collaborated with *Kamsetzer in creating the lovely *Louis-Seize* interiors of the Royal Palace, Warsaw (1776-85), and various buildings in the Royal Park of Ujazdów, Warsaw. Among these were the remodelling of the exquisite lakeside Łazienki Palace (1775-93). Merlini designed the Orangery Theatre (1784-8) with **Jan Bogumił Plersch** (1737-1817) as his collaborator, and the little Lodge in the Park (*c.*1765-74). Other refined works include his Myślewicki Pavilion (1775-7—with curved front, end-pavilions, and a two-storey apsidal entrance), Jabłonna Palace (1775-9), and Królikarnia Palace (1782-6—with *Ionic *portico and domed *rotunda), all in Warsaw. His Jabłonowski Palace, Racot (*c.*1785), is almost *Palladian in composition, but given a rustic flavour.

L & R (1984); J.T (1996); D.Wa (1986)

merlon *Cop. See* BATTLEMENT.

meros, merus Plain surface of a *triglyph between *glyphs.

Merovingian architecture Architecture of the first dynasty of Frankish Kings in Gaul (*c.*500-751/2), derived from *Early Christian Roman prototypes, and usually taken to mean buildings of C5 to the end of C8. Among C5 exemplars are the *baptisteries of Aix, Fréjus, and Mélas, similar to such structures in Italy, and clearly derived from Roman precedents. Surviving buildings include the *crypt of Jouarre near Meaux and the baptistery of St-Jean, Poitiers (both essentially C7).

J.T (1996)

Merrill, John O. (1896-1975) *See* SKIDMORE, OWINGS, & MERRILL.

meshrebeeyah *See* MASHRABIYA.

Meso-American architecture Architecture of the *Aztec, *Mayan, and other Central-American civilizations of the first millennium BC until the Spanish Conquest of C16. Most surviving structures had a ritualistic function, and included flat-topped pyramidal platforms with *ramps and/or steps leading to the summit. Many buildings had sculpted *friezes, borders, and *panels, and the simple rectilinear blocky forms of the temples bore a resemblance to European *stripped Classical buildings of C18 and later, while the formal symmetrical geometry of layouts and complexes (including settlements such as the great city of Teotihuacán (c.C1–C8), near México City) had ceremonial roads and a gridiron plan. Meso-American architecture had a considerable influence on aspects of *Art Deco.

Ck (1996); J.T (1996)

Mesopotamian architecture See ASSYRIAN, BABYLONIAN, SUMERIAN ARCHITECTURE.

Messel, Alfred (1853–1909) German architect, he established (1886) a Berlin practice, designing numerous *apartment-blocks and private houses. His first major work was the *Hessisches Landesmuseum*, Darmstadt (1890s), with rooms decorated in period styles. At the same time he began to carry out work for the **Wertheim** department-store firm: the second store for *Wertheim* on the *Leipzigerstrasse*, Berlin (1896–7), was the first steel-framed building in the capital, and was influential. His later Berlin buildings were in a simplified Neo-Classical style, including the *AEG* office building (1906–7), the National Bank (1907–8), and his well-known Pergamon Museum, designed to house the great *Hellenistic *altar and various architectural fragments (1909–30—built under the direction of **Ludwig Ernst Emil Hoffmann** (1852–1932)).

Blauert *et al.* (2009); J.T (1996)

messuage Dwelling-house, with outbuildings and land assigned to its use. *See* DEMESNE.

mestling *Mastin, mastline,* or yellow metal, e.g. *brass or *latten, used in medieval sepulchral 'brasses'.

Metabolism Japanese architectural movement founded (1960) by *Tange. With members including *Kikutake, *Kurokawa, and **Fumihiko Maki** (1928–), it was concerned with the nature and expression of private and public spaces, with flexibility, and changeable use. *Prefabrication, advanced technology, and industrialization were employed to create small capsules or living-units for private spaces, connected to service-towers and circulation-areas, as in Kurokawa's Nagakin Capsule Tower, Tokyo (1972).

Ku (1972, 1977, 1992); J.T (1996)

Metagenes There were two Ancient-Greek architects of that name. **Metagenes of Athens** (*fl.c.*late–C5 BC) was involved with others in the building of the Periclean *Telesterion*, or Hall of the Mysteries, Eleusis (c.430 BC). **Metagenes of Knossos**, son of *Chersiphron, worked on the great C6 BC *Ionic Temple of Artemis, Ephesus, and contributed to an architectural treatise (now lost).

D (1950); VP (1567), vii, 12, 16, and x, 12

metal structures The first were *bridges, such as the *iron structure at Coalbrookdale, Salop., designed by *Pritchard (1777–9) and various industrial and storage buildings where cast-iron columns carried *beams from which low segmental *brick *vaults sprang. *Schinkel designed cast-iron monuments (e.g. to **Queen Luise of Prussia** (*r.*1797–1810), Gransee (*Gothic *sarcophagus and canopy—1811); the war-memorial at Grossbeeren (Gothic *pinnacle—1817); and the Kreuzberg monument, Berlin (tall Gothic *spire-like cross—1818–21)) and a cast-iron formal interior staircase (at Prince Albert's Palace, Berlin (1830–2)), while iron was also used by many C19 designers including *Baltard, *Bélanger, *Burton, *Fontaine, *Haviland, *Labrouste, *Lanyon, *Menelaws, *Paxton, *Stasov, and *Woodward. *Loudon was a pioneer in the evolution of iron-and-glass *conservatories. Whole cast-iron fronts were designed by John *Baird in Glasgow, and *Badger, *Bogardus, and *Kellum, among others, in the USA. Early iron-and-glass walls were used by *Ellis in Liverpool. Paxton's Crystal Palace, London (1850–1), was the prototype for many C19 exhibition buildings, and there were many conservatories, railway stations, and other structures using iron and glass. (Sir) William *Fairbairn, the Scots engineer, designed (1839) a prefabricated mill erected in Istanbul (1840): later (1854) he brought out his important *On the Application of Cast and Wrought Iron to Building Purposes.* Badger's illustrated *Catalogue of Cast-Iron Architecture* (1865) was also a remarkable compendium. *Viollet-le-Duc, in his *Entretiens* (1858–72), promoted the employment of materials such as metal in architecture, and his work was influential. *Prefabricated iron structures, such as churches (e.g. that published (1856) by **William Slater** (1819–72), a pupil of R.C.*Carpenter), were designed, and kits-of-parts widely available for *industrialized buildings. Metal-framed buildings were evolved, starting with wrought-iron, and then the steel skeleton was developed for tall buildings, including *skyscrapers, notably in Chicago and NYC. Then came the use of steel as an element in *reinforced concrete, and the concept of the completely framed building with a light *envelope of metal and glass, the *curtain-wall. Later structures have included *space-frames, light *trusses, and various developments allowing speed of erection as well as prefabrication, lightness, and adaptability.

Behnisch & G.Hartung (1982); Blanc *et al.* (1993); G & G (1974); N.Jackson (1996); Jodice (1988); Lemoine (1986); Loudon (1834); Mainstone (1975); Marrey (1989); Marrey (ed.) (2002); Roisecco *et al.* (1972–83); Thorne (ed.) (1990)

Métezeau, Jacques-Clément (1581–1652) French architect, brother of Louis *Métezeau, he was involved in town-planning and architectural schemes for the Paris of *Henri IV (r.1589-1610). His designs looked forward to the style of le *Vau, and derive from that of de *Brosse, with whom he worked on the Luxembourg Palace, Paris (1615). Other buildings include the *Place Ducale*, Charleville (1610), the *Orangerie du Louvre* (1617), the *Hôtel de Brienne*, Paris (1630-2), and the *Château de la Meilleraye* (from 1620—destroyed). He was the contractor responsible for the handsome west front of *St-Gervais*, Paris (1616-23), with an *assemblage of *Orders placed on a tall *Gothic church therefore requiring three Orders instead of the two on *Il Gesù*, Rome, by *Vignola and della *Porta. The design of *St-Gervais* has been attributed to de Brosse, but Métezeau may have contributed to it. With **Jean Thiriot** (c.1590-1647) he designed the sea-wall at La Rochelle (1627-8), which gained him renown.

Babelon (1991); Berty (1860); Bt (1982); J.T (1996).

Métezeau, Louis (1559-1615) French architect, brother of J.-C.*Métezeau. He may have designed the *Hôtel d'Angoulême* (begun 1584), the first example of a *Giant Order of *pilasters in Paris, probably inspired by de l'*Orme's *premier Tome* (1567). From 1594 he worked at the Louvre, the Tuileries, and other royal palaces, contributed to the design of the *Place des Vosges* from c.1603 and, like his brother, designed other town-planning schemes for the Paris of *Henri IV (r.1589-1610) with du *Cerceau. He may have been responsible for the south *façade of the *Grande Galerie*, and contributed to the interiors of the *Petite Galerie* and *Salle des Antiques*, all at the Louvre, Paris (1601-8). He worked with *Dupérac on the interiors of the *Hôtel de Jean de Fourcy*, Paris (1601-10). He visited Florence in 1611 to study the *Palazzo Pitti*, an event that inspired the design of the *Luxembourg* Palace, Paris. He made a major contribution to the evolution of French *Mannerism.

Babelon (1991); Berty (1860); Bt (1982); J.T (1996)

metope 1. Plain or enriched slab on the *Doric *Order *frieze between *triglyphs. 2. *Intersectio*, *metoche*, or space between *dentils.

metropolis 1. Seat or see of a metropolitan bishop. 2. Main town or city of a province or district, especially one which is the seat of Government, so a capital city. 3. Very large city with *suburbs, usually one that has absorbed several villages and even towns, like greater London.

Miles (ed.) (1970)

Metz, Odo of (fl.c.792-805) Architect of the Palatine Chapel or *Minster at Aachen, Germany, begun (c.790) under **Emperor Charlemagne** (r.800-14), modelled on *San Vitale*, Ravenna, but made more robust in the process. It may

also have been derived from the C6 *Chrysotriclinion* (Hall of State), Constantinople, an allusion to Imperial continuity.

Ck (1996); D.Wa (1986)

Metzstein, Isi (1928-2012) *See* GILLESPIE, KIDD, & COIA.

meurtrière *Gun-loop.

Mewès, Charles-Frédéric (1860-1914) French architect, Paris-trained, he worked in an elegant Classical (often *Louis-Seize*) style. He developed a large international practice from the 1890s, in association with architects in several countries. In England his colleague was A.J.*Davis, who had worked with him in Paris. Mewès designed the Ritz Hotel, Paris (1898), and (1900) interiors of the Carlton Hotel, London, by **Henry Louis Florence** (1843-1916). **Mewès & Davis** designed the Ritz Hotel, Piccadilly, London (1903-6), a steel-framed building with an elegant Frenchified *façade and tall roofs reminiscent of the architecture of the Paris *Boulevards*. Other joint projects were the Royal Automobile Club, Pall Mall (1908-11), which has a façade reminiscent of *Gabriel's work, and the *Morning Post* Building, Aldwych, Strand (1905-6). Mewès was responsible for the luxurious interiors of the German liners *Amerika* (1905), *Kaiserin Auguste Victoria* (1907-8), *Imperator* (1911-12), *Vaterland* (1913), and *Bismarck* (1914). He also designed the décor in the Cunard liner *Aquitania* (1914).

AR (Boston, MA), xiv/5 (May 1907), 137-48; A.S.Gray (1985); Hamlin (1953); MM & Wa (1989); *RIBAJ*, ser. 3, liv (Oct. 1947), 603-4; Se (ed.) (1975)

mews 1. *Court, street, or yard with stables, coach-houses, and accommodation for servants, at the rear of London town-houses. 2. Group of small *terrace-houses, set close together in a court or *cul-de-sac*, not on a main street-frontage.

Meyer, Adolf (1881-1929) German architect, he worked with *Lauweriks (before 1907), *Behrens (1907-8), *Paul (1909-10), and *Gropius (1911-14 and 1919-25). With the last he designed the *Fagus* Shoe Factory, Alfeld-an-der-Leine, Germany (1910-11), housing at Wittemberg, Frankfurt-an-der-Oder (1913-14), the *Kleffel* Cotton Factory, Dramburg (1913-14), and the Model Factory and Office Building for the *Werkbund* Exhibition, Cologne (1914), all of which are more controlled and elegant than anything Gropius was to produce later on his own. The *Fagus* *curtain-walling and the Cologne curved glazed cases for the stairs were to be enormously influential on *International Modernism. He designed part of the *Zeiss* Factory, Jena (1925), and taught at the *Bauhaus (1919-25).

Casabella, **xlvi** (1982), 40–7; A.Meyer (1925); *Neue Frankfurt*, **iii/9** (1929), 165–82

Meyer, Hannes (1889-1954) Swiss-born Marxist architect, he began teaching (1927) at the Dessau *Bauhaus and succeeded *Gropius as Director (1928-30). Meyer's Collectivist approach alienated many people (he made Marxism and Leninism essential studies), and his insistence that architecture had nothing to do with formal aesthetics caused friction with other teachers. Dismissed (1930), he went to the Soviet Union where he was heaped with honour and privilege until the Stalinist demand for *Classicism made him return to Switzerland (1936-9), after which he spent a decade in México before retiring to Switzerland (1949). His best-known works are the Trade Union School, Bernau, near Berlin (1928-30), and the *Toerten* Housing, Dessau (1928-30).

Hays (1992); H.Meyer (1989); Schnaidt (ed.) (1965); Wingler (1969)

Meyer, Johann Heinrich Gustav (1816-77) German landscape architect, he worked under *Lenné at Potsdam, so knew work by *Schinkel and *Persius, esp. their references to the *Antique. Aware of the benefits of urban *public parks for the proletariat, given the climate of discontent (1840s), Meyer designed for the City of Berlin the parks of Friedrichshain (1846-75), Treptow (1864-76), and Humboldtshain (1869-73), incorporating historical forms and architectonic elements, and adapting them for popular use. His *Lehrbuch der schönen Gartenkunst* (1860) was influential.

Gothein (1966); Hennebo & Hoffmann (1962-5); Meyer (1860); Shoe (2001); Tay (2006)

Mey *or* **Meij, Johann Melchior van der** (1878-1949) Dutch architect, he worked with de *Klerk and *Kramer on the brick- and *terracotta-clad *Expressionist *Scheepvaarthuis*, Amsterdam (1912-16), and designed housing in the *Titianstraat* (1925-30) and *Hoofdorpplein* (1928-30), Amsterdam.

Fanelli (1968); Zuydewijn (1969)

mezzanine Partial low storey (*entresol* if immediately over the ground-floor) introduced in the height of a principal storey, or any subordinate storey intermediate between two main storeys.

MIAR (Movimento Italiano per l'Architettura Razionale) Italian *Rationalism was promoted at an exhibition in Rome (1928) organized by *Libera and *Gruppo 7. A new movement, MAR (*Movimento Architettura Razionale*) was then formed (1930) to bring all Italy's Rationalist architects together and to promote another exhibition (1931), celebrated by the publication of *Manifesto per l'Architettura Razionale* supported energetically

by the Fascist leader, **Benito Mussolini** (1883-1945).

Cennamo (1973, 1976); D & P (1976); Mantero (ed.) (1984); Ve (1953)

Michael of Canterbury (*fl.*1275-1321) *See* CANTERBURY.

Michaud, Joseph (1822-1902) *See* BOURGEAU.

Michela, Costanzo (1689-1754) Italian architect, influenced by *Guarini, he designed several churches in the vicinity of Turin, including the Parish Church at Barone (1729-39), *San Giacomo*, Rivarolo Canavese (1728-33), and *Santa Marta in Agliè* (1739-60). The last is an extraordinary example of complex geometries with three internal volumes (a hexagon contained by convexes and concaves instead of straight lines, a square contained by convex shapes, and a circle), and is an exceptional late-*Baroque masterpiece.

AB, **I** (1968), 169-83; Brinckham (1931); N-S (1986*a*)

Michelangelo Buonarroti (1475-1564) Italian poet/painter/sculptor, he was also the most original, inventive, and influential architect of his time. His architectural career did not really start until he began work on the *façade of the Chapel of **Pope Leo X** (*r.*1513-21), *Castel Sant'Angelo*, Rome (1514), followed by his connection with *San Lorenzo*, Florence, starting 1516, when he prepared designs for a façade (never realized). His first actual building was the New Sacristy (1519-34), the *mortuary-chapel of the **Medici**, the shell of which already was built. For this interior he modelled the wall-surfaces with *cornices and *pediments resting on *consoles without *friezes or *architraves, *panels breaking through open-bedded segmental pediments, and other *abuses of architecture. These *elisions and distortions created a dynamic tension unknown in the Early *Renaissance. *Aedicules seem to press down on the architectural elements below, and each many-layered wall is framed by a *triumphal arch (defined by *pietra-serena* *Orders) over which the *coffered *dome rises on *pendentives that only begin above the cornice over the great arches, with an extra storey slotted in at pendentive level. The darker *pietra-serena* work is conventional, resembling treatment by *Brunelleschi, but Michelangelo erected the walls of white *marble, seeming to crowd and break out of the areas framed by the *Orders.

In his *Biblioteca Laurenziana* (1524-71), *pilasters seemed to carry the structure of the ceiling, the pattern of which was repeated in the design of the floor, unifying the room in a manner not previously seen: *columns in the *vestibule were set in recesses and appeared to sit on consoles, while the *blind aedicules in the wall-panels between the Orders were designed with shafts tapering *towards* the bases. The vestibule-stair (completed by *Ammannati after 1559) is extraordinary, with two external flights and a curious arrangement of steps: it occupies the centre of the space, and was the very first grand stair of the Renaissance period to be treated as a major feature of architectural design. Both the New Sacristy and the Laurentian Library vestibule are examples of *Mannerism.

Michelangelo settled in Rome (1534), where he painted the Sistine Chapel ceiling for **Pope Paul III** (*r*.1534–49). His Florentine architecture had been mostly interiors, with *Quattrocento* treatments of colour, but in Rome his architecture was public, grand, and on a huge scale. He set up (1539) the *Antique statue of **Emperor Marcus Aurelius** (*r*.161–180) on a new base in the centre of a space in front of the *Palazzo del Senatore* on the Capitoline Hill, and designed the genesis of the trapezoidal *Piazza del Campidoglio* as a setting for the statue, though this was not completed until the mid-C17 by the *Rainaldis. He planned a new façade for the *Palazzo dei Conservatori* (completed 1584) which was set at an angle to that of the *Palazzo del Senatore*, and, to balance it, an identical façade on the other side of the *Piazza* that became the front of the Capitoline Museum (completed 1654). In these façades he used a *Giant Order, a device that was to be widely employed thereafter, with a smaller Order carrying the first floor, and an even smaller one in the aedicules. The *Piazza* itself was designed to look like a rectangular space, and in the centre is an elliptical pattern around the statue: both devices are read as a circle and square, and the elliptical element is the first use of this figure in Renaissance design. Both the trapezium and ellipse were precedents for the area in front of the *basilica of *San Pietro* in Rome.

Michelangelo was appointed (1546) to complete *Sangallo's *Palazzo Farnese*, and he first designed the huge *cornicione* over the *astylar façade and redesigned the upper storeys of the *cortile*, introducing some of his perverse Mannerist devices (such as consoles with pendent *guttae* that seem to have slipped down the window-architraves). In the same year Michelangelo was appointed to complete St Peter's in succession to Sangallo and *Giulio Romano, and immediately began to undo some of Sangallo's work in an attempt to return to *Bramante's Greek-cross plan, but in a much more powerful version. His work was largely confined to the outer and upper parts of the building, although he simplified and clarified the basic geometry. For the exterior he unified the façades with a Giant Order based on the one he had used at the Capitol and designed a sixteen-sided drum with paired columns. As built (1588–90) by della *Porta the *dome is higher and more pointed, and the vertical lines of the paired columns are continued in the ribs of the dome and

the *lantern. Michelangelo's proposal for a giant *portico was never realized, as *Maderno built the *nave and façade that muddied the clarity of the great architect's design.

At the *Porta Pia*, Rome (1561–4), named after **Pope Pius IV** (*r*.1559–65), Michelangelo's Mannerist tendencies became more extreme: a broken segmental scrolled pediment with *swag was set inside a triangular pediment, while oversized *guttae* hung below blocks on either side of the *tympanum*; *Ionic capitals, freely interpreted, became copings for the *battlements; aedicules and frames around openings were deliberately oversized and blocky; and panels had broken scrolled pediments holding broken segmental pediments between them. The gate, which faces towards the city at the end of a newly straightened street leading from the *Quirinal*, anticipates the beginning of *Baroque town-planning.

Pius IV also commissioned (1561) Michelangelo to adapt the *tepidarium* of the *thermae* of **Diocletian** (*r*.284–305) as *Santa Maria degli Angeli*, using the ancient vaulting and eight monolithic granite columns of the Roman building: it was remodelled during the C18.

An (1986); Argan & Contardi (1993); He (1996); Lotz (1977); Millon & Smyth (1988); P (1982); Pi (1964); J.T (1996)

Michell, Gordon (1923–2009) English architect and *conservationist, he joined (1962) *Buchanan's study-group which produced the important *Traffic in Towns*, and was responsible for the Bath Conservation Study, one of the investigations which established *urban conservation* as a planning discipline. Appointed (1973) Consultant Architect to the Civic Trust, he advised amenity bodies throughout the country. One of his achievements (1977) was the promotion of the community-led award-winning conservation project for Wirksworth, Derbys. He authored *Design in the High Street* (1986), reports, and studies.

RIBAJ (March 2010), 13; pk

Michelozzo di Bartolommeo *called* **Michelozzo Michelozzi** (1396–1472) Florentine architect/sculptor of the Early *Renaissance, contemporary of *Brunelleschi. He worked first with **Ghiberti** (1417–24) and later with **Donatello** (*c*.1425–32), with whom he designed and made a series of architectural funerary monuments. Around 1427 he designed the *loggia and *court for the **Medici** *villa at Careggi, near Florence, having already remodelled the villa at Trebbio (*c*.1422). The influence of the essentials of Renaissance architecture and Brunelleschi's work is clear from his reconstruction of the *cloister, *refectory, cells, and public rooms at the Church and Monastery of *San Marco*, Florence (*c*.1437–52), including the light, elegant, triple-aisled, vaulted library. Michelozzi's best-known work is the enormous *astylar *Palazzo Medici* (later *Riccardi*), Florence (1444–59), which has the lowest storey faced with rock-faced *rustication and pierced with arched openings, channel-rusticated *piano-nobile* with regularly spaced semicircular Florentine arches, and a top storey of smooth *ashlar, the whole held down under a massive *cornicione*. Behind this powerful exterior he designed an arcaded *cortile* (with echoes of Brunelleschi's Foundling's Hospital) that was to be enormously influential. Michelozzo was also responsible for the remarkable *tribune in *Santissima Annunziata*, Florence (1444–55), one of the first centrally planned domed spaces of the Renaissance, with a polygonal plan off which are radiating apsidal chapels. Inspired by Brunelleschi's unfinished *Santa Maria degli Angeli*, Florence (1434), it is even more strongly related to the *Antique Roman temple of *Minerva Medica*, of *c.*AD 250, and was completed by *Alberti. At *Santa Maria delle Grazie*, Pistoia (from 1452), he used the *cross-in-square plan of central and four subsidiary domed spaces.

Michelozzi was *capomaestro* of Florence Cathedral (1446–55) and supervised the building of the *lantern on the great dome. He designed the fortress-like villa at Cafaggiolo, Mugello (*c.*1452), the much more elegant *Villa Medici*, Fiesole (*c.*1458–61), remodelled the *Palazzo Comunale*, Montepulciano (1440), and designed the Hospital of *San Paolo dei Convalescenti*, Florence (1459). Although he was credited with introducing Florentine Brunelleschian ideas to Lombardy in the Portinari Chapel, *Sant'Eustorgio*, Milan (1460s), based on the Old Sacristy in *San Lorenzo*, Florence, this attribution is now rejected, as is his authorship of the Medici Bank, Milan.

Caplow (1977); Ferrara & Quinterio (1984); He (1996); Lotz (1977); Morisani (1951); P (1982); J.T (1996)

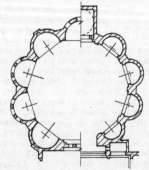

(*left*) Temple of '*Minerva Medica*', Rome (*c.* AD 250). (*right*) East end of *Santissima Annunziata*, Florence, by Michelozzo di Bartolommeo, begun 1444. A Renaissance solution to centralized planning drawing on Roman Antiquity.

Michelucci, Giovanni

Michelucci, Giovanni (1891–1991) Italian architect, influenced by *Piacentini towards the *stripped *Neo-Classicism of *Città Universitaria*, Rome, where Michelucci designed buildings including the *Istituto di Mineralogia* (1932–5). He collaborated with the *MIAR Tuscan Group on the *Santa Maria Novella* Railway Station, Florence (1935–6), a significant examplar of Italian *Rationalism. His *Palazzo del Governo*, Arezzo (1936–9), was an essay in sober Classicism. Among his works after the 1939–45 war were a Church at Collina da Pontelungo, Pistoia (1953–4), the *Casa Ventura*, Florence (1956–7), and *San Giovanni Battista*, Campi Bisenzio, near Florence (1960–3).

Belluzzi & Conforti (eds) (1986); F. Borsi (ed.) (1979); Dezzi Bardeschi (1988); E (1994); Lugli *et al.* (1966); Michelucci (1978); F.Naldi (ed.) (1978); Quaroni (1980); Tafuri (1989); J.T (1996)

Michetti, Nicola *or* Niccolò

Michetti, Nicola *or* Niccolò (*c.*1675–1759) Italian architect, pupil of Carlo *Fontana, he carried Roman *Baroque design well into C18. His elliptical *San Pietro*, Zagarolo, Italy (1717–23), is a conception comparable with designs by *Juvarra. He worked (1718–23) for **Tsar Peter I** ('the Great'—*r.*1682–1725) in Russia and built the Summer Palaces of *Katherinental*, near Tallinn, Estonia (1718–23), and *Strel'na*, near St Petersburg (1720–3). He also designed the enormous gardens with fountains (influenced by French precedents) at *Peterhof* (1719–23). His work was a significant model for *Rastrelli to follow. Back in Rome he designed the west front of the *Palazzo Colonna* (1731–2), with a pavilion containing one of the most impressive C18 non-ecclesiastical interiors in Rome. He designed part of the Theatine

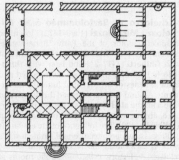

Plan of *Palazzo Medici*, Florence, showing central *cortile*.

Monastery of *Sant'Andrea della Valle*, with its splendid staircase (1755–7).

Millon (1980); P (1982); J.T (1996)

Micklethwaite, John Thomas (1843–1906) English architect, pupil of 'Great' *Scott, he commenced practice (1869), and was later in partnership (1876–92) with **George Somers Clarke** (1841–1926). In his *Modern Parish Churches* (1874) and other writings he denounced *Go, over-pedantic antiquarianism, and vulgar commercialism as the enemies of good architecture, for ugliness and showing off were not signs of originality, taste, or strength. He turned against the architecture of Scott, and, with others of his generation, repudiated almost the whole mid-Victorian *Gothic architectural output as having led nowhere and been an aberration. Advocating a return to rational ecclesiastical design, the study of liturgical requirements to determine the plan and volume of a church, the need to evolve a type of architectural solution for the future, the abandonment of ecclesiological antiquarianism (and dreamy medievalism), and, most significantly, a return to principles of design established by *Pugin and R.C.*Carpenter, he pointed the way forward to the evolution of late-Victorian church-architecture. With Somers Clarke, he designed St Paul's, Augustus Road, Wimbledon Park, London (1888–96), a satisfying mixture of *Second Pointed and *Perp., with the *chancel differentiated by means of a *Rood-screen and more elaborate colouring on the timber roof. Micklethwaite's church architecture was scholarly and correct. A list of his works is given in *ODNB* (2004), but perhaps his most important appointment was to the Surveyorship of Westminster Abbey (1898) on the death of *Pearson. His works of renewal on the south *transept and west front were carried out with W.D.*Caröe, and he aimed primarily at *conservation. He became Master of the *Art-Workers' Guild in 1893.

C.Brooks & Saint (eds) (1995); J.Curl (2007); Micklethwaite (1874); *ODNB* (2004)

Middle Pointed The *Second-Pointed or *Decorated style of the late C13. It seems to refer more to early Second Pointed of the *Geometrical* variety rather than to the later *Flowing* or *Curvilinear* type, so comes just after the *First-Pointed so-called *Lancet style.

Middleton, Michael Humfrey (1917–2009) Appointed Secretary and then Director of the Civic Trust on its foundation (1957), he led battles to preserve quality and character; protect amenity and historic buildings; and oppose ugly shop-fronts, badly designed street-lighting, demands of traffic, obtrusive advertising, and insensitive 'redevelopment' threatening towns and cities. One of his first successes was the campaign against appalling proposals for Piccadilly Circus by **Jack Cotton** (1903–64). Under Middleton's direction, the Trust pioneered regeneration of derelict industrial land, and had an international influence.

The Times (13 Aug 2009), 53

Mies van der Rohe, Ludwig (1886–1969) German architect, one of the most influential of *International Modernists. Without formal architectural education, he went to Berlin (1905) to work for Bruno *Paul: in the following year he designed the Riehl House, Neubabelsberg, near Berlin (completed 1907), which drew on English *Arts-and-Crafts exemplars revealed by *Muthesius in *Das Englische Haus* (1904–5). He joined (1908) the *atelier* of *Behrens, where he met *Gropius and Adolf *Meyer, among others, and absorbed something of Behrens's style, mingled with a strong flavour of the severe architecture of *Schinkel, Behrens's hero. Several suburban *villas followed, including the Perls (later Fuchs) House, Zehlendorf, Berlin (1911), in which the precedent of Schinkel's domestic architecture was clear. He also designed a monument (unrealized) to **Otto, Prince von Bismarck** (1815–98) for a rocky promontory at Bingen-am-Rhein, which anticipated the *stripped Classicism of *Speer later in C20. Indeed, from 1911 his designs were influenced by a simplified *Classicism, as displayed at Behrens's Imperial German Embassy, St Petersburg, Russia (1911–12—which Mies supervised). On his own account Mies (as he then was) worked on a project for the Kröller-Müller House and Gallery, The Hague, The Netherlands (1912–13), influenced by Schinkel's work at Potsdam and Glienicke and by F.L.L.*Wright's designs which were known through Wasmuth's publications (notably of 1910) and the 1911 exhibition. He established (1912) his own Berlin practice (even though the Kröller-Müller project fell through) and designed three houses in a *stripped *Neo-Classical style (house at *Heerstrasse*, Berlin (1913), Urbig House, Neubabelsberg (1914), and Mies House, Werder (1914)). Even the Kempner House, Berlin (1920—destroyed), had stylistic similarities to the pre-war houses, but had a flat roof and an arched *loggia* (influenced by Schinkel's *Italianate round-arched style).

After the 1914–18 war, when the political climate in Germany shifted massively Leftwards, Gropius organized (1919) an exhibition of architecture considered suitable for the new era. Mies submitted his 1912–13 Kröller-Müller designs which Gropius (a convinced believer in the *tabula rasa*) refused to accept because of its clear links to historical precedent. The result was a transformation: *Mies* (which has connotations with what is seedy, wretched, and out of sorts, though its cuddly pussy-cat soothing sound in English conjured different associations) became *Ludwig Mies van der Rohe* (which sounds vaguely grand (the pretentious 'van der') as well as suggesting bareness, rawness, and roughness (his mother's name was Rohe)); and the new Mies van der Rohe emerged as a radical Leftist *Modernist. He joined the *Novembergruppe* (1921), becoming its President in 1923. His 'Five Projects' of the period (1921-3) included the unrealized glass-clad *Friedrichstrasse* Office Block, published by Bruno *Taut. Then followed the design for a Glass Skyscraper (1922), the Concrete Office Block (1922—one of the first to have the *International-style strip- or ribbon-window arrangement), the Brick Country House (1923—influenced by van *Doesburg and *De *Stijl* in its composition of cubic volumes), and the Concrete Country House (1923—designed for a sloping site and with a plan resembling a swastika *cross). The last project had powerfully emphasized overhanging horizontals reminiscent of Wright's work, counterbalanced by the big vertical block of the chimney, while the configuration of the L- and T-plan-shapes of the walls of the Brick Country House is one of the first instances of walls being disposed according to the principles of *De-Stijl* composition.

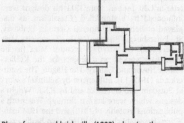

Plan of proposed brick villa (1923), showing the influence of Mondrian and *De Stijl*.

He exhibited at a show (1923) of *De-Stijl* work in Paris, and made contact with the protagonists of Russian *Constructivism and *Suprematism. He also exhibited in Berlin and Weimar (in the latter case at the invitation of Gropius, who was mollified by Mies's conversion to the cause). Nevertheless, he was still designing suburban houses in his prewar Arts-and-Crafts and Neo-Classical modes, a fact concealed in later hagiographies.

With *Bartning, *Behrendt, *Häring, *Mendelsohn, *Poelzig, the *Tauts, and others, he formed *Der *Ring*, which rapidly became a nationwide organization to reject all historical associations and to prepare the ground for an architecture of the new epoch supposedly based (or to *look* as though it were based) on contemporary technology. Mies designed (1926) the monument

(destroyed 1933) to the Socialist and Spartacist **Karl Liebknecht** (1871-1919), the Polish Communist agitator **Rosa Luxemburg** (1870-1919), and the November 1918 Revolution in the *Friedrichsfelde Friedhof*, Berlin: of *brick projecting and receding planes on which the hammer and sickle were predominantly displayed, it was nevertheless based on a steel-frame (so much for 'honesty' of expression in building). In the same year he designed the Wolf House, Guben (destroyed), where blocky masses of brick were pierced with windows, and all *Historicist references were expunged.

Mies and other members of *Der Ring* were elected (1926) to the *Deutscher Werkbund*, which, as a result, shifted ground from its mission to promote good industrial design and crafts to become a bullying pressure-group promoting 'new architecture', i.e. that approved by Mies and his circle. As Vice-President of the *Werkbund* and Director of the proposed *Weissenhofsiedlung* Exhibition, Stuttgart (1927), he consolidated his reputation as leader of the *avant-garde*. The exhibition, for which he designed the master-plan and the long apartment-block on the highest land, contained temporary structures as well as over twenty permanent buildings, including villas, designed by leading German and other Modernists, including *Bourgeois, Le *Corbusier, *Oud, and *Stam. Predominant motifs were long horizontal strips of windows, smooth white walls, and flat roofs: the image of the cult of International Modernism had been found. Mies was also able to exhibit his tubular-steel chair, the earliest of several later variations that were to place him among foremost C20 furniture designers. For the International Exposition, Barcelona (1928-9), shortly after he completed the Lange House, Krefeld, Mies designed the German Pavilion with a flat roof supported on steel columns clad in chromium-plated casings and walls of onyx and *marble (some of which projected beyond the roof).

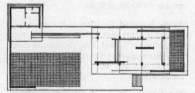

Plan of the Barcelona Pavilion showing structural columns and spaces defined by screen-walls.

This little building (demolished 1929, reconstructed 1983-4), exquisitely and expensively detailed, won immediate approval and became one of the most admired paradigms of the late 1920s. It was furnished with Mies's 'Barcelona

Chair', consisting of a chromium-plated frame with black leather upholstered back and seat. Then followed the Tugendhat House, Brno, Czechoslovakia (1930), with a single storey on the street-frontage and two storeys facing the garden. The living-room was a continuous space with chromium-cased steel columns and free-standing panel, derived from the Barcelona design, while the full-height windows could be fully lowered out of sight, enabling the interior space to extend into the garden-*terrace. Every detail of the house was purpose-made, designed by the architect.

Appointed (1930) to run the Dessau *Bauhaus on Gropius's recommendation following the dismissal of Hannes *Meyer, Mies emphasized instruction within a more clearly-defined pedagogic structure, but the mayhem of mismanagement over previous years had done the damage, and the National Socialist majority in the Dessau Town Council closed the institution (1932). Mies attempted to reconstitute the Bauhaus in a disused factory at Berlin-Steglitz, but it shut in 1933. It has been widely claimed that Mies left Germany because of Nazi hostility to his work, but he remained there for five more years, and was one of the signatories of the Proclamation by leading German artists urging voters to support **Adolf Hitler** (1889–1945) following the death of **President** (from 1925) **Paul von Hindenburg** (1847–1934). Mies and Gropius both joined the Visual Arts section of the Nazi-sponsored Reich Culture Chamber, and submitted designs (predictably decorated with Swastikas) for architecture competitions: some Modernist designs for *Autobahn* service stations by Mies were personally approved by Hitler. Indeed Mies attempted to show that Modernism was apolitical, but this was a complete reversal of his position a decade earlier, and his apostasy did not go unnoticed. However, Hitler (who was uninterested in tedious doctrinal disputes among opportunist architects) saw Modernism as suitable for factories, bridges, airports, *Autobahn* structures, and so on, while a *stripped Neo-Classicism was to be used for State and Party purposes, (because of its austerity, power, and simplicity), and a *vernacular style for housing (especially in the country), a position not much differing from the official line in many other countries (including the democracies) of the period. Furthermore, Mies's gnomic remark that architecture is 'the will of the epoch translated into space' was used, almost verbatim, by Hitler, many of whose *ex-cathedra* sayings were very close to those spouted by the *Bauhäusler*. It soon became apparent, however, that there was not going to be much architectural work in an economy geared increasingly to war, and Mies decided to leave Germany to pursue his career. He settled (1938) in Chicago, IL, where he became Director of the Architecture Department

of the Armour Institute (later Illinois Institute of Technology). From 1940 he redesigned the *campus and buildings, placing rectangular blocks on an overall grid, exposing the steel frames, and designing all the junctions with meticulous care (he claimed 'God is in the detail'). He invented a sophisticated language of metal-and-glass architecture, shown to best effect at the Farnsworth House, Fox River, Plano, IL (1946–50), in which the terrace-slab, floor-slab, and roof-slabs were all raised from the ground and carried on steel stanchions of I-section. This open glass-sided pavilion idea with impeccable detailing was used by Mies on several occasions, e.g. Crown Hall, IIT, Chicago (1952–6), and the National Gallery, *Tiergarten*, Berlin (1962–8). The Lake Shore Drive Apartments, Chicago (1950–1) had steel frames, while the huge Seagram Skyscraper, NYC (1954–8—with Philip *Johnson (who did much to promote the Authorized Version of Mies's career) and *Kahn & Jacobs), was clad in bronze and glass. Mies's influence cannot be overstated, and, with Le Corbusier and Gropius, he completed what might be regarded as the Trinity of Modernism. His impact worldwide is clear, and his metal-and-glass fronted buildings have been extensively (and often unintelligently) copied.

Bill (1955); Br (1977, 1996, 1997); P.Carter (1999); J-L. Cohen (1996); Cuito (ed.) (2002d); Dr (1960); Glaeser (1977); Hilbersheimer (1956); Hi & P.Johnson (1995); Hochman (ed.) (1989); P.Johnson (1978); Neumeyer (1991); Riley & Bergdoll (eds.) (2002); Safran (2001); Schulze (1985, 1989); Schulze & Windhorst (2012); Spotts (2002); Weihsmann (1998); W-H (1989); Zu (ed.) (1986, 1993, 1994); Zu *et al.* (eds) (1987)

Migge, Leberecht (1881–1935) German landscape architect, he joined (1912) the *Deutscher Werkbund*. In *Jedermann Selbstversorger!* (1918) and *Die Gartenkultur des 20. Jahrhunderts* (1913, 1920) he set out his ideas about communal open spaces and the transformation of towns and cities without ruining the countryside. He designed landscapes for *Modern-Movement housing-schemes in the 1920s at Celle (with *Haesler), at Britz, Neukölln, Berlin (with B.*Taut and M.*Wagner) and at Frankfurt-am-Main (with E.*May, with whom he planned the entire area, including cycle ways, paths for pedestrians, and places for recreation). He also worked at Sonnenhof, Worpswede (1920s), and Reemtsma, Altona (1931–3).

Burckhardt (1980); *JUH*, iv/(1977), 3–28; P (1982); Shoe (2001); J.T (1996)

mihrab Semicircular, polygonal, or rectangular *niche or recess, chamber, or slab in the *qibla wall of a *mosque, often elaborately decorated, indicating the direction of Mecca: sometimes the recess is merely suggested on a flat surface. Openings to mihrabs may be flanked by columns from the *capitals of which spring arches, and the hoods of niches may be embellished with *muqarnas.

B & B (1994); Hillenbrand (1994)

Milesian plan Town laid out on a regular grid-iron plan, derived from the Greek colonial city of **Miletus**, and promoted by *Hippodamus, who only publicized rather than invented it.

Wy (1962)

Miletus See HIPPODAMUS and ISIDORUS.

military decoration Architectural ornament representing an arrangement of armour, flags, guns, helmets, swords, etc., known as a *trophy, often used on arsenals, barracks, and the like, as well as on funerary monuments and memorials commemorating military men or war.

L & D (1986)

military garden Garden suggesting fortifications, dispositions of armies, etc. *Vauban and other military-engineers designed gardens incorporating *bastions, *counter-scarps, *ramparts, *scarps, etc. *Lawson, in his *A New Orchard and Garden* (1618), drew attention to *topiary representing soldiers 'ready to give Batell', and *masonry, earth, and topiary in combination offered design possibilities alluding to military architecture. So-called *Troy-towns could suggest *citadels, as at Enghien near Hainault, Belgium (late C17), views of which were published (1685, c.1720) by **Romeyne de Hooghe** (1645–1708) and **Carl Remshard** (1678–1735). *Wise and *London laid out gardens at Hampton Court and Kensington Palaces, London, for **William III** (r.1689–1702) and **Mary II** (r.1689–94), in which cut yew and variegated holly hedges were planted, trimmed to resemble fortifications, and *Switzer and *Langley occasionally suggested defensive structures. Regular avenues of trees might represent troop-formations (Humphry *Repton referred (1803) to military dispositions of planting), and the *quincunx could form 'platoons'. At Castle Kennedy, Galloway, **John Dalrymple** (1673–1747— **2nd Earl of Stair** from 1707) created terraces resembling gun-emplacements, etc., commemorating his military service. *See* BATTLE-GARDEN.

GH, **xi**/1 (Spring 1983), 65–9; D.Green (1956); Hooghe (1685); ISR, **xiii**/3 (1988), 265–81; Lawson (1618); Symes (2006)

Millar or **Miller, John** (1810/11–76). Belfast-born architect, he joined (c.1826) *Hopper's London office from which he exhibited (1828) drawings at the Royal Academy of Gosford Castle, Co. Armagh, and Penrhyn Castle, Caernarvonshire, before returning to Belfast where he designed some Presbyterian churches in an advanced, austerely noble *Greek-Revival style, including the Third

Presbyterian Church, Rosemary Street, Belfast, (1830–1—with cast-iron Greek-*Doric columns (blitzed 1941)), First Presbyterian Church, Antrim (1834—with *Doric columns possibly derived from those of the Temple of Apollo at Delos published by *Stuart and *Revett (1794)), and the splendid Portaferry Church, Co. Down (1841—an amphi-prostyle hexastyle *temple with a similar Order, perhaps derived this time from the Temple of Nemesis, Rhamnus, set on a high *podium, a building in the first rank of Neo-Classical designs in the British Isles, with an interior *Order derived from that of the Temple of *Apollo Epicurius*, Bassae). At Crumlin, Co. Antrim, he designed the pretty *Gothic-Revival Presbyterian Church (inscribed *Ecclesia Scotia* and signed by Millar—1839), and another Neo-Classical church at Castlereagh (the last of 1834–5, with a handsome *in antis* distyle *Ionic Order of *engaged columns (again derived from the Bassae Temple, possibly the earliest use of this Order in the British Isles), with a severe circular *belfry rising from a square base above the front: the building was spoiled (2001) by an inappropriate addition). Millar also designed some fine houses, among them Marino Villas (c.1830—*Tudor Gothic) and Windrush House (formerly Ardville), of c.1845—with a central *bow embellished with a *Giant Order of *engaged *Ionic columns), both at Cultra, Holywood, Co. Down. Millar was called upon (1849) to report on Garron Tower, near Carnlough, Co. Antrim, apparently designed and built by **Charles Campbell** (fl.1825–50) of Newtownards (who also worked at Mount Stewart, Co Down). Millar emigrated to the Antipodes (1854).

Brett (1996, 2002); Co (2008); DIA (2013); P:JRSUA, **iii**/1 (Sept/Oct 1994), 55–7; UA, **xi**/9 (Sept./Oct. 1994), 4–6

Miller, James (1860–1947) Scots architect of Belmont Parish Church, Hillhead, Glasgow (1893), and the charming *Arts-and-Crafts-Free-*Scottish-Baronial building, St Enoch's Square, Glasgow, for the Underground Railway (1896). He won the competition for the Glasgow International Exhibition (1898–1901), and designed Glasgow Royal Infirmary (1907) and the powerful Classical (with Mannerist touches) Institute of Civil Engineers, Great George Street, London (1910). One of the most important commercial architects working in Glasgow after 1900, his houses were also very attractive: Lowther Terrace, Glasgow, and the Village Estate at Forteviot, Perthshire (1908), are among his best. The Peebles Hydro, Borders (1905–7), the Turnberry Hotel, Ayrshire (1904–6), and the Village Hall, Bournville, Birmingham (1908), were also by him.

A.S.Gray (1985); WRH (1990)

Miller, Philip (1691–1771) British horticulturalist/writer, appointed the Society of Apothecaries' gardener-curator (1722–70) at the Chelsea *Physic

Garden, which acquired an international reputation for its collections of rare plants from abroad, prompted by Miller's contacts with **John Bartram** (1699–1777) of Philadelphia, PA. His *Gardener's Dictionary* (1732–68), with abridged editions (1735–71), was important for generic binomial nomenclature derived from the work of **Carl Linnaeus** (1707–78): it was translated into several languages, including a German edn by Johann *Busch (1750–8).

P.Miller (1732–68); *ODNB* (2004); Shoe (2001); Tay (2006)

Miller, Sanderson (1716–80) English amateur architect, he was an important figure in the *Georgian *Gothic Revival (*see* GOTHICK). He embellished his Manor House at Radway Grange, Warwicks., with Gothic features (1744–6), and erected an octagonal *battlemented and *machicolated Gothic Tower at Edgehill, Warwicks. (1745–7). At Hagley Park, Worcs. (1747–8), he designed a 'ruined' castle that to contemporaries had the 'true rust of the Barons' Wars', and very soon the Squire of Radway was being consulted as an expert by many anxious to embrace fashionable Gothicizing for their properties. The motif of a two-storey *bay-window was used at a number of sites, including Radway, Arbury Hall, Warwicks. (*c.*1750–2), Adlestrop Park, Glos. (1750–62), and Rockingham Hall, Hagley, Worcs. (1751). The number of buildings where he was involved was considerable, including Lacock Abbey, Wilts. (1754–5—where he advised on the Great Hall and Gothic Gateway), the *nave and *transepts of Kineton Church, Warwicks. (1755–6), and the *sham Castle at Wimpole Hall, Cambs. (1749–51).

Co (2008); J.Curl (2011a); M.McCarthy (1987)

Mills, Peter (1598–1670) English architect/brickmaker/builder/surveyor, he was involved with Inigo *Jones concerning the Church of St Michael-le-Querne, London (1638), and appears to have designed houses on the south side of Great Queen Street, Lincoln's Inn Fields, London (*c.*1640—an early example of uniform elevations for a group of London houses—demolished), and elsewhere in the capital. His greatest work was Thorpe Hall, Peterborough, Northants. (1653–6), a major monument of *astylar *Artisan Mannerism and the *Protectorate style. He may also have designed Wisbech Castle, Cambs. (*c.*1658—demolished). With *May, *Pratt, and *Wren he was one of the Surveyors employed to supervise the rebuilding of the City of London after the Great Fire (1666). His later work has something of the style of May and Pratt: at Cobham Hall, Kent (1661–3), for example, there was hardly a trace of Artisan Mannerism.

Co. (2008); M & E (1995); W.Pa (1852)

Mills, Robert (1781–1855) American architect, protégé of *Jefferson, he worked with *Hoban and assisted *Latrobe on the Capitol, Washington, DC (1803–8). After Latrobe sent him to Philadelphia (1807–8) to oversee the building of some houses and the Bank of Philadelphia, Mills set up his own practice there. Washington Hall, Philadelphia (1809–16), was in a severe Neo-Classical style worthy of *Ledoux, while the circular Sansom Street Baptist Church (1811–12) and Octagon Unitarian Church (1812–13) drew on an eclectic collection of sources. At the Monumental Church, Richmond, VA (1812–17), there was a centralized octagonal plan with a massive porch featuring distyle *in antis* (*see* ANTA) unfluted Greek-*Doric columns based on those of the Temple of Apollo at Delos, a robust design worthy of Latrobe. This Doric *Order was again used for the Washington Monument, Baltimore, MD (1814–42), where he designed many buildings.

Mills is best known for his monumental architecture in Washington, DC. These include the vast *obelisk of the Washington National Monument (1833–84), the great *stoa-fronted *Ionic Treasury Building (1836–42), the Doric Patent Office Building (1836–40—now the National Portrait Gallery), and the *Corinthian Old Post Office (1839–42). A competent *Greek Revivalist, one of his best buildings was the Lunatic Asylum, Columbia, SC (1821–7), in the Greek-Doric style with south-facing wards and a complete absence of the forbidding severity usually associated with such institutions. He designed several customs-houses and was a pioneer of fire-resistant construction.

Bryan (1976); Gallagher (1935); Hamlin (1964); Hi (1977); P & J (1970–86); P (1982); J.T (1996); W & K (1983); W-L (1985, 1994)

Milton, John (1608–74) English poet/polemicist, his *Paradise Lost* (published 1667) evoked the Garden of Eden, and in *Il Penseroso* (1632) 'arched walks', twilight groves', and a 'peaceful hermitage' of imagined gardens feature. Book IV of *Paradise Lost* was praised by *Addison and *Gilpin in the context of aesthetics and 'naturalness' in the English landscape-garden.

Gilpin (1976); H & W (1988); *ODNB* (2004)

mimbar, mambar, minbar Type of *pulpit in a *mosque, usually at the top of a flight of steps, consisting of a small standing-space with a *parapet enclosing it and with a *canopy above.

minaret Tall, slender tower (circular, rectangular, or polygonal on plan), usually attached to a *mosque, with one or more projecting *balconies from which Muslims are called to prayer.

Bloom (1989); Hilenbrand (1994); J.T (1996)

minchery, myncherie, mynchery Archaic name for a *nunnery.

miniature garden Miniature landscape with dwarf trees, small stones representing rocks, etc., called *bonsai* in Japanese and *shanshui penjing* in Chinese, created in *containers (usually shallow trays).

Bester (tr.) (2003); Koreshoff (1984); Shoe (2001)

Minimalism Style inspired by severe Modern architecture (such as the purest of *Mies van der Rohe's work or the bare images of *Barragán's designs), traditional Japanese architecture, and Zen-Buddhist gardens. Minimalism seeks to avoid clutter, ornament, and even colour, while possessions were stored away. It has sometimes been adopted to suggest exclusiveness and luxury. A feature of the *Modern Movement since the 1920s, it re-emerged in the 1960s and 1980s.

Pawson (1996); A.Tate & C.R.Smith (1986); Toy (ed.) (1994)

minimalist garden Characterized by clean lines, pure form, and a strong sense of place, it employs imaginative ecologically aware planting and sparing use of materials to create tranquil retreats, often quite small (perhaps a spatial extension to the home), sometimes in *courtyards, on roofs, and occasionally featuring water. It is not uninfluenced by *Chinese and *Japanese gardens. Practitioners include *Barragán, **Christopher Bradley-Hole** (1951-), *Noguchi, **John Pawson** (1949-), **Martha Schwartz** (1950-), and **Jacques Wirtz** (1924-2018).

Bradley-Hole (2005)

Minoan architecture Architecture of Ancient Crete, of which the palace at Knossos (C15 BC) is a good example. *See also* CRETAN ARCHITECTURE.

D (1950)

Minorite A friar minor or Franciscan.

minster 1. A *monastery or its church. 2. Abbey- or priory-church, or, more properly, a large *collegiate or conventual church, distinguished from a parish-church or a cathedral.

minstrel gallery *Balcony, *gallery or *loft for musicians, also called a *musician's gallery*, e.g. in a church or hall.

minute 1. Subdivision of a *module, sometimes a sixtieth part of a column-shaft diameter at its base if two modules are equivalent to that diameter, so a minute in this case would be a thirtieth part of a module. 2. Sixtieth part of a degree by which angles are measured.

Mique, Richard (1728-94) One of the creators of the *Louis-Seize* style in C18 France, he trained under J.-F.*Blondel, and worked for a while at Nancy for **Stanisław Leszczyński** (1677-1766), exiled **King of Poland** (*r*.1704-9 and 1733-4).

Called (1766) to Versailles by Leszczyński's daughter, **Marie**, Queen of **King Louis XV** (*r*.1715-74), he designed the Ursuline Convent with its Church (completed 1772—derived from *Palladio's *Villa Capra* near Vicenza); the Carmelite Church, *St-Denis* (1775); and *St-Cloud* Hospice Chapel (1788). He succeeded (1775) *Gabriel as *premier architecte du Roi* and, collaborating with Hubert *Robert, designed the master-plan (1777) for the development of the *Trianon*, Versailles, in the 'English Taste'. He built the *Temple de l'Amour*, the Theatre, the Grotto with Cascade, the Belvedere, and the *Picturesque *Hameau du Trianon* with its exposed timbers and rustic roofs (1778-82) that was a precedent for *Nash's Blaise Hamlet, near Bristol (1811). The interiors of the *petits appartements* at Versailles (1779) were designed for **Marie Antoinette** (1755-93), **Queen of France** from 1774 (*Méridienne*, two Libraries, and the *Cabinet Intérieur* or *Petit Salon*), all in the Neo-Classical style, of which he was an under-sung master. He fell victim to the Guillotine during the Terror.

B (1980); K & L (1972); Morey (1868); J.T (1996)

mirador Garden-building commanding a view, so similar to a *belvedere or *gazebo.

Miralles Moya, Enric (1955-2000). Catalan architect, he established (1984) his practice in Barcelona, collaborating (1983-92) with **Carme Piños** (1954-): works included the Igualada Cemetery, near Barcelona (1985-92—with banks of concrete *loculi); Olympic Archery Range, Barcelona (1992); *Els Hostalets de Balenyá* Civic Centre, near Barcelona (1988-94—which some have linked to *Deconstructivism); and the National Training Centre for Rhythmic Gymnastics, Alicante (1989-93). Miralles won (1998) the competition to design the new Scottish Parliament Building, sited at the foot of the Royal Mile, Edinburgh, in partnership with **RMJM Scotland** (successors of Robert *Matthew, Johnson-Marshall, & Partners), the building and costs of which have not been without controversy. With its pointless, almost unreadable allusions to upturned boats and fatuous claims that applied 'decorations' draw inspiration from *The Reverend Robert Walker Skating*, by **Sir Henry Raeburn** (1756-1823), the building (opened 2004) cannot be said to respond to its context, having no connection whatsoever to Scottish *vernacular architecture, and ignores the great Classical architectural legacy that was such an integral part of Edinburgh. But the *tabula rasa* could well be what it is all about: the obliteration of history.

W.Cu (1996); J (1995a); Mr (1995); E.Miralles (1996); B.Miralles (ed.) (1996)

miserere, misericord 1. *Mercy-seat, subsellium,* or miniature ledge on the underside of hinged medieval *choir-stall seats, so that, when the seats were folded upright, the misericords gave support to a standing person. It had a carved *corbel-like element under the ledge, frequently representing everyday life, comic episodes, fantastic creatures, fables, and even indecencies. Excellent carved medieval misericords survive, e.g. in the Parish Church of St Laurence, Ludlow, Salop. **2.** Room where monastic regulations were relaxed.

M.Anderson (1954); F.Bond (1910); J.Parker (1850); Remnant (1969)

Mission Revival Variant of American *Colonial Revival which drew on the RC mission buildings in CA popularized from the 1890s after the World's Columbian Exposition, Chicago, IL (1893). It is characterized by *arcades, *balconies, courtyards, and towers, with plain rendered walls and pan-tile roofs, and an absence of ornament or frippery. A good example was the Union Pacific Railroad Station, Riverside, CA (1904), by **Henry Charles Trost** (1860–1933).

Weitze (1984)

Mitchell, Arnold Bidlake (1864–1944) English *Arts-and-Crafts architect, he began practice (1886), specializing in parish-halls, houses, and schools. His best works include St Felix School, Southwold, Suffolk (1902), the School of Agriculture, Cambridge (1909–10), and University College School, Frognal, Hampstead, London (1905–7), the last in a robust *Wrenaissance style. His domestic works include the fine 1 Meadway Close (1910) and 34 and 36 Temple Fortune Lane (1908), Hampstead *Garden Suburb, and the outstanding houses in Basil Street, Brompton, London (1900s), with long ranges of *mullioned and *transomed windows and tall *gables (mutilated in the 1939–45 war).

A.S.Gray (1985); M & G (1992)

Mitchell, Ehrman Burkman (1924–2005) American architect, he established (1958) **Mitchell & Giurgola** with Rome-born **Romaldo Giurgola** (1920–2016). Influenced by Louis *Kahn, their work included the Volvo Headquarters, Göteborg, Sweden (1984), the Parliament House, Canberra, Australia (1988), and the IBM Offices, Darling Park, Sydney, Australia (1993).

Beck (ed.) (1988); E (1994); F (1993); P (1982); MGA (1996)

Mithraeum Building dedicated to the cult of **Mithras**, popular during the Roman Empire, often partly underground and planned on an *axis between shelves or *loculi on which followers reclined during the mysteries, and with

an *apse at one end. A good example was discovered (1870) under *San Clemente,* Rome.

mitre Junction of two members at right angles involving *chamfers or *mouldings meeting at a diagonal line. *See* ARCH; MASON's mitre. *Compounds include:*
mitre-head: type of *ogee-headed bulbous top of a *pinnacle or *turret of late *Perp. *Tudor-*Gothic, as in **Henry VII's** (*r.*1485–1509) Chapel, Westminster Abbey, London. The name is derived from its resemblance to a Bishop's head-dress;
mitre-leaf: C18/early-C19 *moulding enrichment featuring a leaf spliced at its base, often found with *beading as *bead-and-leaf* moulding.

Mixed style Eclectic architectural style incorporating hybrid elements from different periods, styles, and even cultures in order to attempt the creation of a new 'style', sometimes called *Synthetic Eclecticism* or *Syncretism*. Although much discussed in the 1970s, 1980s, and 1990s, it was also a phenomenon of other periods notably during the *Regency and late C19.

Crook (1987); D & M (1985); J.Walker (1992)

mixer-courts Forecourts to groups of dwellings used by pedestrians and vehicles.

Mixtec architecture A *Meso-American people, the **Mixtecs** lived in a region in modern México alongside the Pacific shore-line. Unlike the *Aztecs they did not build pyramidal structures. At Mitla, one of their major settlements, there are the remains of large houses, including the Palace of the Columns (*c.*1000) embellished with fine geometrical patterns, suggesting a sophisticated culture capable of producing impressive architecture.

Ck (1996); Kubler (1984)

Miyawaki, Mayumi (1936–) *See* ARCHITEXT.

Mizner, Addison (1872–1933) American architect. After a chequered career in San Francisco he became a gold prospector in northern CA and the Klondike, then a dealer in antiques, settling in NYC (1904). He then designed various buildings in sundry styles for rich clients until the 1914–18 war brought about a reduction in commissions. Settling in Palm Beach, FL, he was fortunate enough to meet **Paris Singer** (*c.*1865–1932), heir to some of the **Singer Sewing Machine** empire, who became his patron. Mizner built the Everglades Club, which was such a success he was then commissioned to design hundreds of houses for rich clients at Palm Beach, mostly erected 1919–26, in a *Picturesque and showy *Saracenic-Spanish style. He also manufactured *terracotta components, artificial-stone ornaments, and iron decorations, specifically to suit his architecture.

The success of his activities at Palm Beach led Mizner to buy land to the south, at Boca Raton, and there he carried out many developments before the property bubble burst (1926). Bankrupted, Mizner ended his life writing his memoirs.

D.Curl (1996); Mizner (1932); Mizner & Tarbell (1928); P (1982)

Mnesicles (*fl.*437–420 BC) Athenian architect of the time of **Pericles** (460–429 BC), he designed the monumental *Doric *Propylaea*, or entrance-gate to the *Acropolis* (437–432 BC). It was a precedent for numerous Neo-Classical gates, including *Langhans's Brandenburg Gate, Berlin, and von *Klenze's Propyläen, Munich. Mnesicles has been credited with the design of the *stoa of *Zeus Eleutherios* (*c.*430 BC) in the north-west corner of the *agora* in Athens, which had projecting *wings at each end: his name has also been associated with the *Erechtheion* (421–405 BC), but evidence is lacking.

Bungaard (1957); D (1950); P (1982); Tiberi (1964)

moat Large steep-sided trench around a town or building for defensive purposes, sometimes filled with water.

Mobile architecture Concept which held that users of buildings and settlements should have a say in plans and changes to them. Architecture would consist of structural frameworks, infrastructures, and services raised above the ground that would be infinitely adaptable. Such views influenced thinking in the 1960s and 1970s, notably *Archigram and *Metabolism.

Y.Friedman (1970, 1975)

Moderne *Art Deco.

Gebhard & von Breton (1969)

Modernism 1. *See* MODERN MOVEMENT. **2.** Style of the 1920s and 1930s described as *Modernist.

Weston (1996)

Modernisme Cultural movement (*c.*1880–*c.*1920) in Catalonia, Spain, divided into conservative *National Romanticism (**La Renaixença**—which promoted and celebrated Catalonian culture and language) and **Progressivism** (which tended to embrace many European tendencies, including the *Arts-and-Crafts movement, *Art Nouveau, and faith in the benefits of scientific investigation, technological advances, and industrialization). Catalan intellectuals saw Progressivism as a release from the stifling centralist structures of Madrid, and so *Modernisme* was associated with an assertion of regional (even nationalist) identity. Its architectural expression lay in the incorporation of eclectic elements derived from historic styles, notably *Moorish and *Gothic; exploitation of materials

(especially *brick and *tile) to express structure as well as to embellish every visible part of the fabric; and exuberant use of enrichment, applied or integral to the structure. Its most celebrated protagonists were *Domènech i Montaner, *Gaudí, and *Puig i Cadafalch.

Boh (1968); Boh *et al.* (1991); M.Freixa (1991); Gh (2000); L (1988); Marfany (1975)

Modernismo Spanish *Art Nouveau, also called *Estilo Modernista*, mostly associated with Catalonia, where it was called *Modernisme*.

Gh (2000); T-M (1967)

Modernist 1. Architectural style (1920s and 1930s) incorporating decorative devices that owed not a little to *Art-Deco, *Aztec, and Ancient-Egyptian styles, prompted by the 1925 Paris Exhibition. Among commoner motifs were *chevrons, canted and *corbelled 'arches', *medallions, wave-scrolls, flutings, *mouldings stepped over surfaces, and geometrical patterns. Colours were vivid, influenced by artefacts discovered (1922) in **Tutankhamun**'s (*r. c.*1332–*c.*1323 BC) tomb, so blacks, vermilions, greens, yellows, blues, and lots of gilt and chrome were *de rigueur*, often in enamels and even glazed openings. *Modernistic* buildings (as they are often called) also incorporated *streamlining and curved walls. A good example of Modernistic architecture is the former Hoover Building, Western Avenue, London (1931–8), by *Wallis, Gilbert, & Partners. **2.** Person subscribing to the doctrine and principles of the *Modern Movement.

Benton *et al.* (eds) (2003); L & D (1986); Hitchmough (1992)

Modernist garden As with *Modernism in architecture, C20 *Modernist landscape architects rejected past styles, though, like architects, often claimed affinities with past masters when it suited them (usually on flimsy grounds). Designers such as *Migge argued that gardens should not be created, but should *grow* to be beautiful, and there was an international tendency to emphasize 'functional' aspects of garden-design. In Scandinavian countries, however, landscape-design was dominated by architects, who created harmonious relationships between buildings and settings (e.g. *Asplund and *Lewerentz's work at Woodland Cemetery, Stockholm), but this sensitive approach was rejected by those favouring more radical design, influenced by *Cubism. The *Vera brothers had divided spaces into chequered designs, using strong colours, in their *Art-Deco-inspired work, but the turning-point seems to have been the *Exposition des Arts-Décoratifs et Industriels Modernes* (1924–5) in which concepts of space were revolutionized by the *Jardin d'Eau* *et de Lumière* designed by *Guévrékian: a pattern of brightly coloured triangles, it was influenced by theories of **Michel-Eugène Chevreul** (1786–1889), and was really conceived as a purely decorative type of triangular *parterre* in strident colours. This *Jardin* was seen by **Arthur-Anne-Marie-Charles, Vicomte de Noailles** (1891–1981) who, with his wife, **Marie-Laure** (1902–70), commissioned Guévrékian to design the garden (1928) of his *villa at Hyères, Var (1923, by *Mallet-Stevens). Noailles had also been patron of the Veras, and the Hyères garden is again triangular, filled with square, rectangular, and triangular brightly coloured compartments. This hard style of pattern-making influenced a generation of Modernists, not least Fletcher *Steele, *Tunnard (in his early career), et al. on both sides of the Atlantic, including *Barragán, *Burle Marx, *Eckbo, *Halprin, *Kiley, and *Noguchi, but was transformed in the process, leading in several directions, some more sensitive to Nature than others. *International *Modernism tended to disdain local conditions, imposing a rigid party line in design, although designers such as *Gibberd (e.g. his own garden in Harlow, Essex), *Jellicoe, et al. attempted a more diverse approach, and F.L.L.*Wright was certainly sensitive to Nature. As International Modernism's tyranny began to be questioned, realization that context (local cultural, climatic, and topographical aspects) really ought not to be ignored, but responded to with greater sensitivity (the firebrand Tunnard mellowed, and was an early convert to this), more complexity, and even contradiction (prompted by **Robert Charles Venturi** (1925–2018) et al.) started to be welcomed in the teeth of opposition, and the works of designers such as *Lutyens, T.H. *Mawson, *Verey, et al., were once again appreciated. Some American landscape architects (e.g. **Peter Walker** (1932–)) have regretted not knowing more about design-history, and draw on precedents from many cultures as a result. *See* NEW HUMANISM.

Adams (1993); Bourassa (1991); Imbert (1993); M & T (1991); Shoe (2001); Treib (1993); Tunnard (1938); Vera (1912, 1919, 1925); R.Vi (1966); W & S (1994); A.Wilson (2005)

Modern Movement C20 disparate architectural tendencies (also called *Modernism*) that sought to sunder all stylistic/historic links with the past, despising context, and demanding a *tabula rasa* so that there could be no comparisons between the New and the Old. While C19 theorists attempted to find a *style* suitable for the times, methods attempted to achieve this involved *eclecticism and mingling to produce so-called *Free or *Mixed styles, the optimistic idea being that something fresh might emerge

from the *mélange*. There were also some for whom function, honest expression of structure and materials, and a rational approach to design-problems from first principles were enough to point the way forward.

Early-C20 movements associated with totalitarianism (such as *Futurism and *Constructivism) sought answers in machinery, technology, and the expression of industrialized power, while the search for a *Machine Aesthetic became at times an end in itself. To some (notably Le *Corbusier), grain-silos, trans-Atlantic liners of the *Titanic* vintage, motor-cars, and aeroplanes were paradigms of a desirable new aesthetic, while others held that all art, all aesthetics, and all refinement were bourgeois affectations and therefore should be rejected. Aims of Modernism were radical, concerned with the suppression of all ornament and historical allusions, counterbalanced by the elevation of *Sachlichkeit* (objectivity) and the widespread adoption of *industrialized methods of building. Some groups, e.g. *De *Stijl*, advocated abstractions and purity of expression, and there were various different emphases within what was never a unified Movement, but virtually all were agreed on the need for 'rational' responses to contemporary needs using modern materials, mass-produced building components, and experimental, industrial methods of construction (which brought in their wake many problems concerning functional failures). Whilst idealistic iconoclasm, allied with Leftist attitudes, was endemic, the more extreme protagonists advocated violence: slogan-making and polemics all too often replaced supposed 'rational' argument. *Functionalism was held to be common ground, but even that faced objections in searchings for an architecture freed from constraints not only of the past and aesthetics, but from use as well. Some advocated that the purest architecture was that which remained on paper, or even in the mind, uncorrupted by the processes of being built, let alone used by untidy humanity.

By 1927 *International Modernism had arrived, and the white rectilinear flat-roofed building with strip-windows in metal frames (e.g. exhibits at the *Weissenhofsiedlung*, Stuttgart (1927), and Le Corbusier's designs) became the exemplar of what Modern-Movement architecture should *aim* to be, no matter if the pristine white walls were rendered *block-work (as they almost invariably were) rather than *concrete or steel. So the Movement that sought to abolish style had simply created a new one, albeit with a decidedly limited vocabulary (and one based on already outdated images (e.g. liners of *c.*1912)), bullying all to conform. Devoted to the destruction of academic architecture and institutions, it constructed its own theories, dogmas, and pedagogic establishment: the *Bauhaus became the model for indoctrination; *CIAM (1928) set the agenda and laid down the creeds; and writers (e.g. *Giedion and *Pevsner) evolved demonstrably dodgy constructs of a continuous, logical, and inevitable development of Modernism from C18 and C19 'Functional' buildings by so-called 'pioneers' of design. Architecture that did not fit neatly into this seamless 'history' was ignored, a chilling parallel to C20 political totalitarianism and its methods. After the 1939–45 war, '*Modernismus', as Reginald *Blomfield called it in the 1930s (a reference to its Teutonic origins), became the doctrine of the architectural establishment until new challenges arose from Modernist apostates (e.g. Philip *Johnson), advocates of contrast and contradiction, the protagonists of *Neo-Rationalist architecture (in particular the *Ticinese School), and the critiques of academics some of whom have identified many strands within a 'Movement' that has not been logical, objective, or homogeneous despite what its apologists believed. What is also clear is that the obsessions of the Modern Movement (which resembled a religion or a cult) with the *image* of what was perceived to be Modernity, killed craftsmanship, wasted energy to a profligate degree, and necessitated high maintenance costs. Modern Movements (there were many strands) promoted an incoherent, limited, non-architecture (with no sound intellectual bases whatsoever), which has not contributed to an agreeable environment, and indeed has succeeded all too well in creating an inhumane, alien, dangerous Dystopia. *See* NEW CLASSICISM; NEW HUMANISM.

Ballantyne (ed.) (2004); Blake (1977); Boyd White (1996, 2003); Brolin (1976, 1985); A.Cm (ed.) (1998); Cu (1996); Dr (1980); F (1980, 1982); Fu (1988); Gn (1967); Henket & Heynen (eds) (2002); Hines (2000); Js (1973a, 1980, 1982, 1988, 1990, 1995b, 2000, 2000a, 2002); Js & Kropf (eds) (1997); Jervis (1984); Khan (ed.) (1998); Lubbock (1995); Peto & Loveday (eds.) (1999); Pe (1960, 1974a); J. Reynolds (2001); Riseboro (1983); Rowland (1973); Salingaros *et al.* (2004); Sharp & Cooke (eds) (2000); Snibbe (1999); T & DC (1986); D.Wa (1977); Wilenski (1957); Wolfe (1993)

Modern style *Art Nouveau.

modillion Projecting bracket resembling a horizontal rather than vertical *console fixed in series under the *soffit of the *cornice of the *Composite, *Corinthian, and (occasionally) Roman *Ionic *Orders, expressive of a *cantilever. Modillions are regularly spaced, their centre-lines relating to the vertical axes of columns, and have *coffers set between them under the *corona. A plain rectangular block in the same position is a *block* or *uncut* modillion, or a variety of *mutule.

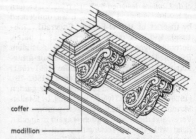

coffer

modillion

Cornice with modillions and coffers between them.

modinature Arrangement, positions, and types of *mouldings appropriate to any building, part of a building, or an *Order.

modular design Based on *modules, or certain standard sizes and multiples of those sizes, often associated with *industrialized buildings and *prefabrication.

module 1. Unit of length used in multiples to determine *proportion, in *Classicism the module is reckoned to be the diameter or the radius of a column-*shaft at its *base, subdivided into 60 or 30 *minutes. **2.** In *modular design a unit of measurement in prefabricated construction, or *industrialized building enabling ease of reproduction of repetitive standard components.

Modulor Le *Corbusier's system of *proportion, in *Le Modulor* (1948), based on the *golden section and on the male human figure (183 cm) with arm raised (total height 226 cm).

J-G (1964, 1968, 1973–7)

Moen, Olav Leif (1887–1951) Norwegian landscape architect, influenced by *Neo-Classicism, Reginald *Blomfield, *Mawson, and *Migge. His most celebrated achievement was the park of the Norwegian Agricultural University, Ås (from 1924), with clearly defined spaces connected by axes, a concept perhaps partly informed by *Schumacher's *Stadtpark*, Hamburg. He also designed *public parks at Mysen, Østfold (1938), Horten, Vestfold (1945), and Harstad, Troms (1947), as well as many private gardens, *cemeteries, and public spaces, all in Norway. He was the first Professor of landscape architecture at the Agricultural University (1939–51).

Shoe (2001)

Moffatt, William Bonython (1812–87) English architect in partnership (1835–44) with 'Great' *Scott: an expert on *workhouses, he designed around 50 (e.g. Great Dunmow, Essex (1840)).

D & M (1985); Morrison (1999); Scott (1995)

Moghul, Mogul *See* INDIAN STYLE; MUGHAL ARCHITECTURE; MUGHAL GARDEN.

Moholy-Nagy, László (1895–1946) Hungarian-born American artist/theorist/teacher. An important figure in the *Bauhaus and supporter of *Gropius, he not only was one of the editors of Bauhaus publications, but wrote two of them himself, including the influential *Von Material zu Architektur* (1929). He went into practice as a freelance designer after Hannes *Meyer took over (1928).

J.T (1996)

Möhring, Bruno (1863–1929) German architect, He was involved in the design of several international exhibitions (e.g. St Louis, MO, 1904), but is remembered primarily as an authority on town-planning, and, with **Alfred Grenander** (1863–1931), as a protagonist of *Art Nouveau (or *Jugendstil), mostly expressed in the bridges and stations of Berlin's elevated tramway system. A disciple of *Sitte, he proposed plans for Greater Berlin (1910), and, with *Gurlitt, founded *Stadtbaukunst alter und neuer Zeit* (from 1919).

Stadtbaukunst alter und neuer Zeit, x (1929), 1–4

molding *See* MOULDING.

molecular structure Building of tubes and balls arranged to resemble a diagram of a molecule, as in the *Atomium* erected for the Brussels Exposition (1958).

L & D (1986)

Molinos, Jacques (1743–1831) French architect, he collaborated with J.-G.*Legrand on a number of projects, including the erection of the huge timber (1782–3 (destroyed 1803)) *dome over the central *court of the *Halle au Blé*, Paris, regarded as progressive at the time. Also with Legrand he designed the *Julien* Garden at Épinay, and the *Théâtre Feydeau* (which influenced F.*Gilly). On his own he built the *Château* of Pulsieux, near Villers-Cotterets (1780–5). As Architect and Inspector of Civil Buildings for the Department of the Seine he produced some experimental but unrealized Neo-Classical designs for *cemeteries and crematoria, including the original proposals for Montmartre Cemetery, Paris (1799). His son, **Auguste-Isidore Molinos** (1795–1850) became an architect in Paris, designing the Churches of *St-Jean*, Neuilly (1827–31), and *Ste-Marie*, Batignolles (1828–9).

Delaire (1907); Etlin (1984); Ga (1972); Ha (1955); M & Wa (1987)

Møller, Christian Frederik (1898–1988) Danish architect. Taught by Kay *Fisker, he worked with the latter (1928–43). With **Povl**

Stegmann (1888–1944) he designed Aarhus University (begun 1932), influenced by Hannes *Meyer's Trade Union School, Bernau, Berlin. Construction (from 1943 Møller's responsibility) went on until 1965, the various buildings (in a yellow *brick) being placed in the undulating landscape for which *Sørensen was consultant. He also designed the Museum of Modern Art, Aarhus (1963–5), and the Carl-Henning Pedersen Museum, Herning, Denmark (1973).

We (1995)

Moller, Georg (1784–1852) German architect. After training under *Weinbrenner in Karlsruhe (1802–7), he became (1810) Director of Architecture for the **Grand Duchy of Hesse-Darmstadt**, and created a Neo-Classical town-centre in Darmstadt itself. His architecture was austerely impressive: it included many houses (1811–25), the Freemasons' Hall (1817–20), the Court Theatre and Opera House (1818–20), and New Chancellery (1826–31). The RC *Ludwigskirche* (1820–7—a drum with an internal *peristyle of *Corinthian columns carrying the *dome), the chaste Palace for **Prince Carl** (1837–41), the *Greek-Revival *mausoleum on the Rosenhöhe (1826–31), the *Doric Victory Column (1841–4), and *Kasino* (1812) were all very fine buildings, but Darmstadt was severely damaged in the 1939–45 war, so little of his work survives.

Outside Darmstadt Moller designed several works of considerable importance, including the Gothic House (1823–4), and the remodelling of the *Schloss* (1825–41), both in Homburg, while at Wiesbaden he rebuilt the *Schloss* (1837–41—now the *Hessischer Landtag*). At Mainz the Theatre (1829–33), with its clearly expressed *auditorium and blocky fly-tower, was derived from *Durand's *Précis* (1802–5), and was reminiscent of F.*Gilly's unexecuted design for a National Theatre for Berlin (1799): with its external *arcades the building influenced *Semper's celebrated Opera Houses in Dresden.

While Moller was one of the greatest of German Neo-Classicists, he was also a pioneering student of medieval architecture. With *Boisserée he discovered (1814) the original plans for Cologne Cathedral that were used as the basis of that building's completion. He published *Denkmäler der deutschen Baukunst* (1815–21) which came out in English as *Moller's Memorial of German Gothic Architecture* (1836), and was of immense importance as a sourcebook for the *Gothic Revival. He was interested in constructional advances, using iron to reconstruct a *dome at Mainz Cathedral, and bringing out publications, including *Beiträge zu der Lehre von den Construktion* (1832–44).

F & S (1959); Haupt (1952–4); Krimmel (ed.) (1978); G.Moller (1815–44); Wa & M (1987)

Mollet Family of French artists and garden-designers. **Jacques** (*fl.*1580s–90s) worked with *Dupérac at the *Château* of Anet, and is credited with the creation of the first *parterre de broderie* there (1580s) although *Boyceau remains a strong candidate for that distinction. Jacques's son, **Claude** (*c.*1564–*c.*1649) worked at Anet, Fontainebleau, Saint-Germain-en-Laye, Monceau-en-Brie, and the Tuileries, Paris, but also left numerous designs for gardens published after his death as *Théâtre des plans et jardinages* (1652). Several of his designs were also published in **Olivier de Serres**'s (1539–1619) *Théâtre d'agriculture et mesnage des champs* (1600), and these were laid out with assistance from his sons, including **Pierre** (d.1659) and **André** (d.1665—whose treatise, *Le Jardin de plaisir* (1651) also came out in German and Swedish, with an English edition (1670), thereby publicizing French formal gardens over a wide area). André designed gardens in England (e.g. Wimbledon House and St James's Palace (1630s and 1640s), The Netherlands (e.g. *Honselaarsdijk* (1633–5)) and Sweden (e.g. the King's Garden, Royal Palace, Stockholm (1646–52)). With his brother **Charles** (*fl.*1600–93), he laid out gardens for **King Charles II of Great Britain and Ireland** (*r.*1660–85) at St James's Park, London, and Hampton Court Palace. André's insistence that shrubs and trees could be planted in an architectural way, and that there should be visual harmony between a building, its gardens, and subsidiary structures, influenced André Le *Nôtre, son of one of Claude Mollet's assistants.

Ht (ed.) (1974); K.Woodbridge (1986)

Mollino, Carlo (1905–73) Italian architect, he designed the offices of the *Confederazione degli Agricoltori*, Cuneo (1933–4), and of the *Società Ippica Torinese*, Turin (1935–9—destroyed). In the latter he freely interpreted aspects of *Neo-Plasticism and *Rationalism with considerable verve and originality. He responded to natural landscapes with sensitivity (e.g. the cable-railway station and hotel, Lago Nero (1946–7), and the cable-railway station, Fürggen, Cervina (1950–3)). At the *Camera di Commercio*, Turin (1968–73—with **Alberto Galardi** (1930–) and **Carlo Graffi** (1925–85)) internal columns were avoided. With others he reconstructed *Alfieri's *Teatro Regio* (1738—destroyed 1936), the modern interior of which was constructed behind the C18 exterior.

Brino (1987); Polano (ed.) (1989); J.T (1996)

Molnár, Farkas (1897–1945) Hungarian architect, associated with *Hungarian Activism, he became a leading member of the *Modern Movement between the wars. At the *Bauhaus he designed his Red Cube House (1922) which was published. At the invitation (1929) of *Gropius, he contributed to the *CIAM conference on 'The Small Apartment', after which he and others formed the Hungarian branch of CIAM. A powerful protagonist of *International *Modernism, Molnár designed several white-rendered blocky houses, with bold *cantilevers and deep *terraces, set in the hills around Budapest, clearly influenced by *De *Stijl. Some of his designs (e.g. Houses on *Cserje* (1931) and *Lejtő* (1932) *utcák*, Budapest) are paradigms of the International Style that gelled at the *Weissenhofsiedlung*, Stuttgart (1927). His Budapest apartment-blocks on *Lotz Károly utca* (1933) and *Pasaréti út* (1937) are also significant. For a brief period in 1933 he collaborated with *Breuer before the latter emigrated to America. Molnár was killed during the Soviet siege of Budapest (1945).

Li (1996); J.T (1996)

Molton, John (*fl.*1524–47) English master-mason, he worked at Westminster (1524–8) and Bath (1526–39) Abbeys, succeeding Henry *Redman as master-mason to the King and to Westminster Abbey (1528). He probably designed the *chantry-chapel of **Abbot John Islip** (1464–1532), Westminster Abbey (1530s), and he worked on Cardinal (now Christ Church) College, Oxford, the Palace of Westminster, and, from 1532, Hampton Court Palace, where he designed the Great Hall. He seems to have been responsible for works at all the major buildings for **King Henry VIII** (*r.*1509–47), including the Palaces of St James, Bridewell, and Nonsuch, and the Forts of Deal, Walmer, and Sandown in Kent, although the last three buildings were designed by von *Haschenperg, with probable contributions from Richard *Lee. He was among the last great English medieval architects.

J.Harvey (1987)

monastery Building or group of buildings arranged for the occupancy of members of a religious Order, or of persons desiring religious seclusion. European medieval monastic architecture derives from C6 types evolved under the rules of the Order founded by St Benedict, of which the C9 plan of St Gall, Switzerland, is the earliest surviving drawn example, with *cloister, *chapter-house and *dorter, *refectory, and infirmary set well away to the south-east. In terms of architectural organization the *Benedictine arrangement was sophisticated, and was the basis for the *Cistercian monastic plan, of which Fountains Abbey, Studley Royal, Yorkshire (mostly C12 and C13), is a fine example.

Braunfels (1972); Horn & Born (1979); J.T (1996)

monastery *or* **monastic garden** During the Middle Ages areas within or adjacent to *monastery precincts were cultivated for growing fruit, herbs, and vegetables (not only for culinary/

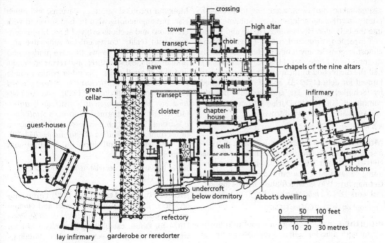

Plan of Fountains Abbey, Yorks.

medical purposes, but to provide commodities for sale): *Benedictines were particularly noted for promoting horticulture. *Dovecotes were built and fish-ponds constructed. The idealized C9 plan of a monastery in the Abbey of St Gall, Switzerland, shows that the rectangular *cemetery was also planted with fruit- and nut-trees. Most monastic communities had areas allocated for meditation, especially *cloisters, but gardens were also provided for spiritual nourishment. *Chinese and *Japanese gardens based on principles of harmony also had profound spiritual dimensions. *See* MEDIEVAL GARDEN.

M.Brown (2012); MacDougall (ed.) (1986); Shoe (2001); Tay (2006)

Monck, Sir Charles Miles Lambert, 6th Bt. (1779–1867) English landowner/architect. After their marriage (1804), he and his wife, **Louisa** (d.1824), visited Greece, where they met *Gell, and saw numerous *Antique remains. They also visited Germany, where Monck sketched several Neo-Classical buildings, including *Langhans's Brandenburg Gate, Berlin. When the Moncks returned (1806) to their estate in Northum. (with a large collection of drawings and a son, appropriately named **Charles Atticus** (1805–56)), they decided to erect a new house at Belsay, and the work was completed (1817), one of the world's outstanding buildings in the *Greek-Revival style (and one of noble simplicity and clarity, happily devoid of pedantry), for which Monck was his own architect, supervising all the work himself.

This fine, austere, and unconventional house has been wrongly attributed to *Dobson, who practised in and around Newcastle upon Tyne: Dobson *advised* Monck on certain aspects such as the details of *Ionic capitals and how to draw them accurately for craftsmen, but otherwise Belsay is entirely Monck's work (his draughtsmanship was, in *Colvin's words, 'neat and accurate'), although he also discussed his work with Gell who seems to have suggested certain refinements. Nowhere in England was the Arcadian vision of Romantic *Neo-Classicism better expressed than at Belsay in its setting, and nowhere may finer *ashlar work be seen. At Belsay, Monck also designed the *stables (with octagonal *lantern based on the Athenian 'Tower of the Winds'), the Greek-Revival lodges, and a remarkable garden in the quarry from which the stone for the house was taken. Monck designed Linden House, near Morpeth (1812–13), with a Greek-*Doric *portico, and a long terrace of houses in the *Italianate style, with arcaded ground floor, at Belsay Village (probably prompted by a visit to Sicily and Italy in 1830–1), and the Old School (1829 and 1841).

Co (2008); Crook (1972a); Grundy *et al.* (1992); Monck papers, NRO, 5/223–6

money pattern *See* COIN.

Moneypenny, George (1768–*c*.1830) Architect who succeeded *Blackburn as the leading designer of English prisons. His work was often distinguished, and even, according to a contemporary, 'terrific', meaning striking *Sublime terror into the beholder. His Sessions House and House of Correction, Knutsford, Ches. (1817–19), was almost as good as anything by *Harrison, and his County Gaol, Leicester (1790-2—demolished), had the distinction of incarcerating Moneypenny himself for debt (1792-3), and of being sketched by *Schinkel (1826). He and Ignatius *Bonomi completed (1811) the Durham County Courts and Gaol after *Sandys's dismissal.

B & R (1993); Co (2008)

Monier, Joseph (1823-1906) Pioneer of *reinforced-concrete construction, he patented designs (1860s), and later (1877) his system for manufacturing *beams and columns, developed by the German firm **Wayss**, which published its theoretical work *Das System Monier* (1887).

Christophe (1902); P.Collins (1959)

monitor Elevated section of a roof with openings at both sides for light and ventilation running its full length (as in a US railway-car or a factory).

monolith Object made of one piece of stone, e.g. an *obelisk or column-*shaft, so *monolithic* means: **1.** made of one piece of stone; **2.** architecture appearing blocky, huge, and uniform; **3.** building constructed of *concrete poured and cast *in situ*; **4.** rock-cut buildings.

monopteron *or* **monopteros** Circular *colonnade supporting a roof, but without walls. *Soane called a *monopteral* building one without walls but with columns, but did not confine it to circular buildings, as he used the term to describe part of his own *mausoleum (on a square plan) in the burial-ground of St Giles-in-the-Fields, Old St Pancras, London (1816).

monotriglyphic *Intercolumniation with one *triglyph on the *frieze between the centre-lines of two adjacent *Doric columns.

Montague, Henry Thomas William (1925-2007) English architect, he made an early career designing television studios before setting up in practice (1963). Working with Frank *Matcham & Partners, he carried out numerous refurbishments of London theatres, including the *Palladium* and the *Lyceum*. He also designed other buildings including a convent, a church, and racehorse-stables.

RIBAJ (Jan. 2008), 61

Montano, Giovanni Battista (1534-1621) Italian architect, of primary importance as a recorder of *Antique Roman architectural remains. Engravings were made of his drawings by his pupil G.B.*Soria, the first volume published as *Scielta di varii tempietti antichi* (1624).

Montano recorded *grottoes, caverns, and much else, but augmenting what he had surveyed with elevations and sections evolved from his imaginings, with reality 'corrected' for subjective aesthetic reasons. He seems to have understood Roman *concrete structures, and recorded *vaults and complicated stairs. His other works include *Diversi ornamenti capricciosi per depositi o altari* (1625), *Tabernacoli diversi* (1628), and *Architettura con diversi ornamenti cavati dall' antico* (1636). His work informed *Cortona's *Santi Luca e Martina* (1634-69) and the design of the *façade of *Bernini's *Sant'Andrea al Quirinale* (1658-70). He was also an influence on *Guarini and *Borromini.

Jervis (1984); *JSAH*, xxxvi/4 (Dec. 1977), 252–5; P (1982); J.T (1996)

Monteiro, José Luis (1849-1942) Portuguese architect, he studied under *Pascal and worked on the reconstruction of the *Hôtel de Ville*, Paris (1874-8), before establishing himself in Lisbon, where he designed several public buildings much influenced by developments in France. His works include the *Rocío* Central Railway Station (1886-7—with a *Manueline-Revival *façade), the *Hotel Palace* (1890-2), the *Liceu Central* (1887), and the Church of the Angels (1908-11). His architectural styles were eclectic, including *Neo-Classicism, French *Second Empire, and even English *Arts-and-Crafts (the latter especially for his private houses). He used metal for the interior of the Railway Station and the *Sala de Portugal, Sociedade de Geografia*, Lisbon (1897). He was Professor of Architecture, *Escola de Belas Letras*, Lisbon (1881-1920), and therefore an influence on later Portuguese architects.

França (1991); R.C.Smith (1968); J.T (1996)

Monteiro, Porfirio Padal (1897-1957) Portuguese architect, he designed several early houses in the *Art Deco style (including 207-15 *Avenida 5 de Outubro* (1929) and the *Cais do Sodré* railway station (1925-8)), the Church of *Rósario de Fátima* (1934-8), and the *Conde de Óbidos* railway station (1945), all in Lisbon.

J.T (1996)

Montferrand, Henri-Louis-Auguste-Ricard de (1786-1858) Russian architect of French birth, he studied in Paris, worked in the office of *Percier & *Fontaine, then under *Vignon on the *Madeleine*, Paris. Having presented (1814) some architectural drawings to **Tsar Nicholas I** (r.1801-25), he emigrated to Russia (1816) where he was appointed Court Architect. Among his most important works in St Petersburg may be cited the *Lobanov-Rostovsky* House (1817-20), St Isaac's Cathedral (1818-58—influenced by *Soufflot's *Ste-Geneviève*, Paris, with an iron-framed *dome (c.1841-2)), the exterior of which has echoes of *Wren's *cupola of St Paul's Cathedral, London, and especially of *Schinkel's *Nikolaikirche*, Potsdam), and the Alexander Column (1829-34). The use of iron in the Cathedral was an important precedent for the later dome of the Capitol, Washington, DC, by *Walter. Montferrand could turn his hand to *Gothic, Russian *vernacular, *Moorish, and *Chinoiserie styles, and designed several interiors of the Winter Palace (e.g. Hall of Peter the Great, Field-Marshals' Hall and Rotunda, and private rooms for the **Tsarinas Aleksandra** and **Mariya**—1827 to early 1830s). He published lavish monographs on the Cathedral (1845) and the Column (1836).

Butikov (1980); G.H (1983); Montferrand (1845); J.T (1996)

Montfort, John (fl.1376-c.1405) English military architect responsible for works at the Castle, Elmley, Worcs. (1391-6), and Warwick Castle, where he built Guy's Tower (1390s) and parts of the East Range.

J.Harvey (1987)

Montigny, A.-H.-V. Grandjean de (1776-1850) *See* GRANDJEAN.

Montoyer, Louis-Joseph (c.1749-1811) Flemish architect, he designed the *Collège du Pape*, Leuven (1776-8), in a late-*Baroque style. He became (c.1780) Architect to **Duke Albrecht of Sachsen-Teschen** (1738-1822), Governor-General of the Austrian Netherlands, where he became a dominant figure in the architectural world of what is now Belgium, designing the Palace of *Schoonenberg*, Laeken (1782-4) and the Church of *St-Jacques-sur-Coudenberg*, Brussels (1776-85). He commenced (1791) the Military Academy of Ixelles, Brussels (not completed), and moved to Central Europe with the Duke where he designed the *Redoute*, Baden (1799), the Temple of Concord in the Park at Laxenburg (1795), major alterations at the *Albertinum*, Vienna (1801-4—to house the Duke's great art-collections), and the Classical Great Hall of the *Hofburg*, Vienna (1804-7). He was responsible for the saloon in the *Palais Rohan*, Prague (1807), one of the best examples of *Neo-Classicism in Bohemia.

G & TK (1960); T & B (1932); W-R (1970)

Montreuil, Pierre de (fl.1239-67) French architect active in Paris. Probably trained at Amiens, his first recorded works were a refectory (1239) and a *Lady Chapel (1245) at *St-Germain-des-Prés* (mostly destroyed). He was *caementarius* at *St-Denis* (1247), but any connection with *Sainte-Chapelle* is tentative. The higher parts of the south *transept at *Notre Dame* (1258-67), were designed and built by him following the death of Jean de *Chelles. His tombstone (no

longer extant) at *St-Germain-des-Prés* acknowledged his status as a Doctor of Masons.

Eudes de Montreuil (fl.c.1250-87), perhaps Pierre's son, was a *Magister Caementarius Operum Domini Regis*, and may have been involved in building fortifications at Jaffa, Palestine. Part of Beauvais Cathedral was attributed to him, but the evidence for this, and for his involvement at the Aigues-Mortes town fortifications, is virtually non-existent.

Branner (1965); W.Pa (1852); P (1982); J.T (1996)

Montuori, Eugenio (1907-82) With other Italian architects in *Terragni's circle, he won the competition to design the new town of Sabaudia, one of five towns planned by the Fascist régime as part of the reclamation of the Pontine Marshes near Rome: the stark, tough architecture was firmly embedded in the *Rationalism and *Neo-Classicism that evolved in 1930s Italy. Montuori designed the concourse for the Railway Station, Venice (1934), the town-plans of Bolzano (1936) and Carbonia (1940), and works in Rome including Classicizing buildings at the University (1935), the *Piazza Imperiale* (1940s), and the *Stazione Termini* (from 1947).

vV (1993)

monument 1. Building or memorial intended to perpetuate the memory of an event or an individual, such as a public memorial or funerary monument. **2.** Structure considered to be an object of historic or architectural interest. *Related terms are*:

monumental: **1.** building intended as a monument, or looking like one; **2.** building that is formal, very large, and permanent, intended to impress;

monumental brass: plate of *brass or *latten *incised with a formalized image and inscription, let into a stone slab as a funerary monument.

moon-door *See* DI XUE. In a *Chinese garden it might be circular, polygonal, or shaped like a gourd or leaf.

Moore, Charles Willard (1925-93) American architect, leading figure of *Post-Modernism. He founded (1970) his own firm, subsequently forming associations with other professionals under **Centerbrook Architects** and various names. His work was varied, full of allusions, and *scenographic. Early buildings included his own house, Orinda, CA (1962), where living-areas were identified by means of historical references, and this set the agenda for later work in which knowledge of architectural history played no small part, for his architecture was often tempered with fancy, myth, and mnemonic associations. Other schemes included the Athletic Club, Sea Ranch, near San Francisco (1964–6—where the buildings recall summer-cottage and sea-shore architecture); Kresge College, University of California, Santa Cruz (1973–4); the *Piazza d'Italia*, New Orleans, LA (1975–80—a stagey composition (almost a *collage) of reminiscences from *Classicism that Modernists found profoundly shocking); St Matthew's Church, Pacific Palisades, CA (1979–83); Humboldt Library and housing, Tegel Harbour, Berlin (1987–8); the Church of the Nativity, Rancho Santa Fé, CA (1989); and the University of Oregon Science Complex, Eugene, OR (1990), all of which had historical references. Moore's use of evocative motifs was powerfully polemical. He also designed several parks (e.g. Hermann Park, Houston, TX (1982)).

K.Bloomer & C.Moore (1977); E (1994); J (1993); E.Johnson (ed.) (1986); Keim (ed.) (1996); Klotz (1988); Littlejohn (1984); Ma (1985); Ojeda *et al.* (eds) (1994, 1997); P (1982); Stern (1977); J.T (1996); Tompkins & Boucher (1993)

Moore, Temple Lushington (1856–1920) Ecclesiastical architect with Ulster connections, he was articled to George Gilbert *Scott Jun. before setting up on his own (1879). His work, a mixture of scholarly *Gothic Revival and ingenious invention, was a link between *Bodley's style and the final phase of the Revival as epitomized in the work of Moore's pupil, Giles Gilbert *Scott: it included St Peter's Church, Barnsley, Yorks. (1893–1911), All Saints' Church, Tooting, London (1904–6), St Wilfrid's Church, Harrogate, Yorks. (1905–14), and Pusey House, Oxford (1911–14—one of his finest and most sensitive works).

AR, **lix** (Jan./Feb. 1926), 12–17, 56–63; Brandwood (1997); C.Brooks & Saint (eds) (1995); J.Curl (2007); A.S.Gray (1985); *RIBAJ*, 3 ser., **xxxv**/14 (26 May 1928), 470–92; *ODNB* (2004); P (1982); J.T (1996)

Moorish arch *See* ARCH.

Moorish architecture *Islamic architecture of North Africa and regions of the Iberian peninsula where the Moors were dominant (711–1492). The most perfect examples were the exquisite *Alhambra*, Granada (mostly 1338–90—which was probably a *madrasa rather than a *palace, with delightful gardens in which geometry, symmetry, water-features, and carefully considered planting played essential parts), and *La Mezquita*, Córdoba (785–987), both in Spain. *Moresque* is architecture like or derived from that of the Moors (*see* HISPANO-MORESQUE), or, more loosely, from Islamic architecture, and the term is especially associated with formal foliate ornament of an interlacing type, also known as *arabesque. Moorish influences had a considerable effect during the C19 enthusiasm for exotic

*Picturesque buildings, and they were exploited by many designers, such as Owen *Jones.

Conner (1979); Danby (1995); Irwin (2004); O.Jones (1868); L & D (1986); W.Pa (1852); S (1901–2); Symes (2006); J.T (1996)

Moosbrugger *or* **Mosbrugger, Caspar Andreas** (1656–1723) With the *Beers and *Thumbs, he was among the most important architects of what is known as the *Vorarlberg School, working in the *Baroque and *Rococo styles in and around the eastern shores of the *Bodensee*. Admitted (1682) as a lay-brother to the *Benedictine Abbey at Einsiedeln, Switzerland, on which he worked (at first under **Johann (Hans) Georg Kuen** (1642–91)) from 1674 until his death, he was one of the first (1680s) Central-European architects to alter the *basilican plan by introducing circular, elliptical, or polygonal volumes. His grandest project was the Abbey at Einsiedeln itself, the design of which dates from the death of Kuen: Moosbrugger's plan bears some resemblance to that of the *Escorial*, Madrid, and after a disastrous fire, construction started (1704). Building of the Church itself began in 1719: it has an interior arrangement that marks its architect as a great original who responded to the challenge of providing not only a hugely impressive Abbey Church, but a place of pilgrimage as well, for it contained a wonder-working statue of Our Lady presented (853) by **Abbess Hildegard of Zürich** (*c.*828–56) to **Count Meinrad of Sulgen** (*c.*797–861). A *Gnadenkapelle* (chapel for the miraculous image) was erected associated with a *monastery of Benedictine Hermits (*Einsiedler*): in due course (C13) the Abbey was created as an independent principality, and, owing to the throngs of pilgrims, became one of the richest in the area. In *c.*1617 *Solari designed a rich *Sanctum Sanctorum* to house the image, and the chapel was associated with the tomb of the founder, by then **St Meinrad**, of the House of Hohenzollern (Solari's work was destroyed (1798) and rebuilt in reduced form to plans by **Jakob Natter** (1735–1815) and *Cagnola). However, the position of the shrine was fixed, and to the east of it was a C17 *chancel: Moosbrugger's solution was to unify the Church by creating an approximately octagonal volume (one side of which is set immediately behind the bowed front) around the *Sanctum Sanctorum*, with a two-bay nave flanked by *aisles and *wall-piers to the east of it. The western volume, accommodating the shrine and pilgrims, has, rising from the shrine, two piers carrying vault-arches, creating complex geometries. Eastwards lie the *choir and *high-altar, and the entire interior seems to be very long, an effect enhanced by refinements of *scenography and by the rich frothiness of the *stucco and other decorations by the *Asam brothers (from 1724).

Moosbrugger was active as consultant architect for several monasteries in the area. He remodelled (1684–1719) the *Romanesque former Benedictine Abbey Church at Muri, Switzerland, creating a Baroque octagonal central space out of the former nave and aisles, and prepared schemes for the Abbey Church at St Gallen, Switzerland, where the central space may have developed from his ideas, although the architect mostly responsible for that great building was Peter *Thumb. Moosbrugger's advice (1685, 1717) on the design of the vast Benedictine Abbey Church at Weingarten, Württemberg (built 1714–24), does not appear to have borne fruit, but his influence may be detected (his involvement is documented) at the former Benedictine Abbey (now *Pfarrkirche*), Rheinau (1702); the *Pfarrkirche*, Lachen (1703); the Benedictine Abbey Church, Engelberg (1704); the former Dominican Convent (now *Pfarrkirche*), St Katherinenthal (1690); the former Monastic Church at Ittingen (1698—with an exquisite interior by **Franz Ludwig Hermann** (1710–97) and others); the Benedictine Abbey Church, Disentis (1696–1712); the former Benedictine Abbey Church, Fischingen (1685, 1706, 1716); and further works in Switzerland. Other Moosbruggers, e.g. **Andreas** (1722–87) and **Peter Anton I** (1732–1806), were producing stucco-work in the 1780s (e.g. the Church at Horgen, Switzerland), and **J.S.Moosbrugger** designed the Neo-Classical high-altar in St Gallen (1810). In 1845–6 **Hieronymus Moosbrugger** (1807–58) executed the *Neo-Baroque Hall of Sessions in the Lower-Austrian *Landhaus*, Vienna.

Birchler (1924); Böck (1989); Bou (1962); E.Hempel (1965); Hi (1968a); Lb & D (1976); On (1973); P (1982); J.T (1996)

Morandi, Riccardo (1902–89) Italian civil-engineer, renowned for his *reinforced-concrete structures, notably the Maracaibo Bridge, Venezuela (1957–62), the Polcevera *Autostrada* viaduct, near Genoa (1960–7), the huge sail-roof of the maintenance hangar, Fiumicino Airport, Rome (1970), and the subterranean car-showroom, Valencia Park, Turin (1959).

Boaga (ed.) (1984); E (1994); Imbesi *et al.* (1991); Masini (ed.) (1974)

Morava School See BYZANTINE ARCHITECTURE.

More, Edmund (*fl*.1523–36) English Freemason. He worked (1523–33) on **Nicholas West's** (*fl*.1475–1533—**Bishop of Ely** from 1515) exquisite *chantry-chapel, Ely Cathedral, Cambs., a sumptuous work in which late-*Perp. and early *Renaissance (especially the vaulted ceiling) merge. Virtually all the images he carved have been destroyed, but if he and his assistant, **Peter Cleyft** (probably German from Cleves), had anything to do with the architectural treatment (which seems likely), they were a remarkable

team, creating one of the loveliest early-C16 spaces in England.

J.Harvey (1987)

Moreau, Charles-Jean-Alexandre (1760–1810) French architect/landscape-gardener. He studied under *Trouard and reconstructed (1803) the Esterházy Palace at Kismarton (Eisenstadt), including the landscape-garden with *Leopoldina* Temple, Steam-Engine House (to shelter the machinery pumping water through the park), and hill-top *gloriette*. He also designed gardens at Pottendorf (Lower Austria) and the park and house at Somlóvár (Doba, now Romania).

Prost (ed.) (2005); Tay (2006)

Moreau-Desproux, Pierre-Louis (1727–93) French architect. He designed the *Hôtel de Chavannes, Boulevard du Temple*, Paris (1756–8), which was praised by *Laugier as an example of the new 'Greek' fashion, although there was precious little Grecian about it apart from the bands of key frets under the first-floor windows. He refronted the *Palais Royal*, Paris, when he reconstructed the *Théâtre de l'Opéra* there (1763–70—destroyed 1781). He was guillotined.

B (1980); M & Wa (1987)

Morel, Jean-Marie (1728–1810) French landscape architect, whose *Théorie des Jardins* (1776) was influential. Morel helped *Girardin to lay out the celebrated *Picturesque garden at Ermenonville, Oise.

W.H.Adams (1979); Racine (ed.) (2001)

Moresque See MOORISH ARCHITECTURE.

Moretti, Luigi Walter (1907–73) Italian architect, his early works were in the *stripped Neo-Classical style of *Rationalist architecture under Fascism, epitomized by the buildings and the plan for the Foro Mussolini, Rome (1927–32), developing by the late 1930s to acquire Grecian references. After the 1939–45 war his buildings became marked by strong horizontals and verticals, and an almost violent juxtaposition of elements. His individuality was marked in the *Astrea Co-operative Building, Monteverde Nuovo (1949), and *Il Girasole* House (1950), both in Rome, and the *Villa la Saracena*, Santa Marinella (1954). He was an important and influential writer (1940s–50s), especially critical of *International Modernism and opposed to the fundamental principles of *Mies van der Rohe and his disciples. He designed the Watergate Complex, Washington, DC (1960–3—which is better known for other than architectural reasons), and (with *Nervi) the Stock Exchange Tower, Montréal, Canada (1961–7).

AR, cxxxix/832 (Jun. 1966), 432–8; E (1994); J.T (1996)

Morgan, Julia (1872-1957) American architect/engineer, she studied architecture at the *École des *Beaux-Arts*, Paris, and became CA's first licensed female architect. Her works include several buildings for Mills College, Oakland, CA, including the *reinforced-concrete *campanile (1903-4), library (1905-6), and gymnasium (1907-8). She was responsible for many private houses (some in *Mission-Revival style) in the San Francisco area and her responses to client-needs were realized drawing on eclectic motifs, often building with local materials, always displaying the assurance in design acquired in Paris. Her Young Women's Christian Association buildings at Asilomar-Pacific Grove, CA (1913-28), are now a State Monument and National Conference Center. Insisting on fine detailing and sensitivity to human beings and sites, she was capable on occasion of creating eclectic fantasies of extraordinary power, among which must be mentioned San Simeon, CA (1919-38), a vigorously composed collection of cultural references at Enchanted Hill, for **William Randolph Hearst** (1863-1951). Her fine *Arts-and-Crafts-inspired St John's Presbyterian Church, Berkeley, CA (1908-10), is now the Julia Morgan Center for Performing Arts.

Beach (1976); Boutelle (1995); C.James (1990); Longstreth (1977); Susana Torre (ed.) (1977); Wadsworth (1990); Winslow (1980); R.Winter (ed.) (1997)

Moro, Peter (1911-98) German-born *Modern-Movement architect, he settled (1936) in England (naturalized 1947), and worked with *Tecton (1937-9). He joined the architect's team of the LCC, and was responsible for the interior of the Royal Festival Hall, London (1948-51). Establishing (1952) his own London practice, he designed several buildings including Moro House, Blackheath Park, London (1957), the Playhouse, Nottingham (1952-64), a Hall of Residence, University of Leicester (1965), the Gulbenkian Centre, University of Hull, Yorks. (1969), and the Theatre Royal, Plymouth, Devon (1977-82).

E (1994); McKean (2001); *The Times* (15 Oct. 1998), 21

Morphew, Reginald (1874-1971) English architect, he designed 111-12 Jermyn Street, London (1901-3), described at the time as a 'Florentine Palazzo', and 7-12 Jermyn Street (1902), which had *Art-Nouveau details on a building in a free, vaguely Tyrolean, style. His work was eclectic, and always interesting.

A.S.Gray (1985)

Morris, Robert (c. 1702-54) English theorist of the second *Palladian Revival, his *Essay in Defence of Ancient Architecture* (1728), *Lectures on Architecture* (1734), *Essay on Harmony* (1739), *Art of Architecture* (1742), *Rural Architecture* (1750),

and *Architectural Remembrancer* (1751) were significant in augmenting *Palladio's work with an aesthetic theory powerful enough to command attention and respect (e.g. from *Jefferson). As an architect he was of small importance, but may have designed the south front of Culverthorpe, Lincs. (c.1730-5).

Co (2008); E.Hs (1990); E.Ka (1955); *ODNB* (2004); Su (1993)

Morris, Roger (1695-1749) London-born architect, significant figure in the history of *Palladianism, the *Gothic Revival, and *Castle style. A kinsman of Robert *Morris, he was associated with Colen *Campbell and Henry *Herbert, Earl of Pembroke, functioning as the last's *amanuensis* and interpreter of his architectural designs. He appears to have assisted Campbell, notably on the designs for Goodwood House, Sussex, before collaborating with Herbert on a number of projects including Marble Hill, Twickenham, Mddx. (1724-9), the White Lodge, Richmond New Park (1727-8), the Column of Victory, Blenheim Palace, Oxon. (1730-1), the Palladian Bridge at Wilton, Wilts. (1736-7), and Westcombe House, Blackheath, Kent (c.1730—demolished). He enlarged Adderbury House, Oxon. (1831), for **John Campbell** (1680-1743—**2nd Duke of Argyll** from 1703), designed the stable-block at Althorp House, Northants. (c.1732-3), with a *Tuscan *portico based on Inigo *Jones's St Paul's, Covent Garden, London (itself derived from *Palladio), and produced his masterpiece, Inveraray Castle, Argyll (1745-60), for **Archibald Campbell** (1682-1761—**3rd Duke of Argyll** from 1743). Earlier, he built Clearwell Castle, Glos. (c.1728) in a castellated *Gothic style, but Inveraray was the precedent for a series of symmetrical *Georgian 'castles', and may be derived from a sketch by *Vanbrugh.

Co (2008); E.Ka (1955); L & C (1973); *ODNB* (2004); Su (1993)

Morris, William (1834-96) English artist/poet/craftsman/medievalist/printer, he had a profound effect on architecture. Early in his career he studied the medieval churches of England and France. Working briefly (1856) in *Street's office, he met Philip *Webb, with whom he became friendly, and was influenced by the ideas of *Ruskin. Disappointed by contemporary architecture and design, he commissioned Webb to build his own dwelling, the Red House, Bexleyheath, Kent (1859-60): with its unpretentious brick walls, *fenestration arranged where needed, and tiled roof, it drew on *vernacular, *Gothic, and other traditions, treated in a very free way, and was influential, especially in the search for a style-less architecture. The difficulties of finding furniture and furnishings for the house led Morris to establish **Morris, Marshall, Faulkner, & Co.,** 'Fine Art Workmen in Painting, Carving, Furniture, and the Metals' in London (1861—after 1874 **Morris & Co.**).

Morris founded the **Society for the Protection of Ancient Buildings** (SPAB—1877) in response to the over-zealous and destructive ideas of church-'restorers'. He was anxious to publicize not only the concept of *conservation (as opposed to wholesale renovation) but the qualities of hitherto unappreciated *vernacular buildings, all of which led him to be regarded as a founding-father of the *Arts-and-Crafts movement, the *Domestic Revival, conservation, and the search for a society in which work would be a joy. His was the inspiration behind the establishment of the *Art-Workers' Guild (1884), the first Arts-and-Crafts Exhibition Society exhibition (1888), and many other late-C19 organizations intended to improve design, craftsmanship, and appreciation of art. His published works include *The Earthly Paradise* (1868–70), various beautifully produced volumes from his Kelmscott Press (which had a great influence on typography), and the Utopian *News from Nowhere* (1891) in which by the end of C21 London was rebuilt in a way inspired by medieval architecture (this suggests that *Gropius's claims to have been influenced by Morris were worse than absurd).

A.Crawford & C.Cm (eds) (1977); C.Harvey & Press (1996); Henderson (1967); Leatham (1994); MacCarthy (1979, 1994); Morris (1966); *ODNB* (2004); Pe (1968, 1972, 1974a); Stansky (1996); P.Thompson (1993)

Morrison, Sir Richard (1767–1849) Irish architect, he specialized in country-houses, drawing on *types established by *Cassels and *Pearce. His *Useful and Ornamental Designs in Architecture composed in the manner of the Antique* (1793), was the first work of its kind to be attempted in Ireland. His houses include the charming Bearforest, Mallow, Co. Cork (1807–8—with elliptical entrance-hall expressed on the main front), the castellated *Tudor-Gothic Castle Freke, Rosscarbery, Co. Cork (c.1814–20—ruined), and Castlegar, Ahascragh, Co. Galway (from 1801—again with elliptical entrance-hall). He designed several handsome Classical public buildings, including the Stables, Castle Coole, Co. Fermanagh (before 1817), the County Court House, Clonmel, Co. Tipperary (c.1800), Sir Patrick Dun's Hospital, Dublin (1803–16), and the County Court House, Galway (1812–15). He collaborated with his son, W.V.*Morrison, on a number of country-houses, notably Ballyfin, Mountrath, Co. Leix (1822—the grandest C19 Classical country-house in Ireland), Baronscourt, Newtownstewart, Co. Tyrone (1835—to which *Steuart, *Soane, and others had contributed), Borris House, Borris, Co. Carlow (c.1813), Fota

Island, Carrigtwohill, Co. Cork (c.1825—with very handsome Grecian entrance-hall) and the *Gothic Shelton Abbey, Co. Wicklow (c.1819—with vaulted gallery). One of his most charming works is the restoration of the *nave and *transepts, and complete rebuilding of the *chancel of the Cathedral of St Carthagh, Lismore, Co. Waterford (c.1810), in a pretty *Georgian-*Gothick style (the delightful Langleyesque gateway appears to have been by **Owen Fahy** (*fl.*1800–31), who worked for Morrison).

B-J (1988); J.Curl (2011a); *DIB* (2009); Graby (ed.) (1989); McP *et al.* (1989); *ODNB* (2004)

Morrison, William Vitruvius (1794–1838) Irish architect, son and collaborator of Richard *Morrison. His work was more Neo-Classical than his father's, but he also carried out a number of *Tudorbethan designs. Apart from the distinguished buildings they designed together (e.g. Baronscourt, Co. Tyrone (from 1835)), W.V.Morrison produced many houses of great interest, including Clontarf Castle, Clontarf, Co. Dublin (1836–7—Tudorbethan), Glenarm Castle and 'Barbican', Glenarm, Co. Antrim (1823–4—*Tudor *Gothic—not unlike his work at Borris, Co. Carlow), Hollybrooke House, Bray, Co. Wicklow (c.1835—Tudor Gothic), and Mount Stewart, Newtownards, Co. Down (1825–8—Neo-Classical, essentially alterations and additions to the house by George *Dance of 1803–6, with later changes by **Charles Campbell** (*fl.*1820–50)). His public buildings include Carlow County Court House (1828—with handsome *Ionic portico and two semicircular court-rooms separated by the entrance and stairs), and Tralee County Court House, Co. Kerry (1828—the plan of which is related to Carlow Court House). His Ross Monument, Rostrevor, Co. Down (1826), a massive *obelisk on an Egyptianizing base, is one of the noblest memorials in Ireland, commemorating **Major-General Robert Ross** (1766–1814).

B-J (1988); J.Curl (2005); *DIB* (2009); Graby (ed.) (1989); McP *et al.* (1989); *ODNB* (2004)

mortar Plastic material to bond stones and bricks together. Before C20 it was usually made from crushed burnt *limestone mixed with sand and water, often with additional brick- or stone-dust. Today, *Portland cement is used with sand and water, sometimes with lime or other additives.

N (1835); W.Pa (1852); S (1901–2)

mortice and tenon A *mortice* (or *mortise*) is a volume hollowed out to receive something, such as a lock or the *tenon* (projection at the end) of another piece of timber.

mort-safe Protective iron railings surrounding and covering a grave or vault.

mortuary 1. Building where corpses are temporarily accommodated, for identification, or autopsies. 2. Burial-place or sepulchre. 3. *Dead-house. *Related terms include*:

mortuary-chapel: 1. *chapel, free-standing or attached to a church, under which is a sepulchre or tomb, often built and used for interment by one family: it may have been built as a pre-Reformation *chantry-chapel; 2. chapel in a *cemetery, or attached to a building (e.g. a hospital), where coffined bodies briefly lie before disposal.

Co (1991); J. Curl (2002a); J.Curl (ed.) (2001)

mosaic Patterned surface on floors, *vaults, walls, etc., consisting of regular squares (*tesserae*) of glass, stone, pottery, marble, etc., embedded in a *cement or *plaster matrix.

Anthony (1968); Pi (1986); J.T (1996)

Mosbrugger *See* MOOSBRUGGER.

Moser, Karl (1860-1936) Pioneer of the *Modern Movement and first President of *CIAM (1928-30). He designed the *Antoniuskirche*, Basel (1924-31), the first church employing exposed *concrete in Switzerland. His earlier work (in partnership with **Robert Curjel** (1856-1925)) is less well known, but in its use of round-arched forms it was influenced by the work of *Richardson in America (e.g. *Pauluskirche*, Basel (1897-1901)). At the *Kunsthaus*, Zürich (1907-10), however, the language was stripped *Neo-Classicism. The main building of the University of Zürich (1911-14) combined round-arched themes with paraphrases of Greek *Doric, and this gives the key to Moser's eclectic approach. His son, **Werner Max Moser** (1896-1970), also had a successful architectural career. His works include several early Modern-Movement buildings with **Emil Roth** (1893-1980)—e.g. Hagmann Boat-House, Erlenbach, Zürich (1929), Eglisee Housing, Basel (1930), and Neubühl Housing, Zürich (1932). He also designed an Old People's Home near Frankfurt (with Mart *Stam—1930), and the Kornfeld Church, Riehen, Basel (1962).

E (1994); Kienzle (1937); P (1982); *Schweizer Rundschau*, xxxvi/8 (1936), 633-9; J.T (1996); vV (1993)

mosque Muslim house of prayer orientated towards Mecca. There are two distinct types: the *masjid* for daily prayers, and the Great or Friday mosque (*masjid al-jámi'*) for communal worship and addresses given by the imam from a *mimbar*. Very large congregational mosques may be of the *hypostyle type (i.e. with many columns, such as the C8 Great Mosque, Damascus); the four-*iwan* type, with one vaulted hall as the entrance leading to a large *court in the centre of each side of which is an *iwan* (e.g. Friday Mosque,

Isfahan, Iran (C11-C15)); and domed mosques, culminating in the centrally-planned mosques with domes or half-domes covering large uncluttered spaces (e.g. the *Süleymaniye Mosque*, Istanbul, by *Sinan (1550-7)). From C8 mosques acquired at least one *minaret, and most modern mosques usually have minarets and domes.

B & B (1994); Frishman & Khan (1994); Hillenbrand (1994)

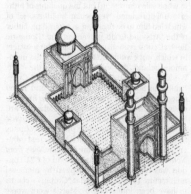

Stylized four-iwan Friday mosque with minarets.

moss hut *Fabrique in a primitive, *rustic style, usually made of branches of trees with the interstices filled with moss, sometimes clad with *thatch or bark. It could be a mnemonic of the *Primitive Hut, or be a simpler *cottage orné*.

Symes (2006)

Mothe, Jean-Baptiste-Michel Vallin de la (1729-1800) *See* VALLIN.

motorway Class of highway with two or more lanes in each direction, designed and regulated for use by fast motor-traffic only. The German super-highway concept dates from 1911, and a small length of express road was opened between Witzleben and Nikolassee, Berlin (1921). In Northern Italy a prototype *Autostrada* was commenced (1922) and opened (1924). In Germany a similar road (*Autobahn*) was proposed linking Hamburg, Frankfurt-am-Main, and Basel, but the German network of motorways quickly got under way after **Adolf Hitler** (1889-1945) came to power (1933), the initial planning having been carried out by private companies during the Weimar Republic (1918-33). *Todt was appointed (1933) Inspector-General of German Highways: he, in turn, employed the landscape architect Alwin *Seifert to take charge of landscaping, and the *Autobahn* between Frankfurt and Darmstadt was opened in 1935. *Bonatz designed *bridges, *viaducts, and other structures: his bridge over the River Lahn at Limburg was typical of his accomplishment in producing works of the highest aesthetic quality. Other bridges and monumental structures were designed by **Friedrich (Fritz) Tamms** (1904–80). It is not generally realized that one of the key reasons for building the *Autobahnen* was propaganda, to create a means by which the beauties of the German landscape could be enjoyed: the new roads would emphasize the *unity* of the Fatherland, dissolving the borders of the former *Länder*, and themselves be works of art as noble as anything the Romans had left.

In the USA national coast-to-coast highways were proposed (1923) by *Manning, but the system of true motorways with limited access was commenced in the 1950s. In the UK and elsewhere in Europe huge motorway systems were constructed since the 1950s, some more successfully landscaped than others, while the pre-war Italian and German networks were expanded.

P.Adam (1992); CoE (1995); Ladret (1974); Spotts (2002); Troost (ed.) (1942–3)

motte Steep artificial earthen mound or *tumulus on which a *keep or fortress stood in a C11 or C12 military structure, usually associated with the Anglo-Normans in the British Isles. It was sometimes surrounded by a ditch, but more often with an enclosed space. *Motte-and-bailey* was a defensive structure consisting of a tower (often of timber) on a motte, sited inside a *bailey enclosed by a ditch, bank, and *palisade.

mouchette C14 *light (often *ogee on at least one side), resembling a curving dagger-like form with *foils at one end in *Second-Pointed *Curvilinear or *Flowing *Gothic *tracery.

mouchette

Mould, Jacob Wrey (1825–86) English-born architect, he emigrated (1832) to the USA. He was said to have been a pupil of Owen *Jones, assisting the latter with the *polychrome decorations of the Crystal Palace, London (1851), and with illustrations for his publications. Mould also worked with Lewis *Vulliamy, designing the great staircase at Dorchester House, London (1850–63—demolished 1929). In NYC he designed the polychrome All Souls' Unitarian Church and Parsonage (1853–5), in an Italian *Romanesque style

(known as 'The Church of the Holy Zebra'), which introduced structural *polychromy to the USA. By the 1860s he was designing in the so-called *High-Victorian style of *Gothic, and with the First Presbyterian Church, Bath, NY (1874–7), he demonstrated a familiarity with *Viollet-le-Duc's illustrations. As assistant to *Olmsted and *Vaux (from 1858), he also designed numerous decorations, including the *Ruskin-inspired carvings for the Terrace, Central Park, NYC (1858–70). He collaborated (1871–4) with Vaux on the design of the Metropolitan Museum of Art and the Museum of Natural History (both before 1874, and both in NYC, although only one *wing of each was completed (1880) to their plans). For a short time in the early 1870s Mould was Chief Architect for Central Park, NYC, where he designed several buildings (some on his own and some with Vaux), many of which no longer exist, although the Sheepfold (1870–1) is now the Tavern-on-the-Green restaurant. Mould was in charge (1875–9) of the Department of Public Works, Lima, Peru, where he designed the *public parks and a polychrome mansion (c.1879). Returning to NYC, he designed the architectural features in Morningside Park (1880–2), and made several designs for the Department of Public Parks (1885–6). Among surviving buildings may be mentioned Holy Trinity Parish School, NYC (1860—later the Serbian Orthodox Cathedral of St Sava), and St Mary's Episcopal Church, Luzerne, NY (1873–80). Many of his purely decorative, non-architectural designs anticipated the *Aesthetic Movement. Mould's career was varied; he was a song-writer and translator of opera *libretti* as well as a designer and architect, and he seems to have been regarded as a genius, although his unconventional, even eccentric lifestyle, put many possible clients off.

C.Cook (1972); *JSAH*, **xxviii**/1 (Mar. 1969), 41–57; Kowsky (1980); P (1982); Su (ed.) (1968); J.T (1996)

moulding *or* **molding** Any continuous projecting or inset architectural member with a contoured profile. It defines, casts shadows, enriches, emphasizes, and separates, and is usually horizontal or vertical, although it occurs around arches and *vaults. It is an essential part of *architraves, *bases, *entablatures, and *string-courses, and is found in virtually all periods of architecture except the *International *Modern Movement from which it was expunged. It occurs in many forms in the Classical *Orders (e.g. *astragal, *bead, *cavetto, *cyma, *fillet, *flute, *ovolo, *scotia, and *torus), *Romanesque work (e.g. *beak-head, *billet, *chevron, hollows, rounds, and splays), and *Gothic (e.g. deep rounds, and hollows, *ballflower, *dog-tooth, *keels, *nail-head, etc.). *See* BOLECTION; BOWTELL; CABLE; CANT; CHAPLET; DANCETTE; DOVETAIL; ECHINUS; EDGE-ROLL; FASCIA; GADROON;

GORGE; HOOD; LABEL; NEBULE; OGEE; ORDERS; PELLET; RESSAULT; ROLL; RUNNING DOG; WAVE.

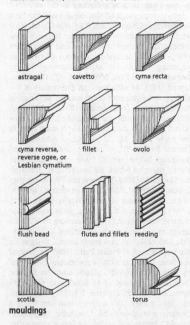

astragal   cavetto   cyma recta

cyma reversa, reverse ogee, or Lesbian cymatium   fillet   ovolo

flush bead   flutes and fillets   reeding

scotia   torus

mouldings

mount Artificial mound of earth, stones, etc., in a garden (usually C16 or C17) to provide a vantage-point from which views might be enjoyed. Advocated (1625) by Francis *Bacon (who had mounts constructed at Gray's Inn, London, and Gorhambury, Herts., both with *banqueting-houses on their tops), some had helical walks winding round them to give access to the summits (often embellished with *gazebos). The gardens of New College, Oxford, still possess a somewhat blurred mount (c.1594), once surmounted by a *summer-house.

Darvill (2008); Tay (2006)

Mountford, Edward William (1855–1908) English architect who designed several *Gothic-Revival churches, but is best known for his public buildings, including the Free-Renaissance style Sheffield Town Hall (1890–7—with elements culled from Spain, France, England, and The Netherlands), and the *Gibbs-Revival style Lancaster Town Hall (1907—with **Thomas Geoffrey Lucas** (1872–1947)). He designed the Northampton Institute, Finsbury, London (1893–6), again in a Free-Renaissance style. The Central Criminal Court, Old Bailey, London (1900–7), is in a grandly *Edwardian-*Baroque style, with a *cupola derived from the work of *Wren.

D & M (1985); A.S.Gray (1985)

mourner See WEEPER.

moving staircase See ESCALATOR.

Moya, John Hidalgo (1920–94) See POWELL & MOYA.

Mozarabic C9–early C11 style of Spanish-Christian architecture under *Moorish rule. It included horseshoe-shaped arches, but was essentially an amalgam of *Romanesque and *Islamic elements, as in *San Miguel de la Escalada*, near León (913), and *Santiago de Peñalba*, near Ponferrada, León (931–7).

Fernandez Arenas (1972); J.T (1996)

mud-and-stud *Timber-framed wall construction filled in with *staves or *battens as a base for a mud finish, also called *clam-staff and daub* or *raddle and daub*.

ABDM (1996)

mud brick See ADOBE.

Mudéjar Style of architecture and decorative art, partly *Islamic (from the *Moorish and *Mozarabic traditions) and partly *Gothic, that evolved in the Iberian peninsula reconquered by Christians (C11–C16). It incorporated horseshoe-shaped arches, *Kufic inscriptions, *arabesques, *stalactite work or *muqarna, and ceramic *tiles. *The Salón de Embajaderes* in Alcázar, Seville (C14), is one of the most sumptuous examples of the Mudéjar style, which persisted well into *Plateresque C16 buildings, and aspects of it were revived in C19 and early C20, usually called the *Moorish style.

CG (1965); Jayyusi (ed.) (1992); G.King (1927); K & S (1959); J.T (1996)

Muet, Pierre Le (1591–1669) French architect, his most important work was *Manière de bastir pour toutes sortes de personnes* (1623), which probably drew on *Serlio's then unpublished sixth book of *Architettura*, and Du *Cerceau's *Trois Livres d'Architecture*, especially the first book (1559). Le Muet's book contains designs for urban dwellings for sites ranging from very small to quite large, was reprinted three times, came out in an English translation (1670), and was superseded (1720) by a collection of designs entitled *Architecture moderne ou l'art de bien bastir pour toutes sortes de personnes*. Of the numerous Parisian town-houses he designed (many of which retained Mannerist tendencies), not much remains intact, apart from the handsome *Hôtel d'Avaux* (later *Saint-Aignan*), 71 *Rue du Temple*

(1644–50—which has a garden-*façade influenced by the Louvre and a *court with façades enlivened with a *Giant Order of *pilasters), and the *Hôtel Tubeuf*, 16 *Rue Vivienne* (1648–54), both of which were elegant essays in *Classicism. Le Muet designed the ground-plan of *Notre-Dame-des-Victoires* (1629), and (1655–66), assisted by Le *Duc, succeeded *Lemercier at the *Val-de-Grâce*, Paris, completing the conventual buildings and the upper *Order and *dome of the Church.

Bt (1982); P (1982); J.T (1996)

Mughal architecture *Islamic architecture, so called after a dynasty of Central Asian origin that ruled (1526–1857) parts of the Indian Sub-Continent. Some fine forts and palaces date from the reign of **Akbar** (1556–1605), and are found in Agra, Lahore, and Fatehpur Sikri, but the reign of **Shah Jehan** (1628–58) saw some beautiful stuff, including the *Tâj Mahal*, Agra, a *mausoleum (1630–53) with a formal garden. Characterized by strict symmetry, the use of the flattened four-centred arch, *chatris, bulbous *domes, and exquisite, regular decorations, it inspired the so-called *Hindoo style (an amalgam of Hindu and Mughal styles) in the West, of which S.P.*Cockerell's Sezincote, Glos. (1805–20) is an example.

Conner (1979); Ck (1996); L & D (1986); M & P (2011); J.T (1996)

Mughal garden Garden associated with Mughal rule in India (1526–1857). Aware of their Central Asian origins, the Mughals always bore in mind the necessity of harnessing mountain-springs to bring life to arid, rugged lands, and to create delightful, ordered, enclosed, formal gardens featuring water, fruit trees, and flowering plants. Early exemplars were laid out as *terraces on steep hillsides, and *Bâbûr drew on memories of these when creating his sequence of verdant well-watered gardens along the banks of the Yamuna River, although terraced gardens of the sort created in Kabul were not possible in the plains of Hindustan. Kashmir provided numerous sites with different levels and plentiful water, and the *chahar-*bâgh layout was embraced, providing settings for *palaces, pleasure-resorts, and *mausolea (*see* PARADISE GARDEN). Plants indigenous to the plains of Hindustan and the mountains of Kashmir were employed to provide floral displays, while fruit trees (including orange, lemon, apple, almond, and mango) afforded shade and symbolized life. Other trees, such as cypress, framed views of distant, snow-clad mountains, and flowing water brought coolness, refreshment, and renewal to the garden. Buildings included *pavilions of the *baradari type. As settings for the living and the dead, Mughal gardens were among the most perfect geometrical creations ever conceived, and were imbued with meaning, not least religious significance.

J.Brookes (1987); Lehrman (1980); M & P (2011); MM & T (1998); Moynihan (1980); Petruccioli (ed.) (1997); Ruggles (2008)

Mulholland, Roger (1740–1818) Distinguished late-C18 Belfast architect/developer, building many houses in Donegall Place and elsewhere in the growing *Georgian town. He designed (probably) the First Presbyterian Church, Dunmurry, Co. Antrim (1779—with *Gibbs surrounds), and the beautiful elliptical Presbyterian Church, Rosemary Street (1781–3—a more definite attribution), the White Linen Hall (1785–1802—again undocumented, and later demolished to make way for the City Hall), the *Sublimely grim House of Correction (1814–18—demolished), and, in Knockbreda Churchyard, definitely the elaborate *mausoleum of **Waddell Cunningham** (1728/9–97) and, probably, that of **Thomas Greg** (*c.*1721–96), all in Belfast.

Brett (1967, 1976); J.Curl (2011a); Larmour (1987); L.Wilson (ed.) (2009)

Muller, Émile (1823–89) French architect/manufacturer. He designed the *Company town outside Mulhouse, a model industrial town with housing (influenced by the pioneering work of his friend, Henry *Roberts) for **Jean Dollfus** (1800–87), begun 1852 under the aegis of the *Société Mulhousienne des Cités Ouvrières*. Muller founded (1854) a factory for making *tiles, designs for which he exhibited (1855): he was responsible for the *polychrome *bricks and tiles used in the *Menier* Chocolate Factory, Noisiel-sur-Marne (1869–72), designed by *Saulnier. Muller went on to design and make durable glazed ceramic architectural kits-of-parts for which he was awarded a prize at the *Exposition Universelle*, Paris (1889).

J.Curl (1983); pk; J.T (1996)

Mullett, Alfred Bult (1834–90) English-born US Government architect (1866–74), he worked in a *Beaux-Arts *Renaissance manner derived from the *Second-Empire style of France (known in the USA as the *General Grant* style because it coincided with **Ulysses Simpson Grant's** (1822–95) term as President (1868–77)). He was in private practice with his two sons after 1875. Typical of his style was the huge Old Executive Office Building (State, War, and Navy), Washington, DC (1871–89), and the Post Office and Custom House, St Louis, MO (1872–84). He designed offices for the *Baltimore Sun* in Washington, DC (1885-6), often claimed as a rival to the first *skyscraper by Le Baron *Jenney. Like many architects before him (e.g. *Latrobe) he was treated appallingly by a parsimonious US Government: facing ruin, he shot himself.

Fitch (1973); Jordy (1976); *JSAH*, xxxi/1 (May 1972), 22–37; Maddex (1973); P (1982); J.T (1996)

Mullgardt, Louis Christian (1866–1942) American architect, he was influenced by the *Arts-and-Crafts movement after a visit to England (1904–5). Establishing (1906) his own office in San Francisco, CA, he designed an Alpine-flavoured *timber-framed house around a brick chimney-core at Mill Valley, CA (1907), but over the next few years the houses that made his name had stuccoed walls, low-pitched roofs, and long bands of *mullioned windows, all in a style strongly reminiscent of *Schinkel and 'Greek' *Thomson. One of his most spectacular designs was the Henry W. Taylor House, Berkeley, CA (1908–10—destroyed). Later works were inventively and freely eclectic (e.g. Theodore H. Davies Building, Honolulu, HI (1917–21), a vast *concrete structure faced with *faïence that recalled the Spanish *Renaissance, freely treated). He produced (1920s) a series of imaginative proposals for San Francisco, including habitable *piers and *bridges connected by 24-lane tiered *motorways. None was realized.

ARe, xxx (Aug. 1911), 1117–34; R.Clark (1966); *JSAH*, xxi/4 (Dec. 1962), 171–8; P (1982); J.T (1996)

mullion Timber, stone, or other vertical between the *lights of a window or *screen, usually moulded. Square timber mullions set diagonally *on plan* in a medieval aperture are called *diamond mullions*; while windows with four or more lights may have subsidiary mullions subdividing the window into lights and larger *king-mullions* corresponding to the aperture proper.

multifoil With many *foils.

multi-storey Building with five or more storeys.

multivallate Defended by three or more concentric banks and ditches, as in a hill-fort.

Mumford, Lewis (1895–1990) American architectural/town-planning critic: a disciple of Patrick *Geddes, his views on urban planning originally stemmed from that source. His *Story of Utopias* (1922) was followed by many books, including *Sticks and Stones* (1924), the widely read *The Culture of Cities* (1938), and *The City in History* (1961). His knowledge and interests ranged far and wide, as is clear from *The Culture of Cities*, *The Brown Decades* (1931), and *Technics and Civilization* (1961), while he contributed articles to many journals, and wrote a perceptive regular column on architecture and the environment for *The New Yorker* entitled 'The Skyline' (1930s–1950s). A critic of the dehumanizing effects of technology, he nevertheless believed in

the need for large-scale regional, even national, plans, and was a founding-member of the Regional Planning Association that sponsored the *Garden-City complex of Sunnyside Gardens, Queens, NYC, and also worked for the New York Housing and Planning Commission. He belonged to the low-density decentralist tradition of Ebenezer *Howard, *Abercrombie, and *Unwin, yet, because of his belief in the need for large-scale planning, found his philosophical position confused. That confusion deepened after he helped to organize the MoMA exhibition, *International Style*, in NYC (1932—with *Johnson, *Hitchcock, and others), for by the 1940s he saw where *CIAM-*Corbusier-inspired dogmas of urban planning were leading, and he became a vociferous critic of them. In his *New Yorker* articles he prophesied the roles that the motor-car and urban *motorways would play in the decay of the city as early as 1943, but his support for large-scale centralized intervention was challenged by others, notably Jane *Jacobs, with whose views on *'urban renewal' he agreed, but when her *The Death and Life of Great American Cities* came out (1961) he was obliged to attack it, apparently confusing urban densities with *high-rise buildings. He insisted that architecture/planning had to be socially responsible, and emphasized the individual's plight in *The Myth of the Machine* (1967) and *The Pentagon of Power* (1971).

AR, clxxxvii/1117 (Mar. 1990), 9; LG & S (1996); D.Miller (1989); L.Mumford (1922, 1924, 1931, 1934, 1938, 1944, 1946, 1952, 1952a, 1961, 1963, 1967, 1970, 1975); *PA*, lxxi (Mar. 1990), 24; J.T (1996); Wojtowicz (1996)

Munday, Richard (*c.*1685–1739) American architect, he designed Colony House (1739–41—an accomplished and pretty work with a *Baroque centrepiece) and Trinity Church (1725–6—a timber building owing something to *Wren's Church of St James, Piccadilly, London, via Old North Church, Boston, MA (begun 1723)), both in Newport, RI. He was responsible for other *Colonial-Georgian buildings (mostly houses) in Newport.

A.F.Downing (1937); A.F.Downing & V.J.Sy (1967); Hi (1939); P (1982); J.T (1996); W.Rotch Ware (ed.) (1923)

Munggenast, Joseph (1680–1741) Tyrol-born architect, he worked under *Prandtauer (his kinsman), and completed Melk Abbey on the Danube, including the graceful upper parts of the western towers (1738), as well as other projects (e.g. the monastic buildings at Herzogenburg and St Pölten). With **Matthias Steinl** or **Steindl** (1644–1727), he worked on the tower of Zwettl Abbey-Church (begun 1722) and on the lovely Augustinian Church at Dürnstein (begun 1718), which has the most handsome *Baroque tower (1721-7) in all Austria. On his own he worked on the monastic buildings at Seitenstetten (from 1718), and reconstructed Altenburg Abbey, Upper Austria (from 1730), casing the medieval Church in a sumptuous Baroque crust, and creating one of the most felicitous libraries of the period (influenced by *Fisher von Erlach's *Hofbibliothek*, Vienna (completed 1730)). He also prepared designs for Wilhering Abbey Church (from 1733), the *Klosterkirche*, Maria Langegg (c.1733), extensions to Geras Abbey (1736-40), rebuilding the Abbey and Church at Mondsee (1736-8), and a new Church at Siebenlinden (1740). One of the leading architects in Lower Austria outside Vienna in the first half of C18, his sons **Franz** (1724-48) and **Matthias** (1729-98) carried on his practice there.

Bou (1962); Brucker (1983); E.Hempel (1965); Karl (ed.) (1991); Mungenast (1963); C.Powell (1959); J.T (1996)

municipal park See GARDEN-CEMETERY; PUBLIC PARK.

munnion *Mullion or *muntin.

muntin 1. Vertical intermediate timbers or *mullions between the *panels of a *door and the outer *stiles, fixed top and bottom to the horizontal *rails. **2.** *Glazing-bar in a window-sash. **3.** Window-mullion.

Müntz, Johann Heinrich (1727-98) Artist of German-Swiss origin, he served as an engineer in the French army. He arrived in England (1755) and was taken up by Richard *Bentley (who designed (1751-61) various elements in Horace *Walpole's Strawberry Hill, Mddx., and recommended Müntz to carry out work there, which included the painted ceiling of the China Closet and several *Gothick features). It was through Bentley (who designed a 'Gothic Cloister' for him) that Müntz created an octagonal Gothick room for Richard *Bateman at The Grove, Bateman's 'half Gothick, half Attic, half Chinese, and completely fribble' *villa in Old Windsor, Berks. (1761-2). Müntz prepared (1762) designs for an 'Egyptian' (actually Gothick with Egyptianizing figures) room at Marino, near Dublin, for **James Caulfeild** (1729-99—**4th Viscount** (from 1734) and **1st Earl** (from 1763) **of Charlemont**), but this does not seem to have been realized, although he made (1768) further designs for Caulfeild. At Kew Gardens he was responsible for the 'Gothic Cathedral' (c.1759—demolished) and probably provided *Chambers with drawings for the *Moorish 'Alhambra' (1758—demolished). An inventive master of the exotic, he proposed (1760) to publish *A Course of Gothic Architecture* which, if it had come out, would have been one of the earliest books on the subject. He designed a *villa for **Prince Stanisław Poniatowski** (1754-1833)

when in Poland (1778-85), and finally settled in Kassel, Germany, where he recorded the gardens, etc. at Wilhelmshöhe.

BL. Add. MS. 6771, fols. 215-16; Co (2008); G (1972); J.Hs (1970); M.McCarthy (1987); Mowl (1996); J.T (1996)

muqarna (*pl.* **muqarnas**) Decorative device in *Islamic architecture, like a small pointed *niche, used in tiers projecting over those below, usually constructed of corbelled *brick, stone, *stucco, or wood. Applied to *cornices, *pendentives, *squinches, and the *soffits of arches and *vaults, with their scalloped surfaces and *pendants they present a very rich sight when seen from below, sometimes resembling *stalactites. The most spectacular muqarnas may be found in C14 rooms in the Alhambra, Granada, Spain, and in the C15 dome of the *mausoleum of Sultan Qa'itbay (c. 1416/18-96), Cairo, Egypt.

B & B (1994); Hillenbrand (1994); J.T (1996)

mural painting Painted decoration applied to an exterior or interior wall-surface. Known in the Ancient World, mural decorations featuring architectural devices, landscapes, and figures, etc. were common in Roman houses, and several spectacular examples have survived from, e.g. Pompeii. Wall-paintings enlivened medieval churches, and many fragments survive, notably of *Dooms, e.g. in England. Murals were enthusiastically revived in C19 throughout the West, notably in didactic and historical painting closely associated with Revivalist architectural movements (e.g. the *Glyptothek*, Munich, and the Palace of Westminster, London). For much mural painting the technique of *fresco was employed, but in France *marouflage* was commonly used. In England, as the progress of the *Gothic Revival demanded more and more historical research and scholarly application, whole interiors were coloured (e.g. Holy Innocents, Highnam, Glos. (1850-71), by **Thomas Gambier Parry** (1816-88), carried out in 'spirit fresco', and St John the Baptist, Tue Brook, Liverpool (1868-71), by *Bodley, superbly restored (1970s) by *Dykes Bower). A revival of mural painting reached its apogee in 1890-1914, when the *Arts-and-Crafts insistence on a complete integration of art, craftsmanship, and architecture found a fertile climate during the years before the 1914-18 war and the dogmas of the *Bauhaus and *International Modernism put paid to it. In the late 1920s there was a new trend towards making art public and accessible as developments in 'Modern' art tended to become more and more introspective and exclusive. Didactic murals were a feature of Fascist Italy, Nazi Germany, and the Stalinist Soviet Union, and attempts were made to promote similar work elsewhere. Interior murals for private houses were occasionally produced (e.g. the dining-room at *Plas Newydd*, Gwynedd, Wales (1937), by **Rex Whistler** (1905–44)), and some artists, e.g. **Stanley Spencer** (1891–1959), painted oil-based murals (1927–32) in the Sandham Memorial Chapel, Burghclere, Hants., dealing with war. Post-*Festival-of-Britain murals were, on the whole, feeble, but political and social issues were unsubtly depicted in such works as *The Battle of Cable Street*, St George's Town Hall, Tower Hamlets, London (1978–83), and (although studiously avoided by most) sectarian gable-end murals in Belfast and Londonderry (called *muriels*) continued to express powerful hatreds and mark tribal/religious boundaries in C21. However, such murals were executed in oil paint on brick or plaster-covered walls. In Central Europe especially, *sgraffito* was (and is) used for murals.

J.T (1996)

Murano, Togo (1891–1984) Japanese architect, he designed the Sogo department store, Osaka (1936—the first modern building of its kind in that city), further such stores in Kobe, Nagoka, and Tokyo, the World Peace Memorial Cathedral, Hiroshima (1953), the New Kabuki Theatre, Osaka (1958), and the Nippon Life Insurance Co. offices, Tokyo (1963), among many other projects.

J.T (1996)

Murase, Robert K. (1938–2005) American landscape architect of Japanese descent, he worked under *Halprin and *Royston before researching gardens in Japan and establishing (1982) a practice in Portland, OR. Among his works were the Japanese–American Historical Plaza, Portland (commemorating internment of Japanese-Americans in the 1941–5 Pacific War); the Town Center Park, Wilsonville, OR; and the Garden of Remembrance, Seattle, WA. In his works meditative emptiness and simplicity, drawing on a long tradition of *Japanese gardendesign, were evident.

Leccese (1997); N & R (2003)

mur de retranchement Wall of entrenchment, part of a fortification; ditch for defence, perhaps ancestor of the *ha-ha*.

murder- *or* **murdering-hole** Small opening in the ceiling of an entrance-*vestibule of a *tower-house or *castle from which intruders or unwelcome visitors would be inspected, or, if needs be, dispatched.

Murphy/Jahn Leading Chicago architectural practice founded in 1959 by **Charles Franklin Murphy** (1890–1985), Chicago, who through his work with *Burnham had a direct connection with the *Chicago School. The German architect **Helmut Jahn** (1940–) joined the firm (1967), and became a partner (1973): the practice was

renamed (1981) **Murphy/Jahn**. The office produced (1960s) several Chicago buildings much influenced by the work of *Mies van der Rohe, including the Continental Insurance Building (1962), O'Hare International Airport (1965), Chicago Civic Center (1965), and Exhibition Building, McCormick Place (1971). After Jahn became a leading member of the firm, its buildings began to incorporate historical references, including *Art-Deco elements. Jahn has been associated with *High-Tech architecture, and his *skyscrapers include the *Messeturm*, Frankfurt-amMain (1991). Jahn also designed buildings for the *Kurfürstendamm*, Berlin, including a steeland-glass block at the junction with *Adenauerplatz* and *Brandenburgische Strasse* (1995). Other works include the *Franz Josef Strauss Flughafen*, Munich (1993–6—with *Arup), and the Post Tower, Bonn, Germany (1999–2003—with curved outer walls composed of two layers of glazing, combining meticulous attention to architectural detail with sophisticated environmental control).

AR, ccxiv/1278 (Aug. 2003), 58–63; Br (1996a, 2002); E (1994); J (1993); J.A.Je (1986); Klotz (ed.) (1986); L (1988); Ma.Miller (1986); Murphy/Jahn (1995, 2001)

muscular Gothic Phase of the *Gothic Revival that embraced a primitive, early *First-Pointed style derived from C13 Burgundian Gothic: it employed *polychrome brickwork, massive, cylindrical *piers, and chunky elements, and was bold, broad, strong, stern, and robust. Some of the work of *Street and *Brooks could be described as 'muscular Gothic' in style.

B.Clarke (1969); J.Curl (2007); D & M (1985); Ea (1970); Smart (1990)

museum Building or part of a building for the display/preservation/study of antiquities/fine and industrial art/natural history/etc. The *Antique *Museum* ('Home for the Muses') was dedicated to the pursuit of learning, of which a celebrated example was the Museum/University created in Alexandria by **Ptolemy I Soter I** (*r.*304–284 BC) and **Ptolemy II Philadelphus** (*r.*285–246 BC): although the Alexandrian model was adopted during the Roman Empire, by the Middle Ages it only survived in historical references, and the term 'museum' was used during the *Renaissance to suggest rooms containing objects, known as *cabinets de curiosité* and *Wunderkammern*. The Ashmolean Museum, Oxford (1683), served as a 'cabinet of curiosities' and laboratory, and institutions such as the British Museum (in Montagu House) were opened to the public, followed by numerous C18 examples (e.g. *Museo Pio-Clementino*, Vatican (1772–3) and the Imperial collections, Vienna (1780s)). C18 advances in ordering knowledge, of which the *Encyclopédie* (1751–65) was a great model, doubtless encouraged the opening of Royal collections to the public in France after 1750, and numerous public museums were established by the French in the early C19. Originally housed in existing buildings, esp. palaces (e.g. the Louvre, Paris), the museum emerged as a distinctive building-type in the latter part of C18, and by 1850 became an essential part of the modern city. The *Fredericianum*, Kassel, by Du *Ry, was one of the first purpose-built examples, and others followed, including those erected from 1816 in Munich to designs by von *Klenze (who also extended the Hermitage, St Petersburg (1839–51)); the mighty British Museum, London, by *Smirke (1823–46); and the *Altes Museum*, Berlin (1823–30), a national Prussian foundation, prompted by proposals by **Aloys Hirt** (1759–1837), designed by *Schinkel. There have been numerous museums of many kinds erected worldwide since then.

The C3 BC Alexandrian Museum had botanical and zoological gardens attached to it, and an example in relatively modern times (C18) was established in the grounds of the British Museum at Montagu House, with gravelled *paths, statues, a raised *terrace, and large grassed areas. Primarily a botanic-garden, with *c.*600 species of plants, a ticket-system had to be introduced (1762) to keep numbers under control. In more recent times *museum-gardens* have evolved as places in which to exhibit: examples include the Smithsonian Institution, Washington, DC, and *Tradescant Garden Museum, Lambeth, London. In C21 the museum-garden is re-emerging in importance.

A:QJBS, xxxii/2 (Summer 2000), 195–231; Caygill & Date (1999); Crook (1972); Pe (1976); J.T (1996)

mushrabeyeh See MASHRABIYA.

mushroom construction Early C20 type of r.c. construction in which the tops of columns are shaped to form a circular disc much bigger than the diameter of the column: the shape is reminiscent of a mushroom-like form, or of the upper part of an Ancient-Egyptian bell-capital, but much more slender. These discs support *floorslabs, and the distribution of loads is such that *beams are unnecessary. *Maillart pioneered it (1908), and F.L.L.*Wright exploited it to great effect in the Johnson Wax Building, Racine, WI (1936–9).

Musō Soseki (1275–1351) Japanese Zen priest, *known as* **Kokushi**, he designed temple-gardens, e.g. those of Nanzenji, Rinsenji, Saihoji, and Tenryuji, Kyoto, et al., which proved influential in the future evolution of the type in his country. Profoundly aware of the part Nature and designed gardens could play in spiritual enlightenment, he created waterfalls, slopes, and placed rugged stones strategically to make harmonious wholes.

See JAPANESE GARDEN-DESIGN; SCHOLAR'S GARDEN; ZEN GARDEN-DESIGN.

A.K.Davidson (2007); Shoe (2001)

Muthesius, Hermann (1861–1927) Attaché at the Imperial German Embassy, London (1896–1903), he surveyed British architecture and design on behalf of the German Government, and his work was brought out as *Die Englische Baukunst der Gegenwart* (1900–2) and *Die Neuere Kirchliche Baukunst in England* (1903) by **Wasmuth**, the distinguished German publishers of F.L.L.*Wright's work. His greatest contribution was *Das Englische Haus* (1904–5), which comprehensively described and illustrated elements, history, plans, styles, and types of English domestic architecture, as well as publicizing works by many architects and extolling the *Arts-and-Crafts movement. The book had a profound influence on Continental (especially German) domestic architecture, and the 'English style' for houses became as fashionable as once the C18 English landscaped park had been. Furthermore, Muthesius's admiration for the simplicity and utility of English domestic buildings and artefacts led to the concept of *Sachlichkeit* and to the foundation of the *Deutscher Werkbund* (1907). By 1914 Muthesius (who had been a powerful official in the Prussian Government for at least a decade, and was to remain influential until his death) was advocating mass-production, standardization, and the development of industrialization for architecture, notions which were completely the opposite of the Arts-and-Crafts position: his stance was opposed by van de *Velde and others, but became an article of faith in the 1920s among those who were to be the protagonists of the *Modern Movement.

Muthesius practised as an architect. His early houses in the Berlin suburbs were seen as 'in the English country-house style', even though they looked far more German than English: among his works may be cited the Freudenberg House, Nikolassee (on a butterfly-plan reminiscent of *Prior's designs), the Bernhard House, Grunewald, the Breul House, again in Grunewald, the Soetbeer House, Nikolassee, the Koch and Velsen Houses, Zehlendorf-West, and the Neuhaus House, Dahlem. He also designed the Stave House, Lübeck, and summer-houses, Travemünde. All these were designed and built 1904–9, and were set in carefully thought-out gardens. He published some of his own work in *Landhaus und Garten* (1910) and *Die Schöne Wohnung* (1922, 1926).

F (1980); H.M (1901–2, 1902, 1903, 1979); H.M (ed.) (1910); F.Roth (200l); Uwe Schneider (2000)

mutilated Broken or discontinued, e.g. a *pediment.

mutule Flat inclined block on the *soffit of the *Doric *cornice, with several *guttae on the underside, placed in line with the *triglyphs and centre-lines of *metopes in the *frieze below. *Tuscan mutules are plain and horizontal. *See also* DORIC ORDER; MODILLION.

Muzio, Giovanni (1893–1982) Italian architect, his *Neo-Classicism was exemplified by the *Ca'Brutta* apartment-block, *Via Turati* and *Via Moscova*, Milan (1919–23), with its simplified *triumphal arch set between vaguely *Mannerist blocks that responded with great success to the urban context and drew on historical references. His other works include the headquarters of the *Banca Popolare di Bergamo*, Bergamo (1924–7); the *Università Cattolica*, Milan (1928–36—adjacent to which is his War Memorial, a version of the Tower of the Winds, Athens); the *Palazzo dell'Arte* (1932–3) and *Palazzo del Popolo d'Italia* (1937–8), both in Milan; the *Palazzo del Governo*, Sondrio (1934–5); *Sant'Antonio*, Cremona (1935–6); and the Basilica of the Annunciation, Nazareth, Israel (1967–9). His work of the 1920s and 1930s was associated with the **Metaphysical** movement in art (of which **Giorgio di Chirico** (1888–1978), with his juxtaposition of the commonplace and the fantastic, was the main exponent), and also with **Fascism** (which led to his interesting, even brilliant, architecture being ignored or denounced after 1945, but it has been reassessed by those with open minds).

Boidi (ed.) (1994–5); D & P (1976); Irace (1994); Me (1974); Seta (1978); J.T (1996)

Mycenaean architecture Architecture in and around Mycenae on the Greek mainland of *c*.1500–1200 BC, of which the *megaron, *propylaeum, in antis* (*see* ANTA) *portico, *court, and *tholos* were features of monumental building. At Tiryns there were two *propylaea* leading to the fortified palace complex: the outer gateway was the model for all the great Greek gateways, including that on the Athenian Acropolis, while in the centre of the palace was a large and impressive *megaron* with *distyle in antis* porticoes. The finest existing *tholos* of Mycenaean design is the so-called Treasury of Atreus (*c*.C15 BC), approached by a *dromos* or open passage lined with *masonry, and constructed of *courses of stone laid on a circular plan, each course a slightly smaller diameter, so that a *corbelled or pseudo-*vault was constructed. At the end of the *dromos* the entrance to the *tholos* was framed by two tapering columns with zig-zags cut in the *shafts. With Mycenaean architecture ordered planning reached a high degree of sophistication.

Ck (1996); D (1950); D.S.R (1945); J.T (1996)

Mylne, Robert (1733–1811) Scots architect, member of a family working as master-masons/architects at least as far back as the beginning of C17. He trained in France and Italy with his brother **William** (1734–90), met *Piranesi, achieved recognition at St Luke's Academy, Rome, and made useful aristocratic contacts. He made drawings of the Greek temples in Sicily which he allowed Piranesi and *Winckelmann to use (1757). Reaching London (1759), he won the competition to build the new bridge over the Thames at Blackfriars (1760, opened 1769, demolished 1868), with a handsome and economical design employing elliptical arches. Thereafter, bridges and canal works became a significant part of his practice. With Robert *Adam and James *Wyatt as contemporaries, Mylne found it difficult to become a fashionable country-house architect, but nevertheless designed several houses (including Woodhouse, near Whittington, Salop. (1773–4)) which have a refinement and restraint that pre-empt the *Neo-Classicism of the 1790s. His interiors have a delicate decorative manner not unlike that of Adam, which may be explained by the fact that he paid Adam's draughtsman, George *Richardson, for drawings on occasion. His finest work is arguably at Inveraray, Argyll, Scotland, where he built the elegant Aray (1774–6) and Dubh Loch (1786–7) bridges, the Church (1795–1800), two groups of tenements, Arkland and Relief Land (1774–6), and the arched screen-wall that is such a memorable frontage to Loch Fyne, and many more structures, all of which are pleasingly well mannered. He carried out extensive redecoration of the principal rooms at the Castle (1782–9), having earlier made alterations to *Morris's windows (1777). Amongst several memorials he designed is the urn in memory of **Sir Hugh Myddelton** (*c*.1560–1631—projector of the New River (Mylne was Surveyor to the New River Company from 1767) to bring fresh water to London) on an island in the New River at Great Amwell, Herts. (1800), perhaps suggested by J.-J.*Rousseau's tomb at Ermenonville.

Co (2008); Kensey (2012); L & C (1973); *ODNB* (2004); A.Rn (1955); Woodley (1999)

Mylne, William Chadwell (1781–1863) Son of Robert *Mylne, he gained early experience with his father and succeeded (1811) him as Surveyor to the New River Company. He laid out the Company's property in Clerkenwell, London, including the pleasant late-*Georgian Myddelton Square, and Amwell, Inglebert, River, and Chadwell Streets, begun 1819. In order to raise the tone of the area, St Mark's Church, Myddelton Square, was built, designed by him (1826–8) in a *Gothic style of the pre-ecclesiological type.

Co (2008); *ODNB* (2004); W.Pa (1852)

nail-head Late-*Romanesque and *First-Pointed *moulding featuring a series of small contiguous projecting *pyramids, so called from their resemblance to medieval wrought-iron nail-heads.

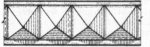

nail-head St Leonard, Upton St Leonard, Glos.

naked Unadorned plain surface of anything, esp. the main plane of a *façade.

naos 1. Inner cell or *sanctuary of a Greek *temple, equivalent to the Roman *cella, containing the deity's statue. 2. *Sanctuary of a centrally planned *Byzantine church. 3. Small *shrine, often portable, e.g. the *battered-sided Egyptian type, carried by a *Naöphorus* figure.

J.Curl (2005); D (1950)

naos (3) (*above*)
Naöphorus (*right*)
(Museo Nazionale, Naples).

narthex 1. Church *vestibule, in *Byzantine exemplars of two kinds: an *esonarthex* (inner narthex), between the outer *porch and the body of the church proper separated from the *nave and *aisles by a wall, *arcade, *colonnade, or *screen; or an *exonarthex* (outer narthex) outside the main wall, sometimes serving as the *portico or part of the cloistered *atrium or *quadriporticus*. 2. Medieval *ante-church often with nave and aisles, sometimes referred to as a *Galilee porch*, as at Durham Cathedral.

Mango (1986); J.Parker (1850); D.Wa (1986)

Nasatyr, Max (1934–2003) South-African-born British architect of Russian descent, he was a significant figure in the *conservation and *community architecture movements, saving the Oxo Tower (1928—by **Albert Walter Moore** (1874–1965)) on the South Bank of the Thames, and drawing up proposals for Coin Street in the teeth of formidable opposition. In his work for the now defunct GLC, most of his designs were for terrace- and courtyard-housing, built of traditional materials.

The Guardian (7 June 2003), Obits; *The Times* (3 June 2003), 27

Nash, John (1752–1835) English master of *scenography/urban designer/architect, he trained with Sir Robert *Taylor before setting up on his own (1775) as a designer/builder of *stucco-fronted houses. Bankrupted (1783), he moved to Wales, where he met Uvedale *Price and was initiated into the cult of the *Picturesque. While there he designed the County Gaol, Carmarthen (1789–92—demolished), and other buildings, and became so busy he had to take on A.C.*Pugin, then a refugee, as a draughtsman. He returned to London (1796) and formed a partnership with H.*Repton, who had ample opportunities to pick up architectural commissions. Between them they remodelled many country-seats and grounds, enhancing their Picturesque qualities, before the partnership was dissolved (1802). Nash went from strength to strength, designing many houses and *villas, including Killymoon Castle, Co. Tyrone (c.1801–3—castellated with round arches), the pretty Cronkhill, Salop. (c.1802—*Italianate), and Caerhayes Castle, Cornwall (c.1808—castellated): these asymmetrical compositions were influenced by Payne *Knight's Downton Castle, Herefs. (begun 1772). Nash built an estate of cottages at Blaise Hamlet, near Bristol (1810–11), the prototype of the Picturesque village, with a heady brew of thatch, *leaded lights, elaborate chimneys, asymmetry, and *rustic architecture loosely based on *vernacular forms.

Appointed architect to the Office of Woods and Forests (1806), from this time Nash was in favour with the **Prince of Wales** (later **Prince Regent** and **King George IV** (*r.*1820–30)). He laid out Marylebone Park, London (an estate that had reverted to the Crown (1811)), with proposals that became (1819) Regent's Park, an agreeably planted area around which were huge stucco-fronted palatial *terraces and private villas. The *façades of Cornwall and Clarence Terraces were designed by Decimus *Burton, and Cumberland Gate and Terrace were built under James *Thomson. Nash designed Ulster, York, Hanover, Kent, Chester, Cambridge, and St Andrew's Terraces, York Gate, Sussex Place, and Park Square (1821-30), Park Crescent was built 1812-22. Of the villas, Nash designed Hanover Lodge, and was responsible for the layout and many of the designs of the Park Villages (begun 1824), really a model suburb, completed by *Pennethorne, and including Italianate and Picturesque barge-boarded inventions. So that the new Park should be connected to Westminster, Nash proposed a new street (Regent Street), linked to the existing Portland Place (1776-90—by James and Robert *Adam) by means of a curved thoroughfare laid out around the ingenious *portico and *steeple of All Souls' Church, Langham Place (1822-5—designed by Nash himself), then crossing Oxford Street and terminating (by means of The Quadrant) at Piccadilly Circus. The palatial blocks along the street were designed as scenographic events (begun 1813, but all destroyed and replaced).

Nash became personal architect to the Regent and remodelled the Royal Pavilion, Brighton, Sussex (1815-21), in the *Hindoo and Chinese styles, exotically intermingled. Once the Prince became King (1820), Nash was ordered to reconstruct Buckingham House (later Palace) on the most lavish scale: much of his work there (1820-30) survives, although the Mall front was twice changed, first by *Blore, then refaced by Aston *Webb. Other designs include the Royal Opera Arcade, Haymarket (1816-18), the Haymarket Theatre (1820-1), Suffolk Street and Suffolk Place (1820s), Clarence House, St James's (1825-8), the United Services Club, Pall Mall (1826-8), the West Strand improvements opposite Charing Cross (1830-2), and Carlton House Terrace, the Mall (1827-33), which has a row of cast-iron Greek *Doric columns on the Mall front. One of his most exquisite designs was Marble Arch, originally designed to stand in front of Buckingham Palace, but moved to its present inappropriate site (1851).

Nash's works have suffered greatly from demolitions and alterations, and of his brilliant scheme linking Waterloo Place to Regent's Park very little remains of the architecture. His eclecticism, charm, scenographic effects, and widespread use of stucco did not find favour with younger architects, concerned as they were with 'purity', 'morality', expression of structure and materials, and the *Gothic Revival. Yet he was the most successful civic-designer London ever enjoyed: he has not had the appreciation he deserves, even from some of those who wrote about him.

Ballantyne (1997); Co (2008); Co (ed.) (1973); T.Davis (1973); Freer (1993); Hobhouse (1975); Mansbridge (1991); M & Wa (1987); Musgrave (1959); P (1982); H.Roberts (1939); Su (1980a); Temple (1979); J.T (1996); Tyack (ed.) (2013)

Nasoni, or **Nazzoni, Nicolau** (1691-1773) Italian architect, he settled in Oporto, Portugal (1723-73), where he introduced the lush forms of late *Baroque and *Rococo. His greatest work is *São Pedro dos Clérigos,* Oporto (1732-50), built on an elliptical plan, with a lavishly decorated and energetic front, complete with spectacular stairs. He also designed the *Palacio do Freixo,* Campanhã (c.1749-54), with grounds descending in a series of terraces to the River Douro, a memorable and theatrical composition.

K & S (1959); Nasoni (1991); R.C.Smith (1966, 1968); J.T (1996)

natatorium, natatory Cold bath of Roman *thermae,* so a swimming-pool, also called *baptisterium* and *piscina.*

National Historicism Architecture influenced by the past (see HISTORICISM), esp. with local or national characteristics, e.g. the English *Domestic Revival and *Queen-Anne styles, Irish *Hiberno-Romanesque, C19 revival of Flemish domestic architecture in Belgium, and aspects of the *Rundbogenstil in Germany (see NATIONAL ROMANTICISM).

National Romanticism Late-C19 and early-C20 movement manifest in the arts of those European countries or regions that once had been subjected to foreign artistic or political domination. Aspects of national or regional historical architecture, including *vernacular sources, were emphasized and used in inventive and eclectic ways. National Romanticism found expression in countries as disparate as Catalonia (see MODERNISME), Finland, parts of the Austro-Hungarian Empire, Norway, Sweden, Germany, and Belgium, but it is a term especially associated with Norway, Sweden, and Finland, where it came to mean the artistic *avant-garde.* Probably the best-known architectural examples are *Östberg's impressive City Hall (1909-23) and *Wahlman's Engelbrekt Church (1906-14), both in Stockholm, but there are many fine buildings which could be included (see NATIONAL HISTORICISM).

Cornell (1965, 1992); J.T (1996)

natural garden Many contemporary gardeners are concerned with natural processes, environmental sustainability, and landscapes that look unforced. The search for a 'natural garden' has embraced differing aesthetics at different times and places, but has roots in the notion of *Arcadia, yet the desire to replicate nature in gardens and parks has always involved carefully considered design, including the planting of trees, shrubs, grasses, flowers, etc., in ways that seem 'natural', being allowed to grow with minimum intervention; the remaking of contours to imitate 'natural' hills, valleys, etc.; placing of rocks and other naturally occurring features (or imitation versions of them) for contrast and effect; and the introduction of architecture and even animals apparently 'natural' to the environment created. *See* ASSOCIATIONISM; BACON; CHINESE GARDEN-DESIGN; CLUMP; ENLIGHTENMENT; JAPANESE GARDEN-DESIGN; LANDSCAPE-GARDEN; LANGE; NATURESQUE; NEW PERENNIALS *or* DUTCH WAVE PLANTING; PICTUR-ESQUE; ROCK-GARDEN; WILD GARDEN; ZEN GARDEN.

Shoe (2001); Symes (2006); Tay (2006)

Naturalism Representation of objects as they are, rather than in a *stylized* or *abstract* manner.

COF (1988); Jervis (1984); J.T (1996)

Naturesque Landscapes (in which natural features are displayed individually or generally) *managed* to exploit the visual possibilities of accidental incidents of Nature (e.g. the blasted oak, outcrops of barren rock, or sudden changes of level), sometimes improved through processes of revealing them or giving them prominence in a view. The essence of the Naturesque is respect for natural features (even old, misshapen trees), displaying them for human recreation. At Hawkstone, Salop., parts of the park could be described as Naturesque, though tree- and shrub-cover has not been managed with sufficient rigour to make the best of natural features. *Compare* GARDEN-ESQUE; PICTURESQUE.

M.W

nautilus-shell Chambered shell of a cephalopod, the spiral form of which is not unlike *ammonite shells, and may have informed the evolution of the *Ionic *volute.

nave Central clerestoreyed *aisle of a *basilican church, or the main body of the church between the western wall and the *chancel, whether aisled or not, used by the laity. The nave was often separated from the *choir by a *screen, and from the aisles by *nave-arcades* which support the *clerestorey. A *nave-chapel* is one on either side of a nave, e.g. in aisles, separated by screens.

Nazi architecture Architecture of the Hitlerian Third Reich in Germany (1933–45), basically of three types: a stripped *Neo-Classicism, as in works by *Kreis and *Speer; a *vernacular style drawing on rural and especially Alpine types; and a simple, utilitarian, industrialized type for factories. Speer's master-plan for the north-south axis of Berlin (1937–45) was unrealized, although his New Chancellery, Berlin (1938–9—demolished), was a fine essay in *stripped *Classicism with an ingenious plan. *March's impressive Olympic Stadium, Berlin (1934–6), was a fresh adaptation of a Classical theme. *Bonatz's *Autobahn *bridges were monumental, with elegant geometries. Apartment-blocks (of which many examples survive) were generally of a standardized type, with *casement windows, grey-rendered walls, and pitched roofs. However, it should be emphasized that the **National Socialist German Workers' Party** had a pluralistic attitude to architecture, and saw no reason to object to the use of steel and glass in factory design. **Adolf Hitler** (1889–1945—who had no time for what he called 'stupid imitations of the past') believed, like all Modernists, that 'form should follow function': Government/State buildings were to be in a simplified, even rudimentary Neo-Classical style; social housing, hostels, etc. would conform to local vernacular traditions; Party schools and buildings around 'Party Forums', or squares for parades, would be cold, stark, and functional; and structures e.g. airports, railway stations, factories, and *Autobahn* service stations and bridges, should be clean and *Modernist. Hitler, it should be remembered, would have nothing to do with Romantic eccentricity or anachronistic buildings: he particularly drew attention, in a conversation with Giesler, to the need for *Autobahn* service stations to declare, by their design, that they 'fuelled autos', not 'gave water' to horses.

P.Adam (1992); L.Krier (ed.) (1985); Larsson (1983); March (1936); Rohrbach (1936); Speer (1970); Speer (ed.) (1941); Spotts (2002); R.Taylor (1974); Troost (ed.) (1942–3)

Nebbien, Christian Heinrich (1778–1841) German landscape-gardener/architect, influenced by 'Capability' *Brown and H.*Repton, most of his works were realized in what was Hungary, but are now in Slovakia. One of his best gardens was *Városliget*, the City Park in Budapest. He believed that the improvement of landscapes had a moral significance outweighing aesthetic or practical aspects.

Buttlar (1989, 1999); D.Nehring (ed.) (1981); Tay (2006)

Nebelong, Niels Sigfried (1806–71) Danish architect, pupil of *Hetsch and *Labrouste, he was an exponent of *Schinkelesque *Neo-Classicism (e.g. J.C.Jacobsen's *villa at Carlsberg, Copenhagen (1852–4)), but later turned to other aspects of *Historicism. He used a *Gothic-Revival style for the new *cloister at Slagelse (1857–8). His social commitment led to his philanthropic housing for the working classes at Christianshavn (1851), influenced by the work of Henry *Roberts in England. His brother, **Johan Henrik Nebelong**

(1817–71) followed his stylistic development. Resident in Norway (1840–53), he designed the Royal Summer Residence, *Oscarshall*, Bygdøy, Oslo (1847–52—*Neo-Gothic with Classical interiors), and many public and private buildings. After he returned to Denmark he collaborated with *Bindesbøll in the design of the mental-hospital at Oringe (1853–7).

M (1951); We (1995)

nebule, nebulé, nebuly *Romanesque ornament, slightly resembling an undulating rounded *chevron moulding, the lower part of which forms a continuous waving overhang, usually found on *corbel-tables.

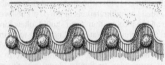

nebule St Peter at Gowts, Lincoln.

neck Upper cylindrical element forming a circular *band at the top of a Roman *Doric or *Tuscan column defined by the *astragal between it and the top of the *shaft and the *mouldings under the *echinus of the *capital. It also occurs in some versions of the Greek-*Ionic *Order, as in the *Erechtheion*, Athens (*c*.421–407 BC), where it is exquisitely ornamented with *anthemion and *palmette. See also HYPOTRACHELION. *Related terms include*:

necking: moulding on a column defining the top of the shaft, dividing it from the capital;

necking-course: any horizontal moulding like a band coinciding with a neck (e.g. at the union of the *finial with a *pinnacle) or continuing along a wall linking necks or necking.

necropolis (*pl.* **necropoleis**) City of the dead, or *cemetery, often partly built above ground, as in the *Staglieno*, Genoa (1844–51), or other Southern-European C19 cemeteries.

Co (1991); J.Curl (2002*a*)

Nedeham, James (*fl*.1514–44) English carpenter/surveyor, he worked (1528–31) on York Place for **Cardinal Wolsey** (*c*.1475–1530) and **King Henry VIII** (*r*.1509–47), and (from 1531) on the Tower of London, where he reconstructed Traitors' Gate (1532). He designed the roof of the Great Hall at Hampton Court Palace, and was involved at Greenwich and Whitehall Palaces as well as being responsible for extensive building-works during the last 15 years of King Henry's reign in his position as Clerk and Surveyor of the King's Works.

J.Harvey (1987)

needle See SPIRE.

Nehring, Johann Arnold (1659–95) *See* NERING.

Neill, John McBride (1905–74) Irish architect, he commenced (1928) practice in Belfast. One of his first important projects was the remodelling of the Savoy Hotel, Bangor, Co. Down (1933), in a *Modernist style with horizontal bands of windows and *streamlined *mouldings. He made his name with a series of cinemas, starting with the *Apollo*, Belfast (1933), with an *Art-Deco *façade, followed by the *Picturedrome* (1934—again Art Deco with much use of *chevrons). With the *Strand* (1935), *Majestic* (1936), *Troxy* (1936), and *Curzon* (1936) cinemas in Belfast, and the *Tonic* in Bangor (1936), he was influenced by the *International style. The *Tonic* was perhaps his most accomplished essay in Modernism (and, with a capacity of 2,250, the largest): its interior was a superb example of the latest in cinema-auditorium design. His later work owed something to *Mendelsohn's *Universum* Cinema, Berlin (1928), which had been widely published. Most of Neill's buildings have been demolished or converted.

P:JRSUA, v/4 (Mar./Apr. 1997), 26–37; Open (1985)

Nelson, Paul Daniel (1895–1979) American-born French architect, he worked in Paris with *Perret and befriended Le *Corbusier. By 1928 he had established his own office there, pioneering research in hospital-design. The *Petite Maison de Santé*, near Paris (1930–2), was one of his first independent designs. With others, he built the France/USA Memorial Hospital, Saint-Lô (1946–50), using his invention of the flexible *curtain-wall. He developed an egg-shaped operating-theatre for hospitals that permitted better asepsis (not having angles that were difficult to clean) and lighting. His best-known project was the *Maison Suspendue* of prefabricated units hung from a steel cage (1936–8), which was exhibited in Europe and the USA. He also designed hospitals at Dinan (1963–8) and Arles (1965–74).

E (1994); Ma (1984*a*); J.T (1996)

Nénot, Henri-Paul (1853–1934) French *Beaux-Arts trained architect, pupil of Charles *Garnier, *Pascal, and *Questel. He designed one of the biggest buildings of his time, the *Nouvelle Sorbonne*, Paris (1885–1901), a splendid display of *Beaux-Arts ideals influential in America, especially on the work of *McKim, Mead, & White. He also designed the *Institut Océanographique* (1910–11) and the *Banque Dreyfus* (1911–12), both in Paris, and the League of Nations Building, Geneva (1927–37).

ABN, cxl (1934), 351 and cxlix (1937), 118–21; M & Wa (1987); Nénot (1895, 1903); J.T (1996)

Neo-Baroque Revival of *Baroque architecture, or of elements drawn from such architecture, especially towards the end of C19 and the beginning of C20. Examples include Brumwell *Thomas's City Hall, Belfast (1898–1906), *Belcher and *Joass's Ashton Memorial, Lancaster (1907–9) (both of which could also be described as *Wrenaissance), *Wallot's *Reichstag*, Berlin (1889–98), and Cass *Gilbert's gaudy Festival Hall for the St Louis, MO, Purchase Exhibition (1904). Neo-Baroque is also known as the *Imperial* style.

A.S.Gray (1985); Pe (1976)

Neo-Byzantine *Byzantine Revival, or a style incorporating certain Byzantine features, as in the C19 *Rundbogenstil*. Good examples of the Neo-Byzantine style are Beresford *Pite's Christ Church, Brixton Road, Lambeth, London (1898–1903), and S.H.*Barnsley's St Sophia, Lower Kingswood, Surrey (1891).

J.Curl (2007); D & M (1985)

Neo-Classicism Dominant style in European and American art and architecture in the late C18 and early C19, essentially a return to the *Classicism of Antiquity as the Italian *Renaissance began to be perceived as offering architectural paradigms that were untrue to the *Antique. Taste was also turning away from *Baroque and *Rococo, and moving towards a greater appreciation of the importance of *archaeology and scholarship to arrive at an architecture that was more true to the spirit of Antiquity. Bodies such as the Society of *Dilettanti of London began to sponsor accurate publications dealing with architecture and antiquities, of which *The Antiquities of Athens* (from 1762) was one of the most important, and a major catalyst of that branch of Neo-Classicism we call the *Greek Revival. Comprehensive excavations led to a huge number of publications dealing not only with Rome and Athens, but with the important Roman sites at *Herculaneum and *Pompeii, leading to the so-called *Etruscan style, and contributing in no small measure to the *Adam and *Empire styles. Appreciation of the architecture of ancient and modern Rome was enhanced by *Piranesi's engraved views published in *Antichità Romane* (1748), *Della Magnificenza ed Architettura de' Romani* (1761), and other works, and also promoted a taste for the *Sublime because Piranesi made his subjects more impressive than they really were by greatly exaggerating their size. The *primitive and the severe began to be explored, especially the baseless *Doric *Order of Ancient-*Greek architecture, which looked strange to eyes accustomed to the refinements of *Palladianism. Promoted by *Winckelmann, Greek art began to be taken seriously, first in studies of the temples at *Paestum and Sicily, and then in Greece itself under the aegis of the Dilettanti by *Stuart, *Revett, and others, leading to the *Doric *Revival and the

use of bold primitive forms in architectural composition. Theorists such as *Cordemoy, *Laugier, and *Lodoli argued for a return to simplicity, rational design free from clutter and unnecessary ornament, and the use of the Orders for *structural* rather than decorative reasons. Furthermore, geometry was to be used for expressive purposes, enabling volumes, parts of buildings, and elements to be clearly seen and understood. **Charles-Nicolas Cochin** (1715–90) and **Jérome-Charles Bellicard** (1726–86) brought out their *Observations sur les antiquités de la ville d'Herculaneum* (1753, 1754, 1756, 1757, 1758) which was influential in promoting Neo-Classical taste, while writers such as Le *Roy and *Peyre moved French architecture towards Ancient Greece for its inspiration and away from Rome. Robert *Adam and *Clérisseau published *Ruins of the Palace of the Emperor Diocletian at Spalatro* (1768), drawing further attention to late-Roman Antique remains. While certain aspects of Neo-Classicism involved scholarly reproductions of Antique buildings and elements, as in the Greek-Revival works by Stuart, *Smirke, and *Wilkins, the movement as a whole was not confined to copying (though accurate quotation was an integral part of it), but favoured clarity, stereometrical purity of form, and a lack of superfluous ornament or fussiness to evoke the Antique. This tendency can best be seen in the works of architects such as *Boullée, *Durand, *Ehrensvärd, *Gilly, *Latrobe, *Ledoux, *Millar, *Monck, and *Soane. The publication of accurate surveys of Ancient-Egyptian buildings from 1802 by *Denon and from 1809 by the *Commission des Monuments d'Égypte* brought further elements into the vocabulary of architects seeking stark, tough, forms (see EGYPTIAN REVIVAL). Neo-Classicism reached peaks of refinement in the hands of *Empire* designers such as *Percier and *Fontaine, and in architecture by von *Klenze and *Schinkel: it also enjoyed a C20 revival as a reaction to *Neo-Baroque and *Art-Nouveau styles, often in very stripped, simplified form, notably in Scandinavia, Germany, and the USA (e.g. work by *Asplund, *Behrens, *Burnham, Tony *Garnier, *Kampmann, *Lewerentz, *Loos, *McKim, Mead, & White, *Muzio, *Perret, *Petersen, *Piacentini, *Plečnik, *Speer, *Tessenow, and many others).

CoE (1972); Crook (1972a); J.Curl (2001, 2005, 2011a); Honour (1977); Jervis (1984); L (1988); L & D (1986); Pariset (1974); Pe (1968); Su (1993); J.T (1996); Traulos (1967); Wa & M (1987)

Neo-Georgian Late-C19 and early-C20 English and American architecture inspired by C18 *Georgian domestic architecture, usually featuring brick *façades with rubbed-brick *dressings, *sash-windows, and *door-cases with *fanlights. Sometimes the inspiration was more *Colonial than English, on both sides of the Atlantic, and *vernacular elements were mixed with the underlying *Classicism. It was especially used to describe architecture of the reign of **King George V** (r.1910–36). Among its most important protagonists were *Erith, Francis *Johnson, *McMorran, and A.E.*Richardson.

A.S.Gray (1985); L & D (1986); Po (ed.) (1987); Stamp (1991); J.T (1996)

Neo-Gothic *See* GOTHIC REVIVAL.

Néo-Grec *Neo-Classical style of the *Second Empire in France (1852–70) in which Graeco-Roman, *Louis-Quinze, *Louis-Seize, *Pompeian, *Adam, *Egyptian-Revival, and other motifs were disposed in a richly eclectic *polychrome *mélange*. A good example was the *Maison Pompéienne*, Paris (designed 1855, destroyed 1891), by A.-N.*Normand. The style enjoyed a vogue in the USA, and had a short-lived impact on interior design in England and elsewhere.

J.T (1996)

Neo-Liberty Italian architectural movement which evolved in the late 1950s as an antidote to *International Modernism, notably where historic town-centres were about to be wrecked by devotees of *CIAM and the *Athens Charter. The term was invented in order to imply (quite fallaciously) that the movement was a mere revival of Italian *Art Nouveau (*Stile Liberty*): those responsible for the attack were largely led by *Banham. However, with architects e.g. **Vittorio Gregotti** (1927–) in the vanguard, and support from figures such as *Aulenti, A.*Rossi, and others, the movement intended to reverse the suppression of truth and distortion of history that had been part of Modernist agendas from the beginning. It was partially successful, especially in parts of Europe and the USA, although the disciples of Banham et al. discounted its importance even at the beginning of C21. It became closely identified with *Neo-Rationalism.

AR, cxxv/747 (Apr. 1959), 231–5; and cxxvi/754 (Dec. 1959), 341–4; Cellini *et al.* (1985); J.T (1996)

Neo-Norman *Romanesque Revival, especially from c.1820, e.g. work by *Hopper.

L & D (1986)

Neo-Palladianism 1. C18 revival of *Palladian architecture by *Burlington and his circle. 2. Late-C20 revival based on earlier revivals.

Whitehill & Nichols (1976)

Neo-Picturesque Spurious revival (1940s) of elements of the *Picturesque in Britain, particularly associated with retention of *ruins after wartime bombing (e.g. *Spence's Coventry Cathedral (1950)). In this sense it is, perhaps, absurd, and a corruption of C18 meanings.

Mellor (ed.) (1987); *Studio*, clxiv/832 (Aug. 1962), 54–7

Neo-Plasticism Associated with **Piet Mondrian**'s (1872–1944) austere abstractions after 1914, the term suggests art freed from any naturalistic tendencies. To this end he confined his designs to straight vertical and horizontal lines and primary colours, with black, grey, and white, reducing three-dimensional forms to simplified, elemental plans which he thought the bases of plastic shapes. Neo-Plasticism was adopted as an aesthetic by *De *Stijl, notably by *Rietveld, and had a profound effect on architectural plans of the 1920s.

COF (1988); Li (1988); Overy (1965); Overy *et al.* (1988)

Neo-Rationalism 1. Italian movement (1960s, 1970s), also called *Tendenza*. Opposed to dogmatic *International Modernism and to prevalent tendencies to treat architecture as a commodity, it stressed the autonomy of architecture and the need to redefine it in terms of *types with rules for the rational combination of all its elements. Rejecting the notion that architecture ends and begins in technology, it insisted on the social and cultural importance of existing urban structures, and reasserted that the huge *vocabulary* of historical forms was a fecund source for fertile *creation*. This offended Modern-Movement orthodoxy, and so the pejorative label *Neo-Liberty was applied to its earlier manifestations by, e.g. *Banham. Important texts of Neo-Rationalism were *Rossi's *Architettura della città* (1966), **Giorgio Grassi**'s (1935–) *La costruzione logica dell'architettura* (1967), and **Vittorio Gregotti**'s (1927–) *Il territorio dell'architettura* (1966). Rossi's *cemetery at Modena is the movement's most celebrated work (1971–85). *Aymonino, the **Krier** brothers (**Léon** (1946–) and **Rob(ert)** (1938–)), *Kleihues, **Bruno Reichlin** (1941–), **Fabio Reinhart** (1942–), and *Ungers have been associated with Neo-Rationalism. In particular, Grassi was influenced by *Tessenow, and his student hostel, Chieti (1976), in the form of a long colonnaded street, recalled, in its severely *stripped *Classicism, the project by *Weinbrenner for the *Langestrasse*, Karlsruhe (1808): he insisted that architecture is made up of elements expressive of their purpose, responsive to social conditions, and that the architect's job is to clarify. He *distilled* his architecture from primary forms. 2. To confuse matters (perhaps deliberately), the same label has been applied to those who (like the *New York Five), it has been claimed, have returned to the 'white' architecture of International Modernism (e.g. the *Weissenhofsiedlung* (1920s)).

A (1994); Bonfanti *et al.* (1973); Botta (1991, 1997); Colao & Vragnaz (1990); DalCo (1987); E (1994); G.Grassi (1982, 1989); Gregotti (1966, 1968, 1993); J (1999a); Klotz (ed.) (1986); Klotz (1988); L.Krier (ed.)

(1978); L.Krier & Pavan (1980); L (1988); Molinari *et al.* (1998); Moschini (ed.) (1984); On (1989); Petit (1994); Pizzi (ed.) (1994-8, 1997); A.Ro (1992); A.Ro *et al.* (1973); Ry (1996a); Sakellaridou (2000); Tafuri (1988); T & DC (1988); Wrede (1986)

Neo-Renaissance C19 revival of *Renaissance architecture from numerous sources, including the *château* style (e.g. Waddesdon Manor, Bucks. (1888-90), by *Destailleur), or the English *prodigy-house (e.g. Mentmore Towers, Bucks. (1851-4), by *Paxton). Luxuriant Neo-Renaissance buildings on the *Ringstrasse*, Vienna (1870s), drew on the *Cinquecento *High Renaissance for sources, directed by *Semper.

Pavoni (ed.) (1997)

Neo-Romanesque *Romanesque or Norman Revival, especially from the 1820s, notably in the works of *Hopper. Aspects of Romanesque occurred in the *Rundbogenstil*, and also in the work of *Richardson in the USA.

L & D (1986)

Neo-Tudor C19 revival of late-English medieval architecture of the period 1485-1547, particularly associated with early-C19 *Gothic Revival, *Domestic Revival, *Old English, and *Tudorbethan styles, and the *Arts-and-Crafts Movement. Tudor *vernacular architecture was also revived (1920s and 1930s).

D & M (1985); Davey (1980, 1995); Oliver *et al.* (1981)

Neo-Vernacular Architecture that drew on brick, *tile, and other traditional materials and even on *vernacular forms in a general reaction against *International Modernism (1960s and 1970s). It was called the *Neo-Shingle* style or the *Shed Aesthetic* in the USA.

Js (1988)

Nering, *or* **Nehring, Johann Arnold** (1659-95) German architect/military-engineer of Dutch descent, he settled in Berlin where he worked on the *Schloss* from 1679, designing *Baroque and *Palladian interiors, all of which have been destroyed. He built the Chapel at *Schloss Köpenick*, near Berlin (1684-5), extended *Schloss Oranienburg* (1689-95), and assisted in the laying out of Friedrichstadt, Berlin, from 1688. His grandest surviving building is the Baroque *Zeughaus*, Berlin (from 1695), evolved from a plan by N.-F. *Blondel, completed by *Schlüter and Jean de *Bodt. He commenced *Schloss Lützenburg*, near Berlin (1695), later altered by *Eosander von Göthe and renamed *Schloss Charlottenburg*. In Saxony he seems to have prepared designs for the *Schloss* at Barby (c.1687).

Borrmann (1893); Geyer (1936); E.Hempel (1965); Nehring (1985); Reuther (1969); J.T (1996)

nerve, nervure *Rib in *Gothic *vaulting.

Nervi, Pier Luigi (1891-1979) Italian civil-engineer, he made his reputation as one of the most gifted C20 designers of *reinforced-concrete structures. Although influenced by Italian *Rationalism, notably by *Terragni, he remained stylistically independent of fashion. His Florence Stadium (1930-2), with its huge cantilevered roof-structure and projecting spiral stairs, was the first of his many buildings to gain international acclaim. From 1932 he headed his own company, and invented a *vault of diagonally intersecting concrete arched forms, the whole resting on leaning columns like flying *buttresses, realized in the huge aircraft hangars at Orvieto (1935-42—destroyed) and elsewhere. He then evolved a system of superimposed steel meshes encased in concrete that enabled him to create prefabricated corrugated elements with high tensile capacity at the Great Hall B, Exhibition Hall, Turin (1947-9). Variations on these techniques were used in Rome at the *Palazzetto dello Sport* (1956-7—with **Annibale Vitellozzi** (1902-90)), and the huge *Palazzo dello Sport* (1958-9—with *Piacentini), where an immense *dome seems to float over the space. Nervi designed the structure for *Ponti's Pirelli *skyscraper, Milan (1955-8), and, with *Breuer, *Zehrfuss, and others, the UNESCO Buildings, Paris (1953-7), where he was responsible for the Congress Hall, with its roof formed of folded ferroconcrete plates. He published *Aesthetics and Technology in Building* (1965) and other works.

P.Collins (1959); Desideri *et al.* (eds) (1979); E (1994); Huxtable (1960a); L (1988); Mainstone (1975); Ma (1984c); Nervi (1956, 1965); P (1982); A.Pica (1969); J.T (1996)

Nesfield, William Andrews (1794-1881) English landscape-gardener, he often collaborated with *Salvin (his brother-in-law), *Burn, and *Blore. His garden-works include Arundel Castle, Sussex, Trentham Park, Staffs., Alnwick Castle, Northum., and elsewhere, and he advised on improvements to London Parks (including St James's, and Kew Gardens). Famous for *parterres (e.g. Castle Howard, Yorks.), he revived box-and-coloured-gravel designs, which he termed 'winter gardens', and favoured *cascades. One of his most celebrated gardens (1859) was for the Royal Horticultural Society in Kensington. He regarded landscape-gardening as the art of painting 'with Nature's materials'.

ODNB (2004); Ridgway (ed.) (1996); Tay (2006)

Nesfield, William Eden (1835-88) English *Arts-and-Crafts architect, son of W.A.*Nesfield. Articled (1851) to *Burn, he soon moved to *Salvin's office and later published *Specimens of Mediaeval Architecture* (1862—the result of several Continental journeys). He established (1863) an office with Norman *Shaw, but practised independently. Many of his finest domestic buildings were in the *Queen-Anne style, starting with the Lodge, Regent's Park, London (1864—destroyed), followed by his masterpiece, Kinmel Park, Denbighshire (1866–74), and then Bodrhyddan, Flintshire, (1872-4), both in Wales. His importance lies in his influence on the evolution of the English *Domestic Revival, and in the charm of his Queen-Anne buildings. One of his finest designs was Cloverley Hall, Whitchurch, Salop. (1862-8—destroyed), which featured *mullioned-and-transomed windows and a free use of *Gothic and C17 features. Other work included Barclays Bank, Market Place, Saffron Walden (1872-5), the enlargement and virtual rebuilding of the Church of St Mary the Virgin, Radwinter (1869–70—with tower etc. by Temple *Moore (from 1886)), and various buildings in the same village (1873–87), all in Essex.

Brandwood (1997); D & M (1985); Ea (1970); Gd (1977); Jervis (1984); P (1982); pk; Saint (1976); Se (1977); Se (ed.) (1975); J.T (1996)

Netherlands Grotesque C16 *grotesque ornament combined with *strapwork, entwined with human figures, invented by Flemish Mannerists such as de *Vries, so should be termed *Flemish Grotesque.*

L & D (1986)

net tracery *See* TRACERY.

Neue Sachlichkeit Term coined (1923) to describe so-called 'New Objectivity' in art/architecture, especially in the German Weimar Republic. Reacting to *Expressionism, it was associated with the development of *Rationalism and the *International-Modernist style.

COF (1988); L (1988); J.T (1996)

Neues Bauen *Avant-garde* architecture in German-speaking countries (1920s and 1930s), originally associated with *Arbeitsrat für Kunst, then with *Häring, and later with new architecture in general, especially of the *International-Modernist style.

L (1988)

Neufforge, Jean-François (1714–91) Born near Liège, he settled (1738) in Paris. His *Recueil élémentaire d'Architecture* (1757–68—the greatest collection of designs in the early Neo-Classical style of the period), with over 900 plates, reinforced his reputation as an archaeological Classicist, so that he was called the *Vignola of the age of *Louis Seize. He also helped with the production of plates for Le *Roy's important *Les Ruines des plus beaux monuments de la Grèce* (1758), one of the early significant influences on *Neo-Classicism and the *Greek Revival.

Jervis (1984); L & D (1986); M & Wa (1987); Neufforge (1757–68); J.T (1996)

Neumann, Johann Balthasar (1687-1753) German architect/military-engineer, one of the greatest of the late-*Baroque and *Rococo eras. He worked mainly in Franconia under the aegis of the **Schönborn Prince-Bishops** in the areas around Bamberg and Würzburg, where his brief covered responsibility for all military, religious, and secular architecture. His first significant major architectural work was on the new *Residenz* at Würzburg from 1719, although Johann *Dientzenhofer, *Hildebrandt, de *Cotte, *Boffrand, and von *Welsch were all consulted about the design. Hildebrandt's influence is clear in the fine central *pavilion (the roof and *pediments resemble his *Belvedere* in Vienna), the *Kaisersaal*, the Chapel, and the fine *Treppenhaus*, although Neumann seems to have finalized the designs *c.*1735. With its ceiling painted (1750-3) by **Giovanni Battista Tiepolo** (1696-1770), the stair at Würzburg is one of the most splendid of the Baroque period, comparable with Neumann's other ceremonial stairs at the *St Damiansburg Palais*, Bruchsal (1728–50), and *Schloss Augustusburg*, Brühl, near Cologne (1740–8). All three are spacious, ingenious, and breathtakingly beautiful.

Neumann's churches are many and invariably interesting. His first was the Schönborn *Mortuary Chapel attached to the *Romanesque Cathedral, Würzburg (1721-6), an adaptation of a building begun to designs by von Welsch. Among other ecclesiastical works were the Parish and *Wallfahrtskirche*, Gössweinstein (1729–39), the *Hofkirche*, Würzburg (1730–43), the *Paulinuskirche*, Trier (1734–54), *Wallfahrtskirche* of the Visitation of Mary (called *Käppele*), Würzburg (1740–81), and the Parish and Mortuary Church of Sts Cecilia and Barbara, Heusenstamm, near Offenbach, Hesse (1739–56).

His celebrated *Wallfahrtskirche* of the Assumption of Mary, *Vierzehnheiligen* (Fourteen Saints), Franconia (1742–72), had been started on site, but the spot where the Fourteen Helper Saints are said to have appeared was left in the middle of the *nave rather than in the *chancel as intended. Neumann turned this error to advantage, creating a large elliptical space around the *Nothelfer* (Helper in Time of Need) *shrine, within a basically cruciform-basilican plan, and making the nave and chancel five overlapping ellipses, three of which had their long axes on the centre-line of the church, and two at right angles to the main axis. The transeptal arrangement consisted of one of the two ellipses at the *crossing, with intersecting circles at either end. The resultant interlocking vaults have almost a *Gothic flavour about

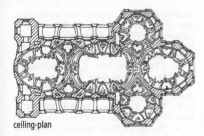

ceiling-plan

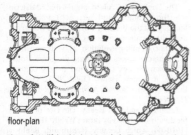

floor-plan

Plans of *Wallfahrtskirche Vierzehnheiligen*, Franconia, showing interpenetrating ellipses, ovals, and circles. The *Nothelfer* shrine is in the centre of the largest ellipse to the liturgical west of the crossing.

them, but this is disguised by the sumptuously joyous Rococo decorations, with which Neumann had no connection whatsoever. It was **Johann Jacob Michael Küchel** (1703-69) who supervised (1762-3) the construction of the vaulting of the church, and contracts were signed (1763) with **Franz Xaver Feichtmayr** (1698-1763), **Johann Michael Feichtmayr** (1696-1772), and **Johann Georg Üblhör** (1703-63) for the *stucco decorations. However, the deaths of two of these in 1763 left J.M.Feichtmayr in charge of the execution of the stucco-work, and **Giuseppe Appiani** (c.1701-86) painted the frescoes. The lovely *Gnadenaltar* (Altar of Grace), a Rococo *tour-de-force* resembling a sedan-chair covered in marine encrustations and standing within an elliptical space to the west of the *crossing, was designed (1762) by Küchel and made by J.M.Feichtmayr and Üblhör (completed 1764). Neumann has been praised to the skies for this building (notably by *Pevsner), but the beauty of the interior owes much to those identified previously, and the plan itself resembles *Guarini's *Santa Maria della Divina Providenza*, Lisbon (c.1656-9), published in the latter's *Architettura Civile* (1737). However, Neumann may have evolved his plan by way of Dientzenhofer's churches in Prague, which he had visited (1738).

Larger and grander was the huge *Benedictine Abbey Church, Neresheim, near Nördlingen

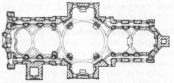

Plan of Neresheim Abbey Church.

(1745-92), completed after Neumann's death by Dominikus and Johann Baptist *Wiedemann. It is a *Wandpfeiler* church, but with some ellipses, two each in nave and choir, one in each transept, and a large one over a vast space at the 'crossing': spatial interpenetration is eloquently demonstrated, as it is in many of Neumann's creations, especially his three great stairs and, perhaps most effectively of all, at *Vierzehnheiligen*. His son, **Franz Ignaz Michael von Neumann** (1733-88) was a pioneer of fire-resistant roof-construction, and proposed an early system of stiffened *concrete vault-construction for Neresheim (not implemented).

Brinckmann (1932); Freeden (1952, 1963, 1981); Hi (1968a); Hubala (1987, 1989); Korth & Poeschke (eds) (1987); Ortner (1978); C.Otto (1979); Pe (1960); Reuther (1960); Teufel (1953, 1957); J.T (1996)

Neutra, Richard Josef (1892-1970) Austrian-born American architect, he worked with *Loos in Vienna (1912-14) and *Mendelsohn in Berlin (1921-3) before emigrating (1923) to the USA, working first with *Holabird and Roche, which gave him material for *Wie Baut Amerika?* (*How Does America Build?*—1927). He met *Sullivan and F.L.L.*Wright, and formed (1925) an association in Los Angeles with *Schindler. Together they built the Jardinette Apartments (1927), using *reinforced concrete, cantilevered balconies, and horizontal strips of metal-framed windows. It was one of the first *International-Modernist buildings in America, and was followed by the steel-framed Lovell 'Health House', Hollywood Hills, Los Angeles (1927-9), largely made of components selected from catalogues. It made Neutra's name.

He became visiting critic at the *Bauhaus and represented America at *CIAM. His most productive years as an architect were the 1930s and 1940s, when he designed several houses for famous Hollywood names (e.g. Josef von Sternberg House, San Fernando Valley, CA, 1935-6—destroyed). The Kaufmann House, Palm Springs, CA (1946-7), was influenced by *Mies van der Rohe. Later works included the US Embassy, Karachi, Pakistan (1959), his own house, Silverlake, Los Angeles (1932-3 and 1963-4), and the Los Angeles Hall of Records (1961). He published *Survival Through Design* (1954) and *Life and Shape* (1962).

Boesiger (1966); Dr & Hines (eds) (1982); Hines (1994); Lamprecht (2000); Leatherbarrow (2000); McCoy

(1960, 1979); Neutra (1954, 1962); P (1982); Spade (1971*b*); J.T (1996)

New American landscape Late-C20 style developed in America involving more sustainable, ecologically sound landscapes, and rejecting 'passive vegetative architecture' in favour of bold massing of perennials and wild grasses, responding to light, wind, and seasonal change: it was paralleled by *New Perennials or Dutch Wave planting. Among its exponents were *Bye and, more recently, **Wolfgang Oehme** (1930–2011) and **James van Sweden** (1935–2013), whose German-American Friendship Garden, Washington, DC, best embodies their design-philosophy, influenced by works of Jens *Jensen.

Oehme & Sweden (1998); A.Wilson (2005)

New Animal architecture *See* ZOÖMORPHIC ARCHITECTURE.

New Brutalism *See* BRUTALISM.

Newby, Frank (1926–2001) Yorkshire-born engineer, he joined the firm of *Samuely and worked on *Festival-of-Britain projects, e.g. *Powell & Moya's Skylon. Later (1957–8), he designed the British Pavilion, Brussels International Exposition, and took over at the Wexford Park Hospital, Slough, Bucks., on Samuely's death (1959). He contributed to the Snowdon Aviary at London Zoo (1962), the architect for which was Cedric *Price, and other projects included *Stirling & Gowan's Engineering Department, Leicester University (1959–63), and *Darbourne & Darke's Stand for Chelsea Football Club (1973).

The Times (18 May 2001), 21

New Classicism Movement involving the study of Classical architecture, to recover a coherent *language* of architecture, something jettisoned by the *Modern Movement. Classical architecture has played a hugely important historical role, renewed with C18 *Classicism and *Neo-Classicism. As a reaction to *Beaux-Arts, *Neo-Baroque, *Neo-Renaissance, and *Art Nouveau, there was a further Classical Revival before the 1914–18 war, leading to the Neo- and *stripped-Classicisms that were so widespread in the 1920s and '30s. Certain Classical elements were used in *Post-Modernism, such as *aedicules, *pediments, *porticoes, and the *Orders, but that in itself does not constitute New Classicism.

In 1952 the American, **Henry Hope Reed** (1915–2013), had the temerity to suggest that most contemporary architecture then was fraudulent, empty of intellectual content, ugly, and illiterate. Convinced that Classicism embraced an architectural language capable of modern use, he published his views in *The Golden City* (1959), and founded (1968) **Classical America** to promote it through exemplars and publications. Among the most effective protagonists in New Classicism were **Robert Adam** (1948–), **Thomas Hall Beeby** (1941–), **Julian Bicknell** (1945–), **Allan Greenberg** (1938–), **Craig Hamilton** (1961–), **Léon Krier** (1946–), **Demetri Porphyrios** (1949–), **John Anthony Simpson** (1954–), **Thomas Gordon Smith** (1948–), **Robert Arthur Morton Stern** (1939–), **John Quinlan Terry** (1937–), and **David John Watkin** (1941–2018): there have been many others, but in a brief entry in a Concise Dictionary, mention of all the personalities is not possible.

The Englishman, **Adam**, argues that Classicism was the common (and very rich) architectural language of the Western world, that it was accessible, had many resonances, and was capable of infinite continuing evolution, as he demonstrates in numerous works, including the Solar House, Wakeham, Sussex (1992), and a new country-house at Ashley, Hants. (1999–2005). He published (1990) *Classical Architecture: a Complete Handbook*.

American architect **Beeby**, Director of Design for the firm founded by **James Wright Hammond** (1918–86) which became **Hammond, Beeby & Babka Inc.** (1977–98), believes that *context* is a major factor in determining form. Two buildings may be cited here. The Harold Washington Library Center, Chicago, IL (completed 1991)—a massive pile with *façades of brick (on a granite *plinth) pierced by huge arched openings, drawing on historical precedents, not least from Florence, Greece, Rome, and C19 metal-and-glass structures, is crowned with an enormous *cornice: particularly successful are the huge metal *acroter ornaments (made by the **Bloomer Studio**) at the corners. From the same period is the Art Institute of Chicago's Daniel and Ada Rice Building: in Beeby's own words, it 'shows a decrease in the level of abstraction with the notion of an increased comprehensibility'. Other works by the firm in which Classicism is evident include the Hale Library, Kansas State University, Manhattan, KS (completed 1997), the James A. Baker III Institute for Public Policy, Rice University, Houston, TX (also finished 1997), and the Meadows Museum, Southern Methodist University, Dallas, TX (finished 2001).

Another English architect, **Bicknell**, has carried out sensitive works (e.g. at the C19 Old Gaol, Abingdon, Oxon. (1972–80)), but his Henbury *Rotunda, near Macclesfield, Ches. (1983–7), is a convincing essay in C20 *Palladianism (based on *Campbell's Mereworth Castle, Kent, and *Palladio's *Villa Capra*, Vicenza). He published (2000) a handsome monograph on his work (which drew on the *Arts-and-Crafts, Classical, and *vernacular traditions, involving close collaboration with craftsmen).

The South-African-born American (since 1973), **Greenberg**, confidently rejected Modernism which has led him to a re-appraisal of Classicism, in the realization of which he has become a distinguished practitioner. His News Buildings, Athens, GA (1992), have an unfluted Greek-*Doric *portico, and an overall authority worthy of earlier Neo-Classicists. Other works by him include a farmhouse in CT (1979–83), offices for Brent Publications, NYC (1985), and several interiors for the US Department of State, Washington, D.C. (1984–7). Also South-Africa-born, **Hamilton**, established in Radnorshire, Wales, has specialized in progressive Classicism, notably in his garden-buildings, monuments, temples, a bath-house, and *Coed Mawr*, his own house in the Welsh hills. In some of his works he has collaborated with the distinguished Classical sculptor, **Alexander Stoddart** (1959–), and among his designs influences of *Bindesbøll and *Schinkel, among others, may be detected. His architecture has a sureness of touch and an integrity that mark it out for greatness.

Luxembourg-born **Krier** has been a champion of *Rational architecture, prompted, perhaps, by *Durand, and has proposed that early-C19 Neo-Classicism provided a suitable means by which the civilized aspects of the European City before mass-industrialization might be recovered. His seductive graphics and powerful polemics have aroused new interest in the qualities of street, square, and urban district, and his work might be seen to be a series of meditations on urban themes in a world where so much has been devalued and forgotten. His view of the city as a document of intelligence, memory, and pleasure is the antithesis of the concept of the disposable, adaptable, plug-in city of *Archigram, *Metabolism, and others, and he has been critical of *Post-Modernism and stylistic *Pluralism, condemning both as unserious, unintellectual *Kitsch. He perceives the de-zoning of activities in cities to be essential, and was fundamentally opposed to *CIAM, *Athens Charter, etc., malign influences still embedded everywhere, despite efforts by Jane *Jacobs and others to excise them. He was involved in the master-plan for the Duchy of Cornwall development at Poundbury, Dorset, England (1988–91), and, with **Gabriele Tagliaventi** (1960–), produced (1988–2002) the master-plan for *Città Nuova*, Alessandria, the provincial capital of Piedmont, a model for civilized urban living, drawing on the strong urban tradition of Mediterranean countries, so has been associated with *New Urbanism.

Greek-born **Porphyrios** has argued passionately that architecture must be grounded in building technology, craftsmanship, and the use of sustainable natural materials, and has been unafraid of returning to the principles of 'firmness,

commodity, and delight' as essentials. At Pitiousa, Spetses, Greece (completed 1993), he created an environment firmly based on traditional European patterns, with houses drawing on Neo-Classical precedents, including paraphrases of designs by Schinkel: the scheme might be regarded as an example of New Urbanism. He has also been associated with *Rational architecture. His house in Chepstow Villas, Kensington, London (1988), is an exquisite testament to his taste. Even younger than Porphyrios, British architect **Liam O'Connor** (1961–) designed two houses in Belgravia, London (1996–2000, 1999–2005), a terrace of houses in Bath, Som. (2002–04); the splendid Memorial near Lichfield, Staffs. (2004–10), to British servicemen and women killed on duty since 1945; and the Memorial to Bomber Command, Green Park, London (completed 2012), in which Greek-Doric plays an important part.

The Englishman, **Simpson**, rejected *International Modernism, and has sought to show how the Classical language of architecture could be employed in new developments. His work is largely influenced by late-*Georgian sources, and he made his name with Ashfold House, West Sussex (1985–8), informed by *Soane's architecture. Simpson made the public aware of New Classicism with the exhibition, provocatively entitled *Real Architecture*, at The Building Centre, London (1987). His works at Gonville and Caius College, Cambridge (1993–8), demonstrate his mastery of colour and detail. In 1999 his firm won the competition to design the Queen's Gallery and Kitchens at Buckingham Palace, London, opened in 2002: this has a Greek-Doric entrance-portico, and the entrance-hall has Homeric *friezes by **Stoddart**.

Gordon Smith's belief in the continuing relevance of Classicism led him to create buildings that engage the intellect and the emotions, achieved not without predictable self-interested opposition. His realized designs include Richmond Hill House, Richmond, near San Francisco, CA (1982–4), the Vitruvian House, South Bend, IN (1989–90), and the Wilson House, Livermore, CA (early 1990s, drawing on Ancient Greek precedents). His Bond Hall, for the School of Architecture at Notre Dame, IN (1994–7), has Greek motifs very much in evidence. He published *Vitruvius on Architecture* (2004).

Stern, like Smith an American, has been a formidable critic of Modernism, advocating an architecture of associations, which can prompt mnemonic perceptions, and is firmly rooted in culture. He has argued robustly for the study of history, and for an eclectic use of forms to give buildings meaning. His works include the Lang House, Washington, CT (1974), the Ehrman House, Armonk, NY (1975), and Point West Place, Framingham, MA (1983–5—with a powerful portico of *primitive square columns and a *pediment like a *section through a *sarcophagus-lid, the whole reminiscent of the work of *Ledoux). Stern has been successful in reviving something of the severe French Neo-Classicism of the late C18 and early C19.

Terry, an Englishman who joined *Erith (1962) and became his professional partner (1967), worked under his own name from 1973. Among his works are the Howard (1983–6), Residential (1993–5), and *Greek-Revival Maitland Robinson (1989–93) Buildings at Downing College, Cambridge. His *Ionic (1987), Veneto (1988), and Regency (2001) Villas, all in Regent's Park, London, are scholarly evocations of *Georgian buildings. He was attracted to C17 Palladian models, as with Waverton House, Glos. (1979–80), Highland Park House, Dallas, TX (2000–4), and Ferne Park, Dorset (1998–2002). In the 1980s he entered the world of major office-developments, popularizing Classicism at the same time, as at Richmond Riverside, Richmond-on-Thames, Surrey (1985–8), allying himself with the ideas of Léon Krier. Terry's RC Cathedral of Sts Mary & Helen, Brentwood, Essex (1989–91), demonstrates his familiarity with the architectural language of *Bramante, *Brunelleschi, and *Wren.

Watkin, English architectural historian, published *Morality and Architecture* (1977), a courageous critique of arguments and criteria of judgement prevalent from the time of A.W.N. *Pugin to that of *Pevsner, exposing the fallacies of an inevitable unfolding logic in architectural evolution leading to the Modern Movement. Among other publications, his books dealing with Thomas *Hope (1968, 2008), C.R.*Cockerell (1974), German Neo-Classical architecture (1987—with **Götz-Tilman Mellinghoff**), *Soane (1996), and Quinlan Terry (2006) may be cited. In 2013 he was honoured with the **Henry Hope Reed Award** by the University of Notre Dame (the School of Architecture of which is unique in that it teaches the practice of Classical and traditional architecture). *See* NEW URBANISM.

AJ, clxxxvii/11 (16 Mar. 1988), 33–51; Anger (1996); Ar & Bi (eds) (1981); Aslet (1986); Bicknell (2000); *CL*, cxcvi/47 (21 Nov. 2002), 80–1; P.Dixon (ed.) (1998); Dodd (2013); E (1994); Economakis (ed.) (1992); Funari (1990); J.-F.Gabriel (2004); Gromort (d) (2001); Huls (1987); Inst.CA (2002); J & C (1983); Js (1977, 1980, 1980a, 1982a, 1987, 1988, 1988a); John (2002); John & D.Wa (2002); Klotz (1984, 1988); Kraft (ed.) (1992); L.Krier (ed.) (1978, 1981); L.Krier & Pavan (1980); Kuspit *et al.* (1986); M & Wa (1987); Musson (2002); information from Mr O'Connor; pk; P & W (1990); Porphyrios (1992); Porphyrios Associates (1999); Po (ed.) (1987); Reed (1959); RdP (1994); Rueda (ed.) (1986); Salmon (ed.) (2008); H.Searing & H.Reed (1981); T.Smith (2004); Stern (1975, 1977, 1982, 1988, 1996, 1997); Stern *et al.* (1995); THB; vV (1993); D.Wa (1968, 1974, 1977, 1979, 1982, 1982a, 1986, 1996, 2001, 2004, 2006); D.Wa (ed.)
(2000); D.Wa & Hewat-Jaboor (eds) (2008); Wa & M (1987)

Newdigate, Sir Roger (1719–1806) As **5th Baronet** from 1734, he became a wealthy landowner with his seat at Arbury Hall, Warwicks., and was a figure of importance in the *Gothic Revival. With the advice and practical help of Sanderson *Miller, Henry *Keene, the *Hiornes, and *Couchman, in the words of *Colvin, he made 'his family seat the Strawberry Hill of the Midlands'.

C.Brooks (1999); Co (2008); J.Curl (2011a); McCarthy (1987); *ODNB* (2004)

newel 1. Continuous vertical member forming the axis of a circular stair. **2.** Upright member set at any turning-point of a stair, or at the top or bottom of a flight, commonly forming part of the framing of the stair, and serving to connect and support the *strings and handrails at a turn or end. *See also* STAIR.

New Empiricism Swedish architecture of the 1940s by *Erskine, *Markelius, and others, perceived as the *New Humanism and 'Welfare-State' architecture.

AR, ci/606 (June 1947), 199–204, and ciii/613 (Jan. 1948), 8–22

New-Essentialist architecture Dutch equivalent of *Bauhaus-inspired *Functionalism or the *International style, 1920–40.

Grinberg (1977)

New Georgians 1. Pejorative term for those who restore run-down C18 houses in inner cities. **2.** Anti-*Modernists who sought a revival of *Georgian *Classicism.

Robinson & Artley (1985)

New Humanism, *or* **Humane Modernism** Associated with *New Empiricism, it suggests the style of Swedish architecture prevalent from the 1940s, which supposedly put the welfare of people first, rather than being derived from abstractions, styles, or dogmas. It refers particularly to the work of a group of British architects, most whom were born in the first two decades of C20, who designed housing influenced by Scandinavian public buildings and private houses, especially exemplars published (1940s and '50s) in *AR*. Its older protagonists included *Casson and *Gibberd (his Somerford Estate, Hackney (1945–7), was a pioneering example), and its younger ones **Philip Powell** (1921–2003—*see* POWELL & MOYA), Ian *Baker, Oliver *Cox, **Leonard Sulla Manasseh** (1916–2017), and *Buzás, all of whom met when students at the Architectural Association. New Humanist architecture (of which the ultimate example was the 1951 *Festival of Britain) was denounced, often viciously, by protagonists of New *Brutalism including *Banham and the

*Smithsons, as *Picturesque and effete, but its impact on younger architects qualifying in the 1950s and 1960s was greater than that of the Brutalists, in part through Manasseh's teaching. The term is also applied to work by architects with similar aims beyond this distinct group (e.g. David and Mary *Medd, *Tayler, and **David John Green** (1912–98)). Most public housing in Britain was profoundly influenced by New Humanism until the late 1950s.

AR, c/606 (June 1947), 199—204, and c/iii/613 (Jan. 1948), 8—22; Harwood (1998); B-C; B-C (2014)

New Objectivity *See* NEUE SACHLICHKEIT.

New Perennials *or* Dutch Wave Planting
Style of planting using hardy grasses, developed by Dutch landscape-gardeners from pioneering work by German plant-breeders (including **Karl Förster** (1874–1970), **Ernst Pagels** (1913–2007), and **Georg Arends** (1862–1952)). Using plants chosen as much for their structure as for their colour, such work is intended to look as natural as possible and does not require intensive maintenance. A practitioner is **Piet Oudolf** (1944–) whose Battery Park (2003) and High Line (2006), both NYC, are representative: his impact on the UK increased with his appointment as Visiting Professor of Planting Design at the University of Sheffield.

Oudolf (2011); Oudolf & Kingsbury (2013)

New Sensualism
Architecture by e.g. *Candela, Le *Corbusier, *Nervi, *Rudolph, *Saarinen, *Utzon, *Yamasaki and others, who, after the 1939–45 war, exploited plastic form and created buildings unlike the style adopted for *International Modernism from the time of the *Weissenhofsiedlung (1927).

PA, xl/9 (Sept. 1959), 141–7, and xl/10 (Oct. 1959), 180–7

Newsom, Samuel (1854–1908), and Newsom, Joseph Cather (1858–1930)
Prolific designers/builders of late-C19 domestic architecture in the USA, the brothers' most celebrated house is the William Carson Residence, Eureka, CA (1884–5), a composition featuring barge-boarded *gables, gouty *colonnettes and extreme ornamentation in what can only be described as an exuberant *Free style. Many designs were published in the *California Architect and Building News*, and Joseph Cather produced a large number of *pattern-books, including *Artistic Buildings and Homes of Los Angeles* (1888), *California Low Priced Cottages* (1888), and *Picturesque and Artistic Homes and Buildings of California* (1890). At the beginning of their partnership (1878) they were building in the *Eastlake or *Stick style, then they turned to *Colonial *Queen Anne, followed by much cribbing from *Richardson, then a flirtation with the Colonial Revival or *Shingle style, the *château style, the

*Georgian Colonial Revival, and *Beaux-Arts Classicism. Later they turned to regional *Mission Revival (based on Spanish Colonial architecture) and c.1900 to the *Arts-and-Crafts style. Clearly all was grist to their architectural mill, and they were never guilty of restraint.

Gebhard et al. (1979); Newsom (1890, 1895, 1895a, 1896, 1981); Newsom & Newsom (1978); P (1982); J.T (1996)

Newton, Ernest (1856–1922)
One of the most successful and influential English domestic architects of his generation, he was articled (1873) to R.N.*Shaw before establishing his own practice (1879). Red Court, Scotland Lane, near Haslemere, Surrey (1894–5), drew on canted *bays, sash-windows, and other features that led *Pevsner to describe it as an 'ominous house with sterile Neo-Georgianism just round the corner', even though it had been described, praised, and illustrated by *Muthesius, no less. Other houses include Steep Hill, near St Helier, Jersey (1898–1900), and Scotsman's Field, Burway Hill, Church Stretton, Salop. (1907–8). He published *Sketches for Country Residences* (1882), *A Book of Houses* (1890), and *A Book of Country Houses* (1903). His son, **William Godfrey Newton** (1885–1949), published *The Work of Ernest Newton R.A.* (1925).

Rod. Brown (ed.) (1985); A.S.Gray (1985); H.M (1979); H.M (ed.) (1910); Nairn et al. (1971)

Newton, William (1730–98)
A native of Newcastle upon Tyne, he had a large practice there as an architect/builder. Among his works were Charlotte Square, Newcastle (c.1769–70), Castle Eden, Co. Durham (c.1760), and (all in Northum.) new *wings and front at Fenham Hall, (c.1770), the *Gothic Kielder Castle (1772–5), the front of Capheaton Hall (1789–90), and the east front of Hesleyside (1796–1800).

Co (2008); *ODNB* (2004)

Newton, William (1735–90)
London-born architect, he worked with Matthew *Brettingham before establishing his own practice by 1764, shortly afterwards visiting Rome, returning to England (1767). He worked for **William Jupp** (1734–88), and assisted (1781) James *Stuart at Greenwich Hospital before succeeding Robert *Mylne as Clerk of the Works. He published (1771) the earliest English translation of the first five books of *Vitruvius under the title *The Architecture of M.Vitruvius Pollio: translated from the Original Latin by W.Newton, Architect*; was the author of *Commentaires sur Vitruve* (in French, but published in London (1780)); and helped to edit and complete the second volume of Stuart & *Revett's *Antiquities of Athens* (1789, although the title-page gives 1787). He then translated the remaining five books of Vitruvius, and a complete

edn was published (1791) by his brother, **James Newton** (1748–c.1804).

Art Bulletin, **xxix** (1947); Co (2008); E.Harris (ed) (1990), 464–6; *ODNB* (2004)

New Towns After the 1939–45 war some of Ebenezer *Howard's ideas were adopted by the new UK Socialist Government (1945–51), and various new towns were built, in theory to take the pressure off large existing cities. London acquired eight (Stevenage, Herts., was the first), and there were others in England, Scotland, Wales, and Northern Ireland. They were not an unqualified success, aesthetically or socially. *See also* GARDEN CITY; SATELLITE TOWN.

Clapson (1998); Cowling (1997); P.Hall & C.Ward (1998); Hardy (1991); Parsons & D.Schuyler (eds) (2002); Whittick (ed.) (1974b)

New Urbanism *International *Modernism produced numerous free-standing box-like buildings deliberately unrelated to their contexts: bits of land (*see* SLOAP) left by the rigidities of Modernist architecture could never be made into urban spaces that meant anything or had any qualities except an ability to dismay those who experienced them. Five thousand years of urban history demonstrate that the complex relationships of streets, squares, parks, monuments, buildings, etc., not only form means of communication, but help identification and orientation, giving the urban fabric a sense of character and place: all that was jettisoned. In reaction, traditional urban blocks, mixed uses, and a coherent, literate, architectural language were promoted by New Urbanists as antidotes to unpleasant, inhumane, threatening, and incoherent environments that were the direct result of the work of devotees of the *Athens Charter, *CIAM, Le *Corbusier, and the products of so-called Schools of Architecture. Among the promoters of New Urbanism may be cited **Sir Jeremy Dixon** (1939–); **Andres Duany** (1949–) and **Elizabeth Plater-Zyberk** (1950–) (e.g. Seaside, Miami, FL (1978–87)); **Edward Jones** (1939–); **Michael Kirkland** (1943–); **Léon** (1946–) and **Rob(ert)** (1938–) **Krier**; **John Anthony Simpson** (1954–); A.*Rossi; and **Demetri Porphyrios** (1949–), among others. It has been denounced by Modernists as 'escapist' and 'historicist': some would argue that, if this is the case, we need more Escapism and Historicism. *See* NEW CLASSICISM.

Katz (1994); Kelbaugh (2002); Krieger & Lennertz (eds) (1991); R.Krier (1979, 1995, 2003); L.Krier & Pavan (1980); P & W (1990)

New York Five Known as the 'Whites' because of their predominantly white buildings (notably those of **Richard Alan Meier** (1934–)), they were a group of American architects (the others were **Peter D.Eisenman** (1932–), **Michael Graves** (1934–), **Charles Gwathmey** (1938–), and *Hejduk) who exhibited in NYC (1969), and were perceived as producing revisions of *International-Modernist white buildings of the 1920s influenced by the works of *Rietveld and *Terragni in particular, so were described, curiously, as *Neo-Rationalists. They were attacked (1973) by the 'Grays', a group of architects including C.W.*Moore and **R.A.M. Stern** (1939–), for pursuing a 'pure' Modernist aesthetic resulting in unworkable buildings respecting neither sites nor users. However, Graves's Public Services Building, Portland, OR (1979–83), and Humana Tower, Louisville, KY (1982–6), broke ranks with controversial work, moving towards *Pluralism, made overt in his Team Disney Building, Burbank, CA (1985–91—with *Snow White* dwarfs standing in for *atlantes in the *Attic storey).

ARe, **clv/2** (1974), 113–16; Bédard (ed.) (1994); Buck & Vogt (eds) (1994); Ciorra (1995); C.Davidson (ed.) (1996); Eisenman (1998, 2003); Eisenman Architects (1995); Eisenman (ed.) (1996); F *et al*. (1975); F & Ry (1993–7, 1999); Graves (1999); Js (1988); *JSAH*, **xxxviii/2** (May 1979), 205–7; J & W (1988); Klotz (1988); Kudalis (1996); K.Nichols *et al*. (eds) (1990, 1995); Sennott (ed.) (2004); J.T (1996); vV (1993); Weissenberger & Levey (1986); K.Wheeler *et al*. (eds) (1982)

Neyelov, Vasily Ivanovich (1722–82) Russian architect/landscape-designer, he travelled in England (1770) before working (1771–8) at *Tsarskoye Selo* (now *Pushkin*), one of the first landscape parks in Russia, assisted by *Busch. He designed several *fabriques* there, including the Siberian Marble Gallery (1772–4), based on the Palladian Bridge at Wilton, Wilts.; the Pyramid (1770–1); the Little Caprice (1770–2); the turreted and pinnacled Hermitage Kitchens (1774–6); the *Chinoiserie* Great Caprice (1772–4); and the 'Admiralty' in Netherlandish *Gothic (1772–7). His son, **Il'ya Vasil'yevich Neyelov** (1745–93), added the Upper (1777–9) and Lower (1778–9) Bath Pavilions in a Neo-Classical style.

Arkhitekturnoye Nasledstvo, **iv** (1953), 73–90; Tay (2006); J.T (1996)

Neylan, Michael (1931–2012) English architect. After a time working with *Chamberlin, Powell, & Bon, he won the competition to design the Bishopsfield housing, Harlow, Essex (1961–6—nicknamed 'The Casbah'), realized with **Bill Ungless**. They also designed the Setchell development, Bermondsey, Southwark (1971–8).

RIBAJ (Nov. 2012), 14; *C20 Magazine*, **iii** (2012), 62

nib Pointed extremity, e.g. the top of a steeply-pitched pyramidal *finial, hence *nib-stone*.

Niccolini, Antonio (1772–1850) Italian architect. Much influenced by French work, he designed the stupendous *façade for the *Teatro*

San Carlo, Naples (1810-12), with a robust, rusticated, arched lower storey and an *Ionic *colonnade on the upper floor beneath a huge *entablature. Six years later, after a fire, he built a new theatre behind the façade. He also built the *Teatro Piccini* and the Church of *San Ferdinando* at Bari, and for the Bourbon Royal Family he builtthe *Villa Floridiana* (1817-19—with gardens laid out in the *Picturesque 'English' style) and the vast stair (1836) to the palace from the *Via di Capodimonte*, much embellished with Neo-Classical and Egyptianizing architectural motifs.

Ms (1966); M & Wa (1987); J.T (1996)

niche Shallow ornamental recess in a wall or *pier, usually to contain a statue, *urn, or other ornament. Classical niches are usually arched, sometimes with a quarter-spherical *head if semicircular on plan, and often with the half-dome carved to resemble a scallop-shell. Some niches are set within *aedicules, and *Gothic niches (called *tabernacles) have *gablets or *canopies over them. A *niche-grave* is a *loculus* in a *hypogeum*, *catacomb, *mausoleum, or a space in a *cinerarium or *ollarium.

Nicholson, Sir Charles Archibald, Bt. (1867-1949) English architect, articled to *Sedding, after whose death he continued to practise with Henry *Wilson. He set up on his own (1893) and was joined (1895) by the Australian **Hubert Christian Corlette** (1869-1956), who had trained with *Belcher. Their first church was St Alban, Westcliffe-on-Sea, Essex (1895-1908—a refined design in a *Free-Gothic style, constructed of *flint and *rubble with red-brick *dressings, and with pretty furnishings inside, including a *Roodscreen and fine *reredos), and they published important papers on the furnishing of ecclesiastical buildings (1907-12). They designed one of the first extensive *reinforced-concrete complexes, Government Buildings and House, Kingston, Jamaica (1910), an extraordinary work with *bays defined by massive *buttresses. Their finest church is arguably St Matthew's, Chelston, Torquay, Devon (1895-1904), where *Arts-and-Crafts influences merged with a freely treated *Gothic Revival. Nicholson contributed to the design of St Anne's Cathedral, Belfast, where he was consultant architect (1924-48).

A.S.Gray (1985); *ODNB* (2004); Bettley & Pe (2007); Cherry & Pe (1989)

Nicholson, Christopher David George ('**Kit**') (1904-48) English Modernist architect, son of the artist, **Sir William Newzam Prior Nicholson** (1872-1949). Among his designs was the Studio, Fryern Court, near Fordingbridge, Hants. (1933), for the painter, **Augustus Edwin John**

(1878-1961), a paradigm of *International-Modernism, complete with spiral stair, *pilotis, and 'flat' roof, all painted light pink. Other works included Kit's Close, Benham's Lane, Fawley Green, Bucks. (1936-7); the Surrealist remodelling (1935-7—with *Casson and **Salvador Dalí** (1904-89)) of Monkton House, near Midhurst, Sussex (originally designed (1902) by *Lutyens), for **Edward Frank Willis James** (1907-84); and the Gliding Club, Tring Road, Dunstable, Beds. (1935-6), influenced by *Mendelsohn's work.

Bingham (ed.) (1996); *RIBAJ* (Dec. 2009), 74

Nicholson, Peter (1765-1844) Scots architect. Settling in London, he published *The New Carpenter's Guide* (1792), which described new methods of constructing *vaults and *niches. This was followed by *The Principles of Architecture* (1795-8) and *The Carpenter's and Joiner's Assistant* (1797). He practised as an architect in Glasgow from 1800, building Carlton Place, Laurieston (1802-18), other buildings in Scotland and Cumb. (he was Surveyor to that County from 1808), and laying out the town of Ardrossan, Ayrshire (1800-8—although the harbour was constructed by *Telford). Back in London (1810) he published his important *Architectural Dictionary* (1812-19), and *The School of Architecture and Engineering* (from 1825, but abandoned). He was assisted in some of his publications by his son, **Michael Angelo Nicholson** (1796-1842), who also brought out several books: their prodigious output constitutes a significant repository of architectural and building knowledge, and includes *An Architectural and Engineering Dictionary* (1835, revised 1852). One of M.A.Nicholson's two daughters married 'Greek' *Thomson.

Co (2008); N (1823, 1835, 1852); *ODNB* (2004); W.Pa (1852)

Niemeyer, Oscar (1907-2012) Brazilian architect, he worked on the Ministry of Education and Health Building, Rio de Janeiro (1936-45), for which Le *Corbusier was consultant. An early devotee of *International Modernism, he departed from *Modernist orthodoxy, admitting he found straight lines uncongenial, preferring 'free-flowing, sensual curves', a stance which earned him the displeasure of Le Corbusier (who, nevertheless, used curves at, e.g., Ronchamp chapel): the 'carnivalization' of Niemeyer's architecture was described in Philippou's study. Early influences on Niemeyer were *Costa (with whom he later collaborated) and *Warchavchik, but his career blossomed under the aegis of **Jusquelino Kubitschek** (1902-76—physician, turned Leftist politician), who commissioned him (from 1940) to design a series of recreational buildings beside the artificial lake at Pampulha (a suburb of *Belo Horizonte*, capital of

Brazil's Minas Gerais State). These included the Casino (set in *Burle Marx's brightly hued gardens) and *São Francisco* Church ('the last with a wave-like roof). When Kubitschek became President of Brazil (1956–61), Niemeyer was appointed chief architect for the new city of Brasília, the layout of which (an aeroplane-shaped distortion of Le Corbusier's *Ville Radieuse* (1935)) was designed by Costa. The centrally-planned Cathedral and Government Offices (1956–64), were all by Niemeyer, and all in stark contrast with the shanty-towns which rapidly sprang up around the island of privilege: indeed, far from being an exemplar of socially imaginative planning, Brasília exacerbated divisions between rich and poor. Furthermore, the slab-like buildings housing bureaucracies were ranged in rigid rows, and, minus *brises-soleils*, were subjected to solar heat-gain rendering unusable the sides exposed to the sun. Niemeyer had been part of the team (which included Le Corbusier (who attempted to claim sole authorship) designing (with W.H.*Harrison and *Abramovitz) the United Nations Headquarters, NYC (1947–53), a complex which perhaps demonstrates the dangers of involving too many cooks. Other works include offices for the Communist Party, Paris (1965–80), the Mondadori Building, Segrate, outside Milan (1968–75), and the Niterói Contemporary Art Museum, Brazil (1991–6).

Botey (1996); Fils (ed.) (1982, 1988); Holston (1989); Hornig (1981); J (2012); L (1988); Niemeyer (1975, 1978, 1997, 2000); *NYRB* (4–14 April 2013), 32–4; Papadaki (1960); Philippou (2008); Salvaing (2002); Segawa (2013); Sodré (1978); Spade (1971a); Underwood (1994, 1994a)

Nietzsche, Friedrich Wilhelm (1844–1900) German philosopher, he recognized the difficulties in European culture when the *Enlightenment undermined religious authority, but failed to replace it. He believed that the Arts might have the potential to liberate Mankind through imagination, and denounced the conflation of Morality with Art (unlike A.W.N.*Pugin's and *Ruskin's stances), holding that Morality served to force everyone to behave like everyone else (the 'herd instinct'), crippling humanity from rising above itself. In arguing the need for independent values and opposition to false 'morality', his notions appealed to late-C19 and early-C20 artists/thinkers. His influence on the visual arts was immense, not least because he criticized *Kant's aesthetic of 'disinterestedness', urging the need to value conflict and innovation. In particular, his ideas permeated *Expressionism and affected Count Harry *Kessler among many others.

W.Kaufmann (2000); J.T (1996); J.Young (2010)

nig To dress stone with a hammer or pick: hammer-dressed *ashlar is therefore called *nigged*.

night-stair *Stair in the south *transept of an abbey-church leading from the *dormitory.

nimbus *See* AUREOLE.

nine altars According to tradition there are *Nine Choirs* or *Orders of Angels*, mediating between God and Man, nine squaring the Trinity. This is reflected in the design of certain *retro-choirs (e.g. Fountains Abbey, Yorks. (c.1205–47), and Durham Cathedral (1242–1280s)).

Whone (1990)

Nissen hut Tunnel-shaped prefabricated hut made of corrugated steel (protected with various substances including bituminous paints and a patented substance called **Arpax**) with a cement floor: it was essentially half a cylinder, sometimes with windows like *dormers projecting from it. Invented by Lt.-Col. **Peter Norman Nissen** (1871–1930), it was widely used in the 1914–18 and 1939–45 wars for military use (e.g. offices, barracks, etc.).

OED Supplement (1987)

Niven, Ninian (1799–1879) Scots gardener, he settled (1827) in Ireland as Head Gardener at Phoenix Park, Dublin. Appointed (1834) Curator of the Botanic Garden at Glasnevin, he only stayed in post until 1838 when he established a private practice as a landscape-gardener and nurseryman, first at Monkstown, then at Drumcondra, where, from 1849, he took on pupils in agriculture and horticulture. He evolved an 'intermediate' style of garden-design, blending English and French principles. Among his realized schemes were works at Santry Court, Co. Dublin (1857, 1863); Templeogue House, Co. Dublin (c.1862); the International Exhibition, Dublin (1863); Ards House, Co. Donegal (1874); and Castle Leslie, Co. Monaghan (1843, 1854).

DIA; Malins & Bowe (1980); Nelson & McCracken (1987)

Nivola, Costantino (1911–88) Sardinia-born sculptor whose technique of 'sand-casting' (pouring of plaster or cement on to sculpted sand) brought him fame. He settled in Long Island (c.1940), creating a 'house-garden' attached to his C18 farmhouse at Armagansett, NY, assisted by *Rudofsky, in which sequences of *'rooms', defined by paths, free-standing walls, fences, and planting as 'interplays of wall-surfaces, sunlight, and vegetation', formed intimate enclosed external spaces. Other works included the wall-relief at the Olivetti Showroom, NYC (1954), and interventions at the McCormick Plaza Exposition Center, Chicago, IL (1959).

Martegani (2003)

Nobile, Pietro (Peter) von (1774–1854) Swiss-born, he became one of the most important C19 architects working in the Habsburg Empire. Having acquired a taste for a rigorous *Neo-Classicism when a student, he was in a position to influence style once he became Director of the Public Works Department in the Austrian port of Trieste (1807–17): during his time there he designed the *Accademia di Commercio e Nautica* (from 1816) and other works, as well as restoring several buildings in Pola and Trieste. Summoned (1817) to Vienna to direct the architectural department of the *Akademie der Bildende Künste*, his austere *Classicism made a huge impact on his students. When in Vienna he designed two significant Neo-Classical buildings: the *Theseustempel* in the *Volksgarten* (1819–22) and the *Burgtor* in the *Heldenplatz* (1821–4)—the former is a miniature version of the *Doric Temple of Hephaestus, Athens, built to contain the sculpture of Theseus and the Centaur (1804–19) by **Antonio Canova** (1757–1822), and the latter a massive gate (based on a severe design by *Cagnola) giving access to the open space in front of the Imperial Palace. Unfortunately, the fortifications in which the gate was set were demolished (1859), so the *Burgtor* is now an isolated structure. Other works by Nobile include the Potocki Chapel, Kraków Cathedral, Poland (1830–2), the *Casa Fontana* (1827–30), *Palazzo Costanzi* (1838–40), and the *Pantheon-inspired *Sant' Antonio Nuovo* (1828–49), all in Trieste.

*L'Architettura, I/*1 (1955), 49–51, *I/*3 (1955), 378–84; Hi (1977); Ms (1966); M & Wa (1987); J.T (1996)

nodding ogee *Ogee *canopy-head. Its *apex projects beyond the springing-line of the canopy, i.e. it is an ogee form in *section as well as in *elevation.

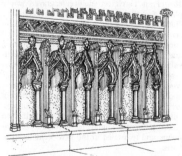

Row of nodding-ogee canopies, Lichfield Cathedral, Staffs., *c.*1320.

nogging Brickwork infill-*panel set in a timber *frame. A *nogging-piece* is a horizontal timber between *posts in a *timber-framed structure

forming part of the frame of an infill-*panel, e.g. of brick nogging.

Brick herring-bone nogging.

Noguchi, Isamu (1904–88) American sculptor, son of a Japanese father and an American mother. He designed the monumental *bridges in *Tange's Peace Park, Hiroshima, Japan (1951–2); sculpture for *SOM's Connecticut General Life Insurance Company offices, Bloomfield, CT (1956–7); the Japanese Garden for *Breuer's UNESCO Building, Paris (1956–8); the garden for the Beinecke Rare Book and Manuscript Library, Yale University, New Haven, CT (1960–4); the *plaza for First National City Bank, Fort Worth, TX (1960–1); the sunken-garden plaza, Chase Manhattan Bank, NYC (1961–4); the Sculpture Garden for *Mansfeld's Israel Museum, Jerusalem (1960–5); and his own Studio and Sculpture Garden, Long Island, NY (opened 1985).

Ashton (1992); M.Friedman (ed.) (1978); Hunter (1979); J.T (1996); W & S (1994); Weilacher (1996)

Noiers, Geoffrey de (*fl.*1189–*c.*1200) Probably the Norman-French master-mason responsible for part of the rebuilding of the *Gothic Lincoln Cathedral from 1192. The vault of St Hugh's *Choir (1192–1200), by him, is perhaps the first case in Gothic Europe where the emphasis was on decorative rather than structural ribs, and he was perhaps also responsible for the three-dimensional blind overlaid arcading on the walls of St Hugh's Choir. However, *Richard the Mason (*fl.*1190s) was also involved, and the original design of the Gothic Cathedral may be his.

J.Harvey (1987)

Nolli, Giovanni Battista (1701–1756) Italian surveyor/typographer/architect, he prepared the plan of Rome that was an accurate and full survey of *Antique remains. He designed *Santa Dorotea in Trastévere* (1751–6), with a concave *façade of monumental gravity, and interior of deceptive simplicity.

Ehrle (1932); P (1982); *W-R-J,* xxxv (1973), 309–42

nook 1. Corner of a room, i.e. interior angle formed by the meeting of two walls. **2.** Piece taken out of an angle, e.g. where a *reveal meets the exterior *face of a wall and a re-entrant angle is formed, giving two *arrises instead of one.

3. Part of the corner of a room beside a fireplace, often with its own window, called an *ingle-nook, sometimes treated as an alcove off a room providing a more intimate space. *Compounds include*:

nook-rib: *rib in the corner of a *Gothic *vault;

nook-shaft: *colonnette set in a nook (**2**), i.e. in the external angle of a building or where the reveal of an aperture joins the external face of the wall;

nook-window: *window in an *ingle-nook, i.e. in the corner of the room next to the fireplace, often recessed.

C.M.Hs (1983); *OED* (1933)

Norberg-Schulz, Christian (1926–2000) Norwegian architect/theorist/historian. Believing (influenced by *Giedion et al.) that *Modernism was the only valid C20 architectural currency, his writings on *Baroque, *Rococo, and the *genius loci are all the more remarkable. Under Giedion's influence, he founded (1952—with *Korsmo, *Fehn, and others) **PAGON** (Progressive Architects Group Oslo Norway) to provide an independent Norwegian delegation to *CIAM, and, with Korsmo, designed three glass-and-steel houses (1953–5) on a hill near Oslo, in which the rigid grid and architectural treatment drew on work of *Eames and *Mies van der Rohe. He edited (1963–78) *Byggekunst*, and (also 1960s) began his long career teaching at Oslo School of Architecture following the publication of his *Intentions in Architecture* (1963), a book in which he investigated the theory of organization of space and built form, emphasizing the importance of visual perception, influenced by *Gestalt* psychology and by the works of **Paul Frankl** (1879–1962), **August Schmarsow** (1853–1936), and **Heinrich Wölfflin** (1864–1945). He developed a method of phenomenological analysis of cities which he described in *Genius Loci* (1979, 1980). Curiously, in *Modern Norwegian Architecture* (1986) and in numerous papers, he celebrated the architecture of his native land, emphasizing *traditional construction*, use of *local materials*, and the virtues of *vernacular architecture, stances very much at odds with his espousal of the *Modern-Movement cult. Influenced by **Charles Alexander Jencks**'s (1939–2019) *The Language of Post-Modern Architecture* (1977), he embraced '*PoMo*' with some enthusiasm, but in the 1990s, stung by growing isolation, he pronounced that *PoMo* had 'dissolved into superficial playfulness', and returned to a study of Modernist 'theory' in his *Principles of Modern Architecture*.

N-S (1963, 1968, 1971, 1980, 1980a, 1982, 1985, 1986, 1986a, b, c, 1988, 1990, 1993, 1996, 1997, 2000, 2000a); N-S & Postiglione (1997)

Norman architecture *Romanesque architecture in Normandy and the British Isles C11–end of C12, generally with massive walls pierced by semicircular-headed windows and doors. There was a short-lived C19 *Norman Revival* (*see* NEO-NORMAN; NEO-ROMANESQUE).

Normand, Alfred-Nicolas (1822–1909) French architect, son of **Louis-Eléonor Normand** (1780–1862), also an architect. After sustained study abroad, he settled (1852) in Paris and became an important designer during the *Second Empire. A confirmed Classicist, he avoided all medieval allusions in his work. His greatest achievement was the *Maison Pompéienne, Avenue Montaigne*, Paris (designed 1855, destroyed 1891), influenced by Roman *villa plans, with a central glazed *atrium. Interiors were revivals of Graeco-Roman, *Pompeian, *Empire, *Islamic, and other styles, juxtaposed in a rich and fruity *mélange*. The house, for **Prince Napoléon-Joseph-Charles-Paul (Plon-Plon) Bonaparte** (1822–91), was a *Néo-Grec* paradigm. Normand also designed the women's prison, Rennes (1867–76), a vast establishment for 1,000 inmates. Among other works were the C17 Revival *Château Latour* at Liancourt-St-Pierre, near Paris (1862–8), the restoration of the *Colonne Vendôme* and the *Arc de Triomphe*, Paris (1871–8), and the Hospital at St-Germain-en-Laye (1878–81). He edited *Le Moniteur des Architectes* (1866–8) and published illustrations of *pavilions erected for the *Exposition Universelle* (1867). His sons, **Charles-Nicolas** (1858–1934) and **Paul-Louis-Robert** (1861–1945) were architects too.

Gary (1979); *GdBA*, NS 5, lxxxvii (1976), 127–34; J.T (1996)

Normand, Charles-Pierre-Joseph (1765–1840) French architect/engineer/engraver, whose plates for *Percier and *Fontaine's *Recueil…* (1801) encapsulated the *Empire* style. His *Nouveau Recueil en Divers Genres d'Ornemens* (1803) contained many *Directoire* and *Empire* themes, and he collaborated with **Pierre-Nicolas Beauvallet** (1749–1828) on *Décorations intérieures et extérieurs* (1803). His most celebrated work was *Nouveau Parallèle des Ordres* (1819), an accurate and exquisitely engraved book of the *Orders of architecture that remains one of the best sources. His son, **Louis-Marie** (1789–1874), published (1832) influential engravings of funerary monuments and mausolea in the new *cemeteries of Paris.

Jervis (1984); L & D (1986); M & Wa (1987); C.Normand (1852); L.-M.Normand (1832); W.Pa (1852)

Norse ornament *See* VIKING ORNAMENT.

Norte, Manuel Joaquim (1878–1972) Portuguese architect, whose individual early-C20 houses in Lisbon were stylistic blends of *Art Nouveau and *Romanesque Revival. Examples included 38 *Avenida Fontes Pereira de Melo* (1914) and a residential block at 206-18 *Avenida da Liberdade* (1915). He also worked in a *Neo-Baroque style (e.g. the school and concert-hall of the *Voz do Operário*, Lisbon (1912)). In the 1930s he employed *reinforced concrete, and embraced *Art Deco themes (e.g. 18/20 *Avenida Barbosa du Bocage* (1931)). In his later years he adopted *National Historicism.

França (1991); J.T (1996)

North, Roger (1653-1734) Aristocratic English amateur architect, he played an important role in negotiations with *Barbon for the rebuilding of The Temple, London, after the fire (1678/9). He designed the Great Gateway from Fleet Street to The Temple (1683-4), and was responsible for a number of other competent Classical designs, including alterations to Wroxton Abbey, Oxon. (1680-5), and to a house at Rougham, Norfolk (1690s—destroyed). An essay, entitled 'Of Building' by him survives in the British Library.

BL Add. MSS 23005, 32510, 32540; Co (2008); *ODNB* (2004)

Northern Renaissance Revival Late-C19 revival (especially in England) of the *Renaissance and *Mannerist styles of Flanders, The Netherlands, and Northern Germany, notably by Sir Ernest *George and other contemporaries, also termed *Pont-Street Dutch or Flemish Revival. It frequently incorporated details made of *terracotta.

D & M (1985); A.S.Gray (1985)

north-light 1. Glazing in a roof facing north, with a pitched roof sloping from the window-head on the southern side. In e.g. a factory, a series of north-lights is often formed with valleys between the bases of the north-lights and the sloping roof, so in *section the roof resembles a jagged saw (hence *sawtooth-roof*). 2. Any large window facing north in e.g. an artist's studio.

north side Side of a church facing north, regarded as the source of cold winds and the haunt of the Devil (hence *Devil's door*, meaning north door).

nose Projecting edge.

nosing Projection formed by a horizontal rounded edge extending beyond an upright *face below, such as the edge of a tread in a *stair, a *cill; or a drip-stone or *label.

notch ornament Ornament produced by cutting notches in series along the edges of a *band, *fillet, etc.

Notman, John (1810-65) Scots-born architect, he worked with W.H.*Playfair before emigrating

to the USA (1831). He designed Laurel Hill Cemetery, Philadelphia, PA (1836-9), one of the finest of all C19 cemeteries of the *Picturesque landscaped type. He followed this with Hollywood Cemetery, Richmond, VA (1848), and Capitol Square, Richmond (1850-c.1860), one of the USA's first *public parks laid out in the informal style. His houses included Nathan Dunn's Cottage, Mount Holly (1837-8—in the *Regency exotic eclectic style), and Riverside, Burlington (1839—in the *Italianate style), NJ; neither survives, but both were published in A.J.*Downing's *A Treatise on the Theory and Practice of Landscape Gardening* (1841). His Prospect Villa, Princeton, NJ (1851-2), was a sophisticated Italianate asymmetrical villa that could easily have been transported from the Edinburgh suburbs. Among his large and always competent buildings were the State House (1845-6—largely destroyed), the New Jersey State Lunatic Asylum (1845-8), both in Trenton, NJ, and the *Athenaeum*, Philadelphia, PA (1845-7), the last a *palazzo no doubt prompted by *Barry's Clubs in London. His best *Gothic-Revival works were St Mark's Church, Philadelphia (1847-52), and the Cathedral of St John, Wilmington, DE (1857-8), but he was equally fluent in the round-arched styles (e.g. St Clement's Church, Philadelphia (1855-9)). He embraced new techniques and at the rebuilding of Nassau Hall, Princeton (1855-9), employed rolled-iron beams, one of the first such instances in the USA. His practice declined from c.1860: the Demon Drink may have played its part in this, as well as in his comparatively early death.

A.Downing (1967, 1967a); Greiff (1979); P (1982)

Nôtre, André Le (1613-1700) Appointed (1657) *Contrôleur Général des Bâtiments, Jardins, Tapisseries, et Manufactures de France* after he had begun work on the design of the gardens at Vaux-le-Vicomte (laid out 1656-61) for **Nicolas Fouquet** (1615-80), his greatest project was the Park at Versailles, with *fountains, *canals, *avenues, and *parterres (1661-87): his work for *Louis XIV (*r.*1643-1715) was enormously influential throughout Europe. For the newly restored **King Charles II of Great Britain and Ireland** (*r.*1660-85) he designed the park at Greenwich (1662—much decayed). He carried out works at Chantilly (1663-88), St-Germain-en-Laye (1663-73), and the Tuileries, Paris. The gardens at Clagny (1674-6), Maintenon (1674-8), Marly (1680-98), Meudon (1654 and 1679-82), the *Palais Royal* (1674), St-Cloud (1665-78), and Sceaux (1673-7), were also his work. He designed (1698) a garden at Windsor, Berks. for **King William III** (*r.*1689-1702). Principles of his designs were recorded by *Dézallier d'Argenville in his *La Théorie et la pratique du jardinage* (1709). His influence straddles continents and centuries: American landscape architects **Peter Walker** (1932-) and *Kiley were among those claiming to be affected by it.

W.H.Adams (1979); DdA (1709); H.Fox (1962); Ganay (1952); Ht (1980); Ht (ed.) (1974); Jeannel (1985); Laird (1992); Mariage *et al.* (1999); Racine (ed.) (2001); Roudaut (2000); V.J.Sy & Baubion-Mackler (1992); J.T (1996); A.Weiss (1995); A.Wilson (2005)

Nourse, Timothy (c.1636-99) English writer, remembered for his posthumously published *Campania Foelix, or, A Discourse of the Benefits and Improvements of Husbandry* (1700): it includes a section *Of a Country House*, in which Italian influences on garden-design are extolled, including *fountains and other water-works, *grottoes, etc., but he also commended the 'negligent order' of the 'Landskip' beyond the garden, suggesting he was looking with a painterly eye and anticipating aspects of C18 English garden-design (*see* PICTURESQUE).

H & W (1988); Nourse (1700); ODNB (2004)

Novembergruppe Association of Left-wing German artists and architects founded immediately after their nation's defeat in the 1914-18 war. It included *Bartning, *Gropius, *Häring, *Hilbersheimer, the *Luckhardts, *Mendelsohn, *Mies, and the *Tauts. Many members were also active in *Arbeitsrat für Kunst*, and the group exhibited and argued in favour of what was to become the *Modern Movement. It ceased to be a force by 1931.

Berlin Exhibition Catalogue, *Die Novembergruppe* (1977)

Novocentismo Group established in Milan after the 1914-18 war: including architects such as *Muzio and *Ponti, it issued a 'call to order' concerned with a return to *Neo-Classicism, and favoured the symbolic use of historical motifs while accepting new ideas concerning space and building technology. Unlike some groups of the period (notably in France and Germany), its members expressed their ideas through architecture rather than through ranting polemic. During the 1920s Classical elements, such as *architraves, recessed arched *panels, and flat, thin layers of ornament, were employed, emphasizing the different planes of walls, but in the 1930s the Classical elements, if present at all, were so paraphrased that they became difficult to detect, and walls became treated with shallow panels, with *piers and projections marking structural *bays and floor-levels. *Novocentismo* merged with Italian *Rationalism by 1933, and was closely associated (almost inevitably) with Fascism.

Etlin (1991); Irace (1994); J.T (1996)

Novosielski, Michael (c.1747-95) Roman-born of Polish parents, he was in London

(1770s), and is supposed to have assisted James *Wyatt when he was erecting the Pantheon. One spectacular development of his may still be enjoyed: this is Fortfield Terrace, Sidmouth, Devon (begun 1792), a *stucco-fronted shallow crescent, never completed. He was also a successful theatrical scene-painter.

Co (2008); ODNB (2004)

Nowicki, Matthew (Maciej) (1910-50) Polish architect, influenced by Le *Corbusier and *Perret. He designed an office-block in Łódź, a sports-centre, Warsaw (both 1938), and the Polish Pavilion, World's Fair, NYC (1938—destroyed). The Dorton Arena, NC State Fair, Raleigh (1948-53—with two intersecting *hyperbolic *parabolas), is regarded as a pioneer of such structural design. He worked with *Saarinen on the master-plan for Brandeis University, Waltham, MA (1948-9), and was engaged on plans for Chandigarh, India (from 1948), when he was killed in an aeroplane crash.

ARe, cxv/6 (1954), 139-49; cxvi/l (1954), 128-35, cxvi/2 (1954), 169-75, and cxvi/3 (1954); 153-9; Mainstone (1975); M & N (1987); P (1982); H.Schafer (ed.) (1973); J.T (1996)

Noyes, Eliot Fette (1910-77) American architect/industrial-designer. He worked with *Gropius and *Breuer (1938-40), then as Director of the Department of Industrial Design, MoMA, NYC (from 1940), and founded (1947) **Eliot Noyes & Associates**, quickly making his reputation as a designer of houses, office-buildings, and interiors, but his industrial-design work for IBM, Mobil Oil, and Westinghouse won international fame. Buildings include the Bubble Houses, Hobe Sound, FL (1953), the Graham House, Greenwich, CT (1970), and the IBM Development Center, Armonk, NY (1980). He published *Organic Design and Home Furnishing* (1941).

E (1994); *ID*, xxiv (Sept./Oct. 1977), 42-3; *PA*, lvi/10 (1975), 80-5

Nüll, Eduard van der (1812-68) Austrian architect, involved in the *Rundbogenstil fashion (1840s). He assisted **Johann Georg Wilhelm Müller** (1822-49) in the design and erection of the Altlerchenfeld Church, Vienna (1848-61), a brick structure in a pronounced and convincing Italian round-arched style with two western towers, an octagonal *cupola, and fine *Historicist interior (the designs for which van der Nüll was responsible). He teamed up with *Siccardsburg to design the *Carl-Theater*, Vienna (1847—destroyed—which had rich C14 and C15 Italian-*Renaissance details on its main *façade). They won (1849) the competition to design the *Kommandantur-Gebäude*, Vienna, with its massive *crenellations and enormous central gateway

(1849–56): part is their work, but others realized much of the rest. Then they won (1860) the competition to design the *Hofoper* (now *Staatsoper* (1860–9)) on the new *Ringstrasse*, the most prominent feature of which is the large block containing the *auditorium and fly-tower. However, for the external treatment they selected a free, but weak, uninspired French *Neo-Renaissance style, severely criticized during construction. The adverse reaction may have prompted van der Nüll's suicide, and Siccardsburg followed him to the grave only two months later: they had been friends and colleagues since 1828, both winning prizes and travelling scholarships, and doing much to set the architectural tone of major buildings in Vienna and the main cities of the Empire from *c.*1850 (their Opera-House (gutted 1945—reopened 1955) influenced those of both Prague (1868–81) and Budapest (1875–84)). They also proposed the Vienna International Exhibition (1873), realized by *Hasenauer.

Auer (1885); Eitelberger (1879); H-C.Ho (1972); *ZdÖluAV*, lxv (1913), 833–7, 849–55

nunnery *Convent where women devote themselves to religious life under certain vows (usually poverty, chastity, and obedience) under a specific rule. *See* MINCHERY.

nuraghe *or* **nuraghi** *See* BEEHIVE.

nut **1.** Any fruit with seed in a hard shell, often found in architectural ornament. Certain nuts, e.g. *acorns, occur as *finials or other *terminations. **2.** Metal piece, pierced and wormed with a female screw, used to make a bolt fast, or at the end of a metal tie.

nutmeg *First-Pointed Northern-English ornament consisting of a series of projections, with a gap between each pair, resembling half-nutmegs, of which good examples occur at St Mary's Church, Nun Monkton, Yorks.

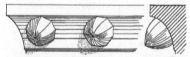

nutmeg St Mary's, Nun Monkton, Yorks. *(after Parker).*

Nuttgens, Patrick John (1930–2004) English architect/educationalist, from 1962 involved in the creation of the University of York, first as Director of the Institute of Advanced Architectural Studies, and from 1968 as Professor of Architecture. Imbued with an *Arts-and-Crafts background

through his parents, he attempted to apply such ideals as first Director of Leeds Polytechnic from 1969 (resigned 1986 shortly before Polytechnics were absorbed in a 'university' system that has not been entirely convincing). Afflicted with poliomyelitis from childhood, he was further damaged by multiple sclerosis, but managed to publish several books and take part in radio and television programmes.

AR, ccxv/1287 (May 2004), 32; *ODNB* (2009)

nymphaeum *Temple, *sanctuary, or *grotto of nymphs, often a feature of *Roman architecture (e.g. **Domitian**'s (*r.*81–96) palace (C1)). Descriptions of *Antique exemplars informed the design of *nymphaea* in *Renaissance and later gardens, often *exedrae* incorporating statuary, pools, and *fountains, or suggesting water by means of *congelated *rustication. Good examples survive in, e.g. *Villa Giulia*, Rome (1551–5), by *Vignola and others, and at the *Zwinger, Dresden, Saxony (1710–32), by *Pöppelmann.

Alvarez (1981)

Nyrop, Martin (1849–1921) Danish architect, his first independent work seems to have been the *rotunda for *Østre Gasværk*, Copenhagen (1881—now a theatre), the *dome of which is almost the same size as that of the *Pantheon in Rome. Influenced by *Dahlerup, *Herholdt, and his travels, his work drew on historical precedents. His buildings include the Vallekilde Training College (1884—with later extensions of 1889), the *Landsarkivet*, Copenhagen (Zealand Public Records Office—1891–2), and a series of country-houses (e.g. those at Gisselfeld (1894) and Vallekilde (1889)). He also designed churches (e.g. *Eliaskirke*, Copenhagen (1905–8), and *Lutherkirke*, Copenhagen (1914–18)), but made his name with the Nordic Exhibition (1888) which established his credentials as a major figure of *National Romanticism. His greatest building, however, is City Hall, Copenhagen (1892–1905), inspired by the *Palazzo Pubblico* and Square, Siena. One of the internal *courts was designed with a glazed roof, possibly a precedent for *Berlage's Merchants' Exchange, Amsterdam, and the building had an immense influence on Northern-European public architecture. His Bispebjerg Hospital (1906–13) drew on the *timber-framed tradition in Denmark, and it was designed on the *pavilion principle.

ARe, xviii (1905), 283–88; Mi (1951); P (1982); Rasmussen (1940); vV (1993); We (from 1994)

O

Oakley, Edward (*fl.*1720-65) English architect/builder, designer of the Chelsea Physic Garden *hot-houses (1732-4). He devoted much energy to *Freemasonry, stressing the importance of architectural knowledge, and publishing (1730) *The Magazine of Architecture, Perspective, and Sculpture*, issued again in 16 instalments (1732-3). His *Every Man a Compleat Builder; or, Easy Rules and Proportions for Drawing the Several Parts of Architecture* came out (1766), with later edn (1774): the latter was culled from *Proportional Architecture* (1733) by **William Robinson** (*fl.* 1730-60).

Co (2008); J.Curl (2011); Hs (1990); Knoop, Jones, & Hamer (eds) (1945); Oakley (1729, 1766, 2010); *ODNB* (2004); W.Robinson (1733)

Oatley, Sir George Herbert (1863-1950) Bristol-born architect, he worked for E.W.*Godwin and **Henry Crisp** (1825-96), becoming Crisp's partner (1888). Oatley is best known for the work he designed for the University of Bristol, including the spectacular *Perp. Wills Memorial Building (1912-25), the Wills Physics Department (1926-30), Wills Hall in Stoke Bishop (1925), and Manor Hall, Clifton (1932). He was also responsible for several mental-hospitals (including the Cardiff Asylum, Whitchurch (1900-08)). Generally, Oatley's Collegiate buildings were Gothic, his banks and offices Classical (e.g. the Scottish Provident Institution, Clare Street, Bristol (1899-1905)), and his industrial buildings as simple as possible. He designed several houses in an *Arts-and-Crafts style, including 'Barton Rocks', Winscombe, Som. (1900-2).

K.Ferry (ed.) (2009); Whittingham (2011)

Obberghen, Antonis van (1543-1611) *See* OPBERGEN.

obelisk Lofty, four-sided, often *monolithic shaft, on a square or rectangular plan, tapering (i.e. diminishing) upwards, usually covered with hieroglyphs, with a pyramidal top. An Ancient-Egyptian form, obelisks were found in pairs, *flanking* axes, such as a *temple *dromos*, but on their introduction to Europe from the time of **Augustus** (*r.*27 BC-AD 14), when the first Egyptian obelisks were re-erected in Rome from 10 BC, they were usually treated as single free-standing objects. They were again set up singly in *Renaissance Rome, this time on *pedestals, where they stand today as the centrepieces of major urban spaces (e.g. *Piazza di San Pietro, Piazza del Pòpolo*), and were widely copied as a form in Northern-European Mannerist work. Subsequently, obelisks were used as *eye-catchers, memorials, and the like, such as *Morrison's Ross Monument, Rostrevor, Co. Down (1826); it (like many C19 European and American obelisks) is not a monolith, but constructed of *ashlar.

J.Curl (2005); Habachi (1984); Iversen (1968); Roullet (1972); J.T (1996)

Obrist, Hermann (1862-1927) Swiss *Arts-and-Crafts designer influential before the 1914-18 war. He was the major figure in the establishment of the *Vereinigte Werkstätten*, Munich (1895): his designs helped to promote *Jugendstil, and influenced *Behrens and *Endell. He published *Neue Möglichkeiten in der bildenden Kunst* (1903) and significant contributions to the journal *Dekorative Kunst*. His designs for tombs and monuments from *c.*1900 were early examples of *Expressionism.

Jervis (1984); P (1982); T-M (1967); Wichmann (ed.) (1968)

observatory 1. Building used for observing natural phenomena, usually astronomical, meteorological, etc., using special instruments, telescopes, etc. **2.** Building commanding an extensive view, e.g. a *belvedere* or *gazebo*.

obtuse *See* ARCH.

O'Connor, Liam (1961-) *See* NEW CLASSICISM.

octagon Eight equal-sided polygonal figure often found as the plan-form for *Antique Classical and later buildings, e.g. *chapter-houses.

octastyle *See* PORTICO.

octopus-leaf *See* ORCHID.

oculus (*pl.* **oculi**) **1.** *Roundel, circular opening or recess, bull's-eye, or *œil-de-bœuf*, as in the *tympanum of a *pediment or at the top of a *dome (e.g. the *Pantheon, Rome). **2.** Button, *disc, or *eye from which the spirals of a *volute progress, e.g. the *Ionic *capital or a Classical *console or *modillion.

odeion, odeon, odeum Small, roofed, Ancient-Greek theatre for musical performances or recitations.

O'Donnell, James (1774–1830) Irish-born architect. Emigrating (1812) to NYC, he designed *Federal-style houses, the Bloomingdale Asylum (1817–21), Fulton Street Market (1821–2), and some churches (including Christ Church (1820–1)). He was responsible for one of the North-American Continent's largest and earliest *Gothic-Revival churches, that of *Notre-Dame, Place d'Armes*, Montréal, Canada (1823–9): it was to have a considerable influence on Canadian church-architecture.

JSAH, **xxix**/2 (May 1970), 132–43; K (1994); P (1982)

Odo of Metz (*fl.c.*792–805) *See* METZ.

oecus Hall or large room in a Roman house, usually with columns around the interior, like an *atrium without *compluvium or *impluvium. *There were four types of* oecus:
oecus Aegyptus: with columns round the sides (an internal *peristyle*) supporting a smaller superimposed peristyle between the columns of which light could enter (so a type of *clerestorey*), and with a walkway over the lower area. Also called an *Egyptian hall*;
oecus Corinthius: with an *Order carrying a vaulted roof;
oecus Cyzicenus: with a view over gardens and the countryside, usually with folding doors;
oecus tetrastylos or -*us*: with four columns carrying the roof-structure.

œil-de-bœuf (*pl.* œils-de-bœuf) **1.** Elliptical ox-eye window, often with four *keystones among the *dressings, and frequently associated with *mansard roofs. **2.** Loosely, *oculus, but only of elliptical, not circular, form.

œillet 1. *Loophole, especially if circular, in medieval fortified walls through which missiles could be discharged. **2.** Triangular sinking at the back of each *cusp-point, in *Gothic *tracery, produced by the intersection of *mouldings.

Oesterlen, Dieter (1911–94) German architect. Some of his work is monumental and jagged, such as at the German Military Cemetery, *Passo della Futa*, near Florence (1961–7). Other designs include the *Filmstudio* Cinema, Hanover (1951–3), Christ Church, Bochum (1957–9), the Twelve Apostles Church, Hildesheim (1964–7), the *Bischof Stahlin* Geriatric Centre, Oldenburg (1974–5), the Post Office Headquarters, Bremen (1979–95), the German Embassy, Buenos Aires, Argentina (1980–3), and the Elia Church Community Centre, Langenhagen, near Hanover (1987–8).

He rebuilt parts of Hanover after the 1939–45 war, including the opera-house.

E (1994)

offertory-window *Lychnoscope.

office 1. Place for transactions of private or public business, e.g. room or department in which paperwork of an establishment is handled. **2.** Building or set of rooms in which the business of a department of Government is carried out, e.g. Foreign Office, Home Office, etc. **3.** Privy (i.e. House of Office). **4.** Authorized form of ecclesiastical service, i.e. Divine Office, Mass, or Holy Communion. **5.** Ecclesiastical tribunal for suppression of heresy (Holy Office, otherwise known as the Inquisition). **6.** In the plural, those parts of a house, or buildings attached to it, used for the kitchens, pantry, laundry, scullery, etc., sometimes including stables, barns, outhouses, etc.

off-set *also* **set-off** Top of a wall, *buttress, etc., created where the wall or buttress above is smaller, usually appearing as a sloping ledge in medieval buttresses or *plinths, and called *weather-table.*

ogee Upright double curve, concave at the top and convex at the bottom, as in the *cyma recta (a *cyma reversa or *Lesbian cymatium, with the convex curve at the top and the concave below, is called *reverse ogee*). Ogee-profiled *mouldings are termed *ogee moulding, ressant, ressaunt,* or *ressaut.* Reverse ogee-headed *canopies or openings are characteristic of *Second-Pointed work, especially over funerary monuments, *niches, *sedilia, and *shrines, as well as in *tracery, where they recurred well into the *Perp. period. A *nodding ogee is a canopy of two ogee arches joined at the apex and bowing outwards from the wall in another ogee double curve, so ogee in *elevation as well as in *section.

ogive Diagonal *rib of a *Gothic *vault, or any arch made up of two arcs meeting at a point. *Ogival* architecture is therefore *Pointed or Gothic architecture.

O'Gorman, Juan (1905–82) Mexican architect. He designed (1920s and '30s) houses and schools, influenced by Le *Corbusier, regarded as paradigms of *Functionalism. He had a very public change of heart (1950s) concerning *International Modernism, and began to incorporate Pre-Columbian and *vernacular motifs into his designs (e.g. the National Library, State University of México, México City (1952–3—covered with colourful *mosaics)).

E (1994); Jimenez (2001); C.B.Smith (1967); J.T (1996)

Olbrich, Joseph Maria (1867–1908) Austro-Hungarian architect, leading figure of the Vienna *Sezession*. A pupil of *Hasenauer and *Sitte, he worked in Otto *Wagner's Vienna office (1894–8), contributing designs for the Vienna *Stadtbahn* stations. Gradually his style moved away from Wagner's dignified and simplified *Neo-Classicism and began to incorporate *Art-Nouveau motifs. He made his reputation with the Club House and Exhibition Gallery (1897–8) he designed for *Sezession* artists: it had something of Wagner's Neo-Classicism on the outside, but with *Jugendstil* decorative effects and a gilded wrought-iron dome-like ornament held between four *battered *pylon-like forms crowning the composition, a motif suggesting the *Ver Sacrum* (title of the influential Sezessionist publication). For the Max Friedmann House, Hinterbrühl (1898–9), Olbrich, influenced by the English *Arts-and-Crafts movement, designed not only the building but all the furnishings and fittings.

The artistic **Ernst Ludwig Charles Albert William, Grand Duke of Hesse** (*r.*1892–1918), invited (1899) Olbrich to the new artists' colony at *Mathildenhöhe*, Darmstadt, where he designed the *Ernst-Ludwig-Haus* (1899–1901) with its pronounced Art-Nouveau entrance flanked by two large Neo-Classical figures looking forward to the 1930s in style. For his own house there (1900–1), Olbrich drew on Austro-German *vernacular forms, enlivened with blue-and-white tile squares (a motif used by Wagner and *Mackintosh) set in the *elevations. Seven of his houses and one by *Behrens (all fully furnished) at *Mathildenhöhe* were ready (1901) for public inspection, the intention being to awaken a sense of modern design in Hesse: it was the first exhibition of its kind. He added further buildings to the *Mathildenhöhe* complex, including the *Hochzeitsturm* (erected partly to celebrate the Grand Duke's second marriage (1905) to **Eleonore Ernestine Marie von Solms-Hohensolms-Lich** (1871–1937)) and Exhibition Building (1905–8). The tower had a top reminiscent of North-German medieval stepped *gables but with semicircular upper parts to the 'steps'.

Olbrich was a founder (1907) of the *Deutscher Werkbund*, and his work became more severe and Classically inspired, including the handsome *Leonhard Tietz* Department Store, Düsseldorf (1906–9), later *Kaufhof*. His *Joseph Feinhals* House, Cologne (1908–9—destroyed), showed the way in which his architecture might have evolved had he lived: it was a powerful Neo-Classical composition with two severe *wings between which was a Greek-*Doric *colonnade, the whole topped by a *mansard roof. **Wasmuth** published (1901–14) a sumptuous set of volumes, *Architektur von Olbrich*.

Darmstadt (ed.) (2000–4); H & K (1988); H & K *et al.* (1988); Latham (1980); Lux (1919); Schreyl (1972); T-M (1967); Ve (1948); W (1901–8); Zimmermann (ed.) (1976)

Old English Architectural style involving the revival of *vernacular elements from the Sussex-Kent Weald, one of the threads of the C19 *Domestic *Revival, *Queen-Anne style, and the *Arts-and-Crafts movement. It was characterized by *tile-hung walls, *diaper-patterns on brickwork, *leaded windows of the *casement type, *timber-framing (sometimes not real, but merely decorative) of elements (often *gables and *jetties), *barge-boards cut with fretwork, rubbed *brick *dressings, steep tiled roofs, and tall ornamental chimney-stacks of moulded brick or *terracotta. Planning was informal and *additive, while composition was *Picturesque. In the USA the *Colonial Revival had similar trends, and led to the *Shingle style.

D & M (1985)

Oldfield, Peter Lawrence (1925–2006) English architect, much influenced by Le *Corbusier and *Niemeyer, who settled (1951) in what was Southern Rhodesia to work on a *New Town near Salisbury (now Harare, Zimbabwe). With **Nick Montgomerie** he practised as **Montgomerie & Oldfield**, designing the National Gallery of Zimbabwe (1955–7), Lusaka Civic Centre (1958), and Victoria Memorial Library, Salisbury (1962).

RIBAJ (June 2007), 82

Old French C19 *Rococo Revival.

Oleaginous style C17 precursor of *Rococo, called *Auricular, Cartilaginous, Dutch Grotesque, Kwabornament*, or *Lobate* style, a branch of *Mannerism. It consisted of smooth flowing lines, folding in on each other, like human ears, intestines, or marine plants. It was invented in The Netherlands, was disseminated in a series of illustrated books, e.g. *Veelderhande Nieuwe Compartemente* (1653), a set of engravings after **Gerbrand van den Eeckhout** (1621–74), and *Cartouches de différentes inventions* (*c.*1620–30), by **Daniel Rabel** (*c.*1578–1637). Its chief protagonists were **Paulus** (*c.*1570–1613), **Adam** (1569–1627), and **Christiaen** (*c.*1600–67) **van Vianen**, and **Jan Lutma the Elder** (*c.*1584–1669) and **Younger** (1624–85 or 89).

H & J (2005); Jervis (1984); L & D (1986); H.O (1970, 1975)

olive Classical ornament, similar to *bay-leaf, laurel, and myrtle, used in *wreaths and *garlands.

Oliveira, Mateus Vicente de (1706–85) Portuguese *Rococo architect, who worked under *Ludovice at first, adopting the latter's grand manner, and then evolved a more exquisite style, of which the *Palácio Nacional*, Queluz, near Lisbon (1747–52), is an example, with its swagged and garlanded window-heads. He designed the *Basilica da Estrêla*, Lisbon (1779–90).

Ck (1996); K & S (1959); R.Smith (1968)

Oliver, Basil (1882–1948) English architect, he established (1910) a practice, and carried ideals of the *Arts-and-Crafts movement into the 1920s and 1930s. Among his works the *Rose & Crown* *public-house, Cambridge (1928) and other establishments for the brewers **Greene King** are cited, many of which contained fittings designed by members of the *Art-Workers' Guild (of which he was Master (1932)). His best-known building is the Borough Offices, Angel Hill, Bury St Edmunds, Suffolk (1935–7), described by *Pevsner as '*Neo-Georgian . . . , tactful, and completely uneventful'. He sensitively repaired Castling's Hall, Groton, Suffolk (1933–4), and served (1912–48) on the Committee of the Society for the Protection of Ancient Buildings. He wrote *Old Houses and Village Buildings in East Anglia* (1912) and *The Renaissance of the English Public House* (1947).

AH, xlvii (2004), 329–60

ollarium (*pl.* **ollaria**) Recess, often arched, in a *columbarium or *hypogeum in which pairs of *cinerary *urns, or ash-chests were placed.

Olmec architecture *Meso-American architecture, of which La Venta, a ceremonial centre situated on an island in the Tonalà River Delta, provides examples (*c.* early C8). Important buildings were laid out formally and symmetrically on axes.

Ck (1996); Kubler (1984)

Olmsted, Frederick Law (1822–1903) One of the most important C19 American landscape architects after *Downing's death, he developed the C18 English *Picturesque style, and was an innovator in the design of *public parks, much influenced by *Paxton's Birkenhead Park, Ches. (1847), as is clear from his admiration for English landscape-design, expressed in his *Walks and Talks of an American Farmer in England* (1852). With *Vaux (who had been associated with Downing) he created Central Park, NYC (from 1858), an ingenious scheme with a wide variety of types of landscape, including *rock-work with *cascades, meadows, and water, and traffic-routes sunk from view (with paths over and under them as the grade required). He designed the *campus for the College of California at Berkeley; Mountain View Cemetery, Oakland, CA (1864); and proposed creating a nature-reserve in the Yosemite Valley, a precedent for the National Parks movement. Again with Vaux he designed Prospect Park, Brooklyn (1865–73), resumed work on Central Park, and planned Riverside, near Chicago, IL (1868), which proposed dwellings around common land, parks, and the beginnings of a scheme that anticipated pedestrian routes. He began the landscaping around the Federal Capitol, Washington, DC (1874),

work completed (1920s) by his son, **F.L.Olmsted, Jun.** (1870–1957), who continued to practise with the elder Olmsted's adopted stepson, **John Charles Olmsted** (1852–1920).

Persuaded to settle (1881) in Massachusetts by H.H.*Richardson (with whom he had collaborated on the design of the State Asylum for the Insane, Buffalo, NY (1871), and on other projects), Olmsted designed the system of parks in Boston, a brilliant scheme forming a meandering trail of greenery and water connecting Charles River to Franklin Park (*see* COPELAND). He contributed to the designs of the campus of Stanford University, Palo Alto, CA (1886); worked with Vaux on the Niagara Falls Reservation, NY (1887); and designed the Louisville Park system, KY (1891). His last large scheme was the World's Columbian Exposition, Chicago (1893), where he created a sylvan setting for the Neo-Classical buildings of *McKim, Mead, & White, Daniel *Burnham, et al. Olmsted's system of transport, roads, and jetties for water-borne visitors was, like most of his work, forward-looking, imaginative, and inventive. He was a prolific writer.

Beveridge (1995); Burley *et al.* (1996); C.Cook (1972); I.Fisher (1986); L.Hall (1995); Kowsky (2013); LeG & S (1996); McLaughlin (ed.) (from 1977); Olmsted & Hubbard (eds) (1973); P (1982); Roper (1973); E.Stevenson (2000); Sutton (ed.) (1979); Todd (1982); J.T (1996); W & S (1994)

onion-dome Pointed bulbous structure on top of a tower, resembling an onion, common in Central- and Eastern-European architecture as well as in The Netherlands. It is usually an ornamented top, made of a timber substructure covered with lead, copper, or tiles, and is not a true *dome.

Opbergen, Antonius van (1543–1611) Flemish architect who worked at the Royal Palace of Kronborg, Helsingør, Denmark (1577–86), and designed the Arsenal in Danzig (now Gdańsk, Poland), one of the great buildings in the Flemish-*Renaissance style (1601–9). He also designed several fine houses in Gdańsk with **Jan Strakowski** (1567–1642), built 1597–1609.

Ck (1996); Kz (1991); Łoza (1954)

open *Compounds include:*
open cornice or *eaves*: Overhanging *eaves with exposed *rafters, visible from below, the ends of which are sometimes shaped to resemble attractive *brackets;
open hall: main living-room of a medieval house, open to the roof, usually with an *open hearth* or *chimney-stack*. An *open-hall* house contained such a hall, and was formerly called a *hall-house* (ABDM (1996));
open-heart: *Romanesque *moulding consisting of a series of overlapping pointed shapes like hearts or spades, with the points upwards,

open-heart moulding 'The Jew's House', Lincoln (*after Parker*).

formed of strap-like elements draped over a *roll-moulding;

open hearth: hearth, usually sited clear of the walls, without a chimney-stack or hood above it, therefore requiring a *femerall, *lantern, or *louvre on the roof;

open-newel or *open-well stair*: *stair built round a *well (i.e. with a void between the outer *strings), unlike a well-less *dog-leg;

open pediment: *see* PEDIMENT;

open plan or *free plan*: space in a building undivided by means of walls or partitions. Areas within it may be defined by means of columns, ceiling-heights, differing floor-levels, *screens, furniture, etc. Inspired by a vogue for things Japanese connected with the *Aesthetic and *Arts-and-Crafts Movements, and with *Art Nouveau, it was adopted (1890s) by F.L.L. *Wright, and by other architects working with the *Shingle style. Le *Corbusier et al. called it *le plan libre*, and it was used to considerable effect by *Mies van der Rohe (e.g. Tugendhat House, Brno (1928–30)). It became a feature of office buildings (Boje (1972));

open roof: open-timbered roof with rafters visible from beneath (i.e. with no ceiling);

open stair: *open-string* stair with *treads visible at the ends, often ornamented below with *scrolls resembling *consoles;

open-string: *open-stringer* or *cut-string* stair with the top of its *string notched so that the treads and *risers can fit within the notches;

open-timbered: 1. exposed *timber frame unconcealed by *pargetting; 2. *open roof*; 3. floor with *joists exposed on the *soffit;

openwork: 1. elaborate perforated ornament, like *tracery, common on *Gothic *canopies, *gables, *parapets, and *choir-stalls; 2. unprotected part of a fortification, such as a narrow entry into a *bastion.

opisthodomos, opisthodomus Recessed *porch or *epinaos* at the rear of a Greek *temple, sometimes enclosed with bronze grilles and used as a treasury. If a porch, it balances the *pronaos at the other end.

D (1950)

Oppenord, Gilles-Marie (1672–1742) French *Régence architect/decorator of Flemish descent. Influenced by work of *Bernini and *Borromini,

he had a considerable role in the evolution of the *Rococo or *Louis-Quinze style. He designed several *altar-pieces (e.g. at St-Germain-des-Prés (1704)), but his most influential work included interiors (working with de *Cotte) in Bonn, Brühl, and Falkenlust, Rhineland, and the *Palais Royal* (1716–20) and *Hôtel Crozat* (1721–30), *Rue de Richelieu*, Paris. From 1719 he was engaged on work at St-Sulpice, Paris, completing the building except for the west portal (which he designed, but which was eventually finished, in greatly modified form, by *Servandoni and *Chalgrin), and designing the *high-altar. Three volumes of engravings (*Livre de Fragments d'Architecture, Livre de différents morceaux,* and *Œuvres*) based on his work were published (1737–51) by **Gabriel Huquier** (1695–1772), thus making his work widely known. By 1755 devotees of *Neo-Classicism (e.g. **Charles-Nicolas Cochin** (1715–90)) saw him as one of those who had 'debauched' Classical architecture. His work also informed the *Rococo Revival* of the 1880s.

Jervis (1984); L & D (1986); P (1982); S (1901–2); J.T (1996)

Oppler, Edwin (1831–80) Architect active in C19 Hanover, he published influential *Gothic-Revival furniture-designs in the journal *Die Kunst im Gewerbe* (1872), of which he was editor (1872–8).

Jervis (1984); J.T (1996)

optical corrections Alterations to planes or surfaces to correct possible perceptions of distortion. They include *entasis*, increasing the height of stone courses with the height of a wall so that the courses appear identical in height, and the slight convex surface of a *stylobate. The work of *Penrose contributed to understanding of optical corrections.

Penrose (1851)

opus Latin for 'work', as intended to designate construction, or arrangement of materials in construction. *The following are the commoner combinations with* opus:

opus albarium: 1. Species of *opus tectorium* (thin coat of burnt powdered *marble, *lime, sand, and water, well mixed) covering a wall and polished after it was set; 2. coating or coatings of pure *lime on a wall;

opus Alexandrinum: type of church-paving found from C4 to C13 consisting of black, *rosso antico*, and other marbles, cut to simple geometrical shapes, inlaid in paving-slabs of a light colour in repetitive geometrical patterns, sometimes with *guilloche, and occasionally including *opus sectile*;

opus antiquum: type of Roman *masonry, called also *opus incertum*, the *face of which has irregularly placed stones of different sizes (*rubble-work, uncoursed), and *bands of *brick or *tile laid to provide horizontal levelling *courses to bind the wall together;

opus caementicium, opus caementum: Roman wall constructed of rough undressed stones placed in a *concrete mix of lime, *pozzolan, sand, and water, also known as *opus structile* or *structura caementicia*;

opus incertum: as *opus antiquum*;

opus isodomum: regular coursed masonry, the courses being of equal height and the *blocks being of equal length, laid with their vertical joints centred on the blocks above and below;

opus latericium or *lateritium*: wall built of thin bricks or tiles; or of concrete faced with bricks, tiles, or a mixture of both, giving the impression that the wall is constructed of these materials rather than merely faced;

opus lateritum: Roman brickwork. *See opus latericium*;

opus listatum: Roman wall constructed of alternating courses of masonry and brick or tiles;

opus lithostrotum: any type of ornamental paving, such as *mosaic, with pictures or abstract geometrical patterns;

opus marmoratum: *plaster or *stucco of calcined gypsum mixed with powdered marble and water, rubbed and polished to a fine marble-like surface when dry;

opus mixtum: wall-facing of brick (*or* tile) and squared *tufa blocks, laid in alternate courses;

opus musivum or *museum*: mosaic-work made of coloured glass or enamelled pieces;

opus polygonum: polygonal masonry;

opus pseudisodomum: *ashlar with the stone blocks of each course alike, but differing from the stones of other courses in height, length, or thickness, so that while continuous horizontal joints were maintained they varied in height, resulting in masonry laid in regular courses of alternating broad and narrow bands. 'Greek' *Thomson used *pseudisodomic* masonry at the Caledonia Road Church, Glasgow (1856), with the narrow bands projecting slightly from the face of the wider bands, emphasizing the horizontal qualities of the building. *See* ISODOMON; PSEUDISODOMON;

opus quadratum: squared ashlar laid in regular courses;

opus reticulatum: concrete wall faced with small squared stones (sometimes the bases of small *pyramids) set diagonally all over the face creating a network or *lattice of *lozenge-shaped interconnected joints;

opus scalpturatum or *sculpturatum*: *inlaid work consisting of a pattern chiselled out of a solid ground, then filled in with thin leaves of coloured marble. A variant was a marble surface with a pattern cut out and filled with coloured *cement or stucco;

opus sectile: pavement or wall-covering of differently coloured pieces (larger than *tesserae in mosaics) of marble, stone, and, sometimes, glass, cut into regular pieces of a few uniform sizes, laid in geometrical patterns;

opus signinum: type of *terrazzo made by mixing fragments of broken pottery or *tiles with lime-mortar, then smoothing it off;

opus spicatum: masonry faced with stones or tiles arranged in herringbone patterns, usually with horizontal courses at various heights to provide bands and to bond the wall together;

opus tectorium: as *opus albarium*;

opus tessellatum: pavement or facing of regular-shaped pieces of differently coloured material (e.g. marbles) in larger pieces than mosaic *tesserae, laid in cement in geometrical patterns;

opus testacaeum or *testaceum*: wall of rubble and concrete faced with whole or broken tiles, usually on both sides;

opus topiarum: *Antique mural-painting or *fresco depicting gardens with *trellis-work, trees, shrubs, etc.;

opus vermiculatum: very fine, delicate Antique mosaic, its tesserae carefully laid in curving serpentine lines, sometimes with emphasis added by darker tesserae suggesting shadow-projections.

orangery Building of the nature of a *conservatory used for the storage in winter of trees in *containers. It usually had large, south-facing windows, and often had architectural pretensions (e.g. at Kensington Palace, London (1704–5)).

M.Woods & Warren (1988)

orans, orant Figure in an attitude of prayer, with arms outstretched and upraised.

oratory 1. Small chapel of any sort, more particularly one for solitary devotion in a private house. **2.** Church and buildings belonging to the Congregation (*not* Order) of **St Philip Neri** (1515–95), constituted *c.*1550 and approved (1575) by **Pope Gregory XIII** (*r.*1572–85), called *Oratorians*.

orb 1. Globe surmounted by a *cross, emblem of power and sovereignty, often placed on top of the *lantern of a *cupola, *pinnacle, or *spire. **2.** Spherical termination or *finial on a *pedestal or *pier. **3.** Circular *knot carved with flowers or herbs (*boss) at the intersection of *ribs in a *Gothic *vault, concealing the junction of *mouldings and acting as an *abutment to them. **4.** Medieval term for a *blind *panel in *tracery, esp. in *Perp. work.

Orbais, Jean d' (*fl.*C13) With **Jean de** *or* **le Loup, Gaucher de Rheims**, Bernard de *Soissons, **Robert de Coucy**, and **Adam de Rheims**, he appears to have been one of the architects responsible for Rheims Cathedral from 1211. He probably drew up the original plan, as he was Master-Mason there (*c.*1211–29).

Bony (1982); Frankl (1962); Gi (1986)

Orbay, François d' (1634–97) Paris-born architect, he assisted Le **Vau at the *Château de Vincennes* (1654–61), and after Le Vau's death executed the designs for the *Escalier des Ambassadeurs*, Versailles (1671–80—derived from a design by **Perrault of *c.*1667–8, but destroyed), and the *Collège des Quatre Nations*, Paris (1662–74—later *Institut de France*). He became **Hardouin-Mansart's draughtsman at Versailles and, according to some, he designed the garden elevations of the Palace there (begun 1668) as well as the Louvre **colonnade, Paris (begun 1667), in which case he was a major figure in the evolution of the **Louis-Quatorze* style. He designed (drawing heavily on **Bullet's work) the *Arc de Triomphe du Peyrou*, Montpellier (1690), built (1691–2) in modified form by **Augustin-Charles d'Aviler** (1653–1700), and the Cathedral of Mountauban (1691–1739—with changes by **Hardouin-Mansart).

Bt (1982); Ha (1949); Laprade (1960); J.T (1996)

Orcagna, Andrea di Cione, *called* (*c.*1308–68) Florentine **Gothic architect, *Capomaestro* of the **oratory of *Or San Michele*, Florence, from 1355, he designed the exquisite gabled domed **tabernacle (*c.*1352–9). At Orvieto Cathedral (1358) he supervised the construction of the **façade **rose-window and may have contributed to the decorations of the front. He was involved as a consultant at the Florence *Duomo* from 1350 and was probably an influence on the final design.

Steinweg (1929); John White (1987)

orchaestra, orchestra 1. Circular space for the chorus and dancers in an Ancient-Greek theatre. **2.** In a Roman theatre, the semicircular level space between the stage and **proscenium and the first semicircular row of seats. **3.** In a modern theatre the space reserved for the musicians. **4.** In the USA the main floor, **parquet, or **stalls of a theatre.

orchard 1. Area for growing fruit trees. **2.** Formerly, a sheltered turfed area surrounded by a barrier, planted with trees. Grassed areas were either flowerless (if used for tournaments, etc.) or stocked with wild flowers, but later descriptions suggested lilies, lavender, columbine, etc., were cultivated in orchards which were really **plaisances, with **arbours, seats, and even **fountains. It is unclear exactly when 'orchard' came to mean a place for growing fruit trees rather than a garden for pleasure, but was probably *c.* late-C15.

Crisp (1924); Symes (2006)

Orchard, William (*fl.*1468–1504) English master-mason, he designed Magdalen College, Oxford (from 1467), the beautiful **vaults of the Divinity School (1480–3), and (on stylistic grounds) probably the **chancel-vaults (*c.*1478–1503) and the **cloisters (*c.*1489–99) at Oxford Cathedral. Both the vaulting schemes have elaborate pendants that look as though they are supports for the structure, the **piers, as it were, having been removed: it is a curious and interesting type of design. He was also responsible for Waterstock Church, Oxon. (*c.*1500–2), and built part of the Cistercian College of St Bernard (now St John's College), Oxford (from 1502). He designed the Harcourt Aisle in Stanton Harcourt Church (*c.*1470), and may be regarded as one of the most distinguished architects of his time.

J.Harvey (1987)

orchid **Romanesque *octopus-leaf,* a leaf-like form with pronounced round fleshy **lobes.

Order 1. In Classical architecture the elements making up the essential expression of a **columnar-and-**trabeated structure, including a column with (usually) **base and **capital, and **entablature. There are eight distinct types of Classical Order: **Greek **Doric, **Roman Doric, Greek **Ionic, Roman Ionic, Greek **Corinthian, Roman Corinthian, **Tuscan (also known as the **Gigantic Order), and **Composite, although before the systematic rediscovery of Greek architecture in C18 the canonical 5 *Orders* (Tuscan, Roman Doric, Roman Ionic, Roman Corinthian, and Composite) were accepted, codified by **Alberti, and illustrated by **Serlio (1537). The Greek-Doric Order has no base, and sometimes (as in the **Paestum Orders of Doric) **entasis is exaggerated and the capital is very large, with a wide projection over the **shaft; the Ionic Order has variations in its base (**Asiatic and **Attic types) and capital (especially in relation to **angle, **angular, and **Bassae capitals where the problem of the corner **volute is dealt with in different ways); and the Greek-Corinthian capital (e.g. C4 BC **Choragic Monument of Lysicrates, Athens) is taller and more elegant than its Roman counterpart. In London, Kent, and Sussex there is a unique type of English Ionic capital known as the **Ammonite Order. **John Outram** (1934–) incorporated services into what he called the 'Robot Order' (*Ordine Robotico*), or 'Sixth Order', not coyly hidden away, but expressed as a new polychrome Order visible throughout the building as the columns and beams were large enough to contain the services, in his Judge Institute of Management Studies, Cambridge (1993–5), an extension and reorganization of Digby **Wyatt's Addenbrooke's Old Hospital. His work was hysterically described as 'sheer terrorism' by a defender of the Modernist faith (although the **Piano–Rogers** *Beaubourg*, Paris, which shows off its service innards, of course, escaped such strictures). *See* AGRICULTURAL, AMERICAN, AMMONITE, BRITANNIC, COMPOSITE, CORINTHIAN, DORIC, GIANT, IONIC, and TUSCAN ORDERS. **2.** *Roman-esque and *Gothic arched opening consisting of several layers of arched openings usually with *colonnettes, each smaller than the layer in front, and forming an *Order Arch.*

Chitham (1985); J.Curl (2001); L & D (1986); C.Normand (1852)

ordinate 1. Of a figure, having all its sides and angles equal (e.g. equilateral triangle). **2.** Any one of a series of parallel chords of a conic section, in relation to the diameter that bisects each. It may be used to form an ellipse, so can be applied to the design of *vaults.

Ordish, Rowland Mason (1824–86) English civil-engineer, he made most of the working-drawings for **Charles** (later **Sir Charles**) **Fox** (1810–74), who was responsible for the construction of *Paxton's Crystal Palace in Hyde Park, London (1851), and supervised the re-erection of the modified Palace at Sydenham. He patented a type of suspension-bridge with the roadway consisting of a rigid girder suspended by inclined straight chains, known as 'Ordish's straight-chain suspension system' (1858). His works include Farringdon Street Bridge, Holborn Viaduct, London (1863–9), St Pancras Train-Shed roof, London (1866–8—with W.H.*Barlow), the Albert Hall roof, London (1867–71), the Franz-Josef Suspension Bridge, Prague (1868), and the delightful Albert Bridge, Chelsea, London (1872–3).

D & M (1985); *ODNB* (2004)

ordonnance 1. Proper disposition of parts of a building. **2.** Selection and application of an *Order of architecture suitable for a building and its *type.

oreillon, orillon 1. Round shoulder at the end of the face of a *bastion next to a flank. **2.** Any ear-shaped appendage.

organ Large musical instrument consisting of many pipes supplied with wind which sound when valves are opened by means of depressed keys. The accommodation of organs in churches and concert-halls requires much space, and the arrangement of pipes has prompted many impressive architectural solutions, notably in the *Baroque period. An *organ-gallery* or *-loft* is one in which an organ is placed, often at the west end of a church, over the *pulpitum*, or to one side of the *chancel.

Organic architecture C20 term used in so many ways it is virtually meaningless. *Organic* suggests organization formed as if by some natural process, so organic architecture may mean governed in its evolution by natural factors rather than by an imposed predetermined plan. F. L.L.*Wright, taking his cue from *Sullivan, who insisted form and function should be one, suggested that the relationship of parts to the whole, and the special relationship of parts, whole, and site, whereby a sense of natural growth was given, constituted organic architecture. *Häring proposed that architecture implied a search, allowing forms to develop during the searching, and that the very discovery of forms was associated with harmony in nature. *Aalto rejected the determination of form by geometrical means, used natural materials in unusual ways (not always successfully), and claimed to respond to the qualities of the sites. *Scharoun's buildings have also been proposed as 'organic' because their design-treatment was not unlike that practised by Häring. Curved *reinforced-concrete shell-structures and tent-shapes (e.g. the work of **Frei Otto** (1925–2015)) have been perceived as organic, while there are those who would claim the use of natural materials, especially those indigenous to an area, leads to organic buildings. 'Organic architecture' also seems to imply the opposite of rational, geometrical architecture, and is probably associated with intuition, irregularity, and a blurring of the man-made artefact with what is natural. The work of *Makovecz has been described as 'Organic', probably because it is difficult to see where rocks, earth, and plants end and structure begins in some of the designs, while **Lucien Kroll**'s (1927–) buildings, evolving slowly as they are required, and altered by their users, have been labelled 'Organic'. The work of the Canadian architects **John** (1947–) and **Patricia** (1950–) **Patkau** has been associated with Organic architecture because of their responses to particularities of local conditions. More recently, with the evolution of so-called *Zoömorphic architecture, and explorations concerned with *biomorphic forms, the term has acquired further confusing associations.

Dvorszky (ed.) (1991); D.Gans & Kuz (eds) (2003); Js (1988); K (1994); L (1988); Patkau Architects (1997); D.Pearson (2001); Pi (2000); Po (1999a); Ree (2000); Wright (1970); Zevi (1950)

Organic Modernism Architecture employing, for example, asymmetrical blob-like forms and multi-directional curves. *See* BLOBISMUS. Organic Modernism was mostly a feature of fabric- and furniture-design in the 1940s and early 1950s (e.g. table-tops).

L & D (1986)

Organo-Tech Style involving free forms, blob-like shapes (*see* BLOBISMUS), and a highly complex (and expensive) structure. It came into vogue at the end of C20.

oriel, oriole, oryel Large *bay-window projecting from the *naked of a wall on an upper storey, supported on brackets, *corbels, a *pier, or *engaged column.

Orientalism Architecture and design drawing on Islamic, Chinese, Japanese, Ottoman, and Eastern styles, such as *Chinoiserie or the *Hindoo style.

Conner (1979); Crinson (1996); Honour (1961); Impey (1977)

orientation Planning, siting, and arrangement of a building with reference to any special point of the compass, especially in relation to the rising and setting of the sun. It was significant in church architecture, where *altars were usually sited to the east. Churches arranged with the *chancel not to the east are nevertheless described as though orientated correctly *(liturgical orientation).*

orillon See ORILLON.

orle, orlet, orlo 1. Narrow *band or series of small *fillets forming a border. Specifically, the fillet beneath the *ovolo of a *capital. 2. *Cincture or fillet at the upper and lower extremities of a column-*shaft, terminating the *apophyge. 3. *Plinth under the moulded base of a column or its *pedestal. 4. Face of the fillet between parallel *flutes of e.g. a shaft.

Orme, Philibert de L', *also given as* **Delorme, De L'Orme**, *or* **de l'Orme** (1514–70) French architect who influenced later generations largely through his books. In Rome (1533–5), he became acquainted with *Classicism, before returning to Paris where he designed several buildings (all very un-Italian), most of which have been mutilated or destroyed. He was responsible (with others) for the tomb of *François Ier (*r.*1515–47) in *St-Denis (1547–58), inspired by the *triumphal arch of **Septimius Severus** (*r.*193–211), Rome, but with an *Ionic *Order substituted. The *Château* of Anet, Dreux (1547–55), was probably his finest building, of which the *frontispiece of the central *corps-de-logis (now in the *École des *Beaux-Arts, Paris) survives, as do the entrance-gate and chapel. The frontispiece has an *assemblage of Orders, its severity and restraint making the contemporary work of *Lescot at the Louvre seem over-elaborate and fussy. The gate is an interesting variation on the Roman triumphal arch, with a Mannerist *Attic storey surmounted by a stag and hounds, motifs that give a foretaste of the complete scheme of iconography related to the hunt and Diana that ran through the *château*, for de L'Orme designed it for **Diane de Poitiers** (1499–1566), mistress (from *c.*1533) of **King Henri II**

(*r.*1547–59). The chapel at Anet (1547–55) is a variation on the circular form, with coffering in the dome shaped like bent *lozenges echoed in the marble floor: it is a master-work of *stereotomy. The celebrated *jubé in St-Étienne-du-Mont, Paris (*c.*1545), is no longer attributed to him. He designed the stone *bridge and *gallery at Chenonceaux (1556–9), completed (1576–8) by *Bullant.

De L'Orme established a French version of *Classicism that was influential until C18, and his work was followed closely by Bullant, Salomon de *Brosse, and F.*Mansart. His published works include *Nouvelles inventions pour bien bastir* (1561) and *Le premier Tome de l'Architecture* (1567 and later editions). Apart from useful practical considerations, some of the published designs for buildings are extraordinary, and include a *basilica with a great arched wooden roof that looks like a C19 train-shed; there are also references to Divine systems of proportion and measurement and the importance of the Temple of Solomon in Jerusalem in tempering the rules of Classicism. He produced his own versions of the Orders, including a column with a pruned tree as the shaft, but his 'French Orders' had decorated *bands to disguise the joints in the drums of the shaft, and this motif he used in his work at the Tuileries Palace, Paris (1564–70—mostly destroyed). French rationalism owed much to de L'Orme, and his system of timber trusses to span great widths was revived by *Legrand and *Molinos for the dome of the *Halle au Blé*, Paris (1782–3). His work inspired *Jefferson in the USA and David *Gilly in Prussia. *Viollet-le-Duc recognized his importance in his *Entretiens* (1858–72).

Berty (1860); Bt (1982, 1997); Brion-Guerry (1960); Ha (1943); M.Mayer (1953); Orme (1567); P (1982); PdM (2000); Potie (1996); Prévost (1948); D.Wa (1986)

ornament Decorative devices, not essential to structure, but often necessary to emphasize or diminish the impact of structural elements, sometimes with iconographic rôles. Most cultures have evolved their own repertoires of architectural ornament, the *sole exception* being the C20 *International-Modern style. In Classical Antiquity, ornament (often repetitive, e.g. *acanthus, *anthemion and *palmette, *egg-and-dart, *paterae, *guilloche, *Greek key, etc.) was an essential part of the sophisticated architectural language of the *Orders, but ornament could be found in the civilizations of Mesopotamia (e.g. cone *mosaics) and Ancient Egypt (e.g. stylized *lotus, *papyrus, etc.) much earlier. *Byzantine, *Romanesque, and *Gothic styles had their own ornament, e.g. transformations from the Classical repertory, *chevron, *beak-head, *dog-tooth, *nail-head, etc., and the *Renaissance period rediscovered Classical ornament, which was often adapted and transformed in *Mannerist, *Baroque, and *Rococo architecture. From the middle of C18, *Neo-Classicism once more turned to archaeologically correct ornament with the works of architects such as *Adam, *Stuart, *Wyatt, etc. When Gothic was revived, medieval ornament was again studied, copied, and then informed a new creativity. From C18 many styles (including oriental, Indian, and Islamic) were adopted in an enthusiasm for exotic *eclecticism, and in C19 publications made a vast range of architectural ornament available in convenient form: among them may be cited the famous *Grammar of Ornament* by Owen *Jones, a vast compendium, with colour-plates. *Ruskin held that ornament was a principal element of architecture (a view that was anathema to *Modernists), endowing it with moral/spiritual qualities that some might find odd. *Semper noted that ornament used in the production of textiles might be used on walls constructed of different materials: he argued that in their transformations, materials used are of no great importance, and that ornament, far from being an afterthought, stuck on a building (as was often the case in C20), was more symbolic and essential to architecture than structure. Ornament, he insisted, was conditioned by tradition, and by millennia of evolution from its origins in patterns that appeared in *Urkunst* (original art, e.g. weaving). Semper was claimed by Modernists for their cause, but they clearly had not read nor were capable of understanding him. *Fergusson claimed that ornament was architecture's poetic element, while structure was altogether more prosaic. Certain architects, such as *Sullivan, suggested ornament should be eschewed for a time, yet were themselves inventive and uninhibited users of it. *Loos, in the *Kärntner* Bar, Vienna (1908), used rich materials and a *stripped Neo-Classical language, while in the Scheu House, Hietzing (1912), the *ingle-nook and library clearly drew on English *Arts-and-Crafts domestic precedents. Yet Loos's fulminations against ornament are always quoted by Modernists, who also refer to his Steiner House, Vienna (1910), as an important work of Modern architecture, despite the fact that the symmetrical plan has Neo-Classical roots, and the interiors, with their exposed beams and joists, again are drawn from English historical exemplars. *Perret used ornament effectively (e.g. *Rue-Franklin* apartments, Paris (1902)), and it was an essential element in works of, e.g. *Hoffmann, *Mackintosh, and *Olbrich (to name but three significant architects). More recently **John Outram** (1934–) has used ornament in an intelligent way, to the displeasure of some.

Brolin (1985); Durant (1986); J.Fergusson (1862–7); Glazier (1926); Gombrich (1979); O.Jones (1868); F.Kroll (1987); L & D (1986); P.Meyer (1944); F.Meyer (ed.)

(1892); Outram (2003); Semper (1860–3); Speltz (1910); J.T (1996); Wornum (1869); Zahn (1864)

Ornamentalism Revival of architectural ornament marking a reaction against the so-called *Machine Aesthetic of *International Modernism from the 1960s. It was one of many aspects of *Post-Modernism.

Brolin (1985); J & C (1983)

O'Rorke, Brian (1901–74) New Zealand-born architect, best known for his *Modernist interiors from the 1930s, including the liner *Orion* (1934–5) and the Mayor Gallery, London (1933). He was appointed Architect of the National Theatre to be erected in London, but the project was abandoned (*Lasdun's National Theatre was erected on a different site and to a much expanded brief). At Derby Hall, University of Nottingham (early 1950s), however, he used a stripped-down Classical manner derived from the work of *Soane that influenced *McMorran & Whitby in their work for the same University.

Harwood (2008); Pe & Williamson (1979); pk

Orsini, Pier Francesco (Vicino), Duke of Bomarzo (*c.*1513–84) Italian connoisseur. He commissioned the celebrated *Parco dei Mostri* at Bomarzo, near Viterbo (begun 1552), which he called *sacro bosco* (sacred wood *or* grove), implying that this *Mannerist garden was far more than a place of relaxation and pleasure. It contained a Classical Temple, a Leaning House, a Mouth of Hell, many garden-sculptures (some extraordinary, even by Mannerist standards), an *exedra, a *nymphaeum*, a *grotto, fountains, and inscriptions from **Lodovico Ariosto** (1474–1533), **Dante Alighieri** (1265–1321), and **Francesco Petrarch** (1304–74). It was, like many *Renaissance gardens, an intellectual construct encompassing all the arts, stimulating the mind and the senses; a place of freedom, yet disturbing; a source of moral instruction, and even an 'Arcadia of Terror'. Several individuals have been credited with contributions to this nightmarishly baffling assemblage, including **Annibale Caro** (1507–66), though the writings of Ariosto may have played some part, and the place itself may have influenced **Torquato Tasso** (1544–95).

JGH, **iv**/1 (Jan.–Mar. 1984), whole issue; Lazzaro (1990); Tay (2006)

orthography *Elevations of a building or any part of it, showing correct relative proportions.

orthostata (*pl.* **orthostatae**) One of several vertical stone posts set in the base of a wall to form part of the facing, sometimes carved, e.g. forming part of the *revetment at the base of a *temple *cella, or as a form of *dado.

orthostyle Series of columns in a straight row.

Osiride *Pier supporting an *entablature or other load, with an *engaged figure of the Ancient-Egyptian god **Osiris** attached to it, which, unlike a *caryatid or a *telamon, does not itself act as a support.

J.Curl (2005)

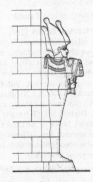

Osiride (from Thebes).

ossature Skeleton of a building, such as a frame or the *ribs of a *vault.

ossuary 1. Bone- or *charnel-house (ossuarium) for the deposit and preservation of remains of the dead disinterred from churchyard grounds to be re-used for burial. **2.** Container for the skeletal remains of an individual.

Östberg, Ragnar (1866-1945) Swedish architect who enjoyed international celebrity in the first three decades of C20 because of the success of his Stockholm City Hall (1908-23), a building of memorable personality with beautifully crafted interiors. Drawing on *Romanesque and *Renaissance elements and certain ideas from Venice (Doge's Palazzo and *Campanile), perhaps suggested by the marvellous waterside site, Östberg combined them in a wholly convincing synthesis of *Arts-and-Crafts architecture, and created a masterpiece of *National Romanticism, drawing on many mnemonics of Sweden's history for the interiors. His first important building was Östermalms Läroverk School, Stockholm (1910), where powerful forms, red *brick, and finely crafted details combined in a satisfying whole. The Swedish Patent and Registration Office, Stockholm (1911-21), began to show Neo-Classical tendencies, while his National Maritime Museum, Stockholm (1936), was more austere, yet reflects Östberg's strivings to create a truly National architecture.

A & B (1992); Ca et al. (1998); Cornell (1965, 1992); Östberg (1908); J.T (1996)

Otaka, Masato (1923-2010). Japanese architect, member of the *Metabolist group, his work has been associated with the search for 'group form', as in the Chiba Prefectural Centre (1967), but later turned to more conventional designs with a hint of traditional styles in them, an example of which is the Fukushima Museum of Art (1984).

E (1994); J.T (1996)

Otani, Sachio (1924-2013). Japanese architect, an early collaborator of *Tange, whose influence can be detected at the Kyoto International Conference Hall (1963-6), with its aggressive display of structure, bold modelling of the masses, and an expression of function. However, the repetition of trapezoidal sections—the result of his use of slanting columns and precast wall-panels—did not create the most serene of internal arrangements. Among later works, the Bunkyo Ward Sports Centre, Tokyo (1986), also exploits angles.

E (1994)

Ottmer, Carl Theodor (1800-43) German architect, trained under *Schinkel. Appointed Court Architect in Brunswick (1829), he brought a robust *Neo-Classicism to that city. He designed several *villas (e.g. Villa Bülow, Cellerstrasse (1839), and 29 Wilhelmtorwall (1841), but his grandest work, the Residenz (1831-8) was a casualty of the 1939-45 war: it had a stunning staircase-hall with squat Greek-*Doric columns and massive *coffering. The Railway Station (1843-5—now a Bank) was a fine conception in the *Italianate style.

Wa & M (1987)

Otto, Frei (1925-2015). See TENSILE STRUCTURES.

Ottoman architecture *Islamic architecture, mainly in Asia Minor, developed from C14, characterized by *domes, thin *minarets, tile-work, and decorations in *relief cut in stone. Typical of early Ottoman buildings was the Yeshil *Mosque, Iznik (1378-92). After the conquest of Constantinople by the Ottoman Turks (1453), Ottoman architecture absorbed *Byzantine influences, notably in the buildings of *Sinan (1489-c.1588), including the Mosque of Sokollu Mehmet Pasha (1570-4) and the Süleymaniye Mosque (1551-8), both in Istanbul. Later architecture of great magnificence was produced, notably the impressive Mosque of Sultan Ahmed, Istanbul (1610-16). The lovely *kiosk of Chinli, Istanbul (1472), has arcaded tile-encrusted elevations of great beauty. Ottoman motifs influenced aspects of C18 and C19 Western design, including some of the orientalizing buildings erected in gardens, e.g. by *Chambers et al.

Conner (1979); Ck (1996); L & D (1986); J.T (1996)

Ottonian style Evolved in the reign (962–73) of **Kaiser Otto I** ('the Great'), and continuing to the late C11, the finest Ottonian *Romanesque churches that survive are *Ste-Gertrude*, Nivelles (Nijvel), Belgium (consecrated 1046), and St Michael's, Hildesheim (1010–33) and the Abbey Church, Gernrode (begun 959–63), both in Germany. The last building was apparently one of the first in Europe to have the *tribune gallery. *See also* CAROLINGIAN; ROMANESQUE.

Conant (1979); Ck (1996); T (1996); D.Wa (1986)

Otzen, Johannes (1839–1911) German architect, whose *Gothic-Revival *brick buildings for the Lutheran Church were influential throughout Northern Germany. His best work was *Johanneskirche*, Hamburg-Altona (1868–73—won in an 1867 competition). He also designed the *Bergkirche*, Wiesbaden (1876–9), the monumental *Heiligekreuzkirche*, Berlin-Kreuzberg (1885–8), the *Apostelkirche*, Ludwigshafen (1892–4), and the *centralized *Ringkirche,* Wiesbaden (1892–4). He was responsible for several *villas in the Berlin suburb of Lichterfelde and elsewhere.

Bahns (1971); J.T (1996)

oubliette 1. Hidden medieval place of imprisonment excavated in the masonry or foundations of a castle, into which unfortunate captives could be dropped. 2. Secret pit where a person could be thrown or his body hidden.

Oud, Jacobus Johannes Pieter (1890–1963) Dutch architect. After collaborating with *Dudok on working-class housing at Leiderdorp, Leiden (1914–16), he became a member of *De *Stijl* and developed an interest in *Cubism and *Futurism under the influence of van *Doesburg. As Rotterdam City Architect (1918–33), he became more concerned with functional, economic planning and design. The *Café de Unie*, Rotterdam (1924–5—destroyed, but rebuilt 1985-6), was composed on the principles of *De Stijl*, and had affinities with the paintings of **Piet Mondriaan** (*or* **Mondriaan** 1872–1944).

Perhaps Oud's most significant designs were the housing-schemes where his growing involvement with *International Modernism was expressed: the terraces of houses at Hook of Holland (1924–7) and Kiefhoek, Rotterdam (1925–9), had the long bands of windows and clean white plain wall-surfaces that formed a non-structural protective skin, while the curved ends of the blocks suggested aerodynamic forms and contemporary ship construction. He designed a row of houses for the *Weissenhofsiedlung Exhibition, Stuttgart (1927), which brought him even more international recognition. However, ten years later, his *Bataafsche Import Maatschappij* (now Shell) Office Building, The

Hague (1938–42), with its symmetry, crude monumentality, and skin of brick and carved sandstone hiding the *reinforced-concrete frame seemed like retrogression. This, the Utrecht Life Insurance Company Office, Rotterdam (1954–61), and the Convention Centre, The Hague (1957–63), suggest that he became disenchanted with the aesthetic of the International style, but was unsuccessful in finding a satisfactory solution to his dilemma. His Bio-Children's Convalescent Home, near Arnhem (1952–60) attempted a return to the architectural language of the 1920s.

Hi (1931); L (1988); Langmead (1999); Mattie (1994); M & N (1987); P (1982); Stamm (1984); Taverne et al. (eds) (2001); J.T (1996); Ve (1953a)

Ould, Edward Augustus Lyle (1853–1909) *See* GRAYSON.

oundy, undy *Vitruvian scroll, *string-course decorated with a wave-like undulating motif, *zig-zag, or the like.

Ouradou, Maurice-Augustin-Gabriel (1822–84) French architect, he studied with *Lebas and *Viollet-le-Duc (whose daughter he married), and worked with him on *Notre-Dame*, Paris, and on the *Château* of Pierrefonds, where he carried out a major reconstruction. He was Diocesan Architect of Châlons.

M & Wa (1987); S (1901–2)

ouroboros, uroboros Symbol of a snake in circular form, eating its tail (or with its tail in its mouth), suggesting an eternal recurring process, or immortality, and therefore often found on *cemetery gates, funerary monuments, etc.

ouroborus

Outram, John (1934–) *See* ORDER; ORNAMENT; POLYCHROMY.

outshot Projection beyond the main line of building, e.g. a *verandah, *oriel, or *jetty, but more usually applied to an extension looking like an afterthought.

over Prefix used in various ways. *Combinations include*:
overdoor: 1. Wall-surface over a *door-case, whether decorated or not. 2. The *sopraporta, only used for internal positions: an exterior *sopraporta* is a *coronet. 3. *Fanlight;

overhang: **1.** projection of part of a structure beyond the portion below, e.g. an *oriel or *jetty projecting beyond the *naked of the wall below; **2.** wall not upright, but with its naked sloping outwards and upwards, i.e. the opposite of *batter; **3.** *corbel;

overlight: square or rectangular equivalent of a fanlight;

overmantel: decorative framed *panel or the architectural arrangement above a *mantel-shelf;

oversail: element projecting over another, so courses of *masonry, each *cantilevered out beyond the *face of the course beneath it, are corbelled or oversailing courses, as in a *cornice or *eaves;

overshot: jetty;

overstorey: **1.** *clerestorey; **2.** upper storey;

overthrow: **1.** ornamental iron structure set between upright *gate-piers or standards and over the *gates; **2.** arched iron support for a lamp between gate-piers or standards.

Over, Charles (*fl.*mid-C18) English land-surveyor in Herts., he published (1758) a volume of charming designs entitled *Ornamental Architecture in the Gothic, Chinese and Modern Taste...*, *for gardens, parks,* ... which included the earliest use of the 'umbrello' as a shelter.

Bendall (ed.) (1997); Co (2008); Over (1758)

ovolo Convex Classical *moulding, often enriched with *egg-and-dart or similar motifs. Greek ovolos were more egg-like in profile, while Roman ovolos were normally quarter-rounds.

ovum Egg-shaped form in Classical *mouldings, e.g. *egg-and-dart.

Owen, Robert (1771–1856) *See* COMPANY TOWN.

Owen, Segar (1874–1929) English architect. He was articled to and later (1896), after a brief time with G.E.*Street, was partner of his father, **William Owen** (1850–1910), architect, of Warrington, Ches. At Port Sunlight, Ches., William refined **William Hesketh Lever's** (1851–1925) plan for the layout of the town, and designed the first 28 cottages and entrance-lodge. W.&S.Owen's designs for houses at Port Sunlight often quoted the *half-timbered gabled *vernacular style of Ches. but also employed *ogee gables, vitrified *diaper-work, and walls of *brick and *terracotta. Among other buildings at Port Sunlight are Hulme Hall (1901) and the very distinguished Gothic Christ Church (1902–4), where the *Perp. style was made more four-square and robust. Segar Owen designed the severe Neo-Classical Art Gallery at Port Sunlight (1914–22). *See* COMPANY TOWN.

Davison (1916); A.S.Gray (1985); Hartwell *et al.* (2011)

Owen, William (1850–1910) *See* OWEN, SEGAR.

Owings, Nathaniel A. (1903–84) *See* SKID-MORE, OWINGS, & MERRILL.

ox-eye *See* ŒIL DE BŒUF.

ox-head *See* BUCRANIUM.

Ozenfant, Amédée (1886–1966) French co-founder, with Le *Corbusier, of *Purism and *L'Esprit Nouveau* (1920–5), the first periodical dedicated to the C20 *Modernist aesthetic in 'all its manifestations'. He contributed to articles with Le Corbusier (on whom he was a formative influence), published in *Vers une architecture* (1923). Probably his most influential work was *Foundations of Modern Art*, first published in English (1931).

Golding (1973); Ozenfant (1952, 1968); Ozenfant & J-G (1975); J.T (1996)

P *See* CHRISMON.

Pabenham, Simon I (*fl.c.*1262–80) English master-mason, in charge of the building of the Church of St Mary's Abbey, York (1270–94). He, or a relative, may also have been involved in building-works at Lincoln Cathedral and York *Minster.

J.Harvey (1987)

Pabenham, Simon II (*fl.*1282–1334) English master-mason, he worked (1280s) at the Tower of London, and, with **John de la Bataile** (*fl.*1278–1300), built (1291–3) the Eleanor *Crosses at Northampton and St Albans. He became Master-Mason at the Tower of London (1307–11), and was involved in the implementation and enforcement of building-codes in the City of London from 1313.

J.Harvey (1987)

pace 1. Part of a floor raised above the general level; a *daïs. **2.** Broad raised step around a tomb-structure, *altar, etc. **3.** Landing in a *stair, especially the area where the stair turns: *half-pace* is a landing where one *flight ends and another begins, involving a turn of 180°; *quarter-pace* is a landing between two flights involving a turn of 90°.

Pace, George Gaze (1915–75) English ecclesiastical architect, his work often sat uneasily between the *Modern Movement and *Arts-and-Crafts principles. His early career was greatly helped by **Eric Milner White** (1884–1963), Dean of York Minster (1941–63), who recommended Pace as architect for the Royal Irish Fusiliers Chapel in St Patrick's Anglican Cathedral, Armagh (1950), his first large commission for integrated furnishings. This was followed by major interventions at Llandaff Cathedral (1949–64), including the parabolic arches on which is the *Majestas* (1954–5) by **Sir Jacob Epstein** (1880–1959), and St David's (Welch Regimental) Chapel (1953–6). The death of Sir Charles *Nicholson, Bt (1949), catapulted Pace into prominence, and he was appointed architect to three cathedrals and numerous churches. With Paul *Paget he

designed the **King George VI** (*r.*1936–52) Memorial Chapel, St George's Chapel, Windsor, Berks. (1967–9). Other works include the Bell-House, Chester Cathedral (1968–74), the organ-case at New College Chapel, Oxford (1967–9), Palace Green Library, University of Durham (1961–6), and a huge number of fittings, furnishings, inscriptions, and vestments, most of which are listed in his son's hagiography.

J.Curl (2013); Pace (1990)

Pacioli, Luca (*c.*1445–*c.*1514) Italian mathematician, his *Summa de Arithmetica, Geometria, Proportioni, etc.* (1494) and *Divina Proportione* (1496, published 1509) set out the mathematical bases of architecture embraced by *Alberti and others, and described the *Golden Section.

COF (1988); H.O (1970); J.T (1996)

Packh, János (1796–1839) Hungarian Neo-Classical architect, trained in Vienna. He assisted his uncle, **Pál** *or* **Paul von Kühnel** (d.1824), in the design and erection of the Cathedral of St Adalbert, Esztergom. Packh was responsible for the *crypt (1823), and after his uncle's death he took over as sole architect to oversee the building of the greatest architectural project within the Habsburg domains at the time: completed (1840–56) by József *Hild, it has a vast *polychrome *dome and a huge *portico. Among Packh's other designs may be cited St Anne's Church, Esztergom (1828–31—a *rotunda with a *Doric *portico), the additions (tower of 1828–32) and extension to the Library (1833–6) at the *Benedictine Abbey of Pannonhalma, and his unrealized proposals for Eger Cathedral (1829), again Neo-Classical, should be cited.

W.Pa (1852); J.T (1996)

packing Filling of interstices with small broken stones embedded in the *mortar between bigger stones in *rubble walls (*see* GALLET).

packing-piece 1. Element, e.g. block of wood, to raise e.g. a beam to the required height. **2.** Timber at the back of a *cruck-*blade to carry a *purlin.

ABDM (1996)

pad 1. Block (also called a *template* or *padstone*) built into a wall or fixed to the top of a *pier on which a *beam or *truss rests. **2.** *Kneeler at the lowest point of a *gable at the *eaves to hold the *cope in place and stop it sliding off, also called *knee-stone* or *skew*. **3.** Short timber across the top of a wall to support a wall-plate or the foot of a common *rafter. **4.** Any large block carrying a load.

Padula, Ernesto Bruno La (1902–69) Italian architect, he became a member of the Italian Movement for Rationalist Architecture (*MIAR). He designed the Knights of Columbus Foundation (1934) and the Palace of Italian Civilization (1938–9—known as the 'Square Colosseum'), both in Rome, two of the most powerful examples of *Rationalism of the Fascist era.

Cennamo (1976)

Paeonius *or* **Paionios of Ephesus** (*fl.*350–310 BC) Ancient-Greek architect, he was partly responsible (with *Demetrius and, possibly, *Deinocrates) for the great Temple of Artemis, Ephesus (*c.*356–236 BC), and, with *Daphnis of Miletus, built the Temple of Apollo at Didyma from *c.*313 BC. Both were huge buildings: the Temple of Artemis employed an elegant *Ionic *Order, and the temple of Apollo was the only Greek-Ionic decastyle temple, but also had *engaged *Corinthian columns at the entrance to the steps leading to the oracular *shrine.

D (1950); La (1983)

Paesschen (*or* **Passe**), **Hans Hendrik van** (*c.*1515–82) Flemish architect from Antwerp, he introduced Italian *Classicism to Northern Europe where *Mannerism was pre-eminent. A contemporary of *Palladio and de L'*Orme, his reputation has suffered because much of his work has been attributed to *Floris de Vriendt, and he is known by many names (e.g. **Hendrik Fleming, Henry Passe**, etc.). He appears to have been selected by Floris to prepare drawings for Antwerp Town Hall (1561–6), while Floris carved the sculptures and dealt with the clients. The *Raadhuis* contains many Italian themes and motifs, as did the *Hanseatenhuis*, Antwerp (1564–6—destroyed 1893—also attributed to Floris, but probably by Paesschen). If, as seems likely, he was involved in the design of the Royal Exchange, London (1566–8—destroyed 1666), Burghley House, near Stamford, Lincs. (1564–87), and Theobald's Palace, Herts. (1560s–destroyed), he must be credited with the introduction of Italian *Renaissance architecture to England before Inigo *Jones was born. He also seems to have designed Bach-y-Graig, Tremeirchion, Flintshire, Wales (1567–9—demolished), in which case he was a Renaissance pioneer there too. His connections

with England and Wales were made through **Sir Thomas Gresham** (*c.*1519–79), founder of the Royal Exchange, friend of the powerful **Cecil** family, and English agent in Antwerp. He may have had a hand in the design of Osterley, Mddx., just outside London. He began Kronborg Castle, Helsingør, Denmark (1574). Later he designed Uraniborg, Hven Island, Denmark (1576), for the astronomer **Tycho Brahe** (1546–1601); the house was crowned with a *dome to aid astronomical observation.

Hubbard (1986); Millar (1987); Mu (1985); J.T (1996); vV (1993)

Paestum Greek colony in Italy, south of Naples, of which a group of ruined *Doric *temples survives (*c.*530 BC–*c.*460 BC). This Doric *Order has the most exaggerated *entasis of any *Antique example, and the very wide squat *capitals on top of the shafts emphasize the *primitive effect. The Paestum Order was much admired by Neo-Classical architects in C18 and C19, and was used where powerful effects were sought.

J.Curl (2001); D (1950); C.Normand (1852); J.T (1996); W-E (2013)

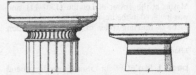

Primitive Paestum Doric capitals (*after Normand*).

Pagano Pogatschnig, Giuseppe (1896–1945) Italian Rationalist Fascist architect/polemicist, a leading player in arguments (1930s) about the renaissance of Italian architecture, largely through his editorship (from 1931) of the influential *Casabella*. His early works had a suggestion of *Perret, *Behrens, and the Vienna *Sezession about them, but with **Gino Levi-Montalcini** (1902–74), he designed (1928) one of the first monuments of Italian *Rationalism, the Gualino Office Building, Turin (1928–9—destroyed). He prepared a plan for the *Via Roma*, Turin (1931—with the Turin branch of *MIAR), designed a standardized industrialized system for building housing (1933) for the Fifth Triennale, and in 1932–5 built the *Istituto di Fisica*, University of Rome (destroyed). The *Università Commerciale Bocconi* (1937–41—destroyed) was remarkable for its adherence to geometry and schemes of proportion throughout the design. He died in Mauthausen concentration-camp, Austria, having renounced (1942) Fascism.

Melograni (1955); P (1982); Seta (1978, 1979); Seta (ed.) (1976); J.T (1996); Ve (1953)

Page, Montague Russell (1906–85) English landscape architect, he designed rock-gardens at a very early age. Influenced by *Jekyll's works and by **Lawrence Johnston**'s (1871–1958) garden at Hidcote Manor, Glos. (from 1907), he began his professional gardening career (1929), collaborated (1930s) with *Jellicoe, and commenced contributing to the journal of the Institute of Landscape Architects. He designed the 'frivolous planting' for the gardens at Battersea Park as part of the 1951 *Festival of Britain (restored 2004). Many commissions followed, many abroad, and he published (1962) *The Education of a Gardener*, one of the most accessible volumes on the topic. Late works include the *courtyard of the Frick Collection, NYC (1977), the sculpture-gardens at Columbus Museum of Art, OH (1979), and PepsiCo headquarters, NY (1981–5).

ODNB (2013); Page (1962); Schinz & VanZuylen (2008)

Pagod *See* MAGOT.

pagoda European term for a tall structure, often polygonal on plan, of several separately roofed stories marked by upturned *eaves, fretwork brackets, and, often, ornaments resembling bells (*campanulae*) suspended from the eaves. Based on Chinese temple-towers, pagodas were used as garden-buildings in the C18 *Chinoiserie manner (e.g. *Chambers's Pagoda at Kew Gardens, London).

Conner (1979); Honour (1961); Impey (1977); L & D (1986); J.T (1996)

Pagot, François-Narcisse (1780–1844) French architect, pupil of de la *Barre, he became Architect to the City of Orléans, where he built (mostly 1820s) the *Palais de Justice*, Grain-Market, Abattoir, Library, and Lunatic Asylum. He also laid out the Botanic Gardens and completed the portal of the Cathedral.

S (1901–2)

Paine, James (1717–89) English architect, he established himself in *Burlington's circle as Clerk of Works at Nostell Priory, Yorks. (c.1737–50), a large Palladian house by **James Moyser** (c.1693–1753) probably based on designs by Colen *Campbell. Paine succeeded (1750s) to the practice of Daniel *Garrett and designed or made alterations to a great number of country-houses. It was said that he and Sir Robert *Taylor 'nearly divided the practice' of architecture between them, for they had few rivals until Robert *Adam appeared on the scene. His architecture was essentially Palladian in that he planned competent, sensible *villas consisting of a central building (often containing a fine *stair) with *wings. At Kedleston Hall, Derbys. (1759–60), he superseded Matthew *Brettingham (who built the east wing) and designed a great central block connected to the wings by *quadrants. His greatest innovation was his proposal for a reconstruction of a *Vitruvian *'Egyptian' colonnaded hall behind the *Corinthian *portico. This would lead to a symmetrically disposed staircase beyond which was a circular *saloon projecting from the south front like a Roman round temple; however, Adam (who, in turn, superseded him) moved the stair to one side and placed a *rotunda in a square block faced on the south front by a *triumphal arch. Paine was no Neo-Classicist: he was scornful of the pursuit of the *Antique, felt foreign travel to be less valuable than practical experience, and considered Greek buildings to be 'despicable ruins'. At Wardour Castle, Wilts. (1770–6), however, he designed a fine staircase under a *Pantheon-like dome. Other works include Sandbeck Park, Maltby, Yorks. (1763–8), and Thorndon Hall, Essex (1764–70). In interior decoration he was one of the first in England to be attracted to *Rococo forms. Much of his work was illustrated in his *Plans, Elevations, and Sections of Noblemen and Gentlemen's Houses* (1767, 1783). From the 1770s his practice declined as the Adam star rose, and despite his fear of foreign travel, died in France.

Co (2008); J.Curl (2011a); E.Hs (1990); Leach (1988); *ODNB* (2004); P (1982); J.T (1996)

Pain, William (c.1730–90) English architect/joiner/carpenter, he wrote many *pattern-books which disseminated the *Adam style, including *The Builder's Companion and Workman's General Assistant* (1758), *The Builder's Pocket Treasure: or, Palladio Delineated and Explained* (1763), *The Practical Builder* (1774), *The Carpenter's and Joiner's Repository* (1778), *The Builder's Golden Rule* (1781), *The British Palladio* (1786), and *The Builder's Sketch Book* (1793). A selection of plates from his books was published as *Decorative Details of the Eighteenth Century by William and James Pain* (1946), with an introduction by A.E.*Richardson. For *The British Palladio* he was assisted by his son, also **James**, who was the father of **James**, **George Richard**, and **Henry Pain**, all pupils of *Nash. **James** (1779–1877) and **George Richard** (1793–1838), assisted for a time by **Henry**, became successful architects/developers in Ireland (James was the *First-Fruits architect for the Province of Cashel), where they designed numerous churches and castellated houses. James Pain's chapel at Cloghjordan, Co. Tipperary (c.1830), is a handsome essay in *Perp., agreeably composed, and, with George Richard, he designed the Parish Church of Buttevant, Co. Cork (1826). The Pains also designed Gothic Anglican Churches at Mallow and Carrigaline (Co. Cork), and produced competent Classical designs for RC Churches at Bantry, Dunmanway, Millstreet, and Ovens, all in Co. Cork, as well as for a convent at Blackrock, Co. Dublin. For Cork

Gaol, the Pains chose a severe Greek-*Doric style, using the unfluted shafts of the Temple of Apollo at Delos as their model (1818–23), and for the Court-House at Cork (1830—destroyed) they used an octastyle *Corinthian Order. Among their houses, Dromoland, Co. Clare (1826—castellated) may be cited.

Co (2008); M.Craig (1982); Graby (ed.) (1989)

Paionios See PAEONIUS.

pair *Flight or series of flights in a *stair from one floor to the next.

pala See ALTAR-PIECE.

palace 1. Official residence of any noble, monarch, or high dignitary, or any grand house of exceptional magnificence. The term derives from the *Palatium*, the Imperial residence on the Palatine hill in Rome. **2.** Large public building, such as a *Palais de Justice*. **3.** Place of entertainment, usually with architectural pretensions, such as a *picture-palace* or *palais de danse*.

palace-front Classical symmetrical main *elevation of a large building or, as in the work of *Wood in Bath (from 1729), where several houses appear to be one palatial composition with emphasis given to the centre and ends by means of *engaged *porticoes, *temple-fronts, end-*pavilions, and the like.

palaestra *Antique wrestling-school or building for athletics, often an open area surrounded by *colonnades, etc.

palatial Italian *Italianate style applied to C19 clubs, banks, offices, making them look like Italian *astylar *palazzi, as in *Barry's Travellers' Club, Pall Mall, London (1829).

palazzo (*pl.* **palazzi**) Italian *palace, corresponding to a town-house (*hôtel*), or to a palace in the sense of a large official residence or municipal building. See ITALIANATE.

palazzo style See ITALIANATE; PALATIAL ITALIAN.

Paley, Edward Graham (1823–95) See SHARPE, EDMUND.

Paley, Frederick Apthorp (1815–88) See SHARPE, EDMUND.

Paley, Henry (Harry) Anderson (1859–1946) See SHARPE, EDMUND.

palimpsest 1. Monumental *brass turned and engraved on the reverse side. **2.** *Mural painting overlapping or obscuring an earlier one.

paliotto *Altar-facing, hanging on all four sides, unlike an *antependium* which covers the front alone.

palisade 1. *Fence of stakes fixed in the ground, forming an enclosure for defence. **2.** Fence of iron railings. **3.** Light fence, or *trellis-work on which trees and shrubs are trained in **espalier** fashion. **4.** Row of trees or shrubs forming a dense barrier of *hedge (*palissade* in French), either solid, pierced with openings, or with the trunks bare and trimmed, but the upper foliage solid, treated as *espalier*-work or *pleached (intertwined or tangled) to create a solid green barrier. **5.** Row of deciduous trees with pleached branches.

Goulty (1991)

Palladian bridge See BRIDGE.

Palladianism Classical style based on work by the C16 Italian architect *Palladio, disseminated primarily by his *Quattro Libri dell'Architettura* (1570), which contained illustrations of his designs, described them and his ideas, and promoted his work. The *first Palladian Revival* was instigated by Inigo *Jones in England in the reigns of **James I and VI** (1603–25) and **Charles I** (1625–49), having studied Palladio's buildings in Vicenza and its vicinity in 1613–14 as well as his publications, notably *Le antichità di Roma* (1554). Key buildings were the Queen's House, Greenwich (1616–35), the Banqueting House, Whitehall, London (1619–22), and the Queen's Chapel, St James's (1623–5). Certain features derived from Palladio's buildings appeared in the works of van *Campen In The Netherlands (e.g. the plan reminiscent of Italian villas at the *Mauritshuis*, The Hague (1633–5)), and *Holl in Germany (e.g. the restrained severity of the *Rathaus*, Augsburg (1615–20)), but the main source for these architects seems to have been *Scamozzi. The *second Palladian Revival* of the early C18 began in Venetia (where it was evident in ecclesiastical and secular buildings) and in England (where it was mostly overt in domestic architecture, especially the grand country-house). The key figures of the English Revival were Colen *Campbell and Lord *Burlington, who also promoted a reappraisal of the first Revival led by Jones. As the high-priest of English Palladianism, Burlington not only designed exemplary buildings but promoted the interests of architects sympathetic to the cause and encouraged publications that established the architectural vocabulary and language that were to dominate (even tyrannize) taste for much of the century. Important in disseminating such elements as the *temple-front and the *serliana were *Vitruvius Britannicus* (1715–25) and *Leoni's *The Architecture of A.Palladio* (1715–20) which remained the standard text-book until *Ware's more scholarly tome (1738). English Palladian ideals were exported, notably to Prussia

(*Knobelsdorff's Opera House on the *Unter den Linden*, Berlin (from 1741—based on Campbell's Wanstead House, Essex), was a fine example, although, influenced by *Algarotti, Potsdam acquired (1750) variants on the *Palazzi Thiene* and *Valmarana*), Anhalt (*Erdmannsdorff's *Schloss Wörlitz* (1769-73—very similar to L. *Brown and *Holland's Claremont House, Esher, Surrey)), Russia (the architecture of *Cameron and *Quarenghi), and the USA (the influence of *Jefferson).

An (1966, 1967); Boucher (1998); J.Curl (2011a); J.Hs (1981, 1994); Köster (1990); Palladio (1570, 1965, 1997); Parissien (1994); Ry (1999); Su (1993); Ta (1991); Whitehill & F.Nichols (1976); Wi (1974a, 1998); Worsley (1995)

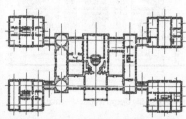

Palladianism Plan and elevation, Holkham Hall, Norfolk (from 1734), by Lord Burlington, William Kent, and Matthew Brettingham. An example of *concatenation*. Each element of the elevation can exist as an independent symmetrical composition, and the various axes establish the order of the plan.

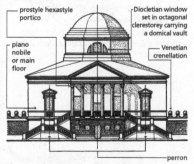

Elevation of Burlington's villa at Chiswick.

Palladian window *See* SERLIANA.

Palladio, Andrea (1508-80) One of the most gifted, professional, and intelligent of architects active in C16 Italy, whose work provided the models for *Palladianism and had a profound effect on Western architectural thinking. Palladio's studies of the architectural remains of ancient Rome led him to attempt to emulate its nobility and grandeur. Interpreting the texts of *Vitruvius in his architecture and theories, he further explored the potential of symmetry in design, and developed various other concerns of the *Renaissance, including the theory of *harmonic proportions. He also drew on precedents provided by Italian architects, notably *Bramante, *Raphael, *Giulio Romano, *Sanmicheli, and *Sansovino.

Born **Andrea di Pietro della Gondola** in Padua, Palladio began his career as a stonemason, and joined (1524) the Guild of Masons and Stonecutters of Vicenza. He became (*c.*1536) the *protégé* of **Count Giangiorgio Trissino** (1478-1550), who stimulated the young man to appreciate the arts, sciences, and Classical literature, granted him the opportunity to study *Antique Roman architecture, and called him 'Palladio' (from *Pallas*, a name for *Athene*, the Greek goddess associated with Wisdom). Palladio won the competition to recase the municipal 'Basilica' (or *Palazzo della Ragione*), Vicenza, and construction started (1549). The design consists of a *screen composed of two storeys employing a version of the arcuated theme at *Sansovino's *Biblioteca Marciana*, Venice (from 1537), and from *Serlio's *L'Architettura* (1537), although ultimately originating with Bramante. Consisting of arches flanked by smaller rectangular openings beneath the *entablatures from which the arches spring, the motif is in essence the *serliana, also called *Palladian* or *Venetian* window. An elegant *tour-de-force* of Classical elements put together with verve and *élan*, the Basilica made Palladio's name, and from 1550 he was fully employed as a designer of churches, *palazzi, and *villas.

His first grand house in Vicenza was the *Palazzo Thiene* (commenced 1542 to designs probably by Giulio Romano), in which the *Mannerism of the heavily rusticated exterior is combined with an interior plan drawing on themes from Antiquity (e.g. the sequence of rectangular rooms with an apsidal-ended hall and octagonal spaces with *niches, clearly derived from the precedents of *Antique Roman *thermae). For the *Palazzo Iseppo Porto* (*c.*1548-52), Palladio planned two identical blocks on each side of a central *court around which was to be a *Giant *Order of columns, evoking the *atrium of a Roman house and the Capitoline palaces of *Michelangelo in Rome. The symmetry and the sequence of rooms (each in proportion to the adjoining) were to become features of Palladio's work. Of the other Vicentine buildings, the *Palazzo Chiericati* (1550, not completed until late C17) deserves mention as it was designed to be a side of a great 'forum', with *loggie as public amenities arranged as two storeys of *colonnades, an unusual and highly original design for C16. The *Loggia del Capitaniato* (begun 1571), opposite the 'Basilica' in Vicenza, again employed a Giant Order, giving the impression that the building was constructed within surviving remains of a Roman temple, and there are Mannerist touches, including windows breaking into the *entablature, *triglyphs acting as brackets carrying balconies, and the side elevation in the form of a *triumphal arch. The last, Roman Antiquity, and tricks of perspective are evoked in the *Teatro Olimpico*, Vicenza (begun 1580 and finished by *Scamozzi), where even the painted sky of the ceiling suggested a theatre of the ancients.

In his designs for villas, Palladio devised a theme with a central symmetrically planned *corps-de-logis, often embellished with a *prostyle *portico. Subsidiary buildings were linked to the main block by means of extended *wings or curved *quadrants containing ancillary accommodation (often associated with the needs of agriculture). Agreeably sited to revive the idea of the Roman love of country life and gardens, the spirit of *Pliny was never far removed from the villas. One of Palladio's most enchanting designs was the *Villa Barbaro* at Maser (c.1560), with a *temple-fronted two-storeyed centrepiece and symmetrical wings on either side consisting of five-bay *arcades terminating in end-*pavilions crowned with *pediments, a fine example of the *villa rustica*. Palladio devised many permutations of his villa theme, including the powerful, almost Neo-Classical boldness of the *Villa Poiana* (c.1549-60); the deceptive simplicity of the *Villa Foscari*, Malcontenta di Mira, near Mestre (c.1558-60); and the remarkable *Villa Capra* (known as *La Rotonda*), a *villa suburbana*, near Vicenza (c.1566-70), with identical hexastyle *Ionic porticoes (temple-fronts) on each of the four elevations and a central circular

two-storey room capped with a *cupola. This employment of temple-fronts or porticoes on villas was based on Palladio's erroneous belief that Antique Roman houses had them: nevertheless, the relationships of porticoes to elements of the composition, including room dimensions, were governed by the concept of harmonic proportion. The *Villa Capra*'s only function was as a pleasure-pavilion or *belvedere from where beautiful views could be enjoyed.

The *façades of Palladio's Venetian Churches of *San Francesco della Vigna* (1562-70), *San Giorgio*

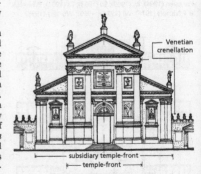

Elevation of *San Giorgio Maggiore*, Venice.

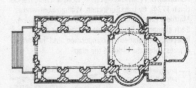

Plan of *Il Redentore*, Venice, with chapels between wall-piers and columnar screen, behind which is the monks' choir.

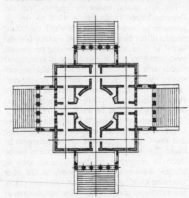

Plan of the *Villa Capra*, Vicenza.

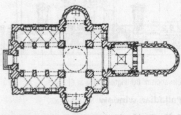

Plan of *San Giorgio Maggiore*, Venice, with monastic choir behind the columnar screen.

Maggiore (1564–80), and *Il Redentore* (1576–80) show ingenious solutions to the problems of placing Classical *temple-fronts on to the *basilican arrangement of *clerestoreyed *nave with lean-to *aisles. High, narrow temple-fronts are placed at the ends of the naves, complete with *pediments, with a wider, lower, pedimented front set 'behind' so that its extremities provide the façades to the aisles. The interior spatial effects in *San Giorgio* and *Il Redentore* have a *gravitas* and complexity unlike other churches of the time.

Palladio published (1554) *Le antichità di Roma* (valued as a gazetteer for two centuries), and *Descrizione delle chiese ... di Roma*. He also provided important illustrations for Barbaro's edition of Vitruvius (1556). He brought out (1570) *I Quattro Libri dell'Architettura*, which publicized his own works, set out his theories, and illustrated and described various important buildings (mostly Roman, including Bramante's circular *Tempietto* at *San Pietro in Montorio*). It also illustrated canonical versions of the Roman *Orders of architecture and a range of his own buildings in *plan, *elevation, and *section, with measurements and descriptive text. Thus the work put his designs on a par with the great buildings of the past, and helped to enhance his reputation. The *Quattro libri*, a more accurate treatise than those by Serlio or *Vignola, appeared in several subsequent editions, but that of *Leoni (1715–20—translated as *The Architecture of A. Palladio* ...) appeared in English, French, and Italian, the first adequate edition since 1642, and the first to substitute large engraved plates for Palladio's woodcuts. The book was a huge success and a second edition was published (1721), a third following (1742), with 'Notes and Remarks of Inigo Jones'. Leoni's remained the standard work until *Ware's more scholarly edition (1738), and it is the last that has found most favour, republished in facsimile (1965) with an introduction by Adolf K.Placzek. The plates, by Ware, were a lot more accurate than Leoni's rather embellished versions, and Ware's *opus* came out in further editions (1767, 1768). Batty *Langley looted these publications for his own books (notably his *City and Country Builder's and Workman's Treasury* (1740)), and a version of Palladio's First Book, augmented with other material by *Muet, was published in the 1740s by Godfrey Richards. It was this Franco-English edition that seems to have introduced Palladianism to America. *See also* PALLADIANISM.

An (1966, 1967); Bonet (ed.) (2002); Boucher (1998); H.Burns (ed.) (1975); Evelyn (2012); Hofberton (1990); Leoni (1742); D.Lewis (2000); Palladio (1570, 1965, 1997); P (1982); Li.Puppi (1975, 1980); Rybczynski (2003); Ry (1999); Ta (1991); J.T (1996); Wi (1974a, 1998); Zorzi (ed.) (from 1959)

palm Palm-leaves occur in Ancient-Egyptian decoration (especially palmiform *capitals). Flat palm-fronds with curved ends appear in a unique type of *Corinthian capital at the Tower of the Winds, Athens (*c.*50 BC), often copied on C18 capitals, *friezes, and other *mouldings.

palmate With fan-like lobes or leaves, as in the *anthemion or *palmette, or with leaves of a palm-tree, as in a *palmiform *capital.

Palmer, Clement (1857–1952) China-based British architect. With **Arthur Turner** (1858–*c.*1945), he built several important *Beaux-Arts-inspired buildings, including the Hong Kong and Shanghai Banking Corporation Building (1921–3). **Palmer & Turner** also designed many other Classically influenced banks, as well as the Sassoon House (later Peace Hotel), Shanghai (1926–8—a vast building clad in granite and embellished with *Art-Deco motifs), and the Sassoon Villa, Shanghai (1930—an essay in the *Domestic Revival emulating timber-framed *Tudor precedents).

Ck (1996)

Palmer, John (*c.*1738–1817) English builder/ architect. In partnership for a time with **Thomas Jelly** (*fl.*1740–81—the competent *Palladian architect who designed King Edward's Grammar School, Broad Street (1752–4), and houses in Abbey and Milson Streets), he erected several buildings in and around Bath, Som. The most important was Lansdown Crescent (1789–93), convex-concave-convex on plan, responding to the contours of the landscape, and combining the Classical and the *Picturesque. He was also responsible for St James's Square (1791–4), the *Gothic Christ Church, Julian Road (1798), and New Bond Street (1805–7).

Co (2008); Ison (1969)

Palmer, John (1785–1846) English architect. Originally an illiterate mason, he taught himself to read and write, and learned the 'rudiments' of architecture from William *Atkinson. He established (1813) a successful practice as an ecclesiastical architect in Manchester (where Atkinson also had an office (1812–16)), specializing in *Gothic-Revival churches. Among his works may be mentioned the ambitious RC Church of Sts Mary and John, Pleasington, Lancs. (1816–19—with a noble circular west window), St Peter's Chapel, Blackburn, Lancs. (1819–21), St Augustine's Chapel, Granby Road, Manchester (1820), the Church (now Cathedral) of St Mary, Blackburn (1820–6—reconstructed and altered after 1831 by *Rickman and others), and Holy Trinity Church, North Ashton, Ashton-in-Makerfield, Lancs. (1873–8). His interventions (1814–15) at the Collegiate Church (now Cathedral), Manchester were disastrous: among other crimes, he covered the *nave interior with *Roman cement. Nevertheless, he published (1829) his *Guide to the Collegiate Church of Manchester*, and contributed a detailed description of that building to Hibbert-Ware & Whatton's *History of the Foundations of Manchester* (1834). Considering his humble origins and late start, some of his work is remarkable for its quality and scholarship.

Co (2008); Hartwell, Hyde, & Pe (2004); Hartwell & Pe (2009); Pollard & Pe (2006)

palmette Stylized fan-shaped *palmate leaf (called *palmetto*), one type resembling a honeysuckle flower and the other a *raceme arrangement, often used in bands with the *anthemion or the *lotus in Classical *friezes, but also on its own to embellish certain elements. It is found incised, in relief, or painted.

(*left*) Egyptian lotus-flower with volutes. (*right*) variant from Cyprus.

palm-house *Conservatory in which palm-trees, etc., are grown and protected.

palmiform Like the top of a palm-tree, with frond-ribs palmately arranged, as in a palm-*capital.

Palmstedt, Erik (1741–1803) Swedish architect, he designed the Stock Exchange, Stockholm (1767–76), the Theatre, Gripsholm Castle (modelled on *Palladio's *Teatro Olympico*, Vicenza—1781–4), the *bridge over the *Riddarholmskanal* (1784), and the monumental German Fountain (1785), Stockholm. He was a major figure in Swedish *Neo-Classicism.

A & B (1986); Ck (1996); T & B (1932)

pamper 1. Representation of vine-stems with grapes, often found draped in spirals around columns, suggesting the twisted *Trajanic or *Solomonic form. **2.** Grapes, leaves, and vine-stems as running undercut ornament in *cavettos and other continuous hollows at the tops of *Perp. *screens called *trail.

B & C (1909)

pan 1. Wall-plate. **2.** Part of an exterior wall, especially the *panel between the structural horizontal and verticals in a *timber-framed building.

panache Approximately triangular surface of a *pendentive.

pan-and-roll *Tile roof composed of repeated patterns formed by two adjacent flat tiles with upturned flanges on each side, the joint covered by tapering semicircular-profiled tiles fitting neatly over the upstanding flanges.

pancarpi Classical enrichments consisting of *garlands or *festoons of fruit, flowers, and leaves.

pane 1. *Light in a window, or a piece of *glass in a *frame forming part of a light. **2.** Side of any large object, such as one face of a *spire or tower. **3.** Space between the structural members of a *timber frame. **4.** Pierced walls of a *cloister facing the *garth.

panel 1. Flat plane surface surrounded by *mouldings or *channels, or by other surfaces in different planes. Architectural panels are generally rectangular, but can be circular, square, quatrefoiled, or other shapes. *Blind *tracery is really a type of panelling. The sunken surface of the panel is often *charged* with ornament, e.g. *parchemin. *See also* BOISERIE. Panels are commonly found in ceilings, doors, *wainscots, etc., and are separated by frames, etc., called *panel-dividers*, while the *beads and other mouldings holding them in their frames are *panel-mouldings* and can be of various types (e.g. *bolection, *ogee, etc). *Types of panel include*:

fielded: with a flat central portion projecting above the edges of the panel, and sometimes beyond the frame;

flush: with the face in the same plane as the frame around it, often with a flush *bead on the edges next to the frame to mask the joint;

linen-fold: decorated with *parchemin plié*;

lying: with its greater dimension horizontal;

raised and fielded: as *fielded*, i.e. with a flat raised surface, but surrounded by a sunken, moulded, or bevelled edge;

sunk: with the face recessed from the frame.

2. Subdivision of a *bay of a *timber-framed wall defined by *studs* and *rails*, called a *pane.

ABDM (1996); W.McKay (1957); J.Parker (1850); S (1901–2)

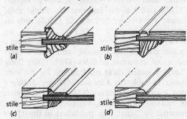

Selection of panels/panel-mouldings. (*a*) *Raised and Fielded* panel secured with two variations of *bolection moulding*; (*b*) *Flush* panel with *beaded* edge secured with *bolection* moulding; (*c*) *Flush* ply panel secured with two varieties of *planted* mouldings; (*d*) *Flush* panel held in *stile* with *solid* or *struck ovolo* upper moulding and *cavetto* lower moulding.

panel tracery *Perp. *tracery.

pane-work Division of an external wall into *panes or *panels, as in a *timber-framed structure.

Pani, Mario (1911–93) Mexican Paris-trained architect, he adopted *Modernist principles, and most of his works were designed with others. Among them were the *Reforma* Hotel (1936); housing-schemes at *Río Balsas* (1944), *Avenida Juárez* (1945), and *Paseo de la Reforma* (1946—destroyed); the National School for Teachers (1945–7); and the National Conservatory of Music (1946), all in México City. His vast *Unidad Habitacional Presidente Álemán*, south of México City (1947–50), consisted of over 1,000 *apartments, with schools, shops, etc., arranged in a scheme of landscaped grounds, and further developments followed, including *Unidad Habitacional Presidente Juárez* (1951–2—partly destroyed (1985)), and the huge *Ciudad Habitacional Nonoalco Tlatelolco* (1964–6—12,000 dwellings in over 100 buildings), the scale of which was perhaps repellent. He prepared (1947) the master-plan for the *Ciudad Universitaria*, and designed the *Secretaría de Recursos Hidráulicos* (1950–3), and the *Rectoría* (1951–2), as well as Acapulco Airport (1954–5). Other Modernist *CIAM-inspired plans were made for Yucatán (1951), Acapulco (1952), Ciudad Satélite (1954), and Ciudad Juárez, Chihuahua (1963). Despite praise bestowed on him, the numbers of demolished projects and failure of his work to age gracefully suggest his reputation, like that of many Modernists, has been inflated.

E (1994); Larrosa (1985); Ma (1983c); P (1982); J.T (1996)

panier 1. As *corbeil. **2.** Bracket or *corbel supporting a *beam or *truss shaped to soften the angle between them, resembling a basket-shape.

panoply Sculpted representation of parts of a suit of armour, with various weapons, arranged decoratively in a heap, in *military decoration.

Panopticon 1. Building, especially a gaol, planned on the radiating principle, with *wings branching from a central control-point, invented by **Jeremy Bentham** (1748–1832). **2.** Exhibition-room or show-room for novelties, etc.

panorama 1. Building containing a large picture arranged on the inside of a cylindrical surface around the spectator at the centre (*cyclorama*) or unrolled or unfolded and made to pass before the spectator so as to show the various parts in succession. If the picture (some parts of which are translucent) is viewed through an aperture, its sides continuing towards the picture, it is called a *diorama*, which can show weather-changes. The *Panorama National*, Paris (1859) is well known. **2.** An unbroken view of the whole surrounding area of a landscape.

Goulty (1991); N (1835); *OED* (1933); W.Pa (1852); S (1901–2)

Pantheon 1. *Rotunda erected by **Emperor Hadrian** (*r.*AD117–38) in Rome, with *coffered *concrete *dome (illuminated by an *oculus at the top) set on a thick circular *drum (the internal diameter of which is the same as the internal height to the top of the dome), and octastyle *portico attached to the drum outside. Any similar building is known as a *Pantheon*. **2.** Building for the general burial-place of or memorial to the great dead, such as the *Panthéon*, Paris (formerly *Soufflot's Church of *Ste-Geneviève*).

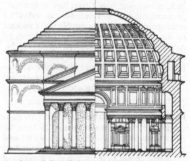

Pantheon (*left*) Half-elevation showing portico and low stepped dome, a type revived by Neo-Classicism. (*right*) Half-section showing *oculus* and *coffering*.

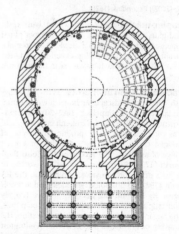

Plan of *Pantheon*.

Pantheon-dome Internally *coffered *dome, with a low, plain, severe, segmental-sectioned exterior surrounded by rings of concentric steps, resembling that of the Roman *Pantheon, much used in C18 and early C19 as part of the vocabulary of *Neo-Classicism, not necessarily with an *oculus.

pan-tile Plain roofing-tile with a profile resembling an **S** on its side (~) giving a corrugated effect when laid.

pantry Room in which provisions are stored. *Compare* BUTLER'S PANTRY.

Paoletti, Roland Romano (1931-2013) London-born of French-Hungarian-Italian extraction, as chief architect of the Jubilee Line Undergound Railway extension from Green Park to Stratford, he commissioned and oversaw the individual architectural practices responsible for 11 stations on the Line. A pupil and assistant of *Nervi, he believed in a seamless marriage between architecture and engineering, and he insisted that the Jubilee Line stations should not be claustrophobic, but be airy, light-filled volumes. He was called 'The Medici of London Transport'.

The Times (22 Nov. 2013), 67

Papendiek, Charles Edward (1801-35) Pupil (1818-24) of *Soane, he exhibited (1823-31) at the RA, and published (*c.*1820) a series of coloured lithographs of Kew Gardens through *Ackermann. He is best known as the author of *A Synopsis of Architecture, for the Information of the Student and Amateur, containing an Enumeration of the most celebrated Buildings of Antiquity*, etc. (1826).

Co (2008); Papendiek (1826)

papier-mâché Paper-pulp mixed with resin and glue, or consisting of shreds of paper glued together and pressed into a mould, used to make ornaments or wall- or ceiling-coverings. Invented *c.* AD 200 in East Asia, it was in use in Europe from C16.

Papworth, John Buonarotti (1775-1847) English architect/landscape architect/town-planner, he laid out the Montpellier (1825-30) and Lansdowne (1825-8) Estates, Cheltenham, Glos., and was one of the most prolific architects of his generation as well as a designer of a wide range of artefacts. The second son of **John Papworth** (1750-99), master-stuccoer, he worked in *Plaw's office for two years, exhibited at the RA from 1794, and promoted new ideas and technologies. By 1800 he had his own practice (largely domestic architecture), was able to take on pupils, and began to produce designs for publication. His drawing of a *Tropheum* to celebrate **Wellington** and **Blücher**'s victory at Waterloo (1815) caused him to be acclaimed as a second *Michelangelo, and he modestly took 'Buonarotti' as his second

name. He designed *conservatories, entrance-gates, coach-houses, stables, and the *Gothic *summer-house at Claremont, Surrey (1816), for **Prince Leopold of Saxe-Coburg** (1795-1865—later (from 1831) **King of the Belgians**) and **Princess Charlotte Augusta** (1796-1817). The latter's untimely death caused it to be adapted as her memorial. He prepared (1817-20) designs for the Park and Palace at Bad Cannstadt, near Stuttgart, for **King Wilhelm I** (*r.*1816-64): only part of the Park (in the English style) was realized, but Papworth was honoured with the title of 'Architect to the King of Württemberg'. He designed (1819) the famous *Egyptian-Revival gallery in P.F.*Robinson's Egyptian Halls, Piccadilly, London (1811-12—demolished), and for **William Bullock** (*fl.c.*1795-1826), builder and owner of the Egyptian Halls, he drew plans (1825-7) for a new town intended to be built by the River Ohio facing Cincinnati: named *Hygeia*, it never materialized. Papworth was responsible for many London shop-fronts and other buildings, and was a pioneer in the use of *iron for construction purposes. His monument to **Lieutenent-Colonel Sir Alexander Gordon** (1786-1815) on the field at Waterloo, Belgium (1815), was an early example of a broken column used as a memorial. He directed the Government School of Design (1836-7), and was a founder (1834) of the Institute of British Architects.

He contributed frequently to *Ackermann's *Repository of Arts* (1809-28). Papers, entitled *Architectural Hints* (1813, 1814, 1816, and 1817), were republished as *Rural Residences, consisting of a Series of Designs for Cottages, Small Villas, and other Ornamental Buildings* (1818, 1832), and he published (1823) designs for garden-buildings as *Hints on Ornamental Gardening. Rural Residences* was far more influential than most commentators have suggested: it appears to have been a stimulant for designs by *Schinkel and *Persius, notably the Court Gardener's House and Roman-Bath complex at Potsdam (1829-37) and the *Gothic Hunting-Lodge at the park at Glienecke (1827-8). In fact, he helped to create the rational Greek style that was so ubiquitous in the period 1815-40, yet his importance has not received the recognition it deserves. Papworth helped (1818-19) **William Henry Pyne** (1769-1843) with the descriptions of Marlborough House, St James's, and Kensington Palace, published as *Royal Residences* (1820), contributed to *Britton and *Pugin's *Public Buildings in London* (1825-8), and edited the fourth edition of *Chambers's *Treatise* (1826), adding much new material; he also wrote *Essay on the Causes of Dry Rot in Timber* (1803). Many designs in *Loudon's *Encyclopaedia* (1833) appear to have originated with Papworth.

His elder son, **John Woody Papworth** (1820–70), was the author of *Ordinary of British Armorials*, and his younger son, **Wyatt Angelicus van Sandau Papworth** (1822–94), founded the Architectural Publication Society and edited its great *Dictionary of Architecture* (1852–92). His pupils included James *Thomson and his brother, **George** (1781–1855—who practised in Ireland (he designed the famous cast-iron bridge (1822–7) over the Liffey in Dublin as well as churches for the Ecclesiastical Commissioners in Connacht)).

Co (2008); Graby (ed.) (1989); McHardy (ed.) (1977); *ODNB* (2004); J.B.Pa (1823, 1832); W.Pa (from 1852, 1879); *Trans. RIBA*, **i** (1835), 111–4

papyrus Decoration based on stylized versions of the flowers and leaves of the paper-reed (*Cyperus papyrus*), often found in Ancient-Egyptian architecture, notably on *capitals.

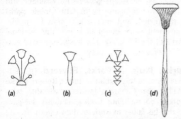

(a)   (b)   (c)   (d)

Stylized representations of papyrus decorations: (*a*) five-branched form indicative of Lower Egypt; (*b*) papyrus-sceptre; (*c*) abstraction of flowering papyrus; (*d*) Egyptian painted papyrus decoration resembling a bell-capital. Stems can vary in length.

parabema Room or area associated with the *bema of a *basilica.

parabola Curve based on a conic section, that is the intersection of a cone with a plane parallel to its side. It resembles a three-centred arch, vertically emphasized.

parade 1. Place (*parade-ground*) where troops assemble for parade. 2. Level space forming the interior or enclosed area of a fortification. 3. Public square or *promenade.

Paradise 1. Cloistered *atrium, *court, or *garth at the west end of a church. 2. West or south *porch of a church, including space above it, sometimes corruptly called a *parvise. 3. Burial-ground of a conventual establishment. 4. *Jerusalem, or innermost part of a *labyrinth or maze. 5. Park containing exotic animals. 6. Pleasure-ground. 7. Topmost gallery in a theatre, called the 'gods', with the cheapest seats.

Paradise garden Geometrical enclosed *Islamic garden of Persian origin with regularly laid out

*canals and paths dividing it into four areas, themselves divided by *paths. The canals represent the rivers flowing out of the Garden of Eden. A good example is the C17 garden of the *Tâj Mahal*, Agra. *See* MUGHAL GARDEN.

J.Brookes (1987); Lehrman (1980); M & P (2011); MM & T (1998); Moynihan (1980); Petruccioli (ed.) (1997); Ruggles (2008)

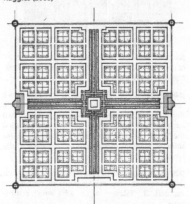

Paradise garden Tâj Mahal garden, Agra, surveyed (1818) by J.G.Hodgson, Surveyor-General of India. The formal geometry is composed of paths, planted areas, and canals.

parametric design Method of designing complex forms using computers in parametric and *algorithmic procedures based on relationships between lines, figures, or quantities: the generation of geometries from families of initial parameters and the design of the relationships of these to each other determine the outcome. By the mid-1960s it became clear that electronics would have a dramatic effect on architecture, for computers were used in the aerospace industries to calculate complicated warped surfaces, and by the 1980s were being harnessed to create shapes such as those found in *biomorphs, *Blobismus, *Deconstructivism, and *Zoömorphic or *New Animal architecture. Some architects have tended to favour ever more wilful distortion, creating alien forms which ignore established context.

Hudson (2010); Lynn (1999); Woodbury (2010)

parapet Low wall or barrier at the edge of a *balcony, *bridge, roof, *terrace, or anywhere there is a drop, and therefore danger of persons falling. Originally a feature of defensive architecture on *castles and town-walls, it often retained *battlements and other features, even when used for non-defensive purposes, e.g. on churches.

Parapets can be ornamented, pierced, or plain. A *parapet-gutter* lies behind the wall, with holes in the wall through which water is discharged.

parapet Pierced parapet with moulded *battlements* or *crenellations*, Sts Peter and Paul, Lavenham, Suffolk, typical of English Perp.

parastas 1. Part of the flanking wall of a Greek *temple *porch projecting beyond the front wall, finished with an *anta. 2. The space between two such flanking walls, outside the *naos, also called the *pronaos, so applied to a *vestibule. 3. *Parastata. 4. Element like a massive *pedestal at the termination of a grand formal *stair.

parastata, parastatica 1. Synonymous with *anta with only very small parts of the return-face exposed. 2. *Pilaster, again with small return-faces.

parchemin C16 development of *linenfold incorporating vines, foliage, etc.

parchemin plié As *linenfold.

parclose 1. *Screen marking off chapels or tombs from the rest of a church, e.g. between a *chancel and the chapel to its side. 2. Front of a *gallery, open or closed.

F.Bond (1908a)

parekklesion *Byzantine chapel.

parge 1. To *plaster. 2. *Parge or parget-work* is pargeting, or external plasterwork on *timber-framed buildings, commonly used in England from the late-*Tudor period, often decorated with patterns (indented or in low relief) produced by the application of carved timber moulds pressed against the *plaster before it dried. *Related terms include*:
parged verge: top of a *gable sealed with *mortar at its junction with a pitched roof where the roof-covering only projects very slightly over the *naked of the wall;
parget: 1. to cover or daub with plaster or ornamental plasterwork; 2. to cover or decorate with ornamental work, e.g. gilding, etc.;
parging: plaster lining inside a *chimney-flue or finishing a gable *verge.

Pâris, Pierre-Adrien (1745–1819) French architect, pupil of *Trouard (whom he succeeded as Architect to the Cathedral of *Ste-Croix*, Orléans, where he worked on the west front (1787–90)), he made his reputation with drawings of *Antique remains in Italy. He designed the interiors of the *Hôtel Crillon*, Paris (1774), and an extraordinary but unrealized palace for the Prince-Bishop of Basel, Porrentruy (1776). His Neuchâtel Town Hall, Switzerland (1784–90), a severe essay in *Neo-Classicism, has an entrance-hall containing baseless Greek-*Doric columns supporting low *vaults, a powerful combination. His taste for the exotic and for archaeology influenced his students *Percier and *Fontaine. He directed some important archaeological surveys in Rome (1806–17).

M & Wa (1987); P (1982); J.T (1996)

park Enclosed outdoor place of recreation, originally used for hunting. From C18 parks were created as *landscape-gardens for aesthetic and recreational pleasure. From C19 *public parks were created, and later larger areas for public enjoyment were designated, e.g. the National Parks of the USA. *See also* BUSINESS-PARK; DEER-PARK; INDUSTRIAL PARK; THEME-PARK.

Parke, Park, *or* **Parks, Edward** (*fl.*1790–1844) Son of the Dublin architect **Robert Parke** (*fl.*1772–92—*Cooley's former assistant, who worked on the Four Courts, Dublin). He succeeded his father to work on the western *façade of the Irish House of Commons (1787–94), to the designs of which **Samuel Hayes** (1743–95) contributed, much improved by *Gandon, later remodelled as the Bank of Ireland (1804) by Francis *Johnston (who filled in Parke's *Ionic *colonnade). He designed the buildings for the Royal College of Surgeons in Ireland, St Stephen's Green West (1806–10); stables and offices at Oriel Temple, Collon, Co. Louth (1812); and (1813) Dundalk Court-House (completed under John *Bowden). He was Architect to the Dublin Society, to the Linen Board, and to the Trustees of the Royal Exchange.

M.Craig (1969, 1982); *DIB* (2009); H.Duffy (1999); *DIA* (website) accessed 8 Jan 2013; McParland (1985)

Parker, John Henry (1806–84) English writer on architecture who published the works of several protagonists in the Oxford Movement, so was of considerable importance to the huge national upsurge of C19 Anglicanism. His 1836 *Glossary of Terms* (which went into several subsequent edns), with *Bloxam's work, must stand as one of the earliest (and most scholarly) influential texts of *Ecclesiology and the *Gothic Revival. He edited the fifth edition (1848) of *Rickman's seminal book, and published (1849) his *Introduction to the Study of Gothic Architecture* which, like his *Glossary*, went through many edns, and played a large part in the instruction of students of medieval architecture. He took numerous photographs of ancient buildings and archaeological sites in and around Rome (1860s and 1870s): they comprise a valuable record, for they show what has been lost since then.

J.Curl (2007); *ODNB* (2004); J.Parker (1850); Rickman (1848)

Parker, Richard Barry (1867–1941) English *Arts-and-Crafts architect, he practised (1896–1914) with his brother-in-law, *Unwin. An early work was 'Woodcote', a house at Church Stretton, Salop. (1896–7), incorporating motifs from English *vernacular architecture, which established his stylistic preferences. **Parker & Unwin**'s first major commission was to build the model village of New Earswick, near York (begun 1902), based on the precedents of Bournville and Port Sunlight, with low-density housing based on *vernacular forms. In 1903 they won the competition to design the first *Garden City at Letchworth, Herts., inspired by the ideas of Ebenezer *Howard, and from 1906 Unwin undertook the planning of Hampstead *Garden Suburb, while Parker contributed designs for several houses there. They published *The Art of Building a Home* (1901), but went their own ways after the 1914–18 war. Parker was involved in the new town of Pacaembu, São Paulo, Brazil (1917–20), and in England was responsible for the Wythenshawe Estate outside Manchester (from 1927) and the smaller Shelthorpe Road Estate at Loughborough, Leics. (1926–39).

Darley (1975); A.S.Gray (1985); Me.Miller (1992, 2002); M & G (1992)

Parker's cement Grey-brown *stucco rendering composed of burnt-clay nodules crushed to powder and mixed with *lime, sand, and water. Patented 1796, sometimes known as *Roman* or *Sheppey* cement, it hardened quickly and was commonly applied to inferior brickwork *façades as a substitute for *ashlar, the 'joints' suggested by scores made before the *cement dried. It was also used (without the addition of lime) for construction under water, as it had the peculiar property of hardening in such conditions: it was superseded by *Portland cement.

Gw (1903); W.Pa (1852)

Parkin, John Burnett (1911–75) Canadian *Modernist architect. He founded **John B.Parkin Associates** with his brother, **Edmund T. Parkin** (1912–94), and **John Cresswell Parkin** (1922–88—no relation—who trained under *Gropius). Among the firm's works are Toronto International Airport (1963–6), Toronto City Hall (1965—with Viljo *Revell), the Union Railway Station, Ottawa (1967–9), and the Trade Centre and Arena, Hamilton, Ontario (1985).

E (1994); K (1994)

parkway Scenic road pioneered in America, laid out in an area of preserved forest or a swathe of enhanced landscape. A precedent was *Olmsted's series of connected suburban *public parks linked by road at Boston, MA, designed with **Charles Eliot** (1859–97), completed 1902. However, the earliest (1913–23) appears to be by G.D. *Clarke from Bronx Park to Kensico Dam, created for recreational motoring, with access prohibited to anything other than private cars. W.H.*Manning's Milwaukee, Minneapolis, and Cincinnati Parkway followed, then Merritt Parkway, CT (1934–40), and S.W.*Abbott's Blue Ridge Parkway (designed 1935) linking the Shenandoah and the Great Smoky Mountains National Parks. The design of parkways was to influence that of *motorways.

Eliot (1902); Radde (1993); US Dept. Commerce (1966); US NPS (1964); Zapatka *et al.* (1995)

Parler Family German master-masons working in Swabia and Bohemia in C14 and early C15. **Heinrich I** (c.1300–71) was *Parlier* (foreman with responsibility for a *Mason's *lodge) at Cologne Cathedral, when the *choir was completed c.1322, but other works proceeded very slowly. He moved to Schwäbisch-Gmünd where he built the *nave (from c.1330) and (probably) the *choir (designed on hall-church principles) of the *Stadtkirche zum Heiligen Kreuz*, one of the most influential buildings of the *Sondergotik style. He may have worked on the choir of the Cathedral at Augsburg, the *Frauenkirche*, Nuremberg, and Ulm *Minster.

Peter Parler (1333/5–99), son of Heinrich, is the most celebrated of the tribe. He worked at Schwäbisch-Gmünd, Cologne Cathedral (possibly), and the *Frauenkirche*, Nuremberg, before being summoned to Prague (1356) by **Kaiser Karl IV** (r.1346–78) to work on the Cathedral of St Vitus (Veit), begun 1344 by Matthias of *Arras: he completed the choir (1385), the Wenceslas Chapel, and later the south *transept. He also designed and built the Charles Bridge over the River Vltava (Moldau), Prague (begun 1357), added the choir to St Bartholomew's, Kolín (1360–78), carried out works at St Barbara's, Kutná Hora (begun 1388), and was responsible for various tombs, shrines, and sculptures.

Johann, Heinrich's eldest son, repaired the Cathedral in Basel (completed 1363), and settled in Freiburg-im-Breisgau where he became Master of the Works at the Minster from 1359 (he may have designed the *chancel). Johann's son, **Michael II** of Gmünd (d.c.1387), who was Master of the Works at Strasbourg Cathedral from 1383, may have been responsible for modifying Erwin von *Steinbach's designs for the west front. He was also involved in the building of the Minsters at Freiburg and Ulm, and probably completed the towers of Basel Cathedral (c.1380). His brother, **Heinrich II** of Gmünd and Freiburg (d.c.1392), worked at Augsburg, Vienna, Cologne, and Prague, and succeeded Michael II at Ulm (1387-91). He also appears to have acted as a consultant for Milan Cathedral (1391-2), a job he probably got through his father-in-law, **Michael of Savoy**, who worked at Cologne.

Wenzel or **Wenceslaus** Parler (c.1360-1404), Peter's second son, worked on the south tower of St Vitus's Cathedral, Prague (c.1375-98). Settling in Vienna (c.1397), he became Master of the Works at the *Stephensdom*, and seems to have been responsible for the lower stages of the south tower. His brother, **Johann the Younger**, of Prague (d.c.1405), succeeded (1398) his father and brother as Master of the Works at St Vitus, proceeding with the erection of the south tower, and completing parts of the south transept. He was also involved at Kutná Hora.

The Parlers were masters of elegant, flowing *tracery, complex vaulting, and fine carving; their works had a profound influence throughout Germany, Austria, and Bohemia in C15 and C16.

A.Legner (ed.) (1978-80); Neuwirth (1890, 1891), Nussbaum (1994); P (1982); Recht (ed.) (1989); Swoboda (1943); J.T (1996)

parlour 1. Apartment in, e.g., a *monastery for conversation with outsiders or among inmates. **2.** Room set apart from a larger hall for private conversations, e.g. mayor's parlour in a town-hall. **3.** Sitting-room in a dwelling-house. **4.** Dining- or supper-room.

Parmentier, André Joseph Ghislain (1780-1830) Born in Enghien, Hainaut, Wallonia (now Belgium), he emigrated to the USA (1824), settling in Brooklyn, NY, where he founded a successful nursery. He was for a time the foremost exponent in the USA and Canada of the English style of naturalistic garden-design, known in America as the *Romantic style: main influences on his work appear to have been *Repton and *Loudon. Only a few design-projects by him have been documented: they include his own horticultural gardens, Brooklyn (from 1824); the Hosack Estate, Hyde Park, NY (1828-9—now the Vanderbilt Mansion National Historic Site); and a *campus-plan for King's College, Toronto (1830—now the University of Toronto), one of the earliest of its kind. A.J.*Downing admired his work.

B & K (2000); Downing (1841); Shoe (2001); Tay (2006)

Parminter, Jane (1750-1811) Architect, she and her cousin, **Mary Parminter** (1767-1849), travelled on the Continent for a decade from 1784, and (1795) decided to build a *cottage orné* as their home, overlooking the River Exe near Exmouth, Devon, possibly helped by their cousin, **John Lowder** (1781-1829), who would have been

serving his apprenticeship when the house (called *A La Ronde*) was started on site. Echoes of *San Vitale*, Ravenna, intermingle with *Regency exoticism in this extraordinary sixteen-sided building with wedge-shaped interconnected rooms set around a central octagonal hall, and the interiors were decorated with *shell-work, paintings by the Parminters, and feathers of game-birds, while furniture was embellished with semi-precious stones and *découpage*. The shell-gallery above the hall was encrusted with bones, glass, lichens, mica, painted decorations, pottery, shells, and stones.

ODNB (2004)

parotis, parotides, prothyrides Refers to *ancons, *brackets, or *consoles resembling the human ear.

parpend *Bond-* or *through-stone* visible on both sides of a wall, and therefore dressed or faced at both ends, as in *parpend ashlar*.

parquet 1. Floor finish of hardwood blocks laid in patterns (often herringbone) on a firm base and polished. *See* PLATED PARQUET. **2.** Orchestra-stalls of a theatre.

parquetry Patterned floor-surface of thin wood veneers, called *inlaid* or *plated* *parquet.

Parris, Alexander (1780-1850) American architect, self-taught largely through publications (e.g. those of *Nicholson and *Pain), he was also influenced by *Latrobe (e.g. in the house (1811-13) for **John Wickham** (1763-1838) at Richmond, VA). His best works were St Paul's Church (now the Episcopal Cathedral), Boston, MA (1819-21—Boston's first large Neo-Classical building), the Faneuil Hall or Quincy Market, Boston (1823-6), and the Stone Temple Unitarian Church, Quincy, MA (1827-8). Parris was involved in the organization of the profession into the American Institution of Architects.

Hamlin (1964); Kilham (1946); P (1982); *PA*, xxxix (1958), 149-52; J.T (1996)

parsonage 1. Benefice or living of a clergyman. **2.** *Rectory. **3.** *Vicarage, or house of an incumbent of a parish.

Parsons, William (1787-1857) Appointed Leics. County Surveyor (1823), he was later responsible for much road- and railway-building, and had a thriving private practice. His works included St George's Church, Leicester (1823-7); the House of Correction, Loughborough, Leics. (1824); Caythorpe Hall, Lincs. (1824-7); the castellated County Gaol, Welford Road, Leicester (1825-8—extended 1844-6); the Leicester and Rutland Lunatic Asylum, Leicester (1837, with additions of 1844—now part of the University of

Leicester); several Leics. *parsonages and *bridges; and the railway stations at Asfordby, Brooksby, Frisby, Melton Mowbray, and Rearsby for the Midland Railway (1846–8). He was in partnership with his ex-pupil, **Abraham Gill** (1803–34), with whom he designed a pair of semi-detached *Greek-Revival *villas, illustrated by *Loudon.

J.D.Bennett (2001); Co (2008); Jane Loudon (ed.) (1846)

parterre 1. Flat *terrace near a house laid out with flower-beds or decorative planting in a regular formation to be read from above. *Types include*:

parterre à l'anglaise: *plat or turfed lawn with a design cut into it. It can also be a large area of grass sparingly cut into to form patterns, surrounded by a path on the other side of which is a border of flowers;

parterre de broderie: *embroidered* parterre with the patterns formed of trimmed-box bordering beds of coloured earth, occasionally with bands of turf;

parterre d'eau: symmetrical arrangement of pools, surrounded by paths, with statuary and fountains;

parterre de compartiment: embroidered parterre symmetrical about two axes.

2. Orchestra-stalls of a theatre (*see* PARQUET (**2**)).

Crisp (1924); Goulty (1991); S (1901–2); Symes (2006)

Parthenon C5 BC Greek *Temple of *Athena Parthenos* on the *Acropolis, Athens, widely regarded as the most refined building featuring Greek *Hellenic *Doric architecture, and the model for much *Greek-Revival work, despite the fact that many details (e.g. the relationships of columns to *soffits) are less than satisfactory. The *Parthenon* had a *peristyle surrounding the *naos* and Virgin's chamber, with seventeen columns on the flanks and eight at each pedimented end. *Metopes* contained exquisite sculptures, as did the *pediments (much is now in the British Museum, London), while subtle optical refinements such as *entasis* and curved *stylobates* further contributed to its stature as a canonic work. Within the Virgin Goddess's chamber were four elegant *Ionic columns, so in some respects it was a synthesis of Doric and Ionic architecture.

M.Beard (2002); Chrisp (1997); D (1950); Korres (2000)

parti Choice, means, or method. *Parti pris* means a bias or a mind made up, so in architectural criticism the *parti* is the assumption made that informs a design as well as the choice of approach when realizing the scheme. *Prendre le parti* is to take a decision, or a certain course, as in architectural design.

Participatory design During the 1960s and 1970s architects and planners involved the public in consultations concerning housing and the environment: in the USA and UK there were many such experiments.

F.Becker (1977); Cross (ed.) (1972)

partition 1. *Screen. **2.** Non-loadbearing wall dividing a space into parts.

party-wall Wall between two buildings (e.g. semi-detached houses) or pieces of land intended for distinct occupation, shared by the two owners, in the use of which each has a partial right. Essentially it is a wall of which the two adjoining owners are tenants-in-common.

parvis(e) 1. Corruption of *Paradise, often, but incorrectly, applied to a room over a church *porch. **2.** Open area, *court, or *atrium in front of a church, or the entire space around a church, especially in France.

Pascal, Jean-Louis (1837–1920) French architect, trained under *Questel. He worked with C. *Garnier on the Paris *Opéra* and, from 1870, with *Labrouste. His buildings include various *mausolea in *Père-Lachaise* Cemetery and additions to the *Bibliothèque Nationale* (1878–81—*Rue Colbert* Stack Rooms—and 1906–17—*Rue Vivienne* Periodicals Reading Room and Stacks), Paris. His most significant building was the *Faculté de Médecine et de Pharmacie, Place de la Victoire*, Bordeaux (1880–8). He promoted an impeccable *Beaux-Arts* *Classicism that had a profound influence from the 1870s to 1914.

RIBAJ, 3 ser. xxi/21 (27 Jun. 1914), 537–44; P (1982); J.T (1996)

Pasqualini, Alessandro (1493–1559) Bolognese architect, he designed the tower of Ijsselstein Church, near Utrecht, The Netherlands (1532–5), with its vertical sequence of *Orders. The *Residenz*, Jülich (*c.*1548–71), which introduced *High-Renaissance motifs to Germany, shows that he was familiar with *Bramante's work.

Ck (1996); J.T (1996)

passage-grave Neolithic tomb-chamber, often covered with a *corbelled roof, with subsidiary chambers on three sides, entered through a long passage lined and roofed with stone slabs: the whole was covered by an earthen mound. A spectacular example is Maes Howe, Orkney. See MEGALITH.

Co (1991); J. Curl (2002a); Grinsell (1975, 1982)

pasticcio As *pastiche.

pastiche 1. Work produced in deliberate imitation of another or others, hence an eclectic composition incorporating allusions to earlier styles, often handled with considerable *originality*.

2. Transfer to another medium of a design, such as a book-cover as a *pasticcio* of a *mosaic. In *neither* (**1**) *nor* (**2**) is the word pejorative.

pastophorium One of two rooms on either side of the *chancel of an *Early-Christian or *Byzantine church.

pastoral column Column resembling a tree-trunk, with branch-stumps and bark, associated with the *cottage orné.

patand 1. Column or *pier-*base. **2.** *Plinth supporting columns, piers, or *pilasters. **3.** Bottom-rail, *cill, *sleeper, or *sole-piece of a *timber-framed wall.

patent-glazing Metal *glazing-bars supporting *glass without putty, employed in roofs and walls. Its dry construction enables speed of erection.

patera (*pl.* **paterae**) Circular or elliptical dish-like Classical ornament in bas-relief, like a shallow *medallion with raised decorated centre, often incorporating *flutes. When further enriched to represent a flower, it is termed *rosette. It occurs in *coffers, on *friezes, and as punctuations on walls, especially in C18.

paternoster 1. Row of bead-like ornaments on *astragals, etc. **2.** Passenger-lift composed of platforms in series fixed to a continuous loop of chains and constantly in motion.

path 1. Walk or track made for pedestrians connecting A to B. In a garden it is often unobtrusive, may afford views, and should aim to be as 'natural' as possible: it can systematically reveal what the designer intended. Moreover, paths may be used to divide various parts of a garden, and can consequently become important features, enabling *fabriques to be seen, features (such as rivers or lakes) glimpsed, or *parterres below inspected. Materials used for surfacing can add to character: paths may be of brick or *tile, laid in patterns; of gravel; of stone; of *hoggin; of pebbles; or of mown grass. Recent trends to lay *tarmac or paving-slabs have reduced the employment of local vernacular materials, with consequent loss of character. Properly designed paths greatly enhance gardens in both practical and aesthetic terms. **2.** *Pavement or footway by the side of a street, called *sidewalk* in the USA.

patio 1. Spanish roofless *courtyard, often with furniture or pools. **2.** Paved area adjoining a house.

Patkau Architects *See* ORGANIC ARCHITECTURE.

Patmore, Coventry Kersey Deighton (1823–96) English poet/essayist. An architectural critic of extraordinary perceptiveness, he realized that all great architecture turns gravitational thrust to aesthetic advantage, expressed in the *Orders and in *Gothic construction. He exposed fallacious arguments about ornament, 'morality' in architecture, etc., and saw clearly that any building only succeeds *as architecture* as an *expression of gravitational control and stability*. He knew that most contemporary architectural critics (e.g. *Ruskin) were hopelessly wrong. What he would have made of *Deconstructivism and C21 critics must remain in the realms of agreeable speculation.

Crook (2003)

patrician house Dwelling belonging to hereditary noble citizens of certain medieval Italian cities, or Orders of Gentlemen of the Free Cities of the German Empire. Some were built as towers for reasons of prestige, e.g. in Bologna, San Gimignano, etc.

Patrington, Robert (*fl.*1352–85) English master-mason, appointed (1368) Master-Mason at York *Minster, where he completed the *presbytery. He was probably responsible for the later parts of St Patrick's Church, Patrington, Yorks. (1368–71), in which case he was one of the most accomplished designers of his time, for the building is unusually beautiful and uncommonly homogeneous.

J.Harvey (1987)

Patte, Pierre (1723–1814) Influential French architect/editor/critic, he continued J.-F.*Blondel's *Cours d'architecture* (1771–7), responsible for many texts and plates dealing with building materials/construction. His most impressive publication, *Monuments érigés en France à la Gloire de Louis XV* (1765), included proposals for sophisticated civic designs for Paris. *Discours sur l'Architecture* (1754), *Études d'Architecture* (1755), *Mémoires* on street-planning (1766), on the building of the west front of *St-Sulpice* (1767), and *Essai sur l'Architecture Théâtrale* (1782), among others, were highly analytical works, and had a powerful effect on late-C18 French rationalist architecture. He analysed *Gothic architecture intelligently, showing that *buttresses, *pinnacles, *ribs, *piers, etc., were part of a logical structural system, using *Notre-Dame*, Dijon, as his exemplar.

M & Wa (1987); P (1982); Patte (1754); S (1901–2); J.T (1996)

patte d'oie Common in French formal gardens, where three, four, or five straight paths radiated out from a central point in a park or garden, so called from its resemblance to a *goose's foot*. It may have originated in town-planning schemes where roads joined in a space, e.g. *Piazza del Pòpolo*, Rome.

Goulty (1991); Symes (2006)

pattée *See* CROSS.

pattern-books Collections of published designs from which builders and craftsmen could copy architectural details. They were largely the means by which Classical architecture, as well as *Chinoiserie and *Gothick tastes, became widespread, notably in C18 and the early C19.

Paty, Thomas (*c*.1713–89) Member of a family of architects/carvers/masons active in C18 Bristol. An accomplished carver (e.g. his work in the Redland Chapel (1741–3)), he also carried out commissions for *Ware's Clifton Hill House (1746) and for **James Bridges** (*fl.* mid-C18) at Royal Fort (*c*.1758–60). Paty was involved in the development of Bath, Bridge, Clare, High, and Union Streets, and he and his sons probably designed the *elevations of the buildings on those streets as well as others in Charlotte, College, Great George, Lodge, and Park Streets, and houses in Berkeley Square and Crescent and Upper Berkeley Place. He executed Bridges's designs for the rebuilding of Bristol Bridge and the Church of St Nicholas (1763–9), where Paty replaced the old *steeple with a *Gothic tower and *spire designed by himself. Other works include the Theatre Royal (1764–6), St Michael's Church (1775–7), the central part of the Royal Infirmary (1784–8), all in Bristol, and other works in Wells, Som., and Glamorgan.

Co (2008); GJ & L (1979); Ison (1978); Roscoe *et al.* (2009)

Paul, Bruno (1874–1968) German member of the *Deutscher Werkbund*, designer of machine-made furniture, the *Typen-Möbel*. His achievements in standardization impressed Le *Corbusier. Stylistically, his architectural work was influenced by the Italian *Renaissance, then the *Sezession, Neo-*Biedermeier, *Art Deco, and finally *International Modernism. He designed the *Jugendstil hunting-room for the Paris *Exposition Universelle* (1900—which made such an impression it was shown again at the 1901 Munich and 1902 Turin Exhibitions); the interiors of several ships (including *Kronprinzessin Cecilie* (1907) and *Prinz Friedrich Wilhelm* (1908)); the beer-hall, restaurant, and other public rooms for the Werkbund Exhibition, Cologne (1914); and *Das Plattenhaus*, Hellerau, near Dresden (1925). As well as numerous interiors (e.g. for the luxurious liner *Bremen* (1927)), he designed many large villas in the Berlin suburbs (e.g. *Villa Warmboldt*, Wilmersdorf (1925–6)—which combined tradition with modern horizontal windows), International-Modernist offices (e.g. Disch offices, Cologne (1929)), and *stripped-Classical buildings (e.g. Gerling Insurance Co., Cologne (1930)). He formed (1929) a brief association with *Mies van der Rohe.

Joan Campbell (1978); Günther (1971, 1992); Jervis (1984); J.Popp (1916); Schäfer (1993); *Stadt*, **xxix**/10 (1982), whole issue; Ziffer *et al.* (eds) (1992)

Paulick, Richard (1903–79) German architect, pupil of *Dülfer and *Poelzig. With **Georg Muche** (1895–1987), he designed the prefabricated all-steel house for the *Bauhaus at Dessau-Törten (1926–7), and assisted *Gropius at that institution (1927–8). From 1929 he joined Gropius's Berlin *atelier*, planning huge housing developments. He emigrated to China (1933), where he taught at St John's University, Shanghai, also working in town-planning, and on railway- and harbour-construction. Returning to Europe (1949), he rose rapidly to positions of influence in the former German Democratic Republic, becoming Director of the Housing Research Institute (1952–4), and designing (from 1952) some of the massive blocks in the *Stalinallee*, Berlin, in the approved Classically inspired style of the *régime*. He directed the reconstruction of *Knobelsdorff's *Staatsoper, Unter den Linden*, Berlin (1951–5—completely redone 2011–15), as well as Dresden, which largely obliterated the old town-plan. He wielded considerable power, and was partly responsible for directing East-German building-construction towards industrialized prefabricated methods, which killed off craftsmanship. He was Chief Architect of a big housing development at Schwedt-an-der-Oder (1962–4), and at the chemical-workers' town of Halle-Neustadt to house 100,000 people, he promoted further his concept of *industrialized building. From 1967 he oversaw the reconstruction of the 'Forum', including the Crown Prince's Palace, *Unter den Linden*, Berlin, and from 1972 directed several institutes developing 'experimental building', which, in essence, meant further promotion of prefabrication techniques. His last works included the reconstruction of the *Nationaltheater*, Weimar (1972–3), and the building of the Town Theatre in Zwickau (1973).

M.Müller (1975); Volk (1983)

Pautre, Antoine Le (1621–79) After Le *Vau and *Mansart, the most inventive C17 French architect. He designed the *Chapelle de Port-Royal*, Paris (1646–8), but his most celebrated work was the *Hôtel de Beauvais*, Paris (1654–60), on an impossibly irregular site with two street-frontages. He imposed order, creating an internal *court on a strong axis, with an impressive variety of invention there and in the main staircase. He published *Desseins de plusieurs palais* (1652–3) and *Les œuvres d'architecture d'Anthoine Le Pautre* (1681), which included proposals for enormous country-houses and palaces even more Baroquely exuberant than those of Le Vau: these publications seem to have influenced *Wren and *Schlüter. His *Baroque *cascade at Saint-Cloud (*c*.1662–4) was one of his finest creations. His nephew, **Pierre Le Pautre** (*c*.1648–1716) worked at Versailles under *Hardouin-Mansart, where he decorated the *Salon de l'Œil de Bœuf* (1701) and chapel (1709–10), significant works in the beginnings of the *Rococo style.

R.Berger (1969); B (1982); Ha (1948); Jervis (1984); K.& L (1972); Kimball (1980); J.T (1996)

pave To lay a surface underfoot with bricks, paving-stones, *tiles, etc. *Related terms include*:

pavé: street, pavement, or *path paved with small blocks of stone in regular patterns, once common in Northern France and Belgium;

pavement: **1.** path surfaced with stones or other materials, including *cement, cobbles, flags, *rag-stones, square-setts, tarmacadam, etc.; **2.** footway for pedestrians beside a road or street used by vehicles, called *sidewalk* in the USA;

pavement-light: solid glass blocks set in a cast-iron frame or cast in a *reinforced-concrete grid bedded in a *pavement*, permitting light to penetrate a *basement;

pavement-pole: stone or metal upright, like a *bollard, linked to others by means of chains or bars, indicating, e.g., the boundary between public and private spaces.

paver: see PAVIOR.

pavilion **1.** Central, flanking, or intermediate projecting subdivision of a monumental building or *façade, accented architecturally by more elaborate decoration (e.g. *Orders, *pediments, or *palace-fronts), or by greater height and distinction of *skyline, as in the Louvre, Paris. **2.** Feature at the angle of a building, or terminating feature of a *wing of a larger structure, as in a symmetrical Palladian composition. **3.** One of several distinct buildings or *blocks, linked by e.g. corridors, as in a hospital or *prison, for reasons of hygiene or security. **4.** Detached ornamental building, such as a *gazebo or a *summer-house, often, but not always, dependent on a larger or principal building. **5.** Building with a *verandah in a sports-ground, e.g. cricket-pavilion. **6.** Temporary building. **7.** Covering or *canopy, so a tent-like structure, such as a canopied litter or the *velarium* over an *amphitheatre. **8.** Small detached building in a park, often associated with relaxation and pleasure, containing a *salon for refreshments, and two chambers: one for storage of provisions, and the other a lavatory. **9.** More elaborate version of (**8**), with several rooms, often treated with elaborate architectural frivolities, e.g. Brighton Pavilion, Sussex. *Compounds include*:

pavilion-ceiling: **1.** ceiling sloping equally on all sides to an apex, i.e. the underside of a pavilion-roof; **2.** *camp ceiling (**3**), also called *comb* or *tent* ceiling, with sloping convex sides, like those of a tent;

pavilion-roof: see ROOF;

pavilion system: as pavilion (**3**), i.e. system used for planning hospitals and similar buildings,

e.g. St Thomas's Hospital, London (1867–71, by **Henry Currey** (1820–1900)—partly demolished), recommended in C18 as a means of controlling infection.

pavior, paviour Brick or stone used to *pave, called *paver*.

Pawley, Martin (1938–2008) Combative English journalist, he had an apocalyptic vision of an urban future, yet that future was arguably the result of the radical *Modernism he espoused. Hating *conservation, tradition, *Post-Modernism, and deriding *Sustainable architecture as 'utterly meaningless', he was impatient with those who did not embrace modern technology with his own evangelical fervour: he foresaw a time when drugs, pornography, and virtual reality would replace social intercourse; all public infrastructures lay in ruins; and the doped populace inhabited minimalist single-person pods with hologram interiors. He laid claim to the mantle of *Banham by entitling one of his books *Theory and Design in the Second Machine Age* (1990), but his prognosis discarded Banham's optimism. He promoted his views in *Building Design* and *World Architecture*, regular contributions to *AJ*, and *The Late Show* (1989–95) for BBC2. Denouncing opinion that regarded architecture as a social service, when clearly it was nothing of the kind, he questioned assumptions that dwellings had to be 'Works of Architecture', and enthused about *High Tech, yet ignored shortcomings among its protagonists: disciples of the High-Tech religion did not tolerate reasoned criticism, and Pawley contributed to the shouting-match. His collected writings were published as *The Strange Death of Architectural Criticism*, a dubious demise with which, if true, he might be associated. On one point, however, he was irrefutably right: universal mortgage-provision inflates the *price* of housing, but that is a view Henry *Roberts held from the 1840s, so was hardly original.

AR, ccxxiii/1334 (2008), 37; Pawley (1971, 1973, 1975, 1978, 1990, 1994, 1998, 2007); *The Times* (28 Mar. 2008), 71; pk

pawn **1.** Anything given as security for a loan, etc. A *pawn-shop* or pawnbroker's establishment is therefore a building where goods are deposited in exchange for cash, to await redemption or sale: some of the earliest were established by C13 Lombards, and many medieval pawn-exchanges (called *Monti di Pietà*) were founded in Italy (e.g. Perugia and a large one in Naples). **2.** Gallery, *colonnade, or covered passage where goods are exposed for sale, especially in a *bazaar.

Paxton, Sir Joseph (1803–65) English gardener/architect. Discovered by **William Spencer** (1790–1858—**6th Duke of Devonshire** (from

1811)), he was appointed (1826) Head Gardener at Chatsworth, Derbys., where he remained for 30 years, cultivating plants, tending and improving the gardens, and designing buildings. Entirely self-taught, his main influences were *Loudon and Payne *Knight. Encouraged by the Duke, he published *The Horticultural Register* (1831–5) and *Paxton's Magazine of Botany and Flowering Plants* (1834–49). He began constructing (1831) *conservatories at Chatsworth, and used the *ridge-and-furrow system of glazed roofs invented by Loudon (1817), patenting his own variation (1850). As a designer he made his reputation with the elegant 'Great Stove' conservatory at Chatsworth (1836–40—destroyed 1920), then the biggest glass-house in Europe, using sheet-glass, the manufacture of which had recently been perfected by **Chance Bros.** of Birmingham. The curved ridge-and-furrow glazed timber roof was carried on arched laminated-timber frames supported on cast-iron columns and buttressed by the side-arches over the flanking *aisles. Although Decimus *Burton was involved in a consultative capacity, the design was essentially Paxton's, who was to turn more and more to architecture.

Paxton created the village of Edensor, near Chatsworth (1838–48), drawing on a range of styles, mostly *Italianate, for the houses (John *Robertson helped to prepare drawings for them), and designed Prince's Park, Liverpool (1842–4), and Birkenhead Park, Ches. (1843–7), the last among the first English *public parks (realized under *Kemp), the layout of which was an influence on *Olmsted. For these works, and also the important *cemetery at Coventry (1845), Robertson again provided collaboration. Paxton constructed (1849–50) a special conservatory for the large-leaved *Victoria regia* (now *Victoria amazonica*) lily, in which that exotic plant flowered for the first time in England. The structural advances in the lily-house helped in the creation of the Crystal Palace for the Great Exhibition, London (designed and built 1850–1), for which Paxton drew on his experiences of greenhouses at Chatsworth. That vast building was remarkable for several reasons: it was designed so that all its constituent parts could be *prefabricated, erected, and dismantled on site, the first example of a very large-scale *industrialized building; it only took just over six months to build; and it was the model for a series of huge C19 exhibition buildings. It earned Paxton his knighthood (1851). After Robertson left Paxton's office, the latter entered into partnership (1847) with his son-in-law, **George Henry Stokes** (1827–74), and together they laid out the gardens beside the re-erected and enlarged (1852–4) Crystal Palace at Sydenham, South London, which were widely admired. From 1851 Paxton concentrated on architectural work, and he and Stokes designed Mentmore Towers, Bucks. (1850–4), a sumptuous country-house in the *Jacobethan style for the **Rothschild** family. He carried out extensive alterations to the Devonshires' Lismore Castle, Co. Waterford, Ireland (1850–8), and designed the house and gardens at Ferrières, near Paris (1853–9), again for the Rothschilds, in a French-*Renaissance style. As noted previously, Paxton was a significant figure in the creation of public parks: among his other designs in this field were those at Dundee, Dunfermline, Glasgow, Halifax, and, of course, Sydenham.

AH, **iv** (1961), 77–92; Berlyn & Fowler (1851); Bird (1976); Chadwick (1961, 1966); Colquhoun (2003); D & E (1994); Hi (1977); Hix (1996); J.McKean (1994); *ODNB* (2004); Pe (1976)

Peabody & Stearns Boston, MA, architectural firm founded by **Robert Swain Peabody** (1845–1917) and **John Goddard Stearns** (1843–1917), whose work was of national importance throughout the USA (*c.*1886–1914). They pioneered the American *Colonial Revival but also influenced *Cram and others with their *Gothic-Revival work. Kragsyde, Manchester-by-the-Sea, MA (1883–5—destroyed), combined the *Shingle style with elements drawn from English *Arts-and-Crafts work, and was one of their best houses. By the 1890s the firm had adopted *Classicism, as in their work for the World's Columbian Exposition, Chicago (1892–3), but several houses drew on the *Federal and Colonial *Georgian styles. Peabody & Stearns created some of the most significant buildings in New England at the turn of the century. They also designed railway stations including Boston, MA (1872–4—destroyed), Jersey City, NJ (1889–90), and Union Station, Duluth, MN (1890–1).

ARe, **I**, (1891), 151–98; D & S (1967); *JSAH*, xxxii/2 (May 1973), 114–31; Ms (1964); P (1982); V.J.Sy (1971, 1974, 1989); S (1971); J.T (1996)

Peach, Charles Stanley (1858–1934) British architect, he worked with H.R.*Gough in London from 1882 before setting up on his own (*c.*1885). Specializing in the design of electricity generating-stations, he advised on several in London and elsewhere, showing considerable ingenuity, such as the raised garden over the electricity transformer-station in Brown Hart Gardens, London, with a splendid *Mannerist domed *pavilion at each end (1904). He designed 127 Stamford Street, London (1915), with Egyptianizing detail. Responsible for the Centre Court for the Lawn Tennis Association at Wimbledon, he used 'board-finished' *reinforced-concrete earlier than Owen *Williams's Wembley Stadium (1934).

A.S.Gray (1985)

pearc, pearch *See* PERCH.

Pearce, Sir Edward Lovett (c.1699–1733) A relative of *Vanbrugh, from whom he appears to have gained (probably 1716–23) some architectural knowledge, Pearce was one of the most important *Palladian architects working in C18 Ireland. His first important commission seems to have been the interior and wings at Castletown, Co. Kildare (c.1726–7), begun by *Galilei: the handsome entrance-hall with columnar *screen was the precedent for several later designs for Irish country-houses. Pearce designed Bellamont Forest, Co. Cavan, (c.1729—Ireland's first mature Palladian *villa), Drumcondra House, Co. Dublin (1727), and the Archiepiscopal Palace, Cashel, Co. Tipperary (c.1727–32), but his masterpiece is unquestionably the Parliament House (now Bank of Ireland), Dublin (from 1729—completed posthumously under the direction of Arthur Dobbs (1689–1765)), with its massive *Ionic *portico and projecting wings. His *obelisk with *grotto at Stillorgan, Co. Dublin (c.1733), was derived from *Bernini's fountain in the *Piazza Navona*, Rome. Appointed (1731) Surveyor of Works and Fortifications in Ireland in succession to *Burgh, he was knighted in 1732. His German assistant, *Cassels, took over his practice after his death.

Co (2008); Co & M.Craig (eds) (1964); M.Craig (1969, 1982); *DIB* (2009); F.Hall (1949); *IAR*, xvii (2001), 96–106; *IARY*, xii (1996), 27–34; McP (2001); *ODNB* (2004); *QBIGS*, xvii/1–2 (Jan.–June 1974), 110–14

pearling Also *beading*. *Moulding consisting of repetitive beads resembling pearls.

Pearson, John Andrew (1867–1940) English architect who settled in Toronto (1888) and trained under *Darling, becoming (1892) his partner. He rebuilt the central block of the Parliament, Ottawa (1916–24), and the Bank of Commerce, Toronto (1929–31).

K (1994)

Pearson, John Loughborough (1817–97) Distinguished English *Gothic-Revival architect, he trained under Ignatius *Bonomi and worked with *Salvin and P.C.*Hardwick before establishing his own practice (1843). At first influenced by A.W.N.*Pugin, by the 1850s he began to draw on Continental Gothic for his precedents. His first significant church was St Peter's, Vauxhall, London (1859–65), a robust essay in early-French *First Pointed, with *vaults of brick and stone ribs, plate-*tracery, an apsidal *chancel, and proportions based on the *Golden Section. His greatest works include his soaring St Augustine's, Kilburn, London (1870–97), with a tower and *spire derived from *St-Étienne*, Caen, Normandy, and internal *buttresses dividing the *aisles into *bays in the manner of Albi Cathedral, France. His Truro Cathedral, Cornwall (1880–1910), again drew on Franco-English sources, and his under-

standing of Gothic vaulting was nowhere better demonstrated. He designed Sts Agnes and Pancras, Ullet Road, Sefton Park, Liverpool (1883–5), one of the noblest Victorian buildings in North-West England, and was also responsible for St John's Cathedral, Brisbane, Australia (from 1886), modified by his son, **Frank Loughborough Pearson** (1864–1947): it was only completed 1988–2001. J.L.Pearson also designed several houses, including Quar Wood, Stow-on-the-Wold, Glos. (1845–9—altered beyond recognition 1954–8), and Roundwyck, Kirdford, Sussex (1868–70). A list of his works is given in Quiney (1979).

J.Curl (2007); D & M (1985); Quiney (1979); J.T (1996)

pebble-dash External wall-rendering made by casting small pebbles on a second coat of *render before it sets, also called *roughcast or *harling. *Other compounds include*:

pebble-wall: wall faced with pebbles bedded in *mortar or constructed of pebbles or uncut *flints;

pebble-work: pebbles set in mortar forming designs on walls or *pavements, often with stones of different colours, found, e.g., in *grottoes.

pecking As *picked.

pectinated Ornamented with narrow parallel elements, resembling the teeth of a comb, as on *friezes, *string-courses, etc.

Peddie & Kinnear Scots architectural firm founded (1845) by **John Dick Peddie** (1824–91) and **Charles George Hood Kinnear** (1830–94—who became a partner (1855)). Peddie had been apprenticed to *Rhind, from whom he imbibed a sound knowledge of Graeco-Roman (e.g. Sydney Place United Presbyterian Church, Duke Street, Glasgow (1857–8—later offices)) and *Italianate (at numerous Banks (e.g. Stirling (1854) and Maybole, Ayrshire (1856)) styles. On occasion both *Romanesque and *Gothic elements were mixed with *Renaissance architecture, as at the Chalmers Hospital (1861), the Royal Infirmary Convalescent Home (1866—later Corstorphine Hospital), and the St Cuthbert's Poor House (1867—later Western General Hospital, much altered), all in Edinburgh. Probably his best work was the *atrium and domed telling-room of the Royal Bank of Scotland Head Office, Edinburgh (1857). Kinnear had been apprenticed to *Bryce, from whom he derived his Franco-Scottish late-Gothic and *Scottish Baronial styles. Among his works may be cited Morgan Hospital, Dundee (1863—later the Academy), the Town House, Aberdeen (1868–74), and several houses (Drygrange, Roxburghshire (1887)). Also Baronial was his Cockburn Street, Edinburgh (1859–64).

The firm designed numerous churches, including the Pilrig Free Church, Edinburgh (1861-3—with *plate-tracery reminiscent of the *Rogue work of *Teulon), and the Blythswoodholme Hotel, Hope Street, Glasgow (1875-7—later offices), which was one of the largest hotel projects in Britain at the time, and reflects the influence of Alexander *Thomson on the practice in the mid- to later-1870s. Also major works were the three hydropathic establishments: Dunblane (1875-8—Italianate); Craiglockhart, Edinburgh (1877-9—Thomsonesque Neo-Classical); and Callander, Perthshire, later Stirling (1879-81—French *Second Empire, with **Francis Mackison** (1822-84)). From 1879 the firm was renamed **Kinnear & Peddie** by **John More Dick Peddie** (1853-1921—Peddie's son, who had worked with 'Middle' *Scott and had studied in Germany) and Kinnear, and after Kinnear's death George Washington *Browne was active in the partnership (c.1895-1907). Later works include the Bank of Scotland, George Street, Edinburgh (1883—an essay in the Italianate *palazzo* style, beefed up with early Renaissance detail), the *Beaux-Arts* Classical entrance to the Caledonian Station, Edinburgh (later (1899-1903) part of the Caledonian Hotel), and the National Bank, Glasgow (1899—a *Baroque confection, later the Cooperative Bank). The younger Peddie designed Westerdunes, North Berwick, Lothian (1908—a fine house in the *Jacobean style). Kinnear was a pioneer in the use of the camera for architectural purposes, inventing (1857) the first bellows camera for portability, a development of a much heavier folding camera invented by Francis *Fowke.

DW; *RIASQ*, **iv** (1922), 6–9, 179–201; J.T (1996)

Pede *or* **Peede, Hendrik van** (*fl.*1516-30) Architect of the *Flamboyant *Gothic *Stadhuis*, Oudenaarde, Belgium (1525-36). He also worked in Brussels from 1516, especially on the *Broodhuis* (1516-36), and remodelled the chapel at the Castle of Leuven, Belgium (1531-2). He was one of the last of the great Gothic architects working in the region.

Bae: *Belgium* (1931)

pedestal Substructure, consisting of a *plinth, *dado (or *die), and *cornice, beneath a column-*base in Classical architecture; used as a support for an *obelisk, statue, *urn, etc.; or found in *balustrades, terminating rows of *balusters, and supporting *vases etc. A Classical *podium is a continuous elongated external pedestal, while inside a building it is expressed as a *chair-rail, dado, and *skirting. *Orders used on *triumphal arches have pedestals for reasons of composition and massing in the combination of *arcuated and *columnar-and-trabeated forms. *See* BALUSTER.

pediment Low-pitched triangular *gable following the roof-slopes over a *portico or *façade in Classical architecture, formed with raked *cornices of the same section as that of the horizontal *entablature at its base and mitring with it in part. *Doric examples often omit the *mutules under the sloping cornices. The triangular *tympanum framed by the raking and horizontal cornices was the *field* left plain or embellished with sculpture in high relief. *Greek or *Greek-Revival pediments were lower in pitch than Roman examples. Pediments may crown subordinate features such as *doorways, *niches, windows, etc., and in such cases are termed *fronton*. The triangular pediment is the most usual, but the *segmental* pediment was evolved in *Antique Roman architecture in AD C1, and found on buildings connected with the worship of Isis, a goddess associated with the crescent-moon. For *pediment-arch see* ARCH. *Types of pediment include*:

broken: with gap in the middle of the lower horizontal cornice and with raking cornices stopping before they can meet, so having no apex;

broken-apex: with raking sides too short to meet at the apex, also called *open* or *open-topped*;

broken-base: with the horizontal base lacking a middle section, also called *open-bed*, often occurring in C18 door-cases with *fanlights breaking upwards into the lower cornice;

scrolled: *open-topped* segmental pediment with segmental tops curling inwards as *scrolls, or with the tops in the form of two *ogees ending in scrolls, called *bonnet*-scroll, *goose-neck*, or *swan-neck*.

J.Curl (2001, 2005)

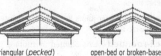

triangular (*pecked*)   open-bed or broken-base triangular (*pecked*)

open-topped or broken-apex triangular (*solid lines*)   true broken or open triangular (*solid lines*)

In both cases the entablature at an angle is *raking*.

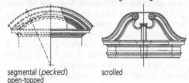

segmental (*pecked*)   scrolled
open-topped
segmental (*solid lines*)
pediment

peel, pele Fortified tower-house with vaulted ground-floor for cattle or storage, found especially in the Border-country between Scotland and England.

Peets, Elbert (1886–1968) American landscape architect, he first met Werner *Hegemann (c.1915), with whom he collaborated on various plans in WI as well as on *The American Vitruvius* (1922), one of the finest C20 books on *urban design. Peets established his own practice (1921), and became a leading critic of landscape architecture. He headed the planning of Greendale, WI, one of the towns sponsored by the Federal Government during the Depression: it was influenced by the work of Ebenezer *Howard, by various historic towns in Europe, and by the *Colonial architecture of Williamsburg, VA. After the 1939–45 war he planned Park Forest, IL, with five neighbourhoods adapted to the undulating site. He was one of the earliest protagonists of what became *New Urbanism.

B & K (2000); H & P (1972); Spreiregen (ed.) (1968); Shoe (2001)

pele *See* PEEL.

pelican *Gothic sculpture of the bird piercing her breast with her beak to draw blood to feed her young, symbolic of Piety and the Eucharist.

Pellegrini, Pellegrino (1537–90) *See* TIBALDI.

pellet *Band enriched with a series of closely spaced *discs or half-balls found in *Romanesque architecture.

pelta Form resembling a wide shield, with sides swooping up and returning as eagle- or ram-heads, often found in *Neo-Classical design (*see* DORIC ORDER).

Pembroke, 9th Earl of (c.1689–1750) *See* HERBERT, HENRY.

pencilling *Mortar-joints in brickwork painted to emphasize them.

pencil-rounded *Arris blunted by rubbing to form a slightly rounded edge.

pendant Fixed hanging ornament, resembling an elongated *boss or inverted *finial suspended from *Perp. fan-*vaulting, *Jacobean ceilings, *posts of timber roof-*trusses, *staircase *newels, or at the mitring of *barge-boards at the apex of a *gable. *Compounds include*:
pendant-post: upright post set against a wall, the lower end resting on a *corbel or *capital, with a hammer-beam or tie-beam fixed to its upper end, as in a *hammer-beam truss;
pendent frieze: *Gothic *cornice, or openwork series of pendants arranged as interlacing C18 *Gothick arches.

pendentive *See* DOME.

pendill Base of a vertical *post in e.g. a *jetty or a *newel in a *stair, ornamentally carved. A *pendant or *pendicle.

Penn, John (1921–2007) English architect. Influenced by the work of *Neutra and *Mies van der Rohe, his plans were often strongly axial: they include houses at Bawdsey Hall (1962–3), Hasketon (1961), Rendham (1966–7), Orford (1967–8), Shingle Street (1967–72), Broomheath, Woodbridge (1963–4), and Westleton (1969–71), all in Suffolk.

C20 (Spring 2007), 39; *Journal of the C20 Society: C20 Architecture* iv (L: C20 Soc., 2000)

Pennethorne, Sir James (1801–71) English architect, most of whose work was for *Nash or the Government. Brought up in Nash's household, he entered Nash's office (1820) and worked with A.C.*Pugin. Later he completed the *Picturesque Park Villages, Regent's Park. Employed (1832) by the Commissioners of Woods and Forests, in 1843 he became Architect to the Commissioners. He designed Victoria Park, Bethnal Green; Kennington Park; and Battersea Park, and prepared many schemes for urban improvements. His best-known public building was the Public Records Office, Chancery Lane, London (1851–70), in which the *module was arrived at by cells made of iron with shallow brick *vaults, the whole of fire-resistant construction. He also designed the sumptuous State Ball Room, Buckingham Palace (1853–5), the Duchy of Cornwall Offices, Buckingham Gate (1854), and what is now the Museum of Mankind, London (1866–70). His brother, **John Pennethorne** (1808–88), was also a pupil of Nash, and made detailed studies of the *optical corrections at the *Parthenon, Athens (published 1844), which prompted *Penrose to pursue the matter.

J.T (1996); *ODNB* (2004); Tyack (1992)

Penrose, Francis Cranmer (1817–1903) English architect/archaeologist, he worked for *Blore before travelling extensively in Europe. He realized the significance of John *Pennethorne's paper (1844) on *optical corrections in Ancient-Greek architecture, and under the aegis of the Society of *Dilettanti made accurate records of the Periclean monuments of Athens (1846–7), working with **Thomas John Willson** (1824–1903). The results of the survey were published (1847), and his vast tome, *Principles of Athenian Architecture* was published (1851), with a further expanded edn (1888). He designed the entrance-gate to Magdalene College, Cambridge, and the Cornish porphyry *sarcophagus of **Arthur Wellesley** (1769–1852—**1st Duke of Wellington** from 1814) in St Paul's Cathedral *crypt, London (1858), among other works.

ODNB (2004); Penrose (1851); J.T (1996)

pent Sloping *lean-to roof, e.g. a *canopy over a *doorway, or over a low building set against a higher one. A pent carried round a building or across a *façade is a *skirt, and a skirt carried round the house supported on slender columns is a *verandah. *Penthouse* or *pentice* is therefore: **1.** structure erected against the sides of another building as a lean-to, that is with a monopitched or pent roof; **2.** covered walkway set against a larger building or buildings; **3.** structure occupying part of the area of a roof of a building used as a select separate dwelling; **4.** protection from the weather over a doorway or window (i.e. same as *pent*).

pentastyle *See* PORTICO.

pepperpot Small circular *turret or *tourelle with a conical roof, called a *pepperbox turret*.

perch Small *bracket or *corbel such as those found near an *altar in a church to carry a reliquary, statue, etc. Also called *pearc* or *pearch*.

Percier(-Bassant), Charles (1764–1838) French *Neo-Classical architect who studied with A.-F.*Peyre and in Rome before establishing (1794) a Parisian architectural practice with *Fontaine. As **Percier & Fontaine** the firm became leading architects of the Napoléonic period, and was largely responsible for the creation of the *Empire style, the epitome of which was at *Malmaison*, with its celebrated *tent-room and other ravishing interiors (1799–1803). The two men were appointed (1801) Architects to the Government, designed the interiors of the Tuileries and St-Cloud Palaces, and extended the Louvre, Paris. They also laid out the *Rue de Rivoli*, Paris, with its arcaded ground-floors, and carried out extensive works at Fontainebleau, Compiègne, and Versailles. Their *Arc de Triomphe du Carrousel* (1806–8) shows their mastery of Roman *Antique *Classicism and refinement of detail. Their *Palais, maisons, et autres édifices modernes dessinés à Rome* (1798) and *Receuil de décorations intérieures, comprenant tout ce qui a rapport à l'ameublement* (1801) were influential throughout Europe and America, and ensured the *Empire* style was widely disseminated.

Biver (1963, 1964); Duportal (1931); Jervis (1994); M & Wa (1987); J.T (1996); D.Wa (1986)

Peressutti, Enrico (1908–76) *See* BBPR.

perforate To form openings in something: a *perforated wall* therefore has openings, often arranged in patterns.

pergola Two parallel rows of columns or *piers carrying *beams and a structure for climbing plants, flanking a *path, set in a garden and often attached to a dwelling.

peri- Enclosing, or surrounding. *Compounds include*:

peribolus: Wall or *colonnade around a Greek *temple or a sacred space, or the space itself;

peridrome: *see peristyle*;

perimeter-block: *apartment-block   designed around an internal *court or garden;

peripteral: of a building surrounded by a single range of columns (*periptery* or *peristyle*);

periptery: row of columns around a temple, also called *peristyle*. A *peripteral building*, e.g. a Greek temple, has a continuous colonnade around it;

peristyle: *periptery, peristasis*, or colonnades surrounding a building or *court. *Peridrome* is the space between the colonnade and the solid wall of the *cell* behind them, e.g. in a Greek temple;

peristylium: inner court surrounded by a colonnade.

perithyrides *See* ANCONES.

perpend *See* PARPEND.

Perpendicular Third and latest of the English *Gothic architectural styles, also known as *Third Pointed or Rectilinear*, it followed from the previous *Decorated* or *Second-Pointed style. Perp. first emerged in designs of *c.*1332 for the *chapter-house and *cloisters of old St Paul's Cathedral, London (destroyed), by William de *Ramsey, and was further developed at Gloucester Cathedral, where the *chancel (*c.*1337–57) displays many of its attributes. An English style, it has no Continental, Irish, or Scottish equivalent, and survived for more than three centuries (the fan-vaulted hall staircase at Christ Church, Oxford, is *c.*1640): it was the first of the Gothic styles to be revived in C18.

Perp. is immediately recognizable by its pronounced verticals and horizontals in *blind panels covering wall surfaces and in *tracery (where the *transoms are often ornamented with miniature *battlements, and *mullions rise straight up to the *soffits of window-openings). Apertures gradually acquired flatter tops, with arches of the four-centred type. *Vaults evolved from the complicated varieties involving *liernes into the *fan-vaults first found at the Chapter House of Hereford Cathedral (destroyed 1769) and the Cloisters of Gloucester Cathedral (both second half of C14), and developing into the spectacular fan-vaulting of King's College Chapel, Cambridge (early C16), and the *Lady Chapel (or Chapel of **King Henry VII** (*r.*1485–1509)) at Westminster Abbey (*c.*1503–12). Rectangular *mouldings framing door- or window-openings formed cusped blind *spandrels (often ornamented) reinforcing the controlled panel-like appearance: those *hood-mouldings terminated in carved *label-stops. Indeed, the panel-motif is one of the most recognizable features of the style, each framed panel having an arched top, often cusped, and is repeated in rows in tracery and over the walls as *blind panels.

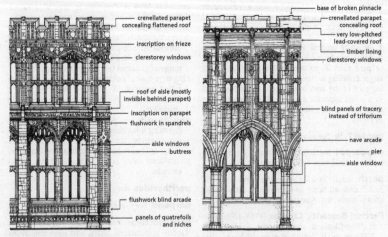

Typical Perp. external (*left*) and internal (*right*) bay, Holy Trinity, Long Melford, Suffolk.

Windows got larger, composed of many *lights (repeating the panel-like forms), and often filled the entire wall between *buttresses. Other characteristics included extensive use of the *bowtell; developed employment of the double-*ogee; quatrefoils set in square compartments; and bases with circular rolls, bells, and cushions over octagonal sub-bases of bell-like form.

The Perp. style is commonly found in parish-churches, especially in East Anglia, the Cotswolds, and Somerset, where great wealth was created by the wool trade. *Clerestoreys were added to existing churches, and they often were vast, airy, and light: as *naves were increased in height to accommodate ranges of large Perp. windows in their clerestoreys, roofs were flattened, and disappeared behind crenellated decorative *parapets. In East Anglia, especially, *chancels were not distinctly compartmented, being part of the main volume of the church, but demarcated by means of elaborate timber *screens, often sumptuously decorated and coloured. Mouldings tended to become mechanical, and foliage less deeply cut than previously: a common moulding was the grapevine or *trail, often found on screens and *canopies.

The use of hood-mouldings, the flattening of roofs and arches, the adoption of widespread crenellations, and the elaboration of lierne- and later fan-vaulting gave the Perp. style its predominant flavour. Perp. architecture from the end of C15 to the beginnings of the *Elizabethan style is often called *Tudor, and frequently featured brick walls ornamented with *diaper-work, very flattened arches, and prominent hood-mouldings. The Tudor

style was revived in C19, often for schools, workhouses, and collegiate buildings.

Harvey (1978); W.Pa (1852); J.Parker (1850)

Perrault, Claude (1613–88) French physician/amateur architect whose fine translation of *Vitruvius (1673) achieved fame, and still commands respect. He played some part (with Le *Vau and Le Brun) in the design of the celebrated east front of the Louvre in Paris (1665–74), an astonishingly 'modern' Classical building for its date, with *coupled *Corinthian columns set on a plain *podium, but he was not solely responsible (indeed his brother, **Charles** (1628–1703), claimed to have conceived the design, and that Claude had used it in the finished building). The noble *façade, which was partly influenced by a design of *Bernini, impressed *Wren sufficiently for him also to use twinned columns on the west front of St Paul's Cathedral, London. Perrault published *Ordonnance des Cinq Espèces de Colonnes* (1683—translated into other languages later) in which he expressed doubts that *proportion could determine beauty, which attracted the opprobrium of N.-F.*Blondel. Perrault was an important figure in the evolution of French rationalism, and indeed one of the fathers of the *Enlightenment.

R.Berger (1993, 1994); Bt (1982); Ha (1948); Hn (1973); M & Wa (1987); Ch.Perrault (1993); C.Perrault (1683); Petzet (2000); Picon (1988); Soriano (1972); J.T (1996)

Perret, Auguste (1874–1954) French architect/building-contractor. He and his brothers **Gustave**

(1876-1952) and **Claude** (1880-1960) were among the first to exploit the architectural possibilities of *reinforced concrete as evolved by *Hennebique. **Perret Frères's** first reinforced-concrete multistorey building was the celebrated apartment-block at 25b *Rue Franklin*, Paris (1903-4), which has **faïence* patterns in the *panels. They built the *Théâtre des Champs Élysées*, Paris (1911-13), loosely based on designs by **Roger Bouvard** (1875-1961) and Henri van de *Velde. Perret and his engineer, **Louis Gellusseau** (1883-1974), evolved reinforced-concrete technology so that the surface of the material itself would be exposed and sufficient thickness of *concrete (theoretically) provided to ensure the internal steelwork was protected from damp. With the war-memorial Church of *Notre Dame*, Le Raincy (1922-4), a truly monumental work of architecture was created, with all the concrete unclad and exposed: the building received widespread publicity and established the reputation of the firm (although by 1985 the steel was rusting, and surfaces of the concrete were crumbling). At the apartment-block, 51-5 *Rue Raynouard*, Paris (1929-32), some of the concrete was finished with *bouchardage* (bush-hammering) to remove the cement film and expose the coarser *aggregate, one of the first instances of this technique. Perret also designed the *Mobilier National* (1934-5) and the *Musée des Travaux Publics* (1936-57), both in Paris, and both concrete buildings. His last works were the master-plan for the rebuilding of Le Havre (1949-56), which had been destroyed in the 1939-45 war, and the central square and centrally-planned Church of *St-Joseph* (1952). In all his works the discipline of *Classicism, even in an extreme, *stripped form, was rarely absent. He published *Une Contribution à une théorie de l'architecture* (1952).

Abram *et al.* (2000); Britton (2001); Champigneulle (1959); J-L.Cohen *et al.* (2002); P.Collins (1959); Do (1982); G.Fanelli & Gargiani (1990, 1991); F (1980); Freigang (2003); Jamot (1927); P (1982); Perret (1959); Perret & Perret (1976); J.T (1996); Zahar (1959)

Perriand, Charlotte (1903-99) French architect/furniture-designer, she was one of the most influential creators of interiors of her time. She collaborated with Le *Corbusier and Pierre *Jeanneret on the *Salon d'Automne* Exhibition (1928), the *Villa Laroche* (1928), the *Pavillon Suisse* (1930-2), and the *Cité de Refuge* (1932), all in Paris, and later (1950s) with *Prouvé on the design of 'serial' furniture (modular wall-units, etc.). She also designed kitchen prototypes for Le Corbusier's *Unité d'Habitation*, Marseilles (1950). With *Goldfinger she designed the interiors of the French Government Tourist Offices (66 Haymarket (1958-60) and 177 Piccadilly (1963-4), both in London). At her *châlet*, Méribel-les-Allues, Savoie, France (1960-3), she married

traditional and Japanese design to the *International-Modernist style.

AD, xxxiii (1963), 601–3; E (1994); Jervis (1984); McLeod (ed.) (2004); Perriand (1985, 1998); J.T (1996)

perron 1. External platform-landing reached by symmetrical flights of steps, leading to the *piano nobile* of a building, a feature of *Palladian architecture. **2.** Steps leading to the platform. **3.** Any platform, base of a *market-cross, sepulchral monument, etc.

Perronet, Jean-Rodolphe (1708-94) French architect/military-engineer, he rebuilt (1745) the *choir of Alençon Cathedral, and was appointed (1747) Director of the *École des Ponts et Chaussées* where engineers and architects were instructed in bridge-, embankment-, and road-construction. He is important because he developed bridge-design in which each arch thrust against its neighbour, enabling spans to be increased, arches flattened, and structures lightened, essentially a principle of *Gothic design, influencing *Telford, among others. He designed *Pont de Mantes* (over the Seine—1757-65), *Pont de Château-Thierry* (over the Marne—1765-86), *Pont de Neuilly*, Paris (over the Seine—1768-74), *Pont des Fontaines*, Chantilly (1770-1), *Pont Biais* (over the Bicheret—1775), the *Ponts de Brunoy* and *de Rozoy* (over the Yères—1785-7), and the *Pont Louis Seize* (now *Concorde*—over the Seine in Paris—1787-91). He also designed the *Canal de Bourgogne* (1775-1832) and wrote *Description des projets et de la construction des ponts de Neuilly, de Mantes, d'Orléans et autres* (1782-3). He championed *Soufflot, so is a founding-father of *Neo-Classicism. With his pupil, **Émiliand-Marie Gauthey** (1732-1808), he sought the best building-stones in France, subjecting them to scientific tests to ensure *Ste-Geneviève* (now the *Panthéon*) would be structurally stable. Perronet is therefore significant in the development of structural theory, experiment, and calculations.

Lesage (1806); M & Wa (1987); Riche de Prony (1829); J.T (1996)

Persian 1. *Telamon sculpted with clothes suggestive of a Persian origin. *Persae* occur e.g. on the portal of the *Friedrichsbau*, Heidelberg Castle (1601-7). **2.** C19 style embracing a range of motifs associated with *Islamic and *Moorish architecture. **3.** For **Persian garden** *see* BÄGH; CHAHAR-BÄGH; ISLAMIC GARDEN; MUGHAL GARDEN; PARADISE GARDEN.

Persic Column with bell-shaped *capital and similarly sized *base, ornamented with *lotus-like forms, derived from *Achaemenian prototypes from Persepolis. It was fashionable in early-C19 *Egyptian-Revival schemes of decoration.

Persico, Edoardo (1900-36) Italian architect/critic, he was invited (1929) by *Pagano to work for *Casabella*, which he helped to transform into a leading architectural journal. He also published polemics in other magazines, including the influential *Domus*. He saw the identification of Rationalists and Traditionalists with Fascism as potentially dangerous, and he was scathing about certain aspects of the *Modern Movement: architecture, he decided, was not a mere engineering solution to an architectural problem (as many Americans thought), nor was its direction to be determined by Le *Corbusier's dogmatic approach, nor by Bruno *Taut's claims for social concerns. Instead, he perceived it as a means of liberating the human spirit, with no doctrinaire overtones. His best works were probably the two Parker Stores, Milan, both of which he carried out (1934-5) with **Marcello Nizzoli** (1887-1969), and the various displays he designed for international exhibitions.

E (1980); Polo (ed.) (1996); Ve (ed.) (1964)

persienne Type of slatted window-shutter either hinged at the side or fixed at the top and hanging loosely.

Persius, Friedrich Ludwig (1803-45) Prussian architect, the most able of *Schinkel's pupils, he supervised the building of the master's *Schloss Glienicke* on the Havel (1824-6) and the exquisite *Charlottenhof*, Potsdam (1826-7). He built the *Römische Bäder*, Potsdam (1834-5), to Schinkel's designs. His masterpieces were the *Rundbogenstil *Early-Christian-*basilica-style *Friedenskirche*, Potsdam (1845-87), and the *Heilandskirche*, Sakrow (1841-4—completed by *Stüler and others), but he also designed a number of charming *villas finished in *stucco and based on a rural Tuscan *vernacular style pioneered by Schinkel, but probably partly derived from *Papworth. He was responsible for the exotic orientalizing Steam-Engine House, Sanssouci, Potsdam, and he constructed the *dome and *turrets of Schinkel's *Nikolaikirche*, Potsdam (1843-50). Under **King Friedrich Wilhelm IV** (*r*.1840-61), with *Lenné, he co-ordinated the transformation of the landscape in the vicinity of the Havel, Potsdam, into one of the most enchanting creations of the first half of C19.

AJ, **xviii** (1928), 77–87, 113–20; B-S (1977); B-H & Hamm (1993); B-S (ed.) (1980); R.Carter (1989); Dehio (1961); Giersberg & Schendel (1982); Persius (1843–9); Poensgen (1930); J.T (1996); Wa & M (1987)

persona 1. *Gargoyle carved as a grotesque mask. **2.** *Antefix, or stop to the ends of the joint-tiles of an *Antique *temple, appearing at the *cymatium or *corona of the *cornice.

personification Representation of a human figure with *attributes to suggest an abstraction, such as Hope with Anchor. **Cesare Ripa's** (*c*.1560-*c*.1645) *Iconologia* (1593) was an important sourcebook for personification.

perspective 1. Method of creating an illusion of recession behind a two-dimensional surface (including gradations of colour, tone, and receding lines). **2.** Technique (invented during the *Renaissance, notably by *Brunelleschi and *Alberti) of representing graphically, by means of lines on paper, an object as it appears to the eye, suggesting three dimensions. It is based on the proposition that parallel lines at 90° to the field of vision (*orthogonals*) seem to join at a *vanishing-point. See also* AXONOMETRIC; ISOMETRIC PROJECTIONS; RENDERING.

FR (1946); Malton (1800); Mohrle (1994); N (1835); Sinisgalli et al. (2000); J.T (1996)

Peruzzi, Baldassare (1481-1536) Italian *uomo universale* of the *High Renaissance, influenced by *Bramante and *Raphael. His first great building was the *Palazzo della Farnesina*, Rome (1505-11), an exquisite house (sometimes referred to as a *villa) with *frescoes by **Ugo da Carpi** (*c*.1480-1532), Peruzzi himself, Raphael, *Giulio Romano, and **Giovanni Antonio Bazzi** (1477-1549—known as *Il Sodoma* (the Sodomite)). Essentially a square on plan, it has a *loggia* between two projecting *wings on the garden-front. He was appointed (1520) Architect (with *Sangallo) at St Peter's, but fled the city after the Sack of Rome (1527), settling in Siena, where, until 1532, he was engaged on strengthening the fortifications, and remodelled the Church of *San Domenico* (1531-3). From 1531 he was again working at St Peter's, Rome, and was appointed (1534) Architect to the *basilica. The *Palazzo Massimi alle Colonne*, Rome (1532-7), however, is reckoned to be his masterpiece: an ingeniously planned building on a difficult site, it has a curved *façade to the street with *Tuscan columns and *pilasters on the ground-floor arranged in pairs. The whole front is rusticated, and the *piano nobile* is separated from the ground-floor by an *entablature. Above the *piano nobile* are two rows of small windows—the lower has architraves with elaborate frames, the patterns of which were to be developed as *strapwork by *Serlio and disseminated through his publications. The *courts which are arranged to be similar to Roman *atria* are on two different axes. Certain details of this *palazzo* (such as the frames of the second-floor windows and the freedom with which the Orders are used) suggest proto-*Mannerism.

R.Adams (1980); M.Fagiolo & Madonna (eds) (1987); C.Fr (1973); He (1996); Lotz (1977); P (1982); J.T (1996); Tessari (1995); Wurm (ed.) (from 1984)

Peruzzi *Palazzo Massimi alle Colonne*, Rome, 1532. An ingenious plan on a difficult site, with internal courtyards: axes are set up on two separate entrances, one for the *Palazzo Angelo Massimi* (*left*), and the other for the *Palazzo Pietro Massimi* (*right*).

petal *Imbrication, petal-diaper*, or *scale-pattern* ornament suggesting overlapping scale-like shapes. It represents roofing-tiles, as on the top of the *Choragic Monument of Lysicrates, Athens (C4 BC), and was often found in Roman work, e.g. *sarcophagi. Petal-diaper patterns* occur in roofing and tile-hanging.

Petersen, Johan Carl Christian (1871–1923) Danish architect who was prominent in the Neo-Classical trend in that country from c.1910. He made an especial study of the works of C.F.*Hansen and M.G.*Bindesbøll. His best work is the exquisite Fåborg Museum, Funen (1912–15—with furniture by **Kaare Klint** (1888–1954)), in which the influence of the earlier masters is clear, and was a manifestation of the return to *Neo-Classicism. He was a vigorous polemicist and prolific writer on architecture, notably in the journal *Architekten*. Some of his projects (e.g. the unrealized proposals for the old railway station area of Copenhagen (1919—with **Ivar Bentsen** (1876–1943)) anticipate the *Neo-Rationalism of *Rossi and others in the 1970s.

Fisker & Yerbury (1927); Pn (1982); J.T (1996); vV (1993); We (1995)

Petersen, Ove (1830–92) Danish architect, influenced by *Herholdt and *Meldahl, he worked in a free Historicist style, and was a powerful force in the revival of interest in Danish brick buildings (e.g. his Hirschsprung Tobacco Factory, Copenhagen, of 1866, with round arches and ornamental brickwork). With *Dahlerup he designed the Royal Theatre, Copenhagen (1872–4), in an Italian-*Renaissance style, the interior of which is

reckoned to be one of the finest works of late-C19 architecture in Denmark.

Mi (1951); We (1995)

Petersen, Vilhelm Valdemar (1830–1913) Danish architect, his early designs were influenced by the work of *Hetsch, but in a heavier Italian style. He designed the Old Meteorological Institute on the *Esplanaden* (1872–3), and the Royal Academy of Sciences, Dante's Place (1894–8—an *Italianate *palazzo*, later rebuilt), both in Copenhagen.

We (1995)

Peto, Harold Ainsworth (1854–1933) English *Arts-and-Crafts architect/garden-designer, he went into partnership (1876–92) with Ernest *George, producing much high-quality domestic and other work. Inspired by his travels, especially in Spain and Japan, he became interested in garden-design, and after the partnership was dissolved, he moved to the country and began to incorporate Japanese and other themes into his landscape architecture. His gardens included those of his own house, Iford Manor, Wilts. (1899–1933); Easton Lodge, Essex (1902—with an Italian and Japanese garden, mostly destroyed); Buscot Park, Berks. (1904); Ilnacullin, Garnish Island, Co. Cork (1910–20s—complete with *Italianate *fabriques*); West Dean House, West Sussex (1910); and several in France on the *Côte d'Azur* (1893–1910).

Grainger (2011); Shoe (2001); Tay (2006); Whalley (2007)

Petri, Bernhard (1767–1853) German landscape-designer, pupil (1782–5) of *Sckell. Under the aegis of **Carl Theodor** (1724–99—**Elector Palatine of the Rhine** from 1742 and **of Bavaria** from 1777) he travelled in several countries (including England): on his return he was appointed Director of Buildings and Gardens at Zweibrücken. When the Palatinate was occupied by French Revolutionary troops, Petri practised as an independent landscape architect from 1791, first in Vienna, where, inspired by the example of Stowe, Bucks., he planned a scheme to celebrate Austrian Worthies, but that did not materialize. Called to Hungary, he introduced the naturalistic style of English gardens, notably at Orczy, Budapest, and Ásványráró (c.1793–6). Mostly influenced by the work of 'Capability' *Brown and *Hirschfeld, he created *Picturesque effects, notably for various gardens in Austria, Bohemia, and Moravia (1803–8), the most significant of which was as Lednice, now Czech Republic (completed 1811).

Becker (ed.) (1795–7); Buttlar (1999); Shoe (2001); Tay (2006)

Petschnigg, Hubert (1913–97) Partner of *Hentrich from 1953.

Petzold, Carl Eduard Adolf (1815–91) German landscape architect, he learned (1831–4) his trade on *Pückler-Muskau's estates, and after further experience at Neuenhof, Thuringia, he travelled, before taking up (1844–52) the post of Court Gardener at Weimar, where he restored *Goethe's Ilm Park, and carried out sundry works. He continued to work as *Parkinspektor* at Muskau (1851–81) for the new owner, **Willem Frederik Karel** (1791–1881), **Prince of Orange**-Nassau, through whose good offices he landed several plum jobs in The Netherlands. His works include some 170 gardens and parks in what are now Germany, Poland, The Netherlands, the Czech Republic, and Belgium. Adopting ideas of H.*Repton in his *Landschaftsgärtnerei* (1862), he also addressed issues of woodland aesthetics and landscaped *cemeteries (e.g. at Zwickau), influenced by *Loudon and by American exemplars. He was also involved in the *conservation of historic parks, and set down sound principles for the maintenance of designed landscapes.

Petzold (1862, 1874); Rohde (1998); Shoe (2001); Tay (2006)

Pevsner, Sir Nikolaus Bernhard Leon (1902–83) German-born British art-historian. A strong supporter of the *Modern Movement, some of his early writings had an undoubted bias, notably the influential *Pioneers of the Modern Movement from William Morris to Walter Gropius* (1936, later reissued as *Pioneers of Modern Design*) and *An Outline of European Architecture* (1942 with many subsequent editions). He had a powerful impact on *AR* in the 1940s (when that journal became a pro-Modern-Movement force and changed the architectural climate of Britain). He originated and edited the *Pelican History of Art* (from 1953), one of the most impressive series on art and architecture published in C20, but his greatest achievement was arguably the county-by-county guides of *The Buildings of England* (from 1951), much of which he wrote himself, although some of his highly subjective comments have been toned down in later editions. His collections of essays published as *Studies in Art, Architecture, and Design* (1968) and *A History of Building Types* (1976) are mines of information. He was devoted to the study of the architecture (especially churches) of his adopted country, and made an incalculable contribution to scholarship. However, the notions he imbibed while a student at Leipzig (especially influenced by his teacher, *Pinder (who was much respected by the National Socialists, not least for his over-estimation of German art in relation to other European countries), including belief in the *Zeitgeist* (spirit of the age)

and in 'national character'), led him to presuppositions that perhaps distorted his sense of history. For example, he argued that among *Gropius's architectural antecedents were members of the English *Arts-and-Crafts Movement: this was typical of his attempts to create links with the past to promote his own heroes, for it is well-known that Arts-and-Crafts architects (e.g. Baillie *Scott and *Voysey) rejected Gropius and all he stood for. Gropius and his disciples did much to destroy traditional crafts-based building (despite Gropius's insistence (to Pevsner) that William *Morris was one of his main sources of inspiration). Nevertheless, his many achievements deserve respect.

Bradley & B.Cherry (2001); B.Cherry (1998); Draper (ed.) (2004); Games (ed.) (2002); Games (2010); S.Harries (2011); *ODNB* (2004); Pe (1960, 1963, 1967, 1968, 1969, 1972, 1974, 1974a, 1976); pk; J.T (1996); D.Wa (1977)

pew Fixed wooden seat with a back and *bench-ends (the latter often elaborately carved with *blind *tracery and finished with *poppy-head *finials) in use in churches from *c.*C13. *Box-pews* were enclosed with high panelled partitions and a door, commonly dating from C18.

Peyre Family French architects active from the reign of *Louis Quinze (1715–74) to that of **Louis-Philippe** (1830–48). The most distinguished members were **Marie-Joseph** (1730–85) and his younger brother **Antoine-François** (1739–1823). Marie-Joseph, pupil of *Blondel, was an innovator who shot to fame with his *Œuvres d'architecture* (1765), which featured several vast *Neo-Classical schemes that affected architecture for the next few decades. In particular, his studies of *Antique Roman remains (with de *Wailly and *Moreau-Desproux) had prompted his advocacy of ingenious internal planning with top-lit rooms, something that was to influence *Adam, the younger *Dance, and *Gondouin, among others. His *Hôtel Leprêtre de Neubourg*, Clos Payen, near Paris (1762—destroyed); was one of the first Neo-Classical buildings in France, and a highly original, compact, modest composition applicable to quite ordinary houses. With de Wailly he designed (1768–82) the *Théâtre-Français* (later *Théâtre de l'Odéon*), a severe Neo-Classical building (rebuilt by *Chalgrin after a fire of 1799). A.-F.Peyre, who taught *Percier, *Fontaine, and A.-L.-T.*Vaudoyer, designed the Electoral Palace and Chapel at Koblenz, Germany (1779–92), for **Prince Clemens Wenzeslaus of Saxony** (1739–1812—**Archbishop-Elector of Trier** 1768–1803): it was a simplified version of the grand scheme (1777) by d'*Ixnard. Peyre also excavated the Roman antiquities at Trier, publishing his findings (1785). He designed the noble *Akademiesaal* in the Electoral

Palace at Mainz (1786–7), and was responsible for part of the new Neo-Classical Clemensstadt (later Neustadt), Koblenz (1782–3). M.-J.Peyre's son, **Antoine-Marie Peyre** (1770–1843), was for a time aide-de-camp to **General M.-J.-P.-Y.Roch Gilbert du Motier, Marquis de La Fayette** (1757–1834), and subsequently had a career as an architect in Paris.

B (1980); M & Wa (1987); J.T (1996); Wa & M (1987)

pharos 1. *Antique lighthouse, such as that at the harbour of Alexandria. **2.** Symbol for a lighthouse. **3.** Any conspicuous beacon or light.

pheasantry Cage or enclosure in which to rear and keep pheasants. The buildings themselves could be ornamental. A polychrome brick example, with polygonal roof-ridge *dovecotes, was built at Haddo House, Aberdeenshire (1884–5).

Philadelphia School Term used to describe architects associated with Louis *Kahn and his disciples, notably *Mitchell & Giurgola.

Philander *or* **Philandrier, Guillaume** (1505–65) French architect whose translation of and annotations on *Vitruvius (1544 and later editions) were greatly respected as major sources for C16 architectural theory and precedent. He is said to have studied under *Serlio, and was Secretary from 1533 to **Cardinal Georges d'Armagnac** (1501–85—Bishop of Rodez), for whom he carried out work at the Cathedral, including the extraordinary *Renaissance additions to the *Gothic west front).

Ha (1948); W.Pa (1852); J.T (1996)

Philo *or* **Philon** (*fl.*C4 BC) Athenian architect, he designed the dodecastyle *portico of the great Hall of the Mysteries (*Telesterion*), Eleusis (330–310 BC) and the huge Arsenal, Piraeus, near Athens (*c.*346–328 BC), intended as a store for the sails, ropes, etc., of the Athenian navy. He was the author of books on *proportion and prepared a description of the Arsenal. Another **Philo of Byzantium** wrote on mechanics and architecture *c.*C2 BC.

Coulton (1977); D (1950); La (1983)

philosopher's garden Ancient-Greek open-air discussions often occurred in gardens associated with *gymnasia (e.g. those of **Plato** (*c.*429–347 BC) and **Theophrastus** (*c.*371–287 BC)): the idea was revived during the *Renaissance (notably by *Alberti who drew on descriptions in *Pliny the Younger's works), and *villa-gardens incorporated geometries and proportional systems reflecting Order, with harmonious relationships of all parts, including the landscape beyond the garden proper. Another influence was *Hypnerotomachia Poliphili*, published 1499, which featured architectural elements in a fabulous landscape. Learned discourse in complex gardens became part of *Humanism's legacy, as in

the Belvedere Court, Vatican, and *Mannerist gardens (e.g. at the *Villa Lante*, Bagnaia, Viterbo). Subsequent impacts of these paradigms during the *Enlightenment were manifest in the *landscape-garden, where places of retreat and contemplation were created, e.g. at Ermenonville (1770s). Furthermore, the tradition of the oriental scholar's garden was beginning to interest Westerners. *See* CHINESE GARDEN-DESIGN; JI CHENG.

Coffin (1960, 1979, 1991); Colonna (1999); Gothein (1966); Hunt (ed.) (1996); Ji Cheng (2012); E.T.Morris (1983); M & T (1991); Shoe (2001); Woods (1996)

photovoltaic cells Silicon-based devices, used to convert solar energy into electricity, which can be integrated into roof- and wall-*claddings as part of an overall energy-strategy for the building. The Autonomous House, Southwell, Notts. (1990–3), by **Robert** (1948–) and **Brenda** (1949–) **Vale** was a pioneering example where such cells were employed.

PS; V & V (1991)

Physick, John Frederick (1923–2013) English architectural historian/expert on sculpture, he spent most of his adult life working at the Victoria & Albert Museum, London (the history of which he wrote), where he oversaw the publication of catalogues associated with important exhibitions, e.g. *Victorian Church Art* (1971), *Marble Halls* (1973), *The Destruction of the Country House* (1974), *Photography and the South Kensington Museum* (1975), *Change and Decay: The Future of Our Churches* (1977), and *The Garden* (1979). He had a passion for sculpture (he was a member of the **Physick Family** of distinguished sculptors (*c.*1769–1906)), was a founder-member of the Church Monuments Society, served for many years on the committee of management for the *Gunnis *Dictionary of British Sculptors, 1660–1851*, and was a founder-trustee of the Friends of Kensal Green Cemetery from 1990.

Physick (1982); Physick & Darby (1973); pk; *The Times* (14 Nov. 2013), 58

physic(k)-garden Garden for the study and cultivation of medicinal plants. **Pope Nicholas V** (*r.*1447–55) set aside part of the Vatican grounds for a garden of such plants to promote study of their properties: this was a forerunner of the celebrated botanical gardens, Padua University (1545). The Chelsea Physic Garden, London (1673), was founded for research, and Edinburgh had its Physic Garden, St Ann's Yards, Holyrood (1670). *See* HERB-GARDEN; MONASTERY *or* MONASTIC GARDEN.

M.Brown (2012); Gothein (1966); Symes (2006)

Piacentini, Marcello (1881–1960) Italian architect, son of **Pio Piacentini** (1846–1928), one of the leading architects in Rome in the first fifty years after Italian Unification (1861–71). Pio's works included the *Palazzo delle Esposizioni* (1880–2), *Palazzo Sforza Cesarini* (1886–8), and the *Ministero di Grazia e Giustizia* (1913–20), all thoroughly competent eclectic buildings. Marcello established his reputation with the *Villa Allegri*, Rome (1915–17), the *Cinema 'al Corso'*, Rome (1915–17), the Palace of Justice, Messina (1912–28), and the centre of the *Garden City *Garbatella*, Rome (1920): his designs of that time were academically sound and eclectically based. He became (1920) Professor of Architecture at Rome, and (1921), with **Gustavo Giovannoni** (1873–1947), founded the journal *L'Architettura* of which he was Chief Editor (1922–43) and was influential in promoting the work of younger architects, including those associated with *Rationalism. When **Benito Mussolini** (1883–1945) came to power (1922), Piacentini became the leading protagonist of a *stripped *Neo-Classicism that was to be virtually the style of State Architecture under Fascism. In fact, he rose to such a position of influence that he has been called 'Mussolini's Albert *Speer'. He was no mean architect, as his *Hotel Ambasciatori*, Rome (1926–7), shows in its powerful *Mannerist *façade. Other significant works include the splendid *mausoleum, Pallanza (1929–30), of **Marshal Count Luigi Cadorna** (1850–1928), the formal *Piazza della Vittoria*, Brescia (1927–32), the War Memorials at Genoa (1927–34) and Bolzano (1926–8), the clearing and redevelopment of the area around the Mausoleum of **Augustus** (*r.*27 BC–AD 14), Rome (1934), the *Casa Madre dei Mutilati*, Rome (1928), the *stripped-Classical Palace of Justice, Milan (1933–40), and the *Grattacielo dell' Orologio* in the *Piazza Dante*, Genoa (1937–41). In 1933 he commenced (with **Attilio Spaccarelli** (1890–1975)) the *Via della Conciliazione* that opened up the vista from *Bernini's *Piazza di San Pietro*, and has been criticized since for its impact on Bernini's scheme as well as for the destruction of historic buildings to facilitate its construction (completed 1950). Piacentini was responsible for the general plan of the *Città Universitaria*, Rome (1932–5), and designed the stripped-Classical Administration Building (1932–3). He worked with *Pagano, *Piccinato, and others on the planning of the *Esposizione Universale di Roma* (EUR) for the projected E42 exhibition (which did not occur because of the 1939–45 war) and worked with *Nervi on the *Palazzo dello Sport*, Rome (1958–9). His *Architettura d'oggi* (1930) was admired at the time, and he also published a work on the buildings of Rome (1870–1952). It is an indictment of architectural commentators that Piacentini has had what is called a 'bad press', unlike the treatment given to convinced Fascists such as Pagano and *Terragni.

Accasto *et al.* (1971); Etlin (1991); GS; Lupano (1991); Ms (1966); Patetta (1972); Piacentini (1930); A.Pica (1936); M.Pisani (ed.) (1996); P (1982); Pi (1968); A.Rose (1995); Scarrocchia (1999); Seta (1978); J.T (1996); Zevi (1973)

Piano, Renzo (1937–) *See* HIGH TECH.

piano nobile Principal *storey of a building containing the apartments of ceremony and reception, usually set over a lower floor, and approached by a *flight of steps from the ground-level, often expressed as a *perron. The *piano nobile* was often of greater height than the storeys above and below, and the architectural embellishments of e.g. windows usually emphasized its significance.

An (1966, 1967, 1990)

piazza 1. Open space, square, or market-place, surrounded by buildings and approached by various streets. **2.** In C17 and C18 a roofed *arcade or *colonnade with buildings above, as at Covent Garden, London, (1631–3), by Inigo *Jones. **3.** Any covered way, colonnaded walk, or *pentice. **4.** Open *porch or *verandah (US).

Piccinato, Luigi (1899–1983) Italian architect/town-planner. Active as a member of the Rationalist tendency in the inter-war period, he worked with *Pagano, *Piccinato, and others on the plans for the *Esposizione Universale di Roma* (EUR) for the E42 exhibition (not realized because of the 1939–1945 war). His town-planning work included schemes for Sabaudia (1936–8) and Catania (1960–2).

Cennamo (1973); Malusardi (1993); Sessa (1985)

picked *Masonry faced with a multitude of small crevices, like *rock-faced work on a small scale (*see* RUSTICATION).

picnostyle, pycnostyle *See* INTERCOLUMNIATION.

picture-rail *Moulding from which pictures are hung in a room: it defines the lower part of a *frieze.

Picturesque Confused and confusing term applied to landscapes which, when seen from specific viewpoints, form framed compositions worthy of a painting or drawing: the word denoted 'as in a picture', and the Italian *pittoresco* was in use by the mid-C17 in relation to architecture, although it had a Dutch equivalent connected with landscape-painting in which buildings, ruggedly irregular scenery, figures, and animals were depicted, so was linked to notions of pleasing the eye with designed landscapes involving carefully positioned elements (including buildings) in gardens and parks. Uvedale *Price published (1794) his famous *Essay*, intended to redefine the nature of Picturesque Beauty made earlier by William *Gilpin: he used the word to describe landscapes evoking sensations not aroused by the *Beautiful or *Sublime categories established (1750s) by Edmund *Burke. To Price, the chief characteristics of Picturesque landscapes were irregularity, variety, roughness of texture, and the power to stimulate the imagination, as found in the wilder, more mountainous regions of the British Isles (previously considered dreary and uninteresting), increasingly visited and appreciated by those following the late-C18 Picturesque cult: to him the rude hut or hovel was more Picturesque than the cottage, and idle peasants more Picturesque than farm-labourers toiling in the fields. In paintings by **Claude Gellée** *called* **Lorraine** (1600–82) he detected the Beautiful; in those of **Salvator Rosa** (1615–73) the Sublime; and in those of **Gaspard Dughet** *called* **Poussin** (1615–75) he found the Picturesque. Payne *Knight responded to Price's views in *The Landscape* (also 1794): whereas Price held that careful positioning of features such as trees and buildings could render a landscape Picturesque, and that Picturesque qualities could be found in objects themselves (a nod to Burke's *Inquiry* (1757)), Knight (who used 'Picturesque' as an adjective) believed that Picturesque aesthetics were dependent on particular ways of *looking* at landscapes, a position which resonated with *Alison's theories of *Associationism. To Price, the Picturesque comprised all the qualities of nature and art that could be discerned in paintings executed since the time of **Titian** (*c.*1485–1576), and he favoured 'natural' beauty, deploring contemporary fashions, such as those established by 'Capability' *Brown for laying out grounds, because their calculated smoothness and tidiness were at variance with all the principles of landscape-painting. As an C18 English aesthetic category, however, largely concerned with landscape and with emotional responses to associations evocative of passions or events, the Picturesque was a standard of taste hugely influential throughout Europe in the design of gardens and parks, helping to create a climate in which asymmetrical and informal aspects of much architectural and landscape-design evolved in C19. Picturesque scenes were full of variety, interesting detail, and elements drawn from many sources, so were neither serene (like the Beautiful) nor awe-inspiring (like the Sublime), but lay somewhere between the two. All this might suggest that the Picturesque was nothing more or less than a milder form of the Sublime, never a *distinct* aesthetic category at all, but rather a *synthesis* of the Beautiful and the Sublime.

In architectural terms, the *freeing* of architectural composition from the *tyranny of symmetry* was undoubtedly due to ideas associated with the Picturesque, which also led to a widespread *eclecticism, and to the *Gothic and other Revivals. *See* ASSOCIATIONISM; GARDENESQUE; NATURESQUE.

Alison (1790); M.Andrews (ed.) (1994); Ballantyne (1997); COF (1988); Co & J.Hs (eds) (1970); Copley & Garside (eds) (1995); Crook (1987); Hunt (1992, 2002); Hussey (1967a); Knight (1794, 1972); Linden (2007); H.O (1970); Pa & Pl (eds) (1977); Pe (1968, 1974); Price (1810); Su (1993); Symes (2012); D.Wa (1982a); Watkins & Cowell (2012); M.W

picture-window Large window containing a single undivided pane of glass.

Pidgeon, Monica (1913–2009) Chile-born (*née* **Lehmann**), as editor (1945–75) of *Architectural Design*, she was influential in British architecture after 1945. Sharing the widespread delusion that architects could shape the world, she was a committed supporter of *CIAM and *International Modernism, later switching allegiance to *Team X, the *Smithsons, and Buckminster *Fuller. Intensely political, she advised the Marxist President of Chile, **Salvador Allende Gossens** (1908–73), on the choice of architects who could help to resolve the country's housing crisis: this resulted in a study by *Pawley, who proposed commandeering the car-industry to manufacture prefabricated homes, but Allende's death ended such efforts. She was a member (1971–6) of a group including Fuller, Louis *Kahn, *Pevsner, and **Moshe Safdie** (1938–), to advise on the re-planning of Jerusalem. At the same time she changed the direction of the magazine to support alternative energy and life-styles, before leaving (1975) to edit *RIBAJ* at the invitation of the then President, Eric *Lyons. She set up (1979) **Pidgeon Audio Visual** to publish packs to promote works of *Banham, *Candela, *Niemeyer, and others of whom she approved.

RIBAJ (Dec. 2009), 14; *The Times* (23 Sept. 2009), 57

pie Ornament resembling a stylized chrysanthemum, or the *rosette.

pièce d'eau Ornamental basin (usually of stone) or pond, esp. the large formal pond at Versailles (1679–82).

piecrust *Rococo scalloped, scrolled, raised border around e.g. a mirror.

piedroit *Lesene, or species of *pilaster without *base or *capital.

pien, piend 1. *Apex, *arris, *ridge, or salient angle. 2. *Hip-rafter in a roof. 3. *Cope. 4. Horizontal and sloping joint in a stone geometrical *stair where one step fits into another to prevent it slipping.

pier 1. Detached mass of construction, generally acting as a support, such as the solid part of a wall between two openings, or a massive element from which arches spring, as in a *bridge. 2. Support, such as a pier in a repetitive medieval *nave-*arcade varying from sturdy, oversized *Romanesque examples to the lighter, taller, more slender, multi-moulded *Perp. types. Piers can therefore be more massive than columns. **3.** Vertical formation in brickwork on the face of a *flint or *rag-stone wall, serving to strengthen it. **4.** Stone, concrete, metal-work, or timber construction jutting out into the sea or other water as a break-water, landing-stage, or promenade. **5.** *Jetty or wharf. *Compounds include*:

pier-arch: arch springing from a pier;

pier-buttress: pier so constructed to resist the thrust of a flying *buttress, thus giving the latter support.

Piermarini, Giuseppe (1734–1808) Italian architect who worked for *Vanvitelli from *c.*1765, and was in Milan from 1769. Then he became Architect to the Archducal Court, and not only designed many buildings but was the arbiter of all matters relating to the work of other architects. He built the enormous *Palazzo Belgioioso* (1772–81), followed by other houses, including the *Palazzo Greppi* (1772–8), the *Palazzo Moriggia* (1770s), and the *Casa Casnedi* (*c.*1776), all in Milan. He designed the *Palazzo Ducale* (from 1773—with interior decorations by **Giocondo Albertolli** (1742–1839)), and the *Villa Ducale*, Monza (1776–80—again collaborating with Albertolli). He was responsible for several theatres including the *Teatro alla Scala*, Milan (1776–9), the *Teatro Canobbiana*, Milan (1777–80), and others at Novara (1777), Monza (1778), Mantua (1782–3), Crema (1783–5—destroyed), and Matelica (1803–12), all in a refined *Neo-Classical style. His work was widely imitated.

Cesarini (1983); Filippini (1936); Ms (1966); Me (1966); M & Wa (1987); J.T (1996)

Pieroni da Galiano, Giovanni Battista (1586–1654) Architect of the *Sala Terrena*, a huge triple-arched *loggia on the Valdštejn Palace, Prague (1624–7), which faces the *Baroque garden designed by Pieroni and **Nicolò Sebregondi** (*fl.*1610–1651/2). This *loggia* (influenced by the work of *Giulio Romano) cannot be matched in grandeur and sophistication by anything of contemporary date in Vienna. Pieroni also designed the Bohemian town of Jičín (from 1623) and numerous fortifications throughout the Habsburg lands.

J.Nn (1970); J.T (1996)

Pierre de Chelles *See* CHELLES.

Pierre de Montreuil *See* MONTREUIL.

Pietilä, Frans Reima Ilmari (1923–93) and **Raili Paatelainen** (1926–) Finnish husband-and-wife team of architects responsible for the Kaleva Church, Tampere (1966), with its inward canted walls and tall window-strips. Among other buildings were the Congregational Centre,

Leisure Centre, and Shopping Hall, Hervanta New Town, Tampere (1979) and the President's House, Mäntyniemi (1984–93).

E (1994); Q (1985); J.M.Ri (1978); Salokorpi (1970); Tempel (1968)

pietra dura Inlaid work with hard stones (agate, jasper, marble, etc.) later used from C16 for *mosaics, also called *Florentine mosaic, opera commesso, pietra commesse,* and *lavoro di commesso*. The *Capella dei Principi, San Lorenzo*, Florence, is decorated with such work (from 1604).

Baldini *et al.* (1979); W.Pa (1852)

pietra serena Dark, slippery, greenish-grey Florentine *Macigno* stone from Fiesole used for the interior *pilasters, *entablatures, and architectural elements by *Brunelleschi at the Pazzi Chapel and *Michelangelo in the Medici Chapel, both in Florence.

W.Pa (1852)

Pigage, Nicolas de (1723–96) French architect, pupil of J.-F.*Blondel. Called (1749) to the Court of **Carl Theodor** (**Elector Palatine** from 1742 and **Elector of Bavaria** 1777–99) as landscape architect, he became Court Architect (1752). He adorned the enchanting gardens at Schwetzingen, near Mannheim (1752–95), with the sumptuous Court Theatre (1752), Temples of Minerva and Apollo (1761), Bath-House (1766–73—with exquisite *Louis-Seize interiors), serpentine bird-bath, water-spouting birds, water-castle, ruined *aqueduct, 'Mosque' (1778–95), and Classical Temple of Mercury. These constitute a collection of some of the finest *fabriques in Europe. He created the beautiful interiors of the Electoral Palace, Mannheim (1752–96—destroyed 1943, rebuilt 1947–72), and realized his greatest work, *Schloss Benrath* and gardens, near Düsseldorf (1755–65), where a restrained *Rococo merges with nascent *Classicism.

Colombier (1956); J.Curl (2011); Heber (1986); Pigage (1805); C.Powell (1959); J.T (1996); Wa & M (1987)

pigeon-house *See* DOOCOT; DOVECOT(E).

Pikionis, Dimitris A. (1887–1968) Greek architect, his work included the Experimental School, University of Salonika (1933–5), a design for the Hotel Xenia, Delphi (1953), the Town Hall, Volos (1961), and St Paul's Church, Ethniki, Estia (1960–8). He designed a number of tombs, but is probably best known for his master-plan and landscape-design for the Acropolis, Athens (1950–7).

Wi.Cu (1996); E (1994); J.T (1996)

pila 1. Plain, unmoulded, undecorated, detached *masonry *pier, square or rectangular on plan, with no allusions to the *Orders whatsoever, also termed *pillar. **2.** *Font on a free-standing *shaft, as opposed to one fixed to a wall or a bracket. **3.** Plain block set on a column, etc., supporting a roof. **4.** *Antique *mortar or plastered finish.

pilaster Roman version of the *anta, except that generally it conforms to the *Order used elsewhere, with *capital, *shaft, *base, and *entablature. It is attached to a wall from which it projects only slightly, and is rectangular on plan, so should not be confused with an *engaged column. In most cases, and correctly, unlike antae, pilaster-shafts have *entasis. Unlike a *pier, a pilaster has no structural purpose, and is used to respond to columns or the design of the *soffit of a ceiling for purely aesthetic reasons. *Terms associated with it are:*

pilaster-face: longest exposed surface of a pilaster, parallel to the wall behind;

pilaster-mass: **1.** pier to which a pilaster is attached; **2.** pier or mass of wall with *impost *mouldings; **3.** as *pilaster-strip* but more massive;

pilaster-side: exposed part of a pilaster at 90° to the wall to which it is attached;

pilaster-strip: *lesene or *piedroit which, unlike an anta or pilaster, has no base or capital, has no entasis, and is not a true pilaster: it is a feature of *Anglo-Saxon work, and with the *plinths and *corbel-table, frames the panels of *Romanesque bays. It is more slender than a *pilaster-mass;

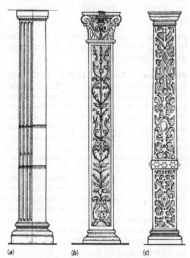

(a)   (b)   (c)

pilaster (*a*) Typical Classical example (*left*) with *flutes* and *cabling*, and (*right*) plain, both with *Attic base*; (*b*) early-C16, with *arabesque* panel monument of Louis XII, *St-Denis*, near Paris; (*c*) Jacobean, Astbury Church, Ches.

pilastrade, pilastra: continuous row of pilasters in series.

C. Normand (1852)

pile 1. Any building with architectural pretensions, such as a castle or country-house. **2.** Mole or *pier in the sea. **3.** Pier e.g. of a *bridge. **4.** Large upright timber *post hammered into marshy or uncertain ground to support a superstructure. Later piles were cylindrical or other hollow forms of iron or steel, and, more recently, of *reinforced concrete. **5.** Row of rooms, hence a *double-pile house is two rooms deep, with or without a corridor between them.

Pilgram, Anton (c.1450–1515) Master-mason, born probably in Brno, Moravia, his first work was the Church of St Kilian, Heilbronn (c.1482–90), much influenced by the work of *Buchsbaum. Involved in the building of the *Pfarrkirche*, Wimpfen-am-Berg near Heilbronn (1493–7), he then worked on the Church of St James, Brno (1502). He designed the *Judentor* (1508) and the staircase to St James's School (1510), also in Brno, both destroyed (C19). He moved to Vienna, where he carved the organ base (1513) and the *pulpit (1514–15), containing self-portraits, in the *Stephansdom*. He designed rooms in the *Niederösterreichisches Landhaus*, Vienna (1513–15), and may have been responsible for the *choir of the *Pfarrkirche*, Freistadt, Austria (1513–15).

Fe (1951, 1978); Oettinger (1951); J.T (1996)

pilgrimage-church Although many great churches were places of pilgrimage (e.g. the Cathedrals of Canterbury and Lincoln) because of the Relics contained therein (St Thomas of Canterbury and St Hugh respectively), the term is especially given to those churches on pilgrimage-routes, e.g. on the way to *Santiago de Compostela*. Examples include *St-Foy*, Conques, *St-Sernin*, Toulouse, and *St-Martin*, Tours. Later examples include the exquisite C18 *Wallfahrtskirche Vierzehnheiligen*, Franconia, Germany, by *Neumann et al.

pilier cantonné *Gothic *pier consisting of a large central core with four attached *colonnettes associated with the springing of the *nave-arcade and *vaults over *aisle and nave.

Pilkington, Frederick Thomas (1832–98) English High Victorian *Rogue *Gothic architect, who worked in Scotland. His best works were the Church of the Trinity, Irvine, Ayrshire (1861–3), and the Barclay Church, Edinburgh (1862–3), both of which have over-emphatic elements in their compositions.

Close & Riches (2012); D & M (1985); GMcW & W (1984)

Pilkington, William (1758–1848) English architect, pupil and assistant of Sir Robert *Taylor.

He supervised the building of Taylor's design for the Council House, Salisbury, Wilts. (1788–95), and then a number of houses in *Neo-Classical and *Tudor styles. His buildings included Otterden Place, Kent (1802—Tudor), Clermont Lodge (now Hall), Norfolk (1812), and Calverton Church, Bucks. (1818–24—*Gothic, with Neo-Norman tower). His younger son, **Redmond William Pilkington** (1789–1844), succeeded his father as Surveyor to the Charterhouse, London, where he built the Preacher's and Pensioners' Courts (1825–30), to the designs of which *Blore contributed.

Co (2008); *ODNB* (2004)

pillar 1. Free-standing unadorned *pila or *pier, *monolithic or built up, usually on a rectangular or square plan. 2. Incorrect term for a free-standing memorial column, such as *Railton's Nelson Column, Trafalgar Square, London (1840–3), and such usage should be avoided. 3. Pier, as in a *nave-arcade in a church, although some commentators find such usage obsolete and confusing.

pillar-piscina Free-standing *piscina set on a short *colonnette.

pillow capital *Capital resembling a cushion, or a cubic capital with the lower angles rounded off, as in *Romanesque architecture.

pillowed *Pulvinated, like a cushion, e.g. a pulvinated *frieze bowing outwards in section.

piloti One of several *piers supporting a building over the ground, thereby elevating the lowest floor to the first-floor level and leaving an open area below the building. It was a favourite device of Le *Corbusier: its widespread adoption in the UK has created many unpleasant spaces.

J-G (1973–7)

pinacotheca *Gallery where pictures are exhibited.

Pinder, Georg Maximilian Wilhelm (1878–1947) German art-historian who specialized in German art of the later Middle Ages. He held (1919–27) a Chair in Leipzig, and there developed his 'generational' theory that style in any period was due to the interaction between ageing and younger artists, that the history of art was the history of ideas, and that in the *Zeitgeist* genius and nationality were responsible for creative movements and styles, a notion that appealed to many, notably *Pevsner. Pinder's overestimation of German art and his perception of its achievements in association with German national history were influential in the post-1914–18-war period.

Games (2010); S.Harries (2011); J.T. (1996)

pine *Finials and *pendants in the form of pinecones, commonly found in Classical architecture. They sometimes resemble the skins of pineapples.

pineapple Ornamental *finial, sometimes used instead of *urns or *vases. *See* PINE. An extraordinary *ashlar pineapple instead of a *dome over an octagonal *Gothick garden-pavilion exists at Dunmore Park, Stirlingshire (probably latter part of C18).

Pineau, Nicolas (1684–1754) French architect, trained under *Boffrand and *Hardouin-Mansart: he settled in Russia where he worked for **Tsar Peter I** ('the Great' (*r*.1694–1725)), for whom he designed a richly decorated *cabinet in *Peterhof* (1721) and his tomb (1725). Returning to Paris (1726), he designed several *hôtels (e.g. *Hôtel Mazarin* (1740)). He was best known as a creator of exquisite *Rococo interiors, for which many drawings survive, some being publicized in J.-F. *Blondel's *De la distribution des maisons de plaisance et de la décoration des édifices en général* (1737–8), while Batty *Langley also reproduced some of his designs for console-tables.

Deshairs (1914); Ga (1972); Ha (1950); Jervis (1984); K & L (1972); Kimball (1980); L & D (1986); J.T (1996)

Pine, John (1690–1756) *See* ROCQUE, JOHN.

pinery 1. *Greenhouse in which *pineapples are cultivated. 2. Plantation of pine-trees (*see* PINETUM).

pinetum (*pl.* **pineta**) Plantation of conifers of various species, for scientific or ornamental purposes. *See* ARBORETUM.

Pingusson, Georges-Henri (1894–1980) French architect/town-planner. After a period with Le *Corbusier he evolved his *Style Paquebot* based on Corbusier's perceptions of passenger-ships as floating apartment-blocks. His main achievements were in the reconstruction of war-damaged areas in the Moselle, Lorraine, and Saar regions, where he planned various industrial towns. He designed the *Hôtel Latitude* 43, St-Tropez (1931–2), the *Pavillon des Artistes Modernes*, Paris Exposition (1937—destroyed), and (with Corbusier), the satellite town of Briey-en-Forêt (1953–9). His *Mémorial des Martyrs de la Déportation*, at the east end of the *Île de la Cité*, Paris (completed 1962), is a severe underground crypt of great emotional impact, commemorating French victims of the Nazi terror.

J.Curl (2002a); pk; Texier (2001)

pinnacle Ornamental *pyramid or *cone, the terminating feature of a *buttress, *parapet-angle, *spire, *turret, etc., often ornamented with *crockets.

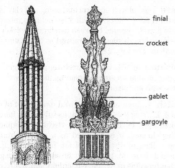

finial

crocket

gablet

gargoyle

pinnacle (a) Early-C13 First-Pointed example, Oxford Cathedral; **(b)** C14 Second-Pointed crocketed, with finial.

Pinsent, Cecil Ross (1884–1963) See SCOTT, GEOFFREY.

Piper, Fredrik Magnus (1746–1824) Swedish architect who introduced a mature English *Picturesque movement (having made studies of Stourhead and other gardens) to Sweden in his landscape-garden at Haga, near Stockholm, with its exotic *fabriques (1780–1820). He designed several Neo-Classical houses, including *Listonhill*, Stockholm (1790–1), and *Bjärka-Säby*, Östergotland (*c.*1796).

A & B (1986); J.T (1996); M.Woods (1996)

Piranesi, Giovanni Battista (1720–78) Venetian engineer/architect/engraver of genius, he had a profound effect on *Neo-Classicism with his *Sublime images of Rome. He produced (1749–50) a series of *Invenzioni* featuring *Carceri*, powerful images of vast spaces and huge structures, drawn to a terrifyingly megalomaniac *scale. Then came the first of the *Vedute di Roma* (1745) revealing a city so overpoweringly Sublime that the plates became influential throughout Europe, but especially among students in the French Academy in Rome. His speculative archaeology led him to design fantasies of considerable originality. Appearing in the *Opere Varie* (1750), they impacted on architects like de *Wailly and the *Peyres. His antiquarian studies led to the *Antichità Romane* (collected in four volumes in 1756), which made his reputation: it was designed to illustrate constructional techniques and the Roman ornamental vocabulary. He took sides in the Graeco-Roman controversy, assuming leadership of the pro-Roman cause against the pro-Greek camp of *Winckelmann. He published (1761) *Della Magnificenza ed Architettura de' Romani* designed to show the supremacy of Roman architecture, followed by *Il Campo Marzio dell' Antica Roma* (1762), dedicated to Robert *Adam, containing a complex

fantasy of urban buildings purporting to show Rome under **Constantine** (*r.*324–37), but far grander than anything created by Ancient Romans.

He reissued (*c.*1760) the *Carceri* plates, reworked, and with some new images, that struck chords among advanced Neo-Classicists, notably George *Dance the Younger, *Desprez, and others. The *Parere su l'Architettura* (1765) argued for a free use of Roman exemplars for the creation of a new style. **Pope Clement XIII** (*r.*1758–69) commissioned him (1763) to design a new Papal *high-altar for *San Giovanni in Laterano*, Rome. Piranesi developed his scheme to include the replacement of the whole structure to the liturgical east of the *transept by a gigantic top-lit apsidal sanctuary, but it was never implemented. Around this time he remodelled the Church and Headquarters of the Knights of Malta, redesigning the *façade of *Santa Maria Aventina* (1764–6—for which detailed account-books have survived), Rome, and creating a formal *piazza one wall of which was embellished with a series of decorative *stelai. The *altar and lighting inside the church were elaborately contrived. This Aventine commission was Piranesi's only building, but it is one of the most powerful and original of C18.

His *Diverse Maniere d'adornare i cammini* (Different Ways of Decorating Chimney-Pieces—1769) was his most important publication for interior design and the applied arts. It was to be significant in the development of Adam's chimney-pieces and *Etruscan style, and also provided *Bélanger and other French architects with motifs. The book contained a series of chimney-pieces in the 'Egyptian' style that provided many ideas for the *Egyptian Revival and indeed influenced aspects of the *Art-Deco style (1920s and 1930s). The book also illustrated Piranesi's Egyptianizing painted interiors of the *Caffè degl'Inglesi*, Rome (*c.*1768). *Vasi, Candelabri, Cippi, Sarcophagi* was brought out (1778–91) and had an enormous following among designers of the *Empire and *Regency periods. It publicized many of the artefacts he had been designing and making since at least the 1760s, as well as Piranesi's activities as a restorer of Antiquities. In spite of his antipathy towards all things Greek, he made superb drawings of the Greek-*Doric temples at *Paestum, which were acquired by *Soane. The engravings made from these, published (1778) as *Différentes Vues ... de Pesto*, had a tremendous impact on the *Doric and *Greek Revivals, and were brought out partly under the aegis of Piranesi's son, **Francesco** (1758–1810), who played an important part in completing his father's later works, notably the *Vasi ...* Francesco Piranesi published a map of the *Villa Adriana*, Tivoli (1781), and added new plates to further editions of the *Vedute, Antichità*, and other works. Most importantly, he issued a massive collection of graphic works in 27 volumes

(1800–7) as well as a three-volume set of *Anti-quités de la Grande Grèce* (1804–7) based on his father's work at Pompeii.

J.Bloomer (1993); Calvesi (ed.) (1967); J.Curl (2005); Focillon (1967); FHL (1967); Lütgens (1994); Nyberg & Mitchell (eds) (1975); P (1982); Reudenbach (1979); Ry (1980); I.Scott (1975); J.T (1996); W-E (1972, 1978, 1978a, 1993, 1994, 2013); W-E & Connors (eds) (1992); Wi (1975)

Pisano, Andrea (*c.*1295–1348/9) Master-Mason of the *Duomo*, Florence, from *c.*1337, where he probably designed the *niche-*stage of the *campanile. He was Master-Mason at Orvieto Cathedral from 1347.

J.T (1996); M.Tg (1971); John White (1987)

Pisano, Nicola (*c.* 1220/5–80) Tuscan sculptor/architect, he influenced the evolution of *Gothic architecture in Italy. He made the hexagonal Pisa *Baptistery *pulpit (1260) and may have designed the second-storey *arcade of the Pisa Baptistery (1260–4). Responsible for the large octagonal pulpit in Siena Cathedral (1265–8), he may have played some part in the design of the west front, commenced by his son, **Giovanni Pisano** (*c.*1248–*c.*1314), Master-Mason there, who built the lower section of the west front (1287–96). Giovanni became (1299) *capomaestro* of Pisa Cathedral, where he designed the pulpit (1302–11).

J.T (1996); John White (1987)

piscina (*pl.* **piscinae**) Stone basin connected with a drainage *channel for carrying away the water used in rinsing the vessels employed at Mass and washing the hands of the Priest. It was usually set in a *niche in the south wall of a *chancel in a church near the *altar, though it was sometimes carried on a short *colonnette or projected from the face of a wall. Piscinae, which were often equipped with a *credence-table for the vessels, were frequently ornamented with an elaborate *canopy, sometimes designed as part of the *sedilia installation, in which case the ensemble was called *prismatory*.

piscina C14 example, St Michael's, Cumnor, near Oxford (after *Parker*).

pisé Type of wall-construction using stiff clay or earth (*pisé de terre*), kneaded, sometimes mixed with gravel, rammed between two lines of wicker-work or boards that are removed as the material hardens. *See* ADOBE; COB.

pishtaq In *Islamic architecture, a rectangular frame around an arched opening, usually associated with an *iwan*.

pitch 1. Amount of slope given to any part of a roof. **2.** Tenacious black resinous substance, hard when cold, becoming a thick viscid semi-liquid when heated: it is obtained as a residue from the boiling or distillation of tar. It is used in its melted form to protect external timbers, e.g. *clap-boarding or *weather-boarding, and, if mixed with ground chalk, sand, and tar, for surfacing roads, etc.

pitched stone Stone with its rough face framed by bevelled edges, so a type of *rustication.

pitch-faced Piece of stone with all the edges of the face trimmed down to true arrises all round so that joints are tight and fine, the remaining part of the face projecting from the margins and left rough. A type of *rustication.

Pite, Arthur Beresford (1861–1934) English architect remembered for several distinguished buildings and architectural fantasies. He worked with John *Belcher for 14 years, also carrying on his own practice and making drawings for *The Builder*. With Belcher he designed the Hall of the Incorporated Chartered Accountants, Great Swan Alley, City of London (1889–90), where sculpture (by **Harry Bates** (1850–99), **Sir William Hamo Thorneycroft** (1850–1925), et al.) was fully integrated with the architecture. The building was to be influential, mainly in Great Britain and Germany, mostly Berlin. Pite's *Mannerism was best seen at 44 and 82 Mortimer Street, London (1890s), where the precedents were in the Florentine work of *Michelangelo. On his own account, Pite travelled in the Middle East, and, influenced perhaps by *Bentley's designs for Westminster Cathedral, London (1895–1903), designed the Parish Hall and Christ Church, North Brixton, London (1901–5), in which *Byzantine, Mannerist, and *serliana motifs are synthesized in one centralized composition. He also designed the Anglican Cathedral at Kampala, Uganda (1913–18), and churches at Entebbe, Uganda, Bucharest, and Warsaw, among other places. Like other architects of the period, Pite turned to *Neo-Classicism, and his office for the London, Edinburgh, and Glasgow Assurance Company, Euston Square, London (1906–19), was the first scholarly *Greek-Revival building in London since the 1850s, using a variation on the *Bassae Order of C.R.*Cockerell. One of his most interesting works, Pagani's Restaurant, Great Portland Street, London (1904–5), with its ceramic-covered *façade, was destroyed in the 1939–45 war. He also designed the rumbustious Piccadilly entrance to Burlington Arcade, London (1911–30).

D & M (1985); A.S.Gray (1985); Se (ed.) (1975); Se (1977); J.T (1996)

Pitt, Thomas (1737–93—**1st Baron Camelford** from 1784) English *Dilettante/amateur architect/ politician/patron, he advised Horace *Walpole on aspects of the internal decoration of Strawberry Hill, himself designing the 'ornaments' of the Gallery and Chapel. Among his works of architecture were the *Gothic cottage, *rockwork *bridge, and a *conservatory at Park Place, near Henley-on-Thames, in Berks. (from 1763); the Palladian Bridge, Hagley, Worcs. (1764—demolished); and the *Corinthian Arch (1765–6) and south front of the house (1772–7), Stowe, Bucks. He was a connoisseur of Gothic, having prepared designs for the furnishings of the *choir at Carlisle Cathedral (1765—removed 1856) and similar work at Norwich Cathedral (1766–7—undone C19). He was an early patron of *Soane and among the first to refute Islamic origins for Gothic architecture.

BuMa (Aug. 1986), 582–4; Co (2008); ODNB (2004)

place See GENIUS LOCI.

plain tile Roofing-tile of burnt clay or *concrete, called a *common* or flat *tile.

plaisance, pleasance, pleasaunce Secluded part of a landscape-garden laid out with lawns, shady walks, trees, and shrubs, as well as architectural elements such as statues on *pedestals, *urns, arches, *fountains, pools, *gazebos and seats.

plaiting Intertwining ornament like a plait, such as the *guilloche on a *band, hence *plait-band*.

plan Horizontal drawn *section through a building showing the arrangement of rooms, etc.: it represents an object in horizontal projection, to *scale, as distinct from those representing vertical sections or *elevations, and might show an exterior of an object as seen from above, as in a *roof-plan*. See also AXIAL; BAY; CELL; CENTRE; DOUBLE PILE; END; ENTRY; E-PLAN; HALL; H-PLAN; LONGHOUSE; OPEN-HALL; SOLAR; WEALDEN.

FR (1946)

planar glazing Frameless glazing system developed by **Pilkingtons** that allows great freedom in the design of *façades.

planceer 1. Underside of any projecting member, e.g. a *cornice. **2.** *Soffit.

plane Flat surface, e.g. a wall or a floor.

plank Long flat piece of timber, thicker than a *board*. *Plank-walling* is a *timber-framed structure, the spaces filled by planks. See STAVE.

ABDM (1996)

plantain Architectural ornament consisting of a wide flat leaf.

planted Anything wrought on a separate piece of stuff, then attached by glueing, nailing, etc., as a *moulding round a *panel.

plaque Metal plate, stone *slab, or any kind of tablet, usually inscribed, fixed to (*planted) or inserted in a wall-surface, pavement, etc., as a memorial, ornament, etc.

plaster Pasty composition of soft and plastic consistency spread or daubed on a surface where it hardens. It was traditionally made of burnt *limestone (quicklime *or* calcium oxide) mixed with sand, water, and hair to provide a smooth surface fit to receive decorations. *Plaster of Paris* is lime sulphate (gypsum) deprived of its natural water-content by heat, ground to a fine powder and mixed with water to form a paste: it sets quickly, expanding at the time of setting, a peculiarity that not only makes it useful for filling cracks, but causes it to take sharp and delicate impressions from a mould. See also STUCCO.

W.McKay (1957); N (1835); W.Pa (1852)

plastic Any of a large and varied class of artificial substances which are usually carbon-based *polymers* (i.e. with molecular structures made up largely or wholly from a great number of similar polyatomic bonded units) derived from synthetic resins or modified natural polymers, and with added substances giving colour and improved performance. They may be obtained in permanent or rigid form after moulding under pressure, extrusion. etc., when they are mouldable or liquid. Although discovered in C19 they were developed from the 1930s, and after the 1939–45 war (when they were employed for numerous purposes, notably in aircraft) were used in buildings for *cladding, *mouldings, pipes, *gutters, etc. Plastics in building are of two general types: *thermosets* (incapable of being softened or melted by heat) and *thermoplastics* (which become soft when heated and rigid when cool, and can be repeatedly reheated and reshaped without any loss of their essential properties). In C20 certain plastics were used to create *tensile structures and transparent *polycarbonates* for use in e.g. *Fuller's *geodesic domes, roofing, etc. Although capable of being formed into curved shapes (e.g. the tubes for the external *escalators at the *Centre Pompidou*, Paris), transparent plastics, though tough, can be scratched, and can look very unsightly after a time. Plastics cause pollution during manufacture, so they are not favoured by advocates of *Environmentally Responsible Architecture, nor do those who argue in favour of traditional building methods approve of them (their appearance (not universally admired even when new) often deteriorates, and, in many cases, they have not lived up to expectations, have discoloured, or failed). However, plastics are widely used in protective coatings (e.g. paints), for electrical and plumbing systems, for insulation, and as waterproof sealants, gaskets, and membranes. Moulded plastic panels reinforced with glass-fibre (GRP) are used for walls and roofs. Whole buildings can be made from moulds on which liquid plastics are sprayed, and the material is being further researched as offering potential in building.

M.Foster (ed.) (1982); T.Newman (1972); Skeist (ed.) (1996); J.T (1996)

plat 1. *Plan, drawing, or instructions for building. 2. Flat area of plain grass in a garden. 3. Map of an estate, landscape-garden, etc.

platband 1. Flat, square-faced *band, *fascia, or *string, with a projection less than its height, e.g. *architrave or *fasciae. 2. Actual or ornamental *lintel. 3. *Fillet or *stria separating the *flutes on the *shaft of a Classical column. 4. Broad step. 5. *Stair-landing. 6. 'Flat' arch or soldier arch.

plate Any timber, e.g. a wall-plate, laid horizontally on *posts or walls serving as the support for other timbers above, its main functions being to provide fixings and to distribute the loads. *Types include*:
aisle-: *wall-plate* of a *timber-framed *aisled building;
arcade-: plate on top of the *posts of an *arcade in an aisled building;
collar-: plate resting on *collars. Called *collar-purlin*;
crown-: plate in a *crown-post* roof, carried on the *crown-posts* and bearing the *collars*. Also called *collar-purlin*;
head-: beam at the top of a timber-framed wall or internal partition;
jetty-: wall-plate of a lower timber-framed storey on which the joists of the jettied floor above rest, really a type of *head-;
sole-: short piece of timber (*sole-piece*) set at 90° to the face of a wall, supporting the foot of a *rafter and *ashlar-piece;
wall-: plate on top of a timber frame or load-bearing wall on which the roof-timbers rest.

ABDM (1996); S (1901-2)

plate-bande *Border of a *parterre de broderie*, either a planted strip of soil edged with box, or a double-strip, one of sand and the other planted (e.g. *Het Loo*, The Netherlands).

plated parquet *Parquet floor with pieces of contrasting wood laid in patterns.

plate-girder *See* GIRDER.

plate-glass High-quality, strong, thick *glass cast in sheets and polished, widely available after the 1830s.

plate-rail Narrow grooved shelf *planted high on the walls of a room to support and display china plates.

Plateresque Intricate highly decorative style of early C16 Spanish architecture, supposedly resembling fine silversmith's work, with enrichments derived from Classical, *Gothic, *Moorish, and *Renaissance sources, extravagantly applied to the walls of late-Gothic buildings and generally unrelated to any expression of construction.

K & S (1959); L & D (1986); H.O (1970)

plate-tracery *See* TRACERY.

Platt, Charles Adams (1861–1933) American architect/landscape-designer. His *Italianate gardens of the 1890s and early 1900s were famous, with buildings and gardens beautifully integrated (e.g. Faulkner Farm, Brookline, near Boston, MA (1897–8), and Gwinn, near Cleveland, OH (1907–8)). He advised on the designs of the *campuses of Dartmouth, Johns Hopkins, and Rochester Universities, and was architect of the Freer Gallery, Washington, DC (1913–18). His earlier architectural work was informed by *Classicism, and especially by Italian exemplars, but he also designed in a restrained *Colonial-*Georgian style, as with the Pratt House and Garden, Glen Cove, NY (1910–13). He designed the campus and buildings for the University of Illinois, Urbana, IL (1919–30—a particularly fine work in which axes, symmetry, and composed vistas are fully exploited), and for the Phillips Academy, Andover, MA (1922–33), the Coolidge Auditorium, Library of Congress, Washington, DC (1925); and the Deerfield Academy, CT (1930–2), among many other distinguished works. He published (1894) *Italian Gardens*, based on his travels (1892), and a monograph on his work (1913).

ARe, xv (1904), 181–244; K.Morgan (1985, 1995); Platt (1913); J.T (1996); vV (1993)

Plaw, John (*c*.1745–1820) British architect, he is remembered primarily for *Rural Architecture: or Designs for the Simple Cottage to the Decorative Villa* (1785 and five other editions), *Ferme Ornée ...etc.* (1795, 1813), and *Sketches for Country Houses, Villas, and Rural Dwellings* (1800, 1803). These publications were among the first of the cottage and *villa *pattern-books that were so influential in the early part of C19. He designed a remarkable circular house on Belle Isle, Windermere, Westmd. (1774–5), based on the *Pantheon; St Mary's Church, Paddington (1788–91); and several buildings in Charlottetown, Prince Edward Island, Canada, where he settled from 1809 (e.g. the Legislative Building and Court-House (1811)).

Co (2008); Darley (1975); K (1994); *ODNB* (2004); Plaw (1785, 1795, 1800); Rosinski (1994)

Playfair, James (1755–94) Scots architect, author of A *Method of Constructing Vapour Baths* (1783). The latest *Neo-Classicism was evident in the powerful Graham *mausoleum at Methven, Perthshire (1793), a Greek temple-front *engaged to *rusticated masonry. At Cairness House, Aberdeenshire (1791–7), his interesting design included a hemicycle of offices, *primitive *Doric columns, and an extraordinary *Egyptian-Revival Billiard-Room. He also designed Farnell Church, Angus (1789–1806), in a precocious *Gothic style.

Co (2008); Crook (1972a); J.Curl (2005)

Playfair, William Henry (1790–1857) Younger son of James *Playfair, pupil of William *Stark, he later worked in the offices of '*Wyatt and *Smirke' (probably **Benjamin Dean** and **Robert**, respectively) before returning to Scotland (1818) to plan the Calton Hill Estate, Edinburgh, where he built (from 1821) Blenheim Place, Brunswick Street, Brunton Place, Carlton Terrace, Elm Row, Hillside Crescent, Leopold Place, Montgomery Street, Regent Terrace, Royal Terrace, and Windsor Street. He also designed Royal Circus, Circus Place, and Circus Gardens (1821–3). For the next three decades, with *Burn and Gillespie *Graham, he was a leading architect in Scotland and gave Edinburgh some of its finest buildings. These include: completion (1817–26) of Edinburgh University (begun (1789–93) to designs by Robert and James *Adam); the splendid *Greek-Revival (with Egyptianesque touches) Royal Institution (1822–35—now Royal Scottish Academy); the unfinished Greek-*Doric National Monument, Calton Hill, based on the *Parthenon (1824–9—with C.R. *Cockerell); Surgeons' Hall, Nicolson Street (1830–2); **Dugald Stewart**'s (1753–1828) Monument, Calton Hill (1831—based on the *Choragic Monument of Lysicrates, Athens); Donaldson's Hospital (1842–54—*Jacobethan); the scenographic *Gothic Free Church College (1846–50); and the *Ionic National Gallery of Scotland (1850–7). He also designed Brownlow House, Lurgan, Co. Armagh (1833–9—Jacobethan); several monuments, including the Rutherfurd *pyramid (c.1852) and his own tomb (c.1857), both in the Dean Cemetery, Edinburgh; and the Greek-Doric Campbell grave-surround, St Quivox churchyard,

Ayrshire (1822). Many of his drawings survive in Edinburgh University Library.

Close & Riches (2012); Co (2008); Crook (1972a); A.Fraser (1989); GMcW & W (1984); Glendinning et al. (1996); Gow (1984); Macaulay (1975); *ODNB* (2004); Youngson (1966)

plaza 1. Public square or market-place, esp. in Spain or Latin America. **2.** Large paved area surrounded by or adjacent to buildings, often embellished with sculpture, fountains, and planting, esp. in North America. **3.** Suburban shopping-area consisting of a huge parking-lot surrounded by shops. **4.** Covered area, often lit from above, for shops, etc. **5.** Area where tolls are collected at a bridge, tunnel, or motorway.

pleach To interlace or intertwine, e.g. branches of young trees to form a 'hedge on stilts' or the like, as in a *palissade* in a garden *allee or *arbour. *See* PALISADE.

pleasance *or* **pleasaunce 1.** Garden, especially that of a medieval *castle, *manor-house, or *monastery. **2.** *As* PLAISANCE.

pleasure-garden 1. Any garden or *pleasure-ground* for relaxation, etc., distinct from a vegetable-garden, *kitchen-garden, or *orchard. **2.** Garden run as a commercial enterprise from the Restoration (1660) until the mid-C19 in London. Spring (later Vauxhall) Gardens was one of the first, with straight walks, regular rows of trees, and secluded areas for dalliance; supper-boxes in the Chinese-*Gothick Taste; various garden-buildings to heighten *perspective; statuary; and a grand-stand for an orchestra. Intended for a wide spectrum of society, pleasure-gardens provided musical entertainment, food, drink, and opportunity for much ogling and quizzing, so acquired a raffish reputation. Other pleasure-gardens included Ranelagh, Chelsea, with its huge Rotunda (designed by **William Jones** (d.1757), opened 1742, demolished 1805) containing an elegant galleried interior where persons of quality could take tea and other refreshments while listening to music. Another fashionable pleasure-garden was Marylebone (or Marybone). Other London gardens (e.g. Bagnigge Wells, Islington Spa, and the somewhat *louche* London Spaw) were associated with springs, supposedly medicinal, which added to their attractions. The London grounds were imitated elsewhere in England and on the Continent (e.g. *Carstensen's Tivoli Gardens, Copenhagen, which, however, was much grander and more sophisticated than the C18 London exemplars).

Coke & Borg (2011); J.Curl (2010); Foord (1910); Sunderland (1915)

pleasure-house *Summer-house or other building used solely for pleasure.

Plečnik, Jože (1872–1957) Slovenian architect, one of the most distinguished and imaginative C20 designers working in the Classical tradition. Ljubljana-born, he trained under Otto *Wagner in Vienna from 1895 and became friendly with *Kotěra. He was appointed (1901) Secretary of the *Sezession, having established (1900) his own office in the Austrian capital, where he designed the Weidmann House, Hietzing (1902), and an office and apartment-block for the wealthy **Johannes Zacherl** in Vienna (1903–5), both of which showed strong Wagnerian influences. His greatest work of the Vienna years was the *Heilig-Geist-Kirche, Herbststrasse* (1908–13), where he used *reinforced concrete, and created a *stripped Neo-Classical exterior and a *crypt employing crystalline, almost *Expressionist forms. Nominated by the Vienna Academy to become Professor of Architecture in succession to Wagner (1911), his appointment was blocked at Court on the grounds that the 'first school' of the Austro-Hungarian Empire should not be headed by a Slovene. Plečnik was invited by Kotěra to teach at the Prague School of Applied Arts (1911), and with the independence of Czechoslovakia (1918), began work on the restoration, adaptation, and enlargement of Hradčany Castle, Prague, as the Presidential Residence (1920–36), where his free use of Classical allusions in the buildings and gardens created one of the loveliest ensembles in all Europe. He also designed the Presidential *Villa and gardens at Lány (1920–30), and the powerful Neo-Classical Church of the Sacred Heart, Vinohrady, Prague (1928–31).

In 1920 Plečnik accepted the Headship of the Architecture Department of the University of Ljubljana, Slovenia (newly part of Yugoslavia), retaining a post as Honorary Architect to the City of Prague. He created a series of masterpieces of *Neo-Classicism in Ljubljana, including the Church of St Francis, Šiška (1926–7); various structures along the river, including *bridges and *colonnades in the Markets Area (1930s); the Slovene National Cemetery, Žale (1937–40); National and University Library (1936–41); and various other buildings. The Church of the Ascension, Bogojina (1925–7), employs the toughest of *primitive *Doric columns inside (with stilted arches), and the Church of St Michael in Barje, Ljubljana (1937–40), has a powerful *campanile and a most elegant interior featuring much timber-work. Throughout his designs from 1920 until his death are free interpretations of the Greek *Orders, including derivations from the *Aeolian and *Ionic forms, suggesting an archaic quality of great power. Unlike those who used the Classical vocabulary with literalness, Plečnik demonstrated what infinite variety and emotional expressiveness could be achieved by developing and extending a rich

language. He should be ranked among the greatest architects of C20.

Achleitner *et al.* (1986); R.Andrews *et al.* (eds) (1983, 1986); B & G (1986); Burkhardt *et al.* (eds) (1989); Krečic (1993); Margolius (1995); Prelovšek (1979, 1997); Svácha (1995)

plenum System of artificial ventilation: fresh air, forced into a building, drives out vitiated air. It is the opposite of the *vacuum system, whereby used air is sucked out. Also used to describe heating and air-conditioning systems.

plinth 1. Plain, continuous projecting surface under the *base-moulding of a wall, *pedestal, or *podium *quadra, connecting the architectural member with the ground or floor. **2.** In the Classical *Orders, the low plain block under the base-mouldings of a column, pedestal, or *pilaster. **3.** Any monumental support for a statue, etc. **4.** Base-course of a wall supporting an *off-set, as when a wall diminishes in thickness. **5.** *Eaves-course. **6.** *Abacus (plinthus) of the Greek-*Doric Order. *Other compounds include*:

plinth-block: simple rectangular base-block against which *architrave, plinth, *skirting, etc., stop to avoid awkward junctions. It is set e.g. between the floor or ground and the architrave, and is the same height as the plinth or skirting;

plinth-course: top, moulded course of a plinth, or the continuous course of *masonry comprising the plinth;

plinthus: used by *Vitruvius for the *abacus of the Greek-*Doric *Order.

Pliny (Plinius) the Younger (Caius Plinius Caecilius Secundus) (AD 62–c.116) Roman politician/orator/writer. From AD 106 he was superintendent of *aqueducts, but his chief importance in architecture lies in his descriptions of his Laurentine and Tuscan *villas that have exercised the imaginations of scholars ever since.

RdP (1994)

ploughshare twist Warped *web of a *Gothic *vault framed by a diagonal *rib and stilted wall-rib, occurring when the wall-ribs are sprung from a higher level than the diagonal ribs, as when accommodating *clerestorey *lights. As the web is distorted, twisted like a ploughshare, it is also called a *plowshare vault.

Plumet, Charles (1861–1928) French architect, he drew on medieval and early French-*Renaissance themes, but used *Art-Nouveau forms in his shop-interiors and furniture-design (with **Tony Selmersheim** (1871–1971)). Interested in reviving the applied and decorative arts in his buildings, he often employed *polychromy, *loggie, and *bay-windows in his *façades. His sumptuous dwellings at 67 *Avenue de Malakoff* (1895), 50 *Avenue Victor*

Hugo (1900-1), and 15 and 21 *Boulevard Lannes* (1906), all in Paris, are typical of his work. He designed the *Château de Chênemoireau*, Loire-et-Cher, France (1901), and an office block at 33 *Rue du Louvre*, Paris (1913-14). Chief Architect of the *Exposition International des Arts-Décoratifs*, Paris (1924-5), he had an influence on the *Art-Deco style.

Badovici (1923); B & G (1978); T-M (1967)

plunge-pool *See* COLD-BATH.

Pluralism 1970s term defining aspects of *Post-Modernism, suggesting drawing on various styles and motifs in eclectic compositions.

Js (1973a); Papadakis (ed.) (1989); Robins (1985)

pluteus Low wall closing the gap between Classical columns, about one-third of their height, in a *colonnade.

plywood *or* **ply-wood** Board composed of three or more thin layers of wood bonded (glued) together with the grain of adjacent layers running at right angles to their neighbours to give increased strength and resistance to warping.

pneumatic architecture Inflatable structures such as balloons and airships have been known for many years, but not until 1917 was the first patent for *pneumatic architecture* taken out by **Frederick William Lanchester** (1868-1946), brother of H.V.*Lanchester, and manufacturer of the Lanchester motor-car. With the development (1940s) of the *Radome* (Radar Dome) to provide protection for microwave antennae, the manufacture of pneumatic structures evolved further, structural stability being achieved by air- or gas-pressure on some kind of membrane or bag, so pneumatic structures are usually curved, often domes or cylinders, or some other form compatible with pressurized construction. Pneumatic buildings have been used for exhibitions, covering stadia, and even formwork for *concrete structures. Pneumatic architecture was proposed by Cedric *Price, among others.

Dent (1971); Dessauce (ed.) (1999); T.Herzog (1977); Horden (1995); Klotz (ed.) (1986); Lim & Liu (eds) (2002); Price (1971); Topham (2002)

Pniower, Georg Béla (1896-1960) German landscape architect, he assisted the Parks Director, **Hermann Kube** (1866-1944), in Hanover before working with the landscape architect **Josef Buerbaum** (1878-1961), in Düsseldorf. From 1922 he headed the design-department of the huge **Ludwig Späth** tree-nursery, Berlin, and by the early 1930s was on the verge of starting an international career when the National Socialists came to power (1933). For a time he worked on the landscaping of the *Autobahnen* before

running foul of the authorities, and was forced to do factory-work until 1945, when he began to rebuild his career, not only as a designer but as a teacher of garden-art and landscape-design based at Humboldt University, Berlin, where he established a new *Institut für Garten- und Landes-kultur*. He was involved in creating exemplary landscapes east of the Harz Mountains, and in research into the need for green spaces as part of Socialist city-planning, not least the greening of rubble- and debris-strewn areas in towns and the recultivation of dumps associated with the mining of brown coal. He was also involved in research related to soil-erosion and ecology.

Gröning & Wolschke-Bulmahn (1997); Shoe (2001); Tay (2006)

Poccianti, Francesco Gurrieri Pasquale (1774-1858) Italian architect, pupil of **Gaspero Maria Paoletti** (1727-1813). As First Architect to the Royal Works in Tuscany (1817-35), he carried out numerous alterations and improvements to Grand-Ducal residences (e.g. *Palazzo Pitti*, Florence (1818-47), the *villa at Poggio a Caiano (*orangery, reservoir, stables, and reordering of the chapel), and the villas at Pratolino and l'Ambrogiana (all *c*.1822-36)). He converted the *Palazzo Strozzi* into offices, designed a new School of Anatomy at the *Ospedale di Santa Maria Nuova* (1818-26), and the extension of the *Biblioteca Laurenziana*, including the domed *Sala d'Elci* (1817-41), all in Florence. He made a huge contribution to the architectural fabric of Tuscany, but his master-work is the massive system of *aqueducts, filters, water-works, etc., in and around Livorno, for which he designed *Il Cisternone* (1829-41—a water-distribution reservoir), one of the most successful realizations of the severe *Neo-Classical style of *Boullée, *Ledoux, and their contemporaries. A plain *façade is fronted by an octastyle unpedimented Roman-*Doric *portico, and above is half a *Pantheon-dome, built in section, as it were, with the interior *coffers showing. He prepared a plan for the expansion of Livorno which is a remarkable expression of Neo-Classical ideals of harmony, balance, function, and rationality.

F.Borsi *et al*. (1974); Matteoni (1992); Ms (1966); M & Wa (1987); J.T (1996)

Pocock, William Fuller (1779-1849) English architect/surveyor, pupil of **Charles Beazley** (*c*.1760-1829), he became assistant to Thomas *Hardwick, and set up in practice on his own account by 1803. His best work was in the *Greek-Revival style, though he also worked in *Gothic. He published *Architectural Designs for Rustic Cottages, Picturesque Dwellings, Villas, etc., with appropriate Scenery* (1807, 1819, 1823—which contained 33 plates of designs for *villas and 'cabbanes ornées', mostly in the 'antient English' character); *Modern Finishings for Rooms: a Series of Designs for Vestibules, Staircases, Boudoirs, Libraries, etc., to which are added some Designs for Villas and Porticos* (1811, 1823, 1837); *Designs for Churches and Chapels* (1819, 1824, 1835); and *Observations on Bond in Brickwork* (1839).

Co (2008); ODNB (2004); Pocock (1807, 2010)

podium 1. Continuous *pedestal with *base, *plinth, *die, and *cornice, such as used to support an *Order of Classical columns high above ground-level in a monumental building. In Classical architecture it is essentially the platform on which stood a Roman *temple or a *peristyle of columns supporting a *dome. **2.** Platform around the arena of a Roman *amphitheatre over which the seats of the nobility were placed.

Poelaert, Joseph Philippe (1817–79) Belgian architect, influenced by *Schinkel and *Visconti, who became (1856) Brussels City Architect. He designed the *Colonne du Congrès* (1850–9) and other buildings in Brussels, but his greatest work was the *Sublime *Beaux-Arts *Baroque *Palais de Justice* (1866–83), a vast *pile of pyramidal composition crowned by a massive *dome, influenced perhaps by *Brodrick's Town Hall, Leeds (1852–8), and by the visionary paintings of **John Martin** (1789–1854). Some of the internal public spaces have an *Antique Roman grandeur worthy of *Piranesi. He also designed the *Neo-Gothic *Notre-Dame de Laeken*, Brussels (1851–65), completed (1865–1907) by von *Schmidt of Munich and others.

Hi (1977); Loo (ed.) (2003); P (1982); J.T (1996); D.Wa (1986)

Poelzig, Hans (1869–1936) German architect. After working under *Häring (1890s), he was appointed (through the influence of *Muthesius) Professor (and Director from 1903) at the Academy of Arts and Crafts in Breslau (now Wrocław), where he also had his own office until 1916. While there he designed the *Expressionist Water Tower and Exhibition Hall, Posen (now Poznań), Silesia (1910–11), a heptagonal steel-framed structure filled with panes of *herringbone brickwork. Other buildings included an office-block in Breslau (1911–12), with horizontal window-strips (anticipating the *International Modernism of the following decades), a Chemical Factory and Workers' Housing at Luban (now Lubań, Poland—1911–12), and several buildings in Breslau (to mark the centenary of the victory (1813) over **Emperor Napoléon I** (r.1804–14, 1815)) in which he used a Greek-*Doric Order simplified and adapted to *concrete construction. He became City Architect of Dresden (1916–20) and Professor

at the *Technische Hochschule* there, where he produced several fantastic Expressionist designs (unrealized), including a proposal for the *Festspielhaus*, Salzburg (1919–20), but built the Dresden Gasworks (1916). In 1918 he joined the *Novembergruppe*, followed by *Arbeitsrat für Kunst, became Chairman of the *Deutscher Werkbund (1919), and was an active participant of *Der *Ring. For **Max Reinhardt** (1873–1943), he converted (1919) the *Schumann Circus* into the Expressionist *Grosses Schauspielhaus*, Berlin, with stalactite vaults in the *auditorium (destroyed). By 1920 he had moved to Berlin, heading a studio in the Academy of Arts there and, from 1923, teaching at Berlin-Charlottenburg: his pupils included *Eiermann and *Wachsmann. Among other buildings the Capitol Cinema, Berlin (1925), the Sigmund Goeritz Factory, Chemnitz (1927), a house for the *Weissenhofsiedlung*, Stuttgart (1927), Broadcasting House, Berlin (1930), and the gigantic *I.G.Farben* Administrative Building, Frankfurt-am-Main (1928–31), the last showing certain tendencies towards a *stripped *Neo-Classicism, deserve mention.

Heuss (1939); Killy et al. (1965); L (1988); Lane (1985); Marquart (1995); Pehnt (1973); Poelzig (1954); Posener (1970, 1992); Sharp (1967); T & DC (1986)

point To fill up and carefully finish, as in *mortar *jointing in brickwork or *masonry. Its purpose is to preserve the material from the weather as well as create an aesthetically pleasing effect. *Related terms include*:
pointed: **1.** rough *masonry finish made by a pick or pointing tool, with a *picked face (i.e. with only the coarsest projections removed) also called *pecking*. **2.** type of arch; **3.** with a capital P, 'Pointed' refers to the *Gothic style, divided into *First, *Middle, *Second, and *Third Pointed, the last most commonly called *Perp. in England. **4.** Brickwork or masonry, the joints of which have been raked out and *pointed* with mortar. *See also* BRICK;
pointing: process, material, or completed finish of mortar-joints in brickwork or *masonry. *See* BRICK.

Bru (1990)

point-block High apartment-building with the circulation and services in the central core and the residential areas grouped around it on several storeys. *See* TOWER-BLOCK.

pointel, poyntell, or poyntill 1. Pavement formed of small *tiles laid diagonally in patterns. *Compare* MOSAIC. **2.** *Pavement of lozenge-shaped tiles.

point of view *Point de vue*, or position from which anything is viewed. *See* EYE-CATCHER.

poivrière Corner-*turret resembling a pepper-pot.

polder **1.** Area of low-lying land reclaimed from sea, lake, or river, protected by *dikes, esp. in The Netherlands. **2.** *pollarded* tree.

policy **1.** Improvement or embellishment of an estate or town. **2.** Buildings, gardens, etc. on an estate. **3.** Enclosed park or *demesne land around a country-house.

polis Ancient Greek city (πόλις) or city-state. It is commonly found combined with other words as a nickname for a town, e.g. *Linenopolis* for C19 Belfast, and with prefixes such as *metro-* it means a capital, mother-city, chief centre, or major city. *See also* ACROPOLIS; NECROPOLIS.

Wy (1962)

Polish hut One of many quasi-national *rustic garden *fabriques* fashionable in C19, built of trunks and branches of trees, still covered in bark and roofed in *thatch, etc., with ceilings and walls covered with kiln-dried *furze* (gorse/whin), etc.). *Papworth designed (*c.*1810) one for **George Spencer Churchill** (1766–1840—**Marquess of Blandford**, later **5th Duke of Marlborough** from 1817) at Whiteknights, Reading, Berks. (all demolished), illustrated in *Ackermann's Repository* (1819), but Papworth credited the *type to **Jean-Baptiste Kléber** (1753–1800), who designed such a *fabrique* for gardens in Alsace. The term seems to have been interchangeable with *Swiss cottage. See* BENGAL COTTAGE.

J.B.Pa (1823)

Polish parapet Type of *Renaissance *parapet ornamented with *blind *arcades, *aedicules, *pilasters, *pedestals, *pediments, *pyramids, etc., concealing the roof, commonly found in Poland. Good examples are the Cloth Hall, Kraków (1555–8), the Town Hall, Chełmno on the Vistula (1567–72), and two remarkable façades in the Market Square of Kazimierz Dolny (1615, 1635).

Zachwatowicz *et al.* (1952)

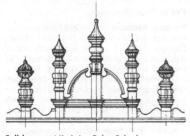

Polish parapet Kazimierz Dolny, Poland.

Polk, Willis Jefferson (1867–1924) American architect, he worked for several architects (including van *Brunt) before establishing himself in San Francisco (1890). He produced a rich array of architecture, the best of which was influenced by the work of *McKim, Mead, & White. He assisted *Burnham in preparing the plan for San Francisco (1904–5), and in the years up to the 1914–18 war his buildings were modelled on Burnham's polished Classical manner. However, Hallidie Building, San Francisco (1917–18), was different, having a fully glazed *curtain-wall hung from the main framed structure, reckoned to be among the very first examples of its kind, although ornamented in the manner of *Sullivan with vaguely *Art-Nouveau details.

ARe, xxxiv (1913), 566–83; *JSAH,* xxx/1 (Mar. 1971), 323–9; Longstreth (1979, 1983); P (1982); J.T (1996); S.Woodbridge (ed.) (1976)

Pollack, Johann Michael *called* **Mihály** (1773–1855) Vienna-born architect, half-brother of Leopoldo *Pollack, he settled (1798) in Pest where he had a successful career as a *Neo-Classical architect (e.g. Evangelical Church (1799–1808)). Most of his work in Pest was for *apartment-blocks and mansions with restrained *façades and internal *courts (e.g. Pollack House, Jossef Attila Street 6 (1822) and Festetits Mansion (1802–6)). He also designed the County Hall, Szekszárd (1828–36), Festetits Palace, Dég, near Enying (1811–15), *Ludoviceum,* Pest (1828–36), and Hungarian National Museum, Pest (1836–46—his masterpiece, incorporating a circular hall with *dome modelled on that of the *Pantheon, Rome). At Pécs (Fünfkirchen) he designed a *Gothic-Revival façade for the Cathedral (1807–25—destroyed when von *Schmidt rebuilt it (1882–91) in a Neo-Romanesque style).

M & Wa (1987); J.T (1996); Zádor (1960, 1985)

Pollack, Leopoldo (1750–1806) Vienna-born architect, he settled (1775) in Milan and assisted *Piermarini on the *Palazzo Ducale.* He designed the *Villa Casati,* Muggiò (1790s), and the *Villa Rocca-Saporiti,* called *La Rotonda,* Borgovico (again 1790s), each of which has an elliptical *salon. His greatest work was the *Villa-Reale Belgioioso,* Milan (1790–6), the elevations of which are derived from *Gabriel's frontages to the *Place de la Concorde,* Paris (1753–75), although the *Order used by Pollack was *Ionic rather than *Corinthian. He also laid out the gardens in a *Picturesque English style, which proved influential, and designed several theatres, including the *Teatro Sociale,* Bergamo (1805—completed by his son, **Giuseppe** (1779–1857)).

L'Arte, xxxviii (1963), 1–20; Me (1966); Ms (1966); M & Wa (1987); J.T (1996)

Pollen, Francis Anthony (1926–87) English RC architect, grandson of J.H.*Pollen, he formed (1956) a partnership with his cousin, Philip *Jebb, and spent most of his career designing houses and ecclesiastical buildings, more often than not through commissions prompted by his family connections. His mastery of *Classicism was demonstrated in the offices for London Assurance, Pall Mall, London (1956), where the influence of *Lutyens was clear. He formed (1959) a new partnership with **Lionel Gordon Baliol Brett** (1913–2004—**4th Viscount Esher** from 1963), by which time he bowed to fashion and became influenced by the work of Le *Corbusier (e.g. at the Lion Boys' Club, Hoxton (1960), and some houses). He also designed several unlikeable churches, including Our Lady Help of Christians, Hurst Green, Sussex (1959), but at Worth *Benedictine Abbey, near Crawley, West Sussex (1989), the Lutyens strain re-asserted itself in its solid forms, scale, and austerity. As his biographer has noted, Pollen's work 'challenges the whole conceptual framework through which architectural judgement is commonly made, based on the assumption that a single sequential development of style is the criterion of integrity'.

The Catholic Herald (1 Sept. 2000), 9; Powers (1999); *The Spectator* (29 Jan. 2000), 53

Pollen, John Hungerford (1820–1902) London-born decorative artist/architect/Anglican clergyman, and RC convert (1852). Through his father-in-law's appeal to **John Henry Newman** (1801–90), then President of the New Catholic University of Ireland, Pollen was appointed Professor of Fine Arts in Dublin, and was commissioned to design the University Church in St Stephen's Green. Inspired by his visit (1847) to Ravenna and Munich (where he saw the almost completed *basilica of *St Bonifaz*, designed by *Ziebland), and determined (like Newman) to avoid *Gothic (by then *Pugin's proselytization had satiated many), he created, in an exquisite *Byzantine style, a master-work (consecrated 1856) with an interior aglow with coloured *marbles. He never again achieved anything as fine, although he designed the *Rundbogenstil RC Church of Our Lady of the Assumption, Rhyl, with Celtic motifs on the *altar (1863–4), and much polychrome decoration (all demolished).

Hubbard (1986); *ODNB* (2004); Pollen (1912)

Pollini, Gino (1903–91) *See* FIGINI.

polos 1. Cylindrical headdress of a *caryatid. **2.** Greek centring-pin or dowel used when jointing the drums of column-shafts.

D (1950)

polychromy Elaborate architectural decoration using many colours, as in Ancient-Greek architecture, revived by *Hittorff, *Bindesbøll, and others. *Structural polychromy* is where the colour is *not applied* after construction, but is provided by the brick, stones, or *tiles used in the building: it was a feature of mature *Gothic Revival. More recently, **John Outram** (1934–) used spectacular polychromy at the Judge Institute of Management Studies, Cambridge (1993–5), thereby enraging Modernists.

Gw (1903); Outram (2003); W.Pa (1852); S (1901–2); J.T (1996); Z (1977)

Polyclitus the Younger (*fl.*370–336 BC) Ancient-Greek architect/sculptor. He designed the theatre and *tholos (*c.*350 BC), Epidaurus, which had very beautiful *Corinthian *capitals on the internal circle of fourteen columns, and a *Doric *Order for the external *peristyle.

Burford (1969); D (1950); La (1983)

polyfoil With many *foils, also *multifoil*.

polygonal masonry Made of smooth many-sided (i.e. with more than four angles or sides) stone blocks closely fitted together. In Antiquity called *opus polygonum*. It is also known as *cyclopean* or *pelasgic* *masonry.

polystyle Composed of many columns.

polytriglyphal *Doric *frieze with more than one *triglyph per *intercolumniation.

pomel *See* POMMEL.

Pomerance, Ralph (1907–95) American architect, he founded (1933) his NYC practice and designed several much-admired houses in the *International-Modernist style (e.g. his own house at Cos Cob, CT (1940)). With *Markelius, he was responsible for the Swedish Pavilion at the New York World's Fair (1939). A single-storey house at Croton-on-Hudson, NYC (1940–1), received acclaim.

PPS

pommel, pomel 1. As *crop. **2.** Ball, *boss, *knob, or *knot *terminal used as a *finial for *pinnacles, pyramidal roofs, etc.

PoMo *Post-Modernism.

Pompe, Antoine (1873–1980) Undersung Belgian architect. His Van Neck Orthopaedic Clinic, Brussels (1910), is a remarkable composition, with ventilation-shafts expressed externally. His low-cost housing projects (e.g. at *Sint-Lambrechts-Woluwe*, Brussels (1922–6)) were sensitively designed and humane, and his private houses (e.g. in *Floridalaan*, Uccele, Brussels (1926–destroyed)) were always interesting. Opposed to the reductivist tendencies of *Functionalism and *International Modernism, he wrote a devastating polemic describing a man who had been disastrously redesigned by a *Modernist architect.

Loo (ed.) (2003); J.T (1996)

Pompeian The Roman town of Pompeii was buried by deposits of volcanic ash when Mount Vesuvius erupted (AD 79), thus partially preserving it for posterity. Rediscovered (1748), it began to be excavated from 1755, and the architecture, artefacts, interior decorations, motifs, and details uncovered there and at *Herculaneum and Stabia had a profound effect on *Neo-Classical design after they began to appear in publications (e.g. *Le antichità di Ercolano esposte* (1757–92), a vast study prepared by the *Accademia Ercolanese*, established under the aegis of **Charles VII, King of the Two Sicilies** (r.1734–59, later **King Charles III of Spain** (r.1759–88)). Pompeian schemes of *frescoed wall-decorations were to provide the main themes, including the bold blacks, greens, reds, and yellows, with finely drawn borders and *grotesques that became an important part of the C18 *Etruscan or *Pompeian* style. *Gell and *Gandy's *Pompeiana* (1817–19 with later editions) was an important source, as were *Die schönsten Ornamente und merkwürdigsten Gemälde aus Pompeji, Herkulaneum und Stabiae* (1828–59) by **Wilhelm Zahn** (1800–71), and *Les Ruines de Pompéi* (1809–38) by **Charles-François Mazois** (1783–1826). Among architects who used the Pompeian style were Joseph *Bonomi at Great Packington, Warwicks. (1785–8), *Schinkel at *Schloss Glienecke*, near Berlin (1824–9), and *Gärtner at the Pompeian House, Aschaffenburg (1842–6), but these are only three examples of very many. See NÉO-GREC.

Gell & Gandy (1852); Honour (1977); L & D (1986); H.O (1970); Panitz (ed.) (1977); J.T (1996); P.Werner (1970).

Ponsonby, Sarah ('**Sally**') (1755–1831) *See* BUTLER, LADY.

Pontelli, Baccio (1450–94/5) Florentine architect/sculptor/engineer celebrated for his impressive fortifications, e.g. those at Ostia, with massive *machicolations (1483–6). He worked on the Ducal Palace at Urbino with F.di *Giorgio Martini and *Laurana from 1479, and settled in Rome (c.1481), where he may have designed (or influenced the design of) *San Pietro in Montorio* (1481–94) and the *Palazzo della Cancellaria* (1480s). The enormous body of work attributed to him by *Vasari seems to be spurious.

G.Fiore (1963); He (1996); J.T (1996)

Ponti, Gio(vanni) (1891–1979) Italian architect, whose earliest work was first influenced by the *Sezession* movement and then by the clear rational architecture of Otto *Wagner (e.g. the house on *Via Randaccio*, Milan (1924–5), and the *Bouilhet Villa*, Garches, near Paris (1925–6), in both of which a simplified *Neo-Classicism may be detected). He was founder-director of the influential architectural journal *Domus* (1928–79), which is perhaps his greatest legacy, and demonstrated his *Rationalist and Classicist credentials with the School of Mathematics, University of Rome (1934). He built the Montecatini Building, Milan (1936–9), in which standardization played a major role (a second block was completed in 1951). His work after the 1939–45 war abandoned all traces of Classical formalism, as in the Pirelli Tower, Milan (1956–8—with *Nervi and others), one of the first *skyscrapers to deviate from the rectangular slab-form common in *International Modernism. Other buildings include the *Bijenkorf* Shopping Centre, Eindhoven, The Netherlands (1967—with others), the Cathedral, Taranto (1969–71), and the Museum of Modern Art, Denver, CO (1972—with others).

E (1994); Ponti (1990); Romanelli (2002); J.T (1996); vV (1993)

Ponting, Charles Edwin (1850–1932) English church architect, who also designed several secular buildings, including the *Carolean-*Edwardian Town Hall, Marlborough, Wilts. (1901–2), with a prominent use of the *Ipswich window. His handsome St Mary's Church, West Fordington, Dorchester, Dorset (1910– 12), is probably his best work.

A.S.Gray (1985)

Pont Street Dutch English Revival of Flemish and North-German *Renaissance architecture (1870s–'80s) featuring high, stepped, shaped, and ornamented *gables, rubbed and moulded brick, *terracotta, and other elements derived from a similar revival in Belgium and The Netherlands, but given particular opulence by Sir Ernest *George and his firm in the Kensington and Knightsbridge areas of London, hence the reference to Pont Street. *Also called* *Northern Renaissance Revival.

J.Curl (2007); Grainger (2011); A.S.Gray (1985); L & H (1993); L & D (1986)

Ponzio, Flaminio (1560–1613) From Lombardy, he settled in Rome (mid-1580s), where he designed a number of late-*Mannerist buildings. The Pauline Chapel at *Santa Maria Maggiore* (1605–11) is much enriched with coloured *marbles, gilded *stucco, and *inlaid work. He reconstructed part of the *Palazzo Borghese*, where the long *elevation is probably his (1605–13), and designed the noble *Acqua Paola* *fountain on the Janiculum (1608–11). Further reconstruction was planned by him at *San Sebastiano fuori le Mura*, including the elegant west front (1609–13), and at *Raphael and *Peruzzi's *Sant'Eligio degli Orefici* (1602).

Hd (1962, 1971); J.T (1996); Waddy (1990)

Poortman, Hugo Anne Cornelis (1858–1953) Dutch garden-designer, he worked (1880–7) under É.-F.*André in Paris before returning to The Netherlands and practice, specializing in parks and gardens for private estates. His style mixed formal and informal layouts in the manner of André. He was co-founder (1922) of the *Bond Nederlandse Tuinarchitecten* (Soc. of Dutch Garden-Architects).

Tay (2006); Zijlstra (1991)

Pop architecture 1. Architecture *popular* with the public. **2.** Buildings the forms of which suggest their function, such as a shoe-shaped shoe-shop; also called 'bizarre', 'illegitimate', 'programmatic', or 'roadside' architecture. **Robert Charles Venturi** (1925–2018) has included 'autoscape architecture' (large illuminated advertisements common in the USA) in the pop-architecture category. **3.** Work influenced by popular architecture, or responding to *High-Tech- and *Archigram-promoted images.

Anderton (1998); J.J.C.Andrews (1985); *AR*, cxxxii/785 (July 1962), 43–6; Js (1979); *RIBAJ*, lxxii/3 (Mar. 1965), 142–3; R.Vi (1966, 1996); R.Vi et al. (1977); Vostell & Higgins (1969)

Pope, Alexander (1688–1744) English poet/garden-designer. He laid out his own garden at Twickenham, Mddx., which exemplified principles of light and shade, grouping and *perspective, and contained a commemorative *obelisk and *urns, so had mnemonic and elegiac overtones. His insistence on respecting the *genius loci led to a growing sensitivity towards the natural features of a site (which even might be enhanced), and his was a powerful influence on the design of the C18 garden.

Batey (1999); D.Coffin (1994); J.T (1996)

Pope, John Russell (1873–1937) American architect, the greatest academic American Classicist of his time. A disciple of *McKim, Mead, & White, he trained at the *École des *Beaux-Arts, Paris (1897–9), began practice (1903), and produced some fine Neo-Classical buildings of national and international importance, including the Temple of the Scottish Rite, Washington, DC (1910—a vast pyramidal composition alluding to the *Mausoleum at Halicarnassus), and his two best-known works, the Jefferson Memorial (1935–43), and the National Gallery of Art (1936–41), both in Washington, DC (and both completed by **Otto Eggers** (1882–1964) and **Daniel Paul Higgins** (1886–1953)). He also designed the Sculpture Hall, Tate Gallery, London (1935–8), and the Sculpture Gallery, British Museum, London (1936–8—built to house the 'Elgin Marbles' from the Athenian *Parthenon): both galleries were donated by **Joseph, 1st Baron Duveen of** Millbank (1869–1939). Pope also designed the conversion of the mansion housing the Frick Collection, NYC (1931–5).

Bedford (1998); Pope & Cortissoz (1924–30); *RIBAJ*, ser. 3, xlv/2 (22 Nov. 1937), 102; J.T (1996); vV (1993)

Pope, Richard (*fl.c.* 1442). English *Freemason, he designed the tower of Dunster Church, Som., and was probably master-mason at St John's Hospital and Sherborne Abbey, Sherborne, Dorset (1440s): if this is the case, he was responsible for the design of the noble *choir at the Abbey. **Thomas** and **Walter Pope** (probably related) worked (first half of C15) at Exeter Cathedral.

J.Harvey (1987)

Pope-Riddle, Theodate (1868–1946) *See* RIDDLE.

Pöppelmann, Matthäus Daniel (1662–1736) German architect, he settled (1680) in Dresden, and from 1705 was in charge of palace rebuildings for **Friedrich Augustus II** ('the Strong'), **Elector of Saxony** (*r.*1694–1733) and **King of Poland** (*r.*1697–1704, 1709–33). His masterpiece is the *Zwinger*, Dresden (1711–28), a space surrounded by single-storey galleries linking two-storey *pavilions and a *gateway of extraordinary inventive *Rococo vitality. Part *orangery, part grandstand, part *nymphaeum, and part *gallery, it was intended to enhance Augustus's status by allusions to Roman theatres, *fora, and *thermae. Richly embellished with architectural sculpture by **Balthasar Permoser** (1651–1732), the *Zwinger* was to be part of a vast new palace designed by Pöppelmann that showed influences from *Hildebrandt and Carlo *Fontana, but the *Kronentor* (1713) of the *Zwinger* was derived from plates 60 and 100 in *Pozzo's Prattica della Perspettiva*, published in a German edition (1708).

The 'Indian' *Schloss Pillnitz*, upstream on the Elbe (1720–3), has charming *Chinoiserie elements, including the roofs, and is one of the largest C18 European buildings in an oriental style. Pöppelmann was in charge of the alterations at the Dutch (later Japanese) Palace, Dresden, from 1715, but was gradually edged out by *Longuelune whose flat elevations were a marked contrast to Pöppelmann's work, and the job was completed by de *Bodt. From 1722 Pöppelmann worked on the alterations and rebuilding of the hunting-lodge, Moritzburg, again completed by Longuelune, and widened the C12 *bridge over the Elbe at Dresden by cantilevering raised footpaths from the edges of the old structure. Iron railings were used to reduce the weight. The bridge (1727) is seen to best advantage in **Bernardo Bellotto's** (1720–80) views of the city. Pöppelmann designed the *Dreikönigskirche*, Dresden-Neustadt

(1731–9), built by Georg *Bähr, who altered the project as it was under construction. His last works were with Longuelune, preparing designs for a huge palace in Warsaw, not realized.

Asche (1978); Gurlitt (1924); Heckmann (1972, 1986); Hempel (1961, 1965); Marx (1989); Pe (1960); P (1982); Sponsel (1924); J.T (1996)

poppy Long recognized as an opiate, the seed-pods and flowers of the poppy were commonly used in *Neo-Classicism as ornaments in bed-rooms and funerary architecture, being associated with the twin brothers, children of Night—Sleep and Death. Poppy-motifs were much used by *Percier and *Fontaine in *Empire design, and they were common elements of *Art Nouveau.

poppy-head Carved *finial of C15 or early-C16 *Gothic *bench- or *pew-ends, resembling the *fleur-de-lys, but often richly decorated with figures, foliage, fruits, and flowers. The term derives from the French poupée (bunch of hemp or flax tied to a staff), and has nothing to do with the *poppy.

Howard & Crossley (1927); J.Parker (1850)

porch 1. Covered place of entrance and exit attached to a building and projecting in front of its main mass, such as the south porch of a medieval church, often with a room over it. 2. Interior volume serving as a *vestibule. 3. *Transept or side-chapel in a church. 4. *Cloister, *colonnade, *Galilee, *narthex, *portico, *stoa, or *verandah (all with columns). A columned porch or portico usually has a *pediment and resembles a *temple-front.

Porcinai, Pietro (1910–86) Italian architect/landscape-designer, much influenced by the Italian-*Renaissance and *Baroque masters, he argued that poetry and science working together were essential ingredients in the creation of successful gardens. He employed *fabriques, sculptures, etc., strategically placed, to trigger responses in the imagination. Among his works were the Villa Fiorita, Saronno, Varese (1952–9) and the Parco di Pinocchio, Collodi, Lucca (1963–76). He contributed to the influential design-magazine, Domus, from 1937.

Porcinai & Mordini (1966)

Porden, William (c.1755–1822) English architect, trained under James *Wyatt. He was employed by the **Prince of Wales** (later **King George IV** (r.1820–30)), for whom he designed the stables, riding-house, tennis-court, and other buildings at the Royal Pavilion, Brighton, Sussex (1804–8), where he introduced the *Hindoo style (he is said to have worked with S.P.*Cockerell). He had a reputation as an architect of *Gothic

buildings, and he built the competent Eaton Hall, Ches. (1804–12—demolished 1870s).

Co (2008); Conner (1979); H.Roberts (1939)

Porphyrios, Demetri (1949–) See NEW CLASSICISM, NEW URBANISM.

porphyry 1. Beautiful, very hard rock quarried in Egypt in Antiquity, deep purplish-red in colour, capable of taking a high polish. **2.** Black or green stones of porphyritic structure quarried in Sardinia, Greece, etc. **3.** Any unstratified or igneous rock having a homogeneous base containing crystals of one or more minerals, e.g. felspar porphyry, claystone porphyry, porphyritic granite, and porphyritic greenstone. The best-known are porfido rosso (deep red with whitish spots), porfido nero (black with white spots), serpentino nero antico (black with lighter oblong spots), porfido verde (very dark, almost black, with fine green shades), porfido di Vitelli (pea-green with small lighter green spots), and a blue porphyry found by the Romans at Fréjus. The so-called rosso antico was not a porphyry, but was a *marble found in Greece or Italy, and was both cheaper and easier to work. The finest rosso antico occurred at Brescia, was fine-grained, deep blood-red or liver in colour, and took a high polish.

Butters (1996); Delbrück (1932); J.Pa (1832)

porta Monumental *gateway of a Roman city or fortress, or any grand entrance (e.g. to a church).

Porta, Giacomo della (1532–1602) After *Vignola's death (1573) this Lombardy-born architect became the leading exponent of *Mannerism in Rome. He supervised the erection of *Michelangelo's Capitoline Hill buildings, completing (with some changes) the Palazzo dei Conservatori (1561–84) and constructing the Palazzo del Senatore (1573–1602): his interventions included modifications to the Piazza and to the great flight of steps. He finished Vignola's noble church of Il Gesù, designing the *façade (1571–3—which was to be of enormous importance as a precedent for Jesuit churches in Italy, Central Europe, and Latin America), *high-altar (1582), and *crossing (1584). As Architect of St Peter's and to the Farnese family from 1573, he carried out various works on the *basilica, and realized Michelangelo's designs for the garden-elevation of the Palazzo Farnese. He collaborated with Domenico *Fontana on the building of St Peter's *dome (1586–92—to which he gave a more pointed profile (like that at Florence Cathedral) than that intended by Michelangelo), and he completed the chapels of **Gregory XIII** (r.1572–85) and **Clement VIII** (r.1592–1605).

He designed the north and south *fountains in the Piazza Navona (1574–8) and many other Roman exemplars; the Churches of Santa Maria *ai Monti* (from 1580) and *Sant' Atanasio dei Greci* (1580-3); the façade of *San Luigi de' Francesi* (1580-4); works at *San Giovanni de' Fiorentini* (1582-1602) and *Sant'Andrea della Valle* (1591—completed by *Maderno, 1608-23); and the *Villa Aldobrandini*, Frascati (1594-1603—completed by Maderno and G.*Fontana). His output was enormous, and he is of singular importance as a transitional figure between the *Cinquecento* and the evolution of *Baroque.

An (1986); He (1996); Lotz (1977); P.Mu (1969, 1986); Onofrio (1957, 1963); P (1982); Tiberia (1974); J.T (1996); Wi (1964, 1982)

portal 1. Entrance-*doorway or *gateway of monumental character, especially if emphasized by stately architectural treatment making it the principal architectural motif of a *façade. 2. Lesser doorway to a gateway-tower. 3. *Portico. 4. Arch over a gateway or doorway. 5. Structural *frame consisting of two *stanchions connected to *beams fixed at angles corresponding to the roof-pitch and rigidly joined at the apex and the tops of the stanchions. 6. Frame of a *gate. 7. Small lobby in a room defined and separated off from the rest of the apartment by *wainscoting.

portcullis Strong door in a fortified medieval gateway, sliding vertically, normally a grating heavily framed of wood strengthened with iron, with pointed iron bars at the bottom. Usually kept in the raised position, it could be dropped suddenly when required for reasons of defence. *See* YETT.

porte-cochère 1. *Doorway to a house or *court, often very grand, to permit wheeled vehicles to enter from the street. 2. Erroneous term for a projecting *canopy or *porch large enough to admit carriages.

Porter, John (*fl.*1423-65) English master-mason, he worked at Lincoln Cathedral before being called to York *Minster (*c.*1542). He was the architect of the handsome *steeple of the Parish Church at Louth, Lincs. (*c.*1431).

J.Harvey (1987)

portico Covered *ambulatory consisting of a series of columns placed at regular intervals supporting a roof, normally attached as a colonnaded *porch to a building, but sometimes forming a separate structure (e.g. James *Stuart's *Doric Temple at Hagley, Worcs. (1758)): the volume so created can be open or partly enclosed at the sides, stand before a building such as a *temple, and have a *pediment over the front, in which case it is described as a *temple-front. A Classical portico can be defined with precision. *The main types are*:

engaged: with the portico not standing in front of the building but with the ensemble of columns,

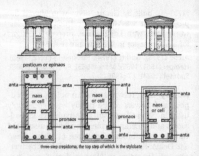

posticum or epinaos

anta — anta   anta — anta   anta — anta

naos or cell   naos or cell   naos or cell

pronaos   pronaos

anta — anta   anta — anta   anta — anta

three-step crepidoma, the top step of which is the stylobate

portico Column arrangements in temples. (*left*) *Amphiprostyle tetrastyle*, or *amphi-tetra-prostyle*, i.e. with four columns in front of and at each end of the cell. (*middle*) *Prostyle tetrastyle*, or *tetra-prostyle*, i.e. with four columns in front of the cell. (*right*) *Distyle in antis*, i.e. with two columns in front of the cell set between *antae* terminating the projecting cell walls, an arrangement found only in small temples, tombs, or shrines.

*entablature, and pediment embedded in the front wall, i.e. *engaged;

in antis: with columns set in a line between projecting walls enclosing the sides of the portico, i.e. between the *antae* (*see* ANTA) of the walls;

prostyle: with columns set in a line standing before and detached from the front wall of the building behind.

In both *in antis* and *prostyle* porticoes the design is further defined by the number of columns visible on the front *elevation: the commonest varieties are *distyle* (2, usually *in antis*); *tristyle* (3); *tetrastyle* (4); *pentastyle* (5); *hexastyle* (6); *heptastyle* (7); *octastyle* (8); *enneastyle* (9); *decastyle* (10); and *dodecastyle* (12). Even numbers of columns are usual to ensure a void on the central axis for the door. A portico with 4 columns standing in front of the main wall of the building behind it is *prostyle tetrastyle*, and if it has 2 set between the *antae* of flanking walls it is *distyle in antis*. *See also* COLONNADE; INTERCOLUMNIATION.

J.Curl (2001)

porticus (*pl.* porticus, porticuses) 1. Entrance-porch of a church. 2. Church *apse. 3. Structure over a medieval tomb (also called *porticulus*). 4. Long covered *ambulatory with a roof carried on *colonnades, sometimes attached to a building, and sometimes a separate structure. 5. Room or side-chapel projecting from the *nave of a church entered through arches in the nave-walls, as seems to have been the case at the *Anglo-Saxon church at Brixworth, Northants., where there was a series of *porticūs* to the north and south of the nave. 6. Arched *arbour (sometimes called *portique*) or garden-walk under a *pergola. **7.** As PORTICO.

Goulty (1991); OED (1933); OED Supplement (1984); pk

Portland Type of white oölitic *limestone from Portland, Dorset, often quarried to provide *ashlar *façades of public buildings from the time of *Wren. *Portland cement*, which is made from chalk or limestone and clay, has a light grey colour, is classed as an *artificial hydraulic cement*, and was invented in *c.*1821. It is very strong and can be used under water.

Gw (1903); W.McKay (1957); N (1835); W.Pa (1852)

Portland, Nicholas (*fl.*1394–*c.*1406) English master-mason, he worked at Salisbury Cathedral from 1394, where he stabilized the *crossing-tower, and was engaged (1396–1405) on the re-building of St John's Hospital, Winchester, Hants., where he may have been responsible for the main *block, apart from the chapels.

J.Harvey (1987)

Portuguese garden Influenced by *Roman, *Moorish, and *medieval garden-design, Portugal's eclectic blend of foreign influences, combined with a climate favourable to the cultivation of gardens, led to some remarkably beautiful creations. The C16 *Quinta da Bacalhôa*, with its *azulejos and huge water-tank, demonstrates the survival of *Islamic design mingled with themes of the Italian *Renaissance. Trade with Japan also impinged to a certain extent on C16 garden-design. At *Bom Jesus do Monte*, near Braga, is an astonishing *Baroque *stair (C18); at Pombal, water, *par-terres, a *grotto, *azulejos*, and even a nod to the *ferme ornée* may be found; and at Sintra, near Lisbon, is a wonderful series of terraced gardens again featuring a spectacular stair and *azulejos*. Also at Sintra is a late-C19 garden with tunnels, grottoes, pools, etc., which may have Freemasonic resonances. There are several *Romantic gardens cultivated by Englishmen, including the C19 garden of Monserrate, near Pena. A spectacular 1930s water-garden is that of the *Parque de Serralves*, Oporto, designed by **Jacques Gréber** (1882–1962), the centrepiece of which is the *Art-Deco *Casa* (1925–1943), designed by **Jose Marques da Silva** (1869–1947), **Charles Siclis** (1860–1942), and others.

Binney & Bowe (1998); Shoe (2001); Tay (2006)

Posener, Julius (1904–96) German-born architect, he moved to Paris (1929) where he became architectural critic for *L'architecture d'Aujourd'-hui*. He emigrated to Palestine (1935), and worked in *Mendelsohn's office. He was an authority on *Expressionism, esp. on *Poelzig.

Posener (1964, 1970, 1979, 1992)

Posokhin, Mikhail Vasil'yevich (1910–89) Russian architect, he worked with *Shchusev (1930s) before establishing a partnership with **Ashot Mndoyants** (1909–66). Projects included the Moscow Council Building (1943–5) and the offices in Znamenka Street, Moscow (1943–5—a heavy Neo-Classical composition). Posokhin adopted Western notions of *urban renewal as can be seen in his brutal destruction of historic fabric and the design of the Kalinin Prospect (1962–8—later New Arbat), with its huge housing and office tower-blocks rising from a base of shops, cinemas, restaurants, etc. It became a paradigm, and was widely imposed throughout the USSR, in climatic and cultural contexts to which it was wholly unsuited.

Ck (1996); J.T (1996)

post Vertical timber supporting a *lintel or providing a firm point of lateral attachment, as in a *gate or *fence. The term is usually applied to a main upright member in *timber-framed and roof-construction, *described as*:

post-and-beam: timber frame consisting of posts supporting horizontal *beams;

post-and-lintel: simple form of construction involving posts carrying horizontal beams or lintels, as in timber-framed work or in *columnar-and-*trabeated architecture (Ancient-Egyptian and Ancient-Greek architecture was of this type, however using stone);

post-and-pane, post-and-pan: timber-framed building with exposed posts, the intervals between them (*panes) filled with *plaster, bricks, etc. Obsolete term for *box-frame construction. *Types of post include*:

aisle-: as *arcade-post*;

arcade-: post in an *arcade, in the sense of a division in a timber-framed building consisting of a row of posts;

crown-: vertical timber on a *tie-beam*, or sometimes on a *collar*, supporting the *crown-plate*;

king-: vertical timber on a *tie-beam* or *collar* rising to the roof apex to support a *ridge-piece: without a ridge-piece it is a *king-strut*;

queen-: one of two posts on a *tie-beam* supporting *plates* or *purlins*.

ABDM (1996); S (1901–2)

Post, George Browne (1837–1913) American architect/engineer who contributed to the origin and development of the early *skyscraper from *c.*1870. Architecturally eclectic and competent, he was noted for his grasp of planning and structural principles. He designed many hotels, and evolved the modern hotel-plan with a bath in each room (e.g. Statler Hotel, Buffalo, NY (1911–12)). He contributed to the design of the Equitable Life Assurance Building, NYC (1868–70—destroyed), one of the very first structures designed with a lift or *elevator, thus helping to develop the planning and organization of tall buildings. The Western Union Building, NYC (1873–5—demolished), was, with *Hunt's Tribune Building, one of the earliest skyscrapers, essentially Classical in its arrangement of a *base, middle section (*shaft), and crowning element (*cornice). The monumental New York Produce Exchange (1881–5—destroyed) was constructed with a complete metal structure within outer load-bearing walls, and influenced *Sullivan. His Stock Exchange, NYC (1901–3—probably his best-known surviving building), has a handsome *Corinthian *in-antis* pedimented *front. Other works included the Vanderbilt House (1879–94), Pulitzer Building (1889–90), and St Paul Building (1897–9), all destroyed, and all in NYC Post's earliest buildings (e.g. the domed Williamsburgh (later Republic) Savings Bank, Brooklyn, NYC (1869–75), and the Savings Bank, Troy, NY (1981–5)), were in a French *Second-Empire style. His State Capitol, Madison, WI (1906–17—Classical) and City College, NYC (1897–1907—*Gothic, with *faïence cladding) were works of some distinction.

Ct (1960, 1961); *JSAH*, xii/1 (Mar. 1953), 13–21, xxxi/3 (Oct. 1972), 176–203, and xlvi/4 (Dec. 1987), 342–55; S.Landau (1998); S.Landau & Ct (1996); P (1982); S (1971a); Helen Searing (ed.) (1983); J.T (1996); W & K (1983)

Post, Pieter (1608–69) Dutch architect, he assisted van *Campen at the *Mauritshuis*, The Hague (1630s), the Town Hall, Amsterdam (1648–55), and supervised the building of the Noordeinde Palace, The Hague (1640s), a dignified and serene building. Post designed the *Huis ten Bosch*, The Hague (1645–51—influenced by *Palladio's *Villa Capra*, Vicenza), with its cruciform domed *Oranjezaal*; the *Waaghuis*, Leiden (1657–9), with a *Tuscan *Order on the rusticated base; and the handsome Town Hall, Maastricht (1656–64). His refined Palladian style can also be seen at the *De Onbeschaamde* House, 123–5 *Wijnstraat*, Dordrecht (1650–3). He may have designed the town-plan and several buildings at Mauritsstad, Brazil (1630s). His style had considerable influence on English architects, notably *May, and he also built in Germany.

Blok (1937); Boogaart (ed.) (1979); Kuyper (1980); P (1982); RSTK (1977); Terwen & Ottenheym (1993)

postern 1. Subsidiary *door or *gate, as in military architecture, where it is very modest and remote from the main gate. **2.** In domestic architecture, it is set near a larger one, such as a door for pedestrians next to a *porte-cochère*. **3.** Rear gate in a city wall used for sorties in war.

postiche Addition to a work of architecture after it has been finished; especially something inappropriate.

posticum 1. Open vestibule in an *Antique Classical *temple, to the rear of the *cella or *naos, also called *epinaos or *opisthodomus, corresponding to the *pronaos, really part of a back *portico. **2.** Inferior, subsidiary, or rear *door in an Antique Roman house.

Post-Modernism Style or styles in architecture and the decorative arts that was or were a reaction to the *Modern Movement, *Modernism, *International Modernism, and the dogmas developed especially at the *Bauhaus. Some have held it began in 1972 when *Yamasaki's Pruitt-Igoe Modernist housing, St Louis (1958), was destroyed after its inhabitants refused to live there any more. Essentially, Post-Modernism (known variously as *P-M, PoMo,* or the *Post*) has been connected with a loss of faith in what were once regarded as certainties (e.g. so-called 'progress', supposed 'rationality', and 'scientific' approaches to design (in reality a search for appropriate *images* to *suggest* all this)) and with a growing acceptance of a bewilderingly large palette of images, signs, and products promoted on a scale never experienced before in the history of the world, which some (e.g. **Robert Charles Venturi** (1925–2018)) welcomed as offering 'complexity' and 'contradiction' in design. In the 1960s *Pop architecture began a tendency away from so-called *Rationalism towards *Pluralism, and later architecture drew on elements that were not themselves archaeologically or historically accurate, but made vague references to once-familiar motifs such as the *Orders, *cornices, *pediments, etc., often brashly and crudely used. Post-Modernism seems to have heralded a major change in Western culture, even a new condition permeating every walk of life, involving cynicism, fragmentation, ill-digested *eclecticism, and what some (e.g. **Fredric Jameson** (1934–)) have called the 'cultural logic of late capitalism'. The label has been loosely stuck to various architects moving away from the Modern Movement and *High-Tech architecture, even though their various responses widely differed. Among architects identified with Post-Modernism are **Ricardo Bofill Levi** (1939–), **Sir Terry Farrell** (1938–), Michael Graves (1934–2015), Hans *Hollein, Philip *Johnson, Charles Willard *Moore, and **Robert Arthur Morton Stern** (1939–), but these have all produced work of great individuality, and the label is far too comprehensive to have much meaning other than to refer to architecture of the late C20 that rejected the certainties of the International-Modern style. In Italy, for example, architects such as *Rossi argued that as cities were organic works of art, their grain, history, and context must be responded to in any architectural intervention, the complete opposite of the International-Modernist position. Architects who subscribed to this paradigm included **Mario Botta** (1943-), **Giorgio Grassi** (1935-), *Kleihues, **Léon** (1946-) and **Rob Krier** (1938-), **Bruno Reichlin** (1941-), *Ungers, and many others, but their work is of a much higher order than the sort of commercial PoMo associated with the vulgarity of advertising and ignorant nods towards a supposed Classicism which was nothing of the sort, and was firmly rejected by the beginning of C21. Such PoMo pseudo-Classicizing should be distinguished from scholarly Classical architecture produced by a few practitioners. *See also* NEO-RATIONALISM; NEW CLASSICISM; TENDENZA; TICINESE SCHOOL.

Appignanesi (ed.) (1986); Jameson (1993, 2009); Js (1977, 1980, 1980a, 1982a, 1987, 1988a, 2002); Js (ed.) (1992); Klotz (1984, 1988); L (1988); M.Larson (1993); Lyotard (1984); Pi (1983); R & K (1984); Sim (ed.) (2001); J.T (1996); R.Vi (1966, 1996); R.Vi *et al.* (1977)

potager *Kitchen-garden, aka *kail-yaird* in Scotland. French *potagers* include the formal example, Villandry, with origins in *monastery-gardens, and the celebrated *potager du roi*, Versailles (1678-83), designed by **Jean-Baptiste de la Quintinie** (1626-88) to be practical, convenient, and ornamental.

Tay (2006)

Potain, Nicolas-Marie (1713-96) French architect, he worked under *Gabriel, and (1754-70) helped to lay out the *Place Louis XV* (now *Place de la Concorde*), Paris. He published (1767) a work on the *Orders of Architecture, and designed the *basilica of *St-Louis*, St-Germain-en-Laye (1764, completed 1823-4), as well as the Cathedral at Rennes (1764-1844), both of which were important examples of *Neo-Classicism in church-design. His work influenced *Thomon (e.g. Stock Exchange, St Petersburg).

B (1980); M & Wa (1987); P (1982); J.T (1996)

potence 1. T- or Γ-shaped element like a crutch, used as a gibbet, support, etc. **2.** Type of *cross, known more correctly as *potent cross*. **3.** Revolving structure inside a circular *colombier, *columbarium, or *dovecote, to enable all the *niches to be reached with ease. **4.** Any *stud supporting a bearing.

Potocki, Stanisław Kostka (1755-1821) Called the 'Polish *Burlington', architect/patron/art-historian, his architectural mentor was **Stanisław Zawadzki** (1743-1806), with whom he designed the Neo-Classical *façade (1783-6) of the *Collegium Nobilium*, Warsaw. He married (1776) **Princess Aleksandra Lubomirska** (1760-1836), whose fortune enabled him to employ *Aigner to improve the Summer residence at Olesin (1776-93): also with Aigner he designed the Palladian

façade of the Bernardine Church of St Anna, Warsaw (1786-8). He carried out significant works at Wilanów Palace, Warsaw (from 1799), adding a *Gothic *gallery designed by Aigner (1802). Like Burlington, he was profoundly influenced by his studies of Italian architecture, but he was also a major figure in promoting the English *landscape-garden, having visited Stowe, Bucks., and other exemplars. One of his most important publications was his adaptation of *Winckelmann's 1764 *Geschichte der Kunst des Alterthums*.

L & R (1984); Łoza (1954); Polanowska (2009); J.T (1996)

Potter, Edward Tuckerman (1831-1904) American architect, influenced by *Viollet-le-Duc's arguments for using iron in architecture, and by English so-called *High-Victorian *Gothic. Indeed, his First Dutch Reformed Church, Schenectady, NY (1861-3), demonstrates how far *Ruskin's writings had affected him, and has certain aspects reminiscent of *Deane & *Woodward's Oxford Museum (1855-60). The Church of the Good Shepherd, Hartford, CT (1867-9), was a good example of his *polychrome style, and his St John's Church, Yonkers, NYC (1871-2), was much admired. One of his most interesting designs was the polygonal Nott Memorial, Schenectady, NY (1858-78), with its exposed-iron interior structure, domed *clerestorey, and *Moorish-Gothic polychrome exterior. He often employed cast-iron *piers in his churches which resemble the work of English *Rogue Goths! His Mark Twain House, Hartford (1873-81), was much influenced by Northern-French domestic architecture, and by the *Stick style, designed with *polychromy well to the fore.

AR, clxix/1009 (Mar. 1981), 162-6; S.Landau (1979); P (1982); Su (1968); J.T (1996)

Potter, William Appleton (1842-1909) American architect, half-brother of E.T.*Potter, he designed several outstanding US equivalents of *High-Victorian *Gothic, including the Chancellor Green Library, Princeton University, NJ (1871-3), the South Congregational Church, Springfield, MA (1872-5—with bold polychrome treatment and a vast *wheel-window of plate-*tracery, probably his finest work), and the Custom House, Evansville, IN (1875-9). He took **Robert Henderson Robertson** (1849-1919) into partnership (1875), and thereafter the firm's work was strongly influenced by that of H.H. *Richardson, notably at the round-arched Alexander Hall, Princeton University (1891-4). The Pyne Library at Princeton (1896-7) and the First Reformed Dutch Church, Somerville, NJ (1895-7), are *Gothic Revival. For his houses he drew on the English *Domestic Revival as well as on American-*Colonial exemplars.

ARe, xxvi (1909), 176–96; JSAH, xxxiii/2 (May 1973), 175–92; S.Landau (1979); P (1982); Su (1968); J.T (1996)

poupée See POPPY-HEAD.

Powell, Geoffry Charles Hamilton (1920–99) See CHAMBERLIN, POWELL, & BON.

Powell & Moya British architectural firm established (1946) by (Sir) (**Arnold Joseph**) **Philip Powell** (1921–2003) and **John Hidalgo Moya** (1920–94) to carry out the Pimlico Housing Scheme (now Churchill Gardens), London (1946–62), much influenced by *International Modernism. Their 'Skylon' vertical monument for the *Festival of Britain (1951—destroyed) received much publicity at the time. Subsequently they designed hospitals, swimming-baths, and other buildings including the Chichester Festival Theatre (1961–2). The firm's much-admired work at Oxford and Cambridge included a building at Brasenose College, Oxford (1962), the Cripps Building, St John's College, Cambridge (1963–7), Blue Boar *Quad and Picture Gallery, Christ Church, Oxford (1966–8), Magpie Lane Annexe, Corpus Christi College, Oxford (1968–9), Wolfson College, Oxford (1972–4), and Cripps Court, Queen's College, Cambridge (1976–8). They were also responsible for the Museum of London, London Wall, Barbican, London (1974–6), the Queen Elizabeth II Conference Centre, Broad Sanctuary, Westminster, London (1980–6), and major redevelopment of the Great Ormond Street Hospital, London (1990–4).

P.Booth & N.Taylor (1970); E (1994); Esher (1981); Mx (1972); Mills (1953); K.Powell (2009); *The Times* (7 May 2003), Obits.

Poyet, Bernard (1742–1824) French architect, pupil of de *Wailly. His Parisian works included the vast circular *Hôpital Ste-Anne* (1788—heavily influenced by *Durand's theories, but never completed), the huge *portico to the *Palais Bourbon*, now the *Chambre des Députés* (1804–8), important urban-design schemes (1790s) around the rebuilt and modified *Fontaine des Innocents*, and proposals for the *Rue des Colonnes* (eventually built to designs modified by *Vestier (1793–8)).

B (1980); Etlin (1984); M & Wa (1987); J.T (1996)

poyntell, poyntill See POINTEL.

Poynter, Ambrose (1796–1886) English architect, he worked (1814–18) in *Nash's office, travelled (1819–21) to Italy, Sicily, and the Ionian islands, and established himself in practice in London on his return. Among his works may be mentioned the Hospital and Chapel of St Katharine, Regent's Park, London (1826–7—a *Palladian *composition* in the *Tudor-Gothic style), and Christ Church, Newmarket Road (1837–9), the Church of St Andrew the Great, St Andrew's Road (1842–3), and St Paul's, Hills Road (1841), all in Cambridge, and all *Perp. Both Christ Church and St Paul's were faced in bright red brick with *diaper patterns, unusual materials for churches of that date. His Christ Church, Westminster (1841–4), was an early design employing asymmetry, *ragstone *cladding, and C13 *Gothic Revival (bombed 1941, demolished 1954). He also designed several buildings for the National Provincial Bank. He was a founder-member of the Institute of British Architects (1834), and was the author of *On the Introduction of Iron in the Construction of Buildings* (1842). He had a large and successful practice until he began to lose his eyesight (1860). His son was **Sir Edward John Poynter, Bt.** (1836–1919), the distinguished painter, whose *Israel in Egypt* (1867) was a fine example of his scholarly and painstaking visions of Ancient-Egyptian subjects. His grandson, **Sir Ambrose Macdonald Poynter, Bt.** (1867–1923), was a successful London architect, responsible for the Royal Over-Seas League, Park Place, St. James's (1906– 8), and many other works.

B et al. (2001); J.Curl (2005); A.S.Gray (1985); ODNB (2004)

Pozzo, Andrea (1642–1709) Italian lay Jesuit, and one of the greatest *Baroque painters of ceilings, exploiting illusion and high drama. His best works were in *Sant'Ignazio*, Rome (1684–94—perhaps the finest ceiling of *quadratura* ever created), San Francesco Saverio, Mondovi (1676–9), and the *Gartenpalais Liechtenstein*, Vienna (1704–8). He settled (1703) in Vienna, where he created a sumptuous *Baroque interior at the *Universitätskirche* (1703–9). His work was influential in disseminating the Baroque style in Central Europe, especially through his *Perspectiva pictorum et architectorum* (1693–1700), which was translated into several languages, including Chinese. He designed several churches and *altars, e.g. the stupendous altar of *Sant'Ignazio, Il Gesù*, Rome (1695–9), the *high-altar of the *Franziskanerkirche*, Vienna (1706), the Church of *Sant'Ignazio*, Dubrovnik, Croatia (1699–1725), and the Cathedral, Ljubljana, Slovenia (1700–5).

Carboneri (ed.) (1961); Feo (1988); Feo & Martinelli (1996); B.Kerber (1971); Marini (1959); Matteucci et al. (1979); P (1982); Pi (1970); J.T (1996); Wi (1982); Wi & Jaffé (eds) (1972)

pozzolan, pozzolana, pozzuolana, puzzolana Variety of volcanic sand with burnt granules resembling powdered brick: it is a siliceous or siliceous and aluminous material which, when mixed with hydraulic limes and water, becomes a cement-like compound capable of setting under water. It was used in Antiquity. Artificial pozzolan was made by calcining fire clay and adding lime, sand, and water, with fine brick dust.

Gw (1903); N (1835); W.Pa (1852); S (1901–2)

Prachatitz, Hans von (*fl.*C15) Architect who completed the south tower and handsome *spire (called 'Steffl') of the Stephansdom*, Vienna (1349–1433), one of the most perfect of German *Gothic *steeples. He may also have designed the stone altar-canopy in the north *aisle (*c.*1437).

Bae: *Austria* (1929)

Prairie School Group of architects in the Mid-West USA inspired by *Sullivan and led by F.L.L.*Wright, active *c.*1890–1920: it included *Elmslie, *Griffin, *Purcell, and others. The term was coined *c.*1914, but was not widely accepted until the 1960s, when the *Prairie School Review* (1964–76) appeared. The long, low, horizontal character of their domestic buildings was seen to derive from the broad, level prairie. See PRAIRIE STYLE.

H.Brooks (1972, 1984); *JSAH*, xix/1 (Mar. 1960), 2–10, and xxv/2 (May 1966), 115–18; Spencer (ed.) (1979)

Prairie style Architectural style evolved in the Mid-West USA, named after a design of F.L.L.*Wright published in *The Ladies' Home Journal* (1901). Characterized by low-pitched roofs with very wide overhanging *eaves, a strongly emphasized horizontality, large hearths separating parts of the living-area, and the use of traditional materials, typical exemplars were Wright's Robie House, Chicago, IL (1909), and *Greene & Greene's Gamble House, Pasadena, CA (1908–9). *Jensen is held by some to have evolved a *Prairie style* of landscape-design. See PRAIRIE SCHOOL.

H.Brooks (1972, 1984); Legler (1999); C.Lind (1994); Wilhelm Miller (2002); Spencer (ed.) (1979)

Prakash, Aditka (1923–2008) Indian architect involved with Le *Corbusier, *Fry, *Drew, and *Jeanneret at Chandigarh from 1952. He designed some sixty major projects in northern India; made some attempts to distance himself from Chandigarh's planning, regarding it as 'escapist'; and published works advocating mixed uses, extensive recycling, the integration of agriculture and animal husbandry into urban systems, and much else of which Corbusier and his disciples would have disapproved. His return to sensible principles of design in India sits uneasily with his earlier enthusiasms.

RIBAJ (April 2008), 14

Prandtauer, Jakob (1660–1726) One of the greatest of Austrian *Baroque architects, related to *Munggenast, he designed the huge *Benedictine *Abbey of Melk (1702–38), high on a cliff-top on the south bank of the Danube, some 50 miles west of Vienna. *Pevsner called it the 'Durham of the Baroque', a judgement with which there can be full agreement, for the architectural composition vigorously exploits the splendours of its site and makes a *Sublime impact. The handsome Church, with its twin towers and high *cupola, is placed between two *wings (in which are the Library and *Kaisersaal*) projecting in front of its *façade and converging towards the cliff-edge. Set on a *podium, these wings are linked in front of the Church by a mighty arch (its form derived from a *serliana), and appear to embrace the *court before the Church.

Prandtauer and Munggenast built the Parish and *Wallfahrtskirche* of Sonntagberg (1706–32), with a façade perhaps influenced by *Fischer von Erlach's *Dreifaltigkeitskirche*, Salzburg. He designed the *Marmorsaal* and very fine open stair at C.A.*Carlone's Monastery of St Florian (1718–24), completed Carlone's *Wallfahrtskirche Christkindl*, near Steyr (1708–9), collaborated with **Matthias Steinl** (1644–1727) and Munggenast at the Church at Dürnstein (from 1717), and transformed St Pölten's *Dom* (from 1722) into a Baroque building. He also built several houses in St Pölten.

Bou (1962); Brucker (1983); Fe (1960); Fe (ed.) (1984); E.Hempel (1965); Millon (1961); P (1982); Pe (1960); Sedlmayr (1930); J.T (1996)

prato Lawn (esp. **prato inglese**) or meadow.

Pratt, Sir Roger (1620–85) English gentleman-architect, one of the C17 pioneers of *Classicism in England (having studied Continental architecture during extended tours and a period of residence in Rome), he was one of the Commissioners appointed to supervise the rebuilding of the City of London after the 1666 fire. He seems to have intended to write an architectural treatise, for his notebooks contain some rules for the guidance of architects as well as on the building of country-houses. He designed four *astylar country-houses: Coleshill, Berks. (*c.*1650–62—demolished 1952), Kingston Lacy, Dorset (1663–5—altered by *Barry 1835–9), Horseheath Hall, Cambs. (1663–5—demolished 1792), and Ryston Hall, Norfolk (1669–72—altered by *Soane 1786–8). The first truly Classical house in London, Clarendon House, Piccadilly (1664—destroyed), was also by him. All his houses were planned on the *double-pile system with a hall and *salon on the central axis. His work influenced later designs, notably Belton House, Lincs. (1685), and Denham Place, Bucks. (1688).

Co (2008); Gunther (ed.) (1928); M & E (1995); *ODNB* (2004); P (1982); Su (1993); J.T (1996)

precast concrete *Concrete cast in moulds before being incorporated in a building.

Pre-Columbian architecture Architecture of the Americas before their C15 discovery by **Columbus**.

predella 1. *Gradino* or step at the top of an *altar supporting the *altar-piece. It may have panels describing events in the lives of Saints and be associated with a *triptych. **2.** Platform or steps on which an altar stands. **3.** Ledge or ledges surmounting an altar to hold the Crucifix, painting, etc.

prefab Bomb-damage during the 1939–45 war obliged the British Government to establish a programme to build temporary housing. This took the form of single-storey dwellings, *prefabricated in factories, with exteriors clad in *aluminium, *asbestos sheets, or *concrete, and with bathrooms and kitchens (though small) fully equipped.

Arieff & Burkhart (2002); Hardy & C.Ward (1984); Vale (1985)

prefabrication Manufacture of parts or all of a building in a factory before they or it are brought to the site. *Industrialized buildings have as many prefabricated parts as possible: units such as complete bathrooms may be made in factories before they are built in and connected. Prefabrication is not new, for *timber frames were often prefabricated and then removed to their site (e.g. early C17 frames constructed in Coleraine, Co. Londonderry, then shipped to the west of the county for erection). *Paxton's celebrated Crystal Palace (1850–1) was an excellent example of a prefabricated structure. Yet there is an argument that there is a prefabricated element in all buildings in that they are made of components manufactured offsite (e.g. bricks, window-frames, etc.), so the line between a prefabricated and non-prefabricated house is often blurred.

Arieff & Burkhart (2002); J.Curl (1986); G.Herbert (1978, 1984); B.Kelly (1964); Klotz (ed.) (1986); R.White (1965)

Prentice, Martin (*fl.*1459–87) English carpenter, he worked at King's College Chapel, Cambridge (1459–62), and became Master-Carpenter there (1480) when construction was resumed. He was responsible for the design of the timber roof above the *vaults.

J.Harvey (1987)

presbytery 1. Part of a church in which the *high-altar stands, at the east of the *choir. It is often raised above floor-level, and is used exclusively by those who minister in the services of the *altar. **2.** Priest's house.

preservation Retention, maintenance, and rehabilitation of buildings, whole areas, and landscapes for historic, architectural, or other reasons. Preservation of ancient fabric was not unknown in Imperial Rome, and, with the rediscovery of Antiquity in the *Renaissance period, the recording, rescue, excavation, and preservation of Ancient-Roman artefacts and buildings became the concern of many (*Raphael was in charge of such operations for a period). In the C18 interest in medieval ruins and standing buildings quickened, and serious study of *Gothic fabric led to several publications recording buildings, tombs, etc. The appalling destruction unleashed by the French Revolution throughout Europe led to an increasing awareness of the vulnerability of ancient fabric, and in several countries attempts were made to record and preserve what remained after the Napoléonic Wars, notably in Prussia, Bavaria, and Hesse-Darmstadt. These efforts, prompted partly by *Romanticism and partly by a growing awareness of Nationalism, led to the study of *Ecclesiology (especially in the British Isles, Germany, and France). Indeed, mindful of the orgies of destruction perpetrated by their fellow-countrymen, the French set up (1830) an Inspectorate of Historical Monuments (**Prosper Mérimée** (1803–70) was inspector-general for nearly 30 years).

The *Gothic Revival brought its own dangers to medieval buildings, for there were plenty of ignorant or misguided architects who did immense damage when zealously 'restoring' ancient churches within inches of their lives when they thought they were 'preserving' them: some *Anglo-Saxon fabric was lost (1850s) at St Wystan's, Repton, Derbys., and 'Great' *Scott's proposals for Tewkesbury Abbey, Glos., galvanized *Morris and others to establish the Society for the Protection of Ancient Buildings (SPAB), which in C20 played an important role in developing a philosophy for preservation and *conservation that would respect as much of the historic fabric as possible. Many ruined ecclesiastical buildings (*abbeys, priories, etc.) and military buildings (*castles, etc.) began to be cared for under the aegis of the Government in the British Isles: these required maintenance to prevent further decay. The National Trust was set up at the end of C19 to preserve places of natural beauty, and from the 1930s started to acquire country-houses, open to the public: nevertheless, there have been many grievous losses.

The disappearance of landscape unspoiled by human encroachment led to the establishment of huge National Parks in the USA, starting with Yellowstone (1872), and the Government may designate areas meriting preservation, even if in private ownership. Furthermore, the loss of fine buildings prompted the founding of organizations to preserve 'landmarks', in the USA mostly through private finance. Catastrophic losses of historic fabric in Europe during the 1914–18 and 1939–45 wars led to a belated recognition that the preservation of historic buildings is of international importance, and from the mid-C20 states started to cooperate to this end. One example of an international rescue was the saving of the Ancient-Egyptian *temples at Abu Simbel and Philae from inundation caused by the erection of the dam at Aswan: this involved (1966–8) dismantling and re-erecting buildings on higher land, and encouraged the creation of a World Heritage List and Fund to protect and preserve the World Cultural and Natural Heritage. In 1964 was founded the International Council of Monuments and Sites (ICOMOS), which has produced guidelines for those involved in preservation, and has encouraged the sharing of knowledge and the training of young people. The World Monuments Fund was set up (1965), which has been involved in preserving several buildings and sites, and it established (1995) World Monuments Watch to decide on what is to be done in the years to come.

Individual buildings are one thing, but often it is desirable to preserve large swathes of towns and cities because of their character. The *Civic Amenities Act* (1967) introduced legislation to designate Conservation Areas in Great Britain, and in France, the USA, and elsewhere such areas have been protected, preserved, and restored to life. Jane *Jacobs was very important in awakening North America to the urban catastrophe (as destructive as any war) being perpetrated by architects and planners under the weaselly misnomer, *urban renewal: she attracted venomous attacks from *Modernists such as *Banham, but gradually several of her ideas achieved acceptance. In some cases, where areas in cities ceased to function (e.g. Covent Garden Market, London, or the *Marais*, Paris), preservation-schemes have revitalized them, yet it is only a few years ago that both areas were threatened with wholesale destruction and 're-development'.

Chamberlin (1979); Fitch (1982); ICOMOS publications (various dates); S.Marks (ed.) (1996); Pressouyre (1996); Sweet (2004)

prestressed concrete Type of *reinforced *concrete, in which steel bars are replaced by steel cables within ducts disposed to enable the tension areas of the concrete to be compressed by stretching them before loading. It allows for accuracy as well as economical use of both concrete and steel.

Allen (1992)

Preti, Francesco Maria (1701–74) Italian architect, he developed *Palladio's laws of *harmonic proportion by further elaborating upon the system. He numbered among his works the completion of the huge Palladian *Villa Pisani*, Strà, Italy, and various outbuildings, begun *c.*1720 to designs by Count **Girolamo Frigimelica** (1653–1732). He was also responsible for the Parish

Churches at Vallà (1730s), Tombolo (1750), Salvatronda (1751–76), and Caselle (1757), as well as for drawing up plans for the Cathedral (1723) and Theatre (1754) at Castelfranco. His theoretical work on musical ratios and architecture was published (1780) as *Elementi di architettura*.

Bae: *Northern Italy* (1913); J.T (1996)

Price, Bruce (1845–1903) American architect, he designed around 40 vigorous *Shingle-style houses at Tuxedo Park, Rockland County, NY (1885–90), with pronounced axes, influencing F.L.L.*Wright and the *Prairie School. His Windsor Station, Montréal, Canada (1888–9), was in a round-arched style strongly influenced by the work of H.H.*Richardson, but his Banff Springs Hotel, Alberta (1886–8), and *Château Frontenac* Hotel, Québec (1892–3), drew on wider ranges of eclecticism (especially from French and Scots exemplars) for their highly effective compositions. One of his last works was the Gould House, Lakewood, NJ (1897–8), a magnificent essay in *Classicism.

Do (1984); K (1994); V.J.Sy (1971); S (1977); J.T (1996)

Price, Cedric John (1934–2003) English architect/innovator/iconoclast, son of the cinema-architect **A.G.Price** (1901–53), he established his practice (1960), and, with *Newby and **Lord Snowdon** (1930–2017), designed the Aviary at London Zoo (1961). The apostle of 'low-cost, short-term, loose-fit' architecture, he projected the Fun Palace (a Utopian C20 version of the Vauxhall Pleasure Gardens—a 'university of the streets' consisting of a structural lattice from which movable capsules (the appearance of which would be determined by what went on within them) were suspended for a wide variety of activities) for **Maudie Joan Littlewood** (1914–2002) at Stratford, East London, one of his most influential (though unrealized) *High-Tech (a term he hated) projects. To Price, in an increasingly changing world flexibility was all: he designed (1967) a range of inflatable plastic chairs, so a favourite armchair might accompany its owner when out for the evening (permanent chairs, after all, took up valuable space in the home). He even proposed a system of air-jets capable of supporting the human body so that beds could be dispensed with. Despite, or perhaps because of, these notions, Price became a guru. He advocated that buildings should be constructed of lightweight, easily dismountable parts in the interests of flexibility and ease of demolition, and he took an anti-aesthetic, anti-stylistic stance, believing that permanence, monumentality, and *preservation in architecture were indefensible: not for him was *Wren's dictum that 'Architecture aims at Eternity'. For example, he advocated the demolition of York Minster because he believed which a building was erected exist no longer, then that building should adapt or die: it did not occur to him that such monuments might have many resonances, purposes, or reasons to be there quite apart from use. An enthusiastic and evangelical believer in the benefits of technology, he was a significant influence on many architects, notably *Archigram. Price's work contained much *imagery* of 'interactive', 'mobile', 'adaptable', 'impermanent' buildings (including the Fun Palace), but it was **Richard George Rogers** (1933-) and **Renzo Piano** (1937-) who captured the headlines with what has been described as their 'noisy interpretation' of Price's ideas, the *Beaubourg*, or *Centre Pompidou*, Paris (1971-7), in which Price's *imagery* was adopted, but for an immobile structure that was, in essence, a monument to **Georges-Jean-Raymond Pompidou** (1911-74) and to the centralized French State. Price predicted (1960s) the impact of Information Technology, and projected (1964) the *Potteries Thinkbelt*, a proposal to invite Government intervention in the retraining of the unemployed in an area of major industrial decline in a 'mobile university'. 1965 saw his 'Pop-Up Parliament', a kind of open-to-all 'supermarket of democracy' to replace the Palace of Westminster (another monument he scorned). He proposed (1972) the Community Centre for the Inter-Action Trust, Kentish Town, a 'flexible' thoroughly serviced structure for communal activities. He reported on air-structures for the Government (1971), further developed 1973. He believed that architecture should be active in preventive health, 'to stop society topping itself': to him, it could be a means of 'dignifying life'. Time will tell how his career should be assessed: he had many ideas (which often fascinated students), but most remained as ideas, floating, without conclusion. *See also* PNEUMATIC ARCHITECTURE.

S.Anderson (ed.) (1968); E (1994); Hardingham (ed.) (2003); R.Landau (1968); Obrist (2003); Price (1971, 1984); *The Times* (22 August 2003), 35

Price, Sir Uvedale (1747-1829) Author of *Essay on the Picturesque* (1794) and important influence on the cult of the *Picturesque (which he defined as a separate *aesthetic category*, identifiable as distinct as *Burke's categories of the *Beautiful and the *Sublime). He, more than anybody, encouraged landscape-gardeners to study the works of celebrated landscape-painters for precedents. He, as well as R.Payne *Knight, *Nash, and *Repton, also influenced the development of 'natural' English landscape-design.

AR, xcv/566 (Feb. 1944), 47–50; Ballantyne (1997); Hussey (1967, 1967a); *ODNB* (2004); Pe (1968, 1974); Price (1810); Su (1993); Wa (1982a); Watkins & Cowell (2012)

pricket 1. Metal spike on which to stick a candle, as on a *hearse, with a rimmed plate fixed below it into which the wax could run. **2.** Top of a *spire.

prick-post 1. A secondary *post in a *timber-framed structure or a *truss, e.g. queen-post. **2.** Short post in a post-and-rail *fence between the two standards into which the horizontal rails are mortised: it is pointed and driven into the ground, giving additional stiffness.

priest's door Entrance to the *chancel of a church, usually on the south side.

Primaticcio, Francesco (1504/5-70). Italian painter/sculptor/architect important as a bringer of *High-Renaissance and *Mannerist design to Northern Europe. He worked with *Giulio Romano in Mantua (1526-31), and then at *Fontainebleau from 1532 for **François Ier** where he designed the *Aile de la Belle Cheminée* (1568) and other parts, including the heavily rusticated *Grotte de Pins* (c.1543) in a style reminiscent of Giulio Romano's work. He also designed the Valois *mortuary-chapel at *St-Denis with obvious influences from *Bramante, da *Sangallo, and *Vignola (1563—destroyed). *Vasari credited him with the first *stucco ornament and the first frescoes of any account in France: certainly his combination of paintings with stucco decorations was influential.

Bt (1982); COF (1988); J.T (1996)

primitive Type of architecture mnemonic of the very beginning, the earliest, original, crude, or fundamental. Suggested by roughness and squatness (as in the primitive *Doric from *Paestum with its exaggerated *entasis), it was a feature of advanced late-C18 *Neo-Classicism.

J.Curl (2001); V (1990)

Primitive Hut C18 architectural theorists, notably M.de *Frémin (1702), J.-L.de *Cordemoy (1706), and M.-A.*Laugier (1753), argued for a greater rationalism in architectural design, and especially for the structural and honest use of the Classical *Orders, avoiding superfluous fripperies and excessive surface-decoration. Laugier, notably, proposed a cleansing of design, a re-examination of first principles, and a study of the origins and sources of architecture which he saw as evolving from a simple structure of four tree-trunks, still growing and rooted in place, with *lintels composed of sawn logs, and branches providing an elementary pitched roof. This was perceived as the prototype for all great architecture, including the Classical *temple, so leading to archaeological endeavours to find the earliest and original exemplars of Classical buildings where the Orders were used for construction rather than applied or *engaged for decorative effects. Inevitably this led to studies of *Antique remains, notably those of Ancient-Greek architecture: *Paestum, for example, provided models of tough, uncompromisingly *primitive *Doric, and the Primitive Hut was regarded as the original form, a *type, so a potent ideal in *Neo-Classicism.

COE (1972); J.Curl (2001); M & Wa (1987); Ry (1981); V (1990)

principal Inclined timber in a roof-*truss supporting a *purlin but not functioning as a common *rafter. *Compounds include*:
principal beam: main tie-beam of a roof-truss supporting the smaller inclined structural timbers;
principal brace: *brace under the *principal rafter*;
principal rafter: principal serving as a common rafter;
principals of a hearse: *turrets or *pinnacles on the central *posts of a *hearse.

print room Interior decorated with prints (topographical engravings, etc.) arranged and stuck to the walls, surrounded by painted or printed frames of wallpaper.

Prior, Edward Schroeder (1852–1932) English architect, articled to Norman *Shaw, he established (1880) his own practice, and was a founder-member of the *Art-Workers' Guild. The Barn, Exmouth, Devon (1895–7), was the first of a series of houses on **X**-shaped (*butterfly) plans, widely copied at the time. He designed St Andrew's, Roker, Monkwearmouth, Sunderland (1905–7), one of the best churches of the *Arts-and-Crafts movement, containing work by **Sir Edward Coley Burne-Jones** (1833–98), Ernest *Gimson, and others. A.Randall *Wells assisted Prior at St Andrew's, and also at Voewood (later Home Place), Kelling, Holt, Norfolk (1903–5), a pioneering house constructed of *concrete faced with pebble *flints and bonded *carstones (Lower Cretaceous *sandstone cemented by iron-oxides, dark-brown in colour, and coarsely gritty in texture, found in Norfolk). In parts of the house exposed *in-situ concrete was used on which the boards of the *formwork are expressed. Among his other works the Music-Schools at Harrow (1890–1) and Winchester College, Hants. (1901–4), deserve especial mention. Prior published *History of Gothic Art in England* (1900) and other works.

AR, cxiv/671 (Nov. 1952), 302–8, and clvii/938 (Apr. 1975), 220–5; P.Davey (1980, 1995); Garnham (1995); A.S.Gray (1985); Cherry & Pe (1989); Pe & Williamson (1985); Pe & Wilson (1997); J.T (1996)

Prisbrey, Tressa (1895–1988) American builder of several small buildings at Santa Susana, CA, made out of old bottles set in *concrete. It was conceived to house her collection of objects salvaged from rubbish dumps, and was surrounded by gardens containing *shrines and miniature *fabriques constructed of other discarded materials

including broken pottery, car head-lights, vehicle licence-plates, etc.

Prisbrey (1967); Walker Art Center (1974), 76–85

prismatic billet *Billet-moulding resembling rows of prisms in series, alternate rows staggered, in *Romanesque architecture. *Related terms include*:
prismatic ornament: C16 and C17 ornament consisting of simple geometric repetitive forms in low *relief, including pyramidal and chamfered *rustication, *jewelled *strapwork, and *lozenges. It returned in favour early C20;
prismatic rustication: *see* RUSTICATION.

prismatory *See* SEDILE.

prison Gaol, jail, or place for confining criminals and segregating them from society. Prisons provided scope for rational planning to ensure efficient control over inmates, and many fine designs date from the late C18 and early C19. *Piranesi's images of phantasy prisons (*carceri*), with their *Sublime volumes, had considerable influence on Neo-Classical architecture and stage-sets. *See* PANOPTICON.

AR, cxvi/694 (Oct. 1954), 251–6; N (1835); W.Pa (1852); Pe (1976); S (1901–2)

Prisse d'Avennes, Achille-Constant-Théodore-Émile (1807–79) French artist/designer/engineer. His publications include *Les Monuments Égyptiens* (1847) and *L'Histoire de l'Art Égyptien, d'apres les Monuments* (1878–9), the latter a sumptuous two-volume set illustrated with chromo-lithographs. He also published *L'Art Arabe d'après les monuments de Caire* (1869–77), a scholarly work that is still a marvellous source for *Islamic decorations, and which influenced *Burges when designing the Arab Hall, Cardiff Castle, Wales (1881).

Clayton (1982); J.Curl (2005); L & D (1986)

Pritchard, Thomas Farnolls (1723–77) English architect, competent in *Rococo and *Gothick styles, he practised mainly in his native Salop., where he designed an enormous number of buildings and other structures, including the first cast-iron bridge in the world, at Coalbrookdale over the Severn (1775). Built (1777–9) by **Abraham Darby** (1750–91), it was illustrated in *The Philosophical Magazine and Annals of Philosophy* (1832) and in **John White**'s (d.1850) *On Cementitious Architecture as applicable to the Construction of Bridges, with a Prefatory Notice of the First Introduction of Iron as the Constituent Material for Arches of Large Span, by Thomas Farnolls Pritchard in 1773* (1832). Among his other works are Hosyer's Almshouses (1758–9), and The Guildhall, Mill Street (1774–6), both in Ludlow, Salop. He made early designs for Payne

*Knight's Downton Castle, Herefs. (1772), one of the key buildings of the *Picturesque, but the Castle as realized was mostly Knight's work.

Ballantyne (1997); Co (2008); J.Curl (2011a); Ionides (1999); Pe (1958); Newman & Pe (2006)

Pritchett, James Pigott (1789–1868) Welsh-born architect, he had an extensive practice in Yorks., where he was responsible for many competent buildings. He designed York Cemetery, including the *Greek-Revival Chapel (1836–7), Huddersfield Railway Station (1846–7), and the *portico of the Assembly Rooms, York (1828).

Co (2008); *ODNB* (2004)

privy garden Private garden for use by its owner. A good example was that at Hampton Court Palace, a formal geometrical layout embellished with an array of *sundials and standards with the King's Heraldic Beasts holding revolving vanes, and by the end of the C16 it had acquired *topiary figures. It also had a bowling-alley, a banqueting-house, and water-features. It was used as a place of retreat from affairs of State by **King Henry VIII** (*r*.1509–47), but, as restored in the 1990s to its 1702 form, it bears little resemblance to the previous *Tudor garden.

processional way Grandly monumental roadway used for ritual processions, as a *dromos before the *pylons of an Ancient-Egyptian *temple.

procession path 1. In monastic churches a line of paving for the marshalling of those participating in the daily processions associated with religious observance. **2.** *Ambulatory, or *aisle to the east of the *high-altar and its *reredos in cathedrals and monastic churches.

prodigy-house Large, showy, late-*Elizabethan or *Jacobean house with North-European *Renaissance detailing and certain post-*Gothic features, such as *mullioned-and-*transomed windows, e.g. Wollaton Hall, Nottingham (1580–8).

Su (1993)

prodomus *or* **prodomos** Open *vestibule at the entrance to the *cella or *naos of a *temple, set behind the *portico proper. Also called *anticum* or *pronaos.

profile 1. Contour or *section of an architectural member, e.g. a *cornice. **2.** Outline of a building showing heights, projections, etc.

projection 1. Representation of a design in *perspective, *axonometric or *isometric projection, or *orthographical means. **2.** Element or elements of a building projecting before the *naked of the main wall of the *façade, such as a *jetty, *cantilever, *oriel, etc.

FR (1946)

promenade 1. Place for walking or 'promenading', especially a paved public walk. **2.** Walkway, often on obsolete (or on the site of) town-fortifications, laid out, gravelled or paved, and shaded with trees, also called *boulevard, an early form of *public park. **3.** Specially constructed walk-way above a beach for recreational walks, as in numerous C19 seaside resorts.

pronaos *Vestibule flanked by three walls and one row of columns between the front *portico and the *cella or *naos of an *Antique *temple, or the space between the *colonnade of a portico and the front wall of the cell. Also called *anticum or *prodomus.

proportion In architecture, a system of relationships of parts to each other and to the whole, often governed by a standard unit of length called a *module based e.g. on half the diameter of a Classical column.

Kruft (1994); Scholfield (1958); Wi (1998)

propylaeum, propylon (*pl.* propylaea, propyla) Imposing monumental entrance *gateway leading to a *temple, sacred *court, or *enclosure, such as a *battered gateway in front of Ancient-Egyptian temple *pylon-towers, or the large *Doric gateway leading to the Athenian *acropolis (called *Propylaea* (*pl.*) because of its complexity).

proscenium 1. *Stage, or part of an *Antique theatre whereon actors performed in front of the *scena.* **2.** In later theatres, the portion of the stage between the curtain and the *orchestra.

prospect tower Tall building on high ground commanding a view, called a *look-out* or *standing tower.* See BELVEDERE; GAZEBO.

Prost, Léon-Henri (1874–1959) French architect/town-planner who won the competition to design the infrastructure plan for Antwerp, Belgium (1910), in which he exploited the canal encircling the old city to make a connection with the engineering complex of Berchem. He also prepared plans for Casablanca, Fez, Marrakesh, Meknès, and Rabat, all in Morocco (1913–17), and for the Paris Regional Plan (1928–39) and Istanbul Master Plan (1936–58).

Académie d'Architecture (1960); J.T (1996)

prostyle Building with a *colonnade in front of it, usually a *portico. A *temple with a portico at each end is *amphi-prostyle.

Protectorate The period of the Commonwealth (1649–60) in the British Isles when **Oliver** (1599–1658) and then **Richard** (1626–1712) **Cromwell** held the title of **Lord Protector** (1653–60). It gave its name to the *Protectorate style* of architecture found in several country-houses of the period, notably Thorpe Hall,

Peterborough (1653–6), built by Peter *Mills. The style was influenced by the architecture of The Netherlands, notably the works of *Vingboons, and also by *Artisan Mannerism from *c.*1630.

M & E (1995); Su (1993)

prothesis Recess on the north side of the *bema or *apse in a basilican church out of which the Bread and Wine were taken for consecration, or a chapel containing the recess.

prothyrides *See* ANCON.

proto- *Primitive, first, early, or precursor of something. *Proto-*Doric* was an early primitive harbinger of the Doric *Order, as in the rock-cut tombs at Beni-Hasan, Egypt (*c.*2133–1786 BC). *Proto-*Ionic* refers to precursors of aspects of the Ionic *Order, especially the *Aeolic type of *capital and certain features from Mesopotamia. *Proto-*Romanesque* is a term embracing various round-arched styles that evolved from *Early Christian and *Byzantine exemplars including *Carolingian, *Lombardic, and *Ottonian architecture. *Proto-*Renaissance* was a late-C11 style in which *Antique elements were copied: examples include the *baptistery, Church of *San Miniato*, and *Santi Apostoli*, Florence, and the late-C13 *façades of Città Castellana Cathedral and *San Lorenzo fuori le Mura*, Rome.

protoma (*pl.* **protomai**) Foremost or upper part of a figure, such as those on the angles of some *Romanesque *capitals.

proudwork *Masonry, found occasionally in *Tudor-*Gothic work, similar to *flushwork, except that the *freestone patterns and *tracery stand in higher relief than the *flint *panels. From *proud*, meaning 'projecting from a plane surface'—probably only used in limited geographical areas.

Prouvé, Jean (1901–84) French pioneer of *prefabrication and *industrialized building, he worked with Le *Corbusier, Tony *Garnier, *Jeanneret, and *Perriand, among others. He developed the concept of the *curtain-wall, metal *cladding systems, and infill *panels for walls (e.g. Roland Garros Aero-Club, Buc (1936–7—destroyed). His adaptable *Maison du Peuple*, Clichy (1937–9—with *Beaudouin and *Lods), and aluminium houses at Meudon (1949–50) were very advanced for their time. He constructed the pump-room at Évian Spa (1956–7—**Maurice Novarina** (1907–2002), architect), and evolved the 'Sahara' prefabricated housing-units (1958). It is revealing that he referred to himself as a *constructeur*, emphasizing his role as inventor/master-builder/engineer, rather than architect.

Clayssen (1983); Coley (1983); E (1994); Huber & Steinegger (eds) (1971); Jervis (1984); P (1982); Prouvé (1988); Sulzer *et al.* (1993, 1995, 2000, 2002)

prow Essential embellishment of the *columna rostrata*, consisting of three sets of prows (*rostra*) and rams of *Antique warships projecting on either side of the column. *Rostra* are also found as sculpture on *keystones or buildings associated with commerce or trade.

Prowse, Thomas (*c.*1708–67) English amateur architect, he assisted Sanderson *Miller in his designs for Hagley, Worcs., and Shire Hall, Warwick. He also designed a number of buildings (often with John *Sanderson as executant architect), including the Church of St John the Evangelist, Wicken, Northants. (1753–67—in Milleresque *Gothick); Hatch Court, Som. (1755—Palladian); enlargement of *Talman's Kimberley Hall, Norfolk (*c.*1755–7—with four corner-towers of the Houghton and Holkham Palladian type, also found at Hagley Hall, Worcs., and Langley Park, Norfolk); the Temple of Harmony, Halswell Park, Som. (1764–5); and Wicken House, Northants. (1765–6). Prowse also seems to have advised *Newdigate on architectural matters.

AH, xvi (1973), 28; BuMa, cxviii (1976), 224, no.61; Co (2008)

Prynne, George Halford Fellowes (1853–1927) Devon-born, pupil of **Richard Cunningham Windeyer** (*c.*1830–1900) of Toronto, Canada, before working as an *improver with G.E.*Street in London. He was also in the offices of **Edward Swinfen Harris** (1841–1924), **Robert Jewel Withers** (1823/4–94), and Alfred *Waterhouse before becoming assistant (1878–9) to E.R.*Robson. He commenced (1879) independent practice and became Architect to the Diocese of Oxford from 1913. He designed the fine *Gothic *screen and *reredos in St Patrick's Church of Ireland Cathedral, Armagh (1913–14), but most of his works are in Devon, drawing upon *Rectilinear precedents, but free from pedantry. Among his ecclesiastical works may be cited St Peter's, Budleigh Salterton (1891–3); Holy Trinity, Exmouth (1905–7); St John the Baptist, Horrabridge (1893); and sundry other jobs in Devon.

The Builder, cxxxii (20 May 1927), 802; J.Curl (2013); RIBAJ, xxxiv (1927), 494

pseudisodomon *Antique *ashlar *masonry consisting of low bonding and high unbonded *courses, thus the taller courses consisted of stones thinner than the lower. *Pseudisodomous* or *pseudisodomic* describes this condition. *See also* ISODOMON.

pseudo- False, counterfeit, pretended, or deceptively resembling something. *Pseudodipteral* refers to a Classical building with the appearance of being a dipteral *temple (with two rows of columns along the longer sides), but with no inner row, leaving a wide passage between *cella and *peristyle. *Pseudo-Gothic* is a pejorative term for C18 *sham *Gothic, and *pseudo-* is also applied to any style used falsely, e.g. *pseudo-Georgian*. *Pseudoperipteral* is applied to a Classical temple with the 'peristyle' *engaged with the cell-wall. *Pseudoprostyle* describes a *prostyle temple without a *pronaos, the *portico *colonnade set *closer than* an *intercolumniation from or *engaged with* the cella-wall behind. *Pseudothyrum* is a false or secret door.

pteroma (*pl.* **pteromata**) In an Ancient-Greek *temple, the area between the *naos or cell walls and the *peristyle *colonnade, so *pteron* is an external *peripteral *colonnade.

public-house 1. *Inn or hostelry providing food and lodging for travellers or members of the general public, licensed for the supply of ale, wines, and spirits. **2.** Today the term (shortened to 'pub') is specifically given to a *tavern* where the principal business is the sale of alcoholic beverages to be consumed on the premises, though it may serve food, but mostly does not have accommodation for travellers.

public park Garden, open space, or park open to and maintained by or for the public. From the time of C18 *Enlightenment the desirability of providing public parks for the well-being of town-dwellers was perceived. *Promenades became available in several European cities, and the Royal Parks in London (e.g. St James's Park) were opened to the public by grace and favour. **Kaiser Joseph II** (*r.* with his mother from 1765, and on his own 1780–90) designated (1766) the huge *Prater Park* outside the fortifications of Vienna as a place of pleasure for the people, and the *fermier* *Watelet (no mean gardener himself) proposed (1770s) that, as in England, the Royal Parks in France should be made more accessible. Indeed, C18 saw numerous proposals for public parks, intended not only as places of recreation for the people, but as agents whereby the tone of society could be elevated: among the most eloquent of those pressing for the creation of public parks was *Hirschfeld. However, *Rumford and *Sckell caused (from 1789) one of the first public parks to be laid out from scratch: this was the *Englischer Garten*, Munich, created under the aegis of **Karl Theodor** (1724–99—**Elector Palatinate** from 1742, and **Elector of Bavaria** from 1777). From the beginning of C19 many redundant town-fortifications in Germany were converted into public promenades and parks (e.g. Frankfurt-am-Main (1807–11)): in Prussia, *Lenné proposed numerous public parks, and under **King Friedrich Wilhelm III** (*r.*1797–1840) created

(from 1824) a park on the old fortifications of Magdeburg. Later, in 1840, **King Friedrich Wilhelm IV** (*r.*1840–61) decreed that the *Tiergarten*, Berlin, which had been beautified by Lenné, should be given to the city for use as a public park. Vienna acquired (1820) its *Volksgarten*, on the site of the fortifications destroyed during the French Wars, and it quickly became a pleasant place of resort. Numerous public parks followed thereafter on both sides of the Atlantic. *Loudon had consistently and often argued in their favour, not just for recreation, but for education (e.g. his Derby Arboretum (1839)), and was to promote the idea of *garden-cemeteries as public parks, embellished with sculpture, funerary monuments, suitable buildings, and varied planting which would be an educational botanic garden and arboretum (of which *Bigelow's Mount Auburn Cemetery, near Boston, MA (opened 1831), and *Hosking's and *Loddiges's Abney Park Cemetery, Stoke Newington, London (1839–43) were outstanding exemplars). English parks created for use by the public included Victoria Park, in the East End of London, by *Pennethorne (early 1840s), *Paxton's parks at Birkenhead, Ches. (1843–7), and the grounds of the Crystal Palace, Sydenham (1852–8), and the Manchester parks (1840s) by Joshua *Major. In the USA *Downing, following Loudon, argued that public parks in growing urban centres would ease social problems and educate those using them, and *Olmsted, who had visited (1850) the Birkenhead Park, was profoundly influenced by English precedents, notably when he and *Vaux designed Central Park, NYC (from 1858), and that, in turn, informed numerous other projects. In the 1850s, under *Haussmann, public parks were created in Paris, notably by *Alphand (*Bois de Boulogne*) and in Vienna (1857) the *Stadtpark* was commenced (designed by **Josef Selleny** (1824–75) and **Rudolf Siebeck** (1812–*after* 1878)) when the old fortifications were demolished to create the famous *Ringstrasse*. The former Imperial garden of the *Hofburg*, laid out from 1810, was opened (1919) to the Viennese public as the *Burggarten*. At the beginning of C20 public parks were features of most cities in Europe (e.g. the *Parque Maria-Luisa*, Seville, Spain (1911), by **C.-N. Forestier** (1861–1930)) and North America, and gradually areas for games and sports were either added or created as separate entities. After the 1939–45 war numerous *plazas and *vest-pocket parks were created in towns and cities, as well as *theme-parks (e.g. the Gas-Works Park, Seattle, WA (begun in the 1970s to designs by **Richard Haag** (1923–)), the *Landschaftspark*, Duisburg (1990s, by **Peter Latz** (1939–))), and the somewhat unnerving **Parc de la Villette**, Paris (1980s and early 1990s by **Bernard Tschumi** (1944–)). Public parks are now found in many guises, with both hard and soft landscapes, and have many connotations.

Chadwick (1966); Conway (1991); J.Curl (2004); B.Elliott (1986); *GH*, **xxiii**/2 (Winter 1995), 201–21; Hirschfeld (1779–85); Loudon (1981); Symes (2006); J.T (1996); Alan Tate (2001)

Pückler-Muskau, Herman Ludwig Heinrich, Fürst von (1785–1871) German landscape-designer. He inherited (1811) his vast estate at Muskau, and transformed it from 1816 into an enormous *landscape-garden, much influenced by what he had seen in England, and helped by J.A.*Repton. He sold this estate (1845), and created (1846–71) a spectacular garden at his family seat, Branitz, near Cottbus: he had lakes formed, and built numerous *fabriques*, including three *pyramids, under one of which he himself was entombed. He also advised on various Prussian royal gardens, including those at Glienecke (again with J.A.Repton) and Babelsberg (the latter was mostly his work, from 1843), and was critical of *Lenné's earlier approach. He also advised on *public parks in Paris from 1852, and influenced both *Haussmann and *Alphand in this respect: the *Bois de Boulogne* owed much to him. He published (1834) his important *Andeutungen über Landschaftsgärtnerei*, which promoted *Repton's ideas (among others), and influenced American landscape-architecture.

Bowe (1995); Emde & Hn (1992); Jellicoe *et al.* (1996); J.T (1996)

pudding-stone Conglomerate, also called *plum-pudding stone*, found, e.g., in Essex, consisting of a mass of rounded *flint pebbles cemented together by a siliceous matrix of a light yellow-brown colour, capable of receiving a high polish, used in inlay and other ornamental work.

W.Pa (1852)

puddle *and* **puddling** Clay, well worked, chopped, and kneaded until a homogeneous mass is formed, used to make ponds, reservoirs, canals, embankments, etc., watertight. Also called *claying*.

pueblo 1. Village in Spain or Latin America. 2. Communal or tribal dwelling, especially in Arizona or New Mexico, USA, usually of *adobe, and sometimes partly constructed in excavations in cliff-faces.

Pugin, Augustus Charles (1769–1832) French-born, he came to Wales during the French Revolution. He became an assistant to *Nash, and made his reputation as a draughtsman, drawing and etching plates for *Ackermann, *Britton, **Edward Wedlake Brayley** (1773–1854), and others. He produced some of the first archaeologically accurate images of medieval architecture in *Specimens of Gothic Architecture . . . at Oxford*

(1816), *Specimens of Gothic Architecture* (1821–3), *Gothic Furniture* (1827), *Specimens of the Architectural Antiquities of Normandy* (1827–8), *Examples of Gothic Architecture* (1828–36), *Gothic Ornaments from Ancient Buildings in England and France* (1828–31), and *A Series of Ornamental Timber Gables, from Existing Examples in England and Wales* (1831). These works were as important for the *Gothic Revival as *Stuart and *Revett's were for the *Greek Revival. With **Charles Heath** (1785–1848) he produced *Paris and its Environs* (1829–31). He made designs for cemeteries, including a layout for Kensal Green Cemetery, London (1830). His pupils included *Ferrey, *Pennethorne, and his son, A.W.N.*Pugin.

Co (2008); J.Curl (ed.) (2001); Ferrey (1861); Jervis (1984); *ODNB* (2004); P (1982); J.T (1996)

Pugin, Augustus Welby Northmore (1812–52) English architect/polemicist, son of A.C.*Pugin, one of the key personalities of the *Gothic Revival: he became an RC (*c.*1835) and soon a leading figure in *Ecclesiology. His *Contrasts; or, a Parallel between the Noble Edifices of the Fourteenth and Fifteenth Centuries, and Similar Buildings of the Present Day; Shewing the Present Decay of Taste* (1836) was a powerful stimulus for a massive shift in Taste. In it he claimed that *Pointed architecture was produced by the RC faith, that Classical architecture was pagan, that the Reformation was a dreadful scourge, and that medieval architecture was greatly superior to anything produced by the *Renaissance or Classical Revivals. The great test of architectural beauty was the fitness of the design to the purpose for which it was intended, and the style of a building should tell the spectator at once what its purpose was. C19 buildings (especially those of the leading architects of the day) were weighed in the balance against those of C14 and found wanting. His other main works, The *True Principles of Pointed or Christian Architecture set forth* (1841), *The Present State of Ecclesiastical Architecture in England* (1843), and *An Apology for the Revival of Christian Architecture in England* (1843), made it clear that Gothic was not a style, but a principle, a moral crusade; and the only mode of building possible for a Christian nation. His arguments and his very deep knowledge of all aspects of Gothic design had an immense impact on *Anglican church-architects: George Gilbert *Scott was to write that he was 'awakened' from his slumbers 'by the thunder of Pugin's writings'.

Pugin assisted Charles *Barry with the details and furnishings of the Palace of Westminster (built 1840–70) and indeed it was Pugin, rather than Barry, who designed the exquisite architectural enrichments and confident colour-scheme for what is one of the great monuments of the

Gothic Revival. As a church-architect, however, Pugin was unfortunate. Most of his churches have a mean and pinched look owing to a shortage of funds, and the RC hierarchy was not always convinced by the furious arguments of its recent convert, but at St Giles's, Cheadle, Staffs. (1840-6), where his patron, **John Talbot** (1791-1852—**16th Earl of Shrewsbury** and **Earl of Waterford** from 1827), paid handsomely (against his better judgement), Pugin was able to create a scholarly and sumptuous revival of a parish-church of the time of **King Edward I** (r.1272-1307), with a glowing *polychrome interior, complete with *chancel-*screen, all in the *Second-Pointed style. Other works by him include St Chad's Cathedral, Birmingham (1839-41), St Alban's Church, Macclesfield, Ches. (1838-41), St Barnabas's Cathedral, Nottingham (1841-4), and St Mary's (or Marie's), Derby (1837-9).

His secular architecture and his polemics were of great importance because he demonstrated by historical argument (e.g. Haddon Hall, Derbys. (C12-C17)) and by his own example (e.g. Alton Castle, Staffs. (1840-52); the complex of the Grange and St Augustine's, Ramsgate, Kent (1843-52—where he is buried); and Scarisbrick Hall, Ormskirk, Lancs. (1836-47)) that the three-dimensional form of the building should grow naturally out of the plan. This he called the 'true Picturesque', while many houses he criticized were sham *Picturesque with 'donjon keeps... nothing but drawing rooms', 'watch-towers... where the house-maids sleep', and bastions 'where the butler keeps his plate'. Such buildings (e.g. G.L.*Taylor's Hadlow Tower, Kent (c.1840)) were 'mere masks' and 'ill-conceived lies', whereas beauty should grow from necessity. *Pattern-books and illustrations of historical architecture, to Pugin, were dangerous because they were mindlessly copied, and bits jumbled together in new concoctions. Such publications, in the possession of architects and builders, were as 'bad as the Scriptures in the hands of Protestants'. His arguments led to the adoption of freely composed asymmetrical buildings (e.g. the vicarages of *Butterfield) and to the *Domestic Revival, and the *Queen Anne and *Free styles.

M.Aldrich (1994); A & W (1994); Belcher (ed.) (2001); Crook (1987); J.Curl (2007); D & M (1985); Ea (1970); Ferrey (1861); G (1972); Graby (ed.) (1989); J.Harries (1994); Hi (1977); ODNB (2004); Pe (1972); P (1982); Port (ed.) (1976); Pugin (1841, 1843, 1843a, 1973); G.Scott (1995); St (1971); J.T (1996)

Pugin, Edward Welby (1834-75) English architect, son and pupil of A.W.N.*Pugin. A gifted *Gothic Revivalist, he designed many RC churches, some in Ireland. Early works included St Vincent de Paul (1856-7), and Our Lady of Reconciliation (1859-60), both in Liverpool, and more lavish churches (e.g. Sts Peter and Paul, Cork (1859-66), Sts Augustine and John, Dublin (1860-93), and All Saints, Barton-on-Irwell, Manchester (1865-8)) attest to his mastery of style. In Belgium he designed the Church of the Immaculate Conception, Dadizeele (1857-9), in Ireland the Cathedral of St Colman, Queenstown (now Cobh), Co. Cork (1868-1919), and in England St Francis, Gorton, Manchester (1864-72). The College of St Joseph, Mark Cross, Rotherfield, East Sussex (1865-6), was in a vigorous polychrome brick Gothic. From 1860-9 he was in partnership with *Ashlin, who continued his practice in Ireland after his death. His practice in Britain continued under his brother, **Peter Paul Pugin** (1851-1904).

A & W (1994); B et al. (2001); J.Curl (2007); D & M (1985); Ferrey (1861); ODNB (2004); J.T (1996)

Puig i Cadafalch, Josep or **José** (1867-1956) Catalan architect, he worked mostly in and around Barcelona, Spain, and was a pupil of *Domènech i Montaner. His *Casa Ametller*, Barcelona (1898-1900), drew on German *Gothic exemplars, even to the quotation of a stepped *gable. Later, he paraphrased *vernacular Catalan architecture for his *Modernisme (see ART NOUVEAU) houses, *Casa Garí*, Argentona (1898), and *Casa Macaya*, Barcelona (1901). From c.1904 his work became more influenced by the Vienna *Sezession, and the *Casa Pich i Pon*, Barcelona (1921), had a flavour of *Sullivan's designs in the USA. His *Fábrica Casarramona* (1911-12) is one of his best works. He published a comprehensive study of Catalan *Romanesque art (1909-18).

Boh (1968); Boh et al. (1991); P (1982); J.T (1996)

Pulhamite Blend of coloured sand, Portland Cement, and industrial clinker applied to a core of rock and brick *rubble, then tooled to look like natural rock, invented by the firm established by James *Pulham. Examples survive at Dewstow, near Caerwent (c.1895-1912), Bawdsey Manor, Suffolk (1890s), and Ramsgate Madeira Walk, Kent (1890s).

Beresford et al. (2008); Hitching (2012)

Pulham, James (1788-c.1838) English entrepreneur, founder of a dynasty engaged in making artificial stone. With his brother, **Obadiah** (1802-80), he worked on several projects for Thomas *Smith. Joined by his son (also **James** (c.1820-98)), he established his firm at at Broxbourne, Herts. (c.1843), and began to manufacture high-quality artificial-stone artefacts made of his own invention, *Pulham's Portland Stone Cement*. In 1865 this James was joined by his son, **James Robert Pulham** (1845-1920), and the company was re-named **Pulham & Son**. They invented *Pulhamite, much used for rock-gardens, ferneries, etc., and the firm was involved in the creation of gardens in the Japanese taste: in fact, it acquired a respectable reputation in the field of garden-design. Pulham & Co made the fine *terracotta canopied funerary monument of the Irish artist, **William Mulready** (1786–1863), designed by **Godfrey Sykes** (1824–66) and exhibited at the 1867 Paris *Exposition Universelle*: today it stands in Kensal Green Cemetery. Pulhams also provided some of the terracotta for what is now the Henry Cole Building of the Victoria & Albert Museum, Exhibition Road, South Kensington (1868–73). Other places where the firm (which ceased trading in 1945) worked are listed in Hitching.

Beresford *et al.* (2008); Corfield (1998); J.Curl (ed.) (2001); Hitching (2012); Tay (2006)

Pullman, George Mortimer (1831–97) American industrial designer/philanthropist. He settled (1855) in Chicago, IL, where he established a thriving business constructing roads and elevating buildings above the water-level of Lake Michigan, then formed a company (1858) to manufacture railway sleeping-cars, and he can be credited with the introduction of comfort, and even luxury, to railway-travel. From 1869 he began to develop land south of Chicago, and, taking his cue from experiments in England at, e.g. Port Sunlight, Ches., and Saltaire, Yorks., determined to build a *Company town for the workforce in his factories, and employed *Barrett as his landscape architect, and *Beman as his architect to achieve this. Pullman, IL, was built 1880–95, and was regarded as an exceptionally well-designed model industrial town.

J.T (1996)

pulpit Partially enclosed elevated desk of wood, *masonry, etc., in a church (usually on the northeast side of the *nave) for a preacher. Often ornate, a pulpit may have a *canopy over (called *tester) functioning partly as a sound-reflector. The Anglican *three-decker* pulpit contains at the bottom level a clerk's stall, a reading-desk above, and at the top the pulpit proper, designed as a whole.

pulpitum 1. Stone *screen in a monastic church between the *nave and *choir, acting as the back of part of the choir-*stalls, over which is a *gallery, *Rood, or organ. 2. In an *Antique theatre the part of the stage used by the actors, also called *proscenium.

pulvin, pulvinata, pulvinus (*pl.* **pulvins, pulvinatae, pulvini**) 1. Form resembling a cushion or pillow, such as the *baluster-like side of an *Ionic *volute, called *balteus. *Pulvination* is therefore a swelling, like a squashed cushion. *Friezes in some of the Roman Classical *Orders are occasionally *pulvinated*, or bulging out with a convex profile, also called *cushioned or swelled*. 2. Impost-block or *dosseret between the *capital and arch in a *Byzantine or *Rundbogenstil* *arcade. 3. *Pulvinus et gradus inferior* were the seat and step below around a warm-water bath in Roman times.

punched First operation to a block of stone before it is finely worked, usually with a pointed chisel.

puncheon *Stud, or vertical timber shorter and lighter than a *post in a *timber frame.

Purbeck Dark-grey or grey-greenish hard *limestone, called a *marble, originating in the Isle of Purbeck, Dorset, England, and almost entirely composed of univalve and bivalve remains fossilized and bound together. It was extensively employed by English medieval architects for *colonnettes, *shafts, monuments, *effigies, and tombs because of its attractive properties, being capable of taking a spectacular polish. Patterned with fossils, the dark shiny *shafts set against ordinary limestone contribute to the sumptuous richness of *First-Pointed interiors such as those of Lincoln, Salisbury, and Winchester Cathedrals, where *clustered or compound *piers may be found featuring the material.

Purcell & Elmslie American architectural partnership of **William Gray Purcell** (1880–1965) and **George Grant Elmslie** (1871–1952), famous first for the various fine houses of the *Prairie School. Elmslie, originally from Scotland, worked for a while with *Adler & *Sullivan and was responsible for the ornament on e.g. the Cage Building (1898–9) and the Carson Pirie Scott Store (1899–1904), both in Chicago, IL. Purcell & Elmslie designed several small Banks for the Mid-West, e.g. First State Bank, Le Roy, MN (1914), which were similar to some of Sullivan's Banks. Their best work was in the field of private houses (e.g. Bradley House, Woods Hole, MA (1911), Owre House, Minneapolis (1911–12), Decker House, Holdridge, Lake Minnetonka, Minn. (1912–13), Purcell House, Minneapolis (1913), Backus House, Minneapolis (1915), and Purcell Bungalow, Rose Valley, PA (1918)). Their Woodbury County Court House, Sioux City, IA (1915–17), was in a robust *stripped Classical style, with certain details reminiscent of *Wright's work in the brick *façade.

W.Andrews (1955); H.Brooks (1972); Ct (1968); Gebhard (1953, 1965a); *JSAH*, **xix**/1 (Mar. 1960), 62–8; P (1982); Spencer (ed.) (1979); J.T (1996)

purfled Ornamented with delicate, lacy decorations, especially on borders or margins: e.g. *Gothic *tabernacles with *finials, *pinnicles, and *tracery.

Purism French artistic movement (*c.*1918–25) linked to the *Machine Aesthetic and founded by *Ozenfant and Le *Corbusier. It claimed *Cubism was becoming concerned with mere decoration, that art needed to reflect the 'spirit of the age', exclude emotionalism and expression, and learn lessons inherent in the precision of machinery. Advocated in *Après le Cubisme* (1918), *L'Esprit Nouveau* (1920–5), and *La Peinture Moderne* (1925), it influenced the architectural theories of *Constructivism and the teachings of the *Bauhaus.

COF (1988); J.T (1996)

purlin Horizontal *beam also called *bridging, rib, side-timber*, or *side-waver*, carried on roof-*trusses in order to give intermediate support to the common *rafters.

putlog-hole Hole in a wall to enable the cross-timbers or horizontal *putlogs* of scaffolding to be supported. The scaffold-boards were supported on the putlogs.

putto (*pl.* **putti**) Unwinged, often obese, male child found in Classical and *Baroque sculpture (frequently on funerary monuments), not to be confused with the winged *Amorino, *Cherub, *Cupid, or Love.

pycnostyle *See* INTERCOLUMNIATION.

pylon 1. *Portal of an Ancient-Egyptian *temple composed of two huge *battered towers, usually decorated with bas-relief sculptured figures and hieroglyphs, flanking a lower framed *gateway which, like the towers, was crowned by a *cavetto or *gorge-*cornice. The towers had the corners finished with *torus mouldings that were continued horizontally at the tops of the battered walls under the gorge-cornices. Some authorities use the terms *pylon, propylon, pylône* for the gateway, but others prefer *pylon* for the gateway and *propyla* for the towers. A *pylon-form* resembles one of the towers, and indeed the term *pylon* is now usually given to the towers, following the precedent set by the editors of the *Description de l'Égypte* (1820s). Pylon-forms (often found in C19 chimney-pots) lent themselves to the towers of suspension-bridges, such as *Brunel's structure over the gorge at Clifton, Bristol (1831–64), and the battered *section was widely employed in C19 dams and *retaining-walls.

2. Tall structure erected as a support, especially a lattice-work metal tower to carry overhead electricity-lines. **3.** Tall structure or *pillar used either as an eye-catcher or as a marker for a boundary.

J.Curl (2005); Ck (1996); Gw (1903); L & M (1986); J.T (1996)

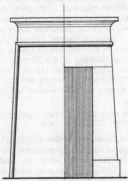

(*left*) Egyptian pylon-form, with *torus* moulding and simple *cornice*. (*right*) The form as an *aedicule* or *door-case*.

pynun- *or* **pignon-table** Sloping stones of a *gable (*pignon* = 'a gable-end').

pyramid Solid figure with a square base and steep *battered triangular sides terminating in an apex. Used in Ancient Egypt for funerary structures, celebrated examples are the pyramids at Giza, near Cairo, Egypt (*c.*2551–*c.*2472 BC). Other types include the stepped form found in both Ancient-Egyptian and *Meso-American *Pre-Columbian architecture, but in the latter region the buildings were temple-platforms rather than tombs: examples include the Ancient-Egyptian pyramid at Saqqara, built by *Imhotep for **King Zoser** (*c.*2630–*c.*2611 BC), and the temple-pyramids of *Meso-American *Aztec and Maya cultures (*c.*C6–C16). Pyramids often featured in Neo-Classical architecture (Roman pyramids included that of **Gaius Cestius** (*c.*12 BC)), and appealed to designers for their stereometrical purity of form, thus responding to *Laugier's admiration for an architecture that was *primitive and pure. Pyramidal compositions for monuments set against walls were common from the time of *Bernini, and countless C18 examples exist. A *pyramidion* is a small pyramid, e.g. that at the top of an *obelisk. For *pyramidal hipped roof see* ROOF; and for *pyramidal rustication see* RUSTICATION.

Carrott (1978); J.Curl (2005); Ck (1996); I.Edwards (1985); Fakhry (1969); Gunnis (1968); Hodges (1989); Lepré (1990); L & M (1986); W.S.Smith (1998); Stadelmann (1985); J.T (1996)

Pythius *or* **Pytheos** *(fl.c.*370–330 BC) *Hellenistic architect, who, with *Satyros, designed and wrote about the *Mausoleum at Halicarnassus (begun c.354 BC), one of the *Seven Wonders of the Ancient World. His Temple of Athena at Priene (334 BC) is one of the finest *Ionic *temples

and therefore he is credited with bringing the Ionic *Order to canonical perfection. His writings have not survived, but the references to him by *Vitruvius suggest he was an important Greek architectural theorist.

D (1950); Fyfe (1936); La (1983); D.S.R (1945); J.T (1996)

pyx, pyxis Box, casket, *shrine or *tabernacle to hold the consecrated Host in a church.

Duffy (1992)

Q

qasr Islamic *castle, *fortress, large house, or *palace.

Qavam al-Din Shirazi (*fl.*1410–38) Iranian architect, he designed the *madrasa* at Herat (1410–11—destroyed) and the *shrine of 'Abdallah Ansari at Gazur Gah, near Herat (completed 1428–9). He was probably responsible for the Friday Mosque and shrine at Mashdad (completed 1417–18). His best-preserved work is the Ghiyathiyya *madrasa*, Khargird (completed 1444–5). His are the architectural master-works of the period of Timurid rule (1370–1506) in eastern Iran and Transoxiana, especially in relation to *vault construction.

Ck (1996); J.T (1996)

qibla Direction towards which every Muslim must turn for prayer. It was originally towards Jerusalem, but from C7 was orientated towards Mecca. In *mosques it is marked by the *qibla wall*, decorated with one or several *mihrabs.

quad Abbreviation of *quadrangle, used in Oxford to describe a college *court surrounded by buildings on all four sides and approached through a *gateway (often set in a tower).

quadra 1. Plain *plinth or *socle of a *pedestal, *podium, etc. 2. *Fillet or *list on either side of the *scotia in an *Attic *base, and especially if used with the *Ionic *Order. 3. Square architectural *moulding framing a sculptured *relief, *panel, *plaque, inscription, etc.

quadrangle 1. Figure with four sides in the same plane. 2. Large rectangular inner *court around which buildings are erected, such as in Oxford colleges, where it is called *quad, and in Cambridge, court.

quadrangular style Building erected in square form around a *court, or on an **H**-plan.

quadrant 1. Fourth part of a circle, hence an object or a street with a plan-form based on a fourth of the circumference of a circle. *Quadrant* was the name given to part of Regent Street, London, designed 1813–16 by John *Nash, laid out on a plan conforming with that shape. A series of buildings the *façades of which form a convex curve is called a *quadrant*, as opposed to that on a concave curve, called *crescent. Quadrants were important in Classical composition as e.g. a means of joining a *corps-de-logis* to *pavilions or *wings, as in *Palladian compositions (*Villa Mocenigo* (1544–64) by *Palladio and Kedleston, Derbys., as designed by *Paine (1757–9)) 2. Medieval term for a *quadrangle or *quad. 3. Octagonal part of a *spire. 4. *Quarter-round.

quadratum *See* OPUS.

quadratura Painted *perspectives of architecture in *Roman, *Renaissance, and (especially) *Baroque ceilings and walls, often very realistic, and frequently (in C17 and C18) extending the actual interior architecture as *trompe l'œil* work of breathtaking technical brilliance, as in the works of *quadraturisti* such as A.*Pozzo.

COF (1988); J.T (1996)

quadrel 1. Artificial stone, perfectly square, made in Italy of a chalky white pliable earth, dried in shady conditions for at least two years. 2. Square *quarrel, or *tile.

quadrifores Roman folding *doors divided in height into two parts, so there were two hinged or pivoted leaves on either side.

quadrifrons 1. Sculptured form, such as an Ancient-Egyptian Hathor-headed *capital, with four heads of the goddess joined at the sides and backs, facing outwards in four directions at the top of the *shaft and under the *abacus, or any other object with four outward-facing heads. 2. *Tetrapylon, i.e. with four equal *gates on four identical *façades, perhaps a structure erected over the intersection of two avenues.

quadriga Sculptured group representing a two-wheeled chariot, with driver, drawn by four horses harnessed abreast, often associated with victory monuments, *triumphal arches, etc. With two horses drawing the chariot it is a *biriga*, while the three-horse type is a *tririga*. A Graeco-Roman motif, it was revived and enjoyed a new lease of life in the Neo-Classical period (e.g. *Cagnola's *Arco del Sempione*, Milan (1806–38)).

quadripartite Divided by the system of construction used into four parts, e.g. a *Gothic *vault on a rectangular plan, with the rectangle divided into four parts by means of intersecting diagonal *ribs.

quadriporticus *Quadrangle with covered *ambulatory, *gallery, or *portico on each side, as in the *atrium of San Clemente, Rome, with *arcades and *colonnades supporting the roofs of structures surrounding it.

quadro riportato 1. Painting on canvas, later transferred to a ceiling, etc. **2.** Ceiling-painting without foreshortening illusionistic effects, designed as though it is to be seen at normal eye-level. It was a Neo-Classical reaction against *Baroque *quadratura and *trompe l'œil work: a good example is Parnassus (1761), Villa Albani, Rome, by **Anton Raffael Mengs** (1728–79).

COF (1988); J.T (1996)

Quaglio Family Italo-Swiss family who designed operatic and theatrical stage-sets for the Electoral Courts of Mannheim and Munich and the Imperial Court of Vienna from C17 to C19. Some Quaglios were also architects. **Lorenzo** (1730–1805) designed some theatres, including the reconstruction of the Schlosstheater (1768) and the building of the Nationaltheater (1777–8), both in Mannheim, as well as (probably) Schloss Wain, Laupheim, Württemberg (1780), and the Rathaus, Lauingen (1783–90). **Angelo** (1784–1815) introduced *Neo-Gothic designs, while **Simon** (1795–1878) produced a series of very fine *Egyptian-Revival sets for the 1818 production of **Mozart's** Die Zauberflöte at Munich, equal in authority to *Schinkel's 1816 designs for Berlin. **Giulio** (1764–1801) decorated the Court Theatre, Dessau (1798), and **Domenico** (1787–1837) was a pioneer of the *Gothic Revival, publishing (1812) some views of old Munich and Denkwürdige Gebäude des Mittelalters, an important work on German medieval art (1818–23). He rebuilt Schloss Hohenschwangau, near Füssen, Bavaria, in a charming Neo-Gothic style (1832–7). **Giovanni Maria**, also called **Johann Maria von** (1772–1813) published Praktische Anleitung zur Perspektive mit Anwendung auf die Baukunst (1811, 1823).

CoE (1972); J.Curl (2005); Quaglio (1823); J.T (1996); Trost (1973)

Quaint style Pejorative term used for *Art Nouveau in its last early-C20 phases.

Quarenghi, Giacomo Antonio Domenico (1744–1817) Bergamo-born architect, working in Russia from 1779, who united developing Russian *Classicism, *Palladianism, and burgeoning *Neo-Classicism. His first significant known work,

the reconstruction of the *Benedictine Church of Santa Scolastica, Subiaco, near Rome (1769–77), is a clever variant on the interior of *Palladio's Il Redentore. After a spell designing for English clients (e.g. an *altar for the chapel at Wardour Castle, Wilts. (1772–4)), Quarenghi left for Russia (where he was patronized by **Empress Catherine II** ('the Great'—r. 1762–96)): there he became a prolific designer, working on the grandest of scales in an impressive Neo-Classical style, and creating a series of important buildings in and around St Petersburg. At the English Palace, Peterhof (1781–9—destroyed), and the Hermitage Theatre (1782–7), for example, he employed a monumental Palladianism, and in both the State Bank (1783–90) and Academy of Sciences (1783–9), St Petersburg, he exploited monumental *colonnades set against simple unadorned stark *elevations. Precision, clarity, and severity were to predominate as his French-inspired Neo-Classicism developed: examples include the Imperial Pharmacy, St Petersburg (1789–96), Jusopov Fontanka Palace (1789–92—with semicircular courtyard), and Alexandrovsky Palace, Tsarskoye Selo (1792–6—with small courtyard embellished with two elegant *Corinthian colonnades set within the main courtyard). With M.F.*Kazakov and **Ivan Petrovich Argunov** (1727–1802) he designed the Sheremetev Palace, Ostankino (1791–8), in which Palladianism and the grandest *Neo-Classicism merge.

Quarenghi used Greek *Doric for his Horse Guards Building (1804–7), and Roman Imperial architecture for his Narva *triumphal arch (1814), which draws on the Antique Roman arches of **Titus** (r.79–81) and **Constantine** (r.324–37) and the refinements of *Percier and *Fontaine's Arc du Carrousel in Paris. His work, which defined the heroic and severe character of early C19 St Petersburg, laid down the direction for the development of Russian Neo-Classicism. Many of his designs were published (1810, 1821).

Burini (ed.) (1995); CoE (1972); G.H (1983); Korshunova (1986); Ms (1996); M & Wa (1987); P (1982); Quarenghi (1821, 1994); D.Shv (2007); J.T (1996); Zanella (1988)

Quarini, Mario Ludovico (1736–c.1800) Italian architect, he collaborated with *Vittone on the latter's buildings and architectural treatises. He designed the *façade of the Church of San Filippo (1759), the side elevation of the Palazzo Comunale (1771), and the façade of San Bernardino (1792), all in Chieri. His later works at Fossano (Annunziata (1777), Palazzo Comunale (1779–80), and Cathedral (1779–81)) were more Neo-Classical, although he never quite shed the *Baroque influence of Vittone.

Atti e rassegna tecnica della Soc. degli ing. e degli archit. in Torino, xii (1958), 153–94; P (1982)

Quaroni, Ludovico (1911–87) Italian architect/ teacher/town-planner, he was a distinguished Neo-Classicist during the Fascist era. He designed a group of small villas, Gaeta Region, Latina (1936), and the *Piazza della Nuova Stazione* Urban Plan, Ostia Lido, near Rome (1937—with **E.Fuselli**). Other works included *Santa Maria Maggiore* (later *San Franco*), Francavilla al Mare (1948–58), a housing development, in which a Roman *vernacular style was attempted, at the *Tiburtino* Quarter, Rome (1950—with *Aymonino, Mario *Ridolfi, and others), and *La Martella* Housing and Church, Matera (1951–2—with others). He published numerous works, including *La Torre de Babele* (1967), *Immagine di Roma* (1976), and *La città fisica* (1981).

Ciorra (1989); E (1994); P (1982); J.T (1996); Tafuri (1964); T & DC (1986)

quarrel, quarry 1. Lozenge-shaped or square piece of glass held in the *cames of leaded *lights. **2.** Approximately lozenge- or square-shaped light in *Gothic *tracery. **3.** Any floor-*tile, lozenge-shaped or square.

quarry-faced *Masonry appearing to be very rough, as though it had not received much attention since being quarried, but squared for the joints, used in *rustication. Also called *rock-faced* masonry.

quarter 1. *Quatrefoil. **2.** Timber *post or *stud in a *timber-framed wall or partition. A series of such posts is called *quartering*. **3.** *See* COMPARTI-MENT. *Compounds include*:
quarter-hollow: concave *moulding or *cavetto, the opposite of a *quarter-round*;
quarter-pace: landing in a *stair between two flights at 90°, so usually square on plan;
quarter-round: convex *moulding or *ovolo, its *section the *quadrant of a circle;
quatrefoil: *see* FOIL.

Quatremère de Quincy, Antoine-Chrysostôme (1755–1849) French *Freemason/architectural theorist/author of *De l'Architecture Égyptienne* (written 1785, published 1803)— an important influence on *Neo-Classicism and the *Egyptian Revival. He wrote much of the architectural content in the *Encylopédie Méthodique* (1788–1825) and many other significant works, including *Dictionnaire Historique d'Architecture* (1832–3). He was also a key figure in the formation of the first landscaped *cemeteries, and was responsible for the conversion of the Parisian Church of *Ste-Geneviève (under the direction of *Rondelet) into the *Panthéon* by blocking up the windows, not to strengthen the structure, as is erroneously supposed, but to give it the character of a *mausoleum (1791–2). As permanent secretary to the *Académie des Beaux-Arts* (1816–39) he had an enormous influence on

virtually all French official architecture. He was among the first to point out the polychromatic aspects of Greek art and architecture (e.g. in *Le Jupiter olympien*) (1814)).

J.Curl (2005); Etlin (1984); M & Wa (1987); P (1982); QdQ (1788–1825, 1803, 1814, 1823, 1828, 1830, 1832, 1834); R.Schneider (1910); J.T (1996); V (1987)

Quattrocento Literally 'four hundred': term for Italian C15 *Renaissance art and architecture.

Queen Anne 1. Period of English architecture during the reign of **Queen Anne** (1702–14), when the English *Baroque style of *Wren, *Vanbrugh, *Archer, and *Hawksmoor came to maturity, notably with Vanbrugh's Blenheim Palace, Oxon. (1705–25), and Hawksmoor's London churches (e.g. Christ Church, Spitalfields (1714–29)). Domestic architecture of the time was derived from *Carolean and Dutch precedents: in London, for example, houses were mainly faced with red brick, had tall *sash-windows and *canopy-like timber *door-cases, while roofs became flatter and hidden behind *parapets. Plainness and dignified restraint marked the domestic architecture in Britain and the American Colonies, and were influential virtues appreciated by later generations, especially *c.*1860–90 and again in C20. **2.** The *Queen-Anne style* or *Revival* evolved from the 1860s, and was not really what its label suggests. Some details were derived from C17 and C18 English and Flemish domestic architecture, but eclectic motifs were drawn from many sources: they included tall white-painted small-paned sash-windows with *rubbed-brick arches and *dressings over and around openings, *terracotta embellishments, open-bed and broken *pediments, steeply pitched roofs (often rising from *eaves-cornices), monumental *chimneys, shaped and *Dutch *gables, white-painted *balustrades, *balconies, and *bay-windows. Such architectural elements were combined with a new freedom of asymmetrical and informal planning derived from the *Gothic Revival and the ideas of A.W.N.*Pugin. In the hands of architects such as G.F.*Bodley, W.E.*Nesfield, R.N.*Shaw, J.J.*Stevenson, and Philip *Webb, the style evolved and began to incorporate elements from *vernacular architecture (e.g. tile-hung gabled walls with *barge-boards, *clap-boarding, and *casement-windows with *leaded *lights). Such developments led to the adoption of the term *Domestic Revival*, while buildings in which Classical motifs predominated were referred to as examples of *Free Classicism* or the *Northern Renaissance Revival*. It should be emphasized that the so-called Queen-Anne style was not a purist scholarly revival, as aspects of the *Gothic and *Greek Revivals had been, but essentially eclectic, drawing on a wide range of motifs from various periods and regions.

It affected domestic architecture in the USA as well, often merging with the *Colonial Revival. **Joseph Mordaunt Crook** (1937–) has called it 'a flexible urban argot', which is as close as one can get to capture its flavour.

Crook (1987); D & M (1985); Gd (1977); A.S.Gray (1985)

Queen-Anne arch *Arch formed of a central semicircular arch flanked by two 'flat' arches constructed of brick *rubbers* set over tall thin side-lights on either side of a wider semi-circular-headed window, a variation on the *Palladian or *Venetian window known as a *serliana (e.g. 39 Broad Street, Ludlow, Salop., *c.*1765). It is commoner in the *Georgian period than in the *Queen Anne.

Ck (1985); Newman & Pe (2006)

Queen-Anne arch With *brick rubbers* and *keystone*, Ludlow, Salop.

queen-post *See* TRUSS.

querelle Square space forming a division or compartment of an *arcade or *colonnade defined by the columns, *beams, structure, and (sometimes) pavement-pattern.

Questel, Charles-Auguste (1807–88) French architect, he studied under **Antoine-Marie Peyre** (1770–1843—*see* PEYRE FAMILY), *Blouet, and *Duban, and began his career with a competent, tough, *Neo-Romanesque design for *St-Paul, Place de la Madeleine*, Nîmes (1835–49). Also in Nîmes the handsome Classical *Palais de Justice* (begun 1838) is by him. His restoration of *St-Martin-d'Ainay*, Lyons, and the furnishings he designed for the same church were much admired when they were exhibited (1855). Later work was much influenced by the *Quattrocento. He designed the Hospital, Gisors, Eure (1859–61), the *Hôtel de la Préfecture* (1862–7), and the *Musée Bibliothèque* (1863–70), the last two both in Grenoble, Isère.

Delaborde (1890); M & Wa (1987); P (1982); J.T (1996)

quincunx 1. Arrangement of five objects, four occupying the corners of a square and the fifth the centre, common in schemes of planting (esp. trees). **2.** Military pattern for deployment of troops, echoed in allusions to battles in gardens (*see* MILITARY GARDEN). **3.** Basis of many *Byzantine churches on a Greek-*cross plan with four barrel-vaulted *bays, central *dome, and corner-bays supporting small domes over angles contained by arms of the cross (*cross-in-square plan).

T.Browne (1658); *ISR*, **xiii**/3 (Sept.1988), 264–81; Mango (1986); Symes (2006); D.Wa (1986)

Typical quincunx arrangement.

quire *See* CHOIR.

quirk 1. Small acute-angled *channel, groove, or deep indent by which a *moulding stands out from its ground, commonly found in *Gothic work: any deep groove separating one moulding from another or from a flat plane or ground. In the latter case a *quirk-bead* would have a quirk on each or one side so that it would be flush with both planes or one. **2.** Re-entrant angle, such as a piece taken out of a regular figure. A rectangular room with a corner boxed in for e.g. a *stair would be classed as having a quirk. **3.** *Quarrel (**1**).

quodlibet Fanciful type of *trompe l'œil* of oddments, often showing letters, paper-knives, playing-cards, ribbons, and scissors, in apparently accidental array, painted on walls, etc.

quoin (*also* **coign, coin, coyn**) **1.** Any external angle or corner of a structure. **2.** Angular courses of stone, etc., at the corner of a building, usually laid as alternate quoin-*headers and quoin-*stretchers, often dressed with *channels around them so they project from the *naked of the wall (*rustic quoins). **3.** One of the *dressed stones used to strengthen the corner of a building. *See* LONG-AND-SHORT WORK.

quonset hut Prefabricated portable building consisting of a semi-cylindrical corrugated metal roof secured to a foundation of steel. Like the *Nissen-hut, it was widely used in the 1939–45 war. It was so called after Quonset Point, RI, USA, and was probably first used in 1941.

OED Supplement, **iii** (1984), 988

R

rabbet, rebate Long rectangular groove formed in the edge of wood, stone, etc., to receive the edge, *tongue, or end of another element, e.g. *door in a *frame.

Rabirius (*fl.* late-AD C1) Roman architect, known from the *Epigrams* of **Martial** (*c.*39–*c.*102), who designed for **Emperor Domitian** (*r.*81–96) a new Imperial Palace on the Palatine, Rome, to the south of earlier buildings erected for Domitian's predecessors. Still occupied as late as C6, it was the origin of the word 'palace': a huge complex, it included enclosed gardens, a *hippodrome, libraries, and many formal rooms for State occasions as well as private apartments. *Vaults and domed constructions of *concrete were used throughout, and the brick-faced concrete walls were clad in coloured *marbles. Rabirius seems to have been partly responsible for the assured application of the *Orders to the new type of vaulted structure in order to create an opulence of unparalleled richness. Throughout the plan, formal axes were handled with deftness, and *apses, octagons, and segments were employed with square and rectangular plan-forms. Rabirius has been linked with architectural works of the period, e.g. the Colosseum, *thermae* of **Titus** (*r.*79–81), Domitian's *Villa near Albano, and others, but evidence is lacking.

W.MacD (1965–86); P (1982); W-P (1981)

raceme Ornament based on a plant where flowers or leaves are borne in succession in the direction of the tip of the plant on an unbranched main stalk (e.g. *anthemion or *palmette).

Radburn Planning principle developed at Radburn, NJ, on lines suggested originally by Ebenezer *Howard and promoted by *Mumford, Clarence *Stein, et al. The proposed town (which was later transmogrified as a commuter-suburb) was designed (1929) to segregate pedestrians and traffic by having *cul-de-sac feeder-roads and *paths on *bridges or in underpasses. This principle of segregation, known as *Radburn planning*, was also used in various New Towns created in Britain and on the Continent after the 1939–45 war.

Schaffer (1982)

radial, radiating Denoting a form based on the radius of a circle. *Compounds include:*
radial brick 1. *Voussoir. 2. Special brick used for walls curved on plan;
radial step: winder in a *stair;
radiating chapels: in a church, projecting chapels arranged radially around the *ambulatory of a semicircular or polygonal liturgical east end (*see* CHEVET);
radiating principle: planning system applied to certain building-types, especially *prisons and hospitals, in which, from a central block or core, wings radiate in several directions (*see* PANOPTICON).

Radical architecture Term used (1960s, 1970s) to suggest extremes of shape, structure, or (more usually) the Leftist political position of its creators, propounded largely by the journal *Casabella*. In reality Radical architecture was often drawn or *collage presentation of projects by certain groups (e.g. *Archizoom), usually involving assaults on architecture conceived as a formal language.

Navone & Orlandini (1974); Sparke (1988)

Radziwiłłowa, Princess Helena (1753–1821) Polish aristocrat, member of the Grand Adoption Lodge of Warsaw, and creator (1776–1821) of the *Garden of Allusions near Nieborów. Called *Arkadia*, with *fabriques* designed by *Ittar, *Zug, and others, it was one of the most interesting C18 gardens with liberal, elegiac, nationalist, and literary mnemonic agendas encapsulated within their boundaries. Three other Polish gardens redolent with meaning were also created by women: Puławy (by *Aigner and the painter **Jan Piotr Norblin** (1773–1830)), Powązki (both for **Princess Izabela Czartoryska** (1746–1835)), and Mokotów (for **Princess Izabela Lubomirska** (1736–1816)).

AQC, cxvi (2004), 83–126; *GH*, xxiii/1 (Summer 1995), 91–112; Piwkowski (1998); Porset & Révauger (eds) (2013)

raffle-leaf 1. Serrated, indented, or crumpled leaf-like enrichment with waving indented frond-like (or *raffled*) edges. *Raffling* is applied to the notched edges of carved foliage in architectural ornament, e.g. the *acanthus-leaf. **2.** Asymmetrically disposed *Rococo curving flowing *scrolling serrated foliage arranged in *ogee- and C-forms, esp. round *frames or *cartouches.

Rafn, Aage (1890–1953) Danish architect, one of the most accomplished C20 Neo-Classicists, he designed the circular *courtyard of *Kampmann's Police Headquarters, Copenhagen (1919–24), and, with **Hans Jørgen Kampmann** (1889–1966), **Christian Kampmann** (1890–1955), Holger *Jacobsen, and **Anton Frederiksen** (1884–1967), completed the great work. He was responsible for other Neo-Classical buildings in Denmark (e.g. 22 Gl. Vartovvej, Copenhagen (1919–20)). His unrealized but ravishing design for a crematorium (1921) won him the Gold Medal of the Royal Academy of Fine Arts. He designed some fine furniture.

Mi (1951); Pn (1982); We (1947)

raft Type of *foundation consisting of a solid *slab, a slab with *beams, or a cellular raft (containing a basement), all in *reinforced concrete. It spreads the load from the building on the ground, and helps to prevent settlement.

rafter One of several long, inclined, rectangular timbers used in the construction of pitched roofs, supporting the roof-covering, e.g. *laths and *tiles. *Types of rafter include*:

angle-: principal rafter under the *hip-rafter carrying the *purlins on which *common rafters* rest. In the USA any rafter at the angle of a roof, whether principal or not, hence either a *hip-* or *jack-rafter* in a *valley;

auxiliary-: in a *truss, a rafter used to stiffen the *principal by doubling it;

binding-: purlin;

common-: of uniform dimensions, placed at regular intervals along the sloping section of a roof, sometimes as intermediate members between principals. A *pair* of common rafters is a *couple*;

compass-: one curved on the lower side, or wholly curved, as in a truss;

compound-: two rafters, one set over the other, separated by *cleats, distance-pieces, or spacers, the inner rafters being *secondary rafters*;

hip-: one set diagonally at the hip of a roof where two slopes at 90° join, supporting the upper ends of the common rafters;

jack-: **1.** one set diagonally at the valley of a roof where two slopes join, such as at a *dormer-window roof, supporting the lower ends of common rafters; **2.** shorter *common rafter* between wall-plate and *hip-rafter*, or between a *valley* and the *ridge*;

principal: large rectangular inclined timber in a sloping roof supporting a purlin also serving as

a common rafter. A principal rafter not serving as a common rafter is a *principal*;

valley-: one set diagonally where two roof-slopes meet in a valley, e.g. at a dormer-window, as in *jack-rafter* (**1**);

verge-: common rafter set beyond a *gable to support the roof-covering beyond the *naked of the wall, itself supported on the ends of projecting wall-plates and purlins.

A *rafter-plate* is a timber by which rafters are supported, e.g. wall-plate.

ABDM (1996); W.McKay (1957)

rag Piece of hard, coarse-textured stone, capable of being broken into thick, flattish pieces, the commonest types being *Kentish rag* (tough, hard *limestone, readily broken into usable pieces), *Rowley rag* (a basaltic stone from Staffs.), and other stones, notably in the USA. Rag-stones are not laid in regular *courses, and mostly used *as facings* to brick or other types of wall. Rag-stone's appearance is net-like, formed of a pattern of approximate polygons, with the mortar-joints coarse (*rough-picked*) or fine (*close-picked*). Kentish rag is commonly found in C19 *Gothic-Revival churches in London and the south-eastern counties of England. Rag is also used in *rubble walls.

W.McKay (1957); J.Parker (1850)

Rageur Style of French C19 architecture in which *Classicism, *Louis-Quatorze, *Italianate, *Renaissance, and *Gothic were promiscuously mixed. A *rageur* is a bad-tempered person: aspects of the *Rageur* style are certainly over-emphatic and outlandishly proportioned, e.g. *Viollet-le-Duc's tomb for **Charles-Auguste-Louis-Joseph Demorny** (1811–65—**1st Duc de Morny** from 1862), *Père-Lachaise* Cemetery, Paris (1865–6). *See* GO; RAGUER.

W.Pa (1887)

raggle Groove or *raglet in *masonry.

Raghton, Ivo de (*fl.c.*1317–39) English master-mason, he appears to have designed the west front of York *Minster including the great window (1338–9) in the *Second-Pointed *Curvilinear style. He may have influenced the design of the east front of Carlisle Cathedral (1318–22), the *reredos at Beverley Minster, Yorks. (1324–34), the east window of Selby Abbey, Yorks. (begun c.1330), the *pulpitum at Southwell Minster, Notts., and the south *rose-window at Lincoln Cathedral.

J.Harvey (1987)

raglet Continuous *raggle or groove in *masonry, *mortar-joints, etc., into which lead *flashing can be set.

Raguer French for 'to chafe' or 'irritate', applied to a phase of the mid-C19 *Gothic Revival in France characterized by perversity, discordance, and aggressive originality owing little to precedent. It had much in common with English and American *Rogue Gothic by *Keeling et al. *See* GO; RAGEUR.

Raguzzini, Filippo (*c.*1680–1771) Celebrated architect working in the *Rococo style in Rome during the Pontificate of **Benedict XIII** (1724–30). He designed the Chapel of *San Domenico* in *Santa Maria sopra Minerva* (1724–5), the *Ospedale di San Gallicano* (1725–6—with a well-considered ventilation system), and *Piazza di Sant'Ignazio* (1727–36), in which five apartment-blocks have *façades rising from plans that are segments of ellipses to enclose the space in front of the huge *Sant'Ignazio*. Other works include the façades of *Santa Maria della Quercia* (1727–31), *San Filippo Neri* (1728), and *Santi Quirico e Giulitta* (1728–30), and his restoration of the Spanish Steps (1731), all in Rome.

Albissini *et al.* (1984); Habel (1981); P (1982); Rotili (1951, 1982); J.T (1996); *TPR*, xiii/3 (1929); 139–48; *ZfGdB*; xi (1981), 31–65

rail 1. Horizontal member of a wall-frame between the *posts or *studs in *timber-framed construction. **2.** Horizontal timber in a *door, panelling, *wainscot, etc. **3.** Horizontal timber or metal bar fixed to upright posts as part of a *fence. Early *compartimenti* or *quarters* were sometimes defined by waist-high rails with latticing down to the ground. *Types of rail include*:

altar-: *see* ALTAR;

chair-: *cornice at the top of a *dado around a room;

clamp-: rebated timber to receive the ends of boards, as in a ceiling, etc., called *batten* or *cleat* in the USA;

dado-: as *chair-rail*;

frieze-: rail in a panelled door corresponding to the *frieze in position;

hand-: rail supported on *balusters, so the top of a *balustrade at the edge of a *balcony, *stair, etc.;

hanging-: rail to which hinges are fixed in a door, window, etc. A rail with hinges at the side of a panelled door is a *stile;

lock-: rail in a framed door into which the lock is fitted, usually corresponding to the top of a dado;

mid-: horizontal timber in a wall-frame placed half-way in a storey, or between a *cill and a wall-plate.

ABDM (1996); GH, xxvii/1 (Summer 1999), 36; Gw (1903); W.McKay (1957); W.Pa (1887)

Railton, William (*c.*1801–77) British architect to the Ecclesiastical Commissioners (1838–48), his economical parsonages and *Gothic-Revival

churches (e.g. St Paul's, Woodhouse Eaves, Leics. (1836–7)) did not win the approval of the ecclesiologically minded. He is best known for the Memorial to **Horatio Nelson** (1758–1805—**Viscount Nelson of the Nile** from 1801), Trafalgar Square, London (1839–43), a *Corinthian column carrying the Admiral's statue. The four lions by **Sir Edwin Landseer** (1802–73), added later (1867), were not part of Railton's design. His account of the 'Temple at Cadachio, in Corfu' was published (1830) in the supplementary volume of *Stuart and *Revett's *Antiquities of Athens*.

Co (2008); *ODNB* (2004)

Rainaldi, Carlo (1611–91) Rome-born late-*Mannerist/*Baroque architect, son of **Girolamo Rainaldi** (1570–1655—architect of *Santa Teresa*, Caprarola (from 1620), and the *Palazzo Pamphili*, *Piazza Navona*, Rome (1645–50)), he worked with his father (Chief Papal Architect, appointed (1644) by **Innocent X** (*r.*1644–55)) on *Sant'Agnese in Agone*, *Piazza Navona* (from 1652): *Borromini took over (1653), but was sacked (1657), after which Carlo Rainaldi was recalled, although *Bernini and *Cortona were consultants. To Rainaldi the plan, front, and huge *piers are credited. Other buildings include the brilliantly articulated *Santa Maria in Campitelli* (1662–75), the front of *Sant'Andrea della Valle* (1656–65), and the apparently twin churches (1662–79) flanking the axis of the *Corso* in the *Piazza del Pòpolo* (one church (*Santa Maria in Montesanto*—Bernini replaced Rainaldi in 1673) has an elliptical *dome to make it appear the same diameter as the dome of its 'twin' because the sites are of different size).

Eimer (1970–1); FdA & C (1977–8); Fasolo (1961); N-S (1986); P (1982); J.T (1996); Va (1986); Wi (1982)

rain-conductor Downspout, leader, or pipe to conduct rainwater from a *gutter or *rainwater-head.

Rainer, Roland (1910–2004) Austrian architect/town-planner, Director of Planning for the City of Vienna (1958–63), he argued for an ecologically aware approach to design. With others, he was responsible for the *Veitingergasse* Housing-Estate, Vienna (1953–4), and the Puchenau *Garden City near Linz, Austria (1964–93), both of which demonstrated his opposition to high-density housing promoted in Vienna in the 1920s by e.g. *Ehn, as well as his advocacy of decentralized developments. He designed Municipal buildings in Vienna (1958), Bremen, Germany (1963–4), and Ludwigshafen, Germany (1962–5), and housing at Kassel, Germany (1980), *Tamariskengasse*, Vienna (1985–93), and *Auwiesen*, Linz (1990–3). His publications include *Livable Environments* (1972).

E (1994); Kamm (1973); P (1982); J.T (1996)

rainwater-head Small cistern of cast-iron, lead, etc., also called *hopper-head*, frequently ornamented, to collect rainwater from e.g. a *gutter behind a *parapet, before it is discharged to a *rain-conductor. Elaborate C17 and C18 cast-lead rainwater-heads are often of great significance on building-façades.

raised and fielded *See* PANEL.

raised moulding Anything raised above its surroundings, such as a *bolection *moulding, or a *panel with its centre higher than its edges.

Raje, Anant Damodar (1929–2009) Indian architect, influenced by *Kahn, his works include the Institute of Forest Management, Bhopal (1984–98—with *Kanvinde), various buildings at the Indian Institute of Management, Ahmedabad (1975–94), and the Indian Statistical Institute, Delhi (1970–6). Raje collaborated with other architects, including *Doshi.

Ck (1996)

rake Inclination or slope of anything, such as the top of a triangular *pediment or a pitched roof. *Raking* is therefore the fact of sloping, and *the word is combined with others*:

raking arch: *see* ARCH;

raking coping: *cope on a sloping surface, e.g. *gable;

raking cornice: *cornice on inclined tops of a triangular *pediment;

raking course: *course of bricks laid diagonally between two normally laid faces of a wall, called *diagonal* (for walls three to four bricks thick) or *herring-bone* (for walls at least four bricks thick) *bond. *See* BRICK;

raking flashing: *flashing of metal (usually lead, but sometimes copper or zinc), following the slope of a pitched roof where it abuts a *chimney-stack, *gable-*parapet, wall, etc., set in a straight line with a *raglet where stepped flashings (as would be usual with brickwork) are not possible (as with *ashlar *masonry);

raking moulding: *moulding on an inclined plane, e.g. raking cornice of a pediment;

raking out: removal of *mortar before *pointing;

raking riser: in a *stair, an inclined or *overhung *riser, making a deeper tread than would be possible with a vertical riser.

Bru (1990); W.McKay (1957)

ram 1. Ram's head or skull on a Classical *frieze: a variation on the more usual *aegicrane or *bucranium. **2.** *Criosphinx. **3.** Reinforced prow or beak (*rostrum*) of an *Antique warship for *ramming* and holing an enemy ship, featured on the *columna rostrata. **4.** To beat down earth, clay, etc., with a heavy implement, to make it hard and firm. *See also* RAMMED.

Ramée, Joseph (1764–1842) French architect/landscape architect, trained under *Bélanger, and influenced by *Ledoux. He designed the *Hôtel Berthault-Récamier, Rue du Mail* (late 1780s–early 1790s), and the great Altar of the *Fête de la Fédération, Champ de Mars* (1790—destroyed), both in Paris. Having fled the Terror, he worked in Germany, where he designed the *Börsenhalle* (1803) and laid out *Picturesque parks with *fabriques in eclectic styles in Hamburg. At Ludwigslust, near Schwerin, he designed a *mausoleum (1806—in an advanced Neo-Classical style with *Doric *portico) for **Friedrich Franz** (1756–1837—**Duke** from 1785, then **Grand Duke** from 1815 **of Mecklenburg-Schwerin**). Ramée also worked in Denmark *c.*1800-6 (*Sophienholm*, a country-house near Copenhagen, is a good example of his work there, with gardens and *Gothic and *vernacular *fabriques*), but he went to the USA (1812) to plan new towns and buildings in NY State for **David Parish** (1778–1826) of Hamburg: the war with the UK ruined those intentions, although Parishtown, NY, acquired a few works erected to his designs. One of his best surviving buildings in the USA is Union College (1813), Schenectady, NY, an early *campus-design which may have influenced *Jefferson when planning the University of Virginia at Charlottesville. Ramée returned to Europe (1816), working first in The Netherlands, then (1823) France, and again (1830s) Hamburg. He spent his declining years preparing works on gardens for publication in Paris: they include *Jardins irréguliers et maisons de campagne, de tous genres et de toutes dimensions* (1823), *Recueil de cottages et maisons de campagne* (1837), and *Parcs et Jardins* (1836). His son, **Daniel** (1806–87), contributed to architectural history and to the restoration of various Cathedrals (e.g. those at Beauvais, Noyon, and Senlis) as well as the Abbeys of *St-Riquier* and *St-Wulfran* at Abbeville. His *Dictionnaire général des termes d'Architecture* (1868), published in Paris by Reinwald, is an impressive volume. He also published books on medieval French architecture, Heidelberg *Schloss*, and practical construction.

GdBA, vii (1860), 110–8; P (1982); Ramée (1836, 1837); J.T (1996); P.Turner (1987, 1996)

Ramírez Vázquez, Pedro (1919–2013) Mexican architect of some of his country's 'muscular Modernist' public buildings, often incorporating Aztec motifs, e.g. the National Museum of Anthropology, México City, with its enormous forecourt featuring *masonry, a cantilevered roof, and a large pond (1963–4). He designed the *shrine of Our Lady of Guadalupe (1975–6—a tent-like structure for 10,000 people inside and 30,000 in the external *court); the House of Representatives and the Senate Building of the

National Parliament (1976–80); and the Aztec Football Stadium (1961–6), all in México City. He developed a prototype for prefabricated school-buildings early in his career, and his system was adopted by UNICEF.

E (1994); Ma (1983b); Pinoncelly (2000); *The Times* (8 May 2013), 50; J.T (1996)

rammed Structure, e.g. wall, made by beating down earth contained between *formwork or *shuttering with a heavy implement. If *cement and other strengthening ingredients are added, the rammed earth is *pisé de terre*. Compare ADOBE; COB; PISÉ.

ramp 1. Inclined plane connecting two different levels. **2.** Part of the hand-rail of a *stair *balustrade with a steep concave upward bend occurring where there is a landing, or where the stair has *winders. Opposite of *knee.

rampant *See* ARCH.

rampart 1. Thick wall in fortifications for defence, with a walkway or platform on top for the defenders, and a *battlemented *parapet. **2.** Defensive mound of earth, with an inclined slope on the outside, its top flat and wide enough for guns and troop-movements, protected by a parapet.

ramping 1. To ascend or descend from one level to another. **2.** Asymmetrical rampant arches associated with the rake of a *ramp or *stair. *See* ARCH.

Ramsey, John de (*fl.*1304–49) English master-mason, son of **Richard Curteys** (*fl.c.*1300—probably **Richard Le Machun**, mason (1285–90), of Norwich Cathedral), he was (1304) Master of the Works at Norwich, when constructing the detached *belfry. He worked on (and may have designed) the south part of the Norwich *cloisters (1324–30), and was probably in charge of building at Ely Cathedral (*c.*1322–26). He seems to have settled in London, where the de Ramseys were engaged in several important projects.

J.Harvey (1987)

Ramsey, William de (*fl.*1323–49) English master-mason. He worked (1320s) on the Norwich Cathedral *cloisters under John de *Ramsey, and probably on St Ethelbert's Chapel over the gate to the precincts. However, he is of major importance for his work in London, where (1323) he was employed at St Stephen's Chapel, Westminster, and (1326–31) was Visiting Master (i.e. consultant) at Norwich Cathedral. By 1332 he was engaged with the *chapter-house and *cloister, St Paul's Cathedral, London. A member of a four-mason Commission charged with reporting on the fabric of the Tower of London (1335), he was

appointed (1336) Chief Mason at the Tower and Chief Surveyor of the King's Works in the Tower and other castles south of the River Trent for life. When the *presbytery at Lichfield Cathedral, Staffs., was being built, he was consulted (1337), and in the same year was put in charge of building at St Stephen's Chapel, Westminster. He was probably involved in the design of the Hall and other buildings at Penshurst, Kent (1341–8). Ramsey is of great importance in the evolution of the *Perp. style, for surviving illustrations and fragments of masonry suggest that the chapter-house at St Paul's (destroyed) was in that style, which first emerged there and at St Stephen's Chapel, Westminster: he was therefore probably one of its inventors, and, if so, he was one of the most influential architects England has ever produced.

J.Harvey (1987)

rand Border, *fillet, margin, or rim, especially in landscape-gardening.

Randall, James (1778–1820) English architect, he published (1806) *A Collection of Designs for Mansions, Casinos, Villas, Lodges and Cottages in the Grecian, Gothic, and Castle Styles* (which includes a country-house in the Egyptian style, with battered corner-piers, Hathor-headed, palm-, and bud-capitals, and hieroglyphic decorations) and a treatise on Dry Rot (1807).

Co (2008); Carrott (1978); J.Curl (2005)

random Irregular in size and shape, unequal. *The word is found combined with others, e.g.:*

random ashlar: *masonry of *ashlars not laid in continuous regular courses, but formed of dressed stones of different heights and widths fitted closely together, otherwise called *broken ashlar, random bond,* or *random range ashlar;*

random bond: as *random ashlar;*

random course: masonry *course of stones of the same height, set in a wall where the courses are of differing heights;

random-jointed: *rubble or random ashlar laid in irregular courses;

random-range: as *random ashlar;*

random rubble: *see* RUBBLE;

random-tooled: ashlar wrought to a surface with irregular tooling, called *random droving* in Scotland.

range 1. *Course of stone in a straight line: coursed regular *ashlar in a straight line is therefore *ranged masonry* or *rangework*. For *ranged rubble see* RUBBLE. **2.** Several bodies standing in a given plane, such as columns forming a *colonnade.

Ransome, Ernest Leslie (1852–1917) English engineer, whose father had patented 'concrete stone' (a type of *reinforced *concrete). E.L.Ransome went to the USA (1869) to exploit this, and designed early reinforced-concrete *bridges in Golden Gate Park, San Francisco, CA (1886-7). Other designs exploiting it include the Borax factory, Bayonne, NJ (1897—the structure of which survived (1902) a huge fire), and the United Shoe Manufacturing Company's factory, Beverly, near Boston, MA (1903-5). These, several grain-elevators, and Albert *Kahn's contemporary Packard factory, Detroit, MI, are among the first fully developed large industrial buildings constructed of reinforced concrete. Ransome's economical exposed frames with glazed panels replacing solid walls served as exemplars for *Gropius and Le *Corbusier, and thus became paradigms of *International-Modernist imagery (1920s). With Danish-born **Henry Alexis Saurbrey** (1886-1967) Ransome published (1912) *Reinforced Concrete Buildings*.

P.Collins (1959); P (1982); Ransome & Saurbrey (1912); J.T (1996)

Raphael (**Raffaello Sanzio** *or* **Santi** (1483-1520)) *High-*Renaissance Urbino-born architect/painter. Trained by his father, **Giovanni Santi** (d.1494), and **Pietro Perugino** (1445/50-1523), whom he later assisted and soon surpassed, one of his early paintings, *The Marriage of the Virgin* (1504—far superior to Perugino's version of the same subject), depicts a polygonal domed building indicating a mature understanding of architecture, notably centrally planned buildings. Moving to Rome (1508), he was commissioned by **Pope Julius II** (*r*.1503-13) to decorate the *Stanza della Segnatura* in the Vatican, including *The School of Athens* showing the ancient philosophers in an architectural setting, a masterpiece of *perspective, evoking *Antique *Classicism.

His first architectural foray was *Sant'Eligio degli Orefici*, Rome (from *c*.1511, with later *dome by *Peruzzi, the whole rebuilt by *Ponzio in C17). This was followed by the *Mortuary Chapel of **Agostino Andrea Chigi** (1466-1520) in *Santa Maria del Pòpolo*, Rome (from 1512), a centrally planned work of great authority owing its present appearance to *Bernini, who completed it (1652-6). The *Palazzo Pandolfini*, Florence (begun *c*.1518), merged the Florentine style of the *Palazzo Strozzi* with the Roman style as epitomized in *Bramante's 'House of Raphael' (*Palazzo Caprini*), and indeed it was from Bramante that Raphael took his precedents. His own buildings, though few in number, were soon recognized as exemplars as significant as *Antique remains and the works of Bramante. Appointed (1515) Superintendent of Roman Antiquities by **Giovanni de'Medici** (b.1475—**Pope Leo X** (*r*.1513-21)), he may have been behind proposals to record all Roman ruins and restore some. The *Villa Madama*, which he

began building near Rome (*c*.1516) for **Cardinal Giulio de'Medici** (b.1479—**Pope Clement VII** (*r*.1523-34)), is ample evidence of his feeling for Antiquity, notably in the *loggia* facing the garden, and aspects of the *villa were derived from recently discovered vaults of the *Domus Aurea* of **Nero** (*r*.54-68) and the so-called *thermae* of **Titus** (*r*.79-81), as well as from *Pliny's description of his Laurentine villa. Embellished with reliefs of *stucco and painted *grotesques by Raphael's assistants (including *Giulio Romano), the ensemble (though only partly completed) was an authoritative evocation of Antique interior *décor*. After Bramante's death Raphael was appointed *magister operis* of St Peter's, and proposed a basilican version of Bramante's plan.

Cable (1981a); Chastel (1959, 1988); C.Fr *et al.* (1984); He (1996); Lotz (1997); P (1982); S.Ray (1974); J.T (1996); Tafuri (1966); R.Weiss (1969); Wi (1982, 1998)

Raphaelesque *Antique type of ornament, the *grotesque, revived by *Raphael and others during the *Renaissance period.

Raschdorff, Julius Karl (1823-1914) German architect. As City Architect of Cologne (1854-72), he restored many of that city's buildings, and evolved an opulent *Renaissance style in which French and German elements were mixed. From 1878 he was Professor at the *Technische Hochschule*, Berlin. He designed the English Church of St George, Monbijou Park, Berlin (1884), and the *mausoleum of **Kaiser Friedrich III** (*r*.1888), **Kaiserin** (*r*.1888) **Victoria**, Princess Royal of England, and two of their children, Princes **Sigismund** (1864-6) and **Waldemar** (1868-79), at *Persius's *Friedenskirche*, Potsdam (1884-9), and built the Lutheran Cathedral in the *Lustgarten*, Berlin (1888-1905—damaged in the 1939-45 war, but restored, although the *dome and *lantern bear no resemblance to the originals), which replaced an earlier structure altered by *Schinkel. The Cathedral contains a large *crypt containing the *sarcophagi of members of the Prussian Royal House, but the whole building's overblown Imperial *Baroque style never gained it much affection. He published volumes describing and illustrating his works as well as a book on Rhenish C16-17 timber-framed buildings.

B-S (1977); J.Curl (2002a, 2011); P (1982); Raschdorff (1879, 1886-1922, 1895, 1896, 1899); J.T (1996)

Rastrelli, Count Bartolomeo Francesco (1700-71) Italian architect, the most distinguished practitioner in mid-C18 Russia, having settled there when his father, **Bartolomeo Carlo** (*c*.1675-1744), sculptor/architect, was called (1715) to St Petersburg. He may have studied (1720s) with de *Cotte in Paris, and possibly travelled in Germany and Italy before returning (1730) to Russia. Under the aegis of **Empress Anna Ivanovna** (*r*.1730-40) and her 'favourite', **Ernst Johann Biren (Biron** *or* **Büh-ren**—1690–1772), **Duke of Courland** from 1737, he rose in the architectural world, designing several important buildings including the Biron Palace at Mitau (Jelgava), Latvia (1736–40). His position as Court Architect continued under **Empress Elisa-beth Petrovna** (*r.*1741–62), when he created many buildings in a *Baroque style of great magnificence. His works include the Andreas Church, Kiev (1747–68), renovations and extensions to the Summer Palace, Peterhof (1747–52), the Vorontsov (1743–57) and Stroganov (1750–4) Palaces, St Petersburg, Smol'ny Cathedral and Convent, St Petersburg (1748–64), the Great Palace, Tsarskoye Selo (now Pushkin—1749–56), and the fourth Winter Palace, St Petersburg (1754–62), the last probably his finest achievement. His work synthesized French, Italian, South-German, and Russian styles, and his sources were many. He was accomplished in creating very long *façades broken up by emphatic vertical punctuations, best seen in the *scenographic Winter Palace. At Andreas Church, Kiev, and Smol'ny Convent, St Petersburg, he drew on C17 Russian exemplars for his Greek-cross plans, dominant central *cupola, and lesser domes. His *Rococo interiors included the famous reconstructed Amber Room, *Tsarskoye Selo* (1753).

G.H (1983); N-S (1986a); P (1982); Ousiannikov (1982); D.Shv (2007); J.T (1996)

ratch(e)ment Curved member resembling a flying *buttress rising from the corner uprights of a *hearse, meeting a similar member at a central upright. Ratchements supported the hangings, valancing, and palls, and often carried *prickets for candles.

rath Earth or stone enclosure, often circular on plan, found in Ireland.

ratha Indian rock-cut temple, heavily encrusted with carved decorations, resembling a huge chariot with massive canopies over it (e.g. Dharmaraja Ratha, Mamallapuram (C7)).

Rational architecture Late-C20 movement that proposed reasonable and buildable responses to design-problems drawing on order in urban fabric and on architectural typology. It evolved from the 1960s, prompted by Aldo *Rossi's *L'Architettura delle città* (1966, 1982) and *Architettura Razionale*, by Rossi and others, published during the XVth Milan Triennale (1973). It embraced *Renaissance theory, severe C18 *Neo-Classicism of the *Enlightenment, and some architectural themes of the 1920s. Its apologists insisted that its essentials, its laws, and its historical continuity confirmed it as an independent legitimate discipline—unlike the theorists of

C20 *Rationalism and of the *Modern Movement, they saw the European historical city as a repository of great riches, composed of *types that were primary, unchangeable, historical essentials in architecture incapable of reduction or subdivision: by rediscovering and redefining the formal vocabulary and language of architecture that had been so thoroughly disrupted (and even corrupted), they sought to reconcile Architecture, the City, and Mankind, for they argued that humans had become alienated by *Functionalism, *International Modernism, and the Modern Movement as a whole. Examples of Rational architecture include Rossi's Apartment Building in the *Gallaratese 2* Complex, Amiata Estate, Milan (1969–73), and **Giorgio Grassi**'s (1935–) Students' Residence, Chieti (1976–84). Among its chief protagonists were **Mario Botta** (1943–), **Rob** (1938–) and **Léon** (1946–) **Krier** (Léon being one of its most powerful polemicists), **Bruno Reichlin** (1941–), and *Ungers. *See* NEO-RATIONALISM; TENDENZA; TICINESE SCHOOL.

Botta (1991, 1997); Dal Co (1987); Ks (1995); L.Krier (ed.) (1978); L.Krier & Pavan (1980); L (1988); Pizzi (ed.) (1994-8, 1997); A.Ro (1982); A.Ro *et al*. (1973); Sakellaridou (2000); J.T (1996)

Rationalism Term employed to mean different things at different times by various groups in the history of C20 architecture, but mostly (and inappropriately) applied to mean the so-called architectural principles behind the *International *Modern Movement led by *Gropius, *Mies, et al., subscribing to the so-called *Machine Aesthetic and to alleged *Functionalism. However, the word has been so loosely used that some expanded explanations are necessary.

Classical and *Renaissance architectural treatises argued that architecture was a science with principles that could be understood on a *rational* basis. C18 and C19 theorists, notably J.-N.-L. *Durand, *Viollet-le-Duc, *Semper, and others also argued for *reasoned* approaches to design derived from the culture of the European *Enlightenment, building on what had gone before. However, those arguing for C20 'Rationalism' were iconoclastic, making assumptions that architectural and urban problems could be solved primarily through an abandonment of *Historicism and of movements such as the *Arts-and-Crafts, *Art Nouveau, and *Expressionism (which they regarded as dead-ends), thus creating a *tabula rasa* on which to start again from scratch. They were messianic in their desire for a 'new world', 'better' architecture, and Leftist political systems: they held quasi-religious beliefs in the inherent rightness of their cause, drawing on a 'Machine Aesthetic' to achieve *images* appropriate to their cause: their position, therefore, was wholly unlike that of C19 theorists, and was based on lack of intellectual rigour, spurious analogies, and false, twisted reasoning.

Advocates of supposed 'Rationalism' evolved certain principles by which their aims were to be met. First, architecture, industrial design, and planning could be used for social-engineering and 'educational' (i.e. conditioning) purposes, and so design had 'moral' meanings (a notion drawn partly from the writings of A.W.N.*Pugin and *Ruskin, both of whom, however, would have been horrified at the inhumane results). Second, strict economy, cheap *industrialized building-methods, *prefabrication, and mass-production at all levels were to be used in the making of the new environment to achieve a *minimum* standard for everyone's habitation, but, even if traditional methods of construction were employed (bricks, after all, are mass-produced, standardized, prefabricated building-components), architecture should *look* machine-made in its pristine state (so brickwork was disguised by being covered with smooth *render). All ornament, of course, was eschewed. Third, wholesale clearances, demolitions, and the destruction of existing urban fabric were deemed to be essential to create the *tabula rasa* and eliminate anything with which modern structures could be compared. Fourth, form itself should be evolved for constructional, economic, functional, political, and social reasons, and so was not (in theory) subject to individual fancy (but in fact was largely determined by a few pre-determined paradigms).

In practice, Rationalism promoted an approved *International style from which all historical and decorative elements were expunged, drawing on influences from e.g. *Constructivism and *De *Stijl, and no deviations from it would be tolerated. Among key buildings were *Gropius's *Bauhaus, Dessau (1925-6), Le *Corbusier's *Maison Stein, Garches (1927), and houses at the *Weissenhofsiedlung, Stuttgart (1927), while theoretical and unifying bases were provided by *CIAM and certain writers, notably *Giedion.

Rationalism flourished in Italy under **Benito Mussolini**'s (1883-1945) Fascist regime (1922-43), and in fact *International Modernism was also called *Razionalismo* by *Gruppo 7. *Terragni was perhaps the most distinguished Italian Rationalist, with his Fascist Party Headquarters, Como (1932-6). *Gruppo 7* expanded to form the *Movimento Italiano per l'Architettura Razionale* (*MIAR), inspired partly by *Futurism. After the 1939-45 war Rationalism was adopted (despite, or perhaps because of, its Fascist-Futurist totalitarian associations), virtually as the *de-rigueur* style of Western Europe and America. Looked at objectively, it was just another style, drawing its motifs from a limited range of features approved in the 1920s, and owing nothing to true rationalism at all, but more to the desire for *images thought to be appropriate* for the times, and that, in any case, were usually only *metaphors* of mass-production, 'modernity', and industrialization.

Behne (1926); Brolin (1976, 1985); Etlin (1991); Gn (1967, 1969); Gropius (1952, 1962, 1965); Hr (1925, 1927a); Ks (1995); L (1988); Mantero (1984); Millais (2009); Pe (1960, 1974a); P & R (1973); T.Sr (1991); J.T (1996); D.Wa (1977); Wolfe (1993)

Rattenbury, Francis Mawson (1867-1935) English architect trained by his uncles, **William** (1828-89) and **Richard** (1834-1904) **Mawson** (who, with *Lockwood, had designed Saltaire, the model *Company town in Yorks. from 1858). Having designed the Town Hall, Cleckheaton, Yorks. (1891), in a *Queen-Anne Revival style, Rattenbury settled (1892) in Vancouver, B.C., Canada. In the following year he won the competition to design the Legislature Building, Victoria, B.C. (1893-8), with a handsome scheme in which English-*Renaissance elements were mixed with massive arches similar to those employed by *Richardson in the USA. He employed *Beaux-Arts, *château, *Scottish-Baronial, and various eclectic styles in numerous works. Notable buildings include the Empress Hotel (1903-8—extended after 1909), the Bank of Montréal (1906-7), Government House (with *Maclure, of 1901-3—destroyed), and the Canadian Pacific Railway Terminal, all in Victoria (1923—with **P.L.James** (1879-1970)). He retired (1930) to Bournemouth, England, where he was the victim of a notorious murder.

AH, xxxvi (1993), 127-44; A.Barrett & W-L (1983); K (1994); J.T (1996)

Rau, Heinrich Heinz (1896-1965) German-born Israeli architect, he emigrated (1933) and opened his own office (1935). His early houses betray a *stripped *Neo-Classicism derived from the work of *Schinkel. He drew up a plan for Jerusalem, concentrating on the new Government precinct and University *campus. Among his works may be mentioned the Synagogue (1957) and the Einstein Institute Mathematics Building (1959), Hebrew University, and the Hebrew Union College (1963), all in Jerusalem. For a brief period in the 1950s he was in partnership with *Reznik.

J.T (1996)

ravelin Outwork in a fortification consisting of two *battered faces forming a *salient angle, constructed beyond the *counter-scarp or slope of the main ditch in front of the *curtain-wall, a common feature in *Renaissance and later military architecture.

Rawlinson, Sir Robert (1810-98) English civil-engineer. He joined (1831) Jesse *Hartley and worked on the construction of harbour-works until he was engaged by Robert *Stephenson for the building of the London and Birmingham railway. He returned (1840) to Liverpool as Assistant Surveyor to the Corporation, where he was primarily concerned with public health: his proposals to supply the city with water drawn from Wales were eventually implemented. He is best-remembered as head of the Commission charged with ameliorating the deplorable sanitary conditions of the British army during the Crimean war (1853-6): thereafter he was mostly involved in improving public health, especially in regard to water-supply and sewerage (on which he published much), and was knighted (1883). Apart from his undoubted national and international importance in this respect, his architectural activities included responsibility for the construction of *Elmes's St George's Hall, Liverpool, from 1841: the structure of this, probably the finest Neo-Classical building in the British Isles, was completed (1851) by Rawlinson, after which C.R.*Cockerell finished the interiors, largely to his own designs (1851-4).

Co (2008); *ODNB* (2004)

Raymond, Antonin (1888-1976) Bohemia-born American architect, he assisted Cass *Gilbert on the Woolworth Building, NYC (1910-12), and then joined (1916) F.L.L.*Wright, later collaborating in the building of the Imperial Hotel, Tokyo (1919-20—destroyed). He practised in Tokyo on his own account (1923-37), designing his own houses at Reinanzaka (1923—an early example of *International Modernism) and Karuizawa (1932-3), Tokyo. In the 1930s he experimented with pitched roofs, but in 1937 left Japan, and after a brief stay in India set up an office in NYC, specializing in Federal, State, and Local-Government work. He returned (1949) to Japan, and, with his house at Azabu (1953), introduced traditional Japanese construction. Among his last works were the *campus of the Nanzan University, Nagoya (1960-6), and the Pan-Pacific Forum, University of Hawaii, Honolulu (1966-9). He influenced Japanese pioneers of the *Modern Movement after the 1939-45 war.

El (1994); Le (2000); Raymond (1973); J.T (1996); vV (1993)

Raymond, Jean-Arnaud (1742-1811) French architect, pupil of J.-F.*Blondel and *Soufflot, he supervised the erection of some of *Ledoux's *Barrières* around Paris from 1785, and designed the *hôtel* and gallery (1784-6) for **Elisabeth Vigée-Lebrun** (1755-1842), the portrait-painter. He became (1798) architect to the Louvre, Paris, rendering parts of it suitably magnificent to provide a setting for the treasures looted by **Napoléon**

Bonaparte (1769-1821) from the rest of Europe, and was succeeded by *Percier and *Fontaine (1805). His main claim to fame was his association with *Chalgrin in the early designs of the *Arc de Triomphe de l'Étoile*, Paris (1805-6—engraved by L.-M.*Normand).

GdBA, ser. 6, lvi (1960), 275-84; W.Pa (1887); S (1901-2)

Raymond du Temple (*fl.c.*1360-1405) French master-mason to Kings **Charles V** (*r.*1364-80) and **VI** (*r.*1380-1422) of France, involved in work at *Notre Dame*, Paris, from 1363. Employed (1364) at the Louvre, Paris, he built the external spiral *stair and made other extensive additions. He was also a consultant at Troyes Cathedral (*c.*1401), and has been credited with the design of the *Château* and Chapel of Vincennes (1370s). He designed/built the *Chapelle des Célestins* (1367-70) and the *Collège de Beauvais*, Paris (1387), including the chapel.

Henwood (1978); W.Pa (1887); S (1901-2)

Rayonnant Style of French *Gothic prevalent *c.*1227-mid-C14. Its first phase was the *Court style, from its association with the reign of **Louis IX** (1227-70), of which the rebuilt Abbey of St-Denis, Troyes Cathedral, and the Chapel at St-Germain-en-Laye are examples (all 1230s). The *Rayonnant* style takes its name from the shapes formed by *tracery-*bars and from the *vault-ribs radiating from *piers shaped with masses of *shafts corresponding to the ribs.

Branner (1965); Kimpel & Suckale (1985); W.Pa (1887); J.T (1996); D.Wa (1996)

Read, Herbert (*c.*1861-1935) British architect. Articled to *George & Peto, he set up (1891) in partnership with **Robert Falconer Macdonald** (1862-1913). They carried out numerous well-crafted designs for the Cadogan and Grosvenor Estates: typical of their work was the group of buildings at the corner of 57-9 Piccadilly (1904), and 45-6 Old Bond Street, all in London.

A.S.Gray (1985)

Read, Sir Herbert Edward (1893-1968). British critic, a leading supporter of *Modernism in the 1930s, he edited *Unit One: The Modern Movement in English Architecture, Painting and Sculpture* (1934). His *The Meaning of Art* (1931), *Art Now* (1933), *Art and Industry* (1934), *Surrealism* (1936), *Art and Society* (1936), and *Education Through Art* (1943) were reprinted several times, and spread the gospel of Modernism in the English-speaking world. His *Concise History of Modern Painting* (1959) and *Concise History of Modern Sculpture* (1964) further enhanced his reputation. He edited the *Burlington Magazine* (1933-9).

COF (1988); *ODNB* (2004); J.T (1996)

rear arch *See* ARCH.

Re/architecture Re-use and refurbishment of old buildings of quality that no longer function as originally intended (e.g. *Hartley's Albert Docks, Liverpool).

Cantacuzino (1989)

rear *or* **rere vault** Internal arch or *vault (called *arrière voussure* or *scoinson arch*) at the head of a splayed *Gothic aperture springing from the *jambs, *corbels, or attached *shafts (*escoinsons*) at the angles of jambs and interior walls.

rebate *See* RABBET.

Rebecca, John Biagio (*fl.*1800–47) English architect of Italian descent, son of **Biagio Rebecca** (1735–1808—the decorative painter), he practised in London and Sussex. He designed Castle Goring, near Arundel, Sussex (c.1795–1815), *Neo-Classical on one side and *castellated on the other. He seems to have specialized in *Tudor *Gothic, but could turn his hand to Greek *Doric to some effect.

Co (2008)

rebus Enigmatical representation of a name, or graphic pun on the name of a person connected with a building, usually in the carved ornamentation, e.g. Alcock *chantry-chapel, Ely Cathedral, Cambs. (1488–1501), with representations of cockerels.

recessed arch *See* ARCH.

recessed balcony Type of *loggia*.

Rechter, Yacov (1924–2001) Israeli architect, son of the Russian-born architect **Ze'ev Rechter** (1899–1960—one of the principal *Modernists in Palestine (e.g. apartment-block, Bet Engle, Tel Aviv (1933)), with whom he was in partnership from 1950. He established (1973) his own office, designing many hotels, offices, educational buildings, e.g. Mivtachim Resort Hotel, Zikhron Ya'aqov (1966–8); Carmel Hospital, Haifa (1976–8); Central Library, Hebrew University, Mount Scopus, Jerusalem (1979–81); the expansion of *Mendelsohn's Hadassah Hospital, also Mount Scopus, of the same period; Promenade and Waterfront development, Tel Aviv (1970–85); and the Graduate School of Business Administration, Technion, Haifa (1981–5).

L'Architettura, **cdiv/8** (1976), 438–56; E (1994); J.T (1996)

reconstruction Rebuilding of structures and their contiguous areas, as distinct from *preservation. When the C14 Bredon Tithe Barn, near Tewkesbury, Glos., burned down (1980), F.W.B. *Charles persuaded the National Trust to permit *reconstruction* based on his own records, and this helped to change purist attitudes opposed to such work. After the 1914–18 war, certain towns that had been pulverized during the fighting (such as

Ieper) were completely reconstructed, using photographs and other records: this was as much for Belgian national pride as anything. A similar (but greater) feat of reconstruction took place in Warsaw after the 1939–45 war, using pre-war surveys by architectural students of the Old Town, etc., as well as photographic evidence, and views of the city meticulously recorded in C18 by **Bernardo Bellotto** (1720–80), Canaletto's nephew: this was deemed essential to keep alive the memory of nationhood. Other celebrated feats of reconstruction include the rebuilding (1912) of the *campanile* in the *Piazza San Marco* after it fell (1902), and in the same city *La Fenice* theatre was restored (2001–3) after it burned down (1996). Gardens, too, can be subject to reconstruction, notably the C17 *Het Loo*, Apeldoorn, The Netherlands, and the late-C18 and early-C19 gardens at *Arkadia*, Poland. *Modernists reject reconstruction out of hand.

Chamberlin (1979); *GH*, **xxiii**/1 (Summer 1995), 91–112; *JGH*, **viii**/2 & 3 (Apr.–Sept. 1988), whole issue

Rectilinear *See* PERPENDICULAR; TRACERY.

Rectory Province or residence of the parson (*Rector*) serving the parochial or common church, who had the right to the great tithes and was holder of a perpetual curacy.

redan **1.** Small *ravelin or fieldwork with two faces forming a *salient angle. **2.** Projection or break at the angle of a *panel. **3.** Step in a wall built on rising ground.

Redman *or* **Redmayne, Henry** (*fl.*1495–1528) English master-mason, son of **Thomas Redman** (*fl.*1490–1516), he worked (1495–7) at Westminster Abbey. With William *Vertue he was consulted (1509) about King's College Chapel, Cambridge, and succeeded his father (1515/16) as Master-Mason at Westminster Abbey, working on the *nave. He rebuilt the *chancel of St Margaret's Church, Westminster (1516–23), where he also designed the tower and porch (1516–22). From 1516 he worked with Vertue on the designs for the new work at Eton College, Bucks., including the west side of the court and Lupton's Tower (1516–20). He became architect to **Cardinal Wolsey** (c.1475–1530), with power of supervision over His Eminence's enormous range of building-projects, including Hampton Court Palace, and by 1525 was at work with *Lebons at Cardinal (now Christ Church) College, Oxford, where they laid out the plan and built the south range and most of the east and west ranges. Among his last works were the *cloister and cloister-chapel of St Stephen's College, Westminster Palace, begun c.1526. He was a pioneer in the use of brick in late-*Gothic architecture of the *Tudor period.

J.Harvey (1987)

redoubt 1. Inner last retreat in a fortification. **2.** Fieldwork or outwork enclosed on all sides, of square or polygonal shape, set beyond the *glacis, known as a *detached redoubt.* **3.** Small work projecting from or within a *bastion or *ravelin. **4.** Public assembly-hall, especially in Germany (e.g. *Redoutensaal,* Vienna).

reduit *As* REDOUBT (1).

reed Small, convex *moulding, smaller than an *ovolo or bead, usually found with several others parallel to it, called *reeding* (decorative moulding of several parallel reeds in a continuous line, an important element of the *Ionic *Asiatic base.

Reed, Henry Hope (1915–2013) *See* NEW CLASSICISM.

reel *See* BEAD.

re-entrant Two faces of a building meeting at an *external angle form a *salient, while two walls meeting at an *internal angle form a re-entrant. An external angle or salient with an internal angle formed in it, as though, on plan, a small square had been removed from the angle of the building, is a re-entrant.

Reeth, Flor van (1884–1975) Belgian *Arts-and-Crafts architect, steeped in Flemish traditional architecture, and influenced by contemporary German buildings. His *Landhuizen Schildersrust, Greta en De Witte Vaas,* Kapellelei in Mortsel (1908–9), were remarkable compositions, typical of his work before the 1914–18 war.

Loo (ed.) (2003)

refectory *Frater-house or dining-hall of a college, *monastery, etc.

refuge 1. Place intended for protection or shelter, e.g. a stronghold. **2.** Place for sheltering the homeless or destitute, i.e. *house of refuge.*

Régence Restrained *Classical style during the minority (*c.*1715–23) of **King Louis XV** of France.

Regency Strictly speaking, the style of English architecture/decoration fashionable during the illness (1810–20) of **King George III** (*r.*1760–1820), when **George, Prince of Wales** (1762–1830), was Regent, but loosely applied to the period from the late 1790s to the accession of **King William IV** (*r.*1830–7). Essentially Neo-Classical, it embraced *Egyptian, *Greek, and *Pompeian motifs, and was much influenced by the *Empire* style of France. Regency taste was showy, eclectic, and opulent, uninhibitedly drawing on Oriental themes such as *Chinoiserie* and *Hindoo, *Gothick, and many diverting styles. It was particularly associated with the *Picturesque and with the architecture of *Nash.

L & D (1986); Morley (1993); H.O (1975); Parissien (1992a); Rn (1914)

regeneration Securing of the repair and *conservation of older structures to ensure their future viability.

Reginald of Ely (*fl.*1438–71) *See* ELY.

reglet *Fillet-moulding e.g. in a *Chinese *fret or *guilloche ornament. Used mostly in *compartments and *panels, it defines and separates parts from each other, or covers joints.

regrating Re-dressing the outer surface of stone to give it a new face, also called *skinning.*

regula (*pl.* **regulae**) **1.** *Fillet beneath the *taenia, in line with the *triglyph above, from which the *guttae hang in the *Doric *entablature. **2.** *Plinth under the base of a column. **3.** *Pedestal under a column.

Reichlin, Bruno (1941–) *See* NEO-RATIONALISM; RATIONAL ARCHITECTURE; TENDENZA; TICINESE SCHOOL.

Reid, John (1656–1723) Scots-born gardener, he learned his craft at Niddry Castle, West Lothian (1673), Hamilton Palace, Lanarkshire (1674), Drummond Castle, and Lawers (aka Fordie), the last two late 1670s, and both in Perthshire. His last work in his native land was Shank, Borthwick, Midlothian (1680–3), where he wrote *Scots Gard'ner,* the first (and highly informative) book on gardening to be published in Scotland. He emigrated to America and became Surveyor-General, NJ (1695).

M.Brown (2012); D & E (1994); Reid (1683)

Reid, Robert (1774–1856) Chief Government Architect in Scotland in the first half of C19. Influenced by the style of the *Adam brothers, his public buildings are less attenuated than theirs. Although castigated by some of his contemporaries for dullness, his contributions do much for the urban fabric of Edinburgh, and include the Law Courts, Parliament Square (1804–40), the Bank of Scotland on The Mound (1802–6—with **Richard Crichton** (*c.*1771–1817)), the exterior of the Signet and Advocates' Houses, Parliament Square (1810–12), St George's Church, Charlotte Square (1811–14—the *cupola of which resembles those by *Gontard in the *Gendarmenmarkt,* Berlin (1780–5), a fact noted by *Schinkel when he visited Edinburgh (1826)), the handsome Custom House, Leith (1811–12), and the layout of the northern extension of Edinburgh New Town, including Cumberland, Dublin, Dundas, Dundonald, Great King, India, Nelson, Northumberland, and Scotland Streets, as well as Abercromby Place, Drummond Place, Fettes Row, Gloucester Place, Heriot Row, Mansfield Place, and Royal Crescent (from 1802). This New-Town layout was prepared with William *Sibbald, but Reid designed the main elevations. He was also responsible for 33-46 Charlotte Square, Edinburgh (1807-15), the Academy, Perth (1803-7), the Prison, Perth (1810-12), and part of Downpatrick Gaol, Co. Down, Ireland (1824-30). The Library and Picture Gallery he designed at Paxton House, Berwickshire (1812-13), is arguably his best work. He published *Observations on the Structure of Hospitals for the Treatment of Lunatics* (1809).

Co (2008); *DSA; ODNB* (2004); Youngson (1966)

Reidy, Affonso Eduardo (1909-64) Brazilian Paris-born disciple of *Warchavchik and Le *Corbusier, he worked with others on the Ministry of Health and Education Building, Rio de Janeiro (1936-49). Appointed (1947) to the Department of Public Housing, he designed *Pedregulho*, a large low-income housing-project in Rio de Janeiro (1947-52), followed by a similar work at Gávea, also in Rio (1950-2). His Museum of Modern Art, Rio de Janeiro (1954-60), was a variation on Le Corbusier's 1937 design for the *Pavillon des Temps Nouveau*.

Bonduki & Portinho (2000); Franck (1960); M & N (1987); J.T (1996)

Reilly, Sir Charles Herbert (1874-1948) London-born British architect, important as a pedagogue. He gained early experience in *Belcher's office before working with *Peach, with whom he designed the Power Station, Ipswich, Suffolk (1900-4). He built up the School of Architecture, University of Liverpool, where he was Professor (1904-33): under his direction it acquired an international reputation, at first promoting *Neo-Classical and *Beaux-Arts styles, with a pronounced American flavour (e.g. Reilly's Student-Union Building (1908) and Gilmour Hall (1910-12), both in Liverpool). Later, Reilly encouraged *International Modernism in London with the Peter Jones Department Store, Sloane Square, London, designed by his former students, *Crabtree, Slater, & Moberley (1934-9). Reilly himself designed few buildings, but those that were realized were of interest: they include St Barnabas's Church, Shacklewell, Hackney, London (1909-29), a crescent of houses in the South-African *Colonial style, Port Sunlight, Ches. (designed before 1914), the Accrington War Memorial, Lancs., and Durham County War Memorial (both 1920). His books include an autobiography, a study of the architecture of *McKim, Mead, & White, and a work on theory and practice.

A.S.Gray (1985); *ODNB* (2004); Reilly (1921, 1924, 1931, 1932, 1938, 1972); Richmond (2001); Sharples *et al.* (1996); Stamp & Harte (1979); J.T (1996)

reinforced concrete *Concrete once set will take a superimposed load that compresses it, but,

if used, say, as a *beam, will fail if heavily loaded, because it is weak in tension. Steel, on the other hand, is strong in tension, so the two materials are combined to enable the concrete to perform well in tension as well as in compression by casting steel rods in the positions where reinforcing is necessary to improve tensile strength, especially in beams, *lintels, etc. Reinforced concrete can be used to construct entire skeletal *frames, floor-slabs, walls, etc., either pre-cast in a factory or *in situ* (on site, i.e. where it will be permanent). Also called *ferro-concrete*, it lends itself to the creation of complex curved forms that may get their stability partly from shape, permitting its use in *bridges and *shell-roofs. *See also* PRESTRESSED CONCRETE.

A.Allen (1988, 1992); Faber & Alsop (1976); Marsh (1907)

Reinhart, Fabio (1942-) *See* NEO-RATIONALISM; TENDENZA; TICINESE SCHOOL.

reja Metal *grille in a Spanish church protecting a chapel or tomb.

relief Projection of a design, or parts of it, from a plane surface in order to give a natural and solid appearance, called *rilievo*. The three main types in architecture are *alto-rilievo* (ornament in high relief, almost detached from its ground); *mezzo-rilievo* (ornament standing out roughly half its three-dimensional form); and *basso-rilievo* (ornament with a projection less than half its three-dimensional form).

relieving arch *See* ARCH.

relieving triangle Approximate triangle above a *lintel where *masonry *courses in a wall are corbelled over each other so avoiding any loading on the lintel (e.g. in Mycenaean work).

reliquary Receptacle in which Relics of Saints are kept. It may be very small, such as a box or casket, or very large, ornate, and magnificent, such as the shrine of **St Edward** (1003-66) in Westminster Abbey. Great medieval churches were often erected to house *shrines or reliquaries, and so may be regarded, by extension, as reliquaries themselves (e.g. Cologne Cathedral, which contains the lovely reliquary of the **Magi**).

Renaissance, Renascence From the French *renaître* (to be born again) and the Italian *Rinascimento* (rebirth), the term is given to the great revival of arts and letters under the influence of Classical precedents which began in C14 Italy and continued during the following two centuries, spreading to virtually all parts of Europe. It is also a convenient label for the style of architecture that developed in, and was characteristic of, that period from the time of *Brunelleschi in Florence (early C15) to the beginnings of *Mannerism (c.1520), and which was based on the architecture of Roman Antiquity. Indeed, it was referred to as *maniera all'antica*, and the style was codified by *Alberti in *De Re Ædificatoria* (begun around 1450), drawing on the exemplary work of *Vitruvius. In architecture the Renaissance includes the *High Renaissance (c.1500–20) in which *Leonardo, *Michelangelo, and *Raphael flourished, but it does not include *Baroque. Elsewhere in Europe, architecture tended to acquire Italian-Renaissance motifs, either from printed sources or from the observations of travellers, but each country or region produced buildings that looked un-Italian: German, French, Flemish, Spanish, and English (the last associated with *Elizabethan and *Jacobean architecture) Renaissance styles all had distinct flavours. English, Flemish, German, Polish, and Scandinavian Renaissance buildings of C16 and early C17 fall into the Northern Renaissance category, but the infusion of Mannerism gave French-Renaissance architecture a different flavour. Only in the early C17 was uncorrupted Renaissance architecture, firmly based on Italian prototypes, introduced in England (*see* PAESSCHEN) by Inigo *Jones, an event that was enormously influential in C18, first in England, and then elsewhere. There were various national Renaissance Revivals in C19 once *Neo-Classicism had become wearisome. There are some (e.g. J.H.*Harvey) who held that the introduction of Renaissance architecture was a disaster, destroying the living, indigenous, and inventive *Gothic tradition of England and Northern Europe.

COF (1988); L & D (1986); H.O (1970); J.T (1996)

Renaissance garden Originating in Italy, it was prompted first by *Brunelleschi's concept of linear *perspective, creating a revolution in garden-design with vistas, avenues, etc. The spirit of *Humanism (by which conscious attempts were made to place Man in harmony with the Cosmos) permeated *Alberti's *De Re Ædificatoria* (1486), and in *Bramante's work at the *Belvedere*, Vatican (c.1502–5), attempts were made to revive the *Antique *villa-garden (none survives intact, so designs were based on descriptions by *Pliny the Younger and *Vitruvius): geometry linked gardens to dwellings in a single design by means of *terraces, *stairs, etc. This new, ordered landscape was suggested in *Hypnerotomachia Poliphili* (1499) in which the illustrations of *fabriques*, etc., were influential, even informing Bramante's work (which was also indebted to the **Emperor Nero's** (*r.*AD 54–68) *Domus Aurea* (c.64–8) and to other archaeological evidence). At the Belvedere, Bramante attempted the reconstruction of Roman Imperial gardens, changing the terrain, and creating architectural elements to provide appropriate settings for collections of Classical Antiquities.

Water also played its part. Spectacular Renaissance gardens include those of the *Villa Madama* (1510s), *Villa Giulia* (1550s), and the *Palazzo Farnese*, Caprarola (also 1550s). By the mid-C16, though, the Italian Renaissance garden was being transmogrified by *Mannerism, but its influence gradually changed European sensibilities over the next century, reaching Scandinavia and the British Isles in C17. It was primarily an *architectural* creation; ordered, harmonious, regular, and geometrical.

Alberti (1988); Colonna (1999); Strong (1979); Tay (2006)

Renard, Bruno (1781–1861) Belgian architect, trained in Paris under *Percier and Fontaine, he designed the *Grand Hornu*, near Mons (1820–32), a huge industrial estate with housing (really a *Company town) much influenced by *Durand and *Ledoux. His gardens by the *Hôtel de Ville* (1822–4) and *Salle des Concerts* (1820–8), both in Tournai (Doornik), deserve note: the latter building had a covered market on the ground floor with the *auditorium above, so was a departure from the usual single-purpose hall. Renard's Tournai abattoirs (1833–5—destroyed 1982) were influenced by French exemplars. A founder-member of the Belgian *Commission Royale des Monuments* (1835), he was active in the *preservation and *conservation of the country's historic fabric. He restored Tournai Cathedral (1840–5), and wrote an account of the work (published 1852).

J.T (1996)

render, rendering 1. Finish applied to a surface not intended to be exposed. The term was given historically to the *first coat*, the second the *float*, and the final the *set*. Common renders are with *pebble-dash, *plaster, and *stucco. **2.** Architectural drawing enlivened by water-colour washes and *sciagraphy to make it more realistic.

FR (1946); R.Gill (1991); N (1835); W.Pa (1887)

Rennie, John (1761–1821) Scots architect/engineer, he made his reputation with the design and installation of machinery at the Albion Flour Mills, Southwark, London (1784—destroyed 1791), and established (1791) his own business, designing *bridges, canals, systems of land-drainage, harbours, light-houses, and docks, all of which are admirable both in architectural and engineering terms. They include the Tweed Bridge, Kelso, Roxburghshire (1800–3), the Dundas Aqueduct, Limpley Stoke, Wilts. (c.1795–7), Southwark Bridge, London (1811–19—with one of the world's largest cast-iron arches—demolished 1913), and London Bridge (1824–31—rebuilt at Lake Havasu City, AZ, USA, 1963–71). The last was constructed under the direction of his sons, **George** (1791–1866) and **John** (1794–1874): the latter, knighted on the completion of the bridge, designed various works in the Royal Dockyards, including the Royal William Victualling Yard, Stonehouse, near Plymouth, Devon (completed 1832), one of the most impressive architectural ensembles ever constructed in England. J.*Britton, in *The Original Picture of London*, claimed John Rennie Jun. was the architect of the Stamford Street Unitarian Chapel, Blackfriars, London (1823), the fine Greek-*Doric *portico of which alone survives: however, **Charles Parker** (1799–1881) has also been credited with its authorship.

Boucher (1963); Co (2008); *ODNB* (2004); Reyburn (1972); Sk (2002); Smiles (1862); Su (1993); J.T (1996)

Renwick, James (1818–95) American architect, mostly active in NYC, best remembered for Grace Church, Broadway (1843–6—one of the first in the USA in which a scholarly feeling for *Gothic Revival of the *Second-Pointed variety was demonstrated), and St Patrick's Cathedral (1858–79). The original design (1853–7) of St Patrick's, the most important building for Roman Catholics in the USA at the time, was an eclectic *tour-de-force* made possible after Renwick augmented his knowledge of Continental Gothic during a study-visit to France (1855), but, as built, was severely modified and skimped, even to the loss of the proposed octagonal *crossing-tower. He also designed the Smithsonian Institution (1847–55—a *Picturesque composition incorporating aspects of English, French, and German round-arched exemplars) and the Corcoran (now Renwick) Gallery (1859–71—in a *Second-Empire style), both in Washington, DC, and Vassar College, Poughkeepsie, NY (1861–5—a simplified version of the *Renaissance Tuileries Palace, Paris).

DAB (1943); Hi (1977); P & J (1970–86); P (1982); Rattner (1969); J.T (1996); W & K (1983)

repeating ornament Pattern capable of infinite extension, e.g. *chequer-board and *diaper-work.

reposoir 1. Shelter of low seats, often covered with climbing plants trained on an open *lattice. **2.** Ornamental arch in a *fabrique*, e.g. the C18 *ogee example in a *pyramid at Wentworth Woodhouse, Yorks. **3.** Wayside *altar.

repoussé Ornamental metal-work with patterns in relief on the exposed surface formed by punching the metal from the back, finished by *chasing.

reprise, reprisal, repryse, reprisse 1. Part of a cill-band or a *cill on which a *jamb or *mullion rests, so it is a seating formed to provide the foot of a window-jamb or mullion, worked in the

same stone as the cill. **2.** Bottom of an *architrave wider than the rest, formed with a curved junction. **3.** Carved stone *corbel supporting a timber roof-*truss. **4.** Recess in *masonry, or the return of stone *mouldings in an internal angle (*see* MASON'S MITRE).

DW; Pride (1996)

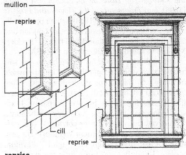

reprise

Repton, George Stanley (1786–1858) English architect, youngest son of Humphry *Repton, he was a pupil of *Nash, and worked with the latter on numerous buildings. He also assisted his father with architectural work. Having opened his own practice (1820), he achieved success with a series of country-houses and extensions to existing buildings. He also designed churches, *parsonages, and other works (e.g. the re-fronting of the Outer Court of Warden's Lodgings (1832–3), New Commoners (1837–9), and Headmaster's House (1839–41), Winchester College, Hants.).

Co (2008)

Repton, Humphry (1752–1818). Leading English landscape-designer after the death of 'Capability' *Brown (1783). He responded to the 1780s fashion for a more truly 'natural' *Picturesque approach than Brown's, and his abilities as a watercolourist enabled him to make his intentions clear to clients by means of 'before' and 'after' views which he presented in his famous 'red books', of which over 70 are recorded. His plantations were denser than Brown's, and he introduced unfamiliar imported varieties of trees and shrubs. He formed (1795) an association with *Nash, and carried out works at Burley-on-the-Hill, Rut. (1795), Corsham, Wilts. (1796–1800), Southgate Grove, London (1797), Attingham Park, Salop. (1798), Luscombe, Devon (1799), and other places. There is no doubt that Repton's ideas had a profound influence on Nash, as can be seen at the latter's Blaise Hamlet, near Bristol (1810–11), and developments at Regent's Park Villages, London, completed by *Pennethorne. Repton had been on good terms with those high-priests of the Picturesque, Payne *Knight and Uvedale *Price, but Knight poured scorn on Repton's red book for Tatton Park, Ches., to which Repton responded by defending his approach to design in *Sketches and Hints on Landscaping Gardening* (1795). He later published *Observations on Landscape Gardening* (1803), *An Inquiry into the Changes of Taste in Landscape Gardening* (1806), and *Fragments on the Theory and Practice of Landscape Gardening* (1818), which profoundly influenced landscape-designers (e.g. *Loudon and Nash in England, *Alphand in France, *Pückler-Muskau in Germany, *Olmsted in the USA).

Although not trained as an architect, he saw architecture as an 'inseparable and indispensable auxiliary' to landscape-gardening, and often introduced architectural arrangements around the houses for which he was preparing land-scape-designs, including *terraces with steps, *conservatories, and 'winter-corridors' (for per-ambulation during inclement weather). He pre-pared a *Hindoo design for Brighton Pavilion, Sussex (1806), but was not a little put out when his former colleague, Nash, supplanted him. With Nash, however, Repton was a pioneer of the cot-tage style that was to be such an important part of the Picturesque movement. Repton's disciple, *Loudon, reprinted (1840) his main publications, with a memoir and reproductions of the Brighton Pavilion designs, in *The Landscape Gardening and Landscape Architecture of the late Humphry Repton*. Repton collaborated with his son **John** on the landscapes of Sheringham Hall, Norfolk (1812–19), and Ashridge, Herts. (*c*.1814). He became increasingly reliant on his sons **John** and **George** for the architectural elements of his designs. His reintroduction of terraces and *par-terres* adjacent to country-houses, and his designs for rose-gardens and aviaries influenced *Victo-rian garden-design.

G.Carter *et al.* (eds) (1982); Co (2008); S.Daniels (1999); Hunt (1992); Hussey (1967a); *ODNB* (2004); P (1982); Stroud (1962); Su (1980a); J.T (1996); D.Wa (1982a)

Repton, John Adey (1775–1860) Eldest son of H.*Repton, he collaborated with his father on a number of projects, especially after the latter was severely disabled (1811). J.A.Repton studied with William *Wilkins, Sen., in Norwich, from whom he acquired a love of medieval architecture. He entered (1796) *Nash's office where he carried out alterations at Corsham Court, Wilts. (1797–8), but Nash appears to have exploited the young man (who was totally deaf from infancy), so he joined his father (1802), and carried out alterations to country-houses where Humphry was improving the gardens. He made extensive changes to a num-ber of Continental estates, including that of *Pück-ler-Muskau at Neu-Hardenberg, near Frankfurt/

Oder (1822), and *Schloss Glienicke*, near Potsdam (also 1822, but begun by *Lenné (1816)). Stylisti-cally he favoured *Elizabethan, but he also used Classical (Sheringham Hall, Norfolk (1813–19)), and *Romanesque Revival (at Holy Trinity Church, Springfield, near Chelmsford, Essex (1842–3)).

Co (2008); Hussey (1958); *ODNB* (2004); P (1982); Stroud (1962)

rere *See* REAR.

reredorter Privy at the back of a *dormitory in a *monastery.

reredos Ornamental facing or *screen behind an *altar in a church, free-standing or forming part of the *retable. In larger churches it separates the *choir from the *retrochoir, *Lady-chapel, and other parts to the liturgical east, and is often found enriched with statues in *niches, *pinna-cles, etc. Another form of medieval reredos was the *triptych.

Resasco, Giovanni Battista (1799–1872) Italian architect. He realized *Barabino's designs (before 1825) for the *Cimitero di Staglieno*, Genoa (1844–61—one of the most spectacular *cemeter-ies in the world), and was responsible for the final appearance of many of the fine *Neo-Classical buildings there, including the Rotunda with its low *Pantheon-like *dome.

J.Curl (2002a); Ms (1966); Resasco (1892)

rescue Project aimed at salvaging historic struc-tures in gross disrepair.

JF

residence 1. Dwelling-place, especially of a person of rank or distinction. **2.** Settlement of traders. **3.** Fact of living in a place for the dis-charge of duties, e.g. the presence of incumbents in benefices, or with reference to colleges, univer-sities, etc. **4.** Seat of a Court (e.g. *Residenz* in Germany, so a *Residenz-Stadt* is a town where a princely Court is based (e.g. Munich, Würzburg, etc.). **5.** *residential quarter* is part of a town pre-dominantly or entirely for housing.

respond *Corbel, half-pier, or other architec-tural element *engaged to a wall at the end of an *arcade from which the first arch springs. In Clas-sical architecture, an *anta or *pilaster-like motif where arcades or *colonnades engage with a wall.

ressant, ressaunt *Ogee.

ressault, ressaut 1. Projection, as of a *chim-ney-breast, *pilaster, or any member or part of a building before a wall or another, e.g. a *moulding projecting in front of another moulding. **2.** In Classical architecture the breaking out of a length of *entablature with two returns, with a column and pilaster, or pair of columns supporting the projection. **3.** *Roll-moulding.

ressaunt *See* RESSANT.

restoration Process of carrying on alterations/repairs to a building or landscape-garden to restore them to their original forms, often involving reinstatement of missing or badly damaged parts, so usually includes replication (new work in an old style). While often necessary after a disaster, it is generally regarded as more drastic than *conservation, which suggests retention/repair/maintenance. *Wyatt's interventions at Hereford (1788–96), Salisbury (1789–92), and Durham (from 1794) Cathedrals were so ruthless that they provoked antiquarian outrage (mostly *Carter's), and were later to enrage A.W.N.*Pugin. *Wyatville's work (1824–37) at Windsor Castle recased almost the whole ensemble, so that what we see now is virtually a creation of the *Regency and **William IV** (*r.*1830–7) periods. The C19 revival of interest in medieval ecclesiastical architecture, and researches into liturgy, had a darker side, for often medieval fabric was destroyed to make the building conform to an architect-approved style (e.g. 'Great' *Scott's 'restoration' of the north nave-arcade at the Church of St Mary de Castro, Leicester). Many churches were stripped of C17 and C18 furnishings, often with unfortunate results. In France, *Viollet-le-Duc attempted to give several medieval buildings a stylistic unity they never had, and his work at *Pierrefonds*, Oise (1858–70), and Carcassonne (1844 onwards—where he rebuilt the walls and fortifications), owed more to his own creative powers than to an archaeological approach. Another drastic (though less successful) French example was *Abadie's work at *St-Front*, Périgeux. *Ruskin, *Morris, *Webb, and others deplored such activities, and, prompted by Scott's proposals for Tewkesbury Abbey, Glos., and drastic Italian notions of 'restoring' *San Marco*, Venice, the Society for the Protection of Ancient Buildings (SPAB) was founded in order to promote a greater sensitivity to the retention of ancient fabric. Although architects such as *Boito urged that 'restoration' should be less comprehensive and destructive, many churches were altered to make them conform to what was regarded as their 'original' state: this often involved the removal of *Baroque and other accretions (even whole *façades) and their replacement with conjectural designs. *See also* RECONSTRUCTION.

Casiello (ed.) (1996); Chamberlin (1979); Crook (1995); J.Fawcett (ed.) (1976a); Morris (1966); Pe (1972); Pugin (1841, 1843, 1973); Ruskin (1903–12)

Restoration The re-establishment (1660) of the Stuart Monarchy in Great Britain and Ireland, so the period following this event, later in the reign of **King Charles II** (1660–85) referred to as the *Carolean period. Restoration architecture was strongly influenced by Continental fashion, the dominant style being *Baroque derived from French and Netherlandish precedents. Typical Restoration buildings were the symmetrical houses of *Pratt and Hugh *May, the grander works of *Talman, and the great contribution of *Wren, whose chief sources were French and Italian.

retable 1. *Screen to the rear of an *altar, rising up behind it, often richly decorated and carved, including the *reredos. **2.** Shelf or ornamental setting for *panels behind a altar. **3.** *Frame around painted or other decorated panels of a *reredos.

retaining-wall 1. Wall, often *battered, also called a *revetment, preventing a bank of earth, etc., from slipping: it is found in the form of battered arched *piers at the back of which are segmental concave walls (like *vaults) to resist the pressure behind them, often associated with C19 railway architecture. **2.** *Dam.

reticulated 1. Constructed or arranged to resemble a net, with the repetition of the same figure all over the surface or plane, as in a *screen or *lattice, or a wall made of polygonal *masonry, such as *ragstone, or constructed of square stones placed diagonally. **2.** With a capital R (*Reticulated*), the term refers to a type of Curvilinear-*Gothic *tracery consisting of a net-like mesh of interweaving *ogees forming a pattern. *See* OPUS RETICULATUM.

retrenchment Work, usually a trench and *parapet, for defence, especially an inner line of defence.

retrieval Process of re-creating historic features, objects, and particularly landscapes to achieve a former condition and appearance.

retrochoir Portion of a large church behind the *retable or *reredos of the *high-altar, in apsidal arrangements including parts of the north and south *chancel-aisles on either side as well as the area to the east. It is essentially the volume bounded by the *sanctuary and the chapels to the east, as in Winchester Cathedral, Hants.

Retti, Leopoldo Mattia (1705–51) German-Italian architect, he trained under his uncle, **Donato Giuseppe Frisoni** (1683–1735), when working on the *Schloss*, Ludwigsburg. He succeeded (1732) K.F.von *Zocha at Ansbach, where he worked on the *Residenz* (begun 1695 to designs by *Gabrieli and continued under the Zochas). Retti designed churches at Weidenbach (1734–6) and Unterschwaningen (1738–43), and at the Court-church at Ansbach he slotted in a new *nave (mid-1730s) between the tower and *choir.

He also built the *Synagogue in Ansbach (1744-6). Called (1744) to Württemberg, he designed the *Neues Schloss*, Stuttgart (begun 1746), completed by *Guêpière.

Arte Lombarda, **xii** (1967), 75–98; Colombier (1956); *Jahrbuch für fränkische Landesforschung*, **ix** (1959), 507–45; *NDB*, **xxi** (2003), 449f

return Any part of a building that turns at an angle (usually 90°) from its principal face, such as the side of a *pilaster or the *jamb of an aperture. A return forming an oblique angle is a *splayed return*. If a *moulding is continued at a different angle to its main direction, as with a *hood-moulding over a medieval window or *doorway returning downwards to a *label-stop, it is referred to as a *returned moulding*. Similarly, the *stalls in a church *choir set against *screens between the choir and choir-aisles and returning at an angle of 90° at the back of the *pulpitum or choir-screen are called *returned stalls*.

reveal, revel Vertical *return or side of an aperture in a wall between the *naked of the wall and e.g. a *door-frame. It is generally set square with the face, the return inwards from the reveal for the door- or window-frame being the rebate, and the inside return the *jamb, often splayed, hence *splayed reveal*.

reveal lining Panelling, shutter-cases, etc., as a finish on the inner *reveal of a window, etc.

Reveley, Henry Willey (1788–1875) English architect, son of Willey *Reveley. He was civil-engineer at Cape Town, Cape Colony, South Africa, from 1826 where he built the *Doric St Andrew's Presbyterian Church (1827) and the *Ionic St George's Church (1828). He then settled in Western Australia, where he designed the Gaol, Fremantle (1830), and the Court House (1837), and erected other public buildings in Perth before returning to England (1838).

Co (2008); *JRWAHS*, **viii/8** (1976), 24–42; Lewcock (1963)

Reveley, Willey (1760–99) English architect, he assisted *Chambers in the building of Somerset House, London, and (1784–89) travelled in Italy, Greece, and Egypt with the antiquary **Sir Richard Worsley, Bt.** (1751–1805), as draughtsman: on his return he established a reputation as an expert on Greek architecture. He designed the Neo-Classical All Saints' Church, Southampton (1792–5—destroyed), and a mansion at Windmill Hill, Sussex (1796–8), illustrated in *New Vitruvius Britannicus* (1810). He edited and prepared the third volume of *Stuart and *Revett's *The Antiquities of Athens* (1794), and made drawings of the *pyramids at Giza (now lost).

Co (2008); *ODNB* (2004); W.Pa (1887)

Revell, Viljo Gabriel (1910–64) Finnish architect of the 'glass palace' office-building, Helsinki (1935—with **Niilo Kokko** (1907–75) and **Heimo Riihimäki** (1907–62)). He assisted *Aalto on the Finnish Pavilion for the 1937 Paris Exposition, and after the 1939–45 war his frequent use of horizontal strip-windows and *pilotis in many of his buildings (such as the *Teollisuuskeskus* office-building, Helsinki (1952), designed with **Keijo Petäjä** (1919–88)) established his credentials as an *International Modernist. With **Heikki Castrén** (1929–80), **Bengt Harald Lundsten** (1928–), and **Seppo Jaako Juhani Valjus** (1928–2014), he won (1958) the competition to design the City Hall, Toronto, Canada, with a design incorporating two curved towers embracing a domed hall (completed 1964): the building was realized in conjunction with *Parkin. He promoted *industrialized building and standardization.

Ålander (ed.) (1966); Hertzen & Speiregen (1973); K (1994); Lundsten (ed.) (1968); M & N (1987); J.T (1996)

reversed zig-zag *Chevron *moulding overlapping another in the opposite direction, forming a series of **Z**- instead of **V**-shapes.

reverse ogee *See* CYMA.

revestry Obsolete term for *vestry.

revetment 1. In *masonry, a thin facing to hide the surface or construction behind, such as the *marble *cladding of *Terragni's *Casa del Fascio*, Como (1932–6). 2. *Retaining-wall.

Revett, Nicholas (1720–1804) English architect, a leading figure in the dissemination of knowledge of Ancient-Greek architecture. With James *Stuart he measured all the principal monuments of Athens (1751–3), and was responsible for the architectural parts of the drawings from which the plates of *The Antiquities of Athens, Measured and Delineated by James Stuart, F.R.S. and F.S.A., and Nicholas Revett, Painters and Architects* were made (the first volume appeared in 1762). This was one of the key publications leading to the *Greek Revival. Stuart bought out Revett's interest even before the first volume appeared, but Revett went on to measure antiquities in Asia Minor (1764–6) under the aegis of The Society of *Dilettanti, and under his editorship *The Antiquities of Ionia* appeared (1769–97). Revett was sufficiently well-off not to have to earn his living, but he turned his hand to architecture on occasion. Among his works are the *Ionic *portico (based on the Temple of Bacchus at Teos) of West Wycombe Park, Bucks. (1771), and Ayot St Lawrence Church, Herts. (1778–9), with a *Doric Order based on the Temple of Apollo at Delos. He seems also to have designed a portico in the garden at Brandeston, Suffolk, which, if

Greek in style, must have been one of the earliest examples of the Greek Revival anywhere (1757).

Co (2008); Crook (1972a); *ODNB* (2004); S & R (1762–1816); Wn (1969)

Revival Resuscitation of any previous style, properly founded on archaeological studies and scholarship, as with the *Egyptian, *Gothic, or *Greek Revivals.

revolving door Door of (usually) four leaves fixed to a central axis, capable of revolving within a cylinder open at opposite sides to permit access and egress. It acts as a baffle for noise and draughts.

Reynolds-Stephens, Sir William Ernest (1862–1943) USA-born British *Art-Nouveau and *Arts-and-Crafts designer. His finest work is the interior of Harrison *Townsend's St Mary the Virgin, Great Warley, Essex (1901–5), with an exquisite Art-Nouveau *Rood-screen and other furnishings, described by *Pevsner as an 'orgy of the English Arts-and-Crafts variety of the international Art Nouveau'.

Bettley & Pe (2007); A.S.Gray (1985); T-M (1967)

Reyns, Henry de (*fl.*1243–53). Master-mason, probably from Rheims in France, but possibly an Englishman who had worked there. He was at Windsor Castle (1243), and advised on the defences of York Castle (1244–5). His chief importance, however, lies in his connection with Westminster Abbey. Demolition of the east end of **Edward the Confessor**'s (*r.*1043–66) church began in 1245, and work started on the new, grander building, with which Henry was to be intimately connected, beginning with the *crypt of the polygonal *chapter-house (1246), and proceeding with the *cloister, *chancel, and *transept. Progress was rapid, for by 1251 *piers were ready to receive their *colonnettes, and by the next year timber was arriving for the roof and *stalls. *Vaults and pavements were being completed by 1253, and all window-*tracery was ready. Henry's work ensured that the eastern parts of Westminster Abbey are French in style, resembling Rheims and Amiens Cathedrals in many aspects, although some commentators hold that details are English, which would be expected, as most of the masons working on the job would have been natives.

J.Harvey (1987); G.Webb (1965)

rez-de-chaussée Ground-floor of a building.

Reznik, David (1923–2012) Brazilian-born architect, he studied with *Niemeyer before emigrating (1949) to Israel, where he worked with **Ze'ev Rechter** (1899–1960) prior to his joining *Rau in partnership. He opened (1958) his own office, designing numerous works (e.g. Engineers'

Institute and Journalists' Association, both in Jerusalem, completed 1966), Israeli Embassy, Brasília (1976), and the Jerusalem Centre for Near Eastern Studies (1986)).

Harlap (1982); J.T (1996)

Rhenish brick Salt-glazed brick made in the Rhineland from the medieval period, especially in C16 and C17, notably in Cologne. It was widely exported, and often decorated.

Rhind, David (*c.*1808–83) Scots architect who studied under A.C.*Pugin and the Edinburgh architect **George Smith** (1793–1877). He set up his own practice (1834), and seems to have had some sort of business arrangement with Gillespie *Graham. He designed the handsome *Doric Monument to **Sir Walter Scott** (1771–1832), George Square, Glasgow (1838), with statue by **Alexander Handyside Ritchie** (1804–70). For the Commercial Bank he designed two great buildings: the head office in George Street, Edinburgh (1843–7—later the Royal Bank of Scotland and later still the Dome Restaurant—with its noble Roman *Corinthian hexastyle *portico and palatial interior with decorations by **David Ramsay Hay** (1798–1866)); and the grandly opulent branch in Gordon Street, Glasgow (1853–7—a sumptuous *palazzo with sculpture by Ritchie, some of which was designed by *Barry's protégé, **John Thomas** (1813–62)). For Daniel Stewart's College, Dean, Edinburgh (1846–8), he chose a lavish *Jacobethan style, and for the head office of the Life Association of Scotland he and Barry designed a lavish Venetian-*Renaissance *palazzo at 82 Princes Street, Edinburgh (1855–9—unhappily destroyed in the 1960s). Rhind designed several houses, the best of which is probably the *Scottish-Baronial Carlowrie Castle, West Lothian (1851–5). Among his town-planning schemes, the *Picturesque residential area of Pollokshields, Glasgow (1849), should be cited.

R.Brown (ed.) (1985); *DSA*; DW; GMcW & W (1984); J.T (1996); WRH (1990)

riad Traditional Moroccan house with interior *courtyard or courtyard-garden.

Blaser (2004)

rib *Moulding on a flat or vaulted ceiling. In medieval work a raised moulding forming part of the *vault, framing the *panels or *webs, often with elaborate *sections, and with their crowning intersections adorned with sculptured *bosses. *Types of *Gothic rib include*:
diagonal: main ribs running diagonally across a square or rectangular compartment;
lierne-: subordinate rib between main ribs, or between the apex (or *clef*) of the vault and the junction of two *tierceron* ribs;

ridge-: rib at the apex of a medieval vault, i.e. horizontal, coincident with the main axis of *nave or *aisle;

tierceron-: secondary rib springing e.g. from *pier to *ridge-rib;

transverse-: rib rising from a pier and set at right angles to the main axis of the nave or aisle, i.e. spanning either of the latter;

wall-: *formeret* or rib *engaged to the wall of a vault-compartment.

Ribart de Chamoust (*fl.*1776–83) French author of *L'Ordre François trouvé dans la Nature* (1776), which contains a curious *French Order consisting of three columns set at the points of an equilateral triangular on plan (∴) with spiral creepers around the *shafts, *capitals similar to those of the *Corinthian Order, and a *pedestal with three *volutes resembling a compressed and inverted *Ionic capital. The analogy with a tree (capital = foliage, shaft = trunk, and pedestal with volutes = roots visible above ground) suggests an extension of ideas from *Laugier. Ribart's first names may have been **Charles-François**, who was author of some works on finance, or (more likely) **François-Joseph**, who probably wrote *Architecture Singulière* (1758) and *Lettre de M. Ribart* (*c.*1770): this latter Ribart was an 'Ingénieur'.

AR, lii/2 (1982), 110–20; J.Curl (2011); CM; PN

ribat 1. Islamic fort or fortified religious establishment. **2.** *Caravanserai.

ribbed With *ribs or *ridges. *Terms include*:

ribbed arch: *arch comprising several *ribs, or moulded to look like a collection of ribs;

ribbed dome: type of *vault resembling a *dome, or where the under-surface of a dome or *cupola is subdivided by radiating *ribs;

ribbed fluting: **1.** flutes separated by *fillets, as in the *shaft of a Classical column; **2.** *cabled fluting;

ribbed vault: any vault with an under-surface subdivided by *ribs framing the *severies or *webs.

ribbon 1. Any ribbon-like strip of decoration, or *riband*. **2.** Lead *came around pieces of glass in a *leaded light. **3.** Representations of ribbons binding *festoons, *garlands, *trophies, wreaths, etc. **4.** Light timber fixed to the faces of *studs forming a continuous tie around the building and supporting the ends of *beams in US *balloon-frame construction. *Compounds include*:

ribbon-border: narrow *bed in a garden (straight or curved) planted with continuous lines of single colours, common in *public parks. *See* BORDER;

ribbon-development: houses built in series along main roads;

ribbon-moulding: ornament in the form of a ribbon loosely spiralling around a thin cylindrical element (*ribbon-and-stick*), often *reeded, and found with *knots, *labels, *rosettes, etc.;

ribbon-wall: *crinkle-crankle wall.

Ribera, Pedro Domingo de (1681–1742) Castilian architect, he worked mostly in Madrid (where he was employed by the municipality from 1719). His late-*Baroque designs included much *Churrigueresque decoration. Typical of his style was the elaborate main portal of *San Fernando* Hospital, Madrid (from 1722), in which *festoons, *estípites*, flame-like forms, *urns, and other motifs tumble over each other in abundance. It was said by Neo-Classicists that he 'filled Madrid with a number of designs that have become the opprobrium of Europe', and his buildings were catalogued as a dire warning to students of architecture: as a result, we know quite a lot about his output, which was remarkably old-fashioned for its date. Among his works may be cited the *Virgen del Puerto* (1718—with octagonal interior and *camarín*), the Church of Montserrat (1732–40), and the *Palacio de Miraflores* (*c.*1725), all in Madrid, and the massive bridge at Toledo (1718–35).

K & S (1959); W.Pa (1887); J.T (1996)

Ricardo, Halsey Ralph (1854–1928) English architect of Portuguese-Dutch Jewish descent. He established (1878) his practice, and was in partnership (1888–98) with **William Frend de Morgan** (1839–1917), for whom he designed *tiles, *vases, and other artefacts. Ricardo advocated the use of *faïence* and other glazed materials to resist the depredations of polluted atmospheres of the C19 city, suggesting that coloured materials would supply the equivalents of shadows and half-tones provided by *cornices, *pilasters, and *mouldings. In this, he anticipated the designs of Otto *Wagner in Vienna, who used coloured tiles set in the same planes as walls and *piers to suggest architectural features. His designs include Howrah Station, Calcutta, India (1901—with a glowing exterior of brick and coloured tiles), and 8 Addison Road, Kensington (1905–8), completely faced with impervious glazed materials, even the roof-tiles. He was an *Arts-and-Crafts architect, whose work was extraordinarily sensitive, imaginative, and original. Among his works his own house, 'Woodside', Graffham, near Petworth, Sussex (1905), deserves note.

A.S.Gray (1985); Jervis (1984); *ODNB* (2004); Sh (1973)

Ricardo of Burgos (*fl.c.*1180–1226) Probably an English master-mason, he designed and built *Las Huelgas* *monastery, near Burgos, Spain, and may have settled in Castile through his connections with **Queen Eleanor of Castile** (1162–1214), daughter of **King Henry II** of England (*r.*1154–

89). It is likely that he was also responsible for the *Santa Maria* monastery, Aguilar de Campóo (finished 1222), and his designs remained influential for several years.

J.Harvey (1987)

Ricchino, Francesco Maria (1583–1658) Milan architect of the early-*Baroque period. His *San Giuseppe* (1607–30), was designed with a main octagonal space, a square *presbytery, and an *aediculated *façade, anticipating later churches in Central Europe. The concave façade he designed for the *Collegio Elvetico* (1627), is one of the first in Italy, while the *cortile* of the *Palazzo di Brera* (1651–86) is a distinguished design.

N-S (1986); Va (1986); Wi (1982)

Rice, Peter Ronan (1935–92) Dublin-born, Belfast-educated engineer, who joined *Arup. Among many schemes on which he worked were *Utzon's Sydney Opera House shell-vaults (1957–73—he was resident engineer on the project from 1963); the structural solution of the design for the *Centre Pompidou*, Paris (1970–7), by **Renzo Piano** (1937–) and **Richard George Rogers** (1933–); Rogers's Lloyd's Building, London (1979–87); **Norman Robert Foster's** (1935–) Stansted Airport, Essex (1981–91); and *Spreckelsen's *Grande Arche*, Paris (1986). In association with Piano his projects included the Stadium, Bari (1988–90), Kansai International Airport, Japan (1988–96), and the Menil Gallery, Houston, TX (1981–6). With **Ian Ritchie** (1947–) and **Martin Francis** (1942–) he was involved in design of the National Museum of Science, Technology, and Industry, La Villette, Paris (1982–5).

AD Profile 2 (1977); *AR*, clxxvi/1053 (Nov. 1984), 70–5; *DIB* (2009); *ODNB* (2004); P.Rice (1994); J.T (1996)

Richardson, Sir Albert Edward (1880–1964) English architect, he worked (1898–1902) in the offices of **Evelyn Hellicar** (1862–1929), *Stokes (1902–3), and *Verity (1903–6—from whom he acquired an enthusiasm for French Classical architecture, particularly *Néo-Grec*). Among his early works were the *façade of the Regent Street Polytechnic, London (executed 1908–9 after he had established his own practice with **Charles Lovett Gill** (1880–1960), and the New Theatre (later Opera House), Manchester (1911–13—in which the influence of C.R.*Cockerell and *Hittorff could be detected). After the 1914–18 war Richardson became Professor at the Bartlett School of Architecture, University of London, a position he held until 1946. The firm of **Richardson & Gill** was responsible for numerous works, including Leith House, Gresham Street (1924), St Margaret's House, Wells Street (1930–2), and Russell Square House (1939–41), all in London, and the Church of the Holy Cross, Greenford, Mddx. (1939–42—a

remarkable building with interesting timberwork). After the 1939–45 war Gill was replaced by Richardson's son-in-law, **Eric Alfred Scholefield Houfe** (1911–c.1995), and several London buildings resulted, including Chancery House, Chancery Lane (1946–53), and 25–35 Grosvenor Place, Belgravia (1956–8—with **Wimperis, Simpson, & Fyffe**, which, despite *Pevsner's predictable view of it as 'almost grotesquely reactionary', stood the test of time). Many of Richardson's domestic commissions were in a refined late-*Georgian or *Regency style, but for his larger works he employed an understated *stripped Classicism reminiscent of some of *Perret's better productions. In his later years (1950s and '60s) he was increasingly reviled by those who had absorbed the dogmas of *International *Modernism: he, however, was contemptuous of the pseudo-intellectual pretensions of the *Modern-Movement cult, and saw clearly that disciples of Le *Corbusier, *Gropius, et al. were creating environmentally disastrous urban deserts. Despite vilification, he produced fine buildings that are becoming appreciated, not least because, unlike much of the stuff he despised, they have worn well. These include the noble Bracken House, Cannon Street (built 1955–9 for the *Financial Times* (Pevsner found it 'puzzling'), with a new core (1987–92) by **Michael Hopkins** (1935–)); the restoration (after bomb damage) and enlargement of Trinity House, Trinity Square (1952–3); the well-considered Livery-Hall of the Merchant Taylors' Company, Threadneedle Street (1953–9); and many distinguished and finely composed works. He also restored several war-damaged churches. His books include *Monumental Classic Architecture in Great Britain and Ireland during the Eighteenth and Nineteenth Centuries* (1914—which helped to foster an appreciation of the work of Cockerell, *Soane, and others, and a return to *Classicism (especially *Neo-Classicism)), *London Houses from 1660 to 1820* (1911—with Gill), *Regional Architecture of the West of England* (1924—also with Gill), *Georgian England* (1931), *An Introduction to Georgian Architecture* (1949), *Southill, A Regency House* (1951), *Robert Mylne, Architect and Engineer, 1733 to 1811* (1955), and (with **Hector Corfiato** (1893–1963)) *The Art of Architecture* (1938) and *Design in Civil Architecture* (1948). He also wrote (with **Harold Donaldson Eberlein** (1875–1942)) *The English Inn Past & Present* (1925).

AR, **cxl/835** (Sept. 1966), 199–205; Houfe (1980); Houfe *et al*. (1999); *ODNB* (2004); P (1982); pk; *RIBAJ*, ser. 3, **xxxi/9** (8 Mar. 1924), 267–74; A.Rn (1914, 1955); Se (ed.) (1975); J.T (1996)

Richardson, Charles James (1806–71) English architect, pupil of *Soane, he seems to have imbibed very little in terms of style or refinement from his master. He designed 13 Kensington

Palace Gardens, London (1851-3—now the Russian Embassy—in a coarse quasi-*Tudor style), and various houses in Queen's Gate, Kensington, London, including 'Albert Houses' (nos. 47-52) of c.1860, in a lavish Classical style. He collected architectural drawings, including work by *Adam, *Tatham, *Thorpe, and *Vanbrugh (now in the Victoria & Albert Museum), and published *Observations on the Architecture of England During the Reigns of Queen Elizabeth and King James I* (1837), *Architectural Remains of the Reigns of Elizabeth and James I* (1840), *Studies from Old English Mansions* (1841-8), *Studies of Ornamental Design* (1848, 1852), *Picturesque Designs for Mansions, Villas, Lodges, etc.* (1870), and *The Englishman's Home from a Cottage to a Mansion* (1871—some plates of which resemble the *Tudorbethan St Ann's Villas, Norland Estate, North Kensington (1840s)). His books gained him a reputation as an expert on *Jacobethan architecture.

Jervis (1984); *ODNB* (2004); W.Pa (1887); Sh (1973, 1975)

Richardson, George (c.1736-1813) British draughtsman/writer/designer, he worked for John *Adam and accompanied James *Adam on the *Grand Tour (1760-3), during which he became familiar with *Antique sources of the 'Adam style'. He appears to have been treated ungenerously by the parsimonious Adams, but nevertheless worked in the London office as he had little hope of establishing a career on his own account. Among the works for which he made drawings were Kedleston, Derbys., and it would seem that he played more than a minor role there, for surviving designs for several ceilings, etc., were signed by him, and by 1765 he appears to have set himself up as a draughtsman, exhibiting under his own name. He probably designed the pretty *Georgian *Gothick churches at Stapleford, Leics. (1789), and Teigh, Rut. (1782), as well as (possibly) the Classical church at Saxby, Leics. (1789). Richardson published several books, including *A Book of Ceilings composed in the Stile of the Antique Grotesque* (1774, 1776, 1793), *A New Collection of Chimney Pieces* (1781), *A Treatise on the Five Orders of Architecture* (1760-3), *New Designs in Architecture* (1792), *Original Designs for Country Seats or Villas* (1795), and the very important *New Vitruvius Britannicus* (1802-8, 1808-10), which promoted fine late-C18 English architecture just as *Campbell, *Woolfe, and *Gandon had championed earlier designs.

Co (2008); J.Fleming (1962); E.Hs (1990); *ODNB* (2004)

Richardson, Henry Hobson (1838-86) Brilliantly gifted American architect, he studied at the *École des *Beaux-Arts (1860-2), and worked in Paris under *Labrouste's elder brother,

Théodore (1799-1885), and *Hittorff, before returning (1865) to the USA. He entered into partnership with **Charles Dexter Gambrill** (1834-80—formerly *Post's partner), who left Richardson more free to design. With his Brattle Square (1870-2) and Trinity (1872-7) Churches, Boston, MA, he established his reputation: the latter is an assured essay in freely treated *Romanesque Revival, with a monumental *crossing-tower, apsidal *chancel, and gritty exterior, clearly influenced by contemporary French round-arched churches such as St-Augustin, Paris, and the works of *Vaudremer, but the emphasized massiveness suggests an influence from *Burges, some of whose publications Richardson had in his collection. With the geometrical possibilities of the semicircular arch, Richardson gradually moved towards evolving his own style, using rock-faced *rustication to give added weight to his buildings, as in the 7-storey Marshall Field Wholesale Warehouse, Chicago, IL (1885-7—demolished 1930). Round-arched too was his Allegheny County Court House and Gaol (1883-8), the staircase of which was thrilling in terms of spatial interpenetration: oversized *voussoirs, clearly derived from Florentine precedents, suggested the *Sublime. Richardson was also attracted to the *Arts-and-Crafts movement, and designed many fine houses, some in the *Shingle style, but all ingenious, beautifully crafted, and organized with great sensitivity to their sites, especially those on the New England coast. Among his best houses were those for Watts Sherman, Newport, RI (1874-5), Paine, Waltham, MA (1884-6), Glessner, Chicago (1885-7), Stoughton, Cambridge, MA (1882-3), and 'Lululaund', Bushey, Herts. (1886-94—for the painter, **Sir Hubert von Herkomer** (1849-1914)—demolished 1939 through anti-German hysteria). His work influenced *McKim, Mead, & White, *Root, *Sullivan, et al.

M.Floyd (1997); Harrington (1993); Hi (1966, 1966b, 1977); *JSAH*, ix/1-2 (Mar. & May 1950), 25-30; Meister (ed.) (1999); L.Mumford (1924, 1931); Ochsner (1982); O'Gorman (1987a, 1997); P (1982); Rensselaer (1969); V.J.Sy (1971, 1974); J.T (1996)

Richard the Mason (fl.c.1195) English master-mason, he seems to be the most likely progenitor of the original *Gothic designs for Lincoln Cathedral, his portrait probably being a carved head in the south-east *transept.

J.Harvey (1987)

Rickards, Edwin Alfred (1872-1920) English architect, he formed a partnership (1896) with **Henry Vaughan Lanchester** (1863-1953) and **James Stewart** (1860-1904), and, as **Lanchester, Stewart, & Rickards**, entered competitions, as a result of which they built the new City Hall and Law Courts, Cardiff, Wales (1897-1905), the first planned civic-centre in Great Britain, in an *Edwardian *Baroque style with sculptures by **Henry Poole** (1873–1928—who also collaborated with the partnership on Deptford Town Hall, London (1908), again Baroque, but leaning towards C17 Anglo-Dutch work of the time of *Wren). After Stewart's death **Lanchester & Rickards** won the competition to design the Wesleyan Central Hall, Westminster (1905-11), one of the most exuberant monuments of the time, with more than a touch of Viennese worldliness about it (again fluently decorated by Poole): a contemporary critic described Rickards's work as 'combining opulence and taste with a touch of refined swagger'.

A.S.Gray (1985); J.Newman (1995); Se (ed.) (1975); Se (1977); J.T (1996)

Rickman, Thomas (1776–1841) English self-taught architect, important in the history of the *Gothic Revival as he was the first (as early as 1811) to subdivide the medieval styles into 'Norman', 'Early English', 'Decorated English', and 'Perpendicular English'. He wrote a long contribution on *Gothic architecture published in *Smith's Panorama of Arts and Sciences* (1812-15), which he later (1817) brought out as a separate volume entitled *An Attempt to Discriminate the Styles of English Architecture from the Conquest to the Reformation*, with many subsequent editions: applying simple scientific methodologies to a subject that, up to then for the most part, had been treated with vagueness, his grasp of detail enabled him to come to reasonably sound conclusions about stylistic progressions. One of his earliest essays in archaeologically correct *Second Pointed was the pretty funerary monument to **Jonathan Henry Lovett** (d.1805) in St Carthagh's Cathedral, Lismore, Co. Waterford: it is signed, and if it is almost contemporary with Lovett's death, is remarkable for its time. He advised **John Slater** (*fl*.1812-23) of Liverpool who remodelled (1812-16) Scarisbrick Hall, Lancs. (later gone over by A.W.N.*Pugin), and, with the iron-master **John Cragg** (*c*.1767-*c*.1854), designed the Churches of St George, Everton (1813-16), St Michael, Toxteth (1814-15), and St Philip, Hardman Street (1815-16—demolished 1882), all in Liverpool, and all with interior cast-iron structural elements.

The publication of his *Attempt* had an enormous impact, gaining Rickman credibility where it mattered, and he took the plunge and opened an office in Liverpool (1817), where he took on *Hutchinson as his pupil. Rickman's expertise in Gothic gained him many commissions, and he acquired a considerable share of work from the Church Building Commissioners: his first churches were really *Georgian preaching-boxes with *Perp. details, but his later essays were more robust, probably through Hutchinson's influence. He opened (1820) a second office in Birmingham (having secured the commission to design St George's Church there (1819–22—demolished 1960)) with Hutchinson (who became (1821) his partner) in charge. Thus Rickman managed to obtain a considerable share of the architectural commissions in the West Midlands and Lancs., and his practice was one of the most successful in England (1820s, 1830s). Among the ecclesiastical works carried out may be mentioned St Andrew's, Ombersley, Worcs. (1825-9), St Peter's, Hampton Lucy, Warwicks. (1822-6), St John's, Oulton, Yorks. (1827-9), and the lovely *belfry and *spire of St Mary the Virgin, Saffron Walden, Essex (1831-2). One of the firm's most successful works was the Gothic New Court, St John's College, Cambridge (1827-31), with its charming 'Bridge of Sighs' designed by Hutchinson. Rickman's grasp of the *Picturesque was also demonstrated at the village of Great Tew, Oxon. (1820-1), where he designed some of the buildings.

His brother, **Edwin Swan Rickman** (1790–1873), had assisted in the Liverpool office, and was a partner (1831-3) in Birmingham, to which the whole practice was transferred, but became mentally incapacitated, and was replaced (1835) by **Richard Charles Hussey** (1802-87). Rickman's son, **Thomas Miller Rickman** (1827-1912) was articled (1842) to Hussey, moved with him to London (1849) when the practice was transferred thither, and remained associated with the firm until 1855. T.M.Rickman compiled a list of his father's works for *Papworth's great *Dictionary*.

BL, Add. MSS. 37793–37802, 37803; Co (2008); W.Pa (1887); Port (1961); Rickman (1848); J.T (1996)

riddel(l) *or* **riddle** In a church, the curtains suspended around an *altar, sometimes from rods fixed into the wall behind, but more often from some means of hanging spanning between *riddel-posts*: there were normally four of the last, polygonal on *plan, coloured and gilded, and crowned by angels, often supporting candelabra. Arrangements of *riddels* behind and around altars seem to have been not uncommon in England towards the end of the *Gothic period, in the decades immediately before the C16 iconoclasm, and were revived (early C20) during the late flowering of the *Gothic Revival, notably by *Comper and Temple *Moore.

Comper (1893, 1897, 1933, 1950); Dearmer (1911, 1931); Dirsztay (1978)

Riddle, Theodate Pope (1868-1946) One of the first (and most distinguished) female architects to practise in the USA, she used materials with intelligence, and her work included housing and educational establishments. Her finest building was the Avon Old Farms School, Avon, CT (1920–9), which drew on English *vernacular prototypes, synthesized with considerable panache.

W.Andrews (1955); P (1982); Paine (1979); Susana Torre (ed.) (1977)

ridge 1. Apex of a pitched roof where two slopes meet, especially the horizontal edge thus formed, often decorated with a *ridge-crest*. 2. Structural top of a pitched roof, including the timber, or *ridge-piece*, against which the upper ends of *rafters abut or pitch. 3. Internal apex of a *Pointed *Gothic *vault, often covered by a *ridge-rib*. **With other combinations, the term includes:**

ridge-and-furrow: 1. roof composed of a series of ridges and furrows, e.g. as used by *Paxton at the Crystal Palace, London (1851); 2. *pan-tiled roof;

ridge-beam: obsolete term for timber against which the upper ends of the rafters below pitch;

ridge-cap: cover of metal, tile, etc., over the *ridge*, sealing the joint between the two sides of a pitched roof;

ridge-course: uppermost course of *shingles, *slates, or *tiles immediately below the *ridge-cap* or *ridge-crest* of a pitched roof;

ridge-crest: ornamental *ridge-cap* or some kind of ornamental *crest fixed above the ridge of a pitched roof;

ridge-fillet: *fillet between two depressions, such as the *flutes in a Classical column-shaft;

ridge-piece: longitudinal timber or *ridge-plate* at the apex of a pitched roof where the rafters pitch against it. It may be rectangular, thin, and upright (*ridge-plank*); square, set square (*ridge-plate*); or square and set diagonally (*ridge-purlin*);

ridge-plank: thin *ridge-piece* set upright;

ridge-plate: square-sectioned timber *ridge-piece* set square under the *ridge*;

ridge-pole: obsolete term for a *ridge-piece*;

ridge-purlin: square-sectioned *ridge-piece* set at an angle under the *ridge*;

ridge-rib: *rib at the apex of a *Gothic *vault running horizontally coincident with the main longitudinal axis of a *nave or *aisle.

ridge-roll: 1. timber roll over which metal is dressed at the ridge, or the metal covering itself; 2. *ridge-tile* or a metal covering over a roll at the *ridge*;

ridge-roof: any roof with sloping sides and *gable-ends, the rafters pitching against a *ridge-piece*;

ridge-saddle: see YELM;

ridge-stone: 1. shaped stone, one of several covering a *ridge* (1), or forming part of a *ridge* (3); 2. curb-stone for a well;

ridge-tile: tile, often like a half-cylinder, but sometimes angular and decorated with *cresting. Also called a *crown-tile* or a *ridge-roll*, it is used to cover the joints between pitched roofs at a *ridge* or *hip: in the latter case it is called a *hip-roll* or *hip-tile*.

ABDM (1996); W.Pa (1887)

Ridinger, or Riedinger, Georg (1568–c.1628) German *Renaissance architect, his greatest work was *Schloss Johannisburg*, Aschaffenburg (1605–14—for **Johann Schweikart von Kronberg** (1553–1626—**Archbishop-Elector of Mainz** from 1604), built round a central *courtyard with four massive towers at the corners, an arrangement possibly prompted by Du *Cerceau's publications. *Gables were decorated with Mannerist devices reminiscent of aspects of *Dietterlin's works.

Bachmann (1970); Hi (1981); Kreisel (1932); Roda (1982)

riding-school Establishment where horsemanship is taught, e.g. the Spanish or Winter Riding School, Vienna (1729–35), designed by **Joseph Emanuel Fischer von Erlach** (1695–1742).

Ridolfi, Mario (1904–84) Italian architect, member of *MIAR. He designed the Post Office in the *Piazza Bologna*, *Quartiere Nomentano*, Rome (1932–3), influenced partly by German *Expressionism and partly by Italian *Rationalism, but soon shed all traces of the former, especially after he formed a professional association with the German engineer **Wolfgang Frankl** (1907–94) that lasted from the 1930s until Ridolfi's death. The Rea Mansion, *Via di Villa Massimo*, Rome (1934–7), for example, designed with Frankl, was entirely Rationalist-Modernist in style. After the 1939–45 war he published *Manuale dell'architetto* (1946) that seemed to favour stylistic *Pluralism, and, with *Aymonino, *Quaroni, and others, designed the *INA-Casa* in the Tiburtino Quarter, Rome, where Pluralist leanings became apparent (1949–54). Yet, in the same period, he designed (with Frankl), the *Casa a Torre*, *Viale Etiopia*, Rome (1950–4), that was unequivocally *Modernist and from which Pluralism was absent. By the 1960s his work became almost wilfully crude (e.g. Infants' School, Poggibonsi (1960–1)).

F.Bellini (1993); Cellini *et al.* (eds) (1979); E (1994); L (1988); Moschini *et al.* (1997); J.T (1996)

Ried or Rieth, von Piesting, Benedikt (c.1454–1534) German architect, the greatest figure in the final phases of *Sondergotik* in Bohemia and Moravia. He is best known for his very considerable works at Hradčany, the Royal Palace in Prague, where his name is recorded (1489). Apart from the massive fortifications and towers, his greatest work there is the Knight's (or Vladislav)

Hall (completed 1502), with its elegant double-curved branch *rib-vaulting that seems to grow out of the wall-piers, and *Renaissance *fenestration. Ried also designed the *vault with *stumps* or cut-off ribs over the equestrian staircase (completed c.1501). Ried contracted to finish the *nave of St Barbara, Kutná Hora, the *choir of which had been virtually completed (with reticulated *vault) by 1499 under the direction of **Matěj Rejsek** (c.1445–1506): Ried's *nave- and *gallery-vaults there are extraordinary, with ribs rising from the *piers to flow and undulate, describing elegant *panels framed by their gentle curves. Ried may have designed the stunning *oratory in Prague Cathedral, with its ribs of decorated branches and twigs, though Rejsek's authorship has been proposed.

Fehr (1961); Hi (1981); Seibt (ed.) (1985); J.T (1996); D.Wa (1986)

Riemerschmid, Richard (1868–1957) German *Arts-and-Crafts architect, founding-member (with *Behrens and others) of the Munich *Vereinigten Werkstätten für Kunst und Handwerk* (1896) and of the *Deutscher Werkbund* (1907), influential in Germany from the turn of the century until the mid-1920s. Works include the *Jugendstil Kammertheater* in the *Schauspielhaus*, Munich (1901), and he contributed (with *Tessenow et al.) to the design at the *Garden City, Hellerau, near Dresden (1907). German *vernacular styles and English Arts-and-Crafts influences were often synthesized in his architecture, as in his own house at Pasing (1896), but at Hellerau (1910) his work was turning to stripped *Neo-Classicism.

DK, xii (1904), 249–83; xiv (1905–6), 265–304; DKuD, xxii (1908), 164–214; xxvii (1910–11), 447–65; Günther (1971); Jervis (1984); H.M (ed.) (1910); Ne (1982); Rammert-Götz (1987); J.T (1996)

Rieth *See* RIED.

Rietveld, Gerrit Thomas (1888–1964) Dutch *De-*Stijl* designer, founder-member of *CIAM: his furniture unequivocally expressed elements of the structure (e.g. the Red-Blue Chair (1918)). From 1921 he worked with **Truus** (G.A.) **Schröder-Schräder** (1889–1985), on the planning of the Schröder House, *Prins Hendriklaan*, Utrecht (completed 1924), in which *De-Stijl* principles were applied to architecture for the first time: with its adaptable interior spaces, removable partitions, asymmetry, white slabs, and large areas of glass it became a *Modernist paradigm. Like his furniture, the house seems to be put together from pieces of card-like elements, with planes overlapping, but it is constructed almost entirely of traditional materials, and expressed its 'modernity' largely by metaphor. He also designed *terrace-houses, *Erasmuslaan* (1934), and the *Vreeburg*

Cinema (1936), both in Utrecht. With others he designed the *Rijksmuseum Vincent van Gogh*, Amsterdam (1963–72).

T.Brown (1958); Buffinga (1971); G.Fanelli (1968); Jaffé (1956); Küper & Zijl (eds) (1992); Mulder & Zijl (1999); Overy (1969); Overy et al. (1988); P (1982); J.T (1996)

right for period Repaired in a way that reflects the design, techniques, and materials current when the building, etc., was first erected.

JF

Riley, William Edward (1852–1937) English architect, he succeeded (1899) **Thomas Blashill** (1831–1905) as Architect to the LCC, and under their direction two major programmes of slum-clearance and rebuilding took place at Boundary Street, Shoreditch (from 1893), and Millbank (from 1897), London. Both were triumphs of humane, well-designed housing, in an eclectic *Queen-Anne style. Riley took over (1904) the London School Board's building programme begun by E.R.*Robson. Some of his team's best works include London Fire-Brigade Stations, including the fine composition opposite St Pancras's Church, Euston Road, London (1902).

A.S.Gray (1985)

rill Small channelled stream in a garden used ornamentally, for irrigation, or to link water-features, e.g. the *serpentine rill at Rousham, Oxon., the straight ones at the Lion Court, Alhambra, Granada, and the *Lutyens exemplars at Hestercombe, Som. (1905).

Rinaldi, Antonio (c.1710–94) Italian architect, trained under *Vanvitelli. Called to Russia by **Kirill Grigoryevich Razumovsky** (1728–1803), he designed a *palace at Baturin, Ukraine (1752–3), and from 1755 was in St Petersburg. From 1756 he was involved in the design of the palace-complex and park at *Oranienbaum* (now *Lomonossow*), where his first building, the small stone palace (1758–60), was decorated in a *Rococo style: he also designed the *dacha* and Chinese Palace (1762–8—with exquisite Rococo and *Chinoiserie* internal decorations) for **Empress Catherine II** ('the Great' (r.1762–96). He worked (1766–81) on the *Gatchina* Palace for **Count Grigory Grigoryevich Orlov** (1734–83)—it was influenced by *Palladianism and *Neo-Classicism. His masterpiece is reckoned to be the Marble Palace, St Petersburg (1768–85), with an exterior partly *Baroque and partly Neo-Classical (perhaps influenced by *Juvarra): it was one of the first major palatial buildings with cast-iron beams.

Ck (1996); G.H (1983); D.Shv (2007); J.T (1996)

rinceau Classical ornament on a *band consisting of a continuous wave of scrolling foliage, often vine. *See* TRAIL.

Ring, Der Architectural pressure-group founded 1923–4 as the 'Ring of Ten' representing *Neues Bauen. Membership was extended (1926) to include *Bartning, *Behrens, *Gropius, *Häring, *Haesler, *Hilbersheimer, *Korn, the *Luckhardts, E.*May, *Mendelsohn, A.*Meyer, *Mies van der Rohe, *Poelzig, *Scharoun, the *Tauts, *Tessenow, and Martin *Wagner, et al., and it acquired its name. It promoted 'new architecture' for the 'new scientific and social' epoch (which, in effect, became *International Modernism) rejecting *Historicism. *Modernists in *Der Ring*, who were in the majority, grouped with Mies to establish the architectural images of the *Weissenhofsiedlung (1927), causing an opposition (*Der *Block*) to be formed by *Bonatz and others.

J.Je & Lauterbach (eds) (1964); J.Je & Plath (1968); Lane (1985); Pfankuch (1974); J.T (1996)

ring Any structure or object having the form of a circle, or set around something. *Combinations with other words include*:

ring-beam: *beam around, e.g., a *drum on which is a *dome, to prevent the dome-base from spreading. A beam around a square or rectangular compartment is an *edge-beam*;

ring-crypt: subterranean passage around a *crypt, semicircular on plan, often with an *annular *vault, usually C8–C10;

ring-fort: area enclosed within a strong circular wall, of which several survive in Ireland;

ring-vault: annular vault;

ring-wall: encircling wall.

ringhiera *Balustrade, hand-*rail, or *parapet, so associated with *balconies from which the public may be addressed.

Riou, Stephen (1720–80) English architect of Huguenot origins, he studied in Geneva, and published *The Elements of Fortification* (1746). He travelled in Italy and Greece, meeting *Stuart and *Revett *en route* to Athens. He also published *Short Principles for the Architecture of Stone Bridges* (1760), and *The Grecian Orders of Architecture delineated and explained from the Antiquities of Athens* (1768).

Co (2008); E.Hs (1990); Wa (2004); Wiebenson (1969)

riparene Classical ornament associated with water. Motifs include *personifications of rivers, *vases pouring water, Neptune, tritons and mermaids, dolphins, fish, reeds and seaweed, frogs, etc. The term is named after **Cesare Ripa** (*c.*1560–*before* 1625), author of *Iconologia* (1593 with later edns, notably 1603 and 1779–80), an influential sourcebook of personifications, *emblems, and decorative motifs.

L & D (1986)

Ripley, Thomas (*c.*1683–1758) English carpenter, he succeeded (1726) *Vanbrugh, no less, as Comptroller of the Works. His meteoric rise was due to the patronage of **Sir Robert Walpole** (1676–1745), whose seat, Houghton Hall, Norfolk, Ripley constructed (1722–5) according to *Campbell's and *Kent's designs. He also acquired the Surveyorships of Greenwich Hospital (1729) and the King's Private Roads (1737), which, for one so untalented, was remarkable. His architecture was unloved by his contemporaries, and has not risen much in estimation since: in particular, his *portico for the Admiralty, Whitehall, London (1723–6), earned him opprobrium, and occasioned the building (1760) of a *colonnaded *screen to Robert *Adam's design to hide it. Wolterton Hall, Norfolk (1727–41), however, was not an ungainly house, suggesting that something of *Palladian grace had rubbed off on him after Houghton. *Pope thought Ripley a model of 'Dulness' compared with *Burlington, *Jones, and *Wren, while Vanbrugh laughed so much when he came across Ripley's name in the public prints that he 'had like to Beshit' himself.

Co (2008); ODNB (2004)

rise 1. Vertical measurement from the *springing-line to the *soffit of an arch or *vault. **2.** Vertical distance between two consecutive *treads in a *stair, or that between landing and landing.

riser 1. Vertical piece between the *treads of a *stair. **2.** Whole vertical part of a step of a stair between treads. **3.** Stone in *rubble-work, usually a *bonder or *through-stone*, also called a *jumper*.

Robe, Sir William (1765–1820) British military-engineer, architect of Holy Trinity Church, Québec, Canada (1803), a variant on *Gibbs's St Martin-in-the-Fields. His work was competent and solid, and he was involved in several improvements and administration in the Province of Québec in the early C19.

K (1994); ODNB (2005)

Robert, Hubert (1733–1808) French landscape-painter/designer, known as **Robert des Ruines** (because he often used *Antique *ruins as central elements in his pictures), he played a minor role in the *Egyptian Revival. He worked on the important gardens at Ermenonville (1770s) for *Girardin, and contributed to the design of one of the most enduring images of the period: the *Île des Peupliers* and tomb of J.-J.*Rousseau. From 1786 he worked on the *Garden of Allusions at Méréville for **Jean-Joseph, Marquis de Laborde** (1724–94), in succession to *Bélanger. He was a key figure in the *Picturesque transformation of the *landscape-garden where sentimental, mnemonic, and moral associations informed the design.

BSHAF (1968), 127–33; J.Curl (2005, 2011); M & T (1991); Nolhac (1910); *L'Œil*, clxxx (Dec. 1969), 30–41, 83, 96; Racine (ed.) (2001); J.T (1996)

Robert de Luzarches *(fl.c.*1220–40*) See* LUZ-ARCHES.

Robert the Mason *(fl.c.*1077–1119*)* Master-mason, responsible for the *transepts, eastern part of the *nave, and the tower of the *Roman-esque Abbey Church (now Cathedral) of St Alban, Herts.

J.Harvey (1987)

Roberto Brothers Brazilian architects, **Mar-celo** (1908–64), **Milton** (1914–53), and **Maurício** (1921–97) were much influenced by Le *Corbu-sier. Their Brazilian Press Association (ABI) build-ing (1935–6) made their reputation. Their designs (e.g. Seguradores Office Building, Rio de Janeiro (1949)) were successful in controlling the intense sunlight of Brazil.

E (1994); Ma (1983*d*); P (1982); J.T (1996)

Roberts, Henry (1803–76) British architect, born in Philadelphia, PA. He worked in *Fowler's and R.*Smirke's office before setting up his Lon-don practice (1830), and won (1832) the compe-tition to design the new Hall of The Fishmongers' Company beside *Rennie's new London Bridge. It was a masterly composition in the *Greek-Revival style with more than a touch of Smirke's influence (Roberts had assisted Smirke on the working-drawings for the British Museum), and included many interesting features such as an ingenious plan, the use of cast and wrought iron in the construction, the inclusion of four unfluted Greek-*Doric columns of polished Peterhead *granite in the entrance-hall and stair (among the first instances of this material being used for such a situation and object), the employment of a huge *concrete *raft for the foundation, and quo-tations from the refined Greek-*Corinthian *Order of the *Choragic Monument of Lysicrates in Athens in the main Hall itself. His pupil and assistant at the time was George Gilbert *Scott. Roberts developed a successful practice, designing coun-try-houses for members of the aristocracy with liberal and Evangelical tendencies. These build-ings were in *Jacobethan, *Tudor-Gothic (Norton Manor, Norton Fitzwarren, Som. (1843)), or pleasing *Italianate (Escot House, Devon (1838)) styles. His essays in *Gothic-Revival churches, however (e.g. St Paul's, Dock Street, Whitechapel (1846)) did not meet with Ecclesiological approval.

However, it is as the architect of a number of philanthropic buildings that Roberts is of world importance. His Evangelical leanings brought him into contact with those who wished to improve society by example. His first essay was the Destitute Sailors' Asylum, Whitechapel (1835), but in 1844 he became Honorary Architect to the Society for Improving the Condition of the La-bouring Classes (SICLC), with which **Anthony Ashley-Cooper** (1801–85—**7th Earl of Shaftes-bury** from 1851) and Prince *Albert were to be so intimately involved. For the Society Roberts designed exemplary buildings, including houses in Lower Road, Pentonville, London (1844—demolished), various lodging-houses, and the epoch-making Model Dwellings, Streatham Street, Bloomsbury (1849–51). The last provided very advanced standards of accommodation, fire-resistant construction using vaulted floors and concrete, and *gallery-access which Roberts argued were elevated streets to individual houses, thus avoiding window-tax which would have been imposed on a large building. As a result of this building and Roberts's arguments the Govern-ment was obliged to abolish both window-tax and other enactments, making it more economical for philanthropic organizations and private individuals to provide dwellings for the labouring classes. Rob-erts developed the plan of a typical apartment evolved at Streatham Street for his 'Model Houses for Four Families Erected in Hyde Park at the Industrial Exhibition of 1851' paid for by the phil-anthropically motivated Prince Consort to further the aims of the SICLC of which he was President. This brilliant design had four self-contained apartments, each with its own lavatory facilities, access from an open *stair, excellent insulation and fire-proof construction, and with a standard of accommodation far in advance of its time. The exhibit (the first of its kind in the world, long before the much-trumpeted 1927 *Weissenhofsie-dlung*) was visited by thousands of people, and the Society published the detailed plans and ele-vations. Roberts's designs were influential throughout Europe and the USA, and versions of his *plans* were still being used in Amsterdam South in the 1920s and 1930s. His designs for model cottages for the country were also pub-lished, and built in numbers throughout the United Kingdom from 1851: most were in a vaguely C17 style, but this could be varied accord-ing to local circumstances and taste. An entire estate of his model dwellings, with a version of the Great Exhibition (or Prince Albert's) model dwellings, was built at Windsor, Berks. (1852), and survives virtually intact.

Roberts was not only a pioneer in the design of accommodation for the less fortunate members of society, but an influential theoretician in the field. His publications include *The Dwellings of the La-bouring Classes* (1850 with a revised edition of 1867 also published in French), *The Improvement of the Dwellings of the Labouring Classes through the Operation of Government Measures* (1859), *The Essentials of a Healthy Dwelling and the*

Extension of its Benefits to the Labouring Population (1862), *The Physical Condition of the Labouring Classes, Resulting from the State of their Dwellings* (1866), and *Efforts on the Continent for Improving the Dwellings of the Labouring Classes* (1874). In these works he laid the foundations for later experiments such as those at Port Sunlight, Bournville, and Letchworth *Garden City, and, in particular, drew attention to the fact that the State and Municipalities would have to intervene to provide housing for those who would never be able to afford to build their own housing. He was opposed to the expansion of Building Societies as he foresaw the effect of easier *loans* would be to inflate *costs*, as the *price* of a dwelling would depend, not on its *value*, but on the amount of money available for loans. In his analyses he has been proved abundantly right.

Co (2008); J.Curl (1983, 2012); Metcalf (1977)

Roberts, John (1712–96) Irish architect, he enjoyed the patronage of **Richard Chenevix** (1697–1779—**Bishop of Waterford and Lismore** from 1746), for whom he designed Waterford Anglican Cathedral (1774—influenced by the work of *Gibbs and *Wren) and other buildings. Waterford RC Cathedral (1790s), Assembly-Rooms (now Town-Hall), the building housing the Chamber of Commerce, Waterford, and the spacious forecourt of Curraghmore, Portlaw, Co. Waterford (*c.*1750–60), were also by him.

B-J (1988); *CL,* **cxli** (15 Dec. 1966), 1627-8; M.Craig (1982); *DIA* [website] accessed Nov. 2012; *Journal of the Waterford and South East of Ireland Archaeological Society,* **ii** (1896), 99ff

Robertson, Daniel (*c.*1778–1849) SC-born architect of Scots descent, probably related to the *Adam family, perhaps a factor in financial difficulties that beset **William Adam** (1820s). Robertson and his (presumably) brother, **Alexander,** were involved (1812) in speculative developments in London which seem, with fecklessness, to have contributed to their bankruptcy (1817). However, Daniel worked (1820s) in Oxford, where he designed the Graeco-Roman University Press Building, Walton Street (1826–7), restored the *Gothic High-Street front of All Souls (1827), rebuilt the west side of the North *Quad, Oriel (1826), and also carried out works at Wadham (1826) and St John's (1826–7) Colleges. He designed two churches in a somewhat starved (hence the local epithet of 'Boiled Rabbit') *Neo-Norman style: St Clement, Oxford (1827–8), and St Swithun, Kennington, Berks. (1827–8—attributed on stylistic grounds). He left Oxford (1829) under a cloud, and settled in Ireland, where he designed some country-houses, including Carrigglas Manor, Co. Longford (1837–45—*Tudorbethan). Castleboro House, near Enniscorthy, Co. Wexford (*c.*1840—Classical, burnt out 1923), and sundry additions to Johnstown Castle, near Wexford (*c.*1833–6—castellated). He was working on the upper terrace at Powerscourt, Enniskerry, Co. Wicklow (1843), where he had to direct the works from a wheelbarrow in a state of inebriation. He was overseeing the completion of Lisnavagh, Co. Carlow, when he finally succumbed to the effects of the Demon Drink. He has been confused with William *Robertson, to whom he does not seem to have been related.

B-J (1988); Co (2008); Craig (1982); *DIA* [website] accessed 6 Nov. 2013

Robertson, Sir Howard Morley (1888–1963) American-born British architect, trained in Paris and the USA, he formed a partnership (1919–31) with **John Murray Easton** (1889–1975), which became **Easton & Robertson.** Their Royal Horticultural Hall, London (1925) exploited the parabolic arch, and the whole ensemble, including the stepped arrangement of windows, recalling *Berg's *Jahrhunderthalle,* Breslau (Wrocław), was as advanced an interior for its date as can be found anywhere. Robertson's admiration for *Mendelsohn was demonstrated in his Metropolitan Water Board Laboratories, New River Head, Rosebery Avenue, London (1938). The firm also carried out the remodelling of the Savoy (1930–9), Claridge's (1935–9), and Sadler's Wells Theatre (1939), all in London. One of their best works was the Bank of England Printing Works, Loughton, Essex (1956), for which *Arup was the consultant. Among Robertson's last buildings was the Shell Centre, York Road, Waterloo, London (1961), a lumpish tower that did not add to his reputation. Among his books were *The Principles of Architectural Composition* (1924), *Architecture Explained* (1926), *Modern Architectural Design* (1932), and *Architecture Arising* (1944). He was Principal (1920–35) of the Architectural Association School of Architecture.

AR, **cxiv**/681 (Sept. 1953) 160–8; M & N (1987); *ODNB* (2004); H.R (1924)

Robertson, John (*fl.*1829–50) *Loudon's draughtsman from 1829, responsible for numerous illustrations in the latter's *Encyclopaedia* (1833), he became *Paxton's assistant, working on designs for Edensor, Derbys. (*c.*1839–45), and later on the *cemetery at Coventry and the park at Birkenhead.

Chadwick (1961); Co (2008)

Robertson, William (1770–1850) English-born architect, active in and around Kilkenny, often confused with Daniel *Robertson. He designed numerous minor country-houses including Jenkinstown, Ballyragget, Co. Kilkenny (early

C19—'cardboard' *Gothick), Rosehill, Kilkenny (1820s—eclectic, but much damaged), and Gowran Castle, Co. Kilkenny (1817–20—Classical). He is primarily remembered for his rebuilding of the ancestral seat of the Ormonde Butlers, Kilkenny Castle (from 1826—castellated), which obliterated virtually all the medieval fabric (the building was subsequently gone over by *Deane & Woodward et al., badly damaged in the Civil War (1922), and drastically worked on in the 1970s by the Board of Works to eliminate dry rot). Robertson appears to have had his eye on Kilkenny for some time, as in 1797 he exhibited a drawing of the Castle.

B-J (1988); Williams (1994)

Robertson, William (1786–1841) Scots architect, he established (c.1823) his Elgin practice, and was active in Morayshire and surrounding areas. An accomplished *Greek and *Gothic Revivalist, he designed several churches and chapels (e.g. RC churches at Wick (Caithness) and Inverness (1830s)); the Public Library (originally Dr Bell's School (1839–41—Greek Revival)), and the former Union Hotel, (1838–9), both in Inverness; and many other buildings. His Banff Academy (1836–8), sundry works at Cullen, Banffshire (Town Hall, Post Office, Seafield Arms, Stables, Houses in the Square, and South Deskford Street, villas at Seafield Place, etc. (1822–5)), and the *mausolea at Bellie, Fochabers, Morayshire (1824–5—Greek Revival), and Inveravon, Banffshire (1829—*Gothic), attest to his ability to design agreeably proportioned and well-mannered buildings. He published a work on Elgin Cathedral ruins (1826).

Co (2008); DSA; Gifford (1996)

Robinson, Peter Frederick (1776–1858) English architect, pupil of *Porden, he later assisted *Holland with the enlargement of Brighton Pavilion (1801–2). He became a prolific provider of eclectic designs suitable for *Regency taste, and could turn his hand to most styles without qualms. He designed the influential 'Egyptian Hall' in Piccadilly, London (1811–12—demolished 1905), a curious concoction of unscholarly Egyptianizing elements on a *façade intended to advertise **William Bullock**'s (fl.c.1795–1826) Museum (*Papworth later added an equally unscholarly interior in a similar style). He carried out developments around Beauchamp Square, Leamington Spa, Warwicks. (1825–6), and was responsible for the original Swiss Cottage, Regent's Park, London (c.1828—demolished). He designed the impressive Gateway, Lodge, and Almshouses, Seaforde, Co. Down (1833), and may have been involved in the design of Seaforde House itself (1816–20—with fine *Greek-Revival interiors). He is best known today as the author of *Rural Architecture* (1823 with subsequent edns), *Designs*

for Ornamental Villas (1825–7, etc.), *Designs for Village Architecture . . . illustrating the Observations contained in an Essay on the Picturesque by Sir Uvedale Price* (1830, etc.), *Designs for Farm Buildings* (1830, etc.), *Designs for Lodges and Park Entrances* (1833, etc.), and other works that were responsible for disseminating his somewhat ungainly ideas of *Picturesque buildings throughout the land and the USA.

B-J (1988); Co (2008); J.Curl (2005); ODNB (2004)

Robinson, Robert (1734–94) Architect/landscape-gardener, trained under 'Capability' *Brown, he established (1760) an office in Edinburgh 'for designing, drawing, and executing all kinds of policy and gardening', in collaboration with **William Boutcher** (fl.1730s–80s). Among his garden-designs were Archerfield, East Lothian (1778), Balbirnie House, Fife (1779), and Banff Castle (1764).

Co (2008); D & E (1994); Tait (1980)

Robinson, Sir Thomas, Bt. (c.1702–77) English amateur architect, a disciple of Burlington's *Palladianism, he rebuilt his mansion at Rokeby, Yorks. (1725–30), to conform (though it also acquired a *portico of baseless *Doric columns, an early example of the use of such an *Order): house and grounds were attempts to re-create *Pliny's *villas in their settings, based on the Roman's descriptions. This expense, together with a somewhat extravagant lifestyle, obliged him to accept (1742) the Governorship of Barbados: there, he erected the Arsenal and Armoury at Pilgrim, which caused further financial embarrassment. Among his works are the landscaped Park and Church (1776) at Rokeby, the west *wing of Castle Howard, Yorks. (1753–9—which did little for the composition), Claydon House, Bucks. (1760–c.1780—of which one wing of Robinson's design remains), the powerful and original *Gothick gateway at Bishop Auckland Castle, Co. Durham (1760), and the Classical Church at Glynde, Sussex (1763–5). For a time Robinson was Master of Ceremonies at Ranelagh Gardens, the fashionable *pleasure-garden in Chelsea.

Co (2008); M.McCarthy (1987); ODNB (2004)

Robinson, William (c.1720–75) English architect. With *Vardy he supervised the building of *Kent's Horse Guards Building, Whitehall (from 1748). He designed the Excise Office Old Broad Street, London (1769–75—demolished 1854), in a *Palladian style. He is best remembered for making the first alterations at Strawberry Hill, Twickenham (1748), and for the *Georgian-*Gothick church at Stone, Staffs. (1754–8).

Co (2008); W.Pa (1887)

Robinson, William (1838–1935) Ulster-born landscape-gardener, he worked at Curraghmore, Co. Waterford, and Ballykilcavan, Co. Laois, before moving (1862) to the Royal Botanic Society's Gardens, Regent's Park, London, where he remained until 1866. By that time he had begun to contribute articles on horticulture to the *Gardeners' Chronicle*, *The Times*, and *The Field*: he also wrote his first two books (*Gleanings from French Gardens* (1868) and *The Parks, Promenades, and Gardens of Paris* (1869)). He then travelled in the Alpine region, Italy, and the USA, and published *Alpine Flowers for English Gardens* and *The Wild Garden* (both 1870) which helped to popularize a taste for hardy plants in mixed borders in natural settings. He founded (1871) *The Garden*, a weekly journal, and *Gardening Illustrated* (1879–1919), which influenced armies of late-Victorian English suburban gardeners, turning them away from the gaudiness of mid-Victorian taste for multi-coloured beds. His most successful book, *The English Flower Garden* (1883), went into fifteen edns during his lifetime, and became the Gospel of 'natural' gardening. He also established the journals *Farm and Home* (1882–1920), *Cottage Gardening* (1892–8), and *Flora and Sylva* (1903–5). One of his most interesting books was *God's Acre Beautiful* (1880), ostensibly concerned with the landscaping of *cemeteries, but which was a powerful polemic in favour of cremation (he collaborated with Ernest *George on the design of the grounds of Golders Green Crematorium, London (1901–5)). Having purchased (1885) the C16 Gravetye Manor, near East Grinstead, Sussex, he created there his model naturalistic garden, with *terraces, woods, water, and a great variety of hardy plants. He recorded his work in *The Garden Beautiful* (1907), *Gravetye Manor* (1911), and *Home Landscapes* (1914). He argued firmly in favour of respecting the *genius loci*, and abhorred paper plans, insisting that gardens should 'grow' out of their sites. He designed the garden at Shrublands, Ipswich, Suffolk (1880), became a close friend of *Jekyll, and was a powerful influence on *Arts-and-Crafts and *Domestic-Revival gardens. Through Jekyll, he influenced *Lutyens and others, though he quarrelled with *Blomfield, who favoured formal gardens. He can be said to have been a revolutionary and popularizer in English garden-design and practice.

HHH (1980); D & E (1994); *DIB* (2009); *ODNB* (2004): Shoe (2001); Tay (2006)

Robinson, Sir William (*c.*1643–1712) English architect/engineer, Surveyor-General of the Fortifications and Buildings in Ireland from 1671, his main works were the redesigning of Dublin Castle from 1684 (completed by Thomas *Burgh and **William Molyneux** (1656–96)), the Royal

Hospital, Kilmainham, Co. Dublin (1679–87— where *Baroque features were of fine quality), and several forts, including Charlemont, Co. Armagh (1673), and Charles, Kinsale, Co. Cork (1677–81). After the Williamite wars (1688–91) he designed St Mary's Church (1701–5) and Marsh's Library (1703–4), both in Dublin. He played a significant part in the development of *Classicism in Ireland, but acquired so many official positions and amassed such a fortune that the suspicion of corruption on an enormous scale is difficult to avoid, the more so when the Privy Council was obliged to pass an enactment (1724) to relieve his creditors long after his death.

CL, clxxvii (9 & 16 May, 1985), 1260–3, 1320–4; M.Craig (1982); *DIB* (2009); *IGSB*, xvii/1–2 (1974), 3–9; *Irish Sword* (1979), 289–98; Loeber (1981)

Robson, Edward Robert (1836–1917) English architect, articled to *Dobson, he worked in 'Great' *Scott's office before setting up on his own. Appointed (1870) Architect to the London School Board, he worked in partnership (1871–6) with J.J.*Stevenson: his school-designs (1872–89—nearly 300 were built) drew on the brick-built *Queen-Anne style that Stevenson et al. were promoting. Among his works were Berger Road School, Hackney (1878), the Royal Institute of Painters in Watercolours, Piccadilly (1881), and the People's Palace, Stepney (1886), all in London. Robson published (1874) his influential *School Architecture*, and in his last years worked with his son, P.A.*Robson.

D & M (1985); Gd (1977); A.S.Gray (1985); E.Robson (1972)

Robson, Philip Appleby (1871–1951) English architect, son of E.R.*Robson. Articled to *Pearson, he worked on Truro Cathedral before joining his father in practice, later working for various Government Departments before establishing his own office. Like his father he built many London schools, but his planning on tight urban sites was even more ingenious. Responsible for a series of handsome *Queen-Anne style tall-windowed brick and *terracotta buildings that enliven parts of London (among them St George's School, South Street (1898–9) and St Gabriel's College, Camberwell (1899–1903)). He also designed Eastbourne School of Art, Sussex (1903–4), and published *School Planning* (1911) and *Architecture as a Career* (1929).

B et al. (2001); A.S.Gray (1985)

Rocaille 1. System of decoration derived from *rock-work, ornamented with pebbles and shells found in *follies and, especially, *grottoes, often associated with water, *fountains, *cascades, etc. **2.** Type of *Rococo *scroll-like ornament, not unlike *Auricular forms, arranged asymmetrically, notably around frames etc., suggesting seaweed and other marine flora.

H.Bauer (1962); Kimball (1980); L & D (1986)

Roche, Eamonn Kevin (1922–) *See* DINKELOO, JOHN GERARD.

rock-cut Building excavated from solid rock, such as an Ancient-Egyptian *temple or tomb.

rock-faced 1. *Quarry-faced *ashlar with a *dressed projecting rough face, as though recently taken from the quarry, also called *cyclopean* *masonry or rock-faced *rustication. 2. Used erroneously for *rock-work.

rock-garden Garden-feature constructed of rocks (real or artificial), providing a suitable environment for growing plants (e.g. Alpines) native to natural rock surfaces. The earliest known in England was constructed at the Chelsea Physic Garden (1773) under the supervision of **William Forsyth** (1737–1804), built with a mix of stone from the Tower of London, Icelandic lava (introduced by **Sir Joseph Banks** (1743–1820)), bricks, and *flint. With the invention of *Pulhamite the development of rock-gardens, *ferneries, pools, and other garden-features was facilitated. Pulhamite rock-gardens included those at Madresfield Court, Worcs., and Lamport Hall, Northants. By the late C19 **Backhouse of York** was a leading builder of rock-gardens (e.g. that created (1896) for **Sir Frank Crisp** (1843–1919—**1st Baronet** from 1913) at Friar Park, Oxon.—a large Alpine fantasy with *grottoes, caves, underground passages, and a scale-model of the Matterhorn topped with crystal to mimic snow (restored in the late-C20 for **George Harrison** (1943–2001))). *See also* ALPINE GARDEN; ROCK-WORK.

Beresford *et al.* (2008); Hitching (2012); Tay (2006); p & g accessed 26 April 2013

rock rash Stone facing composed of a mosaic of irregularly shaped and sized stones, frequently with cobbles, *flints, and *geodes.

rock-work 1. Erroneous term for *rock-faced or *quarry-faced *ashlar. 2. Correct term for a structure in a garden constructed of large fragments of rock, imitation rocks, broken bricks, and other materials, held together with *mortar, the cavities further filled with earth, pebbles, and plants, intended to look 'natural'. Sometimes it was contrived to look like very large rocks, or even natural cliff-like faces as though a path had been cut through rock (but entirely artificial). Rock-work was often associated with *grottoes, *fountains, *hermitages, and *labyrinths in C18 landscaped gardens. Good examples exist at Wörlitz, Anhalt, by *Eyserbeck, *Erdmannsdorff, and the *Schochs.

Rococo C18 decorative style (some (e.g. Pevsner) have denied it as a style at all, but others (e.g. Kimball, Sedlmayr, and Bauer) had no such doubts) originating in France, and coinciding with the *Régence* and *Louis-Quinze* periods, that rapidly spread throughout Europe. It was elegant and frothy, deriving from *Auricular, *Rocaille, and *Baroque themes, drawing on marine- and shell-motifs found in *grottoes, and incorporating *ogee and C-*scrolls, *asymmetrically* disposed around *frames, *cartouches, etc., like a mixture of coral, seaweed, and stylized foliage. Colours were light and pale, often incorporating gold and silver, while the exotic was never far away, for Rococo designs included aspects of *Chinoiserie, *Gothick, and even, in late phases, *Hindoo allusions. Rococo decorations included *bandwork, *diaper-patterns, *espagnolettes, scallop-shells, and *scroll-work, incorporated in schemes of decoration of unsurpassed grace and beauty. In Southern Bavaria and Franconia Rococo reached its finest expression with the interiors of the *Amalienburg, Schloss Nymphenburg*, Munich, by *Cuvilliés and *Zimmermann, and *Wallfahrtskirche Vierzehnheiligen*, Franconia, the architecture of which was by *Neumann, who had nothing at all to do with the marvellous Rococo decorations (*see* NEUMANN). Rococo enjoyed a revival in France during C19, while in America, Britain, and Germany aspects of Rococo re-emerged from the 1820s to the 1860s, and in the late 1880s and 1890s there was another revival which was transmogrified into a synthesis of design in *Art Nouveau.

Bl (1973); COF (1988); Hi (1968a); Kimball (1980); L & D (1986); Loers (1976); M & E (1999); C.Powell (1959); J.T (1996); Zürchner (1977)

Typical Rococo ornament (*after Cuvilliés*).

Rococo garden C18 style of garden suggesting a frivolous, artificial, light-hearted aesthetic akin to that encapsulated in **Jean-Honoré Fragonard**'s (1732–1806) painting, *The Swing* (1767—aka *Les Hazards heureux de l'escarpolette*), sometimes perceived as a transition between *Baroque and *Neo-Classicism. Other paintings featuring dream-like Arcadian landscapes that might be described as *Rococo include works by **Jean-Antoine Watteau** (1684–1721—e.g. his *fêtes galantes*), **François Boucher** (1703–70), and Hubert *Robert. The term seems best-applied to gardens stocked with agreeably diverting, unserious *fabriques*, e.g. those in paintings by **Thomas Robins, Sen.** (1716–70), usually of an exotic type (e.g. *Chinoiserie and *Gothick). In Germany, surviving Rococo gardens include *Veitshöchheim*, near Würzburg (embellished with smiling female Rococo *sphinxes, *putti, *rock-work, etc.), and *Sanspareil*, Bayreuth (with rock-work *fabriques). An early-C19 *Rococo Revival* in garden-design occurred, prompted by *Loudon's reproduction of illustrations from *Dézallier d'Argenville's 1709 *Théorie* in his *Encyclopaedia of Gardening* (first edn 1822). Shell- and rock-work structures at Bowood, Wilts., have suggested *Rocaille influences in the so-called 'Rococo Valley' there.

Dennerlein (1981); DdA (1709); J.Hs (1978); H & H (1962-5); Hunt (2002); Shoe (2001); Symes (2006); Tay (2006); J.T (1996)

Rocque, John (*c*.1704–62) French-born surveyor/cartographer, aka '*dessinateur des jardins*', he published (1734–40) illustrations of country-houses and gardens near London which provide uniquely informative material. He later had a successful career making maps of counties and towns, and was one of the most prolific map-makers of his time. His survey of London (from 1738) was carried out in collaboration with **George Vertue** (1684–1756) and the splendid engravings were by **John Pine** (1690–1756), working with **John Tinney** (*c*.1706–61), published (1746) in 24 sheets. Other large-scale plans of towns surveyed by him include Bristol (1743) and Dublin (1756).

ODNB (2004)

Rode See ROOD.

Rod of Aesculapius Vertical staff or torch round which two snakes are twined, common in Neo-Classical and French *Empire design. An emblem of healing and medicine, it is associated with apothecaries and hospitals. It resembles a *caduceus without wings.

Rodríguez Tizón, Ventura (1717–85) Spanish architect of the late-*Baroque period, whose designs veered strongly in the direction of *Neo-Classicism. He worked under *Sacchetti on the Royal Palace, Madrid (1735–50), and then designed the Church of *San Marcos*, Madrid (1749–53—with plan featuring interlocking ellipses partly derived from *Juvarra's *San Filippo Neri*, Turin (1730–2), internal elevational treatments influenced by *Borromini's works, and a concave *façade reminiscent of *Bernini's *Sant'Andrea al

Quirinale, Rome (1658–70)). He fused Baroque and Neo-Classical themes at Pamplona Cathedral (designed 1783—with *prostyle *tetrastyle *Corinthian *portico set between two towers), but his College of Surgery, Barcelona (commissioned 1760) was severe and stripped, much influenced by French Neo-Classical theory. Among his other works were the Baroque Chapel of the Virgin, *Nuestra Señora del Pilar*, Saragossa (1750), the Chapel of the *Trasparente* in Cuenca Cathedral (1753—influenced by *Tomé's work at Toledo), and several churches in Andalucia.

K & S (1959); Ma (1984d); P (1982); Reese (1976); J.T (1996)

Roebling, John Augustus (1806–69) German-born American engineer. He perfected (1841–9) the manufacture of twisted-wire steel cables which he employed to suspend the Pennsylvania State Canal *aqueduct above the Allegheny River (1844–5). With his son, **Washington Augustus Roebling** (1837–1926), he designed Brooklyn Bridge, NYC (1869–83), then the longest suspension-bridge in the world. J.A.Roebling published *Long and Short Span Railway Bridges* (1869).

Ct (1960, 1968); P (1982); H.Schuyler (1931); J.T (1996); A.Tg (1965); Vogel (1971)

Rogers, Ernesto Nathan (1909–69) Italian *Rationalist architect. Founder, with Banfi, Belgiojoso, and Peressutti, of *BBPR, whose *Torre Velasca*, Milan (1957–60) created much controversy because it did not conform to *International *Modernism. Rogers co-edited *Domus* (1946–7) and *Casabella-continuità* (1953–64): the latter became one of Europe's most influential architectural journals during his tenure.

M & N (1987); J.T (1996)

Rogers, Isaiah (1800–69) American architect, best known for his hotels, the first of which, Tremont House, Boston, MA (1828–9—destroyed 1895), established the USA's pre-eminence in this building-type. He formed his own practice (1826), specializing in the *Greek-Revival style, of which his *Ionic Merchants' Exchange, Wall Street, NYC (1836–42), was his masterpiece, inspired by *Schinkel's *Altes Museum*, Berlin. The great *Pantheon-like *dome over the *rotunda was destroyed when *McKim, Mead, & White drastically altered the building (1907), adding four more storeys. He used the *Egyptian-Revival style for the gates of the Old Granary Burial Ground, Boston (1839–40), and the almost identical gates at Touro Cemetery, Newport, RI (1841–2). Thereafter, he began to favour *Italianate, although St John's Episcopal Church, Cincinnati, OH (1849–52—destroyed 1937), was *Neo-*Romanesque, and the Tyler Davidson Store, also in Cincinnati (1849–

50—destroyed), had a *Gothic *cast-iron front. Posterity has not been kind to Rogers: many of his buildings have been demolished or altered beyond recognition, some have been misattributed, and others attributed to him were not by his hand.

Carrott (1978); Hamlin (1964); R.Kennedy (1989); P (1982); J.T (1996)

Rogers, James Gamble (1867–1947) American architect, he worked in *Jenney's office before enrolling at the *École des *Beaux-Arts*, Paris, where he acquired an understanding of eclectic styles. He designed the Winton Building, Michigan Avenue, Chicago, IL (1904—with *reinforced-concrete frame), and made his name with the scholarly Classical New Haven Post Office and Court House, CT (1911–19). His most distinguished work was at Yale University, New Haven, CT, where he designed the Memorial Quadrangle and Harkness Tower (1916–21), a refined essay in *Collegiate Gothic. He followed this triumph with Sterling Memorial Library (1924–30), Sterling Law Buildings (1926–30), and Hall of Graduate Studies (1927–32), all in an abstracted *Gothic style of great sophistication. Other works include Residential Buildings, Yale University (1928–33), Columbia Presbyterian Hospital, NYC (1923–8), and Butler Library, Columbia University, NYC (1932–4).

AmA, cxx/2379 (1921), 298–314; AF, xxxi/3 (1919), 85–90; ARe, lviii/2 (1925), 101–15; Betsky (1994); P (1982); Perspecta, xviii (1982); J.T (1996)

Rogers, John (fl.1533–58) English *Freemason, he probably designed Thornbury Castle, Glos. (1511–22). He built the upper *stages of the tower, Lavenham Church, Suffolk (c.1523), and worked at Hampton Court Palace (1533–5). He was the King's Master-Mason at Calais and Guisnes (1541), and in the following year inspector of fortifications at Hull and Berwick-on-Tweed (if responsible for the *Tudor military architecture at Berwick, he was the most important architect of such works in the land).

J.Harvey (1987)

Rogers of Riverside, Richard George, Lord (1933–) See ARCHIGRAM; ARUP; HIGH TECH; PRICE, CEDRIC JOHN.

Roger the Mason (fl.1296–1310) English master-mason, in charge of works at Exeter Cathedral, Devon, by 1280; he probably designed the *presbytery (completed 1299) and the *choir (1310) there.

J.Harvey (1987)

Rogue architecture Term (properly **Rogue Elephant**) used by *Goodhart-Rendel to describe works by those *Gothic-Revival architects, addicted to *Go, whose works were not marked by scholarship, serenity, or tact. Among them were *Keeling, *Lamb, *Teulon, and **George Truefitt** (1824–1902), all practitioners, and **Thomas Harris** (1830–1900), whose *Victorian Architecture* (1860) and *Examples of the Architecture of the Victorian Age* (1862) earned opprobrium. Keeling and Lamb designed churches for the Evangelical persuasion—both expressed roof-structures in an outlandish, restless way, seeming to want to jar the eye with repetitive notchings, chamferings, and scissor-shaped *trusses. Their almost frantic originality, debauched acrobatic Gothic, harsh, barbaric *polychromy, and elephantine compositions brought Ecclesiological wrath on their heads. Few have taken their work seriously ever since. See RAGEUR; RAGUER.

AH, xvi (1973), 60–9 and xlii (1999), 307–15; J.Curl (2007, 2012); RIBAJ, ser. 3, lvi/6 (1949), 251–9

Rohault de Fleury, Charles (1801–75) French architect, son of **Hubert Rohault de Fleury** (1777–1846—a fine draughtsman, he designed much but built little (the Barracks, *Rue Mouffetard* (1821–4), was a good example of his austerely grand *Neo-Classicism)). Charles designed in a variety of other styles, including *Moorish (Hippodrome, Paris (1844–5)—destroyed) and *Renaissance (*Pavillon de Rohan* (1853)). A pioneer of iron-and-glass structures, his *Musée d'Histoire Naturelle* (1833–4) was studied by *Paxton. He designed *villas and commercial buildings, was responsible for the plan of the *Place de l'Opéra* and surrounding streets and buildings, and designed the *Grand Hôtel du Louvre* (1855) with *Hittorff and J.-A.-F.-A.Pellechet (1829–1903). Also with Hittorff he designed the layouts and *façades of buildings around the *Place de l'Étoile* (now *Place Charles de Gaulle*), Paris (1857–8). Although he developed plans for a new opera-house, much influenced by *Semper's work, and was appointed (1859) Architect for the new *Opéra*, the **Empress Eugénie** (r.1853–70) called for a competition, won by C.*Garnier. Embittered, Rohault de Fleury abandoned architecture and devoted himself to religious writings, including *La Sainte Vièrge: Études archéologiques et iconographiques* (1878). His son, **Georges** (1835–1905), wrote on medieval architecture and published (1884) a memoir of his father's work.

Gourlier et al. (1825–50); Hix (1996); M & Wa (1987); P (1982); J.T (1996)

Rohe See MIES VAN DER ROHE.

roll 1. *Bowtell* or common nearly cylindrical *moulding, semicircular or more than semicircular in *section. **2.** Rounded piece of wood along a *ridge or *hip over which metal is dressed as a *ridge-cap. **3.** *Volute, or spiral scroll in *Ionic, *Corinthian, and *Composite *capitals. *The word occurs in combinations, including*:

roll-and-fillet: roll-moulding with a *fillet running along its length emphasizing it by means of the extra shadows and lines of the fillet, common in *Gothic work;

roll-billet: one of a series of short *dowel-like rolls with spaces between each set in *cavetto-mouldings, so a type of *Romanesque *billet;

roll-moulding: **1.** as roll (**1**); **2.** *drip-stone, partly cylindrical in section, but with a fillet forming a *throat under it to shed water, in *hood-moulds or *labels;

roll-work: **1.** *Strap-work. **2.** *Cartouche. **3.** *Volute.

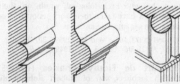

roll (*left*) *Flush-bead* moulding. (*middle*) *Torus* or *half-round*. (*right*) *Angle-bead* or *bowtell*.

Roman, Jacob (1640–1716) Dutch architect/sculptor, he designed (1677) a country-house at Zeist, with interior decorated by *Marot, and the more sumptuous *Het Loo*, near Apeldoorn (1684—now *Rijksmuseum Paleis, Het Loo*), with a similar layout to that of Zeist, with splendid formal gardens, recently restored. He again collaborated with Marot at the fine *De Voorst* (1695), a country-house near Zutphen, for **Arnold Joost van Keppel** (1669–1718—**1st Earl of Albermarle** from 1696). He also designed the *façade of the Stadhuis*, Deventer (1693), and *Meermansburg*, Leiden (1681—handsome *almshouses around a central *court).

Kuyper (1980); J.T (1996)

Roman arch Semicircular arch of wedge-shaped *voussoirs or thin *tile-like bricks.

Roman architecture Knowledge of the architecture of Ancient Rome during the Republic (509–27 BC) is limited, although the Sanctuary and Temple of *Fortuna Primigenia*, Palestrina (Praeneste—perhaps late C2 BC, but more likely *c*.80 BC), has been investigated. It consisted of several *terraces, connected by steps and *ramps, rising up a steep hillside above the *temple, with a semicircular double *portico surrounding a theatre: the climax of the composition was the circular temple at the top of the terraces. It is undoubtedly the finest partly surviving Republican composition, and was clearly of great magnificence. We know more, however, about the architecture of the Roman Empire from the time of **Augustus** (*r*.27 BC–AD 14) to the foundation of Constantinople (AD 330). Not only was Roman architecture of great

significance in itself in the history of *Classicism, the evolution of complex geometries, advances in constructional techniques of the *arcuated type (including *domes and *vaults) using a type of *concrete, and the development of engineering (roads, *aqueducts, *bridges, heating, etc.), but it inspired *Early-Christian, *Byzantine, *Romanesque, *Renaissance, *Baroque, and *Neo-Classical design.

Roman architecture, even that of the Empire at its most advanced, was derived from *Hellenistic prototypes, yet in *Hellenic and Hellenistic architecture the column of an *Order was fully exploited in design, while in Roman work was often reduced in status, becoming *engaged or used decoratively, as in the *pseudoperipteral Temples of *Fortuna Virilis*, Rome (C2 BC *or* probably *c*.40), and the *Maison Carrée*, Nîmes, France (16 BC), both of which are set on high *podia, have deep *porticoes based on the *prostyle *Etruscan type, but with the rest of the surrounding *colonnade or *peristyle usual in a Greek temple engaged with the *cella* walls. From the Greeks, too, came the Orders, but developed as distinctive *Roman* types of *Doric, *Ionic, and *Corinthian. The Roman-Doric Order of the Republican Temple at Cori (*c*.80 BC) was taller and more slender than Greek Doric (with the upper two-thirds of the column-shafts having 18 flutes in the Hellenistic style, the lower thirds cut as 18-sided polygons), and *entablature much less high (with 3 *triglyphs over each *intercolumniation). The distinctive Roman Tuscan-Doric Order (an amalgam of Etruscan prototypes with aspects of Doric, as at, e.g., the Theatre of Marcellus, Rome) only shared triglyphs, *guttae, and *mutules with Hellenic Doric, but capitals were unlike Greek exemplars, and *shafts were unfluted. Roman Ionic was less elegant than Hellenic or Hellenistic precedents, and included the eight-voluted *angular *capital as at the Temple of Saturn, Rome (AD C3 *or* AD C4), that removed the need for a special *angle-capital at the corners of the portico. Such 'diagonal' capitals occurred at *Pompeii, and were in widespread use before AD 79.

The Greeks used the Corinthian Order sparingly (e.g. *Choragic Monument of Lysicrates, Athens (334 BC)), but the Romans adopted it as an all-purpose Order, greatly elaborating the *entablature and applying lavish enrichment with uninhibited zest. To the range of Orders the Romans added the *Composite Order, which was really a type of Corinthian, but with a capital consisting of a luxurious version of the Ionic angular capital set over two rows of acanthus-leaves. Greek Ionic and Corinthian shafts were always fluted, but in Roman Ionic, Corinthian, and Composite Orders the shafts could be fluted or unfluted. In addition to the range of Greek ornament the Romans added a huge repertoire of their own. There was also the simple, unfluted, and robust *Tuscan Order among the five Roman Orders.

Another influence on Roman design from Hellenistic architecture was the tendency to a much wider intercolumniation than that of Hellenic buildings, something that was no doubt partly due to the widely spaced columns of Etruscan porticoes. Wall-surfaces, too, were given considerable attention, not only with finishes (e.g. coloured *marbles, etc.), but by means of the engaged columns and *pilasters so typical of Roman work. One of the most influential Roman innovations was the synthesis of arches (set in substantial blocky structures) and the *columnar-and-trabeated forms of the Orders (applied with very wide intercolumniations), an example of which was the *triumphal arch (c.AD 90) of **Titus** (r.79–81), Rome. This combination was further developed as the *assemblage of Orders applied to several storeys of arcuated walls, as in the *Colosseum*, Rome (c. AD 75–82). The impact of these inventions cannot be overstated, as the history of Classical architecture demonstrates. In particular, they were used in various combinations and transformations from *Renaissance times.

Roman developments in the use of brick, *concrete, and stone led to the construction of enormous arched and vaulted monumental buildings in which interpenetration of volumes based on complexities of plan-form were explored. Rough surfaces were then clad with *stucco, coloured marbles, and other materials, and internal décor of great magnificence was achieved. Good examples of vaulted and domed structures were those at Pompeii in C2 BC, the Roman *Tabularium* with its half-engaged columns (78 BC), **Nero**'s (r.54–68) *Domus Aurea* (AD mid-C1) attributed to *Severus, and the huge complex of Severan buildings on the Palatine by *Rabirius (AD late C1). Vaulted structures with ingenious geometries in the planning include the *thermae* of **Caracalla** (r.212–17) and **Diocletian** (r.284–305) and the *basilica of **Maxentius** (r.306–12), Rome. Highly organized monumental Roman buildings such as the *thermae*, *Domus Aurea*, *Villa Adriana* (**Hadrian**'s (r.117–38) Villa at Tivoli (from c.123)), and the gigantic Palace of **Emperor Diocletian** at Spalato (Salona now Split), Dalmatia (c.300), differ greatly from the architecture of Ancient Greece, yet can be described as 'Classical'. In fact, they can also be seen as having tendencies that anticipated Baroque (although cannot be described as truly Baroque themselves), not only in the geometrical complexities of their plans, but in the elevational treatment, such as the segmental arch rising into the *pediment (called an *arcuated lintel*) in the forecourt of Diocletian's Palace. Furthermore,

vast developments such as the *Villa Adriana*, Tivoli, had different areas and parts intended as mnemonics of various regions within the Empire (such as its *Canopus with Nilotic references), and so were not only important precedents for the C18 *Garden of Allusions, intended to trigger associations, improving thoughts, and sentiments in the visitor, but were forerunners of the eclectic cult of the *Picturesque.

Temples with porticoes at one end only, set on high podia, derive from Etruscan precedents, while temples related to colonnaded forecourts were Hellenistic in origin, and reached heights of magnificence in the Imperial *fora* at the Baalbek complex, Lebanon (formerly Heliopolis—AD C1–3). The Romans also built circular temples (e.g. Temple of 'Vesta' (*probably* **Hercules Victor**) in the *Forum Boarium* (c.C1 BC) and the Temple of 'Vesta' *or* 'Sybil', Tivoli (very likely of the same period, and influential in C18)). Almost proto-Baroque was the circular temple at Baalbek, with entablature arranged in five concave segmental curves on plan over four Corinthian columns. Circular *mausolea, e.g. the Tomb of **Caecilia Metella**, Rome (C1 BC), derived from Etruscan tumuli which were precedents for Imperial mausolea and other circular structures. Possibly the best-known Roman circular building is the Hadrianic *Pantheon (118–28), a thick *drum from which rises a *coffered dome with a central *oculus: attached to the drum is a deep octastyle pedimented portico. Another familiar Roman building-type is the *basilica which, with its *clerestoreyed *nave, *lean-to *aisles, and apsidal end, was one of the most influential of all forms and the precedent for countless churches and halls for the best part of two millennia. Other types included *amphitheatres (of which the *Colosseum* was the grandest and most influential representative); *thermae* (mentioned previously, and including many rooms of different shapes and sizes all combined within one ingenious plan); *circuses and *hippodromes (huge structures, clearly influences in the design of C20 sports-stadia, racecourses, and running-tracks); commemorative columns, e.g. Trajan's Column, Rome (early C2); triumphal arches; and Imperial *fora*, such as Trajan's *forum*, Rome (c.113), designed by *Apollodorus (models for many civic spaces).

Structural and uninhibited use of the arch made great engineering works possible, e.g. *aqueducts (good examples include the *Pont du Gard*, Nîmes (AD C1—which carried the aqueduct and road over the river-gorge), and the *Aqua Claudia*, Rome (AD 38–52—with its *Sublime array of arches springing from massive stone *piers) and bridges (e.g. the *Pons Mulvius (c.109 BC—which crosses the Tiber near Rome and carries the *Via Flaminia*)). Such a command of structure also enabled multi-storey apartment-blocks (*insulae*) to be built, with identical floor-plans throughout, and fire-resistant construction of brick with concrete vaults (e.g. *insulae* at the Roman port of Ostia). From C1 *insulae* often had arcaded ground-floors.

The better type of dwelling-house in towns (*domus*) had origins in Greek and Hellenistic models, and was usually of one or two storeys. Internal planning was based on axes and symmetry, with the main rooms placed around the *atrium* and perhaps other internal *courts* (often with *peristyles*). The *domus* presented blank walls to the street, or backed on to shops that faced the street, as at Pompeii, so it was an intensely private place, keeping the outside world at bay. Bigger houses also had walled gardens attached to them.

Country or suburban houses were called *villas*, the plans of which were looser and often of some complexity, designed to exploit views of the countryside or the sea: the most celebrated example was *Pliny's villa at Laurentum, an elusive building described by its owner that has exercised the imaginations of many who have attempted a reconstruction. However, it must be regarded primarily as a literary phenomenon, and does not represent an archaeological datum, whereas many other Roman villas have been excavated in Italy, France, Tunisia, and England. The villa, unlike the *domus*, was therefore outward- rather than inward-looking, and had rooms of various shapes and sizes, including internal galleries. External *colonnades, connected to the gardens, enabled the pleasures of nature to be enjoyed.

Whereas Greek temples tended to be set on an *acropolis (e.g. the *Parthenon, Athens), remote from the city below, Roman temples were usually sited near or in public places (e.g. *Maison Carrée, Nîmes, and Temple of *Fortuna Virilis, Rome). The triumphalism of Roman architecture was influential in Early-Christian basilican churches, while Roman constructional techniques were passed to the Eastern Empire, and were continued and developed by *Byzantine architects.

Finally, there was the architecture of Death: this included underground *cemeteries (*catacombs); private *hypogea, and *columbaria; linear cemeteries (roads lined with family and individual tombs, often set in funerary gardens (e.g. the Appian Way)); vast Imperial mausolea; cemeteries with built tombs in clusters (e.g. at Ostia); and circular tomb-structures (e.g. *Santa Costanza*, Rome (mid-C4)), that were important models for *martyria and other Christian buildings.

J.Anderson (1997); A.Boëthius (1960); B & W-P (1970); Co (1991); J.Curl (2001, 2002a); W.MacD (1965–86); W.MacD & Pinto (1995); D.S.R (1945); J.T (1996); Tomlinson (1995); Toynbee (1971); W-P (1974, 1981, 1986); D.Wa (1986); Mort. Wheeler (1964); WJ (2000)

Roman brick Long, thin brick (*later*), much larger than modern bricks, requiring approximately 6 *courses for 300 mm wall-height, but even this varies.

Roman bronze Alloy of copper, tin, and zinc.

Roman cement 1. *Cement or hydraulic *mortar made by mixing *lime with reactive siliceous material (in the form of crushed *tiles or volcanic ash), later developing superior strength and water-resistance, used by the Romans. **2.** *Parker's or *Sheppey* hydraulic cement, manufactured from *c.*1796 using *septaria (nodules containing networks of mineral-filled cracks) from Harwich, Essex, and the Isle of Sheppey: calcareous clay nodules were crushed, burnt, then mixed with lime, sand, and water. Setting quickly and hard, it was brownish in colour, and was much used in C19 as a *render for walls, often scored to resemble *ashlar joints. *See* POZZOLAN.

Gw (1903); N (1835); W.Pa (1887)

Romanesque Architectural style of buildings erected (C7–end of C12) in Romanized Western Europe having characteristics similar to those in *Early-Christian, late-*Roman, and *Byzantine architecture, notably the semicircular-headed arch, the use of the *basilican form for churches, and the survival of design-elements such as the Classical *capital (though much coarsened and transformed). Opinion, however, is divided about when the Romanesque style began: some accept C7, drawing *Carolingian and *Anglo-Saxon architecture within the Romanesque umbrella; others hold that true Romanesque began with the *Ottonian Empire in Germany and the evolution of architecture at *Cluny, Burgundy, from 910 and the subsequent rise of the Cluniac branch of the *Benedictine Order. The latter view tends to regard Romanesque as arriving in England with the Norman Conquest in 1066, but this therefore denies the qualities of such unquestionably sophisticated structures as the *crypt of St Wystan's Church, Repton, Derbys. (*c.*827–40—with vaulted roof carried on columns with spiral shafts (clearly associated with the tomb of St Peter in the Basilica of *San Pietro* in Rome) and *pilasters (obviously derived from Classical precedents), and the Old and New *Minsters, Winchester, Hants. (C7–C11—with evident Carolingian-Rhenish prototypes).

Mature Romanesque architecture, mostly surviving in churches and castles, had thick walls and sturdy *piers (often cylindrical); the semicircular arch, as mentioned previously; *vaults based on semicircles, often simple barrel-vaults, but frequently *groin- and *rib-vaults; *plans that were simple in their geometry, including *apses and circular buildings (e.g. Holy Sepulchre Church, Cambridge (*c.*1130)); and clearly defined *bays, square or rectangular on plan, making the construction

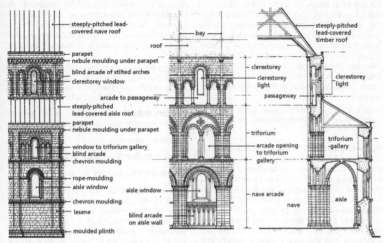

Typical English Romanesque bay, Peterborough Cathedral. (*left*) External elevation. (*middle*) Internal elevation. (*right*) Section.

of vaulted ceilings relatively simple. Bays were often delineated outside the building by means of pilaster-like *lesenes* marking each division between bays, and inside by *shafts rising up to the tops of the walls, or associated with the *springing of arches. Romanesque architecture was therefore clear and logical, the forms and subdivisions comprehensible with ease, both inside and out: this inherent geometrical simplicity also made it impressively powerful.

Grander churches had *ambulatories at the apsidal east end, with *radiating chapels around them (as at Cluny). Barrel- or tunnel-vaults were employed in France (e.g. *Notre Dame*, Clermont-Ferrand, and *St-Austremoine*, Issoire (C12)), and in Spain; groin-vaults were common in Germany (e.g. the *nave of Speier Cathedral (1082–1106)); *domes in parts of France (e.g. Angoulême (1105–30) and Cahors (1119) Cathedrals and *St-Front*, Périgeux (1120)); and rib-vaults in England (e.g. Durham Cathedral (end of C11–*c.*1130)) and Italy (e.g. *San Michele*, Pavia (*c.*1117)). In England and Northern France (where Romanesque is called *Norman*) western fronts of larger churches usually had two towers with a tower over the *crossing (as at Southwell Minster, Notts.). In Italy the basilican *clerestoreyed-nave-and-aisles shape of the west end is often expressed and decorated with ranges of *arcades (as at Pisa and Pistoia); in Southern France the west ends often have *screen-façades (e.g. *St-Gilles-du-Gard*, near Arles, where the Roman *triumphal arch was clearly a precedent); and in

Germany there may be several towers as well as structures (often octagonal) over the crossings (Speier Cathedral (1030–1106) and *Maria Laach* (1093–1156)). In Northern Europe roofs were invariably steeply pitched. In terms of rigid, powerful geometries, German Romanesque was unsurpassed: plans were often composed of a series of square bays in the nave, *transepts, and *chancels, with square bays a quarter of the main nave-bays in the *aisles (e.g. Worms Cathedral (1110–81) and the Church of the Apostles, Cologne (1035–1220)), the three-dimensional compartments of each bay emphasizing rigidity more than in other parts of Europe.

Architectural detail was limited in range, but distinctive. *Capitals were often clearly derived from *Roman and *Byzantine prototypes, but simplified, as with certain examples where the *Corinthian *volutes are still visible (e.g. the *cloisters of Monreale Cathedral (C12)). Basic Romanesque capitals include the *cushion and *scalloped type. *Mouldings and ornaments, too, were simple, and straightforward, including the *beak-head, *billet, *cable, *chevron, *double cone, *nebule, and *reversed *zig-zag.

Romanesque enjoyed a revival in the early C19 connected with a general trend towards *Historicism. In Germany the style was mingled with Early-Christian and Byzantine elements to produce the ubiquitous *Rundbogenstil. In England there were some attempts to create a C19 untainted Romanesque, including *Cottingham's

Church of St Helen, Thorney, Notts. (1846), and some buildings by *Donthorn and Thomas *Hopper. Serious archaeological revival of the style was rare, however, but was a phenomenon in France (with the work of *Abadie and others—e.g. *Sacré-Coeur*, Paris (1874–1919)), and in Ireland, where *Hiberno-Romanesque continued well into the 1960s (e.g. St Oliver Plunket, Blackrock, Co. Louth (1921–3), by **Ralph Henry Byrne** (1877–1946)).

Conant (1979); Ck (1996); Curran (2003); M.Davies (1993); Fernie (1995); Kubach (1986); Pe (1960); J.T (1996); D.Wa (1986)

Roman garden Information occurs in literature (e.g. *Pliny, *Vitruvius, etc.), inscriptions, Roman paintings, and archaeological evidence from *Pompeii, *Herculaneum (from C18), and individual sites throughout the former Empire. Gardens included *courts surrounded by *peristyles, embellished with planting (often in *containers), as part of inward-looking town-houses: the *atrium* (*see* CAVAEDIUM) was also laid out with fruit trees and vines or treated formally, with ornamental planting, statuary, *impluvium*, and *fountains. Larger *villa-gardens were well-stocked with fruit trees, hedges, *pergolas (on which vines, etc., were trained), *colonnades, *exedrae*, etc.: Pliny described these as well as water-features (perhaps not uninfluenced by earlier gardens in cultures such as those of Assyria, Egypt, etc.) and rooms set around gardens planted with boxhedges. Enclosed gardens for herbs, vegetables, and bee-hives were also created close to dwellings, and in country-house grounds influences from Greek *gymnasia- and temple-groves (e.g. **Plato**'s *philosopher's garden of Akademos) were detectable. Imperial gardens from AD C1 were on the grandest scale (e.g. **Emperor Nero**'s (*r.*54–68) palace with park, vineyards, and even lakes, with woods, in the Esquiline and Palatine hills, later expanded as the *Domus Flavia* under **Domitian** (*r.*81–96)). **Hadrian** (*r.*117–138) created a vast garden at the *Villa Adriana*, Tibur (Tivoli) (late C1–early C2), in essence a *Garden of Allusions suggesting various parts of the Empire (e.g. the *Euripus connected with *Canopus, alluding to Egypt). Suburban and rural villas also had courtyard-gardens, but larger premises had extensive parks as well. Temple-precincts were adorned with groves and gardens, and tombs (e.g. on the *Via Appia Antica*, Roma) often had gardens with orchards, vineyards, flowers, etc.: such funerary gardens associated with festivals of the dead might also provide produce which could be sold for the upkeep of the fabric of *mausolea, etc. Some plans of funerary gardens have survived showing geometrical and formal layouts. Roman tombs occasionally featured wall-paintings showing delightful gardens with songbirds, water, and

many trees: interestingly, with the decline of the Empire in the West, gardens associated with Early-Christian churches (e.g. the colonnaded *atria* in front of *basilicas, often featuring fountains, planting, etc.) were referred to as *Gardens of Paradise* or *Eden*.

Bazin (1990); Farrar (1998); Grimal (1984); J.Henderson (2004); Jashemski (1979, 1993); MacDonald & Pinto (1995); MacDougall (1984); MacDougall & Jashemski (eds) (1981); Shoe (2001); Tay (2006); Toynbee (1971)

Roman mosaic *Mosaic with small *tesserae laid in *mortar to form decorative patterns.

Romano *See* GIULIO ROMANO.

Roman Order *Composite Order.

Romantic Classicism *See* ROMANTICISM.

Romantic garden *Landscape-garden influenced by the philosophical principles/aesthetic ideals of *Romanticism in Europe and America in the late C18 and for much of C19. The 'English', 'naturalistic' garden, with *fabriques (notably *ruins), informed many Romantic gardens. *See* LANDSCAPE-GARDEN; PICTURESQUE.

REB (2010)

Romanticism Late-C18–early-C19 artistic movement, its many variations and strands defying any neat definition. The one characteristic found throughout its sundry manifestations was the insistence on individual experience, intuition, instinct, and emotion. Commonly perceived as a reaction against the rationalism of the *Enlightenment, *Classicism, and *Neo-Classicism, it nevertheless shared with Classicism reverence for the *ideal, transcending reality, hence the term *Romantic Classicism* applied to works displaying a Romantic response to the *Antique. A perfect Ancient-Greek *temple in its pristine state would be Classical, but a *ruined* Greek temple, though Classical in one sense, cannot be Classical in another because it is broken, incomplete, partial, and in ruins. Such a *ruin might, however, be perceived as beautiful, and so a Classical building *constructed* as a 'ruin' in an C18 garden could be described as an example of *Romantic Classicism*. Asymmetrical compositions set in the context of the *Picturesque often are purely Classical in detail, such as *Schinkel's exquisite buildings at Potsdam (*Charlottenhof* and the Roman Baths complex), and so can be classed as examples of Romantic Classicism.

Form, in Romantic art, was determined by the inner idea within the subject represented, and the yearning for spirituality and inner meaning allied Romanticism with medievalism, *Historicism, the Picturesque, the *Gothic Revival, and the *Sublime. A new tenderness towards the dead, a love of melancholy, and the cultivation of feelings

were characteristics of Romanticism, creating elegiac gardens, the first *cemeteries, and fuelling
the religious revival that was such an important
part of C19 European and American culture.

COF (1988); Clay (1981); J.Curl (2002a, 2007); Honour
(1979); H.O. (1970); REB (2010); J.T (1996)

Roman tile There are various types, including
Single Roman (rectangular with an upstand on
one side and a slightly tapered *roll on the other
that fits over the narrower part of the roll of the
tile below as well as covering the upstand of the
adjacent *tile); *Double Roman* (large rectangle
with an upstand on one side and two tapered
rolls, one on the other side and the second in
the centre, laid with 'break joints', or staggered,
but requiring special tiles at the *verges to complete the bond); and *Old Roman, basilican,* or
Italian (flat tapered *under* tile with upstands on
both sides, the joints at the upstands being covered by convex tapering *over* or *top* rolls, that
resemble half truncated cones).

W.McKay (1957)

rondel 1. Circular window-opening (i.e. *roundel) or a circular glazed *light. 2. *Bead-moulding
of a *capital around the top of a *shaft. 3. Tower
circular on plan.

Rondelet, Jean-Baptiste (1743–1828) French
architect, he studied under J.-F.*Blondel and assisted *Soufflot during the construction of *Ste-
Geneviève*, Paris, afterwards (with **Maximilien
Bréblon** (1716–96) and **François Soufflot** (*before*
1764–1802)) directing the works. He altered the
building (1791–1812) under *Quatremère de
Quincy when it was converted into the *Panthéon*.
He published *Traité théorique et pratique de l'art
de bâtir* (1802–17), *Mémoire sur l'Architecture*
(1789), and other works, including well over 100
entries on construction for the *Encylopédie Méthodique* (1788–1820).

Chevalier & Rabreau (1977); Middleton & Baudouin-
Matuszek (2007); M & Wa (1987); Rondelet (1790,
1802–17, 1852)

rond-point 1. *Circus where roads converge in
a town or city. 2. In a garden, a circular area
whence paths or avenues radiate.

Rood Derived from the Anglo-Saxon and Mid-
dle-English word (**Rode**) for a *cross, it describes
the large Crucifixion set above the entrance to a
*chancel, sometimes suspended, sometimes sup-
ported on a *Rood-beam* spanning from wall to
wall, and sometimes rising from the *Rood-loft*
over the *Rood-screen*. During the Middle Ages,
Rood-, chancel-, or *choir-screens* were erected in
churches where the *nave ended and the *choir
began: in cathedrals and larger churches they are
usually of stone and called *pulpitum*, while in

smaller churches simply *screens, the tops of
which had *galleries or *lofts, approached from
*stairs, used for readings and chantings. Roods
themselves, usually of wood but sometimes of
stone, consisted of a carving of Christ crucified
on the Cross (often flanked by figures of the Virgin
Mary and St John), occasionally supported on a
base carved with rocks and skulls to represent
Golgotha (a unique *Rood-beam* survives in the
Church of St Andrew, Cullompton, Devon). Timber screens (of which many survive, especially in
Devon) are often richly decorated with *tracery,
painted *panels (excellent examples can be found
in St Edmund's Church, Southwold, Suffolk), and
enrichment, the loft or gallery supported on a
coved, vaulted structure projecting over the
screen proper. Most surviving English Rood-
screens are C15 or C16 in date, though many
were erected during the *Gothic Revival, some of
the most beautiful by *Bodley, *Comper, and
A.W.N.*Pugin. **Terms associated with Roods
include**:

Rood-altar: 1. *nave-altar erected under a Rood;
    2. *altar physically attached to a Rood-screen,
    facing the nave, as in the remarkable altar-
    bases of the *pulpitum* in the Cathedral Church
    of St Kentigern (or Mungo), Glasgow, added by
    Robert Blackadder (c.1445–1508—**Archbishop
    of Glasgow** from 1492);
Rood-arch: 1. central opening or arch in a Rood-
    screen; 2. *chancel-arch, if associated with a
    Rood;
Rood-spire: *flèche or *spire over a *crossing in a
    church;
Rood-tower: *crossing-tower.

B & C (1909); J.Parker (1850); J.T (1996); Vallance
(1947); WRH (1990)

roof Covering of any building by which its fabric
and habitants are protected from inclement
weather. Roofs are here considered as to their
form or *type* and *finish*, the *structure* being dealt
with elsewhere (see CRUCK; TRUSS). *Cladding of
roofs may be of metal (especially *aluminium,
copper, *iron, *lead, *steel, and zinc), *glass,
*slate, stone, *thatch, *tile, turf, wood, or other
materials. Greek *temples had *marble roofs, the
slabs worked to prevent leaks; the Romans used
tiles; medieval churches were clad in lead, tiles, or
thatched; and since C19 a variety of materials has
been used. *Barry's Palace of Westminster, for
example, is clad in cast-iron panels. **Types of
roof include**:

appentice: see LEAN-TO;
barrel: with internal appearance of a barrel-vault,
    like a cylinder;
catslide: *pitched* roof covering one side of a roof
    and continuing at the same pitch over a rear
    extension, commonly found in *Colonial archi-
    tecture in New England (USA), where it is

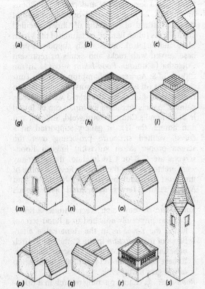

roof (*a*) *common pitched* with *raised gable* (*right*) and *parged verge* (*left*); (*b*) *hipped*; (*c*) *pitched* with *catslide* over extension at a lower pitch; (*d*) *half-hipped* (*left*), and (*right*) with *gablet* or *lucarne* rising from the *naked* of the wall; (*e*) *hipped* with apex *gablets*, incorrectly called *gambrel*; (*f*) *hipped* projection; (*g*) *hipped* with *sprocketed eaves*; (*h*) *hipped curb* or *mansard*; (*i*) *hipped* with central roof-light; (*j*) *pie-ended* platform on *hipped roof* (if the platform is slightly pitched, it is *French*) with *lean-to extension*; (*k*) *mansard* or *curb* with segmental-headed *dormers*; (*l*) *hipped M-shaped*; (*m*) *saddleback* as on a *tower*; (*n*) *Gabled M-shaped*; (*o*) *gabled curb*, *gambrel*, or *mansard*; (*p*) *half-hipped* with same-pitched *catslide*; (*q*) *simple pitched* with *gabled ends* and *gabled M-shaped extension* at right angles to main roof; (*r*) *pyramid* surrounded by *balustrade*; (*s*) *helm*.

referred to as a *saltbox*. A catslide can also be the roof of a *dormer pitching in the same direction but less steeply than the main roof;

compass: see TRUSS;

cradle: see TRUSS;

curb-: *pitched* roof (also *kerb*) with the slopes broken to form two sets of planes on each side, the outer planes being very steeply pitched, called *curbs*. Similar to a *mansard* roof, it is so-called from the horizontal plate, *curb*, or *kerb* at the junction of the rafters at the two pitches, or from the almost vertical lower

part of the roof. It can have either two or four sides, but if only two it is usually called a *gabled curb-roof* or *mansard* in the USA;

cut: see TRUSS;

double-framed: see TRUSS;

French: *curb-roof* with the sides set at very steep angles (almost vertical) and the pitched top part (*gabled* or *hipped*) almost flat;

gable or *pitched*: commonest type, with sloping sides meeting at a *ridge and with a *gable at each end;

gambrel-: in the USA *curb* roof with only the two sides sloping (i.e. a *gabled curb-*roof), but in Britain a *hipped* roof with a small gable or *gablet* under the ridge at one or both ends (this definition is not accepted in all quarters, and indeed is questionable: *hipped roof with gablet or gablets at the apex* would be more accurate);

half-hipped: pitched roof with gables terminating in hipped roofs;

helm-: with four sloping sides joining at the apex, like a *pyramid, set on a square tower with gables the tops of which coincide with the lines of the junctions between the sides of the roof. The sloping sides sweep downwards over the raking tops of the gables, and terminate in points where the gables join;

hipped: with four pitched slopes joining at *hips*, and without gables;

kerb-: see CURB;

lean-to: monopitched *appentice*, set against a higher wall, as over an *aisle and against a *clerestorey of a *basilican church;

mansard-: named after F.*Mansart, a *curb-roof with steeply pitched or curved lower slopes and pitched or hipped roof over, almost invariably with *dormer-windows. Distinguished from the *French roof in having a more steeply pitched upper part, and in the USA called *gambrel*;

M-shaped: with two parallel pitched roofs meeting in a valley or gutter;

pack-saddle: with two pitches and *gable-ends on a church-tower (as **M**);

pavilion-: hipped on all sides to have a pyramidal or almost pyramidal form, as *pyramid*-roof;

penthouse: as *lean-to*, but not necessarily associated with a church, so a simple *monopitched* roof;

pitched: as *gable*;

pyramid-: shaped like a pyramid or a *hipped* roof with a very short *ridge* so that the slopes almost meet at a point, as *pavilion*;

ridge: any *pitched* roof with the sloping sides meeting at a ridge;

saddleback-: ordinary *gable*-roof on top of a tower;

shed-: as *penthouse*;

single-framed: *see* TRUSS;

slab-: flat roof consisting of one slab of concrete or of several concrete slabs joined together and spanning between walls;

span-: *ridge* roof of two equal slopes as distinct from a *lean-to* or *penthouse*-roof;

suspended: web or webs hung on cable-nets stretched between heavy cables fixed to masts and the ground, called a *tent-roof*;

tent-: with a concave surface like a *camp roof, or sloping inwards with a convex surface, such as the roof of a *Regency *balcony or a *verandah;

terrace-: flat roof with imperceptible slope or *fall*, waterproofed, and permitting free use for sitting, etc.;

trough-: **M**-roof;

valley-: **M**-roof, or roof covering a building with projecting *wings requiring valleys where the subsidiary roofs join the main roof.

N (1835); W.Pa (1887); S (1901–2)

roof-garden Plants within buildings (e.g. in *courts or *containers) have been features of architecture since Antiquity. the 'Hanging Gardens of Babylon' were among the *Seven Wonders of the Ancient World, but were probably formed on *terraces (however, we do not know enough about them to establish if they were true roof-gardens, and it seems they were not in Babylon at all). The Romans, with their techniques of massive concrete construction, were able to have gardens on buildings (i.e. on terraces and roofs), and some of the more complex *Renaissance *villas were closely integrated into gardens, *grottoes, terraces, etc. Gardens on the roofs of buildings became part of the imagery of the Modern Movement, notably in drawings by Le *Corbusier, and their creation became possible again with the development of *reinforced-concrete technology. At 101–111 Kensington High Street, London, a remarkable roof-garden was created (1937–8—one of the first in England) at the former **Derry & Toms** department-store (1929–31—in a stripped *Beaux-Arts Classical style): the building was designed by **Bernard George** (1894–1964). Also in the 1930s *Burle Marx designed roof-

gardens, notably at the Ministry of Education and Health Building, Rio de Janeiro (1936–43—by *Costa, with Le *Corbusier as consultant). During the second half of C20 roof-gardens proliferated (e.g. at the Oakland Museum, CA (by *Kiley)).

E (1994); Gollwitzer (1971); K (1994)

room 1. Accommodation, or certain space or area, or interior portion of a building divided off by walls or partitions, esp. a chamber in a dwelling-house. **2.** Clearing in a wood. **3.** Space (*compartment) in a garden defined by walls, hedges, fences, etc.

Roome, William John Waterman (1865–1937) Birmingham-born Belfast architect, his works include the Shankill Road Mission (1898); 'Kingscourt' (1899–1901) and the former **Crymble**'s Music Shop (1903), both in Wellington Place, Belfast; and numerous private houses, including his own house, 'Meroc', Greenisland, Co. Antrim (1902—with a fine *Art-Nouveau staircase).

P:JRSUA, v/5 (May/June 1997), 45–8

Roos, Alexander (c.1810–81) Rome-born German architect, pupil (c.1829–32) of *Schinkel in Berlin, he settled (c.1833) in England, apparently through connections with Thomas *Hope. He designed *Pompeian and other decorations (as well as some of the architecture, where Schinkel's influence was clear) at Hadzor House, Worcs.; much of the *Italianate remodelling of The Deepdene, Surrey (1835–41—where Thomas *Liddell was also involved); and works (including the gardens) at Bedgebury Park, Kent (c.1836–41—again with Hope connections). At Shrubland Park, Suffolk, Roos designed Italianate-Schinkelesque buildings, including the Ipswich and Coddenham Lodges, and various garden-structures (e.g. the *Swiss Cottage). He collaborated with *Burn on numerous country-houses in Scotland, and (1845) was appointed by **John Crichton-Stuart** (1793–1848—**2nd Marquess of Bute** from 1814) to lay out much of Cardiff (including Cathays Park), where he designed *villas, etc. Lists of known and attributed works are given in *GGJ* cited here.

GGJ, xv (2005/6), 11–68; Gow & Rowan (eds) 1998); DWa & Hewat-Jaboor (eds) 2008)

Root, John Wellborn (1850–91) *See* BURN-HAM, DANIEL HUDSON.

rootery Garden-feature constructed of tree-bark, -roots, and -stumps (so called a **stumpery**) arranged upside-down with interspersed soil (usually in a shady place), to enable ferns, mosses, and lichens to establish themselves as well as providing a habitat for wildlife. Suggesting a 'gloomy' and rough effect, it was an alternative to a *rockery. An early example was built (1856) by the artist and gardener **Edward William Cooke** (1811–80) at Biddulph Grange, Staffs.: a more recent rootery has been formed (1980) at Highgrove, Glos.

Symes (2006)

root-house Garden-building constructed or decorated with roots, stumps, branches, and trunks of trees. C18 and C19 pattern-book designs for this building-type included *arbours, 'banqueting-houses', *bridges, *hermitages, and seats: one of the most noted, and still extant, was by Thomas *Wright for the Badminton Estate, Glos. (c.1750). Root-house forms varied from one-roomed *cabins (often with *rustic *porches and *thatched roofs) to two-storey structures. 'Merlin's Cave'—a hermit's *cell by William *Kent for Richmond Park (c.1735)—set a precedent with its thatched roof and *ogee *doorway, a theme Wright continued at Badminton. These ephemeral structures have left few lasting footprints.

B.Jones (1974); Symes (2006); Tay (2006); pk

rope *See* CABLE.

Roper, Lanning (1912–83) American garden-designer/author, he settled in England after the 1939–45 war, and joined (1951) the staff of the Royal Horticultural Society, where he began his writing career, notably for *Country Life*. His first book, *Royal Gardens* (1953), was followed by *Successful Town Gardening* (1957), a tome on the Royal gardens at Windsor (1959), and other works, including the *Sunday Times Gardening Book* (1967). He was garden-correspondent for the *Sunday Times* (1951–75) and garden-consultant to the National Trust: his interventions at Castle Coole, Co. Fermanagh, and Castle Ward, Co. Down, were much admired. He worked on numerous gardens, including the roof-garden of the Ismaili Centre, South Kensington (with *Casson, Conder, & Partners), and the **Prince of Wales**'s gardens at Highgrove, Glos. (1981). Other involvements were at Broughton Castle, Oxon., Waddesdon Manor, Bucks., Scotney Castle, Kent, and many other houses.

ODNB (2004); Tay (2006)

Roriczer *or* **Roritzer Family** (*fl.*C15) Family of German or Bohemian master-masons. **Wenzel** (*fl.*1411–19), who seems to have trained in the *Parler Lodge in Prague, became Architect of the Cathedral of St Peter, Regensburg, Bavaria (c.1411), where he probably designed the lower *stages of the western towers: a surviving drawing may be in his hand or in that of his son, **Konrad** (*before* 1419–77/8), who built the *choir of *St Lorenz*, Nuremberg (1454–66), worked at Regensburg (where he or his father designed the elegant triangular porch (c.1430), was a consultant in Vienna (1462), was involved in the building of the great tower of *St Georg*, Nördlingen (1460s), and advised on the *Frauenkirche*, Munich (1474).

Konrad's son, **Matthäus** or **Mathes** (c.1430–95), worked with his father at Nuremberg, became Master-Mason at the *Lorenzkirche* (1463–6), and worked at Nördlingen on his father's design for the tower. He was again connected with Regensburg (1468–72), and probably worked with *Böblinger on the *Frauenkirche*, Esslingen, designing the *tabernacle there. He built the sacristy at Eichstätt, and (1473) he was in Munich, working on the *Frauenkirche*, before returning to Regensburg (1476) and succeeding his father as Master-Mason. He built the upper part of the west *façade, the *pulpit (1482), the second stage of the north tower (1487–8), the tabernacle (1493), the Eichel *turret, and, perhaps, the Three Kings *altar. His brother, **Wolfgang** (*fl.*1480–1514), completed the west front, added further stages to the towers, and designed the *font and *baldachin. He backed the losing side in a political dispute, and paid with his head.

Matthäus is particularly important as the author of a surviving tract on the design of Gothic *finials (*Das Büchlein von der Fialen Gerechtigkeit* (1486)) as well as a treatise on geometrical resolutions of certain constructional problems published as *Geometria Deutsch* (1486–90). His other surviving publication is a tract on *gables (c.1488–9).

Geldner (1965); P (1982); Recht (ed.) (1989); Shelby (1977); J.T (1996)

rosace 1. Circular aperture or window. 2. *Rose. 3. Rose-window. 4. *Rosette.

rose 1. Conventional representation of a flower (e.g. *fleuron* in the centre of an *abacus-face on a *Corinthian *capital). 2. Circular ornament resembling a *patera, used to decorate ceilings, etc., hence *ceiling-rose* in the centre from which a chandelier or light-fitting is suspended. It is often found ornamented with stylized leaves, and according to its size is termed *rosace* or *rosette*. 3. *Rose-window.

Rose, James C. (1910–91) American landscape architect, influenced by *De*Stijl*, he attempted to apply Modernist principles to garden-design. He was more influential through his writings (e.g. *Creative Gardens* (1958) and *The Heavenly Environment* (1990)) than through his completed works.

J.Rose (1958, 1965, 1990); Snow (ed.) (1967)

rose-ball Stylized tightly petalled rose-flower adopted by C.R.*Mackintosh and his wife for systems of decoration such as stencilled *friezes. It was an *Art-Nouveau motif also favoured by the Vienna *Sezessionists.

Steele (1994); T-M (1967)

Rosenberg, Eugene (1907–90) British architect, born in Moravia, educated in Czechoslovakia, he worked with Le *Corbusier from 1929. He settled in England (1939, forming a partnership (1944) with F.R.S.*Yorke and **Cyril Mardall** (1909–94) which became **Yorke, Rosenberg, & Mardall** (YRM). Rosenberg's credentials were firmly established within *International Modernism, and he quickly became part of the English Modernist circle with *Fry, *Gibberd, and others. Among his works with YRM were the Cowley Peachey Housing Development, Middlesex (1947), Barclay Secondary School, Stevenage, Herts. (1950), Warwick University (1965–71), and St Thomas's Hospital, London (1966–74).

E (1994); P (1992); YRM (1972)

rosette Circular stylized ornament, essentially a *patera* with floral enrichment, occurring on the *soffits of *coffers, and as the *fleuron* of the *Corinthian *abacus*. It is therefore generally smaller than a *rose.

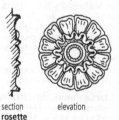

section   elevation
rosette

rose-window *Gothic circular or *marigold window subdivided by complex *tracery radiating from the centre and joining in *foils to form a stylized floral design of great intricacy and beauty, often found combined with the tracery of a large *Pointed window as well as isolated within a circular aperture. It is distinct from a *Catherinewheel *or* *wheel-window, both of which have *colonnettes coincident with the radii, like spokes.

J.Parker (1850); S (1901–2)

Rossellino, Bernardo di Matteo Ghambarelli *called* (*c.*1409–64) Florentine architect/sculptor, he completed the *façade of the *Fraternità di Santa Maria della Misericordia*, Arezzo (1433–5), designed the Spinelli *cloister, *Santa Croce*, Florence (1448–52), and supervised the completion of *Alberti's *Palazzo Rucellai*, Florence (1448–62), including the façade. His masterpiece was the town-centre of Pienza (from 1459), the first *Renaissance *ideal city, which he realized for **Aeneas Silvius Piccolomini** (1405–64—**Pope Pius II** from 1458). It consists of the *piazza* containing the *Duomo*, *Palazzo Piccolomini*,

Palazzo Vescovile, and *Palazzo del Pretorio*, and other *palazzi* and houses. The *palazzi* on either side of the *Duomo* are set at angles to its main axis, like stage wings, and the *Palazzo Piccolomini* has elevational treatment derived from that of the *Palazzo Rucellai*, although the three-storey garden-façade has tiers of *porticoes from which views of the countryside may be had, a concept clearly derived from *Pliny's description of his villa in Tuscany. Some scholars hold that it was Rossellino who designed the façade of the *Palazzo Rucellai* in its final form, and indeed it is almost exactly contemporary with the *Palazzo Piccolomini*, but others suggest Alberti may have contributed.

Carli (1966); He (1996); C.Mack (1980, 1987); P.Mu (1969); Schulz (1977); J.T (1996); Tönnesmann (1990); Tyszkiewicz (1928); D.Wa (1986); *ZfK*, **vi** (1937), 105–46

Rossetti, Biagio (*c.*1447–1516) *Renaissance architect, he worked mostly in Ferrara, where he created one of the most spectacular urban developments of C15, the *Addizione Erculea*, the northern extension of the city that more than doubled its area, complete with the *Piazza Nuova* and the intersection of the *Via Prione* and *Via degli Angeli* (from 1492). Rossetti designed four churches and eight *palazzi*, including the *Palazzo dei Diamanti* (1493–1567), so called because of the diamond-pointed *rustication of its *façades. In the *Piazza Nuova* he was responsible for the *Palazzo Rondinelli* and the *Palazzo Strozzi-Bevilacqua* (both from 1494, with arcaded ground-floors), and the Church of *San Francesco* in the old city (from 1494) on a plan based on *Brunelleschi's *San Lorenzo*, Florence, with nave-ceiling consisting of transverse arches supporting shallow *domes on *pendentives. In the *Addizione* the aisleless vaulted *San Cristofero alla Certosa* (from 1498) was also built to his plans.

He (1996); Marcianò (1991); P (1982); J.T (1996); Zevi (1960)

Rossi, Aldo (1931–97) Italian architect, the most eminent protagonist of *Rational architecture (also called *Neo-Rationalism or *Tendenza*), the theoretical bases of which he set out in *L'architettura della città* (1966) in direct contradiction of the tenets of the *Modern Movement: it was an important stimulus for the evolution of *New Urbanism. Yet in the early 1960s his work had seemed to embrace aspects of *International Modernism, late-C18 *Neo-Classicism of the stereometrically pure type advocated by *Boullée, and a proto-Surrealism reminiscent of the paintings of **Giorgio de Chirico** (1888–1978). Something of the Surreal atmosphere in Chirico's work could be found in Rossi's apartment-blocks for *Aymonino's *Gallaretese 2* Complex, Monte Amiata, Milan (1969–74). With **Gianni Braghieri** (1945–) he designed the *San Cataldo* Cemetery, Modena (1971–6, 1980–8), a master-work of stripped Neo-Classical geometry as severe as any late-C18 or C20 essay, which became a paradigm of Neo-Rationalist architecture. Other important works include the School at Fagnano di Olona (1972-6), apartments in the *Rauchstrasse*, Berlin (1983), housing-blocks for the *Internationale Bauausstellung*, Berlin (1984-7), the School of Architecture, University of Miami, Coral Gables, FL (1986), the *Il Palazzo* Hotel, Fukuoka, Japan (1987-9—with **Morris Adjmi** (1959-)), the *Carlo Felice* New Theatre, Genoa (1983-93—with *Gardella), and the *Bonnefanten* Museum, Maastricht, The Netherlands (1990-4). His *A Scientific Autobiography* (1982) and *Selected Writings and Projects* (1983) set out many of his ideas regarding building typologies and urban morphologies. *See* ANALOGICAL ARCHITECTURE; TICINESE SCHOOL.

Adjmi (ed.) (1991); A (1994); Ar & Bi (1985); Brandolisio (ed.) (1999); E (1994); Ferlenga (ed.) (1987, 1992); Geisert (ed.) (1994); J (1996a); Klotz (1988); Moschini (ed.) (1979); *The Times* (18 Sept. 1997), 25; Pi *et al.* (2000); A.Ro (1982, 1994, 1996); A.Ro (ed.) (1967); A.Ro *et al.* (1973); Savi (1976); J.T (1996)

Rossi, Domenico (1657-1737) Pupil of *Longhena, he made his name as a designer of firework-displays and as an expert on explosives before he turned to the less ephemeral pursuit of architecture after winning the competition to design the *façade of *San'Staè* (*Sant'Eustachio*), Venice (1709-22), a handsome *engaged *temple-fronted composition on the Grand Canal. Thereafter his output was prolific, and included *palazzi* (e.g. *Palazzo Corner della Regina*, Venice (1723-c.1730)), churches, and *villas. Among his many works may be cited the Archiepiscopal Palace, Udine (1708-25), and *Santa Maria Assunta*, Venice (1714-29—with others).

D.Howard (1980); D.Lewis (1979); P (1982)

Rossi, Domenico Egidio (1659-1715) Italian architect, he appears to have played an important role in the development of *Baroque architecture in Central Europe. He probably designed the *Palais Caprara-Geymüller* in *Wallnerstrasse*, Vienna (1687-8), and supervised works at Hradčany Castle, Prague (1690s). He made designs (c.1690) for *Gartenpalais Liechtenstein*, some of which survive, and for the *Czernin* gardens at Leopoldstadt (1696—destroyed), both in Vienna. Other designs included the vast *Schloss Rastatt* (1698-1707—for **Ludwig Wilhelm** (1655-1707—**Margrave of Baden-Baden** from 1677)), the *palace at Durlach (from 1698—for **Friedrich VII** (1647-1709—**Margrave of Baden-Durlach** from 1677)), and other works in Baden. He seems to have sailed close to the wind, had to flee Prague after a brawl (1693), and a warrant was issued for his arrest (1709) for defects at *Schloss Rastatt*.

ÖZK & D, xliii/1-2 (1989), 26-32; J.T (1996); WJfK, xxxiii (1980), 17-19

Rossi, Giovanni Antonio de (1616-95) Roman *Baroque architect, he designed *Santa Maria in Publicolis*, Rome (1641-3), the *façade of which was designed with *scenographic aspects in mind. His *Santa Maria in Campomarzio* (1676-86) and *Cappella Lancellotti* in *San Giovanni in Laterano* (1674-80), both in Rome, deserve mention for their splendour. His best-known work is the *Palazzo Altieri*, Rome (1650-76), with its spectacular four-flight *stair, although his finest work is arguably the *Palazzo d'Aste-Bonaparte* (1658-65), influenced by *Borromini.

C-E (1930); FdA & C (1977-8); Hd (1971); P (1982); Pi (1970); Spagnesi (1964); Wi (1982)

Rossi, Karl Ivanovich (1775-1849) Russian architect and urban planner of genius, working in St Petersburg from 1816, largely responsible for giving the city-centre its monumental *Neo-Classical character. He designed the noble arch of the General Staff building (1819-29) with flanking hemicycle of administrative buildings, the gigantic range of the Senate and Synod (1829-34), the impressive *Mikhailovsky Palace* (1819-33—later the Russian Museum), and the *Aleksandrinsky* (later *Pushkin*) *Theatre* (1827-32). He created formal spaces, an urban fabric of great grandeur, and *Sublime architectural effects by repetition of *colonnades and huge scale.

Egorov (1969); G.H (1983); M & Wa (1987); D.Shv (2007); J.T (1996); Taranovskaia (1980)

Rossi, Marcantonio de (1607-61) Italian architect/military-engineer, his greatest work was the replanning of *San Martino al Cimino* near Viterbo (1648-54), an early instance of comprehensive order and system being imposed on urban fabric. He fortified the *Janiculum*, Rome, for **Pope Urban VIII** (r.1623-44), building the *Porta di San Pancrazio* and the *Porta Portese in Trastévere* (both 1643), and was responsible for the *Acqua Acetosa*, Rome (1661).

B & V (1973); Heimbürger Ravalli (1971, 1977); Onofrio (1978)

Rossi, Mattia de (1637-95) Son of Marcantonio de *Rossi, he assisted *Bernini, notably at *Sant'Andrea al Quirinale*, Rome (1670s). Among his works are the *Palazzo Muti Bussi, Piazza della Pilotta*, Rome (1675—much altered), and *Santa Maria dell'Assunta*, Valmontone (1686-98—with concave *portico flanked by light, airy, *belfries). He also designed numerous *altars, funerary monuments, and chapels.

C-E (1930); FdA & C (1977-8); Hd (1965, 1971); P (1982); Wi (1982)

rosso antico *See* PORPHYRY.

Rosso, Giovanni Battista di Jacopo *called* **Rosso Fiorentino** (1494-1540) Florentine painter, pioneer of *Mannerism in France. From 1530 he was established at Fontainebleau, where he worked for *François Ier (r.1515–47), and, with *Primaticcio, can be credited with the creation of the *Fontainebleau School of decoration (as in the Galerie François Ier). He probably worked as an architect too (he, or Primaticcio, may have designed the doorway to the Pavillon des Armes, facing the Jardin de Diane (c.1530), the earliest piece of Egyptianizing architecture in France).

COF (1988); J.Curl (2005); J.T (1996)

rostral column See COLUMN.

rostrum 1. Bow section of an *Antique Roman warship, resembling a beak, ornamented with an animal-head, buckler, or helmet (acrostolium), forming the projections on columnae rostratae. 2. *Daïs or platform raised above the general level.

Roth, Alfred (1903–98) Swiss architect, he established his position within *International Modernism by collaborating with Le *Corbusier and *Jeanneret-Gris on two houses for the *Weissenhofsiedlung (1927), described in Zwei Wohnhäuser von Le Corbusier und Pierre Jeanneret (1927), and later published reminiscences in Begegnung mit Pionieren (1973). A member of the Swiss *CIAM group, through which he obtained the commission for the Doldertal Apartment Block, Zürich (1935–6), designed with his cousin **Emil Roth** (1893–1980) and *Breuer for *Giedion, from 1934 he edited the CIAM journal, Weiterbauen, published The New Architecture (1939), and edited Werk (1942–56).

J.Gubler (1975); A.Roth (1946, 1973, 1977); J.T (1996)

Roth, Emery (1871–1948) Hungarian-born American architect, he emigrated to Chicago, IL, and worked for *Burnham & Root before joining (1895) Richard Morris *Hunt. Having established his own office (1898), he designed numerous high-rise buildings in NYC, many of them *apartment-blocks or hotels, in which he used a simplified Classicism derived from the World's Columbian Exposition, Chicago (1893), mingled with themes drawn from the *Aesthetic Movement and *Art Nouveau. Works in NYC included 509 West 121st Street (1910–11), 601 West End Avenue (1915–16), Beresford Apartments, Central Park West (1928–9), San Remo Apartments, Central Park West (1928–9), the *Art-Deco Ardsley Apartments (1930–1), and Normandie Apartments (1938–40). His sons **Julian** (1902–92) and **Richard** (1905–88), and grandson **Richard II** (1933–) continued the practice, designing Modernist buildings (e.g. the Look Building, Madison Avenue (1946–50). The firm collaborated with *Yamasaki on the twin-towered World Trade Center, NYC (1964–74—destroyed 11 Sept. 2001).

Ruttenbaum (1986); J.T (1996)

rotunda 1. Building shaped like a cylinder both inside and outside, especially one covered with a *dome, such as the *Pantheon in Rome. It may have a *peristyle around the exterior (e.g. the drum of the Panthéon *crossing-dome, Paris, by *Soufflot) or within it, or both inside and outside (e.g. *tholos at Epidaurus). 2. Hall or room shaped like a cylinder contained within a larger building so that the *drum is not expressed externally as a totality, but may appear partially as a *bow, with or without a *cupola over it.

Rouge, Georges-Louis Le (1707–c.1790) German-born as **Georg Ludwig Le Rouge**, trained as a military-engineer/surveyor, he settled in Paris (c.1740), establishing himself as a book- and map-publisher. An Anglophile, much of his cartographic output was derived from English sources: his engravings (1776–88) of notable C18 gardens included valuable information on French, English, German, and Chinese (based on *Chambers's work) subjects, facilitating comparative studies of developments in European garden-art. They also show places no longer extant or partially destroyed (the 1785 Cahier, e.g., contained 26 illustrations of the Désert de Retz). Appointed ingénieur géographe du roi to **King Louis XV** (r.1715–74), he published numerous city- and town-plans.

Imago Mundi, lii (2000), 124–42; Rouge (1776; 1776–88); Tay (2006)

roughcast Species of external plastering or *render composed of *lime, sand, water, and small particles of gravel, pebbles, or crushed stones, thrown on to an undercoat of render before the latter has dried, also called pebbledash, slapdash, or wetdash. See also HARLING.

rough-setter or **-mason** Worker with stone (also **rowmason**) who only built *rubble-work, unlike a *Freemason capable of dressing and setting *freestones.

round Anything circular, or almost circular, such as a round (i.e. semicircular) arch, round-arched style (*Rundbogenstil), round (as opposed to prismatic) *billet, round church (i.e. circular on plan), round *moulding (e.g. *torus), round *pediment (i.e. segmental or semicircular), round *ridge (i.e. with a half-cylindrical *crest or ridge-tile), round tower (as in Irish exemplars with conical caps and certain other bell-towers in England and Italy), and round window (as in a *Catherine-wheel or *rose-window).

roundel 1. Small circular *panel or window, specifically a deep circular *niche containing a bust. 2. Bull's-eye (*œil-de-bœuf) window or *oculus. 3. *Astragal or large *bead.

Rousseau, Jean-Jacques (1712–78) Swiss-born social philosopher/botanist/protagonist of

*Romanticism. He described the *délicieuse ivresse* (delicious intoxication) experienced by abandoning oneself to the beauties of Nature, and that if only Man could find again a state of innocent, even *primitive*, virtue, greater happiness would result. In his celebrated novel, *Julie, ou la Nouvelle Héloïse* (1761), he described a garden in which 'Julie's' former lover responded to the cool shades, calming effects of running water, many flowers, joyous birdsong, and the apparently haphazard mixing of ornamental and fruit trees. *Julie* was an important influence on contemporary garden-design, prompting the creation of *faux*-Alpine scenery with Swiss-styled *fabriques*: Rousseau was therefore a catalyst in the appreciation of the *Sublime. A friend of *Girardin (whose gardens at Ermenonville were intended as a landscape equivalent of a just and natural social order), Rousseau's writings encapsulated many ideas current at the time, but also impinged on certain gardens, e.g. Hawkstone, Salop. (1780s), Endsleigh, Devon (*c.*1814–20), and Arlesheim, Basel, Switzerland (1785). The Poplar Island at Ermenonville on which Rousseau was entombed became a tourist-attraction, and inspired progeny in numerous gardens (e.g. Arkadia, Poland; and Wörlitz, Anhalt), and also helped to trigger the evolution of the *garden-cemetery. *See* CEMETERY; GESSNER; GOETHE; LANDSCAPE-GARDEN; NATURAL GARDEN; NATURESQUE; PICTURESQUE; SUBLIME; SWISS COTTAGE; THOREAU.

Goethe (1809); H.R.Heyer (1980); Hug (2008); REB (2010); Rousseau (1761, 1782); Rümelin (ed.) (2012); Tay (2006); J.T (1996); Védrine (1989); Velhagen et al. (1993)

Rousseau, Pierre (1751–1810) French architect, much influenced by *Peyre. His masterpiece is the *Hôtel de Salm* (*Palais de la Légion d'Honneur*, 64 *Rue de Lille*, Paris (1782–5)), with its *colonnaded *Ionic *screen containing a central monumental arch. He designed a number of *apartment-blocks, including those at 25 *Quai Voltaire*, *Rue Royale*, and *Rue de Bellechasse* (1770s and early 1780s). He also designed the *Chinoiserie *pavilion of the *Hôtel de Montmorency*, *Boulevard Montmartre*, Paris. Appointed Architect for the town of Clermont-Ferrand he also had responsibilities in the *Département* of Puy-de-Dôme, in which capacity he designed the market-buildings at Issoire and the gaol at Riom.

B (1980); M & Wa (1987); W.Pa (1887)

Rowe, Colin (1920–99) English architectural critic, he established his reputation (1940s) with a series of papers in which he explored a supposed Classical continuity within *Modernism: for example, he demonstrated that Le *Corbusier's proportional systems regulating the structural grid and *façade of the *Villa Stein* at Garches (1926–8) were the same as those used by *Palladio, e.g. at the *Villa Malcontenta*. He held the common view that International-Modern architecture of the 1920s offered paradigms for the second half of C20: however, by 1998, Rowe, like many others, came to regret his championship of the *Modern Movement, finding the study of *Renaissance buildings 'gratifying and refreshing as the spectacle of Modern Architecture' became 'more depressing'. His works included *The Architecture of Good Intentions* (1994), *As I Was Saying: Recollections and Miscellaneous Essays* (1996), and *The Mathematics of the Ideal Villa and Other Essays* (1976). Rowe suggested metaphors and historical references as generators of form, and his belief in links between the Classical past and the Modern Movement affected late-C20 theory and design. He collaborated with **Fred** (Alfred) **H.Koetter** (1938–2017) for *Collage City* (1978) in which he advocated the use of *collage and a wideranging *eclecticism: he appeared to view collage as a method 'for using things and simultaneously disbelieving in them'. It would seem that a manipulation of themes used as collage in design might be a means of enjoyment without depth, for conviction and belief were no longer possible. Rowe's views influenced *Stirling et al.

Wi.Cu (1996); Rowe (1976, 1994, 1996); Rowe et al. (1968, 1984, 2002)

rowmason *See* ROUGH-SETTER or -MASON.

Roy also **Leroy, Julien-David Le** (1724–1803) French architectural historian, who succeeded J.-F.*Blondel as Professor of Architecture at the Academy: he resisted abolition of the School of Architecture when the Revolutionaries closed the Royal Academies during the Terror. His studies of Ancient-Greek buildings had a profound effect on *Neo-Classicism and on the *Greek Revival, although his surveys were not always accurate and attracted adverse criticism. His *Les Ruines des plus beaux monuments de la Grèce* (1758) gave his contemporaries a better understanding of the *Doric Order. He also published *Histoire de la Disposition et des Formes Différentes que les chrétiens ont données à leurs temples depuis le règne de Constantin le Grand jusqu'à nous* (1764), and *Observations sur les édifices des anciens peuples* (1767) which also contained reflections on criticisms of his *Ruines . . . de la Grèce* published in *Stuart and *Revett's *Antiquities of Athens*, the first volume of which had appeared in 1762. His 'reconstruction' of the Athenian *propylaea was the model for *Langhans's masterpiece, the Brandenburg Gate, Berlin. In 1775 he designed an 'English' landscape-garden at Chantilly.

B (1980); Egbert (1980); Eriksen (1974); M & Wa (1987); Ry (1980); Wn (1969)

Royston, Robert R. (1918–2008). American landscape architect, partner of *Eckbo (1945–58).

rubbed, rubber *Rubbed brick, brick rubber, cutter*, or *malm* is a soft brick made of special well-mixed fine loamy clay containing a lot of sand and baked (not burnt) in a kiln, readily sawn and rubbed to the required shape. It is used for making *gauged* brick arches, etc., the extremely fine joints between the rubbers being formed of *lime-putty* rather than conventional *mortar, which would be too coarse.

Bru (1990); N.Lloyd (1925); W.McKay (1957)

rubble Rough, undressed stones of irregular shapes and sizes used in the construction of *rubble-work* walls with the mortar-joints fairly large, often requiring small pieces of stone (*gallets) to be set into the *mortar if the stones are especially irregular and difficult to fit reasonably closely together. *Types of rubble-work include*:

random: constructed of stones not of uniform size or shape laid in apparently random patterns, with no *courses, needing great skill in its bonding so that continuous (and therefore weakening) vertical jointing can be eliminated, and requiring the wall to be sound by means of *bonders* (*bond-stones*), *headers*, or *through-stones* providing the transverse bond by extending through the thickness of the wall. *Random rubble* is also used without mortar (called *dry-rubble* or *dry-stone* walling) for field boundary-walls, the stability of which is entirely dependent on the careful interlocking and bonding of the stones;

random, built to courses: similar to *random uncoursed* rubble in basic construction, except that the work is roughly levelled up to form courses the heights of which coincide with the *quoins or *jamb-stones of a *reveal (often of dressed stones or brick *dressings). Thus courses may be composed of one large irregular stone, then two or three stones set over each other, then two, then one, all laid to form a level upper surface;

squared coursed: rubble roughly formed of rectangular blocks, laid in courses, with the individual stones in a course all the same height, although the heights of courses themselves may vary, also called *regular coursed* or *ranged rubble*;

squared uncoursed: roughly squared stones of different sizes placed in an *uncoursed* arrangement, with *levellers* (stones of low height), *jumpers*, or *risers* as bond- or through-stones, and *checks* or *snecks* to fill in the areas left by the larger stones. It is also called *square-snecked, snecked*, or *speckled*.

In addition there are variations of walling which can be classed under rubble-work. *They include*:

flint-walling: flints or cobbles in *panels framed by *lacing-courses* of brick or stone to bond the wall together;

knapped-flint walls: flints split to expose the hard dark interiors and dressed in pieces roughly square, which are then laid very closely together so that little, if any, mortar joints are visible. Panels of knapped flint are commonly found with dressed stone around them, especially in East Anglian churches of the *Perp. period (*see* FLUSHWORK), and the material always has to be used in conjunction with brick or stone for stability;

Lake District masonry: *slate from Cumb. and Westmd. in flat rough-faced or square-faced blocks dressed and laid in courses bedded in mortar set back from the faces on both sides of the wall, the centre of the wall being packed with dry stones without mortar. Blocks are closely fitted together, spalls being used to pack gaps, and laid tilted (*watershot*) towards the external wall to prevent water-penetration. *Quoins are usually of dressed limestone;

polygonal walling: usually found as a facing using stones such as *ragstone set so that the joints form a net-like pattern all over the wall.

Gw (1903); S.Hart (2000); W.Pa (1887); S (1901–2)

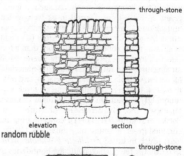

elevation   section
random rubble

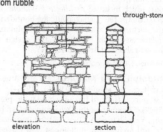

elevation   section
random coursed rubble
rubble

Rubens, Sir Peter (Pieter) Paul (1577–1640) Flemish painter/designer, the greatest and most influential in Northern European *Baroque art of the time. His work blended aspects of the **Cinquecento* with northern realism and appreciation of landscape (derived, perhaps, from the work of **Pieter Bruegel the Elder** (*c.*1525–69), who was deeply affected by Alpine scenery, so was an early appreciator of the **Sublime). In turn, Rubens's work influenced **Francois Boucher** (1703–70) **Gessner, **Goethe, **Jean-Antoine Watteau** (1684–1721) and others, and informed aspects of the **Rococo and **Picturesque garden.

COF (1988); J.T (1996)

rudenture Cabling. *See* CABLE.

Rudnev, Lev Vladimirovich (1885–1956) Architect in the former Soviet Union, one of the team responsible for the gigantic University Complex, Moscow (1948–53), typical of the coarse **stripped **Classicism favoured in the Stalinist era. Similar buildings, with vast towers, were erected in several places in the Soviet bloc during the 1950s (e.g. Palace of Culture and Science, Warsaw, Poland (1951–3)).

CoE (1995); J.T (1996)

Rudofsky, Bernard (1905–88) Moravia-born American architect, he was best known for his championing of buildings based on inherited traditions, passed from generation to generation, without involvement of architects: such 'unpedigreed' structures are referred to as **vernacular, 'indigenous', 'anonymous', 'spontaneous', or 'rural'. Aware that architectural history (if taught at all) was never concerned with more than a few select cultures, he was particularly interested in architectural/cultural aspects (building-materials, life-styles, variable and modular spaces, and relationships between dwellings and natural surroundings) as found in, e.g., traditional Chinese, Japanese, and Mediterranean structures. Rudofsky moved to NYC (1941), concentrating on curatorship of a series of exhibitions (1940s–'60s) which included *Architecture Without Architects* (MoMA 1964), challenging the boundaries of architecture as held by Received Opinion. He collaborated with **Nivola in the design of a 'house-garden' at Armagansett, NY.

Guarneri (2003); Rudofsky (1965, 1977)

Rudolph, Paul Marvin (1918–97) American architect, he studied (1939–43, 1946–7) with **Gropius at Harvard before setting up in practice (1947). Chairman of the Department of Architecture, Yale University (1958–65), he designed the Art and Architecture Building at New Haven, CT (1958–64), with massive towers and many levels joined by **stairs and **bridges, colliding forms, corrugated and chiselled surfaces, and unsettling interiors. The building was partly burned (1969) during student unrest (an episode Rudolph found too painful to discuss): nevertheless it was influential among architects, e.g. some of **Lasdun's work in England. Although never formally associated with New **Brutalism or **Team X, his student housing at Yale (1958–61) came close to expressing similar themes. Brutalist, in the sense of expressing the board-marks on **reinforced concrete, was the Temple Street Car Park, New Haven (1959–62), allegedly a celebration of the motor-car, but in reality a lumpish structure completely dwarfing its surroundings. His Government Center complex, Boston, MA (1962–72), arranged around a public square, was supposedly inspired by the *Campo*, Siena, but resemblances are elusive. Other works include Sarasota High School, FL (1958–9), the Endo Laboratories, Garden City, NY (1960–4), and the core buildings for South-Eastern Massachusetts University, North Dartmouth, MA (1961–3). In the early 1960s he admitted that many of the difficulties experienced in the architectural world stemmed 'from the concept of functionalism as the only determinant of form', which sounds like a possible rejection of Gropius's influence.

Alba (2003); Domin & J.King (2002); E (1994); Moholy-Nagy (1970); Monk (1999); *Daily Telegraph* (13 Aug. 1997); P (1982); Spade (1971c); Stern (1977); J.T (1996)

ruin Carefully contrived specially constructed 'ruins' (sometimes called **folly) or real ruins (e.g. of a **castle or **abbey) were often incorporated within C18 English **Picturesque landscapes, a fashion that spread to Europe. Some architects (e.g **Chambers and **Soane) established their architectural works as worthy of the best Classical **Antique models by arranging for them to be depicted as imaginary ruins, inspired by the **Grand Tour and the influential engravings of **Piranesi.

D.Coffin (1994); D.Jacques (1983); M & T (1991); J.T (1996)

Rumford, Sir Benjamin Thompson, Graf von (1753–1814) British-American soldier/scientist/inventor/philanthropist/administrator/universal man, as a Loyalist, he left America, was elected a Fellow of the Royal Society in London, and decided to further his military career by fighting the Turks in Europe. Settling in Munich, he became Minister of War, Minister of Police, and Grand Chamberlain to **Kurfürst Carl Theodor of Bavaria** (*r.*1777–99). He reorganized the Bavarian Army, did much to improve the condition of the labouring classes, and suppressed mendicity. Created (1791) a Count of the Holy Roman Empire, taking the title Rumford from the township in America to which his first wife's family belonged (now Concord, NH), he concerned himself also with improvements to fireplace-construction and the reduction of pollution from chimneys, and did much to reform hospitals and *workhouses in Ireland. With **Sir Joseph Banks** (1743-1820) he founded the Royal Institution of Great Britain (1799), and himself made the first sketches (now in the RIBA) for the lecture-room of the Institution at 20-21 Albermarle Street, London. In Munich a large tract of land belonging to the Elector was transformed at Rumford's instigation, the designer being *Sckell: it is known as the *Englischer Garten*, is one of the very first *public parks designed as such, and is in the *Picturesque English *landscape-garden style. Rumford published his thoughts on the benefits of public parks in his *Essays Political, Economical, and Philosophical* (1796-1802), with American (1798-1804) and German (1797-8) edns, a work influencing *Downing, *Olmsted, et al. Rumford took (1805) as his second wife **Marie-Anne Pierret Paulze** (1758-1836), widow of the French scientist, **Antoine-Laurent Lavoisier** (1743-94—guillotined during the Terror).

EB (1959); ODNB (2004)

Rundbogenstil German for *round-arched style, it was essentially eclectic, drawing on *Byzantine, *Early-Christian, Italian-*Romanesque (especially North-Italian buildings in and around Como), and Florentine-*Renaissance (e.g. round-arched *palazzi*) precedents. As the name suggests, it developed in C19 Germany, notably in Bavaria, where its chief practitioners were von *Klenze (*Königsbau* and *Allerheiligenhofkirche*, Munich (1826-37)) and von *Gärtner (Court and State Library (1827-43), *Ludwigskirche* (1829-44), and other Munich buildings), and in Prussia, where *Schinkel and *Persius created distinguished architecture in the style (e.g. *Friedenskirche*, Potsdam (completed 1850)). Promoted by *Hübsch, *Rundbogenstil* had considerable success in England, where it was emulated under the aegis of **Professor Ludwig Grüner** (1801-82) and Prince *Albert. It should not be confused with *Neo-Norman or *Romanesque Revival, although the *Rundbogenstil* embraced some Romanesque themes. It should also be emphasized that it was emphatically not an historical Revival, but was derived from abstract notions of utility and rational approaches to design.

Ne (1987); Schinkel (1989); J.T (1996)

runic cross *Celtic *cross.

runic knot Type of intricate interlacing ornament associated with *Anglo-Saxon and *Celtic work, especially *high *crosses, but also found in *Romanesque design.

Rickman (1848); J.T (1996)

running Term describing anything linked in a smooth continuous progression or repeating asymmetrical flowing motifs, set on a *band, each apparently leaning to one side or the other. *Types of* **running ornament** *are*:

running dog: Classical *Vitruvian *scroll or *wave-scroll, like a repeated stylized wave on a band;

running vine: grapevine, *trail, or vignette, common on the upper parts of *Perp. *screens.

rural architecture Buildings associated with the countryside, but esp. C18 and C19 *cottages ornés* and **fermes ornées* or other buildings designed to suggest the rural ideal, as in a *Picturesque landscape, using free compositions, asymmetry, *vernacular detail, and materials such as *roughcast, *thatch, *rubble, etc. *See also* RUSTIC.

Rusconi Sassi, Ludovico (1678-1736) Italian *Baroque architect, works include the *Aedicula, Via del Pellegrino* (1715-16), and the Odescalchi Chapel, *Santissimi Apostoli* (1719-22), both in Rome, in which the influence of *Borromini was apparent. He also designed Chapels in *San Lorenzo in Damasco*, Rome (1732-6), and *Santa Lucia*, Porto Fiumicino (1735).

Fasolo (1949); Grioni (1975); JWCI, xxxvii (1974), 218-48; Zocca (1959)

Ruskin, John (1819-1900) English academic/critic, who had an enormous influence not only on architectural style but on the ways in which standards of aesthetics were judged. He used an Evangelical/polemical tone in his writings that not only reached a mass audience but received Ecclesiological approval. He contributed to *Loudon's earlier publications, but his key works date from the late 1840s and 1850s. The *Gothic Revival was well-established when Ruskin published *The Seven Lamps of Architecture* (1849): an immediate success, it encapsulated the mood of the period rather than creating new ideas. He argued that architecture should be true, with no hidden structure, no veneers or finishes, and no carvings made by machines, and, (absurdly) that Beauty in architecture was only possible if inspired by Nature. As exemplars worthy of imitation (he argued that existing styles were quite sufficient, and that no new style was necessary) he arbitrarily selected Pisan *Romanesque, early *Gothic of Western Italy, *Venetian Gothic, and English early *Second Pointed as his paradigms. In the choice of the last, the style of the late C13 and early C14, he was echoing A.W.N.*Pugin's preferences as well as that of most ecclesiologically-minded Gothic Revivalists. *The Stones of Venice* (1851-3) helped to promote that phase of the Gothic Revival in which Continental (especially Venetian) Gothic predominated. *Deane and *Woodward's University Museum, Oxford (1854-60), is an example of Venetian or *Ruskinian*

Gothic. In particular, structural *polychromy, featuring colour in the material used, rather than applied, was popularized by Ruskin's writings. The *Stones* also contained a section on the nature of Gothic in which Ruskin argued that the admirable qualities of medieval architecture were related to the commitment, creative pride, and freedom of the craftsmen who worked on the buildings. From this idea *Morris developed his theories, and the *Arts-and-Crafts movement began to evolve.

Ruskin found certain styles (e.g. *Baroque) unacceptable because they exploited illusion, and therefore were not 'truthful'. This moral disapprobation to justify an aesthetic stance has been a dangerous weapon in the hands of *International Modernists: *Gropius, for example, *claimed* to have been influenced by Ruskin's writings, something which would have surprised, even shocked, the man himself.

Batchelor (2001); Bell (1978); Blau (1982); M.Brooks (1987); J.Curl (2007); R.Daniels & Brandwood (eds) (2003); Hewison (1976); Hi (1954); *ODNB* (2004); Pe (1969, 1972); Ruskin (1903–12); Sw (1989); D.Wa (1977); Mi.Wheeler & Whiteley (eds) (1992)

rustic, rustick 1. Species of *masonry characterized by surfaces artificially roughened or left rough-hewn, or by having the joints, notably the horizontal ones, emphasized by being deeply sunk or chamfered. *See also* RUSTICATION. 2. Simple, plain, unrefined, and made of rough materials (e.g. roughly-hewn tree-trunks), to suggest *rural architecture or the *Picturesque. *Used with other words, examples are*:

rustic arch: *arch constructed of *rubble in e.g. *rock-work;

rustic brick: facing-brick with surfaces improved by a sand covering or with a scratched texture applied before firing, often with variegated colouring;

rustic joint: in masonry a joint emphasized by the chamfering of the *arrises of the stones;

rustic quoin: at the external angle of a building, one of several stone *quoins with its face roughened and raised (e.g. by chamfering or simply by having a *rock-faced surface surrounded by chamfers) so that it projects beyond the *naked of the wall;

rustic slate: one of many *slates of different thickness imparting a varied uneven appearance to a roof or wall;

rustic stone: *see* RUBBLE.

rustic woodwork: poles and roughly sawn timber with the bark adhering to it used in timber buildings intended to look like humble *rural architecture such as *cottages ornés*, *gazebos, etc., often with decorative touches such as *lattice-windows, twisted *chimneys, thatched roofs, and ornamental fencing and *bargeboards.

rusticated column 1. Column with blocks of plain *ashlar at intervals the length of the *shaft, called a *banded* column. 2. The same, but with the blocks treated with *rustication.

rustication In *masonry, stone cut in such a way that the joints are sunk in some sort of channel, the faces of the stones projecting beyond them. In addition, those faces are usually roughened to form a contrast with ordinary dressed *ashlar. Rusticated masonry enhances the visual impact of *keystones, *plinths, *quoins, and even entire storeys, while its application to *façades can suggest power, solidity, and even the *Sublime. *Rusticating* is the carving or creation of rustication, or the making of a texture on a face. *Types of rustication include*:

banded: plain or textured ashlar with horizontal joints only grooved, giving the impression of a series of *bands;

chamfered: with each ashlar chamfered to create **V**-shaped joints, either all round each stone or, if at the tops and bottoms, to create *banded* rustication with chamfers;

channelled: with a rectangular sunken channel at the joints, formed horizontally only or round each stone;

congelated: *see* FROSTED;

cyclopean: *rock-faced or *quarry-faced ashlar with dressed projecting rough faces, as though recently taken from the quarry, giving a massive, powerful, impregnable effect particularly useful for plinths, *piers of *viaducts, etc.;

diamond-pointed: with ashlar blocks cut with chamfered faces giving the effect in a wall of a series of small *pyramids or hipped roofs set on their sides, also called *prismatic* or *pyramidal* rustication;

frosted or *frostwork*: carved to look like icicles or stalactites, also called *congelated* rustication, normally found on *fountains, in *grottoes, or other situations associated with water;

reticulated: carved with indentations leaving the surface connected in an irregular net-like pattern;

rock-faced: as *cyclopean*;

smooth: with joints clearly shown by some means (e.g. channels or **V**-joints) but the faces flat and plain;

V-jointed: as *chamfered*;

vermiculated: with the face carved as though eaten away in parts, with irregular worm-like tracks and holes all over it, reminiscent of wood or sand.

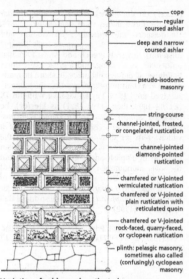

cope
regular coursed ashlar
deep and narrow coursed ashlar
pseudo-isodomic masonry
string-course
channel-jointed, frosted, or congelated rustication
channel-jointed diamond-pointed rustication
chamfered or V-jointed vermiculated rustication
chamfered or V-jointed plain rustication with reticulated quoin
chamfered or V-jointed rock-faced, quarry-faced, or cyclopean rustication
plinth: pelasgic masonry, sometimes also called (confusingly) cyclopean masonry

Varieties of ashlar and rusticated masonry.

Ruusuvuori, Aarno Emil (1925–92) Finnish architect, his work was at first firmly established in *International Modernism and in the 1960s continued in *Rationalism and became more ascetic as *Brutalism was embraced. He often favoured stereometrically pure shapes, such as cubes and *pyramids, as in his Hyvinkää Church and Parish Centre (1961). Other works include the extensions and renovations of the City Hall, Helsinki (1970–84), and proposals for extending the National Museum, Helsinki (1987).

E (1994); K-S (1964); Leiman (ed.) (2000); Salokorpi (1970); Tempel (1968)

Ruys, Wilhelmina Jacoba (Mien) Moussault- (1904–99) Dutch landscape architect, influenced at first by the English *Arts-and-Crafts movement, *Jekyll, and William *Robinson, she veered Leftwards and became involved with *De Stijl and *CIAM. From 1924 she established experimental gardens at Dedemsvaart as a permanent exhibition of model gardens, and, with her husband, **Theodorus Aloisius Maria Moussault** (1888–1974), she published *Onze Eigen Tuin* (Our Own Garden) from 1955, a quarterly gardening magazine, and brought out numerous publications, including *Het nieuwe vaste planten boek* (The New Perennial Book—1973). With *Bijhouwer she wrote *Leven met groen* (Living with Greenery—1960), and (with Rosette Zaandvoort)

Van vensterbank tot landschap (From Window-Cill to Landscape—1981) which summarized her theories and observations on garden-design. A pioneer of the *New Perennial Movement, she carried out over 3,000 commissions, including the *cemetery at Nagele, Noordoostpolder (1956).

She (2001); Tay (2006); A.Wilson (2005)

Ruysbroeck, Jan van (c.1396–1486) Flemish architect of the *spire (c.1449–55) of Brussels Town Hall, one of the most elegant creations of late-medieval *Gothic secular European architecture. Other works include the *lavatorium, Hospital of Our Lady, Oudenaarde (1442–5); the tower of *Ste-Gertrude*, Leuven, (completed 1453); and part of *Sts Pierre & Guido*, Anderlecht, Brussels (1479–85). He worked on the Cathedral, Brussels (1470–85), but on what is not known. To confuse matters, he is also known as **Jan van den Berghe**.

Białostocki (1972); Duverger (1933); J.T (1996)

Ryder, John Gordon (1919–2000) Founder (1953), with **Peter Yates** (1920–82), of the firm of English architects, **Ryder & Yates**. They joined (1948) *Lubetkin's team (which included **Frank Purser Tindall** (1919–98)) in the planning of Peterlee New Town, Co. Durham, but stifling postwar bureaucracy and other frustrations led to the resignation of Lubetkin and his colleagues, and Ryder established (1950) his own practice, joined (1953) by Yates. The firm soon evolved into a multi-disciplinary organization of architects and engineers, designing numerous houses before taking on larger projects, including the Norgas Headquarters (1965), the Engineering Research Station for British Gas (1967), and the Northern Gas Training Centre (1970—much altered), all in Killingworth. From the 1960s the firm was regarded as one of the most progressive in North-East England.

Carroll (2009); Tindall (1998); C20 Soc. *Newsletter* (Spring, May 2001), 22-3; pk

Ry, Paul du (1640–1714) French-Huguenot architect: his grandfather, **Charles** (*before* 1568–*after* 1638), was related to and worked with de *Brosse, and his father, **Mathurin** (d.1674), was Court Architect in Paris. **Paul** trained with N.-F. *Blondel, worked as a military-engineer on fortifications at Maastricht, The Netherlands (from 1665), and, after the Revocation (1685) of the *Edict of Nantes* (1598), was called by **Landgrave Karl of Hesse-Kassel** (r.1670–1730) to design new settlements (the fabric of which was destroyed or badly damaged in the 1939–45 war), including the *Oberneustadt* (Upper New Town), Kassel, for Huguenot refugees. This modest and humanely scaled development in *Baroque and Classical styles had the octagonal *Karlskirche* (1698–1710) as one of its main foci. He also built the *Gartenpalais* and Palace of **Prince Wilhelm** (1682–1760), and designed the town of Karlshafen, Hesse (1699–1720—largely intact). His son, **Charles-Louis** (1692–1757), succeeded his father as *Oberhofbaumeister* and continued the development of the *Oberneustadt*, designing the *canal-system (1739).

Colombier (1955); Diffscheid (1983); Gerland (1895); E.Hempel (1965); J.T (1996)

Ry, Simon Louis (Ludwig) du (1726–96) Son of **Charles-Louis du Ry** (1692–1757), he studied (1746–8) with *Hårleman and J.-F.*Blondel (1752) before settling in Kassel, where he worked for **Landgrave Wilhelm VIII** (*r*.1751–60—who sent him to Italy (1753–6) for further study) and then for **Landgrave Friedrich II** (*r*.1760–85), creating an urban fabric that survived until its destruction in the 1939–45 war. He further developed the *Oberneustadt* originally designed by his grandfather (completed 1776), and linked it (by means of handsome urban spaces

(*places*) on the French model) to the *Altstadt* after the fortifications were demolished (1767). He designed the *Museum Fridericianum* and observatory (1769–79—a purpose-built library/ museum), in which French and Anglo-Palladian influences were strong, and a great many other buildings, all of them of quality. In short, he made of Kassel a charming *Residenzstadt*, which largely survived until 1945. For **Landgrave Wilhelm IX** (*r*.1785–1803, then (1803–1821) as **Elector**), he designed *Schloss Weissenstein* (later *Wilhelmshöhe*), near Kassel (1786–90), the side *wings of which were set diagonally, responding to the landscape beyond: it is a great work of *Classicism inspired by English and French exemplars, but the over-monumental *corps-de-logis* (1791–8) was by *Jussow. He may have designed some of the *fabriques* in the park, and was responsible for the *Ionic *monopteron* marking the spring at Bad Hofgeismar (1792).

Boehlke (1958, 1980); Both & H.Vogel (1973); Dittscheid (1987); Keller (1971); Paetow (1929); P (1982); J.T (1996); Wa & M (1987)

Saarinen, Eero (1910–61) Finnish-born American architect, son of G.E.*Saarinen, he worked with *Eames at Kingswood, *Cranbrook, MI, G.E. Saarinen's Academy, designing furniture. He joined (1937) his father at Ann Arbor, MI, and from 1941 was in partnership with him before setting up (1950) his own practice as **Eero Saarinen & Associates**, having won the competition (1947–8) to design the Jefferson Memorial Park, St Louis, MO, with *Kiley. At first, his architecture was in the *International-Modern style, notably his General Motors Technical Center, Warren, MI (1947–56), designed in collaboration with his father and others, but later, as with many American architects, he attempted to extend the design-vocabulary yet leave buildings valid in terms of so-called *Functionalism. At the Kresge Auditorium, Massachusetts Institute of Technology (MIT), Cambridge, MA (1952–6), the roof was based on a triangular segment of a sphere: the ensemble was criticized for straying from *Modernist principles yet not going far enough to create a new paradigm. Le *Corbusier's chapel at Ronchamp (1950–4) was a precedent for more emotional architecture, and Saarinen was in the vanguard of this tendency in the USA. Although championed by *Hitchcock et al., however, his work, with a multiplicity of shapes and a paucity of ideas, soon dated. For MIT he experimented with massive brick walls at the circular chapel (1952–6), and at Concordia Senior College, Fort Wayne, IN, he also designed the chapel, this time with a pointed roof (1953–8). At the David S.Ingalls Ice Hockey Rink, Yale University, New Haven, CT (1953–9), he spanned the length of the building with a great central arch carrying the curved roof-structure. This was followed by the TWA Terminal Building at Kennedy International Airport, NYC (1956–62), with sail-like vaulted roofs rising from dynamically shaped *piers, supposedly expressive of wings and flight. The Thomas J.Watson Research Center, Yorktown, NY (1957–61), also exploited curves, to be used again at Dulles International Airport, Chantilly, VA, near Washington, DC (1958–63). With the Ezra Stiles and Morse Colleges, Yale University (1958–62), the composition is stepped on *plan and vertical *section, and he used a fragmented, layered geometry

for the treatment of the *façades of the US Embassy, Grosvenor Square, London (1955–60—built in collaboration with *Yorke, Rosenberg, & Mardall). He also collaborated with Kiley, and his practice was continued by Roche and *Dinkeloo.

Gaidos (ed.) (1972); Kuhner (1975); Román (2002); A.Saarinen (ed.) (1968); Spade (1971); Temko (1962); J.T (1996)

Saarinen, Gottlieb Eliel (1873–1950) Finnish-born American architect, he practised (1896–1905) with *Gesellius and *Lindgren, and with Gesellius only until 1907, when he worked on his own, emigrating to the USA (1923). He established an office at Evanston, IL (1923–4), later (1924) moving to Ann Arbor, MI, where he also taught at the School of Architecture, University of Michigan. The firm was joined (1937) by his son, Eero *Saarinen, and then by **J.Robert Swanson** (1900–81), who was a partner (1941–47). His early work in Finland was in the *National-Romantic style to express Finnish identity (when *Neo-Classicism was perceived as the architectural language of Tsarist Russia), and was influenced by late *Gothic-Revival, English *Arts-and-Crafts architecture, and contemporary work in the USA, notably the round-arched buildings of H.H.*Richardson. Saarinen, Gesellius, and Lindgren designed the Finnish Pavilion for the *Exposition Universelle*, Paris (1900), adding touches of vaguely oriental exoticism. Influences from the Vienna *Sezession* were apparent in the Hvitträsk Studio House, Kirkkonummi, near Helsinki (begun 1902), designed for the firm as an idealistic variation on English Arts-and-Crafts themes, with a strong input of American *vernacular, *Shingle style, *Jugendstil*, and national Finnish elements. Saarinen himself won (1904) the competition to design the Helsinki Central Railway Station (erected 1910–14), one of the finest *termini* of the period, comparable with Leipzig (1905) and Stuttgart (1911—which was influenced by the Helsinki exemplar), having massive *masonry walls and a noble composition strongly influenced by the school of Otto *Wagner and the work of the *Wiener Werkstätte*, notably *Hoffmann. He came second in the competition to design the *Chicago Tribune Building* (1922), which made his name in the USA and led to the commission to design the *Cranbrook Academy of Art, Bloomfield Hills, MI. Saarinen designed the Cranbrook School for Boys (1926–30) and the Kingswood School for Girls (1929–30) there, followed by the Institute of Science (1931–3), and Museum and Library (1940–3). This series of *Picturesque buildings was evolved in collaboration with his second wife, **Louise (Loja) Gesellius** (1879–1968), and is freely eclectic, incorporating Expressionist, round-arched, and vernacular elements. He was President of the Cranbrook Academy of Art (1932–42), and was joined by his son, **Eero**, and by *Eames, who both taught there. His published works include *The Search for Form in Art and Architecture* (1985).

Christ-Janner (1979); Gaidos (ed.) (1972); Hausen *et al.* (1990); L (1988); P (1982); E.Saarinen (1931, 1943, 1948); J.T (1996)

Sacchetti, Giovanni Battista (1690–1764) Italian architect, taught by *Juvarra, he assisted his master by building models, preparing drawings, and compiling an important list of his works. He designed several temporary funerary structures for the House of Savoy, and oversaw (from 1734), the building of Juvarra's *San Filippo*, Turin. Sacchetti settled (1736) in Spain where he continued Juvarra's work on the garden-front of the *Palacio Granja*, San Ildefonso, Segovia (1736–42). Sacchetti also worked (1738–64) on the Royal Palace, Madrid, where he expanded Juvarra's proposals, influenced in part by *Bernini's unrealized designs for the Louvre, Paris: it must be ranked among the greatest architectural achievements of the period.

Brayda *et al.* (1966); Ferrero (1970); K & S (1959); P (1982); Pommer (1967); Popelka (1994); J.T (1996)

Sacconi, Count Giuseppe (1854–1905) Italian architect, he designed the elegant *façade of the *Palazzo delle Assicurazioni Generale, Piazza Venezia*, Rome (1902–7) and, as Superintendent of Monuments in Ascoli Piceno and Umbria (1891–1905), carried out many works of preservation/renovation in those regions and in Rome itself. He reconstructed *San Francesco*, Force (1878–83), and restored the *Duomo* of *Sant'Emidio* (1888–90), both Ascoli Piceno, among many other buildings. He is remembered primarily for the gigantic Neo-Classical monument to **Vittorio Emanuele II** (1820–78—**King of Sardinia** from 1848 and **King of Italy** from 1861), a huge pile-up of *masonry (called 'The Typewriter' by irreverent Romans) dwarfing the Capitoline Hill in Rome, much altered after Sacconi's death by others, including G.*Koch and P.*Piacentini. Among his other works may be cited the *quadriportico* of *San Paolo fuori le Mura*, Rome (1893–1910—with *Calderini), the tomb of the assassinated **King Umberto**

I (*r.*1878–1900) in the Pantheon, Rome (completed 1910), and the Expiatory Chapel in memory of Umberto in Monza (1910).

Accasto *et al.* (1971); Acciaresi (1911); David (1990); Maranesi (1929); Ms (1966); Morosini (1929); P (1982); Pi (1968); J.T (1996)

sacellum 1. Small enclosed space or chapel in *Antique Rome where the *lares* and *penates* were venerated, often treated as an *aedicule, called *lararium*. **2.** *Chantry-, *mortuary-, or any other small chapel in a church defined by a *screen. **3.** Unroofed enclosed space associated with an Ancient-Egyptian *temple, or found in Roman architecture in connection with religious rites.

Sackville-West, Victoria (Vita) Mary (1892–1962) English gardener/writer: with her husband, **Sir Harold George Nicolson** (1886–1968), she created celebrated gardens at Sissinghurst Castle, near Cranbrook, Kent (from 1930), retaining and enhancing the formal remains of C16 fabric, and adding informal planting. Individual sections of the garden (influenced by the work of *Lutyens and **Lawrence Johnston** (1871–1958—at Hidcote, Glos.)) were distinguished by colour-schemes (e.g. the 'white garden'), yet they were linked by means of walls, paths, routes, etc. She wrote columns on gardening for *The Observer* (1946–61), material collected and published in book-form. Her vision and sense of the *genius loci*, combined with knowledge of plants and appreciation of colour, informed her skills as a practical gardener.

J.Brown (1987); *ODNB* (2004); Sackville-West (1951, 1953, 1955, 1958); Tay (2006)

sacrarium 1. *Antique chapel, *sacellum, or *shrine. **2.** *Cella or *adytum of a Roman *temple. **3.** That part of the *chancel or *choir in the vicinity of the *high-altar, normally defined by altar-rails, i.e. the *sanctuary. **4.** *Piscina in a church. **5.** *Sacristy.

sacristy *or* **sacristy** Church *vestry near the *chancel in which ecclesiastical garments, utensils used in the services, etc., are stored. It may also be used for meetings.

saddle 1. Cap of a door-*cill or the bottom part of a *door-frame. **2.** Thin timber board, or *threshold, sloping slightly on each side, fixed on the floor between the *jambs. **3.** Short length of structural timber fixed to the tops of two *cruck *blades, forming the flattened top to a ∧ shape, and providing a support for the *ridge-piece. **4.** Any ∧-shaped form suggesting a saddle in *section, usually a splayed capping for a *ridge or a *cope-stone. *Compounds include*:
saddle-back: **1.** *pack-saddle* roof; **2.** cope of triangular *section with a central ridge and slopes on either side;

667   **Salmon, James**

saddle-bar: iron bar fixed horizontally in window-openings to which the *cames of stained-glass windows are fixed to help to support the structure of the leaded *lights;

saddle-board: *comb-* or *ridge-board* at the ridge of a pitched roof;

saddle-coping: saddle-back cope;

saddle-stone: upper or crowning piece of the cope of a *gable. *Apex stone.

Sáenz de Oíza, Francisco Javier (1918-2000) Spanish architect, he won the competition for the Arántzazu *basilica (1949—with **Luis Laorga Gutiérrez**). Shortly afterwards he moved towards acceptance of the *Modern Movement, and in the 1950s his work became openly eclectic, drawing on the works of *Aalto, L.I.*Kahn, and F.L.L.*Wright, leading to his exuberant *Torres Blancas* apartments, Madrid (1959-68). Sophisticated technology was employed in his *Banco de Bilbao*, Madrid (1972-81), and other works include the *Centro Atlántico de Arte Moderno*, Las Palmas (1989), and the massive cylindrical *Torre Triana*, Seville (1993).

AR, clxxix/1071 (May 1986), 47–9; DomenechGirbau (1968); E (1994); P (1982); Sáenz de Oíza *et al.* (1996)

safe-deposit Safe storage for valuables, sometimes with architectural pretensions.

sag To bend or curve downwards in the middle, from pressure or an object's own weight, e.g. *festoon or *swag.

sagitta *Keystone in an arch.

sahn *Court in a *mosque, often surrounded by *arcades, and with a *fountain (*meda*) in the middle (e.g. Mosque of *Ibn Tulun*, Cairo (876-9)).

sail-dome See DOME; VAULT.

sail-over *Jetty or element projecting beyond the *naked of the wall below.

sail-vault See DOME; VAULT.

Saint-George, James of (*fl.*1261–1309) Master-mason, probably from Piedmont (in the service of the **Counts of Savoy** (1260s)), in charge of the construction of **King Edward I**'s (*r.*1272-1307) chain of fortresses in North Wales. He superintended the building of Flint and Rhuddlan Castles, and probably designed Aberystwyth and Builth Castles (1277-82). He then designed the town walls of Conway, Caernarfon, and Denbigh (begun 1282-3), and the Castles of Conway and Harlech. To judge from his rates of pay, he was obviously held in high esteem, and in the 1290s he began to build Beaumaris Castle, Anglesea. By 1302 he was involved in securing the English stronghold of Linlithgow, Scotland, and may have designed the gatehouse at Kildrummy Castle (1303).

J.Harvey (1987)

Saint-Sepulc(h)re Chapel or *church named after Christ's Tomb.

Sakakura, Junzo (1901-69) Japanese architect, he designed the Japanese Pavilion at the *Exposition*, Paris (1937), but his devotion to Le *Corbusier (in whose office he worked (1931-6) later led to massive concrete structures, often heavily over-emphasized (e.g. City Halls, Hashima, Gifu (1959) and Kure, Hiroshima (1962)).

Altherr (1968); M & N (1987)

sala terrena Large, formal room with direct access to a garden gained by one side being open to that garden, especially in C17 and C18 grand houses, frequently embellished with *trompe l'œil* and other decorations to suggest a *grotto. A fine example is that at the Valdštejn garden, Prague (1624-7), by *Pieroni.

J.Nn (1970)

salient, saliant 1. Projection, *jetty, or *sail-over. **2.** Angle pointing outwards, i.e. opposite of a *re-entrant, e.g. gun-emplacement in a fortification.

sally 1. As *salient. **2.** Notch cut in the end of a piece of timber used at the lower ends of inclined timbers, e.g. *rafters.

sally-port *Postern- or side-gate, or a subterranean passage, between the inner and outer works of a fortification, used by defenders to sally forth.

Salmon, James (1873-1924) Scots architect, pupil of **William Leiper** (1839-1916), he was in partnership in Glasgow with his father, **William Forrest Salmon** (1843-1911), from c.1890. The firm was joined by **John Gaff Gillespie** (1870-1926), and became **Salmon, Son, & Gillespie** until 1913. His work had more in common with Continental *Art Nouveau than any of his contemporaries in Scotland (including *Mackintosh). While with Leiper, he worked under **William James Anderson** (1864-1900) on the Italian-*Gothic Templeton Carpet Factory, Glasgow Green (1888-92), and the *François-Ier Sun Life Assurance Building, 38-42 Renfield Street, Glasgow (1889-93). Salmon's best building on his own account was the Mercantile Chambers, Bothwell Street (1896-7), at the time one of the largest steel-framed office-blocks in the city, with sculpture by **Francis Derwent Wood** (1871-1926). He is best remembered for 142-4 St Vincent Street (1898-1900), known as the 'Hatrack' because of the peg-like forms of its exterior: in this remarkably complex building, the entire *façade of which is *cantilevered from an internal steel frame, the external stone *dressings are reduced to a minimum, and most of the details are Art Nouveau in style. Other works include elegant restorations at 79 West Regent Street (1900-4). His Lion Chambers, 170-2 Hope Street (1904-6), used *reinforced-concrete construction based on the *Hennebique system. The firm transmogrified into *Gillespie, Kidd, & Coia.

AH, xxv, (1982), 114–19; DW; A.S.Gray (1985); G & W (1987); O'Donnell (2003); RIBAJ, ser. 3, xcvii/8 (Aug. 1990), 35–40; Se (ed.) (1975); J.T (1996)

Salomónica See SOLOMONIC.

Salomons, Edward (1827–1906) English architect, practising in Manchester, he designed the Reform Club there, in King Street (1870–1), in a symmetrical *Venetian-Gothic-Revival style. Among his works the Crystal Palace, Trafford Park (1856–7—destroyed), the Savings Bank, Booth Street (1872), and the *Saracenic-Moresque Synagogue, Cheetham Hill Road (1874), all in Manchester, may be cited. In London, with **Ralph Selden Wornum** (1847–1910), he designed Agnew's, Nos 42–3 Old Bond Street (1876–8) in the early *Queen-Anne style, and for the same firm, in Dale Street, Liverpool, at the corner of Castle Street, the brick portion with carved ornament.

D & M (1985); Hartwell et al. (2004)

salon, saloon 1. Large, high room, frequently with a vaulted ceiling, and often of double height (i.e. rising the equivalent of two *storeys), serving as one of the principal reception-rooms in a *palace or great house, or as a means of communication through which the main rooms can be reached (called salone in Italian). Sometimes it was circular or elliptical on plan. 2. Large apartment or hall, especially in an *hôtel or other place frequented by the public, adapted for assemblies, entertainments, exhibitions, etc. 3. Public room for a specific purpose, e.g. billiards, dancing, or drinking (saloon-bar) 4. Drawing-room in a house.

Salvart, Jehan (fl.1390s–1447) French master-mason, appointed Master at Rouen Cathedral (1398), he reconstructed (1407) the west portal and enlarged the *choir windows (1430). He was City Architect of Rouen from 1432.

S (1901–2)

Salvi, Nicola (1697–1751) Italian architect, accomplished in *scenography. In the 1730s he entered the architectural competitions arranged by **Pope Clement XII** (r.1730–40), and won that to build the Trevi Fountain (1732–7), his masterpiece, based on a *triumphal arch, the whole composition set on a *rock-work base. He remodelled the interior of Santa Maria dei Gradi, Viterbo (1737), designed the Chapel of St John, St Roch, Lisbon, Portugal (1742), and extended *Bernini's Palazzo Chigi-Odescalchi, Rome (1745).

Onofrio (1957); Pinto (1986); Schavo (1956); J.T (1996)

Salvin, Anthony (1799–1881) English architect, pupil of **John Paterson** (fl.1777–1832), of Edinburgh, with whom he worked on the restoration of Brancepeth Castle, Durham (1817–21). He designed Mamhead, Devon (1826–38—a mansion in the *Tudor style), and established a reputation as an architect of country-houses. His masterpiece is undoubtedly Harlaxton Manor, Lincs. (1831–8), a lavish pile in the *Jacobethan style, at once learned yet inventive, with a heavy *Baroque staircase inside designed by William *Burn. Scotney Castle, Lamberhurst, Kent (1837–44), was a reinterpretation of a more modest C17 manor-house type with cunning massing that made the building look as though it had been added to at various times for the sake of convenience. His Peckforton Castle, Ches. (1844–50), was a brilliant evocation of a C13 castle, conveniently planned, and truly *Picturesque. He took part in the important redecorations of Christ Church, Kilndown, Kent (from 1839), which transformed the *chancel in accordance with the ideals of *Ecclesiology, and indeed was one of the first of its kind in England. He was an authority on English medieval military architecture, and worked on the Tower of London and various castles, including Alnwick, Caernarfon, Durham, Rockingham, Warwick, and Windsor. He built many churches as well as country-houses, ending with the fanciful *Jacobethan Thoresby Hall, Notts. (1864–75). His pupils included Eden *Nesfield, J.L.*Pearson, and R.N.*Shaw.

Ae (1988); D & M (1985); Ea (1970); Hussey (1958); Marsh (ed.) (1999); J.T (1996); J.F.White (1962)

Salvisberg, Otto Rudolf (1882–1940) Swiss-born architect. He settled in Berlin (1908), where he designed the vaguely Expressionist *concrete Lindenhaus, Berlin-Kreuzberg (1912–13). Some of his early works, however, contained eclectic references influenced, perhaps, by the ideas of Camillo *Sitte. Many of his *villas in and around Berlin were influenced by *Jugendstil and *Expressionism, as well as by the *Arts-and-Crafts movement publicized by *Muthesius. In the mid-1920s he adopted *Modern-Movement stances, designing several houses in Berlin-Zehlendorf under the overall direction of Bruno *Taut (1926–31). One of his most luxurious houses was the Villa Flechtheim, Berlin-Grünewald (1928–9). He also designed the Gross-Siedlung Schiller-promenade, Weisse-Stadt development, Berlin-Reinickendorf (1929–31). In 1930 he succeeded Karl *Moser as Professor at the Eidgenössische Technische Hochschule (ETH), Zürich, Switzerland, and designed numerous works, including university buildings, Bern (1930–1), the Machine Laboratory and Heating Plant, ETH (1930–3), and the Hoffman-La Roche Administration Building and Factories, Basel (1936–40), all in a severely rational manner. He was responsible for the Roche Products Factory, Welwyn *Garden City, Herts., England (1939).

Platz (1927); Salvisberg (2000); Wertheim (ed.) (1927)

Sambin, Hugues (c.1520–1601) French architect/sculptor/engineer. Familiar with the works of du *Cerceau and *Vredeman de Vries, as is clear from his portals on the *Palais de Justice*, Dijon (1583), other works attributed to him include *Hôtel Milsand, Rue des Forges* (1561), *Maison Chasseret*, 8 *Rue Stephen-Liègeard* (1560), and *Hôtel le Compasseur*, 66 *Rue Vannerie* (1560s), all in Dijon, and the *Palais de Justice*, Besançon. A master of French *Mannerism, his work was influential. He published *Œuvre de la Diversité des Termes* (dealing with types of *term—1572).

Bt (1982); Castan (1891); Ha (1948); J.T (1996)

Samonà, Giuseppe (1898–1983) Italian architect/town-planner, his prolific output embraced *Expressionism, *eclecticism, *International Modernism, Italian *Rationalism, and much else. He won many architectural competitions during the Fascist era, including that for the Post Office in the Appio Quarter of Rome (1933–6). He was Director (1945–71) of the *Istituto Universitario di Architettura*, Venice, and published much on urban planning. He prepared housing-schemes for several Italian cities including Mestre (1951–6) and Palermo (1956–8), and designed the *Banco d'Italia*, Padua (1968), and the Theatre, Sciacca, Sicily (1974–9).

Aymonino (ed.) (1975a); E (1994); Lovero (ed.) (1975); J.T (1996); Tentori (1996)

Samuely, Felix James (1902–59) Vienna-born Berlin-based engineer (where he collaborated with a number of architects including Arthur *Korn), he settled (1933) in London, and was invited by *Arup to prepare calculations for the Penguin Pool at London Zoo, designed by *Lubetkin: he subsequently joined **J.L.Kier & Co.** on a permanent basis. He also worked with *Mendelsohn and *Chermayeff on the De La Warr Pavillion, Bexhill-on-Sea, Sussex (1934–5), and with numerous other *Modern-Movement architects.

ODNB (2004)

sanatorium 1. Hospital for consumptives or convalescents. 2. Place with an agreeable climate (e.g. hill-station in a hot country) to which invalids and others can resort, i.e. a health-station.

Sancte-cote See BELL-COTE.

Sanctis, Francesco de' (c.1693–1731) Italian architect, best known for one of the most important commissions in C18 Rome, the Spanish Steps (1723–6), linking the *Piazza di Spagna*

to *Santissima Trinità dei Monti*, a master-work of fluid *Baroque urban planning. He also designed the *façade of *Trinità dei Pellegrini*, Rome (1722).

Mallory (1977); Pi (1970); *RJfK*, **xii** (1969), 39–94.

sanctuary 1. Especially holy place within a *church or *temple 2. *Sacrarium, or part of a church in the vicinity of the *high-altar. 3. *Chancel or *presbytery.
sanctuary-garden: 1. piece of consecrated ground, e.g. churchyard; 2. garden used for retreat, for emotional/spiritual rejuvenation/well-being, where inner harmony may be reclaimed. Associated with ideals, e.g. the Garden of Eden, the lost *Paradise garden, and with symbolism, e.g. the *hortus conclusus*, it also has parallels with concepts such as *feng shui and *Zen philosophy. See CHINESE GARDEN-DESIGN; JAPANESE GARDEN-DESIGN; ISLAMIC, MONASTERY, MUGHAL, PHILOSOPHER'S, SCHOLAR'S GARDEN.

Dee (2001); Shoe (2001); Streep (1999)

Sanctus bell-cote See BELL-COTE.

Sandby, Thomas (1721–98) English architect/surveyor, he served in the entourage of **Prince William Augustus** (1721–65—**Duke of Cumberland** from 1726). Appointed Deputy to the Duke in his capacity as Ranger of Windsor Great Park, he acquired financial security, and was assisted by his brother, **Paul Sandby** (1731–1809), in his landscape-gardening activities, including the creation of Virginia Water and several *grottoes and artificial *ruins (completed 1785): these works were published (1754, reissued in 1772). Sandby was appointed Architect of the King's Works in succession to Sir Robert *Taylor, and was one of the original Royal Academicians (1768), first Professor of Architecture, and an honorary member of the newly founded Architects' Club (1791). He designed Freemasons' Hall, Queen Street, Lincoln's Inn Fields (1775–6—demolished 1932), the *Gothic *wainscoting around the *altar of St George's Chapel, Windsor (1782), and the splendid Luttrell's Folly, Eaglehurst, Hants. (c.1780), crenellated and with elegant *Gothick touches.

Co (2008); J.Curl (2011); B.Jones (1974); *ODNB* 2004

Sanders, John (1768–1826) Pupil of *Soane from 1784, he established his own practice (1790), becoming (from 1794) architect to the Barrack Department of the War Office with James *Johnson. His works included the Royal Military Asylum (later the Duke of York's Barracks) at Chelsea (1801–3), and the Royal Military College, Sandhurst, Berks. (1808–12—originally designed by James *Wyatt—with a Greek-*Doric *portico). He retired early, and travelled (1817–19) on the Continent, employing **William Purser** (1788–*after* 1834) as his draughtsman. They met

G.L.*Taylor and *Cresy in Marseilles, and explored the lands around the Mediterranean, measuring and drawing many artefacts, including the *Gothic buildings of Sicily. They discovered (1818) the marble Lion of Chaeronea in Boeotia (c.338BC).

Co (2008); Douet (1998); W.Pa (1887); G.L.Taylor (1870–2)

Sanderson, John (fl.1725–74) English architect, he designed several conventional *Georgian country-houses, and assisted other architects in drawing up detailed plans: among them were Sanderson *Miller, Thomas *Prowse, and Theodore *Jacobsen. His designs for Stratton Park, Hants. (1731), were illustrated in Vitruvius Britannicus (1767), but the building was partly demolished in C18, remodelled (1803–6) by *Dance, and destroyed (1960—see GARDINER). Other works by him included Barrington Hall, Hatfield Broadoak, Essex (c.1735–40—remodelled 1863 in *Jacobean style by Edward Browning (1816–82)); St John's Church, Hampstead (1745–7—much altered and extended); Kirtlington Park, Oxon. (1747–8—with William *Smith, indebted to *Gibbs); Langley Park, Norfolk (c.1750–5—with Prowse); Copped Hall, Essex (1752–8—with *Newdigate and Prowse); completion of the Radcliffe Infirmary, Oxford (1766–70—after the death of *Leadbetter); and the monument to Humphry Smith (d.1743) in Ely Cathedral, Cambs. (carved by Charles Stanley (1703–61), who collaborated with Sanderson on several country-house interiors).

Co (2008); J.Curl (2011a); Woolfe & Gandon (1767–71), pls. 52–5

sandstone Sedimentary rock composed of consolidated sand or grit bound together, with a high silica or calcite content. It can be soft and easily damaged by rain, etc., or it can be very hard. It has a good range of colours, varying from the blue and brown Appleton stones from Yorks. to the salmon-pink Locharbriggs stone from Dumfries, or the red Woolton stone from Liverpool.

W.McKay (1957)

Sandys, Francis (fl.1788–1814) Irish-born architect, he was in the service of Frederick Augustus Hervey (1730–1803—Bishop of Derry from 1768 and 4th Earl of Bristol from 1779), at whose expense he travelled in Italy (1791–6). He built (from 1796) the Earl-Bishop's Palace at Ickworth, Suffolk, consisting of a *Pantheon-domed elliptical *rotunda connected to wings by *quadrants, and apparently based on a design by Mario Asprucci (1764–1804). Ickworth had a predecessor in the Earl-Bishop's great house at Ballyscullion, Co. Londonderry (begun 1787, designed, probably, by *Shanahan, Sandys and his brother

Joseph, and possibly James *Wyatt), influenced by *Plaw's Belle Isle, Windermere (1774–5). The *portico of Ballyscullion now forms the front of St George's Parish Church, High Street, Belfast. Ickworth was a more Neo-Classical version of Ballyscullion. Sandys remained in Suffolk, in Bury St Edmunds, where he built up his practice, designing Finborough Hall, Suffolk (1795), the entrance-lodges at Chippenham Park, Cambs. (c.1800), the Assembly Rooms (now Athenaeum), Bury St Edmunds (1804), the County Gaol, Worcester (1809–13—demolished), Dorchester Bridge, Oxon. (1813–15), and the County Courts and Gaol, Durham (begun 1809 and completed (1811) by George *Moneypenny and Ignatius *Bonomi after Sandys was dismissed following his loss of a legal action by the Durham Magistrates). This event seems to have ended his career by 1814.

Co (2008); Rankin (1972)

Sanfelice, Ferdinando (1675–1748) Neapolitan architect, he was celebrated for *scenographic effects, especially in his staircases, as at the Palazzo Sanfelice, Naples (1723–8), a late-*Baroque arcuated structure between the *cortile and the garden. He designed the scalinata (flight of steps) in front of San Giovanni a Carbonara, Naples (1708—probably a prototype of the Spanish Steps in Rome), and the Palazzo Serra di Cassano (1719–c.1730—a very free and original composition).

N-S (1986a); J.T (1996); A.Ward (1988); Wi (1982)

Sangallo, Antonio da, the Elder (c.1460–1534) Florentine *Renaissance architect/military-engineer/sculptor, also known as Antonio di Francesco di Bartolo Giamberti. The son of the wood-carver and decorator Francesco Giamberti (1404–80), he carried out many works of military-architecture, including the Papal fortress of Città Castellana (1494–7). He built the Loggia dei Servi, Florence (1517–29), giving unity to the Piazza della Santissima Annunziata opposite *Brunelleschi's Ospedale degli Innocenti. His finest architectural work was Madonna di San Biagio, Montepulciano (1518–34), a domed building on a Greek-cross plan resembling *Bramante's designs for St Peter's in Rome, originally intended to have a tower in each of the four *re-entrants formed by the arms of the cross, but only one tower was built. Each arm of the cross is barrel-vaulted, and the dome over the *crossing is carried on a drum supported by *pendentives. It may also have been influenced by Giuliano da *Sangallo's Santa Maria delle Carceri, Prato (begun 1485). For its date it has remarkable clarity, grandeur, integrity, and rigour.

Cozzi (1992); He (1996); Lotz (1977); P (1982); Satzinger (1991); J.T (1996)

Sangallo, Antonio da, the Younger (1484–1546) Aka **Antonio Cordiani**, he became one of the most distinguished architects of the *High *Renaissance in Rome in the second quarter of C16 after the death of *Raphael. He trained with his uncles **Giuliano** and **Antonio the Elder** before entering *Bramante's studio, where he worked on St Peter's. He also assisted Raphael at St Peter's and at the *Villa Madama* (1517–18). He became architect to **Cardinal Alessandro Farnese** (1468–1549—**Pope Paul III** from 1534), designing his monumental *palazzo* in Rome from 1514, a vast block with *astylar external *façades and noble *cortile* with an *assemblage of *Orders based on *Antique prototypes. The *palazzo* was completed (1546) by *Michelangelo and della *Porta, and was influential, especially during the vogue for C19 *Italianate architecture. Among his other secular works the *Palazzi Baldassini* (c.1515–22) and *Sacchetti* (1542–6), both in Rome, deserve notice. When Raphael died (1520) da Sangallo shared responsibility for St Peter's with *Peruzzi, becoming sole architect (1536). His ideas for the building are clear from the model (1538–43), with a rather busy multi-storey façade flanked by tall towers, not executed. There is no doubt that it was aesthetically unsatisfactory, and lacked the sense of Roman grandeur implicit in the Bramante and later Michelangelo schemes. He carried out many works for fortifications in the Roman region, much ecclesiastical design (e.g. the Cesi Chapel, *Santa Maria della Pace*, Rome (1530)), and various schemes for the Vatican (e.g. the Pauline Chapel (1540–6)).

C.Fr & N.Adams (eds) (1994); C.Fr (1973); Giovannoni (1959); He (1996); Lotz (1997); P (1982); Spagnesi (ed.) (1986); J.T (1996)

Sangallo, Giuliano da (1445–1516) Florentine architect/military-engineer/sculptor, born **Giuliano Giamberti**, son of **Francesco Giamberti** (1404–80), and brother of Antonio da *Sangallo the Elder. Influenced by the work of *Brunelleschi, he continued to work in that master's early *Renaissance style well into the period dominated by *Bramante and *Raphael. He was in Rome (1465) working on fortifications where he made a series of studies of *Antique remains (now in the Vatican Library and in Siena). He returned to Florence (1470s), and built the *Villa Medici*, Poggio a Caiano (c.1480–97), one of the very first *Renaissance *villas designed with conscious emulation of Antiquity in mind, notably in its arcaded terrace-platform, *Ionic pedimented porch like a *temple-front embedded in the *façade, symmetrical arrangement, and barrel-vaulted hall. He designed *Santa Maria delle Carceri*, Prato (1484–91), the first realized Renaissance church constructed on a Greek-cross plan with barrel-vaulted arms and domed drum on

pendentives over the *crossing, although the interior owed much to Brunelleschi: it influenced Antonio da Sangallo's designs for *Madonna di San Biagio*, Montepulciano (1518–34). Also influenced by Brunelleschi was the *atrium* of *Santa Maria Maddelena dei Pazzi* (c.1491–5) and the octagonal *sacristy with adjoining vestibule of *Santo Spirito* (1489–95—with *Cronaca), both in Florence. He designed the *Palazzo Gondi* (1490–1501), the façade of which is an elaboration on the *Palazzo Medici-Riccardi*, and constructed a model of the *Palazzo Strozzi* (1489–90), later realized by da *Maiano and Cronaca: that palace was very likely partly da Sangallo's design. Also by him was the *Palazzo Rovere* (or *Ateneo*), Savona (c.1494), but his hopes of preferment when his patron, **Giuliano della Rovere** (1453–1513—**Pope Julius II** from 1503), came to nothing, the plum job of St Peter's going to Bramante. Under **Giovanni de'Medici** (1475–1521—**Pope Leo X** from 1513), however, he shared the responsibility for organizing the building-works at St Peter's with Raphael and Fra *Giocondo, and seems to have had an influence on *Michelangelo's architectural development. He made several unrealized designs demonstrating a sound knowledge of Antique Classical composition, including plans for a Papal palace in the *Piazza Navona*, Rome (1513).

Bardazzi & Castellani (1981); Belluzzi (1993); S.Borsi (1985); He (1996); Huelsen (ed.) (1910); Lotz (1977); Marchini (1943); M & C (1982); P.Mu (1969, 1986); P (1982); T (1996); Tönnesmann (1983)

Sanmicheli, Michele (c.1487–1559) Italian architect/military-engineer, he studied *Antique remains in Verona, and went to Rome (early 1500s) where he learned from *Bramante's work how something of the grandeur of Ancient Rome might be recaptured. He became (1509) Superintendent of the Works at Orvieto Cathedral and built fortifications at Parma and Piacenza (1526) before returning to Verona. With the *Sangallos he is credited with the evolution of massive triangular *bastions and enormous *curtain-walls in military architecture. He applied his expertise to fortifying Verona, where he constructed the bastion of the *Maddalene* and many other impressive structures including the *rusticated gateways with the *Doric Order much in evidence (e.g. *Porta Nuova* (1533–51), *Porta San Zeno* (1547–50), and *Porta del Palio* (1548–59), the last a masterpiece of *Mannerism, with its severe Roman Doric Order in *antis *engaged with a rusticated wall-layer behind which are three recessed rusticated walls into which the gateways are set. The influence of *Giulio Romano's *Palazzo del Tè*, Mantua, is clear). He also designed the *Forte di Sant'Andrea di Lido*, Venice (1535–71). All these works were not only strong, but *looked* impregnable, as did the *façade of *Santa Maria in Organo*, Verona (1547–59).

Sanmicheli's early *palazzi* show influences from Bramante, *Raphael, and *Serlio. The *Palazzo Pompei*, Verona (c.1527–57), for example, has a rusticated ground-floor acting as a *podium for the engaged Doric Order of the *piano nobile*, a variant on Bramante's 'House of Raphael' in Rome, but with the central bay wider and *pier-*pilasters terminating the façade at both ends, thus giving the design greater serenity. At the *Palazzo Canossa*, Verona (begun c.1533), the *Palazzo del Tè* was again the influence in the rusticated base, with its triple arched openings in the centre, while Bramante's work affected the *piano nobile* with its paired *pilasters and para-phrased *serlianas. Much richer is the *Palazzo Bevilacqua*, Verona (late 1530s), with a rusticated Doric podium, the *triglyphs of which project forward as brackets supporting the *piano-nobile* *balcony over which is an elaborately complex façade designed as a series of three overlapping *triumphal arches. His *Palazzo Grimani*, Venice (1556, completed by others), employed the triumphal-arch motif in the centre of the lowest storey, while above, the perceived *naked of the wall was virtually dissolved, and the areas framed by columns and *entablatures contained complicated systems of *fenestration.

He did some ecclesiastical work, including the charming circular domed *Cappella Pellegrini* (begun 1527) at *San Bernardino*, Verona, clearly influenced by the *Pantheon in Rome. It features columns with twisted or spiral fluting which he also employed at the *Palazzo Bevilacqua*. Outside Verona he designed the circular *Madonna di Campagna* (from 1559), the drum pierced by a rhythm of 3 windows, 2 *blind arches, then 1 window, then 2 blind arches, and then 3 windows, demonstrating Sanmicheli's ability to surprise.

H.Burns *et al.* (1995); C.Fr (ed.) (1995); Gazzola (1960); He (1996); Langenskiöld (1938); Lotz (1977); P.Mu (1969, 1986); P (1982); Li. Puppi (1971); J.T (1996)

Sansovino, Jacopo d'Antonio Tatti, *called* (1486–1570) Florentine architect/sculptor, he spent most of his working life in Venice, where he created some of the greatest buildings of the *High *Renaissance, although *Mannerism was not entirely absent from his designs. His finest works were the *Biblioteca Marciana* (begun 1537 and completed by *Scamozzi (1588)—a powerful composition featuring superimposed *Ionic and *Doric *Orders between the columns of which are arcuated arrangements of great sophistication); the *Zecca* (Mint—of 1535–47); and the *Loggetta* (1537–42—a composition of three overlayered *triumphal arches), all near the Doge's Palace, and contributing to the brilliant urban scenery of Venice. The *Biblioteca* (Library of St Mark) was

the first Venetian building in which the *Orders were used in a thoroughly scholarly way, and was recognized by *Palladio as one of the most authoritative buildings erected since Antiquity, and indeed drew on the exemplar of the Theatre of **Marcellus** (23–13 BC) in Rome for its arrangement of Orders. Sansovino also designed *San Francesco della Vigna* (1534—completed by Palladio) and the influential *Palazzo Corner della Ca' Grande* (begun 1537—with a *rusticated ground-floor slightly reminiscent of *Sanmicheli's *Palazzo Canossa*, Verona, but with curiously placed Mannerist *consoles over the openings on either side of the triple-arched centre). Above, the façade has superimposed Orders with arched windows set back behind the plane of the Orders. He also designed (c.1540) the *Villa Garzoni*, Pontecasale, near Padua, with a five-bay arcaded *loggia in the centre over the entrance, a composition of grave serenity worthy of the Ancients.

Boucher (1991); D.Howard (1975, 1980); Lotz (1977); P.Mu (1969, 1986); P (1982); G.Romanelli (1993); J.T (1996); Tafuri (1972)

Sant'Elia, Antonio (1888–1916) *See* FUTURISM.

Santini-Aichel, Jan Blažej (1677–1723) Prague-born, he was one of the most original architects of C18 Bohemia. He mingled *Baroque and *Gothic styles, as at the Church of the Assumption at Sedlec (1701–6), the Cloister Church, Kladruby (1712–26—where he was influenced by *Ried's Gothic vaulting), the Church of the Virgin, Želiv (1713–20), and St John Nepomuk, Zelená Hora, near Žd'ár nad Sazavou (1720–2). Some of his centrally planned churches recall the geometries of *Borromini and *Guarini: *Pevsner called him a 'Bohemian *Hawksmoor'. His palaces have more affinity with the work of *Fischer von Erlach: a good example is *Karlová Koruna*, Chlumec nad Cidlinov (1721–3). His work does not appear to have stimulated further experiment or development.

AR, cxxi/721 (Feb. 1957), 112–14; H.Franz (1962); E.Hempel (1965); J.Nn (1970); N-S (1986a); P (1982); Queysanna (1986); J.T (1996)

SAR (Stichting Architecten Research) Dutch foundation for architectural design that sought to give the inhabitants of urban housing a collective and individual say in its control and evolution. Formed in Eindhoven (1965) by **Nicholas John Habraken** (1928–), it was influential in the so-called *community-architecture movement.

Bosma *et al.* (2000); Habraken (1972)

Saracenic architecture Term given to an exotic style that evolved in Western Europe in C18, derived from *Moorish and *Islamic sources: until recently, it was applied to *Islamic architecture.

sarcophagus (*pl.* **sarcophagi**) Stone or *terra-cotta sepulchral chest to contain a corpse, with or without a coffin, often enriched with sculpture or given architectural form (e.g. Tomb of the Weepers, Sidon, resembling a miniature *Hellenistic temple). A common *Antique type had a pitched roof-like lid with *horns at the angles. *Sarcophagus*-forms were often employed as architectural elements in *Neo-Classicism, especially by *Soane.

sarraime *See* PORTCULLIS.

Sartoris, Alberto (1901–98) Italian architect. Early in his career he was associated with *Futurism, and was a founder-member of *CIAM (1928). In the late 1920s he became involved with Italian *Rationalism, and built numerous structures, mostly in Switzerland. He was associated with *Terragni in the design (1938) of a *satellite city at Rebbio, Como (1938–9). Among his works the *Morand-Pasteur* house, Saillon, Valais (1933–8), earned acclaim for its *International-style aesthetic. A devotee of *Functionalism, he published *Gli Elementi dell' architettura funzionale* (1932, 1936, 1941) and *Encyclopédie de l'architecture nouvelle* (1948–54).

E (1994); J.Gubler (1978); P (1982); Sartoris (1936, 1948–57); J.T (1996); *The Times* (23 Apr. 1998), 25

Sasaki, Hideo (1919–2000) American landscape architect of Japanese extraction. With **Peter Walker** (1932–) he founded (1957) **Sasaki, Walker & Associates** in San Francisco, CA, the first of a series of partnerships that eventually established several offices in the USA and Canada. Among the firm's works of landscape-design may be cited the Golden Gateway Center, San Francisco (1959–60—with *SOM); Foothill College, Los Altos, CA (1960–2); Weyerhaeuser Headquarters, Tacoma, WA (1963–72); Greenacre Park NYC (1970–2); Constitution Plaza, Hartford, CT (1969–73); and the John Deere & Co. headquarters, Moline, IL (1957–63—with buildings by *Saarinen).

E (1994); W & S (1994)

sash Rebated frame, fixed or opening, fitted with one or more panes of *glass forming a window-*light, set in a larger frame placed in the whole window-opening or aperture. Opening sashes can be of the vertical or horizontal sliding type in grooves, or can be hinged or pivoted at the sides, tops, bottoms, or centres. Thus *casements have sashes. A sash capable of being moved up and down is a *hung sash,* suspended from cords or chains and pulleys fixed in the linings of the sash-frame, and counterbalanced by weights attached to the concealed ends of the cords or chains within the *sash-box* of the main window-frame. If only one sash moves, the window is said

to be a *single-hung sash-window,* and if both sashes can be moved, it is *double-hung.* Yorkshire sliding-sashes are moved horizontally.

Sassanian architecture Architecture in Persia (AD 224–631), usually of brick, with much use of arches and *vaults, covered with *stucco. Surviving examples are the palaces at Ctesiphon (probably C6, though some have said it dates from C4, with a mighty brick vault covering the hall), Sarvistan (*c.*350, with a *dome and conical *squinch-arches), and Feruz-Abad (*c.*250—again with domes and conical squinch-arches). Sassanian architecture included the *iwan* and the cone-shaped squinch, later to be important features of *Islamic architecture. As Zoroastrianism was the State religion of the Sassanians, fire-temples were erected, e.g. at Takht-i-Sulayman, Azerbaijan, with high-domed chambers.

Ck (1996); J.T (1996)

satellite town Town, self-contained and limited in size, built in the vicinity of a large town or city to house and employ those who would otherwise create a demand for expansion of the existing settlement, but dependent on the parent-city for population and major services. Although not to be confused with *Garden Cities, satellite towns were influenced by Ebenezer *Howard's theories. A distinction is also to be made between a *consumer-satellite* (essentially a *dormitory-suburb* with few facilities) and a *production-satellite* (with capacity for commercial, industrial, and other production distinct from that of the parent town, so a *New Town).

Beaujeu-Garnier & Chabet (1967); Davidovich & Khorev (eds) (1962); E.Howard (1898, 1902, 1946, 1965); Me.Miller (1992, 2002)

Satyros (*fl.*mid-C4 BC) Joint architect, with *Pythios, or Pythius, of the celebrated *Hellenistic *Ionic *mausoleum of Mausolus at Halicarnassus (begun *c.*353 BC), one of the *Seven Wonders of the Ancient World, with supremely vigorous sculpture, much of which is in the British Museum, London.

D (1950)

saucer-dome *See* DOME.

Saulnier, Jules (1828–1900) French architect/engineer, he designed two celebrated factories: the first was a chemical-works at St-Denis, built (1861–2) of bricks within a metal frame, much admired by Émile *Muller; and the second was the hydraulic mill of the Menier Chocolate Factory, Noisiel-sur-Marne (1869–72—with an iron frame based on the lattice-girder spanning between *piers set in the river, the spaces between iron members filled with *polychrome brickwork, over which the iron diagonals (ensuring structural rigidity) were exposed). This latter factory (probably the first building in which the metal frame was exposed externally) was greatly admired, not least by *Viollet-le-Duc (who mentioned it in his *Entretiens* (1872)), and influenced the design of many iron-framed buildings decorated with polychrome brick that went up in Europe until the early C20: its roof-tiles were manufactured by Muller at his *La Grande Tuilerie d'Ivry* works. Saulnier also designed an estate for the workers at the Menier factory, complete with gardens, decent accommodation, and a day-nursery: for this he was influenced by Muller's designs at Mulhouse, and so, indirectly, by the work of Henry *Roberts.

M & Wa (1987); J.T (1996); V-l-D (1959)

Sauvage, Frédéric-Henri (1873–1932) French architect, trained at the *École des *Beaux-Arts*, Paris, his early work was in the *Art-Nouveau style, much influenced by the Majorelle family with whom (with others, including Frantz *Jourdain) he designed the *Villa Majorelle*, Nancy (1898–1901), one of the finest examples of the Art-Nouveau '*École de Nancy*'. He designed numerous interiors, fabrics, wallpapers, ceramics, and jewellery in the early years of the C20, but gradually moved more towards architectural design from the time of the building of his glazed *Galerie Argentine, Avenue Victor Hugo,* Paris (*c.*1900). This was followed by an inexpensive apartment-block, 1 *Rue Fernand Flocon,* Paris (1901), a building-type which he evolved as founder (with his partner (1898–1912), **Charles Sarazin** (1873–1950)) of *Société Anonyme de Logements Hygiéniques à Bon Marché* to build hygienic model-dwellings (1903). He designed various exemplary blocks, including that at 26 *Rue Vavin* (1912), where he exploited stepped terraces, and treated the walls in a manner derived from the work of *Wagner and his colleagues in Vienna. The *Gambetta* (1920) and *Les Sèvres* (1922) cinemas were built to Sauvage's designs, followed by sundry *pavilions for the *Exposition Internationale des Arts-Décoratifs* (1924–5), after which his work had a pronounced *Art Deco flavour. In 1926 he designed the huge garage at the *Rue Campagne-Première* and, with Frantz Jourdain, the extension to the department-store *La Samaritaine, Rue du Pont Neuf,* Paris (1926–9). His *Magasins Decré,* Nantes, had an overtly expressed steel frame (1931—destroyed).

B & G (1978); E (1980); Minnaert (2002); Sauvage & Sarazin (1904); J.T (1996); T-M (1967)

Savage, James (1779–1852) English architect, he built Richmond Bridge, Dublin (1813–16), and Tempsford Bridge, Beds. (1815–20), both of which demonstrated his command of construction. He is remembered today for St Luke's Church,

Chelsea (1820–4), remarkable for its scholarly (and very early) *Gothic-Revival style incorporating a real stone *vault supported by flying *buttresses. He designed several other churches, including the Classical St James, Bermondsey, London (1827–9), and the *Gothic Holy Trinity, Tottenham Green, Mddx. (1828–9). He was responsible for the Tenterden Union, Kent (1843–7), and other *workhouses. He published *Observations on Style in Architecture…* (1836) and other writings.

Co (2008); Ea (1970); *ODNB* (2004)

sawtooth 1. Ornament consisting of a series of notches, e.g. on a *beam, also called *mouseteeth*. **2.** As *cogging. For *sawtooth roof see* NORTH-LIGHT.

Saxon *See* ANGLO-SAXON.

scabellum (*pl.* **scabella**) High *pedestal for the support of a bust, usually shaped like the lower part of a *gaine or *herm.

scaena, scena, scene 1. *Alley or *portico where theatrical performances took place. **2.** Wall or *screen (*scaena ductilis*) forming the back of the *stage in a theatre. **3.** Richly decorated front (*scena frons*) of the stage, facing the *auditorium. **4.** Entire theatre-stage.

scaffold 1. Temporary platform or platforms supported on poles or trestles to support workers erecting, repairing, or painting a building. **2.** Raised platform to enable orators to address a concourse of people. **3.** Stage for a theatrical performance. **4.** Elevated platform on which executions take place. **5.** Raised platform on which the dead are placed.

scagliola Imitation *marble, known since Antiquity, and much used in C17 and C18 for column- and *pilaster-shafts, etc. It is made of crushed calcined gypsum (*or* selenite), reduced to powder or plaster of Paris, mixed with *isinglass (gelatine) or similar (*Flanders glue* or *size* was commonly used), and then has colours added. Veined marbles were imitated by mixing in different hues. The prepared mix was applied to the intended surface (usually a coat of lime and hair), smoothed, then rubbed down with a pumice-stone and a wet sponge before being polished with *tripoli* (diotomite) and charcoal using fine soft linen, then rubbed with felt dipped in linseed-oil and tripoli, then finally finished off with a rubbing of pure linseed oil. It was also called *stucco lustro*. It should not be confused with *Florentine mosaic* or *opere di commasso* made with thin veneers of marble.

N (1835); W.Pa (1887)

scale 1. In architecture, the proportions of a building or its parts with reference to a *module or unit of measurement. **2.** In architectural drawing, the size of the *plans, *elevations, *sections, etc., in relation to the actual size of the object delineated. **3.** Set of gradations marked along a straight line or a curve on wood, metal, plastic, etc., to assist in the preparation of, or measurement of, a drawing. **4.** A building might disruptively dominate others to the detriment of its context, and its proportions might be such as to render it 'out of scale' and uncomfortable to the eye. The key to appropriate scale is often the human figure seen in relation to the building.

FR (1946); H.R (1924)

scale-moulding *Imbrication* or *petal diaper*, i.e. ornament resembling shaped roof-tiles or the scales of fish, often found on *Antique *sarcophagi-lids. The best-known example is the top of the *Choragic Monument of Lysicrates, Athens (334 BC). In its simplest form it is a pattern of several series of semicircular forms, each row staggered with the centres of each semicircle on the junction of vertical lines struck from the points on which the semicircles spring and other horizontal lines drawn across the top of each arc.

L & D (1986)

Scalfarotto, Giovanni Antonio (1690–1764) Venetian architect who designed the Neo-Classical *San Simone Piccolo*, Venice (1718–38), a domed *rotunda with a *portico fronted by four *Corinthian columns set between square corner-columns.

Ck (1996); D.Howard (1980); Ms (1966)

scallop 1. Classical architectural enrichment derived from the shell of a scallop with many applications including the decoration of the quarter-spherical heads of arched *apses and *niches. **2.** *Romanesque *moulding consisting of a series of convex lobes similar to a *scale-moulding, but in one series only, like the edge of an apron. A variety of it to a very large *scale was used by Neo-Classical architects, often for *friezes.

scallop *or* **scalloped capital** See CAPITAL.

scamilli 1. Plain small blocks or sub-plinths under columns, statues, etc., to elevate them: unlike *pedestals they have no *mouldings. **2.** *Scamilli impares* was a term used by *Vitruvius, and appears to refer to the slight upward curve in the centre of a *stylobate or to the units of measurement required to achieve this *optical correction.

Heyman (1995); *The Times* (21 July 2012), 85

Scamozzi, Ottavio Bertotti (1719–90) See BERTOTTI-SCAMOZZI.

Scamozzi, Vincenzo (1548–1616) Italian architect, remembered primarily as a disciple of *Palladio and as the author of one of the great *Renaissance treatises on architecture, *L'Idea dell'Architettura Universale* (1615), which included an analysis and codification of the Classical Roman *Orders that remained influential for many years. Early in his career he designed the *Vettor Pisani Villa* or *Rocca*, Lonigo (1576–9), a variant of Palladio's *Villa Capra (Rotonda)*, near Vicenza, which Scamozzi completed *c.*1592. The *Rocca* was planned with a *serliana on three elevations, and on the fourth a *loggia behind a *colonnade carrying a *pediment, the four openings giving access to a circular hall illuminated by an *oculus set in a *dome, the whole conceived as an enchanting summer retreat, filled with light and air. *Burlington drew on this building as well as on the *Villa Capra* for his villa at Chiswick in C18. Scamozzi's *Villa Molin*, Mandria, near Padua (1597), also has a great central hall. His finest town-house was the *Palazzo Trissino*, Vicenza (1576–92), in which influences from *Peruzzi and Palladio are clear.

In the late 1570s he travelled to Rome and Southern Italy, visiting Rome on at least three more occasions (1585–6, 1590s). He published (1580) engravings of Roman *thermae, and later prepared commentaries for various topographical prints as *Discorsi sopra le Antichità di Roma* (1582–3). Around this time he produced designs for the Theatine *San Gaetano*, Padua, and won the design competition for the *Procuratie Nuove*, Piazza San Marco, Venice (1592—completed in 1663 by *Longhena). The vast *Procuratie* elevation is based on *Sansovino's Library of St Mark (which Scamozzi was at that time completing), but it has an extra storey (not part of Scamozzi's plans) based on a design by Palladio. He also worked on Palladio's *San Giorgio Maggiore*, Venice, and designed the fixed architectural stage-sets for Palladio's *Teatro Olimpico*, Vicenza (1584–5), an elaborate construction using tricks of perspective and illusion. He designed (1588) a similar theatre at Sabbioneta, and wrote a treatise on *perspective and *scenography (*Dei Teatri e delle Scene—c.*1574), which does not appear to have survived. Scamozzi toured Central Europe and France (1599–1600), making an unexecuted design for the Cathedral of Sts Rupert and Virgil, Salzburg: Santino *Solari retained the apsidal *transepts and certain other features derived from Palladio's *Il Redentore* and *San Giorgio Maggiore* in the realized scheme (commenced 1614). Scamozzi designed and built the Hospital and Church of *San Lazzaro dei Mendicanti* (1601–36), and the *Palazzo Contarini* on the Grand Canal (1608–16), both in Venice.

Barbieri (1952); D.Howard (1980); Muraro (1986); P (1982); Scamozzi (1615); J.T (1996)

scantling 1. Piece of timber, the thickness and breadth of which are of small dimensions. **2.** *Stud.

scapus (*pl.* scapi) **1.** *Shaft of a column. **2.** *Stile of a *door. **3.** *String of a*stair. **4.** *Apophyge.

scarf Type of joint between two timbers meeting end-to-end and designed to appear as one continuous piece: they include *face-halved* (with a rectangular notch taken out of each face); *side-halved* (with rectangular notch on each side); *splayed* (with each piece ending in a *splay* slanted across its length); *splayed and tabled* (with a *splay* broken by a *step*); and *stop-splayed* (with a partial *splay* leaving perpendicular elements at each end of the *splay*, often with further refinements). These complex joints are in the specialist realm of *timber-framed buildings.

ABDM (1996); Hewett (1969, 1980, 1982); W.McKay (1957)

scarp, escarp 1. Pitch or *batter of a bank. **2.** Steep slope below and away from a fortress-wall. **3.** Inner wall or bank of the *fosse.

Scarpa, Carlo (1906–78) Italian architect, he set up his practice in Venice (1927) and there directed (1972–8) the *Istituto Universitario di Architettura*. In the Fascist era he was a devotee of Italian *Rationalism and the *Modern Movement. He made his post-war reputation as a designer of exhibitions, galleries, and museums, starting with the renovation of the *Galleria Nazionale della Sicilia*, Palermo (1953–4). Other works include the extension to the *Gipsoteca Canoviana*, Possagno, near Treviso (1955–7), and interior of the *Museo Civico di Castelvecchio*, Verona (1964). His invention, sense of drama, fine detailing, and use of materials created remarkably successful designs of great intensity. Various works, including the *Villa Zoppas*, Conegliano (1948–53), the *Olivetti* Showroom, Venice (1957–61), and the *Casa Veritti*, Udine (1957–61), demonstrated aspects of his command of volumetric juxtapositions. One of his most successful designs is the Brion Cemetery, San Vito d'Altivole, near Treviso (1970–2), where powerful geometries and stark *concrete are combined.

Albertini & Bagnoli (1988); Crippa (1986); DalCo & Mazziorol (eds) (1985); L.Kahn & Cantacuzino (eds) (1974); Los (1993, 1995); Marcianò (1984); Noever (1989); Olsberg et al. (1999); Saito (1997); Scarpa (1993)

Scarpagnino, Antonio Abbondi, *called.* *See* BON *or* BONO.

scenography *Perspective drawing or scene-painting. The representation of a building in perspective. *Nash's composition of Regent Street, London, was an exercise in *scenographic composition* as his *palace-fronts were designed to be seen in perspective as a series of episodes.

Matteucci et al. (1979)

Schädel, Gottfried Johann (*c.*1680–1752) German *Baroque architect, he accompanied *Schlüter when the latter was called to St Petersburg (1713), and appears to have been responsible for the design of **Prince Alexandr Menshikov's** (1673–1729) Palace at *Oranienbaum* (completed *c.*1725), the first great palace in Russia in the Western-European style, situated overlooking the Gulf of Finland, west of the city. He later worked in Kiev, Ukraine, where he remodelled Kiev Academy (1732–40), designed the *belfries of the Cathedral of the Dormition (1731–45) and the Sophia Cathedral (1744–8), and carried out other works, often merging Baroque and *Byzantine elements.

Cracraft (1988); Grabar et al. (eds) (1960), v, 93–4; G.H (1983); J.T (1996)

Scharoun, Hans Bernard (1893–1972) German architect. Sometimes described as influenced by *Expressionism, he was actually more eclectic, drawing on ideas of 'new building' promoted by *Häring and on the tenets of the *Modern Movement. During the 1914–18 war he worked on reconstruction projects in East Prussia, and later practised there (1919–25). His association with the *Gläserne Kette and Der *Ring led to his building a house at the *Weissenhofsiedlung, Stuttgart (1927). He taught (1925–32) at the *Staatliche Akademie für Kunst und Kunstgewerbe*, Breslau (now Wrocław), and built a residential hall for the *Deutscher Werkbund exhibition in that city devoted to the theme of living- and work-spaces (1929). He prepared plans for the *Siemensstadt* and other housing schemes in Berlin (1929–30): at *Siemensstadt* he was associated with *Bartning, *Gropius, Häring, and others. He produced (1930s) several Modernist houses, including the Schminke House, Löbau, Saxony (1932–3), with huge *cantilevered balconies, much glass, and steel construction. After the 1939–45 war he directed the Building and Housing Department for Greater Berlin, and prepared (with others) plans for the rebuilding of the shattered city. He was also appointed to the Chair of Urban Planning, Technical University of Berlin, which he occupied until 1958, exercising great influence.

He designed a series of residential schemes ('Romeo' and 'Juliet' apartments, Stuttgart-Zuffenhausen (1954–9), 'Salute' block, Stuttgart-Möhringen (1961–3), and dwellings at Charlottenburg-Nord, Berlin (1956–61)), schools, and other structures. His most celebrated building, however, is the *Philharmonie*, Berlin (1956–63), where the *auditorium is surrounded by *foyers and offices, the whole freely composed in a way some have seen as a late flowering of Expressionism, or even as evidence of Scharoun's commitment to *organic architecture. He also designed the Prussian State Library, Berlin (1964–79), sited on the *Kulturforum* that includes the *Philharmonie* and *Mies van der Rohe's National Gallery, but it has to be said that these structures relate neither to each other nor to the city as a place of memory, and ignore one of the most significant historical axes. He also designed the German Embassy in Brasília (1963–71), the Maritime Museum, Bremerhaven (1969–75), and the Town Theatre, Wolfsburg (1965–74), among other projects.

BJ (1995); Bürkle (1993); C & S (1960); Geist (1993); Hoh-Slodczyk *et al.* (1992); Janofske (1984); Kirschenmann & Syring (1993); Marcianò (1992); Messina *et al.* (1969); P (1982); Pehnt (1973); Pfankuch (1974); Syring & Kirschenmann (2004); J.T (1996)

Schattner, Karl-Josef (1924–2012). German architect. Most of his works were carried out in his capacity as Architect to the Diocese of Eichstätt, and he built up his own *Dombauhütte* (Cathedral Workshop) employing a team of craftsmen. The founding of the University at Eichstätt enabled Schattner to conserve and adapt many historic buildings, whereas most of his new works were uncompromisingly radical and modern, erected within the historical context. Influenced by William *Morris's philosophies, he was one of the more sensitive architects working on old buildings in a Germany that rather often favoured wholesale reconstructions. His works include the Archives Building (1989–93), the conversion and extension of *Schloss Hirschberg* (1987–92), and the Episcopal Seminary (1981–93). His rational approach had much in common with that of the *Ticinese School and his Italian contemporary *Scarpa.

E (1994); Pehnt (1999a); pk

Scheerbart, Paul (1863–1915) German writer/fantasist/high-priest of *Expressionism, he was mentor of Bruno *Taut and *Tatlin. In his writings he frequently alluded to an imaginative architecture of glass as an instrument of social change, and indeed his most celebrated work was *Glass Architecture* (1914, 1972), dedicated to Taut, whose famous Glass Pavilion at the *Werkbund* Exhibition, Cologne (1914), was dedicated to Scheerbart.

JSAH, xxxiv/2 (May 1975), 83–97; *Kunstblatt*, iii/9 (1920), 271–4; Sharp (1967); Sharp (ed.) (1972)

Schickhardt, Heinrich (1558–1635) German architect, one of the earliest of the *Renaissance period, and therefore of importance in spite of the fact that very little of his work survives. In his capacity as Architect to the **Dukes of Württemberg** (from 1592), he travelled in Italy to gather ideas for his addition to the *Schloss*, Stuttgart (1600–11—destroyed 1778). It was symmetrical, and employed many *Tuscan columns. Of even greater importance was his layout for the new town of Freudenstadt, originally founded (1599)

for Protestant refugees from Salzburg, and rebuilt after a fire (1632): laid out around a huge square, partly occupied by gardens and surrounded by houses on *arcades, it was based on C16 plans for *Ideal Cities, notably one by **Albrecht Dürer** (1471–1528). A similar design occurred in *Christianopolis* (1619) by the scholar/humanist **Johann Valentin Andrea** (1568–1654). Freudenstadt's Protestant church consisted of two *naves at right angles to each other (one for males and one for females), on an **L** plan, with the *pulpit and *altar in the corner, and a tower at the end of each nave. The town was burned in April 1945 and subsequently rebuilt. Among his other works may be cited the Renaissance *façade of the Town Hall, Esslingen (1586–9); extensions to the town of Mömpelgard (Montbéliard—then part of the Duchy of Württemburg (until 1793)), including the St Martin's (1601–7); and the *belfry of Cannstatt Church, Stuttgart (1612–13).

Hi (1981); J.T (1996); vV (1993)

Schindler, Rudolf Michael (1887–1953) Vienna-born American architect. Early influences were *Loos, Otto *Wagner, and F.L.L. *Wright (in whose office he worked from 1916). He established (1921) his own practice in Los Angeles, and collaborated (mid-1920s) with *Neutra. Most of his work was in the field of domestic architecture, for which (1920s) he used systems of *concrete construction. His Schindler House, North Kings Road, Hollywood, CA (1921–2), was freely composed, with two L-shaped plans containing studios and giving access to external living-areas, but his most celebrated building of the period (influenced by the De-*Stijl movement and by *Constructivism) was the Lovell Beach House, 1242 Ocean Avenue, Newport Beach, CA (1922–6), supported on five exposed concrete frames, with spaces enclosed by prefabricated elements. His work then became more blocky, as in the Buck House, Los Angeles (1934), and he gradually ceased (1930s) using concrete as his main building material, turning to *timber frames and *stucco finishes, and to plywood panels (1940s). He began to express roofs, as in the van Dekker House, Canoga Park, CA (1940), and then evolved an architecture that appeared increasingly fragmented, as in the Janson House, Los Angeles (1949). His individuality, humour, and dislike of the totalitarianism inherent in the *International *Modern Movement led to his comparative neglect, but he was later perceived as a designer of stature.

W.Andrews (1955); R.Ba (1971); M.Darling *et al.* (2001); Gebhard (1980, 1997); Gössel (ed.) (1999a); *JSAH*, xlv/4 (Dec. 1986), 374–88; McCoy (1975, 1979); March & Sheine (eds) (1993); M & N (1987); P (1982); Sarnitz (ed.) (1988); Sheine (2001); Steele (1996); J.T (1996)

Schinkel, Karl Friedrich (1781–1841) Prussian architect, the greatest in Germany in the first decades of C19. He was not only an architect of genius, but a civil servant, intellectual, painter, stage-designer, producer of *panoramas, and gifted draughtsman. His output was prodigious, and his stylistically eclectic work lyrical and logical. He designed many buildings that became paradigms of excellence in the period during which he served his country and King as Prussian State Architect, and he established standards that influenced generations of architects throughout Germany.

Friedrich *Gilly's Graeco-Roman-Egyptian design for a monument to **King Friedrich II** ('the **Great**'—*r.*1740–86), exhibited (1797) in Berlin, fuelled the young Schinkel's ambition to become an architect, and he entered (1798) the studio and household of Gilly's father, David *Gilly, enrolling at the *Bauakademie*, where he received a rigorous training in practical matters as well as absorbing the theoretical bases of *Classicism as expounded by **Aloys Hirt** (1759–1837). Other teachers included *Gentz and *Langhans, and the ethos of the *Bauakademie* included much derived from the teachings of *Blondel and the *École Polytechnique* in Paris, so the young Schinkel absorbed the elements of a rational approach to architecture from which Franco-Prussian *Neo-Classicism evolved.

During his tour of Italy and France (1803–5) he studied *vernacular and medieval architecture and was particularly interested in the structural principles of apartment-blocks in Naples and the *Gothic *vaults of Milan Cathedral. He was less enthusiastic about *Antique remains than about their *Picturesque qualities, and studied *Romanesque and other structures as well as brick buildings (esp. those in Bologna). On his return to Berlin he found lean times, and with the defeat of Prussia by the French (1806) and the occupation of the capital there were no prospects of architectural commissions, so Schinkel occupied himself by producing *panoramas and *dioramas as well as numerous idealized landscapes and other pictures: these made him well known, and attracted the attention of **Queen Luise** (*r.*1797–1810), recently returned (1809) from exile in Königsberg, who commissioned him to redecorate several palace-interiors in Berlin and Charlottenburg. He was appointed (1810) to a post in the Department of Public Works (partly through the influence of **(Karl) Wilhelm, Freiherr von Humboldt** (1767–1835—Minister of Public Instruction and Education)) with responsibility of assessing the aesthetic content of all buildings erected or owned by the State, and began his meteoric rise through the bureaucracy that would later enable him to create architecture to ennoble all human relationships and to express Prussia's aspirations.

The death of the greatly loved Queen (1810) focused patriotic sentiments, and Schinkel, with Gentz and **King Friedrich Wilhelm III** (*r.*1797–1840), designed the Queen's Greek-*Doric *mausoleum at Charlottenburg. He also exhibited an alternative (and enchantingly Romantic) Gothic design in which the supposed 'natural' origins of Gothic were alluded to in the palm-fronds on the *ribs of the *vaults, like a *canopy of peace over the dead Queen, and at that time began to see Gothic as an embodiment of the Germanic soul. It was his synthesis of the Classical and Gothic that gave much of his later work an especial interest. He designed (1811) the cast-iron Gothic memorial at Gransee on the spot where the Queen's coffin had rested on its way to Charlottenburg, a concept suggested by the medieval 'Eleanor crosses' in C13 England. A series of *Sublime paintings followed in which were depicted vast Gothic cathedrals, bathed in light, comparable with aspects of works by **Caspar David Friedrich** (1774–1840) exhibited (1810) in Berlin.

With the galvanizing of the national spirit, the King's proclamation to his people, the collection of gold jewellery for the *Freiheitskrieg*, and Schinkel's design of the *Eiserneskreuz* military decoration (1813), the idea of the Prussian State became associated with economy, fortitude, and self-sacrifice. For the rest of his life Schinkel was to use iron with sensitivity, and indeed his attitudes to new technologies and industrialization were judicious. **Napoléon**'s eventual defeat encouraged a great upsurge of Prussian national pride, partly to be expressed in architecture. Schinkel was promoted (1815) as *Geheimer Baurat* (Privy Building Officer) with special powers to plan Berlin and oversee all State and Royal building-commissions. He also initiated an influential report on the preservation of national monuments that led to State protection of historic buildings throughout Prussia. Among his more important concerns at the time was the commencement of the restoration of Cologne Cathedral (1816) and his investigation of the Marienburg fortress (1309–98), once the seat of the Grand Masters of the Teutonic Order: his recommendations for the latter complex (now Malbork, Poland) were realized after 1845, and the programme he set in motion continued well into C20. His work as a painter and creator of dioramas and panoramas inevitably brought commissions to design for the theatre, and his scenes for Mozart's Die *Zauberflöte* (1815–16) were among the finest conceived, with their *Egyptian-Revival architecture, derived partly from Napoléonic publications, and exotic Meso-American-tropical landscapes inspired by **Friedrich Heinrich Alexander von Humboldt**'s (1769–1859) travels to South America and México (1799–1804), published 1807.

Schinkel's major buildings were designed from 1816, starting with the *Neue Wache* on *Unter den Linden*, Berlin (1816-18), with a free Greek Doric for the portico (there are no *triglyphs and there is a continuous row of *guttae-like elements under the *frieze) set against a plain fortress-like block. This was followed by the monument to the dead of the Napoléonic Wars, Spandau (1816), the Gothic monument (1818-21) on what is now the Kreuzberg, and the *pinnacle-monument in the churchyard at Grossbeeren (1817), all of cast iron. A master-plan for Berlin and series of splendid buildings came next. After the destruction of Langhans's *Nationaltheater*, Schinkel replaced it with the *Schauspielhaus* (1818-21), a brilliant design with an *Ionic portico and a *mullion-and-*trabeated system derived from the Ancient Greek *Choragic Monument of Thrasyllus, Athens, and the square columns of Ancient-Egyptian *temples. This theatre, with the twin churches in the *Gendarmenmarkt*, forms one of the noblest urban ensembles in Berlin. He prepared comprehensive proposals for the *Lustgarten* in front of the Royal Palace, including the reorganization of the waterways, the remodelling of the Cathedral, the construction of various buildings, and the creation of a new bridge linking the *Lustgarten* and *Unter den Linden*. As part of the scheme he worked on the idea of building a new museum, accepted by the King in 1823. This, his masterpiece (very badly damaged in the 1939-45 war, and indifferently treated thereafter), was part of the high-minded programme to raise the tone of society, and consists of a long Ionic *colonnade like a *Hellenistic *stoa behind which a double staircase leads to an open gallery-landing from which views may be enjoyed. Influenced by French theorists such as *Durand, the plan had a clarity and purity worthy of the high ideals of its creator, but in the reconstructed building those qualities are barely discernible. Behind the stair and entrance is a *Pantheon-like *rotunda inside a cubic form.

Meanwhile, he had also built two other great buildings: Humboldt's *Schloss Tegel* (1820-4—west of Berlin, in which he mingled the mullion-and-trabeated style of the *Schauspielhaus*, themes from the *Villa Trissino* near Vicenza, elements from English *Palladianism, and allusions to Antiquity); and the hunting-lodge of Antonin (for **Prince Anton Heinrich Radziwiłł** (1775-1833—Governor of the Prussian Province of Posen)), Ostrow, near Poznań, Poland (1822-4—a five-storey timber-framed and timber-clad octagon with four square *wings, the central area galleried and with a huge Doric column rising in the centre containing the fireplaces and chimney). He also designed the tomb-marker of **General Gerhard Johann David von Scharnhorst** (1755-1813) in the *Invaliden-Friedhof*, Berlin (1820-4).

During the building of the *Lustgarten* Museum (1824-30) Schinkel obtained approval for his Neo-Gothic *Friedrich-Werderschekirche*, Berlin (1824-30), an important example of his work in the Gothic style, after which he set out on a tour of Germany, France, England, Scotland, and Wales, accompanied by **Peter Christian Wilhelm Beuth** (1781-1853), Prussian civil servant. His diaries describe his impressions, notably his interest in English industrial architecture (e.g. London Docks, building-construction, the Staffordshire Potteries, gas-works, etc.). On his return to Berlin he incorporated aspects of fire-resistant construction he had seen at *Smirke's British Museum, and he was instrumental in getting gaslight installed by an English firm in Berlin (1826-7). Then followed an essay in Gothic with the Town Hall of Kolberg (Kołobrzeg), built 1827-32, and the exquisite series of buildings in the park at Potsdam: *Charlottenhof* (1826-7), the Court-Gardener's House (1829-33—evocative of *vernacular architecture in Tuscany), and the 'Roman Baths' (1830). The last three buildings, beautifully integrated with the gardens, drew on ideas of asymmetrical *Picturesque composition pioneered in England, notably by *Nash and *Papworth. With the *Nikolaikirche*, Potsdam (1830-7), Schinkel realized the ideals of stereometrical purity advocated by C18 French theorists with a great cube surmounted by a *drum and dome, an apsidal *chancel, and an *Antique portico. It demonstrates its designer's complete mastery of Greek, Roman, Italianate, and Neo-Classical languages.

An interest in *terracotta and brick, fuelled perhaps by his visit to England, was realized (1828) in the structural *polychrome treatment of the house for **Tobias Christoph Feilner** (1773-1839), a forward-looking design anticipating the ideas of *Hittorff and others. This also led to the *Bauakademie*, Berlin (1831-6), a polychrome brick-and-terracotta structure informed by Classical rigour, Gothic systems of *piers and *buttresses, and English industrial architecture. The *Bauakademie* housed the School of Architecture, Schinkel's living-quarters, and the *Oberbaudeputation*. Until its wholly unwarranted destruction by the Communist authorities (1961), it remained one of his finest creations. Other masterly works in the Classical style by Schinkel include the exquisite New Pavilion, *Schloss Charlottenburg* (1824-5), the Casino, *Schloss Glienicke* (1824-5), *Schloss Glienecke* itself (1824-32), the *Hauptwache*, Dresden, Saxony (1831-3), and the *Grosse Neugierde* (Great Curiosity), *Schloss Glienicke* (1835-7), the last in a Greek-Revival style of enchanting beauty, quoting elements of the Choragic Monument of Lysicrates, Athens (334 BC).

Schloss Babelsberg, near the Havel (1832-49), was conceived in a Romantic *castellated style, based on English exemplars, as was the little-known but charming *Schloss Kurnik* (now *Kórnik*, Poland), a remodelling of an earlier building (1830s), but Schinkel's other great Picturesque Romantic-Classical dream-palaces were never built. These were *Schloss Orianda*, Crimea, Russia (1838—in which the spirit of *Pliny is detectable), and a palace on the Athenian Acropolis (1834): both are among his most imaginative and beautiful designs. With the *Bauakademie* they represent the last phase of Schinkel's career in which eclecticism, mature Classicism, syncretism, and influences from many countries, styles, and periods coalesced. As *Oberbaudirektor* (1831-7), he was placed in charge of all State building-schemes in Prussia, and advised on the conservation of historic monuments, and he became (1838) *Geheimer Oberlandesbaudirektor*, the top post within the State bureaucracy.

Schinkel's funeral (1841) was a national event: he was buried in the *Dorotheenstädtischer-Friedhof*, Berlin, his grave marked by a Greek *stele modelled on his own design (1833) for the scientist **Sigmund Friedrich Hermbstaedt**'s (1760-1833) memorial. **King Friedrich Wilhelm IV** (*r.*1840-61) decreed (1842) that all his works should be purchased by the State. Called the 'last great architect' by *Loos, his publications included *Sammlung Architektonischer Entwürfe* (1819-40), *Werke der höheren Baukunst für die Ausführung entworfen* (1840-8), and (with Beuth) *Vorbilder für Fabrikanten und Handwerker* (1821-7). His most gifted pupils included *Persius, *Strack, and *Stüler, and was a key figure in the evolution of the *Rundbogenstil*.

AJ, cxciii/25 (19 June 1991), 5, 30–49, and cxciv/4, 5 (24 & 31 July 1991), 22–39; Bergdoll (1994); B-H (1977); B & R (1993); B-S *et al.* (2003); B-S & Grisebach (eds) (1981); CoE (1972); J.Curl (2001, 2005, 2011); Forssmann (1981); U.Harten (ed.) (2000); Ibbeken *et al.* (2001); P (1982); Peik (ed.) (2001); Philipp (2000); Riemann (ed.) (1981); Schinkel (1989); Schönemann (1997); Snodin (ed.) (1991); Stemshorn (2002); Wa & M (1987); Zadow (2001); Zu (ed.) (1994a)

Schlaun, Johann Conrad von (1695–1773) German *Baroque architect, most of whose works are in Westphalia. His earliest buildings were uncomplicated churches, but he was appointed (1719) Land Surveyor of Münster by **Clemens August** (1700–61—**Prince-Bishop of Paderborn and Münster** from 1719), who encouraged him to travel, first to Würzburg where he gained further experience under *Neumann (1720-1) before visiting Italy and France in order to broaden his architectural knowledge. He designed *Schloss Brühl* (1725-8—later much changed by Neumann, *Cuvilliés, and others) in a Franco-German Baroque style, and the enchanting brick *Rococo hunting-lodge of *Clemenswerth* (1736-50), with a two-storey building at the centre

and a ring of eight detached *pavilions, one of which contained a *convent and chapel. Most of his notable works were in or near Münster: they include the *Erbdrostenhof* (1749-57—on a triangular urban site with a concave *façade fronting the *cour d'honneur* and with a convex garden-elevation, the whole on an ingenious plan with irregularly shaped rooms); the Bishop's Palace, *called* the *Schloss* (1767-73), built of rose-coloured brick with stone dressings, and containing Neumannesque elements, notably the curved *frontispiece and rounded corners; the *Rüschhaus* (1745-8); and the *Schlaunhaus* (1753-5). The last two both employ brick: the former resembles a Westphalian rural farm-building with a Rococo centrepiece; and the latter has a massive two-storey *rusticated arch in the middle. His *Clemenskirche* (1745-53), is a *rotunda on a triangular site constructed on a six-pointed star of superimposed triangles, clearly influenced by *Borromini's church of *Sant'Ivo* in Rome.

Boer *et al.* (1995); Bussmann (ed.) (1973); Bussmann *et al.* (1995); E.Hempel (1965); Kalnein (1956); Matzner *et al.* (1995); N-S (1986a); C.Powell (1959); J.T (1996)

Schlüter, Andreas (*c.*1659–1714) Claimed as a major *Baroque sculptor/architect by both Germany and Poland, his first works included decorations (1681) at the Royal Chapel, Danzig (now Gdańsk), the *high-altar, Oliva Cathedral, near Gdańsk (1688), and various commissions in Warsaw, to which city he was called (1683) to execute the sculptured decorations of the Krasiński Palace. He also carved the monument of **Adam Zygmunt Konarski**, Frombork Cathedral (1686), made the high-altar for the Czerniaków Church, Warsaw (1690), and the shockingly powerful crucifix for the *Reformati*, Węgrów (a precedent for the 22 'heads of dying warriors' at the *Zeughaus*, Berlin (1696–8)). He made four funerary monuments for the King of Poland, erected in Zółkiev, near Lwów (now in the Ukraine) (1692–4). He moved to Berlin (1694), and was sent by **Elector Friedrich III of Brandenburg** (*r.*1688–1713) on a study-tour to France and Italy. On his return he carved the elaborate heads and *trophies at *Nering's *Zeughaus*, succeeding Nering as architect (1698), the year in which he was appointed to direct building works at the Berlin *Schloss*, in, transforming it from Electoral *Residenz* into the Royal Palace. He also created the equestrian statue of the 'Great Elector' (**Friedrich Wilhelm** (*r.*1640–88)), now at Charlottenburg. The Berlin *Schloss* was Schlüter's masterpiece, and showed the influences of his former Warsaw colleague, van *Gameren, as well as of *Bernini and Le *Pautre. This great Baroque Palace was mostly finished when **Elector Friedrich III** became (1701) **Friedrich I, King in Prussia**: it was completed by *Eosander, badly damaged (1945), and demolished

(1950—an ideologically inspired act that makes nonsense of the historic fabric of the city). As Director of the Academy of Arts (1701-4), Schlüter had immense influence on artistic life in Berlin, and designed the Wartenburg Palace, Berlin (1702-4—later the Post Office—demolished 1889), and *Villa Kamecke*, Dorotheenstadt, Berlin (1711-12—destroyed). Following the collapse of the *Münzturm*, Berlin (1704), he began to fall from favour, was removed (1707) as *Schlossbaudirektor*, and resigned from the Academy (1710). He went to St Petersburg (1713) where he made a major contribution to the planning of the new capital, and prepared designs for the *grotto near the Summer Palace, *Peterhof*, and *Monplaisir*. His work in Berlin influenced *Fischer von Erlach, *Pöppelmann, and *Knobelsdorff.

Gurlitt (1891); W.Hager (1942); E.Hempel (1965); Iwicki (1980); Kz (1991); Ladendorff (1935); Mossakowski (1973); P (1982); Peschken (1993); Peschken & Klünner (1982); J.T (1996)

Schmidt, Friedrich, Freiherr von (1825-91)
Architect of the *Neo-Gothic *Rathaus*, Vienna (1872-82), which resembles a Flemish Cloth or Town Hall. Schmidt established himself as an important exponent of the *Gothic Revival in Austria with his *Fünfhaus Pfarrkirche, Maria vom Siege* (1867-75), built on an aisled octagonal plan, with medievalizing detail. He worked on the continuation of Cologne Cathedral from 1843 (he was an expert on *stereotomy), and taught architecture at Brera, Italy (1857-9). He restored *Sant'Ambrogio*, Milan. Among his other buildings is the *Stephanskirche*, Krefeld, Germany (1854-81).

G (1972); Haiko (1991); Ms (1966); S (1901-2)

Schmitz, Bruno (1858-1916) German architect, remembered primarily for his heroic monuments, including that to **Kaiser Wilhelm I** (r.1871-88) at **Deutsches Eck**, where the Mosel joins the Rhine at Koblenz (1896-7—destroyed in the 1939-45 war, reconstructed (early 1990s)). On the Kyffhäuser Hills, Thuringia, he designed the huge monument (1890-6) to **Kaiser Friedrich I Barbarossa** (r.1152-90). His gigantic *Völkerschlachtsdenkmal*, near Leipzig (1896-1913), is the greatest and most menacingly monumental national memorial of the early C20, built of *reinforced concrete faced with massive *granite blocks: it represents the power of the German peoples who rose in 1813 to drive the French from their lands. Schmitz's brooding work influenced *Kreis.

Ms (1966); Pe (1976); Spitzner (1913); D.Wa (1986)

Schmu(t)zer Wessobrunn (Bavaria) family of architects/stuccoers. **Joseph** (1683-1752) built the *Wandpfeiler Heiligenkreuzkirche*, Donauwörth (1717-22), Oberammergau *Pfarrkirche* (1735-42), and collaborated with his son, **Franz Xaver** (1713-75), on the exquisite *Rococo *stucco decorations at Rottenbuch (1737-50) and Ettal (1744-52), among other places. F.X.Schmu(t)zer also worked at Weingarten Abbey, Mittenwald, and Oberammergau, and evolved a style using many *cartouches and **C**-scrolls with great *élan*. Joseph's father, **Johann** (1642-1701), worked at Wessobrunn Abbey and its many affiliated churches: he designed Vilgertshofen *Wallfahrtskirche* (1686-92), and worked at numerous other sites. Johann's son, **Franz Xaver** (1676-1741), was a renowned stuccoer, and worked at Obermarchtal, Weissenau, Steingaden, etc. The family was one of many groups in the area who created astonishingly lovely things in the first half of C18.

Bou (1962); Dischinger (1977); Hauttmann (1921); Hi (1968a); C.Powell (1959); J.T (1996)

Schnebli, Dolf (1928-2009) Swiss architect. Originally influenced by Le *Corbusier, *Gropius, et al., work produced in his Ticino office moved towards the formal language of the *Ticinese School, notably with his severe *Villa Meyer*, Zürich (1986-7), which owes something to Classical symmetry. His designs for houses at Campione d'Italia and Carabbia, Ticino, aroused interest in the 1960s: other works include Ruopigen Primary School, Littau (1975-6).

Br (1982); E (1994); Schnebli (1998)

Schneckenberg See SNAIL-MOUNT.

Schoch, Johannes, *called* Hans (c.1550-1631) German architect. His most celebrated work is the *Friedrichsbau*, Heidelberg Castle (1601-7), a vigorous essay in *Renaissance architecture, designed for the **Elector Friedrich IV Palatine of the Rhine** (r.1583-1610). He probably worked on the *Neuer Bau* (1582-5) and *Grosse Metzig* (1586-8), Strasbourg. His work may have influenced other early Renaissance buildings in Germany, notably the *Zeughaus*, Amberg (1604), and the *Fleischhalle*, Heilbronn (c.1600), both of which have been attributed to him.

Hi (1981); J.T (1996)

Schoch, Johann Leopold Ludwig (1728-93) Landscape-gardener in the service of Fürst von *Anhalt-Dessau who was one of the creators of the beautiful *Gartenreich* at Wörlitz. His son, **Johann Georg Gottlieb Schoch** (1758-1826), also worked on Anhalt-Dessau estates, and published (1814) an important catalogue of plants growing or raised there.

R.Alex (1988); Quilitzsch *et al.* (1997)

scholar's garden Space designed to nourish the heart, incite poetic reverie, and provide a place of peaceful retreat: a precious terrain feeding the creative imagination, according to C17 Chinese texts. The hermit-like aesthetic life led by the scholar had a profound impact on *Chinese garden-design. See JI CHENG; PHILOSOPHER'S GARDEN; SANCTUARY.

Ji Cheng (2012); E.T.Morris (1983)

Schönthal, Otto (1878–1961) Austrian architect, pupil of *Wagner, for whom he worked, notably on Vienna's *Stadtbahn*, Post Office, and the *Am Steinhof* lunatic-asylum. On his own account he designed several fine buildings, including the *Villa Vojcsik, Linzerstrasse* (1901–2—restored 1975-82). He became (1908) joint-editor of the influential journal, *Der Architekt*, and sole editor (1909–15). He established his own practice with **Emil Hoppe** (1876–1957) and **Marcel Kammerer** (1878–1969) which flourished in Vienna just before the catastrophe of 1914–18. In the inter-war period Schönthal and Hoppe were involved in the huge public-housing programme for Vienna. He designed (1948–50) the *Eiselsberg-Hof*, 40–48 *Wimmergasse*, an essay in which traces of the *Wagnerschule* may be de-tected.

Hoppe & Schönthal (1931); J.T (1996)

Schultze-Naumburg, Paul (1869–1949) German architect/theorist. His work before the 1914–18 war was mostly in historical styles, including *Schloss Cecilienhof*, Potsdam (1913–17), in a free half-timbered English *Arts-and-Crafts style, influenced by *Muthesius's publications, that manages nonetheless to look stolidly German. His books were important, starting with *Kulturarbeiten* (1902–17), *Das ABC des Bauens* (1927), *Kunst und Rasse* (1928, 1938), *Das Gesicht des deutschen Hauses* (1929), *Kampf von die Kunst* (1932), *Kunst aus Blut und Boden* (1934), and *Bauten Schultze-Naumburgs* (1940—which contains a comprehensive list, with plans and photographs, of his buildings). He argued that architecture was expressive of race (an idea then widely held, and not just in Germany), and that German architecture was being corrupted by non-Teutonic influences, notably through the *International-*Modern Movement. During his tenure as Director of the Weimar School that had been the *Bauhaus he removed all Modernists from their posts: it did him no good, as **Adolf Hitler** (1889–1945) thought him a 'stupid imitator of the past', and he had no significant commissions after 1933.

P.Adam (1992); B.Hinz (1979); Lane (1985); Pfister (1940); Spotts (2002)

Schultz, Robert Weir (1861–1951) *See* WEIR, ROBERT WEIR SCHULTZ.

Schumacher, Friedrich Wilhelm, *called* **Fritz** (1869–1947) German architect, he directed the Dresden *Arts-and-Crafts exhibition (1906) and was a founding-member of the *Deutscher Werkbund* (1907). He advised on the *Garden City, Hellerau, designed the crematorium at Dresden, the *Handelshochschule*, Leipzig, and many houses while in Dresden before becoming City Architect of Hamburg (1909–33). His work there was influenced by the North-German traditional brick buildings with steeply pitched *tile roofs, but after the 1914-18 war his designs became angular, hard, and flat-roofed. He published *Die Kleinwohnung* (1917) in which he argued for industrialized mass-production. Other books include considerations of the problems of large conurbations, planning, policies, and style. He was a pioneer of regional planning, notably at Hamburg. His best work is probably the *Hamburg Stadtpark* (1910–24).

AulV (1929); M.Fischer (1977); H.Frank (ed.) (1994); Kallmorgen (ed.) (1969); Kayser (1984); P (1982); F.Sr (1995); J.T (1996); E.Teague (1985)

Schuricht, Christian Friedrich (1753–1832) German architect, pupil of *Krubsacius, he found early employment preparing book-illustrations, including *Theorie der Gartenkunst* (1779–85) by *Hirschfeld, before entering the Saxon State service as Court Inspector (1782). He designed the beautiful domed blue room and other Neo-Classical interiors in the *Römisches Haus* in the *Schlospark*, Weimar, erected to plans by *Arens. Other works include the *Kurhaus* at Bad Wolkenstein, and (with **Karl August Benjamin Siegel** (1757–1832) and others), he was involved in the rebuilding of *Schloss Kuckuckstein*, Liebstadt, near Pirna (1798–1802), both in Saxony. He remodelled *Schloss Gaussig*, near Bautzen, in a *Palladian style, and designed a mansion at Kačina, near Prague (1802), in which Neo-Classical themes became dominant. He also designed the Chinese Pavilion (1804) in the grounds of *Schloss Pillnitz*, near Dresden, and the *Belvedere* on the *Brühlsche Terrasse* by the Elbe, Dresden (1812–14—destroyed 1842), influenced by the severe Neo-Classicism of *Gilly. Appointed Court Architect (1812), he designed the *Neues Palais, Schloss Pillnitz* (1818–26), the roof of which echoed the original theme established (1720s) by Pöppelmann, but the building itself is Neo-Classical with primitive *Doric columns flanking the entrances.

J.T (1996); Wa & M (1987)

Schwarz, Rudolf (1897–1961) German church-architect, pupil of *Poelzig in Berlin. He worked with Dominikus *Böhm on the prize-winning unexecuted design for a church in Frankfurt (1926–7), and Böhm's influence is clear in Schwarz's *Corpus Christi* Church, Aachen (1928–30), a simple white building with a black *altar on a platform reached by a *flight of steps. He published (1938) a work on church-design in which he discussed the relationships of plans, structures, and congregations. After the 1939–45 war he designed a great number of churches, many with *reinforced-concrete frames, the spaces filled with brick, glass, and stone. Chief among his works are St Anna, Düren (1951–6), St Michael, Frankfurt (1953–4), and the Church of the Holy Family, Oberhausen (1956–8). In 1960 he published *Kirchenbau* in which he emphasized the desirability of bringing the congregation into a more intimate relationship with the altar. He was involved in the reconstruction of several German cities after 1945, notably Cologne (where he designed the *Wallraf-Richartz Museum* (1951–7)).

K.Becker (1981); E (1994); Hammond (ed.) (1962); Hasler (2000); K-S (1964); P (1982); Pehnt (1997); R.Schwarz (1958, 1968); M.Schwarz & Conrads (1979); Stegers (2000); E.Teague (1985a)

Schwechten, Franz Heinrich (1841–1924) German architect, pupil of Martin *Gropius, F.A. *Stüler, and J.A.*Raschdorff, he established (1869) his practice in Berlin, specializing in buildings for the railways. He was greatly influenced by the *polychromy of *Schinkel and M.Gropius in his designs for the *Anhalter Bahnhof*, Berlin (1875–80—destroyed). He also designed the railway stations at Dessau and Wittenberg (both 1875–80). His best-known work was the *Romanesque-Revival *Kaiser-Wilhelm Gedächtniskirche*, Berlin (1891–5—of which part remains), and he also designed the Church of the Redeemer, Essen (1905–9), and the *Kaiserschloss*, Posen (1905–10—now Poznań, Poland). He had a successful career, building all over the German Empire.

DB, xlvi (1912), 421–6, and lviii (1924), 427–8; Posener (1979)

Schwitters, Kurt Herman Edward Karl Julius (1887–1948) German artist, he made *collages from detritus collected from dumps and streets (1917) which he called *Merz* (Cast-Off). He then created *Merzbau* (Cast-Off Building) which virtually took over his entire dwelling in Hanover (1923–32—destroyed). The *Merzbau* was wholly unfunctional, and was really an essay in which *Expressionism, De *Stijl, and *Constructivism merged: it, in turn (from pictures and descriptions), seems to have influenced several late-C20 and early-C21 architects. He built a *Merz* mural in Ambleside, English Lake District (1947–8), later moved to King's College, Newcastle upon Tyne.

BaLa (1987); COF (1988); Gumard (2000); Schmalenbach (1970); Steinitz (1968)

sciagraph Representation of a *section. *Sciagraphy* is a branch of the science of *perspective dealing with projection of shadows.

FR (1946)

scissor-truss *See* TRUSS.

Sckell, Friedrich Ludwig von (1750–1823) German landscape architect, son of the landscape-gardener **Wilhelm Sckell** (1722–92), who served **Carl Theodor** (1743–99—**Elector Palatine of the Rhine** from 1742) at Schwetzingen. Having been granted an Electoral stipend to enable him to travel, on his return young Sckell laid out (1777–85) the peripheral parts of the gardens at Schwetzingen in the English style: most of the *fabriques*, however, including the famous 'Mosque', were designed by *Pigage. When **Carl Theodor** became **Elector of Bavaria** (1777), Sckell was summoned to Munich, where, from 1804 he redesigned the *Hofgarten* and the gardens at *Schloss Nymphenburg* (although he retained the powerful central *Baroque axes). He is best-known for the huge *Englischer Garten*, Munich, designed as a *public park, established on the recommendation of *Rumford from 1789: the pools, Monopteros Hill, and streams were all his ideas, and the extensions northwards are based on his plans. Unfortunately, his intended links with the *Hofgarten* were disrupted by building. Other works included the *promenades laid out on the site of the fortifications at Mannheim (1790s), and several parks and gardens in the Rhineland and Bavaria. Influenced first by Capability *Brown, and then by *Hirschfeld (although he seems to have eschewed the latter's enthusiasm for exotic *fabriques*, monuments, and sentimental associations), he published his *Beiträge zur bildenden Gartenkunst für angehende Gartenkünstler und Gartenliebhaber* (1818), which bears small resemblance to his executed designs.

Buttlar (1982, 1989); Dombart (1972); Hanwacker (1992); Probst *et al.* (eds) (1999)

scoinson Interior edge of a window-side, so *scoinson-arch* is that over the interior of a window-aperture on the inside, often much larger than on the outside if the *jambs are splayed.

Scoles, Joseph John (1798–1863) English RC architect, he became interested in medieval architecture through the influence of John *Carter. With Joseph *Bonomi Jun. he travelled in Sicily, Greece, Egypt, and Syria, before setting up in practice (1826). He planned Gloucester Terrace, Regent's Park, London, with the basic elevational treatment by *Nash. He is best known for his RC churches, which were mostly in the *Gothic style, although some were *Romanesque, and a few were Classical: they include St Peter, Stonyhurst College, Lancs. (1832–5—Gothic),

St Ignatius, Preston, Lancs. (1833-6—Gothic), St James, Colchester, Essex (1837—Romanesque), St John, Duncan Terrace, Islington, London (1841-3—Romanesque), Prior Park College Church, Bath, Som. (1844-6—Classical), and his masterpiece, the Church of the Immaculate Conception, Farm Street, Mayfair, London (1846-9—Gothic). He also designed the residential buildings for the Oratory, Brompton, London (1849-53), and the chapel, Ince Blundell Hall, Lancs. (1858-9—Classical).

Co (2008); J.Curl (2007); D & M (1985); *ODNB* (2004); W.Pa (1887)

sconce 1. Earthwork or fort, especially in front of a gate or the main defences. **2.** Protective *screen or shelter. **3.** Screen in the sense of a partition, e.g. to define a chapel, etc. **4.** Squinch (*see* DOME), in the sense of a small arch across the angle of a square room carrying a superimposed mass (e.g. in a church-tower carrying an octagonal *spire). **5.** Decorative lamp-bracket attached to a wall. **6.** Seat or bench fixed in a screen-wall near a fireplace.

scoop-pattern *Band or *frieze ornamented by a series of closely spaced vertical *flutes, normally with the upper ends curved, common in C18 Classical work.

scoop Temple of Jupiter, Rome.

Scotch bond *See* BRICK.

scotia (*pl.* **scotiae**) *Trochilus, or hollow concave *moulding, in e.g. an *Attic *base of a Classical column sandwiched between the *fillets above and below the *torus mouldings.

Scott, Adrian Gilbert (1882-1963) Son of 'Middle' Scott and brother of Sir Giles Gilbert *Scott, he was articled to Temple *Moore, and later assisted his brother in several projects, e.g. Greystanes, Mill Hill (1907). His greatest work was the Anglican Cathedral, Cairo, Egypt (1933-8—demolished), but most of his designs were for the RC Church, including the tower of *Hansom's Holy Name, Manchester (1928), and the centralized Sts Joseph & Mary, Lansbury, Poplar, London (1951-3). He also designed St Leonard's, Hastings, Sussex (1953-61—with lively nautical details and parabolic arches), and St Alban, Holborn, London (1959-61—retaining parts of *Butterfield's earlier church), both of which were replacements of war-damaged buildings. His own house, Shepherd's Well, Frognal Way,

Hampstead, London (1930), was in a chaste *Neo-Georgian style (the front door-case has been removed).

GS; *RIBAJ*, lxx/7 (July 1963), 298; J.T (1996)

Scott, Elisabeth Whitworth (1898-1972) English architect, great-niece of 'Great' *Scott. After the Shakespeare Memorial Theatre at Stratford-upon-Avon, Warwicks., was burned down (1926) a competition was held to select a design for a new building, and Scott won it (1928), so she became the first woman to win a major architectural competition and to undertake an important British public commission. **Alison Sleigh** (*fl.*1920-32) and **J.C.Shepherd** (1896-1978) (whom she later married) helped her with the drawings, and Scott formed a partnership (1929) with Shepherd and **Maurice Chesterton** (1883-1962), in whose office she was working at the time of her success. The theatre was completed (1932), and was severely criticized for its modernity (derived from North-European exemplars). Once the Stratford project was completed, Scott formed a new partnership with **John Breakwell** (*c.*1905-1960), the firm being renamed **Scott, Shepherd, and Breakwell,** which designed the Fawcett Building, Newnham College, Cambridge, finished 1938. Other works included the school at Henley-on-Thames, Oxon. (1935-6), another school in Northallerton, Yorks. (1939-41), and various houses, including one at Morden, Surrey (1933), which was mildly *Modernist. After the 1939-45 war, Scott worked in Bournemouth, and after 1962 she designed *pavilions on Bournemouth and Boscombe piers, Hants.

GS; *ODNB* (2004); J.T (1996)

Scott, Geoffrey (1884-1929) English architect/polymath/writer. He won (1908) the Newdigate Prize with his essay, *The National Character of English Architecture,* forming the kernel of his *The Architecture of Humanism* (1914), in which he defended *Renaissance architecture as a standard, and attacked the multiplicity of styles that had emerged during C19. In Florence, where he met the artistic circle centred on the *Villa I Tatti,* home of the art-historian, **Bernard Berenson** (1865-1959), he set up an a practice with **Cecil Ross Pinsent** (1884-1963), specializing in the design of gardens and *villas in the Renaissance style.

Dunn (1998); *ODNB* (2004); Scott (1914, 1925)

Scott, Sir George Gilbert ('Great') (1811-78) Prolific English *Gothic-Revival architect, articled (1827) to **James Edmeston** (1791-1867—who was better known as a writer of hymns (*Lead us, Heavenly Father, lead us* (1821) was one of his efforts) than as an architect), he later joined (1832) Henry *Roberts, with whom he worked on the new Fishmongers' Hall, London, and on a school at Camberwell (1834). He assisted (1835) *Kempthorne, Architect to the Poor Law Commissioners, but by the end of 1835 Scott was practising on his own, and had formed a working relationship with **William Bonython Moffatt** (1812–87) that developed into a partnership (1838) responsible for over 50 *workhouses and many other buildings. Scott designed the little Gothic church of St Mary Magdalene at Flaunden, Herts. (1838), and thereafter, possibly through the influence of *Blore, greatly expanded his architectural practice. The first real success was when **Scott & Moffatt** won the competition (1840) to design the Martyrs' Memorial, Oxford (1840–2—a finely detailed version of the C13 'Eleanor Crosses'). At the same time, Scott designed a new north (or Martyrs') *aisle for the nearby Church of St Mary Magdalen, the first archaeologically correct piece of C19 Gothic Revival in Oxford, demonstrating that he had acquired sufficient expertise to be considered as a scholarly Goth in his own right. The firm was selected (1842) to design St Giles's Church, Camberwell, London (consecrated 1844—which gained the approval of *Ecclesiologists). By 1841 Scott had immersed himself in the writings of A.W.N. *Pugin (he declared he had been awakened from his slumbers by their 'thunder'), and began to contribute to *The Ecclesiologist*, influential journal of the *Cambridge Camden (later Ecclesiological) Society. Scott & Moffatt entered the competition (1844) to design the Church of St Nikolaus, Hamburg, and came third, but through the influence of *Zwirner, their scholarly *German-Gothic design (with its handsome *steeple which survived the 1939–45 war) was accepted and realized (but, as it was to be a Lutheran Church, gained the architects no credit with Ecclesiologists, who did not recognize the validity of Lutheran Orders). The 1840s also saw Scott developing a career as a restorer of ecclesiastical buildings, starting with Chesterfield, Derbys., and continuing with several major churches, including Ely Cathedral, Cambs. (1848), and Westminster Abbey (1849). Moffatt's extravagance and financial recklessness led to a dissolution of the partnership (1845), the year in which the firm's Reading Gaol, Berks., was completed.

In the 1850s, in common with many of his peers, Scott developed an interest in Continental Gothic. His designs for the Government Buildings, Whitehall, London (1856), drew on Flemish and Italian Gothic exemplars, but he was obliged to Classicize them: the resultant Foreign and India Offices (1863–8) and Home and Colonial Offices (1870–4) are accomplished Italian-*Renaissance essays. Meanwhile he had built the handsome Parish Church of St George at Doncaster, Yorks. (1853–8—one of his best buildings), the Chapel at

Exeter College, Oxford (1856–9—based on *Sainte-Chapelle*, Paris), the huge *Middle-Pointed All Souls, Haley Hill, Halifax, Yorks. (1855–9), St Mary Abbots, Kensington, London (1869–72), and the Cathedral of St John, Newfoundland (1846–80). He also added the Cathedrals of Hereford, Lichfield, and Peterborough to the ever-growing list of buildings in his care. In 1861, *Albert, Prince Consort, died, and Scott's design for his memorial in London (drawn by 'Middle' *Scott) was chosen. Like *Worthington's Albert Memorial in Manchester (1862–3), it was in the form of a canopied *shrine, but Scott's version was in the Italian-Gothic style, glowing with colour and richness (1862–72). For this, the epitome of *High-Victorian Gothic Revival, Scott was knighted (1872). He also enjoyed considerable success as a secular architect. His Kelham Hall, Notts. (1858–62), and Midland Grand Hotel, St Pancras, London (1868–74) have much in common: both are self-confident eclectic brick structures, based on Continental Gothic sources from Ieper, Leuven, and Venice, with a dash of English and French Gothic, and both were almost outrageously opulent and extravagant. He designed the University, Gilmore Hill, Glasgow (1866–70), including Scots *tourelles to give the building a regional flavour, although J.O.*Scott added (1887) the Germanic *tracery-*spire. His Albert Institute, Dundee (1865–7), also employed Scots features such as *crow-step *gables and circular *turrets of the *Scottish-Baronial style. Among his other works the Chapel at St John's College, Cambridge (1863–9), and the Episcopal Cathedral of St Mary, Edinburgh (1874–9), may be mentioned, the latter a noble composition with three spires.

As a church architect, Scott sometimes had his drawbacks. In his *A Plea for the Faithful Restoration of Our Ancient Churches* (1850) and other writings he argued for a sensitivity in dealing with ancient fabric he did not always show in practice. Indeed, his work at St Mary de Castro, Leicester, was mechanical. The Society for the Protection of Ancient Buildings (SPAB) was founded (1877) by William *Morris as a direct result of Scott's draconian proposals for the 'restoration' of Tewkesbury Abbey, Glos. However, he worked on over 300 churches and cathedrals, and often had to swallow his own principles because of the destructive ambitions of clergy and building committees. Among the Cathedrals (in addition to those mentioned previously) he restored were Canterbury (1860, 1877–80), Chester (1868–75), Chichester (1861–7 and 1872), Durham (1859, 1874–6), Exeter (1869–77), Gloucester (1854–76), Ripon (1862–74), and Rochester (1871–4). His work on old buildings was, for the most part, firmly based on scholarship, and he was sensitive to detail: in addition, it should be remembered that he had to adapt them for contemporary worship, at a time when the Anglican Church was powerful, vigorous, and permeated every corner of national life. He was a tireless advocate of Gothic as the only style in which to build, as in his *Remarks on Secular & Domestic Architecture Present and Future* (1857). His *Personal and Professional Recollections* (1879) is entertaining and interesting. Industrious and professionally competent, he was also modest, kind, and generous to pupils and younger architects. His *Gleanings from Westminster Abbey* (1860), was scholarly, and demonstrates his great love for medieval architecture, to the understanding of which he devoted his life.

AH, **xix** (1976), 54–73, and **xxviii** (1985), 159–82; C.Brooks (1999); C.Brooks (ed.) (2000); B.Clarke (1958, 1966, 1969), Cole (1980); J.Curl (2007); Ea (1970); G.Fisher *et al.* (eds) (1981); Hi (1954); Hl & Su (1989); T.Jackson (2003); *ODNB* (2004); P (1982); Pe (1972); P & D (1973); Port (1961); G.Scott (1861, 1995); J.T (1996); Toplis (1987); V & A (1971, 1978)

Scott, George Gilbert, Jun (1839–97) English architect, the eldest of 'Great' *Scott's five sons, called 'Middle' Scott. Articled to his father (1857), he later worked for him as an assistant, carrying out the restoration of St Edward's Church, Cheddleton, Staffs. (1863–6—later adding the new lych-gate, school, and library in the 1870s), and the sensitive restoration and enlargement of the Hall and Combination Room, Peterhouse, Cambridge (1868–70), for both of which jobs he used William *Morris's firm for stainedglass and other decorations. G.F.*Bodley, who had also been the elder Scott's pupil, was a major influence on the younger Scott's architecture, and, with *Garner, *Micklethwaite, *Sedding, and 'Middle' Scott himself, was responsible for altering the thrust of English ecclesiastical design from the 1870s by turning to English- and late-*Gothic precedents instead of the C13 and Continental exemplars that earlier had been *de rigueur*. Indeed, Scott went further than Bodley in championing *Perp., which, from the time of *Pugin's denunciations, had been unaccountably despised as 'decadent'. His masterpiece was undoubtedly the Church, School, and Vicarage of St Agnes, Kennington Park, London (1874–91—destroyed), designed for the English liturgy and Anglo-Catholic ritual. Beautifully furnished, it had the characteristic *nave-*arcade *mouldings 'dying' into the *piers, without *capitals. Other churches included St Mark, New Milverton, Leamington Spa, Warwicks. (1876–9), All Hallows, Southwark, London (1879–92—destroyed), St Mary Magdalene, East Moors, Yorks. (1879–82—supervised and subtly altered by Temple *Moore during construction), and the *First-Pointed St John the Baptist, Norwich (1884–1910, now the RC Cathedral—completed by J.O.*Scott), a scholarly

and satisfying essay in the C13 style. He designed a new building at Pembroke College, Cambridge (1879–83), in a Perp. style, and sensitively enlarged *Wren's Chapel at a time when C17 *Classicism was not appreciated in many quarters. He also designed the new building fronting St Giles's, Oxford, for St John's College (*c.*1881–99). Scott was also a master of the *Queen-Anne style, as demonstrated at his Garboldisham Manor, Norfolk (*c.*1868–83—demolished), and a remarkable group of houses at Westbourne Park, Hull (1876–9), known as 'The Avenues', but they have not been treated well.

Scott published *An Essay on the History of English Church Architecture Prior to the Separation of England from the Roman Obedience* (1881), the year after he himself became an RC, and edited his father's *Personal and Professional Recollections* (1879). His last years were marred by mental instability: outstanding works were completed by Temple Moore, apart from St John's at Norwich. He died in his father's Midland Grand Hotel, St Pancras.

AR, **v** (Dec. 1898), 58–66, and (Jan.–Feb. 1899), 124–32; *BA*, **xv** (1881), 1–2; *BW*, **lv** (1880), 411–14, **v**, 11–14, 51–4; Brandwood (1997); J.Curl (2007); *GS*; P (1982); Ant.Ro (1998); Stamp (2002)

Scott, Sir Giles Gilbert (1880–1960) English architect, son of 'Middle' *Scott, he was articled to the latter's pupil, Temple *Moore, and was profoundly affected by the work of both men. In his early twenties (1903) he won the second competition to design the Anglican Cathedral in Liverpool (1903–80) which occupied him for the rest of his life. Because of his youth and Roman Catholicism, the Liverpool Cathedral Committee insisted that a senior architect should work with him, and *Bodley (who had been one of the competition assessors) was appointed, an arrangement which exasperated Scott, and came to an end with Bodley's death (1907). The beautiful Lady Chapel was immediately redesigned by Scott, who gave the *vaulting a much more German late-*Gothic appearance, something further enhanced by the elaborate *Flügelaltar*. With Bodley out of the way, Scott redesigned the rest of the building, and created a *Sublime monument with breathtaking internal volumes, quite unlike any other work of the *Gothic Revival. He replaced the twin towers of his winning design with a single mighty *battered tower and pairs of *transepts, which also helped to create a huge central space. At the same time he simplified the elevations, contrasting massive unadorned sandstone walls with sumptuous detail, and towering verticality with judicious use of horizontals. The *choir and the first pair of transepts were completed by 1924; the central tower was finished (1942); and the first bay of the nave was opened (1961).

The western parts of the Cathedral were completed under **Frederick Thomas** (1898–1984), who became (1953) a partner in Scott's firm, and senior partner on Scott's death (1960). Thomas continued to be associated with the Cathedral until 1980, but most of the design-drawings for the revised and reduced scheme were the work of **Roger Arthur Philip Pinckney** (1900–90). Even in its smaller realization, the Cathedral is still a scenic prodigy, a mighty monument to the originality and inventiveness of its architect.

Among Scott's other churches may be mentioned the Annunciation, Bournemouth, Hants. (1905–6), St Joseph, Cromer Road, Sheringham, Norfolk (1908–10—in which a tendency to greatly simplify Gothic forms is very marked), the monumental Our Lady of the Assumption, Northfleet, Kent (1913–16—displaying certain design-features that were to reappear at Liverpool Cathedral), St Paul, Stonycroft, Liverpool (1913–16), St Andrew, Luton, Beds. (1931–2), St Francis, Terriers, High Wycombe, Bucks. (1928–30), St Alban, Golders Green, London (1932–3), and the austere RC Cathedral of St Columba, Oban, Argyll (1930–53). One of his most successful churches, with its battered walls, is St Michael, Ashford, Middx. (1927–8). He also designed the completion of the *nave at Downside Abbey, Som. (1917–39), several boarding-houses and the Chapel at Ampleforth College, Yorks. (1922–60), and the very fine Chapel at Charterhouse School, Godalming, Surrey (1922–7—perhaps one of his most successful buildings). At St Alphege, Bath (1927–30), and the Chapel at Lady Margaret Hall, Oxford (1931–2), he employed a simple round-arched style instead of Gothic. After the 1914–18 war he designed the Memorial Court, Clare College, Cambridge (1922–32), in a simplified *Neo-Georgian style, on the central axis of which is the tower of his huge Cambridge University library (1930–4). At Oxford he designed the New Bodleian Library opposite *Hawksmoor's Clarendon Building (1935–46—a great part of which is below ground thus keeping the visible part of the building low), and Longwall Quad, Magdalen College (1928–9).

Among his best-known designs were the 1924 and 1935 versions of the Post-Office cast-iron telephone-kiosk, with tops derived from *Soane's tomb in London. Scott was appointed (1930) consultant architect to the London Power Company for the new generating station at Battersea designed by **James Theodore Halliday** (1882–1932) and **Sir Leonard Pearce** (1878–1947). This huge structure, with chimneys treated like Classical columns, and much *Art-Deco detail, demonstrated Scott's sense of the monumental in composition and his control of massing: even *Pevsner admired it. Other commissions followed, including the Guinness Brewery, Park Royal (1933–5), Waterloo Bridge (1932–45), and

the rebuilding of the House of Commons at the Palace of Westminster following bomb damage (1944–50—a tactful and very intelligent intervention, much hated by *Modernists). He also rebuilt the war-damaged hall of the City of London's Guildhall (1950–4), and designed Bankside Power Station, London (1947–60), his Sublime 'Cathedral of Power' with its chimneys treated as one magnificent *campanile-like tower. This building is now the Tate Gallery of Modern Art, having been converted by **Herzog & De Meuron**, who unhappily altered Scott's handsome stepped main elevation.

Scott's last religious buildings were the Carmelite Church, Kensington, London (1954–9—another replacement of a church lost in 1939–45), an RC Church in Preston, Lancs. (1954–9), and the small but lofty Christ the King, Plymouth, Devon (1961–2). However, his post-1939–45-war work was not appreciated in the climate in which *International Modernism was universally embraced. He himself was impatient of dogma, be it 'unintelligent Traditionalism' or 'extreme Modernism', and stated that he would have been happier about the future of architecture 'had the best ideas of Modernism being grafted upon the best traditions of the past', and if 'Modernism had come by evolution rather than by revolution'. His son, **Richard Gilbert Scott** (1923–2017), became a partner (1952) in the family firm, and designed the extension to Guildhall, City of London (1969–75), as well as the new Art Gallery (1988–2000), which completed his father's scheme for Guildhall's forecourt.

AD, lxix/10–11 (1979), 72–83; Cotton (1964); *CL*, cxcvi/47 (21 Nov. 2002), 58–9; GS; Kennerley (2001); *ODNB* (2004); P (1982); Stamp & Harte (1979); J.T (1996)

Scott, Major-General Henry Young Darracott (1822–83) English military-engineer, he became Secretary to the Commissioners for the Great Exhibition on the retirement of *Cole, and served in the Department of Science and Art in succession to *Fowke. With *Wild et al. he designed the red-brick and *terracotta-faced *Rundbogenstil Science Schools (Henry Cole Wing), Exhibition Road, Kensington (1867–71). With Fowke he designed the Royal Albert Hall, London (1867–71), in which the *Antique, *Renaissance, and *Rundbogenstil combine. He rendered considerable services to the Great Exhibition, London (1862), and other international exhibitions. He contributed papers on types of *cement and on the construction of the Albert Hall as well as preparing plans for the completion of the South Kensington Museum.

D & M (1985); *ODNB* (2004)

Scottish Baronial C19 style evolved during the *Jacobethan Revival in England, with a distinctly Scottish flavour, incorporating *battle-ments, *tourelles, *machicolations, and conical roofs. Derived from medieval fortified tower-houses and castles, among its instigators were William *Burn and his pupil David *Bryce. It was essentially an eclectic amalgam of the traditional fortified domestic architecture of Scotland and asymmetrical compositions common during the vogue for the *Picturesque. The style was popular in Ulster, as in Scrabo Tower, Newtownards, Co. Down (1858), by *Lanyon & *Lynn, and several larger houses.

Billings (1845–52); MacG & R (1887–92)

Scott, John Oldrid (1841–1913) English archi-tect, second son of 'Great' *Scott, he carried out various works with his brother, 'Middle' *Scott, including the spectacular Church of St John the Baptist (now the RC Cathedral), Norwich (1884–1910). He added the German-*Gothic *tracery-*spire to his father's Glasgow University (1887). Scott was responsible for the Church of St John the Baptist, Hythe, Kent (1869), but his mas-terpiece is the *Byzantine-style Greek Orthodox Cathedral of Western Europe, St Sophia, Moscow Road, Bayswater, London (1874–82).

D & M (1985); Ant.Ro (1998)

Scott, Mackay Hugh Baillie (1865–1945) British architect, articled to **Charles Edward Davis** (1827–1902), City Architect of Bath. He moved (1889) to Douglas, IoM, and established (1893) his own practice, specializing in domestic architecture using *vernacular motifs, influenced partly by American work, notably in the *Shingle style, and partly by *Voysey. He began to publish (1895) articles on house-design in *The Studio*, and his work caught the attention of **Ernst Lud-wig, Grand Duke of Hesse** (r.1892–1918), who employed him to decorate/furnish the main rooms of his house at Darmstadt (1897). His entry to the 'House of an Art-Lover' competition (organized by *Koch) won (1901) the highest award, and was published in *Meister der Innen-kunst* (1902)—*Mackintosh was awarded a special prize in the same competition. More commissions followed, including Blackwell, Bowness, Westmd. (1898–9), the White Lodge, Wantage, Berks. (1898–9), and the White House, Helensburgh, Scotland (1899–1900). He built several model dwellings at Letchworth *Garden City, Herts., Hampstead *Garden Suburb, Lon-don, and Gidea Park, Essex, and his work was published and praised by *Muthesius (1904). Other designs include Bill House, Selsey-on-Sea, Sussex (1907), Undershaw, Guildford, Sur-rey (1908–9), and Home Close, Sibford Ferris, Oxon. (1910). Probably his best house, with gar-den and furnishings, was Waldbühl, Uzwil, Swit-zerland (1908–14).

Essentially an *Arts-and-Crafts architect, draw-ing on the domestic vernacular architecture of England, his best works were probably those pro-duced 1901–11, when he seems to have been influenced by *Lutyens. His planning was inge-nious, with volumes freely flowing into each other, and he designed fitted furniture to reduce clutter. This, with his tendency to simplify the exterior treatment of his buildings, gained him a spurious reputation as a proto-Modernist, but this is nonsense: from 1919 he worked in partnership with **Arthur Edgar Beresford** (1880–1952), with whom he collaborated on the second edn (1933) of his 1906 *Houses and Gardens* which *specifically denounced* the *International *Modernism *Pevs-ner et al. ludicrously claim he 'pioneered'.

AR, cxxxviii/826 (Dec. 1965), 456–8; Creese (1992); D & M (1985); *DW*, xxiv (1937), 140–53; Haigh (1995); Jervis (1984); A. (of Darmstadt) Koch (1902); Kornwolf (1972); Me.Miller (1992, 2002); M & G (1992); H.M (1979); H.M (ed.) (1910); *ODNB* (2004); M.H.B.Scott (1906, 1910); Slater (1995)

Scott, Michael John (1905–89) Irish *Mod-ernist, he designed St Laurence's School, Dro-gheda, Co. Louth (1934), Scott House, Sandycove, Co. Dublin (1938), Laois County Hospital, Port-laoise (1936–7), Offaly County Hospital, Tullamore (1937), and Central Bus Station, Dublin (1950–3). Joined (1959) by **Patrick Scott** (1921–2014), **Robin Walker** (1924–91), and **Ronald Joseph Tallon** (1927–2014), they produced *Radio Telefís Éireann* Studios (1959–62), Brown & Polson's factory (1959), and Bank of Ireland headquarters, Baggot Street (1965–73), all in Dublin. Renamed (1966) **Scott Tallon Walker**, the practice designed Carroll's Factory, Dundalk, Co. Louth (1967–70—influenced by *Mies van der Rohe), School of Engineering, Uni-versity College (1980–9), O'Reilly Institute, Trinity College (1986–8), and Civic Offices, Wood Quay (1992–4), again in Dublin.

Architecture Ireland 275/3 (June/July 2014), 15ff.; C & R (1993); O'Regan & Dearey (eds) (1995); M.Scott (1992)

Scott, Richard Gilbert (1923–2017) *See* SCOTT, SIR GILES GILBERT.

scraped 1. *See* SGRAFFITO. **2.** Building from which all additions have been removed. The term was current during the *Gothic Revival when over-enthusiastic 'restorers' would remove virtually everything so that a homogeneous *Mid-dle-Pointed building would result: in the process, all *Perp., *Jacobean, and *Georgian work would be ruthlessly ripped out. This widespread C19 tendency led William *Morris to found the Society for the Protection of Ancient Buildings (SPAB) in 1877 when 'Great' *Scott proposed to over-restore Tewkesbury Abbey. SPAB was known affection-ately as 'Anti-Scrape'.

scratchwork *See* SGRAFFITO.

screen 1. Partition of timber, stone, or metal, not part of the main structure of a church, to separate *nave from *choir (called variously *chancel-, *choir-, *Rood-screen, or *pulpitum), nave from choir- or chancel-*aisle (called *parclose-screen), or to define a *chantry- or *mortuary-chapel, etc. 2. Any other such screen, as in a medieval hall, defining the *screens-passage*. 3. Open *colonnade or *arcade around a *court, e.g. in a *cloister. *Compounds include*:

screen-façade: non-structural *façade disguising the realities of form, size, and structure of a building behind, as in the C13 screens on the west fronts of Lincoln and Salisbury Cathedrals;

screens-passage: space at one end of a medieval hall between the *buttery and kitchen-doors and the screen (placed to conceal activity behind), often with a *gallery over it, common in Oxbridge colleges;

screen-wall: 1. solid unperforated wall hiding something, e.g. a court in front of a house; 2. retaining-wall in a garden, often decorated with *niches, etc.; 3. wall carried up between columns, as in an Ancient-Egyptian *temple.

screw stair Any *newel-, *vice, or circular stair wound about a newel or *pier.

scriptorium Room assigned in a medieval conventual establishment for the copying and storage of texts.

scroll 1. Ornament composed of curved lines like *volutes, often of double flexure passing from one volute to another in series on a *band or *frieze, as in *Vitruvian or *wave-scroll, but sometimes used as a terminal feature, e.g. hand-rail of a *stair *balustrade. 2. Volute of a *console, *modillion, or *capital (e.g. in the *Composite, *Corinthian, and *Ionic *Orders). 3. Type of *Gothic *moulding with a deep scroll-like indentation under a hood-like top occurring on *hood-moulds, *labels, and *string-courses. 4. *Torsade or spiral scroll. *Combinations/related terms include*:

scrolled: participial adjective, meaning curled or in the form of a scroll, so *scrolled heart* = Classical ornament consisting of a repeated heart-shaped form in series formed by two parallel *bands of *wave-scrolls, often occurring on *friezes and borders; *scrolled pediment* = open-topped curved *pediment, its two ʃ-shaped sides ending in scrolls, also called *bonnet-scroll, bonnet-top, goose-neck,* or *swan-neck;

scrolling foliage: architectural ornament of many types, usually combining naturalistic foliage and stems with stylized or even abstract patterns.

scroll-step: bottom *curtail-step in a *flight of *stairs, having rounded ends or ends *scrolled

around the *newel-post, often echoing the scroll of the hand-rail;

scroll-work: any complex ornamental element composed of scrolls or scroll-like forms, such as the C- and S-shapes found in *Baroque, *Celtic, *Jacobean, and *Rococo designs.

sculpture-garden Garden where sculpture either ornaments or serves a primary role. Precedents include *Bramante's *Belvedere* *court, Vatican (completed 1523 to display the Pope's collection of *Antique statuary), and Inigo *Jones's early-C17 court at Arundel House, London, to show off the **Earl of Arundel**'s collection (though there were undoubtedly other examples in Antiquity). During the *Baroque period, sculpture was used to create focal-points, terminate axes, punctuate space, function as *fountains, etc., and with the emergence of the C18 English landscape-garden, sculpture, *fabriques,* etc., became essential elements as part of the *Picturesque (e.g. Stowe, Bucks.). In C20 numerous sculpture-gardens were created to display sculptures to advantage in the open air: examples include those at the Kröller-Müller Museum, Otterlo, The Netherlands (founded 1961); the 'gallery without walls' at West Bretton, near Wakefield, Yorkshire (founded 1977); at the National Gallery of Art, Washington, DC (opened 1999); and at the *Musée Rodin,* Paris (1993). Many museum-directors in C21 now consider sculpture-gardens to be important display-areas.

Beardsley (2006); Js (2011); J.McCarthy (1996); Shoe (2001); Stace (2013); Tay (2006)

Scune, Christopher (*fl.*1505–21) English mason, he succeeded (1505) John *Cole as Master-Mason at Louth, Lincs., and worked on the *steeple until it was almost finished (*c.*1512). He was appointed (*c.*1508) Master of the Masons at Durham Cathedral, and from *c.*1514 he was at Ripon, Yorks., where he carried out all the new works at the *nave of the *Minster (now Cathedral), completed 1520. He was presumably also responsible for the tower and tower-arch at Fountains Abbey, Yorks. (1494–1526).

J.Harvey (1987)

scutcheon *See* ESCUTCHEON.

Searles, Michael (1751–1813) English architect/surveyor, he had a large London practice devoted mostly to the design and building of residential developments south of the River Thames, where he was Surveyor to the Rolls Estate from 1783. His architecture was in a late-*Georgian style, distinguished by his originality of massing and simplicity of detail. His masterpiece is The Paragon, Blackheath (*c.*1793–1807), a series of semi-detached dwellings linked by *colonnades and set out on a *crescent. He also designed

Secession

690

Clare House, East Malling, Kent (1793), with a complex series of circular, elliptical, and octagonal rooms. He was responsible for Surrey Square, Southwark, London (1792–3), and The Circus, Greenwich, London (1790–3).

Bonwitt (1987); Co (2008); Ck (1985); Su (2003)

Secession *See* SEZESSION.

Second Empire Describes characteristic styles of Bonapartist France during the reign (1852–70) of Emperor Napoléon III, or styles influenced by them. Essentially eclectic, the Second Empire was a period of revivals, especially *Baroque, *Empire, *François Ier, *Louis Seize, *Néo-Grec, and *Renaissance styles. The *École des *Beaux-Arts encouraged *Historicism, as can be seen in the Paris created by *Haussmann for Napoléon III, and especially in the extensions to the Louvre, from 1853. High roofs, *lucarnes, and lush ornament gave French architecture of the period an opulent flavour widely appreciated and copied in the USA.

J.T (1996)

Second Pointed Style of *Gothic architecture that emerged in the late C13, known in England as *Decorated*, and developed in C14, during which enrichment became more elaborate, with *diaper-work covering surfaces, and widespread use of the *ogee form. At the end of C13 *First-Pointed *plate-tracery* had evolved, then *bar-tracery* arranged in *Middle-Pointed *Geometrical* patterns. *Nail-head and *dog-tooth ornaments were superseded by *fleuron and *ball-flower enrichment, while *crockets on *pinnacles and *canopies became profuse. Floral/foliate ornament was given naturalistic treatment, nowhere more so than in the enchanting leaves of the *Chapter House of Southwell *Minster, Notts. (c.1290—damaged in the late C20). The later phase of Second Pointed saw the development of *Curvilinear* or *Flowing *tracery, the almost universal adoption of ogee or S-shaped curves, the appearance of *mouchette* or *dagger-forms in tracery, and the invention of *Reticulated* or net-like tracery patterns formed by ogees. Windows became very large, and the flame-like forms of the *lights in the upper parts of traceried windows gave the name *Flamboyant to late (C15) elaborate (especially Continental) Gothic (which continued until the early C16). *Vaults acquired *intermediate* or *lierne* ribs, enabling very complex patterns (some star-shaped) to be created. Celebrated examples of Second-Pointed work include the octagon and *Lady Chapel at Ely Cathedral (first half of C14) and the Percy tomb at Beverley, Yorks. (with its elaborate canopy). Roofs remained steeply pitched.

Bony (1979); Coldstream (1994); J.Parker (1850); Rickman (1848)

secos, sekos *Adytum, *cella, *naos, or *sanctuary in an Ancient-*Egyptian *temple.

secret 1. Intimate, privy, remote, secluded, so a private retiring-room. **2.** Concealed *gutter. **3.** *Stair, often for servants, to provide discreet access. **4.** Chamber in a *temple, e.g. *adytum. **5.** For *secret garden* (*giardino segreto*) *see* HORTUS CONCLUSUS.

section Surface or portion obtained by a cut made through a structure or any part of a structure to reveal its profile, and/or interior. It may therefore show the outline of a *moulding, and a drawing of an imaginary vertical cut through a building will show the *elevations of the walls of internal rooms, the convention being that all beyond the plane made by the intersection of the section is depicted in elevation. A *plan is therefore a section, the section-plane being horizontal, and shows the floors in elevation.

Sedding, John Dando (1838–91) English architect, one of the most inventive of his time. Trained by *Street, he later became much influenced by *Ruskin and *Morris, and his London office became a magnet for all those interested in the *Arts-and-Crafts movement. His assistant, Henry *Wilson, contributed to his later designs. Among early works are St Clement's Church, Boscombe, Bournemouth, Hants. (1871—designed with his brother, Edmund Sedding (1836–68)), but his greatest buildings are in London. His Church of the Holy Redeemer, Exmouth Market, Clerkenwell, London (1887–8), is a remarkable *Italianate early *Renaissance-Revival building, starkly simple, with a west front crowned by a *Tuscan *pediment. Henry Wilson added the *Early-Christian Italian-*Romanesque *campanile. Sedding and Wilson also designed St Peter's, Mount Park Road, Ealing, London (1889–93), an essay using the curvaceous forms of late *Gothic with originality and virtuosity. Their masterpiece is undoubtedly Holy Trinity, Sloane Street, London (1888–90), a work in which late-*Perp., *Byzantine, *Second-Pointed *tracery, Renaissance, *Art-Nouveau, and Arts-and-Crafts elements are found. His nephew, Edmund Harold Sedding (fl.1880–1921), was also an architect.

D & M (1985); Hl & Su (1989); G.Naylor (1971); ODNB (2004); Sedding (1891, 1893); Se (ed.) (1975); Stamp & Avery (1980); H.Wilson *et al*. (1892)

Seddon, John Pollard (1827–1906) English *Gothic-Revival architect who trained with T.L. *Donaldson. He was in partnership (1852–69) with John Prichard (1817–86), and (1884–94) with John Coates Carter (1859–1927). With Prichard he designed the *High-Victorian *Gothic Ettington Park, Warwicks. (c.1856–62). Other works include University College, Aberystwyth,

Wales (1864–90), Powell Almshouses, Fulham, London (1869–70), St Peter's Church, Ayot St Peter, Herts. (1874–5), St Paul's Church, Hammersmith, London (1880–8—with H.R.*Gough), and St Catherine, Hoarwithy, Herefs. (*c.*1874–85—in an Italian-*Romanesque style with *Byzantine detail).

J.Curl (2007); Darby (1983); D & M (1985); Ea (1970); J.T (1996)

sedile (*pl.* **sedilia**) Seat. The plural term is used to describe the series of stone seats (usually three) in a church set in the south wall of the *chancel, often crowned with elaborate *canopies and *pinnacles, used by officiating clergy. *Sedilia*, collectively known as the *prismatory*, may include the *piscina within a series of arched *niches.

sedilia C14 Second-Pointed *prismatory* type incorporating *piscina* and *credence-shelf*, St Swithun's, Merton, Oxon. (*after Parker*).

Seely, Henry John Alexander (1899–1963—**2nd Baron Mottistone** from 1947) English architect, he established in practice (1926) with **Paul Edward Paget** (1901–85), having secured a commission (1925) to restore Mottistone Manor, IoW, for his father. One of the firm's first jobs was the lavish mansion created at Eltham Palace for (**Sir**) **Stephen Lewis Courtauld** (1883–1967) and his wife, **Virginia** (d.1972), with the **Marchese Peter Malacrida** (1889–1980), who created therein some of the most lavish *Art-Deco interiors in the British Isles. Seely was Surveyor of the Fabric of St Paul's Cathedral (1956–63), and was succeeded in this post by Paget, who held it until 1969. **Seely & Paget** carried out numerous schemes of restoration after the 1939–45 war, including Lambeth Palace, the Charterhouse, and Eton College, and designed St Faith's Church, Lee-on-Solent, Hants. (1933), with an interior

*Pevsner described as 'original and impressive', yet the *oeuvre* of the firm, not fitting neatly into *Modernist categories, has been consistently underestimated.

Pe & Lloyd (1967); pk

Segal, Walter (1907–85) German-born architect of Romanian descent, he studied architecture at Delft, Zürich, and Berlin, where he met Bruno *Taut and became interested in *Expressionism. He settled in London, where he established a practice, publishing work in the 1940s and 1950s. His buildings include the *Casa Piccolo*, Ascona, Switzerland (1932), a housing estate, St Anne's Close, Highgate, London (1950), and a house at Rugby Road, Twickenham, Mddx. (1961). During the 1960s he became interested in low-cost housing, specializing in cheap *timber-framed construction. His Timber House, Main Street, Yelling, Hunts. (1970), led to experiments in *community architecture for the Lewisham Self-Build Housing Association, London (1977–80), and it was in the field of cheap, easily constructed housing that he became known.

E (1994); J.McKean (1988); P (1982); *RIBAJ*, ser. 3, lxxxiv/7 (July 1977), 284–95; J.T (1996)

segment Plane figure contained by a straight line and part of the circumference of a circle: a *segmental arch* is therefore the shape of a segment, formed by its centre far below the springing-line.

Seidl, Gabriel von (1848–1913) German architect/engineer, he is best-known for his advocacy of a revival of Bavarian *vernacular architecture (e.g. timber Alpine buildings, or 'Swiss cottages'). He made many designs for *Das deutsche Zimmer der Renaissance* (1880), edited by **Georg Hirth** (1841–1916), which popularized interiors drawing on German vernacular and *Renaissance exemplars. He designed the sumptuous *Villa Lenbach* (1887–9), the *Künstlerhaus* (1893–1900—largely destroyed 1945, rebuilt 1961), the *Romanesque-Revival Church of St Anne (1887–92—restored after war damage), the *Nationalmuseum* (1897–9), and the *Deutsches Museum* (1906–25—an early building in which *reinforced concrete was used for the structure, completed by his brother **Emanuel** (1856–1919)), all in Munich, the Classical *Neues Rathaus*, Bremen (1909–12), and many other works. He influenced Theodor *Fischer and *Schumacher, and his 'Bavarian style' used in domestic architecture continued well into C20: excellent examples were **Emanuel von Seidl**'s *Brey Landhaus*, Murnau, and the *Landhaus* (or *villa) for **Richard Strauss** (1864–1949), Garmisch-Partenkirchen (both completed before 1910). The Strauss villa (where the composer spent the rest of his life) was said to have been built on the proceeds of the opera *Salome* (first given in Dresden, 1905).

Bössl (1966); H.M (ed.) (1910); S.M (1974); J.T (1996)

Seidler, Harry (1923–2006) Vienna-born architect, he studied at Harvard (under *Breuer and *Gropius), and worked briefly with *Aalto in Helsinki, *Niemeyer in Rio de Janeiro, and Breuer in NYC before settling (1948) in Sydney, Australia, bringing aspects of Breuer's style with him, as in the Rose Seidler House, Turramurra, Sydney (1948–9), and other designs conforming to pre-War *International *Modernism. His work includes the Blues Point Tower (1958–61—reviled by some, but considered by Seidler to be his best work), Australia Square Tower (1960–8), MLC Centre (1969–71), Grosvenor Place Tower (1982), all in Sydney; the Australian Embassy, Paris (1973–7), Hong Kong Club and Offices (1980–4), and Riverside Centre, Brisbane (1983–6). He also designed a large public housing-development, the *Wohnpark Neue Donau*,Vienna, Austria (1992–7).

AR, ccxix/1312 (June 2006), 96–7; Blake (1973); E (1994); Forster (2002); F & Drew (1992); Jackson & Johnson (2000); D.L.Johnson (1980); H.Seidler (1954, 1963, 1977); The Times (16 March 2006), 70; J.T (1996)

Seifert, Alwin (1890–1972) German landscape architect. His work integrating *Autobahnen* into landscape was remarkably fine, and, with *Bonatz's *bridges, *viaducts, etc., ensured German *motorways were widely admired.

Spotts (2002)

Seifert, Richard (Robin, *originally* Rubin) (1910–2001) Zürich-born British architect, he achieved notoriety for his huge developments, many of which were realized through his mastery of law relating to planning and building. His most famous tower-block is Centre Point, junction of Tottenham Court Road and New Oxford Street, London (1959–66), which attempted to make the building-type more interesting by means of cruciform precast-concrete elements (with drooping arms) of the *façades, creating straight verticals but repetitive horizontal zig-zags at every floor-level. This restless frame eliminated the need for scaffolding during construction. His National Westminster Tower, Old Broad Street, City of London (1970–81), was, at the time, one of the tallest buildings in Europe, with a plan derived from the Bank's logo. Other works by him include the Royal Garden Hotel, Kensington (1960–5); the Britannia Hotel, Grosvenor Square (1967–9); the Park Tower Hotel, Knightsbridge (1973); the London Forum Hotel, Cromwell Road (1971–2); Space House, just off Kingsway (1964–8—featuring a circular block with cruciform precast concrete members similar to those of Centre Point, the whole supported on splayed stilts); and the

Office Development in the forecourt to Euston Street (1974–8—which demonstrates there would have been plenty of room to retain *Hardwick's Greek-*Doric *propylaeum*, demolished 1960–1 despite widespread protest), all in London. It was claimed that Seifert had made a greater impression on the London skyline than any architect since *Wren: his architecture, however, was somewhat brash (bearing no comparison at all with Wren's), and received little recognition where it counted, although the RIBA Heinz Gallery mounted an exhibition of his work (1984), and he was rarely out of the public prints in the 1960s, 1970s, and 1980s. Centre Point, which became an object of derision because it was seen as a symbol of commercial exploitation and greed (it lay empty until 1975, gaining in value all the time), eventually was listed as being of architectural and historic interest. *Pevsner, in 1973, thought its only merit was that it looked slim from the north and south, but he regarded the zig-zag horizontals as 'coarse in the extreme' and asked of it 'who would want such a building as its image?' Considering that Seifert claimed his work was profoundly influenced by *Gropius, Pevsner's hero, the last's comments are interesting, but Seifert also named Le *Corbusier, *Nervi, *Niemeyer, and *Breuer as his inspirations. Taking his cue from successful transatlantic architects, he built up one of the largest practices of the period.

Bradley & Pe (1997); E (1980, 1994); ODNB (2009); GS; The Times (27 Oct. 2001), 27; pk

Seljuk *or* Saljuk architecture Taking its name from a Turkish Islamic dynasty which, with its branches, ruled in Iran, Iraq, and Syria (1038–1194) and in Anatolia (1077–1307), it consists largely of *madrasas, *caravanserais, and *mausolea, usually executed in high-quality *masonry or brickwork embellished with glazed *tiles. It evolved a type of *mosque with four *iwans facing the *court, with a domed prayer-hall behind the prayer-iwan (e.g. Great Mosque, Isfahan (C11)). Mausolea comprise the most distinctive type of Seljuk architecture: they are towers, often circular or star-shaped on plan (e.g. the cone-capped *Gunbad i Qabus*, Gurgan (1006–7)) with elaborate inscriptions and ornament. *Minarets were often very elaborate, created perhaps more as monuments than as mere towers for calls to prayer (e.g. Ghurid minaret, Jam (1191–8)). Other mausolea are domed, often surfaced externally with brilliantly coloured glazed tiles: a good example is the tomb of Sultan Sanjar, Merv (1157). Seljuk architecture was to influence later *Islamic architecture, especially in Iran and Turkey.

Ck (1996)

Sellars, James (1843–88) Glasgow architect, in partnership (1872–88) with **Campbell Douglas**

(1828–1910) after the latter's collaboration (1860–9) with J.J.*Stevenson ended. When Sellars died, Douglas was in partnership with **Alexander Barr Morrison** (1857–1937), who seems to have developed a drink problem, so Douglas 'found it necessary' to dissolve the arrangement (*c*.1901). Works included the *Greek-Revival St Andrew's Halls (1873–7), Belmont Hillhead Church (1875–6), Belhaven Church (1876–7—later the Greek-Orthodox Cathedral), Kelvinside Academy (1877–9—influenced by the work of Alexander *Thomson), and Anderson's College of Medicine (1888–9), all in Glasgow. His work was either Grecian, *Free-*Renaissance, or French-*Gothic in style. His Glasgow International Exhibition Buildings (1887–8) were exotically oriental, with a *Saracenic influence.

DW; G & W (1987); *SAR*, **ix**/1 & 2 (1967), 16–19, 21–4; WRH (1990)

Selva, Giovanni Antonio (1751–1819) Venetian architect, pupil of *Temanza, he travelled in Italy, France, Austria, The Netherlands, and England before establishing a practice in Venice where he became a leading Neo-Classicist, much influenced by **Antonio Canova** (1757–1822), the Neo-Classical sculptor. His early works show a pronounced *Palladian influence, notably the *Teatro La Fenice*, Venice (1788–92—burnt 1996, and subsequently restored), but his later designs were powerful essays in *Neo-Classicism, and include the grandly Roman *Duomo*, Cologna Veneta (1806–17), and the Churches of *San Maurizio* (1806–10) and *Santissima Nome di Gesù* (1815–34), both in Venice. He also won commissions (1815–19) to design *public parks at Castello and the Giudecca, and the *cemetery on the island of *San Michele*. He prepared works by *Chambers, *Perrault, and *Scamozzi for publication, wrote *Sulla voluta ionica* (On the *Ionic *Volute—1814), and taught *Jappelli.

E.Bassi (1936); D.Howard (1980); Ms (1966); Me (1966); Milizia (1785); J.T (1996)

Semark, Henry (*fl.*1482–1534) English mason at King's College Chapel, Cambridge (1508–15), he worked with *Wastell on the high *vault from 1512. He also contributed to the eastern chapels at Peterborough Cathedral, Cambs., and the Abbey and St James's Church, Bury St Edmunds, Suffolk. It has also been suggested he built the fan-vault under the tower of Fotheringhay Church, Northants. (1528).

J.Harvey (1987)

semi- Half; nearly; partly; incompletely. *Compounds include*:
semi-arch: half-arch, e.g. flying *buttress;
semi-circular arch: *arch with its head a half-circle;

semi-circular dome: *dome with a half-circular *section on its greatest diameter, i.e. half a sphere;
semi-column: *engaged column;
semi-detached: term applied to pairs of houses, separated by a party-wall, but the pair itself is not joined to other buildings, so it differs from a *terrace-house;
semi-dome: *hemi-dome, or quarter-sphere over *apses and *niches;
semi-elliptical arch: **1.** *arch in the form of a half-ellipse; **2.** three- or five-centred arch.

Semiological *or* **Semiotic School** *Semiotics* (the science of *signs* and the study of how signs work) has been perceived as of major significance in architecture, for the built environment may be seen as a communicating-system of signs and symbols. The school of thought (supposedly influenced by *Semper) that recognizes contemporary signs and symbols in design has been termed the *Semiological* or *Semiotic School*.

Broadbent *et al.* (1980); Js (1971); Js & Baird (eds) (1969); Preziosi (1979); J.Walker (1992)

Semper, Gottfried (1803–79) German architect, he is said to have studied under von *Gärtner in Munich (1825), but definitely worked under *Gau in Paris from 1826, where he became acquainted with *Hittorff's theories of *polychromy in Ancient-Greek architecture. He travelled in Southern Europe (1830–4), and published *Vorläufige Bemerkungen über bemalte Architectur und Plastik bei den Alten* (Preliminary Remarks on Polychrome Architecture and Sculpture in Antiquity—1834), a pamphlet dedicated to Gau, which created quite a stir. Partly as a result of this publication he was appointed Professor at the Dresden Academy of Fine Arts the same year. While at Dresden (1834–49) he designed some of his best buildings, including the *Hoftheater* (1838–41, destroyed), a *Cinquecento*-Revival building with an exterior that made clear what were the internal arrangements, not uninfluenced by F. *Gilly's design (1790s) for a National Theatre. This structure was replaced after a fire with the celebrated Opera House, also designed by Semper, built 1871–8 under the direction of Semper's son, **Manfred** (1838–*c*.1914). It was destroyed (1945) but rebuilt (1980s): it is one of the most beautiful theatres in the world. He also designed the polychrome 'Antique' rooms in the Japanese Palace, Dresden (1835), which caused a sensation because of their vivid Classical beauty; the eclectic *Synagogue (1838–40—destroyed 1938) in a mix of *Byzantine, *Lombardic, *Moorish, and *Romanesque styles, with a polychrome interior of great richness; the *Villa Rosa* in a *Quattrocento* manner (1839—destroyed); the sumptuous *Oppenheim Palais* in *Cinquecento* Revival (1845–8—destroyed);

and the *Gemäldegalerie* attached to Pöppel-mann's **Zwinger* (1847–54—restored 1955–6 after war-damage).

Having fallen foul of the Saxon authorities after the 1848–9 revolution, Semper went first to Paris and then to London, where he met (1850) Henry *Cole, through whom he gained valuable intro-ductions, and designed the Canadian, Danish, Swedish, and Turkish sections for the 1851 Exhi-bition in the Crystal Palace. His connections and his book, *Wissenschaft, Industrie, und Kunst* (1852) brought him to the attention of Prince *Albert, who was greatly interested in his ideas about the relationship between architecture, design, industry, and education. Semper taught design while in London, but his most remarkable achievement was his detailing of the great funeral-car for the exequies (1852) of **Arthur Wellesley** (1769–1852—**1st Duke of Wellington** from 1814). He then took up a teaching post at the Zürich Polytechnic, where he remained until 1871: while there he designed the fine *Zürich Polytechnikum* (1855–63—now *ETH*, Zürich), and made designs for **Richard Wagner's** (1813–83) proposed (but unrealized) *Festspielhaus* (1864–7) for Munich which influenced the build-ing (1876) designed by *Brückwald that Wagner eventually succeeded in erecting in Bayreuth. Semper won the competition to design the *Rathaus* at Winterthur, Switzerland (1862—built 1865–70). Semper had published (1851) *Die vier Elemente der Baukunst* in which he identified those elements as hearth, platform, roof and its supports, and non-structural enclosure (of tex-tiles, etc.) to keep out the weather. Having seen a Caribbean hut at the Great Exhibition, he found these four elements perfectly expressed, but believed that each of them could be subject to transformations, together or separately, and that those transformations could become rapid in a period of industrialization and change, as normal evolutionary processes would be subjected to enormous outside pressures. He went on to develop his ideas in his most important book, *Der Stil in den technischen und tektonischen Kün-sten, oder praktische Äesthetik* (1861–3), which proposed that artefacts and architecture acquire meaning from the ways in which they are made and from their functions, so Semper described materials and their uses, investigating how design-motifs appeared and how those motifs were transferred from one material or context to others. In architecture, he noted how traditional and familiar forms retained traces of very early, primitive uses. In Semper's theory he conceived *four* essential categories of making artefacts: *weaving* (producing textiles and patterns); *mould-ing* (creating pottery from clay); *carpentry* (pro-viding essential structures of timber, especially

walls, partitions, and roofs); and *masonry* (involv-ing building with stone for hearth, walls, piers, etc.). To the four processes he added *working with metal*, and came to the conclusion that the greater part of the forms used in architecture actually originated in those processes (now *five*) themselves. From these he derived his theory of style, and argued that architecture was reducible to the materials and processes associated with their uses. Semper believed that long before Man made a building he evolved patterns (e.g. in weaving, which he called *Urkunst*, or original art, meaning the source of art, providing proto-typical models), and that these *preceded the evo-lution of structural form*, so ornament, far from being an afterthought, was *actually more basic and symbolic than structure*. He further developed his theory to postulate how political, religious, and social institutions create conditions by which appropriate and poetic expression is given to architectural forms. Thus architecture should be expressive of its purpose and the parts of a building easily distinguished. This is very far from the 'materialist' and 'functionalist' position he is often held (by those who either have not understood his (admittedly) prolix texts, or who have distorted his meanings for reasons of their own) to have adopted: in fact he stated that his conception of basic forms and their origins was the antithesis of the view which held that archi-tecture was nothing more than evolved construc-tion, a demonstration of statics and mechanics, and a pure revelation of material. For example, he noted that the patterns and ornaments used in producing textiles might reappear on walls con-structed of other materials, while swags or gar-lands on several buildings often reappear as sculpted or painted elements on friezes, and in their transformations the materials used are of no great importance. Claims for Semper as a proto-Modernist are as absurd as those which hold Baillie *Scott, *Voysey, et al. were forerunners of the *Bauhäusler*, for he derided *Viollet-le-Duc as a materialist, and could not accept that monu-mental architecture could be created using iron structures (he did not approve of *Paxton's Crystal Palace). He was, however, claimed as an influ-ence on *Semiotics* (*see* SEMIOLOGICAL SCHOOL).

The final years of Semper's architectural life were spent in Vienna, where his style became more florid than in his Dresden period. He col-laborated with Karl von *Hasenauer on the designs of the *Kunsthistorisches* and *Naturhistor-isches* Museums (1872–81), which face each other across *Maria-Theresien-Platz*: they are fine essays in the Italian *High-Renaissance Revival, and were built under the direction of Hasenauer. Semper and Hasenauer also worked on the *Burgtheater*, in an assured *Renaissance-Revival style (1872–86) with a curved front reminiscent of the Dresden Opera House. The grandiose and triumphal *Neue Burg* (1870–94), where the double columns of the east front of the Louvre, a Roman *triumphal arch, and various Renaissance-Revival motifs are quoted, was planned to harmonize the Imperial Palace with the new Museums: it formed part of a great *Forum*, the plan of which was essentially Semper's, although Hasenauer was mostly responsible for its realization. See FÖRSTER.

AR, cxxxvi/809 (July 1964), 57–60; Bernhard (1992); J.Curl (2002a); Ettlinger (1937); M.Fröhlich (1991); Hn (1984, 1992); Hvattum (2004); *JWCI*, lii, 254 ff.; Laudel (1991); Mallgrave (1996); Mallgrave & Hn (1988); M & Wa (1987); Pe (1972); P (1982); Ry (1973); Semper (1851, 1860–3, 1884, 1966, 1989); J.T (1996); Vogt *et al.* (eds) (1976); W-R (1980); Ziesemer (1999)

Semyonov, Vladimir Nikolayevich (1874–1960) Russian landscape architect/town-planner, he designed several buildings in the spa-resort districts of Northern Caucasus, including the Hotel Bristol, Pyatigorsk, all before the 1914–18 war. He studied architecture and town-planning in London (1908–12), an experience which informed his work at the *garden-city of Prozorovka, near Moscow, from 1913, laid out for workers constructing the Moscow-Kazan railway, a project also influenced by Western *Company-towns. He published numerous books and guidlines on planning, and designed several small rural settlements in the 1940s–'50s, called 'agro-cities'. He produced a detailed scheme for the rebuilding of Rostov-on-Don (1944–6), after damage in the 1941–45 war.

Belousov & Smirnova (1980); P.Clark (ed.) (2006); Shoe (2001)

Senmut or **Senenmut** (*fl.c.*1473–*c.*1458 BC) Ancient-Egyptian courtier, associated with the co-Regency of **Tutmosis III** and **Queen Hatshepsut** (*c.*1479–*c.*1458 BC), who either oversaw or was otherwise involved in the creation of the huge Mortuary Temple at Deïr-el-Bahari (*c.*1479–*c.*1458 BC), with its great ranges of square columns, massive *ramps joining the three main levels, and powerful symmetry. The complex includes columns that are seen by some as proto-*Doric, *Osiride features, and numerous *sphinxes. It is one of the finest and most original of all the buildings of the New Kingdom (c.1540–c.1075 BC), and has had a considerable impact on the *stripped *Classicism of C20, notably some of the works of *Speer and *Rational architecture.

Ck (1996); *JARCE*, vi (1967), 113–18; L & M (1986); J.T (1996); Werbrouck (1949)

Sens, William of (*fl.*1174–80) French architect of the *Gothic *choir from the main *crossing eastwards, including the western *transept,

Canterbury Cathedral, Kent (1174–84). As his name suggests, he had worked at Sens Cathedral (begun *c.*1140), which had some elements similar to those used at Canterbury, and he knew *Notre-Dame*, Paris, and other Gothic buildings in Rheims, Soissons, Arras, Cambrai, and elsewhere in North-West France, notably *Notre-Dame-la-Grande*, Valenciennes (1171). After he fell from the scaffolding (1177) he was incapacitated, and was succeeded by William the *Englishman who completed the choir *vaults, eastern transept, Trinity Chapel, circular chapel at the end of the choir called 'Becket's Crown' or the 'Corona' (1184), and introduced the *triforium-gallery previously used at Laon. Among influential motifs used by William of Sens were shafts of *Purbeck marble set against light Caen limestone, and *sexpartite vaults which draw the *bays into pairs. The prestige of Canterbury ensured the swift adoption of the new style throughout England.

J.Harvey (1987); Newman (2013); *JWCI*, xii (1949), 1–15; Stubbs (ed.) (1879); G.Webb (1965)

sentry-box Enclosure to give shelter to a guardsman before a royal or public edifice. Usually a timber structure, painted, some sentry-boxes are incorporated within the wall of a building.

sepulchre 1. Tomb, burial-place, building, *vault, or excavation made for the deposit of a human corpse. 2. Receptacle for Relics in a Christian *altar. 3. *Easter Sepulchre. 4. *Holy Sepulchre.

serai, sarai 1. Building for the accommodation of travellers (see CARAVANSERAI). 2. Turkish *palace. 3. Incorrect word for a *serail or *seraglio (part of a dwelling reserved for women, or a *harem). 4. *Warehouse. 5. House, or, more usually, commercial premises (e.g. shops), often of two *storeys, grouped round a *court (sometimes with a garden), associated with a corridor lined with shops.

serial See ADDITIVE.

serliana Tripartite window, door, or *blind architectural feature consisting of a central opening with a *semi-circular arch over it springing from two *entablatures each supported by two columns or *pilasters flanking narrower flat-topped openings on either side. Called a *Palladian* or *Venetian* window, it was a common motif in the works of *Palladio and was a feature much used in *Palladianism in C17 and C18 British architecture. It got its name as it was published in *Serlio's *L'Architettura* (1537–75), but probably originated with *Bramante.

serliana

Serlio, Sebastiano (1475–1554) Italian architect/theorist/painter, he is remembered primarily as the compiler of *L'Architettura* (published in instalments (1537–75) and collected in one volume (1584)). The first part to appear was actually Book IV, called *Regole generale* (1537), which outlined the later books, but, most significantly, codified and illustrated the five Roman *Orders of architecture. *L'Architettura* was an enormously important treatise, not only in terms of *Renaissance theory, but because it was a useful tome for architects, essentially because of its excellent illustrations and the fact that it was in a modern language. It was also a model for *Palladio's *Quattro Libri*. Book III (1540) described and illustrated the ancient buildings of Roman antiquity as well as the architecture of *Bramante and *Raphael, but in the work as a whole Serlio covered a huge range of Classical details (including *grotesques and *rustication), discussed the meaning and emotive power of Classical architecture, and, in *Livre extraordinaire* (published in French (1551)), provided illustrations of *doorways, many of which were richly inventive fantasies, and influenced *Mannerism in Northern Europe.

He worked in Rome (*c.*1514) under *Peruzzi, his principal tutor, from whom he acquired many drawings used subsequently in *L'Architettura*. Following the Sack of Rome (1527) he settled in Venice, then a major publishing centre, and an obvious place to live for someone engaged on writing a treatise on architecture. While in Venice he may have designed a few buildings. It is known he participated in the competition to renovate the 'basilica', Vicenza (1539), won by Palladio, whose design was not unlike that submitted by Serlio, and featured motifs similar to the *serliana, which is named after him. Called (1541) to *Fontainebleau, France, he advised on the design of the considerable building-works at the *château*, and designed the *Salle du Bal* there (1541–8—completed by de L'*Orme) in which the influence of Raphael is clear. His *Grand Ferrare*, the house for the Papal Legate to France at Fontainebleau

(1541–8—mostly destroyed), was an important prototype of the *hôtel* in France for the next century, while his *château* of Ancy-le-Franc, Burgundy (1541–50), with its corner-towers and central *court, shows the influence of *Maiano. Serlio's work undoubtedly informed Palladio, while his books had a considerable effect on many generations of designers, initially through the editions of **Pieter Coeck** (1502–50) in Northern Europe, and through the 1611 English edition of **Robert Peake** (*c.*1551–1619) (*The Five Books of Architecture*), which was a major source from the time of Inigo *Jones to the flowering of the *second Palladian Revival* of *Burlington and *Campbell.

AB, **xxiv** (1942), 55–91, 115–55; S.Fr (2004); E.Hs (1990); He (1996); L & D (1986); Onians (1988); P (1982); Rosenfeld (1978); Serlio (1584, 1611, 1663, 1964, 1996); Thoenes (ed.) (1989); J.T (1996)

serpent 1. In *Classical architecture, an emblem of healing, wisdom, and the Messenger (Hermes, St John, etc.), so part of the winged baton or *caduceus. **2.** Arranged in a circle, with tail in mouth, a serpent suggests immortality (*see* AARON'S ROD; OUROBOROS).

serpentine 1 Stone, mainly hydrous magnesium silicate, of a dull green colour with marking resembling those of a *serpent's skin, called 'marble'.

serpentine 2 1. of or pertaining to a serpent; **2.** wavy line associated with **William Hogarth's** (1697–1764) aesthetic theories as propounded in his *Analysis of Beauty* (1753) in which he extolled the superiority of *serpentine* lines over straight ones, the former suggesting freedom of movement, and the latter something static and bound by rigid convention. *Compounds include*:
serpentine path: widely used in Western garden-design from C17, *Langley defined it in the context of *Artinatural* gardens as irregular, described by art, and representing the products of Nature, to be imitated in all woods and *wildernesses, an approach initiated by *Switzer and others;
serpentine rill: *Kent designed *rills at Rousham, Oxon., on serpentine plans, features recurring in *Rococo gardens. The Serpentine Lake in Hyde Park, London (1731), may be the first of its kind;
serpentine wall: *see* CRINKLE-CRANKLE.

J.Archer (1985); Langley (1971); Switzer (1980); Symes (2006); Tay (2006)

Serrure, Louis-Auguste (1799–1845) Antwerp-born architect, much influenced by *Percier and *Fontaine. His masterpiece was the *Passage Dehaen*, a fine Neo-Classical shopping-*arcade, Antwerp (1838—destroyed).

Loo (ed.) (2003); PM

Serrure, Théodore (1862–1957) Belgian architect. Among his realized designs were three fine schools in Brussels, of which that in *Veronesestraat* (1903–7) is a master-work, with *Neo-Classicism wedded to elegant iron-and-glass roof-structures.

Loo (ed.) (2003); PM

Serrurier-Bovy, Gustave (1858–1910) Belgian architect from Luik (Liège), influenced by *Viollet-le-Duc and the English *Arts-and-Crafts Movement. Among his works, the *Villa l'Aube, Avenue de Cointre,* Luik (1902), was freely composed, and his *Château La Cheyrelle,* Dienne, France (1903–9), offered an intriguing mix of natural timber and *polychrome decorations.

Loo (ed.) (2003); J-G.Watelet (2000)

Sert i López, Josep Lluís (1902–83) American architect of Catalan birth, he worked with Le *Corbusier and *Jeanneret-Gris (1929–32) before returning to Barcelona, where he built several structures, including an apartment-block (1931). He was involved in the organization of local groups associated with *CIAM, and designed the Spanish Pavilion at the Paris Exposition (1937—demolished) in the *International-Modern style (the *Guernica* of **Pablo Picasso** (1881–1973) was commissioned for this building). He settled in the USA (1939) where he worked on numerous Corbusier-influenced town-planning schemes (mostly in Latin America). Through the influence of *Gropius he was appointed Dean of the Faculty of the Graduate School of Design and Chairman and Professor of Architecture at Harvard (1953–69), founded (1955) an architectural practice in Cambridge, MA, and designed several buildings, including Peabody Housing, Harvard (1963–5). He was responsible for the US Embassy, Baghdad, Iraq (1955–8), *Fondation Maeght,* St-Paul-de-Vence, Nice, France (1959–64), the Carmelite Convent, Cluny, France (1968–9), and the Miró Foundation Building, Barcelona (1972–5).

Borrás (ed.) (1975a); X.Costa et al. (eds) (1997); E (1994); J.Freixa (ed.) (1979); Mannino & Paricio (1983); Rovira (2004); Sert (1997); VV (1993)

Servais, Charles (1828–92) Belgian architect, celebrated for his eclectic exoticism, including a series of 'temples' he designed for Antwerp Zoo, the best-known of which is the *polychrome *Egyptian-Revival Elephant-House (1855), complete with correct hieroglyphic information about the building.

J.Curl (2005); Loo (ed.) (2003); PM

Servandoni, Giovanni Niccolò Geronimo (1695–1766) Florentine architect/painter, he trained under **Giovanni Paolo Pannini** (1691–1765), the pre-eminent C18 painter of real and imaginary views of Rome. He settled in Paris (1724), where he designed stage-sets, firework-displays, and fêtes, and was also in demand for these skills in a number of European cities, including London, where he designed the fireworks in Green Park to celebrate the Peace of Aix-la-Chapelle (1749—the year in which he also designed various *fabriques* for Vauxhall Gardens, London). He won the competition (1732) to design the west front of the Church of St-Sulpice, Paris, based on an earlier project by Gilles-Marie *Oppenord. This colonnaded *façade of two superimposed *Orders (perhaps influenced by the west front of St Paul's Cathedral in London) was nobler and more severe than anything contemporary built in France, and was recognized at the time as having affinities with the *Antique. It was certainly an early example of the Neo-Classical reaction against *Rococo. He designed numerous *altars and other fittings in various churches, and the interior of the sculpture-gallery at Brandenburg House, Hammersmith, London (c.1751—demolished—but illustrated in *Vitruvius Britannicus,* **iv** (1767), 28–9). His pupils included *Chalgrin and de *Wailly.

Co (2008); J.Curl (2010); Ha (1952); Heybrock (1970); RUA, **xii** (1860–1), 115–18; Ry (1980)

servants' *or* **gardeners' tunnel** Underground tunnel giving access from working-areas (stable-courtyards, etc.) to the basement of the main house *or* from, e.g., kitchen to gardens. The objective was to shield servants from view. An example of the *servants'* type survives at Castle Coole, Co. Fermanagh, and of a *gardeners'* at Calke Abbey, Derbys.

B-J (1988); Gd (1979b); Jackson-Stops (1990); Symes (2006)

set-back 1. *See* BUTTRESS; OFF-SET. Also called *set-off, scarcement,* or *weather-table.* **2.** Upper part of a building, e.g. a *skyscraper, set back from lower storeys to enable light and air to reach the street below. Skyscrapers were sometimes built with several set-backs.

settlement 1. Distortion or disruption of parts of a building caused by unequal compression of its *foundation, or by shrinkage, or by undue weight placed upon them. **2.** Colony. **3.** Group of buildings forming the nucleus of a new village or town.

Seven Wonders of the Ancient World Giza *Pyramids; Hanging Gardens and Walls* 'of Babylon'; *Temple of Artemis,* Ephesus; *Statue of Zeus,* Olympia; *Mausoleum,* Halicarnassus; *Colossus* of Rhodes; and the Alexandrian *Pharos.*

Severus (*fl.*mid-C1 AD) Supposedly the designer (with the engineer **Celer**) of **Emperor Nero**'s (*r.*AD 54–68) *Domus Aurea,* a complex the octagonal hall of which was only rediscovered early in the C20 buried within the substructures of the **thermae* of **Trajan** (*r*.98–117) on the Oppian Hill, Rome. It contained a series of interior volumes of contrasting geometrical shapes illuminated by indirect and top lighting: it is unclear, however, if **columnar-and-*trabeated forms were expunged from the interiors of the vaulted, domed, and **arcuated compartments, as many wishful-thinking Modernists have claimed. Doubtless beguiled by the surviving bare walls and powerful, clear geometries, they perceived the octagonal hall and its ancillary spaces as heralding a 'new aesthetic'. Yet although the basic structure was of **concrete, *Orders were employed for the exterior, and it is likely that Orders were used inside as well, as was the case in the **vestibule of the *'Piazza d'Oro'* at **Hadrian**'s (*r*.117–138) Villa, Tivoli (118–134). The fact that the rich **marble and **stucco finishes have long since disappeared, and with them other internal embellishments (including Orders) does not mean they did not exist. There is no trace of finishes to the **dome itself (though there is evidence that finishes were employed on the walls and elsewhere), but it is likely that the space was covered by a ribbed structure, perhaps of bronze, from which fabric panels were suspended. As **David Hemsoll** has convincingly shown, the octagonal hall of the Golden House, 'far from representing a "revolution" in architecture', seems 'to have been a design that actually was deeply rooted in tradition . . . Modernist aesthetic criteria', such as efforts to define the design as 'an heroic attempt to come to terms with advances in building technology and to free architecture from the constraints of the past', are 'inaccurate and misleading', but typical, one might add. Nero's architects bettered their predecessors by exploiting tradition and established forms, and taking advantage of technological developments. After all, halls and dining-rooms with sophisticated geometries and spatial elaboration were known before Nero's time, and there is evidence from tombs and other building-types of similar ingenious geometrical arrangements before the *Domus Aurea* was built. Severus and Celer may also have played roles in the rebuilding of Rome after the fire of AD 64 and the drawing up of the building regulations that set the agenda. They also proposed a vast canal (begun but unfinished *c*.AD 60) linking Lake Avernus near the Bay of Naples to the Tiber. Severus and Celer's works are described by **Tacitus** (*c*.AD 55–*c*.117) and **Suetonius** (*c*.AD 70–*c*.160), neither of whom was particularly sympathetic to the Imperial idea, yet both were impressed by the *Domus Aurea*'s grandeur, rich interior décor, bathing facilities, and enchanting gardens.

Antiquity, xxx (1956), 209–19; *AH*, xxxii (1989), 1–17; A.Boëthius (1960); W.MacD (1965–86); P (1982); Segala & Sciortino (1999); W-P (1981, 1986)

severy 1. Structural **bay of a building, especially a **vault. **2.** Top of a **ciborium.

Seward, Henry Hake (1778–1848) English architect, articled to **Soane, after which (1808) he became District Surveyor to the parishes of St Martin-in-the-Fields and St Anne, Soho. He entered into partnership (1810) with George **Byfield, and was appointed Joint Surveyor of the estates of the Dean and Chapter of Westminster. He designed several ecclesiastical buildings, including East Witton Church, Yorks. (1809–12—**Gothic), Thorneyburn Church and Parsonage, Northum. (1815–17—Gothic), and Greystead Church and Parsonage, Northum. (1815–17—also Gothic).

Co (2008)

sex- In composition, six: *sexfid* is six-cleft; *sexfoil* is a window, opening, or panel with six **lobes or leaves; and *sexpartite* is parted in six, a term usually applied to vaulting. *See also* VAULT.

Sezession Term adopted (1890s) by several groups of artists in Germany and Austria-Hungary who seceded from the traditional, conservative, academies to show their works. The first group was formed (1892) in Munich, but the most celebrated of the *Sezessionen* was Viennese (1897), and included the artist **Gustav Klimt** (1862–1918) and the architect **Olbrich (1867–1908): the latter designed the exhibition-gallery and premises for the Vienna *Sezession* which made his reputation. The Sezessionists' enthusiasm for **Art Nouveau gave the name *Sezessionstil* to that style in Austria-Hungary.

B & G (1986); Latham (ed.) (1980); Ouvrard *et al.* (1986); Waissenberger (1971); Wiener Sezession (1972)

sgraffito *Scratchwork* made by covering a wall with coloured **plaster on top of which a white coat was applied on which a design was drawn then **scraped or scratched while wet to expose the colour below.

Pericoli-Ridolfini (1960)

Shadbolt, Blunden (1879–1949) English architect, articled (1898) to **Arthur Kelway Bamber** (1869–1949), he completed his training under **George Alfred Hall** (1859–1945). Settling in Horley, Surrey (1901), he formed a partnership with **William Joseph Ballard** (1854–1936), designing several houses, using old bricks, stones, **tiles and oak, all employed to avoid a 'mechanical' appearance, so his multi-gabled buildings look older than they are, with distorted **ridges and **eaves, and external brickwork deliberately laid to avoid accurate horizontal and vertical alignment of courses and joints. Chimneys tended to be over-sized, and walls of rooms were not constructed square. **Gradidge considered Shadbolt one of the greatest of the **Arts-and-Crafts architects of the *Domestic Revival. Examples of his work include Edmundsbury, Beverley Lane, Combe, Kingston upon Thames, Surrey (c.1929), and Whornes Place, Hazel Lane, Petersham, Richmond upon Thames (1925).

B.et al. (2001); Barron (1929); J. of the Thirties Soc., iii (1982); C20 Newsletter (Winter 2009/10), 16

shade- or shadow-house Small C16 or C17 *summer-house sited at the termination of a walk or in a corner of a garden.

shaft 1. Body, fust, or trunk of a *colonnette or column extending from the top of the *base to the bottom of the *capital, in the Classical *Orders diminishing in size as it rises (see DIMINUTION, ENTASIS). 2. Slim cylindrical tall element (often made of *Purbeck *marble or some other material to contrast with the lighter stone of the pier), one of several clustered around a *pier and tied to it by shaft-rings (*annulets, *bands of a shaft, band-rings, bracelets, or *corbel-rings in *Gothic work). 3. *Colonnette set at an angle of a building, e.g. junction of a *jamb with a wall, or framing a *reveal.

Shaker architecture The Shakers (or United Society of Believers in Christ's Second Appearing) were founded by the English-born **Ann Lee** (1736–84), who emigrated to America (1774) and gathered around her sufficient followers to establish a religious sect. Believing that odd or fanciful styles of architecture, with *mouldings, *cornices, etc., should be eschewed, the Shakers created plain meeting-houses in which they could perform their 'round dances' that were part of their ritual, so large areas of floor-space were essential. Believing also that light and cleanliness were the antithesis of evil, buildings had numerous windows. One of the finest is the Round Barn, Hancock, MA (1826—supposedly designed by **Daniel Goodrich** (1765-1835)), and indeed at Hancock are several excellent examples of Shaker architecture. Among the meeting-houses those at New (now Mount) Lebanon, NY (1785—replaced 1824), and Pleasant Hill, KY (designed by **Micajah Burnett** (1791-1829)), deserve mention. Burnett and **Moses Johnson** (1752-1842) seem to have been the most important Shaker architect-builders. In addition to the agreeably serene buildings, Shaker furniture has been admired for its graceful simplicity and excellent construction.

Larkin et al. (1994); Lassiter (1966); Poppeliers (ed.) (1974); J.T (1996)

sham C18 term for a fake *'ruin' or other building erected for effect, e.g. the 'Sham Gothic' of Batty *Langley.

K.Clark (1974)

Shanahan, Michael (fl.c.1770–c.1790s) Irish architect, probably from Co. Cork. He carried out numerous works for the 'edifying' **Frederick Augustus Hervey** (1730-1803—**Bishop of Derry** from 1768 and **4th Earl of Bristol** from 1779). He was involved in the design and construction of Downhill, the Earl-Bishop's great house in Co. Londonderry (begun 1776—unroofed 1950, and now a shell), although James *Wyatt may have produced drawings for it (and there are certain features, e.g. the attenuated *pilasters, which look like Wyatt's work). His masterpiece is the domed circular Mussenden Temple (1783-5) on a headland at Downhill, high above the sea: a distinguished design, it is based on Roman exemplars. He was also responsible for the 'mausoleum' (actually a memorial) at Downhill (begun 1779), which is modelled on the Roman *mausoleum of the **Julii**, St-Rémy, Provence: the upper parts of this charming building were blown down in the 'Great Wind' (1839). He probably designed the Bishop and Lion Gates at Downhill (1784 and 1778-9), both of which have Wyattesque touches, and was also involved from 1787 at the Earl-Bishop's other seat at Ballyscullion, Co. Londonderry. Shanahan may have designed and directed the building of several Anglican churches in the Diocese of Derry (e.g. Desertoghill, near Garvagh, and Banagher (1775-6)).

DIA (2013); Rankin (1972)

shanasheel See MASHRABIYA.

shank Upright (also called leg) between the *glyphs on *triglyphs of the *Doric Order.

Shankland, Graeme (1918-94) See COX, OLIVER JASPER.

shanshui penjing Art of creating miniature landscapes in shallow *containers. See BONSAI; MINIATURE GARDEN.

shaped gable *Gable, its sides formed of convex and concave curves, with a semi-circular top.

Sharawadgi, also Sharawaggi. 1. First used by Sir William *Temple in his Upon the Gardens of Epicurus (1685) to describe the Chinese way of planting in an apparently haphazard manner 'without any Order of Disposition of Parts', the term was popularized in mid-C18 England to describe irregularity, asymmetry, and the *Picturesque qualities of being surprising through grace-ful disorder, and so was applied to irregular gardens, known as *Chinese, or as les jardins anglo-chinois, embellished with Chinese *bridges with *fretwork railings and vermilion-painted *pagodas shaded by weeping willows. However, sharawadgi does not seem to be derived from the Chinese at all, but from a C17 notion of 'Chineses', which includes vague notions of 'The

Indies' or 'The Orient'. The key to the problem seems to be the Dutch East India Company, which had a factory at Deshima, Nagasaki. When Dutchmen, accompanied by the German **Engelbert Kaempfer** (1651-1716), visited the gardens at Kyoto in the late C17, they noted the 'irregular but agreeable' features 'artfully made in imitation of nature', and the Japanese words *sorowaji* or *shorowaji* suggesting asymmetry. It would appear that *sharawadji* is a corruption of the Japanese, filtered through Dutch, probably misheard by the C17 visitors to the Japanese gardens at Kyoto. Temple probably picked the word up from Dutchmen who had visited Japanese gardens. **2.** *Sharawadji* was used (somewhat pretentiously) in town-planning circles in the 1940s to describe irregular, asymmetrical, informal designs.

GH, **xxvi**/2 (Winter 1998), 208–13; C.Mu (1999); Pe (1968)

Sharon, Arieh (1900-84) Polish-born Israeli architect, he settled (1920) in Palestine, where he designed and built several buildings in the *kibbutz* of *Gan Shemuel*. He studied (1926-9) at the *Bauhaus under *Gropius and *Meyer, directed (1929-31) Meyer's Berlin office, and helped to realize Meyer's design for the *Allgemeiner Deutscher Gewerkschaftsbund* School, Bernau. He returned (1931) to Palestine and set up in practice, became (1948) Director and Chief Architect of the National Planning Agency, and was in charge of the Physical National Plan directly under **David Ben-Gurion** (1886-1973—Prime Minister of Israel (1948-63)). With others, he designed the Hillside Housing, Upper Nazareth (1955-7), the Hospital, Ichilov, Tel Aviv (1954-60), the Churchill Auditorium, *Technion*, Haifa (1956-8), headquarters of the Bank of Israel, Jerusalem (1969-74), the Master-plan for Civic Design of the Old City of Jerusalem (1967-9), and the Jerusalem suburb of Gilo (1973-6).

E (1994); J.T (1996)

Sharp, Dennis (1933-2010) English architect, author of *Twentieth-Century Architecture: A Visual History* (1968, 2003), and many other books and articles. He started his career indentured to Sir Albert *Richardson before studying at the Architectural Association (1954-7—where he later taught for many years) and Liverpool University (1960-3). He founded the influential journal, *AA Quarterly*, was a founder-member (1979) of the Thirties Society, and was an authority on the *conservation of *Modern-Movement buildings. Other books by him are cited here. He also edited Hermann *Muthesius's *Das Englische Haus* for the English translation (2007), and published, with **Sally Rendel**, a monograph, *Connell, Ward and Lucas* (2008). A collection of his essays was published posthumously (2011). His own house

at Bayford, Herts., demonstrated some of his concerns about *Sustainable or *Environmentally Responsible architecture.

H.Muthesius (1979, 2007); Sharp (1966, 1967, 1969, 1978, 1981, 1993, 2003, 2011); Sharp (ed.) (1972, 2001); Sharp & Cooke (eds) (2000); Sharp & Rendel (eds) (2008); *The Times* (16 June 2010), 67

Sharpe, Edmund (1809-77) Cheshire-born architect/engineer, much influenced by *Whewell and *Rickman. In France and Germany he studied *Romanesque and *Gothic work before settling in Lancaster where he established his practice, taking on (1838) **Edward Graham Paley** (1823-95—brother of **Frederick Apthorp Paley** (1815-88), the prominent Ecclesiologist) as a pupil, then a partner (1845) when the firm became **Sharpe & Paley** until 1856. Sharpe pioneered the use of *terracotta in what he called his 'pot' churches, notably St Stephen & All Martyrs, Lever Bridge, Bolton, Lancs. (1842-5) of which the openwork *spire (demolished 1936) of which was influenced by that of the Minster at Freiburg-im-Breisgau, and in which even the elaborate *bench-ends were of terracotta. Sharpe's second 'pot' church was Holy Trinity, Platt Lane, Rusholme, Manchester (1845-6), in *Middle Pointed with some *Second-Pointed detail, and his last was the anachronistic *Neo-Norman St Paul, Scotforth, Lancaster (1874-5).

Sharpe withdrew from the practice (1851), and concentrated on writing. His most impressive published works were *Architectural Parallels, ...* (1845-7), the two-volume *Decorated Windows* (1849), and *The Seven Periods of English Architecture* (1851—in which he attempted a revised stylistic and chronological system, a proposal which was violently attacked by J.H.*Parker, publisher of Rickman). Sharpe was also involved in the design and building of railways, in the layout of the tramway system at Geneva, Switzerland, and in urban sanitation (he published *A History of the Progress of Sanitary Reform in the Town of Lancaster, from 1845 to 1875; and an Account of its Water Supply* (1876).

Hubert James Austin (1841-1915) joined Paley (1867), and in the following year the firm became **Paley & Austin**. **Henry (Harry) Anderson Paley** (1859-1946) came on board (1877) as an articled pupil, becoming a partner (1886) when the firm was known as **Paley, Austin, & Paley**: after E.G.Paley died, it was re-named **Austin & Paley**, and as such continued, though seems to have carried out few commissions from the late 1930s, and the offices in Lancaster were sold to the Corporation (1945). In its various guises this firm was one of the most distinguished English architectural practices of the time in the North and the North Midlands. Among the best works it produced were Capernwray Hall, North Lancs. (1844-8), in the *Perp. style; St Peter's, Bolton (1867-71); various buildings at Rossall School (from 1861); sundry structures in Barrow-in-Furness, including the church of St James (1867-9); the huge former Royal Albert Asylum, Lancaster (1868-73—now an Islamic college); and some very fine churches, including St Chad, Kirkby, Merseyside (1869-71), St John the Evangelist, Cheetham, Manchester (1869-71), St Mary, Leigh, Lancs. (1871-3), the tough *muscular Gothic St Mary, Betwys-y-Coed, Caernarvonshire (1872-3—in a noble Transitional style), the very grand St Mary, Dalton-in-Furness, Cumb. (1884-5), and St George, Buxton Road, Heaviley, Stockport, Ches. (1892-7), the largest and most perfect of all the churches, the master-work of **Hubert Austin**, in a free synthesis of Gothic, based on Perp., but highly rectilinear.

Brandwood (2012); Combe (1844); J.Curl (2007); D & M (1985); Price (1998); Sharpe (1848, 1849, 1851, 1876)

Shaw, John (1776-1832) English architect, apprenticed to the elder *Gwilt before establishing his London practice (1798). He became (1803) Surveyor to the Eyre Estate in St John's Wood, and exhibited a proposal (unrealized) for a 'British Circus' of detached and semi-detached houses arranged on either side of a circular road a mile in circumference. Thereafter he and his son, **John Shaw** (1803-70), became developers of suburbs set out on irregular winding roads. He remodelled (1818-c.1830) Newstead Abbey, Nottingham, but is best remembered for the Church of St Dunstan-in-the-West, Fleet Street, London (1831-2—completed by his son), an early example of archaeologically correct *Gothic Revival. The younger Shaw became Surveyor to Eton College (c.1825) and designed the *Tudor-Gothic buildings at Weston's Yard there, also developing the Chalcots Estate, Chalk Farm, London (1840-5), including Adelaide Road and Eton College Road. He was employed by the Church Building Commissioners and published *A Letter on Ecclesiastical Architecture . . .* (1839) in which he proposed the *Romanesque style should be used for churches because it would be cheaper than the Gothic or Classical styles. His work in 'Norman Revival' included Holy Trinity, Gough Square, London (1837-8—demolished), Christ Church, Watney Street, Stepney, London (1840-1—demolished), and St Peter's, Woodford New Road, Walthamstow, Essex (1840—altered), although the last was in a vaguely *Early-Christian-*Italianate *Rundbogenstil.* He designed a number of buildings in a revived *Renaissance style that pre-empted the *Wrenaissance of the end of the century. His best buildings are at Wellington College, near Sandhurst, Berks.

(1855-9—a mixture of *Louis XIII, *Wren's work at Hampton Court Palace, and other Anglo-Dutch elements reminiscent of *Nesfield's *Queen-Anne style at Kinmel Park, Denbighshire some 12 years later), and Goldsmith's College, formerly the Royal Naval School, Lewisham Way, Deptford, London (1843—an astonishing, restrained design of decidedly Italian character that would easily pass for a building of c.1900).

B.Clarke (1966); Co (2008); D & M (1985); *ODNB* (2004)

Shaw, Richard Norman (1831-1912) Scots-born architect, son of an Irish father and a Scots mother. A pupil of William *Burn from 1849, he later travelled (1854-6), joined *Salvin's office (1856), published *Architectural Sketches from the Continent* (1858—the year when he accepted a position with *Street in succession to Philip *Webb). Influenced by A.W.N.*Pugin's writings, but most of all by Street, he acknowledged the latter as his mentor. He set up in practice on his own (1862), and then (1863) with Eden *Nesfield, specializing in domestic and commercial work, each influencing, but working independently of, the other. Shaw's early work included Holy Trinity, Bingley, Yorks. (1866-8—a tough essay in the *Gothic Revival, much influenced by Street's designs, wantonly destroyed (1974) despite *Goodhart-Rendel's opinion that 'no modern church' was 'finer'), but the most important aspect of Shaw's output was his domestic work, in which the Gothic Revival, the *Picturesque, *vernacular architecture, and the *Domestic Revival played their parts, influenced by designs of *Butterfield, *Devey, Nesfield, and Street. Shaw refined and applied elements derived from traditional houses of the Sussex Weald (including tall brick chimneys, much tile-hanging, and mullioned windows with leaded lights) to large country-houses. Early works include Glen Andred (1866-8) and Leys Wood (1868-9 —mostly destroyed), both near Groombridge, Sussex; Grim's Dyke, Harrow Weald (1870-2— perhaps Shaw's finest interpretation of the *Old-English version of the Domestic Revival); and the enormous and eclectic Cragside, Rothbury, Northum. (1870-84). With their use of local materials and vernacular details, these buildings had a profound effect on the evolution of domestic architecture and on the *Arts-and-Crafts movement in general. Shaw's houses were published in *The Building News,* thus making his work widely known on both sides of the Atlantic, and influencing development of the *Shingle style in the USA.

Both Shaw and Nesfield drew on late-C17 Dutch domestic architecture and that of the **William-and-Mary** period in England (1689-1702), so their work of the 1870s began to be called the

*Queen-Anne style. Shaw's chief works in this style were New Zealand Chambers, Leadenhall Street, London (1871-3—demolished), Lowther Lodge, Kensington (1873), 6 Ellerdale Road, Hampstead (1875-6—Shaw's house), Cheyne and Swan Houses, Chelsea (1875-7), and the celebrated Artists' Houses, 8 Melbury Road (1875-6), 118 Campden Hill Road (1876-8), and 31 Melbury Road (1876-7), Northern Kensington. Shaw also worked at Bedford Park, Turnham Green, Chiswick, London, where he designed (1877-80) a club, an inn, shops, several small houses, and St Michael and All Angels (1879-80—an eclectic work, mixing late Gothic Revival with Arts-and-Crafts detail). In New Zealand Chambers and some of the Bedford Park buildings Shaw used the *Ipswich window that was to be widely copied and paraphrased thereafter.

Shaw was assisted (1879-89) by *Lethaby, and the character of his work changed, as in the huge Albert Hall Mansions, Kensington Gore, London (1879-86), the first block of flats in the new red-brick free style that was to be so influential for this type of development. Then there was the very refined 170 Queen's Gate, Kensington, London (1888-90), with early-C18 features (such as the *eaves-cornice and tall *sash-windows) and a *Wrenaissance door-case, the whole ensemble looking forward to a type of *Colonial-*Georgian Revival. At the Alliance Assurance Offices, St James's Street, London (1881-8), he introduced a hybrid style incorporating *Renaissance scrolled *gables, mullioned and transomed windows, and brick *façades with *bands of stone. Striped too were the elevations of New Scotland Yard, London (1887-90 and 1901-7), in which many eclectic elements were mixed, including the *tourelles of smaller French *châteaux*, *Scottish-Baronial architecture, and (a new note) *Baroque *door-cases and gable-*aedicules: similar themes occur at the offices for the White Star Line, Liverpool (1895-8—with J.F.*Doyle). Later, the grand manner of *Classicism became more pronounced, as with Bryanston House, Dorset (1889-94—with its great columns and Baroque details), Chesters, Northum. (1890s), the Alliance Assurance Office, St James's (1901-5—opposite the earlier block mentioned previously), and the huge Piccadilly Hotel, Piccadilly, London (early 1900s).

Two other churches by him deserve mention: All Saints', Compton, Leek, Staffs. (1885-7—wide and broad, incorporating personal interpretations of *Second-Pointed and *Perp. detail, *nave-arcades similar to those of the Bedford Park church, and some furnishings by Lethaby), and All Saints', Batchcott, Richard's Castle, Salop. (1890-3—again with historical detail, some of which was derived from local examples (e.g. the *ball-flowers), the whole composed to give the

impression of having been established and altered over a period). In both these works the influences of *Bodley and of 'Middle' *Scott were apparent. His last works were Portland House, London (1907-8—one of the first buildings with a *reinforced-concrete *frame in England), and studies for the new elevations for the Quadrant, Regent Street, London (1905-8—most unrealized, but finally built to designs by *Blomfield and others).

When he retired (1896), Shaw was hailed as the leading British architect, and his work was internationally known through publications by *Muthesius and others. He published *Sketches of Cottages and Other Buildings* (1878), and (1892) co-edited (with T.J.*Jackson) *Architecture: A Profession or an Art?*, in which proposals to make the registration of architects compulsory were denounced.

Blomfield (1940); D & M (1985); Ferriday (ed.) (1963); Gd (1977); A.S.Gray (1985); H.M (1979); P (1982); Saint (1976); Sh (1973, 1975); J.T (1996)

Shchusev, Aleksei Viktorovich (1873-1949) Russian architect, trained in St Petersburg and Paris, he established his practice in St Petersburg, specializing in ecclesiastical work (e.g. restoration of St Basil's Cathedral, Ovruch, Kiev (1903-11), and the new Intercession Church of the Martha and Mary Mission, Moscow (1908-12)). He designed the Kazan' Railway Station, Moscow (1910-40), in which he employed *vernacular themes and plentiful embellishments derived from C17 *Baroque styles. After the Revolution he settled in Moscow, where he had a successful academic career. In 1924-30 he designed his best-known work, the powerful stripped Neo-Classical *mausoleum of **Vladimir Ilyich Ulyanov** (1870-1924—*known as* **Lenin**), reminiscent of stark Ancient-Egyptian architecture, with its unadorned *columnar and *trabeated architecture set on blocky *podia, the whole forming a stepped pyramidal composition. Shchusev was an important promoter of the official architectural style of the Stalin era, and his architecture set precedents for many buildings throughout the Soviet Union.

Kopp (1978); P (1982); Sokolov (1952); Sorokin (1987); J.T (1996); vV (1993); Vasyutinskaya *et al.* (1974)

shear 1. Force that can break, e.g., a *beam near its point of support, if that force is greater than the strength of a beam. The effect is similar to that of, e.g., a pair of scissors on hair, i.e. the force acts transversely to the axis of a structural member. **2.** If a beam is composed of several horizontal layers, a weight will cause the beam to bend, so the horizontal layers will slide horizontally over each other. *Shearing* is therefore a cutting or sliding process.

shed-roof *Lean-to or monopitch roof abutting a higher element, as in the case of an *aisle-roof and a *clerestorey.

sheet-glass *See* GLASS.

sheeting 1. Also called *sheet-piling*, it consists of timbers driven firmly side-by-side into the earth. Latterly, timbers are usually replaced by steel. 2. Vertical boards lining the walls of a room.

sheila- *or* **sheela-na-gig** Carved nude female figure, legs wide apart, with hands posed so as to draw attention to the genitalia, e.g. carved *corbel on the *apse of the Church of Sts Mary and David, Kilpeck, Herefs.

Shekhtel', Fedor Osipovich (1859–1926) Russian architect, an important designer of buildings in the *Art-Nouveau style, he also exploited iron, glass, and *reinforced concrete in his works which include the sumptuous *Gothic-Revival *Morozova* house, *Spiridonovka Street*, Moscow (1893–6— badly damaged by fire, 1995). He was responsible for the Russian Pavilions (which drew on traditional roof-forms to some extent, and were regarded as 'barbaric' by those who saw them) for the International Exhibition, Glasgow (1901), and the following year he was the leading light behind the 'New Style' Exhibition in Moscow (1902–3), where designs by *Mackintosh and *Olbrich (among others) were shown. At the same time he designed the *Yaroslavl'* Railway Station, Moscow (1902–3), a curious mixture of Art-Nouveau details, vaguely *Historicist roof-forms, and *Classicism, that was rather ungainly taken as a whole. His Mansions for **Stepan Ryabushinsky**, *Malaya Nikitskaya* (1900–2), and **Aleksandra Derozhinskaya**, *Shtatny Lane* (1901–2), both in Moscow, stand favourable comparison with any other comparable European work of the time. The former has an extraordinary Art-Nouveau *stair and hall around which the house is planned, and the latter has elements drawn from *Gothic, the Vienna *Sezession, and especially motifs favoured by Otto *Wagner and his circle. The last influence was overt in the *Villa Kshesinskaya*, St Petersburg (1904–6). The newspaper offices for *Utro Rossii*, Moscow (1907), also had Viennese flavours. Much of his work immediately before the 1914–18 war was elegant and sometimes austere, while around 1910 he began to introduce a severe *Neo-Classicism to Moscow (e.g. his own house, *Bol'-shaya Sadovaya* (1909–10) and the headquarters of the Trading Society (1909–11). More than 50 fine buildings by him survived the Soviet régime, but are under threat (C21) from the need for office-accommodation in Moscow.

Borisova & Kazhdan (1971); Kirichenko (1975); P (1982); *PoA*, **xxiv** (Aug.–Sept. 1996), 58–61; Raeburn (ed.) (1991); J.T (1996)

shell 1. *Concrete structure evolved from work by *Candela, *Freyssinet, *Maillart, *Nervi, *Nowicki, *Saarinen, *Torroja, et al., derived from the exemplar of an eggshell. The *stressed skin or shell operates with the *frame to form a strong structural system. 2. Scallop.

shell-house *See* SHELL-WORK.

shell-lime *Lime made from shells of cockles, oysters, etc. The *spandrels of the *domes over the *aisles in St Paul's Cathedral, London, were made of brick covered with *stucco of cockle-shell lime, which sets as hard as *Portland Stone.

shell-work Arrangements of shells, minerals, mother-of-pearl, etc., in patterns (called *coquillage* or *marine ornament) for decorations of walls of *grottoes, *nymphaea, etc. (e.g. at *Château de Wideville*, Yvelines, France (1635—by Tommaso *Francini)). An elaborate three-chambered grotto at Goldney House, Bristol, Som. (1737–67) is densely set with corals, crystals, exotic shells, fossils, and minerals, and at Goodwood, West Sussex (1740s), the *shell-house* is exceptionally intricately decorated with specimens collected mostly in the West Indies. Other shell-work interiors of great beauty include the exemplar at Curraghmore, Co. Waterford (1754), and the *Chaumière des Coquillages*, Rambouillet (1770–80—designed by **Claude-Martin Goupy** (*before* 1756–1820) and **Jean-Baptiste Pandebled** (*fl.*1780s) in Neo-Classical style). Mrs *Delany also carried out shell-work decorations (e.g. Killala, Co. Mayo), but little of her work survives, and the *Parminters designed shell-work at their charming *A La Ronde*, Summer Lane, Exmouth, Devon (from 1795).

J.Je (1963); L & D (1986); W.Pa (1887); Symes (2006); Tay (2006)

shelter-belt *Windbreak* formed of groups of trees and shrubs to afford protection against prevailing winds.

Shenstone, William (1714–63) English writer/poet/garden-maker, from 1744 he began to transform his estate, The Leashowes, Worcs., into a *landscape-garden (he seems to have been the first to use the term 'landscape-gardening'), a *Picturesque *ferme ornée*, which achieved such fame it attracted the 'envy of the great and the admiration of the skilful': there, he created waterfalls, cleared undergrowth to reveal 'natural' features to be seen from viewpoints, and laid out *serpentine paths with surprise vistas. Believing the rural landscape was never perfect without the addition of buildings, he caused seats, urns, and various *fabriques* (many with inscriptions and an elegiac flavour) to be erected to encourage structured contemplation, and included *Gothick *ruins. Among those who visited The Leasowes were *Girardin and *Watelet, the design of whose own estates was informed by Shenstone's garden. The second volume of Shenstone's *Works* (1764–9) contained 'Unconnected Thoughts on Gardening', among them the definition of 'landskip' as something which 'pleases the imagination by scenes of grandeur, beauty, or variety'. The Leasowes, the melancholy tone of much of Shenstone's writings, and the illustrations of some of the *fabriques* encouraged imitators, and ultimately became catalysts in the late-C18 movement to form *cemeteries.

Etlin (1984); Hunt ((1982); Mowl (2000); *ODNB* (2004); Shenstone (1764–9); Tay (2006); Wa (1982*a*)

Shepheard, Sir Peter Faulkner (1913–2002) English architect, pupil of *Reilly at Liverpool, he later worked on the Greater London Plan for *Abercrombie, and on the master-plan for the New Town of Stevenage, Herts. (1943–7). He set up in practice (1948) with **Derek Lawley Bridgwater** (1899–1983), later (1955) joined by German-born **Gabriel Epstein** (1918–2017) and (1968) **Peter Basil Hunter** (1923–), as architects, landscape architects, and town-planners. The firm carried out a considerable part of the landscape-design for the *Festival of Britain (1951), designed part of the Lansbury area of Poplar, London, around Pekin Street (1950–3), and prepared many other schemes, notably in the East End of London. Other works included the master-plan for the University of Lancaster (1963–71), the new *quad for Hertford College, Oxford (1970s), New Hall, Winchester College (1958–60), and landscaping for London Zoo (1959–67). Fascinated by nature and ecology, he was mindful of the relationship of a building to its site, and always took care to respect the *genius loci. He was one of the first to recognize (1950s) the problems of high-rise housing, and stressed the necessity of creating high-density medium-rise developments (e.g. Royal College Street development, Camden, London (from 1964)): unlike many of his contemporaries, he refused to ape buildings by, e.g., *Gropius and Le *Corbusier, and avoided rhetoric and obfuscatory theorizing. One of his happiest works was the restoration of the garden at Charleston, near Lewes, Sussex (1980s). He published *Modern Gardens* (1953) and *Gardens* (1969).

Downs (ed.) (2004); *ODNB* (2004); *The Times* (15 Apr 2002), 38; pk

Shepherd, Edward (*c.*1692–1747) English architect/builder, he completed Cannons, the great house for **James Brydges** (1674–1744—**1st Duke** of Chandos** from 1719), Mddx. (1723–5—demolished), and carried out building operations for the Duke in London and elsewhere. He appears to have attempted to build a *palace-fronted range in Grosvenor Square (*c.*1728–30—demolished), built houses in Cavendish Square (1724–8), Brook Street (1725–9), St James's Square (1726–8), and South Audley Street (1736–7), and developed Shepherd's Market and adjoining streets in Mayfair (*c.*1735), all in London, but little of his work survives. He also designed Great Stanmore Rectory, Middlesex (1725), and monuments in the De Grey *mausoleum, Church of St John the Baptist, Flitton, Beds. (1739–40).

Collins Baker (1949); Co (2008); *ODNB* (2004)

Shepherd, Thomas (1779–1835) Scots-born landscape-gardener, he emigrated to Australia (1826) where he established a nursery in Sydney, NSW, carried on by his son, **Thomas William Shepherd** (1824–84). He became influential through lectures, published 1835–6, the first books on gardening in Australia which relate specifically to conditions in that country. Extracts from his writings were published by *Loudon.

D & E (1994); *J. and Proc. of the Royal Soc. of NSW*, **xlii** (1908), 60–132; Loudon (1834*a*, 1840 edn); Shepherd (1836); Shoe (2001); Tay (2006)

Sheppard, Sir Richard Herbert (1910–92) British architect, with his first wife, **Jean** (*née* **Shufflebotham** (1911/12–74)), he established (1958) **Richard Sheppard, Robson, & Partners** with **Geoffrey Robson** (1918–91) in London. The firm's work included numerous schools, Churchill College, Cambridge (1959–74), and University buildings at Leicester (1958–62), Southampton (1959–66), Loughborough, Leics. (1961–6), Imperial College, South Kensington, London (1964–8), and City, St John Street, Clerkenwell, London (1969–76). Among other works may be cited West Midlands College of Education, Gorway, Walsall, Staffs. (1964–72), Lymington Road Housing Development, Hampstead, London (1978), the elegant refurbishment of *Arup's offices in Fitzrovia, London (2000–4), and the Salvation Army Headquarters, City of London, between St Paul's Cathedral and the Millennium Bridge (2002–4).

E (1994); Esher (1981); Hitchens (ed.) (1983); *ODNB* (2004); pk

Shereff, John (*fl.*1528–35) English master-mason who completed the upper two stages of the Great Gate, Trinity College, Cambridge (1528–35). He may have undertaken other works in Cambs. and London, but evidence is lacking.

J.Harvey (1987)

shingle 1. Thin timber (normally oak or cedarwood) slab cut to standard sizes, with parallel sides and one end thicker than the other, used instead of *slates or *tiles to cover roofs or clad walls. Called *scandulae* by the Romans. **2.** In the plural, small stones for *roughcast *render, gravel paths, or *aggregate in a *concrete mix.

Shingle style USA version of the *Old-English style of the *vernacular or *Domestic Revival of the 1870s. In England, tile-hung walls and *gables were commonly incorporated in designs of the period, and in America *shingles were substituted. The centenary of the American Revolution (1876) encouraged a revival of *Colonial- *Georgian domestic architecture, with shingle *cladding, *gambrel roofs, and other features which were mixed with the *dormers, *oriels, and elements of the *Queen-Anne style: the result was the *Shingle style*. Examples include the Sherman House, Newport, RI (1874–5) and Stoughton House, Cambridge, MA (1892–3), both by H.H. *Richardson, and Low House, Bristol, RI (1886– 7), by *McKim, Mead, & White. Many Shingle- style houses had ingenious *open plans, anticipating later work by F.L.L.*Wright and *Greene & Greene.

D & S (1967); Harmon (1983); L.M.Roth (1999); V.J.Sy (1971, 1974, 1989)

Shinohara, Kazuo (1925–2006). Japanese architect. His best-known works were the house in Uehara, Tokyo (1975–6), with its massive *truss-like structure inside, a development of the free-standing columnar theme first used in the 'House in White', Tokyo (1966). His designs are characterized by a powerful expression of architectural elements which he uses in symbolic ways, as in the 'Unfinished House', Tokyo (1970). His work gradually became more expressive and extreme, as in the fractured *segments of the Karuizawa house (1975). He attempted to obliterate all sentimentality from his designs, and moved away from his early interest in Japanese *vernacular traditions (e.g. the Tokyo Institute of Technology Centennial Hall (1987)). He published *Residential Architecture* (1964), *Theories on Residences* (1970), *16 Houses and Architectural Theory* (1971), and much else.

E (1994); Shinohara (1976); S & M (1982); D.Stewart (1995)

Shipman, Ellen Biddle (1869–1950) American landscape architect, her work was mostly for private houses, many of them in and around Cornish, NH, often influenced by the *Colonial- Revival style, and frequently employing walls, so axial *paths, rectangular *beds, and *hedges of evergreens were hallmarks of her style, which might also include *topiary and *espaliered fruit trees, *arbours, *dovecotes, *pergolas, and statues. The geometry of her gardens was closely related to that of the houses to which they were attached, and she created 'outdoor *rooms'. She moved to New York (early 1920s, only employing women). Among her non-residential projects the Sarah P.Duke Memorial Gardens, Duke University, NC (1936) may be cited.

B & K (2000); Karson (1995); Shoe (2001); Tankard (1996)

shoin Better class of Japanese house (especially of C16), based on a rigidly applied system of *proportion, with *open plans subdivided by *shoji *screens, etc.

shoji Japanese *screen, the *panels of which were filled with translucent paper, as used in *shoin houses.

Shoosmith, Arthur Gordon (1888–1974) St Petersburg-born English architect, he worked with *Goodhart-Rendel and Sir John *Burnet before moving (1920) to India as assistant to *Lutyens, supervising the construction of the Viceroy's Residence, New Delhi. On his own account, he designed the Lady Hardinge Serai (1930–1) and the boldly massed St Martin's Church, a *Sublime and austerely powerful composition (1928–31).

ODNB (2004); GS; Stamp (1976); J.T (1996)

shopping-arcade Covered walkway, usually top-lit, either by means of a *clerestorey or with a glazed roof, with shops on one or both sides, called an *arcade. It is derived from the Islamic *bazaar. Early European arcades were the Burlington Arcade, London (1815–18—designed by **Samuel Ware** (1781–1860)), the *Galerie d'Orléans*, Paris (1828–30—demolished 1935—by *Fontaine), and the charming *Galerie Vero-Dodat*, Paris (1822— which still survives). One of the grandest of all such arcades is the huge *Galleria Vittorio Emmanuele II*, Milan (1864–7—by *Mengoni—the roof-structure of which is of iron and glass).

Geist (1983); Lauter (1984); Lemoine (1989); MacKeith (1986)

shopping-centre Group of retail facilities in one complex. A C20 type, it originated in the USA (1920s), and was a response to the growing use of the motor-car. The phenomenal growth of shopping-centres in the later C20 has profoundly affected not only shopping habits, but the characteristics and economies of traditional town-centres. Types of shopping-centres are the small neighbourhood centre serving the immediate surroundings; the suburban centre serving a larger area; the larger-scale regional centre with a big range of shops and services, usually situated immediately outside cities; and the urban retail complex intended to compete with suburban shopping centres, often containing a hotel, offices, and residential accommodation as well as shops and car-parks. One of the first large suburban shopping centres was the Northgate Shopping Center, outside Seattle, WA (opened 1950), laid out along a pedestrian mall. At the Northland Center, Detroit, MI (1952-4—by *Gruen), the whole complex was within an air-conditioned structure. At the Southdale Center, Minneapolis, MN (1954-6—also by Gruen), the mall reappeared, but this time it was enclosed, environmentally controlled, two storeys high, and had landscaped interiors. Smaller in-town developments, such as the *Lijnbaan*, Rotterdam (1950-3—by van den *Broek and *Bakema), have not aged gracefully.

Gruen (1964, 1973); Gruen & L.Smith (1960); J.T (1996)

shopping-mall 1. Pedestrianized walkway lined by shops, etc., in a *shopping-centre. **2.** Equivalent of the suburban (or 'out-of-town') shopping-centre, but situated within a town or city, associated with an established commercial centre. Examples include the Midtown Plaza, Rochester, NY (1960-3), and Fox Hills Mall, Los Angeles, CA (1970-5)—both by *Gruen, and the West Edmonton Mall, Edmonton, Alberta, Canada (1981-6—designed by Belfast-born **Maurice Sunderland** (1926-2002)), which included lavish planting, an amusement-park, 19 cinemas, a Deep Sea Adventure Area (with porpoise pool), and a Fantasyland Hotel (with 'theme' rooms). One of the biggest exemplars was the Mall of America, situated next to the airport between Minneapolis and St Paul, MN (opened 1992). Designed by **Melvin Simon & Associates**, it had four large department stores, 350 shops, entertainment centres, and a theme-park. Other malls include the *Haas Haus*, Vienna (1987-90—by Hans *Hollein).

Maitland (1985); J.T (1996)

shore Piece of timber or metal (in reality a *strut) set obliquely against the side of a building as a support when it is in danger of falling, or when undergoing alterations or repairs. *Shoring* is therefore a collection of shores, i.e. some sort of structural framework supporting an unstable wall or building or the sides of an excavated area.

shoulder 1. *Bracket or *console, also called *shoulder-* or *shouldering-piece*. **2.** *Crossette. **3.** Projection narrowing the top of an aperture, as in a *shouldered* arch (*see* ARCH).

Shreve, Richmond Harold (1877-1946) American architect, with **William Frederick Lamb** (1883-1952) he formed a partnership with *Carrère & Hastings (1920), later (1924) dropping the Carrère and Hastings names. They designed various corporate, commercial, and institutional buildings: among their works were the General Motors Building, NYC (1925-7), and the Empire State Building, Fifth Avenue, NYC (designed 1928-29, when **Arthur Loomis Harmon** (1878-1958) became a partner). As **Shreve, Lamb, & Harmon** they designed Brill Brothers Store (1933-4), Hunter College (1939-40—with *Harrison and *Fouilhoux), and many other works in and around NYC. On his own account Harmon designed the Shelton Towers Hotel, NYC (1923-4), a good example of *set-back design.

P (1982); Stern *et al.* (1995); J.T (1996)

shrine 1. *Fereter, often of great architectural magnificence, for Relics. **2.** Building, *feretory*, or *shrine-chapel* in which Relics are deposited.

shrubbery Group of low bushes or other plants (e.g. flowers) designed for aesthetic display, softening transitions, defining winding paths, acting as screens, or presenting punctuations of colour in a landscape that would otherwise be green or brown. In C19 with more plant-varieties being introduced, the achievement of many colourful effects became possible.

Shulman, Julius (1910-2009) American architectural photographer, he illustrated many buildings by Modernist architects in publications. His first pictures were taken (1936) for *Neutra, and from 1945 he was the most-used photographer for the *Case-Study houses of *Arts and Architecture*. Arguably, he made architectural photography an independent art-form.

The Times (31 July 2009), 59

Shurcliff (*originally* **Shurtleff**), **Arthur Asahel** (1870-1957) American landscape architect, he designed gardens at Williamsburg, VA, from 1928, when many C19 buildings were demolished and replaced with *Colonial-Revival buildings based on C18 exemplars. His gardens were based on research to establish what C18 gardens had been like.

B & K (2000); J.T (1996)

Shute, John (*fl.*1550-63) Author of the first treatise on architecture in English, *The First and Chief Groundes of Architecture* (1563), based on his travels in Italy (1550s), and drawing heavily on *Serlio and *Vitruvius. Primarily dealing with the *Orders, its illustrations (probably by Shute himself) are important for their clarity and originality, and the book went into further editions (1579, 1584, 1587).

E.Hs (1990); L & D (1986); Shute (1563); Su (1993); J.T (1996)

shutter Sliding, rolling, or folding *door to close a window on the outside or inside.

shuttering *See* FORMWORK.

Shutze, Philip Trammell (1890-1982) American architect, partner in the firm of **Hentz, Adler, & Shutze**, NYC, from 1926. His works included the English Chambers House (1930), the Hebrew Benevolent Congregation Temple (1931-2), the Whitehead Memorial Annex, Emory University (1945), and his masterpiece, the Citizens' and Southern National Bank (1929—with a stunning interior of Roman grandness), all in Atlanta, GA. Shutze was called (1977) 'America's Greatest Living Classical Architect'. His work deserves more attention than it has been given hitherto.

Dowling (1989); J.T (1996)

Sibbald, William (*fl.*1785-1809) Scots architect/builder, Superintendent of Public Works in Edinburgh from 1790 until his death, he worked with Robert *Reid on the layout of the first extension to the New Town. He designed Lady Yester's Church, Edinburgh (1803), in an early version of the *Jacobean style. His son, **William Sibbald** (*fl.*1800-23), built the Bank of Scotland on The Mound, Edinburgh (1802-6), to designs by Reid and **Richard Crichton** (*c.*1771-1817).

Co (2008); GMcW & W (1984); Youngson (1966)

Siccard von Siccardsburg, August (1813-68) Austrian architect. He studied in Vienna, where he met van der *Null, with whom he later travelled to Italy, France, Germany, and England. They were appointed Professors at the *Akademie* in Vienna (1844), thus influencing later Viennese architects, and designed several Viennese buildings, including the Arsenal and *Kommandantur-Gebäude* (1848-55), but they are best known for the Opera House on the *Ringstrasse* (1861-9). They planned a huge complex for the Vienna International Exhibition (1873), eventually realized with buildings designed by *Hasenauer. Siccard died shortly after van der Null took his own life.

Auer (1885); Pe (1976)

sick-building syndrome Building having disagreeable or unacceptable environmental characteristics.

side *Horn of an *altar, that on the south being the *Epistle side and that on the north the *Gospel. *Compounds include*:
side-chapel: *chapel to the side of a church-*aisle or *choir;
side-light: *margin-light or window to the side of a door or window, usually very narrow.

sill *See* CILL.

silo *See* GRAIN ELEVATOR.

Siloé, Diego de (*c.*1490-1563) Spanish *Renaissance architect/sculptor of Flemish descent, regarded as a master of the *Plateresque style. He travelled in Italy before returning to Burgos (1519) where he designed the symmetrical *Escalera Dorada* (Golden Staircase) in the Cathedral (1515-23) derived in part from *Bramante's work at the Belvedere Court in the Vatican (begun 1505), although much encrusted in a plethora of *grotesque ornament, probably influenced by works of *Michelangelo and *Raphael. He was called (1528) to Granada to complete *San Jerónimo*, and then to design the Cathedral in the Renaissance style, with its huge domed *chancel, which, with *ambulatory and chapels, suggests a centralized building (e.g. *Santa Costanza*, Rome), *martyrium*, or sepulchre, e.g. the Church of the Holy Sepulchre in Jerusalem, the ensemble cleverly joined to a five-aisled *basilica. This brilliant design was to be influential. Other works by Siloé include the arcaded *courtyard of the *Colegio Fonseca*, Salamanca (1529-34), and the plans for *San Salvador*, Ubeda (1536—built by **Andrés de Vandelvira** (*fl.*1536-60) with a *rotunda owing much to Siloé's work at Granada Cathedral).

CG (1953); K & S (1959); P (1982); Rosenthal (1961); J.T (1996)

Silsbee, Joseph Lyman (1848-1913) American architect. His Syracuse Savings Bank (1875) and White Memorial Building (1876), both in Syracuse, NY, were in the *Gothic-Revival style, but he established his reputation with his domestic work, much of it in the Chicago suburb of Edgewater (1886-9). His compositions were fluent, graceful, and eclectic, and he experimented with both the *Shingle style and a round-arched style influenced by the work of *Richardson. Both F.L.L.*Wright and G.G.*Elmslie worked as assistants in his office. For the World's Columbian Exposition, Chicago (1893), he invented the moving sidewalk.

P (1982); Helen Searing (ed.) (1983); J.T (1996)

Silva, Domingos Parente da (1836-1901) Portuguese architect, designer of the fine Municipal Chambers, Lisbon (1865-80), in a *Renaissance style with a strong French influence, and built other important buildings in the capital, including the portal of the *Cemitério dos Prazeres*.

Bae: *Spain & Portugal* (1913); J.T (1996)

Silva, Ercole (1756-1840) Italian landscape architect, he designed (*c.*1799) a *Picturesque 'English' garden at Cinisello, near Milan (destroyed), but his *Dell'arte dei giardini inglesi* (1801 with later edns) was an important Italian work which drew on *Hirschfeld and others while helping to spread the fashion for English-style gardens and exotic plants.

G.Vi (ed.) (1976)

Silvani, Gherardo (1579–1675) Prolific Florentine architect/sculptor, he designed the interiors of the Salviati Chapel (1611—one of the finest examples of late-*Renaissance architecture in the city), and the Calderini Chapel (1618–21—lined with *marble), both in *Santa Croce*, Florence. He also designed the assured *cloister at the *monastery of *San Frediano in Cestello* (1628) and took over responsibility from **Matteo Nigetti** (*fl.*1600–30) for the Theatine Church of *Santi Michele e Gaetano* (from 1628), including the interior, *sacristy (1633–48—in which the influence of his master *Buontalenti is clear), and robustly assured *Baroque *façade (1628–49).

P & P (1940–54); W.Pa (1887); P (1982); J.T (1996)

sima, simatium *See* CYMA.

Simmons, Charles Evelyn (1879–1952) *See* FIELD, HORACE.

Simón de Colonia (*c.*1450–1511) *See* COLONIA FAMILY.

Simonds, Ossian Cole (1855–1932) American landscape-gardener, he worked for a time in *Jenney's Chicago office on Graceland Cemetery, of which he became Superintendent (1881), creating one of the most distinguished 'rural cemeteries' in the USA, with a series of outdoor *rooms, varied surfaces, water, and unifying planting schemes. For several private houses he designed gardens, perceived as part of an emerging *Prairie style created by Jens *Jensen, Walter Burley *Griffin, and Simonds. His practice included parks, residences, and *cemeteries throughout the USA, particularly the Mid-West. A founder of the American Society of Landscape Architects, he established a programme of landscape-design at the University of Michigan, Ann Arbor (1909), and wrote extensively on the subject.

B & K (2000); Shoe (2001); Simonds (2000); Vernon (2011)

Simonetti, Michelangelo (1724–87) Italian architect, he designed most of the *Museo Pio-Clementino* in the Vatican, a master-work of *Neo-Classicism, which provides the settings for many of the greatest treasures in the papal collections. He redesigned the *Cortile Ottagono* (1771–3), the *Sala Rotonda* (*c.*1776–80), the *Sala a Croce Greca* (*c.*1776–9), the *Sala delle Muse* (*c.*1781–2), and the new access-*stairs. In some of this work he collaborated with *Camporese. His use of *Antique elements and clear, logical, expression of structure gave his architecture great authority.

Ms (1966); M & Wa (1987); J.T (1996)

Simon the Mason (*fl.*1301–22) English master-mason, probably in charge of the building of the *nave at York *Minster from 1291, so had control of this virtually from start to finish.

J.Harvey (1987)

Simpson, Archibald (1790–1847) Scots architect, he was responsible for many distinguished buildings in Aberdeenshire. His *Greek-Revival designs include the Aberdeen Music Hall or County Assembly Rooms (1820–2) and Crimonmogate, a country-house at Lonmay (*c.*1825), both built of fine *granite *masonry that gives them a monumental severity. Thainston House, near Kintore (*c.*1847), was in a simplified Classical style, and he also experimented with *castellated architecture (Castle Forbes (1814–15)), *Gothic (Old Aberdeen Free Church (1845–6)), and *Tudor-Gothic (The Gordon Schools, Huntly (1839)). Other works include the handsome Greek-Revival Church of St Giles, Elgin, Morayshire (1827–8). Most of his country-houses and *villas were chastely Greek, with very fine and ingenious Neo-Classical interiors.

Co (2008); *DSA* (2013); J.T (1996)

Simpson, John Anthony (1954–) *See* NEW CLASSICISM, NEW URBANISM.

Sinan (1489–1578 *or* 1588) Master-architect of the Ottoman Empire, holding responsibilities for an enormous range of public works. One of his greatest buildings was the *Süleymaniye* *Mosque in Istanbul (1550–7) which shows how much he had absorbed of *Byzantine forms and construction, especially those of the Church of *Hagia Sophia*, but Sinan improved and rationalized the system of buttressing for the central *dome, and clarified the subsidiary elements. However, the huge complex at Selimiye, Edirne, Turkey (1569–74), in which domed structures and rigorous geometry are thoroughly exploited, is even more successful as a solution to the problem of providing a large domed centralized volume, for the secondary volumes are more closely related to the large domed space, with a logic and clarity carried to their ultimate conclusions. Sinan is credited with around 460 buildings, including mosques, hospitals, schools, public buildings, baths, palaces, bridges, tombs, and grand houses. Among his finest tombs are the *mausolea of **Sultans Selim II** (*r.*1566–74) and **Süleyman I** (*r.*1520–66): the latter's tomb is an octagonal domed structure, exquisitely decorated with tiles, in the *Süleymaniye* complex. His work was a felicitous synthesis of styles in which Byzantine and Turkish themes merged.

E.Egli (1976) H.Egli (1997); Freely & Burelli (1992); G. Goodwin (1971, 1992); Gurlitt (1907–12); Kuran (1987); P (1982); A.Stratton (1972); J.T (1996); Vogt-Göknil (1993)

singerie Style of C17–18 *Chinoiserie*, *Rococo, and *Régence decoration incorporating monkeys (*singe* (French) = monkey) wearing clothes and mimicking humans, set amidst *scroll- and *band-work, sometimes found with *Magots.

singing-gallery 1. Elevated choir-loft, *tribune-gallery, or *cantoria for singers in a church. **2.** *Rood-loft.

single frame Floor of one tier of common *joists, without *girders or binding-beams, or roof with one tier of common *rafters, without principals, but stiffened with *collar-beams, diagonal *braces, etc.

single-hung Window having only one opening *sash.

single-pile house House-plan one room deep, contrasted with a *double-pile plan.

Sirén, Johan Sigfrid (1889–1961) Finnish architect, he designed extensions to *Engel's University (1810) and Parliament Building (both completed 1931), Helsinki, which confirmed him as a leader (1918–39) of Nordic *Neo-Classicism. His Bank of Finland, Vaasa (1943–52), is a noble work of *stripped *Classicism. His son, **Heikki Sirén** (1918–2013), in partnership from 1949 with his wife, **Kaija** (1920–2001), produced paradigms of Scandinavian Modernism, characterized by simplicity and formality. Their Chapel at the Technical College, Otaniemi (1957), was much admired when completed, with its minimalist *altar and cross set against a large window with a background of pine-trees. Other works include *Otsonpesä* Linked Houses, Tapiola (1959), *Brucknerhaus* Concert Hall, Linz, Austria (1974), and the Granite House, *KOP Kamppi* Offices, Helsinki (1985).

E. Bruun & Popovits (eds) (1978); Do (1980a); *MfBuS,* **xxii/1** (1938), 33–40; Pn (1982); J.Sirén (1989); Walden (ed.) (1998)

Sirén, Osvald (1879–1966) Finnish-born, Swedish-educated historian of architecture and art (esp. Chinese), author of two immensely important books on Chinese gardens and their impact on C18 garden-design in England, France, and Sweden.

Sirén (1949, 1990)

Sitte, Camillo (1843–1903) Austro-Hungarian architect/town-planner, pupil of *Ferstel, and admirer of William *Morris and Gottfried *Semper, he designed the *Renaissance-Revival *Mechitaristenkirche,* Vienna (1873–4), and a few other buildings in other parts of the Empire. His importance lies in one work, his well-illustrated *Der Städtebau nach seinen künstlerischen Grundsätzen* (Town-Planning according to Artistic Principles—1889), which emphasized the need to design the urban fabric with aesthetics and composition in mind, and ran into several editions, with translations in French (1902), Russian (1925), Spanish (1926), English (1945, 1965), and Italian (1953). It was one of the first major books

to analyse what became known as *townscape. His work was rediscovered in the 1960s when the reaction against the destruction of towns as a result of the dogmas of Le *Corbusier, *CIAM, and *International Modernism gained momentum, but counts for nothing among Deconstructivists and others in C21.

C & C (1986); H & P (1972); P (1982); Sitte (1965); J.T (1996)

Sixdeniers, C (*fl.*1530s) Builder of the *Ancien Greffe* (Old Registry), Brugge, Belgium (1535–7), in which *Gothic elements were freely mixed with *Renaissance motifs.

Bae: *Belgium* (1931)

Sixteen Principles of Urbanism Agreed with Moscow (1948), the Principles were drawn up in Communist East Germany as a radical alternative to the Le *Corbusier-*CIAM-*Athens Charter dogmas so widely accepted in the West after 1945. Among the Principles were the rejection of urban *motorways cutting swathes through the urban fabric, the abandonment of *zoning that played havoc in Western cities, and the reestablishment of the urban *block and traditional street as essentials, all of which were reassessed at the end of C20 as part of *New Urbanism.

Kostof (1991, 1995); Ministry of Culture of the former DDR; pk

skeleton *Personification of Death, common in funerary architecture.

E.P.Weber (1914)

skeleton-frame Structural *frame of *concrete, metal, or timber supporting floors, roof, and exterior treatment, with spaces between uprights and horizontals filled with a lighter material or having external *cladding (or *curtain-wall) fixed outside the frame. *See also* SKYSCRAPER.

Br (1980)

skew Anything that slopes or is set obliquely, e.g. top of a medieval *buttress or the *cope of a *gable. *Compounds include*:

skew-arch: *see* ARCH;

skew-back: sloping bed, line, *sommering, or surface of an *abutment from which a segmental arch springs;

skew-block, skew-butt, skew-corbel, skew-put(t), skew-table: large stone at the bottom end of the raking top of a gable to hold the cope and stop it sliding off, also called *gable-springer,* *kneeler, *springer, or *summer-stone;

skew-butt: **1.** as *skew-block*; **2.** *rising hinge*;

skew-corbel: as *skew-block*, but especially one projecting beyond the *naked of the return wall of the gable, terminating *eaves, any *cornice, and *gutter;

skew-table: *skew-block.*

Skidmore, Owings, & Merrill (SOM) American architectural firm (founded by **Louis Skidmore** (1897–1962) and **Nathaniel Alexander Owings** (1903–84) in Chicago, IL (1936), and NYC (1937), later (1939) joined by **John Ogden Merrill** (1896–1975) and (1945) *Bunshaft) organized on teamwork principles incorporating ideas from American business-practice. **SOM** won fame with Lever House, Park Avenue, NYC (completed 1952), a 21-storey *curtain-walled *skyscraper slab set on a lower *podium-like building, influenced by the *International-Modern Movement and *Mies van der Rohe, and designed largely by Bunshaft. Their work had a profound effect on the development of architecture in the USA, notably with buildings in landscaped settings (e.g. Connecticut General Life Insurance Company, Bloomfield, CT (1953–7), and the United Airlines Building, Des Plaines, IL (1962)). With the John Hancock Center (1969–70), SOM evolved a tubular structure with diagonal bracing expressed on the exterior, and also designed the Sears Tower (1972–4), both in Chicago. The firm was responsible for a series of office-buildings with large, covered *atrium-halls, including the Fourth Financial Center, Wichita, KS (1974), and the First Wisconsin Plaza Building, Madison, WI (1974). The National Commercial Bank, Jeddah, Saudi Arabia (1982), set new standards for tall office-blocks in very hot climates, while the Broadgate and Canary Wharf developments in London (1990s) have kept the firm in the public eye.

Bruegmann (ed.) (1994); B-B (1984); Bussel (2000); Danz (1962); Dr & Menges (1974); E (1994); Gretes (1984); Krinsky (1988); Menges (1974); SOM (1995); Whyte (ed.) (2000); Woodward (1970)

Skillyngton, Robert (*fl.*1391–1400) English mason, he oversaw the works at Kenilworth Castle, Warwicks., from 1391, including the great hall, towers, and state-apartments. He probably designed the *choir of St Mary's *Collegiate Church, Warwick (1381–96), and the tower of St Michael's Church, Coventry (1373–94). In charge (1397–1400) of the College of St Mary in the Newark, Leicester, he was also (1400) master-mason at Tutbury Castle, Staffs., where he built a new tower and part of the *curtain-wall.

J.Harvey (1987)

skinning *See* REGRATING.

skirt 1. Projection of *eaves. **2.** *Apron-piece under a window. **3.** Plane sides of a room. *Related terms include*:
skirting: timber *skirting-board* fixed to the base of the walls of a room as a finish between the *plaster and the *floor, corresponding to a Classical *plinth;

skirt-roof: *roof around a building, e.g. over a *verandah, between *storeys.

skull 1. Of an animal, an *aegicrane or *bucranium, on *friezes, etc. **2.** If human, represents mortality, transitory life, and vanity, so occurs in funerary architecture, notably as supports for *obelisks.

skylight Glazed opening in a roof or ceiling.

skyline Arrangement of roofs, *chimney-stacks, *spires, and other architectural accessories, creating a pattern against the sky, often *Picturesque.

skyscraper High multi-storey building based on a *steel- or *concrete-*framed or *skeleton structure, evolved in the USA in the late 1880s after the limitations of traditional *load-bearing construction had been reached with ten- or twelve-storey buildings (while it would be possible to build higher load-bearing walls, the huge amounts of material needed would be uneconomic). Important in its evolution was *Post's Equitable Life Assurance Building, NYC (1868–70), designed with a passenger-lift (*see* ELEVATOR): the lift had been invented in the late 1850s, and from *c.*1880 its speed and reliability were greatly improved, enabling the building-type to further develop. *Jenney's Home Insurance Building, Chicago, IL (1883–5—demolished—which incorporated iron columns, *lintels, *girders, and steel *beams), was the model for later architecture of the *Chicago School. Steel and iron, with load-bearing brick, were also used by *Holabird & Roche in the 22-storey Tacoma Building in Chicago (1887–8—demolished 1929), although *Buffington claimed to have originated the whole system on which skyscraper construction was based, and there were earlier experiments by *Loudon, *Paxton, *Saulnier, and others that pointed the way forward. Later important skyscrapers include Cass *Gilbert's Woolworth Building, NYC (1911–13), *Shreve, Lamb, & Harmon's Empire State Building, NYC (designed 1928–9, built 1930–2), *SOM's John Hancock Center (1969–70) and Sears Tower (1972–4), both in Chicago, and **Cesar Pelli's** (1926–2019) Petronas Twin Towers, Kuala Lumpur, Malaysia (1991–7). However, the rapid collapse (11 Sept. 2001) of the twin towers of the World Trade Center, NYC (designed by *Yamasaki with Emery *Roth, 1964–74), following the deliberate attack using passenger-carrying aeroplanes, may cause questions to be asked about the future of steel frames and large areas of glass, although, as **Carol Willis** observed, 'Form follows Finance'.

Bl & Ro (1975); Ct (1952, 1960, 1961, 1964, 1968, 1973); Goldberger (1981); HHS (1985); D.Ho (1988); S.Landau & Ct (1996); Leeuwen (1988); C.Willis (1995); Yeang (1997); Zu (ed.) (1987)

sky-sign Lettering or other advertising material on a metal frame, free-standing or mounted on top of a building, so that it is seen against the sky. It was a feature of *Constructivism and De *Stijl.

O.Shv (1970); Vi *et al.* (1977)

slab Large flat but not very thick portion of any material. Slabs of stone are used for pavements, the *mensa* of an *altar, *cladding, grave-covers, tomb-stones, etc. A *slab-roof* is a 'flat' roof resembling a slab, of *concrete or other material.

slab-block *Multi-storey building, rectangular on *plan.

slab-house Building *clad in rough-hewn timber planks.

slat 1. Thin strip of wood, metal, etc., as in a *louvre, *shutter, etc. **2.** *Slate or roofing-*slab.

slate Sedimentary stone readily divisible into thin plates or *slabs used for *cladding, roofing, paving, tomb-stones, etc. *Slate-hanging, slateboarding*, or *weather-slating* is cladding of a wall with slates.

sleeper Any piece of timber employed to support other timbers, e.g. large horizontal beam (*patand) from which the *posts and *studs of a *timber-framed wall rise from just above ground level, or any *beam under a ground-floor surface supporting the *joists of a larger span. A *sleeper-wall*, usually perforated to allow free passage of air, supports *joists of a timber ground-floor in the case of heavy loads or wide spans between walls of a room; it is also a wall between two structural elements (e.g. *piers) to prevent movement, or a wall supporting a sleeper.

slit and tongue *See* TONGUE.

Sloan, Samuel (1815–84) American architect, he worked mostly in Philadelphia, PA, where he established an office (1849). Among his first works were Bartram Hall, West Philadelphia (1850–1), a luxurious *villa in the *Italianate *Rundbogenstil, several schools, and the Masonic Temple (1853). He also designed many hospitals and lunatic-asylums: at the time of his death there was at least one of his hospitals in every State in the USA. He published *The Model Architect* (1852–3), containing designs for cottages, *villas, and suburban residences, and thereafter brought out many books, including *City and Suburban Architecture* (1859, 1867), *Sloan's Constructive Architecture* (1859, 1867), *American Houses* (1861, 1868), and much else to publicize his work. From 1857 he was assisted in the production of his books by **Addison Hutton** (1843–1916), who was his partner (1864–8): he also edited (with **Charles Jefferson Lukens** (*c.*1827–98)) *The Architectural Review and American Builder's Journal* (1868–70), the

first periodical in the USA devoted wholly to architecture. One of his most extraordinary buildings was Longwood, Natchez, MS (1854–61), an octagonal domed house in the *Indian style. He was uninhibitedly eclectic in his tastes, capable of designing in many styles.

Cooledge (1986); P (1982); Sloan (1867, 1868, 1870, 1873, 1873a); Sloan & Lukens (eds) (1868–70); J.T (1996); vV (1993); Whitwell (1975)

SLOAP (Space Left Over After Planning) Useless bits of ground left between streets and rigidly rectilinear *International-Modernist buildings (which rarely followed traditional street- or urban-patterns).

slurb Combination of 'slum' and 'suburb', the USA equivalent of *subtopia.

slype Narrow passage (*slip*) between *transept and *chapter-house with access from the *cloister in a monastic establishment.

Smeaton, John (1724–92) English civil-engineer/inventor of Scots descent, he travelled on the Continent (1754) to study canals and harbours, and designed (1755–6) his Eddystone Lighthouse, near Plymouth, Devon, using a system of dovetailing the stones together, including the courses and the foundations in the rock: completed (1759), it was replaced (1877–82). He designed several *bridges (the best of which are in Scotland, including those at Banff, Coldstream, and Perth, using *segmental arches, and with circular perforations in the *spandrels), and the Forth and Clyde Canal (begun 1768, completed 1790).

ODNB (2004); Sk (1981); Smeaton (1813, 1837)

Smirke, Sir Robert (1780–1867) English architect, he trained briefly with *Soane (with whom he quarrelled) and the younger *Dance before travelling in France, Greece, Italy, and Sicily (1801–5), after his return (1805) publishing *Specimens of Continental Architecture* (1806). He set up in practice in London, and found favour with the Establishment. Among his first works were the *castellated Lowther Castle, Westmd. (1806–11), and Eastnor Castle (also castellated), Herefs. (1812–20), but he made his reputation with Covent Garden Theatre, London (1808–9—destroyed, replaced 1856–8 by E.M.*Barry), the first public building in the capital to have a pure *Greek-*Doric *portico. Thereafter he became an important protagonist of the *Greek Revival. With *Nash and *Soane, he was appointed (1813) as one of the three Architects to the Office of Works, and gained several important London commissions including the General Post Office, St Martin's Le Grand (1824–9—demolished), the Custom House (1825–7—a rebuilding after the failure of the foundations of *Laing's building), King's College, The Strand (1830–5), and his masterpiece, the prestigious British Museum, Bloomsbury (1823–46). He also designed the Royal College of Physicians (now Canada House), Trafalgar Square (1822–5—remodelled 1925), and the Oxford and Cambridge Club, Pall Mall (1835–8—with his brother, **Sydney**).

He built or altered around 30 country-houses, and designed county-halls for Bristol, Carlisle, Gloucester, Hereford, Lincoln, Maidstone, Perth, and Shrewsbury, all buildings of some personality and presence, but it is as a Greek Revivalist that he produced his best work. The British Museum is one of the greatest buildings in that style in England, with its noble Greek *Ionic *Order, the *capitals based on those of the Temple of *Athena Polias*, Priene (338 BC and later), and the *bases on those of the Temple of *Dionysus*, Teos (c.130 BC), and King's Library (arguably the finest Neo-Classical interior in England). Greek Revival was admirably suited to Smirke's taste for geometrical simplicity and rationalism: a tendency to simplify further and create crisply cubical compositions was apparent at his Kinmount, Dumfriesshire (1812), The Homend, Stretton Grandison, Herefs. (1814–21), and Worthy House, Hants. (1816). One of his best buildings was the *mausoleum and church at Milton, West Markham, Notts. (1831–2), for **Henry Pelham Fiennes Pelham-Clinton (1785–1851—4th Duke of Newcastle under Lyme** from 1795). He was innovative in construction, pioneering *concrete-*raft foundations, fireproof hollow-clay *vaults, and the use of iron in architecture. Among his successful pupils and assistants were *Burn, C.R.*Cockerell, Henry *Roberts, Lewis *Vulliamy, and his own brother, S.*Smirke. Although a conventional designer, his office was regarded as the most progressive of its time, certainly in the 1820s and early 1830s.

AH, **vi** (1963), 91–102; *AR*, **cxlii/847** (Sept. 1967), 208–10; Co (2008); Crook (1972, 1972a); C & P (1973); *ODNB* (2004); P (1982); Su (2003); J.T (1996); *Trans. Newcomen Society*, **xxxviii** (1965–6), 5–22

Smirke, Sydney (1798–1877) English architect, perhaps overshadowed by his older and more famous brother, Robert *Smirke, he nevertheless designed several important buildings. Among his London works were the *cupola of and additions to the Bethlehem Hospital (now the Imperial War Museum—1838–46), and two luxurious clubs; the *Palladian former Conservative, 74 St James's Street (1843–5—with *Basevi), and the Carlton, Pall Mall (1854–6—demolished), an essay in Venetian-*Renaissance Revival with *elevations (in which polished *granite columns were used in the *façade) based on *Sansovino's Library of St Mark. He also assisted his brother with the Oxford and Cambridge Club, Pall Mall (1835–8). His most celebrated building was the domed Reading Room in the British Museum (1854–7), in which

the structure was of cast iron, and he also completed his brother's work at the Museum. He designed the extensions containing the exhibition galleries for the Royal Academy, Burlington House, Piccadilly, London (1866–76), and was Architect to Brookwood Cemetery, Woking, Surrey (1854–6).

Fawcett (ed.) (1976); *ODNB* (2004); W.Pa (1887)

Smith, Arnold Dunbar (1866–1933) English architect. He entered into partnership (1895) with **Cecil Claude Brewer** (1871–1918), and they won the competition to design the Passmore Edwards Settlement (now Mary Ward Centre), Tavistock Place, London (1896–8). It is a delightful building, with influences from *Voysey in the *cornice and roof, Harrison *Townsend in the vaguely *Sezessionist porch, and Norman *Shaw in the fenestration. **Smith & Brewer** designed Little Barley End, Tring, Herts. (1899), and were pioneers of the Neo-Classical Revival with severe National Museum of Wales, Cathays Park, Cardiff (1910), which played an important role in establishing the American *Beaux-Arts* style of *Classicism in England. Their best-known work was Heal's, Tottenham Court Road, London (1916), a reticent *stripped Classical design described by *Pevsner as the 'best commercial front of its date'.

A.S.Gray (1985); J.Newman (1995); Cherry & Pe (1998)

Smith, George (1782–1869) English architect, Surveyor to The Mercers' Company (from 1814), for which he designed York Square and surrounding areas (c.1820–35), Mercers' Cottages, White Horse Road (1854–5), Stepney, London, and buildings on the Company's Estate in Co. Londonderry for which he was assisted by his partner (1836–42), **William Barnes** (1807–68—responsible for the *Romanesque-Revival Parish Church, Kilrea (1841–2), and other buildings in Ulster). Other works included the *Gothic Whittington Almshouses, Highgate, London (1822—demolished 1966), the *Greek-Revival St Alban's Court House and Town Hall, Herts. (1829–33), the *Greek-Doric Corn Exchange, Mark Lane, London (1827–8—demolished 1941), and the Grammar School, Horsham, Sussex (1840–1). He also designed (with Henry *Roberts et al.) London Bridge Railway Terminus (1836), rebuilt several times since then. He laid out the Morden College Estate, Greenwich, where he designed houses (e.g. Brand and Pelton Streets) in a variety of styles.

Co (2008); J.Curl (1983, 1986); W.Pa (1887)

Smith, George Washington (1876–1930) See SPANISH COLONIAL REVIVAL.

Smith, James (c.1645–1731) Scots architect. As a young man he travelled on the Continent, but by 1679 was settled in Edinburgh, married to a daughter of architect/builder **Robert Mylne**

(1633-1710), and was appointed (1683) Surveyor or Overseer of the Royal Works. He built Drumlanrig Castle, Dumfriesshire (*c.*1680-90—probably based on designs by his father-in-law), designed Hamilton Palace, Lanarkshire (1693-1701—demolished), Melville House, Fife (1697-1700), and Yester House, East Lothian (*c.*1700-15), remodelled Dalkeith House, Midlothian (1702-10), and constructed the Mackenzie *mausoleum in Greyfriars churchyard, Edinburgh (*c.*1690-2), among much else. He was responsible for disseminating the Classical style introduced by *Bruce to Scotland, but in his surviving drawings it is clear he was familiar with the works of *Palladio, and he may have been an early and formative influence on Colen *Campbell: in his realized buildings, however, any Palladian tendencies were muted. His works pre-date any *Palladian essays of the *Burlington Palladian Revival which therefore may have originated in Scotland.

AH, xvii (1974), 5-13; Co (2008); Dunbar *et al.* (1995)

Smith, John (1781-1852) Scots architect, he established himself in Aberdeen where he became City Architect (1824), directing building-works there for some 30 years, his only rival being Archibald *Simpson. He designed some distinguished *Greek-Revival structures, including the Schools in Little Belmont Street (1841), but he also carried out work in C16 and C17 *vernacular styles that caused him to be nicknamed 'Tudor Johnny'. He designed the *Ionic *screen, St Nicholas churchyard (1830), and the *Tudor-Gothic Trinity Hall (1845-6), both in Union Street. His son, **William Smith** (1817-91), with Prince *Albert, designed Balmoral Castle in the *Scottish-Baronial style (1853-5).

Co (2008); W.Pa (1887)

Smith, Thomas (1798-1875) Son of **John Smith** (1775-1833—Surveyor of Bridges to the County of Kent (1810-25)), he became County Surveyor of Herts. (1837). His works include the County Hospital, Hertford (1832-3), the remodelling of several country-houses in Co. Louth (including Castle Bellingham (*c.*1834)), Louth County Infirmary, Dundalk (1835—*Tudor-*Gothic, now the Motor-Taxation Office), and five pairs of semi-detached houses in North Crescent, Hertford (*c.*1824-6). With his son, **Thomas Tayler Smith** (1834-1910), he designed Christ Church, Radlett, Herts. (1864), and churches at Cannes, Naples, Nice, and Stuttgart.

Co (2008); Corfield (1998)

Smith, Thomas Gordon (1948-) *See* NEW CLASSICISM.

Smith Brothers Francis (1672-1738) and William (1661-1724) were important master-builders/architects in the English Midlands in the first decades of C18. Francis, known as 'Smith of Warwick', was based in that town, and was largely responsible for its rebuilding after the fire of 1694: the brothers rebuilt (1698-1704) the *Collegiate Church of St Mary, Warwick, to designs by Sir William Wilson (1641-1710), in an airy, vaguely *Gothic style of considerable originality. They carried out numerous ecclesiastical commissions, Francis being responsible for Gainsborough Church, Lincs. (1736-44). William designed Stanford Hall, Leics. (1697-1700), and the brothers were active over a wide geographical area: *Colvin gives an impressive list of their works in his *Dictionary*, and Gomme (2000) covers Francis's *œuvre* in some detail. Francis designed Stoneleigh Abbey, Warwicks. (1714-26), in a *Baroque style, but many of his houses are plain. His Court House, Warwick (1725-30), is in a refined *Palladian style. Francis's son, **William Smith** (1705-47), was also an architect/builder, specializing in a competent *Palladianism: among his works are Catton Hall, Derbys. (*c.*1742-5), Kirtlington Park, Oxon. (1742-7), and Thame Park, also Oxon. (*c.*1745).

AH, xxxv (1992), 183-8; Co (2008); Downes (1966); Gomme (2000); Hussey (1965); Lees-Milne (1970); *Warwickshire History*, ii/2 (1972-3), 3-13

Smithson, Alison (1928-93) and **Peter Denham** (1923-2003) British architects/polemicists, a husband-and-wife team (married 1949), they formed a partnership in London (1950). As members of *Team X and *CIAM they established themselves as leaders of the *Modern Movement in Britain during the 1950s and 1960s. Their steel-framed Secondary School at Hunstanton, Norfolk (1949-54), the panels filled with bricks and glass, owed much to the style of *Mies van der Rohe, and, with its exposed internal services, was claimed in some quarters to be an 'honest' expression of *Functionalism, a rejection of *New Empiricism, and a paradigm of New *Brutalism: it was much admired by *Banham and others, even though its problems were many in terms of solar-heat gain, lack of privacy, distortion of the steel frame through heat, and breakage of windows due to that distortion (all indicative that the building *failed* to 'function', and indeed one contemporary critic suggested that the 'building seems to ignore the children for which it was built'). Their *Economist* Building, St James's, London (1962-4), was perceived as architecture of high quality in an established setting. With developments such as the Robin Hood Gardens Estate, London (1972), their use of exposed raw *concrete derived from Le *Corbusier's work confirmed them as exponents of 'New Brutalism', in a different sense to that used in relation to Hunstanton not unconnected with P.D.Smithson's nickname 'Brutus'. The high-level corridor-streets, making a spurious connection with streets of terrace-housing, together with the character of the buildings, have not been universally admired and indeed have attracted opprobrium. Prolific writers, their publications seem curiously dated, yet were influential at the time: they denounced *Lutyens as 'irresponsible', and adopted similar priggish attitudes to other great architects.

AD, xxxii/12 (Dec. 1962), whole issue; xli/8 (Aug. 1971), 479–81; xliii/8 (Aug. 1973), 524–9 and 621–3; xliv/9 (Sept. 1974), 573–90; xlvi/6 (June 1976), 331–54; Arena, xxxii (1966), whole issue; R.Ba (1966); Domus, dxxxix (1974) 1–8; E (1994); Sn (ed.) (1968, 1982); Sn & Sn (1967, 1968, 1975, 1981, 1982, 1991, 2001); vV (1993); Vidotto (1997); Vidotto et al. (1991); H.Webster (ed.) (1997); Zodiac, iv (1959), 73–83

Smithson, Robert (1938–73) See LAND ART.

smithy Blacksmith's workshop, where metals (especially iron) are worked.

smoke-house 1. Place where meat, fish, etc. are cured with smoke. **2.** Room in a tannery where hides were unhaired.

Smyth, Henry (fl.1506–17) English mason, he collaborated with *Vertue and *Lee at King's College Chapel, Cambridge, from c.1506, and began work (1508) at the hospital of the Savoy, London, where he was engaged when he died. He seems to have been Master-Mason at Richmond Palace, Surrey (1505–9).

J.Harvey (1987)

Smyth, John (fl.1429–60) English mason, he was a lodge-mason at Canterbury (1429), Warden of the Masons at Eton College, Bucks. (1441), and Master-Mason at Westminster Abbey (1453).

J.Harvey (1987)

Smyth, William (fl.c.1465–90) English mason, he carried out works at St John's Church, Glastonbury, Som. (c.1465), and was Master-Mason at Wells Cathedral, Som. (before 1480). He may have designed the *vault under the *crossing-tower, the Sugar *Chantry Chapel (1489), and other parts of the Cathedral. He was probably the architect of Crewkerne Church, Som. (c.1475–90), and may have worked on the vaults of Sherbourne (c.1486–93) and Milton (after 1481) Abbeys, both in Dorset.

J.Harvey (1987)

Smythson, Robert (c.1535–1614) Distinguished English architect of the *Elizabethan period, he worked (1568–75) at Longleat, Wilts., a great house disposed almost symmetrically about both axes, and with very large windows, both features of Smythson's first known independent work, the dramatic *prodigy-house of Wollaton Hall, Notts. (1580–8), a powerful composition

(possibly indebted in part to *Serlio) with much Flemish-derived ornament (probably from de *Vries), tall corner-towers, and a central *clerestoreyed hall (rather than the internal *courts of Longleat) rising high above the surrounding structure. He also designed Worksop Manor, Notts. (c.1585—destroyed); his masterpiece, Hardwick Hall, Derbys. (1590–7—a less frenetic composition than Wollaton); and (probably) Burton Agnes Hall, Yorks. (1601–10). His son, **John Smythson** (c.1570–1634), assisted him, but then worked for the Cavendish family at Bolsover Castle, Derbys. (c.1612–34), Welbeck Abbey, Notts. (1622–3), and (possibly) Slingsby Castle, Yorks. (c.1630). Bolsover is an extraordinary building, very consciously medieval in appearance, and may be classified as an early prototype of the *sham castle so popular in C18. John's son, **Huntingdon** (c.1601–1648), and his son, **John** (1640–1717), were also architects.

Airs (1975, 1995); AH, v (1962), 21–184; Co (2008); Gd (1966, 1983); Lees-Milne (1951); Su (1993); J.T (1996)

snail-mount Cone-shaped spiral-*mount ascended by a helical path, sometimes with a *fabrique at the summit. Known from C16, the form has recurred, notably at the moated garden of the Old Bield, Lyveden, Northants., in Germany (where it is known as Schneckenberg, e.g. at Schloss Machern, near Leipzig (1782–98, originally topped by a *rustic *temple), and at **Charles Alexander Jencks** (1939–2019) and **Maggie Keswick's** (1945–95) Cosmological Garden, Portrack House, Dumfries & Galloway (1990s—where 'energy-curves' derived from ideas in *feng shui principles are also suggested in the modelled *terraces, a complex exemplar of *Land Art).

Gothein (1966); Keswick (1986); N & R (2003)

sneck 1. Lifting-lever of a latch lock. **2.** In squared uncoursed *rubble, a small stone set in the interstices between larger stones preserving the horizontal and vertical *bonds. Snecked harling is a *rendered or *harled wall leaving some stones exposed for effect.

soaker Piece of lead used to make watertight the intersections of sloping roof-surfaces with end-gables or penetrating walls.

Soami (otherwise **Shinso Soami**) (1472–1523/5) Japanese artist, he may have designed the Ryoan-ji garden, Kyoto, celebrated for its stones arranged on a bed of raked gravel.

J.T (1996)

Soane, Sir John (1753–1837) English architect, arguably one of the greatest since *Vanbrugh and *Hawksmoor. Trained in the office of the younger *Dance and at the Royal Academy Schools, he joined the office of Henry *Holland (1772), where he gained valuable experience. Having been awarded (1778) the King's Travelling Studentship, he went to Italy where he met several influential Englishmen on the *Grand Tour. Led to expect employment by the enormously rich but erratic **Frederick Augustus Hervey** (1730–1803— **Bishop of Derry** from 1768 and **4th Earl of Bristol** from 1779), he foolishly ended (1780) his stay in Rome to travel to Ireland where he hoped to design the Bishop's house at Downhill, Co. Londonderry, but this came to nothing. He spent the next four years making good his losses by carrying out small works, some in East Anglia, helped by acquaintances who had heard of his disappointment. Among his designs at this time were lodges and a rustic dairy at Hamels Park, Buntingford, Herts. (1781–3), and a new house, Letton Hall, Norfolk (1783–9). He built up a reputation for probity and competence, exhibited at the RA, made a good marriage, and carried out alterations and additions to Holwood House, Kent (1786–95), for **William Pitt** (1759–1806), cousin of one of Soane's friends from his Roman trip, and Prime Minister (1783–1801). In 1788, the year in which he intended to publish *Plans, Elevations, and Sections of Buildings Erected in the Counties of Norfolk, Suffolk,* etc. (it appeared in 1789), Soane, through his connection with Pitt, gained the Surveyorship of the Bank of England after the death of Sir Robert *Taylor. This appointment gave him status and security, and set him up as a leading English architect. The death of his wife's uncle (1790) brought a legacy that enabled him to build a house at 12 Lincoln's Inn Fields, London (1792–4), and start the great collections of works of art and books that form the contents of his *Museum today. Other official appointments followed. Security also enabled him to evolve an individual style that, while rooted in *Classicism, was yet original, and consisted of certain themes. These included the extensive use of segmental arches; shallow saucer-domed ceilings on segmental arches carried on *piers and sometimes lit from above; cross-vaults carried on piers; top-lit volumes rising through two floors; a *primitive, *stripped language of architecture, sometimes featuring *Orders such as the *Paestum *Doric, but more often the replacement of the Orders by a series of incised ornaments cut into unadorned simple elements; very careful attention to lighting, often involving mirrors (plain and convex) and tinted glass; and, above all, an obsession with the furniture of death in the form of *sarcophagi, cinerary *urns, oppressive vaulted spaces, and the like.

Among his greatest works was the Bank of England in London, with the Stock Office (1792-3—reconstructed by **Higgins Gardner**, 1986–8) and the Rotunda (begun 1796) two of the most remarkable spaces within the complex, both treated without reference to the Orders, but with the *Classicism reduced to simple grooves. The exterior wall was largely a blank wall, enlivened by recesses and *colonnades of the *Corinthian Order from the Temple of Vesta at Tivoli. Virtually nothing of his work at the Bank survived within the exterior wall after the drastic alterations by *Baker (1921–39). After 1800 his work became more intensely personal, as with Pitzhanger Place, Ealing, Mddx. (1800–3), the Dulwich Picture Gallery and *Mausoleum (1811–14, restored 1953—where his architectural language reached a new simplicity and refinement), and his own house, 13 Lincoln's Inn Fields, London (1812-13—now Sir John Soane's Museum), one of the most complex, intricate, and ingenious series of interiors ever conceived, with much top lighting (using coloured glass), mirrors, folding walls, double-height spaces, and parts where the extraordinary obsession with death and the *Antique almost overwhelm. The exterior, with its plain ashlar incised front, shows how far Soane had moved in abstracting his *Neo-Classicism. *Schinkel saw the building (1826), and described the internal spaces as resembling cemeteries and catacombs, with everywhere 'little deceptions'. Schinkel also found Soane's ornamentation at the Bank of England 'strangely simple'.

Soane became (1806) Professor of Architecture at the RA, and gave a series of meticulously prepared lectures. He demanded the highest professional standards, was passionately interested in architectural education, and was very well-read, having one of the finest architectural libraries ever collected. He was clearly influenced by French theorists, notably *Laugier, and by certain architects, including the younger *Dance, *Ledoux, and *Peyre. The impact of Paestum Doric was clear from the entrance-hall at Tyringham Hall, Bucks. (1793–c.1800), and the primitive '*barn à la Paestum*' he designed at 936 Warwick Road, Solihull, Warwicks. (1798). He owned the original drawings of the Paestum temples by *Piranesi, still in the Museum. One of his most beautiful creations was the Council Chamber, Freemasons' Hall, Great Queen street, London (1828—demolished), in which his uses of top-lit saucer-domes, segmental arches, simple incised ornament, and a rigorous unification of walls and ceilings were demonstrated. In spite of the fact that Soane was a convinced *Freemason (a portrait of him in his Freemasonic regalia survives), his biographies have been unaccountably reticent about this, yet much of his personal style can only be explained with reference to Freemasonic concerns with Ancient Egypt, death, and the moral meaning of architecture. The *mausoleum he designed for himself and his wife in the overspill burial-ground of St Giles-in-the-Fields (now St Pancras Gardens), London (1816), with its segmental pediments and much curiously original treatment is indubitably Freemasonic, and was the model for Giles Gilbert *Scott's C20 GPO telephone-kiosks. His other tombs were severe and dignified, and some works, including the stables at Chelsea Hospital, London (1804–17), and the farmhouse at Butterton Grange, Staffs. (1816–17), were even more minimalist, of plain brick treated with the utmost simplicity.

Although Soane had many pupils, including *Basevi, J.M.*Gandy, and *Wightwick, his own work was lampooned by A.W.N.*Pugin, who did considerable damage to his reputation. Earlier, an anonymous attack on him in *The Champion* (1815) turned out to be by his son, **George** (1790–1860), from whom he was thereafter estranged (although knighted (1831), Soane is said to have declined a Baronetcy to prevent his son from inheriting the title). His exacting personality cannot have made him an easy man with whom to deal, and his struggle to evolve a new type of Classicism that was a synthesis of Greek, Roman, Italian, Egyptian, and French Neo-Classicism, handled with scholarship, sensitivity, and originality, did not lead anywhere after his death, although his architecture aroused new interest in the late C20.

AR, clxii/973 (Mar. 1978), 147–55; B & R (1993); Bolton (1927, 1929); Co (2008); Crook (1972a); C & P (1973); Darley (1999); Dean (1999); E.Hs (1990); Js (1999a); M & Wa (1987); Nevola (2000); *ODNB* (2004); P (1982); RdP (1982); M.Rn & Stevens (eds) (1999); Schumann-Bacia (1989, 1990); Soane (1830, 2000); Stroud (1996); Su (1952); Su *et al.* (1983); Waterfield (1996); D.Wa (1979, 1986, 1996); W-E (2013)

Social architecture 1. Architecture intended for use by the mass of people as social beings as a reaction against architecture concerned with form and style supposedly for the dominant members of society. **2.** Schools and other buildings erected after the 1939–45 war in Britain incorporating scientific method, *prefabrication, and *industrialized building as part of the *Modern Movement.

C.R.Hatch (ed.) (1984); Saint (1987); R.Sommer (1983)

Socialist Realism Offically approved styles of art, architecture, literature, etc., in the former Soviet Union and some other Communist countries. In architecture it usually involved a type of coarse *stripped Classicism.

CoE (1995); J.T (1996)

socle, zocle 1. Block of less height than horizontal dimension, without *base or *cornice, serving as a support for a *pedestal, bust, *urn, etc., really an unornamented *plinth. **2.** Base-course of a wall.

soffit(a) *or* (-e) **1.** Ceiling. **2.** Visible underside of an arch, *balcony, *beam, *corona, *cornice,

*vault, or any exposed architectural element. *Compounds include*:

soffit-cusp: *Gothic *cusp springing from a flat soffit or *intrados rather than from a chamfered side, looking like additions;

soffit-roll: *roll-moulding under an arch or soffit in *Romanesque architecture.

Soft architecture 1. Living-spaces with few fixed items or partitions. They would be instantly controlled by computers as required. **2.** Low-energy self-build dwellings.

R.Boyd (1968); Negroponte (1974); Spoerry (1989)

Soissons, Bernard de (*fl.*C13) One of the master-masons of Rheims Cathedral recorded in the *maze (destroyed) on the floor. He seems to have been active *c.*1253–90, but his contribution is never likely to be established with any certainty.

Svanberg (1983)

Soissons, Comte d'Ostel, Baron Longroy. Louis-Emmanuel-Jean-Guy de Savoie-Carignan de (1890–1962) Canadian-born architect, he studied at the *École des *Beaux-Arts, Paris, and at the RA, London. He designed several buildings in England including houses at Bagshot, Surrey (1914), the Earl Haig Memorial Homes, Meadow Head, Sheffield, Yorks. (1928–9), Broom Park and Huxhams Cross Houses, Dartington Hall, Devon (1932–3), and much else, but he is best known for the many buildings he designed at Welwyn *Garden City, Herts. (1919–60), where he introduced a pleasing *Neo-Georgian style with a *Colonial flavour to the second English Garden City.

AR, lxvi/392 (July 1929), 7–16; *ODNB* (2004); *RIBAJ*, ser. 3, xliii/8 (8 Aug. 1936), 975–84

solar, soler 1. *Garret, *loft, or *Rood-loft. **2.** Private upper chamber on the first floor, often in a cross-wing, of a medieval house. **3.** *Bay-window, almost the size of a small room, at the side of the high-table end of a medieval hall, or attached to a late-medieval withdrawing-room or dining-room.

ABDM (1996); Gw (1903)

solar glass Tinted glass to reduce glare from sunlight.

solar house Dwelling heated using energy from the sun's rays.

Solari, Guiniforte (1429–81) Milanese architect, he completed the *Ospedale Maggiore*, Milan, designed by *Filarete, in the *Gothic style and was responsible for the Gothic *nave of *Santa Maria delle Grazie* in the same city (1463–90) to which *Bramante added a domed *crossing and *choir (from 1493). He also seems to have carried out works at the *Duomo*, Milan, and at the *Certosa, Pavia.

He (1996); W.Pa (1887); Welch (1995)

Solari, Santino (1576–1646) Italian architect from the Como area, he was one of the first to bring a mature Italian Classical style north of the Alps into the German-speaking lands. His masterpiece is the Cathedral of Sts Rupert and Virgil, Salzburg (1614–28), with its apsidal *transepts clearly influenced by *Palladio's *Il Redentore* and *San Giorgio Maggiore*, Venice, probably suggested by an earlier design by *Scamozzi. He also designed *Schloss Hellbrunn*, near Salzburg (1613–15), in the early-*Baroque style, and the *Sanctum Sanctorum*, the *shrine of the *Gnadenbild*, or picture of the Black Virgin, at the *Benedictine Abbey, Einsiedeln, Switzerland (*c.*1617–20—destroyed and rebuilt in modified form).

Bou (1962); Fuhrmann (1950); E.Hempel (1965); J.T (1996)

solarium 1. Flat roof, *balcony, or *terrace exposed to the sun. **2.** Room on an upper floor, often opening to a terrace facing east to catch the morning sun. **3.** *Solar. **4.** *Loggia. **5.** *Sundial, often with architectural pretensions.

soldier *See* BRICK.

sole 1. *Cill. **2.** Base-plate supporting a *post: a *sole-piece* is therefore a horizontal timber carrying the *posts in *timber-framed structures. A *sole-plate* is a short timber laid across a wall (i.e. with its length at 90° to the *naked of the wall), supporting the foot of a *rafter and an *ashlar-piece in a timber roof. **3.** Part of anything touching the ground and sustaining a load.

ABDM (1996)

solea 1. Elevated *podium in an *Early-Christian or *Byzantine church linking an *ambo to a *bema. **2.** Step on which stood the *balustrade separating *choir and *sanctuary in a *basilica.

Soleri, Paolo (1919–2013) Turin-born American architect, he worked briefly (1947–9) for F.L.L.*Wright before returning to Italy to design the Ceramics Factory, Vietri-sul-Mare, on the Amalfi coast (1953). He settled (1956) in Scottsdale, AZ, where he established the Cosanti Foundation, building the Earth House (1956–8) to demonstrate the possibilities of alternative technologies. Evolving the concept of *Arcology, fusing architecture and ecology, he designed *megastructures, one of which, called *Arcosanti*, near Scottsdale, intended as an exemplar, was begun in 1970.

R.Ba (1976); Casper (1988); E (1994); LeG & S (1996); Lima (ed.) (2003); Ranocchi (1996); S & S (1976); Soleri (1969, 1971, 2002); Strohmeier (ed.) (2001); *The Times* (13 April 2013), 76; J.T (1996); Wall (1971)

Solomonic column *Barley-sugar, Salomonic, *Salomónica*, spiral, *torso or *twisted column, with a contorted or twisted *shaft, unlike the *Antonine, *triumphal, or *Trajanic column with spiral *band of sculpture wound around it. The form was based on *Antique precedents from the Herodian Temple in Jerusalem in the first century AD, thought to be from the Temple of Solomon. These and others were set up over the tomb of the Apostle in the Constantinian *basilica of *San Pietro*, Rome, and so copies or columns inspired by them became familiar throughout Europe, being often used on *altar-pieces, *shrines, and the like, because they were associated with the gates of Paradise. The earliest English examples are the columns (half-way between the Solomonic and Trajanic type) supporting the *vaults in the *crypt of St Wystan's Church, Repton, Derbys. (C9), but the spiral column was often used in *Romanesque *cloisters, and in *Baroque funerary monuments. The form became widely known in C17 through engravings of the tapestry cartoons by *Raphael showing Christ at the Temple which were brought to England in the reign of **King Charles I** (1625–49).

J.Curl (2001, 2011); L & D (1986); W.Pa (1887)

SOM *See* SKIDMORE, OWINGS, & MERRILL.

Sommaruga, Giuseppe (1869–1917) Milanese architect: with *Basile and d'*Aronco he was a major *Art-Nouveau designer. His works include the spectacular *Palazzo Castiglione*, Milan (1900–3), one of the most important *Stile-Liberty* buildings, elaborately ornamented. He also designed the Aletti tomb, Varese (1898), the Italian Pavilion, International Exposition, St Louis, MO (1903–4), the *Palazzino Comi*, Milan (1906), the *Hotel Tre Croci, Campo dei Fiori*, Varese (1908–12), and the Faccanoni *mausoleum, Sarnico (1907). Many of his works have accomplished *Stile* *Floreale ornamentation (*see* STILE).

Ms (1966); Nicoletti (1978); P & R (1973); Villard (ed.) (1908)

sommering *Skew-back, or the radiating joint between the *voussoirs of an arch.

Sonck, Lars Eliel (1870–1956) Finnish architect. His early work, combining contemporary European styles and *vernacular idioms, was associated with *National Romanticism. His *Villa Sonck*, Finström, Åland Islands (1894), and other houses of the period, drew on traditions of log-construction (e.g. *Villa Ainola*, Järvenpää (1904), for the composer **Jan Sibelius** (1865–1957)). He designed St Michael's Church, Turku (1894–1905), much influenced by German brick-built churches, and his masterpiece, St John's Cathedral, Tampere (1900–7), in which rough-textured stone and sculpted details were successfully integrated.

His monumental Stock Exchange (1911) and Mortgage Society Building (1908), both in Helsinki, showed a tendency towards *Neo-Classicism. In his town-planning work he was influenced by *Sitte. He laid out Kulosaari, a Helsinki suburb (1907-9), and parts of Töölö district (1903).

JSAH, xxx/3 (Oct. 1971), 228–37; Kivinen *et al*. (1990); Korvenmaa (1991); J.T (1996)

Sondergotik German late-*Gothic from *c*.1380, characterized by *hall-churches of immense height, complicated *vaults, fine portrait-sculpture, and highly complex filigree *tracery.

Gi (1986); J.T (1996)

sopraporta *Overdoor*, really a kind of *Attic-storey over the *cornice of a *doorway, often with *scrolls, and other architectural enrichment, sometimes forming a *panel containing a picture or sculpture.

Sørensen, Carl Theodor Marius (1893–1979) Danish landscape architect, he worked (1914–22) with **Erik Erstad-Jørgensen** (1872–1945) before establishing his practice, collaborating (1924–9) with **G.N.Brandt** (1878–1945). He designed the park (1931–53) in which Aarhus University (by *Fisker, *Stegmann, and *Møller) is built. Other works include the *Klampenborg Strandpark* (1931–5), the *Angligården*, Herning, Jutland (1965–6), and the *Vitus Bering Park*, Horsens (1954–6). He exploited the circle in designs, which included several *amphitheatre-shaped gardens (e.g. at Roskilde (1934)). He collaborated with numerous Danish architects (e.g. *Rafn).

S-I.Andersson & Høyer (2001)

Sorensen, Paul Edwin Bielenberg (1890–1983) Danish-born garden-designer, he emigrated to Australia during the 1914-18 war, and established (1920) a nursery and landscape-design practice at Leura, near Sydney, where his 'Everglades' is considered his greatest achievement (now listed as a Heritage Garden). Using dry-stone walls terminating in circular *piers, strong axes, finely crafted steps, paved paths, and *terraces, his work combined *Arts-and-Crafts principles with a use of trees and shrubs as almost architectural elements, for enclosure and to create interpenetrating spaces.

Ratcliffe (1990); Shoe (2001)

Soria, Giovanni Battista (1581-1651) Italian architect, he studied with *Montano, and edited the latter's drawings for publication, including *Scielta di varij tempietti antichi* (1624). In the mid-1620s he began to practise architecture, designing the *façades of the Roman Churches of *Santa Maria della Vittoria* (1625-7), *San Crisógono*, Trastévere (1626), *San Carlo ai Catinari* (1635-8), and *San Gregorio Magno*, Monte Celio

(1629–33), the last a more sophisticated exercise than the previous two, with a two-storey arrangement featuring three arches below and pedimented windows above. He designed the *nave of the *Duomo*, Monte Compatri (1630), the Library of the *Palazzo Barberini* (1635–8), and the façade of *Santa Caterina da Siena* (1638–40), the last two in Rome.

Hd (1962, 1971); W.Pa (1887); Ringbeck (1989); J.T (1996)

Soriano, Raphael Simon (1907–88) Greek-born American architect, he worked (1932–5) with *Neutra before setting up on his own (1936). He made his name with several private houses (e.g. Lipetz House, 1843 Dillon Road (1936), Polito House, 1650 Queens Road (1938), and Ross House, 2123 Valentine Drive (1938), all in Los Angeles, CA). From 1945 he was influenced by *Mies van der Rohe, and designed (1955) a prototype Steel Frame House for Mass Production at Palo Alto, CA, for *Eichler. He contributed to the *Case Study House project (1950).

McCoy (1962, 1983); J.T (1996); Wagener (2002)

Soriay Mata, Arturo (1844–1920) Spanish inventor/civil-servant/town-planner, he devised the linear city-plan along a 'spine' devoted to tracked transport (he ran one of Madrid's tramways), and inaugurated (1894) the *Ciudad Lineal*, Madrid, a linear low-density suburban development that pre-dated Letchworth *Garden City. Soria published the journal *La Ciudad Lineal* (1897–1932).

Collins *et al*. (1968); *NUHG*, xxIx (1970), 1–12; J.R.A. Pereira (1998); P (1982); J.T (1996)

Soseki, Musō (1275–1351) *See* MUSŌ SOSEKI.

Sosnowski, Oskar (1880-1939) Leading Polish architect of the interwar period, he designed the Church of *St Jakob* (1909-23—in a severe monumental cubic *Neo-Romanesque style, much influenced by Finnish, Russian, and Swedish *National-Romantic architecture), and restored the Church of *St Wenceslas* (1916-23), the Garrison Church (1923-33), and the Neo-Classical Paca Palace (1920s), all in Warsaw. His *reinforced-concrete *St Roch*, Białystok (1927–46), was almost an essay in *Expressionism, also incorporating late-*Gothic forms.

Chrościcki & Rottermund (1977); Li (1996)

Sostres (Maluquer), Josep Maria (1915–84) Catalan architect. He and others formed (1952) **Grupo R** to resurrect and promote the *Modern Movement, while he also (an apparent contradiction) galvanized interest in the works of the 'anti-Rationalist' *Gaudí. His architectural output was small, but included the Agustí House, Sitges (1953-5), the *Casa M.M.I.*, Barcelona (1955-8), the *Hotel Maria Victoria*, Puigcerdà (1956-7), the *El Noticiero Universal* Newspaper Offices, Barcelona

(1963-5), and the Xampeny and Campana Houses, Ventola, Gerona (1971-3), all in Spain.

Armesto et al. (1999); E (1994); L (1988); J.T (1996)

Sottsass, Ettore (1917-2007) Austrian-born architect, he established (1947) his own office in Milan, becoming (1959) consultant to the **Olivetti Company**, for which he designed equipment and furniture. Believing that the only design *not* contemporarily valid is that claiming to be 'timeless', with pretensions to some sort of 'moral' mission (e.g. the *Bauhaus 'philosophy'), he rejected conventional *Modernism, and his work became eclectic, drawing on many styles and periods. He created (1981) **Memphis**, an international group of designers: as the name suggests, Egyptianizing, Neo-Classical, and *Art-Deco motifs were brought together in a synthesis, even drawing on trashier elements of popular 'culture' that could be seen as parody or as *Kitsch. Among his works the *INA-CASA* housing at Carmagnola, near Turin, and at Meina, Lake Maggiore (1952-4); the *Galleria del Cavallino*, Venice (1956); and the various projects for *Nonsense* and *Pornographic architecture* (1973-7) deserve note. Sparke detected 'anti-design' and a 'blurring' of boundaries between design-practice and criticism, giving rise to what she called 'meta-design'. **Charles Alexander Jencks** (1939-2019) identified (1971) Sottsass as a *Supersensualist.

AD, xlii/6 (June 1971), 345-7, and xlii/1 (Jan. 1972), 18-21; Bure (1987); Burney (1994); Cable (1985); E (1994); Ma (1985a); Radice (1993); Sottsass (1976, 1983, 1985, 1987, 1988, 1993, 1993a, 1994, 1995, 1997); Sparke (ed.) (1982); The Times (2 Jan. 2008), 41; J.T (1996)

Soufflot, Jacques-Germain (1713-80) French Neo-Classical architect, he studied in Rome (1731-8) before settling in Lyons where he built the *Hôtel-Dieu* (1739-48), the *Loge du Change* (1747-50), and the *Théâtre* (1751-6—destroyed 1826). The last, with its relationship between *stage and *auditorium, was an important paradigm. He was a respected theorist, and after a further nine-month visit to Italy (1750-1), was able to demonstrate his knowledge of Classical antiquities, notably with his up-to-date reports on archaeological discoveries at *Herculaneum and elsewhere. This Italian study-visit, undertaken as part of the entourage of **Abel-François Poisson de Vandières** (1727-81—later **Marquis de Marigny**, brother of **Madame de Pompadour** (1721-64)), was significant in the history of French architecture, for it marked a shift from the *Rococo of *Louis Quinze to the *Neo-Classicism of *Louis Seize (apart from investigating Pompeii and Herculaneum, Soufflot was one of the first to continue his journey south to *Paestum, where he made drawings of the Greek-*Doric *temples from which **Gabriel-Pierre-Martin Dumont** (1720-91) made engravings published as *Suite de plans...de*

trois temples antiques...de Paesto (1764)). Marigny (*Directeur-Général des Bâtiments du Roi* (1751-73) called Soufflot to Paris (1755), where he was made *Contrôleur des Bâtiments du Roi au Département de Paris*, and given the task of designing *Ste-Geneviève*, the first great building of French Neo-Classicism. A Greek-*cross on plan, the *nave and *aisles were defined by rows of *Corinthian columns carrying a continuous *entablature over which rose light *domes and *vaults. Soufflot's pupil, **Maximilien Brébion** (1716-96—who carried out Soufflot's designs for the *drum and dome over the *crossing from 1780), wrote that in building the church Soufflot had reunited, under one of the most beautiful forms, the lightness of construction found in *Gothic churches with the purity and magnificence of Greek architecture. With its Roman *temple-front, elegant columned drum and dome over the crossing, and rational geometry it made a considerable impact, and was much admired as a seminal example of architectural perfection. The *gravitas* of the *Antique was eloquently expressed, especially in the severe *crypt, where the impact of the Greek-*Doric Order from Paestum is clear. The Church was secularized (1791), and altered under *Quatremère de Quincy to become the *Panthéon*, with the character of a *mausoleum (e.g. the lower windows were blocked up, so that the outer walls were blank—*Summerson saw this as a strengthening of the building because the 'factor of safety proved too low', which is serious misinterpretation). Soufflot also designed de Marigny's own house in the *Faubourg du Roule* (from 1769), and various *fabriques (including a fine *nymphaeum) at the *Château de Ménars* (from 1764), in a desiccated Neo-Classical style. He also designed the *sacristy at the Cathedral of *Notre Dame*, Paris (1756-60).

Bergdoll et al. (1989); B (1980); Etlin (1984); Ga et al. (1980); Kalnein (1995); M & Wa (1987); P (1982); Petzet (1961); Rondelet (1852); Ry (1980); J.T (1996); Ternois & Pérez (eds) (1982); D.Wa (1986)

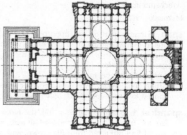

Soufflot Plan of the *Panthéon*, Paris, formerly Ste-Geneviève.

soulace Sloping *brace between common *rafters and *collars.

sounding-board See TESTER.

Southcote, Philip (1697/8–1758) English landscape-gardener, he pioneered (from 1734) the *ferme ornée* at his estate, Wooburn (later Woburn) Farm, near Weybridge, Surrey, which was much visited and admired (notably by Alexander *Pope, *Shenstone, and *Spence). Southcote stressed the importance of *perspective and prospects, and, with William *Kent, can be credited as one of the most important protagonists of the new style of landscape-gardening in his attempts to create an Arcady.

GH, ii/3 (Summer 1974), 27–60; iii/2 (Spring 1975), 3-6; vii/2 (Summer 1979), 82–101; vii/3 (Winter 1979), 9–12; ODNB (2004); Spence (1820)

spa, spau, spaw, spawe Named after the town in present-day Belgium, it is a medicinal spring or well with supposedly beneficial waters, so also a town, locality, or resort possessing such features. Numerous spas flourished in Europe, and even in and around London in C18.

J.Curl (2010)

space 1. Interval between two points, so a linear distance. 2. Superficial extent or area, also a three-dimensional extent or volume. 3. Room or area for some purpose. 4. Extension in all directions from a given point. 5. Area of ground or surface: an expanse. 6. Place where a position is taken up, or a residence. 7. Division, section or portion marked off in some way. 8. Void or empty place. 9. To limit or bound, to divide into sections.

space-frame Complex three-dimensional structural framework, capable of spanning/containing large volumes, constructed using pyramidal, hexagonal, and other geometrical figures, often made of lightweight tubing. It has further advantages of behaving as a single integral unit, and can resist loads in any direction. Space-frame designers included Buckminster *Fuller, Bruno *Taut, and *Wachsmann.

Makowski (1965)

span Distance apart of two supports, especially as applied to the opening of an arch or the width of a space covered by a *beam, *lintel, *truss, etc. *Compounds include*:
span-piece: *collar-beam;
span-roof: roof with two inclined sides as opposed to a *shed-roof* which only has one.

spandrel 1. Quasi-triangular plane, the *hanse* or *haunch*, framed by the extrados of an arch, a horizontal line projected from the crown, and a vertical line rising from the springing, often decorated. 2. Similar plane between two arches in an arcade. 3. *Web of a *vault between *ribs. 4. Triangle formed between the *string of a *stair and the floor. 5. In a framed structure the panel between the *cill of a window and the top of the window below. 6. Approximately triangular space between the curve of a *brace and a *post and *beam in a medieval timber *truss. 7. Space between the *volutes of an *Ionic *capital. 8. Any self-contained approximately triangular surface-area available for decorative use. *Compounds include*:
spandrel-bracket: 1. infilling of the spandrel (6) of a medieval truss, to strengthen or decorate it; 2. one of several *brackets, set in a vertical plane, fixed between one or more curves and the circumference of a circle set in a horizontal plane: it is used to construct ceilings, *cornices, coves, etc., for plasterer's work;
spandrel-panel: 1. part of a wall between the head of a window-aperture and the *cill of the window above in a building of two or more storeys, especially in a *curtain-wall; 2. as *spandrel-bracket* (1); 3. any panel filling a spandrel (1, 2, 4, 6, 8);
spandrel-step: step with an approximately triangular *section, the hypotenuse of which is part of the *soffit of a stone *stair;
spandrel-strut: short timber placed diagonally between an arch-brace and the corner of the main *timber frame;
spandrel-wall: wall built over an arch, forming the spandrel (1, 2).

ABDM (1996); N (1835); W.Pa (1887)

Spanish Colonial Revival Variant of American *Colonial Revival which drew on exemplars from the former Spanish colonies (e.g. Governor's Palace, Santa Fé, NM (1610–14), constructed largely of *adobe). It is distinguished from *Mission Revival by elaborate balcony-rails, carved or cast ornament, Classically-derived columns, and window-grilles, all elements found in Mexican Spanish-Colonial architecture. The Revival became popular after the Panama-California Exposition, San Diego, CA (1915): one of its most successful protagonists was **George Washington Smith** (1876–1930), e.g. Sherwood House, La Jolla, CA (1925–8), Steedman House, Montecito, CA (1922–5), and Maverick House, San Antonio, TX (1927–9).

Gebhard (1964); J.T (1996)

Spanish garden-design Descriptions by **Pliny the Elder** (c.AD 23–79), who lived in what is now Spain, tell us much about Roman gardens, and major archaeological remains have provided information about Roman exemplars. Roman systems of irrigation largely survived to be preserved and extended by the Muslims, whose garden-culture made a profound impact on the Iberian peninsula.

After the C15 Christian Reconquest, the Muslim influence persisted in what is know as *Mudéjar*, and the use of *azulejos* in gardens was a legacy of the 'Moors'. Italian-*Renaissance influences made a considerable impact on Spain, and at *Buen Retiro*, Madrid (early C17), *Baroque tendencies were present, spectacularly developed from 1721 at *La Granja de Ildefonso*, near Segovia, with *cascades, *fountains, etc. Perhaps the C19 was one of the richest periods in the history of Spanish gardens, for Classicism, Romanticism, the Islamic legacy, the Renaissance, and the Baroque all mingled in a heady brew (e.g. *Carmen de los Martires*, Granada). In the C20 the *Parque Güell* (from 1900) was created by *Gaudí, and *Forestier designed *public parks in which he acknowledged the rich traditions of Spanish gardens (e.g. *Casa del Rey Moro*, Ronda (1912)).

Correcher (1993); Shoe (2001); Tay (2006); Valdés (1987)

Spanish Order *Corinthian *Order with *abacus embellished with lions' masks rather than *fleurons.

spar 1. *Rafter. **2.** *Bar, *rail, *stud, etc.

Speckle *or* **Specklin, Daniel** (1536–89) Alsatian architect/engineer/cartographer, he designed fortifications, and wrote a treatise, *Architectura von Vestungen* (1584), which contains a design for an ideal town, the plan of which is like a wheel, with houses laid out along the 'spokes': his ideas about town-plans and fortifications remained influential until well into C18. His *Collectanea* (1587), an architectural history of Strasbourg, has autobiographical information.

Kruft (1994); *Oud-Holland*, xix (1911), 111–17; Rosenau (1975); J.T (1996)

specus (*pl.* **specus**) **1.** Covered *channel of an *aqueduct through which water flowed. **2.** Cave, *grotto, or cavity.

Speer, Albert (1905–81) German architect of the National Socialist period (1933–45), he studied under *Bestelmeyer, *Billing, and *Tessenow, and rose to prominence on the death of *Troost, becoming **Adolf Hitler's** (1889–1945) friend, confidant, and architect from 1934. His interest in archaeology led him to evolve a style of architecture that would be as expressive as anything left by Ancient Rome, and his main influences were *Boullée (for megalomaniac scale) and *Schinkel (for a *columnar-and-trabeated Neo-Classical architecture). He became known for his theatrical staging of Nazi Party rallies, using searchlights to suggest 'cathedrals of light' in the night skies, massed flags, and blocky forms for buildings. His Party Congress-Grounds at Nuremberg, with a vast grandstand and other structures (from 1934—partly destroyed), were impressive in their simplified *Neo-Classicism, drawing on

paraphrases from **Queen Hatshepsut's** (*c.*1479–*c.*1458 BC) Ancient-Egyptian Mortuary-Temple at Deïr-el-Bahari, Roman architecture, and themes derived from work by Schinkel and Boullée. He designed the German Pavilion, World's Fair, Paris (1937—much admired at the time), but his masterpiece was the Chancellery, Berlin (1938–9—destroyed), the plan of which was ingenious and the architecture designed to awe the visitor by suggesting stability, opulence, and power. He remodelled the interior of the German Embassy in 7–9 Carlton House Terrace, London, at the same period: his work there (since 1967 The Royal Society) partially survives. He was in charge of a team to re-plan Berlin with a huge north-south axis joining a gigantic domed hall to a new railway terminus, the whole lined by enormous official buildings, all in a *stripped Neo-Classical style, but vast in scale.

Fritz *Todt was killed in an air-crash (1942), and Speer succeeded him as head of the **Organization Todt**, which carried out the most ambitious and vast construction-programme since the Roman Empire, employing one and a half million men. However, as Jaskot and others have shown, much of the stone and other material was obtained by slave labour (some concentration camps (e.g. Natzweiler, Flossenburg, Mauthausen, and Gross-Rosen) were sited near quarries), and Speer must have known about this. He was also Minister for Armaments and Munitions (1942–3), and was given (1943) responsibility (as Reich Minister for Armaments and War Production) for the direction of the Reich's war-economy, which expanded threefold in two years under the *Speer Plan*. The organizational abilities Speer had demonstrated as architect of the Chancellery were now channelled throughout the Reich and occupied territories. In particular, his planning of the production of synthetic oil enabled the German war effort to continue long after access to naturally occurring fuels had been stopped. He was sentenced to 20 years in prison at the Nuremberg Trials, and afterwards published his memoirs.

P.Adam (1992); Arnst *et al.* (1978); Fest (2001); Jaskot (2000); L.Krier (ed.) (1985); Lane (1985); Larsson (1983); P (1982); Petsch (1978); pk; Scarrocchia (1999); Sereny (1995); Speer (1970, 1976, 1981); Spotts (2002); Stephan (1939); J.T (1996); Teut (ed.) (1967)

Speeth, Peter (1772–1831) German architect, he worked under *Pigage at Frankfurt (1788–94), and (from 1804) for **Carl Friedrich Wilhelm** (1724–1807—1ˢᵗ **Fürst zu Leiningen** from 1779) at Amorbach before moving (1807) to Würzburg, capital of the ephemeral (1806–14) Grand Duchy of the Rhenish Confederation under **Ferdinand of Habsburg-Lorraine** (1769–1824—*r.* as **Grand Duke** 1806–14). There, he designed the curiously forbidding St Burkhardt Gaol (1811, built 1826–7), originally the Guards-Barracks, one of the most radical and startling works of Franco-German *Neo-Classicism, standing below the slopes rising to the *Marienberg* fortress): with its powerful rusticated base punctuated by three semi-circular arches, decastyle *in-antis* *primitive unfluted Greek-*Doric *portico set within a Graeco-Egyptian *battered element surmounted by a plain *pediment set in a blank wall above the rusticated base, over-scaled lion's mask, it has tremendous authority as an example of *architecture parlante*. Speeth designed the *Zellertor* guard-house (c.1813–14—also featuring emphatic *rustication and baseless Doric, and looking rather like one of *Ledoux's Parisian *barrières*) and the *Gerichtsdienerhaus*, 9 *Turmgasse*, (1811–13—but much altered, originally conceived as an Egyptian *pylon-tower in shallow relief, with powerful rustication at the bottom and highly original *fenestration), both in Würzburg. He also designed the Church of St John the Baptist, Unterhohenried, near Hassfurt (1812–17), and the Metropolitan Church, Kishinev, Russia (begun 1826).

Ne (1980); P (1982); Wa & M (1987)

Speirs, Jonathan (1958–2012) British architect, influenced by spectacular lighting-effects in rock-concerts and theatres, he made his reputation with exterior lighting-design (e.g. at St Paul's Cathedral, London). He was a founder-member of one of the first architectural lighting-design practices in Britain (1984). With **Mark Major**, he wrote *Made of Light: the Art of Light and Architecture* (2005).

The Times (14 July 2012), 78

speklagen *Polychrome consisting of redbrick with courses of white stone, so resembling streaky bacon, found in much C19 architecture in The Netherlands and Belgium, particularly associated with the Neo-Flemish *Renaissance style.

Spence, Sir Basil Urwin (1907–76) British architect: a gifted draughtsman, he worked in the office of *Lutyens for a brief period, but made his name when he won the competition for the rebuilding of Coventry Cathedral, Warwicks. (1950–1), regarded as a symbol of Britain's reconstruction after the 1939–45 war. Spence had been Architect for the 'Britain Can Make It' Exhibition (1946–7) and for the Scottish Industries Exhibition (1949). He also designed the Sea and Ships Pavilion for the *Festival of Britain South Bank Exhibition, London (1951). From that time he was able to build up a large and successful practice. Among his works were Undergraduate Residences, Queen's College, Cambridge (completed 1960), buildings for Liverpool and Southampton Universities (1960s), and

the layout and first phase of Sussex University (1962–72). For the last he designed Falmer House, where he used *arcuated forms derived from Le *Corbusier's *Maison Jaoul*. He also designed the Library and Swimming-Centre, Hampstead Civic Centre, Swiss Cottage, London (1964), the Household-Cavalry Barracks, Knightsbridge, London (1970), and the British Embassy, Rome (1971), in all of which he tried to create a degree of monumentality. Spence brought contemporary architecture before the public, and his Coventry Cathedral enjoyed a degree of popularity: his work, however, seems hesitant in retrospect, owing something to Scandinavian sources, yet striving for a grandeur that eluded him, possibly because of reasons of *scale, but perhaps more due to the poverty of the *Modern Movement's architectural language.

L.Campbell (1996); B.Edwards (1995); E (1994); *ODNB* (2004); P (1982); Sp (1964, 1973); Sp *et al.* (1964); Sp & Snoek (1963); J.T (1996)

Spence, Joseph (*pseud.* **Sir Harry Beaumont** (1699–1768)) English biographer/chronicler, his *Anecdotes* is a compendium of opinions and matters concerning his fellow gardeners and their creations. He translated *Attiret's important account of Chinese gardens (1752), made a *ferme ornée* of limited extent at Byfleet, Surrey, and advised on several gardens, influenced by *Southcote.

Attiret (1982); Laird (1999); Mowl (2000); Spence (1820)

spere, speer, spier, spure 1. *Screen, usually treated decoratively, and with one or two doorways, at the lower end of a medieval *hall defining the *screens-passage between hall and kitchen, or separating the *cross-entry from the hall. Its top often coincided with the *tie-beam of a roof-truss above, in which case the screen and *truss were termed the *speer-* or *spere-truss*. **2.** Short screen, check, or heck between a doorway and a fireplace, acting as a baffle.

ABDM (1996)

Spezza *or* **Spazio, Andrea** (*fl.*1600–28) Architect of the *Baroque Valdštejn Palace, Prague (1624–34), for **Albrecht Wenzel Eusebius** (1583–1634), **Graf von Waldstein (Wallenstein)**, commander of the Imperial forces during the Thirty Years War (1618–48). This monumental building, with its five *courts and extensive gardens, was projected by Spezza and realized by G.B.*Pieroni et al., but it was Pieroni who created the enchanting and monumental *Sala Terrena* there, facing the gardens. Spezza also worked at Smiřický Palace, Jičín, from 1625.

J.Nn (1970); J.T (1996)

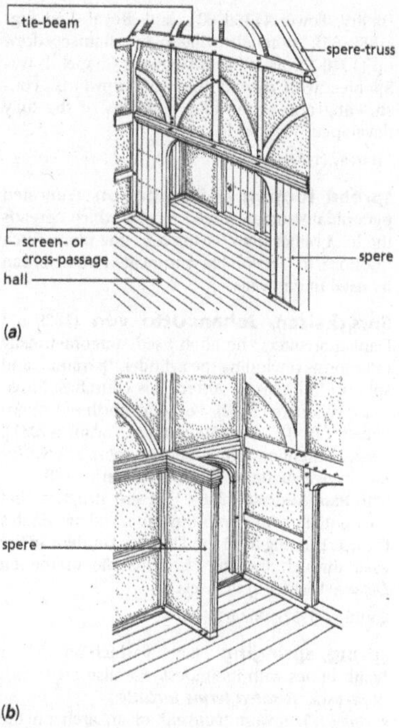

spere (*a*) Spere and spere-truss. (*b*) Free-standing draught spere (*after JJS*).

sphinx Ancient-Egyptian sculptured figure of a recumbent lion's body with a male human head (*androsphinx*), often with the *Nemes* head-dress. Roman sphinxes in the Egyptian style were often made, and the form was revived in the *Renaissance, though by then they were female as often as male, and were commonly used in Neo-Classical architecture, especially during the *Egyptian Revival. Other types include the Egyptian *criosphinx* (ram-headed) and *hieracosphinx* (hawk-headed), and the seated winged Greek sphinx on upright front legs, with the head and breasts of a woman.

J.Curl (2005); Demisch (1977); Dessenne (1957); Roullet (1972)

spike *See* FLÈCHE; PRICKET; SPIRE.

spina Wall or barrier, decorated with *obelisks and other monuments, along the middle of a Roman *circus around the ends of which the contestants turned.

spiral *See* SOLOMONIC COLUMN; STAIR.

spire Tall structure, circular, polygonal, or square on *plan, rising from a roof, tower, etc., terminating in a slender point, especially the tapering part of a church-*steeple. Often of stone, and occasionally of brick, it was also built as a *timber-framed structure *clad with copper, *lead, *shingles, *slates, *tiles, or thin stone *slabs. If square, a spire rises directly from the tower, but octagonal spires required the top of the tower not covered to be occupied by *pinnacles or by an arrangement (*broach) forming a transition between the square and octagon resembling part of a *pyramid and sloping towards the spire (*broach-spire* (***a***)).

Other types of spire include:

crown spire: spire carried on *buttress-like elements, i.e. with the structure fully exposed,

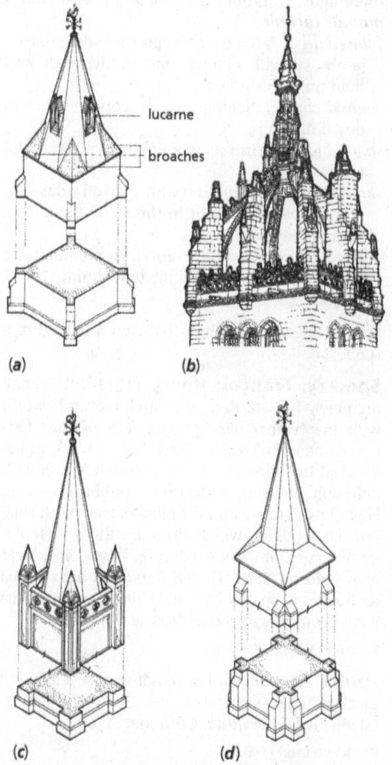

spire (*a*) Broach with lucarnes and weather-cock or -vane on tower with diagonal buttresses. (*b*) Crown (St Giles, Edinburgh, late C15). (*c*) Needle, behind parapet pierced with quatrefoils, attached with flying buttresses to pinnacled clasping buttresses. (*d*) Splay-foot on tower with angle buttresses.

resembling the arched forms at the top of a crown (**b**);

Hertfordshire spike: small needle-spire rising from a tower behind a *parapet;

needle-spire: very tall slender spire rising from a tower behind a parapet, like a *Hertfordshire spike* but much bigger, taller, and finer (**c**);

spike: short spire, *flèche, or spirelet;

spirelet: small *spire, spike,* or *flèche;

splay-foot: spire with a base opening out at a flatter pitch and forming *eaves over the tower (**d**).

Gw (1903); W.Pa (1887); J.Parker (1850); S (1901-2)

spire-light *Gabled *lucarne on a *spire.

splay 1. Any surface, larger than a bevel or *chamfer, making an oblique angle with another surface, such as a *jamb of an aperture admitting more light. **2.** *Embrasure. *See also* REVEAL. *Compounds include*:

splayed arch: *arch over an aperture with splayed jambs, i.e. with a larger span on the inside wall than on the exterior;

splayed coping: *feather-edged *cope pitched in one direction;

splayed jamb: jamb set at an oblique angle to the face of a wall;

splayed mullion: *mullion with splayed sides separating two *lights not in the same plane in a canted *bay-window;

splayed window: window-aperture containing a frame with lights set obliquely within it;

splay-foot: see SPIRE.

split *Engaged, e.g. half-*baluster attached to a *pedestal.

Spoerry, François-Henry (1912-99) French architect, he startled the architectural world with his *vernacular-revival resort of Port Grimaud, near St-Tropez (1967-75), a work much scorned by followers of the *Modern Movement, although enjoying widespread public approval. He followed this with *Port Liberté*, New York Harbor, USA (1984—which drew on the vernacular architecture of New England); *Port Louis*, near New Orleans (1982-4); and *Bendinat*, near Palma de Mallorca, Spain (1982-8). These developments have been categorized as *Soft architecture.

Spoerry (1989); J.T (1996)

spolia Parts of earlier buildings recycled and used in later structures, e.g. Roman column-*shafts in *La Mezquita*, Córdoba, Spain.

Poeschke (ed.) (1996)

Sponlee, John de (*fl.*1350-86) English mason, most of his work was at Windsor Castle, Berks., where he began the *Vestry and *Chapter House (1350), built the Canons' Lodgings (1353), Treasury with vaulted *porch (1353-4), *Cloisters (1356), Spicery Gate (1357-8), New Gate and

*Belfry Tower (1359-60), and Royal Lodgings (1358-65). Although William de *Ramsey drew up (1348-9) plans for St George's Chapel, it was Sponlee who carried the work upwards, constructing one of the first examples of the fully developed *Perp. style.

J.Harvey (1987)

spread footing *or* **foundation** Truncated pyramidal structure under a *pier which spreads the load rather than having it in one place. Such *footings, in *section like a truncated triangle, can be used under walls.

Spreckelsen, Johan Otto von (1929-87) Danish architect, he often used stereometrically pure forms (including the cylinder, *pyramid, and sphere) in his work. Among his churches, *St Nicolai*, Hvidovre (1960), *Vangede*, north of Copenhagen (1974), and *Stavnsholt*, Farum (1981), deserve mention. He is perhaps best known for *La Grande Arche de la Défense*, Paris (1981-9— with **Paul Andreu** (1938-)), a vast structure that is essentially a hollowed-out cube, and terminates the axis running from the Tuileries Gardens in the east, through the *Arc de Triomphe* to the *La Défense* District in the west.

Courtiau (1997); Wi.Cu (1996)

spring, springing Plane at which an arch or *vault unites with its impost. *See also* ABUTMENT; SKEW-BACK. *Related terms include*:

springer: **1.** lowest *voussoir of an arch on the impost; **2.** *kneeler or *skew-block at the lowest end of the raking top of a *gable;

springing-course: impost;

springing-line: horizontal plane from which an arch begins to leave its impost by rising upwards, the first voussoirs on each side being *springers;

springing-wall: *buttress.

sprocket Small triangular or wedge-shaped timber *cocking-piece* fixed to the upper face of a *rafter near its foot to reduce the slope above the *eaves (thus said to be *sprocketed*).

spur 1. Short horizontal timber, one end fixed to a *cruck *blade about a third of its height, and the other fixed to a cruck-stud, to carry the wall-plate. **2.** Short diagonal strut. **3.** Strengthening *pier or sloping *buttress. **4.** Ornamental timber bracket by the sides of *doorways to support a projecting upper floor (e.g. C14 examples in York). **5.** *Salient outwork of a fortress. **6.** Prow-shaped bridge-pier, or *cut-water. **7.** Carved claw, leaf, or *griffe* on the corners of a square *plinth under a medieval pier. **8.** *Spere. *Compounds include*:

spur-beam: horizontal timber over the thickness of a wall (i.e. set with its length at 90° to the *naked of the wall), forming a triangle with the *rafters and *ashlering and fixed to the wall-plate. See SOLE;

spur-stone: upright stone, often circular on plan, like a *bollard, fixed in the road at an angle of a building or on each side of a vehicle-entrance to protect the corners;

spur-wall: wall pierced by an arch constructed transversely across an *aisle: it gives stability to *piers, to the aisle-walls, and to the roof.

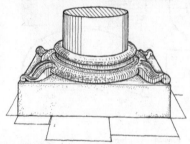

spur (7) C13 example, St Mary Magdalen, Stockbury, Kent (*after Parker*).

square 1. Angle of 90°. **2.** Figure of four equal sides and angles of 90°. **3.** Square or rectangular open space in a town, formed at the junction of two or more streets, and surrounded by buildings, as in the *Georgian squares of Britain, often with gardens in the middle. **4.** *Fillet in a series of *mouldings. *Compounds include*:

square billet: small cube placed in series, often with a parallel row, forming a *Romanesque moulding;

square dome: *cloister-vault* formed on a square plan from which four curved *vaults rise, joined by *groins (not a true *dome);

squared rubble: *rubble with roughly squared stones;

square end: east end of a church on a rectangular plan, common in the British Isles, unlike the Continental *apsidal arrangement;

square-framed: with all angles square, e.g. a panelled *door with *stiles, etc., square, and no mouldings;

square-headed: opening with vertical parallel sides and a horizontal top;

square-turned: member not carved on a lathe, but shaped on four sides, e.g. *baluster square on *plan.

squinch See DOME.

squint See HAGIOSCOPE.

squint corner Angle of a building not 90°.

Squire, Raglan (1912-2004) English architect: with **Rodney Thomas** (1902-96) and **George Edric Neel** (1914-52) he designed the Arcon House, one of the post-1945 *prefabs erected under the Temporary Housing Programme. His firm converted (1948) all the houses in Eaton Square, London, into apartments, for the Grosvenor Estate, retaining the *façades. He carried out numerous commissions in the Middle and Far East, and published *Portrait of an Architect* (1985).

The Times (9 June 2004), 65

stable 1. Building to shelter horses. **2.** Horse-keeping establishment, usually given in the plural.

staccato See CONCATENATION.

stackstand See STADDLE-STONE.

staddle-stone Short tapered vertical stone supporting a rough stone disc sloping all round its top to throw the water off, so resembling a toadstool, forming one of several uprights on which a *timber-framed structure rests. Called *stackstand*, it protected the building from damp and vermin.

stadium (*pl.* **stadia**) **1.** Large open space, often long and relatively narrow, with a rounded end, used for foot-racing in Classical Antiquity. **2.** Modern sports *arena or football stadium.

stage 1. Each of the portions into which the height of a structure (esp. a tower) is divided, i.e. a *storey*. **2.** Horizontal partition. **3.** Raised floor, platform, or *scaffold. **4.** *Pulpit. **5.** Part of a theatre on which the actors, etc., stand. **6.** Roadside *inn, or regular stopping-place on a stage-coach route.

Stainefield, Oliver de (*fl.*1305-10) English master-mason, he was at Beverley *Minster, Yorks., from 1305, and was the probable architect of the *nave, begun 1308.

J.Harvey (1987)

stair Series of *treads* and *risers*, the two making a *step*, in a *flight* of stairs, usually enclosed in a structure or cage (*staircase), providing access from one storey or floor to another. *Common parts of a stair are*:

baluster: one of a series of upright supports for a handrail, also providing protection, also called *banister* (*i*, *j*);

balustrade: ensemble including the *balusters, hand-rail*, and *newels*, also called *banisters*, providing a barrier at the side and a grip for those ascending or descending (*i*, *j*);

cap: top of a *newel* (*j*);

drop: lower end of a *newel* if visible (*j*);

easing: junction between *strings* when the *flight* changes direction;

flight: series of steps between *landings*, or from *floor to floor*, or from *floor to landing*;

stair

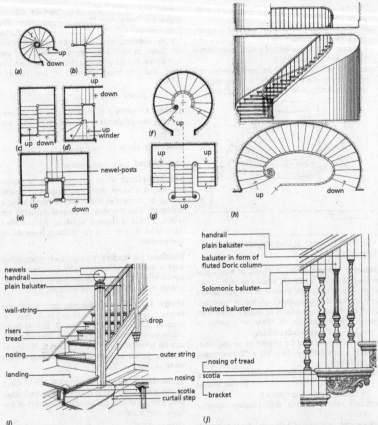

stair Plans of stairs: (**a**) *spiral*, with *winders* and central *newel*; (**b**) *quarter-turn* with *winders* at the turn; (**c**) *dog-leg* with *half-pace landing*; (**d**) *open-well* with *quarter-pace landing* and *winders* at the first turn; (**e**) *open-well* with *quarter-pace landings*; (**f**) *geometrical* with continuous *handrail*: such stairs were often elliptical on plan; (**g**) *geometrical Imperial* with *scrolled handrails*; (**h**) *stone geometrical* or *flying* on an elliptical plan, with each step resting on that below, and with metal *balusters* and moulded continuous *handrail* rising from the ground to the first floor (*after Osborne*); (**i**) *timber closed-string* (*after Osborne*); (**j**) *Georgian cut-* or *open-string* with carved console-like brackets under tread-ends, and with four different types of *balusters* of the period (*after Osborne*).

going or *run*: of a step, horizontal distance between two risers, and of a flight, horizontal distance between the faces of the top and bottom riser;

half-space: *landing* the width of two parallel *flights*, one going up and the other down, involving a turn of 180° (*see* PACE (**3**)) (**c**);

headroom: vertical distance from the *line of the nosings* to the *soffit of the flight over*;

landing: small floor between *flights* (**c**, **d**, **e**, **g**, **i**);

line of the nosings: line drawn through the extremities of all the *nosings*, so parallel to the *string*;

newel: central *pier of a circular stair carrying the narrower ends of each wedge-shaped step, or upright member supporting the *bearer*, *handrail*, *string*, and *trimmer* at the end of a *flight* (**i**);

nosing: projecting front edge of a *tread*, often rounded, overhanging the *riser* (**i**, **j**);

pitch: angle formed by the *line of the nosings* and a horizontal;

quarter-space: *landing* half the size of a *half-space*, where flights are set at 90° to each other (*see* PACE) (*d*, *e*);

rise: vertical dimension between the tops of consecutive *treads*, or between *floors*, or between *landings*, or between *floor* and *landing*, defined as *rise of a step* or *rise of a flight*;

riser: face of a step, sometimes sloping back to the tread under it (thus increasing the size of the tread) (*i*);

scotia: concave *moulding beneath the *nosing* (*j*);

soffit: sloping surface under a *flight*;

spandrel: triangular figure formed between *string* and *floor*;

string: inclined support for the steps, really a raking *beam* (*i*);

tread: horizontal upper surface of a *step* (*i*);

tread-end: smaller dimension of a *tread* projecting over the *string* in a *cut-string* stair, often with a carved *console- or *modillion-like *bracket* below (*j*);

well: void between the outer *strings* of *flights*, or the volume within which the stair rises, its inner strings against the walls of the well, as in a *half-turn* stair (*d*, *e*);

winder: *tread* wider at one end than the other, used when a stair turns (*a*, *b*, *d*, *f*).

Types of stair include:

bifurcated: dividing into two *flights* or *branches*;

caracol: as *cockle*, *spiral*, *vice*, or *winding*;

closed-string: with *strings* from which rise identical *balusters*, the *rake* being parallel to the hand-rail (*i*);

cockle: as *winding*;

cut- or open-string: with *strings* notched to accommodate the *treads* from which *balusters* of differing lengths rise, the *tread-ends* not being parallel to the *hand-rail*, and often having decorative *console-like ornaments under them (*j*);

dog-leg: two parallel *flights*, each rising half a storey, with a *half-landing* joining them but no *well* between the *strings* (*c*);

double-return: stair starting with one *flight* and returning in two from a *landing* (*g*);

flying: with stone steps *cantilevered from the *stair-well* wall without *newels* at the angles or turning points, each step resting on that below. Hand-rails are usually joined by means of short curved portions called *wreaths* (*f*, *h*);

geometrical: *flying* or *wreathed* stair, usually circular or elliptical on plan, the ends of the cantilevered steps forming a curve (*f*, *h*);

half-turn: stair with *flights* on three sides of the *stair-well* with *landings* at the corners (*e*);

Imperial: starts with one straight *flight*, and then, after the *landing*, turning by 180°, with two flights parallel to the first flight, leading to the upper floor. It probably first occurred at the *Escorial*, near Madrid (1563–84), and

spectacular later examples include the staircases at *Schloss Brühl* (1740s) and the *Residenz*, Würzburg (1734) (*g*);

newel: circular stair winding around a solid central *pier or *newel* which carries the narrower ends of the steps (*a*), or a rectangular stair with newels at the angles to receive the ends of the *strings* (*i*);

open-newel: *half-turn* or other stair around a well, as distinguished from a *dog-leg* (*d*, *e*);

open-riser: with no risers, the space between *treads* left open;

open-well: resembling a *dog-leg* but with a gap or *well* between the outer strings, more especially with a larger well, each flight terminating in a *quarter-landing* (*d*, *e*);

perron: unenclosed *flight* of external steps before the entrance to a *piano-nobile* level, or the balcony-landing at the top of a double flight of steps meeting at each end of such a landing;

spiral: as *winding*;

straight-flight: with one flight;

turngrece: as *winding*;

turning: with flights of different directions, so including *bifurcated*, *half-turn*, *quarter-turn*, and *three-quarters turn* stairs;

turnpiece: as *winding*;

vice: as *winding*;

well: within a well rising through more than one storey, with newel-posts forming an open well, as in a half-turn stair (*d*, *e*, *f*);

winder: in *timber-framed buildings rising up one storey, occupying a rectangular space, the top steps *winders*;

winding: any circular or elliptical stair, especially a newel stair (*a*), also called *caracol*, *cockle*, *spiral*, *turngrece*, *turnpiece*, or *vice*.

B & M (1989); Cd'ÉSdlR (1985); C & G (1985); Gambardello (1993); Gw (1903); W.McKay (1957); Templer (1992)

staircase 1. Structure enclosing a *stair, also called the *staircase-shell*, or *stairwell*. **2.** Stair with *balustrade. **3.** Whole stair with supporting framework, *balusters, etc. Grand staircases with architectural pretensions are of considerable antiquity and were known in ancient Crete and Mesopotamia. In Classical Antiquity, curiously enough, staircases were not often exploited as architectural elements, and it was only with the *Renaissance that they began to be developed architecturally, notably with *Bramante's construction at the Belvedere Court, Vatican, and the Imperial staircase at the *Escorial*, near Madrid (1563–84), by Juan Bautista de *Toledo and de *Herrera. *Palladio seems to have been responsible for the *flying* or *geometrical* stair, much used in C18. During the *Baroque period staircase-design progressed to such masterpieces as the *Treppenhaus* in the *Residenz*, Würzburg, by

*Neumann. Staircases were often expressed as powerful architectural elements, notably by *Gropius, *Mendelsohn, and others in the C20.

B & M (1989); Cd'ÉSdlR (1985); C & G (1985); Gambardello (1993); Pe (1960); Templer (1992)

stalactite 1. System of corbelling, called *muqarna, really brick squinches (see DOME) and *vaults with the *soffits elaborately carved to resemble a series of stalactites, in *Islamic, particularly *Moorish, architecture. **2.** Stone or *stucco forms resembling stalactites or icicles, called *congelation, found in *grottoes and *rustication.

stalk In the *Corinthian *capital, the representation of a stem, sometimes with *flutes, from which the *volutes rise.

stall 1. Fixed seat in a *chancel or *choir, one of a number, generally elevated, enclosed at the back and sides, arranged in rows on the north and south sides, and often, in grander churches, surmounted by lofty canopies of *tabernacle-work. Seats were often hinged and had *misericords on the underside. In larger churches the choir-stalls returned at the west end of each row, parallel to the *pulpitum or *choir-screen. **2.** Theatre-seat in the part of the *parquet nearest the stage (*orchestra-stalls). **3.** Division in a *stable equipped with facilities for feeding and drainage.

F.Bond (1910, 1912, 1913, 1916); J.Parker (1850)

Stam, Martinus Adrianus, called **Mart** (1899–1986) Dutch architect, much of his work was carried out with others, notably *Poelzig and Max *Taut (1922), *Brinkman and van der Vlugt (1925–8), and Ernst *May (1930–4). He designed terrace-houses for the *Weissenhofsiedlung, Stuttgart (1927), and was invited by Hannes *Meyer to teach at the *Bauhaus (1928–9). A founding-member of *CIAM, he was firmly of Leftist political persuasion, and worked (1930–4) with May in the Soviet Union on the New Towns. With El *Lissitzky, he was associated with *Constructivism (1924–5). After the 1939–45 war he worked in Dresden and East Berlin until 1952 when he settled for a while in Amsterdam before retiring to Switzerland. His best-known work is the van Nelle Tobacco Factory in Rotterdam, with Brinkman and van der Vlugt (1926–30).

Blijstra et al. (1970); J.Je (1963a, 1976); J.Je & Plath (1968); W.Moller (1997); Oorthuys & W.Moller (1995); P (1982); Rümmele (1992); J.T (1996)

stanchion 1. *Post, or vertical support, such as a structural steel upright in a framed structure. **2.** *Mullion. **3.** *Stud of a *timber-framed wall. **4.** Vertical iron bar between mullions of a *Gothic window.

standing-tower See PROSPECT TOWER.

Stanley, Thomas (fl.1429–62). English mason, he built the tower at Lydd Church, Kent (1442–6), and for some time from at least 1429 was a senior mason at Canterbury Cathedral. He may have designed the towers of Tenterden (1449–61) and Ashford (1460–90) Churches, Kent.

J.Harvey (1987)

staple 1. Obsolete term for a wholesale *market, or a market-place. **2.** Piece of [-shaped iron, driven into the frame of a door, used to catch the bolt or hasp of a lock.

Stark, William (1770–1813) Scots architect, exponent of a refined *Neo-Classicism. He worked in St Petersburg, Russia, in some capacity now unknown (1798), but most of his professional career was spent in Glasgow. Highly regarded in his own lifetime (by Sir Walter Scott (1771–1832), no less, among others), his buildings were distinguished, and included St George's Church, Buchanan Street (1807–8), the Court House, Gaol, and Public Offices, Saltmarket (1809–11—later rebuilt retaining the Greek-*Doric *portico, one of the earliest on any public building in Britain), the handsome interiors of the Signet Library (1812–15—now Lower Signet Library) and Advocates' Library (1812–16—now Upper Signet Library), Parliament Square, Edinburgh, and other refined works. His sensitive Report on the planning of lands between Edinburgh and Leith was published (1814), and contains analyses of what was later called *townscape, as well as the *Picturesque aspects of composition. His pupil, W.H.*Playfair, later realized a plan influenced by Stark's Report.

Co (2008); CoE (1972); GMcW & W (1984); G & W (1987); ODNB (2004); J.T (1996); WRH (1990)

starling 1. Protective *piles round the *piers of a river-bridge, or a pointed projection of the pier called *cut-water. **2.** Breakwater formed of piles driven closely side by side in hydraulic constructions.

Starov, Ivan Yegorovich (1745–1808) Russian architect, pupil of de *Wailly (1762–8), he introduced a sophisticated French *Neo-Classicism to his native land, notably with his *church and *belfry at Nikolskoe (1774–6—partly destroyed) and the Tauride Palace, St Petersburg (from 1783), with its grand Catherine Hall flanked by *Ionic columns. Among his other works the Alexander Nevsky Monastery, St Petersburg (1776–90), and the great house at Pella (1785—destroyed) deserve mention. In the 1770s, 1780s, and 1790s he was involved in urban improvements and in laying out new towns throughout the Empire.

G.H (1983); Kyuchariants (1982); M & Wa (1987); D.Shv (2007); J.T (1996)

starved Classicism Mean, thin, ill-proportioned, non-style, loosely based on *Classicism but displaying no feeling for rules, proportions, details, and finesse, and lacking all *élan*. It is not to be confused with *stripped Classicism, which is usually robust, confident, powerful, and often *Sublime.

Stasov, Vasily Petrovich (1769–1848) Russian architect, pupil of *Bazhenov and *Kazakov, he later travelled in France, England, and Italy, returning to Russia (1808). He designed numerous buildings, some of which were clearly influenced by the severe *Neo-Classicism of *Ledoux. His Victualling-Store, Moscow (1821–35), was understated and plain, but his interesting cast-iron Moscow Gate, St Petersburg (1834–8), was a Greek-*Doric *propylaeum* of great nobility and power. He built several structures at Gruzino in the 1820s, including various towers and a church: the church-*belfry (1822), not unlike Zakharov's Admiralty *spire in St Petersburg, was destroyed in the 1939–45 war.

G.H (1983); Pilyavski (1970); D.Shv (2007); Tyzhnenko (1990)

Statham, Henry Heathcote (1839–1924) English architect, he became (1884) Editor of *The Builder* (then one of the most important influences on architecture throughout the British Empire), and contributed to numerous journals as well as to *Grove's Dictionary of Music* (he was an accomplished musician). Among the many talented men he encouraged in architecture were Curtis *Green and Beresford *Pite. He designed the fronts of *The Builder* office and those of its neighbours in Catherine Street (1903). He wrote *A History of Architecture* (1912) which, with its many excellent illustrations, was once widely used as a textbook by students (revised 1927, 1950). He despised *Ruskin.

A.S.Gray (1985)

station 1. Stages of the Passion, often placed around the walls of a church or in the *cloister, sculpted, painted, etc., usually 14 in number. **2.** Stock farm. **3.** Fixed stopping-place, e.g. *railway station*, so the buildings of such a station. **4.** Local office, depot, or headquarters for a specific purpose, e.g. fire-station, police-station, ambulance-station, etc. **5.** Place of assembly.

statuary Sculptor of statues, funerary monuments, etc., who often made other artefacts, e.g. *marble *chimney-pieces.

stave 1. Upright cleft thick timber, usually with a groove for vertical jointing, used for walls and load-bearing, rather than infilling. **2.** One of several small vertical timbers with pointed ends set between *studs in a *timber frame, placed far

enough apart to accommodate interweaving rods or other backing for infill panels. **3.** Small vertical cylindrical bar used to form hay-racks to feed horses in *stables. **4.** One of many timbers shaped to form wooden barrels.

stave-church *Timber-framed/timber-walled Scandinavian church type (from early C11), built of *staves. Later examples have elaborate tiered roofs.

Bugge (1953); Lindholm (1970)

stay-bar Horizontal iron tie-rod *or* *tirant extending along the tops of *mullions of *tracery to stabilize them.

steel Following the use of cast and wrought iron in buildings, steel (a strong, malleable metal, mostly iron, with added carbon and sometimes small amounts of other metals) was employed for tall structures, notably *skyscrapers in America from the 1880s. One of the first to have a full skeletal frame, supporting all the floors, etc., without the help of brick or masonry stiffeners, was *Jenney's Manhattan Building, Chicago, IL (1889–90), but the frame consisted of cast and wrought iron as well as steel. Jenney had used steel in the upper *storeys of the Home Insurance Company Building, Chicago (1884–5), which was really a prototypical skyscraper, but the structure was a hybrid, and did not have a true steel skeleton. Steel, strong and capable of being assembled quickly, had been proved in *bridge construction and elsewhere, so its potential for *industrialized building and skyscrapers became apparent in the closing years of C19, although full expression of steel structure had to wait until C20. Steel is liable to fail at high temperatures, so it has to be protected against fire, and this seems to have inhibited designers at first, who disguised the frames behind *masonry and other *façades. Elegant uses of steel structures were demonstrated by *Mies van der Rohe much later. *Cor-Ten* Steel, which oxidizes to give a brown finish, can be used for exterior work, as it does not need paint protection.

Blanc et al. (1993); N.Jackson (1996); Mainstone (1975)

Steele, Fletcher (1885–1971) American landscape architect. At Naumkeag, Stockbridge, MA (1925–38), he created an eclectic garden, part Chinese, part rose-garden, part water, with a silver-birch plantation. His writings were influential.

B & K (2000); Karson (1989); Shoe (2001); Treib (ed.) (1993)

Steenwinckel Family Dutch *Renaissance architects/sculptors, they worked for the Royal House of Denmark. **Hans van Steenwinckel the Elder** (*c.*1550–1601) rebuilt (from 1629) the Castle of *Kronborg*, Helsingør, while **Hans van**

Steenwinckel the Younger (1587-1639) and **Lourens van Steenwinckel** (*c.*1585-1619) designed *Frederiksborg*, a huge complex of buildings with elaborate towers and *spires, much influenced by contemporary architecture in The Netherlands. Hans the Younger's masterpiece is reckoned to be the exquisite Stock Exchange in Copenhagen (1619-25) with its curious spire formed of three entwined dragons' tails, long repetitive *façade pierced by large mullioned and transomed windows, and elaborate *lucarnes.

Ck (1996); J.T (1996)

steeple Collective term embracing a church-tower and *spire together.

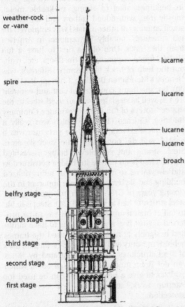

weather-cock or -vane

spire

lucarne

lucarne

lucarne

lucarne

broach

belfry stage

fourth stage

third stage

second stage

first stage

steeple St Mary's, Stamford, Lincs., showing five-stage First-Pointed (C13) tower and Second-Pointed (C14) *broach-spire* with *lucarnes*.

Steffann, Emil (1899-1968) German architect, a close friend of Rudolf *Schwarz, who influenced his thinking, he carried out various works in Lorraine from 1941 and directed the design of housing for the Archdiocese of Cologne from 1947. He made his name with the reconstruction of the Franciscan Monastery, Cologne (1950), and designed many churches, including the *St Elisabeth* Parish Centre, Oplanden (1953-8), and the round-arched Carthusian Monastery of

Marienau, Seibranz (1962-4—with **Gisberth Hülsmann** (1935-)).

Bauwelt, lxx/19 (18 May 1979), 766-87

Stegmann, Povl (1888-1944) Danish architect, pioneer of Danish Modernism, he designed Aarhus University (with Kay *Fisker and C.F. *Møller—1931-3), and taught at Aarhus (1924-37) and Aalborg (1937-44).

P (1982); J.T (1996); We (1952)

Stein, Clarence S. (1882-1975) American architect/planner, he founded the Regional Planning Association to promote solutions to urban overcrowding and applied Ebenezer *Howard's *Garden-City ideas to two important developments: Sunnyside Gardens, Queens, NYC (from 1924), and Radburn, NJ (from 1926), both with **Henry Wright** (1878-1936). The separation of pedestrians from vehicular traffic and the large communal gardens of Radburn were influential, and Stein later promoted these in his *Towards New Towns for America* (1951). He advised on the creation of Chatham Village, Pittsburgh, PA (from 1930), and Baldwin Hills Village, Los Angeles, CA (from 1941). He was associated with *Mumford and others in his work.

JAIA, lxv/12 (1976), 19-29; *JAPA*, xlvi/4 (Oct. 1980), 424-39; P (1982); Schaffer (1982); W & S (1994)

Stein, Joseph Allen (1912-2001) American architect, he collaborated with *Eckbo and *Neutra before settling (1952) in India. He designed several buildings in Lodhi Park, New Delhi, e.g. International Centre (1959-62), Ford Foundation (1965-8), and UNICEF building (1978-81). He formed (1977) a partnership with *Doshi, and designed the Kashmir Conference Centre, Srinagar (1977-89), in which certain *vernacular themes are apparent.

St.White (1993)

Steinbach, Erwin von (*fl.*1275-1318) German architect, his greatest work was at least part of the west front (which survives) and Chapel of the Virgin (destroyed), Cathedral of Our Lady, Strasbourg, France (*c.*1275-1318). In documents he is referred to as **Meister Erwin Werkmeister**: his name may derive from the small village of Steinbach, Baden, and was celebrated by *Goethe in *Von deutscher Baukunst* (1770-3). A drawing, known as *Dessin B*, which survives in the *Musée de L'Œuvre de Notre-Dame*, Strasbourg, dates from *c.*1275, and is probably in Erwin's hand. The Strasbourg *façade, with its exquisite *tracery over the *portals, influenced many German late-*Gothic designs.

Frankl (1960, 2000); Holt (ed.) (1958); P (1982); Recht (ed.) (1989)

Steindl, Imre (1839-1902) Austro-Hungarian architect, his masterpiece is the *Gothic-Revival Parliament-Building, Budapest (1883-1902), situated by the Danube, clearly influenced by Charles *Barry's Palace of Westminster, London, although the style is not English *Perp. but a symmetrically composed essay in Continental Gothic, with a somewhat incongruous *dome possibly derived from George Gilbert and John Oldrid *Scott's entry in the *Reichstag* competition, Berlin (1872).

É & J (1990); Pe (1976)

Steiner, Rudolf (1861-1925) Austro-Hungarian philosopher/artist/architect/scientist/founder of Anthroposophy (knowledge produced by the Higher Self in Man). Much influenced by the writings of *Goethe, he began (1907) designing objects, guided by ideas of empathy, natural philosophy, *Expressionism, and *Symbolism. He believed that spiritual laws and values could be expressed in architecture, and designed seven columns to be set up in sequence within the assembly-hall of the Theosophical Congress, Munich (1907): these represented the seven ancient planetary spheres of influence believed to regulate human development. He designed (1910) an underground chamber for the Theosophical Society in Stuttgart, a windowless elliptical space with two rows of columns supporting arches and *vaults bearing astral and Zodiac signs with a polyhedral glass centrepiece. He began to plan (1912) a domed *auditorium and theatre (in which all the forms would relate harmoniously to each other and have a mnemonic content), realized at the *Goetheanum*, Dornach, Switzerland (1913-20), the epitome of Expressionism with strong Symbolist and *Jugendstil* flavours. This slightly sinister-looking 'temple of spiritual wisdom' burned down (1922), and was replaced by his second *Goetheanum* (1924, completed 1964), a remarkable *reinforced-concrete Expressionist structure.

AAJ, lxxix/873 (June 1963), 371-83; Bayes (1994); Biesantz *et al.* (1980); Br (2002a); Fant *et al.* (1969); Kemper (1966); Messina (1996); Pehnt (1991); P (1982); Sharp (1967); J.T (1996); Zimmer (1971)

stele, stela (*pl.* **stelai**) Ancient-Greek monument consisting of a vertical stone carved with reliefs, inscriptions, and ornament, often a crowning *anthemion, and commonly used as a gravestone. It was a form often used during the *Greek Revival, and a fine example stands over *Schinkel's grave in Berlin.

K & B (1971)

Stell, Christopher Fyson (1929-2014) English architectural historian, his *Inventory of Nonconformist Chapels and Meeting Houses* (1986-2002) is an invaluable record of a C17-C19 building-

type somewhat under-valued before his painstakingly accurate work on the subject. As a senior investigator with the Royal Commission on the Historic Monuments of England (1955-89) his contributions to scholarship were immense. He was instrumental in the establishment of the Historic Chapels Trust (1993): had it not been for his efforts several redundant chapels and RC churches of great historic interest would have been demolished. Among his later works was a volume on *Nonconformist Communion Plate and Other Vessels* (2008). He claimed he was the last person to be employed by the firm founded by A.W.N.*Pugin.

Stell (1986, 1991, 1994, 2002); *The Times* (30 Jan. 2014), 49

Stella, Paolo della (*fl.*1537-52) Italian architect of the beautiful *Belvedere* (Queen Anne's Pavilion), Hradčany, Prague (1535-63), completed by **Hans Tirol** (*c.*1505-75) and **Bonifaz Wohlmut** (*fl.*1522-*before* 1579), an essay in pure *Cinquecento* (consisting of a rectangular block surrounded by an elegant *Ionic *arcade), uniquely sophisticated for its time and location.

Landisch (1968); Wa (1986)

stellar vault *See* VAULT.

stencil 1. Thin sheet of metal, card, etc., in which holes have been cut, of such shape as when a paint-brush is applied, patterns are created on the wall behind. **2.** Pattern produced by *stencilling*, often found in *Gothic-Revival interiors.

step *Tread* and *riser* of a *stair, or a single flat-topped structure, e.g. *door-step*, to enable progression from one level to another.

Stephenson, Robert (1803-59) English railway-engineer, son of the pioneering railway-builder and designer of locomotives, **George Stephenson** (1781-1848). He was mostly responsible for the construction of the main lines from London to Birmingham (1833-8), in the North-East of England, and elsewhere. His greatest works were *bridges, e.g. spanning the Tyne at Newcastle and the Tweed at Berwick (1846-9), but his masterpiece was the Britannia Bridge (1845-50), a tubular-girder structure carrying the Chester-Holyhead line over the Menai Straits. In the detailed design of the last Stephenson was assisted by *Fairbairn and others. He also designed the tubular bridge at Conway, Wales (1845-50). His Victoria Bridge over the St Lawrence, Montréal (1854-9), was for some time the longest bridge in the world.

ODNB (2004); Rolt (1960); Sk (2002); Smiles (1862)

Stephenson, Sam (1933-2006) Irish *Modernist architect. When he and **Arthur Gibney** (1933-2006) won the competition (1961) to design headquarters for Ireland's Electricity Supply Board, their scheme involved the demolition of 17 fine Georgian houses in Fitzwilliam Street, Dublin, outraging conservationists: Stephenson took the predictable Modernist line that Georgian buildings were not worth keeping. Indeed he 'voiced a crude nationalist resentment' towards what he perceived as Dublin's 'colonial' heritage. Stephenson & Gibney were also responsible for the Central Bank of Ireland Tower, Dame Street, Dublin (1971–8), a building some thirty feet higher than the level theoretically permitted by the planning authority, but apart from the impact on Dublin's skyline, the scheme involved the demolition of Commercial Buildings (1796–9), a seven-window-wide *palazzo* designed by Edward *Parke. Despite his antipathy to Georgian architecture, Stephenson regarded himself as the natural heir of *Gandon, a pose not universally accepted.

Casey (2005); *The Times* (22 Nov. 2006), 68; pk

Stephenson, Stephen (*fl.c.*1387–1400) English mason, he worked at the great Abbey at Batalha, Portugal (begun 1388), under **Affonso Domingues** (*fl.*1387–1402). There are so many English influences in the architecture that Stephenson must have made a major contribution to the design.

J.Harvey (1987)

Stephen the Mason (*fl.*1180–1228) English? Mason, he made the wall of the King's Forge at Winchester, Hants. (1180–1), became Master of the King's Works at Corfe Castle, Dorset (1213), and built part of the Great Hall at Winchester Castle (1220s). He probably contributed to the design of the *retrochoirs of Winchester Cathedral (*c.*1202–35) and St Mary Overie (now Southwark Cathedral—1208–35).

J.Harvey (1987)

step pyramid Like a *mastaba* with several more mastabas on top, each one smaller than the one below, so creating a pyramidal stepped structure like that of **King Zoser** (*r. c.*2630–2611 BC) at Saqqara by *Imhotep.

J.T (1996)

stereobata, stereobate (*pl.* **stereobatae, stereobates**) **1.** Top of a foundation or sub-structure, forming a solid platform on which a Classical *temple stands. It is therefore the top of a *crepidoma*, or the *stylobate. **2.** Walls of a Roman *podium supporting a *colonnade. **3.** *Pedestal.

stereometry Art or science of measuring solids, a branch of geometry dealing with solid figures: *stereometric* therefore pertains to *stereometry* or *solid geometry*. Stereometrically pure forms would include the *cone, cube, *pyramid, and sphere, and were important elements in *Neo-Classicism.

N (1835)

stereotomy 1. Craft of cutting and dressing complicated blocks of *masonry such as those for an arch, *vault, or *spiral *stair. **2.** Art of making sections of solids.

Stern, Raffaello (1774–1820) Italian architect, important figure in *Neo-Classicism, he designed the *Braccio Nuovo* (1817–22) which, with the *Sala delle Muse* and the *Sala a Croce Greca* (by *Camporese and *Simonetti), Vatican Museum, contributes to a memorable sequence of spaces based on *Antique precedents.

Ms (1966)

Stern, Robert Arthur Morton (1939–) *See* NEW CLASSICISM, POST-MODERNISM.

Stethaimer *or* **Stettheimer, Hans** (*c.*1360–1432) Also have called **Hans von Burghausen**, he seems to have worked first on the immensely tall *Pfarrkirche*, Landshut, Bavaria (1387), a fine example of a hall-church. He was among the most distinguished of German late-*Gothic architects, and was the designer of the beautiful hall-choir of the *Franziskanerkirche*, Salzburg (1408–60), completed under **Stefan Krumenauer** (*c.*1400–61): it has vaulting with ribs arranged in net-like forms, with star-shaped patterns immediately bursting from the very tall cylindrical *piers, one of which is set on the axis at the east end. Burghausen may also have designed the *Spitalkirche*, Landshut (1407–61), and other churches at Neu-Ötting, Straubing, and Wasserburg.

Brinkmoller *et al.* (1985); Frankl (2000); Fuhrmann (1950); Gi (1986); Liedke *et al.* (1986); D.Wa (1986)

Steuart, George (*c.*1730–1806) Gaelic-speaking Highland-Scots architect, he worked for the **3rd** and **4th Dukes of Atholl**, for whom he designed a house in Grosvenor Place, London (1770—demolished). Most of his significant works are in Salop., where he designed in a refined and attenuated Neo-Classical style. His masterpieces are Attingham Park, near Shrewsbury (1783–5), and the ingenious St Chad's Church, Shrewsbury (1790–2—with a circular galleried *nave, an intermediate vestibule, a large and noble *steeple, and an unfluted Roman-*Doric *portico), one of the most original and pleasing of all *Georgian churches. He also designed the *Ionic *temple at Millichope Park, Salop. (1770), Baronscourt, Co. Tyrone (1779–82—subsequently re-modelled by *Soane and *Morrison), All Saints' Parish Church, Wellington, Salop. (1787–9), and Castle Mona, Douglas, IoM (1801–6).

Co (2008); T.Friedman (2011); *J. of the Manx Museum*, vi (1962–3), 177–9; W.Pa (1887)

Stevens, Frederick William (1847–1900) English architect/engineer, articled to **Charles**

Edward Davis (1827–1902) of Bath, before he settled in India (1867), working under **General John Augustus Fuller** (1828–1902). He designed the Royal Alfred Sailors' Home, Apollo Bunder, Bombay (1872–6—later the Council Hall), and then the spectacularly splendid *polychrome Victoria Railway Terminus, also in Bombay (1878–87—the largest building erected by the British in India at that time). An extraordinary mixture of Venetian and other Continental *Gothic (reminiscent of parts of 'Great' *Scott's Midland Grand Hotel, St Pancras, London (1868–74)), it was also spiced with *Indian and *Saracenic touches, and embellished with superabundant decorations executed under the direction of **John Lockwood Kipling** (1837–1911—Professor of Architectural Sculpture at the School of Art in Bombay, and father of **Joseph Rudyard Kipling** (1865–1936)). Despite the rude condemnation of such architecture by **Aldous Leonard Huxley** (1894–1963) as 'lavatory bricks and Gothic spires', the building was placed (2004) on UNESCO's World Heritage List. He established (1884) his own practice, developing an eclectic Indian-Gothic style, and it continued under his son, **Charles Frederick Stevens** (1872–*after* 1925).

B, lxxviii (1900), 325–6; P.Davies (1985); *JRSA,* cxxix (1981), 358–79; J.T (1996)

Stevenson, John James (1831–1908) Scots architect, he worked in the offices of *Bryce and 'Great' *Scott, and was later (1860–9) a partner of **Campbell Douglas** (1828–1910), and (1871–6) E.R.*Robson. He settled (1869) in London where he worked with Robson on several schools for the London School Board. His Red House, 140 Bayswater Road, London (1871–demolished), was one of the earliest examples of the *Queen-Anne style, and was a catalyst in the move away from *stucco to brick for London houses. Among other works were 42–8 Pont Street, Knightsbridge (1876–8), Lowther Gardens, South Kensington (1878), 14 Melbury Road (1876–8—demolished), all in London, and Ken Hill, Snettisham, Norfolk (1879–80). He also designed the first 'Queen-Anne' houses in Oxford at 27 and 29 Banbury Road (1880–1), featuring red-brick, richer red-brick *dressings, balconies, and white-painted window-frames. He wrote *House Architecture* (begun 1869–70, published 1880).

Aslin (1969); D & M (1985); Gd (1977, 1979); Sh (1973); J. Stevenson (1880); J.T (1996)

Stick style Late-C19 style of domestic architecture in the USA, partially evolved from *Carpenter's Gothic. While many examples were *timber-framed, the name of the style was also given to buildings in which thin *struts or 'sticks' were fixed (sometimes over *clap-boarding) to *suggest* a timber-framed structure. The elements were often very hard, jagged, and angular, and overhanging *eaves and wide *verandahs were frequently employed. It was more influenced by French and Swiss than by English timber buildings. *Hunt's Griswold House, Newport, RI (1861–3), is a good example.

Handlin (1985); V.J.Sy (1971, 1974, 1989)

Stieglitz, Christian Ludwig (1756–1836) German architectural historian, he published many important books including *Encyklopaedie der bürgerlichen Baukunst* (1792–8), *Zeichnungen aus der schönen Baukunst* (1804), *Denkmäler der Baukunst der Mittelalters in Sachsen* (1836–52), *Von altdeutscher Baukunst* (1820), and many other works.

W.Pa (1887); J.T (1996)

stiff-leaf 1. *Gothic late-C12 and C13 stylized three-lobed carved foliage, usually an enrichment of *bosses and *capitals (*see* CAPITAL illustration (*l*)) evolved from *crocketed capital designs, mostly English rather than Continental, and is characteristic of *First-Pointed work. 2. In Neo-Classical ornament, a vertical leaf- or feather-form repeated in series on e.g. *friezes.

L & D (1986); J.Parker (1850); Rickman (1848)

Stijl, De Literally 'The Style', supposedly derived from *Semper's *Der Stil* (1861–3—erroneously believed to advocate Materialism and *Functionalism), it was a Dutch artistic movement and name of a journal founded (1917) by van *Doesburg. Other members included the painter **Piet Mondrian** (1872–1944), *Rietveld, *Oud, and van 't *Hoff. It was influenced by *Cubism, by *Neo-Plasticism, and by a Calvinistic concern with supposed objectivity, simplicity, and truth, and, like many C20 movements, was anti-historical and antagonistic to tradition. It proposed an abstracted clarity of expression, wholly divorced from Nature, advocated straight lines, pure planes, right angles, primary colours, and decomposed cubes, and was one of the most powerful influences on architecture between the World Wars, especially on the *Bauhaus and *International Modernism. Early architectural works of the De-Stijl group included van't Hoff's *Huis ter Heide*, Utrecht (1916—clearly influenced by F.L.L. *Wright's work), Oud's projected but unrealized distillery at Purmerend (1919), and van *Eesteren's and van *Doesburg's axonometric studies for a house (1923). However, the paradigm of De-Stijl architecture was the Schröder House, Utrecht, by Rietveld (1921–4), with its slab-like elements, flat roof, primary colours, and angular construction.

M.Friedman (ed.) (1982); Jaffé (1956); Overy (1969); Overy *et al.* (1988); Padovan (2002); Petersen (ed.)

(1968); Stijl (1998); J.T (1996); Troy (1983); Warncke (1994); Zevi (1974)

stile Upright framing of a *door into which the ends of the horizontal *rails are fixed: they are *hanging* (if fixed with hinges), *middle* or *mounting* (abbreviated to *muntin), and *shutting* stiles or *styles*.

Stile *Stile floreale* is the Italian term for early *Art Nouveau; *Stile Liberty* (after the Regent Street, London, store which did much to popularize it) is the more usual Italian label.

Stilling, Harald Conrad (1815-91) Danish architect, pupil of *Hetsch, he designed the Concert Hall, Bazaar, and other late-Classical buildings at the Tivoli Gardens, Copenhagen (1843), for the entrepreneur *Carstensen. He also designed the Casino (1845-7), later Copenhagen's first commercial theatre (1848), but intended by Carstensen as a 'Winter Tivoli'. Stilling's *Boutique Schwartz*, 3 *Svaertegade*, Copenhagen, was influenced by *Schinkel's work. He wrote on Church Architecture (1870).

Mi (1951); We (1952)

Stillman & Eastwick-Field British architectural firm (1949-2004) established by **John Stillman** (1920-), and **John** (1919-2003) and **Elizabeth** (*née* **Gee**) (1919-2003) **Eastwick-Field**. It was responsible for a number of schools for the Inner London Education Authority, including the Camden School for Girls (1956-7). In Gibraltar, the firm designed the Mackintosh Hall Cultural Centre and Girls' School (1964-7), and in Exeter, Devon, the Residential School for the Partially Sighted (1965-6). Among other works, Hide Tower, Regency Street, Westminster (1959-61—a pioneering work with precast concrete *cladding), and Queen Mary's House, a home for the elderly, Hampstead, London (1991-2), may be cited.

E (1994); The Times (5 May 2003), Obits

stilted Raised higher than normal, a term almost entirely confined to the arch.

Stirling, Sir James Frazer (1926-92) Scots architect, he was in partnership (1956-63) with **James Gowan** (1923-2015). Their flats at Ham Common, Richmond, Surrey (1955-8), featured exposed *concrete *beams with brick infill: influenced by the work of Le *Corbusier, these buildings fell into the category of *Brutalism (a label Stirling detested). The Engineering Building, University of Leicester (1959-63—a *collage of quotations influenced by *Mel'nikov and *Constructivism), with its angular chamfered forms and hard red brick contrasted with much glazing, attracted attention. Thereafter Stirling, practising alone, designed the controversial History Faculty

wing, University of Cambridge (1964-8—subject to many serious problems), Student Residences, University of St Andrews (1964-8), the Florey Building, Queen's College, Oxford (1966-71), housing for Runcorn New Town (1967-76), and other projects.

Joined in partnership (1971) by **Michael Wilford** (1938-), the firm carried out work in Germany, including the *Staatsgalerie*, Stuttgart (1977-84), which paraphrased elements from the work of Ehrensvärd, Ancient-Egyptian architecture, the *primitive, and *Schinkel's Museum in Berlin, but in an apparently whimsical way, owing something, perhaps, to techniques of collage discussed by Colin *Rowe et al. Later works include the *Wissenschaftszentrum*, *Tiergarten*, Berlin (1979-87), Sackler Gallery, Harvard University, Cambridge, MA (1979-84), Clore Gallery, Tate Gallery, London (1980-7), the Performing Arts Center, Cornell University, Ithaca, NY (1983-8), No.1 Poultry, London (1985-97), and the Braun headquarters, Melsungen, Germany (1986-92). His later architecture became increasingly eclectic, containing allusions (some tongue-in-cheek) to historical themes.

Ar & Bi (1984); British Council (1991); Crinson (2012); E (1994); Gd (1998); Js (1973a); Mx (1972, 1998); Mx (ed.) (1998); Mx et al. (1994); C.Naylor (ed.) (1991), 475; Nurcombe (1985); Sudjic (1986); Wilford (1996)

stoa 1. Type of Ancient-Greek *portico of limited depth but great length, with a long wall at the back and a *colonnade on the front, usually facing a public space, used for promenades, meetings, etc. Some were of two *storeys, e.g. Stoa of Attalus, Athens (C2 BC—restored), with *Doric columns on the lower storey and *Ionic above. **2.** *Temple portico with the front columns so much in advance that an extra column is needed between the colonnade in front and the structure behind, i.e. a deep *prostyle portico. **3.** *Byzantine hall with its roof supported on one or more parallel rows of columns.

Coulton (1976); Ck (1996); D (1950); D.S.R (1945); S (1901-2); Wy (1962)

stock brick 1. Hand-made brick moulded on a stock-board. **2.** Ordinary brick of any locality. **3.** The yellowish common brick of London.

Bru (1990); W. McKay (1957)

Stoddart, Alexander (1959-) *See* NEW CLASSICISM.

stoep, stoop Dutch or South-African *verandah.

Stokes, Isaac Newton Phelps (1867-1944) *See* HOWELLS, JOHN MEAD.

Stokes, Leonard Aloysius Scott Nasmyth (1858-1925) English architect, articled (1871-4) to the RC church-architect **Samuel Joseph Nicholl**

(1826–1905), before gaining further experience with *Street, *Collcutt, and *Bodley. He established (1882) his own practice, and designed many buildings for the RC Church in a free *Arts-and-Crafts style. His masterpiece is St Clare's Church, Sefton Park, Liverpool (1888), a fine composition having traceried windows set in powerfully modelled walls, with internal *buttresses resembling those used by Bodley at St Augustine's, Pendlebury, Manchester (1870–4). He favoured long, low, solid compositions on complex plans, as at All Saints' Convent, London Colney, Herts. (1899–1903). He also designed Downside School, near Bath, Som. (1910–12), and the North Court, Emmanuel College, Cambridge (1913–15). His domestic architecture was refined and often impressive: Yew Tree Lodge, West Drive, Streatham, London (1898–9), Thirtover House, Cold Ash, Berks. (1898), and, Littleshaw, Woldingham, Surrey (1902–4), were mentioned by *Muthesius in *Das englische Haus*. His designs were rooted in tradition yet were innovatory and imaginative.

*AR, c/*600 (Dec. 1946), 173–7; D & M (1985); A.S.Gray (1985); P (1982); *RIBAJ*, ser. 3, xxxiv/5 (8 Jan. 1927), 163–74; Se (ed.) (1975); J.T (1996)

Stone, Edward Durell (1902–78) American architect, he absorbed (1920s) the lessons of the *Modern Movement, working on the Rockefeller Center, NYC (1929), where he designed the interior of the Radio City Music Hall. His best *International-Modernist buildings were the Mandel House, Mount Kisco, NY (1932–3), and (with **Philip Lippincott Goodwin** (1885–1958)) the building for the Museum of Modern Art, NYC (1936–9). After the 1939–45 war his work became rather more personal and formal as he turned to regional influences. His US Embassy, New Delhi, India (1954), and Kennedy Center for the Performing Arts, Washington, DC (1961–71), were axial, symmetrical, and paraphrases of *Classicism.

Christopher (1984); E (1994); P (1982); Stone (1962, 1967); vV (1993)

Stone, Nicholas (1587–1647) English sculptor/architect, he worked for **Isaac James** (*fl.*1600—*after* 1624–5), sculptor, of Southwark, London, and then Hendrick de *Keyser in Amsterdam from 1606, whose daughter he married. He settled in London (1613) and established his reputation as a monumental sculptor, much influenced by the *Antique. He was also a master-mason, and was employed by Inigo *Jones to build the Palladian Banqueting House, Whitehall (1619–22). Appointed (1626) Master-Mason and Architect at Windsor Castle, and the (1632) Master-Mason to the Crown, his career in Royal service was interrupted by the Civil War. Other works at that time, however, include the gateways at the Botanic Gardens, Oxford (1632–3), and the remodelling of the north front of Kirby Hall, Northants.

(1638–40). He may have designed the York Water Gate on the Embankment, London (1626), but his connection with the *Baroque south porch of St Mary's Church, Oxford (1637), is tenuous, as it is now known to be by John *Jackson. He possibly designed Lindsey House, Lincoln's Inn Fields, London (*c.*1640). He made (1617) the punning monument of **William Curll** (d.1617), Auditor of the Court of Wards to **Queen Elizabeth I** (*r.*1558–1603), shown curled up in his shroud in St Etheldreda's Church, Hatfield, Herts., and used the shroud-motif again for the figure of **John Donne** (1572–1631) in St Paul's Cathedral, London (1631–2). His primary architectural sources came from *Serlio.

AH, xiv (1971), 30–9; Bullock (1908); Co (2008); Hs *et al.* (1973); J.T (1996); *Walpole Society*, vii (1918–19); Whinney (1964)

stoop, stoup Raised, uncovered platform before the entrance of a North American house, approached by steps. From *stoep. It must not be confused with a *porch or *verandah.

stop 1. Anything serving to keep a *door or opening-*sash from swinging past its proper plane, such as a rebate, stop-*bead, or strip. **2.** Continuous strip or *moulding serving to keep a sliding-sash in its place (*stop-bead*). **3.** Termination of any moulding, e.g. *architrave, *hood-moulding, *label, *skirting, or *string-course: a medieval label over a window, for example, terminates in a *label-stop. *Compounds include*:

stop-chamfer: *broach-stop*, the position of transition between an *arris and a bevel or *chamfer on a medieval timber *beam, often decoratively carved. The term is also applied to the triangular plane, like an inverted *broach*, where an octagonal *pier is transformed into a square block;

stopped flute: *flute cut in the upper two-thirds of the *shaft of a *Classical column, below which the shaft is faceted (i.e. polygonal), smooth, or the flutes contain *cabling.

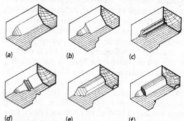

stop-chamfer *Chamfers and chamfer-stops on timber beams: (**a**) plain chamfer; (**b**) plain chamfer with ogee stop; (**c**) moulded chamfer with ogee stop; (**d**) plain chamfer with moulded stop; (**e**) sunk chamfer; (**f**) hollow or concave chamfer.*

storey, story Volume between the floors of a building or between its *floor and roof. Storeys are defined as *basement* (wholly or partly underground), *ground* (in the USA first and in France *rez-de-chaussée*), *first* (or *piano nobile* if containing the principal rooms), *second*, *third*, etc., then *Attic (over the *entablature of the principal *façade). The volume within a roof-space is the *garret rather than the Attic. Entresols and *mezzanines are intermediate floors between the main storeys. Towers have *stages rather than storeys, and, like storeys, are often identified by horizontal *bands of *mouldings, *string-courses, *cornices, etc. Storey-posts are main *posts in a *timber-framed building, rising one storey.

stoup 1. Fixed basin for Holy Water in a *niche, *corbelled out from a *pier or wall, or free-standing on a *pedestal or similar construction, near the entrance to a church. Also called a *Holy-Water stone*, it can be shaped like a *scallop-shell. 2. *See* STOOP.

Stow, Richard de (*fl.c.*1270–1307) English master-mason of the Eleanor Cross at Lincoln (1291–3—destroyed), and Master of the Fabric at Lincoln Cathedral from 1291. He designed (1306/7–11) the *belfry-stage of the Cathedral's *crossing-tower, one of the greatest *Gothic structures in England.

J.Harvey (1987)

Stowell, Robert (*fl.*1452–1505) English Master of the Stonemasons at Windsor Castle, Berks., from 1452, he worked at Westminster Abbey from 1468, becoming Master-Mason (1471). He probably designed the *nave and *aisles of St Margaret's Church, Westminster (1488–1504), by which time he was the King's Master-Mason. He carried out the *vaults of three *bays in the nave of the Abbey (1488–9).

J.Harvey (1987)

Strack, Johann Heinrich (1805–80) German architect, pupil of *Schinkel, he later worked with *Stüler. His designs were often influenced by Schinkel's exquisite *Neo-Classicism, but were sometimes *Italianate, and occasionally explored a confident *Rundbogenstil. Many of his works in Berlin did not survive the 1939–45 war, including the fine *Rundbogenstil* Borsig Factory (1858–60) and *Italianate *Villa for the same family (1868–70). With *Persius he altered and completed Schinkel's *Nash-inspired *Schloss Babelsberg*, near Potsdam (1844–9). For **Crown Prince Friedrich Wilhelm** (1831–88—*r.* as **Kaiser Friedrich III** (1888)) and his wife, **Victoria** (1840–1901), **Princess Royal of Great Britain**, he remodelled the *Kronprinzenpalais, Unter den Linden*, Berlin (1856–8), and with Stüler he designed the handsome National Gallery, Berlin (1866–76). He added the two *pavilions and *wings to the Brandenburg Gate (1868), and designed the *Siegessäule* (1869–73), both in Berlin. He was a sensitive colourist and interior decorator, and published several works.

B-S (1977); Strack (1843, 1858); Strack & Gottgetreu (1857); Strack & Kugler (1833); J.T (1996); Wa & M (1987)

straight arch *See* ARCH.

strainer *See* ARCH.

straining-piece Piece of timber acting in opposition to two equal and opposite forces at its extremities to keep those forces apart, essentially a *strut.

strapwork Common Northern-European C16 and C17 ornament in the form of narrow *bands or *fillets, folded, crossed, cut, and interlaced, resembling narrow leather-straps or thongs. It occurred in an early guise in *Mudéjar* decoration in C15 Spain, but evolved in its most usual forms in early-C16 decorations in *Tudor England and, especially, at *Fontainebleau, France (1533–5). Strapwork became common in Flanders, where complex *Mannerist designs were developed, later published by *Dietterlin, *Floris, de *Vries, and in sundry *pattern-books, and was much used in English *Elizabethan and *Jacobean architecture, especially on funerary monuments in churches. It was often decorated with *jewels, *lozenges, and *roundels.

W-J (1967)

strapwork Caroline strapwork, Crewe Hall, Ches.

Stratford, Ferdinandus (Ferdinando) (1719–66) Glos.-born architect/surveyor, he moved first to London and then to Bristol, where he published an account of how Bristol Bridge might be rebuilt (1760), and designed Bromsberrow House, Glos. (1758–62—demolished). His Market-House (later Town Hall), Newtownards, Co. Down (1765), was one of the many instances in which Bristol-based architects were responsible for works realized in Ulster. He carried out numerous schemes connected with inland navigation.

Bendall (ed.) (1997); Brett (1973, 2002); Co (2008); Ison (1978); Sk (2002)

Strauch, Adolph (1822–83) German-born landscape-gardener, he trained in Vienna, met *Pückler-Muskau, toured Europe (1845), studied in Paris (1845–8), worked in London, and emigrated to the USA (1851), where he practised as a landscape-gardener in Cincinnati, OH. His masterpiece (from 1854/5) is Spring Grove Cemetery, a unified *Picturesque landscape based on a 'lawn' plan, where the landscape architect had control over every aspect of aesthetics, especially the monuments (private enclosures and plantings were discouraged). This ensured that Spring Grove enjoyed a visual unity lacking in other *garden-cemeteries, and influenced later cemetery-designs, e.g. West Laurel Hill Cemetery, Philadelphia, PA. Strauch was greatly respected by both *Olmsted and *Simonds.

B & K (2000); Linden-Ward (1988).

Strauven, Gustave (1878–1919) Belgian architect, whose work in the *Art-Nouveau style was originally influenced by his brief spell (1896-7) in *Horta's office. Among his best works are the Van Dyck House, *Clovislaan* (1899–1902), the extraordinarily exotic Saint-Cyr House, *Ambiorixsquare* (1900–2), and the Apartment-Block, *Louis Bertrandlaan*, Schaarbeek (1906), all in Brussels.

Loo (ed.) (2003); PM

streamlining Aerodynamic design (1920s-1930s) in which curving walls, long strips of windows (often wound around elements of a building), and thin 'flat' roofs with pronounced overhangs were used, often in factories to *suggest* cleanliness and modernity. A characteristic of *Modernism, it was promoted by designers such as *Loewy and *Teague.

Street, George Edmund (1824–81) English *Gothic-Revival architect, pupil (1841–4) of **Owen Browne Carter** (1806–59), of Winchester, Hants., he later worked (1840s) in 'Great' *Scott's office with *Bodley and William *White. His first buildings included St Mary's Church, Par, Cornwall (1847) and a *vicarage in Wantage, Berks. (1847–50): almost from the beginning his work was robust, assured, and satisfying, and he played an important role in the evolution of *muscular Gothic, turning back to a *primitive *First-Pointed style derived from exemplars in Burgundy. He established his own office (1849) and became Architect to the Diocese of Oxford (1852), where he designed some of his best work (the Theological College, Cuddesdon (1852-75), Sts Simon and Jude, Milton-under-Wychwood (from 1854), St Mary, Wheatley (1855–68), St Peter, Filkins (1855-7), all in Oxon., and Sts Philip and James, Oxford (1858-66)). In the last building the Gothic Revival moved emphatically away from English roots to early French exemplars, not uninfluenced by *Viollet-le-Duc. He was assisted for a brief period by William *Morris (1855-6) and Philip *Webb (1852-9) and, having built up a national reputation, moved his practice to London (1856).

Street made several journeys to the Continent, publishing some of his observations on medieval architecture in *The Ecclesiologist* (1850-3), and bringing out his important and influential *Brick and Marble Architecture in the Middle Ages: Notes on Tours in the North of Italy* (1855, 1874) which argued for a rational approach to design, and drew attention to the wide range of Continental precedents. His best works thereafter included All Saints', Boyne Hill, Maidenhead, Berks. (1854-65), St Peter's, Bournemouth, Hants. (now Dorset) (1854–79), St James-the-Less, Westminster (1859-61—with a powerful brick polychrome interior and plate-*tracery), St John the Evangelist, Torquay, Devon (1861-5—First Pointed), St Mary Magdalene, Paddington, London (1867-73—again First Pointed, with structural *polychromy in the tower), the Crimean Memorial Church, Istanbul, Turkey (1863-8), St Paul's, Rome (1872-6—First-Pointed Italian Gothic), and All Saints', also in Rome (1880-1937—completed by **Arthur Edmund Street** (1855–1938)). Both Roman churches employed the striped effects Street admired in his *Brick and Marble*. If Sts Philip and James, Oxford, had demonstrated Street's interest in French First Pointed of the Burgundian type, his magisterial and cleverly planned Royal Courts of Justice, The Strand, London (1866-81), was an accomplished synthesis of Burgundian French, English, and Italian Gothic, one of the last great monuments of the Gothic Revival containing the grandest secular room of the style, the Great Hall. Interventions were sometimes draconian (e.g. Christ Church Cathedral, Dublin (1871-8—which he completely transformed)), sometimes highly creative and scholarly (e.g. Bristol Cathedral (1867-88—where he built a new nave and the two western towers)), and sometimes more self-effacing (e.g. Carlisle Cathedral). He also carried out major works at Kildare Cathedral, and was involved at York Minster.

Other publications included an important essay on the 'proper characteristics' of a town church (1850—which set the scene for those 'citadels of faith' by *Brooks and others), a paper in the *Ecclesiologist* on architecture and its development (1852), *An Urgent Plea for the Revival of True Principles of Architecture in the Public Buildings of the University of Oxford* (1853), an essay (in *The Ecclesiologist*) on the revival of the 'Ancient Style of Domestic Architecture' (1853—which was a milestone in the *vernacular and *Domestic Revivals), and *Some Account of Gothic Architecture in Spain* (1865).

AH, **xxiii** (1980), 86–94; D.B.Brownlee (1984); B.Clarke (1966, 1969); J.Curl (2007); *Ecclesiologist*, **xi** (1850), 227–33, **xiii** (1852), 247–62, and **xiv** (1853), 70–80; E & P (1998); Martley & Urbin (eds) (1867); Ms (1966); P (1982); *RIBAJ*, ser. 3, **lxxvii/1** (Jan. 1970), 11–18;

Stalley (2000); A.Street (1972); G.Street (1855, 1867, 1874, 1969); Su (1970); J.T (1996)

street-furniture Anything erected on pavements or streets, including *bollards, railings, lamp-posts, *pissoirs, post-boxes, street-signs, telephone-kiosks, and entrances to subways or underground railways, often of cast iron.

Design Council (1974); Glancey (1989a); Johannessen (1994); Stamp (1989)

stressed-skin Type of complex structure involving curves and bendings, where the outer skin combines with a *frame to produce a sound, strong, bent, curved structure.

J.Je (1963)

stretcher *See* BRICK.

stria (*pl.* **striae**) **1.** Flat facet in lieu of a *flute on a column-*shaft. *See* STOPPED FLUTE. **2.** *Fillet between flutes of a Classical column. **3.** *Rib in *Gothic *vaults. **4.** Any small *channel, flute, or indentation in a series, separated by fillets, etc.

Strickland, William (1788–1854) A pupil of *Latrobe, he was among the most accomplished of USA-born architects, remembered primarily for his designs in the *Greek-Revival style, although two of his earliest buildings, the Masonic Hall (1808–11—demolished) and Temple of the New Jerusalem (1816–17—demolished), both in Philadelphia, PA, were a rather uncertain *Gothick. He made his reputation with the handsome Second Bank of the United States (1818–24—with a *portico modelled on the Athenian *Parthenon), and followed this with the US Naval Asylum (1826–33—with an octastyle *Ionic portico), the US Mint (1829–33—demolished), and the very beautiful Merchants' Exchange (1832–4—with the Greek-*Corinthian Order from the *Choragic Monument of Lysicrates in Athens wrapped round a drum crowned by a replica of the Monument), all in Philadelphia, PA. Indeed, it is clear that Strickland used *Stuart and *Revett's *Antiquities of Athens* (1762–1830) as his main sourcebook, but with considerable verve and imagination. He again incorporated the Lysicrates Monument as a crowning feature of his otherwise Ionic State Capitol, Nashville, TN (1845–59).

A gifted Neo-Greek designer, Strickland also used the *Egyptian-Revival style for the Mikveh-Israel Synagogue, Philadelphia (1822–5—demolished), and the First Presbyterian Church, Nashville (1848–51—with a stunning *polychrome interior based on the Napoléonic and other publications showing Ancient-Egyptian architecture). It seems that the Nashville church's style was supposed to suggest the Temple of Solomon in Jerusalem. He designed St Mary's RC Cathedral, Nashville (1845–7), and may have been responsible for several *Italianate houses in the same city.

Carrott (1978); Gilchrist (1969); Hamlin (1964); Hi (1977); R.Kennedy (1989); P (1982); P & J (1970–86); St (1968); J.T (1996)

strigil *Flute, usually curved, like an elongated ∫. *Strigillation* refers to repeated upright flutes or *reeds on a flat *band such as a *fascia or *frieze, or repeated closely spaced ∫-shaped flutes, commonly enriching the sides of Classical or Neo-Classical *sarcophagi, *urns, etc.

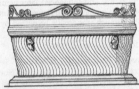

strigillation Roman sarcophagus.

string **1.** One of two inclined *beams (*stringers*) supporting the steps of a *stair. **2.** Horizontal projecting *band or *moulding (*string-course*) on a *façade. **3.** Horizontal *tie in e.g. a *truss.

stripped Classicism Classical architecture from which *mouldings, ornament, and details have been elided, leaving visible only the structural and proportional systems. *Boullée, J.J. *Burnet, F.*Gilly, *Ledoux, *Speer, *Speeth, and *Troost, among many others, experimented with stripped *Classicism (*see* NEW CLASSICISM). It was a feature of late-C18 and early C19 *Neo-Classicism, as well as of the *Rational architecture of C20 (e.g. work of A.*Rossi). Sometimes Classical ornament is merely suggested or implied, as when incisions are used instead of mouldings. With most *stripped* or *diagrammatic* Classicism the *Orders are only alluded to in the most subtle way, but could be added, as the proportions and dispositions of elements would permit this. *Soane's Dulwich Picture Gallery and *Mausoleum, London, is an example. Not to be confused with *starved Classicism.

CoE (1972); J.Curl (2001); M & Wa (1987); Po (ed.) (1987); D.Wa (1996); Wa & M (1987)

stripwork *See* LESENE.

strix *Canalis* (*see* CANAL), *flute, or *strigil.

stroll-garden Japanese garden developed in the **Edo** period (1603–1868): extensive, it featured a central pond around which were *paths constructed to afford the perambulator carefully designed varied scenes alluding to famous landscapes, poetry, Confucian thought, and even villages. Sounds made by contact of shoes with pebbles on paths, wind through bamboo, and running water were important.

Tay (2006)

Structuralism Architecture derived from 'arche-forms' (meaning archetypal or original forms), supposedly involving a creative searching for those archetypes, sign-systems, and indicators that determine, in theory, the history of architecture. Elements of Structuralism have been detected by some in early designs by Le *Corbusier involving an overlay on a pronounced circulation-pattern, and in works by *Kahn and the *Smithsons. It seems to have evolved from discussions by *Team X and *CIAM, and has been used to describe certain Dutch buildings, notably by *Blom and van *Eyck.

B+W, xxxi/1 (1976), 5–40; Ehrmann (ed.) (1970); Js & Baird (eds) (1969); L-S (1963); J.Walker (1992)

strut Any member in compression that keeps two others apart. It is found, for example, in roof-structures between a *tie-beam and a *collar. *Types include*:

king-: vertical timber set on a collar or tie-beam extending to the apex of a pitched roof (with a *ridge-piece, -plate, or -purlin);

queen-: one of two vertical members framed between a tie-beam and a collar;

rafter-: as *raking-strut* but vertical;

raking-: one of a pair of straight or curved members set at an angle on the tie-beam and framed into a principal *rafter, often supporting a *purlin.

ABDM (1996)

Stuart, James 'Athenian' (1713–88) British architect of Scots descent, a key figure in the *Greek Revival. He travelled to Rome (1742—probably supporting himself by acting as a guide and producing drawings and paintings) and to Naples (1748—with M.*Brettingham, **Gavin Hamilton** (1723–98), and *Revett), an expedition on which a scheme to visit Athens (then part of the Ottoman Empire, and difficult to visit) was mooted. Stuart and Revett's proposals for publishing reliable surveys of the antiquities of Athens were taken up by various noblemen and gentry then on the *Grand Tour: finance was raised, and the two young men were elected (1751) to the Society of *Dilettanti under the aegis of which they travelled to Greece. After a dangerous sojourn they returned to England (1755) to prepare material for publication, and the first volume of *The Antiquities of Athens Measured and Delineated by James Stuart, F.R.S. and F.S.A., and Nicholas Revett, Painters and Architects,* duly appeared (1762), some time after Le *Roy's *Les Ruines . . .* (1758), which Stuart criticized for inaccuracy: Le Roy and Stuart continued to castigate each other's efforts for some time thereafter. *The Antiquities of Athens* was the first reliable sourcebook of Greek architecture and was at once recognized as important (even though illustrations of column-shafts ignored

entasis). Stuart bought out Revett's interest, but, being of an indolent disposition, the second volume did not appear until 1789. The third (1795) was edited by Willey *Reveley, while the fourth, issued by **Josiah Taylor** (1761–1834), was published (1816), and C.R.*Cockerell oversaw the last volume (1830).

Stuart designed the garden-buildings at Hagley, Worcs. (1758), and Shugborough, Staffs. (1760s), apparently the first buildings in C18 Europe to have the Greek *Orders. He designed a *Palladian house with Grecian details at 15 St James's Square, London (1763–6—later altered). He was also responsible for the exquisite interiors (including some of the earliest C18 uses of *Pompeian motifs) of Spencer House, Green Park, London (1759–65), Holdernesse (later Londonderry) House, Hertford Street, London (c.1760–5—demolished), the beautiful Chapel at Greenwich Hospital, London (1780–8—assisted by **William Newton** (1735–90)), and (perhaps) the Tower of the Winds, Mount Stewart, Co. Down (1782–3). Had he not been so idle, his command of *Neo-Classicism, including his knowledge of Greek and Roman decorations, together with his flair for synthesizing various schemes of ornament, could have made him a dangerous rival to the *Adam brothers.

AH, xxii (1979), 72–7; Co (2008); Crook (1972a); J.Friedman (1993); E.Hs (1990); *ODNB* (2004); P (1982); S & R (1762–1816); J.T (1996); D.Wa (1982); Wn (1969)

Stuart architecture Architecture of the C17, especially *Jacobean and *Caroline, but also applied to the period of the Stuart dynasty in Great Britain from **James I & VI** (r.1603–25) to **Queen Anne** (r.1702–14). However, the architecture of the reign of **Charles II** (1660–85) is usually referred to as *Restoration or *Carolean, followed by the *William-and-Mary (1689–1702), then *Queen-Anne styles.

Stubbins, Hugh Asher (1912–2006) American architect, he became assistant (1939) to *Gropius at Harvard, established his own practice in Cambridge, MA (1940), and succeeded Gropius as Chairman of the Department of Architecture (1953). His work was influenced by Gropius, *Aalto, and *Breuer: among his buildings may be mentioned the Loeb Drama Center, Cambridge, MA (1957–60), and the Citicorp Center, NYC (1978—with Emery *Roth). His MM21 *skyscraper, Yokohama (1988–92), was the tallest building in Japan at the time of its completion. His Congress Hall, Berlin (1957), with its saddle-shaped catenary roof, was hailed when built, but irreverently referred to by Berliners as the 'pregnant oyster'. He published *Architecture: The Design Experience* (1976).

Do (1987); E (1994); Heyer (1978); Ludman (1986); P (1982); J.T (1996)

stucco 740

stucco *also* **stuc** Slow-setting *plaster known from Antiquity, made of various ingredients. There are basically two types: *common stucco*, classed as a *cement, is a plastered finish of *lime, sand, brick-dust, stone-dust, or powdered burnt clay nodules, mixed with water, used as an external rendering instead of stone, often lined to resemble *ashlar-work, and moulded to form architectural features such as *string-courses, *cornices, etc. *Internal stucco*, widely used in C18, and elaborately modelled, was made of very fine sand, pulverized white Carrara *marble, gypsum (hydrated calcium sulphate), alabaster-dust, and water, often with other additions, such as colouring, provided by mixing in metallic oxides etc.: it was sometimes mixed with size or gum dissolved in lukewarm water, often with the colour also dissolved in the size-water, and when perfectly dry was rubbed and polished. Stucco was widely used by the Romans and in *Islamic architecture, but it reached new heights during the *Renaissance, *Baroque, and *Rococo periods, especially in Southern Germany, where the great masters included members of the Wessobrunn School (notably **J.G.Üblhör** (1703-63) and **J.M. Feichtmayr** (1696-1772)), and *Zimmermann. *Stucco lustro* is fine *scagliola work.

G.Beard (1983); Bt (1978); Garstang (1984); Gw (1903); Jahn (1988); N (1835); W.Pa (1887); Schnell & Schedler (1988); S (1901–2); J.T (1996); Vance (1983)

stud In *timber framing, a subsidiary (usually vertical) member (or *scantling*) in a wall or partition. In *close-studding* the spaces between studs are about the same in width as the studs themselves, a profligate use of material intended for show rather than for any practical purpose. *Herringbone-studding* is set at an angle (usually 45°) to the *posts, filling the space framed by the posts and *rails. A *cruck-stud* is set on and fixed to the outside of a *cruck blade. *Stud-and-panel* is a wall made of studs with panels of vertical planks or *staves slotted into grooves, called also *post-and-plank* or *plank-and-muntin*.

ABDM (1996)

Stüler, Friedrich August (1800–65) German architect, one of the most gifted of *Schinkel's students, he continued designing in a manner reminiscent of the master's style. He supervised the remodelling of Prince Karl's Palace, Berlin (1827), and his first independent work was the inventive *polychrome *Börse*, Frankfurt-am-Main (1839–44—demolished). He made a design (1841) to transform the island in the River Spree behind Schinkel's *Lustgarten* (now *Altes*) Museum as a Cultural Centre with Museums, and the *Neues-museum* was completed to his designs (1843–50) in a Neo-Classical style harmonizing with Schinkel's great building. With *Strack he designed the *Nationalgalerie* near by (1865–76), a Graeco-Roman *temple on a high *podium. He was responsible (with **Albert Dietrich Schadow** (1797–1869—*Hofbaumeister* in Potsdam)), for the Russian-style Church of Sts Peter and Paul, Nikolskoë, *Volkspark Glienecke*, Berlin (1833–7); several *Rundbogenstil* Berlin churches (these, and his writings on ecclesiastical architecture, were influential); the *Quattrocento*-Revival National Museum, Stockholm, Sweden (1850–66); the Officers' Barracks, Charlottenburg, Berlin (1851–9—opposite Charlottenburg Palace); and many other buildings. He designed interiors of the lavish *Renaissance-Revival *Schloss* at Schwerin, erected to plans by *Demmler (1851–7), and for several charming *villas in and around Berlin and Potsdam from 1845.

B-S (1977); B-S (ed.) (1997); Dehio (1961); Evers (ed.) (1995); K-PO-B (1852); *KiDR*, vii (1943), 74–89; P (1982); K.Philipp (2003); Plagemann (1967); Stüler (1853–66, 1861); Stüler *et al.* (1869); Wa & M (1987); *ZfB*, xv (1865), 507–12

stumpery *See* ROOTERY.

stump tracery *See* TRACERY.

stupa Buddhist funerary mound in the form of a hemisphere of earth and *rubble. The earliest (C3–C1 BC) are raised on low drums faced with brick or stone. Stupas are sometimes of bell-like form with a platform at the top (surrounded by stone railings) carrying a mast-like stone upright with one or more canopies resembling umbrellas (*chattra*). Stupa-like elements sometimes occur as ornaments in the *Indian style.

Ck (1996); Glauche (1995); Snodgrass (1985); J.T (1996)

stupa. Stupa surmounted by a *chattravalli*.

Sturgis, John Hubbard (1834–88) American architect, educated in England and on the Continent where he absorbed ideas associated with the *Gothic Revival and the *Arts-and-Crafts movement. He commenced practice (1861) in Boston, MA, and won (1870) the competition for the Museum of Fine Arts, Boston, with a design based on Continental-Gothic exemplars possibly influenced by the University of Oxford Museum by *Deane & Woodward in England. He employed English *terracotta in the design, heralding other *polychrome essays, including the Church of the Advent, Boston (1874–8), in which the influences of *Brooks, *Pearson, and *Street can be detected. He also designed a large number of interesting seaside and country-houses which, after 1870, were influenced by the English *Domestic Revival and the works of Eden *Nesfield and Norman *Shaw, especially those buildings in which the *Queen-Anne style emerged. Sturgis drew on American-*Colonial and *Federal styles to create new and original works. Among his finest domestic designs was the Ames House, 306 Dartmouth Street, Boston (1882).

JSAH, xxxii/2 (May 1973), 83–103; P (1982); *PAIA*, v (1871), 39–43; J.T (1996); vV (1993); Whitehill (1970)

Sturgis, Russell (1836–1909) American architect, he worked for *Eidlitz before a period of study in Munich (from 1859), where he acquired a sound grasp of constructional principles. Setting up in practice in NYC (1863), his works included Farnam (1869–70) and Lawrance (1885–6) Halls, Yale University, New Haven, CT, well-composed *Gothic-Revival essays, and the *Queen-Anne Farnam House, also New Haven (1884). His assistants included G.F.*Babb, C.F.*McKim, and **W.R. Mead** (of *McKim, Mead, & White). He compiled the important *Dictionary of Architecture and Building* ... (1901–2), and built up the Avery Library, Columbia University.

ARe, xxv (1909), 146, 220, 404–10, xxvi (1909), 123–31, 393–416; Do (1985*b*); P (1982); S (1901–2, 1971, 1971*a*, 1977); vV (1993)

Sturm, Der Literally 'The Assault' or 'The Storm', title of a Berlin art-gallery (1912–14) and journal (1910–32) devoted to the avant-garde in Germany, founded by **Herwarth Walden** (1878–1941). Through *Der Sturm* *Futurism and *Expressionism were promoted.

COF (1988); J.T (1996)

Sturm, Leonhard Christoph (1669–1719) German mathematician/architect, he published a treatise on Solomon's Temple in Jerusalem (1694) in which he endeavoured to prove the building's Divinely inspired dimensions and proportions were the basis for Classical architecture (a notion that resurfaces every so often). He

designed parts of the *Lustschloss* of Salzdahlum (1694–1702), with its celebrated picture-gallery. Later, he completed *St Nikolai auf dem Schelfe*, Schwerin, from 1708, after which he published his important *Architektonisches Bedenken von der Protestantischen Klein Kirchen Figur und Einrichtung* (1712 and 1718).

Be (1966); P (1982); W.Pa (1887); Sturm (1694, 1712); J.T (1996); Wl (1915)

Style 1925 *Art Deco.

Style Moderne *Art Deco.

Style Rayonnant *See* RAYONNANT.

stylobate 1. Upper step of a three-stepped *crepidoma* (*see* CREPIDO) forming the platform on which a Greek *temple, any *colonnade, or *peristyle stands. 2. In Classical architecture any continuous *base, *plinth, or *pedestal on which a row of columns is set, properly the uppermost part of a *stereobata.

Suardi, Bartolomeo, *called* **Bramantino** (*c*.1465–1530) Milanese painter/architect, influenced by *Bramante and *Leonardo da Vinci, he worked in Rome (1508–13) where he studied antiquities, and later investigated old buildings in Milan. While his paintings often feature architectural backgrounds, his only surviving building is the octagonal Trivulzio *mortuary-chapel, *San Nazaro Maggiore*, Milan (begun 1512), an early and remarkable example of refined *Classicism.

COF (1988); Suida (1953); J.T (1996)

sub- Prefix meaning under, inferior, etc. *Compounds include*:

sub-arch: *see* ARCH;

sub-base: lowest part of a *base set under the base proper in *Gothic architecture, e.g. *piers;

sub-Order: 1. *Order of architecture inferior to the dominant structural Order, as in *Palladio's *Basilica*, Vicenza, where the subsidiary Order forms part of a *serliana, and the dominant Orders carry the intermediate and crowning *entablatures; 2. in *Romanesque and *Gothic *doorways, with a series of Orders, the smaller or inferior Orders;

sub-plinth: second lower *plinth under the main one, as in column-bases or *pedestals.

Sublime C18 aesthetic category concerned with aspects of Nature and Art (e.g. ruggedness, vastness, overwhelming grandeur, etc., emphasizing Man's relative insignificance in the face of Nature) affecting the mind with an intense sense of irresistible power, terror, and awe, inspiring lofty emotions, and stimulating the imagination. It was therefore distinct from the *Beautiful and the *Picturesque (though some have seen the latter as a *synthesis* of the Beautiful and the

Sublime), and was of profound importance in relation to an appreciation of the visceral violence of natural phenomena and rugged, mountainous scenery, with massive waterfalls, etc. Its chief apologists were *Burke, with his *A Philosophical Enquiry into the Origin of our Ideas of the Sublime and Beautiful* (1757), and *Kant, with his *Observations on the Feeling of the Beautiful and Sublime* (1764). In architecture the Sublime was associated with great size, overpowering *scale, the *primitive (especially the unadorned *Doric *Order), and stereometrical purity (as in much *Neo-Classicism, e.g. *Boullée's work, and the visions of *prisons by *Piranesi).

Burke (1757); COF (1988); J.T (1996)

Subtopia 1. Pejorative term derived from '*suburb' and 'utopia', meaning an area that is neither urban nor rural. *See* SLURB. 2. An idealization of suburban urban fringes and everything they stand for and represent.

Nairn (1955, 1959)

suburb Formed of *sub- and *urbs* (Latin for *town* or *city*), it refers to those residential areas in the outskirts of towns.

Suburbia 1. Residential areas the style of which evolved from C19 ideals associated with the *Arts-and-Crafts and *Aesthetic Movements, and with the *Domestic Revival and *Garden Suburb (e.g. Bedford Park, Chiswick, London (from 1877) and Hampstead Garden Suburb, London (from 1906)), though very often as a travesty, based more on commerce than aesthetics. These low-rise developments on the fringes of towns were supposed to be attempts to combine rural and urban advantages, but those benefits were often so diluted they became meaningless. The *suburb, with its detached and semi-detached houses set in individual gardens, offered a style of living to which many aspired, and became ubiquitous first through the development of railways and tramways, and then through the widespread use of the private motor-car. Suburbia generally lacked shops, *public-houses, etc., which to some was a blessing. Suburbia must not be confused with *satellite towns or *Garden Cities. 2. Pejorative term associated with philistinism, conformity, and dullness, and used by Modernists to promote high-rise urban developments: however, demand for suburban houses (with gardens ever smaller, spaces between buildings ever narrower, and architectural content wholly evaporated) seems insatiable, despite ever-growing problems of pollution caused by car-ownership and over-stretched infrastructures.

H.Barrett & T.Phillips (1987); Fishman (1987); P.Oliver et al. (1981); J.Ri (1973); F.Thompson (ed.) (1981)

Suger, Abbot (1081–1151) Abbot of St-Denis, near Paris (from 1122), when the church there was rebuilt (c.1135–44) in the new *Gothic style. There is no evidence that he was responsible for the design, but he presided over, and wrote about (1144–7), the new buildings which were the earliest in which a mature and consistent *Pointed style was used.

S.Crosby (1987); Panofsky (ed.) (1979); J.T (1996)

Sullivan, Louis Henri (1856–1924) American architect of Irish-German descent, he worked with F.*Furness in Philadelphia, PA (1872–3), before moving to Chicago, IL, and the office of *Jenney (1873–4). He was at the *École des *Beaux-Arts*, Paris, under *Vaudremer (1874) before returning to Chicago (1875). He entered the office of Dankmar *Adler (c.1879), and became (1883) a full partner in the firm of **Adler & Sullivan**. Their first joint work was the Auditorium Building, Chicago (1886–90) containing a 4,000-seat theatre, *hotel, and office-building, the exterior showing the influence of H.H.*Richardson and the interior an eclectic mix of flowing foliate forms containing elements of *Arts-and-Crafts invention as well as *Art-Nouveau themes. Even more Richardsonian was the powerful St Nicholas Hotel, St Louis, MO (1892–4—destroyed). Adler & Sullivan employed (1888–93) the young F.L.L. *Wright (who was devoted to Sullivan, calling him *Lieber Meister*, but designed work on his own account in violation of his contract, which led to his leaving to establish his own practice). Adler & Sullivan's two best-known *skyscrapers, the Wainwright Building, St Louis, MO (1890–1), and the Guaranty Building, Buffalo, NY (1894–5), adhere to Classical principles in that each has a plain *plinth-like base; a series of identical floors above expressed by bands of windows and panels set within recessed strips between *piers, with large corner-piers acting as *antae; and crowning *cornices (the Wainwright Building cornice is particularly lushly enriched).

Sullivan (having set up on his own (1895) after the partnership with Adler was dissolved) built (1898–1904) the Schlesinger & Mayer (later Carson, Pirie, Scott, & Co.) Store, Chicago, which marked a change of direction, in that it did not emphasize the vertical, but created a series of horizontal openings framed by the *skeleton structure of floors and vertical supports. However, he still treated the two lower storeys as a massive plinth enriched with ornament, clad the upper storeys with white *faïence, filled the voids in with *Chicago windows, and capped the whole with an overhanging cornice-like roof. It is the paradigm of the *Chicago School (*see* PURCELL & ELMSLIE).

In spite of his *de-rigueur* remarks in the *Engineering Magazine* (1892) suggesting that ornament should be eschewed for a while, he was an inventive and uninhibited user of architectural enrichment combined with powerful simple geometries and blocky masses, as in the Getty *Mausoleum, Graceland Cemetery, Chicago (1890), and the Wainwright Tomb, Bellefontaine Cemetery, St Louis, MO (1891–2). At the Getty Mausoleum the arch motif looks back to Richardson's work, and strong, simple geometrical forms with well-integrated ornament were themes Sullivan explored in the elegant and colourful series of Banks he designed (e.g. National Farmers' Bank, Owatonna, MN (1906–8), Merchants' National Bank, Grinnell, IA (1913–14), People's Savings & Loan Association Bank, Sidney, OH (1919), and Farmers' & Merchants' Union Bank, Columbus, WI (1919)). Sullivan's ebullient ornament became part of American Mid-West commercial architecture in the early decades of C20, especially in works of the Midland Terra Cotta Company and other firms: its inventiveness is inconvenient for those who insist he was a 'prophet' or 'pioneer' of Modern Architecture.

Sullivan was a prolific writer, his output covering the period 1885–1924, but his prolix texts lack clarity, and his obfuscatory style has been interpreted as indicative of profound thought. In his 'The Tall Building Artistically Considered', published in *Lippincott's Magazine* (1896), he announced that 'form follows function', a dictum eagerly grasped by the protagonists of the *International-*Modern Movement. However, a careful reading of Sullivan's own texts makes clear that his concept of *Functionalism embraces and calls for emotional, expressive, spiritual, and creative values that Modernists wholly rejected. His built work shows that it had virtually nothing in common with the teachings of the *Bauhaus or with the apologists for style that was to be almost universally embraced after 1945.

B-B (1960); Ct (1952, 1964); Connely (1960); *EM*, iii (1892), 633–44; Frei (1992); D.Ho (1988); *JSAH*, xx/4 (Dec. 1961), 3–19; xxvi/4 (Dec. 1967), 250–8, 259–68, and xxxix/4 (Dec. 1980) 297–303; Ed.Ka (1956); *Lippincott's Magazine*, lvii (1896), 403–9; Manieri-Elia (1997); H.Morrison (1998); P (1982); Paul (1962); P & J (1970–86); Schmitt (2002); M.Schuyler (1961); Sprague (1979); Sullivan (1956, 1967, 1980); Szarkowski (2000); C.Taylor *et al.* (2001); Twombly (1986); Twombly *et al.* (2000); Z (2000); Zu (ed.) (1987, 1993)

Sumerian architecture The Sumerians of Mesopotamia were creating sophisticated works of architecture in the fourth millennium BC, almost wholly constructed of brick, and used arches, *domes, and *vaults. The huge Eanna temple-precinct at Uruk (Erech in the Old Testament), the greatest of the Sumerian cities, had two groups of temples connected by a mighty *portico of huge circular columns of brick facing a *court the walls of which were embellished with *engaged columns. Interior wall-faces were decorated with a geometrical pattern of small *terracotta cones of different colours. Other features of buildings were the *buttress-like projections used to articulate walls, a type of wall-treatment that was to extend well into the last centuries BC. By the mid-third millennium BC painted and *relief ornamental schemes were in widespread use, as in the elevated shrine of Al 'Ubaid, where *friezes, free-standing columns covered with *mosaics, copper sculptures, and other enrichment occurred in profusion. The huge *ziggurat at Ur (C22 BC) had enormous battered walls, monumental *flights of *stairs, and a temple on the summit of the platform. The basic principles of Sumerian architecture were absorbed by their successors, the *Assyrians from Northern Mesopotamia, around 2000 BC.

Ck (1996); L & M (1986); J.T (1996)

summer 1. *Lintel, e.g. over a fireplace. **2.** *Beam, also called *breastsummer or bressumer, set on the extremities of *cantilevered joists (*jetty) and supporting the posts of a wall above in *timber-framed construction. **3.** Main beam or *girder in a floor, or any large beam, called a *summer-beam* supporting floor-joists. **4.** Stone at the top of a *pier or *jamb supporting a lintel or arch. **5.** Large stone, the beginning of a *vault. **6.** Lowest stone at the extremity of a *gable, called summer-stone or raked *skew-block at the end of the *eaves against which the first *cope-stone of the *tabling is set to prevent it sliding off. *See* KNEELER.

summer-house Primitive, simple, or *rustic structure in a *garden or park to provide shaded seating during hot weather. It may double as an *eyecatcher.

Summerson, Sir John Newenham (1904–92) Anglo-Irish architectural historian, he began work (1926) as an architect in the office of (Sir) Giles Gilbert *Scott, later assisting Adrian Gilbert *Scott with the working-drawings for the upper stage of the noble tower of *Hansom's Church of the Holy Name, Manchester. He also worked for W.D.*Caröe before becoming an architectural journalist. As assistant editor of the *Architect and Building News* (1934–41) he developed his icy style of criticism, as well as cultivating his support for *International Modernism (though in his 1957 lecture 'The Case for a Theory of Modern Architecture', he made a forlorn attempt to promote a philosophical base for Modernism, recognizing that Classical architecture had always had just that, but his efforts in this respect remain wholly unconvincing).

He made his name with his biography of *Nash (1935, 1949, 1980), yet after the 1939–45 war argued that only a fraction of Nash's *scenographic architecture around Regent's Park should be preserved (a predictable Modernist stance, despite the fact that it would *cease to be scenographic* if fragmented). A founder-member of the Georgian Group (1937), he was also opposed to anything but highly selective retention of C18 and early-C19 buildings. During the war he established, and was Deputy Director of, the National Buildings Record (1941–5), making extensive photographic records of London buildings: with **(Sir) James Maude Richards** (1907–92) he was responsible for *The Bombed Buildings of Britain: A Record of Architectural Casualties 1940–41* (1942, 1947). He brought out his *Georgian London* (subsequently edited (and comprehensively corrected) by *Colvin, reissued 2002–3) in the year (1945) in which he was appointed Curator of Sir John *Soane's Museum, a position he held until 1984. He wrote several perceptive essays on Soane's work, but never produced a major study, probably because he found Soane's architecture and personality uncongenial. On the other hand, he pioneered studies of John *Thorpe, and, under Colvin's rigorous editorship, contributed much material on C16 and C17 architecture to the *History of the King's Works* (1975, 1982). For the *Pelican History of Art* he wrote *Architecture in Britain 1530–1830* (1953), which went into several editions: in that work his appreciation of earlier periods and his ambivalence towards figures such as Nash and Soane were made overt. His attempts to produce a Victorian sequel to *Georgian London* resulted in *Victorian Architecture: Four Studies in Evaluation* (1970), *The London Building World of the Eighteen-Sixties* (1973), and *The Architecture of Victorian London* (1976), with other articles collected as *The Unromantic Castle* (1990), but he was uncomfortable with much Victorian architecture, finding its variety (and, one suspects, its rumbustiousness) unpalatable, but his essays on Inigo Jones, Wren, *Viollet-le-Duc, and others reveal areas he found more to his taste.

Towards the end of his life he modified some of his earlier acerbic judgements: nevertheless, he supported the demolition of Victorian fabric in the City of London to enable new buildings to go ahead, in spite of having admitted that 'cheap modern' was all Britain ever had (a view from which it would be hard to dissent).

AR, cxcii/1151 (Jan. 1993), 9–10; *BuMa*, cxxxv (Apr. 1993), 277–9; Co (1996); *RIBAJ*, c/2 (Feb. 1993), 63; Su (1948, 1952, 1963, 1965, 1966, 1970, 1976, 1980, 1980a, 1986, 1990, 1993, 2003); Su (ed.) (1968); Su *et al.* (1983); J.T (1996)

sunburst 1. Any collection of rods, normally gilded, representing sunbeams, radiating from a centre. In religious contexts it is common in *Baroque architecture, surrounding e.g. a dove, representing the Holy Spirit. **2.** In a secular context, the rods occur around the head of e.g. Apollo, in *Apolline ornament of the *Louis-Quatorze* style. **3.** *Fanlight.

sunburst

sundial Device for telling time by the shadow of the sun cast by the sloping edge of a projecting point (**gnomon**) set on a surface in which the hours of day are inscribed; multifaceted types incorporate moon-dials. During the Middle Ages they were mounted vertically on European churches e.g., St Gregory's Minster, Kirkdale, Yorks. (*c.*1060), and emerged in *gardens from the early C16 (Acton Court, Bristol, *c.*1520). They proliferated during the C17 and continued to be popular throughout the C19 as garden-ornaments, more often positioned horizontally on a pedestal or table.

J.Curl (2011); Symes (2006); S (1902); Tay (2006)

sun-disc Ancient-Egyptian disc or globe flanked by rearing *uraei* (snakes) and outstretched wings commonly found on the *gorge *cornice.

sunk Surface placed on a lower level than that of its surroundings. *Compounds include*:
sunk draft: *margin* round a piece of *ashlar leaving raised the *face framed by it;
sunk face: *panel surrounded by a raised *margin* or *frame*;
sunk fence: *ha-ha;
sunk moulding: *moulding recessed behind the main surface or *naked of a wall;
sunk panel: recessed framed panel;
sunk relief: carved *relief not projecting beyond the *naked of the surface on which it is carved, called *cavo rilievo* or *intaglio rilevato*.

sunken garden Garden set below the level of the surrounding ground, sheltered and secluded, usually surrounded by *terraces, derived from

*Renaissance and *Islamic exemplars, and common in *Arts-and-Crafts gardens. *Lutyens and *Jekyll designed a fine one at Heywood, Co. Laois (1909–12).

super- Above, or on top of. *Compounds include*:

super-abacus: *impost-block, *dosseret, or *super-capital* set on top of an *abacus, common in *Byzantine architecture;

super-altar: **1.** consecrated *altar-slab, or *mensa; **2.** shelf or ledge let into the east wall above and behind the *altar;

super-block: area containing residential accommodation, shops, schools, offices, etc., with public open space (e.g. a green), surrounded by roads and penetrated by *cul-de-sac* service-roads. It is linked to other super-blocks and a town-centre by means of paths over or under the roads (e.g. in *Radburn planning);

super-capital: as *super-abacus*;

supercilium: **1.** *lintel above an aperture (*see* ANTEPAGMENT); **2.** *fillet above a *cyma on a *cornice forming the topmost member of the *entablature; **3.** fillets above and below the *scotia of an *Attic *base. **2.** and **3.** are of doubtful authenticity;

supercolumniation: *see* ASSEMBLAGE OF ORDERS;

superimposed Orders: *see* ASSEMBLAGE OF ORDERS;

supermarket: big, retail, largely self-service store, often associated with *shopping-centres. Supermarkets require space uninterrupted by columns, so many are really nothing more than huge sheds covered by *space-frame roofs, etc.

Supermannerism 1. American style of interior decoration dating from the 1960s employing odd optical tricks, synthetic materials that were either shiny and mirror-like, or transparent, and over-sized elements, so it was referred to as 'mega-decoration', and owed more to images in *Superman* comics than to *Mannerism. **2.** Term applied (1970s) to large *Post-Modernist buildings.

PA, x (Oct. 1968), 148–208; C.R.Smith (1977); J.Walker (1992)

Supersensualism Label given by **Charles Alexander Jencks** (1939–2019) to works by certain designers of the 1970s (e.g. *Archizoom, *Sottsass) which he identified as having excessive sensuality, warped beauty, fantasy, tortured meaning, and technological sophistication, all taken to extremes.

AD, xli (June 1971), 345–7, and xlii (Jan. 1972), 18–21; J.Walker (1992)

Suprematism Russian artistic movement founded (1915) by **Kasimir Malevich** (1878–1935), who produced paintings limited to basic geometric shapes using a sparse range of colour. His *White Square on a White Ground* (1918) was

regarded as the movement's paradigm, and influenced the *International-Modern Movement and *De *Stijl*, though was largely *passé* by 1919.

COF (1988); J.T (1996)

surbase Topmost *moulding of a *dado, *pedestal, or *stereobate. For *surbased arch see* ARCH.

surcharge Arches, *pendentives, etc., can be unstable on their own without superimposed loads. An arch, for example, requires a mass of material at the *haunches for stability, and further *surcharges* over the haunches and arch proper help the structure to settle down.

surmounted 1. *See* ARCH. **2.** Element placed over another part, such as a *door-case *surmounted* by a *sopraporta.

surround Frame of an architectural feature, such as an *architrave around an aperture or a *chimney-piece in front of a fireplace.

suspended Used to describe a structure supported from higher points, such as a *bridge suspended from *piers or a building or *floors hung from a separate structure. A *suspended ceiling* is one hung from the structure above to lower the ceiling and conceal services, etc., and a *suspended floor* is one supported only by its ends.

Sussex bond *See* BRICK.

Sustainable architecture Architecture that does not guzzle energy, require expensive maintenance, or is subject to massive heat-loss or -gain through poor insulation or too much glazing: also called *Environmentally Responsible or *green architecture.

Sustris, Friedrich (*c.*1540–99) *Mannerist architect of Dutch descent who worked for the Electoral Court in Munich, Bavaria, and was a contemporary of *Candid. He may have designed the *chancel and *transept of the huge *Michaels-kirche*, Munich (1583–97—the first large Jesuit church in Northern Europe), and the *Grottenhof* in the Munich *Residenz* (1580–8), a lively composition with statue-filled *niches rather Florentine in style. He carried out alterations at the *Residenz*, Landshut (1570s), and may have designed the former Jesuit College, Munich (1585–90—now the *Akademie der Wissenschaften*).

Hi (1981); W.Pa (1887); Pe (1960); Powell (1959); J.T (1996)

Suter, Richard (1797-1883) English architect. As Surveyor to The Fishmongers' Company he designed the severe Presbyterian churches for Ballykelly (1825-7) and Banagher (1825) on the Company's Estate in Co. Londonderry, drawings of which were exhibited (1827) at the RA. He was also responsible for the Model Farm (1823-4), the

Lancasterian Schools (1828–30), the Company Agent's House (1830-2—now an hotel, much altered), a range of houses on the south side of the main road (1823–4), the lodge in the Presbyterian churchyard (1828), and the Dispensary (1829), all at Ballykelly, and all Classical. As Surveyor to Trinity House Corporation, he designed houses erected (1821-3) by Thomas *Cubitt on a site adjoining Trinity House. For The Fishmongers' Company he designed St Peter's Almshouses, Wandsworth, London (1849–51), and The Old School-House, Gresham's School, Holt, Norfolk (1859), in an Elizabethan style.

Co (2008); J.Curl (1986)

Sutherland, John (c.1745–1826) Landscape-gardener/architect, probably a Scot, active in Ireland from the 1770s, when he was working at Derrymore, Co. Armagh (where he may have designed the *cottage orné*). Later, he designed landscapes influenced by the work of 'Capability' *Brown for five country-houses designed by *Nash: Caledon, Co. Tyrone (1807); Rockingham House, Co. Roscommon (c.1810); Lough Cutra Castle, Co. Galway (c.1812); Shane's Castle, Co. Antrim (c.1813); and Gracefield Lodge, Co. Laois (c.1817). He also designed extensive landscaped parks (e.g. Slane Castle, Co. Meath (1787)). The only urban garden he certainly designed was Mountjoy Square, Dublin (1803).

Lamb & Bowe (1995); D & E (1994); Malins & Glin (1976); Shoe (2001)

Suzuki, Makoto (1935–) See ARCHITEXT.

swag *Festoon on two supports with the suspended element resembling drapery.

Swales, Francis S. (1878–1962) American architect, educated in the USA and Paris, he was imbued with a sound training in *Beaux-Arts *Classicism, and set up (1906) in practice in Chiswick, London. His best-known work (with R.F. *Atkinson and *Burnham as consultant) is Selfridges Store, Oxford Street, London (1907-9), a massive essay in *Beaux-Arts *Neo-Classicism, much influenced by Franco-American architecture, and with a *Giant *Ionic *Order (derived from Philibert de L'*Orme's *Palais des Tuileries, Paris, but with *angular capitals) rising from a massive *plinth to carry an *entablature with windows inserted in the *frieze. The building was constructed on a steel frame designed by the Swedish engineer **Sven Bylander** (1877–1943), who also designed the steel frames for *Mewès & Davis's RAC Club, Pall Mall, and their Ritz Hotel, both in London, and both firmly in *Beaux-Arts Classical styles. Other buildings by Swales included works at le Touquet, Paris Plage, and Boulogne, a hotel in Sandwich, Kent, and the His Master's Voice Pavilion for the Gramophone

Company at the Franco-British Exhibition, White City (1908). He settled in Canada shortly afterwards, where he worked for the Canadian Pacific Railway.

A.S.Gray (1985); K (1994)

swallowtail 1. *Dovetail* or *triangular fret* *moulding consisting of a series of adjacent equilateral triangles, each set alternately with apex and base uppermost, the series framed by a system of *fillets joining at acute angles, and decorating a *band. **2.** Guelphic crenellation. See BATTLEMENT.

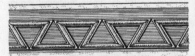

swallowtail Romanesque *swallow-* or *dove-tail* moulding, also called *triangular fret*, Ely Cathedral, Cambs. (*after Parker*).

swan-neck 1. Any member constructed on a double curve, e.g. a *stair hand-rail with a concave curve then bending into a convex curve before straightening out to join a newel-post. **2.** Form of a rainwater-pipe connecting a *gutter to a down-pipe under the *eaves. **3.** *Scrolled *pediment.

Swastika See CROSS.

Swedish hut Quasi-national style of timber *fabrique clad in fir, etc.

swelled chamfer *Vitruvian *scroll.

swelled frieze See PULVIN.

Swiss cottage Quasi-national style of cottage which emerged in France (1778) as a mnemonic *fabrique in a *landscape-garden, and appeared in several countries thereafter alluding to Swiss *châlet architecture. C18 thinkers (including J.-J. *Rousseau), considering their relationship with the natural world, responded to the Swiss Alps as *Sublime and *Picturesque, and travellers on the Grand Tour recalled their journeyings by erecting 'Swiss cottages' on their estates. Numerous examples of *Le Châlet Suisse* (some only nominally Swiss, being just rustic *cottages ornés* (e.g. at Cahir, Co. Tipperary)), were built, including one at Endsleigh, Devon (c.1815), by Jeffry *Wyatville.

Anker et al. (1999); Bernard (1978); Dana (1913); P.F. Robinson (1823); Rousseau (1761); Rümelin (ed.) (2012); *Traditional Dwellings and Settlements*, iii/1 (1 Oct. 1991), 55–64

Swiss garden 1. Garden with real or allusive Swiss elements (buildings, landscape, planting): an C18 example was the miniature rugged 'Switzerland' at Hawkstone, Salop., complete with timber *bridge in a rocky situation (1790s). **2.** Swiss *public parks, gardens, and *botanic gardens attached to the universities of Geneva (1818), Zürich (1834), and Bern (1860) were renowned for their 'neatness' in the C19, while the country's close turf carpet and the grandeur of its mountains rendered all Switzerland a garden in the eyes of travellers, although garden-cultivation as such absorbed stylistic influences from France, Italy, The Netherlands, and England. Until the 1939–45 war Swiss garden-design tended to be traditional, but certain personalities (many associated with the Swiss *Werkbund*) introduced *Modernism: *Bill and *Cramer were two early protagonists.

Heyer *et al.* (1980); Loudon (1834a); Shoe (2001)

Switzer, Stephen (1683–1745) English garden-designer. After early training in Hants., he worked for *London and *Wise in their Brompton nursery, and then created the *wilderness at Castle Howard, Yorks. (from 1706), followed by works at Cirencester Park, Glos. (from *c.*1713), and Grimsthorpe Castle, Lincs. (*c.*1716). The last involved creating an informal park, linking the grounds contiguous to the house with the country beyond: thus he has been claimed as one of the inventors (*or* progenitors) of the English landscape-garden. However, Switzer's reputation rests more on his writings, in which, among other things, he advocated bringing the 'useful' and 'profitable' aspects of gardening (e.g. agriculture, animal husbandry, and forestry) into designs to enhance the 'pleasurable' (e.g. decorative) parts: in this he drew on Classical Roman theory, and proposed the *ferme ornée* as an important feature, both aesthetically pleasing and useful. In short, he advocated that agricultural land, woodlands, uncultivated land, water-features, and grounds for recreation should be designed as a whole, respecting nature and topography. His *Ichnographia Rustica* (1718, 1741–2) is his most important work.

Hunt & P.Willis (eds) (1989); D.Jacques (1983); Pe (1968); Switzer (1980); J.T (1996); P.Willis (ed.) (1974)

Symbolic architecture Term coined (1980s) by **Charles Alexander Jencks** (1939–2019) to describe architecture with a strong degree of *personification or with allusions to cultural ideas, historical references, and other pre-Modernist themes, or in which there were visual jokes, puns, and mnemonic motifs.

Js (1985); J.Walker (1992)

symbol 1. Representation of something, e.g. sacred, such as the elements of the Eucharist. **2.** Familiar object used mnemonically to represent acts, persons, ideas, or anything, e.g. the *Cross for Christianity, the means by which a Saint was martyred (*attribute*) (such as the grid-

iron for **St Lawrence** (d. AD 258), the flaying-knife for **St Bartholomew** (d. AD 50), a dove for the **Holy Spirit**). **3.** Something representing what it is, unlike an *allegory* (a description of a subject under the guise of some other subject of aptly suggestive resemblance: it represents something it itself is not).

G.Ferguson (1961)

Symbolism Artistic movement that flourished in the late C19 as a reaction to *French Impressionism* and *Realism* in painting. The poet **Jean Moréas** (1856–1910) published a manifesto (1886) in which he stated the essential aim of art was to clothe ideas in sensual forms and to resolve the dichotomy between the real and the spiritual world. In painting this often gave expression to mysticism and occultism and the idea that line and colour could express ideas by suggestion and evolution rather than by depiction or description. Symbolist painting was often full of *femme-fatale*-and-death imagery, the erotic, the occult, the diseased, and the decadent. Among Symbolist painters may be mentioned **Arnold Böcklin** (1827–1901), **Ferdinand Hodler** (1853–1918), **Gustave Moreau** (1826–1980), and **Franz von Stuck** (1863–1928). In architecture it was associated with *Art Nouveau and *Expressionism. Perhaps its greatest architectural exponents were *Steiner and van de *Velde.

Cassou (1984); COF (1988); J.T (1996)

symmetry 1. Exact correspondence of parts on either side of an axis, e.g. Greek *temple. **2.** Harmony, proportion, or uniformity between the parts of a building and its whole.

synagogue Building or place of meeting for Jewish worship and religious instruction. Early surviving examples have affinities with Roman *basilicas, with the Ark of the Covenant containing the Scrolls of the Law placed in a *niche or an *apse. Stylistically, Western synagogues conformed to the period and place where they were erected, although late-C19 examples tended to favour a round-arched *Byzantine-*Romanesque style, sometimes with orientalizing detail, especially in Germany and England (e.g. Prince's Road, Toxteth, Liverpool, Synagogue (1874–82) by **George Ashdowne Audsley** (1838–1925)). Many fine examples of *timber-framed synagogues existed in Poland before the 1939–45 war, but the destruction of synagogues during the Nazi domination of Europe was catastrophic.

Chiat (1982); Krinsky (1996); Meek (1994); W.Pa (1887)

synclastic Refers to a surface with the same kind of convex or concave curvature in all directions through all points (as in a hemispherical *dome). *See also* ANTICLASTIC.

synthronus (*pl.* **synthroni**) Joint throne of the Bishop and Presbyters, usually a semicircular row of seats with the *cathedra in the middle behind the* altar in the *apse of an *Early-Christian or *Byzantine church, or disposed on the *bema.

Syrian arch *See* ARCH.

Syrkus, Helena (1900–82) and **Szymon** (1893–1967) Polish architects, they rebuilt (1947–8) the Śleszyńskich Palace, Warsaw, after its destruction in the 1939–45 war. They were better-known, however, for their *International-Modernist buildings of which may be mentioned the apartment-block, *Ul. Waleczynch* (1930—with exaggerated 'functionalist imagery'), and various housing-estates (e.g. *Osiedle Koło WSM* (1947–56), *Osiedle Praga I* (1948–52), and *Osiedle Rakowiec* (1931–6—with others), etc.).

Chrościcki & Rottermund (1977)

Systems architecture 1. Architecture based on prefabricated systems and components variously arranged. **2.** Architecture derived from supposedly logical, rational, analytical procedures related to computerized design (from which unmeasurable aspects of architecture are perforce excluded). **3.** Architecture designed as part of greater (e.g. cultural, social, and urban) systems. In this sense it has been related to *performance-design* based on an analysis of function as well as on the aesthetic, physical, and psychological needs of the users. Fashionable in the 1960s, it has not proved to be the all-purpose solution hoped for by its protagonists.

AD, **xlvl/5** (May 1976); Ehrenkrantz (1989); Finnimore (1989); Handler (1970)

systyle *See* INTERCOLUMNIATION.

t'a _or_ **taa** Chinese name for a *pagoda, probably derived from a *stupa, and occurring in *Chinoiserie work.

tab *Ear, or means of securing a rainwater-pipe to a wall.

tabby Gravel, *lime, and crushed oyster- or mussel-shells mixed with water, forming a type of *concrete.

tabernacle **1.** Portable *shrine, originally a curtained tent, containing the Jewish Ark of the Covenant. **2.** Cupboard with doors containing the consecrated Host on an *altar. **3.** *Pyx. **4.** Canopied *niche containing an image. **5.** Shrine or canopied tomb. **6.** *Baldacchino or *ciborium. **7.** Place of worship distinguished from a church, e.g. meeting-house, especially one with no architectural pretensions, for Nonconformist Protestants. _Tabernacle-work_ is any ornate *openwork *Gothic *canopy over a *cathedra, *choir-stalls, funerary monuments, niches, shrines, etc.

tabia, tapia, tappia Wall-construction of earth *rammed in *formwork, often with added *lime and gravel, finished with several coats of limewash.

table **1.** Flat broad *slab, as on a medieval *altar where it forms the *mensa or top. **2.** Any flat, distinctive, rectangular surface or *panel on a wall, often charged with inscriptions, painting, or sculpture. **3.** *Altar-frontal or -retable. **4.** Protestant *communion-table. **5.** Any horizontal *moulding, e.g. *band, *cornice, or *string-course, usually with a defining word, e.g. *base-table, *corbel-table, etc. _Other connected terms include:_
tabled: **1.** with a flat smooth surface; **2.** *coped or with a horizontal moulding;
table-stone: large, flat stone, as on a *dolmen or _table-tomb_;
table-tomb: **1.** funerary monument consisting of a stone slab supported on e.g. *colonnettes, common in C17 and C18; **2.** *dolmen;
tabling: *cope.

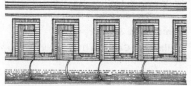

table (5) Romanesque label-table, St Julian's (mostly destroyed), Norwich (_after Parker_).

tablet **1.** Small slab or *panel set into or attached to a wall or other large mass, often framed, and carrying an inscription, usually commemorative. **2.** Horizontal capping or *coping. _See also_ TABLE. _Compounds include:_
tablet-flower: *Second-Pointed ornament like a four-petalled flower, probably a variant on *ballflower;
tablet-tomb: *loculus in a *catacomb or *hypogeum sealed with a tablet.

tablinum, tabulinum Large room in a Roman house connected to the *atrium, often serving as a *vestibule.

tabula **1.** *Niche or cupboard. **2.** Metal or wooden *altar-frontal. A _tabula rasa_ is a *tablet from which the inscription is erased, ready to be written upon again, and can also mean obliteration of history and collective memory.

tabulatum **1.** Floor or *storey. **2.** Timber floor, *wainscot, ceiling, etc. **3.** *Balcony or other projection.

TAC (The Architects' Collaborative) Founded (1945) in the USA by *Gropius: works included the Harvard Graduate Center, Cambridge, MA (1949).

Gropius & Harkness (eds) (1966)

Taché, Eugène-Étienne (1836–1912) Canadian architect of the _Hôtel du Parlement_ (1876–87—based on a plan derived from *Fuller's Ottawa Parliament-Building, but with elevations in a French *Second-Empire style, drawing on precedents from the Louvre, Paris), the Court-House (1883–7—also Second Empire), and the Armoury Building (1884–8—in the *château* style), all in Québec City.

K (1994); J.T (1996)

Tachibana-no-Tohshitsuna (1028–94) Japanese poet/courtier, credited with compiling the *Sakuteiki* (Records of Garden-Making), an account of the main styles of garden-design, defining them as aesthetic endeavours based on poetic feelings. Much of the *Record* is concerned with allusions to sea, water, and the placing of boulders in gardens. See JAPANESE GARDEN-DESIGN.

Kuitert (2002); Takei & Keane (2001)

taenia, tenia See DORIC ORDER.

Tagliaventi, Gabriele (1960–) See NEW CLASSICISM.

tailloir *Abacus, esp. in the *Ionic *Order.

Tait, Thomas Smith (1882–1954) Scots architect, he became (1904) chief draughtsman to J.J. *Burnet, with whom he worked on Kodak House, Kingsway, London (1910–12—an important essay in *stripped Classicism), and the noble Neo-Classical extension to the British Museum (completed 1914). Burnet made him his partner (1918), and the firm designed several buildings, including the Graeco-Egyptian *Art-Deco Adelaide House, London Bridge (1920–5). For a time Tait was strongly influenced by American *Beaux-Arts Classicism, but, with **Frederick McManus** (1903–85), he designed several flat-roofed houses (e.g. Silver End, near Braintree, Essex (1926–8), influenced partly by *Behrens's house for **Wenman Joseph Bassett-Lowke** (1877–1953) at Northampton, and partly by the work of *Dudok), which, with other houses at Tydehams, Newbury, Berks., and Aldbourne, Wilts. (all built 1927–30), were early British exemplars of the *International-Modern style. **Francis Lorne** (1889–1963), who, like Tait, had worked in the USA, became a partner (1930), and several distinguished buildings followed, including the Royal Masonic Hospital, Ravenscourt Park, London (1930–3—where Dutch-American influences are obvious), and the very fine St Andrew's House, Edinburgh (1930–9). Tait was consultant architect for the *Daily Telegraph* building, Fleet Street, London (1927–9), which has *Art-Deco Graeco-Egyptian detailing. Tait was one of the first-ranking architects of the period 1910–39.

GMcW & W (1984); J.T (1996); WRH (1990)

Takeyama, Minoru (1934–86) See ARCHITEXT.

Talenti, Francesco (c.1300–69) Florentine architect, he worked at Orvieto Cathedral (1320s) before succeeding *Pisano at Florence Cathedral (c.1343), where he completed the upper stages of the *campanile*, continued (1351–68) building the

*nave, and helped to finalize the design of the east end, including the octagon. His son, **Simone di Francesco Talenti** (c.1330/5–after 1383), also worked at the *Duomo*, and designed the ground-floor *arcade of Or San Michele (1360s), but his most celebrated building is the *Loggia dei Lanzi*, *Piazza della Signoria*, Florence (1376–81), with **Benci di Clone** (fl. 1337–81) et al.

Kr (1974); P (1982); J.T (1996); M.Tg (1971); White (1987)

tall buildings See SKYSCRAPER.

tallet, tallot, tallus, tallut, talus, talut
1. *Batter, so a *tallus-wall* is a battered *retaining-wall, esp. in fortifications. 2. Any space beneath the pitched roof of a building. 3. Hay-loft.

Talman, John (1677–1726) English architect/artist, son of William *Talman, he spent much of his life recording buildings: on one of his expeditions (1709) to Italy he was accompanied by *Kent, and made a large collection of drawings, while developing contacts with connoisseurs and *virtuosi*. He seems to have supplied images of Italian buildings to several personages, including *Aldrich, and so may have played some part in the *second Palladian Revival* (see PALLADIANISM).

Co (2008); *ODNB* (2004); W.Pa (1892); J.T (1996)

Talman, William (1650–1719) English gentleman-architect, he rose to eminence during the *Restoration period and became (1689) Comptroller of the Works to **King William III** (r.1689–1702). He designed several large *Baroque country-houses in which both French and Italian influences were apparent, favouring *Giant Orders of *pilasters and *entablatures to frame his elevations. Chatsworth House, Derbys., where Talman rebuilt (1687–96) the south and east fronts for **William Cavendish** (1640–1707—**4th Earl** (from 1684) and **1st Duke** (from 1694) **of Devonshire**), heralded a majestic series of houses, including the Baroque redecoration of the interior of Burghley House, near Stamford, Lincs. (c.1688–90), Uppark, Sussex (c.1690—restored 1990–3), the east front of Dyrham Park, Glos. (1698–1704), interiors of the State Apartments and layout of gardens at Hampton Court Palace, Mddx. (1699–1702—where he attempted to undermine *Wren's position), and the south front of Drayton House, Northants. (1702). In the last, he almost achieved greatness with an exquisitely articulated building. He probably contributed more than has been credited to the design of Easton Neston, Northants. (c.1695–1702—usually attributed wholly to *Hawksmoor). Talman was dismissed (1702) from his official posts and fell out of favour with the rise of *Vanbrugh and Hawksmoor.

CL, cxcix/34 (25 Aug. 2005), 52–5; Co (2008); J.Hs (1982); *JWCI*, xviii (1955), 123–39; *ODNB* (2004); J.T (1996)

talon *As* OGEE.

talus, tallus *See* TALLET.

tambour 1. Section of column-*shaft when the latter is composed of *drums. 2. *Bell, ground, or *vase of a *Composite or *Corinthian *capital. 3. *Rotunda, or any circular building, e.g. drum supporting a *cupola. 4. Wall of any circular structure.

Tange, Kenzo (1913–2005) Japanese architect, he joined (1938) *Maekawa's office, where he absorbed influences of Le *Corbusier, but (early 1940s) he began to draw on allusions to traditional Japanese architecture, and won (1949) the competition for the Hiroshima Peace Centre Community Centre and Museum (1949–56), his first major building, which was presented (1951) to *CIAM and announced his arrival on the international architectural scene. Tange developed forms using up-to-date technology, and quickly achieved status as a leader of the *Modern Movement in his country, arguing for a synthesis between Japanese and Western design. His Kagawa Prefectural Offices, Takamatsu (1955–8), relied for its effect on the expression of posts and beams, but the Sports Arena, Takamatsu (1962–4), and St Mary's RC Cathedral, Tokyo (1961–4), were more dynamic, the last with a basic cruciform plan and paraboloids superimposed. His National Gymnasium, Tokyo (1961–4), seating 15,000 people, was protected by a *tensile *catenary roof-structure.

Tange's works included a design for the expansion of Tokyo based on rapid-transit systems, areas of high-density housing, and a major extension of the urban fabric into the sea at Tokyo Bay (published 1960). He also developed schemes for multi-purpose blocks linked in various ways: his Yamanashi Press and Broadcasting Centre, Kofu (1964–7), had 16 cylindrical services- and stair-towers acting as huge columns, with floors spanning between them. This, and the Tokyo plan, were potent influences on *Metabolism. His 1970s designs developed strong affinities with architecture in Europe and the USA: the dynamism of his earlier work was superseded by a refinement of detail, and later buildings included various Embassies (1974–7), Tokyo Prince Hotel (1983–7), City Hall Complex (1986–92), and United Nations University (1990–2), all in Tokyo, and the Japanese Embassy, México City (1976–7). He obliquely criticized *Functionalism, stating that only the beautiful can be functional.

Altherr (1968); R. (1976); Bettinotti (ed.) (1996); Bo (1985, 1995); Borrás (1975); R.Boyd (1962); E (1994); Kulturmann (ed.) (1970); Kulturmann *et al.* (1989); Miyake *et al.* (eds) (1989); Mühll *et al.* (1978); P (1982); Tange (1960, 1970); A.White (1990)

Tanner, Sir Henry (1849–1935) English architect/surveyor, pupil of *Salvin. From 1884 he was responsible for buildings for the post- and tele-graph-services, designing York Probate Registry and Post Office (1885), followed by similar buildings in Bradford, Liverpool, Leicester, and other towns, often with French-*Renaissance touches, but he also worked in *Tudor and *Jacobean styles. His best work was probably the western extension (1908–12) of *Street's Law Courts in The Strand, London, and he was a pioneer in the use of *reinforced concrete, as in the King Edward Building of the General Post Office (1907–10—employing *Hennebique's system in what was then the largest *ferro-concrete building in the world). His son, **Henry Tanner** (1876–1947) ran a prosperous architectural practice, designing several buildings for **J.Lyons & Co. Ltd.**, including the Regent Palace Hotel (1912–15), which acquired splendid *Art-Deco interiors (1934–5) by Oliver *Bernard.

BD (25 Nov. 2011), 11–13; *ODNB* (2004)

T'ao Yuan-ming, aka **T'ao Qian** (365–427) Chinese pastoral poet, he extolled Chinese landscapes and celebrated flowers (notably the chrysanthemum, the flower of retirement and culture).

Davis (1983); Sirén (1949); Shoe (2001)

taper Gradual *diminution in width or thickness in any elongated object towards one extremity or another, e.g. *herm, *obelisk, *spire, or *term. Column-*shafts properly do not taper, as they diminish with height not in a straight taper but a curved *entasis.

tapia *See* TABIA.

Tapper, Sir Walter John (1861–1935) English architect, he worked with *Champneys and then *Bodley & Garner. Although he opened an office in London (1893) he did not leave Bodley until 1901. His churches include the Ascension, Malvern Link, Worcs. (1903), St Mary's, Harrogate, Yorks. (1904), St Erkenwald, Southend-on-Sea, Essex (1905–10), and a large extension to St Michael's, Little Coates, Grimsby, Lincs. (1913). Much of his work was in brick, handled with great integrity, and his style was generally *Arts-and-Crafts *Gothic. He designed exquisite church-furnishings, including the beautiful additions to Sir Arthur *Blomfield's 1883 *reredos in St Wulfram's, Grantham, Lincs. (1901), but in later life he became more of a Classicist, as with the Memorial Carillon Tower, Loughborough, Leics. (1921).

A.S.Gray (1985)

tarmac Mixed material for making roads, *paths, etc., consisting of broken stones or ironstone slag in a matrix of tar, or tar with pitch or creosote.

tarsia *Inlaid wood, usually light on dark, common in the *Renaissance period, and featuring *arabesque or *scroll-work, but especially representing paintings in *perspective, e.g. in *Santa Maria Organo*, Verona (C15).

tas-de-charge 1. Lowest *courses of a group of *Gothic *vault-*ribs, bonded with the wall, forming a solid mass, and receiving the weight of the ribs and panel-work above. 2. In an arch or vault, the lowest *voussoir.

tatami Japanese straw floor-mat. Multiples of its dimensions provided the proportions and sizes of traditional rooms.

Tatham, Charles Heathcote (1772–1842) English architect, he worked for S.P.*Cockerell and then for Henry *Holland who helped him to visit Italy (1794). There, he met many aristocrats/ gentry on the *Grand Tour, including **Frederick Howard** (1748–1825—**5th Earl of Carlisle** from 1758), who became one of his main patrons. He made a study of *Antique remains and ornament, later published as *Etchings of Ancient Ornamental Architecture*, etc. (1799–1800) and *Etchings Representing Fragments of Grecian and Roman Ornaments* (1806) which were used internationally as sourcebooks for Neo-Classical design, notably by *Hope, *Percier, and *Fontaine. His sculpture-gallery at Castle Howard, Yorks. (1800–2), was an exercise in his severe *Neo-Classicism, but his masterpiece is the *primitive Graeco-Egyptian *mausoleum at Trentham, Staffs. (1807–8), one of the most formidable Neo-Classical essays in England. He also designed a mausoleum at Ochtertyre, Perthshire (1809—*Gothic).

Co (2008); *CL*, cli/3905 (13 & 20 Apr. 1972), 918–21, and cli/3912 (8 Jun. 1972), 1481–6; J.Curl (2005, 2011a); *ODNB* (2004); W.Pa (1892)

Tatlin, Vladimir Evgrafovich (1885–1953) Ukrainian painter/sculptor. Influenced by *Cubism and *Futurism he became one of the main protagonists of *Constructivism from 1913. His project (only realized as a large model) for a monument to the Third International (1919–20) consisted of a steel double-helical structure over 400 metres high, with rotating glass buildings containing administrative, legislative, and propaganda facilities for the *Komintern*. Intended as a symbol of 'progress' and technology (based on images of fairground structures and oil-derricks, and painted bright red), this proposal became a paradigm for architects such as *Leonidov, El *Lissitzky, and *Vesnin, and was admired in Western *avant-garde* circles, latterly among those associated with *Deconstructivism.

Andersen (ed.) (1968); J.Harten (ed.) (1993); Milner (1983); P (1982); Punina & Rakitin (1994); Strigalev & J.Harten (eds) (1993); J.T (1996); Zhadova (ed.) (1988)

Tatsuno, Kingo (1854–1919) Japanese architect, one of the first to study abroad (e.g. with *Burges in London). Influenced by Norman *Shaw, he often used red brick with white-stone *dressings. Among his best works were various buildings for the Bank of Japan (Tokyo (1903), Kyoto (1906), and Osaka (1911)), and Tokyo Central Station (1914—partly destroyed).

Ck (1996); P (1982); J.T (1996)

tauriform *Bucranium.

Taut, Bruno Julius Florian (1880–1938) German architect, he worked with Theodor *Fischer (1904–8), then with **Franz Hoffmann** (d.1950), designing several works before gaining critical attention with his Steel Industry Pavilion, International Building Trades Exhibition, Leipzig (1913). In that year he met Adolf *Behne and Paul *Scheerbart, whose ideas about glass in architecture influenced Taut, whose brother, **Max**, joined the firm (1914), which became **Brothers Taut & Hoffmann**. Taut also became adviser to the German *Garden-City movement. At the *Werkbund* Exhibition, Cologne (1914), his polygonal Glass Pavilion with dome-like roof (constructed of a *space-frame with diamond-shaped glass panels) employed glass of various forms and colours, and water-*cascades as well. It caused a sensation, and was his most celebrated work, an Expressionist paradigm.

During the 1914–18 war he published Pacifist polemical works, some of which came out as *Alpin Architektur* (1919), showing the Alps redesigned, as a gigantic task of construction, the antithesis of destructive war. A founding-member of *Arbeitsrat für Kunst* and the *Novembergruppe* in the aftermath of war, he became a leading light of the *avant-garde*, exercising influence through various writings and bodies including the *Gläserne Kette*. However, his utopian and Expressionist tendencies withered as he turned more to *Rationalism from 1921, when he became Director of Building and Planning in Magdeburg. He returned to Berlin (1924), where he designed many huge *Modern-Movement housing-schemes, including the 'Uncle Tom Cabin' development, set among pine-forests at Berlin-Zehlendorf (with *Häring et al.—1926–31) and the *Hufeisensiedlung* (so called after its plan-form), Britz, Berlin-Neukölln (with Martin *Wagner—1925–30).

Taut left Germany (1932), settling first in the Soviet Union (until 1933), then Japan (where he wrote *Houses and People of Japan* (1937) among other works), and finally (1937) Turkey, where he designed various buildings, his own house, and schools in Ankara (1938). His publications were many.

AdK (1963, 1980); Bletter (1979); Boyd Whyte (1982, 1985); Conrads (ed.) (1970); C & S (1960); Wi.Cu (1996); Gisbertz (2000); Junghanns (1970, 1998); Lane (1985); Ne (2001); Offermann (ed.) (1993); Pehnt (1973); Pitz & Brenne (1980); Sharp (1967); Sharp (ed.) (1972); Speidel (ed.) (1995); B.Taut (1920, 1924, 1927, 1929, 1929a, 1930, 1934, 1939, 1958, 1972, 1977); B.Taut (ed.) (1963); B.Taut et al. (1919)

Taut, Max (1884–1967) German architect, he joined his brother, **Bruno**, and **Franz Hoffmann** (d.1950) in partnership (1914), and remained with Hoffmann until the last's death: his designs included a Pavilion for the International Building Trades Exhibition, Leipzig (1913). A founder (1918) of various left-wing groups, including *Arbeitsrat für Kunst, *Novembergruppe, and later Der *Ring, he contributed to Bruno Taut's *Gläserne-Kette group and built the extraordinary Wissinger family-vault, Stahnsdorf, Berlin (1920), one of the few realized Glass-Chain designs. Other works included offices for the Allgemeiner Deutscher Gewerkschaftsbund (1923) and various buildings for trade-unions and similar organizations, one of which (the Verband der Deutschen Buchdrucker—1922–5) he designed with Mart *Stam, where the *concrete *frame was expressed. *International-Modernist style structures by him were two houses at the *Weissenhofsiedlung, Stuttgart (1927), the German Trade Union Building, Frankfurt-am-Main (1931), and the Co-operative Department Store, Berlin (1932). After the 1939–45 war he was active as an architect/teacher, designing the Reuter Housing, Bonn (1949–52), the August-Thiessen Siedlung, Duisburg (1955–64), and an extension to his brother's Hufeisensiedlung, Berlin-Neukölln (1954). He was important in the evolution of *Neue Sachlichkeit.

AdK (1964); Kühne et al. (1984); Posener (1964); Rehm (2002); J.T (1996); M.Taut (1927, 1984); WMfB, xvi (1932), 257–69

tavern See PUBLIC-HOUSE.

Tayler, Herbert (1912–2000) British architect of Scots-Dutch descent. From 1938 he and **David John Green** (1912–98) became professional and domestic partners, and, as **Tayler & Green**, they designed The Studio, Duke's Head Yard, Highgate (1937–40), before moving (1941) to Lowestoft, Suffolk, taking over the practice of Green's father. Two small local-authority housing developments in villages followed (1943), prototypes of the 700-odd houses built for Loddon Council, Norfolk (1945–73), profoundly influenced by Swedish exemplars, so the firm was associated with *New Humanism.

AR, cxxiv (1958), 226–36; Harwood & Powers (1998); ODNB (2004)

Taylor, George Ledwell (1788–1873) English architect. Articled (1804) to **James T.Parkinson** (fl.c.1800–40), he was involved in the building of Montague and Bryanston Squares and other parts of the Portman Estate, London. He and *Cresy travelled in England, France, Italy, Greece, Malta, and Sicily (1816–19), after which they published The Architectural Antiquities of Rome . . . (1821–2, 1874) and The Architecture of the Middle Ages in Italy . . . (1829), an early work extolling Italian medieval architecture. Taylor was appointed (1824) Civil Architect to the Navy, and carried out robust and virile works at the dockyards of Chatham, Sheerness, and Woolwich, responsible also for the Clarence Victualling Yard, Gosport, Hants. (1828–32). He laid out (1840s) a large part of the Bishop of London's Estate in Paddington (e.g. Chester Place and parts of Hyde Park and Gloucester Squares). His most extraordinary work is the huge *Gothic-Revival tower of Hadlow Castle, Kent (c.1840), a *folly to almost rival *Wyatt's Fonthill in extravagance, and he pioneered the modern use of *concrete as a building material in the Proprietary School, Lee, Kent (1836—modelled on the Athenian Propylaea). He published Stones of Etruria and Marbles of Ancient Rome (1859).

Co (2008); ODNB (2004); W.Pa (1892)

Taylor, Sir Robert (1714–88) English architect, with *Chambers and *Paine one of the most gifted of his generation. After an apprenticeship (from 1732) with the sculptor **Henry Cheere** (1703–81), Taylor travelled to Italy before establishing himself in that discipline (1740s), but began practising architecture (1750s) with almost immediate success, thanks to a happy mixture of talent and hard work: it was said that Taylor and Paine divided the practice of architecture between them until Adam 'entered the lists'. He was Surveyor to the Bank of England from c.1764 and became (1769) one of the two Architects of the Office of Works. As a designer of *villas and country-houses his work was original and compact, the plans incorporating ellipses, octagons, and his favourite motif, the *canted *bay (he also favoured octagonal door-panels and window-lights): good examples are Asgill House, Richmond, Surrey (1761–4—with bold *eaves on shaped *mutules and ingeniously shaped rooms inside), and Danson Hill (now House), Bexleyheath, Kent (c.1762–7—with interior completed by *Chambers, virtually derelict for many years, but partly restored and re-opened 2005). At Purbrook House, Portsdown Hill, Hants. (1770—demolished), he designed the first revival of a Roman *atrium in an English house, and so has a place in the history of *Neo-Classicism. His finest country-houses were Heveningham Hall, Suffolk (1778–c.1780—completed by James *Wyatt, damaged (1980s)), Gorhambury, Herts.

(1777–90—later altered), and Sharpham House, Devon (*c.*1770—with a large domed elliptical stair-well). His major works at the Bank of England had segmental arches and side-lit *cupolas that clearly influenced *Soane's later works there, but Taylor's contribution to the Bank was much altered by Soane and obliterated (1921–37) by Herbert *Baker, apart from the Court Room (1767–70), which was reconstructed. He designed the Stone Buildings, Lincoln's Inn, London (1775–7), and the Assembly-Rooms in the Old Exchange, Belfast (1776—later altered by *Lanyon and *Lynn when the building became a Bank). Among other works he designed Osney Bridge, Oxon. (1767), Maidenhead Bridge, Berks. (1772–7), and the *Gothick spire of St Peter's Church, Wallingford, Berks. (1776–7). He made many designs for funerary monuments which survive, together with other material, in the Taylorian Institute, Oxford. The latter was established through Taylor's bequests to the University of Oxford. His pupils included S.P.*Cockerell and *Nash.

Binney (1984); Co (2008); *CL*, cxlii/3670 (6 Jul. 1967), 17–21, cxlii/3671 (13 Jul. 1967), 78–82; *ODNB* (2004); Roscoe *et al.* (2009); J.T (1996)

tea-garden 1. Connected with Japanese rituals in Zen Buddhism from the C15, the setting for the tea-ceremony, emphasizing the spiritual aspects, included gardens (called *roji*) associated with very simple, almost *rustic, tea-rooms as an independent building-type, separated from temples. Gardens had ground-planes of sand or gravel and moss, often with stepping-stones, and were sparingly planted to avoid distractions: they might suggest, within a very confined space, journeyings to a hermit's hut in the mountains. Parallels with C19 European concerns with rustic simplicity are hard to avoid. **2.** Fashionable garden in *Victorian times where ladies might take tea and meet friends: they sometimes contained *mazes. The idea of the European tea-garden was revived between the 1914–18 and 1939–45 wars, sited in orchards/gardens, and provided with 'rustic' furniture.

Shoe (2001); Symes (2006); Tay (2006)

Teague, Walter Dorwin (1883–1960) American industrial designer, he settled in NYC (1903), establishing (1911) his own office specializing in typographical design. He renamed his office an industrial-design firm (1926), and acquired (1927) Kodak Eastman as his client, for which he invented the Baby Brownie camera (1933–4). Other projects followed, including the Marmon Car (designed with his son, **Walter Dorwin Teague, jun.** (1910–2004)), and several *pavilions for the New York World's Fair (1939). Other works included a vast range of designs, from Schaefer beer-labels to the VIP interiors of the Boeing 707 jet. He also developed quality-control for complex missile firing-mechanisms used in the well-known *Polaris*. He analysed modern industrial civilization and the role of contemporary industrial design (1946).

ID, viii (Jan. 1961), 25–9; J.T (1996); Teague (1946)

tea-house Garden-building in which tea was drunk, eg. the C18 polygonal example at Iford Manor, Wilts.

Team X (10) Mid-C20 alliance of architects so called because they combined to organize the tenth *CIAM conference (1956). Believing CIAM had become unwieldy and vague in its aims, they argued for a revitalization of the *International *Modern Movement. Members included van *Eyck and the *Smithsons.

AD, xxxii/12 (Dec. 1962), 559–602; R.Ba (1966); Sn & Sn (1991); Sn (ed.) (1968, 1982); J.T (1996)

tebam *Rostrum or *daïs in a *synagogue.

Tecton Association of London architects established (1932) by *Lubetkin, arguably the most influential *International Modernists in the UK until 1948. Its best-known works are structures for London Zoo, Regent's Park (1932–7), including the Gorilla House (1932) and Penguin Pool (1933–4); apartment-blocks at Highgate, London, known as Highpoint I (1933–5) and II (1936–8); *slab-blocks of flats at Spa Fields, Clerkenwell, London (1939–49); and Finsbury Health Centre, London (1935–8). Tecton also designed several private houses as well as various buildings for Whipsnade Zoo, Beds., and Dudley Zoo, Staffs.

Allan (1992); Allan *et al.* (2002); Coe & Reading (1981); Gould (1977); Hancocks (1971); P (1982); J.T (1996); F.Y (1947)

Tectonic Of, or pertaining to, a building, or construction in general, and therefore, as **Gerard Baldwin Brown** (1849–1932) observed (1903), a 'form produced by the exigencies of construction,—or, to use a convenient term familiar in Germany, a tectonic form'. *Tectonics* is therefore a term for the constructive arts in general. More recently, the word suggests a constructional craft, a notion promoted by **Kenneth Brian Frampton** (1930–), who considered modern architecture to be as much about structure as it is about space and form. Drawing on French, German, and English sources from the C18 to the present, Frampton argued that constructional engineering and innovative tectonics were integral to the evolution of the work of a number of named architects, and that the ways in which these aspects were expressed from one design to another provided a basis for evaluation of an architect's *œuvre*. A *tectonic tradition* he considered to be an essential element in the development of future architectural forms and that taking it into account would mean a major re-evaluation of much supposedly *avant-garde* design.

Brown II (1903), 178; F (1980, 1982, 1995, 2002)

Teige, Karel (1900–51) Czechoslovak Communist architect/critic/polemicist, with others he founded the anti-academic *Devětsil* Group (1920) promoting *Constructivism and other aspects of *Modernism. Opposed to aesthetic considerations predetermining construction, Teige believed that medical science should dictate layout, structure, and planning 'New Architecture'. He edited (1922–8) the *avant-garde* journal *Stavba* (Building), developed relations between Czech Modernists and leading figures abroad (e.g. *Behne, Hannes *Meyer, Le *Corbusier, and the *Vesnins), and promoted housing-schemes for the proletariat, advocating 'dwelling-cabins' for each individual grouped in 'dwelling-hives', also arguing for the abolition of family households (no permanent living together of two persons in one unit was to be possible) and for the complete socializing of children's education (1932). He prepared and edited the general report *Die Wohnung für das Existenzminimum* (published (1937) in book form) for the third *CIAM Congress, Brussels. He chaired the Prague-based Left Front, which he argued was the Czech CIAM group, but its extremism caused dissent within Czechoslovakia and even in CIAM: nevertheless, municipal authorities of Prague and Brno were determined for a time to construct apartments taking into account Teige's anti-family views. However, by 1935, with Czechoslovak architects isolated, and Teige's opinion of architecture as a branch of science no longer fashionable, his influence (so strong for fifteen years or so) waned: opposed to Stalinist *Socialist Realism, he soon became a marginal figure, until the early C21, when his authoritarian Leftism appealed to new generations.

Codeluppi (ed.) (1996); Wi.Cu (1996); Dluhosch & Švácha (eds) (1999); Li (1996); Švácha (ed.) (1990); Teige (1933, 2002)

telamon (*pl.* **telamones**) Straight, *unbowed* male whole figure acting as a column supporting an *entablature on its head. *See also* ATLAS; CANEPHORA; CARYATID; PERSIAN.

Telford, Thomas (1757–1834) Scots mason/surveyor/architect/engineer of genius, employed on the building of Edinburgh New Town before he moved to London (1782). Through the good offices of **Sir William Pulteney, Bt.** (1729–1805), MP for Shrewsbury, Salop., he was employed to carry out certain works in that town, including alterations to the Castle (1787). He built (1787–93) the County Gaol there to designs by **John Hiram Haycock** (1759–1830) with modifications by **John Howard** (*c.*1726–90), the prison-reformer, designed the robust Neo-Classical St Mary's Church, Bridgnorth (1792–4) and the utilitarian octagonal St Michael's, Madeley (1794–6), and pioneered the use of iron for the construction of *bridges (he was Surveyor of Bridges to the County of Shropshire) with his handsome structure at Buildwas (1795–6—demolished), all Salop. His *canal *aqueducts at Longdon, Salop. (1793–4), Pont-y-Cysyllte, near Llangollen, Wales (1795–1805), and Chirk, Denbighshire (1796–1801), are among the finest such structures in the world. Telford designed more than 1,000 bridges, including the Menai (1819–26) and Conway (1821–6) *suspension-bridges, Caernarfonshire, Wales, Craigellachie iron bridge, Banffshire, Scotland (1814–15), and arched bridges at Bewdley, Worcs. (1797–9), Dunkeld, Perthshire, Scotland (1806–9), and Dean, Edinburgh (1829–31). His works as a road- and canal-builder and his designs for harbours and docks (including works at Wick, Caithness (from 1808), Aberdeen, Peterhead, Banff, Leith, and the very important St Katherine Docks, London (1825–8—with severe brick warehouses by *Hardwick (mostly demolished)), were among the most accomplished ever made. He was responsible for over 30 churches and *manses in the Scottish Highlands (1825–34), including those at Acharacle, Ardgour, Portnahaven, and Strontian (all in Argyll), and Ullapool (Ross-shire). He laid out Pulteney Model Town, near Wick, Caithness (1808).

Co (2008); N (1835); *ODNB* (2004); Penfold (ed.) (1980); Rolt (1958); Sk (2002); Smiles (1862); Telford (1838); Thorne (ed.) (1990)

Telmo, José Ângelo Cottinelli (1897–1948) *See* COTTINELLI.

Temanza, Tommaso (1705–89) Venetian architect, his work was Palladian, including the *façade of *Santa Margherita*, Padua (*c.*1750), and the exquisite *Santa Maria Maddalena*, Venice (1760–79—in which influences from the *Pantheon in Rome and *Palladio's chapel at Maser can be discerned). He published *Delle antichità di Rimino* (1741) and biographies of various architects, collected later as *Vite dei Più Celebri Architetti e Scultori Veneziani* (1778), a scholarly work on Venetian architecture and sculpture. He promoted Neo-Classical principles, as is clear from his *Antica pianta dell' inclita città di Venezia* (1781).

D.Howard (1980); Ms (1966); P (1982); Valle (1989); Wi (1982)

temenos Sacred enclosed precinct around a Greek *temple, etc.

temperate house *Conservatory for plants requiring some heat, but not as much as in a *hot-house.

tempietto Small *Renaissance *temple, often circular, e.g. *Bramante's *tempietto* in the *cloister of *San Pietro in Montorio*, Rome (*c.*1510).

template, templet 1. *Pad-stone or any block of timber or stone, or a metal plate, placed beneath the end of a *girder, *truss, etc., to distribute the load, especially the timber block placed under the foot of a *cruck-*blade. **2.** Mould, outline, or pattern to ensure accuracy when forming a profile or *moulding. **3.** *Beam or *lintel.

temple 1. Building for pagan religious observances, or the dwelling-place of a deity. The word was applied to sacred buildings of the Ancient-Egyptians, Greeks, Romans, and others. The *Antique Classical temple was usually rectangular, and consisted of a *cella (*naos in Greek), *sanctuary, and *portico. Greek temples were commonly surrounded by columns (*peristyle) supporting an *entablature, with a *pediment at each end (e.g. C5 BC *Parthenon*, Athens), but sometimes had a portico at each end (*amphiprostyle*) with plain walls (e.g. C5 BC temple of *Niké Apteros*, Athens). Roman temples usually had a deep portico at one end (derived from Etruscan exemplars), a plain *cella* (sometimes with *engaged columns, e.g. C1 BC *Maison Carrée*, Nîmes), and were built on high *podia. Circular buildings of the *tholos* type were built by both the Greeks and Romans (e.g. C1 BC temple of Vesta, Tivoli). Terms used to describe arrangements of columns are described elsewhere (*see* ANTA; COLONNADE; INTERCOLUMNIATION; PORTICO). **2.** *Synagogue. **3.** French Protestant church, or any building for public worship by Nonconformist Protestant sects, especially a large or grand structure. **4.** Mormon place of worship. **5.** Sacred edifice in Jerusalem, seat of the Jewish worship of Jehovah, especially the Temple of Solomon. **6.** Headquarters of the Knights Templars, or a place once occupied by a preceptory of the Tem-

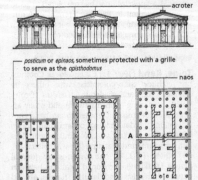

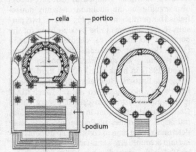

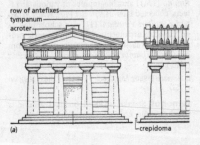

temple (*a*) Greek-Doric *prostyle-tetrastyle* temple-front: note the *anta* terminating the cell wall. (*b*) Various types of Greek-Doric temple plans: (*left*) *peripteral hexastyle*, i.e. with colonnades surrounding the cell, six columns at each end forming the porticoes and carrying the pediments; (*middle*) *pseudo-peripteral septostyle* (or *heptastyle*), i.e. with all columns engaged with the temple walls, and seven engaged columns at each end, resulting in entrances off-centre; (*right*) A half-plan, *dipteral octastyle*, i.e. with two rows of columns surrounding the cell, eight at each end forming the porticoes and carrying the pediments; and B half-plan, *pseudo-dipteral octastyle*, i.e. with a wider space between the walls of the cell and the peristyle, with eight columns at each end forming the porticoes and carrying the pediments. This wide space suggests that further colonnades ought to stand behind the outer ones. (*c*) Plan of Roman 'Temple of Venus', Baalbek, Lebanon (AD C3), showing typical arrangement of podium, portico, and steps, used for a circular structure. (*d*) Plan of Temple of Vesta, Tivoli (*c.* 80 BC), showing circular peristyle.

plars (as in London and Paris). **7.** Building with architectural pretensions for special ritual use, as a Freemasonic *Lodge, related to the Temple of Solomon. *Compounds include*:

temple-front: element of a *façade resembling the front of a Classical temple, with columns or *pilasters carrying an entablature and pediment, applied to an *elevation, as in a *Palladian composition with portico (e.g. *Aldrich's Peckwater *Quad, Christ Church, Oxford (1707–14));

temple-tower: high platform, often stepped, with a temple on top, e.g. in *Meso-American architecture or the Mesopotamian *ziggurat.

Temple, Raymond du (*fl.*1359–1403/4) French master-mason under **Kings Charles V** and **VI** (*r.*1364–1422) of France. He worked (from 1363) at *Notre Dame*, Paris, supervised the building of the *Célestins* Chapel (1367–70—fragments remain), and built (1370s) the celebrated *Vis du Louvre*, an external spiral *stair, one of the first monumental stairs in Western Europe. He was involved in the design and building of the *Collège de Beauvais*, Paris (from 1387), but little of his work survives.

W.Pa (1892); S (1901–2); J.T (1996)

Temple, Sir William, Bt. (1628–99) English diplomat/author/garden-theorist, he created a garden at Moor Park, Herts., containing an early example of *Sharawadgi* (a topic on which he wrote in his *Upon the Gardens of Epicurus*) in the *wilderness through which wound *serpentine *paths. With *Bacon and *Wotton he was receptive to the idea of making visible countryside beyond the garden for aesthetic reasons, anticipating C18 developments. He also advocated creating 'wildernesses' to deceive onlookers to believe they were real *thickets.

H & W (1988); Nourse (1700); Sieveking (ed.) (1908); Temple (1690)

tenaille Low outwork consisting of one or two re-entrant angles in front of the *curtain-wall between *bastions.

tenaillon Work in a fortification strengthening the sides of a *ravelin.

Tendenza 1960s *Neo-Rationalist architectural movement that rose to eminence (1970s), led by *Aymonino, **Mario Botta** (1943–), **Giorgio Grassi** (1935–), **Bruno Reichlin** (1941–), **Fabio Reinhart** (1942–), and Aldo *Rossi, associated with the Swiss Canton of Ticino. It recognized the social and cultural significance of established urban fabric, the importance of historical forms and elements as resources, and the need for architecture to be redefined in terms of rules and *types. Opposed to the inflated pretensions of *Functionalism, the vulgar popularism of *High

Tech, and increasing commercialization by those seen as having betrayed architecture, a return to academic theories propounded by *Quatremère de Quincy and others was proposed. A good example of realized works is Grassi's student residences, Chieti (1976), which drew on proposals by *Weinbrenner (1808). *See also* NEO-RATIONALISM; RATIONAL ARCHITECTURE; TICINESE SCHOOL.

Bonfanti *et al.* (1973); Botta (1991, 1997); B-M (1989); Dal Co (1987); G.Grassi (1982, 1989); Petit (1994); Pizzi (ed.) (1994–8, 1997); A.Ro (1982); A.Ro *et al.* (1973); S & B (1975); Sakellaridou (2000); J.T (1996); Wrede (1986)

tendril Architectural ornament resembling plant-like tendrils, in Classical architecture associated with *acanthus, *anthemion, and *palmette. It recurs in *Celtic and *Anglo-Saxon ornament, medieval grapevine or *trail, *Renaissance and *Mannerist *arabesque and *grotesque, *Art-Nouveau *whiplash and derivations from Celtic and *Norse ornament, and many other styles in various guises and variations.

Gh (2000); T-M (1967)

tenement 1. Land or real property, e.g. a building. **2.** Dwelling. **3.** Portion of a house, or an *apartment or flat tenanted separately. **4.** Block of purpose-built flats.

Tengbom, Ivar Justus (1878–1968) Swedish architect, one of the most influential of his time, he evolved a simplified *Neo-Classicism in the inter-war period, as exemplified in his Concert House, Stockholm (1923–8), in which the building became a blocky mass fronted by a huge *portico of attenuated stripped columns, the whole reminiscent of the work of *Behrens. Early works, e.g. Högalid Church, Stockholm (1911–23), were often in the *National-Romantic style inaugurated by Östberg at the Stockholm City Hall (1909), but Tengbom himself was more influenced by *Nyrop and *Wahlman. Other important buildings include the School of Economics (1925–6) and the Match Company Offices (1926–8), both in Stockholm, and the Swedish Institute of Classical Studies, Rome (1937–40).

A & B (1986); Ahlberg (1925); *AmA*, **cxl**/2598 (1931), 32–7, 98–100; *By*, **vi** (1941), 69–75, **xiv** (1944), 239–60; Ca (1998); T.Hall (ed.) (1981); Östberg (1908); P (1982); Pn (1982); Rasmussen (1940); J.T (1996)

tenia *See* DORIC ORDER.

tenon 1. Projection at the end of a timber, of smaller transverse *section than the timber, so with a shoulder, fitted into a corresponding hole or *mortice in another piece, e.g. timber *door. **2.** Projecting stone at the end of a wall. *See also* TOOTHING-STONES; TUSK.

Tensile architecture Structure formed mostly of components acting in *tension* rather than *compression*: it might include *tents, suspension-bridges, and *suspended roofs (all types where *weight* can determine the *form* of the structure and its very *stability*); *prestressed* membranes and cable-roofs (where form and stability derive from forces in tension created by stressing); and *pneumatic structures (which depend on air to support surfaces in tension). C20 tensile architecture evolved from the design of suspension-bridges (e.g. those by *Brunel and *Roebling): early uses of suspension-bridge technology for buildings were pioneered by **Bedřich Schnirch** (1791-1868) in the 1820s in the then Austrian provinces of Bohemia, Moravia, and Slovakia; in the Naval Arsenal, Lorient, France (1840s); and in the steel pavilions of the All-Russian Exhibition, Nizhny-Novgorod (1895) by **Vladimir Grigor'evich Shukhov** (1853-1939—who also designed the Shabolovskaya Radio Tower, Moscow (1919-22), a parallel to *Tatlin's monument to the Third International. Indeed, nothing like Shukhov's pioneering tent-like structures and suspended roofs was to emerge again until the 1950s. Experimental tensile structures of the 1920s include *Fuller's Dymaxion House (1927-30), and although various proposals were made in the 1930s, there were few examples (e.g. the French Pavilion, Zagreb Fair (1935), designed by **Bernard Lafaille** (1900-55)), largely because the *imagery* demanded by the *International-Style cult inhibited any straying from approved *clichés*. Developments during the 1939-45 war led to a further understanding of tension structures, and this was demonstrated in a series of buildings in which suspended roofs were exploited (e.g. *Saarinen's Dulles International Airport Terminal, Chantilly, VA (1958-63)). *Nervi used a suspension system for the roof of his paper-making factory at Mantua (1961-3), and there were various experiments with structures supported by cable-stays, decks carried from cables hung from masts, and other systems. Tensioned structures using cables were employed by *Nowicki (e.g. Dorton Arena, NC (1948-53)), Saarinen (e.g. David S.Ingalls Hockey Rink, Yale University, New Haven, CT (1953-9)), and *Tange (e.g. National Gymnasia, Tokyo (1961-4)). However, using the tent as his precedent, **Frei Otto** (1925-2015) departed from the suspension-bridge principle with numerous designs (1950s, 1960s), including buildings for the Olympic Games, Munich (1967-72—destroyed): employing flexible, wire-rope, cable-nets (to which covering membranes were fixed) suspended from masts and framed by cables around the edges which transferred the stresses to anchor-points, Otto's work was influential. *SOM used steel *pylons to support radial cables carrying conical tent-like fibreglass roofs at the Háj Terminal, International Airport, Jeddah (1981-2), and there have been other developments. The Aviary at London Zoo (1961-2—by

*Price, **Lord Snowdon** (1930-2017), and *Newby) is an example of Tensile architecture.

Pneumatic architecture (heralded by the design of balloons and airships) has suggested a way by which masts, etc., can be eschewed, air-pressure alone supporting a membrane-envelope, covering the required volume. Separate chambers inflated with air form one type, and a membrane supported by air pressure kept constant by a continuous supply of air form another. Pneumatic structures, introduced (1950s) from the USA to Europe, were developed by Otto, who further experimented with cable-reinforced air-supported membranes, offering many possibilities for enclosing space.

AAQ, 1/2 (Apr. 1969), 56-74; *AD*, xxxviii/4 (Apr. 1968), 179-82; *AR*, cxxxiv/801 (Nov. 1963), 324-34; H.Berger (1996); Drew (1976, 1979); Glaeser (1972); Glancey (1989); F.Otto (1954, 1961, 1963); Scheuermann *et al.* (1996); Schock (1997); J.T (1996); Wilhelm *et al.* (1985)

tent 1. Portable tension structure in which the supports (usually a wooden pole or poles) both carry and are held in place by a membrane of canvas, skins, or cloth stretched over them and fixed by means of pegs driven into the ground. **2.** Portable *compression* structure in which a self-supporting frame or armature is constructed over which a protective membrane is draped. Tents are of great antiquity as a type, and very elaborate examples have evolved for religious, ceremonial, or status reasons. *Tensile architecture was developed from tent-like forms.

Drew (1979); Faegre (1979); Prussin *et al.* (1995); J.T (1996)

tent-ceiling *Camp ceiling: the inward-sagging curved *form* was frequently found in late C18 garden-buildings, especially those in *Chinoiserie* or oriental styles, e.g. *Turkish tent, Painshill, Surrey (c.1760—restored 1990s), and also occurred on *Regency *canopies and *verandahs (not made of fabric, however, but of some more permanent material, e.g. metal). A fine example of a tent-ceiling in fabric was conceived for the blue-and-white *Zeltzimmer* at *Charlottenhof*, Potsdam, by *Schinkel (c.1830).

tepidarium Room of intermediate temperature in Roman *thermae*.

term, terminal 1. Classical head and bust (often with torso) merging with the top of a downward-tapering *pedestal resembling an inverted *obelisk, sometimes with feet appearing under the base of the pedestal (which is proportioned like the lower part of a human figure). A *terminal figure* or *terminus* is a bust or top part of a term. A *terminal pedestal* is like that of a term, but is separate, and a bust stands on it. *Compare* HERM. **2.** Ornamental finish, *terminal*, or *termination*, of an object, e.g. a *bench-end in a church, *finial on a *pinnacle, *knob, *label-stop or anything stopping a *moulding, or an *urn on a pedestal.

terrace 1. Embankment or prepared and levelled mass of earth in e.g. a garden. 2. Any artificial or built level platform for promenading, with a vertical or sloping front or sides faced with *masonry, turf, etc., and sometimes having a *balustrade, often adjacent to a country-house. 3. One of several platforms, as on a hillside or in a *stadium, furnished with seats, or forming part of a *hanging garden. 4. *Loggia or external usable space, e.g. *roof-garden. 5. Series of houses joined together in one row, as in the *Georgian terraces of the British Isles. *Compounds include*: *terrace-garden*: garden laid out in a series of terraces descending a slope, e.g. C17 Lisburn Castle Gardens, Co. Antrim (*see* HANGING GARDENS), and the fine late-C17 exemplar at Powis Castle, Montgom., Powys, possibly by William *Winde; *terrace-walk*: feature of C18 English gardens, designed to facilitate views from it, e.g. Endsleigh, Devon (early-C19, by H.*Repton).

Dalley (2013); S.M (1982)

terracotta Hard unglazed pottery (the term means 'baked' (cooked) 'earth') of which decorative *tiles, architectural enrichment, statuary, *urns, etc., or even components for whole *façades are made. It should be distinguished from *faïence. Widely used in Antiquity, notably by the Greeks and Etruscans, it was also employed in Islamic buildings, but its use in Europe was revived in the medieval period, especially where brick was used (e.g. in Northern Germany). A major C19 revival occurred, when terracotta was manufactured on a huge scale. St Stephen's Church, Lever Bridge, Bolton, Lancs. (1842–5), designed by *Sharpe, was built entirely of terracotta, and a widespread use of the material was prompted by Prince *Albert's admiration of German experiments and by the publication (1867) of *The Terra Cotta Architecture of North Italy*, edited and illustrated by the Prince's artistic adviser, **Professor Ludwig Grüner** (1801–82). Important instances in which terracotta was used include parts of the South Kensington Museum (1856–65), by *Fowke, H.Y.D.*Scott, and **Godfrey Sykes** (1824–66), the Huxley Building, Exhibition Road, Kensington (1867–71—by Scott and *Wild), the Royal Albert Hall (1867–71—by Fowke and Scott), and the *Rathaus*, Berlin (1861–9), by **Hermann Friedrich Waesemann** (1813–79). *Waterhouse was one of the many architects who employed terracotta (e.g. the *Gothic Prudential Assurance Building, Holborn (1878–1906), and the Free *Rundbogenstil* Congregationalist Churches at Lyndhurst Road, Hampstead (1883), and King's Weigh House, Duke Street, Mayfair (1889–91), all in London).

Terracotta was widely used in the USA: its fireproof qualities and decorative possibilities commended it for cladding *skyscrapers, and many such were finished with the glazed and coloured version of terracotta, aka *faïence* (e.g. Wrigley Building, Chicago, IL (1919–24)).

C.Elliott (1992); M.Stratton (1993); J.T (1996); N.Winter (1993)

Terragni, Giuseppe (1904–43) Italian architect, primarily associated with *Rationalism, *Gruppo 7*, and *MIAR, inspired partly by *Futurism, he was active in *CIAM. His first important building (one of the earliest manifestations of *International Modernism in Italy) was the *Novocomum* Apartment Block, Como (1927–8), but his *Casa del Fascio*, Como (1932–6) is regarded as his finest work: with its open grid-like elevation leading to a glass-roofed *atrium* surrounded by four storeys of galleries and offices, it demonstrated Fascist patronage of *Modern-Movement architecture. He also designed the *Sant'Elia* Nursery School (1936–7) and the *Giuliani-Frigerio* apartment-block (1939–40), both in Como; the *Villa Bianco*, Seveso (1936–7); and the *Casa del Fascio*, Lissone (with **Antonio Carminati** (1894–1970)—from 1938–9). A convinced Fascist (a fact ignored by Leftist commentators who find it inconvenient when admiring his impeccable *Modernist credentials), his unrealized design for the Dante Memorial, Museum, and Study Centre, Rome (1938), sums up the essence of architectural expression as favoured by the Party, with its stripped, severe monumentality and dramatic impact. For most of his architecture in and around Como he worked with his brother, the unsung **Attilio** (1896–1958). His *œuvre* influenced *Rational architects and the *New York Five.

AB, lxii (1980), 466–78; Casabella, xxxiv (1970), 38–41; Ciucci (ed.) (1996); Coopmans de Yoldi (ed.) (2000); P.Eisenman (ed.) (1998); Etlin (1991); Galli & Mühlhoff (2000); Germer & Preiss (eds) (1991); Labò (1947); Mantero (ed.) (1969, 1984); Marcianò (1987); P (1982); Saggio (1995); T.Schumacher (1985, 1991, 1993); Ve (1953); Zevi (1980)

terrazzo *In-situ* or *precast finish for floors, *dados, etc., made of small pieces of *marble beaten down into a fairly stiff *cement or lime-mortar, rubbed down, and polished.

Terry, John Quinlan (1937–) *See* NEW CLASSICISM.

Terry, Nicholas John (1947–2008) As head of Britain's biggest multi-discipline firm of architects/engineers/designers, **BDP** (Building Design Partnership), he was involved in significant cultural projects including the refurbishment of the Royal Opera House, Covent Garden (in collaboration with **Sir Jeremy Dixon** (1939–) and

Edward Jones (1939–). Among other works was Millburngate Shopping-Centre, Durham.

The Times (12 Dec. 2008), 92; pk

tessella (*pl.* **tessellae**) Small *tessera.

Tessenow, Heinrich (1876–1950) German architect, prominent member of the *Arts-and-Crafts movement, influenced also by work of *Schinkel and *Thiersch. He published *Der Wohnhausbau* (1909, with later editions), illustrated with his own designs, and laid out several housing-schemes with pitched roofs, modelled on traditional types (e.g. State Electricity Company Workers' Housing, Trier (1906–7), and *Am Schänkenberg*, Hellerau *Garden City, Dresden (1910–11)). His best-known work is the Dalcroze Institute for Physical Education, Hellerau (1910–12), where he employed a rigorous, severe, *stripped *Classicism, especially in the *tetrastyle *in-antis *portico. With his school at Klotzsche, near Dresden (1925–7), and the Heinrich-Schütz-School, Kassel (1927–30), Tessenow showed a tendency to move nearer the prevailing *Rationalism of the period.

The 1914–18 war affected him deeply, moving his interests towards the creation of small towns and communities and drawing on craft-orientated buildings. In 1930–1 he converted Schinkel's *Neue Wache* on *Unter den Linden*, Berlin, into a memorial to war dead. He found it difficult to practise under the Nazi regime, but after the 1939–45 war he resumed teaching in Berlin and concerned himself with the reconstruction of old town centres, notably Lübeck (1947). He was a prolific writer, and interest in his architecture has grown since a major exhibition devoted to him (1961), influencing protagonists of *Rational architecture. He was an influential teacher: among his pupils was *Speer.

K-P.Arnold (1991); J.Campbell (1978); *K & K*, xv (1917), 32–6, xxiv (1925), 55–60; Michelis (1991); J.T (1996); Tessenow (1919, 1921, 1927, 1991); Wangerin & G.Weiss (1976); *WMfB*, ix (1925), 365–81

tessera (*pl.* **tesserae**) One of a great number of small square (almost cubical) pieces of glass, *marble, pottery, stone, *tile, etc., called in the singular *abaculus, *abaciscus, or, if very small, *tessella, embedded in *mortar forming a *mosaic.

Tessin, Nicodemus, the Elder (1615–81) Swedish architect/military-engineer of French origins. After its successes in the Thirty Years War (1618–48) Sweden became a magnet for artists, and enjoyed a period of considerable activity in creative spheres. During the reign of **Queen Christina** (1644–54) Tessin was appointed Royal Architect (1646), travelled to improve his taste and knowledge, and returned to Sweden (1653) armed with the necessary experience, books, and

drawings to become the country's foremost *Baroque architect. Influenced by French designs, he created the gardens at the Royal Palace of Drottningholm as well as the Palace itself, with its system of *pavilions, monumental staircase, and composition in which precedents from France, The Netherlands, and Italy can be detected (1660s). He also designed Kalmar Cathedral (begun 1660), partly influenced by the Roman *Cinquecento and built on a Greek-cross plan with corner *turrets, but with the east and west arms lengthened and with *apses. He was City Architect of Stockholm from 1661 until his death. Among his other works were the noble *Karolinska Grafkoret* at the *Riddarholms-Kyrka* (1671–1740), many houses in Stockholm, and the Bank of Sweden, Stockholm (1676).

A & B (1986); Kommer (1974); Paulsson (1958); P (1982); J.T (1996)

Tessin, Nicodemus, the Younger, Count (1654–1728) Swedish architect, son of *Tessin the Elder. Trained by his father and partly educated in Rome (1673–9) and Paris (1678–80), he thoroughly absorbed Italian and French *Classicism, especially after a second study-tour (1687–8). When in Rome he was introduced to *Bernini and Carlo *Fontana under the aegis of the exiled **Queen Christina of Sweden** (1626–89). He succeeded his father at Drottningholm and as Stockholm City Architect, and built a fine house for himself in Stockholm (1692–1700) that served as a clever advertisement for his skills, demonstrating his mastery of contemporary French and Roman *Baroque, especially with the garden-front. When fire consumed the old Royal Castle in Stockholm (1697), Tessin lost no time in producing designs for the great Palace that stands there today. Building took a long time as Sweden was bankrupted by the disastrous wars against Denmark, Poland, and Russia under **King Charles XII** (*r.*1697–1718), and the Palace was not completed until 1753 by Tessin's son, **Count Carl Gustav Tessin** (1695–1770), and *Hårleman. Nicodemus Tessin the Younger was also responsible for Steninge Castle, Sweden (1681–1712), a country-house much influenced by French and Italian exemplars.

A & B (1986); Josephson (1930, 1930–1); Kommer (1974); P (1982); Snickare (ed.) (2002); J.T (1996); We (1947–52); Wrangel (1912)

tester *Canopy over a *pulpit (called *abatvoix) or tomb.

tetra- Meaning four, it forms the first element of many words adapted from Greek compounds, *examples of which are*:
tetramorph: composite figure combining the *attributes* of the Four Evangelists: it may be a

four-faced creature, and represents the Gospels;

tetraprostyle: Classical *portico of four columns set before the *cella;

tetrapylon: **1.** with four *gateways; **2.** building with four identical (or almost identical) arched *façades set on two intersecting axes (e.g. *Arco di Giano*, near *San Giorgio in Velabro*, Rome (C4));

tetrastoon: **1.** enclosed space with *porches or *arcades on all four sides, as in a *cloister; **2.** building with four porticoes e.g. Temple of the Four Winds, Castle Howard, Yorks.;

tetrastyle: with four columns (*see also* PORTICO);

tetrastyle atrium: *atrium with a column at each of the four corners of the *compluvium*, supporting the roof around the opening.

Teulon, Samuel Sanders (1812–73) English *High-Victorian *Gothic-Revival architect of French Huguenot descent, he commenced practice (1838) and designed several startlingly original churches and other buildings. His masterpiece was St Stephen's, Rosslyn Hill, Hampstead, London (1868–71), with *polychrome brick interior, powerful roof-construction, and a general inventiveness that won admiration from *Eastlake, no less. Ingenious too is St Mary's, St Mary's Road, Ealing, London (1866–74), with an elephantine tower and a galleried interior incorporating a riotously complex roof-structure. More serene and impressive are St James, Leckhampstead, Berks. (1858–60), and St John the Baptist, Huntley, Glos. (1861–3—with fine *polychrome interior). Of his great houses, Tortworth Court, Glos. (1849–53), and the wildly exuberant Shadwell Park, Norfolk (1856–60), deserve especial mention. Interested in model estate-cottages, he designed more than a hundred at Thorney, near Peterborough (1843–63—many of which have been ruined by the insertion of inappropriate modern windows), and other examples may be found elsewhere, e.g. at Sunk Island, Yorks. (1855–7). Teulon is regarded as a *Rogue Goth. For the last five months of his life he was insane, possibly the effects of syphilis. His brother, **William Milford Teulon** (1823–1900), also an architect, founded the City Church and Churchyard Protection Society.

Rod. Brown (ed.) (1985); D & M (1985); Ea (1970); G-R (1949); S.M (1972); *ODNB* (2004); M.Saunders (1982); J.T (1996); Teulon (2000)

thackstane 1. Stone used for covering roofs instead of *slate or *tile. **2.** Stone projecting from a chimney-stack covering the upper edge of *thatch.

thatch Thick roof-covering of reed, rushes, or straw, used in *vernacular buildings, sometimes on medieval churches, and often on structures intended to fit within a *Picturesque landscape, e.g. *cottage orné*.

N.Davey (1961); West (1988)

Thays, Jules-Charles, *called* **Carlos** (1849–1934) Paris-born landscape architect, he studied under É.-F.*André before settling in Argentina (1889) where he became (1891) Director of Parks & Walkways, enabling him to influence the design of urban open spaces. One of his works was the Botanical Garden (1898), named after him as the *Jardín Botánico Carlos Thays de la Ciudad Autónoma de Buenos Aires*. Thays worked on civic projects in other areas of Argentina, including Córdoba, Mendoza, and Mar del Plata, and outside Argentina, including in Uruguay, Chile, and Brazil.

Berjman (1998); Tay (2006)

theatre Building for the public enjoyment of drama, etc. *Antique Classical theatres were planned as segments of a circle, the seats rising in concentric tiers above and behind one another around the *orchaestra* separating the *auditorium* from the stage. *See* AMPHITHEATRE.

thé-au-lait Colour resembling tea with milk often used to describe *terracotta-faced buildings.

theme-park 1960s term for a type of park devoted to a theme, idea, or ideas, which might have some historical, fictional, or other core. It was invented by the Disney organization at Anaheim, CA, where traditional American *vernacular architecture and a main street of *c.*1895 were re-created (1955), together with buildings that evoked Disney's films. Charles *Moore saw it as a powerful lesson in architecture, as a catalyst for a new popularist direction away from *International Modernism, and as an antidote to soulless, ugly environments created as a direct result of the *Athens Charter, *CIAM dogma, and slavish adherence to principles of so-called *Functionalism from which all delight had been expunged. Other 'Disneyland' theme-parks followed, e.g. at Orlando, FL (early 1970s), and Euro Disney, Marne-la-Vallée, near Paris (early 1990s): architects included **Michael Graves** (1934–), Moore, **Antoine Predock** (1936–), Aldo *Rossi, **R.A.M. Stern** (1939–), and **Robert Charles Venturi** (1925–2018), and there is no doubt that the possibilities for creating charming vistas and an element of fantasy helped to promote aspects of *New Urbanism. Disney theme-parks were precedents for European developments, e.g. *Parc Astérix*, Ermenonville, France.

Other types of theme-park include *museums where old buildings are re-erected, or historical architecture is reconstructed, e.g. the Avoncroft Museum of Historic Buildings, Worcs. (founded 1967—where F.W.B.*Charles played a key role), the beautiful *Meiji-mura* architectural museum, Inuyama, near Nagoya, Japan, and the earliest of them all (1890s), the museum at Skansen, near Stockholm (1890s), Sweden. *Jellicoe's garden for the Moody Foundation, Galveston, TX (begun 1983), was conceived as a park explaining the landscape-history of the world and the role of plants in human life. Many other theme-parks have been, or are being proposed, with considerable ranges of allusions.

B.Dunlop (1996); Findlay (1992); Ghirardo (1996); Sorkin (1992)

Theodorus of Samos (d.540 BC) Greek architect, he designed (with **Rhoecus** or **Rhoikos**) the *Ionic *temple of the *Heraion*, Samos (from *c.*575 BC), and wrote an architectural treatise, now lost, one of the earliest of Classical Antiquity. He was also involved in building the fourth temple of Artemis, Ephesus (*c.*565 BC) with *Chersiphron.

D (1950); La (1983); J.T (1996)

Theodotos (d. *c.*360 BC) Greek architect, he designed the *Doric *temple of Asclepius, Epidaurus (*c.*375 BC), celebrated for its sculptures in the *pediments and for the *chryselephantine statue within, and also for the fact that expense-accounts for the building survive.

Burford (1969); D (1950); La (1983)

therapeutic garden One designed to address physical, psychological, and spiritual needs of designated users, usually attached to a hospital, etc.

thermae Public bathing-establishment in Classical Antiquity. The vast Roman *thermae* of the Imperial era embraced not only hot, medium, and cold baths, but luxuriously appointed places for exercise, athletics, and recreation, as well as formal gardens. Furthermore, the *plans included room-shapes of various geometries that were influential on *Renaissance and Neo-Classical planning.

Ck (1996); Heinz (1983); D.S.R (1945); Yegül (1992)

thermal window *See* DIOCLETIAN WINDOW.

Thibault, Jean-Thomas (1757-1826) French architect, pupil of *Boullée, he became a partner of J.-N.-L.*Durand, winning (1790s) several prizes for Government-sponsored projects. He renovated several important buildings, including the *Elysée* and Neuilly Palaces, and worked for a time in The Netherlands, where he adapted the Town Hall, Amsterdam, as a Royal Residence. He published *Application de la Perspective linéaire aux arts du dessin* (1827, 1831, 1833-4).

W.Pa (1892)

Thibault, Louis-Michel (1750-1815) French architect, he studied under *Gabriel, *Mique, and Le *Roy, and was employed (1783) by the Dutch East India Company at the Cape in South Africa. His works include several Neo-Classical buildings in and around Cape Town, including the Supreme Court and Government Offices (1811-15). With *Anreith he brought advanced European architectural ideas to South Africa.

F & C (1978); Lewcock (1963); Puyfontaine (1972); J.T (1996)

Thibiage.— De (*fl.*1840s) French author, probably a pseudonym. His *Histoire pittoresque et anecdotique des anciens châteaux*, etc. (1846), was a significant catalyst in the *Gothic Revival in France and, especially, Germany, where the book was published as *Geschichte der berühmtesten Ritterburgen und Schlösser Frankreichs, Englands, Deutschlands, der Schweiz*, etc. (1846).

Thibiage (1846, 1846a)

thicket Group of trees planted close together; a *wilderness. *See* BOSKET; CLUMP; COPPICE; GROVE.

Thienen, Jacob van (*fl.* early-C15) Flemish architect, he probably designed part of the *Gothic Town Hall in Brussels, Belgium (begun 1402), one of the masterpieces of secular medieval architecture in Northern Europe, although the *belfry (1448-63) was designed by *Ruysbroeck. He may have built the south *aisle of Ste-Gudule, Brussels (*c.*1400).

Duverger (1933)

Thiersch, Friedrich von (1852-1921) One of the most influential architects in Southern Germany, a disciple of *Semper, he designed many buildings, some *Rundbogenstil*, and others combining *Neo-Classicism and *Renaissance influences so common in C19 Germany. Among them were the Munich Palace of Justice (1887-97, 1902-5), remodelling of the *Kurhaus*, Wiesbaden (1904-7—originally designed by **Johann Christian Zais** (1770-1820) in a simplified *Palladian style), and the *Festhalle*, Frankfurt-am-Main (1906-9). His pupils included *Bonatz, Theodor *Fischer, W.*Gropius, Ernst *May, and *Tessenow. His brother, **August** (1843-1916), was also an architect: his best work was St Ursula, Munich (1894-7—*Renaissance-Revival).

Eitel (1952); Marschall (1981); Ne (1977); H.Thiersch (1925)

Third Pointed *See* PERPENDICULAR.

Thirsk, John (*fl.*1420-52) English master-mason, he worked at Westminster Abbey, notably on the *nave, and designed the beautiful *Chantry-Chapel of **King Henry V** (*r.*1413-22) as well as the great *altar-screen (completed 1441). He was appointed (1449) Master-Mason at Windsor Castle.

J.Harvey (1987)

thole 1. *Boss or *escutcheon at the apex of a timber *vault, where the *ribs meet. **2.** *Niche or recess to receive votive offerings in medieval times.

tholobate 1. Substructure for a Greek *tholos, a circular *crepidoma or *stylobate. **2.** Circular substructure of a *cupola.

tholos 1. Circular building with a conical, domed, or vaulted roof, e.g. a circular tomb roofed with a pseudo-dome of *corbelled rings, such as the 'Treasury of Atreus', Mycenae (c.1300 BC). **2.** Ancient *Greek circular building, often with a *peristyle and conical roof, e.g. Tholos of Epidaurus (c.350 BC).

D (1950); La (1983); J.T (1996)

Thomas, Sir Alfred Brumwell (1868–1948) English architect, he won (1896) the competition to design Belfast City Hall, the grandest of all late-Victorian and Edwardian examples of the *Baroque Revival or *Wrenaissance. The interiors, notably the monumental *stair, are as splendid as the exterior, with its great *dome and corner towers modelled on those of *Wren's St Paul's Cathedral in London. Opened (1906), it gained Thomas his knighthood. He followed this triumph with other competition successes, including Stockport Town Hall, Ches. (1903–8), in which a *Beaux-Arts influence is clear, although Wren's themes are not entirely absent. Among other works are Plumstead (now Woolwich) Town Hall (1899–1908—in a florid Baroque style with open-bedded segmental pediments, a tower placed asymmetrically, and a long entrance-hall of great magnificence), the Library, Lewisham Way, Deptford, London (1911–14—again Baroque), the Town Hall, Clacton-on-Sea, Essex (1931—in a *Neo-Georgian style, but with a large central pedimented *portico), and the beautiful Belfast War Memorial (1925–7).

A.S.Gray (1985); Se (ed.) (1975); Se (1977)

Thomas, Francis Inigo (1865–1950) English architect/garden-designer, trained by *Bodley and *Garner. Like other contemporaries, inspired by *William Morris and the *Arts-and-Crafts Movement, he sought to recover the vernacular character and style of the smaller *Tudor and C17 country-house and its surroundings, building up a portfolio of drawings on tours of houses and gardens in France, Germany, The Netherlands, and Britain, and collaborated with *Blomfield in publishing *The Formal Garden in England* (1892), in which most of the illustrations featuring *gazebos, *pavilions, *balustrading, dipping-wells, pools, statues, and clipped yews were by him. Thomas designed several Tudor-style gardens for English country-houses: they include Athelhampton Hall, Dorset (from 1891); Barrow Court, Barrow

Gurney, Som. (from 1892); and Rotherfield Hall, Crowborough, Sussex (from 1897—where he added *terraced gardens, pavilions, and a *nym-phaeum). For the manor-house, Chantmarle, Dorset, he designed (1910) gardens where *canal, pools, and balustrading reflect *Renaissance and *Baroque themes. Thomas was a leading figure in the brief revival of architectural gardens before the 1914–18 war: his work was known in Germany and Austria via *Muthesius's *Das englische Haus* (1904–5).

Blomfield (1892); Fellows (1985), 35–41; Helmreich (2002), 115–25; *JGH*, xiii/1 & 2 (Spring/Summer 1993), 90–103; Muthesius (2007); *ODNB* (2013); Ottewill (1989)

Thomas, John (1813–62) English stonemason/sculptor/architect, he carved sculptural decorations on the King Edward VI Grammar School, Birmingham, to designs by *Pugin, and later *Barry appointed him superintendent of stone-carving for the Palace of Westminster (much work on the north and south fronts was his). He designed Somerleyton Hall, Suffolk (begun 1844) in a *Jacobean-Revival style for the builder and entrepreneur, **Sir Samuel Morton Peto, Bt.** (1809–89—one of the guarantors of the 1851 Great Exhibition), and Preston Hall, Aylesford, Kent (begun 1850—in a more repellent Jacobean style), for Peto's business partner, **Edward Ladd Betts** (1815–72). A *protégé* of Prince *Albert, Thomas made carvings for Balmoral and Osborne House, and was responsible for the Audience Chamber and the Model Dairy, Home Farm, both at Windsor, Berks. He designed the great *majolica *fountain, the centrepiece of the 1862 Great Exhibition.

MFOKGC, **35** (Summer 2004), 11–12

Thomas, William (*fl.* 1770–1800) Architect to the **Duke of Clarence**, and Member of the Smeatonian Society of Civil Engineers. He published *Original Designs in Architecture* (1783) containing images of *villas, *temples, a *grotto, and several of his realized works, all in an elegant Neo-Classical manner influenced by the designs of Robert *Adam. Among extant buildings are the Market House, Mountsorrel, Leics. (1793), and Willersley Castle, near Matlock, Derbys. (1789–90). He taught T.D.W.*Dearn.

Co (2008); Donovan (2005); Thomas (1783)

Thomas, William (1799–1860) English architect, he practised from 1831 in Leamington Spa, Warwicks., where he designed Lansdowne Crescent and Circus (1835–8), the Baptist Chapel, Warwick Street (1833–4), and Victoria Terrace, Pump-Room, and Baths (1837). He suffered bankruptcy after the Leamington Bank failed (1837), and in 1843, the year his *Designs for Monuments* *and Chimney Pieces* was published, emigrated to Canada, where he built up an architectural practice, designing around 30 churches and other buildings, as well as numerous mansions and villas in all the principal towns of Ontario. Among his works were St Paul's Anglican Cathedral, London (1844-6), the District Court House, Town Hall, and Market, Niagara (1846-8), St Michael's RC Cathedral, Toronto (1845-8), and the handsome Brock Monument, Queenston (1853-6—a monumental *Composite column on a high *pedestal). His sons, **Cyrus Pole Thomas** (1833-1911) and **William Tutin Thomas** (1829-92), were also architects. The latter designed the *Gothic St George's Church, Dominion Square, Montréal (1870), and the sumptuous *Italianate Mount Stephen Residence, Drummond Street, Montréal (1881-4).

Co (2008); K (1994); McArthur *et al.* (1996); MacR & A (1963, 1975)

Thomas of Canterbury (*fl.*1324-31) *See* CANTERBURY.

Thomon, Thomas-Jean de (1754-1813) Swiss-born Neo-Classical architect, he studied in Paris under *Ledoux and in Italy, where the Greek-*Doric temples at *Paestum impacted on his sensibilities. He settled (1799) in Russia, where he became (1802) Court Architect to **Tsar Alexander I** (*r.*1801-25) in St Petersburg. His most outstanding work is the *Bourse* (1801-16), a powerful Neo-Classical barrel-vaulted hall surrounded by a Greek-Doric *peristyle of the unfluted type, not unlike *Ledoux's designs for the Stock Exchange and Discount Bank at his imaginary town of Chaux. With its severe unadorned treatment, clear expression of elements, huge *Diocletian windows set within great arches of rusticated *voussoirs, and platform of ramps and podia, it was a major essay in *Neo-Classicism as advanced as anywhere in the world for its date, and also shows some affinity with *Boullée's designs. Among his other buildings are warehouses on the Salni Embankment, St Petersburg (1804-5), the Doric *Mausoleum of **Tsar Paul I** (*r.*1796-1801) at Pavlovsk (1805-8), and the Column of Glory, Poltava (1805-11). He published *Recueil de plans et façades des principaux monuments construits à Saint-Pétersbourg et dans les différentes provinces de l'Empire de Russie* (1809) and a treatise on painting. His watercolours were influenced by *Piranesi's work.

Be (1975); Grabar *et al.* (eds) (1963); G.H (1983); M & Wa (1987); Shuiskii (1981); vV (1993); Vogt (1974)

Thompson, Sir Benjamin (1753-1814) *See* RUMFORD.

Thompson, Benjamin (1918-2002) American architect, one of the founders (1945) of *TAC.

Involved in *urban-renewal projects, he designed the Faneuil Hall Market Place, Boston, MA (1978). Other works included the Harborplace, Baltimore, MD (1980), Fulton's Landing, Brooklyn, NYC (1982-4), and the US Embassy, Ottawa, Canada (1982-4).

P (1982)

Thomson, Alexander 'Greek' (1817-75) Scots Neo-Classical architect, a formidable and original designer, some of whose works have affinities with those of *Schinkel. Known as 'Greek' Thompson because of his frequent allusions to the *Greek Revival in his buildings, his work was nevertheless inventively eclectic, drawing on a variety of sources, including Ancient-Egyptian, Persian, and even vaguely Indian architecture, put together with verve and sureness of touch. He lived and worked for most of his life in Glasgow, starting with a period (*c.*1836-48) with John *Baird before he established his own practice in partnership (1848-57) with another **John Baird** (1816-93—Thomson's brother-in-law (Thomson and Baird married respectively **Jane** (1825-99) and **Jessie** (1827-66), daughters of M.A.*Nicholson), then (1857-71) with his brother, **George Thomson** (1819-78), and finally (1873-5) with **Robert Turnbull** (1839-1905), when the firm was called **A.&G.Thomson & Turnbull.**

Baird and Thomson built a number of villas in the Glasgow suburbs and along the Clyde estuary, some of which were vaguely *Gothic and others influenced by the round-arched styles, but by 1857 Thomson had developed the refined and simplified Greek-inspired architectural language with which he was to be associated thereafter. Among the most outstanding houses are the Double Villa (25 and 25a Mansionhouse Road, Langside (1856-7—illustrated in Blackie's *Villa and Cottage Architecture* (1868)—two identical semi-detached houses facing in opposite directions, composed asymmetrically, with low-pitched roofs and glazing well set back from the stone *mullions)); Holmwood, Cathcart (1856-8—also illustrated in Blackie's publication—a sumptuous *villa at once Classical and *Picturesque, with a circular bay-window featuring a peristyle of inventive columns, and a rich scheme of interior painted decoration and furnishings, also designed by the architect); and Ellisland, 200 Nithsdale Road, Pollokshields (1871—a single-storey symmetrical villa with Graeco-Egyptian detail).

He also designed several terraces of houses. Moray Place, Strathbungo (1857-61), is unquestionably his finest achievement in this respect, and is arguably the most distinguished Greek-inspired group of terrace-houses anywhere. A symmetrical design with projecting pedimented ends (featuring *Giant Orders of square columns), between which is a long *façade with first-floor windows set behind a regular row of square mullions reminiscent of Schinkel's use of the same motif at the Berlin *Schauspielhaus* (1818–21), the form of the building recalls von Klenze's *Ruhmeshalle*, Munich (1850s), and the great *Hellenistic *altar of Pergamon (*c*.180 BC—now in Berlin). Other Thomson terraces include Great Western Terrace (1867–77) and Northpark Terrace, Hamilton Drive (1866), the latter again with a top storey treated with a row of square mullions derived from the Berlin *Schauspielhaus* and ultimately from a synthesis of the *Choragic Monument of Thrasyllus, Athens (319 BC), and the long rows of square columns found in Ancient-Egyptian temples at Elephantine and Deïr-el-Bahari. The very severe *columnar-and-trabeated Walmer Crescent, Paisley Road (*c*.1857–62), a *tenement-block, again uses the Schinkel *Schauspielhaus* motif, the whole composition, with its projecting rectangular bay-windows, handled with rigorous discipline. His Queen's Park Terrace, Eglinton Street (1856–60—disgracefully demolished 1980–1), was an important precedent for subsequent Glasgow tenements.

Thomson's three United Presbyterian Churches, Caledonia Road (1856—mostly destroyed by fire), St Vincent Street (1859), and Queen's Park (1869—destroyed in the 1939–45 war), were among the most original inventions of their time. Queen's Park had pronounced Egyptianizing elements and a hollow *stupa-like top to the crowning part of the composition. At Caledonia Road the *Schauspielhaus* *clerestorey row of square mullions was again used, but at St Vincent Street a complex system of *pylon-forms, high-level *Ionic *porticoes set on tall blocky *podia, and a strangely inventive tower with two Neo-Classical heads facing each other in each **T**-shaped recess over an **H**-shaped (on elevation) lower stage, with much else, suggests some kind of mnemonic programme, perhaps connecting the building with the Temple of Solomon (**T***emplum* **H***ierosolymae*). The platform arrangement also suggests von Klenze's *Walhalla*, near Regensburg (1830–42), a building that may also have influenced Thomson's brilliant but unrealized designs for the South Kensington Museum, London (1864). Furthermore, von Klenze employed *cyclopean (or *pelasgic) and *pseudisodomic masonry in some of his designs, and Thomson also used these at the Caledonia Road Church, possibly for symbolic purposes (e.g. the Rock on which the Church is built). The St Vincent Street Church also has interior cast-iron columns rising from the basement hall to carry the gallery and the clerestorey, while the inventive *capitals employing sharp claws, *acanthus, and stars suggest something exotic and Eastern, perhaps the Solomonic Temple itself.

Among Thomson's designs for commercial buildings are two important exemplars: the Grecian Chambers, Sauchiehall Street (1865–8—with squat Egyptianesque columns along the top storey and an *Attic storey vaguely derived from the Thrasyllus Monument), and the Egyptian Halls, Union Street (1871–3—with a highly complex façade of paraphrases and variations on Graeco-Egyptianizing themes, and a suggestion of a *Renaissance *cornicone capping the whole *Sublime composition).

In 1874 Thomson gave a series of lectures in Glasgow in which he argued for the superiority of *columnar-and-trabeated construction over *arcuated forms, castigated *Ruskin for his selective, illogical utterances, demanded that architects should follow the *example* of the Greeks rather than *imitate* their work, and extolled the 'mysterious power of the horizontal element in carrying the mind away into space and into speculation upon infinity' (in this he appears to have been influenced by the paintings and engravings of **John Martin** (1789–1854)). Although he used the arch in some of his earlier works, Thomson came to reject arcuated construction, insisting that *trabeated building-methods of the Greeks were more appropriate to modern architecture than was the inherently unstable arch. Unlike many Greek Revivalists, he never became a slave to that style, and, unlike Ruskin et al., held that architecture 'in its highest forms does not bear the least resemblance to anything in nature', being 'peculiarly and exclusively a human work'. When the commission for buildings for the University of Glasgow went to 'Great' *Scott, Thomson ridiculed the pretensions of the *Gothic Revival and its protagonists: his sensible views make interesting reading, especially today. The lectures demonstrate that Thomson was widely read and had a deep understanding of architectural styles of all periods as well as their principles. In particular, he analysed the Thrasyllus Monument which was so important in his own architecture. It has become clear that, although he does not appear to have travelled, and built in a small geographical area, he was among the greatest architects of his time.

ATSN, **xi** (Oct. 1994), **xii** (Jan (1995); **xiv** (Dec. 1995), **xvi** (May 1996), **xviii** (Feb. 1997), **xxviii** (Feb. 2001); *AJ*, **clxxxiii/8** (19 Feb. 1986), 36–53; *AR*, xv/90 (May 1904), 183–95; **cxv/689** (May 1904), 307–16; *BA*, **i** (1 May 1874), 274–8, (5 June 1874), 354–7, **ii** (24 July 1874), 50–2, (7 Aug. 1874), 82–4, (30 Oct. 1874), 272–4, (6 Nov. 1874), 288–9, (20 Nov. 1874), 317–8); *B*, **xxiv/1215** (19 May 1866), 368–71; Crook (1972a); J.Curl (2001, 2005, 2007); GS; G & W (1987); McFadzean (1979); Stamp (1999); Stamp (ed.) (1999); Stamp & McKinstry (eds) (1994); WRH (1990)

Thomson, James (1700–48) Scots poet, whose pastoral *Seasons* appeared complete (1730) with illustrations by William *Kent, although subsequent revisions expanded the work (esp.1744): it is an important indicator of C18 attitudes towards landscape and Nature improved by Art, and was inspired by Virgilian pastorals and the philosophical position of **John Locke** (1632–1704) regarding natural laws and toleration. Thomson contrasted the regimented French garden with the freedom of English exemplars, and Kent's illustrations evoked Claudian paintings. His poem enjoyed international success throughout the C18.

H & W (1988); *ODNB* (2004)

Thon *See* TON.

Thoreau, Henry David (1817–62) American writer (among many other things), a pioneer in the appreciation of living the simple life in unspoiled natural surroundings, and an influence on the study of natural history, ecology, and environmental matters. He advocated preservation of wild uncultivated land for recreation.

DAB; M.C.Young (2009)

Thornely, Sir Arnold (1870–1953) English architect, he commenced practice (1898) in Liverpool: with **Gilbert Wilson Fraser** (1873–1954) he designed the Presbyterian Church, Warren Road, Blundellsands (1898–1905), in a free *Perp. style, before entering into partnership (1906) with **Frank Gatley Briggs** (1862–1921), **Frederick Brice Hobbs** (1862–1944), and **Henry Vernon Wolstenholme** (1863–1936). Among their works were the *Wrenaissance Bluecoat School, Wavertree (1903–6), the very showy *Baroque Wrenaissance domed and towered Mersey Docks and Harbour Board Offices, Pier Head (1907), extensions to the Walker Art Gallery (1931–3), and the University Geology Department (1929), all in Liverpool. Thornely's masterpiece is the Northern Ireland Parliament Building, Stormont, Belfast (1927–32), an outstanding, if late, essay in the *Greek-Revival style, with an *Ionic *temple-front in the centre and magnificent scholarly interiors (although some were lost in a fire (1995)). *Knott contributed to the designs. Also at Stormont, Thornely designed the handsome gateways, lodges, and former Provincial Bank at the Massey Avenue entrance to the grounds (1932).

B *et al.* (2001); Larmour (1987); P:JRSUA, vi/2 (Nov./Dec. 1997), 24–35; Pollard & Pe (2006)

Thornhill, Sir James (*c.*1675–1734) Leading English decorative painter in the *Baroque style established by **Louis Laguerre** (1663–1721) and **Antonio Verrio** (*c.*1639–1707), he worked from 1707 on ceilings of the Royal Naval Hospital, Greenwich, notably those of the Painted Hall, and produced (1714–17) scenes in *grisaille on the *cupola and drum of St Paul's Cathedral, London. However, from *c.*1719 he made no secret of

setting himself up as an architect, his skills in which were praised by *Dézallier d'Argenville. *Colvin lists several designs by him, including realized works at Moor Park, Herts. (*c.*1720–8); the interior of the chapel at Dunster Castle, Som. (1723); and remodelling of Thornhill House, Dorset (1720s).

Co (2008); *ODNB* (2004)

Thornton, William (1759–1828) Edinburgh-educated physician, born in the British West Indies, he became (1788) an American citizen, and acquired a reputation as an architect. He designed the Library Company Building, Philadelphia, PA (1789–90—destroyed), based on a plate in volume 2 of **Abraham Swan**'s (*fl.*1745–*c.*1770) *Collection of Designs in Architecture* (1757), and prepared drawings (1792) for the competition to design the US Capitol in Washington, DC, loosely based on plates in *Campbell's *Vitruvius Britannicus* (1715–25). His second design (drawn up (rather unsportingly) after he had been able to peruse some of the entries and submitted *after* the deadline) was accepted (1793), but, having major flaws as a realizable proposition, was revised by *Hallet, who changed Thornton's plans to conform to his own ideas. Thornton produced a third design (1795) when *Hadfield was dismissed as supervising architect, and it is that which forms the basis of the final version, with the central pedimented *portico and *Louis-Quinze elevations (although the Capitol went through several further transformations in the course of its history). He designed the Octagon, a town-house in Washington (1797–1800—which, like his Capitol designs, demonstrates his fascination for elliptical and circular interior spaces), and also a house at Tudor Place, Georgetown, Washington (*c.*1805–10, probably his best work, perhaps influenced by a design by *Soane in *New Vitruvius Britannicus* (1802–3)). He also designed Pavilion VII, University of Virginia, Charlottesville (1817–21). *See also* BULFINCH; HOBAN; LATROBE; WALTER.

G.Brown (1970); *DAB* (1936); C.Hs (ed.) (1995); B.Jenkins (1982); McCue (1976); Maddex (1973); C.Peterson (ed.) (1976); P (1982); Reiff (1977); Stearns & Yerkes (eds) (1976); J.T (1996)

Thorpe, John (*c.*1565–*c.*1655) English land- and building-surveyor (son of master-mason **Thomas Thorpe** (*fl.*1570–96), involved in building at Kirby Hall, Northants.), who also appears to have designed (though rarely supervised) buildings. His book of plans (preserved in Sir John *Soane's Museum, London) containing surveys and projects for country-houses. He probably designed Thornton College, Lincs. (*c.*1607–10), the outer court at Audley End, Essex (*c.*1615), Aston Hall, Warwicks. (1618–35), perhaps Dowsby Hall,

Lincs. (after 1610), and Somerhill, near Tonbridge, Kent (c.1610–13), all showy *Jacobean houses, some with *Palladian hints, but detail derived from French sources (e.g. du *Cerceau). A gallery between the Rosse and Stanton Towers, Belvoir Castle, Leics., for which drawings survive, was by him (1625–7). He may have been responsible for the English version of **Hans Blum**'s treatise (1550) on the *Orders, and also for an English translation of du Cerceau's work on *perspective. He was therefore more than 'an unimportant clerk in the office of works' as some have claimed.

AH, xxiii (1980), 1–39, xxxii (1989), 30–51; *AR*, cvi/635 (Nov. 1949), 291–300; Blum (1550); Co (2008); Lees-Milne (1951); *LH & A*, viii (1973), 13–34, xix (1984), 57–63; *ODNB* (2004); P (1982); Su (1993); *Walpole Society*, xl (1966), whole issue.

Thouin, Gabriel (1747–1829) French garden-designer, trained by his father, **Jean-André Thouin** (*fl.*1745–64), at the Royal Gardens, Paris, he is best known for his book (originally published 1819/20) of hand-coloured plans of numerous types of garden, each of which is accompanied by designs for *fabriques* in various styles, water-features, etc.

Thouin (1838)

three-centred *See* ARCH.

threshold *Cill of a house door, so the entrance to a house or building.

throat Contraction of the flue of a *chimney over the fireplace.

throating Continuous groove or *drip under a *cope or *string-course to prevent water running back towards the wall.

throughstane 1. Flat grave-stone or *slab, also called *thruch*. **2.** *Table-tomb.

through-stone 1. *Bond-stone or *parpend the whole thickness of a wall, binding the *ashlar or facing-stone to the inner or backing-course. **2.** *Throughstane.

thrust Outward pressure of any arch or *vault. It has to be resisted by a counter-thrust provided by another arch, *buttress, etc.

Thumb Family German architects/craftsmen, one of several dynasties from the Bregenz district comprising the *Vorarlberg School: indeed, the Thumb family intermarried with the *Beers. **Michael Thumb** (c.1640–90) was responsible for several important *Baroque designs, including the Priory Church of Wettenhausen (1670–97), *Wallfahrtskirche Schönenberg, Ellwangen (1682–92), and the Premonstratensian *Klosterkirche*, Obermarchtal (1686–92). At Schönenberg he introduced the *Wandpfeilerkirche arrangement, in which

deep internal *buttresses divide the *aisles into side-chapels, the *nave face of each buttress enriched with *pilasters (outside, the position of each wall-pier is marked by a pilaster). Both Schönenberg and Obermarchtal were precedents for other *Wandpfeilerkirchen* incorporating what became known as the *Vorarlberger Münsterschema* (Vorarlberg large-church arrangement), in which galleries connect the wall-piers and form the ceilings of each chapel.

Peter II Thumb (1681–1766), so called to distinguish him from his grandfather, was Michael's son, and married (1707) **Anna Maria Beer** (1687–1754), having supervised the building of **Franz Beer**'s Church at Rheinau, Switzerland (1704–11). He designed the Church and Library of the *Benedictine Church of St Peter in the Black Forest, near Freiburg (1724–53). His greatest work is the exquisite Cistercian Monastery and *Wallfahrtskirche*, Neu-Birnau (1745–51), on the north shores of Lake Constance (*Bodensee*). The church has a large open interior, like a prayer-hall (it does not have the *Wandpfeiler* arrangement, but the *gallery continues all round the volume), with curved eastern corners and diagonals at the west, vestigial *transepts, flattened *vaults, and a partial ellipse for the *sanctuary: its internal decorations are *Rococo, among the loveliest in all Germany, mostly white, but enlivened by subtle colouring. *Stucco-work (1747–50) of the frothiest, lightest kind, was by **Josef Anton Feuchtmayr** *or* **Feuchtmayer** (1696–1770), who also designed and made the enchanting statuary, including the celebrated *Honigschlecker* (honey-sucker, a figure suggestive of the *Antique **Harpocrates**), and the frescoes are by **Gottfried Bernhard Götz** (or **Göz**—1708–74). Thumb contributed to one of the biggest and most sumptuous churches of the period, the Benedictine Abbey of St Gallen, Switzerland, where he also designed the fine Library. *Moosbrugger had already made plans for the Church (1720–1), but Thumb was probably responsible for the nave and domed area, developing the *Wandpfeilerkirche type further, opening it up with an impressive centralized volume.

Other members of the family include **Johann Christian Thumb** (c.1645–1726), who worked with Michael at Schönenberg and Obermarchtal, designed the *Schlosskirche* at Friedrichshafen (1695–1700—with stucco-work by the *Schmutzers), and was also active at Weingarten Abbey Church (1716–24). **Gabriel Thumb** (1671–*after* 1719) worked on the *Pfarrkirche* at Lachen, Lake of Zürich, Switzerland (1707–10), based on a plan by Moosbrugger. Again it was a *Wandpfeilerkirche*. **Michael Peter Franz Xaver Thumb** (1725–69) superintended the completion of his father's Library at St Gallen as well as the nave and rotunda of the same Church.

Bou (1962); H-M.Gubler (1972); Hi (1968a); Lb & D (1976); On (1973); P (1982); C.Powell (1959); J.T (1996)

thumb-moulding *See* GADROON.

thunderbolt Classical ornament, an *attribute of **Jupiter**, in the form of a spiral roll, pointed at both ends, often held in the talons of an eagle, or shown winged, with arrow-headed, forked, or zig-zag lightning-flashes. It occurs on the *soffits of Classical *cornices (e.g. *Vignola's *mutule *Doric *Order) and in *Empire schemes of decoration.

Thura(h), Laurids (Lauritz) Lauridsen (1706–59) Architect to the Danish Court (1733), after a tour of Europe (1729–31), probably the best late-*Baroque architect of his time in Denmark. He designed the exquisite Hunting Lodge, the *Erimitage* (1734–6), in the *deer-park north of Copenhagen, the interiors of which are among the finest of the period in Scandinavia. In 1749–50 he added the *steeple to Our Saviour's Church, Copenhagen, built spireless (1696). The unusual external staircase (gilded to contrast with the copper roof), was probably inspired by *Borromini's *Sapienza*, Rome. He published the Danish *Vitruvius I–II* (1746, 1749), and produced a manuscript of *Vitruvius III*, complete with *cartouches.

Ck (1996); We (1947–52)

Tibaldi, Marchese di Valsolda, Pellegrino *or* **Pellegrini** (1527–96) Bolognese architect/painter, his earliest building appears to have been the *Cappella Poggi* in *San Giacomo Maggiore*, Bologna (1556–8), after which he worked on the fortifications at Ancona. He moved (c.1562) to Milan under the aegis of **Charles Borromeo** (1538–84—**Archbishop of Milan** from 1564, canonized 1610). He designed the *Collegio Borromeo*, Pavia (1564–92—with its elegant two-storeyed *cortile*, a more austere, lighter version of *Alessi's *Palazzo Marino*), and the *Cortile della Canonica* in the Archiepiscopal Palace, Milan (1565–75). Other works include the circular *San Sebastiano* (1557–1617), the Jesuit Church of *San Fedele* (from 1569), the *choir-crypt and screens in the *Duomo* (1567), all in Milan, and the powerfully articulated façade of the *Sanctuario della Madonna dei Miracoli*, Saronno (1583). He carried out major schemes of decoration at the *Escorial*, Spain, from 1586. His brother, **Domenico** (1541–83), reconstructed the *choir of the Cathedral of *San Pietro*, and designed the *Magnani palazzo* (1560s and 1570s), both in Bologna.

He (1996); P.Mu (1986); P (1982); Panizza et al. (1990); J.T (1996); S.D.Torre (1994)

tiburio Tower or *lantern over the *crossing of a church (e.g. Milan Cathedral).

Ticinese School Group of architects working in the Ticino region of Switzerland from the 1960s, concerned with a reconsideration of architectural style, a greater historical awareness, and the promotion of *Rational architecture. Among influential members were **Mario Botta** (1943–), **Bruno Reichlin** (1941–), and Aldo *Rossi. *See also* NEO-RATIONALISM; TENDENZA.

B-M (ed.) (1989); G.Grassi (1982, 1989); Pizzi (1994–8, 1997); S & B (1975)

tide-mill Mill worked by the flux and reflux of sea-tide acting on a water-wheel.

tie Any member that resists a pull, as to prevent the spreading of two sides of a sloping roof. In, e.g. a *truss, the tie-beam is the main transverse timber connecting the feet of the principal *rafters or the *blades of a *cruck truss. *See also* STAY-BAR

ABDM (1996)

tier One of a series of rows placed one above the other, e.g. *galleries or *boxes in a theatre.

tierceron *See* VAULT.

Tiffany, Louis Comfort (1848–1933) American designer, best known for his creations in the *Art Nouveau style. He evolved interiors for *McKim, Mead, & White and *Carrère & Hastings, among others. Works include the Chapel for the Columbian Exposition in Chicago, IL (1893—parts of which survive), the *loggia of Laurelton Hall, NYC (1903–5—re-erected in the American Wing of the Metropolitan Museum of Art), and the Hanley House, Oyster Bay, NY (1921). He designed many glass artefacts, favourably compared with the best French Art-Nouveau works of the period.

Gh (2000); D.C.Johnson (1979); R.Koch (1966); H.McKean (1980); P (1982); J.T (1996); T-M (1967)

Tilden, Philip (1887–1956) English architect, pupil of *Collcutt, with whom he entered into partnership. From c.1917 he established his own practice, specializing in the design of country-houses, gardens, and chapels: interventions include Chartwell Manor, Kent (1923–4); Bron-y-De, Churt, Surrey (1921–8); Port Lympne, Kent (1918–23); Porth-en-Alls, Prussia Cove (1910–14) and Antony House (1945–7), both in Cornwall; and Sydenham House, Devon (1938). He published memoirs (1954).

Aslet (1985); Bettley (1987)

tile Plate of burnt clay: thin flat tiles are termed *plain*, commonly used to clad roofs or walls (in the latter case the wall is referred to as being *tile-hung*); thicker tiles, often of the *encaustic type, are used for paving. Glazed coloured tiles for wall-finishes were employed in Ancient-Mesopotamian architecture, and that tradition continued in *Islamic architecture. In Spain, *Moorish architecture was often decorated with glazed tilework of great beauty (*alicatado*) formed of uniformly shaped *azulejos*. Glazed tiles were employed in France and The Netherlands from C15 to C17, and during C19 were widely used throughout Europe and America, especially in *Art-Nouveau and *Arts-and-Crafts work.

J.Barnard (1972); Berendsen (1967); T.Herbert & Huggins (1995); Lemmen (1993); W.McKay (1957); J.Parker (1850); J.T (1996); Vallet (1982)

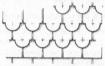

(*top*) fish-scale tiles.
(*below*) plain tiles.

tile-creasing Two or more courses of *tiles laid to protect the surface of a wall below, e.g. in a *cill or *string-course, and, very often, where a tile roof joins a *gable, and does not overhang, the roof ending almost flush with the *naked of the gable-wall.

W.McKay (1957)

timber Wood from conifers (or evergreens) is *softwood* (e.g. pine), and wood from deciduous trees is *hardwood* (e.g. beech, oak). Softwoods are and were widely employed for floor- and roof-construction, and hardwoods (especially oak) were used for structural *timber framing. Prior to the introduction of *metal for structural purposes in C18, timber (or lumber) was the only material used for structural framing.

ABDM (1996); Sunley & Bedding (eds) (1985)

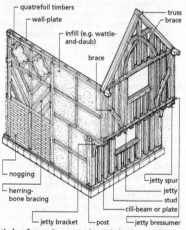

timber frame Composite drawing showing typical elements (*after JJS*).

timber frame Type of building-construction sometimes called *half-timbering*, where walls and partitions are made of a wooden skeleton, set on a *foundation, with the spaces filled with brick *nogging, *plaster, *wattle-and-daub, etc. Timber-framed buildings are frequently *tile-hung*, plastered, *weather-boarded or otherwise protected, as with *mathematical tiles. See BEAM; BRACE; BREASTSUMMER; CILL; COLLAR; CROSS-RAIL; CRUCK; DRAGON-BEAM; JETTY; JOIST; POST; PRINCIPAL; PURLIN; RAFTER; RAIL; STUD; TRUSS; WEALDEN HOUSE.

ABDM (1996); R.J.Brown (1986); Bru (1994); Grossmann (1986); Sobon & Schroeder (1984); J.T (1996)

t'ing Chinese *pavilion, roofed, but with no walls: *Chambers designed one of several examples of *Chinoiserie at Kew, Surrey (c.1760).

Tinney, John (c.1706–61) See ROCQUE, JOHN.

tirant, tiraunt See STAY-BAR.

Tirol, Hans (c.1505–c.1575) See STELLA, PAOLO DELLA.

Tischler, Robert (fl. 1926–58) German architect/landscape-designer, from 1926 he was chief architect of the *Volksbund Deutsche Kriegsgräberfürsorge* (German National War Graves Commission), responsible for the sombre cemetery at Langemarck near Ieper, with a rugged red-sandstone primitivist entrance. He also designed numerous war-memorials, including the massive *Freikorps-Ehrenmal* at Annaberg (Góra Świętej Anny), Upper Silesia (1936–8—dynamited 1945).

Troost (1942–3); pk

Tite, Sir William (1798–1873) English architect, he began his career by designing the Classical Mill Hill School, Mddx. (1825–7), and later laid out the South Metropolitan Cemetery, Norwood, London (1838), with *Gothic-Revival chapels (demolished) and gates. He is best known for the Royal Exchange, City of London (1842–4), an opulent, perhaps rather coarsely detailed building, with a massive *Corinthian *portico. He designed railway stations, including the handsome Classical one at Gosport, Hants. (1840–2). His *Rundbogenstil-*Byzantine polychrome St James, Gerrard's Cross, Bucks. (1858–9), is one of his best buildings, demonstrating he was an accomplished eclectic designer. His Gothic railway stations at Carlisle, Cumb. (1847), and Perth, Scotland (1848), are more successful architecturally than his churches in that style. He laid out the London Necropolis Cemetery, Brookwood, Surrey (1853–4), and built most of the stations on the railway-lines on the Caledonian and Scottish Central Railways and on the line from Le Havre to Paris, France. He designed Government House, Termonbacca, Co. Londonderry, Ireland (1846–8—headquarters of The Honourable The Irish Society of the City of London), and, as a member of the Metropolitan Board of Works, was involved in the construction of the Thames Embankment (1862–70).

B, clxxviii/5578 (1950), 39–42, and 5579, 95–8; Biddle (1973); Binney & Pearce (eds.) (1979); Co (2008); J.Curl (1986, 2000, 2004, 2007); Hi (1954); *ODNB* (2004); J.T (1996)

tithe barn Large medieval *barn for the storage of the tithe-corn, that quota (a tenth part) of the annual produce of agriculture to support the priesthood.

Tivoli window Type of window-opening based on a Roman example in the Temple of Vesta, Tivoli (*c*.80 BC), published by *Palladio. Less wide at the top than at the bottom (i.e. with sloping sides), it has an *architrave with *crossettes crowned with a *cornice, and is sometimes called a *Vitruvian opening.

Todd, Frederick G. (1876–1948) American landscape architect, he commenced his career under *Olmsted, later establishing himself in Canada, where he designed the system of *public parks and *garden-suburbs around Montréal. He designed the park system around Ottawa (1903), the Town of Mount Royal, Québec (a *Garden City—*c*.1910–11), Point Grey, Vancouver (1907), Tuxedo Park, Winnipeg (1906–8), and many other layouts. Involved in the *City Beautiful Movement, he was retained by the Ottawa Improvement Commission from 1902, and was the first resident professional landscape architect and town-planning consultant in Canada.

K (1994)

Todt, Fritz (1891–1942) German engineer, he became (1933) under the Nazis director of the construction of *Autobahnen*, and appointed A. *Seifert as landscape architect. Not a few *viaducts carrying the *motorways are *Sublime constructions, some by *Bonatz. He acquired control (1938) at all waterways, power-plants, military installations, and many other aspects of construction-works/production in the Reich, so by 1940, when he was appointed Minister of Armaments, he had enormous influence. Killed in an air-crash, he was succeeded by *Speer.

P.Adam (1992); CoE (1995); Jaskot (2000); F.Seidler (1986); Speer (1970, 1976, 1981); Spotts (2002); Stockhorst (1967); W-H (1989)

tokonoma *Alcove for seating or for display (e.g. prints, flower-pot, etc.) in a Japanese room.

Toledo, Juan Bautista de (*c*.1515–67) Spanish architect/mathematician/philosopher, he lived in Italy for some time, where he absorbed the essence of *Renaissance architecture. He became (1562) Architect to the *Escorial*, near Madrid, basing the grid-like ground-floor plan on reconstructions of the Temple of Solomon, Jerusalem, and the Court of the Evangelists on *Sangallo's *cortile* in the *Palazzo Farnese*, Rome. The plan is also an allusion to the *attribute of **St Laurence** (d. AD 258), a pot of whose melted fat was enshrined in the Church in the centre of the ensemble. *El Escorial*'s enormous external elevations are models of restraint. After his death the work was completed by Juan de *Herrera.

Ck (1996); J.Curl (2011); FHL (1967); Kubler (1982); K & S (1959); Rivera Blanco (1984); J.T (1996)

Toltec architecture *See* AZTEC ARCHITECTURE.

tomb Monument erected to enclose or cover a corpse and preserve the memory of the dead, so a sepulchral/funerary structure. *See also* MAUSOLEUM; TABLE. ***Compounds include***:

tomb-canopy: *canopy above an *altar-tomb or *tomb-chest*, as though protecting the *effigies that lie beneath, often forming a grand ensemble;

tomb-chest: rectangular stone funerary monument above a tomb, often found in churches (notably associated with *chantry- or *mortuary-chapels), with recumbent effigies on top or *suggested* by figures outlined (incised) on the top *slab or cut into inserts of metal (*brasses). Sides of the chest were often enriched with *quatrefoils, etc., or with *niches containing *weepers (upright or kneeling figures). Canopies and *rails often completed the ensemble. Simplified tomb-chests without weapons, effigies, or canopies were often employed as funerary monuments in churchyards and cemeteries in the C18, C19, and C20;

tomb-garden: garden attached to a tomb, providing a geometrical setting, as in the exceptionally fine C17 *Mughal exemplars (e.g. *Tâj Mahal*, Agra). Tomb-gardens were also associated with tombs in Antiquity, notably Roman *mausolea, etc. The term has been applied to the *garden-*cemetery, of which Mount Auburn, MA, is one of the finest;

tomb-stone: vertical or horizontal inscribed gravemarker or memorial set up over a tomb;

tomb-stone light: small window with lights resembling tombstones with curved tops, often over a *doorway.

Blore (1826); Co (1991); Crossley (1921); J.Curl (2002a); Linden (2007); S (1901–2); Weaver (1915)

Tomé, Narciso (*c*.1694–1742) Spanish architect/sculptor, he worked with his father and brothers on the decorations of the sumptuous front of the University at Valladolid (early C18). His masterpiece, described as a *fricassée de marbre*, is the *Trasparente* in the *capilla mayor* of Toledo Cathedral (1721–32), so called from the glass-fronted receptacle through which the Blessed Sacrament could be seen from the *ambulatory and also permit light to be admitted to the *camarín* behind the *altar itself within the chapel. Around the glass receptacle on the ambulatory side Tomé constructed a wildly extravagant *Baroque confection illuminated from a kind of *dormer set high above the *Gothic ambulatory *vaults from which the *masonry between the *ribs was removed.

CG (1962); K & S (1959); Mallory (1970); N-S (1986a); Pe (1960)

Ton, Konstantin Andreyevich (1794–1881) Russian architect of German extraction, leading figure in the revival of traditional Russian church-architecture, he was closely associated with official Government buildings: his work is variously referred to as 'Russian Byzantine' or the 'Russian style'. His earliest buildings in St Petersburg, including the Main Halls and Chapel of the Academy of Arts (1829–37), were firmly within the Classical tradition, while the monumental Dock in front of the Academy building was an essay in *Neo-Classicism. His first work consciously drawing on five-domed C15 and C16 precedents was the Church of St Catherine, St Petersburg (1830–7), followed by several other churches in the 'National' style. His designs for centralized five-domed churches based on old Muscovite sources were published, proved influential. He was also a pioneer in the study of traditional timber *vernacular domestic architecture. His most important buildings were the Bolshoi Kremlin Palace (1838–49) and the gigantic Church of Christ the Redeemer (1839–83) in Moscow. The last, like many of his buildings, was destroyed during the Soviet period (1934), but reconstructed (1994–7). Ton also designed several railway stations (1844–51) drawing on *Renaissance themes.

Slavina (1989); J.T (1996); vV (1993)

tondo Circular *medallion or *plaque, often set in *spandrels.

tongue 1. Narrow projection or *feather. just below the middle of the edge of a timber board: it fits into a groove or slit along the edge of the adjacent board, in floors, etc., hence *tongued-and-grooved*. **2.** Another name for a *tenon (*See* MORTICE AND TENON).

tooth Late-*Romanesque and *First-Pointed ornament consisting of a series of projecting hollow pierced *pyramids, also known as *dog-tooth, or tooth-ornament, sometimes with the points and bases of the pyramidal form transformed into stylized flowers.

toothing 1. Projecting course of alternate *header bricks under *eaves, *cornice, or *string-course like large *dentils, called *dentilation. **2.** Projecting stones or *tenons, called *toothing-stones* at the end of a wall so that, when required,

another building or wall can be bonded into it to make a continuous surface.

topiary Trees/hedges/etc. (usually box, juniper, privet, and yew), shaped into geometrical forms (*pyramids, cubes, etc.) or figures, animals, birds, etc. Known at least as early as Roman times, it was common in the Middle Ages. Good C17 examples can be seen at *Het Loo*, Netherlands, and Levens Hall, Westmd., and an elaborate C18 scheme existed at Hartwell House, Bucks., shown in paintings (1730s) by **Balthasar Nebot** (*fl.*1730–65).

torana Richly ornamented Indian *gateway associated with the enclosure of a *stupa.

torch Motif, also known as a *flambeau*, often used in Classical ornament. If inverted, it represents the extinguishing of life and therefore occurs in funerary architecture.

tore *As* TORUS.

torii Japanese timber entrance-gateway to a sacred precinct consisting of two cylindrical uprights carrying two projecting cross-beams, the upper of which is usually curved (the lowest part being in its centre).

torii
Typical type.

Torralva, Diogo de (*c.*1500–66) Portuguese architect, perhaps of Spanish extraction. The son-in-law of *Arruda, he nevertheless moved away from the *Manueline style to a more Italian-*Renaissance manner (e.g. the great *cloister of the *Ordem de Christo*, Tomar, Santarém (1554–64), where influences from *Bramante, *Palladio, and *Serlio are clearly displayed in the highly articulated treatment of the *façades). He probably designed the sanctuary of the *Jerónimos*, Belém, near Lisbon (built 1571–2).

K & S (1959); Kubler (1972); R.C.Smith (1968); J.T (1996)

Torrigiani, Pietro di Torrigiano d'Antonio (1472–1528) Italian sculptor. In 1510 he was working in England on the tomb of **Margaret Beaufort, Countess of Richmond and Derby** (1443–1509), mother of **King Henry VII** (*r.*1485–1509), and contracted (1512) to build the funerary monument of the King and **Elizabeth of York** (1466–1503) in the *Lady-Chapel (*Mortuary-

Chapel of Henry VII), Westminster Abbey. He also carried out various other works while in England, much of it portrait-sculpture. His importance lies in the fact that his was the first mature Italian-*Renaissance design to be realized in England.

COF (1988); W.Pa (1892); J.T (1996)

Torroja y Miret, Eduardo (1899–1961) Spanish architect/engineer/designer of *concrete structures, including *shells. His first large project was the Tempul *aqueduct, Guadalete, Jerez de la Frontera, in which he used *prestressed *girders, and he made his name with the concrete shell-roof at the Algeciras Market Hall (1933) and the *cantilevered grandstand roofs in the form of giant *flutes at the Zarzuela Racecourse, near Madrid (1935). He also used steel with great *élan*, as at the roof of the Football Stadium, Barcelona (1943).

Arredonda *et al.* (1977); Boh (1970); Bozal (1978); J.Je (1963); L (1988); M & N (1987); Ma (1983a); Torroja (1958, 1958a)

torsade Twisted *cable-*moulding.

torso Twisted column-*shaft.

torus (*pl.* **tori**) Bold projecting convex *moulding of semicircular *section, e.g. on either side of the *scotia* in an *Attic *base. Larger *tori*, e.g. on the base of a *triumphal column, are often enriched with *bay-leaf garlands.

Total architecture Advocated (1920s) by Walter *Gropius and Bruno *Taut, it pretentiously suggested syntheses of all arts and crafts in a new architecture (based on the composer **Wilhelm Richard Wagner**'s (1813-83) idea of *Gesamtkunstwerk*), but did the opposite by sundering arts and crafts from architecture. In spite of this manifest failure, Gropius published (1955) *The Scope of Total Architecture* (revised edn 1962).

Bildende Kunst, xxxvl/7 (1988), 298–9; Gropius (1962)

Totalitarian architecture Supposedly the officially approved architecture of dictatorships, over-centralized governments, or political groups intolerant of opposition, especially that of Fascist Italy, Nazi Germany, Stalinist Soviet Union, Communist China, etc. As an international style, it often drew on simplified *Neo-Classicism, and sculpture based on C19 realism and *Classicism for massive over-sized State monuments.

P.Adam (1992); COE (1995); Spotts (2002)

touch 1. Black basalt or basanite, capable of being carved, used for *fonts and tombs, e.g. the Tournai fonts of Hants. **2.** Compact dark-coloured stone, such as Petworth or *Purbeck *marble, capable of taking a high polish, used for *Gothic *shafts, tombs, etc.

tourelle *Corbelled *turret, circular on plan, cone-roofed, sometimes containing a circular *stair, set at the angle of a tower or wall at high level, and common in *Scottish-Baronial architecture.

MacG & R (1887–92)

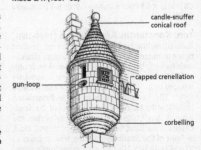

Typical Scots *tourelle*.

tower Tall structure of any form on *plan, high in proportion to its lateral dimensions, often rising in *stages (rather than *storeys), free-standing or part of another building, used in fortifications, as points of reference in the landscape, or as a *belfry attached to a church. Church-towers often have *buttresses, are crowned with *battlements, or support *spires, and have important architectural features. *See* STEEPLE.

tower-block High-rise blocks of *apartments (flats) were widely adopted after the 1939–45 war as a result of Modernist propaganda in order to replace existing low-rise housing with what was perceived as something better. Failure to provide proper supervision of public spaces (entrance-halls, landings, stairs, lifts, etc.), led to their misuse, as well as isolation of flat-dwellers. Other major problems included failure of prefabricated systems, community breakdown, and the loss of the traditional street, prompting a reaction (e.g. *New Urbanism and the re-creation of low-rise housing in streets).

Glendinning & S.M (1994)

tower-house Compact fortified house of several storeys with its main chamber or hall on an upper storey, usually over *vaulted lower floors. Common in Scotland (where many spectacular examples survive) and Ireland, tower-houses were still being built in C17.

Cruden (1963); Dunbar (1966); Glendinning *et al.* (1996); MacG & R (1887–92).

Town, Ithiel (1784–1844) Prolific, influential architect/engineer, a significant figure in the *Greek and *Gothic Revivals in the USA, he may have studied with Asher *Benjamin, and built (1810) the *Federal-style Botanic Garden House, Harvard University, Cambridge, MA. He moved (c.1813) to New Haven, CT, where he built the Center (1812–15) and Trinity (1813–16) Churches, the former a variation on *Gibbs's design for St Martin-in-the-Fields, London (1722–6), and the latter an early example of the Gothic Revival. From 1816 he designed many *bridges and developed a *lattice-*truss or *girder (patented 1820), which brought him fortune (he employed latticed scissor-trusses in his Gothic Christ Church Cathedral, Hartford, CT (1827–8), designed with **Nathaniel Sheldon Wheaton** (1792–1862)). He turned to the Greek Revival c.1820 with several buildings in New Haven, CT, including the *Doric State House (1827–31—destroyed), and moved to NYC (1825) where he carried out work of national importance, mainly in an austere Greek-Revival style, often incorporating massive *anta-like *piers. In partnership (1829–35) with Alexander J.*Davis, practising as **Town & Davis**, the firm produced outstanding work (e.g. the State Capitols at Indianapolis, IN (1831–5—destroyed), and Raleigh, NC (1833–40), and the Custom House, NYC (1833–42)). Town & Davis also designed the first large asymmetrical Gothic house in the USA at Glen Ellen, Towson, MD (1832–4—demolished). Town built up an important architectural library during his career which he was obliged to sell in the 1840s Depression. Among his last works was the main front of the Wadsworth Athenaeum, Hartford, CT (1842–4).

Do (1986a); Hamlin (1964); Hi & Seale (1976); *JSAH*, xiii/ 3 (Oct. 1954), 27–8; J.Kelly (1948); R.Kennedy (1989); Newton (1942); P (1982); P & J (1970–86); J.T (1996); Town (1835, 1842); vV (1993)

town canopy *See* CANOPY.

Townesend, William (1676–1739) English master-mason/architect, he worked in Oxford. He probably designed, and certainly built, the Fellows' Building and Cloister (1706–12) and the Gentleman Commoners' Building (1737), Corpus Christi College, and was the contractor (1706–14) for Peckwater Quadrangle, Christ Church, erected to *Aldrich's designs, the first C18 *palace-fronted English *Palladian composition. He built (under Dr *Clarke's supervision) the front *quadrangle, hall, and chapel (1710–21), as well as the entrance-screen with *cupola (1733–6), modifying *Hawksmoor's designs in the process, at Queen's College. Other buildings erected by him to designs by others include the north-east block of the Garden Quadrangle, New College (1707), Hawksmoor's Clarendon Building (1712–15), the Bristol Buildings, Balliol College (1716–20), Hawksmoor's North Quadrangle, Hall, Buttery,

and Codrington Library, All Souls College (1716–35), and (again under Dr Clarke's direction) the Radcliffe Quadrangle, University College (1717–19). He designed and built the Robinson Buildings, Oriel College (1719–20), and arrived at the final design for New Buildings, Magdalen College (built 1733–4). He carried out works at Blenheim Palace, Oxon., including the Woodstock Gate (1722–3), and the Column of Victory (1727–30), and built Christ Church Library, Oxford, to Dr Clarke's designs (1717–38). In short, he had a hand in the building of almost every important work of architecture erected 1720–40 in Oxford. He was also a sculptor and made several funerary monuments, including that to his father, **John Townesend** (1648–1728), Mayor of Oxford (1682–3, 1720–1) also a master-mason, in St Giles's churchyard, Oxford (c.1728).

Co (2008); J.T (1996)

town garden 1. Small garden to the rear of houses, regularly laid out, with trees, shrubs, and paths, evidence of which in C18 Bath, London, etc., can be found. 2. Garden surrounded by railings, etc., in C18 squares, e.g. London. 3. Front and rear gardens of detached or semi-detached suburban houses, designs of which survive in *Loudon's publications. They became common with the *Garden-City movement, seen as important for family life. Domestic gardens are perceived as extensions to interior living.

townscape Portion of the urban fabric that can be viewed at once. It was a term much used from the 1940s, analogous to *landscape*, in the *AR*, and by **Thomas Wilfrid Sharp** (1901–78) in his *The Anatomy of the Village* (1946), intended to encourage enhancement of the British urban environment. Many historic towns have pleasing townscapes revealed as the pedestrian moves through sequences of spaces, and the *AR*'s campaign proposed that the study of townscape (pioneered by *Geddes, *Parker, *Sitte, and *Unwin) would provide precedents for urban redevelopment as well as for the *New Towns that were planned in Britain after the 1939–45 war. However, *Modernists rejected the concept as *Picturesque, leading to abandonment of its application since 1945, with obvious results.

AD, xlvi/9 (Sept. 1976), 534–6; G.Burke (1976); C & C (1986); Cullen (1973); Me.Miller (1992); Sharp (1946); Sitte (1965); Tugnutt & M.R (1987)

Townsend, Charles Harrison (1851–1928) English architect, he worked in the offices of **Walter Scott** (c.1811–1875) of Liverpool—1867–72, **Charles Barry Jun.** (1823–1900)—1873–75, and E.R.*Robson—1875–77, before commencing independent practice. In partnership (1884–6) with **Thomas Lewis Banks** (1842–1920), but by

1887 on his own, his designs were in the *Arts-and-Crafts tradition, and most were for minor domestic and church work, but he won (1892) the competition to design the Bishopsgate Institute (1891–4), the first of three public buildings in London on which his reputation largely rests, the other two being the Whitechapel Art Gallery (1896–1901) and the Horniman Museum (1901–12). *Muthesius drew attention (1900) to these as among the most significant European works of architecture at the time, with Townsend as one of the two English 'prophets' of the 'new style' (the other was *Voysey). All three show an American influence, derived from the works of H.H. *Richardson, as well as *Art-Nouveau, *Renaissance, and even *Gothic traces. Townsend used artificial stone, *mosaic, and *terracotta to face these buildings, and the use of Art-Nouveau motifs for exteriors was unusual for an English architect. His masterpiece is arguably the enchanting St Mary the Virgin, Great Warley, Essex (consecrated 1904), with a complete Arts-and-Crafts and Art-Nouveau interior, including the *chancel-screen by *Reynolds-Stephens, the *stalls and *pews being by Townsend himself. His best domestic work, inclining to the style of *Devey and Eden *Nesfield, was at Blackheath, Chilworth, Surrey, where he designed several houses, St Martin's Church (1892–5—much embellished with *frescoes), Congregational Church (1893), and Village Hall (1897).

AAQ, vi/2 (1974), 4–12; *B*, lxxxii (1902), 133–6; Bettley & Pe (2007); B *et al.* (2001); D & M (1985); A.S.Gray (1985); L.Miller (1993); *ODNB* (2004); P (1982); P & R (1973); *RIBAJ*, ser. 3, viii/9 (9 Mar. 1901), 221–41; F.Russell (ed.) (1979); Se (ed.) (1975); *The Studio*, iv (1894), 88–92, vi (1896), 24–34, xiii (1898), 239–46; J.T (1996)

Townsend, Geoffrey Paulson (1911–2002)
See LYONS, ERIC ALFRED.

trabeated Constructed on the column-and-*lintel system, as opposed to *arcuated. *See also* COLUMNAR AND TRABEATED.

tracery Arrangement by which *panels, *screens, *vaults, or windows are divided into parts of different shapes or sizes by means of moulded stone *bars* or *ribs*, called *form-pieces* or *forms* in the medieval period. Early-*Gothic windows with more than one *light did not have bars, but had flat stone *spandrels above the main lights (usually two) pierced with a quatrefoil, *roundel, or other figure: this type of tracery is the late-*First-Pointed *plate* variety, consisting of a thin flat panel of *ashlar pierced, like fretwork, with lights (*a*). Starting with early-C13 examples, the flat plate was abandoned, and large lights were divided by moulded *mullions, the *section of which continued at the heads of the window-

apertures to describe circular and other lights, leaving the spandrels open and divided into small lights of various shapes and sizes: this type of subdivision, termed *bar-tracery*, first occurred at Rheims, was introduced to England *c*.1240, and was one of the most important decorative elements of Gothic architecture, with definite stylistic connotations. The possibilities of bar-tracery helped to create the *Rayonnant style of Gothic on the Continent (*c*.1230–*c*.1350), so called from the radiating ray-like arrangement of lights in rose-windows. Simple bar-tracery formed patterns of early *Middle-Pointed *Geometrical* tracery, consisting of circles and foiled arches, with roughly triangular lights between major elements: mullions in Geometrical tracery usually had *capitals from which the curved bars sprang (*b*). After the late-C13 Geometrical tracery came *Intersecting* tracery in which each mullion of the window branched (without capitals) equidistant to the window-head formed of two equal curves meeting at a point: the Intersecting tracery-bars were struck from the same centres as the window-head, with different radii (*c*). Mullions therefore continued in curved **Y**-branches (often found in two-light windows of *c*.1300 and known as *Y-tracery*) to meet the head of the window-opening, thus describing a series of lozenge-shaped lights: the bars and main arches of the window-opening were subdivided into two or (usually) more main lights, each forming a pointed, *lancet-shaped arch. *Cusps and other embellishments were often added to Intersecting tracery, which was common *c*.1300. *Curvilinear*, *Flowing*, or *Undulating* tracery of *Second-Pointed work (*d*) dominated C14, when *ogees were applied to a basic arrangement derived from the geometry of Intersecting tracery, thus creating elaborate net-like constructions of bars at the tops of windows: this type of tracery is called *Reticulated*, because it looks like a net, and was commonly found in work of the first half of C14 (*e*). *Curvilinear* or *Flowing* tracery was developed further, exploiting ogee curves and creating dagger- or flame-shaped lights called *daggers*, *fish-bladders*, and *mouchettes*: such designs evolved throughout C15 in Europe, and became known as *Flamboyant because of the flame-like forms enclosed by the tracery-bars. From the late C14 England began to develop *Perp. or *Third-Pointed tracery, in which the main mullions (often joined by *transoms) continued as straight verticals to the undersides of the main window-arch head, with some mullions branching to form subsidiary arches: this system created *panel-like lights, and so the tracery became known as *Rectilinear* or *panel-tracery. Later still, in C15 and early C16, window-heads became much flatter *four-centred* arches, while ever-larger openings (often filling the entire walls between *buttresses) were subdivided into panels of lights by means of *crenellated transoms, the crenellations really miniature *battlements, each panel having a flattened four-centred arch at its top (*f*). *Other types of tracery include*:

branch-tracery: with ribs that flow from *piers or walls into *vaults without any interruption of a

*capital, evolved from *intersecting* tracery. On the Continent, especially in Central Europe, it means tracery fashioned to resemble tree-branches, as in St Vitus Cathedral, Prague;

drop-tracery: pendent tracery unsupported by mullions, often found on *tabernacle-work,

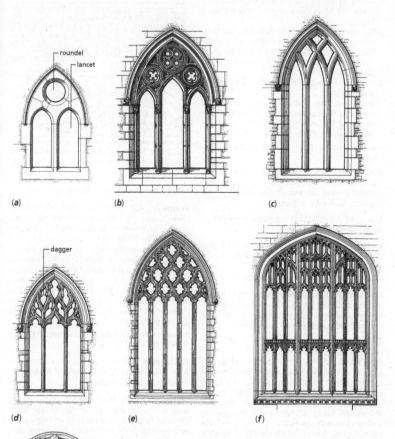

(a)   (b)   (c)

(d)   (e)   (f)

(g)

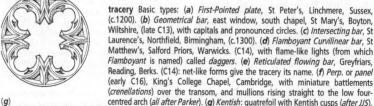

tracery Basic types: (*a*) *First-Pointed plate*, St Peter's, Linchmere, Sussex, (c.1200). (*b*) *Geometrical bar*, east window, south chapel, St Mary's, Boyton, Wiltshire, (late C13), with capitals and pronounced circles. (*c*) *Intersecting bar*, St Laurence's, Northfield, Birmingham, (c.1300). (*d*) *Flamboyant Curvilinear bar*, St Matthew's, Salford Priors, Warwicks. (C14), with flame-like lights (from which *Flamboyant* is named) called *daggers*. (*e*) *Reticulated flowing bar*, Greyfriars, Reading, Berks. (C14): net-like forms give the tracery its name. (*f*) *Perp.* or *panel* (early C16), King's College Chapel, Cambridge, with miniature battlements (*crenellations*) over the transom, and mullions rising straight to the low four-centred arch (*all after Parker*). (*g*) *Kentish*: quatrefoil with Kentish cusps (*after JJS*).

canopied *niches, etc., but also on e.g. the ceilings of the Divinity Schools (finished 1483) and Cathedral (c.1478–1503), Oxford;

fan-tracery or *fanwork*: tracery on the *soffit of a vault with ribs radiating like those of a fan, an invention of English Perp., culminating in the ceiling of King's College Chapel, Cambridge (1508–15). Medieval fan-tracery only occurs in England;

grid-tracery: with a grid of mullions and transoms, common in late-Gothic and early-*Renaissance windows, often found in grand *Elizabethan and *Jacobean houses, e.g. Hardwick Hall, Derbys. (1590–6);

Kentish tracery: with barbs or split cusps between the foils (*g*);

stump-tracery: late-Gothic tracery in Central Europe with interpenetrating intertwined bars truncated like stumps, as in *Ried's Vladislav Hall, Hradčany Castle, Prague (1487–1502).

Gw (1903); W.Pa (1892); J.Parker (1850); Rickman (1848); S (1901–2)

trachelion, trachelium Neck of a Greek-*Doric column between the *hypotrachelion grooves around the top of the *shaft and the *annulets under the *echinus.

trachyte Volcanic rock consisting mostly of sanidine felspar.

tracing-house Place where a medieval mason drew out details of *tracery, *mouldings, etc., for those working under his direction.

Booz (1956); Colombier (1953); W.Pa (1892)

trade-hall Meeting-hall or sale-room in a town for manufacturers or traders. Some medieval trade-halls (e.g. the Cloth Halls of Brugge and Ieper) were of considerable architectural magnificence.

Tradescant, John (c.1570–1638) English gardener/plant-collector employed from 1611 by the Cecil family to acquire plants and lay out gardens at Hatfield House, Herts. He later made further collections in Russia (1618), during an expedition to quell Barbary pirates (1620–1), and on various journeys in Europe. In 1628 he settled in Lambeth, Surrey, where he established gardens well-stocked with exotics, and (1637) was appointed Custodian of the Oxford Physic Garden. His son, **John Tradescant** (1608–62), was admitted a Freeman of The Gardeners' Company, and (1637) made the first of three visits to the Plantation of Virginia, bringing back numerous unfamiliar plants, therefore enriching the palette available to English gardeners.

ODNB (2004)

trail, trayle Continuous horizontal *running enrichment of vine-leaves, tendrils, stalks, and grapes, called also *grapevine, vignette, vine-scroll,* or *vinette,* often found enriching *Perp. *canopies and *screens, e.g. in funerary architecture and *chancel-screens. Several spectacular examples survive in Devon churches. The form was essentially late *Gothic, and recurs throughout Europe.

F.Bond (1908a); B & C (1909)

trail, trayle (*top*) Wells Cathedral, Som. (second half of C15). (*bottom*) St Mary's, Oxford (late C15) (*both after Parker*).

Trajanic column See TRIUMPHAL COLUMN.

Tramello, Alessio (*before* 1470–c.1528) Italian *Renaissance architect, influenced by *Bramante's architecture, he designed the Churches of *San Sisto* (1499–1514—with a barrel-vaulted coffered *nave resembling *Alberti's *Sant'Andrea,* Mantua); *San Sepolcro* (from 1513—with alternate square and rectangular nave-*bays); and centrally planned *Madonna di Campagna* (1522–6—on a Greek-cross plan), all in Piacenza. He was also involved in the building of the *Steccata,* Parma (begun 1521) to designs by **Giovanni Francesco Zaccagni** (1491–1543).

Adorni (1998); Ganz (1968); Gazzola (ed.) (1935); He (1996); P (1982); J.T (1996)

transenna 1. Roman cross-beam. 2. *Transom. 3. *Early-Christian *lattice-work of *marble or metal enclosing a *shrine.

transept 1. Any large division of a building lying across its main axis at 90°. In an *Early-Christian *basilica it was the large and high structure to the liturgical west of the *apse, on occasion so high that the *nave and *aisles stopped against its wall, as in the C4 Constantinian *basilica of *San Pietro,* Rome. 2. In a cruciform church the transept is often of the same *section as the nave, and may have no aisles, or one, or two (called *cross-aisles*): eastern transept-aisles were usually subdivided into chapels. At the position where the transepts branched on either side of the *crossing, often marked by a crossing-tower (e.g. Lincoln Cathedral), *flèche (e.g. many French cathedrals), or *lantern (e.g. Ely Cathedral), the *choir continued eastwards, often divided immediately to the east of the crossing by a *pulpitum* or *choir-screen. Larger medieval cathedrals (e.g. Lincoln) sometimes had secondary transepts at the west end of the nave (really a form of *narthex), and to the east of the crossing, on either side of the *sanctuary and choir-aisles: in both cases they would have had eastern chapels. *Compounds are therefore*:

transept-aisle: aisle on the east or west or both sides of a transept;

transept-chapel: chapel on the eastern side of a transept, usually set in a transept-aisle, but sometimes projecting from it in apsidal arrangements (e.g. Lincoln Cathedral).

Transitional architecture Term used to denote the merging of one style with another, especially the C12 transition from *Romanesque to *Gothic, but sometimes applied to other styles.

Boisserée (1833); Gall (1915); Sauerländer (1987)

transom(e) 1. *Cross-bar or *beam. 2. Horizontal element framed across a window, generally used during the Perp. period, and commonly found in the grid-*tracery of *Elizabethan and *Jacobean houses, dividing the window-aperture into *lights framed by *bars forming the *mullions and transoms. 3. Horizontal piece in a *doorway forming part of the frame, above which is a *fanlight.

transverse arch *or* **rib** Arch or *rib at 90° to the main axis of a vaulted space or outside wall, separating one *bay of a *vault from another.

trap-door Door, sliding or hinged, flush with a surface, in a floor, roof, ceiling, or *stage of a theatre.

Trasparente See TOMÉ, NARCISO.

trave, travis 1. *Cross-beam. 2. Division or *bay, as in a ceiling (thus said to be *travated* or *traviated*) formed by cross-beams. 3. Division between *stalls in a *choir or *stable.

traverse 1. *Screen or barrier, usually a baffle, or to allow a passage from one part to another in privacy. 2. *Transom or horizontal part of an *architrave or *door-frame. 3. *Gallery or *loft, usually screened, for communication between two *apartments, e.g. across a hall.

Travertine Ochre-, amber-, or cream-coloured textured *limestone (also called a *marble*), pitted with irregular holes, and with random dark graining, found in the Tiber Valley near Rome, and used since Antiquity for paving, *cladding, etc.

W.McKay (1957); W.Pa (1892); Rodolico (1953)

trayle See TRAIL.

tread See STAIR.

Treadwell, Henry John (1861–1910) English architect: with **Leonard Martin** (1869–1935) he practised in London (1890–1910), specializing in developing small, narrow-fronted sites in London's West End. Stylistically, their work was a free eclectic mix of *Art Nouveau, *Baroque, late Continental-*Gothic, and dashes of other styles. Among their best buildings were 23 Woodstock Street, 7 Dering Street, 7 Hanover Street, 74 New Bond Street, 20 Conduit Street, 78 Wigmore Street, 106 Jermyn Street, and 61 St James's Street (all early 1900s), and 78–81 Fetter Lane, in the City. They designed the *Rising Sun* Public House, 46 Tottenham Court Road (1897), St John's Hospital, Lisle Street, Leicester Square (1904), the *White Hart*, Windsor, Berks., and St John's Church, Herne Hill (1910).

A.S.Gray (1985)

treasury 1. Room or building in which precious objects are preserved. 2. Building housing the Department of State collecting and managing public revenue.

tree Large piece of timber, e.g. *beam, *lintel, *Rood-beam, *bressummer. *Compounds include*:

tree-house: 1. dwelling built among the branches of trees, affording shelter from floods, wild animals, etc.; 2. *folly, or ornamental *summerhouse built in European gardens from the C16 (e.g. the C18 *Gothick example at Pitchford Hall, Salop.). If (1) had ever been a precedent for (2), the evidence is elusive;

Tree of Jesse: see JESSE;

tree-nail: 1. *gutta; 2. dowel *trenail*, or wooden pin, used to join timbers together;

tree-trunk: pieces of trunks of trees, the branches lopped off, were sometimes used in *Picturesque or *rustic buildings, e.g. *cottage orné*, where a particularly *primitive effect was sought for columns. The form was carved in stone for some *Renaissance and *Mannerist designs.

trefoil See FOIL.

treillage 1. As *trellis (1). 2. More elaborate kind of trellis—the words are interchangeable. It can have architectural pretensions, with *alcoves, columns, *exedrae*, and *wings (e.g. at Versailles and Chantilly (France)). C16 Mannerist *treillage* provided *screens and other elements in gardens, as illustrated by Vredeman de *Vries in his *Hortorum . . . (1583). *Dézallier d'Argenville (1709) illustrated *treillage* elaborated with *pilasters, *entablatures, *cornice, *brackets, and *urns.

DdA (1709); Pa (1892); Symes (1993); Tay (2006); Vries (1583)

trellis 1. Any *screen-work made of thin strips (usually timber laths) crossing each other, either at 90° or set diagonally, forming a *lattice of lozenge-shapes, as in an *arbour or any framework supporting vines or other plants. **2.** Stone enrichment of the *Romanesque period resembling a wooden trellis composed of *fillets, giving the appearance of continuous overlapping *chevron-strips (frequently decorated with stud-like elements perhaps suggesting nails) set between two horizontal framing *mouldings.

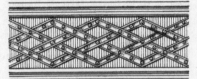

Romanesque studded-trellis moulding, Malmesbury Abbey, Wilts. (early C12) (*after Parker*).

Tresk, Simon de (*fl.c.*1255–91) English master-mason, he supervised the construction of the Angel Choir at Lincoln Cathedral (1256–80), so must be regarded as one of the most important designers of that period.

J.Harvey (1987)

tresse *Interlacing ornament resembling overlapping *guilloches, usually on a *torus *moulding, but also occurring on flat horizontal *bands or *string-courses.

Trezzini, *or* **Tressini,** *or* **Trezini, Domenico** (1670–1734) Swiss-Italian architect. He settled in Russia, having been called by **Tsar Peter I of Russia** ('the Great'—*r.*1682–1725) from Copenhagen at the foundation of St Petersburg (1703). He designed the Summer Palace (1712–33), the Cathedral of Sts Peter and Paul in the Fortress (1712–33), and Government Ministries in a series of buildings linked by a huge open *gallery (1722–41). His relative, **Pietro Antonio** (*fl.*1726–51), re-introduced the *quincunx church-plan to ecclesiastical buildings in St Petersburg.

Cracraft (1988); G.H (1983); K-R & F (1994); Lisaevich (1986); Ousiannikov (1987); D.Shv (2007); J.T (1996)

triangular arch Two flat stones set at an angle of 45° or thereabouts, mitred at the top, and touching each other at the apex of a triangular-headed opening. It occurs in *Anglo-Saxon architecture and is not an arch at all.

triangular fret *See* SWALLOWTAIL.

triangulation 1. Construction in which rigidity is assured by means of *struts and *ties disposed to form triangles in one or more planes. **2.** Setting out of a series or network of triangles from a base-line in order to survey land.

tribune 1. Apsidal part of a *basilica. **2.** *Bema, raised platform, or seat in a basilican building. **3.** Eastern part of a church, especially if apsidal. **4.** *Pulpitum or *ambo, and therefore, by extension, a *pulpit. **5.** *Gallery in a church, usually for seating.

triclinium Dining-room in a Roman house.

triconch *Plan in the form of a trefoil, e.g. space off which there are three *apses.

triforium, triforium-gallery In larger *Romanesque and *Gothic churches, an upper *aisle with its own *arcade forming an important part of the *elevation of a *nave interior above the nave-arcade and below the *clerestorey. **Gervase** (*fl.*late C12), in his account of Canterbury Cathedral, used *triforium* to mean the clerestorey-gallery or any upper passage or thoroughfare, and his usage does not in any way indicate 'three openings', as those at Canterbury were two or four, so the term does not seem to apply to the arcade through which the triforium-gallery is visible from the nave. Probably the most accurate way of describing the arcade would be *triforium-arcade*, or *arcade opening to the triforium-gallery*.

F.Bond (1913); W.Pa (1892); S (1901–2)

triglyph Upright block occurring in series in a *Doric *frieze: flanking *metopes, triglyphs possibly suggest the ends of timber beams. Each triglyph has two vertical V-shaped channels cut in it, called *glyphs*, and the edges are chamfered with *half-glyphs*, hence the three *glyphs* in all. In some versions of the Doric *Order the half-glyphs do not occur, so each block is referred to as a *diglyph.

trilith, trilithon Prehistoric structure composed of two massive upright stones supporting another set horizontally as a *lintel.

trilobate With three lobes: a *trefoil.

trim 1. Frame around an aperture or any architectural feature. **2.** To construct such a frame. **3.** To fit to anything. **4.** Visible timber finish to a building.

trimmer Short timber, also called *trimmer-joist*, fixed to the ends of *joists, and spanning between *trimming-joists*, when an opening is formed in a floor.

tripartite *See* VAULT.

triptych 'Picture or carving in three compartments side by side, the lateral ones being usually subordinate', though connected in subject, 'and hinged so as to fold over the central one' (*OED*), often forming a late-medieval *altar-piece, called *Flügelaltar* in Germany (where some of the finest carved and painted examples can be found). When closed, the part visible (i.e. the backs of the folding leaves) often displayed **grisaille* paintings.

COF (1988); Gw (1903); *OED* (1933)

triquetra Ornament of three interlaced *arcs* or *lobes*, essentially triangular in shape.

trisantia, *also* **transyte, tresantia, tresauns, tressaunte** **Vestibule or narrow passage between a *chapter-house and *transept, or behind the *screen in a hall.

tristyle *See* COLONNADE.

triumphal arch **Type of formal *gateway set over an axis to commemorate a victory or individual. In Roman Antiquity there were two basic kinds: a tall rectangular structure with a single arch (e.g. Arch of **Titus** (*r.*AD 79–81), Rome); and an even grander building containing a large arch flanked by two smaller and lower arches (e.g. Arch of **Septimius Severus** (*r.*AD 193–211), Rome). Triumphal arches were architectural precedents, not least because they combined *arcuated and *columnar-and-trabeated construction. The *Antique Roman type consisted of a large rectangular mass of *masonry pierced by one or three parallel arches cut through the wider sides, with an *engaged or applied *Order, invariably set on *pedestals, and a large *Attic-storey over the *entablature usually carrying a grandiose inscription. In the Titus arch the panel with inscription was set on the Attic over the single wide arch, but in the Septimius Severus exemplar the inscription stretched almost the full width of the Attic. Other versions of the three-arched type include the 'Arch of Tiberius', Orange, France (late C1 BC), and the Arch of **Constantine** (*r.* AD 324–37), Rome.

The triumphal arch was quoted by *Alberti for the front of *San Francesco*, Rimini (from 1446), and for the inside and west front of *Sant'Andrea*, Mantua (designed 1470): it was used on countless *Renaissance *façades in various combinations and transformations as it offered almost limitless possibilities. It was often a centrepiece (e.g. the south front of Kedleston, Derbys., by Robert *Adam (1759–70), and the *Avenue d'Antin* entrance to the *Grand Palais*, Paris, by **Deglane, Louvet, & Thomas** (1900)), but was revived as a free-standing monument during the Neo-Classical period (e.g. *Arc de Triomphe du Carrousel*, Paris, by *Percier and *Fontaine (1805–9)). Some later triumphal arches were designed to have extra arches at 90° to the main axis (e.g. *Arc de Triomphe de l'Étoile*, Paris, by *Chalgrin and others (1806–36), and the Thiepval Arch, Somme, by *Lutyens (1927–32)).

J.Curl (2001); Mansuelli *et al.* (1979); Ms (1966); M.Nilsson (1932); J.T (1996); Wa (1986); Westfehling (1977)

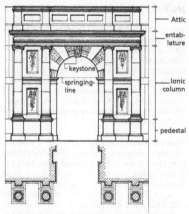

Plan/elevation of C18 triumphal arch (*after Langley*).

triumphal column Very large free-standing column, usually of the *Tuscan *Order (called *Gigantic Order), on a *pedestal, intended as a monument commemorating an individual and events. An example is the **Trajanic column**, Rome (*c.*AD 112–13), with internal winding stair, a continuous spiral *frieze wrapped around the *shaft narrating the Emperor's Dacian wars (AD 101–2, 105–6), and formerly with a statue of **Trajan** (*r.*AD 98–117) on top: the pedestal was Trajan's tomb-chamber. Very similar is the column of **Marcus Aurelius** (*r.*AD 161–80), formerly called the *Antonine column. The form was used by *Fischer von Erlach for the twin columns of the *Karlskirche*, Vienna (1715–25), the spirals recording events in the life of **Charles Borromeo** (1538–84—**Archbishop of Milan** from 1564, canonized 1610), and the columns themselves suggesting the entry to Paradise, the Temple of Solomon, and the *emblems of the Habsburgs. C19 examples include the *Vendôme* Column, Paris, by *Gondoin and *Lepère (1806–10, destroyed 1831, and re-erected 1874). Many commemorative columns, however, have plain or fluted shafts, omitting the spiral (e.g. The Monument (1671–7), and the *Corinthian Nelson Column (1839–42), both in London).

Becatti (1960); H & S (1996)

trochilus *Scotia.

trompe *Vaulted structure over an external angle of a building that has been removed, as when an entrance or *niche is placed at the corner. Thus the vault is really a type of *pendentive or *corbel and carries a load above.

trompe l'œil 1. Literally a deception or trick of the eye, it is usually two-dimensional painting showing an arrangement of objects that look disconcertingly real, often used to suggest architectural elements. **2.** Painted representations of *marble, grained wood, etc. **3.** Applied decoration imitating a surface or texture, such as *grisaille figures in Neo-Classical work imitating *reliefs, *sgraffito decoration imitating diamond-pointed *rustication (e.g. Schwarzenberg Palace, Prague (1543–63)), or *quadratura representing architecture in *perspective.

Troost, Paul Ludwig (1879–1934) German architect, he designed interiors of the North-German Lloyd liners in the 1920s and 1930s, but he is better known for his *stripped Neo-Classical buildings in Munich, including the House of German Art (1933–7) and the two office-buildings with adjacent 'temples of honour' (for Nazis killed in the 1923 Putsch) completing von *Klenze's Königsplatz (1933–7—the offices survive (one of them the Führerbau) but the Ehrentempel structures were destroyed (1947)). His severe square-columned stripped Classicism influenced *Speer.

P.Adam (1992); Lane (1985); *MFBuS*, xviii (1934), 205–12; Speer (1970); Spotts (2002); Troost (1942–3)

trophy 1. Arms and armour hung in an orderly fashion on a tree-trunk and branches to celebrate a victory in Antiquity. **2.** Sculpted representation of (1) in Classical architecture, not to be confused with a *panoply.

L & D (1986); J.T (1996)

Trouard, Louis-François (1729–94) French architect of St-Symphorien de Montreuil, Versailles (1764–70), the earliest of the austere *Neo-Classical *basilican churches erected in and around Paris at the time, with Roman-*Doric *nave-*colonnades carrying a coffered *barrel-vault, and *tetrastyle *portico of the *Tuscan Order. He designed the Chapelle des Catéchismes, St-Louis, Versailles (1764–70), using an *Ionic Order with straight *entablatures. A pioneer of a stripped, Grecian style (e.g. townhouses, Faubourg-Poissonnière, Paris (1758)), he was also an early Goth (e.g. work at the medieval Cathedral of Ste-Croix, Orléans (1766–73)). He taught *Ledoux.

B (1980); GdBA, n.s. 6, lxxxviii (1986), 201–18; M & Wa (1987)

trough-gutter 1. Rectangular-sectioned timber *gutter. **2.** Deep, wide gutter in the middle of an M-sectioned roof.

trough-roof Ceiling like an inverted trough, a term used by *Street et al. Also called trough-vault.

Troy-town 1. *Labyrinth, usually cut in turf with a single path winding in concentric circles: they were developed as hedge-mazes. **2.** *Topiary or artificial 'walls' of planting on *trellis-work and the like to suggest fortifications, as in a *military garden.

Truelove, John Reginald (1887–1942) Articled to **John Robert Hall** (1864–1924) and **William Carter Fenton** (1861–after 1922) of Sheffield, he commenced (1911) independent practice in London. Following service in the 1914–18 war, he designed several military cemeteries, including those at Noyelles-sur-Mer and Vis-en-Artois, as well as the Memorial to the Missing at Le Touret. He left the War Graves Commission (1924) and again set up in practice, designing the Municipal Buildings, Stoke Newington, London (1935–7), a handsome Classical structure unaffected by the *Modern Movement.

GS; Stamp (1977)

trullo (pl. trulli) In Southern Italy, a rough drystone building, circular on *plan, with a cone-shaped *corbel-vaulted roof.

Trumbauer, Horace (1868–1938) American architect. In practice from 1890, he designed numerous houses (Harrison House, Glenside, PA (1892–3), and several others in Philadelphia, New York, and Washington). He was an accomplished *Beaux-Arts *Renaissance-Revival architect, and could turn his hand to scholarly *Gothic. His best works (with *Abele) were the two main *campuses of Duke University, Durham, NC (1927–38), and the Philadelphia Free Library, PA (1917–27). Virtually all his buildings were well crafted and soundly based on precedent.

Maher (1975); P (1982); J.T (1996); vV (1993)

trumeau Stone *mullion or *pier supporting the *tympanum of a wide *doorway, as in medieval *Gothic churches.

trumpet-arch See ARCH.

truss 1. Rigid structural framework of timbers bridging a space, each end resting on supports at regular intervals (often defining *bays), to provide support for the longitudinal timbers (e.g. *purlins) that carry the common *rafters and the roof-covering. Its stability, dependent on e.g. *triangulation, also prevents the roof from spreading. *Types of truss or roof-structure include:*
aisle: in *timber-framed work a complete aisled structure set over the *tie-beams;
Belfast or bowstring: of timber, for spans of up to 15 metres, with a segmental top member joined

to a horizontal lower *chord, *string, or *tie (sometimes slightly cambered) by inclined *lattice-members;

box-framed: complete cross-frame the entire height of the building in a *box-framed* structure;

closed: with spaces between its members filled in (e.g. between rooms or at *gable-ends);

common rafter: type of roof constructed of pairs of common rafters. If common rafters are held together with *collars or tie-beams, the resulting structure is called a *coupled rafter roof* or a

trussed rafter roof, to emphasize the presence of additional components;

compass or *compass-headed roof*: one in which the *braces, rafters, and collar-beams of each truss are arranged and shaped in the form of an arch, thus creating a half-cylindrical underside to the roof-structure;

coupled rafter roof: a *common rafter* roof, but with the rafters connected by collars;

cradle: where the tie from the foot of one rafter is attached to the opposite rafter at a considerable

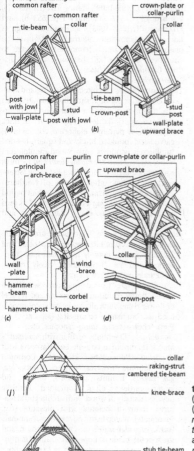

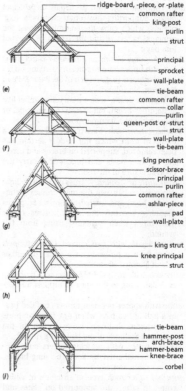

truss (**a**) Common *rafters* connected by *collars*; (**b**) *crown-post roof-truss*; (**c**) *hammer-beam roof*; (**d**) detail of *crown-post* structure; (**e**) *king-post roof-truss*; (**f**) *queen-post roof-truss*; (**g**) *scissor-braced truss* with *king pendant*; (**h**) truss with *knee-principals* and *king strut*; (**i**) *true hammer-beam truss*; (**j**) type of *principal-rafter truss* (there are many variants); (**k**) *false* or *pseudo-hammer-beam truss* (**a,b,c,e,g** after JJS; **d,f, h,i,j,k** RAM, ABDM, CBA).

height from its foot, or the structure has collar-beams and braces as well, thus forming a shape like part of a polygon which, if upside-down, could resemble a cradle, the result is called a *cradle-roof*;

cruck: pair of *cruck *blades with transverse members (e.g. a tie-beam, collar, saddle, yoke, or spur);

cut: truncated, with the part of a truss over the collar-beams flattened off;

double arch-braced: with two pairs of arch-braces forming a continuous curve from where the braces are supported to where they join in the middle of the collar;

double-framed roof: with principals or principal rafters supporting horizontal members (e.g. purlins) which carry the common rafters: the principal rafters divide the length of the roof into bays;

double hammer-beam: as a *hammer-beam* truss, but with upper hammer-beams carrying upper hammer-posts (e.g. Church of Sts Peter & Paul, Knapton, Norfolk);

false hammer-beam: with a transverse timber like a *hammer-beam, but braced to a principal or collar without a hammer-post;

hammer-beam: with transverse timbers, like a tie-beam from which the middle section has been removed, supported on braces and carrying hammer-posts and braces that carry the open structure of the roof;

intermediate or *secondary*: truss of relatively light construction between the main trusses (defining the bays) and carried on horizontal plates spanning between the main trusses rather than on a main structure rising from the ground;

kerb-principal: with two curved *kerb-principals* rising from a tie-beam to a collar on either side of a crown strut;

king-post: with an upright *post set on a tie-beam or collar rising to the apex to support a ridge-piece;

open: with spaces between timbers unfilled (e.g. in a hall of two bays when one truss supports the structure half-way along its length, the trusses at the ends of the hall being *closed*);

post-and-rafter: with principal rafters and wall-posts strengthened by knee- or sling-braces, but no tie-beams;

principal rafter roof: type of structure in which common rafters are supported on plates and purlins, the latter carried on principal rafters forming part of a truss;

queen-post: with paired vertical posts set on the tie-beam and supporting plates or purlins;

scissor-truss: with braces crossing and fixed to each other, thus tying pairs of rafters together;

single-framed roof: constructed with no main trusses, the rafters being fixed to a wall-plate and ridge, or with horizontal members entirely

omitted, so the roof consists *only* of common rafters butting together at the apex of the roof;

spere: set at the lower end of a hall dividing the cross-*entry or *screens passage from the hall itself.

2. Element projecting from the *naked of a wall, e.g. a *console, *corbel, *modillion, etc.

ABDM (1996); Brandon (1860); Gw (1903); W.McKay (1957); W.Pa (1892); S (1901–2)

Tschumi, Bernard (1944–) *See* DECONSTRUCTIVISM.

Tudor Of the time of the Tudor monarchy (of **Henry VII** (*r.*1485–1509), **Henry VIII** (*r.*1509–47), **Edward VI** (*r.*1547–53), **Mary I** (*r.*1553–8), and **Elizabeth I** (r.1558–1603)), although the reign of Edward VI is sometimes referred to as *Edwardine* (associated with much iconoclastic damage to churches), and the *Elizabethan period as distinct. *Compounds include*:

Tudor arch: *see* ARCH;

Tudor architecture: architecture in England during the Tudor period, primarily associated with late-*Perp., very flat *four-centred* or *Tudor* arches (*see* ARCH), domestic architecture of brick with *diaper-patterns, elaborate chimneys of carved and moulded brick, and square-headed *mullioned windows with *hood-moulds and *label-stops. From *Fontainebleau and Flemish sources (especially printed books) came *strap-work and many other aspects of Northern-European *Mannerism. The Elizabethan period is often seen as having a distinct style of its own associated with the early *Renaissance and *prodigy houses;

Tudorbethan: style of domestic architecture involving revival of Elizabethan, *Jacobean, and Tudor elements, notably mullioned and *transomed grid-like *fenestration, freely mixed, sometimes called *Free Tudor*;

Tudor flower: late-*Gothic ornament resembling a flattish trefoil diamond-shaped stylized ivy-leaf or flower rising vertically on its stalk, commonly used as *brattishing or cresting (*see* CRESS) on Perp. *choir-screens, tomb-canopies, etc.;

Tudor garden: Essentially regular with *compartiments*, it combined late-medieval aspects with imported *Renaissance elements. Common were *arbours, *aviaries, *bowers, *knots, *loggie, *mazes, *mounts, *pavilions, *topiary, and larger gardens often contained heraldic devices, usually of wood, with architectural features, many associated with pleasure (e.g. *banquets). Water-features, *terraces, *sundials (some very elaborate), etc., were common, and the *obelisk made its appearance, albeit in miniature. Claims that not much is known about Tudor gardens are exaggerated, for much evidence exists of splendid exemplars, especially in Northants. (where aerial photography has shown up some extraordinarily detailed stuff), and there is no shortage of graphic imagery recording a great deal of information on the topic. Although after the Break with Rome (completed 1534) under Henry VIII, England is supposed to have become insulated from Continental ideas, the *élite* still travelled, and there were published works in plenty about architecture and layouts: their influence permeated the higher levels of society, and it showed in gardens and garden-buildings. *See* PRIVY GARDEN;

Tudor Revival: C19 eclectic revival of Tudor architecture. It had two distinct strands: the style of early *Gothic-Revival cheap churches of the *Commissioners'-Gothic type and of educational buildings (*Collegiate Gothic); and the revival of domestic and *vernacular forms for houses and country cottages associated with the *Picturesque. As Tudor architecture was often of brick, the Revival lent itself to the construction of schools, *workhouses (which gave the style a bad image), chapels, *gate-lodges, and model cottages, often with diaper-patterns, small *casement-windows with leaded *lights, moulded-brick chimneys, and even partially *timber-framed structures. Many books of designs were published that featured such domestic buildings. Later C19 Tudor Revival was part of the *Arts-and-Crafts movement and the *Domestic Revival, and at its best could produce masterpieces, such as the housing in Port Sunlight (1880s–1914) and Thornton Hough (1890s), both in Ches., and both containing brilliant designs by *Grayson & Ould, *Douglas & Fordham, and William & Segar *Owen. A further, not often successful C20 revival occurred, especially in *public-house and domestic architecture (1920s, 1930s).

Airs (1995); F.Bond (1908a); B & C (1909); Bru (1990); Calloway (ed.) (1996); *GH*, xxvii/1 (Summer 1999), whole issue; Glazier (1926); Hartwell *et al.* (2011); Paula Henderson (2005); Hubbard (1991); L & D (1986); A.Langley (1997); N.Lloyd (1925); J.Parker (1850); Strong (1979)

tufa Rough, porous cellular stone, e.g. that from which the Roman *catacombs are cut.

Tuke, William Charles (1843–93) *See* MAXWELL & TUKE.

tumbling-course, tumbling-in Courses of brickwork laid at 90° to the slope of a *buttress, *chimney, or other feature, and tapering into the horizontal courses. It was often employed by C19 architects during the *Muscular phase of the *Gothic Revival, using dense bricks of an engineering type, instead of a *cope. *See* GABLE.

Bru (1990); C-T (1987); N.Lloyd (1925)

tumulus Mound of earth erected over a prehistoric tomb, etc. If made of stones it is called a *cairn*. An elongated mound is a *barrow.

tun *See* CHIMNEY-SHAFT.

Tunnard, Christopher (1910–79) Canadian-born landscape architect. Settling in England (1928) he worked (1932–5) for *Cane, establishing (1936) his own practice, designing gardens for several modern houses, including *Chermayeff's Bentley Wood, Halland, Sussex (1938–9), which he illustrated in his influential *Gardens in the Modern Landscape* (1938), on the strength of which *Gropius invited him to Harvard. The experience seems to have chastened him, for in the 1948 edn of his book he toned down intemperate remarks on C19 garden-design, and, significantly, attacked *International-Modern architecture. His latter years were spent teaching at Yale, working in the field of preserving historic buildings, and writing his history of urban developments in the USA.

B & K (2000); Shoe (2001); Tay (2006); Tunnard (1938, 1953); Tunnard & Pushkarev (1981)

tunnel-arbour *Arbour elongated to form a tunnel covered with climbing-plants over a walkway, similar to a *pergola.

tunnel-vault *See* VAULT.

turba Islamic *mausoleum.

Turin 1902 Exhibition Important international *Arts-and-Crafts exhibition in Turin, Italy, marking the apotheosis of *Art Nouveau in that country (called *Stile Liberty*). The main building, by d'*Aronco, was a *tour-de-force* of Art Nouveau, much influenced by the Vienna *Sezession.

Ms (1966)

Turkish tent Mid-C18 exotic garden-*fabrique*, of which *Keene's *pavilion, Painshill, Surrey is a celebrated example, but the type was also featured at Drottningholm, Sweden, the *Désert de Retz*, France, Vauxhall Gardens, London, and other sites.

turnbout, turnbuckle Fastener of iron or brass, turning on a pivot, to secure a window or cupboard *door.

Turnbull, William (1935–97) American architect. Believing that buildings should respond to sites, and that much that passes for architecture is mere packaging, he attempted to enrich a poverty-stricken environment with buildings that help people to enjoy where they live and work (e.g. his contributions from the 1960s to the Sea Ranch Community, Sonoma County, CA). Among other works may be mentioned the Zimmermann House, Fairfax County, VA (1975), Library and

Cultural Center, Biloxi, MS (1977), Allewelt House, Modesto, CA (1978), Edwards House, Chappaquiddick, MA (1982), St Andrew's Church, Sonoma, CA (1992), and many other buildings.

C.Moore et al. (1998); E (1994); Stout et al. (2000)

Turner, Hugh Thackeray (1853–1937) English *Arts-and-Crafts architect. Articled to 'Great' *Scott, he later assisted J.O.*Scott and 'Middle' *Scott before establishing (1885) a practice with **Eustace James Anthony Balfour** (1854–1911), brother of **Arthur James Balfour** (1848–1930—Prime Minister 1902–5). E.J.A.Balfour was Surveyor to the Grosvenor Estate in London from 1890, and it was in that capacity that **Balfour & Turner** designed Balfour Place, Balfour Mews, and buildings in Mount and Aldford Streets, Mayfair, as well as many other works of distinction for the Estate. They also refaced Wilton Crescent, Belgravia. Turner designed Westbrook, Godalming, Surrey (1902); the impressive *Lethaby-influenced Phillips memorial *cloister, Church of Sts Peter and Paul, Godalming (1913—in memory of the wireless operator who went down with the *Titanic* in 1912); and Wycliffe Buildings (1894), Mead Cottage (1895), and The Court (1902), Guildford, Surrey, among other works of quality.

A.S.Gray (1985); Nairn et al. (1971); Webster (ed.) (2012)

Turner, Joseph Mallord William (1775–1851) Celebrated as a painter, it is little known that he would rather have been an architect: indeed he worked for a time as a draughtsman for Thomas *Hardwick, and was friendly with *Soane. He designed at least two buildings: the first was a gallery he added to his house in Harley Street (now approached from Queen Anne Street West), Marylebone; and the second was his country retreat, Sandycombe (formerly Solus) Lodge, Twickenham (1812–13), a symmetrical *Italianate composition with a two-storey central block flanked by single-storey *wings with rounded corners, suggesting that Soane may have contributed. Some fifty drawings connected with this building survive in various sketchbooks.

Apollo, clxxvi/604 (Dec. 2012), 96–7; ODNB (2004)

Turner, Richard (c.1798–1881) Dublin iron-master/engineer, his earliest-known curvilinear *conservatory (1833) was erected at Colebrook, Co. Fermanagh, and the following year he established ironworks at Ballsbridge where he made iron structures of wrought-iron ribs (based on *Loudon's invention) and cast-iron members, including the east wing of the palm-house at Glasnevin Botanic Gardens (1834) and the wings of the Belfast palm-house (1839–40) designed with *Lanyon, whose beautiful bulbous oblong structure was erected between the two wings (1852—manufactured by **Young of Edinburgh**).

His masterpiece was the palm-house of the Royal Botanic Gardens, Kew, London (1844–8), designed with Decimus *Burton, but his creations were erected in numerous places, and included the central pavilion, National Botanic Gardens, Glasnevin (1847–8), and a conservatory at Bessborough, Co. Cork (1855–60).

DIB (2009); Glasra, v (1981), 51–3; Moorea, ix (Dec. 1990), 3–5; Williams (1994)

Turner, Thomas (1820–91) Irish architect, son of Richard *Turner, pupil of *Lanyon, he designed many buildings in the North of Ireland, some in association (from 1861) with the architect/civil-engineer, **Richard Williamson** (fl.1847–74), who was Surveyor to the County of Londonderry and The Honourable The Irish Society from 1860. One of his earliest works is the handsome *Tudor-Gothic *screen in front of St Patrick's RC Pro-Cathedral, Dundalk, Co. Louth (1849), but his masterpiece is probably the Town Hall in Coleraine, Co. Londonderry, erected by The Irish Society (1858–9). Among his other works may be cited the handsome Northern Bank, Shipquay Place, Londonderry (1866—which looks Glaswegian). He has been credited with The Irish Society's Schools at Balloughy, Coleraine, and Culmore, all in Co. Londonderry, and all 1860s, but the documentary evidence suggests Williamson was mostly responsible for these, although Turner may have had a hand in the designs. With William *Burn, Turner designed Stormont Castle, Belfast (1857–8), a hefty essay in the *Scottish-Baronial style; the conservatory at Ballywalter Park, Co. Down (1863—some accounts suggest he also designed the *Italianate house itself (from c.1847), credited to Lanyon); and Craigavad House (1852—later the Royal Belfast Golf Club). Other buildings have been attributed to him, including Craigdarragh House, Helen's Bay (c.1850).

Brett (2002); CL, dliii/3961 (24 May 1973), 1495–6; J.Curl (1986, 2000); DIB (2009); O Donoghue (2007); Thesis 461 QUB (1989); Williams (1994)

turnpike See STAIR.

turret 1. Small or subordinate tower normally forming part of a larger structure, especially a rounded addition to the angle of a building, sometimes commencing on *corbels at some height from the ground, and usually containing a spiral *stair. 2. Round tower of great height in proportion to its diameter. 3. Small circular tower on the top of a large tower, often at the corners, called *tourelle, usually with a conical or domical roof, so known as a *pepper-pot turret. Such subsidiary turrets are found in *crenellated and *Scottish-Baronial architecture, and may also be capped by *spires, *pinnacles, or *ogee-headed tops.

MacG & R (1887–92); W.Pa (1892)

turret-step Piece of stone with a plan resembling the outline of a keyhole. The circular end forms part of the central *pier or *newel of a circular or winding newel-stair, and the fan-tailed part is the step.

turriculated Building with *turrets.

Tuscan architecture *See* ETRUSCAN.

Tuscan Order One of the five *Roman *Orders of architecture identified during the *Renaissance, and the simplest, also sometimes called the *Gigantic Order after *Scamozzi, probably because a variety of Tuscan column was used for *triumphal columns of the *Antonine or *Trajanic type in Antiquity. It resembles Roman *Doric, but has no *triglyphs on its unadorned *frieze. Its *base is very plain, consisting of a square *plinth-block supporting a large *torus over which is the *fillet and *apophyge creating the transition to the plain unfluted *shaft (often with an *entasis more pronounced than in the other Orders). At the top of the shaft is another apophyge and fillet, then an unadorned *astragal over which is a *neck or *hypotrachelium, then another fillet or fillets, a plain *echinus, and a square *abacus, usually with a simple fillet at the top, but sometimes an unmoulded block. The *entablature has a plain *architrave, plain frieze, and crowning *cornice of simple bed-moulds, and a *cyma recta on top, and there are no *modillions, *dentils, *mutules, or enrichments of any sort. However, in a much more severe version of the Order codified by *Palladio based on *Vitruvius and used by Inigo *Jones at St Paul's Church, Covent Garden, London (1631–3), the conventional frieze and cornice are omitted: instead, there is a very wide overhanging *eaves-cornice supported on long, plain, bracket-like mutules, immediately over the architrave.

W.Chambers (1759); J.Curl (2001); Normand (1852); Spiers (1893)

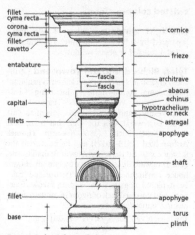

Tuscan Order (*after Palladio*).

Tuscher, Carl Marcus (1705–51) German architect/painter, he worked in Italy (1728–41), where he was influenced by *Juvarra. After a brief period in London (1741–3), he was called to Copenhagen (1743) by **King Christian VI of Denmark** (*r.*1730–46), where he worked mostly as a painter. Impressed by Tuscher's *Abbecedario dell'Architettura Civile* (Primer of Civil Architecture—1743), the King asked him to present plans for the Amalienborg, and it is probably because of Tuscher's influence on *Eigtved that the *Amalienborg Plads* acquired its octagonal form and that the four *palaces were articulated as *pavilions and *galleries.

J.T (1996); We (1952)

tusk, tuss Projecting *tenon or *toothing-stone left in a wall to enable another wall to be joined and bonded to it.

twining stem, twisted stem *Moulding resembling a long, thin, cylindrical rod with a stem wrapped around it, forming a spiral ornament set in a *cavetto between two continuous plain *bowtells, common in *Romanesque work.

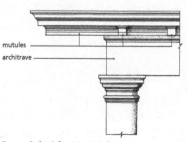

mutules
architrave

Tuscan Order (*after Inigo Jones*).

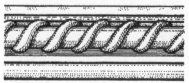

twining stem St Mary's, Wimbotsham, Norfolk (*after Parker*).

twisted column *Torso.

two-light window Window of two *lights separated by a *mullion or (rarely) a *transom, called a *coupled* or *gemel* window.

Tyler, Richard Michael Townsend (1916–2009) English architect, he specialized in restoring/modernizing country-houses, including Forde Abbey, Dorset, Wrotham Park, Herts., Levens Hall, Westmd., and Dochfour near Inverness. One of his best works was the C17 Hall Barn, near Beaconsfield, Bucks. (1968–70—with **Thomas Arthur Bird** (1918–2017)) and he converted the former coach-house and stables at Brahan Castle, near Dingwall, Ross & Cromarty, into an elegant house, leaving the Castle as a *Picturesque *ruin. He deplored slogans such as 'form follows function', and despised lack of rigour in modern architectural 'education'.

The Times (6 Feb. 2009), 75, (11 Aug. 2017), 52

Tylman van Gameren (*c.*1630–1706) *See* GAMEREN.

tympan, tympanum (*pl.* tympana) **1.** Triangular or segmental face of a *pediment contained between the horizontal and *raking *cornices or horizontal and segmental cornices, often enriched with *relief sculpture. **2.** Area above a *lintel over an opening contained by an arch set above it, e.g. in the west doors of *St-Gilles-du-Gard*, near Arles (C12), and the *Madeleine*, Vézelay (C12), both in France.

type 1. Exemplar, pattern, prototype, or original work serving as a model after which a building or buildings are copied. **2.** Something exemplifying the ideal characteristics of, say, a *temple, so some would hold that the *Parthenon* is the very *type* of a Greek-*Doric temple. **3.** *Tester. **4.** Top of a small *cupola or *turret, e.g. the crowning part of a *Tudor turret, such as those of the White Tower, Tower of London (1532). **5.** Form or character that distinguishes a class or group of buildings (building-type), e.g. church, *mausoleum, town-hall, temple.

typology Study of symbolic representation or of *types.

UEC Urban Entertainment Center, American development containing entertainment-facilities (cinemas, etc.) within a *theme-park, *shopping-centre, *shopping-mall, etc.

umbraculum *Baldachin.

umbrella 1. *Chattra, normally on a *stupa but used on its own, in *Hindoo architecture. 2. Type of *dome.

umbrella dome See DOME.

umbrello Garden-*fabrique, a small structure protecting a seat.

Langley (1747)

uncut modillion *Mutule, as in variants of the *Tuscan *Order, or *modillion resembling a bracket or unadorned cantilevered block.

undé, undy *Wave-scroll, *oundy, *Vitruvian scroll, or any *undulating repeated *running wave-like ornament, esp. in Classical architecture: also a late-*Gothic ornament (e.g. *trail).

undercroft *Crypt or vaulted space under a church or other building, wholly or partly underground.

Underwood, Charles (1790–1883) He designed the *Gothic St Augustine's Church, Rugeley, Staffs. (1821–5), before settling in Bristol, where he was responsible for several Classical *villas and *terraces in Clifton, including 1-4 Kensington Place (1842), Worcester Terrace (c.1848–53), and Canynge Square (1840–9). He was engaged for the buildings in the idyllic Arcadian landscape of Arno's Vale Cemetery, Bristol, including the fine *Greek-Revival *lodges (1837–8), Roman-*Italianate Anglican Chapel, and Greek-*Ionic Dissenters' Chapel. Works by him in styles other than *Classicism were less successful (e.g. St John the Baptist's Church, Burley, Hants. (1838–9—brick, with *lancets), and Frocester Manor, Glos. (1857–9—in 'gauche' *Tudor Revival)).

Co (2008); Foyle & Pe (2011); GJ & L (1979); Verey & Brooks (2002)

Underwood, George Allen (1792–1829) Charles *Underwood's brother, many of whose designs show the influence of *Soane. Among his works may be cited Montpellier Spa (1817), stables for Thirlestane House (c.1820), the Masonic Hall, Portland Street (1820–3), and The Plough Hotel, High Street (before 1826), all in Cheltenham, Glos.; and churches in Cheltenham (1820–2), Frome, Som. (1818), and Timsbury, also Som. (1826). Another brother, **Henry Underwood** (1788–1868), was also active in Cheltenham and Bath: in the latter town he designed the *Greek-Revival former Swedenborgian Church, Henry Street (1843–4).

Co (2008)

Underwood, Henry Jones (1804–52) Pupil of *Seward, he later joined the progressive office of Robert *Smirke, who sent him to Oxford (1830) to supervise alterations to the Bodleian Library. He established his own practice in that city, where he designed part of the *Gothic fronts of Exeter College facing Broad and Turl Streets (1833–5); Wolsey's Almshouses, St Aldate's (1834—now part of Pembroke College); the former Botanic-Garden Library and Lecture-Rooms, High Street (1835—now Magdalen College Bursary); the *Greek-Revival St Paul's Church, Walton Street (1836); additions to the County Gaol (1850–2); Sts Mary & Nicholas Church, Littlemore (1835–6—a *First-Pointed essay much admired at the time, even in Ecclesiological circles). He refitted the Laudian Library, St John's College, Oxford, in Gothic style (1838–40). His practice was inherited by **Edward George Bruton** (fl.1845–99).

Co (2008); Pa (ed.) (1892)

undulating 1. Curvilinear or Flowing *tracery. 2. Undulate *band *moulding, *guilloche, *oundy, *undé, undy, *wave-scroll or *Vitruvian scroll.

Unger, Georg Christian (1743–1812) German architect, pupil of *Gontard: together they designed the elegant *triumphal arch at Potsdam (1770), and with *Boumann the Royal Library with its curved *façade to the Forum Fridericianum, Berlin (1774–80). He designed 26-7 Breiterstrasse, Potsdam (1769), based on Inigo *Jones's proposals for the Palace of Whitehall published in Vitruvius Britannicus.

W.Pa (1892); Wa & M (1987); Wendland (2002)

Ungers, Oswald Mathias (1926–2007) German architect. His own house at *Belvederestrasse*, Köln-Müngersdorf (1959), stands out as an unusually crisp and rigorous essay in simple blocky geometrical forms for its time. He became one of the more influential architects of the late C20, as a theorist and a builder of exemplars, and, more especially, as a forceful opponent of *International Modernism. His mature works include the German Architecture Museum, Frankfurt-am-Main (1979–84), Baden State Library, Karlsruhe (1979–92), Alfred Wegener Institute for Polar and Ocean Research, Bremerhaven (1980–4), and the German Ambassador's Residence, Washington DC (1988–94). In these projects Ungers investigated morphologies and transformations, the contexts in which the buildings were to stand, and historical references. His work has a serenity and a geometrical integrity unusual in post-war German architecture. He and *Kleihues have been two of the most influential exponents of *Rational architecture (*or* *Neo-Rationalism) in Germany. Ungers published extensively, including *Quadratische Häuser* (1983): in his belief that architecture must reflect the *genius loci*, history, and evolution, he displayed a rare sensitivity.

B-M (1996); Conrads (ed.) (1970); C & M (1962); E (1994); Js (1988a); Kieren (1994); Klotz (1977); *Das Kunstwerk*, xxxii/2–3 (1979), 132–41; *Lotus*, xi (1976), 12, 14–41; Pehnt (1970); Ungers (1997, 1998, 2000); vV (1993)

Ungewitter, Georg Gottlob (1820–64) German architect, pioneer of the *Gothic Revival. He established (1842) a practice in Hamburg, where his domestic architecture was influenced by *Chateauneuf, but (1845) became convinced that *Gothic could be applied to all building-types, and his attitudes to structure and use of materials drew on arguments advocated by A.W.N.*Pugin and *Viollet-le-Duc. His publications, including projects for town- and country-houses (*Entwürfe zu Stadt- und Landhäusern* (1858–64)), Gothic construction (*Lehrbuch der gotischen Konstruction* (1859–64)), medieval ornament (*Sammlung mittelalterlicher Ornamentik in geschichtlicher und systematischer Anordnung dargestellt* (1866)), and medieval German *timber-framed houses (1889–90) were influential. With **Vincenz Statz** (1818–98) he brought out a *pattern-book of *Gothic (*Gotisches Musterbuch* (1856–61)), also published in French (1855–6) and English (1858–62) edns. He designed churches at Neustadt, Marburg (1859–64), Bockenheim, Frankfurt-am-Main (1862), and elsewhere in Germany.

G (1972); S.M (1974); Reichensperger (1866); Schuchard (1979); J.T (1996)

unit system Very large prefabricated glazing-units which, when fixed to a building's structure, form a *curtain wall.

universal design *See* BARRIER-FREE.

Unsworth, William Frederick (1851–1912) English architect, he worked for both *Street and *Burges before establishing his own office (1875) in partnership first with **Edward John Dodgshun** (1854–1927) and then (from *c.*1908 in Steep, near Petersfield, Hants.) with his son, **Gerald Unsworth** (1883–1946), and **Harry Inigo Triggs** (1876–1923). Among his works were the Art Gallery and Library, Stratford-on-Avon, Warwicks. (1881); Christ Church, Woking (1889—of brick, with *lancets), All Saints Church, Woodham (1893—with a *tile-hung *crossing), and Woodhambury (a fine *Domestic-Revival house (1889)), also in Woodham (all in Surrey); and a series of *Arts-and-Crafts buildings in the model village of Sion Mills, Co. Tyrone, commissioned by the proprietors of **Herdman**'s flax-spinning mills. The last includes the remodelling of *Lanyon's Sion House (1880s) with gate-house and stables, all in a pretty English *half-timbered style, and other attractive structures, among them the Church of the Good Shepherd (consecrated 1909), in an style based on a *Romanesque exemplar in Pistoia, Italy, a curious choice for an Anglican church in Ulster.

B *et al.* (2001); *DIA* (2013); *Irish Builder* (4 Dec. 1884); Rowan (1979)

Unwin, Sir Raymond (1863–1940) English town-planner, the most influential of his time. Influenced by William *Morris and by Socialist ideas, he was later drawn to the theories of Ebenezer *Howard. He formed a partnership (1896–1914) with his brother-in-law, Barry *Parker: as **Parker & Unwin** they designed St Andrew's Church, Barrow Hill, Derbys. (1893), and several houses in the *Arts-and-Crafts style before establishing their reputation by planning (from 1901) New Earswick Village near York for the **Joseph Rowntree** (1836–1925) **Village Trust**. This was followed by the realization of Ebenezer Howard's proposals, the layout of Letchworth, Herts., the first *Garden City (from 1903), where Parker & Unwin also built several houses and other structures. Progress at Letchworth was slow, but at the next project, Hampstead *Garden Suburb, it was rapid (from 1905). Unwin settled in Hampstead, while Parker stayed on at Letchworth. The Suburb was a successful example of the ideals of low-density housing derived from the pioneering development at Bedford Park, Chiswick, and was the prototype for many inter-war suburban developments. The very grand, formal centre at Hampstead, however, consisting of two churches, several houses, and an institute, were designed by *Lutyens (from 1908).

Unwin published (1909) *Town Planning in Practice: An Introduction to the Art of Designing Cities and Suburbs*, a text that had a considerable effect on town-planning for the next three decades. Appointed (1914) Chief Inspector of Town Planning at the Local Government Board (later Ministry of Health), and then Director of Housing for the Ministry of Munitions during the 1914–18 war, he influenced a number of developments, including settlements at Gretna, Scotland, and Mancot Royal (Queensferry), Flintshire (later Clwyd). He was a member of the **Tudor-Walters** Committee on Housing (1918), was consulted for the New York Regional Plan in the USA (1922), and remained a senior civil servant with the Ministry of Health until 1928. He advised on the planning of the Manchester satellite development of Wythenshawe, for which Parker was the main consultant (1927–41): it was one of the most ambitious local-authority housing-schemes of the time, and anticipated the first-generation *New Towns after the 1939–45 war. He was also involved in proposals for London, the fruits of which were the Greater London Plans (1940s). He was one of the founders of the Town Planning Institute (1913) and was President of the Royal Institute of British Architects (1931–3).

AR, clxiii/976 (June 1978), 325–32, 366–75; Ashworth (1954); Creese (ed.) (1967, 1992); F.Jackson (1985); LeG & S (1996); Me.Miller (1992, 2002); M & G (1992); L.Mumford (1961); *ODNB* (2004); P (1982); Sw (1981); J.T (1996); Unwin (1908, 1909, 1918, 1971)

Upjohn, Richard (1802–78) English-born architect, he emigrated (1829) to the USA, settling in Boston, MA, where he established a practice (1834). His earliest works were the serene and pleasing *Greek-Revival houses in Bangor, ME (1833–6), and a *Gothic-Revival house in Gardiner, ME (1835), but he is remembered primarily as a Gothic Revivalist. His masterpiece was the *Second-Pointed Trinity Church, Wall Street, NYC (1841–6), which shows the influence of A.W.N. *Pugin (it resembles the church depicted in Plate H of *The True Principles of Pointed or Christian Architecture* (1841)), and gained critical acclaim. St Mary's, Burlington, NJ (1846), with its handsome *crossing-tower and *broach-spire, was derived from the English medieval Church of St John the Baptist, Shottesbrooke, Berks., illustrations of which, from drawings by *Butterfield, had been published by the Oxford Society for Promoting the Study of Gothic Architecture (later called the Oxford Architectural Society). Upjohn's Church of the Holy Communion, NYC (1844–6), was also Anglo-Gothic in style.

Upjohn produced some buildings in the *Romanesque style, e.g. the Church of the Pilgrims, Brooklyn, NYC (1844–6), Bowdoin College Chapel and Library, Brunswick, ME (1845–55), and St Paul's Church, Baltimore, MD (1854–6), the last more like a true *Rundbogenstil building

based on Lombardic exemplars. He built an enormous number of churches, many of some distinction, and also designed other building types, a fact often obscured by his reputation as a church-architect. He published *Upjohn's Rural Architecture* (1852) which shows something of his grasp of composition and style. He helped to found and was first President of the American Institute of Architects.

P & J (1978); P (1982); St (1968); J.T (1996); E.Upjohn (1939); R.Upjohn (1975)

Upjohn, Richard Michell (1828–1903) English-born American architect, son of Richard *Upjohn. He worked closely with his father, becoming a junior partner (1853). The earliest building for which he alone appears to have been responsible was Madison Square Presbyterian Church, NYC (1853–4). He introduced an almost *Rogue *High-*Victorian *Gothic style to the USA, as at the Grace Church, Manchester, NH (1860), and the spiky, rather frantic north gates of Greenwood Cemetery, Brooklyn, NYC (1861–5). The Connecticut State Capitol, Hartford (1872–8), a showy American interpretation of Continental *Gothic Revival, with many *gables, crested roofs, and an extraordinary (and somewhat incongruous) high *cupola, is his most famous work. He published (1869) an influential paper on *Colonial architecture in NYC and the New England States.

D.Curry & Pierce (eds) (1979); *DAB* (1948); P (1982); *Proc. of the Third Annual Convention of the AIA* (Nov. 1869), 47–51; E.Upjohn (1939)

Urabe, Shizutaro (1909–91) Japanese architect, much of his work was in Kurashiki (his birthplace), near Okayama, the *vernacular architecture of which was largely constructed of beaten earth and brick, to which he responded with sensitivity, reorganizing traditional warehouses and other building-types. His most celebrated work was Kurashiki Ivy Square (1970–4), a conversion of some brick-built industrial buildings into a Cultural Centre for Youth, complete with exhibition areas, refreshment facilities, and lecture-rooms. Other works included the Historical Archives Building, Yokohama (1981), and the Kanagawa Prefectural Archives of Modern Literature, Yokohama Women's University (1984).

E (1994)

uraeus (*pl.* **uraei**) Representation of the sacred asp, cobra, or *serpent, e.g. on the *Nemes* headdress of Ancient-Egyptian divinities and sovereigns, or on either side of winged discs or globes on the *gorge-cornice of Egyptian architecture. *See also* OUROBOROS.

J.Curl (2005); L & D (1986); Roullet (1972)

uraeus Ancient-Egyptian Pharaonic *Nemes* head-dress with (*right*) rearing *Wadjet uraeus* (symbol of kingship and tutelary goddess of Lower Egypt) and (*left*) head of *Nekhbet*, vulture-goddess of Upper Egypt.

urban design Application of certain design-principles relating to the form and use of urban settlements: form is dependent upon mass (buildings, their bulk, modelling, and height, and the land they occupy) and space (e.g. streets and open spaces defined by buildings), and uses of both buildings and spaces (whether intensive or not) also play important roles. Several commentators have agreed that there are five categories of relationships in urban built form: routes (e.g. alleys, streets, canals, etc.); boundaries (e.g. natural or built boundaries, such as water-fronts); districts (e.g. clearly defined residential quarters, central areas, etc.); nodes (e.g. junctions of routes, such as squares, etc.); and landmarks (e.g. built fabric, usually monumental, with significant visual, symbolic, or aesthetic identities). Towns and cities existed in Antiquity: at Ur (present-day Iraq), for example, in the fourth millennium BC, there were routes (alleys and streets), with clearly-defined plots for housing, and important monuments. Settlements laid out on grids (a convenient means of defining land for development) existed in China, Ancient Egypt, México, and Ancient Babylon: in the last, a processional route of considerable magnificence was created. When the Greeks created new cities from scratch (e.g. Miletus, by *Hippodamus (C5 BC)), grids, rationality, and geometry were employed, and theories of urban-design evolved whereby social order could be expressed. Many public buildings and monuments were erected in Athens, but these were not related to each other in formal geometrical ways: the creation of vistas, and the exploitation of geometry to create splendid effects in cities were evolved in *Hellenistic settlements such as Pergamon (C3 BC), although stupendous formal arrangements of processional ways with symmetrically disposed buildings had been created by the Ancient Egyptians in their great temple complexes at Karnak and elsewhere. Geometry was further exploited by the Romans, who developed Hellenistic themes, and who created huge public buildings (e.g. *thermae, fora, *circuses, *arenas, etc.), all treated with great architectural splendour. High-density urban living was possible through the creation of blocks of apartments (*see* INSULA) bounded by streets, and

buildings for large numbers of spectators were erected (e.g., the Colosseum, Rome). By the standards of Antiquity, Rome was a true metropolis, requiring major engineering works to provide it with water and eliminate its wastes. Its defensive walls alone were major undertakings, and its dead were disposed of in linear *cemeteries (e.g. *Via Appia Antica*), in *columbaria, or in *catacombs. In short, Ancient Rome was a remarkable example of a sophisticated and well-organized city that was a precedent for many of the world-cities of C19. The Romans also created many new towns, based on the standard *castrum* plan with two main thoroughfares crossing each other at right angles, a forum in the centre, and public buildings (e.g. *thermae*, temples, etc.) arranged within the logical grid-plan. Constantinople, too, was a world-city, richly embellished with vast churches and public buildings, and with monuments of considerable cultural resonance.

Islamic cities in Central Asia and elsewhere, with their *madrasas, *mosques, etc., also had sophisticated architectural responses to commerce, religion, and social interaction (e.g., at Isfahan), while huge mosques (e.g., the *Mezquita Aljama*, Córdoba, Spain) attest to the importance of geometry and formal axes in the creation of urban monuments. In contrast, urban organization in Western Europe declined after the fall of Rome, and it was not until C12 that some kind of recognizable order in urban design was again apparent in the *bastide* towns and other settlements in France, England, Spain, and Germany (e.g. Villeneuve-sur-Lot, Flint, etc). Generally speaking, however, medieval European towns and cities were densely developed within their walls, with main routes leading from the gates to the centre, where market-places (often containing guild- or town-halls, and surrounded by houses of the more substantial burghers—e.g. Brugge, Antwerp, Brussels) and large churches were built. In Flanders especially, the magnificent *Gothic guild- and town-halls attest to the wealth and power of commerce, and in Northern Italy too, civic aspirations created noble spaces and buildings, as in Siena and Florence.

Around the middle of C15, prompted by the ideas of *Vitruvius (who suggested towns should be centrally planned for defence), many theorists (e.g. *Alberti and *Filarete) proposed formal, geometrical, polygonal town-plans, surrounded by massive fortifications to resist the might of modern artillery. These 'ideal city' plans (e.g. by *Cataneo, *Scamozzi, et al.) were widely published, and had affinities with medieval *labyrinths such as those on the floors of Chartres or Rheims Cathedrals. Palma Nova, near Udine, Italy, was one of the most important to be realized (end of C16—though never finished), and Alberti provided theoretical bases for such plans, advocating a central *piazza*, proportional systems regulating the relationships between spaces and *façades, and emphasizing the importance of what we would term *townscape. Other examples of *Renaissance urban design included the centre of Pienza (late C15) by *Rossellino, and, of course, the transformation of Rome under **Pope Sixtus V** (*r.*1585–90), who caused *aqueducts to be built, *fountains to be erected, ancient *obelisks to be set up in significant positions, and new streets to be laid out (e.g. those radiating from the *Piazza del Pòpolo*). Roman precedents stimulated developments in France, where the *Place des Vosges*, Paris, was created at the beginning of C17 combining an arcaded surround with buildings over, and Inigo *Jones's development at Covent Garden, London, followed, strongly influenced by Italian exemplars. *Hardouin-Mansart's handsome *Place Vendôme*, Paris (from 1699), prompted the creation of regular *Places* in numerous French cities, with accompanying tidying-up of adjacent streets. *Heré de Corny created (1752–6) the splendid *Place Royale*, *Place de la Carrière*, and *Hemicycle*, Nancy, for **Stanisław Leszczyński** (1677–1766)— exiled **King of Poland** (*r.*1704–9, 1733–6) and **Duke of Lorraine and Bar** (*r.*1736–66)), one of the finest examples of *Rococo urban design. At Versailles (founded *c.*1665–71)) the relationship of town to palace (inspired by the *trivium* radiating from the *Piazza del Pòpolo*, Rome) emphasized the Absolutism of **Louis XIV** (*r.*1643–1715), and similar radiating avenues centred on the *Schloss* at Karlsruhe, Baden (from 1715). C17 Mannheim combined massive fortifications, a citadel (similar in layout to Palma Nova), and a grid-plan. Controls to regulate the style, height, and fenestration of façades were imposed in many cities to ensure homogeneity and harmony, as in such huge developments as St Petersburg, Russia, from the early C18. Handsome, regular façades were created by the *Woods at Bath, where streets, a circus, a square, and a crescent provided fine examples of unified urban design. One of the largest developments in Britain where unity of design was achieved was Edinburgh New Town, continuing well into C19. The square, surrounded by brick-fronted terrace houses, with surrounding streets also featuring such dwellings, evolved in C18 London, but when *Nash created his superb scenographic scheme for Regent's Park, Langham Place, Regent Street, and Piccadilly Circus, he chose *stucco to provide varieties of treatment, and a grander, showier architecture. English terraces and squares, of course, were exported to the North-American colonies, e.g. Savannah, GA. At Washington, DC, however, L'*Enfant combined the grid-plan with *Baroque radiating avenues for the new capital of the USA (from 1789).

C19 urban design saw the improvement of many old cities and their embellishment with noble public architecture. Berlin, for example, acquired several fine Neo-Classical buildings and many improvements designed by *Schinkel after the final defeat of **Napoléon** (1815), and from the same period *Gärtner and von *Klenze transformed Munich into the capital city of Bavaria with numerous works of architecture in different styles (*Rundbogenstil*, Neo-Classical, *Renaissance Revival, etc.). Several cities levelled their (by then) obsolete fortifications, and new promenades, avenues, and splendid buildings were laid out on them: the finest example (from 1858) was the *Ringstrasse*, Vienna, designed by *Förster, with buildings by, e.g., *Hansen, *Hasenauer, *Semper, *Siccardsburg, and van der *Nüll. Paris was also transformed into the elegant city of boulevards, parks, vistas, and buildings by *Haussmann et al., and Neo-Classical St Petersburg was further embellished on the grandest scale. Following such works, widely admired for their splendour and elegance, the Classical theory of urban design gained ascendancy, notably at the *École des Beaux-Arts*, Paris. This, in turn, greatly influenced planning in the USA, notably at the World's Columbian Exposition, Chicago, IL (1893). *Burnham applied such a *Beaux-Arts approach to his plan (with **Edward Bennett** (1874–1954)) for Chicago (1909), and the *City Beautiful Movement which was so important in the USA grew from principles established in Paris. But it was not just the creation of grand public buildings and impressive streets that made the C19 city: that century saw a huge change in attitudes towards housing, urban hygiene, and public transport. At the beginning of C19 the means of travel had not changed much since the time of **Julius Caesar** (*c.*102–44 BC), but by the end of it railways, tramways, and steam-powered ships had transformed travel, while gas-light, the emergence of electric power, the provision of clean water, the construction of vast underground systems to dispose of human wastes, and the laying out of huge cemeteries had brought about a revolution in urban comfort and hygiene. Furthermore, the provision of schools, establishments for higher education, *public parks, *museums and zoos to extend knowledge, and places of public entertainment all helped to raise tone and civilize the urban masses. Such changes had been prompted by an awareness of the necessity of doing something about those at the bottom of the social heap: industrialists such as **Robert Owen** (1771–1858) at New Lanark on the Clyde, Scotland (from 1800), and **Titus Salt** (1803–76) at Saltaire, near Bradford, Yorks. (from 1851), had established model *Company towns, and introduced philanthropic ideas to the running of factories, housing the workers, and the education of both adults and children. Such ideas became influential on both sides of the Atlantic, and in

England organizations such as the Society for Improving the Condition of the Labouring Classes built exemplary dwellings (designed by Henry *Roberts) which were widely copied. The C19 saw the development of housing-estates in the suburbs for the middle classes: early examples included Nash's *Picturesque Park Villages, Regent's Park (from 1824—completed by *Pennethorne), and Decimus *Burton's beautiful Calverley Park, Tunbridge Wells, Kent (from 1828). *Loudon's publications not only provided many exemplars for middle-class dwellings, but for workers' cottages, and unquestionably had a profound impact. His promotion of public parks and cemeteries, not only as amenities, but as educational aids, influenced many developments, and he was an early advocate of the *green belt. Architects such as *Davis in the USA owed much to Loudon's ideas and books.

Throughout C19 theoretical writings on the design of cities were published. *Cerdá's work at Barcelona and his *Teoria general de la urbanización* (1867) influenced men such as *Soria y Mata, and he was among the first to attempt to apply scientific principles to urban and rural planning. Soria y Mata's 'linear city' based on a 'spine' of railways, roads, with water-, gas-, and electric-supplies, the sewer system, and possible canals, was conceived as a 510-metre-wide strip linking existing towns, urbanizing the countryside, and ruralizing the towns: conceived on a grand scale, Soria's city might link Cadiz to St Petersburg, and his vision certainly makes economic and aesthetic sense when compared with the uncontrolled explosion of suburbanization that has occurred through almost universal car-ownership. Unfortunately his ideas were never really realized, although a poor relation was created (from 1929) at Magnitogorsk in the former Soviet Union to designs by **Nikolai Aleksandrovich Miliutin** (1889-1942). Soria envisaged linear cities where everyone was within an easy walk of the country, and could quickly reach the linear transport-system nearby to get to work. However, the centralized ideal type of city reappeared in Theodor *Fritsch's *Die Stadt der Zukunft* (1896) which seems to have influenced E.*Howard's *Tomorrow: A Peaceful Path to Real Reform* (1898), although Fritsch's ideas were more developed than those of Howard (who got the first *Garden City started at Letchworth, Herts. from 1903). *Baumeister published (1876) a text on the expansion of cities from technical and economic points of view that was for many years a standard work on the social implications of architectural intervention. **Joseph Stübben** (1845-1936) carried out many urban design schemes, and published (1890, with subsequent revisions) an influential work on the subject. Some commentators were appalled by scientific and empirical approaches, arguing that unmeasurable aspects of symbolism, historical and cultural resonances, and continuity were being ignored: among the most significant publications in this respect were those of *Sitte, who promoted an understanding and appreciation of the irregularities of medieval town-planning, and whose works influenced *Geddes and **Karl Gruber** (1885-1966—whose *Die Gestalt der Deutschen Stadt* was a sensitive study of the form of historic German towns). Other theoretical works of urban design included Tony *Garnier's *Cité Industrielle* (1904), *Hegemann and *Peets's beautiful *American Vitruvius* (1922), *Hilberseimer's *Hochhausstadt* (1924—the inevitable *International-Modernist solution of high-rise glass-clad apartment-blocks along wide streets and linked by bridges), and F.L.L.*Wright's Broadacre City (1931-5—a mostly low-density development of his *Usonian' houses set in their own grounds to provide produce). However, the *Athens Charter of *CIAM (1933), prompted mostly by Le *Corbusier, insisted on rigid *zoning, high-rise apartment-blocks set in parkland, roads for fast-moving motor vehicles, and the abolition of the traditional street: this dogma was accepted (though not by the general public) on a global scale in C20, with disastrous results, leading to considerations of what might be defensible space in increasingly violent and ugly cities. British post-1939-45 war *New Towns (with their low-density housing and uncertain centres) proved not to be the earthly paradises their protagonists claimed, and there were reactions: *Archigram promoted so-called *High-Tech buildings owing something to the imagery of Science-Fiction comic-books (e.g. 'Plug-In City'); the Japanese *Metabolists exploited prefabrication and the idea of capsules fixed to service-towers and circulation-areas; and designers such as *Tange proposed vast new developments such as that to extend Tokyo into the sea (1959-60). *Megastructures made their appearance in British second-generation New Towns (e.g. Cumbernauld (1958-63), where the unlikeable linear town-centre was designed by **Geoffrey Copcutt** (1928-97)).

Aware of problems of pollution and the necessity to control the environment, theorists such as *Fuller and *Soleri attempted solutions, but these were not widely adopted. Several thinkers attempted to recover the street and something of the cultural resonances of traditional European *urbanism (**3**) from disciples of Corbusier (the *Sixteen Principles of Urbanism were a brave riposte), and commentators such as Jane *Jacobs mounted devastating attacks on Corbusier-inspired orthodoxies still (early-C21) being force-fed to students by believers in Modernist Holy Writ. On the other hand, *theme-parks such as Disneyland (with their traditional buildings in different styles and streets) showed that more agreeable environments could be created. Architect-writers such as **Robert Charles Venturi** (1925-2018) began to promote complexity, contradiction, diversity, and even the heretical notion that somewhere as noisily populist as Las Vegas might have something from which to learn. A. *Rossi promoted the architecture of the city, **Léon Krier** (1946-) proposed nothing less than the reconstruction of the European city after its destruction (more by *Corbusier's disciples than by war), **Rob Krier** (1939-) set out theoretical bases for urban design, and Colin *Rowe and **Fred Koetter** (1938-2017) discussed the city as a kind of *collage (an approach that clearly influenced *Stirling in some of his architecture). However, despite these, and a growing interest in the possibilities of the language of *Classicism to reinvigorate urban design (e.g. by those connected with *New Classicism and *New Urbanism), technology-centred schemes were still actively promoted in the architectural press and schools. However, New Urbanism began to emerge in opposition: holding that congested, fragmented, dreary suburbs and disintegrating urban centres were not accidents, but the direct result of zoning and the legacy of CIAM, some architects proposed a return to traditional neighbourhoods with facilities for daily living within walking distances from houses, the provision of a full range of housing-types and commercial opportunities, and the taming of the motor vehicle. Seaside, Miami, FL (1987), by **Andres Duany** (1949-) and **Elizabeth Plater-Zyberk** (1950-) is an example of what might be done.

Braunfels (1988); Broadbent (1990); Calthorpe (1993); Carmona *et al*. (2003); Cerdá (1968); P.Clark (ed.) (2006); Gruber (1977); Gutkind (1964–72); H & P (1972); E.Howard (1898 etc.); J.Jacobs (1961, 1969, 1984, 1996); Katz (1994); Korn (1953); Kostof (1991, 1995); R.Krier (1979); L.Krier & Pavan (1980); Lavedan (1952–60, 1975); LeG & S (1996); Marconi (1973); L.Mumford (1922, 1938, 1946, 1961); O.Newman (1972); P & W (1990); Power (1997); Rogers & Power (2000); Salingaros *et al*. (2004); Schaffer (1982); Sitte (1965); Soria y Puig (1979); Sorkin (1992); J.T (1996); R.Vi (1966, 1996); R.Vi *et al*. (1977); Vercelloni (1994); Whittick (ed.) (1974*b*); Wy (1962)

urbanism 1. Term much used in the 1980s, based on Le *Corbusier's dogmas concerning town-planning. **2.** Urban way of life compared with life in the country. **3.** Approach to *urban design taking into account the need to respond with sensitivity to urban morphologies: **Léon** (1946-) and **Rob** (1939-) **Krier** have been in the vanguard of the movement to treat urban fabric in a more positive and less destructive way than was propounded by *International *Modernism, the *Athens Charter, and *CIAM. The Kriers and their colleagues argued that context was important where sites were being redeveloped, and that it was not just a question of one building, but streets, urban spaces, and, ultimately, whole towns that needed careful design to avoid the visual chaos imposed so destructively on so many cities since 1945: they argued in favour of a sensitivity to *townscape that had been so thoroughly rejected by Modernists. Urbanism (**3**) and *New Urbanism also reject the concept of zoning advocated by Le Corbusier (for the pleasures of urban life suggest a plurality of activities), and accept the necessity of keeping the motor-car at bay. According to Jane *Jacobs and others, people should live in cities, use them, and walk in them, not clutter and pollute them with cars and other vehicles. Urbanism in this sense implies recapturing quality, beauty, pleasure, and civilized living in cities. *See* NEO-RATIONALISM; NEW URBANISM; SIXTEEN PRINCIPLES OF URBANISM.

AD, lvi/9 (Sept. 1986); Calthorpe (1993); Choay (1965); C & C (1986); Glancey (1989); Hertz & Klein (1990); J.Jacobs (1961; Js (1988a); R.Krier (1979); Lavedan (1952–60, 1975); LeG & S (1996); P & W (1990); J.T (1996); Whittick (ed.) (1974*a*)

Urban, Joseph (1872-1933) Austrian-born architect, he studied in Vienna under *Hasenauer, settling in the USA (1911). His best-known building is the New School for Social Research, NYC (1929-30), but he became primarily a designer of interiors and theatres (about which he published a book (1929)).

Architecture, lxix (1934), 250–6, 275–90; G.Carter *et al*. (1992); Kristan (2000); J.T (1996); J.Urban (1929, 1985)

urban renewal Fashionable 1950s American euphemism for large-scale destructive redevelopment, often in association with central or municipal government, offering rich pickings for commercial architects. It was adopted in the UK to mean replanning of towns and urban centres to 'modernize' them and provide access for traffic. More recently it has tended to imply a renewal of urban fabric damaged through neglect or inappropriate intervention.

Doxiadis (1966*a*); Huxtable (1970, 1976, 1986, 1986*a*, 1997); J.Jacobs (1961, 1969, 1984, 1992, 1996)

urilla (*pl*. **urillae**) *Helix or *volute of a *Corinthian *capital.

urn Lidded ovaloid *vase on a circular *plan used in Classical Antiquity to contain cremated remains. It was a form later revived for purposes of architectural decoration, on *balustrade *pedestals, set in *niches, used as garden-ornaments, employed in funerary monuments (often draped, or with a portrait-medallion of the deceased on its side, especially in Neo-Classical examples), shown in relief on *friezes, etc., and sometimes with representations of flames issuing from the lid.

Uroboros See OUROBOROS.

Usonian See WRIGHT, FRANK LLOYD LINCOLN.

Utopian architecture Designs for buildings and cities providing ideal, or supposedly ideal, environments for their users, usually implying development where none previously existed, or where wholesale destruction of built fabric is envisaged. It is associated with social engineering, not usually benign.

AR, cxl/834 (Aug. 1966), 87–91; Choay (1965); Fishman (1977, 1987); Js (1971); Tafuri (1976)

Utopie group Architectural group established (1967) in Paris to promote expendable, inflatable, pneumatic, temporary, transportable structures. It often used *collage* in its publications.

AD, xxxviii/6 (June 1968), 255, 273–7

Utzon, Jørn Oberg (1918–2008) Danish architect. He studied with *Fisker and worked briefly with *Aalto. During 1949 he spent a week at Taliesin East with F.L.L.*Wright (who, with Le *Corbusier, was a major influence on him) prior to visiting Central America, where *Meso-American temple-remains impressed him, notably in his frequent use of the platform or *plinth in his own work. This featured in the Utzon House, Hellebaek, Helsingør (1952–3), and, on the grand scale, in the competition-winning design for the Sydney Opera House and Concert Hall, Australia (1956–74), in which the platform contained all the service-spaces and provided a support for, and visual foil to, the huge sail-like *shell-vaults that soar above the harbour. Developed in collaboration with the engineers Ove *Arup & Partners, the Sydney project proved technically demanding, and Utzon withdrew (1966) when political arguments made his position impossible.

Utzon's most influential designs were for courtyard-houses, a theme he first explored in the unbuilt competition-winning proposals for Skåna in Sweden (1954) and subsequently realized in the Kingo Houses at Helsingør (1956–60) and in a widely-acclaimed development at Fredensborg (1962–3), both in Denmark. The freely arranged site-plans of these schemes used the *additive principle of composition that was also to become the basis of his ideas for more flexible approaches to *industrialized building. These designs included the 'Espansiva' housing system (1969), developed for the Danish timber-building industry and modelled on traditional Japanese houses; a prototype building for a new college in Herning (1967); and the National Assembly Building, Kuwait (1972–85—restored following severe damage in the 1990 Gulf War), built using large-scale components cast on site. Utzon's contract did not however include the interiors, and the only public building realized wholly in accordance with his designs was the Bagsvaerd Church, near Copenhagen (1967–77), where the billowy 'cloud-vaults' form a striking contrast to the modest, system-built exterior. In partnership with his two architect-sons, **Jan** (1944–) and **Kim** (1957–), Utzon realized the Paustian Furniture Store, Nordhavn, Copenhagen (1987), by when he was spending much of his time at 'Can Lis', his house on a cliff-top near Porto Petro, Mallorca, Spain (1971–3). More recently another generation of Utzons (Jan's son and daughter) have become active in the firm: they are **Jeppe** (1970–) and **Kickan** (1971–).

AYB, vi (1955), 173–81; *AD*, xxx/9 (30 September 1960), 347–8; *ARe*, cxli/5 (1967), 189–92; *AR*, clxv/985 (Mar. 1979), 146–9; *Arkitektur*, xiv (1970), 1–48; *B + W*, xx (Sept. 1966), 10–14; Wi.Cu (1996); Do (1983); Drew (1972, 1995, 2000, 2001); Dr (1980); E (1994); T.Faber (1991); C.Floyd & Collingwood (2000); Fromonot (1998); Lasdun (ed.) (1984); Mikami (2001); RW; Weston (2002); *Zodiac* v (1959), 70–105, x (1962), 112–80, xiv (1965), 36–93

Uytenbogaardt, Roelof Sarel (1933–98) South-African architect. His early works (Welkom Church, Orange Free State (1964), and Bonwit Clothing Factory, Cape Town (1967)) were influenced by *Kahn, and during the 1970s (Werdmuller Centre, Claremont, Cape Town (1973), and University of Cape Town Sports Centre (1977)) looked to Le *Corbusier for precedents. He published (with others) *A Comparative Analysis of Urbanism in Cape Town* (1977).

E (1994); J.T (1996)

V *V-joint is a beak-joint*, i.e. **V**-shaped used in straight-joint flooring instead of tongued-and-grooved work. *V-tracery* is like *Y-tracery*, but with straighter sides.

Vaccarini, Giovanni Battista (1702-69) Sicilian architect, influenced by *Borromini, Carlo *Fontana, and (to a lesser extent), aspects of French *Classicism then beginning to percolate into Italy. His appointment (1735) as City Architect of Catania heralded the introduction there of Roman *Baroque, e.g. *San Giuliano* (1739-57), derived from Carlo *Rainaldi's *Santa Maria in Monte Santo, Piazza del Pòpolo*, Rome, while *Sant'Agata* (1735-67) owes something to *Sant'Agnese in Agone, Piazza Navona*, with a *façade slightly reminiscent of that of *San Carlo alle Quattro Fontane*, both in Rome. *Sant'Agata*'s façade is also embellished with carved *valancing like that on *Bernini's *baldacchino* in St Peter's, Rome, and has *pilaster-*capitals decorated with palms, lilies, and crowns, symbols of the Saint's martyrdom. Vaccarini designed the façade of the Cathedral (1730-68), the elephant fountain bearing an *obelisk (1736—a motif also used by Bernini), and many other buildings in Catania, also completing the Town Hall in the *Piazza del Duomo* (1735). Later works, e.g. *Palazzo del Principe di Reburdone* (c.1740-50) and the *Collegio Cutelli* (1748-54), owed less to Baroque and more to Classicism.

Alajmo (1950); Bt (1968); Boscarino (1961); Fichera (1934); N-S (1986a); P (1982); Pisano (1958); J.T (1996); D.Wa (1986)

Vaccaro, Domenico Antonio (1678-1745) Neapolitan architect. His churches, combining octagonal and rectangular volumes, include the *Concezione* at *Montecalvario* (1718-24) and the *choir and *transepts of *Santa Maria delle Grazie*, Calvizzano, Naples (c.1743). In the latter the junctions between *drum and *cupola are blurred by much frothy *stucco. His loveliest creation is the *majolica *Chiostro della Clarisse, Santa Chiara*, Naples (1739-42), in which are vine-clad *pergolas on octagonal *riggiole* (colourful majolica tiles) -clad *piers linked by seats (also majolica-faced). He also designed the *Palazzo Tarsia*, Naples (1732-9), possibly influenced by *Hildebrandt's design for the *Belvedere*, Vienna.

Bt (1975); *CL*, cxcviii/28 (8 Jul. 2004), 88-93; W.Pa (1892); S.Pisani (1994); J.T (1996)

vacuum System of artificial ventilation: vitiated air is drawn out of a volume so that fresh air fills the vacuum. *See* PLENUM.

vagina Lower part of a *term *pedestal with which the bust merges.

Vágó, Pierre (1910-2002) Hungarian-born French architect, whose father, **József Vágó** (1877-1947), and uncle, **László** (1875-1933), were distinguished architects influenced by Otto *Wagner and by *Neo-Classicism. As a pupil of *Perret, construction and its expression was always a strong component in his work. He was editor (1930s) of the influential journal *L'Architecture d'aujourd'hui* which publicized *International Modernism. He set up his own practice (1934) and exhibited a prefabricated steel house at the *Exposition de l'Habitation* in Paris that year. He prepared master-plans for several towns, including Arles, Avignon, and Beaucaire (1945-7), and Le Mans (1947-8), and his buildings included churches, houses, and *villas. He collaborated with *Freyssinet on the design and construction of the huge Basilica of St Pius, Lourdes (1958). He founded (1932) the *Réunions Internationales des Architectes*, a forum which evolved into the *Union Internationale des Architectes* (UIA) after the 1939-45 war, with Vago as its Secretary-General.

E (1994); Merényi (1970); J.T (1996); Vágó (2000)

Valadier, Giuseppe (1762-1839) Rome-born architect/urban-designer of French descent. He designed the *Villa Pianciani*, Terraja, between Spoleto and Todi (1784), and carried out major works of restoration at the *Duomo*, Urbino (from 1789), where he drew on *Palladian precedents, but his rigorous attention to architectural unity was influenced by *Neo-Classicism. From 1800 he worked for **Prince Stanisław Poniatowski** (1757-1833), for whom he built the *villa (and laid out the gardens) on the *Via Flaminia*, Rome (completed 1818), later remodelled (1824-44) by his pupil *Canina. Around the same time he rebuilt the severe gate at the *Ponte Milvio* (1805), was consulted on the design of the *Palazzo Braschi*, Rome (1790-1804), and designed the *façade of

San Pantaleo, Rome (1806), robustly Neo-Classical in style, opposite the *Palazzo Braschi*. His most significant work, however, was the reorganization of the *Piazza del Pòpolo* (designed 1794–1811, built 1816–24), where he created two huge hemicycles (with walls decorated with *sphinxes and other Neo-Classical devices) around the Ancient-Egyptian red-granite *obelisk which **Augustus** (*r*.27 BC–AD 14) had brought to Rome in 10 BC, and which **Pope Sixtus V** (*r*.1585–90) caused to be re-erected (1589) on its present site. Steps and ramps ascend to Valadier's triple-arched *Loggiato* (1816–20) and the terraced garden on the *Pincio* at the top of which he built the *Casinò Valadier* (1813–17), an original design with different elevations on all four sides. This work of eclectic *Picturesque *Classicism, as remarkable as anything by *Jappelli, has Greek-*Doric *loggie surmounted by *Ionic columns, a curved entrance-*portico with Ionic columns carrying a Doric *frieze, and vaulted interiors decorated with Neo-*Antique frescoes.

He also carried out extensive restoration works on various Ancient-Roman buildings, including the arch of **Titus** (*r*. AD 79–81), the Colosseum, the Temple of *Fortuna Virilis*, and **Trajan's** (*r*. AD 98–117) column. He designed the circular *Santa Cristina*, Césena (1814–25), and reworked Palladian themes for church-fronts for his new façade for *San Rocco*, Rome (1833–4), drawing on *San Giorgio Maggiore*, Venice, for his precedent. He published *Progetti* (1807), *Opere d'Architettura e di Ornamente* (1833), etc., some of which deal with his activities as a restorer.

De (1979); De (ed.) (1985); P.Ho (1967); Lapadula (1969); Marconi (1964); Ms (1966); P (1982); Schulze-Battman (1939); J.T (1996)

valance 1. Fall or edging of hanging drapery, e.g. around a *baldacchino, *canopy, or *tester, really a pendent border, as that hung in front of curtain-rails in a room to conceal them and give a suitable finish. It is often simulated, as in the bronze valancing of *Bernini's celebrated *baldacchino* in *San Pietro*, Rome (1624–33). **2.** Vertical timber boards, often pointed or curved at the lower ends, finishing the *eaves of the roofs above C19 railway-platforms.

L & D (1986)

Valle, Gino (1923-2003) Italian architect, mainly of industrial buildings, e.g. the Zanussi Electrical Appliances Factory, Pordenone (1956–61), in which aggressively Modernist tendencies were expressed. He designed the monument to the Resistance, Udine (1959–69—with **Dino Basaldella** (1909–77) et al.); Town Hall, Casarza (1974); Valdadige Prefabricated Schools, Udine and Venice (1978–86); *Banca Commerciale Italiana*, NYC (1981-6); and the *Palazzo di Giustizia*, Padua (1984–94).

Croset (1989); E (1994); J.T (1996)

Vallée, Simon de la (*c*.1590-1642) French architect. Appointed (1637) Royal Architect to the Court of **Queen Christina of Sweden** (*r*.1644–54) in Stockholm, he trained his son **Jean de la Vallée** (1620-96) and *Tessin the Elder, both of whom were to influence the development of *Baroque architecture in Sweden. He designed the exquisite *Riddarhus*, Stockholm (*c*.1641–74—completed by his son and *Vingboons). Jean also gained experience in France and Italy before returning to Sweden in 1650. He was responsible for the Axel Oxenstierna Palace, Stockholm (*c*.1650–4—influenced by the *Renaissance Roman *palazzi of *Raphael and *Peruzzi), the octagonal *Hedvig Eleonora* Church, Stockholm (begun 1656), and the Palladian *Villa Mariedal*, Västergötland (1666), among other fine buildings.

A & B (1986); Ck (1996); Nordberg (1970); W.Pa (1892)

valley Internal angle formed by the meeting of two roof-slopes, the opposite of a *hip. Hence *valley-gutter*, *valley-rafter*.

Vallin de la Mothe, Jean-Baptiste-Michel (1729-1800) French architect. He settled in Russia (1759), introduced French *Classicism influenced by *Palladio, A.-J.*Gabriel, and J.-F.*Blondel (to whom he was related), and taught at the Academy of Arts in St Petersburg. He designed *Gostinyy Dvor* (Merchants' Court), a pioneering work of *Neo-Classicism (1758–85), the Old Hermitage (1764–7), the Classical New Holland Port Gateway and Warehouses (from 1761), and the Academy of Fine Arts (1765–72), all in St Petersburg. In the last building he collaborated with **Aleksandr Filippovich Kokorinov** (1726-72), Director of the Academy of Arts, and himself no mean architect.

A, xxxv/12 (1922), 173–80; B (1980); Ga *et al.* (1980); G.H (1983); Ha (1912, 1952); M & Wa (1987); J.T (1996)

vallum 1. Wall or *rampart of earth or *masonry with *palisades, e.g. Hadrian's Wall in Northern England. **2.** Roman palisaded bank constructed from material excavated from its surrounding ditch, as in a camp or fortress.

valva, valve One or other of the halves or leaves of a double- or folding-door, e.g. a *French window.

Valvassori, Gabriele (1683-1761) Rome-born architect, influenced by *Borromini. He designed *San Salvatori della Corte*, later *Madonna della Luce*, Rome (1730-68), but his most brilliant work was the *Corso* *wing of the *Palazzo Doria-Pamphilj*, Rome (1730-5), one of the few *Rococo palaces where the exterior, abounding in quirky detail, is almost as decorative as the interior. He was also responsible for the Gate at the *Villa Pamphilj*, *Porta San Pancrazio* (1732), and the Convent of *Santi Quirico e Giulitta* (1750–3), in Rome. C19 commentators often found his work 'depraved'.

Capitolium, **x** (1934), 385–98; Fasolo (1949); *IV*, **iv** (1933), 303–4, 428–9; Mallory (1977); N–S (1986a); P (1982); Pi (1970); J.T (1996)

van Alen, William (1882–1954) *See* ALEN.

van Baurscheit, Jan Pieter (1699–1768) *See* BAURSCHEIT.

Vanbrugh, Sir John (1664–1726) English architect of Flemish descent, author of *risqué* plays (including *The Provok'd Wife* (1697), sketched while languishing in French gaols), herald, soldier, and wit. Architecture became his prime interest *c.*1699 when he made designs for Castle Howard, Yorks., for **Charles Howard** (1669–1738—**3rd Earl of Carlisle** from 1692—to whom he was distantly related), supplanting *Talman. Castle Howard (1699–1726) was a virtuoso performance in the *Baroque style, more Continental than English, all the more extraordinary as the work of an amateur. The virile and confident designs were realized with the assistance of *Hawksmoor, who was appointed (1700) Draughtsman and Clerk of Works. Partly as a result of this success (and through his connections), Vanbrugh superseded Talman as Comptroller of the Works (1702), and thus became *Wren's colleague. Quickly perceived as an architect of genius (though apparently without any formal training or experience), the agreeable, clubbable Vanbrugh lost no time in getting himself appointed architect to members of the Whig Oligarchy, replacing Talman whenever possible. For a decade, as Comptroller, he enjoyed not only power but perquisites as well, and made the most of his opportunities. The Tories removed him from his post (1713), but when the Whigs returned to power and **Georg Ludwig** (1660–1727), **Elector of Hanover** from 1698, became **King George I** (1714) he was not only restored to the Comptrollership but knighted as well, and was also appointed (1715) Surveyor of Gardens and Waters. His was a strong personality within the Office of Works, but he failed to succeed Wren as Surveyor in 1718, the job going to *Benson, and towards the end of his life his Baroque style was out of favour, being superseded by *Burlington's *Palladianism.

Vanbrugh gained (1704) his most important commission, Blenheim Palace, Oxon., a great house intended as a symbol of the Nation's and the Queen's gratitude to **John Churchill** (1650–1722—**1st Duke of Marlborough** from 1702), for his victories over the French. There he was able to build on a vast scale, unhampered by penny-pinching, and with Blenheim English Baroque achieved its climax, though it was a Baroque that had no exact Continental equivalent despite the fact that its sources were French, Italian (the arcaded *belvederes at the corner are reminiscent of *Borromini's work), and English (notably the works of Talman and Wren). There was another aspect too, that of Vanbrugh's interest in medieval and *Elizabethan architecture. Something of the dramatic skyline of *prodigy-houses can be seen at Blenheim and at other creations by one of England's greatest architects. Blenheim was completed by **James Moore** (*c.*1670–1726) and Hawksmoor.

Other houses by Vanbrugh were Kimbolton Castle, Hunts. (1707–10—with later additions by *Galilei); King's Weston, near Bristol (*c.*1710–19); Eastbury Park, Dorset (begun 1718—demolished except for one *wing); the *Sublime Seaton Delaval, Northum. (1720–8), and the north front of Grimsthorpe Castle, Lincs. (1722–6). He evoked something of the 'Castle Air' (as he termed it), medieval, and Elizabethan architecture without overt quotation. Seaton Delaval, with a plan combining Classical formalism and a reminiscence of medieval corner-towers, is one of Vanbrugh's most powerful, memorable, and massive creations, with its insistent *banding and *rustication. Vanbrugh's sensitivity towards the past led him to attempt to retain the remains of Woodstock Manor in the grounds of Blenheim, for he recognized the importance of *ruins in a landscape. Indeed, he contributed to the making of the gardens at Stowe, Bucks. (where he designed the Lake *Pavilions, *Rotunda, Temples of Bacchus and Sleep, Cold Bath, and Pyramid (*c.*1719–24—nearly all demolished or altered)), and at Castle Howard, where he was responsible for the Obelisk (1714), Pyramid Gate (1719), and Belvedere Temple (1725–8), and must therefore be regarded as an important pioneer of *Picturesque landscapes. Some of his architecture also had Picturesque qualities, notably his own house at Greenwich (Vanbrugh Castle, from 1718), with crenellated towers and bogus *machicolations, the composition anticipating the *Gothic Revival later in the century.

AH, **x** (1967), 7–88, **xx** (1977), 31–44; G.Beard (1986); C.Campbell (1967–72); Co (2008); Co (ed.) (1976); Co & M.Craig (eds) (1964); Downes (1966, 1977, 1987); D.Green (1951); Hussey (1967A); *JSAH*, **xliii/4** (Dec. 1984), 310–27; *ODNB* (2004); P (1982); F.McCormick (1991); Ridgway & Williams (2000); SS (1990); Su (1993); J.T (1996); Vanbrugh (1927–8); Whistler (1954)

van Brunt, Henry (1832–1930) *See* WARE & VAN BRUNT.

van Campen, Jacob (1595–1657) *See* CAMPEN.

van den Broek, Johannes Hendrik (1898–1978) *See* BAKEMA.

van der Nüll, Eduard (1812–68) *See* NÜLL.

van der Rohe, Ludwig Mies (1886–1969) *See* MIES.

van de Velde, Henri (*or* **Henry**) (1863–1957) *See* VELDE.

van Doesburg, Theo (1883–1931) *See* DOESBURG.

vane Banner-shaped plate of metal, or a *weathercock or -vane, placed on a pivot on a high part of a building, to point towards the direction from which the wind blows.

van Eesteren, Cor(nelis) (1897–1988) *See* EESTEREN.

van Eyck, Aldo (1918–99) *See* EYCK.

van't Hoff, Robert (1887–1979) *See* HOFF.

Vantini, Rodolfo (1791–1856) Italian architect, one of the most accomplished Neo-Classicists of his generation, he designed the noble *cemetery, Brescia (begun 1815), the earliest of the C19 Italian monumental cemeteries: in it he combined a cylinder covered with *Pantheon-dome with the Greek-*Doric Order. Other works include the *Porta Venezia*, Milan (1827–33).

Ms (1966)

Vanvitelli, Luigi (1700–73) Neapolitan architect of Dutch descent, he came to public attention with his entry for the competition to design a new *façade for *San Giovanni in Laterano*, Rome (1732), won by *Galilei. As a result, he was commissioned to design the new *lazaretto* in Ancona, a pentagonal fortress-like building (1733–8), and also built the *Gesù* (completed 1743) and the austere *Arco Clementino* (1733–8) in the same city. He added wings to the *Palazzo Odescalchi* (*c.*1745–50), enlarged *Michelangelo's *Santa Maria degli Angeli* (1748–65—a *tour-de-force*), and designed the *cloister of *Sant'Agostino* (1746–50—where *Borromini's influence is overt), all in Rome.

In 1751 he was called to Naples to build a Royal Palace of great splendour at Caserta for **Carlo VII, King of Naples** & **V of Sicily** (*r.*1735–59—when he became **Carlos III of Spain** (*r.*1759–88)). With its vast internal and external *scenographic vistas and octagonal entrance *vestibule it had *Baroque qualities, but many of the interiors leant towards *Neo-Classicism. The building (the main fabric of which was completed 1774) resembled Robert de *Cotte's unexecuted designs for *Buenretiro* Palace near Madrid (1714–15), while Versailles proved another precedent. Associated with Caserta were

gardens, with elaborate waterworks and ancillary structures designed by Vanvitelli, who was responsible for the *aqueduct system (including the 25-mile-long *Acquedotto Carolino* (1752–64)). The *Annunziata* (1761—completed by his son **Carlo** (1739–1821)) and the *Piazza Dante* (1755–67—influenced by *Bernini's *Piazza di San Pietro*, Rome) were also by him.

Bt (1975); Defilippis (1968); FdA (1863); Fusco (ed.) (1973); Landolfi (1992); Ms (1966); P (1982); Seta (1998); Strazzullo (ed.) (1976–7); J.T (1996); Vanvitelli (1975); Varallo (2000); Wi (1982)

Vardy, John (1718–65) English Palladian architect, he enjoyed a long association with the Office of Works and worked with *Kent, whose Horse-Guards Building, Whitehall, London, he built from 1748 with William *Robinson. He published a volume of engravings entitled *Some Designs of Mr. Inigo Jones and Mr. William Kent* (1744). His greatest work was Spencer House, Green Park, London (1756–65), some of the finest rooms in which were designed by James *Stuart, and he produced several designs in the *Rococo style as well as an essay in *Gothick (Milton Abbey, Dorset, of *c.*1754–5).

J.Brown (ed.) (1985); Co (2008); Co (ed.) (1976); J.Friedman (1993); *ODNB* (2004); Su (1993); J.T (1996)

Vasanzio, Giovanni (*c.*1550–1621) Dutch-born **Jan van Santen** *or* **Zanten** settled in Rome *c.*1583 where he practised architecture, specializing in *fountains, gardens, and *villas. He completed *Ponzio's *façade of *San Sebastiano fuori le mura* (1612), but his best-known work is the *Villa Borghese* on the *Pincio* (1613–15), with a main elevation enlivened with *niches and statuary owing much to *Mannerism. He enlarged the *Villa Mondragone*, Frascati (1615), begun by *Longhi, and collaborated with **Giovanni** (1540–1614) and Domenico *Fontana on the design of the *Fontane di Ponte Sisto* (1613), *dell'Aquila* (1614), and *della Galera* (1620), the last two in the Vatican Gardens.

Hd (1962, 1971); Onofrio (1957); P (1982); W.Pa (1892); J.T (1996)

Vasari, Giorgio (1511–74) Italian architect/author/painter, his *Le Vite de' più eccellenti architetti, pittori, e scultori italiani* (1550, expanded edn 1568) is a prime source of information on *Renaissance architects and architecture. He made important contributions to the designs for the *Villa Giulia*, Rome (1551–5), vetted by *Michelangelo and realized by *Vignola and *Ammannati. He settled (1555) in Florence to work for **Duke Cosimo I de' Medici** (*r.*1569–74): there, he created his masterpiece, the *Uffizi*, Government Offices of the Tuscan State (1560–80s), with *façades influenced by *Bramante's Vatican

Belvedere, Michelangelo's *Biblioteca Laurenziana*, Florence, and *Peruzzi's Palazzo Massimo alle Colonne*, Rome. The *Uffizi* buildings enclose a long *piazzetta* terminated at the river end by a *loggia incorporating a *serliana, and was completed by *Buontalenti, who designed several *Mannerist details, including the *Porta delle Suppliche*.

At Arezzo Vasari designed *Santi Fiora e Lucilla* (1564–86) on a plan resembling that of *San Marco*, Venice, and the handsome loggia in the *Piazza Grande* (1570–96). He also carried out several major alterations of church interiors following the Council of Trent (1545–63) which required unimpeded views of the *high-altar. His drastic work at *Santa Croce* (1565–84) and *Santa Maria Novella* (1565–72), Florence, gave the interiors architectural unity, but removed many medieval features.

Boase (1979); Conforti (1995); M.Hall (1979); He (1996); P (1982); Satkowski (1979, 1993); J.T (1996); Vasari (1912–15)

vase 1. Hollow vessel, unlidded, of decorative character and various forms, with or without handles. **2.** Representation of this for architectural ornament, often in gardens, in *niches or on *pedestals, etc., but distinct from an *urn, commonly found in Neo-Classical designs. Vases were promoted as architectural ornaments by **Enea Vico** (1523–67) in a series of publications, collected 1543, **Matthias Darly** (*fl.*1741–80) in *The Ornamental Architect* (1770), **d'Hancarville** (**P.F.Hugues** (1729–1805)) in *Antiquités Étrusques, Grecques, et Romaines* (1766–7), *Piranesi in *Vasi, Candelabri, Cippi, Sarcofagi* (1778), **Johann Heinrich Wilhelm Tischbein** (1751–1829) in *Collection of Engravings from Ancient Vases* (1791–3), and many other authors. **3.** *Bell or core of the *Corinthian *capital.

Jervis (1984); L & D (1986)

Vásquez *or* **Vázquez de Segovia, Lorenzo** (*c.*1450–*before* 1515) Spanish master-mason/architect who worked on some of the first *Renaissance buildings in the Iberian peninsula. He probably contributed to the design of the *Quattrocento *frontispiece at the College of *Santa Cruz*, Valladolid (1489–91), the heavily rusticated Medinaceli Palace, Cogolludo, Guadalajara (1492–5—modelled on *Quattrocento* Florentine prototypes, though with late-*Gothic *fenestration), and the Mendoza Palace, Guadalajara (before 1507). He probably designed the castle of *La Calahorra*, Granada (1509–12).

CG (1953); K & S (1959); J.T (1996); vV (1993)

Vau, Louis Le (1612–70) French *Baroque architect. With a team of decorators, sculptors, gardeners, and painters he was largely responsible

for creating the *Louis-Quatorze style at the palace of Versailles from 1667. His earliest buildings were Parisian *hôtels particuliers*, notably the fine *Hôtel Lambert* on the *Île-St-Louis* (1639–44), where he designed a formal *stair leading to a landing flanked by an octagonal *vestibule on one side, and, on the other, an elliptical vestibule leading to a long *gallery terminating in a bow-window affording views over the Seine. In 1656 he began *Vaux-le-Vicomte*, a great *château* for **Nicolas Fouquet** (1615–80), with interiors decorated by Charles Le *Brun and others. It incorporated a grand vestibule and stair, with a domed *saloon behind partly projecting on the garden-front, the whole set in formal gardens designed by Le *Nôtre. Le Vau and Le Brun rebuilt the *Galerie d'Apollon* in the Louvre, Paris (1661–4), and, with *Perrault, designed the celebrated east front of the Louvre (1665–74—a harbinger of C18 Classicism) admired by *Wren et al. At the *Collège des Quatre Nations*, Paris (1661–74—later the *Institut de France*), with a pedimented front (behind which rises a tall *cupola) flanked by two *quadrants terminating in *pavilions facing the Seine (so the composition has a concave façade contained by the *wings), Le Vau demonstrated a strong affinity with Italian Baroque, and possible influences from *Bernini and *Borromini. The front and pavilions are graced by *Giant Orders, and the quadrants by subservient superimposed Orders. His most ambitious work, however, was at Versailles, where he remodelled and expanded the *château*. Le Vau's new garden-front can still be seen, although considerably altered and extended by *Hardouin-Mansart. At Versailles and the *Collège des Quatre Nations* he was assisted by François d'*Orbay, who probably contributed to the overall design.

Architectura, vi/1 (1976), 36–46; Ballon (1999); Bt (1982); Bordier (1998); GdBA, lxiv (1964), 285–96, 347–62, cii (1983), 193–207; Ha (1948); Laprade (1960); P (1982); J.T (1996); D.Wa (1986)

Vauban, Sébastien le Prestre, Maréchal de (1633–1707) French military-engineer/architect, he has been credited with the design of over 120 fortresses, and protected France's borders with a series of powerful strongholds, notably those of Lille (1668–74), Maubeuge (1678–81), and Neuf-Brisach (1696–1708). Responsible for planning several new towns, including Sarrelouis (1681–3), Longwy (from 1679), and Neuf-Brisach (1689–99), using regular geometrical layouts, he also designed several accomplished monumental gateways including the *Baroque *Porte de Paris*, Lille (1668–70), complete with *trophies, and the massively severe *Porte de Mons*, Maubeuge (1681). He wrote *Mémoire pour servir d'instruction dans la conduite des sièges* (published 1740 with a memorandum on the defence of fortresses, apparently by another hand), *Traité de l'attaque...* (1737), *De la défense des places* (published with the *Traité de l'attaque* 1828–9), *Véritable manière de bien fortifier* (1702), and sundry other works, including a treatise on building, proposals for fairer systems of taxation (*Projet d'une dix^{me} royale*, 1707), instantly suppressed. He designed the *aqueduct of Maintenon (1684–5) supplying Versailles with water.

Blomfield (1938); Halévy (1925); Lazard (1934); Michel (1879); P (1982); P & V (1971); Rébelliau (1962); Rochas d'Aiglun (ed.) (1910); Sauliol (1931); J.T (1996); Toudouze (1954); Vauban (1910)

Vaudoyer, Antoine-Laurent-Thomas (1756–1846) French architect, pupil of A.-F.*Peyre, his early unexecuted designs demonstrated a concern for stereometrical purity that was a feature of late-C18 French *Neo-Classicism, perhaps influenced by *Boullée and anticipating works by *Ledoux. With L.-P.*Baltard and J.-D.*Leroy he founded (1793) a School of Architecture that became the *École des *Beaux-Arts*. He was an influential teacher, and began (1838) the conversion of the Priory of *St-Martin-des-Champs, Paris, into the *Conservatoire des Arts et Métiers*. With Baltard et al. he published designs for the *Grands Prix* (1806–34), and he himself published much.

AH, iii (1960), 17–180; Bergdoll (1994a) M & Wa (1987); P (1982); W.Pa (1892); S (1901–2); J.T (1996)

Vaudoyer, Léon (1803–72) French architect, son of A.-L.-T.*Vaudoyer. With *Duban, *Duc, and *Labrouste he became (1830s) a leading light in architectural circles, and carried out major work at the *Conservatoire des Arts et Métiers*, Paris (1845–72), in which he synthesized Graeco-Roman and *Renaissance elements and restored much of the surviving *Gothic fabric (the conversion of *St-Martin-des-Champs* into the *Conservatoire* had been started by his father, and was completed by **Gabriel-Auguste Ancelet** (1829–95)). Convinced that the Greek Classical ideal was central to all subsequent architecture in Southern Europe, he attempted in his own designs to demonstrate a further transformation for modern times, as in his *Ste-Marie-Majeure*, Marseilles (1855–72), the overall stylistic effect of which is that of a *Byzantine-*Romanesque *basilica with *polychrome strips recalling the *Duomo*, Siena (the building was completed by **Jacques-Henry Espérandieu** (1829–74), **Henri-Antoine Révoil** (1820–1900), and Vaudoyer's son, **Alfred-Lambert Vaudoyer** (1846–1917)). He also designed the elegant Greek-*Doric monument of **Général Maximilien-Sébastien Foy** (1775–1825), *Père-Lachaise* Cemetery (1825–32), and the Vaudoyer *mausoleum, Montparnasse Cemetery (1846), both in

Paris. He published (1850s) several perceptive articles on *Ledoux in which he referred to *architecture parlante*.

Bergdoll (1994a); Dr (ed.) (1977); Hi (1977); M & Wa (1987); P (1982); J.T (1996); vZ (1987)

Vaudremer, Joseph-Auguste-Émile (1829–1914) French architect, trained in the *Blouet-*Gilbert *atelier*, he worked with *Baltard and *Duban, and was appointed Architect to the XIII and XIV *Arrondissements* of Paris. He designed the *Santé *prison, Paris (1862–85), in the rational manner of Blouet, but his masterpiece is the powerful freely treated *Romanesque-Revival Church of *St-Pierre-de-Montrouge, Place Victor Basch, Paris (1864–72), a building of great presence and dignity that may have influenced H.H.*Richardson. He also designed *Notre-Dame d'Auteuil, Place d'Auteuil* (1876–80—with stone *vaults possibly inspired by work of *Abadie) and the asymmetrical *St-Antoine-des-Quinze-Vingts, Avenue Ledru-Rollin* (1901–3), both in Paris.

Abadie (1984); Dr (ed.) (1977); Egbert (1980); Ha (1957); Hi (1977); M & Wa (1987); P (1982); J.T (1996); Vaudremer (1871)

vault 1. Arch the depth of which exceeds the span, i.e. an elongated arch covering a space, or a structure composed of various curved elements in various combinations, built of *brick, *concrete, *masonry, etc., and sometimes of *plaster and wood to suggest something heavier. It is primarily a ceiling over a space, but may also be a roof, and it may carry a *floor or roof. As with an arch, it is constructed so that the stones or other materials of which it is composed support and keep each other in their places. Any volume covered by means of a vault or *voussure is said to be *vaulted*, while a system of vaults on a ceiling is called *vaulting*. A vault-*bay is defined by transverse *ribs. *Types of vault include*:

annular: *barrel-vault* springing from two concentric walls. See ANNULAR;

barrel, cylindrical, tunnel, or *wagon*: simplest variety of vault, really an elongated or continuous arch like half a cylinder (i.e. with a semicircular *section and a uniform concave *soffit), spanning the distance between parallel walls or other supports. It can also be segmental or half-elliptical in section;

cloister: see DOMICAL;

cross: see GROIN-;

cylindrical: see BARREL;

domical: rises from a polygonal or square base, and is not a true dome, having curved surfaces (*cells, *severies, or *webs) meeting at precise lines (*groins). Also called *cloister*-vault (USA);

fan: late-*Gothic *Perp. form, known only in England during the Middle Ages (though widely

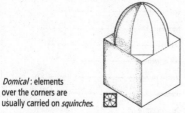

Domical: elements over the corners are usually carried on *squinches*.

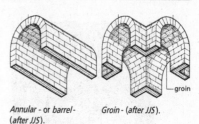

Annular - or *barrel -* (*after JJS*).

Groin - (*after JJS*).

— groin

— trumpet-shaped 'fan'
— flat ceiling in centre of vault

Perp. fan.

copied later), consisting of inverted half-cones or funnel-shapes with concave sides (like *trumpet-bells*), their rims touching at the top of the vault and their visible surfaces covered with *blind *panel-*tracery rising from a *capital or *corbel and diverging like the folds of a fan over the entire surface of the distorted cones. The areas between the circular tops of the fans are flat and form concave-sided lozenge-shapes. At King's College Chapel, Cambridge (1508–15), there are large pendent *bosses in the centres of the distorted lozenges, and at **Henry VII**'s Chapel, Westminster Abbey (1503–*c.*1512—strictly speaking an ingenious fantasy *suggesting* the *form* of fan-vaulting, but actually with ribs only used decoratively, as the vault is essentially of the groin type), the distorted lozenges are covered with blind panel-tracery and there are pendants under the points of each cone as well as in the centres of the lozenges;

groin: formed by the intersection at 90° of two identical *barrel*-vaults (also called *cross*-vaults) creating *groins where they join;

handkerchief: as *sail-dome see* DOME;

hyperbolic paraboloid: *see* HYPERBOLIC PARABOLA;

lierne: ribbed vault with some ribs (*tertiaries* or *liernes*) not running from one of the main springing-points, but from rib to rib, usually joined to them at *bosses;

net: *rib*-vault with ribs forming a net of distorted lozenges all over the surface of the vault, common in late-Gothic work in Central Europe;

parabolic: vault of parabolic *section, resembling a cone cut along a line parallel to its surface angle, usually constructed of a light *shell of *reinforced concrete;

ploughshare: with wall-ribs springing from points higher than those of the diagonal ribs (therefore called a *stilted* vault) so that more light can be admitted from a *clerestorey window, thus distorted and twisted;

quadripartite: bay divided by diagonal and transverse ribs into four cells or webs;

rampant: barrel-vault with one springing-line higher than the other;

rib: with ribs framing the webs and concealing the groins;

sail: *see* DOME;

sexpartite: bay resembling that of a *quadripartite* vault, but further divided by an extra transverse rib so that there are six cells instead of four;

shell: thin self-supporting structure. *See* SHELL;

stalactite: *see* STALACTITE;

stellar: with ribs, including *liernes* (ribs running from rib to rib) and *tiercerons* (rib rising from one of the main springing-points to a position on the *ridge*-rib), forming a star-shaped pattern of ribs;

stilted: *see* PLOUGHSHARE;

surbased: with a section less than a semicircle (i.e. a segment);

surmounted: with a section greater than a semicircle;

tierceron: *see* STELLAR;

tracery: covered with blind *tracery, e.g. fan-vaulting;

tripartite: on a triangular plan with three parts;

trumpet: shapes like the bells of trumpets in *fan-vaulting;

tunnel: *see* BARREL;

wagon: *see* BARREL.

2. Room or enclosed space of any kind covered by a vault. **3.** Any strong place or place of safety. **4.** Burial-chamber or *crypt, vaulted or not. **5.** Cellar.

Gw (1903); N (1835); W.Pa (1892); J.Parker (1850); S (1901–2); J.T (1996)

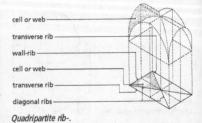

cell *or* web
transverse rib
wall-rib
cell *or* web
transverse rib
diagonal ribs

Quadripartite rib-.

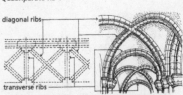

diagonal ribs

transverse ribs

Romanesque rib-, Peterborough Cathedral aisle (mid C12).

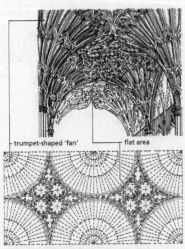

trumpet-shaped 'fan'   flat area

Fan-, Gloucester Cathedral cloister (late C14).

transverse rib   diagonal rib

(left) First-Pointed rib-, Salisbury Cathedral (C13). *(right) First-Pointed rib-, with intermediate ribs,* Westminster Abbey (C13).

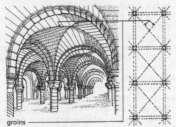

groins

Romanesque groined, Canterbury Cathedral crypt (late C11).

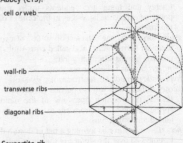

cell *or* web

wall-rib

transverse ribs

diagonal ribs

Sexpartite rib-.

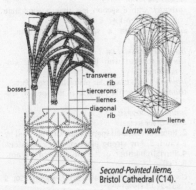

bosses

transverse rib
tiercerons
liernes
diagonal rib

lierne

Lierne vault

Second-Pointed lierne, Bristol Cathedral (C14).

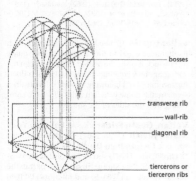

bosses

transverse rib
wall-rib
diagonal rib

tiercerons or
tierceron ribs

Stellar or *tierceron rib-, with bosses.*

vaulting *See* VAULT. *Compounds include*:
vaulting capital: *capital of a *pier or *colonnette (or even *corbel) from which a *vault or *rib springs;
vaulting-cell: area or *web framed by the ribs of a vault;
vaulting pottery: *see* ACOUSTIC VASE;
vaulting shaft: small *shaft or colonnette supporting a vault-rib or group of ribs at their springing. It may rise from the ground or from a *corbel set in the *masonry.

Vauthier, Louis-Léger (1815–1901) French architect/engineer, he settled (1840) in Recife, Brazil, designing the layout for the town's development as well as several buildings, including the *Santa Isabel* Theatre (1840–6). He returned to Paris (1846).

Freyre (1940)

Vaux, Calvert (1824–95) London-born American architect/landscape-designer, pupil of *Cottingham, he assisted A.J.*Downing in laying out the grounds of the Capitol, Smithsonian Institution, and White House, Washington, DC (1850–2). He formed (1851) a short-lived partnership with Downing, and after the latter's death (1852) he collected the partnership's designs for houses (some carried out with F.C.*Withers), and published them (1857) as *Villas and Cottages* (prompted by Downing's successful *pattern-books), and in the same year, with F.L.*Olmsted, prepared an entry for the competition to design Central Park, NYC, which they won (1858): their professional partnership was to last until 1872. Their plan, combining aspects of the English *Picturesque style with ideas taken from *Loudon and *Paxton, and embracing ingenious segregation between vehicles and pedestrians, was influential. Following this success, Vaux prepared further plans for landscapes (including Prospect Park, Brooklyn, NYC (1866–73), which introduced the concept of parkways), and was assisted by the English-born *Mould, who designed many of the architectural features in Vaux's parks, including the *Ruskinian *Gothic Terrace (1858–71) at Central Park. Vaux and Mould worked together on designs for the Metropolitan Museum of Art (1874–80) and the Museum of Natural History (1874–7), both in NYC, but only part of each was realized. Although Vaux's greatest achievements were in the field of landscape-design (e.g. the grounds of the Parliament Buildings, Ottowa, Canada (1873–9)), he was an accomplished domestic architect. He designed the *Gothic-Revival Tilden House, NYC (1881–4), later the National Arts Club. His pupils included his son, Downing *Vaux.

AAAB, Papers, v (1968), 69–106; W.Alex (1994); C.Cook (1972); Francis (1980); *JSAH*, vi/1 (Jan.–June 1947), 1–12; K (1994); Kowsky (1998, 2013); P (1982); H.Reed & Duckworth (1967); Roper (1973); D.Schuyler & Censer (eds) (1992); J.T (1996); vV (1993); Vaux (1970)

Vaux, Downing (1856–1926) American architect/landscape architect, son of Calvert *Vaux, he was named after his father's mentor, A.J.*Downing, and trained partly in his father's office, of which he became a senior member (1887), but by the mid-1890s he was practising under his own name, designing *cemeteries, parks, and institutional, recreational, and residential landscapes. Works included College Hill Park, Poughkeepsie, NY (1898); the Andrew Jackson Downing Memorial Park, Newburgh, NY, with **John Charles Olmsted** (1852–1920) (completed 1897—originally de-signed by the elder *Olmsted and elder Vaux); and many other projects. He urged the cooperation of architect, engineer, and landscape architect from the outset of the design-process, and was active in promoting landscape architecture as a profession.

B & K (2000)

Vázquez, Pedro Ramírez (1919–2013) *See* RAMÍREZ VÁZQUEZ.

velarium Awning over the *cavea* (whole of the area occupied by spectators) of an Ancient-Roman *court, theatre, or *amphitheatre. Fixings for the various segments (*vela*) forming the awning survive at the Colosseum, Rome (*c*.AD 75–82).

Velde, Henry (*or* **Henri,** but this seems spurious) **Clements van de** (1863–1957) Belgian painter/designer/architect, influenced by William *Morris, *Ruskin, and the English *Arts-and-Crafts movement. He built his own house, *Villa Bloemenwerf*, Uccle, near Brussels (1895), and became increasingly interested in *Art Nouveau, designing four rooms for **Siegfried Bing's** (1838–1905) celebrated gallery, the *Maison de l'Art*

Nouveau, Paris (1895-6), and achieved international recognition for the interiors and furniture he exhibited at Dresden (1897). His success in Germany (e.g. interiors for the Havana Cigar Company, Berlin (1899-1901), and for **Kaiser Wilhelm II**'s (*r.*1888-1918) barber, **Haby** (1901), also in Berlin) encouraged him to move there (1900), where he served (from 1901) as art-adviser to **Grand Duke Wilhelm Ernst of Saxe-Weimar-Eisenach** (*r.*1901-18) and published his *Die Renaissance im moderne Kunstgewerbe* (1901, 1903). He designed exquisite interiors for the art-loving Graf Harry *Kessler in Weimar (1903), and the new Grand-Ducal Saxon Schools of Art and Arts and Crafts (1904-11), also in Weimar, directing the latter School from 1908. A founder-member of the *Deutscher Werkbund* (1907), he consolidated his position with sumptuous decorations for the *Folkwang* (later *Karl Ernst Osthaus*) *Museum*, Hagen (1900-2), his finest creations in the curvilinear Art-Nouveau style. Van de Velde's use of curved forms in his buildings (e.g. the Weimar School and the rather eerie theatre for the *Deutscher Werkbund* Exhibition, Cologne (1914—destroyed)), led to a fundamental disagreement within the *Werkbund*, *Muthesius stressing *industrialized building, standardization, and the machine, while van de Velde objected to the restrictions this would place on the individual designer. War in 1914 led to his resignation as an alien at Weimar. He suggested *Endell, *Gropius, or *Obrist as his successor: in the event Gropius was appointed, and the Arts-and-Crafts ethos was destroyed after the 1914-18 war when the Grand-Ducal Schools were merged to become the *Bauhaus.

Van de Velde remained active as a writer and teacher, and from 1923 designed the Kröller-Müller Museum, Otterlo, The Netherlands (erected 1936-54). In 1926 He built up the *Institut Supérieur des Arts Décoratifs*, Brussels (1926), modelled on his earlier Schools at Weimar, and was Director there until 1935. He designed the Library (1936-9) at the University of Gent, where he was also Professor of Architecture. His later career was marked by his claims to have been an early protagonist of the *Modern Movement, and his attitude towards the retrospective 1952 Art-Nouveau Exhibition, Zürich, was equivocal, if not hostile, as it seems he feared it would draw attention to his skills in a style he had repudiated, even though from the start of the C21 it is clear that his best work was carried out before 1914. He published *Déblaiement d'art* (Clearing (i.e. Purifying) of Art—1894), and other works listed here.

AR, cxxxiii/793 (Mar. 1963), 165-8; Curjel (ed.) (1955); Delevoy *et al.* (1963); Dolgner (1996); Fohl (2000); Hammacher (1967); Hüter (1967, 1976); S.Jacobs (1996); Jervis (1984); Kerckhove *et al.* (1993); Lenning (1951); Loo (ed.) (2003); P (1982); Sembach (1989); Sembach, Schulte, *et al.* (1992); J.T (1996); T-M (1967); Velde (1894, 1903, 1907, 1962, 1986)

vellar cupola *Dome like a *sail-*vault*, i.e. with its diameter equal to the diagonal of the square from which it rises, the arched forms between the springing-lines creating an impression of a floating awning or sail billowing upwards. It is really a semicircular dome with four sides sliced off, coinciding with the sides of the square.

Velten, Georg Friderick, aka **Fel'ten, Yury Matveyevich** (1730-1801) Russian architect, son of a German from Danzig. He worked under *Rastrelli, later (1762) succeeding him at the Winter Palace, St Petersburg. He designed part of the Small Hermitage (1765-6) and interiors (1770-9) for *Peterhof*, but his best works are churches (e.g. St Catherine (1768-71), St Anne (1775-9), and the Armenian Church (1770-7), all in St Petersburg). Other designs include the Alexander Institute (1765-75), Old Hermitage (1771-87), granite quays with parapets and steps along the River Neva (1762-80), Palace Square (1779), and many houses, industrial buildings, etc., all in St Petersburg. Stylistically uninhibited, he designed the Gothic Gates (1777-80) and the Chinese Pavilion (1778-86) at *Tsarskoye Selo* (now *Pushkin*), and embraced a graceful *Neo-Classicism when *Baroque went out of fashion.

Grabar *et al.* (1961); Korshunova (1982); J.T (1996)

velum (*pl.* **vela**) Segment of the awning (*velarium*) of a Roman *amphitheatre, etc.

Venetian Of or pertaining to Venice. *Compounds include*:

Venetian arch: see ARCH;

Venetian blind: *jalousie, or sun-blind formed of horizontal laths or slats that can be drawn up or down, and swivelled;

Venetian crenellation: *Palladian type of *crenellation with balls set on a series of curved cops (*see* PALLADIAN) resembling a row of pawns in Chess (e.g. the *piano-nobile* level of *Burlington's *Villa at Chiswick, near London (1726-9)).

Venetian dentil: common Venetian medieval *moulding consisting of a projecting *band with its upper and lower parts cut alternately into notches sloping to the middle of the band, producing the effect of a double row of staggered *dentils;

Venetian door: *serliana used as a doorway;

Venetian Gothic Revival: phase of the *Gothic Revival that drew on exemplars from Venice, featuring *polychrome brickwork, plate-*tracery, and elaborately patterned *arcades. It was promoted by *Street's *Brick and Marble in the Middle Ages: Notes of a Tour in the North of Italy*

(1855, 1874) and popularized by *Ruskin's *Stones of Venice* (1851–3, 1903–12).
Venetian window: see SERLIANA.

Vennecool, Steven Jacobs (1657–1719) Dutch architect, he designed the *astylar Town Hall at Enkhuizen, one of the best late-C17 buildings in The Netherlands (1686–8), and the Manor House (*De Steeg*) of Middachten (1695), with its *battered *basement rising from the moat.

Ck (1996); G & D (1954); Kuyper (1980); RSTK (1977)

vennel *See* GINNELL.

vent 1. Aperture, air-hole, or passage to allow fresh air to enter and foul air to leave. **2.** *Chimney-flue. **3.** Opening-light, hinged at the top or bottom, in a metal window-frame.

Ventris, Michael George Francis (1922–56) English architect/Classical scholar, he worked briefly with the Ministry of Education Schools Development Team under (Sir) **Stirrat Andrew Wilson Johnson-Marshall** (1912–81) with the *Medds. He made his name deciphering the Linear B script of the prehistoric inhabitants of Crete and mainland Greece, and published (1953) his preliminary findings with **John Chadwick** (1920–98), with whom he also collaborated for *Documents in Mycenaean Greek* (1956).

BD (10 May 2002), 17; *J. Hellenic Studies*, lxxiii (1953), 84–103; *ODNB* (2004); Robinson (2002)

Venturi, Robert Charles (1925–) *See* URBAN DESIGN.

Vera, André (1881–1971) French *Modernist landscape architect, close to all that was fashionable at the time, he nevertheless was influenced by Classical French gardens, employing *topiary and *maze-like *parterres in which *broderies were straightened. His linear and extremely rigid geometrical approach to *Art-Deco design was tempered by a belief in using indigenous flora, and drawing on local materials such as pebbles and sea-shells. He argued that house and garden were one (a revival of *Renaissance themes merged with *Arts-and-Crafts precedents), and much of his work was done with his brother, the artist **Paul Vera** (1882–1957). His beautifully illustrated books on gardens (1912, 1919) are packed with information, and his *Modernités* (1925) influenced Le *Corbusier.

Imbert (1993). M & T (1991); Tay (2006); Vera (1912, 1919, 1925)

veranda(h) Light external open *gallery, or covered way, with a sloping or *lean-to roof carried by slender (usually metal) columns or *posts, attached to a building, often in front of the windows of the principal rooms, affording shelter from the sun as well as a pleasant external seating area with access from *French windows. Sometimes it can be very decorative, with *trellis-work and plants, and may extend all round a house, forming a *skirt-roof. It was a popular early-C19 feature.

Verey (*née* **Sandilands**), **Rosemary Isabel Baird** (1918–2001) English garden-designer and historian, wife of the architectural historian **David Cecil Wynter Verey** (1912/13–84) with whom she transformed the garden of their home, Barnsley House, Cirencester, Glos., into a tight architecturally controlled series of *alleys, vistas, paved walks, and contrasting open spaces, influenced by the *Arts-and-Crafts style of other Cotswold gardens. She added (1962) a Classical *temple and (1975) a formal *knot-garden, a *potager, and indulged her taste for creating patterns, vibrant movement, and logical progressions. Her writings include *The Englishwoman's Garden* (1980), *The Scented Garden* (1981), *The Englishman's Garden* (1982), *Classic Garden Design* (1984), *The Garden in Winter* (1988), *Rosemary Verey's Garden Plans* (1993), and *Rosemary Verey's Making of a Garden* (1995). She designed numerous gardens, including work at the New York Botanical Garden.

ODNB (2004); A.Wilson (2005)

verge 1. Slight projection formed by a pitched roof over the *naked of a *gable-wall. The junction between the roof-tiles and the top of the wall has to be waterproof, and this is achieved by creating a tight joint, using *tiles and *mortar (*parged verge*), *tumbled brickwork, etc. If the roof is extended beyond the naked of the wall, with a board fixed under the edge of the roof-covering, that board (often decorated, carved, and cut with *fret-work) is termed *barge- or *verge-board. **2.** *Shaft of a Classical column. **3.** Small ornamental *shaft of a medieval *colonnette, e.g. the *Purbeck-marble shafts on *piers of the *First-Pointed style.

verge-board *See* VERGE.

Verge, John (1782–1861) British architect, he settled (1828) in Australia and designed in a competent, eclectic manner. His best work was probably Elizabeth Bay House, Sydney (1832–5), which incorporated an elliptical staircase and hall, but he also created many fine late-*Georgian houses with very wide *verandahs (often with the roofs carried on Classical (usually *Doric) columns). Other works include Camden Park, Menangle (1831–2), Tusculum, Potts Point, Sydney (1831), and the Homestead, Braidwood, near Canberra (c.1838). He also designed the British Residency, Waitangi, New Zealand (1833–4—*prefabricated in Sydney, and probably the first architect-designed building in that country).

From 1832 he worked with **John Bibb** (1810–62), who took over the practice (1837).

Ck (1996); J.T (1996)

Verity, Francis (Frank) Thomas (1864–1937) English architect, he studied in London and at the Atelier *Blouet, Paris, before becoming (1889) a partner in the practice of his father, Thomas *Verity, specializing in theatre-design (e.g. The Empire, Leicester Square (1893–1904)), and, later, cinemas (e.g. The Pavilion, Shepherd's Bush (1923), and The Carlton, Haymarket (1928)), all in London. His grandest London buildings were his *astylar apartment-blocks in the style of *Champs-Élysées* *façades, Paris, of which Cleveland House, opposite St James's Palace (1905–6), 12 Hyde Park Place, Marble Arch (1908), and 25 and 26 Berkeley Square (1906) were the most distinguished. For a time (1903–6) his assistant was Albert *Richardson, and from 1923 he was in partnership with **Samuel Beverley** (1896–1959).

AJ, lxi/1566 (7 Jan. 1925), 36–59; A.S.Gray (1985); J.T (1996)

Verity, Thomas (1837–91) English architect. Early in his career he assisted *Fowke and H.Y.D. *Scott at the South Kensington Museum and the Albert Hall. He designed the *Neo-Renaissance Criterion Theatre and Restaurant, Piccadilly Circus (1870–4—mutilated), the Comedy Theatre (1881), and, with his son, F.T.*Verity, 96–7 Piccadilly (1891) and the Imperial Theatre (1901), all in London.

B *et al.* (2001); D & M (1985)

vermiculation *See* RUSTICATION.

vernacular architecture Unpretentious, simple, indigenous, traditional structures made of local materials and following well-tried forms and *types, normally considered in three categories: agricultural (barns, farms, etc.), domestic, and industrial (foundries, potteries, smithies, etc.). In England and Germany the great range of *timber-framed medieval and later buildings would largely be classed as vernacular architecture, while humble rural structures, such as cottages, would also fall into the category. It was first taken seriously in the late C18 when attempts were made to re-create it as part of the *Picturesque movement, and it provided exemplars for C19 architects, especially those of the *Gothic and *Domestic Revivals and the *Arts-and-Crafts movement. In the USA *Colonial and simple *clap-boarded buildings provided models for designers, especially for the *Stick and *Shingle styles. It has been contrasted with polite architecture, and even classed as *architecture without architects*, but this is not really true, as most vernacular architecture drew on more sophisticated designs somewhere in its development, while

architects such as *Devey, *Lutyens, and *Webb derived much of their styles from vernacular buildings, so it was never really an isolated phenomenon, an architecture of the proletariat, rural or urban.

ABDM (1996); Alcock (1981); Barley (1961); Beaton (1997); Bru (1987, 1990, 1992, 1994, 1997, 2000); Charles (1967); C-T (1987); Glassie (2000); Kemp (1987); P.Oliver (2003); P.Oliver (ed.) (1997); P & M (2001); Pattison *et al.* (1999); Pennick (2002); J.T (1996)

Vernon, Russell Geoffrey Duddell (1916–2009) English architect. Before the 1939–45 war he worked for his great-uncle, **George Vernon** (1870–1942), who had an extensive London practice. Following demobilization, he joined his uncle, **Frederick Austin Vernon** (1881–1972), becoming (1948) a partner: F.A.Vernon was architect/surveyor to Alleyn's College of God's Gift and Dulwich College, and Russell Vernon (who succeeded (1959) his uncle in these positions) was responsible for the almost complete reconstruction (completed 1953) of *Soane's Picture-Gallery, badly damaged during the war. His development-plan for the Dulwich Estate was approved (1955), and the firm designed well over 2,000 houses there during the 1950s and '60s recognized as among the best examples of speculative housing of that era. The practice also designed numerous buildings for Crawley, West Sussex, and housing at various locations, including Tunbridge Wells, Kent, and Windsor, Berks., as well as social housing for, among other organizations, the Peabody Trust.

The Daily Telegraph (7 Sept. 2009), Obits; *Dulwich Society J.* (29 Sept. 2009), J Archive; *C20* (Winter 2009), 37

vertù, virtù 1. The fine arts as a topic of interest or study. **2.** An antique, article, curiosity, etc. A *virtuoso*, therefore, is a student of objects of *vertù*, a connoisseur, or collector of antiquities.

Vertue, George (1684–1756) *See* ROCQUE, JOHN.

Vertue, Robert (*fl.*1475–1506) English master-mason, he was at Westminster Abbey in a junior capacity (1475–80), and in a more senior one from 1482. Appointed King's Master-Mason (*c.*1487), he carried out works at Greenwich. With his brother William *Vertue, he designed the Abbey Church at Bath, Som. (begun 1501), with its beautiful fan-*vault. Vertue was involved in several works, but among his most important activities was the design of the *Lady Chapel, now **King Henry VII**'s (*r.*1485–1509) Chapel, Westminster Abbey, the foundation-stone for which was laid in 1502/3. Furthermore, Vertue, *Lebons, and *Janyns were involved in the preparation of the sepulchre of the King. He was also engaged at

St George's Chapel, Windsor, Berks., including the fan-vaults. In his will he gave directions that he should be buried in the Abbey Church of St Augustine, Canterbury, Kent, with which he seems to have had connections, probably as Master-Mason; he may have designed the new bell-tower there (1461–1516). His son, **Robert Vertue Jun.** (fl.1506–55), was Master of the Works at Evesham Abbey, Worcs., where he designed the splendid buildings for **Clement Lichfield** (c.1470–1546—**Abbot** 1513–39), including the spectacular *Perp. free-standing bell-tower. For Abbot Lichfield he also designed the *mortuary-chapel in the Church of All Saints, Evesham, shortly before 1513, with a fan-vault resembling the work at King Henry VII's Chapel, which suggests the younger Vertue either had a hand in the Westminster work, had his father's drawings, or knew the fabric well. Also in the Westminster style is the exquisite *chantry-chapel of St Clement in St Lawrence's Church, Evesham (c.1520), also built for Abbot Lichfield. Robert may also have designed Christ Church Gate, Canterbury (1502).

J.Harvey (1987); Brooks & Pe (2007); J.T (1996)

Vertue, William (fl.1501–27) English master-mason, the brother of Robert *Vertue Sen., with whom he worked (from 1501) on Bath Abbey Church, Som. From c.1502/3 the *vaults of the *nave, *aisles, and *transepts of St George's Chapel, Windsor, Berks., were under construction, and it is known William Vertue and John *Aylmer contracted to vault seven *bays of the *choir of the Chapel to follow the design of the nave-vault. They also contracted to build the fly-ing *buttresses, *parapets, *pinnacles, and all carvings. Vertue visited King's College Chapel, Cambridge, on at least three occasions, and there are records he was at a meeting in Cambridge (1507) with Henry *Smyth and others to discuss the resumption of the works there. Vertue again visited (1509) Cambridge with *Redman, probably to act as advisers on the fan-vault, and Vertue and *Wastell are known to have dined in Hall (1512) shortly after Wastell signed the contract to build the vault, so it is reasonable to surmise that Vertue, as one of the great masters of the design of fan-vaults, was called in as consultant. He became (1510) King's Master-Mason at the Tower of London, but his main work at the time was at **King Henry VII's** (r.1485–1509) Chapel, Westminster Abbey, where he was in charge after the death of his brother (1506). He also designed buildings at Corpus Christi College, Oxford (1512–18), may have supplied designs for Thornbury Castle, Glos. (c.1511), and probably designed the Church of St Peter ad Vincula, Tower of London, to replace the earlier structure destroyed in a fire (1512). He and Redman designed the west side of the *Court of Eton College,

Bucks., including Lupton's Tower, and Vertue probably was responsible for Lupton's *chantry-chapel in Eton College Chapel (1515). Humphrey *Coke was also involved in the works at Eton. Vertue designed the *cloister and fan-vaulted cloister-chapel of St Stephen in the Palace of Westminster (1526).

He must be regarded as one of England's greatest architects. His mastery of the techniques and intricacies of fan-vault construction enriched the architectural heritage of late-*Gothic England, and his work at Windsor and Westminster is unparalleled for its beauty: it is fair to say it was the culmination of English medieval architecture.

J.Harvey (1987); J.T (1996)

vertugadin Grassed bank, crescent-shaped on plan, with pointed ends, in a garden.

vesica piscis 1. *Glory*, or *mandorla* of the upright almond-shaped type produced by placing two equilateral triangles above and below a base-line as mirror-images and striking arcs from each end of the base-line passing through the other points of the triangle. This creates two pointed arches base-to-base, commonly found as a vertical *aureole enclosing of figure of e.g. Christ in Majesty. Its resemblance to a fish, or to a fish's bladder, relates it to the *Chrismon. The shape is also found in windows, e.g. the *rose-window in the south *transept of Lincoln Cathedral. **2.** *Light in *Second-Pointed *Curvilinear* or *Flowing* *trac-ery resembling a tadpole or the air-bladder of a fish.

Vesnin Brothers Three Russian architects, **Leonid Aleksandrovich** (1880–1933), **Viktor Aleksandrovich** (1882–1950), and **Aleksandr Aleksandrovich** (1883–1959), they worked together on various projects during the period when *Constructivism was fashionable. Aleksandr co-edited the journal *Sovremenaya Arkhitektura* (Contemporary Architecture) with M.Y.*Ginsburg. The Brothers' design for a Palace of Labour (1923), although not built, was a paradigm of Constructivism, as was the project (by A. and V.Vesnin) for the *Leningradskaya Pravda* (Leningrad Truth) Building, Moscow (1923–4), which exposed the lifts (*elevators), loudspeakers, searchlights, and digital clock on the exterior of the overtly framed structure. Their largest realized works were the *curtain-walled Mostorg Department Store, Moscow (1926–7), the Cultural Palace, Vostochnaya Ulitsa, Moscow (1931–7—later called ZIL—a building that looked to *International Modernism for its style), and the Dnieper Dam and Hydro-Electric Station, Dneprostoi (1929–31).

AAQ, **xi**/2 (1979), 24–35; K-M (1986, 1987); Kopp (1970, 1978); Kroha & Hrůza (1973); Ly (1970); Lodder (1983); O.Shv (1970)

vestibule 1. Enclosed or partly enclosed space (*vestibulum*) in front of the main entrance of a *Greek or *Roman building, i.e. an entrance-court or fore-court. 2. Entrance-lobby or hall immediately between an entrance-door and a building's interior. 3. Ante-chamber acting as a baffle between e.g. a corridor and a room, really a communication-lobby.

Vestier, Nicolas-Jacques-Antoine (1765–1816) French *Neo-Classical architect of the *Rue des Colonnes*, Paris (1793–5), with *primitive unfluted *Paestum-*Doric *arcades, one of the most remarkable designs of the French-Revolutionary period. He also designed houses in the *Rue Mont-Blanc* and *Rue Caumartin*, the *Théâtre Gymnase* (after 1795), the apartment-block at 1 *Rue de Helder*, (in which, as in the *Rue des Colonnes*, miniature Doric columns are used for the *balustrades at first-floor level), the *Passage Delorme* (1808), proposals for a church at Meslay-le-Vidame (1810–16—where square Paestum-Doric columns featured), and the Orphanage, Mont-Valérien (1812–14). Two of his sons, the appropriately named **Archimède** (1794–1859) and **Phidias** (1796–1874), also became Neo-Classical architects. Archimède designed railway stations (e.g. Brest) and grand country-houses in Touraine, while Phidias did the railway station in Tours (1851) and became Inspector of Historic Monuments for Indre-et-Loire.

AJ, cxc/2 (12 July 1989), 32–41; *AAF*, xxiv (1969), 309–21; J.Curl (2001); T & B (1940)

vest-pocket park Tiny urban park. Application of *International Modernism's rigid imagery often meant that street frontages and curved street corners were ignored, so that *SLOAP resulted. Attempts were made to reclaim such waste space as *vest-pocket parks* by means of hard and soft landscaping, notably in the USA.

AF, xxv/3 (1966), 54–63; *LA*, xl/4 (1950), 158–60; *PA*, xli/7 (1960), 108–26

vestry 1. Room adjoining the *chancel in a church where the vestments are kept and clergy vested. 2. *Sacristy, often large, where books, sacred vessels, and vestments are stored, and where meetings may be held.

via 1. Roman paved street or road. 2. Gap between the *mutules of a Roman *Doric or *Tuscan *Order.

viaduct Structure, often a series of arches, carrying a road, railway, etc., over a valley.

vicarage Benefice or residence of the vicar of a parish.

vice, vis, vyse Spiral *stair constructed round a central *newel or *pier.

Vicente de Oliveira, Mateus (1706–86) Portuguese architect, he worked under *Ludovice before establishing himself in practice. He designed the exquisite *Rococo *Palácio Nacional*, Queluz, near Lisbon (1747–60), completed by **Jean-Baptiste Robillion** (*fl.*1758–82), who also designed the gardens. The Basílica da Estrêla, Lisbon (1777–90) was built to Vicente's designs.

Ck (1996); K & S (1959); R.C.Smith (1968); D.Wa (1986)

Vicenzo, Antonio di (*c.*1350–1401/2) Italian architect, he designed the gigantic brick *Gothic *San Petronio*, Bologna (from 1390), and around the same time produced drawings for Milan *Duomo* showing a main vault some 23 metres higher than that realized, although the basic design remained unchanged.

Ck (1996)

Victorian Of the period in which **Queen Victoria** reigned (1837–1901).

Vienna Sezession *See* SEZESSION.

Viganó, Vittoriano (1919–96) Italian *Brutalist architect. His Marchiondi Spagliardi Institute for Difficult Children, Milan (1953–7), with almost every surface of *concrete (inside and out), demonstrated the unsuitability of this material for such a building, and the folly of stylistic intransigence (which incurred the justifiable wrath of critics e.g. *Zevi but the predictable approval of *Banham, who hailed it as an example of *New Brutalism*). Other works by Viganó include the Condominii, *Viale Piave* (1947–8) and *Via Gran Can Bernardo* (1958–9), both Milan, and the Calvi House, Redavalle-Broni (1964–5).

AR, cxxv/747 (Apr. 1959), 231–5; Ck (1996); P (1982)

vignette, vinette 1. *See* TRAIL. 2. Low ornamental metal *rail on a window-*cill or *balconet, to prevent flower-pots, etc., from falling.

Vignola, Giacomo *or* **Jacopo Barozzi da** (1507–73) Born near Modena, he became the most important architect working in Rome immediately after the death of *Michelangelo. With *Ammannati, Michelangelo (as consultant), and *Vasari he designed (for **Pope Julius III** (*r.*1550–5)) the *Villa Giulia* (1551–5), one of the great works of *Mannerism in which *villa, *terraces, hemicycles, and gardens were composed as a whole. It was intended as an elegant retreat for the Pope, the hemicycle clearly intended to be a reflection of *Bramante's *Belvedere* Court in the Vatican (begun 1505). Around the same time he built *Sant'Andrea*, *Via Flaminia* (1550–4), the earliest example of the use of an elliptical *drum and

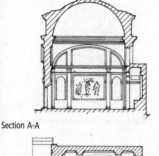

Section A-A

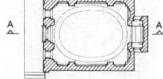

Plan and section of *Sant'Andrea, Via Flaminia*, Rome.

*dome set on a rectangular base: the building's external appearance was derived from Roman tombs and the *Pantheon, while the body of the church had an applied *temple-front of *pilasters carrying a *pediment. His later *Sant' Anna dei Palafrenieri*, Vatican (begun 1572), has an elliptical plan with a dome over it. Both buildings were influential on architects of the *Baroque period, for the ellipse was to become a favoured device, especially in Rome and Central Europe.

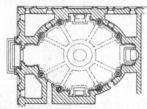

Plan of *Sant'Anna dei Palafrenieri*, Rome.

In 1559 Vignola was appointed by **Cardinal Alessandro Farnese** (1520–89) as Architect of the *Palazzo Farnese*, Caprarola, near Rome, already begun on a pentagonal plan to designs (1520s) by *Peruzzi and *Sangallo the Younger for **Pope Paul III** (*r*.1534–49). It has a circular *cortile in which *rustication and overlapping *triumphal arches feature, and an ingenious, very beautiful spiral staircase with *Tuscan columns and a winding Roman *Doric *string. With its ramps, huge flights of external stairs, and formal gardens, it is one of the most majestic ensembles

of C16, brilliantly connected to the adjoining village. The building's great *cornice, with its plain vertical *consoles, was widely copied, notably in C19. Vignola designed the Mother Church of the Jesuits in Rome, *Il Gesù*, begun 1568 (also for Cardinal Farnese). The plan has similarities to that of *Alberti's *Sant'Andrea*, Mantua, with a tall, tunnel-vaulted *nave, a series of chapels instead of *aisles, and a *façade (begun 1571 by della *Porta) consisting of two storeys of *Orders of *pilasters and columns, with *buttresses hidden behind *scrolls, a device used earlier at Alberti's *Santa Maria Novella*, Florence. The Baroque decorations of the interior were added (1668–73). Churches derived from the exemplar of *Il Gesù* were built all over RC Europe and Latin America, so the Roman exemplar was Vignola's most influential building. His *Facciata dei Banchi, Piazza Maggiore*, Bologna (*c*.1561–5), was his most important contribution to *urban design.

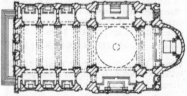

Plan of *Il Gesù*, Rome, showing wall-piers with side-chapels between them instead of aisles.

Vignola was Architect to the Basilica of *San Pietro*, Rome (1567–73), where he carried on Michelangelo's designs. He wrote *La Regola delli Cinque Ordini d'Architettura* (1562) in which (clearly influenced by *Serlio) he established paradigms of the *Orders based on *Antique examples, with clear guidance for setting them out based on a simple modular system. It was an enormously influential book, especially in France, and appeared in many editions in several countries. He also wrote *Le Due Regole della Prospettiva Pratica*, published 1583.

Coolidge *et al.* (1974); E.Hs (1990); He (1996); Lazzaro (1990); Lotz (1977); P.Mu (1969, 1986); Orazi (1982); P (1982); Patetta (ed.) (1990); J.T (1996); Tuttle *et al.* (2002); Vignola (1596); Walcher Casotti (1960); D.Wa (1986)

Vignon, Alexandre-Pierre (1763–1828) French architect of the Revolutionary and Napoléonic periods, pupil of *Leroy and *Ledoux, he was commissioned (1896) to build the *Temple de la Gloire* (after 1813 the *Madeleine*), Paris, on the foundations of an earlier church (1746) begun by *Contant d'Ivry, and revised (1770s) by **G.-M. Couture** (1732–99). It is a grand octastyle *Corinthian building (constructed 1816–28) on a high *podium resembling a rectangular Roman temple

(a *type only revived from C18), with an interior
(1828–40) by **Jean-Jacques-Marie Huvé** (1783–
1852) derived from Roman *thermae.

Biver (1963); *BSHAF* (1910), 380–422, (1933), 258–69;
Ha (1953); Kriéger (1937); M & Wa (1987); J.T (1996);
Vignon (1806, 1816)

Vigny, Pierre de (1690–1772) French architect,
he worked under de *Cotte from whom he inherited various commissions. Among his works may
be cited the *Hôtel de Chenizot, Île Saint-Louis*,
Paris (*c.*1726), the *Cour du Dragon*, Saint-Ger-
main-des-Prés, Paris (1728–32—destroyed 1925),
interiors of the *Hôtel de Luynes*, the Church of *St-
Martin-du-Tertre*, Valois, numerous apartments
in Paris (e.g. 42 *Rue François Miron*), and major
repairs to the Cathedral at Rheims (all 1740s),
and the General Hospital, Lille (begun 1738 but
never completed). He published *Dissertation
sur l'architecture* (1752), in which he expressed
an unfashionable appreciation of the works of
*Borromini, and recommended a pluralist eclec-
ticism instead of an adherence to rigid *Classicism: in this, he anticipated C19 *Historicism.

GdBA, ser. 6, lxxxii (1973), 263–86; P (1982); J.T (1996)

vihara Square or rectangular *court surrounded
by cells occupied by Buddhist monks: opposite the
entrance one cell is usually reserved for a *stupa.

Prip-Möller (1937)

Viking ornament Style of ornament produced (C8–C12) in Scandinavia and in Scandinavian colonies, consisting of *interlacing
elements linked to zoömorphic forms in continuous complex designs. For architectural
purposes there are three main styles: that featuring **S**-shaped intertwined animals, with bodies of even, ribbon-like form (*Jelling*(*e*) style—
mid-C10); that employing semi-naturalistic ani-
mals/birds/dragon-like forms, with influences
from *Anglo-Saxon and *Ottonian decoration
(*Ringerike* style—C11); and that with extremely
stylized ribbon-shaped animals, and snakes, any
animal-heads or -feet being reduced to elongated terminals, forming figure-of-eight and intertwining multiloop *lacertine designs of great
complexity (*Urnes* style—later C11). The last influenced *Celtic, *Hiberno-Romanesque, and
Anglo-Saxon designs. A good example of the
Ringerike type is the carving on the south *doorway of the Church of Sts Mary and David, Kilpeck, Herefs. (*c.*1140–5). Mingled with Celtic
motifs, Viking ornament recurred in *Art Nouveau design.

Glazier (1926); O.Jones (1868); L & D (1986); J.T (1996);
T-M (1967)

(a)

(b)

Viking ornament (a) *Jellinge* style. King Harald's
runestone, Jelling, Denmark (*c.*960–85), showing a four-
legged creature intertwined with ribbon-like serpent.
(b) C11 grave-slab from St Paul's churchyard, London, in
the *Ringerike* style (named after the area near Oslo
where the sandstone largely used for the carvings is
found).

Viking ornament (c)
C12 carving, south
door, Sts Mary and
David, Kilpeck, Herefs.,
showing *Ringerike* style
of the snake-like dragon
forms, also with affinities
to *Urnes* style. (d) C11
carved portal, Urnes
Church, Norway.   (c)   (d)

Villanueva, Juan de

villa 1. *Antique Roman country-house or farm-stead of *three basic types*:

villa rustica: house in the country with spacious accommodation for the owner and his family, and quarters for staff and workers, stores, and animals (the latter called *villa fructuaria*): really a grand farmhouse with refinements;

villa suburbana: house near a town, lacking service buildings (e.g. *Palladio's *Villa Capra*, Vicenza (*c*.1566–70));

villa urbana: essentially a retreat, with spacious rooms, access to agreeable gardens, fine views over the landscape and the sea (if possible), galleries, and parts suitable for summer and winter use. *Pliny's villas were paradigms of this type, which contained all the conveniences, and more, of a town or city mansion.
2. *Renaissance country-house, influenced by concepts of the villa in Antiquity, that was almost a cultural centre, where the like-minded could enjoy civilized life in beautiful surroundings, with fine gardens (fully integrated geometrically and architecturally with the house), works of art, and pleasant views. *Palladio's designs for villas were important exemplars for C18, and led to the creation of some grand country-houses, e.g. *Kent's Holkham Hall, Norfolk, and *Paine and *Adam's Kedleston Hall, Derbys., with landscape-gardens designed with aesthetics (linked to Classical poetry, ideal landscapes captured in paintings, and the beauties of Nature) essential to provide settings for the architecture. **3.** Detached C19 house set in its own grounds on the fringes of a town, often with outbuildings and *wings. *Loudon included several examples of villa-garden layouts and schemes of planting in his comprehensive *Encyclopaedia of Gardening* and *Suburban Gardener*, and **Jane Loudon**'s (1807–58) edited version of her late husband's *Cottage, Farm, and Villa Architecture* also contains much information on the topic. **4.** Small detached house in a modest garden in the suburbs in the late C19 and C20.

An (1967, 1990); J.Archer (1985); D.Arnold (ed.) (1996); B & W-P (1970); D.Coffin (1979); Loudon (1835, 1838); Jane Loudon (ed.) (1846); Mansuelli (1958); D.S.R (1945); RdP (1994); J.T (1996)

Villagrán García, José (1901–82) Mexican architect. Appointed (1923) Chief Architect to the Department of Public Health, he designed the Hygiene Institute, México City (1925–7). Regarded as the father of *Functionalism and *Rationalism in his country, his massive *Instituto Nacional de Cardiología*, México City (1937–44—with later additions), and sundry other works, including the Architectural School at the *Universidad Nacional de México* (1951), demonstrated his debt to the all-pervading influence of Le *Corbusier and *Gropius.

AM, xii/55 (Sept. 1956); Born (1937); Cetto (1961); E (1994); J.T (1996)

Villalpando, Juan Bautista (1552–1608) Spanish Jesuit architect/writer, pupil of *Herrera, he was also influenced by **Jerónimo del Prado** (1547–95), with whom he investigated Solomon's Temple through a study of *Ezekiel*, arguing that Classical architecture derived from the Solomonic Temple, and therefore from God. His *In Ezechielem explanationes et apparatus urbis ac Templi Hierosolymitani* came out (1596) with subsequent volumes (1604). He completed the Jesuit Church, Córdoba (1578), designed the main portal of Baeza Cathedral (1585), and built the College of Saint Hermenegildo, Seville (1587), all Classical, and all restrained.

J.Curl (2011); Rosenau (1979); J.T (1996); Wi & Jaffé (eds) (1972)

Villanueva, Carlos Raúl (1900–75) Venezuelan architect, born in England. As Architect to the Venezuelan Ministry of Public Works (1929–39), he was a tireless promoter of *International Modernism. He designed the enormous housing-estates known as *Dos de Diciembre* (1943–5—with others) and *El Paraiso* (1951–4—again with others), both in Caracas. He designed several works for University City, Caracas: the Olympic Stadium with *shell-concrete *cantilevered elements (1950–2); the *Aula Magna* (1952); and the *Plaza Cubierta* (also 1952). He founded (1944) the School of Architecture, University of Venezuela, designed buildings to house it (1950–7), and taught there for the rest of his life, influencing generations of Latin-American architects to continue on paths that have arguably created huge problems.

Bullrich (1969); E (1994); Hi (1955); Moholy-Nagy (1964); P (1982); Posani (1985); J.T (1996); vV (1993); Villanueva *et al.* (2000)

Villanueva, Juan de (1739–1811) Spanish architect, he worked in the *Churrigueresque and *Baroque styles before visiting Rome (1759–65) when he adopted *Neo-Classicism. He and his brother **Diego** (1715–74) published papers on architecture (1766) in which they promoted a purer form of *Classicism than that currently being practised in Spain. Appointed to work at *El Escorial* by the Jeronymite Order, he soon came to the notice of the Spanish Royal House. **King Carlos III** (*r*.1759–88) and his son, the future **Carlos IV** (*r*.1788–1819), became his patrons. He designed the Palafox Chapel, Burgo de Osma Cathedral (1770–83), the *Casita de Arriba* in the *Escorial* (1771–3), the *Casita del Príncipe*, El Pardo (1784–8), and his masterpiece, the Prado Museum, Madrid (1787–9), a powerful Neo-Classical composition, the finest of its type in all

Spain. He also designed the *Observatorio Astronómico* (1750), and the *cemetery and chapel, Puerta da Fuencarral* (1804–9), both in Madrid.

CG & Miguel (1949); Gaya Nuño (1966); *Goya,* cxcvi (1987), 213–21; K & S (1959); Moleon Gavilanes (1988, 1998); P (1982); W.Pa (1892); Schubert (1924); J.T (1996)

Villard *or* **Wilars de Honnecourt** *or* **Honecort** (*c.*1175–*c.*1240) French draughtsman, author of a portfolio (now in the *Bibliothèque Nationale*, Paris) of some 250 drawings with sections on animals, architecture (only about a sixth part of the collection, containing sketches of buildings and architectural details seen), carpentry, church-furnishings, geometry, human figures (with fine renderings of drapery), masonry, machinery, recipes or formulae, and surveying: it has been claimed that this is the most important medieval architectural treatise to survive. Called the 'Lodge-Book', it has been suggested it was designed to assist apprentices and others: **Paul Frankl** (1878–1962) went so far as to dub Villard the 'Gothic Vitruvius', a grotesque exaggeration, as the drawings demonstrate Villard knew very little about *stereotomy or construction. *Pevsner called Villard an 'architect', claiming his work was 'invaluable as a source': this demonstrates the pitfalls when an art-historian, who obviously knew very little of how buildings were constructed, pontificated on architectural matters. Villard's book is nothing more than an eclectic scrap-book, a record of the interests of a reasonably curious and well-travelled C13 gentleman from Picardy, containing impressions and objects he had actually seen, but it is certainly not a manual of any use whatsoever to 'pupils' or 'apprentices'.

Barnes (1982); Bechmann (1991); Bowie (ed.) (1968); Bucher (1979); J.Curl (2011); Frankl (1960, 2000); Hahnloser (1937); Pe (1960); Recht (ed.) (1989); J.T (1996)

villeggiatura Italian word meaning 'vacation', it was used specifically to suggest the withdrawal from cities, e.g. Rome, to a country residence by the upper classes for reasons of health, pleasure, relaxation, and culture, but it was also associated with agriculture, the celebration of the harvest and the enjoyment of good vintages. It has been eloquently described by *Coffin.

Coffin (1979)

vimana Hindu temple or its sanctuary and superstructure.

Vinci, Leonardo da (1452–1519) *See* LEONARDO.

Vincidor, Tommaso da Bologna (*also known as* **Thomas Vincenz,** *c.* 1495–1534/6) Bolognese architect who had worked in *Raphael's studio in Rome. He designed the courtyard of Breda Castle, The Netherlands (*c.*1534), one of

the first early *Renaissance buildings in that country. He was also responsible for the House of the Salmon, Mechelen, Belgium (1530–4), and for the design of the imposing monument to **Count Engelbert II of Nassau-Dillenburg** (1451–1504) in the *Grote Kerk,* Breda: this work of funerary architecture was the model for the monument of **Sir Francis Vere** (1560–1609) in Westminster Abbey, London (1614).

Bae: *Belgium and Holland* (1905); P.Mu (1986)

vine *See* VIGNETTE.

vinery Building where vines are cultivated (e.g. the charming example at Holkham Hall, Norfolk (1780), by Samuel *Wyatt).

vinette *See* VIGNETTE.

Vingboons, *or* **Vinckeboons, Philip(pu)s** (1607/8–78) Dutch domestic architect who is known primarily for two books (1648, 1674) which proved influential, notably in England. He adapted a Classical vocabulary to tall narrow *façades on the Amsterdam canals, using *pediments, *scrolls, and sparing decoration to great effect: typical of his work are 168 *Herengracht* (1638), 319 *Keizersgracht* (1639), and 364–70 *Herengracht* (1662). His brother **Justus (Joost) Vingboons** (1620/1–98) designed the handsome *Trippenhuis,* Amsterdam (1660–2), with a *Giant *Order of *pilasters rising 2½ storeys, and completed Simon and Jean de la *Vallée's *Riddarhus* (House of the Nobility), Stockholm (*c.*1641–74), also with a Giant Order of pilasters.

G & D (1954); Kuyper (1980); Ottenheym (1989); J.T (1996)

Viollet-le-Duc, Eugène-Emmanuel (1814–79) French architect/theorist, author of the influential *Dictionnaire raisonné de l'architecture française du XIᵉ au XVIᵉ siècle* (1854–68, with a definitive edn (1875)) and the important *Entretiens* (Discourses) on architecture (1863–72). The *Dictionary* helped to consolidate the course of the *Gothic Revival in France (one of its aims was to promote Gothic through logical exposition), and it was scoured for details in England and Germany: *Burges noted that contemporary English Goths 'cribbed' from Viollet-le-Duc, though probably not one in ten read the texts. The fine illustrations helped to create an international taste for French Gothic, especially of the early period. Under the aegis of **Prosper Mérimée** (1803–70), Inspector-General of Historic Monuments, Viollet-le-Duc established a reputation as a restorer of medieval buildings, notably the *Madeleine,* Vézelay (1840–59), *Sainte-Chapelle,* Paris (from 1840—with *Duban), and *Notre Dame* Cathedral, Paris (1844–64—with

J.-B.-A.*Lassus). It was primarily through the study and restoration of historic buildings such as these that the Gothic Revival gained momentum in France, not least through a system of training instigated by Viollet and his colleagues. From 1844 he 'restored' Carcassonne, including the walls and fortifications, but this, and especially his work on the *Château de Pierrefonds*, Oise (1858-70), drew criticism for their dominant, drastic, and conjectural natures.

His interpretation of Gothic was as a rational style, the construction clearly defined by *buttresses supporting *ribs and *vaults, the whole essentially a *skeletal system, with *curtain-walls and *webs really non-structural infill. Forces were transferred to the ground by these systems, and this notion of Gothic became widely accepted, especially by apologists for the much later *Modern Movement (even though surviving ruined Gothic buildings prompt different conclusions). In his *Entretiens* he suggested similarities between iron and Gothic structures, and proposed new techniques to design *framed buildings that would be a modern equivalent of Gothic. His ideas affected many architects, including *Perret and F.L.L.*Wright, especially his insistence on the importance of structure, purpose, dynamics, techniques, and the visible expression of these. In particular he saw parallels between the giving of form to myths in Antiquity and the possibilities in C19 to express mechanical power. Such views made some critics see him as a proto-Modernist, and there can be no doubt about his influence on the architectural worlds of the Continent and the USA.

He published *Dictionnaire raisonné du mobilier français de l'époque carolingienne à la renaissance* (1858-75), *Histoire de l'habitation humaine depuis les temps préhistoriques jusqu'à nos jours* (1875), and many other works, including *L'art russe, ses origins, ses éléments constitutifs, son apogée, son avenir* (1877), translated into Russian (1879), which may have had some influence on *Constructivism. As an architect, his work was often aesthetically coarse, as in the elephantine Morny Tomb, *Père-Lachaise* Cemetery, Paris (1865-6), and the ungainly Church at Aillant-sur-Tholon, Yonne (1864-7), while his drastic reconstructions of historic fabric were among factors that spurred William *Morris to found the Society for the Protection of Ancient Buildings (SPAB) and prompt a nascent *conservation movement.

Auzas (ed.) (1965); Bercé & Foucart (1988); Crook (1981, 1987); Fancelli *et al.* (1990–2); Foucart (ed.) (1980); Heard (ed.) (1990); Leniaud (1994); Marrey (ed.) (2002); Midant (2001); M & Wa (1987); P (1982); Pe (1969, 1972); Su (1963); J.T (1996); Vassallo (1996);

V-I-D (1874, 1875, 1876, 1877, 1959); V-I-D & Narjoux (1979); Vogt *et al.* (eds) (1976); Z (1987)

Viscardi, Giovanni Antonio

(1645-1713) A Ticinese, he settled in Munich where he became (1685) Court Architect. From 1702 he enlarged *Schloss Nymphenburg* by adding *pavilions and began the *saloon. He was involved briefly with E.*Zuccalli (his rival) in the building of the *Theatinerkirche St Kajetan*, Munich (1680s), and designed the *Dreifaltigkeitskirche* in the same city (1711-18). Probably his best work is *Wallfahrtskirche Mariahilf*, Freystadt, near Nuremberg (1700-10), a high-domed centrally planned building, incorporating circle, cross, and octagon, that was to influence *Bähr in his design for the *Frauenkirche*, Dresden. Other buildings by him include the Cistercian Monastery-Church at Fürstenfeldbruck (1701-6), one of the largest and grandest of Bavarian *Baroque churches, a larger version of his Premonstratensian (now *Pfarrkirche*) of Sts Peter and Paul, Freising-Neustift (1700-21).

Bou (1962); Lippert (1969); C.Powell (1959); J.T (1996)

Visconti, Louis(Ludovico)-Tullius(Tullio)-Joachim

(1791-1853) French architect of Italian ancestry, he trained under *Percier, and designed some Parisian *fountains in a robust *Renaissance style, including the *Fontaines Gaillon* (1824-8), *Louvois* (1835-9), *Molière* (1841-3), *Quatre Evèques* (1842-4), and *Saint-Sulpice* (1845-8). He built several large houses, including the *Hôtel Pontalba* (1828). He is best known for two works: the New Louvre, Paris (begun 1852 but redesigned and completed by H.-M.*Lefuel after Visconti's death); and the serene, magnificent, yet dramatic tomb of **Napoléon I** (1769-1821, *r.* as Emperor 1804-14, 1815) under the *Dôme* of the *Invalides* (1841-53), one of the finest *Neo-Classical creations in Paris. He designed a number of handsome tombs in *Père-Lachaise* Cemetery, Paris, notably the elevated *sarcophagus* of the **Duc Decrès** (1761-1821), Vice-Admiral of France.

Aulanier (1953); Hamon & MacCallum (eds) (1991); Lassalle (1846)

visionary architecture

1. The work of certain Neo-Classical architects, notably *Boullée, *Ledoux, and *Lequeu. Boullée's gigantic schemes for *cenotaphs and monuments were noted for their scale and stereometrical purity, while Ledoux's proposals for an ideal city, Chaux, contained many buildings that were expressive of their purpose (*architecture parlante*). 2. Any imaginary scheme featuring fantastic futuristic structures, of which there were many in C20.

AD, xxxi/5 (May 1961), 181–2; Belov *et al.* (1988); Duboy (1987); Feuerstein (1988); E.Ka (1952); L (1982); Rosenau (1976); S & S (1976); V (1990)

vista garden Garden with deliberately designed views, sometimes framed by trees, as in an *allée*, occasionally employing tricks of *perspective, and often involving *eyecatchers revealed in perambulations.

Vitozzi, Ascanio (1539–1615) Italian architect/military-engineer/soldier, he was called (1584) to Turin to serve as architect/engineer to **Carlo Emanuele I** (1561–1630—**Duke of Savoy** from 1580). He designed *Santa Maria del Monte* (or *dei Cappuccini*) (1585–96); *Santissima Trinità* (begun 1598—with a plan based on a star within a hexagon, pre-empting *Borromini's later *Sant'Ivo*, Rome (1643–60)); and *Corpus Domini* (1607), Turin. His greatest work was the huge centrally planned domed *Santuario di Vico*, Mondovì, Piedmont (also called *Vicoforte di Mondovi*— 1596–1736), based on an ellipse and anticipating C17 *Baroque plans. He made a contribution to the urban design of Turin, including the *façades of the *Piazza Castello* (1606) and the adjoining *Contrada Nova* (1615), both of which served as models for subsequent developments in the city. He fortified the town of Cherasco from 1610, and wrote a treatise on fortifications (1589).

Carboneri (1966); P (1982); W.Pa (1892); *RJfK*, vii (1955), 9–99; Scotti (1969); J.T (1996); Wi (1982)

vitrified Converted into a glassy substance by exposure to intense heat, as with certain bricks used as *headers in *diaper-work.

Bru (1990)

Vitrolite Rolled opal glass (ranging from complete opacity through various grades of translucency) with a naturally hard, brilliant, fire-finished surface, first made (1930) in England. Manufactured in black and white and a range of standard colours which were inherent in the glass, it was employed in *cladding as in a *curtain-wall (**4**), usually in *panels beneath panels of clear glass, e.g. Owen *Williams's *Daily Express* building, Fleet Street, London (1932). It was also used to clad the *dado of the Mersey Tunnel (1934), replaced with cream Vitrolite in 1954–5.

McGrath & Frost (1937).

Vitruvian opening Aperture, wider at the bottom than at the top (i.e. with sloping sides), in Classical architecture and *Neo-Classicism, described by *Vitruvius.

lug or ear

architrave

Vitruvian opening
Described by Vitruvius, published by Palladio, has a lugged architrave, based on the example from the interior of the 'Temple of Vesta', Tivoli (*c.*80 BC), so called *Tivoli window*.

Vitruvian scroll Repeated pattern consisting of convolved undulations in Classical *bands, *friezes, *string-courses, etc., resembling a series of *scrolls joined together by a wave-like form, also called *running-dog or *wave-scroll.

Vitruvian scroll

Vitruvius Pollio, Marcus (*c.*80/70–*after* 15 BC). Roman architect/engineer/architectural theorist, author of the only substantial *Antique treatise on architecture to survive. Entitled simply *De Architectura*, it was dedicated to **Emperor Augustus** (*r.*27 BC–AD 14), and is subdivided into ten 'books' or main sections. Although known and copied in manuscript form during the Middle Ages, from 1414, when **Poggio Bracciolini** (1380–1459) publicized the existence of the manuscript in St Gallen Abbey, Switzerland, *De Architectura* began to be taken very seriously, and was the basis for *Alberti's important treatise. The first printed edition (by **Fra Giovanni Sulpitius** or **Sulpizio da Veroli** (*fl.*1470–90)) came out (1486–92), an illustrated version by **Fra Giovanni Giocondo** (1435–1515) appeared (1511), and Italian translations were published from the 1520s, starting with the edition (1521) with copious illustrations and notes by **Cesare di Lorenzo Cesariano** (1483–1543). **Daniele Barbaro's** (1514–70) edition (1556) had plates by *Palladio. Since C15, Vitruvius' text has been published in many forms and translations (e.g. the Nuremberg German version (1528) and *Philander's annotated edition (1544)). It is still an authoritative source for *Classicism, and while the precise meanings of some of its terms and phrases are disputed, it has acquired a wholly unwarranted reputation for obfuscatory dullness: on the contrary, it is a mine of information about Greek and Roman art and architecture, and has been enormously influential since the *Renaissance. One of the most important and encylopedic editions was that by *Perrault (1673). The first English version of the first five books of *De Architectura* was published 1771, and all ten books appeared in English (1791), translated by Newton and edited by his brother, **James Newton** (1748–c.1804). However, a potted Vitruvius in English had been published (1692), but it was so abridged that its usefulness was limited. Newton's edition was superseded by that of *Gwilt (1826), although William *Wilkins had published (1812) *The Civil Architecture of Vitruvius*, with commentaries, but it was incomplete.

As an architect, Vitruvius designed (c.27 BC) a *basilica (destroyed) for Colonia Iulia Fanestris (modern Fano), a new town for army veterans.

E.Hs (1990); Knell & Wessenberg (eds) (1984); W.MacD (1965–86); McEwen (2003); P (1982); T.Smith (2004); J.T (1996); VP (1597, 1960); W-P (1981)

Vittone, Bernardo Antonio (1702–70) One of the supreme masters of Piedmontese *Baroque. He edited *Guarini's *Architettura Civile* for publication by the Theatine Order (1737), but is known primarily for his churches in which the influences of Guarini, *Juvarra (his teacher), and French *Rococo were manifest. His masterworks include the little hexagonal *Cappella della Visitazione*, Vallinotto, near Carignano (1738–9); the octagonal-domed *San Bernardino*, Chieri (1740–4); and *Santa Chiara*, Brà (1741–2). At *Santa Maria di Piazza*, Turin (1750–4), one of his structural inventions may be seen to advantage: the gouged-out *pendentive or inverted *squinch (which opens the form to extra light). This recurred in his *Santi Pietro e Paolo*, Mondovì (1755), and *Santa Croce* (later *Santa Caterina*), Villanova di Mondovì (1755), where the pendentives were virtually eliminated. He experimented with circular, elliptical, octagonal, hexagonal, and longitudinal plans, all ingeniously and assuredly handled, and occasionally threw three *vaults over the space to create a type of domical vault in which the geometries were unusually subtle and complex, creating light and airy effects. His *San Michele*, Borgo d'Ale (1770), combined themes from *Borromini (the convex wall-plans and convex porch) with elements from Guarini.

Vittone published instructive books on civil architecture (*Istruzione Elementari per indirizzo dei giovani allo studio dell' Architettura Civile*

and *Istruzione diverse concernenti l'officio dell'Architetto Civile* (both 1760)).

Brinckmann (1931); Carboneri & Viale (1967); N-S (1986a); On (ed.) (1972); Olivero (1920); P (1982); Pommer (1967); Pi (1960, 1966); J.T (1996); Va (1986); Viale (ed.) (1972); Wi (1982)

vivo 1. *Shaft or *fust of a column. **2.** *Naked of any part of a building, but especially a column or *pilaster.

Voit, August von (1801–70) German architect, he studied under *Gärtner from whom he imbibed an affection for the *Rundbogenstil. He designed the Churches of St Michael, Homburg (1839–41), St Ludwig, Speier (1834–6), and the *Stadtpfarrkirche*, Weissenhorn (1864–9). Called to Munich (1841) by **King Ludwig I of Bavaria** (r.1825–48), he designed the remarkably severe *Glasmalerei-Anstalt* (1843–6—destroyed 1945—influenced by *Schinkel's *Bauakademie*, Berlin), the fine *Neue Pinakothek* (1843–5—destroyed 1945), several *prisons (e.g. Nuremberg (1864–7) and Munich (1866–70))), and the *Glaspalast*, Munich (1853–4—destroyed 1945—inspired by *Paxton's Crystal Palace, London). He also designed (1851–3) a water-garden for **King Maximilian II** (r.1848–64), conservatories in the Botanic Gardens, Munich, and a huge, much-admired winter-garden (1866–8—destroyed 1897) on the roof of the *Residenz*, Munich, for **King Ludwig II** (r.1864–86).

Hütsch (1981); Mittlmeier (1977); Ne (1987); E.Roth (1971)

Volksgarten German *public park, e.g. that in Vienna.

volumetric building Factory-built *prefabricated building, moved whole to the site and there connected to foundations and services.

volute Spiral *scroll, of which there are normally four on the *Ionic capital, eight on the *angular and *Composite capitals, and smaller types, sometimes called *helix, on the *Corinthian capital. It is also a distinctive element of the *ancon, *console, and *modillion, where, like the Ionic capital, it resembles a rolled-up mattress.

vomitorium (*pl.* **vomitoria**) Passage to give ingress to or egress from a Roman *amphitheatre or theatre.

Vorarlberg School Term describing several families of architects/stuccoers/painters/craftsmen, all related, in the Vorarlberg of Austria, west of the Tyrol towards the *Bodensee* (Lake Constance). The main families were the *Beers, *Moosbruggers, and *Thumbs, and they made an enormous contribution to late-C17 and C18 *Baroque architecture in South Germany and

Switzerland. The main general characteristics of churches by the Vorarlberg School were longitudinal plans, often with centralized spaces associated with the *transepts, the *Wandpfeiler* arrangement, vestigial 'aisles' the same height as the nave set between wall-piers (as in medieval *Hallenkirchen* (*hall-churches)), *nave-*arcades almost as high as the *vaults, *galleries between the *piers (often with significant elements placed to draw the eye towards the *high-altar), slight transeptal projections, *choirs narrower than naves, twin-towered *façades, and decoration subordinated to the architecture.

Bou (1962); Lb & D (1976); On (1973); C.Powell (1959)

Voronikhin, Andrey Nikiforovich (1759–1814) Born a serf on the Stroganov Estates near Perm, Russia, he received the patronage of his master, **Count Aleksandr Sergeyevich Stroganov** (1734–1811—possibly Voronikhin's father), who arranged for his formal education and travel. A pupil of de *Wailly, he became one of Russia's most distinguished Neo-Classical architects after his return to his motherland (1790). His main works include the Stroganov Dacha, near St Petersburg (1796–8), remodelling of the State-Rooms of *Rastrelli's Stroganov Palace on the Nevsky Prospect, after fire damage (1790s), the Cathedral of the Virgin of Kazan' (influenced by *Soufflot's *Panthéon*, Paris—1801–11), and the Academy of Mines, with its huge dodecastyle *Paestum-*Doric *portico (1806–11), all in St Petersburg.

Grabar *et al.* (eds) (1963); G.H (1983); M & Wa (1987); J.T (1996)

voussoir *Cuneus, or block (normally of brick, *masonry, or *terracotta), shaped on two opposite long sides to converging planes in what is normally the shape of a wedge, forming part of the structure of an arch or *vault, its sides coinciding with the radii of the arch.

voussure *Vault.

Voysey, Annesley (*c.*1794–1839) London architect/surveyor who, according to *I'Anson Jun., designed the first building in London (*c.*1823) to be used exclusively for offices at the Lombard Street end of Clement's Lane. For a time Voysey was in partnership with Richard *Suter, but went to Jamaica to design Port Antonio parish church, and died there of fever. His grandson was C.F.A.*Voysey, and *Kempthorne was his pupil.

Co (2008)

Voysey, Charles Francis Annesley (1857–1941) English *Arts-and-Crafts architect, much influenced by *Mackmurdo and *Morris. Apprenticed (1874) to *Seddon, he later (1880) worked with *Devey before establishing his own practice (1882). Until the 1914–18 war he designed many medium-sized country-houses, all beautifully sited, informally and asymmetrically composed with exteriors rendered in *pebble-dash, and nearly all with bands of windows subdivided by square unmoulded stone *mullions. *Battered *buttresses, wide overhanging *eaves, and steeply pitched roofs featured in his buildings, which were largely based on *vernacular C16 and early C17 traditions, and also influenced by Devey's work. His fireplaces, furniture, and details were influenced by Mackmurdo, and in turn were precedents for *Mackintosh. Typical of his admired country-houses were Perrycroft, Colwall, Herefs. (1893–4), Broadleys (1898) and Moor Crag (1898-1900), near Windermere, Westmd., in the English Lake District, and The Pastures, North Luffenham, Rut. (1901). Forster House, 14 South Parade, Bedford Park, Chiswick (1888–91 and 1894), owed something to *Art Nouveau, but also to mullioned vernacular architecture and *Regency metal *verandah roofs. His only house in Ireland, 'Dallas', 149 Malone Road, Belfast (1911–12), is very similar to his English domestic work. Voysey's designs were widely publicized in *The Studio* magazine and by *Muthesius in *Das englische Haus* (1904–5), but in the British Isles tended to be parodied in countless speculative houses built in the 1920s and 1930s, although Voysey himself had virtually no commissions after 1918. One of his most interesting designs is the Sanderson Wallpaper Factory, Chiswick (1902), with its bold *piers and glazed-brick walls. *Pevsner admired The Orchard, Chorley Wood, Herts. (1899–1901—Voysey's own house), unaccountably seeing in it and his other houses, with their bold 'bare walls and long horizontal bands of windows', precedents for the *International *Modern Movement, and made spurious claims for Voysey (Master of the *Art Workers' Guild, 1924) as a 'pioneer' of modern design (1937), notably at Broadleys, where Pevsner detected Voysey coming 'amazingly close' to a C20 'concrete and glass grid': Voysey (like Baillie *Scott) dismissed such interpretations of his work as complete nonsense, and was more than irritated by Pevsner's preposterous views. While Voysey had no qualms about using machinery (e.g. to reproduce his wallpaper designs), he actually detested the International style, claiming it could not last and that its Godless creators knew nothing of spirituality and of that which was exalted.

Brandon-Jones *et al.* (1978); Durant (1992); Gebhard (1975); A.S.Gray (1985); Hitchmough (1995); *ODNB* (2004); P (1982); Pe (1960, 1968, 1974a); M.Rn (1983); D.Simpson (1979); J.T (1996)

Vredeman *See* VRIES.

Vriendt, Cornelis Floris de (1514–75) *See* FLORIS.

Vries, Hans Vredeman de (1527-1606) Dutch architect/painter/decorator/prolific writer, his engravings were widely distributed, and his architectural devices, derived from *Serlio, made the style evolved at *Fontainebleau familiar. His treatises on architecture and his *pattern-books were hugely influential throughout Northern Europe, notably in England, where direct quotations of *strapwork and much else informed much *Elizabethan and *Jacobean architecture. His published work demonstrates how important was the Flemish and Dutch contribution to *Mannerism, and includes *Architectura oder Bauung der Antiquen aus dem Vitruvius* (1577), *Variae Architecturae Formae* (1601), and many other books (e.g. *Architectura* (1606—a joint effort with his son, **Paul** (1567—*after* 1630)). *Smythson and *Thorpe drew on his publications, and his designs for *parterres* were adopted in many places (e.g. the celebrated gardens (c.1615-20) at Heidelberg *Schloss*).

Borggrefe *et al.* (eds) (2002); G & TK (1960); Jervis (1984); *JGH*, *l*/1/2 (1981), 67–104, and 179–202; L & D (1986); J.T (1996); Vries (1617, 1651)

Vulliamy, Lewis (1791-1871) English architect of French descent, articled to R.*Smirke before he established his London practice. He designed the sumptuous Italian-*Renaissance Dorchester House, Park Lane, London (1850-63—demolished 1929), and the *Jacobethan Westonbirt House, Glos. (1863-70—with *Renaissance interiors) for the wealthy **Robert Stayner Holford** (1808-92). An eclectic designer, he was competent in any style required of him. Among his churches, St Barnabas, Addison Road, Kensington (1828-9), St Michael, Highgate (1830-2), and St James, Norlands, Kensington (1844-5), are typical of his *Commissioners'-*Gothic style, but he also designed All Saints', Ennismore Gardens, Kensington (1848-9—*Italianate), and St Peter's, Glasbury, Breconshire, Wales (1836-7—*Neo-Norman). The *Greek-Revival Law Institution, Chancery Lane (1828-32), and the *Corinthian frontage of The Royal Institution, Albemarle Street (1838), both in London, were by him. He designed a number of imposing elevations for speculative buildings in Bloomsbury, including the north and west ranges in Tavistock Square (1827) and Gordon (now Endsleigh) Place (1827), and built or altered many country-houses. He published *The Bridge of The Sta. Trinita at Florence* (1822) and *Examples of Ornamental Sculpture in Architecture, Drawn from the Originals in Greece, Asia Minor, and Italy in the years 1818, 1819, 1820, 1821* (1823). Pupils included Owen *Jones, and his nephew, **George John Vulliamy** (1817-86), worked in his office until 1861, when he joined the Metropolitan Board of Works as its Superintending Architect, in which capacity he designed the base, ornaments, and bronze *sphinxes associated with 'Cleopatra's Needle' (c.1468 BC) on the Embankment, London (1878-82).

B *et al.* (2001); Co (2008); *ODNB* (2004)

vulne window *See* LYCHNOSCOPE.

vyse *See* VICE.

Wachsmann, Konrad Ludwig (1901–80) German-born American architect, student (1920–5) of *Poelzig and *Tessenow, before he joined **Christoph & Unmack**, makers of timber buildings and components, becoming Chief Architect (1926–9). He then established his own practice in Berlin (1929–32), where he numbered **Albert Einstein** (1879–1955) among his clients (e.g. the Einstein House, near Potsdam (1929–30)). He exhibited and published designs for timber buildings (e.g. for the *Deutscher Werkbund* Exhibition, 1931), and evolved *reinforced-concrete building systems having set up a practice in Rome (1935–8). In France (1938–9—where he had a short-lived association with Le *Corbusier) he designed tubular steel and plywood-panel construction systems before emigrating to the USA where he joined *Gropius. He moved (1942) to NYC, designing prefabricated building-components for the General Panel Corporation, notably the 'Packaged House' (a housing-system evolved by Gropius and himself), and perfected his '*Mobilar*' *space-frame for aircraft-hangars, making his speciality the design of connecting joints used in cellular structures. Appointed Professor of Design and Director of the Department of Advanced Building Research at the Institute of Design, Illinois Institute of Technology (1949–56), he further developed the '*Mobilar*' system with joints capable of receiving up to 20 tubular members enabling enormous *cantilevers to be constructed so that large areas could be roofed with minimal vertical supports. His work anticipated many later developments, and influenced designers including Buckminster *Fuller. He published *Holzhausbau: Technik und Gestaltung* (1930), *Holz im Bau* (1957), both concerning timber construction, *Wendepunkt im Bauen* (Turning Point in Building—1959), and other works.

E (1994); G.Herbert (1984); Klotz (ed.) (1986); J.T (1996); Wachsmann (1961, 1988); Wachsmann *et al.* (1995)

Wadsworth, Alexander (1806–98) American engineer/landscape architect, he designed Washington Square, Belvidere Village, Lowell, MA, and (with *Dearborn and *Bigelow) Mount Auburn Cemetery, Cambridge, MA (both 1831): Mount Auburn served as the model for other *garden-cemeteries, including Mount Hope, Bangor, ME (1835), Mount Pleasant, Taunton, MA (1836), and Wadsworth's own designs for Harmony Grove Cemetery, Salem, MA (1839–40) and Woodland Cemetery, Chelsea, MA (1850—with **Henry Weld Fuller** (1810–89)). Wadsworth also laid out parks and suburbs in and around Boston, MA.

B & K (2000); Dall (1898); Linden (2007)

Waghemakere Family Flemish architects based in Antwerp. **Herman de Waghemakere** (*c.*1430–1503) was Master of the Works at Antwerp Cathedral, where he was engaged (1474) in building the north-western tower to the second stage, and other works, including the completion of the *nave, north *aisle, and chapel of the Holy Circumcision (1473–1503). His masterpiece is St Jacob's Church, Antwerp, begun 1491, but he was also responsible for much of the fabric of St Gommarus, Lier (*ambulatory, *choir, and *Lady Chapel—1473–85), St Willibrord, Hulst, The Netherlands (1482–7), and the *Vleeshuis*, Antwerp (1501). His son, **Domien** or **Dominicus de Waghemakere** (*c.*1460–1542), assisted Herman at St Gommarus, Lier (1494), completed the upper stages of the north-western tower of Antwerp Cathedral (1502–42), completed the Church of St Jacob, Antwerp (1502–42), and, with Rombout *Keldermans, built the *Maison du Roi*, Brussels (1514–23), the Town Hall, Gent (1517–33), and the *Handelsbeurs*, Antwerp (1531—destroyed).

Białostocki (1972); *DKuDe*, ii/11 (1909), 81–4; Leemans (1972); W.Pa (1892); VTB (1977)

Wagner, Martin (1885–1957) German architect/planner, his reputation was made in the field of low-cost industrialized housing in Berlin, although he himself designed little, and was essentially an enabler. A member of *Der *Ring* and active in the *Deutscher Werkbund, he collaborated with several *Modern-Movement architects, including *Gropius, *Häring, *Mies van der Rohe, *Poelzig, and *Scharoun, and was a pioneer of the *International-Modern style. His best-known housing scheme was the Britz, known as the *Hufeisensiedlung* at Berlin-Neukölln (1925–30—with Bruno *Taut). He also worked with

*Bartning, Häring, and Gropius on the Siemens-stadt Housing Development, Berlin (1927–31). He left Germany for Turkey (1935), and, through Gropius's influence, joined (1938–50) the staff of Harvard University, USA. He published many (usually polemical) works on architecture and planning throughout his career, promoting Leftist views.

J.T (1996); M.Wagner (1918, 1923, 1925, 1929, 1932)

Wagner, Otto Colomann (1841–1918) Austrian architect of great distinction, he studied in Vienna and Berlin (where he absorbed something of *Schinkel's *Classicism), and began practice in Vienna as a competent architect of many *Historicist buildings, drawing heavily on *Renaissance and *Baroque traditions (influenced by van der *Nüll and *Siccard von Siccardsburg). Appointed (1890) to prepare proposals for replanning the city, the only part to be realized was the *Stadtbahn* (1894–1901), with its series of beautiful buildings (stations, bridges, and other structures) in a restrained, economical style, tending to *Neo-Classicism (but where even *Ionic capitals are transformed into machine-like elements), and openly exploiting the possibilities of metal and glass in architecture. The elegant stations at Schönbrunn outside the city and in the *Karlsplatz* in the centre both displayed Baroque and *fin-de-siècle* *Art-Nouveau tendencies.

Among his finest creations in an Art-Nouveau style are the *Majolikahaus* (faced with ceramic tiles), and adjacent apartment-block (with *stucco ornament), on the *Linke Wienzeile*, Vienna (1898–9), while the second *Villa Wagner*, 28 *Hüttelberg-strasse*, Vienna (1912–13), anticipated aspects of C20 Neo-Classicism and even *Art Deco. As a practitioner and Professor of Architecture at the Academy, Wagner influenced the younger generation, including *Hoffmann, *Kotěra, *Olbrich, and *Plečnik, and in his influential *Moderne Architektur* (1896) he argued for forms, style, structures, and materials that would be suitable for the times. His *stripped-Classical *Postsparkasse*, Vienna (1903–12), has a *façade clad in stone fixed with metal bolts, the heads of which are exposed, and the interior of the banking-hall is treated without historical references in a fresh and confident manner, using metal and glass. His mastery of combining new technology and materials with traditional forms is best seen at the *Leopoldskirche, Am Steinhof* (1903–7), on a hill in the grounds of the Vienna State Mental Asylum: there, aspects of *Jugendstil, *Neo-Classicism, and *Baroque combine in a masterly synthesized whole. Wagner's influence extended after his death to the successor-states of the Austro-Hungarian Empire through his many pupils and assistants.

Asenbaum *et al.* (1984); B & G (1986); Geretsegger *et al.* (1983); Graf (1985, 1997, 1999, 2000); Kliczkowski (ed.) (2002); Kolb (1989); Lux (1914); Mallgrave (1993); Ostwald (1948); Ouvrard *et al.* (1986); P (1982); Pintarić (1989); Sheaffer (1997); J.T (1996); Trevisiol (1990); O.Wagner (1914, 1987, 1988, 2002, 2002a)

wagon Term used to describe a curved shape, like a wagon-roof. *Compounds include*:

wagon-chamfer: type of *chamfer consisting of a series of small scoops, like bites, removed from the arrises of a timber of rectangular section, favoured in *Arts-and-Crafts work. A good example is the *balustrade of the Library at the Glasgow School of Art (1907–9—damaged by fire 2014) by C.R.*Mackintosh, where scoops are accentuated with colour;

wagon-headed: having a continuous round-arched ceiling or *vault, as in *barrel-vaulting*:

wagon-roof: *cradle-roof constructed of a closely spaced series of double arch-braced *trusses, suggesting the shape of a covered wagon or barrel-vault. It may be exposed, plastered, or panelled (*wagon-ceiling*);

wagon-vault: as *barrel-* or *tunnel-vault*.

Wahlman, Lars Israel (1870–1952) Swedish architect, much influenced by *vernacular architecture, German *Jugendstil, and the English *Arts-and-Crafts movement (esp. the work of William *Morris and R.N.*Shaw), he also drew on aspects of *Berlage's, *Nyrop's, and H.H.*Richardson's designs. He became celebrated as a designer of houses and churches, and his buildings were important influences on *National Romantics such as *Östberg. His most celebrated works are the powerful Engelbrekt Parish Church, Stockholm (1906–14), Tjolöholm Castle (1897–1906), and Villa Widmark, Lysekil (1902–4).

A & B (1986); Ahlberg (1925); S.Lind *et al.* (1950); P (1982); J.T (1996)

Wailly, Charles de (1730–98) French architect/artist, one of the most distinguished and influential of the *Louis-Seize and Revolutionary periods. He studied under J.-F.*Blondel, Le *Geay, and *Servandoni, and at the French Academy in Rome (1754–7), where he fell under the spell of *Piranesi. His numerous surviving drawings compare favourably with those of Hubert *Robert, and he acquired a formidable reputation as an interior decorator and stage-designer before becoming an urban-planner and architect of several buildings of real distinction, including the austere *Théâtre de l'Odéon*, Paris (1769–82—with M.-J.*Peyre—but subsequently altered), and the *Château de Montmusard, near Dijon (1764–9—only partly realized). The latter, with an ingenious plan and rigorous geometry, was the first country-house in France in which the *Antique flavour was dominant, heralding a severe later *Neo-Classicism of which

*Boullée and *Ledoux were the most celebrated protagonists. His town-houses in the *Rue de la Pépinière*, Paris (1776–8), were resourceful designs, but, like most of his work, no longer exist. For the *crypt of *St-Leu-St-Gilles*, Paris (1773–80), he employed sturdy columns derived from the Greek *temples at *Paestum (but with *reeds instead of *flutes) supporting arches and *vaults, a very advanced design for its date. He also designed the luxurious *Gran' Salone, Palazzo Spinola*, Genoa (1772–3—destroyed), and a theatrical pulpit for *St-Sulpice*, Paris (1788), for which building he also decorated the *Chapelle de la Vierge* (1777–8). **Landgrave Friedrich II** of Hesse-Kassel (*r.*1760–85) invited de Wailly to submit designs for Neo-Classical palaces at Kassel (1783) and Wilhelmshöhe (1785), but neither was realized. In the event, **Landgrave Wilhelm IX** (*r.*1785–1803—when he became **Elector Wilhelm I of Hesse** (*r.*1803–21)) built (1786–92) Wilhelmshöhe to designs by du *Ry and de Wailly's pupil *Jussow. Through other pupils (e.g. *Voronikhin) de Wailly's influence spread to Russia, especially St Petersburg.

B (1980); Ga (1964); M & R (1979); M & Wa (1987); D.Wa (1986); Wa & M (1987)

wainscot 1. Fine oak panel-work for walls. **2.** Timber *dado (USA). **3.** Panelled *box-pews.

walk *Path (traditionally finished with grass, gravel, or sand, within a garden for recreational walking) from which agreeable views may be enjoyed.

Walker, Ralph Thomas (1889–1973) American architect best known for his *Art-Deco *skyscrapers, including the Barclay-Vesey Telephone Building (1923–6) the Western Union Building (1928–9), and the Irving Trust Building (1928–32), all *set-back buildings in NYC. He was an innovative designer of laboratories and of scientific research-centres, including the Bell Telephone Laboratories, Murray Hill, NJ (1937–49), and the Argonne National Laboratory, Chicago, IL (1950–2). He published *The Fly in the Amber: Comments on the Making of Architecture* (1957). His work after the 1939–45 war was not universally admired.

Bosserman (1968); P (1982); R.Walker (1957)

wall Structure of *masonry, brick, etc., serving to enclose a room, house, or other space, and, in most cases, *load-bearing, i.e. supporting the floors, roof, etc. It may also be a *screen-wall for privacy or enclosure. *Types of wall include*:

cavity: with an air-gap between two *leaves to improve insulation and prevent water-penetration;

crinkle-crankle: see CRINKLE-CRANKLE;

curtain: see CURTAIN-WALL;

hollow: as CAVITY, but see BRICK;

partition: wall dividing a space, not usually load-bearing;

party: between adjoining properties, usually load-bearing and fire-resistant;

retaining: prevents earth from slipping, so used in gardens and in excavations;

springing: *buttress;

sustaining: load-bearing or retaining wall, unlike one serving merely as a partition or screen.

Compounds include:

wall-arcade: *blind *arcade;

wall-arch: arch in blind arcade;

wall-base: *plinth, *skirting, or *socle;

wall-column: *engaged column;

wall-coping: see COPE;

wall-dock: wall-insert of timber, the same size as a brick;

wall-dormer: *lucarne with a front continuous with and above the *naked of the main wall below it;

wall-garden: wall with plants growing out of the joints or from specially created hollows, *niches, etc.;

wall-monument: large funerary monument attached to a wall, usually standing on the floor, distinct from a wall-tablet;

wall-piece: **1.** wall-plate, *pan-piece* or *raising piece*; **2.** wall-painting or *fresco with the figures adjusted to fit the shape of the wall;

wall-pier: *Wandpfeiler;

wall-plate: longitudinal timber (*wall-piece*) set on top of a *timber frame or a brick or masonry wall on which roof-*trusses, *joists, *rafters, etc., rest;

wall-press: cupboard or shelving recessed into a wall;

wall-rib: *Gothic *formeret, i.e. *vault-rib set against the outer wall of a *vault-compartment or *bay;

wall-shaft: *colonnette or projecting part of a *pier, like an *engaged column, from which a Gothic vault springs;

wall-string: raking support (*string*) of a *stair nearest the wall;

wall-tablet: inscribed memorial tablet often with an architectural frame.

Wallace, William (*fl.*1615–31). Scots architect, Master-Mason to the Scottish Crown (1617–31) he carried out works including the King's Lodging, Edinburgh Castle (1615–17), the north quarter of Linlithgow Palace, West Lothian (1618–21), and parts of Stirling Castle. He was responsible for Heriot's Hospital, Edinburgh (1628–59), a showy work with Anglo-Flemish *Mannerist decorations. Indeed, he was a major figure in the introduction of this style to Scotland. Among his other designs were Wintoun Castle, East Lothian (*c.*1620–30), and the monument of **John Byres of Coates** (d.1629) in Greyfriars burial-ground, Edinburgh, in which exuberant *strapwork abounds.

Co (2008); Dunbar (1966, 1978); GMcW & W (1984); Mylne (1893)

walled garden Area enclosed by walls used for specific purposes, e.g. for growing herbs, vegetables (*kitchen-garden), flowers, or fruit (often associated with greenhouses, heated walls, etc.). In America, *Shipman's walled gardens were often enclosed with curtains of evergreens.

Wallfahrtskirche *Pilgrimage-church in German-speaking lands.

Wallis, Thomas (1873–1953) English architect. When articled to **Sidney Robert James Smith** (1858–1913), Wallis designed the Tate Gallery, London (1892–97), usually attributed solely to Smith. On his own account his competition-entry (1904) for Herne Hill Public Library was premiated and published (but not executed), and he established (1908) his own practice with **James Albert Bowden** (1876–1949). Several other published designs brought him to the attention of **Moritz Kahn** (1881–c.1939), who had formed (1909) the **Trussed Concrete Steel Company** in Britain to promote the *Truscon* System of *reinforced concrete, but the USA firm (*see* KAHN, ALBERT) needed a British architect who would understand the possibilities and commit himself to the design of industrial architecture. Wallis saw his chance, and set up (1914) a new practice, **Wallis, Gilbert, & Partners:** the identity of 'Gilbert' is not known, but later partners included Wallis's son, **Douglas T.Wallis** (1901–68) and **J.W.MacGregor** (d.1994). From its inception, Wallis, Gilbert, & Partners specialized in industrial buildings that often had attractive and colourful fronts (Wallis was aware of buildings as advertisements) concealing the works behind, and employing systems invented by the *Kahn family: it was one of the most successful British practices of the time, producing bright, clean, light, well-designed factories, among which may be cited the Caribonum, Leyton (1918); Solex, Marylebone Road (1925); Wrigley's, Wembley (1926); Shannon, Kingston (1928); Firestone Tyre, Brentford, Middx. (1928–9—demolished 1980); Pyrene, Western Avenue (1930); the masterly, colourful, Egyptianizing *Art-Deco *Modernistic Hoover Factory, Perivale, on Western Avenue (1931–8—*Pevsner hated it, primly dubbing it 'offensive'); and Klingerit, Sidcup Bypass, Bexley (1935–6—with Dutch-inspired Expressionist brickwork), all in or near London. Other works included the British Bemberg Factory, Doncaster, Yorks. (1931), the Daimler Hire Garage, Herbrand Street, London (1931), Victoria Coach-Station, London (1931–2),

and smaller coach-stations at Amersham, Bucks., Hemel Hempstead and Hertford, Herts., Reigate, Surrey, and Windsor, Berks.

AR, clvi/929 (July 1974), 21–7; Architecture, vii/8 (1929), 61–73; J.Curl (2005); Hitchmough (1992); RIBAJ, ser. 3, xl/8 (25 Feb. 1933), 301–12; Skinner (1997); Twentieth-Century Architecture, i (1994), 12–22.

Wallot, Paul (1841–1912) German architect, pupil of Martin *Gropius, he began his career by designing numerous houses in Frankfurt-am-Main, but made his name with the *Baroque-Revival Reichstag, Berlin 1884–94—gutted 1933, reconstructed with major modifications c.1975–99), which he followed with the Ständehaus (later Landtag), Dresden (1901–7), and a house at the artists' colony, Darmstadt (c.1901).

Hamner-Schenk et al. (2002); Mackowsky (1912); Schliepmann (1913); Schmädecke (1970)

Walpole, Horace (Horatio) (1717–97—**4th Earl of Orford** from 1791) English virtuoso and wit, his importance in the realm of architecture lies in his creation of Strawberry Hill, Twickenham, Mddx. (from 1750), one of the earliest key buildings of the *Gothic Revival, publicized in his A Description of the Villa of Horace Walpole at Strawberry Hill (1774, 1778). This asymmetrical house set precedents for *Picturesque composition. He also helped to make *Gothic fashionable when he published his The Castle of Otranto, a 'Gothic Romance' (1764), an early work of *Romanticism. He included notes on the works of architects in his Anecdotes of Painting in England (1762–71), and he furthered the study of medieval architecture by encouraging James *Essex in his researches.

M.Aldrich (1994); N.Barker (ed.) (2010); G (1972); W.S. Lewis (1960, 1973); M.McCarthy (1987); Mowl (1996); ODNB (2004); J.T (1996)

Walsingham, Alan of (fl.1314–64) Sacristan of Ely Cathedral, Cambs., during the erection of the exquisite *Second-Pointed *Lady Chapel (1321–49—which, before iconoclastic damage in C16, must have been one of the most stunning *Gothic ensembles in England) and the building of the octagon and *lantern (1322–42) over the *crossing after the Cathedral's central tower collapsed. It would appear that the genesis of the design of the octagon came from him, and the works were carried out by the Ely masons **John the Mason** (Cementarius—fl.1322–6) and **John atte Grene** (fl.1334–50), the timber superstructure (1334–50) being by William *Hurle(y).

J.Harvey (1987)

Walter of Canterbury (fl.c.1322) See CANTERBURY.

Walter, Thomas Ustick (1804–87) American architect of German descent, pupil of *Strickland and John *Haviland, he made his reputation with the *peripteral temple-like Girard College for Orphans, Philadelphia (1833–48), one of the finest monuments of the *Greek Revival in the USA, although inspired by the *Madeleine* in Paris, and employing the *Corinthian *Order of the *Choragic Monument of Lysicrates, Athens (334 BC). Thereafter, he designed in a variety of styles. With **John Jay Smith** (1798–1881) he published (1846) *Guide to Workers in Metal and Stone and Two Hundred Designs for Cottages and Villas*. He prepared (1850) designs for the extension of the Capitol in Washington, DC, and until 1865 worked on the building. His greatest contributions were the *wings and the elegant *dome on its cast-iron frame (influenced by *Montferrand's St Isaac's Cathedral, St Petersburg, Russia (completed and publicized 1857)). He was assisted by **August Gottlieb Schoenborn** (*fl.*1850–65) in this work, although **Montgomery C.Meigs** (1816–92) was also involved as engineer-in-charge, and openly challenged Walter's authority (1858). While in Washington Walter also extended the Treasury (1852), Patent Office (1850), Post Office (1856), and Hospital for the Insane (1852). He was responsible for Marine Barracks at Pensacola, FL (1857), and Brooklyn, NYC (1858–9). A parsimonious US Government never paid Walter or his heirs for the last-mentioned works, and he died in straitened circumstances.

Americana, xxxiii (1939), 151–79; G.Brown (1970); Ennis (1982); Hamlin (1964); Hi (1977); *JSAH*, vii/1–2 (Jan./June 1948), 1–31, xvi/2 (May 1957), 22–5, xxxix/4 (Dec. 1980), 307–11; P (1982); J.T (1996); W & K (1983); T.Walter (1984)

Walters, Edward (1808–72) English architect. He was in Constantinople (1832–7) as superintendent of Sir John *Rennie's work on military buildings there, before returning to England where he practised in Manchester from 1839. He designed *warehouses in that city and the Free Trade Hall (1855—*Pevsner called it the 'noblest monument in the *Cinquecento* style in England' but only the *façade survived when a hotel (completed 2004) was built on the site), all of which were in an Italian *Renaissance-Revival style. Perhaps his most accomplished building was the Manchester & Salford Bank (later Royal Bank of Scotland), Mosley Street (1860) a *palazzo* handled with confidence.

D & M (1985); Hartwell *et al*. (2004)

Walton, Walter *or* **Watkin** (*fl.*1381–1418) English mason, *Yeveley's deputy during the rebuilding of Westminster Hall (1394–5). He worked at Porchester Castle, Hants., from 1396, and probably designed the *pulpitum* and *cloisters at Chichester Cathedral, Sussex (*c.*1400–10),

where he may also have been responsible for the detached bell-tower. He became (1397) Chief Surveyor of all stonecutters and masons for the King's Works in England.

J.Harvey (1987)

Wandpfeiler Literally a *wall-pier* or *-column*, the term is given to internal *buttresses forming the walls of side-chapels or pierced with arches to form *aisles in South-German *Baroque churches, especially those of the *Vorarlberg School (e.g. *Thumb's Obermarchtal).

Bou (1962); Lb & D (1976); On (1973); J.T (1996)

Wank, Roland Anthony (1898–1970) Hungarian-born architect, the series of dams and power-houses he produced for the Tennessee Valley Authority, USA (1933–44), are recognized as his finest works. He also concerned himself with public housing: his Grand Street Housing, NYC (1929–30), is his best-known achievement in this field.

AF, cxxxiii (Sept. 1970), 58–9; *AR*, xciii/558 (Jun. 1943), 157; vV (1993)

Warchavchik, Gregori (1896–1972) Odessa-born, he studied in Rome and worked with *Piacentini before emigrating to Brazil (1923), where he became one of the leaders of *International *Modernism. He published (1925) his manifesto on architecture, and designed several houses from 1927 that were much influenced by the blocky cubic forms fashionable in Europe at that time, including his own house in São Paulo (1927–8—the first example of Modernism in Brazil (with some *Art-Deco touches)), and the First Modern House Exhibition, São Paulo (1930). He worked for a time with *Costa.

Correio de Manha (1 Nov. 1925); E (1994); Ferraz (1965); Mindlin (1956); Sartoris (1936)

ward 1. *Bailey or *court of a *castle, protected by a wall, towers, etc. **2.** Large apartment in a gaol or hospital.

Ward, Colin (1924–2010) British anarchist writer on education/architecture/town-planning, originally influenced by the works of *Lethaby, as described in his *Influences: Voices of Creative Dissent* (1991). He saw architects and planners as the *enemies* of good housing, especially in the context of Received Opinion that the 'State should Provide'. In his *Arcadia for All* (written with **Dennis Hardy**) he described housing without control by either the State or the Market, and showed that post-war planning had removed a traditional freedom, grotesquely inflating the price of land. He advocated self-managed, non-hierarchical forms of social organization, admiring Swiss direct-democracy systems where Cantons are run by people who control laws under which they live. Much of his work was concerned with rural housing, over-population, the causes of vandalism (particularly when people's sense of Home had been lost), and the role of the State, bureaucracies, and professions in perpetuating injustices and Dystopia.

R.Bradshaw *et al.* (eds) (2011); *C20* (Spring 2010), 35; C.Ward (1983, 1991, 1996); C.Ward & Hardy (2004)

Ward, Nathaniel Bagshaw (1791–1868) English botanist, he collaborated with *Loddiges in the invention of the *Wardian Case*, a sealed glazed container which dramatically improved the possibilities of importing exotic plants over long sea-journeys.

ODNB (2004); Shoe (2001); N.B.Ward (1852)

Wardell, William Wilkinson (1823–99) London-born architect/engineer/surveyor, he designed (1846–58) nearly 40 RC Puginesque *Gothic-Revival churches (e.g. St. Birinus, Dorchester-on-Thames, Oxon. (1847), and Our Lady of Victories, Clapham, London (1849–51)). He emigrated (1858) to Australia, where he became Chief Architect to the Victoria Department of Works, and subsequently Inspector-General of Public Buildings (1869–78). His *Italianate Government House, Melbourne (1872–6), was influenced by Osborne House on the Isle of Wight, but his two RC Cathedrals (St Patrick's, Melbourne (1857–1927), and St Mary's, Sydney (1865–1940)) were competent Gothic Revival in style. He also designed the Church of St John the Evangelist, Toorak, Melbourne (1860–73), St John's College, Sydney University (1859), and St Mary's Cathedral, Hobart, Tasmania (1876).

Ck (1996); Herman (1954); Jong (1983); J.T (1996)

wardrobe Room or cupboard for storing clothes, also called *garderobe (**1**).

Wardrop, James Maitland (1824–82) London-born, he settled in Edinburgh, where he was articled to **Thomas Brown** (*fl.*1837–68—son of **Thomas Brown** (*c.*1781–1850), Superintendent of the City Works, Edinburgh (1819–47)). Brown Jun. became (1837) Architect to the Prison Board of Scotland, and took Wardrop into partnership (1849). The young man was responsible for the design of several buildings, including the startling Flemish-Italian polychrome *Gothic County Buildings and Town-Hall, Wigtown, Galloway (1862–3), the Flemish-Scottish Sheriff Court-House, Alloa (1862–5), the former County Buildings and Court, Stirling (1864–76—with *crow-stepped *gables, *Renaissance *strapwork, and Gothic porch), and the County Buildings, Forfar, Angus (1869). He designed several large country-houses, including the *Baronial Glenternie House, Peeblesshire (1863–8—reminiscent of the work of *Bryce), and Kinnordy House, Angus (1879–*c.*1881), in a free *Jacobean style with Scottish touches.

DSA (2013); DW

Ware, Isaac (1704–66) English architect, apprenticed to *Ripley, he later became (under *Burlington's aegis) an able devotee of *Palladianism. He published *Designs of Inigo Jones and Others* (1731, 1743—which included many drawings from *Burlington's collection), *The Plans, Elevations, and Sections of Houghton in Norfolk* (1735), and the scholarly translation (and immaculate edition) of *Palladio's *Four Books of Architecture*, dedicated to Burlington (1738). His most important book was *A Complete Body of Architecture*, which came out (1756–7) in weekly parts, with a second edition (1767, re-issued 1768): encylopedic and lavishly illustrated, it became a standard work on *Georgian architectural practice and theory, remaining one of the most influential architectural publications well into the following century. Among his buildings were Clifton Hill House, Bristol (1746–50), and Wrotham Park, Mddx. (1754—now Herts.), the last illustrated in *Vitruvius Britannicus* (**v**, plates 45–6), and clearly derived from Colen *Campbell's Wanstead III. His pupil, *Cameron, carried his influence to Russia.

Co (2008); E.Hs (1990); *ODNB* (2004); P (1982); Su (1993); I.Ware (1756–7); Wi (1974*a*)

Ware & van Brunt Leading USA architectural firm (1863–81), formed by **William Robert Ware** (1832–1915) and **Henry van Brunt** (1832–1903), both pupils of Richard Morris *Hunt in NYC, having studied at Harvard. Their best work was for ecclesiastical and institutional buildings, notably First Church, Boston, MA (1865–7), the Memorial Hall, Harvard (1865–80—perhaps the finest *Gothic-Revival building ever erected in the USA), the Episcopal Theological School, Cambridge, MA (1869–80), Weld Hall, Harvard (1871–2), Third Universalist Church, Cambridge, MA (1875), the stack addition to Gore Hall, Harvard University Library (1876–7—the first example of such book-storage in the USA), and St Stephen's Church, Lynn, MA (1881–2). Their Gothic work was much influenced by *Ruskin, but they designed with considerable flair in the *Queen-Anne and North-European *Renaissance styles.

Ware was appointed Professor and Head of the first US School of Architecture at the Massachusetts Institute of Technology (1865) and later (1881) set up the School at Columbia, NYC, based on *Beaux-Arts* principles. He designed the American School of Classical Studies, Athens, Greece (1886–8), a scholarly essay of considerable distinction. Van Brunt continued to practise, taking **Frank Howe** (1849–1909) into partnership (1881), and moved (1887) the firm to Kansas, MO, from where they designed many railway stations for the Union Pacific railroad (Ware and van Brunt's Union Station, Worcester, MA,

warehouse

824

of 1873-5—destroyed—was an example). Their Electricity Building, World's Columbian Exposition, Chicago, Il (1892-3), was firmly Classical in style.

Ware and van Brunt were committed to high standards of professionalism, and both were distinguished writers and critics. Van Brunt was the first to translate *Viollet-le-Duc's *Entretiens* into English as *Discourses on Architecture* (1875-81), while Ware published several works, including *Greek Ornament* (1878) and *The American Vignola* (1901).

Coles (ed.) (1969); *The Crayon*, vi (1859), 15–20; Hi (1977); P (1982); J.T (1996); W.RotchWare (1866, 1878, 1900, 1912–13, 1977); W & K (1983)

warehouse Building for the storage of goods, e.g. alcoholic drink, grain, etc., often associated with canals and docks, and frequently of considerable interest structurally and architecturally.

Warren, Edward Prioleau (1856-1937) English architect, articled to *Bodley and *Garner, he later wrote the former's biography. He designed a number of distinguished buildings, including the Warren Building, Balliol College, Oxford (1906-8). Perhaps his best work is the range of mansion-flats at Hanover Lodge, St John's Wood High Street, London (1903-4). Other designs include 5 Palace Green (1904), Shelley House, Chelsea Embankment (1912), both in London, and the Fishermen's Institute, Newlyn, Cornwall (1911). Among his churches may be mentioned St Martin, Bryanston, Dorset (1895-8—with a stately tower), St Mary, Bishopstoke, Hants. (1890-1—with an iron *chancel-screen (1903) by **W.Bainbridge Reynolds** (1845-1935)), and St Michael and All Angels, Bassett, Southampton, also Hants. (1897-1910—described by *Pevsner as 'intriguing and distinguished').

A.S.Gray (1985); Pe & Lloyd (1967)

Warren & Wetmore NYC firm of architects (practising 1890s-*c*.1930), founded by **Whitney Warren** (1864-1943) and **Charles D.Wetmore** (1866-1941). Warren's Paris *Beaux-Arts* training was apparent in the New York Yacht Club (1898-9) and the Grand Central Terminal, NYC (with **Charles A.Reed** (1858-1911) and **Allen H.Stem** (1856-1931)—1903-13). Among other works were the Biltmore Hotel, Madison Avenue/43rd Street (1914), Marshall Field Building, 200 Madison Avenue (1920), Equitable Trust Building, Madison Avenue (1918), the Royal Hawaiian Hotel, Honolulu (1927), and the rebuilding (1920) of the University Library, Leuven, Belgium, destroyed by the Germans in the 1914-18 war.

Fitch & Waite (1974); *JSAH*, xlv/3 (Sept. 1986), 270–85; Ms (1964); P (1982); K.Powell (1996); J.T (1996)

Warton, Joseph (1722-1800) English poet, author of *The Enthusiast: or, The Lover of Nature* (1744), an early reaction against the artifice of gardens such as Stowe, Bucks., in favour of less tamed countryside, preferring terrifying precipices to designed landscapes by *Kent, and the *Sublime landscapes of **Salvator Rosa** (1615-73) to the serene Arcadies of **Claude Lorrain(e)** (1600-82). *The Enthusiast* was enlarged and revised in later edns, notably **James Dodsley's** (1724-97) *Collection of Poems by Various Hands* (1782), originally published (1748) with his brother, **Robert Dodsley** (1703-64).

H & W (1988); *ODNB* (2004)

Wastell, John (c.1460-c.1518) Master-mason, one of the greatest of the last phase of English *Gothic architecture. He worked under Simon *Clerk at Bury St Edmunds Abbey, Suffolk (demolished), Saffron Walden Church, Essex (1485), and King's College Chapel, Cambridge, where he was active from 1486, by which time he appears to have been Clerk's partner. However, Bury was his normal place of residence, and he probably spent most of his time there (1480s) working on the Abbey. From 1490 his name recurs in the records of King's College, and he was also called by **John Morton** (c.1420-1500—**Archbishop of Canterbury** from 1486) to Canterbury Cathedral, Kent, where he designed and built the *crossing-tower (1494-1505), one of the finest *Perp. works (known as 'Bell Harry') with fan-*vaults (c.1503) almost identical to the patterns of those at King's College Chapel, Cambridge. He carried out other works for Morton, and was involved in designing buildings at King's Hall, Cambridge, now part of the east range of the Great *Court of Trinity College, and including the lower stages of the Great Gate Tower. He was also engaged at Great St Mary's Church, Cambridge (1491-1514), and, on stylistic grounds, at Dedham Church, Essex (1494), and the lower stages of the tower at Soham Church, Cambs. It has also been suggested that he worked on the *nave at Lavenham Church, Suffolk (1495-1515), and St James's Church (now Cathedral), Bury St Edmunds (1503-21—Dr Harvey confidently attributed the latter to Wastell). He may also have designed the eastern chapels and *retrochoir at Peterborough Cathedral, Cambs. (1496-c.1528), the fan-vaults of which are similar in design to those at King's College Chapel.

Wastell's greatest surviving work was the completion of the latter from 1506, and building operations began in 1508, finishing 1515. He is known to have consulted William *Vertue, John *Smyth, and Henry *Redman about the design and construction, but it must also be remembered that he had had plenty of experience planning and erecting fan-vaults at Bury St Edmunds and Peter-borough. Wastell was responsible for building the *ante-chapel from just above ground level and for completing the *choir, five *bays of which had been roofed in *Clerk's time. He and Henry *Se-mark contracted (1512) to build the vaults, and those and most of the decorative elements, including the *Tudor badges, were made under Wastell's direction. The latter (senior partner in the contract) designed the great west window, the *buttress *pinnacles, and the tops of the corner-*turrets. The entire ensemble at King's is of such high quality that Wastell must be named as among the most gifted architects England ever produced.

J.Harvey (1987); *ODNB* (2004)

Watanabe, Hitoshi (1887–1973) Japanese tra-ditionalist architect responsible for many build-ings in the inter-War years. His best-known work is the National Museum, Tokyo (1931–8), in which European *stripped Classicism mingled with elements taken from indigenous buildings.

Ck (1996); J.T (1996)

Watanabe, Youiji (1923–83) Japanese archi-tect, he caricatured certain tendencies in architec-ture by, for example, designing a paediatrician's house in the shape of a dragon, and an apart-ment-block in the guise of a penguin. Among his works may be cited Dragon Fort, Ito (1968), Sky Buildings (various dates), and the Tanaka House, Naoetsu (1975). To some critics his work was 'heretical' because it punctured the absurd preten-sions of Modernism.

E (1994); Js (1973*a*)

watch-house 1. Small structure to shelter paid persons for security purposes, e.g. to guard bleach-greens in Ulster where linen was left out for whitening (unaccountably also called *watch-towers), or to afford protection to burial-grounds from the depredations of 'body-snatchers'. 2. Lock-up. 3. Police-station.

watching-chamber *or* **-loft** 1. Elevated *gal-lery in a church from which the monks could watch over a holy *shrine, e.g. the beautiful sur-viving timber example in St Alban's Cathedral, Herts. (early C15). 2. Place from which monks could be summoned to the services, appropriately called *excubitorium*.

F.Bond (1908*a*); B & C (1909)

watch-tower 1. Tower or station from which observation is kept of the approach of danger, as on a city wall. 2. As *watch-house (1).

Watelet, Claude-Henri (1718–86) French writer/theorist/painter/landscape architect, his *Es-sai sur les Jardins* (1774) celebrated the 'English' garden as well as his own *Picturesque creation at Le Moulin-Joli near Paris (created 1754–72, based not only on English informality but on Watelet's paintings, influenced by the charming canvases of his friend **François Boucher** (1703–70)). The *Essai* pays due respect to J.-J.*Rousseau, who influenced the design of several French gar-dens, notably at Ermenonville. However, Wate-let's garden (destroyed, among many other beautiful things, in the Revolution of 1789) mixed French *parterres and straight formal *al-lées with wildernesses, meandering paths, and informal 'natural' plantations. His advocacy of working, agricultural landscapes (fields of crops, pastures for animals, and farm-buildings), visible from the more self-consciously designed-for-pleasure garden, brought an appreciation of pro-ductive aspects of the countryside into an aes-thetic of garden-design. Thus the idea of the *ferme ornée* became accepted in French theories of landscape. He may have influenced (directly or indirectly) *Mique's *Hameau de Trianon,* Ver-sailles (1778–82).

Racine (ed.) (2001); J.T (1996); C.-H.Watelet (1774)

water Classical ornament such as the *Vitru-vian scroll may represent waves, while the Ancient-Egyptians used parallel *zig-zag lines to suggest water. Sculpted representations of flow-ing water are associated with *grottoes, *nym-phaea, etc., and are found in *rustication, often frozen, or *congelated. *Compounds include*:

water-bar: small strip, usually of metal, fixed in a *cill so that a door will shut against it, thus stopping the ingress of water;

water-holding base: early-*Gothic *pier- or *co-lonnette- *base with a hollow channel at the top bounded by two *roll-mouldings, as though it could hold water (but not for this purpose);

water-leaf: 1. *Transitional early-*Gothic C12 carved ornament on each angle of a *capital, essentially a large, broad, plain leaf resembling a water-lily or lily-pad, flowing out from above the *astragal in a concave curve, then returning upwards in a convex curve, turning inwards at each angle under the *abacus; 2. Classical orna-ment, often on a *cyma reversa *moulding, re-sembling a series of pointed tongue-like forms pointing downwards, with darts between them, also called *hart's tongue, Lesbian,* or *lily-leaf,* each tongue-form divided vertically by an inci-sion. It is probably related to the *lotus-leaf, or to ivy-leaves; 3. long, feather-like unserrated leaf used by *Palladio in his enrichment of the *Ionic, *Corinthian, and *Composite *Orders, also called *stiff-leaf, and used as a series of vertical ornaments on *friezes, etc.;

water-mill: mill for, e.g., grinding corn, the machinery of which is driven by a wheel turned by water-power;

water-shot: dry-stone wall without *mortar in which the stones are laid to a slope so that water is less likely to penetrate: common in the English Lake District where such walls are often constructed of slate;

water-stair: **1.** steps on the shores of a river giving access to a boat, called *watermen's stairs*; **2.** architectural construction in a garden down which water cascades; **3.** two or more adjacent locks in a canal to facilitate the raising or lowering of boats from one level to another;

water-table: inclined surface on a projection, e.g. a *plinth or *buttress *off-set, called *weathering*;

water-tower: tower supporting high-level *water-tanks* in which water is stored for delivery at suitable pressure over an area lower than the tanks, e.g. in East Anglia, where they are often significant landmarks;

water-wall: a so-called 'curtain' or 'sheet' of falling water, commonly used in C20 landscape-design;

water-wheel: wheel driven by water, either falling from above, or passing underneath;

water-work: **1.** structure to hold water (e.g. tank) or defend against it (e.g. *pier, sea-wall, etc.); **2.** in *pl.* an assemblage of machinery, buildings, etc., to supply water; **3.** contrivance to provide pleasing spectacles, e.g. *fountains, *cascades, etc. **4.** anything concerned with *hydraulics.

water-garden From Antiquity, and in many cultures, water has played an essential part in gardens, not only for practical purposes of irrigation, but for aesthetic reasons (*see* BĀGH; CHAHAR-BĀGH; BAROQUE, ISLAMIC, ITALIAN, MUGHAL, PARADISE GARDEN). A *water-garden*, however, is either part of a garden in which water (in the form of *canals, *cascades, *fountains, pools, etc.) plays a prominent role, often with water-loving plants, or a large garden in which water is dominant (e.g. Hodnet Hall, Salop. (1920s), with its interconnected pools and lake).

Plumptre (2003); Symes (2006); Tay (2006)

Waterhouse, Alfred (1830–1905) English architect, master of rational planning, he made his reputation as the designer of several important secular buildings, starting with the *Gothic-Revival Assize Courts, Manchester (demolished), which he won in competition (1858–9), and gained the approbation of *Ruskin. He consolidated his position by almost winning the competition to design the Royal Courts of Justice, London (1866–7—the buildings were erected to designs by *Street), and by his success in the competition (1867–8) to design the brilliantly planned Gothic-Revival Town Hall in Manchester

(1869–77). Waterhouse designed numerous university buildings including the Master's Lodge and Broad-Street Front, Balliol College, Oxford (1866–9—Gothic Revival), the French *Renaissance-Revival Tree Court, Gonville and Caius College, Cambridge (1868–70), and the Gothic Owen's College (now the University), Manchester (1869–88). Interested in experimentation, he used hard *terracottas, bricks, and *faïences, as in the Natural History Museum, London (1873–81—much influenced by German (especially Rhineland) *Romanesque architecture), the Gothic Prudential Assurance Building, Holborn, London (1878–1906), and the Free *Rundbogenstil Congregationalist Churches at Lyndhurst Road, Hampstead (1883), and King's Weigh House, Duke Street, Mayfair, London (1889–91). His National Liberal Club, London (1885–7), was in a mixture of Romanesque and Italian and French *Renaissance styles, said at the time to reflect the uneasy *pot-pourri* of disparate opinions within the Liberal Party. The spectacular Eaton Hall, Ches. (1870–83), seat of the **Dukes of Westminster** (demolished 1961), was his largest country-house. He also designed the *Tudor-Revival Blackmoor House and Gothic Revival Church, Blackmoor, Hants. (1868–72). His son, **Paul** (1861–1924), studied with him, became his partner (1891), completed his father's University College Hospital, Gower Street, London, and added the Medical School and Nurses' Home (1905). Paul Waterhouse's other works included the Whitworth Hall, University of Manchester (1902) and New Buildings, College Road, University of Leeds (1907–8). Paul Waterhouse was succeeded in the practice by his son, **Michael** (1889–1968).

Axon (1878); C.Cm (2001); C.Cm & Waterhouse (1992); D & M (1985); Ea (1970); J.Fawcett (ed.) (1976); Gd (1990); A.S.Gray (1985); Hi (1977); Maltby *et al.* (1983); *ODNB* (2004); P (1982); Sh (1975); J.T (1996); Waterhouse (1867)

Waterloo church *See* COMMISSIONERS' GOTHIC.

Watkin, David John (1941–2018) *See* NEW CLAS-SICISM.

Watson, Thomas Nicholson (1929–2006) Scots architect, he settled (1952) in East Africa, designing many buildings before (1973) returning the UK. He became Secretary of the Commonwealth Association of Architects (1974), and prepared a report (1978–9) for UNESCO on *conservation in Tanzania. He eventually settled in Edinburgh where he worked for the Royal Fine Art Commission.

RIBAJ (7 July 2007), 78

Watt, Richard Harding (1842–1913) English creator of buildings out of architectural features collected from demolition contractors. He worked with clay models to convey his original ideas to executive architects (including **Walter Aston** (1861–1905), **John Brooke** (1853–1914), **Harry Smith Fairhurst** (1868–1945), **J.H.France** (*fl.* early-C20), and **W.Longworth** (*fl.* early-C20)), resulting in a series of remarkable eclectic buildings in Knutsford, Ches.: among them are the Gaskell Memorial Tower with the adjacent King's Coffee House (1907–8), the Old Croft (1895—with tower of 1907), Moorgarth (1898), the Ruskin Rooms and Cottages (1899–1902), Swinton Square (1902), cottages in Drury Lane, houses in Legh Road, and the laundry in Knutsford Mere (all *c*.1904). Stylistically, the buildings tend to the *Italianate, with *Moorish, Classical, and exotic touches.

A.S.Gray (1985); Hartwell *et al.* (2011)

wattle-and-daub *or* **-dab** Interwoven *staves and twigs used to fill a panel in a *timber frame, providing a backing for a finish of daub (clay, dung, or mud) or *plaster (usually on straw or hair), which is then lime-washed. It is also used in roofs beneath *thatch, in which case it is *under-thatch wattling*.

ABDM (1996); Bru (1987, 1994)

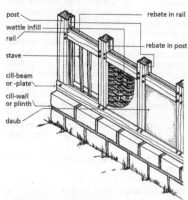

wattle-and-daub (*RAM, ABDM, CBA*).

Watts, Mary Seton (*née* **Fraser-Tytler**) (1849–1938) *Arts-and-Crafts artist, she married (1886) **George Frederic Watts** (1817–1904), and designed the cemetery-chapel, Compton, Surrey (1901–6), in an amalgam of Celtic-Romanesque-Art Nouveau, with richly coloured decorations carried out in *gesso (*Pevsner sniffily thought the 'soporific' interior was unpleasant because of the 'intolerable torpor and weariness of the motifs').

Gould (1998); Nairn,Pe, & Cherry (1971)

wave-moulding *Second-Pointed *moulding consisting of two *roll-mouldings following one

another, as at the base of a *pier, i.e. in profile looking like a wave.

wave-scroll Classical ornament consisting of a series of repeated *scrolls or waves, sometimes like the side-view of a series of overlapping *consoles or long **S**-shapes on their sides, also called *running-dog or *Vitruvian scroll.

Wayss, Gustav Adolf (1850–1917) German engineer who, with **Matthias Koenen** (1849–1924), pioneered scientific calculations in *rein-forced-*concrete construction, thus establishing a theoretical basis for it.

J.T (1996)

Wealden house Medieval *timber-framed dwelling-type found mainly in the South-East of England, and named after the Weald, a district, once forested, between the North and South Downs. It consists of an open hall the full height of the structure with a two-storey *bay on each side of the hall, having a single roof in one direction over the whole, the *ridge of the pitched roof (sometimes hipped) following the length. The upper floors of the end-bays project on *jetties on the front elevation, but the *eaves are continuous, so that part of the roof over the set-back hall wall rests on a flying wall-plate supported on diagonal (often curved) *braces in line with the front of the jettied first-floor wall. A *single-ended* or *half-Wealden* house is similar, but has only one jettied bay.

ABDM (1996); Bru (1987, 1994, 2000)

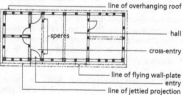

Wealden house The central hall between two-storey bays at each end is the full height of the structure. Stair-positions can vary.

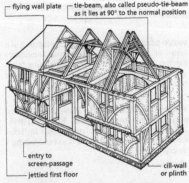

flying wall plate — tie-beam, also called pseudo-tie-beam as it lies at 90° to the normal position

entry to screen-passage
jettied first floor
cill-wall or plinth

Exploded diagram of timber-framed Wealden house (*RAM, ABDM, CBA*).

weather *Compounds and derivatives include*:

weather-boarding: **1.** external wall-cladding of overlapping horizontal timber boards; **2.** true weather-boarding consists of sawn boards of rectangular section (i.e. with parallel sides), as distinct from riven *clap-boards of triangular section;

weather-cock: *see* WEATHER-VANE;

weather-door: *lucarne on a *Gothic *spire;

weathered: **1.** changed by exposure, so means anything from satisfactorily toned down so as not to appear garish and new, to badly worn and eroded; **2.** *weathering*;

weathering: **1.** inclination given to any upper surface, e.g. *off-set; **2.** process of undergoing change caused by action of weather. In some instances the effect of time on a building may be beneficial, giving the surface a beauty that cannot be artificially created (e.g. *limestone *ashlar);

weather-moulding: *moulding projecting from the face of a wall to cast off water, e.g. *label, or anything similar with a sloping top for that purpose;

weather-struck: *pointing in brickwork with the *mortar sloping outwards from the underside of one brick to the face of the one underneath so that water does not lie on the top surface of any brick;

weather-tiling: wall-finish of hung *tiles;

weather-vane: swivelling *vane, often combined with crossed rods to show the compass points, and frequently in the form of a cock, hence *weather-cock*.

web 1. *Cell, compartment, infill, or *severy between *ribs of a *Gothic *vault. **2.** Vertical plate connecting two horizontal flanges or plates in a steel or iron I-beam. **3.** Sheet of lead, e.g. on a roof.

Webb, Sir Aston (1849–1930) English architect, from 1882 in partnership with **Edward Ingress Bell** (1837–1914): the practice was one of the most successful of the late-*Victorian and *Edwardian periods, although the work relied more on bold effects than on refinement of detail. Stylistically, Webb favoured *François Ier early in his career, but later mixed *Byzantine and *Gothic, *Renaissance and *Italianate, and *Palladianism with *Baroque. Among his works were the Victoria Law Courts, Birmingham (1885–91), the French Protestant Church, Soho Square, London (1891–3), the astonishing *Jacobean-Revival house, Yeaton Pevery, Bomere Heath, Salop. (1889–92), Christ's Hospital, Horsham, Sussex (1893–1904), and the Royal Naval College, Dartmouth, Devon (1897–1905), the last two in a *Wrenaissance style. His free eclecticism is perhaps best expressed by the Byzantine-Gothic buildings at the University of Birmingham (1901–9) and the Gothic-Venetian-*François Ier-Renaissance-*Romanesque mix at the main front of the Victoria & Albert Museum, South Kensington (1899–1903). Webb made a major contribution to *urban design with his Queen Victoria Memorial scheme, London (1901): this involved widening and replanting The Mall to make it a grand *Beaux-Arts *boulevard, building the Admiralty Arch (1903–10) on a site between Trafalgar Square and The Mall, and re-fronting Buckingham Palace (1912–13) in a *Louis-Seize style as an appropriate termination of The Mall behind the huge Baroque pile-up of the Queen Victoria monument itself, designed (1904) by (**Sir**) **Thomas Brock** (1847–1922) and built 1906–24 (the *rond-point and architectural elements were designed by Webb). One of his best essays in Classicism was the Royal College of Science, Dublin (1906—with Thomas Manby *Deane (1851–1933)).

Dungavell (1999); A.S.Gray (1985); *ODNB* (2004); P (1982); Se (1977)

Webb, Charles (1821–98) Suffolk-born architect, he worked in *Allom's office before settling (1849) in Australia, where he went into partnership with his brother, **James Webb** (1808–70), as architects/surveyors. Their most important early commission was St Paul's Church, Brighton, Melbourne, Victoria (from 1850), and this was followed by many warehouses, a *synagogue, shops, and other buildings in the Brighton area. Webb practised on his own account from 1858, designing Wesley College (1864), Alfred Hospital (1869), the Royal Arcade (also 1869), Melbourne Orphan Asylum (1878), and the Grand (later Windsor) Hotel (1884).

Bate (1983); *ADB* (2012)

Webb, John (1611–72) English architect, pupil and relative (by marriage) of Inigo *Jones, he assisted the latter when working (1630s) on St Paul's Cathedral, London. He made many drawings for the unrealized Whitehall Palace, and rebuilt (1648–50) the interior (notably the celebrated double-cube room once thought to be by Jones) of Wilton House, Wilts., after a fire (1647-8). After Jones's death (1652) Webb was the unrivalled master of Classical architecture in England, steeped as he was in knowledge of the works of *Palladio, *Scamozzi, and *Serlio, although he seems never to have visited Italy (but may have travelled in France (1656)). His finest surviving works are the *Corinthian *portico and north front of The Vyne, Hants. (1654–6), the earliest domestic portico in England (a motif derived from Palladio's *Villa Barbaro* at Maser), and the King Charles Block, Greenwich Palace (1664–9), the last a masterly composition in which *Baroque devices such as the *Giant Order and the overhanging *keystone were employed to great effect. Probably his finest country-house was Amesbury Abbey, Wilts. (1659–61—rebuilt by *Hopper, 1834–40), described by C.R.*Cockerell as 'of uncommon grandeur', and certainly one of the most outstanding Palladian compositions of C17 (illustrated in *Vitruvius Britannicus*, 1725, and *Kent's *Designs of Inigo Jones*, **ii**, 1727). Much of his other work has been destroyed, although several of his important buildings were published in *Vitruvius Britannicus* (1715, 1717, 1725), where they had a profound influence on the *second Palladian Revival* of *Burlington and his circle. Unfortunately for Webb's reputation, most of his designs were attributed to Inigo Jones by *Campbell and Kent.

Bold (1989); Co (2008); Hs & T (1979); M & E (1995); ODNB (2004); Su (1993); Webb (1985)

Webb, Philip Speakman (1831–1915) Influential English *Arts-and-Crafts architect, specializing in houses: he was one of the leaders of the English *Domestic Revival. His style from the first was deliberately eclectic, drawing on elements from *Gothic, *Queen-Anne, and *vernacular architecture. Initially, his fame grew from his association (dating from his time (1852–9) in the office of G.E.*Street) with William *Morris, for whom he designed the Red House, Bexleyheath, Kent (1859–60), and many artefacts for Morris's firm. Later, he was involved with Morris in the setting up of the Society for the Protection of Ancient Buildings (1877). At the Red House the influence of *Butterfield and *Street is clear, especially in relation to the clear expression of materials and the very free asymmetrical composition: with this building and Benfleet Hall, Fairmile, near Cobham, Surrey (1860), Webb established his

reputation. His best town buildings are the Prinsep House, 14 (formerly 1) Holland Park Road, Kensington (1864–92), 1 Palace Green, Kensington (1868–73—with interior decorations by **Edward Coley Burne-Jones** (1833–98), **Walter Crane** (1845–1915), and Morris), and 19 Lincoln's Inn Fields (1868–9), all in London, in which steep *gables, Queen-Anne *sash-windows, and a few Gothic features are used in free compositions. His country-houses include Smeaton Manor, Great Smeaton, North Riding, Yorks. (1876-9—much altered), and Standen, East Grinstead, Surrey (1891–4), all gabled and freely composed. Clouds, East Knoyle, Wilts. (1876–91), was perhaps his most eclectic composition, with a veritable jumble of styles making the building almost style-less. His one church, St Martin's, Brampton, Cumb. (1874–8), is certainly Gothic, but treated very freely, with ceilings that are more domestic than ecclesiastical in character. Claims that Webb was somehow a precursor of the *Modern Movement do not stand up to serious examination, for his work showed too much of an understanding of traditional materials and vernacular architecture, and his sources lay in historical exemplars. Indeed, his disciples included *Lutyens among their number, none of whom could be regarded as Modernists.

R.Curry & S.Kirk (1984); D & M (1985); Ferriday (ed.) (1963); Garnett (ed.) (1993); S.Kirk (1990, 2002); Lethaby (1935); McLeod (1971); G.Naylor (1971); ODNB (2004); P (1982); M.Rn (1983); Sw (1989); J.T (1996)

webbing *Webs framed by *ribs in a *vault, viewed collectively.

Weedon, Harold (Harry) William (1888–1970) English architect, he commenced practice (1911) in partnership with **Harold Seymour Scott** (1883–1946), designing several high-quality houses in the Warwicks. countryside. He established (1925) an independent office, carrying out commercial and industrial commissions, and laying out housing-estates in the Birmingham area. Following a fortuitous meeting (1932) with the cinema entrepreneur **Oscar Deutsch** (1893–1941), he made his name with numerous cinemas throughout the country for Deutsch's *Odeon* chain, although he employed others to carry out the designs. The name *Odeon* was selected partly because it suggested (**O**)scar (**DE**)utsch and (**ON**), because Deutsch exuded energy and ambition: later, it was claimed to be an acronym for **O**scar **D**eutsch **E**ntertains **O**ur **N**ation. Weedon's first success with Deutsch was the *Odeon*, Kingstanding, Perry Barr, Birmingham (1934–5), designed by **John Cecil Clavering** (1910–2001): with its vertical fins, streamlined look, and crisp modernity, it was an immediate success, and several more

Odeons followed (all opened in 1936) including those at East Parade, Harrogate, Yorks., King Street, Lancaster, Lancs., the very fine building at Birmingham Road, Sutton Coldfield, Warwicks., and the splendid pile at Conway Road, Colwyn Bay, Denbighshire, Clwyd, Wales. However, having designed the last two *Odeons* at astonishing speed, Clavering had had enough, and left Weedon, to be replaced (1935) by the recently-qualified **Robert Arthur Bullivant** (1910–2002), who took over Clavering's designs for the *Odeon* at Scarborough, Yorks. (opened 1936). Bullivant was the job-architect for the cinemas at Chester, Ches., York (1935–6), and other sites, but his masterpiece was the *Odeon*, Leicester (1936–8). Weedon's job-architect for the *Odeons* at Loughborough, Leics., and Hanley, Staffs., was **Arthur J.Price** (1901–53), father of Cedric *Price. Many of these highly successful *Modernistic buildings were enjoyed by the public in a way *International-style architecture was not, and were all influenced to some extent by the works of *Emberton, *Mendelsohn, and *Poelzig, yet were generally unloved by critics devoted to the *Modern Movement. After the 1939–45 war the partnership carried out much commercial and industrial work, but the cinemas were in a superior architectural league: unfortunately, most of them have been ham-fistedly altered, demolished, or otherwise damaged as cinema-going habits have changed.

Atwell (1981); Eyles (2002)

Weeks, John (1921–2005) *See* DAVIES, RICHARD LLEWELYN.

weeper One of a series of mourning figures set around a tomb-chest, usually in *niches, in funerary architecture, common in medieval work (e.g. Beauchamp Chapel, St Mary's Church, Warwick).

Wegmann, Gustav Albert (1812–58) Swiss architect, pupil of *Hübsch at Karlsruhe, and later von *Gärtner in Munich, before settling in Zürich (1836) where he designed several refined buildings, including the railway station (1846–8) and the *Kantonsschule* (1839–42—closely modelled on *Schinkel's *Bauakademie*, Berlin (1831–6)). Other works included the *Rundbogenstil Mädchenschule*, Grossmünster (1850–1), The Freemasons' Temple, Lindenhof (1852—*Gothic Revival), and various residential buildings. Stylistically he was unconfined.

J.T (1996); Vonesch (1980)

Weidenmann, Jacob (1829–93) Swiss-born German-educated landscape architect, he emigrated (1856) to the USA. He designed Bushnell Park, South Common, Cedar Hill Cemetery, and several private gardens, as well as supervising the construction of F.L.*Olmsted and C.*Vaux's

Retreat for the Insane, all in Hartford, CT. He became Olmstead's partner (1874), working on the Buffalo Park system, Mount Royal Park, Montréal, Canada, and the grounds of the US Capitol, Washington, DC. From 1886 he was Superintendent of Mount Hope Cemetery, Chicago, IL, and wrote *Modern Cemeteries* (1888): championing *Strauch's 'lawn' plan. Indeed, Olmsted regarded Weidenmann as the American authority on cemetery-design.

B & K (2000); Favretti (2007); Weidenmann (1876, 1888, 1978)

Weidmann, Leonhard (*fl*.1568–96) German master-builder, he designed and built the *Renaissance wing of the *Rathaus* (from 1570), and was also responsible for the reconstruction of the hospital and *Hagemeisterhaus* (1574–8) as well as the *Baumeisterhaus* (1596—the most important Renaissance building in the town), all in Rothenburg-ob-der-Tauber, Franconia.

Lübbeke (1986); Mayr (1978); J.T (1996)

Weightman, John Grey (1801–72) English architect, trained in the offices of Charles *Barry and C.R.*Cockerell, he commenced practising in Sheffield (*c*.1832), and was in partnership (*c*.1838–58) with **Matthew Ellison Hadfield** (1812–85). As **Weightman & Hadfield**, the firm designed many RC churches, including the Cathedral at Salford (1844–8), based on medieval exemplars at Newark, Howden, and Selby. Among the firm's pupils was George *Goldie.

B *et al.* (2001); D & M (1985); Ea (1970)

Weinbrenner, Johann Jakob Friedrich (1766–1826) The most important architect working in South-West Germany in the first quarter of C19. Having met *Genelli, David *Gilly, and *Langhans in Berlin (early 1790s), he was introduced to the severe Franco-Prussian *Neo-Classicism that was to inform his work for the rest of his life. After a period in Rome (1792–7), he studied the ruined Greek temples of *Paestum and Sicily, and later prepared the illustrations for *Die Baukunst nach den Grundsätzen der Alten* (1809) by **Aloys Hirt** (1759–1837). Most of his buildings were erected in Karlsruhe, which he transformed into the Neo-Classical Grand-Ducal capital of Baden from the time (1797–1826) he was engaged as a State official. He superimposed a sequence of urban spaces over the existing town-plan, including the *Marktplatz* with a *pyramid at its centre, the whole modelled on urban spaces in Antiquity. His *Schloss-strasse* (begun 1799) led to the severe *Doric *Ettlinger Tor* (1803), and was composed as a series of episodes, asymmetrically disposed, giving a varied *Picturesque effect. All Weinbrenner's buildings in Karlsruhe were of an impressively grand, if severe, quality especially the

RC Church of St Stephen (1804-14—inspired by the *Pantheon and Imperial *thermae in Rome—unconvincingly rebuilt 1951-4), and the Graeco-Egyptian Gothic Synagogue (1798—destroyed 1871—one of his most eclectic compositions). His startlingly bold scheme for the *Langestrasse* (1808), with both sides lined by a continuous *colonnade of plain arches carried on slender undecorated *piers, was not realized, but was an inspiration for certain C20 *Neo-Rationalists. He was responsible for six of the major public buildings, including the Sculpture Gallery (1804), and *Kurhaus* (1821-4), Baden-Baden. Weinbrenner published *Architektonisches Lehrbuch* (1810-25) and *Ausgeführte und projektierte Gebäude* (1822-35). His ideas for Karlsruhe and his style were effectively ended by his successor *Hübsch.

D.Brownlee (ed.) (1986); Elbert (1988); Leiber (1991); P (1982); J.T (1996); Valdenaire (1919, 1926, 1976); Wa & M (1987)

Weiner, Tibor (1906-65) Hungarian architect/ town-planner, he worked for a time at the *Bauhaus under Hannes *Meyer, with whom he moved to the USSR (1931), convinced of the messianic role of architecture in the transformation of society. He did not remain for long, and after a spell in Basel and Paris, emigrated to Chile (1939), but returned to Hungary (1948) where he worked on the new industrial town of Sztálinváros (now Dunaújváros) and edited (1952-7) the journal *Magyar Építőművészet.*

Magyar Építőművészet, iii (1965), 57; J.T (1996)

Weir, Robert Weir Schultz (Robert Weir Schultz until 1915) (1860-1951) Scots-born architect, articled to Rowand *Anderson, he later joined the office of Norman *Shaw, where he met *Lethaby, with whom he formed a lasting friendship. After a period with Ernest *George and *Peto, he set up his own practice in London (1890) and worked on several buildings for the 3rd (1847-1900) and 4th (1881-1947) **Marquesses of Bute,** including the reconstruction of Wester Kames Tower, Isle of Bute (1897-1900). Weir studied *Byzantine architecture with Lethaby and Sidney *Barnsley (with whom he collaborated on *The Monastery of St Luke . . . in Phocis* (1901)), and was a leading light in the Byzantine Revival. His Byzantine studies led to the creation of the Chapel of St Andrew and the Saints of Scotland in *Bentley's Westminster Cathedral (1910-15). His greatest work was probably All Saints Anglican Cathedral, Khartoum, Sudan (1906-13—now a *museum), which deserved to be considered, with Lethaby's Brockhampton, *Prior and A.R. *Wells's Roker, and *Bellot's Quarr Abbey, as among the most successful C20 church buildings. He had a thriving country-house practice before

1914, but also designed economical housing at Gretna Green, Scotland (1914-18—under the general direction of *Unwin), and built an extension to a barn at Hartley Wintney, Hants. (1903-12), as his own home. Like many *Arts-and-Crafts architects, he worked with several styles, drawing on many sources, and his smaller domestic buildings were invariably agreeable.

AH, xxii (1979), 88-116; B.Clarke (1958); A.S.Gray (1985); Ottewill (1989); P (1982); Stamp (1981)

Weissenhofsiedlung Literally the 'white house estate', developed by the *Deutscher Werkbund* as an exhibition of workers' housing in Stuttgart, Württemberg (1927). Directed by *Mies van der Rohe, it included buildings by Le *Corbusier, *Gropius, and others, and got its name from the flat-roofed, white-painted minimalist *International-Modern style of the houses which established paradigms for many years to come.

Weissmann, Adriaan Willem (1858-1923) Dutch architect, he became Amsterdam City Architect (1891), designing the *Oosterbegraafplaats* (1892-3) and the *Stedelijk Museum* (1893-4). After he left his position (1894) he designed the *De Vereeniging* Concert-Hall, Nijmegen, and many houses in Amsterdam South (1923-5) for *Eigen Woning,* the housing society to which he became architect (1911). He was opposed to the *Amsterdam School, adopting *Zakelijkheid,* the Dutch equivalent of *Neue Sachlichkeit.*

Hewitt *et al.* (1980), 67-8; Reinink (1975); J.T (1996)

Welch, Edward (1806-68) *See* HANSOM.

Welch, Herbert Arthur (1884-1953) English architect, he made a major contribution to the development of Hampstead *Garden Suburb, London, from 1908, where he designed many houses, including gabled work in Denman Drive. He also designed the handsome curved terraces of shops and apartments in Golders Green Road that demonstrate the early C20 change of style from *vernacular revival to *Neo-Georgian. In collaboration with *Etchells (translator of Le *Corbusier's works into English), Welch, with Nugent Francis Cachemaille-*Day and **Felix J.Lander** (1898-1960), designed the pioneering *International-Modern Crawford's Office Building, High Holborn, London (1930), with long bands of windows subdivided by steel *mullions, much influenced by the *Weissenhofsiedlung.*

A.S.Gray (1985); M & G (1992)

well 1. Spring of water rising to the surface and forming a pool or flowing into a stream. **2.** Spring supposed to have medicinal properties, so associated with a *spa. **3.** Structure erected for convenience in collecting the water. **4.** Vertical excavation, usually circular, of *masonry or brick, sunk to penetrate a water-bearing stratum. **5.** Central open volume containing a winding, spiral, elliptical, or other *stair. **6.** Volume formed by surrounding walls of buildings serving as access for light and air. *Compounds include*:

well-chapel: one enclosing or over a holy well;

well-cover: protective lid over a well-shaft;

well-curb or *-head*: framework around the opening of a well;

well-hole: **1.** volume contained by walls in which a stair is fitted; **2.** opening left in a large winding or other staircase between flights; **3.** opening through floors in a large warehouse through which light comes through a glazed roof;

well-house: small building enclosing a well and any apparatus for raising the water;

well-stair: circular staircase with a hollow centre or *well-hole* between the ends of the steps.

Welland & Gillespie William John Welland (c.1832–95) and **William Gillespie** (1818–99) were appointed joint architects to the Ecclesiastical Commissioners of the Church of Ireland on the death of the former's father, **Joseph Welland** (1798–1860—pupil and assistant of *Bowden, who became (1821) architect to the Board of *First Fruits for the Province of Tuam). When the Board was reconstituted as the Ecclesiastical Commissioners (1833), Joseph Welland retained his position, but his duties were expanded (1843) to take over responsibility for all Anglican Church work in Ireland, thus during the early- and mid-Victorian period he designed over 100 new churches and supervised alterations, repairs, and enlargements to many buildings: there is no Irish county where his works cannot be viewed (e.g. St Swithin, Magherafelt, Co. Londonderry, consecrated 1858). **Welland & Gillespie** inherited this important post before Disestablishment (1870), and carried out an immense amount of new church-building, much of it of very fine quality, often with *plate-tracery and quirky details (e.g. St Matthias, Ballyeglish (1865–8—with *polychrome treatment and apsidal *chancel), and St John, Woodschapel (1860–70—of basalt with freestone dressings), both in Co. Londonderry, and Christ Church, Derriaghy, Co. Antrim (consecrated 1872—with a slim steeple set at 45° to the axis of the nave)).

Brett (1996, 1999, 2002); J.Curl (1986); *DIA* (2013); Rowan (1979)

Wells, Arthur Randall (1877–1942) English *Arts-and-Crafts architect. As Clerk of Works for *Lethaby's All Saints' Church, Brockhampton, Herefs. (1902), he absorbed much of the elder man's style, as is clear from his own St Edward the Confessor and St Mary, Kempley, Glos. (1902–3), with its charming *Rood and exquisite furnishings (1904). He built Voewood (later Home Place), Kelling, near Holt, Norfolk (1903–4), and St Andrew's, Roker, Sunderland, Co. Durham (1906–7—arguably the finest church of the Arts-and-Crafts movement), for E.S.*Prior. Both buildings employed *concrete structure, in the case of the church *reinforced, and at the house mass-concrete faced with *flints and thin tile-like bricks (there are also areas where *in-situ* concrete is left with the board-marks of the form-work exposed as the finish, many years earlier and better handled than fashionable *Brutalism). Wells also designed a prize-winning cottage for Letchworth *Garden City, Herts.

Garnham (1995); A.S.Gray (1985); Me.Miller (2002); Pe & Williamson (1985); Verey & Brooks (2002)

Wells, Joseph Merrill (1853–90) Member of the office of *McKim, Mead, & White, responsible for introducing a revival of the Italian High-*Renaissance style to the firm from 1879. Early examples include the Villard Houses, Madison Avenue, NYC (1882–5), and the Public Library, Boston, MA (1888–95).

Roth (ed.) (1973, 1983); R.G.Wilson (1983)

Wells, The Master of (*fl.*c.1175–c.1215) The part of Wells Cathedral, Som., between the west front and the *choir is unusually of a piece and unified in terms of design and style. Unfortunately the identity of the architect is not known, but he was probably English, for his style has no affinities with French *Gothic, being horizontally emphasized, the *triforium-*arcade treated continuously, and the springing of the *vaults pushed upwards to just below *clerestorey level, quite unlike anything on the Continent. In addition, the *First-Pointed *stiff-leaf *capitals are among the finest and most vigorous in England. The architect is called The Master of Wells, perhaps a Master Thomas who worked at Bath Abbey in the late C12.

J.Harvey (1987); Foyle & Pe (2011)

Wells, Simon de (*fl.*1240–57) English sculptor, he probably carved the statues on the west front of Wells Cathedral, Som., and was at Westminster Abbey (1257) making a design for the tomb of **Princess Katherine**, **King Henry III's** (*r.*1216–72) daughter.

J.Harvey (1987)

Wells Coates, Wintemute (1895–1958) *See* COATES.

Welsch, Johann Maximilian von (1671–1745) German architect/military-engineer, in the service (from 1704) of **Lothar Franz, Graf von Schönborn** (1655–1729), **Prince-Bishop of Bamberg** (from 1693) and **Archbishop-Elector of Mainz** (from 1694), he contributed to the flowering of *Baroque architecture in Franconia. With

*Neumann, von *Hildebrandt, and others, he was involved in the planning of *Schloss Weissenstein*, Pommersfelden (1711–18), the Palace at Bruchsal (1720–52), and the *Residenz*, Würzburg (1719–79). He designed numerous gardens, garden-buildings, and small houses for the German nobility. Among his other works were the Schönborn *Mortuary Chapel, Würzburg Cathedral (1720–1), the Court Chapel, *Residenz*, Würzburg (1720–3), and the Abbey Church, Amorbach (1742–7), all of which had major contributions from others.

Arens (1986); Bou (1962); Lohmeyer (1931); Meintzschel (1963); P (1982); C.Powell (1959); J.T (1996)

Welsh *See* ARCH.

Welzenbacher, Lois (1889–1955) German architect, he studied under Theodor *Fischer and von *Thiersch. His works included various houses: *Settari*, Bad Dreikirchen, South Tirol (1922–3); *Rosenbauer*, Pöslinberg, Linz (1929–30); and *Heyerovsky*, Zell-am-See (1932), all of which had echoes of *Mendelsohn's style. Later, he drew on Alpine *vernacular motifs, as in his *Schmucker* House, Ruhpolding, Bavaria (1938–9). His *Siebel* Factory, Halle-an-der-Saale (1938–41), was *Modernist, giving the lie to beliefs that all architecture in the Third Reich was Classical.

Achleitner (1968); *Prologomena* **xiii**/1 (1984); Sarnitz (1989)

Wentzinger, Johann Christian (1710–97) German architect/painter/sculptor, responsible for the funerary monument (1743–5) to **Franz Christoph von Rodt** (1671–1743) in the Minster, Freiburg-im-Breisgau, he (1757) was awarded the commission to design *Rococo interior-decorations for the Abbey-Church of St Gallen, Switzerland, including the *stucco-work, *frescoes, and statuary. He designed his own residence, the *Haus zum schönen Eck, Münsterplatz*, Freiburg, as well as sundry works at St Blasien in the Black Forest, including the *choir-stalls and *altars (from 1776).

Bou (1962); Hi (1968a); Krummer-Schroth (1987); J.T (1996)

Werkbund *See* DEUTSCHER WERKBUND.

Werkstätte *See* WIENER WERKSTÄTTE.

Weserrenaissance *Renaissance and *Mannerist architecture dating from *c.*1550 in the valley of the River Weser, Germany.

Kreft & Soenke (1964); Stenvert (1990)

Westerley, Robert (*fl.*1421–61) English master-mason, he and 30 other English masons went to Rouen, Normandy (1421), to work on the castle there, and he was employed as deputy mason at Westminster Abbey when construction on the *nave was resumed (1423/4). Appointed King's Master-Mason (1438/9) on the death of *Mapilton, he worked at the Palace of Sheen, near London, and from 1442 was in charge of the works at Tutbury Castle, Staffs., where the south tower at the east end of the hall-range was being built. He also supervised the early works at Eton College, Bucks., from its foundation (1441), and was the architect of the original layout.

J.Harvey (1987)

Westphalen (*or* **Westfalen**), **Arnold von** (*fl.* C15) German architect, called to the Wettin Court at Meissen (1470), and was responsible for many of the late-*Gothic buildings in Saxony. Among his works are *Albrechtsburg* (from 1471), the *Rathaus* (from 1472), and the *Dom* (1472-6), all in Meissen, and part of the *Schloss* in Dresden (from 1471). His influence spread into Eastern Europe, especially to Bohemia.

Białostocki (1972); Hu & Sch (1978); Mrusek (1972)

Westwood, Colin (1920–2004) Architectural photographer, his images of the Herts. County Council schools, *Festival of Britain buildings, *New Towns, work by Eric *Lyons, and the architecture of *Stirling & Gowan provide a unique record of British architecture in the early part of the second half of C20.

RIBAJ (Jan. 2005), xiii

west-work *Westwerk* in German, i.e. massive, wide, tower-like west front of an early *Romanesque or *Carolingian church containing an entrance-vestibule with a chapel and other rooms over it opening to the upper part of the *nave. A good surviving example is the Abbey Church of Corvey-on-the-Weser, Germany (873–5), with its low entrance-hall with massive *piers and circular columns carrying the *vaults over which is a two-storey upper church surrounded by *arcades and *aisles.

Conant (1979); Ck (1996); J.T (1996); D.Wa (1986)

Whately, Thomas (1726–72) English politician/author, his *Observations of Modern Gardening* (1770—a broad-ranging account of mid-C18 garden-design) went into several editions, and was translated into French and German, influencing *Hirschfeld, *Watelet, and others interested in the English style of garden-design, including Thomas *Jefferson when laying out the grounds of Monticello. *Loudon was among his many admirers.

Tay (2006); Whately (1770)

wheel Circular frame of wood, metal, or other material with spokes radiating from a central point (*nave*) attached to an axle around which it revolves, occurring as mill-wheels, turnstiles, or something resembling a wheel. *Derivatives/compounds include*:

wheeler: **1.** winder in a *stair, especially a *newel or spiral stair; **2.** lower part of a *battlement. *Wheelers* (*crenels* or *embrasures*) and *kneelers* (*merlons* or *cops*) refer to *crenellation*;

wheel-head cross: see CELTIC CROSS;

wheel-house: **1.** prehistoric drystone house, approximately circular in plan, with radial partition-walls and a central space (e.g. house at Calf of Eday, Orkney); **2.** structure enclosing a large wheel, e.g. water-wheel;

wheel-step: see WHEELER (**1**);

wheel-window: **1.** circular window-aperture with spoke-like *colonnettes or *bars radiating from the centre, e.g. west front of Chartres Cathedral, France (late C12); **2.** circular part of an early *Middle-Pointed *Geometrical* window with bar-*tracery.

Wheelwright, Edmund March (1854–1912)

American architect, he established his own practice (1883), and was joined (1888) by **Parkman B. Haven** (1858–1943), and later (1912) by **Edward H.Hoyt** (1868–1936). As City Architect of Boston, MA (1891–5), he designed numerous municipal buildings in that capacity. Stylistically eclectic, his architecture drew on numerous and varied historical precedents (e.g. Choate Burnham School, South Boston (1894—Northern Italian *Renaissance); Horticultural Hall, Boston (1900—*Georgian Revival); and Lampoon Building, Harvard University, Cambridge, MA (1909—with red brick treated in the *Tudor-*Gothic manner)).

Chandler (ed.) (1898); J.T (1996)

whelmer and kneeler The former is a *dripstone, the latter its return.

Whewell, William (1794–1866)

Cambridge don, a profound influence on Edmund *Sharpe, and friend of Thomas *Rickman, he published *Architectural Notes on German Churches, with Remarks on the Origins of Gothic Architecture* (1830, with subsequent editions of 1835 and 1842).

Brandwood (2012); *ODNB* (2004); Whewell (1830)

Whidden, William Marcy (1857–1929)

American architect, he entered into partnership with **Ion Lewis** (1858–1933) in Portland, OR (1889), having trained at the *École des *Beaux-Arts*, Paris, before working for *McKim, Mead, & White from 1882. In Portland the firm introduced a sophisticated East-Coast palette of styles, including *Colonial Revival and *Neo-Classicism. Among their Portland works were the Hamilton Building (1893), City Hall (1895—*Renaissance Revival), and Arlington Club (1909).

Marlitt (1989); Vaughan & McMath (1967)

whiplash Decorative element in *Art-Nouveau ornament, a whip-like, flowing, curved line.

Gh (2000); L & D (1986); T-M (1967)

whispering Certain passages or galleries are referred to as 'whispering' on account of the facility and distinctness with which a whisper/low sound is transmitted through its extent, e.g. the circular internal gallery under the *dome of St Paul's Cathedral, London.

Whitby, George Frederick (1916–73)

See MCMORRAN & WHITBY.

White, Stanford (1853–1906)

See MCKIM, MEAD, & WHITE.

White, Stanley (1891–1979)

American landscape architect, who gained his experience under *Olmsted and *Steele, and later taught a new generation of designers, including *Sasaki.

W & S (1994)

White, William (1825–1900)

English *Gothic-Revival architect, he trained in 'Great' *Scott's office (where he met *Bodley and *Street) before establishing (1847) a practice in Cornwall. His works include the All Saints' Church, Notting Hill (from 1852), and St Saviour's, Aberdeen Park, both in London (1865—with a *polychrome brick interior), but his master-work is St Michael's, Lyndhurst, Hants. (1858–70), a big red- and yellow-brick structure in the *First-Pointed style, with odd *tracery, strange cross-gables, and a sumptuous polychrome interior containing work by **Edward Coley Burne-Jones** (1833–98), *Morris, **Lord Leighton** (1830–96), and Street. He also designed several houses, including the Old Rectory, St Columb Major, Cornwall (1849–50), the Vicarage, Little Baddow, Essex (1858), and Humewood, Co. Wicklow, Ireland (1873–7).

J.Curl (2007); D & M (1985); Ea (1970); S.M (1972); Sh (1973); Su (ed.) (1968); B.Wa (1994)

Whitehead, John (1726–1802)

English architect/diplomat, his was the main British influence on the planning and architecture of Oporto, Portugal. He designed houses in the Palladian style in Praça da Ribeira (1774–82), as well as the Factory House (1785–90). His recommendation of *Carr led to the acceptance of the York architect's designs for the *Santo António* Hospital (begun 1770), and Whitehead's pupil, **Joaquim da Costa Lima Sampaio** (*fl.*1790–1830), designed the former Carrancas Palace (from *c.*1795—later the *Museu Nacional Soares dos Reis*) in a style derived from Carr's work. Whitehead was the promoter of the Anglican Cemetery (opened 1788).

Delaforce (1982, 1990)

Whites, The *See* NEW YORK FIVE.

Whitwell, Thomas Stedman (1784–1840) English architect, responsible for numerous buildings in Birmingham and Coventry, most of which have been demolished. He designed (1819) a development to be called 'Southville' at Leamington Spa (with a church that was to be a facsimile of the Athenian *Parthenon*), and (1825–6) the model Utopian town (published 1830) of New Harmony, IN, for **Robert Owen** (1771–1858), but neither scheme was realized. When the roof of his Brunswick Theatre, Goodman's Fields, Whitechapel (1827–8), collapsed three days after the building was completed, with loss of life, his career virtually came to an end. He appears to have detested *Soane, and may have been the author of two attacks (published 1821, 1824) on the great man. His proposed book, *Architectural Absurdities* (the MS of which appears to have been lost), never appeared. However, his book on convection-heating, esp. in fever-wards, was published (1834).

Co (2008); W.Pa (1892)

wichert, whitchet, witchert Variety of chalk marl subsoil found near the Chilterns in Buckinghamshire (especially at Haddenham) which, if mixed with chopped straw, was used for walling. *Compare* ADOBE; COB; PISÉ DE TERRE; TABIA.

Innocent (1916), x,136

wicket Small *door or *gate forming part of a larger door or gate, essentially a door within a door.

Wiedemann Family C18 (German masterbuilders. **Dominikus** and **Johann Baptist Wiedemann** realized J.B.*Neumann's designs for the *Benedictine Abbey Church at Neresheim after the latter's death (1753), one of the finest late-*Baroque churches in all Europe. **Christian Wiedemann** began the Benedictine Abbey Church at Wiblingen (1732), continued after 1750 by J.M. *Fischer, and completed by **Johann G.Specht** (1721–83): he also contributed to the design of the beautiful Baroque Library at Wiblingen.

Bou (1962); H (1968); C.Powell (1959)

Wiedewelt, Johannes (1731–1802) Danish designer/sculptor/writer, one of the first to practise *Neo-Classicism based on a theoretical knowledge of Antiquity. Among his works were the *sarcophagus (1760–8) of **King Christian VI** (r.1730–46) in Roskilde Cathedral, decorations in the gardens of Fredensborg Palace (from 1760), the splendid monument (1769–77) of **King Frederik V** (r.1746–66) in Roskilde Cathedral (1769–77), and numerous memorials and monuments (e.g. Nielsen tomb (1798), Assistens Cemetery,

and the Naval Monument, Holmens Cemetery (1802), both in Copenhagen). He designed the Memorial Grove at *Jaegerspris* (1779–89), and published several books, including a volume on Egyptian and Roman Antiquities (1786) and on Taste in the Arts (1762).

KK; Kryger (1985); J.T (1996)

Wiehl, Antonín (1846–1910) Bohemian architect, pupil of *Zítek. Most of his work consisted of town-houses with *façades in the *Renaissance style, Italian at first, and then from *c.*1882 in the *Czech-Renaissance style, with much *sgraffito* decoration. Among his buildings were the Wiehl House, Wenceslas Square (1895), the Waterworks in the Old Town (1883—now the Smetana Museum), and the Pantheon in Vyšehrad Cemetery (1889–93), all in Prague.

J.T (1996); Wirth (1921)

Wiener Werkstätte Literally 'Vienna Workshop', founded 1903 to emulate English *Arts-and-Crafts workshops, such as the Guild of Handicrafts of C.R.*Ashbee. It grew partly from the *Sezession* exhibition (1900) that included designs by *Mackintosh and Ashbee. By 1905 the *Werkstätte* was employing over 100 people, most of the artefacts being designed by Josef *Hoffmann and **Koloman Moser** (1868–1918). It became the centre for progressive design in Austria-Hungary, promoting a severe rectilinear style. It ceased operations in 1932.

Fahr-Becker (1995); Ouvrard *et al.* (1986); Schweiger (1984)

Wiepking-Jürgensmann, Heinrich Friedrich (1891–1973) German landscape architect, he designed gardens in various European countries, and collaborated with *Mendelsohn (late 1920s) before succeeding (1934) *Barth as Professor at the Agricultural University, Berlin. He designed landscapes associated with the 1936 Berlin Olympics, and was appointed by **Heinrich Himmler** (1900–45) *Sonderbeauftragter* (Minister with Special Responsibilities for landscape-design, land-conservation, and the protection of Nature throughout the *Warthegau* (the huge part of Poland incorporated into Germany in 1939)). In that capacity he published much, enthusing about the possibilities the annexation opened for the profession; designed a 'military-landscape' of north-south deep ditches with shrubs, and hardwood trees to hinder tank-attacks from the East; and continued his academic career (one of his students gained a diploma for the 'greening' of Auschwitz). After the 1939–45 war he established (with others) Colleges for Horticulture in Osnabrück and Hanover (both 1946). He also designed several gardens for private houses, some in collaboration with *Deilmann.

Gröning & Wolschke-Bulmahn (1987, 1997)

Wieser, Ferenc (1812-69) Hungarian architect, trained in Vienna, he worked (1837) for *Hild before travelling extensively in Europe and England. Stylistically eclectic, his work includes the Weber Villa, Buda (1845-8—much influenced by English *Gothic Revival—destroyed); the Pichler House, Pest (1855-7—*Venetian Gothic); and the *spire of the Franciscan Church, Pest (1859-63—English-inspired *Baroque).

Művészttörténeti Értesítő, **xxxvi**/1-4 (1987), 142-54; J.T (1996)

Wiesner, Arnošt (Ernst) (1890-1971) Slovak architect, trained in Vienna, he worked (1919-39) in Brno, where he designed several buildings including the municipal crematorium (1925-30—a chunky pile with echoes of *Expressionism, *Gothic, and ancient *ziggurats) and numerous houses. He settled in England where he taught at the Liverpool and Oxford Schools of Architecture.

Bauforum, **v**/29 (1972), 13-15; *Parametro*, **cxiv** (1983), 12-64; Šlapeta (1981); J.T (1996)

Wiethase, Heinrich Johann (1833-93) German architect, he studied with *Ungewitter before joining (1855) *Raschdorff to work on the reconstruction of the Gürzenich Hall, Köln, and then moved to the office of Freiherr von *Schmidt, who entrusted his unfinished projects to Wiethase when he moved to Italy to teach. Wiethase settled in Köln, where he was active in the *conservation of historic fabric, and designed numerous *Gothic-Revival churches (few of which survived the 1939-45 war).

Grote (ed.) (1974), 175-88; Trier & Weyres (eds) (1980), **i**, 17-193, and **ii**, 555

Wigglesworth, Gordon Hardy (1920-2005) English architect, he worked (1952-4) in Maxwell *Fry's office, became (1957) chief architect at the Department of Education and Science, then director of building development at the Ministry of Public Building and Works (1967-72), and (1972-4) principal architect at the Inner London Education Authority. Appointed housing architect to the GLC (until 1980), responsible for numerous house-building ventures, he promoted research in many publications.

The Guardian (19 August 2005), Obits

Wight, Peter Bonnett (1838-1925) American architect, his works included the Yale School of Fine Arts Building, NH (1864-6—later Street Hall). In partnership (1863-8) with Russell *Sturgis he promoted Ruskinian ideals, advocated honest construction, and promoted *Gothic. His work anticipated the *Arts-and-Crafts Movement in the USA. After Chicago was badly damaged by fire (1871), Wight established a practice there with **Asher Carter** (1805-77) and **William H. Drake** (*fl.*1837-80), designing dwellings and commercial buildings and patenting fireproof iron construction.

ARe, **xxvi** (1909), 123-31; *Brickbuilder*, **vi** (1897), 53-5, 73-5, 98-9, 149-50; Landau (1981)

Wightwick, George (1802-72) English architect, he assisted the elderly *Soane, and published (1827) *Select Views of Roman Antiquities* based on a visit to Italy (1825). He established himself in practice in Plymouth (1829), Devon, joined *Foulston (who was about to retire) in partnership, and became a leading architect in the West of England. He designed a formidable range of buildings in a variety of styles, but his essays in *Gothic did not meet with approval of *Ecclesiologists (who were particularly influential in the Diocese of Exeter from the time the High Churchman **Henry Philpotts** (1778-1869) became Bishop (1831)). Wightwick was a successful architectural journalist, but he also contributed a weighty essay on the use of iron in architecture to J.C.*Loudon's *Architectural Magazine* (1837), and published an eccentric quasi-Masonic book entitled *The Palace of Architecture: A Romance of Art and History* (1840), among much else.

Co (2008); *ODNB* (2004); W.Pa (1892); Wightwick (1840, 1851)

wigwam Type of *tent consisting of a frame of poles converging at the top, covered with bark, matting, or, more usually, hides, to form a cone-shaped shelter. The term is of North-American native origin, in the area of the Great Lakes and eastwards: it is also called a *tepee*.

Wijdeveld, Hendrik Theodorus (1885-1989) Dutch architect: as Editor of the journal *Wendingen* (Turnings—published 1918-31), he encouraged innovatory typography, and was a central figure in promoting the *Amsterdam School. He formed links between German and Dutch exponents of *Expressionism, and publicized work by Eileen *Gray and F.L.L.*Wright. As an architect he was influenced by *Mendelsohn, *Wright, and *Futurism. He designed several housing projects for Amsterdam South (1920s), and a large development on the *Hoofdweg* (1925-6) with tortuously curving complex *façades. He published *My First Century* shortly before he died.

Jervis (1984); Pehnt (1973); Wit & Casciato (1986)

Wild, James William (1814-92) English architect, articled to *Basevi, he was Owen *Jones's brother-in-law, worked on the decorations of the 1851 Great Exhibition, and was Curator of Sir

John *Soane's Museum (1878–92). His most distinguished works include the *Rundbogenstil Christ Church, Streatham (1840–2), a reworking of the *Early-Christian *basilica type, but influenced by C19 German precedents, with decorations (now largely obliterated) by Owen Jones. If the *campanile of the latter is tall, assured, and handsome, it is put in the shade by the gigantic dock-tower, Grimsby, Lincs. (1851–2), based on the tower of the Town Hall in Siena, Italy, but with a crowning *minaret influenced by Wild's travels in Egypt and Syria (1840s). He contributed to the design of the Henry Cole Wing, Exhibition Road, Kensington, London (1867–71), and designed the exterior of the Bethnal Green Museum, London (1873), around the re-sited 'Brompton Boilers', the prefabricated iron structure (by **Charles Denson Young** (1822–87) of Edinburgh) originally erected (1855–6) in South Kensington to house the Museum of Science and Art.

J.Curl (2007); D & M (1985); Sh (1975)

Wilde, Bernard de (1691–1772) Flemish architect, most of whose work was in Gent (now Belgium). His *Pakhuys* (1719—destroyed) showed a pronounced French influence, further demonstrated in the Guardhouse and Guild of St Sebastian on the Kouter square, both of which had *Rocaille* decoration.

J.T (1996)

wilderness 1. Ornamental and agreeable landscape, neither wild nor deserted, carefully planned and tended, planted with trees to form a grove or wood with paths cut through it, often designed in a fantastic way, frequently with a *maze. 2. *Bosket. 3. Land giving the appearance of being wild or uncultivated, a variant on the idea of the *desert. 4. Informally laid out woodland of mixed species and wild flowers, with paths and open areas running through it. *See* BACON, FRANCIS.

D.Coffin (1994); Goulty (1991); *OED* (1933); Strong (1979); Symes (2006)

wild garden Garden where hardy woodland/ meadow plants grow in a supposedly 'natural' way. Advocated by William *Robinson and *Jekyll, the term did not signify haphazard disorder, but a mix of hardy cultivated and wild plants that would flourish without constant attention, e.g. in the less cultivated or neglected parts of grounds. Naturalistic gardens evolved throughout the C20, notably in the work of *Sackville-West and more recently with **Beth Chatto**'s (1923–2018) emphasis of using plants in appropriate habitats and experiments to establish 'natural communities' of plants.

R.E.Davis (ed.) (2011); Jekyll (1984); Oudolf & Kingsbury (2011, 2013); W.Robinson (1870); Shoe (2001); Symes (2006); Tay (2006)

Wilds, Amon (1762–1833) English architect/ developer, he designed and erected a number of houses in Brighton and Lewes, Sussex, featuring the *Ammonite capital, which seems to have been his firm's trade-mark. His son, **Amon Henry Wilds** (1784–1857), with *Busby, laid out the Kemp Town Estate, Brighton, and erected many *stucco-faced terraces and crescents there in a style reminiscent of that of *Nash, including Sussex Square, Lewes Crescent, Arundel Terrace, and Chichester Terrace (1823–*c*.1850). Like his father, he employed the Ammonite capital on his buildings.

Bingham (1991); Co (2008); Dale (1947)

Wilford, Michael (1938–) *See* STIRLING.

Wilkins, William (1751–1815) English plasterer/architect. He carried out many architectural commissions for *Repton (J.A.Repton was his pupil), and was an antiquarian with an interest in medieval architecture. Among his works may be mentioned Donington Hall, Leics. (*c*.1790–7—*Gothic), alterations, including the addition of the *portico, to Calke Abbey, Derbys. (1793–1808), and two houses in Cambridge (38 Newmarket Road, *c*.1795, and Newnham Cottage, Queen's Road, *c*.1800).

Co (2008); W.Pa (1892); Stroud (1962); W-L (1980)

Wilkins, William (1778–1839) English architect, son of William *Wilkins. Educated at Cambridge, he became acquainted with Greek and Italian architecture during his travels (1801–4). He set up his office in London (1809) and quickly established himself as a leading figure of the *Greek Revival. He designed the first pure Greek-*Doric *portico for any English country-house at Osberton House, Notts. (*c*.1805—demolished). This was followed by the East India (now Haileybury) College, Herts. (1806–9), and then Downing College, Cambridge (1807–20—the first of all university *campuses, or separate buildings disposed around a grassed area), both early and important buildings of the Greek Revival. In the latter case, where Wilkins's scheme was selected instead of James *Wyatt's Neo-Classical design, Thomas *Hope was the champion of the Grecian style. Wilkins followed these important schemes with University College, London (1827–8), the Philosophical Society's Museum, York (1827–30), St George's Hospital, Hyde Park Corner, London (1828–9), and the National Gallery, Trafalgar Square, London (1834–8), all Grecian, although the last had a disastrous effect on his reputation for its lack of distinction. Two of his most handsome creations in Greek Revival were the Nelson Column, Sackville (later O'Connell) Street, Dublin (1808–9—destroyed 1966), and the Nelson

Column, Great Yarmouth, Norfolk (1817-20—now marooned in bleakly hideous surroundings).

At Grange Park, Hants. (from 1809), he used Greek Revival for an English country-house, and created one of England's noblest buildings in that style. Elsewhere he succumbed to fashion and designed in *Tudor Gothic, including Dalmeny House, West Lothian (1814-17), Dunmore Park, Stirlingshire (1820-2), and New Court, Trinity College, Cambridge (1823-5). At King's College, Cambridge, however, he responded brilliantly to the great medieval chapel by designing the entrance-*screen, *gateway, and new buildings (1824-8), in *Tudor Gothic of great charm, inventiveness, and delicacy. However, as a Classical (and especially Greek-Revival) architect, Wilkins could be prissy and feeble, for, with the exception of Grange Park, his buildings tend to lack any sense of power in massing, although his detailing was always scholarly, if constricted by his inhibitions as a designer. However, he was among the first to note the optical corrections used by the Greeks in their buildings, and his *The Antiquities of Magna Graecia* (1807) contained accurate illustrations of the Greek temples at Agrigentum, *Paestum, Segesta, and Syracuse. He also published *Atheniensia, or Remarks on the Topography and Buildings of Athens* (1816), as well as *The Civil Architecture of Vitruvius* (1812—an incomplete translation), and *Prolusiones Architectonicae* (1837—essays on Greek and Roman architecture probably based on his lectures as Professor of Architecture at the Royal Academy), among other works.

BuMa, cxiii (1971), 318-29; Co (2008); Co & J.Hs (eds) (1970); Crook (1964, 1972a); M & Wa (1987); *ODNB* (2004); D.Wa (1968); D.Wa (ed.) (2000); Wn (1969); Wilkins (1807, 1816, 1817, 1836, 1837); W-L (1980)

Wilkinson, George (1840-90) *See* WORKHOUSE.

Wilkinson, Leslie (1882-1973) London-born architect, active in Australia, where he settled, having been appointed that country's first Professor of Architecture at the University of Sydney, where he designed several buildings, including the Physics Department (1926). His architecture was restrained, with pitched roofs, lime-washed brickwork, shuttered windows, and sparing Classical detail, a good example of which was his own house at Vaucluse, Sydney.

Arts & Australia, xii/1 (1974), 58-71; Falkiner (ed.) (1982)

Willard, Solomon (1783-1861) American architect, influenced by *Latrobe's work, Willard brought the *Greek Revival to Boston. He designed the United States Branch Bank, Boston (1822-4), the Norfolk County Court House, Dedham (1824-6), and the Suffolk County Court House, Boston (1835), all in Greek *Doric, and all in MA. He was also responsible for the Town Hall, Quincy, MA (1844). He concerned himself (1824-42) with the Bunker Hill Monument, Charlestown, MA, a vast *obelisk with an *Egyptian-Revival base.

Bjelajac (1997); Carrott (1978); W.Edwards (1954); Hamlin (1964); R.Kennedy (1989); Wheildon (1865); W & K (1983); Willard (1843); Winsor (1880-1)

William & Mary Architectural style of the reigns of **King William III** (*r.*1689-1702) and **Queen Mary II** (*r.*1689-94) in Great Britain, coming mid-way between the French-inspired *Baroque of the *Restoration and the *Queen-Anne period. It embraced influences from William's own country, The Netherlands, and was leavened by themes from France brought over by Huguenot refugees after the Revocation (1685) of the Edict of Nantes (1598—which had given French Protestants equality of citizenship). It also included an exotic thread in that it had a taste for oriental motifs from China which led to the beginnings of *Chinoiserie.

JGH, viii/2-3 (1988); Thornton (1984)

William de Ramsey (*fl.*1323-49) *See* RAMSEY.

William of Sens (*fl.*1174-80) *See* SENS.

William of Wykeham (1324-1404) *See* WYKEHAM.

William of Wynford (*fl.*1360-1405) *See* WYNFORD.

Williams, Edward A. (1914-84) *See* ECKBO.

Williams, Sir (Evan) Owen (1890-1969) British engineer. He designed some of the most celebrated buildings in 1930s England, using *reinforced-concrete construction. At the Boots Factory, Beeston, Nottingham (1930-2), he used the *pier-system with a mushroom-like top invented by *Maillart. He was consulting engineer for the *Daily Express* Building, Fleet Street, London (1932—in association with **Ellis & Clarke**), in which a *curtain-wall with black *Vitrolite glass panels was used. He was largely responsible for the Pioneer Health Centre, Peckham, London (1934-6), and for the Dorchester Hotel, London (1929-30—restyled by W.Curtis *Green). Once seen as a pioneer of *Functionalism and of the *Modern Movement, his designs for the M1 Motorway, including the very heavy concrete bridges (1951-9—some of which have the canted arches of the 1920s *Art-Deco style) dimmed his reputation.

AD, xxxix/7 (July 1969), 348; E (1994); Stamp (ed.) (1986); Yeomans & Cottam (2001); *Zodiac*, xviii (1968), 11-30

Williams, Paul Revere (1894-1980) African-American architect, the first to become a recognized architect west of the Mississippi, he practised largely in CA, and designed numerous houses in a variety of styles for show-business celebrities. In the early 1920s he worked for the English-born **John Corneby Wilson Austin** (1870–1963) before establishing his own office. After the war he collaborated with Archibald Quincy *Jones on projects in Palm Springs, including the Tennis Club (1947) and two restaurants (1948). His output was prolific.

K.E.Hudson (1993)

Williams-Ellis, Sir (Bertram) Clough (1883–1978) British architect. Main influences on his work were the *Picturesque, aspects of the *Arts-and-Crafts movement, the Italian *Renaissance, and Mediterranean and English *vernacular architecture. In the years before and after the 1914–18 war, Williams-Ellis had a flourishing practice, designing houses (among which was the precocious Llangoed Castle, Breconshire (1913–19)) and other buildings, but he was also involved in campaigns to build cheap cottages (he published (1919) *Cottage Building in Cob, Pisé, Chalk, and Clay* (revised edn 1947)), and was much influenced by Patrick *Geddes. Among his most felicitous designs of the period were Glenmona House, Maud Cottages, and other additions to the village of Cushendun, and the McNaughton Memorial Hall and School, Giant's Causeway, all in Co. Antrim. He began (1925) his most famous creation, the village of Portmeirion, Merioneth, Wales, a Picturesque composition of individual buildings incorporating Classical details, salvaged fragments, and vernacular elements. Several of the themes explored in Portmeirion were elaborated upon in *The Pleasures of Architecture* (1924, 1954), written with his wife, **Mary Annabel Nassau (Amabel) Strachey** (1894–1984).

He campaigned for effective town- and country-planning, working with *Reilly, *Abercrombie, and others: among his polemics of the time were *England and the Octopus* (1928) and *Britain and the Beast* (1937), and he worked tirelessly for the Councils for the Preservation of Rural England and Wales, the National Trust, and the National Parks. After the 1939–45 war, Williams-Ellis was appointed Chairman of Stevenage New Town Development Corporation, but a growing disillusion with the *Modern Movement (which he had once supported in *Architecture Here and Now* (1934—with *Summerson)) and his independence of mind led to a short-lived association with 'Silkingrad', as wags called the New Town (after **Lewis Silkin** (1889–1972), Socialist Minister of Town and Country Planning who had promoted the *New Towns Act* (1946)). One of his most delightful creations was the garden at *Plas Brondanw*, Merioneth (begun *c.*1913). His

last written works included *Architect Errant* (1971) and *Around the World in Ninety Years* (1979).

Brett (1996); E (1994); Haslam (1979, 1995); *ODNB* (2004); pk

William the Englishman (*fl.*1174–*c.*1214) *See* SENS.

Willis, Browne (1682–1760) English architectural historian active in the Society of Antiquaries of London from 1717. His studies of the Cathedrals of England and Wales (1716–30) were based as much on the evidence of records and registers as on surviving fabric, and they are still of value.

ODNB (2004)

Willmott, Ernest (Ernest Willmott Sloper until 1907) (1871–1916) English architect, he worked with Herbert *Baker in South Africa, notably on the Government Offices at Bloemfontein and Pretoria. He returned to England and established his own practice (1907), much of his work at the time showing a pronounced Dutch-*Colonial influence. He published *English Shopfronts Old and New* (1907) and the useful *English House Design* (1911). His contributions to Hampstead *Garden Suburb included 79 and 81 Hampstead Way.

A.S.Gray (1985); M & G (1992)

Willson, Edward James (1787–1854) Lincoln-born, he worked for some time with his father, **William Willson** (1745–1827), cabinet-maker and master-builder. Through his own observations, young Willson acquired a vast amount of information about *Gothic architecture and ancient buildings in the city. Appointed County Surveyor (1833), he carried out numerous architectural works including St Saviour's Church, East Retford, Notts. (1828–30), and the RC churches of St John, Nottingham (*c.*1825–8), St Mary, Grantham, Lincs. (1832), and St John, Melton Mowbray, Leics. (1840). Willson assisted *Britton with some of his antiquarian publications, and contributed to A.C.*Pugin's works on Gothic architecture. His son, **Thomas John Willson** (1824–1903) was also an architect.

Co (2008); *ODNB* (2004)

Wils, Jan (1891–1972) Dutch architect, he worked (1914–16) with *Berlage, but from *c.*1917 he became involved with De *Stijl, esp. with van *Doesburg (who acted as colour-consultant for Wils's *De Lange* house, Alkmaar (1917)). His town-houses in Alkmaar (1919) were designed on *De-Stijl* principles, but he became known as 'Frank Lloyd Wils' because he drew on aspects of F.L.L.*Wright's work (e.g. the housing development, *Daal en Berg*, Papeverhof, Den Haag (1920)). Later designs included the Citroën Building (1929) and Cinema City Theatre (1935), both

in Amsterdam, and the Chamber of Commerce, Den Haag (1956–9).

Blotkamp et al. (1982); Godoli (1980)

Wilson, Charles (1810–63) Scots architect. He entered (1827) the progressive office of David *Hamilton, and obtained the commission to design the Gartnavel Mental Hospital, Glasgow (1841), in the *Tudor-Gothic style. When carrying out research for this building he travelled in France and England, and from that time he began to experiment with round-arched Classicism, although *Italianate themes still informed his work (e.g. Breadalbane Terrace (now Hill Street) and Windsor (now Kirklee) Terrace, both 1845, and both in Glasgow). He designed Glasgow Academy (1846—influenced by von *Klenze's work in Munich), the Free Church College, Woodlands Hill (1856—where German and Lombardic influences are apparent), and the layout of Woodlands Hill, including Park Terrace (1854) and Park Circus (1855), one of the most dramatically successful pieces of *townscape in the British Isles. His one large country-house, Lewis Castle, Stornoway, Western Isles (1848), was in a Neo-Tudor style. Like his friend 'Greek' *Thomson, he was influenced by the work of *Schinkel, and in turn exercised an influence on the Classicism of later generations of Glaswegian architects, including his assistant John *Burnet.

DW; G & W (1987); Sinclair (ed.) (1995); J.T (1996); WRH (1990)

Wilson, Sir Colin Alexander St John (1922–2007). English architect, he and J.L.*Martin were influential at the School of Architecture, University of Cambridge (where they designed the *Corbusier-inspired brick and raw-concrete blocky Extension C (1958–9)): they were responsible also for several university buildings, including the inward-looking, remorselessly hard terraced brick-built Harvey Court, Gonville and Caius College, Cambridge (1958–62—influenced by *Aalto and *Kahn); the Law, Economics, and Statistics Libraries, Manor Road, Oxford (1961–4—with fragmented *courtyards and stepped *terraces); and the eight-storey brick William Stone Residential Building, Peterhouse, Cambridge (1962–4—betraying Aaltonian echoes). Other designs (by Wilson alone) include two houses, 2 and 2a Grantchester Road (1961–4—described by *Pevsner as 'memorable'), and Spring House, Conduit Head Road (1967—about which Pevsner was muted), both in Cambridge. In London, Wilson designed (1977–9) the West Wing Extension to the British Museum (an uncompromisingly Modernist solution grafted on to *Smirke's distinguished building) and the new British Library, Euston Road, beside *Scott's huge frontage to St Pancras Railway Station. The Library (1982–8) was his largest work,

displaying affinities with some of his earlier designs: the hard red-brick exterior is a dour neighbour of Scott's inventively festive pile, demonstrating the Modern Movement's chronic problems with context, but some interiors almost rise to the occasion.

AR, **cxxvi**/750 (Jul. 1959), 42–8, **clxiv**/982 (Dec. 1978), 336–44; E (1994); F et al. (1997); Hind (ed.) (1997); RIBAJ, ser. 3 **lxxxvi**/3 (Mar. 1979), 107–15; J.T (1996); C.Wilson (ed.) (1988, 1995)

Wilson, Henry (1864–1934) English architect, he worked in the offices of *Belcher, J.O.*Scott, and J.D.*Sedding (whose partner he became and with whom he collaborated on the designs for Holy Trinity Church, Sloane Street, London, where he was responsible for the metal-work, screens, bas-reliefs, and much of the beautiful detail of the interior (1888–c.1901)). He completed Sedding's *Italianate *Renaissance-Revival Church of Our Holy Redeemer, Exmouth Market, London (1887–8), where he added the *campanile, and (again with Sedding) designed St Peter's Church, Mount Park Road, Ealing, London (1889–93), where curvaceous *Gothic forms were used with power and originality.

Wilson's chief claim to fame is as an *Arts-and-Crafts designer of exquisite enamel- and metal-work, jewellery, and sculpture (he was Master of the *Art-Workers Guild (1917) and President of the Arts-and-Crafts Exhibition Society (1915–22)). He had a distinguished career designing church-furnishings, including the decorations (1895–1910) for **Edmund Evan Scott**'s (1828–95) *Sublime Church of St Bartholomew, Ann Street, Brighton, Sussex (1872–4), all of the finest Arts-and-Crafts quality, ample and rich. One of his loveliest creations is the monument to **Canon Edward Douglas Tinling** (1815–97) in Gloucester Cathedral. He also designed the sculpted *frieze over the entrance to Leonard *Stokes's Church of All Saints, London Colney, Herts. (1899), and the monument to **Bishop William Elphinstone** (1431–1514), King's College, Aberdeen. His work was greatly admired before the 1914–18 war in Germany, notably by *Muthesius. He published *Silverwork and Jewellery* (1903) which went into further editions (1912, 1966, 1978), and was Editor of AR (1896–1901).

AR, **vi** (1899), 276–8; A.S.Gray (1985); Manton (2009); RIBAJ, ser. 3, **xli**/10 (24 Mar. 1934), 539; Se (1977); Se (ed.) (1975); T & B (1932)

Wilson, William Hardy (1881–1955) Australian architect, influenced by *Lutyens and *McKim, Mead, & White, he studied surviving *Georgian architecture in Australia, published (1924) as *Old Colonial Architecture in New South Wales and Tasmania*. He established (1911) a practice in Sydney with **Stacey Arthur Neave** (1883–1941):

they designed a series of *Colonial-Revival houses, including Eryldene, Gordon (1913–14—with a *verandah and flanking *pavilions), Purulia, Wahroonga (1916), and Macquarie Cottage, Pymble (1921), all in Sydney. Wilson also designed many gardens, employing axes, *pergolas, and planting-schemes derived from those of the early C19. In the 1920s he introduced oriental exoticism into some of his architecture. The practice continued to design fine Colonial-Georgian buildings almost until the 1939–45 war.

Pearl (1970); C.T.Simpson *et al.* (1980); J.T (1996)

Wimmel, Carl Ludwig (1786–1845) German architect, pupil of **Christian Friedrich Lange** (1768–1833), *Langhans, and *Weinbrenner, he worked in Hamburg from 1814, becoming Director of the Building Department (1841). His earliest buildings for the City included the Greek-*Doric *Steintor* and *Millerntor* (1818–19—both destroyed), and the *arcuated General Hospital (1815–23—destroyed). For the Municipal Theatre (1826–7—destroyed) and the dignified terrace-houses at the Esplanade (1827–30) he chose a refined *Classicism, but his best building, the *Johanneum* (two schools and a library grouped around a *court, of 1837–40—destroyed), was in the rusticated Florentine round-arched style made fashionable by *Gärtner and von *Klenze in Munich. He chose a Neo-*Cinquecento* style for the Exchange (1837–41), designed, like the *Johanneum*, in collaboration with **Franz Gustav Joachim Forsmann** (1795–1878), whose finest work on his own account, the Jenisch House at Flottbeck, near Hamburg (1828–34), survives, a taut Grecian *villa strongly influenced by *Schinkel's work.

Grundmann (1957); Hannmann (1975); Wa & M (1987)

winch Reel or roller, capable of hoisting objects. *Winch-houses* are high-level features protecting winches on the *façades of many tall, narrow Dutch houses. Sometimes the hoisting-mechanisms are set within the houses.

Winchcombe, Richard (*fl.*1398–1440) English mason, he worked at Porchester Castle, Hants. (1390s), and thereafter mostly in Oxon. He seems to have designed the *tithe-barn at Swalcliffe (1403–6), the *chancel of Adderbury Church (1408–18), and carried out various jobs at New College, Oxford. He also seems to have run some kind of private practice, and his hand has been detected in various churches, including Bloxham (Milcombe Chapel), Broughton, Deddington, Enstone, North Leigh (Wilcote Chapel), and Thame (*transept), all in Oxon. He may have carried out works at Northleach Church, Glos. but his main claim to fame is the Divinity School, Oxford, begun 1424, later vaulted by William *Orchard.

J.Harvey (1987)

Winckelmann, Johann Joachim (1717–68) German art-historian/archaeologist, he settled in Rome, became librarian to **Cardinal Alessandro Albani** (1692–1779), and established himself as a scholar/antiquarian, advising on the acquisition of the Cardinal's collection of *Antique sculpture (many items of which are now in the *Glyptothek*, Munich). He was an important influence on *Neo-Classicism, and especially on the *Greek Revival. His two great books, *Gedanken über die Nachahmung der griechischen Werke in der Malerei und Bildhauerkunst* (1755—published in English in 1765) and *Geschichte der Kunst des Alterthums* (1764), proclaimed the superiority of Greek art and subjected it to analysis. His art-historical method and his interpretation of Classical Antiquity informed education, especially in Germany, well into C20. His notion of the best of Classical art imbued with 'noble simplicity and calm grandeur' became deeply embedded in Western thought, and he influenced many artists and architects, notably the painter **Anton Raffael Mengs** (1728–79—whose ceiling-*fresco, *Parnassus*, in the *Villa Albani*, Rome (1761), was one of the key works of Neo-Classicism), *Schinkel, and von *Klenze.

COF (1988); Gaehtgens (1986); J.T (1996); Wa & M (1987)

wind The winds are often shown personified, e.g. Tower of the Winds (*Horologium* of **Andronicus of Cyrrhus**), Athens (*c.*50 BC), published by *Stuart and *Revett and copied widely in C18. *Compounds include*:

wind-beam: *collar-beam tying *rafters or *crucks;
wind-brace: *brace, usually curved, set in the plane of a roof, tying a *principal to a *purlin, or otherwise stiffening a roof-structure to prevent it falling sideways along its length.

Winde, William (*c.*1640–1722) English architect/soldier/military-engineer, he appears to have been trained by *Gerbier, and succeeded the latter as architect at Hampstead Marshall, Berks. (*c.*1663–88—destroyed). With *Hooke, *May, *Pratt, and *Talman, Winde was one of the most important country-house architects working in England in the late C17. He rebuilt Combe Abbey, Warwicks. (1682–8), drawing on Pratt's work, and probably designed part of Dingley Hall, Northants. (*c.*1684–8), and Belton House, Lincs. (1685–8). He may also have carried out works at Cliveden House, Bucks. (*c.*1676–8), and Buckingham House, St James's, London (1702–5—swallowed up within Buckingham Palace), both of which had balustraded *Attics instead of steeply-pitched roofs. Buckingham House, with *colonnaded *quadrants and *wings, was the prototype for a formula applied to many C18 country-houses.

AH, xxvii (1984), 150–62; Co (2008); Su (1993)

winder *See* STAIR.

winding stair *See* STAIR.

window 1. Aperture in a wall to allow light and air to enter: if it is divided into compartments by means of, say, *mullions and *transoms, those compartments are *lights. In its simplest form, a window is a mere hole in a wall, with an arch or *lintel at its head. Some Greek windows on important buildings were narrower at the top than at the bottom (*see* TIVOLI WINDOW; VITRUVIAN OPENING), and had *architraves, often with *crossettes, as in the *Philippeion* at Olympia (begun 339 BC).

Roman windows were much larger and more varied in type especially after glazing was readily available by *c.* AD 65, although other materials were in use until the early C18. Thin parchment stretched on a frame, then painted and varnished; parchment painted and coated with linseed-oil; linen painted and coated with white of egg and gum-water and varnished; paper soaked in poppy-oil, mutton suet, or wax; and linen dipped or coated in beeswax were employed. In many cases glazing was found only in the upper part of the window, the lower part having wooden *shutters, and this arrangement was commonly found even in Scotland's Royal palaces until comparatively recently (C18). In Classical architecture, windows not only had architraves, but were crowned with *entablatures with or without *pediments. In grander window-openings, columns or *pilasters may be found on either side supporting an entablature, *gable, pediment, etc., in which case they are said to be *aediculated* (*see* AEDICULE).

Early-medieval windows were small and narrow, often with *splays on *cills and *reveals of *jambs to improve the ingress of light, and this type of construction seems to be of considerable antiquity. It was as much controlled by questions of security as by the problems of keeping out rain. *Anglo-Saxon windows were of this type, frequently crudely arched, or with lintels at their heads shaped on the *soffits to look like small arched openings, or having two stones set diagonally at the top to form triangular heads: in towers of the period, apertures often consisted of two distinct openings between which were turned *baluster-*colonnettes with exaggerated *entasis. *Romanesque windows were larger, but were still of the hole-in-the-wall type, splayed, semicircular-headed, and often decorated with *billet or *chevron mouldings. Romanesque semicircular-headed lights were occasionally paired, separated by a *shaft, and contained within a bigger semicircular-headed opening. Circular window-apertures were common, often in *gables, but sometimes elsewhere, e.g. the *clerestorey lights of Southwell *Minster, Notts. In *First-Pointed,

early window-apertures were tall and narrow (*lancets), almost invariably with splayed jambs, having sharply pointed heads, used singly or sometimes in groups of three or five (as in the eastern gables of *chancels (e.g. the *Lady Chapel of Hereford Cathedral (*c.*1220–40)), but circles, quatrefoils, and other simple figures were used, especially in plate-*tracery. With the transition to early *Middle Pointed came *Geometrical* *bar-tracery and **Y**-tracery. *Second-Pointed work introduced *Curvilinear, Flowing, Intersecting,* and *Reticulated* tracery, the various lights framed by *mullions and bar-tracery. In England, *Perp. windows had mullions and transoms subdividing ever-larger windows into panel-like lights, the design often continuing repeated as *blind panels over the adjacent walls: the main mullions rose from the cill to the head which, towards the end of the medieval period, was usually a very depressed arch, and transoms were often ornamented with miniature *battlements. *Tudor-Gothic window-heads frequently were four-centred arches, but were also fitted within rectangular apertures subdivided by mullions and framed at the top by a pronounced *hood-mould dropping down on either side and terminating in *label-stops. This was the usual arrangement in late-medieval domestic architecture. *Elizabethan and *Jacobean windows in grander houses were often vast, subdivided by mullions and transoms, called *grid-tracery. **2.** Filling of a window-opening with glass fixed in a frame or *sash of wood or metal, with accessories. The frame usually takes two forms: the *casement and the *sash. The latter is a frame holding the glass, fixed or opening, set in a large frame encompassing the whole window-opening or aperture: if opening, the operation is effected by a vertical or horizontal sliding movement or by hinges or pivots at the side, top, bottom, or centre. A casement-window, therefore, has a sash or sashes. Sashes moving up and down are called *boxed sliding, double-hung,* or *vertical sliding.* In C17, window-frames were often cruciform, with the lights held in frames within each opening, the pieces or *quarries of glass secured in lead *cames stiffened by *saddle-bars* fixed to the main frame. One or more of the rectangular sashes were hinged so that they could open in or out, so were referred to as casements.

With the C17 advent of larger panes of crown *glass, the design of windows changed, and the sashes were subdivided into rectangular squares or rectangles formed by wooden glazing-bars into which glass was set. One sash slid vertically in front of the other in grooves formed on robustly-constructed frames, and suspended on cords over pulleys, counter-balanced by means of weights free to move up and down inside the boxes within the main frame. This *boxed sliding* or *double-hung* sash-window appears to have been an English invention (1670s—although some have claimed it originated in The Netherlands), and was employed when earlier windows were replaced in the *Palladian Banqueting House, Whitehall, London (1685). From then, double-hung sash-windows gained in popularity, often replacing earlier types. However, the limitations of techniques of manufacturing glass ensured that individual panes remained relatively small, so glazing-bars were universal in better work, and somewhat obtrusive, being thick. During C18, glazing-bars (called *astragals in Scotland) were refined and acquired moulded profiles, reducing their visual impact. This elegance of *section and improvements in the methods of making glass enabled larger panes to be made, so that in the finest *Georgian sliding sash-windows the obtrusiveness of glazing-bars was minimal, and the bars themselves contributed to the overall appearance of refinement and well-proportioned artefacts. During the first decades of C19, proportions of window-openings changed: C18 apertures had generally been tall and narrow, but with the advent of *Neo-Classicism and, especially, the *Greek Revival, became wider in proportion to height. Extra glazing was introduced at the sides of sashes in narrow strips (*margin-panes) often with tinted glass. Continuing improvements of manufacturing techniques made large panes of glass available at reasonable cost from the 1830s, and this again encouraged a change of proportion as windows could become wider still and glazing-bars dispensed with. In many cases glazing-bars were removed from earlier windows, changing the geometry and destroying the vertical emphasis created by repeated vertical rectangular panes. C18 relationships between pane, sash, window, and façade that had been so important in establishing the proportions of *Georgian domestic architecture were weakened. Furthermore, tax changes in England (e.g. repeal of window-tax (1851)) tended to encourage more and larger windows, further freeing design from the earlier constraints. Historically, window-widths were determined by the size and strength of the lintel or stability of the arch. With the evolution of structural frames, the various changes outlined previously and C19 stylistic eclecticism, traditional relationships of window-openings to solid walls altered. Many contemporary buildings have external *cladding (consisting of glass in some kind of light frame as the *curtain-wall) forming the enclosing envelope around the internal volumes. **3.** Types of window include *bay; *bow; *casement; *Catherine-wheel; *Chicago; *clerestorey; *cross; *Diocletian or thermal; *dormer; *fanlight; *French (or *croisée); *Ipswich; *laced; *lancet; *lattice; leper; low-side; *lucarne; *lychnoscope; *marigold; *oculus; *œil-de-bœuf;

*oriel; *Palladian; *picture; *rose; *sash; *serliana; *skylight; *tracery; *Venetian; *wheel; *Wyatt; and *Yorkshire light. *Compounds include*:
window-back: framing between the bottom of a *window-aperture* and the *floor*;
window-bar: **1.** mullion; **2.** any division between lights;
window-board: inner cill, usually of timber;
window-bossing: recess beneath a window, often used for a seat;
window-box: *container placed outside a window in which ornamental plants are cultivated;
window-case: window-frame for hung *sashes*;
window-embrasure: splay of a *window-opening*;
window-frame: frame set in a *window-aperture* for *sliding-sashes* or rebated as in a *casement-window*;
window-guard: **1.** small *balcony, *balconet*, or *vignette, fitted with a low railing so that flower-pots, etc., do not fall; **2.** grate or bars, protecting a window, especially at ground-floor level;
window-head: **1.** *soffit of an arched top or of a lintel above a window-aperture. **2.** architectural enrichment above a window-aperture;
window-lead: lead *came subdividing the *quarries of glass and holding them in place in a leaded light;
window-ledge: *cill, inside or outside;
window-post: *post in a *timber-framed building on either side of the window-aperture into which the window-frame is to be set;
window-screen: **1.** pierced *lattice-screen or shutter; **2.** any form of closure, e.g. to prevent insects from entering a room through a window-aperture, or to obstruct a view into a room;
window-seat: seat in the recess of a window-aperture between the inner *jambs, floor, and *cill;
window-shutter: hinged leaf hung on either side of a window-opening, inside or outside, in one or more folds, to secure the aperture.

AH, **xxvi** (1983), 49–72; Gw (1903); N (1835); W.Pa (1892); J.Parker (1850); S (1901–2)

Windrim, James Hamilton (1840–1919) American architect, his career blossomed when he won the architectural competition for the Masonic Temple, Penn Square, Philadelphia, PA (1868–73), an eclectic design with many *Romanesque echoes and lavish interiors by **George Herzog** (1845–1913). Other works in Philadelphia include the Academy of Natural Sciences (1872) and Kemble House (1880s—*Italianate, stylistically not unlike *McKim, Mead, & White's Villard House, NYC (1882–6)). As Director of Public Works in Philadelphia he designed the Richard Smith Memorial Gateway, Fairmount Park (1897—Classical).

JSAH, **xxvi** (1967), 278–84; P (1982); Teitelman & Longstreth (1974); J.T (1996)

wind-scoop Funnel-like feature of domestic architecture in the Middle East: air is carried or blown down to the interiors, sometimes into underground chambers and over cold-water tanks, and then up again to the inhabited rooms. It demonstrates sophisticated technical mastery of climate-control in Islamic culture, probably as early as C14.

Ck (1996)

wine-cellar Large wine-cellars were usually constructed underground, preferably approached through another cellar into which goods could be passed down through trap-doors. Once features of most well-appointed houses, they were paved, had vaulted ceilings (to ensure equable temperatures), and had racks for bottles. Fine medieval examples survive (e.g. in Winchelsea and Antwerp).

Winford, William de See WYNFORD.

wing 1. Part of a building, or any feature of a building, projecting from and subordinate to the main, central part. In Classical and especially *Palladian compositions wings are smaller buildings on either side of the *corps-de-logis, perhaps joined to it by means of *quadrants or *colonnades, and projecting forward to partially enclose a *court or *cour d'honneur. **2.** Part of a building with its roof at right angles to the adjacent main range, as in a *hall-and-cross-wing* medieval *timber-framed house, with the hall-range attached to one or two wings. **3.** *Fillet on a *moulding. **4.** Straight or curved projecting wall at each side and end of a bridge, also the retaining-wall at each end of a *bridge to sustain the bank. **5.** One of the folds of a double *door or *screen. **6.** Lateral wall of a rectangular Classical *temple, or the space between the *cell walls and the *peristyle.

ABDM (1996); Gw (1903); W.Pa (1892); S (1901–2)

winged globe Disc or representation of a globe, usually flanked by rearing *uraei, associated with Ancient-Egyptian architecture, and often occurring on the *cavetto or *gorge-*cornice.

J.Curl (2005)

wing-light *Side-light.

Winter, John (1930–2012) English architect, best known for his own house in Swain's Lane, Highgate, London (1967—clad in Cor-Ten oxidizing steel), and the rebuilding of parts of Morley College, Westminster Bridge Road, London (1973–5, 1979–82). An advocate of self-build, he used recycled bricks and old floor-boards (for *formwork), sensibly believing that architects should be practical builders to give them insights as to how buildings are made.

RIBAJ (Dec. 2010), 10

winter-garden 1. Garden for winter display, with evergreens and winter-flowering plants, e.g. the exemplar at Coleorton Hall, Leics., designed (1806) in a disused quarry with advice from **William Wordsworth** (1770–1850). **2.** Garden in a greenhouse, attached to dwellings (e.g. *Loudon's 3–5 Porchester Terrace, London (1823–5), and palaces (e.g. Łańcut and Łazienki, Poland). **3.** On a larger scale, a building for public entertainment (e.g. cafés, restaurants, concerts, balls, etc.) made possible by the development of C19 iron-and-glass structures (e.g. the tired Winter Garden at Eastbourne, East Sussex (1874–6—by **Henry Currey** (1820–1900), where the display of plants was only incidental).

Hix (1996); Koppelkamm (1981); M & T (1991); Pe (1976)

Wintringham, William (fl.1361–92) English carpenter, he supervised the construction of the Great Hall roof, Windsor Castle, Berks. (1361–5), probably designed in general form by William *Herland. He worked with *Yeveley on the Savoy Palace, London (1375), and carried out various tasks at Westminster Abbey, including the roof of the Abbot's Hall. Other projects included a new chapel and houses at Hertford Castle, Herts. (1380s), various roofs and other structures at Kenilworth Castle, Warwicks., including the roof of the Great Hall, then the widest trussed roof before Westminster Hall eclipsed it. Virtually everything he designed or made has been destroyed.

J.Harvey (1987)

Wise, Henry (1653–1738) English nurseryman/garden-designer, he joined (c.1687) George *London at his Brompton Nursery, becoming his partner by 1694. He carried out works at Hampton Court Palace (1689–92—probably based on designs by *Marot), and was appointed (1702) Royal Gardener to **Queen Anne** (r.1702–14), in which capacity he improved St James's Park with new avenues of limes, and widened the lake. He worked (1705–16) on the grounds of Blenheim Palace, Oxon., with *Vanbrugh, and designed the gardens at Melbourne Hall, Derbys. (1704–6—where French influences are clear). He employed a Franco-Dutch style incorporating *parterres, basins, canals, mazes, and straight avenues, and was working on royal parks and gardens until 1727 when his pupil *Bridgeman succeeded him. *Switzer was another able pupil, and, like Bridgeman, an early protagonist of the C18 English style of landscape-gardening. With London he published *The Compleat Gard'ner* (1699—an abridged translation of *Evelyn's translation from the French of **Jean de la Quintinie**'s (1626–88) *Instructions pour les jardins fruitiers et potages* (1690)) and *The Retir'd Gard'ner* (1706—translations of **François Gentil**'s (fl.1588) *Le jardinier* *solitaire* (1704) and **Louis Liger**'s (1658-1717) *Le jardinier fleuriste et histiographe* (also 1704)).

D & E (1994); D.Green (1951, 1956); J.Harvey (1974)

Wit, *or* **Witte, Peter de** (1548-1628) *See* CANDID.

Withers, Frederick Clarke (1828-1901) English-born architect, he worked with T.H. *Wyatt and David *Brandon before emigrating (1852) to the USA at the behest of A.J.*Downing. Withers worked with *Vaux, with whom he formed a partnership (1852-6), then practised on his own. He designed several *Gothic-Revival houses, illustrated in Vaux's *Villas and Cottages* (1857). After the Civil War Withers and Vaux established another partnership in NYC (1863-72), and designed some ecclesiologically-correct churches (e.g. St Luke, Beacon, NY (1869)) and other, more adventurous *polychrome essays (e.g. the Dutch Reformed Church, also in Beacon (1859)). His largest church was the Chapel of the Good Shepherd, Roosevelt Island, NYC (1888—influenced by James *Brooks's architecture). Other works include the Jefferson Market Courthouse and Prison, now the Greenwich Village branch of New York Public Library (1874-8—influenced by *Burges's architecture), the Hudson River State Hospital, Poughkeepsie, NY (1867), and College Hall, Gallaudet College, Washington, DC (1868-75), in the last two of which Vaux and *Olmsted contributed to the landscape-design. With **Walter Dickson** (1834-1903) he designed New York City Prison (begun 1896—destroyed). He published *Church Architecture* (1873).

JSAH, xxxv/2 (May 1976), 83–107; Kowsky (1980); P (1982)

Witkiewicz-Koszczyc, Jan (1881-1958) Polish architect, his first buildings were in the *vernacular style of the Zakopane area pioneered by his uncle, **Stanisław Witkiewicz** (1851-1915). Many of his 1906-25 works were influenced by his studies (1901-4) in Munich, and responded to local conditions, using undressed stone and wood. Among them may be cited the Bath-House (1920-2) and the Building Trades School (1922-5), Kazimierz Dolny, and the House of Art, Częstochowa (1909). From 1925 he was in Warsaw, where he designed the *reinforced-concrete Higher School of Commerce (1925-55—later the Central School of Planning). He was also a significant restorer of historic buildings.

Arché, iv/v (1993), 14–19, 44, and vi (1994), 25–33; Exhibition Catalogue of Works (Kazimierz Dolny: Regional Museum, 1981); Leśnikowski (ed.) (1996)

Witney, Thomas of (*fl.*1292-1342) English mason, he was engaged (1290s) on the first building of St Stephen's Chapel, Westminster, but by 1311 was in Winchester, Hants., working on the Cathedral. He carried out alterations to the *presbytery before being called (1313) to Exeter Cathedral, Devon, where he was in charge by 1316, completing the *crossing, building the *nave, and creating the *reredos and *sedilia (1316-26) as well as the *pulpitum, all of which are in an advanced *Second-Pointed style. The *piers and other aspects of the architecture at Winchester presbytery resemble the style of the Exeter works. He may have designed the *Lady Chapel and associated parts of the *retrochoir at Wells Cathedral, Som. (completed by 1326), and the crossing at Merton College Chapel, Oxford (1330-2).

J.Harvey (1987)

Witte, Jacob Eduard (*fl.*1764-77) Dutch architect/military-engineer, he became Director of Public Works in Amsterdam (1772), and designed the celebrated timber-built theatre on the *Leidseplein* (1773—destroyed 1890), the outer walls of which were doubled, the gap between them filled with sawdust to reduce noise-penetration.

Worp (1920)

Wittet, George (1878-1926) Scots architect, he worked (from 1898) with **John More Dick Peddie** (1853-1921) and G.W.*Browne, then (1902-4) with W.H.*Brierley. Appointed assistant to John *Begg, he succeeded (1907) the latter as consulting architect to the Government of Bombay (Mumbai). His first independent work was the Prince of Wales Museum of Western India, Bombay, in a scholarly version of Deccan Muslim architecture (begun 1904). Among his designs were the Institute of Science, the Custom House, the Small Causes Court, and the Edward VII Memorial Hospital, all in Bombay, and the Agricultural College (1911) and Central Government Office (1915) in Poonah (Pune). He designed his most celebrated work, the Gateway of India *triumphal arch, Apollo Bunder, Bombay (1927), commemorating the landing (1911) of **King George V** and **Queen Mary** (*r.*1910-36) as **Emperor and Empress of India**.

P.Davies (1985); *RIBAJ,* xxxiii n.s. (1926), 618; Stamp (1976, 1981a); J.T (1996)

Wittgenstein, Ludwig Josef Johann (1889-1951) Austrian-born philosopher/architect, British from 1938. With **Paul Engelmann** (1891-1965—a pupil of *Loos), he designed a house at 19 *Kundmanngasse*, Vienna, stripped of ornament, reflecting his own aesthetic stance and architectural tendencies present in the Austro-Hungarian Empire in the early C20.

Malcolm (1984); Monk (1990)

Wittkower, Rudolf (1901-71) German-born British art-historian. Educated in Berlin and

Munich, he worked (1923–33) at the *Bibliotheca Hertziana*, Rome, with the Director, **Ernst Steinmann** (1866–1934), on an annotated bibliography of *Michelangelo (1927) and there acquired his unrivalled knowledge of Italian art and architecture. As a result of his studies he published (with **Heinrich Friedrich Ferdinand Brauer** (1899–)) the important catalogue of *Bernini's drawings (1931), which was to prepare the ground for his *Gian Lorenzo Bernini* (1955—with subsequent editions). It was while labouring on Bernini that he turned his attention to architecture, publishing a learned paper on Michelangelo's *dome of St Peter's (1933, 1964), and followed this with a study of the Laurentian Library, Florence (1934, 1978), in which he discussed *Mannerism and architecture. A British subject through his British-born father, **Henry**, he settled in London, where he was (1934–56) a member of staff at the Warburg Institute, and co-edited (1937–56) the *Warburg Journal*, published many papers, and produced a work on *Rainaldi (1937) and centralized Roman *Baroque church-architecture. Further research on *Alberti (1941) and *Palladio (1944) gathered material that led to his *Architectural Principles in the Age of Humanism* (1949), which made an immediate and lasting impact, not least because it disposed of the purely aesthetic theory of Renaissance architecture, a notion that had crippled previous work. It showed (among other things) the importance of modular systems during the *Renaissance, and especially in designs by Palladio: it also examined centrally planned *Renaissance churches and their meaning in Christian symbolism, as well as *Harmonic Proportion. Other books include *Art and Architecture in Italy* (1958, with subsequent edns.); *Baroque Art: The Jesuit Contribution* (1972— which he edited with **Irma Blumenthal Jaffé** (1916–)); *Studies in Italian Baroque* (1975); *British Art and the Mediterranean* (1948—with **Friedrich 'Fritz' Saxl** (1890–1948)—which revealed debts owed to Italy and France by British art and architecture); and *Palladio and English Palladianism* (1974—a tantalizing foretaste of what might have been his greatest book, a study of *Burlington, which he never finished). He was Professor at Columbia University, NYC (1956–69), where, in the words of *Pevsner (some of whose views and associates rankled with him), his régime was exacting but generous.

AR, **cli/899** (Jan. 1972), 63; FHL (1967); *ODNB* (2004); Wi (1964, 1974, 1974a, 1975, 1978, 1981, 1982, 1998); Wi & Brauer (1970); Wi & Jaffé (eds) (1972); Wi & Saxl (eds) (1969)

Wodehirst, Robert de (*fl.*1351–1401) English mason, he worked at Westminster Palace (1350s), but by 1361 was at Norwich Cathedral, where he rebuilt the *clerestorey of the *presbytery (1361–

9), and was Master of the Works for the *cloisters (1385–6). At Ely Cathedral, Cambs. (1387–93), he built the *reredos of the *high-altar and (probably) the *lantern over the great western tower.

J.Harvey (1987)

Woderofe, James (*fl.*1415–51) English mason. He and his brother, **John,** worked at Norwich Cathedral (1410s–20s), where they vaulted some of the *bays of the *cloister and carried out other tasks. He seems to have designed the Erpingham Gate (1416–25), the remodelled west front of the Cathedral, Norwich (*c.*1426–50), and the west tower of Wymondham Abbey, Norfolk (from 1445). His expertise must have carried some weight, because he was called (1449) to Eton College, Bucks., but on what pretext is unclear.

J.Harvey (1987)

Wohlmut, Bonifaz (*fl.*1522–79) *See* STELLA, PAOLO DELLA.

Wolff, Jakob, the Elder (1546–1612) German architect/master-mason, he seems (from records of 1572) to have begun his career at Bamberg Cathedral, and made alterations and additions to the Marienberg fortress above Würzburg (1600–7), linking the two *wings to create an enormous *court. He and one **Peter Carl** erected (1602–7) the splendid *Pellerhaus*, Nuremberg (a casualty of the 1939–45 war, but partly rebuilt): its *rusticated *Renaissance *façade (inspired by Venetian exemplars) was crowned with an elaborate three-storey gabled confection, and the internal court had superimposed *arcades and much Renaissance enrichment. Wolff's son, **Jakob the Younger** (1571–1620), travelled (early C17) in Italy, acquiring a knowledge of Italian-Renaissance architecture which he employed in the extension to the Nuremberg *Rathaus* (destroyed in the 1939–45 war, but rebuilt), with its long façade incorporating three festive portals (1616–20). After his death the work was completed by his brother, **Hans** (*fl.*1612–22).

Ck (1996); J.T (1996)

Wolff, Johann Caspar (1818–91) Swiss architect, he published a comprehensive book on architecture, *Der Baufreund* (1841). As Building Administrator in Zofingen (1843–50) and Building Inspector to the Canton of Zürich (1851–65), he was responsible for many public buildings, mostly in a restrained Classical style imbibed when he studied (1836–40) in Munich (e.g. the Gaol, Winterthur (1852–4) and the Burghölzli Sanatorium, Zürich (1864–70)). His religious buildings included the Calvinist churches at Wohlen (1851–4—*Neo-Classical) and Töss (1854–5— *Gothic Revival), and the Parish Church, Rüfenach (1863–4—a *mélange* of various styles). He replanned Glarus after the town was burnt down (1861).

Meyer (1973); J.T (1996)

Wölfflin, Heinrich (1864-1945) Swiss art-historian. In his *Renaissance und Barock* (1888), he argued that architecture had expressive force in itself acquiring meanings changing with time, but what he called 'empathy' was not shared by everyone. In his *Die antiken Triumphbogen in Italien* (1893) he examined the development of the Roman *triumphal arch paralleling the general history of architecture (experiment, perfection, and decadence through over-elaboration).

Critical Inquiry, viii (1982), 379-404; Podro (1982)

Wolters, Mathias-Joseph (1793-1859) Belgian architect/engineer, he became (1837) Chief Engineer for Eastern Flanders, in which capacity he carried out many hydraulic schemes. In architecture he was important in the early phase of the Belgian *Gothic Revival. Among his works were the Episcopal Palace, Gent (1841-5), and churches at Viane (1843-7), Heusden (1844), and other places, all in a free *Gothic style, often using *cast-iron components and *stucco. He published studies of historic fabric in the area around Limburg.

Messager des sciences historiques (1859), 388-94; Piron (1860) 469; Poulain (ed.) (1985), 99-100

Wolveston, Richard de (*fl.*1170-82) English engineer/architect, he designed the *Galilee porch at Durham Cathedral (*c.*1170) and part of Durham Castle, including the west doorway of the Great Hall. As an employee of the **Bishop of Durham** until *c.*1182 he must have been one of the ablest professionals of his time. He built the keep of Bowes Castle, Yorks. (1170-4).

J.Harvey (1987)

Wolvey, Thomas (*fl.*1397-1428) English mason. He built the south *chancel-chapel of the Church at Henley-on-Thames, Oxon. (1397), and Westminster Hall (1398), where he built the upper parts of two towers at the north end of the Hall, complete with *battlements, designed by *Yeveley. He appears to have been master-mason of St Alban's Abbey, Herts., for some 30 years, and worked on a number of churches in that county, including St Peter's in St Alban's, Newnham St Vincent, and King's Langley.

J.Harvey (1987)

Wood, Cecil Walter (1878-1947) New Zealand architect, trained under **Frederick Strouts** (1834-1919), he worked for a time in England, first for LCC (from 1901), and then with *Weir Schultz and Leonard *Stokes, before returning to Christchurch, NZ, where he established (1909) his own practice. Early works included several *Arts-and-Crafts houses, but after 1920 he turned to a *Neo-Georgian *Colonial style. An accomplished *Gothic Revivalist and Classicist, his works included the Dining-Hall, Christ's College, Christchurch (1922-5—*Collegiate Gothic); the Gothic churches of St Barnabas, Fendalton (1925), St Paul, Tai Tapu (1930), and St Barnabas, Woodend (1932); and the Public Trust Building (1922—*stripped Classical) and Post-Office Savings-Bank (1937—well-crafted *Modernist), both in Christchurch. In the 1930s he sparingly used *Art-Deco motifs.

Landfall, xxxviii/4 (1984), 466-81; J.T (1996)

Wood, Edgar (1860-1935) English architect, he designed a great number of houses (some noted by *Muthesius), churches, and schools, most of which incorporate *Arts-and-Crafts and *vernacular influences: houses include Halecroft, Hale Road, Hale, Ches., 37-9 Rochdale Road, Middleton, and Westdene, Archer Road, Middleton, Manchester (all 1890s). His First Church of Christ Scientist, Daisybank Road, Victoria Park, Manchester (1903-4), was an idiosyncratic free composition with a circular tower, *buttresses, and inventive fenestration. With **James Henry Sellers** (1861-1954) he designed several buildings, including Elm Street and Durnsford Street Schools, both in Middleton (1909-10).

A.S.Gray (1985); Hartwell *et al.* (2004, 2011)

Wood, Thomas (*c.*1644-95) Oxford master-mason, he designed the old Ashmolean Museum, Broad Street, now the Museum of the History of Science (1679-83), the first public museum in England, one of the most advanced Classical buildings for its date in Oxford. He rebuilt the tower of Deddington Parish Church, Oxon. (1683-5), in a convincing *Gothic style, so he deserves mention as a versatile and competent designer.

Co (2008)

Wood Family English architects/builders. **John Wood the Elder** (1704-54) was one of the developers of the Cavendish-Harley Estates in London, erecting houses in Oxford, Margaret, and Edward Streets, as well as in Cavendish Square. He was also employed at Bramham Park, Yorks., where he laid out the grounds (1722-4). His experience stood him in good stead when he returned to his birthplace, Bath, Som., then (1727) about to enjoy a building-boom. He developed (1728-36) Queen Square, based on London exemplars, sub-leasing the sites of individual houses, but controlling the development so that the contractors had to comply with his *elevations. The result was a unified *Palladian *palace-fronted composition on the north side. Wood followed this with further schemes for Wood, John, and Old King Streets

(1729–31), the North and South Parades, with Pierrepont and Duke Streets (1740–3), and then Gay Street (from c.1750) and the Circus (begun 1754). The last was an important innovation in English town-planning, with unified *façades featuring an *assemblage of *Orders, the whole resembling the design of the Colosseum in Rome, but on a concave instead of convex plan. His proposals for a Royal Forum were not realized, but the general idea was to re-create a mnemonic of a Roman city.

Wood's publications are more interesting for their curiosity value than for their scholarship, and indeed they stray into the realms of bizarre, even insane, speculation. They include *The Origin of Building, or the Plagiarism of the Heathens Detected* (1741) in which he proposed that the three main Roman Orders had been the result of Divine revelation and had been first used in Solomon's Temple in Jerusalem, a notion recurring in *Freemasonry ... and in *Villalpando's *Ezechielem Explanationes ...* (1596–1631). Behind this was the desire to cleanse Classical architecture of any pagan origins. Wood further fantasized about the origins of Bath in *An Essay towards a Description of Bath* (1742, 1749, and 1765), and also published *A Description of the Exchange of Bristol* (1745), *Choir Gaure, vulgarly called Stonehenge ...* (1747), and *Dissertation Upon the Orders of Columns and their Appendages* (1750). His meanderings drew on a curiously dotty volume (*Chronology of Ancient Kingdoms Amended* (1728)) by none other than **Sir Isaac Newton** (1642–1727).

Other buildings by Wood included a Classical church within the ruined *nave of Llandaff Cathedral, Glamorgan (1734–5—demolished c.1850), the handsome Palladian Prior Park, near Bath (1735–48), Lilliput Castle, Lansdown, near Bath (1738), the Exchange and Market, Corn Street, Bristol (1741–3), and the Exchange (now Town Hall), Liverpool (1749–54—much altered). The development of Bath was continued by his son, **John Wood the Younger** (1728–81), who supervised the building of the Liverpool Exchange and completed the building of the Circus in Bath. His greatest contribution was Royal Crescent, Bath, the climax of the handsome sequence of residential developments begun in 1727. The Crescent (1767–75), with its *Giant *Ionic Order rising from a *plinth, was both original and influential, and was widely imitated thereafter. His new Assembly Rooms (1769–71) and Hot Bath (now Old Royal Baths—1773–7) were fine examples of Palladian architecture. He also designed Buckland House, Berks. (1755–8), the Infirmary, Salisbury, Wilts. (1767–71), and the *castellated Tregenna Castle, St Ives, Cornwall (1773–4). He published *Description of the Hot-Bath at Bath ...* (1777) and *A Series of Plans, for Cottages or Habitations for the Labourer* (1781, 1792, 1806, and 1837). In the latter volume he demonstrated a concerned attitude to housing for the working classes unusual for the time.

ArtH, **vi** (1983), 301–14; Co (2008); J.Curl (2001); E.Hs (1990); Ison (1969); M & E (1988); *ODNB* (2004); P (1982); Su (1963, 1993); J.T (1996)

woodland cemetery Early-C20 development of the *landscape-garden, e.g. Woodland Cemetery, Enskede, Stockholm, Sweden, where *Asplund and *Lewerentz enhanced the natural features of the site, including a disused quarry and varied woods. Another example is the larchwood cemetery, Davos Platz, Graubünden, Switzerland (1919–21), designed by **Rudolf Gaberel** (1882–1962). Later exemplars include 'natural' burial-places in woodlands, where memorials are discouraged or forbidden, and ecological aspects are paramount.

woodland garden C19 garden formed in acidic woodland soils, featuring non-native species, e.g. hydrangeas, rhododendrons, etc., augmented in the late C19-early C20 by the introduction of further imported varieties from Asia, etc. An example is Bodnant Garden, Tal-y-Cafn, Colwyn Bay, Denbighshire (early C20).

wood-mosaic Marquetry or *parquetry.

Woodroffe, Edward (c.1622–75) English architect/surveyor. After the Great Fire of London (1666) he was appointed (with *Hooke and *Wren) as one of the three Surveyors to rebuild the City churches. He assisted Wren from 1668 at St Paul's Cathedral and designed houses (1670) in Amen Court, St Paul's, for the Residentiary Canons.

Co (2008)

wood-roll *See* ROLL.

Woods, Harold Joseph (1908–2006) English architect, he made a considerable contribution to hospital-design, not least in the field of landscape, which he saw as an essential element in incalculable therapeutic benefits. Indeed he insisted on the importance of incorporating landscape-design at an early stage of the planning process.

RIBAJ (11 Nov. 2007), 92

Woods, Richard (1715/16–93) Architect/landscape-designer, known for over forty park-commissions, including those at Buckland, Berks. (1758), the 'New Garden Greenhouse and Pinery', Hartwell House, Bucks. (1759–60), and others at Cannon Hall (1760–5), Cusworth (1761–5), Bretton Hall (from 1764), Goldsborough (1763–5), and Harewood (1764–5), all in Yorks. He also carried out works at Wardour Castle, Wilts. (1764–72), Irnham Hall, Lincs. (1768–71), Lulworth, Dorset (1769–72), Wynnstay, Denbighshire

(1770–75), Audley End, Essex (1780), and Brocket Hall, Herts. (1770–4). Woods leaned more towards detail (flowers and features) than to the seamless line of green naturalistic parkland advocated by *Brown. In the 1740s Woods's own property at Chertsey, Surrey, was close to *Southcote's at Woburn Farm, and it is likely that Woods was involved in the development of its seminal *ferme ornée*. His most successful commissions were on a smaller scale (*c.*40–100 acres), and included Wivenhoe (1765–80), Copford Hall (from 1784), and Brizes (from 1788), all in Essex. Woods included *bridges, greenhouses, *pavilions, and *temples in his garden-plans, although his skill as an architect was limited, and many of his ideas are traceable to *pattern-books. Woods was highly regarded in his lifetime; some of his gardens survive in a state close to their original form: e.g. Copford, Cannon, and Cusworth Halls.

GH, ii/3 (Summer 1974), 27–60, 28a; xiv/2 (Autumn 1986), 85–119; & xv/2 (Autumn 1987), 115–35; *ODNB* (2013); Prince (1967)

Woods, Shadrach (1923–73) *See* CANDILIS, GEORGES.

woodshaving pattern Ornament consisting of superimposed *volute-like elements, decorating the sides of *Romanesque *corbels, and resembling partially planed wood-shavings, still attached to a timber.

Woodward, Benjamin (1816–61) *See* DEANE, SIR THOMAS NEWENHAM.

Woodyer, Henry (1816–96) Prolific English *Gothic-Revival architect. Briefly a colleague of *Butterfield (1844), his work featured sharp angles, inventive *tracery, and imaginative use of materials. His best works are perhaps the House of Mercy, Clewer, Hatch Lane, Windsor, Berks. (1853–86), St Michael's College, Tenbury Wells, Worcs. (1853–6—idiosyncratic, with very thin spiky *dormers), St Peter's Church, Hascombe, Surrey (1863–4), and his masterpiece, Holy Innocents Church, Highnam, Glos. (1847–52), with painted *polychrome interior (by **Thomas Gambier Parry** (1816–88) rivalling *Pugin's work at Cheadle, Staffs.). He carried out numerous church restorations and erected vicarages, among them the red-brick and stone one at Toot Baldon, Oxon. (1860).

AH, xxxviii (1995), 192–219; J.Curl (2007); D & M (1985); E & P (2002)

workhouse House for the provision of work for the unemployed poor of a parish, later an institution administered by the Poor Law Guardians, in which paupers were lodged, fed, and those who were able set to work. Workhouses sometimes doubled as 'Houses of Correction', and although the need had long been recognized

for places to house, feed, care for, and work the destitute, a distinction was always made between deserving and thriftless poor. By the early C19 it became clear that parishes should unite for better workhouse-management, and larger buildings known as the Union Workhouses were erected from 1834 under the Poor Laws: the first was built (1836) in Abingdon, Berks., to designs by **Sampson Kempthorne** (1809–73), Architect to the Poor Law Commissioners, who, assisted by 'Great' *Scott, produced several designs for workhouses and schools that were widely copied in the 1840s. In the harsh utilitarian climate of the 1830s the Union workhouses were the only places where able-bodied men and their families could obtain relief in hard times, and, to deter them, the organization of the institutions was made utterly repugnant. Stylistically, too, many workhouses were in a grim, institutionalized stripped *Tudor manner, or even a utilitarian hybrid, but the architecture itself was often as repellent as the régime. It is no accident that Union workhouses were hated and feared, and that even their appearance could chill stout hearts. **George Wilkinson** (1814–90) won the competition to design the workhouse at Thame, Oxon., in 1835, and went on to design others at Witney and Chipping Norton, also Oxon. In *c.*1840 he became Architect to the Poor Law Commissioners for Ireland, and designed numerous workhouses in that country, many of them particularly grim (most that survived were adapted for use as hospitals after 1945).

Co (2008); K.Morrison (1999); M.Gould MPhil Thesis, QUB (2003); W.Pa (1892), *GGJ*, xiv (2004), 104–30

working-drawing Drawings for the proper construction of a building, for carrying out the various trades in accordance with the design or intention of the architect, and for obtaining estimates of cost. They consist of plans, elevations, sections, and details, augmented with specifications.

Worlich, John (*fl.*1443–76) English Master-Mason at King's College Chapel, Cambridge, before Simon *Clerk took over (1477). Before that, he was at All Souls College, Oxford, working under Reginald *Ely on the Chapel. He seems to have been employed at Bury St Edmunds, Suffolk, and had connections with that county. A **Robert Worlich** (*fl.*1492–1524) of Bury St Edmunds, perhaps a son or grandson of John, was one of the Wardens of Masons at King's College Chapel under *Wastell (1508–15).

J.Harvey (1987)

Worlidge *or* **Woolridge, John** (*fl.*1660–98) English writer on horticulture, gardens, and rural crafts, his books generally appeared under

J.W.Gent. His *Systema Agriculturae* (1669) was a systematic and comprehensive account of arable and livestock husbandry, but his *Systema Horti-Culturae, or, The Art of Gardening* (1677 with later edns) stressed the benefits of growing vegetables and fruit, and was also important in its advocacy of Italian gardens, with water-works, *fountains, *grottoes, *obelisks, statues, etc.

H & W (1988); *ODNB* (2004); Worlidge (1677)

Wornum, George Grey (1888–1957) English architect, he worked with **Philip D.Hepworth** (1888–1963) and then (*c*.1921–30) with Louis de *Soissons. He won (1932) the competition to design the London headquarters of the RIBA, an interesting mix of Swedish-inspired *stripped Classicism and *Modernism, beautifully crafted, and with some of the finest surviving interiors of the period. Other works by him include the Ladbroke Grove housing-estate (1936—with Maxwell *Fry et al.), and he was appointed (1938) architect for the first-class accommodation of the new Cunard liner, *Queen Elizabeth*. He was in partnership with **Edward Playne** (*c*.1907–87), incorporating the practice of Aston *Webb.

B, cxcii (1957), 1115; *RIBAJ*, xlii Nov. 1934; *ODNB* (2004); M.Richardson (2004)

Worringer, Wilhelm (1881–1965) German art-historian, whose *Abstraktion und Einfühlung: Ein Beitrag zur Stilpsychologie* (1907) has rarely been out of print. It started with the notion that works of art enhance human capacities for empathy (*see* WÖLFFLIN), and that perception of Beauty is associated with the ability to identify with an artefact. He argued that abstraction (e.g. in Ancient-*Egyptian, *Byzantine, or *Gothic work) was connected with insecurity and pessimism, but that in Classical and Renaissance work, appreciation of images is associated with self-confidence and optimism. He identified Gothic as all Western art not influenced by Classical Antiquity, and as something seeking the transcendental. His identification of 'pure' Gothic with the 'Germanic North' was pounced upon by National Socialists, thus ensuring his relative subsequent obscurity.

Dittmann (ed.) (1985); Finch (1974); Lützeler (1975); J.T (1996)

Worthington, Thomas (1826–1909) English architect, he designed numerous buildings in Manchester including the canopied *Gothic Albert Memorial (1862–7), the Mayfield Baths, Ardwick (1857), the Towers, Didsbury (1868), and the handsome *First-Pointed Brookfield Unitarian Church, Hyde Road, Gorton (1869–71). With his son, (Sir) **Percy Scott Worthington** (1864–1939), who became (1889) a partner in the firm, he designed Manchester College, Mansfield Road, Oxford (1891–3), and the Unitarian

Church, Ullett Road, Sefton Park, Liverpool (1896–1902), the last with much excellent *Arts-and-Crafts detail. Sir Percy Scott Worthington was later joined by his half-brother **Sir John Hubert Worthington** (1886–1963), and his son, **Thomas Shirley Scott Worthington** (1900–81). Sir Hubert was responsible for the Radcliffe Science Library (1933–4), Linacre College (1936), Rose Lane Buildings, Merton College (1939–40), New College Library (1939), the History Faculty Library, Merton Street (1938–56), Lincoln House, Turl Street (1939), Dolphin Gate, St Giles's (1947–8), and the twin block for the Departments of Forestry and Botany (1947–50), all in Oxford.

J.Curl (2007); D & M (1985); A.S.Gray (1985); Hague & Hague (1986); *ODNB* (2004)

Wotton, Sir Henry (1568–1639) English diplomat/collector/writer. As English Ambassador (1604–12, 1616–19, 1621–4) to Venice he was in a good position to purchase works of art and become familiar with distinguished architecture. He published (1624) *The Elements of Architecture*, a work indebted to *Alberti and *Vitruvius, and which famously identified the 'three conditions' for 'well building' as 'Commodity, Firmness, and Delight' (a remark itself derived from Vitruvius). Wotton also described the Roman *Corinthian Order as 'a columne lasciviously decked like a courtesan'. It was the first book devoted to architecture written in English, and may have had some influence on architects such as *Jones and *Pratt. His admiration for *Palladio put his work in good odour with *Burlington and his circle. He was also one of the first English writers to celebrate irregularity in garden-design, anticipating C18 emphasis on variety and surprise. He seems to have influenced **Constantijn Huygens** (1596–1687), whose advocacy of planting in a 'wild' manner occurs in the latter's poetic *Vitaulium: Hofwijck* (1653).

E.Hs (1990); H & W (1988); Huygens (2008); *ODNB* (2004); Morley (1993); Mowl (2000); Pearsall Smith (1907); J.T (1996)

Wouda, Hendrik (1885–1946) Dutch architect, trained by *Berlage and **Eduard Pfeiffer** (1889–1929). Apart from his furniture-designs, his works include interiors of the *Villa Sevensteyn*, Den Haag (1920–1—for which the chief architect was *Dudok), the *Villa De Luifel*, Wassenaar (1924—in which the influence of F.L.L.*Wright was clear), and several houses in which themes from De *Stijl and *Art Deco were present.

Berlage et al. (eds) (1932–3), ix, 38–40, 51; De Fakkel, v (1925), 55–7; J.T (1996)

Wray, Christopher George (1828–1913) Pupil of **Joseph Clarke** (1819/20–88), he designed the Dock Office (now the Town Docks Museum),

Hull (1868–71), a handsome pile in the Venetian-Renaissance style dominating the centre of the city. Among other works the RC Church of St Francis, Maidstone, Kent (1880—a 'funny little building' with flowing *tracery). He became Civil Architect to the Government of Bombay.

B *et al.* (2001); Newman (2012)

wreath 1. Curved portion of the handrail following a turn around each angle of a *geometrical* or *wreathed* *stair (which has no *newels), or the continuous turn of the handrail in such a circular or elliptical stair. 2. Circular or elliptical *garland of flowers, leaves, or ribbons, used in Classical decoration.

wreathed column 1. Column with its *shaft cut with a spiral sinking, generally as a flat band, sometimes with an *annulet or two annulets between which mosaics are set, as in C13 *Cosmati work. 2. Column-shaft with a spiral of leaved tendrils wound around it.

wreathed stair *See* WREATH (1); STAIR

Wren, Sir Christopher (1632–1723) One of the greatest English architects. His father was Rector of Knoyle, Wilts., so he was well connected, but also exposed to a spirit of enquiry, and became a pioneer of experimental learning. While at Oxford, he assisted **Dr Charles Scarburgh** (1616–94), physician/mathematician/anatomist, and himself developed an interest in anatomy and astronomy. He invented a model (the *Panorganum Astronomicum*) to demonstrate various periodical positions of the earth, sun, and moon, and became a skilled maker of models and diagrams. Made a Fellow of All Souls, Oxford (1653), he was appointed (1657) Professor of Astronomy at Gresham College, London. He returned to Oxford (1661) as Savilian Professor of Astronomy, and, although only 28, was highly regarded by his peers. By that time he was becoming interested in architectural matters, and his advice was sought (1663) by the Commission appointed to repair St Paul's Cathedral in London. In the same year he designed the new Chapel for Pembroke College, Cambridge, a pleasant, if unstartling Classical building. This was followed by the Sheldonian Theatre, Oxford (1664–9), based on *Antique exemplars noted in Italian architectural publications. To roof the considerable span, Wren evolved a timber *truss which gained him approbation as an architect, although the *Baroque façade opposite the medieval Divinity Schools is somewhat hesitant, and clumsy in the sum of its parts. He made an important visit to Paris (1665) to see 'esteem'd Fabricks', which influenced his future work.

After the Great Fire of London (1666) he prepared a plan for rebuilding the City that was not adopted, but he was appointed (with *Pratt and *May) as one of the Commissioners to survey and determine how best to proceed with the work. He was also appointed (with *Hooke and *Woodroffe) to rebuild the City churches, and for this task Wren had overall control, although claims that he personally designed each building are exaggerated, and in nearly all cases the furnishings and architectural details were designed by craftsmen, Wren and his colleagues acting in supervisory roles. Designs for the 50 or so City churches either originated in or were vetted by his office, and in most cases accorded with Wren's idea of how ecclesiastical designs should be adapted for Protestant worship. The inventive towers, however, including that of St Dunstan-in-the-East (1697–9—*Gothic), all seem to have originated in, or were modified by, Wren's office. Plans were also varied and interesting, notably the domed St Stephen, Walbrook (1672–9), and St Mary Abchurch (1681–6), a single-volume domed space. The galleried *auditory church was ideally suited to Protestant worship, and the type was perfected at St Peter's, Cornhill (1675–81), St Clement Danes (from 1680), and St James, Piccadilly (1676–84). Wren's greatest achievement was the new St Paul's Cathedral (begun 1675), although he himself wanted a centrally planned church on the lines of the 'great model' (1673). As built, St Paul's was essentially a medieval plan, adapted with a *drum and *dome over the *crossing, and with western towers owing much to Roman-*Baroque prototypes. The western *façade, with its coupled columns, echoes the east front of the Louvre, Paris, and the great drum and dome were a triumphant affirmation of Wren's intellect, invention, and ability. The design of the exterior includes features such as *aedicules with windows below in the *pedestals, and a screening upper storey on the sides that serves to hide the nave *buttresses, both of which have been the subject of adverse criticism for their alleged 'falseness'.

In 1668/9 Wren became Surveyor-General of the King's Works, succeeded (1684) *May as Comptroller at Windsor, was appointed Surveyor at Greenwich Palace (1696), and was Architect in charge of the building of the Military Hospital at Chelsea. The last, with its bold and severe Roman-*Doric *Order (1682–9), was suggested by the *Invalides* in Paris, and also by *Webb's plan for the Palace at Greenwich. When Wren prepared designs for the completion of Greenwich Palace as a Naval Hospital, the need to retain Inigo *Jones's Queen's House led to the solution of building two tall *cupolas on either side of the central axis (from 1696) and the making of the grandest Baroque composition in England, including the handsome Hall (1698), decorated (1708–27) by Sir James *Thornhill. He prepared major schemes for the Palaces of Whitehall (destroyed 1698), Winchester (destroyed 1894), and Hampton Court (south and east ranges (1689-94)) and interior of the King's apartments (completed by *Talman (1699)). Other works include the Garden Quadrangle, Trinity College, Oxford (1668-1728—much altered), the Gothic Tom Tower, Christ Church, Oxford (1681-2), and the very grand Library at Trinity College, Cambridge (1676-84), one of the noblest buildings of its time. He designed Marlborough House, St James's, London (1709-11—later altered on numerous occasions), in which work he was assisted by his son, **Christopher** (1675-1747), who collected the papers that led to *Parentalia, or Memoirs of the Family of the Wrens*, edited (1750) by Christopher Jun.'s son, **Stephen**. Sir Christopher Wren's work was influenced by French architecture, notably that of *Mansart and Le *Vau, and by Netherlands *Classicism and Roman Baroque. He in turn influenced *Vanbrugh, **Christopher Kempster** (1627-1715—master-mason who built the City Churches of St Stephen, Walbrook, St James, Garlickhythe (1764-87), and St Mary Abchurch, and who was responsible for the Town Hall, Abingdon, Berks. (1678-80)), and *Hawksmoor, who was his assistant and pupil.

AH, xiii (1970), 30-42, xv (1972), 5-22, xxxvii (1994), 37-67; Co (2008); Co (ed.) (1976); Downes (1982, 1988); Hauer (ed.) (1997); Jardine (2002, 2003); *ODNB* (2004); P (1982); M.Parker (1998); Sekler (1956); Soo (1998); Su (1965, 1993); J.T (1996); Tinniswood (2001); G.Webb (1937); Whinney (1971)

Wrenaissance Revival of late-C17 architecture (c.1890-1914) in which themes from designs by *Wren were prominent. Its chief protagonists were *Belcher, *Macartney, and Sir Alfred Brumwell *Thomas.

Wright, Edmund William (1822-86) English-born Australian architect/engineer. He emigrated to South Australia (1849), and, in partnership with **Edward John Woods** (1839-1916), designed the Town-Hall, Adelaide (1863-6), and, with Woods again and **Edward Angus Hamilton** (1831-after 1871), was responsible for the General Post-Office, Adelaide (1867-72), both in a *Renaissance-Revival style. With Woods and Hamilton he also designed Brougham Place Congregational Church (1860-72—derived from *Archer's St Philip's, Birmingham) and many other buildings. Later (1879), he was in partnership with **Joseph H.Reed** (1857-1901).

Jensen & Jensen (1980)

Wright, Frank Lloyd, Jun. (1890-1978) American architect, elder son of F.L.L.*Wright. Trained in his father's studio, he helped (1909) to prepare drawings for the celebrated **Wasmuth** portfolio (1910). He later worked for the Boston firm of *Olmsted, then with his father on the Barnsdall Hollyhock House (1916-21) and on the various concrete-block houses of the 1920s, all in CA. His own output included houses constructed of precast *concrete blocks (e.g. Derby House, Chevy Chase, CA (1926)), whilst pre-Columbian and *Art-Deco motifs occurred in the Sowden House, Los Angeles (1926), and the Samuel-Navarro House, Hollywood, CA (1926-8). He was responsible for the *shell-concrete structure at the Hollywood Bowl, CA (1924-5, 1928). The Swedenborg Memorial Wayfarer's Chapel, Palos Verdes, CA (1946-71), in which architecture is integrated with landscape, is arguably his best work.

A & A, lxxxviii (1966), 22-6; E (1994); Gebhard & von-Breton (1971); Long (1996); Weintraub *et al*. (1998)

Wright, Frank Lloyd Lincoln (1867-1959) American architect, he learned the rudiments of his art from **Joseph Lyman Silsbee** (1845-1913), whose essays in the *Queen-Anne and *Shingle styles were competent. He later (1888) became assistant to Louis H.*Sullivan, and remained with the firm of **Adler & Sullivan** until 1893. Whilst revering Sullivan, Wright was also influenced by Owen *Jones, the English *Arts-and-Crafts movement, *Ruskin, and *Viollet-le-Duc (or rather by what Viollet was *said* to have written), interlocking forms (perhaps suggested by the **Froebel** blocks with which he played when a child), and Japanese architecture (prompted by the Japanese pavilion at the Chicago Exposition (1893)). He designed (1889) his first independent building, his own house and studio at Oak Park, Chicago, IL, an eclectic work, with a shingled exterior (altered and extended 1889-1911), and became (1894) a founder-member of the Arts-and-Crafts Society in Chicago. At this time he began to evolve his *Prairie-House type, with volumes developing from a central core, long, low roofs that appeared to float over the structure, corners treated as voids, and enclosing walls that were treated more as independent *screens (techniques he called 'breaking the box'). Furthermore, the main axes within the houses were continued into the gardens and terraces, suggested in the schemes Wright published in the *Ladies' Home Journal* (1901), and devéloped in the series of houses he designed from that time until just before the 1914-18 war. Yet *Lutyens had also been moving in this direction, as with the Deanery, Sonning, Berks. (1899-1902), while *Schinkel had also brought gardens, water, and terraces within his profoundly ordered geometries, as at the Court Gardener's House and Roman Baths complex, Potsdam (1820s). Wright's finest essays in the Prairie-House style were the Willits House, Highland Park, IL (1902), Robie House, Chicago (1908), and Coonley House,

Riverside, IL (1908–12). With the Unity Temple (Unitarian Church), Oak Park (1906), and the Larkin Building, Buffalo, NY (1904—demolished), a severe, monumental architecture evolved, in which a powerful grid-like geometry was well to the fore, while the architectural language seemed to owe something to a *stripped *Classicism reminiscent of aspects of the work of Schinkel, Otto *Wagner, and others (especially the rows of square columns at Unity Temple which recall the Berlin *Schauspielhaus* by Schinkel and some of the Vienna Metropolitan Railway Stations by Wagner).

Wright's work had been widely publicized, and **Wasmuth** of Berlin published (1910) *Ausgeführte Bauten und Entwürfe von Frank Lloyd Wright* as a handsome pair of portfolios, followed (1911) by a volume of illustrations and plans. The introduction was by C.R.*Ashbee, and these publications helped to promote Wright's work. His designs seem to have enjoyed considerable favour in Germany (*Gropius and *Mies van der Rohe were two architects affected) and in The Netherlands, in particular, where van't *Hoff, *Dudok, and some members of De *Stijl were undoubtedly influenced by his work, and it shows. He moved to the Wisconsin countryside (1911), where he built his Prairie-House-based home and studios at Taliesin (burnt down 1914, but rebuilt and extended during the 1920s). There he was the Master with his pupils, a pose he developed further at Taliesin West, mentioned later.

In spite of a scandalous private life he gained two important major commissions: the Midway Gardens, Chicago (1913—demolished); and the Imperial Hotel, Tokyo, Japan (1915–22—with Antonin *Raymond—also demolished). Both had highly organized plans in which axes featured prominently, and both were lavishly decorated with polygonal, triangular, and other sharp-angled forms, including *chevrons, that had already begun to appear on the lead *cames of some of the Chicago houses, and that anticipated *Art-Deco ornament. With the Hollyhock (or Barnsdall) House (1916–21), Los Angeles, CA, he experimented with repetitive stylized motifs (abstractions of hollyhock forms) cast in moulds (the whole house was cement-rendered), and created a building faintly reminiscent of pre-Columbian American architecture, a theme more pronounced in the Ennis House, Los Angeles (1923–4), constructed of decorated concrete blocks, and featuring battered walls set on terraces. He again used concrete blocks in e.g. the Millard House, Pasadena, CA (1923), and Freeman House, Los Angeles (1923–4), but for the rest of the decade his work did not attract the attention his earlier designs had enjoyed. In the 1930s, however, Wright's buildings were once more widely publicized. At the Kaufmann House (1935–48), 'Falling

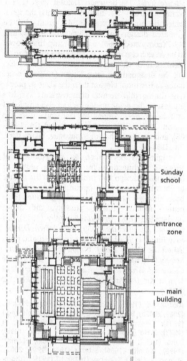

Sunday school

entrance zone

main building

Wright, Frank Lloyd Lincoln (*top*) Plan of Robie House. (*bottom*) Plan of Unity Temple.

Water', Connelsville, PA (1935–48), he gave full expression to horizontals and verticals in a *tour-de-force* constructed over a stream called Bear Run, a design that had superficial resemblances to the *International Modernism of the time, but, with its coursed *rubble walls and hand-crafted detail, owed more, perhaps, to the Arts-and-Crafts tradition, whilst the disposition of elements derived from his Prairie-House type. He designed and built (1936–9) the Johnson Wax Factory, Racine, WI, with a tall interior the roof of which was supported by tapered mushroom-shaped columns, the walls being of brick with glass tubes forming the light-sources. At the same time he developed his low-cost *Usonian houses*, based on vernacular American buildings, that explored the possibilities of prefabrication. The prototype was the Jacobs House, Madison, WI (1936–7), and Wright publicized his ideas in *Architectural Forum* (1938). He also evolved proposals for Broadacre City, a low-density plan in which the Usonian house would feature large. He designed Taliesin West (1937), winter quarters for himself and his disciples, which he built at Scottsdale, AZ. From 1942 he prepared designs for the Guggenheim Museum, NYC (completed 1960), a spiral ramp that proved to be an exercise in formal geometry rather than an ideal form for viewing works of art. At Bartlesville, OK, he designed the Price Tower (1953–6), a tall block rather more elegant than the slabs so prevalent during that period, demonstrating Wright's interest in the acute angles he had also employed at Taliesin West. Among his last works were the Marin County Civic Center, San Rafael, CA (1957–66), and the Beth Shalom Synagogue, Elkins Park, PA (1954–9).

Wright has been seen as an exponent of *organic architecture, by which he seems to have meant design that proceeds from the nature of Mankind and his circumstances as they both change. Although his writings suffer from rather obvious conceit, prolixity, and dense obfuscation (e.g. *An Autobiography* (1943), *An Organic Architecture* (1939), and *When Democracy Builds* (1945)), they were collected and published as *Frank Lloyd Wright on Architecture: Selected Writings 1894–1940* (1941) and *In the Cause of Architecture: Essays by Frank Lloyd Wright for the* Architectural Review *1908–1952* (1975).

Alofsin (ed.) (1999); Bolon *et al.* (1988); Etlin (1994); Fu (2002, 2002a); B.Gill (1987); G & I (1981); Gutheim (ed.) (1941); T.Heinz (1982, 1996, 1997, 1999, 2000); Hi (1973); D.Ho (1988); LeG & S (1996); Levine (1996); Long (1996); McCarter (1997); P (1982); K.Smith (1998); N.Smith (1966); Storrer (1974, 1993, 2002); Stungo (1999a); R.Sweeney (1978); J.T (1996); I.Thomson (2000); Twombly (1979); Wright (1943, 1945, 1970, 1975, 1998); vV (1983); Zevi (1979)

Wright, Henry (1878–1936) American landscape architect/planner, concerned with the segregation of motor-traffic and pedestrians, e.g. *Radburn planning. Convinced that English *Garden-City principles should be adopted in the USA, he was also influenced by *Geddes and *Mumford, and was involved in the laying out of Defense Housing at Newburgh, NY (1918–19), and Yorkshire Village, Camden, NJ (1918), among other schemes. He published *Rehousing Urban America* (1935).

JAIP, xxvi (1960), 293–301; P (1982); Schaffer (1982)

Wright, Henry Myles (1908–2005) English architect, he became (1943) a Ministry of Town and Country Planning research-officer under *Holford, and wrote the influential report on the redevelopment of central areas to be implemented after 1945. He worked with *Abercrombie, Holford, and *Holden on the plan for the City of London, after which he went into practice with Holford, and contributed to plans for Cambridge

(1950) and Corby New Town (1952). Their uninspired proposals for the area around St Paul's Cathedral (begun 1955) were realized, but have since been replaced. Appointed (1954) Lever Professor of Civic Design at the University of Liverpool, he remained there for 21 years. His *Lord Leverhulme's Unknown Venture* (1982) was a history of town-planning in Britain.

RIBAJ (12 Dec. 2006), 62; *The Times* (13 Jan. 2006), 74

Wright, John Lloyd (1892–1973) American architect, son of F.L.L.*Wright. He trained in his father's studio at Oak Park, Chicago, IL, and designed an early *reinforced-concrete structure, the Golden West Hotel, San Diego, CA (1912). His Wood House, Escondido, CA (1912), was a version of his father's *Prairie House designed for the *Ladies' Home Journal* (1901). He assisted his father during the building of the Imperial Hotel, Tokyo (1915–22). Established in his own practice by 1926, he designed several buildings in which aspects of *Art Deco and *Expressionism were well to the fore. From 1945 he developed some of the ideas in his father's *Usonian houses* (e.g. Compton House, La Jolla, CA (1948)), and published (1952) some thoughts on the nature of ornament derived from lichens. He designed (1920) the Lincoln Logs, a children's toy, and the first of his Wright Blocks (1949), inspired by his father's enthusiasm when a child for toy building-blocks.

JAIA, xviii (Oct. 1952), 187–8; *H & H*, i (1952), 136–7; Long (1996); P (1982); *PSR*, vii/2 (1970), 16–19; J.T (1996)

Wright, Thomas (1711–86) English architect/antiquary/landscape-designer and astronomer (he was the first to explain the Milky Way). He published (1748) *Louthiana, or an Introduction to the Antiquities of Ireland,* a pioneering work anticipating many C18 studies. He designed Nuthall Temple, Notts. (1754–7—demolished, but *see Vitruvius Britannicus,* iv (1767)), an elaborated version of *Palladio's *Villa Capra,* Vicenza, and *Scamozzi's *Vettor Pisani* *villa, called *Rocca Pisana* (1576–9). His main claim to fame, however, is as a designer of remarkable garden-buildings, some of which are reproduced in his *Six Original Designs of Arbours* (1755) and *Six Original Designs of Grottos* (1758), intended as the first part of his projected *Universal Architecture* which, regrettably, was never completed. Many of his designs were for *sham castles, *Gothick *follies, gateways, and *eye-catchers, constructed of *rubble and rough materials. He designed the *primitive *Doric 'Shepherd's Grave', a *fabrique* of elegiac character featuring a relief based on **Poussin**'s painting *Et in Arcadia Ego,* at Shugborough, Staffs. (*c.*1756). Several Gothick garden-buildings at Tollymore Park, Co. Down (*c.*1755–80), Dundalk, Co. Louth

(1746–7), and Belvedere House, Co. Westmeath, all in Ireland, were based on his drawings, many of which survive in the Avery Architectural and Fine Arts Library, Columbia University, NYC. He was therefore among the earliest *Gothic Revivalists.

Co (2008); J.Curl (2011a); E.Hs (ed.) (1979); *JGH, I/1* (Jan.–Mar. 1981), 55–66; *JIGS*, xvi (2013), 132–43; M.McCarthy (1987); Rankin (2010); Roden (2005)

Wrighte, William (*fl.*1760s) Obscure English architect, author of the successful and fascinating *pattern-book, Grotesque Architecture or Rural Amusement, consisting of Plans, Elevations, and Sections for Huts, Retreats, Summer and Winter Hermitages, Terminaries, Chinese, Gothic, and Natural Grottos, Cascades, Mosques, Moresque Pavilions, Grotesque and Rustic Seats, Green-houses, etc., many of which may be executed with Flints, Irregular Stones, Rude Branches and Roots of Trees* (1767 and later edns). It explored possi-bilities of different building-materials, and devel-oped notions of the 'rustic' and 'primitive' in natural settings.

Archer (1985); Co (2008); REB (2010)

wrought iron Malleable iron, easily welded, and containing some impurities. It lends itself to decorative work for gates, grilles, balcony-rails, fences, etc.

Wurster, William Wilson (1895–1973) Amer-ican architect with a strong belief that architec-ture should respond to local conditions. As principal of **Wurster, Bernardi, & Emmons,** he was responsible for a great number of 'Regional' buildings in CA, many having *timber frames with pitched roofs, *shingle- or *clapboard-covered walls, and rough carpenter's detailing, collectively called the 'Bay Region School'. Examples of his work were Gregory Farmhouse, Scotts Valley near Santa Cruz (1927); Butler House, Pasatiempo (1934–6); Reynolds House, San Francisco (1946); Stern Hall, University of California, Berkeley (1942); the Medical Plaza, Stanford University, Palo Alto (1959); the Woodlake Residential Com-munity, San Mateo (1965); and the award-win-ning Ghirardelli Square, San Francisco (1962–7), all in CA. With *Belluschi and *SOM the firm planned the Bank of America World Headquar-ters, San Francisco, CA (1970–1).

Ck (1996); E (1994); P (1982); Treib (ed.) (1995); S.Wood-bridge (ed.) (1976)

Wyatt, Benjamin Dean (1775–1852) English architect, eldest son of James *Wyatt. He won the competition (1811) to rebuild Drury Lane The-atre, London (later altered by *Beazley and others), which he published as *Observations on the Design for the Theatre Royal, Drury Lane, as Executed in the Year* 1812 (1813). He succeeded his father as Surveyor of Westminster Abbey

(1813), and built up a flourishing London prac-tice. With his brother, **Philip William** (*c.*1780–1835), he designed Crockford's Club, 50–3 St James's Street (1827—since altered), London-derry House, Park Lane (1825–8—demolished), York (later Stafford, and later still Lancaster) House, St James's (1825–7), the Oriental Club, 18 Hanover Square (1827–8—demolished), and the addition of the *portico and remodelling of the interiors of Apsley House (1828–9), all in London. He was particularly adept at re-creating the *Louis-Quatorze* style which he first used at Crockford's. He redecorated the principal rooms at Belvoir Castle, Leics., and built a *Romanesque *mausoleum in the grounds (*c.*1820–30), in col-laboration with his brother, **Matthew Cotes Wyatt** (1777–1862). He designed the Duke of York's Col-umn, Carlton Gardens, London (1831–4), and car-ried out extensive alterations at Stratfield Saye, Hants. (1838–40). He was declared bankrupt (1833) and died in obscurity.

AR, **clv/926** (April 1974), 217–23; Co (2008); W.Pa (1892); J.Robinson (1979, 2012); J.T (1996)

Wyatt, James (1746–1813) English architect, one of the most outstanding, prolific, and suc-cessful of his time. He spent six years in Italy from 1762 before returning to England where he worked for the family firm, mostly with his brother **Samuel.** He evolved an elegant *Neo-Classicism, possibly derived not only from his time in Italy, but from studies of the work of *Adam at Kedleston, Derbys. Indeed his first architecturally significant house was Heaton Hall, Lancs. (*c.*1772–8), loosely based on a simplified and refined version of *Paine's designs for Kedleston, complete with a central *bow. He made his name, however, with The Pantheon, Oxford Street, London (1769–72—with Samuel), a Neo-Classical domed assembly-room given the *imprimatur* of that arbiter of taste, Horace *Walpole, who declared it the 'most beautiful edifice in England'.

At 26 Wyatt had arrived. He became Surveyor to Westminster Abbey (1776), Architect to the Board of Ordnance (1782), and Surveyor-General and Comptroller of the Office of Works (1796), designed or altered several Royal residences, and carried out many other commissions, in-cluding well over 100 country-houses. However, his interventions with medieval buildings were not universally admired, and he made drastic and certainly controversial alterations to five cathedrals (his work at Salisbury, Wilts. (1789–92), and Hereford (1786–96) earned him the nickname 'The Destroyer', as his approach to medieval fabric was cavalier, speculative, and unarchaeological), and at Durham Cathedral his proposals to demolish the *Galilee and commit other acts of vandalism roused ferocious opposi-tion led by John *Carter.

His Radcliffe Observatory, Oxford (1776-94), drew on the Tower of the Winds in Athens (c.50 BC) for its inspiration, and he completed the interior of Sir Robert *Taylor's Heveningham Hall, Suffolk (c.1780-4), in an elegant Neo-Classical style (damaged in the 1980s). His finest houses are Heaton Hall (mentioned previously), Castle Coole, Co. Fermanagh (1790-7—with an elliptical *saloon expressed as a *bow on one of the *elevations), and the severe Dodington Park, Glos. (1798-1813). Two of his best designs were for *mausolea: that for the **4th Earl of Darnley** at Cobham, Kent (c.1783-4) is a nobly severe Neo-Classical work, whilst that for the **1st Earl of Yarborough** at Brocklesby Park, Lincs. (1786-94), is a refined interpretation of the *Antique Roman Temples of Vesta at Tivoli and Rome, a work of rare beauty that unquestionably is his masterpiece.

As a *Gothic architect Wyatt was fashionably successful, his most *Sublime house in that style being Fonthill Abbey, Wilts. (1796-1812—destroyed), much admired when new. Ashridge Park, Herts. (1802-13), and the additions to Wilton House, Wilts., including the *cloister (1801-11), were also Gothic. One room for his Gothic Lee Priory, Ickham, Kent (c.1785-90—demolished), survives in the Victoria & Albert Museum, London. He provided plans for the Earl-Bishop of Derry's great house, Downhill, Co. Londonderry (built c.1776-9 under *Shanahan's direction—now in ruins), and remodelled Belvoir Castle, Leics. (1801-13) in a castellated Gothic style.

His output was enormous and embraced many building-types, although there is evidence that he accepted more commissions than he was capable of carrying out, and he neglected his official duties to the point of incompetence. Nevertheless, he began to eclipse the *Adam brothers early in his career, and some of his interiors are as delicate as anything they achieved. Particularly felicitous are those of Heaton Hall and the enchanting Brocklesby Mausoleum, Lincs.

Co (2008); C & P (1973); J.Curl (2011a); Dale (1956); *ODNB* (2004); P (1982); J.Robinson (1979, 2012); Su (1993); J.T (1996)

Wyatt, Lewis William (1777-1853) English architect, son of **Benjamin Wyatt** (1745-1818). He trained with his uncles **Samuel** and **James**, and set up in practice c.1805. He published *A Collection of Architectural Designs, rural and ornamental, executed . . . upon the Estates of the Right Hon. Lord Penrhyn in Caernarvonshire and Cheshire* (1800-1), but he is best known as a designer of country-houses. He completed Tatton Park, Ches. (1807-18), begun by Samuel *Wyatt, and built Willey Hall, Salop. (1813-15—probably his best work), both in a *Neo-Classical style. He

used the *Tudor style at Cranage Hall, Ches. (1828-9), and *Jacobean at Eaton Hall, Congleton, Ches. (1829-31—demolished). At Sherborne House, Glos. (1829-34), he emulated a C16 house complete with an *assemblage of *Orders. He published (1816) *Prospectus of a Design for Various Improvements in the Metropolis* in which he argued for a development plan for London, especially the West End.

Co (2008); Pa (1982); W.Pa (1892); J.Robinson (1979, 2012)

Wyatt, Sir Matthew (1805-86) English architect/speculative builder, son of the sculptor **Matthew Cotes Wyatt** (1772-1862) and grandson of James *Wyatt, he designed/built Victoria Square (1838-40), created houses in Stanhope Terrace, Westbourne and Bathurst Streets, and developed land bounded by Connaught, Southwick, and Hyde Park Streets and Hyde Park Square (1830s and 1840s), all in London. Many houses were erected in collaboration with his brother **George** (d. 1880).

Co (2008); J.Robinson (1979, 2012)

Wyatt, Sir Matthew Digby (1820-77) Prolific English architect, younger brother of T.H. *Wyatt, related to the rest of the fecund *Wyatt dynasty. He was Secretary to the Executive Committee for the Great Exhibition (1851), and carried out orientalizing architectural detailing at Paddington Station, London (1852-4), for *Brunel. He designed the *polychrome Addenbrooke's Hospital, Cambridge (1863-5), collaborated with Brunel on Temple Meads Railway Station, Bristol (1865-78), and designed (with 'Great' *Scott) the interior and Durbar Court, India Office, Whitehall (1867-8—perhaps one of the best examples of Victorian *Renaissance Revival). He wrote *Geometrical Mosaics of the Middle Ages* (1848—finely illustrated with chromolithographic plates), edited *Industrial Arts of the Nineteenth Century* (1851-3), and published many other works. When the Crystal Palace was re-erected at Sydenham, Wyatt acted as Superintendent of the Fine Arts Department, and, with Owen *Jones, designed the various 'Courts' demonstrating the characteristics of various periods and styles. One of his most exotic interiors was the spectacular billiard-room at 12 Kensington Palace Gardens, London (1864), in the *Moorish style. He was a pioneer of the Renaissance Revival, the first Slade Professor of Fine Arts at Cambridge (1869), and a prolific author. His Rothschild *Mausoleum in the Jewish Cemetery, Buckingham Road, West Ham, Essex (1866), is a domed building on a circular plan with *Renaissance and *Baroque detail, an example of his 'mixed style'.

D & M (1985); Jervis (1984); *ODNB* (2004); Sh (1973)

Wyatt, Samuel (1737–1807) English architect, the third son of **Benjamin Wyatt** (1709–72). As master-carpenter and later clerk of works at Kedleston, Derbys., he gained first-hand experience of working on a major work of architecture for an important architect, Robert *Adam. He worked with his younger brother **James** on the design and construction of The Pantheon, Oxford Street, London (1769–72), which made James *Wyatt's name. After this, he designed several country-houses in a *Neo-Classical style, often with elliptical or circular rooms expressed as bowed projections. Good examples of his work include Doddington Hall (1777–98), Delamere House (1784—demolished 1939), and Tatton Park (1785–9—constructed by his nephew, L.W.*Wyatt), all in Ches. He designed numerous model farm-buildings, lodges, and cottages, including nearly 50 at Holkham, Norfolk (1780–1807), the Demesne Farm, Doddington Hall, Ches. (*c*.1790), and he was a pioneer in the use of cast-iron construction. He designed the Albion Mills, Blackfriars, London (1783–6—destroyed 1791), the first mill in the world to be powered by steam-engines, and also one of the first to be constructed on a raft-foundation. He also patented (1800) designs for cast-iron bridges, warehouses, and other structures, and prepared systems for constructing prefabricated timber hospitals for use abroad. Other works include lighthouses at Dungeness, Kent (1791), Flamborough Head, Yorks. (1806), and elsewhere; many rectories (e.g. at Wrotham, Kent (1801–2), and Lutterworth, Leics. (1803)) and other medium-sized country-houses, both new buildings and remodellings (e.g. Belmont House, Kent (1789–93), Somerley, Ringwood, Hants. (1792–5), and Hackwood Park, Hants. (1805–7)); the Commissioner's House, Portsmouth Dockyard, Hants. (1784–5); and Trinity House, Tower Hill, London (1793–6—bombed 1940, and restored by Sir Albert *Richardson in 1953). Towards the end of his life he was occupied with major works at Ramsgate Harbour, Kent (1794–1804—all demolished).

Co (2008); P (1982); J.Robinson (1979, 2012)

Wyatt, Thomas Henry (1807–80) English architect, elder brother of Sir Matthew Digby *Wyatt, related to the other architectural *Wyatts. He trained in Philip *Hardwick's office, and entered into partnership (1838) with **David Brandon** (1813–97). Their masterpiece was the Church of Sts Mary & Nicholas, Wilton, Wilts. (1840–6), a convincing *Italianate *basilica with detached *campanile, recognized at the time as a major exercise in the *Rundbogenstil, even in the Viennese journal *Allgemeine Bauzeitung*. It is a remarkable and beautiful building, and contains *Antique black columns (*c*.2 BC) as well as examples of *Cosmati work from Santa Maria Maggiore,

Rome. They also designed St Andrew's, Bethnal Green, London (1841—in a cheaper, less successful *Rundbogenstil), and St Mary's, Atherstone, Warwicks. (1849—*Gothic), and the City of London and Tower Hamlets Cemetery (consecrated 1841), complete with two Gothic chapels and a pretty Gothic gateway and lodge (all buildings demolished following damage in the 1939–45 war). On his own, Wyatt designed Orchardleigh Park, Som. (1855–8), in a vaguely *Jacobean style. With M.D.*Wyatt, he designed the *polychrome *Rundbogenstil St George's Garrison Church, Grand Depot Road, Woolwich (1862–3—gutted in the 1939–45 war and only partially preserved).

J.Curl (2004, 2007); D & M (1985); Ea (1970); Hi (1954); Pe (1972)

Wyatt window Tripartite window resembling a *serliana, but with the arch omitted and the *entablature carried over the wider central window, named after its inventor, James *Wyatt. It may be placed in a segmental-headed recess, or may be capped by a *pediment (e.g. the Radcliffe Observatory, Oxford (1776–94)),

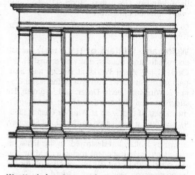

Wyatt window Common domestic type, c.1810.

Wyatville, Sir Jeffry (1766–1840) English architect, born **Wyatt**, the son of **Joseph Wyatt** (1739–85). Apprenticed to his uncle, **Samuel**, he showed early promise as a draughtsman. He joined (1792) the office of his uncle, **James**, leaving (1799) to set up in partnership with **John Armstrong** (d. 1803), building-contractor in Pimlico, London. By the 1820s he had become a highly successful country-house architect (unlike his Uncle James he was thorough, reliable, and highly professional), and began work (1824) for **King George IV** (*r*.1820–30) at Windsor Castle, Berks., not completed until 1837. He raised the *keep, battlemented and *machicolated the towers, and converted the old fortress into a residence for the Sovereign. He virtually rebuilt the

Upper Ward with a new George IV Gateway, reconstructed the State Apartments on the north side around a new staircase (replaced (1866) by *Salvin), and built new apartments on the east (garden) side. The *Picturesque appearance of the Castle today is largely due to Wyatville, who was knighted in 1828 (he had been permitted to call himself 'Wyatville' from 1824). An account of his works at Windsor (in which he was assisted by *Baud) was published in *Illustrations of Windsor Castle by the Late Sir Jeffry Wyatville* (1841).

Most of his country-houses were in Picturesque *Tudor-Gothic or *Tudorbethan modes, and he could design in the Grecian style. Among his works were the County Gaol, Abingdon, Berkshire (1805-11), the completion of and additions to Ashridge Park, Herts. (c.1814-17—*Gothic), the Brownlow *Mortuary Chapel at Belton Church, Lincs. (1816), major alterations and additions, including the library, north wing, tower, and various estate buildings at Chatsworth, Derbys. (1820-41), the remodelling of Sidney Sussex College, Cambridge (1821-2 and 1831-2—Tudor Gothic), extensions to the castellated Fort Belvedere, Windsor Great Park, Berks. (1828-9), and many other building works.

Co (2008); Linstrum (1972); *ODNB* (2004); J.Robinson (1979, 2012)

Wykeham, William of (1324-1404) English ecclesiastic and builder. He was named (1356) Clerk of the Royal Works at Henley and Easthampstead, and later Surveyor of the Royal Castles at Windsor, Leeds, Dover, and Hadleigh. He superintended the erection of the Royal apartments east of the *keep at Windsor Castle (1360-9), and built a new castle on the Isle of Sheppey, called Queenborough (1361-7), known from plans drawn by Hollar, but destroyed. In the 1360s his rise as an ecclesiastic was meteoric, and he was showered with livings. He was responsible for the foundations of New College, Oxford (1379) and Winchester College, Hants. (1382). Both were erected on similar plans, with hall, chapel, and sets. They were the models for later establishments including Eton and King's, Cambridge. Wykeham does not appear to have been an architect, however, and obtained the services of William of *Wynford to act in that capacity. Wykeham's name is primarily associated with major works at Winchester, where he was Bishop from 1366. There, using Wynford, he remodelled the *Romanesque *nave from 1394 in the *Perp. style, which explains the abnormally substantial *piers.

J.Harvey (1987); Hayter (1970); *ODNB* (2004)

Wyman, George Herbert (1860-c.1900) American architect, responsible for one major work, possibly inspired by fiction: the Bradbury Building, 3rd Avenue and Broadway, Los Angeles, CA (1889-93), was a steel-framed structure which had a superb light-filled inner *court with exposed lifts, stairs, and iron galleries.

AIA J, xlviii/5 (1967), 66-9; *Art & Architecture*, lxx/4 (1953), 20, 42-3; Bellamy (1967); Jordy (1976); McCoy (1990); Morgan (ed.) (2012)

wynd *See* GINNELL.

Wynford, William of (*fl.*1360-1405) English master-mason. He was working (1360) at Windsor Castle, Berks., under *Sponlee and William of *Wykeham (then Clerk of the Works there), and probably built the Great Gate and Royal Lodgings. Appointed (1364/5) Master-Mason at Wells Cathedral, Som. (where Wykeham had been Provost since 1363), he built the south-west tower (after 1386) and carried out other works. He may have designed the handsome tower of St Cuthbert's Church, Wells (c.1385-1400), and sundry ecclesiastical structures in the county, including the church-towers at Banwell, Cheddar, and Shepton Mallet. He favoured set-back *buttresses, and seems to have established a pattern for handsome C15 towers in the South-West of England. He was working at Abingdon Abbey, Berks. (1375-6), on Corfe Castle, Dorset (1377-8), and strengthened the fortifications at Southampton (1378-9). With Hugh *Herland and Henry *Yeveley he supervised the building of parts of Carisbrooke Castle, IoW (1384-5).

For Wykeham he designed New College, Oxford (begun 1379/80), and Winchester College, Hants. (begun 1387), on a similar plan. With Herland and Yeveley he repaired and strengthened Winchester Castle (1390s), and it is known he worked at Orford Harbour, Suffolk (1370s), so he obviously had a comprehensive grasp of engineering and military-architecture as well as of other building-types. He began (1394) the great work of transforming the *Romanesque *nave of Winchester Cathedral into a *Perp. space without actually rebuilding it, creating a high lierne-*vault, leaving the steeply-pitched early-medieval roof, and casing-in the huge *piers, thus creating a curiously chunky type of architecture for the period. He probably had a considerable part in the design of the exquisite Perp. *chantry-chapel and tomb of Wykeham in Winchester Cathedral, with its cusped lierne-vault (early C15).

J.Harvey (1987); W.Pa (1892); J.T (1996)

X 1. Mnemonic of Christ, the first letter of ΧΡΙΣΤΟΣ. *See* CHRISMON. **2.** Roman numeral symbol for 10. *See* TEAM X.

xenodocheion, xenodochium Guest-house in a *monastery, etc.

Xylonite Fibrous vegetable matter (e.g. cotton and flax waste and old rags), dissolved in acid and neutralized, which produced a substance called *Parkesine*, named after its inventor, **Edmund Alexander Parkes** (1813–90), of Birmingham. In its liquid state it was used as a waterproofing agent, in its plastic form for insulation, and, with the addition of oils, glues, and colour, for making objects, e.g. tubes and architectural enrichment. Capable of being coloured, and susceptible to a high polish, it was first exhibited at the International Exhibition, South Kensington, London (1862). It was developed (1890s) as a substitute for *plaster *cornices, *friezes, *mouldings, and other decorations in rooms, and was supplied in accurately moulded prefabricated 3-metre lengths which were then fixed to timber grounds by means of screws. Its extreme light weight made it easy to handle and fix.

ODNB (2004); W.Pa (1892)

xylotechnigraphy Decoration of wood by staining, graining, and finishing to resemble a more expensive and finer wood, patented in England *c.*1871.

xystum 1. Open *path, wall, *promenade, or *alley. **2.** *Ambulacrum, *atrium, or *parvis in front of a *basilica.

xystus 1. Roman garden planted with groves of plane-trees, usually laid out with flower-beds and surrounded with a *colonnaded *ambulatory, like a *cloister. **2.** Long covered *portico, open-sided colonnade, or *court used for athletic exercises in Ancient Greece. **3.** Covered *promenade. **4.** Church ambulatory. **5.** Long *loggia or *verandah. **6.** *Hypaethral walk, shaded by trees. **7.** Part of a Roman house, bigger than an *atrium, surrounded by a *peristyle, and planted in the middle.

Y *See* TRACERY.

Yamada, Mamoru (1894-1966) Japanese architect, founder of a Secession group influenced by German *Expressionism, the *Sezession, and *Art Nouveau. His early works (e.g. The Central Telegraph Office, Tokyo (1925-6—destroyed)) demonstrated such sources, but his later designs (e.g. Communications Industry Hospital, Tokyo (1937)) tended towards the *International-Modern style.

Koike (1954); Kulturmann (1967)

Yamasaki, Minoru (1912-86) American architect of Japanese descent. He and his partners **George Francis Hellmuth** (1907-99—until 1954) and **Joseph William Leinweber** (1895-1993—until 1959) made their names with the Lambert Airport Terminal Building, St Louis, MO (1953-6), the main concourses of which are covered by intersecting *concrete-shell barrel-*vaults. His grim public housing, Pruitt-Igoe, St Louis (1950-8), predicatably won architectural awards, but made history by being detested by those living there (it suffered several arson attacks), and was demolished (1972), an event many have seen as the beginning of *Post-Modernism as a reaction against the *Modern Movement. Later buildings tended to have *screen-like elements in the *façades that disguised the structural grids. With **Emery Roth & Sons** he designed the twin-towered World Trade Center, NYC (1964-74—destroyed 11 Sept. 2001).

Wi.Cu (1996); E (1994); Heyer (1978); vV (1993); Yamasaki (1979)

yard 1. Uncovered piece of ground, surrounded by walls or buildings, without the architectural pretensions of a *court or *quadrangle. 2. Linear measurement equalling 3 feet (approx. 90 cm.). 3. Enclosure set apart for some trade or business, e.g. *brick-yard*, *dockyard* (for ships), *shipyard*, *tan-yard*, etc. 4. *Spar or *rafter of a roof.

Yates, Peter (1920-82) *See* RYDER, JOHN GORDON.

Ybl, Miklós, *or* **Nikolaus von** (1814-91) Austro-Hungarian architect, pupil of *Gärtner.

He formed (1840s) a partnership with **Ágoston Pollack** (1807-72), and designed numerous buildings in a Neo-Classical style influenced by *Schinkel. His first major commission was for a church, school, *mausoleum, and parsonage at Fót (1845-57), in a *Rundbogenstil influenced by Gärtner's work in Munich. Numerous houses followed (e.g. the Unger House, 7 Muzeum Boulevard, Budapest (1852)), and in the 1860s, like his contemporaries in Vienna, he turned to a *Renaissance-Revival style, as in the First National Savings Bank (1868) and the Customs and Excise Building (1870-4—now the School of Economics), both in Budapest: his greatest work in that style was the Opera House, Budapest (1875-84), much informed by developments on the *Ringstrasse*, Vienna. Influenced by his visit to the International Exhibition in London (1862), he designed two manor-houses at Parád (1862-88) and Parádsasvár (1880-2), both near Gyöngyös, and a *Romanesque-Revival parish-church, Bakáts Square, Budapest (1866-79). He carried out major works at the Royal Palace, Buda (from the 1860s), and worked on the building of the sumptuous *basilica of St Stephen, Pest (1851-1906), after *Hild's death.

Bae: *Austria* (1929); W.Pa (1892); J.T (1996); Ybl (1956)

Yeates, Alfred Bowman (1867-1944) *See* GEORGE, SIR ERNEST.

Yefimov, Nikolay (**Yefimovich**) (1799-1851) Russian architect. He restored the Winter Palace, St Petersburg, after the 1837 fire but he is best known for his new buildings (e.g. Ministry of State Property (1844-50—with **Nikolay Leont'yevich Benols** (1813-98)) and the House of the Minster (1847-53—completed by **Lyudvig Lyudvigovich Bonshtedt** (1822-85)), both of which are in a refined *Renaissance-Revival style); significant elements of St Isaac's Square; and the City Duma (1848-52—also completed by Bonshtedt). In his ecclesiastical work he incorporated *Byzantine motifs.

J.T (1996)

yellow metal Alloy of three parts of copper to two of zinc, used for covering *domes, roofs, etc., because of its malleability.

yelm Straight bundle of reeds or straw for *thatch.

Yenn, John (1750–1821) English architect, pupil of *Chambers, he was Clerk of Works at Somerset House, London, from 1776. A fine draughtsman, probably the best among any C18 English architects, he designed the Temple of Health (1789) at Blenheim Palace, Oxon., and, with **Henry Hake Seward** (*c.*1778–1848), rebuilt the west *façade of the King Charles Block, Greenwich Hospital, London (1811–14), having succeeded Sir Robert *Taylor as Surveyor.

Co (2008); W.Pa (1892)

yett Grated iron door, *portcullis, or *screen, its horizontals passing through alternate vertical bars, and its verticals passing through alternate horizontal bars.

Yeveley *or* **Yevele, Henry** (*c.*1320/30–1400) English master-mason, possibly hailing from Yeaveley, Derbys., he may have learned his craft at one of many Midlands building-projects, perhaps Lichfield Cathedral, Staffs., but was in London (1353) and rose rapidly in fame and fortune. Employed *c.*1357 by **Edward, the Black Prince** (1330–76), at Kennington Manor, he worked at St Alban's Abbey, Herts., around the same time. By 1360 he was active at Westminster Palace, the Tower of London, Queenborough Castle, Kent (1361–7), and various other castles and properties of the Crown: e.g. with *Sponlee and *Wynford on the fortifications at Southampton (1370s).

He designed several funerary monuments: the magnificent tomb (1374–8—destroyed) for **John of Gaunt, Duke of Lancaster** (1340–99), and his first wife, **Blanche of Lancaster** (d.1369), which stood in old St Paul's Cathedral, London (it appears to have been enclosed in a canopied *chantry-chapel); the noble tomb of the Black Prince, Canterbury Cathedral, Kent (1375–6); most likely the monument (1386) of **King Edward III** (*r.*1327–77) in Westminster Abbey, closely resembling the tombs of **King Richard II** (*r.*1377–1400) and **Cardinal-Archbishop Langham** (*fl.* 1339–76), also in the Abbey, which we know were by Yeveley; and (probably) the canopied tomb of **Prior Rahere** (*fl.*1120–44) in St Bartholomew-the-Great's Church, Smithfield, London (or his work may have influenced the finished artefact). The great Neville *screen of *Caen stone, Durham Cathedral (early 1370s), made in London and shipped north, is stylistically similar to John of Gaunt's destroyed chantry-chapel mentioned previously; James *Wyatt wanted to remove it in the 1790s. By 1378 Yeveley had developed his connections with Canterbury, designing the West Gate of the city, and was involved (1381)

with Wynford as a consultant for some of William of *Wykeham's architectural projects. As he had begun building the Charterhouse in London (1371), he was well-placed to advise on collegiate establishments, and it seems likely he was consulted about the design of New College, Oxford. By 1385 he was spending much time in Canterbury, where he designed the *nave of the Cathedral (*c.*1380–1405), one of the most beautifully proportioned of any in England. While in Kent he may have provided designs for Meopham Church (1381–96), the gate-house of Saltwood Castle (*c.*1383), and the new Church and College at Maidstone (founded 1395).

At Westminster Abbey he worked on the nave, generally following the (by then rather old-fashioned) lines set down by Henry de *Reyns. He commenced work (1394) on Westminster Hall, one of the grandest secular rooms of the Middle Ages, with a great timber roof by Hugh *Herland (completed 1400). He also acted as a consultant on numerous works, including Leeds and Rochester Castles, Kent, Winchester Castle, Hants. (with Wynford and Herland), Orford harbour, Suffolk, and many other places.

Yeveley was an important medieval architect (some have called him the *Wren of C14, and Dr Harvey said he was the 'greatest English architect'), whose output was prodigious. Fortunate in having the patronage of **Kings Edward III** and **Richard II**, he was able to bring English *Perp. to maturity. As a designer of funerary architecture he was in the premier division.

Crossley (1921); J.Harvey (1946, 1948, 1952, 1978, 1987)

ymage Medieval term for a statue.

yoke 1. Short timber linking two other timbers, especially the tops of *cruck *blades. 2. Horizontal timber forming the top of a frame for a *double-hung* *sash-window.

Yorke, Francis Reginald Stevens (1906–62) English architect, one of a handful devoted to the *Modern Movement in England in the 1930s. A founder of the *MARS Group (1932), his use (from 1933) of *reinforced concrete testified to his *Modernist credentials, as did his *The Modern House* (1934) publicizing Continental *International Modernism. With *Holford et al. he designed (1933) a pair of houses (conventional in plan but conforming in *image* to the paradigms promoted at the *Weissenhofsiedlung*) for the Modern Homes Exhibition at Gidea Park, East London (held 1934), and built (1935) a more sophisticated reinforced-concrete house at Nast Hyde, Hatfield, Herts. (destroyed 1980s). In the same year he formed a partnership that lasted until 1938 with the former *Bauhaus teacher, *Breuer, designing an exhibition house for the

Royal Show, Bristol (1936), and Sea Lane House, East Preston, Sussex (1937—in the *International-Modern style, with *pilotis). With Arthur *Korn, he built some flats in Camberwell, London (1940). He published *The Modern House in England* (1937), *The Modern Flat* (1937—with *Gibberd), *A Key to Modern Architecture* (1939—with **Colin Troughton Penn** (1907-97)), and *The New Small House* (1951 and 1954—with **Penelope Muriel Wesbrough Whiting** (1918-2017)) all of which had a powerful effect on British architecture after 1945. With Eugene *Rosenberg and **Cyril Sjöström Mardall** (1909-94) he formed one of the most successful practices in England after the 1939–45 war (**Yorke, Rosenberg, Mardall** (YRM)). Their many schools (e.g. Barclay Secondary, Stevenage, Herts.—1950), housing-schemes, factories (e.g. Sigmund Pumps, Gateshead, Co. Durham—1948), offices, and hospitals were fairly typical of architecture in Britain in the 1950s and 1960s, but with their own offices at Greystoke Place, London (1960-1), St Thomas's Hospital, London (from 1966), and University of Warwick (also 1960s) they introduced an architecture clad in white tiles.

E (1994); Melvin (2003); ODNB (2004); Po (1992); vV (1993); F.Y (1947, 1951); F.Y & Penn (1939); F.Y & Whiting (1954); YRM (1972)

Yorkshire lights *Mullioned two-*light window, one light fixed and the other a *sash sliding in grooves in a *horizontal* direction.

Yoshida, Isoya (1894-1974) Japanese architect, he made his name as a designer of timber houses, often discarding the logic of historical types, e.g. when creating windows in the corners of the buildings where traditionally they would have *posts. From the 1950s he designed several public buildings, using *concrete. Among his works the Sekiya House (1931), Shinkiraku Restaurant (1940-62), Ryuzaburo Umeharo Studio-House (1951-8), Inomata House (1967), Manganji Temple (1969), and Prince Chichibu House (1972), all in Tokyo, may be cited. He sought to create a truly modern national architecture, freed from *International *Modernism and other non-Japanese influences.

E (1994); P (1982); J.T (1996)

Yoshizaka, Takamasa (1917-80) Japanese architect, he worked in Le *Corbusier's studio in Paris (1950-2), and subsequently designed in a manner suggestive of the latter's *Brutalism at the Maisons Jaoul (e.g. Yoshizaka House, Tokyo (1955)), although he moved away from that tendency in later years. Among his works were the City Hall, Gozu (1961—in which the office-block supported on trellis-like forms resembled a large bridge).

E (1994); Yoshizaka (1984-7)

you Ancient Chinese hunting-park containing artificial *mounts (on which the Emperor would perform *rituals) that evolved into gardens where birds, fish, and livestock could breed and plants with symbolic meanings could be cultivated to provide agreeable settings and habitats. It evolved into the *yuan. See CHINESE GARDEN-DESIGN.

Li Zongwei (2011)

Young, Ammi Burnham (1798-1874) American architect, his early work was in a restrained *Federal style, but his Vermont State House, Montpelier (1833-6), with a Greek-*Doric *portico and a low *Pantheon-like *dome (destroyed), was an essay in *Neo-Classicism. He turned to the *Gothic Revival for St Paul's Church, Burlington, VT (1832), then back to Greek Doric and a Pantheon-dome for the Custom House, Boston, MA (1837-47—overwhelmed by extensions carried out by *Peabody & Stearns (1915)). Appointed (1852) First Supervising Architect at the Treasury Department, he designed numerous Federal buildings, many of which were in *Italianate styles: e.g. Custom House and Post Office, Windsor, VT (1856-8), where iron was used structurally as well as for external and internal ornament. Many of his designs were published in *Plans of Public Buildings in Course of Construction for the United States of America* ... (1855-6).

Hamlin (1964); JSAH, xix/3 (Oct. 1960), 119–23; xxv/4 (Dec. 1966), 268–80; R.Kennedy (1989); P (1982); J.T (1996); Vermont History, xxxvi (1968), 55–60; Wodehouse (1970)

Young, Edward (1683-1765) English poet, his *The Complaint: or, Night Thoughts on Life, Death, & Immortality* (1742-50) was acclaimed as a masterpiece, and was translated into every European language (it was *Goethe's English reader). Most importantly, the episode of 'Narcissa's Burial' in *Night III* (in which the difficulties of burying non-RCs in *ancient-régime* France were powerfully described) touched chords throughout civilized Europe, and was a catalyst in the transformation of the *landscape-garden into the *garden*-cemetery.

JGH, xiv/2 (Summer 1994), 92–118

Young, Lamont (1851-1929) British architect/town-planner, he produced visionary but unrealized plans for Naples, where he designed several buildings, including Castello Grifeo (c.1875—later Curcio), in a *Gothic-Revival style, with a garden-tower *fabrique built as a *ruin, and the Palazzina Grifeo (1877—in a *Renaissance-Revival style, seasoned with *Georgian and *rustic motifs). Castle Lamont (1902-4—later Aselmeyer), on a hill in Naples, was embellished with *Tudor elements, and had a complex system of massing; the Villa Hebe (built after the 1914-18 war) was a phenomenally late essay in Gothic Revival, with interior furnishings in a similar style. His highly imaginative architecture has generally been ignored.

Alisio (1984)

Young, William (1843-1900) Scots architect, he made designs for many town- and country-houses throughout the UK. One of his most resplendent interventions was at Robert *Adam's Gosford House, near Longniddry, East Lothian, Scotland (completed 1891), while at Elveden Hall, Suffolk, he enlarged the already extravagant house in a *Baroque style (1899-1903). He is remembered primarily for the Glasgow Municipal Chambers, George Square (1883-9), an opulent pile of French, Flemish, Venetian, and Spanish *Renaissance styles, with eclectic influences from *Sansovino to 'Greek' *Thomson: it made his reputation, and he was commissioned to design the New (now Old) War Office, Whitehall, London (1899-1906), a confident *Wrenaissance essay, with corner *cupolas. The ensemble made such an impression at the time that it was virtually copied by **Samuel Stevenson** (1859-1924) for the exterior of the Belfast College of Technology (1900-7). The War Office was completed by Young's son, **Clyde Francis Young** (1871-1948), after William's early death. William Young was responsible for the proposal to create Kingsway and Aldwych to connect The Strand to Holborn, London. He published several books, including *Town and Country Mansions and Suburban Houses* (1879).

D & M (1985); A.S.Gray (1985); McWilliam (1978); Pe & Radcliffe (1974); Se (1977); J.T (1996); WRH (1990)

Young & Mackenzie Belfast firm of architects founded 1870 by **Robert Young** (1822-1917—pupil of *Lanyon) and **John Mackenzie** (1844-1917), later (1880) joined by Young's son, **Robert Magill Young** (1851-1925): it was prolific, and works include Fitzroy Presbyterian Church (1872-4—*Gothic Revival), Robinson & Cleaver's store (1886-8), Anderson & McAuley's store (1890), the Scottish Provident Institution (1897-1902), Ocean Buildings (1899-1902—a Gothic office-block, unusual for its date), and the Presbyterian Assembly Buildings (1900-5), all in Belfast.

Brett (1967); Larmour (1987); J.T (1996)

Youngman, Peter (1911-2005) English land-scape architect, he worked on the *Festival of Britain (1951), on the master-plan for Cumbernauld, North Lanarkshire (1956), and on various projects with **Shankland Cox** (*see* cox), Colin *Buchanan, et al. He was involved at Milton Keynes, Bucks.; Gatwick Airport, Surrey; and Sizewell nuclear power-station, Suffolk.

The Guardian (17 Jun. 2005), Obits

Y-tracery *See* TRACERY.

yuan In Chinese garden-design the *you was gradually transformed into the *yuan* which included forests, lakes (for pleasure-boating, naval exercises, and aesthetic reasons), pastures (including areas for breeding and raising animals), and *pavilions placed throughout the whole of the landscape (really a large park). Aspects of this transitional landscape influenced the subsequent evolution of *Chinese garden-design.

Li Zongwei (2011)

yurt Felt- or hide-covered Central-Asiatic *tent, with a cone-shaped top, a form repeated in certain C11 Islamic brick-built *mausolea.

Zabludovsky Kraveski, Abraham (1924–2003) Polish-born Mexican architect, a devotee of *International Modernism, from 1968 he began working with **Teodoro González de León** (1926–2016), notably on the *Delegación Cuauhtémoc* (1972-3—with others), the *INFONAVIT* headquarters (completed 1975), and new buildings for the *Colegio de México* (1974-5), all in México City. Independently, Zabludovsky designed the *Centro Cultural Emilio O. Rabasa*, Tuxtla Gutiérrez, Chiapas (1983), two multi-purpose *auditoria, two theatres, and a conference-centre (all early 1990s).

Noelle (ed.) (1994); J.T (1996)

Zachwatowicz, Jan (1900–83) Polish architect/architectural historian, Director of the Warsaw Department of Architecture from 1939, he taught students clandestinely throughout the Nazi occupation and terror, always in great personal danger. Nominated (1945) General Conservator of Historical Monuments, he was appointed to the Chair of Polish Architecture, Warsaw Polytechnic. Not only did he organize a national *conservation structure, but evolved strategies for the reconstitution of buildings and historic town-centres that had been reduced to rubble, all the more difficult when Nazi barbarism had been replaced by Stalinist repression. The 'Polish School of Conservation' (a label he disliked), of which, nevertheless, he was the leading light, held that reconstruction should be based as much as possible on reliable *historical* evidence (documentary, architectural, and archaeological). Under Zachwatowicz's guidance impressive reconstruction achievements in Poland were internationally recognized. The entire Old Town of Warsaw was painstakingly and brilliantly recreated, together with its churches, and the rebuilding of the Royal Palace (completed 1981—with others, including **Professor Stanisław Lorentz** (1899–1991)) can only be regarded as a triumph (especially as the Communist authorities proposed erecting a large *Modernist building on the site to create the predictable *tabula rasa*). Other historic centres (e.g. Gdańsk, Poznań, and Wrocław) were also repaired and rebuilt according to principles established by Zachwatowicz and his team. An outstanding scholar, he had over 200 major publications to his credit.

Puget (ed.) (1994); Zachwatowicz *et al.* (1952); Z-J

Žák, Ladislav (1900–73) Czech architect, he made his name with the *Herain, Čeněk*, and *Zaorálek* houses at the Czechoslovak *Werkbund* Second Exhibition, Baba, Prague (1932), all in a crisp *International style. Other houses followed: for **Dr Hain**, Prague-Visočany (1932-7), for **Martin Frič**, Prague-Hodkovičky (1934-5), and for **Lída Baarová**, Prague-Dejvice (1937), all in the same mode. After the 1939–45 war he specialized in landscape-design.

Li (1996); *Sborn.N.Tech.Muz.Praze*, **xiv** (1975), 189–225; Y (1934)

Zakharov, Andreyan, *or* **Adrian Dmitriyevich** (1761-1811) Russian architect, trained in St Petersburg and then (1782-6) under *Chalgrin in Paris. His reputation rests on the massive *Neo-Classical buildings he designed for St Petersburg, including the New Admiralty (1806-23): a huge structure, probably the largest Neo-Classical building in the world, it was influenced by Pierre *Rousseau's arch at the *Hôtel de Salm*, Paris (1782-5), as well as by designs of *Boullée and *Ledoux. The entrance-block is capped by a massive *Ionic *peristyle (based on descriptions of the Mausoleum at Halicarnassus) supporting a very tall gilded needle-*spire. The severe end-*pavilions with arched cubic blocks surmounted by *drums and flanked by Roman-*Doric *colonnades are among the most *Sublime buildings informed by late-C18 French Neo-Classicism. He was also responsible for standardized administrative buildings for the Russian provinces, and a range of warehouses facing the River Neva on Proviantsky Island territory (1806-9). He was involved (with *Voronikhin) in the planning of the handsome *Bourse* in St Petersburg (1801-16), designed by de *Thomon.

A & O (1980); Grabar *et al.* (1963); Grimm (1940); C.H (1983); M & Wa (1987); P (1982); D.Shv (2007); J.T (1996); vV (1993)

zakomara Semi-circular *gable often expressing the *vault of a *Byzantine church but sometimes merely ornamental.

Zanobi de Gianotis *or* **Gianotti, Bernardino** (*fl.*1520–41) Italian architect/sculptor, most
of whose work was in Lithuania and Poland. He
assisted **Bartolomeo Berrecci** (*c.*1480–1537) on
the *Renaissance sepulchral-chapel of **King Sigismund I** (*r.*1506–48) in Kraków Cathedral (1519–
26). With **Giovanni Battista Cini** (*fl.*1530–65) and
Filippo da Fiesole (*fl.*1530–40) he designed and
built the *basilica at Płock (1532–41), an early
importation of an Italian *type north of the
Alps. They also built the Cathedral at Vilnius
(1536–*after* 1546), Neo-Classicized by *Gucewicz
(1780s). Zanobi himself designed and executed
several distinguished funerary monuments.

Biuletyn Historii Sztuki, **xxi** (1959), 151–74; *Kwartalnik
architektury i urbanistyk*, **xxvi** (1981), 294–306

Zanth, Karl Ludwig Wilhelm von (1796–
1857) Born **Zanik**, son of the Jewish doctor to
Jérôme Bonaparte (1784–1860—**King of Westphalia** (*r.*1807–13)), he studied in Paris with *Percier and *Hittorff, collaborating with the latter
(1822–30) on *Architecture antique de la Sicile*
(1827) and *Architecture moderne de la Sicile*
(1835) in which Hittorff's work on *polychromy
was published. Later, Zanth received his Doctor-
ate for his work on *Pompeian domestic architecture. Settling in Stuttgart (*c.*1830) as Court Architect, he enjoyed the patronage of **King Wilhelm I
of Württemberg** (*r.*1816–64), for whom he built
the *Villa Wilhelma* (1837–51) in the Royal Park of
Rosenstein: an asymmetrical composition, with
rich structural polychromy in the *Moorish style
(published in colour (1855)), it was his best work.
He designed several town- and country-houses in
and around Stuttgart, and taught **Christian Friedrich Leins** (1814–92), who built the *Königsbau*
(1857–60), Stuttgart, designed earlier (*c.*1857) by
Johann Michael Knapp (1793–1861). Leins also
designed (for **Crown Prince Karl of Württemberg**, who later reigned as **King Karl I** (1864–
91)) the charming *Italianate *Villa Berg*, near
Stuttgart (1844–53), influenced by *Schinkel's
work.

Hittorff & Zanth (1827, 1835); W.Pa (1892); Wa & M (1987)

Zanuso, Marco (1916–2001) Italian architect/
furniture-designer responsible for the Olivetti
Office Buildings in Buenos Aires, Argentina, and
São Paulo, Brazil (1955–9), the latter with a thin
*shell-vault covering the central element. His
Vacation-House, Arzachena, Sardinia (1963–4),
was constructed of local red, yellow, and white
granite, giving it a fortress-like appearance that
seemed to grow naturally from the rock. Among
later works the Water Tower, Reggio Emilia
(1985), may be mentioned. He was Chief Editor
of *Casabella* (1947–9).

Casabella, **ccxvi** (1957), 59–71; E (1994); Giorgi (ed.)
(1999); Jervis (1984)

Zapotec architecture The Zapotec civilization of *Meso-America produced buildings that
were similar to those of the *Maya, Toltec,
*Aztec, and other groups, with a clear distinction
between the substructure and superstructure.
The religious centre of the Mixtec-Zapotec peoples in the valley of Oaxaca, México, was the
Palace of the Columns, Mitla (*c.*1000), with an
impressive platform the walls of which were decorated with elaborate geometrical patterns.

Ck (1996); Kubler (1984); J.T (1996)

Zarudny, Ivan Petrovich (*fl.*1700–27) Ukrainian architect, he probably designed the *Baroque Church of the Archangel Gabriel, Moscow
(1701–7—aka Menshikov Tower). He may have
been involved in other ecclesiastical works, and it
is known he designed the *triumphal arches (e.g.
the Synodal Gates, Nikol'skaya Street (1709)) and
*iconostases (e.g. in the Cathedral of Sts Peter and
Paul, St Petersburg (1722–7)).

Arkhitektura SSSR, **x** (1953), 30; *Arkhitekturnoye
Nasledstvo*, **ix** (1959), 157–68; D.Shv (2007)

Zarza, Vasco de la (1499–1524) Spanish archi-
tect/sculptor, he introduced *Renaissance elements from Italy to New Castile, notably in Ávila.
By 1508 he was working on the *cloister at Ávila
Cathedral, and he designed and made the funerary monument (in the form of a *triumphal
arch) of **Don Carrillo de Albornoz** (d.1514) in
the chapel of St Ildefonso, Toledo Cathedral
(*c.*1515). He was also responsible for the *El Tos-
tado*, the monument of **Bishop Alonso Fernández de Madrigal** (*c.*1400–55), in Ávila Cathedral
(1517–18), and advised on building-works at Salamanca Cathedral (*c.*1523).

Azcárate (1958a); Checa (1983); Parrado del Olmo
(1981)

zecca Italian mint for making coins, e.g. the fine
C16 example in Venice by *Sansovino.

Zehrfuss, Bernard-Louis (1911–96) French
architect. He designed many buildings in Tunisia
(1943–8), and, with others, was responsible for
planning much subsequently realized in that
country. Back in France he designed, with *Breuer
and *Nervi, UNESCO Headquarters, *Place de Fon-
tenoy*, Paris (1952–8), and, on his own, the French
Embassy, Warsaw (1970), and the Gallo-Roman
Museum, Lyons, France (1975–6). The National
Centre for Industry and Technology, *La Défense*,
Paris (1955—with **Robert Camelot** (1903–92),
*Prouvé, and **Jean de Mailly** (1911–75), with a
large vault by **Nicolas Esquillan** (1902–89) based
on a preliminary design by Nervi), was severely
(and justly) criticized for destructively impacting
on Paris's skyline. In the 1980s he advocated
comprehensive redevelopment of parts of Mont-

parnasse, with proposals not distinguished by sensitivity.

E (1994); J.T (1996)

Zemtsov, Mikhail Grigor'yevich (1686/8–1743) Russian architect, pupil of *Trezzini, he supervised the realization of the *Baroque *Yekaterinthal Kadriorg* palace and park (1718–25) at Reval (now Tallinn, Estonia). He designed the Church of Sts Simeon and Anna, St Petersburg (1730–4), was in charge of the works at *Peterhof* from 1724, and planned (1740s) the palace and park at *Tsarskoye Selo* (now *Pushkin*). With others, he worked on the *Kunstkammer*, St Petersburg (1718–34). He appears to have been one of the first to arrange for the proper education of architects in St Petersburg.

Cracraft (1988); Iogansen (1975); D.Shv (2007)

Zenetos, Takis Ch. (1926–77) Greek architect. Believing that housing should be elaborate, even luxurious, he opposed prevailing tendencies in the West to provide poor-quality low-cost accommodation to minimum standards, and abhorred box-like Modernist housing. His works include 21 Xanthou, Glyfada, Attica (1961), the *apartment-block, 34 Amalias, Athens (1959—with **Margaritis Apostolidis** (1921–2005)), and the renovation of the Fix Brewery, 53 Syngrou, Athens (1957—with Apostolidis).

J.T (1996)

Zen garden-design Term coined in the West which seems to refer to many types of Eastern-inspired gardens supposedly influenced by Zen Buddhism, esp. *Japanese garden-design. Examples would include the *tea-garden, the *stroll-garden, and sundry sand- and stone-gardens (*karesansui*—mentioned in the *Sakuteiki*) which have had such an impact on Western gardens. Chief characteristics included understatement, economy of means, *borrowed landscapes, rock-placings, water, representations by means of *rock-work of mountains, and responses to drawings of landscapes. Zen Buddhism focuses on *meditation* rather than prayer as a means towards Enlightenment, and so Zen garden-design evolved to provide suitable environments conducive to this activity, providing peace, beauty, and no distractions.

Ji Cheng (2012); Kuitert (2002); Shoe (2001); Tay (2006)

zeta 1. Upper storey. **2.** Watch-tower. **3.** Garden *summer-house. **4.** Small chamber above a church-*porch.

Zettervall, Helgo Nikolaus (1831–1907) Swedish architect, influenced by *Viollet-le-Duc, best known for comprehensive restorations of Lund (1860–80—which involved considerable rebuilding in which stylistic uniformity prevailed over *conservation of historic fabric) and Skara (1886–94) Cathedrals, but at Uppsala Cathedral his faith in *concrete mixes as an alternative to traditional *masonry of freestones was misplaced. As Chief of the National Board of Public Building in Stockholm, he produced many eclectic works, and, as a church-architect, he built All Saints', Lund (1861–91), St Matthew's, Norrköping (completed 1892), and the Oscar Fredrik Church, Göteborg (1887–93). He published on church-restoration, and designed many fine ecclesiastical furnishings (e.g. at All Saints', Lund).

A & B (1986); Åman (1966); Jervis (1984); P (1982); J.T (1996)

Zeugherr, Leonhard (1812–66) Swiss architect, he worked for a brief period with *Rickman in England before settling in Zürich where most of his distinguished *oeuvre* may be found, including the earliest large shops (*Hechtplatz*, 1835) and apartment-blocks (e.g. *Escherhäuser* (1836–40)). His church at Neumünster (1837–8) betrayed the influence of the *Inwoods, and from *c.*1837 he designed several refined Neo-Classical houses as well as *Renaissance-Revival *villas in Zürich (e.g. the beautiful *Villa Wesendonck* (1835–7) and *Zur Seeburg* (1843–7)). Other works include the dignified *Knabenschule*, Winterthur (1836–42).

Zeitschrift für schweizerische Archäologie und Kunstgeschichte, **xxix** (1972), 82–105; *Zuger Neujahrsblatt* (1988), 63–84

Zevi, Bruno (1918–2000) Italian architectural theorist, he studied at Harvard University, USA (1939–43), before returning to Italy. His works included *Towards an Organic Architecture* (1945, 1955), *Architecture as Space: How to Look at Architecture* (1948, 1980), *Storia dell' architettura moderna* (1950, 1973), and *The Modern Language of Architecture* (1973, 1978). Opposed to *International Modernism, *Post-Modernism, *Classicism, and *Neo-Classicism, he advocated a vaguely defined *organic architecture (partly influenced by F.L.L.*Wright) and a return to drawing on natural forms: he stated that architecture can only be called organic when it aims at human happiness, and seems to have advocated a popular idiom that would be contemporary and unindebted to past styles to achieve this. He also contributed major publications on *Michelangelo (1964), *Mendelsohn (1970), and F.L.L.Wright (1979).

Wi.Cu (1996); Zevi (1950, 1960, 1973, 1974, 1978, 1979, 1980, 1980a, 1985, 1999); Zevi et al. (1981)

Zhilyardi, Domenico (1788–1845) *See* GIGLIARDI.

Zholtovsky, Ivan Vladislavovich (1876–1959) Belorussian architect, he practised in Moscow from 1900, and was devoted to *Classicism, translating *Palladio's *Quattro Libri* into Russian (1936). He saw St Petersburg *Neo-Classicism as *the* Russian style, but his fine Tarasov House, Moscow (1909-10), looked back to Palladio's *Palazzo Thiene*, Vicenza (c.1550). He designed the All-Russian Exhibition for Agriculture and Home Industries, Moscow (1922-3), firmly Classical in form; the Residence, Mokhovaya Street, Moscow (1932-4), based on the *Giant-Order arrangement of Palladio's *Loggia del Capitaniato*, Vicenza (1571-2); the Housing Complex, *Bolshoi Kaluzhskoi*, Moscow (1940-9); and the huge Apartment Block, Smolensk Square, Moscow (1947-53), a powerful Neo-Classical composition, the style of which was identified with *Socialist Realism. After Stalin's death (1953), Zholtovsky was denounced (predictably) for his adherence to Classicism.

Ck (1996); Kopp (1978); Musgrove (ed.) (1987); Oschep-kov (1955); P (1982); J.T (1996)

Ziebland, Georg Friedrich (1800-73) German architect, pupil of Karl von *Fischer, he completed Fischer's *Hoftheater*, Munich (from 1820), *Quaglio's charming *Gothic *Hohenschwangau*, near Füssen (1832-50), and the *Mariahilfkirche*, Au, Munich (from 1831), all in Bavaria, but his chief importance lies in his contribution to the *Rundbogenstil*, notably his splendid brick-and-*terracotta (with stone *dressings) fusion of *Early-Christian and *Byzantine architecture at the *Bonifaziusbasilika*, Munich (1828-40), which drew on exemplars in Ravenna and Rome (e.g. *San Paolo fuori le Mura*). He also designed the *Corinthian exhibition-building opposite von *Klenze's more lively *Glyptothek* in the *Königsplatz*, Munich (1838-45).

Ne (1987); P (1982); Reidelbach (1888); Stubenvoll (1875)

ziggurat Ancient Mesopotamian staged temple-tower of pyramidal form in which each successive *stage is smaller than that below it, leaving a *terrace all around it. Each stage was connected by formal ramps. The form was first evolved by the Sumerians in what is now southern Iraq c.2600 BC.

Ck (1996); L & M (1986); J.T (1996)

zig-zag 1. *Romanesque decorative **Z**- or **V**-and inverted **V**- (∧) shaped device (*chevron or *dancette), either incised or in relief, occurring in a continuous *band or *string (as at Southwell *Minster, Notts.), as an ornament around an arch or series of arches (*see* ORDER), or cut into the drum of a *pier (as at Durham Cathedral). It has several variations (*see* HERRING-BONE). **2.** Planform of fortifications with gun-emplacements built outwards with *salient angles.

Ziller, Ernst (*called* **Ernestos**) **Moritz Theodor** (1837-1923) German-born Greek architect, he studied in Dresden (1855-8) and worked in Vienna with T.von *Hansen (1858-9), who brought him to Athens to build the Academy of Sciences (1861-4). Following travels in Italy and a further period of study in Vienna (1864-8), Ziller settled in Greece, was eventually naturalized, and became the most influential architect working in that country during the reign of **King George I** (1863-1913). One of his best buildings was *Iliou Melathron* (1878-80), the residence of **Heinrich Schliemann** (1822-90—the discoverer of Troy), which became the Greek Supreme Court. Other works included the house of **Pavlos Melas** (1884—later the Post Office), the New Palace (1890-7), and the Royal (now National) Theatre (1895-1901), all in Athens. He also designed the Neo-Classical Town Hall, Ermoupolis, Syros (1876), several country-houses in a mixture of Bavarian Alpine *vernacular and Neo-Classical architecture (e.g. the Summer Residence of King George, Tatoi (1870), and the Ziller Settlement, Kifasia (1909-13)), and some *Rundbogenstil ecclesiastical buildings (e.g. *Hagia Triada*, Piraeus (1915-16), and *Hagios Athanasius*, Pyrgos (1911)). He designed numerous architectural details (columns, *caryatids, etc.) which were manufactured in *terracotta and were widely used throughout Greece. He contributed to archaeological discoveries in his adopted country (e.g. excavations of the Stadium (1869-70), and his work on the Theatre of Dionysos (1862), both in Athens).

M & Wa (1987); Russack (1942); J.T (1996); T & B (1932)

Zimbalo, Giuseppe (*fl.*1659-86) Italian *Baroque architect of the *Prefettura* (1659-95), *Duomo* (1659-82), *Sant'Agostino* (c.1660-3), and Rosary Church (1689-91), all in Lecce. His somewhat overblown style was continued into C18 by his pupil, **Giuseppe Cino** (1645-1722).

Calvesi & Manieri-Elia (1970)

Zimmermann Brothers Bavarian artists, sons of **Elias Zimmermann** (1656-95), stuccoer/ mason, they were masters of the South-German *Rococo style. Born near Wessobrunn, where the Abbey was the centre of one of the most important and innovative schools of workers in *stucco, they probably trained under Johann *Schmu(t)-zer, the leading C17 Wessobrunn architect/ stuccoer. The Zimmermanns usually worked independently, but joined forces to create some of their best work (e.g. Steinhausen and *Die Wies* *pilgrimage-churches). They acquired and evolved a light, delicate, and elegant style perhaps influenced by French exemplars, but certainly far removed from the heavy C17 German *Baroque of some of Schmu(t)zer's creations. **Dominikus Zimmermann** (1685-1766) was a stuccoer/*scagliola-worker before emerging as one of the most gifted architects of the first half of C18 in Southern

Germany. His older brother, **Johann Baptist Zimmermann** (1680–1758), was not only a stuccoer/worker in *scagliola*, but a fine *fresco-painter as well. J.B.Zimmermann's exquisitely delicate stucco decorations in the *Amalienburg* (1734–9), *Nymphenburg* (1755–7), and *Residenz* (1733–7), all in Munich, were among the most beautiful of their kind in Europe.

Dominikus's first church was at Mödingen, near Dillingen (1716–21), for which he also carried out stucco decorations, while his brother did the frescoes and other parts of the stucco-work. The fully developed Rococo style of the Zimmermanns, however, was first evident at Our Lady of Sorrows *Wallfahrtskirche*, Steinhausen, near Biberach, Württemberg (1727–35—signed by Dominikus as architect/stuccoer in an inscription beneath the organ-gallery), a large elliptical volume surrounded by a continuous *aisle, with the *high-altar and tower placed at either end of the long axis (an arrangement perhaps suggested by an earlier proposal by *Moosbrugger, and probably by C.D.*Asam's design for Weltenburg). Colouring is predominantly white and gold, with a superb ceiling-fresco by J.B.Zimmermann, while Marian imagery and colouring are found throughout the church, all marvellously integrated within the total design. Steinhausen has been called the first true Rococo church.

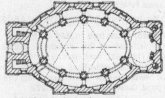

Plan of *Wallfahrtskirche* Steinhausen.

Dominikus Zimmermann's next important solo work was the *Frauenkirche*, Günzburg on the Danube (1736–41), downstream from Ulm: from outside the nave appears to be rectangular, but the positions of columns and curving elements produce an elliptical space further defined by the siting of the side-altars. The Günzburg church, however, lacks the *élan* of Steinhausen, but at the pilgrimage-church of Christ Scourged (1744–54), set in charming meadows (hence the popular name, *Die Wies*) not far from Füssen, Dominikus Zimmermann again achieved greatness: many hold *Die Wies* in high esteem as the triumph of South-German Rococo. Like Steinhausen, it consists of a large, almost elliptical, space surrounded by an aisle, but has a vestibule behind the convex wall of the entrance-front and a long, narrow, rectangular *chancel on the long axis. However, unlike Steinhausen, the plan of the main body of the church

for the pilgrims is not elliptical, but consists of two semicircles on either side of a rectangle, and is separated from the aisle and vestigial *transepts (at each end of the rectangle set on a cross-axis) by paired columns instead of piers, enhancing the delicacy and elegance of the interior. Above the central congregational volume is a ceiling-fresco by J.B.Zimmermann, a vision of the Heavens depicting the moment just before the Last Judgement, with Christ on the Rainbow prior to being seated on the Throne. Christ's Scourging is symbolized by the columns of white and blood-red *scagliola* in the *choir, and the Evangelists by the high-altar have their Gospels open at the passages describing that event. Otherwise, *Wieskirche* is mostly white, colouring being confined to altars, the remarkable *pulpit (one of D.Zimmermann's most effervescent creations), and the ceilings. The architectural arrangements permit generous lighting, enhancing the extraordinary brilliance and delicacy of the interior, a joyous ensemble that is essentially an outpouring of creative energy to astound and enchant.

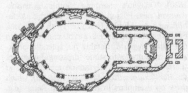

Plan of '*Die Wies*'.

The Zimmermanns, with some of their contemporaries, the brothers **Franz Xaver** (1698–1763) and **Johann Michael** (1696–1772) **Feichtmayr** and **Johann Georg Üblhör(r)** (1703–63), invented a regional Rococo that was one of the most delicious and elegant styles ever evolved.

H.Bauer & A.Bauer (1985); Bou (1962); L.Hager (1955); Hi (1968, 1968a); Kasper & Strache (1957); Lamb (1964); Lampl (1959); P (1982); Rupprecht (1959); Schnell (1981); Schnell & Schedler (1988); J.T (1996); Thon (1977)

Zion, Robert L. (1921–2000) American landscape architect, he became a partner (1957) of **Harold A.Breen** (1923–95), and designed the first *vest-pocket Paley Park, East 53rd Street, NYC, transforming *SLOAP into a granite-paved planted area, softened with ivies and a *water-wall. Among other works may be mentioned the *plaza at the base of the Statue of Liberty, NYC (1986).

W & S (1994); pk

Zítek, Josef (1832–1909) Bohemian architect, pupil of van der *Nüll and *Siccard von Siccardsburg, in whose Vienna office he worked (1857–8) on competition-drawings for the Savings Bank,

Prague, and the Stock Exchange, Vienna. He is mostly remembered for the National Theatre (*Národni Divadlo*), Prague (1866-81), an essay in *Renaissance-Revival much influenced by the *Ringstrasse* buildings in Vienna: it was reconstructed (1881-3) by his pupil, **Josef Schulz** (1840-1917), after a disastrous fire. Zítek was also responsible for a number of other buildings in his native country, including the *Rudolfinum*, Prague (1875-84—also with Schulz), and the *Mühlbrunnen* Colonnade, Karlovy Vary (Karlsbad) (1871-8).

Bae: *Austria* (1929); Landisch (1968); J.T (1996)

Zitterbarth Family Hungarian architects active from the late C18 to the late C19. Among their works can be cited the *Rundbogenstil *Synagogue, Kecskemet (1864-71—by **János Zitterbarth** (1826-82)), and the Pest County Hall (1838-41) by **Mátyás Zitterbarth** (1803-67—probably the most distinguished architect of this family, who also designed numerous apartment-blocks in Pest in a dignified Neo-Classical style).

Epités-Epitészettudomány, iii (1972), 417-8; Zádor & Rados (1943)

zocco, zoccolo, zocle *Socle, *plinth, or any support (less in height than breadth) under the *mouldings of the bases of *pedestals, etc.

Zocha Family German gentlemen-architects. **Johann Wilhelm von Zocha** (1680-1718) directed works at the *Residenz*, Ansbach, from 1715, and after his death, his brother, **Karl Friedrich von Zocha** (1683-1749), who had studied under de *Cotte in Paris, took over, designing two *elevations and some interiors in a restrained Classical style: he was also responsible for the Orangery (1726-7), where Gallic influences from *Hardouin-Mansart and *Perrault were obvious. He designed several Lutheran churches, including those at Wald (1722) and Lahm (1728-32). His Frenchified style was continued by his pupil, **Johann David Steingruber** (1702-87).

Jahrbuch für fränkische Landesforschung, xvi (1956), 455-91; *JGH*, v/4 (Oct.-Dec. 1985), 336-59; Raschzok (1988)

Zocher, Jan David (1791-1870) Dutch architect/town-planner/landscape   architect, trained by his father, **Jan David Zocher Sen.** (d.1817), and by *Lebas at the *École des *Beaux-Arts*, Paris, he promoted the English style of landscape-gardening in The Netherlands, and transformed numerous redundant town-fortifications into landscaped areas. He and his son, **Louis Paul Zocher** (1820-1915), designed the *Vondelpark*, Amsterdam. Much of his architecture was in a *Romantic-Classical style, much influenced by English exemplars, but little of it survives.

Beek (1984); Klopfer (1911); J.T (1996)

zone of transition That part of the interior surface of an Islamic building lying between the vertical walls of a square or polygonal room and the *dome over: it may be covered with *muqarnas.

Ck (1996)

zoning In town-planning and *urban-design, designations of parts of cities/towns for purposes of land-use (e.g. industry, housing, etc.) or for certain restrictions of height or volume. Originally intended, e.g., to keep noxious industries separated from residential areas, its rigid application, as promoted by the *Athens Charter and *CIAM, has been disastrous to the life of towns, as Jane *Jacobs demonstrated, because it killed diversity and any chance of the development of a living urban organism.

J.Jacobs (1961, 1969, 1984)

zoological garden (zoo) Open-air enclosed area for keeping, displaying, studying, and breeding animals. The type is ancient, for animals were kept in gardens in Ancient Egypt, Mesopotamia, and China for purposes of providing game for hunting, food, and impressing visitors. *Menageries to show off species discovered in explorations were developed from *Renaissance times, but the animals were caged rather than allowed the freedom of open-air habitats, and in the C18 royal menageries were opened to the public, including the *Tiergarten*, Schönbrunn, near Vienna. The Zoological Society's Garden opened (1828) in Regent's Park, London, set in landscaped grounds, and many other cities followed suit, including New York (1860s). In the C20, with concerns about *conservation and improved knowledge about animals' welfare, natural habitats were created, so the modern zoo promotes horticulture to provide them.

J.Fisher (1966); Hoage & Deiss (eds) (1996); Shoe (2001)

zoömorph Representation of an animal form. *Zoömorphic ornament* is anything featuring stylized animal forms (e.g. in *Art-Nouveau, *Celtic, and *Romanesque design).

Zoömorphic or **New Animal architecture** Late-C20/early-C21 architecture characterized by wavy and flowing lines, loose, amorphous blob-like shapes, and, sometimes, with exteriors resembling carapaces. Examples might include Selfridge's Building, Birmingham (2001-3—*see* KAPLICKY), and **Sir Peter Frederic Chester Cook** (1936-) et al.'s *Kunsthaus*, Graz, Austria (2000-3): such structures are foreign to established urban fabric, and are anathema to protagonists of *New Urbanism. *See* BIOMORPH; BLOBISMUS.

Aldersley-Williams (2003); K (1994); Patkau Architects (1997)

zoöphoric column Column supporting an animal form, e.g. that in the *Piazzetta*, Venice.

zoöphorus, zophorus Classical *frieze, especially (but not always) embellished with reliefs of human/animal forms.

Zopf und Perücke German term (literally *Pigtail and Periwig*) for a style of late-C18 *Rococo architecture, also called *Zopfstil*.

Zoroastrianism Iranian religion derived from the teachings of **Zoroaster** (**Zarathustra**) (c. early-second millennium BC), which still has devotees (e.g. the Parsees of India). The most important architectural remains are *fire-temples: they provided precedents for later Islamic *mausolea and elements of *mosque design.

J.T (1996)

zotheca 1. *Alcove or *niche, especially one containing a statue or an *urn. **2.** Small dayroom or study, usually entered from a larger room, so a kind of large alcove or *carrel.

Zuazo Ugalde, Secundino (1887–1970) Spanish architect/town-planner, his work was stylistically eclectic, and included several post-offices (e.g. Bilbao, Madrid, and Santander—1924–7), where Viennese influences may be detected, perhaps more strongly expressed in the *Casa de las Flores* housing, Madrid (1930–2). Influenced by his studies of *El Escorial*, near Madrid, he reorganized the inner-city of Bilbao, prepared plans for Greater Seville, and provided designs for the new stretch of the *Avenue Castellana*, Madrid (opened 1933), on which new Government Ministries were to be erected (1930–7). However, Zuazo's vision of a 'hymn to the soberness and nobility' of stone-built architecture was not shared by the architects of the realized buildings which were in a bleak *stripped-Classical style not unlike 1930s official architecture in Fascist Italy and Nazi Germany. A competent Classicist himself, he designed the *Palacio de la Música* (1924–6), and the *Casa Domingo Ortega* (1946–7), both in Madrid, in that style.

Arquitectura, cxlvi (1971); FL (1961); P (1982); T & DC (1986)

Zuccalli, Enrico (1642–1724) Member of a family of architects from the Italian-Swiss Canton of Grisons. Appointed (1672) Court Architect to **Elector Ferdinand Maria of Bavaria** (r.1651–79) in succession to *Barelli, he enjoyed the favour of **Elector Maximilian II Emanuel** (r.1679–1704; 1715–26) so that he was the pre-eminent architect working in Munich for some time, successfully transplanting Italian, French, and Austrian *Baroque styles to Bavaria (one of his first works was the centrally planned pilgrimage-church at Altötting, which, although building ceased (1679), introduced modern Roman Baroque ecclesiastical planning). He took over from Barelli (1674) the building of the *Theatiner-* or *Kajetaner-kirche*, Munich, designing the twin-towered *façade (completed 1765–8 by *Cuvilliés, who made changes to it during its building), the tall *cupola over the *crossing, and the interior. His greatest work was *Schloss Schleissheim*, near Munich (1684–1704). The layout there began with *Schloss Lustheim* (1684–9), set in gardens, and continued with the main palace (completed by *Effner) which stands at one end of a long canal, *Schloss Lustheim* being sited at the other. Zuccalli supervised the making of some interiors of the Munich *Residenz* (1679–1701—destroyed in the 1939–45 war, but partly restored), including the *Kaiserzimmer*, *Alexanderzimmer*, and *Sommerzimmer*. His extensions to *Schloss Nymphenburg*, Munich (begun 1701), consisting of *pavilions linked to the main block, were based on the designs by *Marot for *Het Loo*, The Netherlands. He built the *Palais Fugger-Portia*, Munich (1693–4), and extended (1697–1702) the *Residenz* in Bonn, completed by de *Cotte. His last major commission was the rebuilding of *Kloster* Ettal, near Oberammergau (1709–26), including the design of the curved façade and the domed space of the church itself.

Bou (1962); Brucker (1983); L.Hager (1955); L.Hager & Hojer (1976); Hauttmann (1921); E.Hempel (1965); Heym (1984); Lieb (1941, 1976, 1992); P (1982); Paulus (1912); Riedl (1977); J.T (1996)

Zuccalli, Giovanni Gaspare *or* **Johann Kaspar** (c.1654–1717) Cousin of Enrico *Zuccalli, he designed two centrally planned *Baroque Salzburg churches: the *Erhardskirche* (1685–9), on a Greek-*cross plan (derived from *Cortona's *Santi Luca e Martina*, Rome) with a circular *drum carrying the *cupola; and the more interesting Theatine *Kajetanerkirche* (1685–1711), with its elliptical cupola derived from *Bernini's *Sant' Andrea al Quirinale*, Rome. These two buildings may have influenced the design of *Fischer von Erlach's *Dreifaltigkeitskirche*, Salzburg (1694–1702), and his later *Karlskirche*, Vienna (from 1716). The *Schloss* at Aurolzmünster (1691–1711), near Ried-im-Innkreis, Austria, is also probably by him.

Bou (1962); Ebhardt (1975); Fuhrmann (1950)

Zucker, Paul (1888–1971) German-born American architect/architectural historian/theorist, he was involved (1920s) with *Arbeitsrat für Kunst and *Novembergruppe, and taught at various institutions. Among his many works were shops for the *Etam* (1921–2) and *Festa* (1928) chains, the *Bankhaus Lewinsky, Taubenstrasse* (1924), the Henkel House, *Hagenstrasse*, Grünewald (1927), and the Posnansky Studio-cum-Boathouse, *Kleiner Wannsee* (1930), all in Berlin, but his best buildings were probably the *villas in the western suburbs of that city. Zucker's copious writings include *Town and Square: From the Agora to the Village Green* (1959) and numerous contributions on architectural theory in various journals, mostly dealing with aspects of urban space.

AAAB, Papers, **xii** (1977), 53–145; *JSAH,* **ii/3** (Sept. 1942), 6–13, **x/3** (Sept. 1951), 8–14; P (1982); Ven (1989); *WMfB,* **iv** (1919–20), 83–6; Zucker (1959)

Zug, Simon Gottlieb *or* Szymon Bogumił
(1733–1807) Saxon architect, he settled in Poland where he designed many distinguished *Neo-Classical buildings, including the Guardhouse of the Wilanów Palace, Warsaw (1775–6), and the circular domed Protestant Church, Warsaw (1777–81—destroyed 1939, rebuilt 1950), with its severe *Doric *portico, the first example of a Neo-Classical church in Poland. For **Kazimierz Poniatowski** (1721–1800) he designed at Solec (1772) the first of a series of charming landscape-gardens influenced by English models, and for **Princess Izabela Czartoryska** (1746–1835) he laid out the *jardin anglais* at Powązki, near Warsaw (1770s—now the Cemetery), with **Jan Piotr Norblin** (the French landscape-painter **Jean-Pierre Norblin de la Gourdaine** (1745–1830)), and contributed an article on Polish gardens to *Hirschfeld's Theorie der Gartenkunst* (1785), one of the seminal works on late-C18 gardens in Europe. At Natolin, near Warsaw, he designed the beautiful *pavilion (1780–2), with its main elliptical domed room half-open to the garden through a screen of *Ionic columns, an idea perhaps derived from de *Wailly's *Montmusard* (1764). His most interesting work (again with Norblin) is *Arkadia,* near Nieborów (1777–98), the *Picturesque garden laid out for Princess Helena *Radziwiłłowa: it has a lake, various *fabriques,* including a *Gothic House, an eclectic 'high priest's sanctuary', a megalithic grotto of the Sybil, *arcades, a 'Greek' arch, an *aqueduct, an *Île des Peupliers* complete with *cenotaph as a mnemonic of J.-J.*Rousseau's tomb at Ermenonville, France, and a 'Temple of Diana' with a curious interior of curved rooms. He also designed a block in Warsaw (1784–5) with a ground-floor featuring *primitive unfluted Greek *Doric columns supporting arches, reminiscent of the work of *Ledoux.

AQC, **cxvi** (2004), 83–126; J.Curl (2011); *GH,* **xxiii/1** (Summer 1995), 91–112; L & R (1984); Łoza (1954); M & T (1991); Piwkowski (1998)

Zwinger
1. *Bailey or outer *court, as in a castle. 2. Place for dog-kennels etc., attached to a grand house. 3. Large arena for entertainment, e.g. for jousting, processions, etc., or bear-baiting,

usually a formally designed space with grandstands around it for spectators. Hence the C18 *Zwinger* Palace, Dresden, Saxony, by *Pöppelmann, an extraordinary composition, with a festive gate (*Kronentor*), *pavilions, galleries, *orangeries, and a *nymphaeum* grouped around a large court.

Zwirner, Ernst Friedrich
(1802–61) German architect, pupil of *Schinkel (who demonstrated his confidence in the young man by supporting his appointment (1833) as *Dombaumeister* for the then unfinished medieval Cathedral of Cologne). Building on research by *Boisserée, he prepared designs for the Cathedral's completion before the momentous decision was taken to do so (1842), and thus was in an excellent position to realize what was to be his greatest achievement: his proposals were published in *Daly's *Revue Générale* (1856), although the building was not completed until 1888 (under the aegis of **Vincent** (or **Vincenz**) **Statz** (1819–98) et al.). He also designed the *Gothic Church on the *St Apollinarisberg,* near Remagen (1839–43), the Drachenfels Monument (1857), and the Cologne *Synagogue (1859–61—before its destruction one of the finest essays in C19 *Moorish-*Byzantine *Rundbogenstil*). Several of his other churches were in a Rhenish-*Romanesque style.

Zwirner was a key figure in the German *Gothic Revival not only because of the exemplary nature of his own work, but because he trained several successful practitioners, including Statz (who became (1863) Diocesan Architect of Cologne) and Friedrich von *Schmidt. Zwirner was called in to advise on the competition to design the *Nikolaikirche,* Hamburg (1844): he recommended that 'Great' *Scott's design (placed third by the jury, with schemes by *Semper and *Strack winning first and second places respectively) should be declared the winner, and that Scott should be appointed architect. As this is what happened, it is clear his views carried considerable weight. He published *Vergangenheit und Zukunft des Kölner Dombaues* (1842) and contributed regular reports on progress in *Kölner Domblatt* which were published in translation in *The Ecclesiologist,* arousing considerable interest in Great Britain and the USA.

Borger (ed.) (1980); G (1972); Hoster & Mann (eds) (1973); Mann & Weyres (1968); *Rheinische Lebensbilder,* **iii** (1968), 173–89; Zwirner (1842)

Zwitzel Family
German architects. **Jacob Zwitzel** (*c.*1470–1540) carried out several projects in the Tirol, mostly ecclesiastical work, and built a monumental column and fountain in Augsburg (1515–16), where he designed several city buildings. His son, **Bernhard Zwitzel** (1496–1570) designed the main *façade of the *Stadtresidenz,*

872

Landhut (from 1536), and the *Stadtsbibliothek* (1562–4) and *Geschlerstube* (1563), both in Augsburg, and both destroyed. With *his* son, **Simon Zwitzel** (*fl.*1548–93), and **Wilhelm Egckl** (*fl.*1558–88), he designed the *Antiquarium* of the *Residenz*, Munich. Simon succeeded him as Director of Building Works in Augsburg (1570), responsible (with others) for the Augustus Fountain on the

Perlachplatz and considerable works for the wealthy Fugger family.

Egg (1974); *Lebensbilder aus dem bayerischen Schwaben*, **viii** (1961), 84–107; *Verhandlungen des Historischen Vereins für Niederbayern*, **xcvii** (1971), 90–9; *Welt im Umbruch* (1980–1), 121

zystos *See* XYSTUS.

More History titles from OUP

The Oxford Companion to Black British History
David Dabydeen, John Gilmore, and Cecily Jones

The first reference book to explore the full history of black people in the British Isles from Roman times to the present day.

'From Haiti to Kingston, to Harlem, to Tottenham, the story of the African Diaspora is seldom told. This Companion will ensure that the history of Black Britain begins to take its rightful place in mainstream British consciousness.'

David Lammy, MP, former Minister for Culture

A Dictionary of World History

Contains a wealth of information on all aspects of history, from prehistory right up to the present day. Over 4,000 clear, concise entries include biographies of key figures in world history, separate entries for every country in the world, and subject entries on religious and political movements, international organizations, and key battles and places.

The Concise Oxford Dictionary of Archaeology
Timothy Darvill

The most wide-ranging, up-to-date, and authoritative dictionary of its kind.

'Comprehensive, proportionate, and limpid'

Antiquity

OXFORD